# Time-Saver Standards
# for Building Types

# TIME-SAVER STANDARDS FOR BUILDING TYPES

Joseph De Chiara  Editor

Michael J. Crosbie  Editor

Fourth Edition

McGRAW-HILL

Boston  Burr Ridge, IL  Dubuque, IA  Madison, WI  New York  San Francisco  St. Louis
Bangkok  Bogotá  Caracas  Kuala Lumpur  Lisbon  London  Madrid  Mexico City
Milan  Montreal  New Delhi  Santiago  Seoul  Singapore  Sydney  Taipei  Toronto

*McGraw-Hill*

*A Division of The McGraw-Hill Companies*

**TIME-SAVER STANDARDS FOR BUILDING TYPES – FOURTH EDITION**
International Edition 2001

20  19  18  17  16  15
15  14  13  12  11  10
CTP  BJE

**Cataloging-in-Publication Data is on file with the Library of Congress**

ISBN 0-07-016387-1

**When ordering this title, use ISBN 0-07-120241-2**

Printed in Singapore

# Contents

Previous and Current Contributors ix
Organizations xi
Preface to the Fourth Edition xiii
About the Editors xv

## 1. RESIDENTIAL 1

Dimensions of the Human Figure 3
Single-Family Homes 6
Apartments 43
Apartment Buildings 51
Seniors Housing 63
Housing for People with Disabilities 78
Group Homes 88
Manufactured Housing Developments 92

## 2. COMMERCIAL 103

Retail 105
Supermarkets 117
Regional Shopping Centers 119
Automobile Dealers 145
Automobile Service Centers 163
General Offices 172
Medical Offices 200
Law Offices 225
Research Laboratories 232
Television Stations 248
Radio Stations 255
Funeral Homes 265

## 3. HOSPITALITY 271

Restaurants and Eateries 273
Food Service Facilities 279
Commercial Kitchens 292
Conference Centers 298
Hotels 305
Hotel Space Allotments 325
Motels 337
Motel Planning 340
Motel Site Planning 353

## 4. EDUCATIONAL                                                        357

Planning for Educational and Administrative Technology    359
Safety and Security                                       364
Early Childhood Education Facilities                      369
Planning Elementary and Secondary Schools                380
Organization and Design of Schools                       387
College Student Housing and Residence Halls              446
College Student Centers                                  455
College Classrooms                                       462
Academic/Research Libraries                              479
College Gymnasiums                                       497
College Laboratories                                     506

## 5. HEALTH CARE                                                        517

Hospitals (General)                                      519
Surgical Suites                                          528
Diagnostic X-Ray Suites                                  536
Pharmacies                                               543
Physical Therapy Departments                             545
Occupational Therapy Departments                         549
Community Mental Health Centers                          553
Laboratories                                             555
Labor-Delivery Suites                                    559
Outpatient Activity Centers                              563
Emergency Activity Centers                               573
Rehabilitation Centers                                   575
Mental Health Centers                                    592
Long-Term Care Facilities                                601
Medical Schools                                          609
Dental Schools                                           635
Nursing Schools                                          655

## 6. CULTURAL and ENTERTAINMENT                                         675

Museums                                                  677
Libraries                                                693
Performing Arts Spaces                                   713

## 7. GOVERNMENTAL and PUBLIC                                            757

Municipal Buildings                                      759
Fire Stations                                            772
Police Stations                                          779
Police Facilities                                        791
Recreation Centers                                       799
Courthouses                                              806
Correctional Facilities                                  825
U. S. Embassies/Chanceries                               850

## 8. RELIGIOUS BUILDINGS      871

Churches, General      873
Churches, Lutheran      883
Churches, United Methodist      889
Temples and Synagogues      900
Chapels      913
Church Schools      915

## 9. TRANSPORTATION      923

Airports and Terminals      925
Airport Cargo Facilities      966
Parking Garages      974
Parking Lots      990

Index      995

Richard M. Adler, AIA
Glenn Arbonies, AIA, Arbonies King Vlock Architects
Egmont Arens, Industrial Designer
Leslie Armstrong
James W. Atz, American Museum of Natural History
Geoffrey Baker, Architect
Vilma Barr
Herbert Behrend, P.E.
Richard M. Bennett, AIA
Frederick Bentel, FAIA, Bentel and Bentel Architects
Maria Bentel, FAIA, Bentel and Bentel Architects
Chester Arthur Berry, Ph.D.
Glenn H. Beyer, Housing Research Center, Cornell University
Charles M. Bolden, Conrad Associates
Raymond C. Bordwell, AIA, Perkins and Will, Architects
William M. Breger, AIA
Charles E. Broudy
Gladys L. Brown, Health, Physical Education, and Recreation
     Consultant
Peter Brown, Perkins and Will, Architects
C. William Brubaker, FAIA, Perkins and Will, Architects
Harold Burris-Meyer
Robert Campbell
Charles A. Chaney
Alonso W. Clark, AIA
Harold Cliffer, AIA
F. G. Cole
Walter L. Cook
William J. Cronin, Jr.
Laurence Curtis
Marvin Cutler, AID
T. P. Deis, Architect
William DeJong, Ph.D., DeJong and Associates
Clyde H. Dorsett, AIA
Lathrop Douglas, FAIA
John W. Dreiling, AIA
Max Fenger, Architect
W. R. Ferguson
A. Peter Florio, Designer-Consultant
John J. Fruin, Ph.D.
Bruno Funaro, Architect
Richard C. Gambrill, AIA
Francis W. Gencorelli, AIA
Bryant Putnam Gould
Noyce L. Griffin, E.E.
John J. Grosfeld, AIA
Victor Gruen, AIA
J. L. Gruzen, AIA, Gruzen and Partners
Don Halamka
Raymond Harrison
Louis Hartman, HarleyEllis Architects
Morton Hartman, AIA, Perkins and Will, Architects
Ernest J. Hasch

Keith I. Hibner, AIA
John Hill, Hill Glazier Architects
August Hoenack, U.S. Public Health Service
Douglas R. Hoffman, AIA, The Arris Group
Joseph Horowitz, P.E., Columbia Broadcasting Systems, Inc.
George A. Hutchinson, AIA, Perkins and Will, Architects
Emmet Ingram, AIA, Perkins and Will, Architects
David Jones
David Karlquist, TAMS Consultants, Inc.
Edward A. Kazarian
Aaron N. Kiff, Architect
Alexander Kira, Housing Research Center, Cornell University
Joseph Kleinman, Architect
Robert L. Knapp, AIA, Charles Luckman Associates
A. Frederick Kolflat, AIA, Perkins and Will, Architects
J. J. Koster, Gruzen and Partners
Lendal H. Kotschevar
Jeffery A. Lackney, R.A., Ph.D.
Alan Lapidus, AIA
Morris Lapidus, AIA
Betsy Laslett
Fred Lawson
Stanton Leggett, Education Consultant
Ronald Mace, FAIA
James Mackenzie
John Macsai
Jain Malkin
Francis Joseph McCarthy, FAIA
William McCoy, AIA, Perkins and Will, Architects
Gordon P. McMaster, Architect
Glenn Meeks, Meeks Technology Group
Frank Memoli, Architect
Emmanuel Mesagna, Architect
Keyes D. Melcalf
Jo Mielziner, Stage Designer
William A. Mills, Architectural Consultant
Maurice Mogulescu
Bruno Molajoli
Roger Morgan
George Muramoto, Architect
Richard Muther
Barbara Nadel, FAIA, Architect
Clifford E. Nelson, M.D.
Oscar Newman, Architect
James H. Ogden, R.A., Swanke Hayden Connell Taylor-Clark
     Architects
Raymond C. Ovresat, AIA, Perkins and Will, Architects
James A. Paddock, Dober, Paddock, Upton and Associates, Inc.
Michael Palmer, AIA, Perkins and Will, Architects
Julius Panero, Architect and Urban Planning Consultant
W. Russell Parker, Architect
Richard H. Penner
Robert Perlman

Luis F. Pitarque, HDR Architecture, Inc.
Frank Harrison Randolph, P.E., Cornell University
Kenneth Ricci, Architect
Scott Turner Ritenour
H. W. Robinson, University of Oregon
Herbert Ross, Industrial Designer
Richard F. Roti
Walter A. Rutes
Christine F. Salmon, AIA
F. Cuthbert Salmon, AIA
Maurice R. Salo, AIA, Consulting Architect to the Lutheran Church
    in America
Paul Scarbrough, AMS Acoustics
Ben Schlanger, Architect and Theater Consultant
Myron E. Schoen, F.T.A., Commission on Synagogue Administration
Richard Schoenhardt, Schoenhardt Architects, Inc.
Max B. Schreiber, Architect
Walter E. Schultz, Architectural Consultant
Samuel Selden
Alex Shirshun, HarleyEllis Architects

Peter C. Smith, RIBA
R. Jackson Smith, AIA
Bernard Spero
William Staniar, M.E.
Mark D. Stumer, AIA, Mojo Stumer Architects
Chris Suffecool, Perkins and Will, Architects
Wilbur R. Taylor, Architect
Margaret E. Terrell
James G. Terrill, Jr.
George H. Tryon
Donald B. Tweedy
Howard P. Vermilya, AIA
Sandra Vlock, Arbonies King Vlock Architects
Joshua H. Vogel, AIA
James Wentling, FAIA
Donald C. Westphal, Donald C. Westphal Associates
Mildred C. Widber
Philip Will, Jr., AIA, Perkins and Will, Architects
Mary Worthen, Architect
Martin Zelnik, AIA

American Association for Health, Physical Education, and Recreation
American Association for State and Local History
American Association of Port Authorities
American Association of Zoological Parks and Aquariums
American Bar Association
American Library Association
American Medical Association
American Psychiatric Association
American Trucking Associations, Inc.
American Youth Hostels, Inc.
Association of College Unions International
The Athletic Institute
Boy Scouts of America
Boys' Clubs of America
Brunswick Corp.
Canada Mortgage and Housing Corporation
Canadian Museum Association
Center for Architectural Research, Rensselaer Polytechnic Institute
Civil Aeronautics Administration
Conference Board of Mathematical Sciences
The DeVilbiss Company
Educational Facilities Laboratories
Eno Foundation
Federal Aviation Administration
Federal Housing Administration
Foreign Buildings Office, U.S. Department of State
General Motors Corporation
General Services Administration
Housing and Home Finance Agency
Housing Research Center, Cornell University
Humble Oil & Refining Co.
Institute of Outdoor Drama, University of North Carolina
Institute of Traffic Engineers
Interfaith Forum on Religion, Art, and Architecture
International Association of Chiefs of Police
International City Managers' Association

International Youth Hostel Federation
Kelley Company, Inc.
Manufactured Housing Institute
Michigan State Housing Development Authority
Mosler Safe Company
Motor Vehicle Manufacturers Association of the U.S., Inc.
Music Educators National Conference
National Association of Engine and Boat Manufacturers, Inc.
National Council on the Aging
National Crushed Stone Association
National Education Association
National Fire Protection Association International
National Fisheries Center and Aquariums
National Foundation of Funeral Service
National Golf Association
National Institute of Mental Health
National Office Products Association
National Recreation and Park Association
National Swimming Pool Institute
New York City Housing Authority
New York State University Construction Fund
Philadelphia Housing Association
Rite-Hite Corp.
Society for College and University Planning
Sustainable Buildings Industries Council
Texas A&M University School of Architecture
United Methodist Church, Board of Global Ministries
U.S. Department of Health and Human Services
U.S. Department of Housing and Urban Development
U.S. Department of the Navy
U.S. Public Health Service
University of California
University of Oregon
University of Washington, Bureau of Government Research and Services
Urban Land Institute
Western States Arts Foundation

*Time-Saver Standards for Building Types* is a handbook providing basic data for the architectural planning of buildings. It provides general criteria for the initial planning and development of the most common building types, such as housing, educational facilities, and cultural institutions. More specifically, it provides the necessary information to establish basic architectural programs, space allocation, and functional relationships for a building's components. The material in this publication is intended to be used to assist in the process of planning and organizing the many varied elements of a building to ensure that the facility functions properly for its intended use. This book does not, as most architectural books, suggest the final esthetic expression of a particular building type. The finished buildings shown are often the work of the knowledgeable professionals who have written or reviewed the various chapters herein, and are included as examples of the application of the principles discussed in the text.

This fourth edition of *Time-Saver Standards for Building Types* continues the tradition of a unique and significant architectural publication. The first edition, published in 1973, established for the first time a comprehensive source of reference material dealing with the functional analysis and standards of all major building types. As a milestone, it made available to the architect and other related design professionals an extensive amount of essential planning data to analyze and organize the planning of successful functional buildings. The second edition, published in 1980, greatly expanded the scope and depth of the material. It added new building types and updated the criteria for those already presented. The third edition, published in 1990, continued to refine and update the current planning data and building criteria. It also added more building types that had evolved over the previous decade. The use of computers and the Internet is significantly affecting our society and the building environment.

New ways of using buildings, accessing information, and new functional programs are affecting architectural design.

A word of caution on the use of this handbook. The material represents basic or general principles, spatial relationships, and design criteria for each building type. This information should be used only as a reference point from which individual or specific design solutions can be established. This material is not intended to give definitive schematics, rigid formulas, or final designs that will automatically provide the solution to a specific design problem. Rather, these design standards and criteria should be only the starting point for further analysis, evaluation, and review of the interrelationships of the elements of each building type. Primarily, the material in this handbook is intended to be used by the architect, related design professional or student in the following manner:

• To assist in developing building programs
• To establish preliminary space allocations
• To study general and specific functional relationships
• To assist in the preparation of preliminary architectural designs
• To assist in the evaluation of architectural proposals and projects

Today, many new and exciting challenges are facing the architect and the entire design profession. The most significant are, of course, the computer, the Internet, e-commerce, and wireless communication. They are changing the way we conduct our daily lives, learn in our schools, and operate our businesses. In turn, the organization and functions of our buildings are being significantly affected. Therefore, we must be fully prepared to meet these emerging challenges; hopefully, this handbook will provide a solid base for these efforts.

*Joseph De Chiara*

JOSEPH DE CHIARA, B.A., M.S., is a practicing architect and city planner in New York City. He has taught at Columbia University, Pratt Institute, Cooper Union, the New York Institute of Technology, and the State University of New York at Farmingdale. He is the coauthor (with Lee E. Koppelman) of *Time-Saver Standards for Site Planning*, the author of the *Handbook of Architectural Details for Commercial Buildings*, and the editor of *Time-Saver Standards for Residential Development*, all published by McGraw-Hill. He received a Bachelor of Architecture degree from Pratt Institute and a Master of Science in city planning from Columbia University.

MICHAEL J. CROSBIE, PH.D., R.A., has made significant contributions to the field of architectural research, journalism, teaching, and practice. He received his Doctor of Philosophy in Architecture from Catholic University and is a registered architect in Connecticut. He has previously served as technical editor for *Architecture: The AIA Journal* and *Progressive Architecture*, is contributing editor to *Construction Specifier* and *ArchitectureWeek.com*, and is the editor-in-chief of *Faith & Form* magazine. He is an associate with Steven Winter Associates, Inc., an architectural research and consulting firm based in Norwalk, Connecticut. He is the author of more than a dozen books on architecture, is an editor of *Time-Saver Standards for Architectural Data*, and has written several hundred articles which have appeared in a number of professional journals. He has been a visiting lecturer/critic at the University of Pennsylvania, Columbia University, University of California–Berkeley, University of Wisconsin–Milwaukee, Yale University, and the Moscow Architectural Institute. He is currently an adjunct professor of architecture at Roger Williams University.

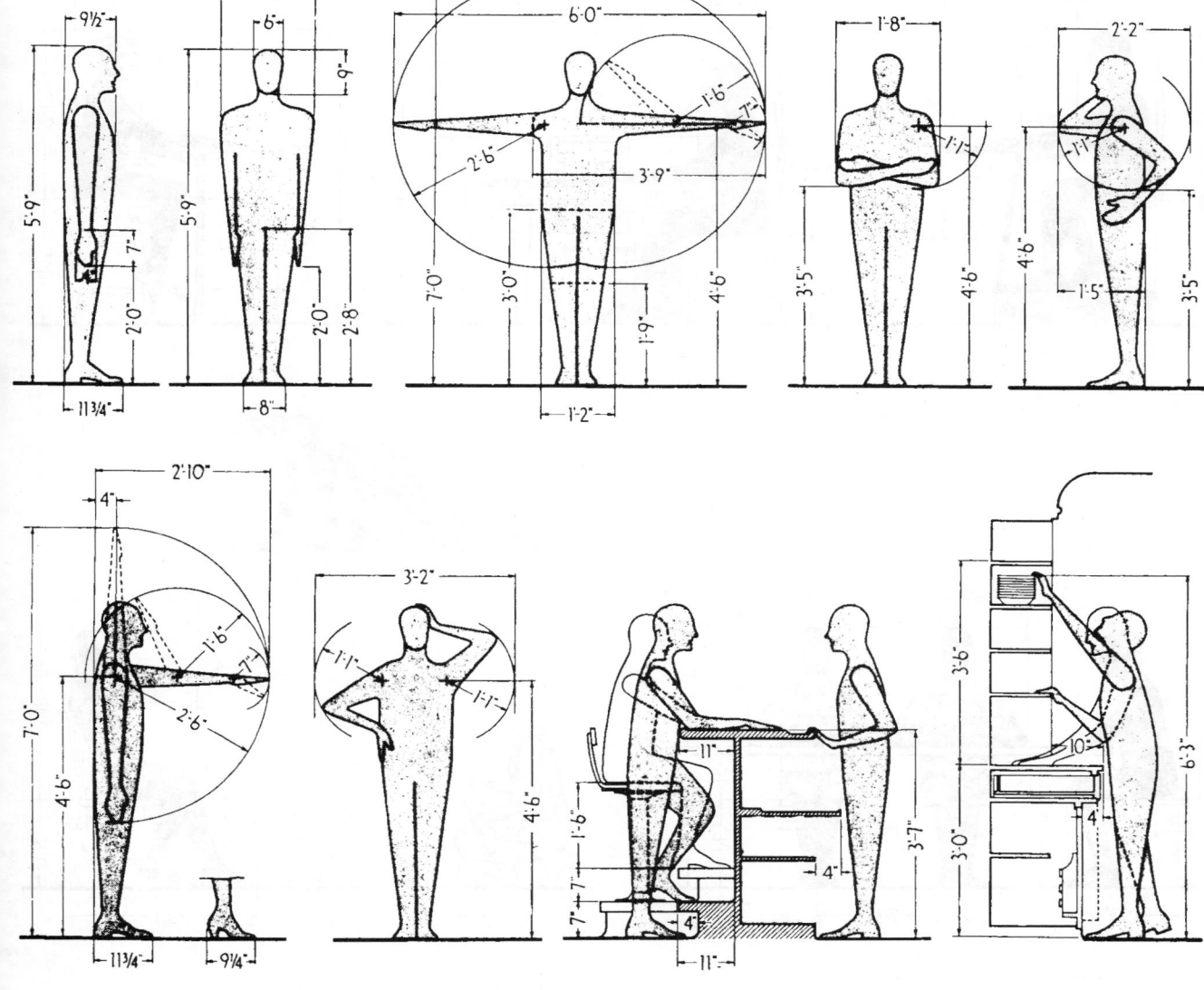

**Fig. 1. Dimensions and clearances for adults**

# DIMENSIONS OF THE HUMAN FIGURE

### DIMENSIONS OF ADULTS

The dimensions and clearances shown for the average adult (Fig. 1) represent minimum requirements for use in planning building layouts and furnishings. If possible, clearances should be increased to allow comfortable accommodations for persons who are larger than average. The height of tabletops shown in Fig. 1 is 2 feet-5 inches; some authorities prefer 2 feet-6 inches, or sometimes 2 feet-6½ inches.

*Reviewer:* James Wentling, FAIA

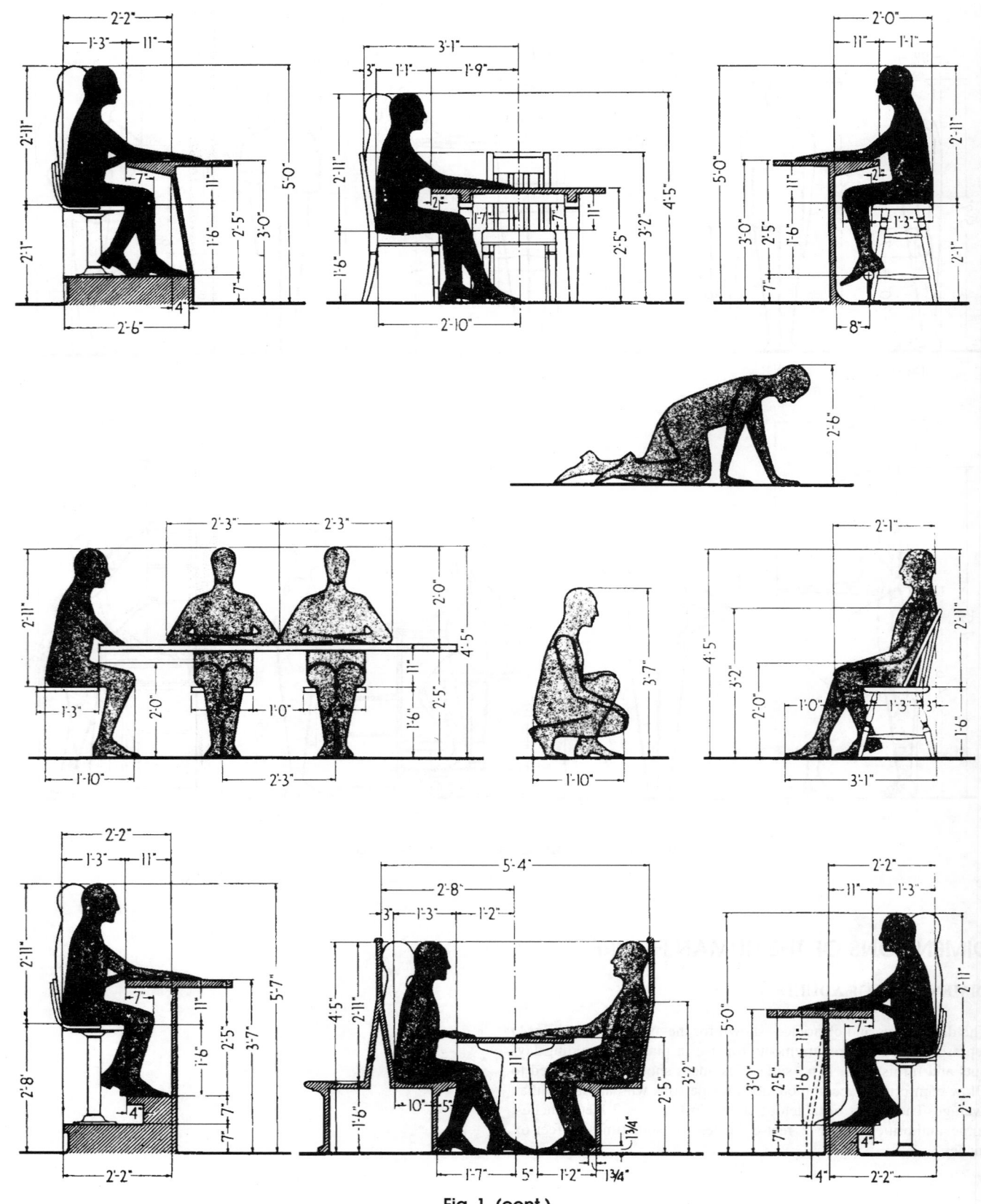

**Fig. 1. (cont.)**

## DIMENSIONS OF CHILDREN

Children do not have the same physical proportions as adults, especially during their early years, and their heights vary greatly, but their space requirements can be approximated from Table 1 and from Fig. 2.

**Table 1** Average height of children

| Age | Height, inches | Age | Height, inches |
|-----|----------------|-----|----------------|
| 5   | 44             | 11  | 56             |
| 6   | 46             | 12  | 58             |
| 7   | 48             | 13  | 60             |
| 8   | 50             | 14  | 62             |
| 9   | 52             | 15  | 64             |
| 10  | 54             | 16  | 66             |

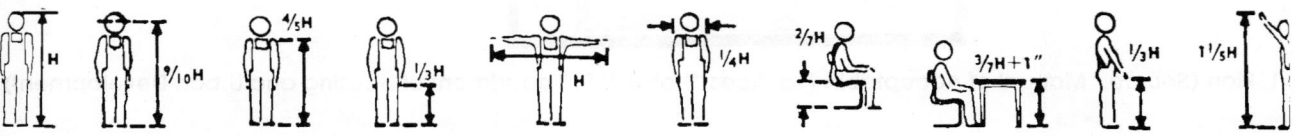

**Fig. 2. Dimensions and clearances for children**

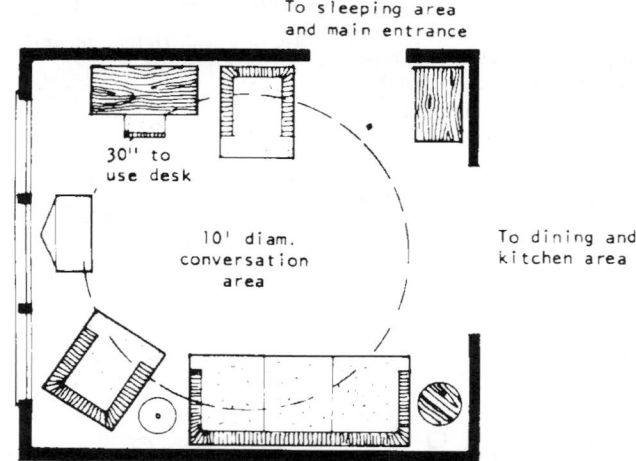

**Fig. 1. Plan** (*Source:* "Manual of Acceptable Practices," Vol. 4, U.S. Department of Housing and Urban Development)

## SINGLE-FAMILY HOMES

### LIVING AREAS

Typical furniture groups in the living and/or family rooms are as follows:

- *Primary conversation group*: Chairs and sofa grouped around a fireplace, window, or view
- *Secondary conversation group:* Chairs and love seat at end of room or in corner
- *Reading group or groups:* Chair, Ottoman, lamp, table
- *Writing or study group:* Desk, lamp, one or two chairs, bookcases
- *Music group:* Piano, bench, storage space
- *Game group:* Game table and four chairs
- *Media group:* Home entertainment center and seating for several people

According to the price of a house and the cubic feet allotted to the living room, two or three or all of the furniture-group units may be included.

### Planning Considerations

- Through traffic should be separated from activity centers.
- Openings should be located so as to give enough wall space for various furniture arrangements.
- Convenient access should be provided to doors, windows, electric outlets, thermostats, and heating, ventilation, and air-conditioning (HVAC) supply grills.

### Furniture Clearances

To assure adequate space for convenient use of furniture in the living area, not less than the following clearances should be observed:

- 60 inches between facing seating
- 24 inches where circulation occurs between furniture
- 30 inches for use of desk
- 36 inches for main circulation
- 60 inches between home entertainment center and seating

Seating arranged around a 10-foot-diameter circle (Fig. 1) makes a comfortable grouping for conversation. Figure 2 indicates clearances, circulation, and conversation areas.

### Space Function

Primary and secondary activities that usually take place in living rooms or spaces are as follows:

| **Primary Activities** | **Secondary Activities** |
|---|---|
| Entertainment | Dancing |
| Watching television | Hobbies and crafts |
| Listening to music | Eating |
| Reading | Sewing |
| Writing | Playing music |
| Studying | Parties |
| Relaxing | Using home computer—Internet |
| Resting | |
| Children's play | |

### Furniture Requirements

If occupants are to be able to carry out their normal activities in a living area, the size and configuration of the space must accommodate both the furniture and its use. Passive activities, such as listening to music and watching television, will not require as much space for movement in front of furniture as will less sedentary activities, such as entertaining or playing (Figs. 3 to 8).

*Reviewer:* James Wentling, FAIA

to kitchen
36" for main trafficway
Main Traffic through Living Area
10' diameter conversation area
to sleeping
36" for main trafficway
30" to use desk
to Kitchen
Traffic through Living Area
entrance
to sleeping
Main Traffic by passes Living Area
10' dia. conversation area
24" for circulation
30" to use desk.
To kitchen, dining & sleeping
Entrance
36" for main trafficway
Traffic through Living Area
30" to use desk.
closet
entrance

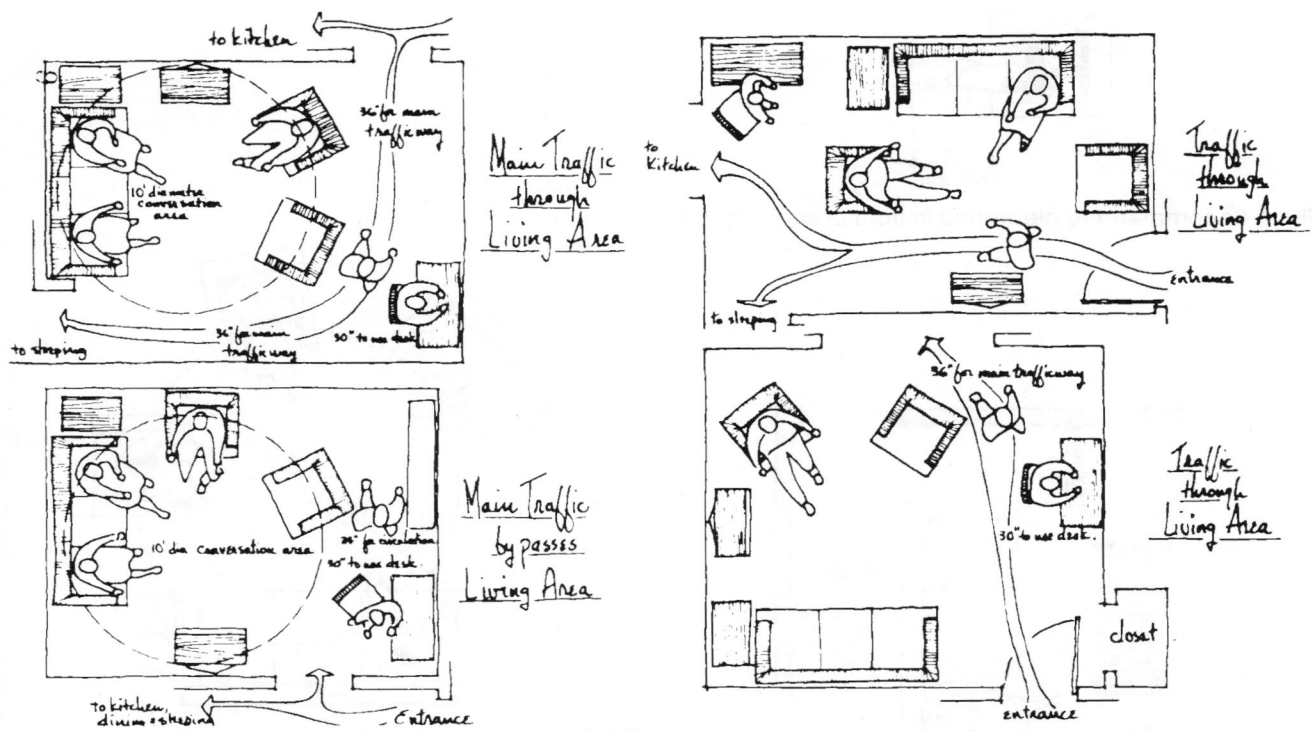

Fig. 2. Minimum clearances, circulation, and conversation areas for living rooms

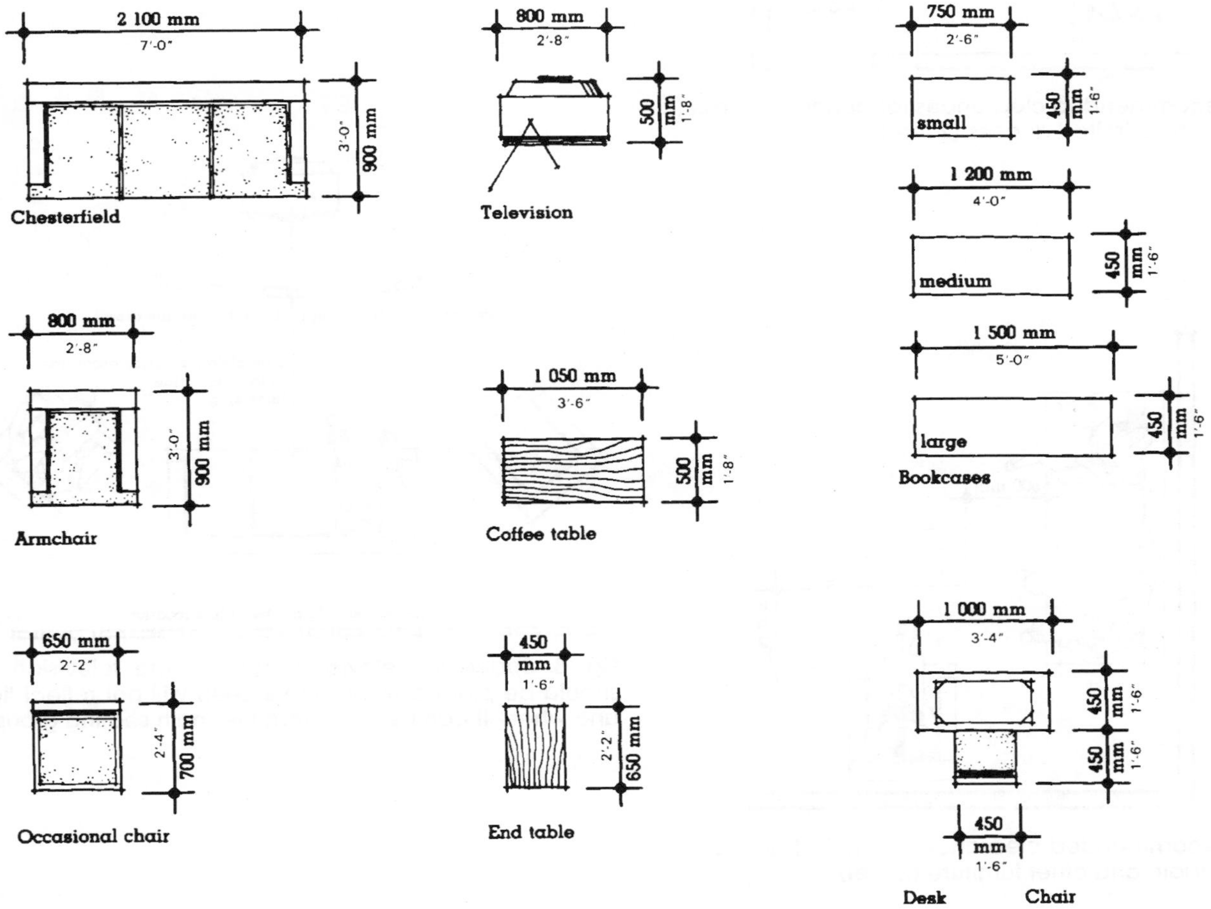

2 100 mm
7'-0"
3'-0"
900 mm
Chesterfield
800 mm
2'-8"
500 mm
1'-8"
Television
750 mm
2'-6"
450 mm
1'-6"
small
1 200 mm
4'-0"
450 mm
1'-6"
medium
1 500 mm
5'-0"
450 mm
1'-6"
large
Bookcases
800 mm
2'-8"
3'-0"
900 mm
Armchair
1 050 mm
3'-6"
500 mm
1'-8"
Coffee table
650 mm
2'-2"
2'-4"
700 mm
Occasional chair
450 mm
1'-6"
2'-2"
650 mm
End table
1 000 mm
3'-4"
450 mm
1'-6"
450 mm
1'-6"
450 mm
1'-6"
Desk
Chair

Fig. 3. Typical living room furniture

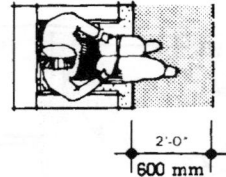

**Fig. 4. Recommended clearance in front of seat (2 feet)**

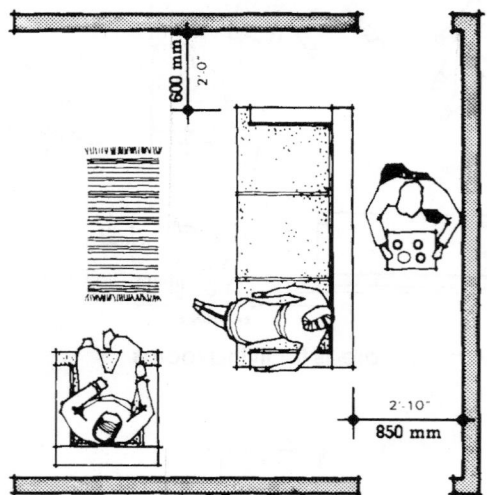

**Fig. 5. Recommended clearances for general access (2 to10 feet) and limited access (2 feet)**

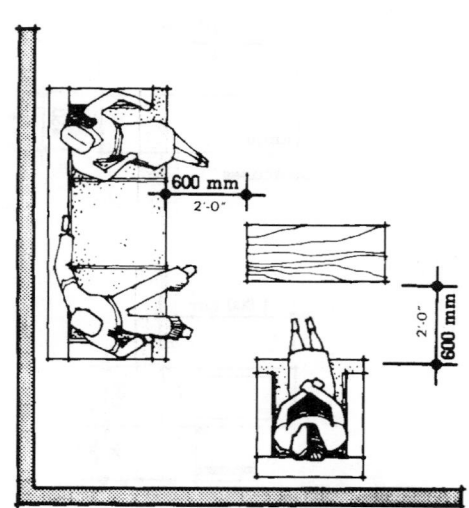

**Fig. 6. Recommended clearance for limited access between a table and other furniture (2 feet)**

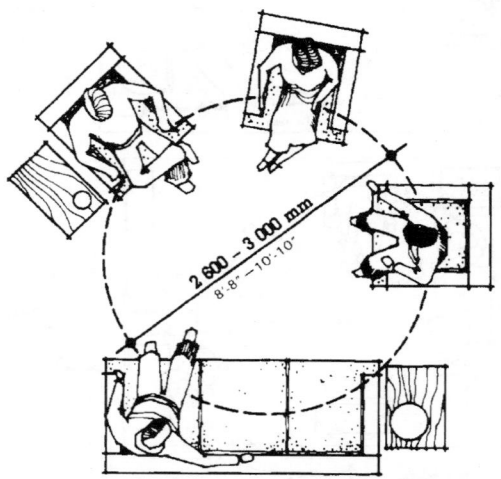

**Fig. 7. Recommended clearance for grouping of seats for social interaction (8 to 10 feet)**

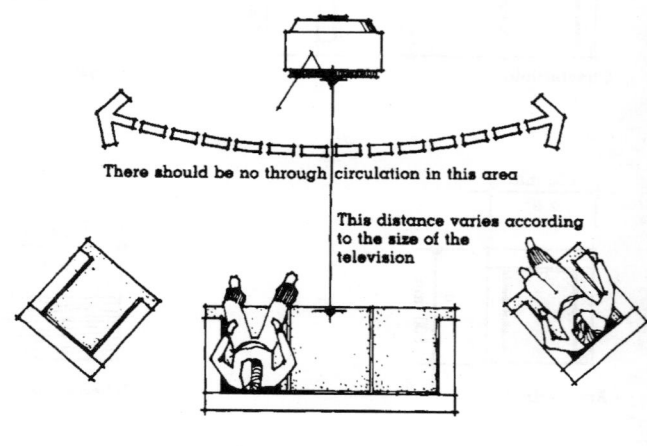

There should be no through circulation in this area

This distance varies according to the size of the television

Windows should not be in this location

**Fig. 8. Space for television viewing. The television set should be placed where the screen will not reflect light and where it can be seen from the main seating group**

## DINING AREAS

### Space Function

Primary and secondary activities that usually take place in dining rooms or spaces are as follows:

| Primary Activities | Secondary Activities |
| --- | --- |
| Setting the table | Children's play |
| Serving food | Reading |
| Eating | Writing |
| Cleaning up after meals | Studying and homework |
| Storing dishes | Entertainment |
| | Board games |

The principal factors to be considered in planning the dining area are as follows:

- Number of persons to be seated
- Space used at the table
- Space for chairs and for passage behind them
- Seating arrangement
- Size and type of furniture
- Storage space for china, glassware, silver, and linen

Recommended space dimensions are provided in the following text.

### Size of Place Setting

The minimum width needed for each place setting is 21 inches; however, a width of up to 29 inches is desirable for greater freedom of movement. A 25-inch width is usually adequate; this permits chairs 19 inches wide to be placed 6 inches apart. The minimum depth for place setting is 14½ inches. These dimensions allow space for china, glassware, silver, and elbow extension (see Fig. 1).

### Passage Behind Chairs

The minimum space recommended for passage behind chairs is 22 inches; a satisfactory range is 22 to 25 inches. If passage behind the chairs is not required, a minimum of 5 inches plus the depth of the chair must be provided for pushing back the chair when leaving the table (see Figs. 2 to 4).

### Size of Table

The minimum width recommended is 36 inches; a satisfactory width is 36 to 44 inches.

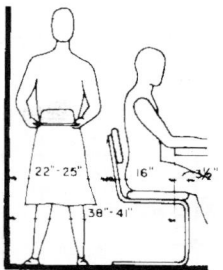

**Fig. 2. Passage behind chairs**

If 25-inch-wide place settings are provided and if one person is seated at each end of the table, then minimum and recommended table lengths are as follows:

| Persons | Minimum, inches | Recommended, inches |
| --- | --- | --- |
| 4 | 54 | 60 |
| 6 | 79 | 84 |
| 8 | 104 | 108 |
| 10 | 129 | 132 |
| 12 | 154 | 156 |

If no one is seated at either end of the table, the length may be reduced by approximately 4 inches.

### Space for Total Dining Area

With the same conditions noted previously and with an ample 42-inch space for passage on all sides of a 42-inch-wide table, required sizes are as follows:

| Persons | W × L, feet | = Area, square feet |
| --- | --- | --- |
| 4 | 10½ × 12 | = 126 |
| 6 | 10½ × 14 | = 147 |
| 8 | 10½ × 16 | = 168 |
| 10 | 10½ × 18 | = 189 |
| 12 | 10½ × 20 | = 210 |

### Storage Space

Linear feet of shelf space required for both moderate and liberal supplies of dishes and glassware for everyday and guest use is as follows:

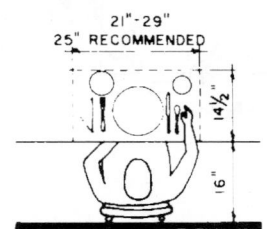

**Fig. 1. Size of place setting**

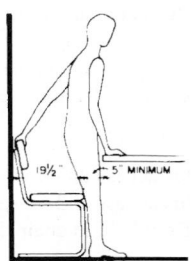

**Fig. 3. Leaving the table**

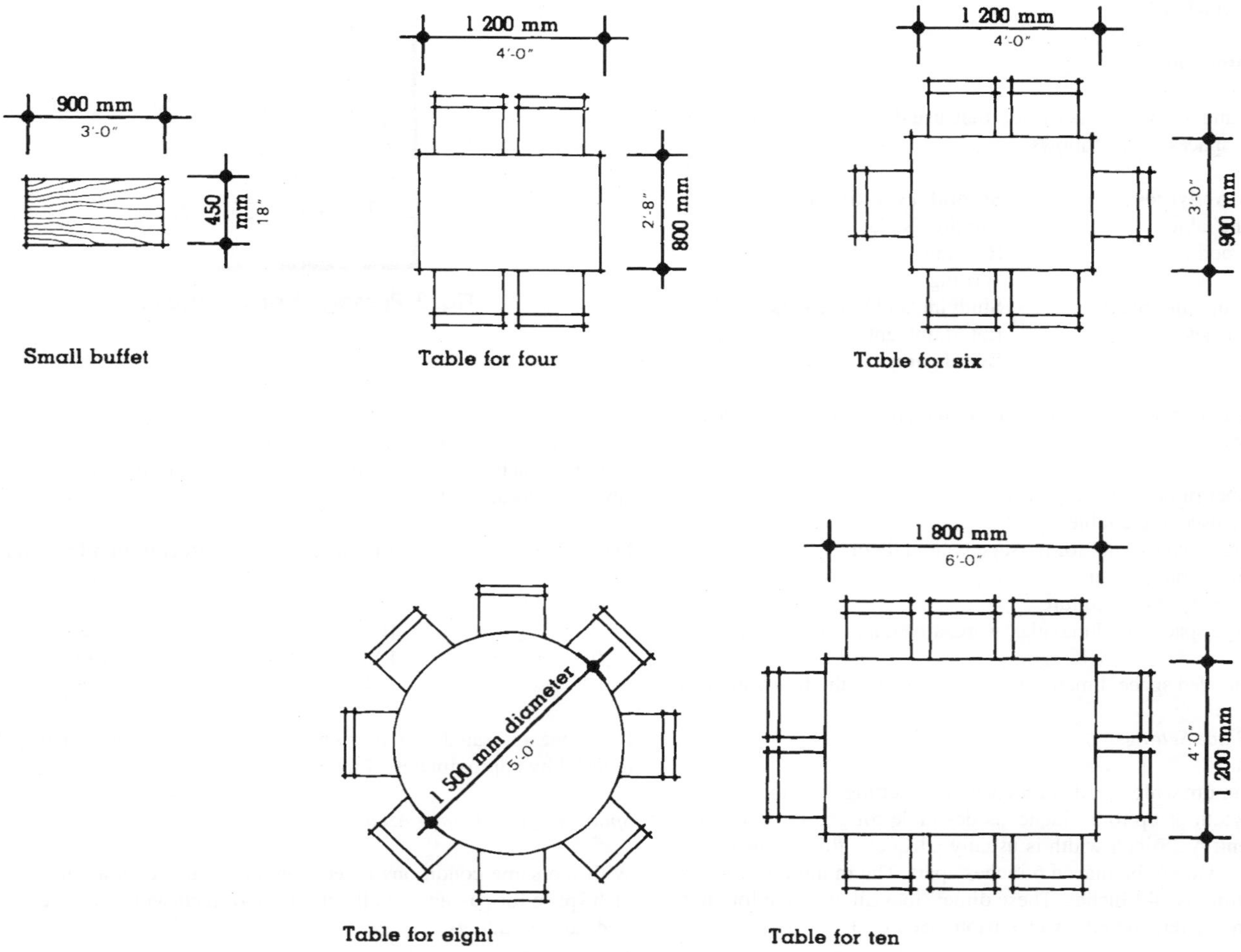

**Small buffet**

900 mm
3'-0"

450 mm
18"

**Table for four**

1 200 mm
4'-0"

800 mm
2'-8"

**Table for six**

1 200 mm
4'-0"

900 mm
3'-0"

**Table for eight**

1 500 mm diameter
5'-0"

**Table for ten**

1 800 mm
6'-0"

1 200 mm
4'-0"

Fig. 4. Typical dining room furniture

| Supply | 12-inch shelves, feet-inches | 20-inch shelves, feet |
|---|---|---|
| Moderate | 21-0 | 2 |
| Liberal | 36-9 | 2 |

**Clearances**

Clearances should be provided in front of and sometimes around furniture in the dining room to allow activities to take place efficiently and in comfort. In some cases, greater clearances are required to accommodate the needs of elderly people, wheelchair users, and those with disabilities.

Recommendations for clearances around furniture are shown in Figs. 5 to 8. Recommendations for net area are shown in Figs. 9 and 10.

To assure adequate space for convenient use of the dining area, not less than the following clearances from the edge of the dining table should be observed.

- 32 inches for chairs plus access thereto
- 38 inches for chairs plus access and passage
- 42 inches for serving from behind chair

- 24 inches for passage only
- 48 inches from table to base cabinet (in dining kitchen)

Figures 11, 12, and 13 illustrate proper clearances.

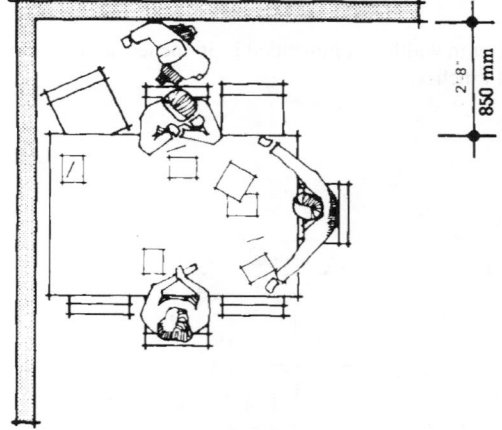

2'-8"
850 mm

Fig. 5. Limited access behind a chair in corner circulation space

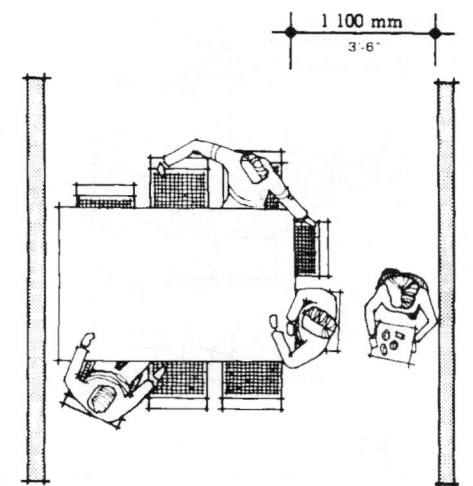

**Fig. 6. Access behind a chair in through circulation space**

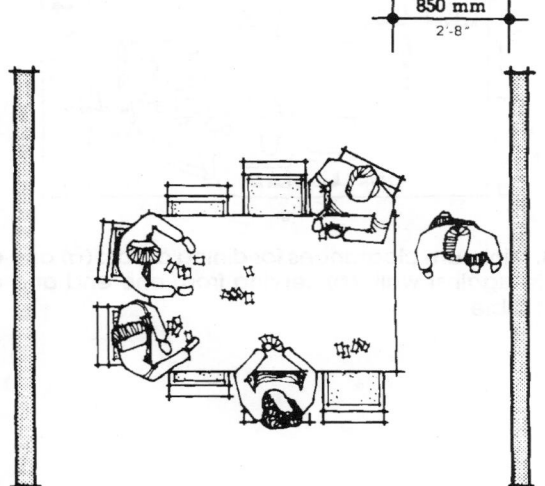

**Fig. 7. Access behind a table and a wall**

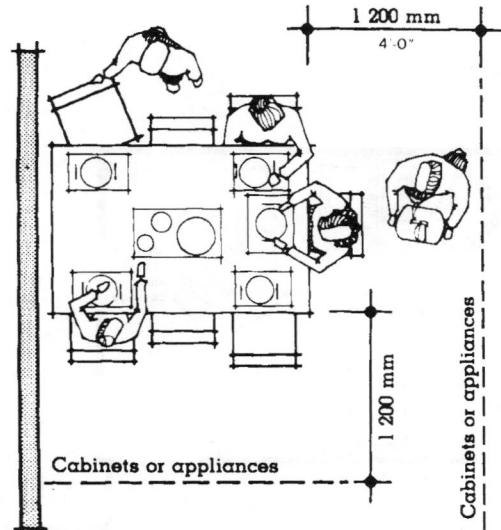

**Fig. 8. Access behind a chair and cabinets or appliances**

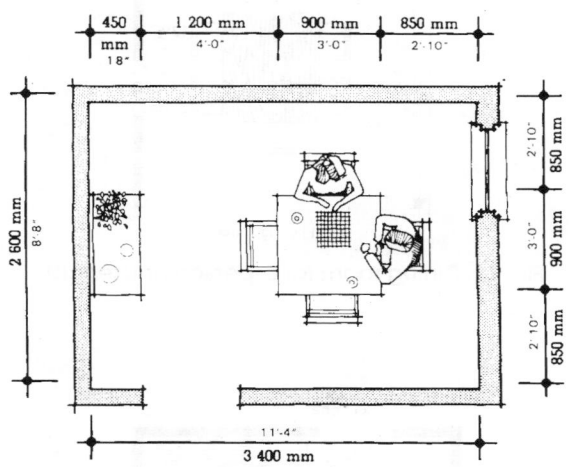

**Fig. 9. Recommended net area for a 2-person household (8.84 square meters)**

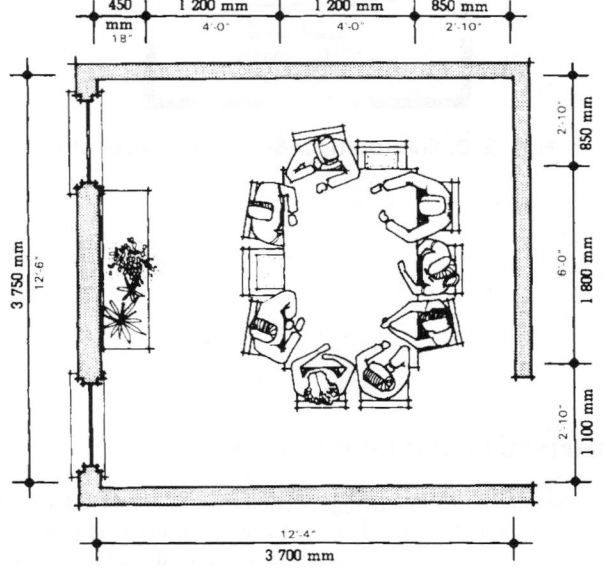

**Fig. 10. Recommended net area for an 8-person household (13.87 square meters)**

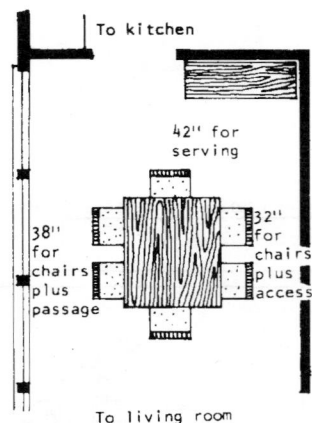

Fig. 11. Dining room for 6-person household

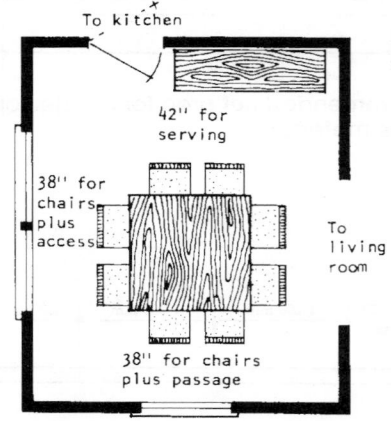

Fig. 12. Dining room for 8-person household

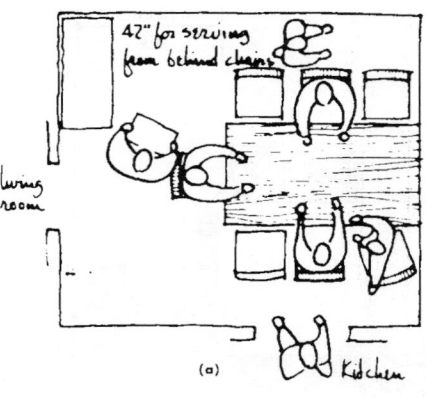

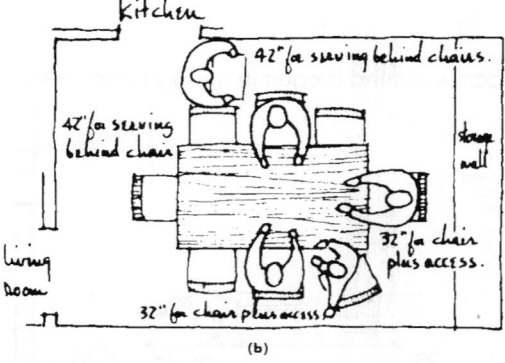

Fig. 13. Minimum clearances for dining areas: (*a*) one end of table against wall; (*b*) serving from one end and one side of table

## COMBINED LIVING-DINING SPACES

Often several compatible living functions can be combined advantageously in a single room. Less space is used, but it is used more intensively. The room's functions can be changed, making it a more flexible and serviceable space. It is adaptable to varied furniture arrangements, while visually it can be made more interesting and seem more generous than if the same functions were dispersed into separate rooms.

For adjacent spaces to be considered a combined room, the clear opening between them should permit common use. This usually necessitates an opening of at least 8 feet. Figures 14 and 15 show combined living-dining rooms.

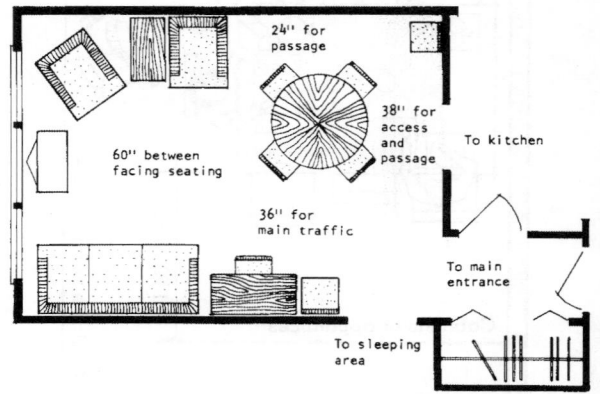

Fig. 14. Combined living-dining room

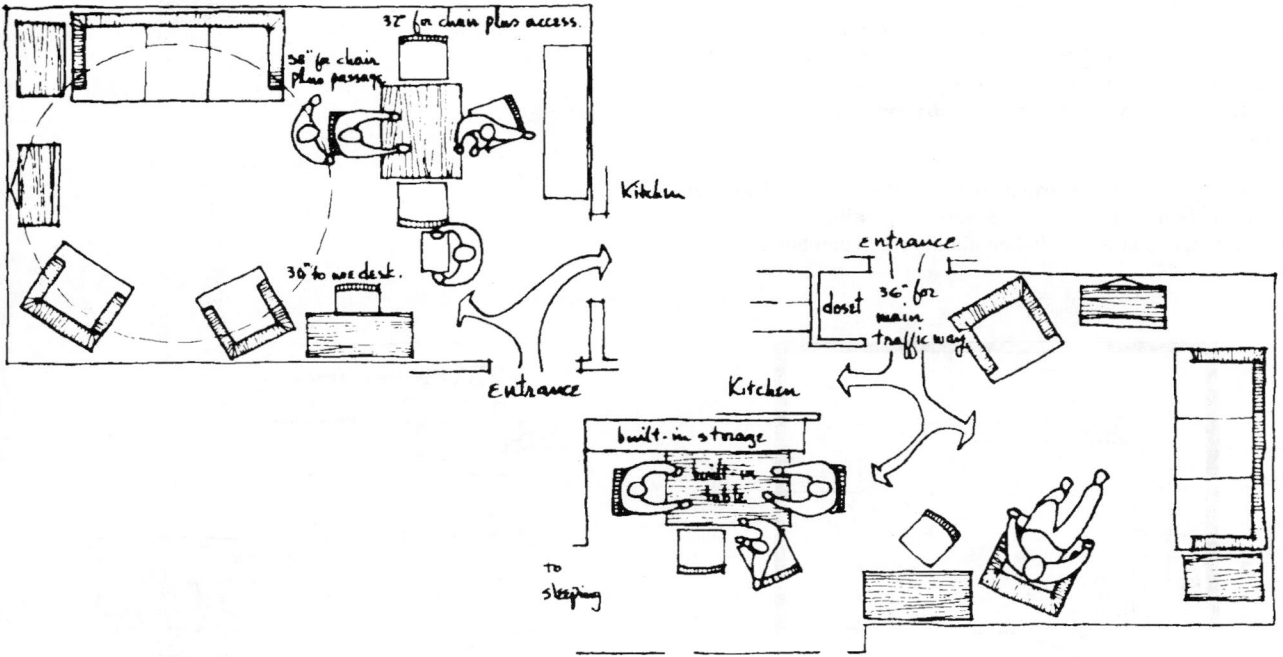

**Fig. 15. Minimum clearances and circulation for combined living-dining areas** (*Source: "Housing for the Elderly Development Process," Michigan State Housing Development Authority*)

## COMBINED DINING AREA–KITCHENS (EAT-IN KITCHENS)

A combination dining area–kitchen or eat-in kitchen is preferred by some occupants of small houses and apartments. This arrangement provides more usable living space throughout the interior (see Figs. 16 and 17).

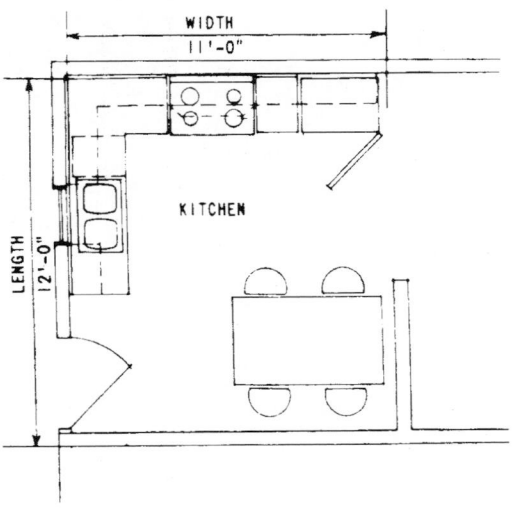

**Fig. 16. Combination dining area-kitchen**

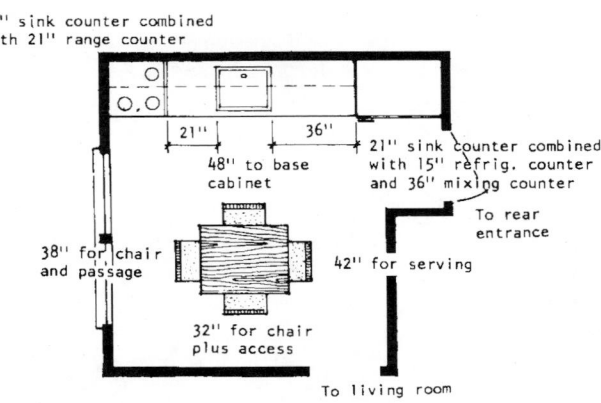

**Fig. 17. Combined dining area-kitchen, 2-bedroom living unit**

One of the primary functions of the kitchen has been to provide a place for informal dining. This is different from formal dining in a separate dining room or area. Informal dining generally consists of breakfast, lunch, snacks, or just serving coffee to a neighbor. This eating area should be clearly defined as a separate functional area (Fig. 18).

A frequent and desirable arrangement is the combined kitchen–dining area. Figure 19 shows the various possible arrangements. Another arrangement is the kitchen–family room combination.

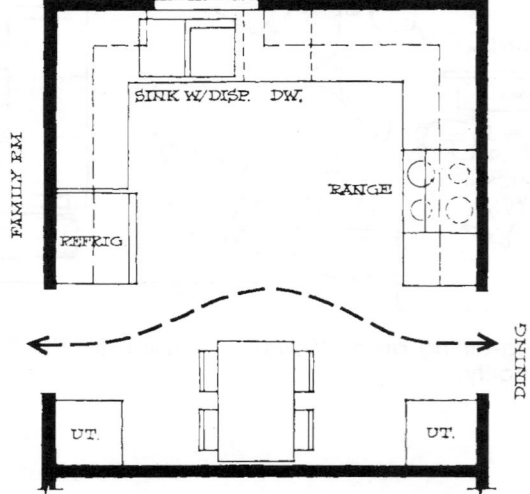

**Fig. 18. Combination dining area-kitchen**

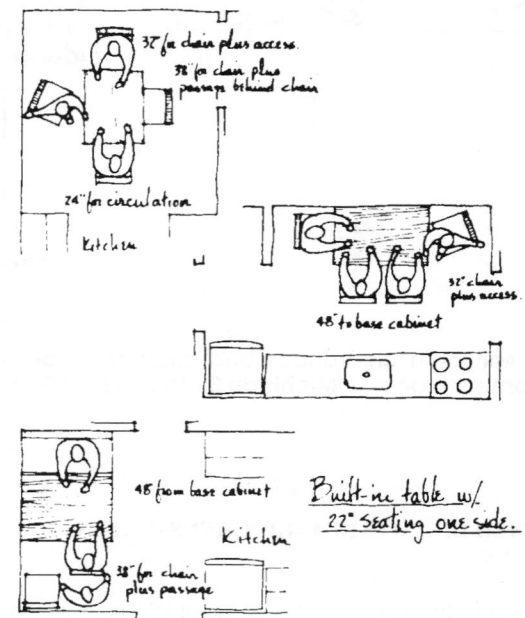

**Fig. 19. Minimum clearances for dining area in kitchen**

# BEDROOMS

## Space Function

Primary and secondary activities that usually take place in bedrooms are as follows:

| **Primary Activities** | **Secondary Activities** |
|---|---|
| Sleeping | Reading |
| Dressing/undressing | Writing |
| Storing clothes | Studying |
| Personal care | Working |
| | Watching television |
| | Home computing/Internet |
| | Listening to music |
| | Children's play |
| | Caring for infants |
| | Ironing |
| | Telephoning |
| | Drawing and painting |
| | Sitting and entertaining |
| | Exercising |
| | Resting and convalescing |
| | Hobbies and crafts |
| | Storing bulky items and seasonal clothes |

## Furniture Requirements

There are minimum requirements for furniture and space if occupants are to be able to carry out their normal bedroom activities.

There are two basic types of bedrooms:

1. *Single-occupancy bedrooms,* which will accommodate one single bed
2. *Double-occupancy bedrooms,* which will accommodate one double bed or two single beds

### Clearances

Clearances should be provided in front of and around furniture in bedrooms so that primary activities can take place efficiently and in comfort (Figs. 1 to 11). In some cases, greater clearances are required to satisfy the needs of elderly people, wheelchair users, and people with disabilities.

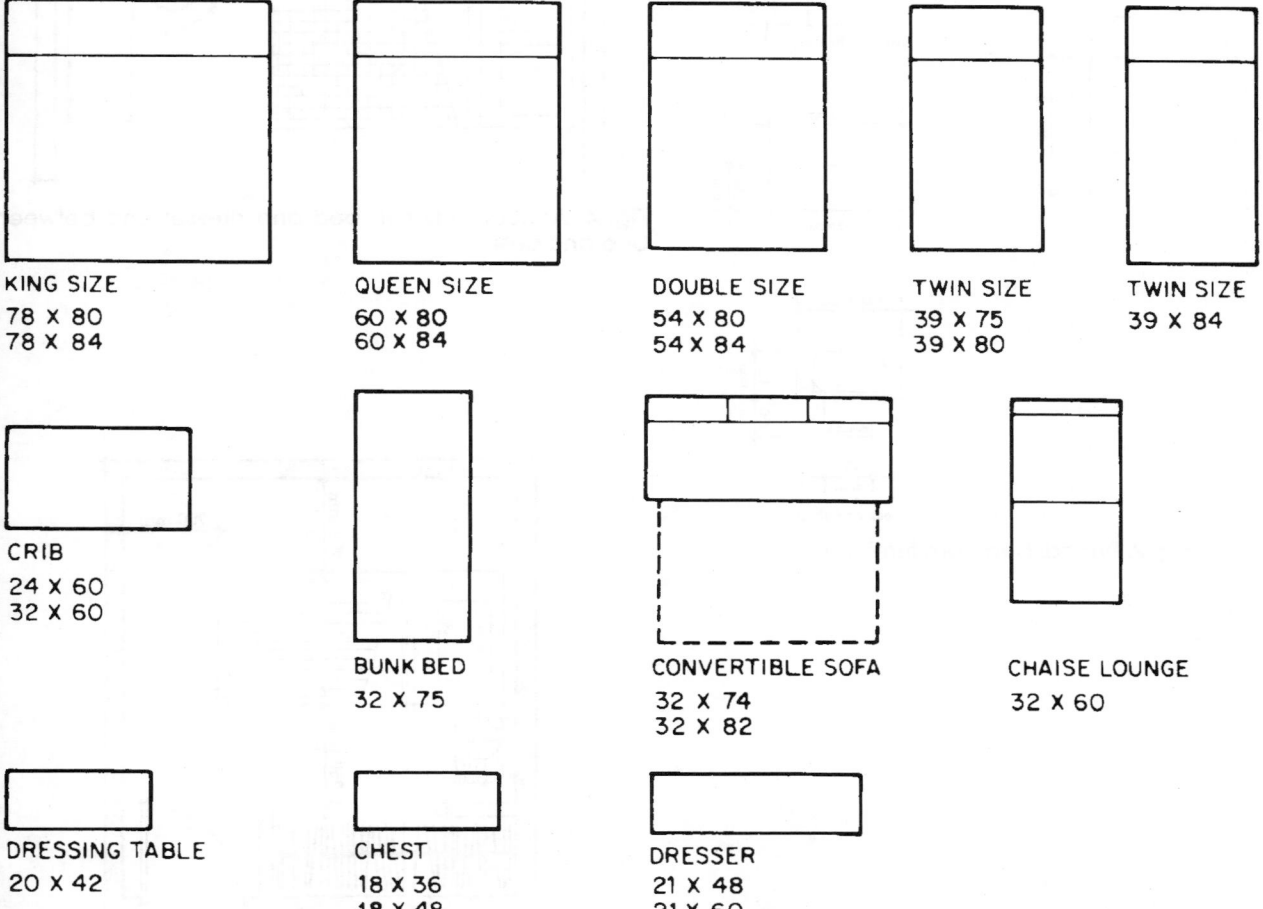

KING SIZE
78 X 80
78 X 84

QUEEN SIZE
60 X 80
60 X 84

DOUBLE SIZE
54 X 80
54 X 84

TWIN SIZE
39 X 75
39 X 80

TWIN SIZE
39 X 84

CRIB
24 X 60
32 X 60

BUNK BED
32 X 75

CONVERTIBLE SOFA
32 X 74
32 X 82

CHAISE LOUNGE
32 X 60

DRESSING TABLE
20 X 42

CHEST
18 X 36
18 X 48

DRESSER
21 X 48
21 X 60

**Fig. 1. Typical average furniture sizes**

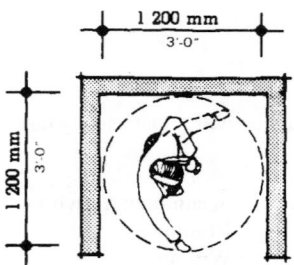

Fig. 3. Space for dressing

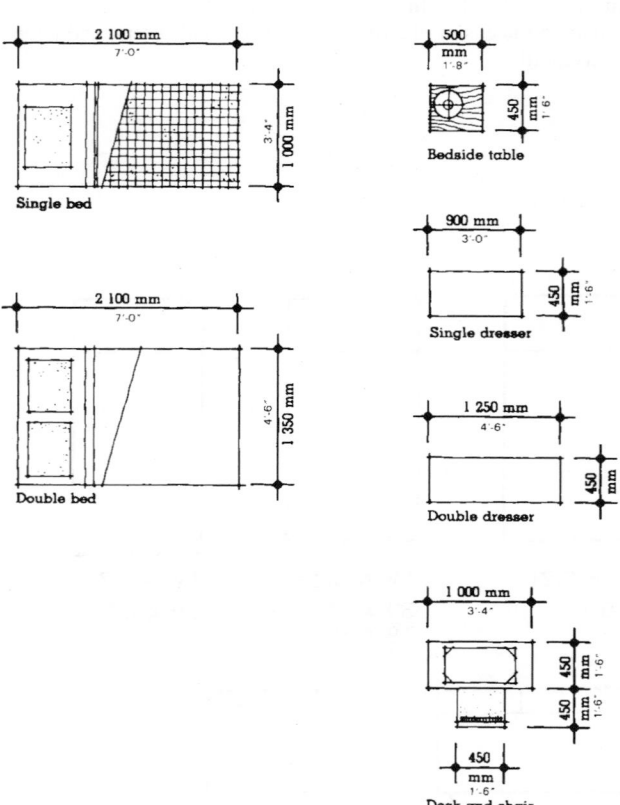

Single bed

Double bed

Bedside table

Single dresser

Double dresser

Desk and chair

Fig. 2. Typical bedroom furniture

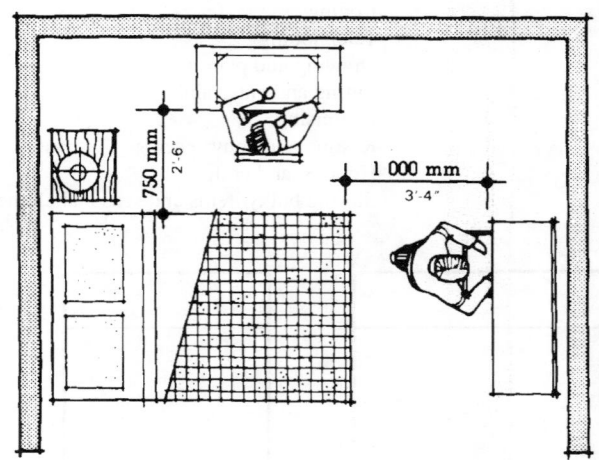

Fig. 4. Access between bed and dresser and between bed and desk

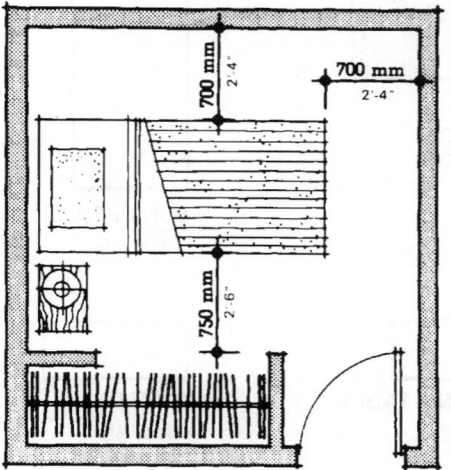

Fig. 5. Access between bed and closet and between bed and wall

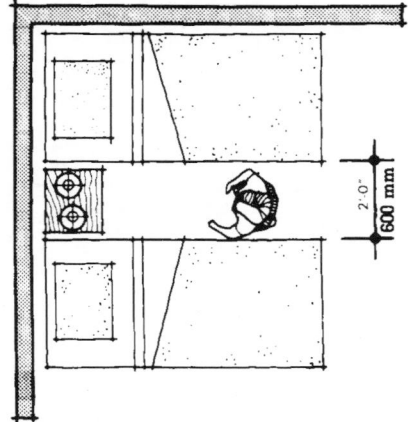

Fig. 6. Access between beds

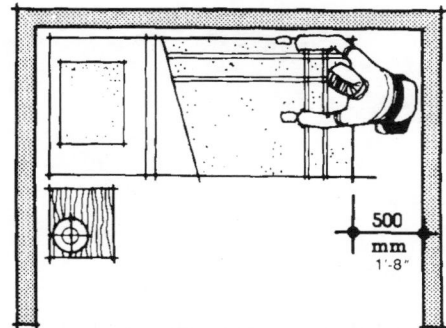

Fig. 7. Space for making beds

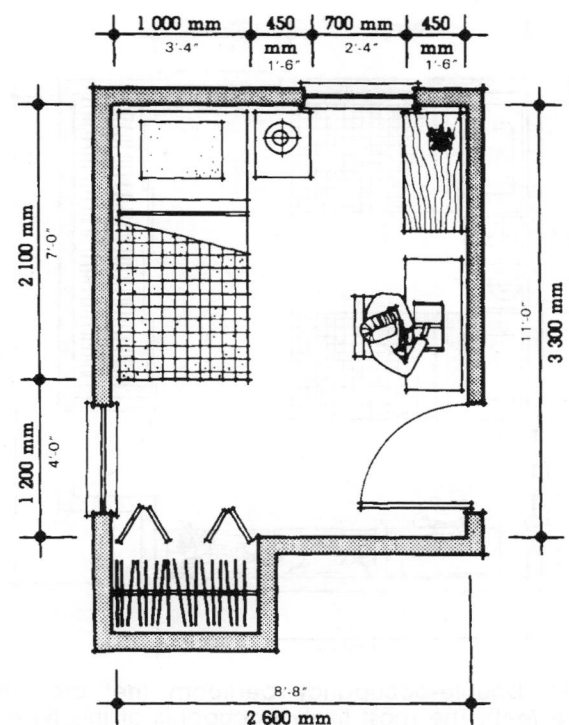

Fig. 9. Single-occupancy bedroom (net area 8.5 square meters). The most likely occupants of this bedroom type are elderly people, adults, teenagers and preadolescent children (i.e., school age children 9 to 12 years old)

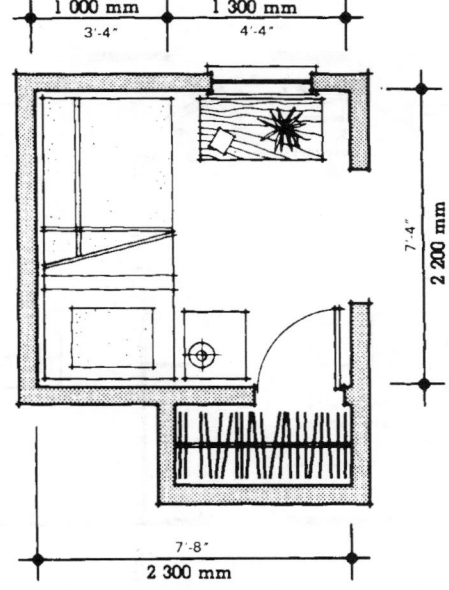

Fig. 8. Single-occupancy bedroom in combination with another space (net area 5 square meters). Adults are most likely to be found in this type of bedroom

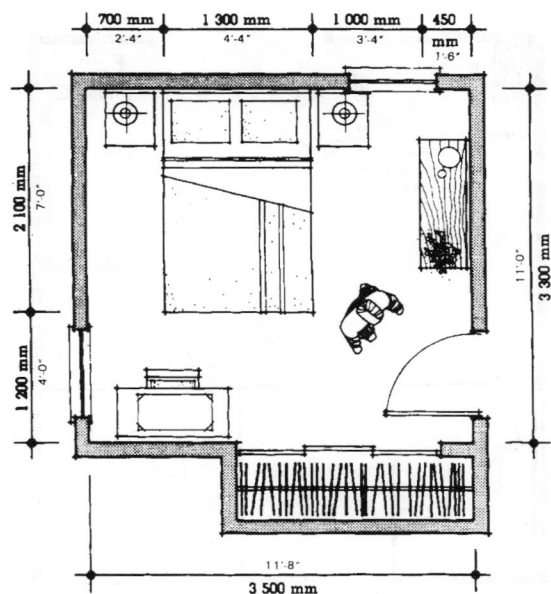

Fig. 10. Double-occupancy bedroom (net area 124 square feet). Adults are the most likely occupants of this type of bedroom

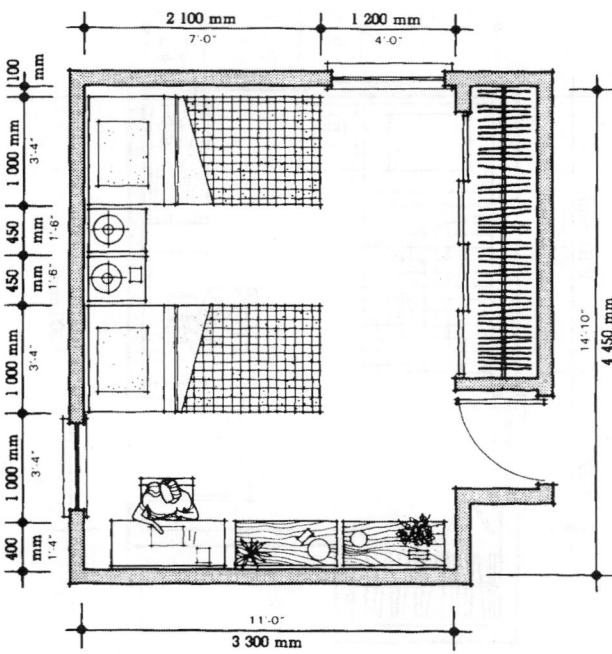

**Fig. 11. Double-occupancy bedroom (net area 160 square feet). The most likely occupants of this type of bedroom are adults, school-age children of the same gender, children of different genders who are less than 9 years old, and preschoolers**

## COMBINED LIVING-SLEEPING AREAS

A bed alcove with natural light and ventilation and which can be screened from the living area is desirable in a studio living unit (Figs. 1 and 2).

In housing for elderly people or people with disabilities, the units suitable for wheelchair users often can be placed advantageously on the ground floor (Fig. 3). Omission of an easy chair is acceptable to give more space for the occupant's wheelchair (Fig. 4).

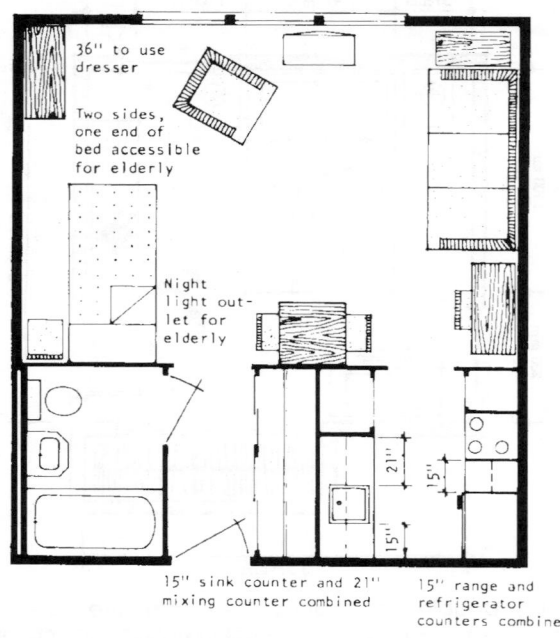

**Fig. 1. Studio living unit**

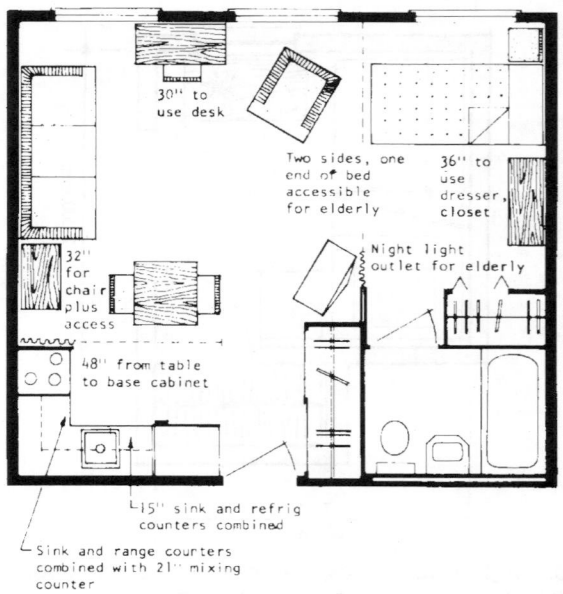

**Fig. 2. Studio living unit with sleeping alcove**

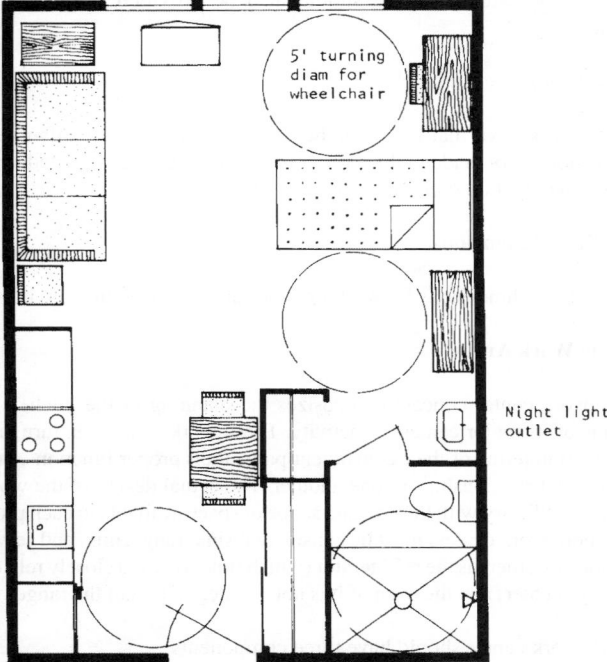

**Fig. 3. Studio living unit for wheelchair user**

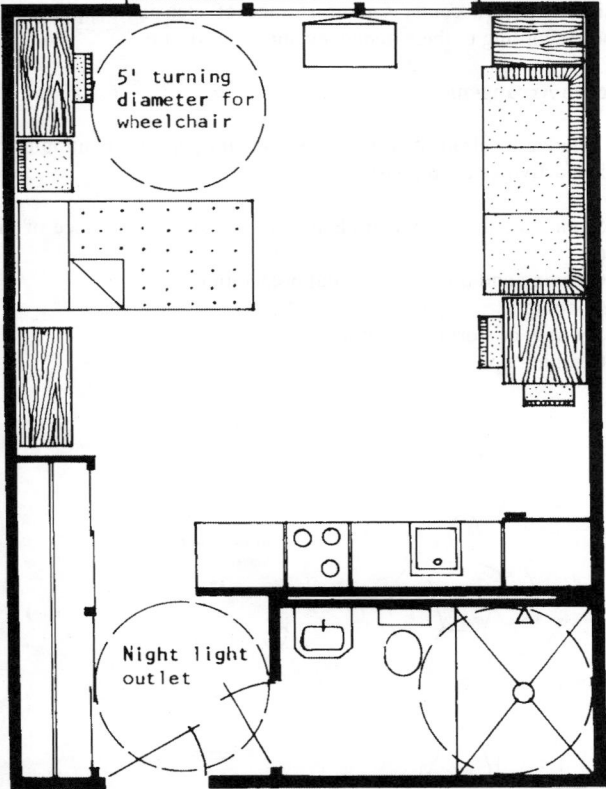

**Fig. 4. Bedroom living unit for wheelchair user**

## HOME OFFICES

A combined sitting-work area permits the user to rotate 180° for ease of access to a lateral file drawer in the rear. If the minimum clearance is not met, access to the file drawer is inhibited, and more awkward body motions or positions for file access are required. The minimum overall dimension to accommodate such a workstation is 96 inches.

If the typical workstation is expanded into the basic U-shaped configuration, the work-activity area dimension range is 46 to 58 inches; additional space is needed to allow for extension of the lateral file drawers. The lateral file unit not only provides more storage, it is generally the same height as the work surface and is often utilized as a supplementary work surface. The distance between this unit and the primary work surface must be sufficient to allow for movement and rotation of the chair.

## KITCHENS

### Food Preparation

*Arrangement*

It is important to keep the basic work area of the kitchen compact, even if the kitchen is open to adjacent living areas. It is common for more than one person to be working there. The arrangement of counters and appliances will vary according to the size and shape of the space available, but one should always keep the working relationships of the kitchen in mind.

*Traffic Lanes*

Traffic lanes through work areas should be avoided. Arrange any secondary entrances from the outside or garage and access to the basements, powder rooms, and the like so that traffic that is not essential to food preparation can bypass the work area.

*Storage*

Kitchen design should be functional in the sense of minimizing reaching and stooping. Storage facilities should be no higher than a person can reach with both feet flat on the floor. There should be sufficient space to store items so that they may be easily seen, reached, grasped, taken down, and put back without excessive strain. With proper planning, stored items can be located close to where they are first used, and some items can be kept out of sight. Storage space should be sufficiently flexible to permit its adjustment to varying amounts, sizes, and kinds of food, supplies, and utensils.

*Counters and Working Surfaces*

The height of counters and working surfaces should permit a comfortable working posture. The worker should be able to sit while doing certain kitchen tasks. Often a desk area may be incorporated into the cabinet layout, to be used as a mini–office space within the kitchen. Continuous lines and surfaces permit ease of movement and are easier to keep clean.

*Authors:* Glenn H. Beyer and Alexander Kira
*Reviewer:* James Wentling, FAIA

*Servicing and Replacement of Appliances*

Consideration should be given to ease of servicing and replacement of major appliances, especially built-in units.

*Materials*

Materials and finishes that minimize maintenance and cleaning should be used, and they should be sufficiently light in color to create a pleasant work atmosphere.

*Lighting*

Good lighting helps to prevent fatigue, as well as promoting safety and a pleasant atmosphere. Comfortable levels of light, with a minimum of shadows, should be planned throughout the kitchen. Adequate daylight or artificial lighting makes the room more agreeable and attractive than a dark or poorly lighted room.

*Ventilation*

The kitchen should be well ventilated, with an exhaust fan to remove odors. An operable window is commonly provided over the sink to allow for a view while working, as well as fresh air.

*Safety*

Burns, scalds, falls, and explosions should be *designed out* of the kitchen. Sharp corners, exposed handles, and control knobs on kitchen equipment should be avoided. Safety catches on doors and drawers limit the exploratory activities of young children.

*Circulation*

There should be easy access to the front and back doors, the laundry area, a telephone, and a powder room from the kitchen.

*Decoration*

Color, texture, and decoration should be used to create an atmosphere that is attractive, cheerful, and restful.

**Other Kitchen Activities**

*Nonworking Areas*

Nonworking areas should be segregated from working areas. Avoid interruption of work areas by breakfast nooks, general storage closets, rest areas, and other areas that are not essential to normal-food preparation activities.

*Eating Facilities*

Most families want to eat everyday meals, particularly breakfast, lunch, and snacks, right in the kitchen. A breakfast area or counter space with seating should be included, even if a separate dining room is also provided.

*Children's Play Area*

In younger families, especially, there is likely to be at least one child who wants to be near the parents. Provision should be made for a play area out from underfoot, but where adequate supervision is possible. Storage space should also be provided for toys and games.

*Infant Care*

It is well known that many kitchens are used to care for infants. If provision is not made in the bathroom for infant care and related supplies, then it should be made in the kitchen.

**Critical Dimensions**

The critical dimensions for working space are illustrated in Figs. 1 to 4.

**Basic Work Areas**

The work center concept emphasizes the planning of the kitchen in terms of its major centers of activity. These work centers, in turn, are planned in terms of their constituent parts, their proper functions, and their ideal relationships to one another. The actual design of the work centers will vary with the size and shape of space available in each project. Four work centers must be considered: sink, range, mix, and serve. In addition, there is the refrigerator (which functions as a closely related storage center) and the oven, if it is not an integral part of the range.

Each work center should have three components:

1. Adequate storage space for the various items used there
2. Adequate counter space for the work to be accomplished
3. Necessary utilities and facilities, such as water at the sink, heat at the range, outlets and space for appliances, and adequate lighting at each center

Equip each work center for the storage of utensils, supplies, and dishes according to their frequency and order of use.

**Kitchen Arrangement**

The relative location of work centers should permit a continuity of kitchen activities as follows:

- Storage (gathering materials needed for the performance of the task)
- Cleaning and mixing (or initial preparation)
- Cooking
- Serving, or storing for future use
- Cleaning up

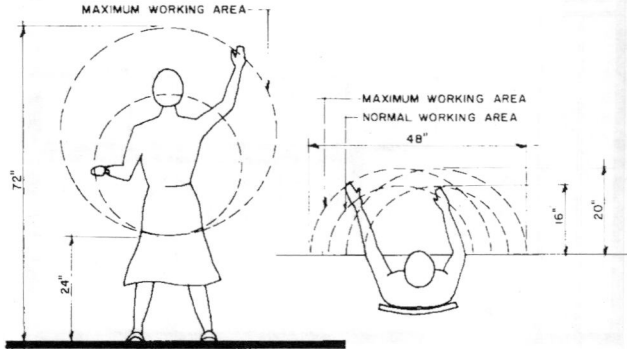

**Fig. 1. Vertical and horizontal limits of reach**

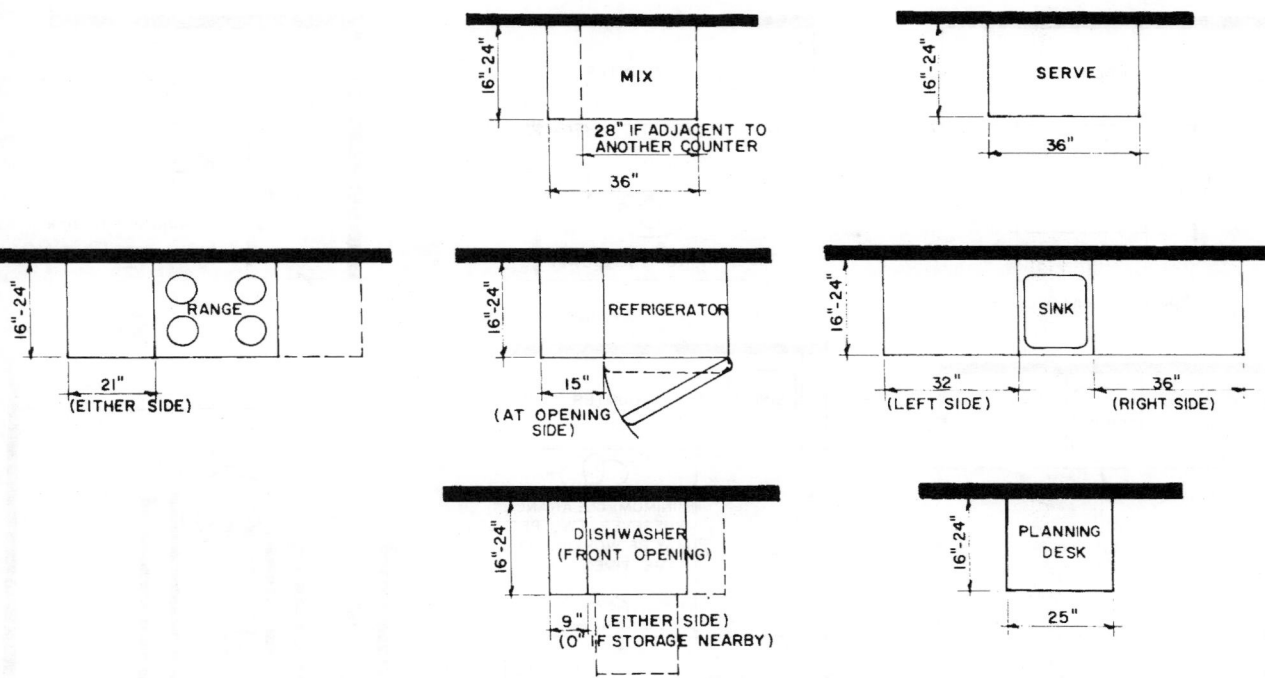

**Fig. 2. Minimum counter-width dimensions**

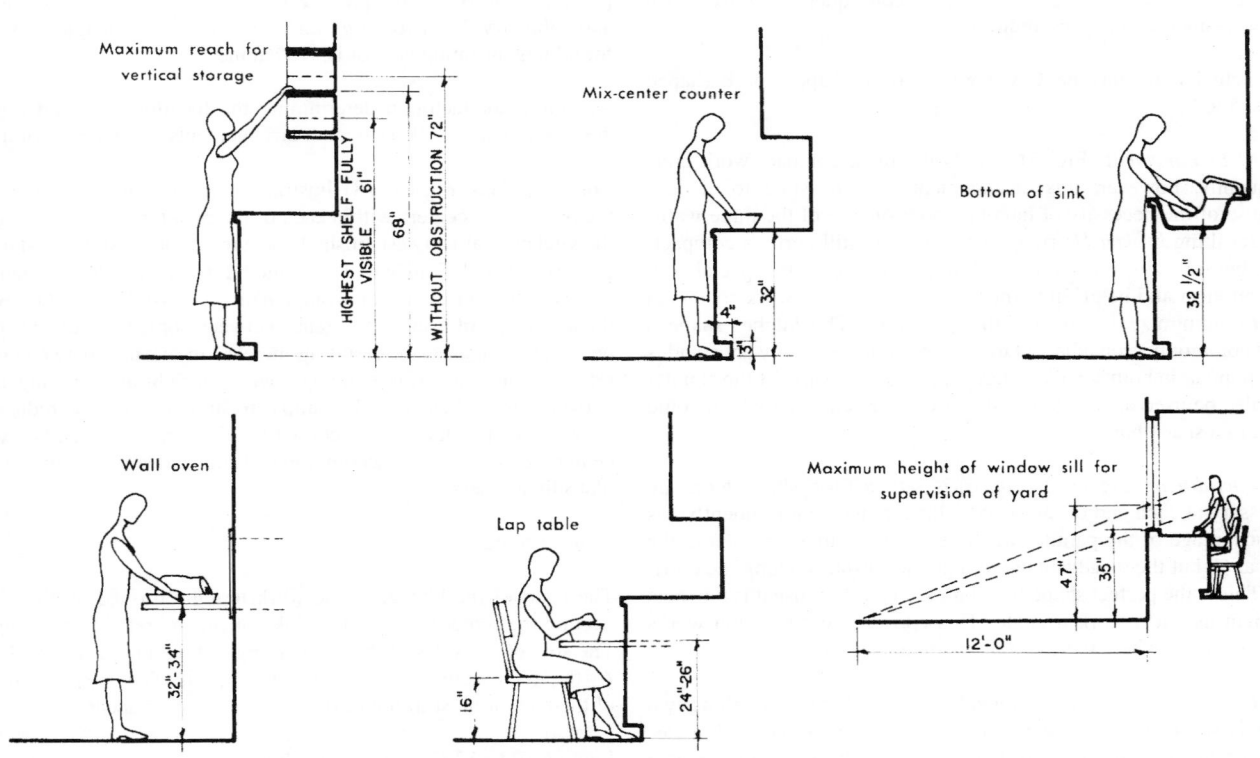

**Fig. 3. Comfortable working heights**

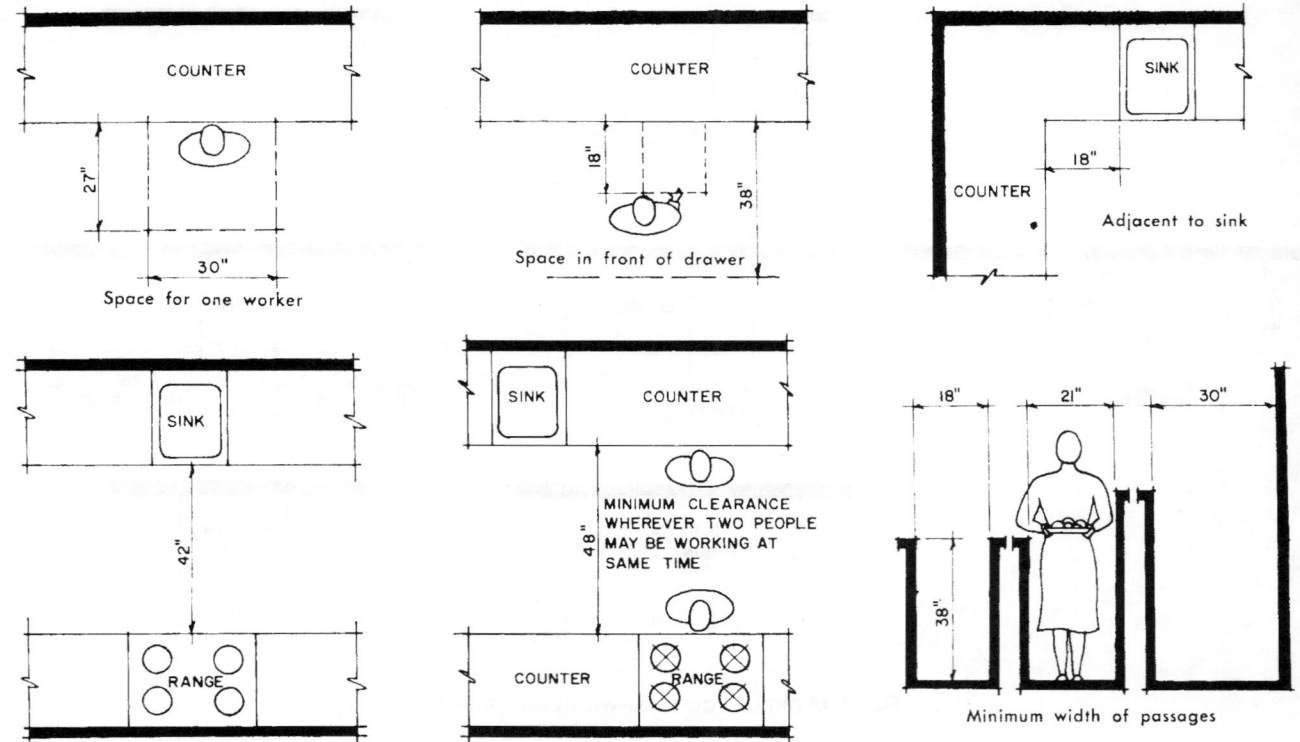

Fig. 4. Minimum clearances—horizontal and vertical

In principle, any plan that interrupts this continuity with doors, or with nonworking areas or facilities, is faulty because extra steps are required every time the gap is crossed; consequently, convenience and working efficiency are reduced.

The actual plan may be U-shaped, corridor-shaped, or L-shaped (Figs. 5 to 8).

The *U arrangement* (Fig. 5) affords the most compact work area. Frequently, however, this arrangement is impossible to achieve because of the necessity of having a door on one of the three walls. The resulting *broken-U* arrangement (Fig. 7) still permits compactness, but traffic is allowed through the area. Therefore, special consideration should be given to the arrangement of the work centers in order to minimize the effect of through traffic. This kitchen shape is most commonly seen adjacent to a dining room or family area, and is very popular in both small and large kitchens. One arm of the counter can also be used as an island cabinet or as a peninsula which could serve as a snack bar.

The *corridor arrangement* (Fig. 6) is satisfactory where doors are necessary at each end of the space. This arrangement frequently has the advantage of the parallel walls being closer together than in the typical U, but the disadvantage of a greater distance along the corridor. This is the perfect shape for small kitchens because it is the most efficient use of a work triangle. This corridor configuration works best, however, where there is a light amount of traffic.

The *L arrangement* (Fig. 8) is ideally suited where space along two walls is sufficient to accommodate all of the necessary work areas. This arrangement has the advantage of concentrating the work area in one corner, thus minimizing travel, but it has the disadvantage of

necessitating longer trips to the extremities of the L. This relationship between refrigerator, sink, and range makes an unbroken traffic flow possible. The two walls provide many options for both appliances and cabinetry. Ideal for large kitchens, this work triangle is perfect for adding an eating area or island cabinet.

An important factor in determining the location of specific work areas within any of these overall arrangements is frequency of use.

The floor plans (Figs. 5 to 8) illustrate some possible arrangements of the basic work centers within each of the plan types. If the space for the kitchen is already established, the number of possible satisfactory arrangements obviously will be limited. If the space is being planned, however, greater choice of arrangements is possible. In either event, the advantage of a shorter distance between some related areas must be balanced against the resulting increase in distance between other related areas. An end-to-end alignment or a right-angle arrangement between areas of close relationship can eliminate trips and reduce the overall travel distances. Functional relationships between key work centers are, of course, accommodated more ideally in some of the plans than others.

**Work Triangle**

The heart of the kitchen is the work triangle formed by lines connecting the center fronts of the sink, range, and refrigerator (Fig. 9). The sum of the sides of the work triangle should not exceed 23 feet. As the major activity area in the kitchen, this triangle should be out of the path of most traffic through the room to adjacent areas.

Figures 10 to 12 show kitchen cabinet dimensions, floor plans, and work flows.

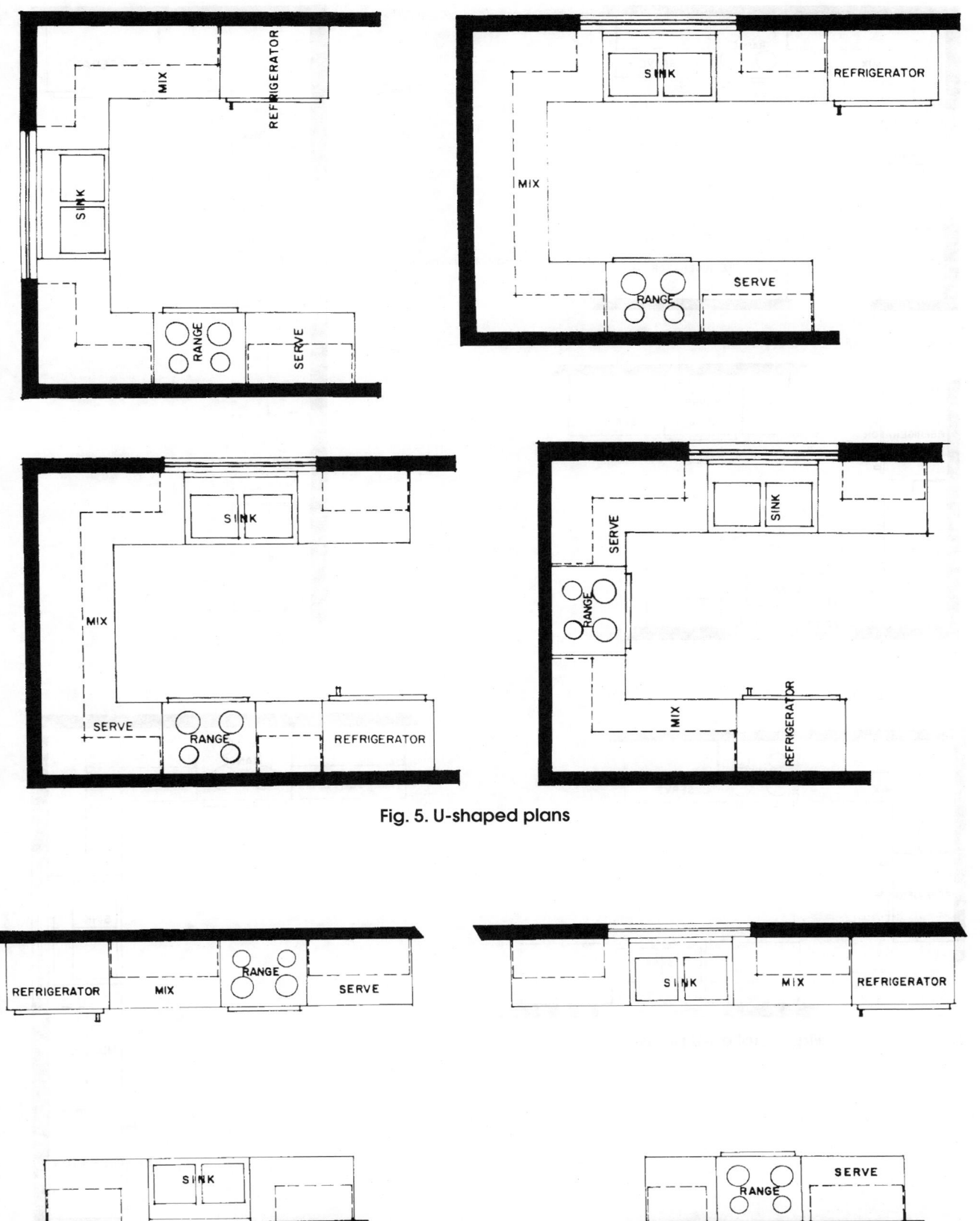

Fig. 5. U-shaped plans

Fig. 6. Corridor plans

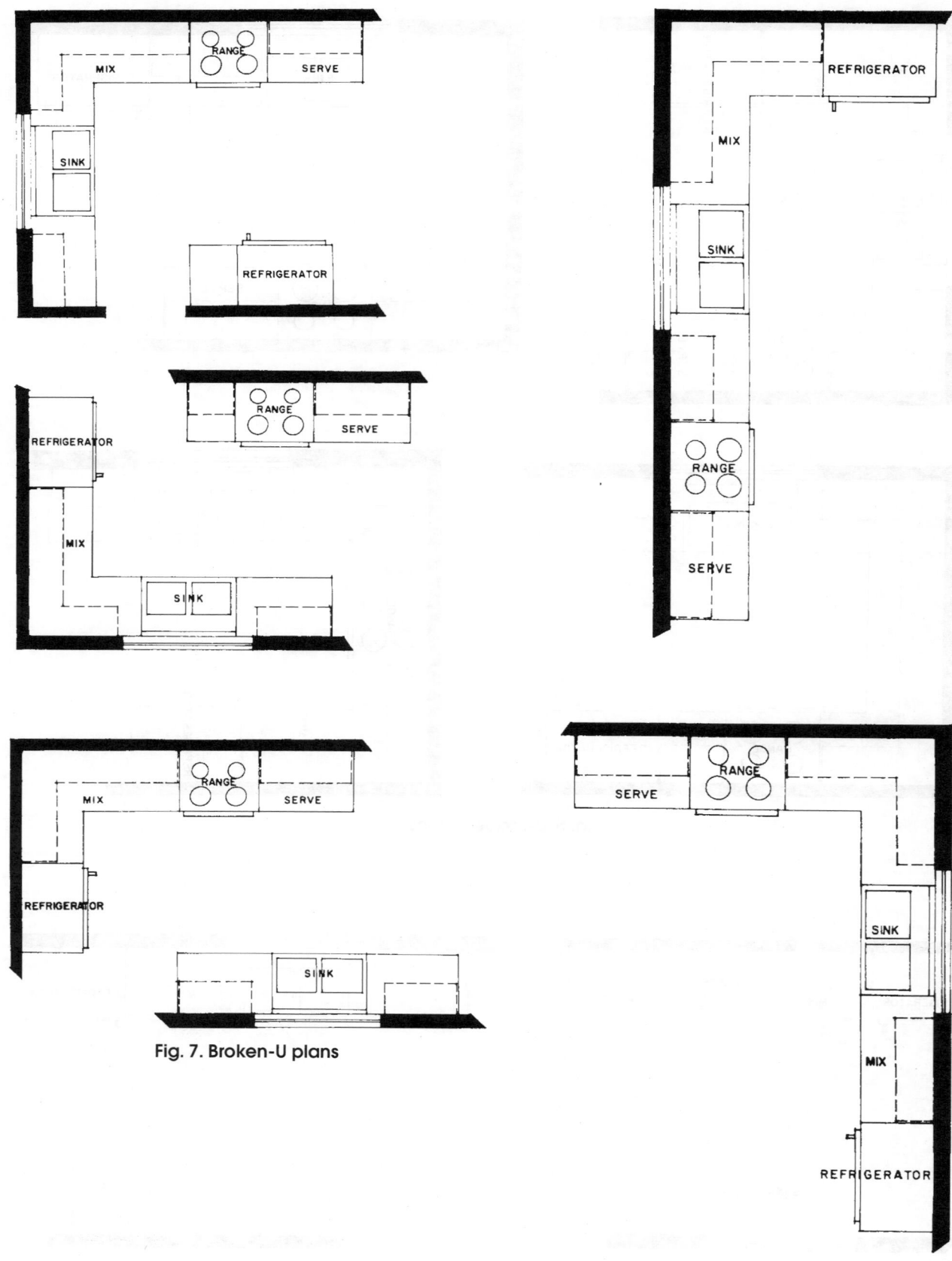

Fig. 7. Broken-U plans

Fig. 8. L-shaped plans

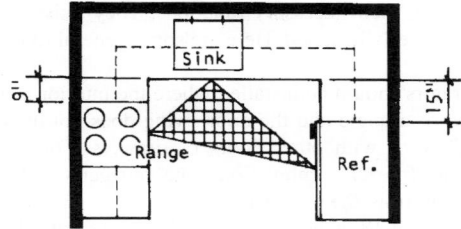

**Fig. 9. Minimum distances from appliances to inside corners of base cabinets**

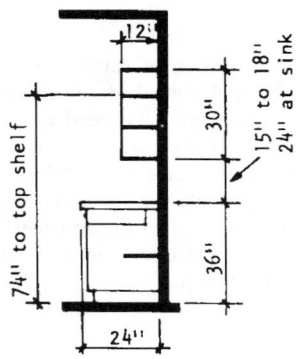

**Fig. 10. Typical cabinet dimensions**

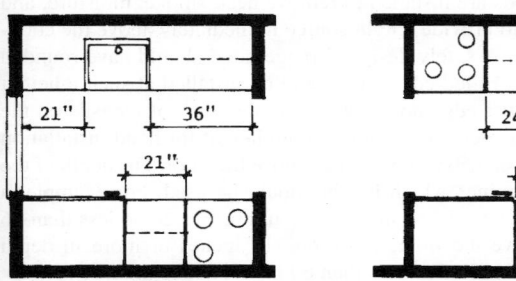
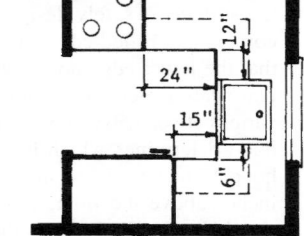

**Fig. 11. Kitchens for small single-family houses or apartment units (with minimum storage, counter area, fixtures)**

## Traffic Flow

Most traffic through a kitchen is bound for the yard or an adjacent dining room or meal-serving area. A combination of hot dishes, appliances, kitchen utensils, and traffic flow can cause accidents. Good planning will keep traffic out of the work area and provide adequate clearance between fixtures and appliances. A minimum of 48 inches should be provided between cabinets and appliances placed opposite each other. When such fixtures are placed at right angles to each other and separated by a passageway, they should be spaced a minimum of 30 inches apart. In an L- or U-shaped kitchen, the minimum edge distance between an appliance and an adjacent corner should be 9 inches from the edge of the sink, 16 inches from the refrigerator, and 14 inches from the center of the nearest range burner. These recommended distances allow people to pass each other safely while using the fixtures, carrying hot food, and opening and closing cabinet and appliance doors and drawers.

## Kitchen Storage

*Total shelf area:* 50 square feet minimum; not less than 20 square feet in either wall or base cabinets.

*Total countertop area:* 11 square feet minimum. (If a 39-inch range is provided, it may be counted as 4 square feet of base-cabinet shelf area and 2 square feet of countertop area.)

*Total drawer area:* 11 square feet minimum.

*Wall shelving:* 74 inches maximum height.

*Countertop:* 38 inches maximum height, 30 inches minimum height.

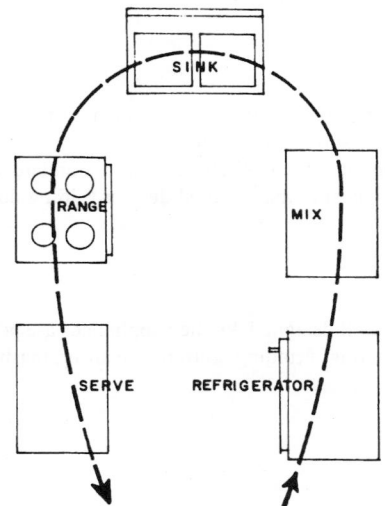

**Fig. 12. Flow of work in food preparation**

*Height between wall cabinets and countertop:* 24 inches minimum over range and sink, 15 inches minimum elsewhere. (Shelving may be closer if it does not project beyond a line drawn from the front edge of the wall cabinet at an angle of 60° to the bottom of the cabinet.)

*Depth of shelving:* Wall shelving—4 inches minimum, 18 inches maximum; base shelving—12 inches minimum, 24 inches maximum; countertop—15 inches minimum, 24 inches maximum.

*Spacing of shelving:* If depth of shelf is 4 to 6 inches, allow 5 inches minimum spacing; if 6 to 10 inches allow 6 inches; if 10 to 15 inches, allow 7 inches; if 15 to 24 inches, allow 10 inches.

*Backsplash (required where countertop abuts walls):* 4 inches minimum height.

*Exhaust fan (required in ceiling or wall near range, or in hood over range):* 15 air changes per hour minimum capacity.

## Cabinets

The size, number, and location of cabinets should be determined while the kitchen is being designed. Base cabinets and countertops with wall cabinets above should not exceed 24 inches in depth. This permits easy access to the rear of wall cabinets without standing on stools or possibly dangerous makeshift climbing aids. For countertops without wall cabinets above, a 30-inch depth is the recommended maximum. The top shelves of cabinets should be placed no more than 72 inches above the floor, and wall-cabinet depth should not exceed 12 inches maximum.

## Countertops

Cabinet countertops should be flush with installed appliances to provide a smooth, clear work area. For convenience and efficiency, a height of 36 inches from the floor is recommended. Most manufacturers design appliances and fixtures for this level of operation. The trim used on countertop edges should be free of sharp edges, burrs, and points.

## Doors

Door swings that conflict with or restrict the use of appliances should be avoided. Doors should be installed to swing against the side or end of a cabinet or out of the kitchen. Where standard hinged doors would present a hazard, the use of sliding or folding doors is recommended.

## Appliances

No matter how well designed, kitchen appliances are potentially hazardous when heating, grinding, cutting, shearing, mashing, or otherwise performing their necessary functions. They must be carefully located and properly installed. Here are some general rules:

- Refrigerators should be installed where the interior is accessible to the work triangle and the door swing does not interfere with traffic flow or with other doors or drawers. For double-door refrigerator/freezer combinations, the refrigerator door should swing away from the work triangle.
- A minimum of 18 inches of counter space on each side of ranges or 24 inches on at least one side of separate oven units provides adjacent space for setting hot utensils, with room for their handles.
- Choose a range with controls located at the front or side and eliminate storage areas above the burners. This reduces the risk of burns from spattering grease, boiling water, or steam and the danger of garments catching fire when reaching over hot burners.
- Range hoods are installed to remove heat, smoke, moisture, and odors and to provide a light source immediately above the cooking surface. A safely designed range hood should have rounded corners and rolled edges. It should be installed at such a height that the lower edge does not restrict the view of utensils on the rear heating elements. The optimum height for hood installation varies between 56 and 60 inches above the floor. The depth of the hood determines which height should be used. For example, a hood 17 inches or less in depth should be placed no less than 56 inches above the floor, while one 18 inches or more in depth should be installed no less than 60 inches above the floor.
- Exhaust systems incorporated within the hood should mechanically direct their flow to the outside atmosphere and not into the attic or other overhead unused space in the house.

## Adaptable Kitchens

Figures 1 to 10 show features of adaptable kitchens.

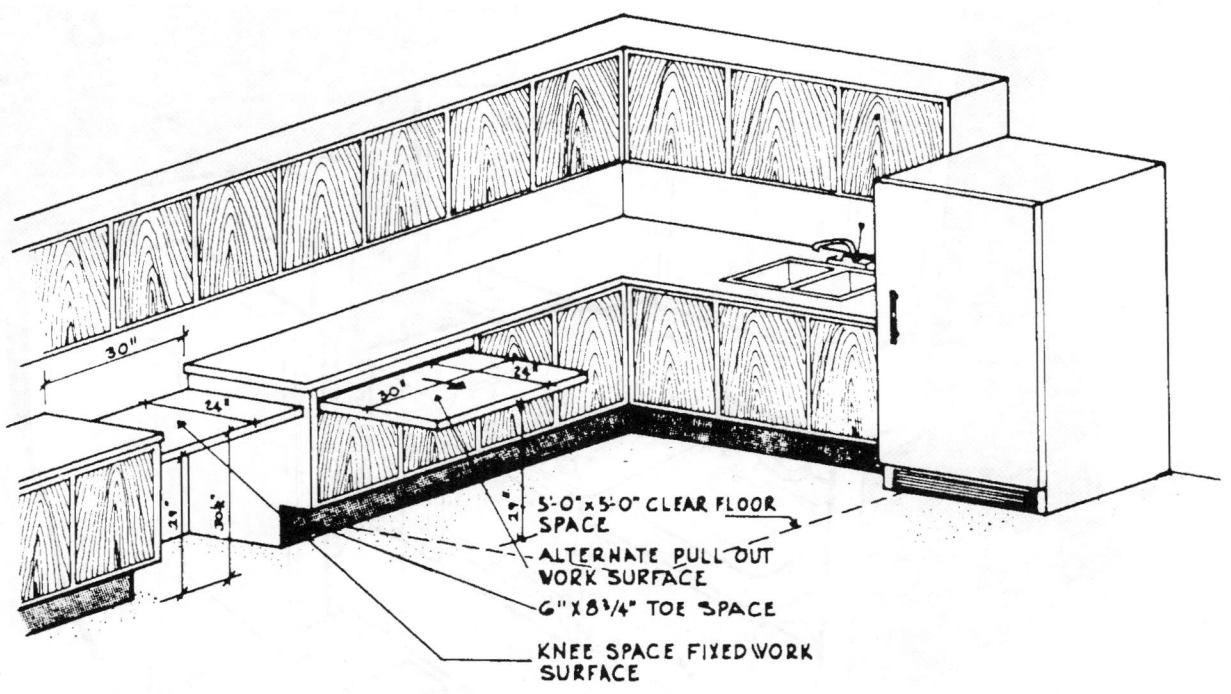

30"

24"

24"

21"

30½"

21"

5'-0" x 5'-0" CLEAR FLOOR
SPACE
ALTERNATE PULL OUT
WORK SURFACE
6" x 8¾" TOE SPACE
KNEE SPACE FIXED WORK
SURFACE

**Fig. 1. Adaptable kitchens**

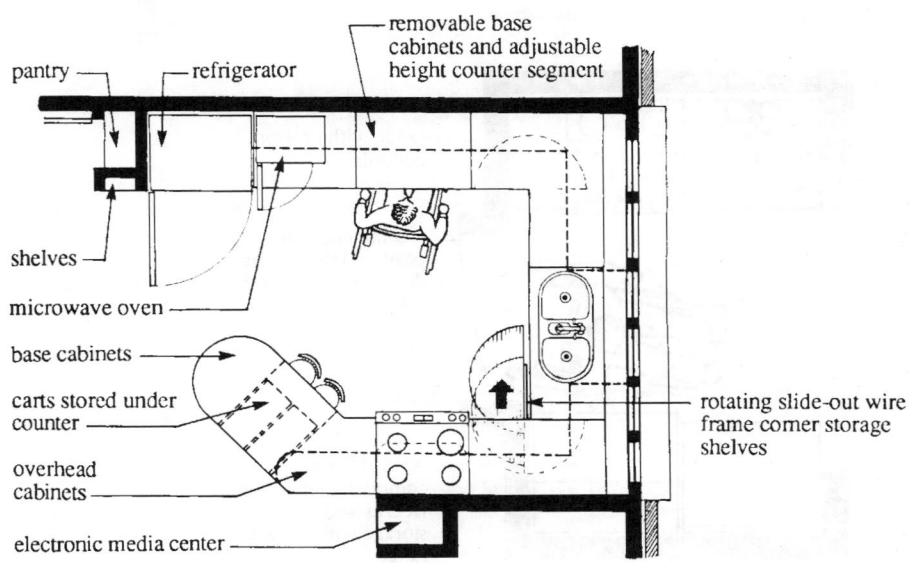

pantry

refrigerator

removable base
cabinets and adjustable
height counter segment

shelves

microwave oven

base cabinets

carts stored under
counter

overhead
cabinets

electronic media center

rotating slide-out wire
frame corner storage
shelves

**Fig. 2. Plan of elaborate kitchen with adaptable features**

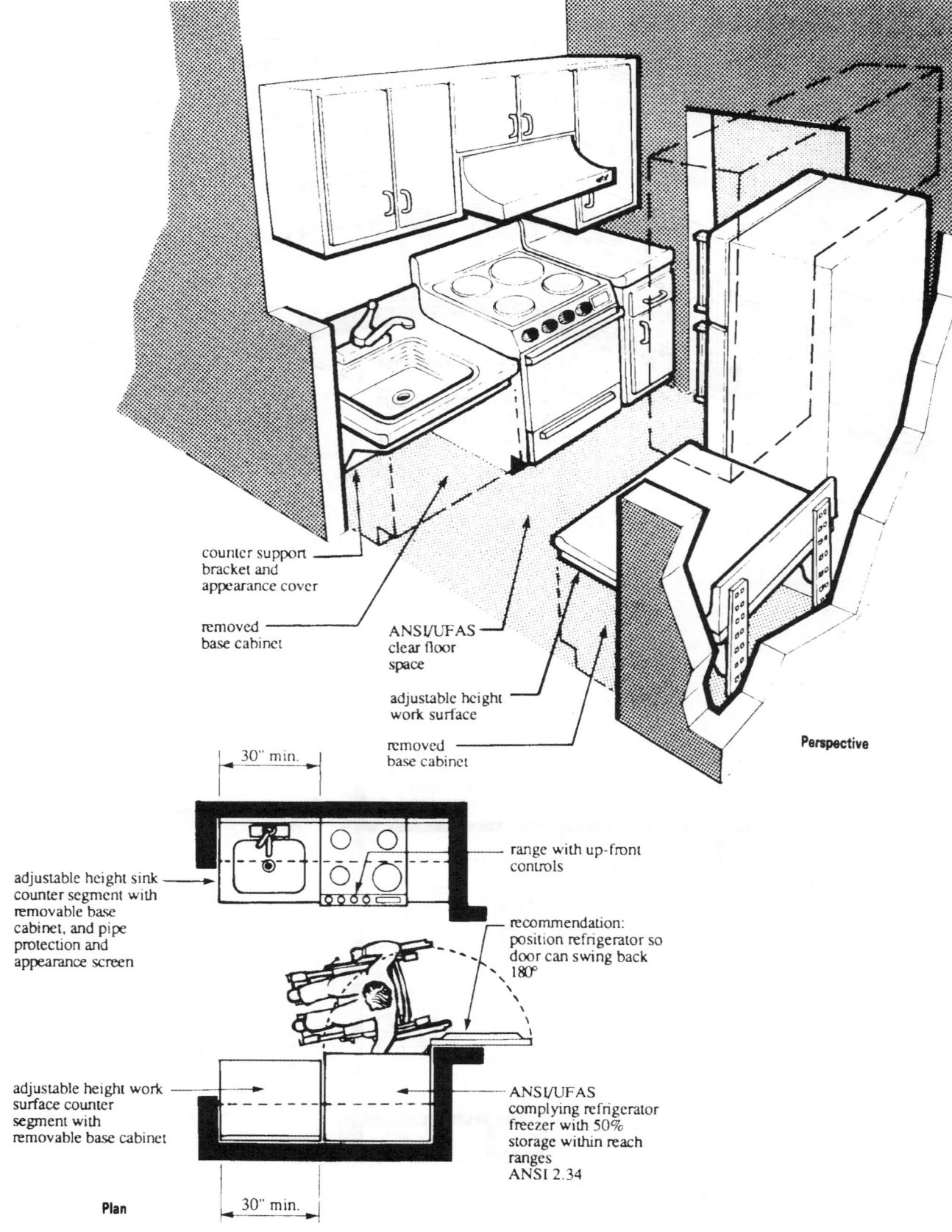

counter support
bracket and
appearance cover

removed
base cabinet

ANSI/UFAS
clear floor
space

adjustable height
work surface

removed
base cabinet

**Perspective**

30" min.

range with up-front
controls

adjustable height sink
counter segment with
removable base
cabinet, and pipe
protection and
appearance screen

recommendation:
position refrigerator so
door can swing back
180°

adjustable height work
surface counter
segment with
removable base cabinet

ANSI/UFAS
complying refrigerator
freezer with 50%
storage within reach
ranges
ANSI 2.34

**Plan**

30" min.

**Fig. 3. Small kitchen with adaptable features**

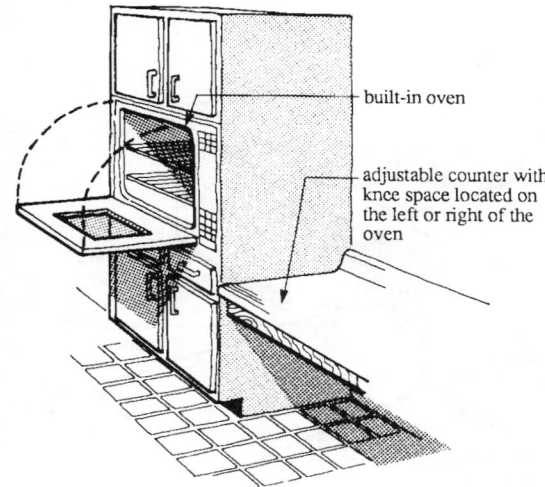

**Fig. 4. Work surface at non-self-cleaning oven with drop-front door**

- built-in oven
- adjustable counter with knee space located on the left or right of the oven

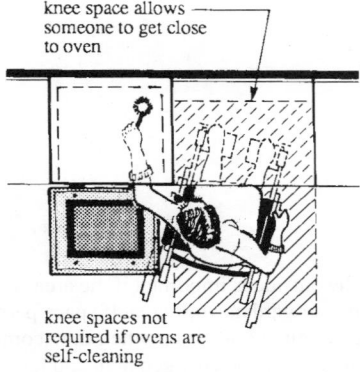

- knee space allows someone to get close to oven
- knee spaces not required if ovens are self-cleaning

**Fig. 5. Use of knee space next to oven**

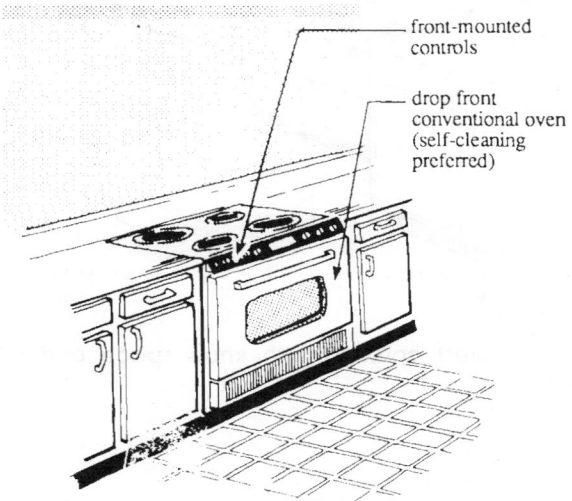

- front-mounted controls
- drop front conventional oven (self-cleaning preferred)

**Fig. 7. Standard range**

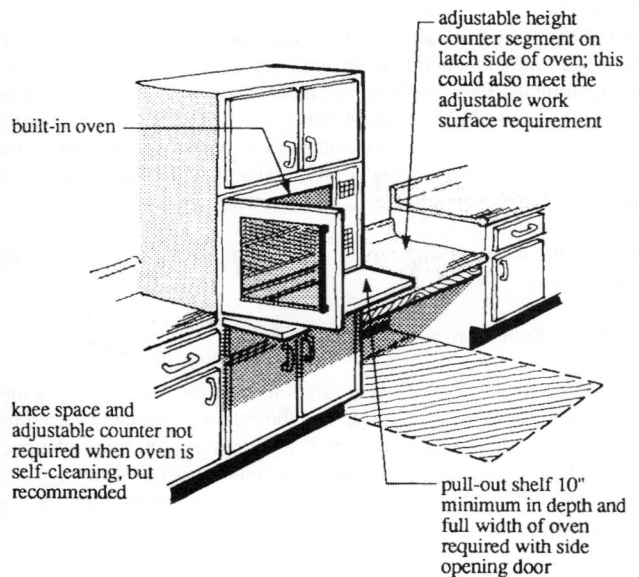

- built-in oven
- adjustable height counter segment on latch side of oven; this could also meet the adjustable work surface requirement
- knee space and adjustable counter not required when oven is self-cleaning, but recommended
- pull-out shelf 10" minimum in depth and full width of oven required with side opening door

**Fig. 6. Pull-out shelf at non-self-cleaning oven with side opening door**

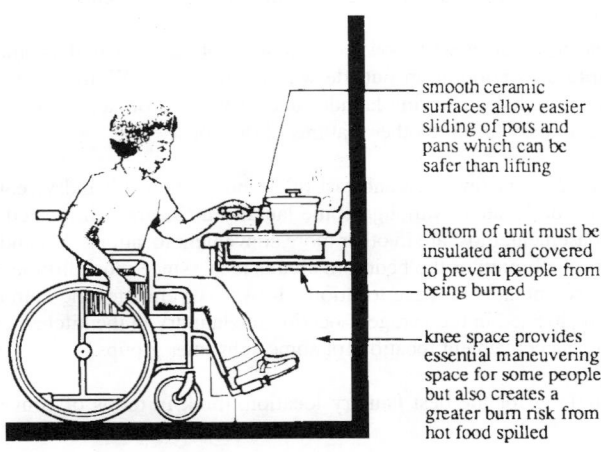

- smooth ceramic surfaces allow easier sliding of pots and pans which can be safer than lifting
- bottom of unit must be insulated and covered to prevent people from being burned
- knee space provides essential maneuvering space for some people, but also creates a greater burn risk from hot food spilled

**Fig. 8. Use of cooktop with knee space**

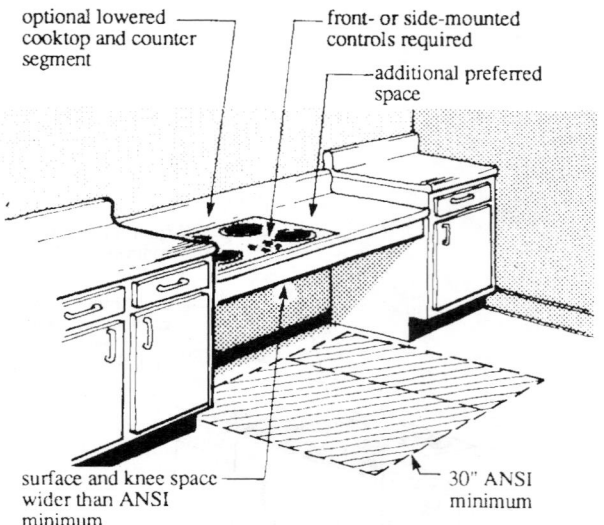

**Fig. 9. Lowered cooktop with knee space and wide counter**

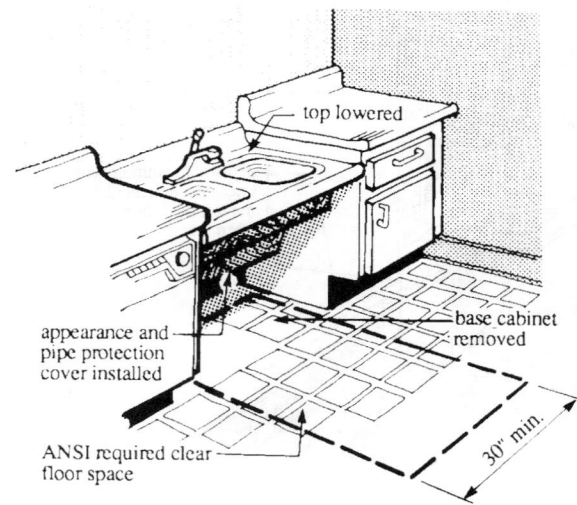

**Fig. 10. Sink in minimum-width adjustable counter segment**

## LAUNDRY AREAS

### Location

Changes in laundry equipment, new developments in fabrics, new consumer preferences, and available space all influence where the laundry center will be located. Other considerations are venting, noise, bedroom locations, and servicing of the equipment.

Some house plans will show a central location for the laundry; others require a location at an outside wall of the house. While a central location reduces carrying laundry and serves lots of steps, this may be secondary to some other features of the house.

There are very few hard-and-fast rules about where a laundry center should be located. Although some laundry areas are still located in the basement, most are in other more convenient locations. A laundry near a bathroom or the bedroom area is ideal, since most dirty laundry accumulates in these locations. In warmer climates the laundry can be located in the garage. Locating the laundry in the kitchen can also be a convenient location for some consumer groups.

In looking for the best laundry location, think in terms of convenience.

### First-Floor Utility and/or Mud Room

A utility room, right off the kitchen, is an excellent location for laundry facilities. It can share plumbing facilities with the kitchen. Sewing and crafts work also might be located here. This location allows for the messiness typically associated with entering the house, hence the name *mud room*. This area is usually adjacent to the kitchen so it is possible to maintain activities in both areas at the same time.

Direct access to the outside is important if the area is to serve as mud room, cleanup area, or garden work area. If space permits, a sink can be provided so children can wash up when they come in from play. Muddy or dirty clothes can be changed here and left for laundering.

### Kitchen

Putting the laundry center in or near the kitchen concentrates the location of two busy work areas of the home. Having the washer and dryer in or near the kitchen area helps in dovetailing with household tasks. Also, plumbing lines are close and there is water available for diluting laundry products and pretreating, if necessary. If a wall or corner of the kitchen is used for the laundry center, some type of partition or peninsula should separate the laundry and food preparation areas for sanitation reasons. The laundry area needs its own work space and storage.

If outdoor laundry drying is planned, convenient access to the outside is important.

### Bedroom–Bath Area

The bathroom is a logical accumulation point for soiled clothing and linens. Plumbing lines are close, and the existing sink can be used for diluting laundry products and for any pretreating that might be necessary. In addition, the floor, wall, and counter surfaces are the same type as recommended for a laundry—moisture resistant, durable, and easy to clean.

If space is available in a smaller home or can be planned into a new or remodeled home, the bedroom hallway is an excellent location. It s at the hub of the bedrooms and bath where most laundry is collected and the bathroom plumbing is nearby. The hallway itself can provide the floor space needed for working in the center. Pass-through storage directly to the rooms behind the laundry center is also quite feasible.

The laundry center could be in a corner of a bedroom or along one wall that backs up to a bathroom. This permits utilization of existing plumbing, thus cutting down installation costs. A spare bedroom could be turned into a combination laundry/general activity room. The area can be attractively hidden from view with sliding or folding doors.

But laundry equipment does not operate silently, so occupants may not want it next to the bedrooms. A separate room is highly desirable, especially if one develops a complete clothes-care center.

### Basement

For cost concerns, the laundry center can be placed in the basement. Other advantages are the removal of the noise from the rest of the house and proximity to the source of the hot-water supply and other plumbing lines. However, a basement laundry center is not recommended for most larger houses. Carrying heavy loads of laundry up and down stairs is an inconvenience.

A clothes chute from the upper floors helps eliminate the extra labor of carrying the clothes down to a basement or first-floor location.

### Family Room

This room frequently provides pleasant surroundings for laundry facilities because of the other activities that take place there. It often has a wall or corner that can be utilized for a laundry center. A sink could serve both for the laundry work and for convenience when entertaining guests. Depending on the floor plan of the house, one should keep in mind these disadvantages of a family-room laundry: transporting the laundry from the point of accumulation to the laundry center may involve considerable walking and one or more flights of steps; also, plumbing lines may not be readily available. On the other hand, a family room might make the task more pleasant and encourage some volunteer help.

### Patio, Breezeway, Carport, or Garage

In warm climates, one of these locations may be the best choice for a laundry center, particularly if it is located near the bedroom, bath, or kitchen areas of the home.

Keep in mind that a laundry center needs hot- and cold-water lines, a drain, electricity and, with a gas dryer, a gas connection.

### Other

A hall, closet, or pantry location usually is not satisfactory, because the available space is not adequate to develop a complete and efficient laundry center.

## Location Advantages and Disadvantages

The ideal location of the laundry space is a matter of preference. The laundry area may be separate or combined with the bathroom, the kitchen, the utility space, or the corridor. The most frequently mentioned advantages and disadvantages of these various options are listed in the following text.

### Separate Laundry

**Advantages**
- A separate space can be used for other activities such as sewing and hobbies, if it is large enough.
- Clothes may be hung for air drying without interfering with other household activities.
- Noise from laundry appliances can be shut off from the rest of the dwelling.
- Temporary holding or storage of clothing to be washed or ironed is made easier.

**Disadvantages**
- Providing this extra room increases the cost of the dwelling.

### Laundry in Combination with Bathroom

**Advantages**
- When the bathroom is located near the bedrooms, the washer and dryer are close to where most laundry originates. This facilitates gathering soiled articles and putting away clean linen and clothing.
- Combining the laundry space with a half bathroom adjacent to the kitchen provides many of the advantages of a separate laundry room.
- The tops of the laundry appliances provide useful horizontal space on which to lay clothes.
- Floor and wall finishes in bathrooms are usually resistant to high humidity.
- Additional plumbing costs are usually minimal.
- Bathroom sink may be used for hand-washing clothes.
- Mechanical ventilation can be provided economically for both functions.

**Disadvantages**
- A bathroom will usually accommodate only washing and drying facilities. Other laundry related activities, such as ironing, will have to be carried out elsewhere in the dwelling.
- Occupants may wish to use the bathroom while laundry is being washed or dried.

### Laundry in Combination with Kitchen

**Advantages**
- Suitable in housing for young families because the person doing the laundry can keep an eye on the laundry while doing other jobs and supervising children.
- Direct access to the outside for clothes drying is likely to be easier than from laundries located in a basement or on a second story.
- Additional plumbing costs are usually small.

**Disadvantages**
- Danger of cross-contamination through the handling of dirty laundry during food preparation.
- Grease and cooking smells can be passed on to clean clothes.
- Noise generated by running appliances cannot easily be shut off from the rest of the dwelling.

*Laundry in Combination with Basement Utility Space*

### Advantages

- Generally, as much space as needed can be provided.
- Noise generated by running appliances can be easily shut off from the rest of the dwelling.

### Disadvantages

- Laundry must be carried up and down stairs.

*Laundry in Combination with Corridor*

### Advantages

- Space is used more economically.
- Space above the appliances may be used as a linen closet.
- Appliances can be hidden from sight when they are not in use; they can be recessed into the wall and enclosed with doors.

### Disadvantages

- Noise generated by running appliances cannot be easily shut off from the rest of the dwelling.
- An alcove adjacent to a corridor will accommodate only a minimum-sized laundry area. Other laundry-related activities, such as ironing, will have to be carried out elsewhere in the dwelling.

## BATHROOMS

Activities commonly performed in the bathroom include washing of hands, face, and hair, bathing, elimination, and grooming, and also such activities as hand laundering and infant care. Often it is also used as a dressing room. Major problems in bathroom design include planning for optimum convenience and privacy of all bathroom functions for all members of the household, adequate provision for storage of supplies and equipment, and ease of cleaning.

Some general planning guides are as follows:

### Arrangement

Facilities should be conveniently arranged, with special attention given to clearances. The room arrangement should permit more than one family member to use its facilities at the same time.

### Illumination

Lighting should be adequate for all of the activities performed. For grooming, direct sources of light are essential in order to illuminate the face from all angles. High strip windows, clerestory windows, and skylights provide excellent overall illumination in the daytime, while still affording privacy.

### Ventilation

Good ventilation is essential in bathrooms, both to reduce humidity and to dispel odors. If a window is relied upon as the sole means of ventilation, care should be taken in its selection and placement to minimize drafts and to permit easy access. Exhaust fans in the wall or ceiling are often used to supplement natural ventilation. In interior bathroom spaces, a mechanical exhaust is essential and required by code.

### Sound Control

Lack of acoustical privacy is one of the most common complaints with regard to bathrooms. Noise can be reduced by proper placement of the bathroom in relation to other spaces, by the use of closets and storage walls as sound barriers between it and adjacent spaces, and by the use of soundproof partitions and tightly fitted doors. Acoustical treatment of the ceiling makes the room more comfortable to use and reduces somewhat the amount of sound transmitted through the walls.

### Storage

Adequate storage should be provided for current and reserve supplies. Articles in current use should be located near their place of first use. A closet opening from the bathroom and hallway or laundry is convenient for such items as bathroom linen and cleaning supplies. Medicine cabinets should be large enough to hold a number of toiletries and medicines. Hamper space is desirable for soiled linen and clothes. Install a cabinet with a self-contained hamper, or, in two-story houses, install a chute from the second floor to the laundry.

*Authors:* Glenn H. Beyer and Alexander Kira
*Reviewer:* James Wentling, FAIA

## Increased Countertop Space

Larger lavatories and increased countertop surfaces provide excellent facilities for light laundry, hair washing, and bathing.

## Children's Convenience

Children's height should be considered in the placement of accessory equipment. A dental lavatory can double as a child's lavatory. If a combination lavatory–dressing table is installed, a step-up retractable stool should be provided for children's use.

## Mirrors

An atmosphere of luxury and spaciousness is created by mirrors. A full-length mirror is always desirable. Also recommended is a medicine cabinet with a three-way combination of mirrored doors on either side and a mirror in the center.

## Safety Features

Grab bars should be used vertically for bathtub and shower and should be located for convenient use. They should be of adequate size and securely fastened to sturdy backing or studs. Use nonskid finishes for flooring. Install a door lock that opens automatically from the inside, and from the outside in case of emergency. Locate light switches out of reach of the bathtub or shower—preferably just outside the bathroom. Electric or radiant heaters should be recessed or protected. Provide a lock for medicine compartments.

## Drying Facilities and Accessories

Add extra racks for drying women's garments and other light laundry. Racks may be concealed in well-ventilated cabinets, which, if desired, may include a receptacle for a low-wattage light bulb to facilitate drying. Sufficient robe hooks, bag hooks, and toothbrush holders should also be provided.

## Accessibility

A bathroom should generally be accessible to each bedroom without requiring passage through another room. A bathroom is desirable near principal indoor living, work, and play areas, and for guest use.

## Basic Dimensions

Space is required not only for the use of particular fixtures but also between fixtures for cleaning purposes and for assisting another person (such as a small child or elderly adult). These last two factors are often completely overlooked. For economy of space, required clearances for each fixture may sometimes overlap (Fig. 1).

## Planning Data and Fixture Arrangements

A bathroom should have enough area to accommodate a lavatory, a water closet, and a bathtub or shower (Fig. 2). Arrangement of fixtures should provide for comfortable use of each fixture and permit at least 90-degree door swing unless sliding doors are used.

The bathroom should be convenient to the bedroom zone and accessible from the living and work areas. Linen storage should be accessible from the bathroom, but not necessarily located within the bathroom.

Each complete bathroom should be provided with the following:

1. Grab bar and soap dish near the bathtub
2. Toilet-paper holder at water closet
3. Soap dish at lavatory (may be integral with lavatory)
4. Towel bar
5. Mirror and medicine cabinet or equivalent enclosed shelf space
6. Shower rod or shower door in all cases where shower head is installed

Each half bathroom should be provided with items 2 to 6.

*Lavatory*

See Fig. 2.

A. Mirror and medicine cabinet. Size is governed by use of shelf or shelf-topped lavatory; mirror should swing 7 inches over any shelf. (A.1) Fixed mirror is desirable immediately above lavatory for children 7 to 14 years.
B. Shelf. Preferably recessed flush with wall. May be part of medicine cabinet or part of lavatory.
C, D, and E. Soap, toothbrush, and tumbler holders. May be separate units or combined; flush or projecting type.
F. Receptacle for electric razor and hair dryer. Should be above and to right of lavatory.
G. Towel bars. May be at level of shelf or lavatory top. If space is tight provide upper bar for face cloths, lower bar for towels.

*Shower*

See Fig. 2.

A. Shower head. Height is governed by client's preferences; may be overhead for men only.
B. Shower valves or mixing valves. Always place near entrance to shower.
C. Shower curtain rod. Alternate: glass shower enclosure door; place hinges on edge opposite shower control valves.
D. Combination soap and sponge holder and grab bar. Use draining-lip type. May be on rear wall or on side wall opposite shower head.
E. Shower ventilator. Desirable to remove steam; may function as vent for bathroom.
F. Shower stall light. Optional; must be waterproof fixture.

*Bathtub*

See Fig. 2.

A, B, and C. Shower head, shower controls, bath valves, and spout. Location is optional with client but must be accessible from outside of tub. See shower stall for recommended heights.
D. Combination soap and sponge holder and grab bar. Draining-lip type preferred.
E. Vertical grab bars. Optional but recommended.
F. Towel bar. Do not use over tub equipped with shower.
G. Curtain rod. Keep within inside face of tub. (G.1) Alternate: glass shower enclosure in place of curtain. Various types, with and without doors, are available.

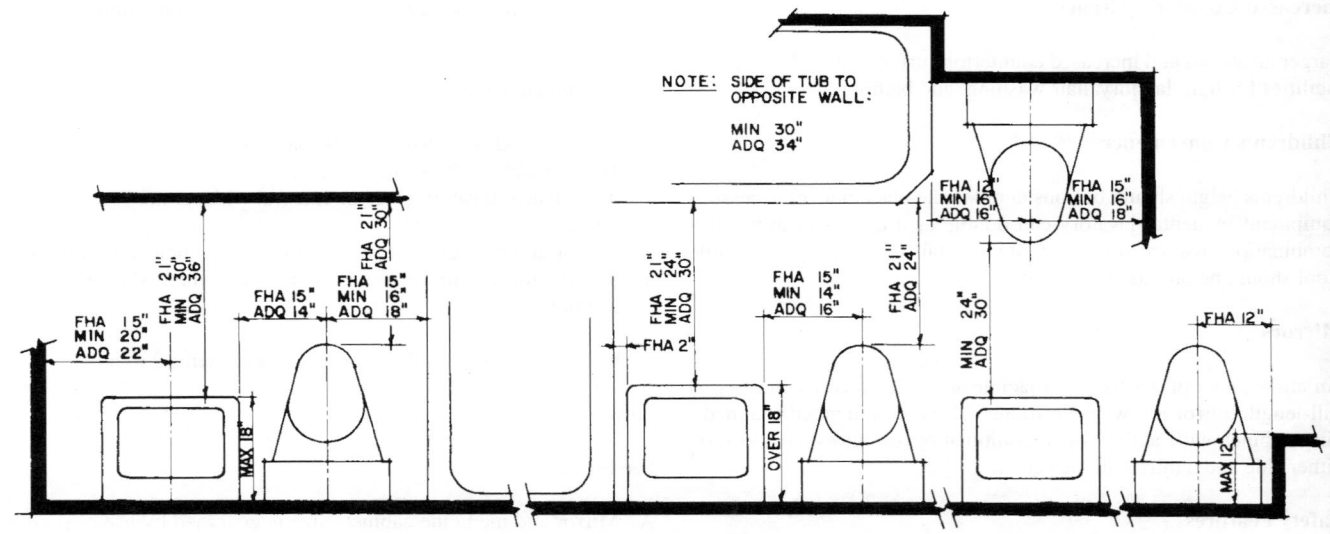

**Fig. 1. Fixture clearances (dimensions in inches)**

*Not Illustrated*

- Full-length mirror. Usually on door.
- Bathroom scale. May be built-in or portable.
- Linen hamper. Optional; may be part of cabinet-type lavatory, built-in or portable.
- Auxiliary heater. Built-in radiant type desirable; should radiate toward open floor space.

**Accessories**

The medicine cabinet should be related in size to the type of bathroom or toilet. For guest baths or toilets, space is needed only to accommodate guest accessories. A bath serving several bedrooms may require a complete supply of medicines in addition to the items mentioned previously. Every bathroom should have a storage closet for cleaning utensils and supplies and for reserve stocks of toilet paper, towels, and sundries.

Floor space should be left in every bathroom for portable accessories desired by the owner or needed on occasion for the care of infants or people with disabilities. Also consider allowing space for such items as scales, stool or seat, infant's bath and dressing table (portable type requires about 3 by 4 feet of floor space in use), soiled-linen hamper, exercise devices, and dressing table or vanity with bench.

Towel bars should be ample in number and length to serve the needs of each member of the family regularly using the bathroom, or of guests likely to use its facilities, before supplies can be replenished. For each person regularly using the bathroom, there should be separate bar space for bath towel, face towel, and face cloth, as well as an additional rack for guest towels.

Linen storage may consist of towel cabinets recessed in the thickness of plumbing walls (either over fixtures or as full-height cabinets) or may be expanded into complete linen closets. Dressing-room baths may include completely fitted wardrobes.

**Lavatory/Water Closet for People with Disabilities**

See Figs. 3 to 6.

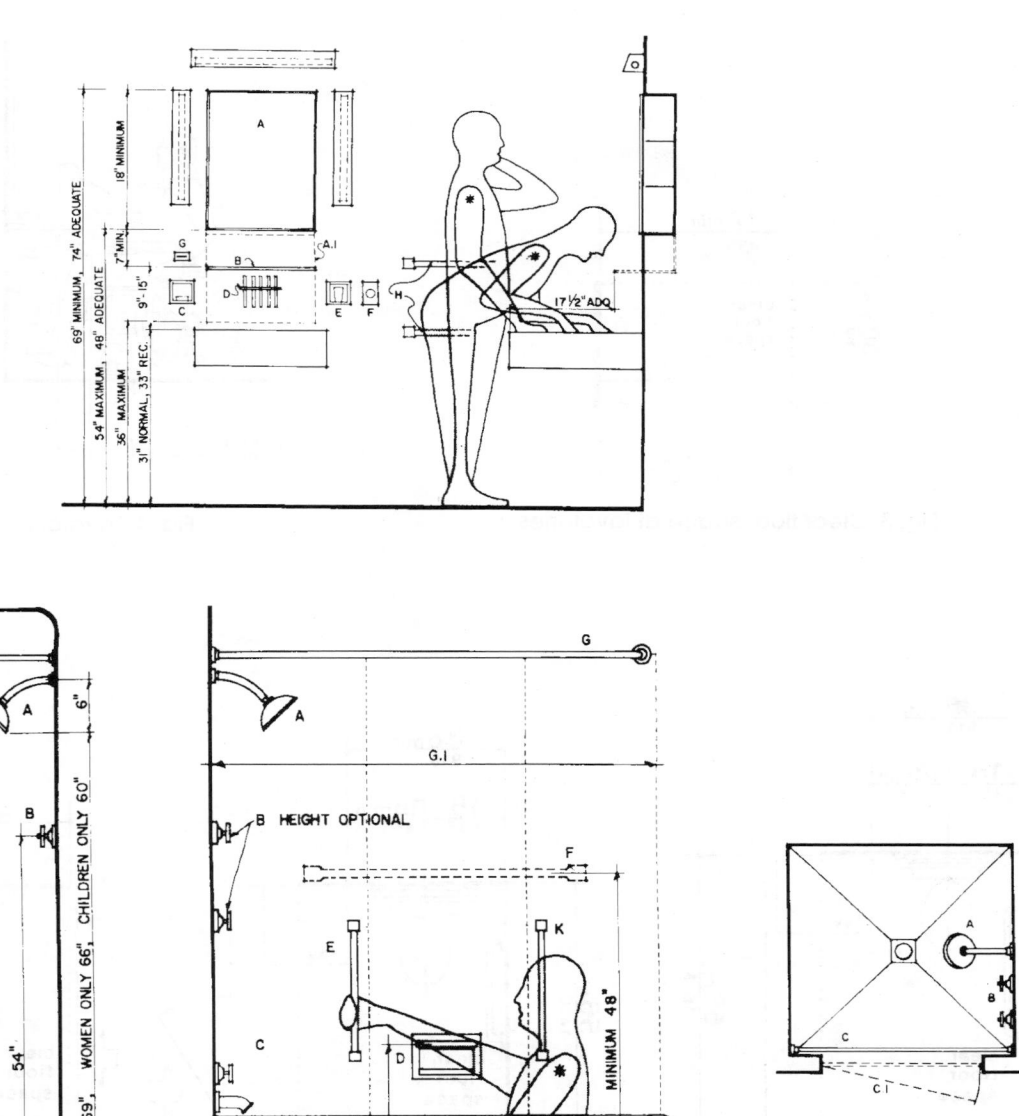

**Fig. 2. Dimensions at lavatory, shower, and bathtub**

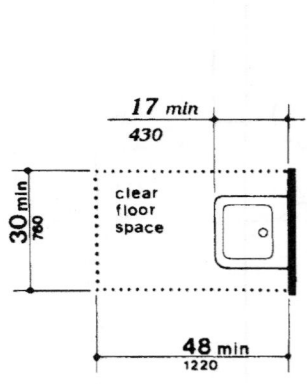

Fig. 3. Clear floor space at lavatories

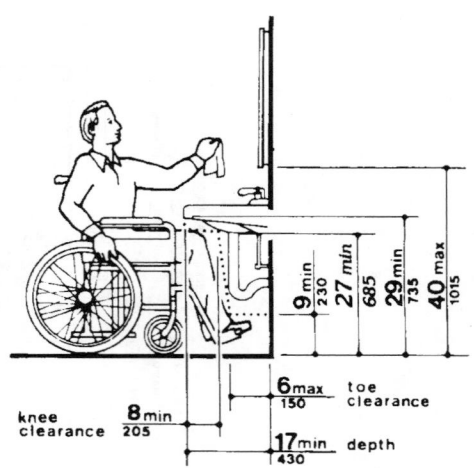

Fig. 4. Lavatory clearances

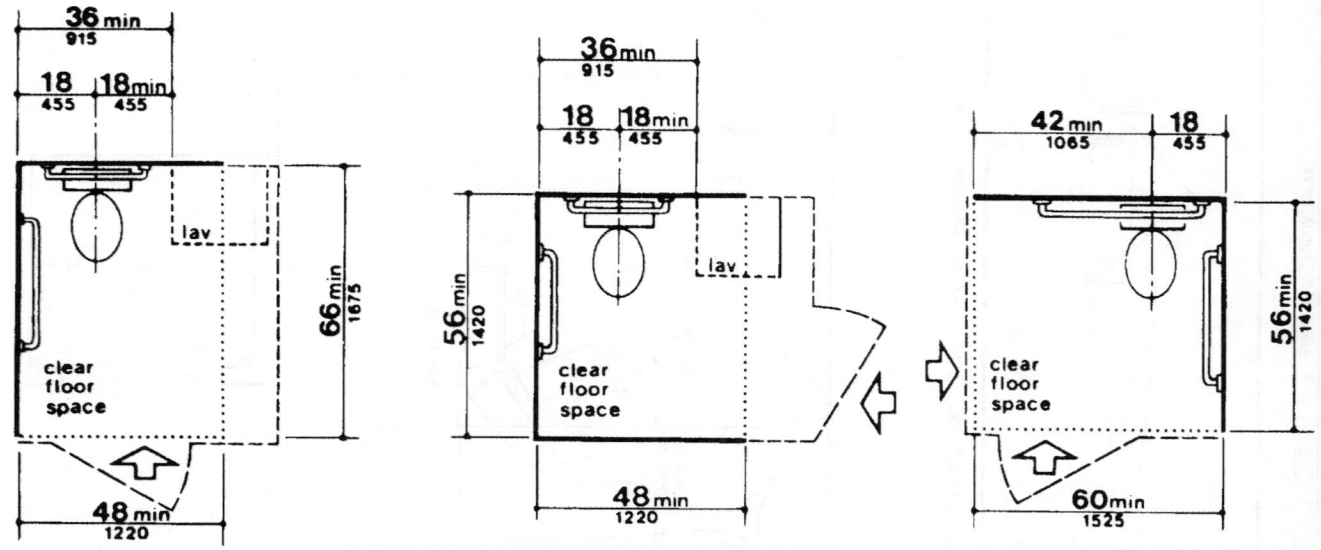

Fig. 5. Clear floor space at water closets

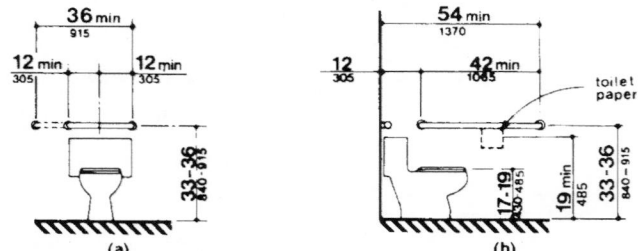

Fig. 6. Grab bars at water closets: (a) back wall; (b) side wall

**Adaptable Bathrooms**

This sample bathroom (Figs. 7 and 8) meets the minimum space requirements of both ANSI and UFAS; note, however, that the space is very small and many wheelchair users will have difficulty using such a bathroom. More space should be allocated when possible.

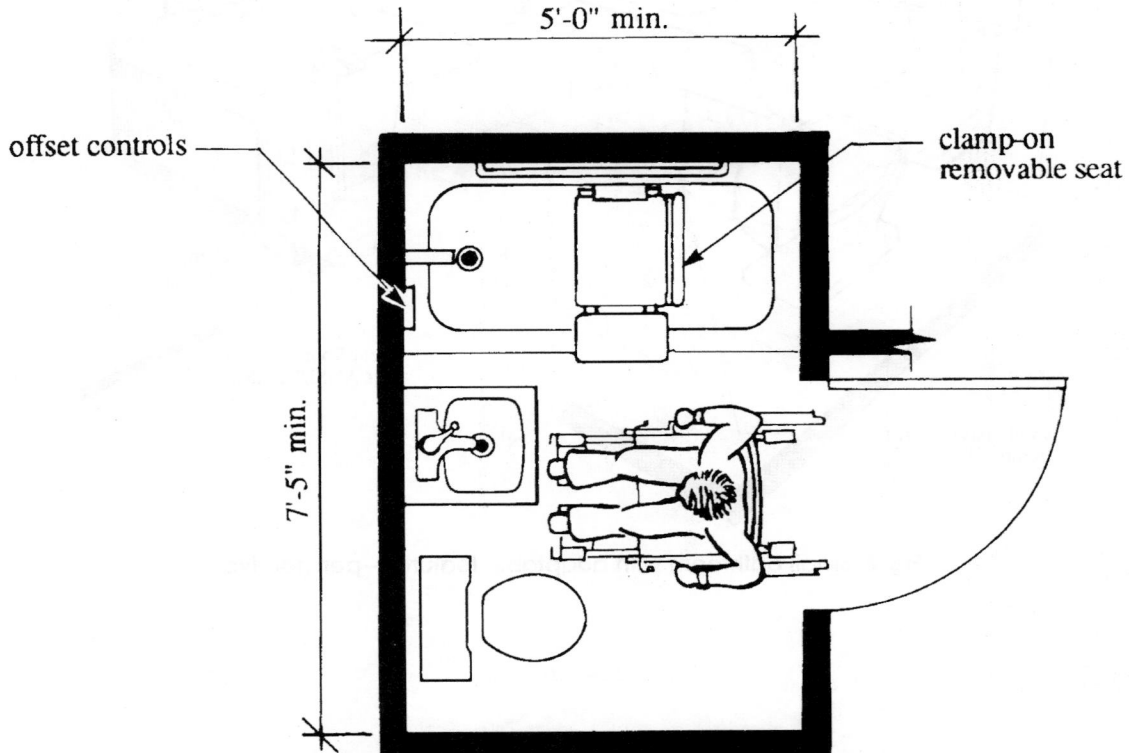

**Fig. 7. Small bathroom with adaptable features—plan**

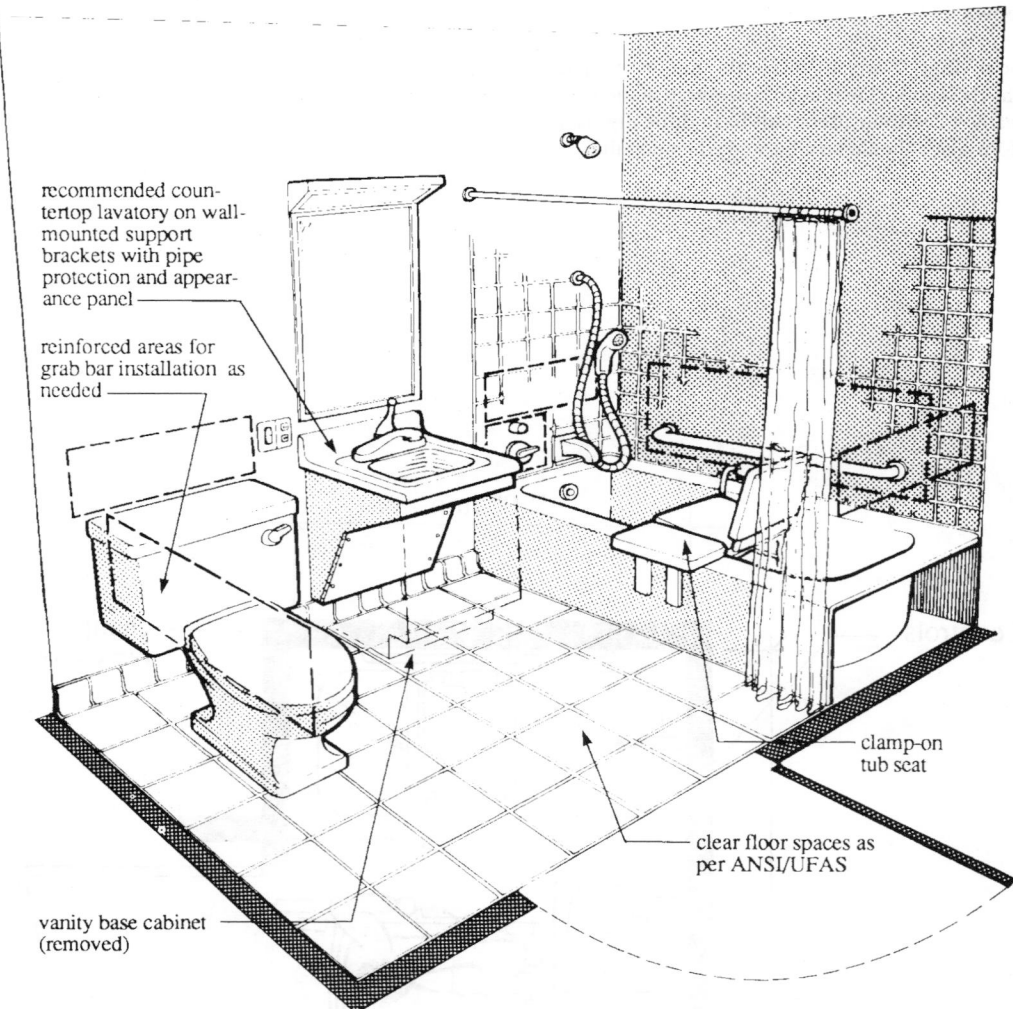

recommended coun-
tertop lavatory on wall-
mounted support
brackets with pipe
protection and appear-
ance panel

reinforced areas for
grab bar installation as
needed

clamp-on
tub seat

clear floor spaces as
per ANSI/UFAS

vanity base cabinet
(removed)

**Fig. 8. Small bathroom with adaptable features—perspective**

# CLOSETS

## Types of closets

Closets are required for various purposes, in different parts of the house. Closets must also be provided for the storage of clothing, bedding, cleaning equipment, books, magazines, CDs, videos, toys and other recreation equipment, and certain items such as luggage that are used only seasonally or infrequently. The discussion here relates only to *active* storage space.

*Clothes Closet*

For clothes closets in bedrooms or dressing rooms, 2 feet is standard depth, or 2 feet-6 inches if a hook strip is to be used (see Fig. 1). This permits clothing to be on hangers on poles, with sufficient clearance. Clothing lengths are shown in Fig. 2. Clothes closet width, parallel to the doors, should be from 3 to 6 feet per person, depending on amounts of clothing and whether drawers or trays are to be provided in the closet or wardrobe for such items otherwise kept in bureaus or other pieces of furniture. Suggested layouts for bedroom closets are shown in Fig. 3.

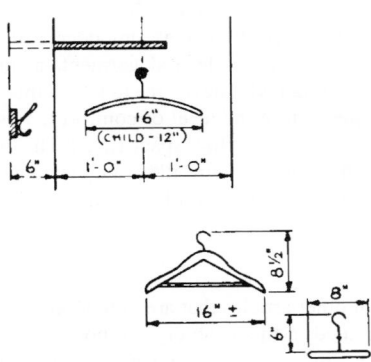

**Fig. 1. Closet depth and hanger sizes**

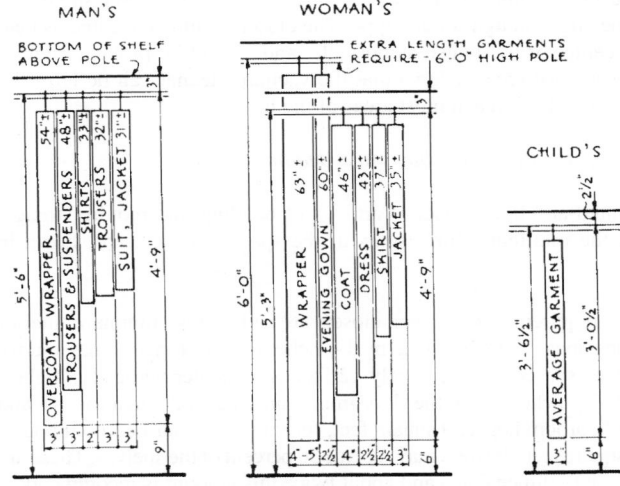

**Fig. 2. Sizes of clothes hung in closet**

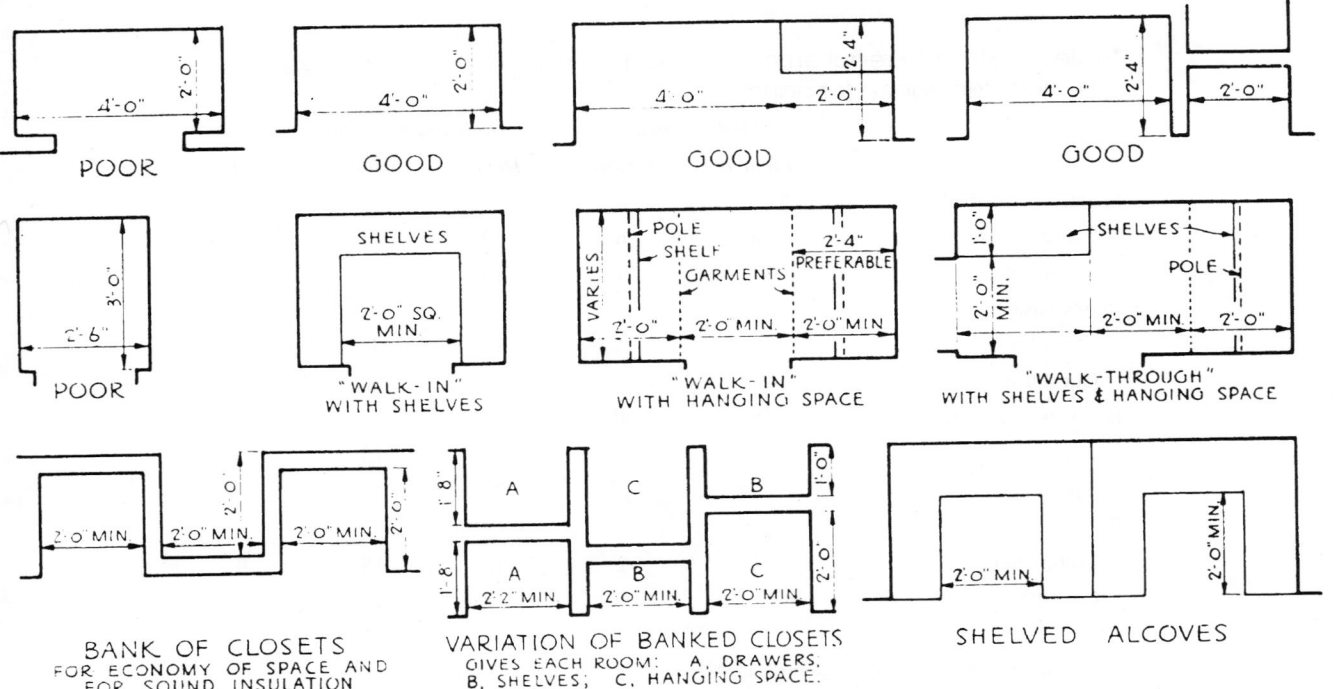

**Fig. 3. Typical closet plans**

*Coat Closet*

Located near the entrance doors, these are sometimes made 2 or 3 inches deeper than bedroom closets, to allow for the bulkiness of some overcoats, and to permit better air circulation around the garments, which are often damp when hung in the closet.

*Closet for Cleaning Equipment*

The dimensions of the storage space needed for cleaning equipment will depend in large part upon the type of vacuum cleaner used: horizontal, upright, or canister. Since families may change from one type of vacuum cleaner to another, the cleaning closet should be made large enough for any type. The closet should be located as near the center of the house as possible, and should be provided with a convenience receptacle so that the vacuum cleaner can be left connected and can reach most areas of the house.

*Storage for Bedroom Linens and Bedding*

Limited and liberal lists of articles of bedding that require storage, and the minimum dimensions of the space required, are shown in Table 1.

FHA requirements for linen closets are as follows: minimum interior dimensions, 18 inches wide by 14 inches deep (24 inches maximum); shelves spaced approximately 12 inches on center vertically; highest shelf 74 inches above the floor; minimum total shelf area for one and two-bedroom house, 9 square feet, for three and four-bedroom house, 12 square feet; drawers may replace 50 percent of the shelves. These are minimum dimensions, and about twice this amount is recommended, especially if both bedroom and bathroom linens are to be stored.

Figures 4 and 5 show the vertical clearances related to male and female closet and storage facilities. Wherever possible or practical, the closet shelf should be located within human reach. The height shown for the high shelf has been established based on fifth-percentile male and female data in order to place it within reach of individuals of smaller body size. Any shelf located at a greater distance above the floor should be used primarily for storage that requires only infrequent access. The location of the shelf just above the rod is essentially a function of rod height. The clearance between the bottom of the shelf and the top of the rod should allow for easy removal of the hanger.

Figure 6 illustrates two various types of walk-in storage facilities. Undoubtedly, it can be argued that the 36-inch clearance shown between the hanging garment and the storage shelf or between opposite garments could be reduced about 50 percent. The authors contend, however, that in order to achieve any degree of comfort in the selection and removal of the desired garment, a minimum of 36 inches should be maintained. The degree to which this dimension can be reduced is a question of the level of comfort the user is prepared to tolerate in exchange for the floor space saved. The two drawings of the plan view of the human figure illustrate clearances required for donning a coat or putting on a pair of stockings.

**Miscellaneous Storage**

A large variety of other articles that are in regular use must be stored somewhere. Included in this category are books, magazines, tables and chairs, games, toys, sports equipment, and tools. If adequate and conveniently located built-in storage is not provided, then portable units (furniture) will have to be used for this purpose.

Book storage is usually required in the living room, study, and each bedroom. Most books (85 percent) can fit comfortably on shelves 8 inches deep (front to back); some books (10 percent) need 10-inch shelves, and a few (5 percent) require 12-inch shelves. Vertical spacing between shelves varies from 8 to 16 inches, with the greatest use in the 10- to 12-inch range. Horizontally, books average 7 to 8 volumes per linear foot of shelf.

**Table 1** Storage requirements for bedroom linens and bedding, including allowance for handling

| Article | Median number | | Minimum dimensions, inches | | |
| --- | --- | --- | --- | --- | --- |
| | Limited | Liberal | Depth | Width | Height* |
| Sheets, double bed | | | | | |
| Everyday use | 6 | 6 | 12 | 14 | 12 |
| Guest use | — | 4 | 12 | 14 | 9 |
| Pillow cases (pairs) | | | | | |
| Everyday use | 5 | 5 | 12 | 8 | 8 |
| Guest use | 3 | 3 | 12 | 8 | 6 |
| Blankets, comforters, quilts | 4† | 4† | | | |
| Pile of 4 | | | 23 | 19 | 26 |
| 2 piles of 2 | | | 23 | 38 | 14 |
| Bedspreads, double bed | | | | | |
| Cotton damask | 2 | 2 | 16 | 15 | 9 |
| Chenille | 1 | 1 | 18 | 16 | 8 |
| Pillows | | 3 | 18 | 26 | 17 |

*For storage on fixed shelves. For storage on sliding shelves or in drawers, deduct 1 to 2 inches.

†Number of warm bed coverings owned is normally larger than this, but balance can be stored in less accessible location than linen closet.

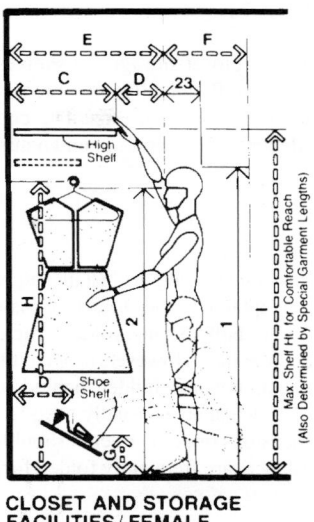

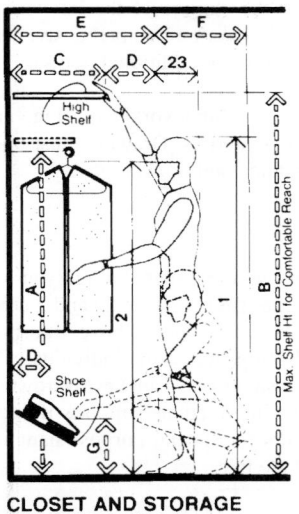

**CLOSET AND STORAGE FACILITIES/MALE**

**Fig. 4. Closet and storage facilities—male**

**CLOSET AND STORAGE FACILITIES/FEMALE**

**Fig. 5. Closet and storage facilities—female**

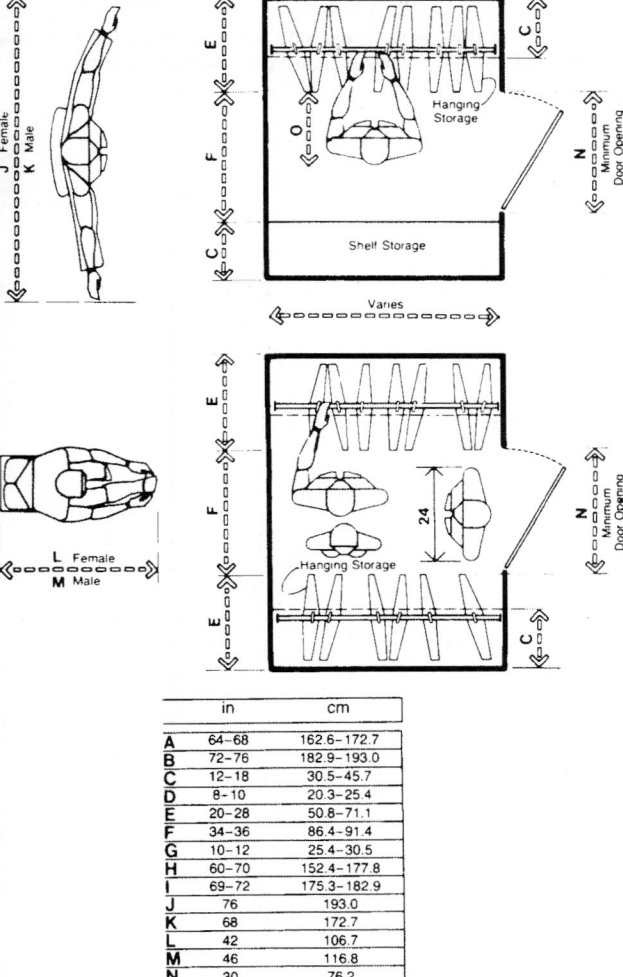

| | in | cm |
|---|---|---|
| A | 64–68 | 162.6–172.7 |
| B | 72–76 | 182.9–193.0 |
| C | 12–18 | 30.5–45.7 |
| D | 8–10 | 20.3–25.4 |
| E | 20–28 | 50.8–71.1 |
| F | 34–36 | 86.4–91.4 |
| G | 10–12 | 25.4–30.5 |
| H | 60–70 | 152.4–177.8 |
| I | 69–72 | 175.3–182.9 |
| J | 76 | 193.0 |
| K | 68 | 172.7 |
| L | 42 | 106.7 |
| M | 46 | 116.8 |
| N | 30 | 76.2 |
| O | 18 | 45.7 |

**Fig. 6. Walk-in closet and storage facilities**

Card tables are usually 30 inches square but may be as large as 36 inches, and are 2 to 3 inches thick when folded. Folded chairs vary widely in dimension, but a fair average is 30 by 16 by 3 inches. Space should also be provided for cards, score cards, rule books, poker chips, and chess sets.

Toy and game storage should be provided in children's bedrooms and wherever the toys are regularly used. Toy storage should be designed for future conversion to other use.

Sports equipment, especially golf bags, skis, and camping equipment, may present a serious storage problem. For some families, a separate closet for this purpose may be justified. Such a closet should be located near the outside entrance which is most used by the family.

Tools and associated items should, of course, be stored in the workshop or utility room.

General storage is required for bulky, seldom-used items, such as trunks, boxes, and extra furniture.

Outdoor storage (i.e., directly accessible from outdoors) is required for lawnmowers, wheelbarrows, sprays, rakes, and other garden tools and equipment; for snow shovels and sleds, ladders, screens, and storm windows; for outdoor furniture, barbecues, hammocks, croquet sets; for bicycles, tricycles, skateboards, and so on.

These last two types of storage (general and outdoor) were provided in the traditional house by the basement, attic, and garage. Some houses may have none of these spaces, and in such cases the architect should take particular care to provide adequate general and outdoor storage space. FHA minimum requirements are 200 cubic feet plus 75 cubic feet per bedroom, of which at least 25 percent and not more than 50 percent should be indoors. Again, it should be emphasized that this is a minimum requirement; much more is recommended.

## Basic Elements

The standard elements of closet storage are shelves, drawers, poles, hooks, and special fixtures. Practically any object can be stored efficiently by one or another of these means. The choice and arrangement of the fixtures depend on the amount and nature of the materials to be stored.

### Shelves

Shelves are simple and inexpensive to install, require a minimum of effort to use, and are adaptable to the storage of many types of things, especially those of odd or bulky shape, folded articles, and, of course, books, magazines, and the like. However, if open, they are exposed to dust. Also, small objects become hidden behind one another if the shelves are deep. A 12-inch shelf is usually adequate for most things. Articles of larger dimensions or greater depth should have their special places; linens, for instance, are frequently folded for a 16-inch shelf.

### Drawers

Drawers accommodate numerous articles with a minimum of space and a maximum of convenience. They provide practically dust-free storage and present a neat appearance even when carelessly used. Drawers of different widths and depths make possible classified filing of different items, thus providing a great saving in time and an incentive to orderliness. A cabinet made up of a battery of standard drawers, selected for the storage of the known possessions of the user, can easily be made from a comprehensive list, with allowance made for the accumulation of additional items.

Drawer construction is cabinetwork requiring both skillful craftsmanship and the best materials. Drawers must operate freely under all seasonal and climatic conditions.

### Poles

Hanging pole length can be estimated roughly at 3 inches per hanger for men's suits (4 inches for heavy coats) and 2 inches per hanger for women's clothing. Height of pole above floor should average 64 inches, but should be adjusted to the individual. Clearance between pole and shelf above should be 3 inches. Hardwood poles 1 inch in diameter should have intermediate supports if over 4 feet in length. Consult manufacturers for special-purpose hanging rods, extension poles, brackets, and the like.

### Hooks

A variety of hooks is available.

### Special Features

Such special features as shoe and hat racks and miscellaneous racks are on the market and greatly increase convenience in storage.

**Fig. 1. Typical apartment building**

# APARTMENTS

## BACKGROUND

In an apartment building (Fig. 1) the spaces themselves must be simple and universal enough to adapt to a variety of life styles. As far as the movement through the apartment is concerned, far more specific criteria can be established relying on basic circulation patterns that are valid for most living conditions.

A well-planned apartment provides maximum privacy for various activities and makes movement to any room possible without crossing another.

*Entering the Apartment*

In inclement weather outer clothing should be taken off at the entrance and put away; umbrellas and boots should be stored to prevent dirtying the floors of other rooms; space should be provided to accommodate packages.

*Entering with Groceries or Leaving with Garbage*

Connection between entrance and kitchen should be as direct as possible; preferably through the entry hall and not the living space. A secondary entrance directly into the kitchen solves this problem ideally.

*Children Coming in from Play*

Children should be able to reach the bathroom or their own rooms without crossing the living space.

*Deliveries*

Packages should be taken without having the delivery person enter the living space.

*Children Entering While Adult Activity is Taking Place in the Living Space (or Vice Versa)*

Children should be able to get to their bedrooms without crossing the living space.

*Passing from Bedroom to Bathroom*

It should not be necessary to cross the living space. Ideally, one should not be seen at all.

*Passing from Kitchen to Bathroom*

This should be done, if possible, without crossing the living space.

*Serving from Kitchen to Dining Room*

Service should be as direct as possible without crossing any other space (except occasionally the entry hall).

Ideal circulation criteria are achieved by proper planning of the rooms around the core of the apartment, which consists of the entry hall and the bedroom corridor. In fact a well-planned apartment can be divided into two zones, living zone and sleeping zone, separated by the entry hall.

Neither this simple geometric division nor the ideal circulation pattern is always possible. Corner apartments, quadruplex walk-ups, and townhouses often require functional compromise to achieve economy.

Equally important as the relation of each room to the other is the relative position it occupies in relation to daylight and fresh air (Fig. 2). Ideally, every room in an apartment should have exterior exposure to ensure light and air. To plan this way, however, would increase the perimeter of the building to an extent that it would not be cost effec-

*Reviewer:* James Wentling, FAIA

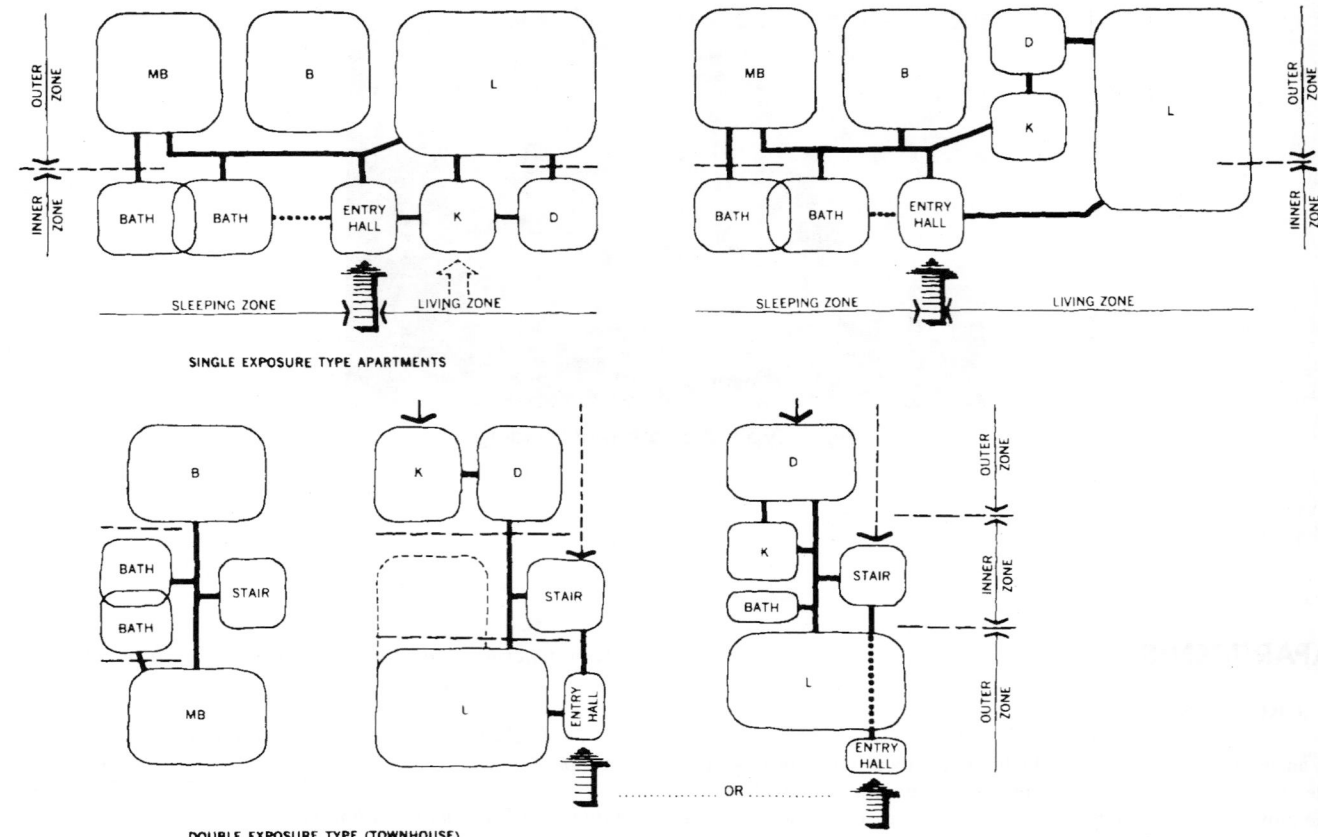

**Fig. 2. Apartment exposure types**

tive to build. Therefore bathrooms, invariably, kitchens, often, and dining rooms, sometimes, are handled as interior spaces. This is possible because building codes allow bathrooms and kitchens to be mechanically ventilated, because an inside dining alcove is really an extension of the living space, and because the kitchen can be situated to borrow light from the living or dining room. Thus the apartment plan is divided into outer and inner zones. Units within double-exposure townhouses, duplex walk-ups, and exterior gallery-type buildings can have kitchens and dining rooms in the outer zone without difficulty.

The approximate size and proportion of the rooms themselves must be included in the program. Extreme care must be taken with public or federally assisted housing because minimum dimensions given as guidelines cannot be accepted without scrutiny.

In the private consumer housing market, market conditions and competition are the best gauge of room sizes. Awareness of the local housing market is essential, for market conditions vary considerably not only from city to city but from neighborhood to neighborhood. As an example, the Chicago market demands a separate alcove as a defined dining space; in New York the entry hall is often substituted, thus serving a dual function and increasing the space allotted to the total living area. Considerably larger rooms are called for along Chicago's Lake Shore Drive than in Old Town, just a few blocks away.

The architect's most reliable guide is a thorough analysis of the function, furnishings, and circulation pattern of each space. In this respect HUD guidelines for minimum furniture requirements are quite reliable, assuming naturally that proper circulation space is provided (see Table 1).

## LIVING ROOMS (LIVING-DINING ROOMS)

The living room should be conducive to general family life and should allow for group activities as well as individual relaxation: entertaining, reading, writing, listening to music, and watching television (see Fig. 3).

The following furniture as a minimum should be accommodated:

- One couch, 3 feet by 6 feet-10 inches
- Two easy chairs, 2 feet-6 inches by 3 feet (one for efficiency apartment, three for four or more bedroom units)
- One desk, 1 foot-8 inches by 3 feet-6 inches
- One desk chair, 1 foot-6 inches by 1 foot-6 inches
- One television set, 1 foot-4 inches by 2 feet-8 inches
- One table, 1 foot-6 inches by 2 feet-6 inches

The living room is the most impressive and largest of all rooms in the apartment, which is why many housing developers like it to be visible from the entry hall.

**Table 1** Minimum room sizes

| | Minimum area, square feet | | | | | |
| Name of space | LU with 0 BR | LU with 1 BR | LU with 2 BR | LU with 3 BR | LU with 4 BR | Least dimension |
|---|---|---|---|---|---|---|
| *Minimum room sizes for separate rooms* | | | | | | |
| LR | NA | 160 | 160 | 170 | 180 | 11 ft-0 in |
| DR | NA | 100 | 100 | 110 | 120 | 8 ft-4 in |
| BR (primary) | NA | 120 | 120 | 120 | 120 | 9 ft-4 in |
| BR (secondary) | NA | NA | 80 | 80 | 80 | 8 ft-0 in |
| Total area, BR's | NA | 120 | 200 | 280 | 380 | — |
| *Minimum room sizes for combined spaces* | | | | | | |
| LR-DA | NA | 210 | 210 | 230 | 250 | |
| LR-DA-SL | 250 | NA | NA | NA | NA | |
| LR-DA-K | NA | 270 | 270 | 300 | 330 | |
| LR-SL | 210 | NA | NA | NA | NA | |
| K-DA | 100 | 120 | 120 | 140 | 160 | |

*Abbreviations: LU = living unit, LR = living room, DR = dining room, DA = dining area, 0 BR = LU with no separate bedroom, K = kitchen, NA = not applicable, BR = bedroom, SL = sleeping area.*

To serve as a guide, the living room in the average middle-income 2-bedroom apartment is about 260 to 300 square feet; combined living-dining room is about 400 square feet. When the living room is also used for dining, its proportions, with minimum waste, become critical. Typical square (20- by 20-foot) living-dining rooms are far less efficient than the oblong (15 by 26 feet) of the same square footage.

**DINING ROOMS**

A truly separate dining room can be afforded only in townhouses or luxury apartment housing. The most common arrangement takes the form of an alcove off the living room (Fig. 4). Although this alcove can occupy an inner zone, a windowed area is preferable even though it creates a larger building perimeter and consequently increases costs. When a large group of diners is to be accommodated, the table can be expanded into the living room and space should be provided for it without having to move heavy furniture.

The table and chair requirements in the following list should be considered not only with proper circulation space and pattern of food serving in mind but also in relation to space for storage.

- Efficiency or one bedroom, two persons: 2 feet-6 inches by 2 feet-6 inches

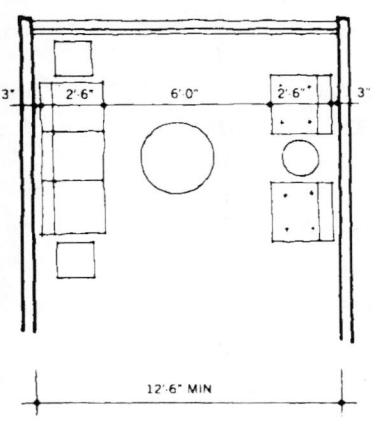

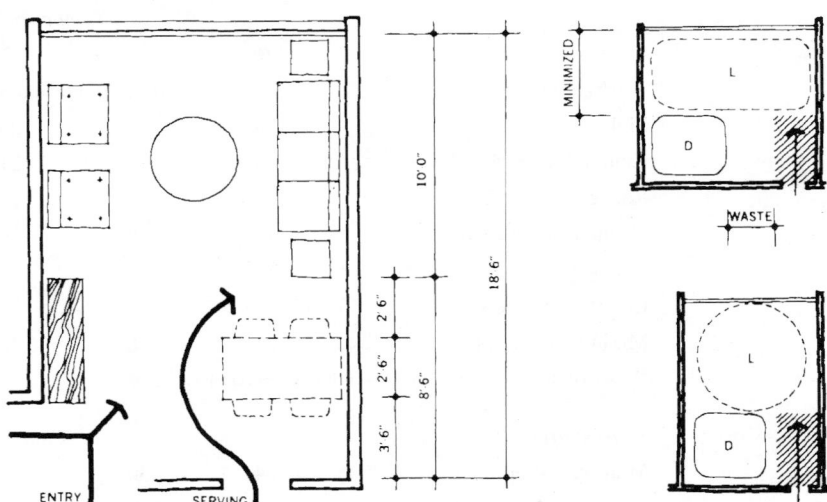

**Fig. 3. Living-dining room layouts**

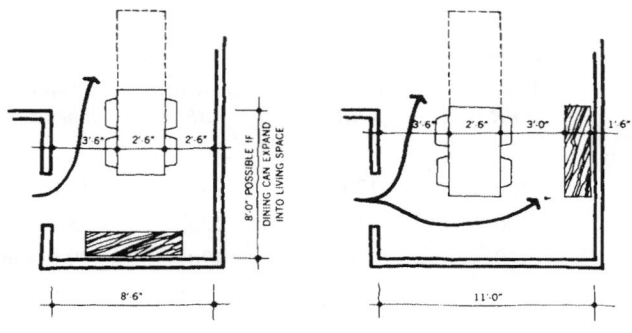

Fig. 4. Dining area

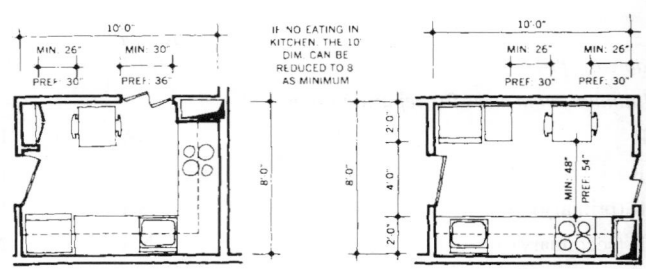

Fig. 5. Kitchen layouts

- Two bedrooms, four persons: 2 feet-6 inches by 3 feet-2 inches
- Three bedrooms, six persons: 3 feet-4 inches by 4 feet, or 4 feet round
- Four or more bedrooms, eight persons: 3 feet-4 inches by 6 feet or 4 feet by 4 feet
- Dining chairs: 1 foot-6 inches by 1 foot-6 inches

In middle-income 2-bedroom apartments, an average dining alcove is about 100 square feet and a separate dining room is about 140 square feet.

### BALCONIES

There is some controversy about the need for balconies in apartment buildings. Besides the balcony's aesthetic factor (it allows strong exterior building articulation) and its symbolic significance (a visible indication of the presence of human beings), its functional role has pros and cons. Those who argue for it stress the delight of sitting out-doors when the weather is pleasant. Its proponents call attention to

the visual extension of the living space, to extra storage space, and to the opportunity to grow plants. Those who oppose balconies claim that they cut off daylight, that they are dirt catchers and hard to keep clean, and in many regions can be used only part of the year.

Balconies must be wide enough for proper use (not less than 5 feet) and have adequate privacy.

### KITCHENS

To provide for the most efficient food preparation, storage, and service, careful planning is required (Fig. 5 and Table 2). Storage space normally provided in cabinets or utility closets can be expanded by the addition of shallow pantries: floor-to-ceiling shelving behind hinged doors.

Unless space is extremely tight, kitchens should be equipped with a small eating space to augment the regular dining room or alcove. When the kitchen is part of a combined kitchen–dining or kitchen–

### Table 2  Countertops and fixtures

| | Number of bedrooms | | | | |
|---|---|---|---|---|---|
| | 0 | 1 | 2 | 3 | 4 |
| Work center | Minimum frontages, linear inches | | | | |
| Sink | 18 | 24 | 24 | 32* | 32* |
| Countertop, each side | 15 | 18 | 21 | 24 | 30 |
| Range or cooktop space | 21 | 21 | 24 | 30 | 30 |
| Countertop, one side | 15 | 18 | 21 | 24 | 30 |
| Refrigerator space | 30 | 30 | 36 | 36 | 36 |
| Countertop, one side | 15 | 15 | 15 | 15 | 18 |
| Mixing countertop | 21 | 30 | 36 | 36 | 42 |

*When a dishwasher is provided, a 24-inch sink is acceptable.

| Storage area[†] | Square feet | | | | |
|---|---|---|---|---|---|
| Minimum shelf area | 24 | 30 | 38 | 44 | 50 |
| Minimum drawer area | 4 | 6 | 8 | 10 | 12 |

[†]Wall cabinets over refrigerators and shelves above 74 inches should not be counted as required storage area.

family room, the food preparation and cooking space should be screened from the dining or family area. When planning kitchens, the basic sequence of refrigerator-sink-stove, starting from the door and progressing toward the serving and eating areas, should be observed. The method of connecting with the dining room or alcove, pass-through or door, needs special attention. Well-planned kitchens in an inner zone should borrow daylight from the living or dining space to make working conditions in the kitchen pleasanter.

In middle-income 2-bedroom apartments, an average kitchen with minimum eating space is about 100 square feet.

## BEDROOMS

Each bedroom should have enough space for double occupancy (Fig. 6) and provide for the following basic furniture:

- Two twin beds, 3 feet-3 inches by 6 feet-10 inches
- One dresser, 1 foot-6 inches by 4 feet-4 inches
- One chair, 1 foot-6 inches by 1 foot-6 inches
- One crib, 2 feet-6 inches by 4 feet-6 inches

It should be kept in mind that night tables must also be accommodated. Because the bedroom often serves as an extra work area, space for a computer is not a luxury.

In middle-income 2-bedroom apartments, average bedroom sizes (exclusive of closets) are 150 square feet for secondary bedrooms and 180 square feet for master bedrooms.

## BATHROOMS

For the sake of economy, a back-to-back arrangement of bathrooms is preferred, either in the same apartment or with one that is adjacent (Fig. 7). When there is only one bathroom, a tub and shower combination is standard equipment; when there are two, the second usually contains a stall shower.

When an apartment has two or more bathrooms, one is customarily attached to the master bedroom; the others serve the remaining bedrooms. A powder room or lavatory is sometimes substituted for the second bathroom, although the savings are nominal compared with the convenience of having two baths. In luxury housing, compart-

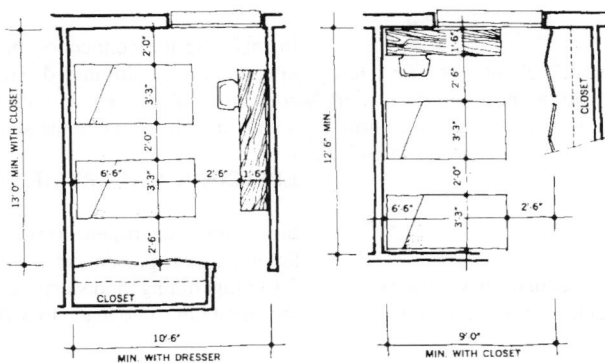

**Fig. 6. Bedroom layouts**

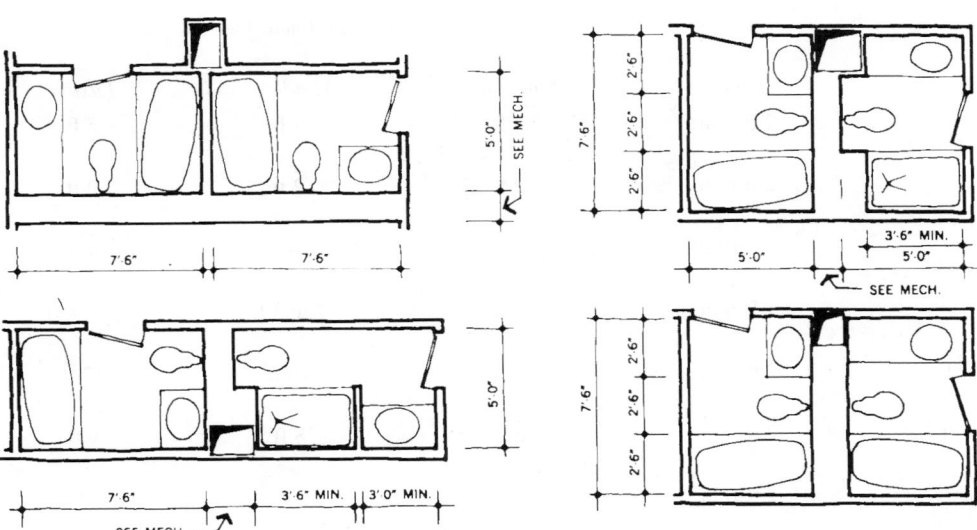

**Fig. 7. Bathroom layouts**

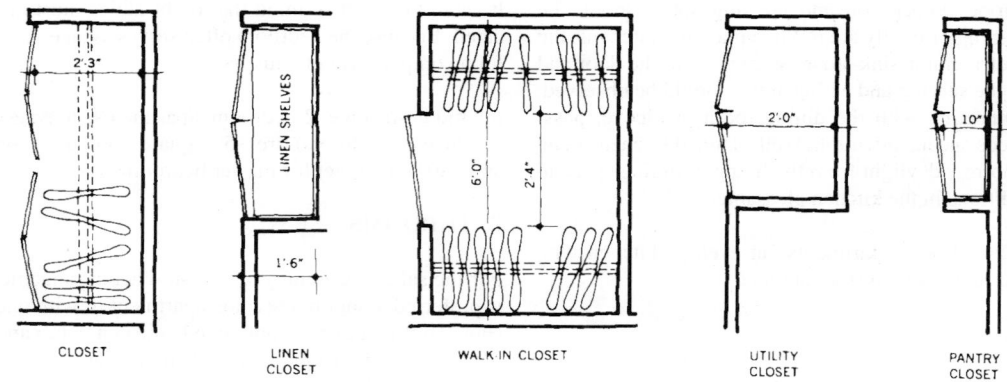

**Fig. 8. Closet layouts**

mentalization is an advantage that allows simultaneous multiple use.

## CLOSETS

Although overall apartment size is stated in a client's program, few clients pay attention in the early design stages to the amount and kind of closet space that is provided (Fig. 8). It is generally accepted however, that it is never enough for the tenant or buyer. Table 3 is a guide to closet sizes at various rental levels.

## ENTRY HALLS

Certain building codes require that large apartments have two exits to the public corridor and that access be made easy to either one with-

out having to pass through the bedrooms (Fig. 9). The ideal location for the second exit is in the kitchen (though it may make its planning more difficult).

In this case the connection between the regular entry hall and the kitchen may be eliminated. The second exit, depending on the local code, may also open directly onto the stair landing (with B-label door), though not when the stair is a smoke-proof tower.

## EFFICIENCY APARTMENTS

In efficiency apartments (Fig. 10) not only room functions but circulation patterns present different problems. Because one space serves for living, dining, and sleeping, precise demarcation is difficult. Still, an attempt must be made to define these areas. The kitchen is usually

## Table 3 Closet sizes at various rental levels

| Location | Depth | Length, linear feet* | | | HUD minimum |
| --- | --- | --- | --- | --- | --- |
| | | Low rental | Middle | Luxury | |
| Guest closet (in or near entry hall) | 2 ft-3 in | 3 ft | 4 ft | 5 ft | 2 ft |
| Utility closet (in or near kitchen) | 2 ft-0 in | 2 ft | 2 ft | 2 ft | 2 ft |
| Pantry (in kitchen) | 8 to 10 in | — | — | 4 ft | — |
| Linen closet (in bedroom hall) | 1 ft-6 in | 2 ft | 2 to 3 ft | 3 to 4 ft | 1 ft-6 in |
| Master bedroom closet (in bedroom) | 2 ft-3 in | 8 ft | 10 ft | 12 ft | 5 ft |
| Second bedroom closet (in bedroom) | 2 ft-3 in | 6 ft | 8 ft | 9 ft | 3 ft |
| General storage closet (in entry or bedroom hall) | 2 ft-0 in | — | — | 4 | — |

*Or equivalent linear feet in a walk-in closet.

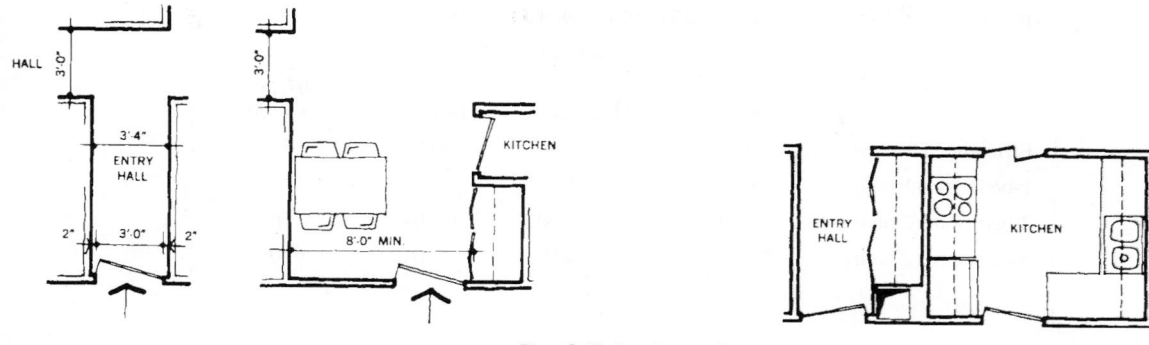

Fig. 9. Entry layouts

considerably smaller than those found in regular apartments, and because there is no bedroom, the bedroom-closet should serve as a walk-in dressing room.

Obviously there is a close relation between room sizes and the total dimensions of the apartment. As a rule of thumb all room areas (living, dining, bedrooms, kitchen, bathrooms, and closet spaces (but not entry hall), can be added to reach a total that should constitute 80 to 85 percent of the gross size, leaving 15 to 20 percent for circulation (entry hall and bedroom corridor), walls, columns, and shafts. Efficiency apartments naturally have less circulation space. In two-story apartments the space occupied on each floor by the stairs should also be taken into consideration as circulation space. It should

be kept in mind that the most efficient apartment is not necessarily the largest but one that has the largest rooms within the smallest gross square-foot area and therefore the smallest possible circulation space. Although good, differentiated circulation is important, it should be handled with a minimum of wasted space.

What one developer considers a small apartment another may find medium; what would be considered medium in a plush suburb may be placed in the luxury class in Greenwich Village. Nevertheless, it is possible within the broadest parameters to propose some guidelines (the HUD minimums in Table 4 were arrived at by adding up HUD minimum room sizes and closets and adding 20 percent to them for circulation).

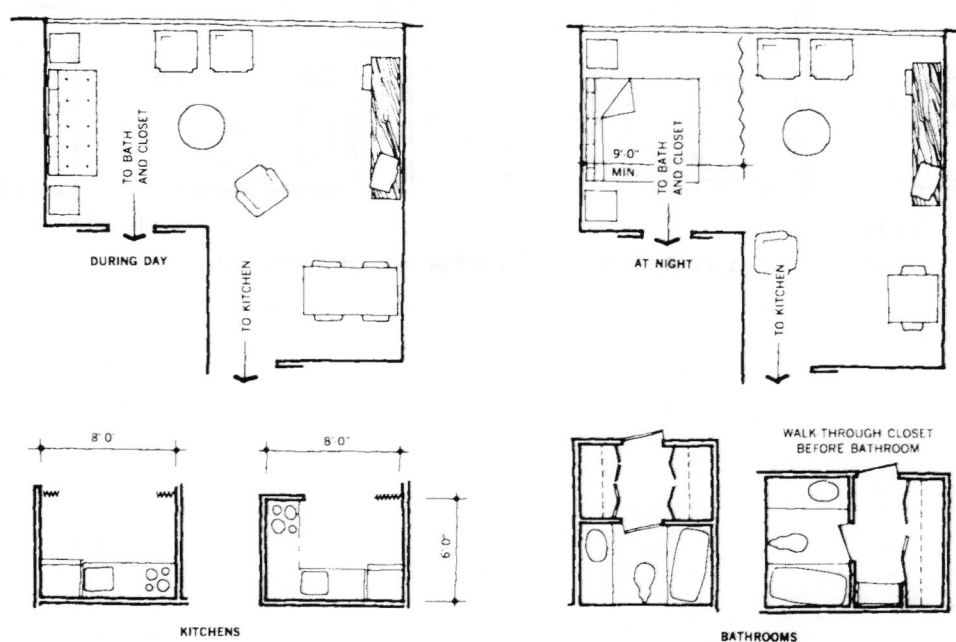

Fig. 10. Efficiency layouts

**Table 4.** Minimum dimensions of apartments

| | Gross size, square feet | | | |
|---|---|---|---|---|
| Unit | Low | Medium | Luxury | HUD minimum |
| Efficiency (1 bath) | 450 | 500–550 | 600+ | 380 |
| 1-bedroom (1 bath) | 650 | 700–800 | 900+ | 580 |
| 2-bedroom (2 baths) | 950 | 1100–1200 | 1250+ | 750 |
| 3-bedroom (2 baths) | 1,250 | 1350–1450 | 1600+ | 900 |

It is useful to know how apartment sizes are figured: from the exterior face of the exterior wall (in condominiums) and from the interior face of the exterior wall (in rentals) to the center line of the corridor partition, and from center line to center line of party walls (partitions between the apartments). Balconies are not included in these dimensions.

Apartments for elderly people fall into a special category (and are covered in detail in the Seniors Housing section of this book). These apartments are generally small (550 square feet for 1 bedroom is not unusual) and are mostly 1-bedroom units or efficiencies. This limited size demands taut, imaginative planning. Because of the frequent use of wheelchairs, wider doors (2 feet-8 inches) are used throughout the apartment, including the bathroom (Fig. 11), and bedrooms should be furnished to permit clear passage around each bed. Bathroom layouts are for ease of wheelchair manipulation and kitchen cabinets are built to be reached with minimum bending and stretching. Because many elderly tenants are house-bound, northern orientation, in which no sunlight can reach the interior, should be avoided.

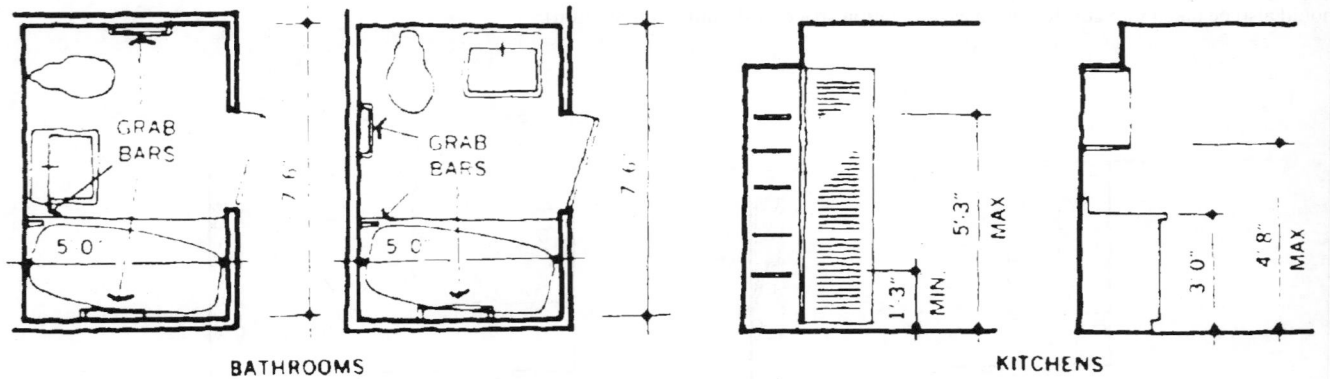

**Fig. 11. Bathroom and kitchen for elderly tenants**

**Table 1**   Process of designing apartment buildings

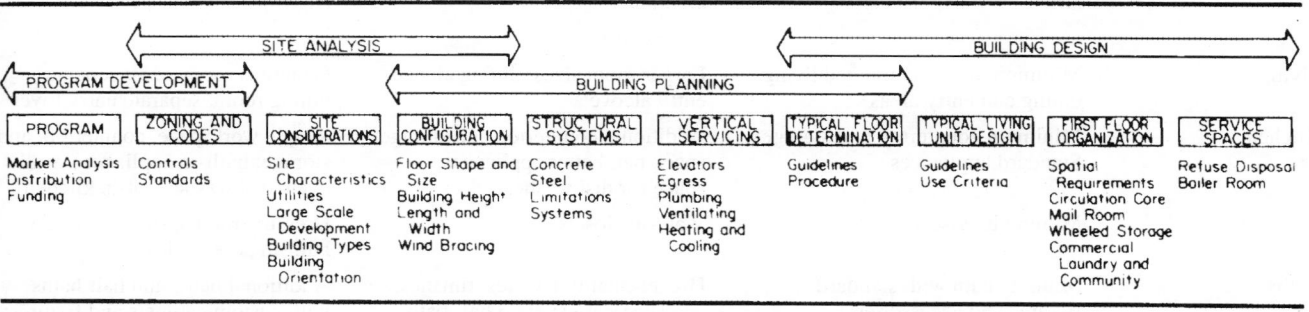

# APARTMENT BUILDINGS

## GENERAL

The process of designing an apartment building may be graphically depicted in a general way as in Table 1. It must be borne in mind that, as with any design development, the evolution of an apartment building design is not a sequential process but a process of continuing interaction, feedback, and reevaluation, and that the number and complexity of events will vary according to the program, scope, and funding sources involved. The sequences shown are labeled as *program development, site analysis, building planning,* and *building design.*

*Program development* is for the most part evaluation of information over which the architect has relatively little control but which shapes the project in a relatively basic way.

*Site analysis* involves evaluation of physical data which must be recognized, identified, and weighed by the architect in making basic design decisions dealing with site use, allocation, and development.

## PROGRAM

### Market Analysis

A market analysis and program formulation may precede the retention of an architect; however, to an increasing degree clients solicit the aid of an architect in these areas. An investigation of the potential market should consider existing market conditions and trends with regard to the following:

1. Type of occupancy
   - Rental
   - Cooperative
   - Condominium
2. Price (rent, maintenance, *etc.*)
3. Amenities
4. Apartment size (area and number of rooms)
5. Building types
6. Vacancy rates
7. Public facilities (transportation, schools, shopping, recreation)

Program items to be resolved include the following:

- *Price range:* What segment of the market is the project to be aimed at?
- *Amenities:* Identified in Table 2 as support facilities and closely interrelated with price range.
- *Scope:* How many units?
- *Distribution:* Percentage of each type of unit.
- *Building type or types.*

### Density

Figure 1 compares relative densities of various urban and suburban situations. It is helpful to have a feel for the physical reality of density figures as an aid in visualizing possible solutions and to anticipate implications of decisions which are made during program formulation.

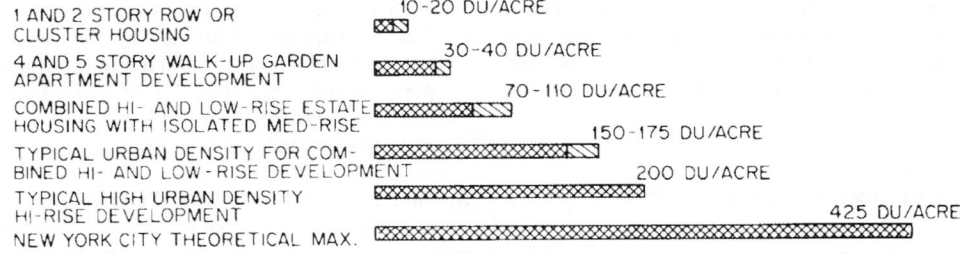

**Fig. 1. Comparative densities**

*Authors:* J. L. Gruzen and J. J. Koster, Gruzen and Partners
*Reviewer:* James Wentling, FAIA

**Table 2**  Comparative program elements—market range

|  | Low | Medium | High |
|---|---|---|---|
| | | *Living unit* | |
| Living | Minimum areas: combined living, dining and entry areas | Larger room sizes: dining alcove, entry alcove | Generous room sizes: separate dining room, separate entry foyer |
| Kitchen | Minimum countertop and storage; Standard appliances | Additional countertop and storage; snack bar, better appliances, space for dishwasher | Ample workspace, countertop, and storage; built-in appliances, wall oven, dishwasher, eat-in kitchen |
| Bedrooms | Minimum closets | Walk-in closets | Dressing rooms, storage closets, built-in accessories |
| Baths | Minimal bath with standard fixtures and accessories; minimum finishes | Higher-quality fixtures, finishes, and accessories; extra half bath at entry or master bedroom | Additional baths and half baths with custom cabinets and fixtures; stall showers, etc.; powder room; luxury finishes |
| | | *Support facilities* | |
| In apartment | Few extras limited to security | Intercom, door signal, balconies, unit air conditioners | Doorman and telephone, large balconies, central air conditioning service entrance, servants' quarters |
| In building | Laundry facilities, minimum lobby | Laundry room, commercial space, community room, central storage | Attended parking, convenience shopping, service elevators, doorman, closed-circuit TV security system, valet service, meeting rooms, health club, sheltered swimming facilities |
| Site | Open parking, drying yard | Secure open or sheltered parking, outdoor play and sitting area, swimming pool | Gardens, recreation areas, country club amenities, swimming pool |

## ZONING AND CODES

### General

Zoning and building codes are of basic importance to any project; of all types of projects, those which involve housing tend to be regulated to a greater degree by zoning ordinances and codes.

Appropriate local and regional authorities should be contacted in order to determine the type and extent of limitations or controls which may be imposed on a project and, further, to gauge the discretionary powers and flexibility of the governing authorities. To an increasing degree, the philosophy of zoning is changing from one of restrictive limits and controls to an approach which attempts to lead and influence community growth. Many communities and regional authorities have guiding master plans which deal with long-range development and evaluation. The conceptual and planning freedom of the architect is linked with these considerations.

### Controls

Zoning is concerned principally with questions of use, bulk, density, and location.

- *Use, bulk, and density* are usually controlled on the basis of districts which are generally shown on maps and explained in an accompanying text (Fig. 2).
- *Uses* may be designated as, for example, residential, commercial, manufacturing, and, in some cases, park or recreational. Mixed

uses are frequently allowed. For large housing projects, it is considered advantageous to incorporate retail shopping, entertainment, and dining facilities into a program.

- *Location* of buildings is controlled in order to prevent oppressive proximity of building masses. Formulas or diagrams which relate to variables such as building height and density are applied to locate buildings with respect to property lines and/or one another (see Figs. 3 and 4).
- *Density* regulations limit the number of people per site-area unit. The basis for density determination will vary from regulation to regulation. Density may range from a low of 10 or fewer people per acre in low-density districts to a high of up to 1,500 or more per acre in the highest-density districts.
- *Bulk is* frequently controlled by floor-area ratio, which limits total buildable floor area as a multiple of the site area. In contemporary zoning regulations, floor-area ratio for apartment buildings will range from a low of 1 or less to a high in the range of 14 to 18 in dense metropolitan areas.

Building codes are less regional and vary less than zoning regulations. Many localities adopt national or state building codes as their standard. Such codes are concerned with health and safety requirements such as light and air, access, egress, construction standards, minimum dimensional standards, fire detection and protection, and fire equipment access. (*Note:* Local fire departments and fire insurance groups may exert more restrictive controls than the previously mentioned codes.)

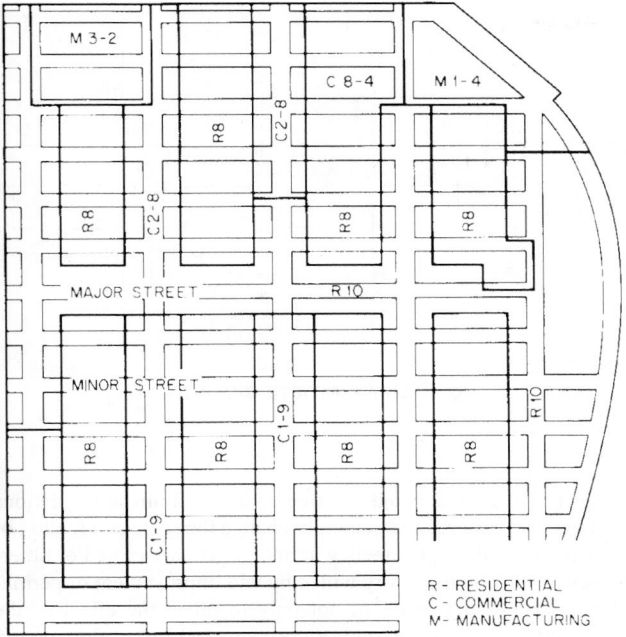

**Fig. 2. Zoning map example**

R - RESIDENTIAL
C - COMMERCIAL
M- MANUFACTURING

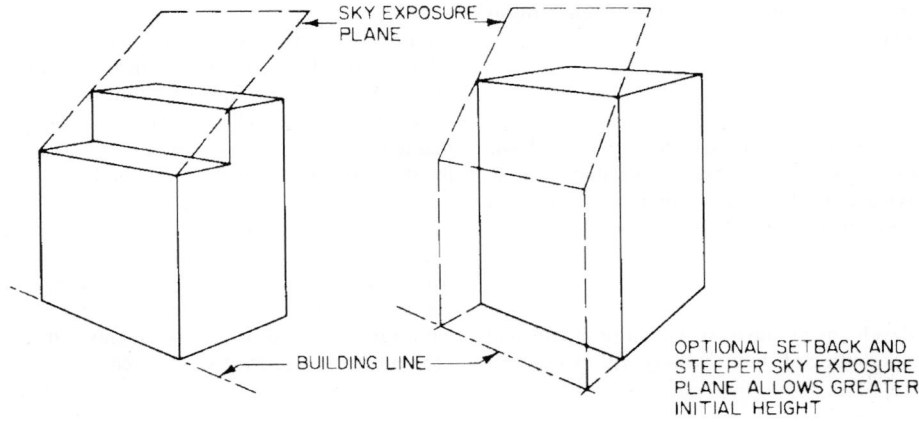

SKY EXPOSURE PLANE

BUILDING LINE

OPTIONAL SETBACK AND STEEPER SKY EXPOSURE PLANE ALLOWS GREATER INITIAL HEIGHT

**Fig. 3. Setback diagrams**

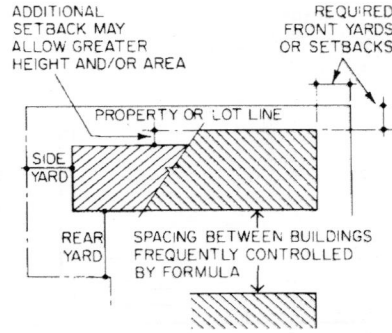

ADDITIONAL SETBACK MAY ALLOW GREATER HEIGHT AND/OR AREA

REQUIRED FRONT YARDS OR SETBACKS

PROPERTY OR LOT LINE

SIDE YARD

REAR YARD

SPACING BETWEEN BUILDINGS FREQUENTLY CONTROLLED BY FORMULA

**Fig. 4. Building spacing and location diagram**

## Standards

Similar to zoning and codes and equally important in many cases are governmental agency standards, which apply when public or semi-public funding sources are involved (or mortgage standards when private funding is involved).

The need for a thorough initial investigation and continuing review for conformance with controls imposed by zoning, codes, and agencies cannot be overemphasized.

## SITE CONSIDERATIONS

### Site Characteristics

Physical characteristics of a site may impose limitations on a building program; therefore, an early analysis of site data and conditions should be undertaken by the architect in order to ascertain and evaluate such limitations.

Borings and samples taken at the site will provide information regarding location and extent of rock, bearing capacity of the subsurface strata at various levels, and the level of a water table.

A survey indicating boundaries, contours, or spot elevations is necessary, and in the case of difficult sites, such a survey may indicate terrain and other conditions which will strongly influence design decisions. Limitations imposed by difficult terrain—in addition to those imposed by local laws or ordinances—may limit such items as location of driveways and parking entrances.

### Utilities

Availability, adequacy, and location of site utilities enter into basic decision making. A building or buildings may be located so as to minimize expensive service runs. Inadequacy or unavailability of certain services may require on-site generation or disposal facilities.

### Large Scale

Large-scale residential developments involve special problems and opportunities. Closing or rerouting of streets wholly within a project

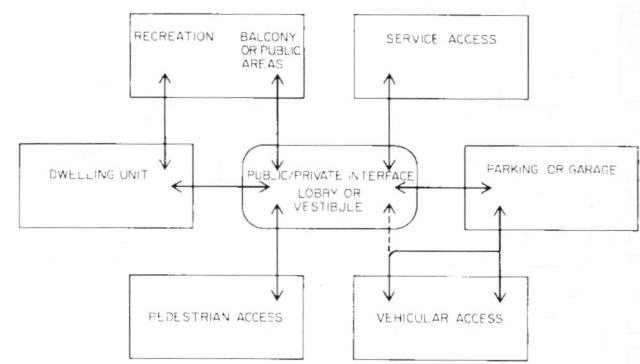

**Fig. 5. Site element diagram**

is frequently undertaken and can free up area, eliminate restrictions of a street grid pattern, and generally change the scale and feeling of a project. When through streets within a project are closed or otherwise restricted, compensatory widening and improvement of peripheral roads is usually in order, not only to offset the effect of the closings but also to accommodate the increased traffic flow generated by the project itself. Similarly, shutting down a utility line and adding to demand generally requires compensatory improvement.

### Site Elements

Figure 5 diagrams possible relationships among site layout elements which normally occur in apartment development. As suggested by the diagram, it is desirable to limit cross traffic among circulation elements, such as vehicular access and pedestrian access, and to maintain proximity or easy access among activity elements, such as the dwelling unit, recreation, and parking.

The relationships may be horizontally or vertically arranged, depending on density or tightness of a site. Emphasis on the importance of certain relationships may vary with the program; however, the basic elements and relationships remain. Fig. 6 shows examples of different arrangements of the site elements—arrangements which reflect program density relative to site area.

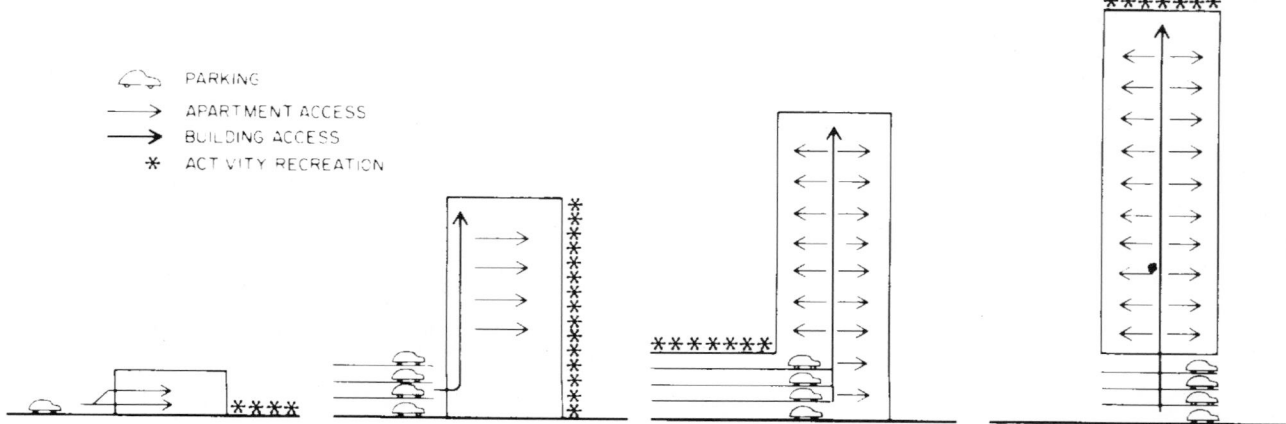

**Fig. 6. Site element relationships**

## Building Access

Figure 7 diagrams various means of building access and internal circulation, each with different advantages and degrees of suitability to specific design solutions.

## Building Orientation

Building orientation may be influenced by a number of factors, such as site, view (desirable or undesirable), sun, and prevailing winds. Closely interrelated to building orientation is the question of internal circulation and floor layout of the building. Figure 8 indicates how different layouts lend themselves to solutions of site problems.

## BUILDING CONFIGURATION

### Floor Shape and Size

The shape and size of an apartment building can have significant influence on the cost and consequently the feasibility of a project.

The shape of the repetitive typical floors influences the cost of constructing and enclosing the floors. For purposes of economy and efficiency, building shape should be such that expensive exterior walls are minimized in ratio to area enclosed and that breaks and direction changes in the perimeter are minimized.

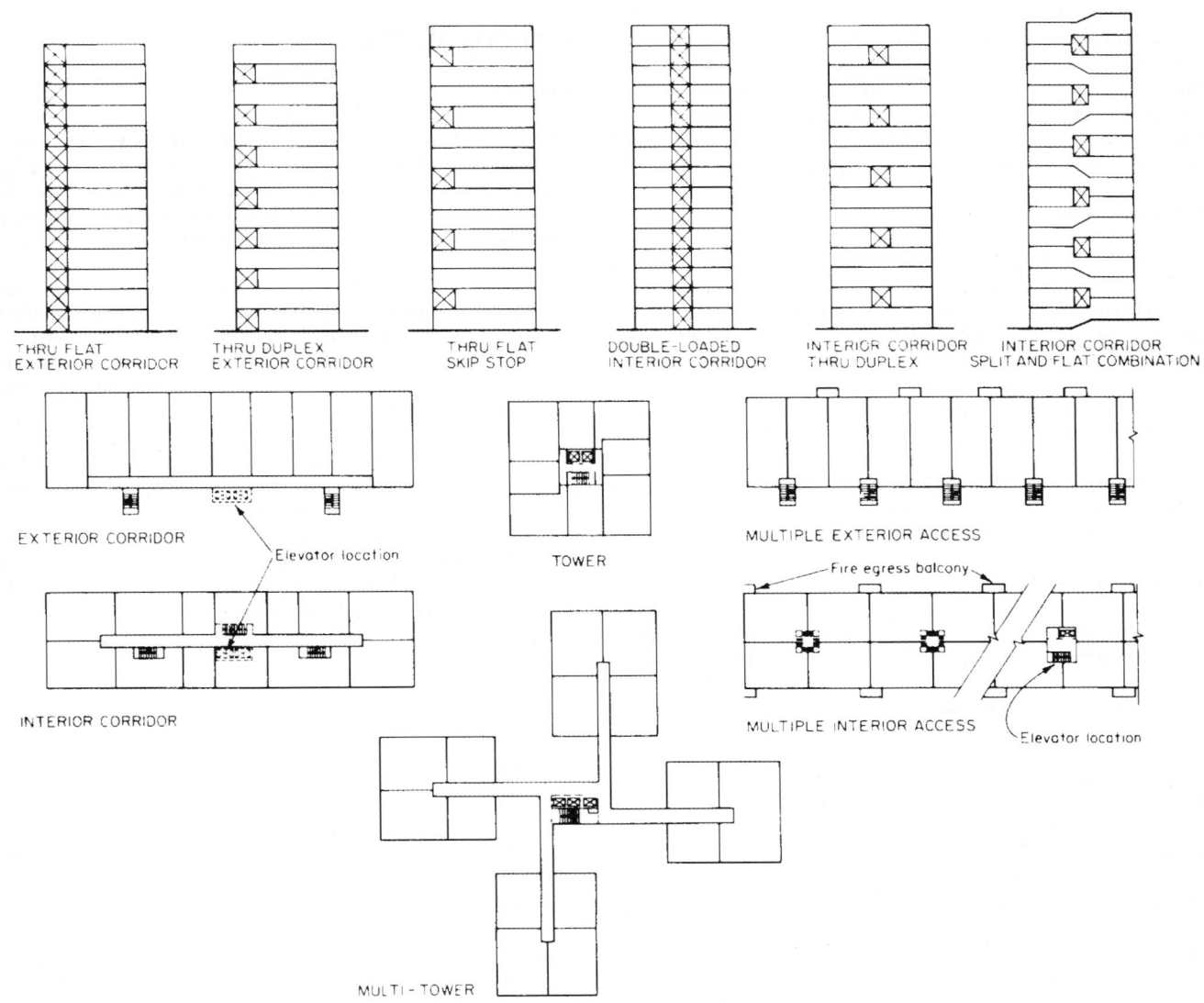

Fig. 7. Building types

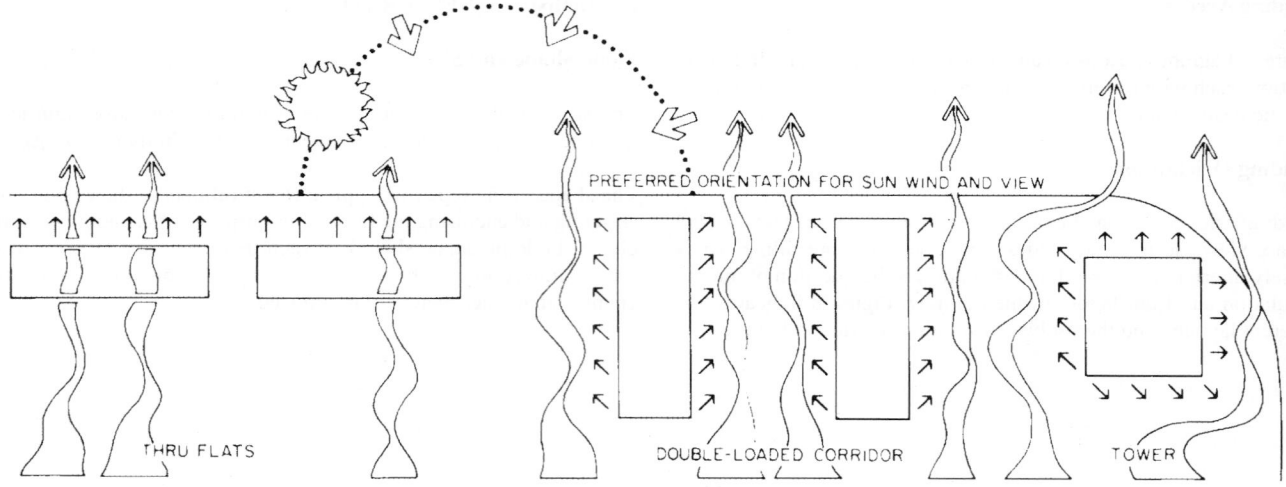

Fig. 8. Orientation influences

The area of a typical floor may affect costs. For example, pouring of a typical tier in a cast-in-place concrete building is a continuous process and requires a full concrete crew throughout. The area of a typical floor or part thereof should be such as to efficiently utilize the day's productivity of a concrete crew. Similar analysis and considerations should be applied to other building techniques or systems.

**Building Height**

The cost of a building may be affected by building height. A building may be of such height that it exceeds prevailing capacities in terms of available construction equipment and contractor experience. In addition to considerations of what is possible, there are considerations of what is practical and efficient from a cost standpoint. Of the various mechanical systems which serve an apartment building, each has various increments and step-up points. For example, there is a situation such that the addition of a single extra floor could require a substantial increase in elevator service either through an additional elevator or an expensive increase in elevator speed. Similar situations exist for heating, cooling, plumbing, and ventilating systems, and opinions of the various consultants in these areas should be solicited.

**Length and Width**

Additional costs resulting from an increase of building length or width are generally proportionate to increase in area. However, as with other such items, there are step-up points at which there are disproportionately large increases in cost for slight dimensional increases.

**Wind Bracing**

Wind bracing becomes a structural design consideration in buildings beyond the 10- to 12-story range, and one must then consider measures which may be introduced to resist the overturning tendency due to wind loads. Wind bracing may be achieved by introduction of various structural measures. The extent and, therefore, the expense of these measures may be reduced if the building shape itself contributes to wind bracing. As the diagrams (Fig. 9) indicate, certain building shapes obviously have a greater inherent resistance to overturning.

## STRUCTURAL SYSTEMS

### Concrete

The most common structural system presently employed for medium- to high-rise apartment construction is flat-plate cast-in-place reinforced concrete with randomly placed columns. This structural approach has certain advantages which make it particularly adaptable to apartment construction (Fig. 10).

1.   The horizontal services normally required in apartment construction may be imbedded within the concrete slab, thereby eliminating the need for a hung coiling and allowing the flat underside of the slab to serve as the finished coiling of the space below. This reduces floor-to-floor and overall building height and eliminates the separate construction of a hung coiling.

2.   The possibility of placing columns randomly adapts well to the inherently irregular module generated by a typical apartment floor layout. Columns may thus be "buried" in convenient locations within an efficient layout.

3.   As a rule, openings for vertical services may be located at will in this type of structure; however, large openings near columns should be handled with care so as to assure continuity of vertical and horizontal reinforcing.

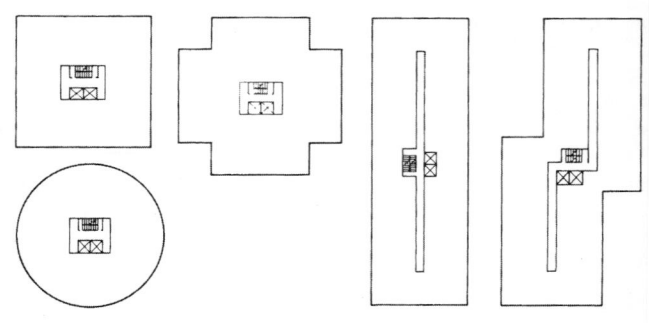

Fig. 9. Building shapes

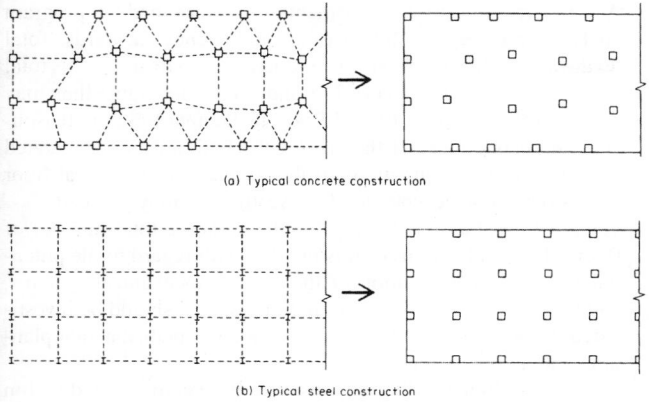

(a) Typical concrete construction

(b) Typical steel construction

**Fig. 10. Steel and concrete structural systems**

## Steel

Although much less common than cast-in-place concrete, steel-frame structures are also employed in the construction of apartment buildings.

The advantages of strength and relative simplicity of erection may recommend steel for use in extremely tall structures or for use in locales where there is limited experience in the use of concrete.

Steel structural frames tend to be laid out in a regular grid pattern, and this in turn regularizes the apartment layout. One should bear in mind that in this type of structure mechanical and structural lines may not coincide.

## Limitations

As a rule of thumb, spacing between concrete columns may economically be in the range of 12- to 18-foot centers and spacing for steel columns may range from 16 to 24 feet.

The smallest dimension per side considered acceptable for concrete columns is 10 inches, and 4 feet is the limit which normal concrete framework can easily accommodate. Columns with larger dimensions become, in effect, walls and are formed differently.

## Egress and Safety

Except in rare circumstances, relatively little in the realm of egress and safety is left to the discretion of the architect. In general, the architect may choose only among accepted and approved procedures as set down in codes.

In most codes, two means of egress must be provided within specified distances from each dwelling unit (Figs. 11a to 11c) except in the case of duplexes, which frequently require an additional means of egress off the corridors, usually by means of an escape balcony (Fig. 11e).

Figure 11d diagrams a scissor stair which, as shown, is an arrangement which allows for construction of two stairs in one fire enclosure. This is an efficient and cost-saving solution to the two-egress requirements. Most codes, however, effectively preclude the use of scissor stairs, in many cases by limiting the allowable length of dead-end corridors. Fire escapes are usually required for construction that is not fireproof, and sprinklers, smoke doors, fire detectors, and alarms are additionally required for various classifications of construction in some codes.

## Plumbing

Vertical plumbing risers and waste lines (or plumbing stacks) are expensive due to both material and labor costs. Reduction in the number of stacks saves money and is, therefore, to a greater or lesser extent advantageous and advisable.

Reduction in the number of plumbing stacks is accomplished by doubling or even tripling up on each stack at each floor. Figure 12 shows common bathroom and/or kitchen layouts with order-of-magnitude dimensions shown.

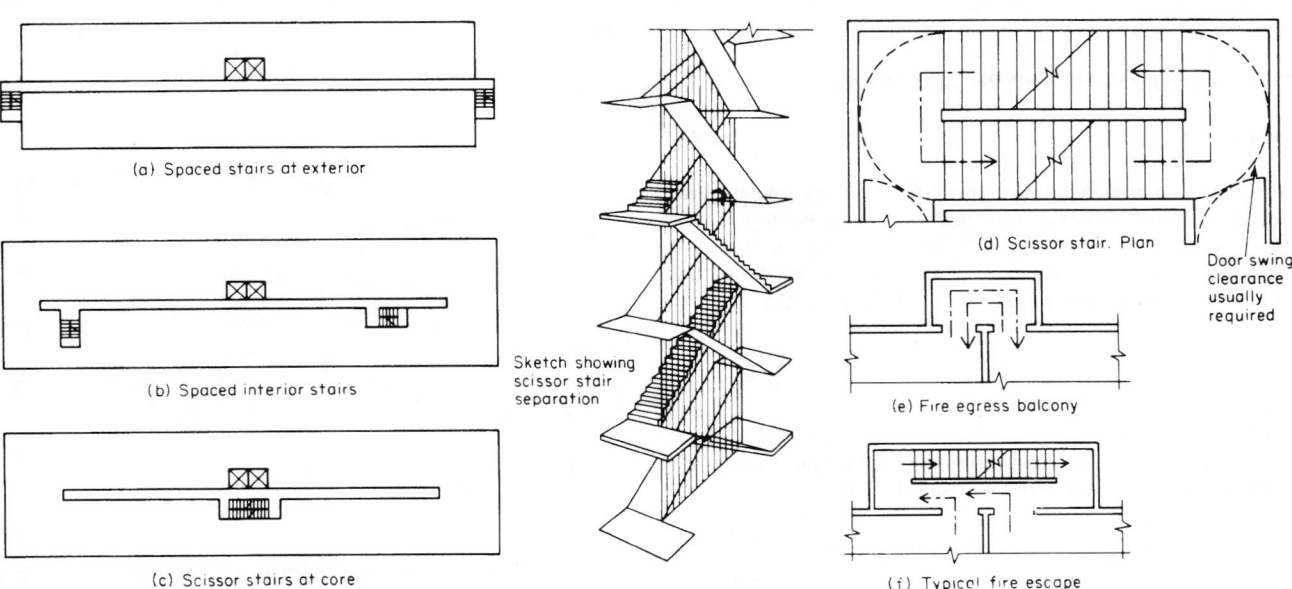

(a) Spaced stairs at exterior

(b) Spaced interior stairs

(c) Scissor stairs at core

Sketch showing scissor stair separation

(d) Scissor stair. Plan

Door swing clearance usually required

(e) Fire egress balcony

(f) Typical fire escape

**Fig. 11. Types of stairs**

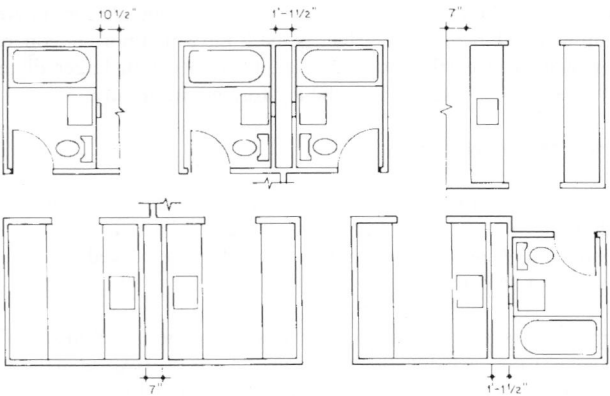

**Fig. 12. Plumbing chases**

*Note:* Dimensions shown are clear dimensions for high-rise buildings up to 25 to 30 stories. These dimensions, it should be remembered, are for rough layout purposes only and should be verified by consultants.

### Ventilation

Interior spaces such as bathrooms, interior kitchens, and public halls require mechanical exhausting.

### Heating and Cooling

In most cases, planning and spatial layout are not significantly influenced by heating and/or cooling units and their lines of supply. The most common exception is the case in which ducts deliver conditioned air from either a central source or a unit in the apartment. In such a case, ducts may be of such size as to become a planning factor. Otherwise, heating or cooling units are served either by hot and/or chilled water pipes or electric conduit.

### DETERMINATION OF A TYPICAL FLOOR

### General

In discussing determination of a typical floor and specific apartment layouts, the most common structural type—poured-in-place flat-plate concrete construction with repetitive typical floors—is assumed. The principles of the procedure which will be outlined may, however, be applied to any construction technique or system, bearing in mind the unique characteristics of that technique or system (Fig. 13).

### Procedure

Sequentially, the steps in the determination of a typical floor (in an ideal case) could proceed as follows (see also Fig. 14):

1. Investigate program with regard to the total number and types of apartments.
2. Identify repetitive groups, with each group possibly representing a typical floor.

3. Assign area figures to apartments as determined in program analysis or as required by governmental agency standards. Total up the area of the apartments in a repetitive group and to this total add 10 to 15 percent for corridors and cores. This figure then may represent the area of a typical floor. If the area figure is reasonable and economical, if the size of the building thus generated conforms with various limits of the site, and if the typical floor area is otherwise acceptable, the investigation may proceed.
4. Tentative acceptance of a typical floor fixes a total number of floors. The implications of this number with regard to the potential for efficient utilization of the various mechanical systems, soil bearing characteristics, zoning limits, etc., should be investigated. If the number of floors checks out acceptably, actual planning and layout may proceed.
5. The typical floor distribution must now be accommodated within the tentatively accepted area and within reasonable dimensions. The elevator core and stairs should be located and apartments laid out around them.

### TYPICAL LIVING UNIT DESIGN

Figure 15 diagrams interrelationships among component elements of a typical living unit.

Although many apartments tend to have much the same layout as the diagram, there are many alternative arrangements which retain the essential component relationships. Apartments may be arranged as corner or floor-through units. In addition to flats, or apartments on one level, layouts may be on two or three floors or on split levels (see Fig. 16).

As the diagram indicates, it is considered desirable to have ready circulation from the entrance foyer to the activity elements of the kitchen, living room, and sleeping areas and at the same time to maintain degrees of separation among these three elements.

Ideally, each space in an apartment should have access or exposure to the outdoors. However, application of this principle could result in an excessively expensive building type. Therefore baths, foyers, and frequently kitchens and dining areas are usually developed as interior spaces (see Fig. 17).

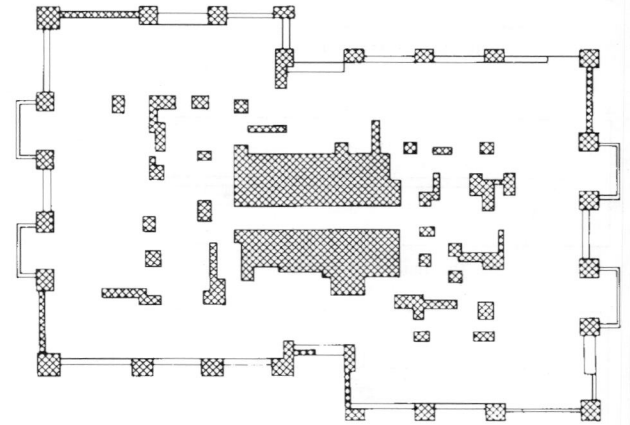

**Fig. 13. Plan of 44-story apartment building with hatched areas indicating space devoted to vertical service element**

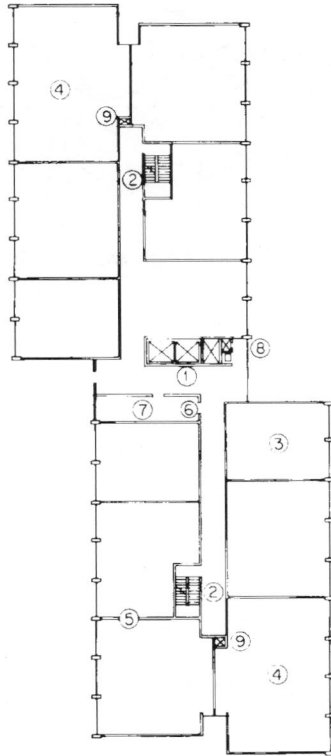

Fig. 14. Typical floor. (1) It is generally desirable to group vertical services such as the elevator, incinerator or refuse chute, flue, standpipe, and, if possible, stairs so as to minimize above-roof construction. (2) Stairs may be spaced to avoid corridors with lengthy dead ends. (3) Efficiency apartments, probably with higher-than-average late-night traffic, may be best located near the elevator. (4) Multibedroom apartments are best located at corners. Larger multibedroom units lay out more compactly with two exposures. Larger apartments at corners also can cut down on required public corridor. (5) An attempt should be made to back up similar units, such as bedrooms, as well as similar mechanical services. (6) It may be necessary to allow space for electric closets (i.e., electric distribution panels) at every sixth or eighth floor. If electric heat is used, closets may occur more frequently. (7) Community balcony, laundry, vending machines, stroller storage, or tenant storage may be provided at each floor or only on certain floors. (8) A janitor's closet is usually located on each floor at the refuse room. (9) If the corridor has no window, mechanical ventilation is indicated. Delivery and exhaust ducts should be planned to be remote from one another

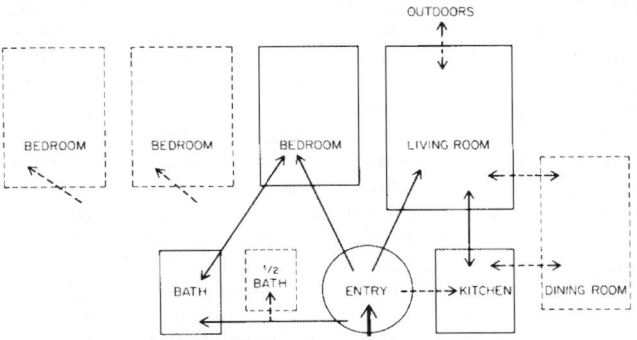

Fig. 15. Apartment element diagram

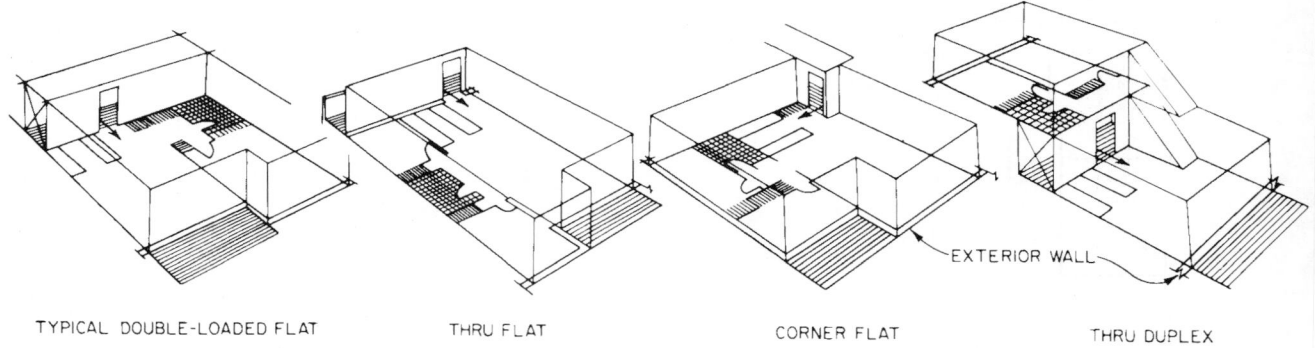

TYPICAL DOUBLE-LOADED FLAT        THRU FLAT        CORNER FLAT        THRU DUPLEX

**Fig. 16. Typical apartment types**

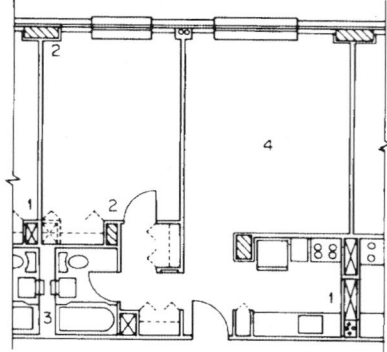

**Fig. 17. Typical apartment layout. (1) It is advisable to back up similar (kitchen and kitchen, bath and bath) ducts where possible. This allows one fan and fireproof enclosure to serve two ducts but requires measures to avoid excessive sound transmission between backed up spaces. Ducts may be "buried" in closets, kitchen, etc. Kitchen exhausts are best located near the range and close to the ceiling. Bathroom exhausts should, if possible, be placed away from the door in order to pull as much bathroom air as possible. Ducts are not necessary in kitchens or baths with windows. (However, baths with windows, like top-floor baths, should be heated.) (2) The structure should be spaced as regularly as practicable and within economical center-to-center distances. Columns built into closets or kitchens should assume the dimensions of the closet or cabinet. Column size should be reduced at upper stories of tall buildings. Slab openings along an entire column face should be avoided. (3) Plumbing backup is recommended. Dissimilar uses may be backed up, and it is possible to back up plumbing for more than two spaces. (4) Depth of rooms is sometimes limited by building codes. In any event, room depth relative to window size and location and natural light should be considered**

## FIRST-FLOOR ORGANIZATION

### General

The first floor of an apartment building fulfills a number of different program requirements. It serves as a connection between the dwelling portion of a building and the outdoors; it relates and interacts with both the outdoor functions and the dwelling units; and, further, it accommodates the physical transition between the dwelling units and the first floor.

Figure 18 illustrates possible interrelationships of first-floor functions with both the outdoors and the dwelling units.

Program requirements for typical first-floor spaces frequently call for larger unobstructed areas than occur at dwelling floors above. Common methods employed to achieve the unobstructed space at the first floor are as follows:

- "Push out" the walls at the ground floor and enclose a larger space with an appropriate structure.
- Hang a ceiling in the first floor and collect and redirect various vertical services which would otherwise break up space at the ground floor. This is a common method used in the case of plumbing, heating, and electrical lines and is not unusual for ventilating ducts. If there is substantial advantage to be gained, structural columns may be picked up and carried on girders concealed by the hung ceiling.

### Vertical Circulation Core

For purposes of security and convenience, elevators should be well illuminated and visible from the lobby area. At least one exit stair should empty directly to the outside (but not necessarily at the lobby level).

It should be borne in mind that the stair layout in the lobby will frequently differ from that of a typical floor due to a greater first-floor ceiling height.

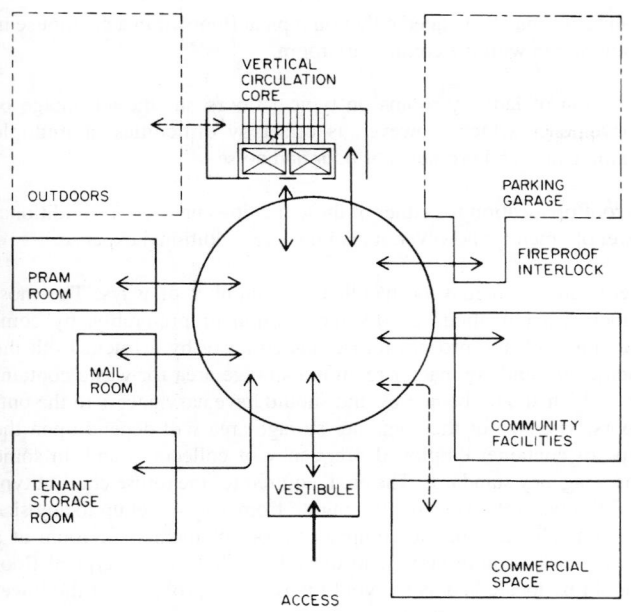

**Fig. 18. First-floor diagram**

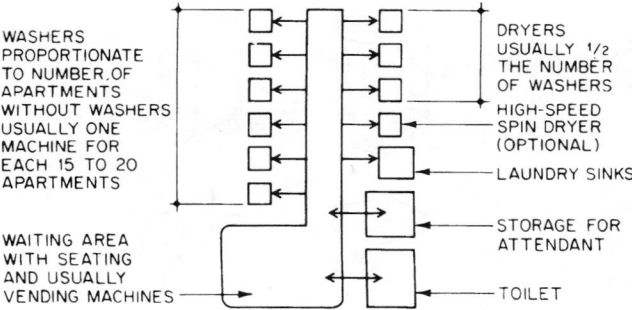

**Fig. 19. Laundry room diagram**

## SERVICE SPACES

### Mail Room

Mailboxes as well should be highly visible. If boxes are rear-loading, a locked room behind the boxes should be provided for the mail carrier's use. Front-loading boxes require no such room. However, in either case, an additional secure area for packages and deliveries may be advised. Current federal requirements which govern matters such as maximum and minimum height of boxes and size of mail rooms should be consulted.

### Wheeled Storage and/or Stroller Room

Paths of travel from the main entrance to these areas should be short, direct, and without steps. Layout of the rooms for purposes of security should be such that all parts of the room are visible from the entrance. Lock rails, to which equipment may be secured, should be supplied.

### Commercial

Shops and service facilities at the ground floor provide many advantages in terms of activity and convenience. However, much of the advantage to the building may be diminished if the shops face away from the lobby and provide either no access or poor backdoor access from the apartment building itself. On the other hand, easy circulation between a commercial establishment and the lobby may cause security problems which must be considered.

### Laundry and Community Room

Laundries and community rooms are frequently found at the first floor for convenient servicing and public access and in order to utilize the additional story height. These facilities should be on a short, direct path from elevators, with as little cross circulation with other activities as possible. (See Figs. 19 to 23.)

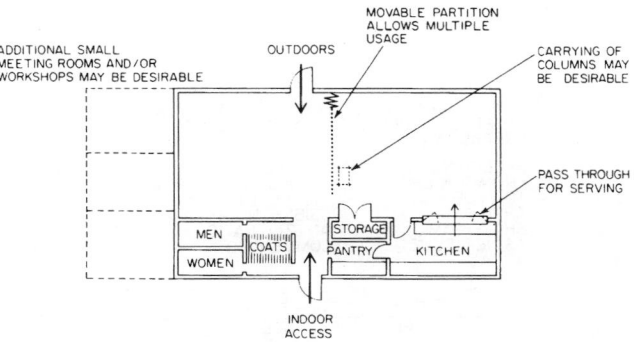

**Fig. 20. Community room layout**

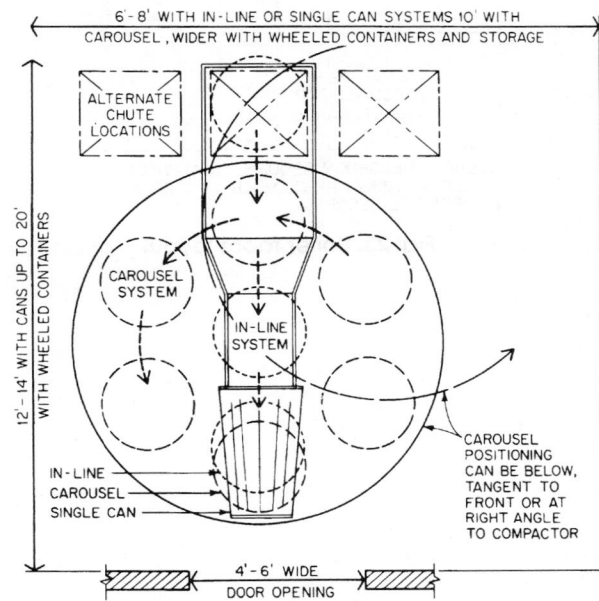

**Fig. 21. Compactor room layout**

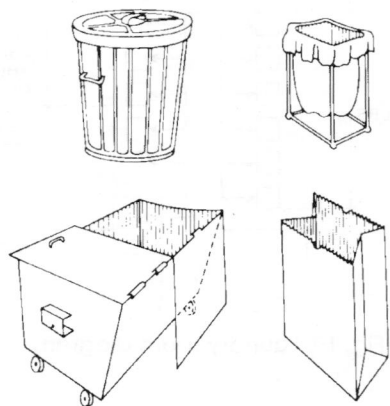

**Fig. 22. Typical refuse containers. Consult and coordinate with refuse collection agency to ensure acceptability of system regarding weight and size of containers**

Laundries may be located either on typical floors or in a penthouse in conjunction with the community room.

Location of laundry rooms on typical floors has the advantage of convenience which, however, is offset by difficulties of multiple maintenance and problems of odor and noise.

A rooftop location for either of these facilities provides an additional level of amenity; however, it also involves additional expense.

Refuse disposal may be handled in a number of ways. The most widely used methods are by incineration or preferably, by compaction, with the process refuse hauled away by a truck. Both the incinerator and compactor require a storage area for waste containers, which should be nearby and should have easy access to the outdoors. The size of the container storage area will depend upon the type of container employed, frequency of collection, and, in some cases, agency standards. The area required for the refuse chute at typical floors is relatively small, ranging from 4 by 4 feet up to any size desired. The area of the compactor room or incinerator room at a lower level is quite large, and the refuse chute at the typical floor should be located so as to avoid interference problems at the lower levels.

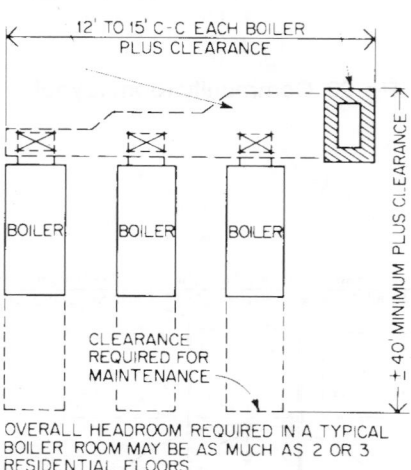

**Fig. 23. Boiler room layout**

Fig. 1. Seniors housing public entry

# SENIORS HOUSING

## ENTRY/EXIT

The entry/exit (or front door, Fig. 1) is the critical transfer point from the least public area of the development to the least private area of the dwelling unit. If properly designed, it will ensure the privacy of unit activities and contribute strongly to the sense of home. It must be a place, not just a door in a wall which opens directly into the living area or other such space (see Figs. 2 and 3).

## Accessibility

The entry/exit area should be directly accessible to the following less private areas of the unit:

- Food preparation
- Living area, with spatial differentiation between the two functions
- Storage and utility

The entry/exit area should be indirectly accessible (minor intermediate activity or a circulation path) to more private areas of the unit:

- Dining
- Private outdoor (optional)
- Personal hygiene
- Sleeping and dressing

The entry/exit area should have both visual and audio contact with visitors outside of the entry door; but visitors should not have visual contact and only controlled audio contact into the entry area of the dwelling unit. This maximizes the ability of the resident to keep out unwanted visitors and allows the resident to control the space just outside the unit.

All of the previously mentioned spaces with direct physical access to the entry/exit area should have visual and audio contact with this area for control and security within the unit. Other areas should have audio but not visual contact to minimize disruption of privacy.

## Orientation

The orientation of this activity toward view and sunlight is governed by more essential concerns related to building type and the functional organization of other activities.

## Furnishings

The furnishings and equipment necessary for this area are as follows:

- Storage for outer wear, that is, coats, boots, umbrellas, etc.; a closet at least 3 feet by 2 feet-2 inches should be provided
- A place to sit while putting on outerwear

## Spatial Characteristics

The space should have sufficient wall area to accommodate a mirror; there should also be a clear dimension area of at least 3 feet-6 inches to 4 feet square for putting on coats as well as greeting guests.

## FOOD PREPARATION

The physical characteristics of the aged hamper the normal functions of food preparation, cooking, food and utensil storage, trash disposal, dish washing and drying, and eating. If appropriate physical design adaptation is not made to the food preparation space and facilities, cooking and related activities will become unpleasant, tedious, and possibly dangerous. The net effect will be the creation of a psychological barrier which deters the user from cooking and eating. This situation is particularly unacceptable because dietary problems can become acute for the aged.

## Accessibility

The food preparation area should be directly accessible to the main entry/exit of the dwelling unit to facilitate carrying of bundles. It should also be directly accessible to the dining area. If the dining area is outside of the kitchen, a small eating surface in the kitchen for

*Reviewer:* James Wentling, FAIA

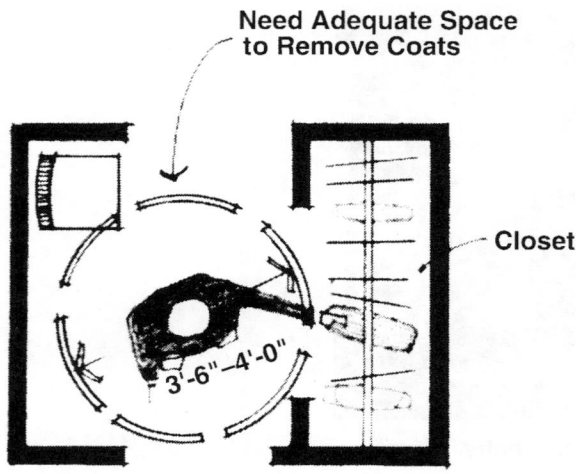

**Fig. 2. Unit entry/exit**

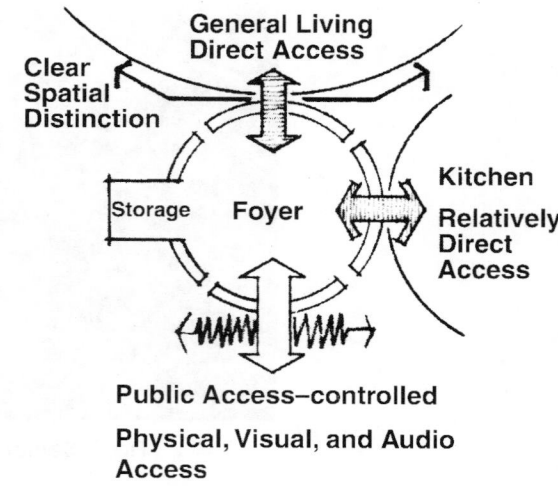

**Fig. 3. The foyer**

breakfast or light meals should be provided. This can be a small table, counter, or pull-out shelf about 24 by 24 inches, set at table height and usable from a wheelchair. The food preparation area should be indirectly accessible to but visually screened from the living, sleeping, personal hygiene, and private outdoor areas of the dwelling unit. Of these, access should be most direct to the private outdoor space. In all cases, indirect access should be through easily traversed intermediate spaces or corridors.

Visual and audio contact to the entry/exit area should be maintained, while audio contact to the living, sleeping, and personal hygiene areas should be minimized (see Fig. 4).

**Orientation**

Often food preparation areas are located at the rear of dwelling units, but, where possible, this should be avoided. The kitchen should be located on an outside wall with an interesting view from a window, and it should have morning sunlight if possible.

**Furnishings and Equipment**

The necessary equipment for food preparation and related activities is as follows:

- Ventilation, both mechanical and natural, to eliminate heat and odors
- Sinks and associated work space
- Cooking unit and oven with associated work space
- Refrigerator and freezer with associated loading and unloading counter space
- Storage consisting of wall and base cabinets and pantry
- Dishwasher (optional, but should be included where possible)
- Dining counter (where formal dining space is outside of the kitchen)
- Clothes washer and dryer (location in the unit is optional, but the kitchen is a good location)

An example of a desirable organization of kitchen activities is shown in Fig. 5.

An L- or U-shaped kitchen is preferable to the pullman or corridor-type kitchen. The corridor type is inconvenient for elderly people who, with advancing age and motor and sensory losses, find it difficult to repeatedly turn from one counter to another as they work. Table 1 and Figs. 6 to 8 give necessary clearances and dimensions.

Equipment should be placed so that there is sufficient operating room between it and any adjacent corner cabinet. At least 12 inches from

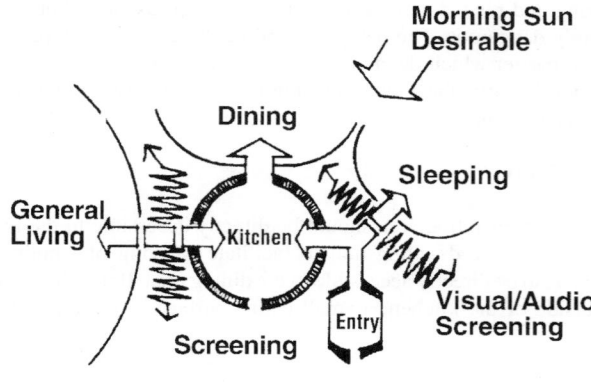

**Fig. 4. Kitchen area**

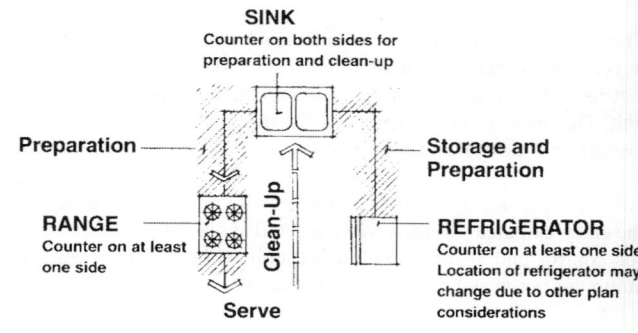

**Fig. 5. Kitchen activity pattern—meal preparation and cleanup**

**Table 1** Frontages for work centers

| Work centers | One bedroom | Two bedroom |
|---|---|---|
| Sink | 24 in | 24 in |
| Counter and base cabinet at each side | 18 in | 21 in |
| Range | 24 in | 24 in |
| Counter and base cabinet at one side | 18 in | 21 in |
| Refrigerator (space) | 30 in | 36 in |
| Counter at latch side | 15 in | 15 in |
| Mixing | | |
| Base and wall cabinet | 30 in | 36 in |

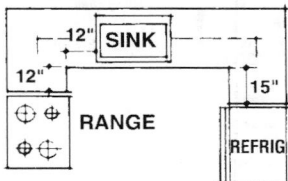

Fig. 6. Minimum corner distances

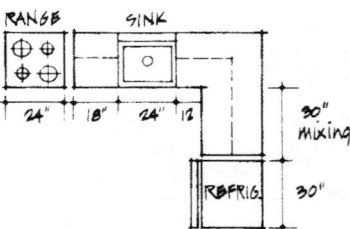

Fig. 7. Minimum frontages and edge distances for one bedroom

the edge of the sink and range and 15 inches at the side of the refrigerator are recommended.

A minimum of 42 inches should be provided between base cabinets or appliances opposite each other. This same minimum clearance applies when a wall, storage wall, or work table is opposite a base cabinet.

Desirable kitchen layouts and work area frontages are illustrated in Figs. 6 to 8. There should be no through circulation in the kitchen work area.

**Spatial Characteristics**

To ensure that this space is enjoyable to work in, it is necessary to provide adequate artificial light at all work areas and to create a spatial volume of appropriate scale. These criteria can be translated to mean that the ceiling height should be no lower than 7 feet-6 inches. Color should be used carefully and be tied to visual identification. It should not create the impression of a closed-in, constricting place. Where ductless range hoods are used, another means of ventilation should be used to carry away cooking heat. Where main dining is combined with food preparation, there should be clear spatial distinction between them, perhaps even a difference in ceiling height.

**DINING**

There must be a permanent dining place within each dwelling unit for independent elderly residents. Depending on the program, the space may be eliminated from units which are part of formal congregate care programs. This place may be within or outside of the food preparation area. Secondary activities will naturally occur within this area, such as table games, paperwork, and hobbies (see Figs. 9 and 10).

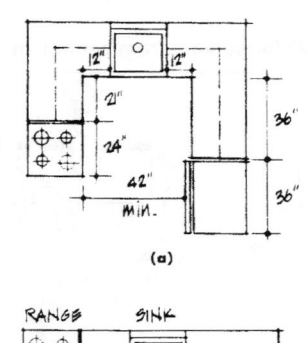

(a)

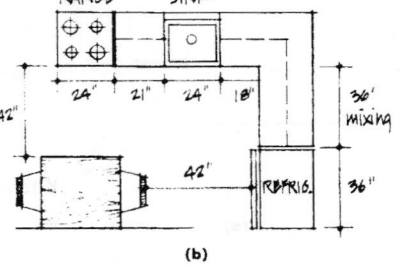

(b)

Fig. 8. Minimum frontages and edge distances for two bedrooms

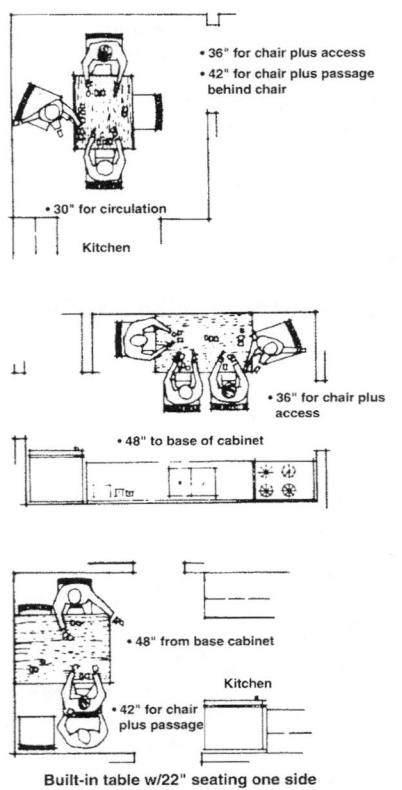

**Fig. 9. Minimum clearances for dining areas in kitchens**

### Accessibility

Because of the array of activities that will be carried out, the dining area should have direct accessibility to the following areas:

- Food preparation area, to facilitate serving of food and cleaning of dishes
- Living area

The dining area may have only indirect (minor intervening activity or circulation path) accessibility to the following areas:

- Entry/exit area
- Private outdoor area

These relationships should be subordinated to the requirements of relationship to the food preparation and living areas. There should be no direct accessibility between the dining activity and the following areas:

- Sleeping and dressing areas
- Personal hygiene areas

There should be direct visual and audio accessibility between the dining and the food preparation areas. Dependent upon unit organization, there may be a direct visual and audio relationship between the dining and living areas; however, in such a case there should be no visual connection between the food preparation and living areas through the dining area. Visual and audio contact between the dining area and very private areas such as the sleeping and dressing and personal hygiene areas should be minimal or entirely eliminated.

### Orientation

Wherever possible, the dining area should have views out of the dwelling unit and should also have morning sunlight. Where the ori-

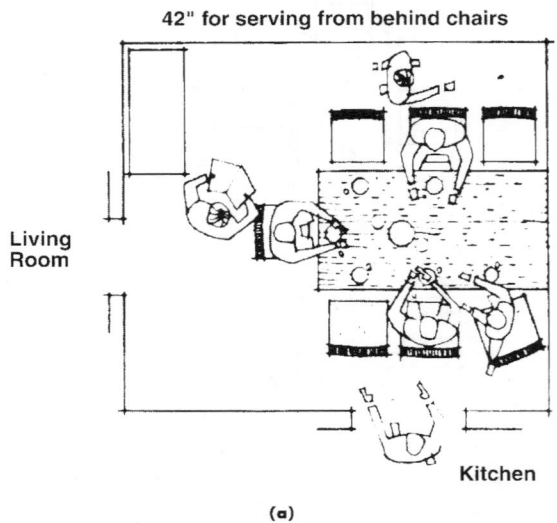

(a)

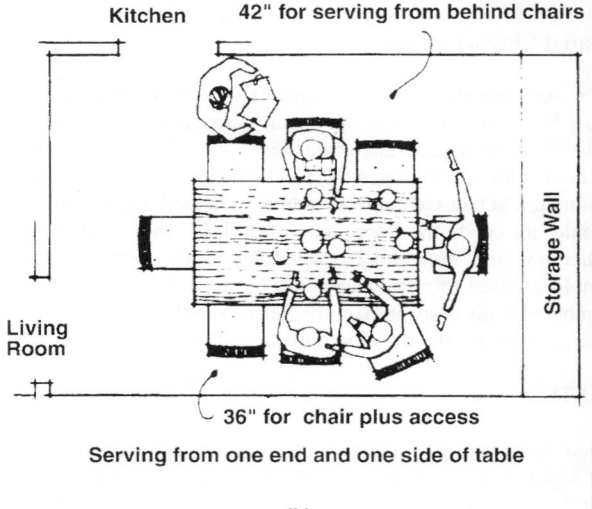

(b)

**Fig. 10. Minimum clearances for dining areas: (*a*) one end of table against wall; (*b*) serving from one end and one side of table**

ntation is western, it is important to control the harsh effects of the etting sun. Because other functional relationships must be achieved such as entry/exit to the living and food preparation areas, and the ood preparation area to the dining area) these orientation criteria must be subordinate and may not be achievable. At the very least, views out should be possible through other activity areas.

## Furnishings

Each dining space must contain sufficient space to accommodate four people. It is desirable that sufficient space be available to expand this accommodation to six persons for special circumstances. Appropriate space should be provided for the storage of china and large dining articles. There should be space to accommodate the following items of furniture:

Dining table with a minimum width of 3 feet, and 2 feet of edge length for each diner (tables should be no less than 3 by 3 feet square, or 3 feet-6 inches in diameter)
Dining chairs of 1 foot-6 inches by 1 foot-6 inches sufficient for the number of diners that can be accommodated
Buffet or storage unit of 1 foot-6 inches by 3 feet-6 inches

Size of the individual eating space on the table should be based on a frontage of 24 inches and an area of approximately 2 square feet. In addition, table space should be large enough to accommodate serving dishes.

The following minimum clearances from the edge of the table should be provided:

- 36 inches for chairs plus access thereto
- 42 inches for chairs plus access and passage
- 42 inches for serving from behind chair
- 30 inches for passage only
- 48 inches from table to base cabinet (in kitchen)

In sizing a separate dining room, provision should be made for circulation through the room in addition to space for dining.

## Spatial characteristics

As previously noted, the dining activity space may be located separately or combined with living or food preparation spaces. Because of economic considerations, a separate dining space seems unlikely, but, nevertheless, it is desirable that developments offer both arrangements to provide a variety and choice in responding to the differences between formal or informal lifestyles of various tenants.

The ceiling height of the dining space in a dwelling unit may be raised or lowered for spatial effect; it should, however, be no lower than 7 feet-6 inches.

The dining table location should be permanent, requiring no rearrangement of furniture at mealtimes, and use of this space should not infringe upon other activities. Wall area should be available for hanging pictures and the like. It should be possible to see the outdoors from the dining table.

Where cabinets are used to separate the food preparation area from the dining area, some of the cabinets should open from both sides to facilitate table setting.

## GENERAL LIVING

Each dwelling unit should have an area or areas which are organized and furnishable for a wide range of activities, such as the following:

- Conversation
- Entertaining
- Reading
- Television viewing
- Stereo/CD listening
- Contemplation
- Lounging

In most units, more than one of these activities will be provided for in a single space. In larger than standard units or in 2-bedroom units, however, it may be desirable to provide more specialized spaces.

### Accessibility

Direct physical accessibility (no intervening spaces) should be provided to the following areas:

- Entry/exit area (planning can be too open; therefore, there should be a definite spatial distinction between living area and entry/exit)
- Private outdoor area, for the extension of general living activities
- Dining area (where these spaces are combined, accessibility should not impair either activity)

Indirect physical accessibility (minor intervening activity or circulation path) should exist between the following areas:

- Food preparation area
- Personal hygiene area for visitor use (this accessibility should not impair the privacy of the sleeping and dressing areas)
- Storage and utility areas
- Sleeping and dressing areas

Visual and audio contact with equally active areas (entry/exit and private outdoor) should be encouraged. Visual and audio contact to the food preparation area should be either minimized or controllable so that it can be minimized or maximized as desired by the resident. The visual and audio relationship between the dining and living areas will vary with the location of the dining area. Visual and audio contact to sleeping and dressing and personal hygiene spaces should be minimized.

### Orientation

Living spaces will be occupied many hours of the day and should, therefore, be provided with interesting views out of the unit. Windows should be located so that a seated person can see out. In first- and second-floor units, windows should also be carefully located to avoid loss of internal privacy from outside of the unit. On upper floors, close views from one unit to another should be avoided.

Sunlight is important to both physical and mental conditions; therefore, planning should ensure that living spaces will receive some sunlight during each sunny day (probably no less than 30 percent of the day). Northern orientations should be avoided. Reference should be made to Fig. 11 for acceptable sun orientations.

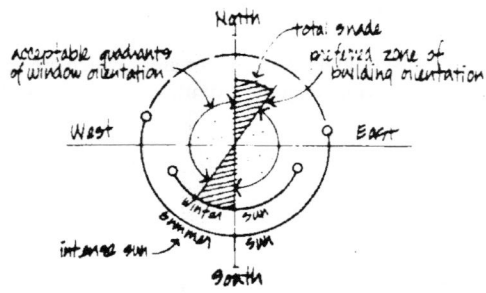

**Fig. 11. Sun orientation**

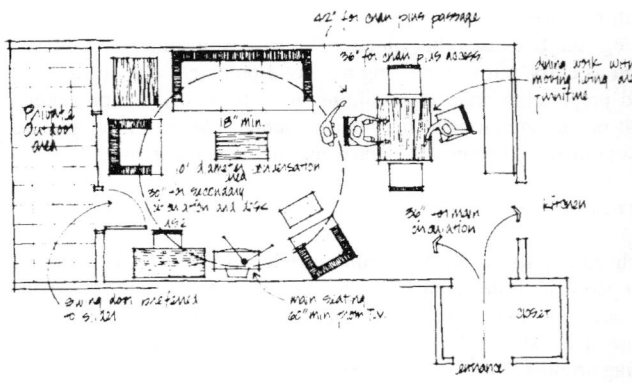

**Fig. 12. Minimum clearances, circulation, and conversation areas for living rooms**

## Furnishability

Furniture that should be accommodated in the living area should include the following items (sizes are minimums) for 1-bedroom units:

- One couch, 3 feet by 6 feet-10 inches
- Two easy chairs, 2 feet-6 inches by 3 feet
- One television set, 1 foot-4 inches by 2 feet-8 inches
- One table, 1 foot-6 inches by 2 feet-6 inches

For 2-bedroom units, one easy chair should be added as well as the following:

- One desk, 1 foot-8 inches by 3 feet-6 inches
- One desk chair, 1 foot-6 inches by 1 foot-6 inches

Because of the diversity of activities which may occur in this space or spaces, and because provision must be made for a wide variety of lifestyles, special provision should be made in the design process to allow for many alternate furniture types and arrangements. The location of doors, windows, and other openings should be carefully considered so as not to unnecessarily limit furniture arrangement. A substantial amount of uninterrupted wall length is required. It should be remembered that many elderly residents will come from single-family or larger rental housing and many of them can be expected to have much more furniture than described here.

The following specific design criteria should be used:

- 60 inches minimum clearance should be provided between facing seating.
- 30 inches minimum clearance is required for use of a desk.
- 60 inches minimum distance is necessary between the television set and seating. The designer should make sure that it is possible to locate the set opposite the main seating area.

People gather during social activities in rather small groups and a desirable conversation distance is rather short; an area approximately 10 feet in diameter is workable.

Figures 12 to 14 illustrate the desired circulation and furnishing requirements.

The living area or areas will most probably have to sustain both intra- and interspace circulation. Adequate circulation space which is direct and nondisruptive is important because of the tendency toward infirmity of movement and loss of visual acuity in elderly people. The following criteria pertain:

- 36 inches minimum clearance should be possible for main traffic paths. This dimension will also accommodate a wheelchair.
- 30 inches minimum clearance should be allowed where secondary circulation occurs between furniture.

## Spatial Characteristics

The living area is likely to become the focus of the dwelling unit for many residents. The size of the space, however, is often not as important as good planning which effectively accommodates the living activity while also accounting for circulation, doors, windows, and furniture. This does not mean, however, that a small space is desirable; in fact, the living area should be of sufficient size as to allow some excess in floor area for such temporary activities as exercise,

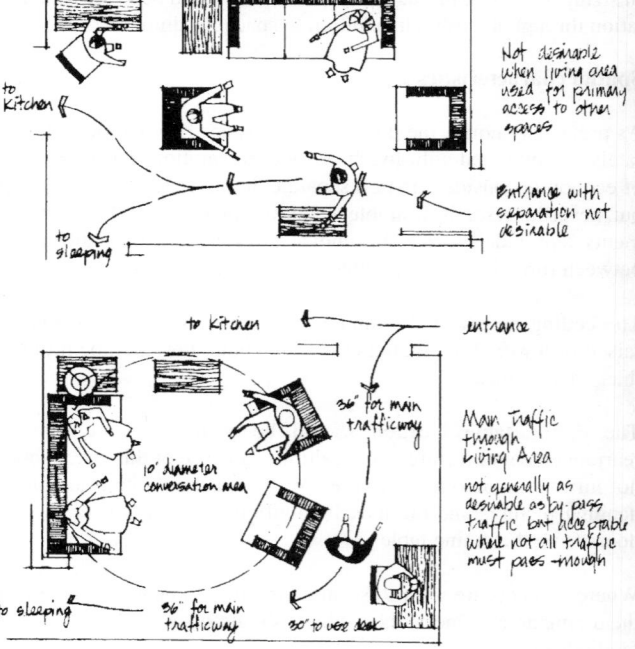

**Fig. 13. Living room circulation approaches**

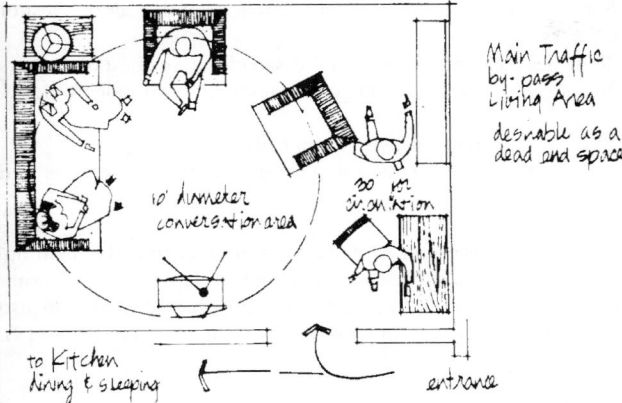

**Fig. 14. Living room circulation approaches**

roning in front of the television set, and the like. Provision of floor area beyond the minimum space required by the furnishability test will also ensure the accommodation of a wider range of lifestyles and activity patterns.

The living activities area may be greatly enhanced in spatial character by a higher than normal ceiling if the building type permits.

As a general rule, it has been found that a width of less than 12 feet is difficult to utilize effectively. It has also been found that rectangular rather than square space is easier to furnish and to zone for different activities.

Consideration should be given in dwelling units of larger than standard size to subdividing the living activities area into two separate areas, such as a living room and den–sewing room combination. This can also be accommodated by room configurations (such as L-shape) which are easily subdivided by furniture arrangement. This approach is particularly effective where there are two residents in a unit who wish to carry on different activities simultaneously.

## SLEEPING AND DRESSING

Elderly people make greater use of the bedroom than any other age group except infants. An efficient and commodious bedroom is important for any household, but for older people it is absolutely necessary. This is partly because of the need for rest periods, but as people grow older, many also become more susceptible to illness and are bedridden more frequently than younger people.

### Accessibility

This activity is one of the most private in the dwelling unit. In dwelling units containing two residents it is essential that one resident be able to carry on normal living activities (including entertaining visitors) without serious loss of privacy to the other person in the bedroom. Because of this basic need, direct physical accessibility (only minor intervening space) should exist only between the sleeping and dressing area and the following areas:

• Personal hygiene area
• Personal clothing storage

The bathroom may also be accessible through a hall.

In some cases, provision for personal living activities may be located within the bedroom. Direct accessibility to private outdoor space may also be acceptable under some circumstances.

Indirect accessibility (through intervening circulation) should exist to the following areas:

• Food preparation area
• Storage and utility area

No direct accessibility should exist between the sleeping and dressing area and the following areas:

• Entry/exit area, for protection of privacy
• Living area
• Dining area

Because of the privacy factor and the desire to be able to entertain guests without having to make the whole dwelling unit tidy, the sleeping and dressing area should be isolated from most visual and audio contact with other areas in the dwelling unit. The level of visual and audio contact between the bathroom and the sleeping and dressing area should be controllable to ensure bedroom privacy when a guest uses the bathroom. It is desirable that a circulation space serve as a buffer between the sleeping and dressing area and the rest of the dwelling unit.

Like the living area, this area should have excellent views from its windows. Windows should be placed so that a person can easily see out while lying in bed. This space requires direct exposure to the sun for at least 30 percent of the day. Reference should be made to Figs. 11 and 15 for desired sun orientation.

### Furnishings

In addition to the sleeping and dressing functions, the bedroom should have provisions for such passive living activities as:

• Television viewing
• Reading
• Sewing
• Computer use

The minimum furniture to be provided for is as follows:

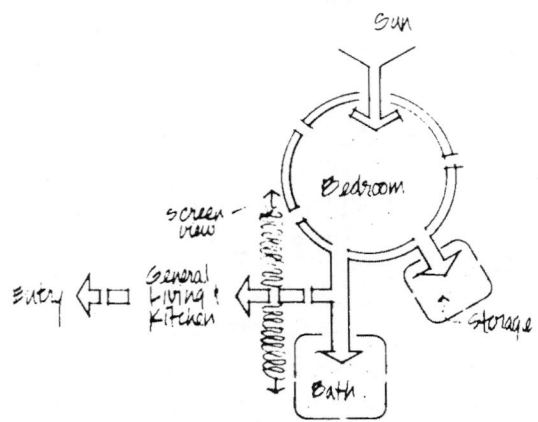

**Fig. 15. Space orientation**

- Two twin beds, 3 feet-3 inches by 6 feet-6 inches, or one double bed, 4 feet-9 inches by 6 feet-6 inches
- One dresser, 1 foot-6 inches by 4 feet-4 inches
- One chair, 1 foot-6 inches by 1 foot-6 inches
- One table, 1 foot-6 inches by 2 feet-6 inches, for sewing or other work (optional)
- Two night stands, 1 foot-6 inches by 1 foot-6 inches
- One portable television set

Where both bedrooms of a dwelling unit are primary (as in unrelated occupancy), the preceding requirements apply to both.

Twin beds should be possible even in the bedroom of a unit programmed for single-person occupancy.

A secondary bedroom for single occupancy should have circulation space and accommodate furniture of the following sizes:

- One twin bed, 3 feet-3 inches by 6 feet-6 inches
- One dresser, 1 foot-6 inches by 3 feet-6 inches
- One chair, 1 foot-6 inches by 1 foot-6 inches
- One night stand, 1 foot-6 inches by 1 foot-6 inches

The location of doors, windows, and closets should be planned to allow for the best placement of the bed and other furniture.

The closet should be placed next to the door into the bedroom because the use of available wall space is minimized in this way (Fig. 16).

For reasonable access to and use of bedroom furniture and equipment, the following minimum clearances should be observed:

- 42 inches at one side or foot of bed, for dressing
- 24 inches clearance for least used side of double bed

- 6 inches clearance from side of bed to side of dresser or chest of drawers
- 36 inches clearance in front of dresser, closet, or chest of drawers
- 30 inches clearance for major circulation path (door to closet, etc.)
- 24 inches clearance between twin beds
- 18 inches clearance between twin bed and wall for ease of bed making

It should not be necessary to move beds in order to make them up. Bedrooms should be sufficiently large and so designed as to permit alternate arrangements of furniture if at all possible. There should also be space provided for working privately or resting (see Figs. 17 to 19).

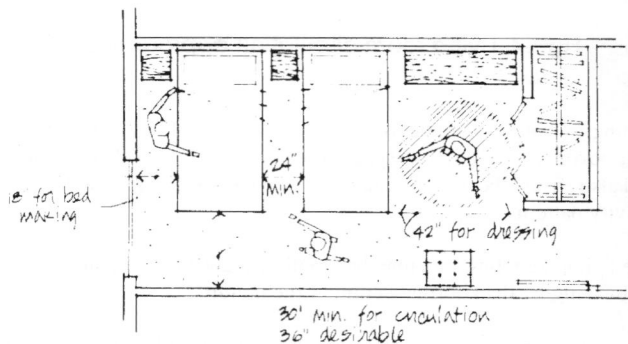

**Fig. 17. Typical standard bedroom with twin beds**

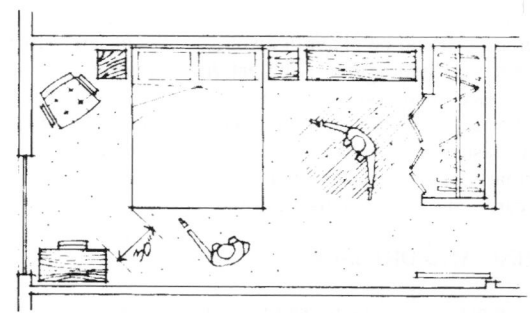

**Fig. 18. Typical standard bedroom with double bed**

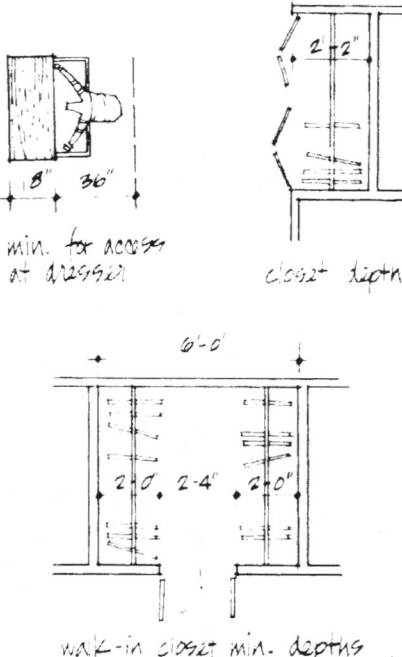

**Fig. 16. Closet depths**

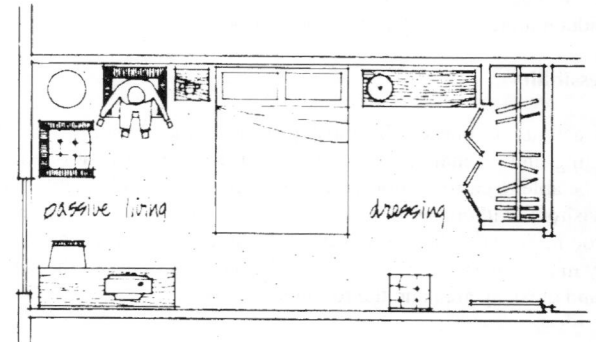

**Fig. 19. Larger-than-standard bedroom—may be applicable in larger-than-standard unit or in 2-bedroom unrelated occupancy**

# PERSONAL HYGIENE

The bathroom is the subject of much public and private research. What is set forth here is not ideal but rather an attempt to synthesize the most current thinking on the subject as it relates to the elderly user. In addition, requirements for adoption of bathroom facilities for use by permanently disabled persons are included. These requirements shall apply to at least 10 percent of the units in developments of 100 units or more. Application to smaller projects will be determined individually for each case.

In general, bathrooms in developments for elderly residents should be given great care in design as this space can, if poorly conceived, cause both serious health hazards and, through its inconvenience, great frustration. The general lack of mobility and slow reaction time of elderly people make it mandatory that hygiene spaces be inherently safe from sharp edges and slippery floor surfaces and that they do not require excessive bending, leaning, or twisting to carry out necessary activities.

### Accessibility

In addition to more frequent than normal use during the day, frequent use of the bathroom at night is common. Therefore, consideration should be given to direct accessibility between the bedroom and the bathroom. Hopefully, this accessibility would not require passage through an intervening circulation space. If it does, the route should be direct, unobstructed, and of sufficient width for a wheelchair to pass easily. Indirect accessibility should also exist between the bathroom and the more general living areas of the unit for use of the bathroom by guests.

Visual and audio contact between the bathroom and other areas should be minimized. It should not be possible to see into the bathroom from the living, dining, or food preparation areas (see Fig. 20).

### Orientation

Views to the outside and natural light are not necessary to bathroom functions. Where windows are used, the following criteria pertain:

- The designer should make sure that no loss of privacy occurs.
- Windows should not be located over bathtubs.

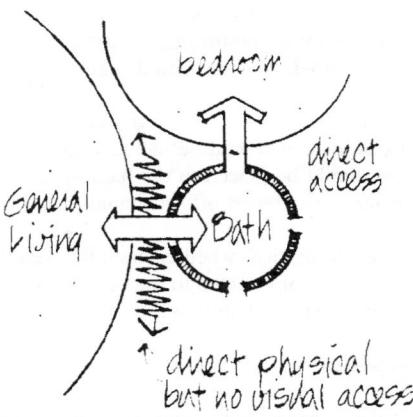

**Fig. 20. Accessibility of bathroom**

### Furnishings and Equipment

All personal hygiene spaces should have the following equipment:

- Lavatory basin (preferred in a vanity countertop)
- Water closet
- Bath or shower
- Appropriate grab bars
- Storage space and mirror
- Toilet-paper holder
- Towel bars

It is essential for the successful functioning of the bathroom or lavatory that certain minimum clear working areas be provided around fixtures (see Fig. 21). These requirements are as follows:

- *Lavatory basins:* 3 feet-6 inches by 3 feet-6 inches; the sink should be centered on one dimension and at the extreme of the other.
- *Water closet:* 2 feet-6 inches by 4 feet-4 inches; the water closet should be centered on the 2 feet-6 inches dimension and located at the extreme of the 4 feet-4 inches dimension.

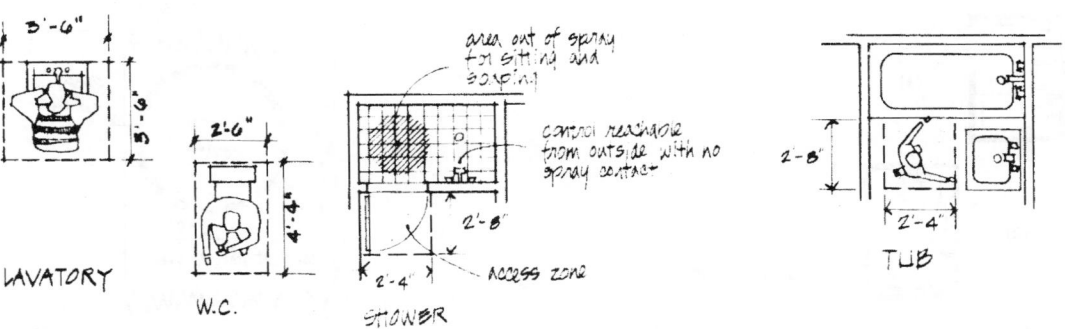

**Fig. 21. Minimum clearances—personal hygiene**

- *Tub and/or shower:* 2 feet-4 inches clear dimension extending out from access point of fixture and at least 2 feet-8 inches along its length; the length dimension should begin from the central end of the fixture.

An emergency call system should be included in all developments. An alarm button should be placed in the bathroom in a convenient place, but not where it can be set off accidentally.

All bathrooms and lavatories, whether naturally ventilated or not, should have air exhaust fans vented to the outside and sized according to the code for an interior bathroom.

### Spatial Characteristics

All personal hygiene spaces, both bathrooms and lavatories, should have privacy locks which can be easily unlocked from the outside in case of emergency. The key type of emergency release is not desirable because there may not be sufficient time to locate the key in an emergency. Outward-opening doors should be used so that people can get in easily to help someone who is lying on the bathroom floor, perhaps unconscious or helpless.

Nonslip, easily maintained floor surfaces which are free from changes in level should be provided.

The vertical surfaces of bathrooms should be free from sharp corners and edges, unnecessary projections, and breakable materials. This requirement has particular bearing on room layout and the location of bathroom accessories, such as towel bars, paper holders, etc.

Many bathroom layouts are possible but two are the most common, offering solutions to a wide range of concerns. Each has its own advantages. These layouts (Fig. 22) are described here for illustrative purposes.

- *Layout 1:* In the first layout, the toilet is placed by the wall with the lavatory next to the bathtub. This arrangement allows easy placement of the toilet-paper holder and grab bar on the wall while, at the same time, the edge of lavatory can be used as a support for getting into and out of the bathtub.
  A vertical grab bar mounted on the wall near the bathtub in addition to grab bars on the bathtub wall is recommended. An angled grab bar should also be provided on the wall by the toilet.
- *Layout 2:* In the second layout, the bathtub is placed against the wall opposite the lavatory and toilet. As in Layout 1, separate grab bars should be provided for the toilet and tub. In this layout

the lavatory can be installed in a vanity countertop with sides. The vanity arrangement can support a toilet-paper holder next to the toilet, a towel rack, and perhaps a small grab bar.

## PRIVATE OUTDOOR

Many older people, either by choice or by limitations of their physical conditions, are largely confined to their dwelling units, and access to a private outdoor space over which they have control is very desirable. It offers a welcome change of atmosphere, a chance to grow flowers, cook out, and enjoy the sun. In the event of fire, a balcony can provide refuge and access to fresh air. Provision for private outdoor activities may take the form of balconies or patios.

### Accessibility

The private outdoor space should be directly accessible to the main general living area of the dwelling unit. If possible this area should also be directly accessible to the food preparation area; however, if this is not possible, the indirect accessibility between the outdoor space and the food preparation area should be via a noncircuitous circulation path. Accessibility to all other areas should be indirect and placed as dictated by the functional organization of the dwelling unit, except that there may also be direct accessibility to the sleeping and dressing area.

To protect the privacy of each private outdoor area on the ground floor, direct access from it to the public outdoor area should be avoided by creating an identity for the outdoor private areas. There should be no direct accessibility between the private outdoor areas of separate dwelling units (see Fig. 23).

Visual accessibility between the private outdoor area and interesting views on and off the site should be maximized, while at the same time loss of privacy from views outside the outdoor area should be minimized. The visual accessibility between the general living area of the unit and the general outdoor area should not be impaired by the design of the private outdoor space.

### Orientation

The configuration and orientation of the outdoor space should be such that sun falls on the space for at least 30 percent of each day during the prime spring, summer, and fall months.

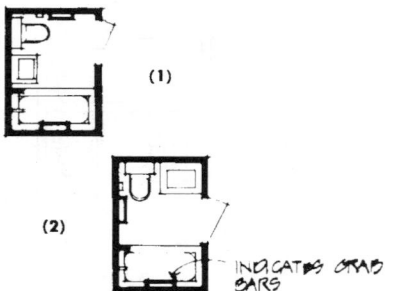

**Fig. 22. Illustrative hygiene space layouts—all doors 2 feet-8 inches**

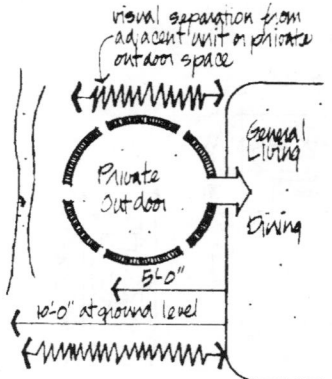

**Fig. 23. Privacy at ground level**

## Furnishability and Spatial Characteristics

On-grade patios and/or private areas should be well defined. Location and design should provide spatial privacy from other living units and from adjacent walks or drives in public space.

Overhead protection of balconies should be fully draftproof and should not be the only source of natural ventilation to the room. The door sill should be kept as low as possible. Passage doors of the swing type are preferable to sliding glass doors and should be required when economically feasible to eliminate large sills.

Balconies or terraces above the twelfth floor are generally undesirable and should not be provided except in special or unique circumstances. Where private balconies are not provided for all the dwelling units on a floor, a common balcony shall be provided at a central location.

All balconies, terraces, and patios should be provided with artificial lighting which is switched on within the dwelling unit. At least one duplex electric receptacle which is weatherproof should be provided in each outdoor space.

The criteria for minimum privacy require that screening walls at the sides of outdoor spaces be provided to protect the space from being overlooked by adjoining dwelling units and their private outdoor spaces. The side of the space opposite the building may be partially closed and/or defined by planting.

On-grade private space should have a dimension of at least 12 feet and include a paved patio of at least 100 square feet. The remaining area should be lawn or planting beds.

Private on-grade outdoor spaces may become a security problem if their design provides the potential intruder with a space completely free from observance and control. Therefore, completely enclosed patios should themselves be secure. Partially enclosed patios should be designed so that they can be controlled visually from public areas.

The paved surface in outdoor spaces should be smooth and free from unexpected changes in level. All steps required to provide a transition from unit floor level to ground level should have handrails.

Private outdoor spaces above grade (raised terraces and balconies) should be included in the integral design at the beginning of the design process and not added later as an afterthought. Only in this way can the problems traditionally associated with balconies be overcome. Balconies should have a clear dimension of no less than 5 feet and a total clear area of no less than 50 square feet for 1-bedroom units and 60 square feet for two-bedroom units. Because the elderly are particularly concerned about security and heights, balconies must not only be safe, but they must also feel safe. The use of solid balustrades is desirable. Where this is not possible, a sturdy railing with a large solid top rail should be used. In either case care should be taken to avoid obscuring views out from the interior of the dwelling unit. For this purpose a solid balustrade to a height of 24 inches with an open handrail above is a good solution. Railings or balustrades should have a minimum height above the balcony surface of 36 inches and should extend completely along all open sides of the balcony (Fig. 24).

Whenever possible balconies should be recessed behind the main face of the building because this technique provides a strong sense of

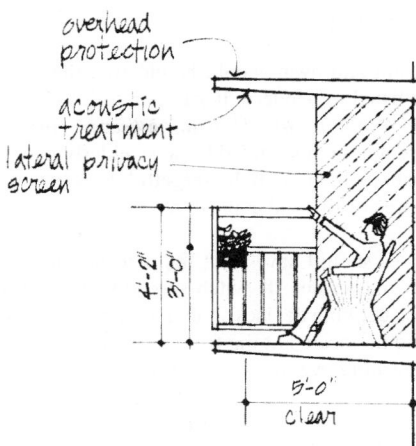

**Fig. 24. Example of balcony**

enclosure, privacy, and security. Where this is not possible, and where there are adjoining balconies or the balcony is exposed to broad public view, balconies should be provided with screening walls or devices at their sides that achieve privacy and security.

## FOOD PREPARATION EQUIPMENT

This section deals with equipment and facilities in the food preparation area of the dwelling unit in terms of quantities, sizes, and detailed location. The question of the functional organization of the food preparation area and its relationship to other areas of the dwelling units is discussed earlier. The discussion here is divided into two parts. The first deals directly with the minimum standards against which all proposed developments will be measured and to which all must comply. The second begins with the minimum standards as a base and develops optimum standards for the various components of the food preparation area where appropriate. These optimum standards are not mandatory, and the achievement of some may not be economically feasible within the context of low- and moderate-income housing programs; however, developments which approach or meet some or all of these standards may be given financing priority over those which only satisfy the minimum standards.

### Minimum Standards

*Refrigerator*

The refrigerator should be an upright freestanding model. The minimum acceptable sizes are 10 cubic feet for a 1-bedroom unit and 12 cubic feet for a 2-bedroom unit. The freezer compartment should be located on the top or the side of the refrigerator. Refrigerators of the undercounter type are unacceptable because of the excessive stooping required in their use.

The refrigerator should be of the self-defrosting type (this is a designated amenity). The general storage shelves of the refrigerator should pull out on roller guides and should be removable for ease in cleaning.

*Cooking Unit and Oven*

The cooking unit and oven should be electric; they should be both approved and listed by Underwriter Laboratories (UL) in the publication *Electric Appliance and Utilization Equipment List.* Gas cooking devices are not recommended because elderly people often have a poor sense of smell and may be forgetful, thus becoming vulnerable to the hazards of fire and explosion.

Cooking devices should have pilot lights to visually indicate when they are on. A master cutoff switch should be provided if possible. The controls on cooking devices should be easily read by sight; touch controls should be located at the front of the device to eliminate the necessity of reaching over hot cooking surfaces.

Where an integral cooktop and oven unit (stove) are used, the oven should be located below the cooktop. Stoves with ovens that are overhead or at eye level are not acceptable because of the reaching required (Fig. 25). The door on the oven should be hung on the side and swing out if such units are available. This type of oven door is safer and also allows the oven to be used by someone sitting in a wheelchair.

All cooktops must have a hood and exhaust fan mounted directly above the cooking surface. Ceiling-mounted exhaust fans are unacceptable. The cook top should have four burners and have a minimum width of 24 inches.

*Sink*

The kitchen sink should be of stainless steel and mounted on the countertop. The minimum overall dimensions are 24 inches by 21 inches. Where countertop area permits, a sink with a double compartment equal to the capacity of a sink with a single compartment is preferred (Fig. 26).

*Cabinets, Shelves, Counters, and Closets*

Each kitchen or kitchenette should have the following features:

1. Accessible storage space for food and cooking and eating utensils
2. Sufficient space for average kitchen accessories

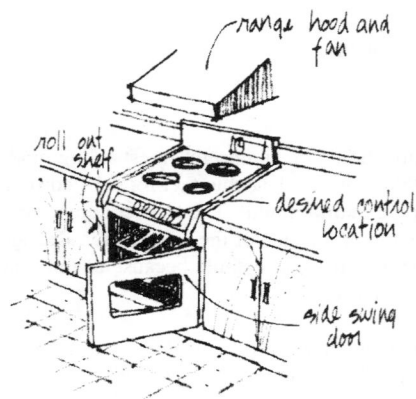

**Fig. 25. Lower oven doors allow easier accessibility**

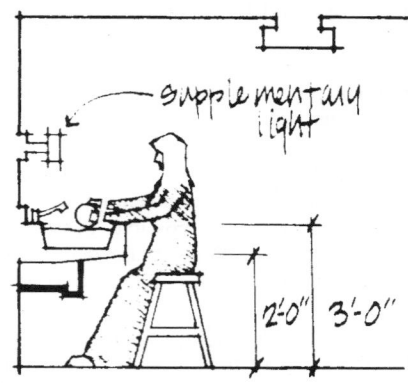

**Fig. 26. Desirable knee space at kitchen sink**

3. Sufficient storage space for those items of household equipment normally used and for which storage is not provided elsewhere, such as brooms, mops, and soap.
4. Sufficient work surface area for the preparation and serving of food and the cleanup of cooking and eating utensils

Kitchen storage should be provided in the form of wall and base cabinets as follows:

• *Shelving:* 40 square feet
• *Drawers:* 7 square feet

Kitchen storage should be designed to satisfy the following requirements (Fig. 27):

1. Usable storage space in or under stoves, or under wall ovens, when provided in the form of shelves or drawers that roll out, may be included in the minimum shelf area.
2. Conventional base cabinets over countertops should not be deeper than 12 inches and the highest shelf should be no more than 66 inches from the floor.
3. No cabinet or shelf space should be located above refrigerators.
4. The minimum clearance between countertops and wall shelves should be 24 inches at the sink and 15 inches in other locations.
5. At least 80 percent of all shelving should be enclosed by cabinetry or a pantry. Cabinet doors should have rounded edges.

No less than 10 square feet of countertop work surface should be provided in kitchens. Countertops should be approximately 24 inches deep and no higher than 36 inches above the floor. In calculating the length of the countertop, the length occupied by sinks and cooktops may not be counted. Countertops should have rounded leading edges. Where possible, supplementary countertop space should be provided at tabletop height so that a resident can use this space for food preparation and for eating light meals. In apartments designed for tenants with disabilities, half of the required counter space should be at worktable height.

Storage of household equipment (Fig. 28) should be provided by a broom closet at least 3 square feet in floor area. These closets should have shelves for the storage of cleaning materials, and they should have a clear area of sufficient height to accommodate an upright vacuum cleaner and brooms.

A separate compartment with a door should be provided in each kitchen for a garbage and trash container.

*Garbage Disposal*

All kitchen sinks should be equipped with garbage disposals that are fully insulated for sound.

**Optimum Standards**

The following modifications can be made to optimize kitchen facilities.

*Refrigerator*

A horizontally shaped refrigerator that is hung on the wall and mounted in the range of 34 to 72 inches greatly improves usability by eliminating stooping (Fig. 29).

*Cooking Unit and Oven*

A separate cooktop mounted on the counter and an oven mounted on the wall greatly increase flexibility of placement and enhance functional organization and usability. The cooktop should be mounted no higher than 34 inches above the floor, while the oven should be mounted at waist level (that is, the bottom of the oven should be 27 inches above the floor).

*Sinks*

Sinks should be mounted 34 inches above the floor.

*Cabinets, Shelves, Counters, and Closets*

Many elderly people tend to develop a stoop and are, consequently, shorter than the average adult. As noted earlier, they also have trouble bending and reaching. Therefore, while maintaining the storage requirement of the minimum standards and increasing the work surface area to 12 square feet, the following changes in location and configuration should be made to optimize storage and work-surface facilities:

- Countertops should be located 34 inches above the floor. This counter area should be supplemented by some counter area at table height to accommodate light dining and food preparation from a sitting position (4 to 6 square feet). Pull-out counters could provide for this need.
- Shelves 12 inches or deeper should not be mounted higher than 55 inches above the floor when the shelf is above a counter, or 63 inches above the floor when no counter interferes. Shelves of this depth should not be located lower than 27 inches above the floor.
- Approximately 50 percent of the kitchen storage space should be provided by pantry cupboards or a closet. Shallow pantry shelves (less than 12 inches) may be mounted as low as 21 inches above the floor (Fig. 28).
- Storage space under counters should be in the form of deep drawers on roller guides rather than cabinets with shelves.
- Sliding cabinet doors should be substituted for doors of the swing type in the optimally designed kitchen. Where cabinet doors cannot be avoided on cabinets that are 34 inches or higher above the floor, they should be limited to no more than 15 inches in width.
- All sharp corners and edges should be rounded off cabinet doors.
- Wall-mounted hanging devices for cooking utensils such as pots, pans, and large spoons should be provided at convenient locations.

**PERSONAL HYGIENE EQUIPMENT**

The following requirements are the minimum equipment specifications for developments for elderly tenants; they are also applicable for adoption for use by tenants with disabilities. Each requirement is accompanied by location and size parameters.

*Lavatory Basin*

Each bathroom or lavatory should have a lavatory basin firmly supported to withstand pulling or leaning loads of up to 300 pounds. Vanity cabinets are not recommended as they require excessive stooping and leaning to be used. Vanity countertops are desirable. Provision for storage should be made in wall-hung cabinetry where necessary.

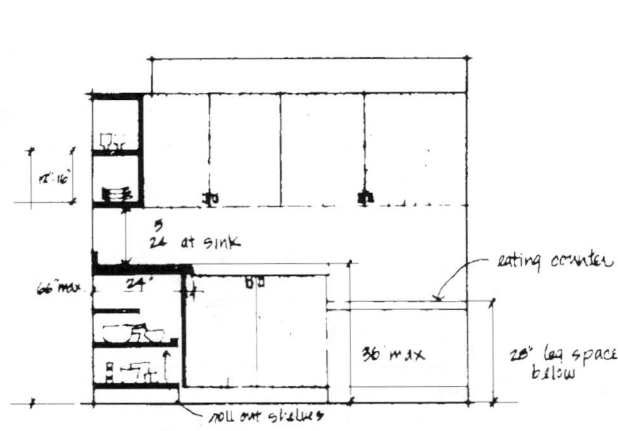

**Fig. 27. Kitchen storage and counter space**

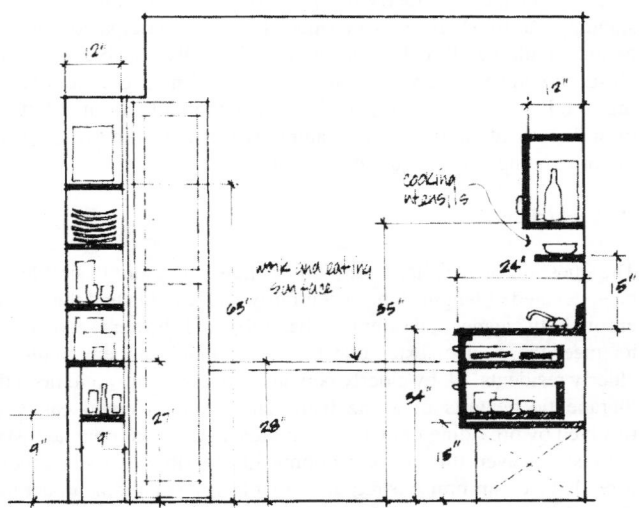

**Fig. 28. Kitchen storage**

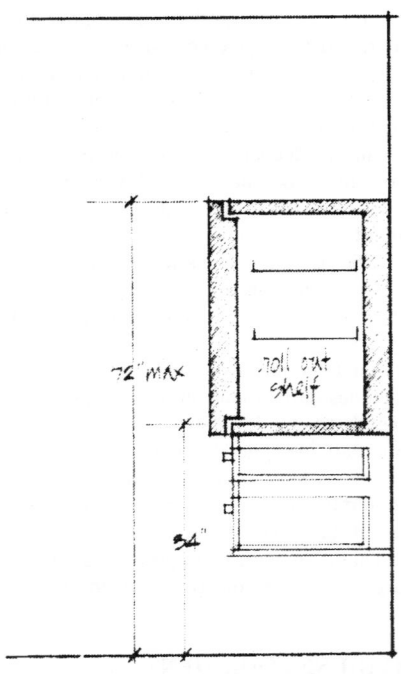

**Fig. 29. Wall-hung refrigerator**

tubs are provided on each occupied floor (1 tub for 20 dwelling units).

Bathtubs should have controls that are easily operated from outside of the tub without excessive leaning or stretching and should include an automatic mixing valve with an upper temperature limit of 120°F. Tubs should have a flat bottom with a nonslip surface. Abrasive tapes and heavy, sharp textures should be avoided. The sides of the bathtub should not be higher than 15 inches and the lengthwise dimension should not be less than 60 inches.

Where showers are provided instead of bathtubs (that is, where centralized bathtubs are available), they should be of sufficient size to allow the bather to stand or sit outside of the area of the spray while soaping up. The shower enclosure should be equipped with a folding seat, as sitting showers prolong independence for those who either require assistance in standing or who are completely infirm. As mentioned, the shower head should be variable in height and preferably of the detachable type with a flexible head. The highest shower head position should not exceed 60 inches.

Shower controls should be easily reachable from outside the shower stall and should include both an automatic mixing valve limiting the maximum water temperature at the head to 120°F, and a water temperature testing spout to be used by the bather before entering the shower. The soap dish and grab bar should be conveniently located 51 inches above the floor of the shower. Where technically feasible, the raised entrance curb should be eliminated. If glass is used in the shower enclosure, it should be tempered for safety.

Soap dishes and similar attachments should be recessed. Water controls should be placed so that they are not a hazard either in normal usage or when the bather slips.

Bathtubs should be equipped with shower heads. The shower head should be adjustable in height and, preferably, detachable with a flexible head. There should be several wall positions for the head to fix it

Basins should be of the cantilever type, either wall-mounted on chair hangers or mounted in a vanity top. An installation of this kind is more easily used by someone in a wheelchair. The most desirable mounting height for basins will provide a minimum clear dimension below the basin and/or vanity top of 2 feet - 2 inches and place the top of the basin and/or counter 2 feet - 9 inches above the floor. Water taps on basins should be low profile with cross-shaped or lever handles. Round knobs should not be used (see Fig. 30a).

*Water Closet*

Each bathroom or lavatory should have a water closet with a seat height of 17 inches (elderly people have difficulty with seating and standing motions). If users in wheelchairs are anticipated, the seat height should be 20 inches. Where economically feasible, the water closet should be of the wall-hung type for convenience in floor cleaning (see Fig. 30b). The toilet-paper holder should be located in front of or directly at the side of the water closet, in a position where leaning or twisting is not required to use it.

*Bath and Shower*

The question of whether a bathtub or shower is more desirable has been debated at length. It has been fairly well established that showers are both cleaner and safer than bathtubs, and showers seem to better meet the goal of extending the span of independent living for elderly residents. Many elderly persons, however, enjoy and need the therapeutic benefits of a sitz bath. The situation could easily be resolved by providing both a shower and a bathtub in separate installations; however, this is not economically feasible. It seems, therefore, that a compromise is required, that is, a specially manufactured tub and shower combination. This compromise is the recommended solution, although showers should be considered where central bath-

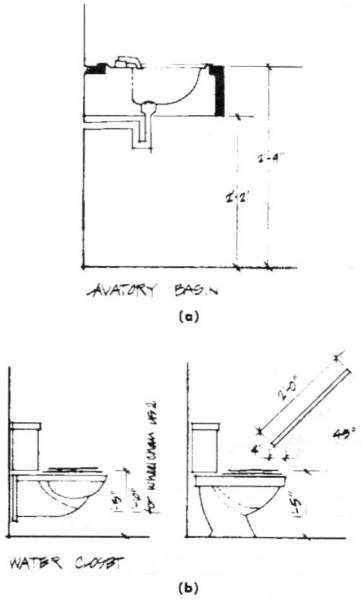

**Fig. 30. (*a*) Lavatory basin; (*b*) water closet**

at various heights. Bathtubs should be equipped with a detachable seat which allows the bather to shower sitting down. A grab bar and soap dish placed at a high level about 51 inches from the bottom of the tub will avoid the necessity to bend down for soap or to use the shower curtain for support when taking a shower. Glass enclosures instead of shower curtains are not advisable as they further restrict getting in and out of the tub.

*Grab Bars*

Grab bars are generally overused and sometimes bear little relationship to the anatomy of the human body. If improperly located, they not only fail to serve the user but they can also become a hazard if the user should slip. Grab bars should be used judiciously and wherever possible located to serve more than one bathroom position. Bars should be approximately 1 inch in diameter, be capable of withstanding a pulling or hanging load of 300 pounds, and be fixed to structure members rather than to wall finishes or materials. There should be at least one grab bar at the water closet and another in the bathtub or shower, located and in the configuration shown in Fig. 31.

*Storage and Mirror*

The preferred provision for storage needs is a large mirror behind the lavatory (not a medicine cabinet–mirror combination) and a separate storage unit, built into a wall, large enough to hold medicine, toiletries and towels. The storage unit should be located so that reaching across countertops is not required. If towel storage is located externally in a linen closet, the bathroom should have a mirror behind the lavatory and a separate medicine cabinet which is convenient to the lavatory but placed so that excessive reaching is not required.

*Electric Outlets*

A convenient duplex outlet should be located adjacent to the mirror and lavatory approximately 6 inches above the height of the lavatory and positioned so that reaching across the lavatory or countertop is not required.

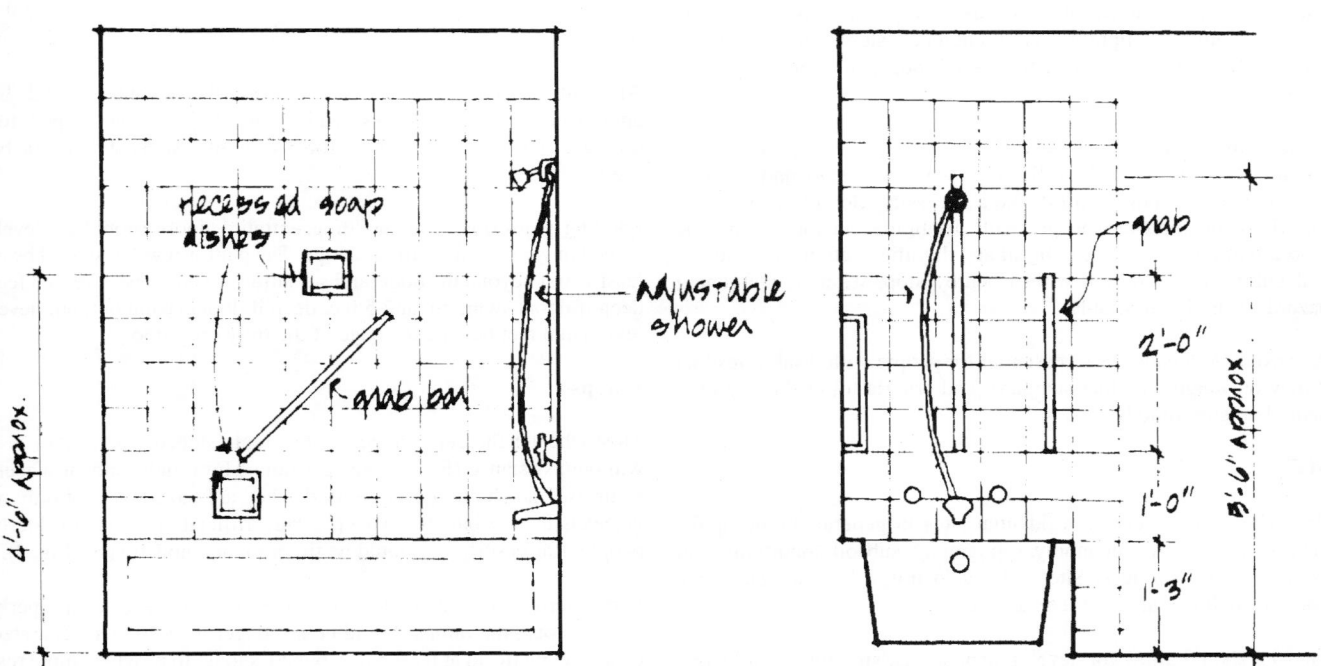

**Fig. 31. Bath and shower**

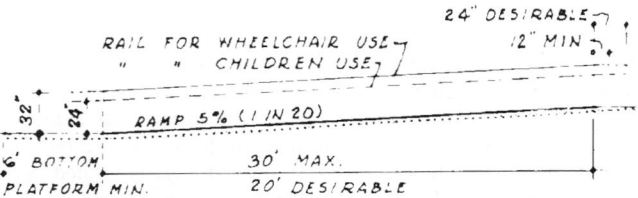

**Fig. 1. Single-run entrance ramp**

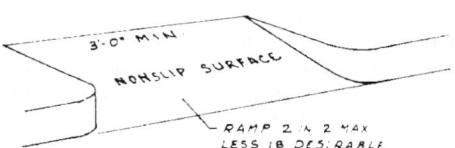

**Fig. 2. Street-curb ramp for wheelchair**

# HOUSING FOR PEOPLE WITH DISABILITIES

## NEIGHBORHOOD

Accessibility to community services and facilities is the first factor to consider in site selection.

Primary services and facilities include employment opportunities; clinics; vocational rehabilitation programs; inexpensive private and public recreation (such as movies, parks lively with activities for participation and view, libraries, etc.); churches; stores including drug, grocery and variety; barber and beauty shops; inexpensive restaurants; and schools.

Another important factor is accessibility to public transportation. To employed people with disabilities, as well as to staff and visitors, good public transportation may be a necessity. Good transportation may keep unemployed people with disabilities in touch with the world, participating in meaningful and dignified activities. Economical public transportation with a nearby stop, without intervening hazards, is highly desirable.

A convenient location is so essential for people with disabilities that it may outweigh the other standards and criteria for evaluating residential neighborhoods.

## SITE

The criteria for selecting residential sites in general should apply. (These criteria cover economy, topography, subsoil conditions, and existing utility services. Sites subject to traffic hazards, excessive noise, or polluted air should be avoided.)

The site should allow for development so that structures can be oriented to give residents the advantages of local climate.

An important special consideration is slope of the site. For people with physical impairments, a comparatively flat site is needed.

It is important to have outlooks, both natural and created, that provide interest or beauty and contribute to pleasant living. Many tenants will undoubtedly spend more time at home than would a comparable group of able-bodied individuals. Views of such things as wooded areas, hills, nightlights, and distant traffic of planes, boats, trains, and automobiles are desirable and count as positive factors in site selection.

Consideration should be given to the existing and proposed approaches to the site (street improvement, widening; surface; sidewalks) and public utilities.

## ACCESS, RAMPS, AND PEDESTRIAN WALKS

### Access

All building entrances to be used by the tenants should be approached by paved walks, with a nonskid surface, sloped for drainage, but not over 1 in 20 (or 5 percent). Steps should not be used.

Landing platforms at all building entrance doors should be level, sloped only as required for drainage. The platform width should be at least 1 foot beyond the door jambs. Platforms should be at least 3 feet deep if doors swing in, and 5 feet deep if doors swing out, but never less than 3 feet beyond the edge of the fully open door.

### Ramps

Most wheelchair users can negotiate a ramp sloped 5 percent or less without assistance (Fig. 1). Steeper ramps limit independent wheelchair use and should never be used. They are hazardous not only to wheelchair users but also to people with artificial limbs and to elderly people. Ramp surfaces should be fireproof and nonslip (see Fig. 2).

If the vertical height requires two ramps to achieve the properly graded slope, the ramps should be no longer than 20 feet, separated by a level platform at least 5 feet-6 inches long, to provide ample rest space. Such two-run ramps may be in a straight line; however, a more desirable and safer arrangement would be a 90- or 180-degree turn at the platform.

When more than two ramp lengths are required, the descent should be broken by turns to be negotiated on level platforms.

The recommended width for a one-way ramp is 3 feet between handrails. At least 6 feet should be provided for two-way circulation.

Handrails and anchors should extend at least 18 inches (24 inches is preferable) beyond the beginning and end of the ramp to assist per-

*Reviewer:* James Wentling, FAIA

ons with poor vision, and they should be returned to a wall or an upright post for safety.

Handrails installed specifically for children should be at a height of 24 inches. Local codes or special safety objectives might necessitate the installation of additional, higher rails.

### Pedestrian Walks

Pedestrian walks at street curbs should be ramped. The ramp should not protrude onto the street but be indented into the curb; it should have a nonslip surface colored orange, or curb jambs should be colored to assist those with poor vision. Greater slopes than 2 in 12 could hinder wheelchair use.

### Parking

The parking areas should be moderately sized and conveniently located to provide easy and safe access to entrances (see Fig. 3).

There should be no steps or curbs from the parking area to the dwelling buildings or to community space.

For wheelchair users, the minimum width of parking bays is 11 feet (12 feet is desirable). Other orthopedic equipment users will require at least a 9-foot width. The wider bays should be nearest the building entrances. For these tenants, covered parking is desirable.

Parking bays for people with disabilities may have a minimum width of 8 feet-6 inches under unusual, restricted circumstances. However, the general rule should be 9 feet. Parking areas should not be permitted to obstruct or dominate views from indoor recreation areas or dwellings.

### OUTDOOR AREAS, LIGHTING, AND PLANTINGS

Outdoor facilities and areas (walks, ramps, drives, parking and recreational areas, etc.) should be sloped for drainage and be properly illuminated for safe circulation.

Existing trees, streams, or rock outcropping of the site should be retained where possible in order to preserve natural beauty. Plantings, with emphasis on recreational and sitting areas, contribute to

enjoyment and create a more pleasant environment. Plantings around parking areas will enhance the site.

The surfaces of concentrated use areas should be paved for maximum safety, use, and interest. For large paved areas, several materials of varied color, design, and texture are recommended to provide a pleasant visual diversity. Nonslip surfaces are desirable—rough surfaces generally present in fieldstone are not recommended.

Rest or sitting areas should be protected from winter winds and excessive summer sun. Some of them should provide a view of the street or of other places where there is animated activity. The best way to provide shade is to use large trees or small, attractive shelters, or both.

Flowering trees and shrubbery can enhance pleasantness and potential enjoyment of the setting.

One-story dwelling buildings and other structures, where appropriate, should have outdoor flower planting areas for the tenants, preferably at or near entrance door.

Every effort should be made to have a sheltered bus stop located at the development. A mail depository box at the same location would be desirable.

### DWELLING STRUCTURES

#### Entrances

Entrance doors (Fig. 4) to multifamily structures, community centers, and other public-use space should provide a clear minimum width passage of 3 feet. Entrance doors to individual dwellings should provide a clear minimum width passage of 2 feet-10 inches. Thresholds that project above the floor should be avoided when possible. If a projection is unavoidable, it should be no higher than 1/2 inch, featheredged to the floor, and 5 to 6 inches wide.

Hinged entrance doors to dwellings are the most economical and safest. Revolving doors should never be installed; they must be collapsed for wheelchair users and are particularly hazardous for users of other orthopedic equipment. For entrance doors to a multifamily building, it is best to have automatic door openers. Such mechanisms

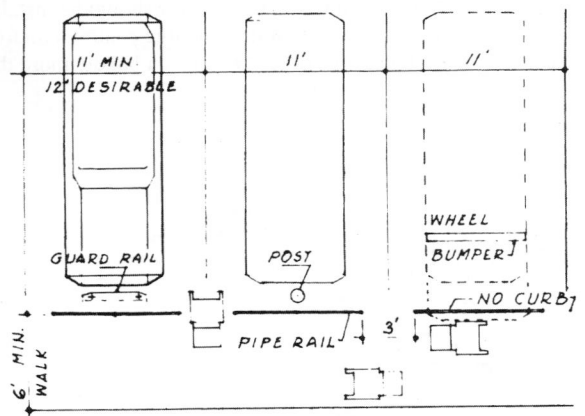

**Fig. 3. Parking (wheel bumper not recommended as car overhangs vary)**

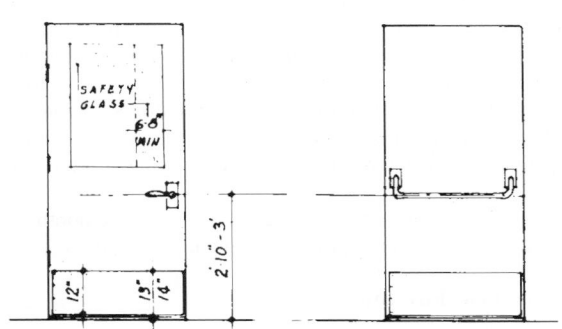

**Fig. 4. Building entrance doors to public space should have vision panels**

should fully open the door without restricting the clear 3-foot mini-mum passage. If the opening mechanism fails to function, the door operation should automatically revert to manual operation. Mainte-nance of the automatic door opener can usually be reduced by flank-ing the automatic doors with hinged doors for use of people who are physically unimpaired.

For those who have poor vision or are blind, the floor directly inside or outside the entrance doors to multifamily buildings should either be slightly ramped or have a finish of a different color, distinguish-able from the surrounding floor and of a different texture that will provide more grip for shoe soles, thus suggesting caution. Recessed floor mats meet these requirements.

Exterior doors should be covered by a canopy or hood of ample width. A porte-cochere may be feasible. A canopy or roofed-over service entrance also should be provided for ambulances if the devel-opment is for people who are elderly or have disabilities. Other entrances may be made from the parking areas and grounds. If a clinic is included, a separate entrance should be provided so that peo-ple outside the project who come to the clinic will not use the main entrance lobby.

The operating hardware of entrance doors should be 2 feet-10 inches to 3 feet above the floor. Door checks or closers should be the adjustable-tension type, set for minimum pull to assist persons using wheelchairs and other orthopedic devices. Pull handles, push bars, and panic hardware bars with curved ends are best because they con-tain no hooks or sharp angles to catch clothing. A lever handle that curves close to the door surface is a most suitable operator for latch or lock. Kickplates 12 inches high help to reduce door maintenance by preventing abrasions caused by footrests and axle hubs on wheel-chairs. In multifamily buildings, entrance doors normally used by tenants should be provided with key locks that can be set to operate as latches (no keys needed) for daytime use and as key locks at night. A tenant's key would operate these locks and the apartment door lock. Master keys should be provided for management use.

### Public Corridors and Galleries

In mild climates, galleries might be appropriate and desirable for cross ventilation, tenant circulation, relaxation, and visiting. Gal-leries should be at least 7 feet wide to allow enough room both for tenant sitting space and two-way traffic of persons using crutches or wheelchairs. Handrails of a bright color or material in bold contrast to the walls should be provided on corridor walls. Such handrails are especially helpful to people who have poor vision or are blind.

To avoid hazards, doors should not swing into public corridors. Doors to public corridors should be identified by raised, brightly col-ored letters to aid people who are blind or have poor vision. An important safety precaution is identification of doors not intended for normal use which would expose blind persons to danger if used. Such doors, when key locked, may provide sufficient protection.

No columns, radiators, drinking fountains, telephone booths, pipes, or other projections should protrude into public corridors.

### Public Stairs or Fire Towers

There should be no stairs or steps in the structure except those con-tained within fire towers for emergency use. Even such stairs should be especially planned. Single-run stairs between floors are not desir-able; at least one landing should be used, two in floor-to-floor height over 9 feet. Straight runs between floors are not advisable; runs with 90- or 180-degree turns at landings are recommended. The most desirable stair would have a 6- to 6½-inch riser and an 11-inch mini-mum tread. The 11-inch tread places the ball of the descender's foot inside the stair nosing. A safety nosing should be used which does not project beyond the riser and which is distinct in color from the rest of the tread, preferably lighter. Risers should slope forward between 1 and 1½ inches to permit the ascender's heel to rest safely on the tread (see Fig. 5).

Stair wall handrails should continue around the platform to help any-one using the stair who is blind or has poor vision. The rails should carry a 6-inch marking for hand feel 2 feet before the first down riser at both floor and landing levels. Steel pipes can be marked by deforming, or by a continuous raised welding, ground smooth, or by a smooth welded strip. Wooden rails can be shaved, notched, or marked with domed-end wood dowels.

Open or grating-type fire escapes are not recommended.

### Steps and Stairs

Steps and stairs should have nonprotruding nosings so that people with stiff joints, braces, artificial legs, or other stability problems will not catch their toes as they climb.

Handrails should be oval or round with 1½ inches hand clearance between the rails and the wall: 1½ inches clearance will provide ease of grip but will prevent the hand or wrist from slipping between the handrail and the wall if the person loses balance. Handrails should be positioned on both sides of steps and stairs and should extend beyond the first and last steps on at least one side (preferably on both) to allow people with long leg braces to pull themselves beyond these points. To guard against falls and to help children, some codes require another lower handrail.

### Laundry Facilities

Laundry facilities should be either in one central area or grouped in several areas.

Conveniently located group laundries are usually preferred by ten-ants who have disabilities or are elderly and are recommended.

One automatic washing machine and batch dryer should be installed for each 20 one- and two-person families. In large central laundries, it is possible to use cabinet-type dryers which can handle more than

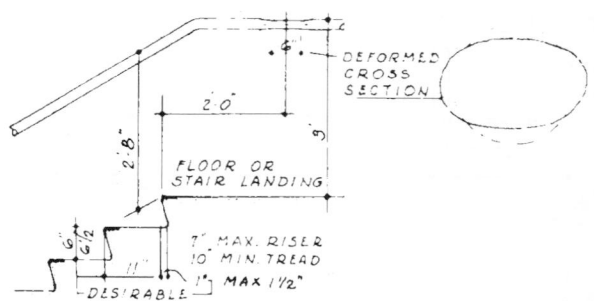

**Fig. 5. Interior stair**

one batch. In multifamily buildings, group laundries may be located on each floor or on some floors and not others, whichever is required to meet the demand.

Laundry rooms must accommodate the necessary equipment: work table, ironing board which is adjustable for standing or sitting, hanging rack, table, and chairs for rest and sociability.

**Tenant General Storage**

Central storage is not recommended for dwellings with 1- and 2-person occupancy. The general storage provided within the dwellings will suffice.

**Mailboxes**

In developments where mail is delivered to the individual dwelling unit, a mail receptacle must be provided. The best type is the mail slot with a receiving box inside, the top of which is 2 feet-10 inches to 3 feet above the floor. Tenants with disabilities should not be expected to pick up mail from the floor. A mailbox mounted outside

is not desirable. Mail slots should not be located in entrance doors where locked screen doors may make them inaccessible to the mail carrier or the inside box would interfere with the door opening at least 90°.

Mailboxes in a multistory structure are usually installed in rows stacked above each other. Sometimes, because of limited wall space, the top rows are beyond the reach of wheelchair users; the locks to their boxes should not exceed 4 feet-3 inches above the floor. The local post office should be consulted when planning this feature.

Separate mailboxes for community space staff workers are desirable, especially when the management office, where they would otherwise receive their business mail, is located at some distance from the community space.

**Living Room**

In general, dwelling entrance should be by way of the living room. The space should be planned to permit circulation by people using wheelchairs or crutches (see Figs. 6 to 9). Entrance through the

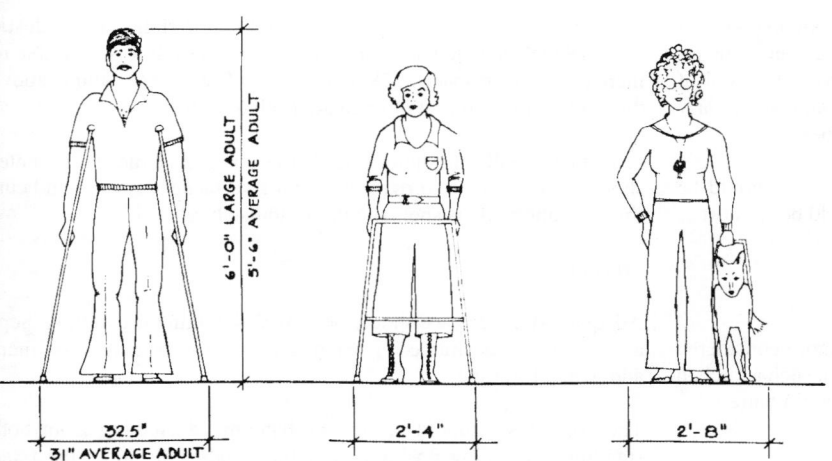

**Fig. 6. Average clearances**

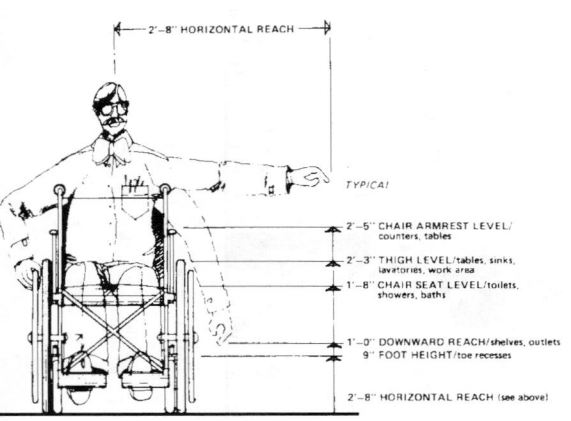

**Fig. 7. Typical dimensions**

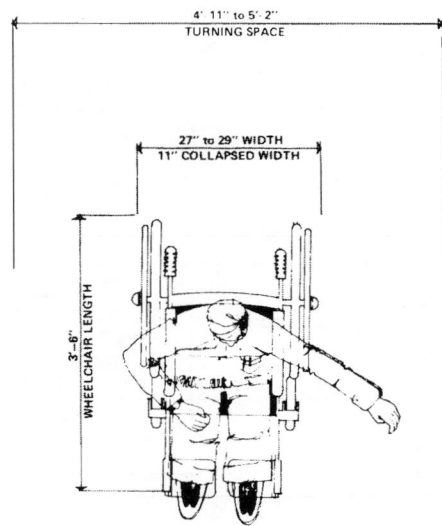

**Fig. 8. Wheelchair dimensions**

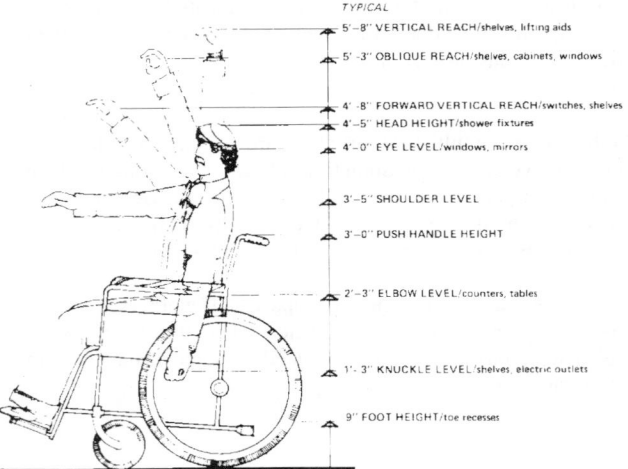

**Fig. 9. Typical dimensions**

TYPICAL

5'-8" VERTICAL REACH/shelves, lifting aids

5'-3" OBLIQUE REACH/shelves, cabinets, windows

4'-8" FORWARD VERTICAL REACH/switches, shelves

4'-5" HEAD HEIGHT/shower fixtures

4'-0" EYE LEVEL/windows, mirrors

3'-5" SHOULDER LEVEL

3'-0" PUSH HANDLE HEIGHT

2'-3" ELBOW LEVEL/counters, tables

1'-3" KNUCKLE LEVEL/shelves, electric outlets

9" FOOT HEIGHT/toe recesses

kitchen is not desirable. For families without children, a combined living-dining room arrangement is preferable to a kitchen–dining room combination. A wheelchair requires at least 2 feet-6 inches seating space at the dining table. Dining by a window, the stool of which is no higher than the dining table, is pleasant, and particularly desirable for people who are elderly or have disabilities.

Food service from the kitchen to the living-dining area should be direct, without turning corners, and the distance should be as short as possible.

**Kitchen**

The kitchen for residents with disabilities requires more considered attention than any other room. Unlike the living room, such a kitchen requires more space than one for residents who are nonimpaired.

A 5-foot minimum width should be provided for wheelchair turns between counters on opposite walls or between counter and opposite wall.

Countertops should be set 2 feet-10 inches above the floor, a workable height from both wheelchair and standing positions.

Base cabinets should have a recessed toe space 6 inches deep and 8¾ inches high to allow the wheelchair user to get close to the counter and to permit maneuverability. A minimum open space 2 feet-4 inches wide should be provided under the sink. The swing spout should have a built-in aerator to prevent splash, especially in a shallow sink. The sink waste line should have a close-fitting elbow leading to the trap installed near, and parallel to, the back wall (Figs. 10 to 11).

One unit could be used for hanging utensils from a peg board (see Figs. 12-20).

The other, if installed, could be used for supplies and should have adjustable shelves. Space for the storage of additional supplies should be provided on the counter or in wall cabinets directly in front of the work center.

Another work center arrangement would be the right-hand pedestal 16 to 18 inches wide with drawers, no left pedestal; it is desirable to increase the open space to 28 or 30 inches. The storage cabinet above the counter may consist of open adjustable shelves.

A lapboard pull-out shelf beneath the counter at the work center should be installed to provide a working surface for mixing and cutting operations. This shelf should be adjustable.

**Storage**

Adequate storage space should be provided within the dwelling. Separate units are desirable for hanging coats and for bedroom, linen, and general storage.

The coat closet should permit the hanging of clothing from both standing and sitting positions. For the standing position, the fixed shelf height at 5 feet-6 inches with the clothes-hanging pole below is

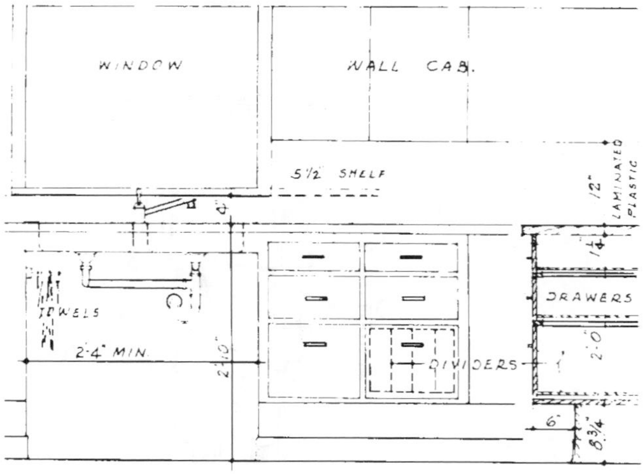

**Fig. 10. Kitchen sink and base cabinet elevation and section**

WINDOW
WALL CAB.
5½ SHELF
12"
LAMINATED PLASTIC
DRAWERS
TOWELS
2'-4" MIN
2'-10"
DIVIDERS
6"
8¾"

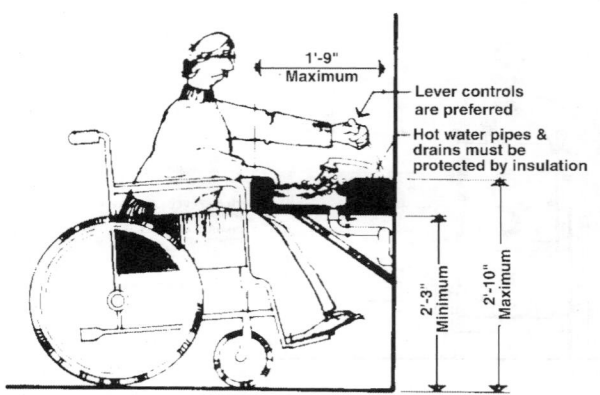

1'-9" Maximum

Lever controls are preferred

Hot water pipes & drains must be protected by insulation

2'-3" Minimum

2'-10" Maximum

**Fig. 11. Sink with knee space**

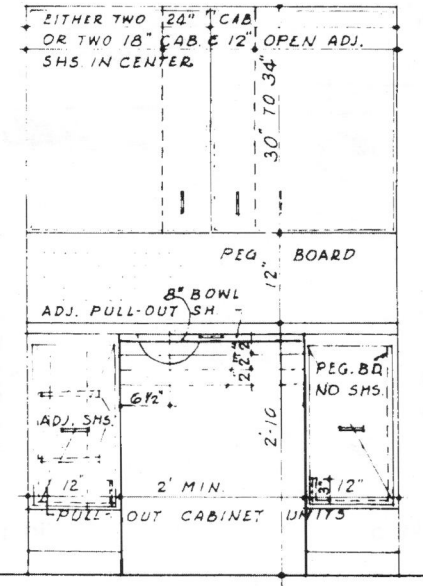

**Fig. 12. Work center elevation**

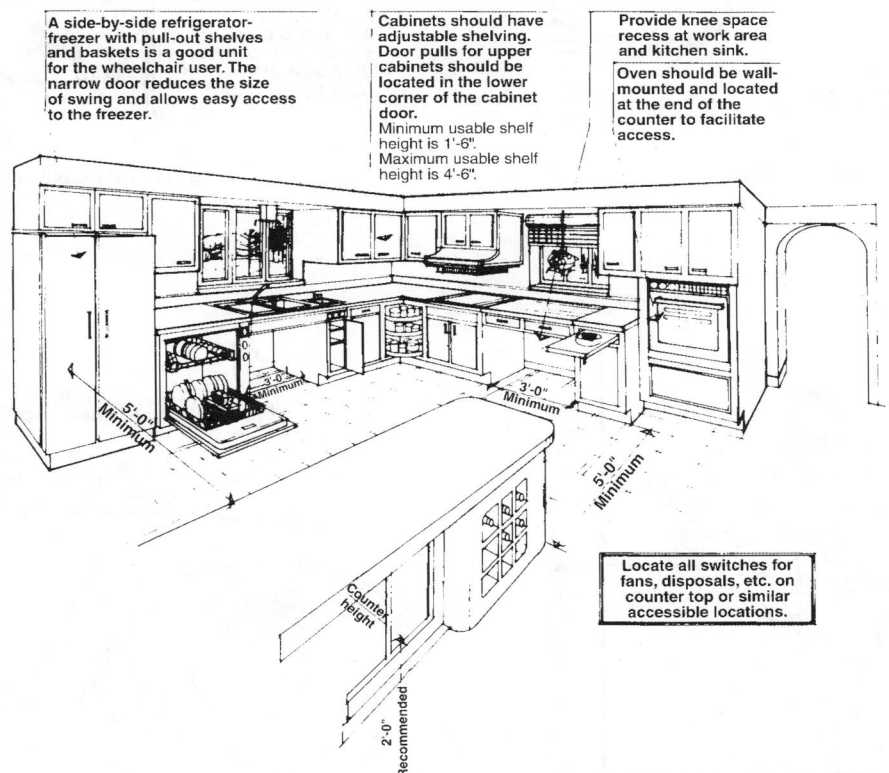

A side-by-side refrigerator-freezer with pull-out shelves and baskets is a good unit for the wheelchair user. The narrow door reduces the size of swing and allows easy access to the freezer.

Cabinets should have adjustable shelving. Door pulls for upper cabinets should be located in the lower corner of the cabinet door.
Minimum usable shelf height is 1'-6".
Maximum usable shelf height is 4'-6".

Provide knee space recess at work area and kitchen sink.

Oven should be wall-mounted and located at the end of the counter to facilitate access.

Locate all switches for fans, disposals, etc. on counter top or similar accessible locations.

**Fig. 13. Kitchen arrangements**

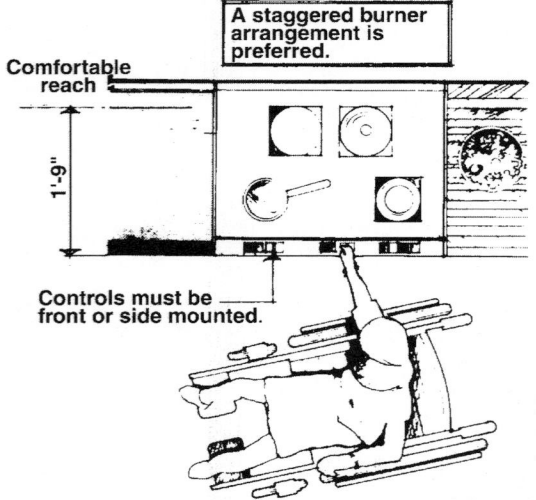

Fig. 14. Counter-mounted cooktop

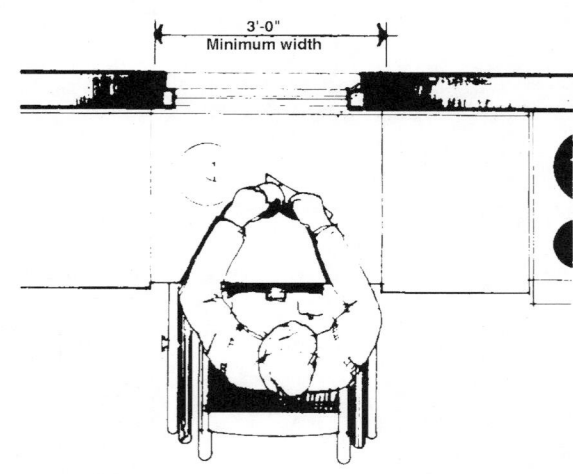

Fig. 15. Knee-recess work area

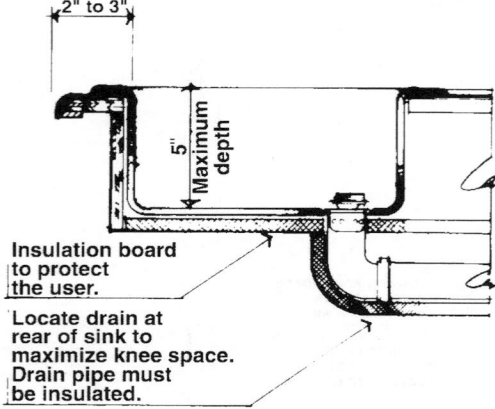

Fig. 16. Sink

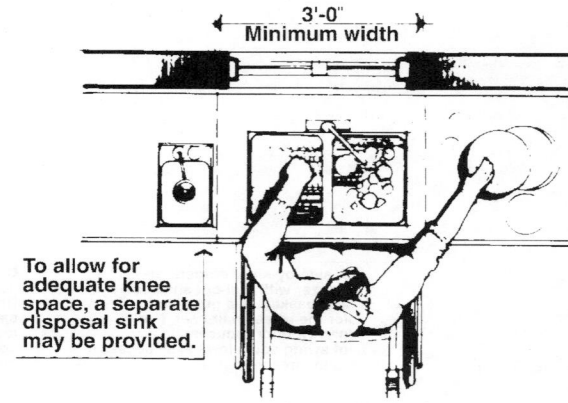

Fig. 17. Disposal sink

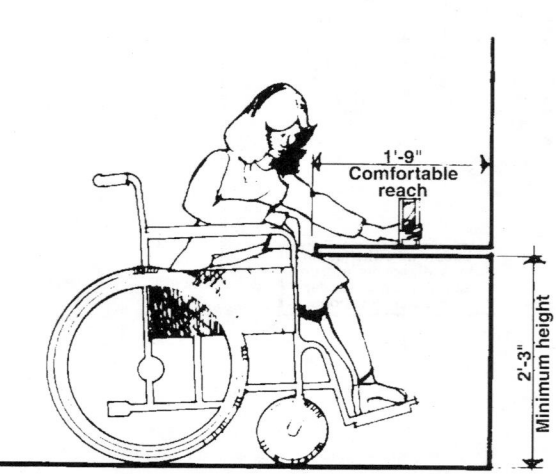

Fig. 18. Knee-space clearance

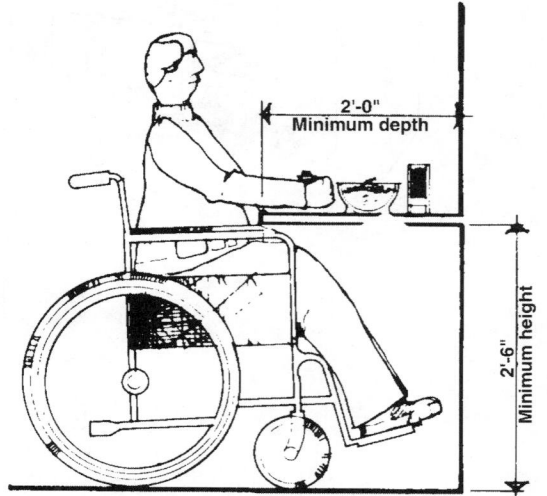

Fig. 19. Armrest clearance

standard. For the wheelchair position, 4 feet to 4 feet-6 inches is most convenient. The lower shelf and pole unit should be adjustable from 4 feet to 5 feet-6 inches (see Fig. 20).

For 1-person dwellings, the coat closet shelves and pole should be made adjustable. For larger dwellings, both the standing position height and the adjustable wheelchair height should be provided by dividing the closet with a wood partition (see Figs. 21 and 22).

The bedroom clothes closet should be divided into two sections, one with shelves and pole for the standing position height and the other adjustable for the wheelchair user.

The linen closet shelves should be adjustable in height, from the baseboard up. Persons in a sitting position can easily reach low shelves, but low shelves are difficult for those on crutches. The linen closet often stores items other than linen, such as clothes hamper, bathroom supplies, and the like. Adjustable shelves provide the needed flexibility.

A general storage area and kitchen storage space may be combined if located conveniently to the kitchen.

Although the general storage area is not primarily designed for the storage of excess furniture, it should be large enough to store foot lockers, suitcases, vacuum cleaner, large and seldom-used cooking utensils, work clothes and work shoes, and—in large family units—folded baby furniture and unused toys.

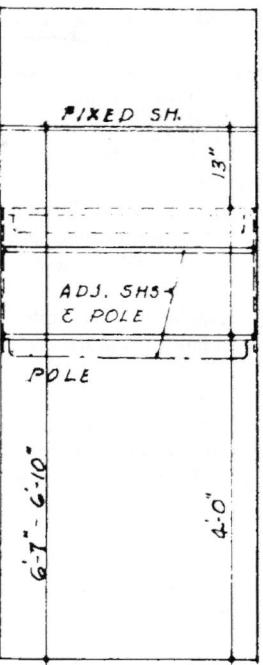

**Fig. 21. One-person bedroom closet (coat closet same but smaller)**

Increasing the amount of storage space does not always economically resolve the storage problem. The best use of available space can be made by careful arrangement of varying shelf widths adjustable for height and use of hook strips for hanging such items as brooms, mops, vacuum cleaner hose and so on.

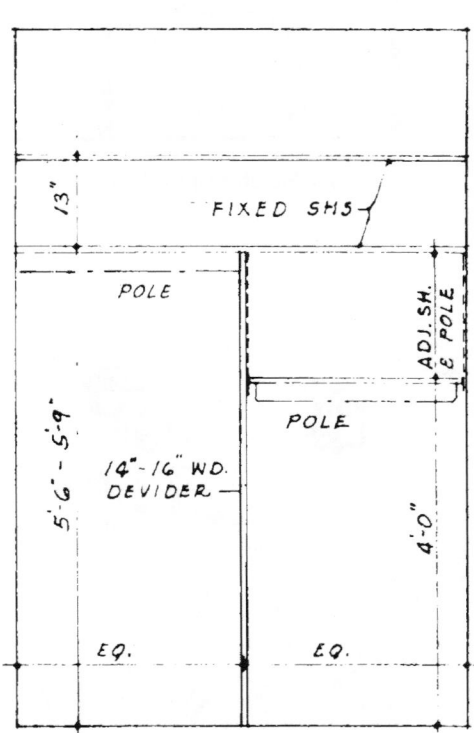

**Fig. 20. Two-person bedroom closet (coat closet same but smaller)**

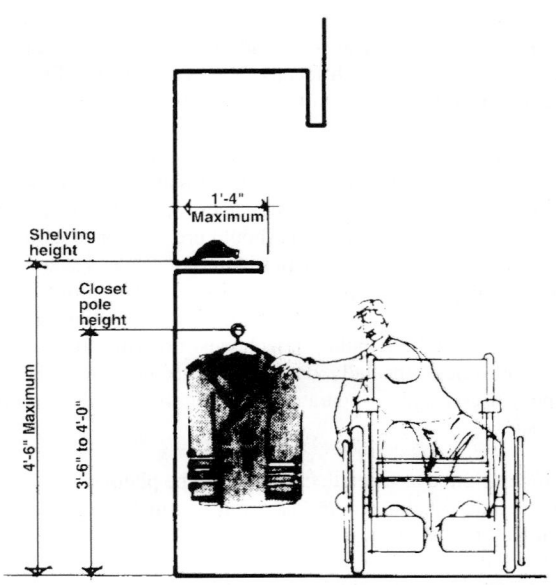

**Fig. 22. Closets**

## LIGHTING, TELEPHONE, AND ELECTRICAL OUTLETS

All light fixtures should be controlled by wall switches. The switches should be uniformly located 2 feet-10 inches to 3 feet above the floor and not over 8 inches from door jamb at latch side of door. A receptacle (not switch controlled) should be combined at some locations with switches, for convenient use of a vacuum cleaner. Tap-type or rocker switches are best for persons with hand impairments. Light fixtures located at a height permitting the tenants to replace light bulbs without using a stepladder are desirable. One way to eliminate this hazard is by the use of a floor or table lamp for room lighting. For this purpose, one receptacle of a wall duplex outlet, conveniently located, should be switch controlled at the room entrance (see Figs. 23 to 25).

Adequate light should be provided outside entrance doors so that residents can easily locate their door locks at night. Higher-than-normal lighting intensity is needed by most elderly people and some people with disabilities, especially in the kitchen and bathroom.

Wall receptacles should be uniformly placed 18 to 24 inches above the floor to reduce the physical effort of bending. Only those wall receptacles placed above kitchen counters and in dining areas should be mounted higher.

## COMMUNITY SPACE

### General

The following recommendations apply particularly to multiuse community space and to those less specialized community facilities most frequently developed in conjunction with residential housing developments. Local considerations will govern the number and nature of specialized community facilities developed in combination with a residential facility for people with physical impairments. Because the range of possibilities in such specialized facilities is so vast—from health clinics to sheltered workshops offering specific types of employment opportunities—anyone undertaking to design them should consult with program directors.

Before the architectural plan and functional layout of the community space can proceed, the local need and available services should be explored in cooperation with local agencies which will finance the staffing and operate the space after it is constructed.

Since the maximum space permitted is determined by the number of families in each development, it is not possible to provide in all developments, especially the smaller ones, space for all activities. The space planning for some areas should provide for functional use of the maximum number of activities. Areas or spaces generally considered desirable are a lounge combined with the entrance lobby; group recreational space with kitchen; craft area; library; clinic; facilities such as toilets, public telephones, drinking fountains, and vending machines especially designed or arranged for orthopedic equipment users; and a separate space for the resident children's activities.

Space to be allotted as a health clinic should be planned as a separate functional unit. Health clinic space rarely can be combined with recreational or other space.

Indoor community space should be closely related to outdoor recreational areas, with easy access and no intervening stairs or steps.

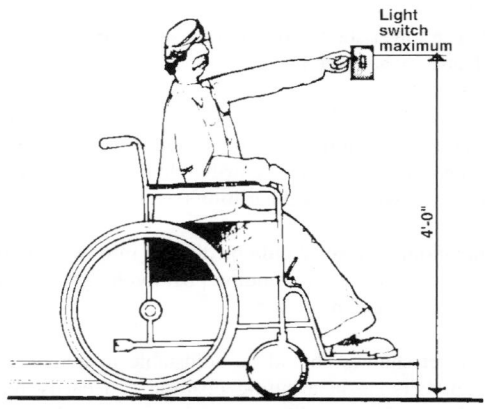

**Fig. 23. Wall switches**

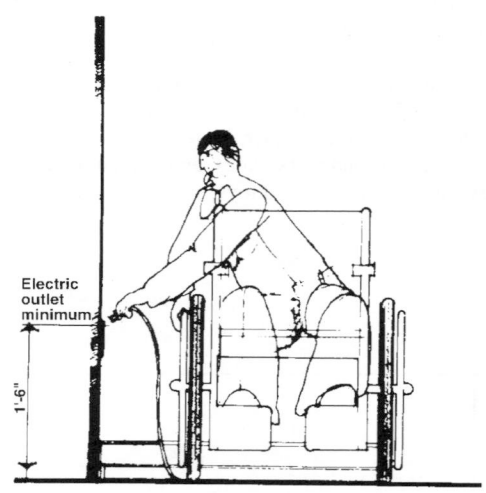

**Fig. 24. Electrical outlets**

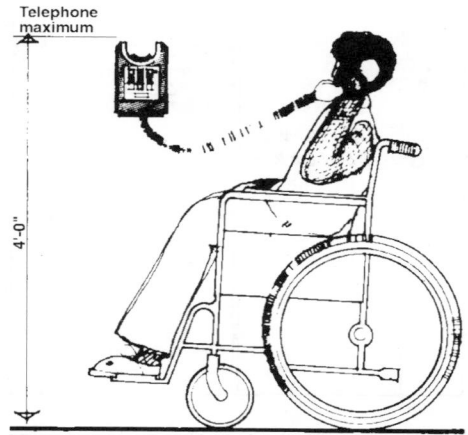

**Fig. 25. Telephones**

Indoor space should have natural light and ventilation, with pleasant outward views. It is not desirable to locate community space in basements or on rooftops detached from outdoor recreational areas.

There should be no hazards within the community space, such as thresholds, freestanding columns, pilasters, projecting radiators, or drinking fountains.

Air-conditioning of all community space used by physically impaired or elderly should be considered.

## Lounge

When combined with the entrance lobby of a community building or the elevator lobby of a multistory structure, a lounge provides increased activity and interest. Residents enjoy watching the going and coming of tenants and visitors. In cold climates a vestibule entrance is necessary.

Locating the mail delivery room in the elevator lobby near the lounge is recommended.

Selection of chairs and sofas for tenants who have physical impairments, especially those who are semiambulant, deserves special consideration. Seat height 18 inches above floor is best. Sturdy arm rests help people with disabilities to rise. Chairs should not overbalance when weight is applied on the arm rest. Deep seats (over 20 inches) are undesirable. Semistiff, upholstered furniture is recommended.

## Recreation or Multipurpose Room

This space may be subdivided by sliding or folding soundproof dividers or doors—the ceiling should be acoustically treated. The space should be suited for meetings, movies, concerts, plays, lunches, and the like. Because of the nature of such activities, convenient storage space for tables and other items should be provided. An inventory of the items is needed to adequately plan orderly and functional storage—flexibility of use with adjustable shelves is desirable.

Building codes may require emergency exits, but at least one exit door may be desirable for departing guests after evening affairs.

Structural columns or other obstructions within this space should be avoided or eliminated if possible in order that the space may function as one room for certain occasions.

## Kitchen

A kitchen should be provided adjacent to the recreation room. Equipment and arrangement should facilitate efficient and functional food preparation and cleanup. The kitchen may be used by the tenants.

The kitchen should be planned and designed to be useful in demonstrating and instructing on food preparation, in planning balanced diets, and in conducting various consumer education activities. For this purpose, the division between the recreation room and kitchen should be a sliding or folding divider or doors which can be locked or secured.

A kitchen service entrance should be planned to accommodate delivery of supplies, catering service, and garbage and trash removal. A garbage grinder may be installed in this kitchen—the continuous-feed type is recommended.

Floor and wall surfaces should be of easily cleaned materials and finishes. Wall cabinets should have adjustable shelves. At least one closet, with lock, for storage of staple supplies should be provided, as well as a cabinet for mops, brooms, and cleaning materials.

## Craft Activity Area

The space for craft activities should have maximum flexibility for varied arrangement. Fixed partitioning of cubicles is *not* desirable—no flexibility. It is best to concentrate the craft space in one room. This provides for multiple use of space and permits adapting space size to tenant interest and various activities.

## Library

The larger community spaces may provide, if need is established, an area for a branch of the city library, which will furnish book stacks. When the book stacks can be locked or otherwise segregated from the rest of the library, then the area generally used for reading could on occasion be used for small gatherings or other uses—again, flexibility. If possible, this space should be large enough for tables and chairs. Since smaller projects seldom can afford a separate library, the lounge may be provided with adjustable shelves for books and periodicals. This same idea, while less desirable than a separate library, may be considered for large projects.

## Health Clinic

A clinic can contribute substantially to the welfare and continued independence of people who are elderly or have physical impairments. Clinic space may be provided when such facilities are not available near the site.

In small developments, the permissible clinic space may consist of an office and examination room for the use of doctors and nurses who visit during scheduled periods.

In larger developments, space for a variety of health services may be provided, including physical therapy and hydrotherapy, a special need of people with physical impairments. Occupational therapy may be conducted in the craft activity area. This type of clinic would generally be active each workday and should have a waiting room with a separate outside entrance permitting nontenant patients to come and go without traversing the lobby or lounge.

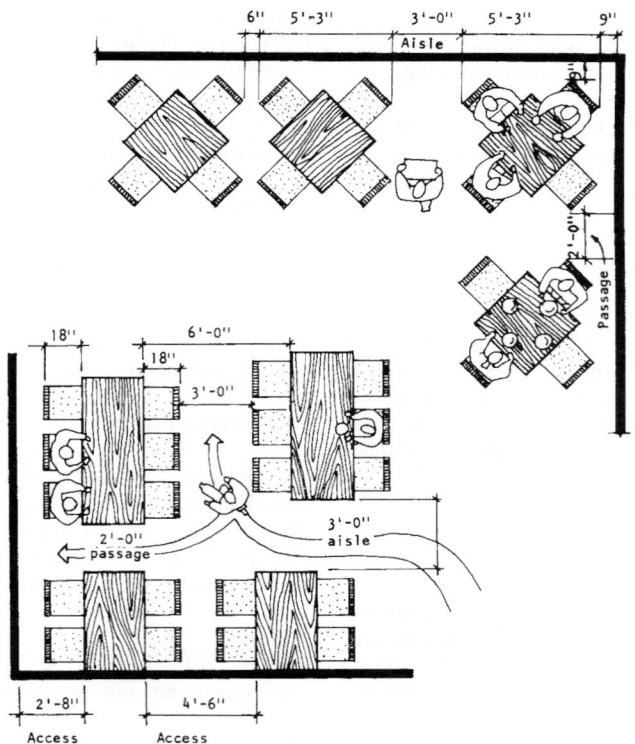

**Fig. 1. Clearances for central dining**

# GROUP HOMES

## SPATIAL REQUIREMENTS

### Building

Approximately 6,650 square feet for a 12-person home and 7,400 square feet for a 16-person home are allotted. This area includes space for the garage and basements. The building can be arranged on one level or on two full or partial levels.

### Entry

*Major*

This spatial requirement varies according to the inclusion or exclusion of the vertical circulation element within the space. Normally, an area of approximately 90 square feet should be sufficient. A closet with a minimum of 6 linear feet of hanging space should be adequate.

*Minor*

The size of this space varies; however, it should be adequately sized for ease of circulation through it.

### Living Space

This space varies in size. In a typical 16-resident group home, it is approximately 400 to 500 square feet.

### Recreation Room

This space varies in size. In a typical 16-resident group home, it is approximately 400 to 500 square feet and as previously indicated should be sized to seat all residents. It is required that direct access suitable for use by people with physical disabilities be provided from the main living area and to the common outdoor activity area.

### Kitchen

The area designated for food preparation should meet all of the requirements of the Michigan Department of Public Health, Michigan Department of Social Services, and the applicable portion of the FHA Minimum Property Standards for Multifamily Housing. The typical kitchen is equipped with the following appliances:

*Reviewer:* James Wentling, FAIA

- Refrigerator
- Freezer
- Microwave
- Commercial dishwasher
- Cooktop range with exhaust hood
- Double oven
- Disposal

## Dining

The dining space should have a glazed area of at least 10 percent of the floor area. The following clearances and sizes should be assumed for design purposes:

- 2 feet for table edge for each diner
- 3 feet minimum table width for tables seating 4 to 6 persons
- 3 feet-3 inches for larger tables
- 4 feet minimum clearance between the table edge and obstruction where seating and circulation occurs
- 3 feet for circulation clearance
- 2 feet-6 inches for seating clearance table to obstruction

Clearances are shown in Fig. 1.

## Powder Room

This space should be sized to accommodate residents with physical disabilities. A water closet and a lavatory without vanity base should be provided.

## Bedroom

No resident room should accommodate more than three persons. Each occupant of a room should be provided with a separate storage closet of at least the following:

- 4 feet by 2 feet-2 inches clear and an opening width of at least 3 feet clear.
- The closet should be equipped with a shelf and hanging rod.
- The bedroom should be equipped with windows whose glazed area is at least 15 percent of the floor area of the room.
- Windows should be operable and have a free air ventilation area equal to half the glazed area.
- Resident bedrooms should accommodate at least the following:
  2 beds, 3 feet-3 inches by 6 feet-6 inches minimum
  2 dressers, 3 feet by 1 foot-6 inches minimum
  1 lounge chair, 1 foot-10 inches by 1 foot-10 inches minimum
  2 bedside tables, 1 foot by 1 foot
- Specially designed desks and storage units may be used. Minimum clearance should be maintained as follows:

1 foot-6 inches between wall and the side of bed that is least used
3 feet in front of dresser
3 foot-6 inch diameter area for dressing
2 feet-6 inches for access to and use of table as a desk
3-foot door opening
2 feet-6 inches general circulation

The bedroom should be designed to provide a clearly defined area within the room for each occupant. It is preferable if one occupant does not have to violate the area of another in order to get to or from the room entrance or the bedroom.

If possible, the room should be designed so that there is a visual separation between the sleeping areas. Generally, resident rooms should be grouped together and served from common halls or foyers. These halls should provide direct access to shared facilities for the residents without the necessity of going out of doors. The room specially adapted for residents with disabilities should have such access only via level floors or elevators. The acoustic separation of party walls and floors of a given resident room should have an STC rating of 45 and INR rating of +5. The ceiling height should be at least 7 feet-6 inches (8 feet preferred).

## Bathroom

One bathroom should serve every two resident bedrooms, that is, a total of four residents. The bathroom should contain a water closet and a vanity base with a pair of lavatories with cabinets mounted on it. The homes specially adapted for residents with physical disabilities should have a stall shower of sufficient dimensions to allow soaping out of the spray instead of a tub. Lavatories should be located in vanity tops without a base. Tubs may be allowed if equipped with appropriate grab bar.

The bathroom should open directly off the resident's room. All bathrooms should be finished with nonslip materials and should include a storage space for each individual's personal toiletries.

## Office

The office should contain no less than 100 square feet in area. It should have walls, floors, and ceilings with a rating of 45 STC and +5 INR to ensure privacy during counseling.

## FLOOR PLANS

Figures 2 and 3 show floor plans for 12-person and 16-person group homes.

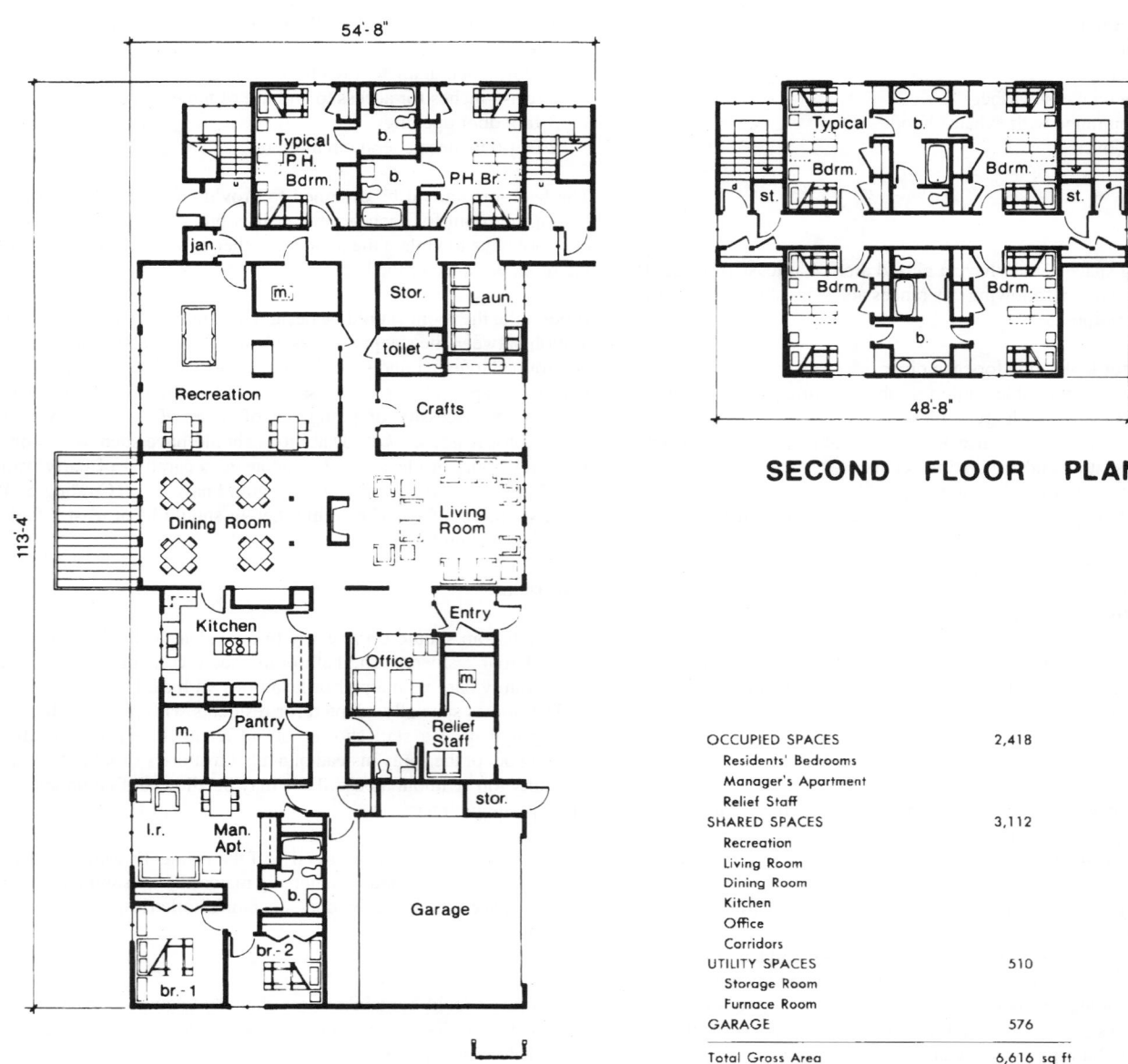

**FIRST FLOOR PLAN**

**SECOND FLOOR PLAN**

| | |
|---|---|
| OCCUPIED SPACES | 2,418 |
| Residents' Bedrooms | |
| Manager's Apartment | |
| Relief Staff | |
| SHARED SPACES | 3,112 |
| Recreation | |
| Living Room | |
| Dining Room | |
| Kitchen | |
| Office | |
| Corridors | |
| UTILITY SPACES | 510 |
| Storage Room | |
| Furnace Room | |
| GARAGE | 576 |
| Total Gross Area | 6,616 sq ft |

**Fig. 2. 12-person group home**

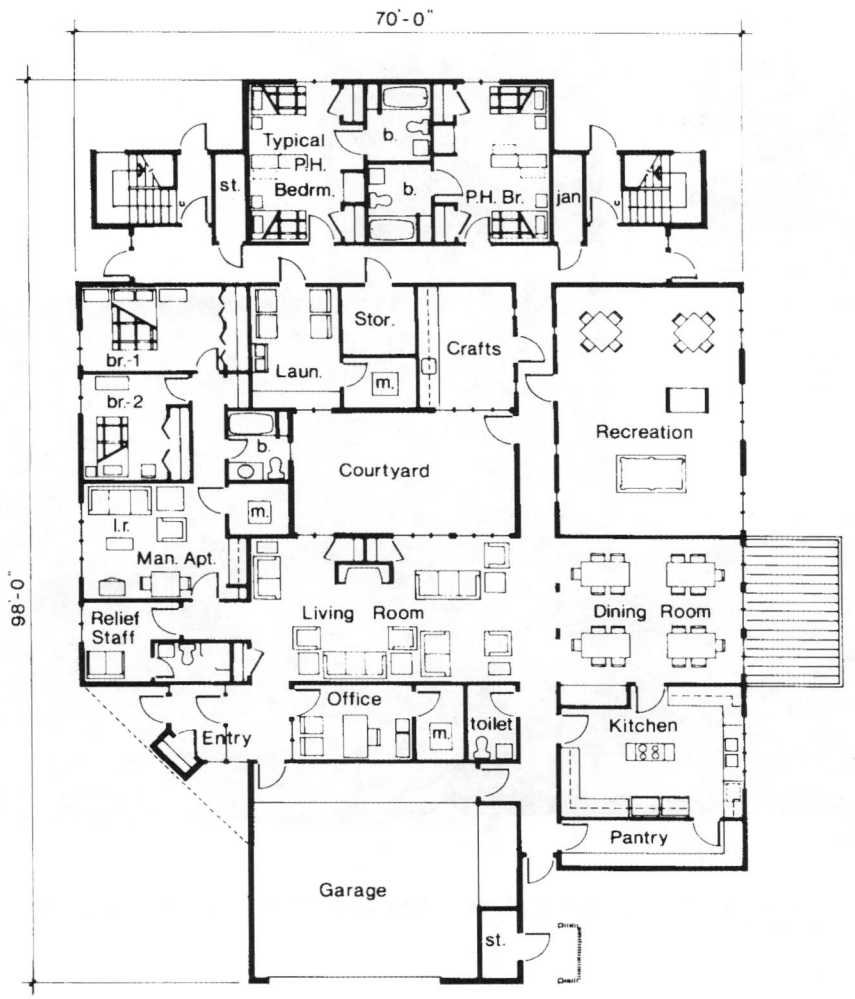

## FIRST FLOOR PLAN

| OCCUPIED SPACES | 2,954 |
| Residents' Bedrooms | |
| Manager's Apartment | |
| Relief Staff | |
| SHARED SPACES | 3,416 |
| Recreation | |
| Living Room | |
| Dining Room | |
| Kitchen | |
| Office | |
| Corridors | |
| UTILITY SPACES | 600 |
| Storage Room | |
| Furnace Room | |
| GARAGE | 576 |
| Total Gross Area | 7,546 sq ft |

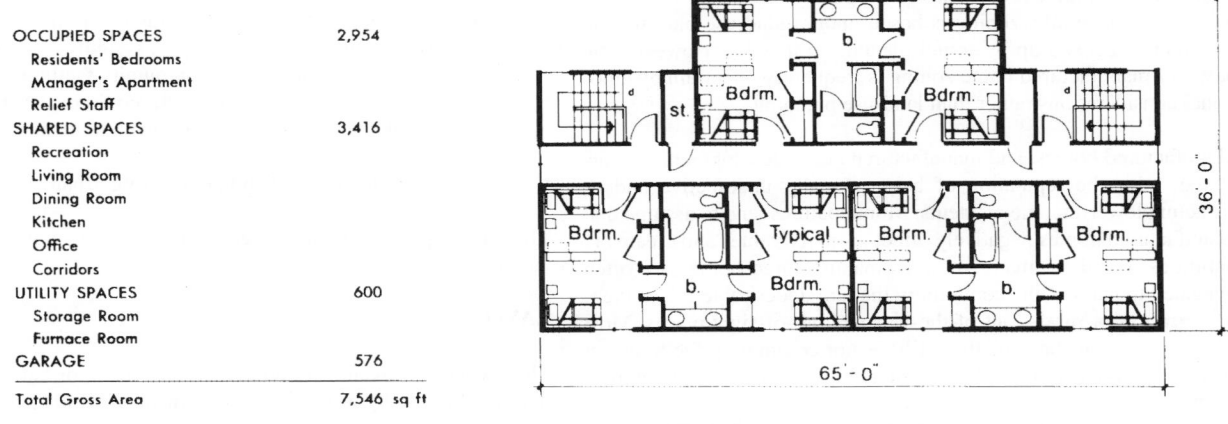

## SECOND FLOOR PLAN

**Fig. 3. 16-Person group home**

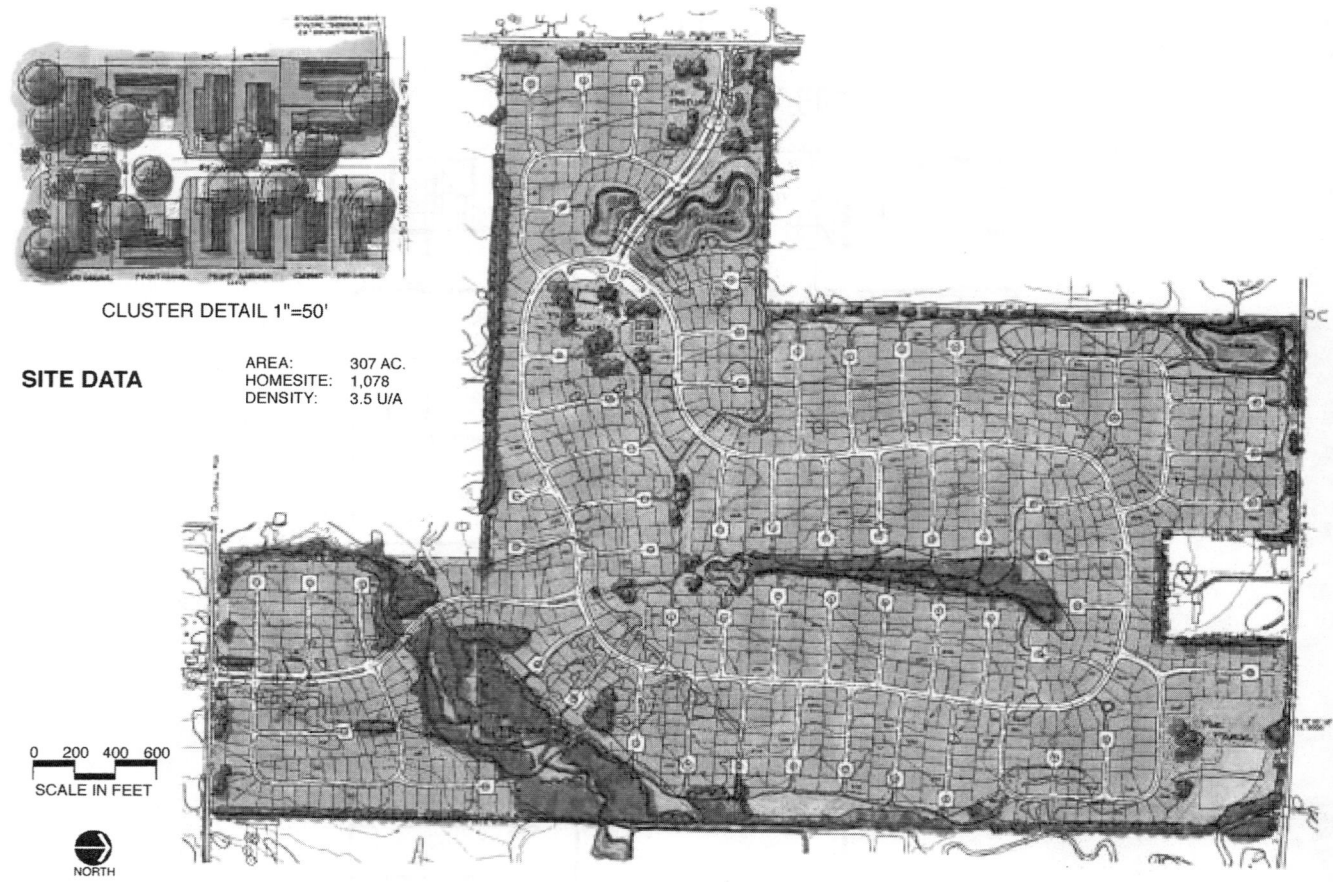

CLUSTER DETAIL 1"=50'

**SITE DATA**

| AREA: | 307 AC. |
| HOMESITE: | 1,078 |
| DENSITY: | 3.5 U/A |

0  200  400  600
SCALE IN FEET

NORTH

**Fig. 1a. Manufactured home community sketch plans: White Oaks Crossing (Donald C. Westphal Associates, landscape architects and site planners)**

# MANUFACTURED HOME DEVELOPMENTS

### LOCATION

The location of manufactured homes (also known as HUD-Code homes) and manufactured home developments is usually controlled by zoning. Generally, zoning is based upon a land-use plan for the community, backed up by sound planning principles. However, the basis for manufactured home zoning is frequently underlain by emotional considerations rather than land-use planning.

Manufactured homes, and manufactured home developments in particular, have the reputation of being visually unattractive and of attracting lower-income residents. Municipalities tend to assume that manufactured homes negatively affect property values and create tax liabilities. For these major reasons, manufactured homes are often relegated to parts of the community that are undesirable for residential purposes or rural—out-of-the-way and out-of-sight places. Most of these locations have neither utilities nor community facilities yet they are designated to be developed as high-density living environments.

Manufactured home developments are rarely allowed or encouraged in areas well suited for residential development. The normally accepted planning principles for residential land-use planning are to locate residential uses in areas:

* of compatible land use and surrounding environments;
* with adequate utility and road support systems;
* with reasonable convenience to community facilities;
* of similar density such as a manufactured home density of 4 to 7 dwelling units per acre, much like townhouses and low density apartments; and
* of logical extension or infilling of existing urban growth pattern.

These principles are often ignored with regard to manufactured home zoning.

### LAYOUT

The layout of a manufactured home subdivision or land-lease community is normally a gridlike arrangement of parallel roads, linked

---

*Reviewer:* Donald C. Westphal, Donald C. Westphal Associates, landscape architects and site planners

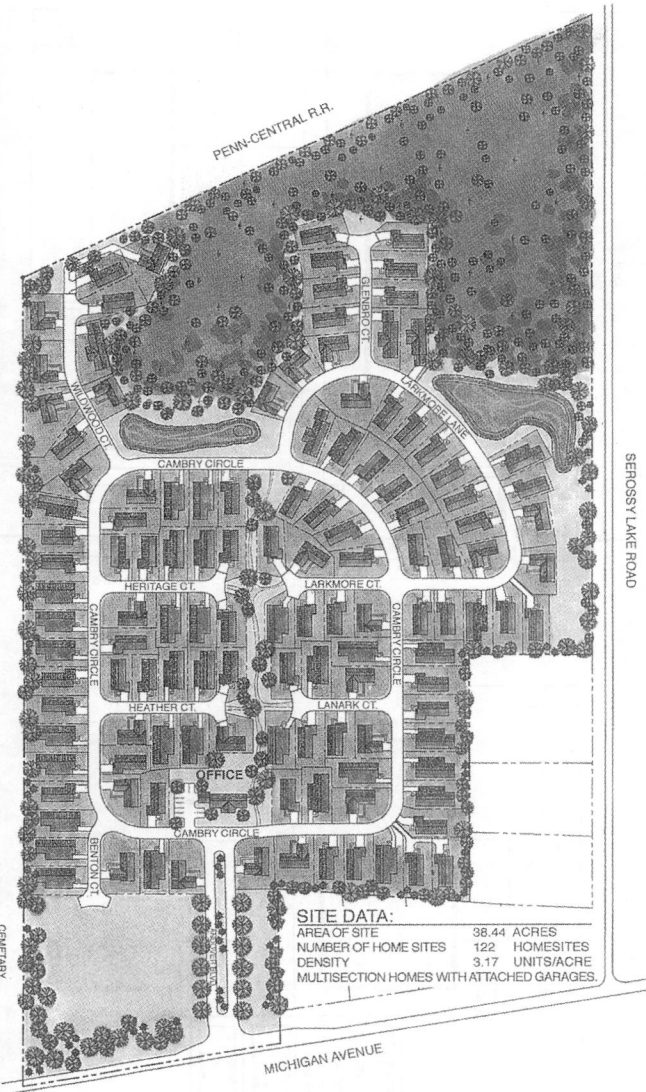

Fig. 1b. Manufactured home community sketch plans: Andover (Donald C. Westphal Associates, landscape architects and site planners)

together by other local or collector roads. This arrangement is used because most development costs are determined by the amount of road frontage required for each lot. Lining the manufactured homes up perpendicular to the road requires the least road frontage and is the most economical arrangement of lots.

However, in recent years plans for manufactured home developments have begun to reflect the sensitivity to the land and creativity of design seen in many quality site-built residential projects (see Figs. 1a and 1b).

Common facilities like swimming pools and community buildings, when provided, are usually centrally located within the development and often serve as a focal point of the entrance drive. These facilities are maintained by the developer or homeowners' association and each resident is charged a monthly rate for use and maintenance.

The typical lots in newer developments are sized to meet ordinance requirements and home sizes anticipated in the local market. Lots accommodating single-section homes range in size from 4,000 to 5,500 square feet while multi-section home sites can contain 5,000 to 6,500 square feet. The lots will front on a road built to local specifications, but may not actually be dedicated to the municipality. When dedicated to the municipality, the road right-of-way width is usually a minimum of 50 feet and contains a 24- to 30-foot paved cart-way. Roads in land-lease communities most often remain under private ownership and maintenance and are not usually in a dedicated right-of-way. Lot dimensions and home sizes (see Fig. 2) can vary based on local requirements and market conditions.

### INDIVIDUAL MANUFACTURED HOME LOT

The manufactured home lot is the land area, large or small, upon which the home is placed and which provides space for all of the belongings and activities of its occupant.

**Required Functional Areas**

The individual manufactured home lot consists of six component areas that reflect the basic functions of the manufactured home site—pad, parking, entrance, outdoor living, utility corridor, and storage. The arrangement of these six functional components of the lot is somewhat variable, but typically looks like Fig. 3.

The only component of this arrangement that is fixed is the utility side of the home, which is always on the right side when facing the manufactured home hitch. The other areas are variable, but depend primarily on the lot size and the home's orientation on the lot.

Each manufactured home lot is not usually required, by ordinance, to provide the pad, parking area, outdoor living and storage areas. Existing standards vary, but typically define a minimum lot size and minimum yard areas. Such requirements often do not give the flexibility minimum required to accommodate the many sizes and shapes of manufactured homes available. Standards, which set a minimum distance between homes and minimum setbacks, allow greater lot size flexibility.

**Convenience in Relationship of Use Areas**

The arrangement of the six functional component areas of the lot should be determined by the floor plan of the home, the characteristics of each site, and the logical and convenient relationship of on-lot

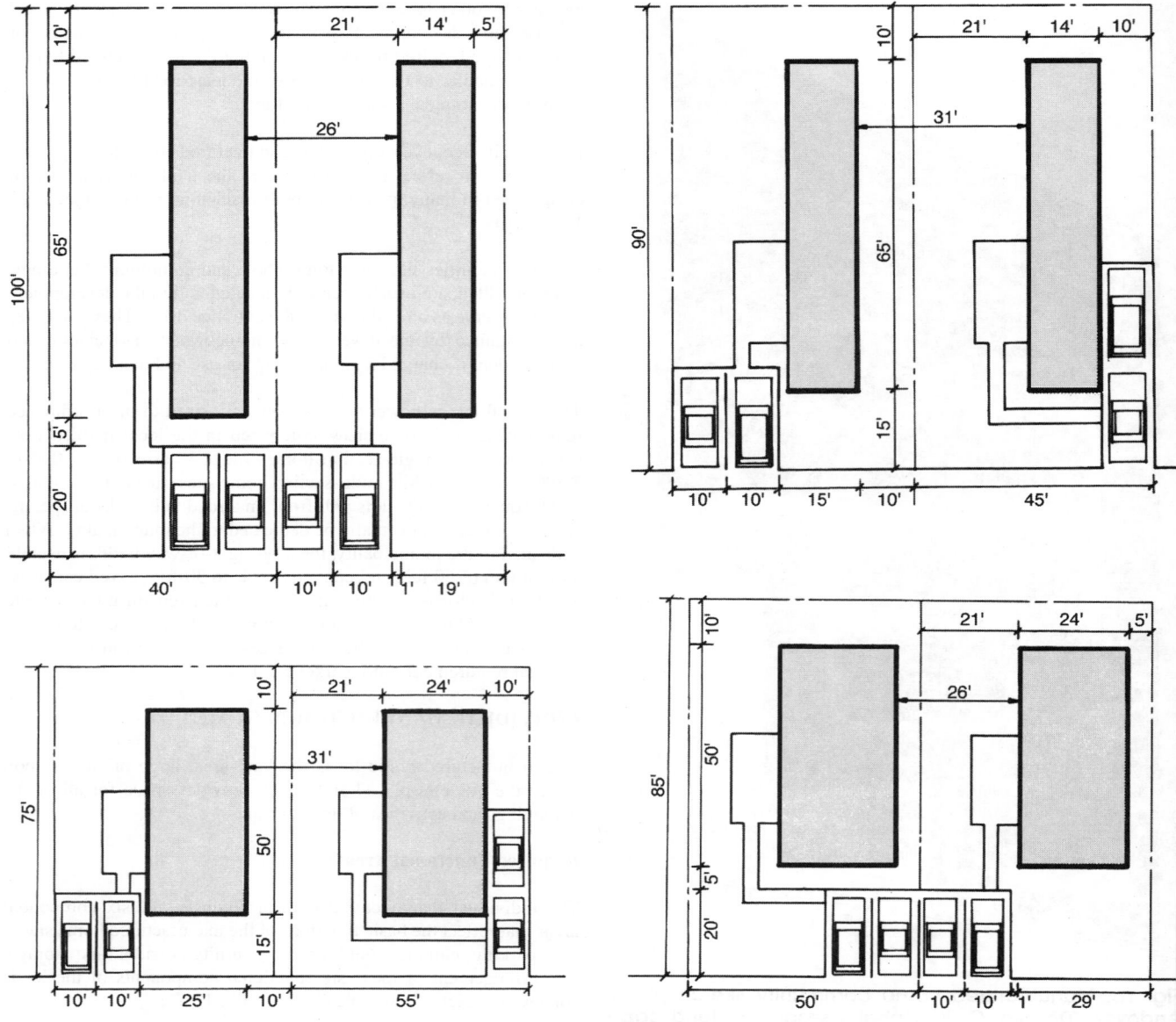

**Fig. 2. Typical lot layouts**

space. The sequence in which residents use the component areas should be supported in the lot arrangement. The occupant arrives at home by car, moves from the car to the door, and enters the home. Or, the occupant spends the majority of their time in the house and occasionally moves to the outside of the home to the yard area—the outdoor living space. Logically, parking should be between the street and one of the doors. The outdoor living area should be adjacent to the home and near one of the two entrances (see Fig. 4).

**Circulation—Hierarchy of Streets**

Streets within a manufactured home development, which is served by an arterial, can be grouped into four functional categories (see Fig. 5):

1. courts, places, cul-de-sacs
2. local streets
3. sub-collectors
4. collectors

**Courts, Places, or Cul-de-sacs**

These are very minor residential streets, the primary purpose of which is to serve individual lots and provide access to local or higher traveled streets. A place may be a dead-end, cul-de-sac street, or court with no through traffic and with limited on-street parking. Local streets are generally short and may have cul-de-sacs, courts, or occasionally two or three branching places. The purpose of a

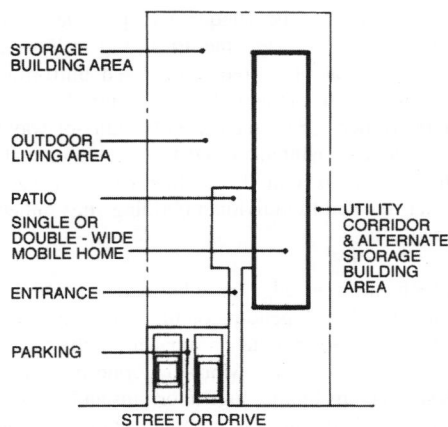

**Fig. 3. Typical individual manufactured home lot**

rial streets outside the residential areas. A well-planned community maximizes the number of homes located on either local streets or courts, places, and cul-de-sacs where there is a limited amount of through traffic. Homes having direct access to subcollectors and collectors are allowable, but should be minimized. Local streets and courts are safe and desirable places to live; living areas are dominant and traffic movement is subordinate.

Each of these four street categories should be designed with the following issues in mind:

*Street alignments* should be based upon sight distance and probable roadway speeds using computation methods endorsed by the Institute of Traffic Engineers. Generally, a minimum practical curve radius in residential areas is 100 feet, with 30 feet acceptable on minor streets. Street alignment at intersections is especially critical. The preferred angle of street intersections is 90 degrees; for safety purposes, streets should never intersect at angles less than 80 degrees. When two streets intersect the same street, they should either form a through intersection or be offset by at least 100 feet.

local street is to connect traffic to and from dwelling units to subcollectors.

## Local Streets

These connect the places, courts, and cul-de-sacs to collectors, subcollectors, and the larger municipality. They have slightly higher volume than cul-de-sacs, courts, and places.

## Sub-collectors

These provide access to local streets and courts, places, or cul-de-sacs and conduct this traffic to an activity center or a collector street. A sub-collector may be a loop street connecting one collector or outside arterial street at two points, or conducting traffic between collector streets or arterial streets.

## Collectors

These are the principal traffic arteries within residential areas and carry fairly high traffic volumes. They conduct traffic to major arte-

*Street gradients* affect the visual character, safety, and accessibility of the manufactured home development. Generally speaking, grades between 2 and 7 percent are the most desirable; and a minimum of 0.5 percent is necessary on all curbed streets to prevent pooling of water. If gradients must be less than the minimum in very flat areas, special subgrade compaction and street construction controls are necessary. Streets of less than 2 percent grade are visually perceived as flat. Moderate slopes of 2 to 7 percent usually result in a more interesting streetscape and encourage more imagination in the siting of homes.

Streets should generally not exceed the norm for the area. Where steep road gradients are unavoidable, care must still be taken to flatten grades at intersection areas; gradients within 100 feet of intersections should not exceed 10 percent, with 4 to 6 percent preferable in snow or ice areas for a distance of 50 feet.

*Circulation layout* determines the accessibility of the manufactured home site within each development. In properly designed residential neighborhoods without through traffic, travel distances from residences to collector streets are short, actual traffic speeds are low, lane

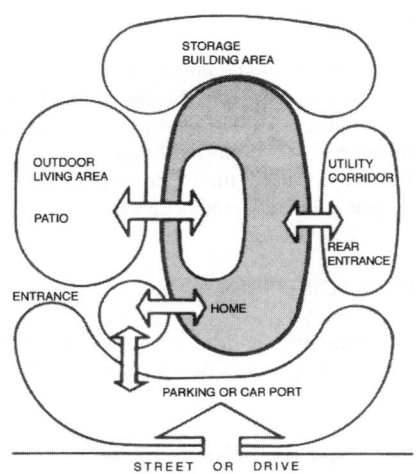

**Fig. 4. Relationship of use areas**

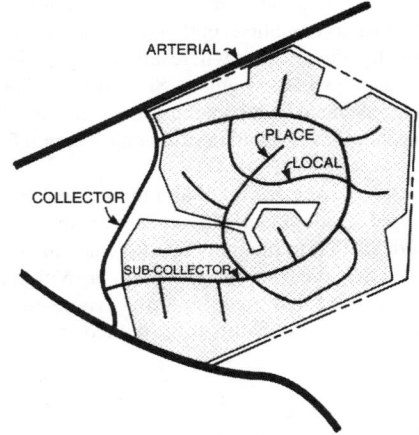

**Fig. 5. Street categories**

capacity is not a controlling design factor, and inconvenience or short delay is a minor consideration.

In conventional single-family residential neighborhoods, traffic speed should be slow; approximately 25 miles per hour. In manufactured home areas where density is higher, speed should not exceed 15 miles per hour. Momentary delays to allow other traffic to pass around parked cars is acceptable and it is customary to drive slowly to avoid children and pets.

*Pavement widths* should be determined by considering probable peak-traffic volume, parking needs, and limitations imposed by sight distance, climate, terrain, and maintenance requirements. It is senseless for streets to be wider than absolutely necessary; excessive widths only increase development costs which are passed on to the lot renter or owner. Also, from an ecological point of view, avoiding excessively wide streets means less impervious surface which results in less storm water runoff. The special problem of delivering manufactured homes to lots is not a major consideration in determining street widths. Spacing between the homes, street setback, and the grades from street to lot are of much greater concern. Movement of manufactured homes from their original placement on a lot is uncommon. When homes are to be moved through narrow streets, notice may be given to remove parked cars from the street.

Where streets also serve as pedestrian walks, they should be built with a cartway 2 feet wider than otherwise required. All entrance streets and other collector streets with guest parking should be at least 22 to 30 feet wide; this provides for two moving lanes and no on-street parking lane. Collector streets without parking should be 24 to 26 feet wide. Minor streets with parking on one side should be 26 feet wide; and local streets, courts, plazas and cul-de-sacs with no parking should be 20 feet wide. A 20-foot wide pavement is the minimum width which generally offers year-round utility and convenience where snow and ice control is not necessary.

One-way streets may be allowed at 11-foot widths in the following situations: (1) adequate off-street parking is assured; (2) the climate is mild, and snow and ice control problems are not likely; (3) total loop length will not exceed about 500 feet; (4) no more than about 25 dwelling units are served; (5) adequate longitudinal sight distances can be provided; and (6) vehicle speeds may be reasonably expected in the 10–15 mile-per-hour range. A 16-foot-wide pavement may be a practical loop street alternative in difficult terrain where cross-pavement ground slopes are severe, where vehicle speeds will not exceed 10 miles per hour, and where other above-outlined considerations can be met. Under the various conditions outlined, the 16-foot-wide pavement can be functionally effective, but will result in a higher level of resident inconvenience than a wider pavement. Sixteen feet cannot be considered a desirable pavement width but must be conceded to be acceptable under certain conditions to avoid destruction of natural features.

*Street rights-of-way* are a consideration unique to the manufactured home land-lease development. Streets within these developments simply aren't dedicated to the municipality since the entire property is privately owned by the community developer. Within the manufactured home subdivision, the streets and street rights-of-way are dedicated or retained in the ownership of the homeowners' association or the municipality.

When roads are to be dedicated, they have to meet the same standards applied to all roads within residential areas. This generally means that a 60-foot right-of-way is required.

Street rights-of-way must be adequate to provide required street pavements, sidewalks, drainage facilities, and utilities as needed. Right-of-way widths are too frequently fixed uniformly by local ordinances, regardless of the actual space required to accommodate necessary improvements. Excessively wide rights-of-way waste land and result in avoidable maintenance costs to the municipality; a community realizes no tax revenue from street rights-of-way. This land would be better devoted to individual building sites rather than public right-of-way.

*Sidewalks* along the road edge in suburban residential areas vary from location to location depending on the amount of pedestrian use. Placement of sidewalks immediately adjacent to the road isn't really safe unless curbs are provided. More elaborate developments have interior pedestrian paths linking logical origins and destinations such as clusters of individual homes to community facilities or to convenience commercial areas. Paths or sidewalks other than these are not necessary in low-traffic-movement areas.

*Drainage facilities* may include either grassed swales or curb gutters and subsurface storm drainage structures. Where roadside drainage swales are used, they normally require a right-of-way at least 10 feet wider than the pavement width. Thus, if a 28-foot pavement is used and swales are located on both sides, a total right-of-way of 48 feet would be required. If streets are curbed, there may be no justifiable reason for right-of-way widths to be much wider than roadway pavements.

*Dead-end streets* must have turn-around areas. Turn-around areas in most conventional single-family subdivisions are cul-de-sac streets with a 75- to 80-foot-diameter paved area. It is fairly common in manufactured home communities to eliminate the turning circle for streets with fewer than 25 homes, substituting a "T" or "Y" turn-around incorporated into a parking lot cluster. "T" and "Y" turn-arounds should utilize an 18-foot-minimum radius on all turns. The residential dead-end turn-around is basically for automobile use, but larger vehicles must sometimes be accommodated. Residential streets will also be used, in decreasing order of frequency, by refuse collectors, delivery trucks, snowplows, moving vans, and fire trucks. Experience has shown that circular paved turning areas 75 to 80 feet in diameter function very well.

*Curbs* along residential streets are usually used for three reasons: (1) prevent the roadway pavement from breaking down, (2) control traffic from encroaching beyond paved surfaces, and (3) concentrate and channel storm-water runoff.

The decision to use curbs should largely be based on how effectively storm water can be removed from the site without causing harmful on- or off-site impacts. The feasibility of using swales can be explored as an alternative over the use of curbs during the early planning phase. If curbs are used, the rolled or mountable curb may be more desirable due to the numerous crossovers required for frequent on-lot parking areas.

## COMMUNITY FACILITIES*

The need for community facilities is related to the density of the development and the make-up of the residents. Community facilities

*Source: *Guidelines for Improving the Mobile Home Living Environment,* Office of Policy Development and Research, HUD, Washington, D.C.

are especially important in small-lot developments where private outdoor space is limited; they are somewhat less critical where lots are large enough to allow many activities in individual yards. At higher densities, community open space can compensate for small private exterior living space.

Some regulations for community facilities require that at least 8 percent of the gross site area be devoted to recreational facilities. A community building, storm shelter, meeting room, toilets, and a management office may be provided. Depending on the size of the development, however, all of these facilities may not be desirable or necessary.

Tot lots and areas for children to play away from the homes are especially necessary for safety and to minimize disturbance of the individual residents' outdoor living areas. In developments where lots are greater than 10,000 square feet, there is less dependence upon community space, but playground and park areas for large-scale activities are desirable as in any residential area.

The entrance and community areas should have a park-like atmosphere compatible with residential living environments. Community buildings and structures should also be designed in a manner more compatible with a residential living environment than a commercial development (see Fig. 6).

Public outdoor open space commonly consists of two types: "structured" and "unstructured" facilities. Structured facilities include formal playgrounds, golf courses, shuffleboard courts, tennis courts, swimming pools, and related facilities. Structured facilities are normally in a complex with a community building. Equally important are the unstructured public open spaces which can be as simple as open grass areas for spontaneous team games and other activities. The type of community facilities necessary for any manufactured home development should be determined by the occupants to be served. For example, a family-oriented development may require more extensive outdoor open space for active recreation, whereas a retirement community may require less space but a greater variation of activity areas. Community facilities commonly include such things as swimming pools, community buildings, vehicle storage areas, pedestrian paths, tot lots, and court games.

**Community Building**

A community facility common to most new manufactured home developments is the community building. It usually contains more than one activity and serves more than one function (Fig. 7). Uses commonly built into a community building include: meeting rooms, recreation rooms, and (in case of the family-oriented parks) day-care centers. The building is normally constructed as part of a complex

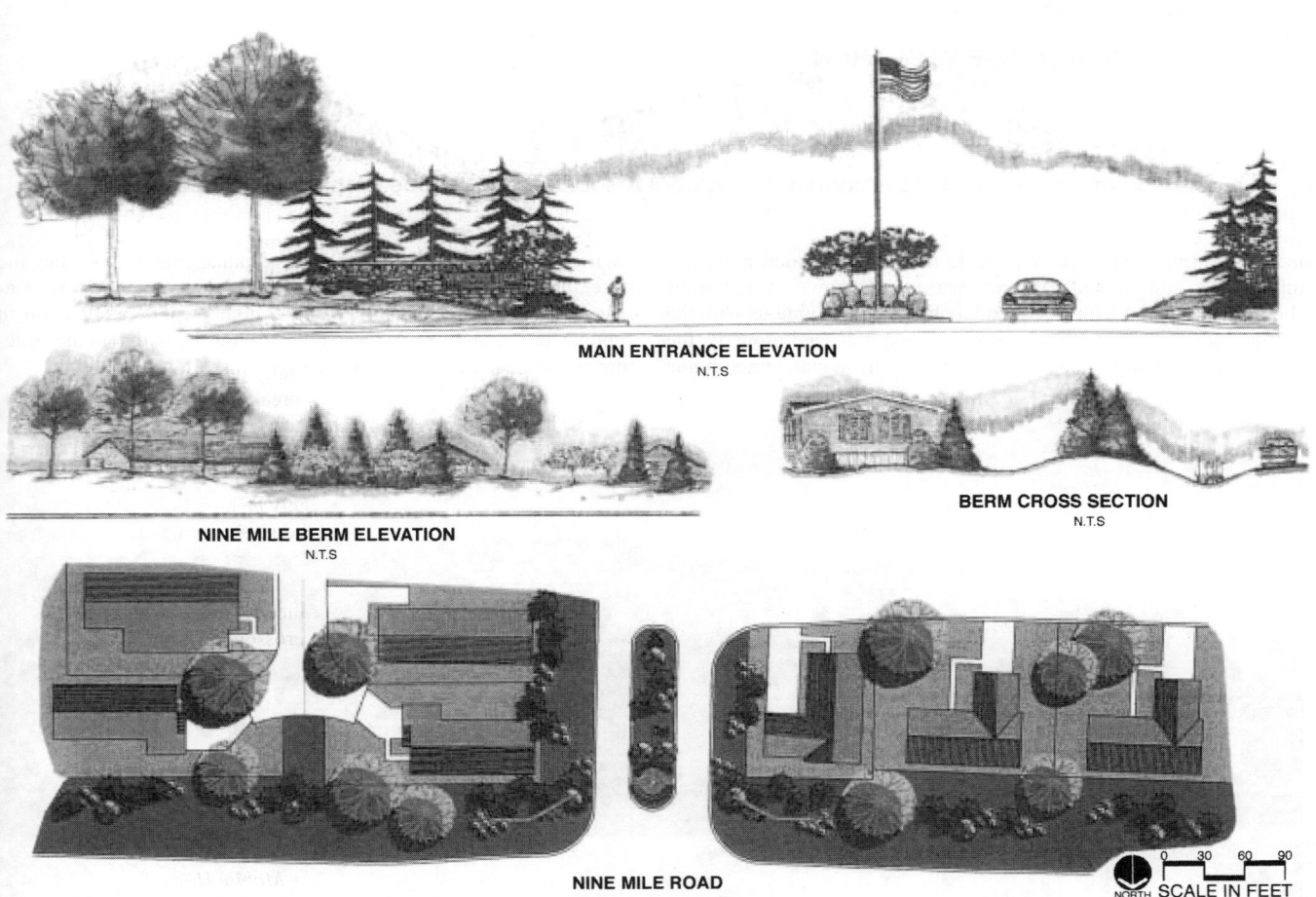

**MAIN ENTRANCE ELEVATION**
N.T.S

**BERM CROSS SECTION**
N.T.S

**NINE MILE BERM ELEVATION**
N.T.S

**NINE MILE ROAD**

SCALE IN FEET
0  30  60  90
NORTH

**Fig. 6. Community entrance sketch plans (Donald C. Westphal Associates, landscape architects and site planners)**

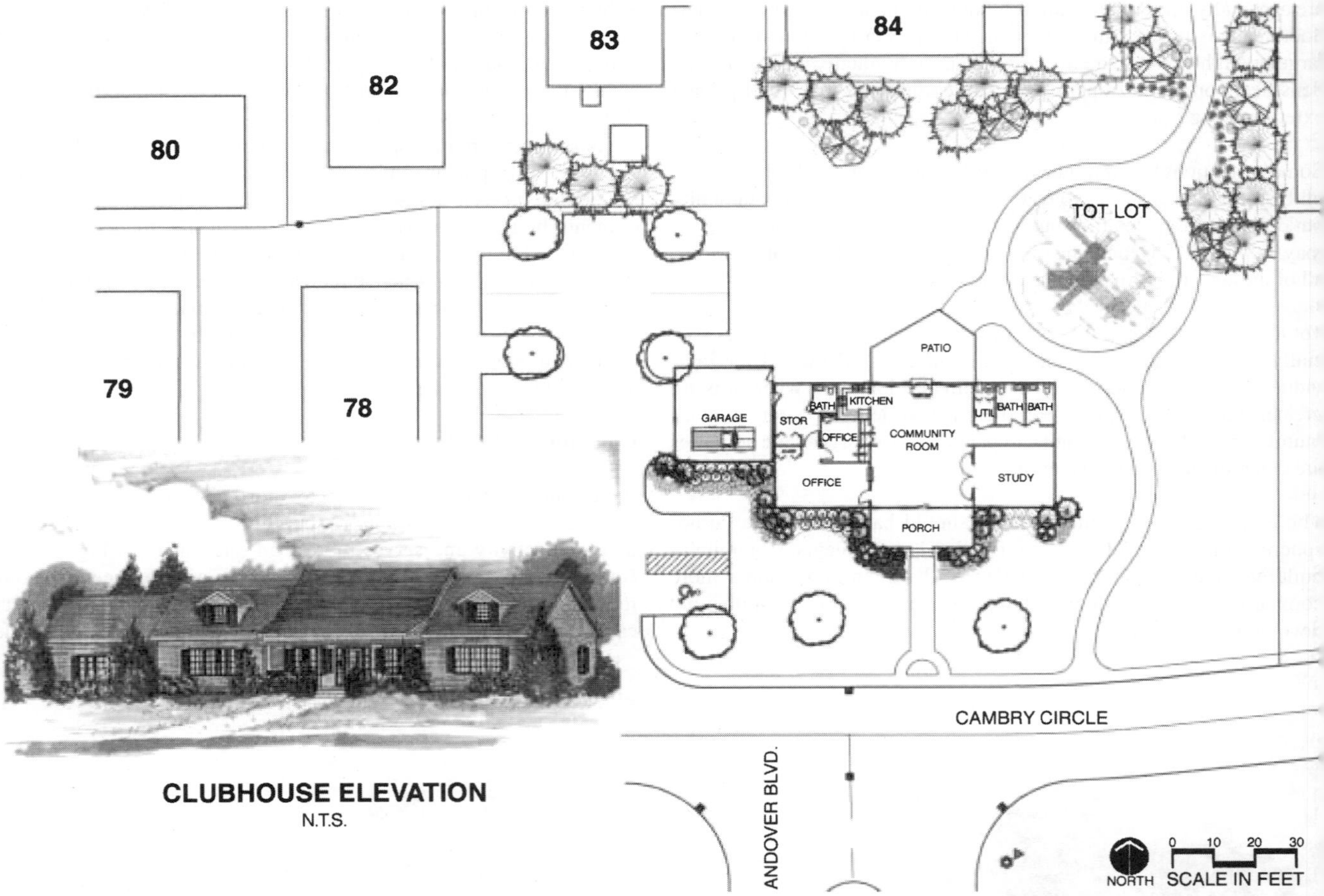

**CLUBHOUSE ELEVATION**
N.T.S.

**Fig. 7. Community building plan (Donald C. Westphal Associates, landscape architects and site planners)**

including structured outdoor recreational facilities, such as swimming pools and limited off-street parking. Community buildings should be designed with a residential character harmonious with the development (Fig. 8). When constructed and managed properly, the community building can be a major asset to the manufactured home environment. The key word becomes "management," for after the development is established and the community building is constructed, it is the responsibility of the homeowners' association in subdivisions, and the operator in communities, to maintain the structure and operate the activity programs.

**Fig. 8. Community building completed (Donald C. Westphal Associates, landscape architects and site planners)**

A secondary, but very important, function of the community building is that of storm shelter for residents. In areas of the country where dangerous storms often occur, a structurally adequate community building of ample capacity must be provided for the residents' safety.

## Common Vehicular Storage Area

Much of the clutter and disarray in manufactured home parks is due to the lack of a defined storage area for seldom-used vehicles or recreational vehicles. Provisions for storage of these vehicles should be included in the development, especially where lots are small. In many communities residents have more leisure time than their conventional housing counterparts; recreational equipment, snowmobiles, boats, and travel trailers are sometimes abundant. Recreational vehicles generally take up too much space to be stored on each individual home site. Common areas accessible to all residents of the development are necessary to store such vehicles or equipment. The storage area should be separated from the living areas of the site and should be a gravel or hard surface area enclosed by a security fence and adequately screened from sight.

## Swimming Pools

Swimming pools do much to enhance the image and livability of a community. In fact, most high-quality communities include a swimming pool or some equivalent structured recreational facility. Swimming pools are usually located near a community building and other structured facilities, and should be designed to accommodate the anticipated usership without undue crowding. An estimate of participation during typical summer weekends provides the basis for determining an appropriate pool size. This rate of participation varies with the expected population characteristics of the development. Approximately one-quarter of the persons at the pool will be in the water at any one time, and the pool should be designed to provide 10 to 15 square feet of water surface for each wader and 30 square feet for each swimmer. Deck area equal to or larger than the pool surface area should be provided. Most participants also desire a large, fenced in turf area of equal size for sunbathing.

## Tot Lots

Tot lots are small playgrounds consisting of several pieces of play apparatus especially for use by young children. They should be located close to the homes which they serve or within the community recreation area where they can be easily observed and supervised. Ideally, a small tot lot could be established for each grouping of home sites so that children could use them without crossing collector streets in the development. Tot lots also work well when located adjacent to adult recreation areas so that children may be observed by adults using other facilities.

## Court Games

Basketball and tennis courts are popular facilities for adult recreation. They can often be incorporated into a centralized recreation clubhouse complex where they are easily accessible via streets and pedestrian paths. Both facilities require much space, serve a limited number of people at any one time, and can benefit from night lighting which increases the number of people who can be served.

## General Court Games

* Provide a variety of facilities to serve various age groups including:
  basketball courts (hard surface)—50 users per half court, daily capacity
  volleyball (in lawn area)—72 users per court, daily capacity
  shuffleboard (hard surface)—20 users per court, daily capacity.
* Lighting for night use of court areas is desirable and will increase daily capacity by 20 to 30 percent.

## Tennis Courts

* Provide a fenced, low-maintenance, all weather (hard-surface) court.
* General capacity is 20 participants per day per court.
* Lighting for night use is desirable and will increase capacity by 40 percent.

## Utilities

(See Figs. 9 and 10.)

## Manufactured Home Community Cluster Plans

(See Figs. 11 and 12.)

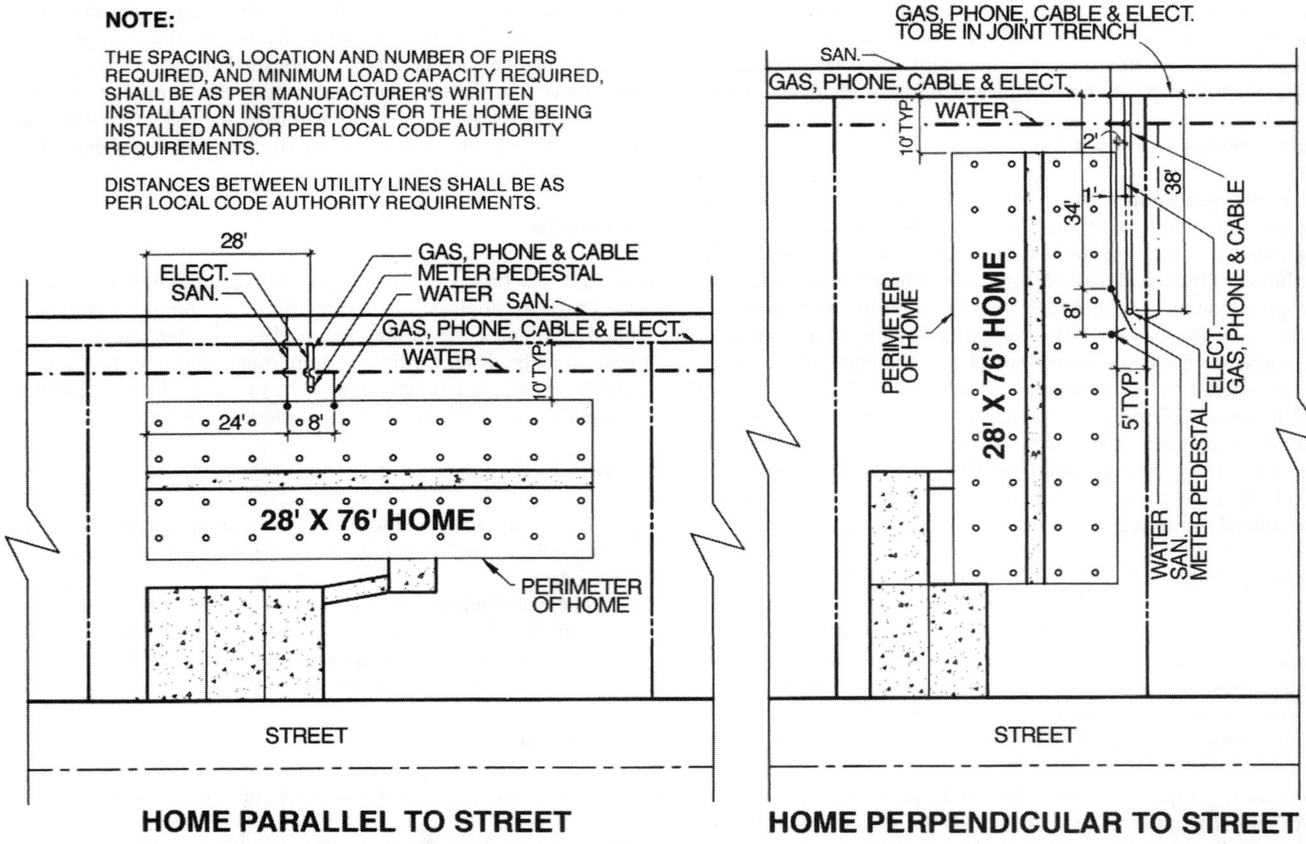

NOTE:
THE SPACING, LOCATION AND NUMBER OF PIERS REQUIRED, AND MINIMUM LOAD CAPACITY REQUIRED, SHALL BE AS PER MANUFACTURER'S WRITTEN INSTALLATION INSTRUCTIONS FOR THE HOME BEING INSTALLED AND/OR PER LOCAL CODE AUTHORITY REQUIREMENTS.
DISTANCES BETWEEN UTILITY LINES SHALL BE AS PER LOCAL CODE AUTHORITY REQUIREMENTS.
28'
ELECT.
SAN.
GAS, PHONE & CABLE
METER PEDESTAL
WATER
SAN.
GAS, PHONE, CABLE & ELECT.
WATER
10' TYP.
24'
8'
28' X 76' HOME
PERIMETER OF HOME
STREET
HOME PARALLEL TO STREET
GAS, PHONE, CABLE & ELECT. TO BE IN JOINT TRENCH
SAN.
GAS, PHONE, CABLE & ELECT.
WATER
10' TYP.
2'
38'
1'
34'
8'
5' TYP.
PERIMETER OF HOME
28' X 76' HOME
GAS, PHONE & CABLE
ELECT.
GAS, PHONE & CABLE
METER PEDESTAL
SAN.
WATER
STREET
HOME PERPENDICULAR TO STREET

**Fig. 9. Typical utility location detail (Donald C. Westphal Associates, landscape architects and site planners)**

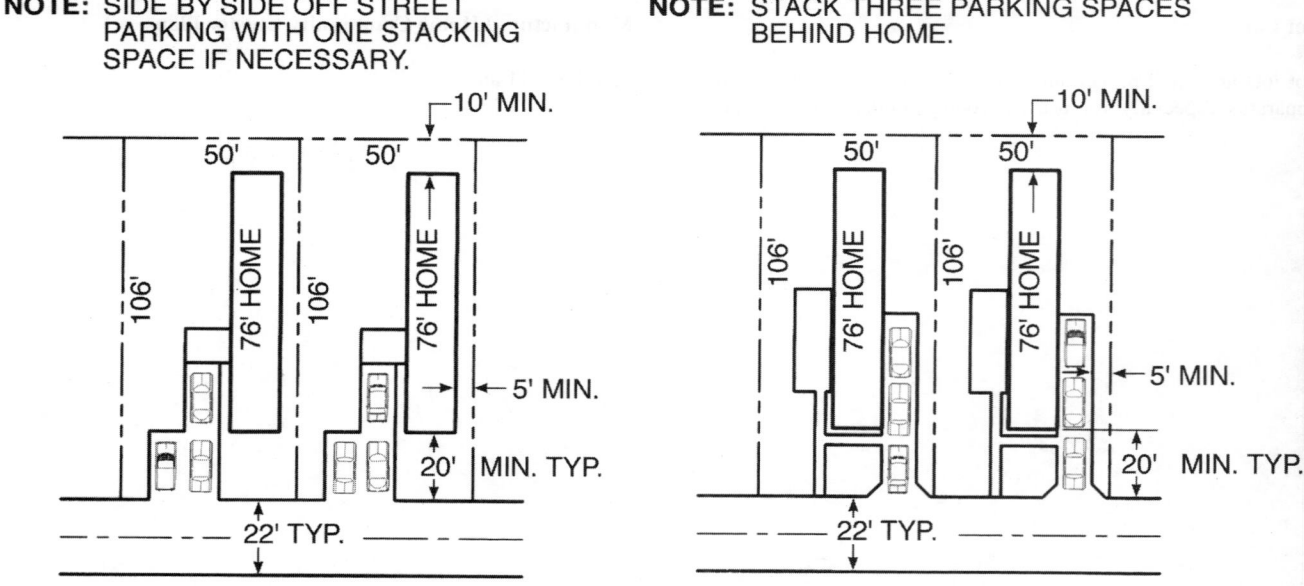

NOTE: SIDE BY SIDE OFF STREET PARKING WITH ONE STACKING SPACE IF NECESSARY.
10' MIN.
50'
50'
106'
106'
76' HOME
76' HOME
5' MIN.
20' MIN. TYP.
22' TYP.
NOTE: STACK THREE PARKING SPACES BEHIND HOME.
10' MIN.
50'
50'
106'
106'
76' HOME
76' HOME
5' MIN.
20' MIN. TYP.
22' TYP.

* SIMILAR DETAIL COULD BE UTILIZED WITH MULTI-SECTION HOMES BY ADJUSTING LOT WIDTHS.

**Fig. 10. Typical lot detail (Donald C. Westphal Associates, landscape architects and site planners)**

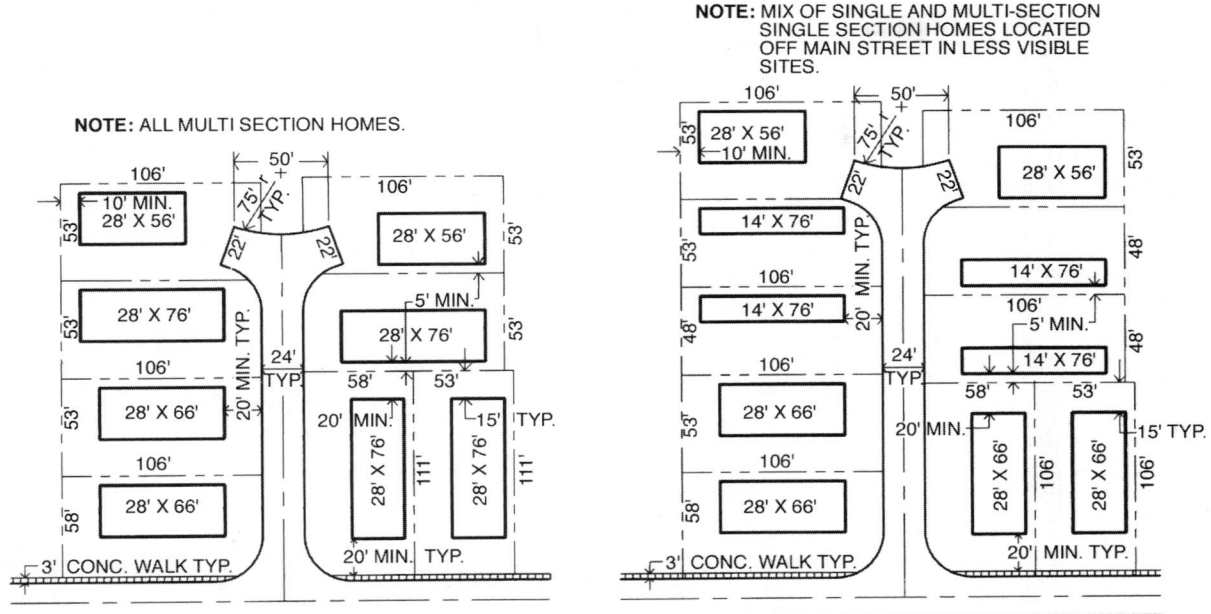

**Fig. 11.** Typical lot clusters and details (Donald C. Westphal Associates, landscape architects and site planners)

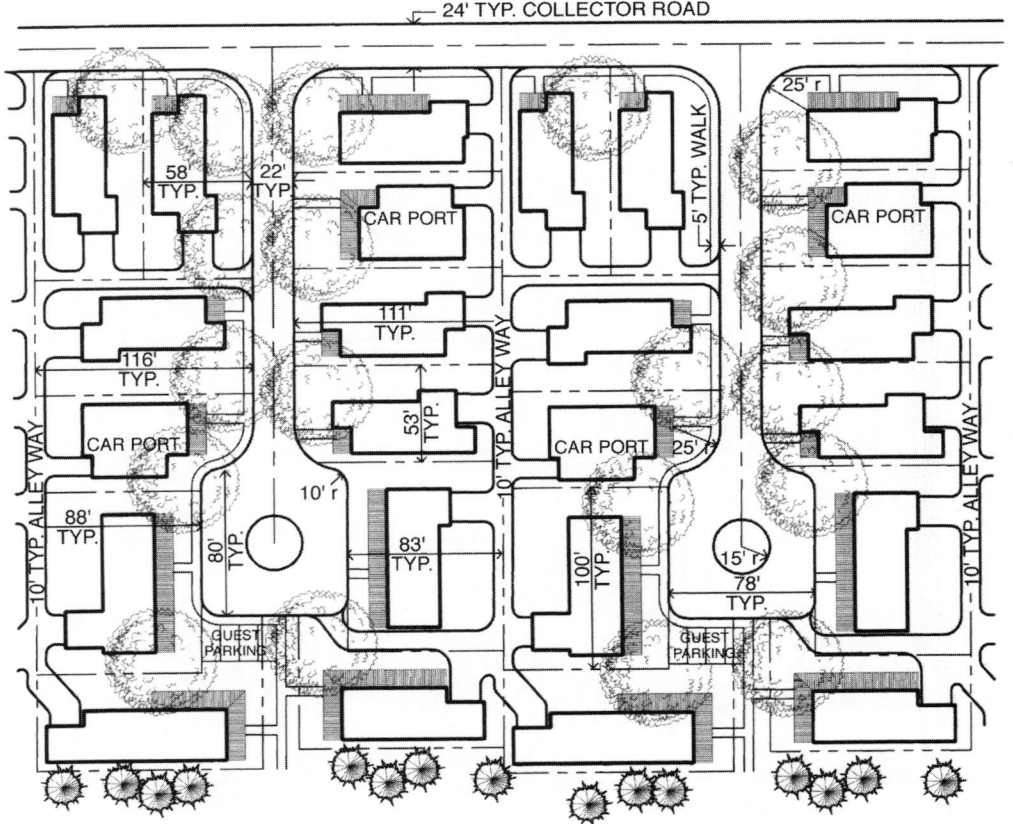

**Fig. 12.** Typical lot clusters in community (Donald C. Westphal Associates, landscape architects and site planners)

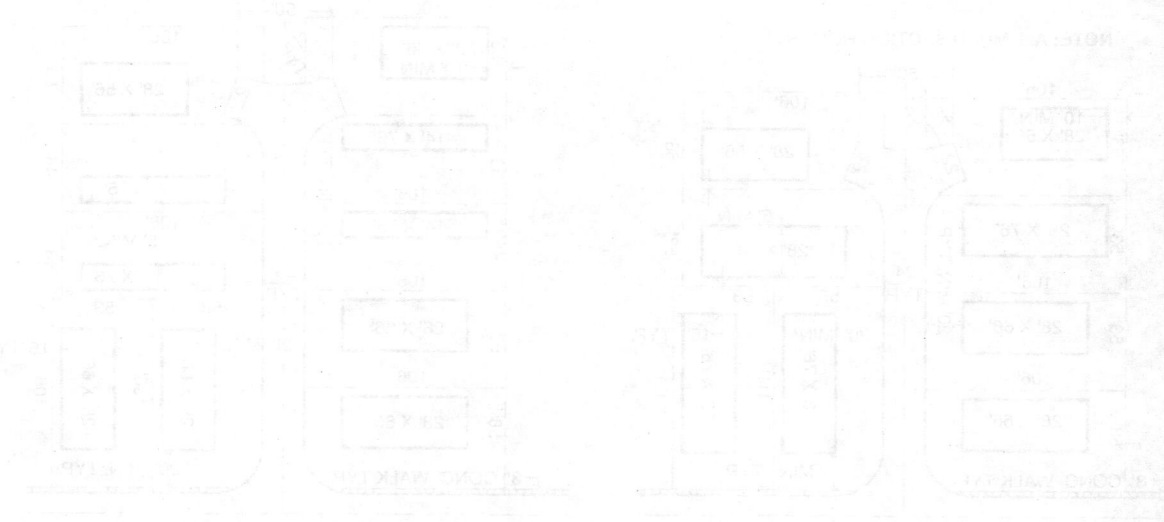

Fig. 11. Typical of clusters and details (Donald C. Wandmacher Associates, landscape architects and site planners)

Fig. 12. Typical lot of area in community (Donald C. Wandmacher Associates, landscape architects and site planners)

Fig. 1. Retail interior (Mojo Stumer Associates; photo: Frank Zimmermann; courtesy of the architect)

# RETAIL SHOPS

## GENERAL

People love to look, window-shop, and buy. Shopping as an experience should provide fun, which in turn provides profits. A successful store or shop is one that is designed to merchandise in addition to looking good (Fig. 1). A store can be divided into two principal parts: the exterior, which gives identification, encompasses the storefront, show windows, and displays; and the interior, where the promise of the storefront display is delivered. Briefly stated, the storefront initiates the sale, and the interior consummates it.

The storefront and the design of the facade must be attractive in order to catch the shoppers' attention and to draw the customers in from the street or from the mall in shopping centers. Graphic identification—with bold color, lighting, lettering, and logos—and attractive display of merchandise are the initial steps (Fig. 2).

In enclosed malls, the glass-enclosed show windows are often eliminated or minimized. The "show window" displays are set up in a large vestibule, perhaps elevated or on portable platforms, and become part of the interior. Hence the demarcation between the exterior and the interior is not physical; rather, the two are integrated and it is difficult to define where one ends and the other begins. This is particularly true in enclosed shopping malls. The open or no front generally promotes more impulse buying; department stores will often make their entrances an extension of the mall so that the shopper will be easily enticed into the store. When doors are used, either on the street or on the mall, they should be well marked and easy to find. Entrance to the interior should be easy, related to interior traffic flow and layout, and should be accessible to vertical transportation, if any.

## PRINCIPLES OF RETAIL DESIGN

In order to design satisfactory shops, the first requirement is an understanding of those portions of current merchandising theories which affect the design problem. Briefly, "merchandising psychology" consists of, first, arousing interest; second, satisfying it.

With staple goods the first phase is almost automatic. When nonstaples, accessories, or specialties other than "demand" goods are to be sold, methods of arousing interest may become more complex.

The second phase—the actual sale—involves factors of convenience that are desirable in order to make buying easy, to satisfy customers completely, and to achieve economy of space and time for the store management.

Both phases affect the design of retail shops, and are closely interrelated. In some cases the planning problems involved cannot be segregated. The steps in the merchandising process, as they affect shop design, are as follows.

### Attracting Customers

This can be accomplished by means of advertising, prices, show-window displays, or new or remodeled quarters, which occupies

*Author:* Murray S. Cohen, Architect
*Reviewer:* Mark D. Stumer, AIA

**Fig. 2. Storefront (Mojo Stumer Associates; photo: Frank Zimmermann; courtesy of the architect)**

much of a merchant's efforts. Of these, storefronts and display windows are important to the store designer.

### Inducing Entrance

Show windows, in addition to attracting passersby, should induce them to enter the store (Fig. 3). Show windows may be opened up to display the shop's interior, or closed in to give privacy to customers within. Door locations require study in relation to pedestrian traffic flow, grades of sidewalks and store floors, and interior layout of the shop. In colder climates drafts and outdoor temperature changes can be controlled at the door.

### Organizing Store Spaces

Organizing store spaces, and consequently the merchandise to be sold, into departments enables customers to find objects easily and permits storekeepers to keep close check on profits or losses from various types of goods. Store lighting and "dressing" are simplified. Even small shops benefit from a measure of departmentalization; in large shops, the practice becomes essential as methods of training salespeople, of handling, controlling, and wrapping stock become more complex.

### Interior Displays

Interior displays require particular attention in specialty shops. Types range from displays of staple goods, which assist customers in selection, to displays of accessories, which the sale of staples may suggest

to the customer. Problems of arrangement with regard to merchandise, departments, and routes of customers' approach are involved.

Relief from the repeated impact of merchandise sales efforts and displays is necessary in most shops. Experienced salespeople can tell at a glance the customer who is satiated with shopping and too bewildered to buy. After he or she has been refreshed by a brief rest, the customer's interest can be recaptured quickly. Such relaxation may be mental or physical, or both.

### Conveniences

Conveniences intended primarily for the customers' benefit, while not strictly allied to the problems of attracting trade or selling goods, are necessary to some types of shops. A florist, for instance, provides a card-writing desk or counter in her shop. In other shop types, particularly those whose prices are above the average, such extra provisions are often highly desirable. Conveniences of this kind include: telephone booths, drinking fountains, lavatories, desks for writing cards or checks, stools or chairs at counters or in special sales rooms, and vanity tables or triplicate mirrors for certain types of apparel fitting rooms.

In regard to finishes and equipment, the idea may be extended to include: floor surfacing for comfort; acoustic treatment of ceilings and possibly walls; and illumination of pleasant, sometimes special, features. All these have been found profitable investments in various cases. Their necessity or desirability depends to an extent on the type of shop and its location.

**Fig. 3. Inviting retail interior (Mojo Stumer Associates; photo courtesy of the architect)**

# INTERIORS

The successful retail shop is an efficient selling machine or sales factory. In addition to servicing the customers, the employees have to be considered so they can give better service to the customer.

Merchandise and space must be organized to help the customer in making a selection and to help the salesperson in selling. Easy circulation and exposing the customer to the maximum amount of merchandise are part of good design (Fig. 4). Avoid monotony in circulation and display of merchandise. Where possible, do not hesitate to be bold or even shocking. This stimulates the customer and her urge to buy.

The location and design of the cashier and wrapping unit are important and provide for several persons to be serviced. Often this acts as a control center.

Flexibility so that fixtures and departments can be moved or modified is part of merchandising. Fixtures should be minimized and merchandise emphasized. Design and use fixtures so that full attention is thrown on the merchandise. Surveys must be made for each particular type of store, its merchandise, operation, and personnel to determine actual sizes and requirements. Do not design fixtures so that a salesperson has to reach merchandise on too high a shelf or stoop too low.

Determine what customer accessories are required: seating in general, counters, tables, mirrors, telephones, drinking fountains, rest rooms, special lighting, and floor coverings. Accessories will vary, depending on the store's location and the type of customer, as well as the nature of the merchandise.

Location of stock rooms, or of reserves, must be carefully considered so that the salesperson does not have to leave a customer for too long a period.

Fitting and dressing rooms should be located conveniently near the item being sold.

## Departmentalization

Benefits to be derived from segregation of merchandise by types have been touched upon previously. All these are factors in decreasing the average time per sale, an important figure in large-store accounting and in small stores with rush periods (Fig. 5).

Within each department, and as a guide when relating departments to each other and to the path of the typical customer through the store, merchandise and services can be analyzed by classification. Most objects can be placed in one of the following classes, relating them to the needs of customers:

Impulse or luxury goods are high-profit articles, usually (but not necessarily) high in price.

Convenience items are stocked for the passerby who happens in, but who may return for other purchases if properly impressed. Often these are not in themselves strictly profitable merchandise.

Demand goods are also staples, like conveniences, but are articles which the customer starts out with a definite idea of purchasing. These attract her to the store and she buys them—other goods must be sold to her.

These classifications necessarily overlap; but, in a shop whose type of customer can be forecast, divisions along some such lines are possible. Signs are not always necessary; each department may be designated by display of typical articles as a kind of poster.

## Customer Flow

The accompanying diagrams based upon analyses of traffic indicate the possibility of organizing departments in relation to the flow of customers through the store.

Interest in articles on display was found to be inversely proportional to the number displayed after a low limit had been reached. A central location in a group seemed to lead to increased interest in a picture.

**Fig. 4. Retail display (Mojo Stumer Associates; photo: Frank Zimmermann; courtesy of the architect)**

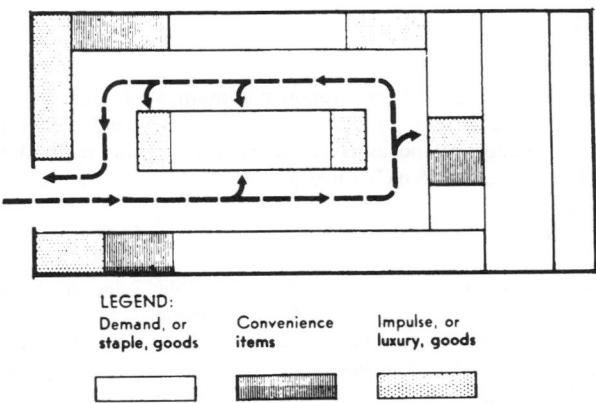

LEGEND:
Demand, or staple, goods
Convenience items
Impulse, or luxury, goods

**Fig. 5. Principles of shop design. Merchandise is located according to classification: staple goods are unobtrusively yet accessibly placed; luxury items are spotted where the prospective customer cannot help but be attracted to them. White counter areas are allocated to services: cashier, wrapper, information, etc.**

One important conclusion is that what a customer sees is more influenced by the arrangement of the space and the walking habits of customers, than by the intrinsic quality of the objects exhibited. Tendencies to turn to the right, to be attracted by doorways, to choose the wider of two aisles, and to be fatigued by too much material on display are all of utmost importance to the store planner.

Store services must also be analyzed in relation to customer flow.

### Self Service

Operators of large stores know that self service speeds up selling. For that reason their stock is easily accessible to the shopper. Often, too, customers insist upon handling merchandise, and are more easily sold when they can get these first-hand impressions. As a result, few stores now sell-over-the-counter (which decreases free sales space) but rely upon open wall fixtures, wall displays, and display tables whenever possible.

In direct contrast to this technique is the exclusive shop, which keeps its stock in closed fixtures or in the stockroom, permitting selection of merchandise only by sample displays. Some specialty shops work entirely on this basis.

### Shop Sizes

These are far from standardized. However, as determined by real estate values and merchandising, structural, fixture, and aisle space requirements, shops with one customer aisle only are usually 12 to 15 feet wide by 50 to 60 feet long in large cities; and 15 to 18 feet wide by 60 to 80 feet long in smaller cities. These dimensions apply particularly to shops in 100 percent retail districts.

Heights are more easily determined. Basements 8 to 9 feet high, in the clear, permit economical stock storage. Ground floors are preferably approximately 12 feet high if no mezzanine is included; mezzanines at least 7 feet-6 inches above floor level will accommodate most fixture heights. The height from mezzanine floor to ceiling may be as low as 6 feet-6 inches if used for service space only; 7 feet is the preferred minimum for public use.

### Typical Counter and Case Layouts

#### Center Island

Type illustrated, L = 13 feet average minimum; W = 9 feet-6 inches to 13 feet. Islands composed of showcases only, L = 10 feet minimum; W = 5 feet-10 inches to 6 feet-3 inches. For floor tables, L = 4 to 7 feet; W = 2 feet-6 inches to 3 feet.

#### Aisle Widths

For clerks, minimum: 1 feet-8 inches; desirable: 2 feet to 2 feet-3 inches. For main public aisles, minimum: 4 feet-6 inches; average: 5 feet-6 inches to 7 feet; usual maximum: 11 feet. Secondary public aisles: 3 feet to 3 feet-6 inches.

### Displays

The segregation of displays in areas specifically designed for the purpose, and in locations selected with respect to entrances and customer traffic flow, is easily accomplished in departmentalized store planning (Fig. 6).

#### Display Surfaces

Locating display surfaces perpendicular to the line of entrance may result in angular plans, or in the use of screens or freestanding display cases, as indicated in the diagram. Locations for display niches, alcoves, etc., may depend on space requirements of the various shop departments and upon the relationship to customer flow lines.

In a shop, "architecture" is preferably secondary in importance to the merchandise displayed. This does not mean that every inch of space must be crowded with goods on display, because such practice causes loss of customer interest.

#### Scale

An important factor in display is the relation between the possible viewing distance and the scale of the merchandise. Thus a stairway side wall or narrow passage is suited for small-scale display only (Fig. 7). Vistas, on the other hand, and displays opposite doorways have more carrying power and consequently can be bolder. Vistas or a sense of perspective can also be created by lighting emphasis. When a lighted display is placed at the rear wall under a mezzanine space that is slightly darker than the store proper, a spatial relationship is set up that depends more upon the relative intensities of light than upon actual distance. It is possible to dramatize objects on display, to make them stand apart from their neighbors, and in this way suggest that they are more desirable. On the other hand, it is not always best to separate costly and inexpensive objects. Low-priced merchandise may often be sold by contrast with high-priced objects, and vice versa. Choice of method depends to an extent on the problem under consideration.

Accessible zones, rather than low or high displays, are particularly valuable in self-service portions of the shop. Just as show-window bulkheads are rising and glass heights decreasing, so the fixtures inside the store are bringing merchandise within reach and concentrating it for emphasis.

**Fig. 6. Display areas (Mojo Stumer Associates; photo: Frank Zimmermann; courtesy of the architect)**

**Fig. 7. Small-scale display (Mojo Stumer Associates; photo: Frank Zimmermann; courtesy of the architect)**

**Fig. 8. Retail lighting (Mojo Stumer Associates; photo: Frank Zimmermann; courtesy of the architect)**

*Show Windows*

These elements are designed primarily with the effect upon potential customers in mind; ease in changing displays is also important. Windows must be "dressed" quickly; if they are hard to work with, they will not be changed as often as merchandising policies indicate to be necessary. Variety and timeliness of displays are considered essential.

Glazing types that do not interfere with vision will materially increase the show window's value. Patented systems, which eliminate reflections, are available; so are types of glass suited to special conditions, such as heat-resisting glass.

Window backs may be closed or open, depending on the type of shop and the degree of customer privacy desired. When backs are open, confusion of display and shop interior may be avoided by using temporary or permanent screens or panels as backgrounds.

Window dressing may be done in full public view in certain types of shops, such as jewelry or gift shops. In other cases, blinds or other types of glass curtains may be required. Apparent size of glass area may be changed to accommodate varying displays by using variable valances and side-pieces.

Storage space is required for display accessories, forms, blocks, platforms, panel backgrounds, and seasonal changes of floor pads or carpets.

Ease of window dressing may be aided in several ways. Access panels should be large enough for easy passage for personnel and materials. Access passages, segregated from the shop's interior, may be provided. Dummy windows may be provided, sometimes on rolling platforms.

*Show-Window Lighting*

In many stores other than specialty shops, light intensities have been increased far above requirements for ordinary vision, in an effort to overcome reflections (Fig. 8). This has also been considered a means of competing with adjacent store windows.

## LAYOUTS AND DIMENSIONS

There are two basic planning guidelines for laying out a retail sales floor:

1. Use 100 percent of the space allocated.
2. Do not sacrifice function for esthetics.

Successful plans combine both to the fullest. Six basic plans can help the designer to carry them out. These are certainly not the only plans that can be developed, but they form the foundation on which others can be created.

The six basic plan types are:

> Straight
> Pathway
> Diagonal
> Curved
> Varied
> Geometric

### Straight Plan

The straight plan (Fig. 9) is a conventional form of layout that utilizes walls and projections to create smaller spaces. It is an economical plan to execute and can be adapted to any type of store, from gift shops to apparel outlets, from drug and grocery stores to department stores.

Variety in the straight plan can be introduced by creating niches with the merchandise. To define transitions from one section of the store to the other, displays can be placed to help lead customers. Elevate floor levels for a change of pace.

This plan lends itself well to pulling customers to the back of the store. In a bookstore, for example, special sale merchandise can be placed at the rear, with signage informing shoppers of the items and directing them in the right direction.

### Pathway Plan

Applicable to virtually any type of store, the pathway plan (Fig. 10) is particularly suited to larger stores over 5,000 square feet and on one level. The pathway plan, a good architectural organizer, gets shoppers smoothly from the front to the rear of the store.

This plan is recommended for clothing stores because of its ability to minimize the cluttered feeling that tends to discourage or disturb shoppers who do not care to fight their way to the racks in the back. This plan also focuses the shopper's attention to other merchandise on the path. The designer can create designs off the path using the floor or ceiling as directional elements.

### Diagonal Plan

For self-service stores, a diagonal plan (Fig. 11) is optimal. The cashier is in a central location, with sight lines to all areas of the space. Soft goods or hard goods stores, including drug and food stores, can take advantage of the diagonal plan.

Visually, the plan has an exciting and dynamic quality. Because it is not based on a straight line, it invites movement and circulation.

### Curved Plan

For boutiques, salons, or other high-quality stores, the curved plan (Fig. 12) creates an inviting, special environment for the customer. It also costs more to construct than angular or square plans.

The curved theme can be emphasized with walls, ceiling, and corners. To complete the look, specify circular floor fixtures.

### Varied Plan

For products that require back-up merchandise to be immediately adjacent (shoes and men's shirts, for example), the varied plan (Fig. 13) is highly functional. It is a variation of the straight-line plan with sufficient square footage allowed for box or carton storage off the main sales floor with perimeter wall stocking.

As shown, the varied plan has a "bellows" effect, a tapering back or space delineation that focuses on a special-purpose area in the back. Service departments in stereo, jewelry, or hardware stores can be located in this narrow end. For a tobacco shop, it is a fine place for the humidor.

### Geometric Plan

The designer creates forms with shapes derived from showcases, racks, or gondolas in a geometric plan (Fig. 14). This plan is the most exotic of the six basic plans, and the designer can use wall angles to restate the shapes dominating the sales floor.

The geometric plan comfortably allows for fitting rooms without wasting square footage; this benefit makes the plan especially suitable for apparel stores. Also, it can nicely accommodate adjacent stock, making it an alternative to the varied plan for shoe stores and gift shops.

Figure 15 shows the clearances required for a medium height display counter. The suggested seat height of 21 to 22 inches requires a footrest for the seated customer. The counter height shown will allow the display to be viewed by both the seated customer and the standing sales clerk. The customer activity zone allows adequate space for the chair. Knee height, buttock-knee length, popliteal height, and eye height sitting are all significant human dimensions to consider in the design of counters to be used by a seated customer.

The drawing in Fig. 16 is of a low 30-inch display counter also for use by a seated customer. The anthropometric considerations are the same. Although the counter height is responsive to the anthropometric requirements of the seated customer, it is less than ideal for the standing clerk. For the standing user's optimum comfort, the counter height should be about 2 or 3 inches below elbow height. This will allow a person to handle objects comfortably on the counter surface or use the counter as support for his or her arms. The 30-inch height is too low to permit such use.

Figure 17 shows the clearances involved for a 42-inch-high counter to service a seated user. By filling the recess with an additional display, however, the counter can also be used exclusively as a typical sales counter. It should be noted, however, that although sometimes used for special display situations, such a counter height is not recommended. Both the customer and the sales clerk of smaller body size would find coping with such a height uncomfortable anthropometrically, particularly when one considers that the counter would be

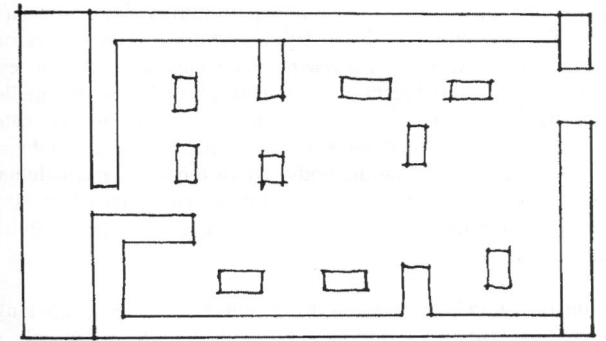

Fig. 9. Straight plan uses walls and projections to create smaller spaces and is economical.

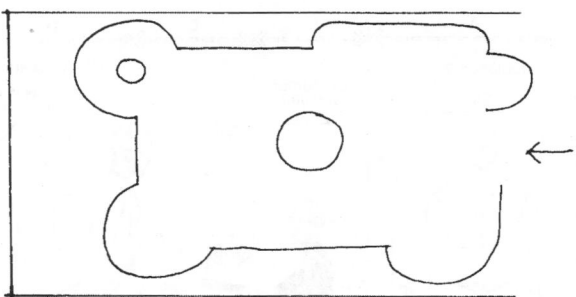

Fig. 12. People respond to circular and curved shapes such as those shown here, which soften the angular and square plan.

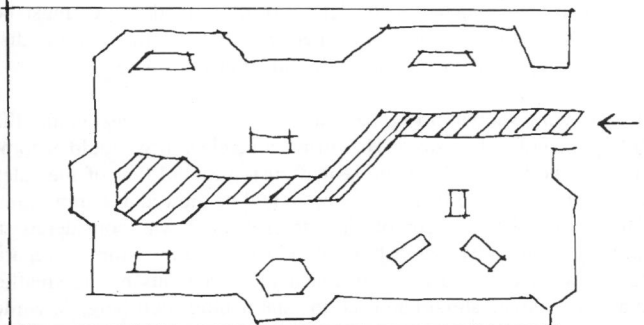

Fig. 10. Pathway plan pulls patrons through the store to the rear without interruption by floor fixtures. The merits of such a layout are that the path can take any shape and that it creates a design pattern.

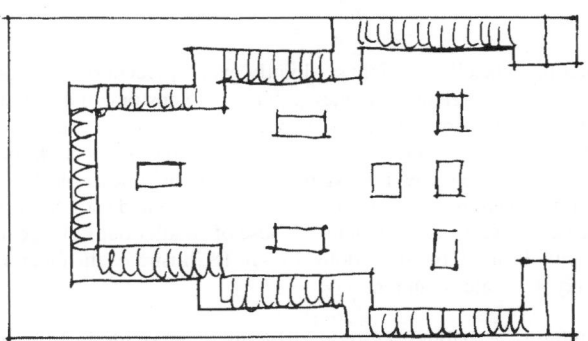

Fig. 13. Varied plan illustrates added variety of forms which can work to a designer's advantage.

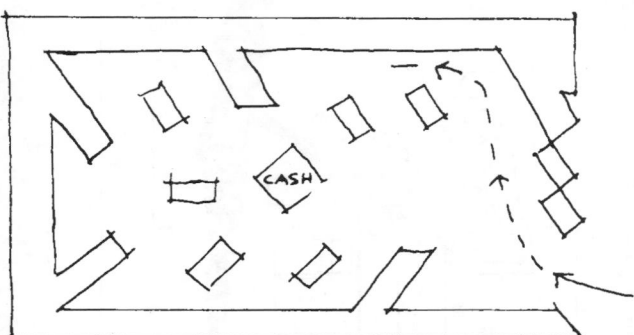

Fig. 11. Diagonal pattern permits angular traffic flow and creates perimeter design interest and excitement in movement. Central placement of the cash-wrap permits security and vision.

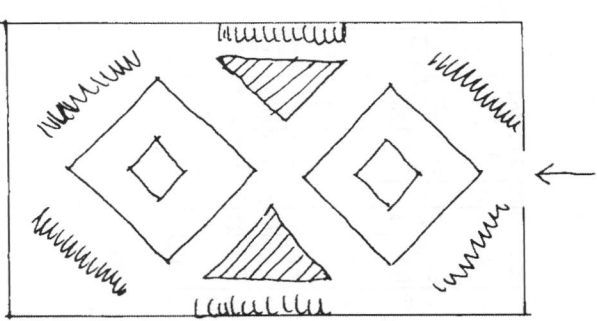

Fig. 14. Geometric plan can establish interest without excessive cost, it the store's product can accept it. Ceiling and floors can be lowered or raised to create zones and departments.

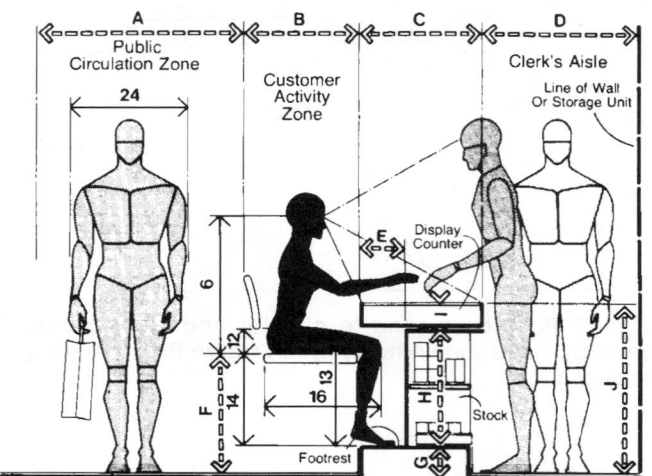

**SEATED CUSTOMER / DESIRABLE COUNTER HEIGHT**

**Fig. 15. Seated customer/desirable counter height**

only must the merchandise be within reach anthropometrically, but it must be fairly visible as well. The heights established must therefore be responsive to vertical grip reach dimensions as well as to eye height. In establishing height limits, the body size data of the smaller person should be used. Since in retail spaces departments may cater exclusively to members of one sex or the other, two sets of data are presented. One is based on the body size of the smaller female and the other on the body size of the smaller male. The suggested heights reflect a compromise between reach requirements and visibility requirements.

The illustration in Fig. 20 shows the clearances involved in hanging-type merchandise cases. Rod heights should be related not only to human reach limitations, but in certain cases to the sizes of the merchandise displayed. There is usually no conflict in respect to garments.

The drawing in Fig. 21 concerns book and magazine displays and suggests the anthropometric considerations involved. The rationale is essentially the same as that indicated for the general merchandise shelving on the preceding pages. In regard to books, however, the question of visibility is even more critical. To perceive the basic form, shape, and color of general merchandise may be sufficient, but for books and magazines the legibility of printed matter must be taken into account. The distance between the customer and the display lighting, and angle of sight should all be considered.

The drawing shown in Fig. 22 deals with human dimension and the fitting area of a shoe store. The fitting zone clearance should accommodate the body size of the seated customer and that of the sales clerk. The 60- to 66-inch clearance should be viewed as a minimum. The buttock-heel length of the larger person was considered in anthropometrically establishing the clearance dimension. In regard to the workzone, vertical grip reach measurements of the smaller male and female should be used in establishing shelf heights, while maximum body breadth and maximum body depth of the larger person should be considered in establishing clearances.

higher than the elbow height of slightly over 5 percent of the population. From a merchandising viewpoint, where customer convenience is of paramount importance, it would be unwise to exceed 39 to 40 inches as a counter height. In addition, the smaller sales clerk forced to tend such a counter for extended periods of time could be subjected to severe backaches and pains. Getting on and off a high stool for elderly and disabled people, or those of smaller body size, can be not only difficult, but hazardous. Figure 18 illustrates the clearances for a typical sales counter.

Shelving is probably used more than any other single interior component for the storage and/or display of merchandise (Fig. 19). Not

|   | in | cm |
|---|------|------|
| A | 36 | 91.4 |
| B | 26–30 | 66.0–76.2 |
| C | 18–24 | 45.7–61.0 |
| D | 30 min. | 76.2 min. |
| E | 10 | 25.4 |
| F | 21–22 | 53.3–55.9 |
| G | 5 | 12.7 |
| H | 23–25 | 58.4–63.5 |
| I | 4–6 | 10.2–15.2 |
| J | 34–36 | 86.4–91.4 |
| K | 30 | 76.2 |
| L | 16–17 | 40.6–43.2 |

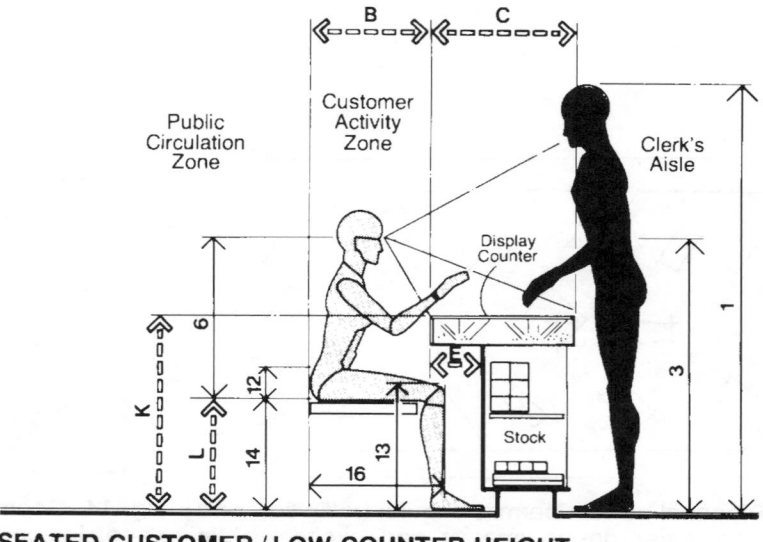

**SEATED CUSTOMER / LOW COUNTER HEIGHT**

**Fig. 16. Seated customer/low counter height**

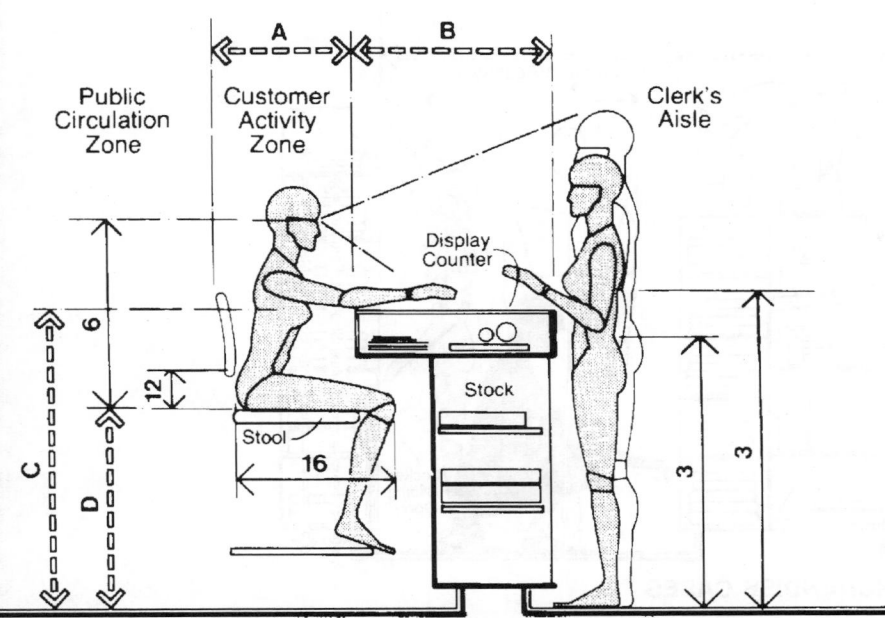

## SEATED CUSTOMER / HIGH COUNTER HEIGHT

Fig. 17. Seated customer/high counter height

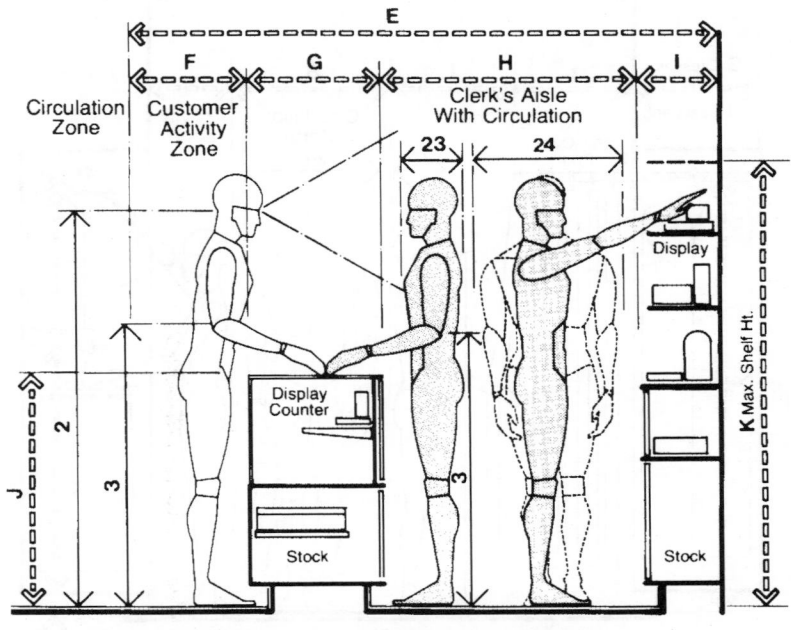

## TYPICAL SALES AREA / STANDING CUSTOMER

Fig. 18. Typical sales area/standing customer

|   | in | cm |
|---|---|---|
| A | 26–30 | 66.0–76.2 |
| B | 18–24 | 45.7–61.0 |
| C | 42 | 106.7 |
| D | 28 | 71.1 |
| E | 84–112 | 213.4–284.5 |
| F | 18 | 45.7 |
| G | 18–24 | 45.7–61.0 |
| H | 30–48 | 76.2–121.9 |
| I | 18–22 | 45.7–55.9 |
| J | 35–38 | 88.9–96.5 |
| K | 72 | 182.9 |

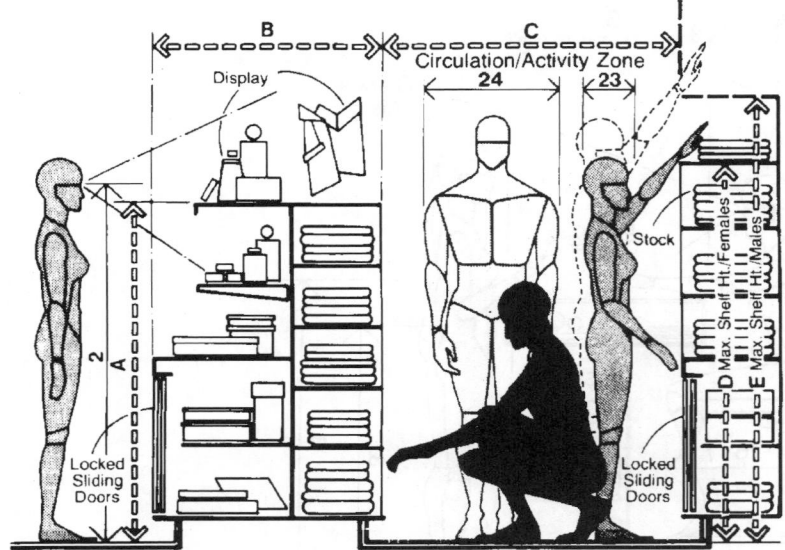

**TYPICAL MERCHANDISE CASES**

Fig. 19. Typical merchandise cases

| | in | cm |
|---|---|---|
| A | 48 max. | 121.9 max. |
| B | 30–36 | 76.2–91.4 |
| C | 51 min. | 129.5 min. |
| D | 66 | 167.6 |
| E | 72 | 182.9 |
| F | 84–96 | 213.4–243.8 |
| G | 20–26 | 50.8–66.0 |
| H | 28–30 | 71.1–76.2 |
| I | 18–24 | 45.7–61.0 |
| J | 18 min. | 45.7 min. |
| K | 72 max. | 182.9 max. |
| L | 4 | 10.2 |
| M | 42 | 106.7 |
| N | 26 min. | 66.0 min. |

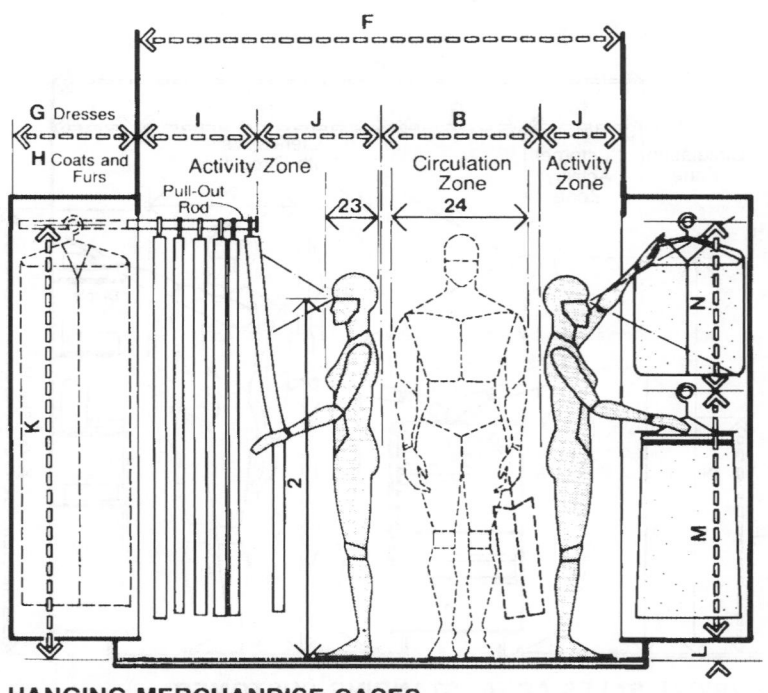

**HANGING MERCHANDISE CASES**

Fig. 20. Hanging merchandise cases

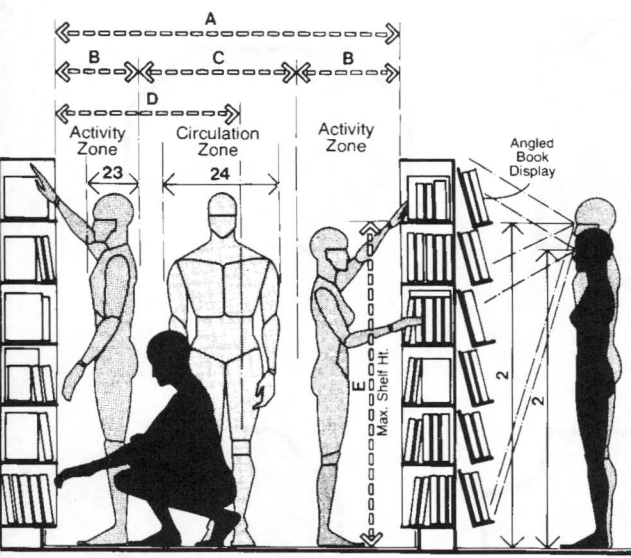

BOOK STORE / DISPLAY AREA

**Fig. 21. Book store/display area**

## Shop Entrances and Displays

Show windows cannot stop at merely attracting and stopping passersby. Patrons must be induced to enter the shop, and displays should be aligned with entrances (Fig. 23). Angular walls also create niches for displays (Fig. 24). Steps are considered inadvisable. When a change in grade is necessary, and it is too great for a ramp, the steps may be inside the store, well lighted. However, provisions must be made to satisfy the ADA Accessibility Guidelines.

It is necessary to provide some form of protection from drafts at entrances, particularly in cold climates. Vestibules offer such protection, and may be made removable in summer months. Revolving doors are often essential where wind pressures are high, when volume of traffic is great, or when air conditioning is used. In order to maintain the air conditioning system's efficiency at a maximum, a seal between indoor and outdoor air may be needed.

### Wrapping and Cash Register Counter

Locations for these require study. The type of shop will determine whether these services should be out in the open or concealed, near or remote from the door; positioned to permit a salesclerk to make

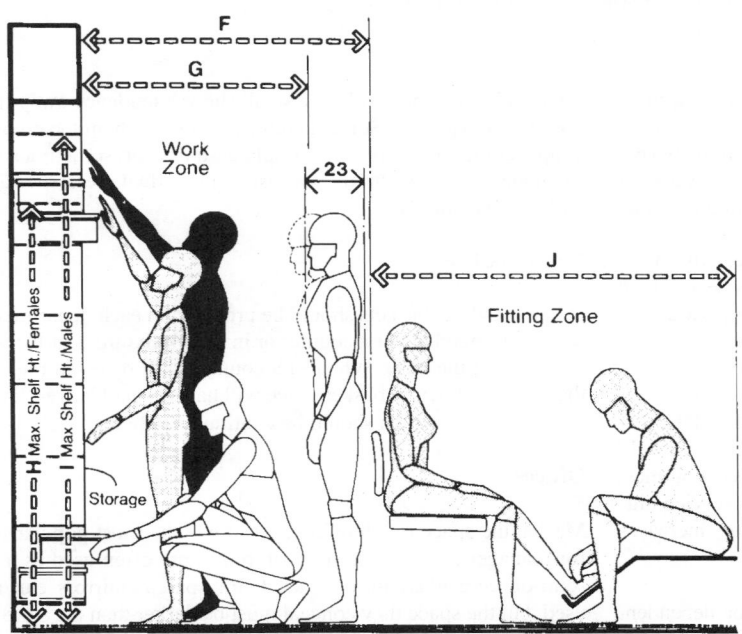

SHOE STORE / FITTING AREA

**Fig. 22. Shoe store/fitting area**

|   | in | cm |
|---|---|---|
| A | 66 min. | 167.6 min. |
| B | 18 min. | 45.7 min. |
| C | 30 min. | 76.2 min. |
| D | 36 | 91.4 |
| E | 68 | 172.7 |
| F | 48 | 121.9 |
| G | 36 min. | 91.4 min. |
| H | 66 | 167.6 |
| I | 72 | 182.9 |
| J | 60–66 | 152.4–167.6 |

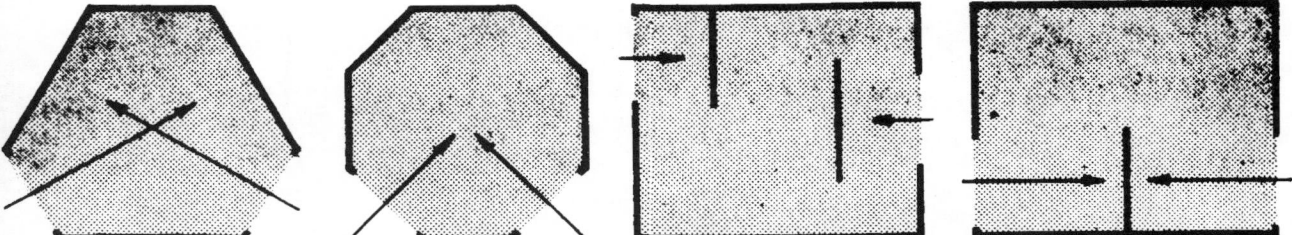

**Fig. 23. Displays opposite doorways**

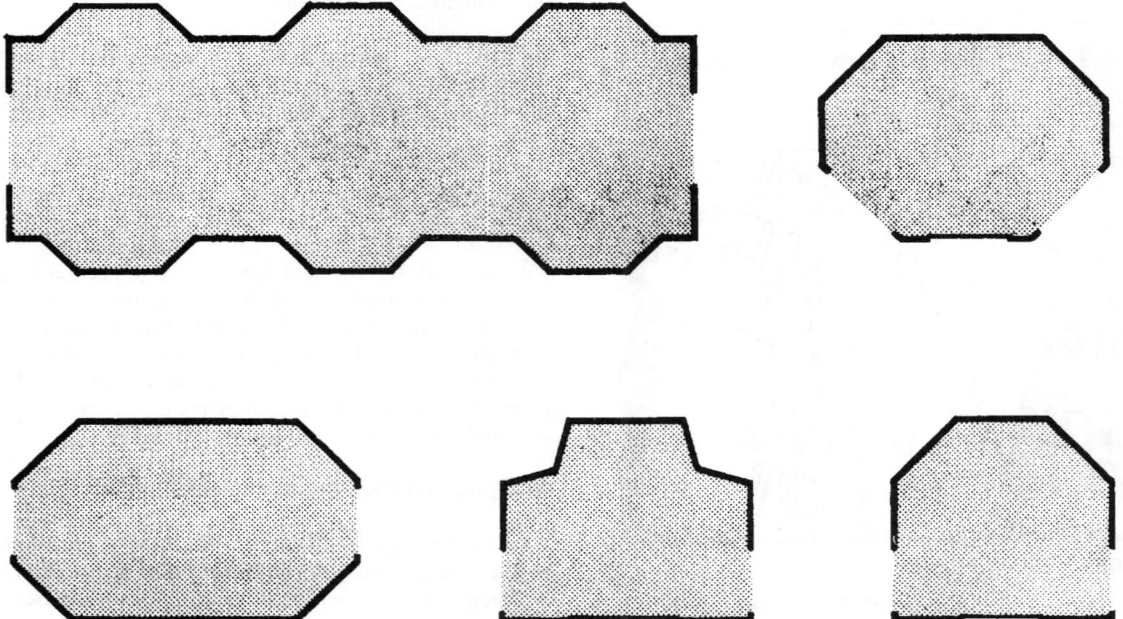

**Fig. 24. Isolation of displays by angular planning**

change while facing the doorway, or, as some managers prefer, to do nothing else when ringing up sales. To other shops, a cashier is considered to provide better control and efficiency. Some shops have a separate room or curtained alcove for wrapping and cashier space, or a basement or mezzanine served by dumbwaiter and pneumatic tube.

A cash register and wrapping counter in an alcove near the door, which permits the clerk to face the shop and doorway, is desirable in small shops where business is hurried, or where for long periods one clerk must sell, order, wrap, ring up sales, make change, and watch the shop. A store with a narrow entrance might better have these services remote to avoid crowding at the doorway. The separate wrapping room, basement, or other space is used in stores with a more leisurely trade, or when (as in many gift shops) goods are fragile and rarely carried out by the customer. It is less confusing and less "commercial" in appearance for the shop as a whole to have this service outside of the selling space. However, such planning increases customers' waiting time.

Proper location of the cash register for safety may also be dependent upon a wide variety of factors such as the number of salespeople, the type of show-window back (open or closed ones, which conceal the shop from the sidewalk), and the type of neighborhood (busy or quiet).

There is in the more exclusive small shops a tendency away from the use of cash registers. Some merchants consider them too commercial in appearance and provide a simple cash drawer, sometimes without a bell alarm. This naturally is a case of individual preference and reliability of personnel.

**Waste Baskets**

Space for waste baskets should be provided in each department. This can be arranged under a counter or in a back fixture near the wrapper by omitting the base. When in a counter with recessed toe-space at the front, such waste basket space will have a small ledge—the top of the toe space—which should be continuously braced.

**Offices**

Mezzanine space overlooking the store is the most popular location for management offices. Venetian blinds are often used as a screen; semi-obscure glass may be used; transparent mirrors can also be used, but the space they conceal must be darker than the store side. A practical way of doing this on a mezzanine used for working offices is to run the corridor along the front of the mezzanine, separating the mirror-screen from the offices.

Fig. 1. Supermarket display of goods

# SUPERMARKETS

Architecturally, the supermarket is a large scale emporium of merchandise (Fig. 1) that doesn't have to shout to be noticed.

## STORE SIZE

Properly situated on its site, the supermarket and any "satellite shops," attached or not (shops which can be entered from the market or from a separate outside entrance), offer a parking ratio of 3.6 square feet to 1 square foot of total store area. To obtain the necessary parking area in neighborhoods with high land costs, rooftop and basement parking should be considered. The satellite shops such as convenience grocery stores, liquor and drugstores, and a carry-out food shop remain open after the supermarket has closed for the day.

New, free-standing supermarkets (Fig. 2) average 22,700 square feet to 31,000 square feet with 75 to 80 percent of the total store devoted to selling space and the remaining 20 to 25 percent of floor space devoted to service areas such as storage coolers, prepackaging areas, grocery storage, etc.

About 50 percent of the supermarket's total equipment and fixture investment is in refrigeration equipment—meat, dairy, produce, frozen food, delicatessen, and the storage coolers necessary for each department (Fig. 3). The remaining 50 percent is devoted to grocery items—half of which can be nonfood items, such as housewares, soft goods, glassware, health, and beauty aids. The most important square footage is that required by the check-out stands—one for each $10,000 of projected weekly volume plus an additional check-stand for future expansion (this is only a rule of thumb figure and varies with the region of the country and the type of service the market provides the customer). The accompanying plan (Fig. 4), adapted to the

individual operation requirements, provides a practical guide in the layout of a supermarket.

## CONFIGURATION AND LAYOUT

Assuming proper location of the store on the site—one which makes it most accessible to traffic and parking—the next step would be to decide on the configuration of the store.

Generally, free-standing markets tend to be rectangular in shape, with the narrower portion forming the front-to-rear dimension. Since most often the deliveries are at the rear, the various back room areas (preparation and storage) are located at the rear of the building, leaving the selling space more or less square.

At this point, the method of construction must be considered, particularly the location of any columns. Ideally, these should be kept out of the shopping aisles (Fig. 5). Assuming a 7-foot aisle between 4-feet-wide shelving islands, columns spaced in a multiple of 11 feet will keep the columns out of the aisles. (Shelving can be cut to fit around columns, and this is preferred to columns in the shopping aisles.)

Although refrigerated fixtures have been and can be located almost anywhere on the sales floor, most often they are located at the walls. They tend to be too large and bulky to be placed in any central location, where they would obstruct the overall view of the store. The refrigerated cases should be placed as near as practicable to their associated work rooms and storage coolers. This also applies to the service departments such as the delicatessen, in-store bakery, and snack bar.

Since all merchandise purchases must be funneled through the check-out counters, they are all located in one location (usually at the front of the store near the exit door).

*Author:* Herbert Ross

**Fig. 2. Supermarket facade**

**Fig. 3. Refrigeration equipment**

## REFRIGERATION EQUIPMENT

The size of today's supermarket makes the use of self-contained refrigerated cases (with a few exceptions) impractical. Therefore, a centralized refrigeration system is employed. (All major refrigeration equipment manufacturers offer a form of centralized refrigeration system and all are basically alike.) Such a system utilizes a bank of compressors and condensers (air- or water-cooled) located in one room with liquid refrigerant running to the individual cases and the heated gas being returned to the condensers.

## SUPERMARKET DISPLAY

Good vision arc demands that top shelves be not over 5 feet-3 inches high, permitting an angle of view not more than 15 degrees above the horizontal. The easy-to-reach zone starts at about 15 inches above the floor, the minimum height for the bottom shelf. Face of cans or packages should be as nearly at right angles to eye as practical. Cans for bottom shelves are now designed to be legible lying on their side.

The length of "super island" units varies, 9 feet being the longest in common use. Distance between shelf supports varies about a norm of 2 feet-6 inches. Supports should be set back to permit an appearance of uninterrupted merchandise.

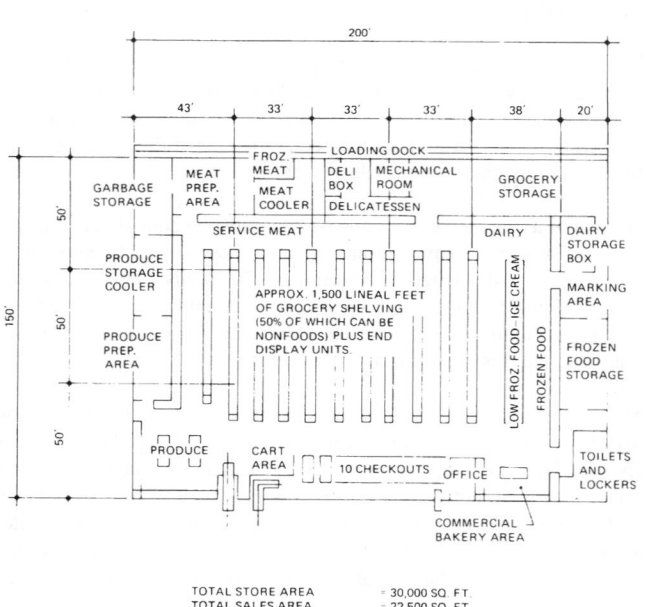

**Fig. 4. Typical free-standing supermarket plan**

**Fig. 5. Well-lit shopping aisle**

*Author:* Egmont Arens

Fig. 1. Shopping center (Mojo Stumer Associates; photo courtesy of the architect)

# SHOPPING CENTERS

## BASIC HISTORY AND TRENDS

A shopping center is a complex of retail stores and related facilities planned as a unified group to give maximum shopping convenience to the customer and maximum exposure to the merchandise. The concept is not new. The agora of the typical city of ancient Greece was essentially a shopping center in the heart of the business district. The Emperor Trajan's architect, the Greek slave Apollodorus, built a shopping center adjacent to the Roman Forum in AD 110. It had a two-level enclosed and ventilated mall lined with open-fronted shops startlingly similar to today's concept. The typical Arabian souk, or market, of the Middle Ages also had narrow, weather-protected malls lined with open-fronted shops.

Several factors have led to the shopping center (Fig. 1). Population growth has led to outward expansion of the cities and the growth of not only suburbs, but "exurbs"—residential communities in formerly rural areas. Downtown congestion weakened the downtown merchants and prompted them to set up branches in the expanding periphery in order to be more convenient to their customers. Major shopping centers have grown along with the suburbs and exurbs. They are now megacenters, complete with department stores, "big box" retail chain stores, office buildings, hotels and motels, entertainment, and, of course, parking facilities. Meanwhile, depressed central business districts are reaching out to the suburbs and exurbs with connector routes to downtown and construction of major downtown renewal projects, also complete with stores, offices, hotels, entertainment, and parking facilities, usually in decked garages due to the high downtown land cost.

## TYPES OF CENTERS

### Neighborhood Center (Suburban)

This is a row of stores customarily (but not always) in a strip, or line, paralleling the highway and with parking between the line of store-fronts and the highway. Service is by alley in the rear. Ranging from 20,000 to 100,000 square feet, these projects usually contain a supermarket and a drugstore, often a variety store, and a half-dozen or more service-type stores. They cater to a very limited trade area and are not normally competitive with the major centers. A few of the centers have their retail units clustered around an enclosed "mini-mall."

### Intermediate or Community-Size Center

This also is usually a strip of stores but substantially larger than the neighborhood center and usually containing a so-called "junior" department store as the major unit. This type is vulnerable to competition from the larger centers and hence has declined in desirability. The parking pattern is normally similar to that of the neighborhood center.

### Regional Center (Suburban)

This contains one to four department stores plus 50 to 100 or more satellite shops and facilities, all fronting on an internal pedestrian mall, or shopping walkway. Parking completely surrounds the building group so that all stores face inward to the mall with their "backs" to the parking (Fig. 2).

With today's rising land costs and diminishing supply of suitable large tracts, there has been a trend toward double-decked parking to save land area. It is simply a matter of the relation between the land cost and the cost of the parking deck (Fig. 3).

There is also a strong trend toward double decking of the stores themselves so that the central pedestrian mall has two interconnecting levels, each lined with shops. The double-level mall is also due, in part, to the need to keep horizontal walking (shopping) distances

*Author:* Lathrop Douglass
*Reviewer:* Mark D. Stumer, AIA

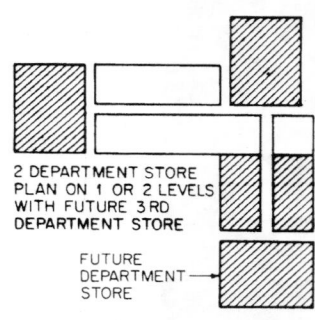

2 DEPARTMENT STORE PLAN ON 1 OR 2 LEVELS WITH FUTURE 3RD DEPARTMENT STORE

FUTURE DEPARTMENT STORE

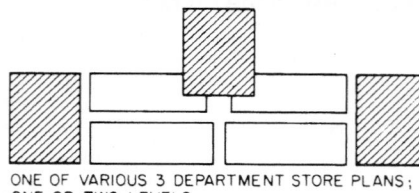

ONE OF VARIOUS 3 DEPARTMENT STORE PLANS; ONE OR TWO LEVELS

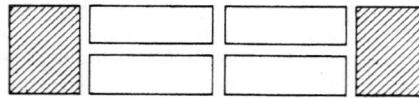

CLASSIC 2 DEPARTMENT STORE PLAN; 1 OR 2 LEVELS. PLANS WITH ONE DEPARTMENT STORE ARE RARELY UNDERTAKEN

ONE OF VARIOUS 4 DEPARTMENT STORE PLANS; 1 OR 2 LEVELS

▨ DEPARTMENT STORE
☐ SHOPS

**Fig. 2. Regional center diagrams**

within reason. As land costs continue to rise and projects to grow larger, three- and four-level malls will become more common.

### Renewal Projects (Downtown)

Partly a product of the Neo-Traditional Development movement, the trend is toward a close integration, on two or more shopping levels, of department stores, shops of all sorts, restaurants, etc. The multi-level malls may connect directly or by bridges to other shopping facilities, hotels, office buildings, theaters, and parking garages. Because of high land costs, all parking is normally multidecked and can be above, below, or, better, laterally contiguous to the shopping facilities. Downtown developments often have a multilevel pattern interconnecting the essential parts of the central business district.

### DEVELOPMENT AND FINANCING

Shopping centers are customarily promoted and owned by developers whose primary motive is a return on their investment and, to a lesser extent, by department stores or other merchants who are looking for new outlets to increase their sales volume. There is also participation in ownership by institutions, such as insurance companies, who in the past confined their activity merely to lending money to the developer or merchant.

Customarily the developer, regardless of what individual or group she represents, can, with good judgment and skill, set up the project on the basis of, let us say, a 10 percent investment of her own money and the remaining 90 percent as a long-term loan from an insurance company or other institution. As the long-term loan usually does not become available until completion of the project, the developer borrows needed interim money, or short-term financing, usually from a bank. The dollar value of the long-term loan is primarily calculated as a multiple of the anticipated rent roll; that is to say, it is based on a certain number of times the total projected annual rent collectible from all the committed tenants who have acceptable credit ratings. As the loan is based primarily on the rents and, therefore, is not affected by overruns in the construction cost of the job, it is obvious that the construction budget becomes of utmost importance. With only, say, 10 percent of the total job cost as her investment and 90 percent borrowed, an overrun of 10 percent will, in actuality, double the amount of money that the developer must invest. Otherwise, she will have to sell out, go bankrupt, or cut every possible cost she can, even if it damages the popularity of the project. The vital importance, as a result of this pattern, of a realistic and inviolable budget should be clear.

### Professional Team

At the earliest possible stage in the concept of the project, preferably even before acquisition of the land, a developer, i.e., owner, should assemble her professional team. For a small neighborhood center, such a team might consist solely of the owner and the architect, especially if the owner is experienced in this type of leasing.

For regional centers and downtown development programs, however, the essential team involves, in addition to the developer (who may be an individual or a large development corporation), the architect; the market analyst; the leasing agent; the mortgage broker; the engineers (usually retained by the architect and including mechanical, structural, and site); the attorney; the public relations advisor; and other occasionally needed specialists. The larger and more complex the proposed project, the more necessary it is that each of these members

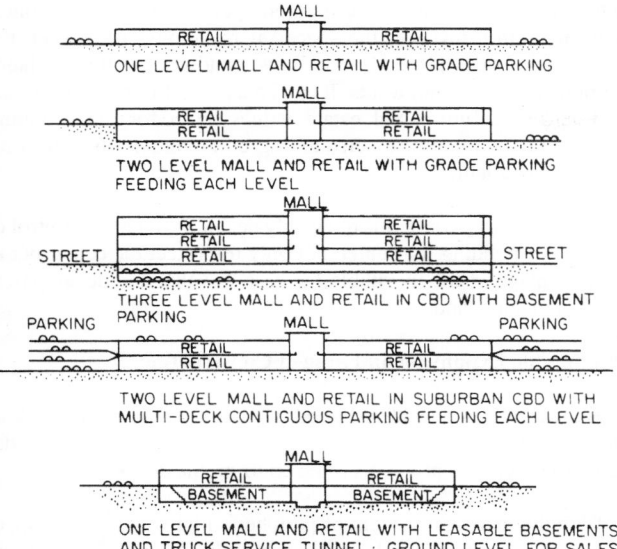

ONE LEVEL MALL AND RETAIL WITH GRADE PARKING

TWO LEVEL MALL AND RETAIL WITH GRADE PARKING
FEEDING EACH LEVEL

THREE LEVEL MALL AND RETAIL IN CBD WITH BASEMENT PARKING

TWO LEVEL MALL AND RETAIL IN SUBURBAN CBD WITH
MULTI-DECK CONTIGUOUS PARKING FEEDING EACH LEVEL

ONE LEVEL MALL AND RETAIL WITH LEASABLE BASEMENTS
AND TRUCK SERVICE TUNNEL; GROUND LEVEL FOR SALES
ONLY; BASEMENTS FOR SERVICES

**Fig. 3. Sectional view of regional shipping center**

of the team be experienced not only in his own profession but also in the specific field of shopping center development. It is desirable, in fact, that they participate, as part of the team, in major decision making.

**Economic Survey or Market Analysis**

Prior to any planning activity and often prior to acquisition of the land, the market analyst makes a complete survey of the anticipated trade area surrounding the proposed site for the center. The boundaries of the trade area customarily depend on acceptable automobile driving time to the center. Frequently the trade area is broken into a primary area, where a high percentage of the inhabitants would shop at the center, and one or more secondary areas where, due to competition or to driving times or other reasons, a smaller percentage would be anticipated. The analyst assembles data on existing population, future population trends, income levels, car ownership, existing shopping facilities and their probable future competitive effect, and also projected facilities already announced or likely to be announced by other developers. She estimates the probable mortality rate of these proposed projects—i.e., how many will never be built—and the competitive effect of any survivors. The analyst, from available statistical records, and based on the income level, population, ethnic origins, and other characteristics of the trade area, then makes estimates of the amount of family income likely to be allocated to such categories as food, drugs, furniture, women's and men's clothes, shoes, department store purchases, etc.; and, from these estimates prepares charts indicating the recommended total amount of floor area to be built and how much of this floor area should be devoted to the various kinds of merchandise and services. These data then form the basis for the architectural programming. No major project should be undertaken without an analysis.

It is axiomatic that success goes to the developer who "gets there the fastest with the mostest," as the saying goes. If the project is too slow in coming to fruition, a competitive center, securing a firm hold on the available business, may be built.

If a project is too large for the trade area, it cannot be sufficiently rented, and the unrented space may cause it to fail. If it is too small for the trade area, it will invite the construction of competitive centers and may lose out due to this competition. In the past this determination of size, i.e., total store area, was perhaps the most vital decision to be made and one that could be readily pinpointed from a thorough market survey by a firm of sound judgment. Today, however, with increased mobility it has been conclusively established that trade area boundaries no longer can be pinpointed. Today every aspect of a center's concept, planning, and design must be of the best for survival in the face of competition.

A school can be nonfunctional, but the children still have to go to school. A home may have many bad features, but the family will still live there. A shopping center, however, depends on the whims of its customers for its success. If, because of inconvenience or unsuitable merchandise or for any other reason, it does not have the proper appeal, the customers simply will not go there to shop, and the project may fail.

**SITE SELECTION**

The following criteria normally apply:

- A site available for development and located within the trade area recommended in the market analysis.
- Location easily accessible to at least one existing or shortly to be constructed major highway, preferably to two or more major highways. A location literally bordering on one or more major highways is desirable for its advertising impact on passing cars, but this is not necessary if suitable access roads exist between the highway and the site.
- Adequate present and future capacity of adjacent highways for through traffic piles to be generated by the center.
- Land cost in proper relation to total capital cost and to obtainable rents.
- Adequate size and suitable shape to permit proper planning of the merchandising area and a proper number of parking spaces. Where acreage is limited and high land costs are justified, parking can be on decks and the whole project can be multilevel.
- Zoning suitable for proposed use or at least a reasonable chance that such zoning may be obtained. Zoning changes are often difficult, expensive, and time-consuming to make.
- Utilities available or installable at acceptable cost.
- Subsurface ground conditions that can be overcome at acceptable cost, such as rock, swamp, trunk sewers, streams, etc.
- No easements or other legal restrictions that will interfere with proper planning.
- Topography that will permit as near to an ideal plan as possible without incurring excessive grading or drainage costs. It is noted, however, that it is usually better in principle to move a million yards of earth than to compromise a plan that will give maximum customer convenience and proper store relationships.

Other criteria that are desirable but not essential include:

- Adequate site area for future expansion and inclusion of supporting facilities, such as office buildings, motels, etc. There is little risk in the acquisition of such additional land, as land values always go up with the construction of a major center.
- Proximity to public transportation (in the case of larger cities).
- Possibility of integrating the land with other mutually beneficial uses such as town centers, recreation, housing, etc.
- Suitable zoning of adjacent land.

## SCHEMATIC PLANNING

Following acquisition of the site and completion of the economic survey, it is customary for the developer to retain a suitably experienced architect who proceeds to work out, from the market survey and physical information pertaining to the property, a simple schematic solution. This shows building sizes and arrangement, gross leasable areas, malls and public space, parking layout, access roads, method of servicing, and other basic aspects of the concept, including all pertinent statistics. This material, in conjunction with the economic survey, is then used by the developer in approaching the department store prospects. The architect's work normally is suspended at this point until the department stores are committed. Many projects never go beyond this stage and, in any case, there is usually a substantial lapse of time before the project goes ahead.

The major principles of schematic planning, in addition to conforming to the leasable area recommendations of the economic survey, are:

• Convenience and comfort for the customer
• Maximum merchandising potential for the tenant stores

Customer convenience demands ease of vehicular access to and from the site; ease and adequacy of parking; reasonable walking distances; simple, direct pedestrian shopping routes with minimum obstructions and inconveniences. It is axiomatic that a shopper rarely goes where there is inconvenience of any sort.

Maximum merchandising potential means giving each tenant in the project a reasonably equal opportunity to capture a portion of the customer's trade. The means of achieving this is normally based on the concept of "anchors," or "pulls," that is to say, those merchandising units that have maximum appeal to the customer. The typical shopper is usually attracted to a center primarily by the type and range of merchandise offered by the major department stores. This appeal is supplemented by the opportunity for convenient comparison shopping in the many smaller or satellite stores. Because of the customer activity generated by the appeal of the department stores, these major units are spaced at strategic spots, such as at each end of a one- or two-level pedestrian mall whose length is lined on each side with the smaller satellite stores. The flow of customers from these major units to each other then draws people past the smaller stores, where they stop en route for impulse and comparative shopping.

The key to this planning is the avoidance of any dead ends or out-of-the-way locations for the smaller stores and the concentration of all shopping on clearly defined routes connecting with major anchors, or pulls, i.e., the department stores.

### Integration with Community

For many years the typical shopping center has been a low, flat building mass resembling an island surrounded by a vast, barren ocean of asphalt. Landscaping has been inadequate, and integration of any sort with the community has been completely lacking. With the competitive need, however, for increasing the size of centers and including within their general scope office buildings, hotels, housing, etc., more complex planning requirements have given rise to a better opportunity, as well as to greater urgency, for the true integration of the stores and parking within a larger, major complex, which is integrated with the existing neighborhood. Plan integration with the neighborhood has, in fact, become a must for large

centers and a factor not to be ignored even for the smallest ones. Such integration involves the space interrelationship between the neighborhood and project's buildings, roadways, parking, landscaping, and pedestrian walks. It can be a powerful means of assuring long-range future real estate values, both for the shopping project and for the entire surrounding community, whether commercial or residential.

Where land costs permit, it is obviously desirable to obtain control of the land surrounding the center, not only to protect the center but to take advantage of the inevitable increase in value and development potential of such land.

### Planning for Expansion and Staged Construction

It has always been considered good practice to build retail space as nearly commensurate as possible with market survey recommendations. However, two problems often confront the developer:

1. With the increasing extent of peripheral highways and the spectacular growth of suburbs and exurbs, it has become increasingly difficult to estimate the future potential of a particular center and hence the amount of future space needed to maintain its competitive position.
2. With the increasing number of centers with two to four department stores, the situation arises in which one or more such stores (however necessary they may be to the project and however eager they may be to be included) may, for good reasons of their own, want an opening date a year or more later than the official opening date set for the center.

Therefore, it has become more and more customary to do either or both of the following:

• Plan for a more or less indeterminate expansion at some unspecified future date.
• Plan for one or more specific stages of construction, each to be undertaken as a successive part of a more or less continuous construction operation.

In the latter case, i.e., two or more specifically scheduled construction stages, the problem becomes more one of leasing than of planning. The project is planned for the final stage, and it becomes the leasing broker's problem as to how much space can be leased at top rents in the first stage and how much it becomes necessary to leave for the later stage or stages due to the initial absence of one or more department stores.

There also arises the problem of the construction contract. If stage one is completed before stage two is sent out for bid, then the bidding can be truly competitive. But when the second stage begins before completion of the first stage, it may be difficult to secure bids or to negotiate a reasonable price with the contractor already on the job. A method occasionally used on large centers, and one which applies in this situation, is for the general contractor or the owner's building organization to clearly establish that more than one subcontractor in each major trade will be utilized and thereby to ensure a continuing competitive atmosphere. This procedure also has the advantage of allowing smaller subcontractors to bid on parts of large jobs.

In the case, however, of providing for expansion at some undetermined future date, the situation is different and much more difficult to resolve. Merely to provide excess land area for future use is usually an unacceptable solution. This is because proper integration of the future unknown facilities with the existing center may turn out to be difficult if not impossible. This, in turn, weakens the trade potential of the overall enlarged project. The proper procedure usually is to master-plan the entire available site so that a thoroughly acceptable final project can result. It is noted, however, that any master plan for the enlargement of a center at some indeterminate time (say, three years or more in the future) must in every case take into consideration that the most critical time for any center is the year it opens and usually the succeeding two years of its life. It either becomes a success within those years, or it becomes (for the time being at least) a failure. Few developers with their small equity investment and mortgage payments can afford to retain ownership of a losing operation for a sufficient length of time to take advantage of any ultimate success.

Therefore, the master plan for the site must provide for as nearly perfect an initial stage as is possible. If, then, in 5 or 10 years the center becomes so popular that the developer decides to enlarge it, the center's popularity and sales potential are already clearly established and the perfection of the final plan is of much less importance.

Expansion of individual stores is a different problem. Special provision for such expansion may be made by:

- adding future floor(s)
- lateral contiguous construction
- use of areas held in reserve for this purpose in basements and mezzanines
- eliminating adjacent tenancies and taking over their space

In all cases involving an increase in the project's gross leasable area (GLA), parking must be added to compensate and maintain proper ratio of GLA to car stalls.

Regardless of the program of phased construction or of future expansion, there are two additional items that must at all times be taken into consideration in any schedule:

1. A shopping center does by far its greatest amount of business in the two months before Christmas. Its next busiest season is before Easter, and the next busiest, after that, is prior to "back to school." Therefore, shopping centers in general and department stores in particular customarily set opening dates that are inviolable. Any serious postponement can jeopardize the heavy investment in merchandise for that particular season. It is customary, therefore, in all shopping center operations to schedule the work backward from the mandatory and inflexible opening date and allow adequate time for completing and stocking the stores.

2. For public impact and general public acceptance in a shopping center's early years, it is generally desirable to schedule the leasing, planning, and construction so that all stores can open at once. This avoids the public inconvenience and bad public relations of a mall with many barricades due to unfinished stores, as well as the unfavorable customer reaction from limited merchandise.

## GENERAL DESIGN AND PLANNING CRITERIA

### Column Spacing

A significant dimension is column spacing, as this involves the widths, i.e., frontages, of stores (Fig. 4). Often used spacing widths

are 20, 25 and 30 feet, with the last the most flexible. The dimension from the mall to the rear of the store can be set by the most economical structural system. It is essential to arrive at the most economical structural system, as the roof is a major cost factor.

### Store Depths

For one-story stores in America, buildings are usually 120 to 140 feet deep, sometimes more to accommodate larger stores. If there are basements or mezzanines, the depth dimension usually can be reduced 20 to 25 percent. In European centers and others with many very small stores, there is a problem in how to achieve shallow depth without incurring higher costs from greater mall lengths in relation to floor area. One often used and desirable device is to "dog leg," or "ell," a larger store around a smaller store.

### Clear Heights

These vary from 10 to 14 feet or more, with 12 feet a good average. Above this clear height, there must be adequate space for air-conditioning ducts, recessed lights, structural system, etc.

### Ducts and Shafts

The shells of the buildings must be flexible enough to accommodate any reasonable tenant requirements. It is essential that the mechanical engineer set up a schedule of the location and sizes of the principal duct runs and shafts to avoid serious future space problems. This requirement includes special exhaust ventilation through the roof and all other mechanical items that can be anticipated.

### Central Plant Versus Individual HVAC System

Regardless of which method is used, the space to be occupied by all equipment must be determined, both in size and location, in the earliest planning stages. Central plant equipment can be in a separate building, on the project roof, or elsewhere so long as it is economical as to design and length of runs. Individual plants in each store require roof space, cooling towers, etc. The inexcusable eyesores of equipment on the roof can be avoided by proper coordination of work between the leasing agent, the architect, and the mechanical engi-

**Fig. 4. Frontage and column spacing (Mojo Stumer Associates; photo courtesy of the architect)**

neer, and the resulting provision of properly located and designed roof screens and enclosures.

### Exterior Walls

As these may have, depending on each store's requirements, service doors, public entrance doors, trash rooms, show windows, etc., a modular design that can suitably accommodate for visual effect any of these features is very desirable. Show windows and public entrances are rare on parking lot facades, as it has been found that the great majority of customers enter stores from the mall rather than directly from the parking lot. Public entrances from the parking lot usually occur only for department stores, for stores open on Sundays, and for such tenants as restaurants, drugstores, and the like.

### Anarchy Versus Regimentation

In the earliest shopping centers there often was no design control at all, with a resulting anarchy of signs, materials, and design. This situation gradually changed to one where so much rigid control was exercised that the projects became far too monotonous. Proper design calls for a homogeneous whole with the widest possible latitude for individual design of each store. Generally the greatest possible latitude (in good taste) should be given to the mall facades, with fairly severe restrictions placed on the exterior facades. This gives interest to the interior, where it is desirable, and unity of design for the exterior.

### Traffic

The car capacity of all contiguous roadways used for ingress and egress must be sufficient to accommodate present and future through traffic plus the traffic generated by the shopping center. Proper signal controls, reservoir lanes, divider strips, and other traffic control features must be provided. It should always be kept in mind that a center with, say, 5,000 parking spaces and an average turnover on Fridays of, say, four cars per parking space, accommodates a total number of cars per day that would stretch, if traveling in a line on the highway, all the way from New York to Boston. Because of the complexity of the traffic problem, the developer or the architect fre-

quently hires a traffic engineer to assure that the highways have adequate capacity and that the center can accommodate smoothly the ingress and egress of customers' cars. The traffic engineer is, however, interested in speed and smooth flow of traffic, while the architect for the project should be more concerned with convenience, simplicity, and customer's freedom of choice in selecting the route and parking procedure (Fig. 5).

### LEASING ARRANGEMENTS

Customarily the satellite stores and all other facilities, retail or otherwise, with the exception of the department store, are leased by the developer. The developer may lease one or all the department stores and build them to the tenant's requirements, or may sell or lease the land to one or more, in which case the department store designs and constructs its own facilities within the established limits and requirements of the overall project.

The satellite leases usually provide for a minimum annual rent (on which the mortgage calculation is based) plus or against an overage rent consisting of a percentage of the store's gross annual sales. It is the latter provision which makes the success of each individual store so important to the developer and which compensates him for future inflation. It puts the developer and tenant into a sort of partnership.

It is obvious that the individual rent terms must reflect not only the cost of the land and overall project costs but also the amount of special work done by the developer for the individual tenant. In the past, the developer installed much of the tenant's special requirements and received a proportionally higher rent. Today, however, it is more common for the developer to supply the shell of the premises only, with each tenant installing (at their own expense) the ceiling and floor finishes, decor, mall storefront, and some of the air-conditioning equipment items. Trade fixtures, except in unusual circumstances, are always installed by the tenant.

As the leasing program takes time to consummate, it is absolutely essential that the leasing proceed simultaneously with the architectural design and drawings and that the leasing agent and the architect and his engineers keep in continuous communication. Otherwise, long delays and expensive changes ensue.

In view of the importance of the department stores in generating customer traffic for the project, their lease terms usually provide only a minimum (if any) profit for the developer. The profit on the development as a whole must then come from proportionally higher rents from the satellites. For this reason, when the owner of a center is a developer and not a department store, it is essential that at least half the total retail area be occupied by high-rent satellites.

### Tenant Mix

Tenant "mix" is the name for the plan relationship to each other of the various types of stores and facilities. Proper tenant mix exposes the customer to a varying sequence of differing types of merchandise. If each store type is properly located in relation to every other store type, it has been demonstrated that each store will receive its maximum sales volume. In such cases, the center will be successful and all tenants, plus the developer, will profit. If the relationships are not correct, many of the stores may not receive their fair share of the customer's dollar, and both the individual store and the developer will suffer. The developer may not, in such cases, receive any rent based on percentage of sales volume, and the strength of the center as

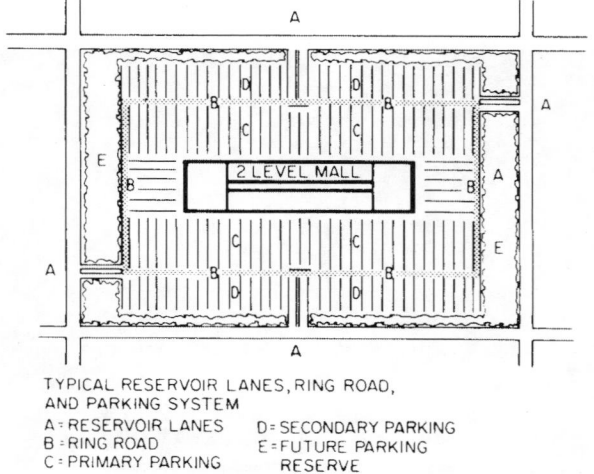

TYPICAL RESERVOIR LANES, RING ROAD, AND PARKING SYSTEM
A = RESERVOIR LANES    D = SECONDARY PARKING
B = RING ROAD    E = FUTURE PARKING
C = PRIMARY PARKING       RESERVE

**Fig. 5. Typical reservoir lanes, ring road, and parking system**

a whole will be weakened. There are many theories on proper tenant mix. It has been fairly well established, however, that with few exceptions and regardless of length of malls or number of mall levels, a generally mixed pattern of high and low prices, soft goods and hard goods, retail and services produces the best individual sales volumes and overall success

## MALLS

The pedestrian mall has become the feature of today's shopping center, whether the project is in the suburbs or in the central business district. The pedestrian mall has the following characteristics:

- The mall usually consists of the principal mall, the major pedestrian shopping street of the project (Fig. 6), and one or more subsidiary approach malls or access routes connecting the main mall with the parking areas or adjacent streets.
- With few exceptions, all stores have their principal entrance on the main mall or, less desirably, on approach malls, whether or not these stores have additional entrances to parking lots or adjacent streets.
- The mall can be on one level or on two or more superimposed levels. Each mall level should, however, avoid slopes or steps within its own walkways to avoid hindrance to shopping and a source of accidents.
- The mall can be open, with weather protection consisting solely of continuous canopies along the store fronts; or completely covered but open to the air; or completely enclosed, necessitating climate control.

The trend has been toward enclosed malls except where weather conditions are ideal or some other factor makes the open mall preferable.

Enclosed malls have been in the form of huge courts; they have been wide, narrow, straight, circuitous, empty, or filled with amenities; they have had one level or two or more levels; and they have been lighted by skylights or solely by artificial means (Fig. 7).

The trend has been away from wide malls and court-type malls. Widths of 30 to 40 feet are outnumbering widths of 50 feet or more. The wider malls require more landscaping and features to avoid a barren atmosphere. They also require more cubage and hence are less economical despite the possibility of high rents from kiosks and similar features spotted along their lengths. Furthermore, and most important, narrow malls facilitate back and forth comparison shopping from one side to the other and hence significantly aid the customer's exposure to the merchandise. A logical trend is toward stretches of narrow mall, generally devoid of amenities, punctuated by moderate-sized courts in front of department stores or elsewhere which become customer magnets. The courts have greater lighting intensity, greater height, and spectacular features such as fountains, lush landscaping, and monumental sculpture.

The length of malls generally should not be more than 800 feet (preferably less) between department stores or other major features; but, in the case of more than two department stores, total length can be substantially more.

Because of the high downtown land costs and increasing land costs in the suburbs, plus the shortage of sites of adequate area, two-level malls are a standard solution; malls of three levels or more are becoming more common. Such multi-levels make the shopping area much more compact and walking distances shorter.

In connection with any two-level (or more) mall, it is mandatory that each level be as important as every other level; otherwise, one level will become the prime level, all the stores will want to be on that level, and the other level will be second choice, will command lower rents, and hence, in all probability, will not economically justify its construction.

To achieve this equality of desirability, of customer appeal, and of rent balance, it is essential that both (or all) levels have:

- Equally convenient accessibility from parking areas by means of two or more levels of immediately adjacent parking, whether on grade or on decks or by means of other devices to equalize the parking convenience.
- No mall dead end on any level without a department store as its terminus.
- Adequate vertical transportation between levels, usually one or more sets of escalators and several sets of convenient stairs (Fig. 8).

**Fig. 6. Mall pedestrian street (photo courtesy of John M. Maher)**

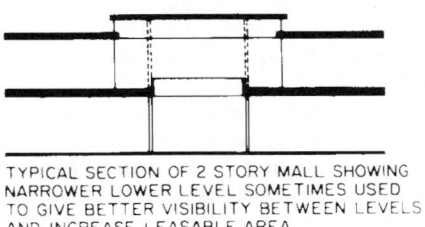

TYPICAL SECTION OF 2 STORY MALL SHOWING NARROWER LOWER LEVEL SOMETIMES USED TO GIVE BETTER VISIBILITY BETWEEN LEVELS AND INCREASE LEASABLE AREA.

**Fig. 7. Typical section of 2-story mall**

Fig. 8. Vertical transportation (photo courtesy of John M. Maher)

- Visual interconnection of levels through the maximum use of open wells permitting maximum visibility of one level's shops and customers from the other.

## Mall Amenities

With the advent of the pedestrian mall came the need to give it interest and glamour as an enhancement to the overall customer appeal of the center. This interest or glamour is normally non-income producing; but, in the case of small retail kiosks for such items as keys, stockings, photo supplies, and soft drink facilities, very high rents can be obtained because of the conspicuous and high-exposure locations.

Mall amenities generally include, in addition to landscaping, which will be elaborated on in another section, most of the following items:

- Trash and ash receptacles, a mandatory aid in preventing litter.
- Directories of one sort or another to facilitate finding specific stores.
- Public telephone installations.
- Seating groups and individual benches for resting, although many planners believe it is better to have frequent coffee stands both for better control and to produce income. Many also believe that, in downtown areas, it is often better to avoid benches so as to discourage loitering by undesirable elements.
- Fountains (Fig. 9), properly designed for public protection from water hazards. (Water seems to have a universal appeal.)
- Kiosks of various sizes and shapes, generally less than 250 square feet (although there is a trend to larger ones).
- Lockers (occasionally) for storing purchases while continuing to shop.
- Food courts, offering a wide variety of hot and cold dishes and refreshments.
- Sculpture or other art forms as major design features.
- Miscellaneous items occasionally used to catch the public interest, such as bird cages, kiddy mazes, fashion mirrors, closed-circuit TV, clocks, continuous music, fashion platforms, exhibit areas, etc. It is noted that in the case of exhibit areas, it is necessary to provide adequate mall-access doors for bringing in large items to be exhibited.

Mall lighting should be low-keyed and incandescent, should lend interest to dark or monotonous areas, and should, except in major courts, allow the storefronts to be the main attraction. Natural light is often used in moderation to give variety of effect and sometimes to save energy cost, but generally natural light must be limited in order to avoid dilution of the impact of the storefronts along the mall. As malls are customarily open late afternoons and evenings, adequate artificial illumination must be provided regardless of the extent of the natural light.

Mall materials are of great importance. Generally speaking, they should reflect the quality level of the project, be sturdy enough to resist vandalism, and require minimum maintenance. As an example, floor materials on projects vary from hardened cement to terrazzo, tile, or marble, and, occasionally, to carpeting. It is noted that the floor of a mall is very conspicuous and the character, quality, and ease of maintenance of its surface materials should be primary considerations.

## Mall Storefronts and Signs

Open malls require glazed storefronts, and hence their requirements are similar to those of the typical city street. Enclosed, climatized malls can have open storefronts, i.e., the major part of the store's frontage can be without show windows and completely open, so that the shopper can enter the store virtually without being aware she has done so. At night the store is protected by sliding glass panels or roll-up grilles.

Generally speaking, except for certain limitations on use of materials and, more particularly, on store signs, the tenant is encouraged to use as much imagination and variety in her store frontage as possible to give glamour, interest, and appeal not only to her own store but to the mall as a whole. Customarily the storefront as well as the store interior is designed by a firm retained by the individual store rather than by the developer.

Except for whatever devices are used to achieve overall unity and harmony, the mall frontage can be treated completely at the will of each tenant, subject only to such restrictions as are recorded in the lease terms. It is essential, however, that such terms give the developer and the architect the right of final approval at their sole discretion. Signs are primarily either for store identification or for general

Fig. 9. Mall fountain with seating (photo courtesy of John M. Maher)

advertising of the store (Fig. 10). The former has a legitimate place in the shopping center concept. The latter generally does not. The larger the store, the greater the justification for a sign, as the larger stores are the magnets that attract the public. Endless exterior signs for the smaller stores are confusing, unsightly, and useless to store, owner, and customer. The passerby cannot read the confusion of smaller signs, and the shopper who has already parked gets no identification value from small-store exterior signs as there is literally no way to relate any such sign to its own store once she has parked and has entered the mall.

Signs, on the other hand, are a necessity within the mall to identify the individual stores. Signs should be simple, easily grasped, in good taste, and so arranged as to be visible at close range as well as at a distance. Too often store identification to the passing potential customer is omitted in favor of huge signs legible only at a distance that may not exist. Properly designed and lighted signs can greatly enhance the interest and appeal. Sign regulations should accompany each lease, and all signs must be subject to final approval from the owner and the architect to ensure proper harmony.

Signs or pylons on the exterior to identify the shopping center itself are a common practice but of dubious value. A regional project with its half-mile of construction is so conspicuous that anything more than simple identification is usually unnecessary.

### Exterior Facades

Some of the major satellite stores desire storefronts on the exterior of the complex, i.e., parking lot facades. The trend, however, whether by store preference for simpler control or by developer preference for economy, is to reduce to a minimum the number of show windows and public entrances on the exterior facade. Experience has shown that the public does not like to enter a mall through anything but the regular mall entrances or else through major stores such as department stores. Furthermore, the whole theory of the present-day shopping center is to get the customers as quickly as possible into the mall, from which the shopping process originates. Department stores insist on having direct entrances on the parking lot as well as the mall, but here again, exterior show windows are usually cut to the minimum.

Even in projects in central business districts, where some of the stores front on both city streets and the mall, experience has shown that the majority of the shoppers enter the stores from the malls rather than from the city streets, and many street entrances have been closed off.

In the matter of materials, the trend is toward permanence through good but not elaborate quality and the use of masonry and related types of material.

A major problem that requires careful solution is that resulting from the fact that there may be several department stores, in addition to the satellite stores, each designed by a different architect. Achievement of harmony of design can, therefore, become difficult.

The problem of visible mechanical equipment is always a serious one. Mechanical design and drawings should always be carefully checked for visual aspects, and when such equipment is visible, consideration has to be given to suitable methods of concealment, whether by masonry screens or whatever.

### Servicing

Servicing involves the delivery of goods to the various stores and also the removal of trash and garbage. In the simple strip shopping center, the servicing is customarily by an alley in the rear of the strip of stores. It is desirable to conceal the alley from adjacent neighborhood areas by a wall or landscaping.

In the one-level regional shopping center, servicing is customarily by one of the following:

- *Underground service tunnel.* This is usually under the mall, connecting directly to tenant-leased basements which connect, in turn, to the stores above. This system avoids all unsightly trash, keeps parked trucks out of the way, and avoids allocation of prime parking space to servicing. It also relegates non-selling activities to the basement, reserving the main floor for sales. The tunnel adds, however, 3 percent or more to the total cost of the construction and more or less necessitates the inclusion of basements. This, in turn, calls for realistic leasing and financing of these basement areas if they are to be self-supporting financially.
- *Service courts on the periphery of the building complex.* These are usually partially shielded from public view by masonry walls 6 to 10 feet high or higher. Their cost is minimum, but they occupy space that is expensive if land costs are high and that could otherwise be utilized for prime parking. The interiors of the courts are objectionable in appearance and can rarely be adequately screened. Furthermore, these courts can usually be made directly accessible to only a portion of the stores present. This type of project normally has no basement space.
- *Over-the-curb and sidewalk directly from the street.* This is the cheapest solution and uses the least land, but it requires rigid enforcement of cleanliness by the project management, delivery of merchandise and removal of trash generally before or after business hours, and the mandatory inclusion of trash rooms in each store.

Generally speaking, markets, department stores, restaurants, and drug and variety stores have the greatest demand for adequate service facilities.

Service trucking routes on the site are often separated from customer routes, but this arrangement is generally not necessary, as the relatively few number of trucks per day in a typical shopping center presents no traffic problem. In the case of sidewalk delivery, the parked

**Fig. 10. Mall signage (photo courtesy of John M. Maher)**

trucks pose problems, and policing may be required to prevent the accumulation of trash.

In multilevel projects, the use of strategically placed freight elevators is necessary. These usually connect to fireproof passages at the rear of the stores (whether on an upper level or below grade) and often serve also as fire exits. With this type of project, necessitating service corridors, service courts can usually be fewer and more concentrated.

Mezzanines are occasionally used to provide storage and non-selling space. Such facilities have value in that they reduce the depth of space required and hence the land occupied, but they rarely produce savings in construction cost because of the need for greater height of store-building roofs for adequate clearances.

### Climate Control

Virtually all commercial space such as stores, offices, hotels, and pedestrian malls are maintained year-round within certain limits as to temperature and relative humidity. In most climates this means heating and humidification in the winter, cooling and dehumidification in the summer, and at least ventilation in the intermediate seasons.

The problem of cooling is proportionately more important than heating, even in relatively cold climates, because of the necessity to compensate for the body heat and moisture emitted by crowds of people and the heat from electric lighting, especially the incandescent type. It is not uncommon, even in the north, for the cooling system of a department store to operate almost into the winter season.

In the past, cooling equipment such as compressors, fans, and cooling were installed in basements, on mezzanines, and on roofs. Roof installations, necessary both for lower cost and engineering requirements, are large and unsightly. This led to efforts to concentrate the equipment as much as possible and to surround it with lightweight or, preferably, masonry screen walls creating penthouses on the roofs.

With a central cooling and heating plant for the entire project, the developer installs the central plant, all the equipment for the mall, and the distribution lines for the heated and chilled water to the individual tenant spaces. Usually each tenant and/or store owner then installs the heat exchanger, fans, and distribution ducts within her own premises. The developer buys electric power at low rates because of the large amount purchased, and the individual tenant pays the developer for the water used at a lower rate than that which she would have had to pay in the case of her own individual plant. However, the tenant still pays enough to allow the developer to make a profit on the overall central plant operation. Because of this demonstrable and sometimes very substantial annual profit from the sale of heated and chilled water, the developer can finance the central plant so that it does not increase the equity investment.

In some states the developer can go even further and set up a total energy plant, producing the electricity itself by means of gas or other fuels. Such systems are, in effect, private utility companies and subject to state law.

Should the developer wish to stay out of the problems of negotiation with tenants and operation of the central plant, there are companies that will undertake, for suitable remuneration, the construction, operation, and ownership of the system on behalf of the developer. In this case, it is obvious that financial and engineering responsibility of the operating company must be clearly established.

It is always essential that design provision be made in the earliest stages of the planning for all items of mechanical equipment, with allowance for floor space, for weight, for ceiling clearances, and for suitable visual effects of supply and exhaust grilles, especially in malls.

### Parking and Traffic

The need for parking was one of the primary factors leading to the development of the shopping center concept. Provision of adequate and convenient parking is, in fact, a basic requirement of any shopping center, regardless of its size or location. In suburban areas where almost all the trade comes by automobile, a ratio of between 5 and 6 car spaces per 1,000 square feet of leased store area is mandatory. In the central business district, where mass transportation and walk-in trade can be counted on for a substantial part of the clientele, the ratio can go down to as low as 2.5 to 3 cars per 1,000 square feet.

In strip centers, customer parking is generally between the roadway and the line of storefronts.

In regional suburban centers, the parking normally is on grade and completely surrounds the shopping complex. Where land costs approach the cost of parking decks, it is feasible to deck at least a portion of the site area, often where topography aids the situation.

In central-business-district projects, because of very high land cost, parking usually has to be multidecked and is preferably contiguous, connecting directly with different levels of the shopping center. It can also, for further economy of land use, be above the retail floors on decks as roof parking; or, more customarily, it can be below the retail levels in basement or partial basement locations. Though basement parking is the least desirable from the viewpoint of the shopper's normal psychology and is also least desirable from the construction cost point of view, it is a relatively common arrangement due to inadequate land area and to the legal aspects of the federal urban renewal programs. In such programs, in order to conserve land area and cost, the developer frequently can build the complex on air rights over multidecked garage facilities built by one or another government agency.

It has been stated by authorities on the subject, however, that for customer acceptance it is better to have parking above grade, even up to six or eight levels, than to have it more than one or two levels below grade.

In the matter of parking layout, car stalls can be set at angles (say, 70 degrees) to the lanes, which then requires one-way traffic; or stalls can be at 90 degrees to the lanes, permitting two-way traffic. The former is easier for the actual positioning of the car in the stall but more complicated and inflexible for the customer, due to the one-way pattern. Although both are commonly used, the 90-degree arrangement is somewhat more frequent for grade parking whereas the angled system is more customary for garages and decks.

Parking lanes, including the stalls on each side, range from 60 to 64 feet wide for 90-degree parking and from 56 to 58 feet for angled parking. In any decked parking layout, it is important that deck widths be multiples of these standard dimensions. Otherwise, wasted deck area substantially increases the cost per car of the parking without any offsetting advantages. In the case of multi-use central-business-district structures, the proper column spacing, requirements of parking, merchandising, offices, and hotel use vary considerably, and the planning becomes very involved. Practical decisions must be made as to which facility governs, and in no case must the "tail be allowed to wag the dog."

In the typical shopping center, parking is provided by the developer. In the case of central-business-district renewal projects, however, parking may be provided by a parking authority, renewal agency, or others. It may or may not be leased to the developer, or it may be built by the developer and leased to a parking authority or others.

In the case of double-level malls in the suburbs, topography can be an aid rather than a hindrance through provision of on-grade parking at two different levels: one parking area at the level of the upper mall, the other at the lower, thus equalizing the parking access and convenience for each level of the mall.

There are a number of ramp systems for decked parking and various patterns of parking lanes or bays for both ramped and grade parking. In the case of grade parking, lanes or bays should generally be at right angles to the building facades to enable shoppers to walk directly to the building complex without threading through parked cars, as with lanes parallel to the facades.

## Landscaping

This visually important element of shopping center design rarely receives the attention and budget its importance deserves. Most suburban customers have gardens and are landscape-conscious. Nevertheless, there are literally hundreds of shopping centers that are surrounded by barren oceans of monotonous asphalt. The primary reason for this situation is that the landscaping is installed last, is not related directly to the building construction operation, and consequently is vulnerable to "corner cutting" by the developer, especially if the project cost is running over the budget

The landscaping in the regional, suburban shopping center usually has two components: interior, i.e., the landscaping in the mall; and exterior, i.e., that outside the buildings and in the parking areas. Because of the climate control in the typical enclosed mall, tropical planting can be maintained provided that adequate light, water, and drainage are supplied and there is proper maintenance. Although mall landscaping should not be luxurious to the point of blocking views of stores and interfering too much with cross-mall shopper traffic, mall landscaping can become a very powerful attraction to shoppers and provide a great deal of advertising and public relations value (Fig. 11). When conditions are not suitable for living plants, good results can sometimes be obtained with properly fabricated artificial material.

For the exterior landscaping of the project, the principal problems are:

• budget
• proper scale and effect in relation to the buildings
• suitable maintenance, including the problems involved in snow removal
• necessity for obtaining maximum visual impact the first year of the center's operation

As to this last item, the developer is not so concerned with how the planting will look in 10 years because the first 3 years of the center's operation are the most critical. It is during those years that everything must be at its best.

**Fig. 11. Landscaping and signage (Mojo Stumer Associates; photo courtesy of the architect)**

As to scale and effect, it is difficult to obtain satisfactory results when a building mass may be as much as 2,000 feet long and only 20 feet high, and where vast acres of parking must be laid out with maximum convenience for those parking their cars (Fig. 12).

The following basic criteria, if used with imagination and a reasonable budget, can produce maximum effects for minimum costs:

• Mass effects through close spacing of several trees or bushes in clumps or rows. Better to group five trees a few feet apart than to spot them singly, such as at ends of parking lanes, where they will be lost visually.
• Concentration of the planting near the buildings where it will have the most effect, and not on the periphery.
• Use of long lines of hedges (not less than 3 feet high, and of inexpensive plant material if necessary) wherever the parking pattern will permit. The hedges cut the line of sight from the normal eye level at 5 feet and, especially inside a car, at 4 feet. If the hedges are properly located, they can effectively conceal from view large areas of the parking pavement. This can go a long way toward preventing the "sea of asphalt" effect.
• Installation of the maximum-sized plant material the budget will permit. Better to omit parts of the planting and use cheaper varieties of material than to have to wait 10 years for the plants to produce the proper effect.

As the regional centers must grow larger, more complex, and more glamorous to maintain their competitive positions, the quality and extent of the landscaping on future projects should steadily improve.

## List of Stores by Locations

For reference purposes, the alphabetically arranged lists below represent a checklist of stores that the Council* considers suitable for the several categories of real estate location in shopping areas.

*Community Builders Council of the Urban Land Institute

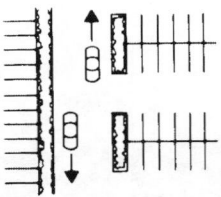

IDEAL LOCATION FOR HEDGES
(3 FT. MIN. HEIGHT) TO
CONCEAL "OCEAN OF ASPHALT."

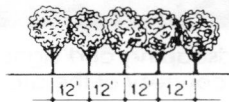

SPACING FOR CONTINUOUS
TREE HEDGE

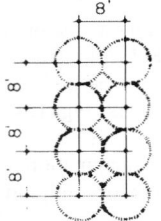

SPACING FOR BOSQUE
OR FORMAL MASS OF
SMALL TREES.

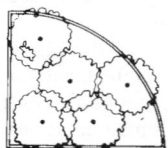

COMPACTED MASS OF
TREES FOR SCALE
EFFECT

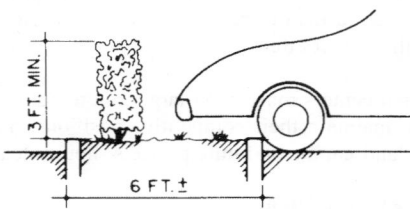

SIMPLE CONTINUOUS HEDGE FOR CONCEALING
"OCEAN OF ASPHALT."

**Fig. 12. Landscaping scale and effect**

### No. 1 Locations (100 Percent or "Hot Spot")

1. Bakery
2. Boys' clothing
3. Candy store
4. Children's wear
5. Cosmetics and perfume
6. Costume jewelry
7. Department store
8. Drugstore
9. Florist
10. Gift shop
11. Girls' apparel
12. Grocery
13. Handkerchiefs and handbags
14. Hosiery shop
15. Infants' wear
16. Jewelry
17. Leather goods and luggage
18. Lingerie
19. Men's clothing
20. Men's furnishings
21. Millinery
22. Novelties
23. Optical shop
24. Paperback book store
25. Photographic supplies and cameras
26. Popcorn and nuts
27. Prescriptions (may not be possible because of drugstore)
28. Restaurant
29. Shoes, children's
30. Shoes, men's
31. Shoes, women's
32. Sportswear, women's
33. Tobacconist
34. Toilet goods
35. Variety store
36. Women's wear

### Either No. 1 or No. 2 Locations

1. Cafeteria
2. Delicatessen
3. Dry goods
4. Newsstand
5. Service grocery

No. 1 locations should be held largely for shops that keep open on certain common nights.

### No. 2 Locations (Near the 100 Percent Area)

1. Art store and artists' supplies
2. Athletic goods
3. Auto supplies
4. Bank
5. Bar
6. Hair stylist
7. Bookstore
8. China and silver

9. Cleaners and dyers (pick-up)
0. Electrical appliances
1. Fruit and vegetable market
2. Glass and china
3. Linen shop
4. Liquor store
5. Maternity clothes
6. Electronics
7. Sewing machines and supplies
8. Sporting goods
9. Stationery and greeting cards
20. Woolens and yarns

A bank should not be in a no. 1 location, as it has limited open hours and when closed has a deadening effect on adjacent shops.

## Either No. 2 or No. 3 Locations

.  Gas, power, and light company offices
.  Theater
.  Ticket offices
.  Toy shop

## No. 3 Locations

1. Army surplus store (or No. 4 location)
2. Art needlework shop
3. Baby furniture
4. Chinese restaurant
5. Christian Science Reading Room (or second floor in No. 2)
6. Dance studio (or No. 4 location)
7. Doctors and dentists
8. Drapery and curtain shop
9. Electronics repair
10. Express delivery service office
11. Furniture (pays low rent per square foot)
12. Hardware
13. Health food store
14. Hobby shop
15. Interior decoration
16. Ladies' and men's tailor (or second floor in No. 1 or No. 2 locations)
17. Mortgage loan office (or second floor in No. 2 location)
18. Office supplies and office furniture
19. Optometrist and optician (or No. 1 or 2)
20. Paint store
21. Photographers (or second floor in No. 1 or No. 2 locations)
22. Piano store
23. Pictures and framing
24. Post office
25. Power and light offices
26. Real estate offices
27. Shoe repair
28. Ticket offices
29. Travel bureau (or No. 2 location)

## No. 4 Locations

1. Automatic family laundry service
2. Bowling alley
3. Carpets and rugs
4. Veterinarian
5. Drive-in eating places
6. Radio and television broadcasting station

## REGIONAL SHOPPING CENTERS*

### Selecting the Site

*Location*

For the purposes of this discussion, the term "location" indicates the general area in which to select a shopping center site. The merits of location, whether the land has already been acquired or is being sought, must always be subjected to careful economic analysis. If the site has already been acquired, the economist directs the study toward the economic characteristics of the location in an effort to decide whether the particular property should be developed as a shopping center project, and if so, what its size and character should be. If the site has not yet been acquired, the economist must make a study of the general area within which the most suitable location can be pinpointed. This over-all study may involve as large an area as the metropolitan area of a large city.

First, an analysis is made of the total available economic potential of the general area. The search is gradually narrowed down through analysis of various segments of the larger area; a specific area within the chosen segment that seems to offer the most advantageous potential is then examined, and finally, a defined location within this specific area is chosen. If properly undertaken, this procedure will usually establish the most suitable location for a shopping center.

Inherent in any economic analysis is a study of the following factors:

- Population
- Income
- Purchasing power
- Competitive facilities
- Accessibility
- Other related considerations

Attention must be paid not only to the existing population but also to prospects for future growth, which may be forecast by reference to past growth rates, the trend of population shifts, and the availability of remaining suitable land for residential development.

*Population*

In forecasting the population trend for 10 or 15 years, consideration must be given to such factors as existing population density, zoning

*Author:* Victor Gruen
*Reviewer:* Mark D. Stumer, AIA
* The illustrations and certain other material in this section have been represented, with permission, from *Shopping Towns USA,* by Victor Gruen and Larry Smith, published by Reinhold Publishing Corp., New York.

restrictions, physical or man-made barriers to the development of new residential areas (mountains, waterways, industrial areas, public parks, cemeteries, airports), and other land uses that would forestall residential development.

*Trade Area*

The term "trade area" is normally defined as "that area from which is obtained the major portion of the continuing patronage necessary for the steady support of the shopping center."

The defining factors used in delineating a trade area vary from center to center. They include, but are not limited to, the size and influence of the proposed retail facilities, planning and design characteristics, travel time to and from the location, the existence of natural or man-made barriers—such as railroads and rivers—that would limit accessibility either in fact or psychologically, and the existence of competitive facilities. Thus the trade areas for various locations will not necessarily assume similar sizes or shapes (Fig. 13).

Shown in the plan are trade areas, means of access, and various barriers to accessibility.

*Site Qualifications*

It is important that the land to be used possess, to the greatest degree possible, the following qualifications:

- The site must be located in the most desirable general area as established by the economic survey.

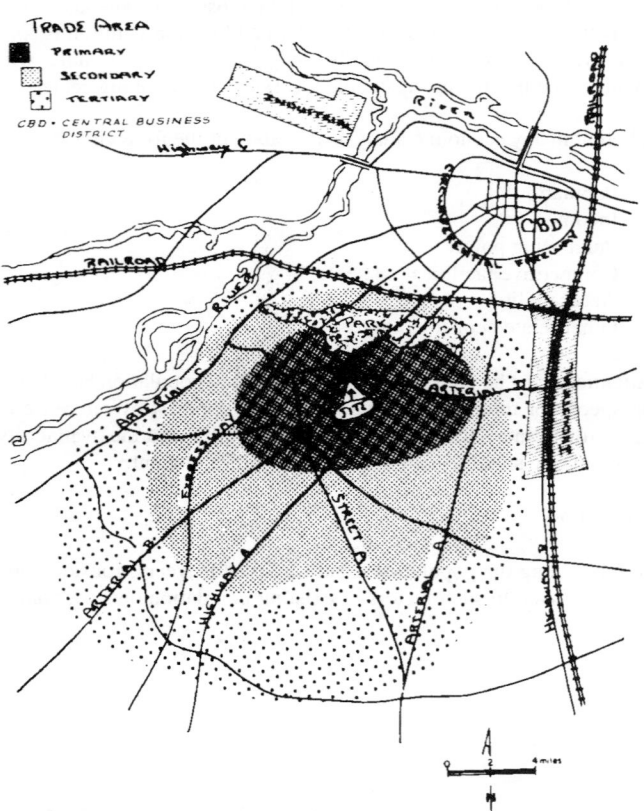

**Fig. 13. Schematic plan of a shopping center location**

- The site must be owned or controlled by the developer, or offer the possibility of acquisition.
- Land cost must be in keeping with overall economic considerations.
- Existing zoning must permit shopping center development, or a reasonable likelihood of rezoning must exist.
- The site must contain sufficient land to permit construction of facilities to meet the sales potential.
- The land must be in one piece, free of intervening roadways, rights-of-way, easements, major waterways, or other obstacles that would force development in separated portions.
- The topography and shape of the site must permit advantageous planning and reasonably economical construction.
- The surrounding road pattern and accessibility must allow full utilization of the business potential.
- The structure must be visible from major thoroughfares.
- Surrounding land uses should be free of competitive developments, and, if possible, should be of a nature that enhances the operation of the shopping center.

Rarely will a site completely fulfill all the above requirements, and advantages will have to be weighed and balanced against shortcomings. If the site already exists, it is sometimes difficult to separate the affection an owner may have for it from the hard facts of suitability, but it is well to remember that most poorly operating centers in the U.S. are located on just such "accidental" sites. It is, of course, possible that an existing site may also fulfill the standard requirements, but determination should be made only after the same thorough scrutiny and analysis that would be given to a site to be purchased.

The following list indicates the relative importance of various considerations in site selection:

| *Location* (value of 50) | Value |
|---|---|
| Population within 1 mile—quantity | 5 |
| Population within 1 mile—quality | 3 |
| Population within 5 miles—quantity | 7 |
| Population within 5 miles—quality | 4 |
| Population from rural area— quantity | 2 |
| Population from rural area—quality | 1 |
| Pedestrian traffic shopping at adjacent stores | 4 |
| Pedestrian traffic nearby for other purposes | 3 |
| Public transportation | 5 |
| Automobile traffic—quantity | 4 |
| Automobile traffic—availability | 4 |
| Direction of population growth | 8 |

| *Area* (value of 15) | |
|---|---|
| Size of plot | 15 |

| *Physical characteristics* (value of 25) | |
|---|---|
| Shape of plot for design | 4 |
| Plot not divided by traffic lanes | 8 |
| Location on arterials for ease of traffic control | 4 |
| Cost of clearing and grading | 2 |
| Cost of utilities and drainage | 2 |
| Visibility | 3 |
| Surrounding areas | 2 |

| *Availability* (value of 10) | |
|---|---|
| Ease of acquisition and time | 6 |
| Cost | 4 |
| | 100% |

### Zoning

Contrary to 19th-Century precepts of strict separation of industrial and residential land, brought about by rapid industrialization, most planners and zoning boards today recognize that not all types of nonresidential activities are necessarily undesirable in predominantly residential areas.

The shopping center that integrates commercial, business, entertainment, and cultural facilities within a carefully planned framework, separates various modes of traffic from one another, and provides for the protection of surrounding residential areas from any objectionable uses, has made a significant contribution in this direction.

The developer may encounter any of the following zoning conditions:

The site is commercially zoned, or zoned for a "lower" use, in which case there is no problem.

The community has not yet adopted a zoning master plan, and the local planning board is willing to grant suitable zoning.

The entire site area is zoned residentially, or only a small portion, usually a narrow strip along the highways, is zoned for commercial use. The owner will then have to apply for rezoning of all or part of the site.

### PLANNING TEAM

Depending on the size and complexity of the project, the planning team might, in neighborhood and intermediate centers, consist of the developer, the architect, and in some instances a leasing consultant or lease broker. In projects of greater complexity and size, such as regional shopping centers, it may be well to add to the team an experienced consultant in real estate matters, well versed in shopping center economics (Fig. 14).

### Planning Schedule

Shopping center planning is a lengthy process in which each step must logically follow from the previous one. Impatient or snap decisions may result in catastrophe. First, a tentative planning and construction schedule is outlined which may be divided into five phases:

1. Exploratory phase
2. Preliminary phase
3. Final planning phase
4. Construction phase
5. Opening phase

For regional centers, each of these phases is likely to be clearly defined and even subdivided into various stages; for smaller centers the activity may be consolidated into fewer stages.

1. *Exploratory phase:* All pertinent circumstances and conditions are thoroughly probed, and the conceptual image of the shopping center is established.

2. *Preliminary phase:* Negotiations with major tenants and financing institutions are undertaken, and necessary adjustments are made. Preliminary drawings indicating all architectural and engineering

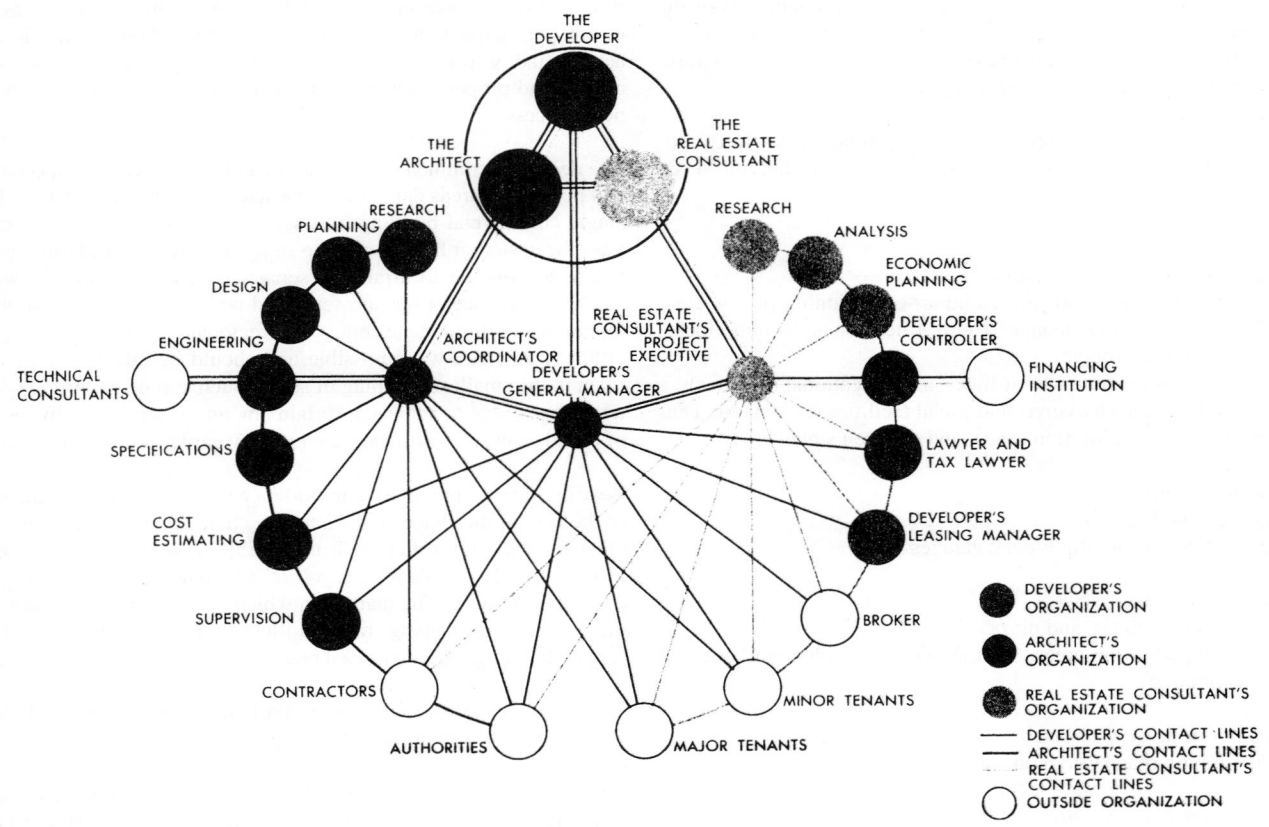

**Fig. 14. One version of a planning team**

aspects are completed. Preliminary specifications are written, and a reliable preliminary cost estimate is arrived at.

3. *Final planning phase:* Working drawings and specifications are completed, establishing a reliable basis for competitive bidding and for construction. Building permits are obtained. Invitations to bid are written.

4. *Construction phase:* Contracts are awarded. The architect is engaged in general supervision, supported by clerks-of-the-works who are usually retained by the developer. The architect chooses materials, selects colors, and integrates landscaping and art work. The developer and the economist are active in completing leasing, getting the center on an operational basis, and preparing for the opening.

5. *Opening phase:* The opening is an important event that calls for imagination as well as careful planning. Shopping centers of varying size throughout the country have been opened with ceremonies ranging from the quiet, unobtrusive opening of a few stores at a time, to mass opening ceremonies lasting for several days and featuring various kinds of promotions.

**Space Allotments**

The architect's work starts with the planning of the site. For this task she must have at her disposal the findings of the economic analysis establishing the total rental area that can be supported by the shopping potential, broken down into main merchandising categories. She must have some idea of other uses to which the land should be devoted, and an idea of other probable zoning problems. On the basis of feasibility studies, she now has a general idea of traffic and accessibility, as well as full information about physical conditions of the site (including a topographic survey) and, as a result of test borings, about soil conditions. Sometimes she also knows the basic requirements of the potential major tenant or tenants.

With this information, the architect begins planning by carefully allocating portions of the land to specific uses. These uses fall into seven basic categories:

1. *Structures*
- For retail purposes (retail areas)
- For service purposes (heating and air-conditioning plants, electric substations, maintenance shops, truck roads, loading docks, and equipment storage)
- For other commercial uses (offices and recreational facilities)
- For public use such as civic and social facilities (community center auditorium, exhibition space, and children's play areas)

2. *Car storage areas*
- Surface parking lots
- Double-deck or multiple-deck garages

3. *Pedestrian areas*
- Malls, courts, lanes, and plazas
- Covered pedestrian areas, such as public corridors and covered malls or courts

4. *Automobile movement areas*
- Distribution road system on site

5. *Public transportation areas*
- Bus roads, bus terminals, and taxi stands

6. *Buffer areas*
- Landscaped areas separating car storage areas or service areas from the public road system
- Areas separating parking areas from one another or parking areas from service areas

7. *Reserve areas*
- Portions of site to be held in reserve for the planned growth of the shopping center

**Site Planning Principles**

The allocation of space for these and possibly other uses should be guided by certain planning principles in order to attain the highest feasible productivity of the land over an extended period of time:

- Expose retail facilities to maximum foot traffic
- Separate various mechanized traffic types from one another and from foot traffic
- Create a maximum of comfort and convenience for shoppers and merchants
- Achieve orderliness, unity, and beauty

**Foot Traffic**

Exposure of all individual stores in a shopping center to the maximum amount of foot traffic is the best assurance of high sales volume. Suburban business real estate often has been evaluated on the basis of passing automobile traffic—an evaluation that overlooks the fact that automobiles do not buy merchandise. It is only after the driver of even the most expensive car leaves it and becomes a pedestrian that she can become a buyer. Therefore, if shopping centers are to prosper, dense foot traffic must be created. Shopping traffic, the act of walking from store to store, creates the lifeblood of a shopping center; and proper circulation of this shopping traffic ensures business success.

The degree of completeness of the separation between transportation and pedestrian areas depends on the size of the shopping center. In a single commercial building, this separation becomes effective only after the customer has entered the store. If there are two buildings, it might be possible to arrange a separated pedestrian area between them. The chances to create separated pedestrian areas are slightly higher in an intermediate center. In a regional center, complete separation is almost always possible and should be effected (Fig. 15). Even in the smallest grouping of stores, such as a neighborhood center, it is possible to achieve a certain amount of separation by means of broad sidewalks with landscaping, low garden walls, and the like.

Bearing in mind the relative importance in each instance of the size of the center, the shape of the site, the character of the tenancy, and other related circumstances, it is possible to weigh the advantages and drawbacks of various types of site planning to achieve the desired foot traffic. The manner in which site planning can influence the quantity of shopping traffic is illustrated in the schematic plans (Figs. 16 through 22) discussed below.

The following are a number of parking arrangements and their impact on the shopping center:

*Strip center with curb parking (Fig. 16):* In this plan, the shopping center is comprised of a row of stores extending 2,000 feet along the highway. The shopper parks at the curb in front of the store, transacts

Fig. 15. Separation of pedestrian and vehicular areas (Mojo Stumer Associates; photo courtesy of the architect)

■ SHOPS

├———┤ PARKING

Fig. 16. Strip center with curb parking

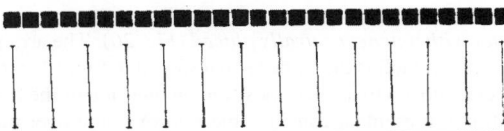

Fig. 17. Strip center with off-street parking

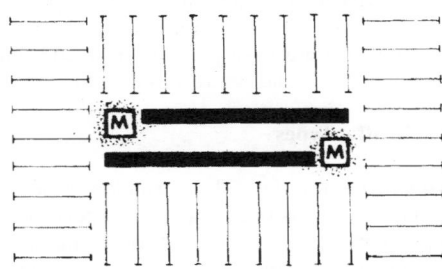

Fig. 18. Double-strip center with off-street parking

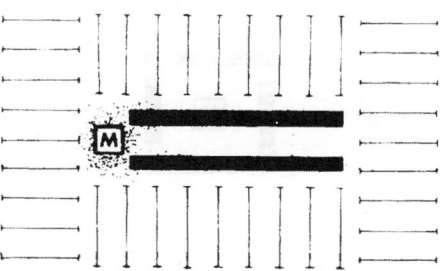

Fig. 19. Mall center with only one magnet

her business, and then is likely to enter her car and drive off. Shopping or foot traffic is limited.

*Strip center with off-street parking (Fig. 17):* This shopping center consists of a 2,000-foot-long row of stores set back from the highway sufficiently to permit parking in front. The sidewalk, or covered walkway, encourages foot traffic along the store fronts. This plan generates a certain amount of shopping traffic and thus is clearly superior to the type shown in Fig. 16. Shopping traffic is nevertheless limited chiefly because of the 2,000-foot distance between the extreme ends of the strip. The shopper may return to her car after each transaction and drive to the next store on her list, ignoring intervening merchants.

*Double-strip center with off-street parking (Fig. 18):* Here, the strip is divided into two rows of stores, facing each other along a pedestrian mall, with parking on four sides. A "magnet" (department store, junior department store, or other major tenant store) is placed at each end. The 2,000-foot strip of stores is now divided into two 1,000-foot-long strips. With the distance between the two magnets now only half as great, foot traffic will be greater and the intervening stores will profit accordingly. Also, the creation of a highly desirable pedestrian area shielded from the noise, smells, confusion, and hazards of automobile traffic will contribute to greater shopping traffic.

*Mall center with only one magnet (Fig. 19):* In this plan, the existence of only one magnet, located at the extreme end of the pedes-

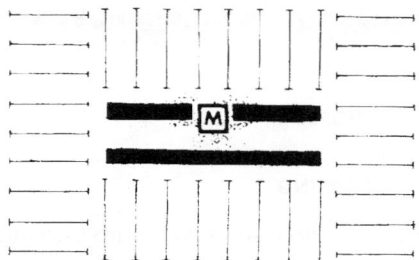

**Fig. 20. Mall center with magnet centrally placed**

trian mall, reduces shopping traffic because of lack of interchange. The stores farthest from the magnet will participate very little in the traffic it generates.

*Mall center with magnet centrally placed (Fig. 20):* The arrangement of the pedestrian mall is the same as that shown in Fig. 19, except that the magnet is moved to a center position on one side of the mall. This modification represents a considerable improvement over the previous example.

*Cluster-type center (Fig. 21):* The major tenant is placed in the center of a cluster arrangement. Nearly all stores thus become neighbors of the most powerful shopping—traffic puller.

*Introverted center (Fig. 22):* This type exemplifies what might be called the "introverted" center, in which all store fronts are turned toward the inside of the building cluster. Entry into individual stores directly from the parking lot is diminished or completely excluded. Shopping traffic is funneled through a limited number of entrance arcades into pedestrian areas—a plan that markedly increases the density of shopping traffic and controls its direction.

**Separation of Traffic Types**

*Pedestrian from transportation:* The separation of pedestrian areas from transportation areas is one of the cornerstones of good planning. The constant movement of vehicles within transportation areas inevitably creates a certain amount of danger, noise, fumes, and confusion, which distract the shopper and diminish shopping enjoyment.

*Service from customer traffic:* Service traffic in shopping centers represents a considerable portion of mechanized traffic. Even in the smallest shopping center, service vehicles for deliveries, pick-ups, garbage and trash collection, repair crews, construction and fixture contractors, and utility companies create a significant portion of the over-all traffic. Separation of service traffic from customer traffic is essential and may be accomplished on one or two levels.

Service areas on the merchandising or ground level in the form of truck roads, service courts, and other types of loading facilities, are practical in the neighborhood and intermediate centers. Good planning principles demand that such areas be properly shielded by screen walls or landscaping and that service vehicles be able to enter or leave without interference from automobiles or pedestrians.

Service areas on nonmerchandising levels permit the most productive space to be totally freed from service functions. Only the large center can achieve this separation, for which there are a number of possible arrangements. The truck tunnel under the shopping center mall is an expensive solution that is more talked about than used. Service roads located at the basement level provide a less expensive solution and are widely used. Where subsurface or topographical conditions make the construction of basements impractical, service and storage areas may be placed above the merchandising level and connected to it by ramps.

*Public transportation from customer traffic:* Separation of public transportation from customer traffic is essential. The designer must also consider the space needs for public transportation. Generous arrangements for public carriers with well-located and well-protected waiting areas will encourage transportation companies to use them. Space requirements for existing and future public transportation facilities should be discussed at the outset of site planning work, and if possible, provisions should exceed the required minimum. Storage space for buses should be provided on or near the site so the transportation company can make extra facilities available for peak periods, especially at closing hours.

The plan shown in Fig. 24 represents the architect's suggestions for the surrounding land use for the same shopping center shown in Fig. 23. The revisions ensure control of the surrounding land by the developer.

**Planning for Expansion**

Planning for expansion should be considered if the shopping center is located in a steadily growing area. In such a situation the department store and other major stores will often express the desire to enlarge when their sales volume reaches a stated figure.

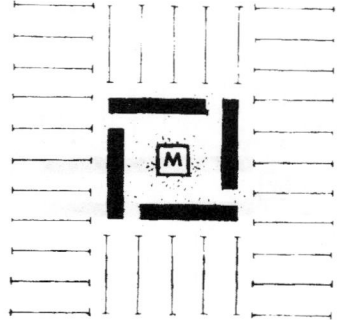

**Fig. 21. Cluster-type center**

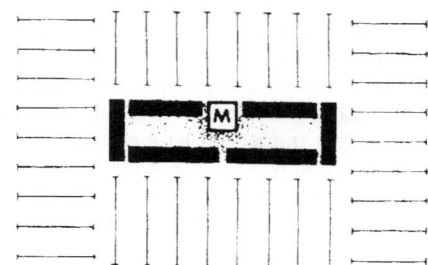

**Fig. 22. "Introverted" center**

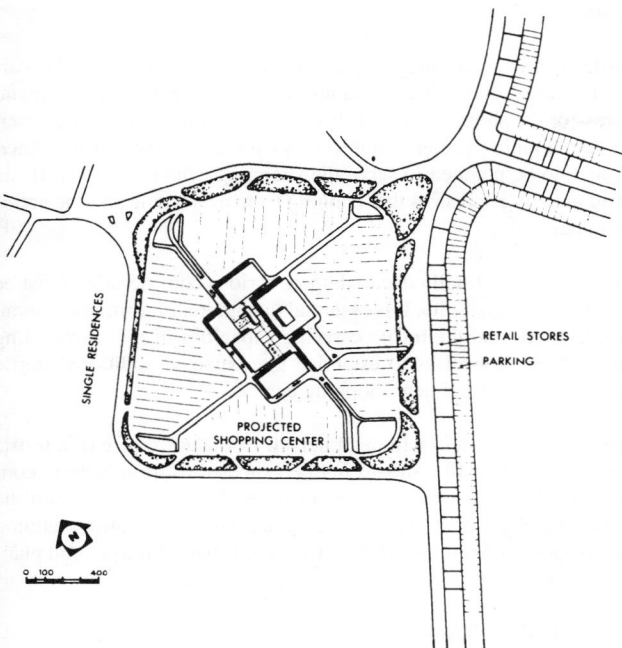

SINGLE RESIDENCES

RETAIL STORES

PARKING

PROJECTED
SHOPPING CENTER

0   100   400

**Fig. 23. Original zoning plan**

In order to make planning for expansion feasible, certain prerequisites must exist:

- The carrying potential of surrounding public roads must be sufficient to absorb additional traffic loads.
- The site must be large enough to permit the developer to hold space in reserve for additional building, parking, and traffic areas.
- Additionally created income must be such as to justify capital investment for double-deck or multiple-deck parking structures at the time of enlargement.
- Most important, the developer must be reasonably certain that the growing buying potential of the area will not be more efficiently served by existing or future competition. For example, if suitable shopping center sites exist within the trade area, the likelihood of such future competition is great.
- These and other related factors must be carefully considered before making a decision to plan for expansion.

If it is decided to plan with a view to expansion, certain measures must be taken:

- Since the desire of department stores and other major tenant stores for growth is usually best met by provisions for vertical additions, the construction of larger foundations and heavier columns as well as roof slabs strong enough to carry future floor loads are required.

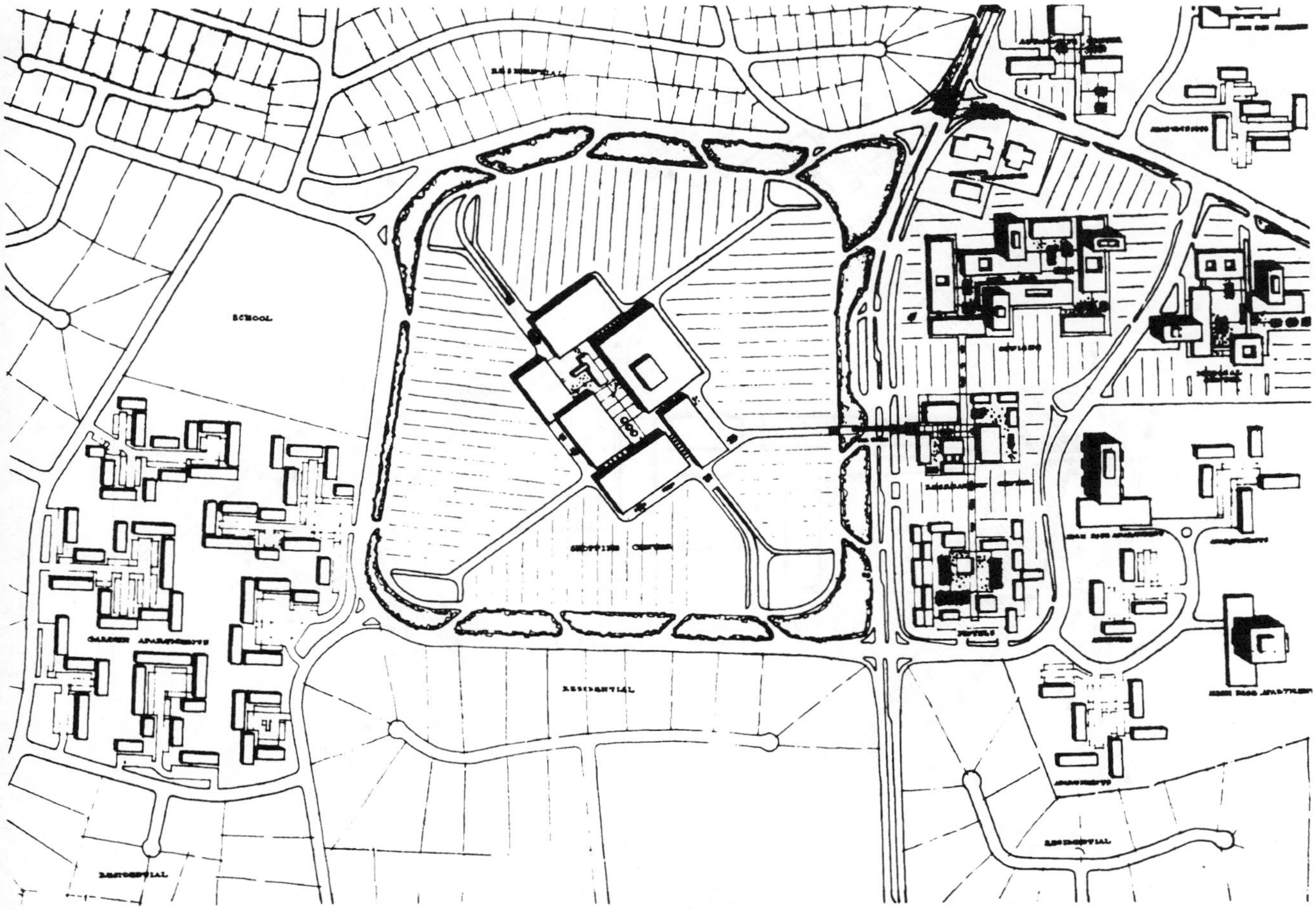

**Fig. 24. Revised zoning plan**

- Horizontal growth is difficult to accomplish without destroying the relationship between shopping center buildings and other elements. Land must be held in reserve for the enlarged parking needs that will be created by expanded shopping facilities. When the original construction is completed, these reserve areas will have to be properly landscaped in order not to mar the overall appearance of the center.
- Central air-conditioning and heating-plant structures must be dimensioned to provide space for additional equipment, and all underground utility lines should be of sufficient size to meet ultimate needs.
- The general plan shown in Fig. 25 indicates existing structures and provisions for expansion.

### Planning for Development in Stages

Planning for development in stages should be considered if the shopping center site is located in an area that has not reached its ultimate population potential and if a quick acceleration of population growth may be expected. Another motivation for development in stages may be the desire of a land owner to make some immediate use of the land even though full utilization will be practical only in future years.

Planning for development in stages can be successfully accomplished only if a total master site-use plan is completed before construction or even detailed planning of the first stage is undertaken.

### Traffic

Traffic planning, an integral part of planning the site and the surrounding area, plays an important role in the proper functioning and success of the shopping center. It should be borne in mind, however, that the shopping center is not to be planned to serve traffic; rather, traffic is to be planned to serve the shopping center (Fig. 26). Basic traffic planning concerns the planning team as a whole and the architect in particular.

Before the site is finally decided upon, serious consideration must be given to its accessibility. It is essential to gather all information about existing roads and the traffic-carrying capacities of the surrounding road system, as well as to establish the expected additional traffic load generated by the new shopping center.

Although the architect will avail herself of the assistance of a traffic engineer, the specialist should not be expected to furnish basic concepts but should assist the architect in finding solutions within the framework of general and specified planning aims. Traffic planning is the responsibility of the architect since it is part of the general planning of the center.

### Aims of Traffic Planning

*Easy traffic flow on surrounding road system.* The existence of enterprises that would result in a constant entering and exiting of cars

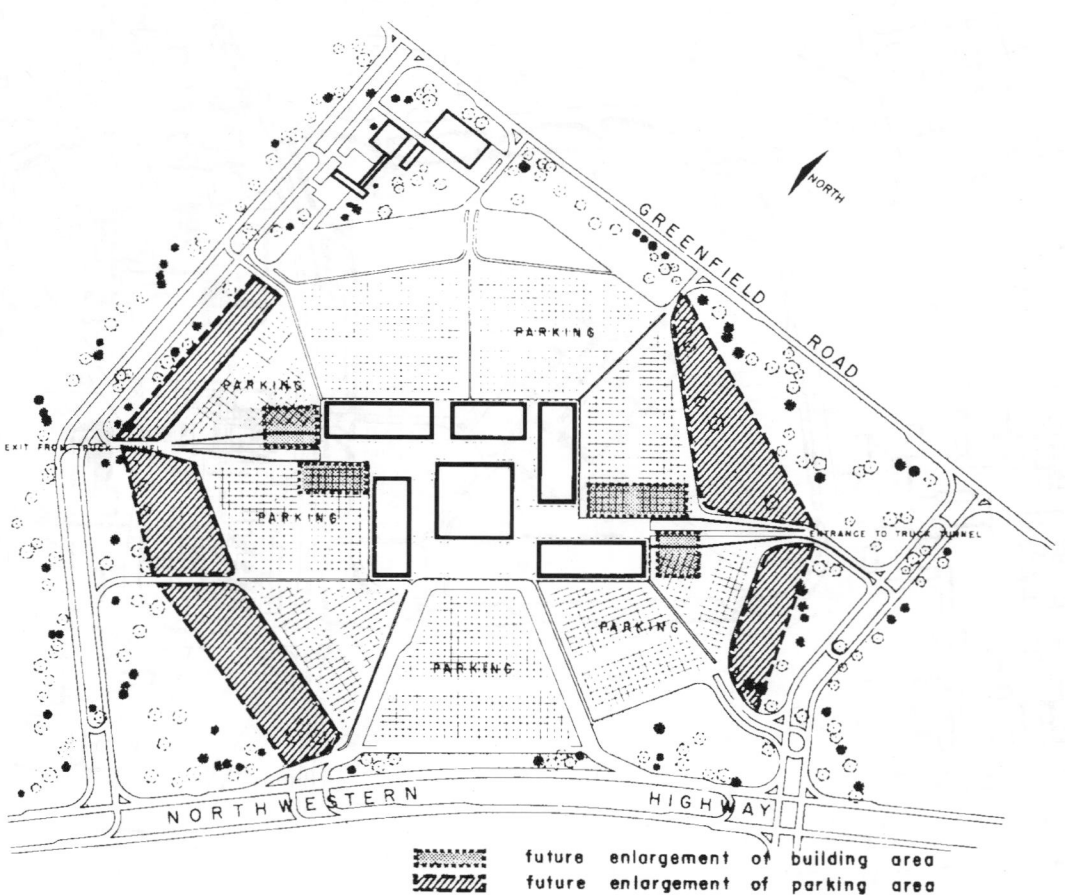

**Fig. 25. Plan for expansion Northland Center, Detroit (Victor Gruen Associates, Architects)**

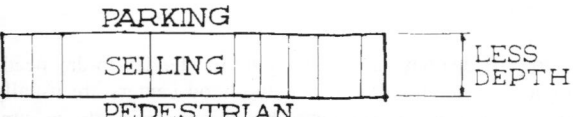

Small depth is needed if service facilities are in basements and pedestrian traffic moves only on one side of structure

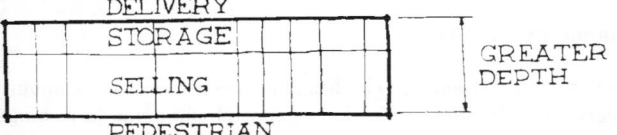

Greater depth is needed if delivery is at back of store on ground level and storage facilities have to be provided on **ground level for each tenant**

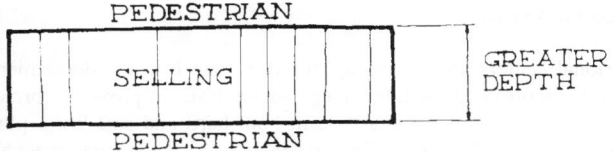

Greater depth is needed if shopping traffic moves on both sides of individual stores

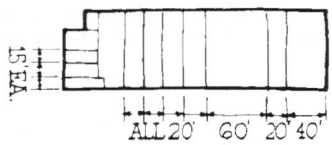

Stores of varying depth and width can be arranged between multiple-tenant structures by skillful division and orientation of stores

**Fig. 26. Depth requirements for tenant stores according to traffic and access**

along the roads opposite the shopping center would disrupt the flow of traffic and is therefore highly undesirable. (This is one reason why proper planning of the surrounding area is so important.) The existence of many side roads opposite the shopping center would also interfere with good traffic flow. The planner's main task is to see to it that automobiles can enter the site without slowdowns.

*Effective transfer of road traffic onto the site.* If automobiles are driven directly from an adjoining highway onto parking-lot lanes, chaos will result. The circulatory road that functions as a turn-off lane from the highway, making possible a gradual change of speed from fast-moving traffic to slower parking-lot traffic, plays an extremely important role.

*Even and effective distribution of traffic on the site.* The customer should be free to drive to any of the parking areas that surround the center so that she may come as close as possible to the store where she will make her first purchase. Secondary traffic movements within the parking area must be facilitated. In larger centers, arrangements must be made to guarantee the easy flow of circulatory traffic, avoid-

ing any interference with pedestrians walking to and from the center's structures.

*Convenient and efficient arrangement of car storage facilities.* The aim of the parking-lot layout should not be to achieve the greatest possible number of parking stalls, but rather to ensure the greatest possible turnover of cars during a given period. Parking capacity is a valid measuring stick only if it denotes the number of conveniently arranged and dimensioned parking stalls.

Walkways for pedestrians provide greater safety for shoppers and will eliminate the slowing down of vehicles, but will reduce the number of parking spaces in any area. Surfacing of good quality will speed parking and reduce maintenance costs. Lanes should be clearly numbered with signs visible to the motorists when entering the lot as well as when returning from shopping. Proper illumination is essential for safety and speed of parking operations.

No formula for proportioning parking area to sales area is recommended. Existing successful shopping centers provide from 3 to 9 car spaces per 1,000 square feet of rental area; however, each project must be decided on its own merits. An allowance of 400 square feet per stall, including drives, walks, and landscaping, is recommended. Wide stalls arranged at a 45-degree angle permit the fastest and most comfortable parking. The maximum size recommended for a single parking lot is 800 cars.

*Separation of service vehicles from customer car traffic.* For service vehicles (trucks, trailers, and garbage and trash collecting vehicles), separate roads, branching off from the general road system at points removed as far as possible from the shopping area, should be provided. Ideally—and this can be accomplished in large regional shopping centers—separate entrances and exits to the public road system should be planned. If this arrangement is not feasible, the service roads should branch off from the perimeter circulatory road or, in smaller centers, from general entrance and exit roads before such roads take on the characteristics of parking lanes. Under no circumstances should service vehicles cross roads that directly serve parking operations. Public transportation vehicles should be similarly separated from customer car traffic.

**Character of Buildings**

The shopping center establishes a new environment resulting from the banding together of individual businesses in cooperative fashion with the aim of creating greater commercial effectiveness through unified endeavor. It is important that the individual characteristics of the participants not be suppressed, but encouraged. It is equally important, however, that a strong common denominator be created to tie the individual enterprises into a homogeneous unit (Fig. 27). These dual aims can be achieved by skillful planning and design. Buildings for single tenancy, for example, are planned not only in accordance with the specific requirements of the specific tenant, but also in harmony with the character of the overall shopping center architecture. Such buildings thus offer a variation of the main theme rather than the introduction of a new one.

Regimentation is as much to be shunned as anarchy. Complete control of store-front design results in monotony and dullness, and diminishes the enjoyment of window shopping, which thrives on excitement created by ever-changing designs and colors. The cooperative spirit is best expressed if individual design of tenant stores is encouraged within established limits; around these individual design

**Fig. 27. Strong architectural character (Mojo Stumer Associates; photo courtesy of the architect)**

areas there must be a framework of architecturally controlled areas large enough and treated with sufficient forcefulness to hold the varying expressions firmly together (Fig. 28).

### Pedestrian Areas

Open spaces must be more than narrow lanes between long rows of stores. They must be busy and colorful, exciting and stimulating, must make walking enjoyable and provide places for rest and relaxation. All the senses should be rewarded. Trees, flowers, fountains, sculpture, and murals, as well as the architecture of freestanding structures, are vital parts of the over-all scheme. Public events such as holiday celebrations and exhibitions are all parts of the life in these open spaces, as are outdoor cafes and restaurants.

Shopping must thus be understood as more than a utilitarian activity. The environment should be so attractive that customers will enjoy these trips, will stay longer, and return more often (Fig. 29). This will result in cash registers ringing more often and recording higher sales.

### SHOPPING CENTERS

Within the industry, centers are generally classified by functional type categories that are usually related to size but are not controlled by it.

### Neighborhood Centers

Designed to provide convenience shopping for the day-to-day needs of the immediate neighborhood, neighborhood centers are usually anchored by a supermarket supported by stores offering drugs, sundries, and personal services. The majority of neighborhood centers range from 90,000 to 100,000 square feet of gross leaseable area (GLA) and are sited on 3 to 10 acres.

### Community Centers

In addition to convenience goods and personal services, community centers typically offer a selection of apparel and home furnishings. Anchors commonly consist of a junior department store and/or a large variety store in addition to one or more supermarkets. The size ranges from 100,000 to 300,000 square feet of GLA and the land area from 10 to 30 acres.

### Regional Centers

Regional centers are always anchored by one full-line department store (or more) and include enough other stores to provide a broad selection of general merchandise in both hard and soft lines, plus food and personal services. Regional centers are designed to meet all the shopping needs of a large residential area and usually range in size from about 300,000 to 1,000,000 square feet of GLA, occupying 30 to 50 acres. Although they account for less than 5 percent of all United States shopping centers, regional centers have had an enormous impact on the industry and were the first to challenge downtown shopping districts.

### Superregional Centers

Similar to regional centers, but are bigger and draw upon a larger trade area, superregional centers include three or more full-line department stores and well over 100 tenants. They offer a wide variety of personal services; food outlets, often in the form of a food cluster; and general merchandise in both soft and hard lines. Superregional centers, which usually cover 50 or more acres, comprise at least a million square feet of GLA and some are larger than 2.5 million square feet.

### Specialty Centers and Theme Centers

Generally appealing to a relatively narrow segment of the total market, specialty and theme centers are almost always anchorless and their tenants are mainly local stores rather than chains. Frequently, such centers are located in high-tourist and/or high-income areas, and restaurants contribute greatly to their drawing power. Sometimes located in historic landmark buildings or districts, they use existing or newly constructed space in unusually creative ways. Because their regular customers come from only a limited area, most are kept relatively small, usually less than 250,000 square feet of GLA and often in the 50,000 to 70,000 square foot range.

### Mixed-Use Centers

Mixed-use centers typically combine at lead three revenue-producing uses from among retail, office, parking, restaurant, hotel, residential, and entertainment facilities. They may be built in suburban or urban areas, and in the latter often contribute significantly to the revitalization of inner cities. In downtown areas, where land costs are high, a multilevel or high-rise, single-mass design is commonly used to min-

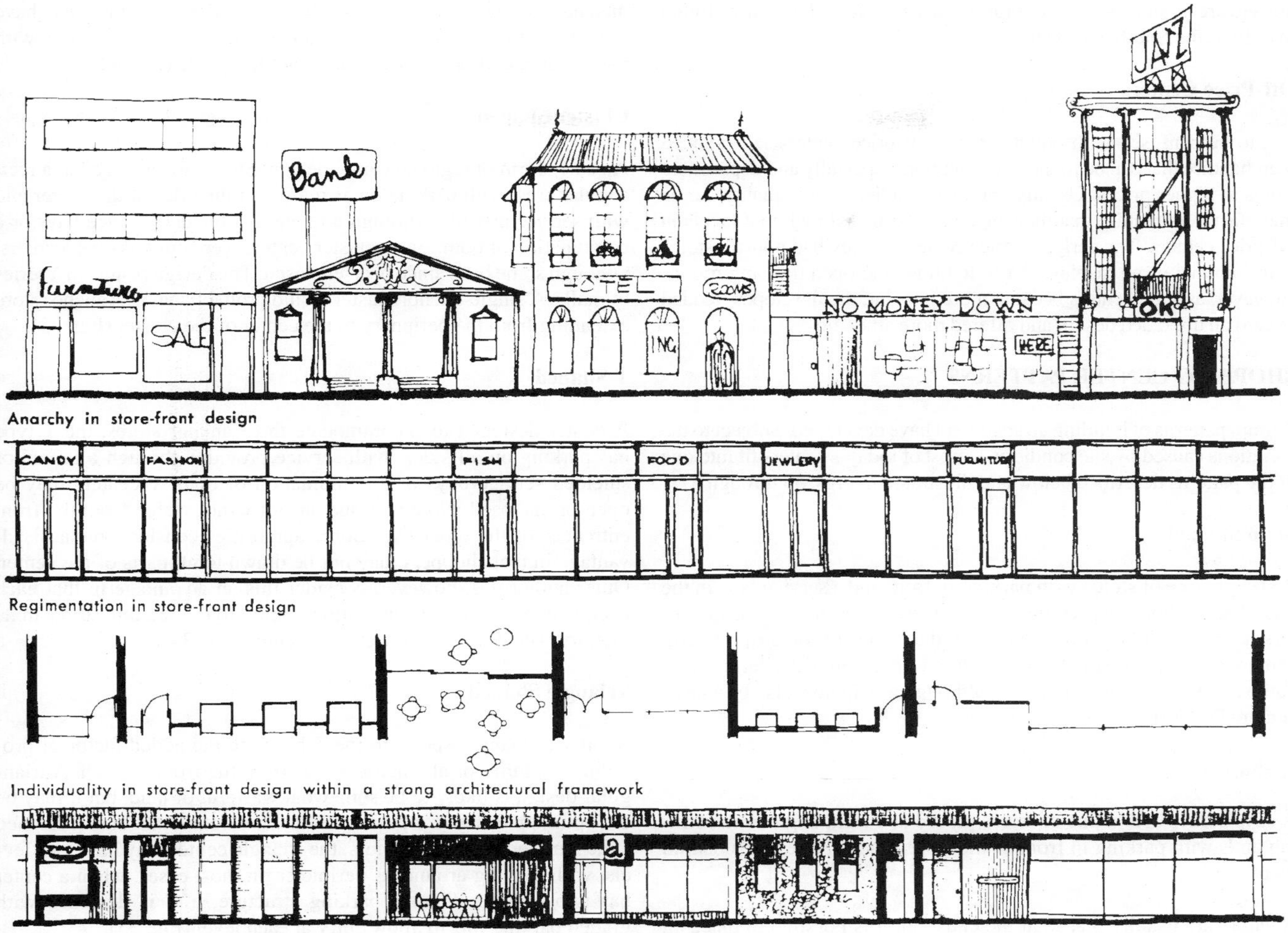

Anarchy in store-front design

Regimentation in store-front design

Individuality in store-front design within a strong architectural framework

**Fig. 28. Storefront design**

imize the land area needed. A key requirement for the success of a mixed-use center is that even though the uses work synergistically to enhance one another's performance, each use must be independently successful.

## Urban Centers

Also contributing to the revitalization of downtown areas, urban centers are usually part of a city's urban-renewal program. They usually include a pedestrian mall and/or covered walkways (particularly in areas of climate extremes) and are built right in the traditional shopping district. Characteristically, urban centers feature a parklike atmosphere, absence of cars, freedom to move about among a variety of retail stores, and, in many cases, a food court.

## Outlet Centers

Designed to sell goods at lower-than-normal prices outlet centers are of two types: One is the factory, or manufacturer's outlet where retail stores are owned and operated by manufacturers and sell the manufacturers' own irregular or overrun merchandise. The other sells many kinds of merchandise bought on consignment or as factory overruns, irregulars, or overstocked items. A majority of outlet centers sell clothing; but others carry luggage, books, home textiles,

**Fig. 29. Attractive shopping environment (photo courtesy of John M. Maher)**

housewares, and home decorating accessories. They are found mostly in the South and East.

### Off-Price Centers

Not to be confused with outlet centers, off-price centers sell branded merchandise that can be found in conventional specialty and department stores at higher prices. Usually, the merchandise is first-quality. Some manufacturers require that their merchandise be sold without labels in off-price centers. The early off-price centers usually had nonfrill stores with minimal or no displays, basic lighting, and open dressing rooms. However, as such centers became more popular, the developers tended toward an upgraded design and offered more amenities.

### SHOPPING CENTER PATTERNS

Certain patterns of building arrangement have developed. Subject to the variations caused by site conditions, most of today's centers fit into one of the patterns described below and illustrated in Figs. 30 through 37.

### Strip Shaped

A straight line of stores with parking in front and a service lane in the rear. The anchor store, commonly a supermarket in small strip centers, is placed either at one end or in the center of the strip. A strip center is usually a small neighborhood center and the terms have come to be used interchangeably; although a strip may also be a large center (Fig. 30).

### L Shaped

A strip center with a line of stores placed at a right angle to it, forming an L with parking in front of the stores and service lanes behind them.

Anchors are usually pieced at the ends, but it is possible to place an anchor in the crook formed by the two lines of stores. The L shape is adaptable to corner locations and is used widely for both neighborhood and community-type centers (Fig. 31).

### U Shaped

A strip center with two lines of stores placed at right angles to the strip, forming a U, with parking in front of the stores and service lanes behind them. U-shaped centers usually have more store space than a strip of L's and consequently tend to be community-type rather than neighborhood-type centers. Because of their size, they may have as many as three anchors, one at each end and one in the middle, with the major anchor generally located in the middle (Fig. 32).

### Cluster Shaped

An early form of regional center design. Stores are arranged in a rectangular area, with parking on as many as four sides of the center and with service provided through a tunnel or shielded service bays or a combination of both. Early cluster centers were built as open centers, although some have since been enclosed. The design results in a series of malls. A single-anchor cluster would probably have its anchor store extending from the periphery to the center of the cluster (Fig. 33).

### T Shaped

A center designed to accommodate three anchor stores, the T type has parking on all sides, with service provided through a tunnel or shielded service bays or a combination of both. T centers may be open or enclosed. Note that one anchor is not viable from the front entrances of the other two. Some authorities consider this a disadvantage in that shoppers may not be drawn to all parts of the center. Other authorities, however, consider this an advantage in that each anchor store provides an attraction helpful to the satellite stores in its vicinity. The T may be a two-level center (Fig. 34).

### Triangle Shaped

Similar in many respects to the T but with the added factor of providing visibility of all anchor stores from the front of each. A triangular design is likely to be somewhat wasteful of land, but it may be the optimum design for those sites that are not rectangular. Designed to accommodate three anchors, the triangle center may have two levels, with parking around its perimeter. In most cases, when a center has two levels without a parking structure, a U is designed with graded parking lots to allow entry at each level (Fig. 35).

### Dumbbell Shaped

A double strip of stores placed face-to-face along a mall, with anchor stores placed at both ends of the mall, and with parking on all sides. The dumbbell is designed so that the anchors draw traffic along the mall in an effort to achieve maximum interchange of shoppers (Fig. 36).

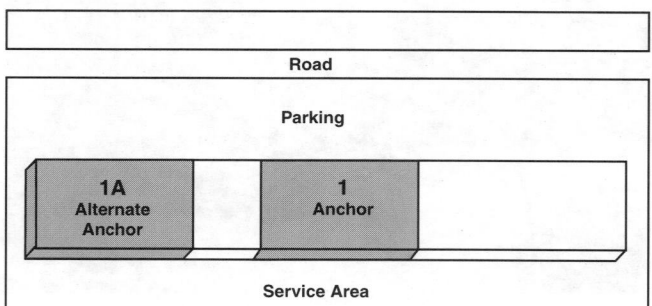

Fig. 30. Strip shaped

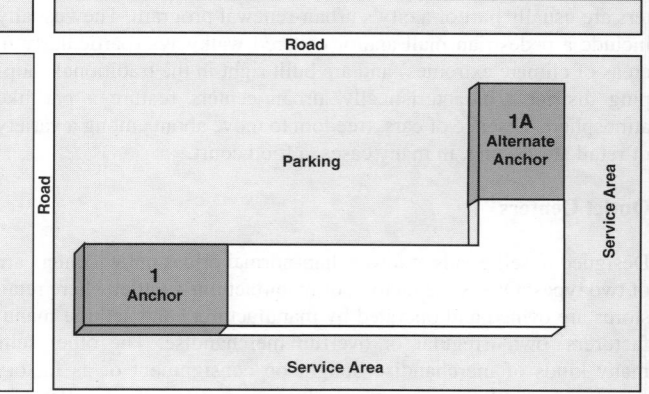

Fig. 31. L shaped

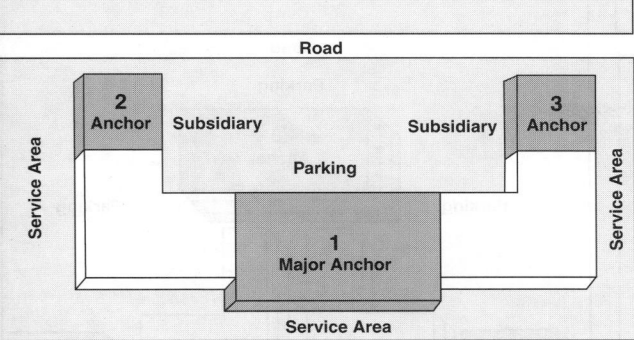

Fig. 32. U shaped

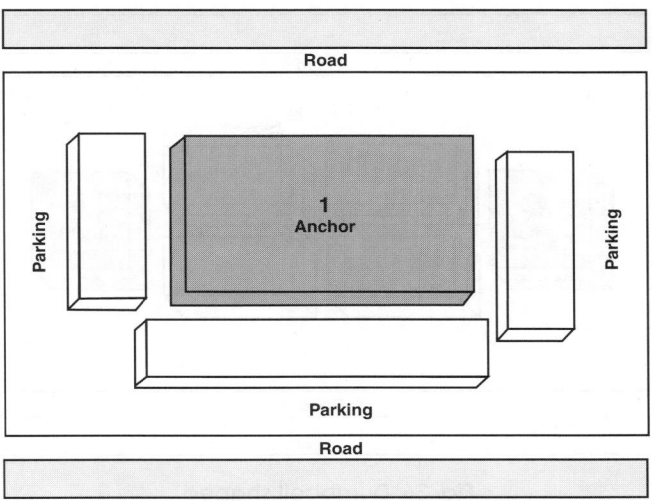

Fig. 33. Cluster shaped

## Double-Dumbbell Shaped

Essentially a dumbbell-type center. One dumbbell runs longitudinally and a second dumbbell runs latitudinally, forming malls that cross in a central court. This design accommodates four anchor stores and provides parking on four sides of the center and in the intervening U-shaped areas. Service to stores is available through a tunnel or service bays (Fig. 37).

## Vertical Shaped

Among the newer shopping center patterns, the high-rise mall has escalators and elevators to carry people from floor to floor. Frequently, the stores are placed around a central atrium. Such centers are usually in downtown areas or close to other high-density developments.

Large centers built in years past had open malls. Those being built today are almost invariably closed-mall centers.

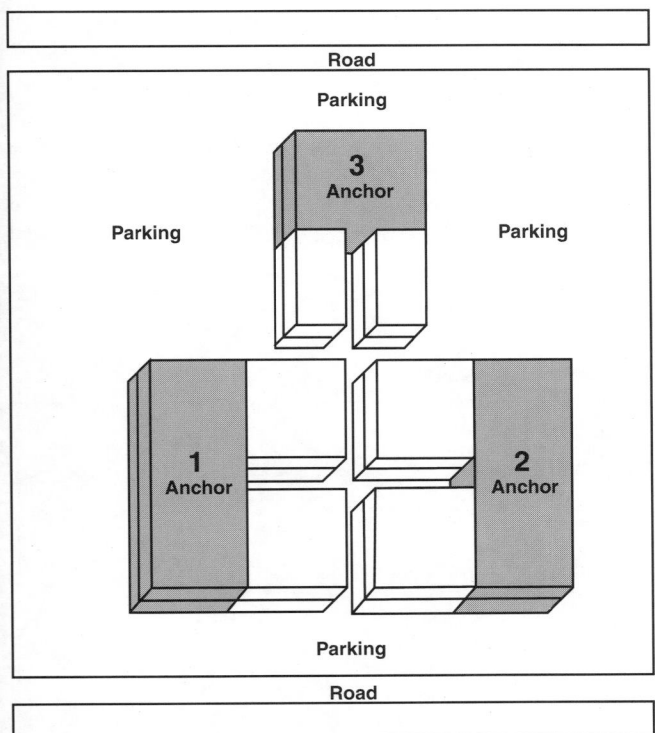

Fig. 34. T shaped

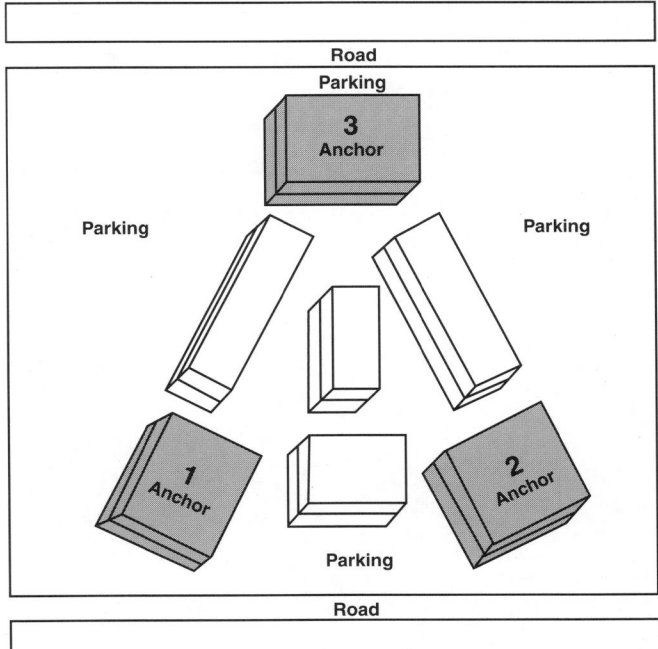

Fig. 35. Triangle shaped

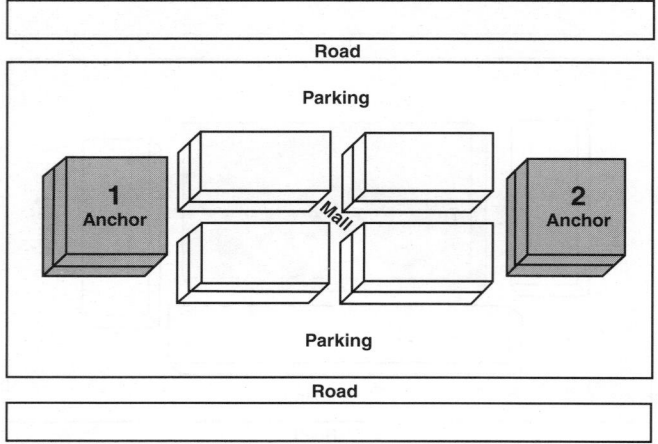

Fig. 36. Dumbbell shaped

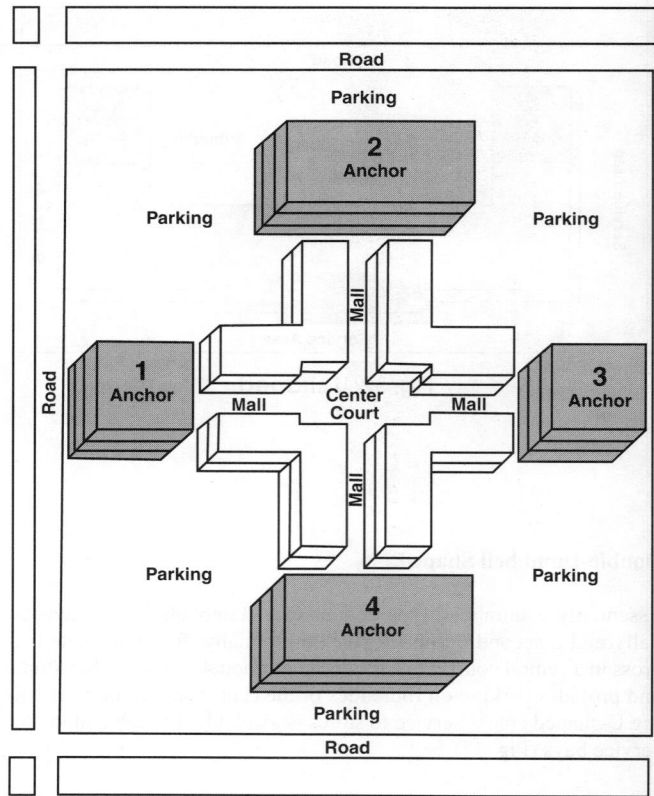

Fig. 37. Double-dumbbell shaped

Fig. 1. Auto dealer (Mojo Stumer Associates; photo: courtesy of architect)

# AUTOMOBILE DEALER CENTERS

### SITE

The ideal site is a wide, level, rectangular lot on the corner of a primary thoroughfare. If an interior lot must be used, it should have wide frontage for display purposes (Fig. 1) and sufficient depth for future expansion. While in some cases the suburbs may provide the ideal dealership site, in metropolitan areas with space limitations it may be necessary to plan on expanding upward, by adding levels to present facilities, to relieve growing pains.

### Space Allocation

The site selected should contain sufficient usable space to provide for an adequate building and the necessary outside lot area. Ordinarily, the space allocation is approximately 60 percent outside area and 40 percent inside or under roof area. The inside space of a dealership is ordinarily apportioned into four major areas approximately as shown in Table 1.

### Table 1  Inside Space Proportions

| Inside area | Percent total inside space |
| --- | --- |
| Service department | 70 |
| Parts department | 14 |
| Showroom | 11 |
| Administration offices | 5 |

*References:* Planning Guides, General Motors Corporation, Detroit, Michigan
*Reviewer:* Mark D. Stumer, AIA

These figures in Table 1 are basic averages, and therefore will not be exactly the same in all cases. Slight upward revisions in space allocation should be provided in the service department area for dealerships doing a large service business.

Outside space apportionment generally takes into consideration the requirements for car display (Fig. 2), service parking, new car storage, and employee parking. Space allocation among these four areas varies according to the sales volume set up in the planning potential of the dealership. In general, twice as much space is allotted to service parking as employee parking, and used car display requires roughly twice the space needed for new car storage.

## SPACE ANALYSIS

The illustrated building layout (Fig. 3) was prepared as an example, in accordance with recommendations for a conventional dealership building design (see also Table 2).

|  | Square feet |
| --- | --- |
| Total building area | 46,200 |
| Showroom and administrative offices | 7,200 |
| Parts department | 6,500 |
| Service department | 32,500 |
| Number of service stalls | 66 |

### Planning Potential

A dealership's planning potential is a reasonably expected annual new car sales potential, which a properly located dealership with adequate facilities, and effective personnel and management, should be expected to retail profitably over the business cycle. Planning potential is a measure of the sales potential, based on the actual high price group market within the dealership's area of sales responsibility and, as such, is not necessarily a measure of the dealership's past or expected retail unit sales performance. It is against this planning figure that space guides are recommended.

## SHOWROOM

The new car showroom performs a merchandising and advertising function for the entire dealership. The exterior should be designed, decorated, and lighted so it will stand out from its immediate surroundings in an appealing way as well as identify the business quickly and be inviting to potential customers. It represents the basic physical image of the dealership as it first appears to the customer, influencing not only his original valuation of the facility as a place of business but also his continual impression of it. It exerts an immeasurable but certain pressure on owner relations.

### Locating the Showroom

The showroom should be located in a position of unobstructed visibility—one that will readily attract the attention of people passing by (Fig. 4). It should present at a glance an impressive and appealing view of the new cars on display. If the building site is on a corner, the showroom should be on the corner facing both streets for maximum visibility of its interior. On an inside lot the showroom should be projected in front of the major portion of the facilities to increase visibility and exposure time. Always provide maximum customer visibility.

Additional new unit display, if desired, can be provided outside the showroom under a canopy or roof extension, adjacent to the customer service reception area or through use of a landscaped patio display area. These types of new unit display areas are relatively inexpensive to provide and can be very effective.

The minimum space guide for inside showroom display is 500 square feet per unit. Leave at least 5 feet open around each car. This will allow space so that the customer may walk around and open the hood, doors, and trunk freely. Allow as much extra space as possible around the display, so that customers can stand back and get a good view of the car from all angles.

**Fig. 2. Display area (Mojo Stumer Associates; photo: courtesy of architect)**

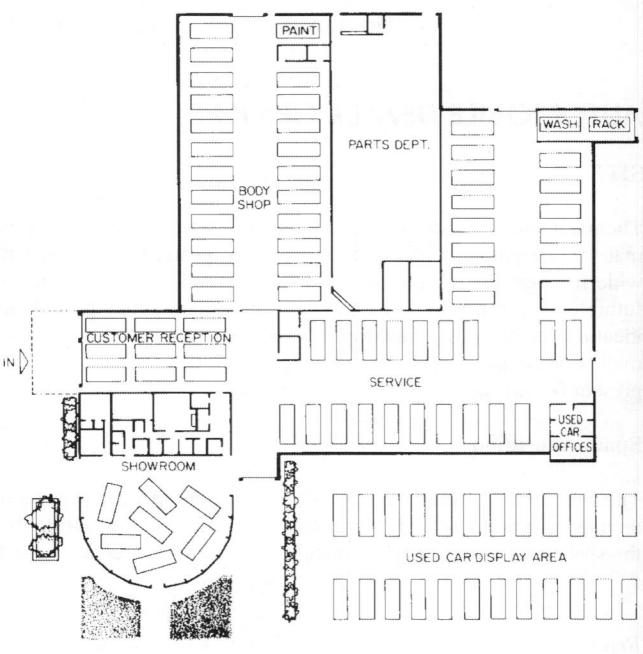

**Fig. 3**

## Table 2 Minimum space recommendations

| Planning Potential | Total Building | Total Lot | Total Building and Lot | Suggested Reception Stalls | Productive Service Stalls | Service Area* | Parts Area | Suggested Display Units | Showroom & Office Area | Service Parking Units | Service Parking Area | Demo & Employe Parking Units | Demo & Employe Parking Area | Used Car Display Units | Used Car Display Area | New Car Storage Units | New Car Storage Area | 5% Of Actual Lot Requirements** |
|---|---|---|---|---|---|---|---|---|---|---|---|---|---|---|---|---|---|---|
| 0- 25 | 3,750 | 5,850 | 9,000 | 1 | 4 | 2,000 | 1,000 | 1 | 750 | 8 | 2,500 | 8 | 1,280 | 3 | 960 | 3 | 750 | 300 |
| 26- 50 | 5,700 | 10,640 | 16,340 | 1 | 7 | 3,500 | 1,200 | 1 | 1,000 | 14 | 4,480 | 7 | 2,240 | 6 | 1,920 | 6 | 1,500 | 500 |
| 51- 75 | 6,600 | 12,770 | 19,370 | 1 | 8 | 4,000 | 1,400 | 1 | 1,200 | 14 | 4,480 | 8 | 2,560 | 9 | 2,880 | 9 | 2,250 | 600 |
| 76- 100 | 7,600 | 16,850 | 24,450 | 2 | 9 | 4,500 | 1,600 | 1 | 1,500 | 18 | 5,760 | 9 | 2,880 | 13 | 4,160 | 13 | 3,250 | 800 |
| 101- 125 | 8,200 | 18,980 | 27,180 | 2 | 10 | 5,000 | 1,700 | 2 | 1,500 | 18 | 5,760 | 10 | 3,200 | 16 | 5,120 | 16 | 4,000 | 900 |
| 126- 150 | 9,300 | 22,490 | 31,790 | 2 | 11 | 5,500 | 1,800 | 2 | 2,000 | 22 | 7,040 | 11 | 3,520 | 19 | 6,080 | 19 | 4,750 | 1,100 |
| 151- 175 | 9,900 | 25,260 | 35,160 | 2 | 12 | 6,000 | 1,900 | 2 | 2,000 | 24 | 7,680 | 12 | 3,840 | 22 | 7,040 | 22 | 5,500 | 1,200 |
| 176- 200 | 11,000 | 28,030 | 39,030 | 2 | 13 | 6,500 | 2,000 | 2 | 2,500 | 26 | 8,320 | 13 | 4,160 | 25 | 8,000 | 25 | 6,250 | 1,300 |
| 201- 225 | 11,700 | 30,900 | 42,600 | 2 | 14 | 7,000 | 2,200 | 3 | 2,500 | 28 | 8,960 | 14 | 4,480 | 28 | 8,960 | 28 | 7,000 | 1,500 |
| 226- 250 | 13,400 | 34,730 | 48,130 | 3 | 16 | 8,000 | 2,400 | 3 | 3,000 | 32 | 10,240 | 16 | 5,120 | 31 | 9,920 | 31 | 7,750 | 1,700 |
| 251- 275 | 14,100 | 36,860 | 50,960 | 3 | 17 | 8,500 | 2,600 | 3 | 3,000 | 32 | 10,240 | 17 | 5,440 | 34 | 10,880 | 34 | 8,500 | 1,800 |
| 276- 300 | 14,800 | 40,840 | 55,640 | 3 | 18 | 9,000 | 2,800 | 3 | 3,000 | 36 | 11,520 | 18 | 5,760 | 38 | 12,160 | 38 | 9,500 | 1,900 |
| 301- 350 | 17,300 | 47,540 | 64,840 | 4 | 21 | 10,500 | 3,300 | 3 | 3,500 | 42 | 13,440 | 21 | 6,720 | 44 | 14,080 | 44 | 11,000 | 2,300 |
| 351- 400 | 19,300 | 53,080 | 72,380 | 4 | 23 | 11,500 | 3,800 | 3 | 4,000 | 46 | 14,720 | 23 | 7,360 | 50 | 16,000 | 50 | 12,500 | 2,500 |
| 401- 450 | 20,900 | 58,720 | 79,620 | 4 | 25 | 12,500 | 4,400 | 4 | 4,000 | 50 | 16,000 | 25 | 8,000 | 56 | 17,920 | 56 | 14,000 | 2,800 |
| 451- 500 | 23,500 | 65,890 | 89,390 | 5 | 28 | 14,000 | 5,000 | 4 | 4,500 | 56 | 17,920 | 28 | 8,960 | 63 | 20,160 | 63 | 15,750 | 3,100 |
| 501- 550 | 25,400 | 72,590 | 97,990 | 5 | 31 | 15,500 | 5,400 | 4 | 4,500 | 62 | 19,840 | 31 | 9,920 | 69 | 22,080 | 69 | 17,250 | 3,500 |
| 551- 600 | 27,800 | 79,190 | 106,990 | 6 | 34 | 17,000 | 5,800 | 4 | 5,000 | 68 | 21,760 | 34 | 10,880 | 75 | 24,000 | 75 | 18,750 | 3,800 |
| 601- 650 | 29,700 | 85,790 | 115,490 | 6 | 37 | 18,500 | 6,200 | 4 | 5,000 | 74 | 23,680 | 37 | 11,840 | 81 | 25,920 | 81 | 20,250 | 4,100 |
| 651- 700 | 31,100 | 92,000 | 123,100 | 7 | 39 | 19,500 | 6,600 | 4 | 5,000 | 78 | 24,960 | 39 | 12,480 | 88 | 28,160 | 88 | 22,000 | 4,400 |
| 701- 750 | 33,500 | 98,600 | 132,100 | 7 | 42 | 21,000 | 7,000 | 4 | 5,500 | 84 | 26,880 | 42 | 13,440 | 94 | 30,080 | 94 | 23,500 | 4,700 |
| 751- 800 | 35,400 | 105,200 | 140,600 | 8 | 45 | 22,500 | 7,400 | 5 | 5,500 | 90 | 28,800 | 45 | 14,400 | 100 | 32,000 | 100 | 25,000 | 5,000 |
| 800- 850 | 37,800 | 111,800 | 149,600 | 8 | 48 | 24,000 | 7,800 | 5 | 6,000 | 96 | 30,720 | 48 | 15,360 | 106 | 33,920 | 106 | 26,500 | 5,300 |
| 851- 900 | 39,700 | 119,070 | 158,770 | 9 | 51 | 25,500 | 8,200 | 5 | 6,000 | 102 | 32,640 | 51 | 16,320 | 113 | 36,160 | 113 | 28,250 | 5,700 |
| 901- 950 | 41,100 | 124,710 | 165,710 | 9 | 53 | 26,500 | 8,600 | 5 | 6,000 | 106 | 33,920 | 53 | 16,960 | 119 | 38,080 | 119 | 29,750 | 6,000 |
| 951-1000 | 43,500 | 131,310 | 174,810 | 9 | 56 | 28,000 | 9,000 | 5 | 6,500 | 112 | 35,840 | 56 | 17,920 | 125 | 40,000 | 125 | 31,250 | 6,300 |
| 1001-1100 | 44,800 | 141,040 | 185,840 | 10 | 58 | 29,000 | 9,300 | 6 | 6,500 | 116 | 37,120 | 58 | 18,560 | 138 | 44,160 | 138 | 34,500 | 6,700 |
| 1101-1200 | 47,100 | 151,060 | 198,160 | 10 | 61 | 30,500 | 9,600 | 6 | 7,000 | 122 | 39,040 | 61 | 19,520 | 150 | 48,000 | 150 | 37,500 | 7,000 |
| 1201-1300 | 48,400 | 161,090 | 209,490 | 11 | 63 | 31,500 | 9,900 | 6 | 7,000 | 126 | 40,320 | 63 | 20,160 | 163 | 52,160 | 163 | 40,750 | 7,700 |
| 1301-1400 | 50,200 | 170,150 | 220,350 | 11 | 65 | 32,500 | 10,200 | 6 | 7,500 | 130 | 41,600 | 65 | 20,800 | 175 | 56,000 | 175 | 43,750 | 8,000 |
| 1401-1500 | 52,000 | 180,080 | 232,080 | 11 | 67 | 33,500 | 10,500 | 6 | 8,000 | 134 | 42,880 | 67 | 21,440 | 188 | 60,160 | 188 | 47,000 | 8,600 |
| 1501-1600 | 53,800 | 190,200 | 244,000 | 12 | 70 | 35,000 | 10,800 | 7 | 8,000 | 140 | 44,800 | 70 | 22,400 | 200 | 64,000 | 200 | 50,000 | 9,000 |
| 1601-1700 | 55,600 | 200,030 | 255,630 | 12 | 72 | 36,000 | 11,100 | 7 | 8,500 | 144 | 46,080 | 72 | 23,040 | 213 | 68,160 | 213 | 53,250 | 9,500 |
| 1701-1800 | 56,900 | 209,290 | 266,190 | 12 | 74 | 37,000 | 11,400 | 7 | 8,500 | 148 | 47,360 | 74 | 23,680 | 225 | 72,000 | 225 | 56,250 | 10,000 |
| 1801-1900 | 58,700 | 219,120 | 277,820 | 13 | 76 | 38,000 | 11,700 | 7 | 9,000 | 152 | 48,640 | 76 | 24,320 | 238 | 76,160 | 238 | 59,500 | 10,500 |
| 1901-2000 | 61,000 | 229,340 | 290,340 | 13 | 79 | 39,500 | 12,000 | 7 | 9,500 | 158, | 50,560 | 79 | 25,280 | 250 | 80,000 | 250 | 62,500 | 11,000 |
| 2001-2100 | 62,500 | 239,170 | 301,670 | 14 | 81 | 40,500 | 12,500 | 8 | 9,500 | 162 | 51,840 | 81 | 25,920 | 263 | 84,160 | 263 | 65,750 | 11,500 |
| 2101-2200 | 64,500 | 248,430 | 312,930 | 14 | 83 | 41,500 | 13,000 | 8 | 10,000 | 166 | 53,120 | 83 | 26,560 | 275 | 88,000 | 275 | 68,750 | 12,000 |
| 2201-2300 | 65,700 | 258,060 | 323,760 | 14 | 85 | 42,500 | 13,500 | 8 | 10,000 | 170 | 54,400 | 85 | 27,200 | 288 | 92,160 | 288 | 72,000 | 12,300 |
| 2301-2400 | 68,000 | 268,280 | 336,280 | 15 | 88 | 44,000 | 14,000 | 8 | 10,000 | 176 | 56,320 | 88 | 28,160 | 300 | 96,000 | 300 | 75,000 | 12,800 |
| 2401-2500 | 71,000 | 277,810 | 348,810 | 15 | 90 | 45,000 | 15,500 | 8 | 10,500 | 180 | 57,600 | 90 | 28,800 | 313 | 100,160 | 313 | 78,250 | 13,000 |
| 2501-2600 | 72,500 | 287,270 | 359,770 | 15 | 92 | 46,000 | 16,000 | 9 | 10,500 | 184 | 58,880 | 92 | 29,440 | 325 | 104,000 | 325 | 81,250 | 13,700 |
| 2601-2700 | 74,000 | 296,900 | 370,900 | 16 | 94 | 47,000 | 16,500 | 9 | 10,500 | 188 | 60,160 | 94 | 30,080 | 338 | 108,160 | 338 | 84,500 | 14,000 |
| 2701-2800 | 76,500 | 307,320 | 383,820 | 16 | 97 | 48,500 | 17,000 | 9 | 11,000 | 194 | 62,080 | 97 | 31,040 | 350 | 112,000 | 350 | 87,500 | 14,700 |
| 2801-2900 | 78,000 | 316,950 | 394,950 | 17 | 99 | 49,500 | 17,500 | 9 | 11,000 | 198 | 63,360 | 99 | 31,680 | 363 | 116,160 | 363 | 90,750 | 15,000 |
| 2901-3000 | 79,500 | 326,210 | 405,710 | 17 | 101 | 50,500 | 18,000 | 9 | 11,000 | 202 | 64,640 | 101 | 32,320 | 375 | 120,000 | 375 | 93,750 | 15,500 |
| 3001 + for each 100 P.P. | | | | ••• | 2.25 | ••• | 500 | ••• | ••• | 4.5 | ••• | 2.25 | ••• | 12.5 | ••• | 12.5 | ••• | ••• |

*Does not include reception stall area.

**For landscaping, building setback and lot entrance driveways.

•••As required.

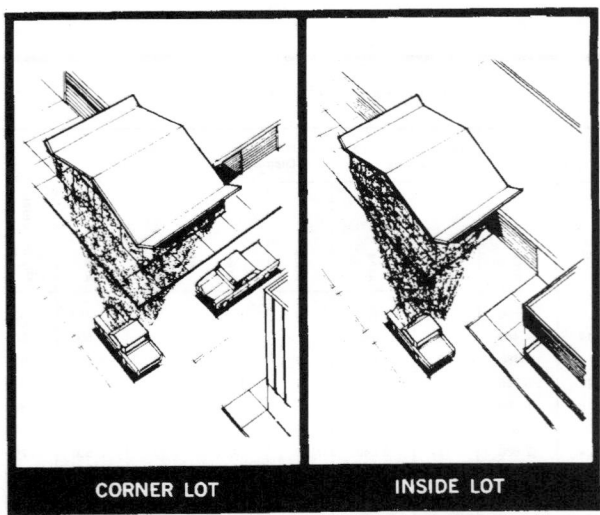

**Fig. 4**

**Table 3** Average office size

|  | Average size, ft | Area, sq ft |
|---|---|---|
| Dealer | 12 by 15 | 180 |
| General manager | 12 by 15 | 180 |
| Sales manager | 10 by 12 | 120 |
| Owner relations manager | 10 by 12 | 120 |
| Truck manager | 8 by 10 | 80 |
| Used car manager | 8 by 10 | 80 |
| Sales closing office | 8 by 8 | 64 |
| Men's and Ladies' rooms | 8 by 8 | 64 |
| Meeting room | 20 sq ft per person | |
| General office | 100 sq ft + (60 sq ft × number of office employees) | |

## OFFICES

Most dealers have their own preference for the location of offices (Fig. 5). As a general rule, the office of a department manager should be placed close to the activities of her department (Table 3).

Additional consideration should be given to the following areas: waiting room, custodian closet closet, walk-in vault, file and record rooms, telephone equipment room. Sizes of these rooms should be in accordance with individual requirements. If vending machines are considered, install them in the service area near a waiting room.

### General Offices

The general office should be in a central location, convenient to all operating departments, with adequate lighting, heating, and cooling for maximum productivity (Fig. 6).

The size of the general office is determined by the number of employees and the amount of office equipment. Sufficient space should be provided for the storage of stationery, office supplies, and promotional literature.

### Vault

A built-in vault adjoining the general office is customary for storage of valuable documents. If this is not possible space should always be provided for fire-resistant equipment to protect important records (Fig. 7).

## SERVICE DEPARTMENT

Just as capacity is the key to profitability, overall organization and appearance determines the operating efficiency and sales appeal of the service department. Dealers have to create a balanced service

**Fig. 5. Auto dealer showroom and offices (Mojo Stumer Associates; photo: courtesy of architect)**

**Fig. 6. Auto dealer office (Mojo Stumer Associates; photo: courtesy of architect)**

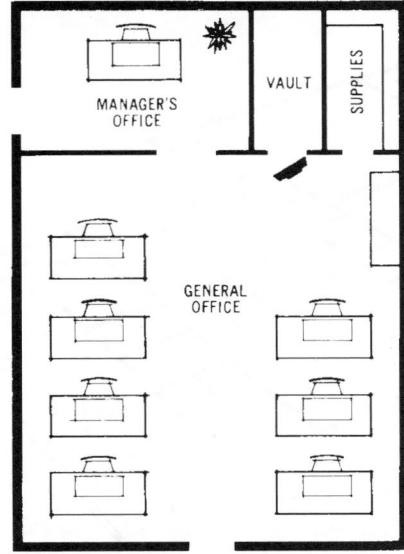

**Fig. 7. Office Layout**

environment that serves the customer's needs as well as the dealer's. The service department is a "salesroom" for service and should be treated as such.

## Basic Considerations

The following are features that should be considered basic elements in the service environment: the covered, out-of-the-weather reception area, well-positioned signs that spell out traffic flow, the service tower that provides visual control, including a view through the service entrance and into the street and over the reception area and into the work areas, the customer lounge and cashier at one location, convenient access to the lounge without the need to wander through the service department to find it, wide entrance and exit lanes, and uncrowded write-up areas with sufficient room for customer convenience.

The type of building shown in Figs. 8 to 10 requires 120 square feet per stall for access area, which results in an average of 420 square feet per stall (work area plus access area). An average of an additional 80 square feet per stall is required for other nonproductive service-related areas such as a tool room, locker room, service manager's office, and other utility areas. This results in an average area requirement per stall for a conventional 70-foot (inside dimension) center-aisle type of building of 500 square feet per stall.

The space and stall needs of the service department are determined by expected business. However, the size and shape of the lot and building will sometimes dictate the service department general layout and arrangement. For best efficiency, a service building width of 70 to 72 feet is suggested. It is wide enough for two rows of cars and an aisle, and can accommodate a few truck stalls. For two rows of work stalls and an aisle, the 70-foot width is considered an absolute minimum.

A width of 80 feet is recommended if the dealer specializes in truck service and does not want a building with direct drive-in stalls. Rec-

ommended width for a building with a single row of direct drive-in stalls is 30 feet for passenger cars and 35 feet minimum for trucks. Recommended width for buildings with a double row of direct drive-in stalls is 60 feet for passenger cars and 70 feet if exclusively used for trucks. Recommended width for buildings with two rows of stalls, an aisle, and a 30-foot extension on one side, with direct drive-in stalls, is 100 feet. Recommended width for buildings with two rows of stalls, an aisle, and a 30-foot extension on each side, with direct drive-in stalls, is 130 feet.

## Customer Reception

The reception area should be immediately inside the service entrance, decorated, well lighted, and equipped to create the best possible impression and selling atmosphere.

It is strongly recommended that the customer reception area be removed from the productive service area. This concept has the following advantages:

- Keeping vehicles out of the productive area until they are ready to be worked on
- Outside (canopy) reception area can be considered, which is less expensive than inside roof area
- Customers prefer a clean, quiet atmosphere to the normal noise, dirt, and congestion of the shop area.

Straight-through reception area is preferable and more conducive to service selling. Traffic control also is much more efficient, with congestion and car maneuvering kept to a minimum.

Where local climate permits, outdoor covered reception areas may be desirable as a building economy. The outdoor reception area can be designed to attractively complement the building architecture.

### Customer Waiting Room

A special waiting area should be provided for customers who wait for service repair on their cars. Comfortable chairs, table, TV, and a public telephone are desirable. Some dealers provide a waiting area in the showroom. However, a separate room, near the customer reception area and cashier, is desirable. The room size will be determined by the potential business.

### Doors

The service entrance door for the customer reception area should be 16 feet wide and 12 feet high. A two-lane traffic door should have a minimum width of 24 feet. Wide doors make it easier to move cars into the stalls just inside the service entrance. Single service exit doors should be 14 feet wide and 12 feet high.

### Service Control Tower

The service control tower should have sufficient space for efficient operation and the necessary equipment to control and schedule the service.

### Write-up Area

The write-up desk adds a professional touch to the service selling function. It is desirable to have the desks located on the driver's side of the car entering the reception area.

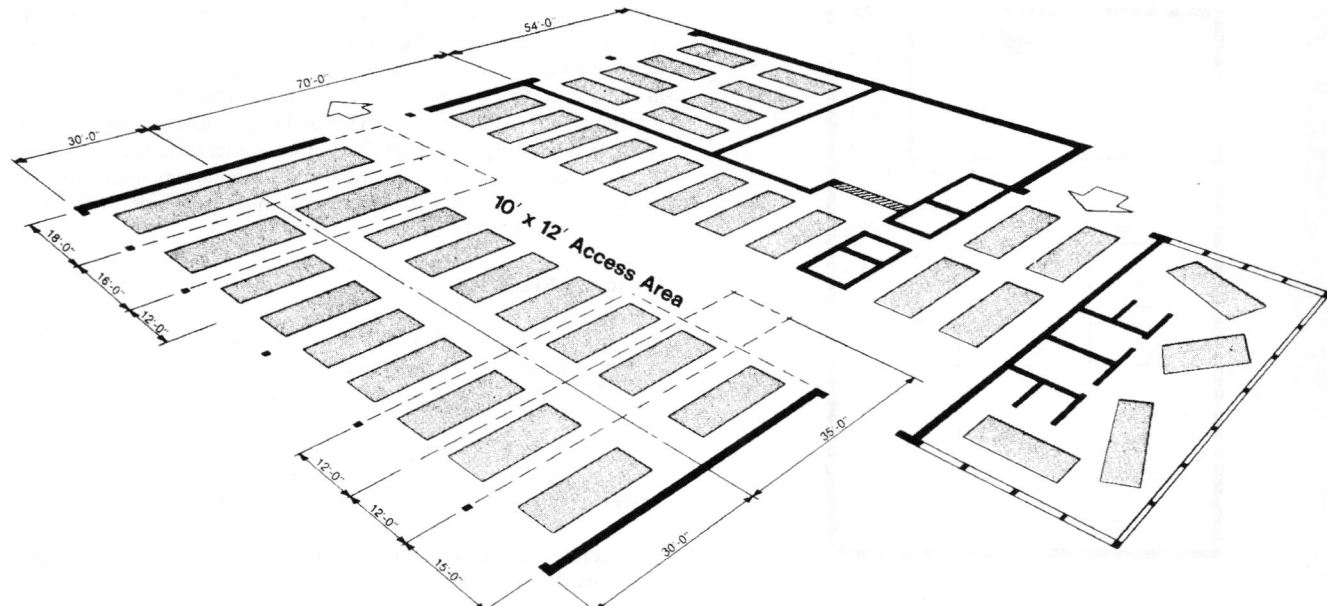

**Fig. 8. Combination conventional center-aisle and drive-in stall with heavy-duty drive-in truck stalls**

**Traffic Flow**

The layout of the service department should be planned so that entrances and exits permit one-way traffic flow. Traffic flow should be a combination of dealership aisle patterns coordinated with traffic movement on public streets and alleys.

The arrangement of stalls to obtain an efficient traffic pattern is one of the most critical factors in planning an efficient service department.

**Stall Arrangement**

Productive stall arrangement depends on size of operation, number of specialized technicians, and the dealer's preference. However, here are a few fundamentals to keep in mind:

- Convenient location of entrances and exits
- Easy access to quick service stalls from customer reception area
- Parts counter convenient to lubrication and quick service stalls
- Separation of body shop

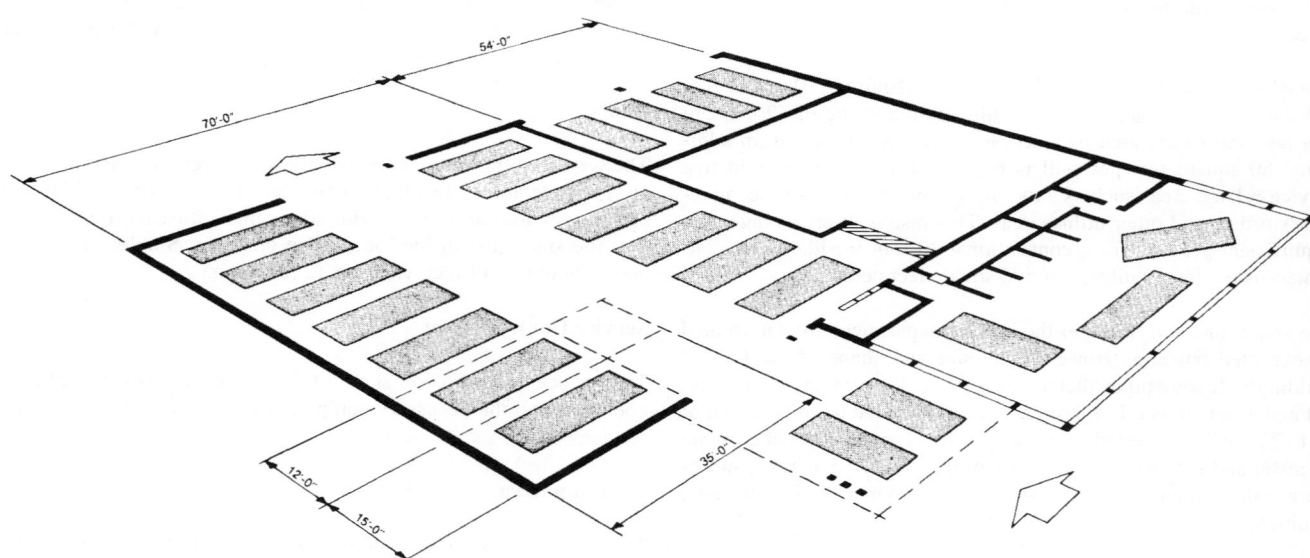

**Fig. 9. Conventional 70-foot-wide center-aisle service building**

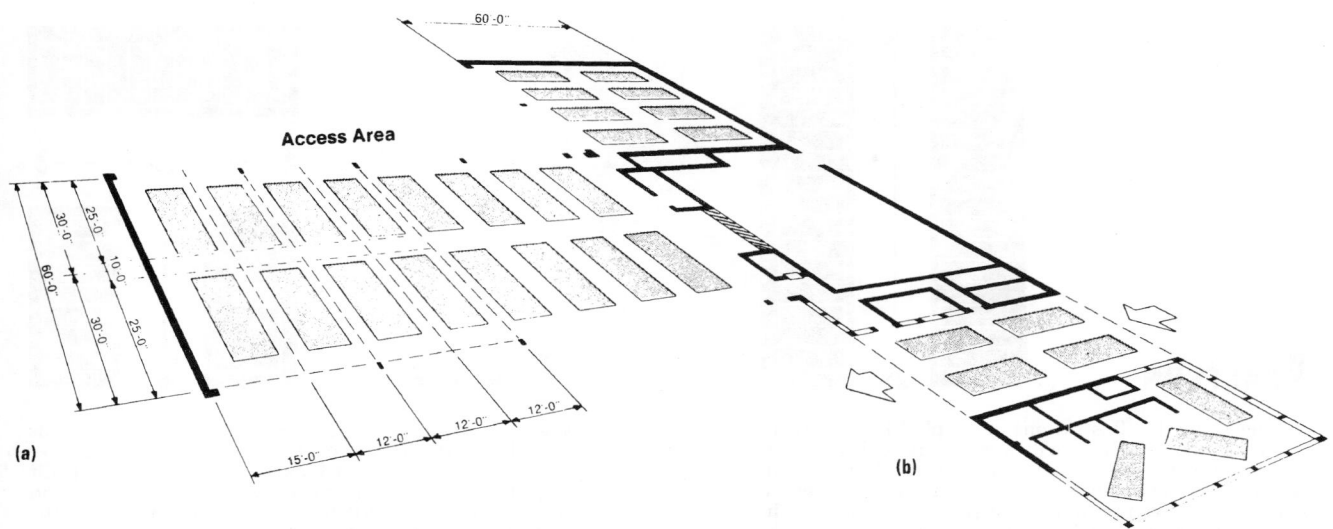

**Fig. 10.** (*a*) Drive-in stall 60-foot-wide service building; (*b*) 70-foot center-aisle service building

- Maximum efficiency of aisle space by having one access aisle serving two rows of productive stalls (Fig. 11)

*I-Pattern*

As shown in the illustrations, a simple I-pattern is the most efficient. This will work in most dealerships if the site permits such an arrangement. However, it cannot be considered a "cure-all." If the number of stalls needed results in an excessive overall length, it makes supervision difficult and places many stalls too remote from the parts department.

*L-Pattern*

The L-pattern is the second most efficient stall and aisle arrangement. It is normally used in those instances where straight through traffic is not possible. Note: It is necessary to sacrifice two stalls in order to accommodate one of the entrances.

*U-Pattern*

The U-pattern is used in large service operations or where no other arrangement is permissible because of existing neighboring structures or public streets. The U tends to centralize service traffic for more efficient control and accessibility to supporting departments.

*T-Pattern*

The T-pattern permits the same number of stalls as the L-pattern. However, it is not suggested over the L-pattern since it makes car movement difficult into the two end stalls near each exit. This stall and aisle pattern is useful in cases where an exit in the rear wall is impossible and the location of an alley makes two side exits more practical.

The standard 70-foot-wide pattern shown in Fig. 12 provides the most efficient use of covered service space when an aisle is required. Long and narrow, it works best in small and medium-size operations. With only two main doors, heating costs are low; and when land is ample expansion is simply a matter of adding on—without the need for major structural work.

However, if the number of stalls needed results in an excessive overall length, it makes supervision difficult and places many stalls too remote from the parts department.

Service facilities with a high percentage of "fast in–fast out" customers find the T-pattern efficient. Notice that the write-up area does not conflict with the productive stall traffic flow area. Cars can be moved directly into stalls—or optionally, straight through to the service parking area ensuring one-way traffic flow. Clear-span width is 70 feet. Like the I-pattern, expansion is relatively simple (Fig. 13).

With doors on one side, it is suggested that the building should be 30 feet wide. With doors on both sides the recommended width is 60 feet. Direct drive-in stalls provide a maximum number of stalls in a minimum floor area and are very economical to construct. Although these buildings occupy less space than the 70-foot-wide buildings, they require more space on the lot for service drives and entrance to the building. The 60-foot-wide building is ideal for truck service because each double truck stall can accommodate the largest bus or tractor-trailer. Often a combination of a 70-foot-wide building with a 30-foot extension on one or both sides can be used very advantageously. The larger span of the roof beams can be 70 feet because the necessary columns do not interfere. This creates a double row of stalls on each side of the central aisle. The cars in the 30-foot extension enter and leave through overhead doors in the side of the building. Here the double stalls can be used for servicing buses or tractor-trailers and, if there is a double wash rack, it can be used for washing these large vehicles (Fig. 14).

**Stall Dimensions**

The width of stalls is made up of "car width" plus working space on each side of the vehicle. The total width varies from 10 feet to 14 feet according to stall function (Table 4).

Whenever a stall is next to a wall, add 2 feet to its width. Local building or fire codes supersede these recommendations if they conflict.

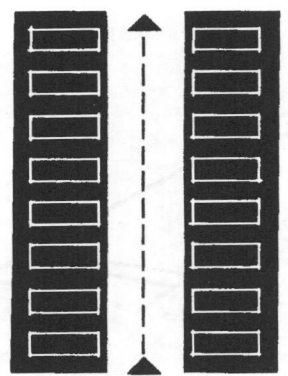

# I PATTERN

As shown in the illustrations, a simple "I" pattern is the most efficient. This will work in most dealerships if the site permits such an arrangement. However, it cannot be considered a "cure-all." If the number of stalls needed results in an excessive overall length, it makes supervision difficult and places many stalls too remote from the parts department.

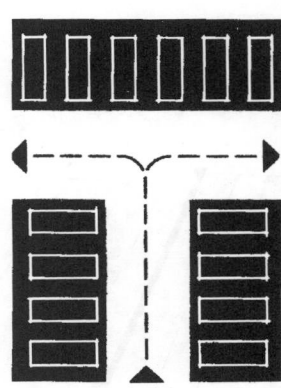

# T PATTERN

The "T" pattern permits the same number of stalls as the "L" pattern. However, it is not suggested over the "L" pattern since it makes car movement difficult into the two end stalls near each exit. This stall and aisle pattern is useful in cases where an exit in the rear wall is impossible and the location of an alley makes two side exits more practical.

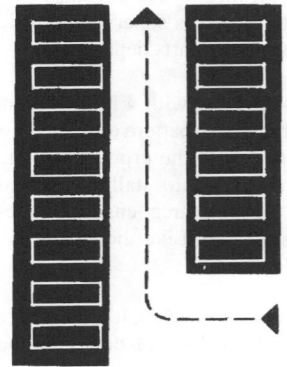

# L PATTERN

The "L" Pattern is the second most efficient stall and aisle arrangement. It is normally used in those instances where straight through traffic is not possible. Note: it is necessary to sacrifice two stalls in order to accommodate one of the entrances.

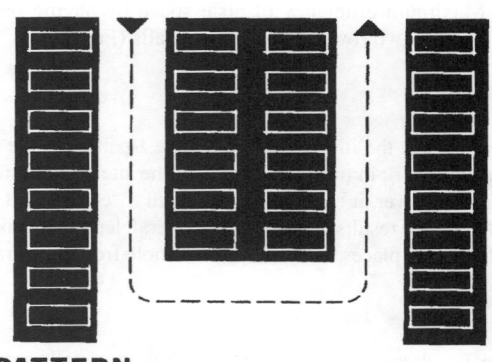

# U PATTERN

The "U" pattern is used in large service operations or where no other arrangement is permissible because of existing neighboring structures or public streets. The "U" tends to centralize service traffic for more efficient control and accessibility to supporting departments.

**Fig. 11. Stall layouts**

**Table 4**  Stall dimensions

| Stall function | Width, ft | Length, ft |
|---|---|---|
| Customer reception (aisle) | 14 | 25 |
| Lubrication (overhead equipment) | 12 | 24 |
| Mechanical repair | 12 | 24 |
| New car conditioning | 12 | 24 |
| Polishing and sheet metal | 12 | 24 |
| Paint spray booth | 14 | 26 |
| Wash rack | 14 | 25 |
| Parking | 10 | 20 |

## Service Stall

General-purpose service stalls should be 12 feet in width. In special situations, an 11-foot width may be acceptable, but only when structural requirements or land limitations impose the need. In buildings with direct drive-in stalls, 12-foot widths are mandatory, since lack of an aisle means minimum walk-around and working areas. Figure 15 provides general dimensions and locations for equipment.

If the work load is light and space is at a premium, a single-stall station might be appropriate. In this suggested layout (Fig. 17), the brake testing is done on the road. Wheel alignment, front suspension hoist or jack area, and headlight testing and aiming are provided through careful arrangement in a single lane. This could be either a drive-through or drive-in-and-back-out system.

The drive-in-and-back-out safety test area could be designed around an existing front-end pit. Wheel alignment and under-vehicle inspections are made in one lane and visual inspection, brake testing, and headlight testing in the other. Suggested layout could possibly be realized by the relocation of existing equipment (Fig. 18).

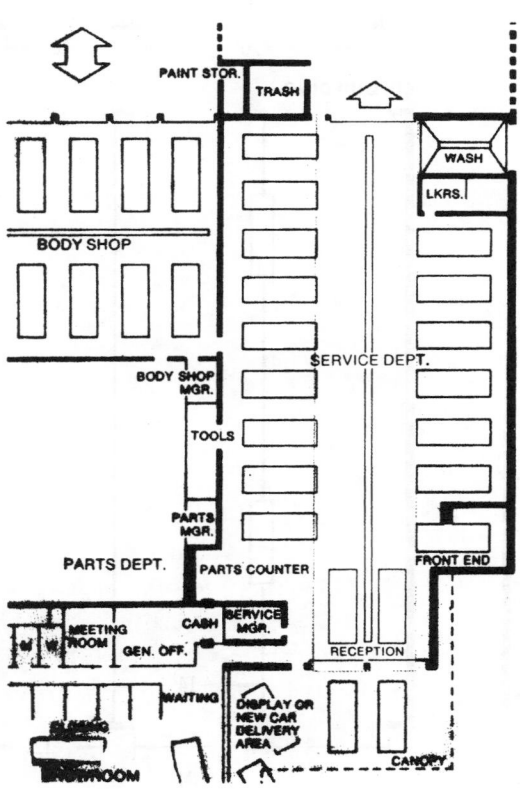

Fig. 12. Center-aisle I-pattern

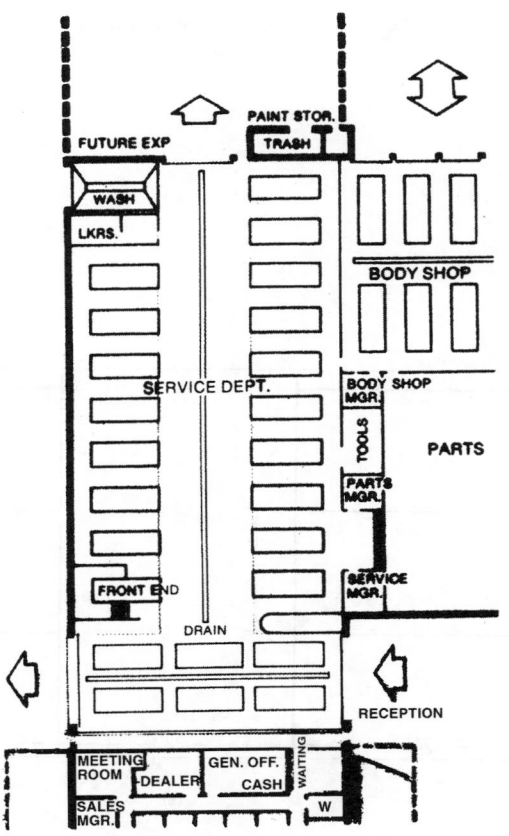

Fig. 13. Center-aisle T-pattern

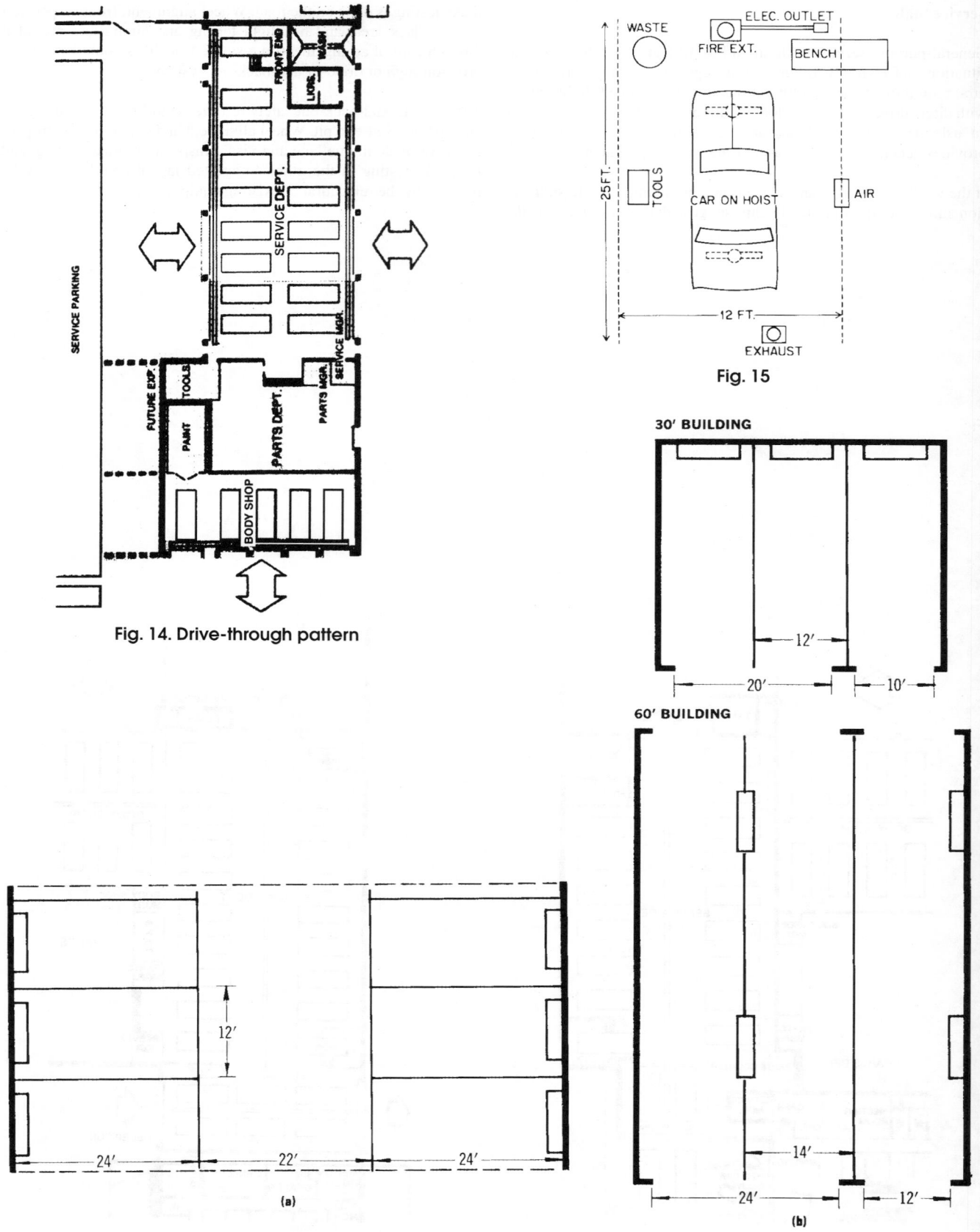

Fig. 14. Drive-through pattern

Fig. 15

Fig. 16. (a) 90-degree stalls; (b) drive-in work stalls

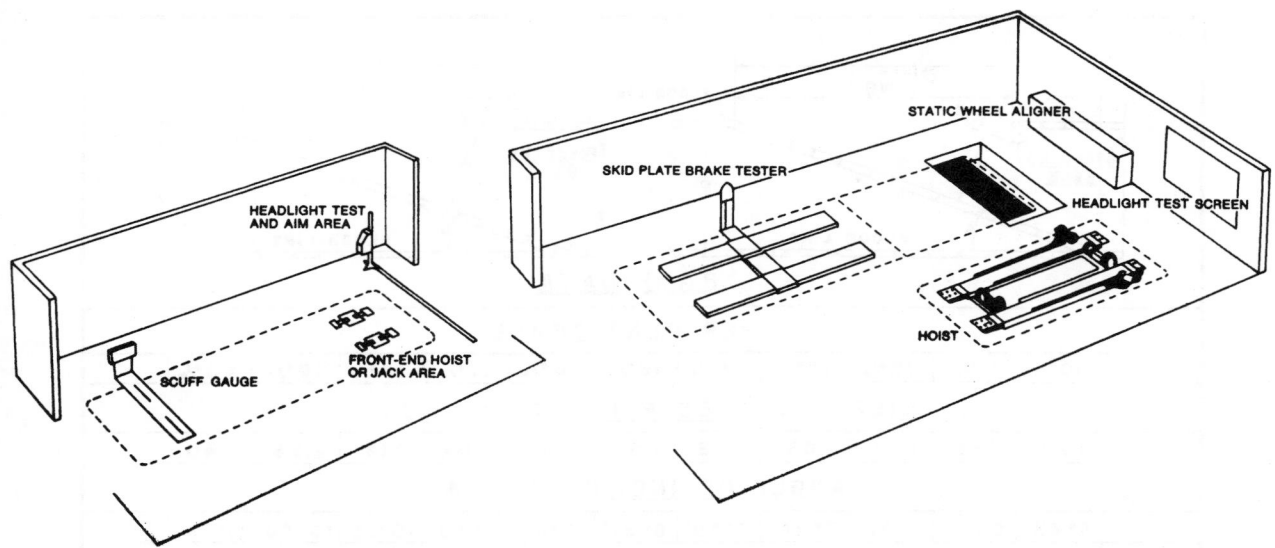

**Fig. 17. Single-bay safety inspection station**

**Fig. 18. Two-bay safety inspection station**

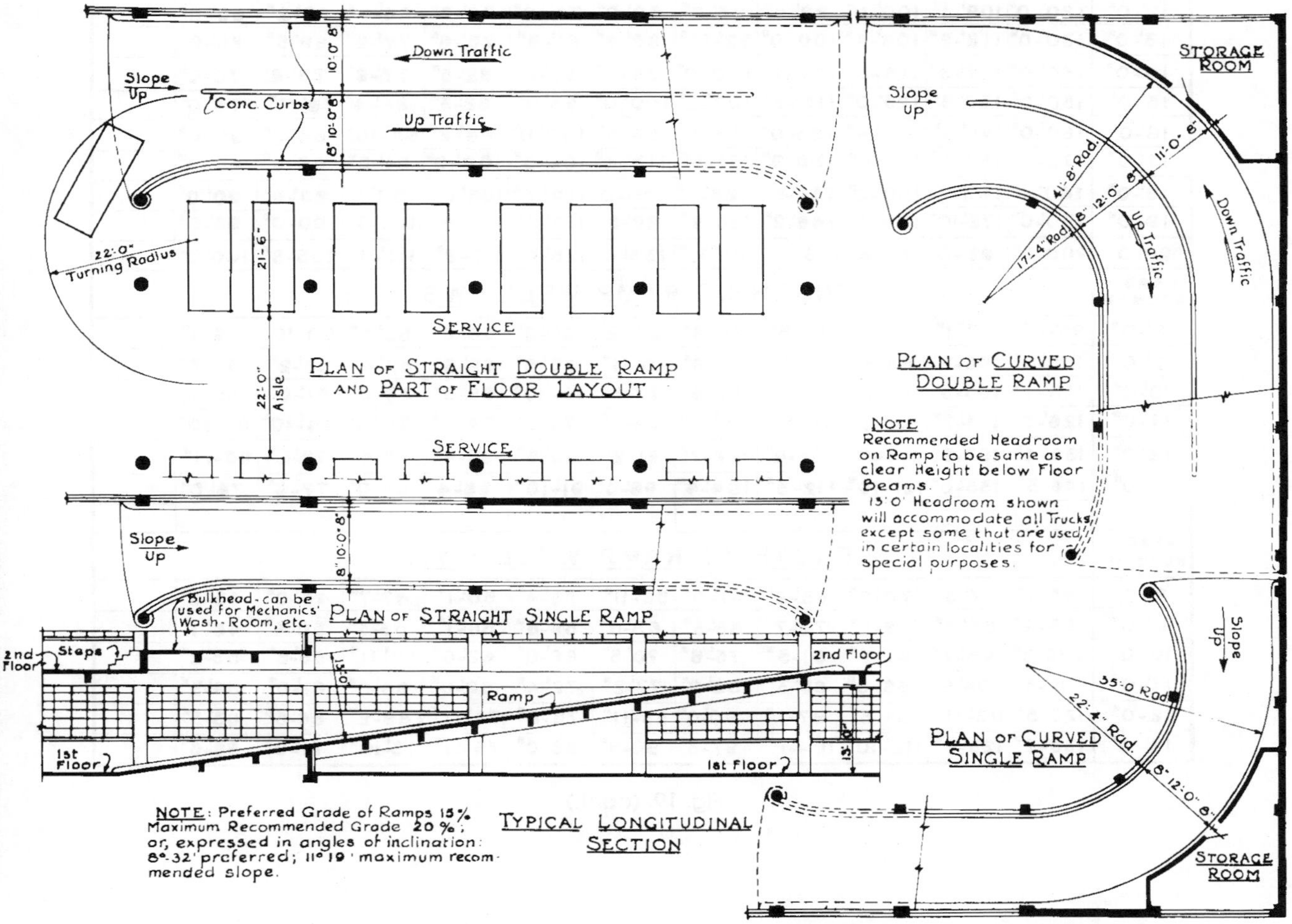

**Fig. 19. Ramp design (Chevrolet Motor Division, Building Department, Detroit, Michigan)**

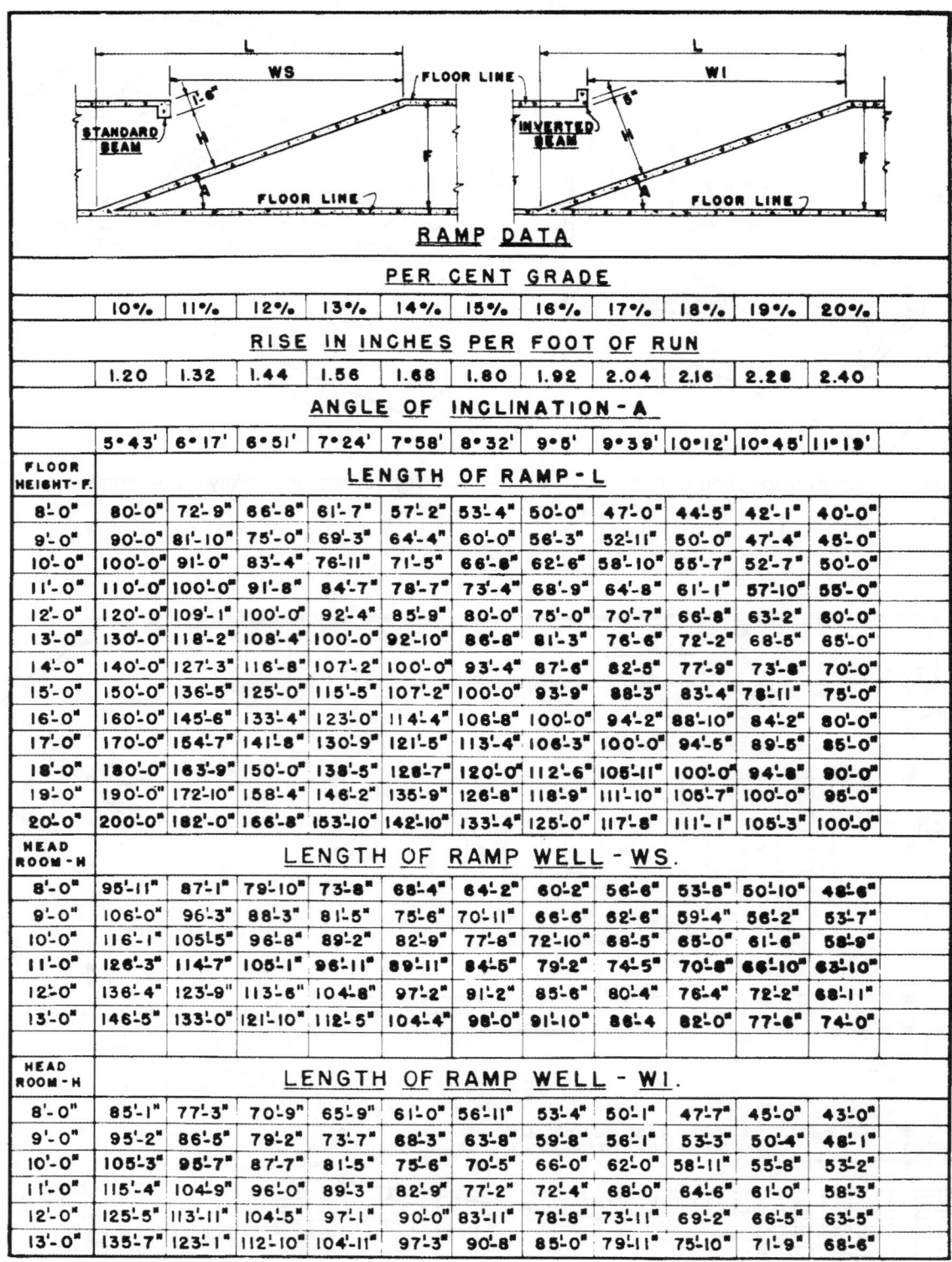

## RAMP DATA

| PER CENT GRADE | | | | | | | | | | | |
|---|---|---|---|---|---|---|---|---|---|---|---|
| 10% | 11% | 12% | 13% | 14% | 15% | 16% | 17% | 18% | 19% | 20% | |
| **RISE IN INCHES PER FOOT OF RUN** | | | | | | | | | | | |
| 1.20 | 1.32 | 1.44 | 1.56 | 1.68 | 1.80 | 1.92 | 2.04 | 2.16 | 2.28 | 2.40 | |
| **ANGLE OF INCLINATION - A** | | | | | | | | | | | |
| 5°43' | 6°17' | 6°51' | 7°24' | 7°58' | 8°32' | 9°5' | 9°39' | 10°12' | 10°45' | 11°19' | |

| FLOOR HEIGHT-F. | LENGTH OF RAMP - L | | | | | | | | | | |
|---|---|---|---|---|---|---|---|---|---|---|---|
| 8'-0" | 80'-0" | 72'-9" | 66'-8" | 61'-7" | 57'-2" | 53'-4" | 50'-0" | 47'-0" | 44'-5" | 42'-1" | 40'-0" |
| 9'-0" | 90'-0" | 81'-10" | 75'-0" | 69'-3" | 64'-4" | 60'-0" | 56'-3" | 52'-11" | 50'-0" | 47'-4" | 45'-0" |
| 10'-0" | 100'-0" | 91'-0" | 83'-4" | 76'-11" | 71'-5" | 66'-8" | 62'-6" | 58'-10" | 55'-7" | 52'-7" | 50'-0" |
| 11'-0" | 110'-0" | 100'-0" | 91'-8" | 84'-7" | 78'-7" | 73'-4" | 68'-9" | 64'-8" | 61'-1" | 57'-10" | 55'-0" |
| 12'-0" | 120'-0" | 109'-1" | 100'-0" | 92'-4" | 85'-9" | 80'-0" | 75'-0" | 70'-7" | 66'-8" | 63'-2" | 60'-0" |
| 13'-0" | 130'-0" | 118'-2" | 108'-4" | 100'-0" | 92'-10" | 86'-8" | 81'-3" | 76'-6" | 72'-2" | 68'-5" | 65'-0" |
| 14'-0" | 140'-0" | 127'-3" | 116'-8" | 107'-2" | 100'-0" | 93'-4" | 87'-6" | 82'-5" | 77'-9" | 73'-8" | 70'-0" |
| 15'-0" | 150'-0" | 136'-5" | 125'-0" | 115'-5" | 107'-2" | 100'-0" | 93'-9" | 88'-3" | 83'-4" | 78'-11" | 75'-0" |
| 16'-0" | 160'-0" | 145'-6" | 133'-4" | 123'-0" | 114'-4" | 106'-8" | 100'-0" | 94'-2" | 88'-10" | 84'-2" | 80'-0" |
| 17'-0" | 170'-0" | 154'-7" | 141'-8" | 130'-9" | 121'-5" | 113'-4" | 106'-3" | 100'-0" | 94'-5" | 89'-5" | 85'-0" |
| 18'-0" | 180'-0" | 163'-9" | 150'-0" | 138'-5" | 128'-7" | 120'-0" | 112'-6" | 105'-11" | 100'-0" | 94'-8" | 90'-0" |
| 19'-0" | 190'-0" | 172'-10" | 158'-4" | 146'-2" | 135'-9" | 126'-8" | 118'-9" | 111'-10" | 105'-7" | 100'-0" | 95'-0" |
| 20'-0" | 200'-0" | 182'-0" | 166'-8" | 153'-10" | 142'-10" | 133'-4" | 125'-0" | 117'-8" | 111'-1" | 105'-3" | 100'-0" |

| HEAD ROOM-H | LENGTH OF RAMP WELL - WS. | | | | | | | | | | |
|---|---|---|---|---|---|---|---|---|---|---|---|
| 8'-0" | 95'-11" | 87'-1" | 79'-10" | 73'-8" | 68'-4" | 64'-2" | 60'-2" | 56'-6" | 53'-8" | 50'-10" | 48'-6" |
| 9'-0" | 106'-0" | 96'-3" | 88'-3" | 81'-5" | 75'-6" | 70'-11" | 66'-6" | 62'-6" | 59'-4" | 56'-2" | 53'-7" |
| 10'-0" | 116'-1" | 105'-5" | 96'-8" | 89'-2" | 82'-9" | 77'-8" | 72'-10" | 68'-5" | 65'-0" | 61'-6" | 58'-9" |
| 11'-0" | 126'-3" | 114'-7" | 105'-1" | 96'-11" | 89'-11" | 84'-5" | 79'-2" | 74'-5" | 70'-8" | 66'-10" | 63'-10" |
| 12'-0" | 136'-4" | 123'-9" | 113'-6" | 104'-8" | 97'-2" | 91'-2" | 85'-6" | 80'-4" | 76'-4" | 72'-2" | 68'-11" |
| 13'-0" | 146'-5" | 133'-0" | 121'-10" | 112'-5" | 104'-4" | 98'-0" | 91'-10" | 86'-4" | 82'-0" | 77'-6" | 74'-0" |

| HEAD ROOM-H | LENGTH OF RAMP WELL - WI. | | | | | | | | | | |
|---|---|---|---|---|---|---|---|---|---|---|---|
| 8'-0" | 85'-1" | 77'-3" | 70'-9" | 65'-9" | 61'-0" | 56'-11" | 53'-4" | 50'-1" | 47'-7" | 45'-0" | 43'-0" |
| 9'-0" | 95'-2" | 86'-5" | 79'-2" | 73'-7" | 68'-3" | 63'-8" | 59'-8" | 56'-1" | 53'-3" | 50'-4" | 48'-1" |
| 10'-0" | 105'-3" | 95'-7" | 87'-7" | 81'-5" | 75'-6" | 70'-5" | 66'-0" | 62'-0" | 58'-11" | 55'-8" | 53'-2" |
| 11'-0" | 115'-4" | 104'-9" | 96'-0" | 89'-3" | 82'-9" | 77'-2" | 72'-4" | 68'-0" | 64'-6" | 61'-0" | 58'-3" |
| 12'-0" | 125'-5" | 113'-11" | 104'-5" | 97'-1" | 90'-0" | 83'-11" | 78'-8" | 73'-11" | 69'-2" | 66'-5" | 63'-5" |
| 13'-0" | 135'-7" | 123'-1" | 112'-10" | 104'-11" | 97'-3" | 90'-8" | 85'-0" | 79'-11" | 75'-10" | 71'-9" | 68'-6" |

Fig. 19. (cont.)

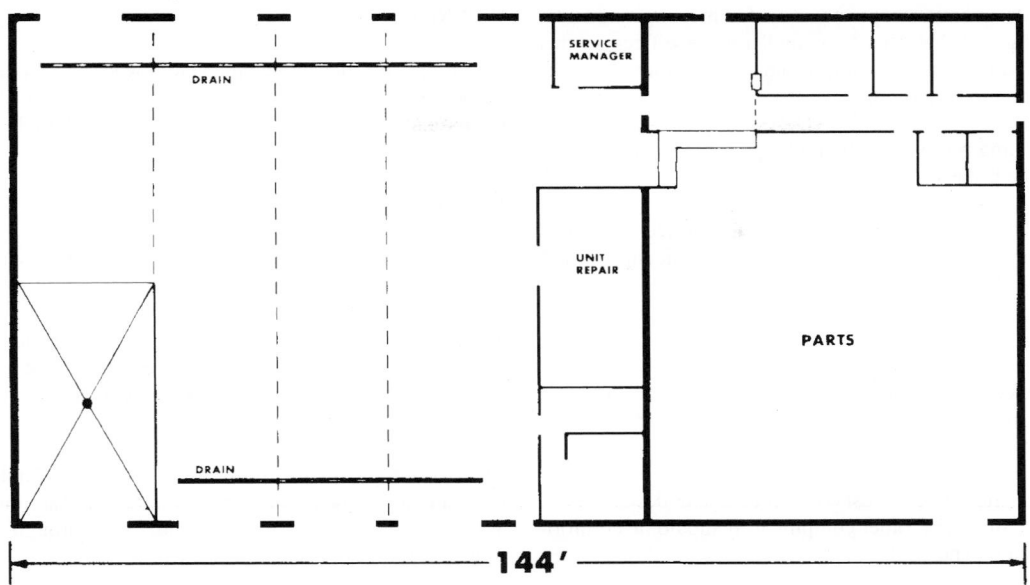

**Fig. 1. Layout for small dealer**

# TRUCK DEALER AND SERVICE FACILITIES

## AREAS

### New Truck Display

Truck sales profit from good interior display, particularly light-tonnage trucks sold to families as second cars or recreation vehicles.

However, because of the wide variation in size between truck models, and because the sales of larger units are frequently made away from the dealership, indoor truck showroom displays are usually limited in size.

If there is to be an interior display area, make sure that it is large enough for at least one pickup, with adequate room to walk completely around it (1,000 square feet). The display should occupy at least 3 percent of the dealership's total area.

The display should face the majority of traffic that moves past the dealership, and be placed so that a driver does not have to turn her head to see it.

For a driver to see a display easily, it should be within 30 degrees to the left or right of her straight-ahead forward vision, and close enough to catch her eye.

Display area windows should be large, but do not have to be slanted. Having strong enough lights inside the display area will usually minimize any natural glare or reflections on the outside of the glass.

Many truck dealerships rely entirely on exterior display.

This may be under a canopy or not. The advantage of the canopy is that the vehicle stays cleaner longer, doesn't spot as easily from rain or snow, and is sheltered from the sun and weather.

The disadvantage of the canopy is cost and the fact that vehicle movement can be hampered if the placing of the canopy supports is not carefully planned.

### Private Offices

The dealer's or general manager's office should be the largest in the dealership. The office should be able to accommodate four or five visitors. It should have closet and storage facilities, and if desired, its own rest room.

Consider the possibility of allowing this office to double as a meeting room for the sales staff (Table 1). If the dealership also has a sales manager, she should have an office. Offices for individual sales personnel can double as closing rooms.

### Meeting Room

A meeting room is not a luxury in a truck dealership. When facilities have lunchrooms, these are frequently used as meeting rooms.

*Reference: Profitable GMC Dealership Expansion,* General Motors Corp.

If it is not possible to have a separate room for meetings, consider installing a folding wall between two small private offices so that they can be opened up into a meeting room. Or consider using the dealer's office for a meeting room.

Wherever the meeting room is, it should be possible to darken it so that pictures can be projected.

Equipment for VCRs and 35-mm sound slide film projection should either be permanently set up or be stored in a convenient cupboard. A blackboard and/or chart stand will also be useful.

### General Office

If the cashier works in the general office, then the office should be adjacent to the parts counter and the service reception area, so that the cashier's window can serve both.

The general office should be furnished with adequate desks, chairs, files, business machines, and other equipment. It should be comfortable, reasonably quiet, and well lighted.

Storage should be provided in the room for current operating records and daily supplies. Old records and infrequently used supplies can be stored somewhere else.

### Vault and Storage

A vault should be provided for cash and valuable business records. If no vault is provided, essential records should be kept in special fire-resistant files or fireboxes.

Stationery, sales promotion material, model literature, and seasonal dealership decorations should be given a storage area. Obsolete records can also be stored here. This space can be in a basement, mezzanine, or on the same floor but in an out-of-the-way location.

### Rest Rooms

Rest rooms for men and women employees and for customers should be provided. While local codes will dictate much of the design and equipment for these rest rooms, try to select durable and economical as well as attractive fixtures.

### Floor Plan

The most functional type of layout for a truck service department is one with drive-through stalls (Figs. 1 and 2).

Trucks of varying lengths can be easily handled, including those with extremely long wheelbases. Each vehicle can be moved in or out without disturbing the others. And since no aisles are required, more floor space is useful space.

The two things that can prevent the use of this kind of stall are climate and a narrow property with limited turn-around space outside. Where the climate is extremely cold, drive-through stalls can be too drafty and too expensive to heat.

Where there is not enough room outside for vehicles to move freely at both sides of the building, such as at some in-town locations, drive-through stalls are impractical. However, a practical layout in this situation would be stalls where you drive in and back out through individual doors.

To preserve heat in very cold areas, it may be necessary for the department to use a common entrance door, with the trucks turning into individual stalls after entering the building. If these stalls are angled, more floor space will be required for each stall, although less will be required for the aisle.

One-way traffic through a service department door is more efficient than two-way traffic. If a common entrance must be used, try to provide a common exit at another point.

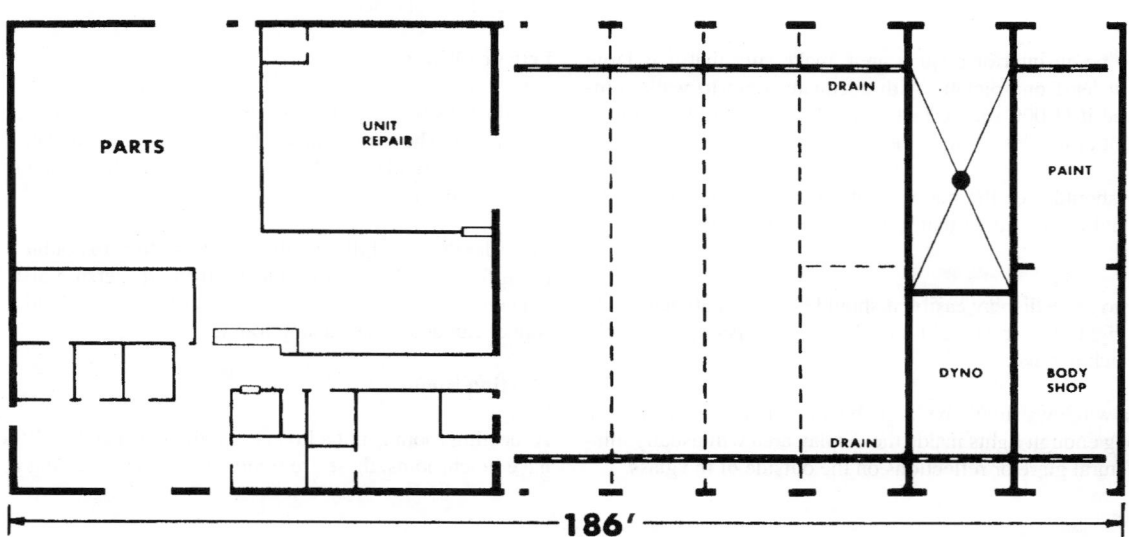

Fig. 2. Layout for medium-sized dealer

**Table 1**   Sales area and building

| Area | Space allowance |
|---|---|
| Interior display | |
| Showroom | 1,000 sq ft, plus 600 sq ft for each vehicle over one |
| Entrance door | 10 by 12 ft (pickups) 12 by 14 ft (larger trucks) |
| Offices (minimum) | |
| Dealer or general manager | 180 sq ft |
| Sales manager | 120 sq ft |
| Salesmen | 90 sq ft per man |
| Closing office | 64 sq ft |
| Used truck office | 120 sq ft |
| General office | 100 sq ft per person |
| Ceiling height | Offices—9 ft 6 in |
| Meeting room | Allow at least 12 sq ft for each person to attend meeting, plus room for speaker and for projection equipment |
| Other areas | |
| Rest room | 30 sq ft minimum |
| Hall or aisle | 5 ft wise |
| Janitor closet | 32 sq ft minimum with deep sink |
| Customers' waiting room | Variable |

## FLOW FACTORS

Four groups of things move or "flow" through the department while it is working. How logically and easily each of these groups flows determines much of the department's ability to turn a profit. The four flow factors are:

1. Flow of traffic
2. Flow of people
3. Flow of parts
4. Flow of repair orders

### Flow of Traffic

Start by planning where the customer traffic will wait before it gets to the service salesperson or write-up personnel. There must be adequate standing room outside where waiting vehicles will not get in the way of other dealership customers or street traffic.

From the service salesperson, traffic must flow either to another waiting area, or to a stall where work is to be done. If the vehicle will have to go to more than one stall (such as from diagnosis to a work stall), it should never have to backtrack. When the work is done, the vehicle should move out to be road-checked by dynamometer and parked.

Before finalizing any service department layout, mentally move a day's traffic through it to see where the bottlenecks might appear.

### Flow of People

The customer should be able to get out of her vehicle, talk with the service salesman, go to the driver lounge or out of the dealership, go to the cashier, and pick up her vehicle without getting in the way of sales, service, or parts employees.

The mechanic should be able to get the tools and parts she needs without going through customer areas or getting in the way of other workers.

### Flow of Parts

Parts shipping and receiving should not have to be made across the flow of incoming service traffic. Parts customers should not have to wait for service customers.

Parts access for the service department should be convenient, both for the mechanic and for the parts department. To get parts, the mechanic should not have to travel far or travel through customer waiting areas. Departmentally, quick service and tune-up stalls should be nearest the parts counter.

Stalls doing work that normally requires fewer parts per day (such as heavy repair) should be farther away than stalls doing general repair and maintenance.

### Flow of Repair Orders

Trace the physical movement of repair order originals and copies in the current maintenance system. Bad flow here will cause wasted mechanic time, slower billing with increased customer dissatisfaction, and poorer cost accounting and maintenance control. In larger buildings a system of pneumatic tubes between offices aids in the efficient flow of paper work.

## ROOMS AND AREAS

### Service Manager's Office

The service manager's office should provide privacy and relative quiet, so that it can be used to handle customer complaints. It should be closed off from the working area to keep out dirt as well as noise. It should have windows and be located so that the service manager can easily see the main service entrance and the work areas of the department that return the highest profit.

Direct supervision from the service manager's office improves work quality and reduces idleness. Being able to see diagnosis and service stalls usually improves profit and promotes better care of the special equipment used. In large operations, a raised office that allows the service manager to look across the entire department is effective.

### General Service Area

The number and type of stalls are determined by the services (Tables 2 to 4).

### Quick Service Area

Quick service is normally limited to jobs that can be done in one hour or less. An area set aside for quick service usually produces more profit per square foot because it creates a high parts volume with rel-

**Table 2**   Service areas

| Area | Space allowance or dimensions |
|---|---|
| Service manager's office | Usually 120 sq ft |
| Paint department office (if separate) | Usually 120 sq ft |
| Drivers' lounge | 100 sq ft plus 20 sq ft for each person over 5 |
| Lunch room | 300 sq ft plus 20 sq ft for each person over 10 |
| Showers, rest rooms, lockers | 60 sq ft plus 10 sq ft for each person over 5 |
| Unit repair | Minimum of 300 sq ft |
| Detroit diesel injector repair | Minimum of 48 sq ft |
| Toro-Flow diesel fuel pump | Minimum of 80 sq ft |
| Entrances: | |
|    Individual service doors | 12 ft wide, 14 ft high |
|    One-way main service doors (or reception door on drive-through layouts) | 16 ft wide, 14 ft high |
|    Two-way main service doors | 24 ft wide, 14 ft high |
| Ceiling height: | |
|    General service area | 15 ft minimum—floor to roof truss clearance |
|    Over lifts | 17–18 ft |
| Center aisles: | |
|    With 90° stalls | 22–24 ft wide for small trucks only 26–28 ft wide for large trucks |
|    With 60° stalls | 25 ft wide for large trucks |
|    With 45° stalls | 23 ft wide for large trucks |

•The entire service department normally occupies 65 to 70 percent of the total area of the dealership building.

**Table 3**   Stall dimensions

| Drive-through-type building | | |
|---|---|---|
| Stalls | Dimensions | Total |
| Two deep (70-ft building) | 15 by 35 ft | 525 sq |
| Three deep (80-ft building) | 15 by 26 ft | 390 sq |
| Three deep (90-ft building) | 15 by 29 ft | 435 sq |

| Drive-in-type building | | | |
|---|---|---|---|
| Stall angle | Dimensions | Aisle width | Total |
| 90° | 15 by 35 ft | 28 ft | 945 sq ft |
| 60° | 17 by 35 ft | 25 ft | 1,020 sq f |
| 45° | 21 by 35 ft | 23 ft | 1,218 sq f |

| Other areas | Dimensions |
|---|---|
| Front-end stalls | 20 ft wide, 35 ft long |
| Wash rack | 20 ft wide, 35 ft long |
| Lubrication stalls | 20 ft wide, 35 ft long |
| Dynamometer stalls | 20 ft wide, 35 ft long |
| Paint preparation, drying, and cleanup stalls | 18 ft wide, 40 ft long |
| Sheet metal and body repair stalls | 20 ft wide, 40 ft long |
| Paint spray booth | 20 ft wide, 40 ft long |
| Floors | 6-in. wire-mesh-reinforced concrete slab. Cmpressive strength of not less than 3,000 psi at 28 days. Exposed floors should be treated with floor sealer. Floor should slope ⅛ in per foot toward drain. |
| Compressed air lines and fittings | Designed for operating pressure of 175 lb |

atively short labor times. Specific quick service jobs fall into these areas:

- Engine tune-up
- Cooling system
- Exhaust system
- Clutches
- Brakes
- Transmissions
- Front end
- Brake linings
- Wheel balance
- Wheel bearings
- Shock absorbers
- Universal joints
- Electrical
- Tires
- Lubrication
- Body
- Trim

Quick service can be done in a limited way in any service operation just by setting aside a stall for that purpose. However, the most prof itable quick service results from using special methods, tools, and equipment and from reducing the time required to get parts.

**Unit Repair**

A separate unit repair room can speed the rebuilding of engines and other assemblies. This room is usually most effective when separated

**Table 4**   Parts areas and dimensions

| Area | Dimensions |
|---|---|
| Parts office | 120 sq ft minimum |
| Parts lobby | 200 sq ft minimum |
| Customer counter | 42 in high, at least 12 ft long |
| Mechanic's counter | 42 in high, at least 5 ft long |
| Storage and obsolete files | 100 sq ft minimum |

from the general repair area. It also has all the necessary tools and equipment for overhaul of units. As a result, the work done there usually produces more reliable assemblies.

By having repair stands, test equipment, and special tools in one location, close to the parts department, a specialist can do the required work in the least time.

The unit repair area should be set off from the rest of the department by wall or screen fencing. It should have a lockable door or sliding 5-foot gate.

## Injector Repair

Where frequent Toro-Flow or GM Diesel work is available, a diesel injector and fuel pump repair room is profitable (Fig. 3). Since this precision work must be done in a dirt-free area, the room must be completely enclosed, easy to keep clean, and pressurized slightly to keep outside dust from seeping in.

Smooth-surfaced walls, windows with flush sills, and benches enclosed to the floor reduce dirt traps and the time required to clean the room. Light-colored wall enamel also improves illumination.

To pressurize the room, use a fixed fan to draw air in through a glass fiber filter, such as those used in many air conditioners. To let air out of the room, a hood and stovepipe with a damper can be placed over the solvent pans. This will carry out solvent fumes as well. A roof fan can also be used to exhaust air that is drawn in through filters placed at opposite ends of the room.

The room also requires an air supply to dry injector parts. The air filter and moisture trap for the air line should be placed outside the room.

## Body and Paint Shop

A well-managed truck body shop will usually produce more profit per dollar invested than the dealership's general repair area. Consult local paint and equipment companies for advice on the best possible layout for the equipment to be used and the services to be offered. Local codes strongly govern what you can and cannot do.

If possible, plan to separate the body and paint shop from the main service building. This allows the avoidance of excessive noise, fumes, display of damaged vehicles, fire hazard, and increased fire insurance premiums that can come from an attached body and paint department (Fig. 4). If the department has to be under the same roof, it must be isolated from the main service area by a firewall. Whether the body and paint shop is attached or separate, an isolated fireproof room for paint storage and mixing will lower insurance costs.

At least four stalls should be planned for complete body work: one for sheet metal repairs, one for heavy metal work and straightening frames, one for painting, and one for drying and cleanup. In a separate facility, also provide office space, wash-up areas, and storage for body parts.

Proper placement of the paint spray booth is a job for an expert. The booth cannot function satisfactorily if the filter doors open directly to the outside of the building. A booth exhausts 7,000 to 14,000 cubic feet of air a minute. This air should not be reused because it contains volatile fumes. It must be replaced without creating a draft through the body department. Consult an expert.

## EQUIPMENT

### Monorail

A monorail is helpful in moving engines and other major truck components to and from the steam clean area and unit repair room. However, a monorail alone is insufficient for engine removal, as it can lift only vertically, and many truck designs require several lift positions to get the engine out.

Minimum capacity for a monorail should be 3 tons. The rail should be suspended from the ceiling structure 20 to 25 feet inside the service doors on a drive-through layout, or near the front of a row of drive-in-back-out stalls. One end of the rail should be in the wash rack and the other end in the unit repair area.

### Hoists

Large truck dealerships use hydraulic floor hoists extensively for quick service and general repair services, since their use improves

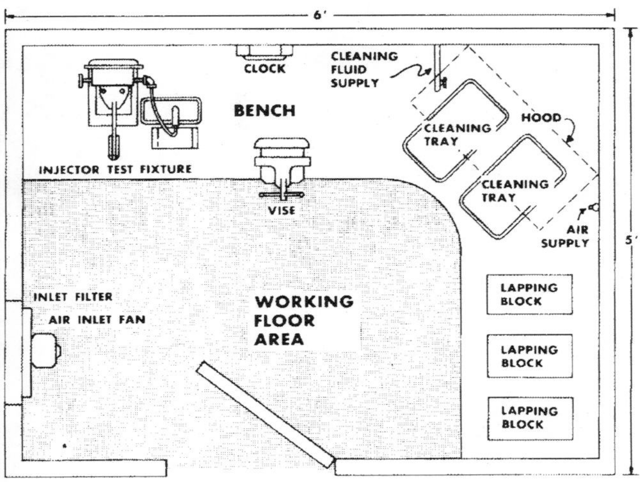

**Fig. 3. Typical fuel injector repair room**

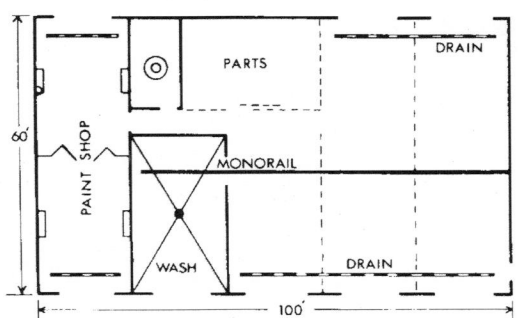

**Fig. 4. Typical auxiliary paint and body shop**

mechanic efficiency. Hoist work also helps attract the best grade of mechanic to the business by providing better working conditions.

Where hoists are used, the best choice is one of the disappearing types. This way a creeper can be used in the stall when the hoist is not being used.

Most mechanical truck services can be provided without the use of hydraulic hoists. Transmissions and power train components can be repaired with the truck front or rear axles up on stands. To get the unit onto the stand, a fork lift, an A-frame hoist, or a boom lift can be used. The major advantage is that all of these are portable and can move from stall to stall.

Since there is generally ample room underneath most large trucks, work may be done without any lift at all. However, hydraulic lifts can be highly advantageous.

**Dynamometer**

Any dynamometer needs to be isolated with sound-deadening material because of engine and tire noise.

**Fork Lift**

A fork lift can be a good investment for the service department and the parts department. In the service department, it can be used to remove and install heavy truck components and to carry them to repair and cleanup areas. In the parts department, it can be used to carry large items such as transmissions and for the shipping and receiving of stock. The fork lift should have an 11-foot vertical beam and a capacity of at least 3 tons.

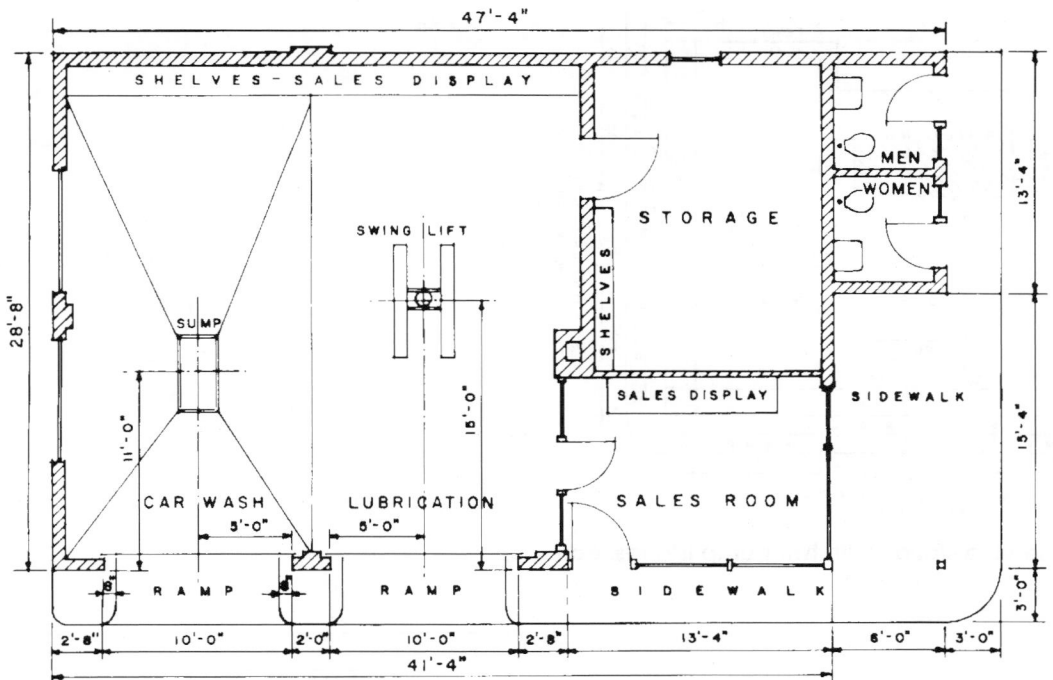

**Fig. 1. Plan of typical two-bay service station building**

## AUTOMOBILE SERVICE STATIONS

Figures 1 to 15 show the standard plan of a major oil company for a two-bay service station. Additional bays may be added for larger installations. Minimum recommended dimensions for bay door opening is 10 by 10 feet. Overhead type doors are the most effective. Servicing pits have become obsolete, the mechanical lift being considered more practical.

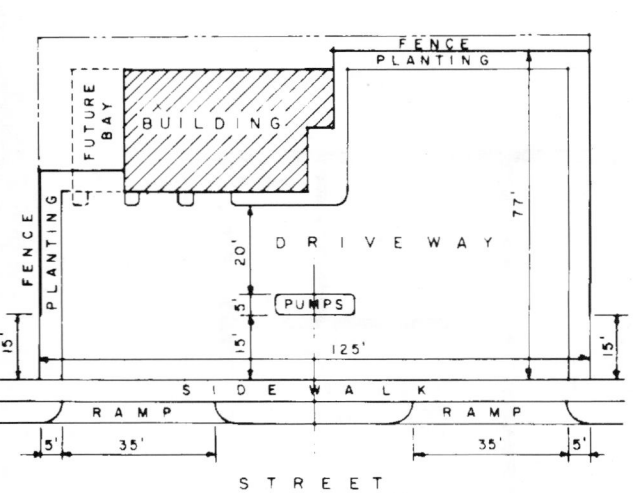

**Fig. 2. Plan of service station with one pump island, mid-block location**

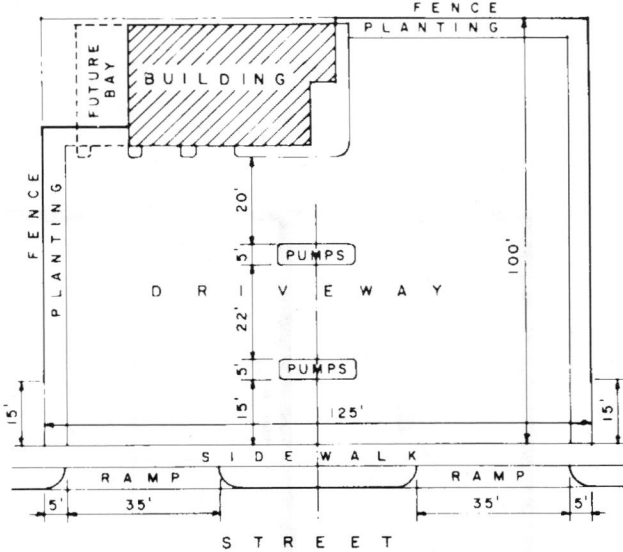

**Fig. 3. Plan of service station with two pump islands, mid-block location**

Compiled and edited by William J. Cronin, Jr., Marketing Department, Humble Oil & Refining Co.

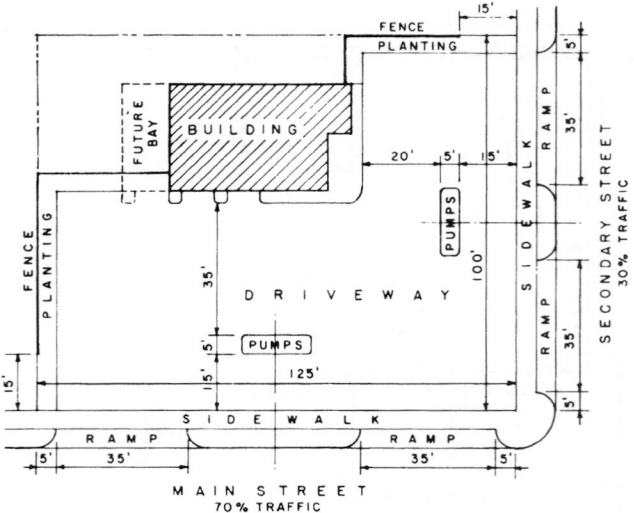

**Fig. 4. Plan of service station with two pump islands, corner location**

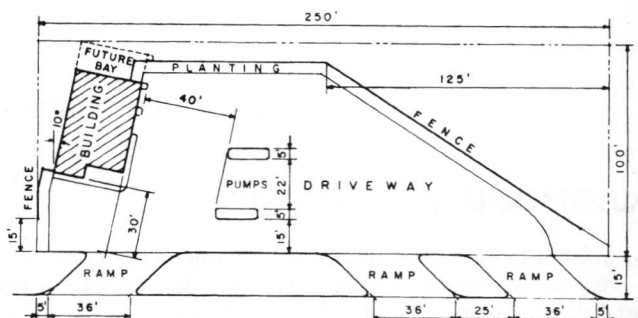

**Fig. 5. Plan of service station with two pump islands, highway location**

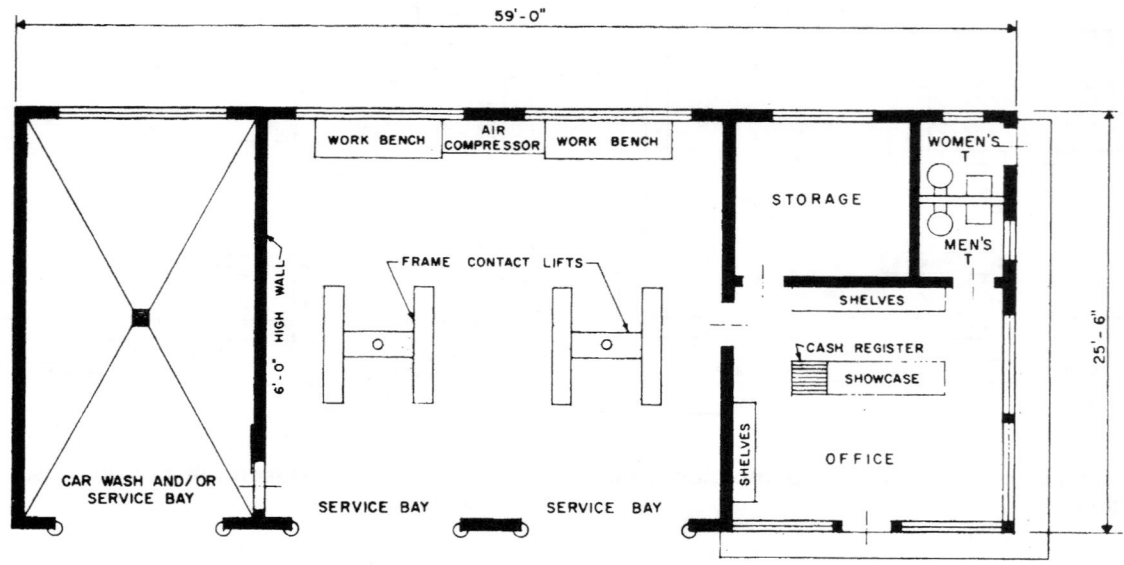

**Fig. 6. Two- and three-bay stations**

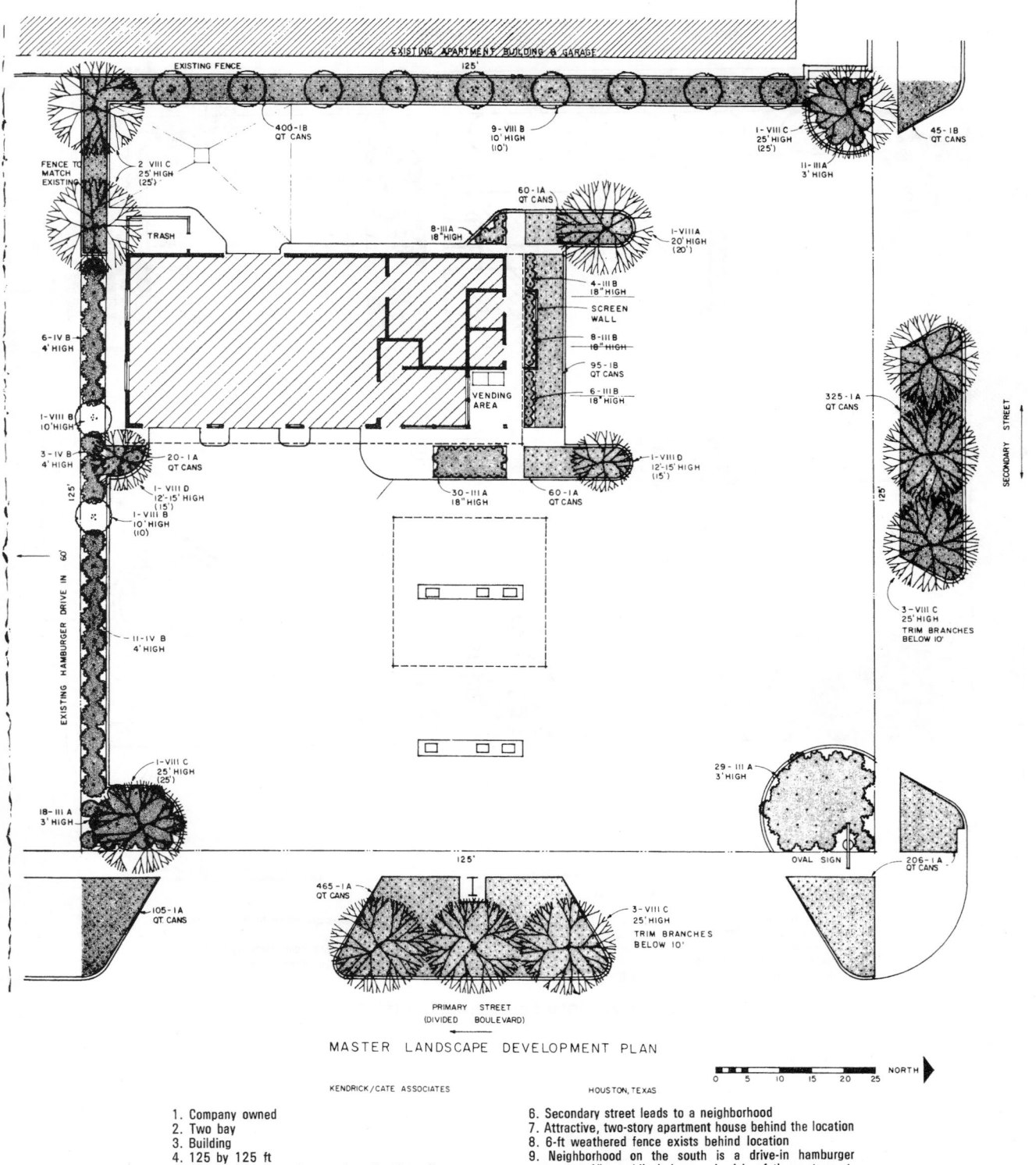

MASTER LANDSCAPE DEVELOPMENT PLAN

KENDRICK/CATE ASSOCIATES                    HOUSTON, TEXAS

1. Company owned
2. Two bay
3. Building
4. 125 by 125 ft
5. Primary street, four-lane boulevard with median

6. Secondary street leads to a neighborhood
7. Attractive, two-story apartment house behind the location
8. 6-ft weathered fence exists behind location
9. Neighborhood on the south is a drive-in hamburger restaurant. View while being serviced is of the restaurant.

**Fig. 7. Existing neighborhood (light commercial) location**

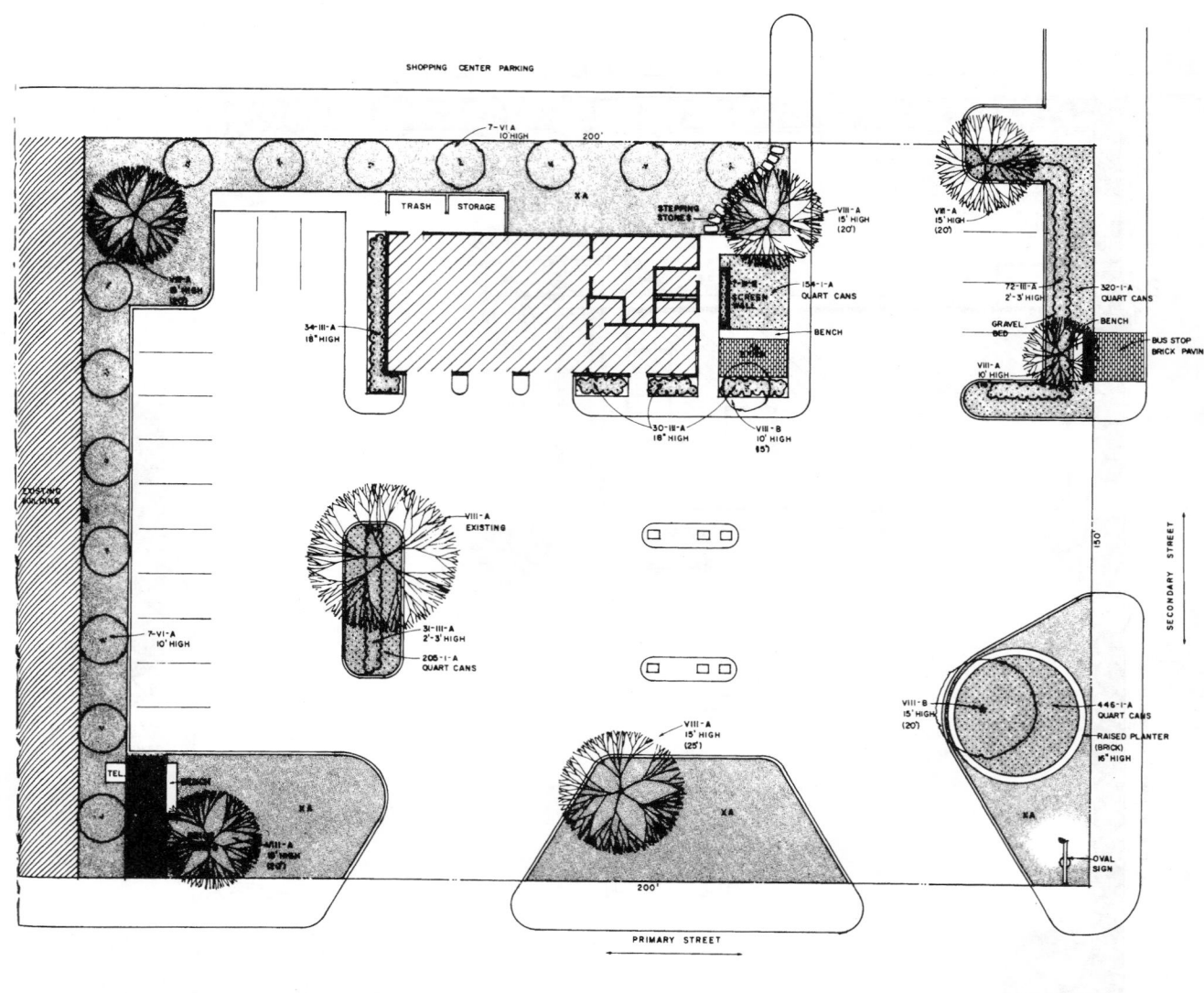

MASTER LANDSCAPE DEVELOPMENT PLAN

NEW URBAN LOCATION

KENDRICK/CATE ASSOCIATES      HOUSTON, TEXAS

1. Company owned
2. Two bay, contemporary design
3. Field stone
4. Business district 200 by 150 ft
5. Large shopping center and parking lot to the rear

6. Neighbor on the west, three-story office building, extending to the sidewalk
7. Considerable foot traffic to and from shopping center
8. Purchase agreement specifies opening to parking lot

**Fig. 8. Proposed new urban location**

# AUTOMOBILE SERVICE STATIONS

## Automotive Shop

## Gas-Filling and Service Stations

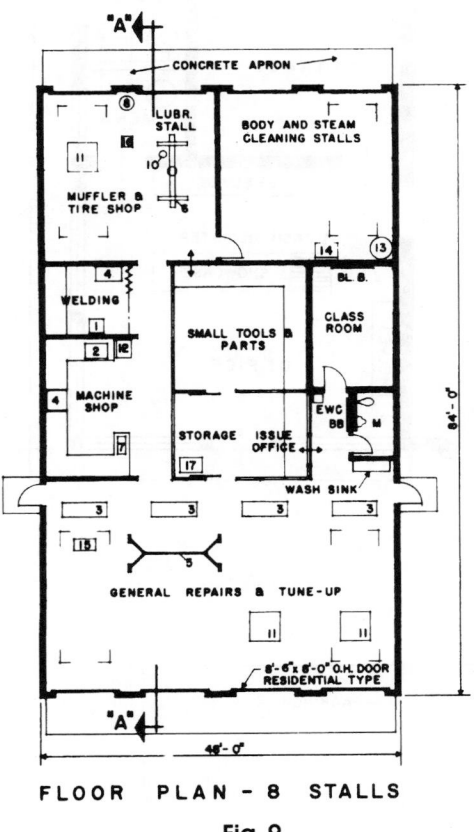

FLOOR PLAN - 8 STALLS

Fig. 9

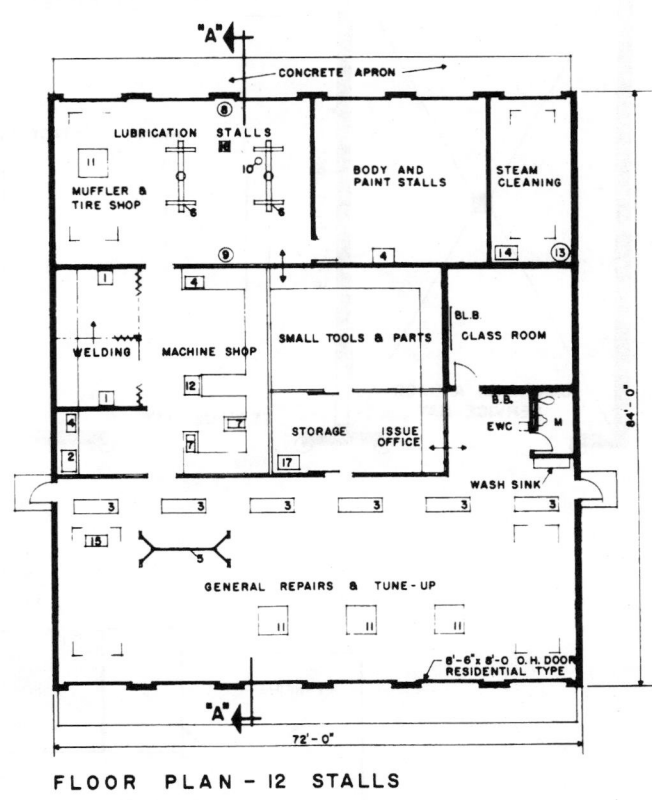

FLOOR PLAN - 12 STALLS

Fig. 10

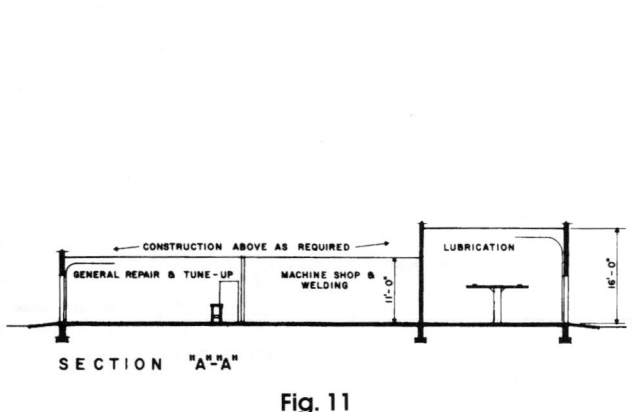

SECTION "A"-"A"

Fig. 11

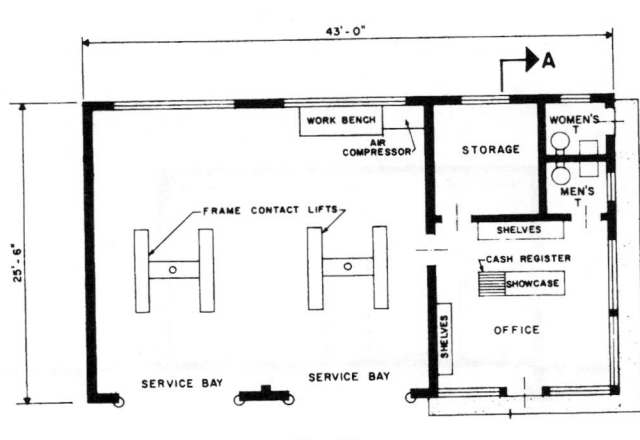

Fig. 12

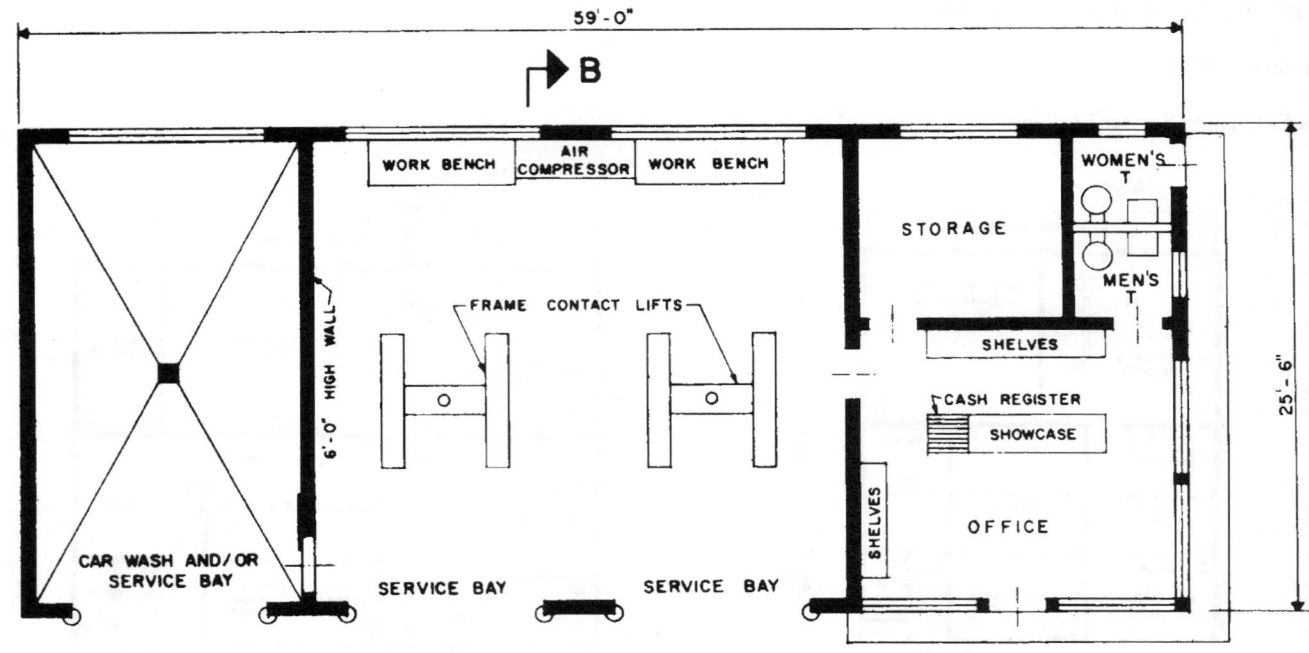

Fig. 13

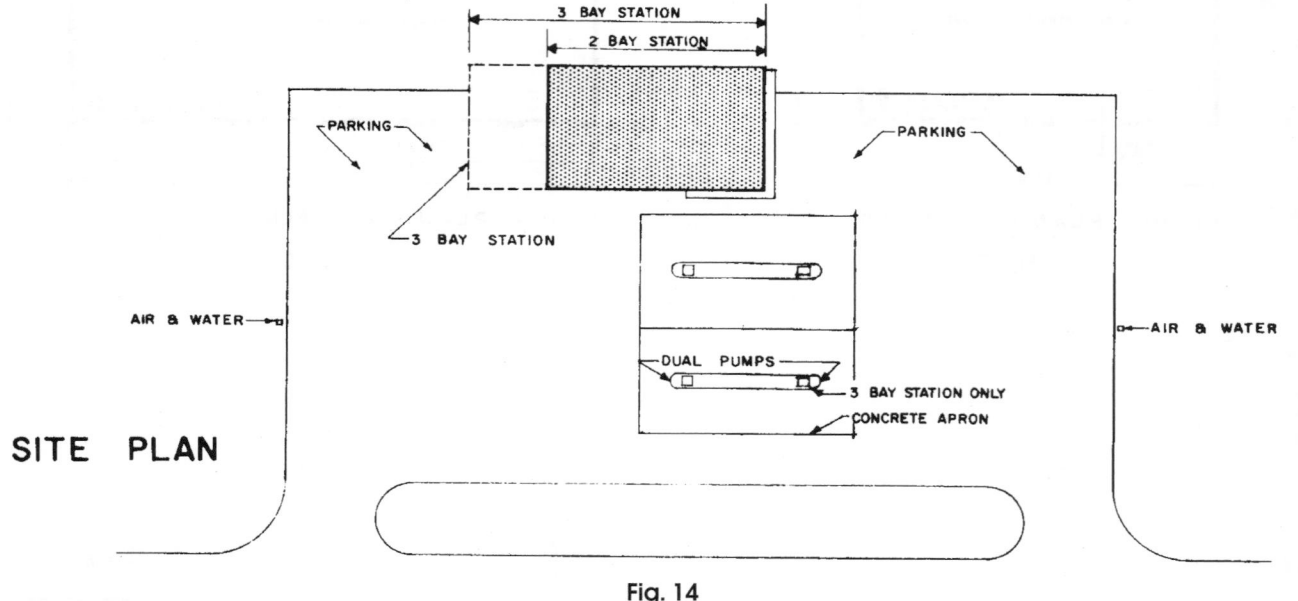

SITE PLAN

Fig. 14

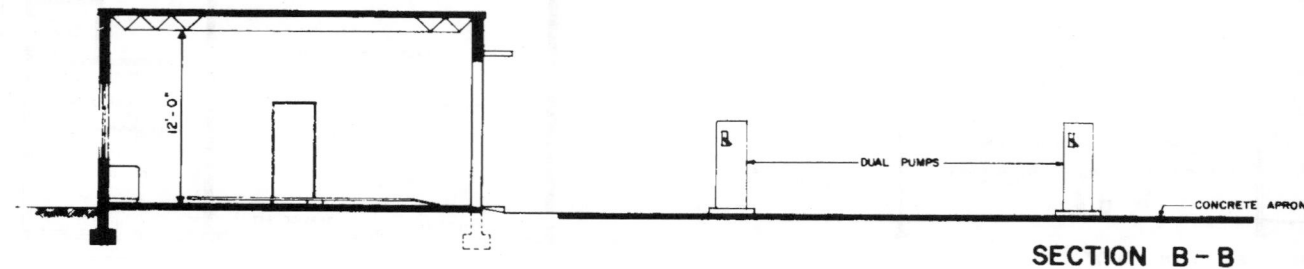

SECTION B-B

Fig. 15

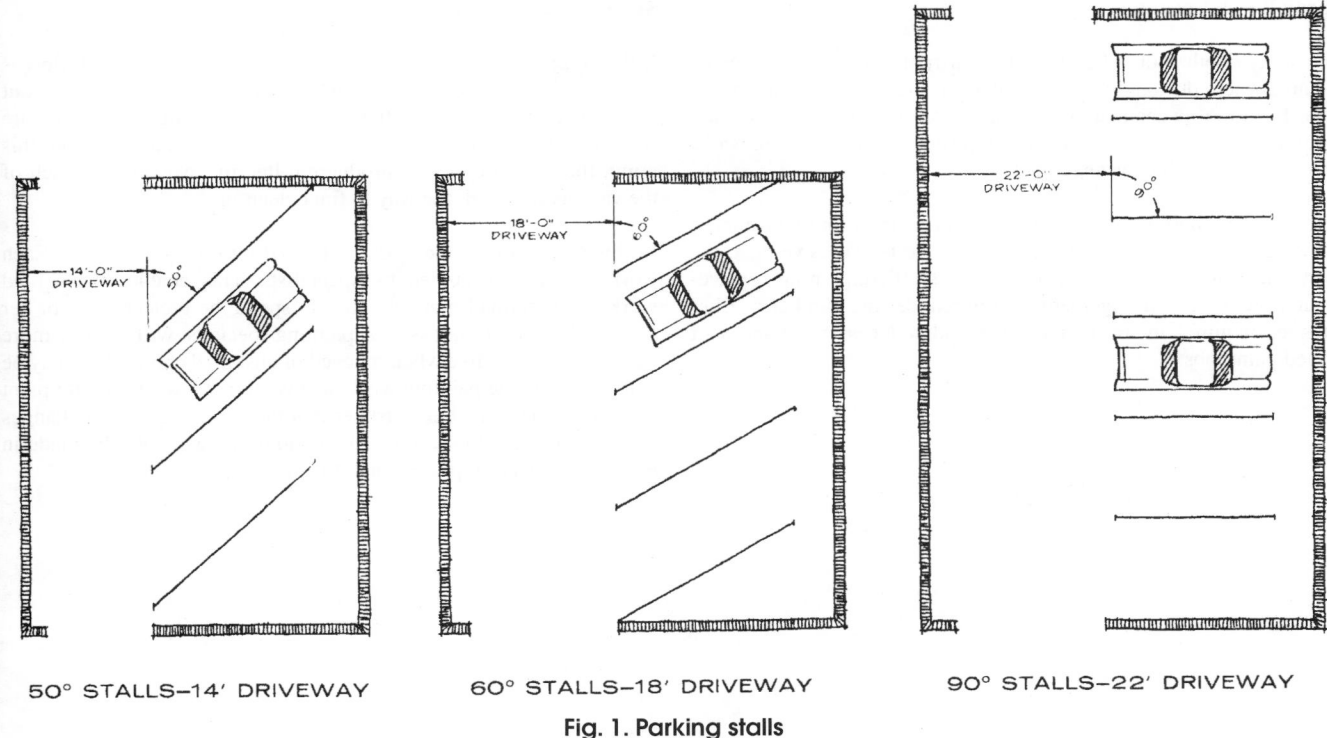

50° STALLS—14′ DRIVEWAY     60° STALLS—18′ DRIVEWAY     90° STALLS—22′ DRIVEWAY

**Fig. 1. Parking stalls**

# AUTOMOBILE BODY SHOP

### STALL SIZES

Production stalls (Figs. 1 to 3) are those in which body or paint work is performed. There should be an additional outdoor parking space for each production stall to accommodate the bank of jobs to come or the jobs completed.

The general rule for stall sizes is 5 feet in front of the car for tools and work space, or 24 feet for average cars with at least 4 feet of work space between cars. This means a stall width would be the approximate width of the car plus 2 feet on either side. For stalls against the wall, add an extra foot for a 3-foot aisle between car and wall.

Stalls for passenger cars, small trucks, and vans should be 12 feet wide and 24 feet deep. This size can be decreased if the shop is predominantly for compacts. Or, a ratio of compact work to the total can be determined and smaller stalls set aside for this work. Special stalls for frame straightening and other body equipment will have to be sized according to the specific piece of equipment used. Generally, 14-foot stalls are adequate for heavy metalworking. Stalls for cleanup, masking or other light duty work that does not require heavy tools may be 10 feet wide and 24 feet deep.

### Estimating

Since estimating may take place in many different areas, depending on the extent of the damage, it may be well to consider a separate well-lighted area for estimating.

### Office

A guide for planning office space allows 48 square feet for each person who will be using the office. If insurance adjusters will be using office space as well, add 48 square feet for each one.

### Paint Storage

A separate, isolated, fireproof room for paint storage and mixing may be required by national or local codes. It will also help to control inventory and be easier to keep clean. Paint should be stored at room temperature year-round.

### Parts Storage

If the body shop is separate from the mechanical service shop, consider stocking body parts in the body shop and allow space accordingly. Overhead or mezzanine storage offers a good solution without taking up added floor space.

### Driveway Widths

Driveways for 90-degree parking should be a minimum of 22 feet. This width can be reduced to 18 feet with 60-degree angle parking and 14 feet with 50-degree angle parking.

Angle parking should be used only where it cannot be avoided. The awkward triangular spaces at both ends of the car and the building can seldom be used efficiently.

## Spray Booth Location

The spray booth should be located as far removed as possible from the area where dust and dirt is prevalent. Therefore, it should be isolated from the mechanical and metal-working portions of the shop wherever possible. This can be accomplished with partitions, walls, or a separate building arrangement.

When a spray booth must be located in the same room with metal-working stalls or other locations where there is excessive dust, the intake air can be drawn from the outdoors utilizing an air replacement system. This arrangement greatly reduces the number of filter changes required in the booth doors and reduces the chances of ruined paint jobs.

## Straight-Line Work Flow

If the volume of paint work is sufficient, a straight-line work flow is recommended. Utilizing a drive-through type spray booth, this layout is designed for maximum efficiency of work and equipment. Jobs are started in the metal-working stalls in the normal manner. From this point, the work flows in a production-line manner through each of the various stages all the way to final clean-up.

In this arrangement, the work is divided into its components. Each work station is occupied by specialists. This enables the skilled worker (painter and metal worker) to spend the greater share of her time on the tasks of her skill. A painting specialist will become more skilled and productive when relieved of unskilled chores. She may be able to handle the painting work of several metal workers with paint preparation personnel to assist her. Another advantage is that changes in work load due to seasonal fluctuations can generally be made in the easiest area of replacement—the unskilled worker.

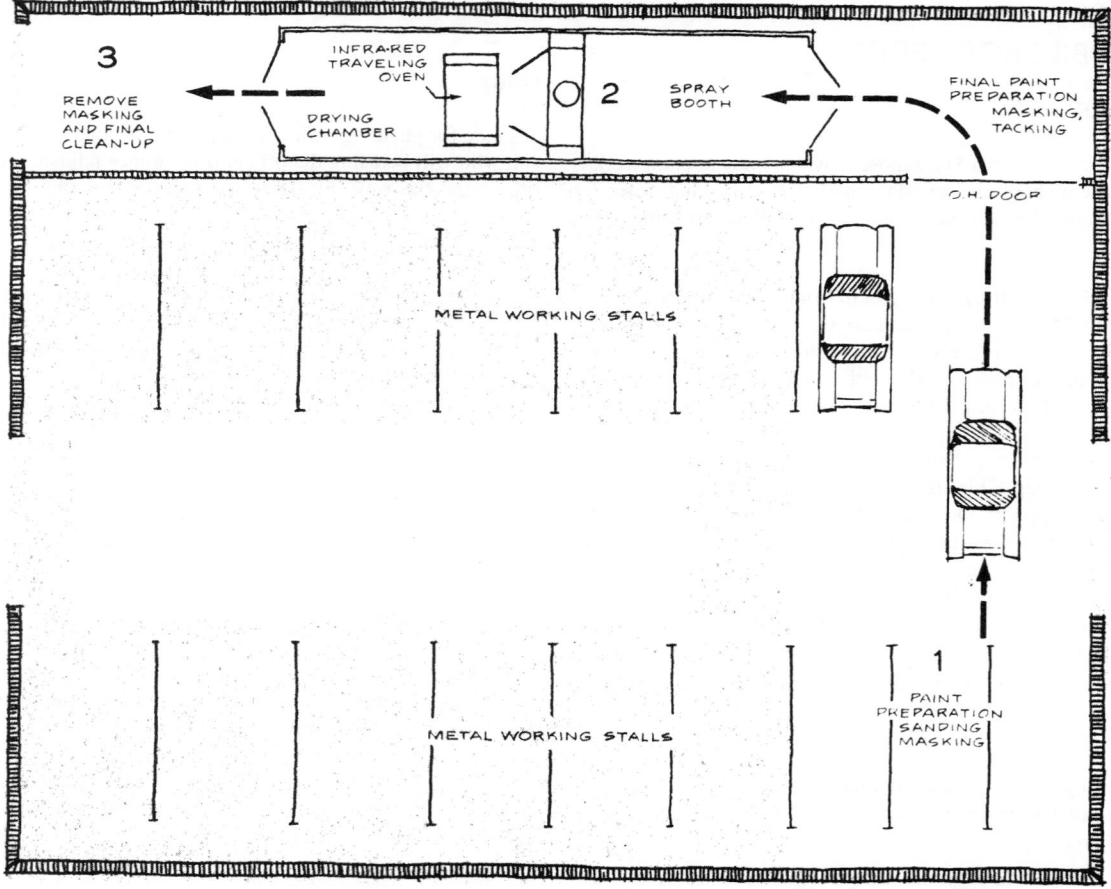

**Fig. 2. Typical body shop layout showing straight-line work flow finishing operation**

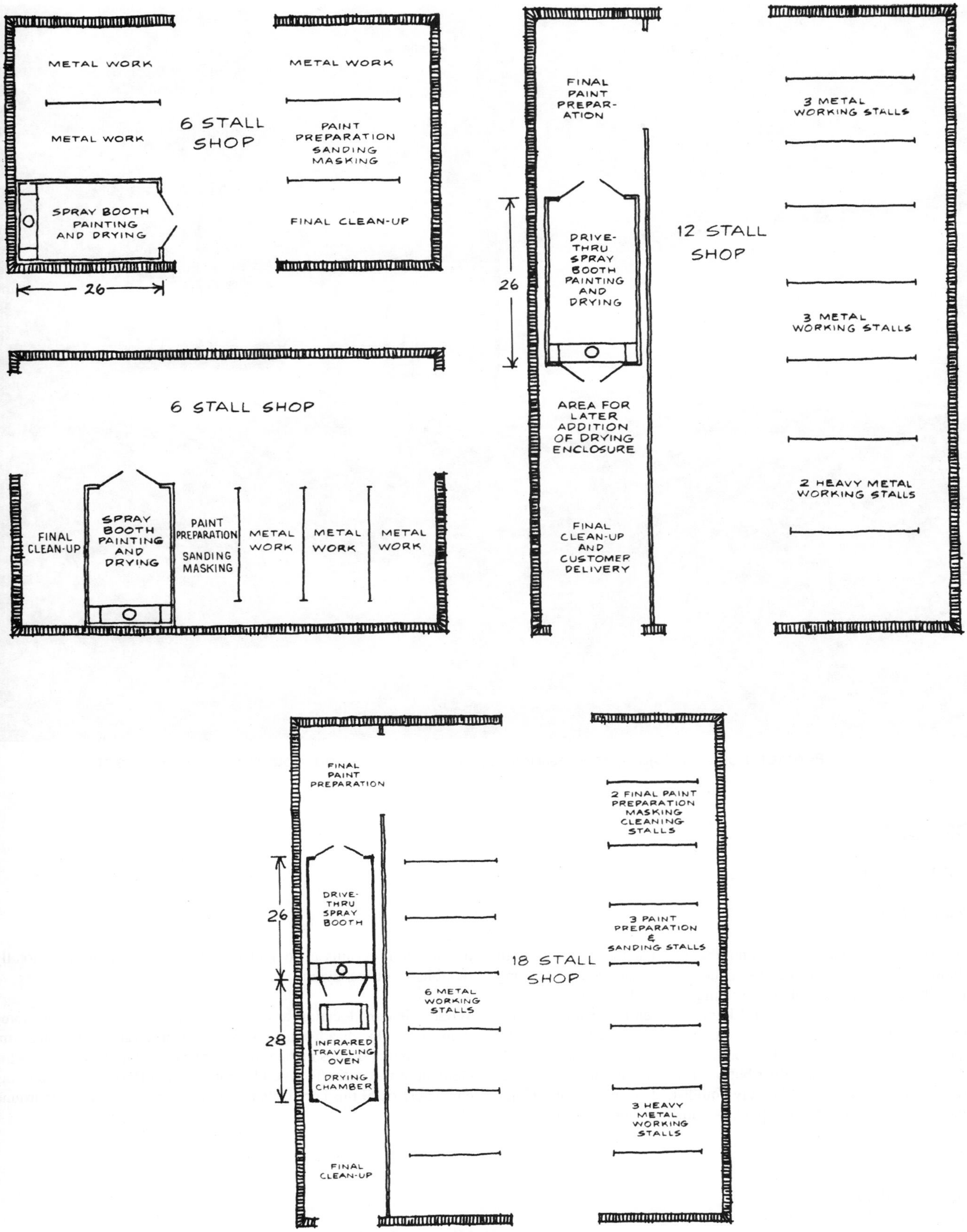

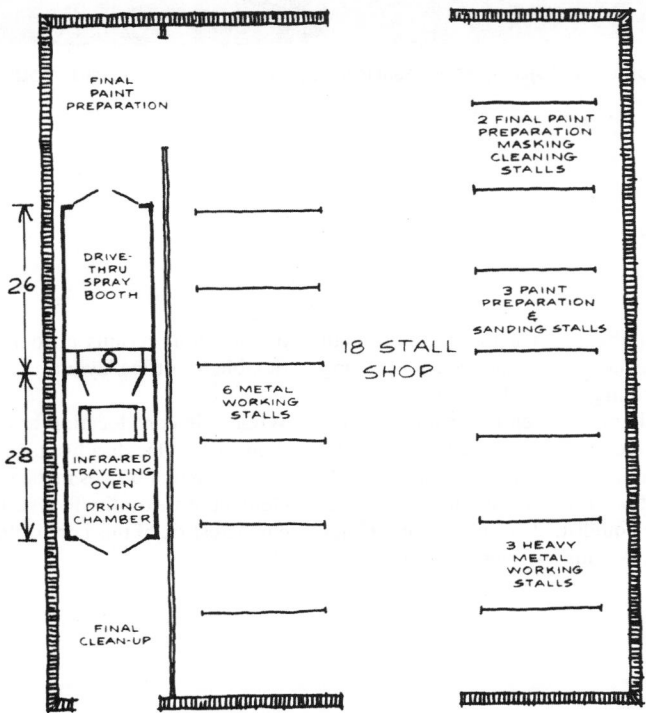

**Fig. 3. Typical body shop layouts**

**Fig. 1. Perimeter office (Mojo Stumer Associates; photo: Mark Samu, courtesy of the architect)**

## OFFICES

### CORE LOCATION

#### Central (Interior)

This location for the core has a number of advantages. It allows all window space to be utilized as rental office space and depending upon the configuration of the building plan will permit offices of varying depths to receive natural light. The central location is also extremely convenient in terms of access and in some cases may be equidistant for all sides. This simplifies area division and provides good flexibility of tenant distribution in the same way. Horizontal utility runs may also be relatively equidistant from the core. Combined with a square building plan, bearing exterior, and core walls, this location permits a floor plan free of columns and thus totally flexible for office layout.

While this core location has definite advantages, it also has some drawbacks. One disadvantage is that the central interior location limits the depth of offices in the midzone of each floor, thus affecting the element of flexibility in office layout. Another floor-area-consuming characteristic of this core is that it requires an access corridor around its perimeter.

*Author:* Frank Memoli
*Reviewer:* Mark D. Stumer, AIA
*References:* Guide for Space planning & Layout, General Services Administration Public Buildings Service, Washington, DC.

## Off-Center (Interior)

Like the central-interior core, the off-center interior core permits all window or building perimeter space to be used for offices (Fig. 1). However, it presents somewhat more flexibility in maximum depth and arrangement of spaces. This can be particularly desirable where large open spaces such as secretarial or clerical pools are required. It also affords the opportunity of developing small secluded spaces in the relatively narrow portion of the floor plan where the core is closest to the exterior wells.

This core location may present some problems of access. Because it is off-center, it is somewhat remote and thus less convenient to the far sides and corners of the building. If there is multiple-tenant occupancy on any given floor, a long access corridor will be required as will be a perimeter corridor around the core itself. The off-center location may also lessen flexibility of tenant distribution.

## Split (Interior)

The principal advantage of a split core is that it virtually eliminates the need for a peripheral corridor on the core. Access to this core is from the area between its split elements and not from the area around its edges. This permits more flexibility of floor-area division, leaving even the area immediately adjacent to the core available for office space. Depending on the width of the access space in the center of the core, this space may be put to different of the on different floors. At the ground, or entry, level this area can become a lobby, while on floors where elevators do not stop this space can be used for additional office space.

## Exterior

Unlike the three interior core locations discussed, the primary advantage of an exterior core arrangement is that it leaves the entire floor area of the building available for tenant use. In addition, the core does not complicate the floor plan either functionally or structurally. With this type of arrangement, maximum flexibility is achieved with respect to tenant distribution, office depth, and layout. Since the core creates a "dead wall" or portion thereof, it may be used as a buffer between the building and an adjoining property which may have objectionable characteristics. Location on the outside of the building also permits the core to act as a point of transition between one building and another of possibly different scale.

Some problems are also created by placing the core on the outside of a building. The primary drawback is that, in the case of multi-tenant occupancy, the core requires a long access corridor lessening flexibility of tenant distribution. In addition, the core occupies desirable window space so that the offices immediately adjacent to the core may not receive any natural light.

## GENERAL DESIGN PRINCIPLES

### Work Flow

The relationship of individuals, as determined by operating procedures, must be the governing factor in any layout. The development of a layout which conforms to and complements the predominant work flow requirements of an office is perhaps the most important phase of space planning. By the systematic study of the operations, processes, and procedures involved in individual (or group) tasks, the planner can assist management by providing work station patterns which ensure a smooth, straight-line flow of work. It should be understood that space planning does not conflict with or overlap the field of methods and systems analysis. The role of the space planner is to gain a knowledge of the functions, as developed, and to translate them into the best space layout possible within the limitations imposed by building characteristics, fiscal allotments, etc.

### Straight-Line Principle

In a well-planned office, paper goes from one desk to another with the least amount of handling, traveling, and delay. Work should progress in a series of straight lines with a general forward movement, avoiding criss-cross motions and backward flow. When the layout is being developed, the flow pattern can be traced from desk to desk. Caution must be exercised, however, since the straight-line work principle cannot be adapted to all activities, particularly those headquarters or departmental offices whose staff activities do not lend themselves to assembly-line processing.

### Work Stations

All work stations, whether in a private office or in open space, are reduced to units of furniture and equipment. The basic units of work stations are desks, and therefore they require the most consideration. The following general rules are applicable in positioning desks:

- Desks should face the same direction unless there is a compelling functional reason to do otherwise. The use of this technique provides for straight work flow patterns, facilitates communications, and creates a neat and attractive appearance.
- In open areas, consideration should be given to placing desks in rows of two. This method will permit the use of bank-type partitions as a divider for those activities which require visual privacy while still obtaining maximum utilization.
- Desks should be spaced at a distance of 6 feet from the front of a desk to the desk behind it. This distance should be increased to 7 feet when desks are in rows of two, ingress and egress is confined to one side of the aisle, or in instances where more than two desks side by side cannot be avoided.
- In private offices the desk should be positioned to afford the occupant a view of the door.
- In open work areas the supervisor should be located adjacent to the receptionist or secretary. Access to supervisory work stations should not be through the work area.
- Desks of employees having considerable visitor contact should be located near the office entrance (Fig. 2). Conversely, desks of employees doing classified work should be away from entrances.

### "Executive Core" Concept

Most office building designs produce a block-type structure that is well lighted and air conditioned, and which is divided by a few access corridors radiating from a central service core. This type of construction permits development of space plans based on the "Executive Core" concept. This concept, or technique, places all or a majority of the private offices in the core area and allocates space along the building perimeter for others. It has proved very satisfactory in many cases where it has been used and has potential in most new buildings in which large, or relatively large, groups of "lower echelon" employees will be housed (Fig. 3).

This concept arises from the premise that employees performing routine tasks that keep them at their desks almost the entire work day

**Fig. 2. Desks near office entrance (Mojo Stumer Associates; photo courtesy of the architect)**

**Fig. 3. Office open to perimeter (Mojo Stumer Associates, photo courtesy of the architect)**

require the psychological advantages of window space. On the other hand, supervisors and executives are frequently called upon to leave their offices for meetings, supervisory tours, etc., and interior offices, if properly designed and decorated, are completely acceptable for them. Also, the occupants of private offices generally receive the greatest number of visitors; in fact, the need to receive many visitors is perhaps the justification most frequently given for private offices. The location of private offices in the core facilitates the handling of visitors and keeps them from the general work areas.

**Other Planning Considerations**

The application of the following considerations will assist the space planner to attain functional effectiveness in the final layout:

* Employees performing close work should be in the best-lighted areas. Glaring surfaces which affect vision should be identified and corrected.
* Clothes lockers in an office layout are out of date and wasteful. Large rooms or open areas should be provided with hanging space for coats and shelves for hats, packages, and other material. Space not suitable for work stations should be used whenever possible.
* Heavy equipment generally should be placed against walls or columns in order to avoid floor overloading.
* Be safety conscious. Do not obstruct exits, corridors, or stairways. Comply with fire safety codes governing aisles, exits, etc.
* Where frequent interviews with the general public are required, as in personnel offices, the use of interview cubicles should be considered. Such cubicles need only be large enough for the interviewer, the applicant, and a small desk or table.
* In operations that require employees to work away from their office, with only infrequent visits there to file reports, etc., consideration should be given to assigning two or more employees to each desk. Other considerations include the provision of 45-inch desks and the use of common work tables, with the assignment of file cabinet drawers to each employee in which to keep papers, etc.

**Private Offices**

The private office is the most controversial problem facing the space planner. The assignment of private offices and the type of partitioning to be used are issues to be settled by top management acting on the advice and recommendations of the space planner. Private offices should be assigned primarily for functional reasons, i.e., nature of work, visitor traffic, or for security reasons. When private offices are provided, they should be only large enough for the occupant to conduct his normal business with a reasonable degree of dignity (Fig. 4). The following are some of the factors requiring consideration prior to making the assignment:

* The necessity for a private office cannot be directly related to the classification grade of the employee.
* Supervisors who are working with their employees, rather than planning for them, should generally be in the same room or open space with them. The supervisor may be separated from the balance of his section by a distance of several feet which permits a degree of privacy.
* A frequent justification for a private office is to impress visiting representatives of industry, and the general public, with the importance or dignity of the official being contacted. However, studies of office planning in private industry tend to refute such a

position. They show many highly paid employees housed in attractive open space. Moderately sized private offices are provided only for upper echelon officials. The offices of many top executives of large, nationally known companies are less than 250 square feet each. The provision of a private office, or too large a private office for a government official, for example, may give the taxpayers an adverse impression.

- The space planner hears many reasons why people in offices need places where confidential discussions can be held and a variety of suggestions as to how this should be accomplished. The private office is the most popular, if not always the most practical, solution. A federal establishment undoubtedly has a greater problem in this respect than many branches of business. In addition to the security requirements, the government is faced with privacy situations involving investigative agencies and other activities which have occasion to inquire into the most confidential aspects of individuals' personal lives and the operations of business concerns. There is no question as to these persons' entitlement to reasonable privacy regardless of whether they are summoned to the office, appear voluntarily to render assistance, or avail themselves of services offered by the agency. There are alternatives, however, in determining the methods to be used to satisfy the various requirements.
- It is desirable that private offices be a minimum of 100 square feet and a maximum of 300 square feet each in size, depending upon the requirements of the occupant. See sketches of most widely used private offices (Fig. 15). Only in cases where it is necessary for the occupant to meet with delegations of 10 or more people at least once a day should the size approach 300 square feet. For the average government function, the private office should not exceed 200 square feet.

## Semiprivate Offices

The semiprivate office is a room, ranging in size from 150 to 400 square feet, occupied by two or more individuals. These offices can be enclosed by ceiling-high, three-quarter-high, or bank-type partitions. Examples of semiprivate offices are shown in Fig. 17. Because of the loss of flexibility introduced by the use of the partitions

required to enclose these offices, the same rigid review given private offices should be employed. Generally, the need to house members of a work team or other groups of employees assigned to a common task is an acceptable justification for semiprivate accommodations.

## General or Open Space

The following factors affect good office layout in general or open space:

- "General office space" refers to an open area occupied by a number of employees, supervisors, furnishings, equipment, and circulation area (Fig. 5). Large open areas permit flexibility and effective utilization, aid office communications, provide better light and ventilation, reduce space requirements, make possible better flow of work, simplify supervision, and eliminate partition costs. In many cases, however, open-space housing for more than 50 persons should be subdivided either by use of file cabinets, shelving, railing, or low bank-type partitions.
- The space allocated to open-area work stations is based on the furniture and equipment necessary to perform the work assigned as well as on circulation area. The space assigned to any specific work station may be increased due to special furniture and equipment requirements associated with the particular position.

## Circulation

This is the area required to conveniently permit ingress and egress to work stations. The size of an aisle should be governed by the amount of traffic it bears. The following standards with regard to internal circulation will be applied in space planning surveys:

- Aisles leading to main exits from areas which carry substantial traffic (main aisles) should be 60 inches wide.
- Aisles which carry a moderate amount of traffic (intermediate aisles) should be 48 inches wide.
- Aisles between rows of desks (secondary aisles) should be approximately 36 inches wide.

**Fig. 4. Private office (Mojo Stumer Associates; photo courtesy of the architect)**

**Fig. 5. General office (Mojo Stumer Associates; photo courtesy of the architect)**

### Conference Requirements

Conferences, meetings, and assemblies are an important part of office operations. Since there is no established standard suggesting the number of conference rooms based on the number of people, the needs will vary widely among companies or agency components, depending largely on the nature of their work. Whenever possible, the establishment of conference rooms should be based on need established from past records and experience, rather than on anticipated needs. Unnecessary conference space is often allowed because planning is not based on such records of demonstrated need. The space planner should always evaluate the utilization of existing conference rooms before recommending others.

Conferences are best conducted in space designed for that purpose. Conference space should not be provided in private offices. In lieu of large offices, it is desirable to provide a conference room adjoining the office of a top executive who holds a large number of conferences and nearby conference rooms for employees with more limited requirements. Separate conference rooms permit maximum utilization through scheduling at an appropriate level of management (Fig. 6). Where feasible, training and conference requirements should be pooled and conference space used as auxiliary office area for visitors.

The conference room should be centrally located to the users. Interior space, which is not the most desirable for office purposes, is well suited for conference use. This location eliminates outside distraction and the need for window coverings during visual presentations. Access to conference rooms should be through corridors or through reception areas.

Conference rooms should be designed to accommodate average but not maximum attendance. Extra chairs can be used to achieve additional seating. See illustrations of preferred layout of conference rooms of various sizes.

### Reception Areas and Visitor Control

Visitors receive their first impression of an organization from the decor and layout of the reception area. It should be attractive, neat,

businesslike, and above all, adequate to accommodate normal visitor traffic (Fig. 7). An allowance of 10 square feet for each visitor to be served may be used for space allocation. For example, if space is required for a total of five visitors at any given time, a total of 50 square feet should be used in planning the space. Size, decor, and equipment will depend largely on the type and volume of visitor traffic; thus special planning will be required to meet specific needs. The receptionist should be placed so as to command a clear view of those entering and be easily accessible to visitors.

### General Office Areas

General office areas are the spaces that accommodate workstations. There are three basic approaches to planning general office areas: closed plan, open plan, and modified open plan.

### Planning Approaches

The primary considerations in identifying the most appropriate approach to planning general office areas:

- Amount of planning flexibility required
- Amount of visual and acoustical privacy required for personnel
- Initial and life-cycle construction and furniture costs

In a *closed plan* (Fig. 8), full-height walls or partitions divide the space into offices and support space by floor-to-ceiling partitions (walls) with doors. Private offices typically are located along the window wall. Administrative support is housed in workstations along corridors or in shared rooms.

**Fig. 6. Conference room (Mojo Stumer Associates; photo courtesy of the architect)**

**Fig. 7. Reception area (Mojo Stumer Associates; photo: Frank Zimmermann; courtesy of the architect)**

*Advantages*

> Controlled environment
> Security
> Visual privacy
> Physical separation
> Traditional and systems furniture applications

*Disadvantages*

> Less efficient than open plan
> Lack of flexibility
> Cost of relocation
> Restricted individual and group interaction
> Views
> More extensive mechanical systems required

An *open-plan concept* (Fig. 9) locates all workstations in open space with no division by floor-to-ceiling partitions with doors. Support spaces are located in floor-to-ceiling-partitioned rooms with doors.

*Advantages*

> Efficient space utilization
> Greater planning flexibility
> Views
> Ease of communication
> Life cycle cost lower

*Disadvantages*

> Higher initial cost
> Less environmental control
> Visual privacy

*Modified open plan* (Fig. 10) combines elements of both open plan and closed plan by locating certain workstations in open plan with systems furniture and others in private offices. In a modified plan, support spaces are also located in enclosed rooms.

### Work Stations

The two elevations (Figs. 12 and 13) illustrate the major anthropometric considerations for the seated male and female user at both workstation and keyboard return. What should be noted is the seat height of the chair (a function of popliteal height) and its relationship to the specific task. When the work surface is lowered to accommodate a specialized function, as in the case of the typing return, special attention must be given to the requirements for thigh clearance. Most standard office keyboard returns have been geared to the anthropometric requirements of the female user. The popliteal height and thigh clearance requirements of the larger male user may not be readily met.

The plan (Fig. 14) shows the typical workstation expanded into the basic U-shaped configuration. The work/activity zone dimension range is shown as 46 to 58 inches; additional space is needed to allow for drawer extension of the lateral file. Not only does it provide more storage, the lateral file unit is generally the same height as that of the work surface and is often utilized as a supplementary work surface. The distance between this unit and that of the primary work surface must be sufficient to allow for movement and rotation of the chair.

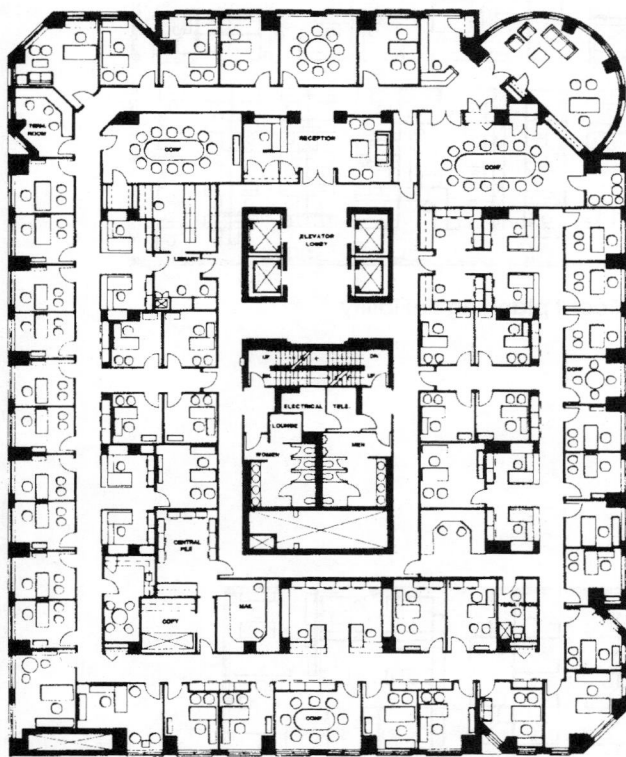

**Fig. 8. Closed plan is an appropriate planning approach for organizations with strong privacy requirements and for which planning flexibility is not a priority**

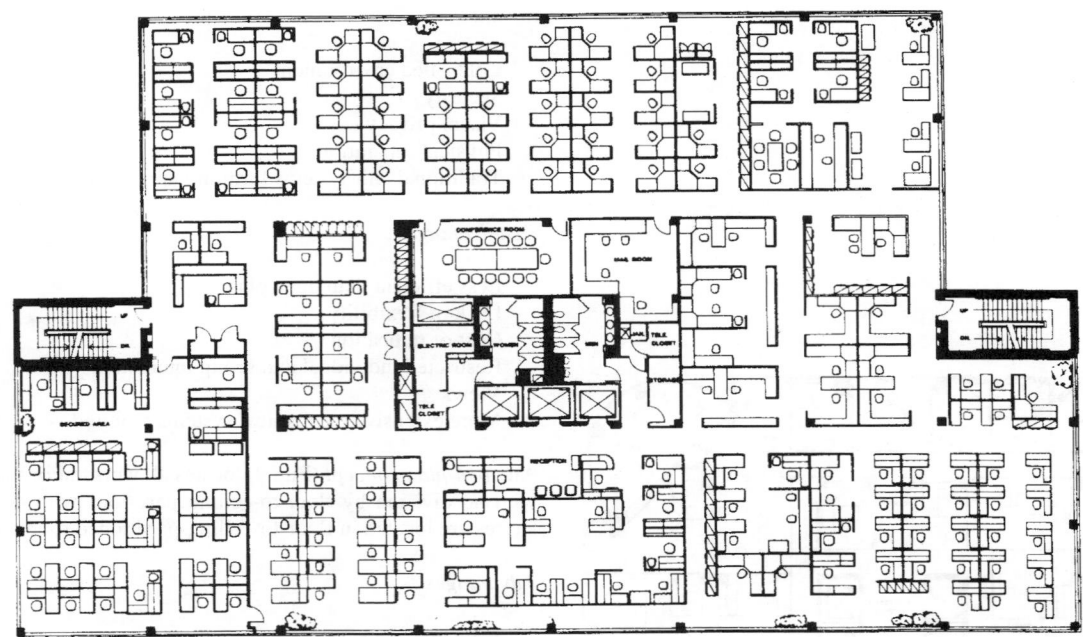

Fig. 9. Open plan provides significant planning flexibility

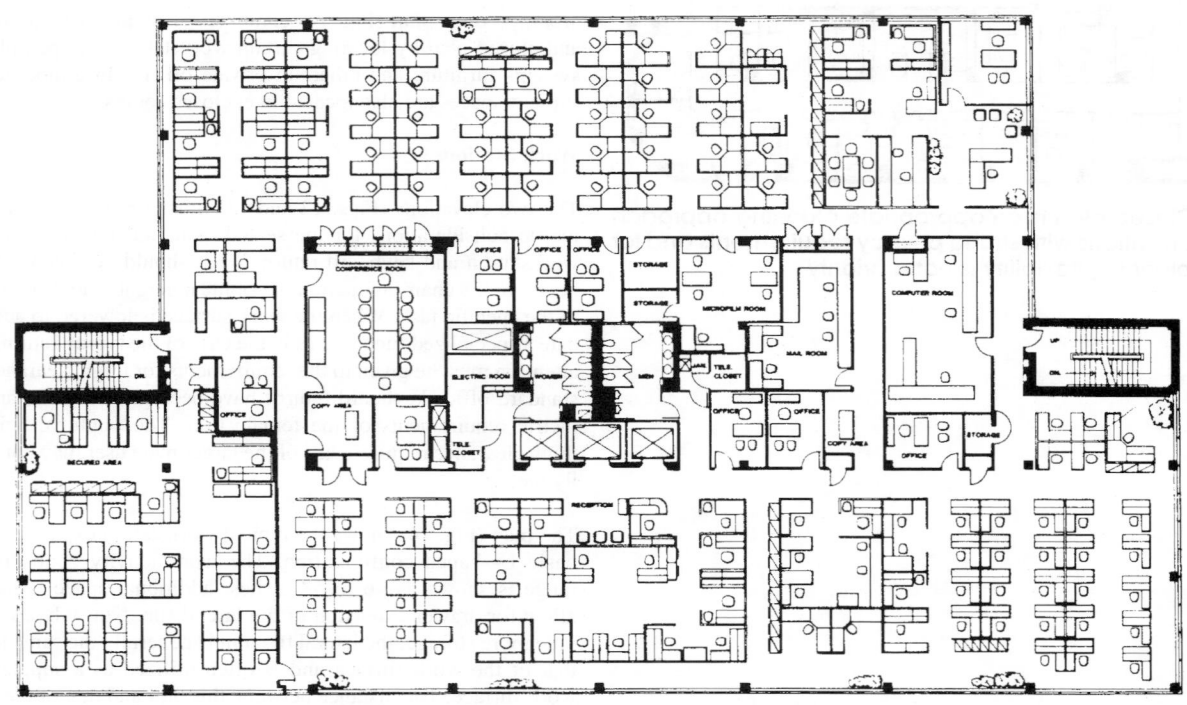

Fig. 10. Modified open plan. This modified space planning concept integrates open planning for general office areas with closed planning for conferencing and other support areas

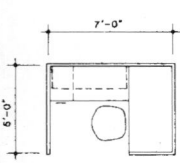
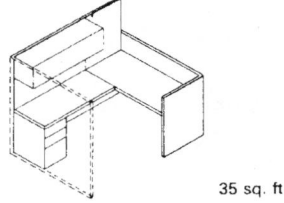

35 sq. ft.

30x60   Primary worksurface
24x54   Secondary worksurface pedestal
54 inch   Overhead storage

**WORKSTATION TYPE A**

TASK PROFILE:
Wordprocessor as primary tool
Limited storage capacity
Partial visual privacy

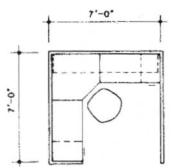
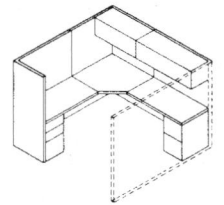

24 sq. ft.   Worksurface
2   Pedestal
84 L. inch   Overhead storage

**WORKSTATION TYPE E**

49 sq. ft.

TASK PROFILE:
EDP equipment as primary tool
limited storage capacity
full visual privacy

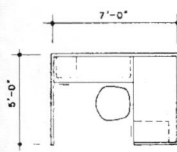
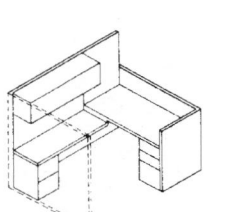

35 sq. ft.

30x60   Primary worksurface
18x54   Secondary worksurface pedestal
54 inch   Overhead storage

**WORKSTATION TYPE B**

TASK PROFILE:
Nonautomated task
Limited storage capacity
Partial visual privacy

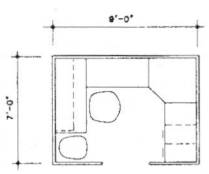
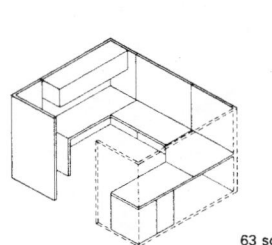

63 sq. ft.

1   Guest chair
24 x 60   Primary worksurface
24 sq. ft.   Secondary worksurface
2   Pedestal
60 L.inch   Overhead storage

**WORKSTATION TYPE F**

TASK PROFILE:
Limited conference capability
ADP equipment as secondary tool
Limited storage capacity
Full visual privacy

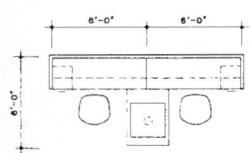
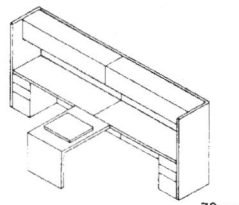

72 sq. ft.

24x72   Primary worksurface
30x45   Shared worksurface pedestal
72 inch   Overhead storage

**WORKSTATION TYPE C**

TASK PROFILE:
Shared tasks
Limited storage capacity
Partial visual privacy

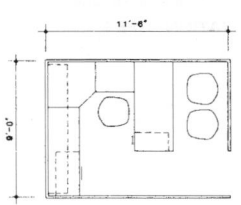
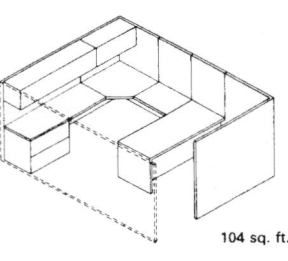

104 sq. ft.

2   Guest chair
30 x 72   Primary worksurface
25 sq. ft.   Secondary worksurface
1   Pedestal
2   Lateral drawer

**WORKSTATION TYPE G**

TASK PROFILE:
Extended conference capability
EDP equipment as secondary tool
Moderate storage capacity
Full visual privacy

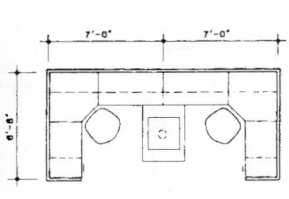
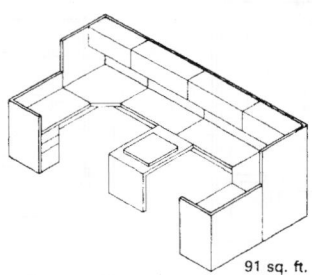

91 sq. ft.

25 sq. ft.   Primary worksurface
30 x 45   Shared worksurface
1   Pedestal
84 L. inch   Overhead storage

**WORKSTATION TYPE D**

TASK PROFILE:
Individual EDP equipment
additional shared tasks
limited storage capacity
partial visual privacy

**Fig. 11. Workstations types A-L**

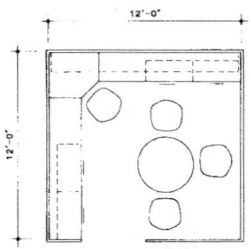

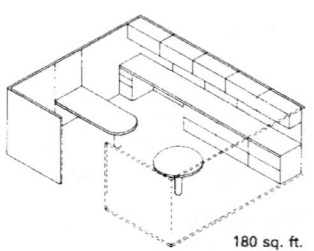

144 sq. ft.

| 3 | Guest chair |
| 42 dia. | Conference table |
| 44 sq. ft. | Worksurface |
| 8 | Lateral drawer |
| 144 L. inch | Overhead storage |

**WORKSTATION TYPE H**

TASK PROFILE:
Extensive conference capability
DP equipment as secondary tool
Extensive storage capacity
full visual privacy

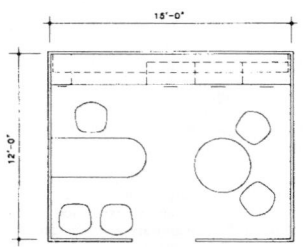

180 sq. ft.

| 4 | Guest chair |
| 42 dia. | Conference table |
| 30 x 72 | Primary worksurface |
| 30 sq. ft. | Secondary worksurface |
| 1 | Pedestal |
| 6 | Lateral drawer |
| 180 L. inch | Overhead storage |

**WORKSTATION TYPE I**

TASK PROFILE:
Extensive conference capability
ADP equipment capability
extensive storage capacity
full visual privacy

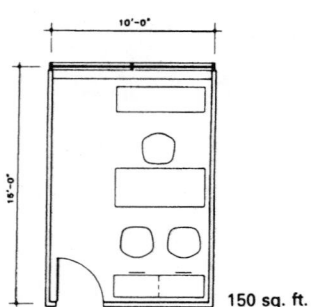

150 sq. ft.

| 30 x 66 | Double pedestal desk |
| 18 x 66 | Credenza |
| 2 | Lateral file |
| 1 | Desk chair |
| 2 | Guest chair |

**WORKSTATION TYPE J**

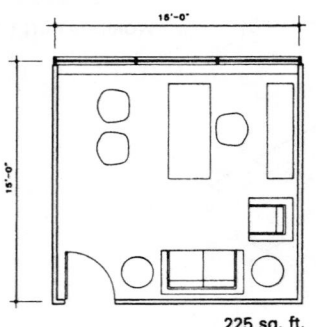

225 sq. ft.

| 30 x 72 | Double pedestal desk |
| 18 x 72 | Credenza |
| 1 | Desk chair |
| 2 | Guest chair |
| 1 | 2-Seat sofa |
| 1 | Lounge chair |
| 2 | End table |

**WORKSTATION TYPE K**

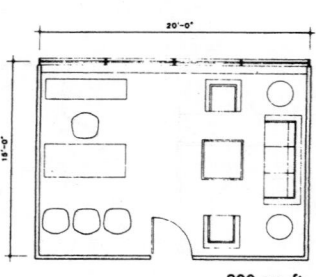

300 sq. ft.

| 30 x 72 | Double pedestal desk |
| 18 x 72 | Credenza |
| 1 | Desk chair |
| 3 | Guest chair |
| 1 | 3-Seat sofa |
| 2 | Lounge chair |
| 36 x 36 | Coffee table |
| 2 | End table |

**WORKSTATION TYPE L**

**Fig. 11. (cont.)**

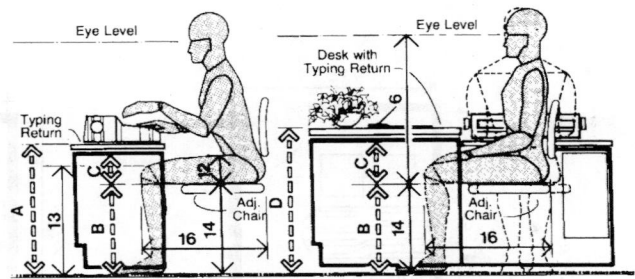

Fig. 12. Keyboard return and desk / male user

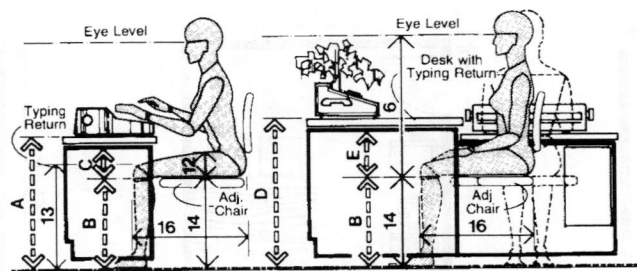

Fig. 13. Keyboard return and desk / female user

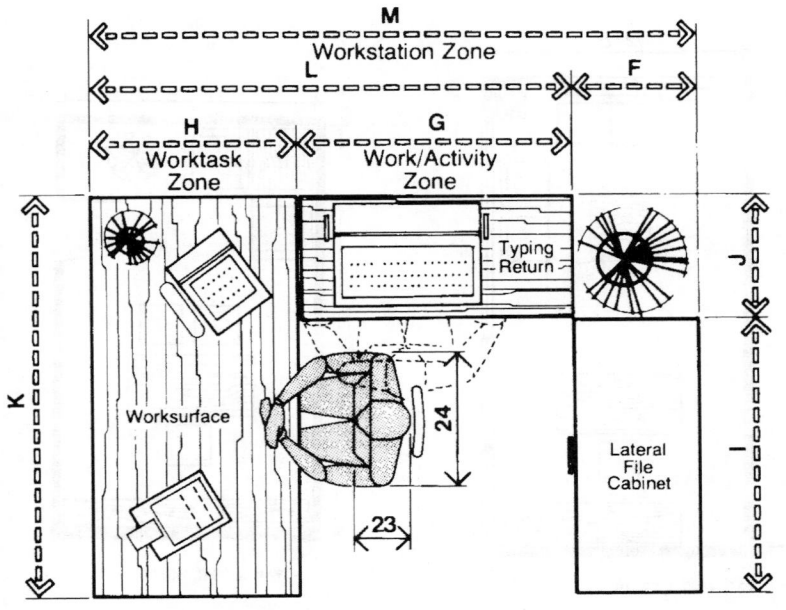

| | in | cm |
|---|---|---|
| A | 26–27 | 66.0–68.6 |
| B | 14–20 | 35.6–50.8 |
| C | 7.5 min. | 19.1 min |
| D | 29–30 | 73.7–76.2 |
| E | 7 min. | 17.8 min. |
| F | 18–24 | 45.7–61.0 |
| G | 46–58 | 116.8–147.3 |
| H | 30–36 | 76.2–91.4 |
| I | 42–50 | 106.7–127.0 |
| J | 18–22 | 45.7–55.9 |
| K | 60–72 | 152.4–182.9 |
| L | 76–94 | 193.0–238.8 |
| M | 94–118 | 238.8–299.7 |

Fig. 14. Basic U-shaped workstation

## PRIVATE OFFICES

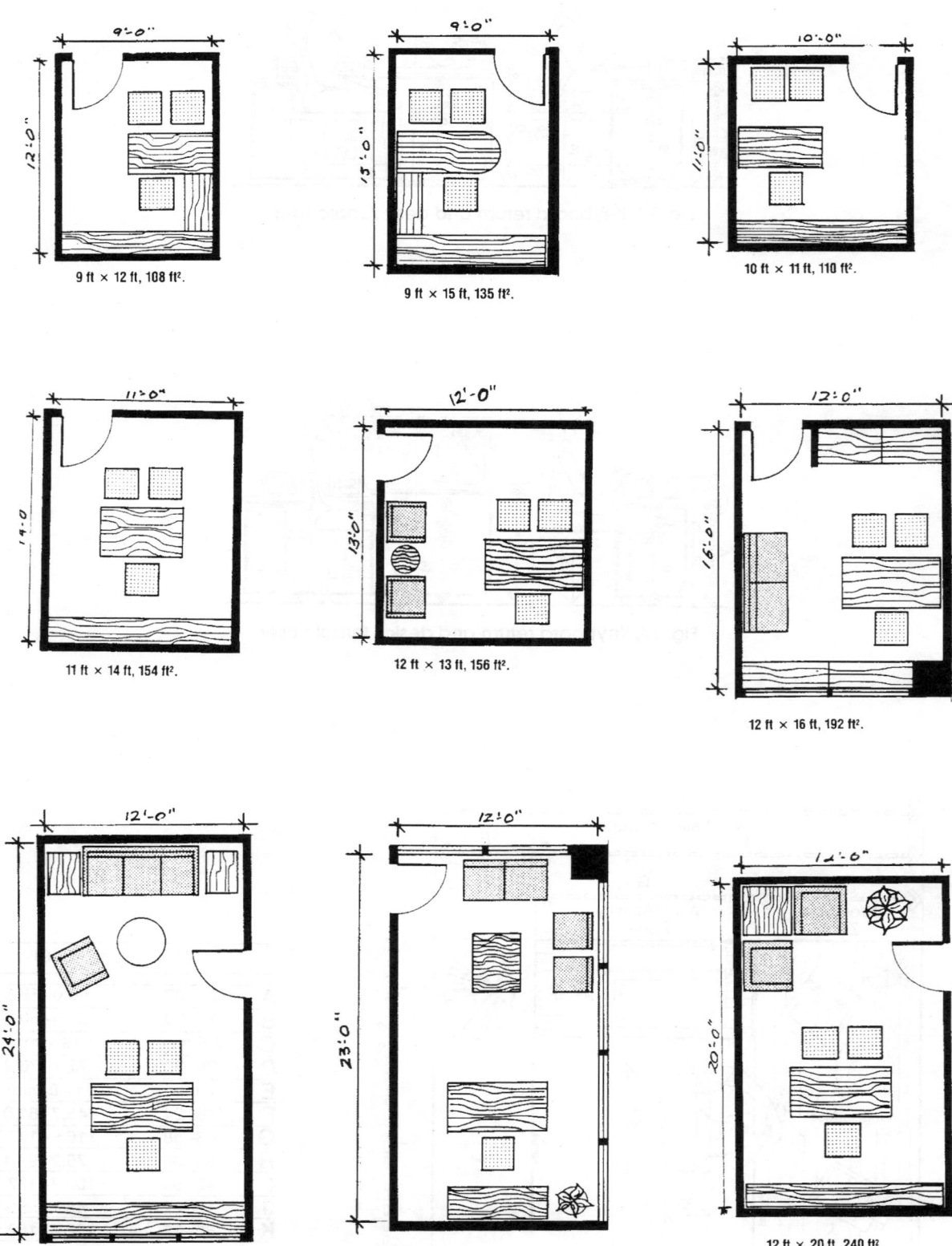

9 ft × 12 ft, 108 ft².

9 ft × 15 ft, 135 ft².

10 ft × 11 ft, 110 ft².

11 ft × 14 ft, 154 ft².

12 ft × 13 ft, 156 ft².

12 ft × 16 ft, 192 ft².

12 ft × 24 ft, 288 ft².

12 ft × 23 ft, 276 ft².

12 ft × 20 ft, 240 ft².

**Fig. 15. Private office arrangements**

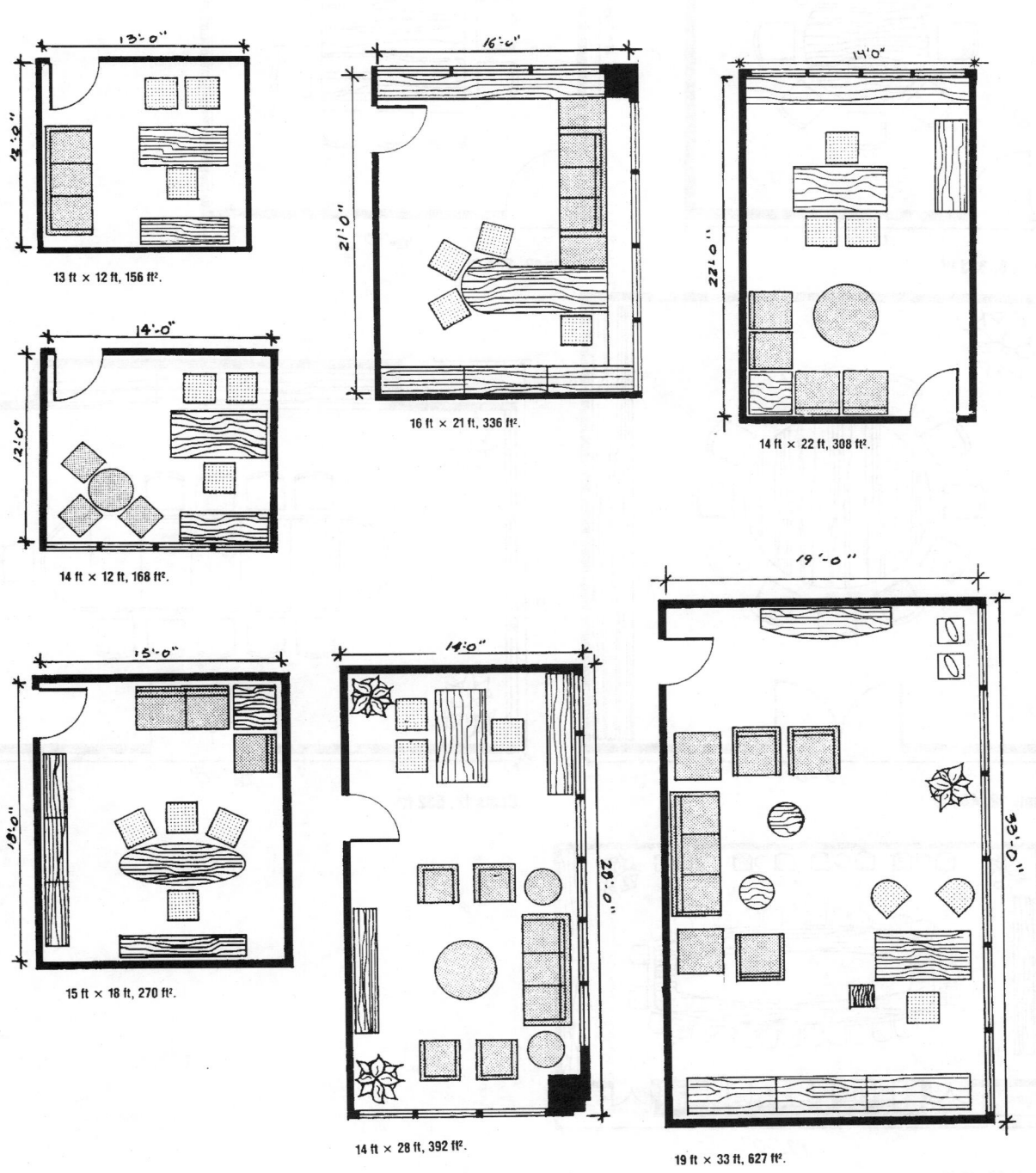

13 ft × 12 ft, 156 ft².

14 ft × 12 ft, 168 ft².

16 ft × 21 ft, 336 ft².

14 ft × 22 ft, 308 ft².

15 ft × 18 ft, 270 ft².

14 ft × 28 ft, 392 ft².

19 ft × 33 ft, 627 ft².

**Fig. 15. (cont.)**

## CONFERENCE ROOMS

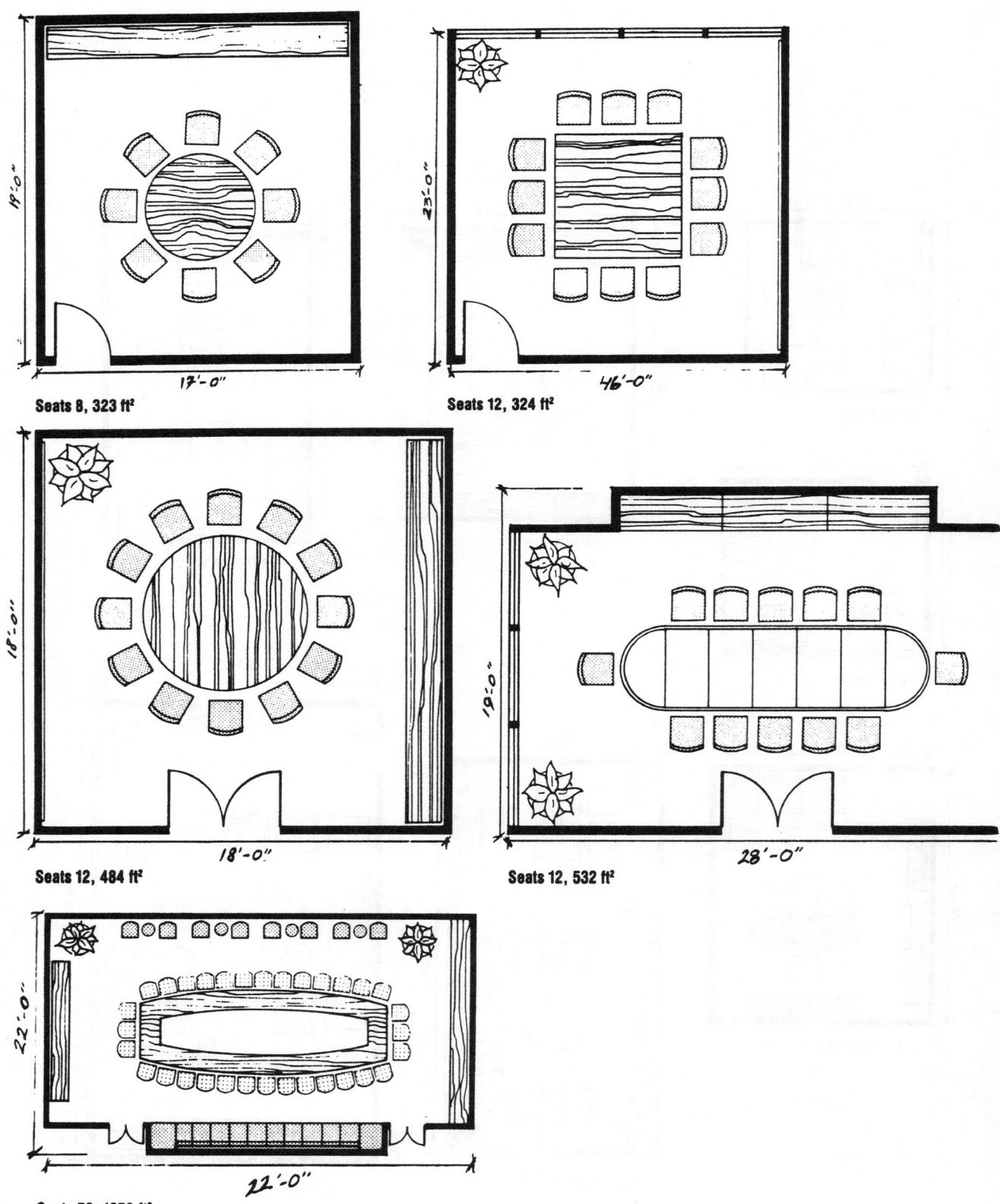

Seats 8, 323 ft²

Seats 12, 324 ft²

Seats 12, 484 ft²

Seats 12, 532 ft²

Seats 50, 1058 ft²

Fig. 16. Conference room arrangements

# GENERAL OFFICES AND MULTIPLE WORKSTATIONS

It is not unusual to have two or more persons share an enclosed office space. In planning shared office space, both circulation and clearance become critically important. Door swings, the extension of file drawers and points of entry must all be carefully considered.

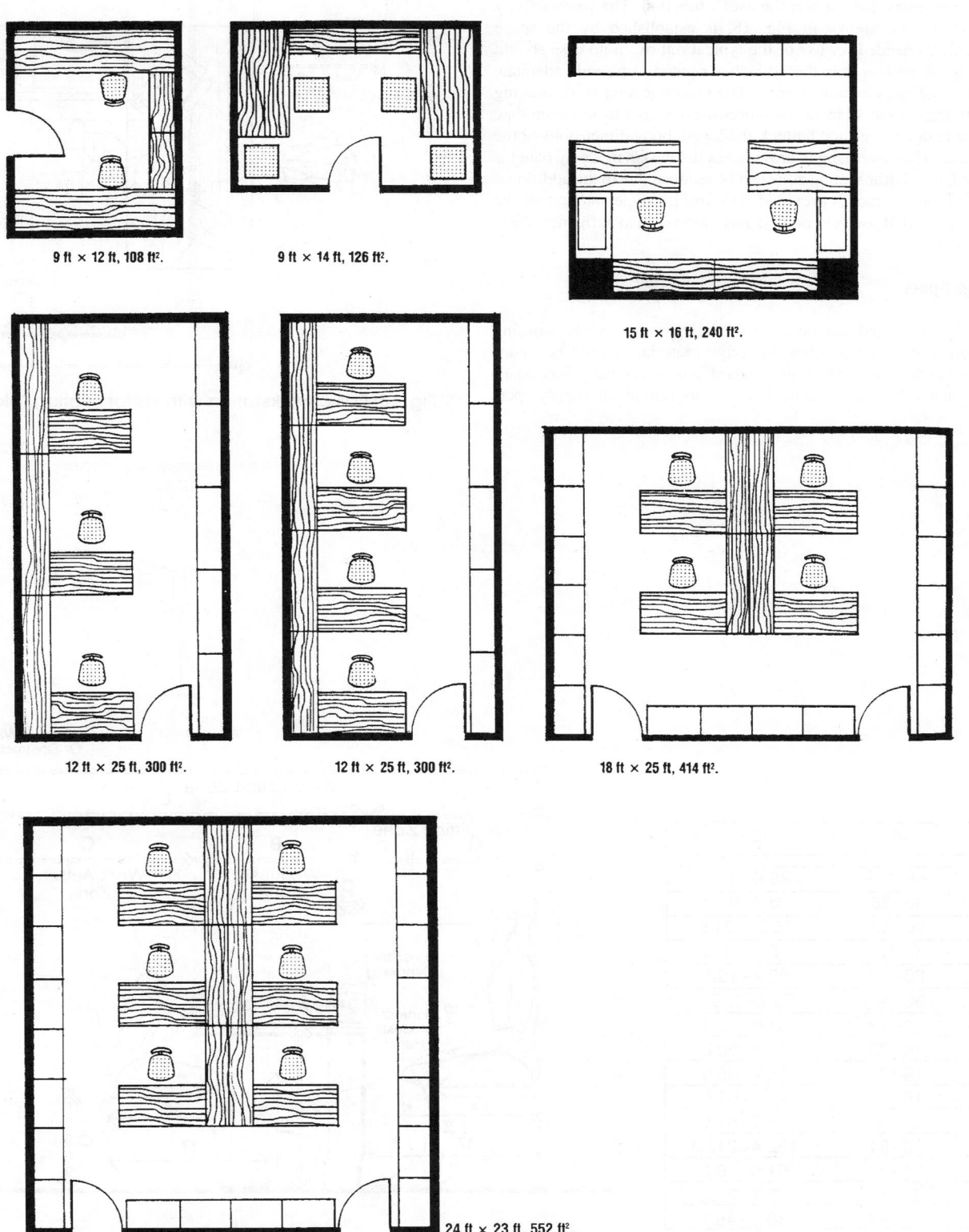

9 ft × 12 ft, 108 ft².

9 ft × 14 ft, 126 ft².

15 ft × 16 ft, 240 ft².

12 ft × 25 ft, 300 ft².

12 ft × 25 ft, 300 ft².

18 ft × 25 ft, 414 ft².

24 ft × 23 ft, 552 ft².

**Fig. 17. Shared enclosed office arrangements**

The basic workstation (Figs. 18 and 19) is the fundamental building block in understanding the anthropometric considerations for the planning and design of the general office. The work task zone must be large enough to accommodate the paperwork, equipment, and other accessories that support the user's function. The work/activity zone dimension, shown in Fig. 18, is established by the space requirements needed for use of the typical return. In no case should this distance be less than the 30 inches needed to provide adequate space for the chair clearance zone. The visitor seating zone, ranging in depth from 30 to 42 inches, requires the designer to accommodate both the buttock-knee and buttock-toe length body dimensions of the larger user. If an overhang is provided or the desk's modesty panel is recessed, the visitor seating zone can be reduced due to the additional knee and toe clearances provided. The specific type and size of the seating (i.e., if it swivels or if it has casters) also influence these dimensions.

## Storage Space

Office space should not be used for bulk storage. Only working inventories of office supplies and other materials should be maintained in offices, preferably in standard supply cabinets. Secondary space, such as basement areas, should be used to locate supply operations.

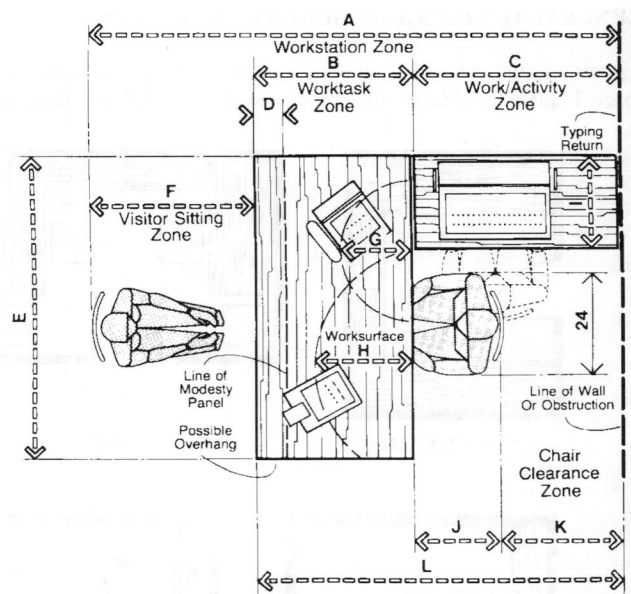

**Fig. 18. Basic workstation with visitor seating (plan)**

| | in | cm |
|---|---|---|
| A | 90–126 | 228.6–320.0 |
| B | 30–36 | 76.2–91.4 |
| C | 30–48 | 76.2–121.9 |
| D | 6–12 | 15.2–30.5 |
| E | 60–72 | 152.4–182.9 |
| F | 30–42 | 76.2–106.7 |
| G | 14–18 | 35.6–45.7 |
| H | 16–20 | 40.6–50.8 |
| I | 18–22 | 45.7–55.9 |
| J | 18–24 | 45.7–61.0 |
| K | 6–24 | 15.2–61.0 |
| L | 60–84 | 152.4–213.4 |
| M | 24–30 | 61.0–76.2 |
| N | 29–30 | 73.7–76.2 |
| O | 15–18 | 38.1–45.7 |

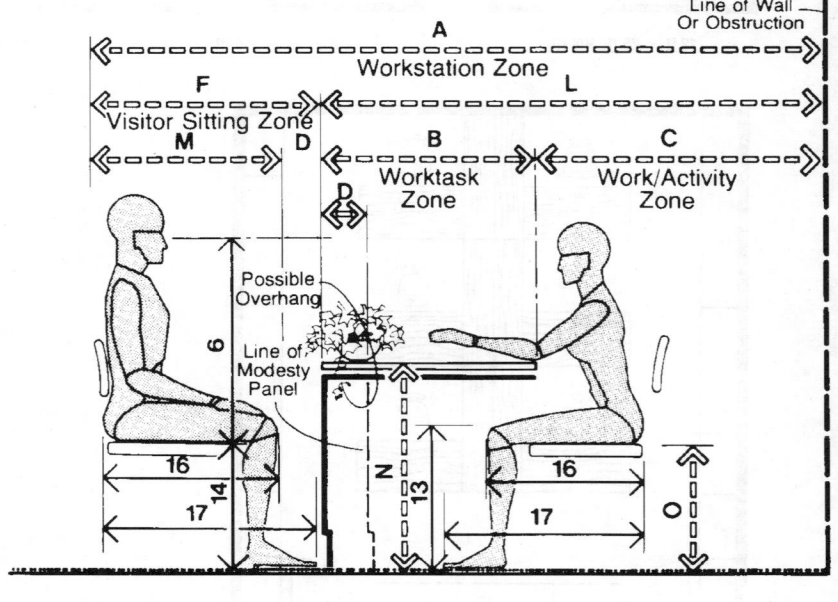

**Fig. 19. Basic workstation with visitor seating (elevation)**

# OFFICE LAYOUT BY FUNCTION

The office operation is like a large machine which needs to have all of its parts synchronized and moving smoothly. Each office function must mesh smoothly with the others with a minimum of friction.

The office machine's source of power is information, and it is the purpose of good office layout design to permit this information to flow smoothly, avoiding unnecessary turns and traps. There is certainly no one office layout that will fit all companies, any more than there is an all-purpose machine, but there are some reasonably good principles of layout by function that could be applied to any office situation.

## Six Basic Office Functions

If you were to make a list of the typical office functions, you would find it quite a long one. Every office needs management, communications, filing, billing, payments, payroll, purchasing, and accounting. Other functions are added according to the purpose of the business, such as production, production engineering, quality control, shipping and receiving, cost accounting, industrial engineering, data processing, inventory, etc.

However, all office functions can be cataloged into one of these six groups:

1. Management
2. Finance
3. Sales
4. General services
5. Technical services
6. Production

Here are some pointers for placing these groups in the best office layout position to permit smooth operation.

## Management

The top management group is usually arranged together, often in a sort of chain of command. They will be reasonably isolated from general office traffic and casual interruptions. They are frequently around the edge of the office, but they may also be in the center. The top official is perhaps the chair of the board or the president, and she naturally will have the largest and best-appointed office. The top executives need more space not only for prestige but because they have more than the usual amount of visitors and meetings. If a conference room is used, the size of the individual offices can be reduced somewhat. There is a trend away from the overabundant office for the top executives, undoubtedly encouraged by the high cost of office space rental. Space-saving furniture, however, makes the reduced space practical from an efficiency standpoint. It is not unusual in the newer offices to find the top management personnel in offices about 12 by 15 feet in size.

## Finance

Although the financial executives have responsibilities that extend into the general office and involve a considerable percentage of the clerical force, the executives need not be on the spot. Supervisors can run the show with little more connection to the boss than through intercoms or interoffice mail.

It is probably more important to put the accounting function near where it picks up the orders from the sales department. The accounting functions usually line up according to the system procedure, going in a straight line through such activities as credit checks, order processing, inventory control billing, and accounts receivable.

The purchasing department has a lot of contact with vendors, so it should be near the entrance or reception room to avoid excessive traffic. Part of purchasing has to be tied to the accounting function through the handling of requisitions, shipping notices, and vendors' invoices.

The personnel department is usually close to the reception area so that they can interview job applicants and other callers without general disruption of the office area.

The data processing activity usually comes at the end of the line, but it should be out of the traffic swirl and in a spot where the noise can be confined.

## Sales

Most firms have some sort of a sales function that starts the activity of the company. For this reason there is a considerable amount of communication between it and all the other functions of the office. The sales group frequently has visitors and needs a lot of space for catalogs and specification files, so that each person there probably has a little more than the average amount of floor space. Pricing, estimating, and correspondence are large functions in the sales group. Many sales groups need a conference room or an all-purpose room that can be used for training, meetings, demonstrations, and conferences with the engineering and product development group.

## General Services

This is the group that provides general services for all of the other functions, such as central files, stenographic service, library, mail handling, duplicating, and general communications.

The reference functions like central files, the library, and data processing are normally in the center of all the other functions in the office (Fig. 20). The mail handling is at either end of the office work flow. Duplicating services are normally isolated because of the noise and fumes, and may be near the function that calls most frequently for this service, such as shipping and receiving rooms.

The communications center is part of the job of the receptionist, and is naturally in the reception area. In a more complicated communications setup it might be in a center by itself, convenient to the other office activities.

## Technical Services

Technical services such as the engineering, drafting, and design people are normally located near the activities they assist, such as manu-

*Reference: How to Plan Your Office Space,* National Office Products Association, Washington, DC.

**Fig. 20. General office (Mojo Stumer Associates; photo courtesy of the architect)**

facturing, sales, and production. When they deal with production and systems work they are frequently out in the plant.

### Production

The production group is usually in a second office, set up out in the production plant. It is just as important to the business as the general offices and should have the same amount of considerations, dignities, and facilities. This is not always the case, unfortunately, but where it has been the policy to put this office group on a par with the general offices, an improvement in work and general morale has been accomplished.

In any large-scale planning, other factors besides available space will naturally influence the decision for the final placing of any particular department. The shipping and receiving departments, for example, could hardly be placed on the top floor even though their space requirements would fit perfectly into a given area on the top floor.

### Organization Chart

The arrangement of the office functions will actually be a projection of the organization chart of the firm, located with respect for the flow of work and the physical requirements of each department.

The organization chart will show the departments and sections which make up the firm, like the executive, offices, sales, accounting, engi-

neering, production, research, and purchasing. The chart will also give a clue to the interrelationship of the departments.

Relatively minor activities are better placed around the major office activities rather than integrated with them. When more space is needed, the major activities can be expanded with less disruption simply by moving a minor activity over a desk or two.

Each department and division has a good reason for being in one location rather than another. Here are 10 guides for determining what that location should be. When the department is properly assigned to a major area, minor changes can be made later without an upheaval in the basic pattern. Some departments will naturally qualify in several of these guides, and then it will be a matter of choosing the locations which seem to offer the best compromise.

- *Convenience to the Public:* Those departments having the greatest number of visitors should be located so that the visitors have a short, direct, and convenient route from the main entrance to the department sought. The sales, purchasing, and employment or personnel departments usually have the most visitors. Convenient access is not only enjoyed by the visitors but it offers the least disturbance to the work of employees.
- *Flow of Work:* Departments having the closest working connections should be placed closest together. When this is done, the work flows with a minimum waste of time between operations. Sales and advertising departments normally work together; so do the sales and credit departments, cost and payroll departments. When they are too far apart, unnecessary walking time is increased or the telephone system or intercoms are overworked.
- *Equipment Used:* Some departmental operations require the use of special equipment requiring extensive wiring, plumbing, or ventilation equipment. Moving departments of this type requires expensive alterations. Obviously, two such departments should not be located together because of the difficulty of later expansion. Some sections of a department may use noisy equipment. They may use various business equipment, reproduction equipment, and similar specialized equipment. Data entry sections, because of their concentration, will produce a higher noise level than a similar number of machines scattered throughout the area. To minimize disturbance to the rest of the employees, these sections are commonly segregated into sound-treated rooms.
- *Centralized Functions:* Sections and facilities that serve the entire office should be centrally located and easily accessible to all who use them. Data processing, central files, and cost accounting are examples. Of course, rest rooms, water fountains, and supply cabinets should be provided in sufficient numbers and conveniently located.
- *Confidential Areas:* Certain functions of a business may be of a confidential nature that requires them to be isolated from others in the office and from the general public. Central files, payroll, the controller, and legal offices are examples.
- *Conference Rooms:* Conference and training rooms should be reasonably near those departments that use them the most. If the office is air conditioned, the room can be in the interior of the space to eliminate the distraction of windows and to provide more wall display area.
- *Freight Elevators:* Departments receiving and delivering large quantities of materials should be located near the freight area for ease of handling, less time and labor, and less distraction of other

workers. Mail, stockroom, and machine departments are in this category.

- *Shipping Dock:* Shipping and receiving activities and mail rooms should obviously be near the point of entrance and exit of material.
- *Service Facilities:* Eating, medical, and lounge facilities are generally on the lower floors to reduce elevator traffic. The number and type of employees in a particular department might be considered in locating it near these facilities.
- *Passenger Elevators:* When an office occupies more than one floor, elevator service will be more effective when the departments with large clerical forces are on the lower floors.

The fundamental unit (module) for office space planning is the individual worker, seated at his or her desk or work station. The space allowance assigned to each worker can be either liberal or economical depending upon space limitations or the kind of atmosphere desired in the office.

In larger offices where there are many routine jobs, space standards tend to be economical. Where the work is specialized, where there are many visitors, or where high morale is promoted, space assignment is apt to be more generous. Larger firms tend to be more economical than smaller ones, for the extra space means extra rental costs or more buildings. Smaller firms have fewer routing operations and tend to have more generous space allowances.

In the general office area, allotment of 100 square feet per clerical worker is generally considered a liberal standard; 65 square feet is an economical standard. Eighty square feet would be a reasonable average.

## FIVE GUIDES FOR SPACE ALLOWANCES

Good space utilization does not necessarily mean allocating the least possible working space per person. On the contrary, too little working space may reduce the worker's efficiency and waste many times the savings made by any reduction in the square-foot rental costs. Good space utilization, in its broad meaning, allots more space to those positions whose activity justifies it, and reduces the space where there is a surplus.

There is no accurate scale of space allowances which will make layout planning automatic. Here, however, are some guidelines that have been established from a large number of surveys made of offices, both commercial and governmental. These suggestions will help you make a broad estimate of your space requirements or will serve as a check against your own utilization of space.

The types of space required in the typical office fall into five categories:

1. Office space
2. File space
3. Special equipment
4. Storage space
5. Special rooms

### Office Space Allowance

The following typical allowances include space for departmental aisles, space to move about, space for occasional visitors and consultation, rest rooms, drinking fountains, special files, general office equipment, bookcases, and coat racks. It does not include main aisles, corridors, or the space covered by the other four space categories.

|  | Square feet |
|---|---|
| Top executive | 400–600 |
| Junior executives | 100–200 |
| Supervisors | 80–100 |
| Worker at 60-inch desk | 55 |
| Worker at 55-inch desk | 50 |
| Worker at 50-inch desk | 45 |

Workers are assumed to be at desks side by side, two in a row. Add space for file and side chair if needed.

The use of L-shaped furniture for work stations will give more surface room than the standard desks, but the floor space will be roughly equivalent when the width is the same as desks above.

### File Space Allowance

The actual space taken up by a file cabinet and its open drawer is easily measured. It is difficult to estimate how much should be added to these measurements for working area until decisions are made on arrangement of the filing area.

In general, each open file cabinet will require the following space allowance without consideration of any working area in front of the open drawer

|  | Square feet |
|---|---|
| Standard letter file | 6 |
| Standard legal file | 7 |
| Side-opening letter file | 6½ |
| Side-opening legal file | 7½ |

### Special Equipment Allowance

Certain special types of office machines require more space than normally allowed in an estimate based on the average clerk or word processor position. Any space taken up by the following equipment and their personnel should be added to that considered for the regular office space.

    Computer equipment
    Duplicating equipment
    Communications equipment
    Time-clock space
    Other special equipment

### Storage Space Allowance

Storage requirements depend on the nature of the firm's work, its age, and the inclination of the administration to retain records. Here are some storage space requirements which should be considered:

    Vaults
    Stockrooms
    Transfer files
    Shelving
    Janitor supplies and equipment
    Stock rooms
    Coat rooms

### Special Rooms Allowance

Depending on the type of business, offices will require rooms of a size matched to their use. These will include:

Reception room
Waiting room
Interviewing room
Examination room
Conference room
Exhibit room
Medical room
Lunch room
Employee lounge
Rest room
Mail room

The more common rooms will have the following typical space allotments, based on their use by 15 people.

| | **Square feet** |
|---|---|
| Reception room | 400 |
| Waiting or interviewing room | 200 |
| Conference room | 500 |

Add approximately 10 square feet for each additional person to be provided for.

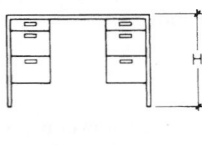
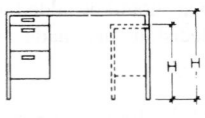
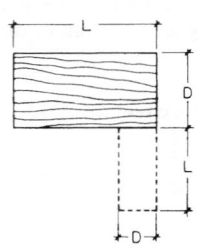

DESK DIMENSIONS

| | DESKS | | | | RETURNS | |
|---|---|---|---|---|---|---|
| | DOUBLE PEDESTAL | | SINGLE PEDESTAL | | FOR EXECUTIVE DESK RETURNS ARE AVAILABLE AT SAME HEIGHT AS DESK | |
| | STANDARD | RANGE | STANDARD | RANGE | STANDARD | RANGE |
| D | 2'-6" | 2'-0"–3'-3" | 2'-6" | 2'-0"–3'-3" | 1'-6" | 1'-3"–1'-8" |
| H | 2'-5" | 2'-4"–2'-6" | 2'-5" | 2'-4"–2'-6" | 2'-2" | 2'-1"–2'-3" |
| L | 5'-0" | 4'-6"–7'-0" | 5'-0' | 3'-9"–7'-0" | 3'-0" | 2'-0"–5'-0" |

DESKS - SINGLE OR DOUBLE PEDESTAL

WORK TABLES ARE OF SIMILAR DIMENSIONS.
FOR EXECUTIVE DESKS WITH RETURNS, RETURNS ARE AVAILABLE AT THE SAME HEIGHT AS THE DESK SURFACE.
A MINIMUM CLEAR WIDTH OF 22" SHOULD BE PROVIDED FOR KNEE ROOM, 24" IS NORMAL.

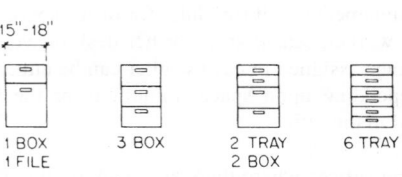

1 BOX 1 FILE    3 BOX    2 TRAY 2 BOX    6 TRAY

VARIOUS DRAWER ARRANGEMENTS FOR PEDESTALS

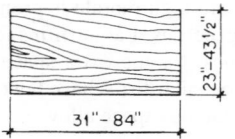

ARTIST AND DRAFTING DESKS OR TABLES

PEDESTALS FOR SECRETARIAL RETURNS WILL BE REDUCED IN HEIGHT THE EQUIVALENT OF ONE PENCIL DRAWER.

**Fig. 21. Office planning: desks—sizes**

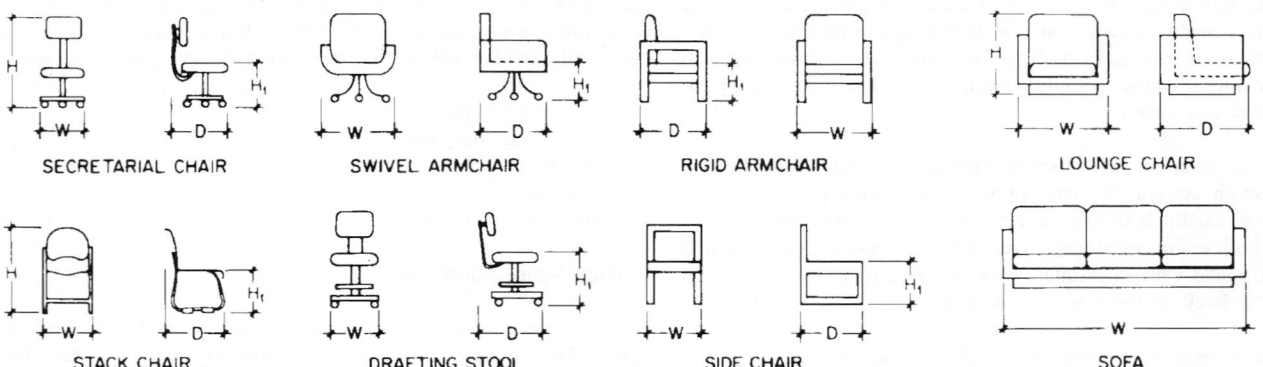

SECRETARIAL CHAIR    SWIVEL ARMCHAIR    RIGID ARMCHAIR    LOUNGE CHAIR

STACK CHAIR    DRAFTING STOOL    SIDE CHAIR    SOFA

CHAIR DIMENSIONS

| | SECRETARIAL | | SWIVEL ARMCHAIR | | RIGID ARMCHAIR | | STACK CHAIR | | RIGID AND ADJUSTABLE DRAFTING STOOL | | SIDE CHAIR | |
|---|---|---|---|---|---|---|---|---|---|---|---|---|
| | STD. | RANGE | STD. | RANGE | STD. | RANGE | STD. | RANGE | STD | RANGE | STD. | RANGE |
| W | 1'-5" | 1'-4"–1'-8" | 2'-4" | 1'-8"–2'-6" | 1'-10" | 1'-6"–2'-3" | 1'-9" | 1'-6"–1'-11" | 1'-6" | 1'-5"–2'-0" | 1'-8" | 1'-4"–2'-0" |
| D | 1'-7½" | 1'-6–2'-0" | 2'-3" | 1'-8"–2'-6" | 1'-10" | 1'-7"–2'-8" | 1'-9" | 1'-7"–1'-10" | 1'-8" | 1'-6"–2'-0" | 1'-10" | 1'-6"–2'-8" |
| H | 2'-6" | 2'-5"–2'-10" | 2'-9" | 2'-6"–3'-0" | 2'-6" | 2'-4"–2'-10" | 2'-6" | 2'-4"–2'-9" | 3'-0" | 2'-11"–3'-6" | 2'-6" | 2'-4"–2'-10" |
| H₁ | 1'-5" | 1'-4"–1'-8" | 1'-5" | 1'-4"–1'-10" | 1'-6" | 1'-4"–1'-7" | 1'-5" | 1'-5"–1'-6" | 2'-4" | 1'-5"–2'-10" | 1'-6" | 1'-5"–1'-7" |

LOUNGE CHAIR AND SOFA DIMENSIONS

| | LOUNGE CHAIR | | SOFA |
|---|---|---|---|
| | STD. | RANGE | |
| W | 2'-6" | 2'-6"–3'-4" | D, H AND H₁ SIMILAR |
| D | 2'-7" | 2'-2"–3'-4" | 2 SEATS-5'-0"–6'-7" |
| H | 2'-6" | 2'-1"–3'-4" | 3 SEATS-6'-0"–7'-6" |
| H₁ | 1'-3" | 1'-0"–1'-6" | 4 SEATS-7'-8"–9'-0" |

**Fig. 22. Office planning—sizes**

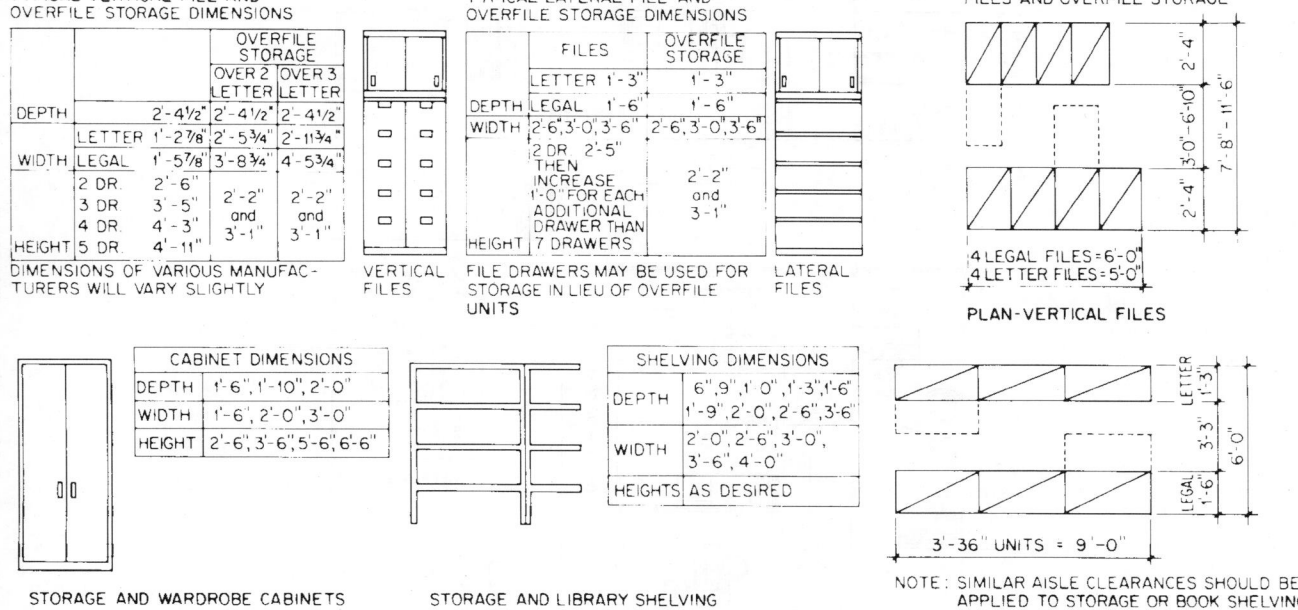

**Fig. 23. Office planning: files and storage—sizes**

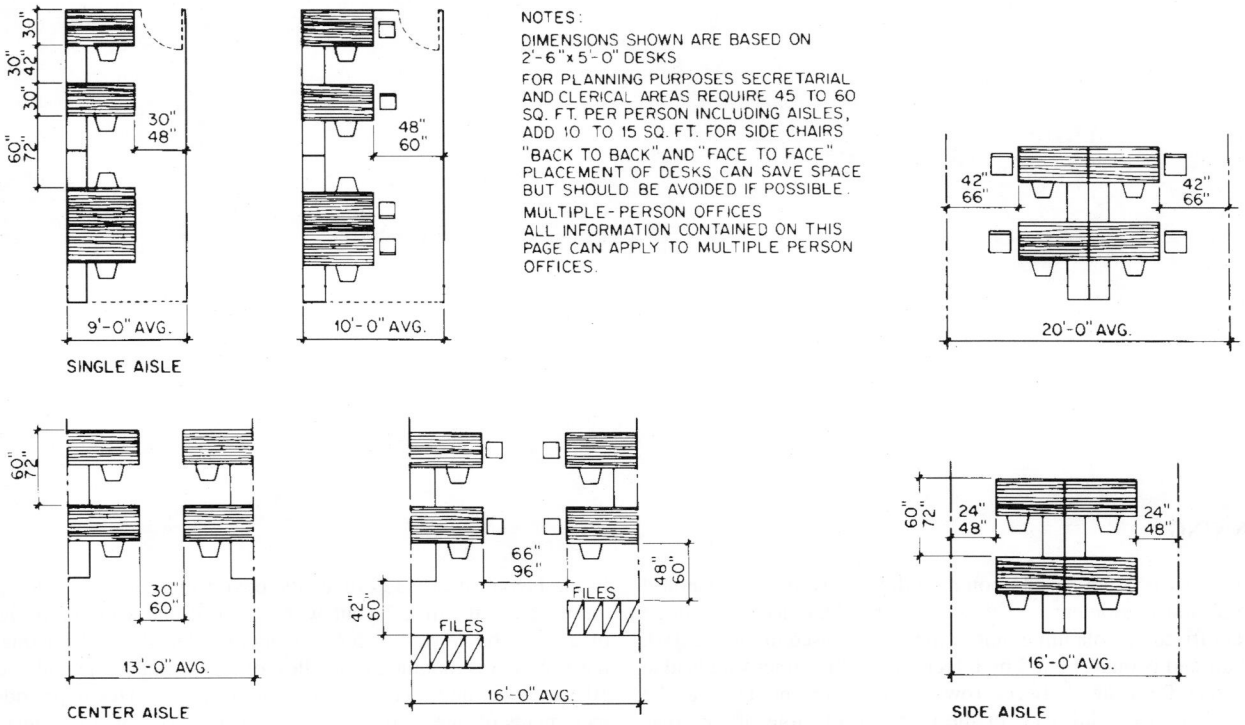

**Fig. 24. Office planning: clearances for secretarial areas and general clerical offices**

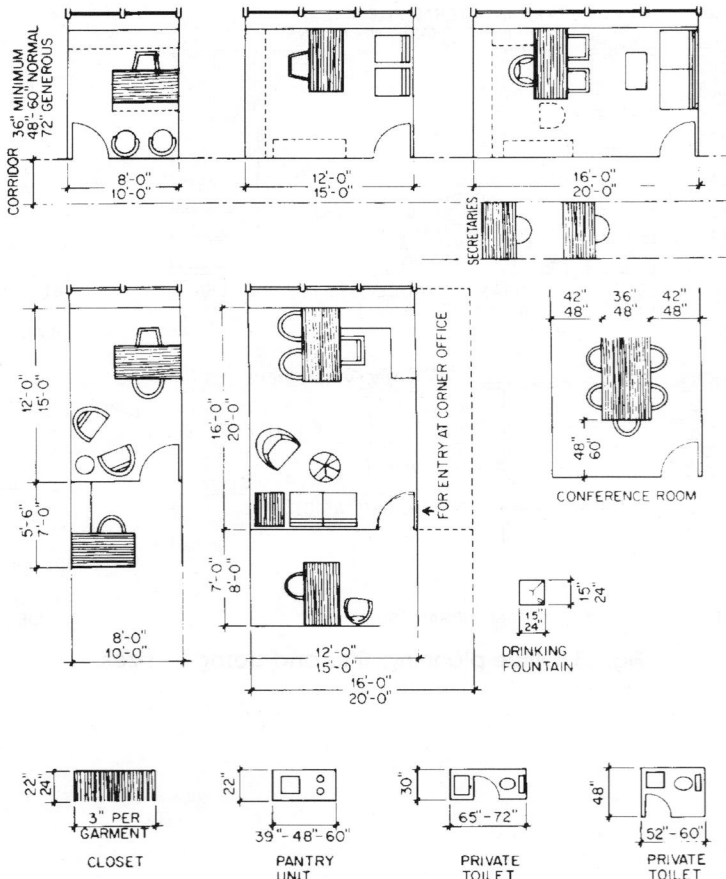

**Fig. 25. Office planning: layouts for private offices**

## PLANNING

Office layout is often based upon a module derived from standard furniture and equipment and the necessary clearances. For large general offices, the planning unit or module is based upon one desk and chair and is thus about 5 by 6 feet. Since this dimension is also satisfactory for aisles between rows of desks the module can be used to form a regular grid for the planning of large office areas (Fig. 26).

In the layout of private offices the controlling factors are the minimum practical office layout with the wall and window design. A planning module of 4 to 5 feet works reasonably well for this purpose. With this module the smallest office (2 modules) would be 8 to 10 feet wide, and a convenient range of office sizes is provided in increments of one module (Fig. 27). If the exterior wall consists of continuous windows, one module in width, then the office widths are limited to even modules. If windows alternate with solid walls, then office widths do not have to be in even modules but may vary widely (Fig. 28). This type of wall design permits greater flexibility in office layout at the expense of less natural light in the offices.

The planning module and the exterior wall module must be reconciled with the structural module or column bay. If all these modules coincide, then the wall or window units adjacent to the column must be smaller than the intermediate units (Fig. 29a). If the wall units are kept uniform in size, then the planning module is interrupted by the column width (Fig. 29b). If the columns are set inside the walls, they do not interfere with the wall module but they create a serious limitation on the layout of private offices (Fig. 29c). If the columns are

set outside the walls, then the planning module and the wall module are not affected by them (Fig. 29d).

Column spacing most frequently used in multistory steel-framed office buildings is around 25 feet, center to center. The recent trend is toward larger spacing; 30 to 35 feet is not uncommon. Flexibility of interior space is so important in office building design that the extra cost of clear span framing with the elimination of all interior columns is sometimes considered worthwhile; clear spans of 60 to 70 feet have been used.

Efficiency of an office building design is measured by the ratio of rentable space to total space. Average efficiency is about 70 percent; maximum possible is about 85 percent. The nonrentable space consists of the elevators, stairs, and toilets and their associated lobbies, corridors, pipe and duct shafts, and custodian's closets. These facilities are usually planned in a compact unit called the service core. For preliminary assumptions, the number of elevators required may be estimated on the basis of one elevator per 25,000 square feet of rentable area. Elevator lobbies should be 6 to 9 feet wide if elevators are on one side only; 10 to 12 feet if elevators are on both sides. Corridors are usually 5 to 6 feet wide (Fig. 30), wider if very long, narrower if very short.

Since the floor space within 25 to 30 feet from the exterior wall brings premium rentals, office buildings (site or zoning consideration aside) tend to assume a slablike shape, 60 to 70 feet wide by 150 feet or more long, with the service core in the center (Fig. 31). For greater flexibility in the rental space, the service core may be moved completely outside the office space. When this scheme is combined with clear span framing, the ultimate in flexibility is achieved (Fig. 32).

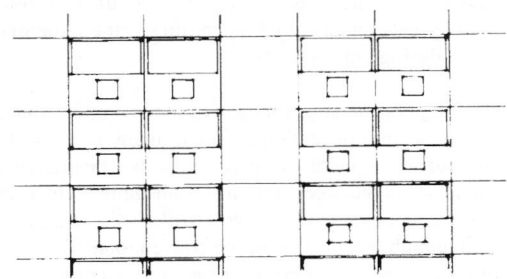

**Fig. 26. Planning module for layout of general office space**

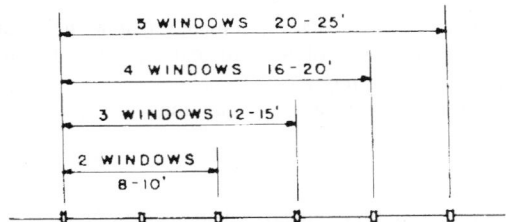

**Fig. 27. Private office widths using a module of 4 to 5 feet with continuous windows**

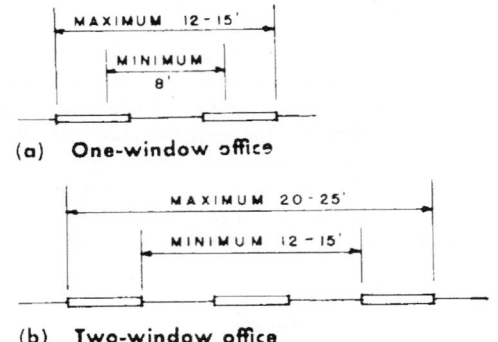

**Fig. 28. Private office widths using a module of 4 to 5 feet**

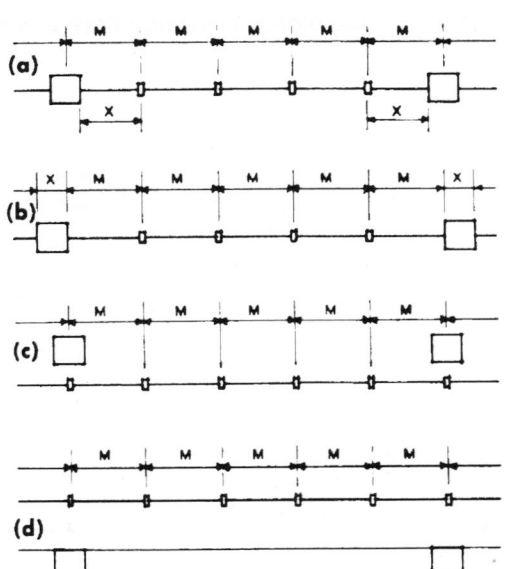

**Fig. 29. Relation of planning module and wall module to column spacing and location**

*Author:* Joseph Kleiman, Architect, Freidin, Kleiman, Kelleher, New York, New York
*Reviewer:* Mark D. Stumer, AIA

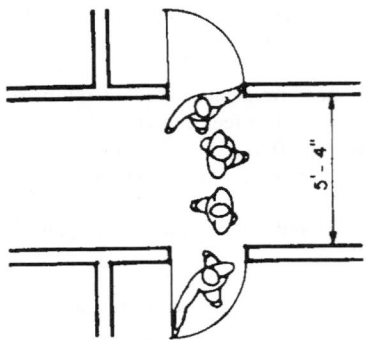

**Fig. 30. Corridor width based on requirements of human figures**

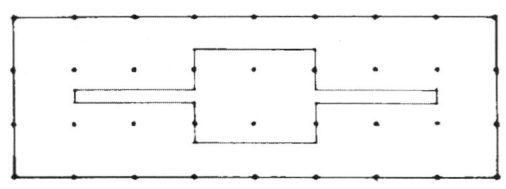

**Fig. 31. Typical slab plan with service core at center**

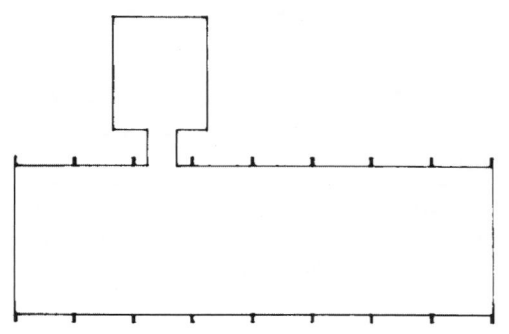

**Fig. 32. Maximum flexibility of rental area achieved by use of clear-span framing and core moved to tower**

Floor-to-floor heights are usually about 12 feet, ranging from 11 to 14 feet. Finished ceiling heights are generally about 8 to 8.5 feet. The space above the ceiling is required for ducts and recessed lighting. In order to avoid excessive depths in this utility space, girders are sometimes designed with openings in the web to permit the passage of ducts.

**Office Planning Concept**

The office planning concept has a strong effect on design. The concept is properly dealt with in programming, since it influences building size and form. Two main concepts may be considered: the conventional plan in which most of the building perimeter is taken up by fully enclosed private offices and the open plan, which assigns all or most occupants to spaces enclosed by low screens or modular furniture. Of course, the concept is closely related to the decisions made when creating space standards and, accordingly, the issue may need to be discussed during data collection.

There are several pros and cons for each of the two main concepts. As implied by its name, the conventional plan for many years has been the customary way of arranging office space, and it may be ingrained in the attitudes of at least the older generation of management. In a corporate headquarters, where the ratio of managers to clerical and technical people may be quite high, application of the conventional plan may result in the use of almost the entire perimeter for enclosed offices.

The *advantages* of the conventional plan are:

• Visual and aural privacy can be provided for the offices of executives and managers.
• The plan is well suited for a company that wishes sharp lines drawn between ranks of its staff and that considers a private office a measure of promotion.
• The need for conference space is minimized.

The *disadvantages* include:

• Partitions must be demounted or demolished when space changes are necessary.
• Natural light and a view of the exterior are denied to those working in the interior.
• The energy savings made possible by directing natural light to the interior are minimal.

The open plan has its ultimate application in the office landscape concept, whereby even senior executives are situated in open areas screened by low partitions or plantings. While open planning is widely used, a few headquarters today are designed without enclosed offices for senior executives and high-level managers. In the resulting compromise plan, managers below a certain level may be assigned to comfortably sized work stations. Inherent in the open planning concept is the need for an acoustical environment that affords aural privacy.

The *advantages* of the open plan are:

• Most employees enjoy natural light and a view of the exterior.
• The plan is highly flexible. Space can be rearranged or offices moved with relative ease.
• By using modular work stations, variations in the user's needs can easily be accomplished.
• The plan is compatible with energy-conserving design.

*Disadvantages* include:

There is, inevitably, some loss of aural and visual privacy.
The plan is not feasible in buildings with narrow wings or many obstructions.
Orientation for visitors may be more difficult than in the conventional plan.
More conference space may be necessary than for the conventional plan.

As noted above, most office plans represent a compromise between the two basic concepts. This usually requires that part of the management staff be assigned to open locations. However, such offices can be placed on the perimeter to preserve the intent of the conventional plan. Another compromise involves the executive core concept, which places fully enclosed offices (with glazed wall sections) at the interior, thus keeping the perimeter open to the interior.

## Office Planning Module

The space allocations in the facilities program are usually based on a consistent space module. The module is derived from analysis of needs, compatibility with manufacturers' standards, and an existing module if a headquarters building is being expanded. The modular approach is most applicable to offices, so the office module will control the planning of the building.

The greatest advantage of modular planning is the flexibility that can be attained. The basic module is extended to the structural grid and to ceiling and underfloor systems, thus making for ready change or interchange of space. There is a minor penalty in overall space in modular planning versus exact sizing of individual spaces. However, considering a headquarters' vulnerability to change, the benefits outweigh the disadvantages.

The 5 foot by 5 foot office-planning module is commonly used, and it is the basis for sizing most partitions, work stations, and ceiling and underfloor systems.

A 5 foot by 5 foot grid, using a consistent depth of 15 feet for the larger offices, affords a good range of sizes and requires minimum perimeter for average-size spaces.

It is usually necessary to depart from the module at corridors and core spaces in which case a "half module" should be used.

The Type D offices are the smallest that should be considered for rooms with full-height partitions. Placing them on the perimeter necessitates breaks in aisles, or wasted space, unless the offices occupy a full end or side of a floor.

The types of offices on the perimeter should be kept to a minimum number; avoid, if possible, creating a variety of sizes using half-modules.

Different grades of offices can be created by varying the furniture and furnishings within spaces of similar size.

Staying on the module is most important for spaces with full-height partitions. Working positions in regular office areas should be planned in general conformance with the grid, but some latitude is possible in a flexible underfloor system.

## Typical Office and Work Station Arrangements

The programmed allocations for all occupants of office space result from analysis of the users' needs. A number of factors, including modularity, dictate a degree of uniformity in the types and arrangements of working spaces for all but the senior executives in a headquarters.

Usually, the items of furniture in each office are assumed and the typical spaces are tested by making layouts showing alternate arrangements (Fig. 33 shows such a study).

The availability of a wide variety of modular work stations affords almost limitless opportunities for adapting individual spaces to the users' needs. However, space management and inventorying are greatly simplified if all or most of the occupants' needs can be satisfied by a few typical work stations. In making this determination, it is well to establish a basic type that serves the largest number of users. Variations can then be made for the atypical needs of certain groups. Usually, a careful study discloses commonality in the requirements of many office occupants. Three or less typical work stations can often fulfill the needs of such users as analysts, accountants, auditors, computer programmers, and supervisors, with only minor variations in equipment and storage units. Fig. 34 shows two such typical work stations for a headquarters. The basic types shown are suitable for assistant managers and all professionals below that rank. Fig. 34 also shows two work stations designed for secretaries and clerical workers.

Considerations in establishing typical work stations:

• A program is usually written before a work station manufacturer is decided upon. The typical stations should therefore be based on units that can be supplied by several vendors.

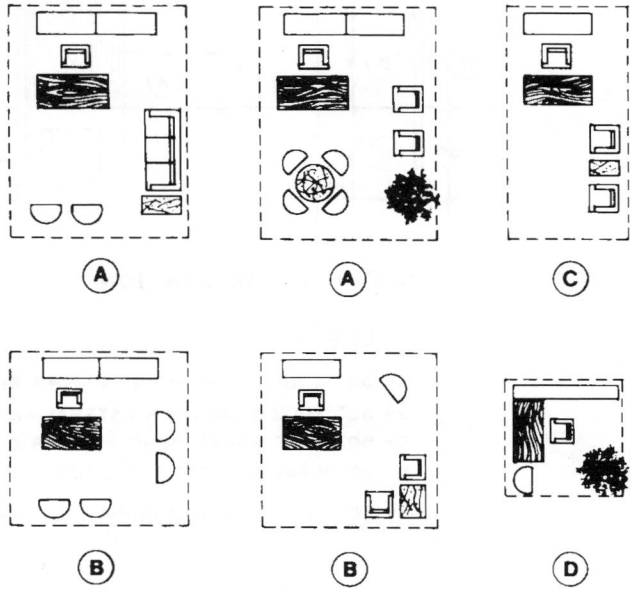

**Fig. 33. Alternate furniture arrangements in typical offices**

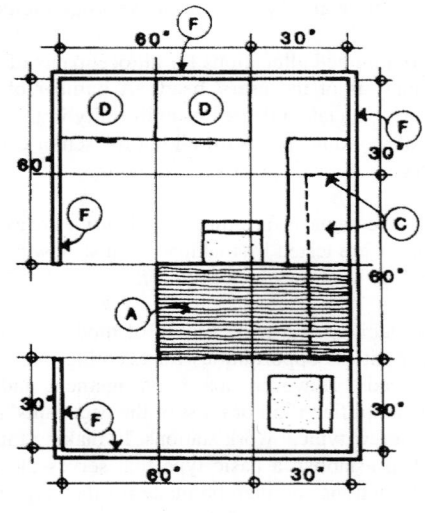

**WORK STATION 2**

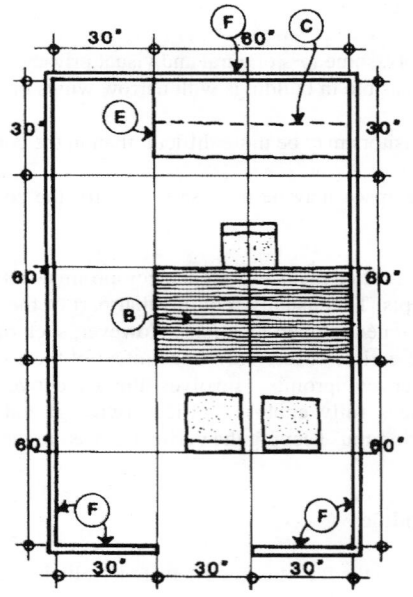

**WORK STATION 1**

● **LEGEND**

A- 30" x 60" L DESK W/42" ± EXECUTIVE HEIGHT RETURN

B- 30" x 60" DOUBLE PEDESTAL DESK

C- FLIPPER DOOR PANEL HUNG CABINET W/TASK LIGHT UNDER

D- 30" WIDE 2 DRAWER LATERAL FILE (FREE STANDING)

E- 60" WIDE CREDENZA W/STORAGE CABINET AT CENTER BOX
    & FILE DRAWER EACH SIDE

F- 66" H.± ACOUSTIC STRUCTURAL PANELS, WIDTH AS NOTED ON PLAN

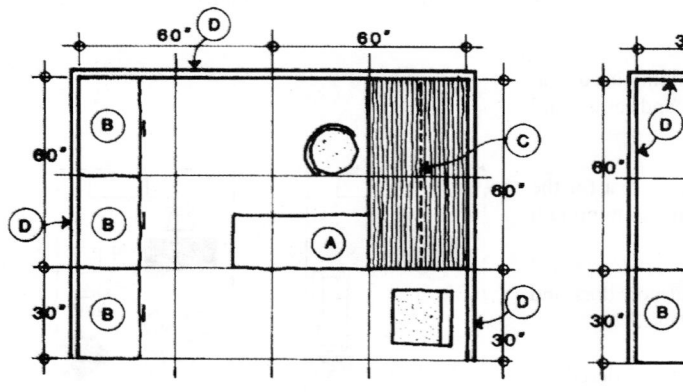

**SECRETARIAL STATION**

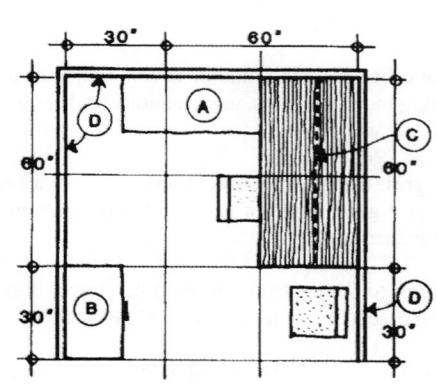

**CLERICAL STATION**

● **LEGEND**

A- 30" x 60" DESK W/42" TYPING RETURN

B- 30" WIDE 2 DRAWER LATERAL FILE (FREE STANDING)

C- 60" WIDE PANEL HUNG FLIPPER DOOR CABINET W/TASK LIGHT UNDER

D- 66" H.±ACCOUSTIC STRUCTURAL PANELS , WIDTH AS NOTED ON PLAN

Fig. 34. Typical work stations: managers and analysts, secretaries, and clerks

- A basic determination involves whether a work station employs freestanding desks, credenzas, and other furniture; or whether a "hang-on" system is contemplated that attaches all furniture and equipment to the space-dividing screens. The former method allows existing furniture to be used, while the second offers the great versatility and high degree of standardization made possible through integrated furniture/partition systems.
- Modular systems can be extended to work stations for secretaries, clerks, equipment operators, and other workers in a general office.
- Groups of work stations can be arranged in clusters, pinwheels, or linear fashion. Screens or storage units can be employed to define the groups, or to give a degree of privacy.

## Space Allocations for General Office Areas

The term general office applies to space used primarily by secretaries, data entry personnel, clerks, and the like. In an open plan that uses work stations, there may be a blurring of the distinction between private and general office areas, except that the private offices will be larger and provided with a different grade of furniture. However, the general office areas require space allocations for items other than desks and chairs, and it is important that the program reflect allowance for these items.

Typical plans for conference centers and training centers are shown in Figs. 37 and 38.

## Open-Office Landscaping

The principal feature of open-office landscaping (OOL) is space that is free, or almost free, of conventional walls, corridors, private offices, and straight-line passageways between rows of desks and office equipment. Instead, the available space is divided into "clusters" or work centers, and individual workstations are delineated by high, medium, and low screens and cabinets, plants, bookshelves, modular furniture, and fixtures designed to suppress noise and promote working efficiency. Instead of in rows, desks are arranged at various angles to each other as dictated by the natural lines of work flow and communications.

In the typical landscaped office, eye appeal is also a main objective, but such other environmental considerations as lighting, acoustics, air conditioning, noise abatement, functionally designed furniture, and the use of color and decorations such as plants, statues, and other artwork are incorporated in OOL designs. Apart from environmental considerations, the absence of fixed partitions between work centers and, in most cases, private offices permits a maximum degree of flexibility in the initial OOL design, as well as making it possible to accommodate new activities, or extend those already in existence, at minimum cost and inconvenience.

## OOL Elements

A principal feature of OOL is entirely open office space, free of conventional walls and corridors.

Workstations comprise movable elements such as desks, chairs, freestanding screens, shelving, files, and foliage usually without relocation of fixed installations such as light fixtures, heating and air conditioning outlets, partitions, or floor covering. Each individual grouping of workstations is arranged without regard for windows or other conventional constraints, in non-uniform fashion, usually dictated by natural lines of information flow and one-to-one personal communication.

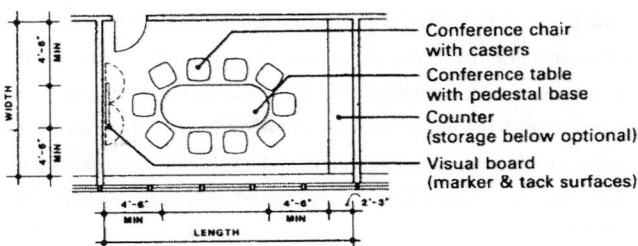

**Fig. 35. Typical conference room plan**

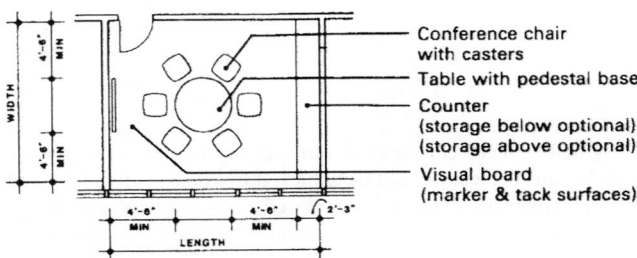

**Fig. 36. Typical workroom plan**

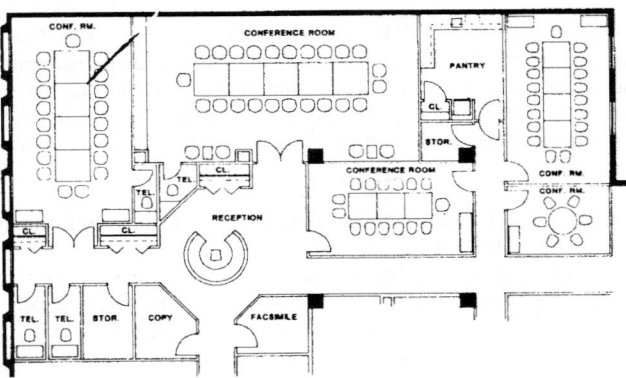

**Fig. 37. Typical conference center**

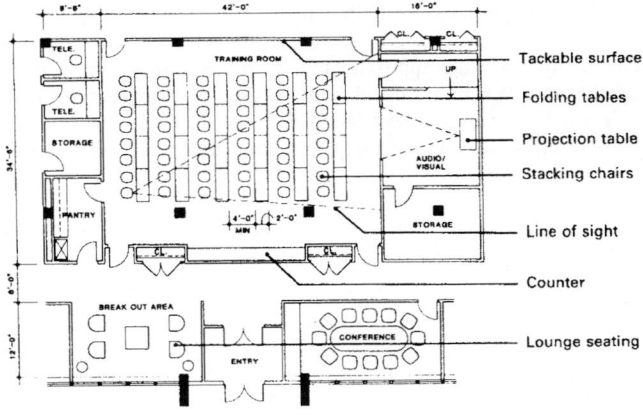

**Fig. 38. Typical training center**

## Table 2  Open-office landscaping design guidelines

A. Recognize (and act accordingly) that the open plan requires total planning before, during, and after implementation.

B. Consider both present and expected personnel and equipment needs when determining space requirements.

C. Consult with the workers who will be affected by the conversion to the open-plan concept.

D. Educate office personnel about the advantages of the open plan over the conventional office layout.

E. Face the issue of privacy and noise in relation to the psychological and physiological needs of the workers and those of the organization as a whole.

F. Exercise control over unauthorized rearrangements whereby office workers abuse the open plan by encroaching on their neighbors' space and unnecessarily disturbing others.

G. Locate noisy equipment such as telex, word processing printers, and dupicators in well-insulated, enclosed rooms to avoid disturbing others in open-plan modules or enclosures.

As originally conceived, the OOL office plan provided for no private offices because privacy could be achieved by the use of foliage and movable sound absorbing screens wired for electricity and sometimes for optionally located telephone and/or computer connections. The original OOL plan has been somewhat modified (referred to as the American Plan) so that higher-echelon executives may have walled-in offices to provide a greater degree of privacy for confidential conferences and concentration and as recognition of their higher organizational status.

The status of workers in OOL, as compared with executives, is determined more by their work assignments than by their locations. Upper-echelon personnel, however, may have a greater amount of floor space, a distinctive color of desk top, and possibly a differently shaped desk. Beyond these, there are few visible signs of organizational rank.

Perhaps the most significant characteristic of the OOL plan is that it provides flexibility for layouts that shift as work assignments shift. Only simple tools are required to rearrange the panels and component parts that make up each workstation. Furthermore, the cost of relocating the parts of the OOL plan to create new designs is substantially less than the cost of rearranging offices with fixed partitions.

Approximately 20 percent fewer light fixtures are needed to light a particular work center, since the reduction of walls between offices allows a more efficient placement of the fixtures. Further, it is estimated that a lighting system that is part of an OOL plan reduces energy consumption by about 40 percent.

Construction costs are approximately 50 percent lower when using the OOL plan. When the cost of furnishings and equipment is added, the cost differential narrows, since OOL-plan furniture and component parts are somewhat more expensive than traditional office furniture and equipment. It should be noted, however, that the cost is partially offset by the OOL's greater flexibility and the lower cost of later rearrangement.

The amount of usable space, expressed as a percentage of the gross available space, is greater than the conventional grid layout with its usual rows of desks, files, etc. In the landscaped office, the usable space may run as high as 80 to 90 percent. This means that square footage under the OOL plan can be reduced by as much as 20 to 30 percent. In turn, the rental cost per square foot of usable space is much less than in a traditional fixed-wall office. To illustrate, through the use of workstations that utilize vertical space for storage, the OOL plan reduces the amount of floor space required for each workstation while at the same time providing for a more efficient work area for the individual.

The psychological effect on employees of removing physical barriers is pronounced. Their positive feelings about OOL are manifested in productivity measure of the success of the plan (Table 2). It is contended that when walls are torn down, the communication barriers between managers and employees tend to diminish. Employees in clusters or groupings seem to feel freer to ask questions and come into a supervisor's workstation to discuss problems. Managers and supervisors, too, have more opportunity to observe interactions among employees, since they are less isolated in private offices and more in touch with their workers (see Fig. 39).

**Cost**

Both the initial cost of an OOL-plan application as well as continuing maintenance are lower than those of conventional arrangements, while employee morale has usually improved, except in a few cases where executives have felt that being deprived of a private office has lowered their status in the eyes of their subordinates and peers.

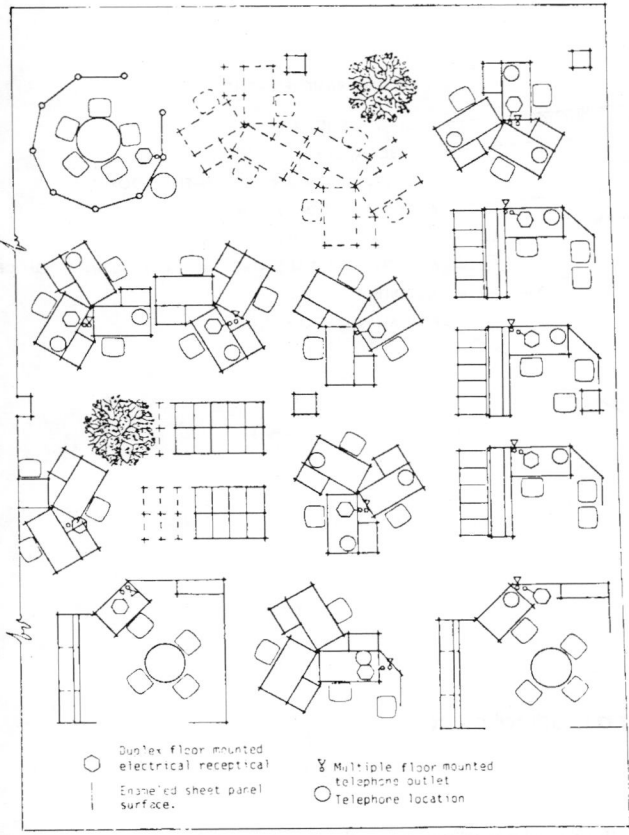

Fig. 39. Example of open-office landscape concept

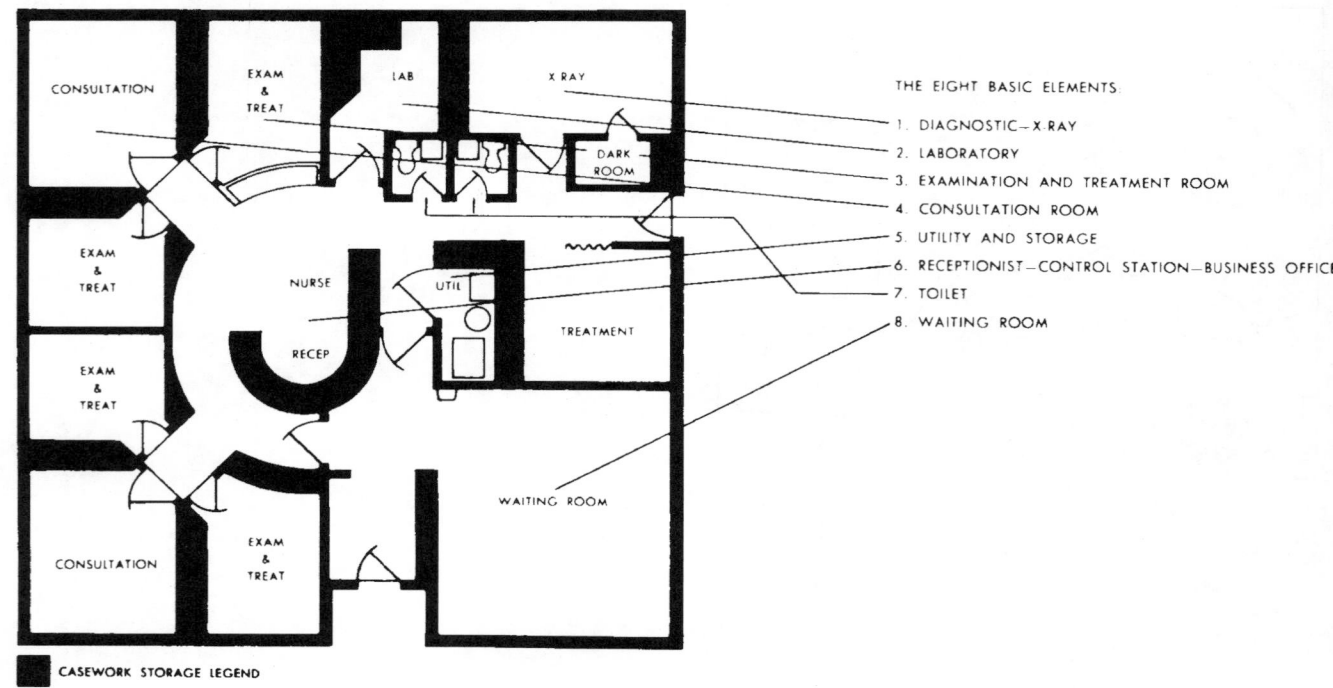

**Fig. 1. Basic elements of a medical office**

## MEDICAL OFFICES

The eight basic elements of a medical office are:

> Receptionist—control station—business office
> Waiting room
> Consultation room
> Examination and treatment room
> Laboratory including EKG and BMR
> X-ray
> Utility and service areas
> Toilet

A medical practice facility can have no fixed, ideal plan. First, no two individuals or groups of individuals think alike or work alike. Second, the physical and geographical limitations which characterize a medical practice facility, whether for a new building, a remodeled building, or rental space, do not permit the adoption of any single plan. Each facility must be custom-made to express the individuality and to satisfy the working habits of those who will use it.

The eight basic elements found in nearly all medical offices can be thought of as the "building blocks." While these eight elements may change in size and shape depending on methods of operation, they are always integrated in the medical practice facility, or their counterpart is conveniently available (Fig. 1).

In the following pages will be found drawings and explanations of each of the eight elements, and further examples of how they can be combined and expanded.

### RECEPTION AND BUSINESS OFFICE

The receptionist, who in the small medical practice facility is also the doctor's assistant, the bookkeeper, and the bill collector, is the hub around which the office revolves. The receptionist should be so placed that he can keep an eye on all the workings of the office. He should see and acknowledge the arrival of the patient and must follow the progress of the doctor so that the patient flow has proper direction. If the receptionist discusses bills and appointments, the space should be large enough for others besides himself, and private enough that his conversations are not generally overheard.

For the larger office the functions mentioned above may be split among two, three or even more persons. Receptionists still should be able to see the entrance and the waiting room. If they are too far removed to watch the progress of the doctor they have to be informed by the nurse assistant of this progress so they can keep the flow of patients coming.

If there is a separate business manager bookkeeper, a private space should be provided for working on records and discussing bills with patients.This office should be located so that it is accessible to outgoing patients. The exit from this office should permit patients to leave without backtracking or going through the waiting room. Proper relationship to the entrance will also assist in the control of deliveries to the office (Fig. 2).

*Reviewer:* James H. Ogden, R.A.
*References: A Planning Guide for Physicians' Medical Facilities*, edited by the American Medical Association and published through a grant made by the Sears-Roebuck Foundation.

## Reception-Waiting Room

The patients receive their first impression from the waiting room (Fig. 3). Its appearance may indicate the type of care they can expect to receive. A wait in a crowded, out-of-date room can depress and disgruntle even the best and steadiest of patients.

The chairs, tables, and lamps should be adequate in number and well spaced so as to make reading possible and to give the patients a feeling of freedom. The patient load provides the only criterion for the number of chairs you must provide. If the schedule is always well maintained, the waiting area need only be a minimum. If the doctor is burdened with emergency calls and extended house or hospital calls, then the waiting room should be more ample.

Needless to say, some educated thought should be given to decoration: the walls, upholstery, pictures, and window treatments. Tasteful, harmonizing colors that are cheery rather than drab are desirable. The overall effect should be homelike and restful.

The waiting room preferably should permit a view of the outside and, if possible, the view should be a pleasing one. Flowers, trees, or distance are the best, but when this is impossible an interesting view of people and activity is the second choice (Fig. 4).

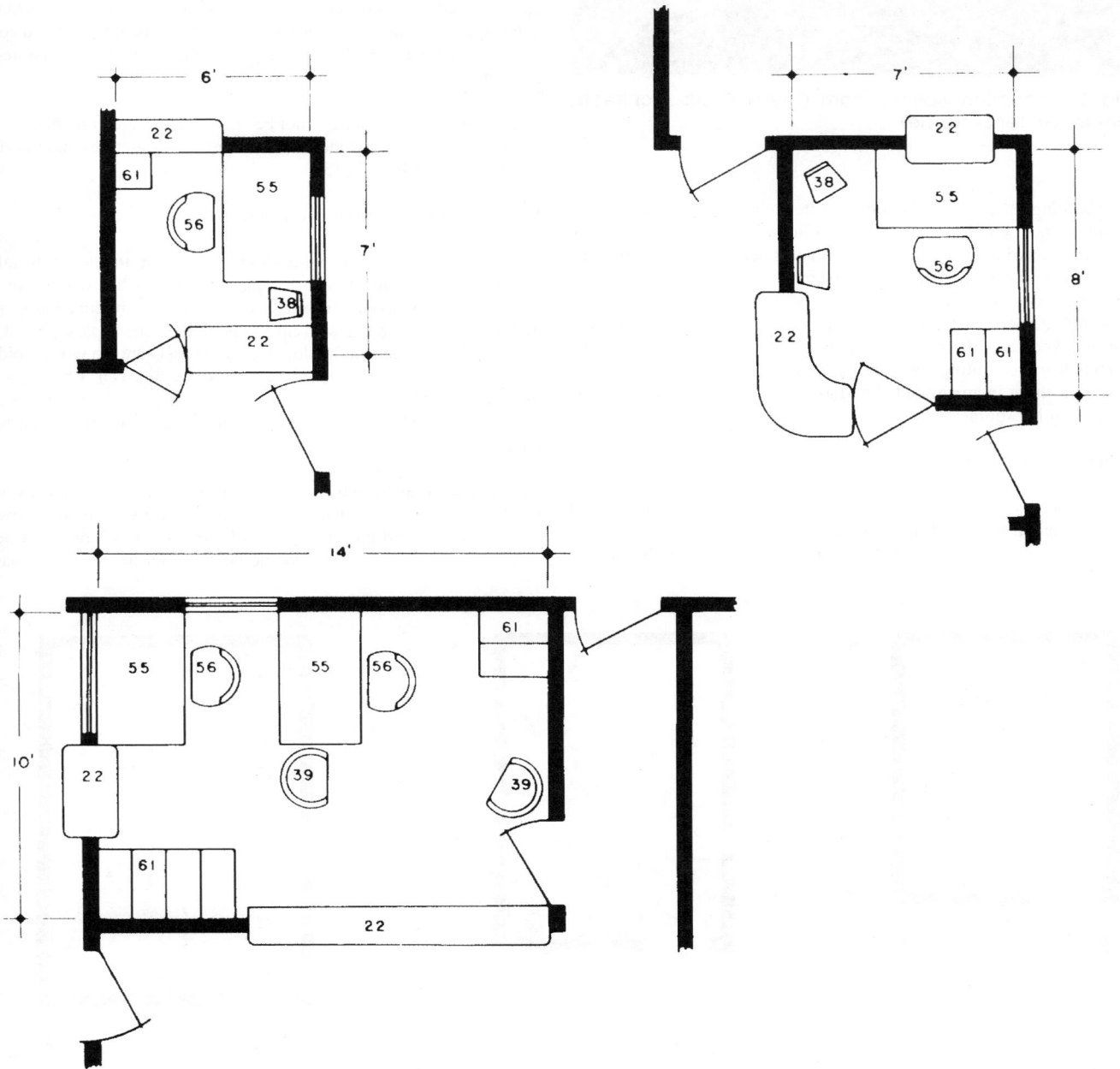

**Fig. 2. Reception and business office**

**Fig. 3. Reception-waiting room (Taylor Clark Architects; photo: Walter Dufresne)**

The waiting room should be removed from the actual office activity. It should not be a thoroughfare for traffic, nor should it be an office for the discussion of bills and appointments between the receptionist or office manager and patients. If one enters the office directly from out-of-doors, it is well to have a lobby to prevent drafts. If the business office opens on the lobby, it may well serve to receive the visitor and to determine her business. This, in turn, allows some to be directed to the waiting room and others to be taken directly to the doctor without incurring hurt feelings and complaints from patients in the waiting room.

**Consultation Room**

This space is generally the stopping point, at some time, for all patients passing through the office. The patient is usually directed there first for a discussion of symptoms and progress and for simple

examinations. She is then sent to an examination or treatment room, from which she may return to the consultation room for further discussion and prescription. However, there seems to be a trend to simplify and speed up this procedure, in a majority of instances, by concentrating the entire patient visit in the examination room.

This enables the physician to utilize another room for patient examination and treatment.

The theory that all space be used for examination and treatment or for purely professional use has merit. However, the average examining room is sparsely equipped and very impersonal. Patient discussions and diagnostic reviews are better handled in more comfortable and professional surroundings. A properly furnished consultation room can have a beneficial effect on both the patient and the physician. In addition physicians are called on by many professional detail specialists and other individuals in the medical field. Such contacts are better handled in a nicely furnished—but not elaborate—consultation room.

The consultation room need not be spacious, but a cramped, closed-in feeling should be avoided. Tasteful furniture, pictures and interior colors are desirable (Fig. 5).

**Examination and Treatment Room**

It is in this room (Fig. 6), with its variations, that the doctor usually has her closest contact with the patient. This is her workroom. It needs, first of all, to be efficient. In other words, it should be properly and adequately lighted, with all the equipment necessary placed in such a way as to permit the doctor and her assistants to work rapidly and easily. Here space cannot be wasted; neither can it be reduced beyond a certain minimum. Unnecessary steps must be eliminated; yet there should be room to move around easily and without interference.

This is one room in which the design must be determined by the needs and the working habits of the doctor. These must be investigated carefully and thoroughly in order that he may have what best meets his needs and desires. While he has been trained to do many

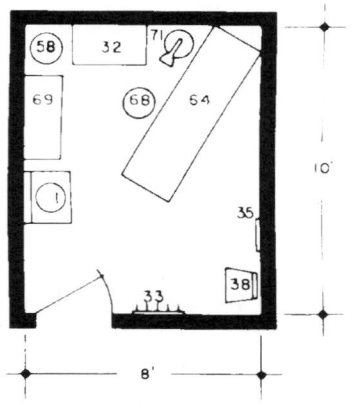
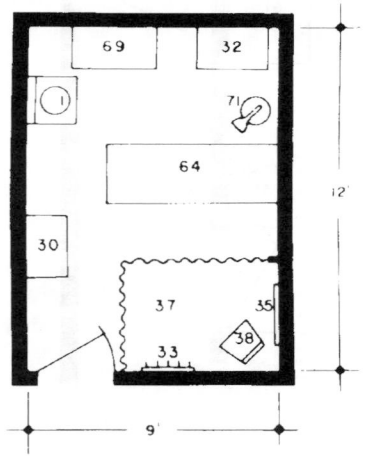
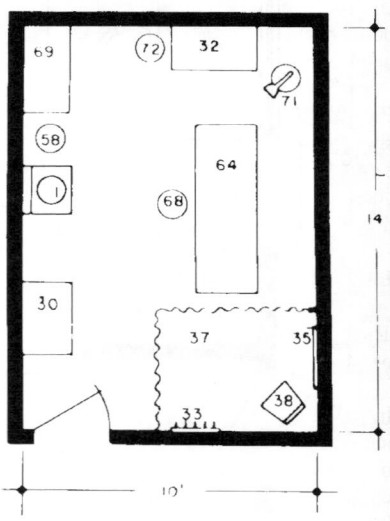

**Fig. 4. Reception-waiting room**

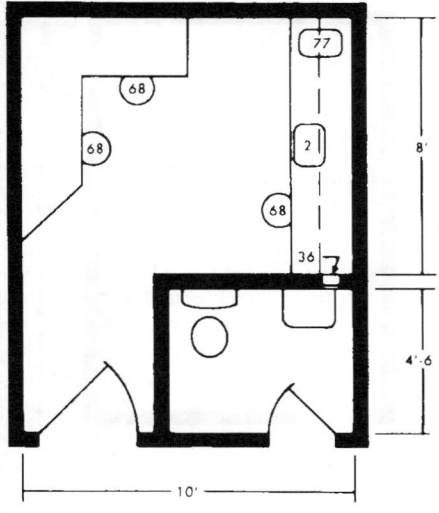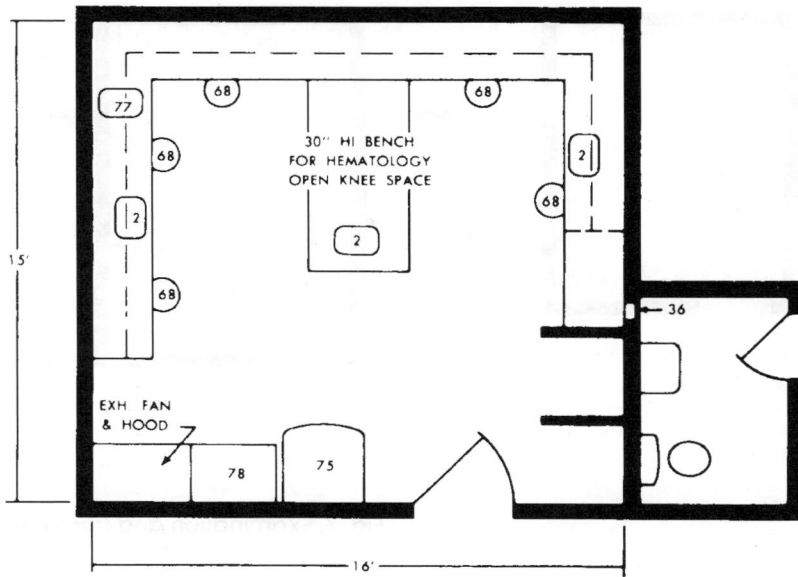

**Fig. 5. Consultation room**

things well, despite adverse conditions and scanty equipment, there is no need to handicap him on his home grounds.

Seldom is one examination and treatment room enough. Two rooms can often more than double the doctor's capacity, and some doctors have as many as eight. Where there are several rooms, patients can be prepared ahead of time by the assistants. Furthermore, a number of procedures can be handled by the assistants, on direction of the doctor, while she is putting her time to better use with other patients. When this practice is followed intelligently and it does not slip into an impersonal production line technique, it results in increased efficiency.

Where the examination and treatment room is used for most of the doctor-patient contacts, it is necessary to provide a few things not formerly found there. It is also necessary to provide for the patients' comfort and convenience. For the doctor, a desk or writing space, and perhaps a satisfactory chair for use during discussions with the patient, may be ample additions.

For the patient, dressing facilities, cubicle, mirror, clothes hooks, slippers, chairs or low bench in or immediately adjacent to the examination-treatment room are a great convenience. A comfortable chair is also advisable to ease the patients' waiting time when the doctor is delayed with some other patient (Fig. 7).

**Laboratory**

This room varies from a few shelves, sink, sterilizer, etc., in the corner of the examination room to a complete laboratory in a separate room.

In the smaller office it is best combined with other uses for the saving of space and of steps. The nurses' workroom, the store room, the recovery room, and a spare examination room are all possible elements which can, under certain conditions, be combined with the laboratory. The ideal, of course, is a room designed for specific laboratory procedures with adequate equipment and supplies. However,

the extent to which each doctor desires to carry on her own procedures determines the extent to which this ideal is approached.

In planning laboratory space, it is best to keep two factors in mind. A common mistake is to provide too little counter space, so be generous with it. Secondly, regardless of size, laboratory space should be contiguous with toilet facilities and a pass-through should be provided between the two areas (Fig. 8).

**X-Ray**

If the doctor is planning to use an x-ray machine, provisions for housing it must be made in the planning stage. It is best to decide early exactly what kind of x-ray, darkroom, and developing equip-

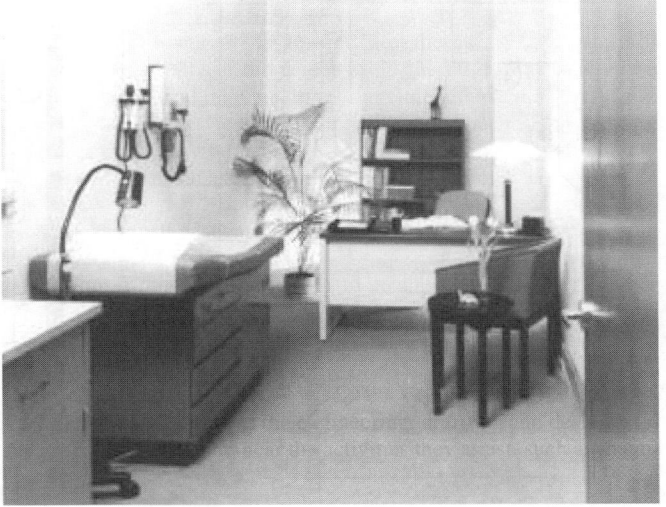

**Fig. 6. Typical examination and treatment room (Taylor Clark Architects; photo: Walter Dufresne)**

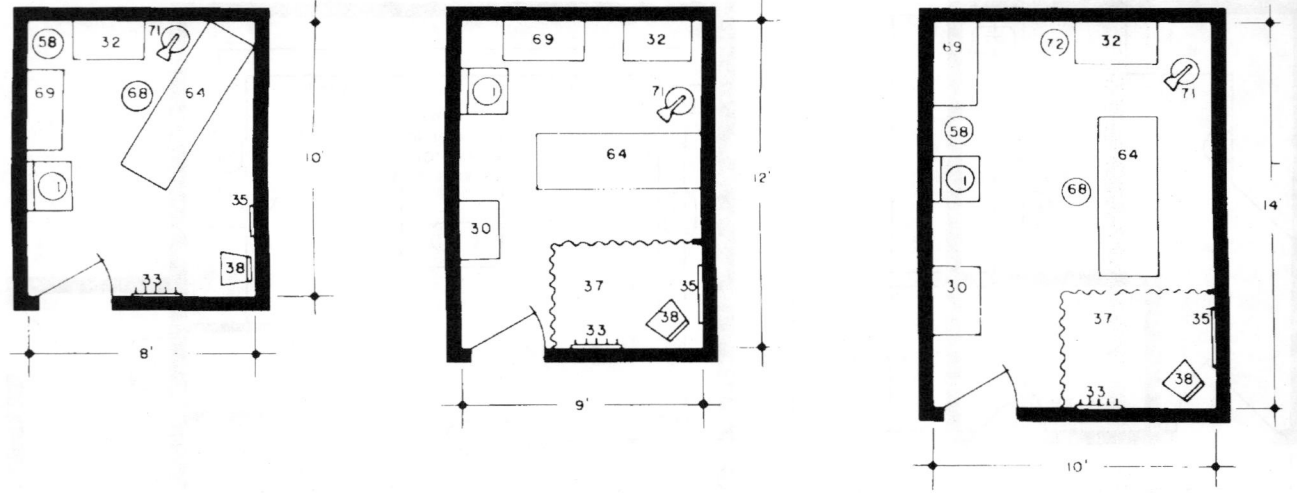

**Fig. 7. Examination and treatment room**

ment the doctor will use. The representatives of the manufacturers can be a part of the planning team then, working closely with the architect or consultant in the preliminary stages of planning.

Nearly all state and city codes now require lead or concrete protection in all interior walls and doors of rooms housing x-ray equipment. If spaces above or below are inhabited, protection is also required in floors and ceilings. Exterior walls need not be protected.

Likewise, there are rather stringent code requirements for the wiring of x-ray rooms and equipment—including separate entrance service in many cases. This should be checked carefully. In most cases, the manufacturer's representative will be familiar with wiring requirements, but if she is not a local resident, she may not be familiar with all the local rules. For this reason, it is best to have this reviewed independently. If a pass-through system is to be installed, or the through-wall immediate developing system used, the viewing room must be located adjacent to that wall of the darkroom (Fig. 9).

**Equipment List**

The numbers appearing in the drawings refer to the equipment list below. This list should be used in conjunction with the diagrams.

1. Lavatory with mirror and towel bar
2. Sink with gooseneck spout
3. Water closet
4. Shower stall
5. Gas line
6. Air line
7. Vacuum line
8. Piped oxygen
9. Sink disposal unit
10. Sterilizers—stills, etc.
11. Ceiling light
12. Convenience outlets, 110
13. Convenience outlets, 220
14. Wall light
15. Intercom systems and buzzer calls
16. Telephone system
17. Heating controls
18. Air-conditioning controls
19. Radiological devices
20. Special operating lights
21. Room dividers
22. Receptionist's desk and counter
23. Special desk

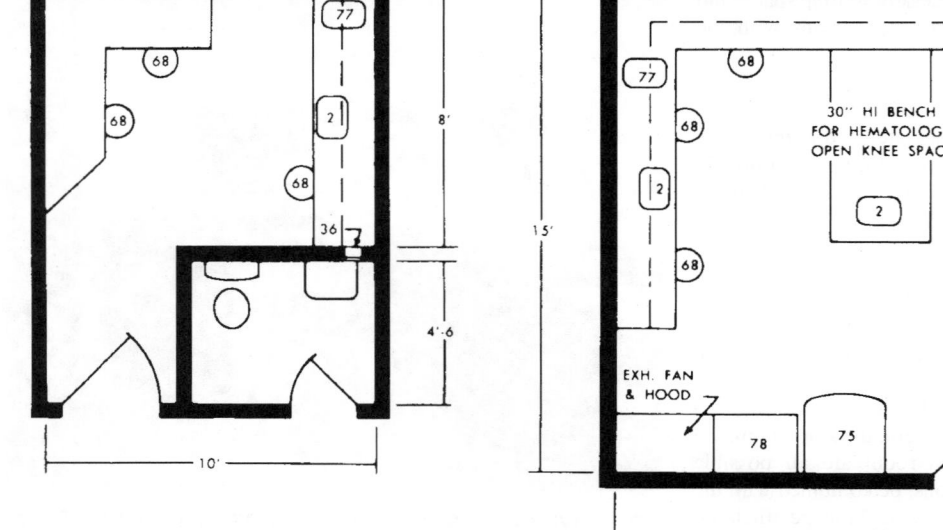

**Fig. 8. Laboratory**

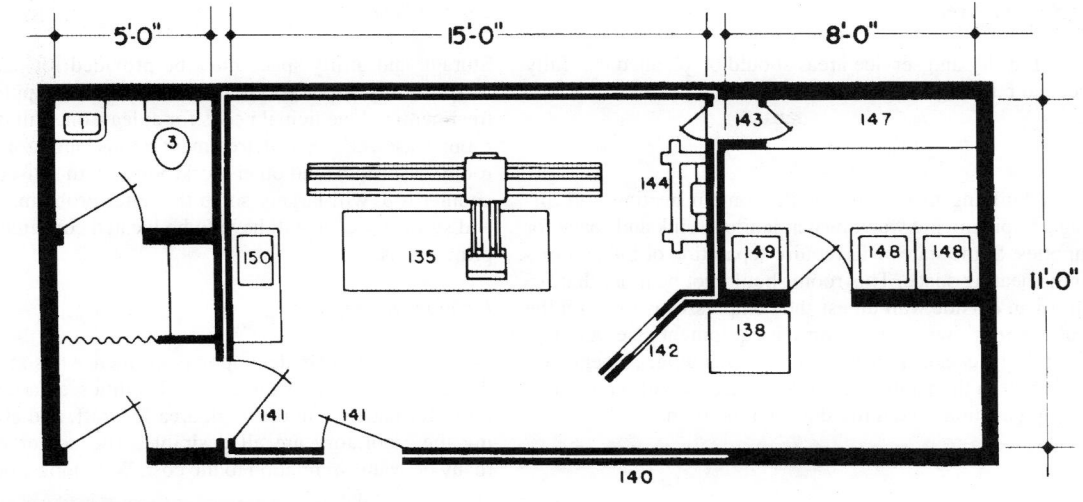

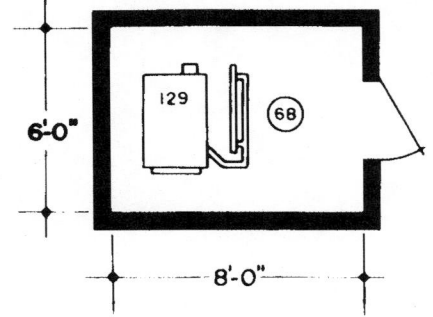

**Fig. 9. Typical radiologist's office**

24. Bookcases
25. Counter open where stool is shown
26. Backsplash
27. Reagent shelf
28. Wall-hung shelf
29. Wall cabinet
30. Wall-hung charting desk
31. Instrument case
32. Equipment table or stand
33. Hook strip
34. Dressing table with mirror
35. Mirror
36. Specimen passbox
37. Dressing cubicle
38. Straight chair
39. Occasional chair
40. Easy chair
41. Small couch
42. Sectional seat
43. End table
44. Magazine table
45. Occasional table
46. Floor lamp
47. Table lamp
48. Coat rack
49. Umbrella rack
50. Toy cabinet
51. Play desk
52. Children's chair
53. Executive's desk

54. Executive's desk chair
55. Secretary's desk
56. Secretary's chair
57. Bookcase
58. Waste receptacle
59. Work table
60. Desk lamp
61. Filing cabinet
62. Supply cabinet
63. Step stool
64. Treatment table
65. Treatment chair-table
66. Physiotherapy table
67. Couch
68. Adjustable stool
69. Instrument and supply cabinet
70. Instrument sterilizers
71. Examining light
72. Waste receptacle with foot lever
73. Clinical scale
74. Instrument treatment chair
75. Refrigerator (biological)
76. Pegboard with drip pan
77. Pressure sterilizer
78. Incubator
79. Serological water bath
80. Paraffin oven
81. Laboratory table
82. Centrifuge

83. Bunsen burner
84. Hot plate
85. Basal metabolism apparatus
86. Electrocardiograph
87. Portable operating light
88. Operating table
89. Mayo table
90. Specialist's chair
91. Cabinet with suction pump and compressed air
92. Ultraviolet lamp
93. Infrared lamp
94. Diathermy short wave unit
95. Electrosurgical unit
96. Audiometer
97. Accessory table
98. Woods light
99. Baby scale
100. Examining table
101. Urological x-ray table
102. Irrigator unit
103. Proctoscopic examining table
104. Irrigator unit
105. Instrument and supply cabinet with suction equipment
106. Galvanic unit
107. Plaster cart
108. Wheelchair
109. Whirlpool bath
110. Paraffin bath
111. Stall bars
112. Shoulder wheel
113. Pulley weights
114. Timing device
115. Couch
116. Reading light
117. Eye operating light
118. Greens' refractor
119. Binocular ophthalmoscope
120. Lens case on cabinet
121. Vertometer
122. Vision chart

123. Tangent screen
124. Chin rest
125. Slit lamp
126. Kertometer
127. Troposcope or synoptophore
128. Perimeter
129. Fluoroscope
130. Film illuminator
131. Stereoscope
132. Movable lead-lined screen
133. Film filing cabinets
134. Film storage bin
135. Radiographic and fluoroscopic combination unit
136. Superficial x-ray therapy unit
137. Deep therapy unit
138. Control unit (current control)
139. Movable lead-lined screen
140. Lead protection
141. Lead-lined door (light-proof)
142. Leaded glass view window
143. Cassette pass box
144. Cassette changer
145. Film dryer
146. Storage cabinet (4½ feet high)
147. Loading counter with film storage bin and cabinets below, safe light and film rack above
148. Developing tank with (size)—(timer) and (safe light) above
149. Film washing tank, with illuminator above; without illuminator above
150. Barium sink in counter, cabinet below, recessed cabinet above
151. Folding screen

## Utility and Service Areas

The location of utility and service areas should be planned carefully in every medical building. These areas include:

### Utility Room

In a one-story building this room should contain heating and air-conditioning equipment, hot water heater, janitor's sink and space for janitor's supplies. Some states will require separation of the janitor's space from the heating space. This room should not be more than 15 to 20 feet from an outside wall unless the compressor is to be on the roof. Size of the room will depend on the equipment size, and this should be carefully checked in preliminary planning. A pegboard wall will be handy in the janitor's area. Some states will require one or two fire-wall partitions and a fire door in this room.

### Storage Spaces

Storage and utility space must be provided for patient wraps, staff wraps, utility paper goods and towels, office supplies, old files, and treatment and medicinal needs for at least one full day in each workroom. Casework walls in treatment rooms laboratory, EKG and BMR room, cast room, and other workrooms, with self-contained sink and counter top, will largely solve the latter problem. The other closets and storage spaces will have to be located convenient to the place of principal use.

### Lavatory Rooms

The number is dependent upon convenience desired and the expense the doctor wishes to undertake. Facilities adjacent to the waiting room for patients, in the work area for staff, and at least one adjoining the laboratory are all desirable. The doctor must decide how many he wants in relation to the cost. Wall hung stools and lavatories are recommended.

RADIOLOGY

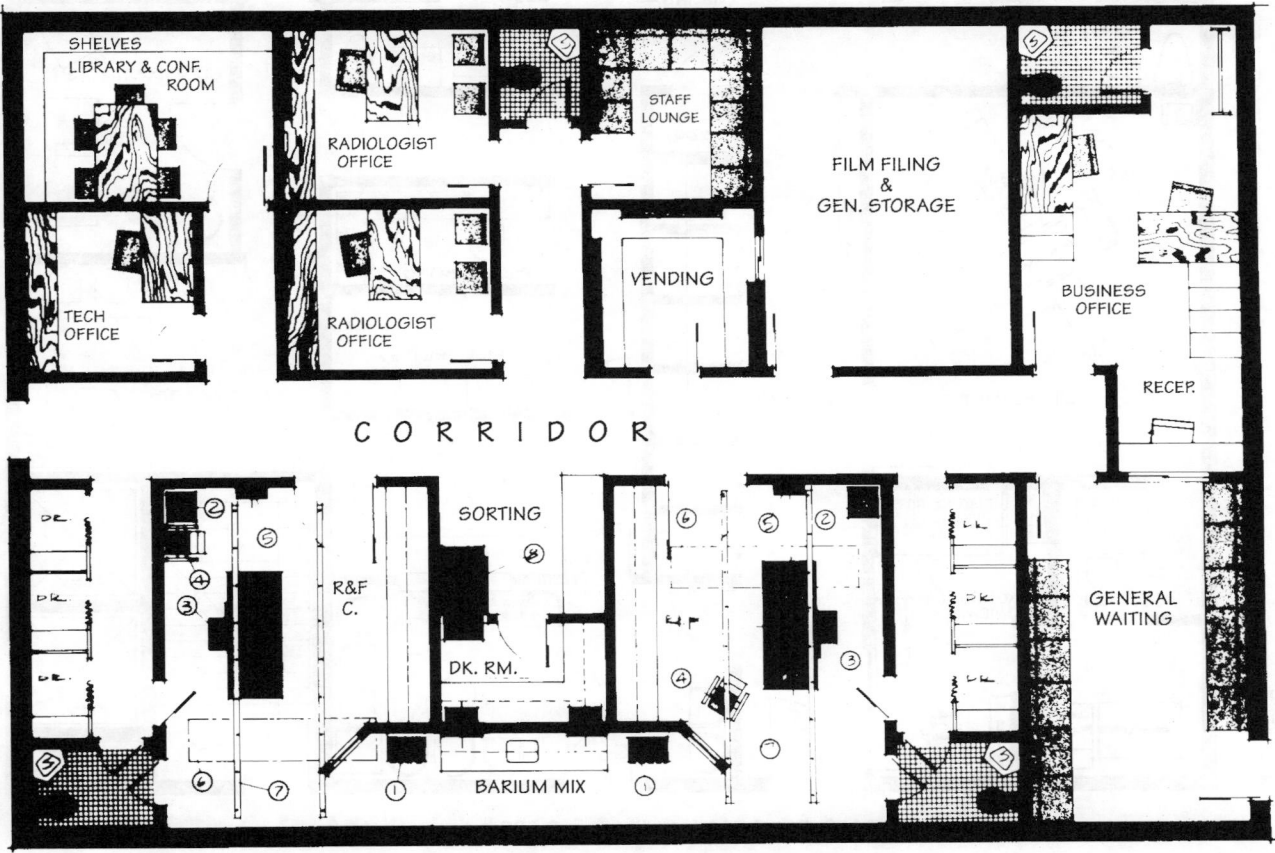

Equipment list
1. Control
2. X-ray transformer
3. Table
4. TV monitor on mobile cart
5. Cassette holder
6. Overhead tube conveyor
7. Ceiling-mounted rails
8. Autoprocessor

**Fig. 10. Typical radiologist's office**

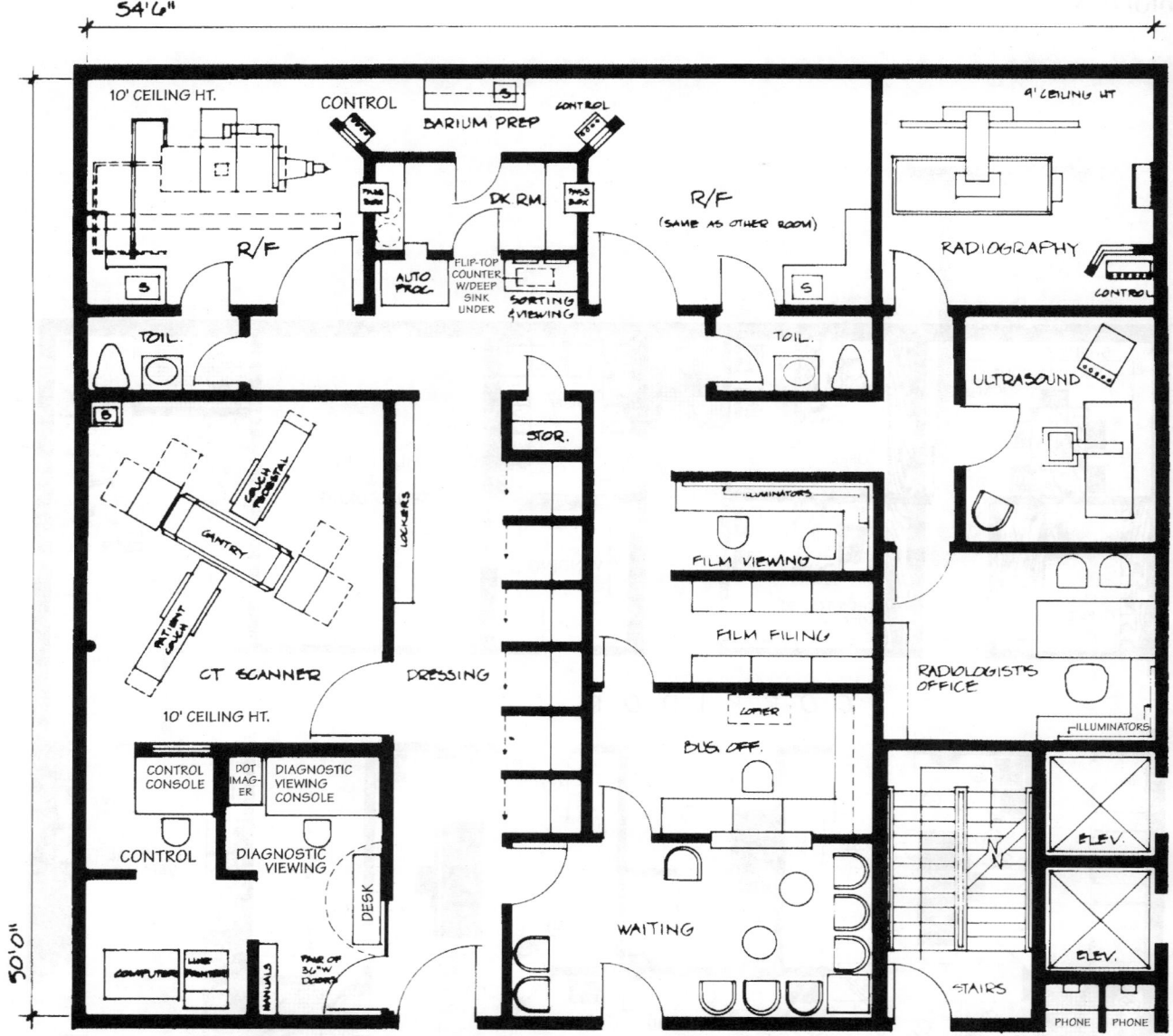

Fig. 11. Suite plan for radiology, 2,522 square feet

# GENERAL PRACTICE

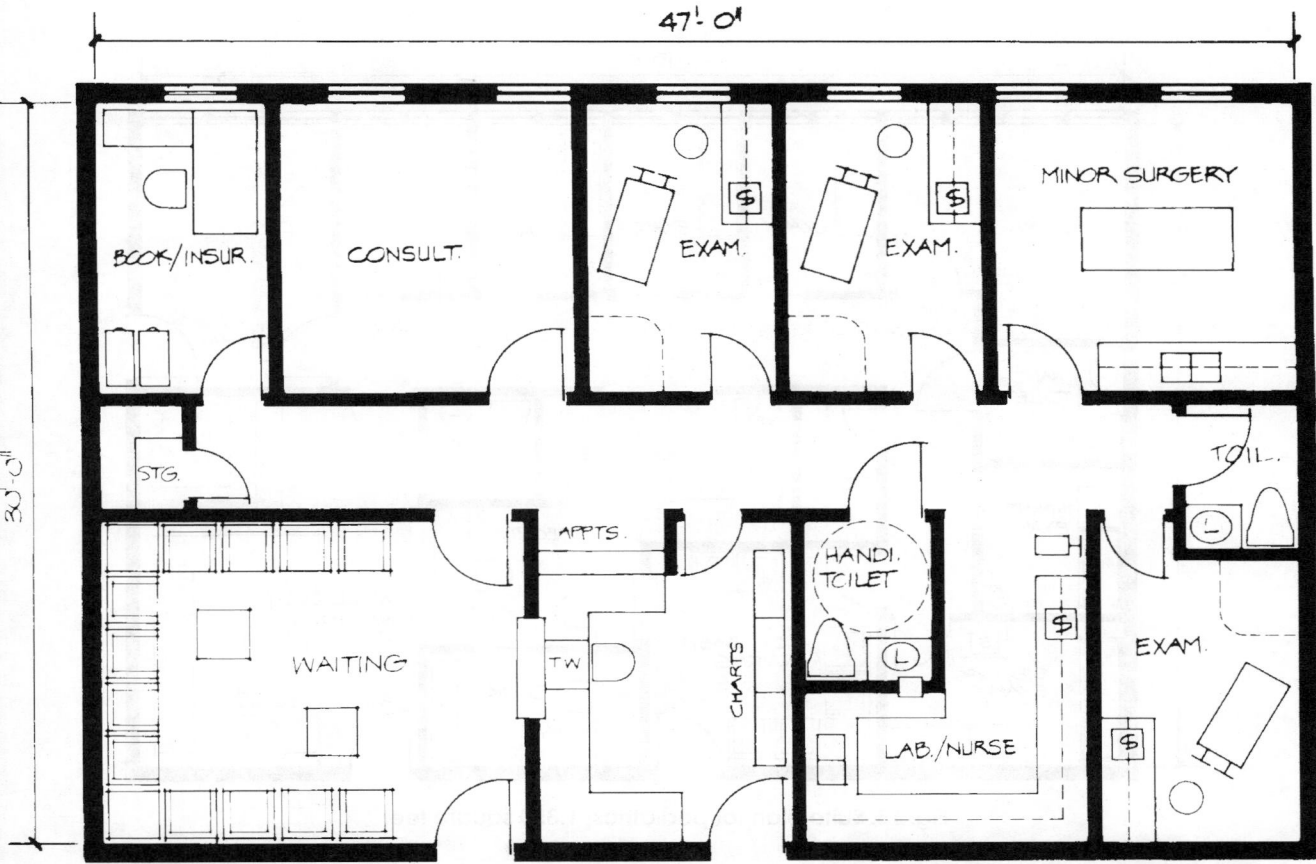

**Fig. 12. Suite plan for general practice, 1,380 square feet**

**Table 1** Analysis of program: General practice

| No. of Physicians: | 1 | 2 | 3 |
|---|---|---|---|
| Consultation | 12 × 12 = 144 | 2 @ 12 × 12 = 288 | 3 @ 12 × 12 = 432 |
| Exam Rooms | 3 @ 8 × 12 = 288 | 6 @ 8 × 12 = 576 | 9 @ 8 × 12 = 864 |
| Waiting Room | 12 × 14 = 168 | 14 × 18 = 252 | 20 × 24 = 480 |
| Business Office | 12 × 14 = 168 | 14 × 16 = 224 | 18 × 30 = 540[a] |
| Nurse Station | 8 × 10 = 80 | 10 × 12 = 120 | 12 × 12 = 144 |
| Toilets | 2 @ 5 × 6 = 60 | 2 @ 5 × 6 = 60 | 3 @ 5 × 6 = 90 |
| Storage | 4 × 6 = 24 | 6 × 8 = 48 | 8 × 10 = 80 |
| Cast Room | Use Minor Surgery | Use Minor Surgery | 12 × 12 = 144 |
| EKG | Use Minor Surgery | Use Minor Surgery | 8 × 12 = 96 |
| Staff Lounge | — | 8 × 12 = 96 | 10 × 12 = 120 |
| Minor Surgery | 12 × 12 = 144 | 12 × 12 = 144 | 12 × 12 = 144 |
| X-ray Area[b] | — | 12 × 20 = 240 | 12 × 20 = 240 |
| Laboratory | — | 8 × 10 = 80 | 16 × 16 = 256[c] |
| Subtotal | 1076 ft² | 2128 ft² | 3630 ft² |
| 15% Circulation | 161 | 319 | 545 |
| Total | 1237 ft² | 2447 ft² | 4175 ft² |

[a]Includes insurance clerk, bookkeeper, and office manager.
[b]Includes darkroom, control, film filing, and dressing area.
[c]Includes lab, waiting, and blood draw.

**PEDIATRICS; INTERNAL MEDICINE**

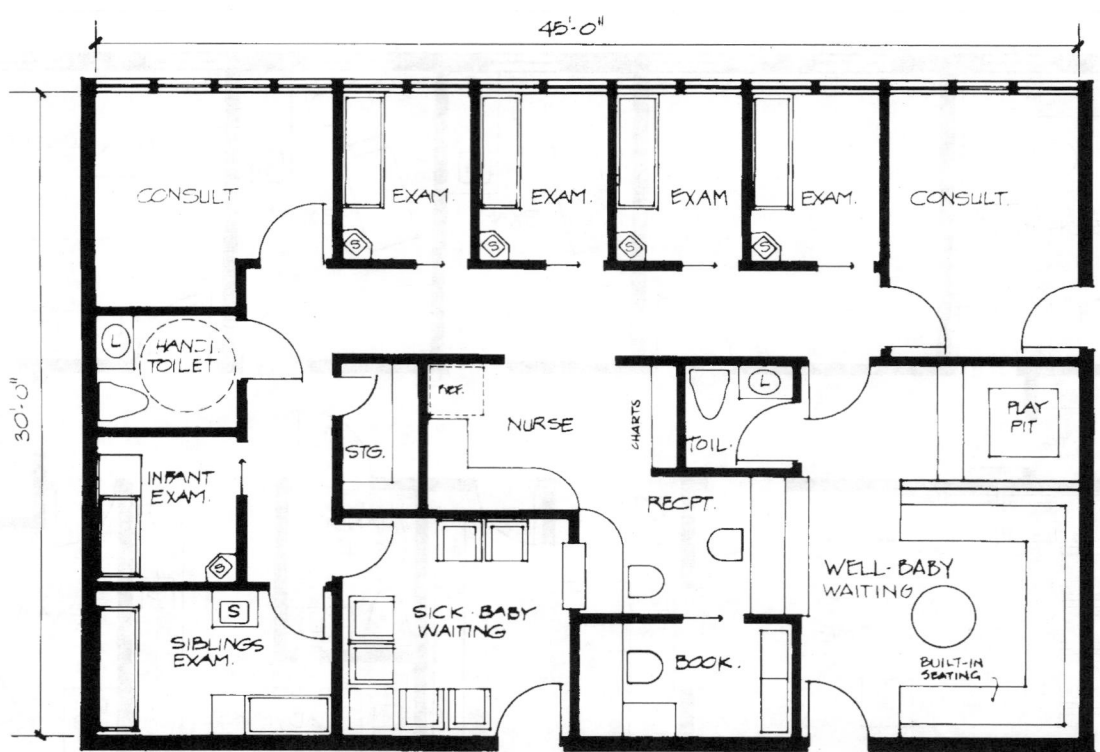

Fig. 13. Suite plan for pediatrics, 1,350 square feet

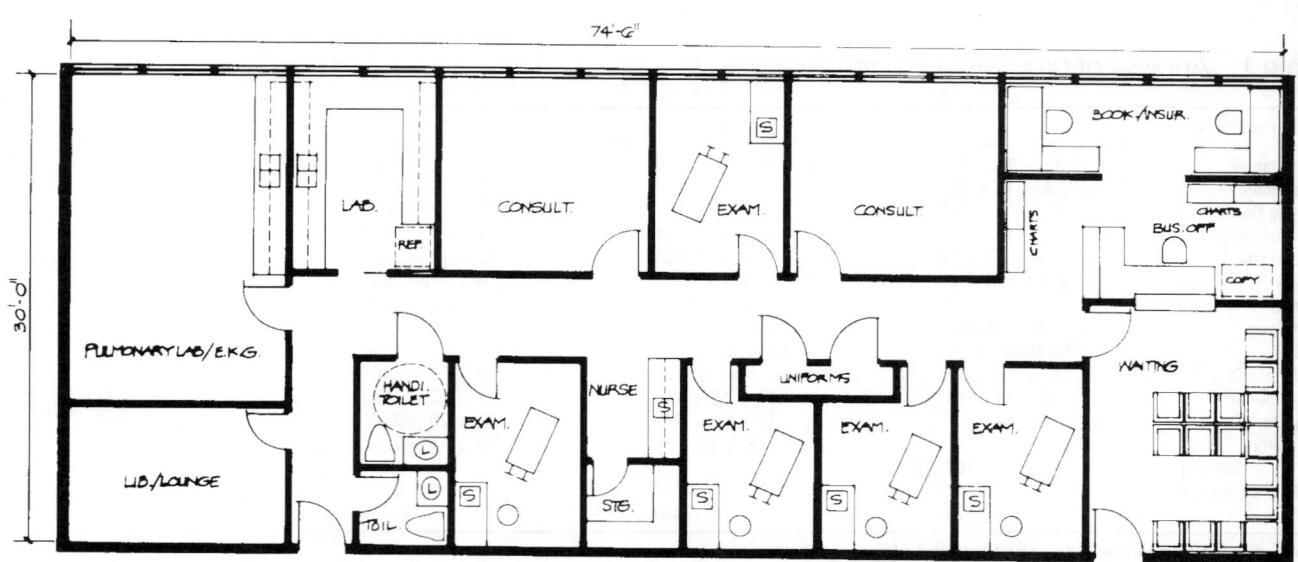

Fig. 14. Suite plan for internal medicine, 2,238 square feet

**PLASTIC SURGERY**

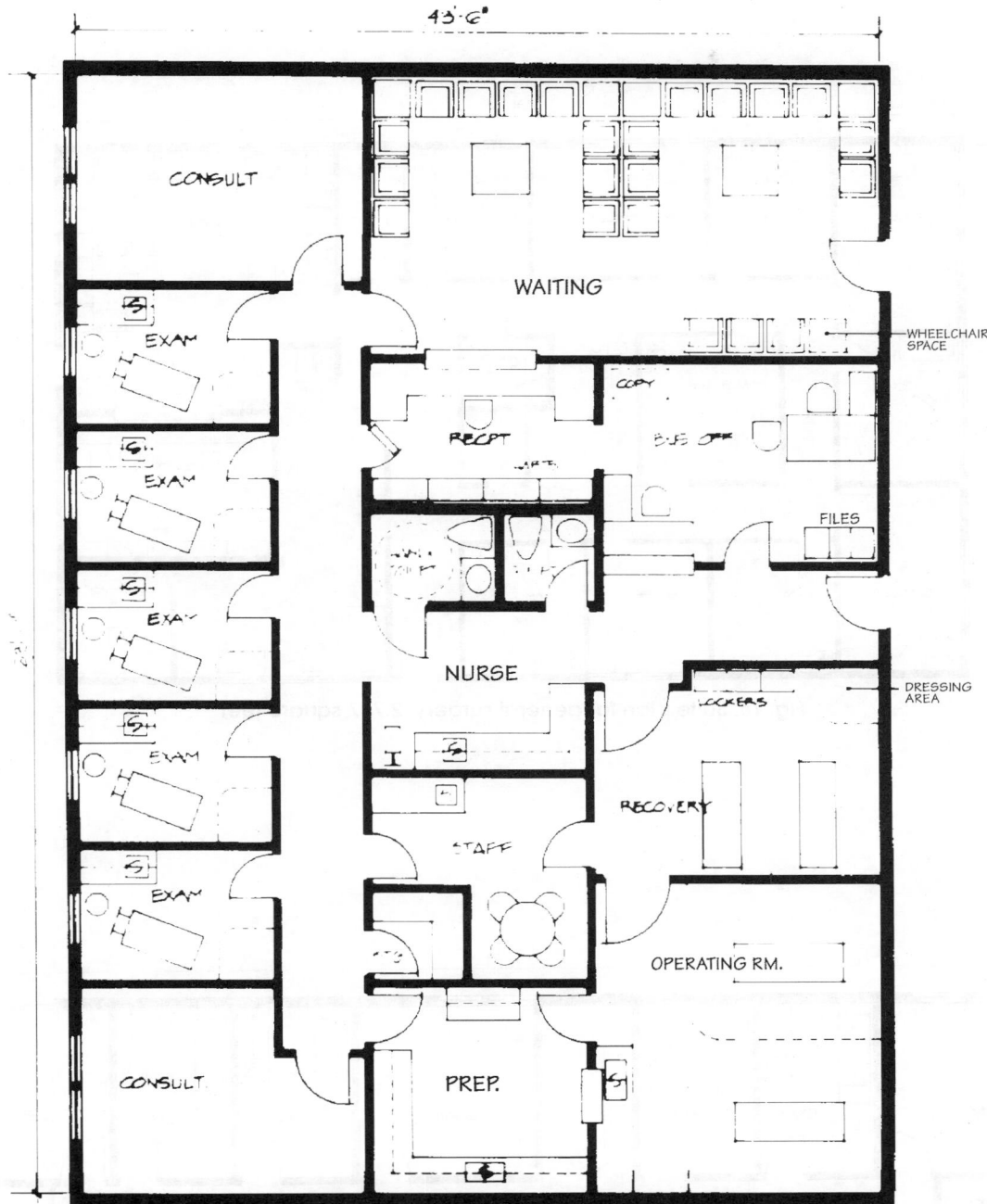

43'-6"

CONSULT

EXAM

EXAM

EXAM

EXAM

EXAM

CONSULT

WAITING

WHEELCHAIR SPACE

RECPT

COPY

B.S. OFF

FILES

NURSE

LOCKERS

DRESSING AREA

STAFF

RECOVERY

OPERATING RM.

PREP.

Fig. 15. Suite plan for plastic surgery, 2,750 square feet

## GENERAL SURGERY; ORTHOPEDIC SURGERY

**Fig. 16.** Suite plan for general surgery, 2,747 square feet

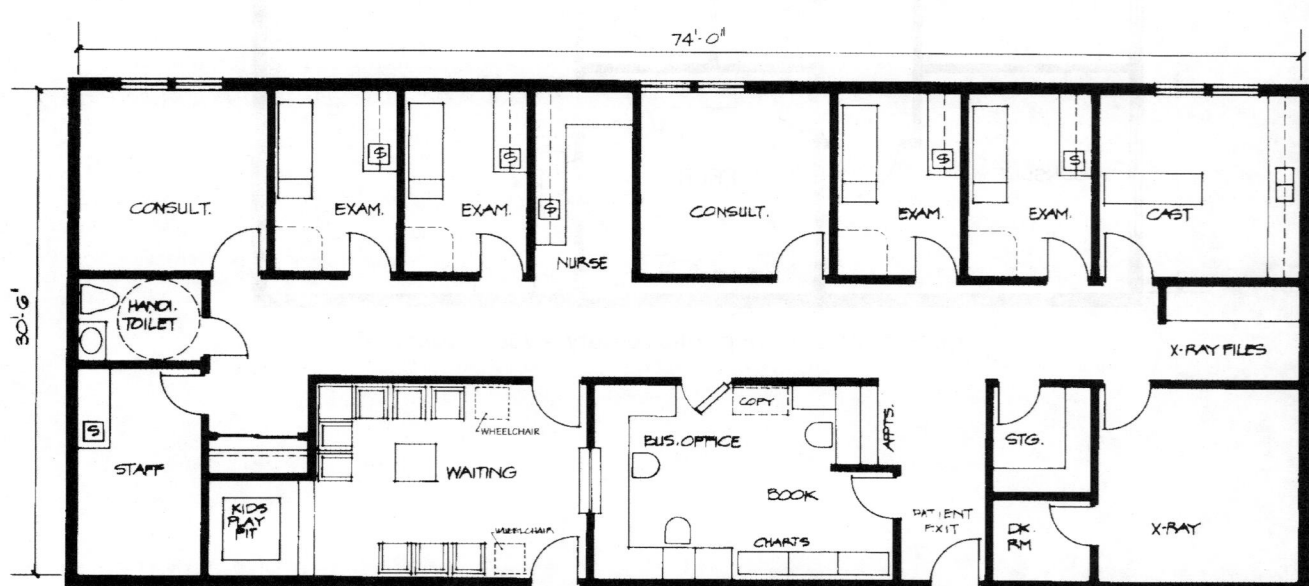

**Fig. 17.** Suite plan for orthopedic surgery, 2,257 square feet

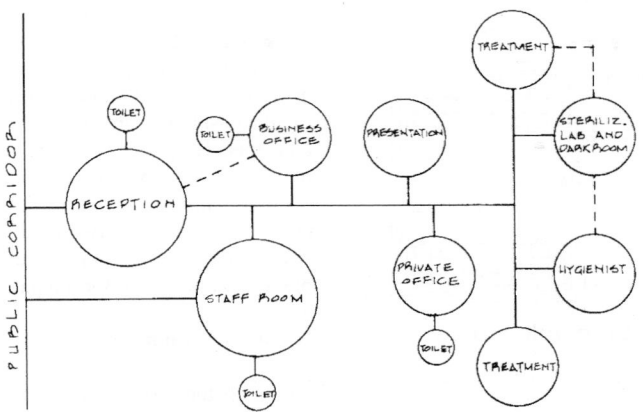

**Fig. 1. Dental office flow diagram**

# DENTAL OFFICES

## ELEMENTS OF A DENTAL OFFICE

Reception (waiting area)
Business office
Auxiliary business area
Consultation or study areas
Audiovisual, patient education
Hygienist (variable)
Treatment rooms (variable)
Laboratory (variable)
Darkroom
X-ray (variable)
Sterilizing area (variable)
Staff lounge
Preventive area (patient education)

### Environment and the Professional Image

The dentist, as opposed to a physician (unless a specialist), is locked into her environment. In order for a dentist to treat her patient, she must use extensive tools and dental equipment which require fixed or semi-fixed plumbing and other built-in operating instruments and services. The plumbing services that are necessary to facilitate the operation are water (filtered), air (dry, filtered), suction (wet or dry), waste (vented), and electricity. These are basic and essential input and output elements.

The proper location of services to be performed is essential. The relationship, volume, and use of each area will vary according to individual concepts and needs. Whether the dentist is a general practitioner or a specialist, training and developed concepts or working habits vary, often greatly (Fig. 1).

With semi-fixed or flexible equipment, the dentist can change or modify his operative procedures. With both the increase in patients and constantly changing dental concepts, the need for flexibility in the office is essential.

### Reception

The ideal area for a single practitioner should be approximately 150 square feet minimum, with three walls unbroken by doorways. This allows perimeter of space for maximum seating of five to seven people. Lighting should be incandescent and diffuse. Both recessed and below-ceiling light sources should be used.

### Business Office or Secretarial Area

This is the key or control point in the management of the office. Figure 2 reflects the position the receptionist assumes in relation to the waiting area. Full visual control is maintained through closed sliding glass window. Appointment and financial arrangements are consummated at this point. All traffic and flow control is regulated by the nurse/secretary.

### Private Office

In many offices the private consultation room serves multiple functions, particularly when the cost of space has become so prohibitive and the doctor is interested in increasing the number of treatment rooms within a small overall space. Consultation room desks may take on several shapes (Fig. 3), depending on the practice concept of the doctor. She may wish to maintain a formal relationship whereby she faces the patient, who sits opposite the desk. She may prefer an informal arrangement where she and the patient sit around a "table" rather than a formal desk. Active study models and diagnostic models should be located in shallow desk drawers in the desk or in the nearby storage system (Fig. 4).

### Treatment Room

The heart of any dental practice is the treatment room. Storage, instrumentation, and comfortable arrangement of equipment and instruments vary with each doctor and doctor's concept as well as with field conditions. The main consideration is to permit the doctor to work in a stressless or comfortable working position and environ-

*Author:* Marvin Cutler, AID
*Reviewer:* James H. Ogden, R.A.

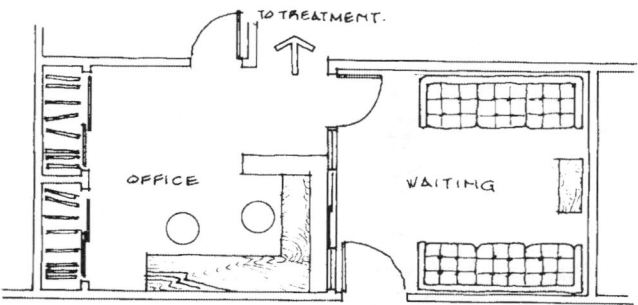

**Fig. 2. Business office and reception room**

ment. The use and placement of one or two sinks depend upon doctor's concept. Figs. 5 and 6 show a fair amount of storage for supplies and instruments. Adequate work space and counter permits doctor to do bench work without interfering with his chair-side assistant. During the past few years, doctors have experienced a constant change in concepts. Therefore, a degree of flexibility must be reflected in the planning. A mobile instrument cabinet can be tucked under the counter. This is necessary to allow the doctor a greater degree of change in his position while treating his patient. The emphasis in the treatment room should be on efficiency, ease of maintenance, and a pleasant atmosphere for the patient, doctor, and staff.

### Hygienist's Room

Although the size and function of the hygienist's room may differ from those of the regular treatment room, it is not uncommon to equip this room in the same way as the regular treatment rooms. This will allow the dentist to use this room, when needed, as an additional treatment room (Fig. 7).

### Sterilizing Area

The location of the sterilizing area is determined by various factors: dental procedural concepts, the available space in the office, and the psychological image the doctor wishes to obtain. The materials used here should be about the same as those in the laboratory. There should be adequate storage space for trays and supplies, including the pre-prepared trays as well as those which will be cleaned up at various intervals during the normal working day. The autoclave should be placed out of the reach of children, and the ultrasonic cleaners can be used more efficiently if recessed into the work-counter tops.

The size and location of support areas such as sterilizing, laboratory, dark room, x-ray area, etc., will depend in part on doctor's concept as well as the logistics of the space. A small laboratory unit is merely used for model pouring, trimming, and storage. The size of many labs is often larger to accommodate expanded technical skills and services. Some doctors split lab duties into two areas.

**Fig. 3. Private consultation room furnishings (Taylor Clark Architects; photo: Walter Dufresne)**

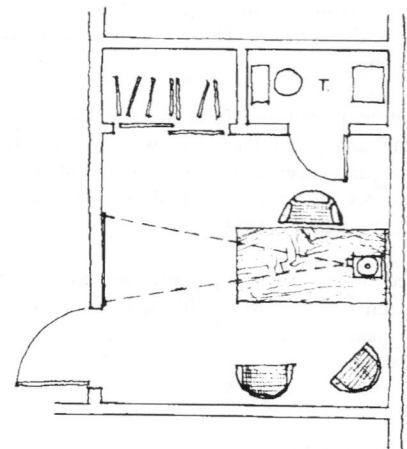

**Fig. 4. Private office**

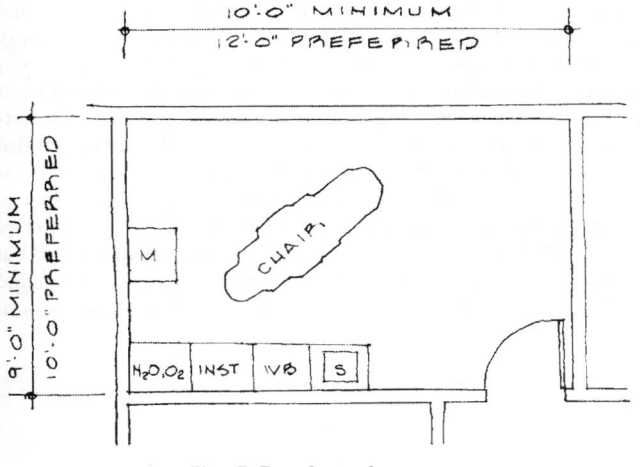

**Fig. 5. Treatment room**

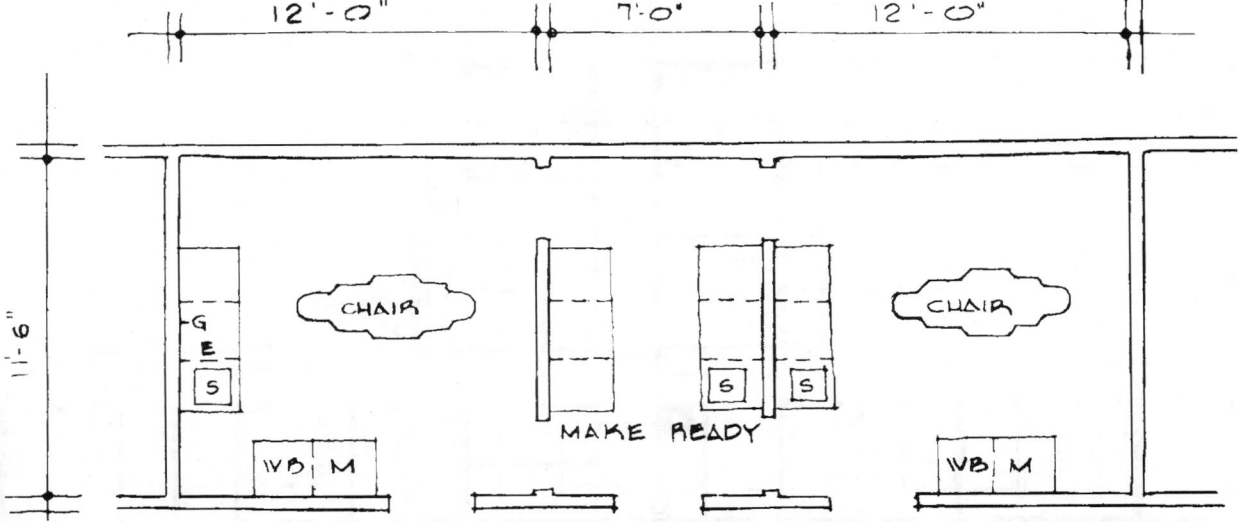

**Fig. 6. Treatment rooms**

In conclusion, the dental office is a professional home. Like it or not, the dentist spends the most productive years of her life in it—more than half her waking moments. The office does, therefore, reflect her personality as well as her professional image. It can either assist the doctor to aspire to greater success and satisfaction, or it can sentence her to a professional life of mediocrity and apathy.

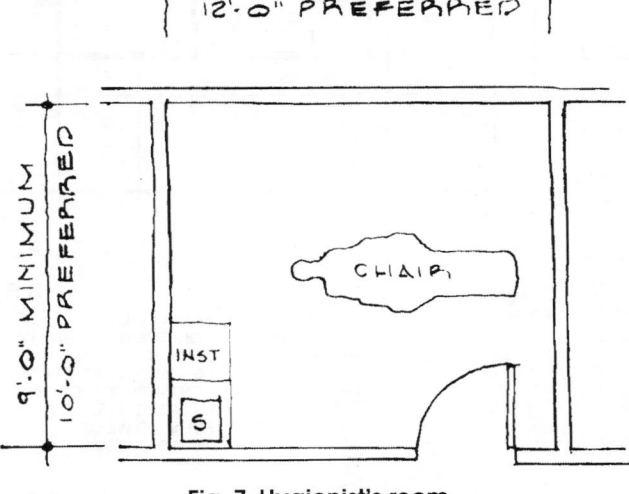

**Fig. 7. Hygienist's room**

## GENERAL DENTISTRY

### Office Circulation Patterns

The traffic flow within a dental office is from waiting room to X-ray (either a special room for this purpose or located in a standard operatory) to operatory (Fig. 8). The patient should be able to enter the operatory and sit down on the right side of the chair (for a right-handed dentist) without walking around the chair or through the assistant's work area (Fig. 9). At the end of the procedure the patient walks to the reception area, books a future appointment if required, and pays for services.

The dentist's circulation is from private office to operatory and between operatories. He or she should be able to enter the operatory without having to walk around the chair or through the assistant's work area, wash hands, and be seated on the patient's right (if he or she is right-handed), as in Fig. 9. The assistant's path is from the sterilizing area to the operatories, darkroom, and lab. The assistant (also called the auxiliary), in most cases, will have to walk the greater distance in order to reach his work area since it is more important to maximize production that the dentists have the shortest route (Fig. 10, Plans A, C, D, and Fig. 11, Plan F). The office should be laid out to save as many steps as possible. Since the dentist and assistant are working in such confined areas, it is critical that these spaces be well

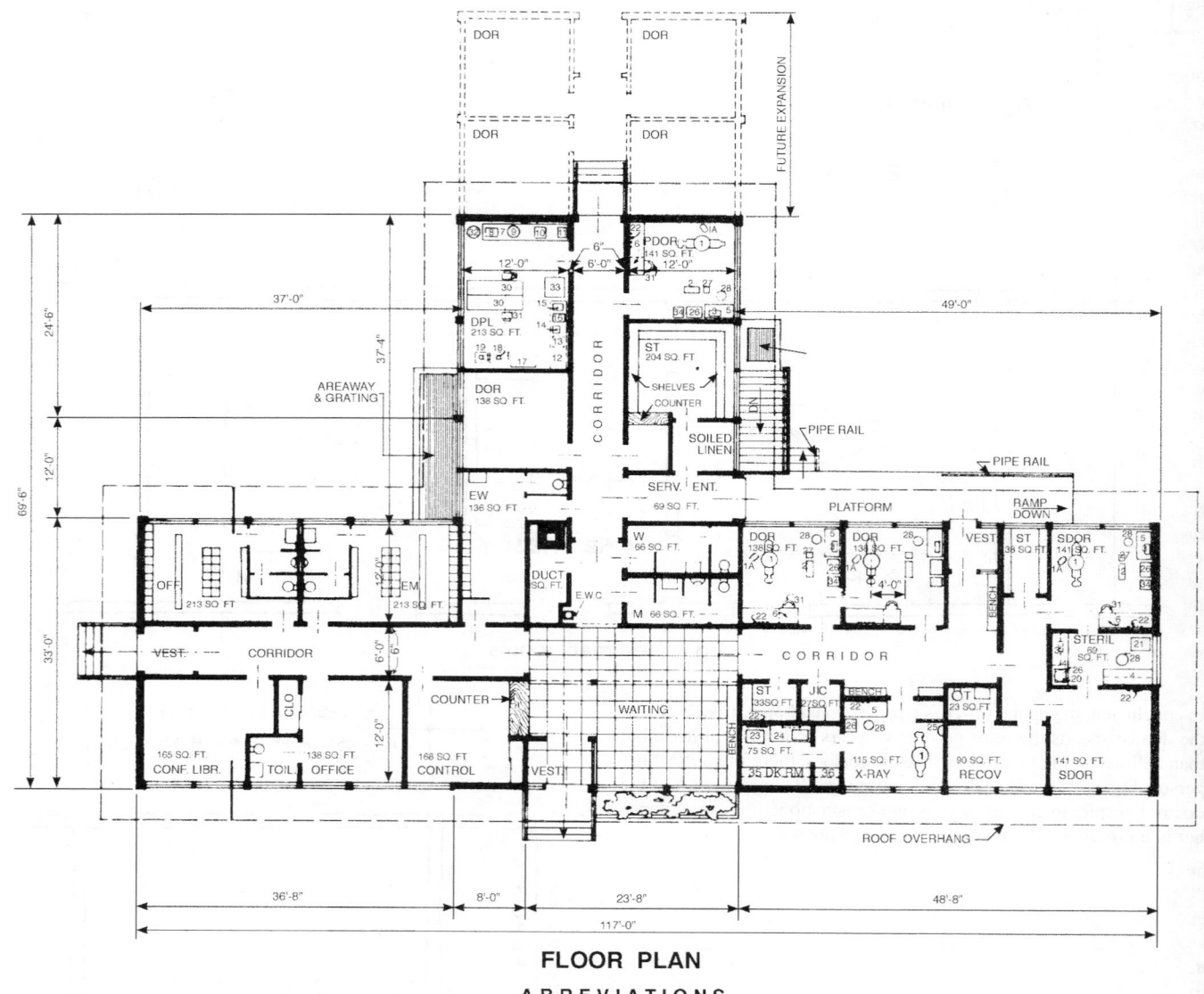

## FLOOR PLAN

### ABREVIATIONS

| | | | |
|---|---|---|---|
| ADMIN | - ADMINISTRATION | OFF | - OFFICERS |
| CONF - LIBR | - CONFERENCE - LIBRARY | PDOR | - PROSTHETICS DENTAL OPERATING ROOM |
| DK RM | - DARK ROOM | RECOV | - RECOVERY |
| DOR | - DENTAL OPERATING ROOM | SDOR | - SURGICAL DENTAL OPERATING ROOM |
| DPL | - DENTAL PROSTHETICS | ST | - STORAGE |
| EM | - ENLISTED MEN | STERIL | - STERILIZATION ROOM |
| EW | - ENLISTED WOMEN | T | - TOILET |
| JC | - JANITOR'S CLOSET | VEST | - VESTIBULE |
| M | - MEN | W | - WOMEN |

**Fig. 8. Dental clinic plan**

planned and efficient. As with a medical office, a dental office should have a private entrance/exit for the staff and dentists so that they do not have to pass through the waiting room.

## Dental Assistant

The dental assistant or auxiliary performs many duties. Among them are cleanup of operatories, seating of patients in dental chair, preparing tray setups, taking X-rays, sterilizing instruments, loading anesthetic syringes, pouring impressions, mixing amalgams, charting and numbering teeth, handling suction, air, and water syringe, and assisting the dentist in dozens of restorative and surgical procedures.

## Design Operatories for Flexibility

A right-handed dentist will work to the patient's right and a left-handed dentist to the patient's left. Traditionally, operatories were designed either for a right-handed dentist or a left-handed one. Today, flexibility is the key. New equipment is designed to accommodate change. In a practice composed of right-handed and left-handed dentists, an ambidextrous operatory can be designed (Fig. 12) in which the utilities are brought up under the toe of the chair and are mounted near the chair on a swing-away bracket that is designed to swing to either the left or the right of the chair. The X-ray head should be mounted over the fixed cabinet behind the patient, and the mobile cabinet used by the assistant may be used on either side of the chair. The mobile cabinet would slide into an opening in the fixed cabinet when not in use, and the hoses for water, compressed air, and suction would come from the wall behind the fixed cabinet or from a swing-away bracket on the chair, negating the need for a mobile cabinet.

## Size of Operatories

Operatories may be as small as 8 by 10 feet or as large as 10 by 12 feet, 100 square feet is the average size. Figure 13 shows the minimum distances between the dental chair, cabinetry, and perimeter of the room. Dentists used to prefer small operatories when they worked alone so that while seated (or standing) they could reach everything they needed without walking. Now that most dentists use an assistant and the trend is toward longer appointments (it is more efficient to do a lot of work at one sitting), many dentists feel more comfortable working in a large operatory. If the dentist uses large mobile cabinets, a more spacious operatory is desirable so that the cabinets can easily be moved to any position in the room.

## Number of Operatories

There is no rule governing the number of operatories per dentist since the dentist's temperament and practice methods have a lot to do with it. A dentist who works slowly or who does a lot of restorative work with long appointments can be comfortable with two operatories. A dentist with many short appointments will need four operatories in order not to lose time during the change of patients and the preparation or cleanup of operatories. A rule of thumb is three operatories per dentist in a general practice.

## Design of the Dental Operatory

This is the most important room in a dental office. Although analogous to the physician's examination room, it is far more critical to a dentist's practice than the medical exam room is to a physician's practice since the physician has ancillary rooms for diagnosis, testing, and treatment, but the dentist has only the operatory. In terms of economics, the physician has the opportunity to enhance his or her income from laboratory tests, X-ray films, and the use of medical aides to give injections, administer EKGs and EEGs, or to do physical therapy. But the dentist has only the operatory plus the laboratory and X-ray work from which to derive income. For this reason many time and motion studies focusing on operatory efficiency have been published in dental journals. And certain major changes have evolved as a result of these studies. Patients now recline in a contour chair with the dentist working from a seated position at the side of the patient. If right-handed, the dentist will be seated to the right of the patient and will work in an area that could be designated at from 9:00 to 12:00, imagining the face of a clock surrounding the patient. Most dentists use an assistant, which is called four handed dentistry. Some dentists use two assistants. Fig. 9 illustrates the optimum traffic flow pattern for an operatory. However, the exigencies of the fixed structure of the space, the location of windows and other "given" features, have an impact on the layout of the space, and compromises sometimes must be made.

## Instrumentation

There are four categories of instrumentation:

1. *Handpiece Delivery System*  This is composed of rotary tools with drill bits that are used to cut and shape teeth.
2. *Evacuation System*  Blood, debris, and water are removed from the mouth usually by suction (a vacuum system). This is normally performed by the dental assistant.
3. *Hand-held Instruments*  These tools include probes, scalers, forceps, etc.

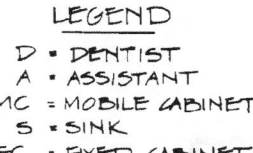

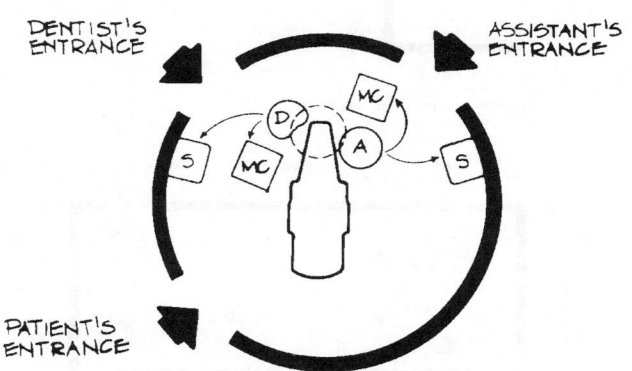

OPTIMUM TRAFFIC FLOW PATTERN FOR OPERATORY. DOTTED LINE INDICATES INSTRUMENT TRANSFER ZONE.

**Fig. 9. Optimum traffic flow pattern**

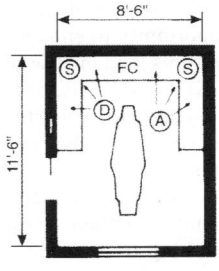

**PLAN A**

"U" DESIGN OPERATORY
DENTIST AND ASSISTANT WORK
OFF OF FIXED CABINETS

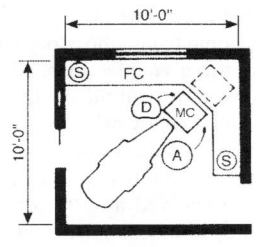

**PLAN B**

DIAGONAL CHAIR PLACEMENT
WITH SINGLE MOBILE CABINET
BEHIND PATIENT'S HEAD OFF OF
MOBILE CABINET

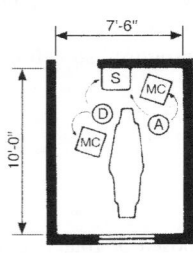

**PLAN C**

ASSISTANT AND DENTIST
WORK OFF OF SPLIT MOBILE
CABINETS. NO FIXED CABINETRY
IN ROOM.

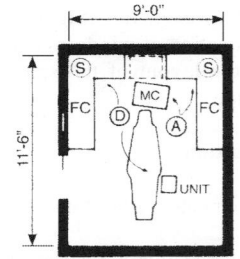

**PLAN D**

MODIFIED "U" ARRANGEMENT
WITH OPENING IN FIXED CABINETS
FOR STORAGE OF MOBILE CABINET.
ASSISTANT WORKS OFF OF MOBILE
CABINET BEHIND PATIENT AND DENTIST
WORKS OFF OF A DENTAL UNIT WITH
INSTRUMENTATION DELIVERED
OVER THE PATIENT'S CHEST.

**Fig. 10. Plans A, B, C, D**

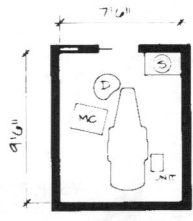

**PLAN E**

AN OPERATORY FOR A DENTIST
WHO WORKS WITHOUT AN ASSISTANT.

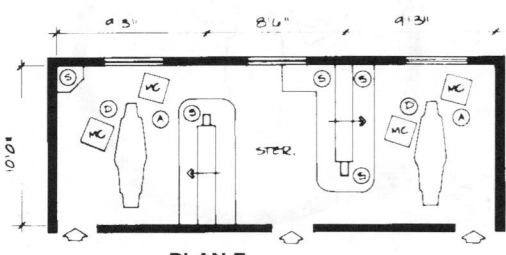

**PLAN F**

DENTIST AND ASSISTANT WORK OFF MOBILE CABINETS
BOTH OPERATORIES HAVE PASS-THROUGH FEATURE WITH
STERILIZATION AREA WHICH PERMITS CLEAN TRAY SET-UPS
TO BE PLACED IN OPERATORY (AND DIRTY ONES REMOVED)
WITHOUT ENTERING THE ROOM.

**Fig. 11. Plans E, F**

4. *Three-way Syringe*   Often used by both the dentist and the assistant for spraying water, compressed air, or a combination thereof. In a well-equipped operatory, the assistant will have her own three-way syringe for drying or moistening preparations as well as for washing debris from the patient's mouth.

**Methods of Delivery**

The instrumentation can be delivered to the oral cavity of the patient by three methods:

1. *Mobile Delivery System*   The utilities (water, air, suction, electricity) can be delivered via mobile carts in split fashion (the dentist's cart has the handpieces and syringe, while the assistant's cart has a syringe and suction), or via a single cart from which the dentist's as well as the assistant's instruments are delivered. The single cart is usually located to the rear of the patient (Fig. 10, Plan B), while the split cart (for a right-handed dentist) would be located just below the patient's right shoulder and the split cart for the assistant would be located to the left of the patient's head (Fig. 9 and Fig. 10, Plan C).
2. *Rear Delivery System*   Both the dentist's and the assistant's instrumentation are delivered from behind the patient's head from a fixed cabinet (Fig. 10, Plan A) with the systems built in. Delivery of instrumentation from a mobile cabinet behind the patient is discussed above.
3. *Over-the-Patient Delivery System*   Instruments and utilities are delivered from an area near the patient's left or right elbow or over the patient's chest. These kinds of delivery systems are usually attached to the chair so that even as the chair is adjusted up or down, the relationship of instrument location with respect to the oral cavity is constant (Fig. 10, Plan D and Fig. 11, Plan E).

There are combinations of the above delivery systems as well as other variables that must be considered. Two such items are the use of the cuspidor versus the more efficient central suction, and the number and placement of sinks in the operatory. Cuspidors can be purchased with central suction operation or with gravity drain. However, most modern dental offices use central suction with no cuspidor. The suction hoses at each operatory work off of a vacuum pump located in an equipment room near the operatories.

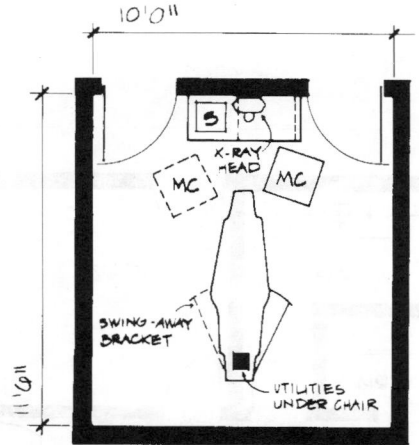

THIS ARRANGEMENT SERVES A PRACTICE
COMPOSED OF RIGHT- AND LEFT-HANDED
DENTISTS. THE X-RAY HEAD IS MOUNTED
BEHIND THE PATIENT. UTILITIES ARE UNDER
THE TOE OF THE CHAIR AND THE ASSISTANT'S
MOBILE CART CAN MOVE TO EITHER SIDE.

**Fig. 12. Ambidextrous operatory**

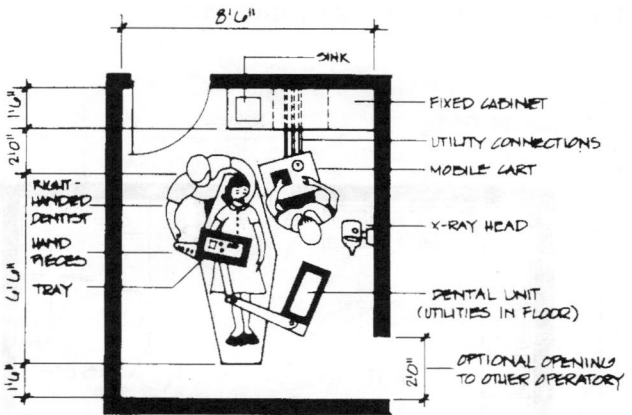

**Fig. 13. Optimal size of operatory**

## GENERAL DENTISTRY; ORTHODONTICS

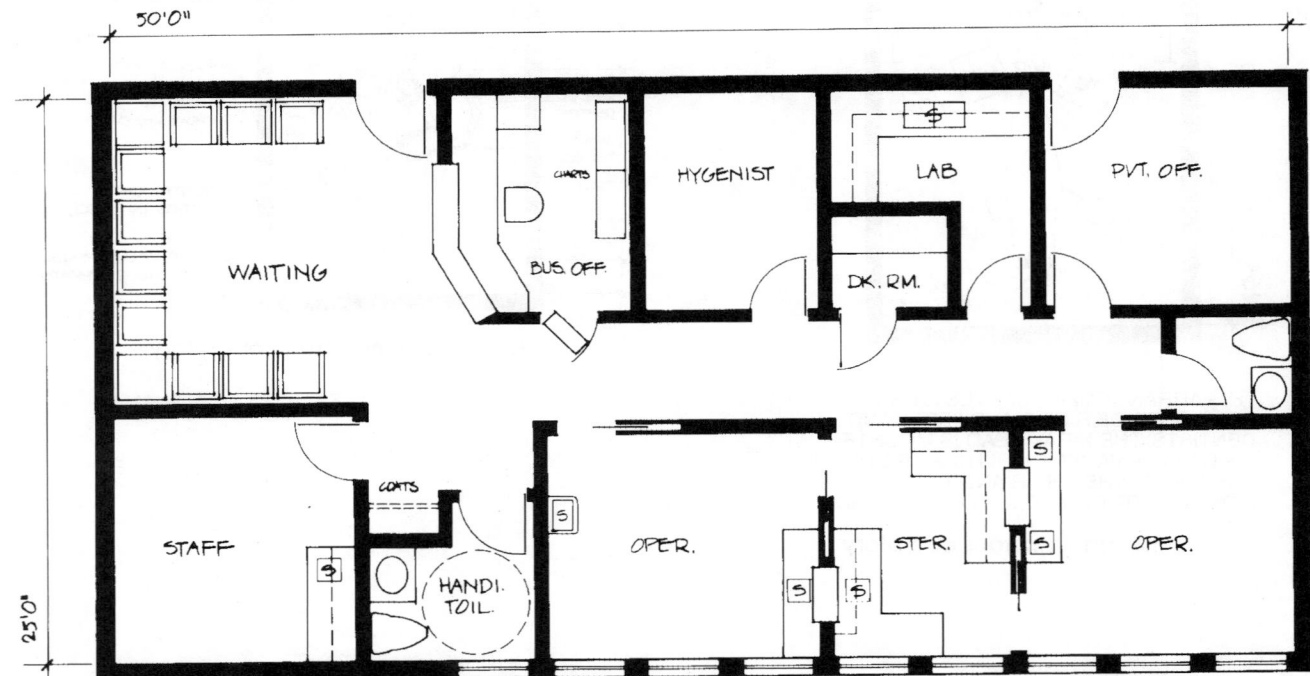

Fig. 14. Suite plan, 1,250 square feet

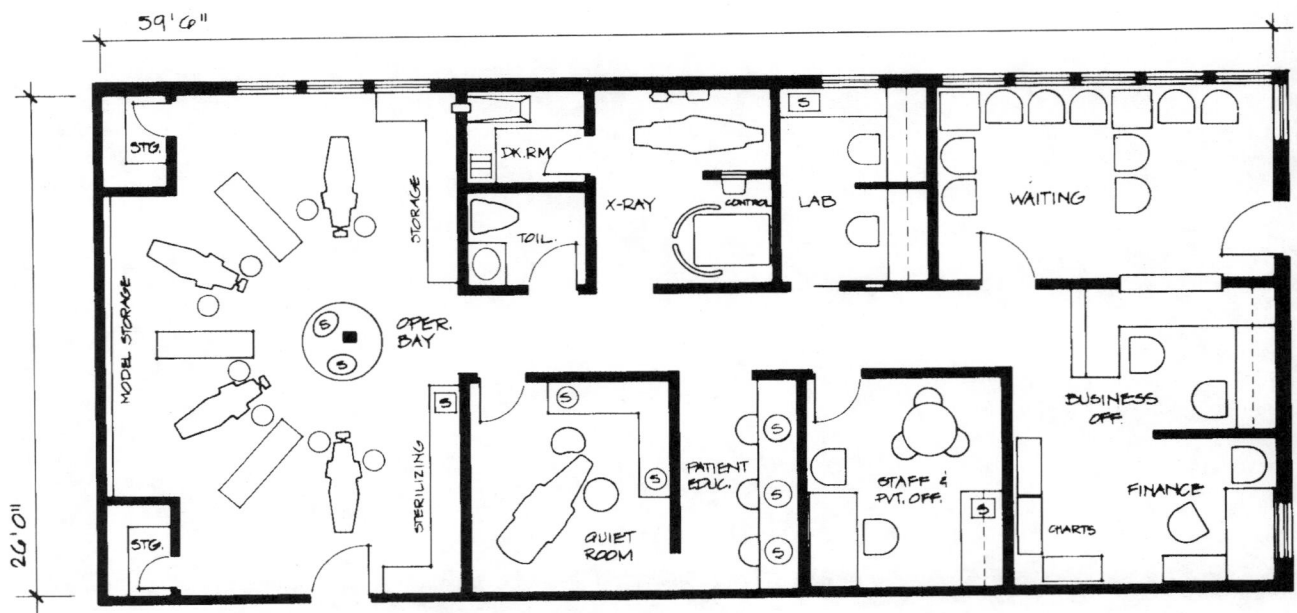

Fig. 15. Suite plan for orthodontics, 1,547 square feet

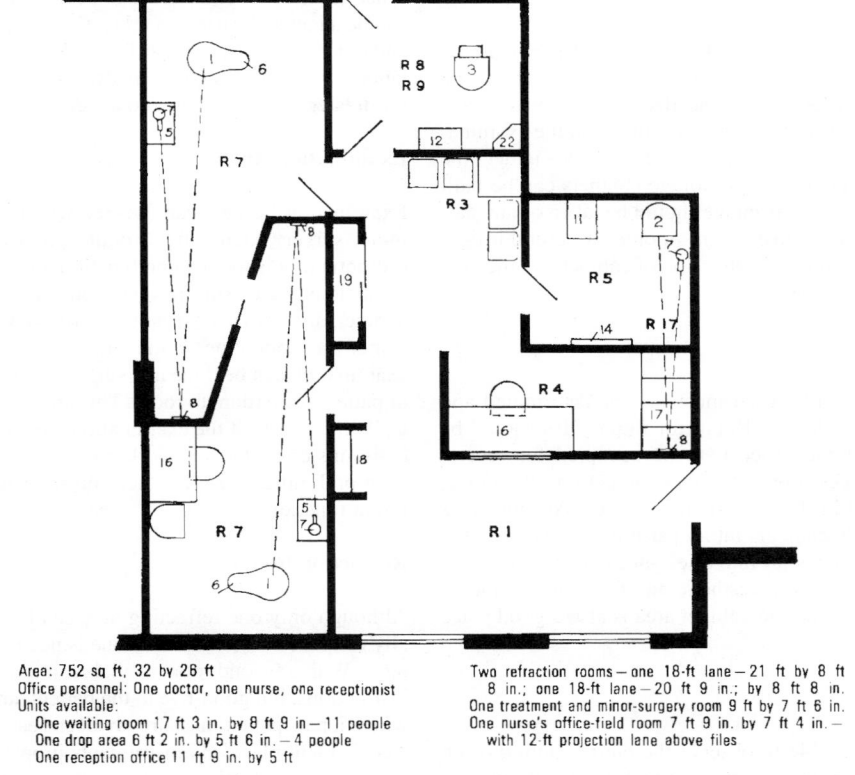

Area: 752 sq ft, 32 by 26 ft
Office personnel: One doctor, one nurse, one receptionist
Units available:
   One waiting room 17 ft 3 in. by 8 ft 9 in — 11 people
   One drop area 6 ft 2 in. by 5 ft 6 in. — 4 people
   One reception office 11 ft 9 in. by 5 ft

Two refraction rooms — one 18-ft lane — 21 ft by 8 ft
   8 in.; one 18-ft lane — 20 ft 9 in.; by 8 ft 8 in.
One treatment and minor-surgery room 9 ft by 7 ft 6 in.
One nurse's office-field room 7 ft 9 in. by 7 ft 4 in. —
   with 12-ft projection lane above files

**Fig. 1. Plan for one-doctor ophthalmological office**

# OPHTHALMOLOGICAL OFFICES

Efficient office layout calls for the use of certain basic principles which must be modified to meet the requirements of available space, personal habits, and individual preferences. What might be considered efficient by one practitioner is not necessarily so deemed by the next. It is axiomatic that the ones who seem most pleased with their office layouts are the ones who have worked in one or more offices before designing their final suites. Their layout better serves their own habit patterns. Therefore, it is wise to consider each factor as an individual problem and solve it according to the individual requirements as well as to limitations of space.

**Waiting Room**

The size of the waiting room depends on the practitioner's style of operation. Some adhere closely to their appointment schedule; others do not. Some must accommodate a great many children or expect a family group with many patients. Some use a production-line modus operandi in which assistants process the patients through drop areas or other checkup stations; others prefer to do all patient workup themselves. So perhaps a "kiddie area" or a "drop area" or both are required. In general, the busy practitioner should be able to accom-

modate from 10 to 12 people and provide emergency space for 3 or 4 more. About 2 feet of wall space is needed for each person. The idea that waiting room space is nonproductive and therefore wasteful is a fallacy. Few practitioners decrease their waiting room space in subsequent offices; most of them increase it.

If the waiting room is inadequate to contain the patient load, it is helpful to use a system of traffic control in which patients are transferred from the waiting room, in proper order, to operational rooms to await the doctor. This means that extra refraction rooms or combination refraction-treatment rooms are required—or even a field room, a muscle room, or a photography room, if these functions are to be performed independently.

**Closets**

Space must be provided for patients' wraps. If the space available does not lend itself to installation of a clothes closet, then racks or decorative wall-mounted clothes hangers can be used. Although less efficient, cloakroom facilities can be placed in the receptionist's quarters or in the passageways into the doctor's working areas.

*Authors:* Bernard Spero and Ernest J. Hasch
*Reviewer:* James H. Ogden, R.A.
*Credits:* "International Ophthalmology Clinics," *Efficient Office Management*, Little, Brown and Company, Boston, MA

## Storage

Storage is an important, and often forgotten, item in office planning. A multitude of supplies are essential to sustain a busy practice, and they should be readily available when needed. Professional accessories and adjuncts are usually kept in small cabinets in the examination rooms, but general office supplies should be under the commission of the nurse or secretary. Storage cabinets can be built along corridors or above files. Advantage should be taken of any natural structural indentations due to columns or other structural irregularities; these are most useful for construction of cabinets, as they are normally waste space otherwise.

## Files

The type of record charts to be used must first be determined and then the appropriate files selected. Room for future files should be apportioned, especially if the office is to be occupied for several years. Files should be accessible to the receptionist and the nurse, and are generally located in the receptionist's office. At times it is advantageous to recess file cabinets into a partition so that only the fronts show, while their bodies jut into a less-needed area of a contiguous room. This can have both aesthetic and functional value. If other space is not available, the file-cabinet area is also a good place for a small refrigerator.

## Receptionist

The receptionist should be able to observe the entire waiting room and also control the flow of traffic of patients. After registering the patient, the receptionist usually pulls the record chart or starts a new one if necessary. The chart is placed at the doctor's disposal by means of the particular system used. Different systems are used. The chart can be placed in a rack outside the examination room to be used next, or on a desk in the examination room; some prefer just to select the chart from a rack or a counter top in the reception area or passageway.

Depending on the locality of the practice, the habits of the community, and the duties given the receptionist, one of several reception arrangements can be used. If the practice is located in a community where an informal relationship between public and profession is the rule, the receptionist can be placed behind a desk right out in the waiting room or behind a counter top. Office fees, if uniform, can be quoted and collected over a desk or a counter top. But if histories are to be taken, it is normally advisable to install the receptionist at a desk behind a partition, or to compromise with a half partition.

If the practice is large, or expected to be, it is advisable to provide space for two staff in the receptionist area. This is particularly true if the location is considered a permanent one. If not, a small business office should be planned for any future exigency.

## Consultation Room

This is an arbitrary feature dependent on availability of space and on personal preferences. Many physicians prefer to interview patients initially in a private office. Others do so in the examination rooms, thus saving the time involved in transferring the patient from consultation room to examination room. Those who work straight through and then must dash off to other commitments have little need of a private office, per se; but those who wish to stop and rest during the day need the privacy of some office to which they can retire. If excessive

space must be taken in order to acquire a particular suite, one room can be adapted for use as a relaxation room, with a cot and beverages and other comforts; or it can be used as a dressing room for the assistants. A room of this type can always be converted to an examination room later, if the need should arise.

## Examination Rooms

Examination rooms can be refraction rooms, treatment rooms, minor-surgery rooms, field rooms, photography rooms, muscle and orthoptic rooms, or any combination thereof. There was a time when refractions were done in one room, treatment in another, fields in another, and perhaps slit-lamp microscopy in yet another. Now, there is more consolidation, so that practically all phases of a complete eye examination can be done in a single room, thus obviating the transfer of patient from room to room. This arrangement is a time-saver, especially if all parts of the examination are done by the eye doctor; but if assistants do part of the work-up, such as fields or muscle testing or even preliminary visions, there must be separate rooms for the different functions.

## Refraction Room

Although only one refracting lane can be used at a time, it is generally conceded that more than one is needed by the busy ophthalmologist. With a second room available, it is a simple matter to give final instructions, bid good-bye to the patient, and step into the next room, where a new patient has already been seated, with records laid out in a convenient place and instruments properly positioned for immediate use. Someone else can assist the departure of the patient just finished. This is not a very important item when the practice has just started, but as it flourishes, time becomes extremely important.

If it is not possible to have two identical refraction lanes, it is helpful to set up a second lane in a smaller room, perhaps a treatment room, which can be used when the patient load gets unduly heavy. Mirrors or special visual charts can be used, and still the room can be devoted primarily to some other function.

The size of a refraction room depends not only on the space available, but also on the predilections of the practitioner. Some insist on at least a 20-foot lane; others feel that this is relatively unimportant. Most feel that a visual lane of from 15 to 20 feet is satisfactory. Disregarding other factors, the characters on vision charts can be sized appropriately for any distance used. The size of projected characters can be altered by optical means; charts with reverse characters can be used in conjunction with a mirror; charts with direct characters for a 10-foot distance are available; and sometimes it is feasible to use a two-mirror setup, in which one of the mirrors becomes a secondary projector to gain length of projection.

If the longer visual lane is considered necessary, and space is limited, it is sometimes feasible to use tunnels to attain the desired distance and yet conserve space. Tunnels can extend from floor to ceiling, or can even be constructed above files, which open out into a different room. In any case, if there is no objection to the so-called "tunnel effect" in the mind of the eye doctor, many space-saving arrangements are possible with this method.

As mentioned before, many doctors now prefer to do a complete eye examination, including treatment, in a single room. Then there must be room for the visual lane with the routine examining equipment (chair, stools, trial lenses, refracting accessories, slit lamp) as well as some field equipment (perimeter, tangent screen) and, no doubt, a consultation desk. There should also be room for medicines, treatment cabinet, and perhaps a treatment table. This would require a minimum of 150 square feet.

The type of equipment selected will determine, to some extent, the size of the space needed or, conversely, the space available determines, to some extent, the type of equipment which should be used. If the larger "deluxe-type" patients' chair is used, it should be positioned about 4 feet from a wall in order to utilize its adjustable and reclining features; and then a treatment table might not be considered necessary. On the other hand, the smaller, less adjustable chair can be placed close to the wall; but a treatment table is needed for tonometry, treatment, and minor surgery unless these functions are to be done in another room.

Sometimes the positioning of the projector (for vision lanes) presents a problem, perhaps because of corners or extraneous paraphernalia around the patient's chair. Remote-control projectors can be mounted in an out-of-the-way position and be completely controlled by fingertip switches on or around the lens cabinet. With this arrangement, there is no need to reach in front of a patient, or turn awkwardly, to change the characters projected.

If two refraction rooms are to be used, it is better to have them adjacent or adjoining, or separated by no more than a smaller treatment or minor-surgery room.

**Miscellaneous Rooms**

Since the various services required of the ophthalmologist are so interrelated, refraction rooms now usually contain some treatment facilities. But it is still helpful to have a room available, possibly smaller, which can be used for treatment, minor surgery, and fields. One such room for every two refraction rooms should be adequate, even in the larger multimanned practices. It is advisable to have a vision lane in the miscellaneous rooms whenever possible. Almost any distance can be used to create a satisfactory vision lane.

Minor surgery can be done in any chair with a headrest and a reclining back, but a chair-table or a stationary treatment table is considerably more comfortable to the patient. The examining chair, which can be converted into a flat treatment table, can serve several purposes. It can serve as a general treatment chair for tonometry or minor surgery; it can be a refraction chair; and it can be positioned at the prescribed distance from a tangent screen so that central fields can be taken from the same chair, thus making efficient use of a smaller room.

Orthoptic rooms, as such, are seldom used unless the volume of the practice affords the use of an orthoptist. The diagnostic work performed by most eye doctors is done in one of the other operational rooms; but if orthoptic treatments are to be given, a separate orthoptic room is indicated.

Treatment, minor surgery, and fields can usually be done in a room of about 100 to 130 square feet, with smaller rooms serving well for any single one of the functions.

Fig. 1 is a plan designed to give the nurse and the receptionist complete control of the traffic flow. The receptionist controls the patients in the drop area and refers them to the nurse, who does primary workups. Then the patients are directed to one of the doctor's refraction rooms. The refraction rooms are identical, and should be equipped

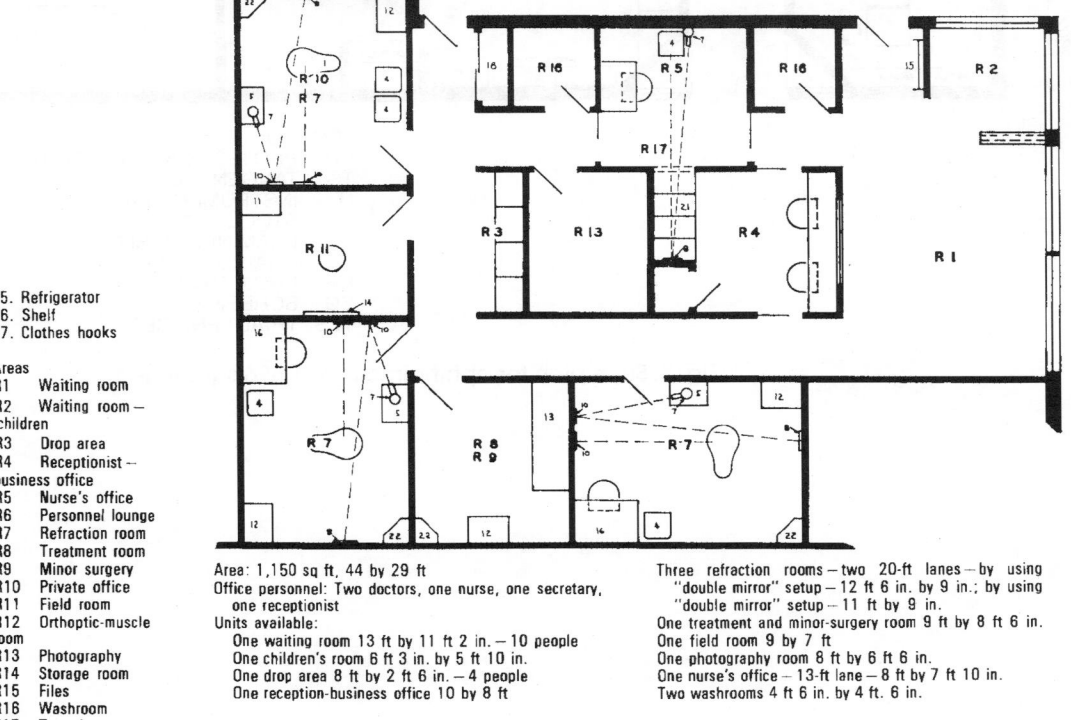

**Furnishings**
1. Deluxe refracting unit
2. Small adjustable chair
3. Reclining treatment chair
4. Casual chair
5. Lens cabinet
6. Slit lamp
7. Projector
8. Screen
9. Vision chart
10. Mirror
11. Perimeter
12. Treatment cabinet
13. Treatment table
14. Tangent screen
15. Clothes rack
16. Desk
17. Files
18. Clothes closet
19. Storage cabinet
20. Storage cabinet 40 in. high
21. Storage cabinet over files
22. Sink
23. Wall mount

25. Refrigerator
26. Shelf
27. Clothes hooks

**Areas**
R1  Waiting room
R2  Waiting room — children
R3  Drop area
R4  Receptionist – business office
R5  Nurse's office
R6  Personnel lounge
R7  Refraction room
R8  Treatment room
R9  Minor surgery
R10 Private office
R11 Field room
R12 Orthoptic-muscle room
R13 Photography
R14 Storage room
R15 Files
R16 Washroom
R17 Tunnel

Area: 1,150 sq ft, 44 by 29 ft
Office personnel: Two doctors, one nurse, one secretary, one receptionist
Units available:
One waiting room 13 ft by 11 ft 2 in. – 10 people
One children's room 6 ft 3 in. by 5 ft 10 in.
One drop area 8 ft by 2 ft 6 in. – 4 people
One reception-business office 10 by 8 ft

Three refraction rooms – two 20-ft lanes – by using "double mirror" setup – 12 ft 6 in. by 9 in.; by using "double mirror" setup – 11 ft by 9 in.
One treatment and minor-surgery room 9 ft by 8 ft 6 in.
One field room 9 ft by 7 ft
One photography room 8 ft by 6 ft 6 in.
One nurse's office – 13-ft lane – 8 ft by 7 ft 10 in.
Two washrooms 4 ft 6 in. by 4 ft. 6 in.

**Fig. 2. Plan for two-doctor ophthalmological office**

identically. There is a room for treatment and minor surgery, and the nurse could also use it in addition to her field room. Storage is centrally located in the corridor.

Fig. 2 shows three refraction rooms, one nurse's office, and three miscellaneous rooms to facilitate processing a large practice through this suite. The nurse and any other assistants have access to all parts of the suite, and the nurse has a 13-foot vision lane over the files. A similar layout is seen in Fig. 3. All assistants to the doctors can cooperate efficiently to route patients properly according to the system used, and still oversee the overall operation from various vantage points. The doctors, under a proper system, will have several rooms in which they can perform the various functions required. For instance, the photography room, which is seldom used as such, can be used for topography, gonioscopy, and orthoptics, or even as a personnel lounge. The children's waiting room can be kept under constant surveillance.

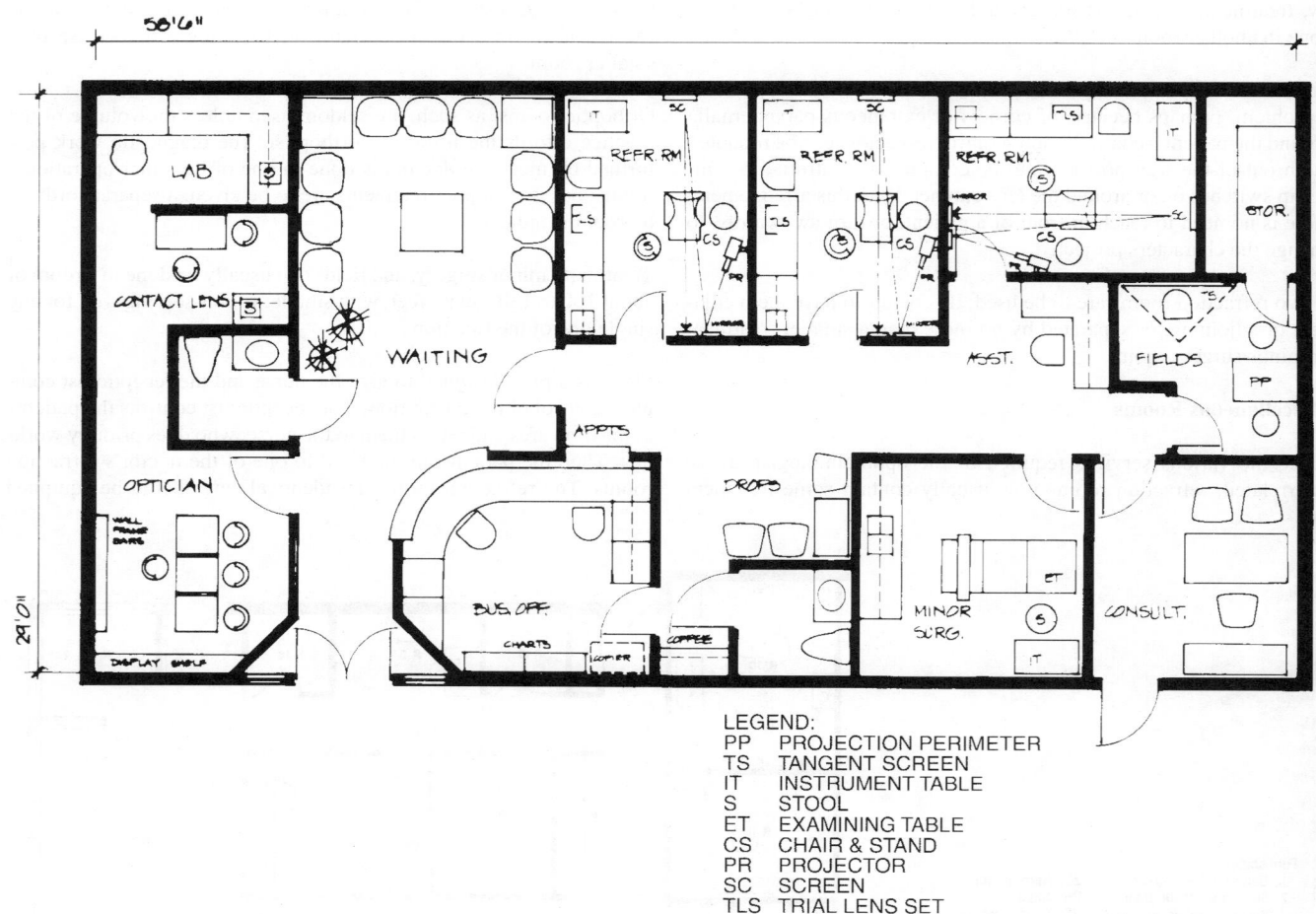

LEGEND:
PP  PROJECTION PERIMETER
TS  TANGENT SCREEN
IT  INSTRUMENT TABLE
S   STOOL
ET  EXAMINING TABLE
CS  CHAIR & STAND
PR  PROJECTOR
SC  SCREEN
TLS TRIAL LENS SET

**Fig. 3. Suite plan for ophthalmology, 1,696 square feet**

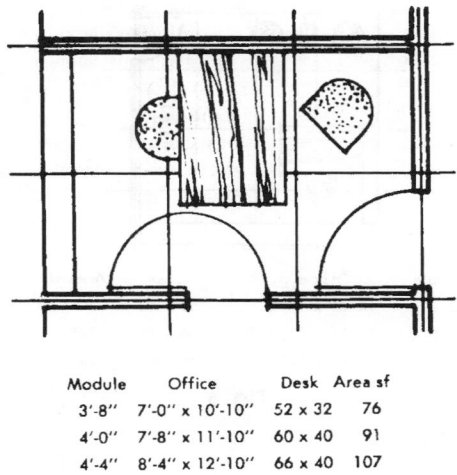

| Module | Office | Desk | Area sf |
|---|---|---|---|
| 3'-8" | 7'-0" x 10'-10" | 52 x 32 | 76 |
| 4'-0" | 7'-8" x 11'-10" | 60 x 40 | 91 |
| 4'-4" | 8'-4" x 12'-10" | 66 x 40 | 107 |

**Fig. 1**

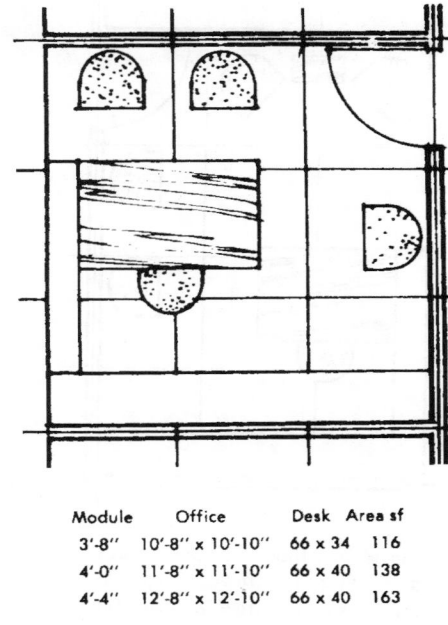

| Module | Office | Desk | Area sf |
|---|---|---|---|
| 3'-8" | 10'-8" x 10'-10" | 66 x 34 | 116 |
| 4'-0" | 11'-8" x 11'-10" | 66 x 40 | 138 |
| 4'-4" | 12'-8" x 12'-10" | 66 x 40 | 163 |

**Fig. 2**

# LAW OFFICES

The rental area per lawyer varies from 230 to 1,212 square feet. The median is 455 square feet, and the average is 484 square feet.

A minimum-size office is illustrated by Fig. 1, which is two modules wide by three modules deep. If a 48-inch module is adopted, the clear dimensions without allowance for partitions will be 8 by 12 feet. The clear dimensions (with partitions 4 inches thick) are given in feet and inches, the maximum desk size is given in inches, and the net area is given in square feet. Larger offices are illustrated by Figs. 2 to 8, and suites are illustrated by Figs. 9 to 20. With each illustration of a suite of rooms comprising a law office, the dimensions and the following square-foot areas (using a 48-inch module) are given:

Rental area as customarily measured
Architectural area as measured for preliminary cost estimates
Area (rental) per lawyer

The following abbreviations and symbols are used with these diagrams:

P—Private office
R—Reception room or area
S—Secretary
F—File room or space
L—Library or library and conference room
C—Conference room
V—Vault
U—Utility, storage, or work room
T—Toilet room
→ Exit

*Reference: Law Office Layout and Design*, Committee on Economics of Law Practice of the American Bar Association

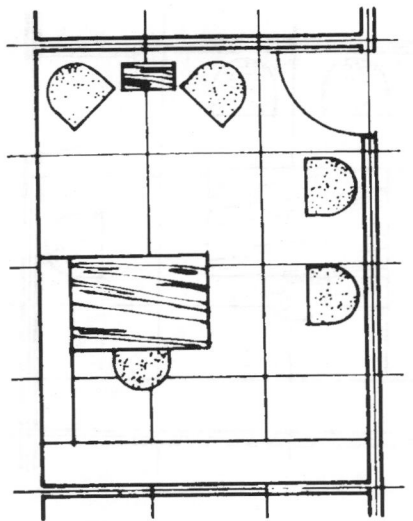

| Module | Office | Desk | Area sf |
|--------|--------|------|---------|
| 3'-8'' | 14'-4'' x 10'-10'' | 60 x 40 | 155 |
| 4'-0'' | 15'-8'' x 11'-10'' | 60 x 40 | 185 |
| 4'-4'' | 17'-0'' x 12'-10'' | 60 x 40 | 218 |

Fig. 3

| Module | Office | Desk | Area sf |
|--------|--------|------|---------|
| 3'-8'' | 7'-0'' x 14'-6'' | 52 x 32 | 102 |
| 4'-0'' | 7'-8'' x 15'-10'' | 60 x 40 | 123 |
| 4'-4'' | 8'-4'' x 17'-2'' | 66 x 40 | 142 |

Fig. 4

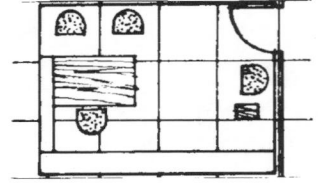

| Module | Office | Desk | Area sf |
|--------|--------|------|---------|
| 3'-8'' | 10'-8'' x 14'-6'' | 60 x 34 | 155 |
| 4'-0'' | 11'-8'' x 15'-10'' | 66 x 40 | 186 |
| 4'-4'' | 12'-8'' x 17'-2'' | 66 x 40 | 217 |

Fig. 5

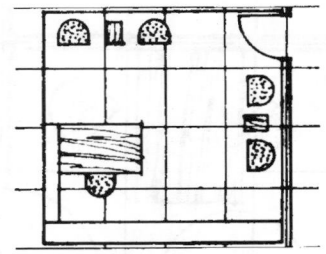

| Module | Office | Desk | Area sf |
|--------|--------|------|---------|
| 3'-8'' | 14'-4'' x 14'-6'' | 66 x 40 | 208 |
| 4'-0'' | 15'-8'' x 15'-10'' | 66 x 40 | 248 |
| 4'-4'' | 17'-0'' x 17'-2'' | 66 x 40 | 290 |

Fig. 6

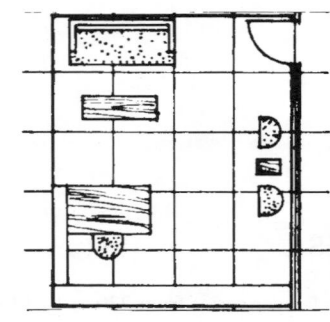

| Module | Office | Desk | Area sf |
|--------|--------|------|---------|
| 3'-8'' | 18'-0'' x 14'-6'' | 66 x 40 | 256 |
| 4'-0'' | 19'-8'' x 15'-10'' | 66 x 40 | 312 |
| 4'-4'' | 21'-4'' x 17'-2'' | 66 x 40 | 357 |

Fig. 7

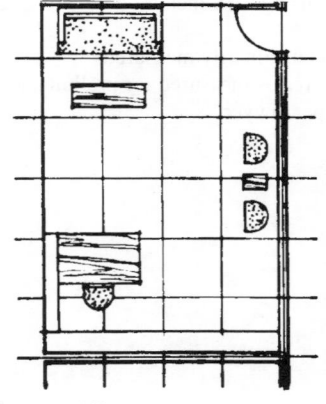

| Module | Office | Desk | Area sf |
|--------|--------|------|---------|
| 3'-8'' | 21'-8'' x 14'-6'' | 66 x 40 | 314 |
| 4'-0'' | 23'-8'' x 15'-10'' | 66 x 40 | 378 |
| 4'-4'' | 25'-8'' x 17'-2'' | 66 x 40 | 438 |

Fig. 8

## Small Office

Fig. 9 shows possible arrangements for a firm composed of only one lawyer. If a single lawyer's office must serve as a library and conference room, and perhaps also accommodate the files, it should be large enough for a conference-type desk and four or five chairs. It is almost essential to have a second room for use as a reception room and secretary's office. It is better to have a separation between the secretary's space and the reception space (Fig. 10). The files may be of sufficient volume to require a separate file room.

Figure 11 illustrates arrangements for two lawyers (either partners or cooperators). In Fig. 11c, with a combination library and conference room, the private offices could be somewhat smaller. Fig. 12 shows offices for three lawyers. Files should be separated from the reception room and convenient to the clerical employees as in Fig. 12a, or in a separate room as in Fig. 12b. If one office is large enough for conferences and the book collection not too large, the library and conference room may be eliminated. On the other hand, some firms with only two principals have a large enough collection of books to warrant inclusion of a sizable room for use solely as a library as in Fig. 11c. Figure 11a is suitable for a separate building and Figs. 11b and c are for rental space in an office building.

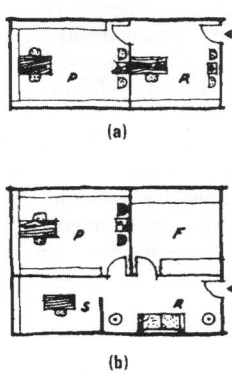

Fig. 9. Offices for one lawyer. (a) Rental area: 366 square feet, 12 by 28 feet. (b) Rental area: 560 square feet, 20 by 28 feet

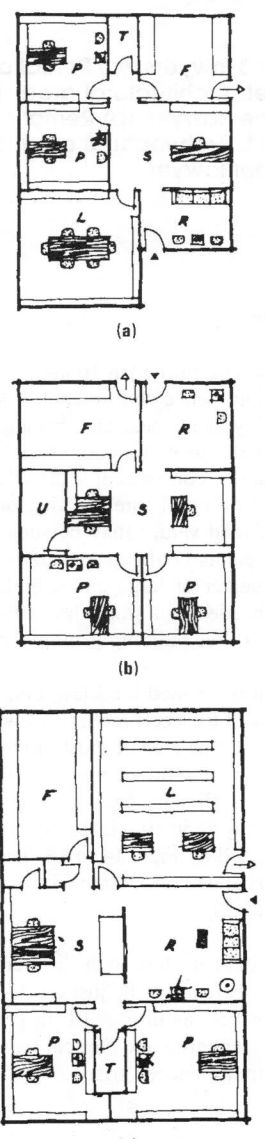

Fig. 11. Offices for two lawyers. (a) Rental area: 1,008 square feet, 36 by 28 feet. Architectural area: 1,140 square feet, 504 square feet per lawyer. (b) Rental area: 1,008 square feet, 36 by 28 feet. Architectural area: 1,140 square feet, 504 square feet per lawyer. (c) Rental area: 1,536 square feet, 48 by 32 feet. Architectural area: 1,600 square feet, 768 square feet per lawyer

Fig. 10. Law office reception (Elkus/Manfredi Architects; photo: Peter Vanderwarker, courtesy of architect)

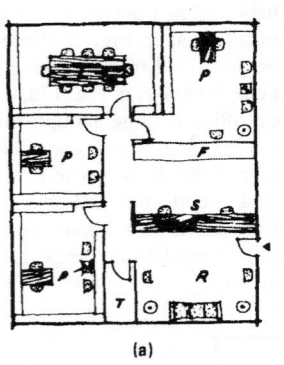 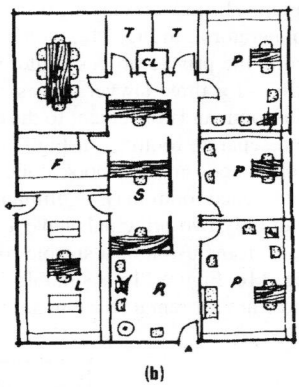

**Fig. 12. Offices for 3 lawyers. (a) Rental area: 1,152 square feet, 36 by 32 feet. Architectural area: 1,292 square feet, 384 square feet per lawyer. (b) Rental area: 1,584 square feet, 44 by 36 feet. Architectural area: 1,748 square feet, 523 square feet per lawyer**

## Medium-Size Office

While firms composed of more than 10 lawyers generally carry on a diversified practice and hence choose central locations, some firms of 5 to 10 lawyers may locate near their principal clients. The selection of space in the first story of a commercial building or the erection of a building may be considered. If the clientele is concentrated in a suburban center or small satellite city, or a city of 50,000 or smaller, the scale of land values may be such that first-story space near the commercial center could be considered. Because of the high cost of land in the center of large cities, buildings, to be feasible, must be larger than needed by a single law office; hence selection of space in a multistory office building is often the only answer.

The same area which is planned for 3 lawyers, as is indicated in Fig. 12a, may be rearranged to accommodate 5 lawyers, as indicated by Fig. 13a. As rearranged, the area of most of the private offices is too small for conferences with more than one or two visitors, and secretarial space may be insufficient; but where rental rates are high this degree of crowding may be justified. Offices for firms with from 5 to 12 lawyers are indicated by Figs. 14 to 18. The arrangement shown in Fig. 18 may be expanded or contracted to provide for as few as 4 lawyers or as many as 20.

Secretaries' desks should be close to the lawyers' offices. Some firms prefer each lawyer's secretary to be just outside the office door or in an adjacent private office, as in Fig. 18. In general, however, more use can be made of secretarial and clerical employees if some are in a pool to be drawn upon as needs arise.

## Large Office

The planning of space for a large law office may be influenced by the size and shape of the space available. The possibility of securing adequate, well-planned space is enhanced when the firm actively participates in the promotion of an office building.

Figure 19 indicates possibilities of planning large spaces. The same scheme with larger offices could provide for 11 to 18 lawyers, or

could be enlarged to accommodate up to 40 or more lawyers. The plan should be based upon a study of the special needs of each lawyer and the relations between members of the firm.

### Space for a Cooperative Group

In buildings planned for occupancy by a number of law firms, facilities may be pooled, such as library, vault, utility space, and reception room. Files should be kept in the separate offices and secretaries' spaces (Fig. 20).

### Plan Elements

The most desirable orientation for offices and workrooms varies in different locations, but north is generally preferred. Outside exposure is desirable for offices and advantageous for large work areas, conference rooms, library, and rest rooms. Central locations are preferred for library, file room, and conference rooms.

The size of rooms is determined in part by the purpose and effect desired, and the furniture chosen. The desirability of commodiousness may be weighed against the rent or its equivalent. If space is air conditioned, smaller spaces may be tolerated. Lack of commodiousness may be offset by the use of rich materials and effective decoration.

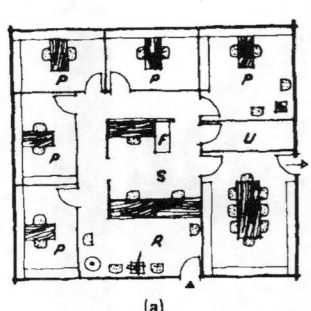 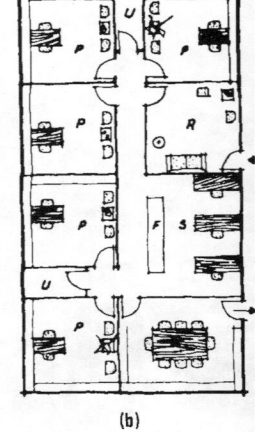

**Fig. 13. Offices for 5 lawyers. (a) Rental area: 1,152 square feet, 32 by 36 feet. Architectural area: 1,292 square feet, 230 square feet per lawyer. (b) Rental area: 1,456 square feet, 52 by 28 feet. Architectural area: 1,620 square feet, 291 square feet per lawyer**

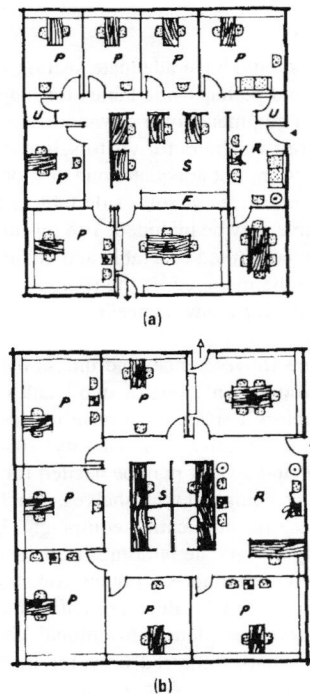

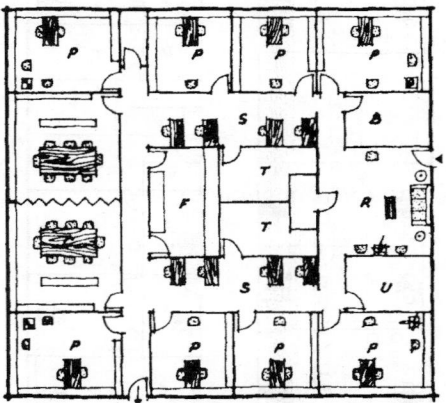

Fig. 14. Offices for 6 lawyers. (a) Rental area: 1,440 square feet, 40 by 36 feet. Architectural area: 1,596 square feet, 240 square feet per lawyer. (b) Rental area: 1,760 square feet, 44 by 40 feet. Architectural area: 1,886 square feet, 293 square feet per lawyer

Fig. 16. Offices for 8 lawyers. Rental area: 3,120 square feet, 52 by 60 feet. Architectural area: 3,348 square feet, 390 square feet per lawyer

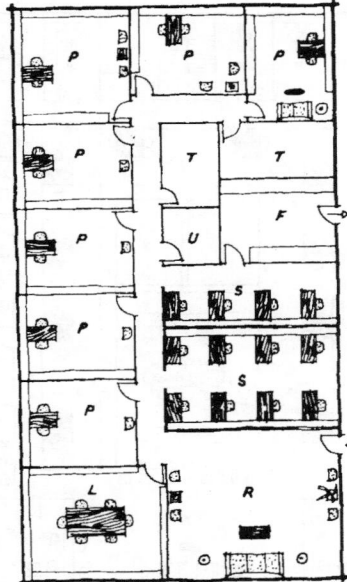

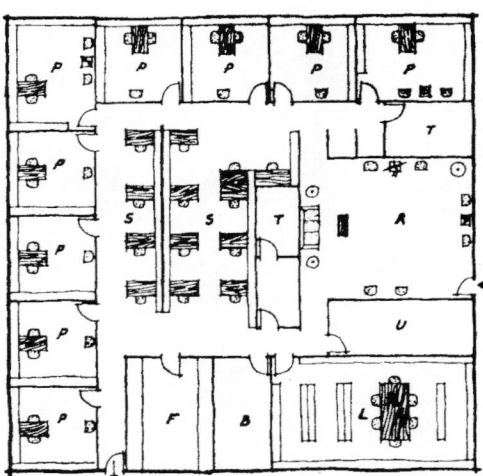

Fig. 15. Offices for 7 lawyers. Rental area: 3,250 square feet, 80 by 44 feet. Architectural area: 3,772 square feet, 503 square feet per lawyer

Fig. 17. Offices for 9 lawyers. Rental area: 4,096 square feet, 64 by 64 feet. Architectural area: 4,356 square feet, 455 square feet per lawyer

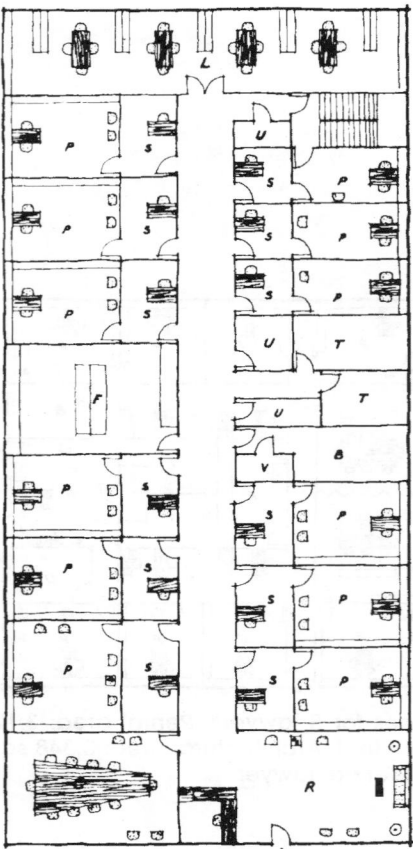

Fig. 18. Offices for 12 lawyers. Rental area: 6,720 square feet, 56 by 120 feet. Architectural area: 7,076 square feet, 560 square feet per lawyer

## Furniture

The reception room should have adequate seating in addition to the receptionist's desk, and perhaps side tables for magazines and journals. The minimum equipment for a private office is an executive's desk and chair, one or two chairs for visitors, and desk-height bookcases. If desk drawers are not adequate, one or more letter files may be required. For large offices, a sofa, side tables, coffee table, and even a conference table may be included. The furniture of conference rooms (Fig. 21) may be limited to a table and chairs, but some ornamental furniture may be included. If the room may be divided by a folding partition, two tables may be needed.

Lawyers' libraries are for reference, and unless they are to be used also as conference rooms, only one or two small tables are needed (Fig. 22). Each secretary's space must have its desk and chair, and files should be placed nearby. For security, file rooms may be included in the plan, and a vault may be needed for valuable papers. Storage spaces may be equipped with shelves, coat hooks, etc., combined with work space for duplicating equipment. Utility rooms are usually required only in separate buildings (rather than rental space) for heating and air conditioning equipment, transformer vault, main switch and meters, etc. A small kitchen or coffee bar may have a hot plate and sink, or more complete conventional kitchen equipment. Toilet facilities are usually required only for large law offices or when the offices occupy complete separate buildings. A couch should be provided in the women's toilet room or in a separate rest room.

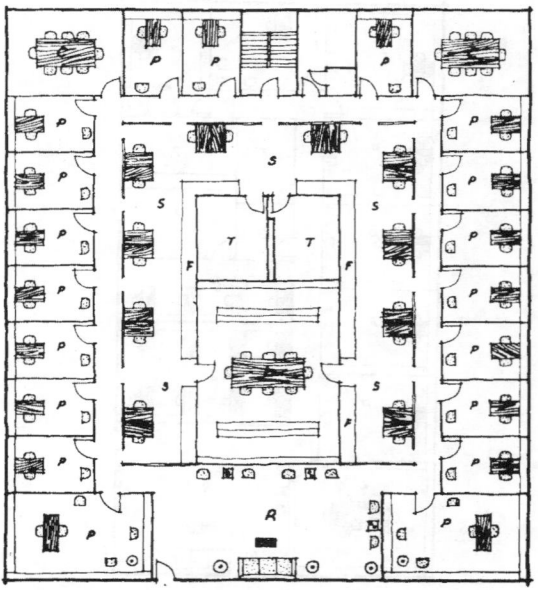

Fig. 19. Arrangement for large firms: 19 lawyers. Rental area: 23,040 square feet, 144 by 160 feet. Architectural area: 23,652 square feet, 1,212 square feet per lawyer

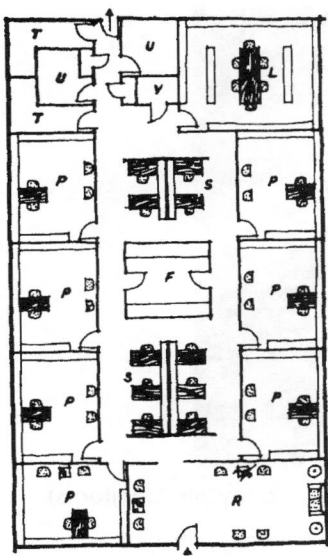

Fig. 20. Cooperative building for 7 lawyers. Rental area: 3,340 square feet, 44 by 76 feet. Architectural area: 3,588 square feet, 477 square feet per lawyer

Fig. 21. Conference room (Elkus/Manfredi Architects; photo: Peter Vanderwarker, courtesy of architect)

## Interior Design

Lawyers' offices require little interior decoration, but there is a discernible tendency to make offices homelike. Accessories used should be carefully selected. The most common wall decorations found in lawyers' offices are the certificates of admission to the bar and diplomas. These serve the purpose of assuring clients of the lawyer's qualifications.

Fig. 22. Law firm library (Elkus/Manfredi Architects; photo: Peter Vanderwarker, courtesy of architect)

**Fig. 1. Oakland University Science and Engineering building (HarleyEllis Architects)**

# RESEARCH LABORATORIES

The following criteria establish a minimum basis for the design of research facilities. The research facility designers' expertise and creativity is critical in creating research facilities that provide the desired physical environment.

**Flexibility and Capability**

The term flexibility is frequently used in discussing the design characteristics of research laboratory buildings. Flexibility in laboratory building design should be all-inclusive, including mechanical, electrical, and structural systems. The structure's capability to meet varying ventilation needs for different research functions, its ability for temperature control of varying heat loads, its capability to meet the needs for fume hoods, air supply, and exhaust in different concentrations with time in various areas in the building are all critical. The ability to supply electric power in high concentrations to any localized area without the need to reposition electric distribution lines within the building is a measure of the facility's flexibility and capability to meet the needs of the research program that will eventually occupy the building.

**Building Shapes**

Planners and designers sometimes try to meet laboratory functional needs with esoteric shapes and dimensions. Although circles, hexagons, and tall slim towers may have esthetic appeal, none of them are as efficient as, or have the capability of, rectangular designs. Rectilinear laboratory equipment and office furniture and the anticipated continual interplay between rooms call for utilitarian solutions. Buildings with simple rectangular configurations, commensurate with standard laboratory equipment and furniture, and with unrestricted accessibility to mechanical utility systems, are the easiest to adapt to the changing needs of research.

To a large extent, the design of a laboratory building will be dictated by the heating, ventilation, air-conditioning systems, and the utility

distribution layout. If these factors are carefully planned, the laboratory building design will be an efficient one, and it will still be possible to plan for flexibility and growth needs as well as for engineering capability.

**Physical Environment**

The physical environment of the research facilities is a key component of recruiting and retaining research staff. It is important that the research facility presents an appropriate image and provides a high quality internal work environment.

**Work Environment**

The quality of the work environment within a research facility is influenced by many factors including:

- Appropriate laboratory furnishings and equipment
- Daylighting and views to the outdoors
- Sound levels
- Quantity and quality of illumination
- Indoor air quality
- Collaborative environment and informal interaction areas
- Comfort

**Image**

The image presented by research facilities (Fig. 1) must be consistent with the owner's stature in the research field. Facilities should provide an inviting and professional appearance and be an asset in recruiting and retaining research staff.

**Health and Safety**

Research operations often involve the use of potentially hazardous materials. It should be the designer's goal to provide research facili-

---

*Reviewers and authors:* Alex Shirshun and Louis Hartman, HarleyEllis Architects

ies that when used within the parameters that they were designed to accommodate provide a healthy and safe working environment.

## Building Systems

Building systems are a critical component of a research facility. In addition to comfort control they play a key role in maintaining a safe and healthy work environment, and are critical to supporting research operations. Reliable electrical power, standby electrical power, high purity water systems, and data systems are examples of key utility systems that the research facility design must provide.

## Security

Research facilities need to provide a secure environment for research staff and the scientific equipment. Animal facilities need special security considerations.

## Accessibility

The Americans with Disabilities Act, along with the local Barrier Free Codes, prescribe accessibility standards that must be met in the design of research facilities. Special attention to provisions that exceed these minimum requirements should be given to research programs involving clinical and human performance testing activities.

## Signage and Wayfinding

Graphics and signage must be provided to help visitors and employees find their way through a research facility. Directional graphics and signage should be functional and in harmony with the architecture of the building. Special attention is required for research facilities involved with clinical activities.

## Hazard Assessment

Laboratory operations potentially involve some degree of hazard. The nature, quantity, and hazard of experiments and the materials in use combined with the types of operations dictate the overall safety protocols, containment devices, and safety equipment required for a particular research laboratory. Before the laboratory and the laboratory utility systems are designed a comprehensive hazard assessment must be completed. This hazard assessment needs to be performed with the researcher and the appropriate health, safety, and loss prevention officers.

## Maintenance Considerations

Research laboratories, the facilities they are housed in, and the systems that support their operation must be maintainable.

Materials used in research laboratories need careful consideration of the specific research activities. Items effecting the material selections include the specific chemicals being used, processes, equipment weights, etc.

The design of utility systems should allow for normal maintenance activities to be conducted without disruption of the research activities. For research activities that require long duration of uninterrupted service stand-by equipment should be provided.

Research activities commonly involve the use of potentially hazardous materials. The utility systems that support the research activ-

ities are commonly utilized to contain these substances and transport them to points of collection or discharge from the building. System design, layout, and specific equipment selection must minimize the potential of exposure of maintenance personnel to these potentially hazardous materials.

## PLANNING THE RESEARCH LABORATORY

### Programming

A research laboratory building must have the capability to satisfy research operational needs, allowing for variation both in research projects and in occupancy, for at least 10 years. Planners and designers must recognize that the structure will have to meet a variety of functional needs, rather than the specific requirements of a single group of occupants.

The most effective administrative device for planning a research facility that will meet both current and future requirements is a written description of the building. Generally called the Program of Requirements (POR), this written description lists the functions and operations that will be housed in the structure, the design criteria for those functions, and their space needs. It also provides information on the projected staffing and the equipment, which will be needed in the building. This written POR is most valuable if it is prepared before any drawings and preferably should precede the preparation of space function relationship diagrams.

### Functional Understanding

These guidelines provide information relative to required input that the designer must seek, the planning goals and objectives that the design of new and renovated facilities should accomplish and design criteria that should be considered during the design process.

There are a number of codes, standards, and guidelines that cover different aspects of the design of research facilities. Designers of research laboratories need a complete understanding of the applicable criteria and should not exclusively rely upon this guideline. The laboratory designer must seek input from the researchers, safety officers and facilities personnel.

Individual researchers must be consulted during the development of the technical requirements of the research facility. The function of the laboratory is important in determining the appropriate space allocations, casework selection, containment devices, utility needs, and safety equipment. It is imperative that the designer seeks a comprehensive understanding of the specific science and research activities that the laboratory is expected to house. Research initiatives vary greatly and the facilities to support these activities must provide for the uniqueness of these individual activities.

Performance criteria for the utility systems that support the research activities must be thoroughly discussed with the researcher. Examples of typical utility system parameters include:

- Environmental setpoint
- Range of adjustable setpoints
- Acceptable variance ranges from setpoint
- Sensitivity of specific research to air currents
- Air particulate (clean room / space)
- Quantity and quality of high purity water
- Quantity, quality, and pressure of compressed gases

- Quantity and level of vacuum
- Quantity, quality, and pressure of compressed air
- Quantity of electrical power
- Electrical power conditioning or isolation
- Instrument grounding
- Uninterrupted electrical power service
- Back up, emergency power source
- Data networking
- Special alarms and monitoring

### Space Function Relationship Diagrams

A challenge that is faced in the early planning stages is the translation of the written space program into a schematic design that reflects functional issues such as required lines of communication and movement of personnel, equipment and supplies. Space function relationship diagrams assist in establishing and visualizing functional relationships and systematically translate the written program into a graphic analysis that is clear to understand.

Space function relationship diagrams (Fig. 2) consist of two-dimensional flow diagrams, drawn to approximate scale, which are used to illustrate the relationship of one operational group to another or the interrelationship of spaces within a specific group, without the distraction of architectural details that have little bearing on the overall effectiveness of the proposed plan, such as furniture replacement, window location, or door swings. Space function relationship diagrams focus on broader functional issues such as required lines of communication and movement of personnel, equipment and supplies. Compromises, conflicts and potential inefficiencies of proposed schemes are readily seen and changes or adjustments can be made quickly.

### Area Required—Net Area

The square foot area expressed in diagrams are representative of net areas defined in the program. This refers only to the area actually required to perform the function, which the program defines. A factor, gained from experience with various building types, is added to the sum of net areas to determine the gross area or total departmental and building area.

Requirements for future expansion for specific functions also can be shown graphically on the space function relationship diagrams.

### Relationships and Traffic Patterns

The functional areas described are arranged to express a priority of adjacencies by their juxtaposition on the diagram. They are connected by flow lines, which terminate at appropriate areas with an arrowhead. These flow lines represent the movement of public, staff, supplies, equipment or other traffic generating elements of the program. The arrowhead represents the desired penetrations into, out of, or through a functional unit. These penetrations may be finally interpreted as doors, openings, or passages in the schematic floor plan (Fig. 3) subsequently derived from the diagram.

### Laboratory Planning

Laboratory planning is generally regarded as one of the most difficult assignments with which an architect can be confronted. It involves the development of a layout to meet an exacting set of conditions, and the integration of complicated engineering services.

The planning of space within an individual laboratory and the clus-

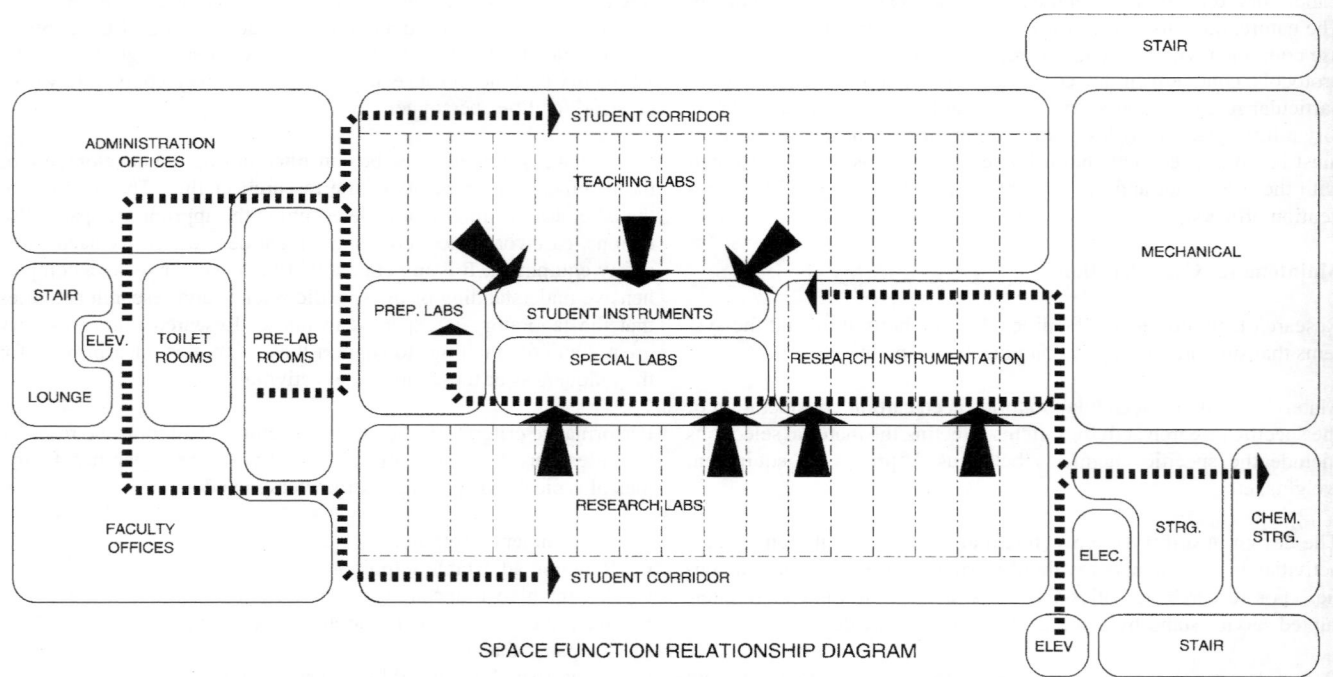

SPACE FUNCTION RELATIONSHIP DIAGRAM

**Fig. 2. Space function relationship diagram (HarleyEllis Architects)**

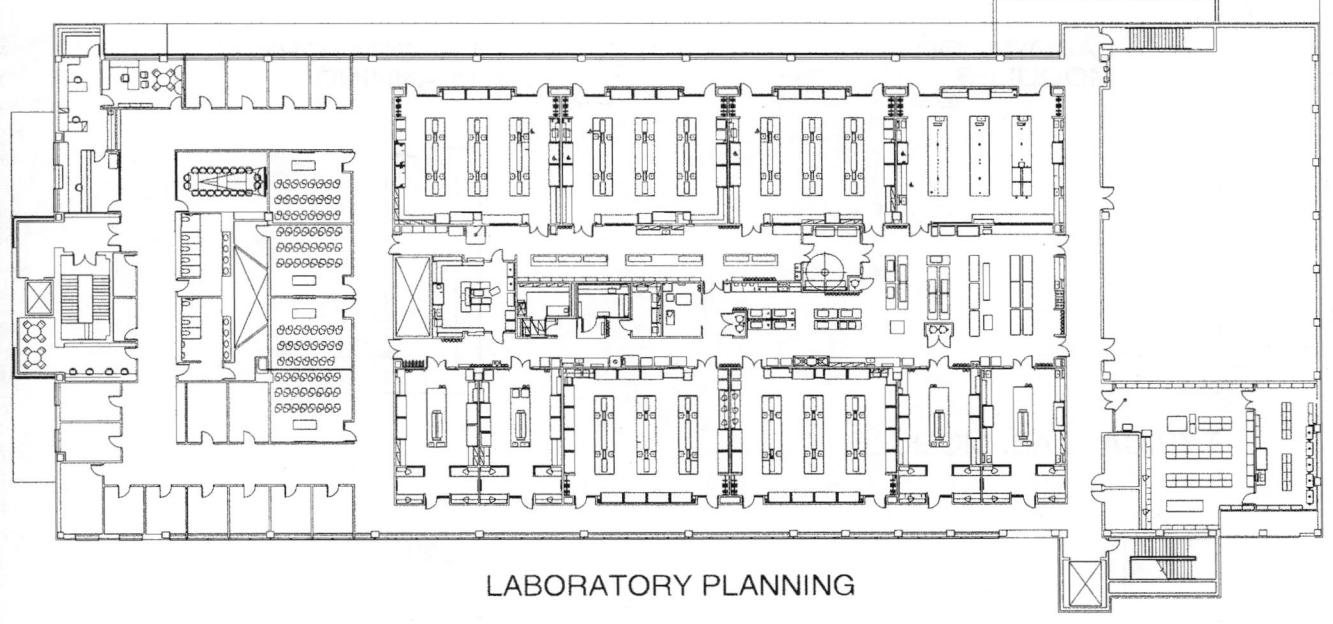

LABORATORY PLANNING

**Fig. 3. Laboratory floor plan (HarleyEllis Architects)**

tering of individual laboratories to form overall building floor plans and circulation paths should be based on a modular approach. This approach begins with a planning module size that recognizes the special spatial requirements of laboratory casework. This planning module is then arrayed to form circulation paths and overall floor plans. Utility system distribution must recognize the modular space planning and be configured in a consistent fashion.

Research facilities should be based on a planning module that is repetitive and regular. These planning modules are usually between 10 and 11 feet in width and vary in length from 24 to 35 feet in length, dependent upon the research function.

It is essential that the module and layout of the individual laboratories be considered in detail before even preliminary sketch plans are prepared. This can best be done in the following sequence.

### Module

A module width of 10 to 11 feet is recommended; this is the distance from center to center of two peninsular or island benches, and it is based on a bench width of 5 to 6 feet with a space of 5 feet between (Fig. 4). In a one-module laboratory it is the distance between the center of one partition and the center of the next; it is based on a wall thickness, a bench on both sides maintaining a 5-foot ± aisle. Generally an entirely satisfactory and functional layout can be planned with the 10- to 11-foot module. Of course, the module is dependent on the width of the benches and the space between them.

### Width of Bench

In chemistry laboratories, the generally accepted width of benches fitted with reagent shelves is 2 feet-6 inches for wall benches and 5 feet for peninsular benches. In physics laboratories, widths of 3 feet

and 6 feet are sometimes preferred, with a wide shelf for electronic equipment.

### Space Between Benches

As building costs rise, it is expected that the distance between benches will receive closer scrutiny. Some research laboratory planners maintain that the increasing use of mobile equipment justifies the adoption of a 6-foot space.

The distance should be determined by considerations of convenience and safety, i.e., one person should be able to pass another (working at the bench) comfortably and without risk of collision if the latter should step back unexpectedly. Experience has shown that 4 feet-6 inches to 5 feet is ideal; 4 feet is cramped.

In student and routine laboratories where there is less bench space per person and often two people will be working back to back immediately opposite each other, the space between the benches should be greater than 5 feet so that there is room for others to walk down the center.

### Adoption of a Basic Laboratory Layout

Every effort should be made to develop a basic layout, which is standard throughout the building. This is not easy because on every job there is generally at least one scientist who, without any real justification, insists that her office or bench be in a different position, and she will advance reasons why her idea of layout is necessary for some particular investigation. If she wins her argument and her laboratory layout is nonstandard, it so often happens that the research project stops, or she leaves, and it is almost certain that her successor will require a different layout. On the other hand, there are some situations where it really is necessary to meet particular requirements, but these can and should be met by variations within the basic layout.

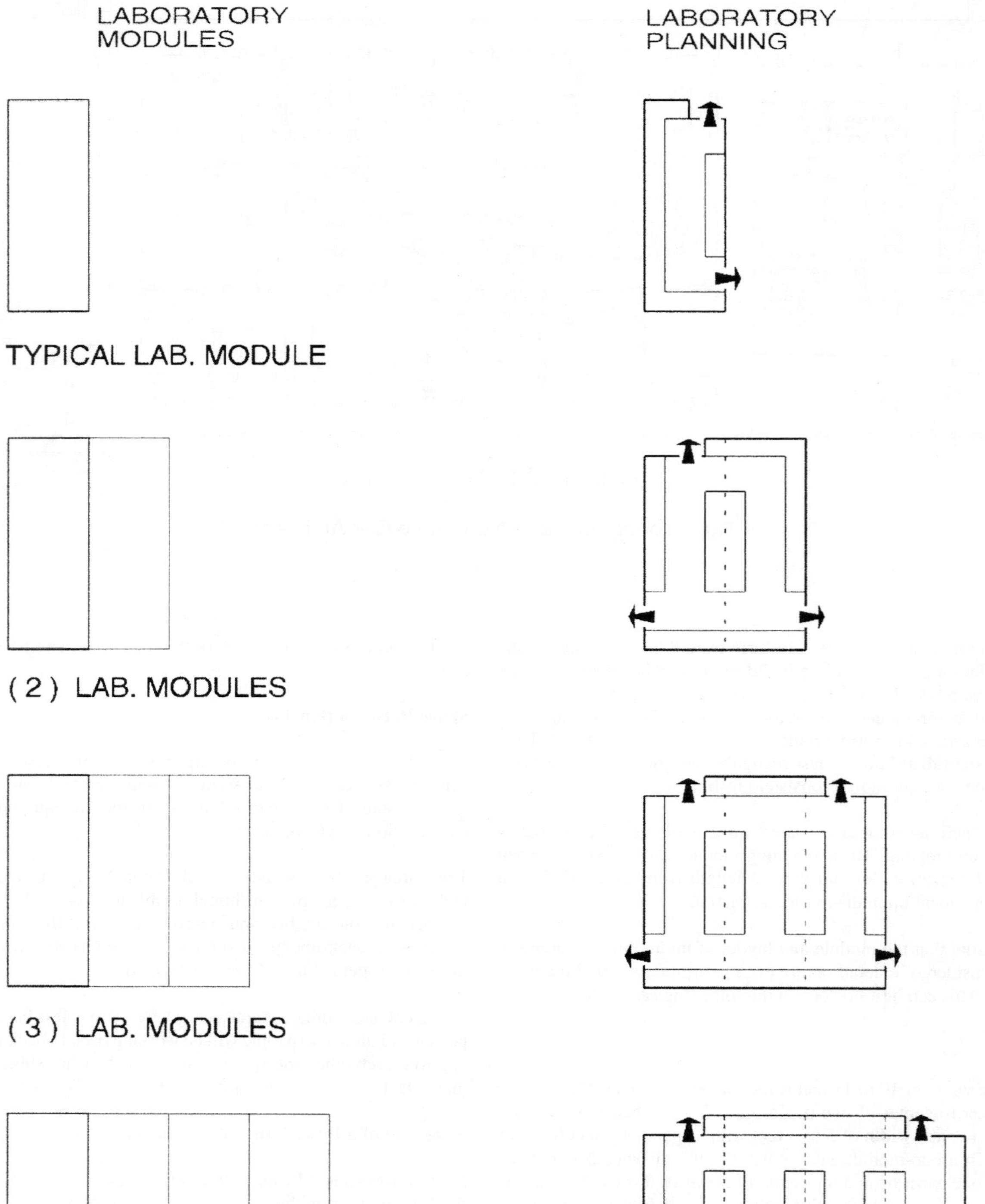

LABORATORY
MODULES

LABORATORY
PLANNING

TYPICAL LAB. MODULE

( 2 ) LAB. MODULES

( 3 ) LAB. MODULES

( 4 ) LAB. MODULES

**Fig. 4. Modular laboratory planning (HarleyEllis Architects)**

The establishment of a basic layout requires some firm decisions by the officer in charge, and these must be applied with a certain amount of ruthlessness if this proves necessary.

## Windowless Laboratories and Offices

Given a choice, most people would prefer to work in a laboratory with windows (Fig. 5); it is very pleasant to be able to look out on a garden or landscape, or even to get a glimpse of the sky. There is a prejudice against working in rooms without windows because it is thought that they create a sensation of being confined. The objection to this feeling of lack of contact with the outside world can be partially overcome if it is possible to "look out if you want to." For example, in some double-width laboratories, the door to the internal laboratory is opposite the door of the external office, and both are in line with the window; the doors have clear-glass top panels.

## Prototype Laboratory or Bench

For large projects, it is a very good idea to have a prototype laboratory, and for small schemes at least a prototype bench. If these are to achieve their real purpose, they should be complete with services and accurate to the smallest detail. Most scientists can read plans very well; however, there are always some that can't visualize the finished product, and for them, and for the builder and the subcontractors, a prototype is a great help. Invariably, after examination and discussion, some improvements or economies are affected.

## Layout of Building

While the planning of each laboratory building has its individual problems, the range of layouts can be narrowed to a few which have been found satisfactory. Depending on the size of the project, the type of work, and the space available, any one of the following can be recommended (Fig. 6).

### Off-Center Corridor

This layout has wide application for relatively small schemes; for instance, from a single-story building 100 feet long to several two- or three-story buildings about 200 feet in length. It has the great advantage that all the laboratories can have a south-facing aspect, and the two room depths provide flexibility in planning.

### Central Corridor

This layout is more suitable for larger schemes. It has the advantage that the grouping of laboratories is more compact because they are on both sides of the corridor. Also, as the same width corridor is serving a wider building than in the case of the off-center layout, it provides a greater assignable space.

### Double Corridor

This layout provides a good interrelationship between laboratory, laboratory office, and service laboratory, and it sometimes offers the best solution when the width of the building is fixed within certain limits. It has the advantage that, as the service laboratories are windowless, it is easier to obtain accurate temperature control; in many cases, the absence of natural light is an asset.

### Service Corridor

The double-width layout is especially suitable for large schemes. As laboratory services become more complex, and temperature control more critical, it is likely that this type of layout will be more widely accepted. The increased area at one level contributes to more efficient operation because the scientific staff is brought closer together and the sharing of equipment is facilitated.

## Assignable Area

The gross area is the overall area of the building. The assignable space combined with the area of entrance halls, corridors, stairs, toilets, ducts, and wall thickness make up the gross area. The "use factor" is the ratio of assignable area to gross area, and it ranges from approximately 50 to 70 percent.

The best utilization of space is obtained by having one corridor serving rooms on both sides. For example, in the simplest type of three-

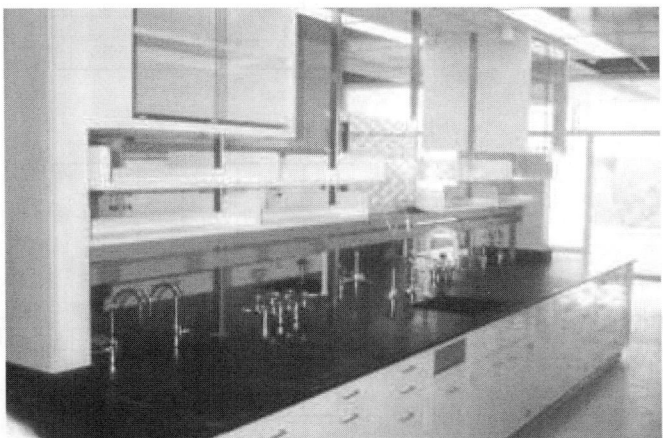

**Fig. 5. Daylight in Pfizer laboratory (HarleyEllis Architects)**

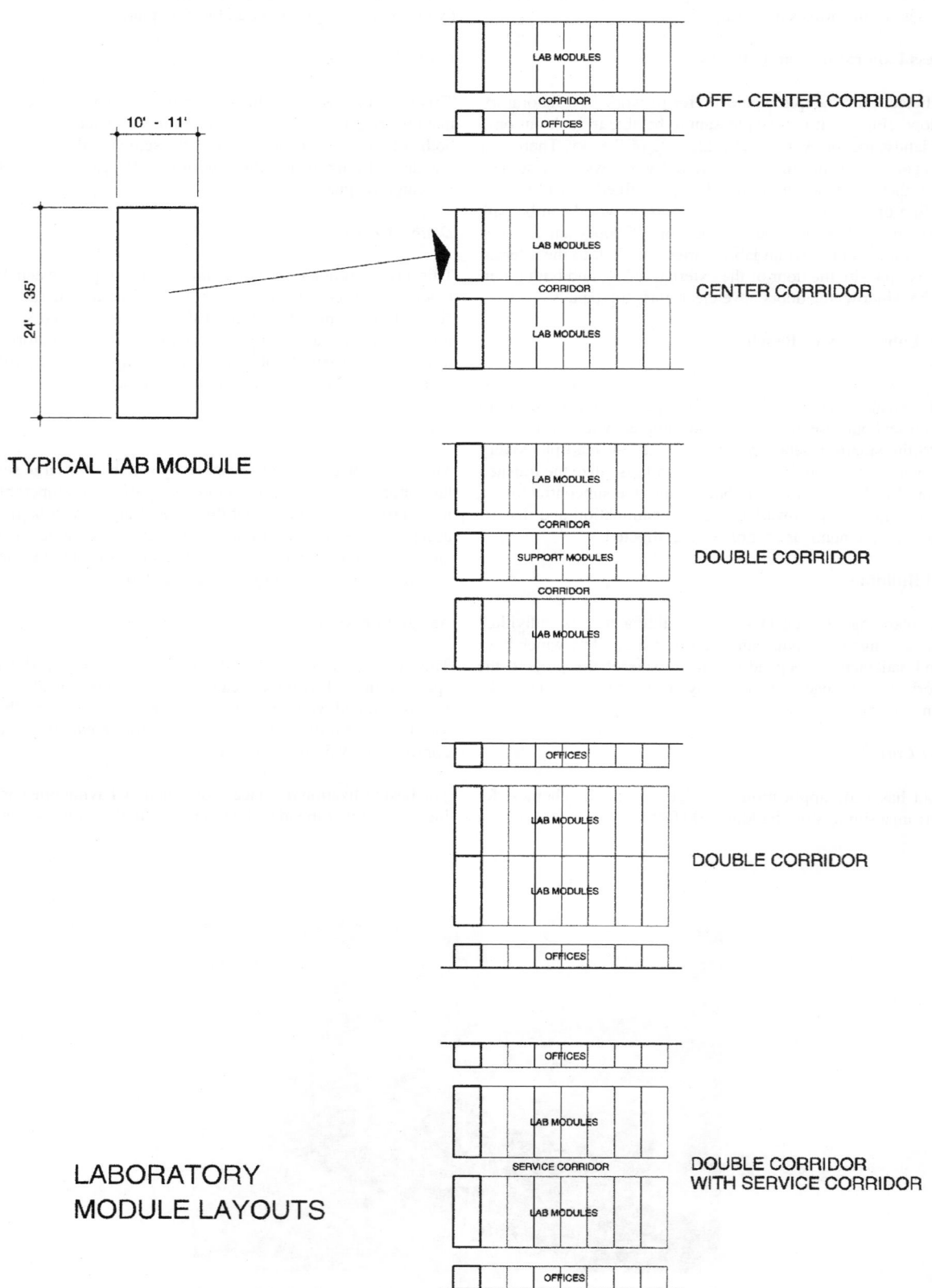

TYPICAL LAB MODULE

LABORATORY
MODULE LAYOUTS

Fig. 6. Laboratory module layouts (HarleyEllis Architects)

story building with minimum entrance hall, a 5 foot-6-inch corridor with 24-foot-deep laboratories along one side and 14-foot-deep service laboratories along the other.

Obviously, a corridor serving rooms on one side only, or two corridors serving three rooms, decreases the ratio of assignable to gross area and therefore increases the cost.

## Floor Space per Person

The space required by scientists varies greatly. Most require a laboratory, a laboratory office, and access to several service or support laboratories, but quite a number need additional facilities such as glass-houses, animal pens, or large areas for pilot-plant investigations or the preparation and storage of many hundreds of specimens. Then again, some scientists use equipment which is small and commercially available, while others must have large equipment which often has to be specially designed and fabricated in workshops on the site.

## LABORATORY DESCRIPTIONS

The research initiatives can be very diverse and the types of laboratory functions are equally different.

### Biological

Biological laboratories are those that contain biologically active materials or involve the chemical manipulation of these materials. These include laboratories that support such disciplines as biochemistry, microbiology, cell biology, biotechnology, immunology, botany, pharmacology, and toxicology.

### Chemical

Chemistry laboratories support both organic and inorganic synthesis and analytical functions. They may include laboratories in the material and electronic sciences.

### Animal

Animal laboratories are areas used for manipulation, surgical modification, and pharmacological observation of laboratory animals. They include holding rooms, which have a different set of performance requirements.

### Physical

Physical laboratories are associated with physical experimentation and include a wide variety of functions. Common physical laboratories support the use of lasers, optics, nuclear material, high and low temperature material, electronics, dynamometers, etc.

## LABORATORY SUPPORT AREAS

Adequate laboratory support space should be provided to house special and shared equipment. The amount of laboratory support space shall be sufficient to eliminate the need to locate laboratory equipment in non-laboratory functional areas. Consideration should be given to locating noise-, heat-, and vibration-producing equipment in laboratory support space adjacent to research laboratories. These support spaces may be dedicated or shared spaces, alcoves, or securable rooms as required.

### Autoclave Rooms

An autoclave is an industrial appliance that utilizes pressurized steam to sterilize laboratory instruments, glassware and other hard materials, and infectious waste. An autoclave room requires overhead exhaust, floor drains, equipment alarms, electricity, hot/cold water, steam, and air conditioning. All finishes and materials must be moisture resistant. Doors must accommodate larger pieces of equipment. Adequate access to the autoclave for maintenance is required. Special considerations are required for autoclaves using ethylene oxide.

### Glasswash Rooms

Glasswash rooms provide space for glassware washing, drying appliances and carts. All areas of the room shall have cleanable walls, ceilings, and epoxy floors. Space must be provided for staging clean and dirty glassware. Utilities include air conditioning, electricity, overhead exhaust, cold water, high purity water, vacuum, and equipment alarms.

### Environmental Rooms

Environmental rooms are generally prefabricated units used for providing internal conditions below or above normal laboratory conditions. Rooms used as working laboratories should be provided with appropriate amounts of ventilation for the occupants. Rooms should be configured so that the mechanical units are accessible from outside the room. Rooms used to hold material below ambient may required insulated flooring, usually recessed in the concrete slab for handicap accessibility. On-grade rooms used for holding materials below freezing may require frost prevention.

### Darkrooms

Darkrooms will generally require casework, counters, worktables and sinks. Specific requirements need to be determined during the programming phase but commonly include a light tight enclosure, cylinder doors, hot/cold water, compressed air, vacuum, electricity, spot exhaust, and air conditioning.

### Shared Instrument and Equipment Rooms

Much scientific equipment is shared between researchers and needs to be housed in separate dedicated areas. These areas need to be designed to support varying and changing scientific equipment. Often shared equipment generates a high heat release to the room and sufficient cooling must be provided. Some shared equipment will also generate significant sound. Cooling requirements must be developed on an application specific basis. Heat release rates may be 35 watts per square foot or higher. Utilities required often include 110 and 220 volt electrical power, emergency power, equipment alarms, cooling water, hot/cold water, compressed gases, and vacuum.

### Tissue Culture

Equipment located in tissue culture rooms includes biological safety cabinets and incubators. Access to refrigerators, freezers, autoclave, sink, environmental room, and liquid nitrogen is often required.

### Offices and Shared Use Areas

Office and administrative areas shall be adequate to provide areas outside of the laboratory with a quiet, aesthetic environment that is sized to support the appropriate number of researchers. It is desired to provide laboratory staff with office space that is physically separated, but adjacent to the laboratory work area. Administrative and clerical support areas should be provided with adequate storage for files, records, etc.

### Offices

Research staff should be provided with dedicated enclosed offices located outside of the research laboratory. Offices should be located so that the views to the outdoors are available. Adequate work surface, bookshelves, file space, and computer connectivity must be provided. The overall work environment should be consistent with the stated goals for the research facility physical environment.

### Technician Offices

Research technicians should be provided with dedicated adjacent workstations physically separated from research laboratories using hazardous materials. The workstations should be configured to provide file space, adequate work surface, and computer connectivity. The overall work environment should be consistent with the stated goals for the research facility physical environment.

### Small Conference Rooms

Small conference rooms suitable for up to 8 people should be provided throughout research facilities to encourage collaborative interaction between researchers and to provide for space for research staff to meet with outside visitors. Conference rooms should be provided with communication and computer connectivity.

### Break Rooms

Since consumption of food and beverage is not allowed in research laboratories where hazardous materials are used, break areas (Fig. 7) must be provided throughout the research facility. Break areas should be appropriately sized to support the number of research staff in the area.

### BUILDING SUPPORT AREAS

### Circulation

To the extent possible circulation (Fig. 8) should provide for separate flows of people and materials. Inherent in some research operations is the need to transport potentially hazardous materials from receiving and storage areas to the research laboratories. The flow of this material must be considered in the design of facilities and may require special considerations. These considerations should be identified as part of a comprehensive hazard assessment.

### Vertical Transportation

Research facilities should be equipped with both passenger and freight elevators. Elevators used for the transportation of potentially hazardous materials should be equipped with appropriate safety controls and alarm systems.

### Loading Docks and Receiving Areas

The loading dock should be covered and must be securable after hours. An outdoor telephone or doorbell shall be provided. Exiting

should be arranged so that the loading dock is not a required means of egress from other than the dock or receiving areas. Marshaling space shall be provided adjacent to the loading dock for the temporary and limited storage of materials. Separate spaces for holding medical, hazardous, radioactive, general, and recycling waste should be provided.

The loading and receiving space should be provided with a toilet and hand wash sink and be equipped with eyewash and emergency showers.

Receiving areas should also be provided with appropriate space and counter space for inventory control computers and bar coding devices.

### Material Storage

Many of the materials used in research operations present potential health and safety concerns. Storage facilities for these materials must be provided that are designed for the materials being stored. Specific storage requirements will vary greatly dependent upon the nature of

**Fig. 7. Pfizer laboratory building (HarleyEllis Architects)**

he research activities. The specific storage facility requirements must be determined during the programming phase.

### Flexibility and Adaptability

It is desirable to have research facilities that are flexible to accommodate different research initiatives and easily adaptable to accommodate evolving research initiatives. To the degree possible, generic spaces with the ability to readily accommodate changes in function without requiring significant physical or infrastructure changes should be provided. Individually planned, non-generic, or customized spaces should be provided only where absolutely required to accommodate unique research operations.

### Expansion Considerations

Designs for new research facilities can include considerations for future expansion including horizontal and vertical expansion potential. Reserve capacity should be planned into primary building systems to accommodate future growth and research mission changes within budgetary constraints.

## LABORATORY FINISHES AND MATERIALS

Materials selected for the construction of laboratories must be durable and cleanable, and contribute to the creation of a comfortable, productive, and safe work environment. Design features should promote cleaning, maintenance, and storage while minimizing pest access.

### Windows and Window Treatments

Windows should be non-operable and must be sealed and caulked (Fig. 9). Light-tight treatments will be provided in conference rooms, laboratories, and other spaces that may need to be darkened. Window systems should be energy-efficient glass.

### Doors and Door Hardware

Doors into laboratories from main corridors can accommodate personnel, equipment and material distribution. Common door assemblies have a 3-foot-wide active leaf and a 1-foot-6-inch inactive leaf. The doors should be a minimum of 7 feet high and be supported in

**Fig. 8. Michigan Biotechnology Institute (HarleyEllis Architects)**

**Fig. 9. Pfizer laboratory building (HarleyEllis Architects)**

hollow metal frames. Typical door frames should be 7 feet-2 inches high or 7 feet-4 inches in masonry conditions.

In laboratories where the use of larger equipment is anticipated, wider/higher doors or removable transoms should be considered. Laboratory doors should be recessed and swing outward in the direction of egress. They should be provided with locks and closures for security/safety. Door assemblies must comply with all applicable codes. Vision panels should be provided in the active leaf of laboratory doors.

Laboratory doors should be fitted with hardware, hinges, kickplates, keys, closures, etc. appropriate for their function and service. Door closures should be provided for all laboratory doors.

The key and lock system should be based on several levels of master keys. Grand master and great-grand masters should be provided for functional zones and modules.

### Flooring

Floor materials must be nonabsorbent, skidproof, resistant to wear, and resistant to the adverse effects of acids, solvents, and detergents. Materials may be monolithic (sheet flooring) or have a minimal number of joints such as vinyl composition tile (VCT) or rubber tile. The base may be a 100-millimeter vinyl or rubber material (if readily cleanable) with an integral cover base when sheet vinyl flooring is used.

### Walls

Wall surfaces should be free from cracks, unsealed penetrations, and imperfect junctions with ceiling and floors. Materials must be capable of withstanding washing with strong detergents and disinfectants and be capable of withstanding the impact of normal traffic. Corner guards and bumper rails should be provided to protect wall surfaces in high traffic/impact areas.

### Ceilings

Laboratory ceilings should provide easy access to utilities above the ceiling. Ceilings such as washable or easily replaceable lay-in acoustical tiles should be provided for most laboratory spaces depending on laboratory activity. Ceiling heights should be a minimum of 9 feet in laboratory and laboratory support spaces and a minimum of 8 feet in administrative spaces. Gypsum board with epoxy paint and equipped with access panels should be provided in glassware washing and autoclave rooms or other laboratories, where the potential for high moisture exists.

### Casework Systems

Wood or metal casework would be appropriate for use in typical laboratories (Fig. 10). Laboratories with sensitive materials or special functional requirements may require the use of stainless steel or polypropylene casework.

Countertop materials will vary depending upon usage. Typically chemical-resistant, plastic laminates will be used. Epoxy resin will apply for most applications where corrosive chemicals are used or for sinks where heavy water usage occurs. Stainless steel shall be used for radioisotopes, perchloric acid, glassware washing, and cold rooms.

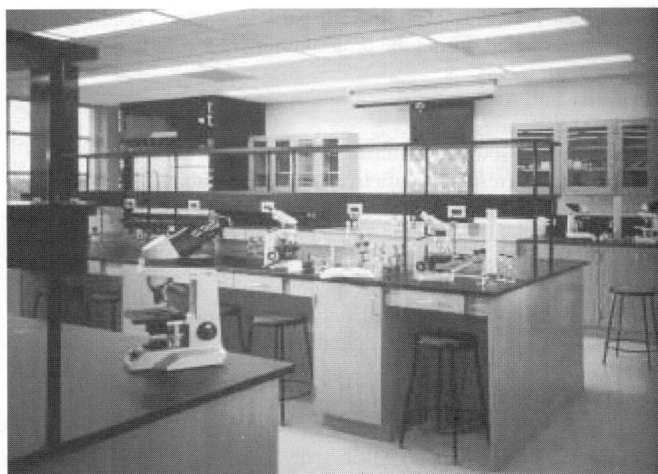

**Fig. 10. Casework in Oakland University Science and Engineering building (HarleyEllis Architects)**

Chemical-resistant plastic laminates can be used in laboratories with low exposure to corrosive chemicals and water use.

Casework systems should have modular unit widths to facilitate renovation and reuse. Racked equipment, mobile casework on "wheels," or other options, which minimize costs and maximize flexibility, may be considered due to the tremendous changes in research requirements.

### Chemical Fume Hoods

Fume hoods (Fig. 11) function as ventilated, enclosed workspaces, designed to capture, confine and exhaust fumes, vapors and particulate matter produced or generated within the enclosure. Design fume hoods so that, when connected to an exhaust system that provides proper exhaust volume under normal laboratory conditions, they will operate in a safe, efficient manner, within acceptable tolerances for face velocities specified.

Chemical fume hoods may be constant-volume, variable-volume, or restricted bypass exhaust hoods depending on user and facility management considerations of function, first cost, and life-cycle cost issues. All containment devices must be located in the laboratory to avoid entrapment, blocking of egress, or safety hazard to the lab occupant.

The following lists physical styles of fume hoods:

- *Benchtop:* Benchtop fume hoods should be designed to accommodate laboratory activities at normal benchtop height.
- *Distillation (high bay):* Distillation fume hoods should be designed with a low bench height and a tall interior and sash opening. The hood may accommodate tall complex distillation apparatus and large benchtop equipment required to be in a hood environment.
- *Walk-in:* Walk-in fume hoods should be designed to accommodate large and complex apparatus. The hood can allow walk-in entry of a user and the ability to roll-in equipment.
- *Accessible:* Accessible fume hoods should be designed to accommodate physically disabled users. The hood must comply with

**Fig. 11. Fume hoods at Michigan Biotechnology Institute (HarleyEllis Architects)**

The selection of a BSC is a combined effort between the designer, the user and the owner's safety officer. Depending on the class and type selected, laminar flow biological safety cabinets can offer the following protection:

- *Personnel protection:* To protect personnel from harmful agents inside the cabinet.
- *Product protection:* To protect the work, product, experiment, or procedure performed inside the cabinet from contaminants in the laboratory environment or from cross-contamination inside the cabinet.
- *Environmental protection:* To protect the environment from contaminants in the cabinet.

**Flammable, Acid, and Ventilated Chemical Storage Cabinets**

Certain materials used in the laboratory environment present physical and environmental hazards that mandate the use of special cabinetry to facilitate their storage. Special cabinets shall be provided for the storage of flammables, acids/bases and odor-producing materials.

**Miscellaneous Laboratory Equipment**

In addition to casework, fume hoods, biological safety cabinets, service fittings, etc., the laboratory designer should incorporate into the design all the miscellaneous laboratory equipment required (Fig. 12). The following list provides a range of equipment that is normally designed and specified by the laboratory designer:

- Laboratory benchtops
- Laboratory sinks
- Glass-drying racks
- Laboratory adjustable wall shelving
- Island superstructure support frames
- Service drops
- Exhaust snorkels (Fig. 13)
- Exhaust manifolds
- Canopy hoods
- Gas cylinder restraint straps and racks
- Stainless steel shelving
- Wire shelving
- Utility storage shelving

the criteria of the Americans with Disabilities Act and the code requirements of the applicable local or state accessibility codes.
- *Glass-sided student workstations:* Glass-sided student workstation fume hoods shall be designed to provide maximum visibility of hood interior from all sides. The hood must have a work surface at normal benchtop height.
- *Two-sided (California hood):* Two-sided fume hoods shall be designed to facilitate access from both faces of hood. The hood should be a walk-in, benchtop, or distillation type as required.
- *Demonstration:* Demonstration hoods must be designed to have a clear, unobstructed view of procedures inside the hood to an audience.
- *Custom:* Custom fume hoods can be designed to comply with the requirements for special lengths, heights, depths and configurations as required.
- *Radioscopic fume hoods:* Provide fume hoods specifically designed to handle radioactive isotopes.
- *Perchloric acid fume hoods:* Provide fume hoods specifically designed for handling perchloric acid.

**Safety Considerations**

- Locate fume hoods to permit unrestricted exit from the lab in the event of fire or explosion.
- Locate hoods away from high traffic lanes.
- Provide sufficient aisle space in front of the hood to avoid interference with passersby—at least 5 feet.
- Locate safety devices, such as drench showers, eyewash stations, fire extinguishers, first aid kits, and fire blankets convenient to each fume hood.

**Biological Safety Cabinets**

Biological safety cabinets (BSCs) are safety devices that are used for primary containment of biohazardous materials. These units are uniquely different from other types of laboratory hoods, and installation involves specific design consideration. BSCs are classified as Class I, II, or III.

BSCs are not to be confused with chemical fume hoods. These safety devices have specific criteria for installation, decontamination, and certification that should be followed.

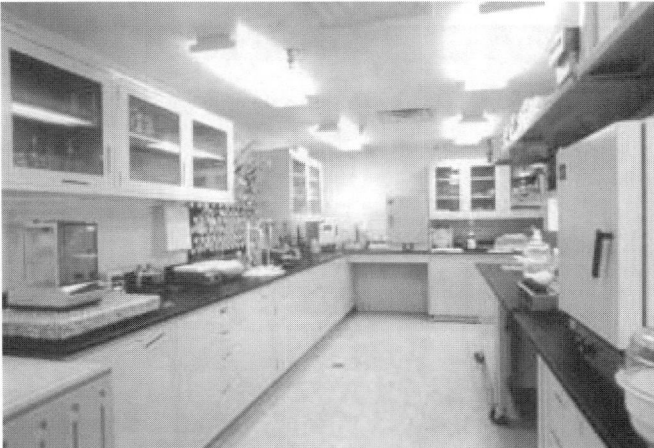

**Fig. 12. Lab equipment at Baxter Hyland Immuno Biotechnology Center (HarleyEllis Architects)**

- Unistrut framing
- Lightproof curtains
- Fire resistant curtains
- Sticky mats and sticky flooring
- Photography processing sinks
- Backdraft hoods

## UTILITY DISTRIBUTION

### General

Utility services within a research laboratory building require a great deal more emphasis than is customary in the design of the average building. Heating, ventilation, and air conditioning systems and the multiple pipes of the various laboratory services such as water, gas, vacuum, and oxygen create a demand for cubic space as well as floor space. In more recent designs, utility systems have taken a higher percentage of the gross area, with consequent reduction in net space. This special aspect of the research laboratory building sometimes comes as a surprise to architects and engineers whose experience has been mainly with commercial buildings, which need much less utility service capability. Associated with this need for additional space for utility services is the need to provide functional space for the unseen occupants of the building: maintenance and operating engineers, and the craftsmen who provide the continual changes and adjustments in utility systems which mark an active research program.

### Selection of Systems

Selection of the utility distribution systems strongly influences the configuration, design, and cost of a research laboratory building. The type of utility system used should be selected as early as possible in the planning process. Room arrangement and equipment location should be designed to work in conjunction with the utility distribution pattern once this has been standardized.

Planning a nonstandard room arrangement makes it difficult to visualize – without elaborate mockups – the configuration of space and equipment in the completed building. Then too, successive occupants are not always happy with the room arrangements selected by the first occupants. The rearrangement of plumbing and duct systems to meet preferences of successive occupants is usually costly unless these systems are installed on the standard repetitive pattern. Then a minimum of time and materials is required to rearrange the ventilation, lighting, and the plumbing and draining systems.

### Standard Configuration

Utility services should be laid out with an identical configuration for every floor. This layout should be designed to meet the capability needs of the programs that will occupy the building over its life and with appropriate consideration of costs. Where it is not practical to provide an identical layout in each floor, a standard utility layout should be established for the floor that requires maximum utility services, and this standard should be used for all the other floors, with deletions made where it is anticipated the services will not be needed for a considerable time. The arrangement of utilities should be such that installation of missing portions of the plumbing and duct systems can be made with a minimum of labor and materials.

It may be difficult for the architect and the initial user to accept an arrangement of space based on a standard utility and mechanical system distribution system rather than on the preferences of the first occupants of the space. This is somewhat similar to installing water mains, gas lines, and electric power lines along the streets of the city, and then building the houses on lots in such a way that they can connect to the public utility systems. It would be uneconomical and exceedingly difficult to maintain adequate service in the future if the building utility supply mains were installed in the streets according to the needs of each individual home.

## TYPES OF SYSTEMS

Utility services are usually provided within a research laboratory building by either a horizontal or vertical distribution system or a combination of the two. Five systems are generally used to distribute laboratory utility services:

1. Utility corridor system
2. Multiple interior shaft system
3. Multiple exterior shaft system
4. Corridor ceiling with isolated vertical shafts
5. Utility floor system

### Utility Corridor System

In the utility corridor design all service mains and ducts are brought to the various floor levels by means of a vertical central core which distributes the utilities by vertical mains, usually from a basement, sometimes from a room mechanical room. The horizontal distribution of utilities from the central core may be at the ceiling and downward to individual casework or it can be directly along the floor through the wall in the pipe space behind the case cabinets.

This design provides access for maintenance and service personnel to the utility piping and duct work throughout the life of the structure. It has a high degree of flexibility for meeting the needs of changes in research program and has a high capability to meet a wide range of criteria with regard to environmental control and ventilation, temperature controls, lighting, electric power, etc. Its efficiency in terms of the net assignable area and the gross area is not high. It usually runs somewhere between 50 and 60 percent.

The utility corridor design is most applicable to multistory buildings and should be used with reservation for laboratories with only one or

**Fig. 13. Exhaust snorkel at Oakland University Science and Engineering building (HarleyEllis Architects)**

two floors. This system results in functionally efficient laboratory buildings. It is extremely useful where future expansion, whether horizontal or vertical, is planned and is particularly adaptable to those arrangements where offices with window exposure are separated from the interior laboratory units.

*Advantages*

- Excellent flexibility
- Moderately high initial cost
- Low modification cost
- Low replacement cost
- Low cleaning (maintenance) cost
- Permits full utilization of walls
- Modifications do not interfere with conduct of work in adjacent modules

*Disadvantage*

- Fair net to gross area efficiency

**Multiple Interior Shaft System**

This system provides for concealed utilities with duct work and plumbing services in a series of regularly spaced shafts located either on both sides or on one side of a circulation corridor. All service mains and ducts are brought vertically to the various floor levels either upward or downward from the mechanical room. The shafts are located in each (or alternate) laboratory module or room on both sides of the central corridor. Distribution of utility services from the vertical shafts into the laboratory working areas is generally in the pipe space behind the laboratory benchwork. With the exception of the plumbing drains, in some designs the utility services are extended from the utility shaft above the ceiling in the laboratory and then downward to the laboratory benches. The interior utility shaft system is not a good selection for buildings with only one or two stories; it is most efficient in multistory buildings (Fig. 14) and is frequently found in those with a long rectangular shape.

*Advantages*

- Good flexibility
- Moderate net-to-gross-area efficiency
- Moderate initial cost
- Moderate modification cost
- Moderate replacement cost
- Easier to service than the exterior shaft system

*Disadvantages*

- More expensive and not as flexible as exposed systems
- Servicing interferes with traffic flow in corridors

**Multiple Exterior Shaft System**

This system brings service mains and ventilation duct work to the individual floor levels by a series of exterior wall vertical shafts located at each or alternate laboratory room or modules. Utility services are distributed from these exterior shafts into the laboratory rooms by means of the pipe space behind the base cabinet of the fixed equipment, or at the ceiling level. The multiple exterior utility shaft system generally should be considered only for multistory laboratories since its cost does not justify it use for one- or two-story buildings.

*Advantages*

- Good flexibility
- Moderate net-to-gross-area efficiency
- Moderate initial cost
- Moderate modification cost
- Moderate replacement cost
- Low cleaning (maintenance) cost
- Permits full usage of walls
- Utilities are common with duct work and drainage systems
- Good appearance

*Disadvantages*

- More difficult to service or modify than other recommended systems
- Requires removal of one section of case work
- Modifications interfere with conduct of work in adjacent modules
- More expensive and not as flexible as exposed systems
- Available space usually does not permit individual supply and exhaust of fume hoods.

**Corridor Ceiling Distribution**

In this system, utilities are located in the corridor ceiling and in some cases above the ceiling of the rooms on each side of the corridor and are supplied by one or two vertical pipe shafts. Distribution from the ceiling mains to the laboratory areas may be downward to the floor and upward

**Fig. 14. Baxter Hyland Immuno Biotechnology Center (HarleyEllis Architects)**

through the floor above in order to supply two floors from one ceiling distribution arrangement. Generally, it is preferable to provide the distribution downward within each room to avoid perforation of the floor slab and consequent leaks and flooding due to accidents in later years.

This system is commonly used in research buildings with only one or two stories or where a single research floor is inserted in a multistory building primarily designed for other than research purposes. Designs employing exposed utilities are ideal for two story or one-story-and-basement buildings where economy of construction is a major consideration.

*Advantages*

• Excellent flexibility
• Low first cost
• Low modification cost
• Low replacement cost
• High net-to-gross-area efficiency
• Modifications do not interfere with conduct or work in adjacent modules

*Disadvantages*

• Requires increased ceiling height for same clearance
• Limits installation of wall cabinets

### Utility Floor Distribution System

This system probably provides the maximum of flexibility and capability in research laboratory structures. Utilities, consisting of the duct work and the plumbing systems, are in separate floors. From the supply, the service mains and trunk ventilation ducts are brought to each individual utility floor by means of a centrally located vertical shaft or tower. Then distribution is made laterally on each utility floor with final distribution made by penetrating the floor below or above to service the research laboratory areas. Although this system has almost unlimited flexibility, its cost is high and it has an extremely low new gross area of efficiency. This system is primarily suitable only to multistory buildings and is not a good selection for one or two stories.

*Advantages*

• Excellent flexibility to any portion of room
• Low modification cost
• Low replacement cost
• Modifications do not interfere with conduct of work in adjacent modules
• May be used with up-feed at every floor or may be combined with down-feed and located at every third floor

*Disadvantages*

• Very high first cost
• Low net-to-gross-area efficiency

### STRUCTURAL CONSIDERATIONS

### Relationship to Modular Laboratory Planning

The dimension of the structural bay, both vertical and horizontal, must be carefully evaluated with respect to the laboratory planning module, mechanical distribution, and future expansion plans. Due to

the importance of the laboratory-planning module to functional and flexibility issues, the laboratory planning module should be considered as the primary building module in laboratory facilities.

The horizontal dimension of the structural bay must be a multiple of the laboratory-planning module dimension to provide for maximum flexibility and regular fenestration, and to allow uniform points of connection for laboratory services with respect to the laboratory planning module.

### Vibration Considerations

An analysis of vibration response of the structure should be made. Consideration must be given to vibration of floor-framing systems caused by mechanical and electrical equipment such as pumps, chillers, fans, emergency generators, and transformers and other sources such as foot traffic, parking garage traffic, and movement of heavy equipment.

Because vibration can interfere significantly with sensitive laboratory instruments, designers must take every opportunity to control vibration and to locate vibration sources away from activities sensitive to vibration. It may be necessary to have specific vibration recommendations made by an experienced vibration consultant. Steel structures should not be precluded for use in structural design relative to vibration without analysis.

New building construction should be analyzed for noticeable vibration and limited in pedestrian areas to "slightly noticeable." Where laboratory and special room requirements exist, coordinate allowable vibration limits with owner or equipment manufacturer.

To control vibration transmitted into laboratory space, the architect/engineer might consider the following items during the early design phases:

• The structural system should be relatively stiff so that any vibration that is transmitted occurs at high frequencies. Vibrations occurring at higher frequencies are more easily dampened with instrumentation vibration dampening systems and isolation tables than vibrations occurring at lower frequencies.
• The structural system should have relatively short column spacing.
• Laboratory spaces should be isolated from sources of vibration.
• Vibration-sensitive equipment should be located on grade-supported slabs.
• On framed floors, vibration-sensitive equipment should be located near columns.
• On framed floors, the combining of corridors and laboratory spans in the same structural bay must be avoided.

### Floor Loads

Existing buildings should be analyzed for new load requirements in building code effective at time of review. Building loads must meet either minimum code requirements presently in effect or anticipated occupancy loads, whichever is greater.

Where additions or extensive renovations are planned for a structure, existing facility should be analyzed for current lateral wind and seismic analysis.

New buildings must be designed in accordance with either minimum code allowable or anticipated occupancy loads. Buildings should be analyzed and designed for lateral wind and seismic loading in accordance with latest code provisions. New buildings should make use of current design practices including ACI 318-99 for concrete and AISC LRFD Second Edition for steel design. Analysis of existing buildings may use AISC ASD Ninth Edition for existing steel building use. In all cases, stress ratio should not exceed code allowable stress increases for loading parameters.

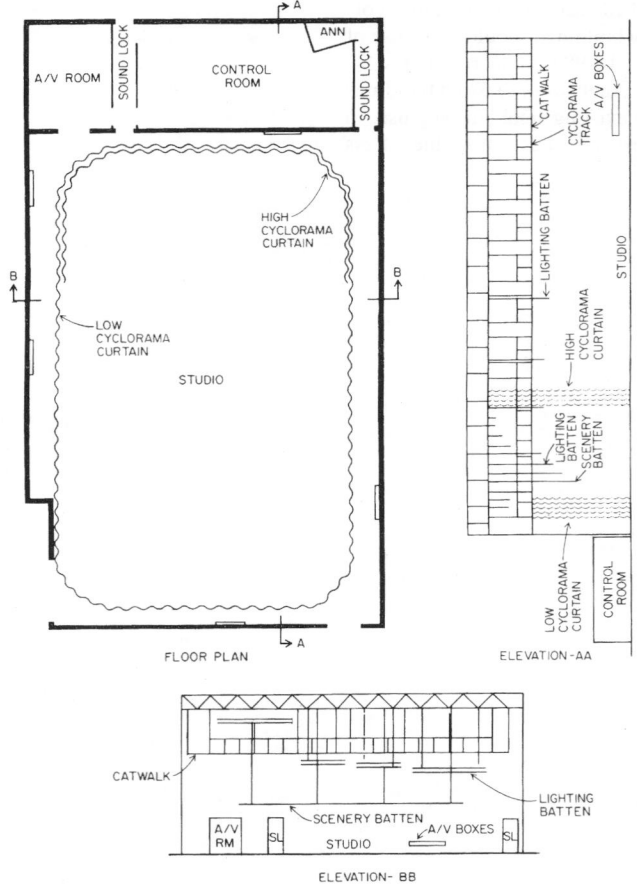

**Fig. 1. Typical studio layout**

# TELEVISION STATIONS

### TELEVISION BROADCASTING FACILITIES

#### Scope

Television broadcasting facilities range from tiny stations serving a small community to a major network facility with multiple studios and extensive supporting facilities providing programming to hundreds of city and regional markets. Because of the wide variation in requirements, this article will be limited to basic planning considerations plus a brief description of each of the facilities that may be required. Emphasis is on program origination facilities; transmitter installations are covered only briefly.

#### Classification

Television facilities may be classified as to purpose, type of programming, and extent of audience involvement. These factors, plus the size and budget of the station, determine the facilities to be provided and their relationships.

#### Purpose

- *Local Station.* A local television station serves a defined geographical area as authorized by FCC licensing. Programming will reflect the size of the market (area served) which may range from a small town to a large metropolitan area. Many local commercial stations are affiliated with one of the major networks, which provides a large portion of their programming. Another common source of outside programming is syndicated tape and film.
- *Network.* Program origination facilities for a television network differ from those of a local station in that they are usually larger, with a greater variety of supporting services. They originate program material for use by affiliated local stations.
- *Cable Television (CATV).* Facilities for cable television consist of a receiving antenna and a small head end building containing the associated electronic equipment. Incoming programs are distributed over a network of cables to subscribers. Some CATV operators have austere studios suitable for local news and interviews.

*Author:* Joseph Horowitz, P.E.

• *Other purposes.* Schools and industrial concerns are making increased use of television for educational and training purposes and have set up studio facilities for this purpose. Programs may be broadcast or distributed over closed circuits. In addition, a number of cassette-type media are available on which programs are recorded for later playback on closed circuit.

## Type of Programming

A basic planning factor is the extent of locally originated programming material as opposed to network-supplied or syndicated material. Locally originated programs require a studio; studio type and extent of supporting facilities will depend on nature of programming planned.

• *News* studio requirements are usually quite simple. Supporting facilities will include news gathering services, plus storage and editing facilities for film and videotape. Coverage of local news events will require remote equipment.
• *Interview and panel discussions* can be handled with the simplest of studios and minimal support facilities.
• *Dramatic programs* (such as soap operas) call for elaborate facilities, extensive sets, props, makeup, wardrobe, and other support facilities. Studio lighting is also more elaborate.
• *Music and entertainment programs* are the most demanding. Studios must accommodate anything from a single performer to a large group and require great flexibility in lighting, scenery, properties, etc. Supporting facilities are similar to those for dramatic programs, but usually there is less opportunity for reuse of materials in subsequent programs.
• *"Remotes,"* or broadcasts originated outside the station's studios, include coverage of sports events, political conventions, news, and other public events. Facilities required for this type of operation (in addition to control room and other technical facilities required for on-premises programming) are described below.

## Audience and Public Involvement

Studios may be further classified as audience or nonaudience. An audience studio is a cross between a theater and a studio, with the usual theater considerations of sight lines, audience acoustics, and public safety complicated by the requirements for camera operation and lighting.

The public may be involved in television facilities in ways other than as studio audiences. A station planning to encourage visitors to view the behind-the-scenes operations should make ample provision for such circulation.

Another case is the special-purpose facility which has as a major function, the training of television technicians and operating personnel. Here, control rooms and other supporting facilities must be planned to do double duty as classrooms.

## Other Planning Factors

In addition to the classifications described, the following factors must also be considered:

• Hours of operation
• Union regulations affecting technicians, stagehands, etc.
• Management decisions on contracting out versus work done in-house. Examples are rental of scenery props and costumes and outside film developing and storage.

## Site Selection

Site selection has much in common with radio studios, but it will also depend on the planning factors previously enumerated. The site for an audience studio is planned much as is that for a theater, with considerations of parking, transportation, and audience egress.

All studios require truck loading facilities for delivery and removal of heavy cameras and electronic equipment and—if dramatic or variety programming is planned—scenery and properties. Insofar as possible, avoid a site subjected to vibration, such as that caused by a highway.

## FACILITIES

The listing which follows includes spaces required in a larger station, a network, or a college facility where exposure to all facets of television broadcasting is desired. Smaller stations will require fewer and less elaborate facilities.

### Studios

A television studio is any room where television cameras are used (Fig. 1). Studios range in size from that of a regular office (with the camera shooting in through a window or open door) to large studios of 100 by 100 feet used for dramatic or variety programming. Because of its importance, a brief discussion of studio planning is included here.

### Control Rooms

Control rooms contain electronic equipment for monitoring and controlling the studio output. They may have separate compartments for sound (audio), picture (video), and lighting control. An announcer's booth incorporated with the control room must be acoustically isolated, since it contains a live microphone.

Control rooms must usually be accessible to the studio which they serve; direct visual contact may or may not be necessary, depending on operating practices (Fig. 2).

Acoustical considerations are similar to those for radio control rooms. Lighting should be adjustable to permit observation of television monitors.

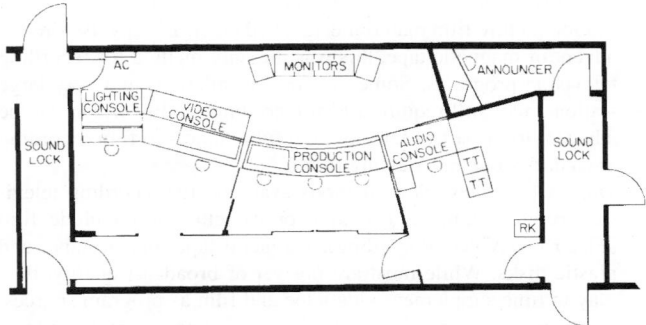

**Fig. 2. Studio control room. Note that the control room shown has no visual contact with the studio; wall space is used for television monitors**

## Technical Facilities

Technical facilities house the extensive electronic equipment which supports broadcasting operations. Because of the space required and the fact that some of this equipment is noisy, only the smallest stations locate it in the control rooms.

To facilitate maintenance, the technical facilities are often grouped together in a Central Technical Area (CTA). CTA need not be adjacent to the studios, provided good communications are available. A dust-free temperature-controlled environment is essential. Following are the facilities that make up CTA:

- *Equipment (Rack) Rooms.* The equipment room houses ancillary electronic equipment that does not require attendance or adjustment during programming, such as audio and video equipment, switching devices, transmission equipment, etc. A separate room facilitates maintenance and simplifies design of the control room. The rack room need not be adjacent to the control room(s) but should be convenient to the maintenance shop.
- *Videotape Recording (VTR).* The usual medium for television recording is magnetic tape using a device called a videotape recorder (VTR), which resembles a very elaborate magnetic sound tape recorder. The VTR area for a local station may contain from two to six machines. Central network facilities will have more.
- *Telecine.* Despite the advantages of magnetic tape, some television programming will originate as motion picture film. In addition to the popularity of full-length feature film as television fare, off-station news and special events are usually easier to record with portable video cameras. As the name implies (tele-television, cine-cinema), telecine contains assemblies that combine motion picture and slide projectors with a television camera. Size will depend on the number of machines to be housed.
- *Master Control.* Larger stations with several studios may require a central or master control for final switching and monitoring of the on-air operation.
- *Maintenance Shop.* This is an electronics workshop with considerable space for spare parts. It must be as convenient as possible to the central technical area. Ideally, it should also be convenient to the control rooms, but this is not always possible.
- *Telephone Equipment Room.* For large stations and network facilities, telephone equipment associated with transmission of television programming requires a substantial floor area which is usually close to or a part of the central technical area. (This equipment is distinct from that used for normal telephone communications.)
- *Film Recording.* This area contains equipment for recording on motion picture film material originated electronically. Before the advent of magnetic tape, this was the only method for recording television programs. Some network installations and very large stations may still require a film recording facility which can be adjacent to or part of telecine. Useful adjuncts to film recording are a darkroom and viewing room.
- *Video Cartridges.* New methods available for recording television programming in cartridge or cassette form include film (Electronic Video Recording), magnetic tape, plastic tape, and plastic disks. While most are not yet of broadcast quality, they may in time supplement videotape and film as program sources, much as tape cartridges and CDs now supplement records in commercial radio studios.
- *Program Control.* This is a room resembling a control room without a studio where television signals from various sources—such

as telecine, VTR, or live remotes—are combined electronically to produce a complete program. It is useful where studios are heavily used and much off-premises work is anticipated. A program control room is required only for the largest stations or network facilities.

## News

Even the smallest station will have local news. The following facilities would be required for a large station or a central network facility:

- *Newsroom.* This is similar to a newspaper "city room" with desk and telephone space for news reporters. It usually contains or is adjacent to wire service printers and is usually equipped with TV monitors.
- *Library and Archives.* Just as a major newspaper will maintain a file of clippings, a large news operation will have a library of film and tape as well as reference books and other resources. This should be accessible to the newsroom.
- *Special News Studios.* Since the live "action" in a news broadcast is usually limited to a person at a desk, larger stations may want a small studio opening directly off the newsroom from which news programs may originate without tying up one of the regular studios. When not in use as a studio, it serves as an office.
- *Graphic Arts.* This is a facility for rapid production of charts, photos, and other visual materials. It is used extensively for news as well as other programming. It may vary from a single artist's desk in a small operation to a large room with many artists and facilities, such as a Statmaster, for photo developing and printing, and several computer terminals.

## Studio Support Facilities

The following rooms are basically similar to corresponding spaces in legitimate theaters and will not be discussed in detail. Need for them depends on the type of programming.

- Rehearsal halls (these are best kept away from the studio to minimize sound problems).
- Wardrobe rooms.
- Dressing rooms (individual and group).
- Makeup rooms.
- "Talent" lounge for performers (convenient to studios and dressing rooms). This is often called a "green room" after a similar green-painted room in a well-known concert hall.
- Multipurpose rooms. These are rooms about the size of a chorus dressing room which can be used, as the occasion demands, for dressing rooms, rehearsal of small groups, lounge, music origination, etc.
- Ready storage for scenery and props. This must be available as close as possible to the studios to minimize handling.
- Crew's lounge. This should also be convenient to the studio area.
- Storage for cameras, microphones, and lighting equipment. This should be convenient to studios, and if possible, to the maintenance shop.

## Scenery

Facilities for a large station or network will include scenic design (art studio with possibly blueprinting or photostating services), production (carpenter shop, paint shop, stage electrical shop), scenery and property (prop) storage, and facilities for disposal of unwanted scenery.

Facilities to be provided depend on business decisions as well as station size and programming, since many of these functions can be contracted out. Some networks maintain a central scenery fabricating department from which materials are trucked to and from off-premises studios. Whether made on premises or off, scenery and props constitute a significant materials handling problem. The general flow is shown graphically in Fig. 3.

### Film

Facilities for processing (developing), editing (cutting), and storage of film are identical to those in commercial film laboratories and in many cases these functions (except possibly editing) are performed for the station by a commercial film laboratory.

Film storage and handling facilities are usually strictly regulated. In the absence of local codes, refer to National Fire Protection Association pamphlets.

### Sound Effects

Central sound effects rooms—similar to small radio control rooms—are required only in the larger facilities. They need not be adjacent to the studios provided good intercommunications are available.

### Music Origination Rooms

These provide musical background to a studio program. If the instrument (piano, organ, etc.) does not appear visually, it may be located in a separate room to avoid cluttering up the studio. Usually, very close microphone techniques are used, so that acoustical requirements are not severe.

### Viewing (Screening) Rooms

A viewing room may be anything from a room with a 16 mm projector on a table for previewing films to an elaborate miniature theater for showing programs to prospective sponsors. The latter type should be easily reached from sales and executive areas and convenient to rest rooms and offices. They are not usually related to the studio or technical facilities. Viewing rooms should have facilities for 16 mm and 35 mm motion picture film (if possible, with a separate projection booth), video tape, as well as television monitoring.

It is often possible to arrange viewing rooms so that two rooms share a single projection booth. Local code requirements will influence planning and design. The viewing room may also be designed to double as a conference room.

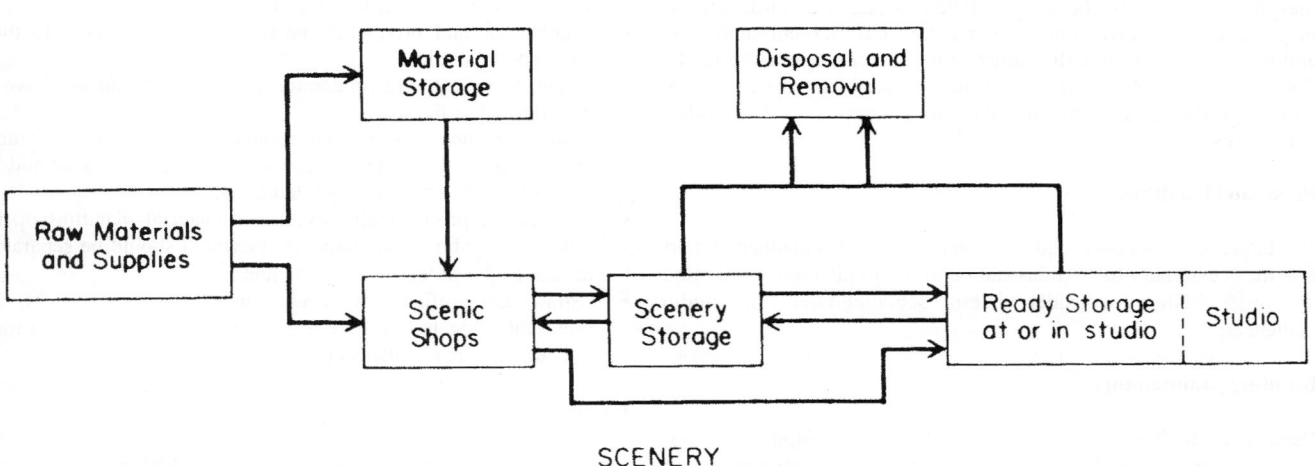

SCENERY

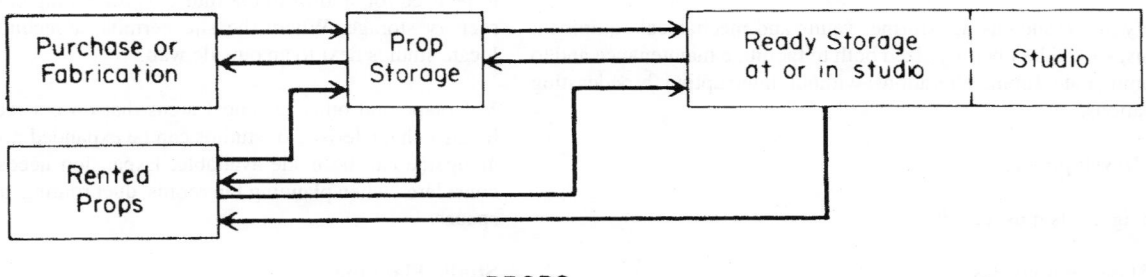

PROPS

**Fig. 3. Materials flow, scenery and props storage**

### Facilities for Outside (Remote) Program Origination

By contrast with radio, facilities for remote (off-premises) television broadcasting are quite elaborate. A station planning such activities will require the following:

- Garage or parking space for the mobile vans containing remote equipment. Since these may be taller than ordinary vehicles, a careful check of overhead clearances is required.
- A field shop for maintenance of the equipment and for storage of gear. This must be convenient to the garage area, since some of the equipment cannot be readily removed from the vans for servicing.

For a station with much off-premises work, an extra control room (without a studio) is useful. This permits putting together a remote without tying up one of the regular studios.

### Echo Chambers

Echo or reverberation effects are obtained in one of two ways: using "natural" echo chambers (highly reverberant rooms) or by means of artificial reverberation devices. The natural (physical) echo chambers require isolation from surrounding noise, otherwise they can be located anywhere. Need for reverberation sources depends on the type of programming contemplated.

### Offices

With the exception of those directly related to production, offices may be remote from the studios (even in another building), but they should be convenient to viewing rooms. Executive offices and conference rooms will require closed-circuit television feeds. For major network facilities, consider offices for outside "show units" (producer, director, and their assistants) as well as other employees.

### Personnel Facilities

The larger activities may require cafeteria, first aid, and other support facilities customary in an industrial building. In planning circulation and toilet facilities, consider visitors, schoolchildren, and studio audiences.

### Building Maintenance

Because of the heavy investment in facilities and equipment, television facilities are usually intensely used. Similarly, continuity of air conditioning, electric power, and other building services is essential. These factors dictate allocation of adequate space to building maintenance such as cleaning, repair shops, and spare parts storage.

Utility areas, such as transformer vaults and mechanical equipment rooms, should be liberally sized both to facilitate maintenance and to accommodate future alterations without interrupting broadcasting operations.

### Site Development

Parking needs must consider:

- Station employees
- Visitors on business, such as customers, performers, and tradespeople

- Studio audiences
- General public (guided tours, schoolchildren, etc.)
- Station vehicles

Off-street loading facilities are essential for scenery and properties as well as heavy cameras, dollies, and electronic equipment. Access is required from the loading facilities to shops, storage area, and studios.

Some stations make special use of their outside facilities for programs such as farm or animal shows.

## PLANNING CONSIDERATIONS

### Circulation

Organization of a typical television station is shown schematically in Fig. 4. A television broadcasting facility includes quite divergent functions. Flows of people and materials that may be in conflict must be separated as in a manufacturing plant. Some of these flows are as follows:

- Office personnel require access to production or technical spaces only rarely. Executive and sales personnel require ready access to conference and viewing rooms.
- Visitors should be controlled. Sponsors and other official guests should have ready access to offices and screening rooms without going through production or technical areas.
- "Talent" (performing artists of all types) require access to studios and studio support facilities (see Fig. 5).
- Technicians and production personnel require access to their areas and to studios.
- Talent, technical, and production personnel should not have to pass through office areas.
- Studio audiences, where used, should have access only to studio and toilets. Visits to production or technical spaces should be carefully controlled, as on guided tours.
- Scenery and props involve significant materials-handling operations. Fig. 3 shows the major flows which should be separated, insofar as possible, from the "people" flow.
- "Show unit" offices (producer, director, and their staffs) are preferably located within easy access to studio facilities, although this is not always possible.

### Expansion

Studios and technical rooms are very difficult and costly to expand unless expansion is contemplated in the original construction. One approach is to build the basic shell large enough to accommodate all anticipated requirements. Interior finishes are deferred and the space to be used for studios in the future is, for example, used initially for scenery storage. Where the site permits, a second approach is to locate studios next to an outside wall.

Videotape and other technical areas that do not require the ceiling heights characteristic of studios can be expanded provided the space alongside can be made available. Expansion needs should also be considered when planning fan rooms, duct routing, and other utilities spaces.

### Studio Planning

The studio is the heart of original programmed television.

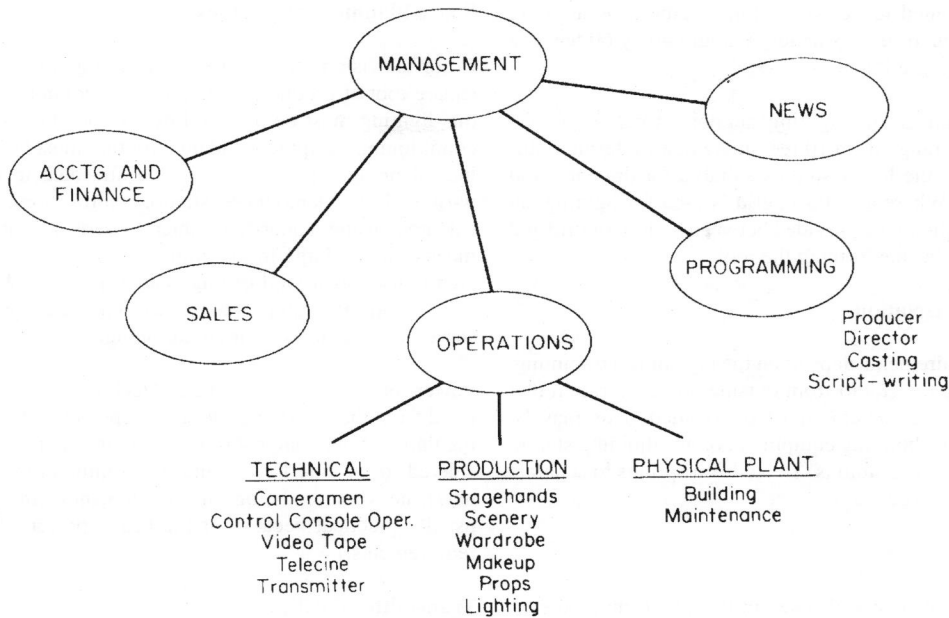

**Fig. 4. Television station—schematic organization**

## Audience Studio

Audience studios present a particular challenge, since camera operation conflicts with the theater requirements for unobstructed sight lines. The resulting studio is usually a compromise. For a production facility with only occasional audience use, removable bleacher seating may be considered.

Television studios require a substantial camera maneuvering space between the production area and the audience seating. Camera runways project out into the seating area to permit long camera shots. Seating area is usually sloped for better audience viewing. Note that

it must be possible to aim cameras at the audience as well as at the stage. Musicians are located at the same level as the rest of the production area and are usually enclosed for acoustical reasons.

Audience studios are "places of public assembly" in building code terms, with seat spacing, egress, and other aspects of audience safety and comfort to be considered.

### Dimensions

Studios can range from 20 by 25 feet for a very small station to 100 by 100 feet or more for a large facility suitable for all types of pro-

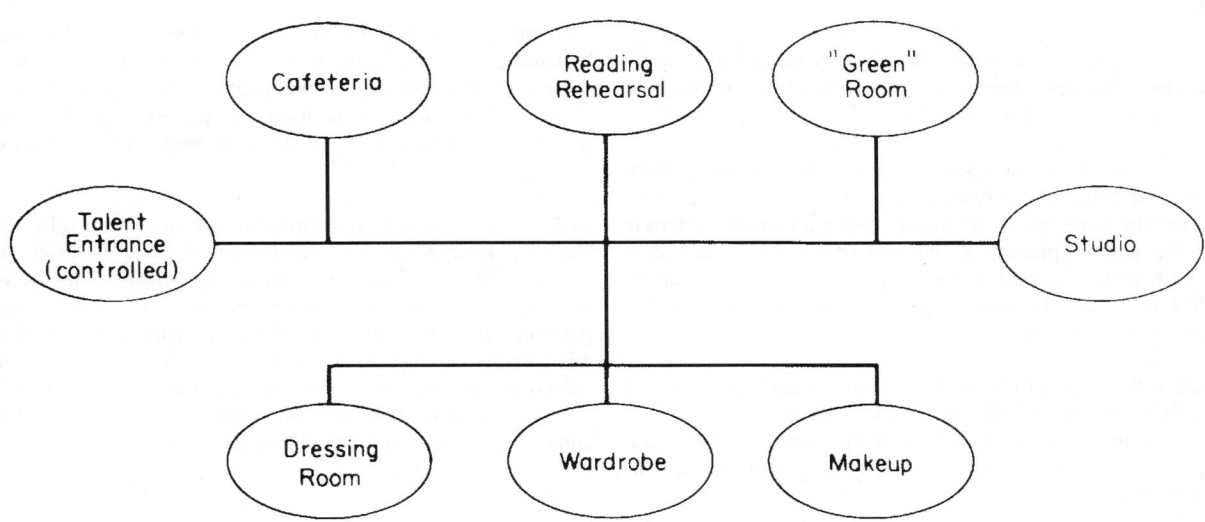

**Fig. 5. Performer ("talent") flow**

gramming. Studios limited to news or similar static programming with little movement can be even smaller. A studio 40 by 60 feet is a good size for an average station.

Minimum clearance under the lighting support structure or air-conditioning ducts can range from 10 feet in the news-interview studio to 15 or 20 feet in the larger studios suitable for dramatic and variety programming. Where a walk-on grid is used for lighting, an additional 7 feet or so should be provided between bottom of grid and underside of trusses or beams forming the roof.

### Sound and Vibration Isolation

Interior acoustical requirements depend on the type of programming. In addition to isolating the studio from outside noise, vibration that could be felt by sensitive cameras must be avoided. This may be caused by outside traffic, building equipment, or an adjoining studio. In extreme cases, the entire studio is "floated" on springs to separate it from the building structure.

### Materials Handling

Scenery, props, and other materials used in the studio may be both bulky and heavy. Entrance for large scenery flats is essential, as well as facilities for delivery of heavy items such as an automobile.

### Floor Loading

Floor loadings should accommodate the type of programming anticipated, as well as the weights of the cameras which, with their moving carriages (dollies) can be quite heavy. A live load of at least 100 pounds per square foot is recommended for maximum flexibility in large studios, and some authorities recommend 125 to 150 pounds per square foot. Finished floors require greater than usual freedom from irregularities and waves which would affect a rolling camera.

### Cyclorama

The production area of the studio is usually surrounded by a cyclorama: a thin, opaque curtain which provides a backdrop to scenery and conceals the walls or any storage outside the production area.

### Lighting

For smaller studios, lighting is provided by a combination of overhead and floor-mounted luminaires. Greater flexibility is obtained with an electrified raceway of the Litespan type.

For the larger studios, some type of lighting grid from which light fixtures may be hung is usually necessary. This may be serviced by ladders from the floor, but in the major studios a catwalk system is provided that permits placement and adjustment of the luminaires entirely from above. Individual light pipes or battens that can be raised and lowered are also used (see Fig. 1) permitting adjustment of lights from the studio floor.

Associated with the lighting system is a patch panel, an oversized version of a telephone switchboard, used for making lighting connections. Dimming equipment may be in the studio or centralized elsewhere and remotely controlled by a lighting console in the control room or studio.

### Space Planning for Utilities

Color television requires very intense lighting—50 to 75 watts per square foot of production area is not uncommon. Heat generated by this lighting must be removed by air conditioning. Location of air-conditioning equipment and duct routing must be considered in original planning. Space must also be allocated to the very extensive wiring which interconnects studio, control room, and central technical area, using under-floor ducts, overhead cable trays, or other means. In one large installation, the ceiling of the central technical area is used as a kind of huge cable tray, with bundled cables laid directly on the grating that serves as the ceiling. (The ceiling also serves as a plenum for air conditioning.)

Power for electronic equipment ("technical" power) should be separated from that serving building equipment and may require voltage regulation. For a major station, emergency generators should be considered to provide for continuity of minimal broadcasting, such as news, network feeds, or film. (Emergency studio operation is not usually practical because of the heavy power and air-conditioning requirements.)

### Transmitter Facilities

Transmitter facilities consist of the broadcasting antenna and the transmitter building or room. As with FM, the radiating element (antenna) is mounted on a separate tower or mast, whose function is purely structural.

There is no ground radial system as with AM radio transmitters except for lightning protection. Several antennas may be mounted on a single mast or tower.

TV transmission is primarily a line-of-sight phenomenon and is affected by buildings, mountains, etc. For this reason, antenna height is a major consideration; many television towers are more than 1,000 feet tall.

Because of these heights, particular consideration must be given to falling ice and drifting paint spray when the tower is repainted. In general, physical site planning has much in common with radio transmitter planning.

Planning for the transmitter room also resembles that for radio transmitters, but the equipment and plant facilities are larger and more complex. Detailed requirements depend very much on the transmitter equipment to be used, and particular attention must be paid to transmitter cooling (UHF equipment usually requires water cooling).

In the past, most television transmitters have been fully manned, requiring kitchen and toilet (and even sleeping facilities in some cases). While unattended transmitters are permitted, the transmitter building will still be occupied for a part of each day, requiring some personnel support facilities. On the other hand, provision should be made for remote monitoring of building services—temperature, fire detection, electric power, etc.—for use during those periods when the station is unmanned. Where continuity of broadcasting is essential, emergency power should be provided.

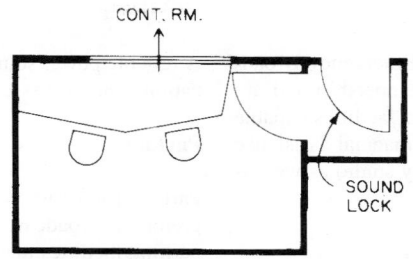

**Fig. 1. One- or two-person studio (newscast, disk jockey, etc.)**

# RADIO STATIONS

## PLANNING RADIO STUDIOS

### Scope

The term "radio studios" is used in the broad sense of facilities for the origination of radio programs. Broadcasting facilities intended for police or other radio communications are not included. Application of broadcasting equipment to stadiums, arenas, concert halls, etc., is a specialized topic and will not be covered here.

Discussion will center on planning an individual station, which may be commercial or noncommercial, but principles are also applicable to centralized network facilities. Except as otherwise indicated, criteria apply to both AM and FM facilities.

### Planning Factors

Planning of a radio station, while constrained by the technology of broadcasting, is determined to a large extent by the station's operating practices. It is essential to realize that, while all stations perform the same basic functions, there are wide divergences of operating practices and philosophy. Planning, therefore, starts with a careful analysis of the station's method of operation.

Following is a checklist of basic planning factors which must be known or established in order to plan the facility.

### Type of Programming

The most important single influence on facility requirements is the type of programming. In current practice this will usually consist of one or more of the following:

- Music
- News and public features
- Interview and panel discussion
- Production of advertising commercials

Some stations may have special requirements for dramatic or audience participation shows, but this is no longer common. Many music-oriented stations use automated programming, which means, basically, that not only the music but announcer's commentary, time

checks, station breaks, etc., are all prerecorded and all switching is handled automatically. This has significant impact on both layout and power requirement. For all stations an important planning question is the extent of "live" versus recorded programming.

### Hours of Operation

Stations are restricted by their FCC license provisions. Commercial stations must provide certain minimum hours of operation daily.

### Relationship to Talent Sources

The term "talent," as used here, refers to the persons who participate in programs, whether as performing artists, employees, interviewees, etc.

### Relationship to Public

Some stations view themselves as a kind of program "factory" and limit visitors to persons having specific business with the station. Others encourage visits from schools and community groups and make elaborate provisions for them, such as viewing windows from which visitors (or passersby) can view station operations. This decision affects circulation patterns, support facilities, and security provisions.

### Government Regulations

All stations are licensed by the Federal Communications Commission, whose very detailed regulations influence every aspect of operation and hence planning. Regulations, which require constant monitoring of certain devices, influence the configuration of the control room. Most stations are familiar with these requirements, but for a new station, use of an outside consultant may be desirable. As an example, an FCC regulation requiring separate AM and FM programming has generated the need for FM program facilities separate and, in some cases, apart from the AM facilities in some stations that were formerly combined.

*Author:* Joseph Horowitz, P.E.

### Emergency Broadcasting System (EBS)

Another area of government involvement is the Emergency Broadcasting System (EBS). Stations that agree to membership and are designated as primary EBS facilities must provide facilities capable of operation during an emergency. Government financial assistance may be available for equipment for the emergency studio as well as for emergency generators.

### Relationship of Studio and Transmitter Facilities

Studios and transmitter may be at the same or separate locations. Similarly, stations (such as an AM and FM) may share certain facilities.

### Operating Procedures

Most larger commercial radio stations are highly unionized. Work rules vary from one locality to the next and can have significant influence on planning of studio facilities. In some locations a disk jockey may actually operate the tape player or turntable. In other areas, this work requires a studio engineer or even a separate "platter spinner." Where regulations are less restrictive, one may act as engineer and announcer if she meets the licensing requirements. In all cases, a careful study of operating procedures is essential.

### Site Selection

Broadcasting facilities are usually quite compact and are often located within a building having other primary functions, such as an office or school. Following are some of the factors to consider in selecting a site.

### Location

Location is largely a function of planning factors such as type of programming, relationship to talent sources, and relation to the public. If extensive interviews or panel discussions are planned, the station should be convenient to the prospective participants (show business personalities, sports, or government figures). Where the station desires maximum exposure to the general public, it should be easily reached by public transportation. Sales activities of commercial radio stations likewise point to a "downtown" location.

Where these factors are less significant or good transportation is available, advantage may be taken of lower-cost suburban areas. Where studio and transmitter are combined in one building, the technical requirements of transmitters will govern the site selection (see section on planning radio transmitter facilities.) This arrangement, while economical, creates a location conflict, at least for AM stations, since the ideal site for an AM transmitter is rarely convenient as a studio location.

### Environment

Although studio design can compensate for a hostile noise environment, reasonable freedom from excessive noise and vibration is desirable. Within a building, the area selected for studios should be free of overhead building pipes and ductwork to prevent noise and water leaks. It should also have adequate headroom, both for acoustic purposes and to accommodate air-conditioning ductwork. Surrounding tenancies should be free of objectionable noise. Otherwise, environmental factors are similar to those for an office.

### Utilities

A reliable power source and access to telephone and telex communications lines are essential.

### Parking

Parking (or garage space) for station vehicles used for "remote" (off-premises) broadcasting is particularly important. Desire for liberal parking facilities may conflict with the need for a "downtown" location convenient to visitors, talent sources, and VIPs.

## DESCRIPTION OF FACILITIES

Radio broadcasting (studio) facilities may be considered under the following groups:

- Technical (on-air) facilities
- Other broadcasting facilities
- Support facilities
- Personnel facilities
- Facilities for off-premises operations

### Technical (On-Air) Facilities

The on-air facilities include the studios and control rooms that form the heart of the station's operation, along with other facilities.

### Studio

A studio is any room used for originating broadcast material—one in which there is a live microphone. With proper acoustical design, studios can be made just large enough to contain the desired number of persons. A two-person studio (disk jockey, newscaster) is shown in Fig. 1; Fig. 2 shows an interview studio. In contemporary radio, music is almost always prerecorded, and broadcasts involving the public are likely to be recorded off-premises at theaters, concert halls, legislatures, etc. For these reasons large studios suitable for music or audience participation are not required in the station itself. In the exceptional case of an audience studio, the room would be designed primarily as a theater or auditorium with provision for taping or live broadcasting. This would be a facility apart from the radio station.

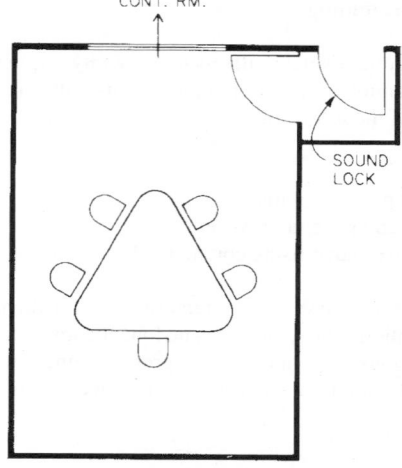

**Fig. 2. Interview studio**

Floor areas for studios may range from 100 square feet for the minimum studio (news, recorded music) to 270 square feet for a six-person studio suitable for panel discussion.

## Control Room

The control room, as the name implies, contains a control console and other electronic equipment for monitoring and controlling the output from a studio. In addition, it may house tape players, turntables, and automatic switching devices as well as a small amount of disk and tape storage. Plan dimensions are dictated by the equipment to be used; occupants are one or two persons. Figure 3 shows some of the devices that may be contained in a well-equipped control room.

Many smaller stations have so-called "combo" operations, in which the engineer doubles as announcer, disk jockey, etc. In this case, the control room is also a studio and has the same sound requirements. Even when the control room does not contain a live microphone, sound characteristics are still important. The technician monitoring the program must make critical decisions based on what she hears from the loudspeakers, and any distortion caused by room acoustics will be reflected in improper adjustment of controls.

## Equipment Storage

Electronic equipment is usually mounted in cabinets or racks, roughly the size of file cabinets. In a large station, they may be grouped for easy maintenance into a single equipment or rack room. In smaller stations, they will be located in the control rooms. In either case, access for servicing is essential. Racks are sometimes used to form the outside wall of one of the control rooms, but this is not suitable for the combo arrangement in which one room serves as both studio and control room.

## Maintenance Shop

The maintenance shop is an electronics workshop and must be convenient to control and rack rooms. In addition to the usual work-benches and test equipment, space must be available for spare parts and portable equipment for use on "remotes" (off-premises broadcasting). A 10- by 12-foot space is adequate for a small or medium-sized station. Usual occupants: one.

## Telephone Equipment Storage

In addition to the telephone equipment associated with voice communications, switchboard, etc., considerable floor space is required for telephone equipment associated with audio (sound) communications lines, including transmission to the transmitter area and receipt of incoming transmissions such as those from a radio network, etc. Local telephone company representatives should be consulted for requirements early in the planning process.

Automation equipment may be located in a control room or in a separate space. There are no special listening requirements. However, if the equipment includes card punching or tabulating equipment (used to program the automated switchers), the room can be noisy, and acoustical treatment on ceiling and walls is desirable. A glass partition will permit monitoring of the equipment while helping to contain the noise. No standards can be given for room size as this depends entirely on the equipment to be used.

## OTHER BROADCASTING FACILITIES

The following facilities will not be required in all stations, but where used, they are usually closely associated with the on-air facilities.

## Newsroom

Similar in appearance and function to the city room of a newspaper, the newsroom is the central point for gathering and editing of news stories prior to broadcast. In some cases, news may be broadcast directly from the newsroom. Special tables permit close contact between correspondents and conserve space. Newsrooms will include television monitors, an assignment board, bulletin board, and mailboxes. In some cases, particularly in large networks, separate

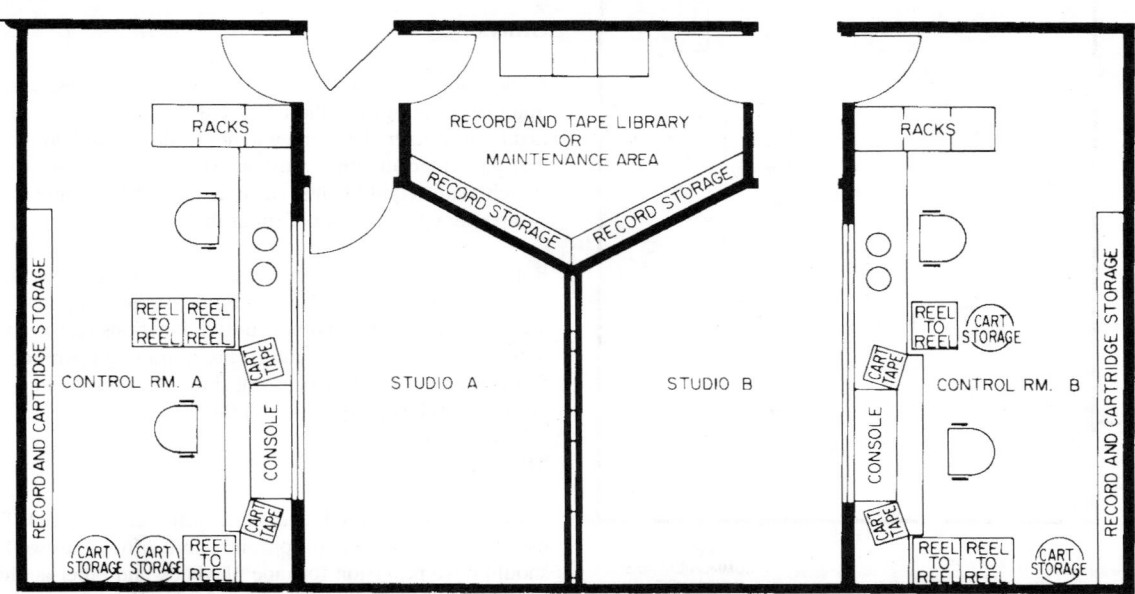

**Fig. 3. Two-studio layout for a music-oriented FM station (designed by Fenwick S. LaBoiteaux)**

offices are required for certain correspondents and writers; these should open onto or be not far from the newsroom.

From a construction standpoint, design of the newsroom is similar to a large, very busy office. Even where news is broadcast directly from the newsroom, the background noise is usually not objectionable. (At least one all-news station plays recorded news-printer sound as background to its news broadcasts.) News facilities will vary depending on the extent of news operations at the station:

- The most elementary is the "rip-and-read" operation, so-called because the announcer or disk jockey leaves her post only long enough to tear off a sheet from the wire service teleprinter, which she then reads on the air. Here, the only "facility" is a printer in a closet.
- A typical music and news station might have a news staff of five, most of whom would be out on assignments. A room about 15 by 25 feet with three desks would suffice.
- An all-news station might have a staff of about 14, plus an editor. Desk space for each staff person is necessary. This type of newsroom is shown in Fig. 4.

An important feature of the newsroom is the bank of teleprinters representing various wire services, weather, etc. These must be readily available to the newsroom, but since they are noisy, are often enclosed in a separate room acoustically treated to reduce clatter.

If operating personnel insist on locating the printers within the newsroom, consider enclosing them in a sound-proof container with hinged covers. Telex or TWX machines should also be isolated, if possible.

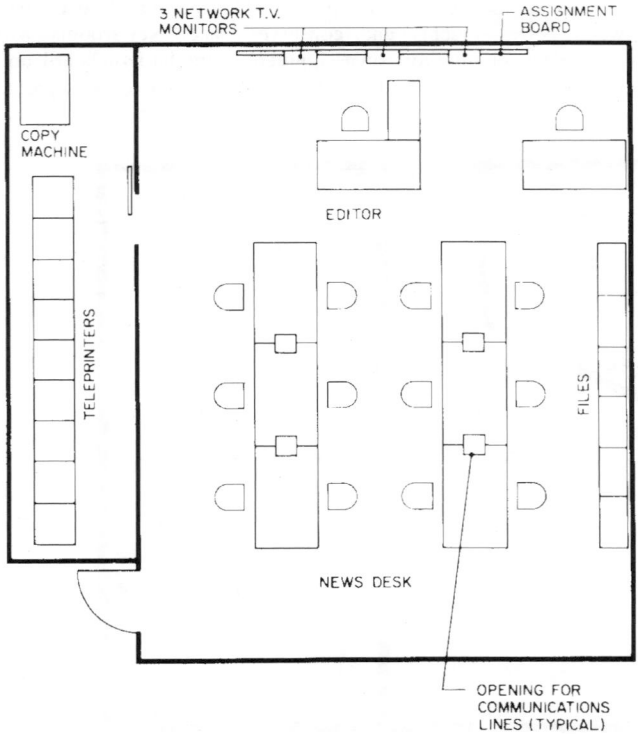

**Fig. 4. Newsroom for all-news station**

### Tape and Record Library

Ideally, the CD, tape and record library should be convenient to the studio, especially for music-oriented stations. However, since the studio area may be congested, it may be necessary to locate this elsewhere; the extent to which this can be tolerated is very much a variable and depends on local operating practices (Fig. 3).

For a station featuring popular contemporary music, a space 10 by 15 feet should suffice. A station with a very extensive library of classical music may require a much larger area. Normally, the library will be used by only one or two persons at a time.

Standard cabinets used for storing 12-inch diameter long-playing records can accommodate approximately 60 records per foot of shelf, allowing enough space to permit easy insertion and removal. Tapes come in three forms: reels, cartridges and cassettes. Reels are stored in cardboard boxes; cassettes and cartridges do not require a separate container. CDs offer the most compact storage of recorded material, and can be stored in conventional shelving or specially designed and fabricated CD racks.

As part of the library, or closely adjacent to it, should be facilities for auditing or listening to tape and records. Again, layout is a function of operating practices. If station personnel will use earphones, listening can be done in the library itself; if they insist on loudspeakers, the listening rooms should be separate and isolated acoustically from surrounding spaces, particularly studios. Provision for one or two listening positions is sufficient.

### Editing Room

Most program editing is done in the control room. However, some larger stations can effectively utilize an editing room, which is a facility akin to a control room but somewhat less sophisticated acoustically. Editing rooms are usually a part of the studio complex.

### SUPPORT FACILITIES

### Offices

Station offices will include facilities for executives, sales, programming, accounting, scheduling, operations, etc. Planning is similar to that for any other office and will not be discussed here, except to note that particular attention must be given to mailroom and telephone switchboard requirements, since activity in these areas may be high compared with a business firm of the same size.

Relation of offices to studios will depend on the size of the station and its method of operation. Some stations operate with sales, accounting, and other administrative functions remote from the studios (even in another building). Programming operations, and other functions related to broadcasting should be convenient to the studios but need not be contiguous with them.

### Meeting Rooms

For most stations, good meeting facilities are essential. They will be used for contact with sponsors and public officials as well as staff and should have provision for tape playback and other audiovisual presentations. Some stations make effective use of a conference room designed to double as a studio.

## Reception Areas

Planning and design of reception areas depends on whether visitors are limited to persons on official business or will include the general public, schoolchildren, etc. If the latter, a large lobby is desirable where groups on tour can assemble and be met by a guide. The reception area must control access effectively while still providing a welcome to bona fide visitors. Unless a receptionist or guard is on duty 24 hours a day, after-hours access presents a difficult problem. One solution is card access (similar to the system used in some parking garages) for night operating personnel, plus a night bell for other after-hours visitors. The receptionist may double as switchboard operator.

## PERSONNEL FACILITIES

### Rest Rooms

Plan toilets and rest rooms as for an office. Consider after-hours access. If public tours of the facility are anticipated, size toilet facilities for the visitors.

### Cafeteria

Need for a cafeteria depends on the size of the station and the availability of other food service facilities. However, even if a complete cafeteria is not to be provided, consideration should be given to a snack bar with vending machines. This is particularly important for after-hours use when other food service facilities are not available or for operating personnel whose duties do not permit them to leave the station. The snack bar can do double duty as a lounge.

### Parking

Parking needs are a function of local conditions, including the availability of public transportation. Planning is similar to that for offices. Parking needs may include the following:

    Station employees
    Visitors
    General public
    Station vehicles

### Facilities for "Remote" Operation

Availability of lightweight, portable recording equipment has led to an increase in the amount of programming material originated outside the station. It is likely that this type of activity will increase and most stations will have one or more vehicles specially equipped to handle remote (off-station) operations.

Facility needs include garage space for station vehicles and storage space for portable equipment used in remote operations. Storage should be convenient to vehicle parking areas and safe from pilferage. The garage should have AC power, and space should be available for minimum maintenance or troubleshooting of mobile equipment that cannot readily be removed from the vehicle.

## LAYOUT PLANNING

### On-Air Facilities

The on-air facilities form the heart of the station and should receive primacy in planning. Since these facilities share common utilities and personnel and require sound isolation from the rest of the building, they are usually grouped together in a tight "island." This makes for operating convenience but is inflexible for changes.

### Number of Studios

Two studios and two control rooms permit one studio to be used for editing or recording while the other is on-air. Some small stations get by with a single studio, using a second microphone position in the control room. Similarly, automation may obviate the need for the second studio. A larger station's needs can be determined only by careful study of its operations, including the amount of original programming planned.

### Layout

Layout of the on-air complex requires understanding of the station's method of operation. Usually, direct visual contact is desired between studio and control room. Flexibility is provided by making it possible for each control room to handle more than one studio. Studio doors should not open directly into adjoining rooms or general corridors; where this is unavoidable, provide a sound lock at the entrance.

Although this is undesirable acoustically, operating personnel may require studio windows to the outside, either to permit the announcer to observe weather conditions or to give passersby a view of operations. A good solution in this case is use of a glassed-in corridor between studio and outer wall. Figure 5 illustrates a station where this system was employed.

### Sound Isolation

There is an important trade-off between space requirements and complexity of construction. Isolation between adjoining rooms may be accomplished by using dividing partitions or by separating the two rooms involved. While cost is lower, the second scheme requires more floor area. Figure 6 shows a hypothetical layout for the on-air facility using corridors for sound isolation.

### Allowance for Growth

Expansion of the on-air facility after the station is in operation is both difficult and costly. Accordingly, it is well to anticipate the need for an additional on-air facility. As an example, a room can be built to studio standards but used as a listening room, library, or office until it is required for studio purposes.

### Three-dimensional Planning

Planning of on-air facilities requires consideration of the third dimension. In studios, maintenance of a minimum inside height of about 9 to 10 feet is important for proper acoustics. At the same time, space of 4 feet above the ceiling is desirable to accommodate ducts and other ceiling utilities.

### Newsroom

The newsroom must be accessible to the studio complex. A news-oriented station may insist on direct visual contact between newsroom and studio for signaling of "hot" news items. One solution is to place the newsroom on the opposite side of a corridor to the studio, with windows in both walls.

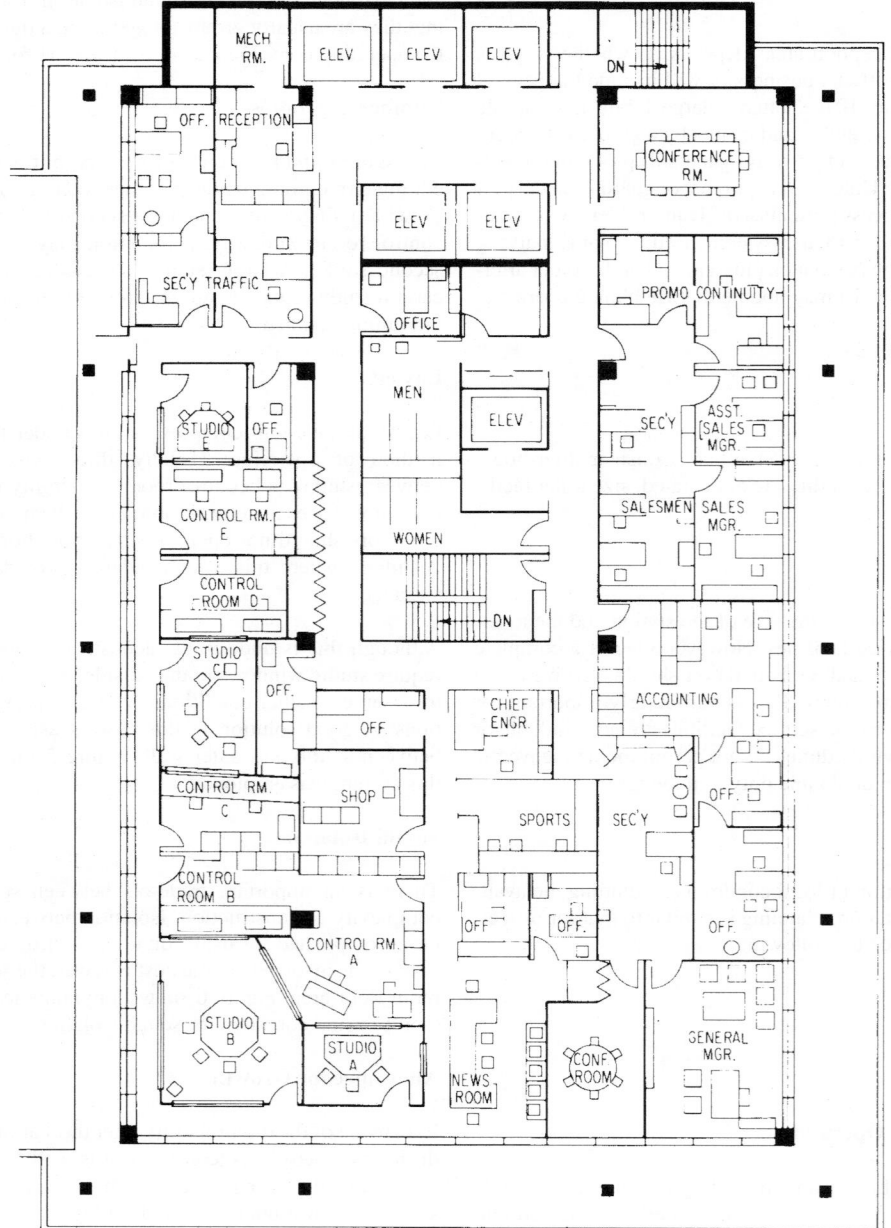

**Fig. 5. Floor plan of a station serving a large metropolitan area. Files, storage, and copier are on another floor (not shown)**

### Circulation

Circulation should be around, rather than through, the on-air complex. Visitors can view operations through soundproof windows. Corridors can be used to provide separation between the studio complex and adjoining spaces as well as a sound lock between the technical spaces.

### Studio Acoustics

Acoustical design of studios, control and editing rooms requires the services of a specialist, particularly for the architect unfamiliar with

such work. However, this section will touch on some of the points about which he should be consulted.

### Objectives of Acoustical Design

Basically, there are two objectives in the acoustical design of on-air facilities. The first is to attenuate or exclude unwanted sound from the room, and the second is to provide the desired acoustical characteristics within the room for the sounds reaching the microphone. The latter requirement has been simplified by extensive use of prerecorded music, since acoustical requirements for speech are less critical. Attenuation is still critical, particularly in stations

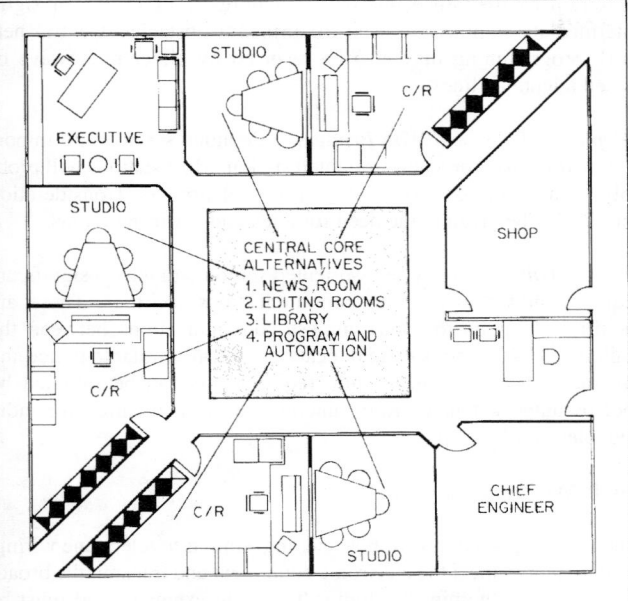

**Fig. 6. Hypothetical layout for a radio studio built around a central core (designed by Fenwick S. LaBoiteaux)**

offering rock, where listening in adjoining rooms is done at high sound levels.

Each of these objectives will be considered in turn. In either case, the key planning factor is the nature of the broadcasting operations. It is most important that station management participate in setting acoustical design targets.

Acoustical design for control rooms is similar to that for studios. The objective is to have the sound (from loudspeakers or earphones) reaching the control operator's ear match that originated in the studio (or prerecorded) as closely as possible.

### Room-to-Room Isolation

*Attenuation:* To exclude sounds, each studio and control room is designed as a separate "envelope," independent of the basic building structure. The first step is to establish, for each room, the permitted level of residual noise, usually expressed in noise criteria (NC) levels. Typical NC levels are 20 for studios and 25 for control rooms.

The next step is to identify sources of hostile sound and to establish required room-to-room attenuation factors. Attenuation, expressed in decibels, represents the sound power loss from one space to another and determines the design of partitions, hung ceilings, windows, etc., and the need for independent "floating" floors. It should be established only after the most careful consultation with station management. As an example, if adjacent studios will be used only for news and interviews, the room-to-room attenuation may be about 40 dB—using construction similar to a good private office. Where music is played loudly, required attenuation can reach 60 dB or even higher, with significant effect on cost and complexity of construction.

On the other hand, planning should also consider future program changes, since it is very difficult to upgrade a studio without total reconstruction.

*Floor Isolation:* Successful radio studios have been built using a common floor slab. Again, this is very much a function of the sound levels expected within the rooms. Where extreme sound levels are unavoidable, each studio must be placed on its own floating floor supported on springs or neoprene isolators. Note that where used, the floating floor will also support the entire studio envelope: inner walls and ceiling.

*Doors:* Doors are the Achilles' heel of every studio installation. A sound lock is an arrangement of two sound doors separated by a small vestibule. It is analogous to a light lock at the entrance to a photographic darkroom in that it prevents accidental sound leakage into a studio if the door is opened while the studio is in use. "Hostile" sounds, such as those that may become a problem when there are two separate studios, should be separated by at least two doors which should, if possible, not be opposite to each other.

Doors should be sound rated and equipped with gaskets or seals, including drop seals at the threshold. They should have hydraulic closers and handles (instead of latches) and should be provided with small viewing ports.

### Design Details

- Windows must be tightly gasketed. Multiple-pane windows are common; whether they are actually needed is a function of room-to-room attenuation. For most purposes, two panes are sufficient; but to be effective, the two panes must be in independent frames and must be of different thickness to prevent resonance.
- Fluorescent lighting, if used, should have remote ballasts.
- Particular attention must be paid to penetrations through the envelope; entries for ductwork, conduit, cable trays, and other services must all be designed and not left to the contractor if they are not to defeat the carefully planned envelope.
- Corridors within the on-air complex should be carpeted to minimize foot-impact noise. Consideration should also be given to carpeting areas above the studio complex. Opinion differs on the need for carpeting within the on-air facilities themselves. While absorbing foot noise, it makes movement of equipment difficult.
- Studio tabletops should be of cork or felt to minimize paper-shuffling noise, and to prevent unwanted reflections of the "talent's" voice.

### Room Acoustics

Room acoustics require the proper balance between "hard" (sound-reflecting) and "soft" (sound-absorbing) surfaces, which is a function of the type of sound (speech, music, etc.), the room size, and the type of microphones that will be used. The tendency is towards very "dead" (absorbent) studios and control rooms. (If reverberation is desired, it can be added electronically.) Absorbent wall treatment and closely held microphones reduce the problem of reflection from parallel, hard surfaces that used to require skewing of opposite walls. Highly directional microphones may also prevent unwanted echos or "slap" from hard glass surfaces. Where a naturally "live" (reverberant) studio is required, walls should be skewed.

It is also important that sound absorption be uniform over the frequency spectrum. This is done by spacing out absorbent material such as fiberglass over a portion of the walls and ceiling.

A traditional rule of thumb for studio acoustical design is that the height, width, and length should be in the ratio of 3:4:5.

## UTILITIES AND SERVICES

### Electricity

*Power Source:* For a radio station, the most important utility is a reliable power source. Incoming service should be stable as to both voltage and frequency and free from interruptions.

*Technical Power:* This should be fed from electronic equipment or a separate "technical" or "clean" power feeder. No lights or building loads should be placed on this feeder. Where voltage fluctuations are expected, provide voltage regulators for the technical power feeder. Secondary wiring from a technical power panel within the room to the electronic equipment is usually part of the radio equipment installation, but the architect may have to provide the necessary conduits or raceways.

*Emergency Power:* Even with a reliable power source, outages and "blackouts" are still possible. The most common emergency power source is a diesel engine generator equipped with controls to start automatically when voltage drops to a predetermined level. An automatic transfer switch shifts from normal to emergency power and prevents simultaneous connection to both sources. A brief off-air period can usually be tolerated, so that the cost of no-break power is not warranted. If the station is a member of the government-sponsored Emergency Broadcasting System (EBS), it will require a two-week fuel supply.

### Air Conditioning

Air conditioning is required in the studio's control and equipment rooms to protect sensitive equipment, as well as for comfort, and it is usually provided in other areas in keeping with modern practices.

Special consideration must be given to acoustical requirements to prevent ductwork from carrying unwanted sounds from one room to another and to exclude fan and duct noises. Proper acoustical design of the air-conditioning system starts with equipment selection and its isolation from the building structure. It includes careful duct routing to avoid short circuiting of sound from one area to another with mains located outside the on-air complex. It also includes proper use of sound traps, turning vanes, flexible connections, and duct insulation to remove residual duct noises. Finally, careful attention to wall penetration is essential.

Air distribution inside these areas must be at low enough velocity to keep air and duct noises within the noise criteria (NC) levels selected for the space. As a rule of thumb, air velocities in branch ducts should not exceed 400 feet per minute at the point where the duct enters the studio. Velocity out of the diffusing element should not exceed 300 feet per minute; 200 feet per minute is preferred. In addition to maintaining this low velocity, diffusers must also be of a type that will not in themselves generate noise.

### Communications

*Audio Signal Feeds:* Except where studios and transmitter facilities share a single facility, broadcasting signals are transmitted from the studios to the transmitter by microwave, leased telephone lines, or a combination. Where microwave is to be used, a study must be made

of terrain profile, since microwave requires a direct line of sight. Intermediate stations are used to surmount obstacles. Central network programming may also be received by either microwave or leased telephone lines.

*Telephone, Telex, and Wire Printers:* Telephone services are important, particularly for a news-oriented station. Most stations will probably require one or more wire service teleprinters. Consideration should also be given to the need for telex and fax installations.

*Point-to-Point Radio:* A news-oriented station will have a significant requirement for local radio communications facilities. These are facilities for point-to-point wireless communications between the station and its reporters in field locations and are similar to police and fire radio. Usually transmission requirements can be satisfied by roof-mounted antennas. Roof antennas are also required for radio and television pickup.

### Audio Wiring

Audio wiring is the low-voltage cabling, similar to telephone wiring, used to interconnect the electronic equipment and transmit the broadcasting signals within the studio. It is quite extensive and must be considered in design. Audio wiring may be distributed by one or more of the following:

- Floor trenches with removable covers
- Underfloor duct, conduit, or raceway
- Hollow, elevated floors similar to those used in computer rooms
- Overhead cable trays or raceways
- Horizontal baseboard raceways

Floor channels and underfloor ducts do not lend themselves to future changes in equipment layout. Cable trays or "ladders" are the most flexible from the maintenance standpoint, since cables are easily removed and inserted but are acceptable only if permitted by local codes. Cable system routing must be carefully checked for the interference with ducts and lights (if in the ceiling) and to avoid compromising the acoustical "envelope" surrounding each studio and control room.

### Other Systems

Following is a brief checklist of some of the other systems that may be required:

- Compressed-air and central vacuums systems. Large stations and networks may require central systems serving control rooms, rack rooms, and maintenance shops. They are used for cleaning and general maintenance.
- Loudspeaker system
- TV monitor system
- Clock system.

## RADIO TRANSMITTER FACILITIES

Radio transmitters may be attended or unattended. In some smaller stations, transmitter and studios share a single building; but for AM facilities, this usually means a less than optimum location for one or the other. The following discussion assumes that studio and transmitter facilities are separate.

Besides the transmitter building, the main feature of a transmitter installation is the broadcasting antenna. For AM stations, the antenna is usually one or more radiating towers. For FM, the tower serves as a support on which a separate radiating antenna is mounted.

## AM Transmitters

For an AM transmitter, the main structures will include the towers and their foundations, the guy anchorages (usually three, spaced radially at 120 degrees about each tower base), and the transmitter building, which will be discussed subsequently. There is also a small building, of concrete or block, at the base of the tower, known as the "tuning house" or "coupling house," which houses equipment for matching the transmitter and its transmission line to the impedance of the antenna.

An important but less obvious feature of AM installations is the ground system. A copper-mesh screen, about 40 by 40 feet, is centered at the base of the tower. Buried copper cables extend outward radially from the mesh every three degrees. These are generally 6 to 12 inches below ground surface.

If the antenna is "directional," i.e., designed to broadcast in a particular, nonuniform pattern, multiple antennas (an "array") must be used instead of a single tower. Tower height is a function of the station's assigned wavelength, with most AM towers between one-quarter and five-eighths of a wavelength in height. As an example, a station with a frequency of 600 kilohertz (kHz) (1 kHz = 1,000 cycles per second) has a wavelength of 1,640 feet and could have a tower height of between 400 and 1,050 feet.

Because of the cost and land area required for an AM transmitter, some competing stations have joined forces to operate from a single tower. This arrangement calls for highly specialized design of the tower, and services of a professional radio engineer become essential.

## FM Transmitters

FM facilities are limited to the antenna, which is usually mounted on a tower or mast, plus the transmitter itself. It is common for several FM stations to share a single mast or tower as well as for FM antennas to be mounted on a TV or AM antenna tower.

The main requirement for an FM antenna is height to clear the surrounding terrain. FCC regulations control the relationship between height and allowable broadcasting power, which depends on the class of station. Most FM antennas are between 200 and 1,000 feet high.

## SITE SELECTION

### Location

Transmitter location is determined by antenna requirements, which differ sharply for AM and FM. For AM transmitters, a rural location is usually necessary to achieve the required ground conductivity and avoid interference with reception in nearby homes, as well as to find the space needed for the ground system. FM antennas, on the other hand, require mainly height and have been successfully located in cities, on top of tall buildings.

### Area Required

For an AM station, the site must be large enough to contain the antenna array plus the guys and ground radials. Tower guys require a radius of about two-thirds the tower height, while the ground radials should be about half the length of the station's wavelength. In the

example given above of a station with a frequency of 600 kHz, the ground radials for a single tower should be about 820 feet long.

For an FM station, the site need only be large enough to contain the tower base (or the guys, in the case of a guyed tower) plus a small transmitter room. Thus, a tall building that can support the required mast makes a good FM transmitter site. A TV tower that can carry an additional antenna is also a good location.

### Technical Considerations

Site selection for a transmitter facility is highly technical and is best entrusted to a consulting engineer specializing in this kind of work unless the station itself possesses the necessary expertise. In addition to studies of ground conductivity (for AM), careful analysis must be made of potential interference with other stations, all in accordance with detailed FCC regulations. Air traffic patterns must also be considered, as must local zoning regulations.

### Other Considerations

In addition to the necessary technical considerations, the site should have:

- All-weather access
- Reliable power supply
- Reliable telephone service
- Parking space

It should lend itself to proper security. It should be possible to provide water and sanitary sewage either from public utilities or on-site facilities.

### Site Planning

The ground area required by the spread of the guys and the need to accommodate the ground radial system can be quite extensive. Some of this acreage can be sold or leased out provided provision is made in the lease or deed for protection and maintenance of the ground system. Similarly, the area between the tower base and the guy anchorages, which is largely unused, can be devoted to grazing or other uses that will not disturb the ground system.

Safety should be considered in locating the transmitter building. Although structural tower failures are rare, collapses caused by accident (aircraft) or sabotage are not unknown. If possible, the transmitter building should be so placed that, in the event of such a catastrophe, the tower would be likely to fall clear of the building. An AM transmitter may be located some distance from the antenna.

FM transmitters must be as close to the tower as possible, to minimize line losses. Concern over continuity of broadcasting has led some stations to provide an auxiliary antenna. This is costly both in terms of construction and land area. Perhaps a better solution is an agreement with other stations permitting some kind of dual use of their facilities in the event of an emergency.

## CONSTRUCTION

### General

*Grounding:* For an AM facility, all structures within the transmitter area, including the transmitter building, must be properly grounded and tied into the ground radial system. In concrete buildings, reinforcing steel must be made electrically continuous and bonded to the ground radial system.

*Soil Condition:* AM antennas have been located in marshy or waterfront land, to take advantage of good soil conductivity. This may require pile foundations for towers and buildings. In swampy areas, consideration must be given to possible land subsidence which could affect the grounding system.

### Towers

A ground-supported tower is usually designed as a slender mast, pinned at the base and braced by one or more levels of guys. Fixed-base or cantilevered towers (without guys) are now used only for masts on the roofs of buildings. The tapered shape of a self-supporting tower is also undesirable for an AM transmitter where, as previously indicated, the tower itself is the radiating element. Electronic considerations will determine the height and general arrangement of the tower.

AM towers, which are usually of steel, are given a heavy coating of zinc galvanizing. This serves to protect the tower, but its primary purpose is to provide electrical conductivity. At radio frequencies, the "current" flows mainly along the outside periphery of the tower. Sections of the tower must be electrically bonded together for the tower to function properly.

FM towers serve only to support the separate antennas and are designed purely for structural considerations. All towers require aviation marking (alternate white and orange striping) and obstruction lighting; details are found in FCC regulations.

### Transmitter Building

In addition to space for the transmitter itself, there should be space for the associated equipment racks, maintenance, spare parts storage, and toilet facilities. Even an "unattended" facility is occupied periodically for inspection and maintenance. If the station is quite remote, minimal kitchen facilities and a shower may be desirable.

The amount of equipment that must be contained in the transmitter building depends on the station's assigned operating power. This can vary from 250 watts for very small stations to 50 kilowatts for the larger commercial stations. For the larger stations, equipment may be quite heavy, so that floor loads must be checked, particularly when locating the transmitter in an existing building.

In cold climates a carport may be desirable to protect the operator and his vehicle against ice falling from the tower. This can be a more serious hazard than it may at first seem.

When two or more stations share a single antenna system, the need for separate transmitter buildings or rooms will be determined by local operating preferences; both systems work well. Fig. 7 shows the layout for an unattended transmitter in a rural location.

### Utilities

*Communications:* Program signals may be brought to the transmitter by leased telephone lines, microwave, or a combination. Microwave requires a series of direct lines of sight.

*Power:* Some transmitters have two primary power services from different substations and feeders for greater reliability; usually automatic switching between services is included. Emergency power is required for Emergency Broadcasting System (EBS) stations and may be desirable for others, particularly where the primary power source is subject to interruptions. If provided, it should be sized to handle minimal lighting, tower obstruction lighting, and transmitter ventilation as well as the transmitter itself.

*Heating, Ventilating, Air Conditioning:* The transmitter generates considerable heat, which must be removed by mechanical ventilation. This system consists of a filtered intake with a ducted exhaust connected directly to the transmitter. Dampers are arranged so as to reduce the amount of outside air during the winter and make use of the transmitter heat. Supplemental heat is usually required to maintain comfortable working conditions in winter. Air conditioning is not required unless the transmitter plant will be occupied for a large part of each day.

*Lighting:* Good lighting (office levels) should be provided to facilitate housekeeping and maintenance.

*Site Development:* Since an AM tower is dangerous when in operation, its base must be fenced, as should each of the guy anchor blocks, to discourage tampering with the guys. Fencing of the entire area and security lighting may also be desirable. Planting or other erosion protection for the ground around the tower should be provided.

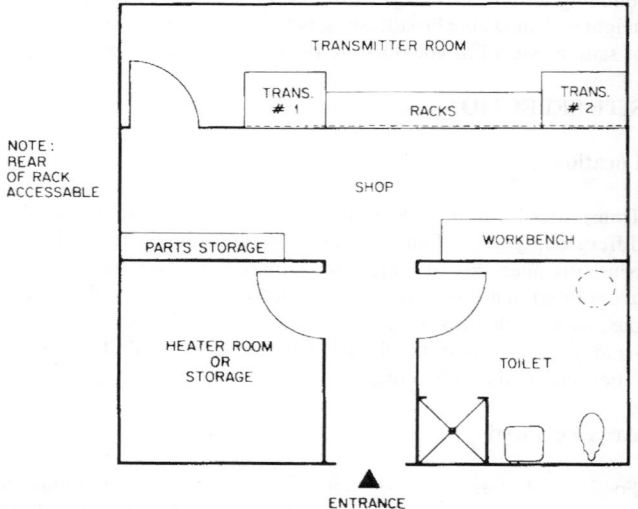

**Fig. 7. Small AM or FM transmitter building**

**Fig. 1. Newbaker Funeral Home, Blairstown, NJ**

# FUNERAL HOMES

## GENERAL COMMENTS

1. The information included here highlights the unique aspects of the funeral home building type. As with any project design, common planning techniques need to be incorporated.

2. Often the structures used as funeral homes are former residences. This function is appropriate due to the common desire of funeral homes to project an image and feel of comfort and warmth.

3. In the planning of funeral homes, the step-by-step process of receiving the body to its ultimately being taken from the home should be the central thrust for the design of the facility.

4. Another critical aspect of the funeral home, which is often overlooked, is creating a building that provides appropriate spaces, whether formal or informal, for social interaction of the home's guests.

5. Future expansion of the building should always be anticipated and can include the potential enlargement of the chapel and visitation areas, space for additional preparation equipment, as well as additional staff and increased parking accommodations.

6. Since it is often the elderly who are the most frequent guests to a funeral home, special attention should be given to the ease of movement through the facility and meeting their needs during a visit. The design principle commonly known as "universal design" can be particularly important for these facilities, and they should be designed to meet the Americans with Disabilities Act Accessibility Guidelines.

7. In smaller funeral home facilities, certain functions listed separately below can be combined for greater efficiency.

## THE SITE

### Location

The site for a funeral home should be accessible by the public and should be easily found by out-of-town guests. Consideration should also be given that hospitals and other individuals might find the view of a mortuary objectionable. Access to cemeteries and churches should also be readily available.

### Lot Size

In order to accommodate the building with ample parking and landscaping, and to provide for possible future expansion, a site of two acres in area with at least 300 feet of frontage is recommended as minimum.

### Parking

An ample and efficient parking layout (Fig. 1) is essential and should accommodate processional departure following a funeral service. It should provide at least one parking space for every four seats of capacity plus one space reserved for the clergy. The most convenient spaces can be designated for family members and for the required accessible spaces. Consideration of drainage and snow removal should be made as well. Separate parking for staff can be provided near the service entrance.

*Reviewer:* John W. Dreiling, AIA.
Prepared from Frank Memoli's adaptation of the "Checklist for Mortuary Planning," by Dr. Charles H. Nichols, National Foundation of Funeral Service, Evanston, Ill.

Fig. 2. Service entrance, Newbaker Funeral Home, Blairstown, NJ

Fig. 3. Signage at Newbaker Funeral Home, Blairstown, NJ

### Service Entrance

A discreetly located or screened service area (Fig. 2) should provide for receiving bodies, caskets, flowers, and other deliveries. An area for washing hearses, vans, and cars should be located here as well.

### Site Lighting and Signage

Since the majority of visitations occur at night, ample lighting of the parking area and the paths to and from the building should be provided. An appropriate and well positioned site sign (Fig. 3) will assist guests in finding the facility. Lighting for the sign and the exterior of the building can also be provided.

### THE BUILDING

### General Comments

All doorways through which caskets will pass must be at least 48 inches wide, and the corridor system must be free of sharp, narrow turns.

If the facility allows for cremation, an area adjacent to the cremation equipment with a window for viewing, with blinds, should be provided.

### Reception Area

This area (Fig. 4) is a focal point of public activity in the funeral home and, while it affords access to all other areas (Fig. 5), it should project an air of comfort and welcome. In the event that no foyer or vestibule is practical, this area will serve as a buffer against weather, dirt, and noise. Bear in mind that a lot of casual conversation occurs in this area and should be accommodated.

Since the building is often staffed by one person, a vantage point should be provided to see any activity at the entry doors. It is also helpful to have other office related functions adjoining this space.

A form of signaling device, such as an intercom, is useful to be notified of deliveries at another part of the building or to let another staff member know they have a visitor.

Fig. 4. Main entrance, Newbaker Funeral Home, Blairstown, NJ

## Visitation or Reposing Rooms

These rooms should be readily accessible from the preparation room and the reception area and should be at least 12 by 14 feet in dimension. The rooms may be of different sizes but must all be sufficiently flexible to double as chapels and to accommodate a variety of religious rites.

Where possible, they should be adjacent to one another, separated by folding partitions, for use in combination. When used separately, each room should have reasonable privacy and be individually accessible for guests.

Each visitation room must provide for attractive casket placement with spotlights overhead, and floral displays around.

## Chapel

The chapel must be directly accessible from the reception area and convenient to the parking area for the post-service movement of casket, flowers, etc. A minimum clear ceiling height of 10 feet-6 inches is desired. The space should be relatively free of columns and other structural elements. A center aisle with a minimum width of 5 feet is needed.

The chapel must accommodate all types of religious services, and be void of any denominational symbols. A dignified air of reverence and comfort should be apparent.

Provision must be made for a pleasing setting for the casket, a pulpit or rostrum, flower arrangements and memorial stand, which should occupy a dominant focal point.

An area for unobtrusive but effective video and audio recording needs to be incorporated. Also, an area for the storage of chairs and other necessary equipment should be readily accessible.

## Family Room

The family room should be screened from public view in the chapel, have a private entrance and exit, allow the family to see the casket, and yet enable the family to be aware of what is going on within the chapel.

It should be more than large enough for the average extended family and should be provided with the necessary accommodations to occasionally serve as a visitation room.

Restrooms and first-aid facilities should be nearby.

## Minister's Lounge

This quiet, secluded room should be conveniently located near the front of the chapel.

It should be a place for members of the clergy to prepare for the service and to robe and disrobe.

Toilet facilities should be in close proximity.

## Audio/Visual Room

This room should be located adjacent to the chapel and serve as the control point for all amplified sound in the chapel, as well as the recording of services by audio or video tape.

## Preparation Room

This room should be located well apart from public areas of the building, convenient in terms of movement of bodies, and readily accessible to the visitation rooms. If the preparation room is not on the ground floor, an elevator large enough for a casket should be located nearby.

Allow an area of approximately 14 by 16 feet for each one-table room.

Each room should contain sufficient cabinet space for lockable chemical storage, a sink or drain bowl at the foot of each table, an arrangement for an aspirator, hot and cold water sources at the head of each table, convenient sink and sterilizer location, cleanup facilities (possibly including a shower), and adequate clothing hooks and storage space.

Floors should be of tile or vinyl with the surface extending partially up the walls of the room. Floor drains should be provided.

A special exhaust system is needed to move ample air and prevent the build-up of fumes.

Wherever possible, windows should be omitted.

Convenient sanitary facilities for refuse disposal are required.

A provision for emergency power and lighting may be desirable.

## Dressing Room

Directly adjacent to the preparation room, the dressing room serves as the area to do final preparations of the body prior to viewing.

Clothing hooks or rods should be provided for clothing to be used.

A countertop with sink is needed for make-up and accessories.

Enough space is needed to allow the transfer of the body from a gurney to a casket.

## Business Office

This area should be planned as the central control post for the entire operation. It should be readily but separately available for those who come to conduct business only.

Typical activities that occur in this office will be typing, filing, bookkeeping, mailing, accounting, etc. A safe will be required, as will sufficient storage space for business records and supplies.

## Arrangement Office

This office should be private enough to be free of all disturbances during the discussion of family arrangements and should afford access to the selection room. It should be separate from the general business office but in reasonable proximity.

The room should contain a closet for storing information as well as coats and have ready access to drinking water and first aid.

## Selection Room

This room should be privately accessible from the arrangement office and conveniently located, especially for elderly or disabled

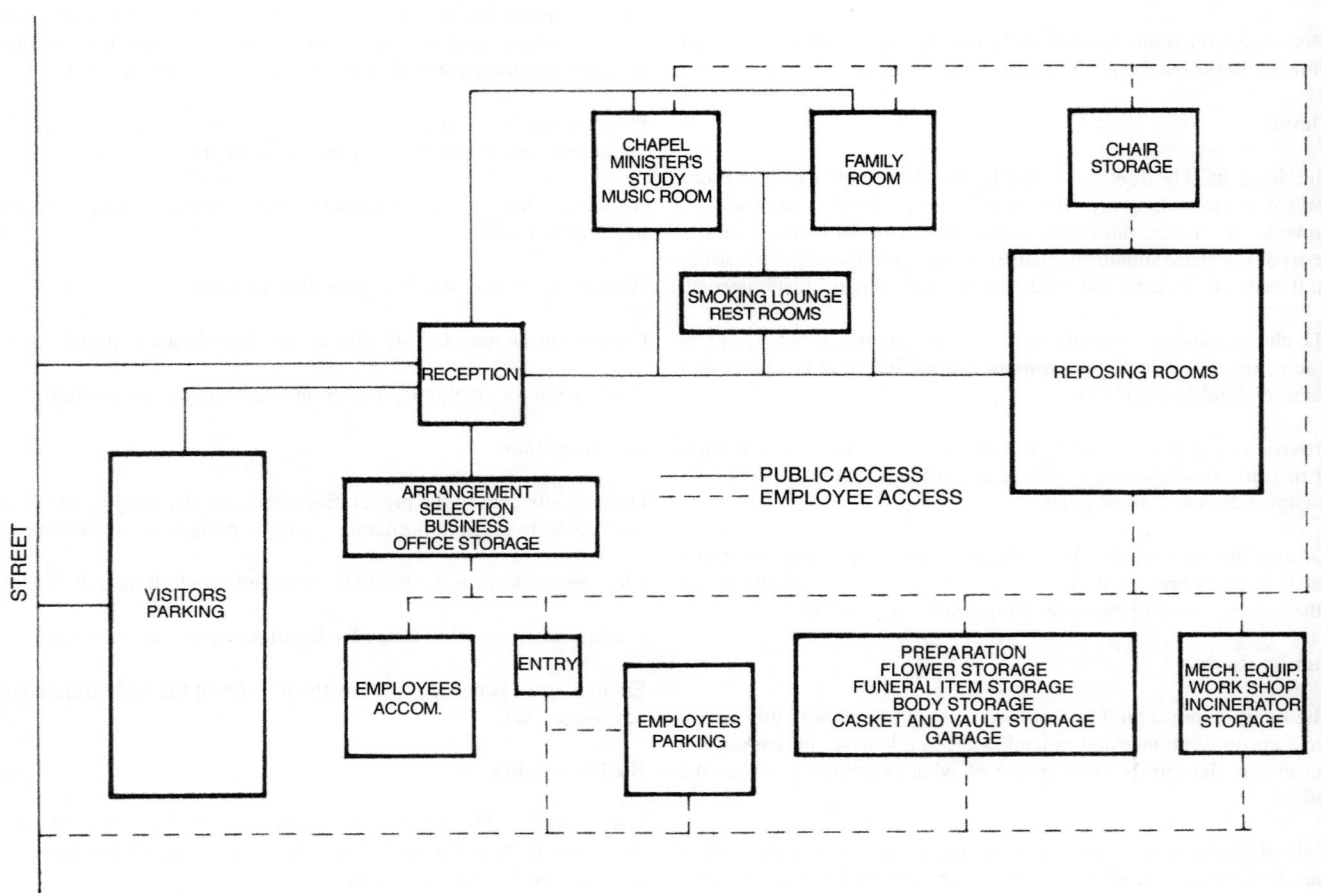

Fig. 5. Funeral home flow diagram

persons. Its function should be clearly marked to prevent unintentional access.

In sizing the selection room, allow approximately 60 square feet per casket for non-stacking displays. The floor space should be free from unnecessary partitions and obstructions and the wall space relatively large and unbroken.

Doors into the room need to be at least 48 inches wide.

Windows are not a necessity, but if provided, they should be screened from public views in.

Sufficient lighting levels should be maintained. Built-in display cabinets for garments and urns may be necessary, as may be a separate vault selection room.

## Flower Room

Located near the service entrance, this room should be equipped to receive and store flower arrangements until their use in the visitation rooms and the chapel.

A sink with ample countertop space should be provided and a series of tall shelves for storing the arrangements.

Storage is needed for vases, racks, and plant stands.

A hard, slip-resistant flooring is recommended.

## Restrooms

These must be conveniently located, especially with respect to the visitation rooms and chapel. Separate rest room facilities may also be provided for the staff near the service entrance area.

A smoking area may also be incorporated and needs adequate ventilation.

## Staff Lounge

Located away from the public areas, this room should be a place where employees can relax during off-duty periods or periods of waiting.

Accommodations can include a staff toilet with shower, television set, phone, kitchen countertop with microwave oven and dining table, and day bed.

## Garage

A multi-vehicle garage is should be provided and equipped for indoor car washing in bad weather, general repairs, and maintenance.

Often a space for a washer and dryer is included.

Allow space behind a hearse for the full width of the rear door to be open and still allow access around the rear of the vehicle.

One end of the garage can be used for the storage of caskets and other miscellaneous equipment such as a lawn mower, garden hoses, rakes, and snow removal equipment (if necessary).

## Utility Rooms

Provide for a mechanical equipment room containing heating and air conditioning equipment, and for the appropriate electrical panel board locations.

A flow diagram (Fig. 5) is helpful in understanding how all the services discussed here interrelate.

# 3
# Hospitality

**Loews Ventana Canyon Resort (Hill Glazier Architects; photo: courtesy of architect)**

# RESTAURANTS AND EATERIES

## SPACE REQUIREMENTS

Adequacy of space will influence building and operating costs and efficiency. When space is too small, labor time and effort are likely to increase and the volume and quality of output decrease. When it is too large, building and maintenance costs are excessive.

Decisions pertaining to space allowance may be strongly affected by the limitations of investment funds and available space. Ample space is sometimes provided by means of low-cost materials and equipment of such inferior quality that they have short and unsatisfactory service life. In other instances, space is restricted to a point where it prohibits profitable volume or the best utilization of labor. Space allowances in relation to investment should be balanced in terms of:

*   proposed permanence of the facility
*   acuteness of need for the specific operation
*   essentials for operating efficiency
*   desirable standards in terms of appearance, sanitation, and good quality of production and service
*   immediate and future costs, depreciation, upkeep, and maintenance

Facts peculiar to the particular establishment should be used as the basis for determining space needs. Requirements will vary for facilities of a given type and volume. Production and storage requirements will be affected by location; type of operation; clientele; frequency of deliveries of supplies; kind of food used, such as fresh, frozen, or canned; and the completeness of processing to be done. The policies of those in charge will have an influence. Certain general information such as numbers to be served, turnover, arrival rate, and type of service will be helpful in deciding dining area needs.

Study is required to clarify immediate and future needs in food production. Choices should be made between meat cutting or portion-ready meats, a baking section or use of commercially baked products, and the use of unprocessed versus processed foods. If enlargement is probable, studies made before the building is planned as to how space may be added and how the initial plan should be designed to minimize ultimate cost will be helpful.

It is well to block out space allowances according to functions that the facility is to perform. Calculate area requirements in terms of:

*   volume and type of service
*   amount and size of equipment to be used
*   number of workers required
*   space for needed supplies
*   suitable traffic area

The dining area location and space allowance are usually determined first, the production areas next in terms of specific relationship to the dining area, and the other sections as required to these. Planners should be careful in accepting general space recommendations. There are many variations.

## DINING AREAS

Space for dining areas is usually based on the number of square feet per person seated times the number of persons seated at one time.

## SPACE REQUIREMENTS

The patron's size and the type and quality of service should be considered. Small children may require only 8 square feet for a type of service in which an adult would need 12 square feet for comfort. A banquet seating allowance might be as little as 10 square feet per seat

*Authors:* Lendal H. Kotschevar and Margaret E. Terrell
*Reviewer:* John Hill, Hill Glasier Architects
*Reference: Food Service Planning,* John Wiley & Sons, New York

and that for a deluxe restaurant as much as 20 square feet. The amount of serving equipment in the dining area and lineup space will influence needs. Lost space must be considered.

The diner's comfort should govern allowance. Crowding is distasteful to many people. It is likely to be tolerated more readily by youngsters than by adults. It is more acceptable in low-cost, quick-service units than in those featuring leisurely dining. Both young and old enjoy having sufficient elbow room and enough space so that dishes of food and beverage are not crowded. Place settings for adults usually allow 24 inches and for children 18 to 20 inches (Table 1).

All of the areas in a dining room used for purposes other than seating are a part of the square footage allowed for seating. This does not include waiting areas, guest facilities, cloakrooms, and other similar areas. Excessive loss or use of space for other than seating in the dining area will, however, increase needs. Structural features of the room should be considered. Width and length of the room, table and chair sizes, and seating arrangements affect capacity.

Service stations may be estimated in the proportion of one small one for every 20 seats or a large central one for every 50 to 60 places. The advisability of having a central serving station will be influenced by the distance of the dining area from the serving area. It is of special value when production and dining are on different floors. Location of the stations will be influenced by plumbing and wiring and whether supplies are delivered mechanically. Small substations for silver, dishes, napery, beverages, ice, butter, and condiments may measure 20 to 24 inches square and 36 to 38 inches high. The size of central stations varies from that for a small enclosed room to that of a screened section measuring approximately 8 to 10 feet long by 27 to 30 inches wide by 6 to 7 feet high.

Table size will influence patron comfort and efficient utilization of space. In a cafeteria, for example, where patrons may dine on their trays, it is important that the table be of adequate size to accommodate the number of trays likely to be there. Four trays 14 by 18 inches fit better on a table 30 inches by 48 inches than on a table 42 inches square. Small tables, such as 24 or 30 inches square, are economical for seating but are uncomfortable for large people. They are only suitable in crowded areas with fast turnover and light meals. Tables having common width and height allowing them to be fitted together will give flexibility in seating arrangements. These are particularly good for banquette or cocktail-type bench seating along a wall. Tables for booths are difficult for waitresses to serve if they are

longer than 4 feet. The width of booths including seats and table is commonly 6 feet. A lunch counter will have a minimum width of 24 inches and a maximum width of 30 inches. The linear feet are calculated on the basis of 20 to 24 inches per seat. The maximum area best served by one waitress is generally 16 feet of counter. This will give 8 to 10 seats. U-shaped counters make maximum use of space and reduce travel. Space in depth of 8 feet-6 inches to 11 feet will be required for every linear foot of counter. This will provide 3 to 4 feet of public aisle, and 4 feet (ACA) of aisle space for employees. A width of 4 feet-6 inches is desirable where employees must pass.

Calculate aisle space between tables and chairs to include passage area and that occupied by the person seated at the table. A minimum passage area is 18 inches between chairs and, including chair area, tables should be spaced 4 to 5 feet apart. Aisles on which bus carts or other mobile equipment is to be moved should be sized according to the width of such equipment.

The best utilization of space can often be arrived at through the use of templates or seated models. Diagonal arrangement of square tables utilizes space better than square arrangement and yields a more trouble-free traffic lane. Lanes that pass between backs of chairs are likely to be blocked when guests arise or are being seated.

Table heights in schools should be chosen for the comfort of children. In units patronized by many grades a compromise height will be needed between the 30 inches normally used for adults and the 24 inches suitable for children, or two sizes may be used in different sections of the room. A table length to seat four, six, or eight is preferable to longer ones.

### 'Number of Persons' Allowance

The number of persons to be seated at one time is the second point of information needed for calculation of the dining room size. The total number of seats required at one time, multiplied by the space required for each seat, will give the total number of square feet needed in the dining area. The number of times a seat is occupied during a given period is commonly referred to as "turnover." The turnover per hour, times the number of seats available, gives the total number of patrons who can be served in an hour. If peak loads, or number to be served at one time, are known, the number of seats required can be estimated.

Turnover rates tend to vary, for they are influenced by such factors as the amount of food eaten, the elaborateness of the service, and the diner's time allowance. A breakfast meal of few foods may be eaten more quickly than dinner, and a simple fare faster than a many-course meal. Turnover is quickest in dining rooms where food has been prepared in advance for fast service and where patrons serve themselves and bus their soiled dishes. The turnover time is sped up 10 percent by patrons removing their soiled dishes so that tables are quickly available for other guests. Deluxe service for leisure dining, involving removal and placement of several courses, takes the longest time. Although specific turnover may vary from 10 minutes to 2 hours, actual eating time is normally 10 to 15 minutes for breakfast, 15 to 20 minutes for lunch, and 30 to 40 minutes for dinner.

The calculation of occupancy of seats in a dining room must take into consideration a certain percentage of vacancy, except where a given number are seated at one time according to assignment. In table-service dining rooms this has been estimated as 20 percent of total capacity, in cafeterias from 12 to 18 percent, and for counter opera-

**Table 1** Square feet per seat used for various types of food operations

| Type of operation | Square feet per seat |
| --- | --- |
| Cafeteria, commercial | 16–18 |
| Cafeteria, college and industrial | 12–15 |
| Cafeteria, school lunchroom | 9–12 |
| College residence, table service | 12–15 |
| Counter service | 18–20 |
| Table service, hotel, club restaurant | 15–18 |
| Table service, minimum eating | 11–14 |
| Banquet, minimum | 10–11 |

ons 10 to 12 percent. Many factors influence this percentage, such s patrons arriving at different times, irregular rate of turnover, and eluctance to share a table with strangers.

he table sizes used in the dining room will affect occupancy. It is ften desirable to provide for groups varying from 2 to 8, with a predominance in most dining rooms of those for 2 people. The "deuces" may be of a size and shape that can be put together to form tables for arger groups. In metropolitan areas where many tend to dine alone, all bench-type seating (banquet) and tables for two with a center dge or line denoting space for one have been used successfully.

he utilization of seating capacity tends to be greater for cafeterias han for table service. The patron may spend 25 to 50 percent of the me while seated at the table waiting for service. The cafeteria diner may begin eating as soon as he is seated. One cafeteria line can serve to 8 patrons per minute depending on:

    speed of the servers
    the elaborateness of food selection
    convenience of the layout
    type of patrons

t these rates, 240 to 480 patrons will need to be seated within an our. If the turnover rate is two per hour, then from 120 to 240 seats ill be used. However, if 15 percent of the total capacity at the peak eriod remains unfilled, then between 140 and 280 seats will be equired. An additional 14 to 28 seats or 10 percent would be needed f the patrons do not bus their soiled dishes.

atronage estimates for facilities of different types may be guided by he number of persons in residence, enrollments in a school, an ndustry's payroll, the membership of a club, or the amount of traffic n an office or shopping area. In each case a certain percentage may ormally be expected to dine in the facility provided. The percentage ill be influenced by such factors as its location in relation to other acilities, the patron's buying power, the price plan (on the basis of ubsidy or profit), patron's mealtime allowance, and convenience of ne location.

he patronage estimate for a college cafeteria should take into consideration the number of students who live at home, are members of a live-in group, such as an organized house, and the number of other dining facilities available on or near the campus. A college residence providing table service may have to allow a seating capacity that is 10 percent of occupancy if a policy exists for having "special guest" occasions and seating all at one time.

A corporate cafeteria may serve as few as 25 percent and as many as 50 percent. Management knows that a quality cafe will attract and etain quality staff. If the staff are corporate officers, engineers, or ales staff the only participation factor is nearness to the dining acility.

The size of a dining room in a hospital should be determined as to whether it is to be used for employees, patients, or guests, or any combination of these. The type of hospital and the number of ambulatory patients should also be considered. The type of hospital will also influence the number of personnel employed. The ratio of personnel to patients will vary from one to three, depending on how much special care is required or how much teaching and research are done. Good food and reasonable prices will attract a high percentage of those eligible to dine in the facility.

School lunch participation varies 25 to 75 percent and a good percentage for planning is 50 percent of enrollment. Any participation above 50 percent will depend on the number of students in the school whose meals are free or reduced-price.

Banquet seating requires planning because maximum seating potential means maximum profits. Folding tables 30 inches wide are popular. These are obtained in varying lengths, but 72 and 96 inches are commonly used. The spacing for the legs should be such as to allow for comfortable seating when the tables are joined end to end and place settings are laid on 24-inch centers.

Restaurant operators should consider space in relation to patronage volume essential for a profitable business. Labor, food, and operating costs must be met and a profit realized that covers risk-bearing effort expended and return on investment. Essential income is weighed in the light of probable patronage and probable average check. The number of seats provided in planning must cover this need.

Flexibility in seating capacity is often desirable. People do not like to be crowded nor do they enjoy the lonely experience of being seated in a huge area occupied by only a few. Sparse patronage creates an impression of poor popularity. Separate rooms, folding doors, screens, or other attractive devices can be used to reduce size of an area during slack periods. Sections left open should be those easiest to serve. Balconies, back rooms, or other less desirable space can often be used for overflow numbers that occasionally require service.

A common experience in many college dining room operations is the need for more seating at dinner. This may be due either to increased numbers or different turnover rates. A residence cafeteria serving 600 people has an overflow room seating 100, which it uses only at dinner. The night meal is larger and eaten in a more leisurely fashion. College students on meal plans may not get up for breakfast, are at class for lunch, and most always eat dinner.

Commercial restaurants located in shopping or office areas often have a heavier demand at noon than at the dinner hour. Rooms used for general patronage at noon may be closed at night or provide space for private dinner parties. Entrances to these rooms should not require passage through the main dining room. Convenience for special service is important.

## MEAL PRODUCTION AREAS

A frequently used rule for allotting space for the kitchen is that it should be one-half the area of the dining room. But it has been found unsatisfactory to go by a set space allowance for this area. Detailed study of space allocations leads to the conclusion that percentages in relation to the dining area are "completely unrealistic and unreliable." An analysis of specific needs is required. Many factors influence space requirements, such as:

• Type of preparation and service
• Amount of the total production done in the unit
• Volume in terms of the number of meals served
• Variety of foods offered in the menu
• Elaborateness of preparation and service
• Amount of individual service given, as in a hospital tray service
• Seating and service plan, whether on one floor or many

The cost of providing space, equipment, and labor is sufficient to merit careful calculation of the best type of operation before planning. New products on the market, new cooking methods, and new equipment available should be evaluated. The use of preprocessed products has made a pronounced change in the amount of space allotted for bake shop, meat cutting, and vegetable preparation areas. The use of large quantities of frozen foods also affects storage needs. The cost and quality of market products, their availability, and the frequency of deliveries are all to be considered. Fresh food will require more refrigeration and less freezer space.

**Impacts on Space**

Variety in menu selection and elaboration of foods tend to increase space needs in work areas and storage. Small amounts of numerous items do not permit stacking and bulk packaging. Elaboration of food often involves individual portion treatment, with individual casseroles, for example, as compared to bulk steam table pans. A hospital food service requiring many special diets serves as a common example of menu variety and individual portion treatment imposing special space requirements.

The equipment provided will affect the space needs. Garbage and refuse, for example, may require a sizable area for storage awaiting pickup. Disposal units for food garbage, such as a pulper/hydroextractor or compactor, and a crusher for tin cans will greatly reduce the amount to be held. Frequency of garbage collection will minimize the space needs, but increase collection cost.

Structural features of the building may influence the utilization of space. The shape of the kitchen, location of ventilation and elevator shafts, support columns and partitions should be considered in rela-

tion to an efficient layout for work. The location of entrances and exits for a good flow of traffic, window placement, suitable space, and relationship of sections need consideration. Eliminate partitions whenever possible; this will reduce space needs and also permit easier supervision of production areas.

Kitchens serving a smaller number require a larger square footage per meal than those serving a larger number. The data in Table 2 for industrial cafeterias show the rate at which space needs per meal tend to decrease as the number served increases.

Planners are often asked to make estimates of space needs before having an opportunity to make policies or detailed plans for operations. Figures that will be found useful in making such estimates are given in Table 3. These figures pertain to average kitchen areas found in different types of food facilities. Their use is to be regarded as tentative and to be measured carefully in terms of specific needs. The square footage given is to be multiplied by the maximum number of meals estimated per hour of service, in order to find the total space requirement.

**Area Sizes**

After production policies have been established, work areas may be blocked out in terms of the equipment needs and the number of workers required to do the work in a section. Linear space, depths, and heights for work centers should be controlled in terms of average human measurements. This will include the reach to and grasp of material or equipment used in working. The length and width of the work table is adjusted in terms of the amount and size of equipment that will rest on it during the progress of work. The linear measurement will vary in terms of the number of workers using it at one time.

The width of the table may be 24 to 30 inches unless dishes or food containers are to rest at the back of the table. Tables 36 inches wide are preferable when the back of the area is used for such storage. Where two workers work opposite each other, a table 42 inches wide may be used. A work area of 4 to 6 linear feet will be within convenient reach of the average person. Tables 8 to 10 feet long are used if two people are working side by side. A height of 34 inches, commonly used as a working height, should be evaluated in terms of specific work done and equipment used.

Aisle space should permit free, easy movement of essential traffic. The minimum width for a lane between equipment where one person

**Table 2** Variation in space needs in relation to numbers served

| Meal load | Square feet per meal | Variation in square feet |
|-----------|---------------------|--------------------------|
| 100–200 | 5.00 | 500–1,000 |
| 200–400 | 4.00 | 800–1,600 |
| 400–800 | 3.50 | 1,400–2,800 |
| 800–1,300 | 3.00 | 2,400–3,900 |
| 1,300–2,000 | 2.50 | 3,250–5,000 |
| 2,000–3,000 | 2.00 | 4,000–6,000 |
| 3,000–5,000 | 1.85 | 5,500–9,250 |

**Table 3** Square feet of kitchen space per meal for food facilities of different type and size

| | Estimated maximum meals per hour | | | | |
|---|---|---|---|---|---|
| Type of facility | 200 or less | 200–400 | 400–800 | 800–1,300 | 1,300–7,500 |
| Cafeterias | 7.5–5.0 | 5.0–4.0 | 4.0–3.5 | 3.5–3.0 | 3.0–1.8 |
| Hospitals | 18.0–4.5 | 12.0–4.5 | 11.0–4.5 | 10.0–4.0 | 8.0–4.0 |
| Hotels | 18.0–4.0 | 7.5–3.0 | 6.0–3.0 | 4.0–3.0 | 4.0–3.0 |
| Industrial lunchrooms | 7.5–5.0 | 4.0–3.2 | 3.5–2.0 | 3.0–2.0 | 2.5–1.7 |
| Lunch counters | 7.5–2.0 | 2.0–1.5 | | | |
| Railroad dining car | 1.6 | | | | |
| Restaurants (service) | 7.0–4.0 | 5.0–3.6 | 5.0–3.6 | 5.0–3.0 | 5.0–3.0 |
| School lunchrooms | 4.0–3.3 | 3.3–2.2 | 3.0–2.0 | 2.5–1.6 | 2.0–1.6 |

works alone is 36 inches, and 42 inches where more than one is employed and where workers must pass each other in the progress of work. However, ACA requires a 44-inch aisle open at both ends and a 60-inch aisle if closed at one end. Where mobile equipment is used, 48 to 54 inches are recommended. At least 60 inches are needed for main traffic lanes where workers regularly pass each other with mobile equipment. If workers or equipment must stand in the lane while working, appropriate space should be allowed for this. Thought should be given to space for doors opening into an aisle and for handling large pieces of equipment, such as roasting pans, baking sheets, and stock pots.

Main thoroughfares should not pass through work centers. Compactness is essential for step-saving. It is well for the work centers to be in close proximity to main traffic lanes, with easy access to them. It is important both to avoid distraction from outsiders passing through work centers and to conserve space. Work centers at right angles to traffic lanes are efficient (Fig. 1).

The percentage of floor area covered by equipment varies according to production needs and the type of equipment used. A satisfactory layout may claim less than 30 percent of total space for equipment while work areas, traffic lanes, and space around equipment for easy operation and cleaning may require 70 percent or more.

For hospital production and service areas, 20 to 30 square feet per bed is suggested. The need is reduced as the number of beds increases—approximately 30 square feet per bed for a 50-bed clinic, and 20 square feet per bed for a 200-bed hospital. This allowance does not include major storage areas, dining rooms, employee facilities, or floor serving and retherm pantries.

## SERVING AREAS

Space allowance of serving areas should be adapted to the needs of the specific facility. The menu, organization of work, and number served will influence size. The type of service will also be influential in dictating space needed.

In cafeterias the counter length should be regulated by the variety and volume. Excess space partially filled is unattractive, but crowding is also undesirable. An estimate that may be used for allotting width is 14 feet. This allows for 4 feet as patron lane space, a 1-foot tray slide, a 2-foot-6-inch counter width, 44 inches for workers, and 2 feet-6 inches for a back bar. The width of the tray slide should be 1 foot if it is a lower height than the counter top. However, the counter top and tray slide can be the same height with a 3 foot-6-inch-deep counter. The average length of counters in college residence halls and hospitals is found to be 10 to 12 feet, while those in school lunchrooms average around 30 feet and are double-sided self-service "speed line" buffet counters with packaged food. Schools may have lower counters so that children may see the food and push their trays along a slide as they are served. For children, 28 to 30 inches is desirable, with counters narrow enough for servers to reach over and assist a child. A solid tray slide tends to result in fewer accidents than those made of bars or tubing. Plastic trays measuring 9 by 12 inches, compartmented, and of pastel colors are popular. Slides for these may be on the servers' side of the counter for ease of service and to eliminate spillage or accidents. The child picks up the completed service at the end of the line. The number of food court stations and cashiers is determined by the number of seats.

Hospital service space will depend upon whether cook-serve or cook-chill issued trays are set up in serving pantries, and modified diets are set up in line or in a diet kitchen. Space must be allowed for bulk food trucks, tray trucks, small tray carts, or special dispensing units used.

Fast food units where food moves directly from production to the consumer require the least service space. The need for an intermediate station is eliminated. Step-saving compactness saves space. The units requiring the most space are those furnishing elaborate or highly individualized service.

## RECEIVING AND STORAGE AREAS

Space allocation for receiving and storage must be based on specific needs. The volume and type of items received and stored should be considered. Although the average operation may find a dock 8 feet deep and 12 feet long sufficient for receiving items, this would not be sufficient for a large one. The space requirement in square feet for food storage for 30 days has been calculated by some as approximately one half the total served or, if 1,000 are served, 500 square feet may be used as a tentative figure for total food storage needs. Cases of 6/10's stacked 6-cases-high on flat trucks will have a bearing weight of approximately 250 to 300 pounds per square foot. Skid sizes should be 3 feet by 2 feet-6 inches by 8 to 12 inches high. One case of 6/10's, 24/2-1/2's or 24/2's weighs approximately 50 pounds and occupies 1 cubic foot.

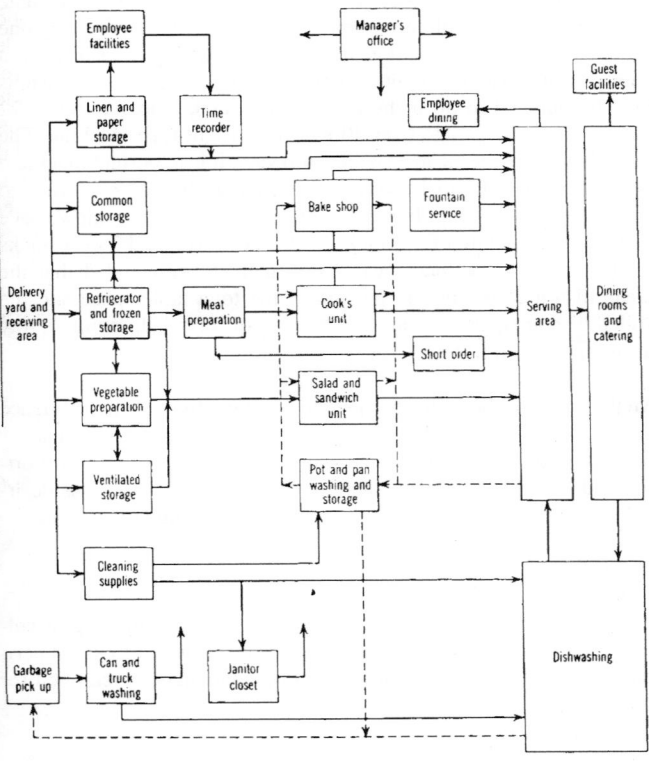

**Fig. 1. Flow diagram showing functional relationships**

## Common Storage

The volume of canned food needed to serve 100 persons three meals daily for one month is estimated at approximately 45 cases of 6/10's or equivalent. The maximum stack height will be 8 or 9 cases or approximately 72 inches. Accessibility of items that differ, as well as volume, will govern the number of stacks needed. A total of 3 cubic feet per stack is estimated to include floor space covered by a case of canned food, plus a share of aisle space. One thousand cases piled 8 high in 125 stacks will require 375 square feet or a storage area approximately 20 by 20 feet. Storeroom aisles may be as narrow as 36 inches, but 42 or 48 inches are preferred. Wider aisles may be required if trucks are used. A 3-foot skid on a hydraulic jack needs maneuvering room. If rolling bins or garbage cans on dollies are used for storage, plan locations for these. If cans or bins are under shelves, adjust height of bottom shelf to clear and allow for work space for removing food from these containers. Fixed shelving will be best when planned to suit the sizes of items stored. Consider both interspace and depth suitable. Condiment bottles, cereal packages, and canned goods differ in package sizes and in stacking quality. The depth of a shelf should accommodate either the width or length of the case, and the interspace should be adequate for the number to be stacked one on top of another. Allow 1-1/2 to 2 inches as free space for ease of positioning. Add thickness of shelving to interspace when stating measurements between centers.

Position heavy items to reduce lifting and facilitate dispensing. Table surface and scales should be located for convenient issuing of dry stores. Plan to have all products at least 6 inches above the floor or movable to facilitate cleaning of storage area. Limit height of top shelf for easy reach without aid of stool or stepladder. The average vertical reach of men is 84.5 inches and of women 81 inches. Use of the top shelf for light, bulky packages, such as cereal, is recommended.

## Refrigerated and Low-Temperature Storage

There are many factors affecting space needs for refrigerated and low-temperature foods. Across-the-board figures generally should be used only in preliminary estimates. The quantity stored at one time will dictate the storage needs. Variation in the type of storage also will be indicated by the types of items to be stored. Allocation in preliminary planning may be as follows: 20 to 35 percent for meat (portion-ready meats require a half to a third less space than carcass or wholesale cuts); 30 to 35 percent for fruits and vegetables; 20 to 25 percent for dairy products, including those in serving areas; 10 to 25 percent for frozen foods; and 5 to 10 percent for carry-over foods, salads, sandwich material, and bakery products.

A requirement of 15 to 20 cubic feet of refrigeration per 100 complete meals has also been used by some planners. Others state 1 to 1.5 cubic feet of usable refrigerator space should be provided for every three meals served. Analysis of a number of award-winning installations indicated that approximately 0.25 to 0.5 cubic feet of refrigerated walk-in space was provided per meal served, and frozen walk-in space approximated 0.1 to 0.3 cubic feet per meal served. Additional low-temperature or refrigerated space in terms of reach-ins was not calculated. In some climates, refrigerated space must be provided for dried fruits, nuts, cereals, and other foods to prevent weevil and insect infestation.

A walk-in refrigerator becomes feasible for an operation serving over 200 meals per day. A walk-in 5- to 6-feet-wide does not permit storage on both sides with adequate aisle space. Storage space of 1 foot-6 inches to 2 feet should be allowed on either side of the aisle. If crates or cases are stored, this may have to be increased. Aisles of 30 inches are usually too narrow; 42 inches are desirable. If mobile equipment is moved in and out, aisles may have to be wider. Walk-ins that are 8 feet wide and about 8 feet long are minimum size. This allows for two storage areas 30 inches wide with a 3- to 4-foot aisle. If added width is desired for storage space in the center, allowance for storage areas of about 3 feet wide and 42-inch minimum aisles should be provided. Large walk-ins may be designed for lift truck operation, with doors opening from the receiving dock on one side and into the kitchen opposite. If this is done and lift trucks are used, space must be provided in storage aisles for their working and turning around.

Doors should be a minimum of 43 inches wide to admit large crates and containers or be sized to suit mobile equipment. Doors to low-temperature areas are most often planned to open into a refrigerated area. If this is not done a heating device may have to be installed on a door opening into a warm area to prevent its freezing tight from condensation. About 12 to 15 square feet must be kept free for every door opening. About 45 pounds of frozen food, if stacked in cases, can be stored per cubic foot. About 30 to 35 pounds of refrigerated food can be stored per cubic foot. Refrigerators and freezers that store pallets of food may be designed to allow the pallet racks to be structural support for the insulated structure. Aisles need to be 9 feet wide to accommodate forklift trucks.

## SANITATION AREAS

### Dishwashing Area

The space required for the dishwashing operation depends on the methods and equipment used. In all instances there must be adequate room to receive the volume of soiled dishes likely to arrive at any one time, plus space for scraping, stacking, and placing in baskets on a conveyor of a machine or into a prerinsing operation. The dimensions may be only 30 to 36 inches for a single tank machine, 60 to 72 inches for sinks, or 7 to over 30 feet for a flight-type machine. The requirements in the clean dish area will vary. It is important that there be enough space for dishes to be exposed to air for sufficient time to air-dry before stacking. For a rack machine, it is well to allow space equal to that occupied by 3 racks, a stack of trays, and 3 or 4 stacks of dishes. For rack machines, it is usually recommended that the clean dish area occupy 66 percent of the total table space and the soiled dish area, 40 percent. Self-bussing of trays will require a tray accumulator conveyor.

Methods used for transporting and storing dishes will influence space needs. Where mobile storage equipment is used, more space is needed for the several units than where one cart is used for transporting and is repeatedly loaded and unloaded. A table surface is desirable for sorting, treating, or inspecting silver and other tableware.

### Pot and Pan Section

Provide a soiled utensil collection area adequate for the largest volume that normally arrives in the section at one time. The busiest periods are likely to occur when preparation containers are emptied for service.

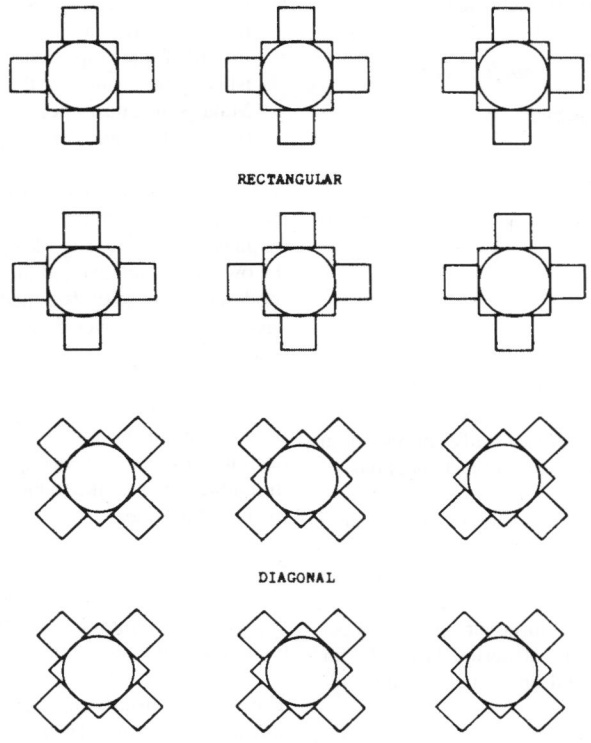

**Fig. 1. Rectangular and diagonal arrangement of tables**

# FOOD-SERVICE FACILITIES

## INTRODUCTION

Accurate determination of the space requirements for a food-service facility is a very difficult problem, involving considerable research and computation. The space required for each functional area of the facility is dependent upon many factors which are not constant for all types of operations. The factors involved include the number of meals to be prepared; the functions and tasks to be performed; the equipment requirements; the number of employees and corresponding workplaces required; storage for materials; and suitable space for traffic and movement. The importance of accurately evaluating these factors cannot be overemphasized. Overestimating or underestimating any of them can lead to an excess or a shortage of space for the facility.

## SPACE ESTIMATES

The general guides and "rules of thumb" that will be given are to be used for preliminary space estimates only. They are to be regarded as strictly tentative and subject to easy change. The "rules of thumb" are used to get a general idea of the overall size of a facility in order to make preliminary cost estimates for feasibility studies, or to determine approximate land requirements for the building. One problem with using guides and "rules of thumb" is that the figures given are usually based on existing operations and do not reflect newer methods of food-service operation. Another difficulty is that these figures are not given for all types of food-service operations and conse-

quently they would be of little use for certain types of projects. Most of the figures available are for general facilities that have no unusual space requirements.

### Total Facility Size

Depending upon the type of food service to be planned, a general estimate of the total building size can be obtained by relating it to the number of seats to be provided. The estimated square footage of total space per seat is given in Table 1. These figures can be related to the number of meals to be prepared by considering the turnover rate for a particular meal period. A range of space estimates is given to allow for variations in the methods of operation. The smaller figures are used for limited menu and limited-space operations; the larger figures are suitable for operations with extensive menus and allow more spacious areas.

Figures for estimating the total facility size of other types of food service such as tray service, car service, or take-out service are not available because of the great variations that exist in these types of operations. The only guides available would be to evaluate similar existing operations and make adjustments as needed.

### Dining Areas

Estimating the space required for dining areas is based on the number of persons to be seated at one time and the square feet of space allowed per seat (Table 1). The number of persons to be seated at one time is determined by considering the total number of customers to

*Reviewer:* John Hill, Hill Glazier Architects

**Table 1**  Estimated total facility space for food-service facilities

| | Area per seat | |
|---|---|---|
| Type of operation | ft² | m² |
| Table service | 24–32 | 2.23–2.97 |
| Counter service | 18–24 | 1.67–2.23 |
| Booth service | 20–28 | 1.86–2.60 |
| Cafeteria service | 22–30 | 2.04–2.79 |

be served for a given time period, and the turnover. Turnover refers to seat usage and is expressed by the number of times a seat will be occupied over a given time period. Turnover is usually expressed on a per-hour basis, although it can be determined on a per-meal basis.

The turnover is determined by estimating the average time a seat is occupied for the time period desired. For example, if the turnover is to be expressed on a per-hour basis and the average estimated time the seat is occupied is 20 minutes, the turnover is three. If the average seat occupancy time is 30 minutes, then the turnover rate is two per hour. Determining the turnover rate per meal period is useful for determining the total seating capacity based on estimated sales volume.

Turnover rates are affected by the method of serving and serving time as well as by the type of customer, menu offerings and the dining atmosphere. Typical turnover rates for some types of food-service operations are shown in Table 2.

Turnover rates can be increased to some extent by many design and operational factors. This is not to suggest that all facilities should be designed for high turnover rates. However, if high turnover is one of the basic objectives, then the planner and subsequent manager can do the following to accomplish this:

- Use menu items that require short processing times, or use predominately preprocessed items.
- Provide ample production space and equipment to handle the peak periods.
- Use well-lighted and light-colored painted areas for serving and dining.
- Arrange dining tables in close proximity to each other.
- Develop a somewhat uncomfortable dining seat design.

- Provide sufficient service personnel so guests are served promptly after they are seated.
- Provide for prompt clearing of the tables when a customer is finished with a course or the entire meal.
- Make sure guest checks are presented to customers as soon as they are finished eating.

Note that a number of factors identified above are characteristic of the management policy after the facility has been built. This again emphasizes the close working relationship that has to exist between the owner or manager and the planner during the planning process. A food-service facility designed for high turnover must also be managed for high turnover if the anticipated volume of sales is to be generated.

The square footage of space allowed in the dining areas is governed by the amount of comfort desired. Crowding in dining areas is not desirable except in some quick-service fast-food operations. Most individuals would like to have sufficient elbow room and table space to enjoy their meal.

Suggested space requirements for dining areas are given in Table 3. The figures on the high end of the range are used where ample space or leisurely dining are to be provided. The figures on the low end of the range will result in minimum space requirements.

The estimates for dining areas include space for tables, chairs, aisles, and service stations. They do not allow for waiting areas, rest rooms, or other similar areas. Space requirements for these areas have to be determined separately. The size and arrangement of tables, chairs, booths, and counters selected for the dining area are important to the efficient use of the space allowed.

**Production Areas**

The space estimates for production areas include room for all the functional areas, such as receiving, storage, preparation, cooking, and warewashing, that are required to produce the menu items. Estimates for production areas for typical foodservice facilities are given in Table 4.

Facilities that will be processing primarily fresh items should use the higher space estimates. This allows for the additional equipment and worker space needed. The smaller figures are used for operations using preprocessed foods and require minimal production space.

A suggested percentage breakdown of the production space for general table service operations is shown in Table 5. These percentage

**Table 2**  Turnover rates for food-service facilities

| Type of operation | Turnover rate (per hr) |
|---|---|
| Commercial cafeteria | 1½–2½ |
| Industrial or school cafeterias | 2–3 |
| Counter service | 2–3½ |
| Combination counter and table service | |
| Leisurely table service | ½–1 |
| Regular table service | 1–2½ |

**Table 3**  Estimated dining area space for food-service facilities

| | Dining space per seat | |
|---|---|---|
| Type of facility | ft² | m² |
| Table service | 12–18 | 1.11–1.67 |
| Counter service | 16–20 | 1.49–1.86 |
| Booth service | 12–16 | 1.11–1.49 |
| Cafeteria service | 12–16 | 1.11–1.49 |
| Banquet | 10–12 | 0.93–1.11 |

**Table 4** Estimated production space for food facilities

| Type of facility | Space per seat | |
| | ft² | m² |
|---|---|---|
| Table service | 8–12 | 0.74–1.11 |
| Counter service | 4–6 | 0.37–0.56 |
| Booth service | 6–10 | 0.56–0.93 |
| Cafeteria service | 8–12 | 0.74–1.11 |

**Table 5** Estimated percentage of production space allowed for functional areas

| Functional areas | Space allowed (%) |
|---|---|
| Receiving | 5 |
| Food storage | 20 |
| Preparation | 14 |
| Cooking | 8 |
| Baking | 10 |
| Warewashing | 5 |
| Traffic aisles | 16 |
| Trash storage | 5 |
| Employee facilities | 15 |
| Miscellaneous | 2 |

Figures assume a typical operation using fresh products. Baking of rolls, pastries, and cakes is also assumed to be done in the facility.

## SPACE CALCULATIONS

Another approach to the problem of determining space requirements is to calculate the space needed for each of the functional areas separately. This is done by identifying and determining the pertinent variables involved for the different functional areas. It is assumed at this point that the individual workplaces and pieces of equipment for the facility have been determined and will now be grouped together. The space required for the flow of materials and workers between the workplaces and pieces of equipment is added as needed to develop the space to allow for each function.

A brief discussion of some of the functional areas and the variables affecting their space requirements will be given to illustrate this procedure. Computational operations are presented as applicable. Consideration of the traffic aisles is one of the common variables for all areas and is therefore included.

## Traffic Aisles

Traffic aisles are used for the movement of materials and workers, and should not be confused with work aisles that provide floor space for workers to perform tasks. The primary purpose of traffic aisles is to allow easy movement between workplaces, equipment, and functional areas. Since traffic aisles are not productive space, they should be kept at a minimum both in numbers and size. Traffic aisles should

be just wide enough to provide easy movement of the materials and workers required for efficient operation of the facility.

In general, work aisles and traffic aisles should be separated as much as possible. This can usually be accomplished by locating traffic aisles perpendicular to the work aisles. In some instances, combined work and traffic aisles may be used if the traffic is light and if they offer a better solution to the design problem. Traffic aisles that serve two or more functional areas will minimize the amount of space required. Placement of traffic aisles along walls and other perimeter locations is not desirable for the same reason.

The width of traffic aisles is dependent upon the type of traffic to be accommodated. If it consists of only people who are not carrying anything, a minimum aisle width of 30 inches will allow persons to pass without difficulty. However, if ACA standards are followed, the minimum aisle must be 44 inches wide. For workers who will be carrying containers and materials or pushing mobile carts and trucks, an aisle width of 24 inches plus the width of the container or material carried or the mobile cart width will allow enough space. For example, if one worker has to pass another worker pushing a 20-inch-wide cart, an aisle width of 44 inches (24 plus 20) would be needed. The traffic aisle widths required for special types of movement such as carrying large trays have to be sized accordingly.

In those instances where a combined work and traffic aisle is needed, a minimum of 42 inches is required to allow one person to pass another person at the workplace. Aisles where there are persons working in a back-to-back arrangement have to be a minimum of 48 inches wide to allow passage of people between them. An important point to remember is that the less movement required to operate the facility, the less aisle space is needed.

### Receiving Area

The main variables affecting the amount of space needed for the receiving function are the number, type, and size of deliveries that are to be handled at one time. Many operations can have deliveries scheduled so they will have to handle only one delivery at a time. The types of materials to be received are considered because of the variety of containers and packaging methods available. Ease of opening, checking, moving, and stackability all have a bearing on the space required.

The size of deliveries to be handled may depend on the storage space available in the facility, and is determined in conjunction with storage space requirements. Storage space in turn can be modified by the frequency of deliveries. A greater frequency of deliveries can reduce the size requirements of the receiving area as well. Therefore, storage space and receiving space requirements should be determined together after these factors have been evaluated. Needless to say, all equipment and work areas for the receiving function must be provided for.

### Storage Areas

The amount of dry, refrigerator, and freezer space required for the facility is determined by the number of days of storage to be provided for. A general recommendation for dry storage of foods is to provide space for one to two weeks supply, depending on the availability of the food items. The total volume of goods to be stored can be estimated as follows. First determine the number of meals for which storage is to be provided. An operation planning on serving 600 meals per day and desiring a two weeks supply will need storage for 8,400 (600 meals per day x 14 days) meals. Next, estimate the weight per meal of items that will be stored in the dry storage area. This calls for an evaluation of all menu items. A general estimate between 0.25 and 0.5 pounds per meal may be used; it is based on a total weight estimate per average meal of 1 to 1.5 pounds. These figures are for full meals and adjustments for partial meals have to be made. If an estimate of 0.5 pounds per meal is used, then the total weight to provide storage for is 4,200 pounds (8,400 meals x 0.5 pounds per meal). The total weight computed is then divided by an average density of 45 pounds per cubic foot, which will give the total volume of goods to be stored. In this example, the total volume in cubic feet is 4,200 pounds ÷ 45 pounds per cubic foot = 93.3 cubic feet. This indicates that space for 93.3 cubic feet of goods, exclusive of aisle space, will be needed.

If the goods are to be stored on shelves, the total square footage of shelving can be computed by considering the height to which the materials can be stored on the shelf. If the materials can be stored to a height of 1 foot, then 93.3 (93.3 cubic feet ÷ 1 foot) square feet of shelving will be needed. If a height of 1 foot-6 inches can be used, then 62.2 (93.3 ÷ 1.5) square feet of shelving is required. The length of shelving is computed by dividing the square feet by the width of shelving to be used.

This same method of computation can be used for the refrigerator and freezer storage areas. The weight per meal of items that will be stored in the refrigerators and freezers will vary between 0.75 and 1 pound. The average density of refrigerator items can be assumed to be 30 pounds per cubic foot. Items that will be stored in freezers can be assumed to have a density of 40 pounds per cubic foot.

The number of days of storage for refrigerator items may vary from one day to a week or more, depending on the method of operation used for the facility. Freezer items can be stored for longer periods of time and are determined by the frequency of deliveries available. An economic lot size analysis may be made to determine the optimum size of storage to provide. The analysis compares ordering, purchasing, and receiving costs to the cost of the storage.

**Serving Areas**

Serving areas for most table service facilities are planned as a part of the main cooking area and separate space determinations are not usually needed. The pick-up area is included in the space requirements for the main cooking area. Additional serving stations for table service can be considered in computations for the dining area.

Cafeteria operations require separate space for the serving function to allow room for the serving counter, room for guests, and room for servers. Variables affecting the size of the serving area are the number of people to be served and the serving time allowed. Serving line rates vary from 2 to 10 persons per minute for straight-line cafeteria counters. The serving line rate is dependent on the number of choices and the number of servers. Food court or marche-style serveries can handle up to 20 or more persons per minute.

The length of cafeteria counters is determined by the variety and volume of food items to be displayed. Adequate space for merchandising food items should be allowed.

The space required for straight-line counters may be roughly estimated at 10 to 15 square feet of floor space for each linear foot of counter. This provides room for the counters, customer aisles, room for servers, and backbar equipment. Food court/marche arrangements generally require 8 square feet of floor area for each seat in the dining room.

The sizing of serving facilities for cafeterias is directly related to the capacity of the dining area. Ideal design results when the flow of people from the serving facility is balanced with the seating available in the dining room. At equilibrium conditions, the flow rate of people leaving the serving areas and entering the dining area should equal the flow rate of people leaving the dining area. In other words, the number of seats provided in the dining area has a direct relationship to the rate of people leaving the serving line for a given average eating time. This relationship can be expressed by the equation:

$$R = N/T$$

R = rate of people leaving serving area
N = number of seats in dining area, and
T = average eating time

For example, a 200-seat dining room where the average eating time is 20 minutes should have serving facilities capable of handling 10 (R = 200/20) persons per minute. If the eating time is 30 minutes, a serving facility must be able to handle 6.7 (R = 200/30) persons per minute.

**Dining Areas**

Calculating the space requirements for dining areas can be difficult because of the many choices available. A rule of thumb is 15 square feet per seat. The final space required for a dining room is dependent upon the following variables:

- Types of seating to be provided:

  a. tables and chairs
  b. booths
  c. counters
  d. banquettes
  e. combinations

- Table sizes desired
- Table shapes desired
- Pattern of table arrangements
- Aisle space desired
- Number of service stations needed

A suggested approach that allows a planner to evaluate these variables and their effect on the dining space per seat is the modular concept. For this situation the module contains space for the table, the seats, and the appropriate share of the service and access aisles. The modular concept enables designers first to evaluate the space requirements for different choices that may be made before reaching their final decisions.

The following example will illustrate this concept for a dining room that will use tables and chairs only. The first step in the modular concept is to select the size and shape of table to be considered. This is done in relation to the customer, the menu, the type of service, and the type of atmosphere desired in the dining room. Some typical sizes and shapes of dining tables are given in Table 6.

The second step is to select the aisle spaces to be used. Aisle space in dining areas may be divided into service aisles and access aisles. Ser-

**Table 6**  Typical sizes and shapes of dining tables

| Type | Shape | Minimum size (in.) | Spacious (in.) |
|---|---|---|---|
| Tables for 1's or 2's | Square | 24 × 24 | 30 × 30 |
| | Rectangle | 24 × 30 | 30 × 36 |
| | Round | 30 | 36 |
| Tables for 3's or 4's | Square | 30 × 30 | 42 × 42 |
| | Rectangle | 30 × 42 | 36 × 48 |
| | Round | 36 | 48 |
| Tables for 5's or 6's | Rectangle | 30 × 60 | 42 × 72 |
| | Round | 48 | 60 |
| Drop leaf tables | 30 × 30 in. opening to 42 in. round | | |
| | 36 × 36 in. opening to 52 in. round | | |

vice aisles usually range from 2 feet-6 inches minimum for a limited menu operation to as wide as 4 feet-6 inches for a dining room featuring cart service or table side food preparation. Access aisles are provided to allow people to get into and out of the chairs easily. Thus the type of customer, size of chairs and the desired atmosphere (crowded vs. spacious) are the critical factors in selecting the access aisles. Access aisles are generally 1 foot-6 inches to 2 feet wide as a minimum. Combined service and access aisles or aisles for cafeterias where people carry their own trays are usually sized from 44 inches to 4 feet-6 inches.

Having selected the table size and shape and the desired aisle space, the next step is to consider possible table arrangement patterns. Square or round tables may be arranged into a rectangular or diagonal pattern, as shown in Fig. 1. The diagonal pattern is more efficient in the use of space than the rectangular pattern.

The module used for evaluating the factors mentioned is drawn as illustrated in Fig. 2. The module contains one-half of the aisle space selected. The following choices were used for the module:

- Square table, 36 x 36 inches for four diners
- 18-inch seating space (occupied position)

- Combined service and access aisle of 44 inches
- Rectangular pattern of table arrangement

The module size for this example is 9 feet by 9 feet, which results in a total area of 81 square feet. Considering that the module is for four persons, the space per seat for this module is 20.25 square feet per seat. If this module were to be used for a dining room with 100 seats, the total area required would be 2,025 square feet.

The module for a diagonal pattern of table arrangement using the same choices for the table size, seat space, and aisle space is shown in Fig. 3. The size of the module for the diagonal pattern is 8 feet-4 inches by 8 feet-4 inches, which gives a total area of 69.44 square feet. The space per seat is 17.36 square feet per seat, which is 2.89 square feet less than for the rectangular pattern. For the 100-seat dining room, the diagonal pattern would require 1,736 square feet, which is 289 square feet less than the rectangular pattern.

Similar modules for other sizes or types of seating arrangements can be developed. Care must be taken when using different size tables so that the modules developed for each size table are compatible at least on one side. For example, when tables for twos and tables for fours are to be used, the modules can be adjusted by selecting table shapes

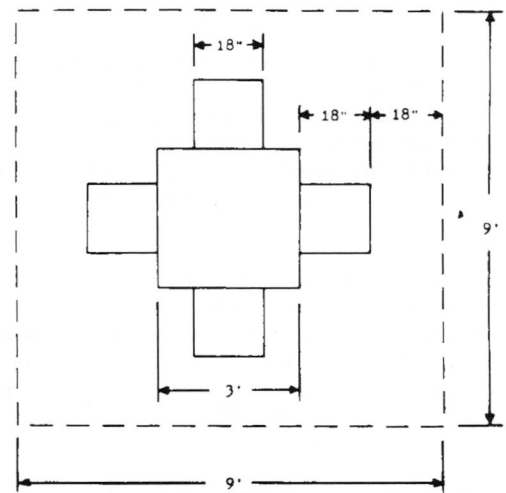

**Fig. 2. Module for a square table to be arranged in a rectangular pattern**

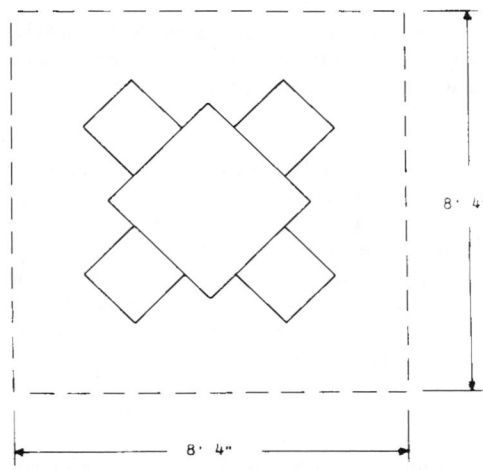

**Fig. 3. Module for the square table to be arranged in a diagonal pattern**

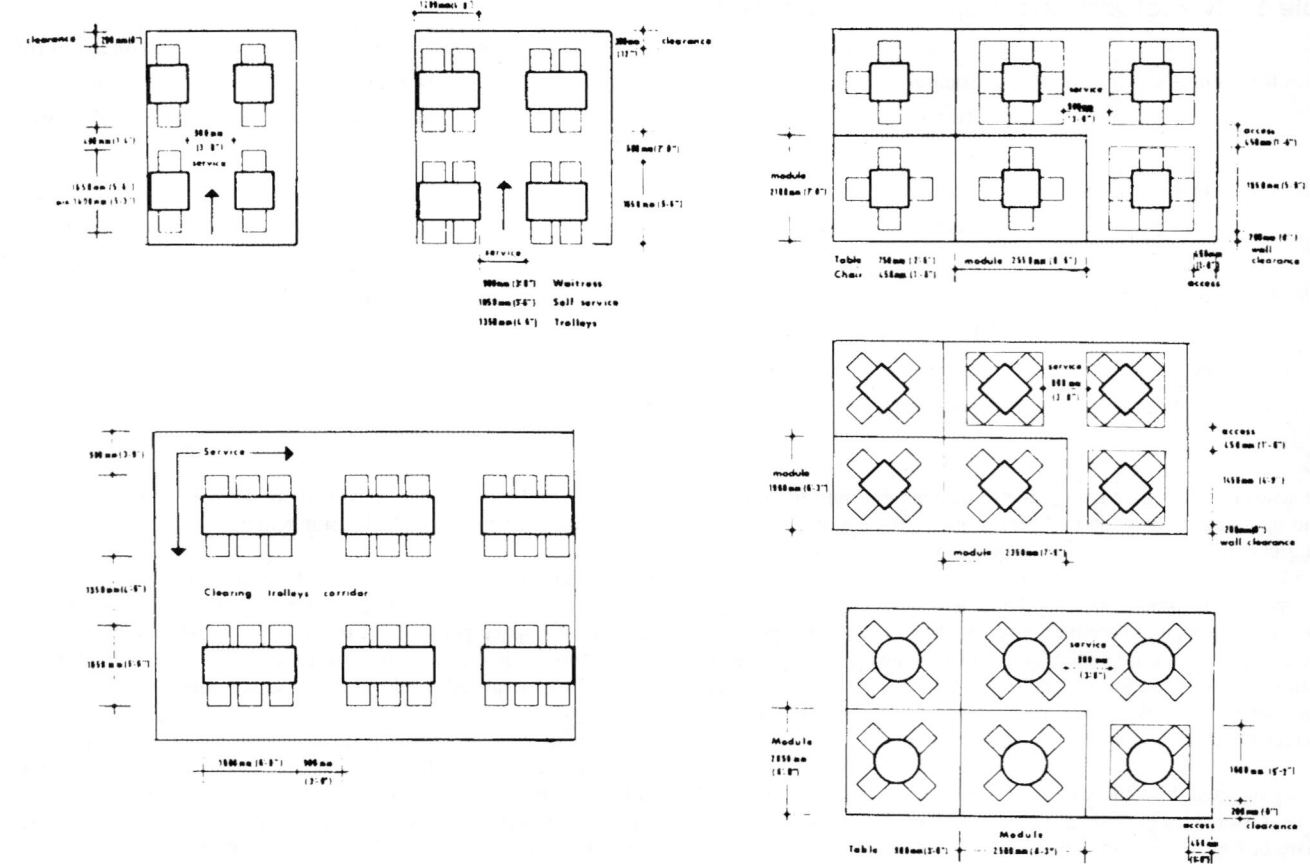

**Fig. 4. Seat groupings around rectangular and circular tables**

or sizes that give the same module dimension along one axis. This would allow a mixing of the tables without affecting the pattern of aisle ways in the dining area.

The possible seating configurations for dining areas are endless, and careful planning is required to make the most efficient use of space (Figs. 4 to 7).

These procedures illustrate the preferred method of arriving at space requirements for a foodservice facility. Each type of food facility to be planned will have differences that will result in different space requirements.

Figure 8 indicates some of the basic clearances required for a typical counter: 36 inches for workspace behind the counter; 18 to 24 inches for the countertop; and 60 to 66 inches between the front face of the counter and the nearest obstruction. The bottom drawing shows a section through the counter and back counter. Most counters are about 42 inches in height. The clearance from the top of the seat to the underside of the counter top and the depth of the counter top overhang are extremely important. Buttock-knee length and thigh clearance are the key anthropometric measurements to consider for proper body fit. Footrest heights should take into consideration popliteal height. In most cases this is ignored, and 42-inch counters are provided with 7-inch footrests that are 23 inches below the seat surface, which cannot work. The popliteal height of the larger user, based on 99th percentile data, is only about 20 inches. Therefore, the

feet dangle unsupported several inches above the footrest and the body is deprived of any stability. The footrest shown on the drawing, although higher, only serves a portion of the seated users and is intended primarily for standing patrons. The most logical solution is a separate footrest, integral with the stool.

**Bar Sizes**

To ensure proper circulation and interface, adequate clearances in front of the bar are illustrated in Fig. 9. A customer activity zone of 18 to 24 inches should be provided to allow for seating, standing, and access, in addition to a general circulation zone of at least 30 inches. If a supplementary drinking surface or shelf is provided, a smaller activity zone of 18 inches is suggested in front of the shelf. The shelf can be 10 to 12 inches deep.

The distance between bar and back-bar should allow adequate workspace. A minimum of 36 inches should provide space for one bartender to serve and another to circulate behind him. Maximum body depth and maximum body breadth are the primary anthropometric considerations in establishing clearance. A one-bartender operation would require a 30-inch clearance. If ACA standards are being followed 44 inches will be required.

In regard to bar stools, clearance between the stool seats is more critical than centerline spacing, and it should allow patrons of larger body size a comfortable side approach and departure from the stool

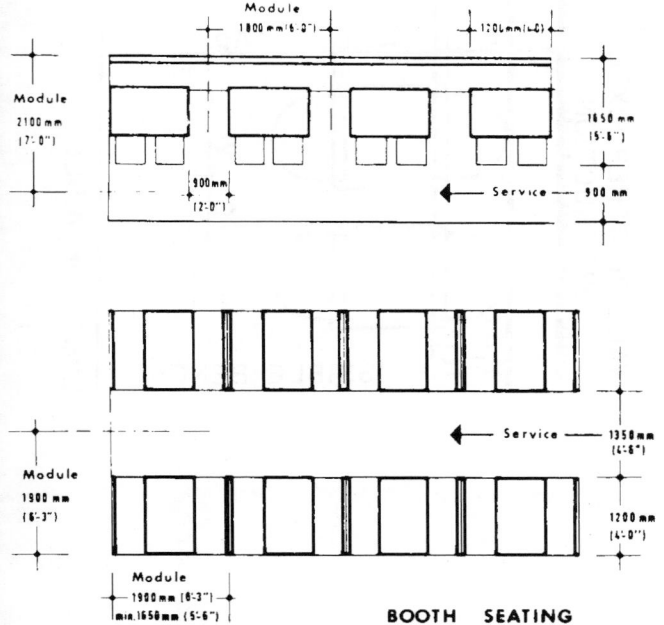

**Fig. 5. Banquette seating arrangements and limiting dimensions including space for access and service (Reference: Fred Lawson, *Restaurant Planning and Design*, The Architectural Press, Ltd., London)**

without body contact with the next person. A 12-inch-wide stool on 24-inch centers, which is quite common, will allow only less than 5 percent of male users access to the stool without disturbing the next patron, while a 30-inch spacing will accommodate 95 percent of the users. The tradeoff, however, would be the loss of two seats for every 120 inches of bar length. A spacing of 12-inch stools on 28-inch centers is suggested as a compromise. The ultimate decision is an individual one and must reconcile human factors with economic viability.

Layouts for a cashier's area and check room are shown in Fig. 10.

### Miscellaneous Sanitation Areas

When allowing space for the pot and pan section, 40 square feet is generally regarded as a minimum for the smallest unit. The free work aisle between the sinks and other equipment should be 4 feet wide. The space allowance above the minimum will vary widely depending upon the type equipment used and the volume of pots and pans handled. Less space in relation to the maximum load may be required where a mechanical washer is used and fewer labor hours will be spent in handling a large volume per unit handled.

For washing mobile equipment, space is needed where splashing can be confined and that has satisfactory drainage. This area may be adjacent to the dishwashing section or to the place where can washing is done. The size and type of equipment to be handled will govern the space needs.

A storage area for emergency cleanup equipment is needed in convenient relationship to dining rooms and work sections. Spillage and breakage create unsightliness and are accident hazards. Immediate

care usually does not require heavy or large equipment but may be handled by a small broom, dustpan, small mop, and bucket not used for major cleaning. A mobile unit may be designed to carry these things, or a small closet may be provided.

Major cleaning equipment required will depend on the floors, finishes, and furniture to be cleaned. Determine whether a power sweeper, scrubber, and waxer are to be used. Space may be required for storage of janitor supply carts and for miscellaneous replacement items, such as light bulbs. Provision will be needed for storing, emptying, cleaning, and filling mop trucks and for cleaning and air-drying wet mops.

### Employee Facilities

Facilities for employees may include locker and lounge area, toilets, time clock, hand basins near work areas, and dining rooms. An employee entrance should be so located that the employees may go directly to the dressing rooms without passing through the dining room or production area.

### Locker and Lounge Area

Employee possessions should be protected in a suitably safe and sanitary condition while the employees are at work. Whether individual lockers or common cupboard, sufficient space should be allowed for personal clothing to hang without crowding or wrinkling. If linen cabinets are used for clothing, a separate space should be afforded for street clothing and for uniforms, and individual parcel lockers should be provided for storage of purses and other valuables. The height of the space for clothing should permit the longest garment to hang straight without wrinkling. The depth from front to back should be a minimum of 20 inches.

Suitable size for an employee lounge depends largely on scheduling of workers and the policies of individual establishments. Many operators discourage lounging in the dressing room and recommend the employees' dining area for this. Others having broken shifts on their schedules favor an extra room for lounging. In all cases, benches or chairs are to be provided upon which workers may sit while changing clothes and shoes.

### Toilets

The location of toilet facilities near work areas is preferred over a remote location in promoting good health habits, lessening loss of labor time, and permitting closer employee supervision. Separate facilities should be provided for men and women. They should be separated from food areas by a hallway or double entrance. Supply one wash bowl for every 8 to 10 workers, one toilet stool for every 12 to 15 women, and one urinal and one toilet stool for every 15 men. Toilet compartments measure approximately 3 by 4 feet-6 inches to 5 feet.

The type of employees, the climate, kind of work, and conditions of work will influence the need for shower facilities.

### Time-Clock Area

Provide space for a time clock near and within view of the office. Wall-hung card racks of sufficient capacity are recommended for the number of workers, both full and part time, who are likely to be employed during an accounting period. Estimated space for a time clock is

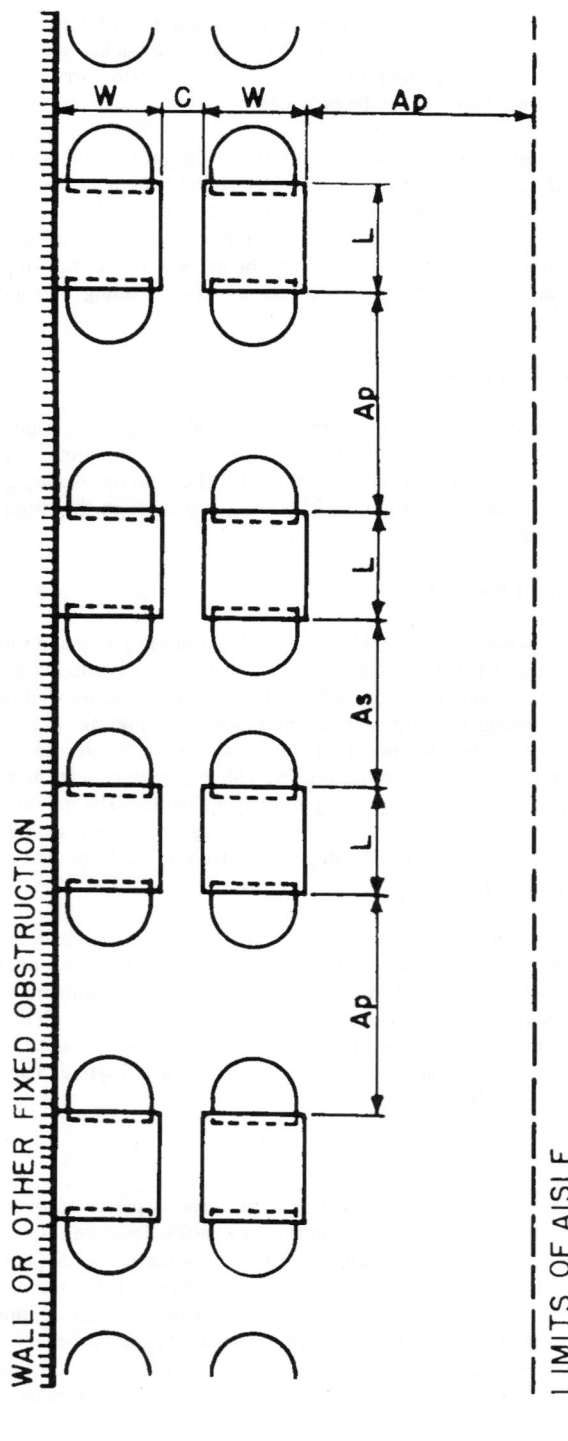

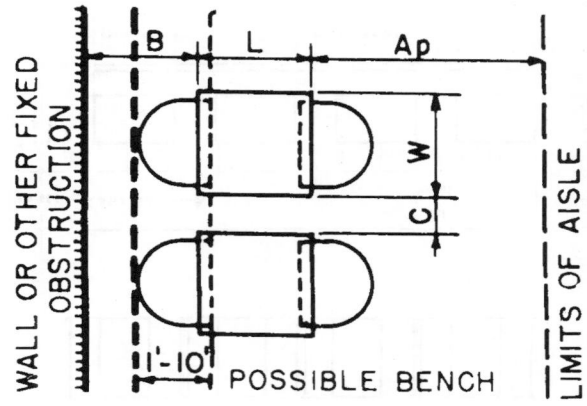

| | | Abs. Min. | Des. Min. | Comfort-able |
|---|---|---|---|---|
| **Ap** | Public circ'n | 3–0 to 4–6 | 3–6 to 5–0 | 3–9 to 5–0 |
| **As** | Service aisle | 3–6 to 4–6 | 4–0 to 5–0 | 4–0 to 5–6 |
| **B** | To wall | 1–8 to 2–0 | 2–0 to 2–6 | 2–0 to 3–0 |
| **C** | Between units | 0 to 8 | 6 to 1–0 | 1–0 |
| | Length | 1–8 to 2–0 | 2–3 to 2–4 | 2–4 to 2–6 |
| | Width | 1–8 to 2–0 | 2–2 to 2–3 | 2–4 to 2–6 |

all dimensions in feet and inches

| | | Abs. Min. | Des. Min. | Comfort-able |
|---|---|---|---|---|
| **Ap** | Public circ'n | *1–10 to 4–6 | 2–3 to 5–0 | 3–0 to 5–0 |
| **As** | Service aisle | 3–0 to 3–6 | 3–6 to 4–0 | 3–9 to 4–0 |
| **C** | Between units | 0 to 3 | 4 to 6 | 6 |
| | Length | 1–8 to 2–0 | 2–3 to 2–4 | 2–4 to 2–6 |
| | Width | 1–8 to 2–0 | 2–2 to 2–3 | 2–4 to 2–6 |

*Lower range only if chairs, etc., do not project into aisle

## Fig. 6. Table and chair units

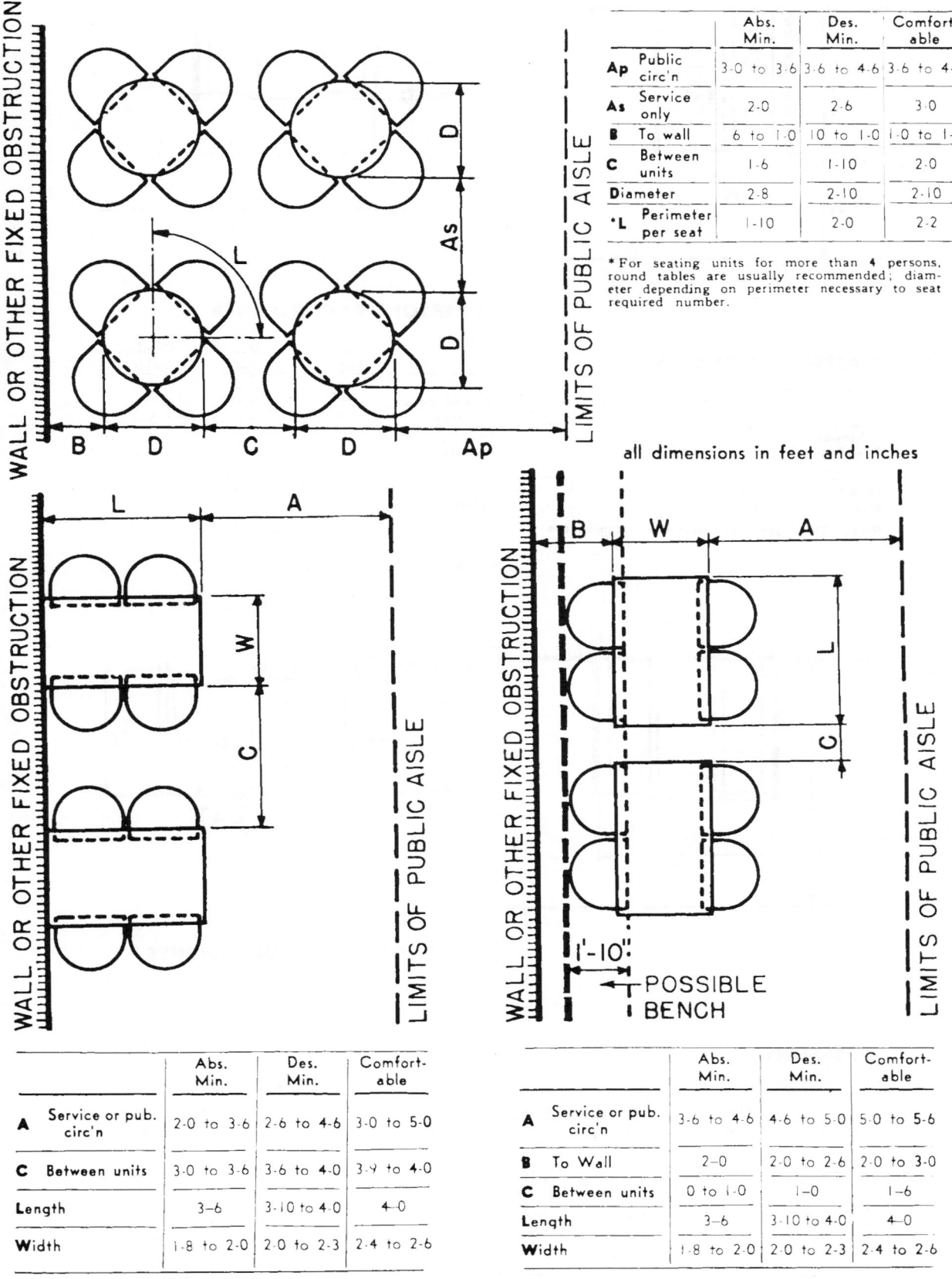

| | | Abs. Min. | Des. Min. | Comfort-able |
|---|---|---|---|---|
| Ap | Public circ'n | 3-0 to 3-6 | 3-6 to 4-6 | 3-6 to 4-6 |
| As | Service only | 2-0 | 2-6 | 3-0 |
| B | To wall | 6 to 1-0 | 10 to 1-0 | 1-0 to 1-3 |
| C | Between units | 1-6 | 1-10 | 2-0 |
| Diameter | | 2-8 | 2-10 | 2-10 |
| *L | Perimeter per seat | 1-10 | 2-0 | 2-2 |

* For seating units for more than 4 persons, round tables are usually recommended; diameter depending on perimeter necessary to seat required number.

all dimensions in feet and inches

| | | Abs. Min. | Des. Min. | Comfort-able |
|---|---|---|---|---|
| A | Service or pub. circ'n | 2-0 to 3-6 | 2-6 to 4-6 | 3-0 to 5-0 |
| C | Between units | 3-0 to 3-6 | 3-6 to 4-0 | 3-4 to 4-0 |
| Length | | 3-6 | 3-10 to 4-0 | 4-0 |
| Width | | 1-8 to 2-0 | 2-0 to 2-3 | 2-4 to 2-6 |

| | | Abs. Min. | Des. Min. | Comfort-able |
|---|---|---|---|---|
| A | Service or pub. circ'n | 3-6 to 4-6 | 4-6 to 5-0 | 5-0 to 5-6 |
| B | To Wall | 2-0 | 2-0 to 2-6 | 2-0 to 3-0 |
| C | Between units | 0 to 1-0 | 1-0 | 1-6 |
| Length | | 3-6 | 3-10 to 4-0 | 4-0 |
| Width | | 1-8 to 2-0 | 2-0 to 2-3 | 2-4 to 2-6 |

**Fig. 6. (cont.)**

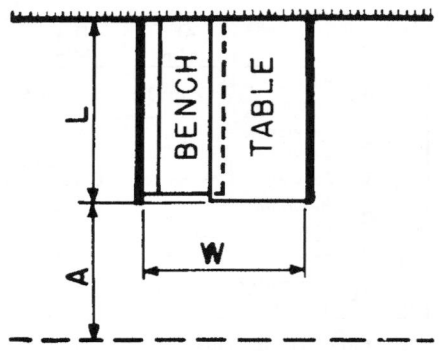

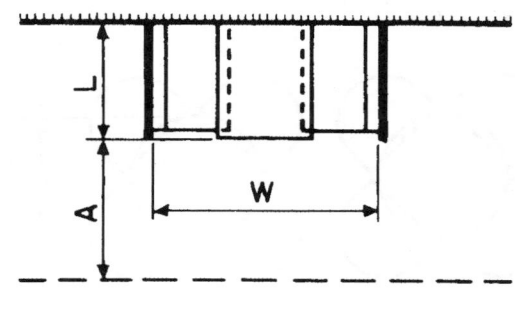

## 2 PERSONS FACE TO FACE

| | Abs. Min. | Des. Min. | Comfort-able |
|---|---|---|---|
| Service A and pub. circ'n | 2–6 to 3–0 | 3–0 to 4–0 | 3–6 to 5–0 |
| Length | 2–0 | 2–2 to 2–6 | 2–6 |
| Width | 4–10 to 5–6 | 5–2 to 5–6 | 5–8 to 5–10 |

## 2 PERSONS SIDE BY SIDE

| | Abs. Min. | Des. Min. | Comfort-able |
|---|---|---|---|
| Service A and pub. circ'n | 2–6 | 3–0 | 3–6 |
| Length | 3–6 | 3–9 | 4–0 |
| Width | 3–0 | 3–3 | 3–6 |

Note: This type not ordinarily recommended.

dimensions in feet and inches

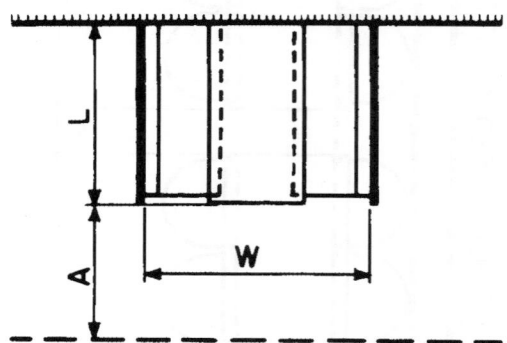

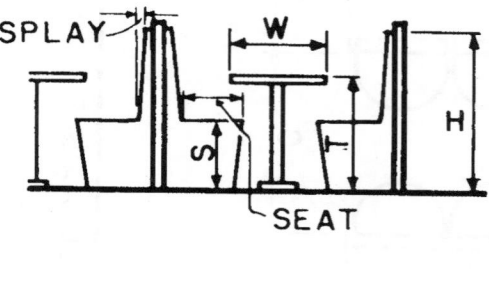

## BOOTH FURNITURE HEIGHTS

| | Abs. Min. | Des. Min. | Comfort-able |
|---|---|---|---|
| H | 3–0 to 3–6 | 3–6 | 4–0 |
| S | 1–5 to 1–6 | 1–5 to 1–6 | 1–6 |
| T | 2–5 | 2–5 to 2–6 | 2–6 |
| W | 1–8 to 2–0 | 2–0 to 2–2 | 2–4 to 2–6 |
| Seat | 1–4 to 1–5 | 1–5 to 1–6 | 1–6 to 1–8 |
| Splay | 0 to 0–3 | 0–2 to 0–3 | 0–3½ to 0–4 |

## 4 PERSONS

| | Abs. Min. | Des. Min. | Comfort-able |
|---|---|---|---|
| Service A and pub. circ'n | 2–6 to 3–0 | 3–0 to 4–0 | 3–6 to 5–0 |
| Length | 3–6 | 3–9 to 4–0 | 4–0 to 4–2 |
| Width | 4–10 to 5–6 | 5–2 to 5–6 | 5–8 to 5–10 |

Fig. 7. Booths

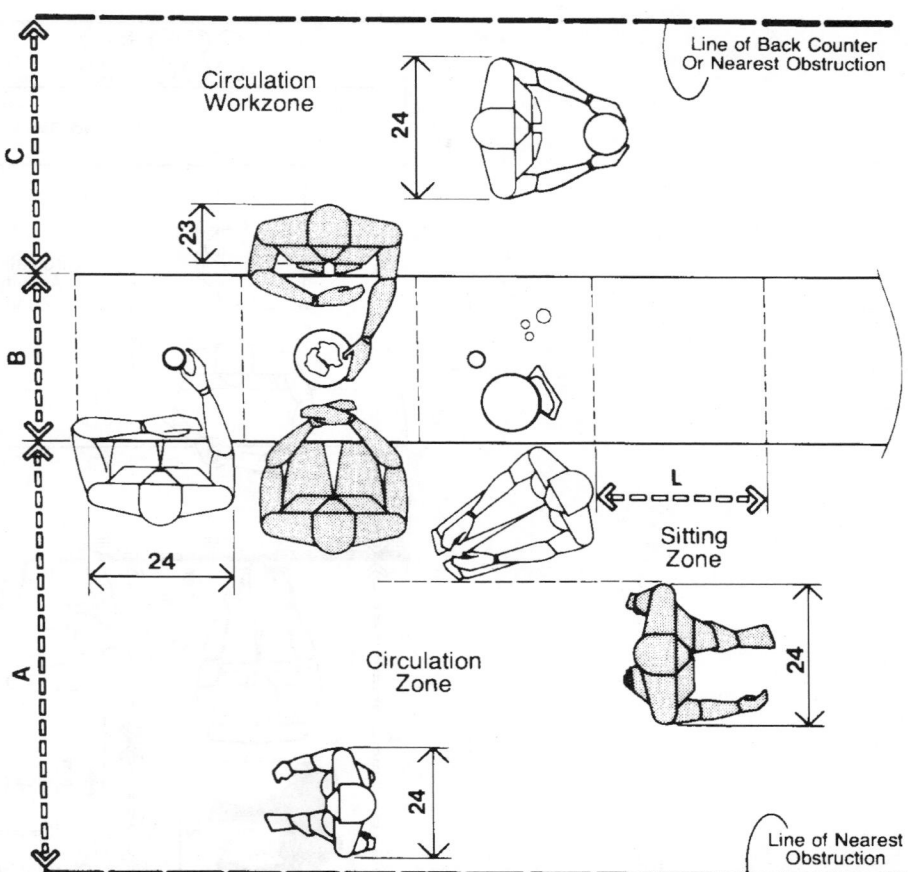

## LUNCH COUNTER

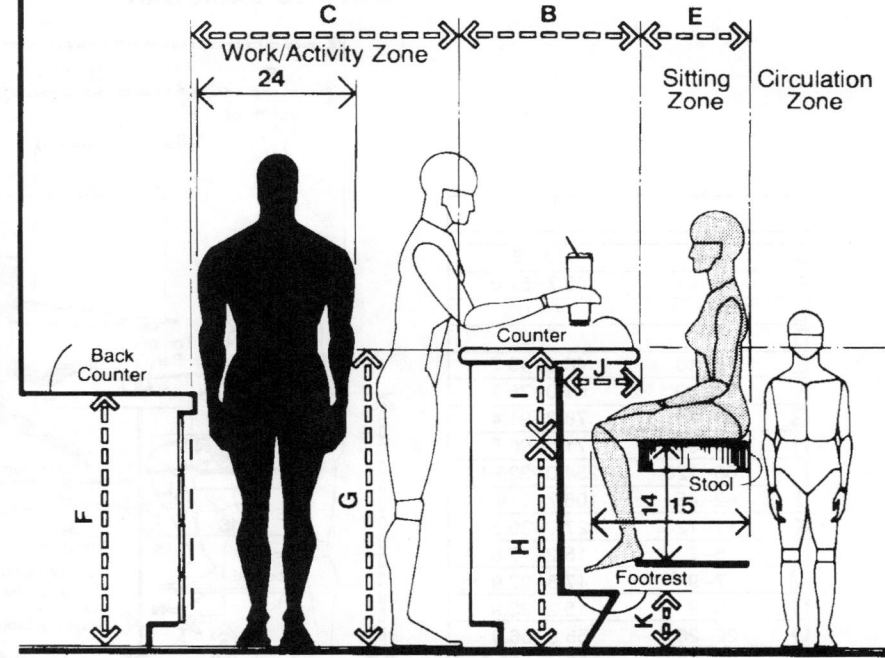

| | in | cm |
|---|---|---|
| A | 60–66 | 152.4–167.6 |
| B | 18–24 | 45.7–61.0 |
| C | 36 | 91.4 |
| D | 24 | 61.0 |
| E | 12–18 | 30.5–45.7 |
| F | 35–36 | 88.9–91.4 |
| G | 42 | 106.7 |
| H | 30–31 | 76.2–78.7 |
| I | 11–12 | 27.9–30.5 |
| J | 10 | 25.4 |
| K | 12–13 | 30.5–33.0 |

## LUNCH COUNTER

**Fig. 8. Counter service**

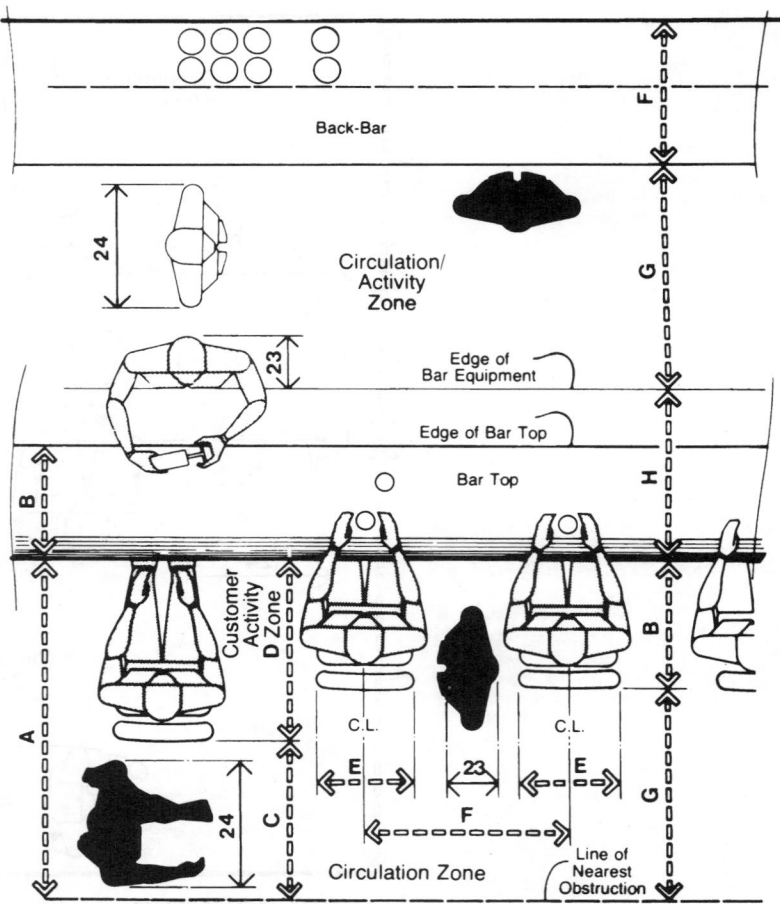

**BAR AND BACK-BAR**

| | in | cm |
|---|---|---|
| A | 54 | 137.2 |
| B | 18–24 | 45.7–61.0 |
| C | 24 | 61.0 |
| D | 30 | 76.2 |
| E | 16–18 | 40.6–45.7 |
| F | 24–30 | 61.0–76.2 |
| G | 30–36 | 76.2–91.4 |
| H | 28–38 | 71.1–96.5 |
| I | 100–128 | 254.0–325.1 |
| J | 42–45 | 106.7–114.3 |
| K | 11–12 | 27.9–30.5 |
| L | 6–7 | 15.2–17.8 |
| M | 7–9 | 17.8–22.9 |
| N | 6–9 | 15.2–22.9 |
| O | 22–26 | 55.9–66.0 |
| P | 60–69 | 152.4–175.3 |
| Q | 36–42 | 91.4–106.7 |

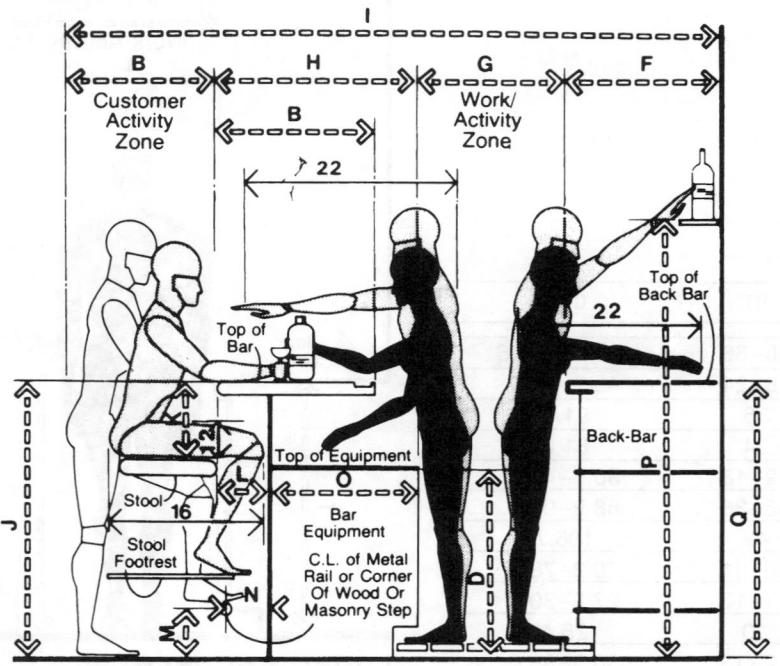

**BAR / SECTION**

Fig. 9. Bar and back-bar layout

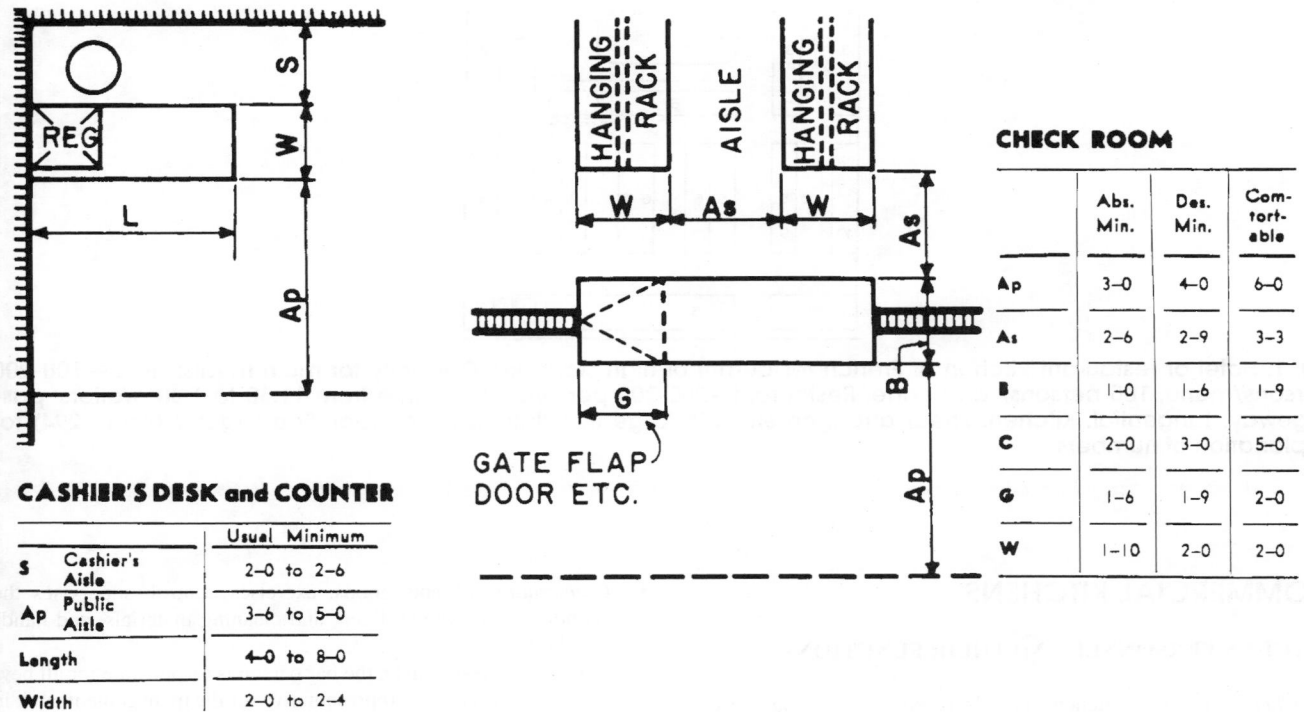

## CASHIER'S DESK and COUNTER

| | | Usual Minimum |
|---|---|---|
| S | Cashier's Aisle | 2–0 to 2–6 |
| Ap | Public Aisle | 3–6 to 5–0 |
| Length | | 4–0 to 8–0 |
| Width | | 2–0 to 2–4 |

## CHECK ROOM

| | Abs. Min. | Des. Min. | Comfortable |
|---|---|---|---|
| Ap | 3–0 | 4–0 | 6–0 |
| As | 2–6 | 2–9 | 3–3 |
| B | 1–0 | 1–6 | 1–9 |
| C | 2–0 | 3–0 | 5–0 |
| G | 1–6 | 1–9 | 2–0 |
| W | 1–10 | 2–0 | 2–0 |

**Fig. 10. Nondining spaces**

approximately 18 inches wide by 12.5 inches deep and 18 inches high, and a rack of 50 cards approximately 1.5 by 2.5 by 34.5 inches.

### General Considerations

The size of employee facilities has been found to vary widely. Small operations may not supply lockers and may have only a toilet and lavatory for workers. Some do not provide separate dining areas. Expediency in allowing ample space may be tempered by cost of space, available room, and the acuteness of need. Total space used may be increased where main toilet and locker areas are remotely located and additional facilities are provided near work area. It may be decreased where the food facility is a part of a larger organization providing facilities for other workers as in a hospital or in a hotel.

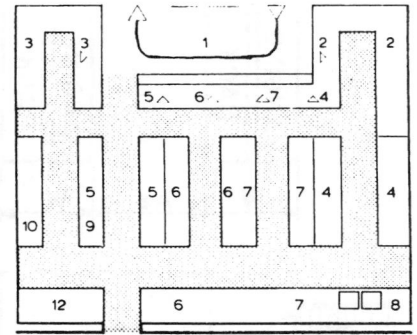

**Fig. 1. Hotel or restaurant kitchen or French restaurant of high standard. Capacity for main meals: Hotel—100-200 persons/menu, 100 persons/ à la carte. Restaurant—200-300 persons / mealtime from 11:30 to 1:30. Waiters' passageway: tangential. Kitchen: linear arrangement with large installations in the rear. See Legend (page 294) for explanation of numbers**

# COMMERCIAL KITCHENS

## KITCHEN PERSONNEL AND THEIR FUNCTIONS

- *Chef de cuisine* (kitchen chef) is responsible for purchase of goods, cost control, setting up the menu, and supervision of personnel and hygiene in the kitchen area.
- *Sous-chef* (kitchen chef's assistant) represents the kitchen chef in his absence; in a large organization, she takes over some of the chef's duties.
- *Saucier* (sauce cook) prepares all sauces and the meals that go with them, as well as all fish dishes (although in large organizations there is a poissonier); she is responsible for the work at the kitchen range, and in medium-sized establishments she assumes the functions of the chef's assistant.
- *Rotisseur* (roast, fry, and grill cook). In large restaurants, there is, in addition, a grilladin.
- *Entrémetier* (soup, vegetable, and side-dish cook). In large restaurants a potagier prepares soups and broths.
- *Garde-manger* supplies the ready-to-cut meat and fish preparation, the cold appetizers, hors d'oeuvres, and salads. In large restaurants, this work is divided between the hors d'oeuvrier (appetizer cook) and the boucher (butcher).
- *Pâtissier* makes cookies, cakes, ice cream, and other desserts. In large restaurants, the work is divided among the glacier (ice cream maker), confiseur (fine pastry cook), and boulanger (baker of bread, rolls, and other baked goods).
- *Commis* (junior cook) is available to chefs of sections.
- Salad person produces and serves various kinds of salads and in some restaurants is responsible for the smorgasbord (hors d'oeuvres) and is subordinate to the garde-manger.
- *Casserolier* cleans, cares for, and services all pans, cooking equipment, and kitchen machines.
- Kitchen person cleans the kitchen, helps with the preparation of dishes, and has other duties.
- *Contrôleur* is in charge of supplies, controls their placement and storage, and does the inventory bookkeeping.

- *Gouvernante* accepts goods, exercises control, supervises the economat dry storage, linen, and cleaning materials, and hands out staples.
- In European restaurants, the bar person is responsible for all beverages and often is the representative for the management, and, in smaller restaurants, oversees the waiters.
- *Argentier* is responsible for the care of silver.
- Office person.
- Dish washer.

Figures 1 to 15 present kitchen layouts for different commercial uses.

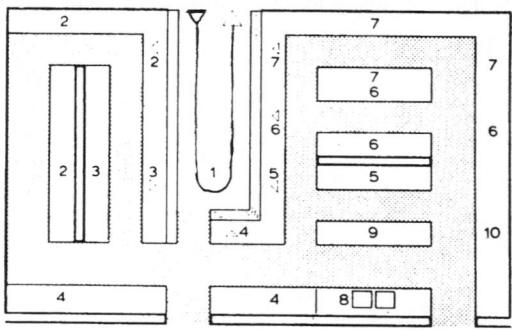

**Fig. 2. Hotel or restaurant kitchen. Capacity: With this layout, 200-seat restaurant will be able to handle three full sittings. This layout can also take care of a hotel with 100 guests and can also accommodate a restaurant open to the general public, an outdoor restaurant, and a private dining area for parties and conferences (altogether, 400 guests). Waiters' passageway: in the center. Kitchen: linear arrangement with large installations in the rear. See Legend (page 294) for explanation of numbers**

*Author:* Max Fengler
*Reference: Restaurant Architecture and Design,* Universe Books, New York.

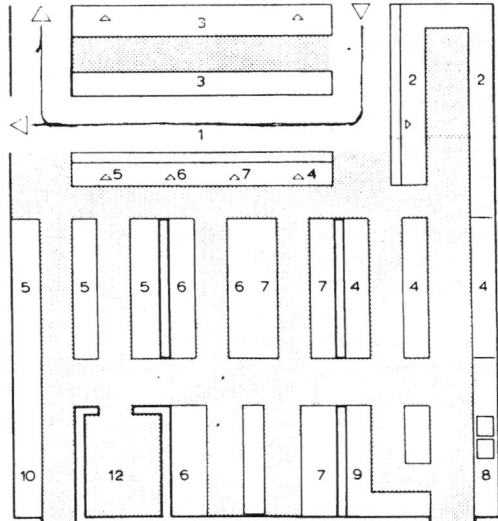

**Fig. 3.** Large restaurant kitchen for restaurants with many private party and conference facilities or with commissary and catering capacity for other businesses. Suitable also for large hotel with large restaurant for the general public. Capacity: 800-1,000 persons. (e.g., 200 seats and fourfold reoccupancy). Waiters' passageway: tangential, with food buffet situated in front. The waiter has access to beverages and other items from the waiters' passageway in the kitchen and from the dining room side as well. The buffet looks over the dining rooms. Kitchen: linear arrangement with fitted berths for large apparatus. See Legend (page 294) for explanation of numbers

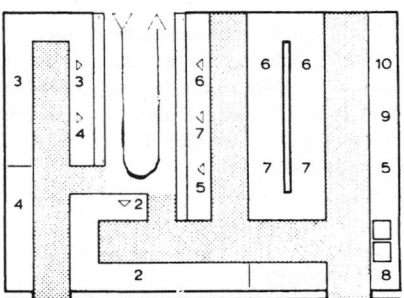

**Fig. 5.** Restaurant kitchen. Capacity: This arrangement is conceived for a very busy city restaurant of good quality (approximately 600 persons e.g., 150 seats with four-fold reoccupancy). Waiters' passageway: in the center. Kitchen: The cooking, roasting, grill, and frying apparatus are planned as wall structures. See Legend (page 294) for explanation of numbers

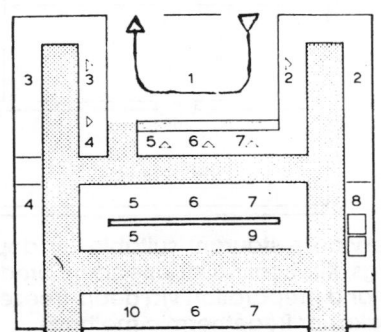

**Fig. 4.** Restaurant kitchen especially suited for city or excursion restaurants. Capacity: as in Fig. 1. Waiter's passageway: tangential. Kitchen: The cooking, roasting, grill, and frying apparatus are planned as wall structures. See Legend (page 294) for explanation of numbers

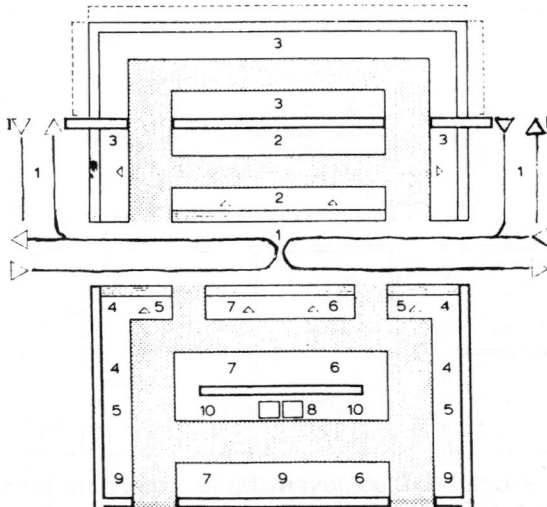

**Fig. 6.** Large restaurant kitchen for restaurants with many auxiliary rooms, bowling alleys, garden, and a snack bar projecting into the main dining room. Suitable for a highly frequented city restaurant or for an excursion spot with various conference rooms, etc. Capacity 1,000-1,200 persons. Waiters' passageway: tangential. Buffet and washing-up zone (dish return) placed in front. The waiter can pick up drinks and other items at two places in the kitchen, the drinks coming pertly from the bar. Kitchen: Warm kitchen as wall structure with central serving area; cold kitchen and pastry area divided with two serving areas each, symmetrically arranged. See Legend (page 294) for explanation of numbers

## Legend (Figs. 1 to 6)

1. Waiters' passageway—meal and beverage counter—dish return
2. Dishwashing area (dishes, glasses, silver)
3. Beverages—preparation and serving
4. Pastry (cookies, cakes, ice cream, dessert)—preparation and serving
5. Cold kitchen (cold appetizers, salad, fish)—preparation and serving
6. Warm kitchen—saucier/rôtisseur area (sauces, roasts, grill, fish)—preparation including large apparatus area and serving
7. Warm kichen—entremétier area (soups, vegetables, entrees)—preparation including large apparatus area and serving
8. Pot and pan washing—casserolier area
9. Vegetable preparation
10. Meat preparation
11. Vegetable cold storage
12. Meat cold storage
13. Economat (dry storage)
14. Beverage cold storage
15. Linen, dish, cleaning supplies storage
16. Staple goods storage
17. Goods acceptance and control
18. Empty goods and garbage collecting rooms

5. Garde-manger
6. Saucier/ rôtisseur
6/7. Range
7. Entremétier
7a. Cooking vat and high-performance steam cooker
6/7b. Warming cupboard and warm serving counter with warming lamps
8. Pot and pan washing
11. Storage, empty goods, office; instead of cold storage rooms—cold storage and freezer cupboards
19. Employees' toilets
G1. Bar counter—also for meals
G2. Dining room with table seating
G3. Guests' toilets / make-up room / telephone booths

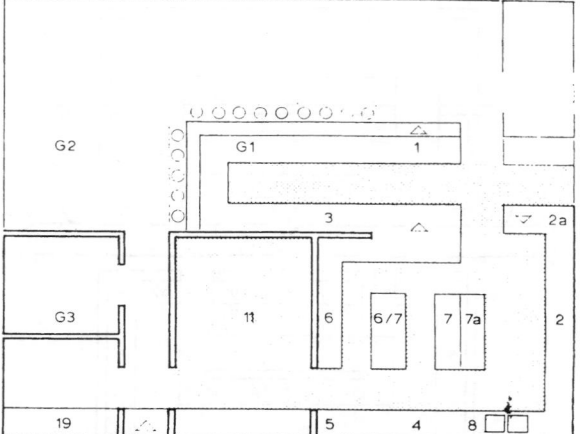

Fig. 7. Snack bar (Pub, tavern, bistro, café, or restaurant). Capacity: 55-60 seats (five- or six-fold reoccupancy over lunchtime, two-fold in the evening; at other times, a well-run café, cake, and snack business). The kitchen deals primarily with ready-to-serve articles. In a city business with daily delivery, the storage space does not have to be especially large

## Legend (Fig. 7)

1. Meal and beverage serving counter
2. Dishwasher
2a. Dish return
3. Beverage buffet with mixer, toaster, ice-cream container, etc.
4. Oven and small pastry station

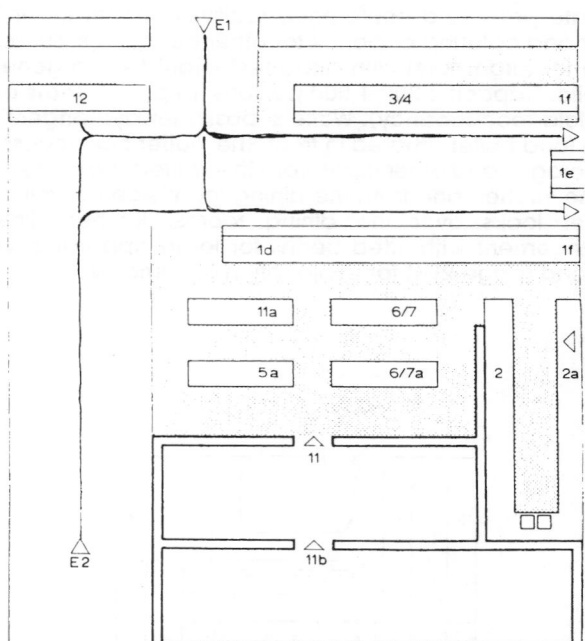

Fig. 8. Self-service restaurant suitable for department or office buildings. Kitchen: no independent production; outside delivery and preparation via deep-freeze, boiling-in-the-bag (Nacka) or Régéthermic methods

## Legend (Fig. 8)

1d. Self-service buffet with grill and fry unit
1e. Salad dressings, spices, cutlery reserves
1f. Cashier
2. Dishwasher
2a. Dish return
3/4. Sandwich unit, cakes, ice cream, coffee, beverages; service available at an outdoor café
5a. Cold preparation table
6/7. Defrosting, warming-up apparatus front, serviceable on two sides (convection ovens, heating appliances for Nacka system or Régéthermic ovens)

11. Cold storage and storage (varies in size according to system of servicing and rhythm of delivery)
11a. Refrigerator front, serviceable on two sides
11b. Delivery, empty goods, intermediary storage, personnel cloakroom
12. Kiosk—sales on the inside and to customers on the street
E1. Entrance from street
E2. Entrance from building (department store, office building, etc.)

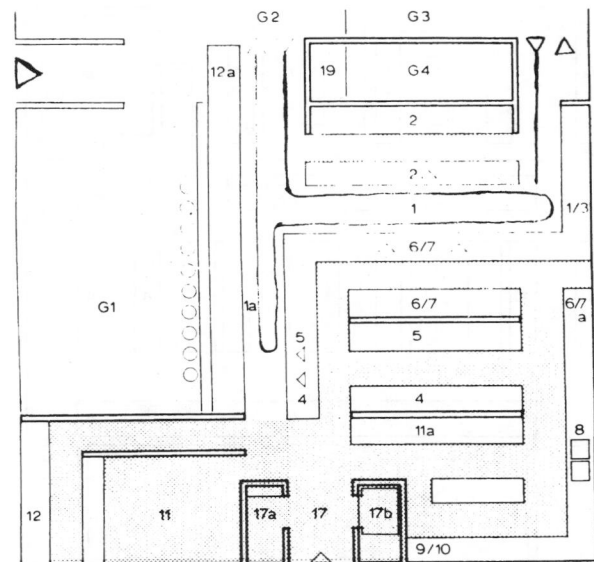

**Fig. 10. Restaurant for travelers (highway restaurant, or café-restaurant at a busy intersection in the city). Capacity: Snack—45-50 seats (200 persons every hour); restaurants—80 seats (two- or threefold reoccupancy during meals; at other times, coffee, ice cream, pastry and sandwich service); grill—40 seats (one- or twofold reoccupancy, high standard service) Kitchen: Linear-wall arrangement, approximately equal balance between freshly prepared meals and ready-to-serve meals. Storage, empty goods, and personnel cloakrooms in the cellar**

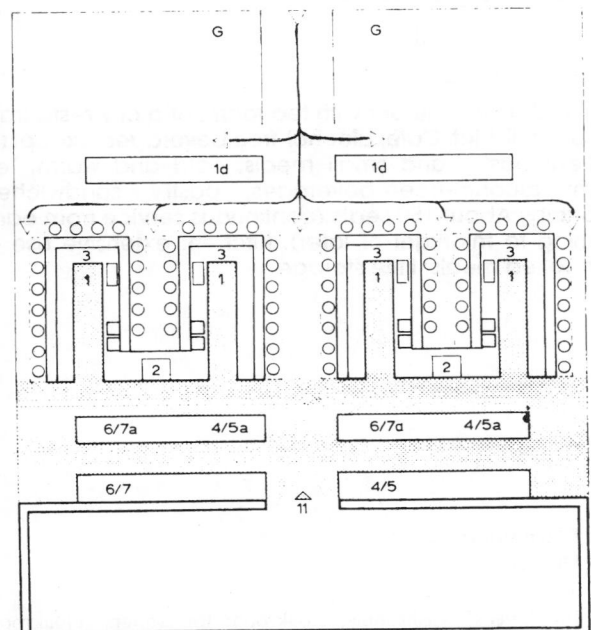

**Fig. 9. Restaurant with finger-shaped bar and automats for quick lunch service in restaurants for passersby, cafeterias, department stores, highway restaurants. Capacity: 500 persons per hour. Kitchens: preparation of precooked meals, salads and ice cream**

## Legend (Fig. 9)
1. Service passage for U-shaped or finger-shaped counter
1d. Automats for self-service
2. Connection of two fingers with dishwasher having two covers, serviceable on both sides; adjoining are two sinks each
3. Coffee machine, refrigerators, soup vat storage
4/5. Salad and ice cream preparation
4/5a. Cold counter—salad, ice cream, dessert
6/7. Frying pan, soup cooker, and other cooking equipment
6/7a. Warm counter—bain marie, fryer, grill plates
11. Economat, cold storage, and freezer space, staples room (delivery, empty goods room, office, personnel cloakrooms, and washrooms not included)
G Guest rooms with standing room and seats (automat service with disposable dishes)

## Legend (Fig. 10)
1. Waiters' passageway
1a. Service corridor for snacks, and cold meal and pastry-serving counter for restaurant
1/3. Waiters—Beverage self-service
2. Dishwashers
4. Pastry
5. Cold kitchen
6/7. Warm kitchen (roast, grill, fry), bain-marie in the serving counter
6/7a. Cooking and frying apparatus (2 vats, 1 pan)
8. Pot and pan washing
9/10. Meat and vegetable preparation
11. Storage for the day
11a. Cupboard group, cooled and not cooled
12. Kiosk facing the street
12a. Cigarette machine
17. Goods delivery
17a. Office
17b. Elevator to cellar
19. Employee toilets
G1. Snack area with about 40 seats and seats at the bar
G2. Restaurant
G3. Grill restaurant, possibly with small bar for espresso, aperitifs, whisky and other spirits
G4. Guests' toilets

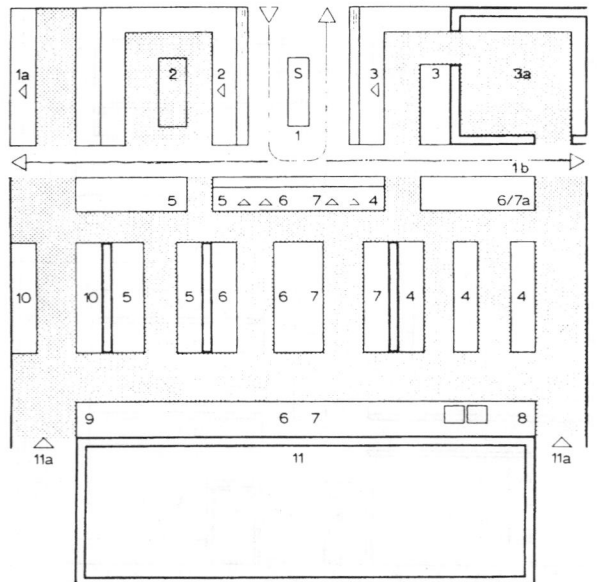

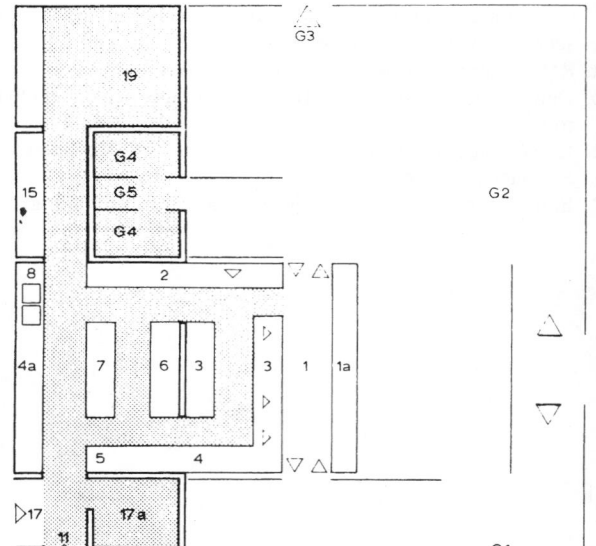

Fig. 11. Large hotel-restaurant kitchen also for large restaurants with some auxiliary rooms and with outside deliveries or production for other organizations (variant of Figs. 3 and 6). Capacity: 800–1,000 persons. Waiters' passageway: in the center, with a special serving link to the garden (or, for instance, to a bowling alley) and directly connecting to the auxiliary rooms. Kitchen: Linear arrangement with rear side of large apparatus

Fig. 12. Café-restaurant with tea room, or a city restaurant in a busy district. Café: alcohol-free beverages, except for bottled; pastry and small meals, cold and warm. Tea room: alcohol-free beverages, pastry, sandwiches. Capacity: About 150 seats (continuous service from early morning to midnight or later). Kitchen: extensive use of precooked meals; little storage

**Legend (Fig. 11)**
1. Waiters' passageway
1a. Meal and beverage serving to garden
1b. Access to auxiliary rooms
2. Dishwashing area
3. Beverage serving area.
3a. Beverage cold storage (day cellar)
4. Pastry
5. Cold kitchen
6. Warm kitchen—saucier/ rôtisseur area
7. Warm kitchen—entremétier area
8. Pot and pan washing
9. Vegetable preparation
10. Meat preparation
11. Cold storage and storage rooms
11a. Accesses to delivery, empty goods room, and intermediary storage, office, personnel cloakrooms, and toilets
S Service accessories (cash register)

**Legend (Fig. 12)**
1. Waiters' passageway
1a. Serving stations and cash register
2. Dishwasher
3. Beverage buffet with mixer, toaster, ice cream container, etc.
4. Pastry
4a. Pastry oven
5. Sandwich unit
6. Defrosting and heating equipment, soup vats
7. Oven, grill, frying apparatus
8. Pot and pan washing
11. Day stores, empty goods (staple goods in cellar)

15. Linen storage
17. Delivery
17a. Office
19. Employees' washrooms, cloakroom for waiters (cloakroom and washrooms for kitchen employees in cellar)
G1. Tea room
G2. Café restaurant
G3. Terrace or garden
G4. Washrooms
G5. Telephone booths

**Legend (Fig. 13)**
1a. Platter and cutlery trolley
1b. Distribution help, regulation of conveyor-belt speed, dietary food storage
1c. Conveyor belt for standard menu
1d. Self-service buffet menu:
    1 soup of the day
    1 stew
    1 standard menu
    1 dietary food
    2 cold meals
various salads
various desserts
dairy products
5 cold beverages (beer, wine, carbonated beverages, juice)

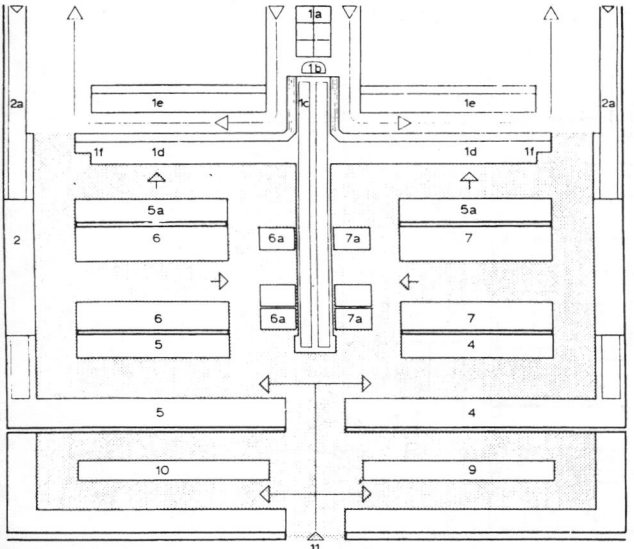

**Legend (Fig. 14)**
1d. Self-service buffet—menu as in Fig. 13
1e. Circular device for salad dressings, condiments, extra cutlery, etc.
1f. Cash register
1g. Preparation table with trolley stand
2. Dishwasher
2a. Soiled-dish return
11. Standard or conveyor-type elevator connection to kitchen

**Fig. 13.** Student dining hall or cafeteria with two-sided self-service buffet and conveyor belt. Capacity: 12 per minute x 2 = 24 persons. Without cash payment, hourly capacity: 1,400 persons. With cash circulation, hourly capacity: 1,100 persons. Seating: at least 340 seats. Kitchen: fully equipped linear arrangement, planned for automatic equipment

1e. Salad dressings, condiments, cutlery
1f. Cash register
2. Dishwasher
2a. Soiled-dish conveyor belt
4. Pastry
5. Garde-manger
5a. Portioning table for cold meals, salads, and desserts
6. Roast kitchen, possibly roasting automats
6a. Warm-storage trolleys—portioning of meat, sauces, dietary foods
7. Cooking kitchen, possibly with automatic steam cookers
7a. Warm-storage trolleys for portioning of vegetables, entrées
9. Vegetable preparation
10. Meat preparation
11. Access to the storage rooms, delivery and auxiliary rooms

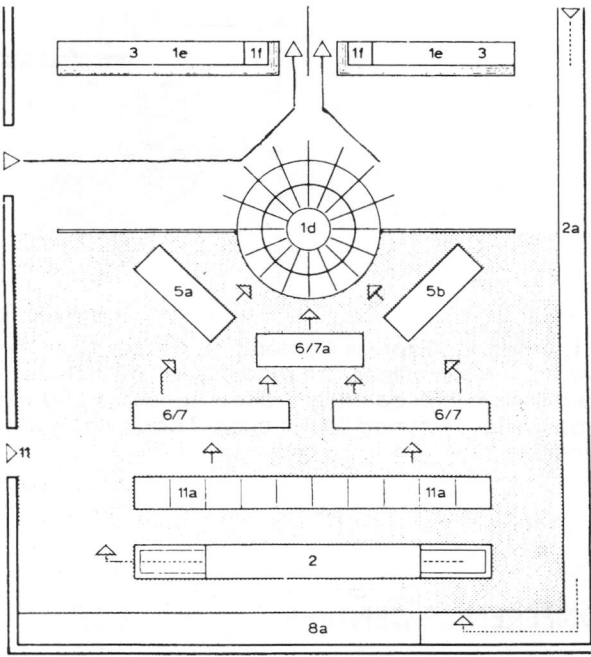

**Fig. 15.** Student dining hall or cafeteria with self-service carousel. Capacity: after the initial phase, 1,400 persons per hour. Seating: at least 400 seats. Meal delivery from a central kitchen—deep freeze, boil-in-the bag (Nacka), and Régéthermic system

**Legend (Fig. 15)**
1d. Self-service, three-tier carousel.
   Below: 2 cold dishes, various salads, desserts (partly on ice)
   Center: warm meals, 3 warm dishes, 2 grilled or fried dishes (with warming lamps above)
   Above: sandwiches, pastry, etc.
1e. Salad dressings, condiments, extra cutlery, etc.
1f. Cash register
2. Dishwasher (stacking area, 3 tanks, drying zone)
2a. Soiled-dish conveyor belt
3. Beverage self-service area
5a. Portioning table for cold dishes and salads
5b. Portioning table for desserts, sandwiches, etc.
6/7. Warming and defrosting appliances
6/7a. Portioning table for warm meats
8a. Trolley storage
11. Meal delivery from central kitchen, access to the supply and auxiliary rooms
11a. Storage cupboards for cold goods and other goods delivered from the central kitchen

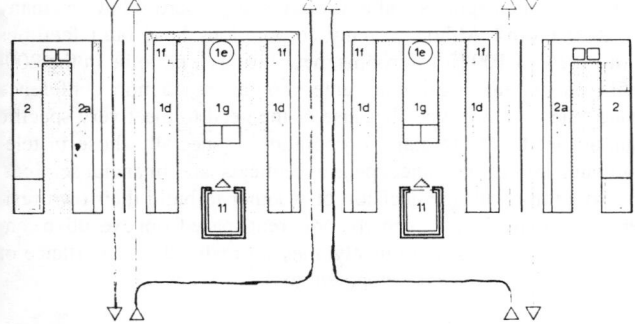

**Fig. 14.** Student dining hall or cafeteria with four self-service buffets. Capacity: at least 1,500 persons per hour. Seating: at least 400 seats. Kitchen: outside delivery of meals with standard or conveyor-type elevator

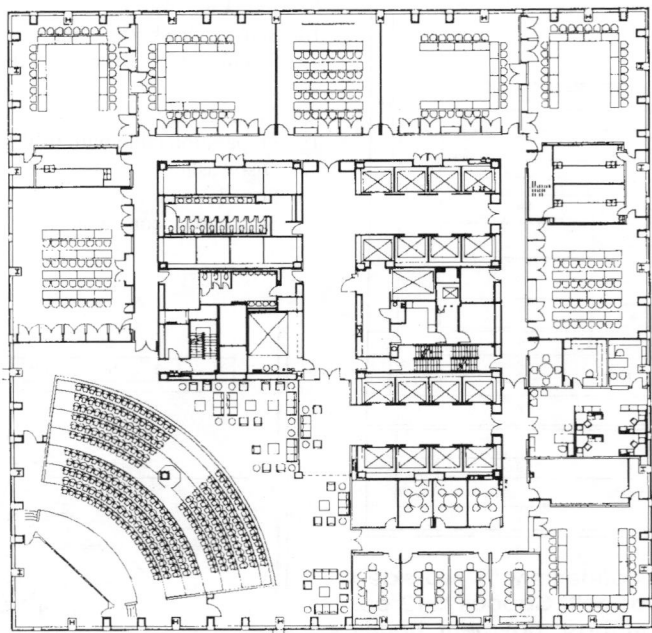

**Fig. 1. American Express Conference Center, New York City. Located on the twenty-sixth floor of American Express' lower-Manhattan offices, the meeting facility includes eight exterior meeting rooms, nine small breakout rooms, and an auditorium with carefully crafted acoustics and closed-circuit television connections to the neighboring training rooms. The foyer formed by the curved back wall is used for receptions and social events. (Architect: Swanke Hayden Connell)**

## CONFERENCE CENTERS

Table 1 identifies the principal types of conference centers, the typical meetings they attract, and their general physical characteristics. Figure 1 shows a nonresidential center.

The *executive conference center* is the most typical midrange facility (although not necessarily midprice). It is oriented toward corporate meetings, including both training and management development. Such centers feature a relatively large number of conference rooms—only the largest corporate training centers have more. Most executive centers are located in the suburbs around the larger cities, such as New York, Washington, Atlanta, and Chicago. With increasing competition and land costs, the main concern of both developers and operators should be whether a proposed facility has the potential to attract weekend conferences or social business, both of which are necessary to ensure profitability.

Many of the *resort conference centers* have evolved from executive properties by marketing and promoting their recreational facilities. They are designed for the same type of management meetings, as well as for sales and incentive groups. Resort conference centers vary in size but most new properties are in the 350- to 500-room range, in

order to support the recreational infrastructure. Usually they have somewhat less meeting space than do executive centers, but more food and beverage and recreational facilities. New resort centers are being built in both suburban locations and the more traditional resort destinations, such as Arizona and California. These often are joint-venture developments because of the extreme cost in acquiring the land and building the center and recreational amenities. In addition to these new properties, existing resort operators are adding conference center buildings to extend their seasons, and attract additional markets.

*Corporate conference and training centers* are physically the largest of the several categories and a few existing properties have as many as 1,000 rooms. Although many corporations have built facilities with as few as 100 to 150 rooms, new entities tend to be in the 200- to 500-room range. Corporate centers contain much more conference space than do other types because of the need to meet very specific training needs. Many major corporations, especially those in telecommunications, insurance, pharmaceuticals, and financial services, are struggling with the decision of whether to build their own residential or nonresidential centers, or to rent space from executive centers or at other sites. Fortunately, they all realize the importance of training and employee development to their success.

*Author:* Richard H. Penner
*Reviewer:* John Hill, Hill Glazier Architects
*Reference: Conference Center Planning and Design,* Whitney Library of Design

**Table 1** Conference center characteristics

| Type of Center | Typical Meeting Uses | Facility Characteristics |
|---|---|---|
| Executive | Mid- and upper-level training and management development; management planning; sales meetings | Suburban locations; 225–300 midsize to large guestrooms; multiple dining and beverage outlets; moderate number of mid-size conference rooms; large number of breakout rooms; moderate recreational facilities |
| Resort | Mid- and upper-level management meetings; incentive trips; sales meetings | Resort destination or suburban locations; 150–400 large rooms; multiple dining and beverage outlets; small to moderate number of conference rooms; additional banquet rooms; extensive recreational amenities (especially outdoors) |
| Corporate | Technical and sales training for low- and mid-level employees; management development meetings; outside conferences if company policy permits | Suburban or headquarters locations; 125–400 rooms of varying sizes; limited dining alternatives; extensive training or conference rooms to meet corporate objectives; specialized rooms; auditorium; moderate to extensive recreational facilties |
| University | Executive education for middle managers; scientific meetings and continuing education programs | On-campus location; 50–150 small to midsize rooms; limited dining and beverage options; small to moderate number of conference rooms; amphitheater; auditorium (at continuing education centers); recreation located elsewhere on campus rather than as formal part of center |
| Nonresidential | Low- and mid-level employee education; middle and upper management development | Urban or corporate headquarters location; no guestrooms; one limited-service dining room-café; generic conference and breakout rooms; limited special-purpose rooms; no recreation |
| Not-for-profit | Religious, educational, and government staff training; association and foundation meetings | Often at remote location; 25–100 rooms; single dining room; small to moderate number of generic conference rooms; large multipurpose room; limited recreation (primarily outdoors) |

*University conference facilities* meet three different needs: some of the most luxurious are designed for dedicated business school executive education programs; others provide for campus visitors and educational conferences, or for growing continuing education programs. The university centers generally are no larger than 150 to 200 rooms, and feature amphitheaters or an auditorium as well as the more typical conference rooms. These centers exist because the large research universities realize that their reputations are, in part, dependent on the types of executive and adult education programs they run, and on their abilities to bring business executives to campus on a regular basis.

The *nonresidential centers* most often are corporate operated, either for low- and mid-level training or for upper-level management development. They may be constructed near the corporate headquarters or at a site convenient to the training department. Most contain fairly standard conference rooms and may be available to the public for day meetings, depending on the corporate policy

The most highly variable group are the *nonprofit centers*, which may be owned by religious or educational organizations, associations and foundations, research centers, or private humanitarian and arts groups. Their facilities reflect the differing missions of their respective owner groups and offer the public or specific interest groups the opportunity to meet in, for example, a spectacular mountain setting or near a historic landmark.

The following sections discuss each of the conference center types and illustrate a variety of planning and design solutions. Later material investigates the various complex programming and planning

issues of the individual functional areas, including guest rooms, public areas, conference core, and recreational facilities.

## PLANNING THE MEETING FACILITIES

One key difference between hotels and conference centers, and certainly the one that developers and operators feel is most central to their success, is the planning and design of the conference and training areas. The conference center industry has grown around providing a superior meeting product, including better service, fewer distractions, and an all-inclusive price. However, these attractions give little real advantage if the meeting facilities design does not provide sufficient dedicated conference space organized for effective meetings.

The earliest conference centers developed a core of meeting space balanced between multipurpose rooms to meet the varying needs of different users and single-purpose spaces dedicated to conferences, audiovisual presentations, private dining, and so forth; developers eventually learned which types of rooms established the most salable mix between these two divergent approaches. Today, most conference center operators emphasize the single-purpose spaces, further strengthened by increased marketing and management abilities. Also, over the last two decades, operators have found that attendees want and expect more generously sized rooms, and so space requirements have escalated. For example, breakout rooms that might have once been 250 square feet are now 400 to 500 square feet; meeting rooms for 30 participants have increased from 750 to 1,000 square feet. As a result, among the most important decisions is to evaluate the expected conference user, and to design rooms for their specific needs.

## ESTABLISHING THE CONFERENCE SPACE PROGRAM

The architectural program for salable conference and meeting spaces is essential to defining the conference center product. This can best be done in three steps:

1. Consider the types of general and special purpose rooms that are required
2. Determine the optimum and maximum capacity for each
3. Establish the number of each type

The difference with hotels is obvious. Convention hotels contain one or more large ballrooms and a number of smaller meeting and banquet rooms, usually multipurpose and subdivisible; not much space is dedicated to small and midsize meetings. The current standard for conference centers, on the other hand, is to provide many more conference rooms, few of the smaller spaces subdivisible, a high number of small breakout rooms for working groups, and such dedicated rooms as amphitheaters, auditoriums, and computer facilities. In addition, assembly and refreshment spaces, conference services staff offices, and projection and audiovisual needs are essential to meeting customer expectations. Because different developers and management companies use varying terminology (for example, an "auditorium" may be a large, multipurpose conference room or a sloped-floor theater), it is necessary to define the terms used generally throughout the conference center industry.

### Auditorium

The auditorium is a sloped floor, theaterlike room for formal presentations, sometimes with additional balcony seating. It generally includes a stage and front screen (and occasionally rear-screen) projection capability. Auditoriums are most common in corporate training facilities, with room capacities of 150 to 300, and in university continuing education centers, with capacities as high as 1,000. Space requirements: 8 square feet (7 square feet per person by code for occupancy calculation) per seat for the auditorium seating and aisles; 10 to 12 square feet per seat overall, including the stage and a small projection room.

### Amphitheater

The amphitheater is a tiered room incorporating built-in work surfaces, which are often curved to focus seating on the speaker or horseshoe-shaped to allow better eye contact among attendees. It features front-screen projection in university executive education centers and rear-screen projection in executive facilities. Capacity at university centers is limited to between 40 and 60, depending on the class objectives, and between 90 and 125 at executive conference centers. Space requirements: 25 square feet per seat.

### Multipurpose Conference Room

This is a large, flexible meeting room, often with subdivisible partitions, a flat floor, and a 200- to 500-seat capacity. The character of this room can vary greatly, depending on the type of conference center, with some more resembling a junior ballroom and others little different from a standard conference room. Most incorporate either front- or rear-screen projection. Space requirements are 15 to 24 square feet per seat for executive theater and classroom setups.

### Conference Rooms

These dedicated conference rooms for 20 to 50 people form the majority of the meeting facilities. They have flat floors, simple built-in systems, including writing and tackable surfaces, projection screens, and presentation rails. Some include front-screen projection. Space requirements: 18 to 26 square feet per seat for executive theater and classroom setups; 34 to 42 square feet per seat for hollow square and U-shaped arrangements.

### Breakout Rooms

Breakout rooms are small conference rooms for up to 12 people with limited features, usually including tackable walls, a whiteboard, and a projection screen. Space requirements: 25 square feet per seat; larger rooms are often used, but still for no more than 10 to 12 people.

### Boardroom

The boardroom is a special, upgraded conference room with a fixed table, executive chairs, high-level finishes, front and/or rear-screen projection, and a private lounge or anteroom. Usual capacity is about 16 to 24. Space requirements: 40 square feet per seat, increased by 50 percent when providing a projection room, pantry, or anteroom.

### Computer Room

This special training room, found mostly in corporate and university centers, incorporates several rows of work stations, each with the capability of exchanging information between the instructor and the students. Many of these rooms are part of a larger building or campus network. Space requirements: 30 to 40 square feet per seat.

Of course, the exact number of each room type and its respective capacity will be the result of the market study and operational objectives of the owner and operator. For example, the program may call for many similar 40-person conference rooms and 10-person breakout rooms designed to meet a general set of design criteria. In addition, it may establish specialized requirements for individual larger rooms, or for those with distinctive audiovisual or computer requirements. A computer company, for example, certainly will have different requirements for a presentation room in a training center than a university business school will have for its executive education case study room—both of which may essentially be a tiered-floor amphitheater for 30 people.

## ESTABLISHING THE ASSEMBLY AND SUPPORT AREAS PROGRAM

In addition to determining the necessary conference and training spaces, the team must establish the program for the prefunction areas and such support functions as conference services, audiovisuals, coffee pantries, and (in corporate and university projects) offices for faculty and program directors. The assembly spaces are of several types, from a separate lobby for day attendees, to major prefunction areas outside the larger rooms, to smaller refreshment areas and outdoor terraces. The assembly areas should total between 30 and 50 percent of the salable conference space.

The support areas add further complexity to the program definition. The principal components include:

*Conference services:* Space is needed for offices for the conference concierge, the conference service manager, and conference and A.V. planners, and a lounge for meeting with clients; some operators include an audiovisual display room and work areas adjacent or nearby.

*Audiovisuals:* Rear- and front-screen projection rooms, the latter being the more common; office and workrooms for the audiovisual technicians; a "head-end," or central distribution room.

*Graphics:* Reproduction capability for handout material is essential; larger centers provide a complete print shop to reproduce course materials, signs, name badges, and so on, and include a full photographic darkroom.

*Storage areas:* Space is needed for conference room furnishings, including tables, chairs, lecterns, and risers; portable audiovisual equipment; food service supplies; and client materials sent in advance of meetings.

*Coffee pantry:* Include a service area for brewing coffee and tea, holding cold drinks, preparing and holding pastries and fruit, storing soiled dishes, and so on.

*Faculty and trainer offices:* Requirements include offices, staff workrooms, and resource rooms for the instructors and program managers. These are most common in university executive education and corporate training centers; executive and resort conference centers may provide two or three small offices for the client meeting planner.

If there are no extensive offices for instructors, the support areas range from about 15 to 30 percent of the salable conference space. The major variant is the amount of audiovisual support space required for projection rooms and the central audiovisual-graphics services. Throughout the program phase, the owner and operator must fully discuss whether added capabilities and service levels justify higher capital expenses (for both space and equipment) and the eventual correspondingly higher payroll cost. And a separate audiovisual program should address the equipment duplication implied by a major investment in audiovisual support space.

## TYPES OF CONFERENCE AND TRAINING ROOMS

Each of the typical conference rooms has a number of unique planning criteria to consider early in the design. These require the collaborative effort of all members of the design team, especially the architect, interior designer, audiovisual consultant, and operator. A room-by-room examination follows.

### Ballroom

The conference center ballroom serves dual functions as the principal banquet room and, for larger groups, as the meeting room for general sessions. Its design, therefore, includes sophisticated audiovisual systems, one or more projection booths, increased ventilation, larger foyer and breakout areas, and high-quality soundproof divisible partitions. Many of the decorative touches common in hotel ballrooms (the expansive chandeliers, delicate wall sconces, or boldly patterned carpet) are absent, but the conference center ballroom still offers the potential for attracting weekend social business, and so should have enough design character to capture this secondary market.

The ballroom's "split personality" raises a number of difficult planning and design questions:

- Should the ballroom be located in the conference core or nearer the restaurants?
- How should it be decorated?
- Does it need the same sophisticated systems of the largest meeting rooms?

Each project team needs to assess the anticipated conference market and determine where the ballroom falls on the continuum between function room and meeting room. For example, Westfields' three large subdivisible ballrooms each offer highly sophisticated computerized audiovisual systems, and the management provides the full range of conference services at each one.

Several resort properties include two ballrooms oriented to different uses: One is designed principally as a function room; the second equipped as a large meeting room, including rear-screen projection. Although, either room can be used for any type of meeting or function, the developers established a primary use and designed and equipped the rooms accordingly.

### Large Conference Room

Large conference rooms (those greater than 1,500 square feet; see Fig. 2) are most often used for presentations requiring little audience involvement through discussion or questions. These rooms are set up theater or classroom style, in straight rows facing the speaker. Because the room depth usually exceeds 50 feet and the rows number at least ten (often 20 or more), it may be necessary to provide a stage or riser. This is an important consideration because it influences

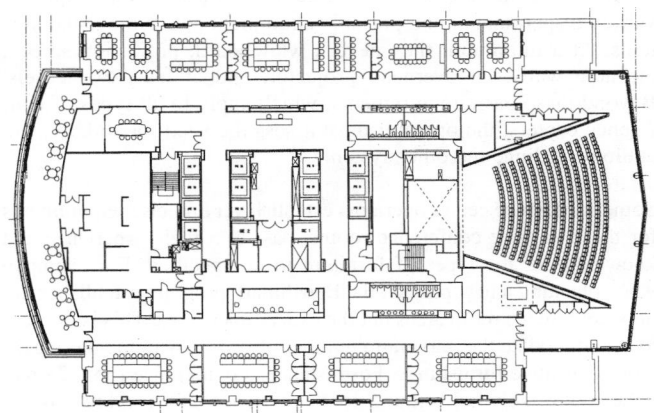

**Fig. 2. Shearson Lehman Brothers Conference and Training Center, New York City.** Located on two upper floors of a Wall Street office building, the Shearson center contains 23,000 net square feet of dedicated conference space. Guests are greeted at a reception area on the lower floor and directed to one of 25 meeting rooms, including a 393-seat auditorium, four computer labs, and two rooms with rear-screen projection. Except for the computer rooms, all the conference and breakout spaces have windows with spectacular views of the harbor and lower Manhattan. Window coverings include three layers—drapes, blackout curtains, and a lighter sun screen—all electrically operated by the instructor. A small dining room is available for lunches and special receptions. (Architect: Skidmore, Owings & Merrill)

the design of the front presentation wall and, as a result, the planning of such support areas as a rear projection room.

Unfortunately, the larger rooms often are subdivided, an alteration that creates significant difficulties because these rooms have the greatest need for sophisticated audiovisual and sound reinforcement systems. Audiovisual capability often is compromised, or redundant systems are required in subdivisible rooms. These rooms more often have specialized audiovisual presentations, and it is therefore imperative for the speaker to be able to darken the room with a minimum of effort; if the rooms include windows, it is important to provide electronic blackout shades or drapes.

Also, the larger rooms require substantially greater ceiling heights, which influences the rooms' location in the building. Rather than combining higher and lower ceiling spaces in the same zone (resulting in unusable volume above the finished ceiling of the smaller rooms), the larger rooms frequently are located in a low structure extending beyond the guest room tower, or on a lower level that can accommodate the two-story volume.

### Medium Conference Rooms

These rooms, in the 1,000 to 1,500 square foot range, are the mainstay of today's properties. For example, among the corporate projects, the Pitney Bowes training center includes 30 out of 46 conference rooms at this size, and the IBM Advanced Business Institute has 18 of 21. These midsize rooms, used for highly interactive training, management development, marketing, and executive education, need to allow practically any type of room arrangement: theater, classroom, hollow square, U-shaped, or small-group configurations (Fig. 3). In addition, these rooms require a variety of permanent and portable equipment and audiovisual systems. At a minimum, they need a whiteboard, projection screen, tackable walls, an overhead projector, and at least two easels. Beyond these basic requirements, which apply to all types of conference centers, the operator must assess the need for slide, video, audio recording, and other systems.

Some conference center operators establish very precise requirements for these midsize conference rooms, based on their experience and knowledge of the types of furniture to be specified. For example, when planning a new project, the Benchmark program establishes not only conference room areas but the exact dimensions. This is in order to accommodate the maximum number of people with the more generous executive furnishings. For instance, a conference room 28 feet wide comfortably holds four 5-foot conference tables and two 4-foot side aisles; a narrower room would force the elimination of one table in each row or would require a single center aisle. A slightly wider room would provide more generous aisles but no increase in capacity.

### Small Conference Rooms

Centers expecting to attract groups of 20 to 30 people may program a large number of smaller conference rooms in the 500 to 1,000 square foot range. While these smaller rooms offer less flexibility and may encourage crowding of slightly larger groups, many operators bemoan the lack of a sufficient number of smaller rooms. A careful analysis of the needs of the primary users and of competitive centers may establish the right mix for a new project.

These rooms should be equipped similarly to midsize rooms. Each space should have a permanent projection screen, whiteboard, and

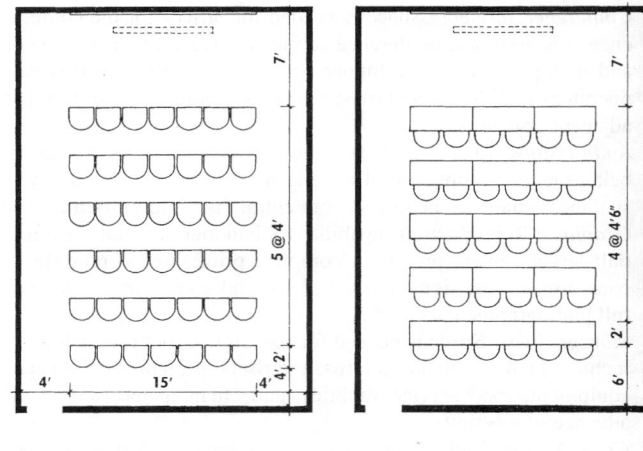
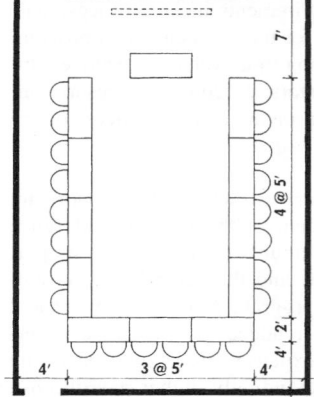
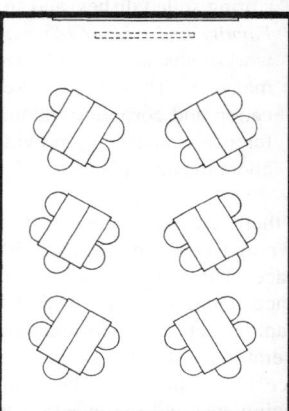

**Fig. 3. Conference room layouts. Conference center operators are alert to the potential variations in capacity of different layouts. The illustrated rooms, 23 by 33 feet or 760 square feet show maximum seating and fairly tight spacing, especially between seating and the walls. Theater layout (top left) offers the most seats; classroom (top right), U-shaped (bottom left), and cluster (bottom right) arrangements accommodate about equal numbers but will vary slightly depending on the room dimensions**

walls that can accommodate sheets torn from a flip chart. Some operators install a hanging rail, offering wide flexibility to meet the needs of each client.

### Breakout Rooms

Another distinguishing feature of conference centers is the provision of a high number of breakout rooms, often equaling the total of the other conference rooms. The size of these rooms varies dramatically among centers, some allowing no more than an office-sized space, say 150 to 200 square feet; other operators insist on breakout rooms large enough for groups of 8 to 12 and set a minimum size of about 400 square feet. The addition to Scanticon-Princeton included seven breakout rooms of 450 square feet each. The larger rooms are more flexible, of course, accommodating larger groups as well as those needing to work on extended projects, bring in computers or video equipment, role-play, or otherwise spread out.

Breakout rooms require the same minimal equipment as do smaller conference rooms. Most have little specialized audiovisual equipment; executive centers may provide audio and video jacks to accommodate transmissions to or from a central control room.

## Boardrooms

Most executive and resort conference centers include one or two boardrooms. The developer needs to determine whether a boardroom is desired as a marketing tool or is necessary to meet actual demand for such a room. While the boardrooms require relatively little floor area (500 to 800 square feet for the room itself), many developers choose to add private lounges, toilets, projection rooms, and other accessory areas, which increase the space program. In addition, the boardroom is expensive to furnish and equip, often running two to three times the cost of a standard conference room. Much of this expense comes from the additional millwork: movable wall panels, to hide writing and tackable surfaces or coat closets, oversized custom tables, built-in buffets, and similar luxuries.

If security is a major concern, the boardroom may need to be physically separated from the other conference rooms, fully soundproofed, and totally private; for example, switches may be installed to cut off audio transmissions to the central control room. Such characteristics need to be defined early in the programming phase.

## Amphitheater

Some resort and university centers include an amphitheater (Fig. 4). These custom-designed spaces are expensive to provide, in part because they are not sufficiently flexible for different types of seating arrangements, which means groups that are the right size for the amphitheater may not choose to use it because they prefer a different layout. In fact, instructors who like one design (the horseshoe shape common in business school case study rooms, for instance) often refuse to use the slightly curved amphitheaters found in resort and executive centers because of the lack of eye contact among the participants. In addition, amphitheaters' construction, furnishings, and equipment costs are high because of the change in floor levels, ceiling articulation, millwork counters and railings, special lighting, upgraded executive chairs, and audiovisual and computer connections. The feasibility study should establish early on whether there is legitimate need for an amphitheater.

An amphitheater, if eventually programmed, requires about 25 square feet per seat, or about the same amount of space as a more typical conference room. Most rooms will have either a front- or rear projection room equipped for most media, including slides, video, and film at the very least. If multimedia or multiple-image presentations are anticipated, the front wall needs an oversized screen.

One of the most difficult design tasks is the organization of the amphitheater's presentation wall, which needs to accommodate a writing surface (business schools may require multiple whiteboards), tackable surface, presentation rail, projection screen, and speakers. Scanticon provides two or more screens, one for the projection systems and a second that can be tilted for use with overhead projectors.

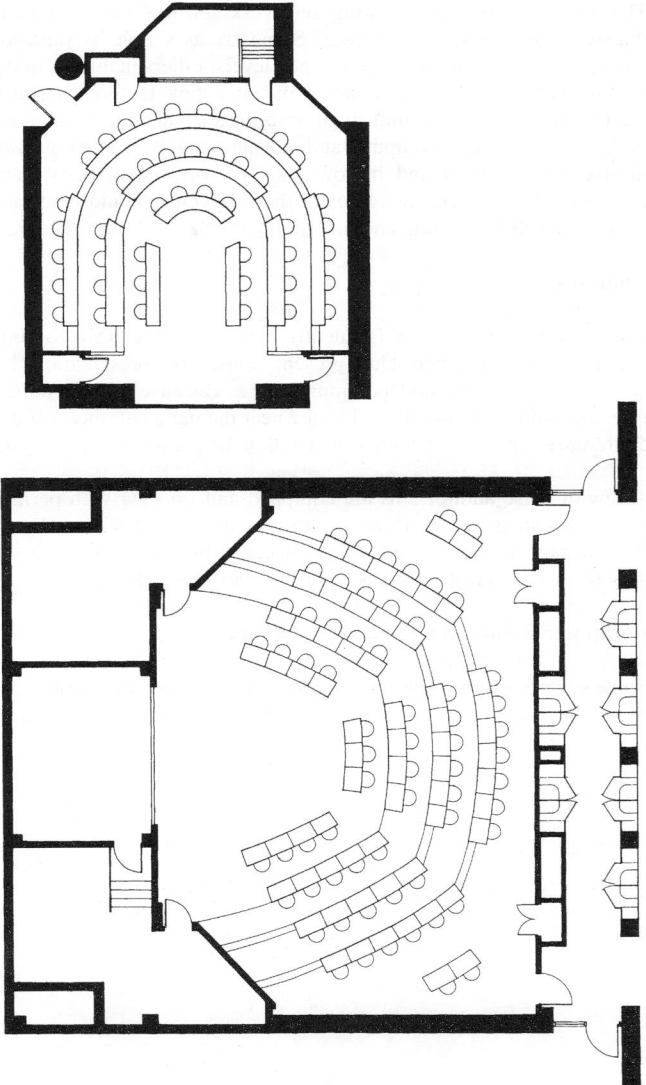

**Fig. 4. Amphitheater layouts. Special-purpose rooms offering less flexibility may be essential for particular instructional objectives; many centers provide amphitheaters—either gently curved or horseshoe-shaped—to enhance participation among the attendees. Top: Steinberg Center, University of Pennsylvania (Architect: The Hillier Group); bottom: IBM-Palisades (Architect: Mitchell/Giurgola)**

Some presenters may want to combine two systems—showing slides and, at the same time, writing notes on the board, for example.

Controls need to be positioned at several locations. Room lights are switched at the door; the other systems, including lights, projection, audio, window drapes, and so on, are controlled at the lectern (which often is connected into a floor box), at the front wall, and in the projection booth. Wireless remote control is possible for most applications.

The design of the tiered seating and work surfaces varies tremendously among conference centers. Some are as simple as standard conference tables bolted to the stepped levels; others include a fairly simple work surface and modesty panel; a few feature carefully crafted custom millwork units incorporating such details as electrical outlets, microphones, computer and translation jacks, leather writing inserts, undershelves and narrow slots for displaying participant name boards. The relative values of these features should be established at an early meeting and incorporated into the design criteria.

### Auditorium

Corporate training centers frequently include a large, 150- to 300-seat auditorium for major class presentations, other presentations by company executives, and community use. Because of this public role, the auditorium usually is located near the main entrance, off the conference center lobby, rather than within the main conference core.

A few of these auditoriums are equipped and finished with permanent work areas; most, however, are typical theaters with a sloped floor, a stage, a balcony, and projection capability. Translation booths may be provided if the need is identified early enough.

### Computer Rooms and Special Classrooms

Some centers will include specialized spaces to meet their individual market needs. Many of the university executive education facilities, for example, feature a computer room, which is used both for instruction and as a student resource when classes are not being conducted. Generally these are limited to 15 to 20 stations because of the difficulties of conducting computer exercises for larger groups.

The program should allow at least 35 to 40 square feet per person to accommodate the computer stations and the associated printers, reference materials, software, and supplies. Most computer rooms are designed so that the instructor's computer display is projected on the front wall. More sophisticated arrangements allow the instructor to retrieve any student's work onto her computer or onto the projection screen for discussion and comment. Ambitious centers may include a computer network, so that the software and instructional systems are available at each classroom and even in the individual guest rooms.

Other centers feature unique rooms equipped for highly specialized needs. Merrill-Lynch has installed five telephone laboratories at their conference and training center in Princeton, where financial consultants are trained in telephone sales techniques, cold prospecting, and closing deals, a three-week course that follows a 14-week field program. Designed like a computer lab, the multipurpose phone lab features rows of carrels with adjustable front and side panels which provide the flexibility of open, semi-private, or full carrel configurations.

**Fig. 1. Shutters on the Beach Resort (Hill Glazier Architects; photo: courtesy of architect)**

# HOTELS

## BASIC THEORIES OF HOTEL PLANNING

Before an architectural office begins planning and designing a hotel, it should know exactly how a hotel operates. Every type of building must function smoothly and economically to achieve the end result that the client is seeking. The primary function of a hotel has not changed from the earliest recorded hostelry to the present-day hotel, whether that be a hotel of 100 rooms or 3,000 rooms, whether it be an in-city hotel or resort hotel (Fig. 1), whether it be a convention hotel or a family-type hotel.

The earliest hostelry offered "bed and board" as well as pleasant surroundings in which to enjoy both commodities. The earliest hostelries and caravansaries worked on the some principle. The front half of the house included the reception area and the public rooms, or the covered arcades in the caravansaries, where the guests gathered to dine and to socialize. The other half of the house, or to use a form which is still applicable, the back of the house, was where food was prepared and where the guests' service amenities were taken care of, such as laundering, the shoeing of horses, or the repair of harness and traveling gear.

This duality of a hotel must be thoroughly understood by an architect before starting design. For convenience's sake and for ease in preparing a preliminary study, we will assume that all those services take place on one level. Figure 2 indicates the flow of services and hotel personnel. For the time being, we will ignore the actual rooms and concern ourselves only with the level where the "greeting" takes place and where the services are rendered. The "greeting areas," for future reference, will be known as the *front of the house*, and the place where services occur will be known as the *back of the house*. It must be borne in mind that, as far as planned circulation is concerned, there must never be a mingling of the front-of-the-house services with those

of the back of the house. At no time should the guest be aware of everything that is taking place at the back of the house, but at the some time, the smooth operation of the front of the house is completely dependent upon what is taking place at the back of the house. The two functions must be kept separate and yet so interrelated that both function smoothly, efficiently and economically.

Hotels are designed and built so that the client, owner, or operator of the hotel will get a satisfactory financial return on his investment. In order to achieve the greatest return for each dollar invested, we again face a dual problem. In the first instance, the guest must feel completely comfortable and at ease from the moment she steps through the entrance doorway, checks in, goes to her room and partakes of the food and beverages available, spends a comfortable night in a well-appointed, scrupulously clean room, and returns the next day to a room which is as fresh and inviting as it was the moment she first entered it after checking in.

Everything for the guest's creature comforts should be carefully considered, whether it be the ease of finding the registration desk, the cashier, the bars and dining rooms, the elevators that will take her up to her room, and finally the room itself. The service at the registration desk, in the bar, and dining rooms, and in the guest room itself as well as in the corridors must be such that the guest finds her every want courteously and efficiently taken care of. The physical environment becomes an important part of the guest's creature comfort. These factors include color and decor, lighting, proper air temperature, comfortable furnishings and, above all, a pleasant and relaxed atmosphere.

Everything that the guest expects and should get will be a result of what takes place at the back of the house. It is only in this area that everything that will keep a guest contented during her stay is arranged for and so ordered that everything the guest is seeking is accomplished unobtrusively and, what is most important, economically.

*Authors:* Morris Lapidus and Alan Lapidus, Morris Lapidus Associates
*Reviewer:* John Hill, Hill Glazier Architects

## Hotel Economics

Economic operation of a hotel depends upon the initial cost of the hotel and the back-of-the-house services. Since these services are primarily concerned with hotel personnel, the plan must be so arranged that maximum efficiency from each hotel employee can be achieved without taxing the employee and without allowing the guest to feel the drive for efficiency that dictates every phase of hotel planning.

The economics of a profitable hotel venture brings us to the third duality of which the architect should be extremely conscious or aware during every phase of the planning stage. This involves the economics of a new hotel, which will center upon the cost of construction and furnishing. These costs represent, together with the cost of the land, the amount of money that is to be invested. They are the base upon which the hotelier will figure his financial return. A rule of thumb devised many years ago by a prominent hotel architect still seems to be a sound rule to follow. At that time, it was stated that for every dollar of income per room, $1,000 should be spent in the construction of that room. We must bear in mind, of course, that when we speak of a room we are speaking figuratively, with the knowledge that the cost of a room would also carry its proportionate share of every other part of the structure, such as the hotel lobby, the dining rooms, the bars, the corridors, the offices, the laundry, the kitchens, and all the other facilities that will be found in a hotel.

Using that rule of thumb (that is, $1 income per $1,000 invested), a room that costs $100,000 to build should bring in $100 for a night's lodging. Unfortunately, with rising costs of operation, this balance of $1 per $1,000 will not always hold, but it is still good rule of thumb. With hotel rooms now going at from $85,000 to over $400,000, we find that a $100-per night room is a rarity and an average of $100 to $200 is more common, while luxury hotels run as high as $300 and even $600 per night's lodging. From the above, it becomes obvious that the architect should know approximately what type of hotel her client wants, as expressed in terms of cost per room per night, in order to establish some sort of rough budget for the cost of the hotel.

At this point, it should be pointed out that we are talking of cost of construction, which does not include furnishing and equipping the hotel. Another fact which does not really affect the planning of the hotel but which the architect should be keenly aware of is that preopening expenses are sizable. They are, in fact, a part of the original investment and should be charged to cost per room. More will be said of this at an appropriate place.

## Hotel Operation

The second part of the financial consideration in the design of a hotel is the cost of operation. We now know what it will cost to build the hotel, and so some sort of preliminary budget becomes feasible. The architect may not know what it will cost to operate the hotel, but she should understand every facet of hotel operation and develop plans to achieve maximum economies in the operation of the hotel. This includes the hours spent by such personnel as maids, porters, housekeepers, chefs, cooks, dishwashers, laundry workers, bellhops, receptionists, bookkeepers, reservations clerks, banquet managers, and executive staff. If we would, for a moment, think of a hotel as a plant that turns out a finished product, we would think of the finished product as the creature comforts of the guests (bed and board) and of the kitchens, laundries, and service areas as the machines. The hotel personnel would be the workers who operate the machines in order to achieve a fine product at the lowest possible cost. With these thoughts

in mind, we can now take up each facet of hotel operation—front of the house and back of the house—so that each part of the jigsaw puzzle which forms a hotel can be fitted into place to achieve a smoothly functioning and financially profitable operation.

First let us clear up the question of preopening expenses, which should be considered as a part of the total cost of the hotel. Before a hotel is put into operation—in fact, months before the first guest arrives—certain hotel personnel are employed who will eventually be charged with the operation of the hotel. Such employees include a manager, chief chef, a controller, an advertising and/or a public relations firm, and an engineer who will be operating the mechanical equipment of the hotel. These people will usually be found on the site of the hotel under construction anywhere from six months to one year before the hotel is completed. Their salaries are part of preopening expenses.

Another factor in preopening expenses would include stationery and other supplies that various key personnel will need before the opening of the hotel as well as, ultimately, the cost of hotel stationery, computer, bookkeeping machinery, and office supplies. Another preopening expense will be a cost allocated for opening ceremonies, which often include receptions and banquets for people from the news media and civic organizations as well as for civic authorities. All these costs are considered preopening expenses. One other item that must be considered in preopening expenses is the training of the personnel that will service the hotel. This will include maids, housekeepers, chefs and cooks, waiters and waitresses, and front-office and clerical personnel. There also will be others, such as maintenance people, bellhops, and porters. These can add at least 30 percent or more to the construction cost.

Another facet of costs, which the architect may or may not be involved in, involves furnishings for the hotel. In this category will be found not only the actual beds, dressers, chairs, tables, and floor coverings in the guest rooms but also the furnishings, floor coverings, wall coverings, special lighting fixtures, and decor items needed for all public spaces. These fall into the categories of the "public spaces": lobbies, dining rooms, bars, cocktail lounges, coffee shops, meeting rooms, banquet rooms, spas and recreational spaces and other facilities which will be found in hotels.

Another large portion of the costs that normally would not be a cost of construction would be the equipment for all kitchens and bars as well as the equipment, if such a facility is to be included, of laundries and valet service. Going further, we will need lockers for employees and other amenities for the service personnel.

Finally, we come to a group of items which will include glassware, china, silver, pots and pans, linens, pillows, and uniforms for maids, bellmen, waiters, etc., which are generally categorized as "operating supplies."

When we lump preopening expenses together with all the items enumerated above, we will find ourselves adding anywhere from 50 to 75 percent or more to the actual construction costs. All these figures will not influence the budget for construction, but it would be wise for an architect designing a hotel to be conscious of these additional expenditures.

## BACK OF THE HOUSE

Though rarely seen by a guest, the back of the house is the most crucial part of the plan. It must be laid out with two paramount objecives: control and efficiency. Foodstuffs, housekeeping supplies, and a great many other items must be received out of sight of the hotel guests. Such receiving is usually done at a loading dock, which should be covered so that deliveries can be made regardless of the weather. An operating hotel, even a small one, will have deliveries going on throughout the day. The receiving of shipments as well as the checking of whatever comes into the hotel and, finally, sending the various items received to their proper destination must be under tight control. This is usually the function of a receiving department that should be located directly on or adjacent to the loading dock. Tight control must be exercised in two directions. In one direction, it is not uncommon for material to be delivered and, within a short time of its having been left on the dock unchecked, for the management to find that this material has disappeared or that some parts of the shipment have gone astray.

The second part of the control is to make sure that, once these shipments have arrived, they go directly to their destination without a chance of becoming lost on the way. As an example, let us say that a shipment of liquor is delivered to the hotel. It is a very simple thing to pick up a case and remove it from the loading dock before the receiving clerk has checked the shipment through his control point. It is also a very simple thing to have a case of liquor disappear on its route, once it has been checked in and before it gets to the liquor storage room. This type of pilferage will apply not only to liquor but to almost every item, including linens, foodstuffs, and even items of furnishings. A good back of the house plan will be worked out in such a way that the flow of supplies is tightly controlled by the security that the architect works into the design.

Another example will suffice: It would be poor planning to have a valuable item such as liquor carted through a passageway and past an employees' locker room on its way to the liquor storage room. It would take but a moment for a case to disappear from the cart into the locker room. A tight, well-planned back of the house will have circulation patterns that will provide the utmost in control. It is this type of planning that is definitely the province of the architect.

There is one further item in the control area which, at first glance, might seem highly unimportant: namely, the movement of garbage out of the hotel to a point where it will be picked up by garbage trucks. Experience has indicated that a good deal of pilferage in hotels is accomplished through the medium of garbage removal. Well-wrapped steaks and cans of food can be concealed in garbage and removed by an accomplice before the garbage haulers pick up the refuse. In the larger hotels, garbage destructors or compressors may be used, in which case, tight surveillance is necessary only in the garbage receiving area. Where garbage is shipped out, it is wise to have the garbage rooms so placed (and, incidentally, refrigerated) that the receiving office has this space in full view to discourage an outside accomplice or an employee who is leaving the hotel from entering the garbage room to filch what was placed there previously by someone in the kitchen or the supply areas.

Another form of control that must be exercised, and becomes a part of the architect's planning, is the flow of personnel into and out of the hotel. Hotel personnel usually come through at a point close or adjacent to the receiving area. This is not necessarily a must, but it is advisable because the same control office can observe the coming and going of the help. Usually time control is through the medium of a time clock, which is punched by the employees. It is not uncommon for thieves to attempt entry through the service area and to work their way up through service elevators to accomplish what they came for.

Tight control at the point of entry and egress of all employees is highly desirable and can easily be accomplished if it is the same point as that at which food and other hotel supplies are brought in. Once again, the architect's careful planning will make it possible for employees to reach their various dressing and locker areas with a minimum of travel time lost.

It must be borne in mind that there is class distinction in hotels and, as an example, that dishwashers and porters are not placed in the same locker rooms as head waiters and reception clerks. The distinction here is far from a fine line. The mix of hotel employees will be dictated by the hotel operator, and she may determine whether waiters and bellhops are to be placed together or separated. Maids and waitresses may or may not be in the same locker room, depending on the hotel operation. Locker rooms should be provided with ample toilet facilities and showers.

Once the personnel have changed into their uniforms, the plan of the back of the house will make it possible for the people to get to their work stations with little time lost. Maids and porters will want to get to service elevators along the shortest possible route. Chefs, cooks, and dishwashers should get to their work areas without going through long, tortuous passages. It is usual to issue uniforms in an area as close to the locker rooms or the point of entry as possible.

In this phase of planning, it should be borne in mind that uniforms are usually under the control of the housekeeper, so that the proximity of the uniform issuing room to the housekeeping department becomes a most important consideration. It should also be borne in mind that the housekeeper controls soiled and clean laundry as well as clean uniforms ready for reissue. The interplay of all of these activities will dictate a finesse in planning to bring all these activities together and to achieve as little loss in time and motion as possible. At this point, let us sum up this portion of the back of the house.

The flow diagram (Fig. 2) for a typical back of the house indicates that the service entrance is located out of view of the main entrance to the hotel but has direct access to a street or road capable of handling truck traffic. The loading dock should be protected from weather so that food, laundry, and supplies will be offloaded and stored and not get rain-soaked while waiting to be checked in. All personnel will enter the hotel at this point. At least two small offices will probably be located here, one for the steward (or receiving clerk) and another for the timekeeper. Outside the steward's office there should be a floor scale to check the weight of produce as it enters. If the food storage and preparation kitchens are located on a different level, a sidewalk lift or conveyor belts should be provided. The timekeeper will check the employees in and out and help to discourage those who may be tempted to steal. Immediately past the timekeeper, the employees should be separated into two different traffic flows, one for the food service personnel, the other for everyone else. Once food service personnel enter their traffic flow, they should have no contact with either guests or other house personnel with the obvious exception of waiters. All this is simply a matter of security. If there is any deep dark secret of successful hotel service design, it is a built-in security system, which is a direct outgrowth of the architect's plans.

Uniform issue is related to the housekeeper, the housekeeper to the laundry room, and the laundry room to the soiled linen room. The soiled linen room connects by vertical linen chute to the service room on every typical floor, and every typical floor is connected by a service elevator that opens to the lower-floor service area convenient to the scrutinizing gaze of the steward and the timekeeper. For conve-

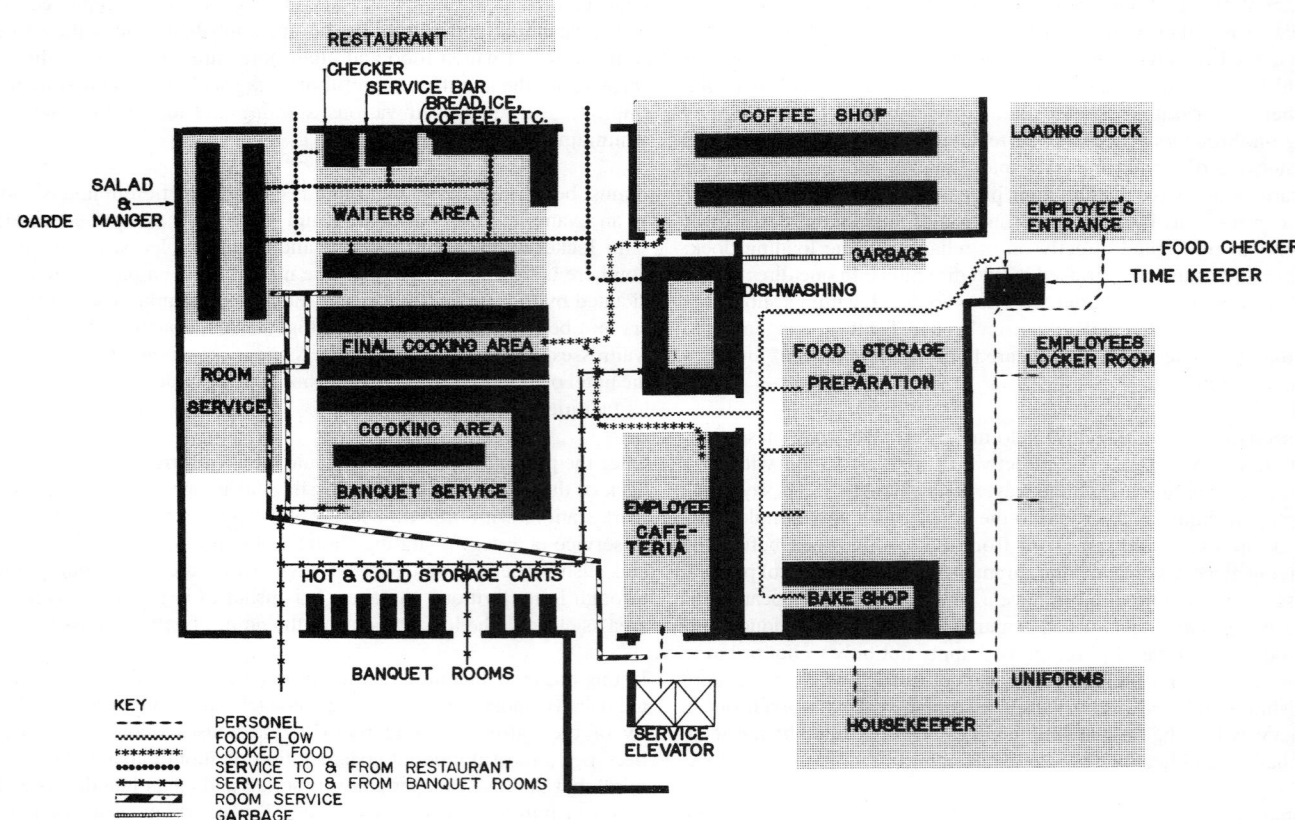

**Fig. 2. Flow diagram of service areas**

nience, a trash chute (Fig. 3), going from every typical floor service area, should be located next to the linen chute. This will force an arrangement where the trash room is close or adjacent to the soiled linen room and both of these are near the service entrance for ease in pickup.

**Laundry Facilities**

A laundry is a usual adjunct of most good-sized hotels. Many hotels avail themselves of city laundry service, in which case there is no laundry room at all or only a small laundry which handles towels only. A hotel laundry that does its own uniforms and flatwork (sheets, pillowcases, linens, etc.) requires a good-sized space for washers, dryers, drum ironers, and various pressing machines—each suitable for its own type of flatwork, uniforms and guests' laundry, and men's and women's wearing apparel. If the laundry is done by a laundry service out of the hotel, then items like towels require a comparatively small space for washing and drying, since only washers and fluff dryers are necessary, together with an area for folding and stacking the clean towels. Larger hotels will maintain their own cleaning department for dry cleaning and pressing of woolens and similar garments. Such a cleaning and valet service is usually a part of or close to the laundry area, and it is definitely under the supervision of the laundry manager.

It may be that, in the not-too-distant future, experiments with disposable sheets, pillowcases, and uniforms will do away with laundry services in hotels. Presently, the disposable types that have been pro-

duced are still not of sufficient strength and durability for hotel use, although the future may produce exactly that. At present some "no iron" linens are in use, thus eliminating some of the large ironers.

**Housekeeping Department**

The housekeeping department, having several functions, is the province of the chief housekeeper, who will usually have assistant floor housekeepers. Under the housekeeper's strict control and supervision will be all the maids and porters. These people, after donning their uniforms, will come to the housekeeper for instructions and very often for supplies to take with them to the various guest-room floors. Some operators have employees arrive in uniform or have a hanging rack to exchange the uniform and street clothes to reduce locker area requirements. The porters will deliver to the service areas on the guest-room floors all linen and soap as well as facial tissue, toilet paper, matches, room service menus, and ashtrays. (Most hotels use inexpensive ashtrays that carry the hotel name and that the guests may take along as souvenirs.)

The housekeeper's area is also a storage area, for here are kept all the supplies that become a part of housekeeping. Aside from such obvious things as a stock of linen, paper goods, soaps, etc., the housekeeper will carry in his warehouse storage area additional lamps (which are easily broken by guests) and small items of furnishings which are easily removed or destroyed. In the housekeeper's department there will usually be a place for a seamstress to mend those sheets, pillowcases, and drapes that need repair. It might be useful for

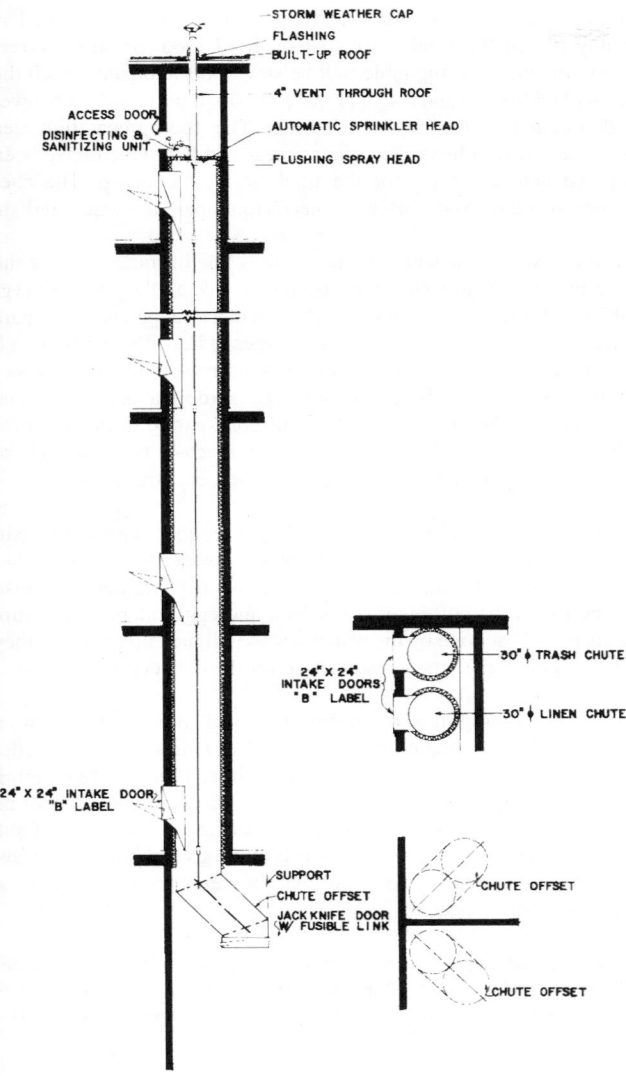

**Fig. 3. Trash or linen chute**

kitchens and food preparation areas are planned by experts known as kitchen engineers. It is not the architect's province to plan a kitchen, but it is certainly helpful for the architect to have a good working knowledge of what takes place in the food preparation area and in the kitchens. It will make for better communication between the architect and the kitchen engineer when they are discussing the planning of these spaces.

Just one word of caution—each expert will want more space than the plan can possibly allow. They don't really need that much space. The kitchen engineer will conjure up visions of irate chefs stalking off the premises, but experience has indicated that the architect's knowledge of what the requirements are will temper the demands of the kitchen engineer.

*Food Flow*

Let us follow the flow of the raw food from the time it is delivered to the steward until it is finally cooked and ready to be picked up by the waiters or the waitresses.

After the comestibles have been weighed in, checked, and signed for, they are sent to either dry storage or liquor storage (a room with a locked door) or to one of the various cold holding rooms or boxes. Canned food and other bottled or packaged food that does not need refrigeration will be sent to dry-storage rooms. In this storage space will also be kept the various condiments that the chef will need in the preparation of food. Vegetables will be sent to an area where they will be stored ready for preparation. A refrigerator box of the proper temperature will be needed, as well as work space, sinks, and cutting boards where vegetables will be prepared for the chefs as needed. The peeling of potatoes, cleaning of carrots, trimming of lettuce, etc., are done in the vegetable preparation area and not in the kitchen area.

Dairy products will go to their own cold-storage boxes. Fish, fowl, and meat will go to a separate area where boxes must be arranged with proper temperatures for their storage. Some of these items will be kept frozen, others in aging boxes, and others in simple cold storage. Fish preparation needs its own space. The hotel, in its purveying department, may buy cut and trimmed meat or portioned meat and fowl. In the latter case, only a storage area is necessary, since no preparation takes place. Where a hotel does its own butchering, it is necessary to know what size cuts the hotel intends to buy (halves, quarters, etc.), and it may be necessary to provide ceiling rails to transport them. Once again, it must be borne in mind that all these facilities are under tight control.

Once the food has safely reached its destination in the rooms just described, there must be no place for it to go except into the kitchen where it will be used by cooks and chefs. Freezer, refrigerator, and cold storage boxes require heavy insulation. Slab sinkages in these areas should be provided for. If this is not done in advance, then boxes will be set on top of the slab, therefore requiring a ramp from the work area to the box. This is something that is far from desirable in a smoothly functioning kitchen. If the architect does not attend to this detail before construction starts, it may be necessary to depress the entire slab in this area and then, after the boxes have been placed, use fill to bring the working area up to the level of the boxes.

At this point, a word or two should be said about the bakery facilities. The bakery shop should be a separate entity, having its own refrigerator boxes as well as all the pertinent equipment that a baker will use in his art—and an art it is, indeed. The baker will be called upon to

the architect to know how many rooms a maid can make up during her daily tour of duty. In some areas unions control the number of rooms, and it may be as little as 12 per maid. It rarely goes beyond 15. One porter is usually assigned to each maid. In addition to the regular daytime maid, there will be, in most hotels, a night maid who will make up beds for guests ready to go to sleep. This entails the removal of the bedspreads, straightening of the room, the supplying of additional soap, toilet paper, etc., all for the guests' convenience. One night maid usually can handle twice as many rooms as a day maid handles.

## Food and Beverage Service

We have now taken care of the bed portion of the "bed and board." Now let us examine the "board" part of a hotel service. *Board* refers to the old English trestle table where guests took their meals. In the earliest hostelries, the innkeeper's wife took care of the cooking, maids took care of the serving, and a large board or table sufficed for the guests. Today's food operation is a highly complicated one, and an architect should be familiar with the entire operation. Most hotel bake not only the everyday bread and rolls and the run-of-the-mill cakes and pastries but also unusual designs in birthday cakes, wedding cakes, etc., and he may often be asked to carve ice figures for elaborate food displays or buffets. Here again, one should be reminded that the bakery should be close to the actual food service area so that not too many of these goodies find their way into the locker rooms or out of the hotel entirely.

*Food Preparation*

We now have everything delivered, prepared, and ready for expert transformation by cooks, chefs, and garde-mangers who will be preparing soups, ragouts, roasts, epicurean sauces, and hors d'oeuvres.

Let us take a walk through what would be an ideal kitchen, assuming that everything is happening at one level (see Fig. 4). The food brought in from the various prep areas consists of fish, meat, fowl, vegetables, and condiments. The food from the prep area is brought to the various points where it is to be used. One of the first areas to which a good part of the prepared food will go is the rough cooking area. Here we find the big soup kettles, the vegetable steamers, the ovens, and the hot tops where most of the bulk foods will be prepared. Since many large pots are used in this area, there is usually a pot-washing area close to the rough or preliminary food cooking area. Rough cooking is usually backed up to the finished cooking area. In this finished cooking area, the chefs will be preparing sauces and gravies as well as broiling and frying and applying final flame to various types of meats, fish, and fowl.

Between the chefs' ovens, broilers, and fryers, which are aligned in a straight line, there will be an aisle for the chefs. On the other side of this aisle will be the serving tables from which the waiters will pick up the finished food. At the bottom of these tables will be plate warmers, which the waiter picks up and sets on the table so the chef can place the order of the specific dish that is required. Also on this table will be *bains-marie*, which are pans immersed in circulating warm or hot water into which are put already prepared vegetables, gravies and soups, all kept at the proper temperature, so that the chef

can ladle the required portion of food onto the dish where she has already placed the steak, broiled fish, fried food, or other entree. Above this long serving table will be small pots and pans which the chef will take down and use to prepare the small portions of whatever food is called for on the waiter's order. This food preparation area will have reach-in boxes for cuts of meat and fish which have been prepared and are ready for the final stage of cooking. The chef reaches in and takes out what she needs to prepare the required dish.

Off to one side, somewhere in the waiter's line of traffic, will be the garde-manger section. Here have been delivered all the prepared vegetables and fruits so that the garde-manger can arrange salads, prepare cold desserts, and work up the various types of hors d'oeuvres as well as seafood cocktails and other cold items for the start of a meal or salads that accompany the main dish. The garde-manger, on special occasions, will prepare special trays of cold, exotic dishes used for buffets or banquets. He will have his own reach-in boxes for all the types of fruits, vegetables, seafood, garnishes, etc., that are used.

Farther along the waiter's course will be a section, close to the exit, where such items as bread and rolls, butter, coffee, tea, ice, and other items are stored. Bread and rolls may be in a roll warmer. Here also will be found the coffee urns, toasters, and egg boilers. This entire area is for self-service by the waiters, who will pick up the items they need on their way to the guest waiting for the delivery of her food.

The waiter, coming into the kitchen, places his orders and follows a definite path along the cooks' and chefs' serving tables, the garde-manger's serving tables, and the pick-up area. Then before entering the dining room, he will usually go by a checker's desk where he presents a check indicating the items that he is taking out of the kitchen to the diner. A checker controls all foods and beverages leaving the kitchen area to make sure that the items are correct and the prices properly indicated.

One other space will usually occur in our ideal kitchen—a service bar with a bartender who will prepare the drinks that the waiter has ordered. Here again, it must be on the direct path of travel, so that after

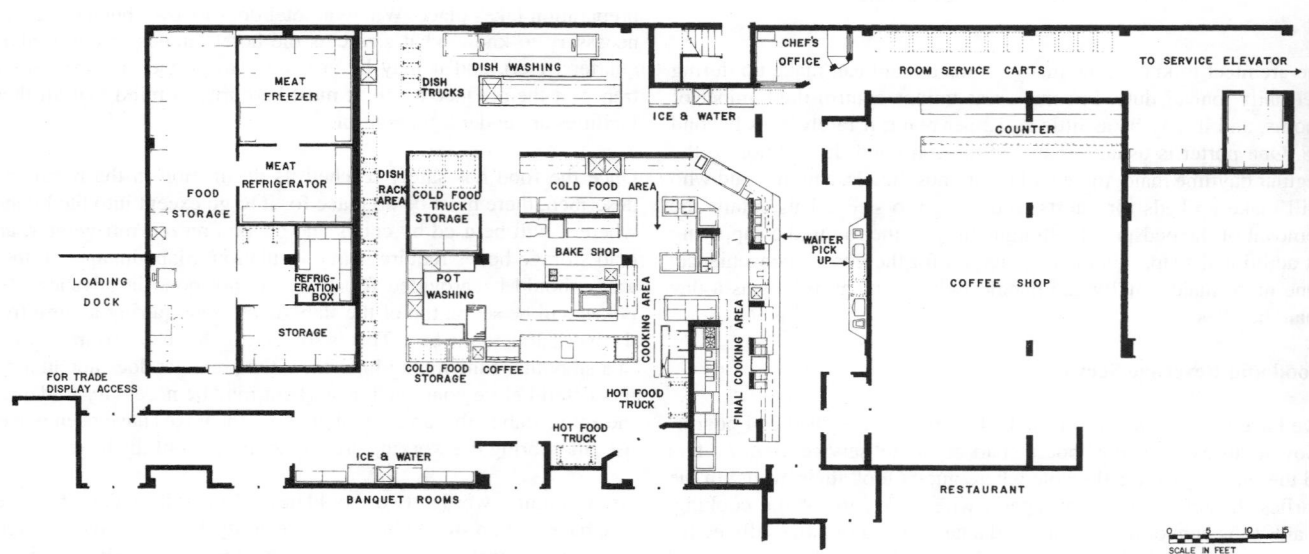

**Fig. 4. Main kitchen, Paradise Island, Nassau, B.W.I.**

the prepared drinks have been picked up by the waiter, he will pass the checker, who will check off the drink items as to quantity and price.

*Bussing and Washing*

Now let us, for a moment, leave the kitchen and go into the dining room. A bus person has picked up the soiled dishes after a guest has completed her meal. He brings the soiled dishes into that kitchen area which is allocated for dishwashing. In some cases the waiter will pick up his own soiled dishes and deposit them in the dishwashing area. This is a very noisy operation in which sound should be carefully baffled; but because of the need to get the dishes from the dining room to the dishwasher, the dishwasher is usually placed close to the dining room area so that the dishes can be disposed of as soon as the waiter or busboy enters the kitchen.

The dishwashing area is, of necessity, not only noisy but also a rather untidy operation, so it must be kept fairly isolated from the actual cooking and serving area. The reason for keeping it within the kitchen is obvious, since the dishes, as soon as they have been properly cleaned, will be brought back into the kitchen area for the service of freshly prepared food.

*Kitchen Support Spaces*

Before leaving the kitchen, there are other areas that we will usually find. There will be a chef's office, which is set where the chef can observe all the activities in the kitchen. Her office is usually enclosed with glass to give her aural privacy but complete visual control. Here the chef will prepare and plan menus. She will place orders for food and will generally operate a rather complicated and meticulous part of the hotel service.

In addition to the chef's office, there may be two other areas (once again, assuming that everything is happening on one level). The first of these is the room service area. Here there must be sufficient space for a fairly large number of room service rolling tables, which are set and ready to carry the dishes that have been ordered by the guest via telephone. These tables are usually set up with their linen, glassware, and silver. In the warming compartment below the tablecloth, the room service waiter will place the hot dishes, and on top of the rolling service table he will place the cold dishes. The room service area is always close to the cooking and garde-manger area.

Much of the room service will consist of breakfasts or sandwiches and salads. Whenever a hot dish is called for, the room service waiter will pick it up at the chef's cooking area. The room service area should, of necessity, be as close to the service elevators as possible. These, of course, must come down to the kitchen from the service areas on each of the guest floors. Normally, we will find a room service operator, who sits at a telephone taking calls from the guests. These calls are especially numerous in the morning, when many guests are calling in for their breakfasts rather than coming down to the dining room. The cooking area, consisting mainly of griddles, will be manned by short-order chefs who are ready to prepare various hot breakfast dishes, and the garde-manger section will be manned by a crew who are expert in the preparation of breakfast menus. For the rest of the day, sandwiches and salads coming from the garde-manger will be most in demand.

Another part of the kitchen will be devoted to the banquet area. We are assuming that this hotel is not too large and does not require a separate banquet kitchen but rather a banquet serving area. We will see again

that the chefs will prepare the banquet food, managing their schedule so that it does not interfere with lunch or dinner. In the banquet area there will be mobile cabinets that take trays. These are electrified cabinets arranged to keep dishes either hot or cold. These banquet cabinets can be stocked before a banquet for certain types of menus. In other instances, where steak and roast beef are on the banquet menu, there must be areas in which the chef can broil the steaks or large ovens where a number of roasts can be prepared at the same time.

A large banquet area in a hotel will require a separate banquet kitchen with its own cooking facilities as well as its own dishwashing area. Here the architect must review the food service requirements and, working with the kitchen engineer, determine the location of the banquet cooking and service area. Very often the banquet facilities are not on the same floor as the dining rooms, in which case there would have to be an elevator connecting the main kitchen with the banquet area.

The kitchen floor should be of some material which can be easily cleaned. In the past, the better kitchens used ceramic tile. There are many new types of floor preparations like epoxy, which can be applied directly over the concrete slab and lend themselves to easy cleaning as well as offering a firm foothold to prevent slipping on wet spots. The walls in most kitchens were usually ceramic tile. By all means, every effort should be made to dampen the noise level in the kitchen, and this is best accomplished by using a perforated and washable metal ceiling with acoustic insulation above or a ceramic-treated acoustical material. Hoods over all cooking areas are a must, and the architect should check with the building code to see that the hoods conform with the standards not only of the code but also of the National Fire Underwriters to prevent the spread of fires, which often occur when a dish flames up while cooking.

It is an excellent idea to have toilets and washrooms for kitchen help, so that it isn't necessary for them to return to their locker rooms, which may be at some distance. It is always advisable to keep the kitchen help within the kitchen during their stint of duty. Doors to dining rooms (and there may be several dining rooms serviced by the one kitchen) should be strategically placed and baffled so that the diners do not see or hear what is going on in the kitchen.

*Employee Food Service*

There is another phase in the food area which may or may not be considered in a hotel, namely: food service or dining for the hotel help. Larger hotels will provide an employees' cafeteria. This space is usually planned to be close to the help's locker rooms and yet contiguous to the main kitchen. If such a plan can be worked out, the food prepared for the employees' cafeteria comes from the main kitchen, and it is served as it would be in any normal cafeteria. Employees go through a self-service line, picking up hot and cold foods as well as drinks as they go along. They are checked by the checker or cashier and carry their trays to the tables. Attention should also be paid to the fact that the dirty dishes that come out of the employees' cafeteria must be returned to the dishwashing area. If at all possible, a pass-through should be arranged whereby the dirty dishes can be passed directly to the main dishwashing area in the kitchen.

The beverage service area may be a bar room or a cocktail lounge (Fig. 5). In any case, there will be a bar with stools (if local codes permit) and an area for cocktail tables and chairs. A cocktail lounge must be serviced just as the kitchen is serviced. To the bar must be brought not only liquor and bottled goods but also the usual peanuts, pretzels, etc. The bartender will also need from the commissary area

**Fig. 5. Loews Ventana Canyon Resort (Hill Glazier Architects; photo: courtesy of architect)**

oranges, lemons, limes, tomato juice, etc. Cocktail lounges will also serve cocktail canapés and, very often, sandwiches. Arrangements must be made in the plan for the delivery of all of these items to the bar without too much possibility of losing something on the way. Ideally, the delivery should be made directly to the back bar through pass-throughs from the kitchen. This will not always be possible.

There is a great deal more to be known about full food and beverage service in a hotel, but a general knowledge on the part of the architect will suffice. She must depend upon the kitchen engineer for advice, plans, and details, just as she must depend upon the electrical engineer, the mechanical engineer, and structural engineers for the information needed to complete the plans for a hotel. It must be borne in mind that most hotels consider food service as a necessary evil. The percentage of profit on a food operation is always very small. Profit on beverages is much higher, and so beverage service is quite desirable as an adjunct to a food operation. A well-planned food and beverage setup, where control and efficiency are the guiding principles, will increase the rather meager profits on this hotel function. It is in this area that the architect, working with the hotel operator and a staff of experts—including chefs, managers, etc., as well as the kitchen engineer—can bring to bear her talents in creating an entity which will function at top efficiency.

### Mechanical and Maintenance Spaces

Another area that should be considered in designing the back of the house spaces will be the boiler or mechanical room. In this area will

be found the various pieces of equipment for heating and cooling as well as all the tanks and pumps to keep all the mechanical systems in operation. Each mechanical room will be of a size and shape that will satisfy the requirements for all the creature comforts that a modern hotel has to offer. In this area will also be found all central switch gear that controls electric current for every purpose in the hotel complex. This domain belongs to the house engineer and, naturally, there should be provision for an engineer's office, with a mechanical repair shop close by.

There are a number of other shops that probably will be located in this area of the hotel. These would include a carpentry shop, an upholstery shop, and an area for a locksmith. Somewhere in the area, where they are easily accessible, will be storage rooms in which will be kept a multitude of spare parts to service the hotel. Some of this storage space will be used for mechanical equipment replacements, and other storage areas will contain spare parts for the furniture, carpet replacements, wallpaper replacements, cleaning materials, and cleaning equipment that will be used by the house porters.

There will be another area which, technically, belongs to the back of the house. This area will be occupied by personnel that very often come in contact with the guests, and the strategic location of these back-of-the-house facilities will be controlled entirely by what happens in the front of the house. Included in these areas you will find accounting and bookkeeping offices (which back up the front cashiers); reservations offices (which back up to the front registration desk); and offices for management, which will include a reception area, a manager's office, and an assistant manager's office. In this part of the hotel complex one would usually find the head of the food and beverage department, who may double as the banquet manager. There will be a mail sorting room, which might well be placed behind the registration desk, since guests' mail is delivered at this point. More will be said about all these spaces when front of the house operation is discussed further. There will probably be a clerical support area to handle all the spaces that have been enumerated above. We will be referring to all the above spaces as the *administrative area*.

### FRONT OF THE HOUSE

We have now established the activity which controls the plan of a hotel as far as the back of the house is concerned. We will now examine what happens in the *front of the house*—that area which concerns itself with the guest. It must be borne in mind that a hotel, like Janus, wears two faces. The guest or the paying customer sees only the front of the house, and this must be all that she desires—a wish fulfillment, an ego builder, a status symbol, and above all else a pleasant and satisfying place in which she will spend a night, a week, or a month.

The back of the house, which has already been discussed, is where all that makes this happen takes place. These are the areas of burnishing, butchering, baking; of boilers, motors, compressors, and ovens. The guest never sees all this, but these unseen spaces will precisely determine her degree of contentment. These are the areas that will ultimately dictate whether the hotel will run at a profit or a loss. The front of the house comprises every area that the guest will see; lobbies, dining spaces, rest rooms, passenger elevators, corridors, hotel rooms, etc. These spaces must be handled and planned with one thought in mind: the convenience and continued approbation of the guests.

Let us now accompany our arriving guest from the time her car or taxi pulls up to the main entrance. As the guest enters the main entrance (and there should be only one main entrance), she should be

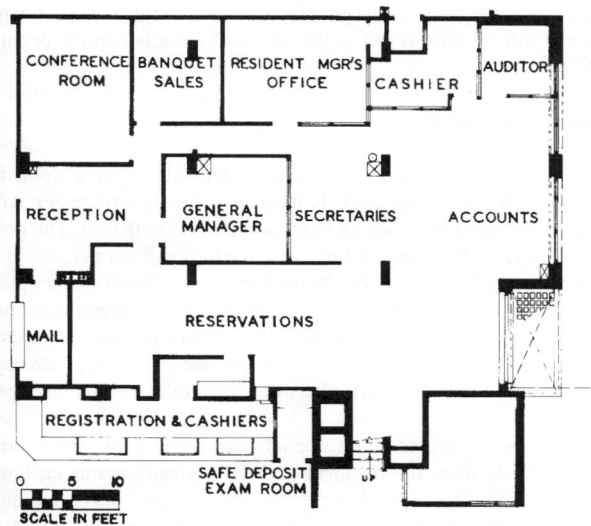

**Fig. 6. The Churchill Hotel, London**

overcome with a feeling of serenity, welcome, and definitely a complete absence of confusion. The registration desk and the elevators should and must be immediately apparent. The registration area consists of a front desk or sit-down desk, or even several registration "pods," behind which are registration clerks, behind whom is the key and mail rack, and behind that the various administration spaces. At this point let us consider the registration process itself (see Fig. 6).

### Guest Registration

A hotel registration desk must be located so that it is immediately visible as one enters the hotel lobby. The size of the desk will be determined by the size of the hotel. There is no special rule to be followed except that a hotel of let us say, 2,000 rooms might have anywhere from four to six registration clerks, while a hotel of 100 to 200 rooms will have one or at most two spaces at which guests may register.

There are certain requirements for the clerk behind the desk as far as equipment is concerned. The simplest arrangement will call for a suitable file containing advance reservation cards requesting space, so that the clerk can quickly check what room has been reserved for what particular guest. Another mandatory piece of equipment is a slip or card file which, at a glance, indicates which rooms are occupied and which rooms are open. Occupied room spaces will have a card with the name of the guest and probably the date when the guest intends to leave. As soon as the guest checks in, a card is slipped into the space for the room, indicating that the room is now occupied. This, the simplest form of registration, is applicable to the smaller hotels.

Larger hotels have far more sophisticated equipment, much of it electronically controlled, which serves to indicate time of arrival of guests who have made reservations, time of departure of guests who are already checked into the hotel, and systems whereby the registration clerk can also be informed whether the room has been vacated and whether the room has already been made up by the maid on the floor and is ready to receive a new guest. The architect should acquaint herself with the requirements of the front desk and also be aware of certain companies who manufacture the filing systems and the electronic equipment which is used for reservation and guest control.

### Advance Reservations

The hotel industry depends primarily on advance reservations to keep its rooms filled. The traveling public is aware of this fact, and most travelers will book their reservations in advance. Chain hotels and chain motels have developed complicated and efficient electronic systems for advance reservation bookings which are made from any point within the chain. The systems employed are very much like the systems now being used by airlines for bookings and reservations. Terminal points in the larger hotels have automatic electric equipment which types out the name, date of arrival, anticipated length of stay, and type of accommodations requested. Whether the system be the involved electronic system or whether it be a reservation made by telephone or over the Internet, a reservation clerk within a reservation office in the hotel will take care of all these requests for rooms.

Since questions do arise at the time when the guest is checking in, the location of the reservation office must obviously be as close to the front desk as the plan will permit. This will enable a reservation clerk to go back to the reservation department to check on a questionable reservation or to adjust any problems which may arise at the time that the new guests are checking in.

### Mail and Keys

There are two other services that the front or registration desk must perform. The first and obvious one is to serve as the place where the room keys are kept. Some of the larger hotels have room-key clerks whose functions consist only of receiving keys from guests as they leave the hotel and giving the incoming guests, either upon registration or during their stay, the keys to their rooms. If the registration clerk handles the keys, then obviously the key rack is directly behind the desk, easily accessible to the registration clerk. If the hotel is large enough to require a separate area and separate personnel for handling of keys, this function will usually be alongside the actual registration desk.

Since it is comparatively simple for someone to ask for a key who is not entitled to it and who may be using that key to enter and rob an absent guest, it behooves the architect to realize that some control is necessary in the handing out of keys to make sure that keys are given only to the registered guests for that particular room. Mail is also handled in most hotels at the registration desk, which dictates that keys and mail slots are designed as one unit and placed directly behind the registration desk.

Where a hotel is large enough to require special key clerks, the same clerks will probably handle all incoming mail for the guests. If at all possible, mail sorting and handling should be done in an area where the guest does not see this operation take place. Ideally it would be behind the mail and key rack. A well designed unit will be worked out so that a mail clerk can place the mail into the individual mail slots from behind, rather than working in the front and interfering with the activity of the registration clerk.

### Cashier

The average hotel usually has the cashier's counter located adjacent to the registration desk. There is no hard and fast rule concerning this close interrelationship. The larger hotels may place cashiers in the front desk area, but somewhat remote from the actual registration desk. There are times in large hotels, especially those catering to conventions, where one convention is checking out while another is checking in. This will make for traffic congestion and some confusion. Such a situation can be avoided by planning the registration and cashier facilities so that lines forming in front of the registration desk do not conflict with lines forming at the cashier's counter.

The cashier in the smaller hotels will handle most of the bookkeeping. This is done by means of today's quick and efficient electric bookkeeping machines. Very often the night cashier will handle a good deal of the bookkeeping, relieving the daytime staff of this chore. Larger hotels will have a complete bookkeeping department. This will require more than just the actual cashiers, who remain at their stations, while the bookkeeping department handles all entries and bookkeeping for the guests. It is obvious that this bookkeeping department should be close to, if not backed up to, the front desk cashiers so that any questions of charges can be quickly checked and adjusted by the cashier, who will contact the bookkeeping department for clarification or corrections in the guests' bills.

Conveniences will usually be found in the cashier's area for guests who bring valuables with them, such as cash, jewelry, or important papers. Guests are requested by hotel management to leave such valuables in the hotel's safe deposit boxes or vault. It is desirable to have the guest transfer his valuables to a cashier out of sight of the public occupying the main lobby. Therefore, a small closed room is normally provided. The guest enters this room and gives the valuables to the cashier through a pass-through window. This pass-through window should have a view of the vault or the safe so that the guest can watch his valuables being deposited properly. Where safe deposit boxes are furnished by the hotel, the cashier will hand a key to the guest. The same procedure will be followed when the guest wishes to withdraw his valuables from the safekeeping of the hotel. This convenience is especially useful in large resort or convention hotels where guests will be wearing jewelry on special occasions. A closed room makes it possible for the guest to deliver and receive the jewelry without being observed.

A hotel cashier must also handle the cash from restaurants and coffee shop. The cashiers in these facilities will be bringing their cash receipts to the central cashier. In a small hotel, this can be done directly without any concern about the transfer of the funds from the restaurant and coffee shop to the cashier. In large hotels, where there are a number of restaurants and other facilities which entail cash payment, special arrangements should be made for the handling of this cash and, in some instances, safety deposit boxes or vaults are provided so that the money can be stored when it is brought to the cashier space at off hours and held until normal cashier operations begin in the morning, at which time receipts from the night before are taken out and properly credited. This system is very much like a night depository in a bank.

Checks for food, beverages, etc., which have been signed by the guests, should be transferred as quickly as possible to the cashier. This is especially important when a guest is checking out a short time after having signed a check for food or beverages or such items as laundry and valet. More and more hotels are installing pneumatic tube systems for the transfer of guests' checks directly to the cashier. These checks will be coming from various dining rooms and cocktail lounges as well as from the coffee shop and from the room service area. Charges for telephone calls will have to be forwarded to the cashier also. Most hotels monitor guest calls via computer, which indicates the number of calls made by the guest while occupying his room. These indicators function automatically but must be supple-

mented whenever long-distance calls are made by guests. Such supplemental information is fed to the cashier by the telephone department.

## Administrative Area

The administration of a hotel operation depends entirely upon its size. A small hotel will most likely have an office for a manager, who may have his secretary working in the same room with him. The door to his office faces the public lobby, and an additional door is provided so that he can go from his office to the front desk. This is the simplest operation and is found only in the smaller hotels. A larger, medium-sized hotel will have a manager and an assistant manager and, as a rule, there will be a reception office where one or two typist/receptionists will be acting as a buffer between the public and the manager.

As a hotel project grows larger, the administrative area grows more complex. Aside from the manager and the assistant manager, there may be an office for a food and beverage manager and a banquet manager. A larger hotel, with sizable convention facilities, will also have an office for the convention manager and his assistants. Obviously, as the complexity of the office and administrative area grows, a more careful and detailed study is, perforce, made to arrange a smoothly functioning suite of administrative offices together with secretarial pools, bookkeepers, computers, a mailroom for incoming mail and for voluminous outgoing mail, etc.

It must be borne in mind that this front of the house works closely with the back of the house. Many of the people in the administrative area will deal with guests as well as hotel customers seeking to arrange for luncheons, banquets, and conventions. Accessibility to the public, therefore, is of the utmost importance.

## Restaurant Facilities

Every hotel, whether it has 50 rooms or 2,000, must consider the feeding of guests. Small hotels may get by with a pleasant coffee shop restaurant. This is more popular in the smaller hotel where feeding facilities are kept to a minimum. Such a facility would be the type where quick coffee shop service could be offered a guest, either at a counter or at a table, and where, within the same space, more leisurely dining could be provided. The difference between the two is achieved primarily through decor and atmosphere rather than any physical or structural arrangement. In such a facility, it is possible to take care of a large breakfast business using the entire facility. There are occasions when a visual separation between coffee shop and restaurant is made movable, so it can be taken away during the breakfast-hour rush. For luncheon, the division is reestablished, making it possible to serve quick meals for those in a hurry in the coffee shop area and more leisurely luncheons in the restaurant portion. In the evening, it is possible to get a more permanent type of separation between coffee shop and restaurant by pushing the coffee shop separator around the counter area, thus allowing for maximum table and seating arrangements in the so-called restaurant area when the coffee shop is doing a minimum business.

Under normal situations there will be a cocktail lounge or beverage bar even in the smallest dining facility. The larger hotel will have a pleasant 3-meal restaurant or "all-day dining" restaurant for simpler meals, and a "specialty" restaurant, with its appropriate decor for more leisurely dining (Fig. 7), will offer a more varied menu with probably higher cost per meal than in the coffee shop. The cocktail or lobby lounge will usually be found close to the dining room so that

area of the hotel. The same hotel kitchen can prepare almost any type of special food including Chinese, Polynesian, seafood, or gourmet dishes. The important thing to remember in laying out these spaces is that the decor must be developed to entice the hotel guests to eat in the hotel rather than outside in other specialty restaurants.

Supper clubs or nightclubs may also be found in the larger hotels. When faced with this type of dining and entertainment feature, the plans must include not only a stage of sorts, together with the attendant stage lighting, but also dressing rooms for performers and a room for the orchestra. It is highly desirable to keep such an adjunct as close to the main kitchen as possible. In the planning of large hotels that encompass all the dining facilities already mentioned, it may not be possible to operate out of one central kitchen. In this case there may be several kitchens, preferably on a horizontal core, so that there is the possibility of vertical distribution of food from the preparation areas which would probably be on the lower level.

## Lobbies

Every hotel, regardless of its size, must have a public lobby. The size of the lobby is largely determined by the number of guest rooms as well as by the type of hotel. The lobby may be larger in a resort or convention hotel. A hotel catering to conventions needs a large lobby because there is a constant gathering of conventioneers before they go off to lectures, seminars, meetings, luncheons, and dinners. There is no rule of thumb to determine the size of a lobby. One must proceed by making a careful study of similar types of hotels and arrive at decisions after discussions with hotel operators and managers. A hotel lobby sets the mood for a hotel. This space, more than any other, creates the first and sometimes the most lasting impression. Furnishings, color, finishing materials, lighting, and decor must create the proper ambiance regardless of whether the hotel is large or small, in a city or a resort, moderately priced or expensive. The interior designer plays a most vital part in planning and designing hotel lobbies.

## Elevators

Except for one- and two-story motels, every multi-storied hotel and motel will use elevators, and sometimes a grand stairway, to take guests from the point at which they have checked in up to the floor where the guest's room is located. Elevators should be located so that they are immediately visible, either from the entrance of the hotel or from the check-in or registration area. Another consideration in the planning of elevators is that of their location on the guest-room floors. It is advisable to place them centrally so that the distance walked by a guest in any direction is reduced to a minimum.

The number, size, and speed of the required elevators is best determined by the elevator companies themselves. It would not be wise for the architect to make a determination as to these factors. Elevator companies can determine elevator need and capacities given project design information, and it is they who will inform the architect what the number and size as well as the speed of the elevators should be. Most elevator companies have computerized this information and can furnish it to the architect within a matter of hours.

The designer should bear in mind that the elevator is part of the hotel atmosphere and, just as it is important to create the proper ambiance in the lobbies, it is important to create and to carry out this pleasant feeling in the elevators, since they are the transitional points from lobby to guestroom floor.

**Fig. 7. Shutters on the Beach Resort (Hill Glazier Architects; photo: courtesy of architect)**

hotel guests can pause for a cocktail before lunch or dinner, or while waiting, before going to the dining room, to meet friends or other guests. Where convention facilities are offered within a hotel, it is wise to have a bar placed close to the convention facilities. Conventioneers seem to have a propensity for a cocktail before or after meetings. This impulse-type of beverage buying is boosted tremendously if beverage facilities are placed in the normal path of traffic. Large convention and banquet facilities usually provide a fixed or portable bar arrangement in the preassembly or foyer areas to take care of pauses between meetings and seminars and to fill those pauses with a facility that will provide a "pause that refreshes."

There is no special requirement for the design of hotel restaurants, bars, cocktail lounges, and coffee shops which are in any way different from the standard requirements for any such facility. Attention is called to the fact that people staying at hotels have a tendency to seek out highly touted specialty restaurants within an area rather than eating their meals in the hotel. This is especially true for evening dining. Toward that end, hotels more and more are turning to specialty restaurants whose specialty is not only food but also decor, so that they can compete favorably with individual restaurants in the general

Under no circumstances should guest elevators be used for service. Service elevators are separate and apart. Many hotel designs indicate the service elevators within the same general area as the passenger elevators, but this need not necessarily be so. Each bank of elevators should be strategically located to best service the front of the house (guests) or the back of the house.

Before leaving the subject of lobby design, attention is called to the location of the bell captain's station. The bell captain's station should be located so there is a commanding view of the hotel entrance, the registration desk, the cashier, and the elevators. If the hotel is to render the proper kind of service, it is up to the bell captain to see that the arriving or departing guest is properly taken care of. He must see to it that there is a bellhop available for the luggage going into the hotel and the luggage going out of the hotel. Incidentally, this is also a form of safeguard to see that guests departing the hotel stop at the cashier and take care of their bills before leaving.

The bell captain should have at his disposal a storage space for small parcels which may be left for absent guests and which he will eventually deliver when the guests return to the hotel. Somewhere in the lobby there should be a rather large storage space for luggage which may be left by guests after checking out but prior to departing. In very active hotels with a high occupancy, there is a mandatory check-out time. Very often the guest is not going to leave the hotel until several hours after the check-out time. Under those circumstances, the guest will leave her luggage with the bell captain after checking out, but she will remain in the hotel until it is time to depart.

**Guest-Floor Corridors**

We will now accompany our guest from the elevator to the guest's room. As the elevator doors open, the guest should find herself in an area which can be designated as an elevator foyer. This may be a large open space or a space slightly wider than the corridor itself. Whatever its size, it should, by its width, denote the fact that it is the elevator foyer. It is wise to remember that no guest-room doors should be placed opposite the elevators. Guests coming or going late at night, coming out or getting into the elevators, may talk loudly or may be too noisy, in which case they would be disturbing guests whose doors open off this area.

The foyer should be further demarked from the guest-room corridor by its decor and lighting. It is always a thoughtful touch to have certain appurtenances which indicate consideration for the guest in the total overall planning. One of these appurtenances would be a small bench or some type of seat for guests who may want to wait in the foyer for the elevator or who may be waiting to meet someone else on the floor. it is also a thoughtful gesture to have a full-length mirror in this area; men as well as women guests appreciate the chance to have a took at themselves before descending to the main lobby floor. There should obviously be a good-sized ash receiver for cigarettes, cigars, and other trash that the guest may want to discard before getting into the elevator.

The guest-floor corridors are transitional spaces between the public space, which has already been discussed, and the guest room, which will be discussed further below. The first problem the architect faces is a question of dimension-width and length. Let us consider the advisable length of a corridor first. Good practice indicates that a corridor should, if at all possible, not be over 100 feet in length. It sometimes occurs that, because of the size of the hotel or its configuration, corridors may be longer. There are a number of hotels where corridors stretch out for over 200 feet. The architect would be well advised to introduce an interruption of some sort in the corridor plan to keep the guest from feeling as if the approach to the room were an endless path. The interruption may be by means of a change in dimension or, if the plan permits, a change in direction. The long look of a corridor may be relieved by means of appropriate lighting and decor. Where a corridor turns at right angles or at any angle, it would be well to arrange for a secondary foyer effect to give the guest a second breath, so to speak, before continuing along the corridor to her room.

There is very little choice in the width of a corridor. Normally, 5 feet-6 inches is considered an adequate width, although some hotels have made do with only 5 feet. This could well suffice if the corridor was a rather short one. Another expedient, which may be used either in a narrow corridor or a standard-width corridor, would be the device of recessing the bedroom or guest-room doors. Setting doors back from the corridor wall 1 foot or even as much as 2 feet gives an apparent width to the corridor and, what is more important, it gives each room entrance its own sense of privacy and individuality. It is normal to pair guest-room doors and therefore the recess or door alcove would normally be the width of two doors and casings.

An expedient that always helps a corridor to appear shorter is that of creating a change in the height or color of the recesses, which under ideal conditions would be opposite each other on either side of the corridor. If this is possible in the plan, and it usually works out that way, a break in the carpet color or design in this area as well as a change in the color scheme for each entrance-door alcove creates a pleasant feeling of pause or interlude along a long corridor.

Lighting will also play an important part in making corridors seem more interesting and less stretched out. Illuminating the alcove areas is always a pleasant device. In the first place, it makes the numbers of the doors immediately visible, and in the second place, it gives the guest a sense of comfort to know that no one could be lurking in the door alcove where deep shadows might hide him. Lighting always creates an ambiance of hospitality, and lights would be best placed in these door alcoves. This is not a hard and fast rule. In many instances, the interior designer or the architect may decide that lighting along the blank wall between the guest-room doors would serve this purpose better. All this, of course, is a matter of individual taste as well as of the wishes of the hotel operator.

Another small but important factor is the design of the guest-room door itself. A flush panel door is the least expensive but also the least desirable type of door for a guest room. If only a flush door is used, color might be helpful, or the use of natural wood finishes. If at all possible, some form of decor on the door will create a sense of inviting hospitality for the arriving guest. Another thing to be borne in mind is that the guest must be able to recognize his room number, and such a room number might well be an attractive decorative adjunct in this area. Some hotels have used room numbers placed to the side of the door rather than on the door itself. Here again, the ingenuity of the designer comes into play.

Wall covering and wall colors in corridors are most important. It must be borne in mind that along these corridors pass endless numbers of pieces of luggage carried by the guest or the bellhop. Luggage may also be transported by means of trolleys. In any case, the lower portion of the wall will be subjected to brutal abuse by being banged with luggage or trolleys. The lower portion of the wall, therefore, might well be designed as a dado made of a bruise- and shock-resistant material or merely marked off with a contrasting color or wall covering. Thus the lower walls in the corridor can be repainted or repapered when they have been sufficiently scuffed while the upper walls may remain as they are. This can result in considerable savings to the hotel operator.

## Guest Rooms

Everything that has been said about hotels thus far may be considered peripheral to the prime product that a hotel has to offer, namely, the guest rooms (Fig. 8). This is the final product that is to be sold. In connection with this thought, it is well to remember (although this may not have any influence on the planning or the architecture of a hotel) that, unlike an item on a merchant's shelf, a guest room that is not sold one night means a complete loss. It would be as if a grocer were forced to throw out each day's unsold supply of boxed cereal and to lay in a fresh supply every morning. That is a precise analogy to the situation of the hotel owner and the guest rooms. The room that is not sold and the revenue that is lost can never be recovered.

Now let us have a look at the guest room itself (Fig. 9). The first consideration is that of size. The accompanying illustrations of guest rooms in hotels show as wide a variety of dimensions as an architect may encounter. For the moment, let us eliminate the space taken by a bathroom and a closet and consider the actual room itself. The length and width are determined by the amount of furniture that is to go into the room and by the degree of luxury that the hotel operator wishes to achieve. Let us consider the latter first. It is an obvious truism that the luxury of space is an expensive one when considered in the light of construction costs. Space, however, does convey a feeling of luxury and, where an operator is aiming for the high-priced market, it would be well to create rooms that are sized not for the actual furniture requirements but for the sheer luxury of spaciousness.

The first design premise concerns what furniture should go in and what size room should accommodate the furnishings. In order to understand furniture requirements, it is important to have a knowledge of the various types of rooms that a hotel or motel offers guests. The most common room in the hotel field today is the king or stadium room. Then we have the possibility of a double occupancy (king, queen or twin-bedded) room, and, lastly, suites. The double occupancy room, generally, will vary in length depending on the type of beds that the operator wishes to install. Economy in space and

**Fig. 8. Shutters on the Beach Resort (Hill Glazier Architects; photo: courtesy of architect)**

length of room can be achieved by placing beds side by side, but although such an arrangement is often used, it is not the best one.

The next consideration is the size of the beds themselves. There are single beds which are 3 feet-6 inches wide, a full-sized bed which is 4 feet-6 inches, a queen-sized bed which is 5 feet wide, and a king-sized bed which is 6 feet wide. Presently, all beds are still being made in a 6 feet-6 inches to 7 foot length. Since the average American is growing taller, it would be wise to consider 7-foot beds as a standard. One reason for the king-sized bed is the comfort of the guests. Many guests would appreciate the extra width of a king-sized bed, and it is possible for families traveling together to have an adult and a child sleep in the same bed.

In connection with beds, it is wise to remember that the headboard, which seems like an anachronism in home furnishing, is a most important feature in hotels. Guests like to read in bed, and because of the widespread use of hair preparations, the headboard portion of the bed is subjected to heavy wear and soiling. Whether a headboard is provided or whether some other device such as a flat cushion against the wall or any other ingenious arrangement that the interior designer may come up with is used, headboards are definitely a part of hotel equipment. Beds, as a rule, come on glides or coasters in one form or another so that they can be moved when the maid comes in to make up the beds. Movement of beds is most important, so that maids and porters can clean under them. Nothing is more disturbing to a guest than to look under a bed and see an accumulation of carpet fluff and discarded cigarette butts.

Now that we have discussed beds, we know that we must have at least 7 feet-6 inches from the wall to the front edge of the 7-feet beds. If at all possible, there should be a 3-foot to 3-foot-6-inch isle and, because furniture is placed opposite the bed, the minimum width of the room is generally more than 12 feet. When furniture is placed on the wall opposite the bed, such furniture will most likely consist of a dresser or cupboard with drawers. Such a piece of furniture requires a minimum of 18 inches in width and most likely an optimum width of 24 inches. It must be remembered that drawers have to be opened, and the guest will need room to stand in front of the dresser to open the drawer without being forced to sit down on the bed while doing so. These are minimum dimensions, and if the plan and the budget permit, widths may be increased up to 15 feet clear.

Let us now consider the length of the room. This dimension will vary depending upon the types of beds used—queen, king, or standard twin—but this is only part of our consideration. It is necessary in each room to provide not only sleeping facilities but also sitting facilities.

Another area that will need good lighting is the area which we will call the writing and makeup area. This is usually some sort of table arrangement where a guest may sit and write, or apply makeup. It has become rather standard to combine the dresser with its drawers and another piece of furniture which is called the dressing-writing table. This type of case goods is most often used, but it is by far the least desirable for a well-appointed room. Another piece of fixed furniture that is desirable is a luggage stand. Many hotels overlook this useful piece of furniture and supply folding luggage stands. These will serve adequately but, since the guest will usually leave his piece of luggage in the room, it is far more desirable to have a pleasant piece of furniture than a folding luggage rack.

Before leaving the furnishing of the standard room, it should be noted that there is often one more chair in the room. This could be a

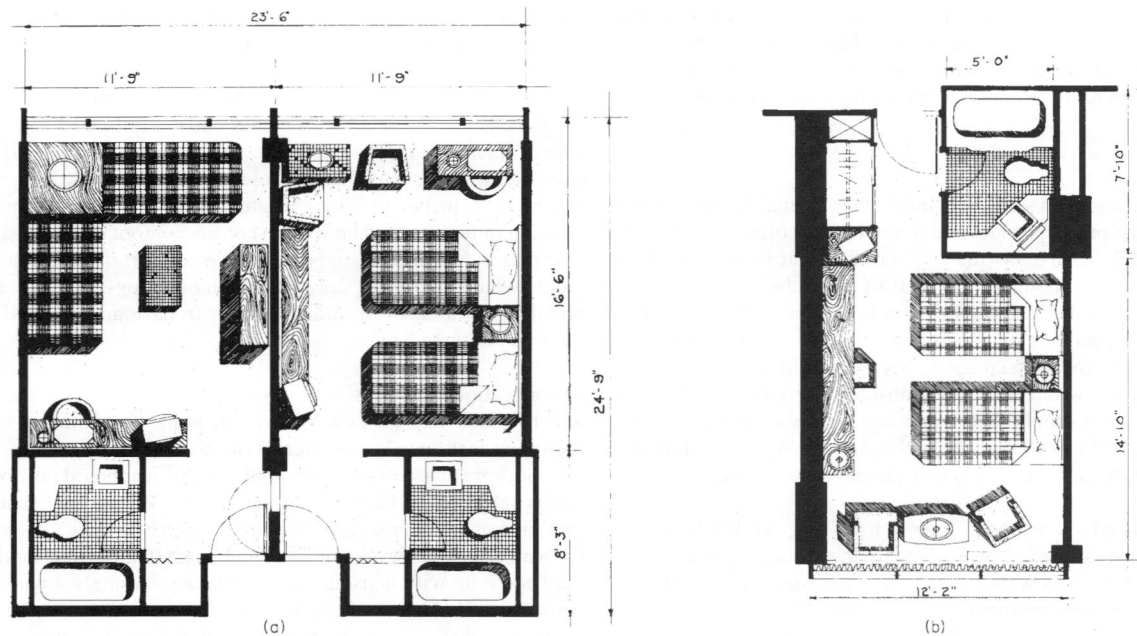

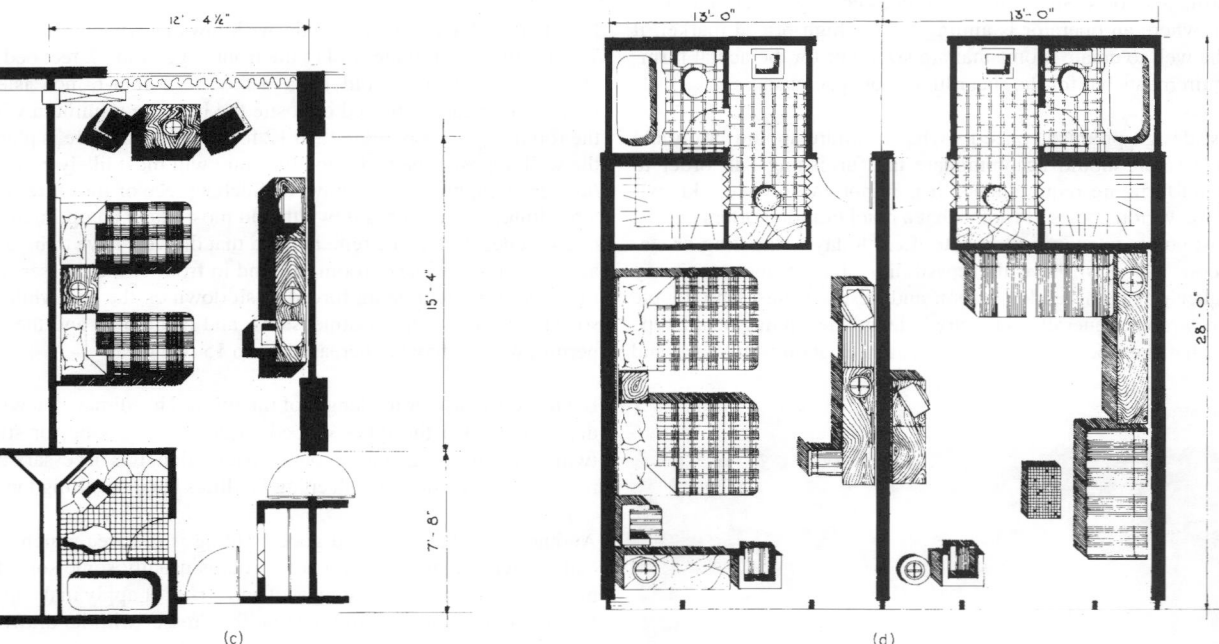

**Fig. 9.**
(*a*) Uris Brothers Hotel, New York
(*b*) Americana Hotel, New York, typical tower room
(*c*) Loews New York Motel, typical room
(*d*) Causeway Inn, Tampa, Florida

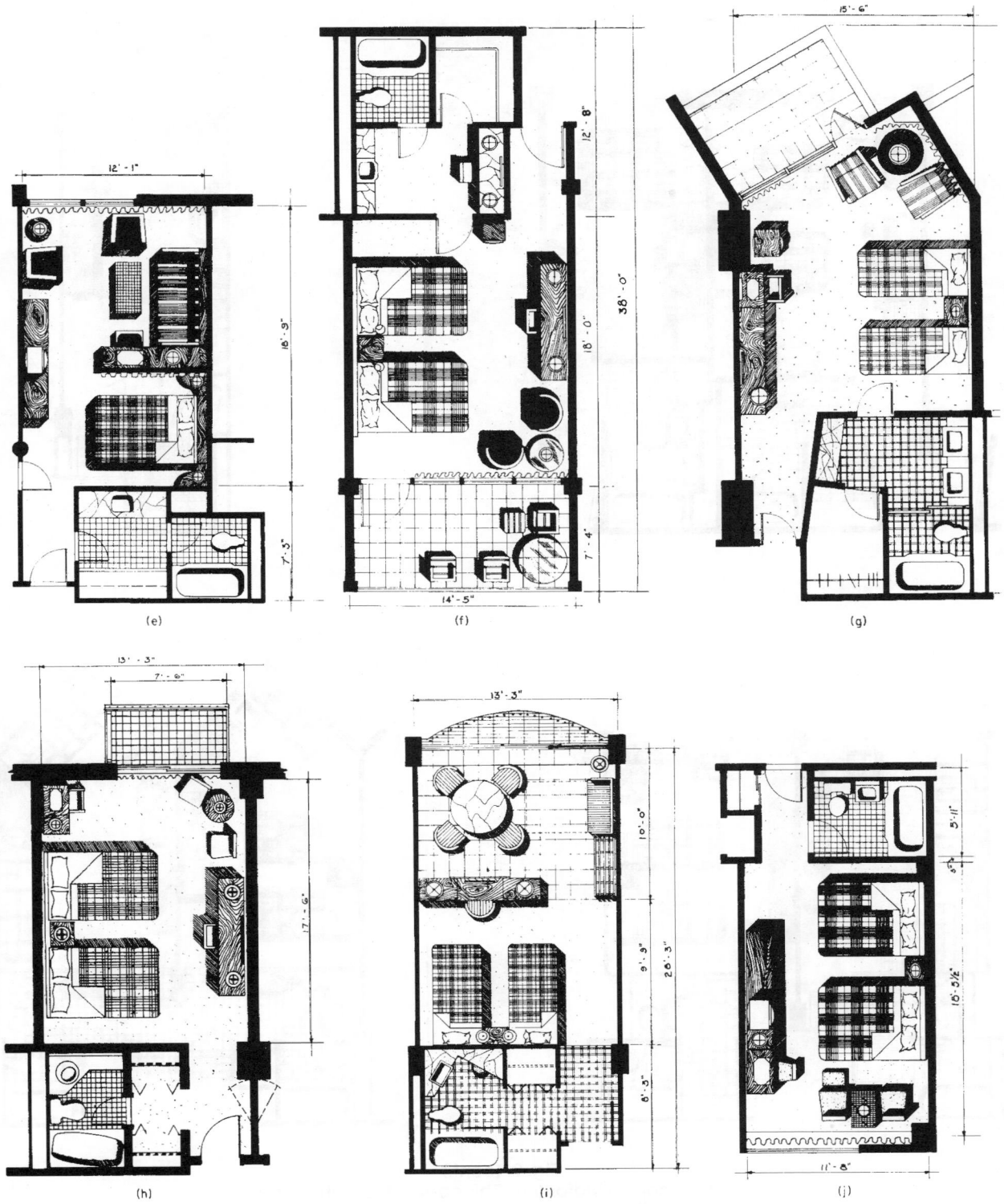

**Fig. 9. (cont.)**
(*e*) Tampa International Inn, Tampa, Florida
(*f*) Indies House, Duck Key, Florida
(*g*) Americana Hotel, Bel Harbour, Florida
(*h*) Paradise Island Hotel, Paradise Island, Bahamas
(*i*) Americana of Puerto Rico, typical room layout
(*j*) Massena Motor Inn, Massena, New York

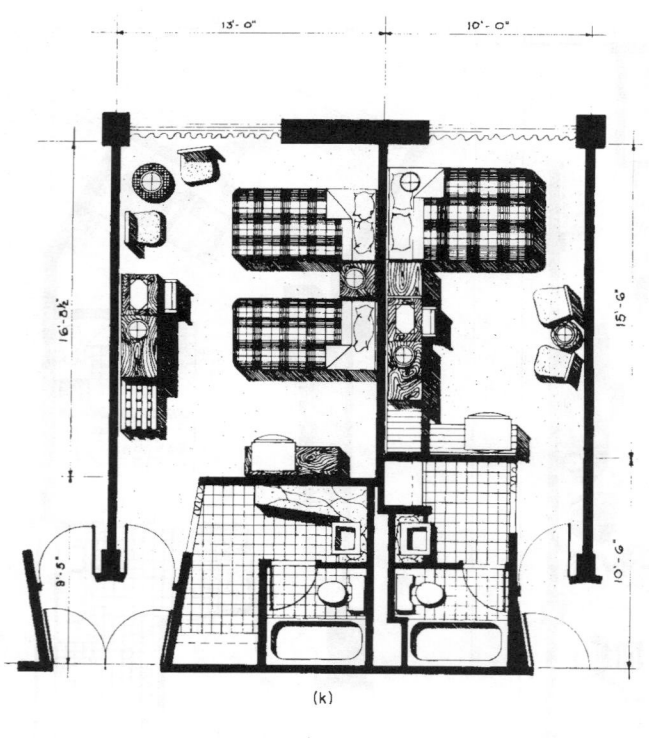

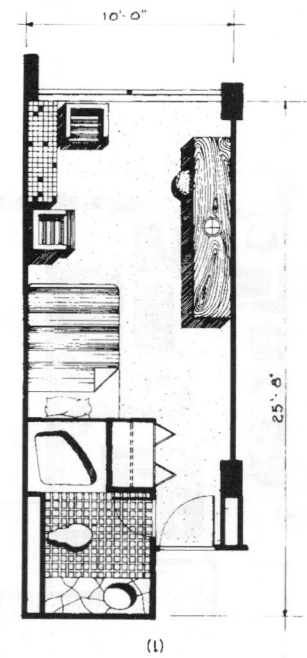

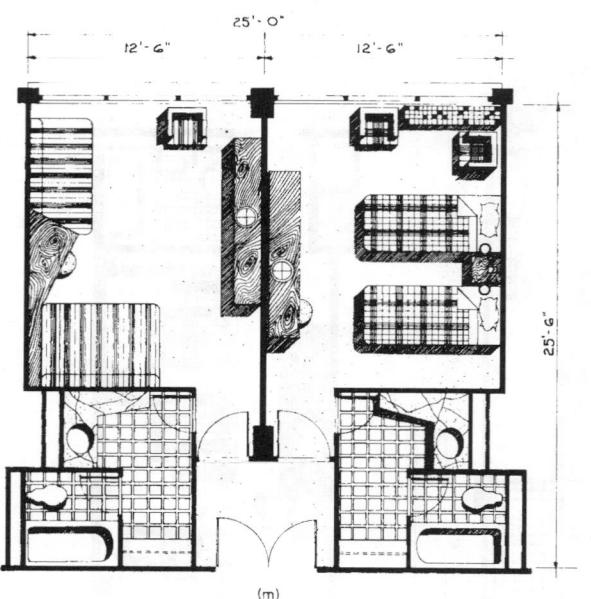

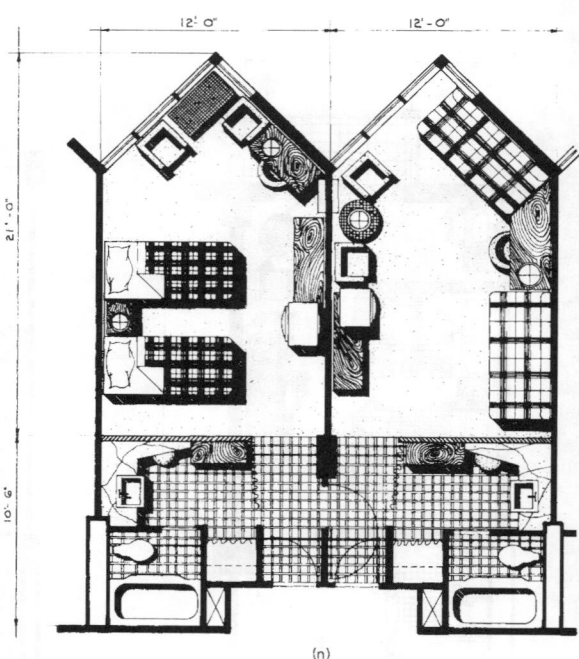

**Fig. 9. (cont.)**
(*k*) Chicopee Motor Inn, Chicopee, Massachusetts
(*l*) and (*m*) Thomas Circle Motor Hotel, Washington, DC
(*n*) Riverview Motor Hotel, New York

straight-backed chair or a stool placed in front of the writing-makeup able. This will provide for three sitting pieces. If at all possible, a ourth chair should be considered. It is far pleasanter to have four people sitting on chairs than to have three people supplied with chairs while the fourth visitor or guest has to sit on one of the beds. Between a pair of twin beds, the nightstand with a small storage space below s standard. A clever interior designer can improvise and create far better furnishing arrangements than the standard nightstands—arrangements which will give the room additional storage space. The cocktail table may well give way to a dining table, which will serve he purpose far better because it can be used for setting down a drink or a book or a package and also for serving a meal (rather than depending upon the room service trolley). In connection with the room service trolley, the designer should bear in mind that if a dining able is not provided, there must be sufficient space in the room to set up a room service table. This is wheeled in by the waiter, and it must hen be possible to arrange at least two and sometimes more chairs around it for the guests who wish to dine in their rooms.

The luggage stand has already been mentioned, but at hotels where he guests may be staying for as long as a week or more (this obviously will be the case in resort hotels), the designer should bear in mind that they will come with more than one piece of luggage. Some travelers carry four and six pieces, and where to put them in the standard room becomes a serious problem.

Lighting in the room, which has been partially covered, will depend upon the interior designer. The necessary luminaires have already been discussed, but these may be supplemented with additional light to create a pleasanter ambiance in the room (Fig. 10). The control of these lights must be carefully considered. The simplest type of control will call for a switch at the door which will turn on one or two or even all the lights in the room. Most hotels and their designers give entirely too little thought to the switching arrangement for the control of lights. This leads to confusion on the part of the guest, who has to explore the room to discover which lights are controlled at their source. A great source of annoyance is the arrangement in which all the lights are controlled by one switch at the door and then each luminaire has its own ON and OFF switch. It presents an annoying and puzzling problem to the guest coming into the room or the guest who wants to turn out the lights when going to sleep. This problem has been solved in many hotels by placing one light switch at the door to turn on one of the lights and then providing a battery of light switches at the bed which control the other lighting in the room. If this is not carefully thought out, a fuming guest will often comment that one has to be a lighting engineer in order to understand how to work the intricate switching arrangement. This is especially true if two-way switches are used, one at the door and one at the bed; then you may be sure that the guests will become quite thoroughly confused. Such switching arrangements are prevalent in European hotels, but there the problem is overcome by using graphic symbols on each switch to make it possible for the traveler to figure out the intricacies of the light controls. Here we can give no advice other than to consider the problem carefully as if it were a problem in logistics. In today's world data and communications compatibility's are more important then ever. It has now become common practice for hotels to have at least two phone lines into each room and higher technical capabilities such as T-1 lines, in-room faxes, and portable phones are now common.

Thus far we have been speaking only of guest rooms with normal twin- or single-bed arrangements. Another popular arrangement in

Fig. 10. Four Seasons Resort Hualalai (Hill Glazier Architects; photo: courtesy of architect)

hotels is that of the so-called "studio room" or "alcove suite." Dual sleep pieces have been developed that are comfortable sofas during the day and perfectly comfortable beds at night. The purpose of a studio or alcove arrangement is to enable the guest to use his room as a true sitting room. Many travelers use their rooms during the day to conduct business or to visit with friends. Obviously it is much more pleasant to sit in a room that looks like a living room than to ignore the beds, which may or may not have been made up when the guest receives company. Another reason for having these studio rooms is that they may double as sitting rooms for suites by having one room, which is a normal bedroom or guest room, adjoin another room which is furnished as a studio room. Thus the hotel can provide a two-room suite (obviously, connecting doors must be provided between these two accommodations).

Before leaving the question of adjoining rooms, the architect should determine with the hotel operator how many rooms will have adjoining doors. These doors are a source of annoyance because, unless the finest type of sound barriers are used on them, these doors become a nuisance in that sound will travel more easily through doors than through walls. This is true in spite of the fact that a good installation will call for one door in each room, so that actually every connecting opening has two doors. Wherever the budget permits, a high-rated door is desirable. A gasketing device and drop seal should be employed to cut the sound transference from one room to another. With regard to sound transference, the electrical plans must indicate that base outlets and telephone outlets may not back up to each other. This is one of the most troublesome ways of transmitting sound from one room to the other. It is economical to back up electrical and telephone outlets, but it is a bad policy in hotels. Outlets should be staggered to avoid sound transmission. The architect should definitely consider the decibel rating of the wall construction to try and cut sound transmission from one room to another, which is generally 50-56 STC horizontally and vertically. This usually adds to the cost of the hotel, but it is highly desirable.

Every hotel should have arrangements for suites of a permanent nature. Suites will be furnished like fine sitting rooms (Fig. 11). They are used not only by the affluent traveler because she can afford it but also by travelers who do a good deal of entertaining, especially business travelers who entertain clients and customers on their arrival in any given

**Fig. 11. Shutters on the Beach Resort (Hill Glazier Architects; photo: courtesy of architect)**

city. If a hotel offers convention facilities, it will require an inordinate number of suites. Conventions will mean that there will be a good deal of entertaining going on, and companies whose representatives are guests in the hotel will want good-sized suites for entertainment. These large suites, incidentally, may double at times as seminar or conference rooms. In this context the hotel may be asked to move most of the furniture out of the suite living room and bring in seminar chairs for meetings. If such will be the case, the planner should provide for a storage room on each floor capable of holding alternate types of furniture to suit the requirements of guests using large suite-sitting rooms. These suites are also often used by two couples or by a large family, in which case the sitting room of the suite may be used for sleeping at night. In this case, dual sleep pieces will be required, but they will usually be the type that is referred to as a "davenport," or the type of sofa which opens out to become a comfortable double bed (never as comfortable as a true bed). Some of these suites may have a good-sized dining table with a sufficient number of chairs, provision for an adequate desk (since some business may be carried on in that room), a sufficient number of comfortable lounge chairs, and an accessory table. The decor of the room will depend upon the interior designer and the hotel operator, who usually knows what he would like in these suites. It is a good practice to arrange the sitting room of a suite so that it connects with at least two bedrooms and, if at all possible, three. This will require some intricate

planning. Suites will usually be found in the corner or upper floors of a building, which makes it possible for the planner to join up several bedrooms.

There are times when suites are not used, and the hotel should be able to rent each of the rooms in the suite separately. This means that each room will have its own separate key. A foyer which connects the bedrooms and the sitting area or connection doors makes this separate keying of rooms possible. A single door or a pair of doors leading to the foyer of the suite will be on one key, but by opening these doors temporarily (the plans should be devised so that the doors can be swung back and out of the way), the foyer becomes part of the corridors and each room, including the sitting room, would have its own key. This option can allow for maximum flexibility, so that the sitting room can be rented on an individual basis. Many times a complete bathroom (shower in lieu of tub) is planned for each of the sitting rooms of a suite to make it possible to rent the rooms out singly. Even if the room is not rented singly, a bathroom or lavatory facility certainly is needed in each living room or sitting room of a suite. Plumbing connections might well be arranged so that a bar can also be introduced in the sitting room in the larger suites. Since this room will be used for entertaining (either business or private), a bar with water connection becomes a pleasant adjunct.

There is a growing tendency in hotels and motels to create greater flexibility in meeting and seminar rooms that would be available to conventions. "Hospitality rooms" are so designed that they can be used as bedrooms when not required for meetings or other purposes when a convention is in the hotel. Under this concept usually two rooms are divided by a foldaway partition, so that the two rooms can be thrown into one if a larger room is required. On other occasions, the one guest room may be used for very small meetings without being opened up to the adjoining guest room. In view of the fact that these rooms are designated for meetings, whether singly or in pairs, their furnishings are different from those of the standard guest room. At the outset it must be determined that this will probably be used as a single room rather than a double room. The bed itself is placed in the wall. It is the type that swings up and is hidden in the wall. There are a number of manufacturers today who make hideaway beds, which are quite satisfactory for hotel use. It is possible, if so desired, to have two hideaway beds, in which case the room becomes a double room. The rest of the furniture is carefully considered so that it can be moved out of the way to open up the room for meetings or, at best, is sized so that it will not interfere with meetings in these rooms. Obviously, these rooms will be placed on the lowest floors so they can be close to the public spaces for the convenience of those who are going to use them for meetings or seminars in connection with a larger convention or meeting taking place in the hotel.

**Guest Bathrooms**

The minimum bathroom will have a combination tub-shower, a lavatory, and a water closet, although some operators are experimenting with an oversized shower in lieu of a tub. Since the traveling public is very conscious of bathroom accommodations, the architect should give a good deal of thought to this feature in the hotel. The accompanying plans show various arrangements of bathroom accommodations.

European hotels invariably have not only the tub, water closet, and lavatory but also a bidet. This is a particularly European custom, and we are finding that in a few hotels in America the bidet is being introduced, but generally only in larger suites. Obviously, this addiional feature is found only in the most luxurious hotels. Taking the water closet as the first of the fixtures in the bathroom, there is one word of caution. A noisy flushing toilet is a disturbing noise element not only to the occupants of the room but also to the occupants of the adjoining rooms. Flushometers are not desirable because they are noisy. There are noiseless flushometers, but they are quite expensive. The average hotel uses a silent tank-type of toilet as the most expedient type of water closet for hotels. A wall-hung unit makes cleaning of hotel bathrooms easier for the maid, but again, its economics will determine whether this fairly expensive type of installation is warranted. The tub in a guest room is normally a 5-foot tub. A good hotel installation will go for the additional expense and the additional dimension by installing 5-foot-6-inch tubs. The higher-quality hotels invariably have at least a 5-foot-6-inch tub, and there are many luxury hotels with 6-foot tubs. The normal shower head becomes standard in all hotels, although there is a growing tendency to using the so-called "telephone shower head." This is a hand-operated shower head.

Bathroom countertops should be wide enough to allow ample space for toiletries, shampoo, etc. In high-end hotels, it is preferable to have a glass or stone ledge on which toiletries may be placed, where they are conveniently reached, and where, obviously, they will not be left when the guest checks out. There are a number of appurtenances that will be placed in the washing area, but here again the tendency is to leave out these pieces of hardware, although a receptacle for toilet tissues is desirable and should be included. Obviously, a G.F.I. electrical convenience outlet must be placed in this area for electric shavers, electric toothbrushes, and other electrical gadgets that today's traveler takes with him.

Towel bars must be strategically placed so that the guest can reach for a towel regardless of whether she is stepping out of the tub or washing at the lavatory. A well-run hotel should keep an ample supply of bath towels and face towels in each guest room, and sufficient space for these should be allowed together with the necessary hardware arrangements. Hooks are often omitted, these are necessary in higher-end hotels for a guest's pajamas or bathrobe. Of course, the ubiquitous bottle opener should not be forgotten. Another nicety which might be provided is some form of clothesline, which is often located in the tub area.

Finally, the treatment of the walls and floors of a bathroom becomes the province of the interior designer. Tile or stone are the two most frequently used wall and floor materials. It usually is found around the bath enclosure and usually on the floors because they are so required by sanitary building codes. There are many new materials on the market, and such old materials as thin-slab marble may be used. Where code permits, some hotels are actually using washable synthetic carpets in bathrooms for floors. The walls are definitely no longer tiled, but some form of scrubbable wall covering material is prevalent in most hotels today.

It need hardly be said but it should be noted that good lighting is an essential in a bathroom. This, together with ample mirror services, is an indisputable must. A wall-hung mirror which is an enlarging mirror on one side and a normal mirror on the other is a very nice touch for guests.

Much has been said about the bathroom, but Americans are a bathroom-conscious people. A hotel designer should realize that pleasing the guest is his prime purpose and that the bathroom can be a great guest pleaser.

## Guest Room Closets

We now come to the final requirement in the guest room, namely, the closet. The size of a closet will be determined by the type of hotel. Obviously, such an accommodation in a motel is of little use. Most motels expect guests to stay only overnight, and therefore they need very little accommodation for hanging clothes. Many motels, in fact, have no closets at all but provide a neat hanging space to make sure that the motel guest who likes to check out early in the morning does not forget any clothes in the closet, which might be closed when she is leaving. The longer the guest-room stay that is anticipated, then the larger the closet. The larger walk-in closet should certainly be considered in high-end hotels or where guests will be staying for any length of time. This is especially true in resort hotels, where the guest will be arriving with many pieces of luggage and the closet should be large enough to accommodate the emptied luggage during the guest's stay. It should be possible to store the luggage out of sight in the closet without diminishing the available hanging space, or shelf space.

Whether the closet is a flat reach-in type or a walk-in type, the door should be such that, when the closet is opened, there are no hidden recesses where clothing may be forgotten because it cannot be readily seen by the departing guest. Another thought to be borne in mind is that closet doors can become a nuisance when opened, and their strategic location to avoid banging into open doors is definitely the province of a hotel planner. A good closet will have a hang rod with sufficient space to hold clothes, a shelf for packages, pillows, etc. A walk-in closet must, of course, have a good source of light. A reach-in closet should also have light inside or outside the closet so that the guest can see what is inside.

## Guest-Floor Service Space

Every guest-room floor will have a service area. A service area serves several functions. Primarily, it is a place where linen is stored and where the maids' carts are kept. We must bear in mind that each maid will handle anywhere from 12 to 15 rooms and that each maid will need a cart. The number of rooms on the floor will, therefore, determine the number of maids and, in turn, the number of carts. A closed storage area should be provided for the storage of linens. In addition to the maids' and linen supplies, sufficient space should be left for the storage of room service carts. These carts will be brought to this area by the waiters after the guests have finished their meals. They may have to remain on the floor for some time waiting for the service elevator or elevators. Obviously, the service elevators will open out to this service area, so that all this activity takes place out of the sight and hearing of the hotel guests. Some hotel operators still insist on providing toilet facilities for the help in this area.

## Banqueting Facilities

Most hotels and motels include meeting and banquet facilities. The smaller hotels may provide only a few meeting rooms, which may also be used for luncheons and dinners. Larger hotels will have a more diversified arrangement for meetings, luncheons, dinners, and banquets. The largest hotels are usually designed with a full banqueting and convention facility. The extent of these facilities will be determined by the hotel operator who, in turn, will convey her requirements to the architect. It is wise for the architect to have a thorough knowledge of what the feeding and space requirements for these facilities are.

The normal meeting room requirements are rather simple. The rooms will vary in size to accommodate anywhere from 10 to as many as 100 people. In most instances, wherever it is feasible, the meeting rooms will be arranged in a straight line, so that the walls separating one room from the other can be made movable. Movable, separating walls make it possible to achieve a great flexibility in the size of the rooms to accommodate meetings of various sizes. Thus, if two meeting rooms which normally might seat 25 people are thrown open to one, the meeting room could now accommodate 50 people; and if another wall is opened, it would seat 75 people, and so on. (The numbers used are not necessarily those that will be found in hotels, they are merely used for convenience, as an example.) In larger rooms, which normally qualify for conventions or large banquets, it is also possible to subdivide the space by the use of movable walls to create smaller rooms when a large room is not required. A large space which might seat 1,000 people when all folding walls have been moved back can be cut up into anywhere from four to six spaces, allowing for meeting rooms that can accommodate 150 to 250 people. In many instances both arrangements will be found in a hotel, so that there are lines of meeting rooms of a smaller nature, all subdivisible, and a really large space that is also subdivisible.

Thus far we have spoken of these spaces as meeting rooms. Most of these spaces will also be used to serve meals. These meals may consist of small luncheons or dinners for 10 or 12 people and go on up to accommodate as many as 1,000 people for dining. Of course, in the really large convention halls, it will not be unusual to seat 3,000 or more people in one large convention banquet hall. Realizing that food must be brought to all these rooms, their juxtaposition to serving kitchens is highly important in arranging the plan. For the most part, food should be brought directly from banquet kitchens to the banquet spaces. In subdividing these spaces, the subdivision must be so planned that each space is contiguous to the kitchen and has its own doors to enable waiters to come and go between the banquet spaces and the banquet kitchen. In some instances, this is not completely possible, and it is an accepted practice, where small meeting rooms cannot be placed contiguous to the actual banquet kitchen, to arrange to serve through the same corridors that will be used by people coming and going as diners in these smaller spaces.

If the architect, working with his client, the hotel operator, has come to the conclusion that the subdivision of these spaces by means of movable walls is what will be included in the plans, it behooves the architect to make a careful study of the various types of movable walls available for use in such hotel facilities. There are many manufacturers who make these walls. The architect should be careful in arranging these walls so as not to interfere with the overall concept of opening up clear spaces by moving walls.

The acoustical value of the walls must be carefully studied. Nothing is more disturbing than to have two meetings in adjacent rooms where the sound transmission is of such a high-level that what happens in one space can be clearly heard in the other. Sound isolation is of the greatest importance, and this applies not only to the decibel rating of the panels themselves but also the arrangement of the joints between the sections or panels of the movable wall. The architect must also be aware of what happens above the panel as it comes up to the ceiling track and what happens to the panel as it glides along the floor. Sound isolation should be carefully studied in all these spaces, which will allow, if not properly controlled, sound to be transmitted. There are practically no walls which can guarantee absolute sound isolation when the sound reaches a high enough decibel rating. In such instances, it has been found expedient to use two sets of walls with an air space between them, which will ensure almost total sound isolation. These movable walls or panels can be operated by hand or by motor. *Sweet's* catalog carries all the pertinent information from manufacturers, and an architect is well advised to carefully study not only the operation and construction of these movable wall panels but also the sound isolating devices that the manufacturer specifies.

In fairly large meeting, banquet, and convention facilities, space must be provided which is normally called "prefunction assembly space." Actually, this is a sort of foyer or gathering place for people before they go to the various meeting rooms or where they may congregate before going into a banquet hall. Since most of the people who are standing are those who will eventually be seated, the proportions of the preconvention foyer space will be determined by the number of people who will be eventually seated. As a rule of thumb, a person standing in fairly close quarters will take up approximately 7 square feet. A person seated at a table will take up anywhere from 10 to 15 square feet. A person seated for a seminar or a meeting will require 8 or 9 square feet. It thus becomes apparent that the ideal prefunction, prebanquet, or assembly space should be at least one-third of the area of the actual dining and meeting spaces. This one-third is arrived at empirically by comparing the amount of space required sitting or standing and by allowing for a diversity factor, knowing that not all the people who will eventually be seated will be standing, since some of them will be latecomers and will arrive after many of the people have already gone in to be seated for their meetings or their meals. Even the one-third proportion may not be possible, and it has been found proper, in some operator's opinion, to use as little as 25 percent of the space for this preassembly foyer. Coat check areas, restrooms, and telephones are conveniently located off prefunction areas to support visiting and meeting.

It has been previously noted in this discussion of hotel design that it is good policy to have a bar within this preconvention, premeeting space. Such bars do an excellent business. A fixed bar would be a very nice feature, but in many very large hotels it is normal practice to have movable bars set up. Very often there may be two or three bars to accommodate large groups of people.

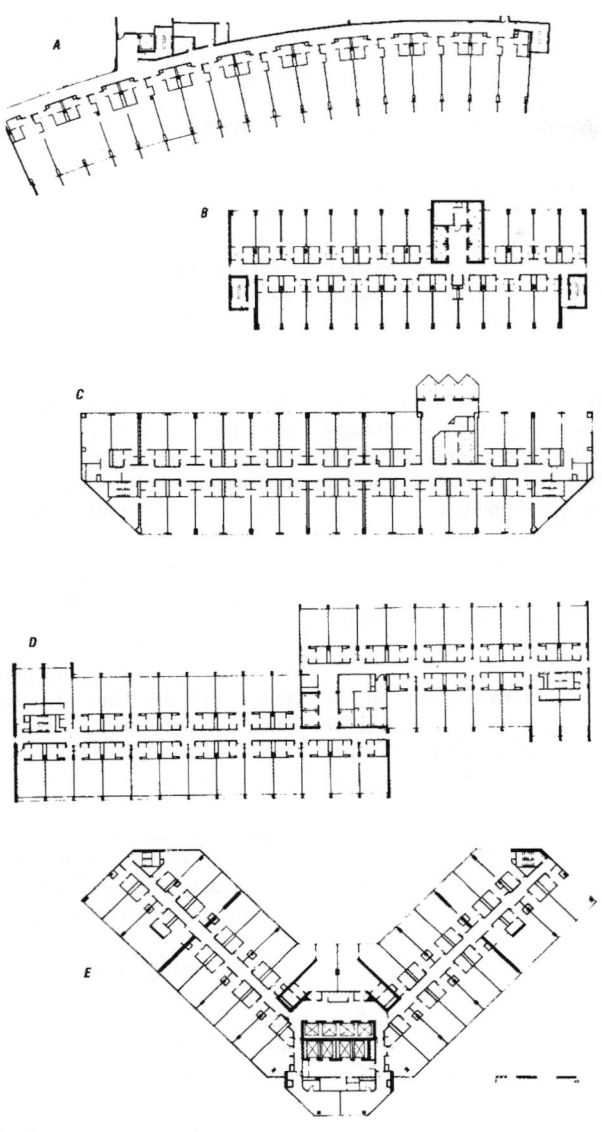

**Fig. 1. Slab Configurations**

A. Single-Loaded Plan (Alameda Plaza Hotel, Kansas City, MO). Plan represents typical single-loaded design with elevators and stairs unrelated to guestroom, structure.

B. Double-Loaded Plan (Sheraton Hartford, Hartford, CT). Layout illustrates economical elevator core with service area "behind" the public elevators.

C. Double-Loaded Plan (Hyatt Regency Flint, Flint, MI). Design features elevators pulled out of the tower, stairs in bathroom zone at suite.

D. Double-Loaded Offset Slab (Westin Hotel, Tulsa, OK) The core, equivalent of three guestrooms, is positioned in center of offset, stairs accommodated by extending end rooms.

E. Double-Loaded Slab (Boston Marriott Hotel/ Copley Place, Boston, MA). Layout includes elevators buried at corner of L shape creating economies similar to offset arrangement.

# HOTEL SPACE ALLOTMENTS

## SCHEDULE OF SPACE ALLOTMENTS

The following example of applying the statistics to a proposed typical commercial hotel of 100 rooms is presented as a guide (Table 1).

First the general data indicate the overall characteristics of the hotel. These data are followed by more specific space allotments.

The schedule shows a preliminary estimate of 59 percent productive area and 41 percent nonproductive area, which is a more favorable ratio than is generally realized in practice.

*Author:* Frank Harrison Randolph, P.E., hotel planning consultant and professor of hotel engineering, Cornell University

During the preliminary planning stage, it may be decided to allocate the 1,500-square-foot area to the coffee shop, thus eliminating the main dining room and reducing the size of the main kitchen by about 250 square feet. The banquet-ballroom, together with its three auxiliary rooms, might be omitted or, if demand for these facilities is assured, placed in the basement. The laundry would probably be omitted, although it was placed in the schedule as a possibility.

From the standpoint of efficiency, it might be convenient to have almost all areas on the ground floor. However, to make the ground-floor and basement area approximately equal, those areas designated "B" have been consigned to the basement.

Thus the area of the ground floor including 500 square feet for stairways and elevators, but omitting the 800-square-foot coffee shop and deducting 250 square feet from the main kitchen, amounts to 10,590 square feet. This figure compares satisfactorily with the preliminary overall estimate of 10,000 square feet for the ground floor.

The area of the basement including the banquet-ballroom facilities, but omitting the laundry, and allowing 2,500 square feet for corridors and the like, amounts to 10,440 square feet. This figure is about the same as the ground-floor area.

The typical floor has 17 guest rooms. Two stairways, the elevator shaft, and maid's closet increase the floor area by an equivalent of three guest rooms, making a total area equivalent to 20 rooms per floor. Ten rooms on each side of the corridor and each room with an assumed average frontage of 12 feet gives 120 feet as the approximate length of the typical guest floor. The width is usually about 50 feet. Thus the area of the typical guest floor (120 feet by 50 feet) is 6,000 square feet, which checks with the estimate previously made under "general data."

The summary of areas is as follows:

| | |
|---|---|
| 6 typical guest floors, each 6,000 square feet | 36,000 square feet |
| Ground floor, figured at 10,590 square feet | 10,500 square feet |
| Basement, figured at 10,440 square feet | 10,500 square feet |
| Total approximate floor area | 57,000 square feet |

- Guest-room areas
- Public Spaces
  - Lobby
  - Food & Beverage
  - Meeting Space
- Back of House
  - Kitchen
  - Laundry
  - Service Areas

The floor assignments are designated as follows: basement (B), ground floor (G), and typical guest floor (T).

## GUEST-ROOM FLOOR

### Planning Efficiency: Maximum Guest-Room Area

In order for the operator to realize profits, the design team must maximize the percentage of floor area devoted to guest rooms and keep to a minimum the amount of circulation and service space (service elevator lobby, linen storage, chutes, and vending). Although esthetic issues cannot be ignored, a simple comparison among alternate plans of the percentage of space allocated to revenue-producing guest rooms leads to the selection of more efficient solutions (Table 2).

Analyses of scores of different hotel tower plans show that some configurations yield more efficient solutions than other types. The choice of one configuration over another can mean a saving of 20 percent in gross area of the guest room tower and of nearly 15 percent in the total building. For example, the three principal plan alternatives—the double-loaded slab, the rectangular tower, and the atrium—using the same net guest-room dimensions, will vary from 460 to 575 gross square feet per room.

The study also indicates the affect of subsequent minor decisions on the efficiency of the plan-standard groupings of pairs of guest rooms, double- or single-loaded circulation, grouping of public and service elevators, and efficient access to end or corner rooms (the most difficult planning problem in certain configurations). Because guest rooms account for such a major part of the total hotel area, the designer should establish a series of quantitative benchmarks for the efficient design of the guest-room floors.

The relative efficiency of typical hotel floors can be compared most directly by calculating the percentage of the total floor area devoted to guest rooms. This varies from below 60 percent in an inefficient atrium plan to more then 75 percent in the most tightly designed double-loaded slab. Clearly, the higher this percentage the more options are available to the developer and the architect: Additional guest rooms can be built; larger rooms can be provided for the same capital investment; the quality of the furnishings or of particular building systems can be improved; other functional areas of the hotel can be enlarged; or the total construction and project cost can be substantially reduced.

The following sections contain a description, for each of the basic guest-room configurations, of the planning decisions that have the most influence on creating an economical plan. In some plans, it is the number of rooms per floor, in others it is the location of the elevator core, whereas in others the shape of the building is most critical. In general, the most efficient configurations are those where circulation space is kept to a minimum, that is, in structures with either double-loaded corridors or compact center-core towers.

## GUEST-ROOM FLOOR PLANNING OBJECTIVES

### Orientation/Siting

- Consider solar gain; generally N/S preferable to E/W exposures
- Analyze wind loading
- Study the potential for guestroom views
- Site the structure to be visible from the road
- Assess the relative visual impact and construction cost of various guest-room plan configurations.

### Floor Layout

- Organize plan so that guest rooms occupy at least 70 percent of gross floor area
- Locate elevators and stairs at interior locations rather than on exterior wall
- Develop corridor plan to facilitate guest circulation

**Table 1**   Space allotments and floor assignments for typical hotel of 100 rooms

*General data and approximations*

| | |
|---|---|
| Height of building above ground (ground floor plus 6 typical guest floors) | 7 stories |
| Ground-floor area | 10,000 sq ft |
| Typical guest-floor area | 6,000 sq ft |
| Guest rooms per typical floor | 17 rooms |
| Stairways on the typical floor | 2 stairways |
| Elevators ( 1 guest and 1 service car) | 2 elevators |

The first four factors listed above are of course all interrelated and must be organized as a compatible group.

| | Productive area, sq ft | Nonproductive area, sq ft |
|---|---|---|
| Public space | | |
| Lobby and front office | | 1,100(G) |
| Lounge | | 600(G) |
| Corridors adjoining (total of above, 1,900 sq ft) | | 200(G) |
| Men's toilet for guests | | 150(G) |
| Women's toilet for guests | | 100(G) |
| Women's restroom for guests | | 100(G) |
| Coat checkroom | | 120(G) |
| Bellman's checkroom | | 40(G) |
| Concession space | | |
| Barber shop | 180(B) | |
| Valet shop | 100(B) | |
| Subrental space | | |
| 3 rented stores, (each 800 sq ft) | 2,400(G) | |
| 3 storage rooms (each 200 sq ft) | 600(B) | |
| Food and beverage service space | | |
| Main dining room (90) seats | 1,500(G) | |
| Main kitchen | | 1,100(G) |
| Bake shop | | 200(G) |
| Coffee shop (50) seats | 800(G) | |
| Bar and cocktail lounge | 750(G) | |
| Private dining rooms (250 + 500 sq ft) | 750(G) | |
| Banquet-ballroom | 1,400(B) | |
| Banquet-ballroom foyer | | 450(B) |
| Banquet-ballroom storage | | 140(B) |
| Banquet serving pantry | | 350(B) |
| Employees' dining room | | 220(B) |
| Steward's storeroom | | 400(G) |
| Beverage storerooms | | 180(B) |
| China, glass, and silver storage | | 300(B) |
| Receiving room | | 180(G) |
| Garbage room | | 80(G) |
| Guest-room space | | |
| 102 rooms (each 250 sq ft; including bath, closet and vestibule) | 25,500(T) | |
| Auxiliary space (add 40 per cent of above for corridors, stairs, elevators, maid's closets, walls, and partitions | | 10,200(T) |

**Table 1**  Space allotments and floor assignments for typical hotel of 100 rooms (continued)

| | Productive area, sq ft | Nonproductive area, sq ft |
|---|---|---|
| General service space | | |
|     Manager's office | | 140(G) |
|     Secretary's office | | 100(G) |
|     Accounting office | | 150(G) |
| Sales and reservations office | | 140(G) |
|     Mimeograph room | | 40(G) |
|     Linen room | | 350(B) |
|     Laundry (700 sq ft; omitted) | | |
|     Men's toilet and locker room | | 360(B) |
|     Women's toilet and locker room | | 360(B) |
|     Maintenance shops | | 400(B) |
|     Furniture storage | | 250(B) |
|     Records storeroom | | 250(B) |
|     General storeroom | | 200(B) |
|     Boiler room | | 600(B) |
|     Water-heater tank space | | 150(B) |
|     Fuel storage | | 200(B) |
|     Transformer vault | | 100(B) |
|     Refrigerator compressor room | | 400(B) |
|     Fan rooms, ventilation equipment | | 400(B) |
| Total productive area | 33,980 sq ft | |
| Listed nonproductive area | | 20,800 sq ft |
|     Add for basement corridors, walls, stairways, and elevators | | 2,500 sq ft |
|     Add for ground-floor stairways and elevators | | 500 sq ft |
| Total nonproductive area | | 23,800 sq ft |
| Grand total of areas | 57,780 sq ft | |

- Provide elevator lobby in middle third of structure
- Locate ice/vending near public elevators
- Provide service elevator, linen storage, and chutes in central location
- Plan corridor width at 5 feet minimum, 5 feet-6 inches preferred
- Plan guest-room distance to exit stairs at 150 feet maximum (if fully sprinklered) or as directed by local code
- Design guest rooms back to back for plumbing economies
- Locate guest rooms for guests with disabilities on lower floors and near elevators.

The design of the guest-room floors, which often represents three-quarters or more of the total hotel, is critical to the efficiency of any project. Planning objectives, which help the architect assess the relative success of any particular design concept, include the points in the checklist.

**Slab Plans**

The "slab" configuration (Fig. 1) includes those plans that are primarily horizontal, including both single- and double-loaded corridor schemes (see accompanying plans). The planning variables are few; they are concerned primarily with the shape (straight or L-shaped), the layout of the core, and the location of the fire stairs. The architect must address the following issues:

- Corridor loading: Given site conditions, are any single-loaded rooms appropriate to maximize views or other site conditions?
- Shape: Which particular shape (straight, "offset," L, "knuckle," courtyard, or other configurations) best meets site and building constraints?
- Core location: Should the public and the service cores be combined or separated and where in the tower should they be positioned?
- Core layout: What is the best way to organize public and service elevators, linen storage, chutes, and vending?
- Stair location: Where should the fire stairs be located?

The high degree of efficiency of the slab plan is based primarily on the double loading of the corridors; single-loaded schemes require 4 to 6 percent more floor area for the same number of rooms. For example, only where external factors, a narrow site dimension, or spectacular views suggest single-loading should it be considered.

Table 2  Guest-room floor analysis

| Tower configuration | Rooms Floor | Dimensions, ft (m) | Guestroom (%) | Corridor, sq ft (sq m) | Perimeter × room width | Comments |
|---|---|---|---|---|---|---|
| Single-load slab | Varies 12–30+ | 3 × any length (10) | 65 | 80 (7.5) | 2.2–2.4 | Some economy in that vertical core can be absolute minimum—not affected by room bays. |
| Double-loaded slab | Varies 16–40+ | 60 × any length (18) | 60 | 45 (4.2) | 1.6–1.8 | 200 feet (61 m) plus deadend corridor for two stair scheme; can be turned into L or T. |
| Offset slab | Varies 24–40+ | 80 × any length (24) | 72 | 50 (4.6) | 1.4–1.6 | Core is buried creating lower perimeter factor; higher corridor because of elevator lobby; also other shapes. |
| Rectangular tower | 16–24 | 110 × 110 (34 × 34) | 65 | 60 (5.6) | 1.5–1.7 | Planning problems focus on access to corner rooms; fewer rooms/floor make it difficult to plan core. |
| Circular tower | 16–24 | 90 × 130 diameter (27–40) | 67 | 45–65 (4.2–6) | 1.05 | Smaller diameter for 16 rooms per floor; larger for 24 rooms; corridor area varies tremendously; perimeter of 16–19 feet (4.9–5.8 m) |
| Triangular tower | 24–30 | Varies | 64 | 65–85 | 1.4–1.8 | Central core inefficient because of triangular shape; corner rooms easier to plan than with square shape. |
| Atrium | 24+ | 90+ (27) | 62 | 95 (8.8) | 1.6–1.8 | Open volume creates spectacular space, open corridor balconies, opportunity for glass elevators; requires careful engineering for HVAC, especially smoke evacuation; can be shaped into irregular configurations. |

Each guest-room floor configuration has certain characteristics which affect its potential planning efficiency. The table shows the basic building dimensions, the usual percentage of floor area devoted to guest rooms, the amount of area per room needed for corridors, and a "perimeter factor," a multiple of the room width required for the exterior wall. For example, the table shows that double-loaded slabs (and the "offset slab" modification) are the most efficient in terms of guest-room area percentage and that the atrium plans are the least economical in providing guest-room space.

While slab plans as a category are the most efficient, experienced hotel architects and management company staff have found approaches to further tighten plan layouts. Configurations that bury the elevator and service cores in interior corners have several advantages. They slightly reduce the non-guest-room area, substantially reduce the amount of building perimeter, and increase the opportunities for creating architecturally interesting buildings. The "offset slab" plan, for example, is especially economical because the public and service cores are combined and, in addition, because no guest rooms are displaced from the building perimeter. The "knuckle" configuration, which bends at angles, creates interestingly shaped elevator lobbies, provides compact service areas, and breaks up the slab's long corridors.

The core design is complicated by the need to connect the public elevators to the lobby and the service elevators to the housekeeping and other back-of-house areas. This often necessitates two distinct care areas at some distance from each other, although in many hotels they are located together. One common objective is to position the elevator in the middle third of a floor so as to limit walking distances. Rather than integrate the vertical circulation into the body of the tower, the designer may, for planning reasons, add the core to the end of a compact room block or extend it out from the face of the facade.

The actual layout of the core is another determinant of efficiency in the typical plan. In most slab-plan hotels, the vertical cores require space equivalent to two to four structural bays. Usually, the area can be kept to a minimum; certainly fewer guest-room bays are displaced if service areas are located behind the public elevators, rather than beside them or at some distance. Clearly, the efficiency of the plan is improved when the core displaces the fewest number of guest-room units.

Surprisingly, the addition of a distinct elevator lobby is often found in the more efficient layouts. As well as creating an attractive foyer space and isolating the noise and congestion of waiting people from the guest rooms, plans with an elevator lobby tend to have many fewer awkwardly shaped and designed rooms and are required by most building codes. Thus, efficiency in the core layout comes down to the successful integration of public elevators, service elevators, linen storage, chutes, and vending into a compact vertical core.

The most frequent solutions to the placement of the fire stairs are to locate them at both ends of the corridor, as part of the elevator cores, or within the usual bathroom zone of certain rooms, thereby reducing the guest-room size. These rooms, then, require especially careful planning or are combined with others to form suites. Combining the stairs with one or both of the elevator cores often results in a more efficient overall plan than adding them to the ends of the building.

One limiting factor to the number of rooms on the guest-room floor is the typical building code requirement that there be no more than, say, 150 feet (unsprinkled or 300 feet sprinkled) between stair exits. Therefore, one goal in planning the repetitive guest-room floor is to create a layout that does not require a third fire stair. Experienced hotel architects have evolved techniques for lengthening the slab, adding rooms, and manipulating the stairs and corridors to increase the building's overall efficiency.

**Tower Plans**

A second major category of guest-room floor plans are the vertically oriented towers (Fig. 2), which are generally organized with a central core surrounded entirely by a corridor and guestrooms (see accompanying plans). The exterior architectural treatment of the tower can vary widely as the geometric shape of the plan changes from square to cross-shaped, circular to triangular. The planning considerations for towers raise similar issues for the designer:

- Number of rooms: How many guest rooms economically fit a particular layout?
- Shape: Which shape is most efficient and permits the desired mix of rooms?
- Corridor: How is hallway access to corner rooms arranged?
- Core layout: How are the elevators, linen storage, and stairs organized – minimum separation between stairs?

Unlike the other plan configurations, selection of the tower shape creates specific limitations on the number of rooms per floor. For the most part, towers contain between 16 and 24 rooms, depending on the guest-room dimensions, the number of floors, and the optimum core size. With 16 rooms, the core is barely large enough for two or three elevators, fire stairs, and minimum storage; on the other hand, designs with more than 24 rooms are so large at the perimeter that they contain too much central core area to be efficient.

In most building configurations, efficiency is improved by adding rooms to a floor in which the core and services are only minimally enlarged, if at all, to support them. With the tower configuration, the opposite is true. The analysis of a large sample of actual hotel designs shows that, surprisingly, the fewer the number of rooms per floor, the more efficient the layout becomes because the core by necessity must be extremely compact and, as a result, the amount of corridor area is kept to a bare minimum. Inefficient layouts often result from adding rooms and by extending single-loaded corridors into each of the building corners.

The shape of the tower has a direct effect on the appearance of the structure and on its perceived scale. The efficiency of the plan, also, is a direct result of the shape because of the critical nature of the corridor access to the corner rooms in the rectangular towers and because of the design of the wedge-shaped guest room and bathroom in the circular towers. Those plans, which minimize the amount of circulation and, in addition, create unusual corner rooms, exemplify the best in both architectural planning and interior layout.

For the circular towers, the measures of efficiency are judged by the layout of the room as well as the core design. Typically, the perimeter of the wedge-shaped guestrooms is about 16 feet, whereas the corridor dimension may be less than 8 feet, thus challenging the designer's skill to plan bathroom, entry vestibule, and closet.

While the design of the core in both rectangular and circular towers is less critical than the arrangement of guest rooms, certain specific issues have to be resolved. Generally, the core is centrally located, and the vertical elements are tightly grouped. The smaller hotels, those with only 16 rooms per floor, generally do not feature an elevator lobby (however, lobbies are required by most building codes), and the guests in rooms opposite the elevators must tolerate noise from waiting guests.

In the larger tower plans with 24 rooms per floor, inefficiently arranged guest rooms often create excessively large central cores. Simply, the space within the corridor may be larger than is needed for the elevators, stairs, and service areas. Some hotels have "sky-lobbies" to make this wasted space appear to be a positive feature, or they add conference rooms on every guest floor. Unfortunately, these solutions only show up the problems resulting from poorly conceived and designed guest-

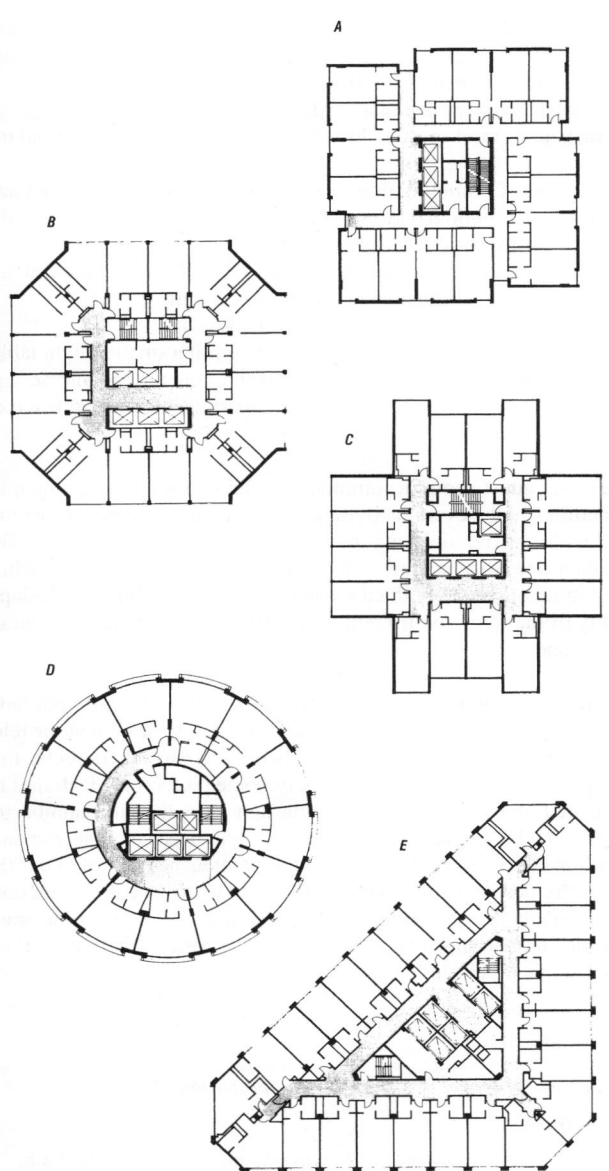

**Fig. 2. Tower Plans**

**A. Pinwheel Plan (Berkshire Common, Pittsfield, MA):** Plan illustrates simple arrangement of 16 rooms in 4 equivalent blocks, the core is extremely efficient with scissor stair, but corridors extended to corners are excessive.

**B. Square Plan, H Corridor (Noble Inn, Tampa, FL):** Design features extremely economical circulation and core, all bathrooms back to back, unusual yet easily furnished corner rooms.

**C. Cross-Shaped Plan (Holiday Inn, Ontario, Canada):** Layout exemplifies economical corridor plan but increased building perimeter.

**D. Circular Tower (Westin, Seattle, WA):** Arrangement shows efficient plan with very compact core and well laid-out guest bathrooms.

**E. Triangular Tower (New Otani, Los Angeles, CA):** Design illustrates well-organized and well-configured core with good access to the ends of the tower.

room planning. The efficient design of hotel towers requires the simultaneous study of the core layout and of the ring of guest rooms around it, with attempts to compress both as much as possible.

### Atrium Plans

A third major category of guest-room floor plans is the atrium design, which was reintroduced by architect John Portman for the Hyatt Regency Atlanta hotel in 1967. The atrium prototype had been used in the past century in both Denver's Brown Palace, and San Francisco's Palace. The true atrium configuration has the guest room arranged along single-loaded corridors, much like open balconies overlooking the lobby space. The following issues must be addressed by the architect:

- Shape: What configuration is to be used for the guest-room structure?
- Public elevators: How are scenic or standard elevators to be arranged?
- Service core and stairs: Where are they to be located?

In addition to the open lobby volume, each atrium hotel is distinguished by the plan of the guest-room floors. While the basic prototype is the square plan with scenic passenger elevators that provide the guest with an ever-changing perspective of the lobby activity as the elevator moves to the upper floors, many of the most recent atrium designs are irregularly shaped to respond to varying site constraints. This sculpting of the building contributes to creating a unique image for the hotel, a primary goal of most developers and architects who select the atrium configuration and who accept the fact that, because of the single-loaded corridors, it is by far the least efficient of the plan types.

Practically all atrium hotels feature scenic or glass elevators, which provide views of the lobby as well as add animation to the space itself. Often these are located on an additional bridge or platform, thereby increasing the amount of circulation on each floor. In some cases, scenic elevators are placed opposite conventional ones, creating the anomaly of two very different experiences.

Service elevators, the housekeeping support functions, and the exit stairs are generally located at both ends of the wings and have relatively little effect on the efficiency of the overall plan. At a practically unfeasible 60 percent usable guest-room space, architects have sought ways to gain the prestige benefits of the atrium while increasing its efficiency. One technique that has been successful in several hotels is to combine an atrium space with double-loaded wings. This effectively and appropriately draws together the architectural excitement of the atrium space-usually on a smaller and more personal scale than in the larger atrium volumes with the necessary economies of the double-loaded plan.

### GUEST-ROOM DESIGN

#### Furnishings

The definition of the market determines not only the most appropriate bed combinations but also all the other furnishings for a particular hotel. Generally, hotels include a mixture of rooms with two beds (generally double beds), one oversized bed (either a queen or king), and suites of various types. The more common alternatives are listed in Table 3. While it is uncommon in the United States to have hotel guest rooms furnished with single, twin, or only one double bed, some hotels recently have introduced oversized twin beds in place of two double beds (primarily in convention hotels) in order to provide a more residential atmosphere and to allow more room for other furnishings (Table 4).

The selection of a proper room mix is important because it influences the hotel's ability to rent 100 percent of its rooms and to generate the maximum revenue. For this reason, rooms with great flexibility—a king-size bed plus a convertible sofa, for example—are increasingly popular. Typical room mix percentages for different types of hotel are provided in Table 5.

The full list of furnishings can be determined by analyzing the guest room function—sleeping, relaxing, working, entertaining, dressing—and their space requirements. The typical double-double room has several zones: The bathroom and areas for dressing and clothes storage are grouped next to the corridor entrance; the sleeping area is in the center of the guest-room module; and the seating and work areas are located near the window. New layouts combine the several functions in different ways or find techniques for separating them more fully. For example, suite characteristics are provided in a standard room by adding a screen to separate the sleeping and sitting portions of the space. Or a compartmentalized bathroom is created by isolating the bath and toilet area from the sink and dressing function. Such guest-room zones are shown in Fig. 3.

With the continuing increase in construction and furnishing costs, it becomes more important to find new solutions to the guest-room layout that is, designs which combine function and comfort within realistic budgets. One basic approach is to use fewer individual pieces of furniture or to scale them slightly smaller so as to give the perception of a larger or more luxurious room. The designer might include the following:

- Queen or 72-inch king-size bed: Beds smaller than the 78-inch kings create more open space.

- Convertible sofa or wall-bed: These provide more open space and flexibility, either as the second bed with a double, queen, or king, or as the only bed in a parlor.
- Adequate luggage/clothes space: Sufficient drawers, luggage rack, and closet space reduce the clutter of clothes throughout the room.
- Armoire: Combining drawer space with a television cabinet and possibly a pullout writing ledge in a single unit eliminates the need for two or three separate pieces.
- Lounge/desk chairs: Lounge chairs designed to be used at the work surface eliminate the straight desk chair.
- Mirrors: They enlarge the space visually.
- Wall-mounted bedside lamps: These permit a smaller night table.
- Bathroom: Designs should expand the countertop, mirror, and lighting as much as possible and compartmentalize the tub and/or toilet.

The hotel guest room accommodates one to four or more people, sometimes with several activities occurring at one time (for example, bathing and dressing or sleeping and watching TV). The designer needs to be alert to techniques for separating some while combining others, in both cases increasing the flexibility and adaptability of the room to different users. The plan illustrates five guest-room zones.

Several details in the room arrangement and furnishing do not have any "best" solution. For example, many operators insist that the telephone should be located next to the beds, whereas others prefer that it be placed at the work area. Similarly, some prefer that the drapes be laminated and combined in a single unit to reduce the number of drapery tracks, whereas others insist on separate sheer, blackout, and overdrape to allow easy cleaning and maintenance. Throughout the room, the designer must balance the conflicting needs of function, safety, maintenance, comfort, and budget and, at the same time, must consider the varying requirements of the several different markets that a single hotel tries to attract.

**Table 3**   Hotel guest characteristics*

|  | Guest characteristics | Purpose for travel | Guest-room design factors |
|---|---|---|---|
| | | Business | |
| Group | Single or double occupancy; 2–4 night stay; 75% men, 25% women (rising); somewhat price insensitive. | Conventions, conferences; professional associations; sales and training meetings | King, twin, double-double; bath with dressing area; lounge seating with good work area. |
| Individual | Single occupancy; 1–2 night stay; 85% men, 15% women; very price insensitive | Corporate business; sales; conventions conferences. | King; standard bath with shower; lounge area with exceptional work area. |
| | | Pleasure | |
| Family | Double-plus occupancy (includes children); 1–4 night stay; longer in resort areas; budget or midprice. | Family vacations; sightseeing; sports, family activity. | Double-double, king sofa, or adjoining rooms; lounge area and television; generous, compartmentalized bath; balcony, deck, outside access. |
| Couples | Double occupancy; 1–7 night stay; midprice to upscale. | Tours, clubs, associations; sightseeing; sports, family activity. | King; dining, work surface; moderate storage; compartmentalized bath. |
| Singles | Single occupancy; young professionals, midprice to upscale. | Tours, clubs, associations; culture, arts, theater; shopping. | Queen; dining, work surface; standard bath. |

*Guest-room design must reflect the needs of the lodger. Commercial hotels, for example, have a high rate of single occupancy and, therefore, need few rooms with two double beds. For the same reasons, they do need better designed and larger work surfaces for the businessperson and full hotel services. The table identifies the principal hotel guest markets, their characteristics, and their influence on the room design.

## Table 4  Guest-room bed types†

| Type | Size |
|---|---|
| Twin | 2 twin beds 39 × 80 in. (1 × 2m) |
| *Double-double | 2 double beds 54 × 80 in. (1.35 × 2m) |
| Queen | 1 queen bed 60 × 80 in. (1.5 × 2 m) |
| *King | 1 king bed 78 × 80 in. (2 × 2 m) |
| California king | 1 king bed 72 × 80 in. (1.8 × 2m) |
| Oversized twin | 2 twin beds 45 × 80 in. (1.5 × 2 m) |
| Queen-queen | 2 queen beds |
| Double-studio | 1 double bed and convertible sofa |
| Queen-studio | 1 queen bed and convertible sofa |
| *King-studio | 1 king bed and convertible sofa |
| *Parlor | 1 convertible sofa |
| Wall bed (Sico room) | 1 wall bed |

†Guest-room bed types: Bedrooms come in a great variety of arrangements, generally defined by the type of beds and by the number of room bays. The table provides a comprehensive listing of hotel guest-room types (the more common being identified with an *) and standard bed sizes.

## DIMENSIONS

The guest-room design decision which most influences the rest of the hotel plan is the selection of the room's net width. This establishes the structural module throughout the building, including the public and service areas on the lower floors. The most common dimension is 13 feet, as a standard. It was designed to accommodate the furniture needed in the roadside motor inn: two double beds against one wall and a desk/luggage rack/ TV stand against the opposite wall, with adequate aisle space between. While the room has undergone some minor changes in the last quarter-century, the industry's standard room today is essentially the same one pioneered by founder Kemmon Wilson's Holiday Inns and immediately adopted by Howard Johnson and other companies.

Until then, even the newest and best convention hotels built in the post-World War II period included a variety of room sizes, including a large percentage that were narrower than this 12-foot standard. These hotels, many of them still operating and competing with properties 50 years newer, are greatly limited by the smallness of their guest rooms. In the United States and Canada, no first class or chain-affiliated hotels (except for the budget inns) are built today with rooms less than 13 feet wide, unless, as in the case of renovations of older hotels, the size of a few rooms is limited by unavoidable architectural constraints.

Guest-room dimensions have become fairly well standardized for different quality levels within the industry (see Table 6). While a few hotel operators have tried to provide noticeably larger rooms than their direct competitors, guestroom size, quality, and room rate remain closely linked because of the overriding influence of construction and furnishing costs.

The guest-room layouts in Fig. 4 illustrate the standard room design alternatives as well as a number of more innovative solutions. The budget chains have slightly reduced the 12 feet by 18 feet motor inn room to lower construction costs, shortening it to between 14 and 16 feet, which is sufficient to accommodate two double beds. On the other hand, operators who are selling a more luxurious room have experimented with larger guest-room spaces, including more sumptuous bathrooms. Increasing the width of the room module to 13.3 or 15 feet permits one major change in the room layout: two twin beds, or a queen or king-size bed can be positioned against the bathroom wall instead of the side wall, permitting many other arrangements of the furnishings. For example, several designers have placed the bed diagonally instead of against a full wall.

Generally, there is little advantage to increasing the guest-room width beyond 14 feet. Even this slightly larger space does not provide improved arrangements, and construction costs are increased dramatically by the increased circulation space and exterior wall area. However, at a room width of 16 feet or more a new set of design alternatives arises: the bed or beds can be positioned against one side

## Table 5  Guest-room mix for different hotel types*

| Type of hotel | Percent of total guest rooms | | | | Comments |
|---|---|---|---|---|---|
| | Double-double | King | King-studio | Parlor | |
| Budget Inn | 100 | 0 | 0 | 0 | |
| Motor Inn | 60 | 28 | 10 | 2 | Trend away from all double-double |
| Conference center | 40 | 40 | 15 | 5 | Single occupancy, except needs couples' weekend business |
| All-suite | 10 | 90 | 0 | 100 | All rooms connect with a parlor |
| Super-luxury | 20 | 70 | 0 | 10 | Double-double replaced with oversize twins |
| Commercial | 20 | 60 | 10 | 10 | Limited double occupancy |
| Resort/family | 80 | 8 | 10 | 2 | Provide room for cots |
| Resort/couples | 20 | 70 | 5 | 5 | |
| Convention | 55 | 35 | 5 | 5 | Trend toward replacing double-double with oversize twin |
| Mega-hotel | 55 | 35 | 5 | 5 | Double-double provides greatest flexibility for family/ group business markets |
| Casino hotel | 40 | 50 | 0 | 10 | Depends on strength of tour markets |

*Guest-room mix for different hotel types: Hotel operators have established guidelines for furnishing guest rooms based on the history of the types of guests who stay at a particular type of hotel or resort. This table establishes the room mix objectives for particular types of classes of hotels.

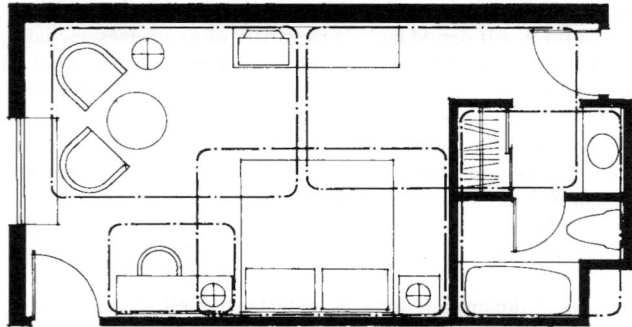

**Fig. 3. Guest-room activity zones**

D. Typical double-double—finishes plan: Vinyl wallcovering (VWC), paint (P), carpet (C), ceramic tile (CT) identified and keyed to legend.

E. King-studio (Holiday Inn): Standard layout with armoire unit and large lounge area including a convertible sofa.

F. Parlor (Holiday Inn): Convertible sofa and small conference area and adjoining typical king and double rooms.

G. King room—diagonal bed placement (Sheraton Plaza, Palm Springs): Resort layout, larger room size, with bed splayed to reduce institutional look.

H. Luxury room (Four Seasons, Montreal, Canada): Room with wider window dimension than depth including luxurious lounge group and oversized four-fixture bath.

I. Reversed layout (Sheraton, Washington, DC): Unusual room with bed placed in front of window and lounge area near bathroom.

J. Luxury king room (Sheraton Grande, Los Angeles): Oversized room with shelf/ledge in place of headboard, large desk surface and lounge area; four-fixture bathroom.

**Suites**

One principal way that a hotel can provide different qualities of accommodations is to include a number of guest-room suites in the room mix. A suite is defined simply as a living room connected to one or more bedrooms (Fig. 5). Larger hotels frequently provide a hierarchy of suites, from single-bay living rooms with a sleeping alcove to multiple-bay living rooms with perhaps six adjoining rooms, including dining/conference rooms and several bedrooms. A typical suite breakdown is shown in Table 7.

Hotel suites, which make up about 10 percent of the total guestrooms, are usually positioned on the upper floors of the tower, but they may be stacked vertically where unusual conditions occur. For example, suites may be used to fill larger structural bays of the typical floor, with mini-suites tucked behind stairs or elevators and others located where the building form provides uniquely shaped rooms.

Over the years, several new amenities have been added to hotel suites. One of these is the inclusion of express checking and concierge services on the upper floors. In some hotels, these services occur in a single room near the elevator lobby, where the staff serves light hors d'oeuvres, sells beverages, and makes newspapers available. In other hotels, this service has been expanded so that guests on

wall and the lounge and work area against the opposite wall. Also, the greater width permits unusually luxurious bathroom arrangements, often with four or five fixtures, as well as larger entry vestibules. Most four and five-star hotels are now 14 to 15 feet wide.

The wedge-shaped rooms characteristic of circular towers present their own design problem in the layout of the guest bathroom. The smaller towers have a corridor frontage of only 6 to 8 feet, the larger plans a more reasonable 10 feet. Although many of these room plans show such positive features as compartmentalized bathrooms (out of necessity), minimum foyer space, a large lounge area, and expansive window wall, increasing competition in room size and upscale furnishings has made the smaller cylindrical towers virtually obsolete.

The room layouts illustrate a variety of solutions to accommodating the family and business markets in hotels, ranging from budget to convention and luxury types. The larger rooms generally provide better lounge and work areas and oversized bathrooms.

A. Budget double-double (Day's Inn). Small room layout with outside rather than corridor access, limited seating (AC unit used for end table), sink and hanging clothesrod in dressing area,

B. Typical double-double: Standard motor inn and hotel room; beds take up 70 percent of living area, limited seating space.

C. Typical double-double—electrical/mechanical plan. Identify all electrical outlets, TV, phone, HVAC units; outlets and cable connections should be planned around proposed furnishings.

**Table 6** Guest-room dimensions

| | Living area* | | Bathroom | | Total guest room | |
|---|---|---|---|---|---|---|
| | Dimensions, feet | Area | Dimensions, feet (meters) | Area | Dimensions, feet (meters) | Area |
| Budget | 11'6" × 15' (3.5 × 4.5) | 172 (16) | 5' × 5' *1.5 × 1.5) | 25[†] (2.3) | 11'6" × 20'6" (3.5 × 6.2) | 236 (21.9) |
| Midprice | 12' × 18' (3.6 × 5.5) | 216 (20.1) | 5' × 7'6" (1.5 × 2.3) | 37 (3.4) | 12' × 26' (3.6 × 6.6) | 312 (29) |
| First class | 13'6" × 19' (4.1 × 5.8) | 256 (23.8) | 5'6" × 8'6" (1.7 × 2.6) | 47 (4.4) | 13'6" × 28'6" (4.1 × 8.6) | 378 (35.2) |
| Luxury | 15' × 20' (4.5 × 6.1) | 300 (27.9) | 7'6" × 9' (2.3 × 2.7) | 71 (6.6) | 15' × 30' (4.5 × 9.1) | 450 (41.8) |

*Living area does not include the bathroom, closet, or entry.
[†]Bathroom of budget guest room includes tub/shower and toilet; sink is part of dressing area.

**Fig. 4. Guest-room plans**

**Table 7** Different types of suites

| Suite type | Living room | Bedrooms | Keys | Bays | Percent |
|---|---|---|---|---|---|
| Mini-suite | One bay | Alcove | 1 | 1.5 | 2* |
| Conference suite | One bay | 1 | 2 | 2 | 3 |
| Junior suite | One bay | 2 | 3 | 3 | 4 |
| Executive suite | Two bays | 2 | 3 | 4 | 1 |
| Deluxe suite | Three bays | 2 | 2 | 5 | 0.5 |

*Percentage of total rooms, that is, two mini-suites per 100 rooms.

**Fig. 4. (cont.)**

**Fig. 5. Suite plans**

Hotel suites combine separate living and sleeping areas and are generally furnished with upgraded fabrics and casepieces. The largest suites may extend for 10 or more structural bays and combine numerous bedrooms and living areas. A range of suites includes:

(A) The mini-suite, containing a single bay living room plus a king bed alcove created by adjacent stairs or elevators. The divider between the two rooms houses the TV and a built-in dressing table.

(B) The junior suite (Westlake Plaza, Westlake, CA) is equal to the area of two typical rooms. The living area, on an area rug over parquet floors, includes seating and dining areas, while the bedroom features a luxurious compartmentalized bathroom.

(C) Hospitality suites are intended for large groups, such as at conventions where they are the focus of corporate entertaining. The suites show two distinct lounge areas in addition to the conference/dining area with its own pantry; one or more bedrooms generally interconnect.

the club floors or towers section bypass the busy lobby registration area and check in at the club floor. The more extensive of these tower club lounges may extend over several bays and contain space for the concierge/registration service, an office, a small seating/television lounge, a conference room, and a large lounge used for continental breakfast, afternoon tea, and cocktails.

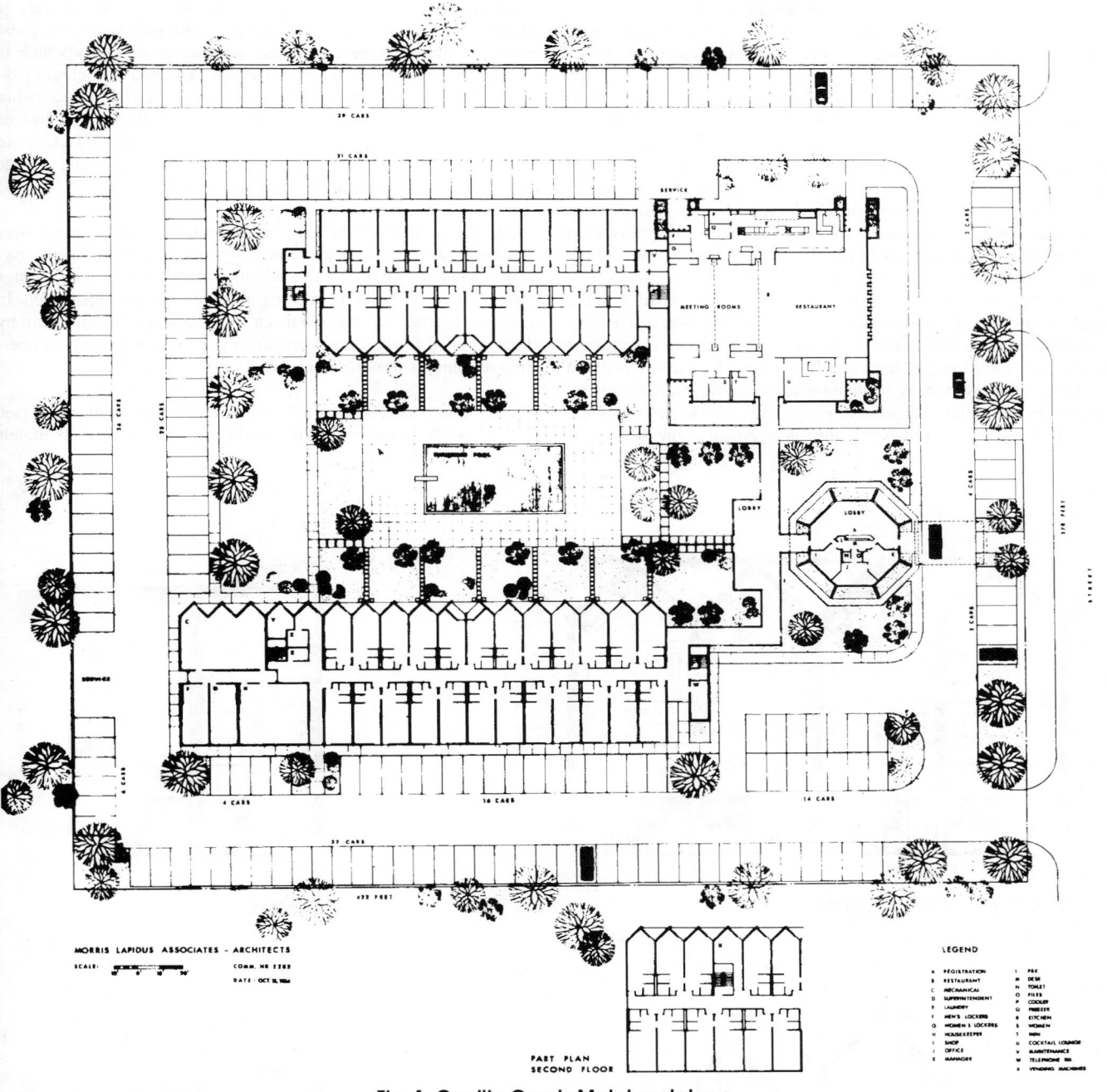

**Fig. 1. Quality Courts Motel prototype**

# MOTELS

Much of what is discussed in the preceding section on hotels will apply to motels. The term motel is rather loosely used. There are many so-called motels within cities which are, in fact, multilevel hotels providing more than the average parking found in a hotel. Where such a project occurs, it would normally be called a motor hotel.

Parking may be provided in an adjacent garage, in several levels below grade, or in several levels above grade with guests rooms starting on an upper floor above the garage levels. If property values permit, there may be an open parking area or a two- or three-story open parking garage. Whatever arrangement is eventually used, these

*Authors:* Morris Lapidus and Alan Lapidus, Morris Lapidus Associates
*Reviewer:* John Hill, Hill Glazier Architects

structures should properly be called motor hotels rather than motels. Aside from the parking, everything that will be found in these motor hotels will be the same as what has been discussed under hotels.

A true motel is one which is normally found on a main highway, at an important intersection of several highways, or, finally, at a highway which enters a city and therefore is close to the city and yet not a part of it. The obvious reason is that land values within cities are too high to permit the spread that a true motel will require. Motels usually provide open parking and as a rule are only one-, two-, three-, or at most four-stories-high. Usually most of the rooms will be entered from an open corridor, although this is not a hard and fast rule. There may be a combination of open corridors and closed corridors. The parking, by preference, should be placed as close as possible to the actual room that the guest will be occupying. The great advantage that motels have is the ability of guests to park close to their rooms and to carry their luggage back and forth without the assistance of a bellhop. Bellhop service is available when required, but many guests arriving by car prefer to handle their own luggage. The option should be with the guest rather than with the management of the motel.

In the highway motel the lounge and registration area as well as administration offices may be within the buildings housing the guest rooms, or they may be completely separate as an entity which is reached from the motel rooms by means of covered or enclosed passages. Housekeeping and maintenance spaces may be placed within the management and registration area, attached to the motel wings, or housed in a separate small building to handle laundry, housekeeping supplies, locker rooms for help, and maintenance shops and storage for taking care of the grounds, the swimming pool, etc.

The restaurant that will be a part of the normal motel complex may be attached to the management and registration area or, again, may be in a separate building or in a building attached to the motel wings rather than to the building housing management and registration. In many motels the food operation is a lease arrangement and is run by chains of food and beverage companies that make a specialty of operating restaurants for individual motels or for motel chains.

Quality Court Motels are used in this context as an example (see Figs. 1 and 2). In the case of this particular chain, where the motels

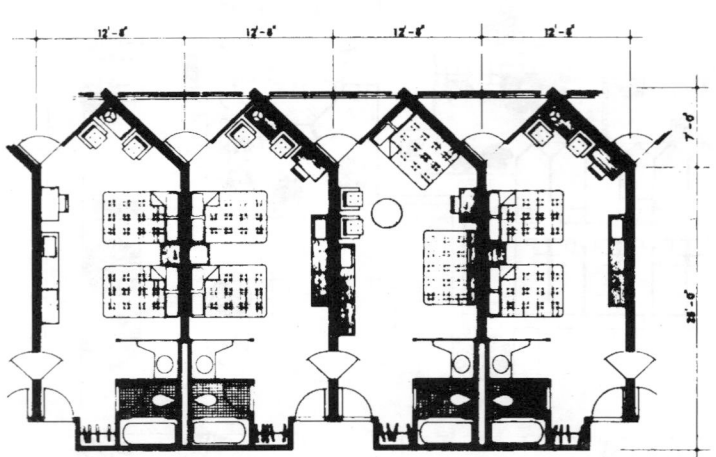

**DOUBLE – WITH BALCONY**

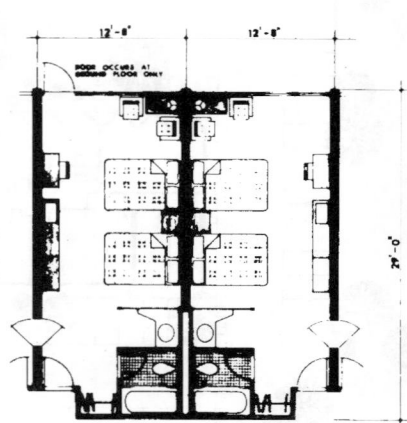

**DOUBLE**

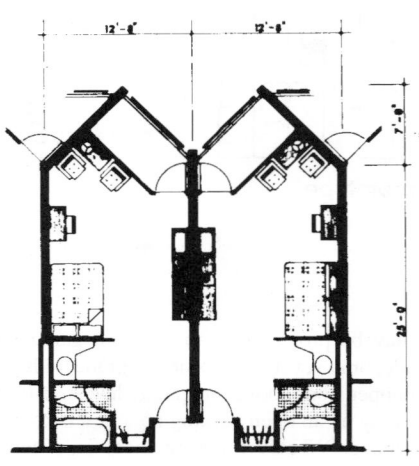

**SINGLE – WITH BALCONY**

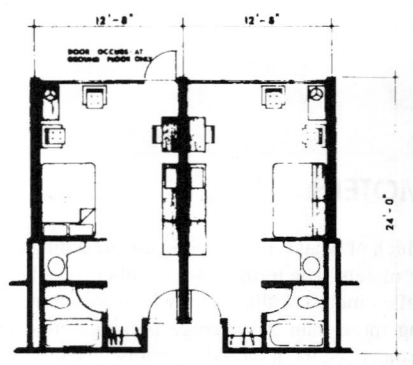

**SINGLE**

Fig. 2. Typical rooms, Quality Courts Motel prototype

re usually individually owned and operated under a franchise, the
ood operation is a lease operation, but in every respect each of the
otels contain the same basic element: namely, the registration and
dministrative building and a restaurant varying in size depending
pon the size of the motel. A standard feature of every motel is an
dequate swimming pool and pool deck (an amenity which is invari-
bly found in all highway motels), ample parking to take care of all
he guest rooms, and sufficient parking for restaurant guests who
nay not be staying at the motel.

Motel guest rooms differ somewhat from hotel rooms. Motels cater
o two distinct clienteles. One type is the traveling businessperson
using a car for transportation. She usually travels alone. All she wants
s a small room for her overnight stay. The other guest accommoda-
ion is for a traveling family. Here a large room is wanted. It will have
wo king-size beds to accommodate the parents and two children. A
areful study of the location will yield the clue that will determine
he mix of small and large rooms.

Drawer space is not a necessity; several shelves and luggage stands
are of prime importance. Closets may be and usually are omitted.
Most motels are designed for single overnight stays. The use of an
additional lavatory is suggested. This amenity permits a family to
complete its toilet rapidly for the usual early morning start (see Figs.
3 and 4).

A space should be provided for vending machines that dispense hot
and cold drinks, candy, snacks, and magazines. An ice maker is a
must, as well as insulated ice buckets for each room. Self-service of
traveler comforts and needs by means of vending machines is an extra
boon for the road-weary traveler who is anxious to get a night's rest.

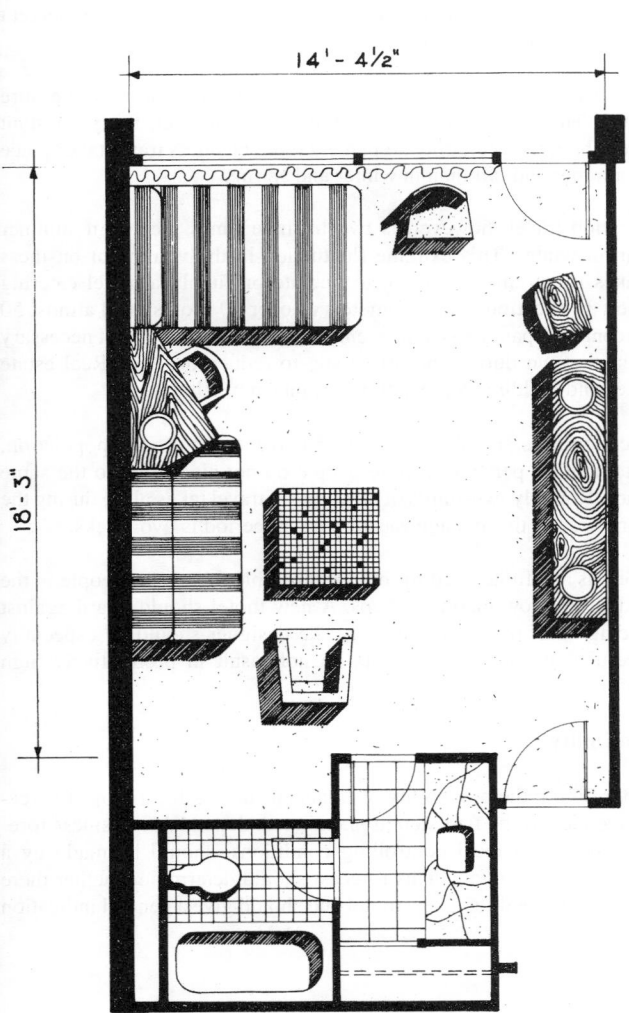

**Fig. 3. Tampa International Inn, Tampa, Florida**

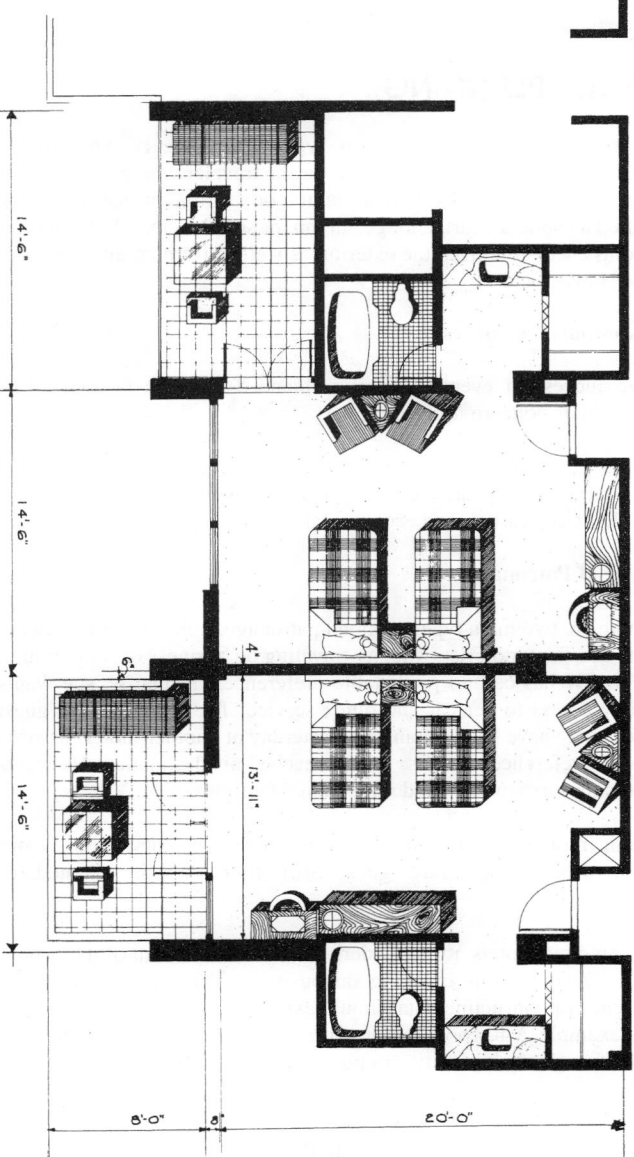

**Fig. 4. Arawak Hotel, Jamaica, B.W.I.**

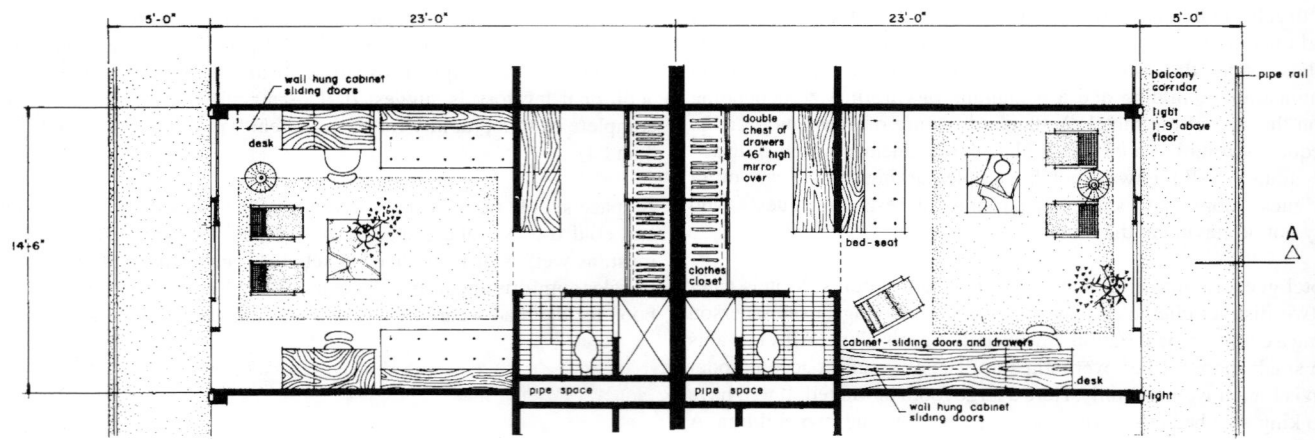

**Fig. 1. Motel rooms—exterior entrance**

# MOTEL PLANNING

A motel can be defined as any type of sleeping accommodation designed and operated especially for the traveler who travels by car. It may be the most primitive structure, or a virtual palace. It may be called a cabin, a court, a lodge, an inn, or simply a motel. It can offer rooms accessible from the exterior, as well as from an interior corridor (Figs. 1 and 2).

## Essentials for Success

The success of every motel is influenced by three factors, all of immediate concern to the designer:

1. Good location
2. Attractive appearance
3. Quick, pleasant, and economical service.

## Type of Patronage

There are two main types of motel patronage: transient and terminal. The transient motorist, whether traveling on business or for pleasure, generally has certain predictable preferences. Primarily, she wants ready access to her car and quick service. The "longer stay" guest (who may have been a transient yesterday at another motel) has different preferences because he has reached his destination. He wants pleasing surroundings and recreational facilities.

Some motels are designed primarily for transients; others cater only to the "longer stay" guest. Still others must be planned for both types.

Commercial hotels normally derive at least 85 percent of their room sales from persons traveling on business. The city motel, in the absence of conflicting data, should expect about the same. As a typical example, a 40-room motor court, although 2 miles from the center of a good-sized city, found that business people supplied 85 percent of its annual business. And it was a popular motel—its average of 80 percent room occupancy for the year was nearly 10 percent above the national average.

Business travel is much greater in volume than vacation or pleasure travel. The volume of business travel is, moreover, fairly constant throughout the year: only 25 percent more business travel takes place in summer and fall than in winter and spring.

Vacation travel, however, is two to three times greater in summer than in winter. This extreme fluctuation in the volume of business makes it extremely difficult to operate profitably a motel catering solely to vacationers. Most motels of over 50 rooms need almost 50 percent occupancy to break even. Thus some motels find it necessary to shut down during the off-season to reduce the loss. Real estate taxes and building depreciation continue nevertheless.

Vacation trips are taken by over 75 percent of our adult population, but about 60 percent of these people do not always go to the same place. Roughly two-thirds of all vacation travel takes place during the summer, and the average vacation travel period is two weeks.

There is a definite need for more acceptable motels for people in the middle and low-income groups. A new motel should guard against pricing itself out of the market. The designer should be especially careful that construction costs do not result in prohibitively high rental rates.

## Feasibility

Determining the probability of financial success for a project is recommended as the first step in planning. A dependable business forecast, based on local controlling conditions, should be made by a competent consultant. This forecast should determine whether there is adequate need for a new motel and should give a general indication

*Author:* Frank Harrison Randolph, P.E.
*Reviewer:* John Hill, Hill Glazier Architects
*References:* Hotel Planning Consultant and Professor of Hotel Engineering, Cornell University

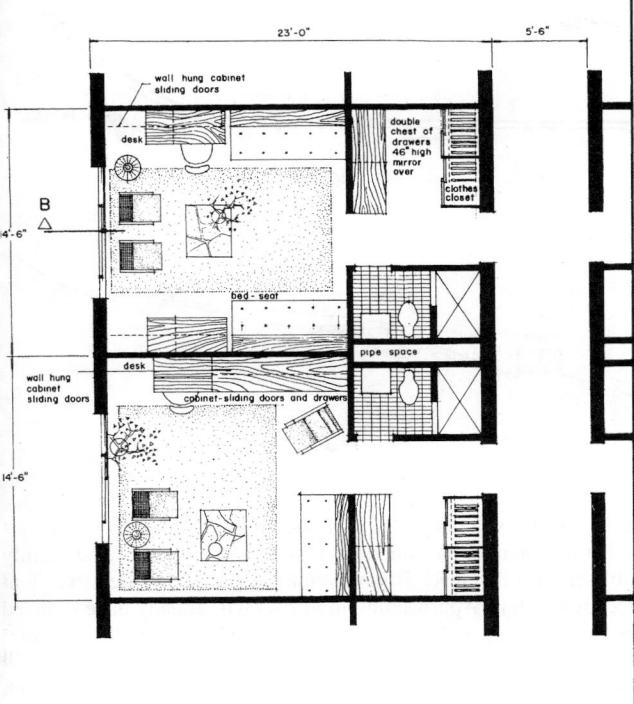

23'-0"    5'-6"

wall hung cabinet
sliding doors

desk

double
chest of
drawers
46" high
mirror
over

clothes
closet

B

4'-6"

bed-seat

pipe space

wall hung
cabinet
sliding doors

desk

cabinet-sliding doors and drawers

14'-6"

**Fig. 2. Motel rooms—interior corridor**

of the number of guest rooms and the type and extent of services to be provided. The forecast should be followed by selection of the site, working out of the financial plan, and finally, determination of the functional scheme: the number, types, and sizes of guest rooms, public spaces, and food and beverage facilities, the type of building construction, and the extent of mechanical services. Only after these preliminary steps have been completed is the project ready to be started on the drawing boards. Otherwise, much time, money, and effort may be lost in developing specific ideas that are impractical and yet difficult to discard.

### Basic Economic Survey

Many factors will require careful study by a qualified financial advisor, such as a firm experienced in hotel and motel accounting. Ever-increasing costs of construction and operation are vital considerations. The rapidly expanding and shifting pattern of major highways should be evaluated for its effect on the site. The possibility of an overabundance of motels in the area must not be overlooked. The soundness of the title to the land may be questionable. The decision of whether to purchase the land, build on leased land, or select a sale-and-lease-back arrangement may well have a considerable effect on taxes.

It will aid greatly in planning to have in advance an idea of the type of traveler expected, the probable length of his stay, and the seasonal fluctuations expected in the volume of business. Such a survey is unquestionably a help in determining the financial feasibility of a project. Seasonal variations may require a break-even point at close to 50 percent occupancy.

Horwath & Horwath Hotel Accountants and Consultants stress the importance of determining:

- rate of economic growth of the area
- probable future development of the community
- status of existing or contemplated transient housing and feeding accommodations.

### Location

Site location is of paramount importance. Geographically, it should be at the end of a day's run for the motorist in order to attract transient business. The average motorist is not interested in stopping for the night except at the end of the day's run, so the site should be a day's run (or a multiple of this) from one or more reservoirs of potential transient business. The typical motorist covers about 300 miles in a day, plus or minus up to 100 miles, depending upon personal preferences and highway conditions, which need individual analysis for a given area. Obviously the motorist will travel considerably farther in a day on limited-access express highways than on the usual improved routes.

Traffic surveys showing the daily volume are of value only if they indicate the number of potential customers passing the site during the critical few hours at the end of the day. The total 24-hour volume of trucks, local passenger traffic, and whatever else comes along means very little. A tally of all passenger-car license plates that passed in each direction during the end-of-the-day period, disregarding, if possible, those issued within a radius of about 200 miles, would give the most helpful indication of potential business for the day or days on which the count was taken. It would give no guarantee of volume, however, for another season or for future years.

Major highway routes are constantly changing, both in pattern and in condition. An excellent location today can become almost worthless next year because a new highway has bypassed it, taking virtually all of its long-distance passenger traffic. Or the condition of a long major route might be so greatly improved that, although the motel was formerly a normal day's drive from a potential reservoir of transient business, it would now be reached by most potential customers by midafternoon—at least two hours before their stopping time. Future highway conditions are difficult to forecast, since highway plans are often changed for unpredictable reasons with disastrous consequences for the motel, which may become virtually stranded. Careful checking with all the various planning agencies, especially the state highway department, is a precaution that must not be overlooked. Indeed, selection of the proper site requires the combined judgment of persons in many fields. The state highway department can forecast traffic characteristics. The chamber of commerce is familiar with recent civic development and building and population trends. The real estate broker knows land values. The construction engineer can report on soil conditions, excavation, and drainage, and indicate probable difficulties in building. The architect experienced in motel design will have a wealth of practical advice. The accounting firm that made the economic survey should be satisfied that the site is properly qualified. The finance company or bank that is to loan the necessary funds must be convinced of the apparent soundness of the venture. If a particular site is vetoed by any one of these qualified parties, the success of the enterprise must be considered open to serious question. There is no satisfactory substitute for an excellent location that meets these various criteria.

When the typical motorist, thinking she has traveled long enough for the day, realizes there is some difficult driving a short distance ahead, and then encounters an attractive motel, she will be conditioned to decide to stop for the night. The difficulty may be the heavy traffic of a large city, a winding road over a mountain, or a tedious long stretch of road through barren country—something she would rather postpone until morning. Situating the motel suitably in advance of such an obstacle can be definitely rewarding (Fig. 3).

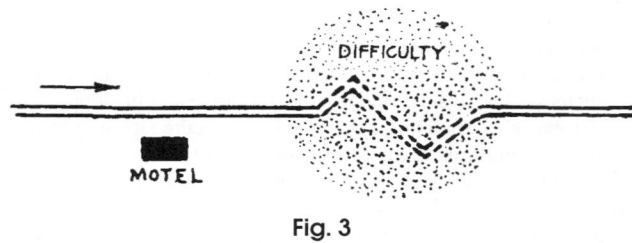

Fig. 3

Some motels successfully intercept the traveler just outside a city where she had thought to find lodging (Fig. 4). If several motels are already grouped along the highway leading into a city, a new motel can be expected to be more successful if it joins the group than if it selects an isolated location. Prospective guests tend to be favorably impressed by a large group of motels, which by its very magnitude suggests abundant hospitality and a popular motel area. Once she stops, the traveler is almost certain to stay at one or another of these places (Fig. 5).

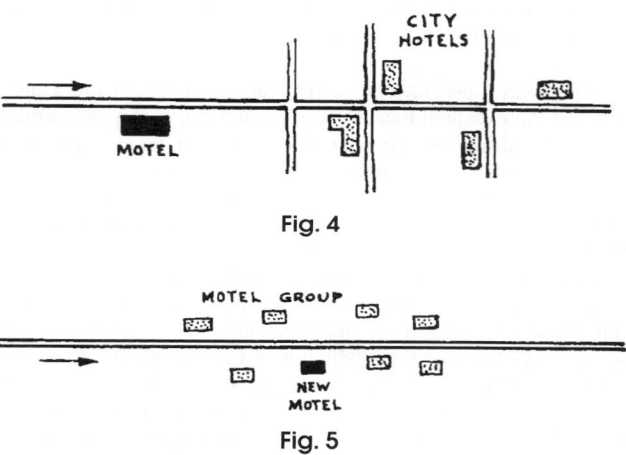

Fig. 4

Fig. 5

If possible, the motel should be on the right-hand side of the road, especially if traffic is at all heavy, since drivers would rather not make a left turn (Fig. 6). If the highway curves, place the motel on the right of a left-hand curve, so that it will be directly in line with the driver's vision (Fig. 7). If the site selected slopes upward from the highway, the hillside location of the motel will add to its prominence (Fig. 8).

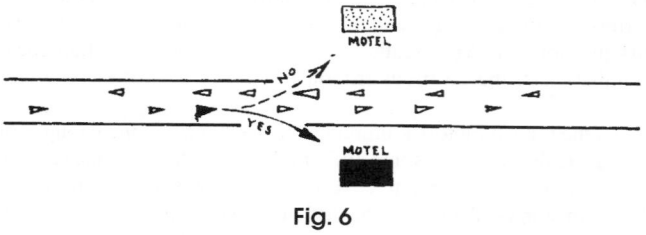

Fig. 6

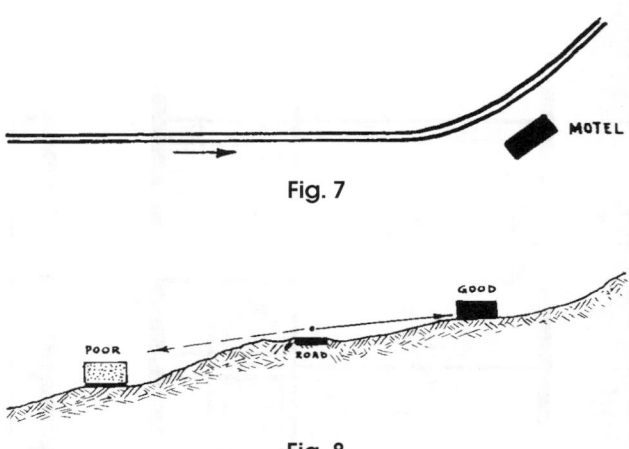

Fig. 7

Fig. 8

The best motel site is the one with the greatest appeal to the largest number of potential customers. The site should of course be plainly visible from a distance. Highway intersections are often excellent places for motels. Approaching motorists will already have reduced speed and be prepared to stop, and can readily size up the situation before reaching the intersection. The order of preference of several possible site locations at an intersection may be influenced by such factors as the slope of the land and the presence of existing or future buildings (Figs. 9, 10, 11).

If travel is about equal in both directions, the motel should aim for those who are going rather than those returning, because of the opportunity for repeat business. Twenty-five percent of the guests of some motels are repeat customers.

If a town is bypassed by the main traffic route, the motel may be placed on the right-hand side of the road leading to the town, but should be plainly visible from the main highway (Fig. 12). If two towns are not far apart on the highway, the motel should be placed to intercept the major volume of traffic before it reaches either of them. Putting the motel between the towns generally proves unsatisfactory, since most motorists would not be in the mood for stopping on such an in-between stretch (Fig. 13).

It is important to determine well in advance whether the highway department will permit the desired location. Encroachments, set-back regulations, deceleration lanes, and access drives must all be considered. The highway department may not permit direct access from deceleration or acceleration lanes. Definite approval of specific plans should be obtained from the authorities at a very early stage in the planning.

Advance signs advertising the motel and directing the motorist are essential. Often the authorities have very severe restrictions on the placement of such signs; therefore, sign locations must be assured and permissions obtained before the site may be said to be satisfactory.

**Types of Motels**

Motels can be differentiated by their location and purpose. The most common types are as follows:

- *City motels* are built in town or on the edge of town. They are intended primarily for commercial travelers with business in the

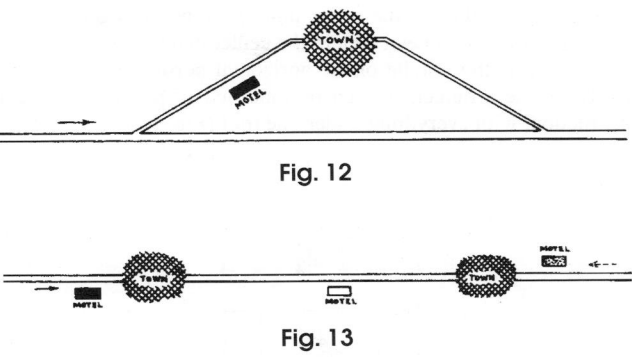

Fig. 12

Fig. 13

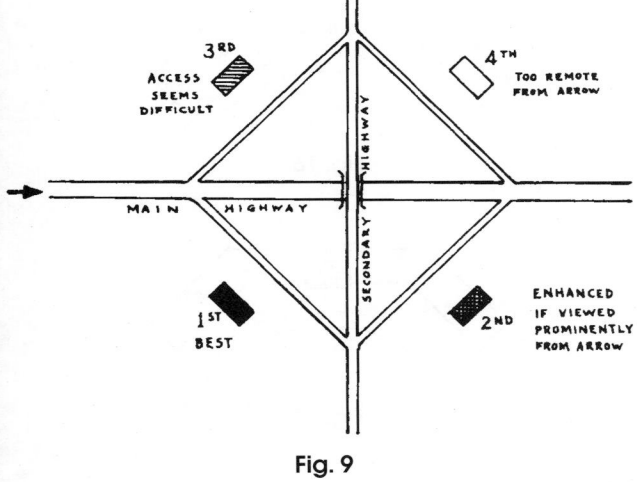

Fig. 9

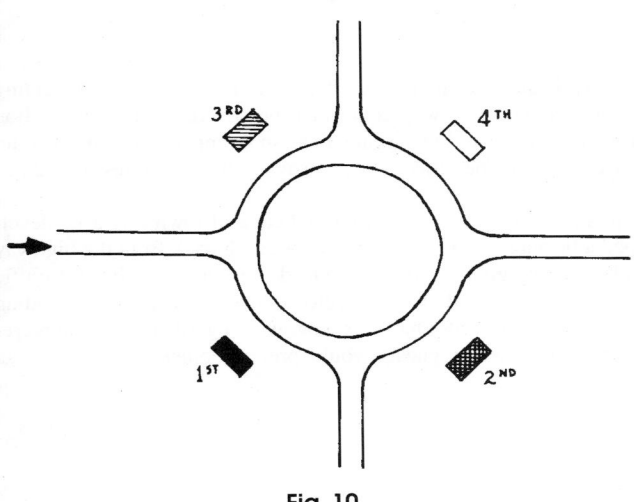

Fig. 10

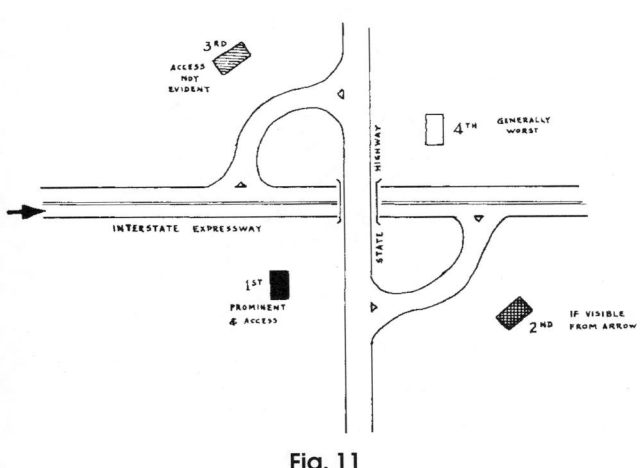

Fig. 11

downtown area. They generally involve expensive land, a restricted site, and a structure at least three stories high. Nearly the entire site is used for buildings and parking.

- *Motor annexes* adjoin an existing hotel in the city. Whether the motel emphasizes its connection as an annex will depend on the reputation of the hotel and its advertising, location, services, utilities, supervision, and maintenance staff.
- *Highway motor hotels* furnish room-side parking for the traveler en route. This type of motel is usually one or two stories high, with a site of at least three acres. If space permits, not more than 15 percent of the site area is used for buildings and parking.
- *Resort motels* are intended primarily for guests who have reached their destination, and usually require ample facilities for recreation. Closing during the off-season may also be necessary. The site, ideally spacious, can be small if necessary.
- *Airport inns* are built at a major, usually intercontinental, airport. Relatively large, high-class operations, these motels often have 150 to 300 rooms, two-story guest-room buildings, and a site of at least 10 acres. Business is supplied by airline patrons, motorists, and guests from the metropolitan area served by the airport. The size of such a motel permits full-scale food and beverage facilities, function rooms, and often as extensive recreational facilities as are found in resort motels. The location usually borders on the outlying industrial area, within easy driving distance of both the suburban residential area and the city.

**Site Plan**

Pertinent factors include the size of the buildings, the area for parking, size of the site, contour of the land, and the extremely important traffic patterns for guests, employees, supplies, and refuse. The ideal arrangement should combine "pull" with privacy—two items that are difficult to attain simultaneously in any site plan. The "pull" or drawing power of an attractive appearance from the highway should be converted to privacy for the guest after arrival. Drawing power is linked with proximity to the highway; privacy is associated with quiet surroundings. Some compromise must be made on the basis of the variety of motel, the type of guest, and the site conditions. One operator may want the motel set far back from the highway; another may want the swimming pool right out in front. The designer must know the preferences of the motel owner and operator in order to produce the results desired.

If the motel is to be located on a high-speed thoroughfare, it should have a frontage of at least 500 feet. The motorist going 60 miles an hour will need about that distance to slow down comfortably in order to turn off the highway.

For a small installation, the guest units may be arranged in a U-shaped pattern, with a lawn area in the center and the guest registration building at the middle of the horizontal portion of the U (Fig. 14). The same arrangement can be modified to provide unbroken construction, with everything under one roof (Fig. 15).

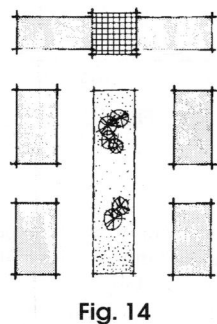

**Fig. 14**

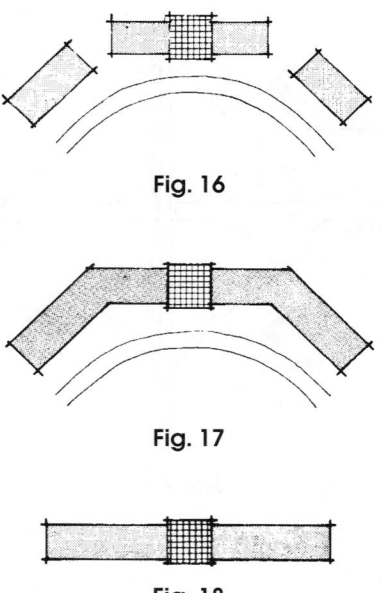

**Fig. 16**

**Fig. 17**

**Fig. 18**

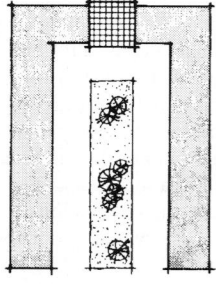

**Fig. 15**

way, the U may advantageously be broken by a driveway connecting the streets. The driveway could then be covered at the registration office and access to the parking areas so arranged that control could be exercised by the office over all arrivals and departures (Fig. 23).

A relatively long, narrow site on the edge of town might be developed advantageously by setting the building back from the highway and providing good visibility, roomside parking, and efficient traffic patterns (Fig. 24). If the site were somewhat deeper, the building might be designed as a half-hexagon, with a garden court and recreation area. Whether guests would prefer roomside parking or an

A crescent-shaped arrangement is often quite appealing. The central registration building may be flanked by guest units (Fig. 16). If built as a simple structure, this arrangement usually takes the shape of a half-hexagon (Fig. 17). Or the motel might be designed as a long, straight building, with equal wings extending from the registration office (Fig. 18).

For some sites, a T-shaped structure might be most suitable. With that design, however, the service entrance can be difficult to locate (Fig. 19). The L-shaped layout is deservedly popular. Placing the registration office toward the highway extends an obvious welcome to the motorist. The sight of other cars in the parking area will also be an inducement to the prospective guest. In addition, the garden and pool area will be secluded, so that the guest can escape the noise and confusion of the highway (Fig. 20). Or the position of the L might be reversed, and the ground areas adjoining the building attractively arranged. The swimming pool, for example, could be placed out in front as an inducement to the traveler (Fig. 21).

If the site is approximately square, and located near or in town, the registration office may best be placed at the tip of one side of a U. This familiar solution is both well-ordered and attractive (Fig. 22). If the site is longer and has access to a rear street parallel to the high-

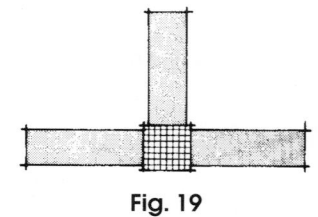

**Fig. 19**

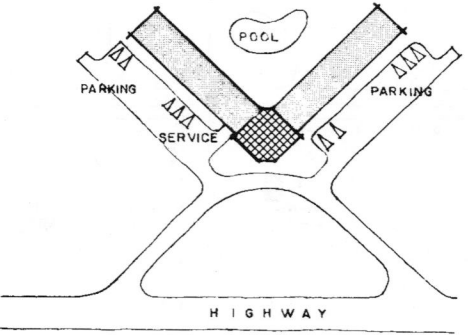

**Fig. 20**

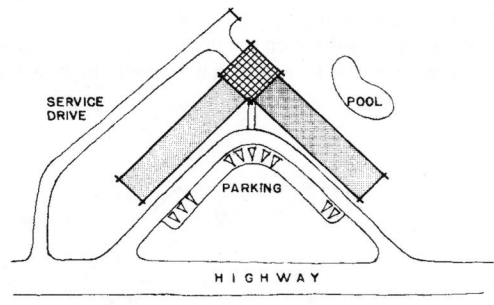

**Fig. 21**

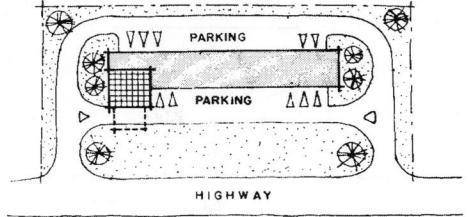

**Fig. 24**

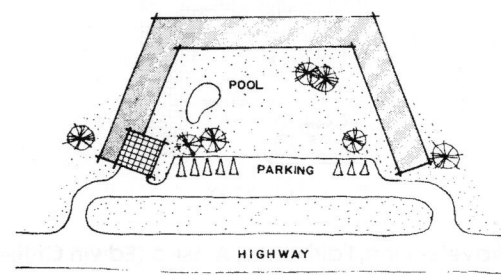

**Fig. 25**

adjacent garden court and recreation area depends on such circumstances as the purpose of their visit, length of stay, climatic conditions, and the view from windows not facing the court (Fig. 25).

A large motel in the downtown area may take the form of a hollow rectangle. The example shown in Fig. 26 provides a wide scope of services, including a restaurant, ballroom, shops, room service, year-round swimming pool, and an attractive central garden area. Street-level parking is provided under the guest rooms. A similar pattern is followed in the 68-unit motel shown in Fig. 27. The registration office, gift shop, coffee shop, cocktail lounge, and restaurant are located in the portions of the building nearest the highway. The inner court provides parking space around an island lawn with trees. This arrangement permits good control of cars entering and leaving, brings the cars near the guest rooms, and may thus seem the obvious solution to parking problems. The noise of cars arriving and departing, however, often late at night or early in the morning, will affect all guest rooms facing the court, where the noise is accentuated by reverberation. Also, the headlights of arriving cars will rake the windows

facing the court. In northern climates, snow removal can be a difficult problem as well, with the hollow-rectangle arrangement.

The 150-room airport motel shown in Fig. 28 uses the inside of the enclosure for the garden, recreation, and swimming-pool area, with parking facilities around the outside. Business comes from both airline and motor travelers. Service is comparable to that of large hotels in the city. The circular building contains a dining room and cocktail lounge on the ground floor, and a second floor meeting room.

Individuality is an asset to the motel illustrated in Fig. 29. On a site of moderate area, this motel has a convenient, covered entrance for the motorist and an adjoining circular restaurant building, backed up by an L-shaped, two-story guest section. The outside dining terrace overlooking the lawn and pool is especially inviting with its open, yet secluded atmosphere. Separate parking areas are provided for restaurant patrons and for guests.

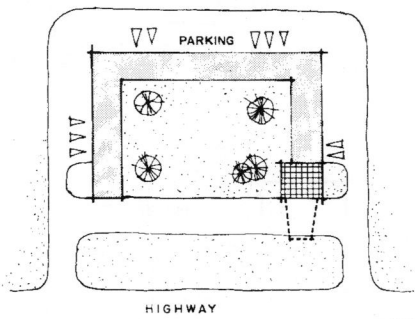

**Fig. 22**

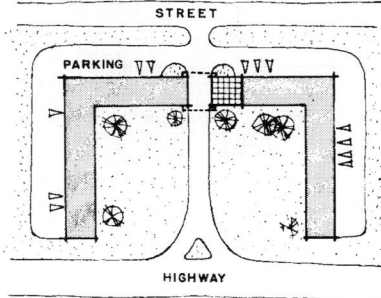

**Fig. 23**

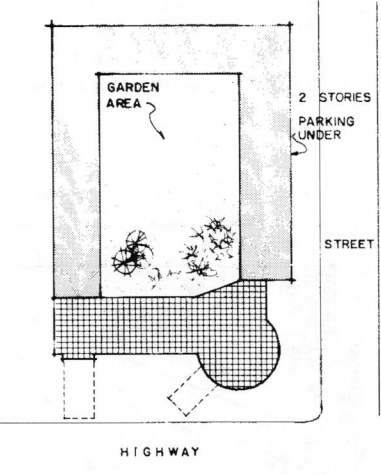

**Fig. 26. Manger Motor Inn, Charlotte, North Carolina (Finn-Jenter, Architect)**

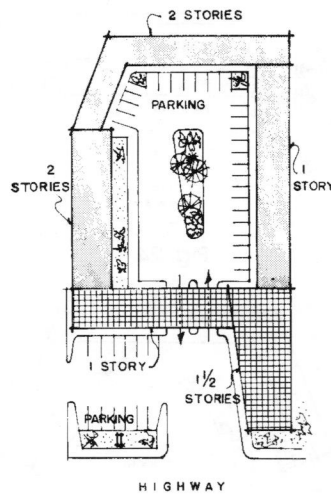

**Fig. 27. Travelers Inn, Fairbanks, Alaska (Edwin Crittenden, Architect)**

A motel may be built on a narrow strip of valuable land between the highway and the ocean, as is frequently done in Florida. The example in Fig. 30 concentrates the three stories of guest rooms (with a double-loaded corridor) perpendicular to the shore line, providing an ocean view from every room. All guest rooms have private balconies. A garage in the semibasement accommodates self-service parking. The single-story lobby, bar, and coffee-shop portion includes a dining terrace that overlooks the circular outdoor dance floor, the pool, and the ocean. The arrangement is open, uncluttered, and inviting.

**Room Groups and Parking**

Designed for the convenience of the motorist, each room of the motel should have, if possible, at least one window with a desirable view or private outlook on a quiet area (for which landscaping may be required). Bathrooms and clothes closets should be placed along the driveway side of the rooms. The room layout should follow the usual hotel guest-room arrangement, with the central guest corridor replaced by an access driveway. Convenience, privacy, and rooms that are both quiet and cheerful are the objectives. The shape, orientation, dimensions, and topography of the individual site, of course, may necessitate some deviation from the ideal layout.

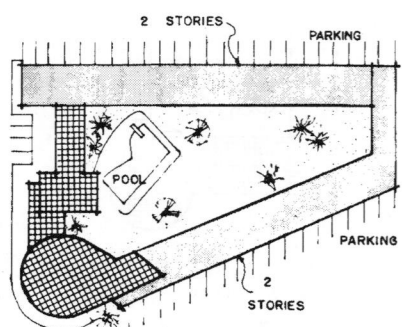

**Fig. 28. Avis Motel, Midway Airport, Chicago (Design, Inc., Architect)**

Ideally, one side of a row of guest units would take full advantage of the view, with the access drive on the opposite side of the row. Bathrooms on the entrance side would have small, high windows to

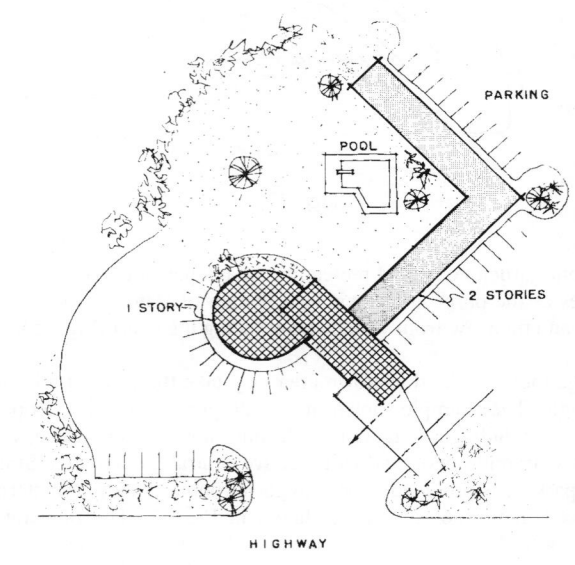

**Fig. 29. O'Hare-Chicago Motor Hotel, Chicago International Airport (A. P. Swanson Associates, Architect)**

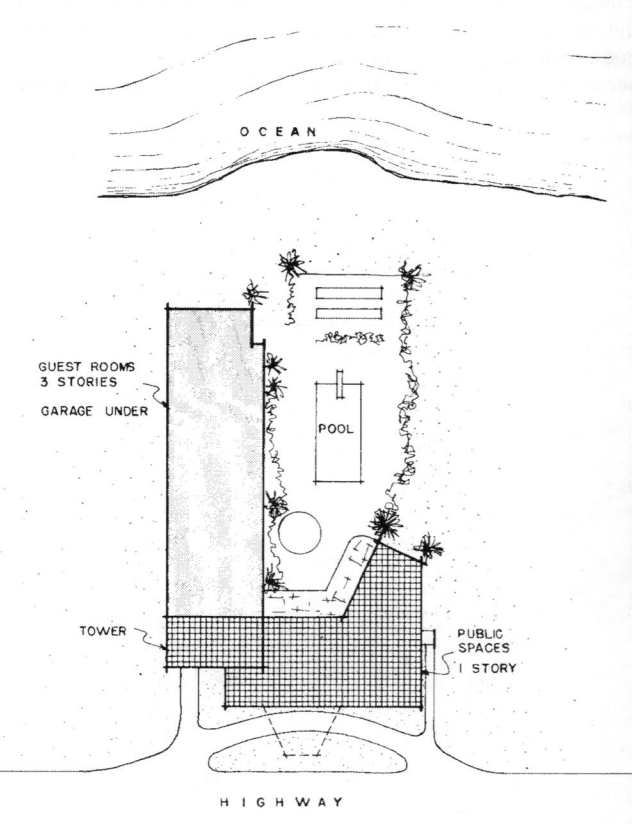

**Fig. 30. Pan American Motel, Miami Beach, Fla. (Carlos B. Schoeppl & Associates, Architect)**

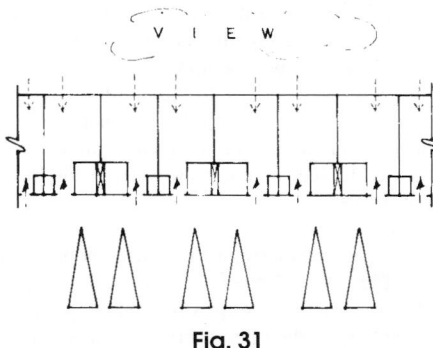

Fig. 31

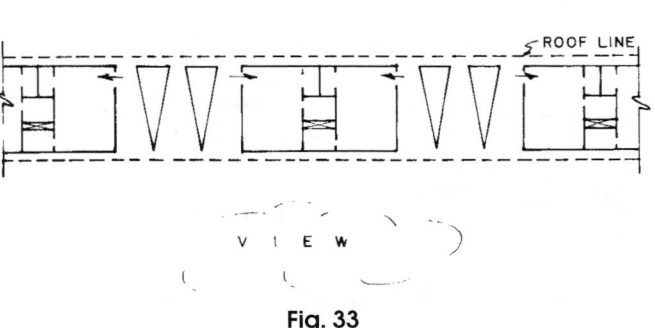

Fig. 33

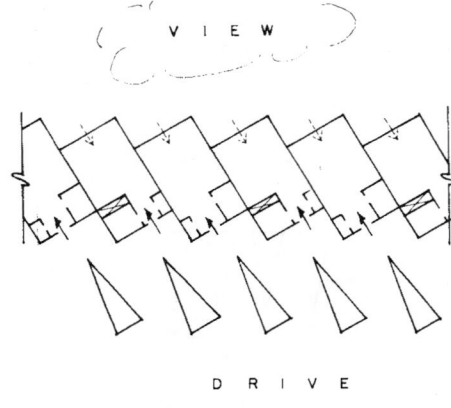

Fig. 34

increase privacy and reduce noise, whereas the guest rooms might have large picture windows to capitalize on the view. An extra doorway on the side with the view might be desirable. (See Fig. 31, 33, 34, 36, 38, 42.)

If the strip of land available for guest units is narrow, either because of dimensions or topography, the best solution is generally to set the units well back from the road. The effect from the road will be impressive (Fig. 42). If the strip were about 25 feet wider, better results would be obtained by setting the guest units 25 feet back from the parking area, and landscaping the area between.

A level strip on a hillside, even as narrow as 43 feet, can readily accommodate both a drive and a single row of parked cars. Placing each guest room over its parked car solves the problem nicely: The cars are protected from the weather, and each guest is provided with a private balcony (Fig. 43). If the site continues downhill, it may be desirable to sink a guest room into the bank and park its car on the roof (Fig. 44). This arrangement provides privacy and a good view of the valley.

If there is no desirable view and the patronage will be mostly transient, the more economical back-to-back arrangement may be justified, despite its lack of privacy and cross-ventilation (see Figs. 32, 35, 37, 40, 48, 50). Two- or four-room units are often arranged with parking space between them, serving to break the monotony and add visual interest (Figs. 32, 33, 36). Another alternative is a four-room unit with all four cars parked in a row (Fig. 37).

Rooms on different levels may be advantageous, depending upon the topography and dimensions of the site, and the number of units required. Guests handling their own luggage generally do not welcome climbing a full story height, but seldom object to half that amount (Figs. 39, 47).

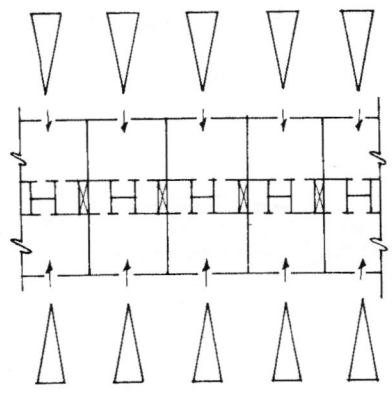

Fig. 35

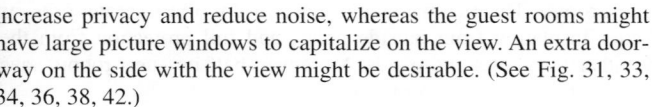

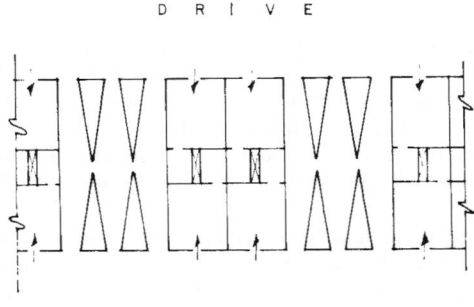

Fig. 32

### Corridors

An interior corridor will protect the guest in bad weather and be a great help to maid service. With protected inside corridors, a maid is customarily assigned 14 to 16 rooms; if only an outside entrance is provided, one maid would probably handle only 10 to 12 rooms. Moreover, a single interior corridor will make it easier for the management to exercise desired control; the guests, also, will probably feel more secure.

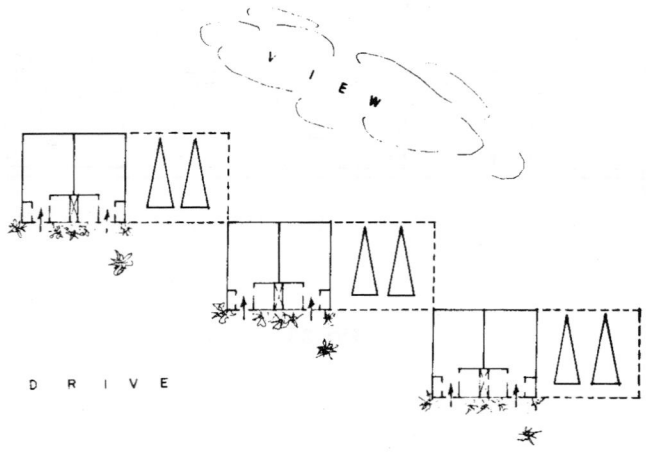

**Fig. 36**

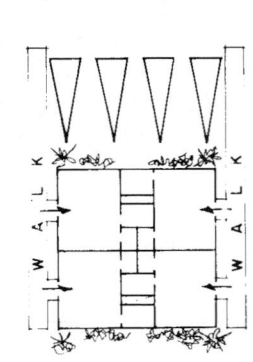

**Fig. 37**

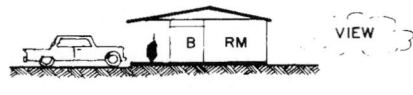

**Fig. 38**

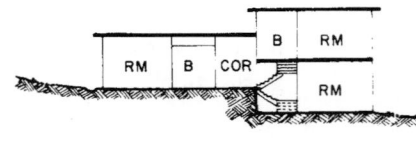

**Fig. 39**

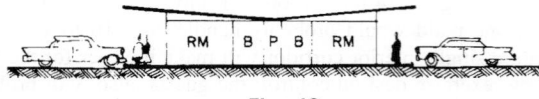

**Fig. 40**

On the other hand, if the only entrance to a room is through an outside doorway, the guest can enjoy the feeling of having a private cottage. That feeling, however, will be appreciably reduced if the open corridor or public walkway is close to the building and protected by an overhanging roof, despite high windows, venetian blinds, or similar remedial devices. Privacy would be greatly improved by placing the public walkway 15 feet or more away from the building, with suitable planting between.

Compare the arrangement of two-story guest-room buildings with open corridors in Fig. 48, with the one with interior corridors in Fig. 49. Note that the construction requires floor slabs of the some width for each. An advantage of the open-corridor plan is that a quarter of the rooms have direct access to parking. The corridors, however, extend along the only windows, and thus reduce the privacy of all the guest rooms. The plan with the inside corridor offers greater privacy, better insulation from outside noise, and full protection from the weather for guests and maids. Moreover, half its guest rooms have either a private balcony or terrace.

A narrow site requiring two guest floors to secure the necessary number of rooms may necessitate putting the building on stilts, with parking below the guest rooms. (Such an arrangement, however, increases the building height, and adds unwelcome stair climbing—or elevator problems.) With two stories, two access drives are preferable, one on each side of the building. If two drives are not feasible, however, it is possible to use a central driveway, a solution often employed in garages (Fig. 50). Both guest floors can be served by an interior double-loaded corridor, or by open corridors (one on each side) with a pipe-and-vent shaft between the guest bathrooms.

**Guest Rooms**

The motel guest wants much the same things in her room as she would want in a hotel. Reference should be made to previous pages concerning typical hotel rooms: types, sizes, design principles, and representative layouts. A motel will often increase the length and width of a similar room by a foot or two, however, to provide a greater spaciousness than would be feasible in a commercial hotel in the city. Some experienced motel operators say that 12 by 13 feet of net bedroom area is the best minimum size for a room to accommodate two persons.

*Kitchenettes*

Motel guests who have arrived at their destination often want cooking facilities on a modest scale. If the motel will cater primarily to overnight guests, however, the probable demand for kitchenettes should be determined by a careful study, involving a check of other motels in the neighborhood. Representative layouts including kitchenettes are shown in Fig. 51.

Complete factory-assembled kitchenettes are available in 30 to 72-inch lengths. Features included are a range top with 2, 3, or 4 burners (either gas or electric), with an oven underneath; a sink, with a utensil storage cabinet underneath; and a worktable area, with a refrigerator underneath. A storage cabinet for china and nonrefrigerated foodstuffs is usually provided on the wall above the unit.

The kitchenette unit may be placed in an alcove sized to fit it, with louvered doors or an equivalent device to screen it off or even lock it up when not desired by the guests. Or a separate room might be provided.

### Wall Partitions

Partitions between guest rooms should be of any construction that will reduce sound transmission by at least 45 decibels, a reduction that is usually adequate. In wood-frame construction, 2x4s are often staggered on 8-inch centers, with a sound-insulating blanket between them. In selecting the method of construction, the designer should consider materials, labor, suitability, fire hazards, transmission loss, and cost.

### Number of Guest Rooms

Several motel chain organizations have made careful studies to determine the minimum number of guest rooms that would be economical to operate. Their conclusions run from 64 rooms for the less elaborate forms of operation to 100 rooms for those organizations that intend all guest conveniences and services to be distinctly superior.

### Space Allotments

Space allotments in motels follow, in general, the pattern for allotments in hotels. Data taken from over a dozen motel plans were used to establish the space allotments listed in Table 1. Consideration was also given to the typical values for hotels. Space allotments are directly proportional to the number of guest rooms; the figures provided below for a typical 100-room motel can be adjusted to suit any other size. (For a 60-room motel, multiply by 0.60; for 130 rooms, by 1.30.) Other modifications may be necessary to meet individual requirements. No adjustment should be made, however, for the manager's office and the secretary's office, as each would still need about the same area.

### Food Service

Food service is not a lucrative part of the motel business; money invested in rooms pays better dividends. The motorist, however, will want food service handy; if not actually on the premises, then only a step away. She generally dislikes to go more than a few hundred yards to find a restaurant. Therefore, unless adequate food service is already adjacent, it is advisable to provide it.

For the motel requiring strictly minimum facilities, a good solution is the factory-assembled roadside "diner" with a dozen or more seats, which can be handled by a single employee during slack hours. For the more ambitious but still rather small motel with little outside patronage, the best solution may well be a coffee shop, possibly supplemented by a bar. Such an arrangement helps to keep investment and labor costs within bounds. For the larger motel, a dining room, coffee shop, and bar with cocktail lounge may all be needed. If the motel is near a city, private dining rooms are usually added as well. Outside patronage is necessary to make extensive restaurant operations pay. The larger, more spectacular motel restaurants may derive as much as 75 percent of their business from persons who are not overnight guests (Fig. 52).

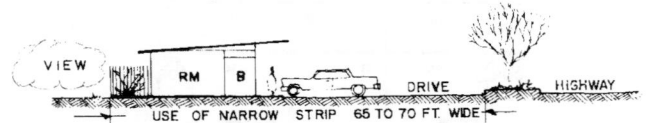

Fig. 42

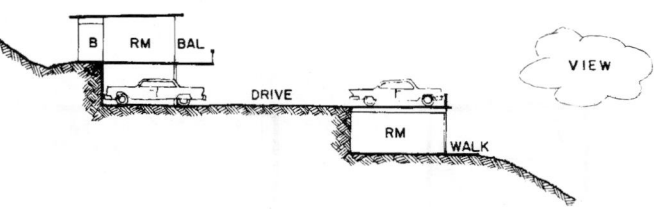

Figs. 43 and 44

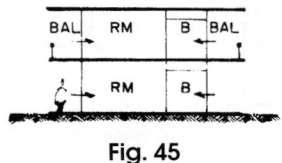

Fig. 45

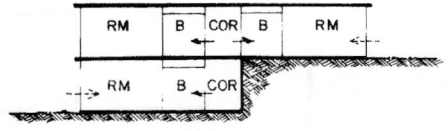

Fig. 46

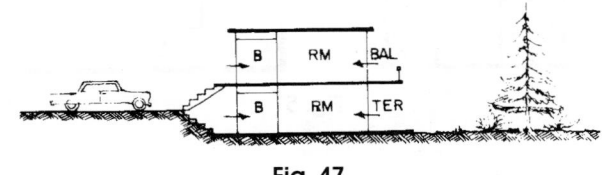

Fig. 47

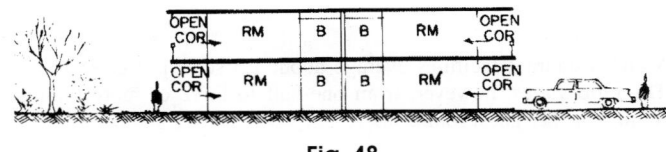

Fig. 48

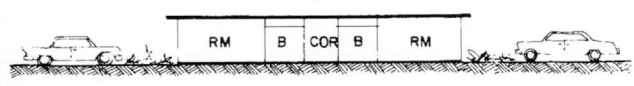

Fig. 41

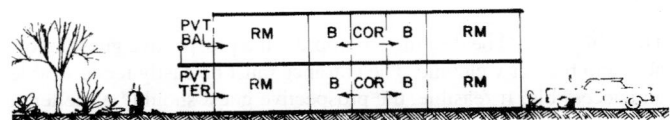

Fig. 49

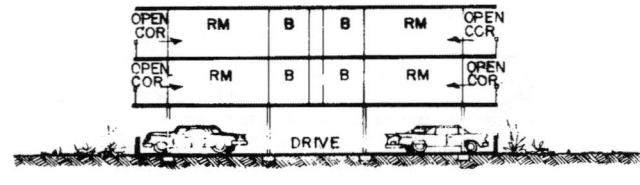

**Fig. 50**

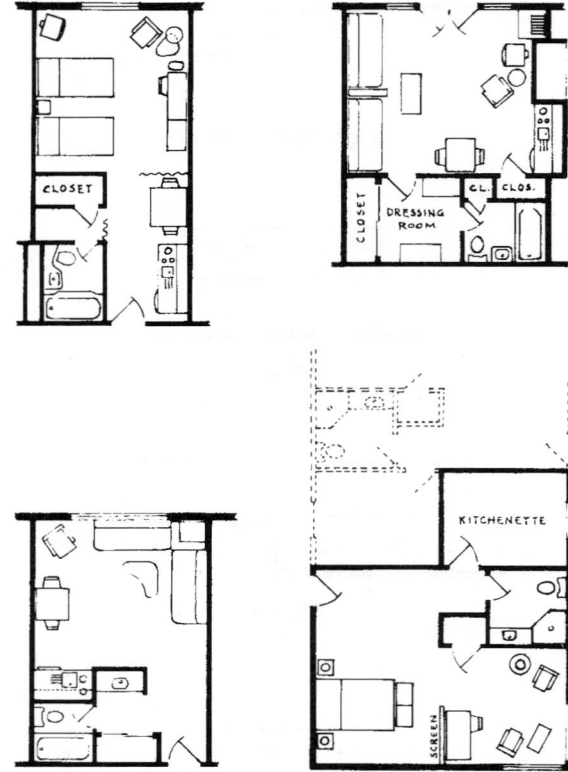

**Fig. 51**

**Table 1**   Space allotments for typical 100-room motel

| Category | Area, square feet |
|---|---|
| Public space | |
| Lobby | 1,100 |
| Front office | 100 |
| Lounge | 500 |
| Corridors adjoining | 300 |
| Men's toilet for guests | 140 |
| Women's toilet for guests | 120 |
| Women's restroom | 100 |
| Coat checkroom | 100 |
| | |
| Concessions and subrentals | |
| Rented stores | 2,000 |
| | |
| Food and beverage service space | |
| Dining room (110 seats) | 1,700 |
| Coffee shop (70 seats) | 1,100 |
| Bar and cocktail lounge (50 seats) | 800 |
| Private dining rooms (75 seats) | 900 |
| Employees' dining room (20 seats) | 260 |
| Kitchen | 1,300 |
| Steward's storeroom | 300 |
| Walk-in refrigerators | 150 |
| Beverage storage | 180 |
| China, glass and silver storage | 200 |
| Receiving room | 200 |
| Garbage room | 100 |
| | |
| General service space | |
| Manager's office | 130 |
| Secretary's office | 90 |
| Accounting office | 130 |
| Linen room | 350 |
| Laundry | 600 |
| Men's toilet for employees | 100 |
| Men's locker room | 150 |
| Women's toilet for employees | 120 |
| Women's locker room | 170 |
| Maintenance shops | 600 |
| Furniture storage | 250 |
| General storage | 600 |
| Boiler room | 750 |
| Transformer and switchboard room | 150 |

Extra items (if needed)
   Garage for motorized lawn mowers and snow plows
   Swimming pool filters, chlorinator, pump, and heater
   Storage for lawn furniture and recreation equipment

Motel restaurant facilities average about 1.5 seats per guest room. The ratio varies, however, from one-half to three or more dining-room seats per guest room.

Care should be taken in applying the schedule of space allotments to ensure that, if any food-service area is modified, the effect on auxiliary facilities is considered.

The lobby should be designed to impress the prospective guest favorably and bid her welcome. The entrance must be easily recognizable and accessible. If feasible, the prospective guest should be sheltered from the weather, from her car to the entrance doors. Within the lobby, the registration desk should have a relatively central location,

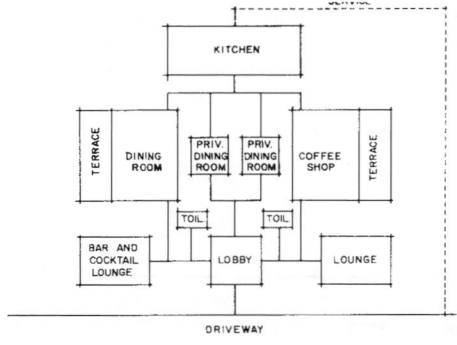

**Fig. 52. Schematic layout for motel with full dining service**

or it is the main control point of motel operation. If the guest, standing at the registration desk, can look through a large plate-glass window and see the swimming pool, attractive landscaping, or a scenic view, room sales will be greatly aided.

## Parking

Parking spaces, preferably in separate areas, are generally required as follows:

- 1 parking space for each guest room (may sometimes be reduced to 0.8 per guest room);
- 1 parking space for every 5 restaurant seats;
- 1 parking space for every 3 employees;
- 2 parking spaces for delivery and service trucks (in addition to space for a truck at the service entrance).

These allotments, of course, should be modified if circumstances warrant it. A motel that is filled to capacity, with a good restaurant, bar, and banquet business from nonguests, may need 2 parking spaces per guest room. On the other hand, a downtown motel, with parking available nearby and many guests arriving by taxi, might get along with parking space equal to two-thirds the number of guest rooms.

## Entrance Drive

The turnoff from the highway to the motel should be at an angle of 30 to 45 degrees; sharper turnoff angles are inadvisable. The driveway should be 20 to 25 feet wide, and the radius of the curb on the driver's right should be at least 50 feet. If a restricted site frontage should require a right-angle turnoff, then the driveway should be 25 feet wide and the curb have a 30-foot radius. A curb radius of less than 30 feet is inadvisable under any circumstances.

A slope of 6 percent is the usual maximum for turnoffs from state highways. A slope of 12 percent is customary for ramps, but can be as much as 15 percent. The parking lot should be nearly level. The central driveway may be crowned, with a 1 percent slope to the edges, so that persons on foot will find it relatively free from water after rain or from ice in winter.

## Landscaping

Landscaping is important—it is one of the things the guest sees first. Well-kept, neatly defined lawns and drives will make a favorable impression; the parking arrangement should be logical and practical. Hard-surfaced walks should be so arranged that lawns may be preserved; retaining walls should be installed to prevent erosion and enhance appearance. The right varieties of trees will provide attractive shade. Undesirable views should be screened by dense plantings, trimmed hedges, stone walls, or louvered fences.

## Outdoor Advertising

Signs are the most effective means of attracting the attention of prospective customers. Most people stop at a motel because they like its sign.

Signs should be neat, bold, brief, and distinctive. Their message must be grasped at a glance. The entrance sign should be plainly visible a good hundred yards from the turnoff, with letters at least 18 inches high. Copy should be reduced to a bare minimum, and only unusual services advertised.

A distinguishing emblem, trade mark, or coat of arms should be unique and easily remembered. Select one that can be used at the motel entrance, in the lobby, and on stationery, menus, and souvenir match books. Avoid using too many colors in a sign. Simplicity is effective.

Signs should be durable and suited to the climate of the location. Night illumination is essential, at least for the sign in front of the motel, but care should be taken that guests will not be annoyed by beams of light, glare, flashing off and on, or other features that might bother a person wanting to sleep. The sign at the motel customarily has a "Vacancy-No Vacancy" indication.

## Swimming Pool

Most motels include swimming pools, even those in the downtown area of the city. Although the pool may be actually used by only a minority of the overnight guests, many more will enjoy watching the activities. Thus the pool should be surrounded by a suitable terrace at least 10 feet wide with a depth of generally 4 feet-6 inches maximum. Grass areas beyond the terrace are also recommended.

The motel pool should generally be of the recreation type. A free-form pattern, either kidney-shaped or oval, is usually suitable, but of course is subject to topography and the designer's judgment. The minimum size recommended for the pool is 20 by 40 feet, which is large enough for about 15 people in the water and 20 to 30 bathers around the edge. One motel chain prefers a 24 by 48-foot pool. Another chain, operating motels of 150 rooms and more, considers 35 by 75 feet to be the minimum.

A separate wading pool is often provided—sometimes with spray fittings or a small fountain to enhance its appearance. A fairly wide terrace should surround the pool, with benches on the terrace for parents.

Toilet facilities for men and women bathers should be accessible from the pool area. Such facilities are required by law in many states. Provision should also be made, within 40 feet of the deep end of the pool, for housing the necessary water filters, pumps, purification equipment, and heater. A water heater can extend the use of the pool over a longer season.

Other planning considerations concerning the pool and surrounding area include food and beverage service and adequate illumination for evening activities.

The inclusion of a cabana club may be considered if there is sufficient local demand. In addition to membership fees, the cabana club may bring other profitable business to the motel. Since cabana club members are not overnight guests, however, provision must be made for dressing rooms, lockers, showers, and toilets. The members will also expect an ample poolside terrace area with tables and chairs, umbrellas, and reclining lawn chairs, in addition to the cabanas. The cabanas themselves, though, may serve as a windbreak, and thus help to prolong the pool season.

## Recreation Areas

Although the pool will probably be the most popular recreation area, a children's play yard, and areas for adult games may also be desirable. Some such games are listed below; the dimensions indicate the area for the game, including the usual surrounding border.

| Game | width × length, feet |
|------|----------------------|
| Shuffleboard | 10 x 60 |
| Clock golf | 40 x 40 |
| Croquet | 50 x 95 |
| Horseshoes | 12 x 60 |
| Table tennis | 12 x 20 |
| Tennis | 60 x 120 |
| Handball | 30 x 45 |

Barbecue facilities may also be desirable. An area of about 15 by 20 feet is generally ample. The play yard for small children should be enclosed by a fence. Suitable modern equipment should be selected and installed.

Indoor recreation facilities may include a television room, one or more card rooms, reading room and library, table tennis, video arcade, movies, etc. These facilities should be discussed and decided upon in the early planning stages, because it is often impossible to fit them into a completed plan at the last minute.

**Heating and Air Conditioning**

Guest rooms are best served by a central plant, with individual room temperature controls provided. A system favored by some of the more experienced organizations circulates water through convectors concealed beneath the guest-room windows. The circulating water is heated in winter and chilled in summer, the water temperature being varied in accordance with weather conditions. Each guest-room conditioning cabinet has a multispeed, manually controlled, motor-driven fan to blow air over the coils. The guest can regulate the fan speed to vary the rate of heat transfer.

Other parts of the building—such as the lobby, restaurant, kitchen, and employees' quarters—should be divided into "zones," according to their hours of use and type of air treatment needed. Each zone will have its own separately controlled equipment to supply heat or air conditioning. Air conditioning is supplied in the summer for public spaces, restaurant, and bar facilities frequented by guests. Ample exhaust ventilation will be needed for the kitchen and the employees' locker rooms and toilets. Care should be taken to avoid having to operate an entire zone of rooms with short hours of use just to accommodate one or two that will be used many hours a day.

**Fig. 1. Four Seasons Resort Haulalai (Hill Glazier Architects; photo: courtesy of architect)**

# MOTEL SITE PLANNING

The basic element of design in motel site planning is not the rental unit alone—i.e., a living room, bedroom, and bathroom—but the rental unit plus parking space, plus an access roadway, plus pedestrian walkway, plus a certain quality which can be summed up in the term "amenity." This latter will include outlook, privacy, protection from noise, and character (Fig. 1). All except the last will usually imply space. In the case of outlook one may visually poach on neighboring land, but this will not in the long run be dependable without control over the development of this land.

As the basic element of design is not simple and easily defined, as might at first appear, so in its use it may be equally difficult to classify and analyze. Being composed of so many elements, it will vary greatly from one case to the next. A change in one element will change the whole balance of relative importance. We have therefore attempted to simplify and sharpen the most common requirements of this site geometry by concentrating upon a typical rental unit strip of near-minimum dimensions placed in a number of different and typical situations to demonstrate the considerations which should control the site planning of a small roadside motel. These diagrams will also provide the data for a preliminary quick check on site area and shape, as related to possible density of development and efficient utilization of the land with various types of plans.

### Rental Unit Strip Dimension

The basic planning element in these simple site plans is made up of the rental unit, a pedestrian walkway, parking space, and access roadway. Not shown here, because it is too difficult to measure or reduce to a type, is amenity space, which includes outlook. The size of each of these elements will vary from one case to another, but each dimension shown here is typical.

### Shallow Site Parallel to the Highway

This will almost inevitably be best served by an elementary type of strip plan with front parking. Such a site is too narrow for the units to be turned at right angles to the highway, and if they were moved far enough forward for rear parking, the rooms would be unpleasantly close to the highway (Fig. 2).

If there is an opportunity for some outlook in the rear, even onto someone else's property, then the plan can be greatly improved by keeping access and parking on the highway side and opening up big outlook windows to the rear.

*Reference:* From *Motels*, Geoffrey Baker and Bruno Furno; © Litton Educational Publishing, Inc., New York.

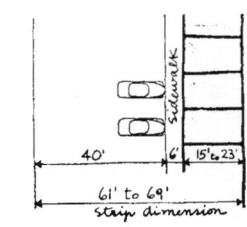

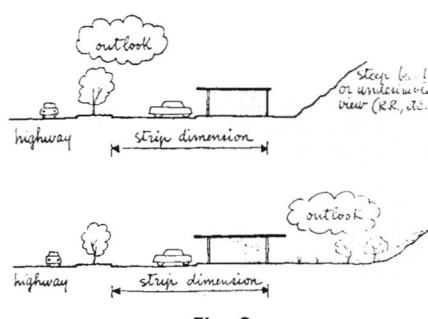

**Fig. 2**

## Narrow Site at Right Angles to the Highway

This must be wider than the minimum strip dimension to allow for the side yards normally required by local building and zoning regulations. There is nothing to prevent one or both of these side yards from being incorporated into the parking space (Fig. 3).

For more intensive use of this sort of site, the strip is normally turned at the end to form an "L." A corresponding wing might be added at the highway end, but is seldom done because it would close off the motel from the view of motorists on the highway. Such wings upset the parking ratio of a typical strip; space must be found for these extra cars possibly at the rear of the wing units.

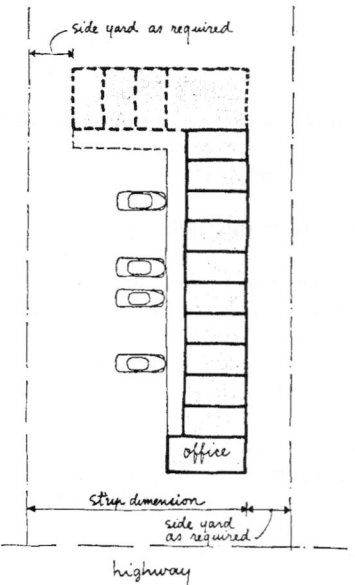

**Fig. 3**

If the view to the rear beyond the lot line is pleasant, then it would be better to do without the rear wing. If the view is undesirable, the wing can effectively close it off, and the inside of the "L" can create an environment of its own.

## Greater Density

On a similar deep narrow site at right angles to the highway, a common plan is to pile the units two or more stories high, facing outward from a central bathroom spine. Access and parking is on each side, with access balconies along the face of the upper stories, so that pedestrian traffic is channeled immediately in front of the outlook windows, eliminating privacy.

The parking space must be enlarged to take care of the units above the first floor. The side yards can be usefully employed as part of the parking area. But if the second-story access balconies are reached by stairs at each end of the rental unit block, then parking space for the second-story units is most convenient if concentrated in this same area at each end of the building (Fig. 4).

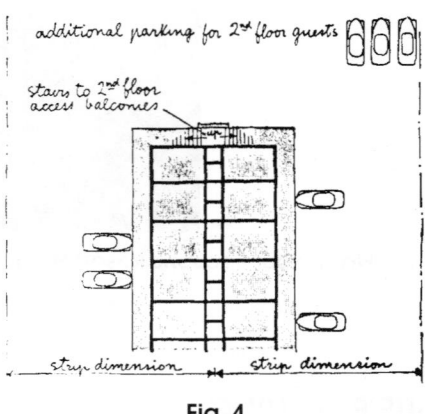

**Fig. 4**

If parking need not be at the unit entrance, a larger number of rental units can be fitted more successfully onto a long narrow lot by concentrating the parking area at one end. Where the central garden court becomes very narrow (Fig. 5), the only way to obtain privacy of outlook is to divide it down the center with screens or high planting.

In the plan (Fig. 6), the disadvantage of a road down the center is counterbalanced by the convenience of unloading baggage at the entrance.

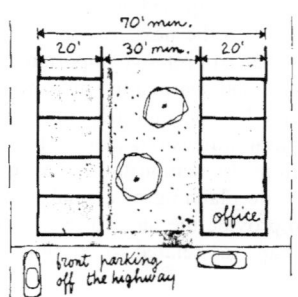

**Fig. 5**

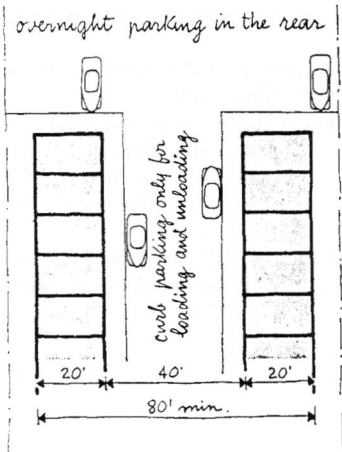

Fig. 6

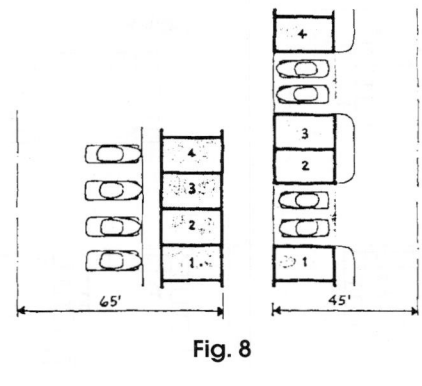

Fig. 8

Bathroom spine plan may be improved, if all parking space is concentrated at the highway end of the long narrow lot, each unit has a private fenced garden. Access is by a perimeter covered walk (Fig. 7). Plan suggested by Mayfair House, Carmel, California.

**Road Parking Strip and Carport Strip Compared**

Alternating unit pairs and double carports gives a longer but narrower strip than the conventional. For a more spacious lawn and easier drive-in, the carport strip is in practice usually made wider than shown in Fig. 8.

It's the corners that count. When a strip plan is bent into a court, the more corners, the more waste of space; often this is of small importance. With parking on the outside front (Fig. 9) there is space for a car outside the door of each unit. With parking on the inside front (Fig. 10) there cannot be space enough for all the cars expected and corner units are left without parking stalls. The visual values of the open corner could well be combined with a road through, so that the U becomes two L courts (Fig. 11). The larger a plan, the less important are the corners.

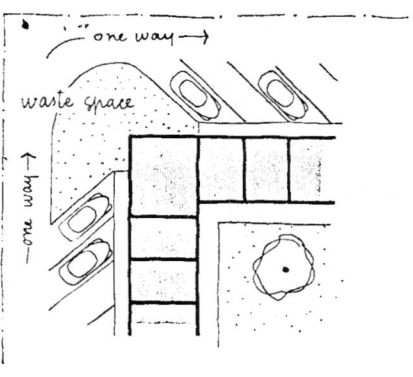

Fig. 9

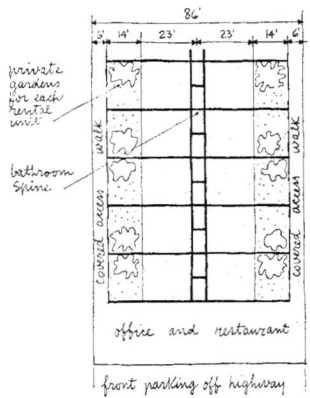

Fig. 7

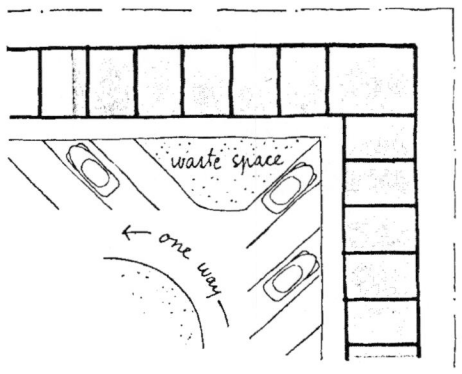

Fig. 10

Fig. 11

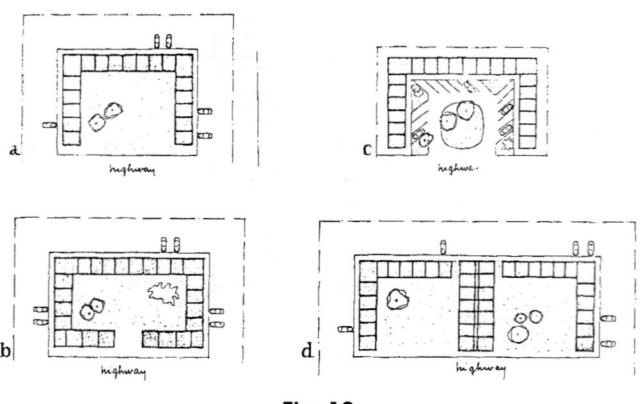

**Fig. 12**

The U court comes in all patterns and all sizes, as shown in Fig. 12.

a. Opens an attractive central garden court to the highway, using this as an advertising feature.

b. Almost closed to the highway, is of less advertising value, but guests have more quiet and privacy.

c. By parking inside the "U," the same number of units can be packed onto a smaller lot. Noisy and without privacy. Worst on a small scale.

d. For more units the "U" becomes "E." Center line does not have parking directly outside door but can be served by interior corridor or covered walk.

# 4
# Educational

Woodlands High School, Conroe, Texas (Perkins and Will, Architects; photo: Jud Haggard, courtesy of the architect)

# PLANNING FOR EDUCATIONAL AND ADMINISTRATIVE TECHNOLOGY

## TECHNOLOGY: VEHICLE OF CHANGE

Technology is one of the key elements in transforming the industrial age schoolhouse into a more viable model reflecting the needs of today. Just as technology is reshaping most other institutions, it has the potential to reshape educational facilities and the disconnect that often exists with the broader society. Technology offers exciting new ways of meeting student learner needs, teaching methods, and the very operations of the physical plant schools.

The technology available in the past has had a substantial impact on a school's ability to deliver small group or individualized instruction, often limiting it only to teacher facilitated. The trend of schools adapting technology originally developed for other high-technology industries was beginning to develop.

Advancements in technology will continue to affect society. Addressing these changes is part of the answer but may also fuel even greater changes in the way school facilities are designed. Keeping up with technology means keeping up with software as well. This is where the future of Internet access may be the most cost-effective way to stay ahead of the curve.

Internet resources developed for and by educators, teachers, and even students are expanding. Increasingly, schools are accessing the World Wide Web and creating a presence. Technologies and tools supporting collaborative activities over the Internet are enabling shared workspaces, off and on-line conferencing facilities are also offering a variety of options. Students from different schools, perhaps in distant countries, working together will perform project and small group work. There are many signs that this technology will be available, affordable and accessible for students, teachers, and the community.

The challenge for educators, planners, designers, and citizens of integrating instructional technologies is to recognize the magnitude of changes likely to occur over the next generation and to develop facilities capable of receiving those changes.

### General

The implementation of a voice, data, and video telecommunications system throughout the institution or school facility is as much of a building's infrastructure as the electrical, plumbing, and heating/cooling systems. Appropriate and strategically designed technologies greatly enhance the teaching and learning of basic skills and position a school to take advantage of technological developments in the future.

To take advantage of these technologies schools need comprehensive staff development programs, student access to technology applications, home-to-school access, technical support personnel at school level, and a system of "security" that encourages use and protects the investment.

Technology skills and applications should be articulated in feeder schools and other community facilities to meet post graduation expectations. All classrooms should be multi-use/multi-purpose with technological support. Lastly, there should be a seamless web of technology to support the classroom management between administration, teachers, students and the home. A student-learning interface with technology is expressed in Fig. 1.

### Learning Space Components

Contemporary learning environments use systems design that merges three basic systems in an all-digital network. This voice, data,

*Authors:* Raymond C. Bordwell, AIA, Perkins and Will, Architects and Glenn Meeks, Meeks Technology Group

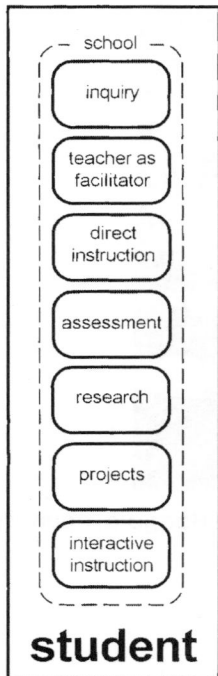

**Fig. 1. Student-learning interface**

puter systems such as laptops increases and the cost becomes more affordable, more students will be using these as their primary computing device and support a portable computing environment. This will push the need for electrical and power sources in non-traditional space such as hallways, libraries and other informal learning environments.

Technology systems support multiple instructional designs:

- *Whole Group Instruction Space (25-30 students):* This includes the use of overheads, VCRs, LCD displays, video stills, and various forms of computer display techniques.
- *Small Group Instruction Space (6-8 students):* This includes areas in the classroom and in shared common spaces, which a teacher or another resource person can work with groups of 6-8 students. The technology is essentially the same as whole group instruction technology, the only difference being the size of the groups.
- *Self Directed Learning Space (1-2 students):* This is primarily a computer-based instruction design where students interact with a computer workstation. As all forms of technology become more and more digitized, it is envisioned that these will become multimedia workstations that integrate voice, video, and data formats.
- *Informal Instruction Space (1-3 students):* This includes areas in hallways, libraries and other shared common spaces,

**Typical Learning Environment (Classroom)**

It is recommended that all learning environments (classrooms) (Fig. 4) have voice, data, and video accessibility. This will enhance the flexibility of the learning environment to respond positively to alterations in the use of space. The wiring and other infrastructure components should be the first priority since terminal devices can be added later. The facility should have surplus electrical power capacity to permit expansion of technology. Infrastructure, systems and cabling are typically funded as capital projects.

and video system is likely to be implemented through an all fiber-optic network.

- *Voice:* This system makes telephone and voice communications available in every learning space, office and workroom throughout the entire building.
- *Data:* This system makes data retrieval possible in every learning space, office and workroom throughout the building including access to district-wide and to other external databases.
- *Video:* Video distribution in every learning space, office, workroom and selected public spaces throughout the building with interactive video capabilities to support whole and small group instruction, distance learning, and providing access to a wide range of internal and external resources.

**Multimedia Technology Applications in 21st Century Schools**

Voice, data and video systems provide leadership, instruction, data management, and student services, which go far beyond the systems in schools that were constructed as recently as the late 1980's. Advances in technology are becoming increasingly useful and appropriate to the student and the educator. Fig. 2 represents the four areas of technology to be accommodated by the instructional and administrative technology system.

**TECHNOLOGY AND LEARNING ENVIRONMENTS**

The four primary applications shown in Fig. 2 have the potential to have a positive impact on every aspect of the educational processes found in school. Fig. 3 provides the planning concept of how the four primary applications interface with each other and some examples of educational applications in each area. As the power of portable com-

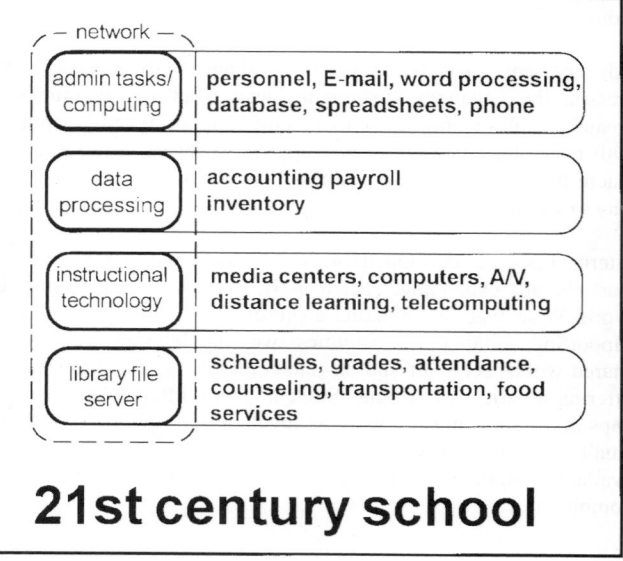

**Fig. 2**

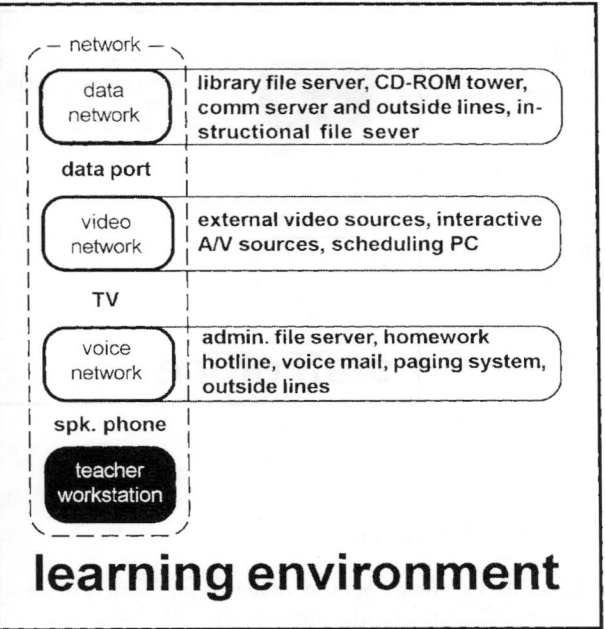

**learning environment**

Fig. 3

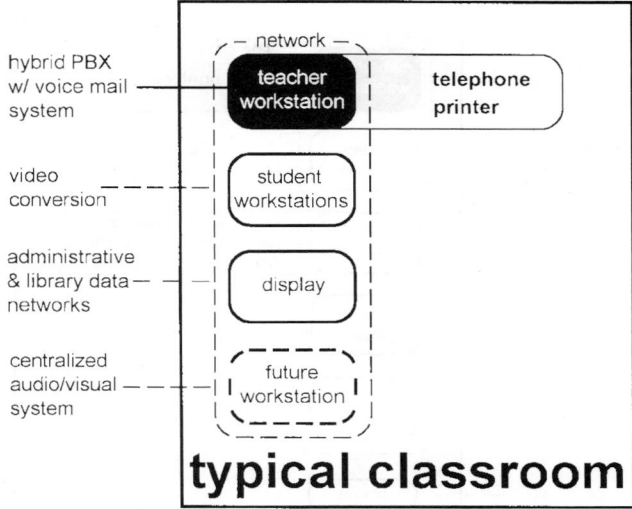

**typical classroom**

Fig. 4

The following components should be included in each learning environment and are based on a class size of up to 30 learners:

- One instructor's workstation with voice, data, and video
- Six data drops for student computer workstations
- Electric power availability (one quad type outlet per drop) and/or raceway wiring system to support 4-6 student computers
- One video drop with mounted video monitor
- One voice drop with telephone
- Preparation for future (25-30 data drops)

Careful attention should be given to furnishings, i.e., student desks specialized or customized cabinetry, location of data ports, white boards, and monitors.

Fig. 5 is representative of the typical ports/hardware for all instructional spaces:

- Two data drops
- Video drops and monitors
- Electric power availability (1 quad per drop) and /or raceway wiring system
- Voice port and one telephone
- Preparation for future data connections

**Media Retrieval/Media Center**

Media retrieval equipment includes all of the devices to operate or control the video, data, and voice communications system. This equipment should be located in an area (Fig. 6) easily accessed by the media specialist. It will include devices such those listed here; the number and type are a function of the size of the school:

- Telephone operating equipment
- Video control systems

- VCRs
- Laser discs
- CD interactive
- File servers
- Video still players

**Office Space**

Office areas (Fig. 7) have the following needs per user planned in the space:

- One voice and data drop
- Electric power availability (quad per drop)
- Capability to support computer, printer (shared), and telephone
- One telephone (removable)
- One computer (removable)

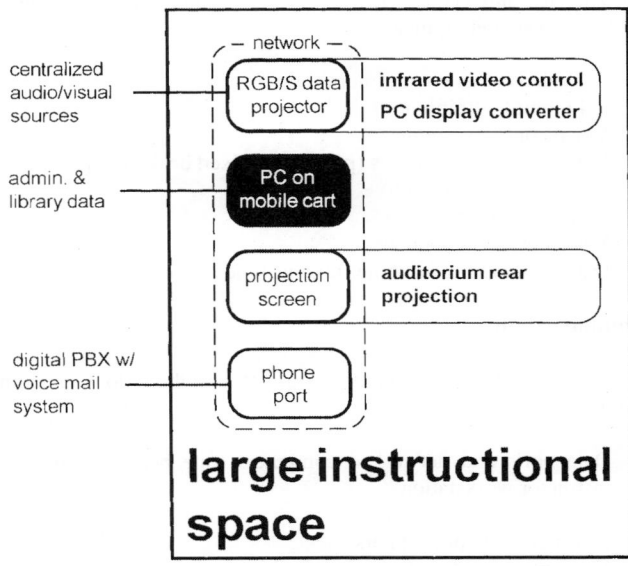

**large instructional space**

Fig. 5

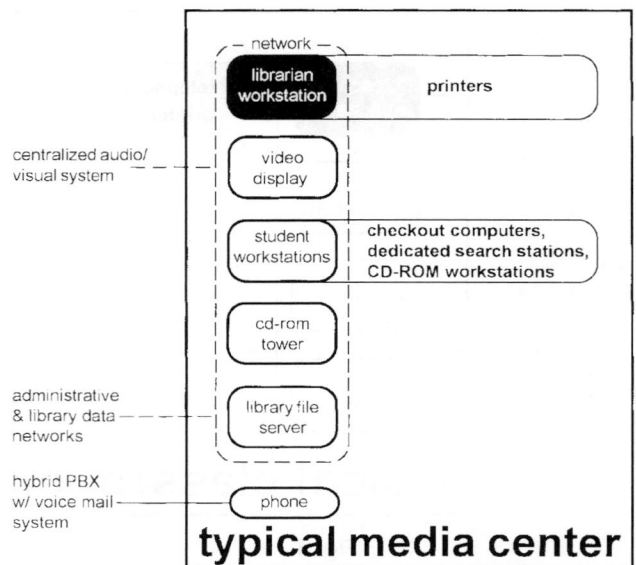

**Fig. 6**

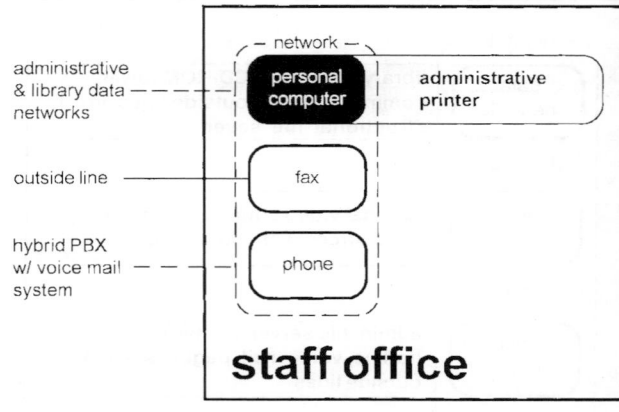

**Fig. 7**

## Conference Areas

Conference areas should include a minimum of:

- Video, voice, and data drops
- Electric power availability (quad per drop)
- Capability to support computer, printer, telephone operations, and video monitor
- One telephone (removable)
- One computer (portable)
- One video monitor (removable)

## Distance Learning Center

Distance learning centers (Fig. 8) typically require varying amounts of the following equipment:

- 2-4 video cameras (minimum)
- 2-4 monitors (minimum)
- Video control systems
- Networked work stations (portable or fixed desktop type)
- Printers (one minimum)
- Projection system
- Voice port and telephone
- Data port and fax machine (fax machine optional)

## Computer Lab

A computer lab (Fig. 9) usually requires at least the following equipment:

- Data ports and networked computers (one per user plus one instructor workstation)
- Scanner (one minimum)
- 2 or more network printers
- Voice port and phone
- Projection system

## Typical Cafeteria/Commons

To enhance the experience of the user and assure a variety of secondary uses of the cafeteria and commons (Fig. 10), these areas often incorporate the following equipment:

- Video ports and monitors that can be used for video displays of electronic bulletin boards
- Data ports throughout
- Video projector on mobile stand
- Video monitor on mobile stand
- Large, electric front screen

## Physical Education Space

Gymnasiums (Fig. 11) should have the following equipment:

- Video ports and monitors that can be used for video displays of electronic bulletin boards

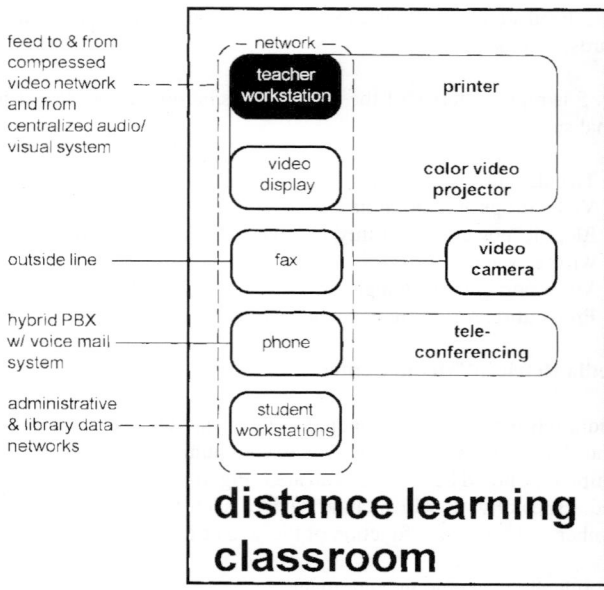

**Fig. 8**

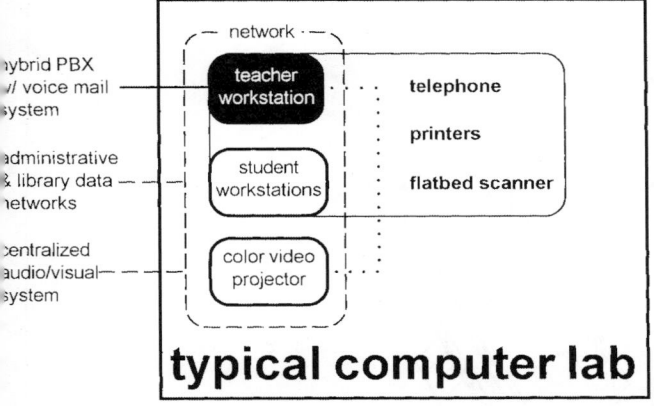

**Fig. 9**

Maintenance and upgrades in most states is typically funded as a line item in the yearly budget, and may include:

- Expansion of video network resources (adding more VCRs, LCDs, CD-IS, CD-COMs, etc.)
- Expansion of data network resources
- Upgrading specific computers for specific curriculum tasks
- Replacing obsolete computers, televisions, etc.
- Upgrading media production systems

Staff development in most states is typically funded from the operating budget, and includes:

- In-service training on technology
- Special training activities for advanced users (stipends and summer grants)
- Attendance at regional and national shows
- Time for developing applications
- Special grant funds for new application development and experiments

Staff support in most states is typically funded from the operating budget, and includes:

2-3 video and data ports
Video projector on mobile stand
Video monitor on mobile stand
Large, electric front screen

**Funding and Implementation**

Courseware in most states is typically funded through capital project or state grants and includes:

- Professional productivity software
- Student workstation software
- Computer lab applications
- Library automation software
- Reference resources (computer and A/V)
- Curriculum-specific software
- Curriculum-specific A/V media

- Technology director hired to implement plan(s) for instructional focus
- Data network administrator
- Technology technicians - repair and maintenance
- Campus-level technology coordinator
- Media production staff

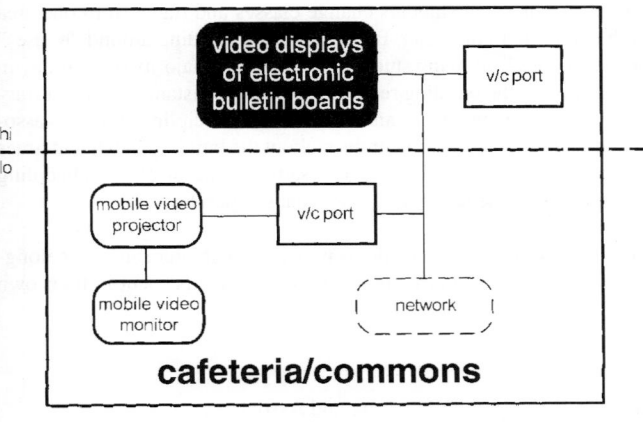

**Fig. 10**

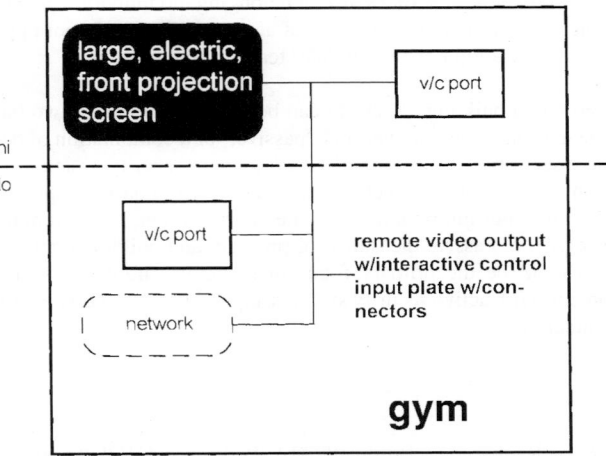

**Fig. 11**

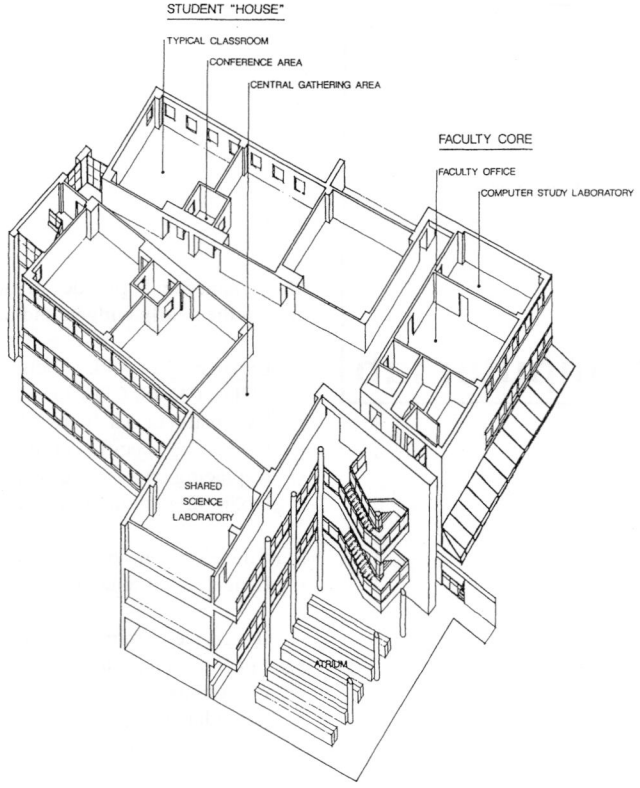

**Fig. 1. Student "house"**

# SAFETY AND SECURITY

### GENERAL

Society demands our schools provide an inviting and deinstitutionalized facility, which is also a safe environment for students, staff and community who use school facilities. Security and safety problems and their causes are multi-dimensional. Some can be addressed through building planning and others cannot. Causes can include family problems, lack of a sense of belonging, no individual identity, problems of communication, lack of accountability, and poor opportunities to develop positive student/ teacher relationships.

Improving a building's security can be addressed through two basic strategies known as "active" and "passive," or a combination of both. Active security is based on utilizing hardware security systems such as cameras or motion detectors. Passive security is based on program and facility design, building and site configuration, and community participation. Passive measures for program and building configuration should be the primary focus in reducing safety and security problems with active security systems applied where necessary as the secondary focus.

### PASSIVE SECURITY CONCEPTS

Whether an inner city school or one located in a far suburb, building organization can have a major impact on student behavior and help alleviate certain safety concerns. The architect and school district should consult a CPTED (Crime Prevention Through Environmental Design) specialist. This can prove a great up-front cost saving and minimize the need for security hardware where passive measures were not sufficient. In general, the greatest numbers of discipline problems in schools occur when students change classes and travel from one area of the building to the other. By organizing a building around "houses" or "academies," allowing students to spend the majority of their day in one section of the building reduces the average distance a student travels for class changes. This can result in fewer discipline problems associated with student movement throughout the building in what at times can be overcrowded hallways. The same is true of block scheduling that minimizes the number of class changes per day.

In this planning strategy students may have a greater sense of belonging and identity when the majority of their day is spent in their own

*Authors:* Raymond C. Bordwell, AIA, Perkins and Will, Architects and William DeJong Ph.D., DeJong and Associates
*Reference:* National School Safety and Security Services, Inc., Cleveland Ohio, http://schoolsecurity.org/

house." In the example (Fig. 1) students may spend up to 65 percent of their day in their own "area."

Teams" of teachers who have responsibility for the same group of students helps improve the student/ teacher relationship and results in greater continuity and monitoring of behavior issues. Decentralized administrative offices, counseling, and teacher preparation areas place staff in closer and more direct contact with students. Another benefit of schools as community centers allows for increased use of the facility by the public at large and brings more adults on campus. Allowing opportunities for these various groups to interact with students can increases mentoring and leadership contact with students.

## Building Layout

As discussed above, the building organization can have a significant impact on building security and operations. One of the most important aspects might involve how a student or the community at large enters the building. Almost all office buildings have some kind of desk where a visitor is greeted. Schools almost never have one. Lobby design may need to look more like the entry to a library complete with a check in and check out desk (Fig. 2). Other passive concepts that can help promote a safe learning environment include:

- Planning that avoids blind spots, unnecessary corners, and corridor recesses greater than 12 inches.
- Locating administrative and teacher preparation areas or offices with good visual contact of major circulation areas (i.e., corridors, cafeteria, bus drop-off, parking).
- Locating actively programmed elements around the periphery of the school building so that there is "natural surveillance" from within the school to outdoor areas such as parking lots and playgrounds.
- Minimizing windowless, blank walls at the periphery of the building, particularly when these uses face residential, play areas, and parking lots (again, maximize "natural surveillance").
- Planning spatial relationships in such a manner that there are natural transitions from one location to another (i.e. locker bays and rest rooms near classrooms).

**Fig. 2. Interior of Capital High School, Santa Fe, New Mexico (Perkins and Will, Architects; photo: Greg Murphy Photography, courtesy of the architect)**

- Locating rest rooms in close proximity to classrooms within houses or academies.
- Locating areas likely to have significant community (after school) use close to parking and where these areas can be closed off from the rest of the building.
- Providing for natural integration of students and staff during class changes.

## ACTIVE SECURITY CONCEPTS

Active security systems should ideally be used only when passive measures are not sufficient. Hardware can play an important role in reducing the risk of security problems. The architect should consult a specialty consultant or systems supplier to assist in the design of any "active" system. However, here are a few guidelines related to planning an active security system:

- Begin planning the system during the programming and planning phases of the design process. This will allow for input from a wide range of constituents to help determine an appropriate strategy, as active systems can sometimes be a sensitive political issue.
- A security consultant can help with system design and device location and should be consulted during the programming phase with increased involvement during schematic design.
- A major benefit of using an "active" security system is in "risk management" by providing a "recorded history" of events that took place in or around the facility.
- When planning a security system, it is necessary to include a provision for accessing cameras and recorded data remotely in the event the building was to become inaccessible.
- Auto-connecting systems to police and fire authorities when an alarm is tripped is advisable.

### Uses of Technology

New and renovated schools are currently being planned to have extensive technology systems for instructional and administrative purposes. These same infrastructures and technology components can be used to enhance building security by:

- Providing phones in every instructional and support area
- Building-wide public address system designed to be heard throughout the school and on the play fields when needed
- Motion or infra-red detectors, which can also be configured to conserve lighting costs
- Video cameras that are used for instructional purposes could also be used for security and risk management purposes during non-school hours

## SITE PLANNING, VEHICULAR AND PEDESTRIAN TRAFFIC

Site size and planning practices can vary widely between urban, suburban and rural school districts. For example, a suburban high school with 75 acres will require vastly different site requirements than urban high school on 5 acres. In the urban example, the building enclosure will most likely be part of defining the site boundary or edge. Some basic considerations are:

- The bus drop-off area may be at the curb or in a public right-of-way and should be "connected" to the building entries by wide, well illuminated open walkways.

- The building envelope should be sensitive to how it responds to the proximity of pedestrian walkways (Fig. 3). Consider window size and location, climbing access to the roof, etc.
- Exterior play areas and open space should be rectilinear, with a minimum of "blind" spots.
- Clear signage to indicate public entries with easily controllable entry lobbies.

Larger sites may have additional issues of site utilization related to play fields and vehicular use. In addition to those items listed above, additional guidelines in planning the site are:

- A bus drop-off area separated from other vehicular traffic
- Separate student, staff and community parking areas
- Separate student (pedestrian) site circulation flow from roadways

### Landscaping and Lighting

Landscaping can enhance the learning experience by providing environmental study opportunities and enhanced aesthetics. Additionally these guidelines will help with security related site concerns:

- High trees and low bushes (less than three feet high) to deter hiding
- Aesthetically pleasing fencing around the site perimeter
- Building placement along the site perimeter to protect on site open space
- General, non-intrusive site lighting of all parking, pedestrian and entry areas
- Security lighting at selected building and parking lots with photocell timer with on/off capacity
- Separate athletic fields from informal gathering areas
- Locate athletic facilities away from building, isolated by fences

### SUMMARY

School safety may be as much of a community issue as it is a school issue. Better communication is necessary between school officials and the community at large. Our school officials need to be informed, alert, and proactive in preventing and, if necessary, in managing incidents that if left unattended can escalate into much larger problems.

Fig. 3. Exterior of Capital High School, Santa Fe, New Mexico (Perkins and Will, Architects; photo: Greg Murphy Photography, courtesy of the architect)

# LIFE SAFETY CONSIDERATIONS

Schools, by the nature of their occupancy and use, require higher standards of safety than other types of buildings. Provisions for life safety has the highest priority and affects the entire design in plan, construction, and choice of materials. All phases of health and safety become pervasive program elements that unavoidably add to the complexity and cost of schools and greatly determine their form and plan organization and appearance.

Building codes generally have separate and specific requirements for school construction. Many states and counties have school safety codes established by departments of education, health, and public safety. Architects and engineers are obligated to inform themselves of all reviewing authorities and applicable codes in a given locality. In addition to special local requirements, the local codes usually incorporate one of the national model codes, such as the BOCA National Building Code, Uniform Building Code, Standard Building Code and/or National Fire Protection Association (NFPA) Codes. In addition to the American with Disabilities Act Accessibility Guidelines (ADAAG), the local accessibility codes must be consulted. The following are some of the safety considerations of concern:

## Structural Safety
- Material strengths and factors of safety
- Fireproof and fire resistive structures
- Windstorm resistance
- Earthquake resistance

## Fire Safety
- Provision and protection of exits, corridors, and stairs
- Fire detector and alarm systems
- Sprinkler systems
- Materials and finishes with low flame-spread rating and nontoxic combustion characteristics

## Health Safety
- Ventilation systems and standards
- Lighting standards and electrical code
- Plumbing fixture requirements and plumbing code
- Swimming pool and locker room requirements
- Food service area health requirements

## Special Emergencies
- Emergency lighting systems
- Tornado or hurricane protection and shelter

## Accident Protection
- Nonslip surfaces (especially stairs, ramps, shower areas, pool decks)
- Vision panels, door swings, and hardware
- Hand rails and guard rails
- Safety glass in doors, sidelights

# ACCESSIBILITY PROVISIONS

Accommodations are required throughout the school for use by persons with disabilities. Considerations for accessibility by both adults and children should be made in a school.

Sensible corridor planning and location of stairs and exits to handle traffic flow without congestion will usually provide appropriate fire exit facilities. However, codes must be checked to ensure proper corridor widths, travel distances, and smoke barriers at suitable intervals. Stair enclosures are required for all stairs connecting more than two levels and are recommended for stairs generally. Most stairs are used for exit purposes and have detailed code requirements which must be met such as width and ratio of tread-to-risers.

## School Exits

Exits and emergency exits should be clearly marked so that at no time is there any doubt or hesitation as to their purpose. A sign indicating the nearest exit should be visible from every point in the corridor. Two or more exits should be provided from any area within the school. Some states require two exits from each classroom.

It should be possible to open every door from the inside at all times, even after school is closed for the day. Doors should swing in the direction of travel, and may require panic device hardware.

## Stairways

One of the most critical parts of school traffic design is the stairway, which should be located in relation to the overall traffic pattern, keeping in mind load distribution, safety, destination of students between periods, and elimination of cross traffic. The stairways should be designed for easy, fast, and safe movement.

Stairways not only provide egress to and from various floor levels, but they are used every period for the vertical circulation of students changing classes. It is important that stairways are designed so that students with books under their arms may walk side by side to avoid

*Reviewed by:* Michael Palmer, AIA, Perkins and Will, Architects

congestion; a width of 4 feet-8 inches to 5 feet between handrails is recommended. In a large school, the major stairways will probably need to be wider than the code requirements. Stairways should be of fireproof construction, leading directly to the outdoors. They should be provided with smoke-control facilities, separating the stairwells from the corridors that they serve.

Standard dimensions of stair treads and risers should be used in schools. Odd dimensions increase the stair hazards for children as well as adults. A non-slip surface should be used. Surface-mounted edge strips are unsatisfactory.

Handrails are necessary on both sides of all stairways in accordance with most building codes and the ADA Accessibility Guidelines. They should be installed with attachment brackets permanently anchored in a masonry wall.

## Corridors

A well-designed school has corridors that accommodate the free and informal movement of students. A narrow corridor requires formal, regimented, and supervised traffic flow, which is impractical in today's school environment.

The walls of corridors should be free of all projections. Heating units, drinking fountains, fire extinguishers, lockers, doors, and display cases should be recessed in the interest of student safety (Fig. 4).

Acoustical properties are desirable to reduce hall noise. Corridors should be well lighted, with emergency provision in the event of main power failure. Floor covering should be durable, slip resistant, and easy to maintain.

The maximum length of unbroken corridors should not exceed 150 to 200 feet. Longer sections can give an undesirable perspective.

## Doors

Boys and girls are not expected to use caution in opening and closing doors. The hazard of striking students with doors can be reduced by including a vision panel in the door and by recessing the door. The location of this panel should be in proportion to the varying heights of children. Use of tempered or wire glass will provide safety.

Classroom doors should always swing out into the corridor, regardless of the size of the room. Door placement must also adhere to the ADA Accessibility Guidelines and local accessibility code.

Vision panels placed next to doors allow students to see someone approaching the door from the opposite direction. These panels should be designed with mullions at suitable intervals to clearly identify them as windows, not passageways.

Covered walkways to accommodate interbuilding traffic should be designed to protect students and not for appearance alone. The roof deck should be wide and low. Provision should be made to carry off roof water. Proper outside lighting will be necessary under the roof deck.

Efforts to minimize barriers between instructional areas and corridors by glazing with ordinary glass or by eliminating portions of corridor walls run counter to traditional safety requirements, but have been accomplished through special provisions of sprinkler systems, plan organization, and building material use. Open planning for large instructional areas accommodating several groups with no designated corridor areas and with flexible divisions provided by movable partitions and divider units also presents special problems of safety. Planning of this type will require cooperation with public safety officials to obtain agreement on acceptable provisions for safety.

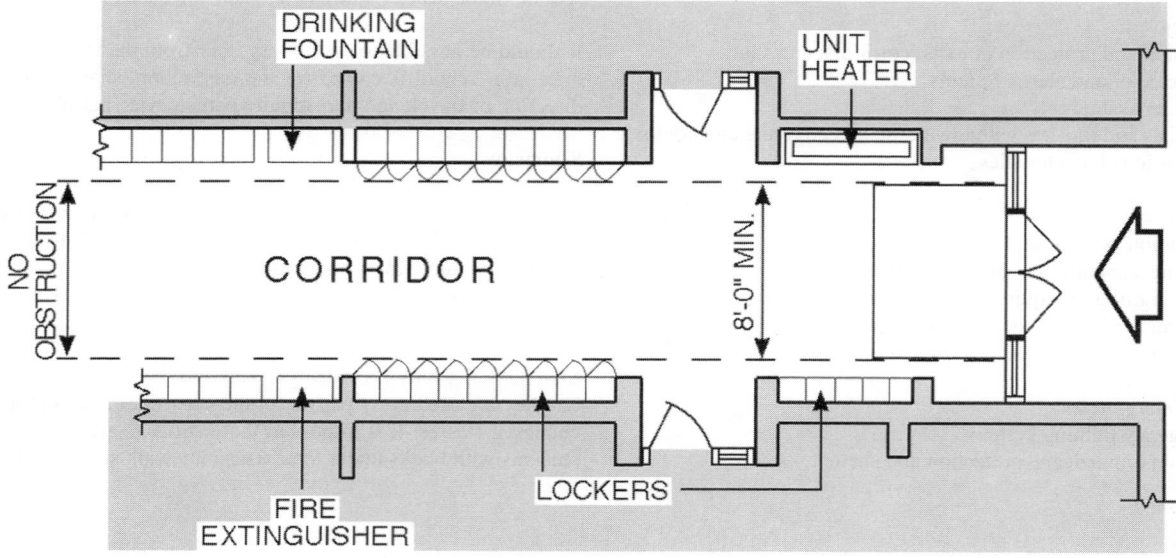

**Fig. 4. Corridor diagram**

**Fig. 1. Anthropometric information**

# EARLY CHILDHOOD EDUCATION FACILITIES

## INTRODUCTION

Recent studies of young children's cognitive development emphasize the importance of providing stimulating educational environments. Theorists contend that safe, nurturing spaces offering a wide variety of learning opportunities enhance the early development of the neurological connections that spark emotional interest and provide the pathways for learning. Optimal learning environments directly motivate students to enjoy the process of learning and help teachers to facilitate the learning process.

By definition well-designed classrooms are motivational places that create new opportunities for learning by providing educational and physical stimulation and a variety of settings (math, art, music, etc.) within a classroom. The brief summary that follows provides a general overview of typical spaces found in early childhood education classrooms and centers. Individual centers and teaching methods determine the combination of elements utilized in a particular facility but the guidelines below will help to determine how to design spaces to create the ideal educational environment for young children.

### General Classroom Requirements

The compositions of early education classrooms vary across the U.S. Pre-kindergarten and daycare programs can now be found within schools, corporate offices, community centers or strip malls serving anywhere from 3 or 4 children in a private home to facilities serving 400 or more students. The center can serve infants (birth to 12 months), toddlers (12 - 36 months) and pre-school children (3-5 years old). Along with the variations of size and locations of programs, age groups within programs may also differ. Exact teacher-to-student ratios will vary by state so it is important to check with your state government's requirements for early childhood facilities. Examples of staff to child ratios based upon age can be found in Table 1.

Similar to the student teacher ratio, space allocations for an early education classroom will also vary by state requirements. The space program of the facility should reflect the expected age range of the children in attendance. Outlined in Table 2 are generally accepted space requirements for early education facilities classroom size. These requirements do not include washrooms, kitchens, staff areas, etc.

### Classroom Environment

The classroom environment should contribute to a child's concept of order and space as well as provide a rich, stimulating and safe environment where children can develop a variety of skills. To create this type of nurturing environment, the design of the classroom must reflect an appreciation of children's scale (Fig. 1) in the design of individual spaces as well as the choice of furnishings. The early educational classroom should also provide a maximum of natural lighting and few acoustical distractions. The colors and wall textures of a classroom are important, and they can be used to differentiate quiet areas from active areas, identify classrooms, and display student work or seasonal decorations. It is important for each child to have a personalized space such as a cubby or mailbox where they can leave coats, bags, or projects to bring home.

The overall space allocation of a classroom will largely be determined by the curriculum used by the educational facility. In a broad sense, the classroom should be a flexible environment that has specified spaces for active and passive play as well as group learning. In addition, the space plan of the room should facilitate the teacher's visual supervision of the students at all times.

The National Association for the Education of Young Children (NAEYC) recommends that classroom space be divided into a Discovery Area which would include sand and water play, a large motor area, art area, music area, house area, reading/listening area, manipulatives area, block building area, woodworking/construction area, science area, and math/computer area. The division and use of these active and passive spaces within a room will vary based upon a

*Author:* Perkins and Will, Architects

**Table 1**  Recommended staff-child ratios within group size

| Age of Children | Group Size | | | | | | | | | | |
|---|---|---|---|---|---|---|---|---|---|---|---|
| | 6 | 8 | 10 | 12 | 14 | 16 | 18 | 20 | 22 | 24 | 28 |
| Infants (birth–12 mos.) | 1:3 | 1:4 | | | | | | | | | |
| Toddlers (12–24 mos.) | 1:3 | 1:4 | 1:5 | 1:4 | | | | | | | |
| 2-year-olds (24–30 mos.) | 1:4 | 1:5 | 1:6 | | | | | | | | |
| 2½-year-olds (30–36 mos.) | | 1:5 | 1:6 | 1:7 | | | | | | | |
| 3-year-olds | | | | 1:7 | 1:8 | 1:9 | 1:10 | | | | |
| 4-year-olds | | | | | 1:8 | 1:9 | 1:10 | | | | |
| 5-year-olds | | | | | 1:8 | 1:9 | 1:10 | | | | |
| 6- to 8-year-olds (school age) | | | | | | | 1:10 | 1:11 | 1:12 | | |

Child Care Center Design Guide, PBS 3425-13, Chapter 4: NAEYC AND OTHER STANDARDS, Table 4.1 (pg. 4-6), U.S. General Services Administration, Public Buildings Service, Child Care Center of Expertise, PBS-P140 - June 1998

school's curriculum. Whichever curriculum is used by an early educational center it is important that the classroom environment foster a climate conducive to the educational objectives of the program.

In addition to specific curriculum-related areas within the classroom, early education rooms should have an architecturally defined entrance, cubby storage, teacher storage, diapering station and storage, toilet areas, sleeping, and nursing areas (for infants). Classrooms should also provide ample space for children to display their own work. The display areas should be within a child's realm of visual awareness. Any display areas higher than 4 feet-6 inches is beyond the small child's usual range of awareness.

Acoustical control is a fundamental concern in designing early education classrooms because children's voices are naturally high-pitched, and many activities, both noisy and quiet, take place simultaneously within the room. A carpeted floor is recommended for acoustical purposes, however, state mandates may restrict your use of carpeting within the room. In messy areas of the room it is important to have floors that can be easily cleaned. If area rugs are used, it is important to have non-slip backings to prevent injury.

**Table 2**  Space requirements for early education facilities classrooms

| Age Group and Class Size | Suggested Minimum (square feet/student) | Suggested Optimal (square feet/student) |
|---|---|---|
| Infants | 35 | 50 |
| Toddlers | 35 | 50 |
| Pre-school | 35 | 60 |

Regarding the number and placement of windows, consideration ought to be given to the view outside the window. Where the school setting affords a pleasant, changing view, windows might be included as integral parts of the classroom. Windows should be low enough for the children to see through so they may appreciate the world outside of the center, with a minimum of 18 inches beneath the window sill for placement of furniture or equipment along the exterior walls. Natural light is an important element in any classroom; where possible, use a combination of windows and skylights to maximize sunlight. By combining natural light with artificial light, the sharp contrasts from direct sunlight are softened and the artificial light can be used to create interest in the room.

**EDUCATIONAL AREAS**

**Large Motor Area**

Every classroom will contain a large motor area where children can move about freely and gather together as a class. Over the course of a day, this area may be incorporated into the smaller learning areas of the overall room, such as the reading area or music area. For this reason, it is important that the area remains flexible. Specific design requirements for the large motor area will vary based upon student age, but in general, this area is used to develop eye/hand coordination, large and small motor skills, and positive self-image.

**Infants**

Infants require a soft, print-rich environment where they can crawl and explore the room. Creating nesting areas and crawl spaces will provide the infants with different environments within the large motor area thus scaling the room down to their size. To provide additional stimulation within the infant's scope of comprehension, place mirrors approximately 17 inches above the finished floor so children

an see and play with their reflection. Be sure that the mirror mate-
ial is shatterproof with edges that will not cut or puncture the skin.
n addition to items of interest on the floor level, it is important to
provide infants with something to look at when held on an adult lap
or lying in their cribs.

Children within the infant age group will begin to experiment with
the process of walking by pulling themselves up to a standing posi-
ion. To aid this development, it is important to provide low grab bars
that are 17.3 inches above the floor that the child can use for leverage
or support as they begin walking.

## Toddlers

Large motor areas for toddlers should have a hard surface flooring
with non-skid area carpets available for quieter areas or in colder climates. As with infants, the motor area should leave space for toddlers
to explore and wander. It is important to create pathways wide
enough for small groups to navigate and to create areas of interest
such as small lofts. While creating these intimate spaces keep in
mind that the teacher must be able to maintain visual contact with the
child. It is through visual supervision that early education instructors
maintain order and ensure safety within their classroom.

## Discovery Area

The discovery area is also often called the sand and water area of the
room. It is in this area that children explore the materials of the world
around them through play while developing concept formation,
experimentation, exploration, sensory development, eye/hand coordination, and small motor skills. The main components of this area
are tubs – one filled with sand and the other water – placed on free-
standing 24-inch-high tables. The flooring surrounding the tubs
should have an impervious floor finish, and, if possible, a floor drain
to facilitate clean-up. If a floor drain is not a possibility within the
classroom, it is suggested to place the discovery area close to the art
area sink.

In addition to the tubs, the space should contain hooks for students'
smocks and towels as well as shelving for storage of tools that might
be used while playing.

## Art Area

In the art area, children paint pictures, make finger paintings, collages, and mobiles, or play with clay, modeling compound, paste,
crayons, marking pens, and an assortment of other material such as
soda straws, pipe cleaners, and popsicle sticks.

The art area is placed near a water source and, like the water and
sand area, must have easily cleanable floors. A sink must be provided in this area to facilitate clean up of art materials and students.
The guidelines for day-care facilities in federal buildings requires
the art area be equipped with a stainless steel sink with a goose neck
faucet and wrist handles. The sink handles are placed at 22 inches
above the floor for toddlers and 26 inches above the floor for preschoolers.

The art area is equipped with shelving that is within easy reach of the
children for paper storage such as newsprint (usually 18 x 24 inches)
and colored construction paper. The construction paper should be
organized so that each child can take one color without disturbing the
other stacks. This storage space might also be used to store markers,

paint brushes and crayons. A second storage area for items such as
scissors, paint and paint cleaner should be closed and out of reach of
the children. The storage cabinets can also serve as room dividers.

The art area should have space enough for two or more children to
paint at one time. A regular easel with room for painting on either
side is satisfactory; or three or four easels side by side could be provided by sloping a long piece of plywood or masonite out from a wall
or room divider. The latter arrangement has the virtue of providing
more work area in less space, and it allows the young painters to
admire each other's work. Easels should be easy to clean, and the tray
that holds the paints and brushes should be removable for cleaning.

A table is important in this area. It should be large enough to accommodate four children playing with clay, using finger paints, or past-
ing collages. The table should be about 18 inches high and have a
work area of 15 square feet or more.

A drying rack provides an area to store just completed pictures while
an extensive display area, positioned at a child's height, provides a
place where children can hang and see completed works. It is important to place the display area within a child's scope of vision to
enhance their feeling of ownership and importance related to a completed project.

## Music Area

Important studies have found interesting linkages between music and
other cognitive developmental skills such as mathematics. Easily
incorporated into the larger motor area the music area provides students with musical instruments, stereo equipment, and toys that can
be used during musical play (balls, scarves, etc.). If possible, supply
students with a recording device so that they can make tapes of themselves or classmates and play back the recorded sound. Children
should have room within this area to sit and listen to music as well as
dance or move around the larger motor area.

## House Area

The house area encourages role-playing or make-believe among children. By participating in this form of socio-dramatic play, children
develop their oral language skills, positive self-image, self-expression
and vocabulary.

Providing child-size duplicates of home furnishings enables students
to mimic reality within a known environment: the home. When
organizing this space provide students with a child-size sink, stove,
refrigerator, table and chairs, doll bed, high chair, mirror, and a space
for hanging up dress-up clothes. The dress-up area is usually of great
interest to the children. It should include a child-size chest of drawers and either hatboxes or open shelves for dress-up clothing (shoes,
hats, jewelry, material suitable for belts, trains, capes, veils), a full-
length mirror, and a telephone connected to another telephone elsewhere in the room. One telephone should be placed so that the child
can look into the mirror while talking. The second telephone need not
be fully enclosed, but neither should the child be able to see or hear
(except through the receiver) the one to whom he is talking.

## Reading/Listening Area

Children need a place within the classroom specified for quiet or
down time. The reading/listening area should be a welcome escape
from the noise and motion of the classroom. It is within this area that

children develop articulation skills, auditory discrimination, concept formation, oral language skills, self-expression, and vocabulary.

The reading and listening area should be a quiet place well away from the more active areas of the classroom such as the block area, art area, and house area. The space should be well defined either by walls and dividers, by cabinets, or by a difference in ceiling height, floor elevation, lighting, or color and texture on the floor and walls. In addition, the floor should have carpeting and be sure to supply plenty of comfortable seats. This area could be elevated two or three steps above the general area, an arrangement that would convey a feeling of its being special, separate and cozy. If elevated, it can also serve as a platform for dramatic activity, and the children can sit on the steps when they are being read to.

The reading/listening area requires sufficient display-shelf space for showing the front cover of each of 20-25 books. The highest shelf should be no more than 3 feet-6 inches from the floor, preferably only 3 feet. If the shelving cannot be adjusted, there should be at least 14 inches between the two shelves. Thirty-two linear feet of shelving provides enough space for books. There should be a place to display one book and related small objects and pictures. An adjacent bulletin board adds to the display.

### Block-Building Area

Blocks provide a wide variety of learning opportunities. These opportunities include development of cooperation, eye/hand coordination, self-expression, problem solving, and perceptual motor development. Building structures that are shared with and admired by peers and teachers help the child view herself positively. If possible, the block area should be located near the house area with enough room for storage of the building blocks and space for small groups of children and their projects. The block area could be a little alcove (24 to 30 square feet) outside of the major traffic area but opening onto the general area. This arrangement creates a protected space where children can build something that won't be inadvertently knocked down by children engaged in other activities, and it also provides the necessary space for several children to play with the blocks simultaneously.

Unpainted, rectangular unit blocks, uniform in height and width but varying in length, are used, along with blocks of various shapes: triangular, curved, and so on. Blocks of the same shape and length are stored in separate stacks with enough space between the stacks to make them easy to arrange. The lengths of the blocks, which vary, are exposed rather than the ends, which do not vary. Silhouettes painted on the shelves help the children to find and replace the blocks themselves.

### Manipulatives Area

Play with manipulative toys complements and enhances some of what children learn when playing with the blocks. By playing with colored pegs and pegboards, lockboards, small unit blocks, rods puzzles, felt boards and geometric forms children can learn colors, develop perceptions of size and form, develop small motor skills, develop eye/hand coordination and develop concept formation.

The manipulative toy area is basically a quiet area where children work individually. It can be by itself or part of the area for reading and listening. Two or three two-shelf, open cabinets are sufficient to display the manipulative toys. Puzzles are best displayed on sloping shelves so the children can see them all as they select the ones they want to use. Most children can select their own books or puzzles if

the top shelves are not higher than 3 feet-6 inches. A cabinet above the manipulative toy area is a good place to store toys and puzzles not currently in use; the number and complexity of toys and puzzles are increased as the year progresses. A table should be located near this toy area so children have a place to bring their puzzles while working with them.

### Woodworking/Construction Area

Similar to the educational goals of the block area, the construction area lets children use child-sized versions of typical woodworking tools when building their creations. Since the use of tools such as hammers, screwdrivers, and saws will lend themselves to noisy play, place the construction area near the art area. Furnish the construction area with a child-sized workbench and a variety of accompanying tools and materials such as bolts that will fasten together two pieces of pegboard. Storage in this area should include shelves, bins for smaller tools and hooks for items such as hammers and saws.

### Science Area

The science area of the classroom is an ideal opportunity for children to experiment, observe, develop their prediction, concept formation, problem-solving, and sensory skills. The science area should be placed adjacent to the outdoor play area so children can easily perform nature studies. To assist in different science activities, this area should have plenty of shelving and low counters or tables where the students can observe plants growing, store collections of leaves, flowers, etc. and participate in simple science projects led by the teacher. The science area is often used to house the class's small pets such as a rabbit, a hamster or fish. The animal cage or tank must be placed in a position where children may observe the animal without causing harm. A child should not be able to remove the animals from their cages without teacher supervision.

### Math and Computer Area

The computers in an early education center must be set up for young children. Each computer should be placed on a child-sized desk (20 - 28 inches high) with room for one to three students to use the computer together (Fig. 2). Wires, cables and outlets must be carefully organized and kept out of reach of the children. Software programs and on/off switches should be clearly labeled to allow children access to programs without constant adult supervision. In addition to computers, this area can supply children with math games that will develop their basic mathematical skills such as counting, measuring and problem solving.

**Fig. 2. Computer table by Childcraft**

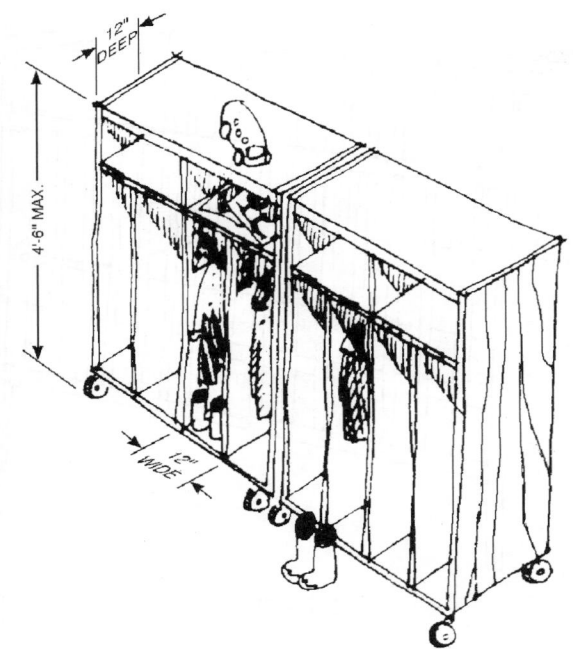

**Fig. 3. Individual cubicles**

## ANCILLARY CLASSROOM AREAS

### Storage Cubbies

Each child should have a place of his own in which to hang his hat and coat, set his boots, and store things that belong to him. These cubicles, or cubbies, should be about 1 foot deep, 1 foot wide, and 4 feet-6 inches high. The child should be able to sit down in or near her cubicle to put on her shoes (see Fig. 3).

### Toilets

Where rest rooms for the children are not adjacent to the classroom, inordinate time is wasted in moving children to and from the rest room. If rest rooms are integral parts of the classroom, children can use them independently and develop self-reliance.

The theory that the fixtures should resemble those in the children's homes has merit, but the overriding considerations are convenience and utility. The wash basin and toilets should be appropriately sized for children. Refer to www.access-board.gov/rules/child.htm for information regarding ADA requirements for building elements designed for the use of children (Table 3).

### Kitchenette

Where a central kitchen is not provided for the entire facility, consideration should be given to providing small kitchen areas in each of the classrooms for the storing and preparation of snacks and meals. This is especially important in infant and young toddler classrooms where reg-

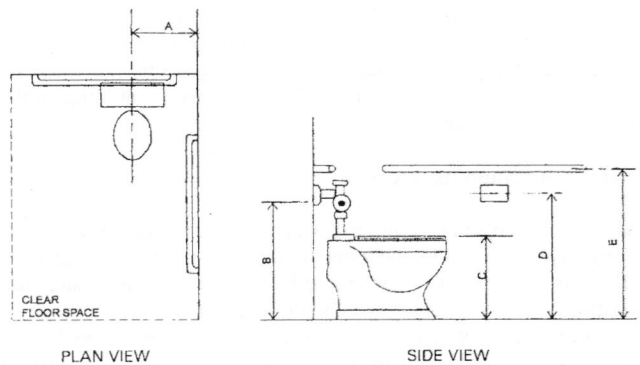

PLAN VIEW          SIDE VIEW

**Plan view, side view**

**Table 3** ADA requirements

|   | Ages 3–4 | Ages 5–8 | Ages 9–12 | Ages 12+ |
|---|----------|----------|-----------|----------|
| A | 12 in (30.5 cm) | 12–15 in (30.5–38 cm) | 15–18 in (38–45.5 cm) | 18 in (45.5 cm) |
| B | 36 in (91.5 cm) | 36 in (91.5 cm) | 36 in (91.5 cm) | 44 in (112 cm) |
| C | 11–12 in (28–30.5 cm) | 12–15 in (30.5–38 cm) | 15–17 in (38–43 cm) | 17–19 in (43–48 cm) |
| D | 14 in (35.5 cm) | 14–17 in (35.5–43 cm) | 17–19 in (43–48.5 cm) | 19 in (48.5 cm) |
| E | 18–20 in (45.5–51 cm) | 20–25 in (51–63.5 cm) | 25–27 in (63.5–68.5 cm) | 33–36 in (84–91.5 cm) |

A   Distance from centerline of toilet to side walls or partition on which the side grab bar and toilet paper dispenser are located. All other requirements of ADAAG's Section 4.16(1)—Clear Floor Space remain in effect. See www.access-board.gov/bfdg/fig28.html.

B   Maximum height allowed for flush controls. Controls must be mounted on the open side of the toilet and must be hand operated or automatic.

C   Height of toilet seat above floor. Seats that are equipped to spring back to a lifted position are prohibited.

D   Mounting height of toilet paper dispenser measured from floor to the centerline of the dispenser.

E   Mounting height of grab bars located to back and side of toilet. See the following section "Grab Bars" for additional specifications.

Adapted from: Architectural and Transportation Barriers Compliance Board, *Americans with Disabilities Act (ADA) Guidelines for Buildings and Facilities; Building Elements Designed for Children's Use, 1998.*

ular and frequent feedings occur and where individual bottles need to be stored and heated. The size and outfitting of kitchens will depend on whether or not students bring their own food and the type of program offered by the school. Kitchenettes are typically equipped with residential equipment including: a refrigerator/freezer, a microwave and a stainless steel sink and should be placed near activity areas offering the teacher clear views of the classroom. Standard adult-height base and wall cabinets should be utilized and equipped with child-proof latches or locks. In infant classrooms, consideration should be given to providing a gated separation of the kitchen to prevent crawling children from entering the area. Food preparation areas must be separated from diapering station, toilet, and hand washing areas.

**Diapering Station**

Each classroom serving infants or toddlers should have a diaper changing station and diaper storage located in an easily accessible area. This station consists of a changing table, storage area for diapers and other supplies, and a hand-washing sink. When diapering, the teacher should be able to maintain visual control over the entire classroom and the children should also be able to see the teacher. Additionally, the teacher should be able to reach all needed diapering supplies while maintaining direct physical contact with the infant. Removable stairs to help toddlers climb to the changing station are required and help prevent unnecessary back strain by the teachers. Consideration should be given to providing exhaust ventilation at the station to remove odors.

**Sleeping and Napping Areas**

Since infants and some young toddlers sleep more frequently during the day, separate areas for sleeping are required for these age groups. While it is important for teachers to be able to maintain visual and acoustical access to this area, it should be located away from active areas of the classroom and can be separated with a low, 30-inch-high defining wall. The sleeping area should be quiet and have dimmable light fixtures – indirect up-lighting should be considered to avoid direct light in the eyes of sleeping infants. The sleeping area should be sized to provide room for one crib per infant spaced according to state requirements (Fig. 4).

Quite often older toddler and pre-school classrooms will not have a separate sleeping area although cots or mats will be provided for napping (Fig. 5). Storage should be provided for the cots in the classroom.

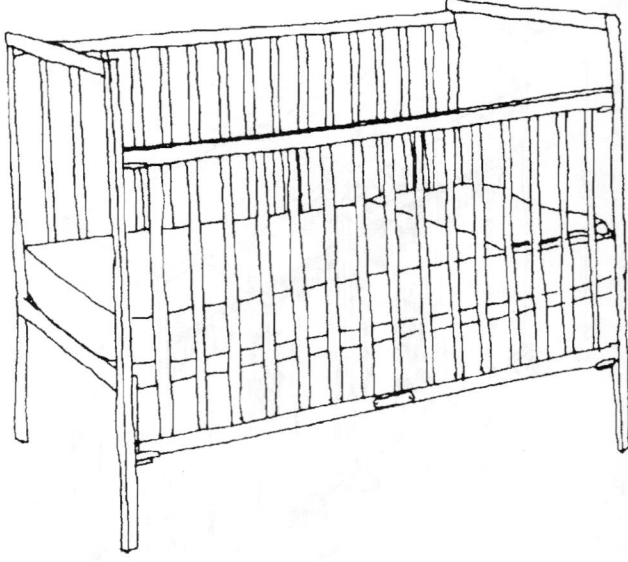

Fig. 4. Crib

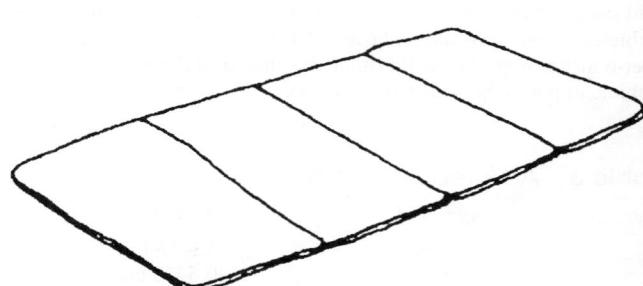

Fig. 5. Rest mat

# SAMPLE FLOOR PLANS

The following floor plans (Figs. 6 to 10) are provided as sample facilities that incorporate many of the recommendations made in the text.

## COMMON AREAS

### Entry

The entry into the early education facility should be welcoming to the children and their parents while providing maximum safety and security for the building. To accomplish these goals, the entry should provide views of the short-term parking lot through windows with sills low enough for children to look in or out of the building. Ideally, children should be able to see other children in classrooms to help allay anxiety. Double sets of doors should be used at the entry for maximum security and energy conservation.

If the center is located in an area with snow and ice during the winter months, an ample roof overhang will decrease the risk of falls. Designers should also refer to ADA standards for disabled access requirements.

### Reception

Once inside the building, the reception area should be a warm, bright, and welcoming area. To make children feel comfortable they should be able to see the person sitting behind the reception desk or table. The reception desk can be a full-height desk that serves several functions. For example, the reception desk can house teacher/parent mailboxes, sign-in facilities, fee box for tuition checks, and announcement boards. Additional furnishings within the reception area include a sofa, chairs, end table, and small coffee table. Looped pile carpeting or oriental–style patterned rugs will increase students' association of the reception area with the home environment. As with rugs used in the classrooms, be sure to use non-slip backing.

### Office

The director's office will provide a space for administrative tasks, interviews and meetings with parents, staff members, children, or visitors. It should be located in a quiet space near the reception area and be easily accessible to visitors. From the office, the director must have excellent views of the building entry, reception area and as many classrooms as possible. The facility's size and the number of administrative staff will determine the size of the director's office.

Within the office a small isolation area can be created where children may go to receive their medications or where a sick child can rest while waiting for a parent to arrive. The isolation area should have a small cot where the child may lie down without feeling completely isolated from the office staff.

### Resource Storage Room and Resource Center

A centrally located resource storage room can be used for bulk storage of curriculum materials, supplies, books, and audio/visual equipment. This larger storage area will supplement the smaller storage units within the classrooms, and it will permit the teachers to rotate toys, props, and lesson materials throughout the year. The resource storage room should have adequate lighting, open shelving, lockable and closed door storage, filing cabinets, and, where possible, a workcounter and counter-height stool.

If space is available, an early educational facility may wish to create a resource center adjacent to the storage area. The resource center would serve as a common library for students, teachers, and parents.

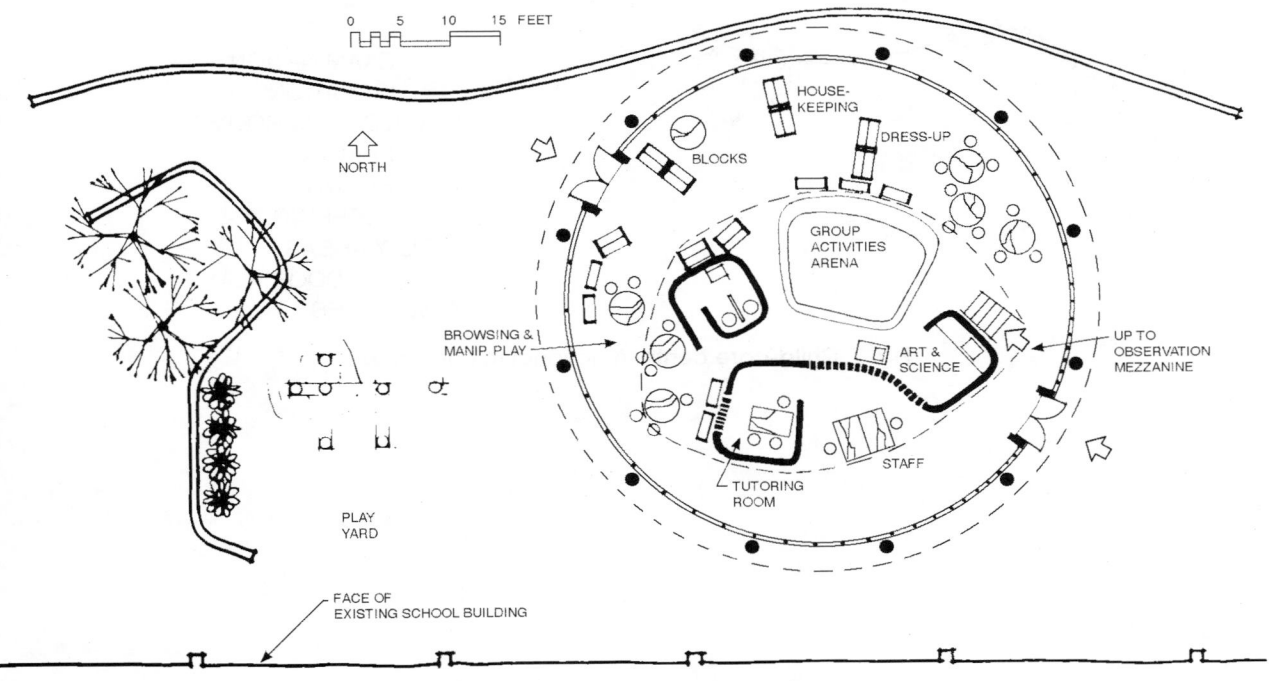

**Fig. 6. Typical child-care center**

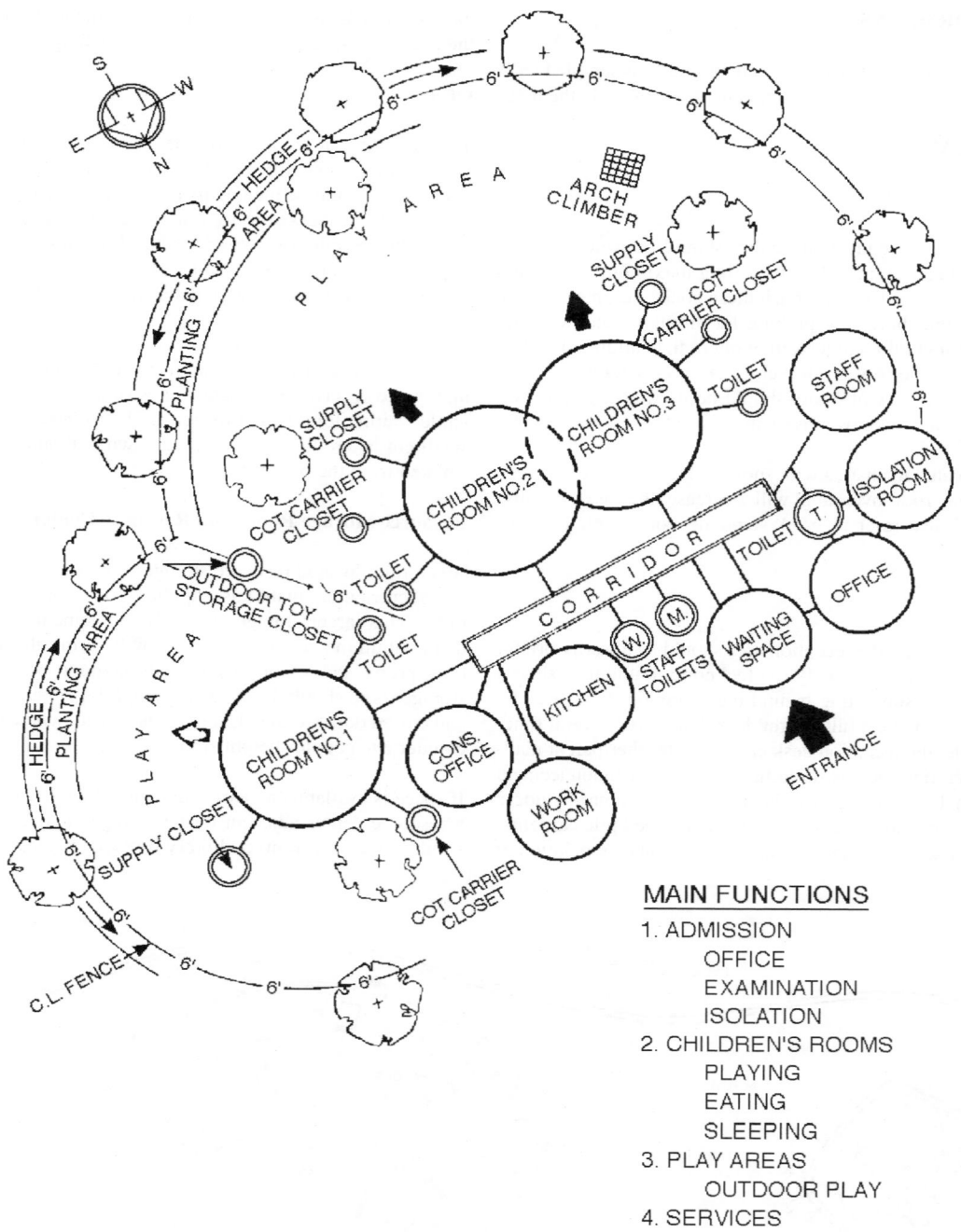

**MAIN FUNCTIONS**

1. ADMISSION
    OFFICE
    EXAMINATION
    ISOLATION
2. CHILDREN'S ROOMS
    PLAYING
    EATING
    SLEEPING
3. PLAY AREAS
    OUTDOOR PLAY
4. SERVICES

**Fig. 7. Child-care center functional relationships**

```
0 4 8  16      32
```

**Fig. 8. Child-care center plan**

Students and parents could borrow books, music, and videos from the resource center for use at home.

**Indoor Play Area**

Facilities with ample indoor space should also consider providing an indoor activity area where children may go during bad weather. An indoor play area would be located near the playground and provide approximately 800 square feet of space for children to use. The indoor play area can also serve as a large gathering place for performances, movies, and other social events where several classes and/or parents would be brought together.

**Laundry**

Accessible only by adults, the laundry area will be used to clean bedding, smocks, and toys. The laundry room should be located near the infant/toddler classroom with a lockable door that can be opened from inside. Ideally the room should be located near an exterior wall to minimize the run of the dryer exhaust vent. Since the dryer exhausts contain combustible materials it is important that the dryer is vented separately from other building exhaust systems. The size of the early child-care center will determine the equipment needed in the laundry area. A folding table, however, must be provided as well as shelves for drying toys. Cleaning supplies must be kept in wall lockable cabinets.

**SITE PLANNING**

When building a new early childhood center, site the building to provide positive orientation and safe circulation. The scale and character of the building should appear welcoming and friendly to a child.

Vehicular traffic around the building should be carefully planned during the design phase of a project. It is important that the building be visible to cars and pedestrians, particularly children, as they approach the building. Traffic should be directed away from the playground areas of the facility and to a well-defined entry point. Parents may decide to either park their cars in a longer term parking area when spending time at the school, or, they will wish to quickly park, walk their child to her classroom and immediately leave the grounds. Traffic patterns around the site will need to be designed to meet both these needs as well as the needs of service vehicles and buses or small vans that transport children to the facility. To ease the flow of traffic around the building a pull-off area should be created for the quick drop-off and pick-up of children. It is important that the view from the long-term parking lot is to a clearly defined entrance into the building. Service vehicles should be directed to a separate service apron away from other motor traffic.

Security is extremely important in an early childhood facility, and by sound safety planning during the initial design phases, an early education building can easily aid in maintaining a safe and secure educational environment. According to the CPTED (Crime Prevention Through Environmental Design), the three basic principles of a well-designed building are:

1. *Natural surveillance* or the ability to observe and be observed in the course of normal everyday activities.
2. *Natural access control* that denies easy access to potential crime targets or creates a perception of risk in offenders.
3. *Territorial reinforcement* where the properties clearly indicate ownership and acceptable behavior for all spaces.

For additional information about creating building security through design, please see the section above on safety and security.

**Play Areas**

Outdoor play areas are essential to the early childhood education environment. A well-designed playground is an extension of the classroom and is designed for the age group it serves. The overall outdoor space should be zoned in response to site conditions, age groups and activities, and the entrances from each age group area should provide a physical and visual connection between the building and the yards.

Similar to the classroom, the outdoor play area is divided into active and quiet areas. Each age group's play area should be separated with a fence at least 3 feet-3 inches high that does not contain any sharp points or rough edges. In order to prevent children's heads from becoming entrapped in the fence, spaces between pickets must be less than 3.5 inches or greater than 9 inches. Spaces less than 3.5 inches must be large enough to prevent finger and hand entrapment but should not prevent fingers from poking through the fence.

The playground area should be designed with separate yet linked activity pockets and clear circulation. Paved pathways within the play area encourage walking and provide hard surfaces for wheeled toys. By working with the natural layout of the play area provide sun pockets as well as shady areas. In addition, make sure all plants found within the playground are non-toxic and safe for children.

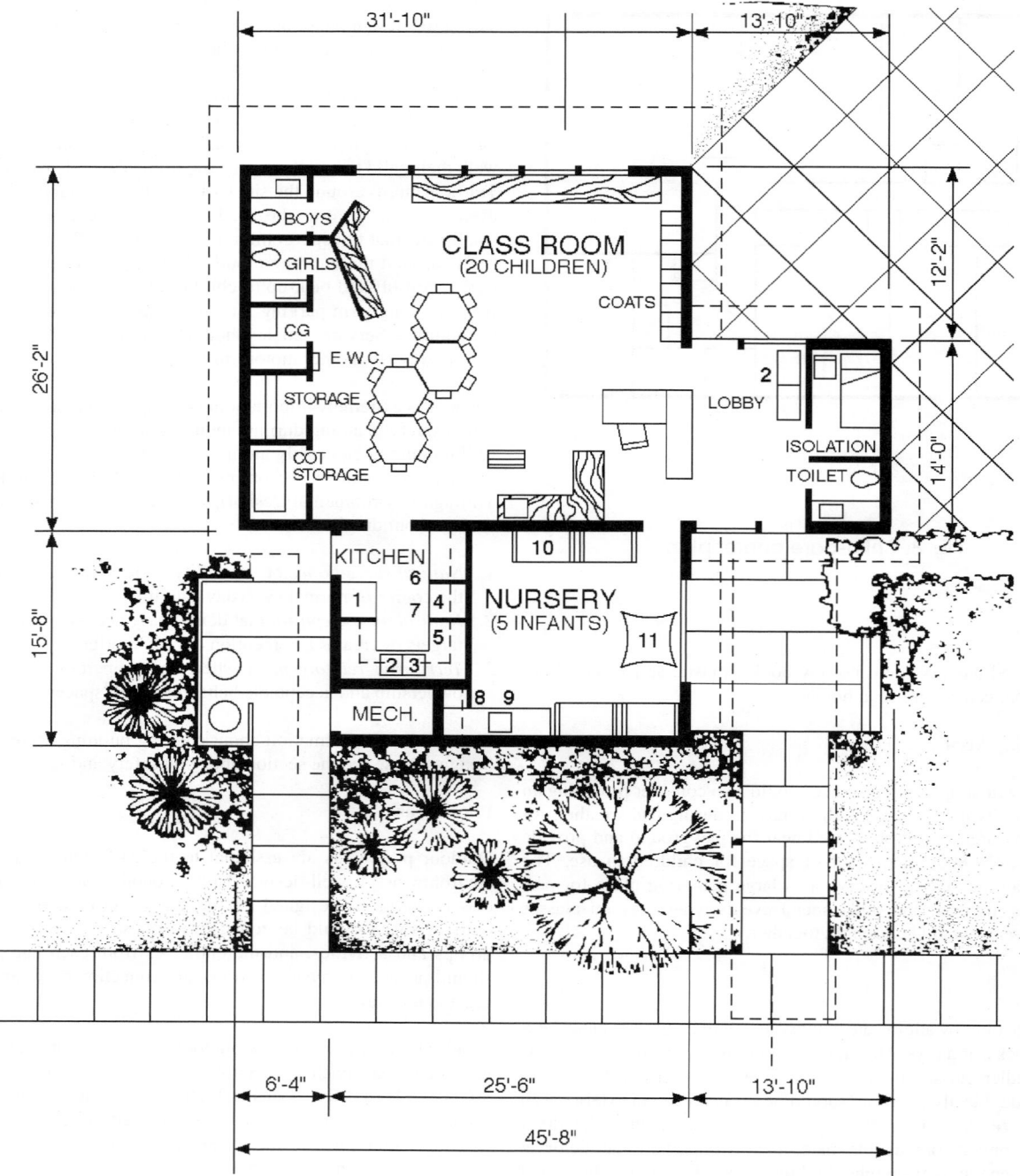

**Fig. 9. Care center for 25 children**

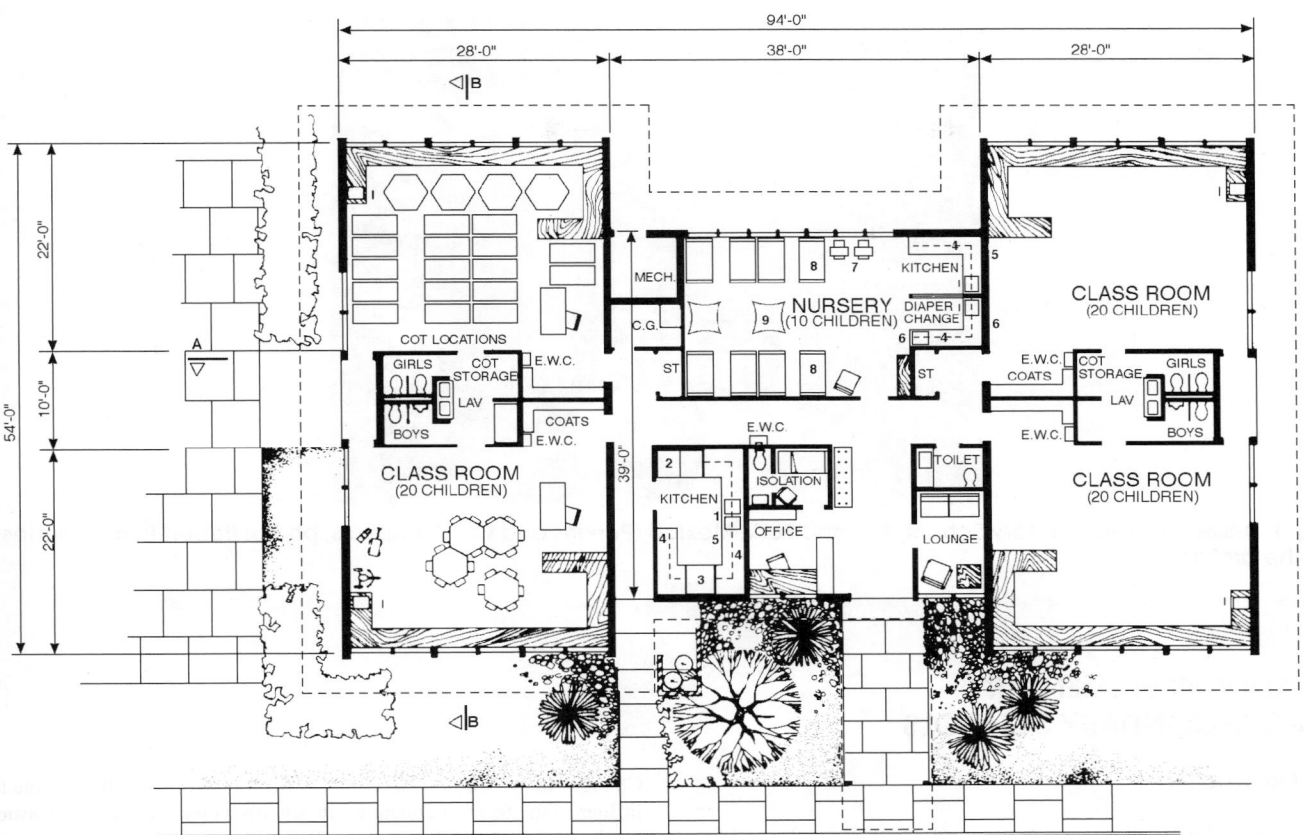

**Fig. 10. Care center for 50 children**

Fig. 1. Desert View Elementary School, Sunland Park, Mexico (Perkins and Will, Architects; photo: Robert Reck, courtesy of the architect)

# PLANNING ELEMENTARY AND SECONDARY SCHOOLS

### INTRODUCTION

The school facility plays an important role, both symbolic and functional, in support of the educational process. Symbolically, the school building represents the values each community places on education. Functionally, the building acts as a stage for learning, either supporting or limiting the activities of teaching and learning (Fig. 1).

School buildings are symbolically reflective of the educational philosophy driving the educational program. In turn, educational institutions are intimately affected by changes occurring in the society within which they are embedded. Issues such as future employment trends often affect educational and facility directions. Understanding these changes can provide both the architect and the educational client with a critical context for planning, programming, and designing a truly flexible and adaptable facility that meets the present day needs of learning communities while anticipating future trends in education.

Demographic shifts in population in and out of a school district's school site attendance areas can have short- and long-term influence on school attendance and socio-cultural diversity of the student body of a particular school. The trend, for instance, toward an "aging society" in North America is having a dramatic effect on the nature of education in general with an increased focus on adult and community education as well as community use of various recreational facilities. This trend has influenced the planning and design of school buildings into becoming more like community centers than specialized school buildings for a particular developmental age group.

Changes in the cultural structure of society have and will continue to influence the form of education in schools as well. Changes in structural patterns of family, work, and community are all contributing to a variety of educational responses. Flexibly scheduling the school day has become a central concern for many schools. Extended day programs such as daycare and after-school programs accommodate the needs of two working parents. A plethora of alternative, magnet, charter, and choice programs increasingly appeal to the growing diversity of interests in many communities, while simultaneously responding to defacto segregation in urban areas. These social trends have also influenced the planning and design of school buildings for both specialized and multiple purposes, influencing issues such as security, zoning, and accessibility.

Changes in the economic structure of our society have always influenced public and private education. From the establishment of the common school during the Industrial Revolution, to the restructuring of business in the 1980s influencing reform in school governance and the emphasis on national standards, economics has been a powerful influence on the form of education. Economic trends have influenced how school buildings are planned and designed by encouraging creative solutions such as partnerships with other community organizations. Identifying partnership opportunities in the sharing of school and community facilities to save on both capital improvement costs and operating costs has now become a first step in school planning.

Technological advances have influenced both the content and process of education. The use of information technology in deliver-

*Authors:* Philip Will, Jr., and Raymond C. Ovresat with the assistance of C. William Brubaker, Morton Hartman, George A. Hutchinson, Emmet Ingram, A. Frederick Kolflat, William McCoy of Perkins and Will, Architects, and Stanton Leggett
*Reviewers:* Raymond C. Bordwell, AIA, Perkins and Will, Architects and Jeffery A. Lackney, R.A., Ph.D.

ng education has encouraged both advances in cooperative learning and self-directed learning, while providing additional tools such as distance learning for more traditional forms of teaching such as lectures. Educational research recognizing the diverse needs of learners has effected a change in both curricula and instructional methods. Curricula are becoming more integrated and authentic, while instructional methods have developed beyond the lecture-style instruction to include small-group cooperative learning, project-based and activity-based learning, and self-directed learning. Many of these changes have been possible with the help of information technology. Technology, and the educational response to technology, have the potential to radically modify both the planning and design of school buildings as well. Beyond the obvious changes necessary in infrastructure to accommodate technology, the site of a school facility itself may change from a singular building to a network of multiple sites linked by distance learning. With the development of wireless technology, learning can take place anywhere in the building or grounds suggesting that the building design accommodate an ever more diverse set of formal and informal learning settings beyond the self-contained classroom.

## Conducive Environments for Learning

Educators are aware of the need to provide what they refer to as "conducive environments for learning." Often this phrase emphasizes the need for safe, healthy, and clean environments. In addition, educational research indicates that the school building can provide much more support for learning. And "environments for learning" include a broad range of special qualities, evidenced by characteristics of a building's design. The ambient environmental qualities of the environment - those relating to thermal, visual, and auditory comfort - may be relatively well controlled by known methods of engineering. Those environmental qualities which affect attitudes of satisfaction and behavior are far more difficult, but not impossible to accomplish through building design. Designing for developmental age through scale; providing a sense of familiarity through homelike elements; creating an environment rich in sensory experience that elicits warmth, excitement, and repose are recognizable attributes of a building that promote real responses from its occupants.

Providing spatial flexibility that supports changing forms of learning activity is a critical criterion for environments conducive to learning. Ideally, the physical setting of a school should be one that actively stimulates the development of human beings as a whole – socially, intellectually, physically, as well as emotionally. Creating a "place" for learning, and not just a "space," should not be a bonus, but rather an essential requirement in providing great settings for learning.

## STRATEGIC PLANNING

In order to ensure success in the planning and design of a school building, the initial planning should be derived from the school district's broader educational strategic plan. With this in mind, the architect (and her facility planner) should, when feasible, seek to provide pre-design services early in the planning stages prior to conventional building design and construction. In this way, the architect can contribute with the best of her experience and technical knowledge in the processes of strategic visioning, site selection, preparation for bond issue referenda, time scheduling, programming, and budgeting. During the early planning stages the architect will gain insight into the philosophical attitudes of the learning community including staff, school board members, administrators, and the surrounding community or neighborhood for which facilities are needed.

The architect should know the community she serves. Contextual issues might include:

- Demographics, rates of growth and cultural diversity of the surrounding neighborhood population
- The physical character and quality of the residential, commercial and industrial structures within and around the neighborhood surrounding the school site
- The presence of significant environmental issues or influences such as water, air, or noise pollution
- Programs that may be required to anticipate the educational, cultural, and social needs of members of all ages in the surrounding community
- The potential community-based organizations and private businesses willing to explore partnership opportunities with the school, and
- The opportunities for joint-use that exist for community organizations.

All these contextual issues must be understood to support the building program and eventual design of the school building. Once these community issues are addressed, the "educational specifications" can then be prepared. The educational specifications will address optimal school size, organizational configurations (graded, multi-aged, looped), student-teacher ratios (class size) and learner groupings, scheduling (conventional vs. block, year-round schooling), organization of the educational program (school within-a-school, house plan), and instructional methods (disciplinary vs. interdisciplinary instruction, group versus individualized instruction). It is often the case that a building will need to accommodate a variety of these methods either on a changing basis or simultaneously. The specifications will also clarify all the mechanical, electronic, and audio-visual equipment and printed material and resources necessary to supplement the educational process. Finally, performance and visual arts, physical education, competitive athletics, recreation, cultural, and specific social needs should be addressed as well.

## BUILDING ECONOMICS

The programmatic functions discussed above influence the size, shape, and form of the school building (Fig 2). The school board, administration, citizens committees, and architect must consider these functions in establishing priorities for space, quality, and cost, which governs the design and construction of new school facilities. In theory, the parameters of space, quality, and cost must be balanced in order for a facility to be feasibly constructed. In applying the space x quality = cost formula, only two factors can be fixed by the client. The architect must be allowed to control the third; i.e., if space and cost are rigid requirements, the only variable then is *quality* of materials and construction. Inefficient planning can rob the administration of space urgently needed to meet the requirements of desired programs. Unless appropriate materials, equipment, and finishes are used, the board of education will be forever burdened by excessive maintenance and operation costs. Additionally, through lack of discipline over these factors of space and quality, the project cost exceeds the funds available.

The common strategy to ensure high quality in school facilities is to employ long-term economic planning theory. The largest single cost of the school system resides in teachers' salaries and related educational expense. Even if schools cost nothing to build, the effect on a citizen's tax bill for education would be relatively trivial. The budget for the building and financing of the physical plant over its lifetime

**Fig. 2. Exterior of Troy High School, Troy, Michigan (Perkins and Will, Architects; photo: Hedrich Blessing Photography, courtesy of the architect)**

varies from 5 to 15 percent of the cost of educating a child. Of this cost approximately half is chargeable to financing—the interest paid on bonds. Inexpensive and inadequate educational facilities save some dollars initially but in the long run these buildings become poor investments and permanently disable the educational process.

## EDUCATIONAL SPACE PROGRAMMING

In order to state the needs of an educational institution and to relate a facility more closely to the educational program, communities, schools, and colleges increasingly use an educational consultant as a primary member of the planning team. A school planning project, whether for a new building or for a master plan for an institution, should be used to construct a good facility and provide a setting for the effective study of educational programs. The schedule should allow time for examining new perspectives of learning and the resulting effect on facilities planning. This may best be achieved by close personal contact between a consultant with wide experience and a faculty that searches its collective soul long before the concrete is poured.

### Procedure

As in education, planning is a *process*. While the assessable outcomes of a facility planning procedure are most important, dollars for consulting services can be used twice: once for the building product and once for the process of building consensus among the many people who will be involved in the planning and decision-making process.

Greatest advantage can come by designating a planning cadre that will ultimately take over operation of the new institution. Alternatively, a group of potential operators of the educational system could be involved. Further options include general participation by parallel staff members from other schools.

When groups are identified to participate and be involved, one useful device is to select a steering committee. Ideally, a steering committee will include a cross section of the people who will be involved, with optimistic but not necessarily similar views. Also it should be composed so that it will give credibility to the work of the committee. The steering committee should steer. The consultant should become the working staff for the committee.

The planning process should involve as many people as possible, and the consultant must be responsive to the direction of the educational institution. The consultant is a temporary employee of the school system. The school system should induct the consultant into the problem, providing wide opportunities for him to get to know *where* the institution is going, *what* the educational aspirations of the community are, and *how* the new facility should help the system achieve its goals.

While the process of induction is going on, where many people tell the consultant about the problem, opportunity, or purpose, the consultant is making her contribution. This is, essentially, to widen the spectrum of choices or options that are considered by those involved in the planning process. Viewing and discussing ways to meet objectives should go on for some time—long enough so that all the participants feel that they have explored and participated, but not so long that frustration of "delay" or "inactivity toward the goal" sets in.

Somewhere in the process the consultant takes on another role as the "organizer of chaos." It is her task, as temporary staff to a decision-making organization, to develop a first document, which states the problems and offers a set of alternatives to consider in decision making about general directions. Such a report should be made widely available to the staff or the involved group to review, critique, revise, edit, and add to. A program of needs for a building are the base for a master plan evolved from the basic study and evaluation of options, through successive revisions to descriptions of spaces in terms of numbers, sizes, and characteristics.

### Educational Specifications

Development of the formal educational specifications document for new facilities is now accepted practice in approaching the construction of educational projects of all consequences. The document is designed to formally organize the needs of the users so that the design can be developed to house these needs.

### Outline of Educational Program Document

*Educational vision:* A brief statement should be made of the educational vision, mission, goals, and purposes driving the facility program. Discussion of the educational philosophy to be followed is necessary. Make a general description of the facility and its basic elements. Draw up a statement of design objectives.

*Activity program and space requirements:* Make a general description of the assumed academic curriculum, instructional methods, and other activities to be housed in the facility. Make a general description of types of space required to meet these needs of the curriculum and instruction. Data are to be summarized in four charts:

1. Space requirements and utilization chart
2. Area summary chart
3. Activity program chart
4. Environmental conditions chart

*Detailed area and equipment requirements:* For each activity area, write a narrative outline of how the various spaces in it will be used, their relationship to each other, and their relationship to other parts of the facility. For each activity area, provide a detailed list of all spaces, giving areas and equipment for each. Data are to be summarized on two standard forms:

1. Space list
2. Equipment list

## Flexibility and Change

All schools must be as flexible as possible. The spaces in them must be easily adaptable to new uses and arrangements in the future. The types and division of spaces given in the program should not imply structures that cannot be modified for changing needs in the future.

The operative idea in the traditional view of educational specifications is *specific*. It is a road map that a school can "freeze" at a fixed point in time and whose elements are held constant while the architect begins the journey of design. Change an element or direction on the "map" and the design process must change, for the "program" has changed. The school facility is an envelope for change. The objective is to develop a building that provides the environment for that growth and change.

## Process

Educational specifications are a set of "agreements" upon which securing an appropriate building are based. Ideally, the arrangement of the space, staffing, and the deployment of the resources should be left up to the occupants who will eventually use the school. The educational specifications will be the beginning of the planning process that will continue through the design process and eventually throughout the life of the school.

During the design process the architect should create models and simulations of learning environments so that the planning team (students, educators, parents, community) can make value judgments about the use of space. People learn a great deal from simulations, it is in this manner the consequences of actions or decisions are seen graphically and realistically.

Educational specifications can help by being constructed on a modular basis and by including examples of the options that exist within the more generalized requirements. The architects can contribute greatly by graphically representing the wide variety of ways people can organize themselves within the pliable, yet not anonymous, environment the architects have created for them.

The educational consultant may not be the architect, or *vice versa*. As the planning process moves from words toward lines, the consultant's role changes. The planning organization, of which he is a part, responds to the designs of the architect. For this is a team process and good teams use all the qualities of the participants as fully as possible, shifting roles unobtrusively, but responsibly.

## Architectural Programming

Architectural programming is the specific defining and analysis of physical needs. It is also the defining and analysis of constraints (such as budget, code, site, and time schedules). Architectural programming follows and evolves from the planning team's educational specifications.

The prime objective is to define the problem: to clearly state the physical spaces required, the uses of these spaces, the functional relationship between them, and the occupancy and equipment needs of each space, all in a format understood and approved by the client.

## Procedure

The first step is to determine who will participate in the planning process to follow. Included should be the owner, educational consultants, the architect, and any others who may have a direct influence on the end result. These representatives should have the authority to make the day-to-day decisions on the formation of the program. In the case of a larger project, such as an urban high school, additional consultants may be required. They should be brought into the programming process as soon as possible so that the end result benefits best from their expertise when their recommendations of basic philosophy and policy are incorporated.

Second, a time schedule should be set with a final target date. This is essential. It should go beyond the programming phase and relate to an overall schedule including completion of construction and occupancy. Adherence to a schedule from the very outset imposes a constructive discipline and a healthy sense of urgency encouraging interaction among the participants. Modification or change of a schedule can then be appraised in light of the overall effect on time of occupancy. The time schedule clearly defines those points in time when approvals and reviews are required or desirable.

Third, there should be a sequence and methodology establishing the aims, organizing and collecting the facts, seeking out meaningful inherent concepts, and determining the prioritized needs consistent with realistic constraints. The prioritized needs should then be stated in terms of interior and exterior spaces, site, budget, and time schedule.

Fourth, there should be a format and technique that graphically portray the parts. A picture may convey an idea more than words can. The technique should be consistently followed so that the continuing experiences can be added and their implications made clearly visible.

Finally, meetings should be scheduled in a "neutral" location. Meetings do not have to take place in the school building. In fact, there may be fewer interruptions elsewhere, and new ideas might be generated best in new surroundings where inhibitions are left behind.

## Content

A complete architectural program should contain the following information:

- *Statement of use by owner:* Educational and community programs that may have a direct bearing on the planning of schools.

In some urban schools, for example (Fig. 3), specialized instruction in one school serving students throughout the city might require much more ample access into the site, as well as extraordinary circulation and toilet requirements. The complete, intended use of the facility should be made clear, as well as its place in a total educational system since that too may affect its future use.

- *Basic concepts of teaching/administration:* What the approach to teaching and administering will be has critical influence on space needs, size, and building type. Team teaching and differentiated staffing would call for large open space and a variety of space sizes. Modular scheduling in a variety of time periods dramatically affects space utilization. Will it be an open campus with students free to leave the building during "free" periods, or must the entire student body be housed in the building's spaces during all periods? Will there be study halls or free library or lounge access? Will the school be divided into independently operating sub-schools? Particularly in larger schools and school systems the matter of food service can influence decisions on plan organization and program organization. Counseling arrangements can be related to the administration offices or faculty-department grouping. The whole concern of administrative centralization versus decentralization can pull a plan one way or another.

- *Spaces to be provided:* All details of the space requirements should be recorded, their size, how many of each size, the number of occupants in each space, the number of teaching stations, the equipment demands, their relationship and functions, and

**Fig. 3. Interior of Troy High School, Troy, Michigan (Perkins and Will, Architects; photo: Balthazar Korab, courtesy of the architect)**

other special comments should be noted. With even a minimal experience in school design, a format can be developed to cover all basic types of school facilities as a checklist in developing a particular program. Through experience, certain guidelines and "rules of thumb" have been developed for school planning. Unit areas have gradually increased over the years, with the trend toward more individualized instruction, more specialized and diverse course offerings, and greater reliance on special equipment. Typical basis for calculation includes number of students per teaching station, area per student by types of space, gross square feet per student, and cost per student.

- *Graphic representation:* It is most useful and makes clear to everyone relative sizes and priorities for consideration if the individual program parts and their numbers are graphically illustrated. All interior spaces and exterior spaces like playfields and parking lots should be shown to give a good overall picture of what the total space needs are in relation to land available and what various parts of the program physically represent in area relation to others. Some initial bulk areas may be additionally included to represent circulation, storage, and service requirements, and to indicate the relationship between net and gross areas.

- *Limits/constraints:* List various constraints on the programming process, such as budget, time schedule, codes, insurance provisions and ratings, zoning and special use requirements, net-to-gross area limits or projections, and any special considerations (e.g., required review processes by government or other review agencies). Soil borings, site surveys, and information about utility services should be a part of the program data as well.

- *Architectural design statement:* Just as the owner's intended use and teaching-administrative philosophy will significantly guide the formation of the program, so the architect's basic planning approach to the particular problem should be written and recorded as part of the programming process. The incorporation of the architect's design statement into the programming document can serve as an important guide for the others who will be involved in making decisions that should relate more clearly to a common philosophy and assure a more consistent and better end result. For reviews by various approval groups, whether the school owner or a code official, having the rationale stated clarifies understanding and minimizes misinterpretation.

### Summary

The architectural program is the basis for beginning the building, and the more information collected at the outset, and properly evaluated, the more successful the planning process and end result will be. Time and thought carefully spent in programming will bring everyone's ideas together at the outset, give everyone a chance to make his contribution, and advance the project in an orderly manner.

### FINANCING

Very quickly, programming procedures and determinations unfailingly hit financial limitations. Almost invariably the facility program must be adjusted to conform to financial realities. The nature of financing school buildings depends on the type of school and its sponsorship. The task of raising financial resources is becoming increasingly harder as more complex government funding procedures come into effect, tax allocations are spread across consolidated districts, and the trend to more centralized control and management increases. Campaigns for bond issues and tax increases must become more effective, newspaper publicity, coffee klatches, and public o-dos must be more objectively organized to convince an increasingly well informed, interested, but demanding public.

Both new communities and old residential based communities have problems in funding new schools and programs because of the limits of assessed valuation of their total properties. This prompts a search for state and federal support and a concern about the possible loss of local prerogatives. New tax revenues are being sought within the communities by charging for more services and pursuing zoning changes toward a wider mix of community to accomplish a broader tax base.

## Types of Financing

A given project will normally be in one of the following categories, requiring a related type of financing:

*School districts with taxing power:* Major building projects are financed by a bond issue referendum within the limits established by the differential between existing indebtedness and an allowed percentage of current assessed valuation of taxable property in the district.
*School systems under local government:* Project funds are received as appropriations, which may or may not represent proceeds from sales of bonds by the governmental taxing authority.
*State government:* A percentage of the project cost is provided by the state, which is supplemented by the sales of bonds.
*Private schools:* Funding is primarily dependent on bequests, contributions, and mortgage loans. Under special circumstances some facilities may be funded by federal agencies.

These categories, and the traditional methods of financing characteristic of each, generally apply to institutions of elementary, secondary schools, and higher learning. Near exhaustion of traditional financing sources has led in recent years to the development of methods of supplemental aid or procedures for lifting the entire burden of capital investment from the school or institution.

Federal legislation provides grants-in-aid and self-liquidating loans to qualifying institutions through agencies of the Department of Health, Education, and Welfare and to a limited degree through agencies of the Department of Housing and Urban Development. State and local governments have assistance programs of their own. A growing trend is toward the establishment of school building authorities or commissions, which will finance and construct buildings for occupancy by a school on a rentlike basis, with costs paid out of operating income.

It has become a routine obligation of school administrators to keep themselves informed about all agencies and assistance programs which may be available to help in financing a project or, in some cases, to make traditional funding unnecessary.

## Programming and Budgeting

Financing patterns have critical effects on the design and planning of school facilities. If the amount of a bond issue or an appropriation has been established prior to programming or detail planning, the scope of the project will be rigidly limited by that amount. The only flexibility then lies in a supplemental bond issue or appropriation, which is usually not feasible. If planning funds are available, programming and preparation of preliminary plans and estimates should be carried out prior to the establishment of a fixed amount of funds available for the project.

If assistance in financing is obtained from outside agencies, these agencies will become reviewing authorities with their own requirements and standards, which will directly affect the implementation of the program. Such requirements may include any or all of the following:

- A maximum allowable cost per square foot
- A minimum required ratio of net instructional area to gross building area
- Use of governmental specification standards
- Specified bidding procedures
- Designation of construction labor pay scale

In contemplating allowable costs for a proposed project, there must first exist a clear idea of all the costs involved. If there are $10 million to spend, a $10 million building cannot be built. The project budget must cover all costs related to the project, which are chargeable to the capital funds available. A typical project budget would contain allowances for the following items:

- Construction cost of building facilities
- Site development and utility connections
- Fixed and movable equipment
- Technology equipment
- Architectural and engineering fees
- Contingency allowance

Additional budget items might include land acquisition, demolition of existing buildings, landscaping, furnishings, legal fees, special consultant fees, and miscellaneous special expenses. As a rule of thumb, in the average building project, construction cost cannot exceed three-quarters of the allowable project cost amount. If the project requires an unusual amount of furnishings and equipment, or if unusual site conditions add heavily to site-related costs, the allowable ratio for building construction cost will be correspondingly reduced.

### Environmental Conditioning

Not many would disagree students learn and teachers instruct more efficiently in a controlled learning environment. If the building is conditioned for effective 12-month operation and is made attractive for intensive community use, the facility can be more efficiently and economically used.

Certain characteristics of building designs appropriate to total environment conditioning may, if the educational program permits, facilitate more economical construction, particularly if imagination is used in planning. The compact plan, for example, produces minimum exterior wall area, reduces piping runs, uses corridors and service areas most efficiently, and can be substantially more economical to build, operate, and maintain than other plan arrangements.

More efficient and effective use of school buildings is, in itself, an economy to the community. Add to this the broadened educational and cultural advantages to the community at large, and it becomes apparent that the totally comfort-conditioned school is both practical and necessary.

At the beginning of the 1990s, the concept of "green" design began to move to center stage. More commonly known as "sustainable building" design, green construction utilizes design practices and building materials that are recycled, reused, and renewable to create resource-efficient buildings that are conducive to preserving natural resources. These buildings can generally cost less to own and operate due to an increased focus on efficiency throughout the planning process.

Continued concern over the effects of global warming, ozone levels, depleted natural resources, and other environmental problems have focused the attention for new design practices in planning effective, economical schools.

## Functions of Economy

The mechanical systems of space conditioning are not the only consideration for the design of an operationally efficient building. The orientation, the plan arrangement, the design of the building, and the materials used can contribute to the quality of comfort achieved and to the economy of the building operation. Consider the following:

- *Plan:* Less room and exterior wall exposure in a compact, multi-story building will cost less to heat and cool than a sprawling, one-story arrangement of equal area and volume.
- *Orientation:* Classroom windows facing east or west receive excessive heat from the sun. Although this fact assists heating in colder northern climates, the cooling problem is generally greater. As a general rule, it is preferable to face the majority of rooms north or south.
- *Fenestration:* Buildings with reduced window areas are operationally practical: they save on initial cost, maintenance, and heat loss and are free of outside dust, smoke, odors, and noise. However, from the learning environment perspective, this is less than desirable. Windows should be included in all school design. Factors affecting the amount and location of windows may include building orientation, the neighborhood in which the building is to be constructed, security, etc. The benefits of a close relationship to the out-of-doors, and the effect of light and sunshine in the interior environment to one's physical being should not be underestimated.
- *Solar controls:* Wide roof overhangs, solar screens, glass block, and similar devices to control sunlight are some means of reducing solar gain. The use of heat-absorbing glass reduces glare and light transmission and produces economies in the HVAC system design.

- *Space conditioning:* Skillful use of lighting, acoustic materials and color and form in school design are essential ingredients of conditioning space in the learning environment and, properly applied, act upon our senses of sight and hearing to cause reactions conducive to better learning and teaching.
- *Lighting:* Good lighting design involves locating illumination sources so that work areas receive adequate light free of glare and excessive contrast or shadow. Both natural and artificial light must be controllable to eliminate glaring shafts of sunlight or to darken the room for projecting pictures. It is desirable to use some incandescent lighting, strategically placed, to create points of variety and accent in the more conventional all-fluorescent systems.
- *Acoustics:* Acoustical control involves containment, absorption and reflection or reinforcement of sound. According to the circumstances of the listener, sound should be prevented from leaving a space when it will disturb people in adjacent rooms. Certain amounts of acoustically absorbent material must be used to "soak up" noise in such areas as corridors, toilets, and cafeterias. Accurate and comfortable hearing of music in an auditorium depends on projecting sound from reflection from some surfaces, but absorption in others to prevent distracting echoes; a speaker's voice may have to be reinforced by an amplifier in large rooms.
- *Colors:* Color is a psychological aid to learning. Functionally used, it can enhance the environment, engendering a cheerful receptive mood promoting different learning abilities. Bright warm colors stimulate excitement and action in the gymnasium, soft, cool colors create a quiet atmosphere in places of study.
- *Form:* The physical shapes of our surroundings also have psychological effects that can favorably influence learning. Large rooms, such as the library, cafeteria, or auditorium require higher ceilings for a sense of airy freedom than do small offices and conference rooms; corridors should be offset, widened occasionally and given a view in order to avoid the feeling of interminable constricting length; an atmosphere of spaciousness, or lack of confinement, can be created by making some interior partitions of glass. This is particularly important when the plan design involves large areas of interior spaces.

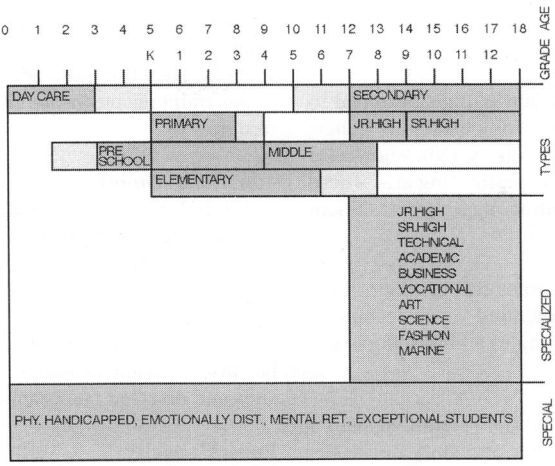

**Fig. 1. Types of school organization**

# ORGANIZATION AND DESIGN OF SCHOOLS

Schools—structured to meet the needs of the students, faculties, and communities they serve—can be organized into elementary, middle, and high schools, community, central, neighborhood, and regional schools, vocational and technical schools, academies, charter schools, international schools, and special schools.

Time, location, organization, methods, and semantics have influenced schools. Elementary schools generally contain grades K-5. Middle schools generally contain 6-8 grades, while junior high schools are commonly structured around a 7-9 program. High Schools usually denote grades 9 to 12, sometimes 10-12. Kindergarten is almost universally a part of the elementary school's program. Preschool education can be divided into a number of types, including day care, nursery, and Head Start programs.

The following glossary, along with Fig. 1, provides clarity in understanding types of school organization and overlapping names and age groups.

## Glossary

*Central and/or regional schools:* Generally found in rural areas where population density does not support adequate school facilities. Children are bused for great distances to allow them to attend facilities that offer them broader programs and opportunities.

*Charter schools:* Public schools operated by private organizations. Depending on the laws within the state, the charter may be issued by the local school district or the state board of education to either not-for-profit or for-profit groups. Funding for operation is generally received on an enrollment basis. Charter schools must be accountable to a performance-based contract.

*Community schools:* Schools that provide facilities for community programs in addition to the typical school program. Community programs range from the use of a gymnasium for basketball at night to a building that could house social agencies; health agencies; extended youth programs; university partnerships; library partnerships; programs for the elderly; and technology programs.

*Day care:* Offers a dual function, provides a care center where working parents can leave their preschool child and provides a group learning experience for the child.

*Elementary schools:* In current practice, generally K-5 or K-6 schools. Traditionally, elementary school included K-8 (grammar school).

*Head Start:* Programs for 3-5 year olds with the overall goal of increasing the school readiness of young children in low-income families. Early Head Start provides child development programs to serve children from birth, pregnant women, and their families.

*International schools:* Global network of schools offering American and Western principles and methods of teaching. The schools are generally organized as K-12 facilities providing high academic and programmatic standards. The schools are comprised of a multinational student body and generally function as a community center for students and parents.

*Junior high schools:* The earlier years of secondary education usually grades 7-9, sometimes grades 7 and 8.

*K-12 school campus:* International, private, or public school systems that combine all of a school district's facilities into one campus. The elementary, middle, and high school programs generally share common amenities while maintaining individual identities. Shared facilities may include library, gymnasiums, fitness facilities, and auditoriums. Usually K-12 facilities also serve as community centers, similar to a community school.

*Reviewer:* Peter Brown, Perkins and Will, Architects

*Kindergarten:* Usual type of introduction to group learning experience in elementary schools.

*Magnet schools:* Schools offering specialty curriculums designed to embrace a subject matter or teaching methodology that is not generally offered to students in the local education system, such as a science-technology school or a school for the performing arts. These schools offer a curriculum capable of attracting diverse student demographics.

*Middle schools:* Usually grades 6-8, sometimes 5-8 or other grade configurations. Program is frequently structured as a secondary school, with a focus on the student's transition to a high school program.

*Neighborhood schools:* Generally smaller schools identified with a specific neighborhood, where busing is neither necessary nor desirable.

*Nursery schools:* May serve the same function as day care, but frequently provide only the group learning experience.

*Primary schools:* The earlier years of elementary education, usually K-3, sometimes K-4.

*Schools without walls:* In downtown urban areas, use of community facilities, office space of business organizations, public libraries, etc. to assist in the delivery of curriculum.

*Secondary schools:* Includes middle schools, junior high schools, and senior high schools, generally grades 5-12.

*Senior high schools:* Usually grades 9-12, sometimes grades 10-12. The later years of secondary education.

*Special schools:* Schools for children who do not fit traditionally into the typical school programs, for example, schools for emotionally and physically disabled, the mentally disabled, or the exceptionally gifted.

*Special schools for secondary education:* These schools are usually found in large urban areas or in more rural areas as special regional schools. They provide a special curriculum for such studies as vocational training, business, art, drama, science, marine, fashion, and design.

*Storefront schools:* These schools identify with people in heavily congested urban areas. Such schools do away with the traditional atmosphere, relating instead to dropout students and other youth that are alienated from a traditional institution. May be housed in buildings not originally designed as schools.

*Urban schools:* Can be structured as any of the schools in this list, but also respond to issues specific to urban areas, i.e. constrained sites and diverse demographics.

**Pupil Capacity**

The size of a school is largely determined by the student capacity. According to *American School and University* in 1999, the median elementary school in the U.S. provided 105 square feet per student, middle schools provided 143 square feet per student, and high schools provide 167 square feet per student.

Before any calculation of school capacity can be made, the school system must have an educational policy establishing the optimum capacity of classrooms. Some schools do not like to exceed 25 pupils per class. In many schools this figure is set at 27, which, when used as an average class size, may mean that some rooms will exceed this number. When a class goes to 32 pupils the recommendation is frequently that the class be divided into two sections with two teachers.

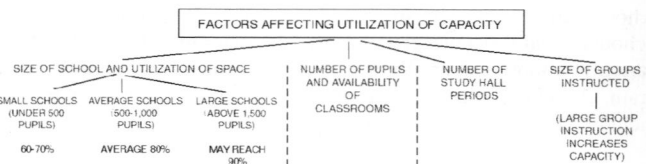

**Fig. 2. Utilization factors for high schools**

**Table 1**  Classroom capacity for high schools

| Type of space | No. of units | Capacity of units | Total capacity |
|---|---|---|---|
| Classroom | 19 | × 27 | 513 |
| Science laboratory | 3 | × 25 | 75 |
| Commercial education | 4 | × 25 | 100 |
| Home economics | 2 | × 25 | 50 |
| Art | 1 | × 25 | 25 |
| Shop | 3 | × 20 | 60 |
| Band or chorus | 2 | × 35 | 70 |
| Gymnasium, playroom | 1 | × 35 | 35 |
| Gymnasium with partition | 1 | × 70 | 70 |
| General education laboratory or study hall | | × 35 | |
| | | Maximum capacity: | 998 |
| | | Optimum capacity at 80 percent utilization: | 798 |

It is also advisable in determining the capacity of an elementary school to consider each grade separately so that there will be no single classroom housing more than one grade. Kindergartens are generally set at 20 pupils in each of the morning and afternoon sessions.

Determining capacity for the secondary school is considerably more complex than on the elementary school level. Capacity in a good secondary school reflects the kind of educational program and the educational goals of the community (see Fig. 2).

The classroom's character and subject are determinants of the classroom size. Physical education classes may run to 35 or 40 students; fabrication labs, prototyping facilities and similar hands-on instructional spaces should not exceed 20 students. Other areas that are likely to support 20 pupils and should not exceed 25 students include science rooms, life skills, and fine arts.

Class sizes may vary from community to community, but for comparative purposes it would be helpful to maintain a standard formula for determining capacity (Table 1).

## Working Space Relationships

An effective school plan responds to the school's organizational structure. The spatial organization should reflect the philosophy of the teaching program and the program needs of the school, logically organizing the program parts. The building's expression can also reinforce the school's organization structure.

Schools can be civic buildings that are used beyond the end of the school day. The building should be zoned to allow appropriate access to public areas without disrupting the academic areas within the facility.

Circulation should be direct and as clear as possible, helping to define the organization of the school. Circulation space should be planned to allow gathering spaces for groups of varying sizes to promote social interaction among students.

The school plan needs to accommodate functional and practical requirements including site and climate conditions, construction phasing, funding, and code issues. Over the life of a school, the organizational structure usually changes; therefore a school's planning should be flexible to extend the serviceable life of the facility.

## Variety in Plan Concept

Many factors affect and determine the concept of a plan. Plans are generally organized around program and functional relationships. Some schools may relate to unusual site conditions, they may place emphasis on unique circulation requirements, or respond to the need of incremental expansion of classrooms or core elements. Plans can be compact with large amounts of internal spaces, they can be linear in organization, and they can form exterior spaces—extending learning areas to the outdoors.

Some plans organize large schools into smaller communities of students. In this model, interconnected classroom groupings organize the plan into a series of smaller elements, called houses, clusters, or academies. Academies provide students more intimate environments, reduce travel distances required for class changes, and can be planned to offer curriculum specific instruction.

## Elementary Schools

Elementary schools generally have simple programmatic requirements, resulting in clear building organizations. Figure 3 illustrates a formal organization with shared functions centralized in the school and classroom wings forming a major entry courtyard. Figure 4 shows a linear organization with clusters of classrooms forming common shared resource areas along the major circulation spine as well as shared outdoor courtyards. Public functions are located near the building's main entrance. Figure 5 is a K-8 facility for an urban setting. The building reinforces the street edge, while forming outdoor play areas for the students. This school is three stories and is organized around academic houses.

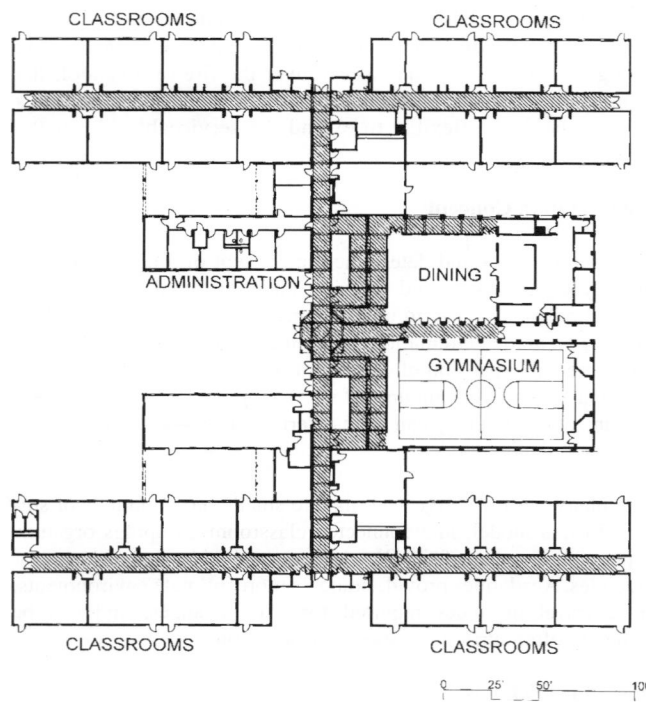

CLASSROOMS　　CLASSROOMS

ADMINISTRATION

DINING

GYMNASIUM

CLASSROOMS　　CLASSROOMS

0　25'　50'　100'

**Fig. 3. Elementary school**

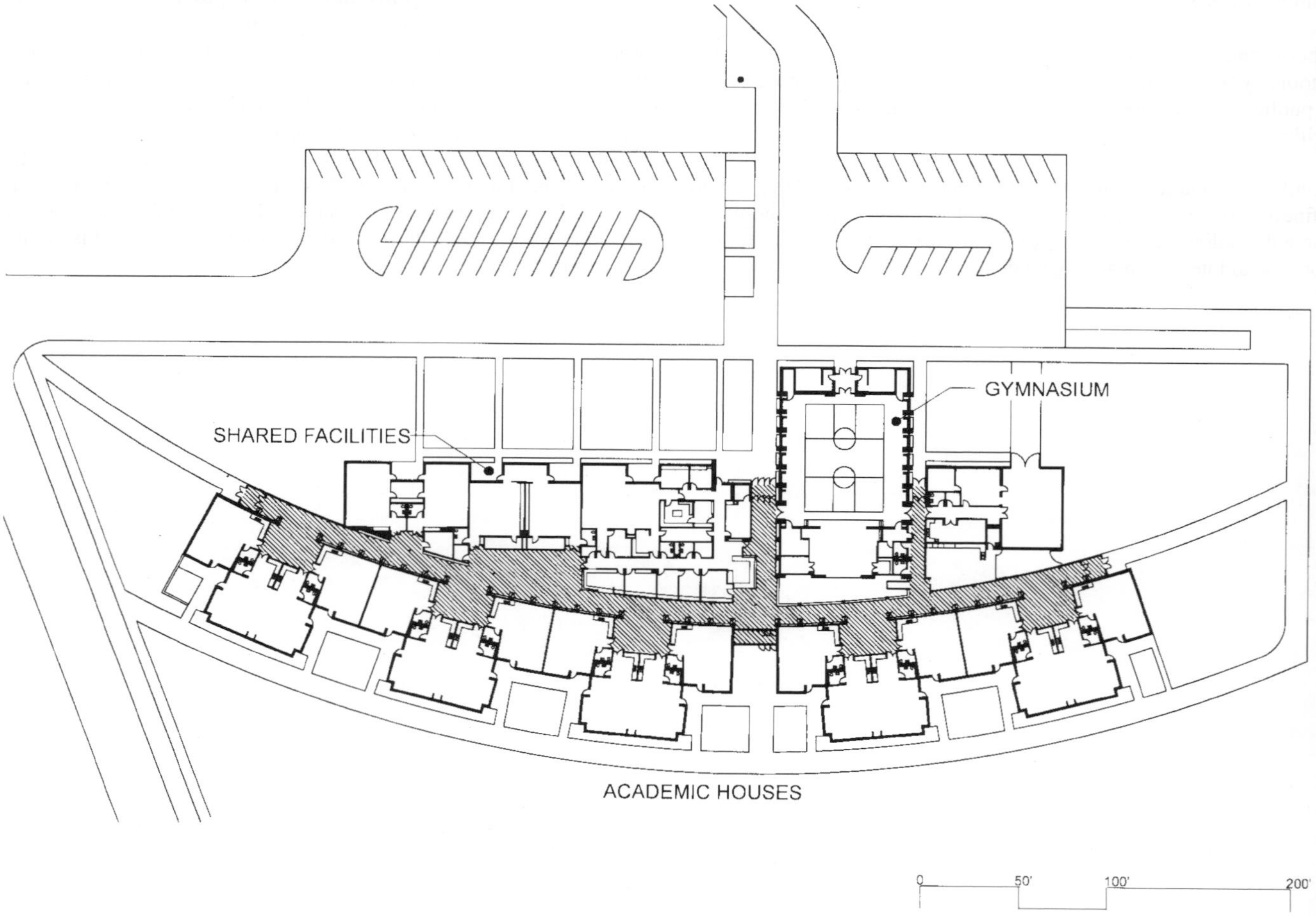

SHARED FACILITIES

GYMNASIUM

ACADEMIC HOUSES

0　50'　100'　200'

**Fig. 4. Elementary school**

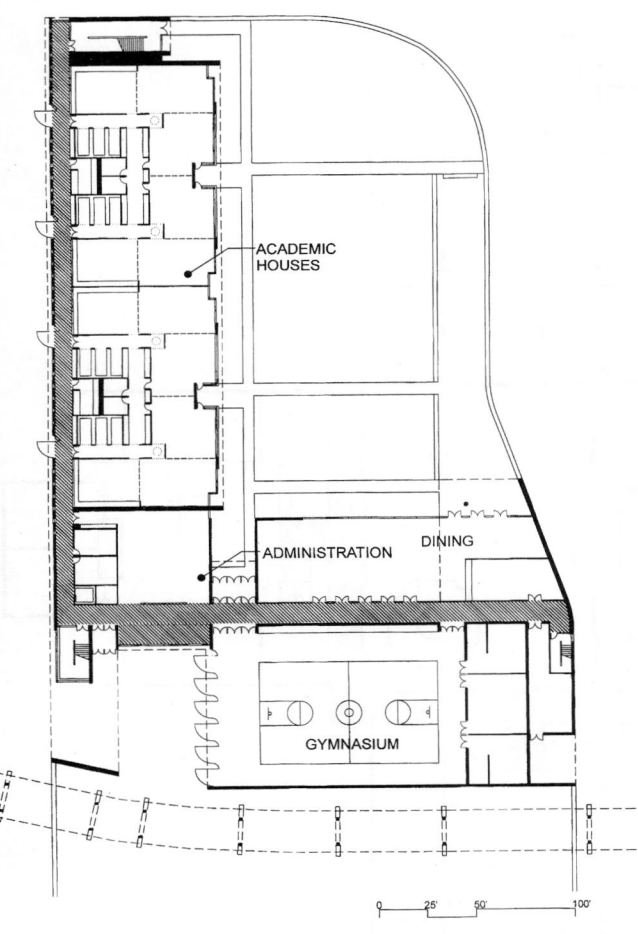

**Fig. 5. K-8 school**

### Middle Schools

Middle school space programs reflect more curriculum specific spaces than elementary schools, and offer students a greater selection in exploring educational interests. Figure 6 is a suburban middle school planned for 1,000 students. The school is organized around academic clusters. The clusters each have a large gathering area for specialized instruction or social interaction. The program also includes a full gym with locker rooms, multi-purpose hall with stage, and a performing arts suite. Figure 7 is a middle school located in a tropical climate, allowing a greater use of exterior areas to meet programmatic requirements. The radial classroom arrangement forms a private courtyard anchored by the library. Shared facilities and specialized classroom extend from the library and terminates with the student cafeteria opening onto the school's play fields.

### High Schools

High schools are usually large—sometimes serving between 1,000 and 3,000 students. Organization needs to be clear and direct with ample circulation to facilitate prompt movement of students. Fig. 8 illustrates a high school with flexible houses planned to offer curriculum specific programs. Houses are organized vertically to provide identity and reduce student movement through the building. Shared facilities are located across a commons area. This high school also provides child care services for students. Figure 9 shows a similar organizational concept placed on an urban site. Academic houses are arranged around a central commons that provides a link to the shared facilities. Figure 10 is a high school designed for an arid climate, making use of outdoor courtyards to link program elements.

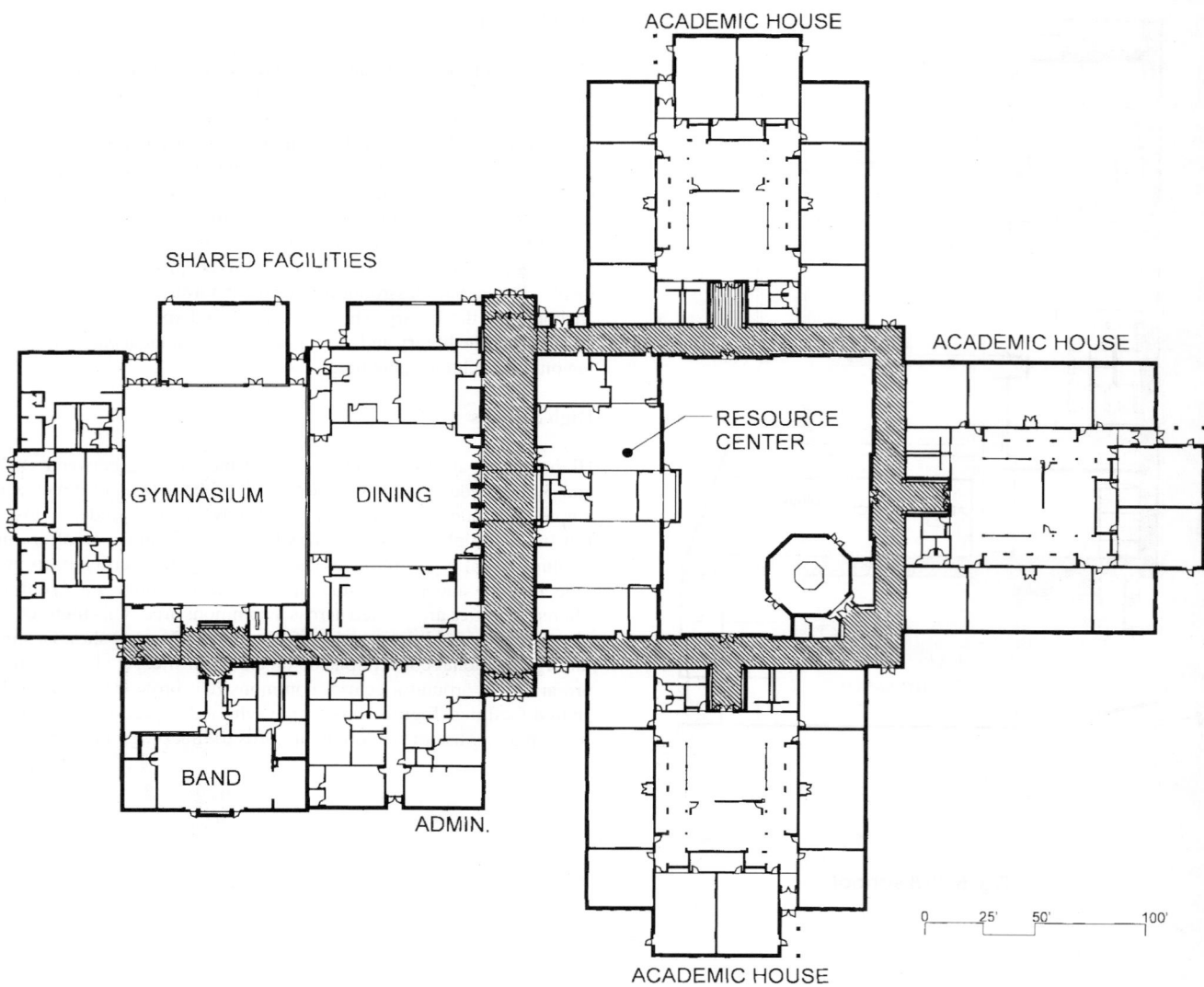

ACADEMIC HOUSE

SHARED FACILITIES

ACADEMIC HOUSE

GYMNASIUM

DINING

RESOURCE
CENTER

BAND

ADMIN.

ACADEMIC HOUSE

0    25'    50'    100'

**Fig. 6. Middle school organized around academic clusters**

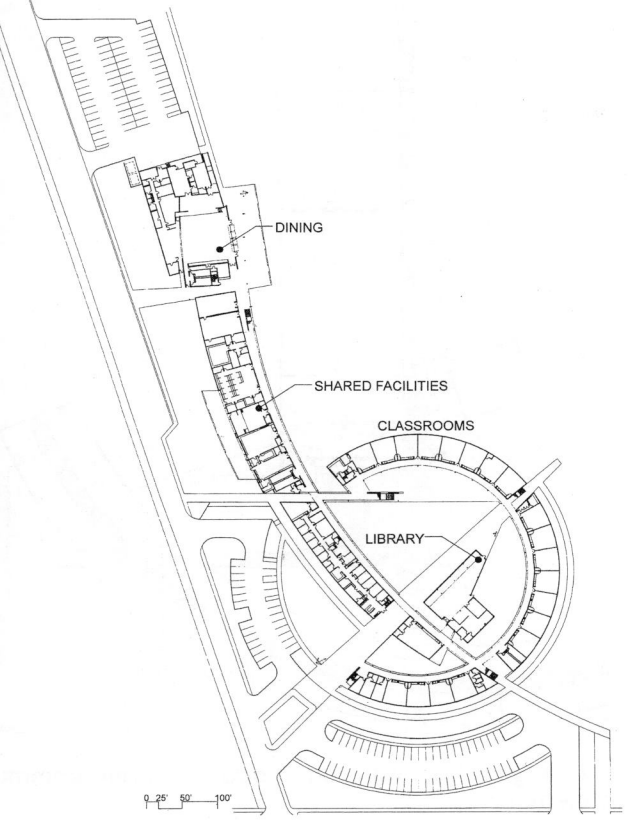

Fig. 7. Middle school in tropical climate

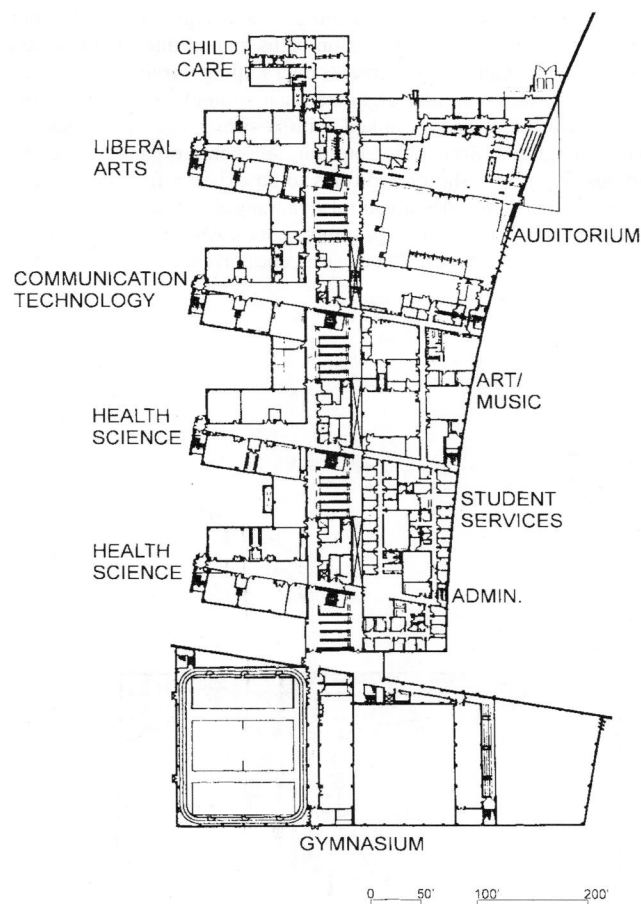

Fig. 8. High school with flexible houses

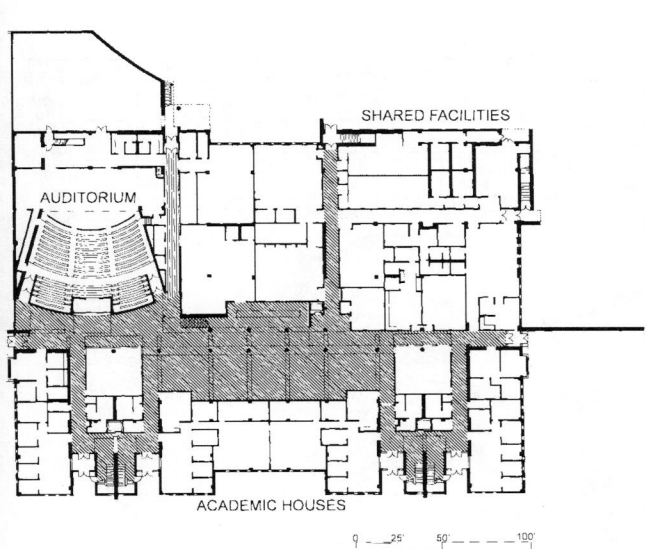

Fig. 9. High school on urban site

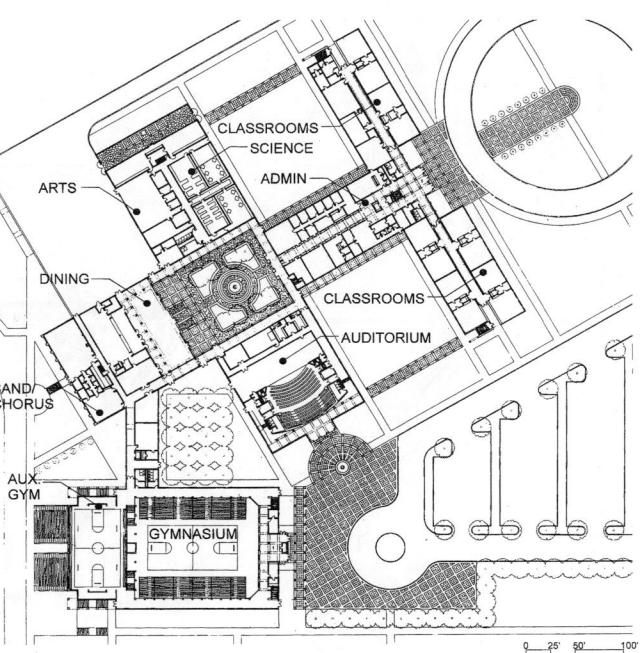

Fig. 10. High school for an arid climate

Figure 11 emphasizes a clear zoning of academic and community elements of the facility. Circulation paths extend into the landscape to define and organize site elements on a sloping terrain, Fig. 12. Figure 13 illustrates a similar organizational strategy, providing a zone for academic classrooms linked with a strong circulation path to shared programs. Sometimes building elements organize an entire campus. Figure 14 shows additions to an existing facility. A radial classroom core provides a central quadrangle and offers a focus to the campus, linking existing program spaces. A wing of shared facilities extends the school to the existing auditorium.

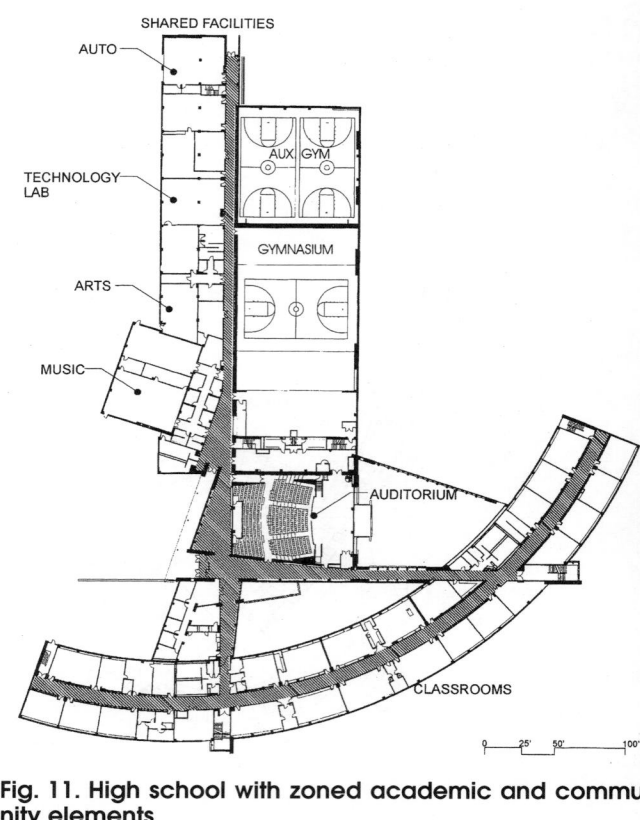

**Fig. 11. High school with zoned academic and community elements**

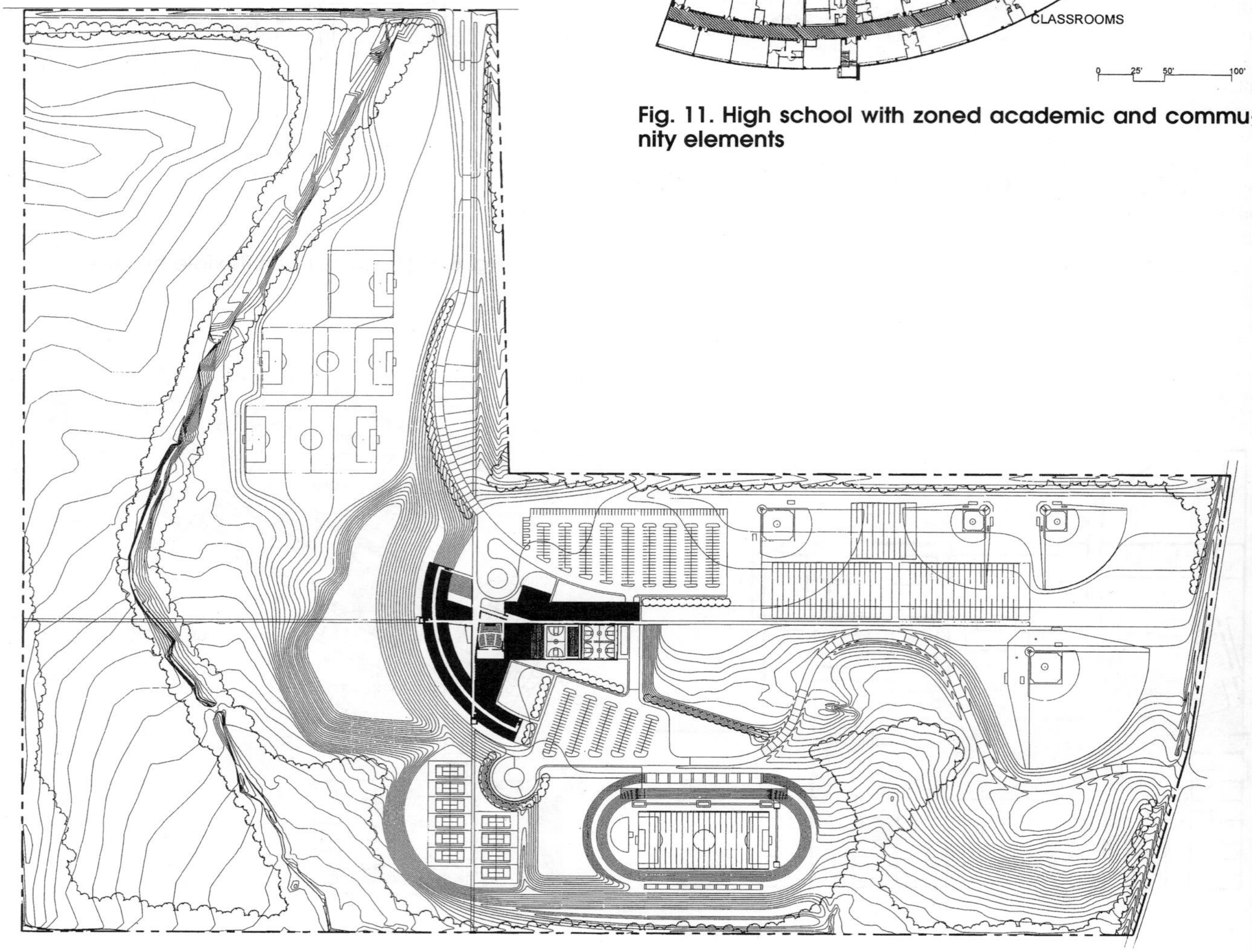

**Fig. 12. Site plan on sloping terrain**

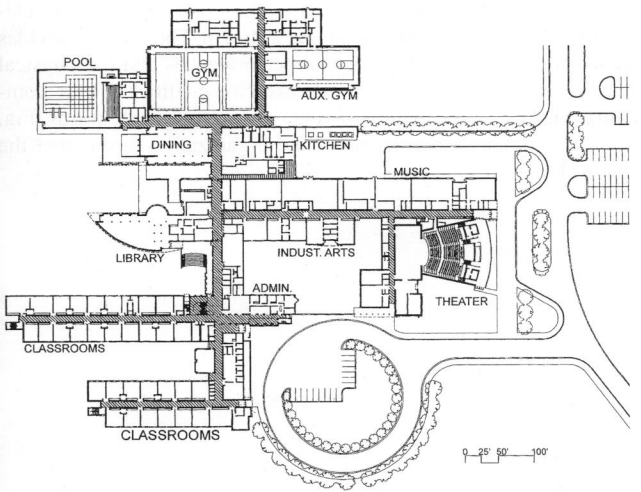

Fig. 13. High school with circulation paths

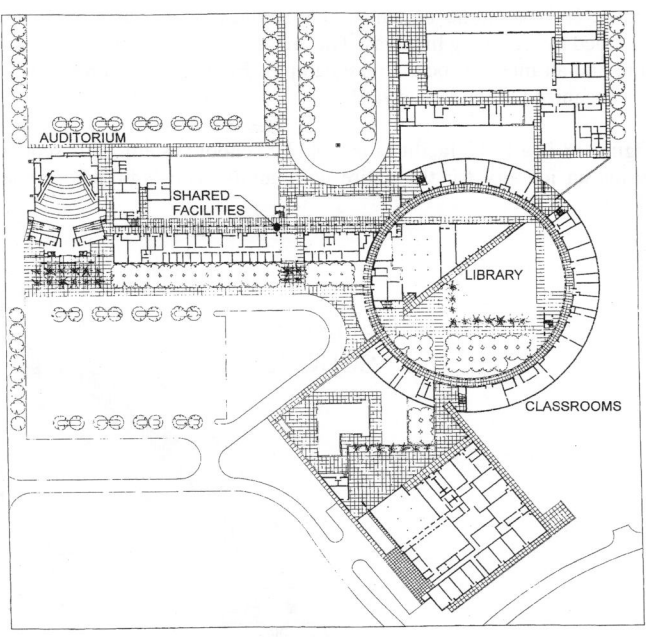

Fig. 14. High school addition

## International Schools and K-12 Campus Facilities

International schools are generally organized into K-12 facilities and provide a community structure for families and students who attend the school. Figure 15 shows an international school with a clear organizational structure. Shared community facilities can be accessed separately from academic areas. Each school within the campus maintains an individual identity while being directly connected to shared areas.

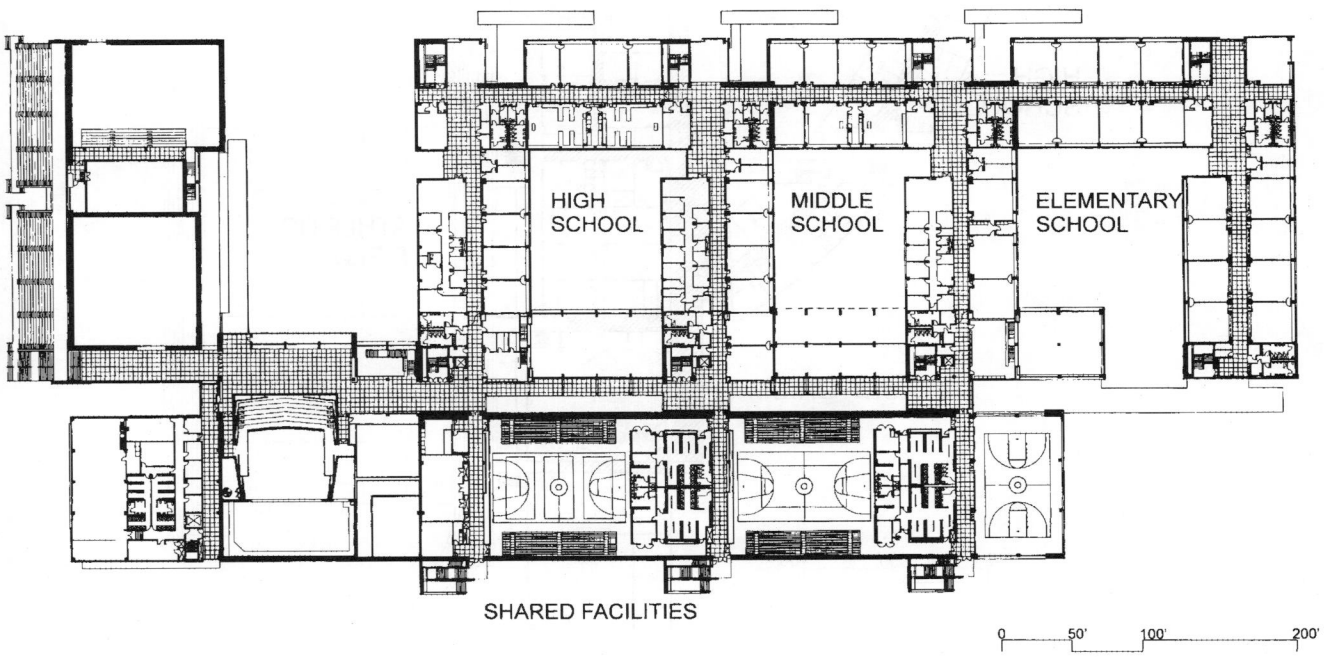

Fig. 15. International school with organizational structure

Figure 16 is a similar organizational strategy on a constrained site, bounded by a curving highway. The arc of the school provides enclosure and an internal focus to the campus. Figure 17 is a linear campus organized around courtyards.

Figure 18 is a K-12 facility for a public school system. This school forms an identity for the entire community. The high school and community buildings are connected to the middle school and elementary school with a bridge spanning a stream. The theater provides a venue for school and professional performances and the physical education wing provides sports and exercise facilities for the community, Fig. 19. A vocabulary of singular and repeatable forms, Fig. 20, provides identifiable elements and organization throughout the campus, Fig. 21.

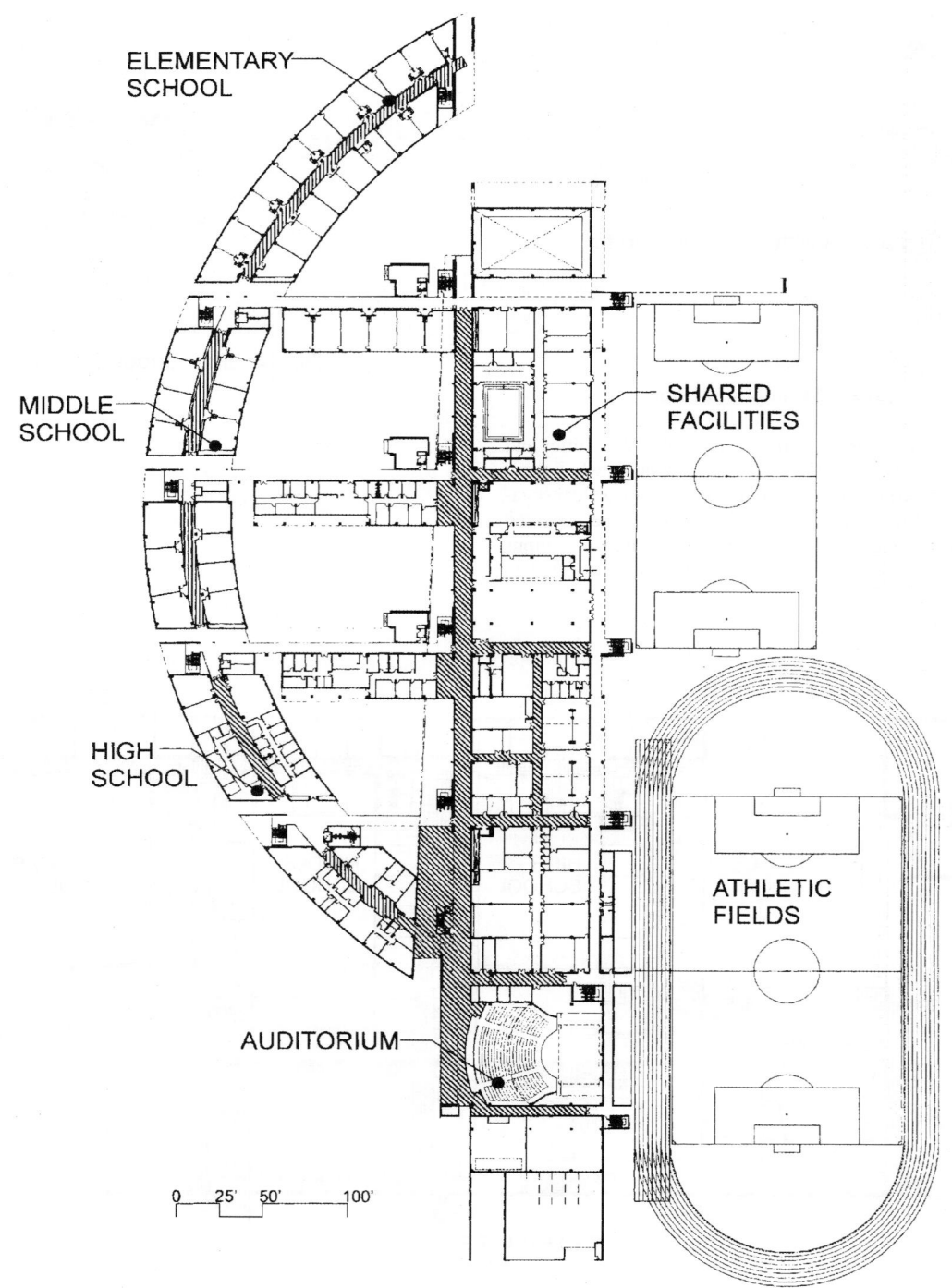

**Fig. 16. International school on a constrained site**

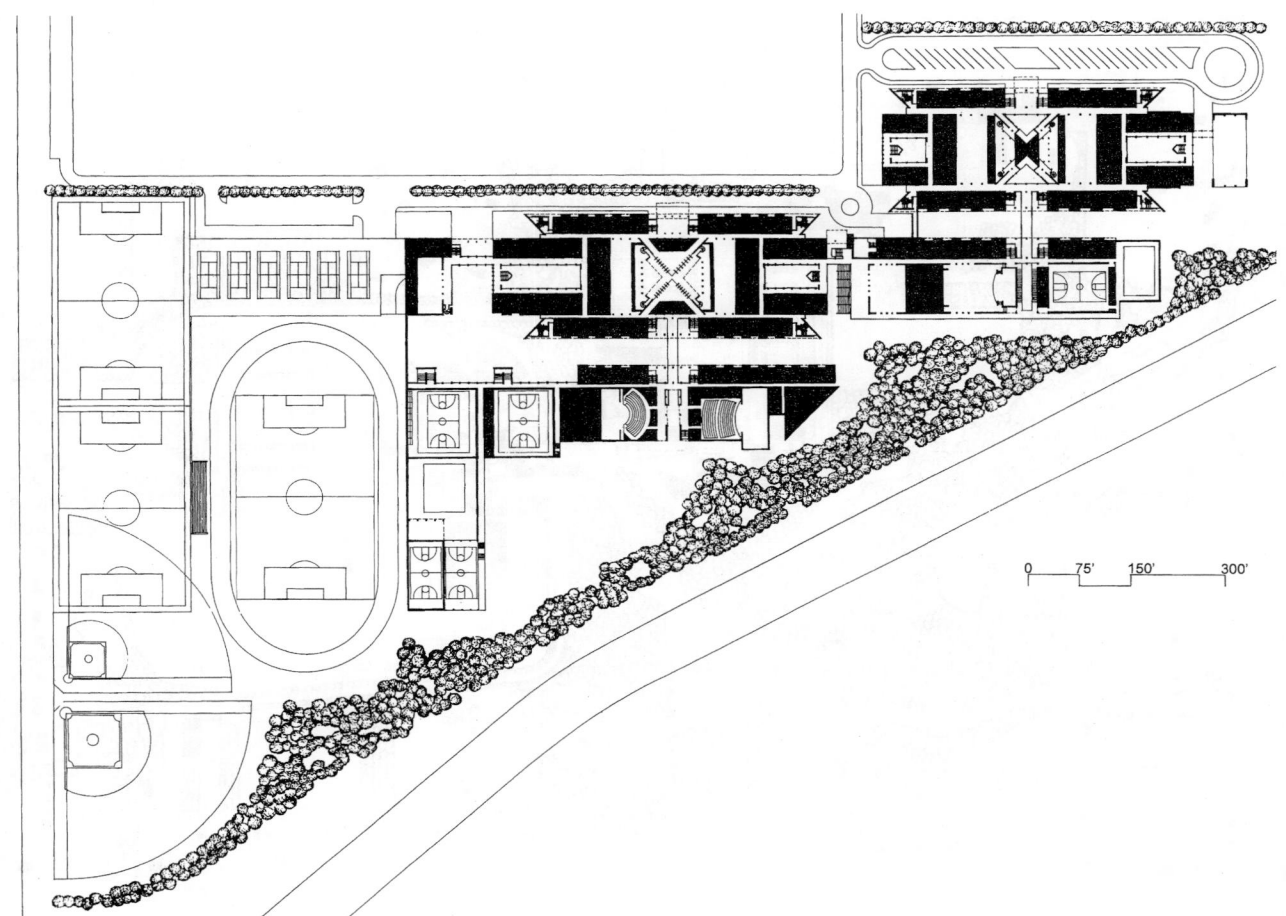

**Fig. 17. International school as linear design**

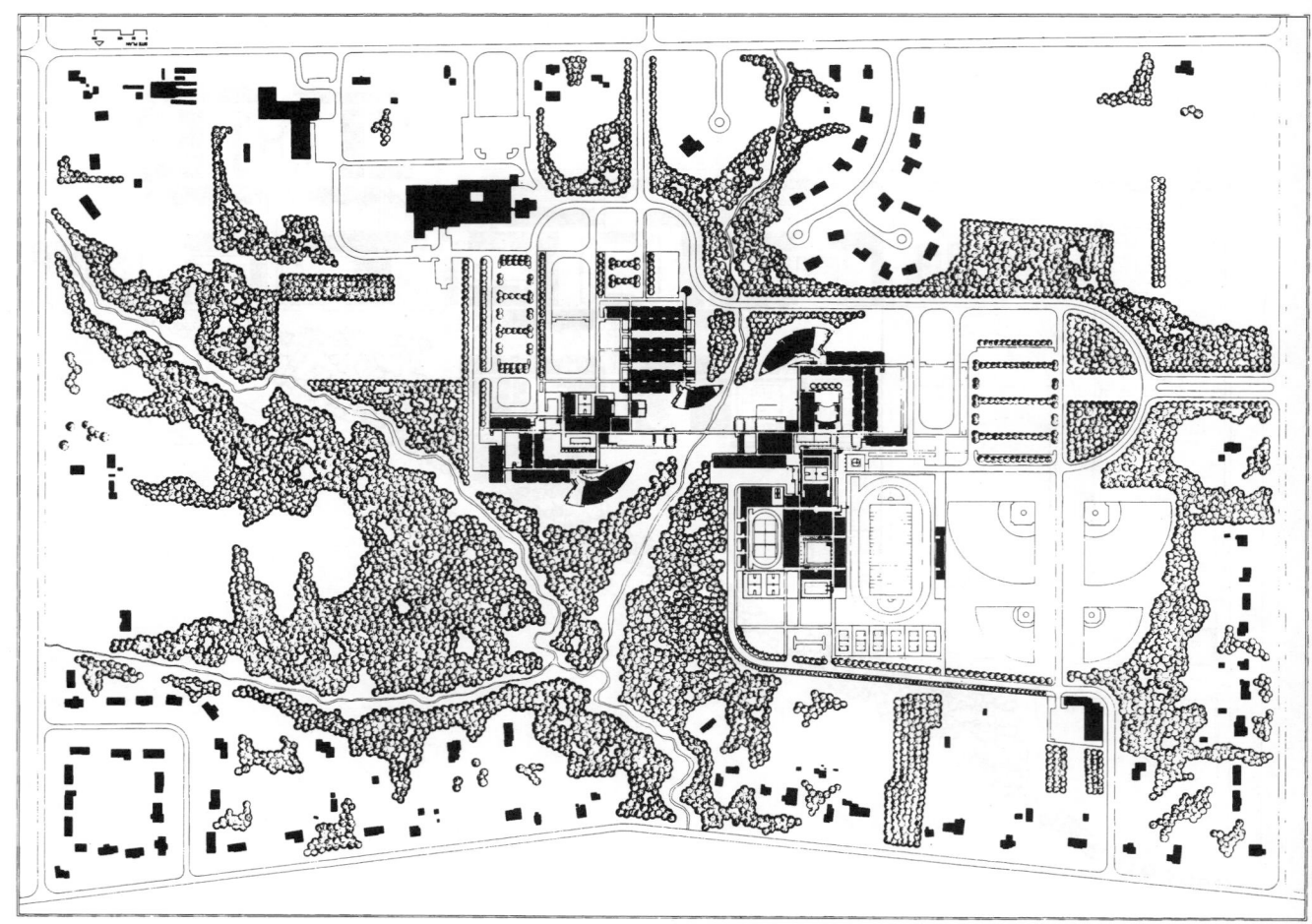

**Fig. 18. K-12 campus**

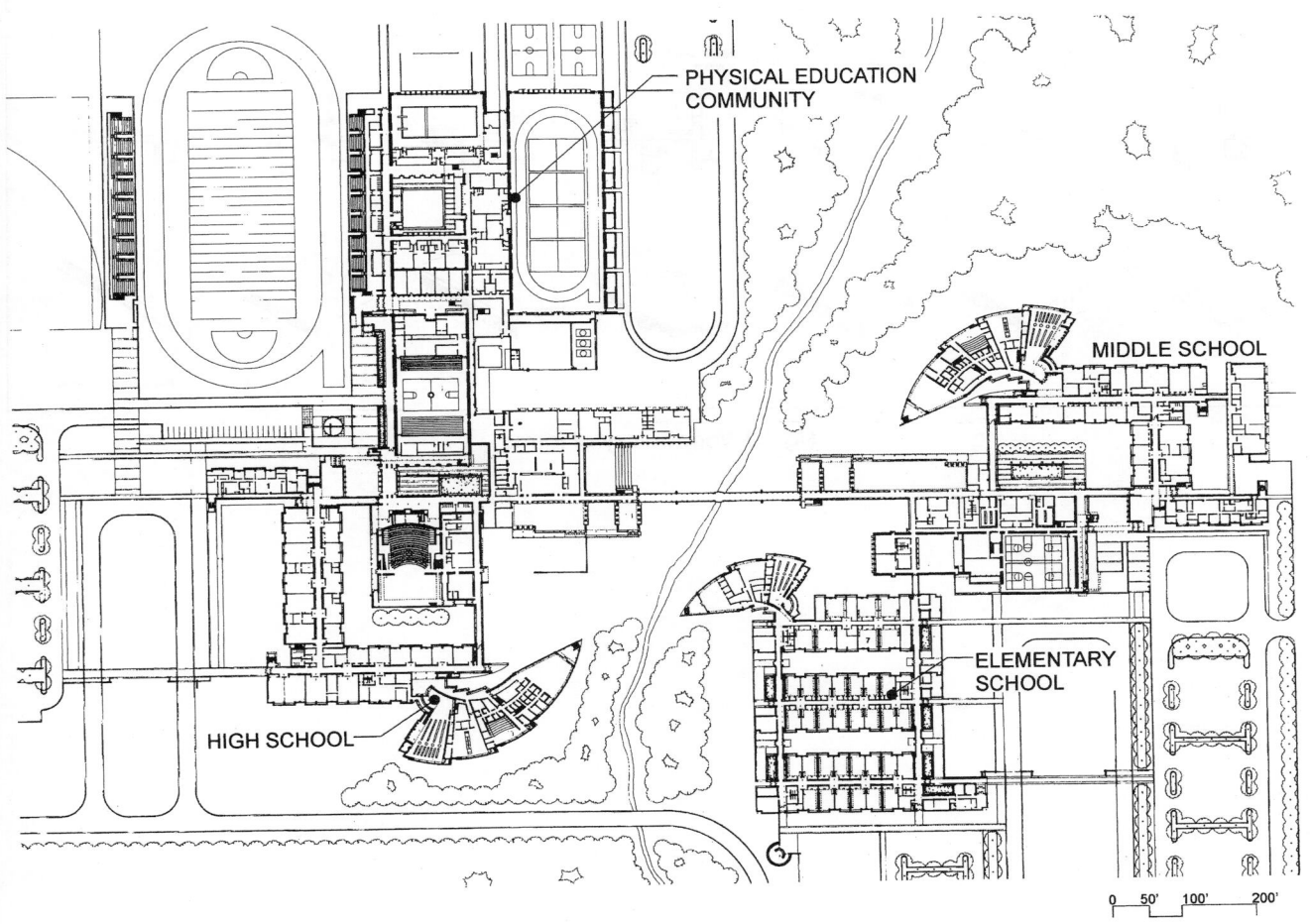

PHYSICAL EDUCATION
COMMUNITY

MIDDLE SCHOOL

ELEMENTARY
SCHOOL

HIGH SCHOOL

0  50'  100'  200'

**Fig. 19. Campus plan**

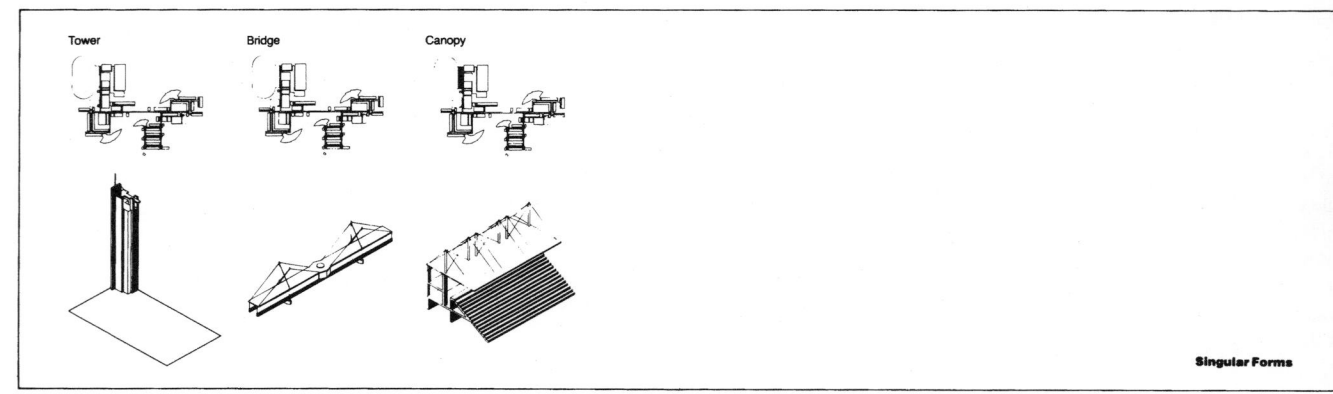

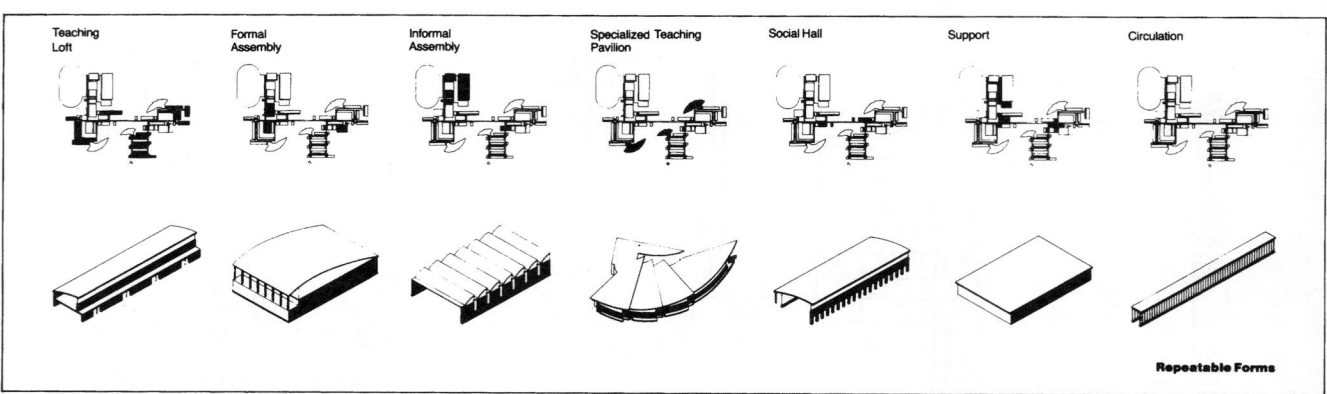

Fig. 20. Vocabulary of forms

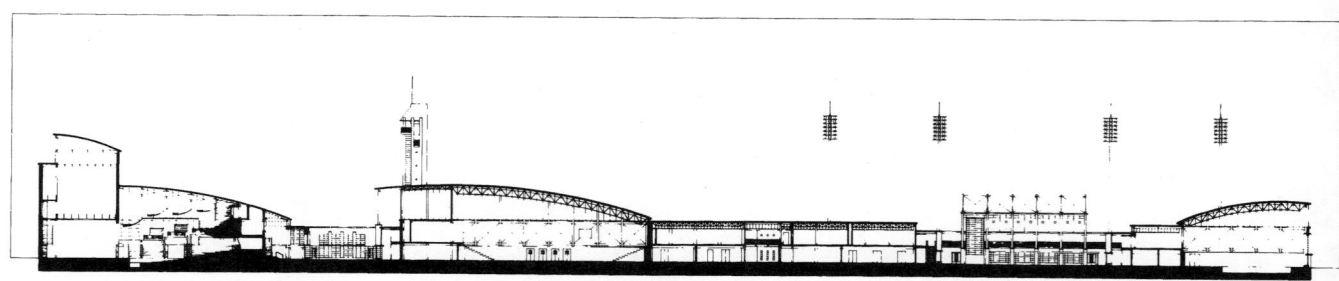

Fig. 21. School section

# SITE DESIGN

## Site Selection

The farsighted school board will project its needs well into the future and select and acquire sites while land is still available and cheap. Such prudent long-range planning is facilitated by consultation with local county or regional planning agencies that possess knowledge and appreciation of the long-term system needs and growth patterns on community development. Frequently, large-scale development builders can be persuaded to dedicate land to community purposes well in advance of need with consequent savings to taxpayers. The following is a list of basic items for use in the selection of a school site.

- *Present and future environment:* Economic, social, and housing makeup of community.
- *Integration with community planning:* Potential housing expansion relative to size, need, and location. Zoning requirements, limitations or restrictions.
- *Role in comprehensive school building plan.* Relationship to high schools and other elementary schools in same district (township, county, or community)
- *Site characteristics:* Site location—urban, suburban, or rural (determines demand for minimum and maximum space required); percent of usability of site for building, recreation and playfields, parking, roads, and services; soil conditions—water table, flood plan, adjacent watersheds, and suitable materials for structural applications
- *Utility service:* Utilities—availability and cost of electrical service, sanitary service (if none, feasibility of sewage treatment plant or septic tank); initial cost of land versus cost of land versus cost of improvements

## Space Allocation

Studies should incorporate all the elements and spaces required by the total developed program. In addition, any limitations, which may be caused by specific site conditions, should be noted.

## Relationships

The relationships of these proposed site elements and spaces to each other and to the site are best developed visually as diagrammatic studies such as those shown in Figs. 22 to 24.

## Circulation

Circulation patterns are continuous from the points of access at property lines to and through the buildings and must be designed as integrated systems. Safety is important, particularly for lower age groups. For safe and efficient movement, separate each different type of circulation. Eliminate or minimize cross traffic between pedestrians and vehicles. Separate drop-off facilities for buses and automobiles. Service vehicles should be excluded from these drop-off areas; if this is not possible, use of service areas should be permitted only at times when pedestrians are not present.

- *Vehicular/Automobile:* Differentiate and provide for the three types of automobile traffic normally found on a school site: faculty, student, and visitor or parent.

- *Vehicular/Bus:* Give careful consideration to number, loading and unloading areas, site access, and storage of vehicles. Plan so that the backing up of buses is never necessary.

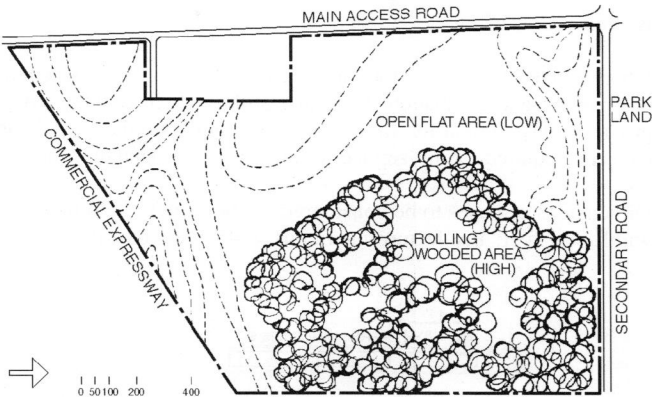

**Fig. 22. Site analysis**

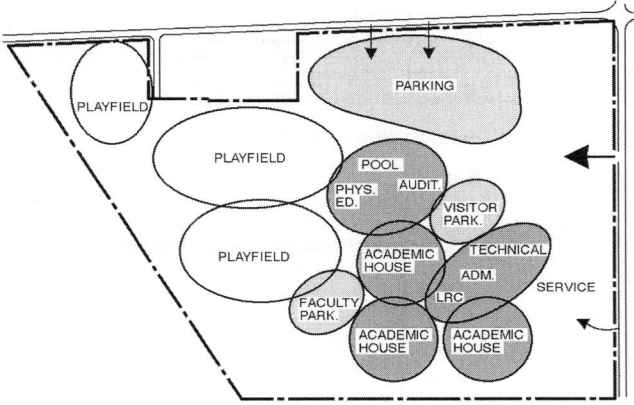

**Fig. 23. Land use diagram**

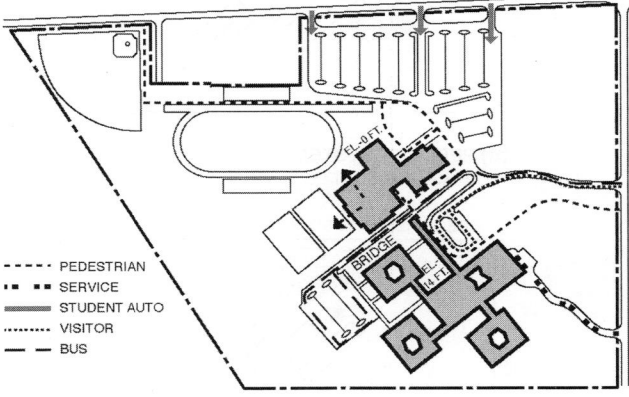

**Fig. 24. Site circulation program**

*Reviewer:* Michael Palmer, AIA, Perkins and Will, Architects

- *Vehicular/Service:* Service-vehicle access and loading and unloading areas should permit as short and direct an approach as possible with adequate maneuvering space. Service areas and access should be separate from other circulation systems.

**Busing**

Figures 25 to 28 represent four approaches to developing a system of bus parking and circulation. Presently, 36 buses will be required to provide transportation for 1,800 students to and from the school site (site area required for this service is significant—see land use studies).

Dimensions of buses to be considered are bus length = 36 feet; bus width = 8 feet; inside turning radius = 45 feet; outside turning

radius = 60 feet.; typical stall size = 12 feet x 14 feet. Buses should not be required to back up (Table 2).

**Pedestrians**

Safety is most important. Walkways of all-weather, nonskid materials, well delineated and arranged to eliminate or minimize conflict with vehicle circulation can be both safe and pleasant. Where

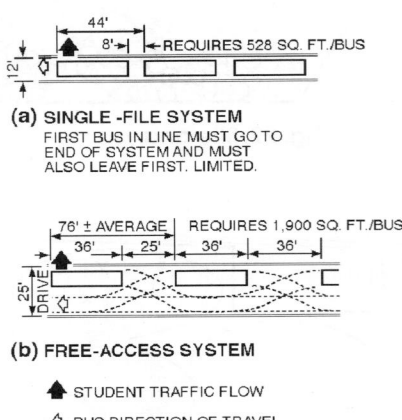

Fig. 25. Parallel bus parking system

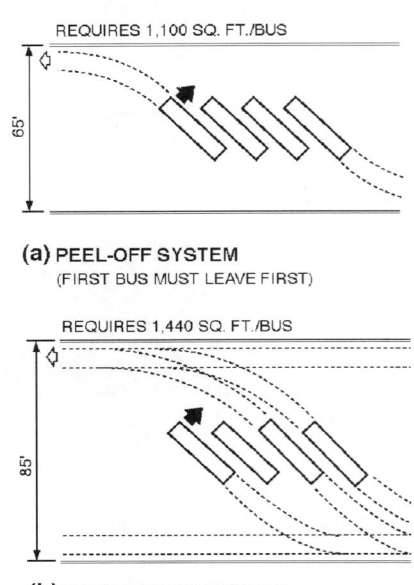

Fig. 27. 45-degree bus parking system

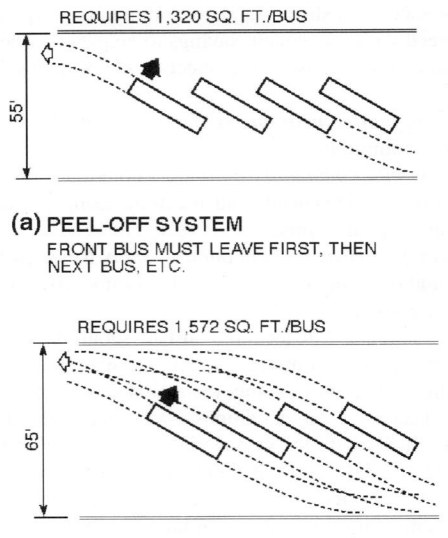

Fig. 26. 30-degree bus parking system

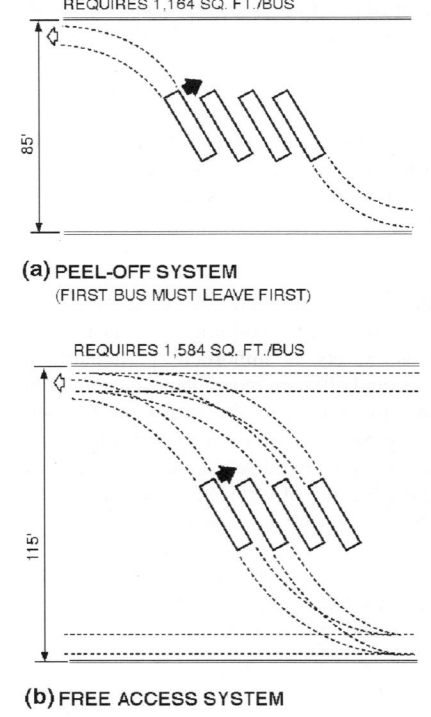

Fig. 28. 60-degree bus parking system

**Table 2**  Comparison of busing study data

|  | Minimum width required | Linear feet required (for 36 buses) | Area required per bus (includes circulation) sq ft* |
|---|---|---|---|
| Parallel single file | 12 ft | 1,584 | 528 |
| Parallel free access | 25 ft | 2,736 | 1,900 |
| 30° peel-off | 55 ft | 860 | 1,320 |
| 30° free access | 65 ft | 860 | 1,572 |
| 45° peel-off | 65 ft | 620 | 1,100 |
| 45° free access | 85 ft | 620 | 1,440 |
| 60° peel-off | 85 ft | 510 | 1,164 |
| 60° free access | 115 ft | 510 | 1,584 |

*Data are approximate.

hanges in grade are necessary, a ramp is generally preferred to steps nd the incline should not exceed 5 percent, especially where snow nd ice are expected and to meet accessibility requirements.

**Parking**

There is usually merit in separation of the three types of automobile parking, with the daytime visitor taking precedence over faculty and student. Parking facilities should be located to consider all their uses, including daytime uses for visitor, parent, faculty, or student, uses for school-related or community events within the school building, and uses relating to various outdoor athletic events. Overflow parking areas may double as paved play areas when properly designed and located.

Access to parking facilities and arrangement of parking lanes should minimize conflict between automobile and pedestrian. Collector walks should be provided and arranged to permit pedestrians to exit vehicle areas as directly as possible.

**RECREATION FACILITIES**

These criteria for recreation areas, such as relation to adjacent property, soil stability, and percolation, existing vegetation, existing topography, etc., are important; however, special attention should be given to the need for large open spaces for field games with adjacent existing vegetation to provide shade, fresh air, and windbreak. In dense urban areas, where ordinary open spaces are scarce, such field facilities can be created on air rights, rooftops, and terraced slopes. Informal play areas, especially for the lower grades, can be created in multilevel arrangements conforming to a steep site; this is not possible with field recreation facilities for the contact sports enjoyed by upper grades. Superimposition of layouts and multiuse helps conserve space when land is at a premium.

**Recreational Facility Layout**

In creating a unique layout for a site, consider these factors:

- Optimum orientation for sun and wind
- Circulation for players and spectators
- Buffer zones between action spaces
- Access from showers, classrooms, student and spectator parking, and buses

- Access from community where multiuse is possible
- Flexibility of layout and accommodation of staging or building expansion
- Programming of play and learning experiences for younger children
- Supervision and safety
- Compatibility of age groups, sexes, and type of activity in contiguous play areas
- Grading and slope for drainage (or underdrainage)
- Existing relationship to nearby community facilities
- Need for balance of action spaces with provision of quiet open spaces
- Fencing

Suggested facilities according to age group and grade:

- *Kindergarten to third grade:* Slides and tunnels, swings, enclosed "forts," climbers and steppers, hopscotch, four-square, kickball.
- *Fourth to seventh grades:* Climbers and jungle gyms, informal group games, little league ball, softball, soccer, basketball, adventure playgrounds.
- *Eighth to twelfth grades:* Softball, baseball, football, touch football, soccer, basketball, volleyball, tennis, track and field events, physical fitness workout course.

**Materials**

Effect of low-maintenance synthetic surfacing and structural materials is significant. Their increased durability under intensive use makes multiuse and community use feasible. All-weather surfaces maximize use; cleaning by hosing, vacuum, and snow blower minimize maintenance. Durable yet flexible play surfaces allow use in cold or wet weather without injury to surface or players. Regrading, reseeding, fertilizing, aerating, spraying, mowing, and weeding are eliminated; however, durability of synthetic surfaces relative to the local climate must be fully investigated prior to any recommendation to the client.

**Drainage**

Proper storm drainage is essential to successful school-site facilities in most areas of the country. Not only do the function and longevity of many facilities and materials depend on good drainage, but also in some cases permanent damage may result from water. Surface and subsurface systems or combinations should be designed to adequately handle the needs of buildings and site facilities. Where possible, an overland emergency system should be incorporated, using the relative grade elevations of the site. When circumstances do not permit this, a standby system of pumps or power generators is recommended. Coordination with the requirements of the local authorities is also very important.

**Planting**

Select materials indigenous to the area where possible, and supplement with ornamental materials that possess special characteristics not obtainable with local materials. Plant materials should also have low maintenance requirements and be compatible with existing growing conditions. Plant material for school sites generally consists of shade trees, ornamental trees, evergreen trees and shrubs, deciduous shrubs, and ground covers. Though some of the ground-covering material on most school sites functionally is mowed grass, this material remains one of the highest maintenance types. It is recommended that its use is kept to the necessary minimum and the use of meadow and prairie grasses and other types of ground-covering materials are considered. This is particularly important on sites where appropriate ground cover material exists and should be carefully preserved. Select plant material on the basis of its mature size and character to minimize excessive shearing and early replacement. Initial sizes should not be less than a reasonable minimum to ensure survival from injury or damage by students and other causes. In addition to providing an aesthetic contribution plant material on the school site can be used to solve many problems such as windbreaks, screens and buffers, sound dampers, sun and light controls, erosion control, and air purification. Security issues should be considered when selecting locations of trees and shrubs; for example, plant material should not create hiding places or dark areas.

**ADMINISTRATIVE SUITES**

The administrative space for a school, whether a single office for a principal and an assistant or a series of offices for a large high school, functions as the control center for the school and as a contact point for parents, students, and faculty members. Here the school records are kept and reviewed, the public address system originates, budgets are established, books are kept, and students are counseled. The office is a first contact point, a crossroads checkpoint and is most always placed near the main entrance.

In order to control access into the school building, visual contact between the office and the main entrance is necessary. Some administration offices share a common vestibule with the main school entrance, routing visitors through the office prior to having full access into the building. In some schools, an information desk is located in the entry lobby as a central point for visitors to register. Other administration suites have small security cameras and speakers located at the entry, allowing voice communication and visual contact by the receptionist.

The administration suite contains groups of offices, conference rooms, work rooms, storage rooms, and sometimes a money vault. Figure 29

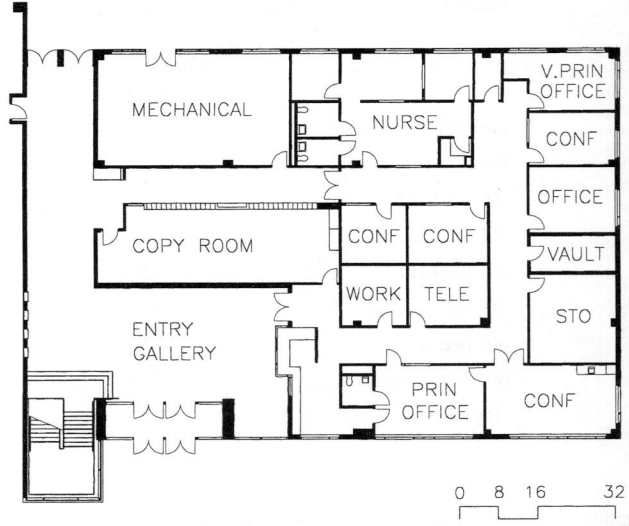

**Fig. 29. High school administration suite**

shows a typical office suite for a high school. Figure 30 shows an elementary school suite, with a large professional development space for teachers and a close proximity to the media director. Figure 31 shows a simple administration suite for a middle school within a K-12 campus.

Figures 32a and 32b are details for faculty mailboxes, allowing service from one side and access from the other. Staff mailboxes can also

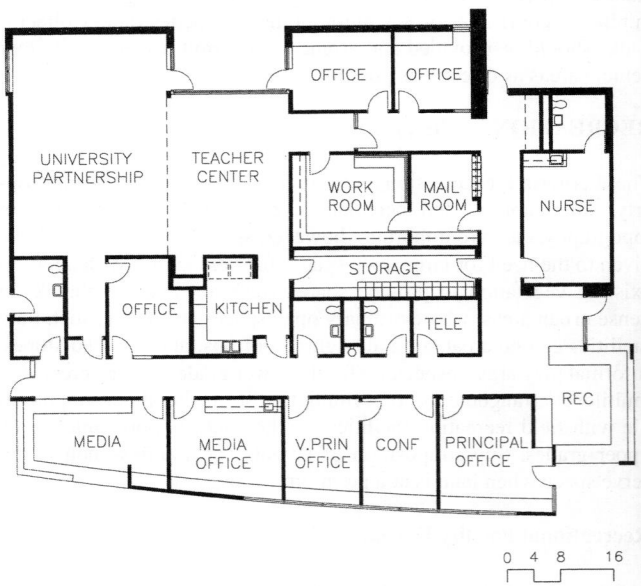

**Fig. 30. Elementary school administration suite**

*Reviewer:* Peter Brown, Perkins and Will, Architects

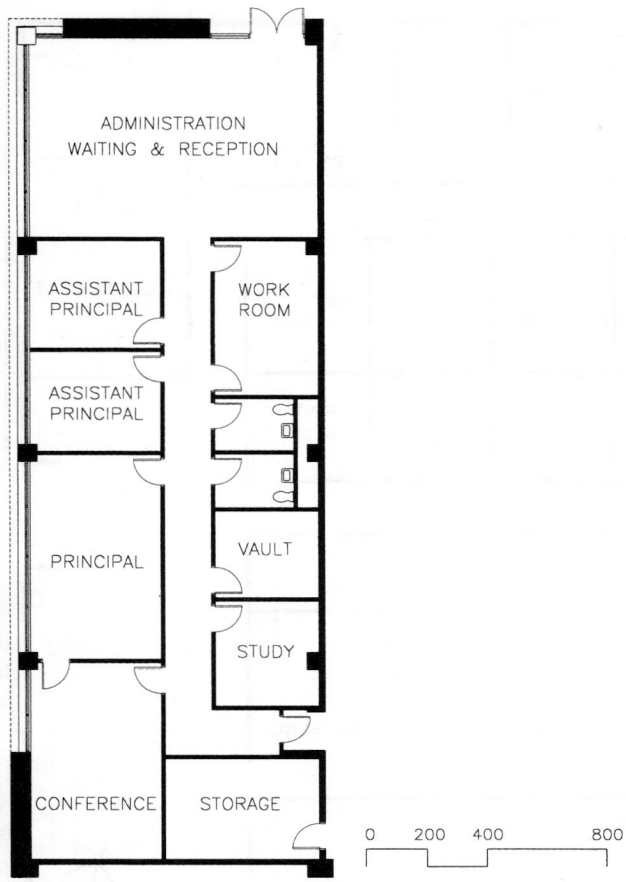

**Fig. 31. Middle school administration suite**

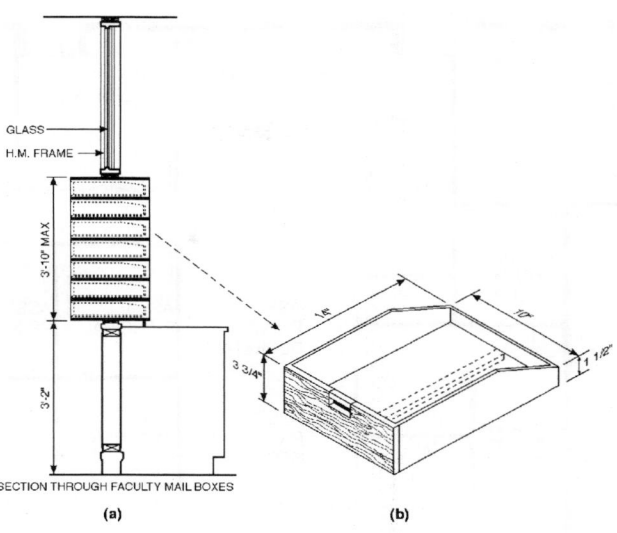

**Fig. 32. Faculty mailboxes:**
**(*a*) section, (*b*) detail**

be specified as a postal specialty product, similar to those used at a post office. Mailboxes should be private, easily accessible, and large enough to hold large mail, magazines, and publications.

In school planning, the floor area for office use is carefully allocated in relation to other program spaces. School districts generally choose to maximize educational spaces while minimizing offices. Careful planning and choice of efficient equipment are especially important. Although minimums are almost invariably exercised, common sense should be used in creating an effective office suite.

## STUDENT SERVICES OFFICE

In large schools, the administrative functions are separated from student support functions. The plan in Fig. 33 shows a high school student services office adjacent to the administration suite, while Fig. 34 is a student services suite separate from the main office area. The student service suite provides a central location within the school for career guidance, student records, student identification, speech and social workers, and special testing facilities. Some schools place truancy and discipline personnel within the student services suite.

### Reception Area

The reception area is provided as a waiting area and as an informal resource area. This room should provide space for a secretary, a receptionist and for one student for each counselor available. In addition, there should be waiting space for 3-4 people. In order to provide a smooth flow of traffic, and to minimize possible embarrassment to those students who appear to have experienced an emotional disturbance during the counseling interview, exits should be provided other than through the reception area.

*Reviewer:* Peter Brown, Perkins and Will, Architects
*Reference: Physical Facilities for School Guidance Services.* Office of Education, Dept. of Health, Education, and Welfare, Washington.

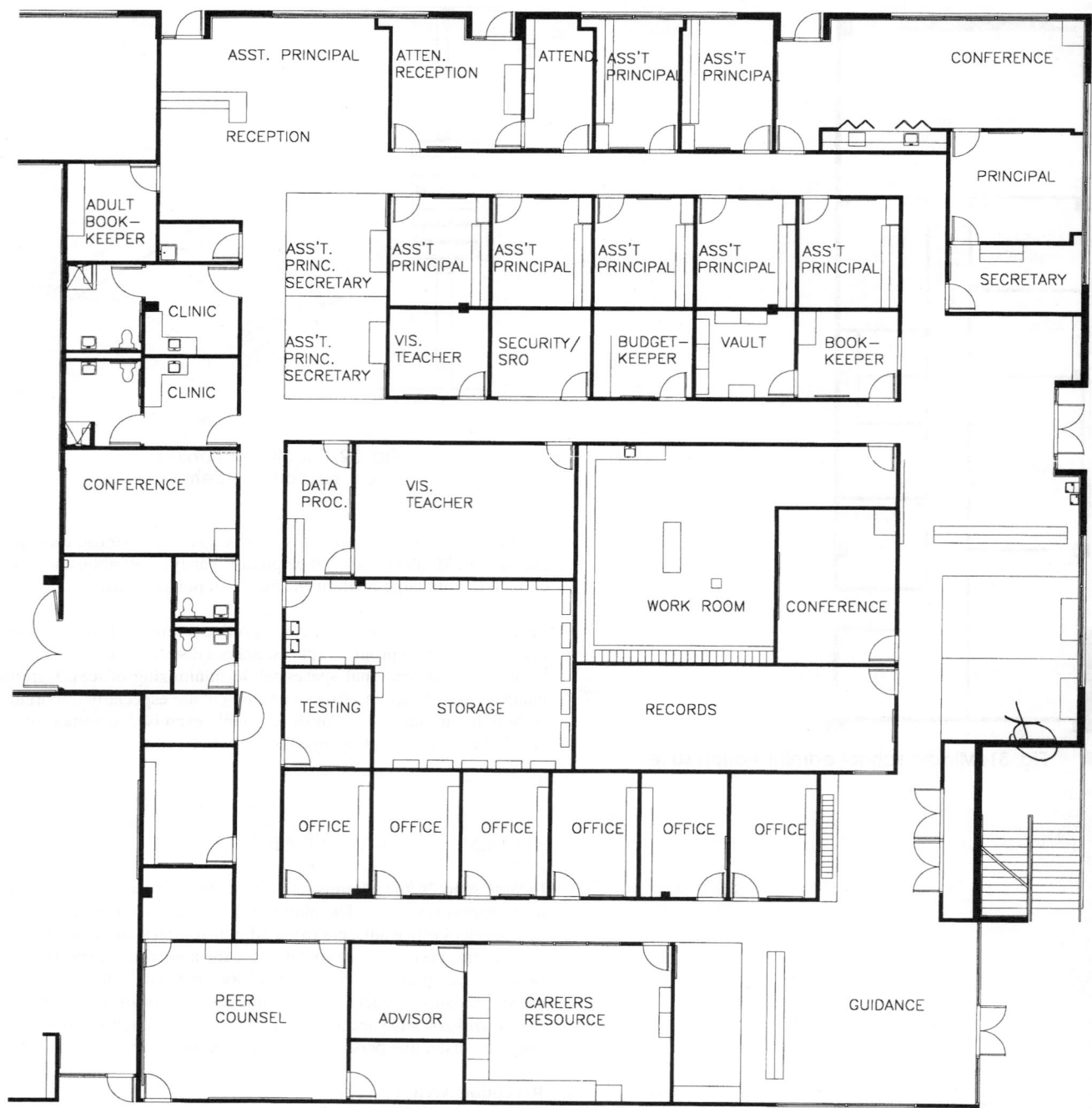

**Fig. 33. Student services and administration**

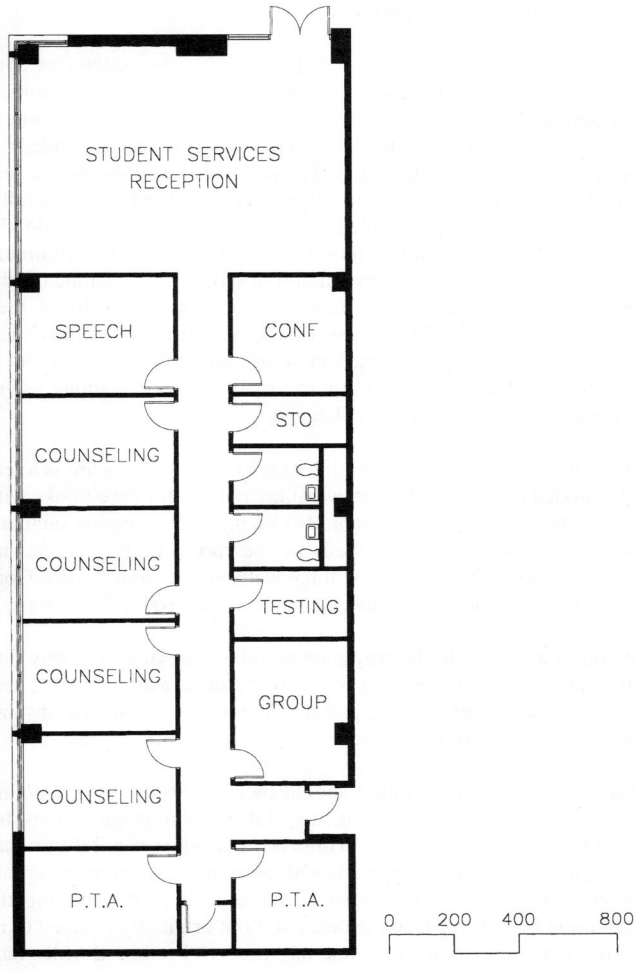

**Fig. 34. Student services**

## Counselors' Offices

The counselor's office should provide desk space for a counselor and two to three side chairs for a student, and others who may attend a conference, such as a teacher, a parent or another professional worker. Since student conferences are regarded as confidential, the office should offer privacy, and be reasonably soundproof. The use of partial partitions is not satisfactory. The door into the room should have a vision glass pane and be equipped with a call button.

## Location Guidelines

The location of the student service facilities should be:

- Near the administrative offices for convenient access to personnel records and certain clerical services.
- Entered directly from corridor, with separate exits from counseling area, if possible.
- Accessible to students and should be near the main flow of student traffic to facilitate contact, scheduling, and communication.
- Accessible from a main entrance for the benefit of parents and representatives of community agencies.
- Reasonably near to related personnel services, such as pupil accounting, health, and psychological services.
- Reasonably near to the library for convenience in use of display and reference materials.

## Space Guidelines

The guidance unit should provide the following amenities:

- Attractive and comfortable reception areas with appropriate reading materials to encourage profitable use of waiting time.
- Private counseling rooms or offices.
- Conference room for such uses as case conferences; individual testing; special staff personnel such as the school nurse, visiting teacher, speech therapist; interviewing by prospective employers and representatives of institutions of higher learning.
- Multipurpose room adjacent to counseling offices for group testing, group procedures, and in-service training activities.

## CLASSROOMS

### Classroom Planning

Changes in the teaching/learning process, extension of classroom activities, and use of group techniques within the classroom have led to new classroom design in recent years. Classrooms that are generally more square in proportion are proving more satisfactory than rectangular ones for small group work and video viewing. The area of the classroom is increasing with the realization that small classrooms of the past have had a large impact on limited future use of classroom space. Today's classrooms are expected to delivery flexibility in a variety of ways. On any given day or any period during the day, the classroom might be arranged to accommodate:

- Small group teams
- Large group lectures
- Use of a wide range of technologies
- Large digital projection
- Television viewing
- Different subjects being studied (is it a math room or an English room? Probably both)

### General Requirements for All Classrooms

In accommodating these required flexibilities, careful attention to a wide range of details is necessary. Here are a few considerations:

*Electrical and Data Access*

Providing sufficient electrical and data port locations so as to not restrict the opportunity to move computers and equipment around the room. When possible a few locations in the floor can offer increased arrangement options. Locate the clock (minimum 8-inch-diameter analogue type clock for elementary, large display digital read for middle and high school), and PA speaker away from areas that can be obstructed by projection screens or other equipment. Telephone should be located near the classroom entry door.

*Air Conditioning and Ventilation*

School use for extended days and year-round make cooling more a necessity than an option. Mechanical ventilation is almost always a requirement. Operable windows provide a connection to the outdoors and offer flexibility in the learning environment. In addition, some codes require classroom windows to serve as emergency escapes.

*Lighting*

Lighting can and should be used to help create a variety of instructional settings. Two levels of lighting controls allow a "dimming" effect for video viewing and other low-light activities. Indirect lighting reduces eyestrain and glare for computer use. Natural lighting reduces lighting costs, while darkening curtains or "black-out" shades help control light and heat gain. Consideration should be given to light control clerestories, skylights, and other sources of light; shades that ride in side channels are usually easier to operate and to maintain than other blinds. Classroom light switches should be located at the door. Switches for corridor lighting should be located so that pupils do not have access to them.

*White Boards and Tack Surfaces*

Chalkboards are rapidly being replaced across the country as concerns about environmental safety and the interference with computers continue to mount. White boards and tack surfaces on a minimum of two contiguous walls (three when possible) are recommended for seating and grouping flexibility. The demands for white boards and tack board vary from subject to subject in the high school. Generally, English and mathematics require more white boards than do the social studies, which in turn require more tack board. The minimum amount of white boards in any classroom should be determined in the programming phase but is generally never less than 16 linear feet, and could be up to 48 linear feet in classrooms used for mathematics. Approximately 16 to 32 linear feet of tack board should be provided. By arriving at a common minimum for all classrooms, future use of the individual rooms will be enhanced.

A display rail extending the entire length of the white board is a recommended teaching aid. Such a display rail should have hooks with clip fasteners. Provisions might also be made for hanging pictures, maps, and charts on other walls of the room. Embedded picture molding should be installed on three walls at a suitable height. Consider designing display cabinets to serve as classroom showcases.

Products available in the corporate world are making their way into the classroom. Wall covering products available with magnetic, projection, and marker surfaces provide continuous writing and display walls over an entire wall surface.

For each room consideration should be given to the type, amount, height, and necessary attachments. Table 3 offers guidelines for working heights of children. However, current accessibility codes and guidelines should be reviewed prior to specifying mounting heights. Flexibility should also be considered in determining the mounting heights of fixed elements; a room originally planned to be a first grade classroom may one day need to become a fifth grade room.

*Projection Equipment*

In the last 10 years video projection and large screen televisions have become common in classrooms. As networks continue toward all digital systems, provision for digital projection should be considered, either ceiling mounted or portable units are both options. This projection device requires both power and a data connection so consider the location carefully when planning the classroom.

### Doors

Doors should be placed at the front of the classroom and should be recessed so that they do not protrude into the corridor. Thresholds should be avoided so that equipment on wheeled tables, such as mounted video projectors and televisions, can be rolled in and out easily. All doors should have a vision panel of code approved tempered or wire glass. Door hardware should be such that doors cannot be locked from inside the classroom.

### Acoustic and Visual Control

Acoustic and visual control from outside sources includes:

*Authors:* Raymond C. Bordwell, AIA, and Peter Brown, Perkins and Will, Architects

**Table 3**  Working height guidelines (inches) for K-12 students

| Item | Elementary Kindergarten Min. | Opti-mum | Max. | Grades 1-3 Min. | Opti-mum | Max. | Grades 4-6 Min. | Opti-mum | Max. | Junior high Grades 7-9 Min. | Opti-mum | Max. | Senior high Grades 10-12 Min. | Opti-mum | Max. |
|---|---|---|---|---|---|---|---|---|---|---|---|---|---|---|---|
| Cabinet, display (top) | | 54 | | | 56 | | | 66 | | | 74 | | | 77 | |
| Cabinet, display (bottom) | | 26 | | | 29 | | | 34 | | | 38 | | | 39 | |
| Cabinet, pupil use (top) | | | 50 | | | 56 | | | 65 | | | 74 | | | 79 |
| Chairs and bench | 10 | 11 | 11 | 10 | 12 | 13 | 12 | 14 | 16 | 13 | 15 | 17 | 14 | 16 | 18 |
| Chalkboard (top) | 68 | 70 | 73 | 72 | 73 | 74 | 76 | 77 | 78 | 79 | 80 | 82 | 80 | 82 | 84 |
| Chalkboard (bottom and chalkrail) | 20 | 22 | 25 | 24 | 25 | 26 | 28 | 29 | 30 | 31 | 32 | 34 | 32 | 34 | 36 |
| Counter, cafeteria | 21 | 27 | 32 | 25 | 31 | 34 | 29 | 36 | 39 | 32 | 40 | 45 | 33 | 42 | 48 |
| Counter, classroom work (standing) | 20 | 24 | 26 | 24 | 26 | 29 | 28 | 30 | 34 | 31 | 34 | 38 | 32 | 36 | 39 |
| Counter, general office | 20 | 27 | 32 | 24 | 31 | 34 | 28 | 36 | 39 | 31 | 40 | 45 | 32 | 42 | 49 |
| Desk and table, classroom | 17 | 18 | 19 | 18 | 20 | 22 | 21 | 23 | 25 | 23 | 26 | 28 | 24 | 27 | 29 |
| Desk, typing | | | | | | | | | | | 26 | | | 26 | |
| Door knob | 19 | 27 | 32 | 24 | 31 | 35 | 28 | 36 | 40 | 30 | 40 | 46 | 31 | 42 | 49 |
| Drinking fountain | 20 | 24 | 27 | 24 | 27 | 29 | 28 | 32 | 34 | 32 | 36 | 40 | 32 | 40 | 44 |
| Fire extinguisher (tank)* | | | | | | | | | | | | | | | |
| Hook, coat | 32 | 36 | 48 | 38 | 41 | 51 | 47 | 48 | 58 | 53 | 54 | 64 | 54 | 55 | 68 |
| Lavatory and sink | 20 | 23 | 25 | 24 | 26 | 27 | 28 | 29 | 31 | 32 | 33 | 35 | 32 | 35 | 38 |
| Light switch | 27 | 27 | 46 | 31 | 35 | 49 | 36 | 40 | 56 | 40 | 46 | 64 | 42 | 50 | 68 |
| Mirror, lower edge | | | 35 | | | 38 | | | 43 | | | 48 | | | 52 |
| Mirror, upper edge | 46 | | | 56 | | | 65 | | | 71 | | | 71 | | |
| Panic bar | 21 | 27 | 32 | 25 | 31 | 34 | 29 | 36 | 39 | 32 | 40 | 45 | 33 | 42 | 48 |
| Pencil sharpener | 20 | 27 | 33 | 25 | 31 | 35 | 28 | 36 | 40 | 32 | 40 | 46 | 32 | 42 | 49 |
| Rail, hand and directional | 20 | 21 | 32 | 24 | 24 | 34 | 28 | 29 | 39 | 31 | 32 | 45 | 32 | 33 | 48 |
| Shelf, hat and books | | 41 | 48 | | 46 | 51 | | 54 | 58 | | 60 | 64 | | 62 | 68 |
| Soap dispenser | 20 | 27 | 33 | 25 | 31 | 35 | 28 | 36 | 40 | 32 | 40 | 46 | 32 | 42 | 49 |
| Stool, drawing | | 19 | | | 21 | | | 26 | | | 28 | | | 29 | |
| Table, drawing | | 26 | | | 29 | | | 34 | | | 38 | | | 39 | |
| Table and bench, work (standing) | 25 | 26 | 28 | 26 | 29 | 32 | 30 | 34 | 38 | 36 | 38 | 41 | 37 | 39 | 42 |
| Tackboard (top) | 72 | 84 | | 72 | 84 | | 72 | 84 | | 72 | 84 | | 72 | 84 | |
| Tackboard (bottom) | 20 | 22 | 25 | 24 | 25 | 26 | 28 | 29 | 30 | 31 | 32 | 34 | 32 | 34 | 36 |
| Telephone, wall mounted | | | 35 | | | 37 | | | 43 | | | 48 | | | 52 |
| Toilet stall, top of partition | 44 | 44 | | 52 | 52 | | 61 | 61 | | 67 | 67 | | 69 | 69 | |
| Towel dispenser | 23 | 27 | 46 | 28 | 31 | 49 | 33 | 36 | 56 | 37 | 40 | 64 | 37 | 42 | 68 |
| Urinal (bottom) | | | | 3 | 3-15 | 17 | 3 | 3-17 | 20 | 4 | 4-18 | 22 | 4 | 4-19 | 24 |
| Wainscotting | 54 | 54 | 54 | 54 | 54 | 54 | 54 | 54 | 54 | 60 | 60 | 60 | 60 | 60 | 60 |
| Water closet (seat) | 10 | 10½ | 12 | 11 | 11½ | 12 | 13 | 13½ | 14 | 14 | 14½ | 15 | 14½ | 15 | 15 |
| Window ledge | | | 29 | | | 30 | | | 34 | | | 38 | | | 41 |

*\* Recessed at baseboard height.*

- Using larger volume spaces such as gymnasiums as a "buffer," locating the classrooms from noises sources such as trains or highways.
- Orientating windows away from "visual noises" such as play-fields or roads.
- Providing surface treatments such as carpet and acoustical ceiling systems.
- Installing insulated glass.
- Depending on the size and proportion of the room, providing ceilings at a minimum of 9 feet high.

## Furniture

When it comes to flexibility furniture can be one of the biggest supporters or a great limitation. Tables and chairs that can be arranged in a variety of configurations are recommended. Testing the location of equipment within the room, allowing for multiple locations, is a good design exercise. Potential equipment includes:

- Projection equipment and screens
- Teacher/presenter computer location
- Video and media players
- Student computers
- Television monitors
- Speakers (if not permanently installed)
- Podium and "lecture" location

## CLASSROOM EXAMPLES

The classroom layouts shown below represent "standard" size rooms with a recessed corridor door and a variety of seating arrangements illustrating flexibility in seating and interior classroom circulation.

Figure 35 illustrates a traditional lecture emphasis classroom with students arranged in rows facing the front of the classroom. A variation is shown in Fig. 36, showing an arrangement for demonstrations. The same space reconfigured for team-project based learning is shown in Fig. 37, and more informally in Fig. 38.

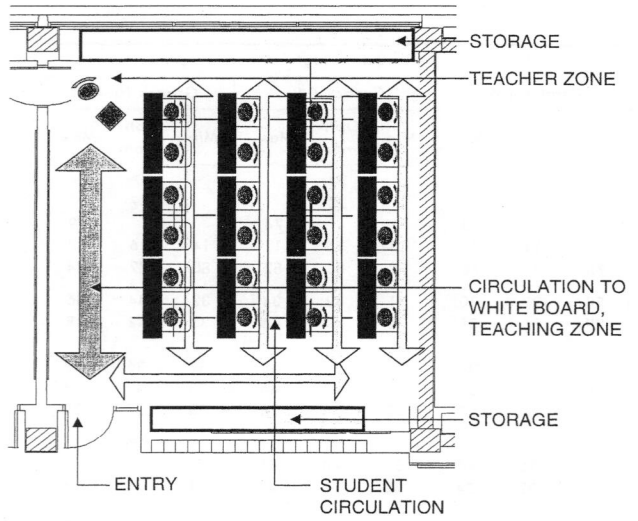

CLASSROOM CONFIGURATION STUDY

Fig. 35. Row arrangement, lecture format

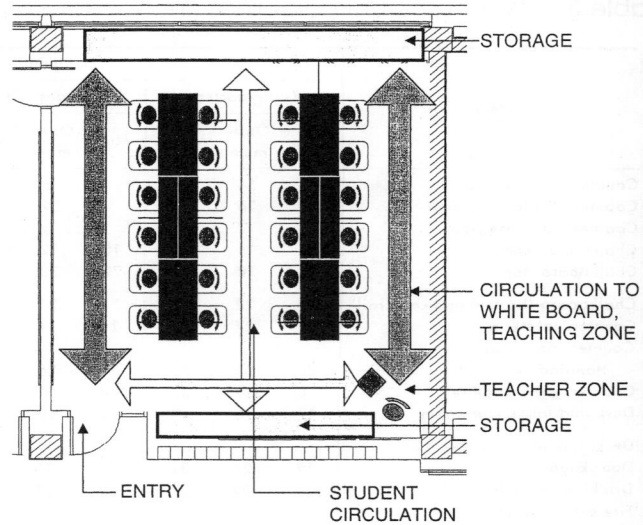

CLASSROOM CONFIGURATION STUDY

Fig. 36. Paired rows, demonstration format

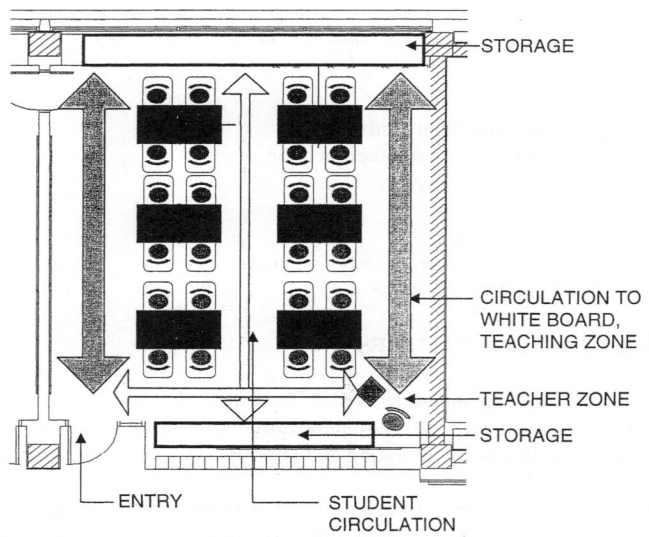

CLASSROOM CONFIGURATION STUDY

Fig. 37. Table arrangement, project teams

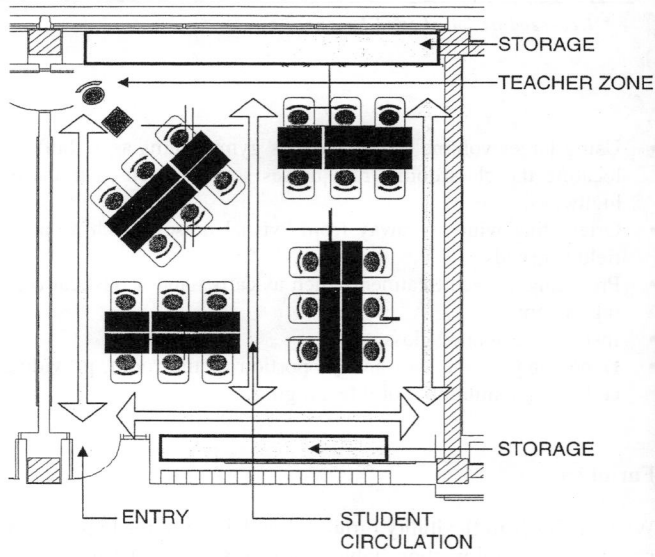

CLASSROOM CONFIGURATION STUDY

Fig. 38. Informal arrangement, project teams

# CLASSROOM FACILITIES

Recommended classroom sizes for elementary schools range from 850 to 1,150 square feet. Middle and high school classrooms may range from 750 to 900 square feet. Schools, regardless of type, that require a high degree of flexibility may provide 1,200-square-foot classrooms. As stated above, large classrooms are more adaptable in re-assigning spaces within an educational facility.

## Elementary Classroom Facilities

Elementary classrooms are much more self-contained than their middle and high school counterparts. This room requires facilities for teaching various subjects, such as English, mathematics, reading, arts and crafts, music, social studies, and science. This area is used exclusively by one group of pupils. Many schools supplement these classrooms with computer and project spaces. Other specialized spaces for music and art are also common.

A student focused elementary classroom (Fig. 39) provides spaces that support a variety of individual activity and group interaction. A large classroom area is provided for group interaction, window seats allow for small group gatherings, a workroom accommodates technology and science projects and the classroom is extended to the outdoors with a garden courtyard.

Storage requirements in elementary classrooms include such items as science projects and equipment, reference books, paints, paper, posters, maps, globes, coats, boots, audiovisual equipment, lunches, and small playground equipment. For kindergarten and primary grades, toilets and coat storage areas located in or adjacent to the classroom are convenient for the teacher to assist the smaller children. Central toilet facilities should be provided for the intermediate grades and above. Drinking fountains in or adjacent to classrooms are desirable.

Several educational activities require such facilities as sink, counter work area, portable stage, hot and cold water, earth bed, and special furniture. Provision should be made for such items in accordance with the educational program when the building is planned.

Figure 40 illustrates a classroom cluster for an elementary school. The classrooms provide similar amenities as those in Fig. 39, however the rooms have been clustered to allow the flexibility of self-contained classrooms and for team-teaching, non-graded programs, or looping. A common study resource area is provided for additional interaction.

## Middle and High School Classroom Facilities

Flexibility and adaptability for these classrooms is key. Fig. 41 diagrams standard classrooms arranged in an academic house structure. The classroom units are self-contained with access to shared project and support spaces.

In supporting this flexibility consider how storage will help accommodate a variety of uses within the classroom:

- Storage space for each group using the classroom should be provided with locks.
- Movable storage (units with wheels) can help in changing the location within a building of a particular subject by simply moving the support materials and their associated storage cabinets.
- Storage is needed for the following items: supplies, such as paper and pencils; books and magazines; special equipment for the subject taught in the room; and the teacher's coat and personal belongings, if not provided for elsewhere.
- A standard storage closet, either of metal or wood, is recommended for all classrooms.

A variation of the diagram is shown in Fig. 42. Two groups of three classrooms are arranged around a common core of storage, rest rooms, and project areas. The grouping is highly adaptable, allowing the possibility of six individual classrooms or a combination of larger, more open classrooms. Furniture is arranged to accommodate a variety of teaching methods. Storage is shown as mobile carts that help spatially define the rooms.

## Display systems outside the classroom

Tack board and display cases should be distributed throughout the school. Display of educational materials and student work will sup-

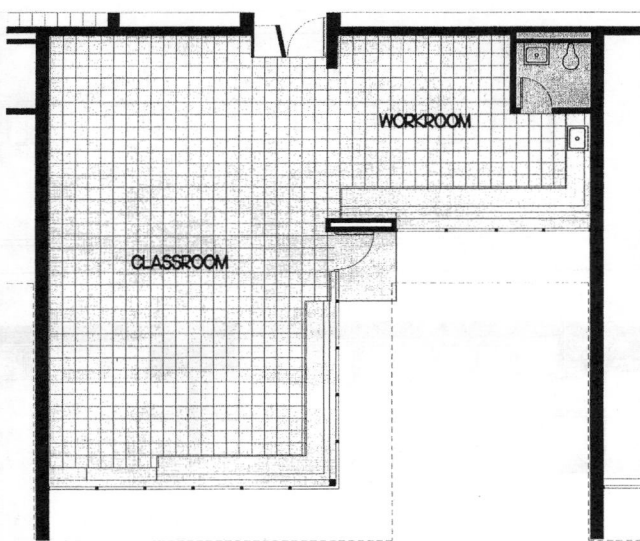

**Fig. 39. Elementary classroom**

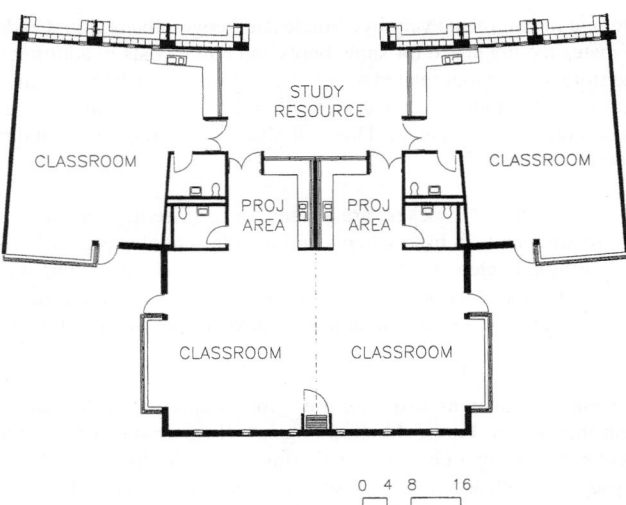

**Fig. 40. Elementary classroom cluster**

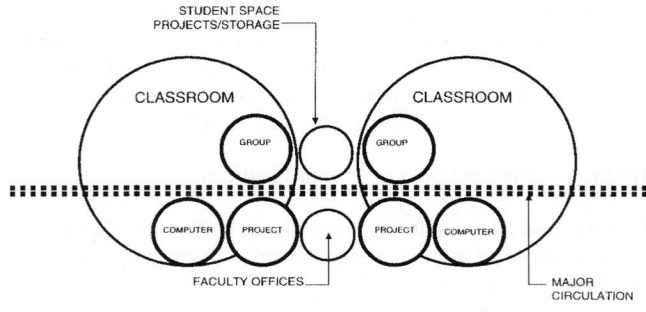

**CLASSROOM RELATIONSHIP CONCEPT**

**Fig. 41. High school / middle school house diagram**

port the educational program. Consider locating video monitors in strategic locations, near entries for example, to display student video work, recorded athletic events, live network feeds of special events, a morning "news" show produced by students or even signals from security cameras for student awareness.

*Lockers and Student Storage Space*

Many different solutions have been developed to store coats and personal belongings of students. In the elementary school, proximity to the homeroom for the purpose of teacher supervision is important. Lockers in the high school should be located for easy access between periods. Circulation in the locker areas should be provided for to prevent congestion. It is generally necessary to provide arrangements whereby students may lock up personal belongings and books. Most high schools also provide security lockers for coats. However, others have been successful in providing small security lockers and open coat racks.

Concern over safety in schools has had an impact on student storage spaces. Personal storage spaces are sometimes restricted or unlocked in schools with violence and controlled substance issues. In some schools, students carry personal belongings in backpacks and rolling luggage carts.

Storage requirements vary by climate and geographic region. Colder climates require space for snow boots and bulky coats in addition to the storage of school related materials. As technology becomes more accessible to students, delivery of curriculum could occur over personal notebook computers. This will also have an impact on student storage requirements.

Prefabricated metal lockers are a standard for meeting student storage requirements in high schools and middle schools, usually lining the corridor. In elementary schools, storage for students is sometimes provided in the classroom as a part of the casework. In schools organized around houses or academies, storage is provided within the house.

Student storage areas also offer great opportunities for informal student interaction. Figure 43 shows open lockers arranged around an alcove, providing an informal gathering space for children. A bench is provided both as a place to visit with friends and to provide a place for boots underneath. Adjustable cubbies are provided to accommodate students of different grade levels.

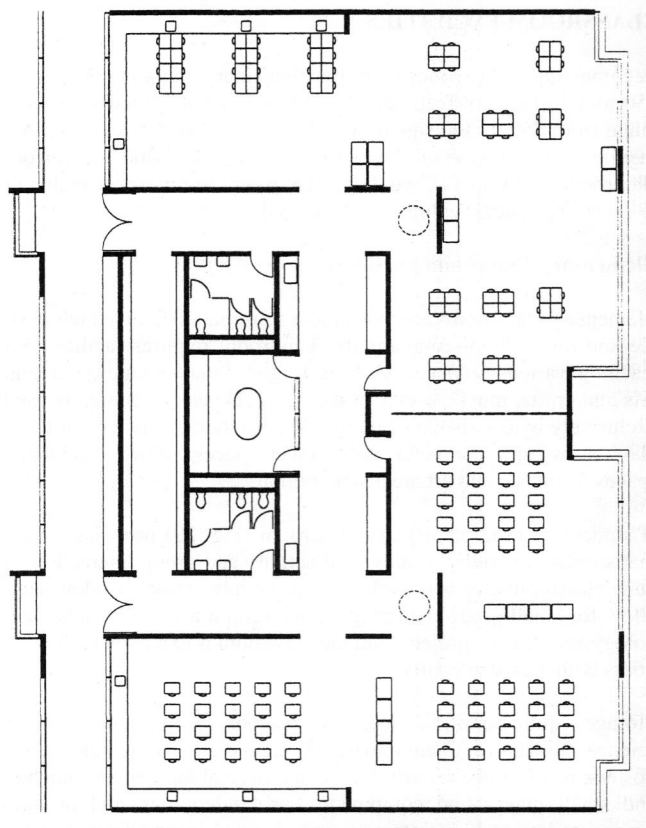

**Fig. 42. High school / middle school house classroom plan**

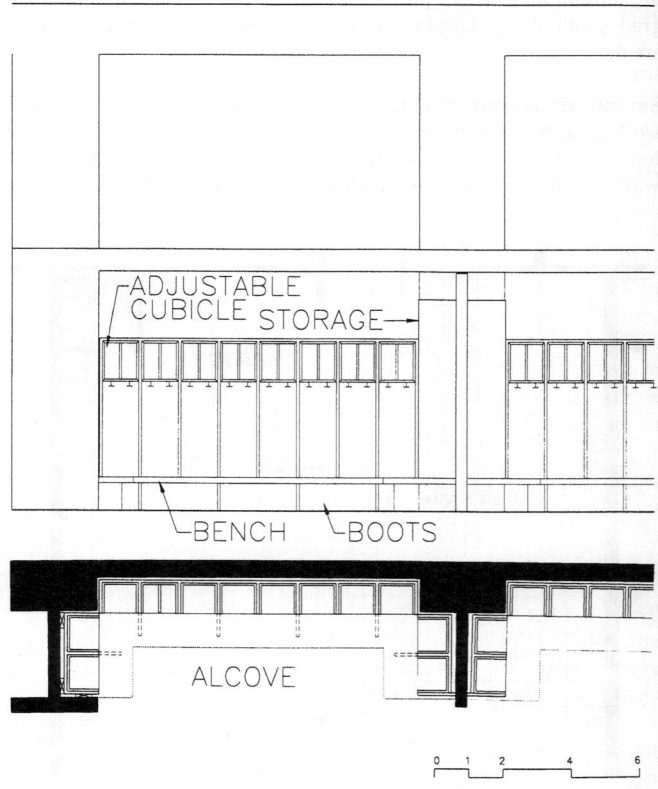

**Fig. 43. Student cubby alcove.**

# ARTS FACILITIES

Working surface, and lots of it, by way of counters and tables is a basic requirement, as is wall space for display and storage cabinetry. Figure 44 shows a typical art room, well-equipped with sinks (X squares) in the perimeter counterwork, allowing flexibility for various table and desk combinations. Fig. 45 shows a larger art suite, with no windows and all kinds of wall space, artificially well lit, with a storage core and peninsula sinks, but otherwise open, flexible space utilizing 7-foot-high storage units as dividers of functions.

Art rooms have unique and stringent storage requirements for a room where working techniques are so important in the activities that take place within the room. As a result, certain special details and ideas have been developed as useful and practical. For example, rooms should be equipped with all kinds of cabinets and counters with as much hanging space as possible. Displaying art work itself becomes a creative and practical challenge. Ample tack surface should be available on the wall. Display devices can be hung from the ceiling, developed as free-standing kiosks, or used in other constructions, even in front of windows to set ceramic pieces on. Track lighting can then be used for highlighting display spaces created throughout the room.

The art room should be an exciting place to be and to work where new projects are created amid completed work or work in progress so that the students are encouraged to compare artwork and increase their own quality. Finishes throughout the room should be practical and spartan, for the art room is a laboratory to work in with freedom to explore and, if necessary, to be messy.

## Arts in Primary Schools

There should be one art room with one art teacher for every 400-500 students. The art room should have at least 55 square feet of work space per student (excluding storage and teacher's work space), and the space should be flexible enough for use with large or small groups and for individual instructional activities (Figs. 46 and 47).

Cover at least one wall with cork-board from floor to ceiling for displaying student work. Display areas such as shelves and cases should also be provided for three-dimensional work like sculpture and ceramics. These areas should be well lighted and equipped with multiple lighting plug-in tracks with movable spotlights.

Adequate in-class storage, accessible to students, is needed as well as at least 350 square feet of lockable storage space for art supplies, equipment and student art works. This latter space should be connected to the art room.

A wet area with a sink is desirable for clay work. If facility planning includes a patio, it should be located near the art room.

## Arts in Secondary Schools

There should be one art room with one art teacher for every 500-600 students. The art room should have a minimum of 55 square feet per student, excluding storage and teacher's work space, and the space should be flexible enough for use with group or individual instructional activities (Fig. 48). Adequate design should allow for ease of traffic flow with adequate space planned for special furniture and equipment such as easels, potter's wheels, floor looms, and darkroom developing tanks and enlargers. A wet area with a sink is desirable

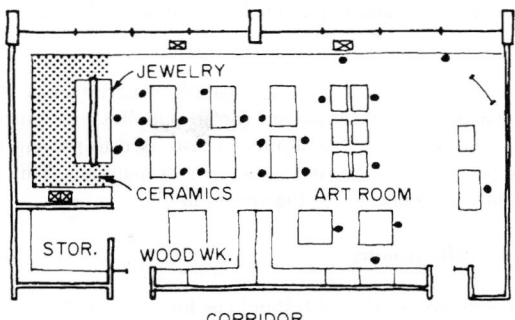

**Fig. 44. Typical art room**

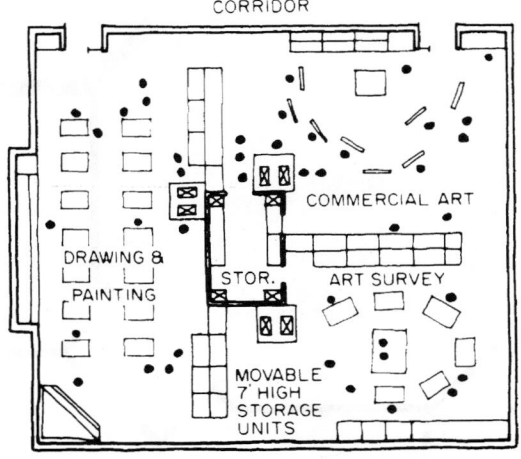

**Fig. 45. Art suite**

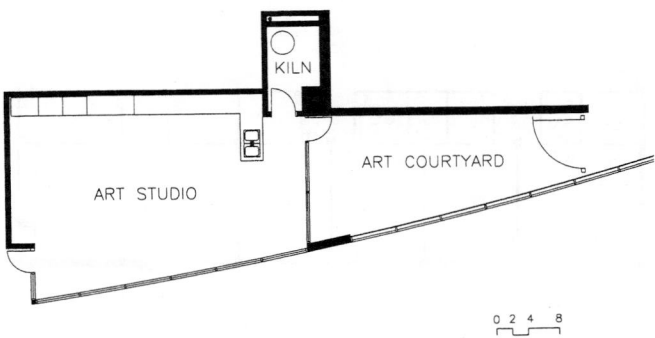

**Fig. 46. Elementary art room**

for clay work. If a patio is provided, the wet area should be located near it.

In addition to in-class storage, at least 400 square feet of lockable storage space should be provided for art supplies, equipment, and student art works. Lockable storage is also used to prevent student access to potentially dangerous equipment or materials. This storage space should be connected to the art room.

### Arts and Crafts Rooms

Arts and crafts rooms (Fig. 49) should be located near the auditorium stage, stagecraft area, homemaking, industrial arts, dramatic arts, and music rooms. The location of art rooms should facilitate delivery of supplies. They should also have an outside door to use when holding classes outdoors and to supply good natural lighting.

The space should be arranged with sufficient imagination so that it is flexible and allows the teacher to vary the curriculum from year to

year. The program involves the use of a number of media. Rooms, therefore, should be conceived of as a series of work centers in which activities with different kinds of materials can be carried forward. There is much need for display space for finished work. Walls should be of material that will receive thumbtacks, to eliminate the need for broken-up wall panels and bulletin board. Avoid breaking up wall

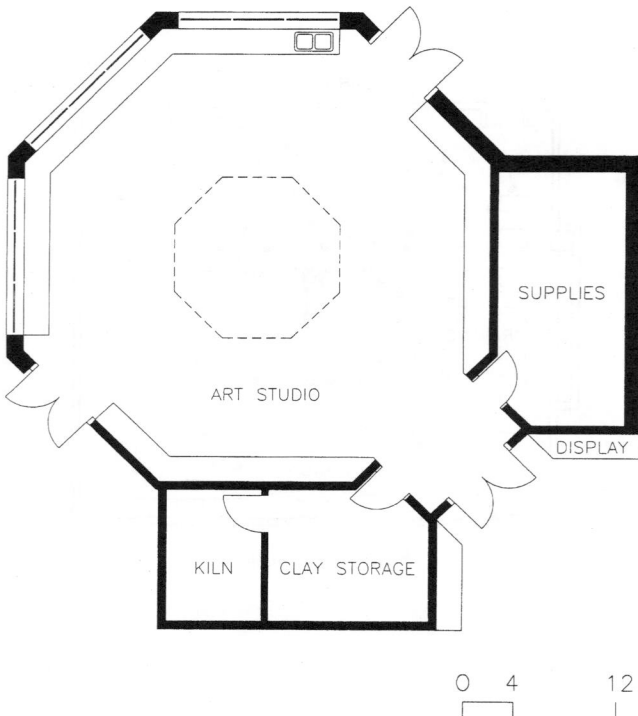

**Fig. 47. Middle school art room**

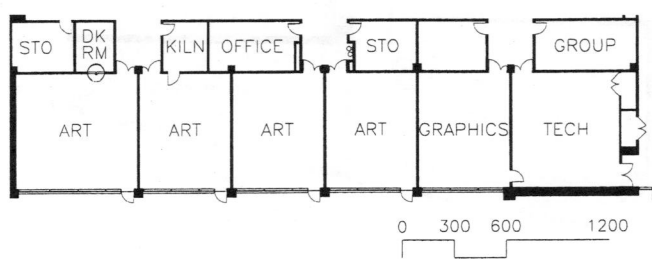

**Fig. 48. High school art room**

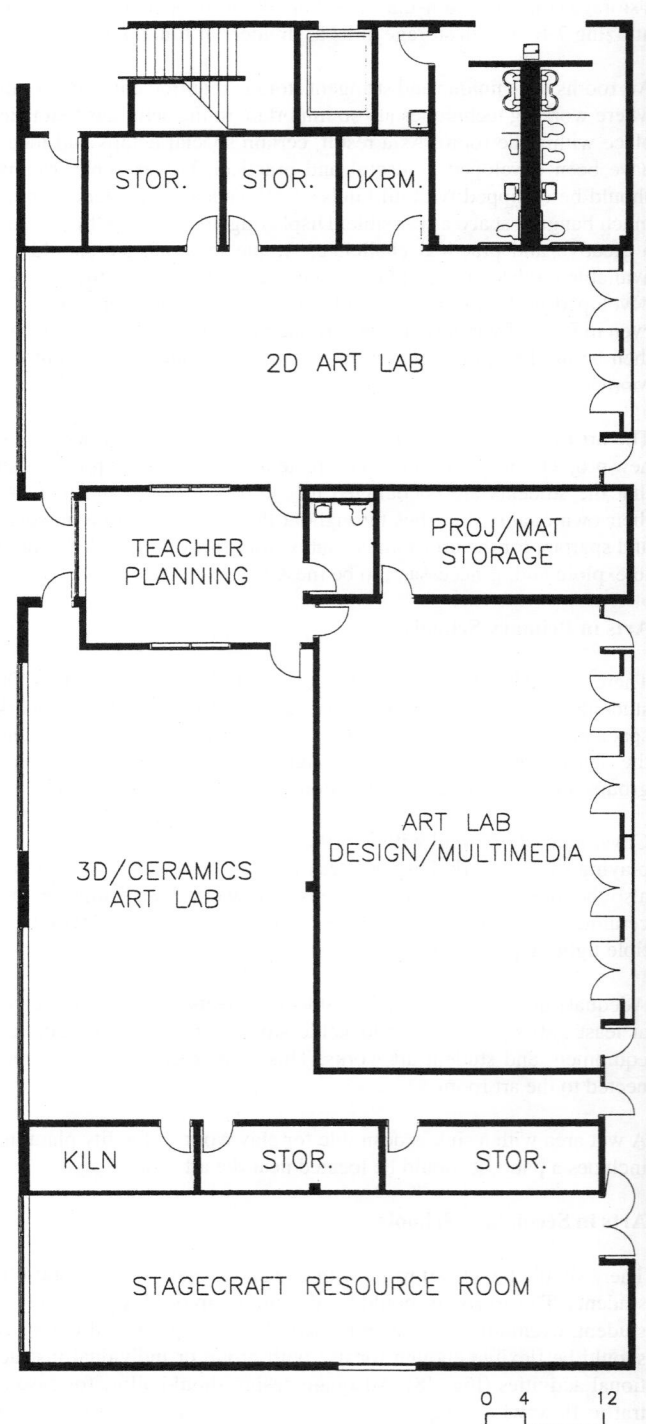

**Fig. 49. High school arts and crafts room**

spaces uneconomically; keep display areas large and simple. Phones, light switches, thermostats, and other necessary electric outlets should be placed where they are accessible but do not interfere with otherwise usable display spaces. Windows should provide adequate light and be high enough for storage and counter space underneath.

Ceilings and/or walls should be acoustically treated. It is preferable to have a vinyl floor in the general art area; in the ceramics area terrazzo or hardened concrete floor is suggested. Finishes should be easily washed and maintained, and they should be resistant to oils and heat. A chalkboard should be placed where it can be seen easily but where it will not produce reflections or shine. For example, it could be incorporated in a cabinet of vertical sliding balanced sections to include two chalkboards, one corkboard, and one projection screen. A bulletin board and opaque drapes or light-tight venetian blinds for darkening the room are also necessary.

Suitable lighting is needed to ensure effective color rendering on dark days and in the evening. Semi-indirect lighting with daylight bulbs is recommended. If the room is located on the ground floor, it will need protection against ground glare in lower sash of windows. Double sinks with hot and cold water; drinking fountain outlet; gas outlets; enough electric outlets around room for projectors and spotlights; and heating by ceiling or floor radiation to save floor and wall space, or at least a minimum allocation of space to this utility, are also recommended.

Room for bulk storage and storage of papers, illustrative materials, models, cardboard, finished and unfinished projects will have to be supplied. The area will require superior protection against fire. Shelving, suspension facilities, and bins should be arranged for great flexibility.

## MUSIC FACILITIES

Music programs in schools generally consist of four parts: choral activities, instrumental activities, classroom activities, and associated performance activities. Planning for these activities varies depending on the type of school being designed.

High school music programs offer a broad curriculum, allowing students to specialize their music experience. Separate choral and instrumental rooms are provided. Music suites usually are arranged around a common core of offices, practice, and storage facilities (Fig. 50).

Middle school programs typically have designated choral and instrumental rooms. Practice facilities are simplified, a designated office may be provided for the music instructor, and storage space is provided for instruments and music.

Elementary schools generally have a simplified program, making use of flexible, multi-purpose spaces. One or two rooms are usually allocated for music—sometimes using the stage of the auditorium as a designated instructional space.

Some schools serve as magnet schools for performing arts, providing professional quality practice and performance spaces to deliver the musical curriculum (Fig. 51).

### Music Suites

Good traffic circulation is essential. The music suite needs to be located and planned to allow convenient movement of large instruments to assembly and performance areas including the stage, playing fields, and buses.

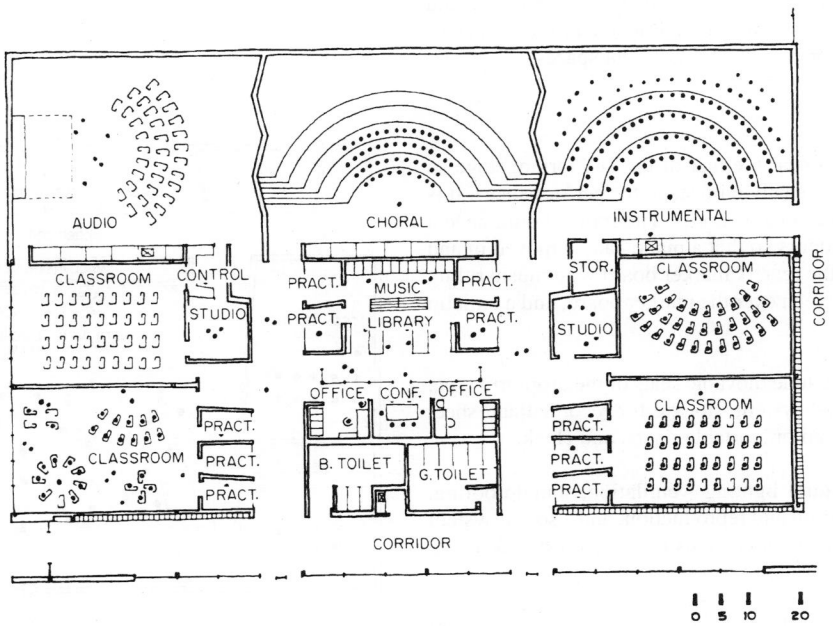

**Fig. 50. High school music suite**

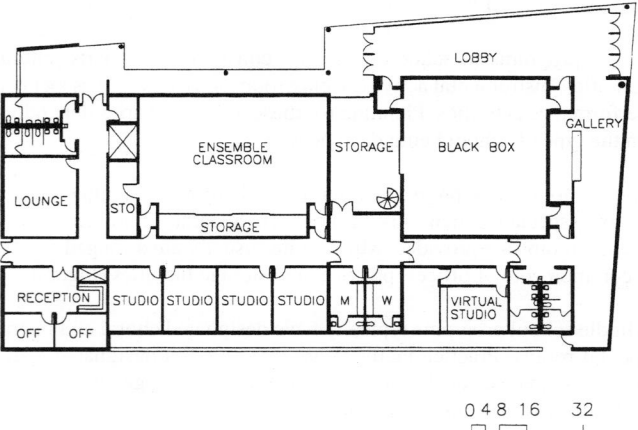

**Fig. 51. Performing arts center**

Planning and design of music and performance areas should aim for the best sound control possible. The size, shape, and construction material are important factors to consider in planning and designing music facilities. It is recommended that a competent acoustical engineer be consulted in preliminary planning stages and retained for consultation as the project is designed and detailed. The designers should aim for rooms that have optimum reverberation time, even distribution of sound, and freedom from undesirable absorption at certain pitches. However, the reverberation period must not be reduced below the point mandatory for correct brilliance of tone. Nonparallel walls or splayed walls and ceilings should be considered; soundproof walls and doors are desirable. Acoustic ceilings and walls should be carefully designed to ensure satisfactory conditions within each room. Storage areas should serve as sound-transmission buffer areas to keep interference between music rooms at a minimum. Structural and mechanical systems need to be planned and detailed to minimize or eliminate sound transmission to and from adjacent spaces.

*Choral Room*

The choral room should be near the rear of the auditorium stage so that choral groups can move easily onto stage for performances. It is used for singing groups and mixed chorus. The room should have a flat floor and 6-foot-wide doors so that a piano can be moved in and out. It may be rounded at the rear. A marker board with music ruling on part of it, a projection screen over the marker board, and a bulletin board are recommended.

Furniture and equipment include movable seats of the drop-arm type, conductor's platform, sound system, storage for recorded and sheet music, piano, television monitor, portable risers, and clock.

The room should have natural lighting, ventilation, soundproofing, provisions for music recording and reproduction, and a sound system with proper live and recorded connections to serve for broadcasting over school public-address system.

Tiers are often built-up from the flat, main-level structural floor in both the choral and instrumental rooms.

*Instrumental Music Room*

Figure 52 shows in more detail an instrument rehearsal room, with student stations shown as dots, and practice rooms across a typical circulation corridor; a very typical, basic situation allowing free use of the practice rooms and easy access to the small instrument storage lockers along the corridor (Fig. 53). Large instruments are stored in the rehearsal room in rolling racks (Fig. 54) to allow for their easy moving for away-from-home performances. The instrument storage area should allow students to quickly and efficiently collect instruments, attend class, and return instruments for storage.

In this scheme, the room steps down from the corridor, allowing the generation of adequate volume in the room without stepping the roof up.

The front wall is made heavily absorbent to sound-simulate playing to an audience: The ceiling is 50 percent reflective and 50 percent absorbent so that one section of the room can hear the other.

Figure 55 shows a related reflected ceiling pattern, and shows some details for soft and hard surfaces, for the rehearsal room in Fig. 52.

The instrumental music room should be near the rear of the auditorium so that the band can move instruments easily onto the stage, near an outdoor entrance so that the band can have access to the field without going through the building, and near practice rooms. It is used for band, orchestra, brass and woodwind ensemble, chamber music groups, and sectional rehearsals.

The space should have a flat floor and doors 6 feet wide to move piano and other large instruments in and out. Doors should be soundproofed. Storage space in back and sides of room, a marker board with music ruling on part of it, projection screen over marker board, and bulletin board are suggested.

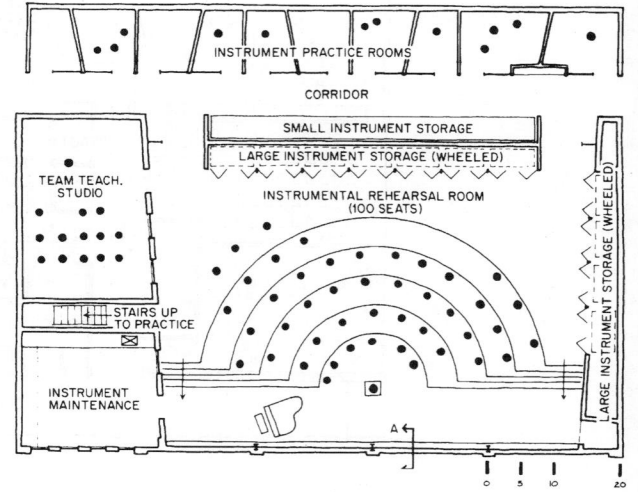

**Fig. 52. Instrument rehearsal room**

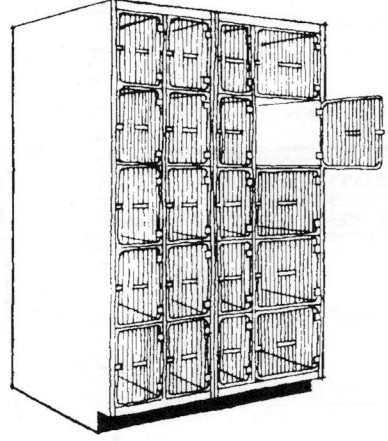

**Fig. 53. Small instrument storage unit**

**Fig. 54. Large wheeled instrument unit**

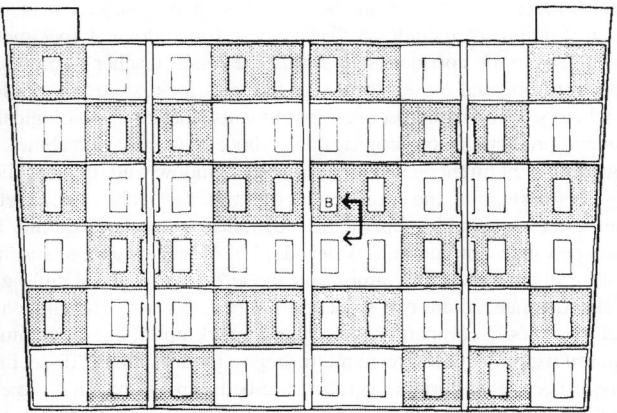

**Fig. 55. Reflected ceiling plan of rehearsal room in Fig. 52**

Furniture and equipment include movable seats, conductor's platform, television monitor, music stands, small sink, counters for books with music slots below counters, storage for musical scores of various size, portable risers, and clock.

The room should have special soundproofing; natural lighting and ventilation, if possible; provision for music recording and reproduction; and a sound system with proper live and recorded connections to serve for broadcasting over school public-address system. The music facility should also have rooms with recording, mixing, and editing capabilities.

Figure 56 illustrates a specialized facility that includes a black box performance space that can be configured for various performance types. A lobby and associated gallery is provided. The performance spaces are separated from the public spaces with light and sound locks.

### Practice Rooms

Practice rooms should be near the band and orchestra room. They are used for practicing and individual instruction. Rooms of varying sizes should be provided (Fig. 57). They may serve as music listening rooms. Soundproof doors, and soundproof windows into corridors, are necessary for supervision.

Equipment includes music rack, small table, music lamp, chairs, clock, and counter for instruments and books. It may have a piano and a connection to the sound system, allowing recorded music to be played in the practice room.

Electric outlets and artificial lighting are needed. Special acoustical treatment is necessary to prevent interference between rooms and with other areas and to deaden reverberation. Special attention should be paid to mechanical ventilation.

### Music Office and Library

The music office and library should be between the choral and instrumental rooms. It should provide good supervision of spaces in the music area. It is used as an office for teacher conference, teacher preparation, record keeping, and as a library for research, reading, studying, and storage of music.

Furniture and equipment include teacher's desks and chairs, wardrobe space, conference table, work counter, adjustable shelves on walls, bookcase, cabinet for records, computer, and sound system.

### Music Storage Room

The music storage room should provide safe, sanitary protection against robe and uniform destruction. Cabinets, 3 feet deep, 30 feet long, equipped with racks and hangers and space above for hats and lockers, for special band equipment such as flags and batons, and with lockable sliding doors are desirable.

Instruments need maximum care and preservation from damage. Adjustable shelving must vary according to instrument sizes. Rollaway racks for bulky instruments are needed. Smaller instruments are best cared for in cabinets. Other provisions include lockers with master-keyed padlocks, student benches, record cabinet, music filing cabinet, piano dolly, and music stands. If possible, a small area for instrument maintenance should be provided: sink with hot and cold water, floor drain, shelves, workbench, gas outlet for Bunsen burner, and counter for instrument repair.

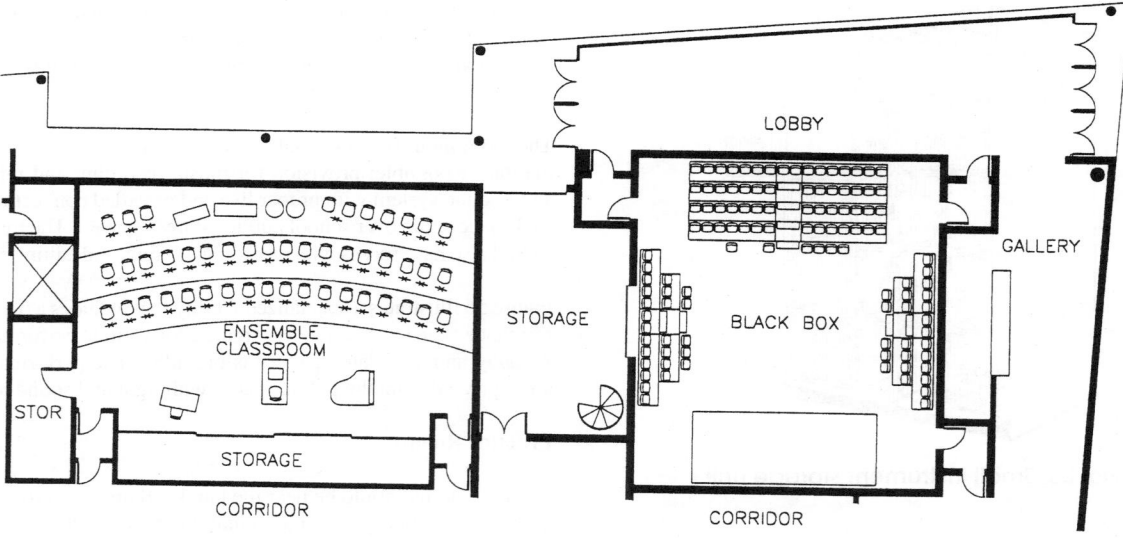

Fig. 56. Black box performanc

## GENERAL SCIENCE ROOMS AND BIOLOGY LABORATORIES

General science rooms and biology laboratories (Figs. 58 to 63) should be located on the first floor, with windows facing south or southwest, a door opening into the preparation room, and a door opening onto the campus so that classes may study outdoors without passing through the building.

Activities include lectures, demonstrations, viewing projected materials, individual and group study, writing, and experimentation with animals and plants.

The front wall should be equipped along its entire length with chalkboard, the center section of that should be reusable. There should be a display rail over everything except the reusable section of board. Provision should be made for a projection screen at the front of the room. Corkboard 4 feet wide should cover the entire width of the back wall above the wainscoting. It is suggested that counters be installed along two sides of the room, one being the window side. Such counters should include several sinks and outlets for gas and electricity.

All laboratory furniture should be acid-resistant and easy to wash and clean. Equipment includes a display case for biological specimens that opens to the corridor from within the room; teacher's combination wardrobe and closet; legal-size file with lock; storage areas for notebooks, aprons, microscopes, instruments, specimens, biologicals, student projects, microprojector, and books. A storage cabinet at counter height might be installed along the window wall. Locked sliding doors extending the entire length of the storage cabinet and metal shelves are desirable. Instructor's demonstration desk should be equipped with hot and cold water, duplex AC receptacle, soapstone sink, upright rods with clamps and wood crossbar, and double gas cock. Also needed are two student biology desks with one cupboard and two book compartments; chairs, mock-up table; herbarium, aquariums; projection screen; microscopes; models, charts; dissecting trays; specimens; portable germinating bed; terrarium; microprojectors; three sinks with towels and soap dispensers; experiment sheet filing cabinet near tackboard; first-aid cabinet; fire extinguisher.

### Music Classroom

The music classroom should be part of the music suite and readily accessible to corridor and office. It is used for class instruction, choral work, and as a dressing room for performances.

Music classrooms should have sound-tight doors, natural lighting, lavatory, and a dressing table. Marker boards ruled for music should be provided. Provision should be made for a sound system and projection television. The door should be large enough to accommodate a piano.

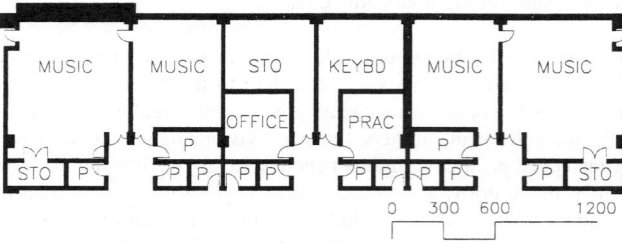

Fig. 57. Practice room layout

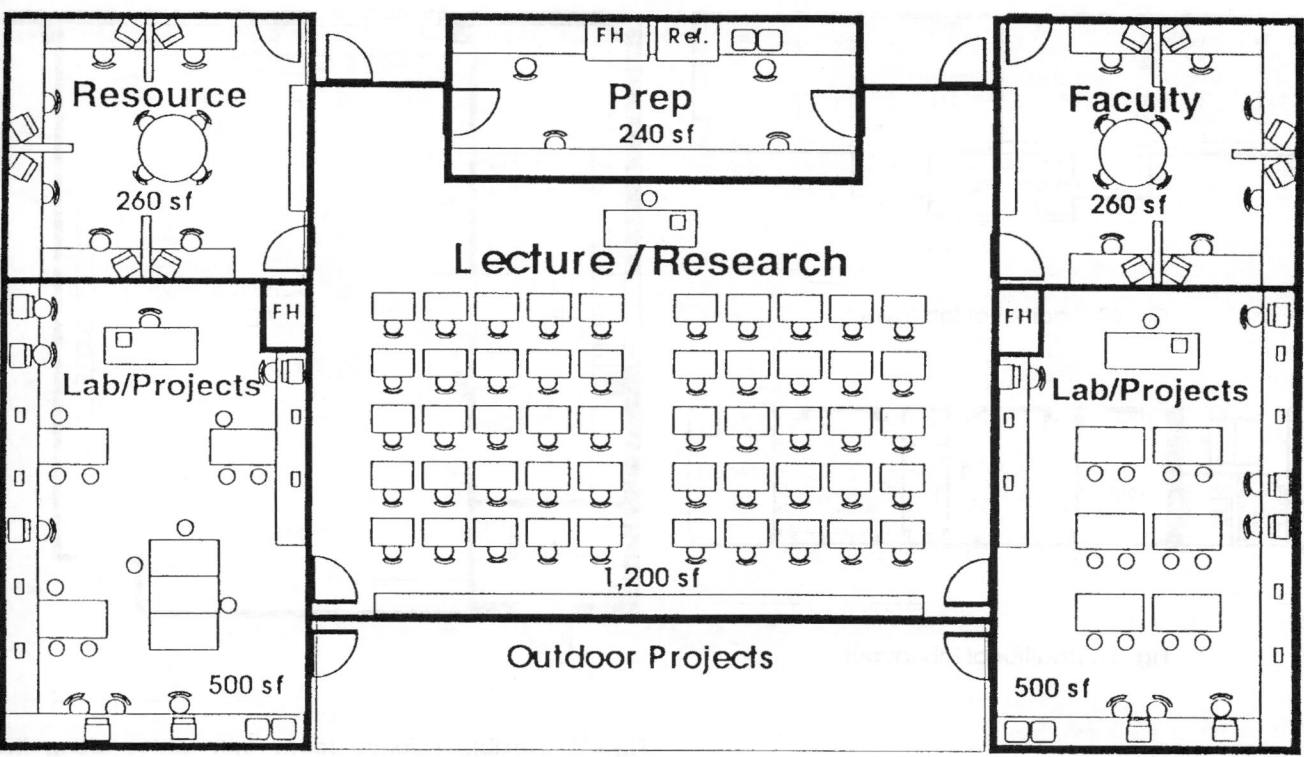

**Fig. 58. Classroom with lecture emphasis**

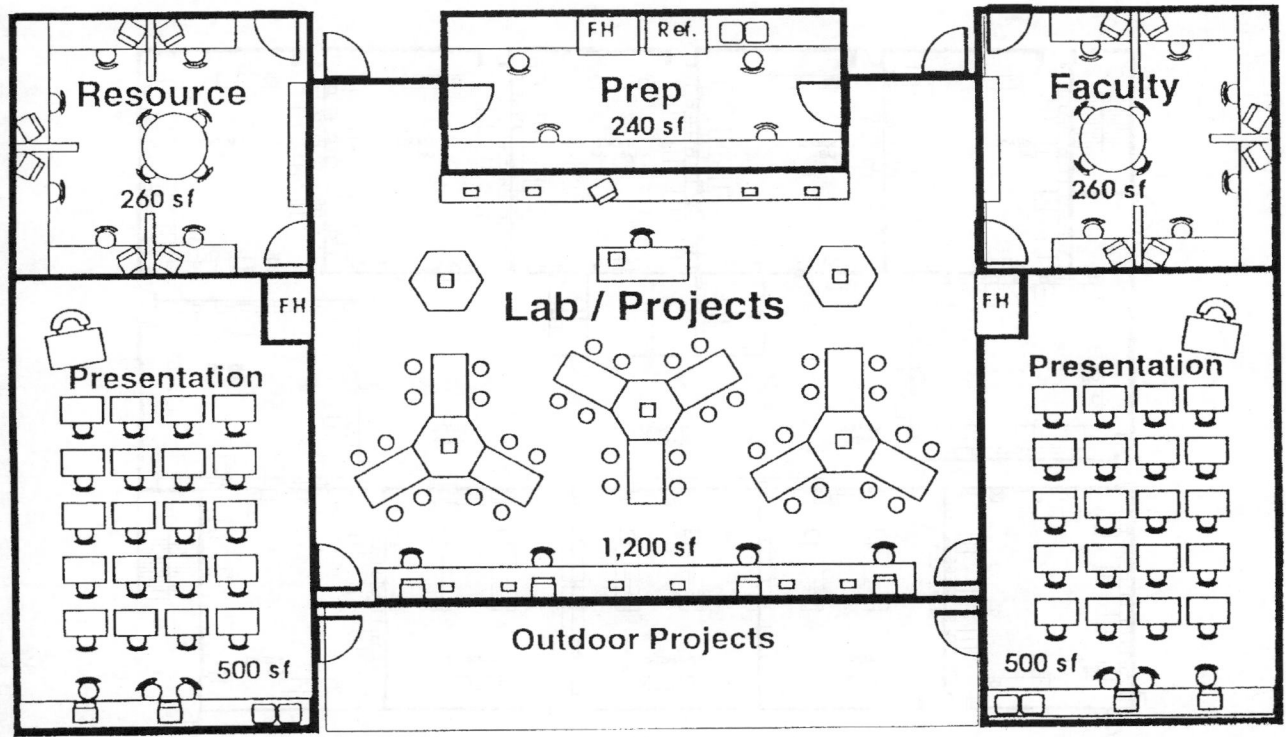

**Fig. 59. Classroom with lab emphasis**

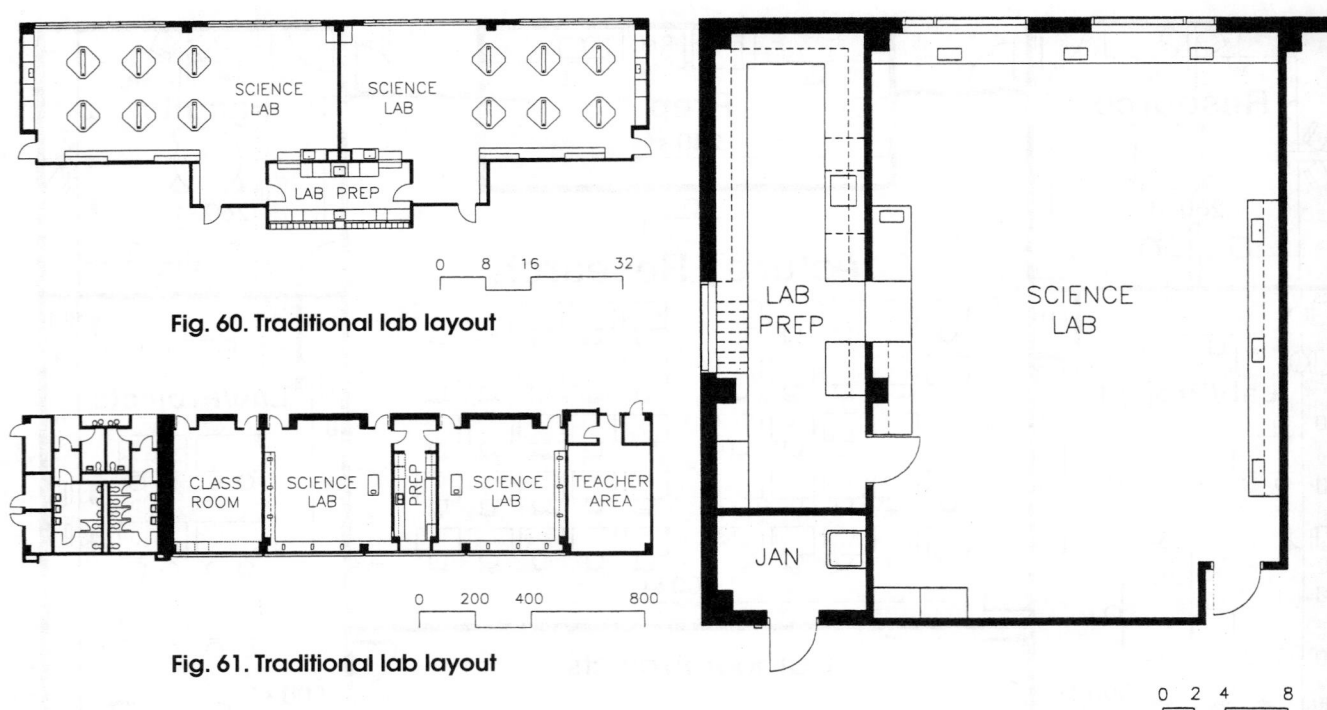

Fig. 60. Traditional lab layout

Fig. 61. Traditional lab layout

Fig. 62. Flexible science room with tables along the perimeter walls

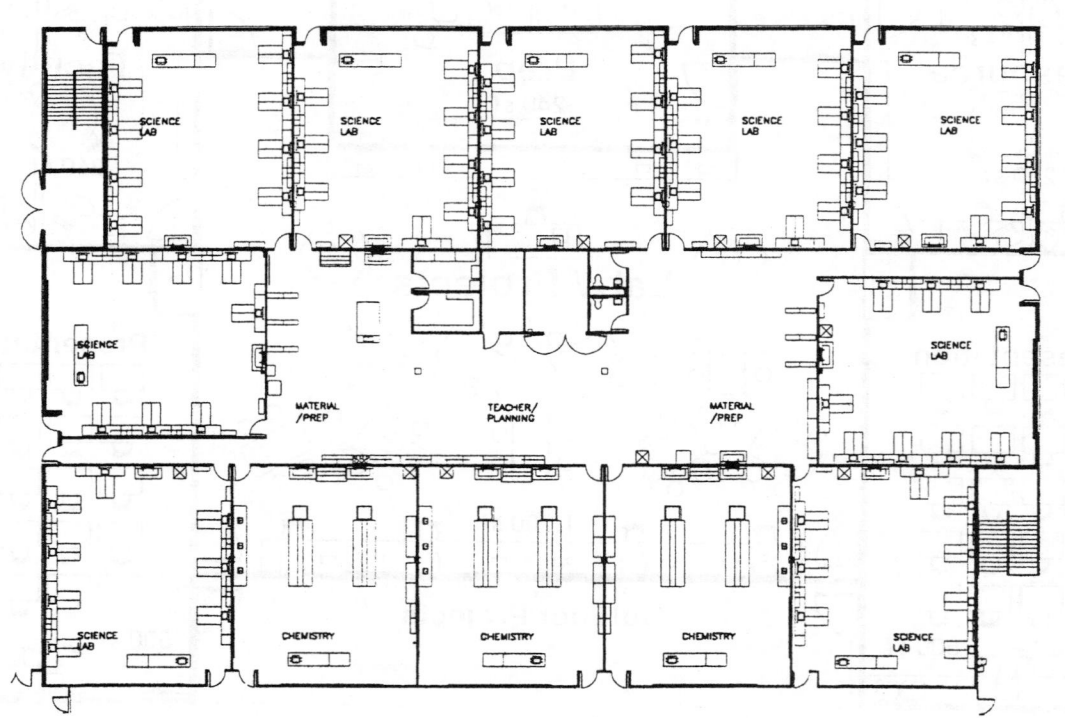

Fig. 63. Science suite with all planning and prep in the center

Electric outlets should be located on each of the walls. If the entire class uses electrically lighted microscopes, tables will need outlets. Sinks and outlets for gas and electricity are needed in counters.

## Storage and Preparation Rooms

Storage and preparation rooms should be adjacent to general science and biology. These rooms are used for teacher preparation, storage of bulk supplies, conferences, and offices.

This area should be lined with storage spaces for materials and equipment of various sizes. There should be provisions for teacher's records and professional books. Room should be outfitted with a sink and gas and electric outlets. Access windows should open into the laboratories.

Storage provision should be made for equipment used in general science and biology. A storage bin, made up of many small drawers, each measuring approximately 4 by 4 inches, should be included for efficient storage of small items of equipment. Also needed are desks and chairs; preparation table on wheels; preparation table with drawers; standing storage cabinet for charts; cabinet with slides; bookcase; shelving to ceiling; sink with hot and cold water; gas and electric outlets.

## Plant and Animal Room

The plant and animal room should be located adjacent to the biology laboratory, possibly adjacent to a biology storeroom. Easy access to the outdoors is desirable. Southern exposure is also desirable. This area should be arranged like a greenhouse, with sanitary finishes and a concrete floor with drain so that the room can be hosed down. In addition to sunlight, the plant room will require special ventilation and heating so that it does not get cold overnight. Special heating, thermostatically controlled and separate from other parts of the building ensures even heating during weekends and holiday periods.

Equipment includes table and racks for plants; growing beds on wheeled tables; animal cages; feeding trays; storage for food, tools, equipment; sink with hot and cold water; hose; pails; hand garden tools; bins for loam, sand, and peat moss.

## Chemistry Laboratories

Chemistry laboratories should be readily accessible from individual research and preparation rooms. Laboratory activities include demonstrations, individual and group study and experimentation, writing, viewing projected materials, and lectures.

At a comfortable height there should be student stations for 24 students, consisting of tables with large free working areas and all services available: AC and DC variable voltage should be provided. The front wall should be equipped for its entire length with a chalkboard, the center section of which should be reusable. There should be a display rail over all but the reusable section of board. On the back wall above the wainscoting level there should be some corkboard and pegboard with hardware. A fume hood, accessible from three sides, should be provided.

One end of the room should contain the teacher's desk and a demonstration area with a 5-inch-high dais for demonstration. Demonstration table should have a stone top, spotlighting, and a roll-away

extension. AJI services should be provided for the demonstration area, including variable AC and DC voltage. Sound cable should be installed in the floor for projection purposes. Provision should be made for darkening the room.

Special attention should be given to the furniture for this space. As a minimum, it should be acid- and base-resistant and easy to wash and clean. It should include tablet armchairs; teacher's combination wardrobe and closet; acid-proof sinks with dilution tank; storage for chemical supplies; storage space in laboratory tables; normal chemistry laboratory equipment for semi-micro techniques; salt and solution cabinets; three rolling tables to service tables; standard reagent storage area; locked cupboards for delicate instruments and dangerous chemicals; fire extinguishers and first-aid kits; storage for notebooks and aprons; experiment-sheet filing cabinet; charts and models; projection screen.

## Physics Laboratories

Physics laboratories are used for lectures, demonstrations, viewing projected material, individual and group study, writing, individual and group experimentation.

Around the room on three sides at a comfortable height (higher than the ordinary table) should be a work station for each student, consisting of a table with a large free working area and all services available. AC and DC variable voltage should be provided to all stations; voltage should be supplied by several portable voltage-regulating units. Sinks should be available. Some attention should be given to permanent or semi-permanent laboratory stands for rigging equipment.

One end of the room should contain the teacher's desk and a demonstration area with a 5-inch-high dais for the demonstration table. The demonstration table should have a stone top, spotlighting, and a roll-away extension. All services should be available. A downdraft ventilator is suggested, but it should be positioned so as to give as much unobstructed broad area on table surface as possible. It should not be centrally placed. Tablet armchairs should be placed in front of the demonstration desk.

The room should have as much chalkboard space as possible, since chalkboard work with problems constitutes a considerable part of class time. Ample corkboard space and some pegboard with hardware are needed.

Attention should be given to darkening the room properly. This is important for the projection of movies and slides, as well as for demonstrations that require a darkened room, and for some laboratory work such as photometry. Sound cable should be installed for projection purposes and cable facilities for television and antennae for radio reception. There should be central control of lighting.

An open joist ceiling has the advantage of permitting hanging of apparatus. A ceiling hook capable of holding a 1,000-pound load should be provided.

One of the main problems for the physics area will be provision of adequate storage space for a vast amount of demonstration equipment and specialized scientific apparatus. Storage space with glass doors for visibility, bookshelves for a reference library, and a cabinet for notebooks should be provided.

## Preparation and Storage Rooms for Chemistry and Physics Laboratories

Preparation and storage rooms should be adjacent to laboratories, with a door leading to corridor and laboratory. They are used for teacher preparation, storage of bulk supplies, and conferences.

The area should be lined with storage spaces for materials and equipment of various sizes (i.e. glass tubing, long items, tall items). All shelves should have lips to prevent slippage, and should be built so that the floor supports the weight, unless the storage area is small and specifically designated for light items.

*Chemistry:* Open shelving of cabinets is favored for storage of bulk chemicals. Special transite-lined volatile closets vented to the outside for volatile reagents, acids, and alkalies should be provided, along with provisions for the teacher's records and professional books. The room should be outfitted with sink and gas and electric outlets. It should also have storage provision for all equipment, a preparation table large enough for six analytical balances, adequate work space for preparation, special storage for charts so that they are kept flat, not rolled, desks and chairs, preparation table on wheels, ladders with rail, and a bookcase.

*Physics:* A storage bin made up of many small drawers measuring approximately 4 by 4 inches for efficient storage of small items of equipment is suggested. Electric outlets similar to those provided in the demonstration table, as well as plentiful 110-V AC outlets, and adequate lighting should be provided. Ladders with rail should be available to reach stored items, and a workbench and sink with drainboard along one side, to repair and set up equipment. The bench should be rugged enough to take considerable hammering.

## Individual Research and Project Rooms for Chemistry and Physics

Research and project rooms should be adjacent to chemistry and physics laboratories and separated from them by half-glass partitions. They are used for individual and small group study and experimentation, instruction, and research.

## Science Shop

The science shop and the darkroom may be built as a unit and placed back to back between the corridor and the window side. The project room should be located on the window side and have a door opening into a laboratory. A glass wall will enable the teacher to supervise the area.

The science shop is used for individual work in making and repairing instruments and equipment. It should have a workbench and sink along one side of the room. The bench, for repair and setting up of equipment, should be rugged enough for metalworking.

The furniture and equipment should include equipment drawers, work counter, drill press, small metalworking lathe, some storage shelves for reference books, tool storage, sink, and ample space for electrical equipment. Electric outlets similar to those provided in the demonstration desk should be available, as well as 110-volt AC outlets.

## Darkroom

The darkroom could be placed back to back with the science shop and located on the corridor side with the door opening into the corridor. It is used for developing film and the storage of darkroom materials and reagents, mounting equipment, and the like.

A vestibule and two-door entrance will prevent light from entering. The area could be divided into a small room near the entrance for weighing and mixing chemicals and a larger room toward the rear for developing and printing.

A counter should be constructed along three sides of the room, 34 to 36 inches high and 24 inches wide. There should be a large chemical-resistant open sink, 24 by 30 inches and 18 inches deep; and a wet bench, attached at either end, draining into the sink. The sink must have both hot and cold water. Stainless-steel surfaces are recommended; finishes must be easily cleaned and stain-resistant.

Shelves 12 inches apart and 10 inches deep should be constructed above the counter. Storage in standard darkroom style should provide tray and chemical storage as well as shelves for dry stock. Since the room will be used for dry work, such as spectroscopy, provision should be made for sit-down as well as standup dry work. Walls should be finished a flat green for eye ease. Serious attention must be given to ensure adequate ventilation of this room.

Furniture and equipment will include retouching table; developing; enlarging, and printing equipment; dryer; print washer; trays; paper cutter; hot plate; safe lights; timer; fire extinguisher; clock.

At least four double electric outlets are needed at the counter. There must be sufficient plugs for all appliances, conveniently placed near all work positions.

## Auxiliary Science Facilities

Special science facilities like animal rooms, greenhouses, and vivariums, are not exclusively part of large science complexes. Sometimes a given instructor will have a special interest, or a local business group or community effort will focus on funding such added programs. As a result, such spaces often get extra special attention in their development from everyone, demand research, turn out to be topnotch, and really excite the students.

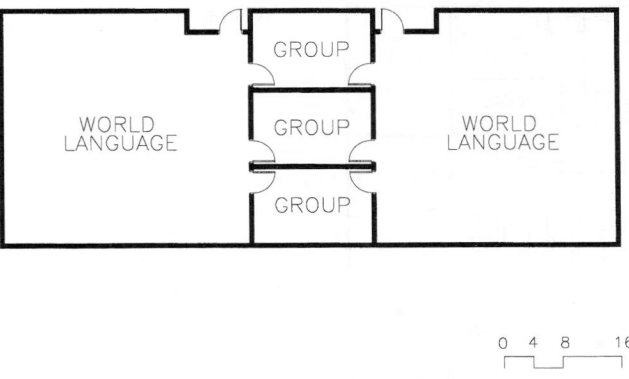

**Fig. 64. World language facility**

## WORLD LANGUAGE FACILITIES

The world language lab is a facility that provides tools and instruction for students to become fluent in world languages. In this area, learners receive both instructional guidance and work self-directed with audio, visual, and recording devices primarily delivered through electronic media. Electronic language tools are becoming more and more common with media distribution systems being introduced into the school's technology plan.

Language labs are similar to computer classrooms (Fig. 64). Students sit at individual workstations and have access to interactive videos and recordings. Language instructors are able to monitor and interact electronically with individual students. The classroom should be equipped to accommodate multi-media presentations. A world language suite may contain shared soundproof rooms for specialized instruction and used for practicing and critique of oral skills.

## INSTRUCTIONAL MEDIA/RESOURCE CENTERS

"Library" may be yesterday's term for yesterday's services. The school library has become the information and resource center for the school, and it is more appropriately now commonly called learning resource center (LRC), instructional materials center (IMC), information resource center (IRC), or instructional media center. In addition to books and periodicals there are now records, tapes and cassettes, CD-ROMs, DVDs, closed-circuit TV programming and production, film, videos, cameras, projection equipment and computers. Alongside the book stacks, chairs, and tables are sight-and-sound-equipped study carrels, listening rooms, earphones and program selectors, film splicers and slide-making equipment, preview rooms, television studios, and computer printers and scanners.

The resource center is now indeed where the action is and should be physically and educationally at the heart/center of the school, as equally accessible as possible to the classrooms, the laboratories, the administrative offices, and the community. It may well be open after school hours and should be located to allow direct access to it.

While the resource center is now a conglomerate of materials and services, and while successful planning seeks the mixture of these elements for the convenience of the users, control of the materials, along with well-related backup preparation and work space, becomes a greater concern and problem. The circulation of the users, the administration of the materials, and the functional accommodation of the materials are the basic planning determinants.

The examples illustrated show various combinations of elements, the constant of the control desk and its more usual relationship to workrooms, reference-periodical areas, and offices. Added required exits are treated as emergency exits with alarm provisions. Areas allocated for books and seating are usually prescribed by state agencies or follow recommendations of the American Library Association. The total program may best be developed with a consultant in the field who is fully aware of equipment needs, current developments, and the proper relation of a program for the resource center to the entire school curriculum.

Though the idea of a quiet reading atmosphere has not been forgotten, the resource center has become a pleasant, busy goldfish bowl kind of place: glassy, on display itself, extending its welcome to students as a comfortable place they like to learn in (Figs. 65 to 68). Whether it may be considered a resource center or still a library, whether it is an alcove off the lobby, a room, or a maze of parts, the real goal is to get the students to use the materials and to learn. Carpeting has become very common, and other surfaces are being upgraded, resulting in good looking functional finishes to which everyone responds well.

Accommodating books remains a basic problem in the desire to visually "open up" a resource center; capacities can be gauged from the illustrations in Fig. 67 and Table 4.

*Reviewer:* Peter Brown, Perkins and Will, Architects
*Reference:* www.worldlanguage.com; www.jonescampbell.com/school.htm

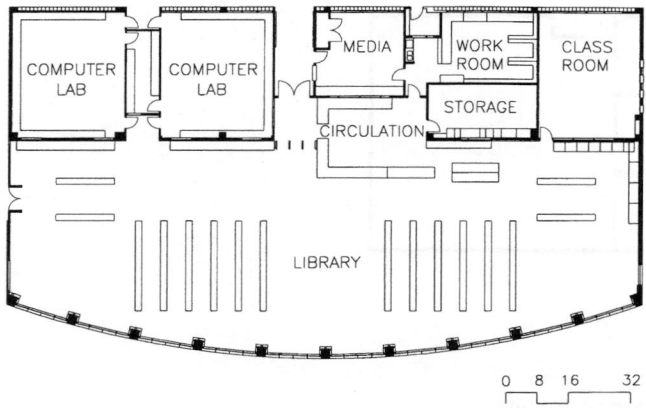

**Fig. 65. High school resource center**

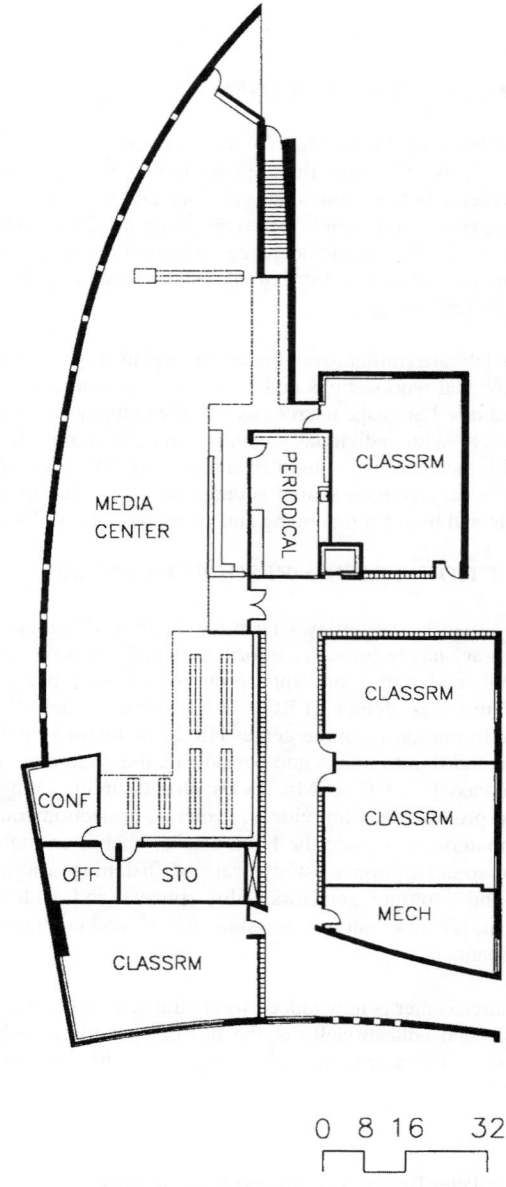

**Fig. 66. Middle school resource center**

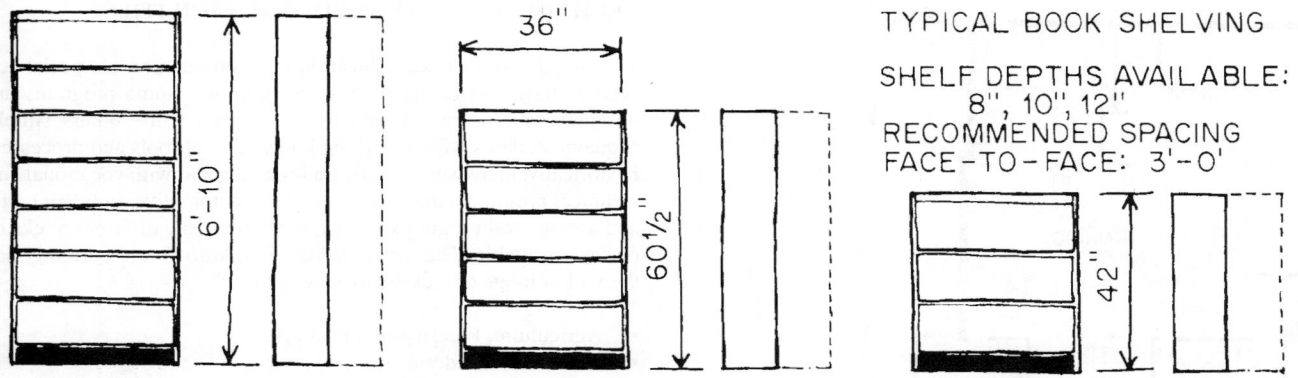

TYPICAL BOOK SHELVING

SHELF DEPTHS AVAILABLE:
8", 10", 12"
RECOMMENDED SPACING
FACE-TO-FACE: 3'-0'

APPROXIMATE BOOK CAPACITY PER 3' SINGLE-FACE SECTION:
HIGH SHELF UNIT: 150; MEDIUM SHELF UNIT: 105; LOW SHELF UNIT: 65

**Fig. 67. Book shelving**

**Table 4** Book shelving capacity (approximate)

| No. of 3 ft sections | Single-face sections | | | Double-face sections | | | Lineal ft of 3 ft shelving sections |
|---|---|---|---|---|---|---|---|
| | High— 7 shelves | Medium— 5 shelves | Counter— 3 shelves | High— 7 shelves | Medium— 5 shelves | Counter— 3 shelves | |
| 1 | 150 | 105 | 65 | 300 | 210 | 130 | 3 |
| 2 | 300 | 210 | 130 | 600 | 420 | 260 | 6 |
| 3 | 450 | 315 | 195 | 900 | 630 | 390 | 9 |
| 4 | 600 | 420 | 260 | 1,200 | 840 | 520 | 12 |
| 5 | 750 | 525 | 625 | 1,500 | 1,050 | 650 | 15 |
| 6 | 900 | 630 | 390 | 1,800 | 1,260 | 780 | 18 |
| 7 | 1,050 | 735 | 455 | 2,100 | 1,470 | 910 | 21 |
| 8 | 1,200 | 840 | 520 | 2,400 | 1,680 | 1,040 | 24 |
| 9 | 1,350 | 945 | 595 | 2,700 | 1,890 | 1,170 | 37 |
| 10 | 1,500 | 1,050 | 350 | 3,000 | 2,100 | 1,300 | 30 |
| 11 | 1,650 | 1,155 | 715 | 3,300 | 2,310 | 1,430 | 33 |
| 12 | 1,800 | 1,260 | 780 | 3,600 | 2,520 | 1,560 | 36 |
| 13 | 1,950 | 1,365 | 845 | 3,900 | 2,730 | 1,690 | 39 |
| 14 | 2,100 | 1,470 | 910 | 4,200 | 2,940 | 1,820 | 42 |
| 15 | 2,250 | 1,575 | 975 | 4,500 | 3,150 | 1,950 | 45 |
| 16 | 2,400 | 1,680 | 1,040 | 4,800 | 3,360 | 2,080 | 48 |
| 17 | 2,550 | 1,785 | 1,105 | 5,100 | 3,570 | 2,210 | 51 |
| 18 | 2,700 | 1,890 | 1,170 | 5,400 | 3,780 | 2,340 | 54 |
| 19 | 2,850 | 1,995 | 1,235 | 5,700 | 3,990 | 2,470 | 56 |
| 20 | 3,000 | 2,100 | 1,300 | 6,000 | 4,200 | 2,600 | 59 |

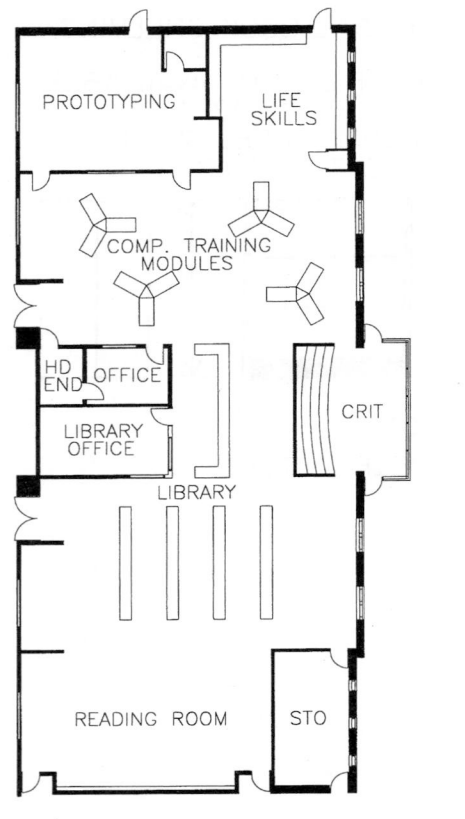

0  4  8    16        32

**Fig. 68. Resource center**

## TECHNOLOGY AND VOCATIONAL FACILITIES

Vocational and technical education is a combination of specialized course study and hands-on business training. Some programs are designed to prepare students for a vocation while others simply acquaint students with a working knowledge of tools and processes. Historically, there were limited trades associated with vocational and technical programs; there may have been automotive, industrial arts and agricultural programs. Today, there are many different tracks or clusters available. The *National Skill Standards Board* currently has the widest range of clusters to choose from:

- Agriculture, Forestry, and Fishing
- Business and Administrative Services
- Construction Operation
- Education and Training
- Finance and Insurance
- Health and Human Services
- Restaurants, Lodging, and Hospitality
- Tourism, and Amusement and Recreation
- Manufacturing, Installation, and Repair
- Mining and Extraction
- Public Admin., Legal, and Protective Services
- Transportation
- Scientific and Technical Services
- Telecommunications, Computers, Arts and Entertainment
- Utilities and Environmental and Waste Management
- Wholesale/Retail Trade, Real Estate, and Personal Services

School-To-Work programs offer a wide variety of vocational implementation. There are three keys to the program:

1. *Work-based learning:* Students gain hands-on training with a local business.
2. *School-based learning:* Academic instruction in the classroom.
3. *Connecting activities:* Students with work-based learning are connected with other community services to ensure a smooth transfer from school into the work force.

Some vocational programs are not limited to secondary education. Tech Prep is a program that requires 2 to 4 years of vocational training in high school and 2 years in post secondary education, such as in a community college. The final example of implementation is the most common throughout secondary education. Vocational courses offered are not reserved only for the vocational program students; all students can take individual courses to fulfill general education requirement credits.

Many vocational clusters can be taught in traditional classrooms or in standard computer classrooms. Courses focusing on topics such as business and administration or finance don't require specialized facilities. However many of the cluster focuses do require labs or teaching facilities beyond the normal classroom layout.

*Authors:* Peter Brown and Chris Suffecool, Perkins and Will, Architects
*References:* Technology Student Association (www.tsawww.org)
Vocational Industrial Clubs of America (www.skillsusa.org)
Business Professionals of America (www.bpa.org)
Family, Career and Community Leaders of America (www.fcclainc.org)
Future Business Leaders of America (www.fbla-pbl.org)

The vocational and technical portion of the building can be planned as an integral part of the total school, physically and philosophically, with an integral relationship to the rest of the school, rather than separate, as often planned in the past.

Traditionally, the industrial arts department was generally isolated from quieter areas of the building. It might have been placed near the cafeteria or physical education facilities, with a service road provided nearby. In this model there may have been an outdoor instructional area, and access to shower and locker facilities. All machines and equipment were arranged so that a sequence of operations could be carried out with the greatest possible efficiency.

Recently, education trends are moving toward a synthesis of technical and academic programs. A resource center may combine the traditional library and a computer learning center with life skills stations, and a fabrication shop. This type of close proximity layout allows students to fully research and execute projects in one area without having to trek across the school for each step of the process.

Accessibility, noise reduction, and the need for specialized equipment are all key issues that need to be addressed in the planning of a vocational section of a school. Related structural and enclosure systems may be appropriately different from the more finished spaces in the school, therefore these systems should not be overlooked. A one-story structure, on grade is most common, though mezzanine space is often developed for storage or seminar use.

Other issues must be considered in planning, such as:

- Special code and safety concerns
- Good lighting
- Sawdust collecting systems
- Overhead hoist systems
- Air exhaust systems
- Ability to move and store large supplies.

The layout of any vocational specific area should follow the logic of its equipment use and its relationship to electrical and mechanical services. It should also be realized that students in these labs are learning on the different types of equipment, and extra clearances should be allowed for joint instructor-learner use.

The specific equipment provided in any vocational facility is determined by the owner and by the various requirements most states have. Sometimes the school leases the equipment, therefore flexibility becomes an issue. Electrical, air, and data service fed down from the ceiling allows flexibility in room configuration. Services through the floor can provide flexibility if planned accordingly. While most finishes must be hard surfaces for maintenance reasons, some acoustic relief can be introduced. The most commonly used materials for sound absorption are acoustic-absorbent blocks, ceiling materials, roof decking, and high wall surfaces.

Figure 69 shows the layout of a high school technology center. In the large open area there are specialized computer learning modules for hands-on work and research. After the research is completed the students simply go to the appropriate room connected to the general tech center, and perform the necessary work to complete their project.

Figure 70 shows the layout of a vocational food service facility. This area is a full-service teaching kitchen adjacent to the cafeteria. It has

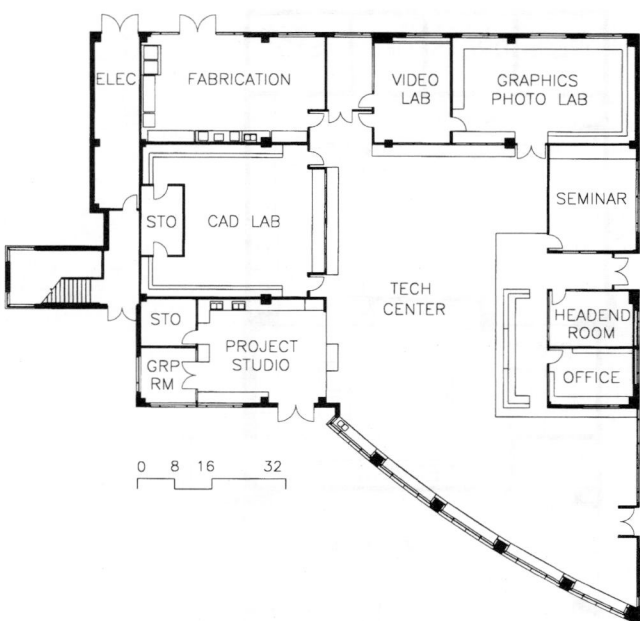

**Fig. 69. High school technology center**

its own dining and service area where student prepared meals are served to faculty and students.

## LIFE SKILLS

Life skills courses teach students about everyday living, home life, cooking, sewing, personal care, and caring for a home and family. Space designed for life skills classrooms should represent the feeling and purpose of the total home in the school.

Facilities comprising a life skills program can range from a single laboratory space serving cooking and sewing classes to a full suite of spaces embracing these, and child development, cosmetology, living-dining, and supportive classroom areas. The various examples shown here illustrate program emphasis, and the many combinations possible, the relationships of one space to another, and the apparent flow of activity functions. Obviously, the larger the facility, the more difficult to avoid an institutionalized character. But it should be realized that certain of these programs are directed toward institutional vocational education, others toward homemakers.

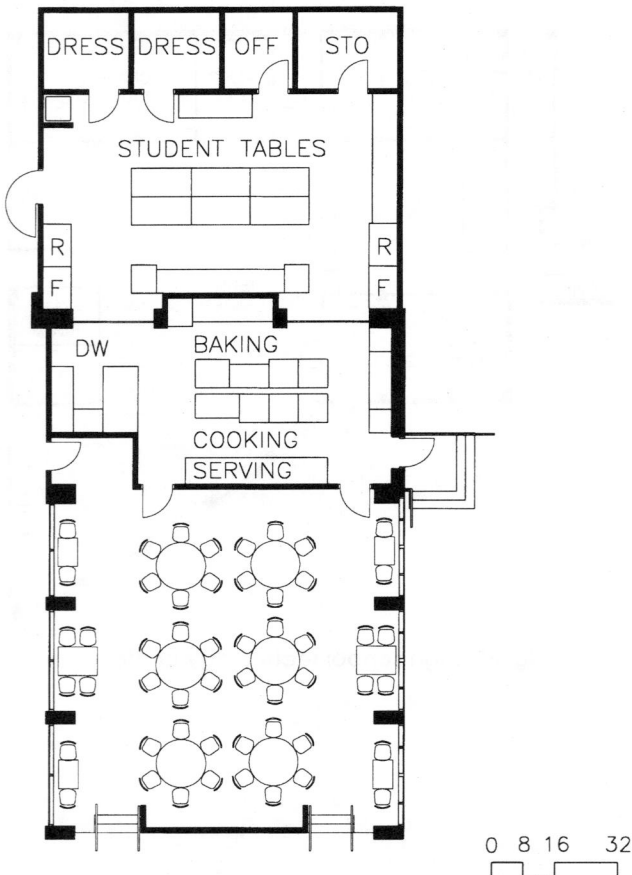

**Fig. 70. High school vocational food service facility**

0  8 16    32

### Food Preparation

The food laboratories may be divided into cooking area, freezing area, laundry, wall storage (for tote drawers, staples, cleaning supplies, and books), and classroom area large enough to accommodate movable desk chairs for students. Grease-resistant asphalt tile or linoleum flooring is necessary. Folding doors or screens could be used to separate areas.

Unit kitchens should contain equipment for about four students and include stoves, double sinks, counter space, and storage cupboards above and below the counters. Enameled-steel upper and lower cabinets with back splashes that are molded into a curved surface rather than joined together with stainless-steel strips are suggested. Movable supply wagons made of materials similar to those of other kitchen equipment can be built to fit into recessed space under the counter surface. Allowance must be made on the window wall for access to windows.

Counters should be made of a durable material with two areas large enough to place two boards 16 by 20 inches next to each other so that two students can work side by side at each area. These should not be located at a corner since this does not allow space for two pupils to stand and work together. Minimum desirable length of counter per pupil is 30 inches. If counter width is 24 inches, minimum desirable size of one unit kitchen should be 11 by 9 feet, or 99 square feet.

Counter heights should be about 33 to 34 inches. To accommodate four students at work, space between counters should be 6 to 8 feet. Just outside each kitchen should be space for a kitchen table and four chairs for serving and eating.

Allowance should be made for adequate ventilation to carry away food odors. An exhaust fan for the entire room is suggested. Two duplex electric outlets should be provided in each cooking area. In the laundry area, provision should be made for a 110/220-volt outlet for clothes dryer.

### Clothing Laboratory

The clothing laboratory should be equivalent in size to a large classroom. It should include a sewing area (preferably along window wall); grooming area; dressing room area (about 8 feet square), walled off by cabinets on at least one side; storage areas (preferably along walls); and fitting area. Folding doors or screens could be used to separate areas.

Storage should be provided for portable machines, notions, tote boxes (5 inches deep by 14 inches wide by 19 inches long), rolls of 36-inch wrapping paper, small articles, textbooks, large fashion magazines, patterns, teacher's wardrobe, four-drawer, and legal-size file with lock. Space is needed for hanging student projects.

Provide adequately keyed electric outlets for machines—suggest one double outlet for each machine—electric outlets for irons and visual-aid machines, one fluorescent light over grooming unit, and adequate light at working surfaces.

### Basic Home Management

Basic home management facilities are used for advanced courses in homemaking: table service, housekeeping, home decoration, selection and arrangement of furniture, entertainment, bed-making, home-care of sick, leisure time activities, family living, money management, child care, and consumer education.

This is the central core of home management facilities. Furniture and equipment should represent advanced solutions of home problems. Space should provide for dining room, living room, and flexible area for home nursing, child care, home furnishing, family living, group discussion, and film viewing. There should be at least one plastered wall for experimentation with wallpapers. Hardwood floors are preferred. Folding doors or screens could be used to separate areas.

Furniture and equipment include upholstered sofa and chairs; side tables and coffee table; lamps and vases; sideboard or hutch; drapes (to be made by class); dining room table and chairs to seat eight; card table and chairs; framed pictures (art project); rollaway bed; built-in storage cabinets for magazines and linens; cleaning supplies; vacuum cleaner; electric drill and attachments for waxing and buffing; samples of home furnishing materials; dishes; silver; table linen; curtain and drapery fixtures; full-length mirrors; home nursing equipment; child-care supplies. Supplies should be stored near area where they will be used.

There should be artificial lighting and switches adapted to house situations; combination outlet for electric iron, pilot light, switch and outlet; electric clock; special lighting on machines; electric duplex outlet spaced at least every 12 feet of available wall space; sink with hot and cold water.

In laying out the prototype kitchen units it should be remembered that there are both instructors and students using them; hence dimensions between counters should be more ample. Figure 71 indicates some minimum dimensions, while Fig. 72 shows a grouping of U kitchens. Figure 73 shows perimeter kitchens, allowing for a sit-down class grouping at the tables in the center in a rather typical combined food-and-clothing arrangement.

Typically, various kitchen-plan types as well as various appliance types are incorporated into a layout to allow the student to experience their differences. Counter and cabinet types and finishes, even flooring, might likewise be varied while realizing some discretion toward enough common denominators to give order to the total space.

Like planning any laboratory, equipment functions, clearances, and their electrical and mechanical service requirements should be carefully understood, and most of the needs are larger extensions of home situations, such as extra lengths of counter and space between appliances. Unit kitchen plans should also be designed to allow for periodic appliance replacement with new models, sometimes provided for specific consignment by local utility companies, such as accommodating ranges at counter ends to allow for size changes.

A few miscellaneous planning aids should be provided:

- A minimum of 2 linear feet of counter space per student (wall cabinet storage is underutilized in the prototype kitchen and can be more minimal)
- Tackboard or wall behind sink
- A well-located teacher demonstration kitchen counter (an overhead mirror helps too)
- Pull-out bread boards (they save on counter-top wear)
- Spread-out storage for student projects, like sewing

- Portable ironing boards (these are better than built-ins)
- Sewing table unit (for use by four works well)
- Corridor exhibit area for display

Summing up, the home arts area (Figs. 74-75) is a place for learning about living; make it as easy and pleasant as life can be for the students starting out.

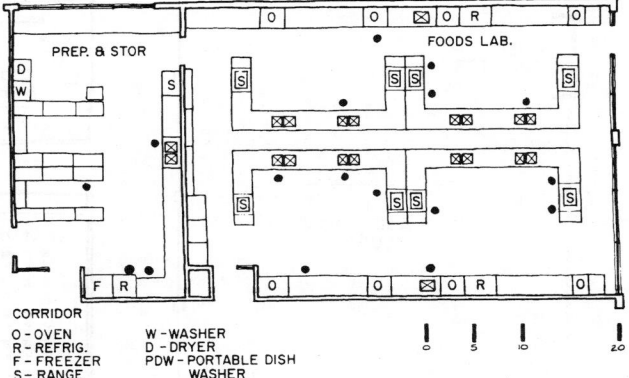

CORRIDOR
O - OVEN    W - WASHER
R - REFRIG.    D - DRYER
F - FREEZER    PDW - PORTABLE DISH
S - RANGE         WASHER

**Fig. 72. U kitchens**

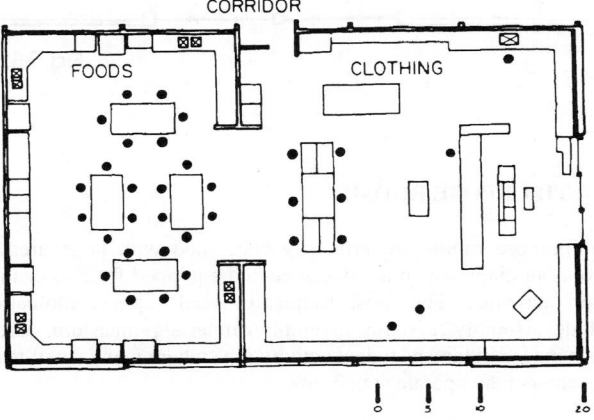

**Fig. 73. Perimeter kitchens**

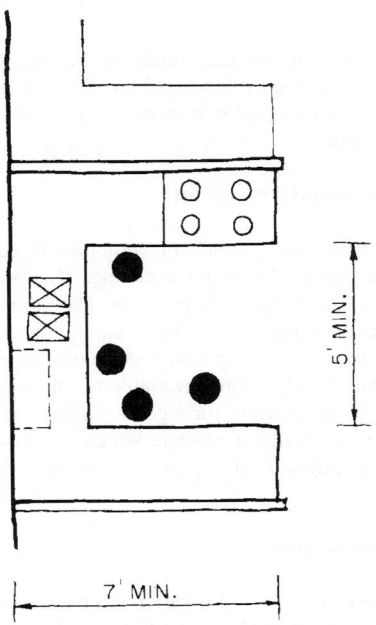

**Fig. 71. Minimum dimensions**

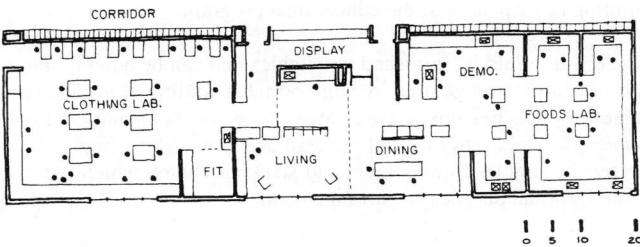

**Fig. 74. Home arts area**

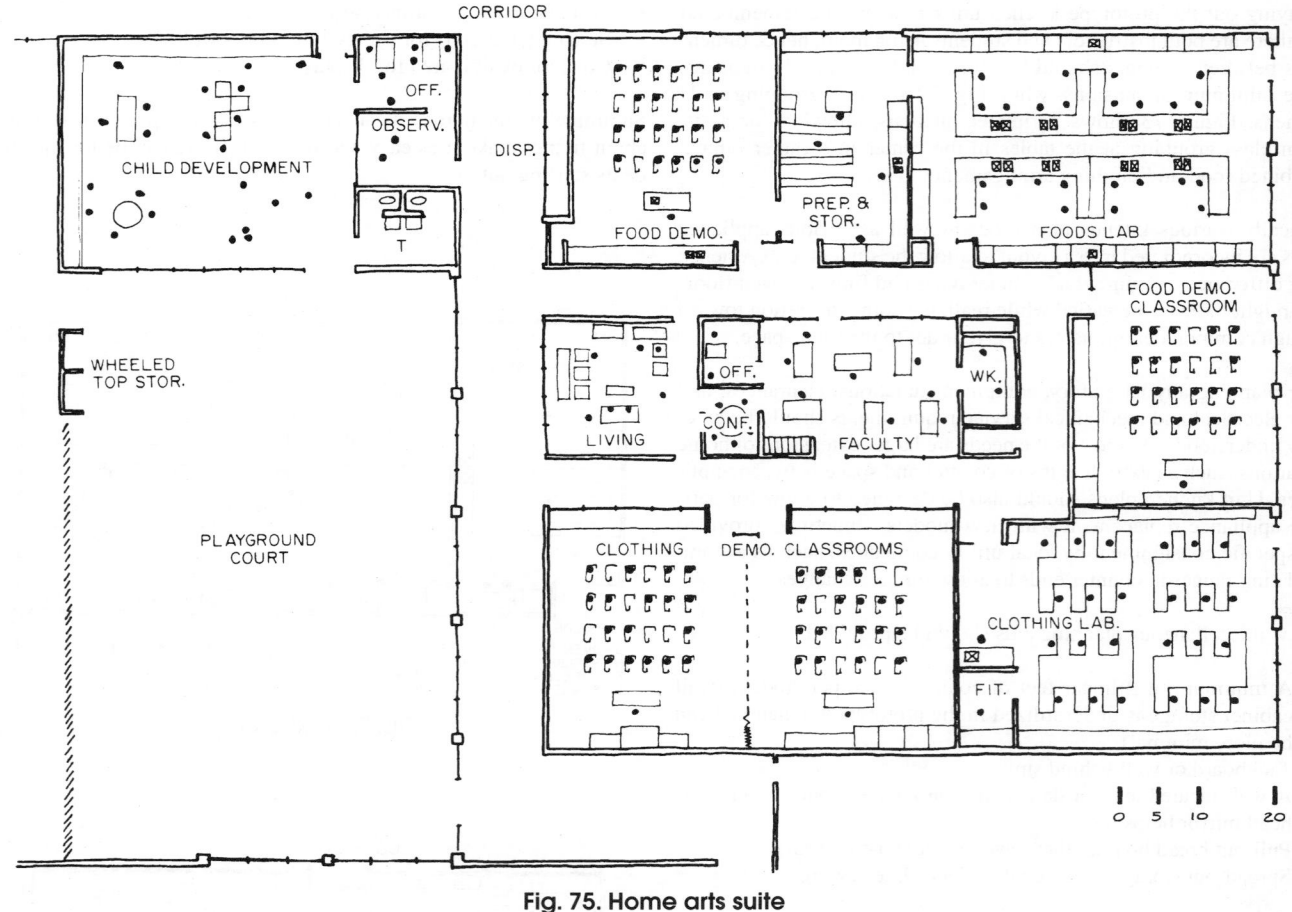

**Fig. 75. Home arts suite**

## MULTIPURPOSE ROOMS

Multipurpose rooms are primarily concerned with large areas in school buildings which are designed and equipped for two or more group activities. The most frequently used room combinations include assembly/cafeteria, assembly/cafeteria/gymnasium, assembly/gymnasium, and a student activity area where many small learning centers may operate at one time.

### Assembly/Cafeteria

The assembly/cafeteria combination is popular because the room can be designed with a pleasing environment for both eating and assembly. This type of room is also more adaptable to scheduling without limiting other phases of the educational program.

The room should be furnished with tables that can be quickly moved into a nearby storage area. A large portable folding unit containing table and benches has proved satisfactory for elementary schools. Tables that fold into the wall are also available. Many high schools prefer the smaller folding table and stacking chairs, which permit a more informal and flexible arrangement.

This type of room should have a stage, stage curtain, backdrops, and adequate lighting for dramatic presentations.

Student traffic flow in this area should be planned. Minimum cross traffic is essential during the lunch period when children are carrying food. During student assembly periods good circulation may reduce discipline problems.

### Assembly/Cafeteria/Gymnasium

The assembly/cafeteria/gymnasium combination can be found in schools where limited funds are available. This arrangement may seriously curtail the educational program. The time necessary to set up the cafeteria furniture, feed the children, clean the room, and remove the cafeteria furniture will consume a large portion of the school day. The remaining time available for physical and assembly activities may be insufficient for a good program. It is also difficult for the architect to design a room in which the atmosphere is conducive to dining, physical education, and assembly productions (Fig. 76).

### Assembly/Gymnasium

The assembly/gymnasium combination is a possible solution to seating the total student enrollment when a small or no auditorium is available. This area should be designed with a stage that can also be

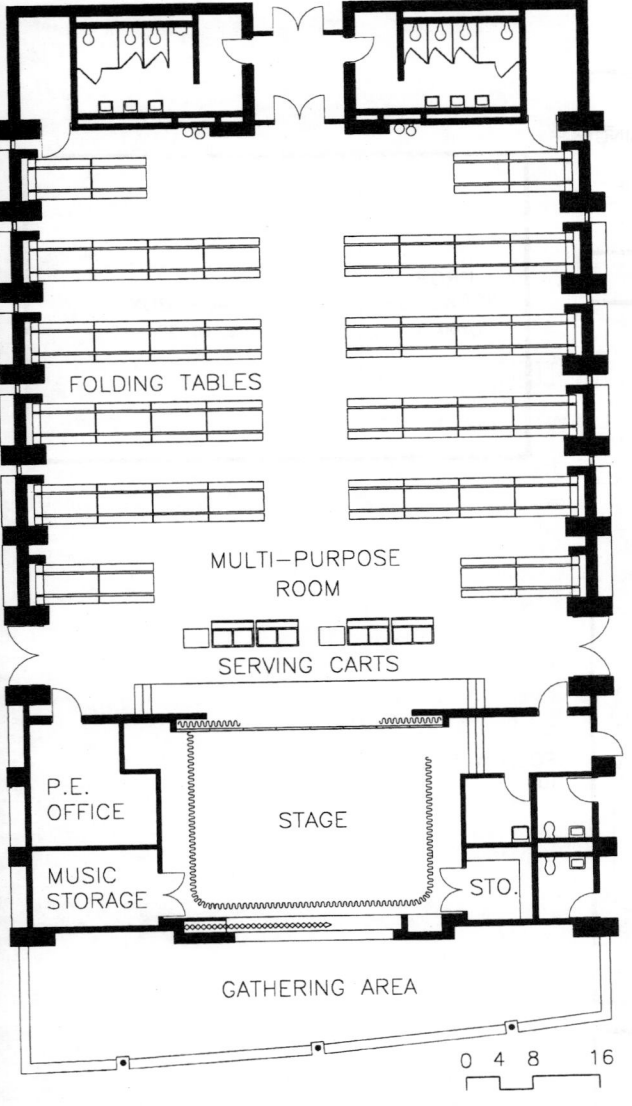

FOLDING TABLES

MULTI-PURPOSE
ROOM

SERVING CARTS

P.E.
OFFICE

STAGE

MUSIC
STORAGE

STO.

GATHERING AREA

0  4  8      16

**Fig. 76. Multipurpose room for elementary school**

used for physical activity. Storage space will be needed for chairs, gymnasium equipment, and stage equipment. Acoustics, lighting, ventilation, and traffic flow should be adequate for assembly and physical education. This arrangement is not considered as satisfactory as the assembly/cafeteria combination.

## AUDITORIUMS

The school auditorium is frequently used as a center for community affairs. It should be designed and equipped so that all groups—amateurs, professionals, youth, and adult alike—may use it effectively. The use of this facility will extend over a wide range, including concerts, plays, motion pictures, forums, and other forms of presentation.

The stage is the essential educational facility, for it is on the stage that young people have the opportunity to learn to present themselves before large groups. It should be designed for ease of movement of performers and stage sets. Areas that support production, such as stagecraft, band room, choral room, storage, dressing rooms, and rest rooms, should be located to give rapid and convenient access to the stage (Figs. 77 and 78).

Many school officials have expressed a preference for auditoriums without any natural lighting. Absolute light control is essential for a good performance. In some schools, windows can be darkened by automatic controls operated from a central point. Stage lighting should be flexible and simple enough to permit amateurs to operate the equipment effectively.

The seating of the auditorium is not as important from an educational point of view as it may be from the community use standpoint. There is no need for the school auditorium to seat the entire student body. It is best designed when the audience is small enough to make participation possible in group discussions and to ensure a reasonably full assembly area under most types of usage. A capacity of 300 to 800 would normally meet all school requirements. Additional capacity would be dictated largely by community use.

The school auditorium in Figs. 79 and 80 will comfortably seat about 650 students. A ticket booth is located in the foyer of the auditorium lobby. This lobby provides ample circulation space immediately outside the seating area. The placement of seats and aisles gives good traffic circulation. The entire seating area has adequate sight lines giving good view of the stage from all seats. The front of the stage platform extends beyond the main curtain, providing area for a speaker or discussion panel while the main stage is being set up for a following performance. Stage curtains, teasers, borders, and cyclorama can support various stage activities. The ample corridor space and doors back stage provide rapid circulation of performers, stage crews, and properties. The band and choral rooms are conveniently located by the stage as is a black box theater. The black box theater expands the types of performance spaces available to support curriculum needs (Fig. 81) while sharing the same support areas as the main auditorium. The auditorium also has direct access to a delivery area, which is convenient when delivering or removing stage properties.

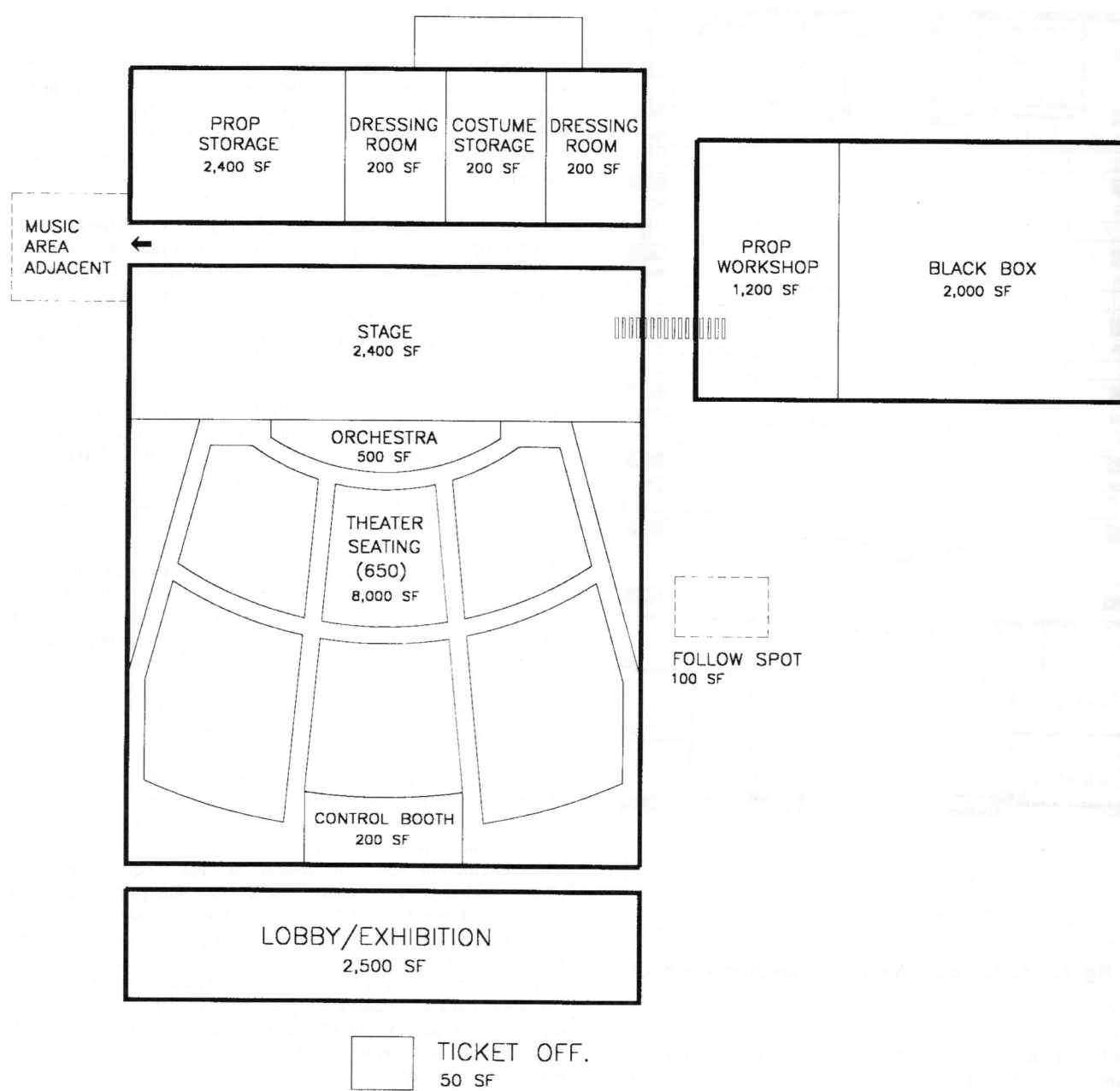

PROP
STORAGE
2,400 SF

DRESSING
ROOM
200 SF

COSTUME
STORAGE
200 SF

DRESSING
ROOM
200 SF

MUSIC
AREA
ADJACENT

PROP
WORKSHOP
1,200 SF

BLACK BOX
2,000 SF

STAGE
2,400 SF

ORCHESTRA
500 SF

THEATER
SEATING
(650)
8,000 SF

FOLLOW SPOT
100 SF

CONTROL BOOTH
200 SF

LOBBY/EXHIBITION
2,500 SF

TICKET OFF.
50 SF

**Fig. 77. Auditorium for 650 planning diagram**

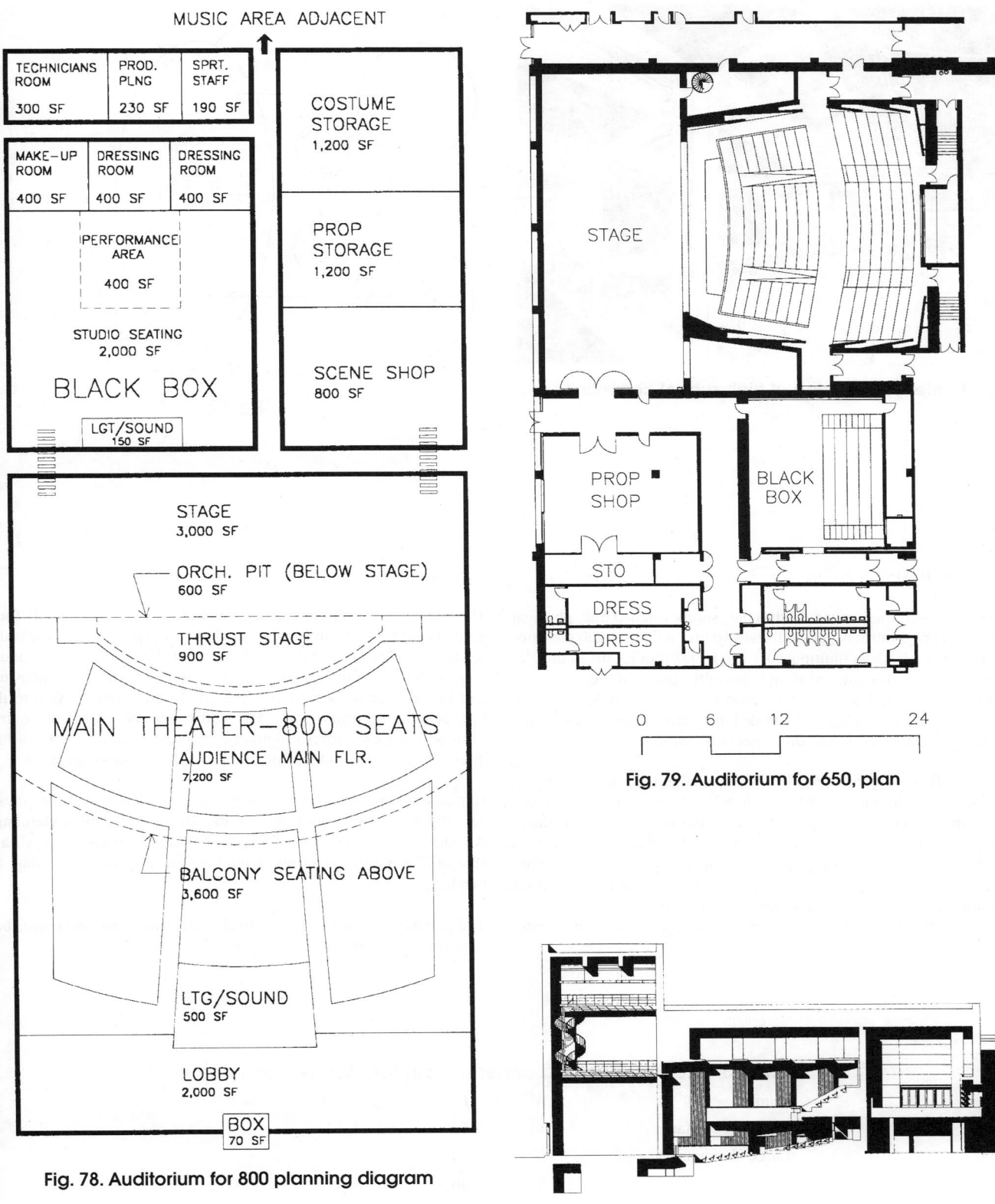

MUSIC AREA ADJACENT

| TECHNICIANS ROOM 300 SF | PROD. PLNG 230 SF | SPRT. STAFF 190 SF |
|---|---|---|

| MAKE-UP ROOM 400 SF | DRESSING ROOM 400 SF | DRESSING ROOM 400 SF |
|---|---|---|

PERFORMANCE AREA
400 SF

STUDIO SEATING
2,000 SF

# BLACK BOX

LGT/SOUND
150 SF

COSTUME STORAGE
1,200 SF

PROP STORAGE
1,200 SF

SCENE SHOP
800 SF

STAGE
3,000 SF

ORCH. PIT (BELOW STAGE)
600 SF

THRUST STAGE
900 SF

## MAIN THEATER—800 SEATS

AUDIENCE MAIN FLR.
7,200 SF

BALCONY SEATING ABOVE
3,600 SF

LTG/SOUND
500 SF

LOBBY
2,000 SF

BOX
70 SF

**Fig. 78. Auditorium for 800 planning diagram**

STAGE

PROP SHOP

BLACK BOX

STO

DRESS

DRESS

0    6    12    24

**Fig. 79. Auditorium for 650, plan**

0    6    12    24

**Fig. 80. Auditorium for 650, section**

**Fig. 81. Interior rendering of high school community theater**

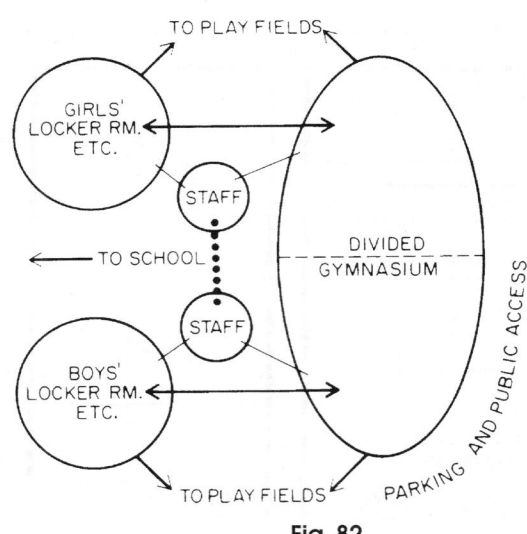

**Fig. 82**

## GYMNASIUMS

In this keep-fit, diet-crazed, body-bent, sports-minded age, physical education programs have gained a new focus, and top-notch facilities are getting built, from multipurpose 40- by 60-foot rooms in the elementary grades to multi-gyms and specialty spaces in the large high schools (Table 5). The basketball court is the common denominator of the gymnasium plan, overlapped by other court layouts and enlarged for other uses including spectator seating.

Factors influencing the right kind of environment are diagrammed in Fig. 82. Places to play should be well designed in all ways, and more than super-space boxes. The gymnasium, the whole physical education unit, is most always a place for other performance use, and so its internal planning relationships must serve its everyday use, but its public use sets other demands for its relation in the total plan. Its great volume begs other considerations for separate, special ventilating systems; structural systems; and related massing concerns of its exterior.

The basic relationship of elements and planning fundamentals for a gymnasium is shown in Figs. 83 to 88. In the typical school the staffs for boys and girls have a working relationship to each other and a responsibility for instructional supervision to both the gymnasium and locker spaces, as well as a preferred, direct relationship to the total school or corridor entry. The staff offices are, in effect, control centers. The locker rooms should be so located and planned to allow direct access to the outdoor playfields as well as to the gym.

Expansion potential should always be considered, and the physical education parts should not be locked into other plan elements. As enrollment increases, additional practice gyms or auxiliary spaces like wrestling rooms, a pool, or more locker space may be needed.

The gymnasium itself develops from many functional and prescribed requirements as are noted in Fig. 83.

**Table 5** Recommended dimensions in feet for gymnasiums

| School | W | L | $W_{I*}$ | $L_{I*}$ | Seats |
|---|---|---|---|---|---|
| Small elementary | 36 | 52 | | | |
| Large elementary | 52 | 72 | | | |
| Junior high school* | 65 | 86 | 42 | 74 | 400 |
| Small senior high school† | 79 | 96 | 50 | 84 | 700 |
| Large senior high school† | 100 | 104 | 50 | 84 | 1,500 |

*$W_I$ and $L_I$ are dimensions of basketball court.

†Use folding partition.

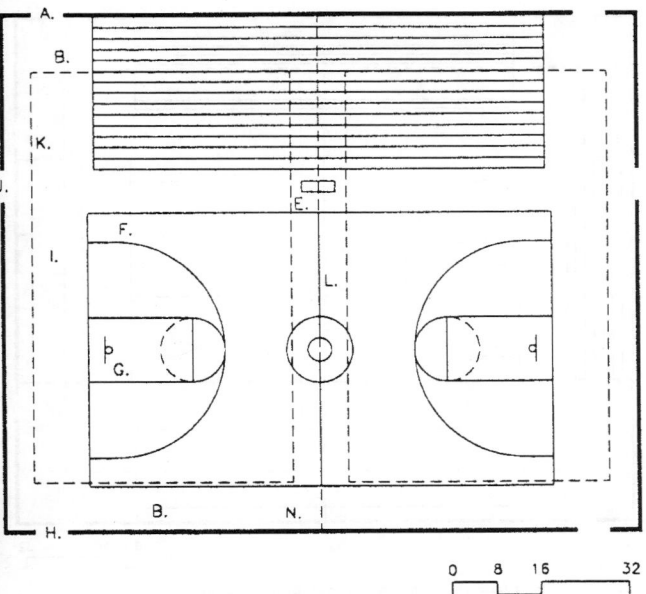

A. ACCESS FROM LOCKER ROOMS.
B. 5' MIN. DIMENSIONS RECOMMENDED—FACE OF BLEACHER OR WALL FROM END OR SIDE LINE OF COURT. 10' PREFERRED.
C. FOLDING BLEACHERS EXTENDED. VARIES DEPENDING ON REQUIREMENTS. FOR BEST SPECTATOR VIEW, RESTRICT BLEACHER LENGTH TO FACE-TO-FACE DIMENSION OF BACKBOARDS.
D. 6' MIN. — 10' RECOMMENDED.
E. SCORER'S TABLE—MAY BE LOCATED IN BLEACHERS. PROVIDE ELECTRICAL AN DATA OUTLETS, MICROPHONE JACK, AND SCOREBOARD CONTROLS.
F. COURT SIZE: JR. HIGH—50' X 74', HIGH SCHOOL—50' X 84'. SOME HIGH SCHOOLS USE COLLEGE SIZE COURT, 50' X 94', FOR VARSITY TOURNAMENT COURT.
G. HIGH SCHOOL BACKBOARD. TRANSPARENT OR NON TRANSPARENT. 1. 6' X 4' RECTANGLE. 2. 6' X 3-1/2' RECTANGLE, OR 3. 54" FAN SHAPED. KEEP WALLS BEHIND BACKBOARDS FREE OF DOORS AND OBSTRUCTIONS
H. EGRESS TO PLAYING FIELDS.
I. 10' RECOMMENDED CLEARANCE FOR TOURNAMENT COURT.
J. ACCESS FOR SPECTATORS. LOCATE TO MIN. TRAFFIC ON GYM FLOOR. (POSSIBLE USE OF CARPET RUNNERS.)
K. PRACTICE COURTS. MAY BE SHORTER AND MORE NARROW THAN STANDARD COURT.
L. STRUCTURE HUNG VERTICAL ROLL NET CURTAIN WITH CANVAS BOTTOM VISUAL BARRIER MAY BE USED.

0   8   16          32

**Fig. 83. Divided gym, seating one side (two teaching stations)**

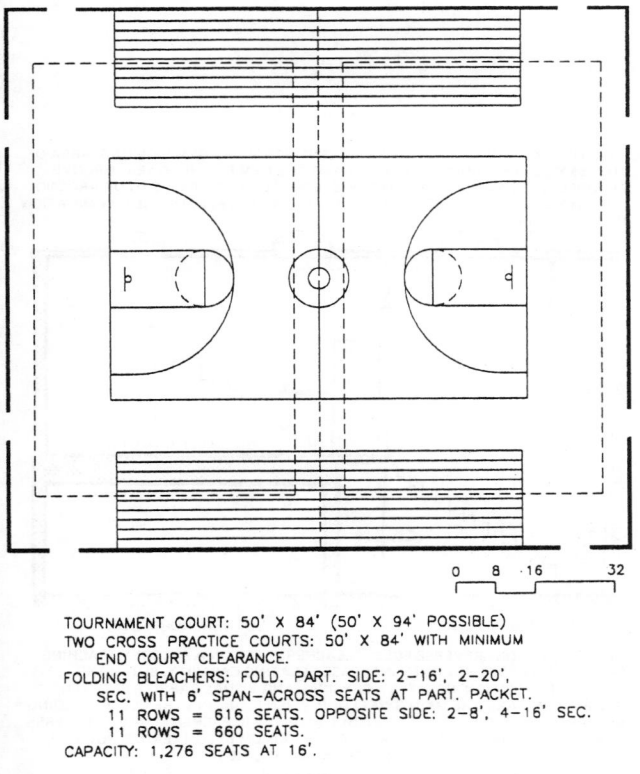

0   8   16          32

TOURNAMENT COURT: 50' X 84' (50' X 94' POSSIBLE)
TWO CROSS PRACTICE COURTS: 50' X 84' WITH MINIMUM END COURT CLEARANCE.
FOLDING BLEACHERS: FOLD. PART. SIDE: 2–16', 2–20', SEC. WITH 6' SPAN–ACROSS SEATS AT PART. PACKET.
    11 ROWS = 616 SEATS. OPPOSITE SIDE: 2–8', 4–16' SEC.
    11 ROWS = 660 SEATS.
CAPACITY: 1,276 SEATS AT 16'.

**Fig. 84. Divided gym, seating two sides (two teaching stations)**

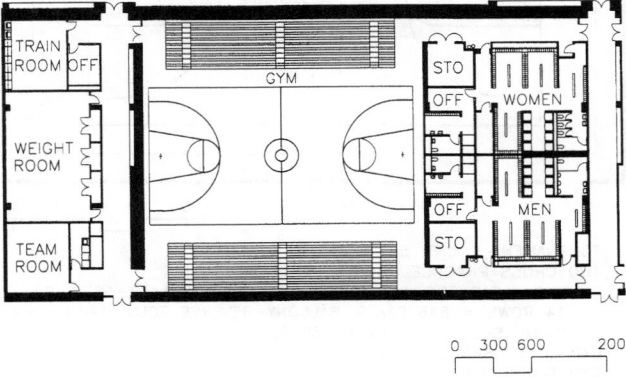

0   300   600        200

**Fig 85. Floor plan based on Fig. 84**

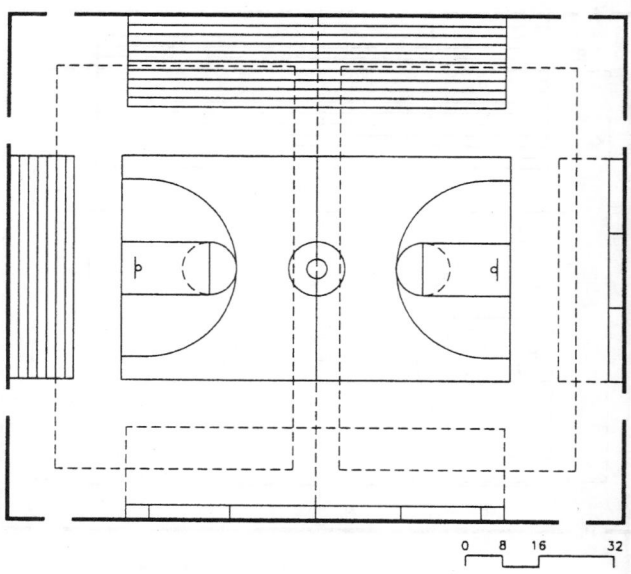

TOURNAMENT COURT: 50' X 84' WITH MINIMUM END AND SIDE CLEARANCE.
TWO CROSS PRACTICE COURTS: 50' X 84' WITH MINIMUM END COURT CLEARANCE.
FOLDING BLEACHERS: FOLD. PART. SIDE: 2–16', 2–20', SEC. WITH 6' SPAN ACROSS–11 ROWS = 616 SEATS.
OPPOSITE SIDE: 4–16', 2–8' SEC., 11 ROWS = 660 SEATS.
ENDS: 3–16' SEC. EACH, 9 ROWS = 648 SEATS.
CAPACITY: 1,924 SEATS AT 16"

**Fig. 86. Divided gym, seating four sides (two teaching stations)**

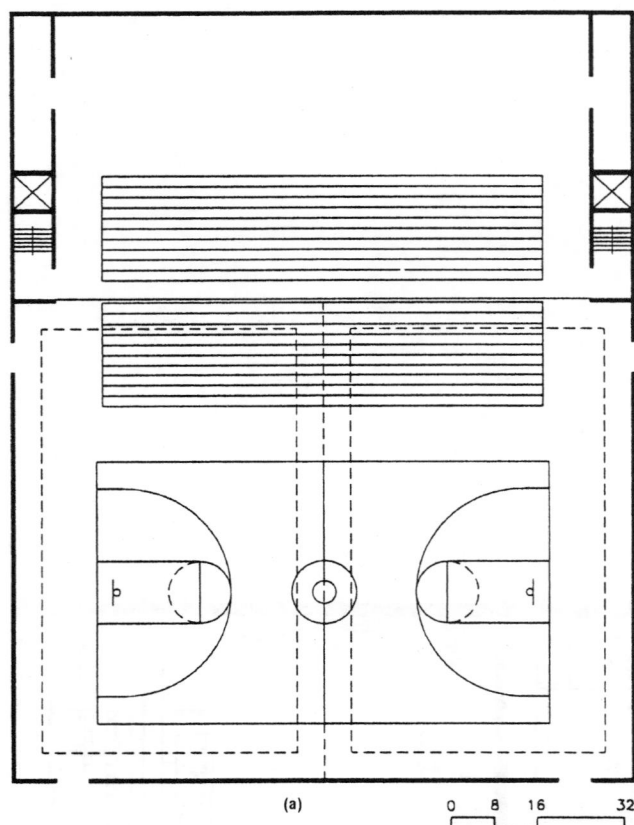

PLASTIC "SKY DOMES" PROVIDE EXCELLENT NONGLARE GYM LIGHTING. AREA OF THE "SKY DOMES" SHOULD EQUAL 4–6% OF THE GYM FLOOR. POWER–GROOVE FLUORESCENT LAMPED LIGHT FIXTURES, GROUPED ADJUSTABLE TO OR AROUND THE "SKY DOMES" PROVIDES A GOOD CLEAN LOOKING ELECTRICAL ILLUMINATION INSTALLATION.

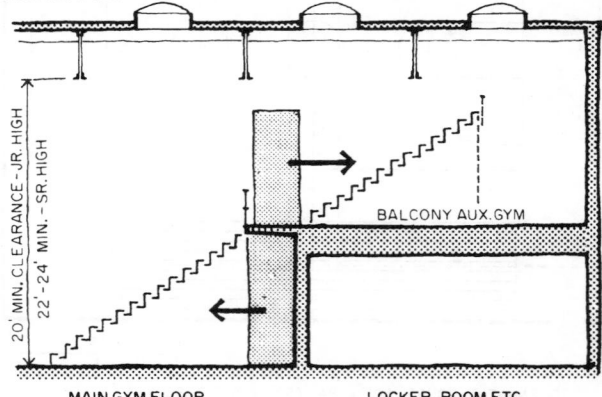

DELAYED ACTION–REVERSE FOLD. BLEACHERS USED ON A BALCONY TEACHING STATION, PROVIDES NOT ONLY INCREASED SEATING CAPACITY, BUT IN THE RETRACTED POSITION, CREATES A PHYSICAL AND VISUAL BARRIER BETWEEN THE BALCONY AND THE MAIN GYM FLOOR. WHEN PLANNING THE USE OF FOLDING BLEACHERS AS SHOWN ABOVE, CONSULT WITH THE BLEACHER MANUFACTURERS FOR CORRECT DIMENSIONS, CLEARANCES, MAXIMUM RECOMMENDED ROWS, OPERATION AND SEAT RISE, FOR OPTIMUM SIGHT LINES.

(b)

(a)

TOURNAMENT COURT: 50' X 94'
TWO CROSS PRACTICE COURTS: 50' X 84'
FOLDING BLEACHERS: GYM FLOOR–RECESSED: 4–14',2–16' SEC. 14 ROWS = 846 SEATS. BALCONY–REVERSE FOLD: 4–14', 2–16' SEC., 15 ROWS = 960 SEATS.
CAPACITY: 1,846 SEATS AT 16".
GYM FLOOR: 94' X 120'.

**Fig. 87. (a) Divided gym with (b) balcony auxiliary gym, seating one side (four teaching stations)**

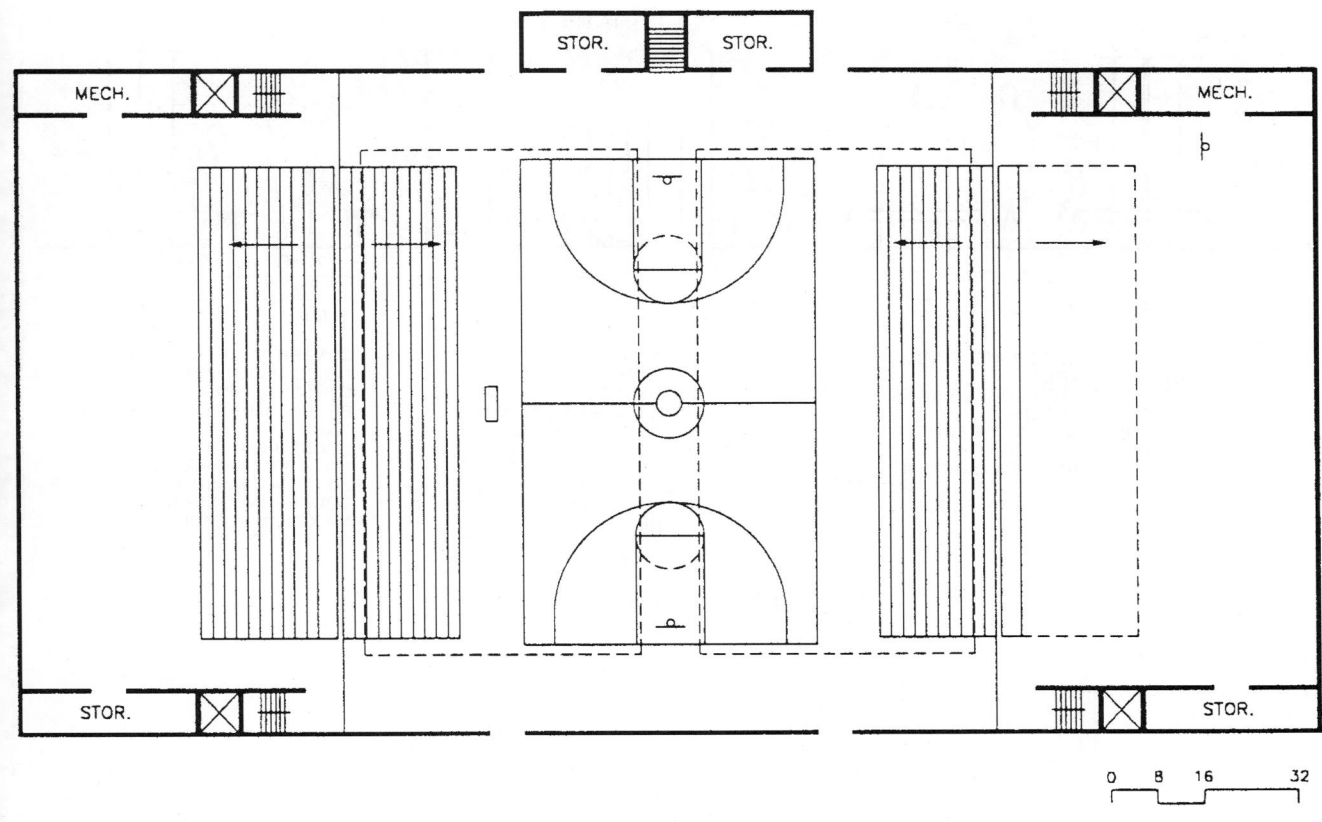

TOURNAMENT COURT: 50' X 84'.
TWO PARALLEL PRACTICE COURTS: 50' X 84'.
FOLDING BLEACHERS: GYM FLOOR-RECESSED: 1-14', 4-16' SEC. -14 ROWS = 812 SEATS ⎤— EACH SIDE
  BALCONY-REVERSE FOLD: 5-16' SEC. -15 ROWS = 900 SEATS. ⎦
  CAPACITY: 3,424 SEATS AT 16".
GYM FLOOR: 104' X 120'.

**Fig. 88. Divided gym with balcony auxiliary gyms, seating two sides (four teaching stations)**

## Locker Rooms

Locker rooms need not be the noisy, steamy, smelly, dimly lit spaces too many have been. Because they are very concentrated areas of complex plumbing and ventilation and hardware requirements, they can be expensive to build and are too often made too minimal to properly function and be maintained.

Locker rooms are busy places for students in a hurry, dressing in never-enough room, with showering humidity, outdoor muck, and emotional pitch and pique as added realities. A very functional plan is a must, one that thoroughly considers traffic flow, the realities of body dressing clearances, locker door swings, clothing storage, systems for towel distribution, uniform drying, and supervision and discipline. Equal concern must be given to good and durable lighting, plumbing, ventilation, and finishes (see Fig. 89).

Unless the increasingly seldom used system of central basket storage is utilized for clothing storage, the number and ratio of gym suit to street clothes lockers are determined by the formula:

$$T \times N/P = S$$

where T = number of students to be enrolled

N = number of times/week student in course

P = number of periods/week that physical education is given (hours/day × days/week)

S = number of street clothes (dressing) lockers required

T also then represents the gym suit lockers needed, and T/S = R, or the ratio of gym suit versus street clothes lockers, varying as shown in Figs. 89, 90, and 91 determining the total space required for lockers.

The standard type of full-length locker should be set on a masonry base to facilitate cleaning. The unit should be complete with two top shelves, ventilating grilles, and four hooks for hanging clothes. Some type of locking device should be furnished.

Wire baskets may be used in place of the small lockers for the storage of gym clothes. Although in some cases the baskets have been mounted in a fixed position, it is more desirable to place them on

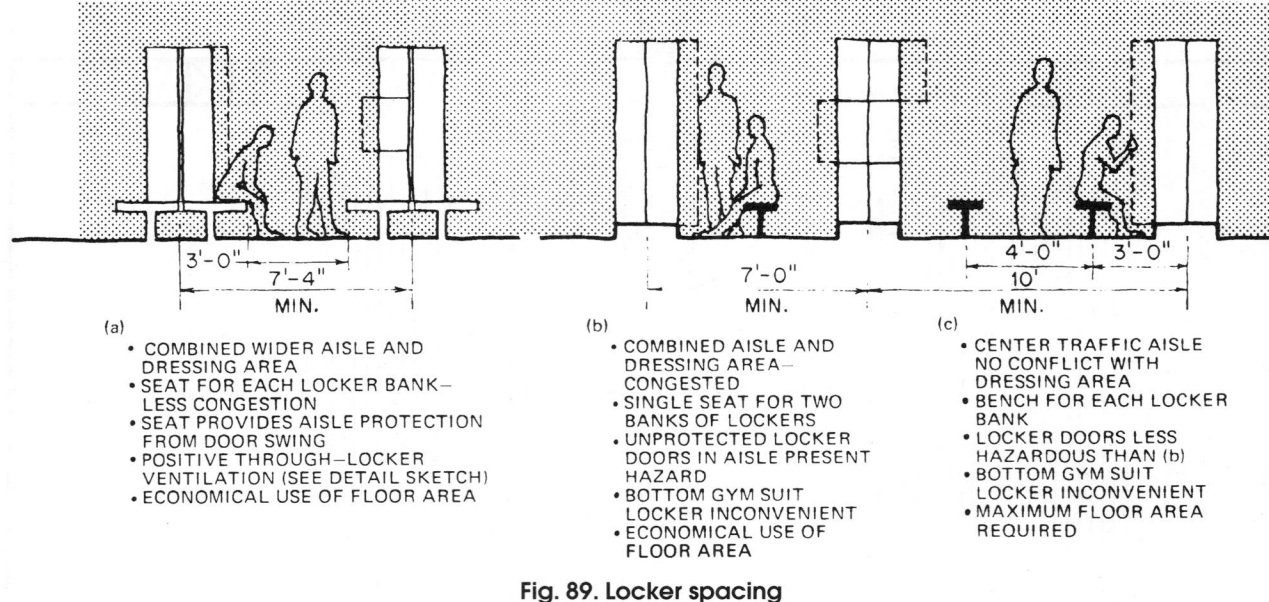

(a)
- COMBINED WIDER AISLE AND DRESSING AREA
- SEAT FOR EACH LOCKER BANK— LESS CONGESTION
- SEAT PROVIDES AISLE PROTECTION FROM DOOR SWING
- POSITIVE THROUGH—LOCKER VENTILATION (SEE DETAIL SKETCH)
- ECONOMICAL USE OF FLOOR AREA

(b)
- COMBINED AISLE AND DRESSING AREA— CONGESTED
- SINGLE SEAT FOR TWO BANKS OF LOCKERS
- UNPROTECTED LOCKER DOORS IN AISLE PRESENT HAZARD
- BOTTOM GYM SUIT LOCKER INCONVENIENT
- ECONOMICAL USE OF FLOOR AREA

(c)
- CENTER TRAFFIC AISLE NO CONFLICT WITH DRESSING AREA
- BENCH FOR EACH LOCKER BANK
- LOCKER DOORS LESS HAZARDOUS THAN (b)
- BOTTOM GYM SUIT LOCKER INCONVENIENT
- MAXIMUM FLOOR AREA REQUIRED

**Fig. 89. Locker spacing**

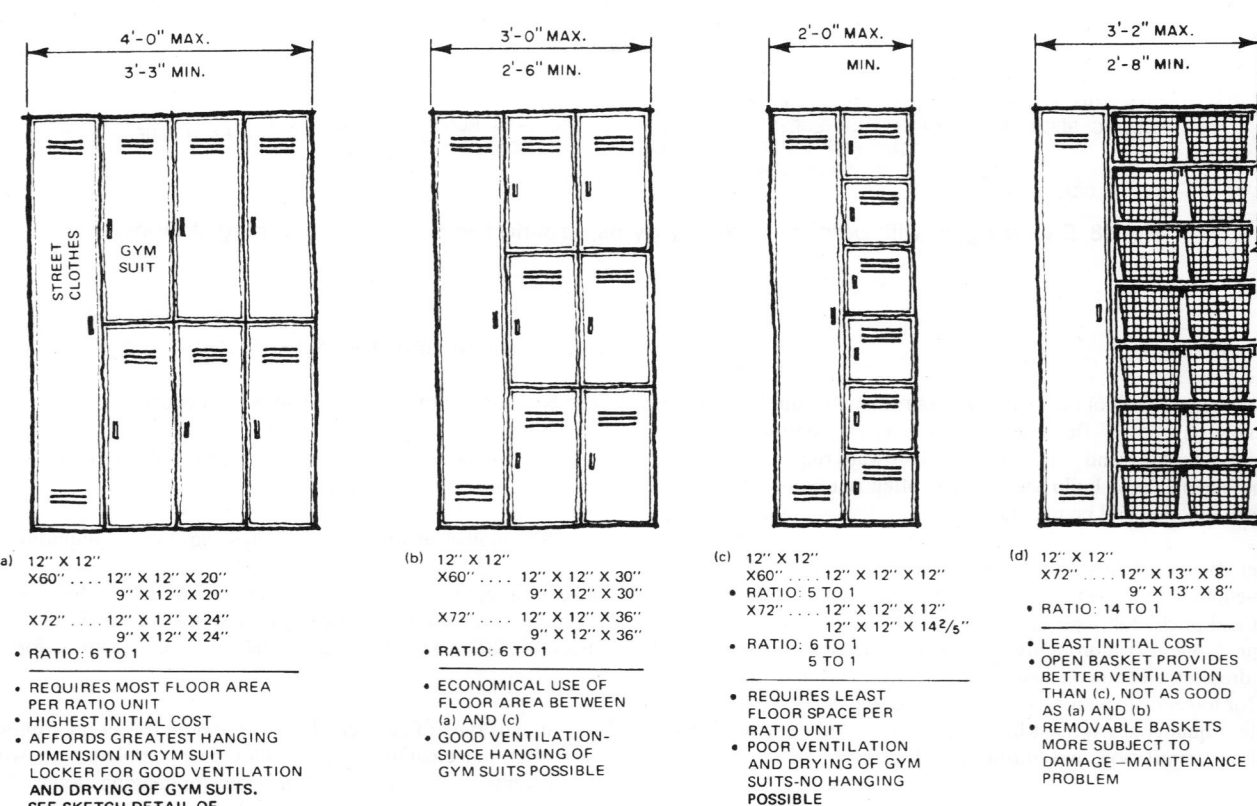

(a) 12″ X 12″
X60″ . . . . 12″ X 12″ X 20″
9″ X 12″ X 20″

X72″ . . . . 12″ X 12″ X 24″
9″ X 12″ X 24″
- RATIO: 6 TO 1

- REQUIRES MOST FLOOR AREA PER RATIO UNIT
- HIGHEST INITIAL COST
- AFFORDS GREATEST HANGING DIMENSION IN GYM SUIT LOCKER FOR GOOD VENTILATION AND DRYING OF GYM SUITS. SEE SKETCH DETAIL OF POSITIVE VENTILATION THROUGH LOCKERS

(b) 12″ X 12″
X60″ . . . . 12″ X 12″ X 30″
9″ X 12″ X 30″

X72″ . . . . 12″ X 12″ X 36″
9″ X 12″ X 36″
- RATIO: 6 TO 1

- ECONOMICAL USE OF FLOOR AREA BETWEEN (a) AND (c)
- GOOD VENTILATION— SINCE HANGING OF GYM SUITS POSSIBLE

(c) 12″ X 12″
X60″ . . . . 12″ X 12″ X 12″
- RATIO: 5 TO 1
X72″ . . . . 12″ X 12″ X 12″
12″ X 12″ X 14²/₅″
- RATIO: 6 TO 1
5 TO 1

- REQUIRES LEAST FLOOR SPACE PER RATIO UNIT
- POOR VENTILATION AND DRYING OF GYM SUITS—NO HANGING POSSIBLE

(d) 12″ X 12″
X72″ . . . . 12″ X 13″ X 8″
9″ X 13″ X 8″
- RATIO: 14 TO 1

- LEAST INITIAL COST
- OPEN BASKET PROVIDES BETTER VENTILATION THAN (c), NOT AS GOOD AS (a) AND (b)
- REMOVABLE BASKETS MORE SUBJECT TO DAMAGE—MAINTENANCE PROBLEM

NOTE: OTHER WIDTHS, DEPTHS AND COMBINATIONS ARE AVAILABLE: THESE SHOWN ARE REPRESENTATIVE.

**Fig. 90**

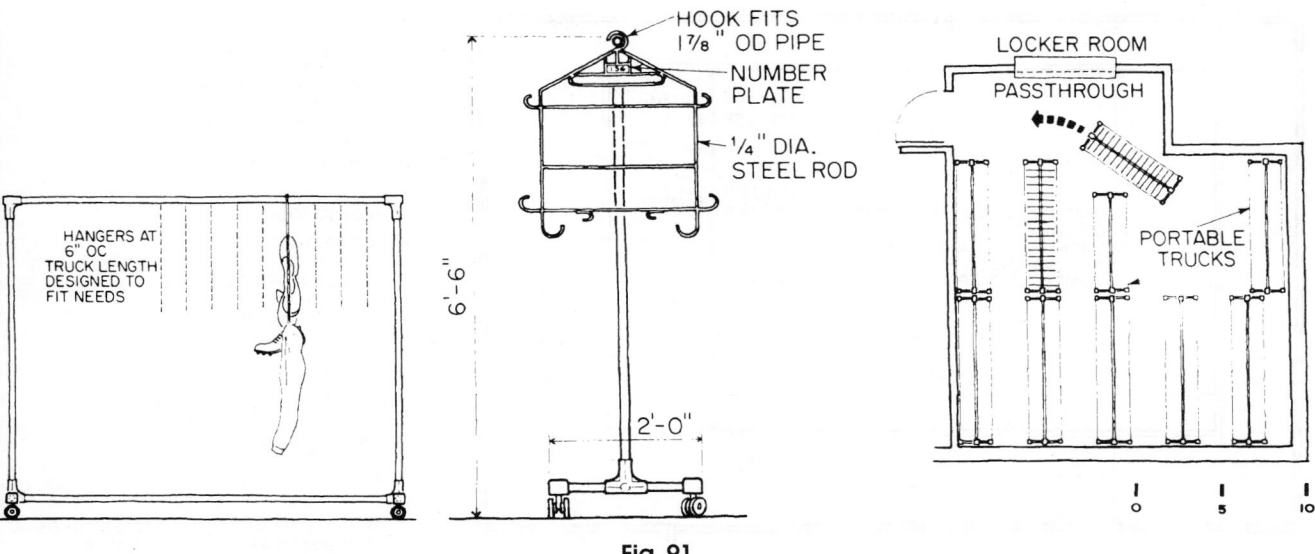

**Fig. 91**

trucks which can be locked in a well-ventilated storage space. The basket system is generally more difficult to manage than the locker system.

A common arrangement is to provide one large dressing locker, together with six storage lockers. This permits the student to have a large locker in which to hang his street clothes and also provides him with a small locker for the storage of gym clothes.

**Swimming Pools**

Swimming pools are a very desirable, but relatively expensive, part of a physical education program. However, with the increasing public interest in participating, more recreational activities are being built as parts of schools or as community facilities.

Swimming programs divide their activities into diving, swimming instruction, and competitive swimming. The more extensive facilities accommodate these three activities into separate, appropriately designed pools or develop diving alcove areas in T- or L-shaped pools.

The basics of pool design are covered in Fig. 92, the various dimensions relating to the age group using the pool. Important also is the amount and location of the surrounding deck area for instructional use, a related advantage of the T- and L-shaped pools (Fig. 93).

Giving spectators a good and comfortable view involves proper sight lines, plus a careful consideration of acoustic and lighting that takes into account the reflectance of the water. Figure 94 shows one solution where the light source has been screened and the ceiling made nonparallel to the floor to minimize reverberation. Figure 95 illustrates other ideas for user comfort and convenience. A way to accommodate supervision and privacy both is shown in Fig. 96.

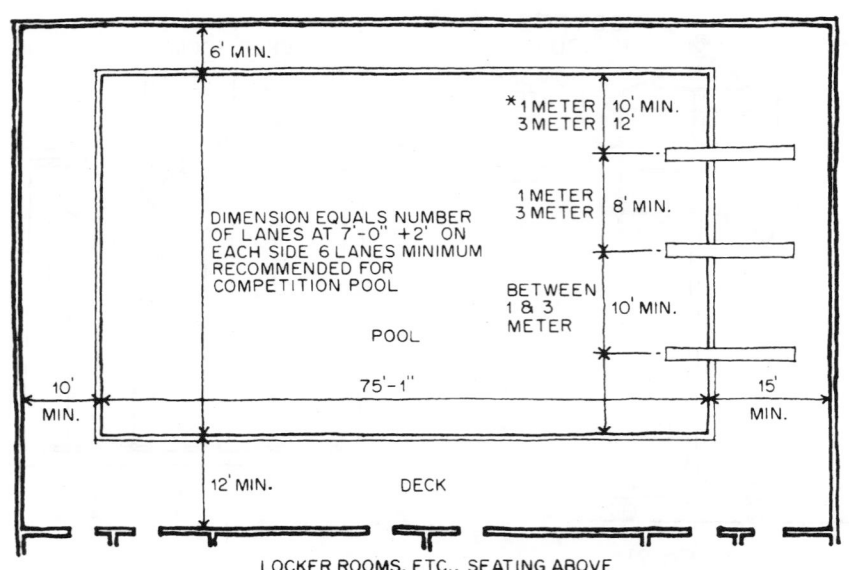

SIZE RECOMMENDATIONS:

ELEMENTARY SCHOOL

WATER DEPTH: 2' TO 4', 4.5'
MIN. WIDTH: 16'
DESIRABLE WIDTH: 20', 25', 30'
MIN. LENGTH: 36'
DESIRABLE LENGTH: 50', 60', 75'

JR. HIGH SCHOOL

WATER DEPTH: 3'–5'
MIN. WIDTH: 25'
DESIRABLE WIDTH: 30', 36', 42'
MIN. LENGTH: 60'
DESIRABLE LENGTH: 75'

SENIOR HIGH SCHOOL

WATER DEPTH: 3'–6'' TO 9' (1M. BD)*
MIN. WIDTH: 36'      12' (2M. BD)
DESIRABLE WIDTH: 45'–46'
MIN. LENGTH
    DESIRABLE:    75'–1''

*4' SHALLOW DEPTH PERMITS FASTER TURNS.
FASTER SPEEDS ARE POSSIBLE IN 5' OR
DEEPER WATER.

**Fig. 92. Recommended minimum pool design dimensions**

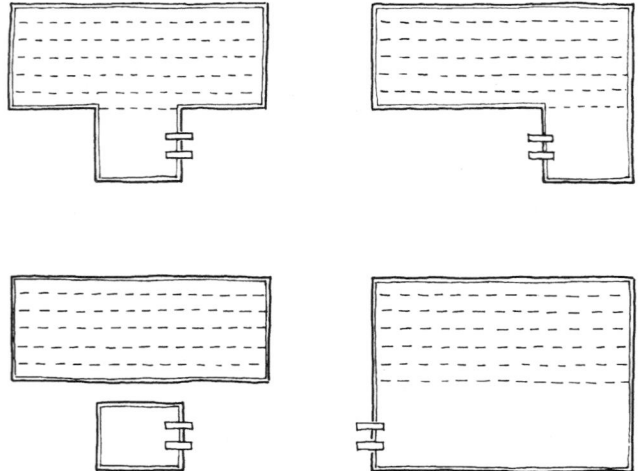

**Fig. 93. Additional pool shapes incorporating separated diving pool**

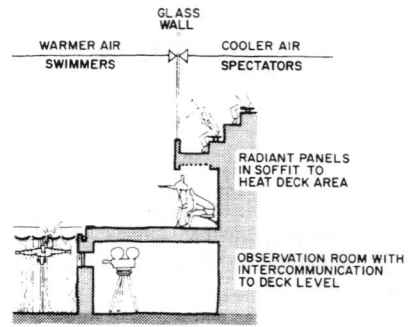

**Fig. 95. Comfort control**

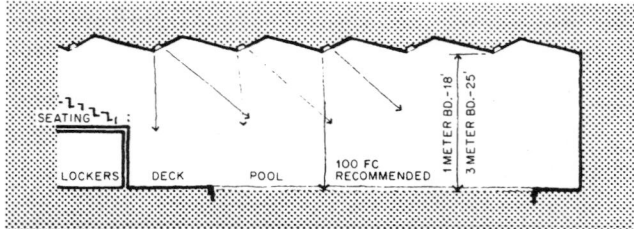

**Fig. 94. Light source not from spectator area**

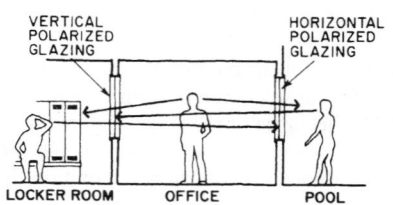

**Fig. 96. Visual control for supervision**

# FOOD SERVICE

Lunch time can and should be break-time, a change of pace in a place different in feeling and fact from the rest of the day. In reality, it is hard to be efficient in the use of space in schools. Most often lunch-rooms must serve other purposes. Time for eating is cut too finely between academic periods. Great numbers must be served in a hurry. In today's schools cafeterias are often doubling as dining rooms and gathering areas or commons. In line with this dual functionality, a trend is developing to create school dining facilities that resemble food courts by creating a social atmosphere while providing a variety of food choices.

All the more reason and need then to try harder while planning to carefully consider the processes of food preparation and serving, together with seating areas and traffic flow, to give the best chance for table manners to survive and a happy shipshape atmosphere to exist amid the hubbub.

There are enough ordinary problems to be solved in planning a din-ing and kitchen area to allow consideration of a unique design approach. Like anything that is architecture, it grows from those human needs it is serving, asking: Whom are we going to serve? What are we going to serve them? How will we go about it?

The program is made up of three factors: patrons, menus, and opera-tion. Particularly in this part of the school, the allocation and arrangement of spaces and the choice of fixtures must develop for specific reasons in order that the total design be functional.

## Conventional Kitchen

The serving counter adjacent to a conventional kitchen requires little or no cartage of bulk food. In Fig. 97 the distance between prepared food and pickup of trays is but the thickness of the wall. Kitchen per-sonnel assemble trays at both sides of this assembly line. There are no conveyor belts. Trays are set up in advance with napkin-wrapped silver. Output of the line is two trays at a time. Snack bars, when they do exist in schools, usually augment cafeteria counter service of a full, hot lunch. Most snack bars serve milk, prepackaged ice cream, apples and cookies, as does the small unit in Fig. 98. Some serve soft drinks. The second or third counter in some high schools is an a la carte service (see Fig. 99).

Clean dishes are needed at the serving station; the serving station is adjacent to the cafeteria. Soiled trays and dishes from the cafeteria are usually deposited by student customers at the dishroom. This cycle establishes the location of dishwashing as adjacent to cafeteria and adjacent to serving, as shown in Figs. 97 and 98.

Large cafeterias utilize conveyor belts because these permit multiple and simultaneous deposit of trays. Fig. 100 shows a belt bringing soiled trays from the student and faculty dining rooms to join trays from a third dining room for scraping near the feed end of the dish-washer. The baffle wall between the conveyor and dishroom in Fig. 101 screens that room's activities and sounds from the dining area. Ample dish- and tray-scraping table, disposer and shelf space can be provided whether or not a conveyor is used.

Flight-type dishwashing machines are commonly employed for patronage numbers as small as 1,000, although conveyor models function efficiently for programs of more than 1,000 people. This choice depends upon many factors, such as the amount of ware to be

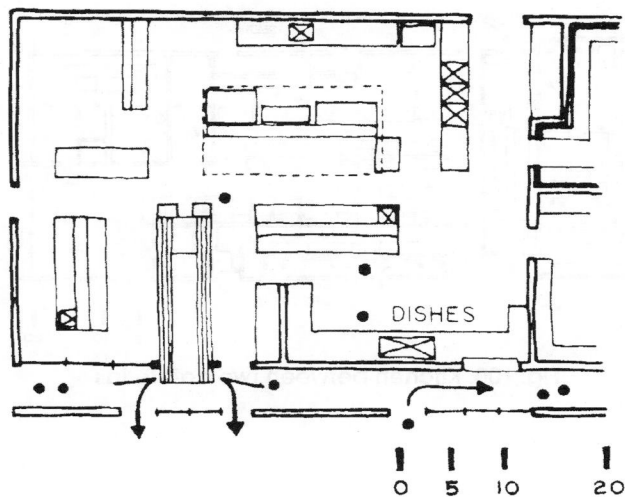

**Fig. 97. Kitchen, serving, dishwashing**

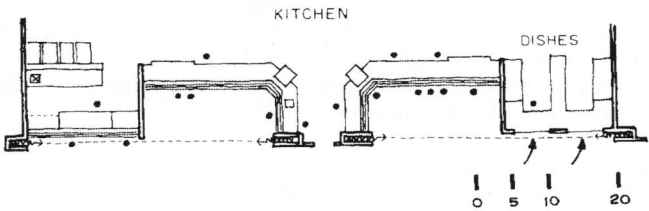

**Fig. 98. Snack bar, serving, and dishwashing**

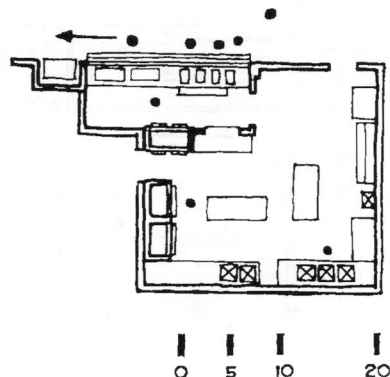

**Fig. 99. Cold food kitchen and a la carte counter**

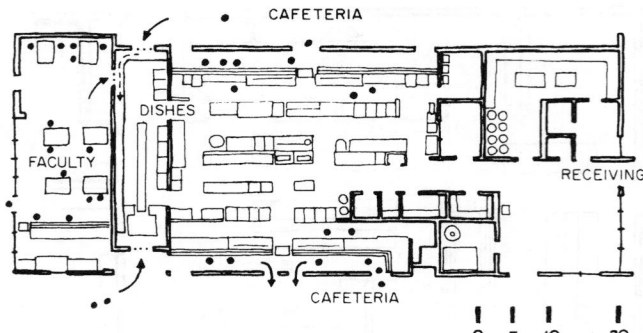

Fig. 100. Kitchen between two cafeterias

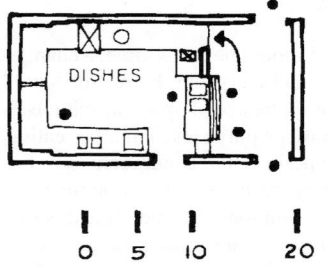

Fig. 102. Remote serving station

stored and handled in racks, the shape of the room available, and the ratio of trays to dishes, etc.

The dishroom is difficult to ventilate effectively. Provide a steam removal exhaust for dishwasher, ample fresh air supply and exhaust, and keep ceiling high for maximum cubic feet of air in circulation.

**Kitchen Central to Site**

Small bulk-food carts can traverse the corridors or elevators from the kitchen to the remote serving station within a building. The hot food, cold food, and pastry carts shown at the serving station in Fig. 101 have been fitted with tongues and hitches. They are pulled by electric tractor from the existing kitchen in the old school building through the new corridors to this location.

Some remote serving stations have dishwashing facilities. The source of clean dishes must be close to the serving station in any plan. Fig. 102 shows a small serving station that includes a counter garaging bulk foods under its top, a back bar with refrigerator and small electric appliances, plus a complete assembly of soiled and clean dish tables with smallest floor-supported dishwasher, a window sill for soiled tray deposit, a disposer, and a silver-soak sink.

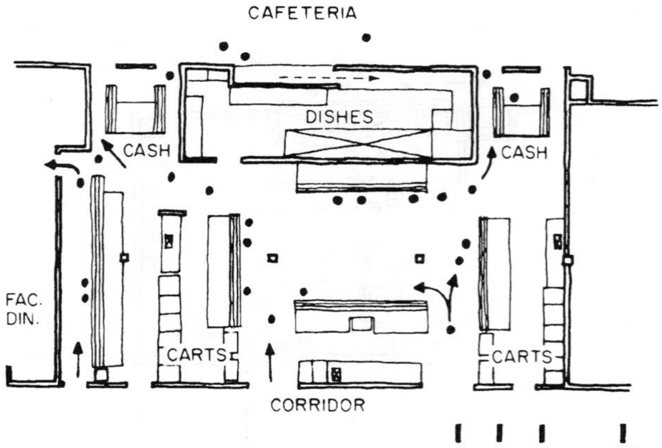

Any remote station also requires some dish-scraping facility; it is not practical to transport garbage. Note the location of soiled tray deposit in the remote serving station of Fig. 103. The plan permits the flow of high school student patrons to circulate around this serving station segment of the building without any turning back or crossing of traffic. Pick-up food and entrance to the dining area are at the left of the plan; exit and tray deposit are at the right. Within the segment, dishes are processed in a direction toward the serving station.

**Kitchens Central to Community**

The conventional kitchen differs from the central kitchen in that it does not have to accommodate, wash, garage, and load bulk-food carts. Kitchens central to the community differ from the kitchen central to a building because community bulk-food carts and kitchen cart spaces are large, and these carts are invariably transported by motor vehicle. Each of those shown in Fig. 104 is strapped into place along with a cart of trays inside a truck. The truck is fitted with a hydraulic tailgate to adjust to the various unloading conditions at community schools. Thus, an adjacent, well-appointed loading-dock facility is imperative. If located in a cold climate, the loading dock can be enclosed.

Compartmented trays used in lieu of dishes travel in carts to the remote serving station in the community and are returned to the central kitchen for dishwashing, as shown in Fig. 104. This largest of carts keeping bulk, hot, and cold food has a serving top. It therefore has many applications as a portable counter, for example for service in the classroom to kindergarten tots and first graders. Fig. 103 shows it substituting for a section of built-in counter.

Fig. 101. Serving and seating arrangements

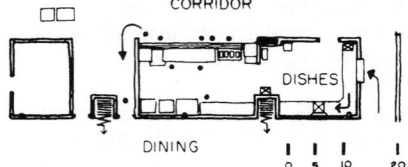

Fig. 103. Remote serving station

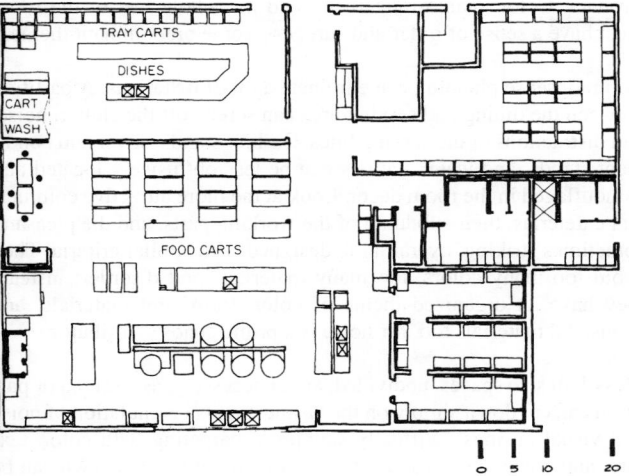

TRAY CARTS

DISHES

CART WASH

FOOD CARTS

0 5 10 20

**Fig. 104. Community central kitchen**

## Anatomy of a Kitchen

An efficient kitchen has a straight-through flow of foods being processed from the raw state to finished and ready to serve. Table 6 suggests space sizes while Table 7 shows the adjacencies.

## Serving Counters

When the menu is simple and everyone receives the same lunch, tray assembly can be employed for fast service. When food choices are offered, the serving counter is needed to stock and display items. The number of seats in the cafeteria determines the total length of serving counter required (refer to Table 8). Bottlenecks in student traffic can occur if counters are not of sufficient size, if there are too few cashiers, or if there are not ample seats. As Table 8 illustrates, a counter (35 feet) is required for every 150 to 200 seats. One to two cashiers per counter is recommended. The quantity of seats required is halfway between one-third and one-half of total patrons daily. This formula provides for the peak load in the cafeteria, which will occur during three seating periods.

**Table 6** Kitchen spaces in square feet

| Department | 500 | 1,000 | 2,000 | 3,000 |
|---|---|---|---|---|
| Receiving | 50–70 | 80–100 | 160–200 | 240–300 |
| Dry storage* | 150–250 | 300–500 | 600–1,000 | 900–1,500 |
| Refrigerated storage | 180 | 180 | 360 | 500 |
| Dishwashing† | 120–150 | 240–480 | 520–720 | 750–780 |
| Trash room | 90–110 | 130–150 | 190–240 | 250–320 |
| Employee lockers and toilets | 65–80 | 100–115 | 230–250 | 330–360 |
| Manager's office | 80 | 80 | 120 | 140 |

*Dry storage has direct relationship to quantity of patrons.

†The dishroom shape and size relate to type pf machine required.

**Table 7** Kitchen adjacencies

| Departments | Relationship |
|---|---|
| Receiving and trash rooms | Near dock |
| Dry storage | Near the receiving area and adjacent to the kitchen |
| Refrigerated storage | Near the receiving area and adjacent to the kitchen |
| Pre-preparation sinks, tables | Between refrigerated storage and vegetable prep |
| Vegetable preparation | Adjacent to the cooking battery |
| Cooking | Adjacent to the cooking battery |
| Baking | Can be remote, adjacent to the kitchen |
| Pot washing | Must be near the cooking area, baking area or both |
| Salad making | Near refrigerated storage, can be remote, adjacent to the kitchen |

It is increasingly necessary, with the advent of modular scheduling of classes, to provide for fast pickup of food. For this reason, "scramble" and other configurations should be contemplated as soon as more than one counter is required. This need not increase the quantity of counters. Sections of counters for categories of foods, such as beverages or cold foods are arranged separately for direct and quick access.

If the scramble system incorporates parallel units, the minimum distance between tray slides is 12 to 13 feet. Duplication of counter sections keeps traffic crisscross at a minimum. The scramble system is most successful in schools or any situations where people eat regularly. The patron who enters the serving area knows where she is going. The scramble layout in Fig. 105 incorporates a beverage island at the center. Two sides of the island are identical. Figures 106 and 107 show examples of elementary school cafeterias.

### Dining Rooms, Seating and Plan Arrangements

While bywords like washable, easily maintained, movable, durable, and economical do and must prevail in selecting furnishings and finishes, the call for character and creativity must then come on

stronger. Color, plan arrangement, and the whole feel of the room must have a sense of order and sureness, some predominant theme.

Commonsense planning can eliminate a lot of irritations. A partition between the dining and serving area can screen off the clutter, noise, and distractions of the serving lines. Cashier stands, silver and condiment stands, and water stations can be less obtrusively located and camouflaged in the room decor. Look at the more attractive commercial cafeterias, their subduing of the working parts, and the pleasant, sometimes striking, overall look designed with similar criteria. They avoid too many colors, too many materials, and disorder; instead, they have an organized theme of color, form, and materials, and acoustical materials too, for noise is a prime chaos contributor.

Mess-hall size spaces, undivided, are unnecessary, as a screen or partition can cut down simply on the vastness and accumulation of noise and visual business. Virtually stainproof carpeting with color, texture, and a whole environmental control and order of its own can be used now to further minimize noise. Or, if the room has to serve for gym or dances, all kinds and colors of resilient flooring materials are available.

**Table 8** Food service space requirements for school, college, and commercial lunch programs

| Planned enrollment or patrons | Seats required | Area designation, sq ft Kitchen | Serving | Number of counters |
|---|---|---|---|---|
| 400 | 170 | 1,500 | 700 | 1 |
| 500 | 210 | 1,650 | 800 | |
| 600 | 250 | 1,800 | 1,540 | 2 |
| 700 | 290 | 1,950 | 1,540 | |
| 800 | 335 | 2,100 | 1,920 | |
| 900 | 375 | 2,250 | 1,920 | |
| 1,000 | 420 | 2,400 | 2,310 | 3 |
| 1,100 | 460 | 2,250 | 2,310 | |
| 1,200 | 500 | 2,700 | 2,690 | |
| 1,300 | 540 | 2,850 | 2,690 | |
| 1,400 | 585 | 3,000 | 2,690 | |
| 1,500 | 625 | 3,150 | 3,080 | 4 |
| 1,600 | 670 | 3,300 | 3,080 | |
| 1,700 | 710 | 3,450 | 3,460 | |
| 1,800 | 750 | 3,600 | 3,460 | |
| 1,900 | 790 | 3,750 | 3,460 | |
| 2,000 | 835 | 3,900 | 3,850 | 5 |
| 2,100 | 875 | 4,050 | 3,850 | |
| 2,200 | 920 | 4,200 | 4,230 | |
| 2,300 | 960 | 4,350 | 4,230 | |
| 2,400 | 1,000 | 4,500 | 4,620 | 6 |
| 2,500 | 1,040 | 4,650 | 4,620 | |
| 2,600 | 1,085 | 4,800 | 5,000 | |
| 2,700 | 1,125 | 4,950 | 5,000 | |
| 2,800 | 1,170 | 5,100 | 5,000 | |
| 2,900 | 1,210 | 5,250 | 5,390 | 7 |
| 3,000 | 1,250 | 5,400 | 5,390 | |
| 3,100 | 1,290 | 5,550 | 5,770 | |
| 3,200 | 1,335 | 5,700 | 5,770 | |
| 3,300 | 1,375 | 5,850 | 5,770 | |
| 3,400 | 1,420 | 6,000 | 6,160 | 8 |
| 3,500 | 1,460 | 6,150 | 6,160 | |
| 3,600 | 1,500 | 6,300 | 6,540 | |

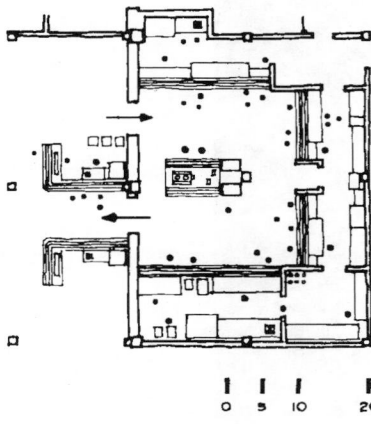

**Fig. 105. Serving**

An outlooking view can provide an outward visual release and can generate calm with the apparent increase of space. Good ventilation is another critical item. Food odors are best controlled by bringing air into the dining room and exhausting it through the kitchen at 30 air changes per hour minimum. In the kitchen itself, 30 to 60 air changes are desirable.

Space and how it is used, though, is the key. A good guide is to allow 12 to 15 square feet per seat in planning the dining space. Smaller tables will use more space, but will encourage more quiet conversation. The small table for four persons, which makes most of floor space and yields the most elbow space when standard trays are placed on its top is 30 x 48 inches. Four standard 14- x 18-inch trays will not fit on a 36-inch square table. Mixing round tables with rectangular ones relieves the monotony of the repetitious, institutional look. Manufacturers provide tables which are 29 inches and 24 inches high for younger children. All kinds of table and seating types—folding, jackknifing, folding into walls, stacking—allow for countless arrangements and flexibility.

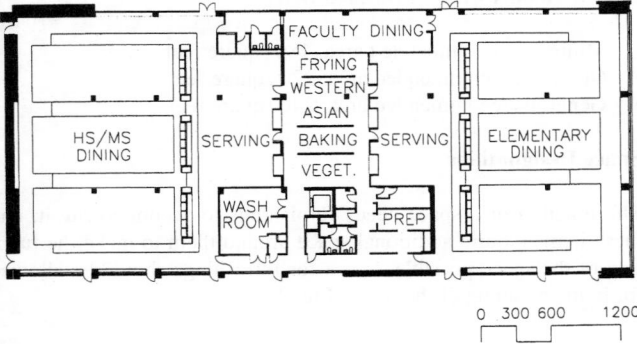

**Fig. 106. Example of cafeteria designed to serve a K-12 community**

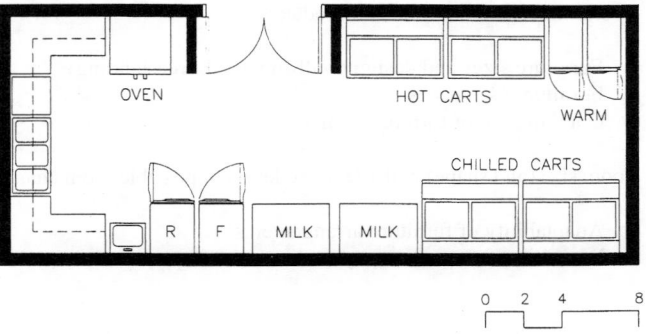

**Fig. 107. Example of an elementary school cafeteria**

**Fig. 1. Monroe Community College (Perkins & Will, Architects; photo: Esto Photographics, courtesy of the architect)**

# COLLEGE STUDENT HOUSING AND RESIDENCE HALLS

## INTRODUCTION

Student housing has become an opportunity to develop and improve the quality of education at most academic institutions. The desire to provide spaces for students that allow active computer interaction, comfortable and convenient living, and opportunities for socialization (Fig. 1) is foremost in university and college planning. Consider all these facets along with the pragmatic spatial needs of furnishings and the integration of efficient effective mechanical, electrical, and plumbing requirements when designing and planning for new student residential buildings.

## STUDENT ROOMS

The student room is the smallest element and the basic space in the housing facility. It is the core environment of the student. In this space the student studies, sleeps, dresses, and socializes. All clothes, books, and personal possessions are stored here except for nonseasonal clothing and larger-size sports equipment. In a very real sense, it is here a student's identity within the university is established. A student's room is the only space on campus that the student can control in any way.

Room dimensions must accommodate:

*   Furniture sizes and design (wall-mounted, freestanding)
*   Furniture use spaces
*   Combination of furniture items

Room size (and shape) will affect two levels of possible room change:

*   Adaptability of furniture arrangements
*   Divisibility of spaces—physical or visual separation of activities

## ROOM AREA REQUIREMENTS

Definitions of terms used:

*   *Minimum:* Access to furniture items; overlap of items and use space; some restriction in the use of furniture
*   *Optimum:* No overlap of items and use space
*   *Generous:* Beginning of space divisibility

### Single Rooms

*   Minimum recommended area: 90 square feet
*   Optimum recommended area: 110 square feet
*   Generous recommended area: 120 square feet

### Double Rooms with Bunked Beds

*   Minimum recommended area: 140 square feet
*   Optimum recommended area: 160 square feet
*   Generous recommended area: 180 square feet

### Double Rooms without Bunked Beds

*   Minimum recommended area: 180 square feet
*   Optimum recommended area: 220 square feet
*   Generous recommended area: 240 square feet

### Space Designations

The function of a space needs furnishings to accommodate it, and these items require additional space around them to make the function of the space possible. Space for furnishings should be allowed for in the planning of the room (Fig. 2).

*Reviewer:* Perkins & Will, Architects

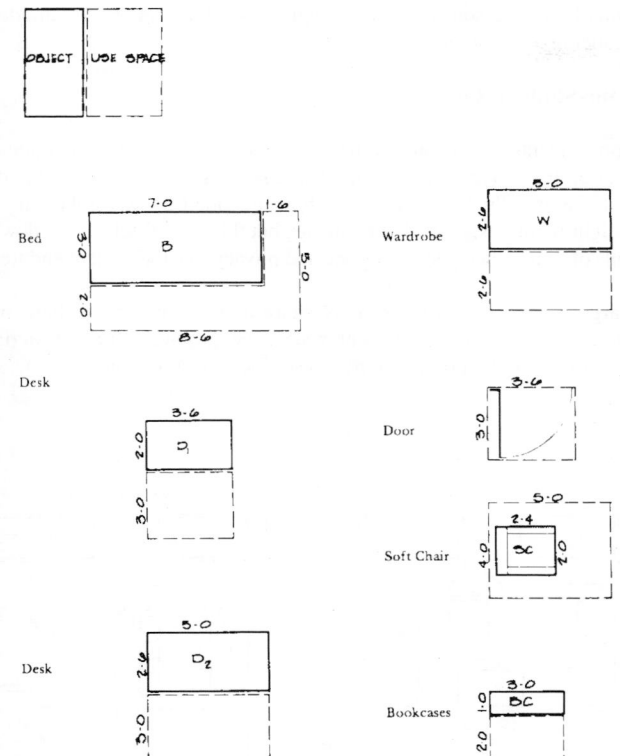

Fig. 2. Furniture sizes and clearances

## Studying

People study in a variety of ways and with a variety of tools. Some engage in long periods of concentration while others apply themselves for relatively short periods interspersed with intervals of social or recreational activity. Some read and take notes manually, while others use a computer both to accumulate information and to process data already gathered. A student's room must plan for as many of these means and methods as possible.

With the increasing realm and influence of technology, it is important to consider the most flexible and the most advanced technological infrastructure available at the time of the design. To assist in accommodating all of the possibilities, it is vital to provide adequate desk space and storage space as well.

The student's desk is used for many of the activities involved in studying. These activities will often require space for specific equipment such as a computer, monitor, keyboard, mouse and mouse pad, stereo, and desk lamp. Along with this equipment, the desk will also need to accommodate space for more traditional means of study. It serves as a spot for reading, note taking, searching though reference materials, and writing. The location of power and data outlets and the location of storage and bookshelves should take all of these factors into account. Combining the space required from the above and adding in room for personal paraphernalia means that a standard 42 inch desk is inadequate.

## Sleeping

The student's pattern of activity is rarely consistent; students may sleep at any time of the day or night. Two occupants of a room very rarely follow the same schedule. Exams and social activities modify their patterns even more extensively. It is the varying patterns that present conflicts in multiple-occupancy rooms. These variables are significant when considering furniture and layout in student rooms.

## Socializing

The student's room has always attracted social discourse. However, with its split emphasis of study and sleep, it presents difficulties as a social environment. Mobile, freestanding furniture allows students the ability to mold the space in a way most effective in meeting their needs. It should be possible to have either intimate conversations or sessions with a number of additional individuals within one's own private room.

## OPTIONAL CONFIGURATIONS

### Single Rooms

The single room provides controlled privacy for its occupant. It may open directly to a corridor and thus provide complete privacy coming and going, or it may be part of a suite or apartment. Privacy for sleeping can be controlled if adequate acoustic separation between adjacent spaces is provided.

The single room should be arranged so that it is possible to study effectively with a second person (Fig. 3). In addition, the student should be able to play music or quiet instruments and to indulge in reasonable recreational activity without creating an acoustical problem for the neighbors.

### Split Double Rooms

The split double room provides the social contact obtained by two students sharing a common space, but at the same time recognizes and solves the problem of conflict of interest in the student's social and study activities. The split double room consists of two spaces with a connecting opening. When connected with a door, there is a degree of acoustic privacy. Without a door, the arrangement provides only visual privacy and shielding from light sources. The provision of two spaces makes it possible for one student to sleep while the other studies or talks with friends.

One arrangement would be to treat each of the two spaces as a single room with direct communication between them. Then the spaces may be separated on an activity basis, with the desks, study, and living facilities in one space and sleeping and dressing facilities in the other.

### Double Rooms

The double room is a common space on college and university campuses. In the past it represented the economical traditional standard in student living. With the increased concern for quality of education and living at these institutes, it is becoming a less desirable option.

At present, the area of a double room varies between 145 and 250 square feet. Within these areas, possibilities for alternative furniture layouts and room shapes are particularly important (Fig. 4). Some room configurations make possible the separation of the two students in their study activities; others situate the desks in parallel arrangements for study. The use of movable wardrobes to shield the beds from desks provides the degree of separation between activities within a room. If double rooms are to be provided, there should be sufficient area to convert them into split double, single, or other types of rooms in the future.

### Triple Room

The triple room is an existing room type at colleges, but not recommended for implementation today. The extra area provided by these rooms allows various manipulations of furniture. However, the situation of three persons living in a single space does not provide an ideal academic environment.

### Four-Student Room

Four students sharing one room have the same constraints as the students sharing triple-occupancy rooms. There is a slight advantage in that the space is usually large enough to be subdivided by wardrobes, lightweight partitions, and other elements, but this doesn't offset the downfalls of diminished personal space and privacy that the student endures.

Large numbers of students may share a space, but more than four require that separate adjacent spaces be provided for conflicting activities. At this point, one must consider the suite plan.

**Fig. 3. Diagrammatic arrangements, rectangular single rooms**

**Fig. 4. Diagrammatic arrangements, rectangular double rooms**

## Suites

A suite is an arrangement in which four or more students share the total space in single and double rooms, with or without a bathroom, and at least one extra common space. In this way, the group of students working and living together have at least one space under their own control which may be used for any of the three major facets of room life: sleep, study, or social activities. The common space within a suite reduces some of the pressures felt by two students trying to share a single room; it also provides for social activities as does a residential living room.

The sharing of a fair amount of space by a group of students makes possible a variety of usage patterns and provides considerable flexibility in room rearrangement.

Typical patterns are a common room also used as a study room; one room used only for sleeping, with separate rooms for study and social purposes; and four single rooms or two double rooms with a common living room (Fig. 5).

Suites composed of single rooms rather than double rooms increase the potential for privacy. However, if one desires a separate room for each student, additional square footage above that normally required for four students will be necessary. This space may be regained through a reduction in public common spaces.

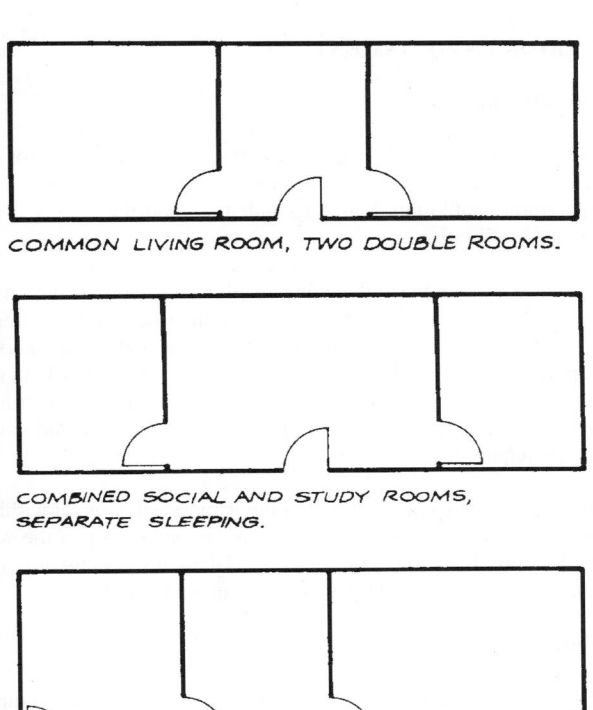

COMMON LIVING ROOM, TWO DOUBLE ROOMS.

COMBINED SOCIAL AND STUDY ROOMS, SEPARATE SLEEPING.

SEPARATE ROOMS FOR STUDY, SLEEPING, AND SOCIAL.

**Fig. 5. Suite organization 1**

Another way to obtain sufficient area for a suite is to incorporate some corridor space in the common room. Ideally, each individual room would be sufficiently acoustically separated from the common space.

Bathroom facilities pose one of the major questions in the design of suites: should these facilities be available just for the suite or for a larger group of students? Although initially it is less expensive to build group facilities for larger groups, long-term economy can be obtained by providing residentially scaled bathrooms for suites wherein students, instead of maids, clean the facility. The reduction in maintenance requirements will more than amortize the increased first cost of smaller bath facilities, while also considerably improving the human quality of the housing environment for the student.

Suites must also be considered for the social impact resulting from them. Students developing a strong social life around the activities of their suite may have less incentive to make friends outside their circle. Objections might be posed for this reason, especially in regard to freshman students who desire maximum opportunities to meet other students.

The shared living room provides a larger base for friends and tends to reduce stress. The value of grouping students into a suite where an ordered pattern of relationships may develop (first with a roommate or perhaps with two or four additional students and then with a larger number) provides some balance in the way outside attachments are formed. Therefore a design approach for the use of suites should consider alterations for future living patterns.

Within the suite it is important to organize the common spaces so that privacy is maintained between the sleeping rooms and the bathroom (Fig. 6). Problems occur when the common rooms in a suite may be open for coed activities and it is necessary to pass through the common area when going between one's room and the bathroom.

With seven or more students in double rooms, more than one common space in a suite is required. At least one separate study as well as a social room should be provided to accommodate privacy for study and the noisy social sessions that inevitably occur within a suite. Obviously, single rooms designed so privacy may be maintained represent the most ideal solution.

If the suite is entered through a common space, this space is useful only for purposes where quiet and privacy are not essential. Attempts to provide a combined living-study room in the suite are not successful because students soon revert to using their bedrooms for study.

### Apartments

An apartment differs from the suite by providing a kitchen. It may consist of single or double rooms built around common spaces as in a suite, or it may have a number of students in a sleeping room with the other spaces in common for social, dining, and study purposes.

Some students believe they get better food at less cost if they do their own cooking and shopping. Therefore, the apartment requires adequate food supply capacity for the number of occupants intended to live in the apartment.

Students living in apartments or off campus often desire alternatives to eating at home. A central food service can provide this option and service for many of the students.

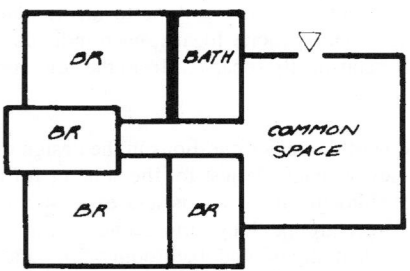

ACCESS TO STUDENT ROOMS
THROUGH COMMON SPACE.

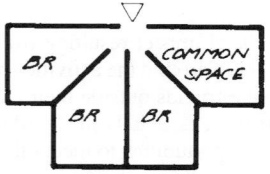

SEPARATE ACCESS TO STUDENT ROOMS
AND COMMON SPACE.

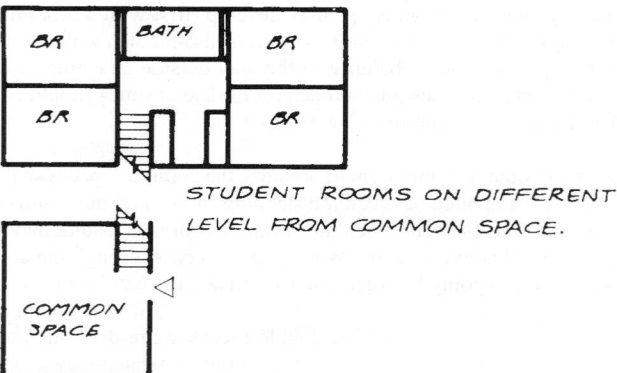

STUDENT ROOMS ON DIFFERENT
LEVEL FROM COMMON SPACE.

**Fig. 6. Suite organization 2**

Much of the attraction of the apartment is its comparative freedom from behavioral control, particularly in regard to coeducational activities. This does not mean complete relinquishment of responsibility on the part of the university but rather the more positive recognition of the student's adult qualities.

Students living in apartments tend to develop a very close relationship with those sharing the space. It is a pattern perhaps more appropriate for upper-division and graduate students than it is for lower-division students. These students have developed a range of acquaintances on campus and now are interested in cultivating specific friendships. Apartments, like suites, can be grouped to provide activities through combined use of spaces for recreation, study, and social affairs so that a wide range of friendship is possible.

Since the key difference between the suite and the apartment is the kitchen, provision could be included in suites for a plug-in kitchenette. This would allow for future change of use and enhanced flexibility.

## SPACE ALLOCATION

Rooms of minimum size should be avoided. The goal in sizing a room should be to strike a balance between the economic needs of the institution and the spatial needs of the student. Studies have found this balance to be in the range of 110 square feet for single-student rooms and 200 square feet for two-student rooms (Table 1).

The layout of the furnishings as built-in or movable will most likely be dictated by a minimum room size. This in turn will restrict self-expression in the room. As the size of the room increases, so does the potential for self-expression through the arrangement of movable furniture.

## INTERIOR ENVIRONMENT

### Thermal Comfort

Student rooms require an appropriate thermal environment for the functions carried on within them. The environment is affected by temperature, ventilation, humidity, radiation, and the quality of air produced by filtration.

The thermal system in student housing allows for individual requirements and the wide range of conditions which personal preference may demand. In a mixed community of smokers and nonsmokers, it is important that the air be kept moving and clean, particularly in student rooms, interior spaces, lounges, and study areas. Because of variations in student hygiene, separate ventilation of individual spaces is required.

Although conventional air-conditioning is more economical within a sealed space, it is important that students be able to open the windows to enjoy fresh air, and in the lower-height buildings to enjoy communication (but not access) through an open window.

### Lighting

The quality of lighting in student rooms is determined by the quantity and brightness of both the light sources and their general surroundings. High illumination levels are appropriate to study; lower levels to social functions. In the daytime, natural daylight may provide much of the necessary illumination if windows are well placed and the glare eliminated.

**Table 1**    Recommended space standards per student

| University | ASF[a] | | OGSF[b] | |
|---|---|---|---|---|
| | Single | Double | No dining | With dining |
| University of California [c] | 100 | 100 | 239 | 265 |
| California state colleges[d] | 94–110.5 | 84–91 | 215.5 | 230.5 |
| University of Guelph[e] | 115 | NR | 230 | |
| University of Pennsylvania[f] | 108 | NR | 271.5 | 290 |
| M.I.T.[g] | 140 | | 470 | 486 |
| Aggregate United States[h] | | | | |
| Men | | 96.7 | 211.1 | 234.7 |
| Women | | 103.5 | 237.4 | 261.4 |

Assignable feet per student.

Outside gross square feet per student.

University of California. UC Standing Committee on Residence Halls, Meeting of August 29 and 30, 1966, Hilton Inn, San Francisco International Airport.

Development Guide for Campus Housing, California State Colleges, July 1968, Table 1, Summary of Project Norms, p. 13.

University of Guelph Student Housing Study, Evan H, Walker, Student Housing Consultant, November 1965, pp. 56–66.

Univeristy of Pennsylvania. Study of Undergraduate Men's Housing system, Geddes, Brecher, Qualls and Cunningham, Architectural Consultants.

Massachusetts Institute of Technology. A Program for Undergraduate Men's Housing, MIT Planning Office, August 1965.

Eugene E. Higgins, M. Louise Steward, and Linda Wright, Residence Hall Planning Aids, Report OE-51004-9A, College and University Physical Facility Series, Department of Health, Education, and Welfare, U.S. Office of Education, Washington, D.C.

Because of the highly-individualized nature of activities performed in student rooms, light from a number of well-placed point sources is far more desirable than light from one central source. Task lighting is required in areas where reading, studying, or writing is most likely to take place, such as student desks and beds. Other sources of lighting could be integrated in the room or left to the students to purchase as an expression of their individual tastes.

**Acoustics**

Quiet is the most desired characteristic of any living arrangement in the opinion of students, so acoustical considerations are of great importance. Fundamental to providing quiet environments are walls, floors, windows, and doors. These elements must be properly sealed to reduce the amount of sound traveling between environments. The simplest inhibitor of noise transfer is good planning of the relationship between rooms. The social space of one student room should be adjacent to the social space of another; likewise, the bedroom spaces should also share a dividing wall. Whenever applicable, group social areas should be as far removed from student rooms as possible.

**Color, Texture, and Materials**

Some materials presently used in dorm rooms are hard, unyielding, and chosen for their durability and ease of maintenance. However, those choices can lead to a depressing, sterile, institutional atmosphere.

The student's need for expression and the university's need for ease of maintenance need not conflict. Walls can be covered with safe, removable wall-covering panels that provide the student with the ability to apply personal decorations to the wall. These panels should be able to withstand the abuse of tape and tacks while still protecting the wall surface beyond.

Carpeting is the best solution as a floor-covering material. Since many study and social activities are performed on the floor, the comfort and quiet provided by carpeting are quite desirable.

**Appliances**

The design, production, and marketing of economical personal appliances have resulted in each student bringing a number of these items to college. This situation has generated problems of general safety, fire hazards, intolerable odors, high noise levels, and frequent interruption of electrical services. The designers of residence halls must anticipate and acknowledge the requirements for dealing with these occurrences.

An anticipated group of appliances falls in the category of personal entertainment—stereos of various shapes and sizes, personal computers, televisions, and video recording equipment are within the economic reach of most students. The presence of such devices and the control they provide makes the dorm room a more likely spot for group social gatherings. Space for such equipment and their social implications as well as their respective power requirements must be considered in the design of rooms.

The other anticipated group of appliances falls in the category of food and drink preparation and storage. This group can include hot plates, coffee pots, popcorn poppers, blenders, refrigerators, and microwave ovens. Appliances in this category can be sources of potential fire hazards and odors. Many institutions have strict rules governing the use of such devices. Should these appliances be allowed, then the proper electrical and storage requirements must be attained. In this situation, an in-room sink becomes a necessity.

New buildings must recognize the evolution of electrical use by providing initial high capacity with provision for easily adding to that capacity with minimum disruption.

## RESIDENCE HALL FACILITIES

### Bathing

The group bathroom is one of the most persistent features of student residence halls (Fig. 7). It has been defended on the basis of economy.

The initial construction cost of one central group bathroom is less than that of smaller installations in several locations. It is also evident that when a bathroom serves more than a few students, maintenance is the university's responsibility. The initial extra expense for smaller baths will actually result in long-term cost savings if the students themselves maintain the smaller bathroom, because it eliminates the need for maid service throughout the life of the building.

Another economic factor against the group bathroom is its inflexibility. Residence halls with group baths are far less appropriate for par-

ticipants in conventions, reunions, and institutes where families or both sexes are involved than are areas with smaller baths serving a few persons.

### Dining

There is universal agreement that the single, large room for hundreds of students is not the satisfactory solution to the problem of student dining facilities. Although the large kitchen with its extensive equipment, service-line arrangements, and building area is the most economical and efficient method of food preparation, the one large dining room for all students negates a congenial atmosphere for social interaction during mealtime.

Dining facilities that combine the best advantage of the large kitchen—efficiency, economy, and flexibility—while at the same time providing a pleasant and social dining environment can be built. Proper planning permits large central areas to be divided by movable walls into smaller or intimate dining rooms. The walls can be moved when a large scale is needed for social events such as dances. For large institutes, another solution to single large dining halls is a central food preparation kitchen servicing several small warming kitchens dispersed around the campus. These warming kitchens can each have a dining area associated with it.

Food preparation in student rooms presents a safety and sanitary problem. This can be resolved to a degree by providing vending machines located strategically in the residence halls or by provision of facilities in which they can prepare snacks themselves. Student food preparation problems cannot be solved by unenforceable prohibitions but only by construction of appropriate areas with a microwave oven and water source.

### Recreation and Social Activity

Recreational spaces and facilities are important in providing environmental support to the personal interaction of students, both new and old. However, care must be taken in the areas programmed for recreation so that they truly accommodate the intended activities. The size of the institution, the provision of space, and the cost consideration of providing recreation facilities in each residence hall often prove prohibitive. Large centrally located (when possible) recreation centers on the campus provide economy of scale and encourage student interaction on a broader level.

Social interaction and student involvement are valuable aspects of each student's learning experience. Providing environmental encouragement for this to occur is vital. Flexibility and variety in space size will give the users opportunities for different types of interaction. Student lounges on every floor for small and large group meetings and as an alternative to the individual room for social gathering are necessary. Plan for lighting and electricity that can supply various settings for activities.

### Cultural

Residence halls can participate in the overall academic environment of the university with the inclusion of facilities for music performance and discussion. It is part of the job of housing to smooth the transition from green freshmen to sophisticated seniors.

Formal academic classes in residence halls present difficulties in mechanical services and density beyond the capability of most resi-

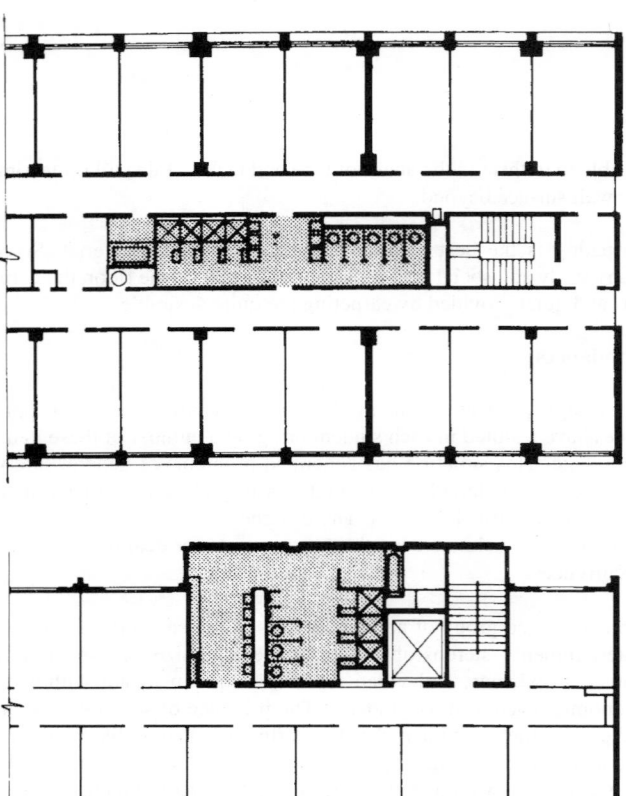

**Fig. 7. Group bathrooms**

ence hall structures, but informal classes and seminars can be successfully held in the social spaces in the hall.

## Service and Storage

The university must provide facilities for the following:

    Maintenance of buildings
    Mechanical and electrical equipment
    Overflow storage from student rooms

Increasing affluence of students and the growth of disposable articles has increased space requirements for efficient trash collection and removal. Central collection facilities and dumping trucks are required to handle present volumes of trash. Too often this involves the ugly exposure of the trash while awaiting collection, as well as the considerable fire hazard.

Efficient maintenance of electrical and mechanical systems requires easy access without the invasion of student privacy. Access panels and equipment need to be located to allow this.

Out-of-season and seldom-used student property is usually stored in inexpensive areas of a building, but these are often the least accessible. More adequate storage provisions in the student room could relieve this situation. Student and service storage should be in separate areas and away from heavy traffic areas such as laundry and recreation rooms. Bikes, surfboards, skis, and scuba gear present spatial storage problems that require careful consideration. All student storage areas must be lockable.

## Circulation and Interrelation of Spaces

The student residence hall is a social organism. The relationship of student rooms one to another and to the public and service rooms makes up a total environment most conveniently studied as a hierarchy of spaces. The hierarchy is determined by the student activities and the physical characteristics of the building. Following is a hierarchy of typical unit sizes in university housing:

| Student unit | Students |
| --- | --- |
| Room | 1–2 |
| Suite | 4–16 |
| Group | 16–24 |
| House or floor | 48–72 |
| Hall, building or college | 120–800 |
| Complex of halls | 1,200–4,800 |
| Campus | 12,000–27,500 |

Unit size is defined by building spaces, activities related to space, and by agents of regulation and control. For example, a number of rooms served by a bathroom constitute a suite, group, or floor. A number of rooms under the direction of a resident assistant will establish a unit. All the rooms on one floor having common access and services may also be considered as a unit.

The predominant traditional pattern is the familiar double-loaded corridor arrangement wherein the unit is one floor of a residence hall (Fig. 8). This plan offers easy control opportunities. With a group of 48 to 72 students, it facilitates the organization of intramural and academic activities. Another source of group size derivation is the optimum number sharing bathroom facilities.

Efficient space utilization requires that the circulation area comprise the smallest possible percentage of the total area. Studies of existing student housing show the efficiency percentage varying from 7 to 25 percent. Although it is advantageous to reduce circulation areas, building safety codes prescribe minimum areas and arrangements.

Economy is the obvious feature of double-loaded corridors because core plans require more circulation area. When each student has a single room, economy of circulation space is difficult since each room must have a window on the periphery of the building. This arrangement, in its simplest configuration, requires extremely long frontages. Irregular building configurations to reduce corridor space must be considered in a cost context also.

Passenger and freight elevators are useful in all buildings and are necessary to comply with various codes.

A major determinant of environment is the access to movement from space to space. Those spaces grouped about a room or wide corridor make up a more residential environment through the use of attractive carpets, colors, and materials. Corridors can be more fully utilized; for example, conversation spaces that do not impede circulation can be provided by window seats and railed landings. Although stairs must conform to fire regulations, their configurations can be a pleasant contribution to the environment.

## PLANNING TYPES

As a frame of reference, student residence halls are classified in five basic plan types (Fig. 8):

1. *The double-loaded corridor:* A series of perimeter rooms on both sides of a 5-foot+ corridor, usually with group bathroom facilities and stairs at either end.
2. *The gallery plan:* A variation of the double-loaded corridor with rooms on one side only of an open or closed corridor.
3. *The extended core plan:* A series of perimeter rooms around four sides of a structure. In the center is a core of service rooms including group toilets, janitor's closets, elevators, and so on. A corridor usually surrounds the core on four sides.
4. *Vertical house:* A series of 4, 6, or 8 rooms or suites. A stair serving one or two such configurations of rooms or suites is provided, creating the feeling of an individual house.
5. *Core plan:* Usually (but not always) high-rise with vertical circulation such as stairs and elevators in a center core along with group bathroom facilities and service rooms. The rooms, suites, and arrangements are on the perimeter. Shared baths are often used with suites of 4, 6, or 8 persons.

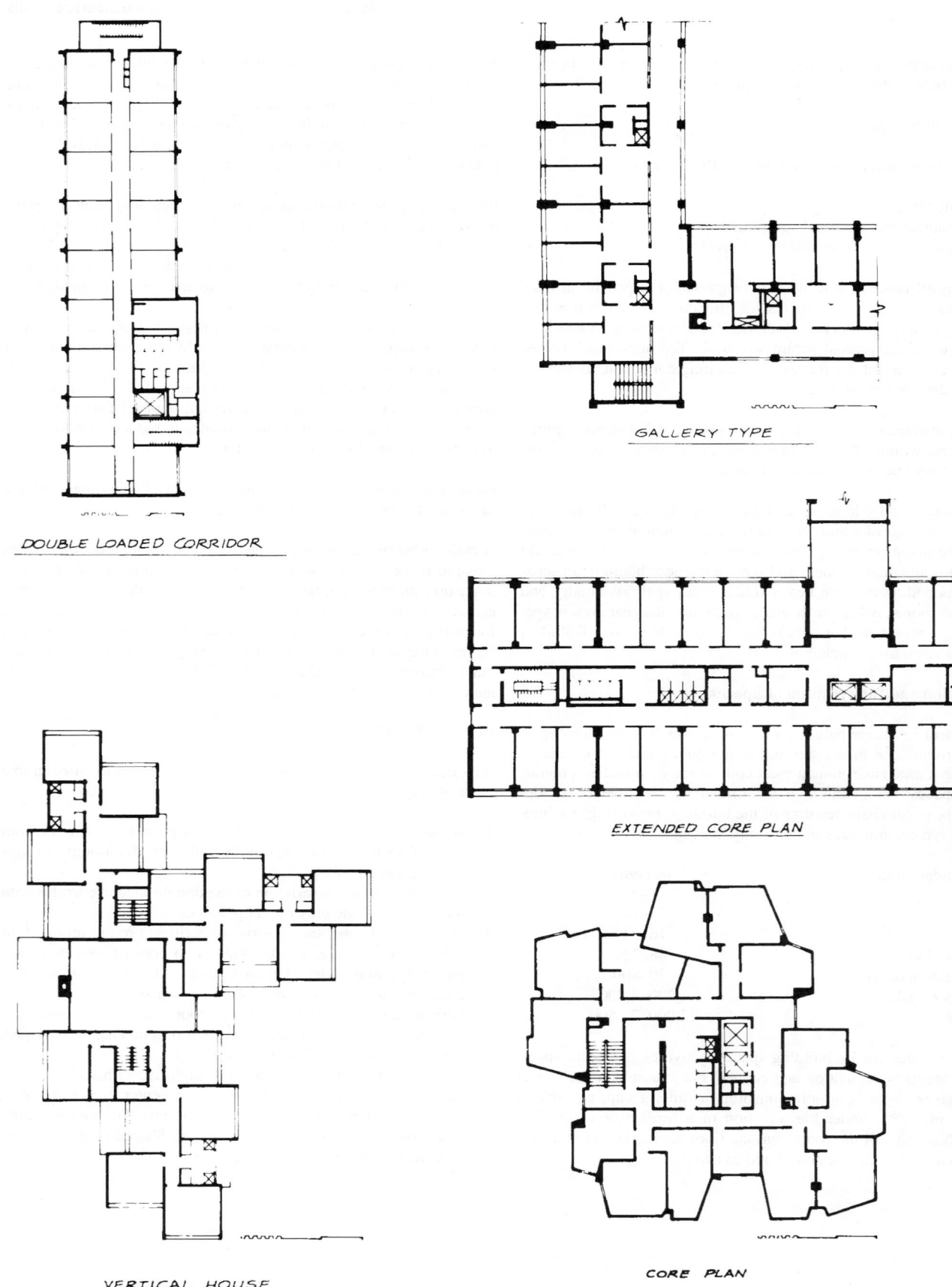

DOUBLE LOADED CORRIDOR

GALLERY TYPE

EXTENDED CORE PLAN

VERTICAL HOUSE

CORE PLAN

**Fig. 8. Basic room-hall plan types**

**Fig. 1. Monroe Community College (Perkins & Will, Architects; photo: Esto Photographics, courtesy of the architect)**

# COLLEGE STUDENT CENTERS

## ORGANIZATION

The organization of students, faculty, and alumni that oversees the student center usually operates with a governing board at its head. This board, which may or may not include representatives of the three groups, is responsible for the operation of the center, although trained staff members handle much of the detail and much of the guiding philosophy is originally that of the professional staff. The board itself is concerned largely with questions of policy and implements its policies through the work of various volunteer committees and the paid staff of the student center.

The committees consist almost entirely of students and may or may not include members of the governing board. Regardless of the titles and varying functions, most of the committees serve as the links that connect the boards with the general campus population. The committees plan and execute programs, attending to such details as scheduling, publicizing, decorating, and budgeting. They may

choose CDs for the music library and prints for the art collection. They may help in freshman orientation or study a proposed change in furniture layout. They may run the table tennis tournament or a book review hour. The committees, sensitive to campus needs and interests, keep the student center dynamic, flexible, and busy.

## BUILDING

The functions housed by the student center building ideally are those needed to make it the focus of the recreational, cultural, social, and civic life on the campus. Needless to say, many existing campus facilities such as the library, art museum, or theater cannot and should not be duplicated in a new student center building, but the inclusion of as many such facilities as feasible is desirable to ensure that the student center gives the widest possible range of educational experiences to the students and faculty.

*Author:* Chester Arthur Berry, Ed.D.
*Reviewer:* Perkins & Will, Architects
*Reference: Planning a College Union Building,* Teachers College Press, New York.

The student center building must efficiently house the facilities and functions required by the center while suggesting its purposes by its appearance and design. If the student center is considered the heart of the campus, it is logical that the environment be warm and welcoming, casual and comfortable to both staff and students (Fig. 1). If it also serves as a convention center and hotel, it might offer a slightly more formal environment; however, such a design approach may result in a building and an operation that do not meet the terms of definition of a college student center. Whatever the local requirements may be, it is important to remember that much of the activity of a student center is informal in nature and that most of the participation in its activities is by informal college students. The nature of a college student center building might be largely informal to reflect the character of the activities that it houses.

A well-planned student center building separates its areas by functions to permit efficient communication, supervision, and operation. It is important in planning to separate quiet zones (such as student services, libraries, and conference rooms) and public zones (such as retail stores, dining halls, and game rooms). By separating yet coordinating the building's components, there is the opportunity for new experiences, so that the walk from the coffee shop to the games area, for example, may lead students past a music room or an art exhibit.

**SPACE REQUIREMENTS AND ACTIVITIES**

The diversity of space requirements and activities of a student center makes their classification into a few major categories difficult. Nevertheless, there are many similar aspects to consider when planning the different types of program spaces (i.e., noise, service, supervision requirements, etc.). Therefore, it may be helpful to use the following

eight general classifications of space requirements and activities of a union building as a guide in planning:

1. Administrative, service, and maintenance
2. Food service
3. Quiet areas
4. Theater
5. Arts and crafts workshops
6. Games
7. Outdoor
8. Miscellaneous

These classifications can be further broken down into specific program areas as listed in the space recommendations (see Table 1). Please note that some program areas listed under one of the general classifications of facilities and activities may be duplicated in another of the eight classifications. Not all of the program areas listed in the space recommendations table may be required in every student center; some programmatic spaces may serve multiple functions (i.e. the ballroom or meeting rooms of a building without a theater may assume many of the functions which are best performed in the theater). Conflicting events might also demand alternate options, such as showing movies in a large meeting room on dress-rehearsal night or holding a club meeting in a rehearsal room on an evening when meeting rooms are at a premium. The classifications are meant as a general guide to planning, and are not intended to limit the flexibility of use of these spaces.

Not all of the space requirements mentioned in Table 1 are discussed here. Some, such as cooperative groceries or ice-skating rinks, occur so seldom in connection with student centers that they are barely

**Table 1** Space recommendations

| Administrative, service, and maintenance | Food service | International center | Ping pong |
|---|---|---|---|
| Offices | Snack bar and grill | Student activities area | Billiards room |
| Coat rooms | Cafeteria | Student organization offices | Cards/checkers/chess room |
| Information center | Private dining rooms | Art room | Bowling alleys |
| Bookstore | Service dining rooms | | |
| Hairdresser | Coffee shop | **Theater** | **Outdoor** |
| Post office | Faculty dining rooms | Auditorium | Cement slab |
| Mail center | Commuter's lunchroom | Stage | Sun decks or patio |
| Maintenance shop | Banquet room | Dressing rooms | Picnic and dining areas |
| Lobby | Offices | Shops | Parking |
| Retail stores and shops | Kitchen | Lobbies | |
| Lost and found | Dishwashing room | Projection booth | **Miscellaneous** |
| Copy and production area | Refrigeration room | Stage house | Ballroom |
| Rest rooms | Trash room | Costume shop | Music recital room |
| Janitorial spaces | | Costume storage | Music practice room |
| Bulletin boards | **Quiet areas** | Rehearsal room | Television room |
| Bank or ATM | Meeting rooms | Ticket office | Convention hall |
| Delivery area | Lounges | Offices | Swimming pool |
| Trash rooms | Music listening room | | Ice-skating rink |
| Elevator | Library | **Arts and crafts workshops** | Cooperative grocery |
| Mechanical rooms | Guest rooms | Photographic studio and | Campus newspaper |
| Storage | Dormitory | darkroom | College yearbook |
| Employee locker and rest rooms | Chapel | Arts workshop | Student government |
| Pay phones and fax service | Study rooms | Crafts workshop | Student radio station |
| Paging system | Other faculty space | | Religious counseling |
| | Commuter's lockers | **Games** | |
| | Commuter's sleeping rooms | Video game room | |

onsidered as recommended facilities. Others, including bookstores, aculty spaces, hotel units, swimming pools, university administrative offices, hairdressers, or chapels, are facilities that may or may not be included in the student center building program based on specific local and campus requirements.

### Administrative, Maintenance, and Service Areas

A glance at Table 1 reveals that student center program activities are infrequently held in most of these spaces. The program potential of the hairdresser and coat checkrooms, for example, is not very high. Closer examination of the table shows that nearly all of the activities are service oriented, and most are probably provided by paid staff members. If the student center board has its offices located away from the administrative offices, the function of staff members is even more important, since many of the services rendered, such as interviewing and training building committee applicants, are carried on in the student offices.

### Food Service

Since dining service is one of the main sources of student center revenue and caters regularly to a large segment of the campus, it is extremely important that it be planned, constructed, and operated properly. A food service consultant might be brought on board the design team to offer expertise in this area.

#### Functionality

As in other student center facilities, the functions of food service areas vary with the institutions. The existence of other eating facilities on and off the campus, the policies of such facilities (à la carte, 5- or 7-day board/meal plans, semester contracts), the location of existing places as well as that of the student center building, the prevalence and size of conferences and conventions, and the institution's future plans are some of the items which should be considered.

#### Food Area Components

An all-inclusive union food operation embracing grills; cafeteria; private, banquet, and service dining rooms; coffee shops; and commuters' lunchroom includes many components in common with other food operations elsewhere, since the flow process is basically the same. Such components include receiving, storage, meat cutting, vegetable preparation, cooking, baking, ice cream storage, salad making, service (cafeteria counter or wait-staff pantry), dining, pot washing, dishwashing, garbage and trash storage, maintenance, employees' facilities, rest rooms, coat rooms, and offices. When planning for these food area components, keep in mind that all student centers may not need or be able to afford such a comprehensive plant, and only the largest can use all components.

#### Receiving

The receiving facilities for the food service area do not necessarily need to be separate from those for the rest of the student center building. If the various receiving areas are combined (due to limitations of site, space constraints, etc.), the employment of a receiving clerk may be required. A central storeroom for nonperishable items may be provided, and therefore may make it possible for even the smaller student centers to utilize a receiving clerk. Obviously, both vertical and horizontal transportation is needed in such an operation, and, since the frequency and perishability of food deliveries are high, the receiving room should be located near the food service department.

#### Storage

Storage in the food area includes dry stores or nonperishables, day stores, refrigerated stores, frozen stores, and garbage and trash storage. Some may include several subdivisions such as freezers for meat, fruit, vegetables, and ice cream or dairy and meat, fruit, and vegetable refrigerators. Location of storage areas should be adjacent or in close proximity to dining halls and food service areas.

#### Service areas

Service areas should be directly adjacent to the various food preparation and dining areas. Typically, the food is placed on the individual plates and distributed at a staging area; these staging areas may take the form of a cafeteria counter, a serving kitchen or pantry, a wait-staff station, a serving counter in the kitchen, or a station in a short-order kitchen. Food must be kept hot or cold, dishes must be stored, and food must be dispensed for consumption in the dining area. Slight variations of this basic operation may be required according to the type of food service being offered at the student center.

The prepared food in larger student center buildings may be transported in several directions from the central kitchen. Cafeterias, counters, banquet service kitchens, soda fountains, coffee shops, employees' cafeteria counters, private and public dining room kitchens, and commuter lunchrooms may all be served from this single area, with auxiliary food preparation completed at the serving scene.

#### Dining Rooms

The variety of dining facilities found in the larger student centers attests to the variety of dining functions demanding service. As mentioned earlier, students are demanding greater variety and level of food service, as well as branding and retail restaurants and stores on campus. Some types of dining facilities found in student centers include cafés and snack bars where a quick bite or cup of coffee may be obtained; coffee shops, with or without table service, for a relaxed meal or casual entertaining; the cafeteria, for low-priced meals three times a day; and the dining room which typically offers a more formal atmosphere where students can come for a full-course meal, a special occasion, or dinner with their parents. The banquet hall is typically utilized for numerous student, faculty, and other organizational dinners that occur throughout the year, and private dining rooms cater to luncheon or dinner meetings for groups, classes, guests, and so on.

### Quiet Areas

All the quiet areas of the student center do not need to be connected, but they should be isolated from the noisier program areas such as kitchens, workshops, or game areas. Actually, quiet areas subdivide quite easily by function to permit separation. For example, the living quarters such as guest rooms, guest dormitories, or commuters' sleeping rooms should be separated from the busier lounges and meeting rooms, and their close proximity or combination permits more efficient operation, supervision, and housekeeping. Student activity areas (rooms with desks and files not permanently assigned) and student offices (permanently assigned spaces) should be located together for ease of communication and supervision. The facilities for day or commuter students, if they are distinguished from those normally used by all students, should be adjacent or in close proximity to the facilities provided for the rest of the student population, including their lunchroom and lounge. Meeting rooms located near each other permit flexibility of use, easy transfer of furniture and equipment, proper supervision and maintenance resulting from concentration of people, and economy of time between meetings. Lounges may be spread throughout the building to serve various needs and populations.

*Meeting Rooms*

Table 1 shows that student centers typically demand a wide variety of uses for meeting rooms and lounges, and that it is recommended that these spaces be designed and planned to be interchangeable and flexible for both formal and informal gatherings. However, if the decision makers for the student center prefer that lounges be utilized only for spontaneous, informal use, the number of meeting rooms required would be substantially increased.

Typically, both small and large meeting rooms need to be provided in a student center to accommodate a variety of functions. The need for many small meeting rooms, however, does not eliminate the demand for larger ones. The larger meeting rooms may be subdividable with moveable partitions to increase the flexibility of each room. Some small meeting rooms, equipped with tables and seating, may double as conference rooms, and the tables themselves may serve as podiums for meetings as well as conference tables. Storage should be provided for folding tables and chairs adjacent or in close proximity to these meeting and conference rooms.

*Lounges*

A variety of lounges (student, faculty, commuters', etc.) may be included in the student center, and, as previously mentioned, they should be planned to be flexible and adaptable for both formal and informal meetings, etc. To a certain extent, the kind of institution involved determines the kinds of lounges that are desirable. For example, a residential college does not need a commuters' lounge, and a women's college probably finds a men's lounge superfluous, although it may wish to have a room available that can be converted to serve such a purpose on special occasions. The existence and location of a faculty club may determine the desirability of a faculty lounge, and the facilities and entertaining regulations in residence halls and dormitories may have an impact on the size and number of mixed lounges. The presence and availability of other lounges on campus should also be considered in planning the number of student center lounges.

*Reading Rooms*

Reading rooms or browsing libraries are often utilized by students as convenient alternatives to the libraries provided elsewhere on campus to study or read. It is important to create comfortable surroundings with proper HVAC, relaxing lounge furniture, adequate lighting, and so on in order to attract students.

The normal functions most likely to be carried out in the browsing room are reading, group and/or individual study, and book, periodical, and newspaper storage. Book storage and shelving units need to be provided and separated from furnishings and equipment (such as printers, copiers, computers, fax machines, etc.) by an aisle wide enough to permit students to select their books easily. Periodicals and newspapers require less browsing room and may be incorporated in a lounge arrangement of furniture by use of standard racks, or by storage on coffee or other tables. Electrical outlets and teledata ports should also be provided for students to easily plug in their laptops

and work. Areas for group study might be provided in adjacent enclosed spaces so as to prevent noise from distracting or bothering the other students using the reading and browsing room.

*Music Rooms*

Changes are constantly occurring in the field of music listening. CDs, minidiscs, DVDs, MP3 players, and radio have tremendously increased the interest in recorded music and have offered student centers a real opportunity for improving the level of musical understanding and interest of their students. At the same time, problems of control and usage have been raised since the equipment required is costly and complex, CDs are easily damaged, and the noise potential is great enough to disturb the so-called quiet areas of the student center.

The whole music listening program must be thought out well in advance, because this aspect of the student center is dependent to a great extent on the manner in which the program functions. Students may listen to music in soundproof booths or small rooms or lounges of varying sizes, or they may use headphones at listening stations (standing or sitting). They may play the music themselves or may request selections from an attendant who plays from a control point. The various music selections may be kept with the player and used by anyone, they may be issued by an attendant, or they may be private property. Planned group listening such as coffee hours may be held in a multipurpose lounge equipped with a player or a speaker from a master system, or it may take place in a music lounge specifically designed for music listening, both recorded and live. Other items to be considered when planning music rooms are storage racks, acoustics, equipment, furniture, electrical, phone, and teledata outlets, glazed doors for supervision, and cataloging methods.

*Commuters' Areas*

Nonresident students at colleges near or in metropolitan centers afford many challenges to student centers, a number of which focus around their nonparticipation in most of the center's programs and activities. The commuter's demands on the college naturally differ from those of the residents: they need parking space on campus; a place to eat a bag or light lunch; storage area for books, laptops, and lunches; a spot for resting; or, perhaps, occasional overnight accommodations. While the student center is not necessarily the only location on the campus where these types of services may be provided, it seems to be the logical place for many of them. Furthermore, many of the day students are quite likely to eat in the dining halls and food marketplaces in the student centers and utilize the building as their home away from home; therefore, it seems appropriate to plan to meet as many of their demands as possible in advance. If the student center building is to be a gathering place on campus for all students, it must be prepared to serve the nonresident segment of the student body.

*Guest Rooms*

Many student centers contain overnight guest facilities, which may range from a single room or suite to large barracks-like halls to elaborate hotels with full commercial and hospitality service. The facilities may be intended primarily for university guests such as convocation speakers, for visiting groups such as athletic teams, for parents or returning alumni, for the guests of students, or for conventions. These guest facilities add to the service aspects of the building, and the university may provide training to student employees and to students who are majoring in hotel administration. The need for inclusion of guest rooms in the union building depends on many diverse elements, such as present and future needs of the campus, other existing facilities on campus, nearby hotels, curricular development, operating hours, operating costs, and other student center facilities.

### Student Activities Area

The student activities area in the student center is a room or a series of rooms that houses desks, chairs, computers, phones, and filing cabinets that can be used by various student organizations for a portion of the academic year. Groups that do not need an office or room of their own can be accommodated with a minimum of space allocation, by sharing or hotelling these areas with other organizations. When planning for a student activities area in a student center the number of groups and activities on each campus that might use such an area should be a large factor in determining its size.

### Theater

Like many other parts of the student center building, the theater must be designed and planned to meet the programmatic needs of its campus. A student center located near a contemporary, well-equipped theater can probably utilize its facilities and not need a theater of its own. However, the demands on such a theater by dramatic and other groups may render the theater unavailable for the variety of activities which Table 1 indicates may be required, thus making the inclusion of a theater in the student center desirable.

There are three basic types of theater configurations—proscenium, thrust, and arena (theater in the round). Of these, the proscenium configuration is the most flexible for the varied activities of a student center theater, and allows the facility to accommodate both theatrical activities (such as drama and dance performances, talent and fashion shows, orchestral and choral concerts, etc.) and nontheatrical activities (such as film projection, lectures, conferences, convocation, etc.).

To function properly, the student center theater should include of the following program areas:

| | |
|---|---|
| Auditorium | Projection booth |
| Stage | Sound system |
| Forestage | Screen |
| Orchestra pit | Stage house |
| Proscenium arch | Lobby |
| Dressing rooms | Ticket office |
| Scene shop | Scenery storeroom |
| Costume shop | Control board |
| Light booth | Rest rooms |
| Makeup room | Coatroom |
| Rehearsal room | Lounge or green room |

Some of the facilities listed, such as lounge, coatroom, rest room, or rehearsal room, may already be a part of the program for the student center building, and might be able to serve multiple purposes for different program areas of the center.

### Arts and Crafts Workshops

The student center workshops can provide areas for a wide variety of arts and crafts (Fig. 2). Some of these offerings, such as photography, demand specialized facilities and equipment; others, such as leather-

work or jewelry making, require little specialized facilities and can be accommodated in a general shop area. The tools of some crafts may be used in common by participants in other student center activities, so that the scene, maintenance, and woodworking shops may use the same power tools and central materials sources and photography and campus publications the same darkrooms and studios. The size of the student center building itself, the size of the university, and the organizational requirements and expected use of the various workshops would determine the possibility of such multipurpose spaces. Some typical arts and crafts activities that a union might accommodate are as follows:

Painting
Poster making
Silk-screening
Clay modeling
Drawing
Plastic work
General woodworking
Picture framing
Metal and jewelry work
Ceramics
Photography
Leatherwork

While supporters of nearly each art or craft could develop a list of reasons why their favorite activity should be allocated separate space and equipment, (i.e., those with special requirements such as north light for sketching or humidity control for clay modeling), enough compromises and combinations can be effected to provide a variety of activities within reasonable and oftentimes shared areas.

### Games

The extent to which the games area should be developed is dependent in large degree on what is available elsewhere on the campus. Typically, the university's recreation centers, gymnasiums, and field houses accommodate most organized activities and games; however, it would be beneficial to provide an informal games area and room

**Fig. 2. Monroe Community College (Perkins & Will, Architects; photo: Esto Photographics, courtesy of the architect)**

for outdoor activities directly adjacent to the student center where students could gather and participate in spontaneous activities.

## INTEGRATION OF STUDENT CENTER AREAS

Some student center facilities must be located at the street level; others operate most efficiently on other levels. There are strong reasons for placing the food services, information center, mail center and post office, bookstore, ticket offices, ballroom, and administrative offices on the ground floor, while other areas, such as the publication offices or student activity offices may be in less accessible locations. Guest rooms, which receive relatively little traffic and function better in quiet areas, fit nicely into higher floors and more remote locations. Reality may dictate that such revenue-producing facilities as a bookstore or coffee shop take precedence in location over a music room or browsing library, even though it may be educationally desirable to expose, at least by proximity, those entering the building to the latter rather than the former. Some seldom-used facilities (which are determined by the campus) such as a ballroom or arts and crafts shops, may also need to be placed in a remote location of the student center because other functions in the building may take precedence.

## SEGREGATION BY FUNCTION

Whenever practical, areas should be separated by function, where supervision, instruction, and equipment control for all areas are possible. The placement of such areas within the student center may assist the utilization of other areas when properly located (i.e., a self-contained game room receives players from a nearby coffee shop, and the presence of such a shop induces gamesters to stop for refreshments when leaving).

The following are examples and guidelines for combining various program areas of the student center into shared spaces:

- The game room tends to be noisy; therefore, it should not be adjacent or in close proximity to sleeping rooms or private dining or meeting rooms.
- The information center should be near the main entrance of the student center, to be visible and accessible for visitors and guests.
- The theater should have its own entrances and exits and is probably best situated in its own wing or section of the student union. Similar or related activities (i.e., ballroom–banquet room or theater–radio station) may be grouped together or shared.
- The browsing, music, and art rooms might be located together so that they are easily serviced and supervised by one central control point.
- The kitchen should connect with the ballroom and with some or all of the meeting rooms and lounges (depending on what is required for food service), even if only by conveyors, dumbwaiters or elevators, to provide adequate service for receptions, coffee hours, intermission refreshments, and possibly banquets. Therefore, those areas served by the kitchen, but not located on the same level, must be vertically aligned with the kitchen if they are to be serviced by dumbwaiter. Kitchens also demand considerable delivery, removal, and storage services; hence they should be located near driveways, storerooms, and receiving spaces.

### Public Spaces

As mentioned in the preceding section, the food areas or marketplace are best located primarily on the ground level of the student center

for convenience and accessibility by students, faculty, staff, and visitors; game rooms should be located near refreshment areas; and some meeting rooms and lounges should be placed directly above, or in close proximity to, the kitchen for food service. The theater crowds at intermission may utilize the refreshment service if it is fairly close by, and service facilities such as coatrooms, toilets, and public telephones are also required. If the costume and stage shops are to share any facilities or equipment with the arts and crafts workshops, the latter should be located in this section of the building, and if the darkroom facilities are to be used by the campus publications, these offices should be located here too.

### Reception Area

The lobby and information center should be located near the main entrance of the student center. In some buildings the information center includes ticket and other sales, a lost-and-found service, and some office functions. Smaller student centers may have the reception area serve multiple purposes, such as the issuing and supervising center for the music and browsing rooms or the concierge desk for the guest quarters. They may also require that administration offices be located directly adjacent to reception. Many centers may also have a large lounge or banquet hall for receptions next to the main entrance. Coatrooms and pay phones should be adjacent to this area, and toilets should be located nearby.

### Administrative Spaces

If the advantages of adjoining offices outweigh those of decentralized offices, an administrative suite can be planned wherein equipment and personnel can be used with flexibility. Some office space is needed in the various departments, but it can be reduced if centralization is adopted. Should decentralized offices be used, the social director might be placed in the student activities section where the various student government organizations, union committees, and publications are located. By locating these program areas adjacent to one another, communication among the various groups and with the social director is improved, and a relatively quiet group of activities is kept together. If decentralization of offices is adopted, other offices besides the social director's can serve dual purposes. For example, if the business office is located near the food or bookstore area, it can offer closer supervision and emergency assistance. A maintenance superintendent's office near the maintenance shop or a reservation office near the information center can benefit the efficiency of operation of the student center in the form of added service.

### Quiet Areas

The quiet areas of the student center should be located away from the noisier, highly trafficked ones. Offices, conference and meeting rooms, lounges, and art, music, and browsing rooms might benefit from being located together in a quiet section of the building, but they cannot entirely be separated from the noisier sections. For example, meeting rooms may occasionally introduce some noise to an otherwise quiet facility, particularly when larger rooms are in use. Larger meeting rooms and lounges may be best accommodated in the noisier section of the student center, which includes the food services, while smaller meeting rooms, lounges, and conference rooms are placed together in a quiet section of the building which houses offices and other less noisy facilities. While outside noise can interfere with the music room, the considerable amount of sound that originates inside makes the music room an unlikely component of a quiet area unless it is well soundproofed.

Primarily, the quiet areas of the building present most of the demands for late or vacation-time operation. Guest rooms, administrative and publications offices, and the campus radio station are quite likely to function late at night or during the winter and summer vacations, and locating these together with separate access permits their use after the student center's normal operating hours. Separate use of other areas of the building late at night or during vacation time (i.e., the theater) should also be considered in planning.

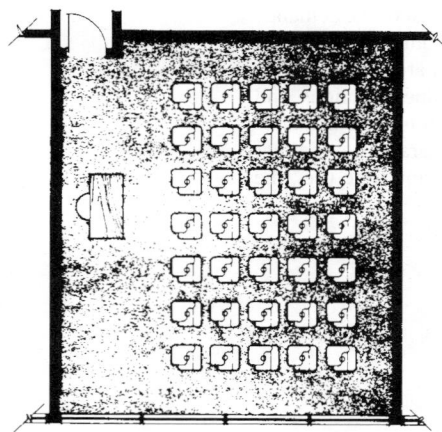

**Fig. 1. Seating arrangement in a classroom for 35 students**

# COLLEGE CLASSROOMS

Major factors to be considered in designing a classroom for college-level instruction are the following:

- Teaching methods – type of curriculum relevant
- Seating, writing surfaces, and laptop computers
- Space and furnishings for the lecturer
- Use of wall space, including marker boards, screens, size and location of windows, and so on
- Facilities for projection and television
- Coat racks, storage, and other conveniences
- Acoustics and lighting
- Heating and air-conditioning
- Aesthetic considerations

**Classroom Seating**

The seating arrangement is the most important feature in determining the size and shape of a classroom. Seating arrangements in a class-room should provide all students with a good view of the front marker board; ready access both to the seats and to marker boards on other walls; an adequate, well illuminated writing surface at each seat; a place to set books and papers; reasonable comfort; and privacy in taking examinations. In a class of 50 or fewer students, where a long front marker board is desirable, it seems better to have the front wall longer than the side walls. This presupposes that there are more students in a row of seats than there are rows; for example, visibility is better in a classroom having five rows of seven seats than in one having seven rows of five seats.

In a room measuring 26 feet by 30 feet (Fig. 1), with separate tablet armchairs for 35 students, the seven seats in a row might have a spac-ing of 3 feet-6 inches between seat centers laterally and 4 feet-6 inches between the end seat centers and side walls (6 × 3 feet-6 inches + 9 feet = 30 feet). Spacing from front to back in a column might be 3 feet between seat centers with 4 feet behind the back-seat

center and 10 feet between the front-seat center and the front marker board (4 × 3 feet + 14 feet = 26 feet). This pattern allows for aisles of about 20 inches between columns, a width just under the 22-inch *unit width* used as a standard in estimating the number of persons who can walk abreast in a corridor or stair hall. This arrangement requires about 22 square feet of space per student. Lecture halls whose seats have folding tablet arms may allow 15 square feet or less per student.

Close-packed seating arrangements are not the most desirable, but sometimes are necessary because larger rooms are not available. Laws in some states provide that no person shall have to pass more than six others to reach an aisle; hence 14 persons in a row between aisles is an absolute maximum. If 10 to 14 students sit next to each other in a row behind a long strip table or writing ledge, the ledge should be at least 12 inches wide and should provide at least 2 feet of length per person. An arrangement whereby the nearer half of the writing surface in front of each person can fold up and away from the writer gives more room for students to pass. A spacing between rows of 42 inches between seat centers is adequate for most seating arrangements that use strip tables for writing.

Tablet armchairs are commonly used for seating in college class-rooms and permit rows to be spaced every 3 feet. They are satisfac-tory for most classes that do not make use of special equipment, provided they have a large writing surface and a shelf underneath for books and papers. Tablet armchairs may be found either fixed to the floor, fastened together in sets of two to six that can be moved as a group, or individually movable. When chairs are fixed to the floor, the arrangement should be one that permits good visibility and ready access. Good visibility may be achieved in three ways: by sloping the floor, by staggering seats in consecutive rows, or by wide spacing.

An arrangement permitting a class of 30 to spread out for examina-tion purposes in a 26-foot by 26-foot classroom seating 40 students would be the following (Fig. 2): in each of five rows, spaced 3 feet

Reviewers: Perkins & Will, Architects

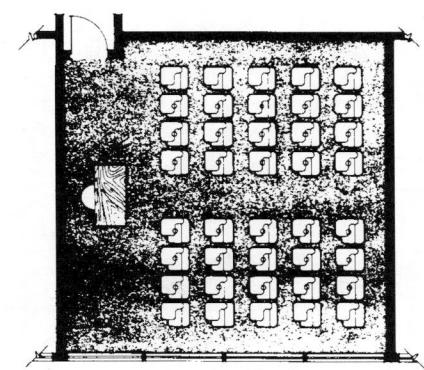

**Fig. 2. Classroom for 40, with 10 side seats movable**

part from front to back between seat centers, let two triples of seats ·e placed with seat centers 2 feet apart laterally and with a 4-foot ·entral aisle from front to back between triples. In 5-foot aisles at the ·ides, let movable tablet armchairs be placed next to the fixed seats ·or lectures and recitations (keeping the 3-foot aisle by the walls), but ·et these chairs be moved over next to the walls during examinations. ·f the center chair in each fixed triple were left vacant, there would ·till be 30 widely spaced chairs available for an examination. ·Another pattern involves joint activity by two instructors whose ·djoining classrooms are separated by a folding partition, and can be ·ombined into a larger room for 60 for appropriate portions of the ·nstruction (Fig. 3).

**·RONT PLATFORM**

·n front of the students' seating area, there should be enough space ·or the lecturer to walk back and forth before a long marker board. In ·ooms with more than five rows of seats there is an advantage in hav-·ng a platform, possibly 8 inches above the floor and extending the ·ull width of the room, on which the teacher may walk the length of ·he board without danger of failing off the end. The marker board ·hould then be raised correspondingly higher above the classroom ·loor for better visibility. The teacher needs a table to place lecture ·notes and papers, but it is better to have this table either movable on ·casters or fixed at the side of the platform where it does not block the ·view of the marker board from the first two rows of students. If a pro-

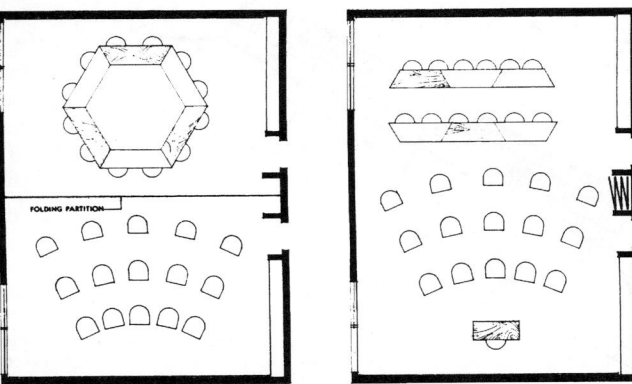

**Fig. 3. A classroom divisible into two seminar rooms**

jector is to be used, there must either be a place where it can be mounted permanently at the front of the room, or there must be pro-vision for rolling it in on a cart and connecting it electrically. In the latter case, the front platform might be slightly lower and be accessi-ble by a ramp. The teacher seldom sits during a lecture but may wish to sit down during an examination. There should be a chair near the table or desk for the teacher.

A lecture room should be so placed in a building that it is accessible to students without overcrowding of corridors or stairways. Coat racks, adequate bulletin boards lining the corridors, and ample toilet facilities should be provided nearby. The room itself should be arranged so that the audience can see well, hear well, and be com-fortable. In part this depends on temperature, humidity, background of light and sound, and seating space. Accessibility provisions in classrooms should be addressed.

**PROJECTION SYSTEMS**

The large lecture room should be built to accommodate a variety of projection systems. An overhead projector requires a screen properly mounted to ensure that the entire class has good visibility with mini-mum distortion. More screens or a wide screen may be needed to enable the lecturer to use two or more overhead projectors at once. If movies, films, or slides are projected from the rear of the room and reflected from a front screen, the room should have a projection booth, or at least a suitable stand and electrical outlet for the projec-tor. Remote controls for operating the projector are desirable. Shades may be required for darkening a room with windows. If the rear-screen method of projection is to be used, in which the image is thrown onto a translucent screen mounted in the front wall from a projector in an adjacent room beyond the front wall, the building plans must include adequate provision for this projection room.

A room or space for the preparation of visuals related to a lecture is a corollary of their use. Copies of lecture material can be posted after the lecture for inspection by students. Storage for such materials must also be provided, as well as for any materials distributed to stu-dents to supplement their lecture notes.

Provision for receiving and transmitting television is also an impor-tant consideration in planning a lecture room for large group instruc-tion.

**SEATING AND VISIBILITY**

Good visibility depends not only on the arrangement of marker boards and of projection screens and equipment, but also to a large degree on seating arrangements. Factors to be considered are avoid-ance of obstructions, slope of the floor and height of the speaker's platform, viewing distance, and the extreme vertical and horizontal viewing angles. It is clear that a good lecture room will not have columns or supports so placed as to block the front screen and marker board from any seat in the room. However, when a large demonstra-tion table stands on a platform between the marker board and the audience, the lower 12 to 18 inches of the board often cannot be seen by people in the first few rows. In this case, vertically sliding marker boards are needed so that the writing may be raised to a level where it can be seen by all.

A sloping floor in a lecture room will generally add somewhat to the cost of construction, but in many instances it will be worth the extra cost in providing good visibility for all. The object of a sloping floor is to make it easier for a person to see over or around the heads of those in front and to give the impression of a smaller room. If the seats in successive rows are staggered so that the line of sight from one seat to the lecturer goes directly between the centers of two seats in the next row, the rise required per row may be reduced by half. Closely interdependent are the slope of the floor and the height of the speaker's platform. The use of a raised platform for the teacher has advantages in increased visibility in any room seating more than about 40 persons, provided that the table or other furniture on the platform does not block the marker board for those in the front rows (an example of a plan is shown in Fig. 4).

Studies of distances and angles for satisfactory viewing indicate that seats should be placed at a distance from a screen not less than 2 nor more than 6 times the width of the screen image to be viewed and that the distance from a person to the marker board should not exceed 400 times the size of the smallest letter or digit being written. Thus, if the back row of students is 64 feet away, the lecturer should make her letters and digits at least 2 inches high. Similar studies indicate that the angle of elevation from the eye to the upper part of an object on the screen or marker board should not exceed 30 degrees (see Fig. 5). If lecture rooms are built in a fan shape instead of a rectangular shape, the minimum angle between line of sight and the blackboard should be at least 30 degrees and preferably more than 45 degrees. These limitations of viewing distance and angle impose restrictions on the placement of seats for adequate viewing.

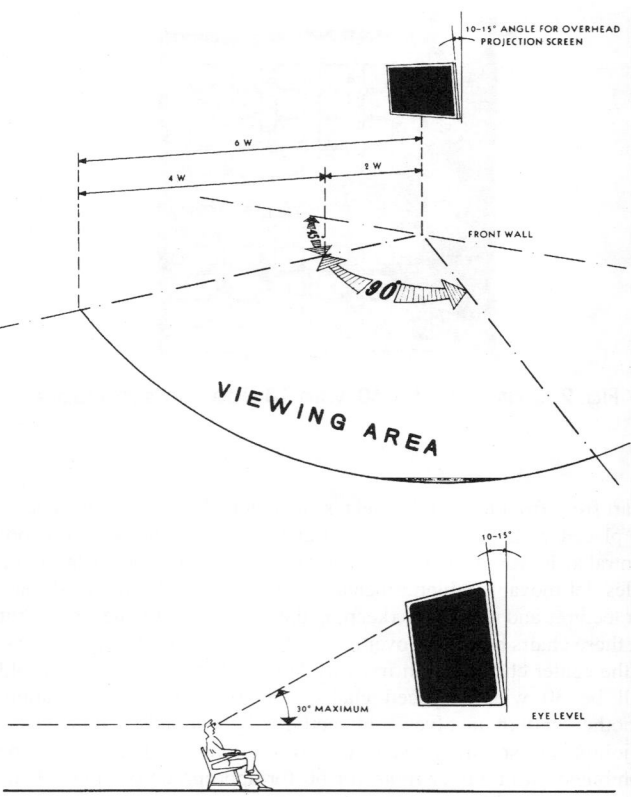

**Fig. 5. Optimum viewing angles**

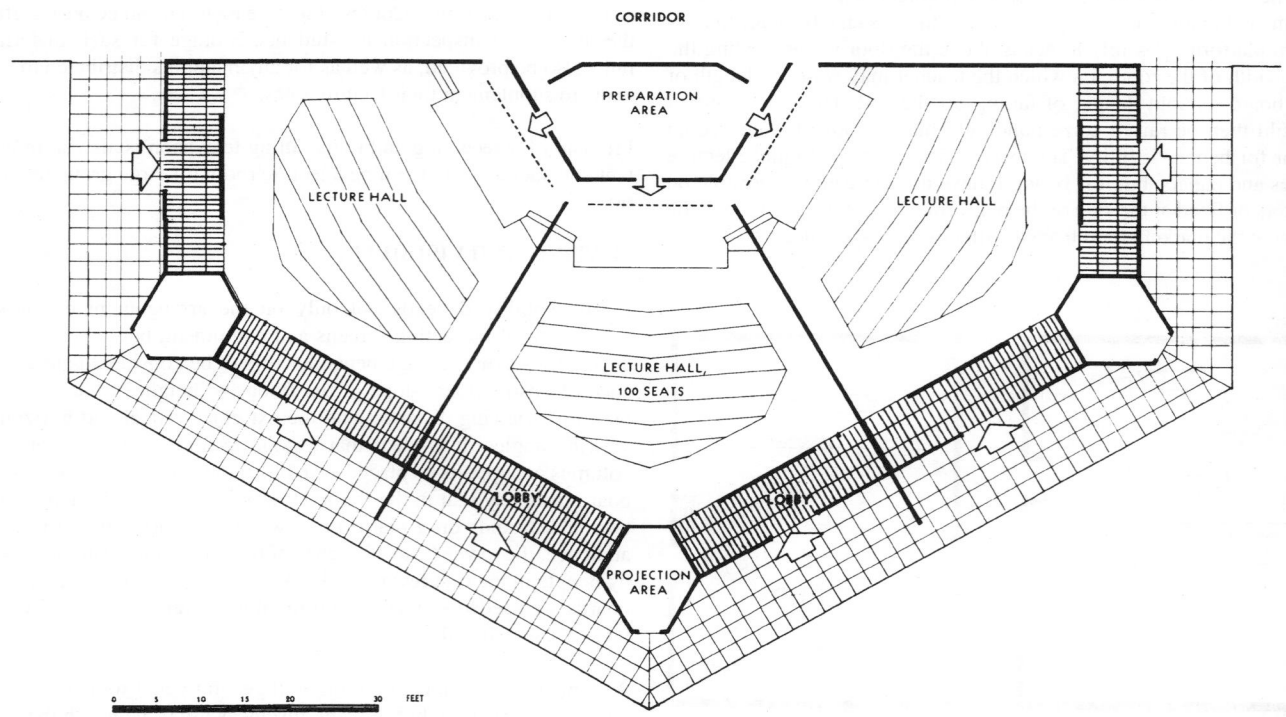

**Fig. 4. Three auditoriums with common preparation room**

# THEATER ARTS LABORATORY TEACHING STATION

There are many types of space facility which may be employed in the theater arts program. The theater arts laboratory teaching station is primarily a classroom which is designed for, and specifically allocated to, the teaching of theater arts subjects. It is presumed that this room will probably be assigned to a single teacher or to a small group of teachers employed in a team-teaching concept. With only slight expansion, however, it might serve in some instances as a very comfortable and pleasant place for public performances. It is not designed primarily as a replacement for a conventional school auditorium. Its existence, however, will emphasize the fact that the well-appointed auditorium is not essential for the successful pursuance of a theater arts program. Under ideal circumstances, such a facility is employed on a day-to-day basis by the teacher in the normal progress of instruction, and therefore may be considered a supplement to the auditorium employed for the larger public performances. In addition to the normal daily class functions, it is entirely appropriate to employ the teaching station, on occasion, for public presentation of material adapted to this space, if the seating will accommodate a small invited, or even paying audience.

Although some dimensional data are provided, it should be remembered that they represent only a suggested treatment and that, in specific instances, a room might change its shape perceptibly and be increased or decreased in size. The basic concept of this room implies that its primary function is that of a classroom, and a continual enlargement of this facility approaching a small auditorium would be undesirable. The term *teaching station* is employed rather than *little* or *studio theater* in an attempt to emphasize its classroom function.

## Separate Service Facilities

If the school has separate auditorium facilities, it is recommended that the teaching station be nearby in order that some of the service areas might be employed by both of these theater units. As an example, it would be possible for the teaching station and the auditorium to use the same dressing rooms, the same lobby space, the same ticket offices, the same rest rooms, the same shop area, and some of the same storage area (see Fig. 6). Although it is true that on occasion both of these producing units might be in performance simultaneously, it is not probable that this would occur frequently enough to warrant complete duplication of all these service areas. However, such support space is absolutely essential, and, if it is not provided in connection with some other function of the building, it will be necessary to plan it in connection with the teaching station. In the description which follows, it will be apparent that there are a number of advantages to having the teaching station accessible from four sides. The dimensional data suggest the possibility but do not demand that the teaching station occupy space equivalent in size and shape to two standard classrooms. The recommended plan includes space for normal classroom function, space for arena-type presentation, space for proscenium and thrust stage presentations, and allows all of this space to be converted to other multiple-theater purposes.

The area designated as the teaching station divides roughly into three parts (see Figs. 7 and 8):

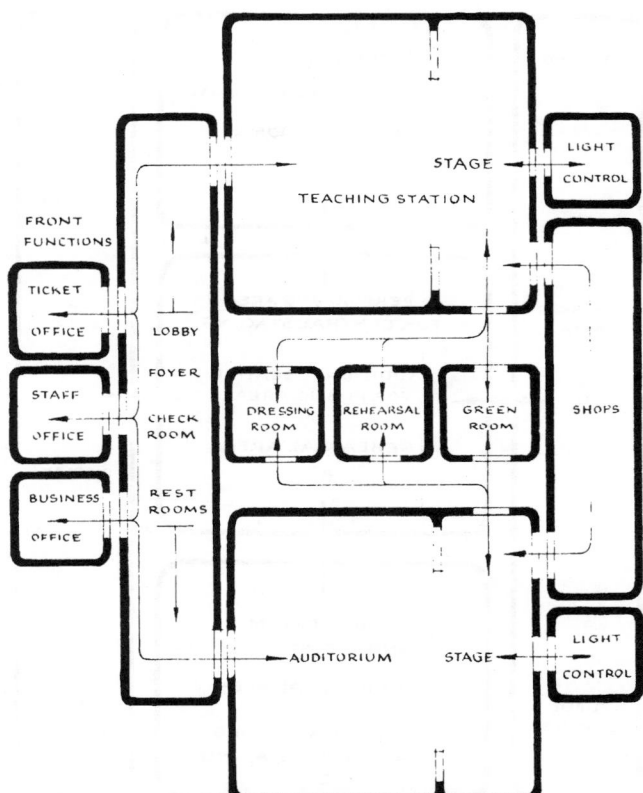

**Fig. 6. Functional and space relationships of auditorium to teaching station. It is highly desirable, as the text indicates, to have both a stage-auditorium and a teaching station in an efficient academic theater plant. If both are provided, it is not necessary to duplicate all of the support functions; avoiding unnecessary duplication will save space and construction costs. This diagram illustrates the desirable functional and positional relationships between the two complementary theater forms**

*Source: Architecture for the Educational Theatre,* H. W. Robinson, University of Oregon. Reprinted by permission.

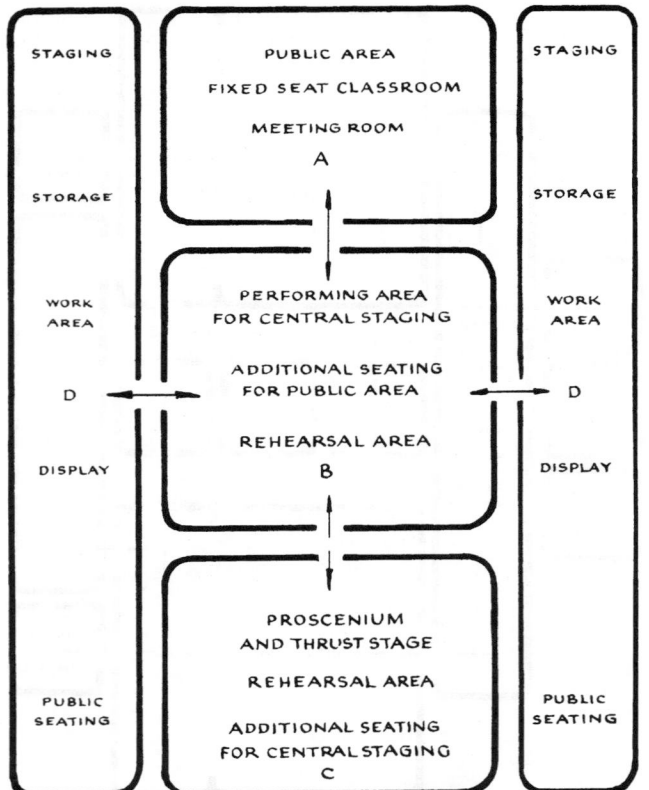

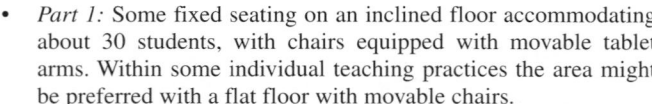

Fig. 7. Teaching station. The teaching station provides space for all theater functions such as work areas, rehearsal areas, classroom, and public seating for all three basic theater forms: thrust, arena, and proscenium. It is multifunctional in terms of space, but can seldom accommodate more than one function at one time. The basic concept calls for three major tandem spaces (A, B, and C), and two flanking spaces (D); all are multifunctional. The dimensions of these spaces are optional (see text). This diagram shows the interrelationship of the spaces and their function, and introduces the plan presented in Fig. 8

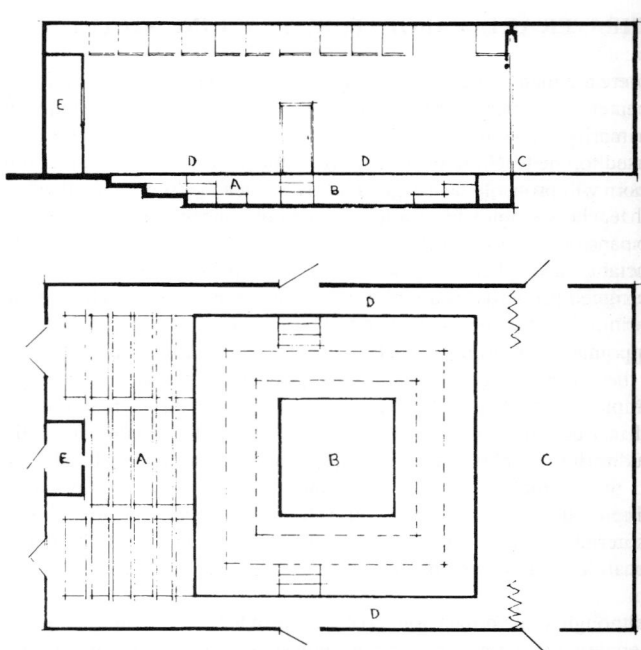

Fig. 8. Teaching station section and plan: (A) fixed seating; (B) potential arena staging; (C) elevated stage, no fixed proscenium; (D) elevated walkways on each side of the room serve as work tables and arena seating and provide chair and platform storage underneath; (E) projection room

- *Part 1:* Some fixed seating on an inclined floor accommodating about 30 students, with chairs equipped with movable tablet arms. Within some individual teaching practices the area might be preferred with a flat floor with movable chairs.
- *Part 2:* An elevated stage, presumably at the opposite end from the fixed seating just described, and with the usual physical and electrical equipment. When employed as a proscenium stage, there would be space for seating approximately 80 in the fixed seating described combined with the temporary seating in the space next described.
- *Part 3:* A flat floor area between part one and part two for rehearsal, demonstration and arena staging, a playing area of at least 14 by 18 feet, and with the usual lighting and mechanical equipment. When this area is employed for arena staging, and all other areas adapted to seating, it can accommodate approximately 140. The minimum width of this room is 24 feet; widths up to 36 feet would prove desirable. The total length of the room, if the areas described are laid end-to-end, is about 70 feet.

If the fixed seating plan is employed for some 30 to 50 seats, and if they are on a raked (inclined) or terraced floor, it is recommended that there be at least a 5-inch differential in the height of the rows. Back-to-back spacing of 36 inches is recommended for rows, and 20 to 22 inches for individual seat widths. Other seating to be provided should be of padded metal folding chairs with arm rests. Linkable chairs have some advantages in terms of ease of movement, for regrouping, and for cleaning.

The center area of the room is recommended for general demonstration, classroom space, and as an arena playing area for productions to be viewed from four sides. It is suggested that the recessed space might be 21 to 24 inches below that of the surrounding areas, including the service halls. This provides a depressed area for the arena stage with some seating at that level, with other raised seating on all sides, and it also allows for the elevated proscenium and thrust stage to be above the central floor area. Although the raised stage at the end of the room may be employed as a proscenium stage, it should not be thought of as that exclusively. Its design lends itself to other, flexible treatment. There is no fixed proscenium—the bounding edges of the opening are established by movable sections of wall or by a simple curtain framing. This stage space should be the full width of the room at that end, and should be at least 14 feet deep. Although more-than-usual classroom height is desirable over the stage area, it is not necessary to provide the usual stage house or fly space. It is suggested that two levels (each 3 feet deep) running the full width of the stage be provided in front of the fixed platform area with one-third stage height differential for each, namely 7 or 8 inches. These levels can be created by separate, collapsible, or nesting boxes and reemployed as terraced seating spaces for the arena concept, or as variable forestage space as suggested by the accompanying diagrams (see Fig. 9).

A projection room may be provided at the end of the room opposite that of the fixed stage, to serve as a sound room and a listening room, as well as to accommodate projection equipment.

The ceiling of this room should be approximately 14 feet above the stage level, and should provide, in addition to standard room lighting, other arrangements for the hanging of special stage-lighting instruments and other hanging units. These supporting members can be exposed or concealed above a false ceiling. Lighting control may be located either in the offstage area on the fixed stage floor or in the projection room previously described.

A walkway at least 42 inches wide should be provided on the two long sides of the room which connect the stage level at one end with the entrance level at the opposite end. For classroom use, these levels will be employed as display and work areas at low table height. When the room is employed for arena staging, they serve as elevated rows of seating on the two sides. For end staging, they serve as additional side stages or for walkways approaching the stage for entrance, tableau, or processional purposes. If slightly enlarged, the space beneath these walkways may be employed for storage for seating or other theatrical equipment.

No attempt will be made here to specify a minimum of equipment for this teaching station, but it is obvious that it must have the usual complement of front traveler, cyclorama, switchboard, and lighting equipment.

Although it is not planned that all three of these areas will be used simultaneously in a classroom teaching station, it is possible to have on stage the fixed stage scenic, lighting, and property elements to be used for a public presentation or for the use of another class while the teacher lectures or conducts a demonstration in the central area without having to clear this material. In the same way, a setup can remain in the arena section and the teacher will still have a lecture area and a drill or rehearsal area unencumbered.

The essential features of this classroom teaching station are designed specifically to serve the purposes of theater instruction, but if, in scheduling, it appears that the room will not be in continual use, it may be employed quite effectively in the true multiple-function sense. Although specifically designed for theater purposes, it has not

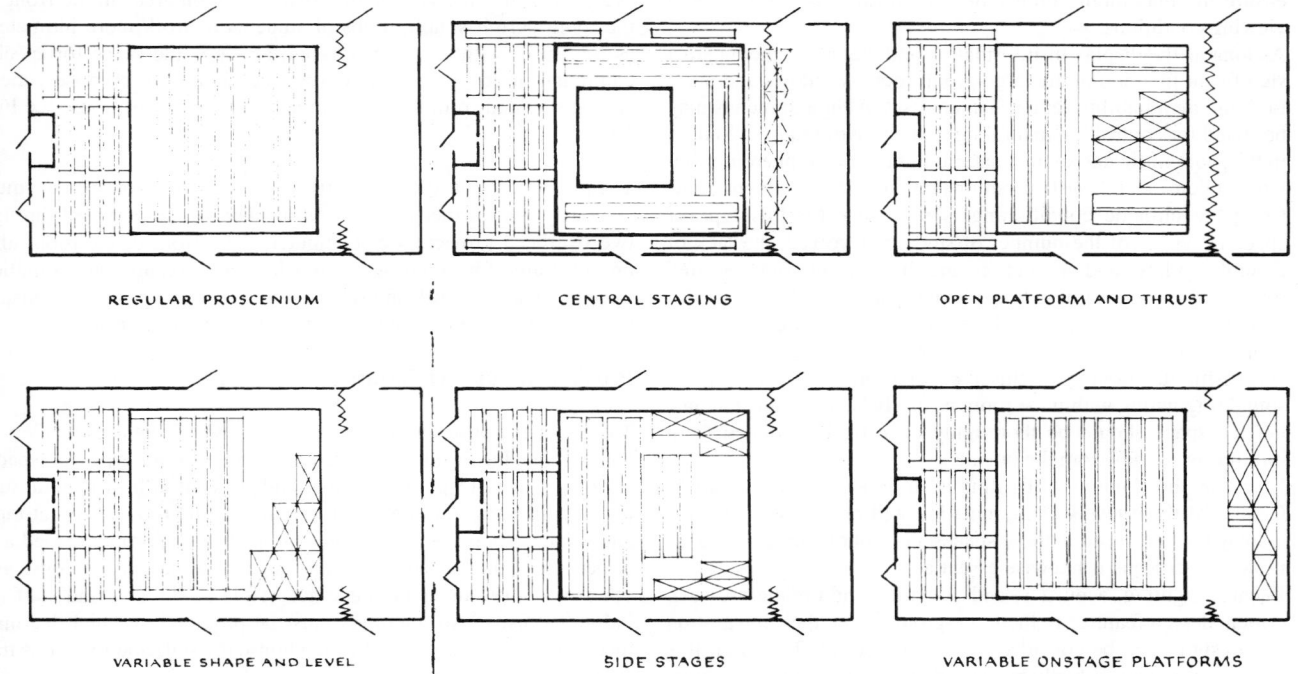

REGULAR PROSCENIUM    CENTRAL STAGING    OPEN PLATFORM AND THRUST

VARIABLE SHAPE AND LEVEL    SIDE STAGES    VARIABLE ONSTAGE PLATFORMS

**Fig. 9. Teaching station platform and seating alternatives. The standard teaching station is readily convertible to many staging forms. A few of the alternates are suggested in this diagram. Portable platforms of standard modular dimension, such as 3 by 6 feet, may be used as a base for audience seating on varying levels or stacked to change the height of playing levels. These units are stored, when not in use, under the forestage and under the elevated walkways at each side of the room. Stair units of compatible height increase the flexibility of the system. Infinite variety is available with the exercise of imagination (note that the fixed seating remains the same for each alternate)**

lost its usefulness as a general classroom regardless of subject matter. It has a raised stage for any type of classroom performance, a large flat floor space for activities such as dance, and may even be used as a small lecture hall.

## LARGE-GROUP FACILITIES

An examination of the planning of large-group facilities with media is essential, particularly because the design criteria and planning considerations in large-group facilities with media are probably the most critical of any type of space that might be provided. The following points summarize these design and planning criteria:

- An optimum viewing area, as defined by the various display surfaces that are considered critical for student viewing, will determine the most effective room shape. This optimum area is not a fixed function of the combination of screens and/or monitors but will vary with the type of material presented, the duration of the presentation, the quality of the equipment, the type of screen, and other factors of environment (see details of projection systems and viewing areas).
- Stepped or sloped floors will always be required in order to provide optimum viewing conditions. Both horizontal and vertical sight lines in these rooms are major design factors. Also, raised seating introduces more intimacy in these rooms and may allow the interaction desired for case presentations and discussions.
- Once the viewing area has been established, the actual capacity of the large-group space becomes a function of the seating type and arrangement. Seating types run the gamut from loose seats to fixed seats and built-in counters. Whenever possible, aisles and circulation spaces should be kept out of the viewing area to ensure the maximum number of seats located within optimum viewing conditions.
- As long as the display of information and the use of media are a significant function in the large-group room, windows and natural light are a liability rather than an asset. Although means may be found for controlling natural light, the size of required images in the room mitigates against natural light with its inherent problems of control and washed-out images caused by ambient light.
- Complete climatic conditioning is necessary for this type of space by virtue of the number of students involved, the lack of natural windows and ventilation, and the concentration required by this type of learning experience. Such conditioning will include cooling, air change, filtration, and humidity control.
- Proper acoustical design, from the outset, is necessary for the successful functioning of this type of room. Not only should sound originating within the room be easily heard by all students, but the space should be thoroughly acoustically isolated from interfering sounds from the outside.
- Likewise, the planning of lighting is an important consideration. Generally, three levels of illumination will be necessary for the display methods used in these spaces; control of ambient light on projection screens is likewise essential.
- Because lighting, acoustics, and climatic conditioning are such critical design features in the large-group room, their integration and design must be considered from the outset. Too often this kind of space suffers badly because these design features are neglected until too late in the planning process.
- Educationally, the key to the proper functioning of this type of space is the integration of technology. The studies which follow illustrate the fact that the display surfaces are an integral part of the room, and that equipment should be located for proper functioning and not to interfere in any way with the process of learn-

ing. This consideration includes the location and planning of the teacher's lectern or control center and suggests that lighting and equipment be tied in and controlled from this lectern.
- Finally, the success of these rooms will depend on the inclusion and relationship of adjunct storage, projection, and preparation areas. This is particularly true when rooms are to be used for science courses requiring equipment and demonstrations. In addition, these adjunct spaces may include project areas, conference rooms, and other smaller group activities used to complement large group presentation.

Large-group instruction can include learning functions other than the simple presentation of information. Manipulative and laboratory types of experiences have been employed for many years, and this study suggests a combination of laboratory and lecture-demonstration functions within the same facility. The resulting *lecture laboratory* permits the experimental and information presentation functions to be carried on simultaneously and without changing rooms. The advantages of being able to demonstrate and present information to a group of students seated at laboratory stations is one that may help overcome the problems of amalgamating media and instruction in science areas.

The lecture laboratory is a suite of facilities including a large area containing over 100 student laboratory-desk stations, two smaller demonstration and special equipment areas, a rear projection area, a special projects room, and storage and preparation space serving all parts of the facility. The student area is arranged on three platforms with a ramp at one side for wheeling in special equipment, reagents, and other materials for student use. Each laboratory station consists of a stand-up, sit-down work area with complete utilities serving every two students. The smaller demonstration areas in the front of the room permit small groups of students to work more intimately as a team or with an instructor, and also provide space for special equipment used by students during the laboratory exercises; these can be shielded from the larger area by movable partitions (see Fig. 10).

The projection area allows two 10-foot images to be projected simultaneously, and further information display can be provided through two overhead projectors or computers. The front of the room also provides area for demonstrations which are prepared and supplied from the adjacent work and storage room. These types of demonstrations are also recorded and projected on the projection screen.

### Production-Support Facilities

To reiterate a basic point, the effective and efficient utilization of learning media in education requires three broad types of space: learning spaces, resource facilities, and production-instructional support facilities. In addition to classrooms, lecture rooms, laboratories, and seminar rooms designed and equipped with appropriate media, it is necessary that video, slide, and tape materials, technology, and other media resources be made accessible to students and staff for individual use. Also, facilities must be provided in which learning media may be produced and which house the staff and functions that support the teaching faculty in their work.

Production and support functions and, in turn, their facilities vary in complexity and size with their location and level within the educational system. Within an academic department or "little school," simple facilities should be available for teachers and students to produce transparencies, photocopies, slides, multiple copies, graphs, com-

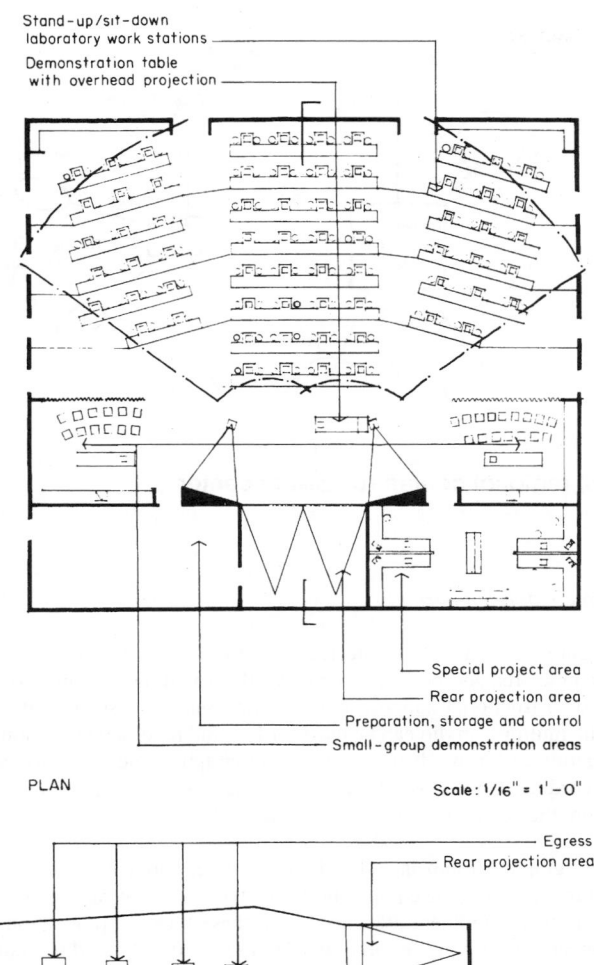

Stand-up/sit-down laboratory work stations
Demonstration table with overhead projection

PLAN                    Scale: 1/16" = 1'-0"

— Special project area
— Rear projection area
— Preparation, storage and control
— Small-group demonstration areas

— Egress
— Rear projection area

SECTION

**Fig. 10. Lecture laboratory plan and section views**

puter presentations, and charts. Usually, this local, simple production area will be located within the resources center or instructional materials center.

At the other end of the spectrum may be a very large and complex production facility as part of a large regional service and production center. Such facilities may form a part of the regional service center or educational laboratory. In between these two extremes are production centers which will serve a university, a college, a large high school, several schools within a district, an entire school district, or all the institutions located in an educational park.

The important objective is to provide several echelons of production and support ranging from the very large and complex covering a region to the very simple and local serving a few teachers. Also, to adequately support the uses of media, all of these echelons of production and support should eventually be represented so that the instructional staff has many levels to draw upon, depending on the complexity and needs of the particular learning situation.

Production support centers may be composed of a variety of components, each of which is related according to the echelon of production and the types of services to be offered. Some of these components are as follows:

> Graphic arts production
> Photographic production
> Motion picture production
> Audio recording
> Animation
> Television origination
> Television control, distribution, and recording
> Film editing and processing
> Graphic materials production and assembly
> Scene, set, and model production
> Equipment storage and repair
> General storage
> Administration and offices for production staff and visiting faculty and teachers
> Conference and preview facilities
> Film and tape materials and equipment storage and distribution

In programming an instructional support center, it is the manner in which these components are arranged and placed together that creates the appropriate center for a particular institution.

The instructional support center can perform several major services in addition to producing films, slides, tapes, and other instructional materials:

- It can design and produce materials that are not commercially available but which are needed for specific instructional purposes.
- It can provide technical assistance to teachers and professors in using instructional technology effectively. It is this type of assistance which helps teachers overcome a fear of mechanical devices about which they have little knowledge.
- It can be the catalyst that causes teachers to begin planning instruction and learning together. Producing televised instruction may bring cooperation among teachers who otherwise would always function as independent entities.
- An instructional support center can provide pedagogical assistance to teachers in designing learning. The learning systems designers—the pedagogical consultants—would logically be housed within this center.
- These facilities can provide the professional focus for teachers and faculty members by making available professional references, material, journals, and consultants.

Instructional support facilities may be an integral part of an educational plant or a separate, free-standing building or unit. In either case, consideration should be given to designing the area to permit changes in areas and relocation of walls, services, and cables. Flexibility of this type is very important, as the functions, staff, and faculty develop. A loft space, free of interior partitions and permitting economical changes, may be the best type of space.

One of the changes anticipated here involves the planning of television studios. Often when studios are initially planned, the faculty will wish to provide for a class of students to be present in the studio during production. However, as the faculty becomes more comfortable with television, the need for students in the studio is less significant. The building should be designed to permit this evolutionary change.

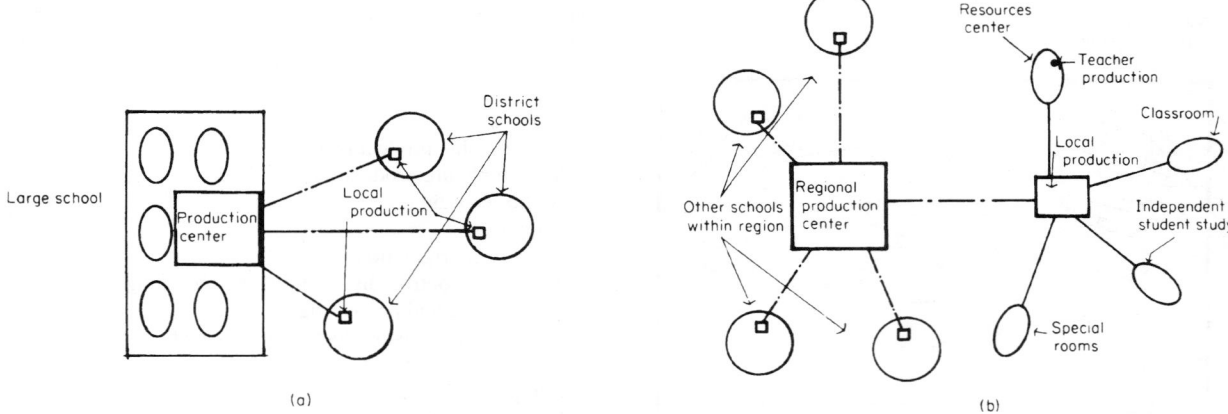

**Fig. 11. Production and support centers: (a) regional center; (b) district center**

Obviously there is no single instructional support facility that solves all needs at all levels. There are many, many different systems of production and support which can be diagrammed. Fig. 11a indicates a regional center that supports a number of subcenters within schools throughout the system. From the subcenter, further production and support activities are provided to individual classrooms, resources center, independent study facilities, and special rooms. It should be noted that within the resources center there is the small, simplified production area for teacher use. The same diagram might illustrate the activities within a college or university campus where, from a central location, major production and support feeds out into schools and departments and then into individual facilities and areas.

Fig. 11b illustrates a center within a large central school which not only supports that school but feeds into other, smaller schools throughout a school district. This might be the appropriate diagram to illustrate production-support facilities within an "educational park."

*Production-Support—1*

Figure 12 shows the basic facilities to support uses of television, graphic arts, and projected media while providing the administrative and instructional support activities necessary for such a situation. The multiuse studio can be used for live and recorded television production, film production, still photography, and possibly audio recording. Control of all of these production activities would come from the central control and distribution room.

The graphics room includes drafting space, copying machines, film editing and copying equipment, computers, assembly and work tables, and other equipment associated with these types of production. The preparation and storage area adjacent to the studio is used for building and storing sets and models; next to it is maintenance and repair area for audiovisual equipment used both within this production facility and throughout the schools it serves. The administrative facilities include waiting and exhibit areas, preview and conference rooms, and offices.

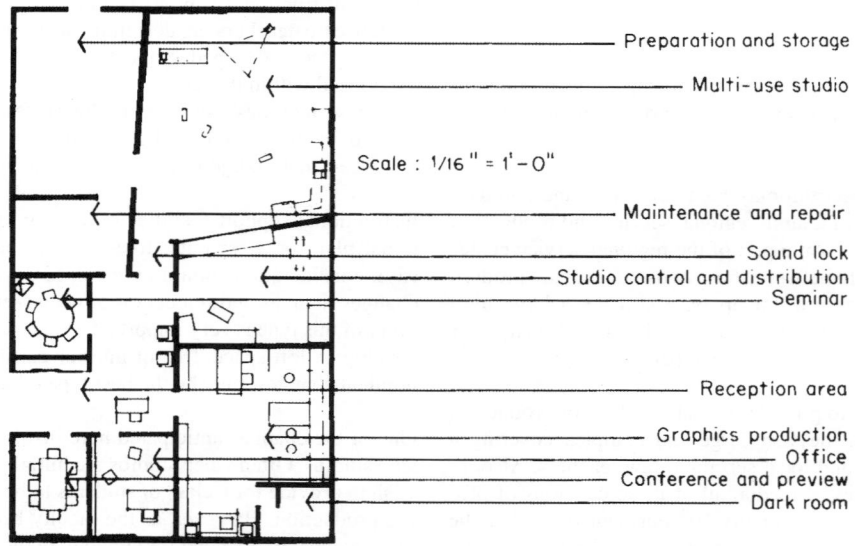

Preparation and storage
Multi-use studio
Scale : 1/16 " = 1'-0"
Maintenance and repair
Sound lock
Studio control and distribution
Seminar
Reception area
Graphics production
Office
Conference and preview
Dark room

**Fig. 12. Media facilities plan**

*Production-Support—2*

Figure 13 illustrates a center producing basic institutional aids and media, with an emphasis on film production. The production process is initiated by a conference between faculty and production staff, at which time the nature and instructional requirements of the materials are defined and a production schedule is set up. After production, the finished materials are distributed to the faculty concerned. Eventually the material may be deposited in the library of resources center where it is available to the student for review; it may also be distributed to cooperating institutions.

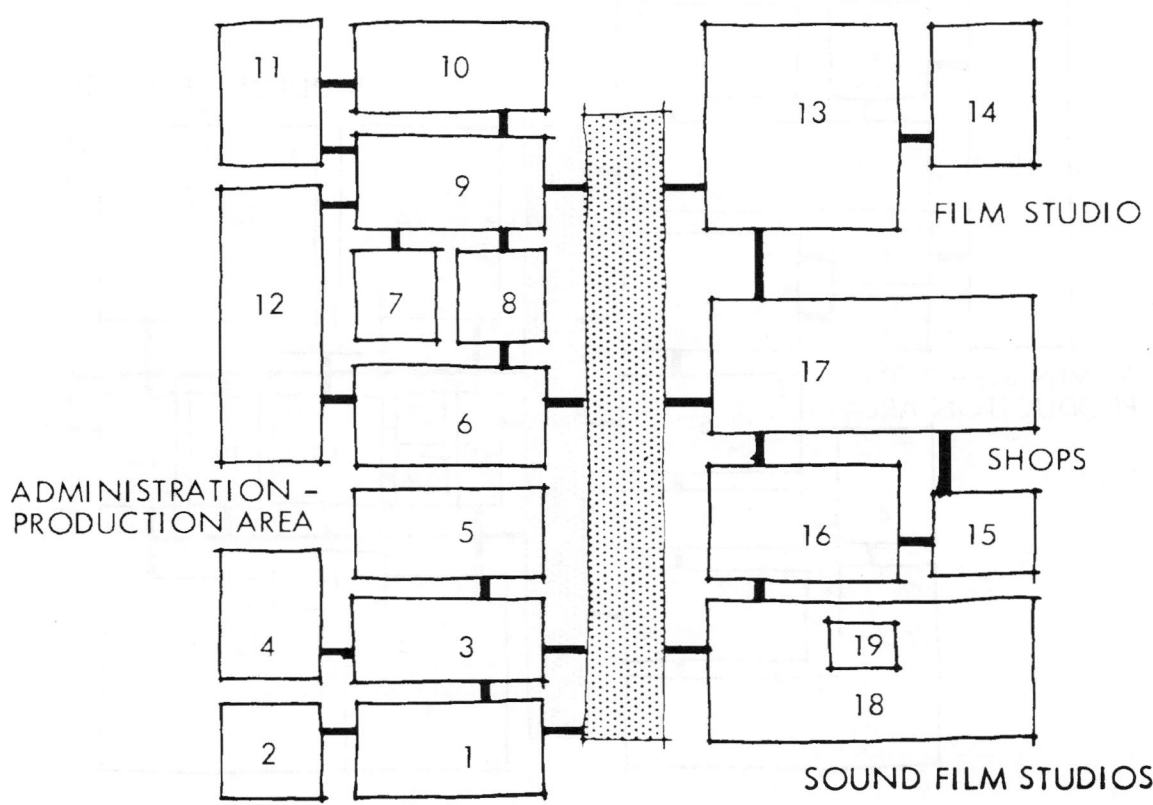

1. clerical and shipping – location of receptionist, secretaries and personnel involved in distribution of materials.

2. film vault – storage of completed film materials.

3. conference-rehearsal – rooms for faculty-production staff conferences, rehearsals prior to recording or filming, and periodic staff conferences.

4. production staff offices.

5. recording and radio studios – making of audio-tapes, dubbing of sound on films and possibly radio broadcasting.

6. graphic-art studio – production of graphs, charts, "visuals" and some slide materials for both direct classroom and film production use.

7. still photography.

8. animation – filming of art work.

9. processing – darkrooms for limited developing and printing of film materials.

10. editing-assembly – editing of motion pictures and assembly of all instructional materials.

11. previewing – small projection rooms for viewing incomplete as well as finished film materials.

12. offices, storage, and toilets – located as needed adjacent to the various production areas.

13. film studio – a large, open studio for the filming of silent motion pictures on which the sound may later be added. The studio can be flexibly divided into filming areas by using demountable flats. This will permit simultaneous filming of one or more productions.

14. external slab – concrete slab (possibly covered) adjacent and accessible to the studio for exter-

nal filming. It may also be used as a receiving platform for materials taken directly into the studio.

15. model and set shop – production of models and demonstration apparatus for direct instructional or production uses, and the making of sets and flats for use in the studios.

16. storage – a large area for storage of materials used in the studios or awaiting distribution for classroom use.

17. equipment receiving, storage and maintenance.

18. sound studios – several studios in which both the sound and image are recorded simultaneously. This permits only one production at a time per studio.

19. control-engineering – glass-fronted booths accessible to each studio for control-engineering personnel and equipment.

**Fig. 13. Film studios and administration-production area**

*Production-Support—3*

Figure 14 illustrates a center designed for originating televised instruction for distribution to a number of receiving points on the campus or to cooperating institutions. This center may fulfill a number of related functions, such as reception and distribution of off-the-air programs, recording of televised instruction (videotape or kinescope), distribution of film materials, and coordinating of remote origination from labs, research centers, and other potential studios. These related functions affect space considerations only as far as requirements of engineering and control, and storage of materials and equipment. Distribution of the television image may be by open or closed circuit or both; the method of transmission does not basically affect the design of the facility. Such a unit would probably serve an entire campus or, in the case of the large university, one or more colleges on the campus.

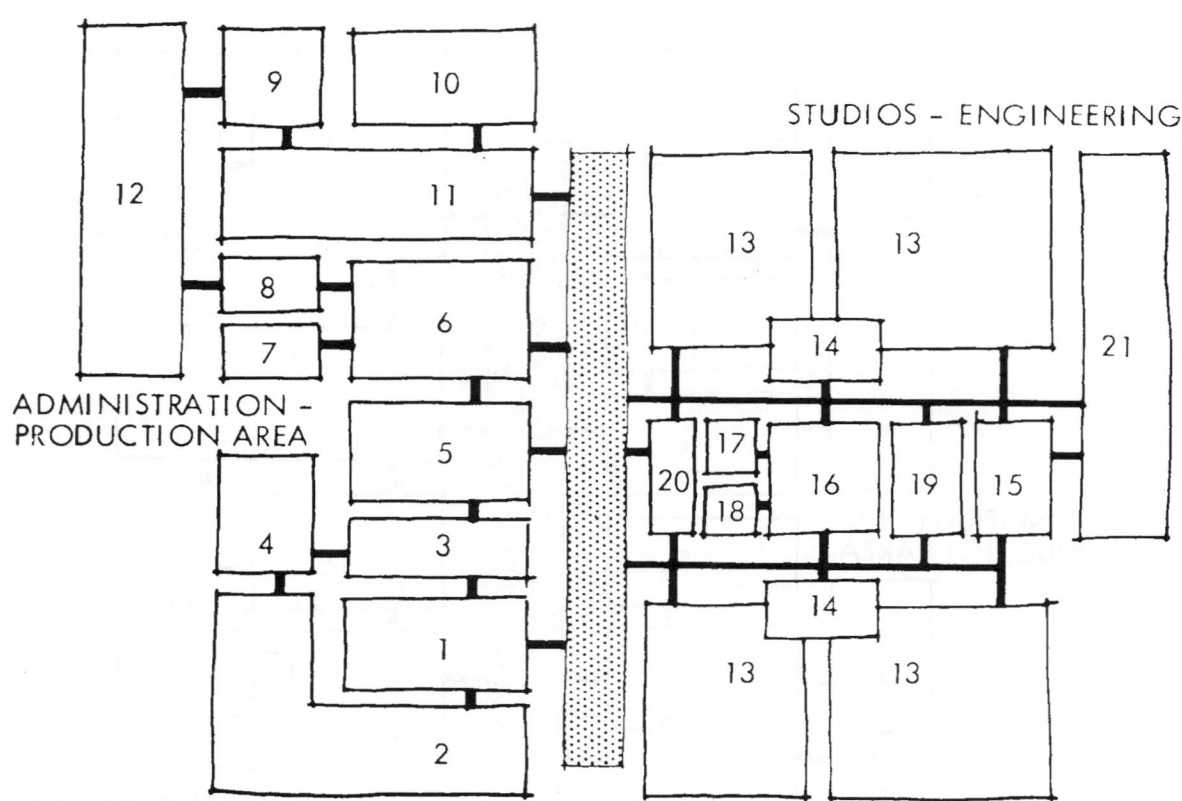

1. reception and secretarial – space for secretarial staff and reception area for visitors.

2. TV faculty offices – offices for faculty members instructing by television and provided to permit coordination between "on-camera" faculty and production staff. (The faculty may also have academic office elsewhere on the campus).

3. production staff offices.

4. conference rooms – spaces for planning

5. film and graphic materials storage – storage of materials used by the faculty in preparation and presentation of televised instruction and includes space for previewing projected materials.

6. graphic arts studio – production of art work

7. still photography.

8. processing – darkrooms for limited processing of film materials.

9. workshop – making or assembling of models, sets, flats and apparatus for studio use.

10. equipment shop – receiving, maintenance and storage of camera, sound, control, lighting and other production equipment.

11. storage – large area for flats, sets, apparatus, and other production materials.

12. offices, storage, toilets and mechanical equipment areas – located as needed throughout the unit.

13. television studios – origination of televised production. The size, location and functioning of the studios will vary depending on the philosophy and scope of televised instruction.

14. studio control – glass-fronted booths which serve one or more studios and house the producer-director and control equipment. (Booths do not require direct visual contact with studios; control may be handled by monitors.)

15. storage – adjacent to the studios to avoid loss of production areas within the studios given over to storage.

16. central control, engineering and distribution – electronic "nerve center" for receiving "off-the-air", coordinating remote and studio signals, and maintaining control of all origination and distribution.

17. projection – location of camera chains for distribution of film, slide, and opaque materials.

18. recording – location of kinescope or video tape recorders.

19. equipment storage – storage of camera equipment available for studio use.

20. dressing and make-up areas.

21. external slab – televising of equipment and apparatus too large or cumbersome to be moved into a studio.

**Fig. 14. Engineering studios and administration-production area**

*Production-Support—4*

An institution venturing into a broad program utilizing the aids and media may well consider providing a single facility that combines all the production functions. In the long run such an approach can probably be justified from the standpoint of economy of space, equipment, and personnel, as often a single activity will support several production processes. A graphic arts studio, for example, can produce not only visual and graphic materials for direct classroom use but also the materials used in film production and television production. This total, more complex center is represented in Fig. 15.

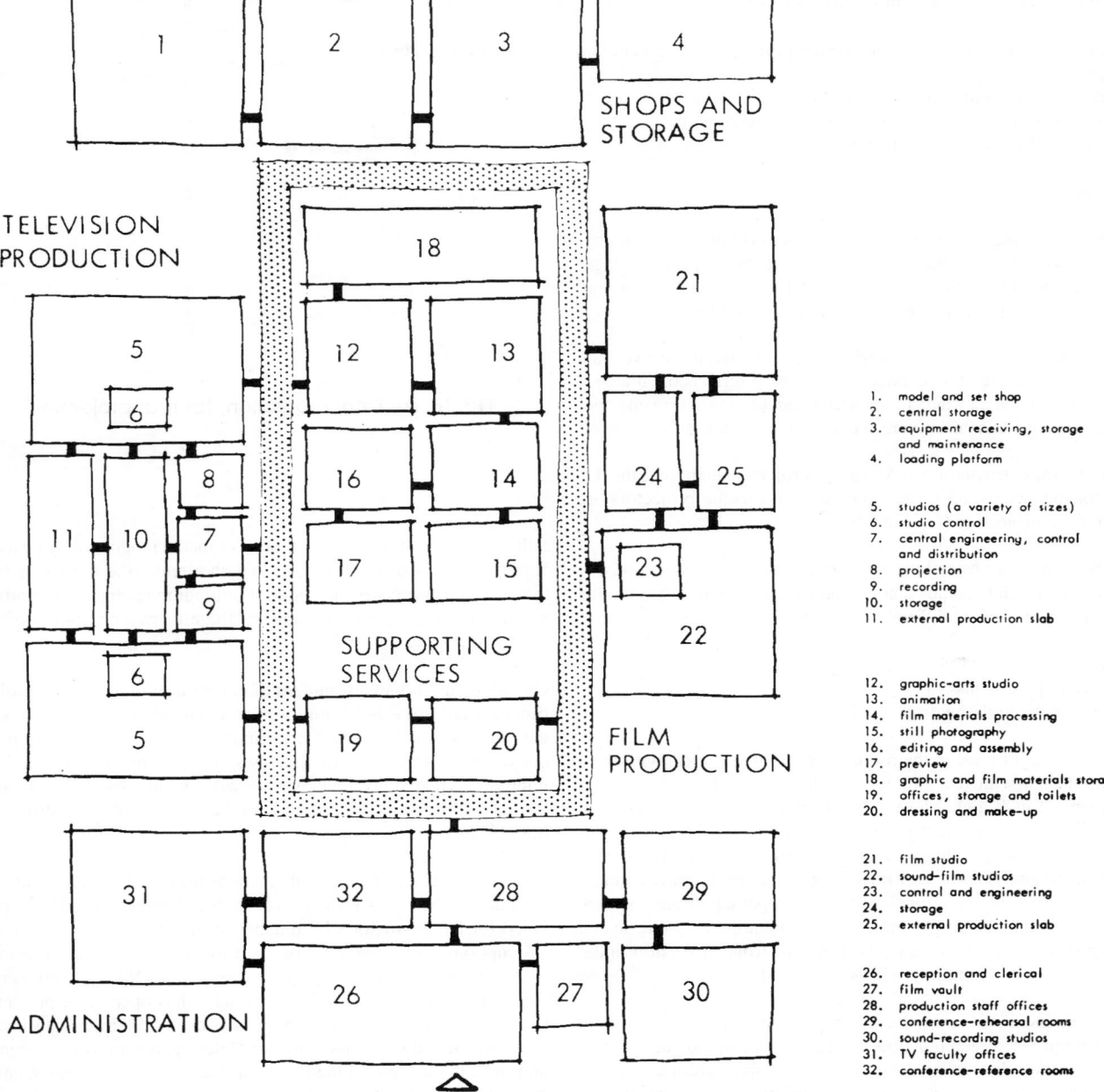

SHOPS AND STORAGE

TELEVISION PRODUCTION

SUPPORTING SERVICES

FILM PRODUCTION

ADMINISTRATION

1. model and set shop
2. central storage
3. equipment receiving, storage and maintenance
4. loading platform

5. studios (a variety of sizes)
6. studio control
7. central engineering, control and distribution
8. projection
9. recording
10. storage
11. external production slab

12. graphic-arts studio
13. animation
14. film materials processing
15. still photography
16. editing and assembly
17. preview
18. graphic and film materials storage
19. offices, storage and toilets
20. dressing and make-up

21. film studio
22. sound-film studios
23. control and engineering
24. storage
25. external production slab

26. reception and clerical
27. film vault
28. production staff offices
29. conference-rehearsal rooms
30. sound-recording studios
31. TV faculty offices
32. conference-reference rooms

**Fig. 15. Total media production-support center**

## Projection Systems

Too frequently the hardware used in audiovisual presentations is regarded as a collection of individual items—a projector, a screen, and a speaker—each performing its function more or less independently. A much broader concept is essential if media are to be used with maximum effectiveness. Not only these hardware items but also the seating area and the environment itself must be considered as integrated components of a system, each influenced by and depending on all of the others in producing the total effect. None of these components, even the hardware, can be selected on its merits alone.

Regardless of the projected material or method, the effectiveness of the presentation depends upon the ease with which the viewers receive the message. With any normal audience, the quality of viewing conditions is chiefly determined by four factors:

1. Appropriateness and efficiency of the projection equipment and screens
2. Quality of the projected material
3. Location of the viewer in relation to the screen
4. Visual and auditory environment

### Front and Rear Projection

Before considering any of the above matters, it is important to recognize that two different methods may be used for projecting images onto a screen, and that the choice of method will influence the design of a projection system. These two methods are as follows:

- *Front projection,* in which both the projector and the viewers are on the same side of an opaque screen which reflects the image
- *Rear projection,* in which the projector and the viewers are on opposite sides of a translucent screen upon which the image is displayed

Either one may be used for any type of projector, including the TV projector, but customarily the overhead and opaque projectors are used in front projection (see Fig. 16).

Both front and rear projection have their inherent advantages and disadvantages, which become clear by comparing them in respect to the most important areas of difference. These are as follows:

- Affect of ambient light
- Space requirements
- Interference with the projected image

The ambient light level in the room is much more critical with front projection than with rear projection. This means that with present equipment a much higher level of room lighting can be tolerated in the viewing area when rear projection is employed. This is considered to be the chief advantage of rear projection, particularly in larger rooms. In rooms where small image sizes are appropriate, ambient light effects may not be critical providing proper equipment is used. Current developments in the improvement of equipment indicate that the size of acceptable images possible with front projection under useful levels of ambient light will be increased.

An undeniable disadvantage of rear projection is that additional space behind the screen must be provided to accommodate the projectors and their throw distances. To conserve space, projectors with short focal length lenses are desirable, and mirrors may be used to "bend" the projection rays.

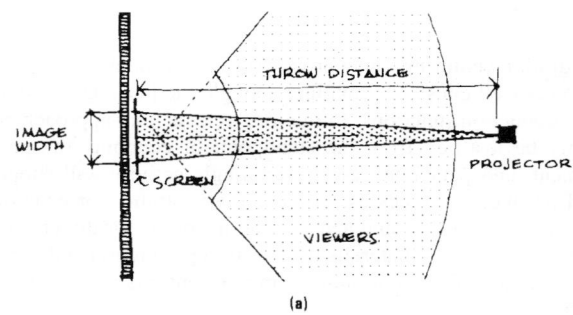

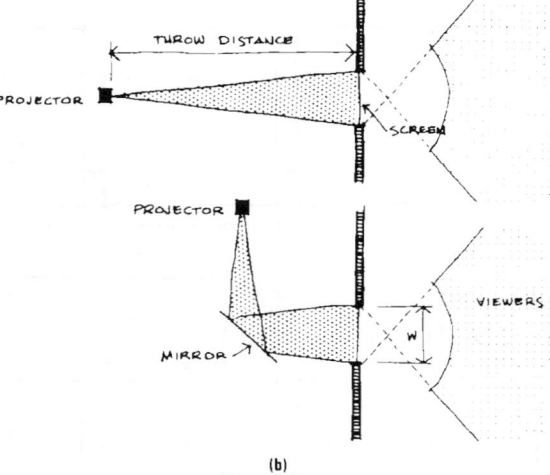

**Fig. 16. (*a*) Front projection; (*b*) rear projection**

Self-contained screen-projector units or media modules may be used. It must be recognized, however, that shortening the focal length of the projector decreases the width of optimum viewing areas, and the use of mirrors generally diminishes the effective brightness of the projected image.

One of the important advantages of rear projection is that the projection rays are protected from interference by either the instructor or the viewers. The instructor can stand in front of the image to point out details without casting shadows. With front projection this is impossible; distracting shadows are cast by any object or person in the path of the projection beam, and the freedom of the instructor is limited accordingly.

It has been assumed that in both methods the projectors are located in reasonably soundproof enclosures and that remote control is provided for the instructor who remains at the front of the class. Such assumptions are frequently not valid for front projection, however. With relatively small groups of viewers, portable front projection equipment is often used, and the instructor may operate the projector. Used in this way, front projection has several additional disadvantages which should be recognized. Unless precautions are taken to minimize it, the noise of the projector is distracting to viewers, and if the instructor must double as an operator, the instructor's effectiveness as a teacher is necessarily diminished.

## Screen

The design of any projection system must necessarily recognize the human factor—the needs and limitations of the observer. The impact and effectiveness of the image displayed largely depend on such matters as its brightness, its legibility, and its contrast values.

The human eye can tolerate and adjust to a remarkably wide range of conditions, but if eyestrain is to be avoided, these critical variables must be controlled within established limits of acceptability. The projection screen is a major component in determining visual comfort.

A variety of screen types are available for both front and rear projection. They differ significantly in their characteristics, affecting both the appropriate size of viewing area and the tolerable level of ambient lighting.

### Space for Rear Projection

In designing for rear projection, one of the problems the architect faces is the allowance of the correct amount of space for the location of the projection equipment. Figure 17a shows a projector located at a throw distance of 1 width of the screen W and indicates the maximum bend angle for seat A as over 75 degrees. This is unsatisfactory for this seat; the allowable bend angle is established by the screen characteristics, and at present, the maximum bend angle is 60 degrees. Figure 17b shows a 2W throw distance and a maximum bend angle at seat A of about 60 degrees, which is satisfactory. Figure 17c shows a total depth of rear projection area as 1W, but by using a mirror, it still permits a 2W throw distance and a 60-degree bend angle.

### Mirrors Reduce Light

The use of mirrors, however, has its drawback in that about a 10 percent loss of image brightness occurs. One must also be careful of reflections of ambient light of other projectors or classroom light passing through other screens and affecting either the mirror or the screen. This can be combated by locating black drapes to mask the projectors from this stray light.

### General Rules

A few general rules are helpful in locating projectors and establishing space for rear projection equipment:

- The larger the screen, the longer the throw distance.
- Conversely, the smaller the screen, the shorter the throw distance.

- Mirrors may be used to fold the projection beam for space saving with smaller screens or with projectors with high lumen output on larger screens.
- For initial schematic design a 2W depth behind all the screens should be allocated for the rear-projection area.
- The use of extra close-up lenses decreases the viewing area, and may result in some distortion around the edge of projected images.

### Viewing Area

*Viewing area is not critical in most classrooms:* Before projected materials were introduced, the objects to be viewed in the usual schoolroom were the instructor, the marker boards, and sometimes maps and charts. The instructor was free to move about the room, and the other objects of visual attention were usually distributed over several wall areas. All of them received their illumination by the general lighting of the room itself. With no fixed area of attention, sight lines and viewing were not critical as long as the general lighting was adequate.

*Projected images restrict viewing area:* For the effective use of visual aids, the requirements for good viewing are much more demanding. The projected image necessarily occupies a fixed position, and, except on the TV receiver, is in a flat plane. Whereas a three-dimensional object may well be viewed from the side, a flat picture can be seen intelligibly only within the limits of a *cone of view*. To see the image properly, the viewer must be within the limits of this cone, and neither too near the image nor too far from it. The area defined by these limits is referred to as the *viewing area*. Its importance in the planning of spaces for image viewing is fundamental, whether the space be a small informal conference area or a large formal lecture hall.

*Shape of the viewing area:* The shape of the viewing area, then, is approximately as shown. Its size is always based on the size of the image to be viewed. The human eye comprehends detail only within a limited cone angle (about 2.5 minutes of arc), and the length of chord subtending this arc (e.g., the image width varies with its distance from the observer). Thus, an object 20 feet away and 6 feet long appears the same as a similar object 10 feet away and 3 feet long. The size of the viewing area is determined by three dimensions, as shown in Fig. 18.

- Minimum distance (1), which is the distance from the nearest part of the image of the eye of the closest viewer

- Maximum distance (2), which is the distance from the furthermost part of the image to the most distant viewer

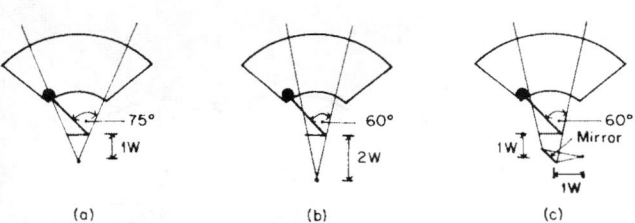

**Fig. 17. Projector location:** (*a*) 1*W* throw distance; (*b*) 2*W* throw distance; (*c*) 2*W* throw distance achieved with a mirror

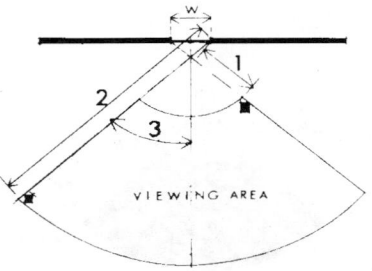

**Fig. 18. Viewing area**

• Maximum viewing angle (3), which is the angle between the projection axis and the line of sight of a person located as far from this axis as one can be and still see all image detail in proper brilliance

*Two ways of establishing viewing angle:* Whether the apex of the maximum viewing angle should be located at the screen or at some other point on the projection axis is a moot point. There is some disagreement among authorities, too, as to how it should govern the side limits of the viewing area. Some prefer the use of the *edge angle,* while others use the angle at the center of the screen. By either approach, the limits defined are essentially similar. In this study, an edge angle of 40 inches has been used in laying out viewing areas for rear projection, since it is felt this best represents average screen characteristics. With front projection, the use of the *center angle* is probably more common practice, and its values range from 20 degrees to possibly as high as 50 degrees. The maximum value of the angle used in determining the viewing area for receiver TV is 45 degrees.

## Minimum and Maximum TV Viewing Distances

| Size of TV tube | Min viewing distance, 4W | Max viewing distance, 12W |
|---|---|---|
| 17 in | 4 ft-11 in | 14 ft-9 in |
| 19 in | 5 ft-1 in | 15 ft-2 in |
| 21 in | 6 ft-4 in | 19 ft-0 in |
| 23 in | 6 ft-6 in | 19 ft-4 in |
| 24 in | 7 ft-5 in | 21 ft-5 in |
| 27 in | 9 ft-8 in | 24 ft-5 in |

*Defining minimum and maximum viewing distances:* Practical minimum and maximum distances are both expressed as multiples of the image width *W*. They vary both with the medium being used and with the type and quality of material being projected, and may be affected also, in some degree, by personal preferences. They have not yet been precisely determined by scientific methods, and it is doubtful that such data would have much practical value anyway. The generally accepted values, resulting from numerous studies, are these (see Fig. 19):

| | *Film, Slides, and Projected TV* | *TV Receivers* |
|---|---|---|
| Minimum distance | 2W | 4W |
| Maximum distance | 6 to 10W | 12W |

*Relation of screen size and viewing area:* Since the size of the viewing area is a function of the image width, it follows that the proper screen size for any given space will be determined by the number of

viewers intended. Conversely, a given type and size of screen automatically establishes the size of the viewing area, and consequently the size of audience that can be properly accommodated. The viewing area is the pattern which determines the seating arrangement in any learning space where projected images are to be used, and in the larger spaces, at least, it also influences the shape of the room (Fig. 20).

**Planning the Projection System**

Whether front or rear projection is to be used, the design of the projection system itself involves determining the following:

• Size of viewing area required
• Appropriate screen size
• Proper type of screen
• Appropriate projector(s)—the required lumen output, focal length and location
• Maximum permissible level of ambient lighting on the screen

The desired audience size is usually predetermined. In some cases, the size of the viewing area, too, may be established by existing conditions. Otherwise, its size and shape should be tentatively approximated in accord with the principles already discussed. Because of the relationship between its dimensions and the width of screen to be used, the inexperienced designer necessarily proceeds by trial and error until arriving at a satisfactory arrangement accommodating the specified audience in proper relationship with the screen. Sometimes, the problem may be reversed, requiring a determination of the optimum audience and seating arrangement for projection equipment already at hand.

**Standards**

Professional standards accepted by the Society of Motion Picture and Television Engineers have been developed for viewing front- and rear-projected images. These standards provide excellent images. However, for the purpose of economy in classroom use of projected media, it is felt that some standards based on the poorest seat in the room can be lowered, particularly for large images. The following

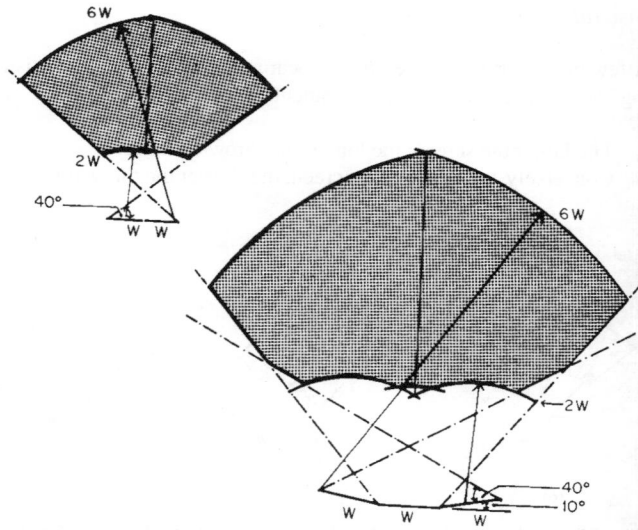

Fig. 20. Viewing areas for two- and three-screen projection

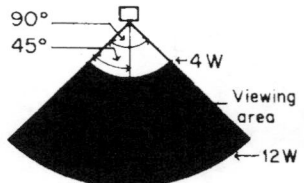

Fig. 19. Viewing area

resume of standards indicates by asterisk (*) those that are less than the professional standards.

*Screen Brightness*

*Motion pictures:*

> 5 feet L—minimum* (gross images)
> 10 feet L—satisfactory
> 15 feet L—excellent
> 20 feet L—maximum (flicker threshold for some observers)

*Slides:*

> 2.5 feet L—minimum* (gross images)
> 5 feet L—minimum for slides with detail
> 10 feet L—satisfactory
> 20 feet L—excellent

*Projected TV:*

> 2 feet L—minimum* (gross images)
> 20 feet L—maximum (flicker threshold for some observers)

*TV monitors:*

> 100 lumens per square foot

*Brightness ratio:*

> 2:1—excellent
> 3:1—very good
> 10:1—acceptable* under some conditions

*Contrast ratio:*

> 100:1—pictorial scenes
> 25:1—good legibility of printed characters
> 5:1—white letters on black background
> 30:1—minimum* contrast ratio for poorest seat dictated by higher levels of classroom light and many types of projected materials

Contrast ratio is determined in part by nonimage brightness which, in turn, is related to screen reflectance and room ambient light. Therefore, controlling the amount of ambient light reaching the screen is important. For large screen installations, if the amount of ambient light occurring at the screen is held to 1 to 2 footcandles, the contrast ratio will normally be adequate.

*Writing Surface Lighting Levels*

Ideally, an average ratio of 1:1 between writing surface brightness and screen brightness should be maintained, while not spilling excessive ambient light on the screens. Since screen brightness varies for each seat in the viewing area, the average condition of brightness for each broad class of projected material should be approximately satisfied. For a medium- to large-size room, three lighting levels would be in the following ranges:

> 5 to10 footcandles—projected TV and films
> 10 to 20 footcandles—slides
> 30 + footcandles—other class activities

**Media Module**

The study led to the design and development of a self-contained media cabinet which might be used in many types of small and medium group situations. These media modules can be of several types:

- A fixed cabinet with self-contained equipment, rear projection screen, and several additional swing-out display surfaces.
- Same as above, only the entire media module would be mobile.
- A basic fixed cabinet with rear-projection screen and swing-out display surfaces. Projection equipment would be mounted on mobile carts which would roll into the cabinet and which would permit the interchanging of projectors.
- Same as above with both the basic cabinet and the equipment carts mobile.
- Any of the above, but with a cabinet and a rear-projection screen sized to accommodate two rear projected images side by side.

Media modules have several attractive features. They can be fabricated in a shop and installed in existing classrooms with little disruption of normal class meetings; in this way, media modules can quickly and inexpensively convert existing facilities for uses of media. Both in building new facilities and remodeling old, the media module is a relatively inexpensive answer initially, which also readily adapts to new and improved equipment. Mobile units can be designed for flexible spaces where the regrouping of students frequently is an important functional requirement; fixed installations of media might not be feasible in such circumstances. As illustrated in this study, media modules can be used to increase the utilization of facilities such as dining rooms and gymnasiums by also allowing them to be used for instruction.

Figure 21 shows one type of media module that was designed and built. The basic cabinet with screen and display surfaces could be either fixed or mobile. Various types of projectors can be mounted in the cart, which is rolled into position for projection on the rear projection screen. Remote controls operate the equipment and the rear screen is of the flexible type. This media module has a screen surface 32 inches square and the entire unit stands 6 feet-8 inches high. Naturally, these dimensions will vary from module to module.

**Furniture**

Planning for furniture is an integral part of the design process. For effective uses of media in education, the manner in which classrooms, seminar rooms, independent study facilities, and other learning spaces are furnished is an important design decision. Unfortunately, too

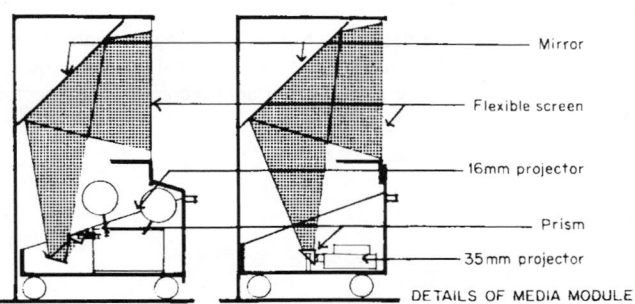

**Fig. 21. Media module**

often the selection and purchase of furniture are left until too late in the planning process when energies, funds, and professional services have been expended. Furniture, as part of the learning environment, should be considered an integral part of any space in which media are to be employed; its selection should be based on careful study and professional advice early in planning. Attention should also be paid to required technology connections (data and power) by a student's desk. Most important, functional, aesthetic, and economic criteria should be established during the programming stages when the functional requirements of the spaces are spelled out.

Many types of seating for learning spaces are available, but their individual appropriateness varies from space to space. Of the three basic types of seating (fixed, movable, and combined), fixed has had the advantage of guaranteeing that, once properly positioned, every student will always be in the proper relationship to screens and other display surfaces. Of the various types of fixed seating, the continuous counter with individual fixed chairs provides a desirable surface for writing and for holding references. This is particularly important in secondary and higher education where the learning process may require extensive use of various types of materials and resources during a class. Also, a continuous counter works well when portable audiovisual equipment, small demonstrations, or various forms of teaching machines are to be used by students at their seats, or when student response systems, requiring the use of a response panel at each station, are to be installed initially or planned for later installation. This type of seating does require more floor area per unit than most other types of fixed seating, but this may be compensated for by the provision of cross aisles between each row of seating, allowing students to move freely to and from their seats.

There are many kinds of so-called theater-type fixed seating, employing a seat with a folding or lifting individual writing surface. Unfortunately, many of the tablet arms provided with this type of seating have the disadvantage of being too small to accommodate writing and reference materials. Lately, some improvements in seating have resulted in folding tablet arms that are adequate in size. Generally, fixed seating of this kind requires less floor area than the continuous counters, but student access to individual seats is more limited. Also, the necessary moving parts to raise and lower the tablet arms can create maintenance and upkeep problems. Installation of response devices and outlets for equipment can be handled in seating with movable tablet arms, but this again introduces maintenance problems.

*Movable Seating*

Movable seating also introduces a variety of alternatives, and again the provision of an adequate writing surface is extremely important. In rooms where regrouping of students is important, separate table units or seat-table units that are modular to allow conference and discussion groupings are desirable. Movable seating mitigates against the use of any individual student instructional device requiring wiring, such as response systems, portable recorders or projectors,

and power-operated teaching machines. Particularly with movable seating, seating should be scaled and designed with the age and character of the students in mind.

*Combined Seating*

Combined seating is basically of one type—continuous counter with loose seats. This type has the advantages of flexibility, accommodation to many body postures, and reduced cost over the continuous counter with fixed seats. However, the interpretation of building codes may prohibit continental seating in large rooms.

*Seating Mix*

In many instances, several types of seating in one space may best meet functional needs. For instance, loose tables and chairs on a flat floor area at the front of a large teaching room can be used for case studies, moot courts, and other instructional methods, while the remainder of the seating is fixed on a sloped or stepped floor. Also, in rooms requiring raised seating, rows of seating may alternate between riser-mounted and floor-mounted types. Particularly in medium group spaces, various types of loose seating may meet the varying requirements dictated by multiage, multiclass, and nongraded approaches to learning.

*Sight Lines*

Certainly in rooms where projected media are to be used extensively, good sight lines from all seats to all screens are important. Where 40 or more students are involved, this will generally require stepped or sloped floors. However, steep slopes such as seen for years in college lecture halls or amphitheaters are not always necessary. These slopes have usually been dictated by a functional requirement that every student be able to see the top of a demonstration table at the front of the room. Rather than thus increasing the volume of the room, and the cost of the room, electronic means of magnification should be employed which shifts the functional requirement from viewing a demonstration table to the more easily accommodated viewing of screens. By offsetting the rows of seating, and by using platforms containing two rows of seating each, the volume of the room can be reduced without impairing the viewing of screens and information display surfaces.

*Continental Seating*

In laying out seating in the larger rooms, continental seating, which allows cross aisles between the rows of seats, should be explored. This arrangement can move aisles outside the viewing area, can allow longer rows of seats, and can permit students to move to and from their seats without disturbing other students. The square footage per seating unit based on the total room area may not be much greater than that for more conventional arrangements. Each such solution must be judged in accordance with the applicable building code.

**Fig. 1. Library, Lansing Community College, Lansing, Michigan (Perkins & Will, Architects; photo: Gary Quesada, Hedrich Blessing Photography, courtesy of the architect)**

# ACADEMIC AND RESEARCH LIBRARIES

Libraries (Fig. 1) are a crucial feature of colleges and universities.

## FORMULAS AND TABLES

The figures given in this section are only approximations and may be altered by local conditions. Please also check with local conditions regarding accessibility standards.

The following four issues are dealt with:

1. Column spacing
2. Ceiling heights and floor size areas
3. Reader accommodations
4. Book storage (excluding problems that are affected by column spacing)

## COLUMN SPACING

### Stack Areas

No one size is perfect for column sizes or column spacing. Other things being equal, the larger the bay size, the better. Column spacing—that is, the distance between column centers—is generally more important in concentrated stack areas than in combined stack and reading areas because in the latter suitable adjustments are easier to make.

Clear space between columns (this is not the space between column centers) in a column range should preferably be a multiple of 3 feet (plus an additional 4 inches to provide for irregularities in the column sizes and for the end uprights in the range).

Range spacing and range lengths have a greater effect on book capacity than the distance between columns in a column range. The reduction of space between range centers by 1 inch increases book capacity by approximately 2 percent. The reduction of space used for cross aisles at right angles to the ranges is also of importance (see Fig. 2).

If practicable, columns should be no greater than 14 inches in the direction of a range, and the dimension in the other direction should be kept down to 18 inches. If over 14 inches in the direction of the range is necessary, the column might almost as well be 32 inches in that direction. It could then occupy the space of a full stack section and perhaps enclose a heating duct. If a column is wider than the range, it will jut into the stack aisle. Irregular length stack sections are inconvenient, and can often be replaced to advantage by a lectern or consultation table.

Tables 1 and 2 deal with standard layouts in commonly used module sizes.

The following comments may be useful in connection with Tables 1 and 2.

- Spacing 3 feet-9 inches or less should be used for closed-access storage only, with ranges not more than 30 feet long and not more than 18 inches deep.
- Spacing 3 feet-9 inches to 4 feet-1 inch can be used to advantage for large, little-used, limited-access stacks with ranges up to 30 feet long. Closed-access ranges up to 60 feet long have been used successfully with ranges 18 inches or less deep, 4 feet or 4 feet-1 inch on centers.
- Spacing 4 feet-2 inches to 4 feet-6 inches can be used for open-access stacks, preferably held to 18 inches in depth, with the range length based on the amount of use.
- Spacing 4 feet-6 inches to 5 feet is generous even for heavily used open-access undergraduate stacks if ranges are 15 feet long and 4 feet-6 inches on centers, and in some circumstances up to 30 feet if 5 feet on centers.

*Reviewers:* Perkins & Will, Architects

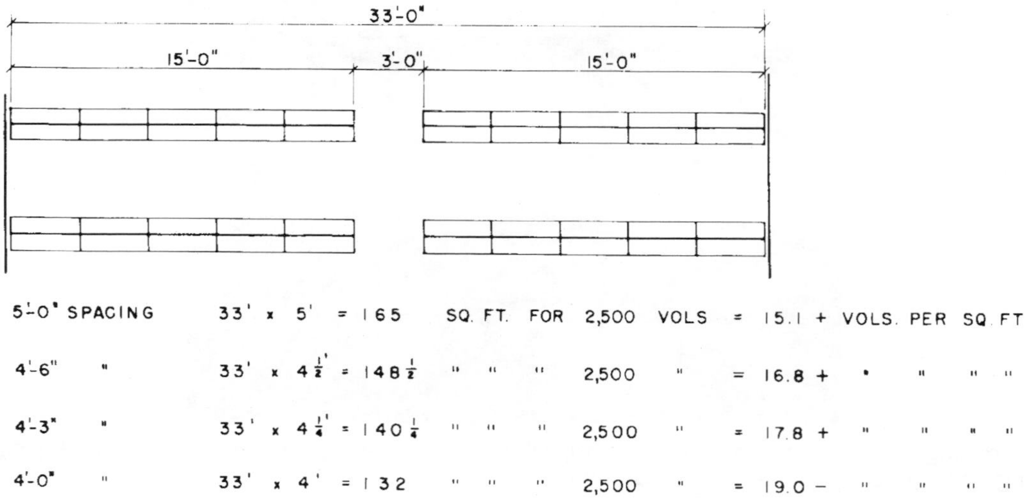
33'-0"
15'-0"
3'-0"
15'-0"
5'-0" SPACING 33' x 5' = 165 SQ. FT. FOR 2,500 VOLS = 15.1 + VOLS. PER SQ. FT
4'-6" " 33' x 4½' = 148½ " " " 2,500 " = 16.8 + " " " "
4'-3" " 33' x 4¼' = 140¼ " " " 2,500 " = 17.8 + " " " "
4'-0" " 33' x 4' = 132 " " " 2,500 " = 19.0 − " " " "

**Fig. 2. Stack capacity. Diagram indicates different range spacing and minimum cross aisle; cross aisle = 1/11 area**

**Table 1** Square modules with the column spacing a multiple of 3 feet (plus 18 inches for the column itself)*

| *Bay size* | *Sections between columns, standard 3 ft* | *Ranges to a bay* | *Range spacing on centers* |
|---|---|---|---|
| 19 ft-6 in by 19 ft-6 in | 6 | 4 | 4 ft-10½ in |
| | 6 | 3 | 6 ft-6 in |
| 22 ft-6 in by 22 ft-6 in | 7 | 6 | 3 ft-9 in |
| | 7 | 5 | 4 ft-6 in |
| | 7 | 4 | 5 ft-7½ in |
| 25 ft-6 in by 25 ft-6 in | 8 | 7 | 3 ft-7 5/7 in |
| | 8 | 6 | 4 ft-3 in |
| | 8 | 5 | 5 ft-1 1/5 in |
| | 8 | 4 | 6 ft-4½ in |
| 28 ft-6 in by 28 ft-6 in | 9 | 8 | 3 ft-6¾ in |
| | 9 | 7 | 4 ft-0 6/7 in |
| | 9 | 6 | 4 ft-9 in |
| | 9 | 5 | 5 ft-8 2/5 in |

*Columns should not be wider than the depth of range. 14 by 14 inches up to 14 by 18 inches is suggested.

**Table 2** Square modules with column spacing multiple of 3 feet*

| *Bay size* | *Sections between columns, standard 3 ft* | *Ranges to a bay* | *Range spacing on centers* |
|---|---|---|---|
| 18 by 18 ft | 5 | 5 | 3 ft-7⅕ in |
| | 5 | 4 | 4 ft-6 in |
| | 5 | 3 | 6 ft |
| 21 by 21 ft | 6 | 6 | 3 ft-6 in |
| | 6 | 5 | 4 ft-2⅖ in |
| | 6 | 4 | 5 ft-3 in |
| 24 by 24 ft | 7 | 7 | 3 ft-5⅐ in |
| | 7 | 6 | 4 ft |
| | 7 | 5 | 4 ft-9⅗ in |
| | 7 | 4 | 6 ft |
| 27 by 27 ft | 8 | 8 | 3 ft-4½ in |
| | 8 | 7 | 3 ft-10 2/7 in |
| | 8 | 6 | 4 ft-6 in |
| | 8 | 5 | 5 ft-4⅘ in |
| | 8 | 4 | 6 ft-9 in |

*Columns should not be wider than the depth of the range; 18 by 32 inches is suggested.

- Spacing 5 feet to 5 feet-10 inches is unnecessarily generous for any regular stack shelving and is often adequate for periodical display cases and for heavily used reference collections.
- Spacing 6 feet or greater is adequate for newspaper shelving and generous for periodical display cases.

Square bays are more flexible than those that form a long rectangle and are generally somewhat cheaper if the ceiling height is limited. But if the latter are used, the number of suitable sizes can be greatly increased. Table 3 shows possibilities with 22 feet-6 inches in one direction and different spacing in the other one.

**Table 3** Long rectangular modules, 22 feet-6 inches in one direction*

| *Bay size* | *Ranges to a bay* | *Range spacing on centers* |
|---|---|---|
| 22 ft-6 in by 18 ft | 4 | 4 ft-6 in |
| 22 ft-6 in by 20 ft | 5 | 4 ft |
| 22 ft-6 in by 20 ft-10 in | 5 | 4 ft-2 in |
| 22 ft-6 in by 21 ft-8 in | 5 | 4 ft-4 in |
| 22 ft-6 in by 24 ft | 6 | 4 ft |
| 22 ft-6 in by 25 ft | 6 | 4 ft-2 in |
| 22 ft-6 in by 26 ft | 6 | 4 ft-4 in |
| 22 ft-6 in by 27 ft | 6 | 4 ft-6 in |

*A bay of this size will give seven sections 3 feet long between 14-inch columns in the direction of the column range. The column sizes suggested in Table 2 are suitable here.

Similar tables can be prepared for long rectangular bays 18 feet, 19 feet-6 inches, 21 feet, 24 feet, 25 feet-6 inches, 27 feet, and 28 feet-6 inches in one direction.

If section lengths are changed from 3 feet to some other size, such as 3 feet-1 inch, 3 feet-2 inches, 3 feet-3 inches, 3 feet-4 inches, 3 feet-5 inches, or 3 feet-6 inches, tables comparable to Tables 1, 2, and 3 should be prepared with those lengths as a base.

**Seating Accommodations**

Column spacing is of less importance in connection with seating accommodations than with shelving. Tables 4 and 5 show the maximum number of carrels available on one side of standard-size bays and the number of studies available in such bays.

### Table 4  Carrels*

| Bay size | Open† | Double- or triple-staggered‡ | Small closed§ | Large closed¶ |
|----------|-------|------------------------------|---------------|---------------|
| 18 ft    | 4     | 4                            | 4             | 3             |
| 19½ ft   | 4     | 4                            | 4             | 3             |
| 21 ft    | 5     | 4                            | 4             | 4             |
| 22½ ft   | 5     | 5                            | 5             | 4             |
| 24 ft    | 6     | 5                            | 5             | 4             |
| 25½ ft   | 6     | 5                            | 5             | 5             |
| 27 ft    | 6     | 6                            | 6             | 5             |

*A carrel, as used here, is an area in which a reader is cut off from any neighbor who is closer than 3 feet on either side or front and back and one side. The minimum desirable width of an adequate carrel working surface is 2 feet-9 inches, which is as useful as 3 feet for each person at a table with two or more persons sitting side by side. Minimum depth suggested is 20 inches.

†Distance apart on centers should be not less than 4 feet-3 inches, unless the front table leg is set back 4 to 6 inches and armless chairs are used, in which case the distance on centers can be reduced to 4 feet. Any distance over 4 feet-6 inches is unnecessarily generous. A clear space of 27 inches or more between working surface and partition at the rear is recommended. A shelf above the table interferes with overhead lighting and makes a deeper table desirable.

‡Distance between centers should seldom be less than 4 feet-6 inches; 5 feet is preferred, anything greater is unnecessarily generous. With triple-staggered carrels, the back of the center one should be held down to no more than 10 inches above the tabletop.

§The distance between centers should be not less than 4 feet-6 inches; 5 feet is preferred. Watch out for ventilation. A window is psychologically desirable. Closed carrels are not recommended for undergraduates or any student not actually engaged in writing a dissertation. Glass in the door or grills should be provided for supervision.

¶A room less than 6 feet long at right angles to the desk will permit shelves above the desk or a bookcase behind the occupant but preferably not both. One less than 6 feet parallel to the desk will not permit a 4-foot-long desk, and a second chair, and may make it necessary to open the door outward.

### Table 5  Faculty studies and small multipurpose rooms

| Bay size | Small faculty study* | Small conference room or generous faculty study† |
|----------|----------------------|--------------------------------------------------|
| 18 ft    | 3                    | 2                                                |
| 19½ ft   | 3                    | 2                                                |
| 21 ft    | 3                    | 2                                                |
| 22½ ft   | 3                    | 2                                                |
| 24 ft    | 4                    | 3                                                |
| 25½ ft   | 3                    | 2                                                |
| 27 ft    | 4                    | 3                                                |

*A room of this size can house a large desk, shelving, a filing case, and permit a door to open in.

†This will provide for conference rooms for four, an adequate small staff office, or a generous faculty study. It should be at least 8 feet in the clear in one direction and have a total area of over 70 square feet.

Any small room will seem less confining if it has a window, and since window wall space is generally at a premium, a room can well have one of its short sides on the window wall.

## CEILING HEIGHTS AND FLOOR AREAS

Minimum and maximum ceiling heights and floor areas involve basic functional and aesthetic problems. Suggestions from the functional point of view are proposed as an aid in reaching decisions.

### Ceiling Heights

Table 6 suggests functional minimums and maximums.

### Floor Areas

Both the number of floors in a library and the area of each floor may be important functionally and aesthetically. Decisions in regard to them may properly be influenced by the site surroundings, the slope of the ground, and the value of the property.

Table 7 makes suggestions, which at best are only approximations, as to the percentage of the gross square footage of a library building which functionally should be on the entrance or central-services level in a typical academic library.

**Table 6**   Clear ceiling heights

| Area | Suggested minimum* | Suggested functional maximum† |
|---|---|---|
| Book stacks‡ | 7 ft-6 in | 8 ft-6 in |
| Stacks with lights at right angle to ranges§ | 8 ft-4 in | 8 ft-9 in |
| Stacks with lights on range tops functioning by ceiling reflection | 9 ft-0 in | 9 ft-6 in |
| Reading areas under 100 sq ft | 7 ft-6 in | 8 ft-6 in |
| Individual seating in large areas | 8 ft-4 in | 9 ft-6 in |
| Large reading rooms over 100 ft long broken by screens or bookcases | 9 ft-6 in | 10 ft-6 in |
| Auditoriums up to 1,500 sq ft | 9 ft-6 in | 10 ft-6 in |
| Entrance or main level with over 20,000 sq ft | 9 ft-6 in | 10 ft-6 in |
| Floor with mezzanine¶ | 15 ft-6 in | 18 ft-6 in |

*Heights lower than specified have been used successfully on occasion, but ceiling lights should be recessed and good ventilation assured. Financial savings will be comparatively small.

†Greater heights may be useful aesthetically and provide added flexibility by making areas available for a wider range of purposes.

‡7 feet-8 inches is the lowest height which permits an adequate protective base and seven shelves 12 inches on centers (standard for academic libraries) with suitable clearance at the top. The top shelf will be 6 feet-4 inches above the floor, the greatest height that can be reached without difficulty by a person 5-feet tall. Space above 7 feet-6 inches is not useful for storage of open-access collections and will be confusing if used for other shelving.

§This height used with fluorescent tubes, at right angles to the ranges, permits stack ranges to be shifted closer together or farther apart without rewiring, and is high enough so that heat from the tubes will not damage the books on the top shelf. If the fixtures are flush or nearly flush with the ceiling, the clear height can be reduced a few inches.

¶Mezzanines provide inexpensive square footage if they occupy at least 60 percent of the floor area (building codes may prohibit them unless mezzanine is partitioned off and made a separate unit), and if the overall height of the two resulting levels is not much more than 6 feet greater than would be provided if there were no mezzanine.

**Table 7**   Suggested formulas for percentage of gross square footage functionally desirable on the central-services level

| Gross building area, sq ft | Size of collections in volumes | Minimum percentages of gross area on central-services level* |
|---|---|---|
| Under 20,000 | Under 100,000 | 40–50 |
| 20,000–45,000 | 100,000–250,000 | 33⅓–40 |
| 40,000–80,000 | 250,000–500,000 | 25–33⅓ |
| 75,000–150,000 | 500,000–1,000,000 | 20–30 |
| 135,000 + | 1,000,000 + | 16⅔–25 |

*Central services as used here include the main control point, circulation and reference services, reference and bibliographical collections, the public catalog, and acquisition and catalog departments.

These computations are approximations only, but smaller figures than those in the last column will often necessitate shifting part of the central services to other levels and incidentally may add considerably to staff payrolls.

## READER ACCOMMODATIONS

Seating accommodations for readers and the service to readers are the largest space consumers in most libraries. The required areas depend on the following factors:

- Number of accommodations provided
- Types of accommodations and the percentage of each
- Dimensions of the working surfaces for each type of accommodation
- Average square footage required for each type of accommodation
- Additional space required for service to readers

The formula for determining the percentage of students for whom seating accommodations are required should depend on the following factors:

- Quality of the student body and faculty. The higher the quality, the greater the library use.
- Library facilities provided. The more satisfactory the seating accommodations and the services provided, the greater the use.
- Quality of the collections. Superior collections increase use.
- Curriculum. In general, students in the humanities and social sciences use the library more than do those in the pure and applied sciences.
- Emphasis placed on textbook instruction. This tends to reduce library use.
- Whether the student body is resident or commuting and, if the former, whether the dormitories provide suitable study facilities. Heaviest library use in most residential institutions is in the evening; in commuting ones, during the daytime hours.
- Whether the location is rural, suburban, or urban. Large population centers tend to decrease evening use because of other available activities and attractions.
- Whether the institution is coeducational or for one gender only. Coeducation tends to increase library use, particularly in the evening.
- Emphasis placed by the faculty on the library and on nontextbook reading.
- Percentage of graduate students and the fields in which they work.
- Institution's policy in regard to use by persons other than those connected with it.
- Departmental library arrangements which may make available other reading facilities and reduce the use of the central library.

Table 8 suggests formulas for percentage of students for whom seating is suggested.

### Types and Percentage of Seating Accommodations

*Undergraduate Students*

- *Tables for four or more:* Not more than 20 percent. Should be largely restricted to those in reserve-book and reference rooms.
- *Lounge chairs:* Not more than 15 percent. Should in general be restricted to lounge areas, smoking rooms, and current-periodical rooms, or used to break up unpleasantly long rows of other types of accommodations. In many libraries 8 to 10 percent of seating of this kind is adequate.
- *Individual accommodations:* Up to 85 percent. These should provide in most cases for working surfaces cut off from immediately adjacent neighbors, by aisles or partitions on one, two, or three sides. The partitions should be high enough—52 inches for

**Table 8**  Formulas for percentage of students for whom seating accommodations are suggested

| Type of institution | Percentage |
| --- | --- |
| Superior residential coeducational liberal arts college in rural area or small town | 50–60 |
| Superior residential liberal arts college for men or women in rural area or small town | 45–50 |
| Superior residential liberal arts college in a small city | 40–45 |
| Superior residential university | 35–40 |
| Typical residential university | 25–30 |
| Typical commuting university | 20–25 |

men—so that heads do not bob up or down above them and cause visual distraction. These accommodations may include the following:

- Tables for one. These can be quite satisfactory along a wall or screen if the readers all face in the same direction.
- Tables for two with partitions down the center (see Fig. 3b). For limited use only.
- Tables for four or more with partitions in both directions (see Fig. 4). A great improvement over a table for four without partitions.
- Pinwheel arrangement for four (see Fig. 5c). Satisfactory, but requires more space than tables for four or more.
- Double carrels with readers facing in different directions (see Fig. 3b). Not as satisfactory as double-staggered carrels.
- Double-staggered carrels (see Fig. 6a).
- Pairs of double-staggered carrels on both sides of a screen (see Fig. 6b).
- Triple-staggered carrels in place of three stock ranges or in a large reading area.
- Rows of single carrels at right angles to a wall in book-stack or reading area (see Fig. 7a).
- Single carrels in place of last stack section at the end of a blind stack aisle (see Fig. 7b).
- Typing carrels similar to single carrels at end of stack aisle, but with special acoustic protection.
- Rows of double carrels in a reading area or in place of two stack ranges (see Fig. 8).

Closed carrels are rarely recommended for undergraduates. Shelves in carrels tend to encourage undesirable monopolization. A shelf outside the carrel with an open or locked cupboard provides for books and papers to be reserved and makes possible longer hours of carrel use.

*Graduate Students*

- *At tables for multiple seating:* Not recommended.
- *Open carrels of any of the types proposed in Fig. 7:* Graduate carrels may have shelves over the working surface, but this will require deeper table tops because of lighting problems, unless the shelves are installed at one side (see Figs. 9a, b, and c).
- *Closed carrels.* See following sections for working surface dimensions and square-footage requirements. Closed carrels require special care for satisfactory lighting and ventilation. Unless larger than necessary to provide adequate working surfaces, claustrophobia tends to result. A window for each carrel or an attractive grill on at least one side will help.

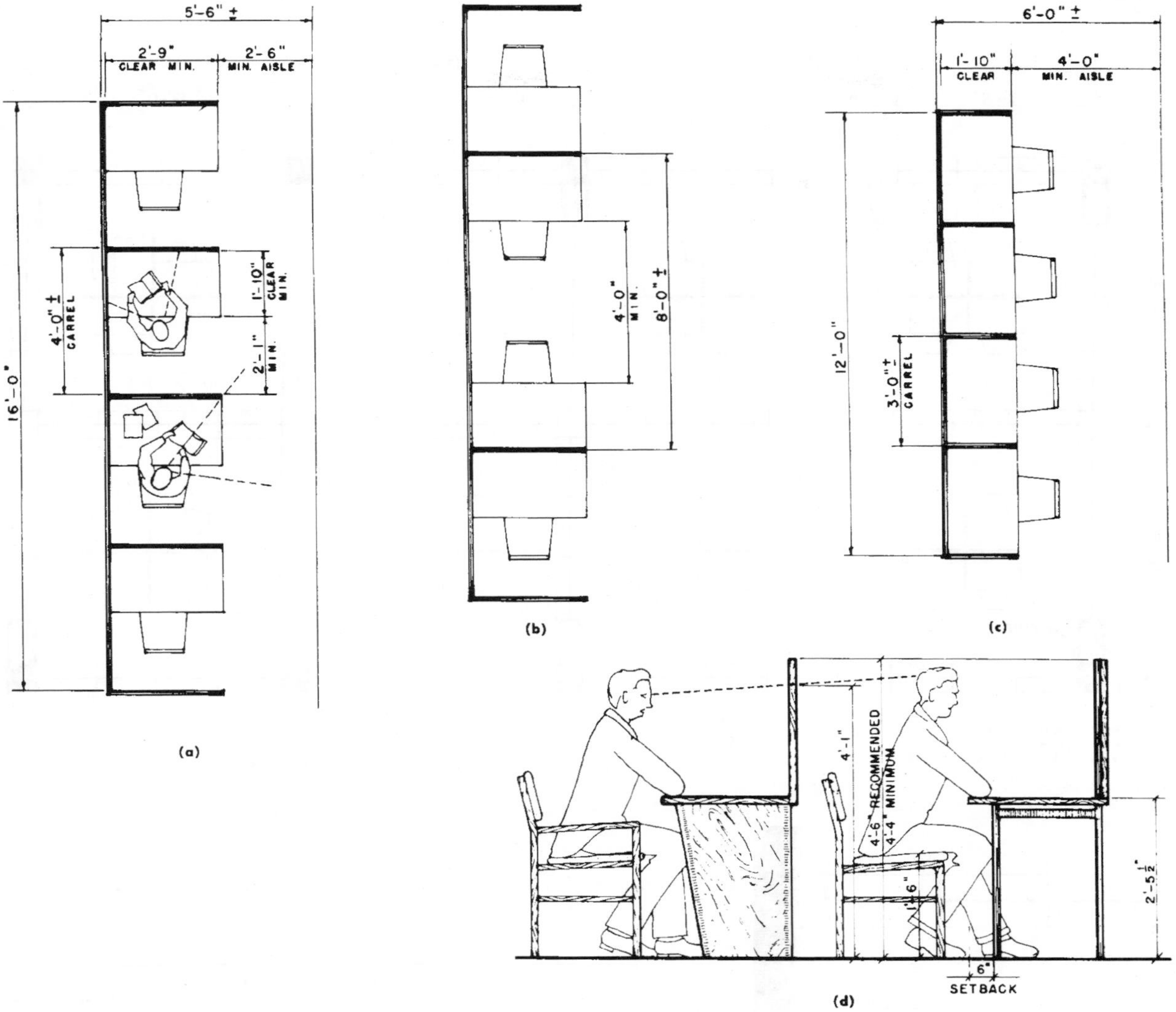

**Fig. 3.** Open carrels along a wall or a partition at least 52 inches high; (*a*) carrels along a wall all facing the same way (recommended); (*b*) carrels along a wall in pairs (possible, but they back up to each other unpleasantly); (*c*) carrels facing a wall (not recommended—if there are side partitions, reader has "blinders," and if reader leans back, neighboring reader is close at hand); (*d*) carrel elevation to show desirable height of partitions to prevent visual distraction (left-hand carrel shows a rounded type of construction and the right-hand one a square type)

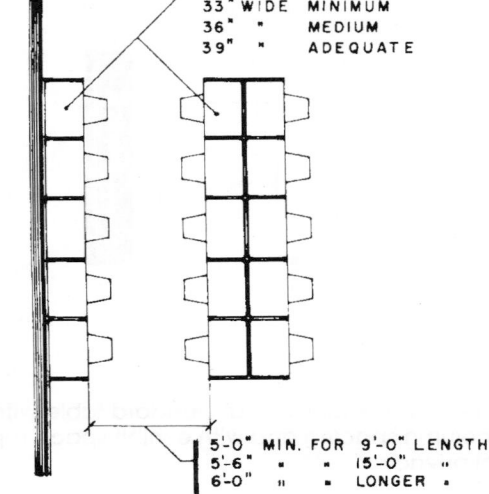

**Fig. 4.** Reading-room table with dividing partitions. Not very satisfactory if table seats more than four and reader is hemmed in on both sides. If reader leans back, reader is too close to neighboring reader. If light is hung from the partition, it tends to cause an unpleasant glare. If partitions between readers sitting side by side are extended on both sides to provide more privacy, they become too confining

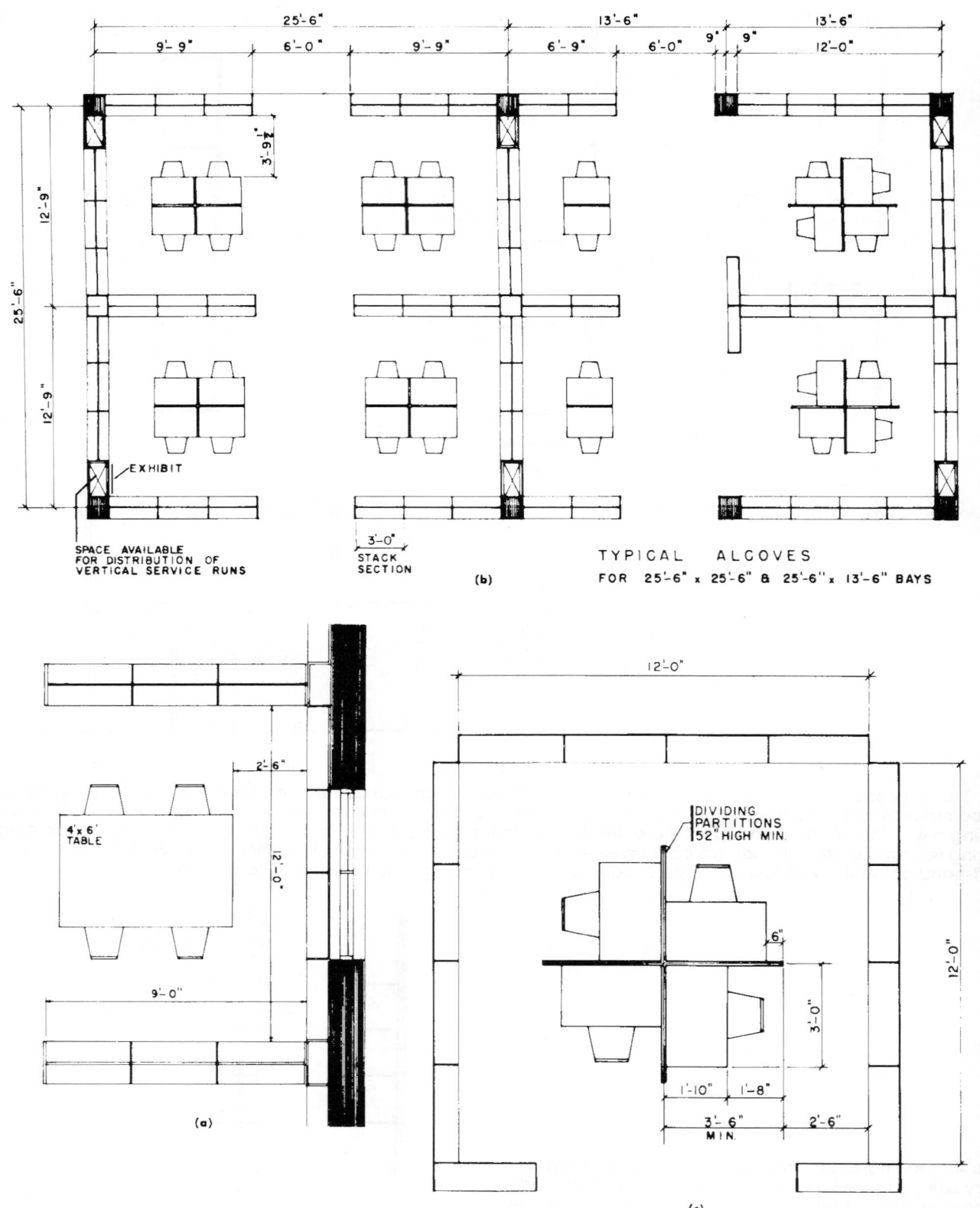

Fig. 5. Tables in book alcove: (*a*) standard table with no partitions; (*b*) tables for 2 to 4 persons, with partitions fitted in different column spacing and with exhibit space replacing a short section; (*c*) nest of tables in pinwheel form to give additional privacy

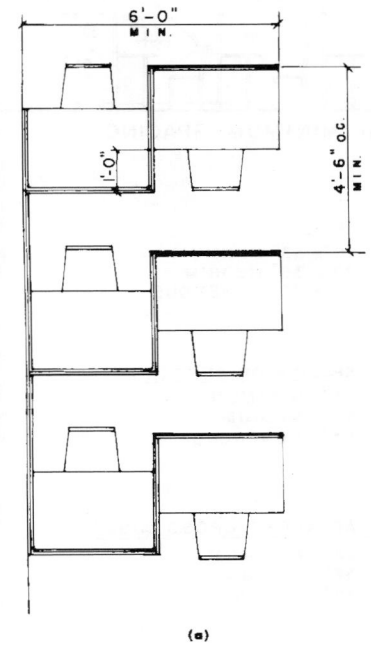

(a)

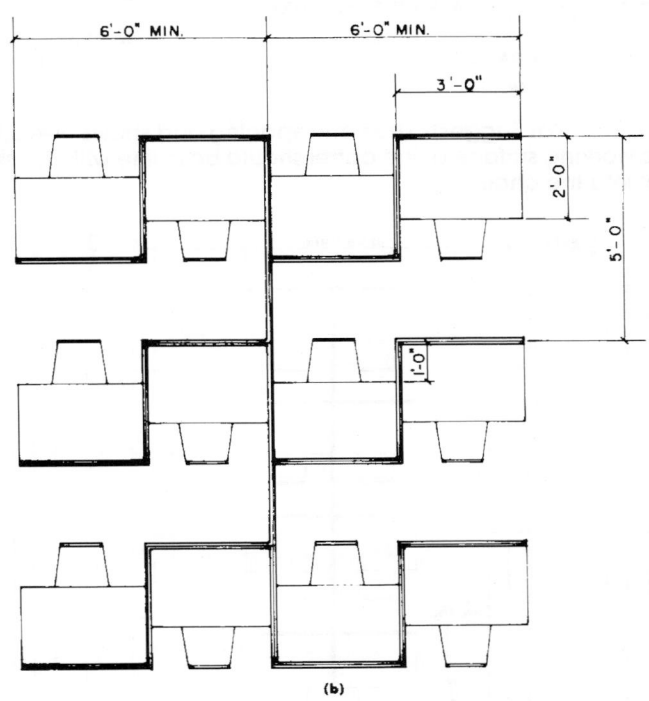

(b)

Fig. 6. Double-staggered carrels. (*a*) Double-staggered carrel adjacent to a wall. The carrel by the wall will be helped by a window. Partitions should be 52 inches high or higher (recommended). (*b*) Double-staggered carrels on each side of a screen or partition. A space saver, but recommended only when necessary to provide required seating capacity. The backs of the inside carrels should be no more than 40 inches high

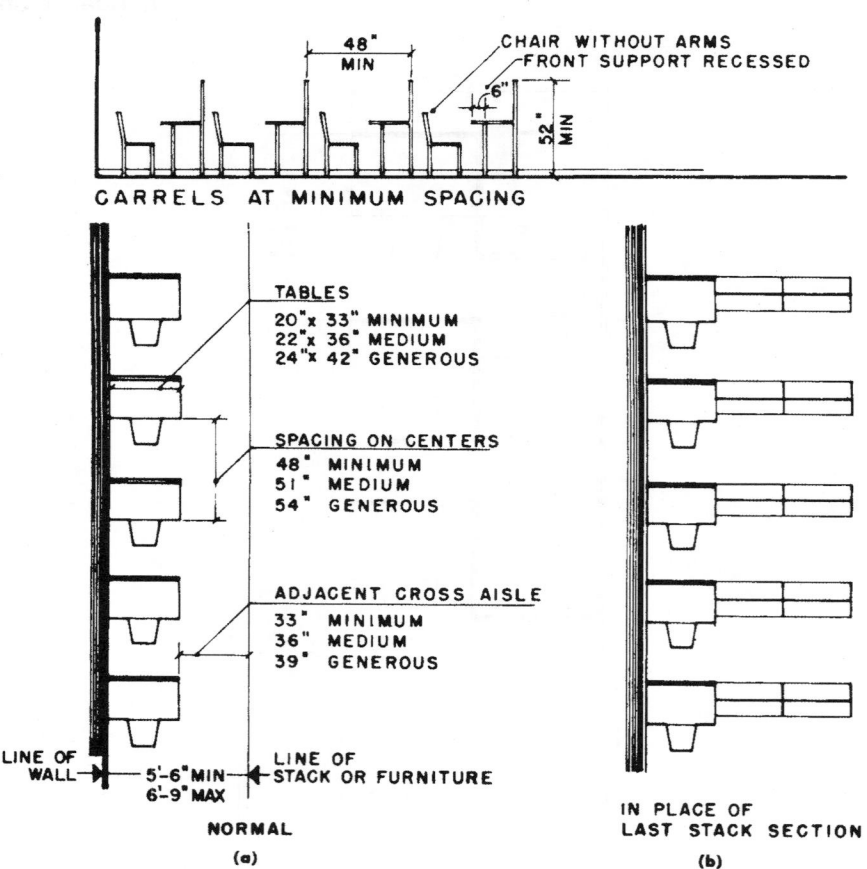

**Fig. 7. Carrels at right angles to a wall.** (*a*) Suggests sizes and spacing and shows elevations. (*b*) Carrel in place of last stack section next to a wall. The working surface of the carrel should be in line with the stack range instead of the aisle in order to make it easier to get into the chair

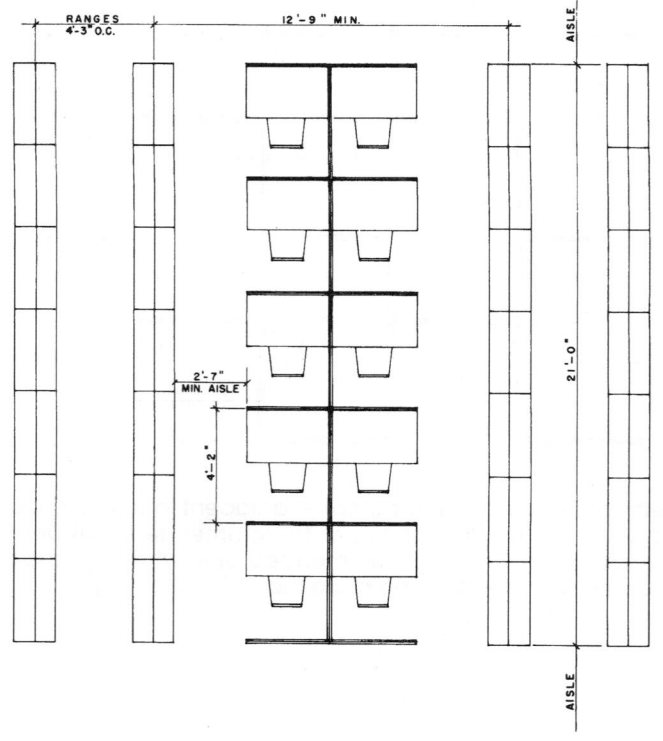

**Fig. 8. Double rows of carrels in bookstack or reading area in place of two stack ranges**

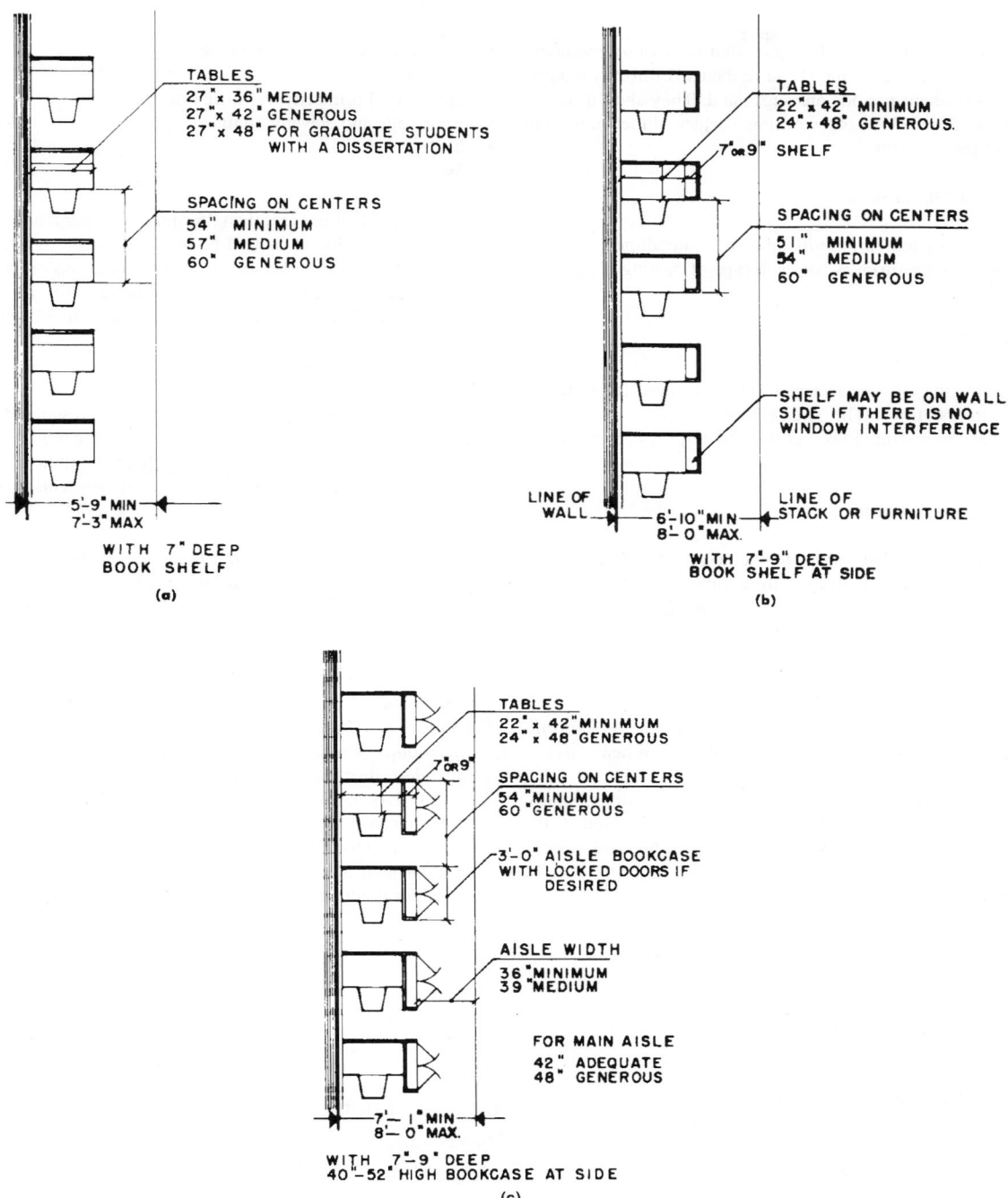

**Fig. 9. Carrels with shelves.** (*a*) Shelf in front of reader. The table should be 5 inches deeper than one without a shelf, and adequate spacing between carrels may be difficult to arrange. (*b*) Shelf at one side instead of in front (it can be at either side). This requires more width but less depth. (*c*) Shelf at one side facing the aisle. This can provide more shelf capacity and greater privacy; it also demands greater total width

*Faculty Accommodations*

If possible, closed studies should be provided for faculty members engaged in research projects which require the use of library materials. Limited assignment periods are suggested. They should not be used as offices. See below for working surface dimensions and square-footage requirements.

### Working Surface Dimensions

Table 9 gives suggested minimum and adequate dimensions for dimensions of working surfaces for each type of seating accommodation.

### Required Square Footage

Table 10 presents the average square footage required for different types of accommodations. The square-footage requirements suggested are at best approximations, but may be helpful in preliminary stages of planning.

### Reader Service Space Required

Additional space required for service to readers, such as direct access to seating accommodations is dealt with in Table 10 and elsewhere. Additional space requirements include the following:

*Assignable Areas*

- Public catalog
- Space around the bibliographical and reference and current-periodical collections, which is required because of heavy use.
- Public areas outside service desks.
- Special accommodations for microfilm reproductions, maps, manuscripts, archives, and other collections not shelved in the main stack area. These may include audiovisual areas of various types.
- Staff working quarters.

*Nonassignable Areas*

- Entrances, vestibules, and lobbies
- Corridors
- Areas used primarily as traffic arteries
- Stairwells and elevator shafts
- Toilets
- Walls and columns

It is suggested that not less than 25 square feet per reader in assignable or nonassignable areas will be required for the services in these groups, and that unless the special accommodations previously mentioned are held to a reasonable minimum and careful planning is provided throughout, this may need to be increased to 35 square feet.

### Seating Arrangements

As an aid in planning layouts, suggestions are presented for arrangements for seating accommodations in reading areas and book stacks. Remember that academic and research (not public) libraries are under consideration, and the sizes and arrangements suggested are for academic and research use.

- *Single open carrels with the long axis of the tabletops at right angles to a wall:* These may be in reading areas, or in book stacks with walls on one side, a subsidiary cross aisle on the other, with the end of stack ranges beyond the aisle, or they may take the place of the last stack section in a range. Single carrels should preferably be fastened to the wall or floor in some way so as not to get out of position (see Fig. 7a and b).
- *Single closed carrels along a book-stack wall and opening into a subsidiary stack aisle:* These are quite similar to the open carrels just described, but have partitions and a door and, unless considerably larger, they may be difficult to ventilate and to light and tend to cause claustrophobia. Partitions to the ceiling are not recommended for undergraduates, but if the area, including the adjacent aisle, is at least as much as 5 feet by 6 feet-8 inches, it can be used for graduate students if there is glass in the door. Light from

**Table 9** Suggested working surface area for each person

| Types of accommodation | Minimum size | Adequate size |
|---|---|---|
| Table for multiple seating | 33 by 21 in* | 36 by 24 in |
| Individual table or open carrel for undergraduate | 33 by 20 in† | 36 by 22 in |
| Open carrel for graduate student without book shelf over it | 36 by 24 in‡ | |
| Carrel, open or closed, for graduate student writing dissertation, with a book shelf | 36 by 27 in§ | 48 by 30 in |
| Faculty study | 48 by 30 in | 60 by 30 in if there is shelving over it |

*Recommended only for reserve-book use or for a college for women.

†A space of 33 by 20 inches goes farther in an individual accommodation than at a large table because others do not intrude on the space.

‡Shelves are not recommended over open carrels because they make it easier for an unauthorized student to monopolize one.

§A shelf over a carrel table requires additional depth because it interferes with lighting. A closed carrel should preferably have a window, glass in the door, and more space around the table than an open one, or claustrophobia may result.

**Table 10**  Approximate square-footage requirements for different types of seating accommodations[a]

| Type of accomodations | Requirements, sq ft | | |
| --- | --- | --- | --- |
| | Minimum | Adequate | Generous |
| Small lounge chair[b] | 20 | 25 | 30 |
| Large lounge chair[c] | 25 | 30 | 35 |
| Individual table[d] | 25 | 30 | 35 |
| Tables for four[e] | 22½ | 25 | 27½ |
| Tables for more than four[f] | 20 | 22½ | 25 |
| Individual carrels[g] | 20 | 22½ | 25 |
| Double carrels[h] | 22½ | 25 | 27½ |
| Double-staggered carrels[i] | 22½ | 25 | 27½ |
| Triple-staggered carrels[j] | 22½ | 25 | 27½ |
| Double row of carrels with partitions between, placed in a reading room or in place of two stack ranges[k] | 22½ | 25 | 27½ |

[a]The figures used here include: (1) area of working surface if any; (2) area occupied by chair; (3) area used for direct access to the accommodations; and (4) reasonable share of all the assignable space used for main aisles in the room under consideration.

[b]These chairs if in pairs should be separated by a small table to prevent congestion and to hold books not in use.

[c]Large lounge chairs are expensive, space-consuming, and an aid to slumber. Rarely recommended.

[d]Individual tables are space-consuming, are generally disorderly in appearance because they are easily moved, and result in a restless atmosphere from traffic on all sides. Not recommended except along a wall or screen.

[e]Tables for four are the largest ones recommended, unless pressue for additional capacity is great.

[f]Tables for more than four are space savers, but few readers like to sit with someone on each side. They will avoid using them as far as possible.

[g]Individual carrels are economical in use of space if placed at right angles to a wall, adjacent to an aisle that must be provided under any circumstances. They reduce visual distraction if partitions 52 inches or more in height are provided on at least two of the four sides. See Figs. 3a and 3d.

[h]Double carrels are useful, but the staggered ones are prefererred.

[i]Double-staggered carrels are as economical of space as tables for four and reduce visual distractions. See Fig. 6a.

[j]Triple-staggered carrels are as economical of space as tables for six or more and reduce visual distraction.

[k]Double rows of carrels are economical in space use and reduce visual distraction. See Fig. 8.

an outside window will help. Figure 10b shows a closed carrel with a door.

- *Single carrels in place of a stack section at the end of a book range (see Fig. 7b):* As far as space use is concerned, this is the most economical way to provide a seating accommodation, and it gives a great deal of seclusion, which many readers want. It presents four problems, however, as follows:

1. The space from front to back is limited to the distance between range centers, which in some cases is minimal.
2. Unless the table top is specially designed to occupy the full depth of the double-faced range, as shown in Fig. 4, it may be difficult to get into the chair because the table top will jut out into the aisle.
3. Some readers, particularly if there is no adjacent outside window, will feel too shut in for comfort.
4. Since the seat is at the end of a blind aisle, the length of the range should not be more than half that of a range with cross aisles at both ends.

- *Single seats facing a reading room or stack wall or a high partition down the center of a regular reading room table:* Sometimes this arrangement has a high partition at the sides projecting 6 inches beyond the table top into the aisle, to shield the user from neighbors. There is no place to look out, except directly at the neighbor to the right or left when leaning back in the chair. They

are not recommended, except in an open area in groups of four where the reader can look out in at least one direction, because few students enjoy facing a blank wall, unless they can look out at least a few feet on one side without seeing a neighbor close at hand (see Fig. 4). Single carrels in a sawtooth, or what is known as a *dog-leg* arrangement, shown in Fig. 10c, are preferable to those directly facing a wall, as the reader can look out on one side and still is protected from neighboring readers. They require no additional space.

- Double carrels in rows in a reading room separated by partitions which are at least 52 inches in height in the front and on one side of the working area. Partitions in front can be limited to no more than 3 to 10 inches above the table top because a full view of one's neighbor all the time is less distracting than a head bobbing up and down occasionally; but 52 inches above the floor is preferable (Fig. 3d).
- *Double carrels in rows in place of two stack ranges:* A size of 33 by 22 inches can be used in place of two stack ranges when ranges are 4 feet-3 inches on centers. A size of 36 by 22 inches can be used comfortably with ranges 4 feet-6 inches on centers. By placing one or both end pairs at right angles to the others, the carrel range and the stack range length can be made to match with table tops and distances between centers of standard size (see Fig. 8).
- *Double-staggered carrels with the adjacent table tops overlapping by one-half their depth:* These should be placed along walls, with 4 feet-6 inches minimum on centers and 5 feet preferred.

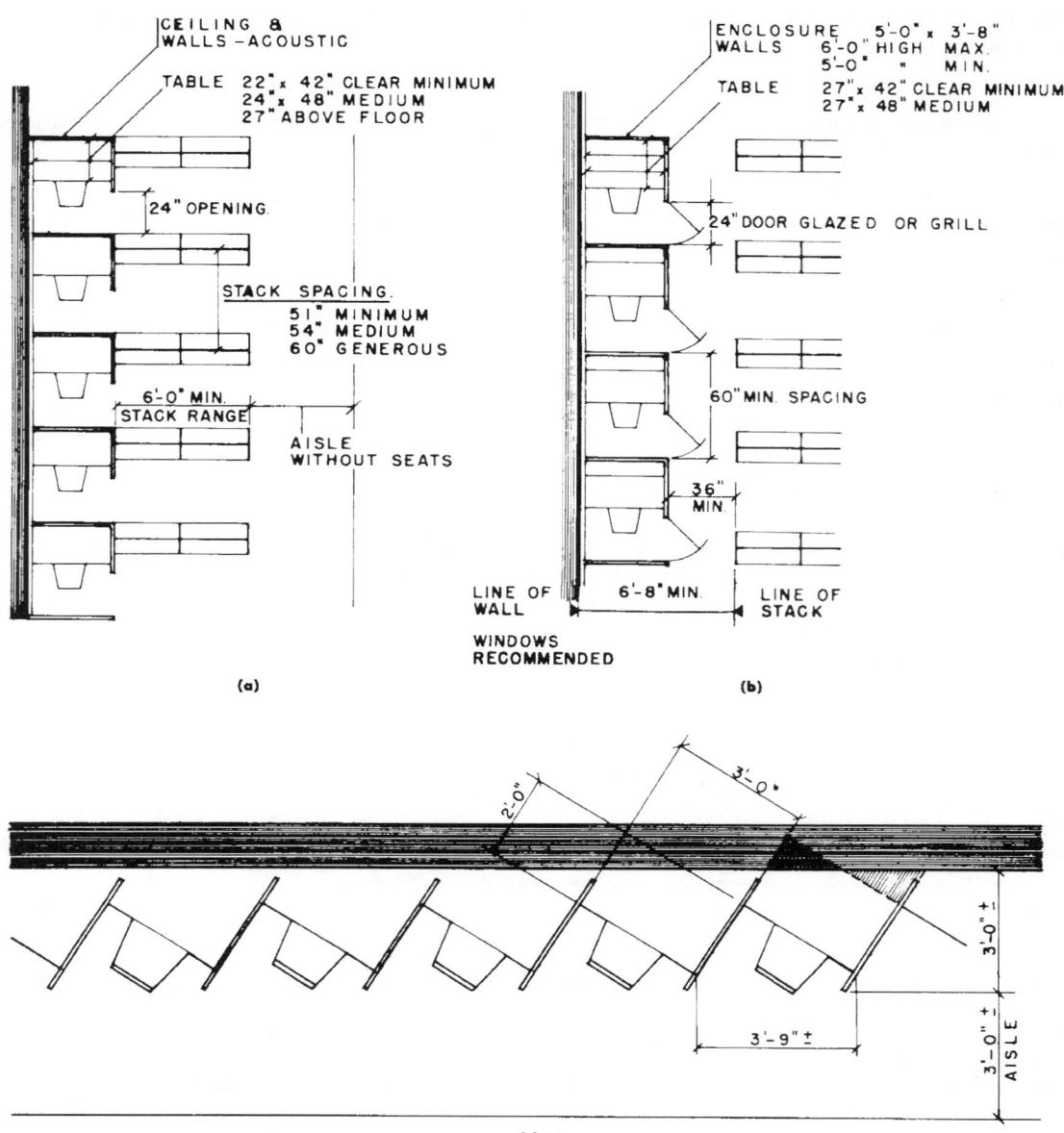

**Fig. 10. Other types of single carrels.** (*a*) Partly open typing carrel in place of lost stack section with acoustically protected walls and coiling aided by adjacent books. Absence of other seating close at hand makes doors unnecessary. (*b*) Closed carrel with door and shelf. If there is no window, wider spacing is desirable to prevent claustrophobia. Ventilation and lighting will present problems. (*c*) A dog-leg carrel is a compromise for one facing a wall, which is disliked by many, if partitions are extended enough to provide seclusion. The carrel is open an one side

*"Pinwheel" groups of four carrels, preferably in a reading alcove:* If the alcove is 12 by 12 feet in the clear, tabletops 22 by 36 inches are recommended, with partitions at least 52 inches in height, which extend 6 inches beyond the end of each table. Shelves are ordinarily not recommended for these cases, particularly if the tabletop is less than 27 inches deep. This arrangement fits perfectly in a 27-foot column spacing with two alcoves to a bay. If the module size is 25 feet-6 inches, the space in each alcove will be reduced a total of 9 inches, and one of the shelf sections will be only 27 inches. It can be used for shorter shelves or set up as wall space for a bulletin board or for a picture or other decoration. If ventilation is adequate, alcoves can be partially closed in on the fourth side by a single or double-faced book section, which may help to use space to advantage and make possible the best utilization of the available bay size. The main aisle between double rows of alcoves can be as narrow as 4 feet-6 inches (see Figs. 5*b* and *c*). Pinwheel groups have been successful in large reading areas, but they tend to give an impression of disorderliness when not in an alcove.

- *Carrels in alcoves with tables for four:* These should be installed with 52-inch-high partitions in each direction. These alcoves may be as little as 9 feet deep and 11 feet-3 inches to 12 feet wide in the clear. With a 25 foot-6 inch bay and a 4 foot-6 inch main aisle, an unusually large capacity is possible (see Figs. 5*b* and *c*). With a 27-foot bay, the space utilization is still good, and the main aisle can be widened to 6 feet.

## BOOK STORAGE

Book-stack capacity is based on the following:

- Number of volumes shelved in a standard stack section
- Square-footage requirements for a standard stack section.

### Number of Volumes Shelved

The number of volumes that can be shelved in a standard stack section depends on the book heights and the number of shelves per section, the book thickness, and what is considered a full section.

- *Book heights and shelves per section:* Stack sections in academic libraries are considered standard if they are 7 feet-6 inches high and 3 feet wide. Sections of this height make possible seven shelves 12 inches on centers over a 4-inch base. This spacing is adequate for books which are 11 inches tall or less, which, as shown in Table 11, includes 90 percent of the books in a typical collection. It is suggested that most of the remaining 10 percent will be concentrated in a comparatively few subjects, that 70 percent of this 10 percent will be between 11 and 13 inches tall, and that six shelves 14 inches on centers will provide for them.
- *Book thickness and the number of volumes that can be shelved satisfactorily on each linear foot of shelving:* No two libraries are alike in this connection. The average thickness will depend on the definition of a volume; binding policy, particularly for pamphlets and serials and periodicals; and the collection under consideration. A commonly used formula for thickness of books is shown in Table 12.
- *The decision on when a section is full:* In Table 10 a suggested number of volumes per single-faced section is proposed. It is evident that if books are shelved by subject, it is unwise to fill the shelves completely, and any estimate must be an approximation. For many libraries 125 volumes per stack section is considered safe.

### Standard Stack Square-Footage Requirements

The square-footage requirements for a standard stack section depend primarily on range spacing, range lengths, the number of cross aisles

### Table 11   Book heights*

| | |
|---|---|
| 8 in or less | 25% |
| 9 in or less | 54 |
| 10 in or less | 79 |
| 11 in or less | 90 |
| 12 in or less | 94 |
| 13 in or less | 97 |
| Over 13 in | 3 |

*Adapted from *Rider's Compact Storage*, p. 45, which was based to a considerable extent on research done by Van Hoesen and Kilpatrick on the height of books in academic libraries.

### Table 12   Volumes per linear foot of shelf for books in different subjects*

| Subject | Volumes per foot of shelf | Volumes per single-faced section |
|---|---|---|
| Circulating (nonfiction) | 8 | 168 |
| Fiction | 8 | 168 |
| Economics | 8 | 168 |
| General literature | 7 | 147 |
| History | 7 | 147 |
| Art (not including large folios) | 7 | 147 |
| Technical and scientific | 6 | 126 |
| Medical | 5 | 105 |
| Public documents | 5 | 105 |
| Bound periodicals | 5 | 105 |
| Law | 4 | 84 |

*This table is in common use by stack manufacturers

and their widths, cross-aisle area charged against adjacent reader accommodations, and nonassignable space.

- *Range spacing:* Range spacing should be based on column spacing, stack aisle widths (which is discussed shortly) and on shelf depths. Shelf depths as used here are based on double-faced bracket shelving with 2 inches between the back of the shelf on one side of the range and the back of the shelf on the other side. Shelf depths specified by stack manufacturers are 1 inch greater than the actual depth; that is, a 7-inch actual shelf is called an 8-inch *nominal* shelf, because 8 inches is available if half the 2 inches noted above is assigned to the shelves on each side of a double-faced shelf section. Table 13 shows depths of books. A shelf with 8 inches actual depth, together with the space available between shelves on the two sides of a double-faced section, will provide for practically any book that does not have to be segregated because of its height, and 8-inch actual-depth shelves (designated by the manufacturers as 9-inch shelves) are recommended in place of the 7- or 9-inch actual-depth shelves which are commonly used. In many libraries, a 7-inch actual-depth shelf is suitable for a large part of the collections.
- *Stack-aisle widths and stack-range lengths:* Stack-aisle widths should be based on the amount of use by individuals and by trucks and the length of the ranges before a cross aisle is reached. Other things being equal, the longer the range, the wider the aisle should be. Table 14 suggests desirable stack aisle widths in conjunction with stack-range lengths under different types and amounts of use. Do not forget that stack-aisle widths must be based, indirectly at least, on the column spacing, and are affected as well by the shelf depths previously discussed, if columns are not to obstruct the aisles. The distance between column centers should be an exact multiple of the distance between the center of parallel stack ranges within the stack bay, which in turn is determined by the sum of the depth of a double-faced range and the width of a stack aisle.
- *Widths for main and subsidiary cross-stack aisles:* Cross-aisle widths should be based on amount of use and are inevitably affected by the column spacing. Column spacing often makes it difficult to provide any cross-aisle widths except 3 feet or a multiple of 3 feet. Table 15 suggests desirable cross-aisle widths under different types and amounts of use.

**Table 13** Percentage of books in an academic collection below different depths measured from the back of the spine to the fore edge of the covers*

| 5 in or less | 25% |
|---|---|
| 6 in or less | 54 |
| 7 in or less | 79 |
| 8 in or less | 90 |
| 9 in or less | 94 |
| 10 in or less | 97[†] |
| Over 10 in | 3 |

*Adapted from *Riders Compact Book Storage*, p. 45.

[†]An 8-inch actual, i.e., a 9-inch nominal depth shelf, will house a 10-9-inch-deep book without difficulty, unless there is another deep book immediately behind it. Most books over 10 inches deep will be more than 11 inches tall and should be segregated on special shelving which is more than 9 inches in nominal depth.

- *Cross-aisle area charged against adjacent reader accommodations:* The effect on square-footage requirements per stack section and volume capacity per net square foot of stack area, resulting from the provision of reader accommodations in the form of stack carrels, is shown in Figs. 2 and 11. These indicate that the assignment of one-half of the adjacent cross-aisle areas to reader space when carrels are on one side of the cross aisles and book-stack ranges are on the other may increase rather than decrease book capacity per square foot of net stack area, and in addition provide desirable and economical seating accommodations adjacent to the books (see Table 16). It is evident that a large number of variables are involved in book-stack capacity. Table 16 is based on the square footage required for a single-faced standard section in stack layouts, with different range spacing, range lengths, and cross-aisle widths, as well as stack carrels. Table 17 shows stack capacity per square foot of area if 100, 125, 150, or 160 volumes per standard stack section is used in connection with 7, 8.5, 9, or 10 square feet occupied by each section.

**Table 14** Suggested stack-aisle widths and stack-range lengths*

| | Aisle width, in[†] | | Range lengths[‡] | |
|---|---|---|---|---|
| Typical use of stack | Min. | Max. | Min. | Max. |
| Closed-access storage stack | 24 | 30 | 30 | 60 |
| Limited-access, little-used stack for over 1 million volumes | 26 | 31 | 30 | 42 |
| Heavily used open-access stack for over 1 million volumes | 31 | 36 | 30 | 42 |
| Very heavily used open-access stack with less than 1 million volumes | 33 | 40 | 15 | 30 |
| Newspaper stack with 18-inch-deep shelves | 36 | 45 | 15 | 30 |
| Reference and current-periodical room stacks | 36 | 60 | 12 | 21 |
| Current-periodical display stacks | 42 | 60 | 21 | 21 |

*These are suggestions only and not to be considered definite recommendations. Circumstances alter cases.

[†]Stack-aisle widths of 24 inches should be considered an absolute minimum and are rarely justifiable. Anything under 26 inches is difficult with a book truck, even when the use is light. The minimum range lengths suggested.

[‡]Stack-range lengths are often determined by available space, rather than by their suitability. The maximum lengths shown in the table should generally be used only with the maximum aisle widths suggested.

**Table 15**  Suggested cross-aisle widths*†

| Typical use of stack | Main aisle | | Subsidiary cross aisle‡ | |
|---|---|---|---|---|
| | Min. | Max. | Min. | Max. |
| Closed-access storage | 3 ft | 4 ft-6 in | 2 ft-6 in | 3 ft-6 in |
| Limited-access stack | 3 ft | 4 ft-6 in | 3 ft | 3 ft-6 in |
| Heavily used open-access stack | 4 ft | 5 ft | 3 ft | 4 ft |
| Heavily used open-access stack for large collection and ranges 30 ft or more long | 4 ft-6 in | 6 ft | 3 ft-6 in | 4 ft-6 in |

These are suggestions only and not to be considered definite recommendations. Circumstances alter cases.

In determining minimum or maximum widths, keep in mind the length and width of the book trucks used, as well as the amount of use. Minimum width stack aisles should not be accompanied by minimum cross aisles. From the widths shown in the table, up to 4 inches may have to be subtracted to provide for adjacent stack uprights and irregularities in column sizes.

If open carrels adjoin a subsidiary aisle, they will make it seem wider, but traffic will tend to be disturbing to the carrel occupants.

If closed carrels open from a subsidiary aisle, they will make it seem narrower.

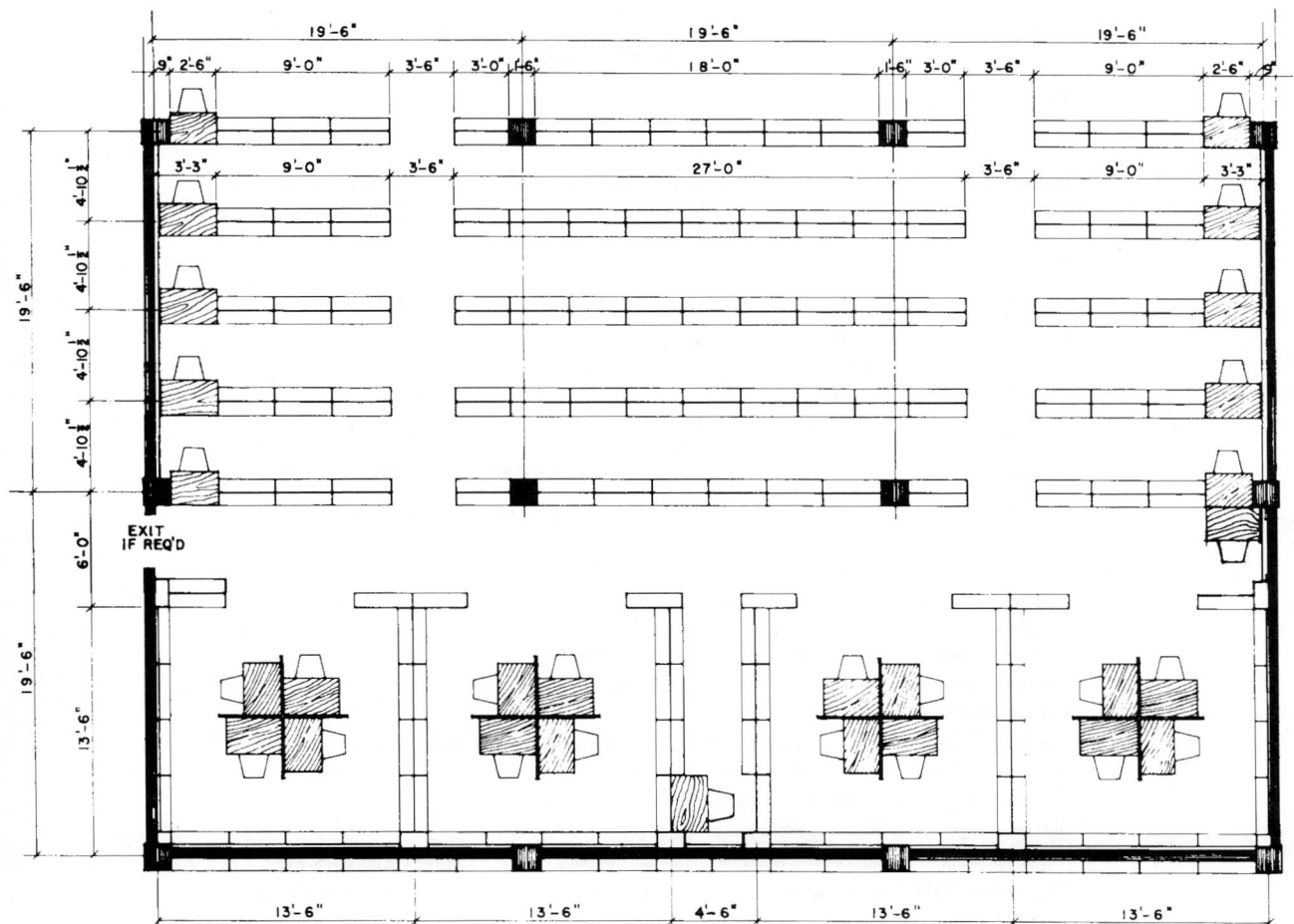

**Fig. 11. Stack combined with stack alcoves. Nonstandard bay sizes can sometimes be used to advantage without seriously affecting capacity per square foot**

- *Nonassignable space:* Nonassignable space includes, as far as its effect on book capacity is concerned, the floor space occupied by columns, mechanical services, and vertical transportation of all kinds. It is mentioned here simply to call attention to it. In a carefully designed stack for 25,000 volumes or more on one level, nonassignable space should not amount to more than 10 percent of the gross stack area, and with a larger installation considerably less than that.

**Table 16**  Square footage required for one single-faced standard section

| Range spacing | Square feet with minimum cross aisles* | Square feet with generous cross aisles† | Square feet with adequate cross aisles combined with carrels‡ |
|---|---|---|---|
| 5 ft-0 in | 8.25 | 9.00 | 8.4375 |
| 4 ft-6 in | 7.425 | 8.10 | 7.60 |
| 4 ft-3 in | 7.0125 | 7.65 | 7.225 |
| 4 ft-0 in | 6.60 | 7.20 | 6.75 |

*Based on Fig. 2, with a 15-foot blind-aisle range on each side of a 3-foot center aisle.

†Based on two 3-foot side aisles and a 6-foot center aisle separated by 30-foot stack ranges.

‡Based on 3-foot side aisles between carrels and 30-foot stack ranges, the latter separated by a 4 foot-6 inch center aisle. One-half of the side aisles are charged against the carrels, but even on 5-foot centers the carrels occupy only 22½ square feet, and square footage for a section is low.

**Table 17**  Volume capacity per 1,000 square feet of stack area with different number of square feet and different number of volumes per section

| Square feet per section[a] | No. of sections in 1,000 sq ft | Volumes per 1,000 sq ft with different no. of vols. per section[b,c] | | | |
|---|---|---|---|---|---|
| | | 100[h] | 125[i] | 150[j] | 160[k] |
| 10[d] | 100 | 10,000 | 12,500 | 15,000 | 16,000 |
| 9[e] | 111 | 11,100 | 13,875 | 16,650 | 17,760 |
| 8⅓[f] | 120 | 12,000 | 15,000 | 18,000 | 19,200 |
| 7[g] | 143 | 14,300 | 17,875 | 21,450 | 22,880 |

[a]Examination of Table 16 and Figs. 2 and 11 should help in determining area to allow for a single-faced section. This matter is covered under Standard Stack Square-Footage Requirements.

[b]Volumes per section is covered under Number of Volumes Shelved.

[c]If a period is used instead of a comma in the volume count in the last four columns shown above, it will give the number of volumes per square foot available under different conditions.

[d]10 square feet per section is the cubook formula proposed by R. W. Henderson.

[e]See Table 16 for an example.

[f]The author suggests that this is a satisfactory and safe figure to use for a large collection accessible to graduate students and a limited number of undergraduates.

[g]Adequate for a very large collection with limited access.

[h]100 volumes per section is the cubook formula.

[i]The author suggests that this is a safe figure for comfortable working capacity in an average library. See text.

[j]The number of 150 volumes per section is too often proposed by architects and librarians. While it is a possible figure, it should be realized that it approaches full capacity and should be used only in cases where additional space is immediately available when capacity is reached. The time to consider what comes next will have passed.

[k]The number of 160 volumes per section should not be considered for most academic libraries, unless the collection has an unusually high percentage of abnormally thin volumes and individually bound pamphlets.

Fig. 1. Recreational center, Hamilton College (Perry Dean Rogers + Partners, Architects; photo: Richard Mandelkorn, courtesy of the architect)

# COLLEGE GYMNASIUMS

## Basic Considerations

The type and size of gymnasium facilities required for a given college or university depends upon many factors, one of the most important of which is the anticipated enrollment of the institution. A gymnasium planned to serve 2,000 students will, obviously, be considerably smaller than, and different in design and construction from, a facility planned for a university of 10,000 or more students. Planning must be done with current and future enrollment in mind, and as part of the master plan for the college or university. If the enrollment ceiling is indefinite, however, the structure should be planned so that additions to the building are feasible. Most universities or colleges should plan for and build for some expansion, ideally for enrollments of at least 10 years in advance. Universities of 15,000 or more students may find it desirable to build multiple gymnasiums and recreation centers, each servicing an area of the campus.

Another factor that affects the type of building constructed is the philosophy of the administration concerning athletics and physical education. Many questions need to be answered before planning begins:

- Will all students be required to take physical education for one or more semesters?
- Is the required program in physical education to be broad in scope?
- Is faculty training in physical education to be part of the program?

- What responsibility does the college or university take for the physical education, recreation, and fitness of its faculty?
- Is it anticipated that research in physical education, health, and recreation may become an important aspect of the program?
- What is the scope of the varsity athletic program? (The facility requirements are considerably different if varsity teams are to be fielded only in the major sports.)
- What will be done to provide facilities for expanded intramural and extramural programs?

### GYMNASIUM LOCATION

If physical education and athletic facilities are used by all of the students at a college or university, the gymnasium facility and additional recreation centers (Fig. 1) must be sited to accommodate easy access from both the academic buildings and student housing. Physical education facilities that serve as teaching stations must be close enough to academic buildings to make it possible for students to move from the classroom into the gymnasium and back within the time provided between classes.

Buildings used only for intramural and intercollegiate activities may be located farther from classrooms and housing than a general-use gymnasium would be. This is especially true if the activities promoted in these buildings are scheduled. If the building is to be used for

*Reviewer:* Perkins and Will, Architects
*Reference: Planning Areas and Facilities for Health, Physical Education and Recreation,* rev. The Athletic Institute, Merchandise Mart, Chicago, Illinois, American Association for Health, Physical Education, and Recreation, Washington, D.C.

unscheduled participation of students, however, the amount of use will vary inversely with the distance from housing and other campus buildings. Providing public transportation may increase this usage.

## GENERAL PRINCIPLES OF GYMNASIUM PLANNING

The selection of appropriate facility types and the allocation of square footage will be determined by the scope of the athletic and intramural programs, as well as the students' physical education requirements. Campus circulation should be carefully studied during the initial planning process.

Locker rooms must be centrally located in the building so that they may serve all activity areas. Easy access should be provided from the locker rooms to indoor facilities and to the playing fields adjacent to the building. Adequate planning will permit easy access to all areas from both the men's and women's locker rooms. This type of planning permits the flexibility necessary for efficient utilization and control.

The space used for permanent seating of spectators at athletic events should be kept to a minimum unless space and funds are available. Rollaway or folding bleachers can be used in order to utilize efficiently the space available. Most colleges and universities cannot afford to invest large sums of money nor give large areas of space to permanent seating which is used only a few times each year.

Storage rooms for equipment and supplies must be carefully planned and functionally located. These rooms should be of four types:

1. Central receiving storage room, to which all equipment and supplies are delivered. The warehouse storage room should be accessible by truck.
2. Utility storage rooms located adjacent to gymnasiums so that bulky equipment may be moved to the floor and back to storage with limited difficulty. Overhead doors or double doors should be large enough to permit free movement of heavy equipment.
3. Supply rooms with an attendant's window opening to the locker rooms.
4. Off-season storage and reserve storage. The type of equipment to be moved and stored will dictate the dimensions of the room and doors size required.

The health and safety of those using the building will be a prime consideration in planning of all activity areas. Applicable state and federal codes for life safety and accessibility for disabled persons must be consulted.

## SPACE REQUIREMENTS

Those involved in planning college and university facilities for physical education, intramural sports, intercollegiate athletics, and recreation should consider the standards found in Table 1.

It has been estimated by intramural leaders that graduate students participate in physical recreation 25 percent as extensively as undergraduates. Consequently, it is suggested that planners add 25 percent of the graduate enrollment in using the standard.

## MAIN GYMNASIUM

The primary criteria for determining the size of the main gymnasium are the following:

- Nature of the total physical education program
- Student load as determined by enrollment and attendance requirements per week
- Spectator interest
- Anticipated enrollment growth

The physical education building should include one main gymnasium to be used for general physical education, intramurals, and intercollegiate athletic activities in basketball and wrestling. Ideally, the size of the main gymnasium floor for an average enrollment of 4,000 students would be approximately 20,000 square feet (use a rectangular proportion if the facility will be heavily used for spectator sports.) This size would provide for one official and three junior-size (35- by 84-foot) basketball courts, with adequate space between the courts and between the courts and walls. If desirable, folding partitions can be used to provide three practice gymnasiums, each of an approximate size of 48 by 140 feet. For the basketball courts, backboards that swing up to the ceiling can be used to prevent interference with court usage for volleyball and other net sports. Moveable partitions or nets may be used to divide the space for more activities.

The varsity basketball court should be laid out lengthwise in the center of the gymnasium. If the dimensions of 114 by 145 feet are provided, 25 feet is left on either side for bleachers. A minimum of 5 feet should be left between the first row of seats and the outside boundary line of the court.

The height from the floor to the beams in the main gymnasium should be such that in normal use of any of the courts, the balls will not strike the lowest ceiling beam. This height should be a minimum of 22 feet to accommodate basketball, volleyball, and rope climbing.

If the gymnasium is to be used for intercollegiate athletics, seating must be provided for spectators (3 square feet per person). Portable folding bleachers, which can be easily moved, are recommended for seating. Portable knockdown bleachers are not recommended because they interfere with activities while they are being erected, used, and removed. The number of seats to be provided will be determined by the size of the student body, the college community, and the degree to which there is public demand for admittance. The seating capacity should be set at a minimum of one-half to two-thirds of the student-faculty population. In larger institutions, it may be necessary to install rollaway bleacher seats in a balcony, which, when combined with the bleachers on the main floor, will provide the required number of seats. Where a permanent balcony is required, it is necessary to plan the line of vision so that the sidelines of the varsity basketball court are plainly visible to the spectators. In this case, the folding bleachers on the floor should be planned to conform to the same line of vision. With the use of rollaway bleachers, additional activities can be provided in the balcony area.

Where intercollegiate basketball is played, there should be adequate provision for reporters, sports broadcasters, and scouts. The placing of tables adjacent to playing courts is not good design practice; a press box and/or soundproof broadcasting booth is recommended if conditions permit. Provisions should be made for telephone and Internet connections, cable TV access, and for the operation of a public-address system, including music. Scoreboards and timing devices should be of sufficient number and be so placed that players and all spectators can see them readily. They should be easy to operate and readily accessible for maintenance purposes.

**Table 1**  Summary of Space Requirements by Facility

| Facilities | Space Requirements | Uses | Breakdown |
|---|---|---|---|
| *Type A—Indoor teaching stations* | | | |
| Gym floors, mat areas, swimming pools, courts, etc. (adjacent to lockers and showers and within walking distance of academic classrooms) | 8.5 to 9.5 sq ft per student (total undergraduate enrollment) | Physical education class instruction, varsity sports, intramural sports, informal sports participation, student and faculty recreation, etc. | A1—Large gymnasium areas with high ceilings (22 ft minimum) for basketball, badminton, gymnastics, apparatus, volleyball (≈55%) A2—Activity areas with lower ceilings (12 ft minimum) for combatives, therapeutic exercises, dancing, weight training (≈30%) A3—Swimming and diving pools (≈15%) |
| *Type B—Outdoor teaching stations* | | | |
| Sports fields of all types (adjacent to lockers and showers and within walking distance of academic classrooms) | 70 to 90 sq ft per student (total undergraduate enrollment) | Physical education class instruction, varsity sports, intramural sports participation, student and faculty recreation | B1—Sodded areas for soccer, touch football, softball (≈60%) B2—Court-type areas for tennis, volleyball, etc. (≈15%) B3—Specialized athletic areas for track and field, baseball, archery, varsity football, golf, etc. (≈25%) B4—Swimming pools (included in B3) |
| *Type C—Sports fields and buildings; intramural and general outdoor recreation areas* | | | |
| Playing fields and athletic buildings of all types; softball diamonds, tennis courts, arenas, field houses, etc. too far removed from general student lockers, showers, living quarters, and academic buildings for use as teaching stations; maximum distance from major residence areas 1 miles) | 120 to 140 sq ft per student (total undergraduate enrollment) | Intramural sports, varsity sports, informal sports | C1—Sodded areas for soccer, touch football, softball (≈40%) C2—Court-type areas for tennis, volleyball, etc.(≈10%) C3—Specialized athletic areas for track and field, baseball, archery, varsity football, golf, camping demonstrations (≈45%) C4—Swimming pools (included in C3) C5—Sports and intramural buildings, locker rooms, play space, office space, lounges (≈5%) |
| *Type D—Informal recreation areas* | | | |
| On-campus picnic areas (maximum distance from residence areas: 1½ miles) | Included in C3 | Picnics, outdoor activities, cooking, etc. | |
| *Type E—Off-campus outdoor education, camping, and recreation area* | | | |
| Outdoor camping and outdoor education center, off-campus golf course, university country club, etc. (maximum distance from heart of the campus: 25 miles) | Variables in climate, topography, distance from the heart of the campus, and emphasis on outdoor education make a square-feet-per-student standard difficult to establish. | Overnight camping, picnics, outing activities, camping demonstrations, golf, archery, boating, canoeing, outdoor swimming, formal classes taught outdoors | |
| *Ancillary areas* | | | |
| Locker rooms, equipment storage, supply rooms, and offices | Approximately 40% of the play or activity area | | |
| *Tare* | | | |
| Hallways, stairways, wall thickness, lobbies, public toilets, bleachers for public use, custodial space, and space needed for service conduits | Approximately 80% of the activity or play area | | |

When an area is designed for an activity that will require the use of a piano or audiovisual (AV) equipment, a lockable space should be provided for storing this equipment. It is preferable to have a space recessed in the side wall near the place where the instructor will stand to lead the class. Electrical and data lines will be needed for such equipment. In addition to the AV storage niche, there should be a storage room adjacent to the main gymnasium of sufficient size to accommodate the storage of all types of gym equipment, such as roll-away standards, mats and gymnastics apparatus, and chairs. Additional audiovisual aids can include movie projectors, projection screens, televisions, scoreboards, clocks, chalkboards, and teleconferencing computer systems.

Certain materials are traditionally used in gymnasium construction; however, new products are frequently tested and introduced, and research will be required during the design process. Concrete with sleepers of 2 by 2 inches up to 2 by 10 inches laid on edge is commonly used as a base in constructing the floor of the main gymnasium. Maple tongue-and-groove is a popular type of wood finish, although many other durable, resilient finishes are acceptable. It is suggested that a wainscot be carried up to a height of 7 or 8 feet to protect the wall surface. Hanging pads or ceramic tile are commonly used. In addition to natural light, mercury-vapor or fluorescent lights with diffusion panels can be used to provide satisfactory illumination.

### Entrance/Lobby

The purpose of the lobby is to furnish an area for the control of admission, distribution of traffic, and the provision of information and tickets. Entrances, with vestibules for climate control, should be located with reference to parking facilities and traffic approaches.

Public telephones, ticket booths, and toilet facilities should be located in or adjacent to the lobby entrance. Additional toilet facilities in sufficient number for men and women spectators should be provided in close proximity to the seating areas. The space may contain well-lit, lockable, and recessed display cabinets, bulletin boards, and directories. Adequate stairways or ramps should lead from the main lobby to balconies or other spectator areas above the first floor.

A coatroom should be placed adjacent to the direct line of traffic, in an alcove or a side room in order to prevent congestion. The location and arrangement of the coatroom should serve the daily needs of the building as well as the needs for special occasions. Shelves and racks, numbered for checking coats, hats, packages, and bags, should be provided.

The general administrative offices of the building should be located near the lobby. Corridors should lead from the lobby to locker rooms and spectator areas. Walls and flooring should be constructed of durable materials that are easy to maintain.

### Offices

The central administrative offices serve as the nerve center of the entire physical education department. They should be located in close proximity to the building entrance, since many who have business with the department will first come to these offices. The director's office and those of the various faculty members should be adjacent to a large central office which can serve as the workroom for the administrative staff, as a repository for all departmental records, and as a reception center.

The work area of this central office should be separated from the reception-waiting room area. The reception area should open into the main corridor of the building. A large closet should be provided adjacent to the work area for the storage of office supplies and records. The administrative head should have an office in or near the central administrative suite. This office should be of sufficient size to accommodate an executive desk, chairs, file cabinets, and a small worktable, equaling approximately 200 square feet.

The central administrative office unit should include a conference room near the office of the administrative head. It should be furnished with a conference table large enough to seat the entire physical education faculty, if possible, or the administrative staff in a larger university. Other members of the faculty with major responsibilities should be provided a private office. Ideally, each of these offices should occupy a minimum of 120 square feet and be equipped with necessary office furniture. A workroom with space for an administrative pool should receive serious consideration. A coat closet and rest rooms should also be located near the conference room, in addition to a kitchenette for convenience.

### Locker Rooms

Facilities may include dressing areas with lockers, benches, vanity counters with mirrors, toilets, sinks, showers, steam room, and sauna. An additional dressing room with lockers and adjoining shower and toilet facilities should be provided for staff members. Game officials can also utilize these accommodations. Wall and floor finishes in wet areas should be ceramic tile or stone for easy maintenance, though carpet may be used on the floor in changing areas.

Some gymnasium locker room facilities include a steam bath and sauna installation. If a steam room is constructed, a satisfactory size is 8 square feet, with a ceiling 10 feet high. A door containing a window should open outward. The room should be equipped with two or three movable benches of sturdy wood construction. The steam valve used should be a type that can be set to prevent the temperature in the room from exceeding 130°F.

### Classrooms

The physical education complex should include sufficient classroom space designed primarily for lectures, discussion, and demonstrations. The number, size, and types of rooms will depend upon the anticipated enrollment and curricular offerings. Institutions offering teacher-training programs in health, physical education, recreation, and safety will have need for more specialized rooms than will those concerned primarily with service and basic instruction courses and varsity athletics.

The sizes of classrooms may well vary to accommodate from 10 to 150 persons. The space per student may vary from approximately 20 square feet per student in smaller rooms to 12 square feet per student in rooms for 100 or more persons. Standard classrooms normally seat an average of 40 students. The smaller rooms lend themselves more readily to seminars, conferences, and informal discussions, while an assembly room big enough to combine large groups for professional lectures, clinics, and demonstrations is essential.

If the gymnasium is to serve the needs of students enrolled in a major professional program, the inclusion of small-group study rooms is recommended. Study rooms should occupy approximately 150 square feet and should be equipped with a large table and sufficient chairs to accommodate a maximum of 8 students. These rooms may serve a variety of educational needs in addition to small-group on-campus study.

In smaller classrooms, movable tablet or desk armchairs may be used, or conference tables and straight chairs may be preferred. Large lecture halls and assemblies should be equipped with numbered tablet or desk chairs secured to the floor and so arranged as to provide visual efficiency. It is highly desirable that convenient recessed cabinets and closets be provided for storing instructional materials and equipment.

Windows should be equipped with effective room-darkening treatment, which are easily operated. A speakers' platform or podium is frequently desirable in rooms designed for larger groups. Large assembly rooms might well be equipped with a projection booth. A rectangular room is more satisfactory for film projection. Transmission and reception of television and teleconferencing equipment should be considered when planning modern physical education facilities.

## AUXILIARY GYMNASIUMS

In addition to the main gymnasium, field house, and recreation center, other spaces may be required for the following programs:

- Physical therapy
- Gymnastics
- Weight training
- Wrestling and personal defense
- Dance
- Aerobics
- Rock Climbing
- Tennis
- Swimming and Diving

### Physical Therapy Facilities

Two separate areas should be planned for this specialized program:

- An exercise-therapy room, which can be used as a clinic, designed for individual ameliorative exercises
- A gymnasium for adapted activity

The exercise-therapy room should be on the ground floor or be accessible by elevator. The number of students needing this special attention determines the size of the room. Approximately 70 square feet of floor space is required per student. To accommodate equipment, the minimum size of the room should be 1,600 square feet. Office space should be located within this area, and the office should be equipped with large glass windows for adequate supervision of the room. An accessible locker room with toilet facilities should be close to the physical therapy room.

Permanent equipment installed in the exercise-therapy room should include stall bars, wall weights (pulley), press bar, weight racks, shoulder wheel, finger ladder, hanging bars, overhead ladder, push-up bars, wall charts and anatomical drawings, single and triple mirrors, and walking rails.

Removable equipment should include plinths (treatment tables) 26 by 72 by 30½ inches; stall-bar benches; incline boards 7 feet by 30 inches by 3 inches; ankle exercisers; a bicycle (stationary); weights (dumbbells); weights (barbells); exercise mats; iron boots (single); iron boots (double); parallel bars (low); orthopedic stairs; rowing-machine stools; scales; an Elgin table (or improvisation of quadriceps exercise table); wrist rollers; neck-traction halters; cushions or pillows; crutches; a wheelchair; dynamometers (hand, spring cable); goniometers; a chalkboard; and a skeleton.

The equipment in an adapted-activities gymnasium should be the same as in a regular gymnasium, with necessary adaptations. This gymnasium should be in close proximity to the physical therapy room so that a student can utilize both facilities.

### Gymnastic Facilities

In addition to the main gymnasium where gymnastic meets, exhibitions, and other competitions are held before a viewing public, a separate gymnasium should be provided for the permanent installation and storage of apparatus and equipment and for instruction in gymnastics. The dimensions of this gymnasium should be determined by space requirements needed to accommodate the apparatus and equipment to be installed, by space needs for performance in gymnastics, and by total school enrollment and interest in gymnastics. Ideally, the size of this gymnasium should be 120 by 90 feet, with a minimum ceiling height of 23 feet. This height permits a clearance of 22 feet for the rope climb and is ideal for hanging the various mechanical systems used in gymnastics. Some have found it desirable to install tracks on the ceiling supports to make it possible to use trolleys for moving equipment and for attaching safety belts used in the instruction of trampoline jumping and tumbling.

The safety of performers and instructors should receive major consideration in planning the location and installation of apparatus, equipment, and wall fixtures. Apparatus used in performance should be located so that performers do not interfere with each other when going through their routines. Flying rings should be located so that there is at least 15 feet of free space allowed at each end of the swinging arc. All equipment should be installed according to a plan that will permit, without interference, a full range of movement, including the approach. Mats should be laid completely around the area of performance on horizontal and parallel bars. A landing pit, filled with sponge rubber—for use with parallel bars, horizontal bars, still rings, and tumbling—may also be incorporated.

Floor plates for attaching equipment should be recessed and flush with the floor. It may be necessary to reinforce the floor to install floor plates adequately where tension is unusually severe. Additional wall reinforcement should be installed when equipment is attached to it. Apparatus suspended from the ceiling should be securely attached to additional structural supports.

The ceiling should be acoustically treated. Lights should be shielded and adequate for the program. Doors should be constructed wide enough and without a threshold so as to accommodate the movement of equipment to other areas. The facility should be air-conditioned and ventilated in accordance with standard gymnasium specifications. Wall and flooring construction should be of the same materials as recommended for other gymnasiums.

A common failure in planning is to overlook the need for adequate and conveniently placed storage space for gymnastic equipment. If multiple use of this equipment is expected, transportation carts and dollies should be provided. Specifications on size and installation of the various pieces of apparatus and equipment may be obtained from the manufacturers. Ideally, the gymnasium for gymnastics should be equipped with the following types of apparatus: side horses, horizontal bars, long horses, parallel bars, bucks, trampolines, mats, rings, and other special apparatus.

## Weight-Training Room

This room should provide adequate floor space for the practice of official events in competitive weight-lifting, as well as training equipment including free weights, weight machines and cardiovascular equipment. The weight-lifting area should be separated and should be approximately 15 by 15 feet for the practice of official lifts. Several full-length mirrors should be installed on the walls. Barbell and weight racks should be attached to the walls so that the room may be kept clear. It is recommended that the floor of this room be covered with a durable, resilient material. A flooring of this type makes it unnecessary to use weight platforms, which are used to protect a maple or other wood flooring.

## Wrestling and Personal-Defense Room

This room is designed for wrestling and all other personal-defense activities. The ceiling should be of acoustical material and should be a minimum height of 12 feet. The room should be rectangular in shape and should contain two square 40- by 40-foot mats. The floor area not covered by the regulation mats should be covered wall to wall with some type of mat material. The room should be at least 40 by 80 feet. A satisfactory standard is 40 square feet per student during peak usage.

The floor of the wrestling room should be constructed of, or covered with, resilient materials to prolong the life of the mats. Concrete is not recommended. The mats should be of highly resilient, easily cleaned materials, and should cover the floor and the walls up to 5 feet on all sides. Adequate indirect lighting and forced ventilation are essential in this room.

## Dance Studios

Dance areas should be provided to serve the departmental and student needs and to afford opportunity for individual and departmental development. Some of these areas are specific and may be limited to forms of dance activity. Other dance areas are versatile and may serve several purposes. Large colleges and universities with a variety of courses may need to plan for one or more of each of several dance-activity rooms. Classes should be advantageously scheduled for the purposes of floor maintenance or equipment moving. The types of dance areas suggested are as follows:

### Main Dance Studio

This studio, which should measure no less than 56 by 56 feet, will provide for a class of up to 36 students in modern dance, ballet, or some other dance form performed in bare feet or with soft-sole dance shoes. The floor, which should be of conventional gymnasium construction, tongue-and-groove maple, should be free of floor plates, plugs, and other installations. The ceiling height should be 22 feet to be proportional with the room and to give the feeling of height in leaps.

The room should have wall mirrors (6 feet high, minimum) along at least one wall. The mirrors should have a draw drapery controlled by cord pulls. Ballet bars (hand rails) should be installed on two oppo-site sides of the room at ascending heights of 3 feet, 3 feet-6 inches, and 4 feet above the floor.

Audiovisual equipment should include a tackboard, a chalkboard, a hook rail, and a bulletin board. A stereo and amplification system on a rollaway table should be recessed into a lockable cabinet. Other cabinets should provide space for musical instruments, records, music, costumes, and other properties. Some dance studios may have a grand piano; however, it may be desirable to have an area where a grand piano or an upright piano can be stored when removed from the floor. Storage cabinets for stage equipment, levels, and other items should be provided since floor storage of materials not actively used markedly diminishes the floor space usable for dance activities.

### Auxiliary Dance Studio

An auxiliary dance studio of 56 by 40 feet with a ceiling of 22 feet can be located adjacent to the main dance studio on the side opposite from the balcony and can be separated by appropriate folding doors and draperies. This studio can serve as a stage for small concert productions or class projects. Traveling draperies suspended from the ceiling can be run on tracks and can be controlled electrically to serve as the traditional flats used in staging and in making up a backdrop behind which dancers can cross over. When not used, the draperies can be withdrawn from the staging area and can be stacked along one wall. Stage lighting can be developed to give illumination from the ceiling, from the stage side of the divider, from projecting semicones in the ceiling of the main dance studio, and from spots in the balcony.

This dance studio will need to include those features desirable for the program needs as are included in the main dance studio: ballet bars, mirror, cabinets for classroom materials, and a rollaway table with stereo equipment. In addition, there may be a need for piano and equipment storage rooms.

### Dance Rehearsal Room

One or more dance rehearsal rooms of a minimum of 400 square feet each will contribute to the development of students in dance who need small-group practices and extra rehearsals. A chalkboard, tackboard, and moveable sound system should be provided in such rooms. The table should be housed in a recessed, lockable cabinet. Other lockable cabinets will provide needed storage space for dance practice materials. Ballet bars and mirrors will add to the usefulness of such a room.

### Dance Property Construction and Storage Room

Flats, levels, and other properties can be made and stored in a room of approximately 25 by 30 feet. This room should be located adjacent to the main dance studio and should have wide double doors to allow sets and properties to be moved in and out. The room should have a high ceiling to allow sets to be constructed and moved to a vertical position or to the finished position for painting. Drawers and cabinets, some lockable, a sink with hot and cold water, lumber racks, work counters and tables, and electrical power are essential in the planned structure of the room. Tackboards, bulletin boards, and lockable, glass-front display bulletin boards are desirable.

### Dance Costume Construction and Storage Room

The size of this room will vary according to the program needs for costume construction and the storage needs for costumes made and etained in the department. Having cabinets in close-order banks, somewhat as bookcases are placed in the stacks in a library, will probably best use the room. This will free one end of the room for clothing construction. Costume-storage cabinets should have racks for hanging and bins and drawers for storage. Units can be planned to be comprised of several components, which may be used as desired for separate assignment to clubs, groups, or projects. Cabinets for material and equipment storage, wall-attached ironing boards, an automatic washer-drier, a three-way mirror unit, a washroom basin, a large cutting table of 4 by 8 feet, and a counter sink are additional necessities.

## Ball Courts

One or more courts should be provided for handball, squash, and racquetball. The official size of each type of court can be obtained from the rulebook for that particular game. When more than a single battery of courts is to be constructed, the batteries should be arranged so a corridor approximately 10 feet wide and 8 feet high separates the back walls of each battery. A corridor located immediately above, and at feast 12 feet high, may serve an instructor or be used as a spectator gallery. Corridors and galleries should be illuminated with indirect light.

The back wall of a single court need not be higher than 12 feet. Shatterproof glass may be used to enclose the remainder of the back wall. The use of wire mesh for this purpose is of questionable value. Many courts are satisfactorily used with an open upper rear wall.

Depending on the size of the institution and the expressed interest in handball, one or more batteries of four-wall handball courts should be provided. The official size of a handball court is 20 feet wide by 40 feet long by 20 feet high. Specifications for handball courts can be found in the official handball rulebook.

Handball court walls may be finished with gypsum wallboard, concrete, shatterproof glass, or a nonsplintering durable wood. While gypsum wallboard is recommended, other materials are preferable from a maintenance standpoint. Glass courts provide maximum spectator participation, but the initial cost may be prohibitive. Hardwood construction is most satisfactory. Courts constructed with a high proportion of glass walls obviously allow for a large number of observers. Open-balcony construction interferes with individual-court air-conditioning.

Front walls may be constructed of hard maple laid on diagonal wood sheathing. Studding should be placed close enough to prevent dead spots. A maximum of 16-inch centered studs is recommended. A costly but desirable front-wall construction is to lay maple on edge grain.

Side and back walls may be of nonsplintering durable wood such as yellow pine or hard maple. Some side and back walls constructed with 1-inch tongue-and-groove marine plywood have been satisfactory and economical. Hardwood floors of standard gymnasium construction are recommended. Plaster ceilings have proved satisfactory. All interior surfaces should be painted with a durable, easily cleaned finish.

Entrance doors should open toward the corridor and be provided with flush-type pulls and hinges. A small shatterproof window installed flush with the interior surface of the door should be located at approximately eye level.

A single light switch to control all lights in each court should be placed on the corridor side and near the entrance door. Warning lights, located outside each court, should indicate when a court is being used. By use of a sturdy push button, lights can be turned on when an entrance door is closed.

Air-conditioning, or at least forced ventilation, is essential for individual courts. The ventilation switch can operate in conjunction with the light switch. Climatic conditions may dictate separate switches.

Single and double squash courts may also be provided for in the physical education program. A singles court is 18 feet-6 inches wide by 32 feet long by 16 feet high. A doubles court is 25 feet wide by 45 feet long by 20 feet high. The number of courts should be determined by the interest in this activity in a given community.

It is possible to install movable metal telltales across the front of handball courts so they can be used for squash. Construction features of squash courts are similar to those of four-wall handball courts relative to floors, walls, ceilings, lighting, heating, and ventilation. The official rules of the United States Squash Racquets Association and the National Squash Tennis Association should be consulted in planning and constructing squash courts.

### Rowing-Practice Facilities

In certain colleges and universities, it may be desirable to construct facilities for indoor crew practice. Colleges engaging in competitive rowing will require either fixed rowing machines with accompanying mirrors to reflect the action of the rowers, or a rowing-practice tank. The rowing machines may be installed in a special activity room. If there is space underneath the spectator area in the main gymnasium, they may be installed there. In every case, the area should be well lit and ventilated.

The rowing tank, when used, should simulate the conditions to be found in open-water rowing. The water should be mechanically circulated in such a manner as to make possible the actual introduction of the oar into the water and the completion of the stroke. The crew should be seated on a rigid platform that spans the pool at actual shell height.

All the specifications for indoor rowing equipment may be obtained from the manufacturers, and the details of the construction of a rowing tank are available through the office of the Intercollegiate Rowing Association.

### Health Research Laboratory

College and university health, physical education, and recreation programs are becoming increasingly involved in research. Graduate studies and faculty research cannot thrive unless space is allocated for this work in the gymnasium building where exercise and sports areas are convenient.

Research in physical education may be of many different types. Some colleges and universities emphasize one or more areas. The research in physical education programs is in the following categories: kinesiologic, tests and measurements, organic (metabolic, cardiovascular, and chemical analysis, etc.), and statistical.

A laboratory providing opportunities in the kinds of research mentioned requires a minimum of 2,800 square feet of space for the basic equipment needed. The maximum space needs will depend on the number of faculty and students involved and the complexity of the research program. Research laboratory space may be provided in one large room or in several smaller rooms. It is suggested that a separate room of 300 square feet be used for a statistical laboratory.

## FIELD HOUSE

### Function

The field house provides enclosed and unobstructed space adaptable to indoor and outdoor sports activities. It is not intended as a substitute for the gymnasium; it is complementary and supplementary to other facilities for indoor and outdoor physical education and recreation activities.

Typical functions of the field house for a college are as follows:

- Instruction in the service program in physical education
- Practice for intercollegiate athletics (football, track and field, baseball, basketball, tennis, soccer, lacrosse, and other sports)
- Intramural and intercollegiate competition
- Informal play
- Horseback riding
- Demonstrations and exhibitions which attract large crowds of spectators
- Commencement exercises
- Registration
- Final examinations
- Community uses may include interscholastic games, matches, meets and tournaments; band concerts; exhibits; and mass meetings

The total physical education program, including co-physical education and co-recreation, should be considered when plans are developed, so that facilities for activities such as tennis, volleyball, badminton, and golf practice may be provided. Unless provided in the gymnasium, handball and squash courts should be constructed in the field house. A survey of available facilities for activities common to modern physical education programs will serve to determine the number and type of activity units to include in the field house.

### Location

The field house should be placed in an area contiguous to athletic fields and where parking problems are not critical. If space is not available in proximity to the gymnasium, the field house will serve well for intramural activities and intercollegiate sports, even though it is constructed in a peripheral area of the campus. If needed for class instruction, the preferable location for the field house is adjacent to the main gymnasium building and the natatorium.

### Size

The size of the field house should be determined by careful study of its functions; consideration should be given to the size and number of groups (classes, squads, teams) likely to participate simultaneously in the program. There should be a minimum of interference of groups with each other. Programmatic elements may include the following:

- Quarter-mile track around the perimeter
- Regulation basketball court
- Tennis courts

- Broad-jump, high-jump, and pole-vault runways and pits
- Shot-put area
- Press, radio, and scout accommodations
- Public-address system
- Entrance vestibule
- Locker and shower rooms
- First aid and training room
- Lounge and trophy room
- Concession booths
- Equipment storage area

The minimum length of the field house should accommodate a 60-yard straightaway track plus sufficient distance for starting and stopping. A wide door at the end of the straightaway to permit competitors to run outside the field house would prevent injuries and eliminate a hazard where space is limited. Six regulation lanes are desirable. The track around the portable or permanent basketball floor should be of such size as to be a convenient fraction of a longer standard distance.

### Balconies and Bleachers

When permanent balconies are planned, they should be constructed without supporting columns that would interfere in any way with the playing or visual area. Temporary bleachers, when placed in front of and below the permanent balconies, should continue the sight lines of the balconies. Bleachers can be placed inside an eighth-mile track on both sides and ends of a basketball court to accommodate approximately 5,000 spectators.

The field house should be so designed that normal flow of traffic will not encroach upon the activity areas. It is essential that this be done in order to avoid interference with instruction and participation and to decrease maintenance costs.

### Service Units

If the field house is adjacent to the main gymnasium building and the natatorium, the requirements for lockers, showers, and toilets can, in some instances, be reduced. An underpass from the gymnasium to the field house may be desirable in order to make the gymnasium service units available to some participants in the field house. If the field house is not adjacent to the gymnasium, consideration should be given to design for dressing areas, showers, and toilet facilities.

Convenient and accessible dressing units equipped with chalkboards and tackboards for the home and visiting teams should be provided. When the field house is to be used for interscholastic basketball tournaments and indoor track meets, consideration should be given to providing separate locker rooms with adjoining shower and toilet facilities. These units could be used regularly throughout the year by intramural participants and intercollegiate squads.

### Lighting, Heating, and Ventilation

Windows should be equipped with means to prevent the interference of sunlight with player performance at any time during the day. Condensation problems should be given major consideration, particularly where there are extremes of temperature, where sprinkling of surface or dirt areas is required, and where large crowds witness events in the field house. As a means whereby some of the excess condensation may be reabsorbed, the building should be heated by the circulation of warm air in addition to fixed radiation. Adequate means should be provided to supply fresh air and to exhaust air. The walls inside and outside should be impervious to vapor pressure. Mechanical heating, ventilating, air-conditioning and lighting problems should be referred to a consulting engineer.

**Floors**

The floor of the field house should be of an all-weather-resistant construction. Rubber asphalt and several patented resilient synthetics should be considered. A portable wood floor for basketball may be used.

**STUDENT RECREATION CENTERS**

A new supplemental sports facility, called the student recreation center, began to appear in the early 1980s. The program for this facility was developed in response to a new prominence of athletics, more women participating in sports activities, higher student expectations for quality of sports facilities, and a clearer distinction between intramural and intercollegiate sports. This shift in students' values, prioritizing health and fitness, combined with faculty and staff participation in fitness, contributed to the development of this new building type.

As with gymnasiums, the size and program of the student recreation center will vary with the size and needs of each college or university. Institutions may decide to have one large facility or several smaller satellites. Programmatically however, these facilities differ greatly from the older, prototypical gymnasiums. In addition to housing

needed supplemental sports spaces, there is also a social aspect to the student recreation center. Programmatic elements may include the following:

- Single, controlled-access entrance/lobby
- High-bay court space for basketball, volleyball, etc.
- Weight training and exercise rooms with free weights, weight-training machines, and cardiovascular equipment
- Courts for squash, racquetball, and volleyball
- Multipurpose rooms of various sizes for aerobics, combatives, and yoga
- Indoor elevated jogging track
- Administrative offices and conference rooms
- Locker and shower rooms
- Equipment check-out and storage
- Lounge spaces for social events and activities
- Aquatic facility (Fig. 2), composed of swimming pools, a diving well, spectator seating (fixed and retractable), motorized curtains, and backdrops, for shared use
- Secondary spaces: wellness center, climbing walls, sauna, whirlpool, first-aid center, and computer study rooms

Although this type of facility requires a great deal of square footage for programmed spaces and parking, the current demand requires that it be centrally located on campus. Because it is considered a valuable tool for student recruitment and retention, and because students are often willing to contribute financially to its operation, a larger budget is often allotted for the student recreation center. This additional budget typically allows for more creativity in planning and design.

*References: Special Planning for Special Spaces*, Persis Rickes, Editor.
"The Outburst of Student Recreation Centers," David Body, Society for College and University Planning, Ann Arbor, MI 1997.

**Fig. 2. Swimming pool, Hamilton College (Perry Dean Rogers + Partners, Architects; photo: Richard Mandelkorn, courtesy of the architect)**

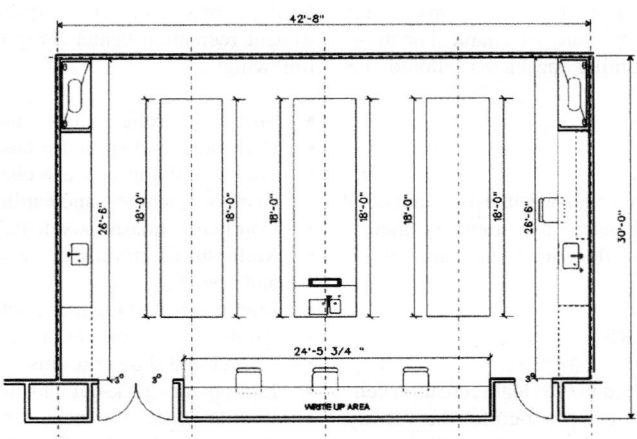

**Fig. 1. Laboratory module**

# COLLEGE LABORATORIES

## PROGRAM REQUIREMENTS

The goals and objectives of a new college laboratory building or renovated space are initially outlined in the building's program. A laboratory building program is a report that describes and quantifies the physical characteristics and components of a research or teaching laboratory facility. A facility program is intended to provide a comprehensive profile of a building, calculating the physical space needs and operational requirements of the facility or space. The building program is prepared by a project team, which ideally includes administrators, users (including principal investigators and research staff), and facility management staff from the institution, in addition to planning and design professionals. The program defines and describes all aspects of the physical environment of the building, including what spaces and facilities are required, how functional spaces and activities should be organized, and where spaces should be located in relation to each other.

### Programming Quantities and Numbers

Space requirements and occupant counts of a laboratory building are typically identified during initial programmatic interviews at the outset of the design process of a particular project. Detailed and specific programmatic information is best attained by interviewing participating occupants, based on functional needs and desired capabilities, and confirmed by commonly observed laboratory protocols and settings. Quantitative information is gathered and analyzed in order to implement the development of a desired building plan and laboratory-planning module.

General area standards are used to determine the amount of research, support, instructional, and administrative space for each investigator and research team, instructor, and support staff. Primary space standards that define area among the various experimental science activities and disciplines are: Office or administrative; laboratory; and laboratory support area per investigator and per research team or program. The following are definitions used in describing and quantifying such spaces within a typical laboratory building:

*Building support facilities*   Include reception areas, toilets, change rooms, locker and shower rooms, health and first-aid offices, lounges, meeting rooms, dining facilities, kitchens, and indoor recreation areas. They also include shipping and receiving areas, and areas for handling chemical or biological hazardous wastes.

*Gross area*   The total building floor area. It includes the area occupied by the structure, exterior walls, partitions, and vertical shafts, plus all usable area.

*Interstitial space*   A floor constructed between any two occupied floors of a building that is dedicated to mechanical, electrical, and plumbing distribution systems. Interstitial space is not included in building gross area.

*Laboratories*   Prime spaces, often modular, catering to research and teaching functions.

*Laboratory support facilities*   Include equipment and storage rooms that may be located near the laboratories they serve; balance and special instrument rooms, data-processing facilities, glassware-washing rooms, sterilization facilities, preparation rooms for media and solutions, sample processing and distribution rooms, machine shops, electronics shops, darkrooms, fluorescent microscopy rooms, and electron microscopy suites.

*Net assignable area (NAA)*   The floor area, excluding interior partitions, columns, and building projections, that lies within the walls of a room or the total area of all rooms and spaces assigned to a specific occupant, group, or function, such as to a principal investigator or to a department. Net area may refer to the total assigned floor area within all rooms and spaces except personnel and building support.

*Office or administration*   Facilities that do not directly support research program activities include private offices, group offices and secretarial pools, business offices, personnel records offices, and data processing offices that are assigned to administration of the building or to general administration of the institution. Other administrative facilities include libraries, conference rooms, seminar rooms, and mail rooms.

---

*Authors:* Perkins and Will, Architects

## TOTAL AREA CALCULATIONS

Laboratory building configurations show variations of 40 to 80 percent in net assignable laboratory area on a typical lab floor. Total net area must be converted to gross area in order to estimate the amount of actual building area that will be constructed to accommodate all the programmed functions. Net-to-gross ratios vary from 45 percent for intensive chemistry laboratory buildings with a high proportion of laboratory area to 65 percent for the most efficient laboratory building.

Buildings containing a low proportion of laboratories to nonlaboratory areas may achieve even higher efficiencies. Buildings that do not have mechanical penthouses or expansive mechanical equipment rooms—when utilities such as steam, hot water, and process chilled water are supplied from an external source—experience higher net-to-gross ratios than lab buildings which are mechanically free-standing.

Table 1 lists special standards that quantify typical research spaces by disciplines (per researcher and research team).

### Laboratory Module

The laboratory module (Fig. 1) is the foundation for planning and designing research and teaching laboratories. A *single laboratory module* is defined as a basic unit of space of a size commonly referred to as a *two-person laboratory*. Formulation of the internal organization of the laboratory building begins with a decision on the dimensions of the laboratory module. This task redirects the planning focus from the large scale of the total facility down to the small scale of the single laboratory module.

### Laboratory Dimensions

Over 35 years ago, dimensional criteria were established for individual laboratory work areas. Specifications for optimal dimensions of a standard laboratory aisle were derived from ergonomic factors related to reaching across and above the work surfaces, equipment, benches, and utilities, where laboratory personnel essentially spend their workday.

The aisle between benches, work surfaces, or equipment should be a minimum of 60 inches so that one person can pass behind another working at a bench. The maximum clearance in a research laboratory should be no more than 72 inches because wider aisles tend to get clogged with freestanding equipment and other obstructions set up by researchers to make maximum utilization of the space close at hand. The average width of an array of benches and equipment on both sides of an aisle varies widely. Typically, a bench with a utility chase behind may be 30 inches from the face of the bench to the wall. Freestanding equipment typically ranges from 2 to 3 feet wide; when there is a built-out utility chase behind, total width can be over 45 inches. Table 2 assumes an average 36-inch width. To ensure that there is sufficient space for a single-aisle laboratory at each module, the dimension for the thickness of a standard interior partition should be added to the clear width of each module.

This method provides flexibility to divide a large laboratory into individual single-module laboratories, or an entire laboratory floor into individual laboratories of varied sizes, without reducing the recommended aisle width. Special-purpose laboratories, such as controlled-environment laboratories and pilot plants, have space requirements that may not conform to a standard laboratory module.

Existing structures converted to laboratory use may not have structural module dimensions consistent with division into the recommended module dimensions. To overcome this difficulty, adjustments may have to be made to the depth of benches or in the distribution of utilities to the laboratory floor, but under no circumstances should the clear aisle width be reduced below 60 inches. Table 2 presents laboratory widths for a variety of modular arrangements.

## LABORATORY FUNCTIONS

Academic laboratories are generally divided between two separate functions: research and teaching. Research labs are often geared toward higher-level graduate instruction and faculty or principal investigator research. Academic research labs are often very similar to private-sector and government-sponsored laboratories. Teaching labs are generally used for the instruction of undergraduate students in the basic sciences.

**Table 1** Sample research area standards for a variety of experimental science laboratories (net square feet per full-time researcher)

| | Laboratory area categories | | | |
| Primary activity | Office min.-avg. | Laboratory min.-avg. | Lab Support min.-avg. | Total nsf* min.-avg. |
| --- | --- | --- | --- | --- |
| Molecular biology | 57-90 | 120-130 | 80 | 257-300 |
| Tissue culture | 57-90 | 95-130 | 95 | 247-315 |
| Analytical chemistry | 57-90 | 110-150 | 20-35 | 187-275 |
| Biochemistry | 57-90 | 130-175 | 60-80 | 247-345 |
| Organic chemistry | 57-90 | 150-190 | 40-50 | 247-330 |
| Physical chemistry | 57-90 | 170-200 | 30-40 | 257-330 |
| Physiology | 57-90 | 150-170 | 20-40 | 227-300 |

*Totals do not include area allocations for animal facilities, administration, personnel, or building support.

**Table 2** Laboratory Width by Number of Modules in a Building Unit

| Number of modules | 1 | 2 | 3 | 4 | 5 | 6 |
|---|---|---|---|---|---|---|
| **Number of parallel rows** | | | | | | |
| Aisles | 1 | 2 | 3 | 4 | 5 | 6 |
| Benches or equipment | 2 | 4 | 6 | 8 | 10 | 12 |
| Utility strips | 2 | 4 | 6 | 8 | 10 | 12 |
| **Width of parallel rows** | | | | | | |
| Aisles—60 in wide | 5 ft-0 in | 10 ft-0 in | 15 ft-0 in | 20 ft-0 in | 25 ft-0 in | 30 ft-0 in |
| Equipment—30 in wide | 5 ft-0 in | 10 ft-0 in | 15 ft-0 in | 20 ft-0 in | 25 ft-0 in | 30 ft-0 in |
| Utilities—6 in wide | 1 ft-0 in | 2 ft-0 in | 3 ft-0 in | 4 ft-0 in | 5 ft-0 in | 6 ft-0 in |
| **Total constructed width, center to center** | | | | | | |
| Walls 4⅝ in GWB* | 11 ft-4⅝ in | 22 ft-9¼ in | 34 ft-1⅞ in | 45 ft-6½ in | 56 ft-11⅛ in | 68 ft-3¾ in |
| Walls 5⅝ in CMU† | 11 ft-5⅝ in | 22 ft-11¼ in | 34 ft-4⅞ in | 45 ft-10½ in | 57 ft-4⅛ in | 68 ft-9¾ in |

*GWB is a partition type with 3⅝-inch metal studs with one layer of ½-inch gypsum board on each side.

†CMU is a partition type constructed with 6-inch nominal width concrete masonry units (concrete blocks).

The two lab types differ in a variety of functions, capabilities, and physical layouts. The following are several differentiations between teaching labs and research labs:

- Furniture systems and casework for research labs are flexible (moveable tables, adaptable heights, etc.), however, casework for teaching labs often includes the adaptability to morph not only into different configurations, but often different functions (e.g., a mobile lab bench converting to an instructional desk in order to increase utilization).
- There is less equipment and instrumentation in teaching labs compared to research labs.
- Teaching labs often require a specific bench or lectern for lecturing, often with extensive information-technology and audiovisual capabilities.
- Teaching lab benches are oriented toward the professor and marker boards.
- Computer equipment such as electronic cameras, computer boards, and elmos (overhead projectors tied into the computer) are used to enhance the learning environment.
- Storage of student microscopes and other supplies is necessary in teaching labs.
- More people (students) and seating must be accommodated in the teaching lab.
- Prep labs are usually located between two teaching labs. The prep labs allow faculty to set up supplies before classes.
- The number of students within the curriculum or course usually determines the size of the teaching labs, while a preferred research process of grant-funded research programs often drives the size and configuration of research labs.
- Teaching labs have very little interior glass in order to keep students focused on the class.

## REQUIREMENTS BY LAB TYPE

Undergraduate lab spatial requirements depend heavily on the type of science, course level, equipment used, lab type, and the amount of flexibility needed. A typical lab module of 10 feet-6 inches by 30 feet (320 net square feet) will support 4 to 6 students. The following are proposed spatial requirements per student and guidelines for various science disciplines:

| | |
|---|---|
| General biology | 60 net square feet |
| General chemistry | 75 net square feet |
| General geology | 50 net square feet |
| Physics | 60 net square feet |
| Psychology | 40 net square feet |
| Biochemistry | 60 net square feet |

- Shared bench space ranges from 15 to 30 linear feet per teaching laboratory. This space is used for benchtop instruments, exhibits, or glasswear distribution.
- 10 to 20 linear feet of wall space per lab is required for storage cabinets and moveable equipment such as refrigerators and incubators.
- The typical student workstation is generally 3 to 4 feet wide, with 3 to 4 feet of additional bookshelves, file cabinets, and data and electric hookups for computers.
- Teaching labs should include casework that can easily be changed from 30 to 36 inches to accommodate both seated and standing positions.
- The overall size of a teaching lab is based on the amount of space needed per student and the total number of students. A flexible design allows for fluctuations in enrollment sizes.
- A 6-foot-wide fume hood is typically shared by two to three students.
- A separate discussion room shared among several teaching labs may be an alternative to lectures in the lab.
- Minimal travel distances between workbenches and fume hoods lessens the possibility of chemical spills.

Figures 2 to 4 illustrate a variety of teaching-lab planning options. Following these are characteristic descriptions of teaching-lab layouts and profiles for various sciences.

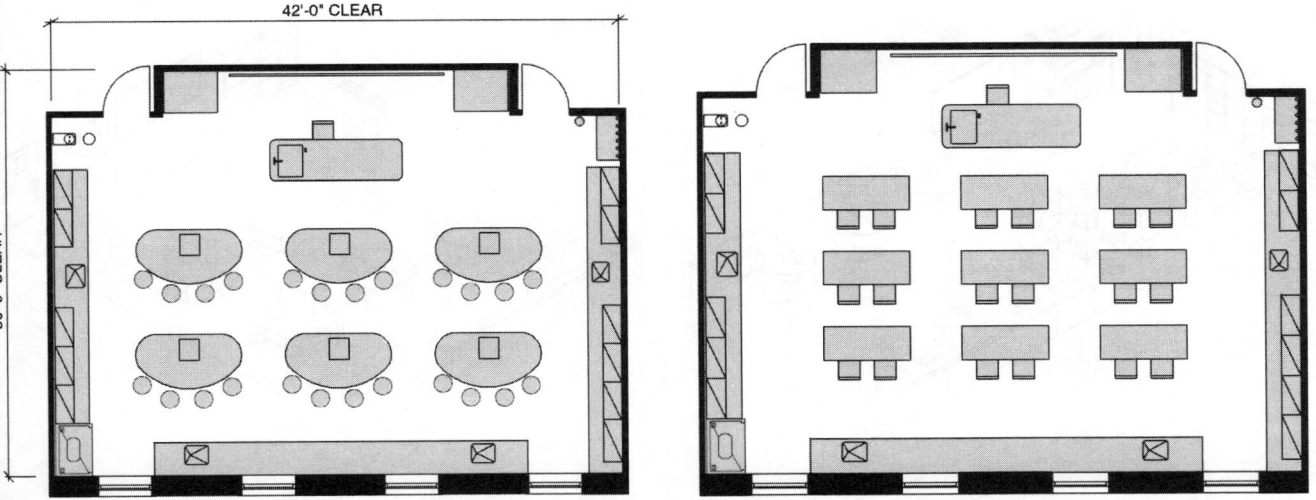

**Fig. 2. Teaching laboratory casework options**

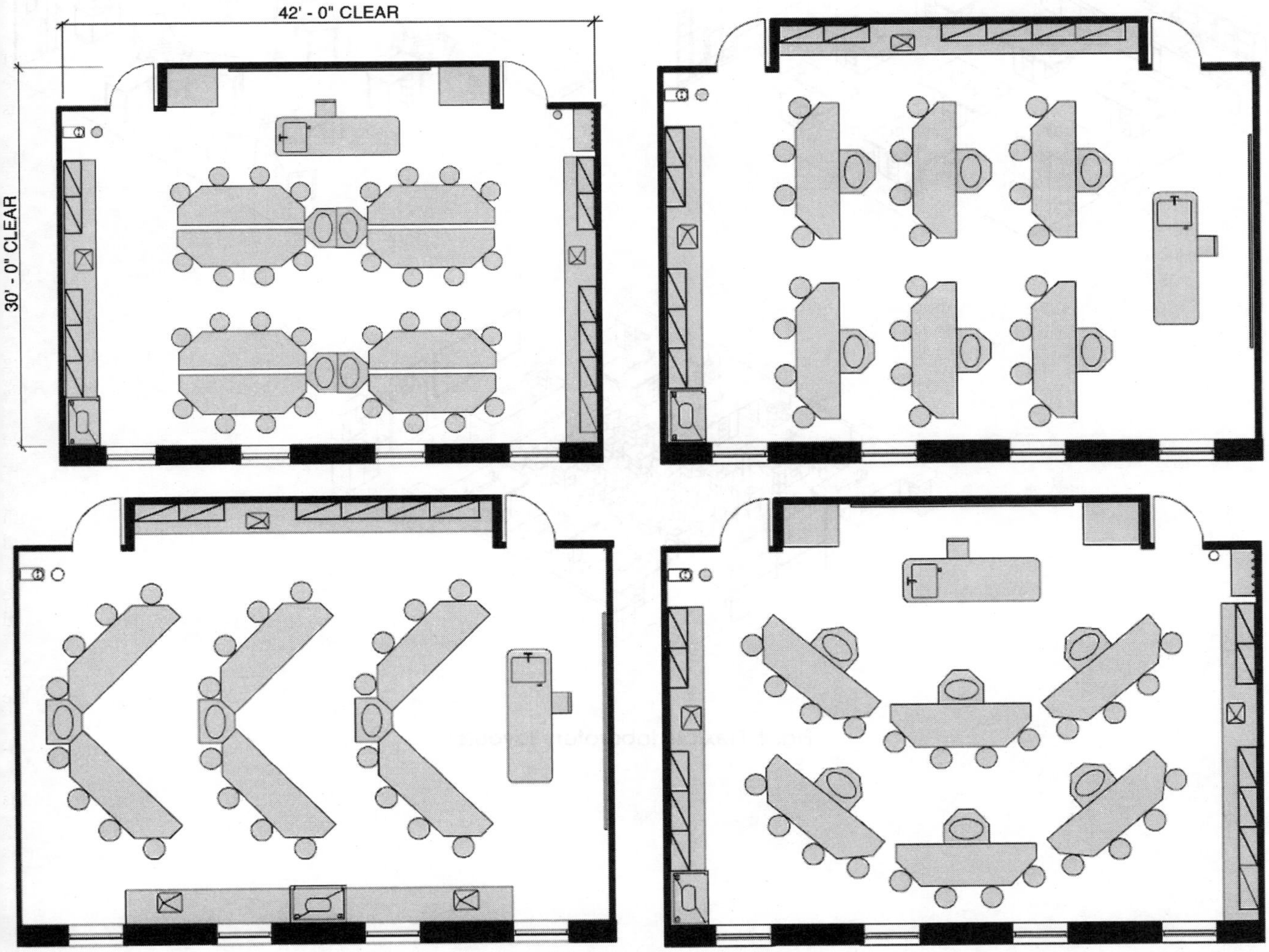

**Fig. 3. Flexible teaching laboratories**

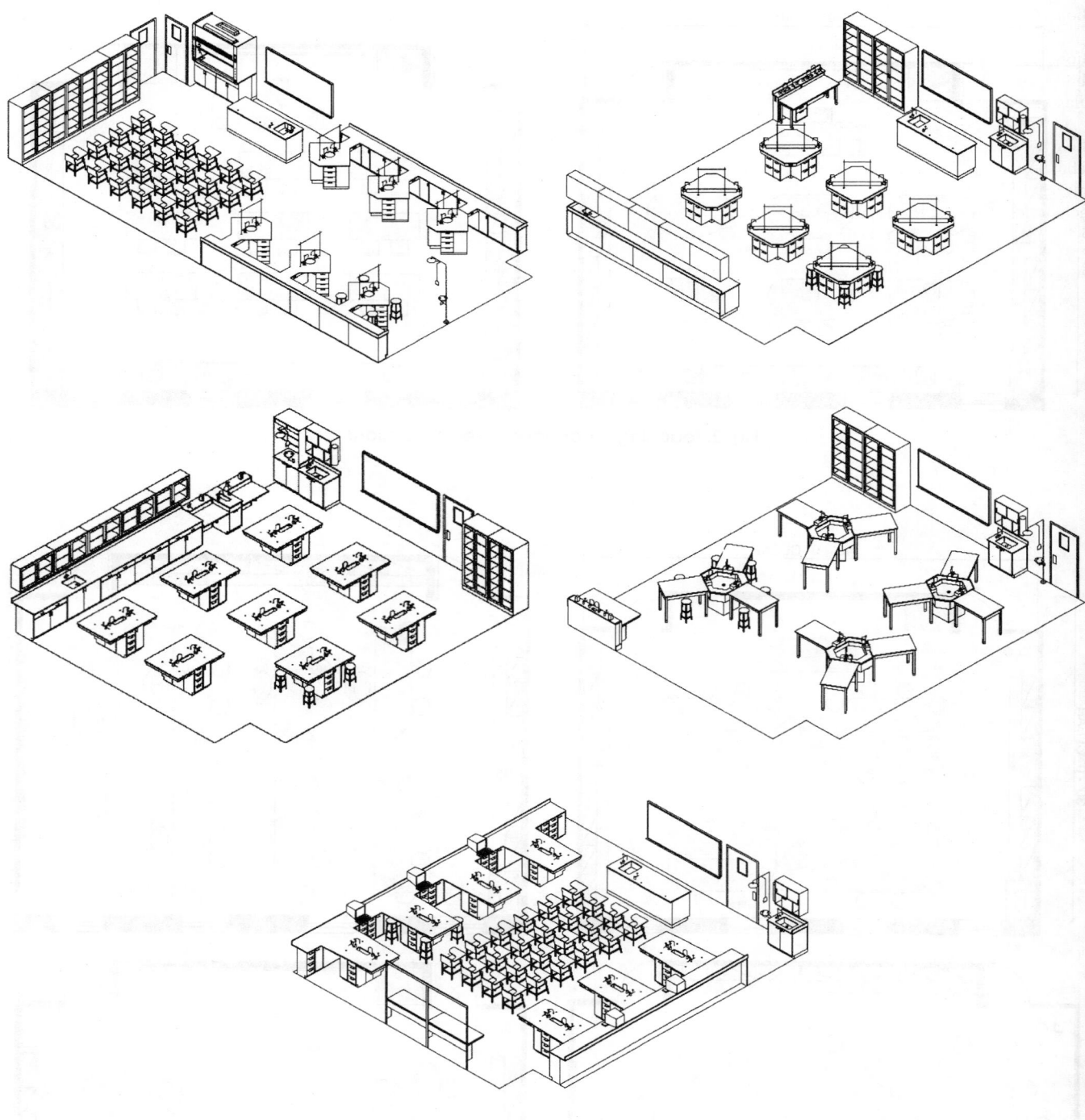

**Fig. 4. Flexible laboratory layouts**

## Biology Labs

Biology labs (Fig. 5) should provide the necessary flexibility, adaptibility and convertibility to accommodate biochemistry, biology, cellular and molecular biology, and genetics.

Biology labs are wet labs which require fume hoods and biosafety cabinets; equipment space to house incubators, refrigerators and freezers; lab benches; and storage space (cabinets and/or shelving—including specialized chemical and fire retardant storage).

Fig. 5. Biology laboratories: (*a*) moveable tables; (*b*) fixed benches; (*c*) moveable tables; (*d*) moveable tables

### Physics Labs

Physics labs (Fig. 6) require significant computer and telecommunications support. Some key design issues for physics labs include the following:

- Noise and vibration control
- Magnetic shielding
- Extensive electrical power requirements
- Durable and mobile casework
- Extensive computer networking
- Flexible workspace

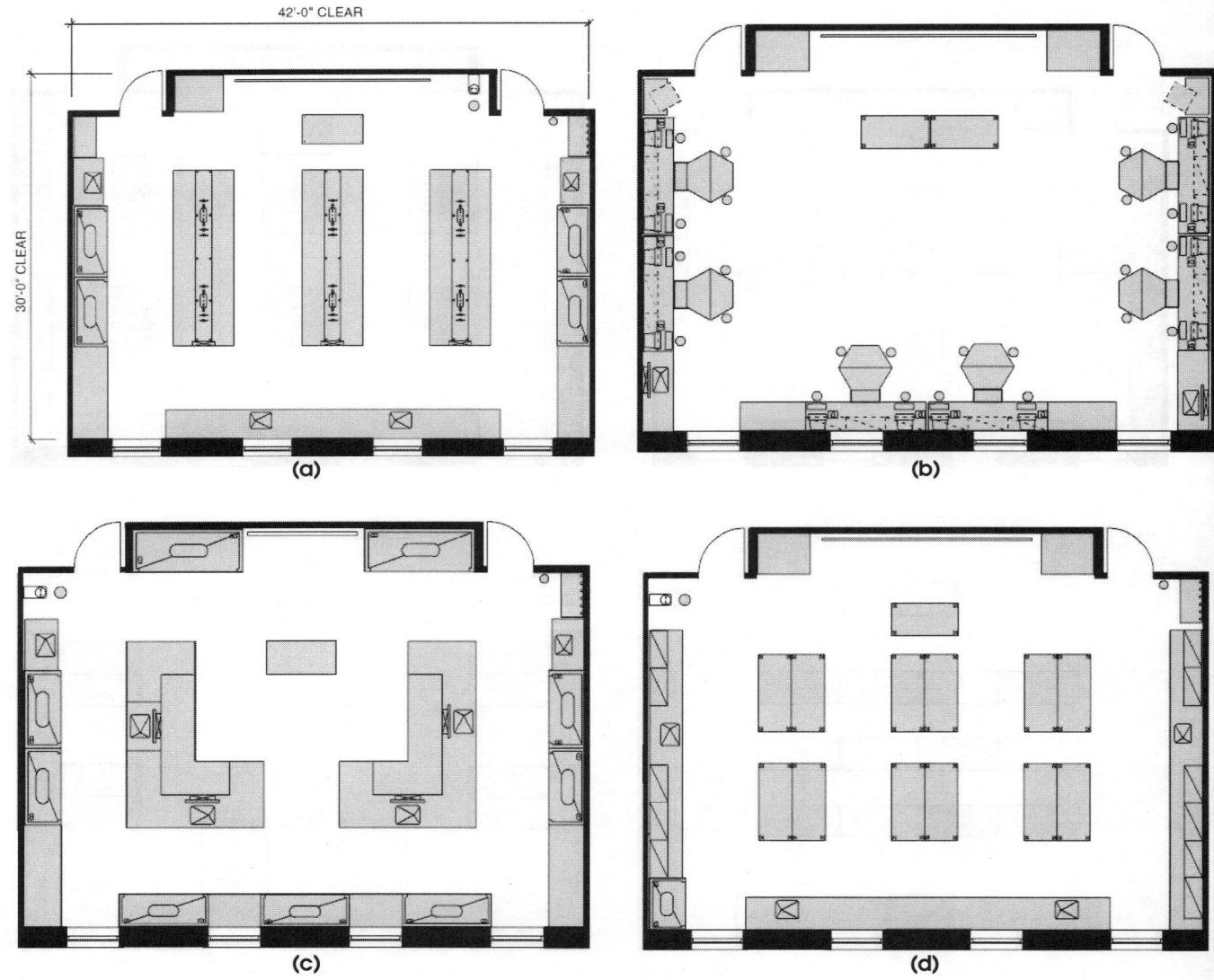

**Fig. 6. Physics laboratories**

## Chemistry Labs

There are usually three areas to focus on in chemistry teaching labs:

Adequate bench space for equipment and instrumentation
Fume hoods along perimeter walls
Write-up areas for documenting research experiences

Synthetic chemistry (organic and inorganic) labs generally require 3 linear feet of fume hood for each student.

All chemistry labs (Fig. 7) are wet labs requiring piped gases, heavy electrical and data services for instruments, and 100 percent outside air.

Chemistry support areas include chromatography labs, mass spectroscopy, nuclear magnetic resonance spectroscopy, and imaging. There may also be requirements for instrument rooms, stock rooms, and shops.

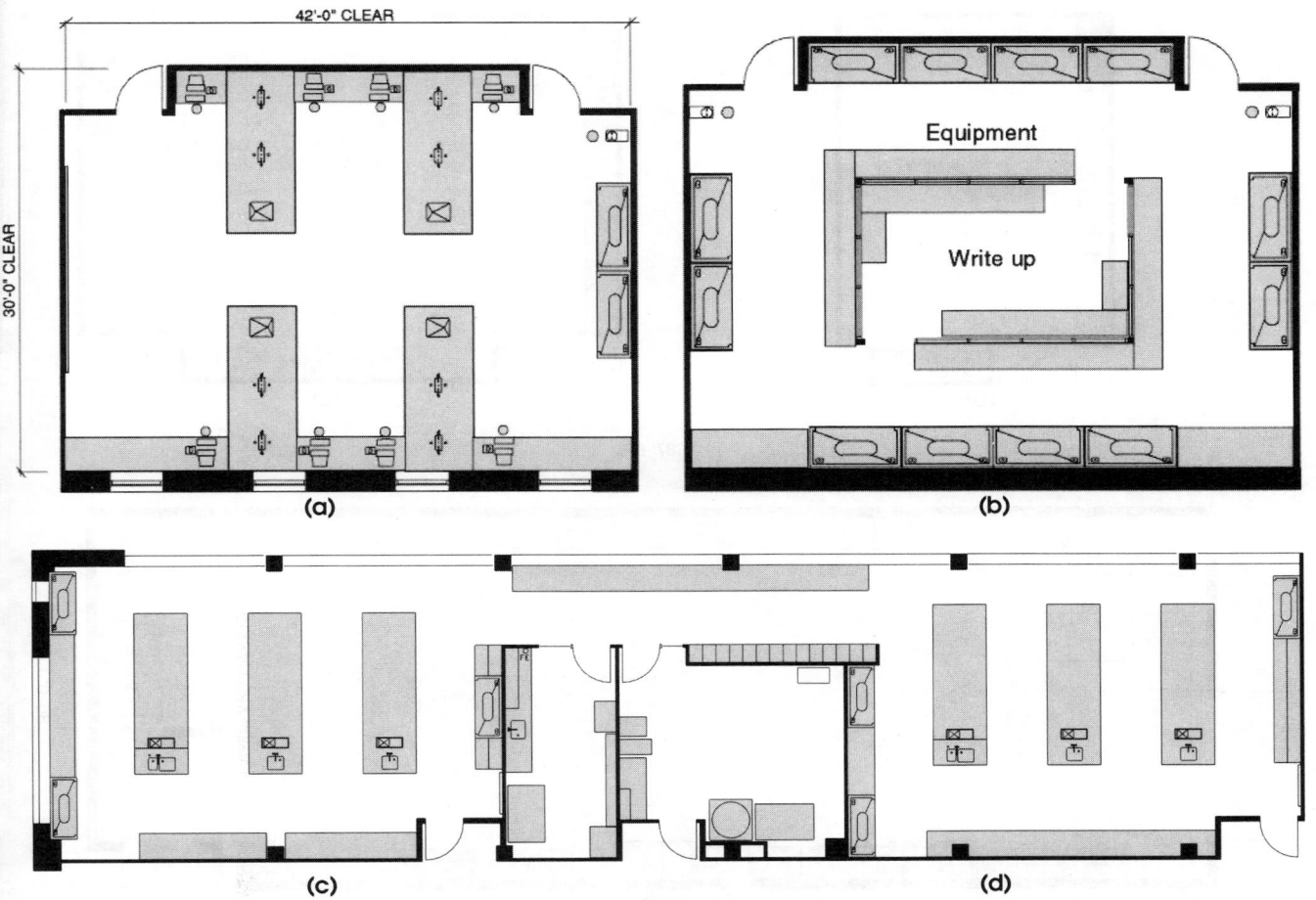

Fig. 7. Chemistry laboratories: (*a*) general chemistry (fixed peninsula benches); (*b*) organic chemistry; (*c*) general chemistry

### Engineering Labs

Engineering labs (Fig. 8) are typically like large workshops. The labs are usually open, with little fixed casework and utility services provided along the wall and from overhead. Engineering labs require large pieces of equipment or custom-made setups.

Key characteristics of engineering labs include the following:

- Flexible open space for large equipment
- More volume space for tall apparatus
- Overhead cranes to move large heavy equipment
- Possible location of labs on the lowest level of the building to accommodate heavy floor loads
- Wide and tall doorways to allow forklifts to haul in equipment

Engineering labs may require fume hoods and 100 percent outside air. There are also many dry labs for engineering research.

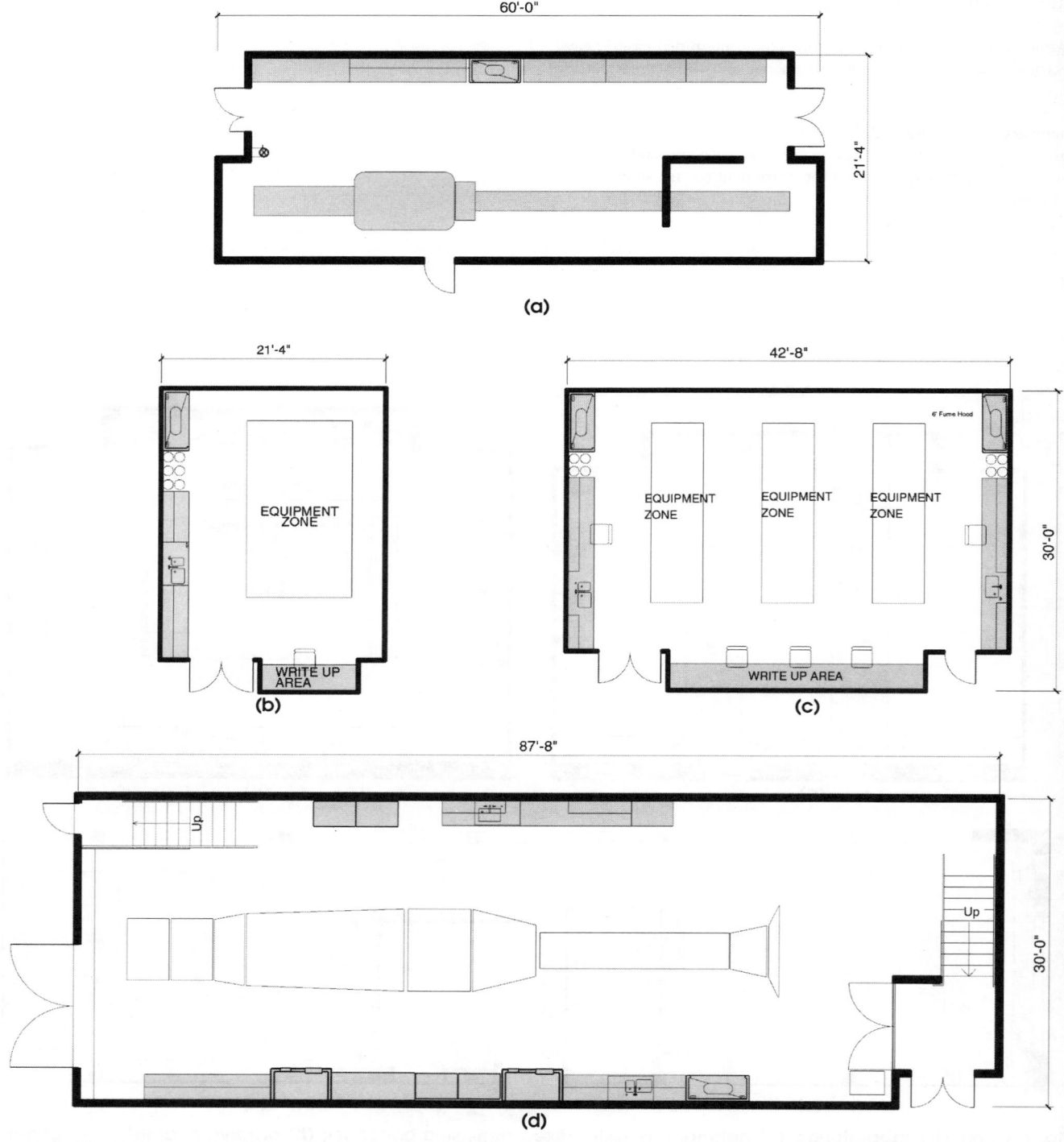

**Fig. 8. Engineering laboratories:** (*a*) gas-gun lab; (*b*) and (*c*) general labs; (*d*) from wind tunnel lab

**ELF Factor**

Another aspect of lab space needs is the equivalent linear footage (ELF) of bench factor. Typically the ELF is based on anything that occupies floor area in the lab such as casework, equipment, or storage. Today's concern for safety and environmental protection dictates the basic minimum allocation for an organic benchtop chemistry station as being no less than 20 ELF. The space consists of 8 feet of fume hood, 8 feet of bench, 2 feet of sink, and 2 feet of refrigerator-freezer. The biology labs, on the other hand, need far less fume-hood space but have a significantly higher need for ancillary equipment such as refrigerators, incubators, centrifuges, and environmental rooms. Therefore, the biology lab's requirements can easily exceed 30 ELF per person.

ELF values per person per discipline are as follows:

| | |
|---|---|
| Organic chemistry | 24 to 28 |
| Physical chemistry | 24 to 33 |
| Instrumental analytical chemistry | 33 to 41 |
| Microbiology and immunology | 20 to 31 |

Net lab square-footage-per-person requirements based on the preceding ELF values (10-foot-6-inch-wide module) are as follows:

| | |
|---|---|
| Organic chemistry | 126 to 147 |
| Physical chemistry | 126 to 173 |
| Instrumental analytical chemistry | 173 to 215 |
| Microbiology and immunology | 103 to 163 |

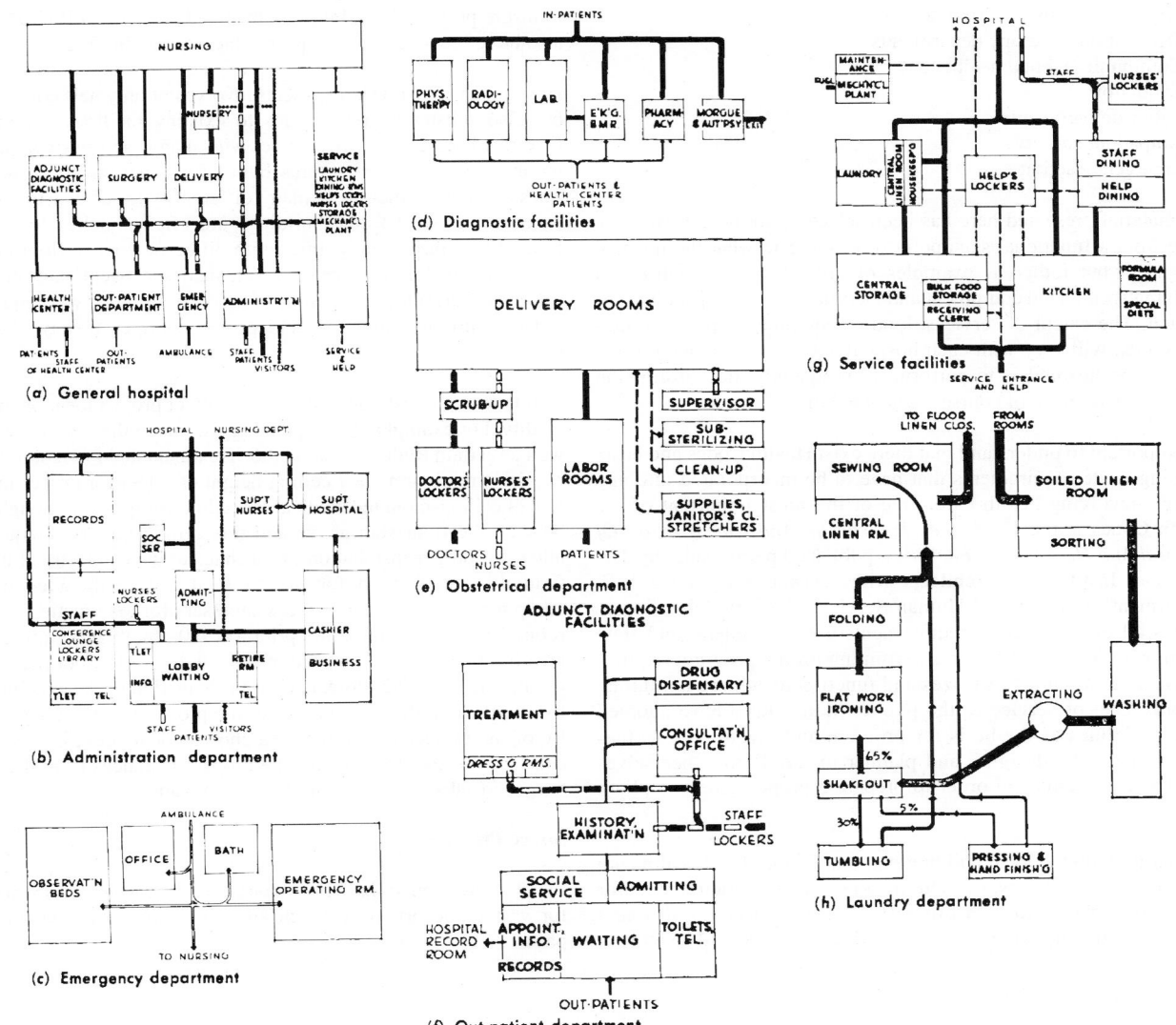

**Fig. 1. Flow charts. From** *Design and Construction of General Hospitals by Public Health Service,* **US Department of Health and Human Services**

# HOSPITALS (GENERAL)

## INTRODUCTION AND FLOW CHARTS

The hospital as a building type is composed of complex components, each of which could well tax the talents of architects, mechanical engineers, and the other professions and skills involved in their design and construction. Material relating to all these components would fill several books. Therefore, the following have been selected for discussion in this section:

Bedrooms
Nursing units
Surgical suite
Nursery
Pediatric nursing units
Diagnostic x-ray suite

*Author:* August Hoenack, Chief, Architectural and Engineering Branch, Division of Hospital and Medical Facilities, Public Health Service, US Department of Health and Human Services.
*Reviewer:* James H. Ogden, R.A.

Physical therapy department
Occupational therapy departments
Community mental health center
Laboratory
Labor-delivery suite
Outpatient activity
Emergency activity

The material presented here has been selected, not necessarily as a guide from a functional standpoint or to indicate what the hospital may need, but rather as examples of critical space organization involving specialized equipment and facilities which are peculiar to a hospital. The extent of services, kind of equipment, space requirements, etc., will vary with each hospital and must be related to the services the hospital is to perform. Consequently, the information presented here must, of course, be adapted in each case.

It is important to understand that there exist Health Codes and basic Building Code requirements that have to be incorporated into any projects involving health care. One of the most important of the Health Codes is the *Guidelines For Design And Construction Of Hospital And Health Care Facilities*, published periodically by The American Institute of Architects with assistance from the U.S. Department of Health and Human Services. This guideline incorporates all of the updated requirements used by federal and state health overseeing facilities in determining proper program requirements and minimum room sizes and function to achieve a minimal uniform level of service to the public. Many states have adopted these guidelines as the basis for program and layout review. It is important for the designer and planner to familiarize themselves with these guidelines in order to prepare a proper code compliant project.

Familiarity with the local building codes and other local health care codes is also mandatory, as there may be specific requirements for health care that have to be incorporated into the project. Local zoning codes are also important to review. The ADA Code should be utilized to insure proper accessibility by the handicapped. NFPA 101 should also be referenced to insure proper facility functioning.

Hospital and Health Care projects involve not only new construction, but also substantial renovations to existing facilities. Often these facilities have evolved over time, with many facilities containing a number of attached structures built over a period of many years. These structures may have many different types of construction; as an example, steel frame buildings are often attached to concrete framed structures, many times with different floor to floor heights, with many different types of mechanical, electrical, and plumbing services. Careful investigation of an existing facility is required in order to provide adequate and proper services to any alteration project.

Limitations of existing buildings may affect project location and feasibility. For example, new Operating Rooms in the Surgical Suite as well as certain Radiology and other Treatment and Procedure Rooms require a minimum clear ceiling height of 9 feet for proper installation of ceiling-mounted medical procedure equipment. Enough space beneath the floor slab above and this ceiling height is required to allow for proper installation of mechanical ducts, electrical lighting fixtures, steel support for the required ceiling mounted medical equipment, and all other services necessary for the functioning of the room. Existing facilities built prior to 1970 usually have limited clear area from ceiling to underside of slab, and floor to floor height were usually smaller. Therefore, careful investigation of the existing facility is critical in the early phases of the project to determine feasibility of the project within the area chosen for its development. New construction should allow for the proper clearances from the beginning, and subsequently easier future renovations.

**Space Planning**

Fig. 1 shows generalized flow charts for the hospital as a whole and for various departments which are not discussed in the following pages.

## PATIENT ROOMS

It was not the committee's purpose to include an analysis of the number of beds per nursing unit, or the proportions of single, double and four-bedrooms within given units. This study is limited to the individual room per se, to a review of numerous small but often vital details that make either a good room or an unsatisfactory one. These details are fine points that an administrator or architect should be familiar with before departing to something more original, if that should be his wish.

In general, the many room plans reviewed have basic similarities but many variations in detail. Accompanying plans (Figs. 2 and 3) have been specially drawn to illustrate the majority of features that will be discussed. It must not be construed that these represent ideal or minimum standards.

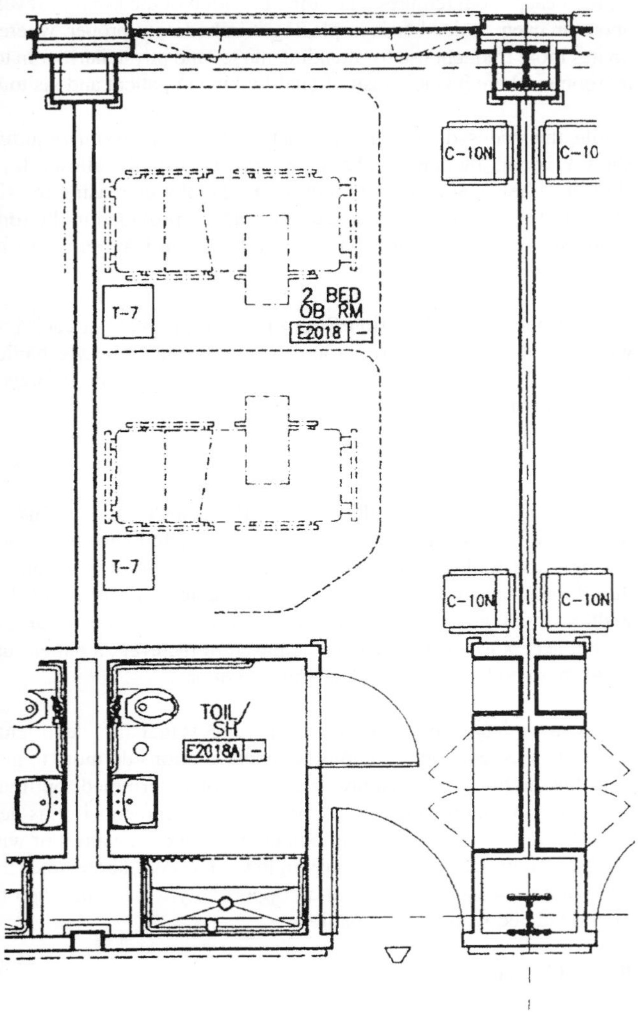

If required by codes or program, separate Isolation Rooms should be provided. These are single bed rooms for the containment of patients with infectious diseases that require separation from other patients. These rooms are usually entered by a small ante-room containing a sink. A separate toilet/shower room opening directly off the room is required.

### Size

First point of interest is the considerable variation in room sizes. Ranges of net clear floor area from corridor door to window stool, not including built-in wardrobes, vestibules, and toilet rooms, are:

Private rooms: 120 square feet minimum
Semi-private rooms: 100 square feet/bed minimum

Usually in new construction, a combination of private and semi-private rooms of two patients maximum is required. Three- and four-bed rooms are not desired, unless renovation of existing facilities does not allow for their exclusion. The arrangements and dimensions of rooms should allow a minimum of 3 feet between the sides and foot of the bed and any fixed obstruction. Multiple bed rooms require at least 4 feet clearance at the foot of the bed. Different layouts are caused principally by varied space requirements of one or two beds in combination with various plumbing facilities—they reflect the endless search for a common denominator which will have flexibility

**Fig. 2. Semi-private room**

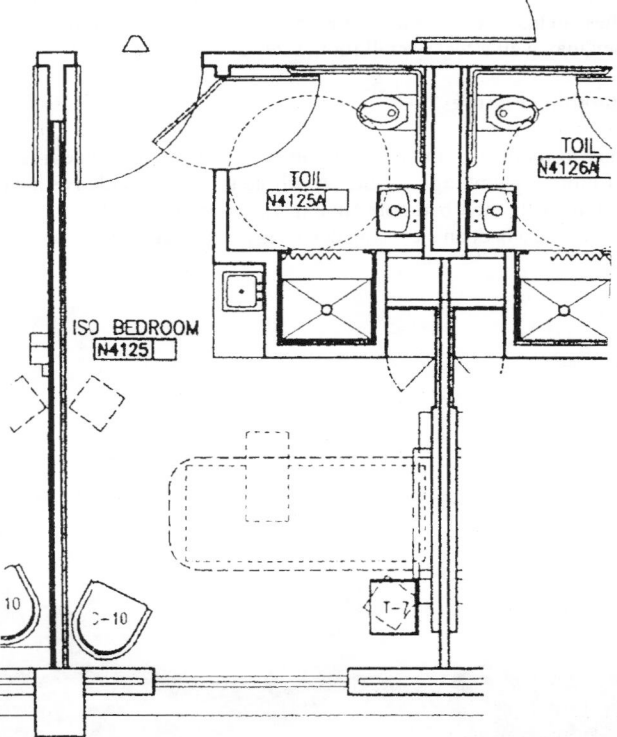

**Fig. 3. Private room**

*References:* Report by the AIA Committee on Hospitals & Health

to accommodate several combinations of room and toilet requirements within a uniform building dimension and fenestration without waste of expensive space. Lavatory, toilet door, or wardrobe door do not encroach into these clear dimensions in these rooms. For renovation work, multiple-patient rooms may have a clear work area of 80 square feet. In single bed rooms, the clear floor area may be 100 square feet.

### Closets

In almost every case individual hanging space is provided for each patient, often in the form of built-in wardrobes. One caution was offered that mirrors should not be so placed as to reflect light into patient's eyes.

### Furniture

There is uniformity in every plan reviewed in the way beds are set parallel to exterior wall, so that patients can look out windows without facing directly into the bright sky. Motor-operated high-low beds are also uniformly popular; it should be noted that they may be a full 7 feet-3 inches in overall length, not including any specialized equipment.

There is no uniformity in position of bedside table. It may be placed on near side of bed as one enters room, or on far side, or sometimes on patient's right or left, whichever way the bed faces. The typical bedside table measures about 16 inches by 20 inches.

Plans reviewed did not concern themselves with other furniture. These items take space and deserve attention in the planning stage as they may well affect overall room size.

### Plumbing Fixtures

Next to room size, the most important architectural problem is disposition of plumbing facilities. A private toilet is regarded as a basic feature with each bedroom. It is perhaps axiomatic that in almost every case a bedpan cleansing device is incorporated. 3 feet to 3 feet-

2 inches by 3 feet-10 inches to 4 feet-10 inches are the dimensions noted for individual toilet rooms, with grab-bars on one or both side walls. Locating water closet slightly off-center in the room allows a little more space on wider side for manipulating cleanser. The latter needs only cold water and is usually on the right as you face back wall. Some plans indicate a bedpan rack or cabinet within the toilet room. Toilet room layouts should generally follow a side-by-side fixture arrangement, with a minimum clearance of 5 feet. A check of local codes should determine the number of disabled accessible toilet/shower rooms required on each nursing unit floor. Proper 5 feet clear turning radius for wheelchairs is required in these rooms.

Several plans were reviewed which showed shared toilets between two single or double rooms. While this arrangement may save some space and expense, it presents its own problems such as added disturbance to patients, special door hardware, and lack of flexibility in room assignment to patients of opposite gender. A shared toilet is valid only in large hospitals in renovation schemes.

At least each room requires a lavatory. Location of the lavatory reveals about an even choice between placing it in bedroom proper, where it invites more frequent use by attending nurses and physicians, or in toilet rooms, where it is less institutional-looking to patient and visitors.

While the codes do not dictate that each patient room require a shower room, modern health care practice usually allows for a shower to be installed in the toilet room, thereby increasing the size of the toilet room to accommodate stall. If not provided in the room itself, then a shower room and separate tub room is required off the patient room corridor.

At least one private Isolation Room is to be provided at each unit, with a separate toilet/shower room off the room itself. Mechanical system has to allow for negative air pressure in the room to prevent spread of contaminated air.

### Doors and Windows

Standard bedroom door width is 3 feet-10 inches or 4 feet. This can be reduced by 2 inches with offset hinges. A slight majority of doors to single and double rooms are hinged on the side toward the beds, so that door when ajar serves to screen the patient. Toilet room door widths are 2 feet-10 inches, swinging both in and out into bedroom, so that access to a patient can be achieved in the event a patient in a toilet room collapses and falls against the door.

The wide variety of window treatments suggest that climate, orientation, esthetics, economics, and other considerations do more to govern this architectural feature than any predetermined optimum standard. It is interesting that administrators' comments in this general area say little about psychological or therapeutic values of wide versus narrow or high versus low windows. The committee notes that low window stools offer patient an opportunity to see out when his motorized bed is in its low position.

### Room Finishes

There is no strong preference for one type of flooring material over another. Usually a resilient flooring material is preferred for cleaning and ease of movable equipment issues. Walls can be either painted or utilize vinyl wall-covering material. Rubber or vinyl bases are preferable. A suspended acoustical system is more valuable for access to mechanical work than for its acoustical properties.

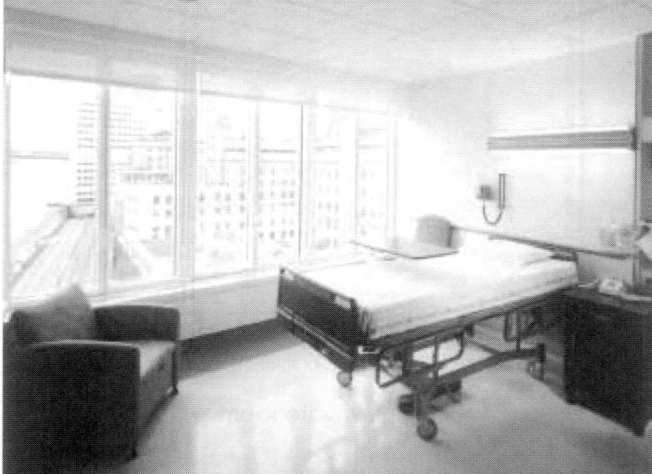

**Fig. 4. Patient room (Taylor Clark Architects; photo: Walter Dufresne)**

## Built-in Equipment

Built-in wardrobe-dresser combinations are provided, although separate movable furniture may be utilized instead. There are a variety of cubicle curtain arrangements in multi-bedrooms, from the simplest cross-room tracks to complete enclosures around each bed.

## Medical Equipment

Space for the required use of medical equipment, such as respirators and monitoring equipment, should be considered. If the nursing unit is to be for a specialized discipline, such as Orthopedics or Oncology, the room should be designed with the function of this equipment in mind, with the proper electrical and medical gas requirements provided.

## Lighting

A study of the rooms shows that no single or double rooms have ceiling fixtures for general illumination. In almost all rooms there is a wall fixture over the head of the bed. There are numerous fixtures on the market today for this purpose, providing varying combinations of direct and indirect light. The one prevailing comment of a number of administrators is that no wall light gives adequate illumination for examining the patient. Another caution is to control light in multi-bedrooms so that it will not shine in another patient's eyes. Almost all rooms have night-lights, either set in wall at a low elevation or incorporated in the over-bed light (Fig. 4).

A special notation for single rooms, where private duty nurses may be in attendance, is a ceiling down-light over a chair near the door into the room, at which location the nurse can guard a patient from unwanted visitors and at the same time read comfortably day or night without bothering the patient.

## Electrical Requirements

The audio-visual nurse's call is almost universal. The call system/speaker is located on the wall over the bed. A light is also used in the corridor outside the patient room door to indicate to staff which room requires attention, while a central control unit at the nurses station provides monitoring. On walls with two beds, each patient should have the ability to contact a nurse by a hand-held control unit.

In many hospitals, audio channels are piped in at the head of the bed, along with the television audio. Most TV sets are portable and are provided through a rental agency.

Emergency outlets are to be provided; check with local codes.

## Medical Gases

Oxygen is piped in from a central source, and delivered to rooms via outlets adjacent to patient. Outlets are 4 feet to 5 feet-6 inches above the floor. There is an even division of opinion concerning the location of oxygen outlets, either near side of bed as one enters room, or on the far side. Vacuum is provided in all rooms. Outlets are either grouped in the same plate with oxygen or they are separate, beside or below oxygen. Piped compressed air in bedrooms is also utilized. A headwall system incorporating these medical gas requirements, along with electrical outlets and emergency electrical outlets, is often used. These units range from a "rail system" attached to the wall above the patient bed to a wall height unit for more complex delivery of services, usually in more critical care areas.

## ADMITTING DEPARTMENT

Figures 5 to 9 from *Administrative Services and Facilities for Hospitals,* Health Services and Mental Health Adm., Dept. of Health and Human Services, Washington, D.C.

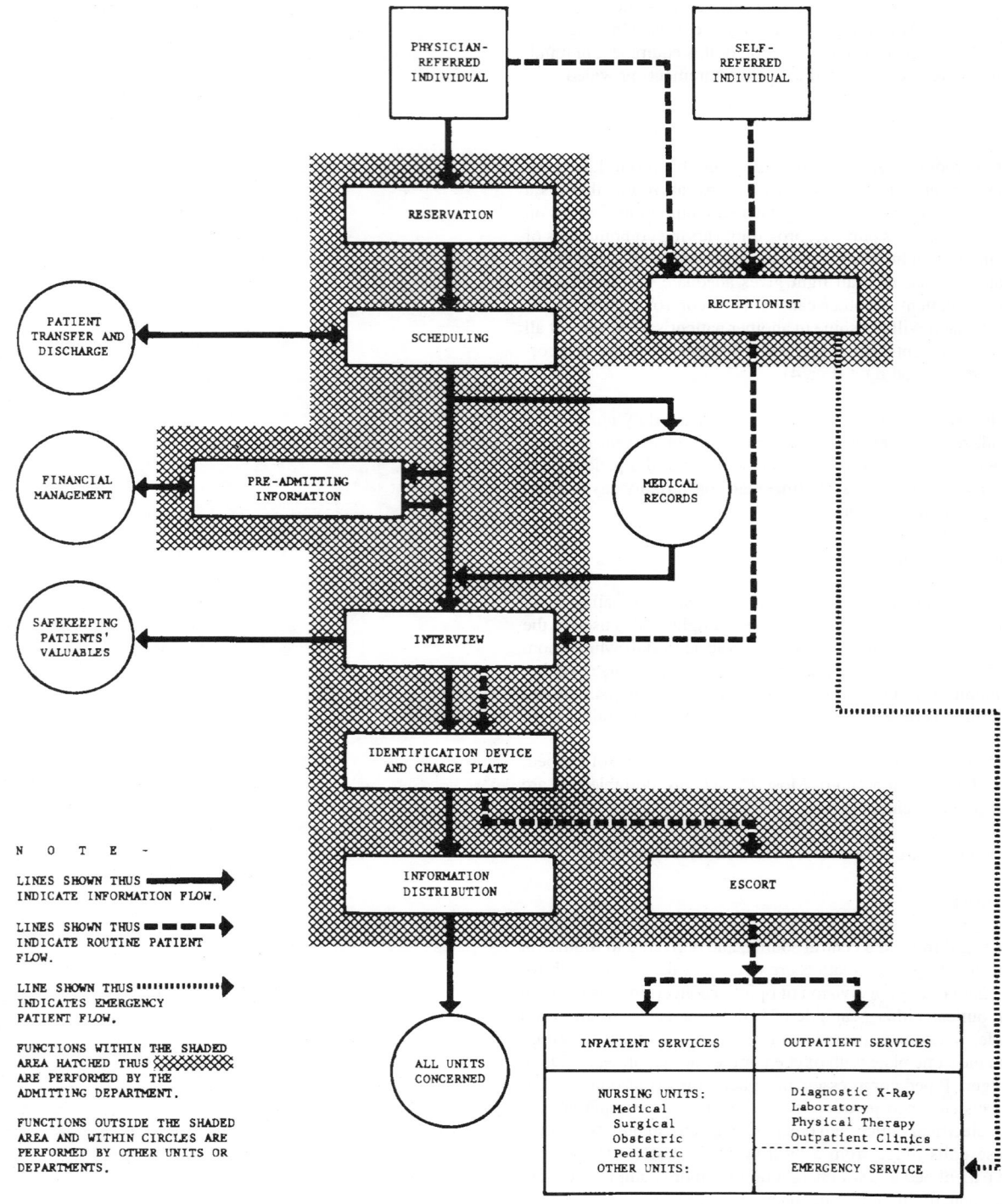

**Fig. 5. Functional flow chart of Admitting Department**

DOCTORS' ROOM

PUBLIC AREA

REVIEW CLERK

INFORMATION CLERK

ASS'T. M.R.L.

M.R.L.'s OFFICE

TRAN- SCRIBERS' ROOM

ADMITTING OFF.

STO.

FILE CLERK

WORK AREA

MEDICAL RECORD STACK ROOM

TOI.

RECEPTIONISTS' AREA

RECEPTION DESK

ADMITTING CUBICLES

COAT ROOM

WHEELCHAIR ALCOVE

MACHINE ROOM

M A I N   O U T P A T I E N T

W A I T I N G   A R E A

M A I N   L O B B Y

PARTITIONS SHOWN WITH DOTTED LINES INDICATE MEDICAL RECORD DEPARTMENT AREAS

NOTE: COAT ROOM AND TOILET ALSO SERVE MEDICAL RECORD PERSONNEL

0    4    8
FEET

### L E G E N D

| | | | | |
|---|---|---|---|---|
| 1. Control counter | 9. Sink top cabinet unit | 15. Wall-hung lavatory |
| 2. Clerical desk | 10. Manual plate printer | 16. Master patient index |
| 3. Secretarial swivel chair | (keyboard controlled) | (elevator file) |
| 4. Straight chair | 11. Plate file cabinet | 17. Appointment index |
| 5. File cabinet | 12. Electrostatic copier | (mobile, visible type) |
| 6. Utility table | 13. Work table with knee- | 18. Current bed occupancy |
| 7. Built in supply closet | hole and base cabinets | index (insert type) |
| 8. Shelf and hanger rail | 14. Supply cabinet | 19. Admittance chair |

## Fig. 6. Central Admitting Department with adjacent medical record department for a 100-bed hospital

---

ADMISSION PATIENTS' WAITING AREA

DIRECTOR & CREDIT MGR.O.

ADMIT. OFF.

ADMIT. OFF.

WORK AREA

WORK AREA

SUPPLY STORAGE

MACHINE ROOM

RECEPT- IONISTS' AREA

RECEPTION DESK

WORK AREA

PRE- ADMISSIONS OFF.

ADMITTING CUBICLES

COAT ROOM

TOILET

WHEELCHAIR ALCOVE

M A I N   L O B B Y

M A I N   O U T P A T I E N T

W A I T I N G   A R E A

0    4    8
FEET

NOTE: COAT ROOM AND TOILET ALSO SERVE MEDICAL RECORD PERSONNEL.

### L E G E N D

| | | |
|---|---|---|
| 1. Lounge chair | 16. File cabinet | 28. Work table |
| 2. Three place sofa | 17. Current bed occupancy | 29. Shelf over work table |
| 3. Lamp table | index (insert type) | for remote tape punches |
| 4. Center table | 18. Bed availability registers | 30. Automatic plate printer |
| 5. Health literature | (illuminated signal type) | (punched tape controlled) |
| display table | 19. Built in supply cabinet | 31. Manual plate printer |
| 6. Control counter | 20. Master patient index file | (keyboard controlled) |
| 7. Secretarial swivel chair | (elevator type) | 32. Electrostatic copier |
| 8. Utility table | 21. Pass window in door with | 33. Imprinter with lister |
| 9. Management swivel chair | hinged shelf | (foot controlled) |
| 10. Management desk | 22. Shelf and coat hanger rail | 34. Shelf truck |
| 11. Clerical desk | 23. Sink top cabinet unit | 35. Shelf truck work position |
| 12. Teletypewriter desk | 24. Admittance chair | 36. Supply cabinet |
| 13. Bookcase | 25. Universal air tube station | 37. Shelving for notification |
| 14. Straight chair | 26. Work table with kneehole | form stock |
| 15. Appointment index | and base cabinets | 38. Trash receptacle |
| (mobile, visible type) | 27. Plate file cabinet | 39. Wall-hung lavatory |

## Fig. 7. Central Admitting Department with adjacent medical record department for a 500-bed hospital

## NURSING UNITS

### Ventilation/Air Conditioning

Individual room units present no problems of cross-contamination of air from one room to another. Central systems do create issues if recirculation is desired. A check across the country indicates that opinion is divided on the extent to which central recirculation should be permitted. Check with local codes to determine the amount of recirculation allowable.

### Organization of Wall Outlets

An overall glance at the numerous room layouts studied by the committee emphasizes the clutter of wall outlets and paraphernalia of many kinds at head of each bed. A checklist for a well-equipped bed in a single room will include some 24 different facilities. In order to minimize the scatter effect at eye level, the committee suggests that half of these facilities could be consolidated in a low-wall outlet through a single flexible cable to bedside table, where many items would be within reach of patient. Only two items might then occur on wall at eye-level: the medical gasses outlets (code requirement) and the over-bed light. The following checklist gives an indication of the thinking of some of the committee on this point:

### Portable Bedside Panel (Patient's Control)

Nurses' call switch, pilot light, monitor light
General room illumination switch, dimmer control
Reading light switch
Duplex convenience receptacle
Jack for pillow speaker
Provision for TV remote control to be clipped onto panel
Provision for telephone instrument (bracket type)

### Nursing Units
*Integral with bed*
Bed control (within patient's reach, but with nurse-controlled cut-off feature)
*High on wall (60 inches or higher)*
Over-bed light fixture (direct and indirect)
Medical gasses outlets
*Low on wall (approximately 24 inches)*
Receptacle for portable bedside panel
Night light (switched from corridor)
Telephone jack
Double duplex receptacle (bed, oxygen tent, portable x-ray, heating pad, etc.)

Remote recording instrument receptacles (temp, pulse, respiratory)

### Double-Corridor Nursing Floor

Figure 9 shows a typical double-corridor nursing unit which is often utilized in hospital planning. It has the following advantages:

- Permits a closer relationship between the patient bedrooms and the nursing station and other service areas.
- Permits greater flexibility in segregation of patients for various medical reasons.
- Much of the staff activity and particularly conversation can be carried on within the service unit complex, thus cutting down noise in the patient corridor.

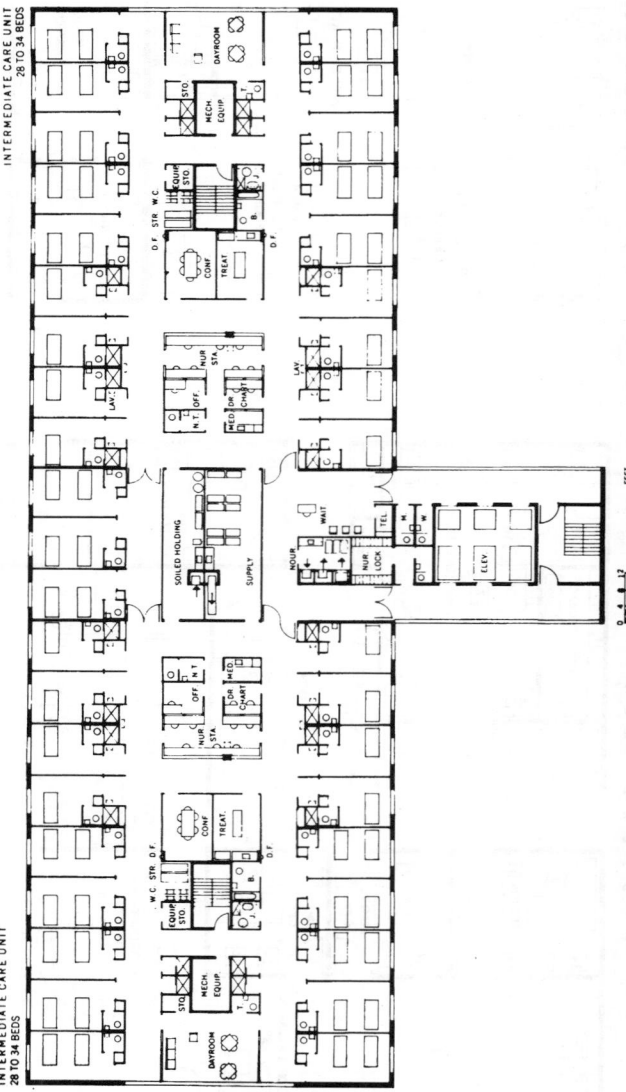

**Fig. 9. Double-corridor patient care floor made up of one 30-bed and one 32-bed unit utilizing centrally located mechanical conveyors for the handling of supplies and food-tray service. From Planning the Patient Care Unit in the General Hospital, U.S. Public Health Service**

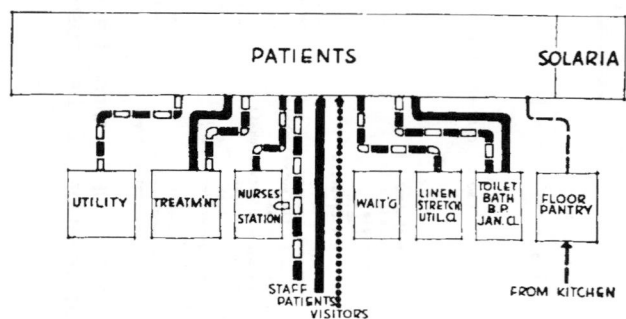

**Fig. 8. Flow chart of nursing unit**

Figure 10 indicates more clearly the nursing station and utility room arrangement. The clean utility is designed to accommodate carts for storing linens, utensils, and other supplies, which would be brought from a central supply and sterilizing unit. Elevators are located outside the nursing unit to cut down on the amount of noise. This would also permit a future nursing unit to be located on the other side of the elevators.

While this nursing floor consists of two 25-bed nursing units, many authorities believe that greater efficiencies are obtained in having a larger ratio of beds per nursing station. This particular nursing floor might easily be extended one or two bays, increasing the capacity to 52 or 70 beds.

This plan also demonstrates how an intensive nursing service can be integrated into the same module or bay which accommodates the typical patient room. One 6-bed intensive care unit is shown, and the adjacent typical double rooms can accommodate intensive-care patients when the need arises.

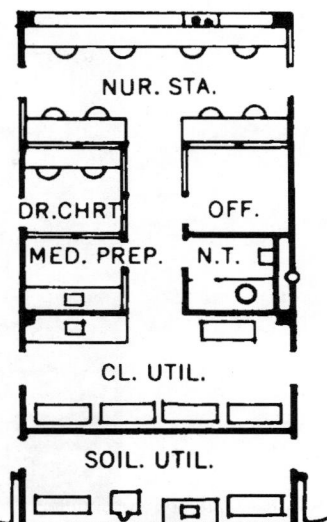

**Fig. 10. Detail of nursing station and utility cart**

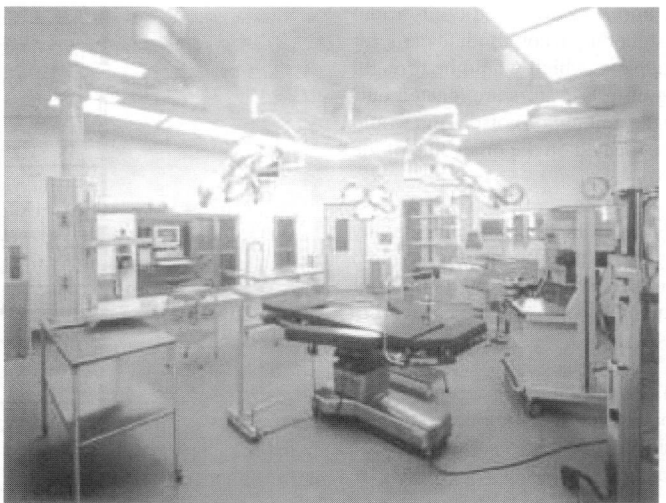

Fig. 1. Operating room (Taylor Clark Architects; photo: Walter Defresne)

## SURGICAL SUITES

The surgical suite of the general hospital is a very complex workshop. It is one of the most important departments of any hospital, and its planning is complicated by the diversities of opinion and experience of the many persons involved in policy decisions essential to development of a good program of requirements.

We say a program of requirements rather than plan. Before any intelligent planning can be done by the architect, there must be a meeting of minds on the size of department; i.e., the number and type of operating rooms and the work methods to be followed in the supportive areas. Administrators, surgeons, anesthetists, surgical nurses, all must participate in the preplanning analysis of needs and functional methods. The architect must have a wide understanding of various management procedures to be sure that all are discussed in reaching any conclusions with the particular group involved.

The number and type of operating rooms is the first major decision. In the general hospital, the tendency is to have all major operating rooms as nearly identical as possible to facilitate scheduling of various surgical procedures. Free floor space should be 400 square feet minimum, with a minimum width of 20 feet. Operating rooms that will contain special procedures such as cardiovascular and orthopedics require a minimum of 600 square feet clear, with a minimum width of 20 feet. Renovation projects may have 360 square feet clear in the general room, and 400 square feet clear in the special procedure rooms.

The planning and equipping of each operating room (Figs. 1 and 2) are based on a series of questions, such as:

Size
Usage
Environmental control*

Lighting—surgical and general illumination*
Intercommunications and signal systems*
Electronic equipment and monitoring system*
Service lines, such as suction, oxygen, nitrous oxide, compressed air (medical gasses)
Provision for x-ray, x-ray control, transformer, and necessary lead protection
Provision for video and other monitoring equipment
Safety precaution in hazardous areas
Cabinet work, supply cabinets and storage for operating table appliances
Need for clocks, film illuminators
Computer accessibility

The rapid development of cardiac and neurosurgery has created a demand for one or more extra-large operating rooms. This type of surgery requires a larger team of surgeons, nurses and technicians, plus a great deal of extra equipment, such as heart-lung machines, hypothermia equipment, etc.; also electronic devices for measuring bodily functions, i.e., electrocardiograph, electroencephalograph, blood pressure, respiration, body temperature, etc. Many architects provide an instrumentation room adjacent to or between two extra-large operating rooms to accommodate such equipment. Through-wall conduits accommodate wires and other leads of various appliances to the surgical field instrumentation room.

In the hospital as a whole, the actual patient area is only a very small percent of the total. The same is true within the surgical suite. The operating rooms themselves will account for only about one-fourth of the total area required for the suite with its supportive functions such as:

* These subjects have many ramifications.

*Authors:* Aaron N. Kiff and Mary Worthen Kiff, Colean, Sounder & Voss (Office of York and Sawyer)
*Reviewer:* James H. Ogden, R.A.

Offices and administration areas
Scrub areas
Work and supply rooms
Laboratory
Processing rooms (radiology)
Post-anesthesia recovery
Holding or induction areas
Lounge, locker, and toilet rooms for various personnel groups
Conference or teaching rooms
Circulation within the department.

The analysis of various suites shows a spread from 1,800 square feet to 2,000 square feet total gross area per operating or cystoscopic room (if included)—and every suite could use more gross floor area for storage, according to comments. Thus, a suite of eight operating rooms averaging 400 square feet each = 3,200 square feet x 4 = 12,800 square feet estimated total.

Within the surgical suite we have three basic zones predicated on three types of activity and circulation involved, and the degree of sterility to be maintained. The preplanning analysis of these areas is just as important as the determination of the number and type of operating rooms.

*Outer Zone*

Administrative elements and basic control where personnel enter the department, patients are received and held or sent to proper holding areas of inner zone: conference, classroom areas, locker spaces, any outpatient reception, etc.

*Intermediate Zone*

Predominantly work and storage areas; outside personnel will deliver to this area but should not penetrate the inner zone. The recovery suite, if completely integrated with the surgical suite, is an intermediate or outer zone activity.

*Inner Zone*

The actual operating rooms, the scrub areas, the patient holding or induction areas. All alien traffic should be eliminated. Here we want to maintain the highest level of cleanliness and aseptic conditions.

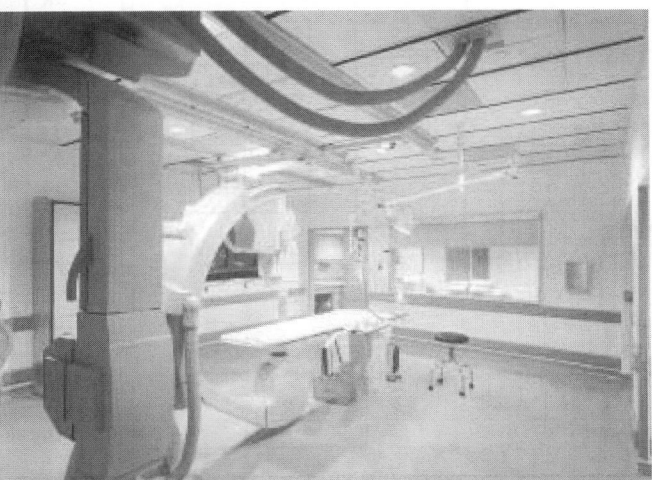

**Fig. 2. Cardiac catheterization room (Taylor Clark Architects; photo: Walter Defresne)**

Outer zone administrative areas have increased in importance. Offices are needed for the surgical supervisor, the clerks who manage scheduling and paper work, the clinical instructor (particularly if there is a school of nursing), possibly the chief of staff. There must be provision for surgeons to dictate medical records.

The patient is the primary concern. Who is responsible for his transportation to the surgical suite, and on whose bed or stretcher? How is he checked in and where does he wait if the room for which he is scheduled is not ready? Who has not seen surgical corridors lined with occupied stretchers for want of adequate holding, preparation, or induction areas? Another factor is added if any ambulant outpatient work is to be done. There must be provision for receiving and controlled waiting, dressing rooms, and toilets.

Lounge, locker, and toilet spaces must be provided for a variety of staff of both genders: surgeons, nurses, technicians, aides, and attendants.

A conference or classroom for departmental meetings and in-service training programs is easily justified.

The access to all these areas should be removed from strictly surgical areas, as people are entering and leaving in street clothes, and should not penetrate into other zones until after changing shoes and clothing.

The planning and equipping of the intermediate zone are based on the method of processing and storing of the thousands of items involved. It is fairly common practice for the central sterile supply department, elsewhere in the hospital, to be responsible for the preparation and autoclaving of all surgical linen packs, gloves, syringes, needles, and external fluids. The storage of these items to be used in surgery becomes the responsibility of the surgical department and adequate space must be provided for a predetermined level of inventory (see Fig. 3).

The method of packing and sterilizing instruments and utensils will determine the size, type, and location of autoclaves needed. Consideration must be given to inclusion of an automated sterilizer for cystoscopes, bronchoscopes and delicate surgical instruments which cannot be sterilized by steam or high temperatures. How and where instruments will be stored is another decision to be made.

Suitable storage space must be provided for:

Clean surgical supplies such as extra linen, tape, bandage materials, etc.
Parenteral solutions, external fluids, or sterile water
Essential drugs and narcotics
Blood supplies, bone bank, tissue bank, eye bank, etc.
Radium and isotopes used in surgery.

It seems impossible to provide adequate centralized garage-type spaces for bulky equipment not in constant use. It has been estimated that an average of 100 square feet per operating room is needed.

The intermediate zone also houses the facilities for handling waste, soiled linen, etc., and janitorial equipment.

The anesthesia service requires adequate space. It may spread over all zones of the surgical suite. Office space is required, work and storage space for equipment. Most important is the decision on where induction of the patient is to take place: centrally to all rooms, locally in induction areas (sometimes referred to as preparation or holding rooms), or in the operating room proper. There are acknowledged

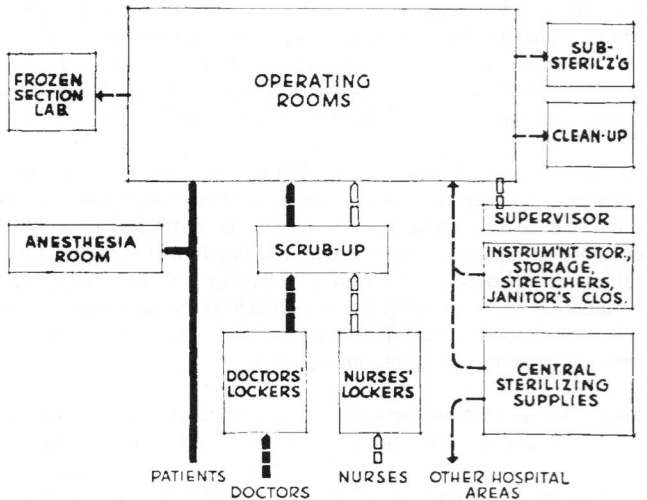

**Fig. 3. Flow chart.** From *Design and Construction of General Hospitals by U.S. Public Health Service,* U.S. Department of Health and Human Services

hazards in moving anesthetized patients and equipment. Induction areas should permit quicker turnover in operating room usage, but they also require more anesthetists and nurses to administer.*

The post-anesthesia recovery room has become an integral part of the surgical suite. The size will vary from one-and-a half to two beds per operating room. There is a close relationship between the anesthesia department and the recovery room.

Any frozen section laboratory should be located near the entrance of the surgical suite so that laboratory personnel need not penetrate the inner zone.

Any film processing facilities should be located to serve those rooms generating greatest load of film, normally the cystoscopic, urological, and orthopedic services. It should be accessible from a corridor to prevent alien traffic through any operating room.

Inner zone planning includes the operating rooms and their essential supportive elements. Decisions must be made on the type of scrub-up sinks or troughs and their location providing minimum travel to the operating room to eliminate chance of contamination after scrub procedure.

*Experience with various suites indicates that what was planned for induction frequently is converted to other causes.

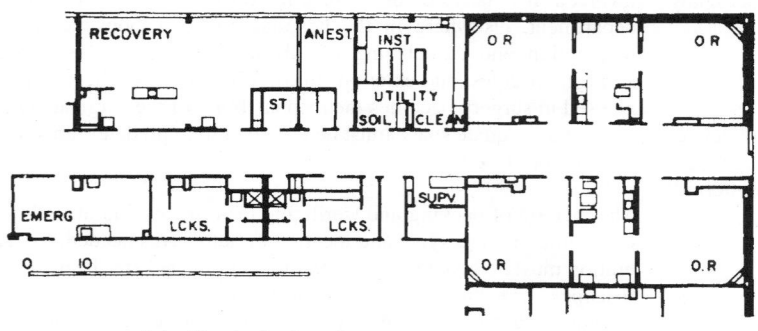

(a) *Sherlock, Smith and Adams, Architects.*

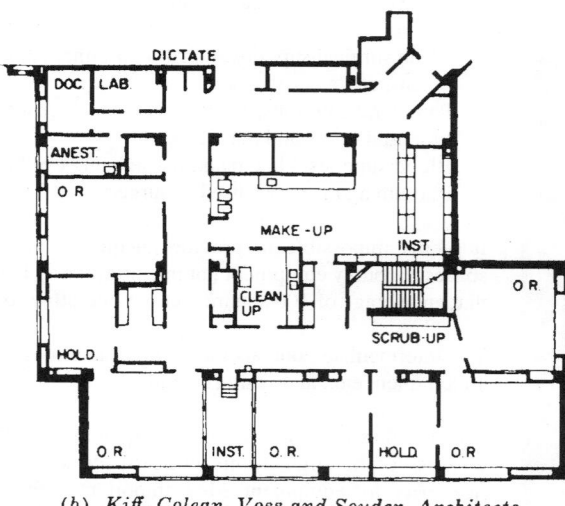

(b) *Kiff, Colean, Voss and Souder, Architects.*

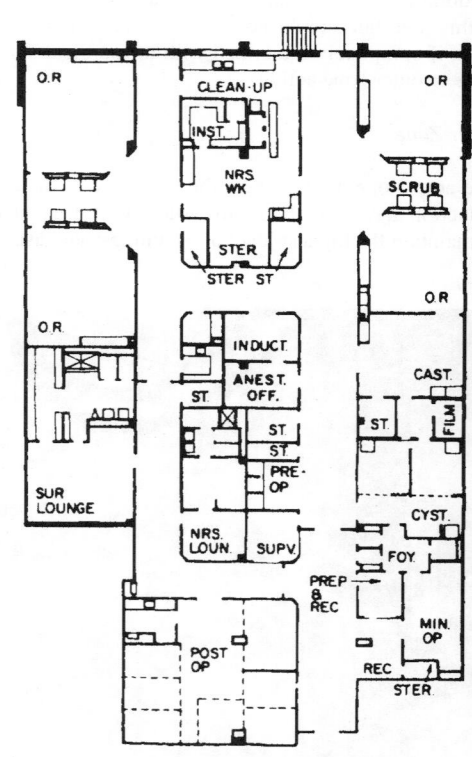

(c) *Louis Allen Abramson, Architect.*

**Fig. 4. Typical plans of operating suites** (*a*) Sherlock, Smith and Adams, Architects (*b*) Kiff, Colean, Voss and Souder, Architects (*c*) Louis Allen Abramson, Architect

The need for local substerilizing rooms is required, even though the trend toward centralization of work areas and sterilizing equipment, and the changing techniques of instrument packaging are reducing the importance of the substerilizing area. Circulation travel distance and work patterns are factors determining the need for decentralized work areas. Provide such areas so there should be staff access for servicing and stocking them without going through an operating room.

The program of need dictates the gross area required for the surgical suite. Recent developments indicate that more efficient departments with minimum travel distances can be planned in bulky square-like or rectangular areas. This tendency has affected the location of the surgical suite in relationship to the hospital as a whole. The suite is on a lower floor where it is more possible to spread out and achieve the desired shape, divorced from the usually narrow structural pattern of a nursing unit.

The surgical suite location (Fig. 4) must mesh with the total circulation pattern so that patients can be moved to and from surgery with a minimum of travel through other hospital services. Its location is also affected by its close relationship to three other major hospital services the x-ray department, the clinical laboratories, and the central sterile supply.

One other important factor in the location of the surgical suite is future expansion. Anticipate ways and means to permit growth in an orderly fashion without upsetting the basic relationship of internal organization or without extending lines of travel to unacceptable or uneconomical lengths.

## NURSERY*

As one of the areas in the hospital where patients are most vulnerable to infection, the nursery should be planned to provide the best means for the care, safety, and welfare of the infants. Although the plans and

*The study from which this article was condensed was prepared for the Division of Hospital and Medical Facilities, Public Health Service, and the Children's Bureau, Social Security Administration, by O. Bernard Ives, architect.

diagrams, shown here, have been developed for hospitals of specified sizes, the principles set forth apply to all hospitals, large or small, new or old.

Basic recommendations for planning nurseries that have been developed, based on clinical experience and study, include: limiting the number of infants in each nursery; wide spacing of bassinets within each nursery; promoting the use of aseptic techniques and individual care by providing, among other things, ample space and handwashing facilities; limiting the number of bassinets served by one nurses' station; separating facilities for premature infants and for observing infants suspected of having infectious conditions; and providing optimum conditions of temperature, relative humidity and ventilation. Figs. 5 to 7 show a variety of nursery plans.

Full-term nurseries (Fig. 8) should be located in the maternity nursing unit as close to the mothers as possible and away from the line of traffic of other than maternity services. An area of 24 square feet per infant is recommended, exclusive of the nurses' station.

The extent of the spread of infection in a nursery can be reduced as the number of infants in each nursery room is reduced. The optimum

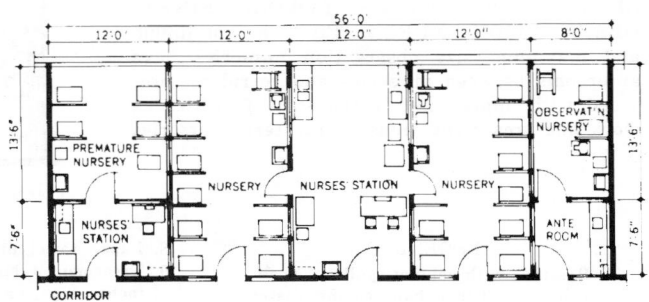

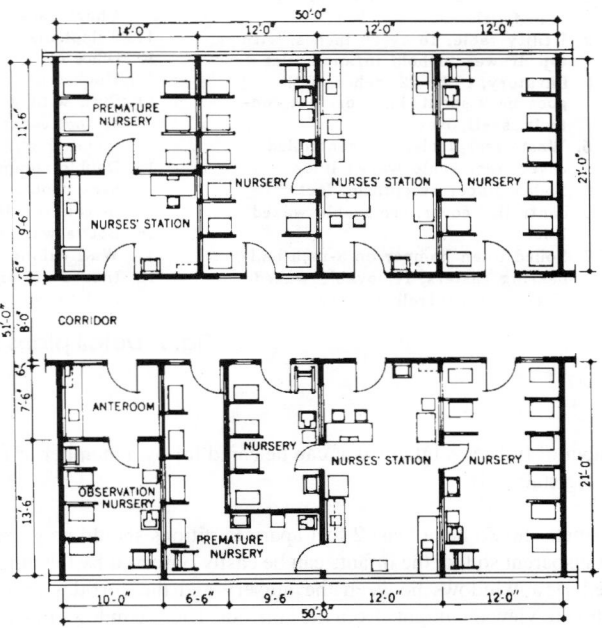

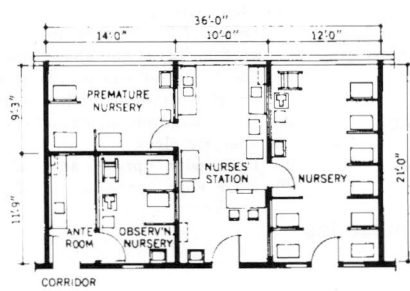

NURSERY FOR 440 LIVE BIRTHS PER YEAR
IN HOSPITAL OF APPROXIMATELY 50 BEDS.
The number of bassinets and maternity beds required is based on number of live births expected in hospital per year, rather than a rule-of-thumb relationship to the over-all bed complement. Six to 8 per cent (up to 12 per cent in poor economic areas) of the total live births will be premature (low birth weight of 5 pounds 8 ounces)

**Fig. 5. Plans for nursery in 50-bed hospital**

**Fig. 6. Plans for nurseries in 100- or 200-bed hospitals**

*References:* U.S. Department of Health and Human Services, Health Service and Mental Health Administration, Division of Hospital and Medical Facilities, Architectural and Engineering Branch.

**DETAIL PLAN, TWO EIGHT-BASSINET FULL-TERM NURSERIES AND NURSES' STATION.** Typical arrangement of a pair of full-term nurseries with nurses' station between allowing two nurses to tend 16 bassinets (or a maximum of 20) from one position. Recommended items of furnishings and equipment are shown located in what is considered their proper relationship to each other and to the complete nursery-nurses' station layout

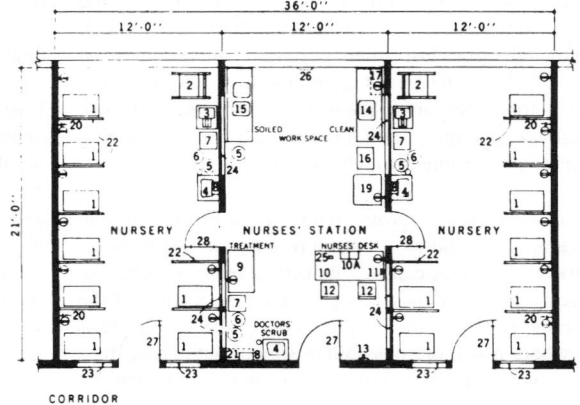

*LEFT:* **DETAIL PLAN, FIVE-INCUBATOR NURSERY WITH NURSES' STATION.** *MIDDLE AND RIGHT:* **MAXIMUM (THREE-BASSINET) AND MINIMUM (TWO-BASSINET) OBSERVATION NURSERIES.** The minimum and maximum size observation nurseries have anterooms between nurseries and corridors, provided with approximately the same facilities as work and treatment areas of full-term nurseries

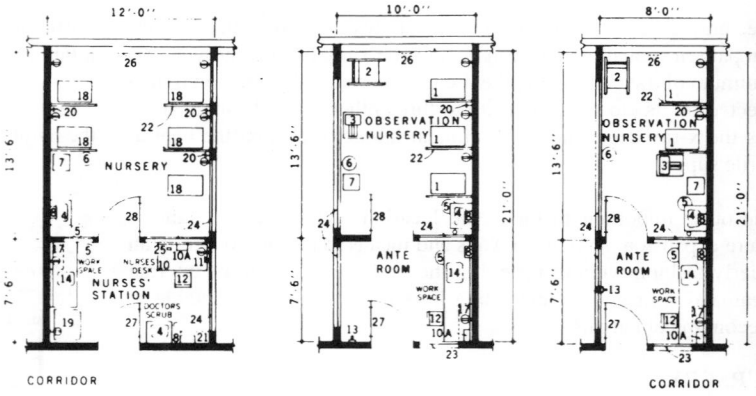

| LEGEND | | |
|---|---|---|
| 1. Bassinet with cabinet, pull-out shelf below, on 3-inch ball-bearing casters, with wheel lock | 8. Paper towel dispenser, enclosed type | 19. Refrigerator, with built-in thermometer |
| 2. Rocking chair with armrests, washable finish | 9. Treatment table, 24 by 36 by 36 inches high, on 3-inch ball-bearing casters, with wheel lock | 20. Double oxygen outlet, one for each four full-term—or each two premature—bassinets |
| 3. Utility table, 16 by 20 inches, with top drawer to hold infant scales | 10. Nurse's desk, 30 inches high | 21. Shelves (three), starting 42 inches above floor, for clean gowns, supplies |
| 4. Lavatory, 18 by 22 inches, with gooseneck spout, knee or foot controls, shelf over | 10A. Chart rack | 22. Cubicle partition, starting 30 inches above floor, with 2-foot-high clear glass or lucite panel, wall- and ceiling-hung metal frame |
| 5. Waste receptacle, foot-controlled cover, removable waxed liner | 11. Telephone outlet | |
| | 12. Office chair, swivel, without arms | 23. Clear wire-glass view panel in steel frame, 1,296 square inches maximum, bottom 42 inches above floor |
| 6. Soiled diaper receptacle, foot-controlled cover, removable waxed liner | 13. Hookstrip | |
| | 14. Sink with gooseneck spout, knee or foot controls, in counter 36 inches high, open below | 24. Clear plate-glass or lucite view panel, bottom 42 inches above floor |
| 7. Soiled linen hamper on 3-inch ball-bearing casters, removable waxed liner, foot-controlled cover | 15. Double compartment sink with gooseneck spout, knee or foot controls, in counter 36 inches high | 25. Hand-wind clock, desk type |
| | 16. Bottle warmer on portable carriage | 26. Electric clock |
| | 17. Wall cabinet | 27. Door with upper panel of wire glass |
| | 18. Incubator, on 3-inch ball-bearing casters, with wheel lock | 28. Door with upper panel of clear glass |

**Fig. 7. Detail plans for two types of nurseries**

number of full-term infants that can be cared for by a member of the nursing staff is 16.

Bassinets should be at least 2 feet apart. Partitions should be glazed or transparent so that the infants can be easily observed by the nurse. Fixed-view windows between the nursery and the corridor permit visitors to view the infants from the corridor. These windows must be safety glass set in steel frames and must conform to National Fire Code requirements. Fixed view windows in partitions between nurseries and the nurses' station or between two nurseries facilitate observation of all infants in the area. These windows may be of clear safety glass and should be as large as practicable.

A door direct from each nursery to the corridor is recommended to permit faster evacuation in case of fire and easier movement of bassinets from the nursery to the mothers at feeding time and to avoid traffic through the nurses' station. This door, hung in a steel frame, should have a safety glass panel and must conform to National Fire Code requirements.

Furnishings and equipment for each full-term nursery should include, in addition to the items shown in the plans, a suction bulb or a mechanical device with a soft rubber tip and individual catheters for individual infants for each full-term (and premature) nursery. Controls of the suction device should include a regulator to limit the suction to avoid injury to the infant. Suction should be provided from a central system.

## Neo-Natal

Premature infants require more specialized care than full-term infants. Thus, a premature nursery room should have a minimum area of 50 square feet per infant. A separate nursery is usually not indicated if less than five infants are to be cared for at one time. In such cases, space for them can often be provided in the full-term nursery. One nurses' station may serve two premature nurseries, or a premature nursery and a full-term nursery if the nurseries are paired.

In a premature nursery where suitable environmental temperature and humidity are maintained, only 50 to 75 percent of the premature infants may require incubators. Furnishings for premature nurseries will be similar to those in full-term nurseries, aside from the incubators.

An observation nursery should be provided for infants suspected of infection. When positive diagnosis is made, the infant is transferred elsewhere in the hospital and placed on isolation precautions. However, if diagnosis is not positive the infant may be returned to the regular nursery provided he has not been exposed to an infected infant in the observation nursery.

The observation nursery should be a completely separate unit, but it should be located adjacent to a full-term nursery with a glazed partition between to permit observation by the nursery staff. A minimum of 50 square feet per bassinet is recommended to provide adequate space for bedside care and treatment of the infant.

An anteroom should be provided between the nursery and the corridor. This area should contain the same facilities as the work and treatment areas for full-term nurseries.

The nurses' station serves as a control point and also provides workspace for the nurse and an area for treating infants. The nurse's desk should be placed so that the entrances from the corridor and from the station to the nurseries can be supervised. The nurseries should be visible through observation windows in the partitions.

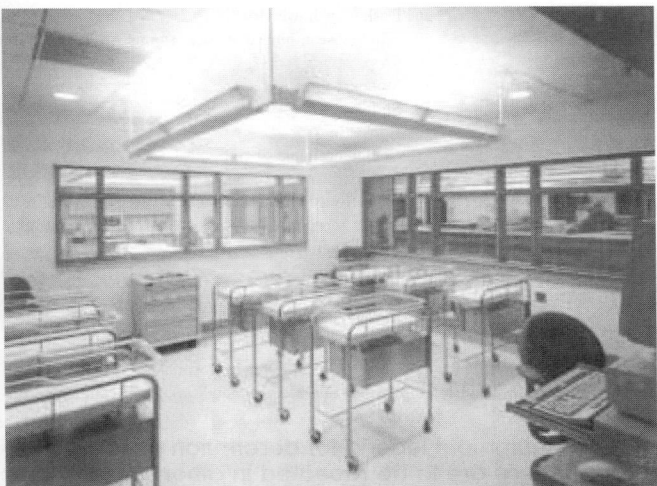

**Fig. 8. Nursery (Taylor Clark Architects; photo: Walter Dufresne)**

A station between two nurseries will require a double desk for two nurses. No more than two full-term nurseries, each housing 8 to 10 bassinets, should be served by one nurses' station.

The nurse's workspace should occupy a separate area at one end of the nurses' station. This arrangement affords the nurse full view of the infants while attending to most activities. The treatment area should be located near the entrance to the nurses' station so the physician need not walk through the workspace. Routine examinations and treatments should be carried out at the bassinets in the nursery. A physicians' scrub area should be located at the entrance of the nurses' station. The description of the full-term nurses' station also applies to premature nurseries, except that the treatment table is omitted. Other necessary areas, not shown in the plans, include formula rooms, nurses' locker rooms, demonstration rooms, and storage.

### Pediatric Nursing Units

The floor plans of pediatric nursing units shown in Figs. 9 and 10 illustrate suggested arrangements of the patient rooms and the supporting facilities described in the text. These plans are designed also to conform with other nursing units of the hospital.

The total bed count in each plan exceeds the recommended maximum of 20 beds per nursing unit because provision has been made for parents to sleep in. The number of sleep-in beds will vary with hospital policy and with the number of parents who are able or who wish to sleep in. All bedrooms are sized and equipped to accommodate full-size hospital beds as well as smaller youth beds and cribs.

Another feature is the extensive use of glass in partitions between rooms and in corridor partitions. This provides the visual control most necessary in pediatric nursing.

Rooms for sick infants and isolation rooms are located for direct observation from the nurses' station. The nurses' station is centered in each unit, thus reducing travel distances and allowing general observation of activity and traffic.

Workrooms are centrally located in the single pediatric nursing unit (Fig. 9) and conveniently accessible to both nursing units as shown in Fig. 10.

An important therapeutic area is the dayroom/playroom which may be used for dining and schoolwork as well. At least 50 percent of the children may use this room. It is located for ready observation and control from the nurses' station and at the same time designed to avoid disturbing patients in their rooms. Furnishings and equipment are selected for multiuse in these various activities.

The dietary facility for the unit is located adjoining the dayroom/playroom to provide convenient and sanitary service of meals.

The library/classroom is located at the quiet end of the nursing unit, convenient to the adolescent patients.

Waiting and interview rooms are located at the entrance to the unit. This provides an office for the physician and a place where the child's medical history may be reviewed with the parent.

See equipment legend for description of items numbered. Items of equipment are identified in only one typical room. These are to be repeated in other similar rooms unless otherwise numbered. The components of this plan are designed to conform with those of other nursing floors of the hospital.

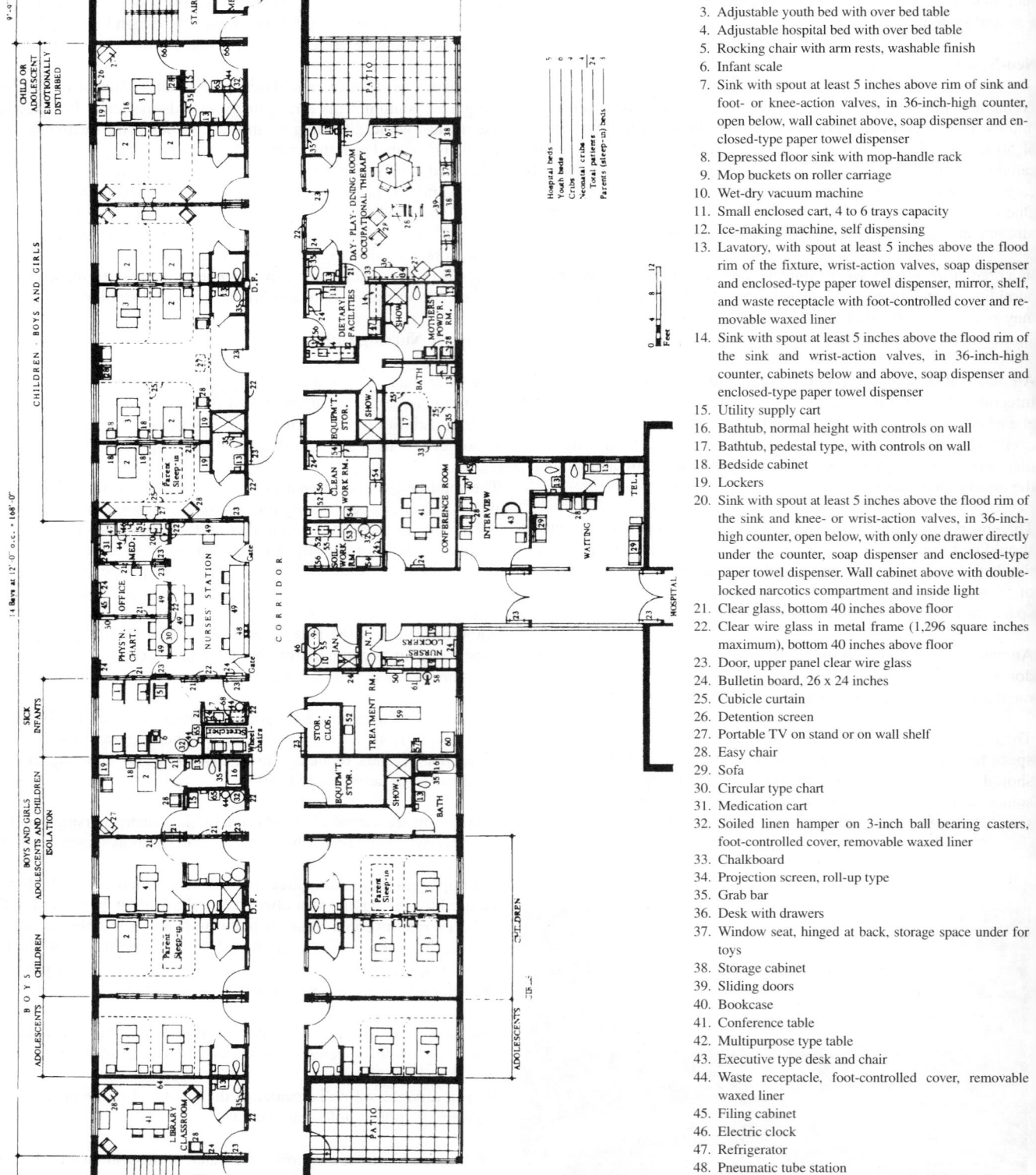

**Equipment Legend for Figures 9 and 10***

1. Sick infant's crib
2. Crib
3. Adjustable youth bed with over bed table
4. Adjustable hospital bed with over bed table
5. Rocking chair with arm rests, washable finish
6. Infant scale
7. Sink with spout at least 5 inches above rim of sink and foot- or knee-action valves, in 36-inch-high counter, open below, wall cabinet above, soap dispenser and enclosed-type paper towel dispenser
8. Depressed floor sink with mop-handle rack
9. Mop buckets on roller carriage
10. Wet-dry vacuum machine
11. Small enclosed cart, 4 to 6 trays capacity
12. Ice-making machine, self dispensing
13. Lavatory, with spout at least 5 inches above the flood rim of the fixture, wrist-action valves, soap dispenser and enclosed-type paper towel dispenser, mirror, shelf, and waste receptacle with foot-controlled cover and removable waxed liner
14. Sink with spout at least 5 inches above the flood rim of the sink and wrist-action valves, in 36-inch-high counter, cabinets below and above, soap dispenser and enclosed-type paper towel dispenser
15. Utility supply cart
16. Bathtub, normal height with controls on wall
17. Bathtub, pedestal type, with controls on wall
18. Bedside cabinet
19. Lockers
20. Sink with spout at least 5 inches above the flood rim of the sink and knee- or wrist-action valves, in 36-inch-high counter, open below, with only one drawer directly under the counter, soap dispenser and enclosed-type paper towel dispenser. Wall cabinet above with double-locked narcotics compartment and inside light
21. Clear glass, bottom 40 inches above floor
22. Clear wire glass in metal frame (1,296 square inches maximum), bottom 40 inches above floor
23. Door, upper panel clear wire glass
24. Bulletin board, 26 x 24 inches
25. Cubicle curtain
26. Detention screen
27. Portable TV on stand or on wall shelf
28. Easy chair
29. Sofa
30. Circular type chart
31. Medication cart
32. Soiled linen hamper on 3-inch ball bearing casters, foot-controlled cover, removable waxed liner
33. Chalkboard
34. Projection screen, roll-up type
35. Grab bar
36. Desk with drawers
37. Window seat, hinged at back, storage space under for toys
38. Storage cabinet
39. Sliding doors
40. Bookcase
41. Conference table
42. Multipurpose type table
43. Executive type desk and chair
44. Waste receptacle, foot-controlled cover, removable waxed liner
45. Filing cabinet
46. Electric clock
47. Refrigerator
48. Pneumatic tube station

*Figures 9 and 10 from Manual for the Care of Children in Hospitals, US Dept. of Health and Human Services, Division of Hospital and Medical Facilities, Architectural and Engineering Branch.

**Fig. 9. Pediatric nursing unit for hospitals in the 200-bed range. See equipment legend for description of items numbered. Items of equipment are identified in only one typical room. These are to be repeated in other similar rooms unless otherwise numbered. The components of this plan are designed to conform with those of other nursing floors of the hospital**

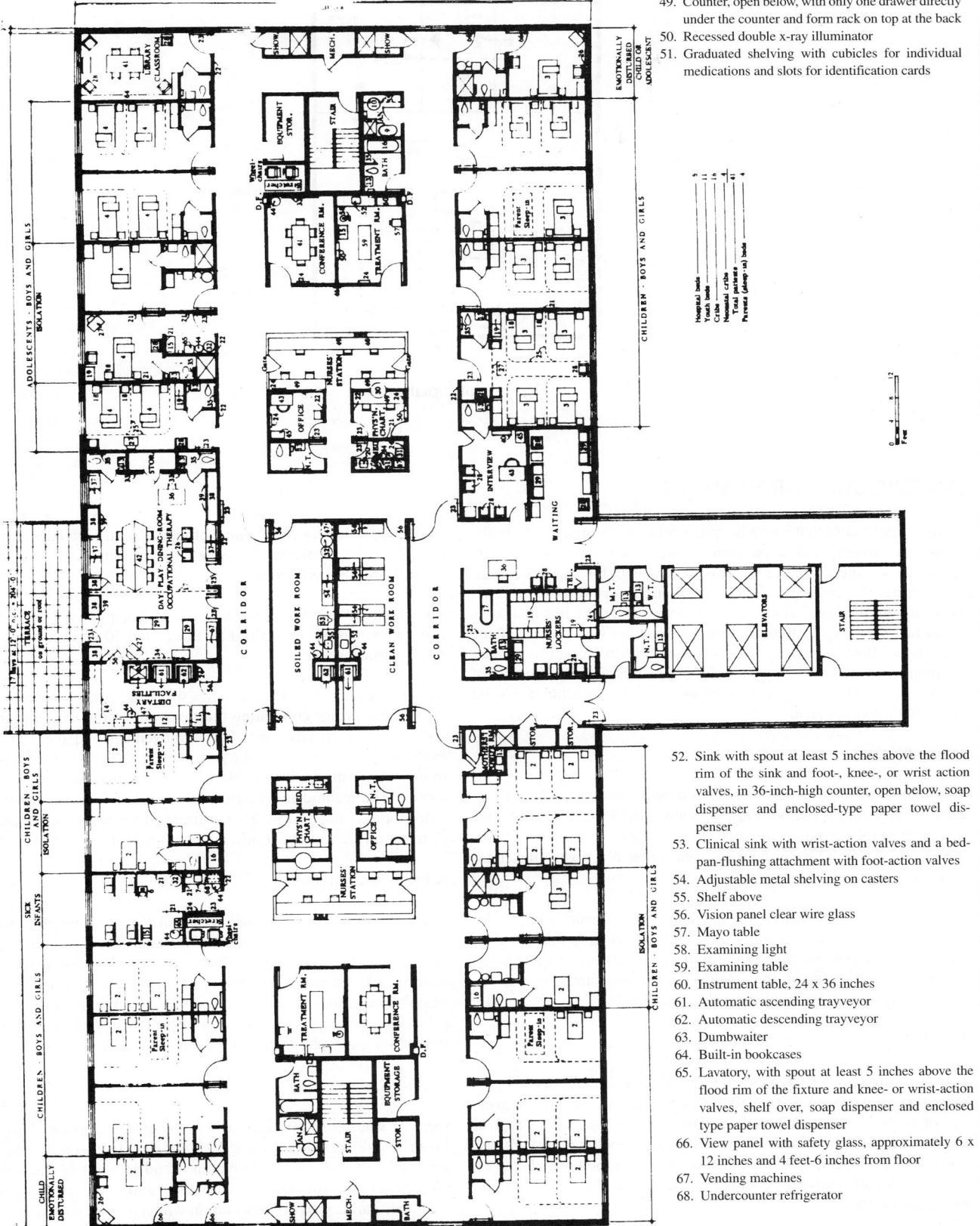

49. Counter, open below, with only one drawer directly under the counter and form rack on top at the back
50. Recessed double x-ray illuminator
51. Graduated shelving with cubicles for individual medications and slots for identification cards

52. Sink with spout at least 5 inches above the flood rim of the sink and foot-, knee-, or wrist action valves, in 36-inch-high counter, open below, soap dispenser and enclosed-type paper towel dispenser
53. Clinical sink with wrist-action valves and a bed-pan-flushing attachment with foot-action valves
54. Adjustable metal shelving on casters
55. Shelf above
56. Vision panel clear wire glass
57. Mayo table
58. Examining light
59. Examining table
60. Instrument table, 24 x 36 inches
61. Automatic ascending trayveyor
62. Automatic descending trayveyor
63. Dumbwaiter
64. Built-in bookcases
65. Lavatory, with spout at least 5 inches above the flood rim of the fixture and knee- or wrist-action valves, shelf over, soap dispenser and enclosed type paper towel dispenser
66. View panel with safety glass, approximately 6 x 12 inches and 4 feet-6 inches from floor
67. Vending machines
68. Undercounter refrigerator

**Fig. 10. Pediatric nursing unit for hospitals in the 400-bed range**

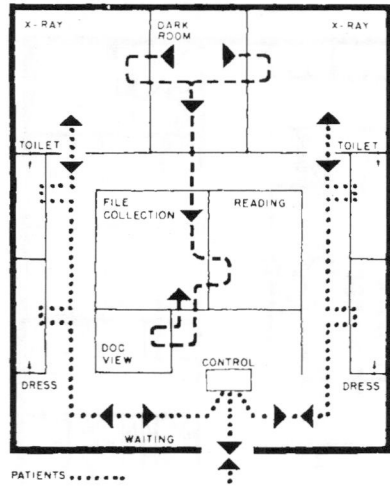

**Fig. 1. Traffic patterns**

# DIAGNOSTIC X-RAY SUITES

Studies have found that many hospitals allot inadequate space to the x-ray department, and expansion is often impractical. Adequate space for waiting, toilets, and dressing rooms helps insure continuous routines in handling patients. An unsatisfactory layout is a detriment to both the hospital and the radiologist since the hospital loses potential revenue, and the radiologist's time, as well as that of the staff, is needlessly wasted. This is particularly important to a small hospital which has a visiting radiologist for it is to the advantage of the hospital and radiologist to schedule as many examinations are possible during his visit.

## LOCATION

The diagnostic x-ray department should be located on the first floor, conveniently accessible both to outpatients and inpatients. It is also desirable to locate the department close to the elevators and adjoining the Emergency Department and near other diagnostic and treatment facilities.

The functional requirements of the department are usually best satisfied by locating the x-ray rooms at the end of a wing. In this location, the activity within the department will not be disturbed by through traffic to other parts of the hospital, and less shielding will be required because of the exterior walls (see Fig. 1).

## PLAN A

Plan A illustrates an x-ray suite that will provide an efficiently operating service for about 8,400 patient examinations yearly, or an average of about 35 examinations daily. This average workload is typical in a hospital of approximately 100 beds (or somewhat more) with an outpatient x-ray service. Unforeseen scheduling problems, of course, will occasionally cause the average of 35 examinations per day to be exceeded (see Fig. 2).

The staff needed for this volume of work usually includes: 1 radiologist, 2 or 3 technicians, 1 secretary-receptionist, 1 secretary-file clerk, 1 orderly (as needed).

This plan will permit the workload to be augmented at least 50 percent by increasing the staff, if no more than 20 percent of the X-ray work is fluoroscopic.

Among the desirable characteristics that this plan attempts to provide for is the need for correlating the functions of the working group to obtain maximum efficiency. The arrangement of patient areas and examination rooms around the perimeter, with the administrative staff in the center, makes it possible for these units to operate more efficiently. The technicians' corridor in the rear of the department provides for easy access to the x-ray rooms, film processing rooms, and distribution areas without interference from patients' cross traffic.

### Administration Spaces

Every radiologist has specific ideas on the most suitable ways for arranging and operating the administrative functions of the x-ray department. Some of the variables involved are assignment of personnel and functions, reception of patients, sequence of patient examinations, film distribution, and staff viewing facilities. This plan provides for flexibility of space arrangements by allowing for variation of several of the operations within the administrative unit.

*Waiting Room*

General waiting space is located at the entrance to the department. From here the patient is directed to an assigned dressing room. A separate area, to the left of the entrance and in sight of the secretary-receptionist, is provided for wheelchair and stretcher patients. This section is partitioned off by a curtain which may be partially drawn to

---

*Authors:* Wilbur R. Taylor, Clifford E. Nelson, MD, and William W. McMaster

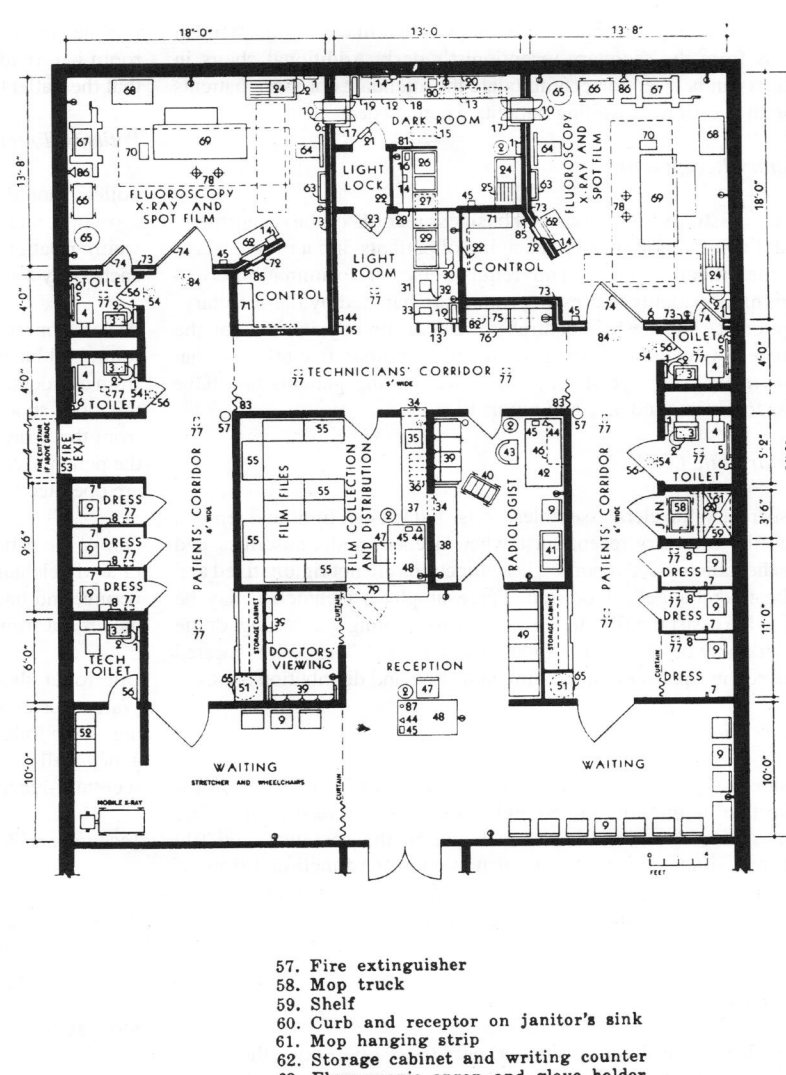

## LEGEND

1. Paper towel dispenser
2. Waste paper receptacle
3. Lavatory
4. Wall-hung water closet
5. Continuous grab bar
6. Emergency calling station (push button)
7. Hook strip
8. Mirror and shelf below
9. Straight chair
10. Cassette pass box
11. Film loading counter
12. Film storage bin
13. Film hanger racks under counter
14. Safelight
15. Ceiling light, white and red
16. Timer
17. Counter with storage cabinets below
18. Cassette storage bins
19. Trash deposit cabinet
20. Cassette cover retainer and wall guard
21. Door with light-proof louver in upper panel
22. Access panel
23. Door with light-proof louver in lower panel
24. Utility sink with drainboard
25. Refrigerating unit under drainboard
26. Developing tank with thermostatic mixing valve
27. Through-the-wall fixing tank
28. Light-proof panel
29. Washing tank
30. X-ray film illuminator (wet viewing)
31. Film dryer
32. Film dryer exhaust to outside
33. Film corner cutter
34. Film pass slot
35. Flush-mounted counter illuminator
36. Film sorting bins above counter
37. Film sorting counter
38. Counter with cabinets below
39. On-wall or mobile film illuminators
40. Temporary film file cart
41. Stereoscope
42. Executive type desk
43. Executive type chair
44. Telephone outlet
45. Intercommunication system outlet
46. Bookshelves, 42 in. by 14 in.
47. Typist chair
48. Typist desk
49. Filing cabinet, letter size
50. Gown storage, open shelves, storage cabinet above
51. Gown storage, open shelving with laundry hamper below
52. Technicians' lockers
53. Fire door
54. Dome light, buzzer and annunciator at receptionist's desk
55. Closed metal film files, 5 shelves high
56. Hook on toilet side of door

57. Fire extinguisher
58. Mop truck
59. Shelf
60. Curb and receptor on janitor's sink
61. Mop hanging strip
62. Storage cabinet and writing counter
63. Fluoroscopic apron and glove holder
64. Fluoroscopic chair
65. Laundry hamper
66. Clean linen cart
67. Cassette changer
68. Transformer
69. Radiographic fluoroscopic unit with spot film device
70. Foot stool
71. Control unit
72. Leaded glass view window
73. Lead lining (or other shielding material) as required
74. Lead-lined door, light proofed
75. Barium sink
76. Barium storage (below counter)
77. Red light for dark adaptation
78. Fluoroscopic ceiling light
79. Counter with gate
80. Film identifier, cabinet below
81. Anti-splash panel
82. Wall cabinet over sink
83. Curtain, floor to ceiling
84. Warning light
85. Microphone
86. Loudspeaker
87. Annunciator (for emergency calling station)

### Fig. 2. Diagnostic radiographic suite, Plan A

provide privacy, yet afford the necessary surveillance of unattended patients from the secretary-receptionist's desk. Additional chairs in this area can be used to accommodate the attendants of these patients or for an overflow of waiting patients when needed.

### Secretary-Receptionist

The administrative functions and business records of the department, scheduling of appointments, receiving of patients, input of the necessary identification forms and requisitions for examinations, and assigning of patients to dressing rooms are handled by the secretary-receptionist. The desk is centrally located, directly in front of the entrance between the waiting room and administrative area, so that the secretary-receptionist may supervise waiting patients and have access to correspondence and report files.

### Secretary-File Clerk

The secretary-file clerk assembles, sorts, and files all films and reports, assists the secretary-receptionist when needed, and transcribes and types the radiologists' reports. These functions are not rigidly fixed and can be interchanged, if desired. For example, a technician may be assigned to assist the file clerk with film assembling and sorting, or the file clerk may be given other functions as needed. The desk is located near a counter-partition in the film collection and distribution area.

### Doctors' Viewing Area

The doctors' viewing area is located near the office of the radiologist so that he may be immediately available for consultation. The room is near the film files, convenient to the secretary and file clerk, and situated so as not to intrude upon the functional flow of the work. Its location within the administrative unit provides privacy so that diagnostic comments and discussions will not be overheard by patients.

### Radiologist's Office

This office is conveniently situated near the x-ray rooms, the secretary receptionist's desk and the filing distribution area, and is less accessible to the public; it is also provided with a door which opens directly to the technicians' corridor.

### Film Files

The film files are located in the collection and distribution area and convenient to the radiologist's office. It is desirable to keep active films for at least five years. After that time, additional storage space elsewhere will be needed for the less active files. Closed front metal x-ray files are recommended. Teaching files may not be needed, but if desired, a section of the active files may be allotted for this use.

## General Facilities

### Dressing Rooms

Dressing rooms for each x-ray machine should be provided so that the equipment and staff can function without delay. Each dressing room should be equipped with a bench, clothes hook, mirror, and a shelf below the mirror. For the protection of patients' valuables, the doors may be equipped with locks, or centrally located lockers may be provided. Where doors are installed, they should swing outward to avoid the possibility of being blocked by a patient and should be at least 12 inches from the floor.

For the convenience of patients in wheelchairs, an outsized dressing room is provided. Instead of a door, it is equipped with a curtain so that the patient can maneuver easily.

### Patients' Toilet Rooms

Toilets should be immediately available for patients undergoing fluoroscopy, and similar facilities should be conveniently available for waiting patients. A minimum of two toilets should be provided for each x-ray room. All toilets should be located near the x-ray rooms.

At least one toilet room should be directly accessible to each x-ray room and have an opening into the corridor. To prevent the patients from accidentally opening the door between the toilet and x-ray room, this door should be equipped with hardware which is operable only from the x-ray room. The doors of the toilet rooms which open into the patients' corridor should be equipped with bathroom locks, which are operated by knob latch bolts and dead bolts from both sides.

One of the patients' toilet rooms is designed to accommodate a patient in a wheelchair. The room is larger than the others, for easy maneuvering, and has a 3-foot door. The lavatory is set on wall brackets 6 inches out from the wall and 2 feet-10 inches from the floor.

One toilet should be provided with a bedpan flushing attachment. Water closets should be suspended from the wall to simplify cleaning. Each toilet room should be equipped with a grab bar. An emergency call station in each toilet room and an annunciator at the secretary-receptionist's desk are recommended.

### Technicians' Toilets and Lockers

During busy periods it is essential that the staff be available at all times. Separate toilet and locker facilities are provided for technicians. This reduces the time technicians must be absent from the area and contributes to the efficiency of the department.

## Storage Facilities

### General Storage

For bulk supplies, a storage cabinet equipped with sliding doors and adjustable shelves is located inside each patients' corridor near the entrance. Materials such as films, opaque solutions, developing solutions, and office supplies are stored here.

### Daily Linen Supplies (X-Ray Rooms)

Clean linen, requisitioned from the hospital central supply, is stored on a cart (No. 66) in each x-ray room; soiled linen is placed in a hamper (No. 65).

### Gown Storage

Open adjustable shelves for gown storage are placed next to each general bulk supply cabinet, just inside the corridor entrance. The shelving for clean gowns starts about 4 feet from the floor, leaving space beneath for a linen hamper (No. 65) for soiled gowns.

### Janitor's Closet

The janitor's closet must be readily available for emergency cleaning and it should be convenient to the x-ray rooms and toilets. The closet should contain a floor receptor with a curb or a janitor's service sink, a mop-hanging strip and a shelf, and provide space for parking the mop truck.

## Diagnostic X-Ray Rooms

### X-Ray Equipment

Both rooms are equipped with combination x-ray and fluoroscopic machines with spot film devices. An overhead-type tube support is indicated in the plan, as this facilitates x-raying a patient in bed or on a stretcher. For reasons of economy, however, it may be desirable to equip one room with a floor-ceiling track. If an overhead mounted track is used, it may be supported from the floor by columns or may be bracketed from the wall, although a ceiling suspension makes a neater installation.

The optimum size of the x-ray room is about 18 by 20 feet. Ceiling height requirements vary for different x-ray machines, but a minimum of 9 feet-6 inches is recommended. The machine and transformer should be placed so as to allow adequate space for admittance of a bed or stretcher in the room. Mounting the transformer on the wall is recommended to save floor space. However, sufficient clearances (at least 2 feet above the transformer) for servicing the transformer should be provided.

The sink and drainboard, for handwashing and rinsing utensils and barium equipment, is equipped with a gooseneck spout. It is located near the foot of the x-ray table.

It is recommended that the control panel be wired to a signal outside each x-ray room to indicate when the machine is on, to prevent other personnel from inadvertently entering the room. An In-Use lighted sign will be satisfactory as a signal for most installations.

### Control Booth

It is essential that the control booth be located to the right of the machine so that the patient may be observed when the table is inclined, since machines with end-pivoted tables tilt to the right. In the plan, no door is shown on the control booth as the radiation will have scattered at least twice before it reaches the control booth area. The arrangement of the control booth to the right and the cassette changer to the extreme left, as shown in the plan, fully meets this requirement. In addition, since the beam is directed toward the outside wall, radiation exposure to other personnel is lessened, and the amount of shielding required is decreased.

If the cassette changers are placed to the right of the machine (on the wall opposite to that indicated on the plan), a door on the control booth or a baffle placed in the room is required to protect the technician in the booth. Furthermore, additional shielding is required to protect films and personnel in the department because the primary beam would not be directed toward the outside wall. In the present scheme, the shielding necessary in the interior walls is principally to safeguard against the scatter radiation.

### Storage Cabinet and Writing Counter

A storage cabinet (No. 62), with a safety light above, serves also as a writing counter for the radiologist and technicians. Shelves in the cabinet provide space for storage of accessory items, measuring devices used with x-ray machines, and disposable items needed for patients' examinations.

## Film Processing and Distribution Area

### Darkroom

This room is located between the two x-ray rooms to facilitate handling of films. Cassettes are loaded and unloaded on the counter (No. 11). Space is provided for loading and stacking cassettes at both ends of the counter.

A utility sink with a drainboard (No. 24), located opposite the processing tank, is provided for mixing chemical solutions and handwashing. A refrigerating unit (No. 25) for the tank is located in the space beneath the drainboard.

X-ray films are processed in an area separated from the loading counter by a partition (No. 81) at the end of the developing tank which helps to avoid accidental splashing and damage to the screens and films on the loading counter. A through-wall processing unit tank permits the radiologist or staff doctors to read the wet films in the lightroom area without interrupting darkroom procedures.

A lightlock between the darkroom and the lightroom, equipped with interlocking doors, is necessary to allow entrance into the darkroom of other personnel during film processing. Although a maze has some advantages over the lightlock, the additional space needed is not justifiable in a facility of this size. Access panels (No. 22), located in the lightlock and in the control space, are provided to simplify installation and servicing of the processing tanks.

### Film Processing Area

To reduce unnecessary traffic, the film processing rooms are located near the collection and distribution area. This layout allows the technician to work without interruption during the processing routine. Processing of films begins at the developing tank (No. 26) in the darkroom, and continues to the final rinsing tank (No. 29) in the lightroom where the films may be wet-viewed at an illuminator, if desired, and then dried. After the films are dried, they are brought to the counter (33) in the technicians' corridor for final trimming, and passed through to the film collection and distribution area.

Another developing process is Daylight Processing. This process involves the use of a self-contained film developing unit, eliminating the need for a darkroom. Cassettes are loaded into the unit from the x-ray room side, pass through the processor unit, and emerge developed from the opposite side, usually in an adjacent sub-room. Film then can be read immediately.

Another type of process is Digital Radiology Imaging, in which x-rays are read directly from the x-ray machine into computer monitors (filmless system). These images can also be read from any computer throughout the hospital if need be.

### Collection and Distribution Area

Film sorting bins (No. 36) are provided above the counter in the collection and distribution area for temporary filing. After all films have been assembled, they are passed through the film pass slot (No. 34) to the radiologist for interpretation. He returns the films in a file cart or through a slot which leads into a box under the distribution counter. The films may then be temporarily filed for viewing by staff doctors or placed in the active files.

### Barium Mixing Facilities

A two-compartment sink (No. 75) in a counter, located in the technicians' corridor and accessible to both x-ray rooms, is provided for mixing barium. A duplex outlet for plugging in an electric mixer or a heating element is located above the counter unit. Barium supplies for daily use are stored in cabinets under the counter; the bulk supplies can be stocked in one of the general storage cabinets located in the patients' corridors.

### Dark Adaptation

Patients must be allowed to become accustomed to the low lighting level in the x-ray rooms and the staff must retain their dark adaptation despite the opening of the doors of the fluoroscopic rooms between patients' examinations.

To facilitate dark adaptation, curtains are shown at the intersections of the technicians' and the patients' corridors. In addition to the illumination normally provided in the corridors, patients' toilet rooms, and dressing rooms, it is recommended that these areas be equipped with an independently controlled dim lighting system of red bulbs for dark adaptation.

### Miscellaneous Services

It is assumed that the central sterile supply department of the hospital will provide all such services for the x-ray department.

The mobile x-ray unit should be stored in the radiology department where it will be under the supervision and control of the department and available when needed.

### Optional Facilities

*Intercommunication System*

Provision of a system within the department increases the efficiency of the staff and speeds up service. Outlets are shown at the desk of the secretary-receptionist, in the x-ray rooms and the darkroom, and in the technicians' corridor. It is recommended that a one-way intercommunication system, with an intercom in the control booth and a speaker at the cassette changer, be installed so that the technician need not leave the control booth to give instructions to the patient at the far end of the x-ray room.

*Refrigerator*

Some items used in the x-ray department require refrigeration. The space under one end of the barium counter at the sink (No. 75) in the technicians' corridor may be used for an under-counter type refrigerator.

*High-Speed Film Dryer*

The plan provides sufficient space for an anhydrator, if desired, in lieu of the dryer shown (No. 31).

### PLAN B DESIGN FOR EXPANSION

This one-machine department, designed to handle a daily average of about 20 patient examinations, could satisfactorily serve a hospital of 50 to 100 beds, depending upon the extent of outpatient services pro-

vided. As in Plan A, its volume of examinations can be increased, depending on the staffing pattern and other factors discussed previously (see Fig. 3).

This plan will result in a functional unit. It has another important advantage in that it may be expanded to include all the features of Plan A. Such expansion is usually indicated when the hospital is served by a full-time radiologist, when the average daily load approaches 30 examinations per day, and when the proportion of time-consuming examinations becomes high.

Expansion problems frequently occur in a hospital of 100 beds or less, where there is only one x-ray machine and a part-time radiologist. As the volume of work increases, the radiologist spends more time at the hospital, and a second machine is installed. Unfortunately, in most of these cases, the lack of planning for a future expansion program and expansion area results in an inefficient layout. This limits the usefulness of the equipment and the efficiency of the staff. Examples of such limitations are: poor location of the darkroom in relation to the new x-ray room, inadequate size of the darkroom, insufficient number of toilet facilities and dressing rooms, lack of office and waiting areas, and limited film filing space.

Remodeling an x-ray department is more expensive than remodeling other areas of a hospital because of the shielding, wiring, and plumbing. Expansion of the x-ray department should be incorporated in the original plan where possible. Roughing in the plumbing and building in the shielding and electrical conduits in the expansion space will result in future savings and an efficient x-ray suite.

Minimum alterations to Plan B necessary to duplicate the facilities of Plan A would be the remodeling of the film collection area to accommodate a new control booth, the elimination of the partition between the light room and reception space, the elimination of the dressing rooms and of the partition behind them.

Until the need for remodeling becomes apparent, part of the administration offices of the hospital may temporarily be situated in the expansion space. When enlarging the x-ray department, other space may then be added to the administration department. The dotted lines on Fig. 4 illustrate how this expansion may be designed.

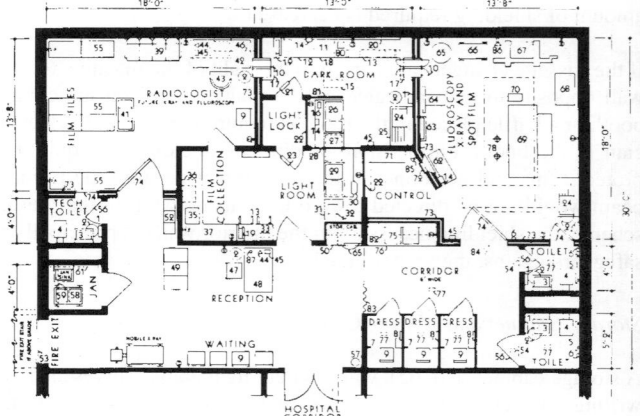

**Fig. 3. Diagnostic radiographic suite, Plan B**

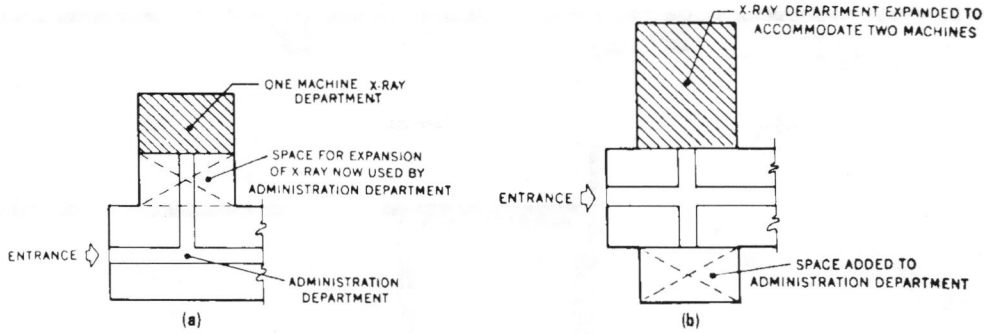

**Fig. 4. X-ray department (a) Before expansion (b) After expansion**

A typical radiographic room is shown in Fig. 5; a typical vascular layout is shown in Fig. 6.

## MRI

Many hospitals provide for an MRI (Magnetic Resonance Imaging), a diagnostic process that involves a patient being analyzed using imaging technology. A patient is placed on a motorized table that slides into the MRI, where a patient is diagnosed using imaging technology. Results are read directly into a computer.

These units are typically setup as suite in the hospital or in an outpatient facility. Proper waiting, patient processing, gowning, and staff areas are necessary. MRI equipment requires its own computer room. The size of the room can range from 400 to 600 square feet.

Proper radiation and electrical interference shielding is required for equipment support. Adequate HVAC and electric is necessary to support these sensitive areas.

**Legend**
1. Overhead tube conveyor (OTC)
2. OTC ceiling tracks
3. Image intensifier carriage
4. Negator with TV and 90-mm cine
5. Table
6. Table
7. Pedestal table
8. Stretcher
9. Control
10. Transformer
11. High-voltage adapter kit
12. Planigraph mounted on ceiling track
13. Franklin headstand
14. Mobile TV monitor
15. Wall-mounted cassette holder
16. High-capacity autoprocessor
17. Cassette transfer cabinet
18. Multibank film viewer
19. Replenisher tanks
20. Wall-mounted cable catch
21. Intensifier power supply mounted on shelf above control
22. TV control mounted on shelf above control
23. Planigraph control
24. High-speed starter mounted on wall
25. Single-plane film changer
26. Program selector
27. Single-plane parked

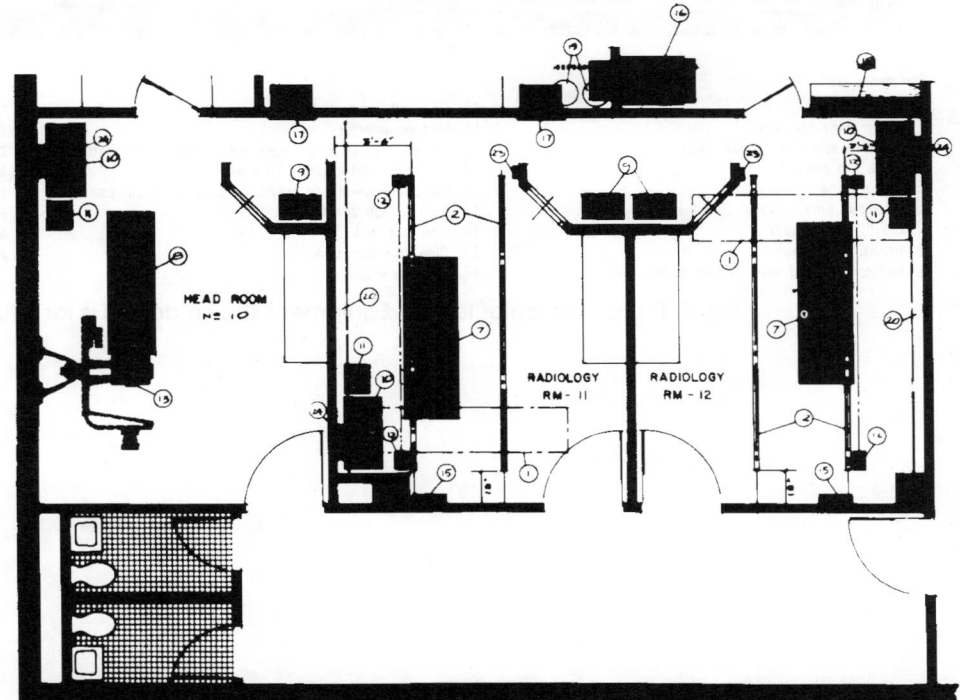

**Fig. 5. Typical radiographic room**

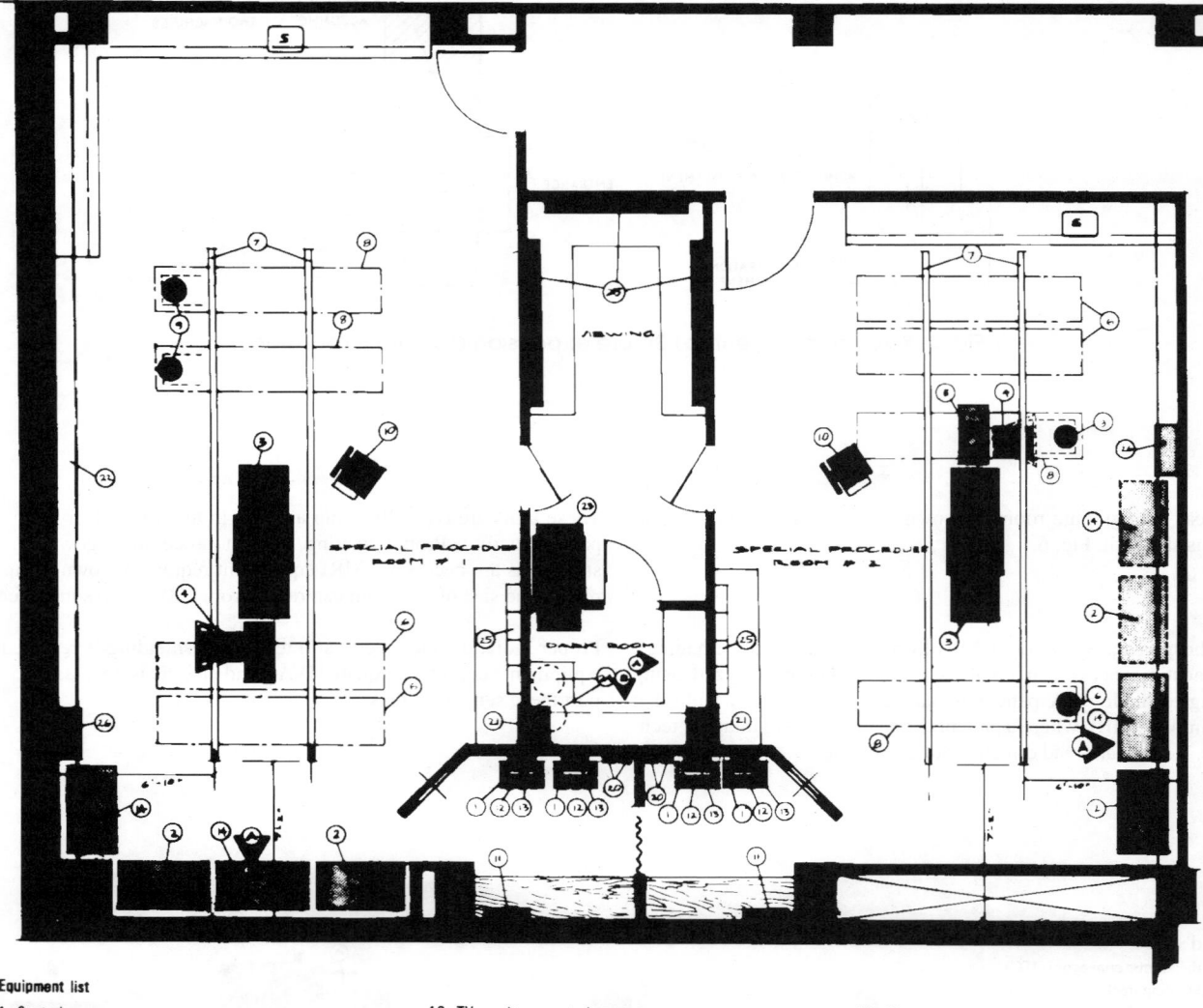

**Equipment list**

1. Control
2. Power units cabinets
3. Spectrum special procedure table
4. Plane film changer
5. Single-plane film changer
6. Overhead tube conveyor (O.T.C.)
7. O.T.C. ceiling track
8. Intensifier carriage
9. Negator mounted with TV and 35-mm cine

10. TV monitor mounted on cart
11. Program selector
12. Intensifier power supply mounted on shelf above control
13. TV control unit mounted on shelf
14. Additional power unit cabinet to house cine equipment
15. High-voltage adapter kit
16. Cine bias tank
17. Cine smoother tank
18. Cine powerstat

19. Cine control cabinet
20. Operator's control
21. Cassette transfer cabinet
22. Wall-mounted cable catch
23. High-capacity processor
24. Replenisher tanks
25. Multibank film viewer
26. Airflex biplane control

**Fig. 6. Typical vascular layout. Equipment shown dotted is for future installation**

# PHARMACIES

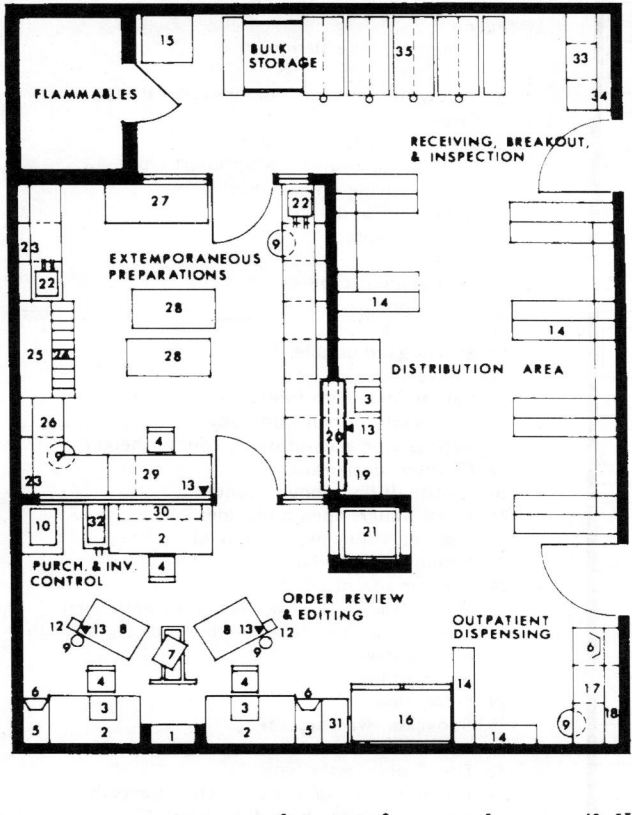

**FLAMMABLES**

**BULK STORAGE**

**RECEIVING, BREAKOUT, & INSPECTION**

**EXTEMPORANEOUS PREPARATIONS**

**DISTRIBUTION AREA**

**PURCH. & INV. CONTROL**

**ORDER REVIEW & EDITING**

**OUTPATIENT DISPENSING**

SCALE 5    0    5    10 FT

*Legend*
1. Pneumatic tube station
2. Desk
3. Typewriter, electric, nonmovable carriage
4. Chair
5. Files, intermediate height
6. Files, swinging panel, strip insert type
7. File, revolving on two levels
8. Table, movable, 2 feet by 3 feet
9. Waste receptacle
10. Photocopier
11. File, 2-drawer
12. Utility pole
13. Telephone
14. Shelving, adjustable, 12 inches
15. Safe
16. Refrigerator, with freezer
17. Counter, with file drawer, bins
18. Shelving, adjustable, 7 inches
19. Counter, dispensing
20. Two-shelf unit above counter
21. Dumbwaiter, open both sides
22. Cabinet, with sink, drain board
23. Cabinet, wall-mounted
24. Bins, on top of hood
25. Hood, laminar airflow, vertical or horizontal
26. Counter, with open adjustable shelving beneath
27. Cart, storage
28. Carts, utility
29. Desk, small
30. Bookcase, wall-mounted
31. File cabinet, 5-drawer
32. File, visible index type
33. Counter, with adjustable shelves beneath
34. Shelving, wall-mounted, 9 inches
35. Shelving, adjustable, rail-mounted

**Fig. 1. Pharmacy department in a 100-bed hospital** (From *Planning for Hospital Pharmacies*, DHEW Pub. No. (HRA)77-4003, U.S. Department of Health and Human Services, Washington, D.C.)

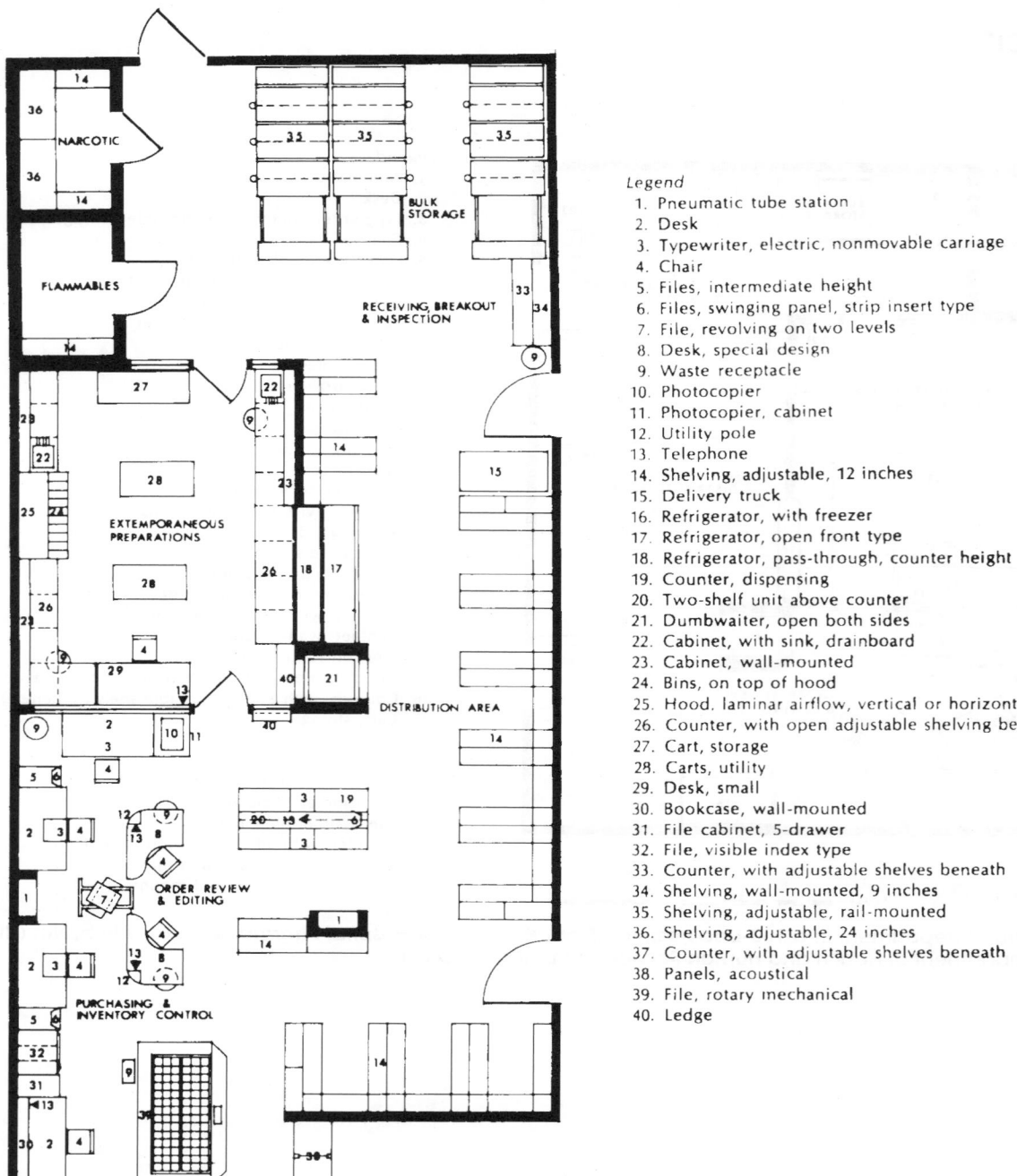

**Legend**
1. Pneumatic tube station
2. Desk
3. Typewriter, electric, nonmovable carriage
4. Chair
5. Files, intermediate height
6. Files, swinging panel, strip insert type
7. File, revolving on two levels
8. Desk, special design
9. Waste receptacle
10. Photocopier
11. Photocopier, cabinet
12. Utility pole
13. Telephone
14. Shelving, adjustable, 12 inches
15. Delivery truck
16. Refrigerator, with freezer
17. Refrigerator, open front type
18. Refrigerator, pass-through, counter height
19. Counter, dispensing
20. Two-shelf unit above counter
21. Dumbwaiter, open both sides
22. Cabinet, with sink, drainboard
23. Cabinet, wall-mounted
24. Bins, on top of hood
25. Hood, laminar airflow, vertical or horizontal
26. Counter, with open adjustable shelving beneath
27. Cart, storage
28. Carts, utility
29. Desk, small
30. Bookcase, wall-mounted
31. File cabinet, 5-drawer
32. File, visible index type
33. Counter, with adjustable shelves beneath
34. Shelving, wall-mounted, 9 inches
35. Shelving, adjustable, rail-mounted
36. Shelving, adjustable, 24 inches
37. Counter, with adjustable shelves beneath
38. Panels, acoustical
39. File, rotary mechanical
40. Ledge

**Fig. 2. Pharmacy department in a 300-bed hospital** (From *Planning for Hospital Pharmacies,* DHEW Pub. No. (HRA)77-4003, U.S. Department of Health and Human Services, Washington, D.C.)

# PHYSICAL THERAPY DEPARTMENTS

Of the many environmental factors that affect physical therapy service to patients, the most important are space, location, and work areas. Ventilation, lighting, interior finish and related considerations also contribute toward providing a suitable environment. The keynote is function.

## Location

Location is closely related to function. The area selected for physical therapy should be centrally located to minimize problems of transporting patients and to facilitate giving bedside treatment when necessary. At least half of the patients treated in a general hospital physical therapy department are likely to be outpatients. With this in mind, special attention should be given to accessibility, and to having as few steps as possible to climb, as few long corridors and heavy doors to negotiate. A ground floor location, convenient for both in- and outpatients and for access to an outdoor exercise area, is desirable.

Physical therapy is frequently placed in an area that includes other outpatient services, such as social service, occupational therapy, and recreation. It is particularly important that physical and occupational therapy be in close proximity.

## Amount of Space

The amount of space needed depends on the number of patients treated, the kinds of disabilities and the treatments required. Also to be considered is the fact that some space-consuming equipment such as a whirlpool bath, treatment tables, parallel bars, etc.—are minimum essentials for even a one-therapist department. These pieces of equipment will not be multiplied in direct proportion to increases in staff and patient load.

Efforts to correlate bed capacity and physical therapy space requirements are not satisfactory. Hospitals with 50–100 beds may serve large numbers of outpatients. The amount of space given over to physical therapy in a small hospital is, justifiably, out of proportion to the bed capacity.

No absolute standard can be recommended as the amount of space needed for physical therapy in a general hospital. The most that can be said is that, if possible, it is desirable to plan for at least a thousand square feet of floor space, free of structural obstructions. About half of that should be exercise area (see Fig. 1).

This does not mean that a hospital cannot begin an effective physical therapy service in smaller quarters. Many have done so successfully, using to full advantage whatever space resources they had.

## Work Space Components

Whatever the eventual size of a physical therapy department, from the very beginning plans must be made to provide certain kinds of work space. These essential components can be expanded, multiplied or refined as the physical therapy department grows but the fundamental requirements are the same for a small or large department. They include:

Reception area
Staff space
Examining room
Treatment areas
Toilet facilities
Storage

Experienced physical therapists have many suggestions for increasing the efficiency of physical therapy departments by giving attention to details of planning and arranging these component work areas. For example:

### Reception Area

Accommodations for inpatients and outpatients, if possible. Adequate space for stretcher and wheelchair patients.

### Staff Space—Private

Office space suitable for interviewing patients, attending to administrative and clerical duties, housing files, etc. Writing facilities for the staff adequate for dictation, record keeping. There should be space for staff lockers and dressing rooms separate from the patient area, either within the department or near to it.

### Examining Room

Floor to ceiling partitions for privacy. Arranged so that necessary examining equipment can remain in the room permanently. Possible to use this space for special tests and measurements or for treatment when privacy is desirable.

### Treatment Area

There are three types of treatment areas: cubicle (dry), underwater exercise (wet) and exercise (open). Each is designed to meet the particular requirements of the special equipment used for different kinds of treatment.

### Cubicle

Each unit large enough for the physical therapist to work on either side of the table without having to move equipment belonging in the cubicle. Preferably cubicles divided by curtains for easier access for wheelchair and stretcher cases, for expansion of usable floor area for gait analysis, group activity, or teaching purposes.

Curtain tracks should be flush with the ceiling and curtains should have open panels at the top for ventilation when drawn. Both curtains and tracks should be sturdy. In or near the cubicles, outpatients need a place or locker for their outer clothing.

### Underwater Exercise Area

All equipment requiring special plumbing and water supply should be concentrated in one section of the department but accessible and adjacent to other treatment areas. It should include a treatment table, especially in the room with a tank or exercise pool. Fixed overhead lifts are absolutely essential for the efficient use of tanks; failure to

References: Planning is by Thomas P. Galbraith and Peter N. Jensen, Hospital Architects of the Architectural and Engineering Branch, Division of Hospital and Medical Facilities Public Health Service.

provide lifts severely limits the usefulness of this valuable equipment. Plumbing and other installation requirements, and humidity call for special care and attention. Electrical and metal equipment in other treatment areas may suffer damage unless the underwater exercise area is carefully planned.

*Exercise Area*

Very flexible open space planned to accommodate patients engaged in diverse individual or group exercise activities. Used extensively by people in wheelchairs, on crutches or canes, or with other disabilities

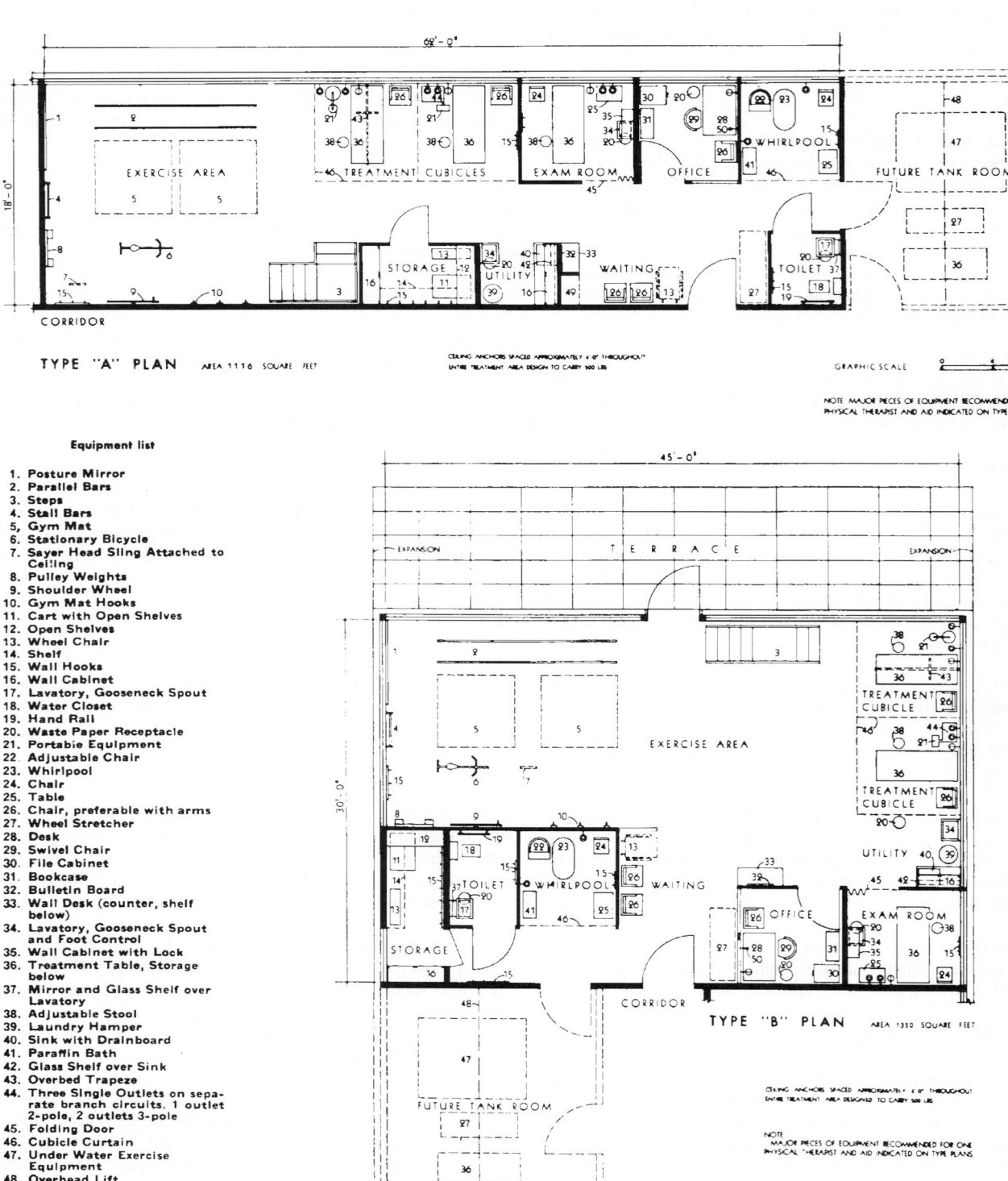

**Equipment list**

1. Posture Mirror
2. Parallel Bars
3. Steps
4. Stall Bars
5. Gym Mat
6. Stationary Bicycle
7. Sayer Head Sling Attached to Ceiling
8. Pulley Weights
9. Shoulder Wheel
10. Gym Mat Hooks
11. Cart with Open Shelves
12. Open Shelves
13. Wheel Chair
14. Shelf
15. Wall Hooks
16. Wall Cabinet
17. Lavatory, Gooseneck Spout
18. Water Closet
19. Hand Rail
20. Waste Paper Receptacle
21. Portable Equipment
22. Adjustable Chair
23. Whirlpool
24. Chair
25. Table
26. Chair, preferable with arms
27. Wheel Stretcher
28. Desk
29. Swivel Chair
30. File Cabinet
31. Bookcase
32. Bulletin Board
33. Wall Desk (counter, shelf below)
34. Lavatory, Gooseneck Spout and Foot Control
35. Wall Cabinet with Lock
36. Treatment Table, Storage below
37. Mirror and Glass Shelf over Lavatory
38. Adjustable Stool
39. Laundry Hamper
40. Sink with Drainboard
41. Paraffin Bath
42. Glass Shelf over Sink
43. Overbed Trapeze
44. Three Single Outlets on separate branch circuits. 1 outlet 2-pole, 2 outlets 3-pole
45. Folding Door
46. Cubicle Curtain
47. Under Water Exercise Equipment
48. Overhead Lift
49. Coat Rack
50. Telephone Outlet

**Fig. 1. Physical therapy facility. Type A Plan, Type B Plan**

hat limit their motion and agility. At least one wall should be reinforced for the installation of stall bars and similar equipment (see Fig. 2).

*Toilet Facilities*

Separate toilet facilities for patients and staff. Patient facilities should be designed to accommodate wheelchair patients.

*Storage*

Designed to meet special needs in and near work areas. Should also be storage space on the unit for equipment and supplies usually needed for bedside treatments. All storage space should be accessible, simple, well lighted. Wheelchair/stretcher alcoves are desirable.

**Special Considerations**

*Ventilation/Air Conditioning*

Adequate, controlled ventilation is of extreme importance in a physical therapy department. Many of the treatment procedures require the use of dry or moist heat, or active exercise, which raise body temperatures. A continuous, reliable flow of fresh air is essential to the comfort of patients and staff. This includes protection from drafts.

*Sinks*

Hospital hand-washing lavatories with hot and cold water mixing outlets, preferably foot operated, should be located at the proper height in convenient places. At least one sink should be of sufficient width and depth to accommodate the care of wet packs and other special washing needs.

*Interior Finishes*

The activity of patients in wheelchairs, on stretchers and crutches subjects floors and walls to heavy wear. Materials which will stand up under such rough usage, remain attractive and require a minimum of maintenance should be specified despite higher costs.

All interior wall surfaces of the department should have a durable and attractive wainscot to protect them against damage by wheelchairs, stretchers and carts. Vinyl wall covering is a popular wainscoting material, and in some cases used for the entire wall. Two weights of the material are available; the heavier weight for areas subjected to severe abuse, the lighter weight for other parts of the wall.

The use of decorative colors for interior finishes and equipment is, of course, highly desirable in this department as it is in other parts of the hospital. Research in color therapy for hospitals adds to decorators' ideas the therapeutic value of combinations of pastel colors. Cool colors, including pastels, green, blue, violet, are considered mildly restful. Some light colors in general are stimulating and may be used to advantage in the exercise area.

*Doors*

For accommodation of stretcher and wheelchair traffic, doors within the department should be at least 36 inches wide. Raised thresholds should be eliminated.

Perspective sketches by William McMaster

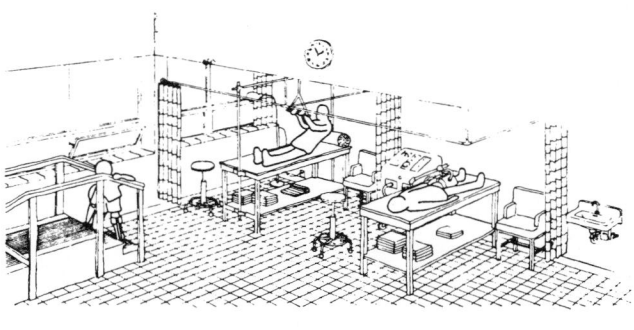

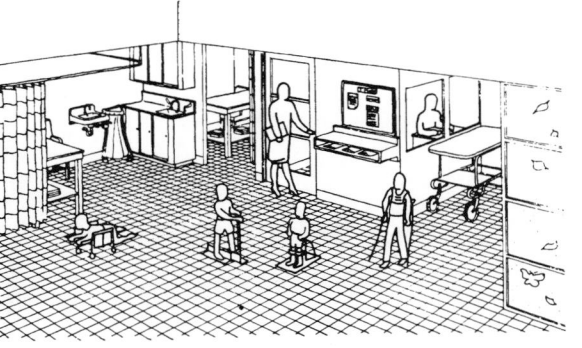

**Fig. 2. Physical therapy uses**

*Ceiling Moorings*

These moorings, strategically located in the ceiling in treatment areas, have been found useful for attaching overhead equipment such as hoists, pulleys, bars, counter balancing equipment, etc. They should be constructed and attached to joists in such a manner that each supports at least 500 pounds.

**Layout**

It is impossible to anticipate all of the practical problems of layout in a particular building or to say in advance that one plan or another is the right one. A few guidelines, however, may be useful in making decisions about layout.

- Expect to expand and plan for it from the beginning. It is impossible to overestimate the value of the exercise area. Give it as many square feet of appropriate space as possible.
- Note the need to have the underwater exercise equipment grouped in one area, separate but adjacent and accessible to the other treatment areas.
- Visit other physical therapy departments and find out what the physical therapists like, or would like to change in the layouts of their own departments.

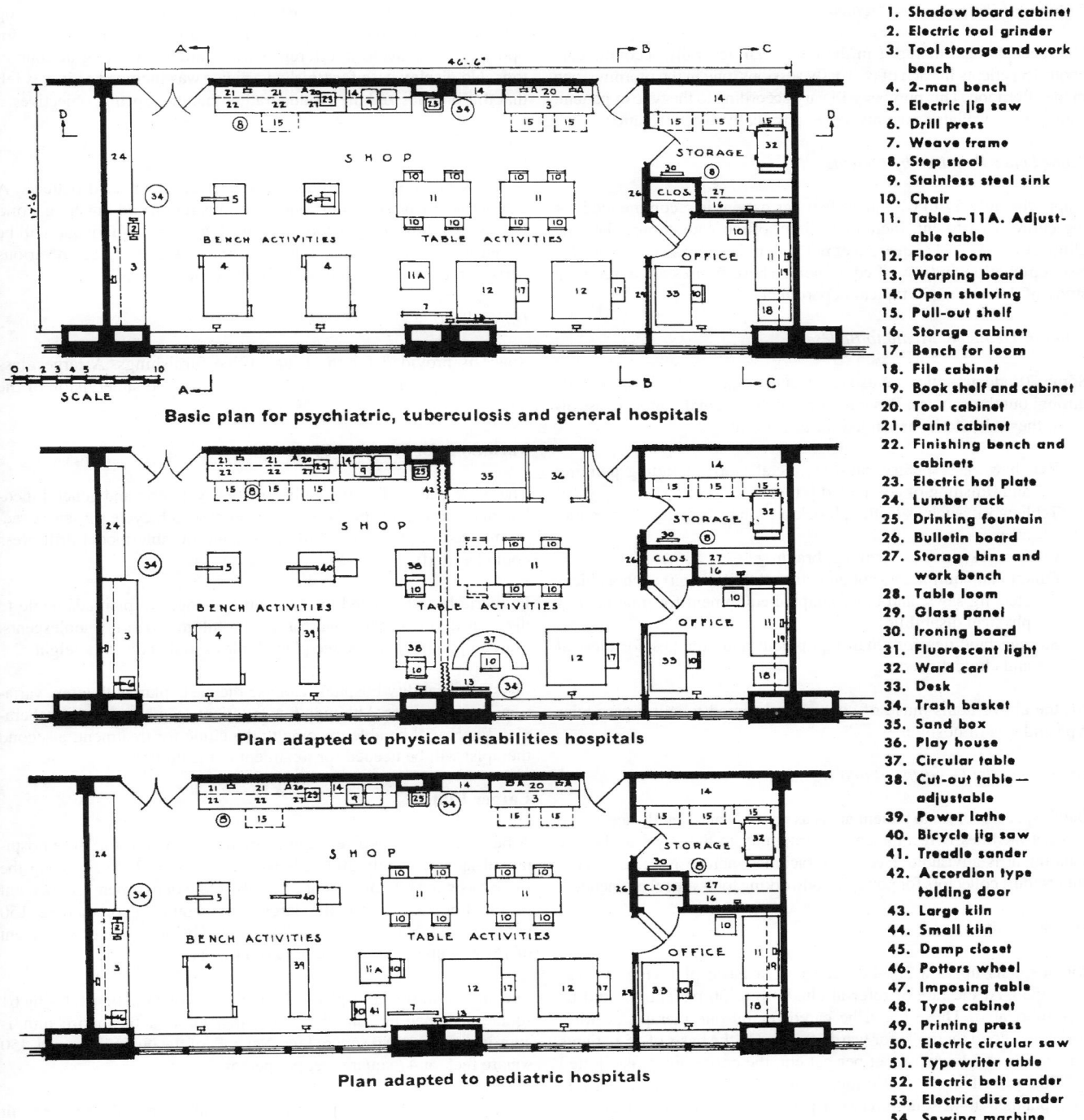

1. Shadow board cabinet
2. Electric tool grinder
3. Tool storage and work bench
4. 2-man bench
5. Electric jig saw
6. Drill press
7. Weave frame
8. Step stool
9. Stainless steel sink
10. Chair
11. Table—11A. Adjustable table
12. Floor loom
13. Warping board
14. Open shelving
15. Pull-out shelf
16. Storage cabinet
17. Bench for loom
18. File cabinet
19. Book shelf and cabinet
20. Tool cabinet
21. Paint cabinet
22. Finishing bench and cabinets
23. Electric hot plate
24. Lumber rack
25. Drinking fountain
26. Bulletin board
27. Storage bins and work bench
28. Table loom
29. Glass panel
30. Ironing board
31. Fluorescent light
32. Ward cart
33. Desk
34. Trash basket
35. Sand box
36. Play house
37. Circular table
38. Cut-out table—adjustable
39. Power lathe
40. Bicycle jig saw
41. Treadle sander
42. Accordion type folding door
43. Large kiln
44. Small kiln
45. Damp closet
46. Potters wheel
47. Imposing table
48. Type cabinet
49. Printing press
50. Electric circular saw
51. Typewriter table
52. Electric belt sander
53. Electric disc sander
54. Sewing machine

**Basic plan for psychiatric, tuberculosis and general hospitals**

**Plan adapted to physical disabilities hospitals**

**Plan adapted to pediatric hospitals**

**Fig. 1. Floor plans for typical occupational therapy department in hospitals up to 250-bed capacity**

# OCCUPATIONAL THERAPY DEPARTMENTS

Occupational therapy is an integral part of many medical rehabilitation programs, and is an increasingly important element of hospital planning. Basic solutions for occupational therapy departments are largely dependent on the following factors:

*Author:* Alonzo W. Clark, AIA with the collaboration of the American Occupational Therapy Association
*Reviewer:* James H. Ogden, R.A.

*Number of Patients to Be Treated*

One occupational therapist in the clinic can generally accommodate about 15 patients in each of two daily sessions, one in the morning, one in the afternoon. This number will vary according to the type of patient, e.g., more psychiatric patients, fewer physically disabled patients.

*Floor Space Required by Patients*

Approximately 54 to 61 square feet per patient is recommended for the entire department, including clinic, office and storage. For the clinic alone, 42 to 47 square feet per patient is suggested to allow for easy circulation and use of equipment. These figures are based on a study of the needs of a typical department.

*Types of Treatment Media to Be Used*

Some 70-odd activities are used in occupational therapy departments throughout the country. Basic requirements for small units are as follows; these should be expanded for larger units:

> Bench work-carpentry, plastics, metal work including painting and finishing of completed projects.
> Table work, such as leather, block printing, fly tying, sewing and art work.
> Loom work, such as weaving, braiding.
> Functional equipment (not an active classification) such as bicycles, jig saws, and other adapted equipment for treatment of physical disabilities.
> Storage facilities for small equipment and supplies for clerical and clinical needs.

All the above items must, of course, be adapted to suit a particular type and size of hospital.

*Location of the Department in a Hospital*

Daylit space as close to patient areas as possible and readily accessible to toilet facilities is recommended. Proximity to the physical therapy department is advisable. Necessary facilities include gas and electric outlets; dust collectors for power woodworking tools are recommended.

**Smaller Unit**

For hospitals up to a 250-bed capacity, a basic plan (Fig. 1) was developed. At the rate of referral cited, up to 30 patients should be accommodated. These could be cared for by one therapist, with a possible second therapist for ward service. On the basis of 15 patients per session at 54 square feet per patient, the entire unit was allotted 813.75 square feet (17 feet-6 inches by 46 feet-6 inches). The clinic area, planned at 42 square feet per patient, totals 638.75 square feet (17 feet-6 inches by 36 feet-6 inches). The minimum basic activities were provided for with 20 work stations for flexibility in selection. Activities requiring bulky equipment such as printing and advanced ceramics were omitted. It was assumed that preparation and finishing could be done in the clinic or on a counter top in the storeroom. The following considerations were made for the three specific areas within the department:

*Clinic Area*

The first obvious requirement is space for free circulation around the required equipment (see general list following). Space for parking at

least three wheelchairs is also necessary. Double doors at shop entrance simplify moving equipment and supplies. Sliding doors for upper cabinets avoid interference with patients working at counter tops. No display case for finished articles was included as it was felt that this emphasized the product rather than therapeutic objectives.

*Storage Area*

Space is provided for a mobile cart for servicing ward patients. A cabinet with work top is included for preparation and finishing work. It is assumed that only 8-foot lengths of lumber and plywood will be stored in this basic unit, and that other closets, rooms, etc. in various parts of the hospital could be used for "dead storage."

*Office Area*

Space is provided for the usual office furnishings. A large glass panel in front of the desk facilitates control and supervision of the unit.

**Variations for Hospital Types**

The basic plan is directly applicable to psychiatric and general medical and surgical hospitals. In the latter case, a bicycle jig saw is recommended in place of a drill press stand (a table model drill press could be used).

Pediatric hospitals need the following changes: a plan adaptable to division into two parts-one for small children, one for adolescents. For equipment changes, see plan. Tables should adjust in height.

Physical disability hospitals can use the basic plan with a few variations in equipment. Although fewer patients can be treated per therapist, fewer will be able to come to the clinic for treatment; a second therapist will be needed for treatment in the units.

**Larger Unit**

A basic plan for a typical occupational therapy unit for large hospitals of approximately 500 beds is shown in Fig. 2. Again using the same basis for rate of patient referrals to the department (30 percent of rated-bed capacity), the large unit should accommodate 150 patients a day. The actual clinic load would be 60 patients (40 percent of 150), or about 30 in each of two sessions.

The unit as presented is planned on the basis of 31 patients. Using 61 square feet per person, the gross area allotted the entire unit is approximately 1,880 square feet. Net area of the clinic is about 1,450 square feet, or 47 square feet per person.

This increased space per person over that allowed in the smaller unit is the result of adding two activities requiring bulky equipment and separate rooms. These are ceramics and printing. It is also deemed essential to have a separate unit preparation room to serve the increased number of patients. To allow for a necessary dispersion factor, 10 extra work stations are provided in the clinic. The larger unit therefore contains the following sections:

> Clinic (including weaving and table activities area, bench activities, printing unit, ceramics unit)
> Office
> Storage
> Unit preparation area

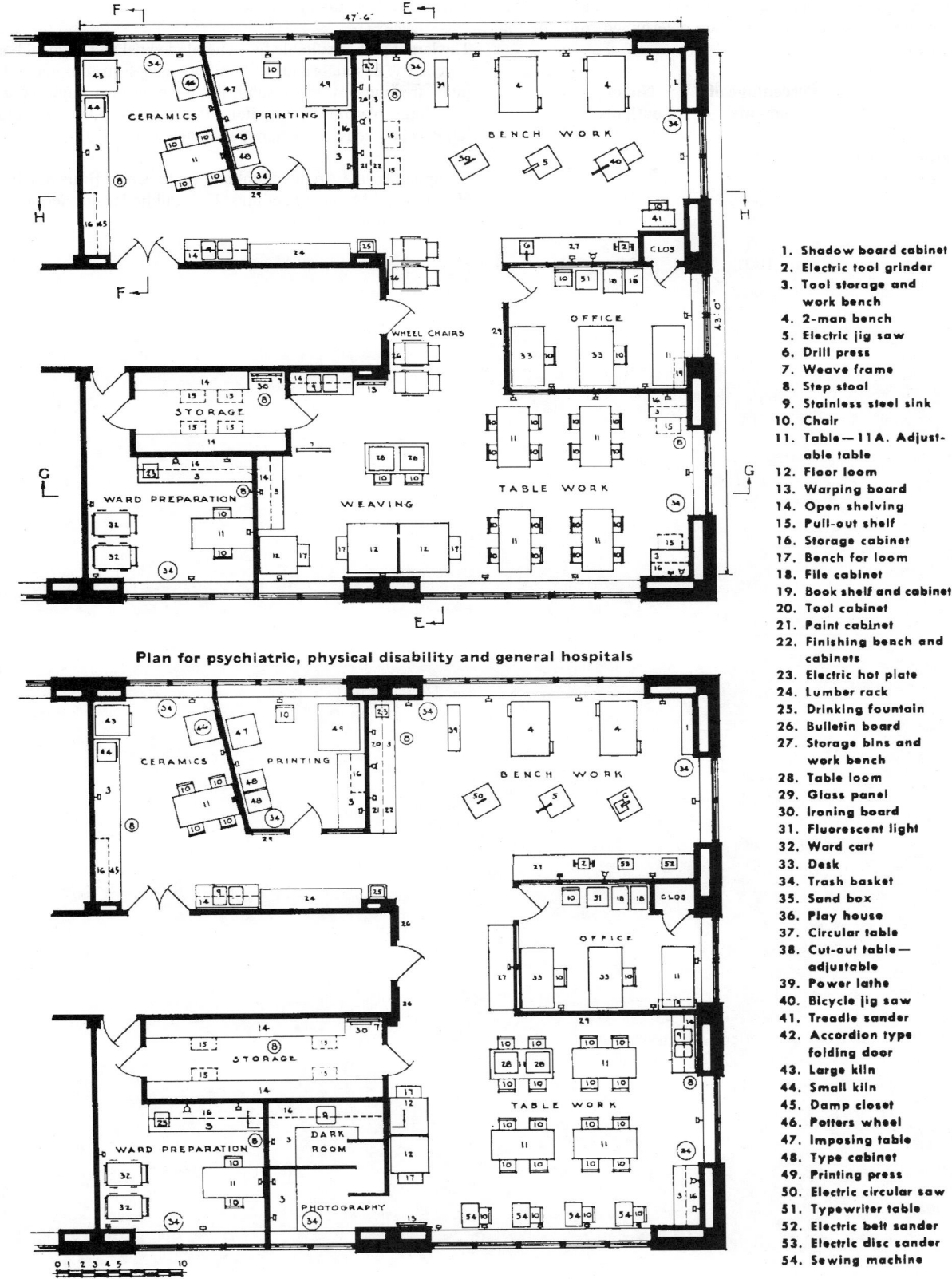

Plan for psychiatric, physical disability and general hospitals

1. Shadow board cabinet
2. Electric tool grinder
3. Tool storage and work bench
4. 2-man bench
5. Electric jig saw
6. Drill press
7. Weave frame
8. Step stool
9. Stainless steel sink
10. Chair
11. Table—11A. Adjustable table
12. Floor loom
13. Warping board
14. Open shelving
15. Pull-out shelf
16. Storage cabinet
17. Bench for loom
18. File cabinet
19. Book shelf and cabinet
20. Tool cabinet
21. Paint cabinet
22. Finishing bench and cabinets
23. Electric hot plate
24. Lumber rack
25. Drinking fountain
26. Bulletin board
27. Storage bins and work bench
28. Table loom
29. Glass panel
30. Ironing board
31. Fluorescent light
32. Ward cart
33. Desk
34. Trash basket
35. Sand box
36. Play house
37. Circular table
38. Cut-out table—adjustable
39. Power lathe
40. Bicycle jig saw
41. Treadle sander
42. Accordion type folding door
43. Large kiln
44. Small kiln
45. Damp closet
46. Potters wheel
47. Imposing table
48. Type cabinet
49. Printing press
50. Electric circular saw
51. Typewriter table
52. Electric belt sander
53. Electric disc sander
54. Sewing machine

Fig. 2. Floor plans for typical occupational therapy department in hospitals up to 500-bed capacity

Three therapists plus three assistants can run clinic and units. Space requirements for the various activities are determined from the following estimate:

| Activity | Percentage of patients | No. of patients |
|---|---|---|
| Wood, plastics, metal | 22 | 7 |
| General crafts (table activities) | 64 | 19 |
| Ceramics | 9 | 3 |
| Printing | 5 | 2 |
| | 100 | 31 |

**Variations for Hospital Types**

The larger plan is suitable for general medical and surgical hospitals, psychiatric hospitals and, with minor changes in equipment, for hospitals treating physical disabilities. Several units might be used for very large psychiatric hospitals. Pediatric hospitals are seldom as large as 500 beds; if so more personnel are needed.

Compiled by the Architectural and Engineering Branch, Division of Hospital and Medical Facilities, U.S. Public Health Service; August Hoenack, Branch Chief.

# COMMUNITY MENTAL HEALTH CENTERS

## CHECKLIST OF SPACES FOR COMMUNITY MENTAL HEALTH CENTER

Facilities listed are those that may be required in the overall programs of mental health centers. They can be in one or several buildings on one or several sites, even under one or several cooperating ownerships. The list is for review by architects and administrators whenever new facilities are planned.

## ADMINISTRATION

Office space for:
1. Director
2. Assistant director
3. Nursing director
4. Secretaries and typists
5. Business office

## ANCILLARY SPACES

1. Record room
2. Staff lounge
3. Library
4. Conference room
5. Lobby and waiting
6. Toilets public, staff

## DIAGNOSTIC AND TREATMENT

*Laboratory*

1. Office
2. Clinical
3. Pathology
4. Bacteriology
5. Washing and sterilizing

*Suites*

1. Basal metabolism and electrocardiology
2. Morgue and autopsy
3. Dental
4. Eye, ear, nose, and throat
5. Electroencephalography
6. Radiology

*Physical Therapy*

1. Electrotherapy
2. Hydrotherapy with exercise
3. Small gymnasium

*Pharmacy Department*

*Occupational Therapy*

1. Space for small woodworking tools and benches for carpentry, metal work, leather work, printing, weaving, rug making, etc.

2. Office
3. Storage room

## OUTPATIENT EXAMINATION AND TREATMENT

*Office Space*

1. Psychiatrists
2. Psychologists
3. Social workers
4. Nurses
5. Health educators
6. Occupational therapists
7. Rehabilitation counselors
8. Recreation ion therapists
9. Clerical operators
10. Aides
11. Research analyst
12. Group therapy and conference (lobby, waiting space, and toilets may be combined with those in the administrative area)

## INPATIENT FACILITIES

Facilities may be required for the following types of patients, grouped in accordance with the local program. (Separate spaces for male and female. Treatment and diagnosis spaces for each category.)

*Patients' Categories:*

1. New admissions
2. Quiet ambulant
3. Disturbed
4. Substance Abuse
5. Criminalistic
6. Day care
7. Night care
8. Children
   a. Emotionally disturbed
   b. Retarded

Each patient care unit:

1. Waiting space for visitors
2. Doctors' offices and examination rooms
3. Offices for psychologists, social workers, therapist or others as required
4. Nurses' station and toilet
5. Conference room
6. Therapy space
7. Day room(s)
8. Utility room
9. Pantry or nourishment preparation
10. Dining room
11. Washroom and toilets
12. Patients' lockers
13. Showers and bathrooms
14. Storage (for recreational and occupational therapy equipment)
15. Supply and linen storage
16. Janitors' closet
17. Stretcher alcove

Minimum room areas (check all applicable codes): 100 square foot per bed

1.  120 square feet in single rooms
2.  40 to 50 square feet per patient in day rooms, preferably divided into one large and one small room

## STERILIZING AND SUPPLY FACILITIES

*(Sufficient to serve both outpatients and inpatients.)*

## SERVICE DEPARTMENT

*Dietary Facilities*

1.  Main kitchen and bakery
2.  Dietitians' office
3.  Dishwashing room
4.  Refrigerators
5.  Garbage collecting and disposal facilities
6.  Can washing room
7.  Day storage room
8.  Staff dining room

*Housekeeping Facilities*

1.  Laundry
2.  Separate sorting room
3.  Separate clean linen room
4.  Housekeeper's office and storage (near linen storage)

*Mechanical Facilities*

1.  Boiler room and pump room
2.  Engineer's office
3.  Shower and locker room

*Maintenance Shops*

Carpentry, painting, mechanical, repair rooms

*Employees' Facilities*

Locker, rest, toilet and shower rooms for various categories

*Storage*

1.  Medical records
2.  General storage (a minimum 20 square feet per bed to be concentrated in one area)

# LABORATORIES

## PRELIMINARY PLANNING

Locate the department as favorably as possible for the laboratory staff and the ambulant inpatients and outpatients. A space on the first floor near an elevator is preferable. Also, another determinant in locating the laboratory is the consideration for future expansion.

In determining the overall size of the laboratory, the first concern is the individual technical units. It is only after the size of these units has been established and an architectural layout has been developed to fit the program that the sum of the areas can accurately reflect the size of the laboratory department.

The square-foot-per-bed ratio is no longer considered a desirable guide in determining the size of a hospital department because of the wide variation of such factors as type and size of hospital, pattern of usage, growth of the community, and medical practice. Plans for the laboratory area should be based on work volumes within specific ranges, such as 40,000 to 75,000 tests, or 75,000 to 120,000 tests. The key to this method is to estimate the work volume and its breakdown into work units for hospitals of different sizes.

The following is an outline of a procedure that may be used to estimate needed laboratory space, based on the number of tests performed, personnel, and equipment.

1. Break down the total volume of work into units, such as hematology, urinalysis, chemistry, as previously noted.
2. Determine the number of technologists required in each department.
3. Determine the necessary equipment and space for the number of technologists required.

## Laboratory Guide Plan

Plan A is a suggested plan for a hospital laboratory service with an estimated workload of 70,000 to 120,000 laboratory tests annually. For planning purposes, this laboratory is designed to serve a general hospital of 150 to 200 beds. The nontechnical staff would include one or more laboratory helpers and a clerk-typist and secretary in the administrative unit (see Fig. 1).

The laboratory services of a general hospital having this work volume would require work areas for six main technical units: hematology, blood bank, urinalysis, biochemistry, histology, and serology-bacteriology.

The block plan has been utilized here, as it provides a good functional relationship for all units. The pathologist's office in the center provides for easy supervision of the work stations: the hematology unit is near the waiting room; the bacteriology unit is at the end of the laboratory, yet near the washing and sterilizing areas; and the histology unit is near the pathologist's office.

Other schemes similar to that shown in Fig. 2, Plan B or a typical wing arrangement with a corridor down the center would also be satisfactory.

In the technical area of Plan A, the open plan arrangement (except for the histology and serology-bacteriology units) has several advantages over the "separate room for each unit" scheme for hospitals of this size. These advantages include: easier supervision; common use of such equipment as desks, refrigerators, and centrifuges; flexible use of personnel; and more available space since many doors and partitions are eliminated. If desired, partitions can be erected between each unit, as indicated on the plan for the histology and serology-bacteriology units.

## Laboratory Module for Technical Area

Maximum flexibility is desirable in the technical work areas of the laboratory department. In the plans, this has been achieved by using a module of approximately 10 by 20 feet, with a similar arrangement for each module. Each one consists of two standard laboratory workbenches 12 feet long, 30 inches deep, with a working surface or counter of about 23 inches, and a reagent shelf. Knee spaces are indicated where needed for personnel who perform tests from a sitting position. Drawers, cabinets, and shelves are provided below the work counter for daily equipment and supplies. This arrangement provides a 5-foot aisle between workbenches, which is considered optimum for movement within the working area. Equipment such as centrifuges, refrigerators, and desks, which may be used jointly by the personnel, is located opposite the units along the interior of the technical work area.

## Technical Areas

### Hematology-Blood Bank Unit

A standard module is assigned to the hematology-blood bank unit. One half of this module is provided with a workbench for procedures such as hemoglobin tests, sedimentation rates, staining, and washing of pipettes (in Plan A, counter No. 7 on left side of unit). Knee space and storage cabinets are provided below the counter. In the other half of the module, a workbench 30 inches high, with three knee spaces, is provided for technologists who are seated during tests, such as those involving microscopic procedures.

The micro-hematocrit centrifuge, because of its noise and vibration when in use, is placed in the general technical area along the interior wall directly opposite the hematology unit. The other equipment needed by this work unit, such as a refrigerator, centrifuge, and recording desk, is located conveniently opposite the unit, where it is shared with the urinalysis and the chemistry units.

It is assumed that the laboratory will obtain blood for transfusions from other sources and, therefore, needs only facilities for blood storage. A blood bank refrigerator is provided for this purpose in the examination and test room. Compatibility tests on the blood are done in the hematology unit. A hospital which operates a self-contained blood bank (that is, collects and does complete processing of all blood) should provide a separate bleeding room, processing laboratory, donors' recovery room, and an office available for preliminary physical examinations.

### Urinalysis Unit

The urinalysis unit is assigned one half of a standard module, consisting of a workbench, 12 linear feet long and 30 inches high, and

*Planning the Laboratory for the General Hospital,* Public Health Service, U. S. Department of Health and Human Services

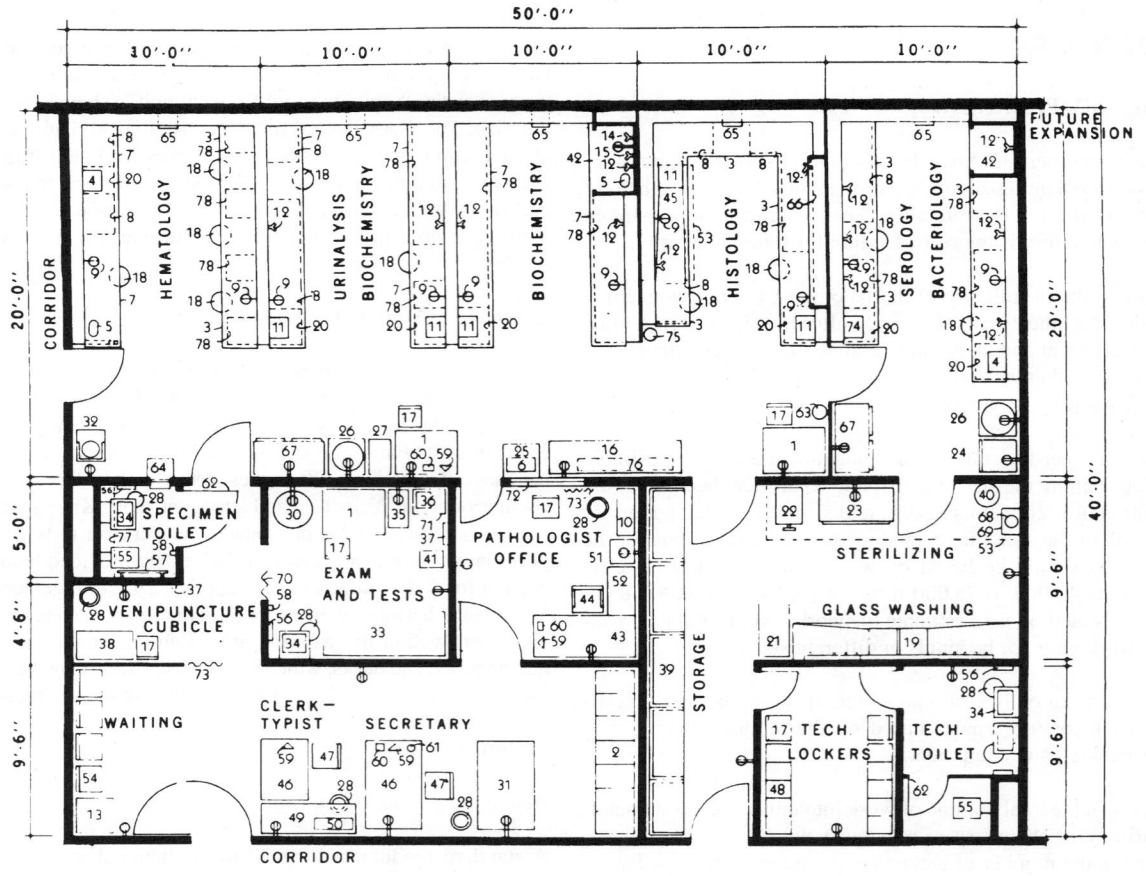

## LEGEND

1. Desk, 30 by 40 in., single pedestal
2. Filing cabinet, letter size
3. Counter, 30-in. high
4. Staining sink
5. Cup sink
6. Analytical balance
7. Counter, 36-in. high
8. Cabinets with adjustable shelves, below counter
9. Electric strip outlets, continuous
10. Bookcase
11. Utility sink
12. Gas outlet
13. Table for magazines
14. Suction outlet
15. Compressed air outlet
16. Table for instruments
17. Straight chair
18. Stool
19. Two-compartment sink 8-in. deep; drainboards-noncorrosive metal; peg boards above drainboards
20. Cabinet with trash receptacle on inside of door
21. Utility cart
22. Laboratory pressure sterilizer
23. Hot air oven
24. Incubator
25. Shelf or table for analytical balance
26. Centrifuge
27. Table for Harvard trip balance
28. Waste paper receptacle
29. Refrigerator, 8 cu. ft.
30. Refrigerator, blood bank
31. Worktable
32. Micro-hematocrit centrifuge
33. Examination table
34. Lavatory
35. Basal metabolism apparatus
36. Electrocardiograph
37. Hook strip
38. Table, 24 by 36 in.
39. Storage cabinets
40. Water still, 2-5 gals. per hr.
41. Adult scale
42. Fume hood
43. Double-pedestal office desk
44. Office chair, swivel, with arms
45. Noncorrosive metal work surface; pitch to sink
46. Typewriter desk
47. Posture chair
48. Technicians' lockers
49. Specimen receiving table
50. Request file with pigeon holes
51. Slide file cabinet
52. Microscope table
53. Exhaust hood
54. Easy chair
55. Wall-hung water closet
56. Paper towel dispenser
57. Grab bar, continuous
58. Emergency call station (push button) connected to buzzer at secretary's desk
59. Telephone outlet
60. Intercommunication system outlet
61. Buzzer at receptionist's desk from emergency calling stations
62. Hook on toilet-side of door
63. Fire extinguisher
64. Pass-through between toilet and laboratory
65. Exhaust air grills near floor
66. Wall cabinet
67. Refrigerator, 11 cu. ft.
68. Pipette washer
69. Shelf, for pipette washer, 10 in. above floor
70. Folding door
71. Table for electrocardiograph
72. Window
73. Curtain
74. Sink with electric waste disposal
75. Carbon dioxide cylinder
76. Gas cylinders under table
77. Shelf for urine bottles
78. Drawers with adjustable shelves, below counter

**Fig. 1. Plan A (70,000 to 120,000 tests annually) for average size of 150 to 200 beds**

erves as the work area for the microscopic and chemical examinations. Five linear feet of the workbench and a knee space are provided for personnel performing the microscopic examinations; the remainder of the workbench is used for the chemical examinations. A sink located at one end of the workbench provides a continuous working surface for the technologists.

*Biochemistry Unit*

The biochemistry unit requires an area that occupies one-and-a-half standard laboratory modules. The half module is shared with the urinalysis unit and is used for the necessary preliminary procedures that are done prior to the actual chemical analyses. A knee space is provided in this workbench for personnel who perform titrations and other procedures while seated. The adjoining module provides workbench area where a variety of chemical procedures may be performed; it includes a fume hood for removal of vapors and gases.

The workbenches for the chemical procedures are about 36 inches high, with drawers and cabinets below. The reagent shelves are used to hold the chemicals needed during the procedures. Two utility sinks are provided, one in each chemistry work area. Apparatus used in this unit is cleaned by the personnel in the unit; test tubes, pipettes, and flasks are sent to the central glass-washing area nearby.

An instrument table 36 inches high is located along the interior wall opposite this unit where chemical apparatus, such as colorimeter, flame photometer, spectrophotometer, and carbon dioxide gas apparatus are placed. Adjacent to the instrument table is an analytical balance on a vibration-free table or other type of support. By placing this apparatus away from the busy preparation and test procedure work areas, personnel can use the apparatus without interference from other procedures. It also lessens the possibility of damage to the equipment by the accidental spillage or splattering of chemical reagents.

A centrifuge, refrigerator, and desk are provided along the interior wall opposite the unit for the use of the personnel in this unit. The desk and refrigerator are shared with the urinalysis and the hematology units.

*Histology Unit*

The histology unit is assigned a standard module, separated from the other units by a partition to prevent odors from spreading to other areas. It is located near the pathologist's office since the medical technologist here works under his direction and supervision.

Along one half of the module, an area is utilized by the pathologist to examine surgical and autopsy specimens and to select the tissues for slide sections to be prepared by the technologist. An exhaust hood is provided over this section, as shown in the plan (No. 53), to draw off odors from specimens and solutions. The remainder of the module is used for the processing and staining of tissues. Knee spaces are provided, one at each of the specialized work areas. The workbench is 30 inches high with a 22- or 23-inch-deep working area, cabinets and drawers below the counter, and a reagent shelf. Wall-hung cabinets are provided for additional storage. A utility sink is provided at the end of the workbench.

*Serology-Bacteriology Unit*

The serology and bacteriology work is combined in one standard laboratory module, where a half module is assigned to each unit. Culture media for use in bacteriology are prepared in the bacteriology work area and sent to the sterilizing unit for sterilization.

The workbenches are 30 inches high with a 22 or 23-inch-deep working area, and are provided with reagent shelves. A knee space is provided in each workbench since most of the procedures are done in a sitting position. A utility sink is provided for the personnel in both units, but the bacteriology unit also requires a sink for the staining of slides. A fume hood is provided to prevent the spread of possible infection to personnel when preparing specimens from suspect cases of tuberculosis, fungus, or virus diseases.

A centrifuge, refrigerator, and incubator are provided along the interior wall within the unit. A desk is also conveniently located for the use of the personnel.

This module is partitioned and separated from the other units by a door to reduce contamination of air and the hazard of infection to personnel in the other lab areas.

**Administrative Area**

The administrative area is separated from the technical work areas so that the non-laboratory personnel need not enter the technical areas. This is the central control and collection point for receiving specimens and is the reception area for the patients and the hospital staff who come to the laboratory.

*Waiting Room*

A waiting area, with conventional waiting room furnishings, is provided for the ambulant patients. In this area, a desk is provided for a clerk. An intercommunication system between the technical areas of the laboratory and the clerk is recommended. This enables him to quickly notify the technical personnel when a patient arrives and also to transfer phone calls for information concerning a laboratory report.

The pathologist's secretary is also located in this area, near the pathologist's office. The secretary handles the pathologist's correspondence, surgical pathological reports, and autopsy protocols.

*Cubicle*

A venipuncture cubicle is provided here; blood specimens are taken from the ambulant patients sent to the laboratory.

*Specimen Toilet*

A specimen toilet is provided in this area for the collection of urine and stool specimens; a pass window opens directly into the technical area near the urinalysis unit.

*Basal Metabolism Electrocardiography Room*

A room is also located here for basal metabolism tests and electrocardiograms, and when necessary, to obtain blood from donors. A writing surface is provided in this room to permit handling of paper work. A lavatory is also provided.

*Pathologist's Office*

The pathologist's office is located so that she may have easy access to the technical areas of the laboratory, particularly the histology unit. This office is separated by a glass partition which permits the pathologist to observe the technical work areas. A draw curtain may be used when she desires privacy. Those who wish to consult the pathologist have access to her office through an entrance from the administrative area.

### Auxiliary Service Areas

The auxiliary service units are located adjacent to the administrative area and are easily accessible to the technical areas.

*Glass Washing and Sterilizing Unit*

The glass washing and sterilizing unit is close to the serology-bacteriology and the biochemistry units which will utilize such services more often than the other units. A separate door leads directly into the serology-bacteriology unit so that contaminated glassware need not be transported through other work areas.

Within this unit are located a water still, pressure sterilizer, sterilizing oven, and pipette washer. Storage cabinets are also provided for stock items of glassware, chemicals, and reagents. A hood over the sterilizers and water still is used to exhaust the heat generated by the equipment. Utility carts used to transport dirty glassware from the various laboratory units to this area are parked in this unit.

*Locker and Toilet Facilities*

Separate locker and toilet facilities are provided within the laboratory department for the medical technologists. This convenience reduces the time personnel must be away from the work areas.

*Optional Services*

Clinical photography, medical illustration, and research facilities are not included in the plan because of their specialized requirements. If these services are to be part of the laboratory department, revision and expansion of the plan will be necessary.

### Guide Plans for Smaller Hospital Laboratories

Plan D presents a design which might be used for a laboratory service in a small hospital. However, more difficulty is encountered in providing as efficient a relationship between the administrative and auxiliary services and the technical laboratory units as in the plans for larger departments (see Fig. 2).

The utilization of the standard laboratory module previously described permits even the small laboratory to be divided into technical, administrative, and auxiliary service work areas where the technologists may work in an area designed for the specific task.

Because of the decreased workload in a laboratory of this size, it is feasible to combine the hematology, bacteriology, and serology units by providing half a module for hematology and the other half for bacteriology and serology. A second module is provided for urinalysis and biochemistry, storage space, and refrigerator. Only the more common and simple laboratory procedures would be done in these units.

A glass washing and sterilizing area is provided directly opposite but apart from the technical work areas.

The administrative area provides a small waiting room where a clerk receives patients and laboratory requests and specimens. In this area, a room is also provided for performing basal metabolism tests and electrocardiograms. This room also can be used for obtaining blood specimens from ambulant patients.

### Utility Services

The utility service systems required in the operation of the laboratory include water, waste, gas, vacuum and compressed air. Because of the importance of these systems, the need for continuity of service, and the probability of future expansion, careful study is necessary in designing them for safety and efficiency.

Piping systems should not be exposed because they create housekeeping problems as dirt collectors and may be hazardous; many are noisy and unsightly. They should be located where they will be easily accessible for service and repairs with a minimum of disruption of normal laboratory services. A sufficient number of valves, traps, and cleanout openings should be installed and should be located so as to permit maximum use of the facilities during repairs.

Laboratory benches (Fig. 3) are usually placed at right angles to and adjoining outside walls to effectively utilize space. This location of the benches simplifies, to some extent, the arrangement of the piping systems by installing vertical lines in the outside wall and mounting the horizontal piping on this wall. This arrangement is particularly advantageous for the waste vent stacks which must be carried vertically to the roof.

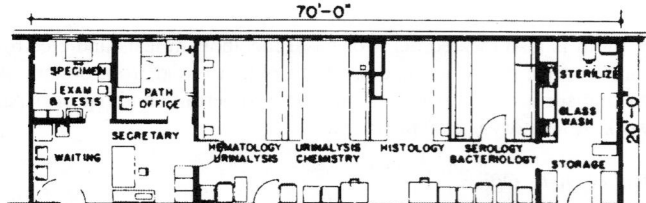

**Fig. 2. Plan B alternate plan (40,000 to 75,000 tests annually)**

**Fig. 3. Perspective view of laboratory for general hospital of 150 to 200 beds**

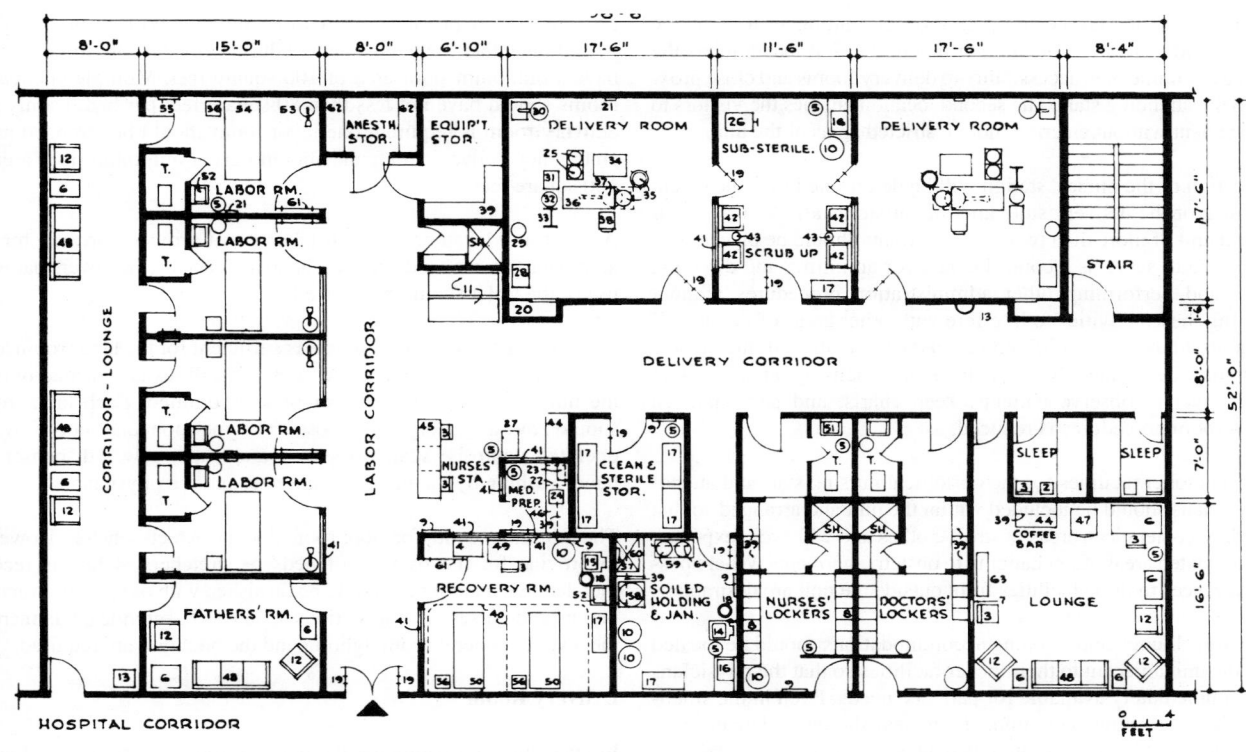

**Fig. 1. Labor-delivery unit for approximately 1,500 births per year**

# LABOR-DELIVERY SUITES

## LOCATING THE DELIVERY SUITE

Since the labor-delivery unit is basically self-sufficient, it may be located adjacent to the newborn nursery and maternity unit or elsewhere in the hospital; wherever possible, it should be located on the same floor. Transportation of mother and infant is reduced and maximum utilization of staff is obtained when all three units are together.

However, in large hospitals requiring more than one maternity nursing unit, another location may be required.

## FUNCTIONAL ARRANGEMENT OF THE DELIVERY SUITE

The delivery suite includes three areas of activity: labor, delivery, and recovery. Proper sequential arrangement of labor, delivery, and recovery areas within the labor-delivery unit facilitates patient care and aids the staff in carrying out proper medical techniques and practices (see Fig. 1).

Labor, delivery, and recovery rooms should be located and related for easy movement of patients from one area to another and for good patient observation. In large suites, locating service facilities on subsidiary corridors may help to reduce and control traffic.

From the standpoint of asepsis, location of delivery rooms and service facilities is critical. A location as remote as practicable from the entrance to the suite will reduce traffic, cause less air turbulence, and provide greater privacy for the patient.

Scrub-up areas should be adjacent to delivery rooms so that attending physicians can observe delivery room procedures and the condition of the patient.

A medical preparation facility serving labor and delivery areas should be convenient to both, accessible only to authorized personnel. This is usually located at the nurses' station or control area.

A soiled holding room should be convenient for preparing the delivery room for a subsequent patient and for retaining soiled articles for disposal, processing, or return to central service.

Since the time of need for the delivery can seldom be determined, labor rooms should be close to delivery rooms but not so close that the two areas are intermixed or that patients in labor can overhear or view delivery room procedures.

A subsidiary corridor, if placed with a separate access to labor rooms, will permit the father to visit in the labor room without passing through the main corridor and may also serve as a lounge area for ambulant patients and authorized visitors.

A recovery room should be located within the unit in an area: (1) adjacent to delivery rooms, or (2) near the main entrance to the unit. The

*References: Planning the Labor-Delivery Unit in the General Hospital,* Public Health Service Department of Health and Human Services.

determining factor may be the policy on permitting visitors to the recovery room. If no visitors are permitted, the first location has the advantage of immediate accessibility to delivery rooms and close proximity to the attending staff. The second location enables the visitors to see the patient without entering more restricted areas of the unit.

The location of the nurses' station will be determined to some extent by the size of the delivery suite and the nursing staff. A nurses' station for a unit of more than two delivery rooms should be placed near the entrance to serve as a control center for admitting and directing patients and performing other administration procedures without permitting these activities to interfere with other areas of the unit. If continuous attendance is difficult because of a small staff, the nurses' station may be located between labor and delivery areas so that nurses' travel to observe patients, keep charts, and participate in delivery room procedures is reduced.

Locker and toilet facilities for the obstetrical nursing staff and attending physicians should be included within the unit and arranged so that they will not enter clean areas in street clothes and will avoid exposure to contaminated areas after changing to obstetric garments. Where possible, entrances to these facilities from outside the unit are desirable.

The doctors' lounge and sleeping accommodations should be located within the unit adjacent to their locker facilities so that the physicians may be immediately available for patients' needs. Even in the smallest hospitals, sleeping accommodations near the labor/delivery unit should be available to attending physicians.

Dictation facilities should be located in or near the doctors' lounge.

**Admitting and Preparation**

Various methods are used to admit maternity patients:

- Through the main hospital admitting desk and then either to a maternity nursing unit or to a labor room in the delivery unit.
- Directly to labor rooms in the delivery suite.
- In an admitting and preparation unit. An admitting and preparation unit is desirable in hospitals where a large daily patient load makes it necessary, after observation, to group patients: those to be returned home, those to be sent to the nursing unit, and those to be admitted to the labor-delivery unit. If such a unit is provided, two locations are feasible: (1) adjoining the hospital admitting area, and (2) adjacent to but not a part of the delivery suite. The first location facilitates the admitting process and permits immediate patient examination, provided the obstetrical staff is available, and it also prevents patients not in labor or those destined for isolation from entering maternity nursing areas. The second location concentrates obstetrical staff activities in a single area of the hospital and allows immediate availability of the delivery suite in emergency cases.

**Labor Rooms**

Labor rooms should provide maximum comfort and relaxation for the patient and should have facilities for examination, preparation, and observation. Unless an admitting and preparation unit outside the labor-delivery unit is available, the patient may be admitted directly to the labor room.

Although traditional practice has permitted two or more beds in labor rooms, single occupancy rooms are also utilized. They eliminate the necessity for a patient preparation room, separate infectious patients,

provide greater privacy, and if in accordance with hospital policy, permit the father to visit the patient during labor. These rooms should have a minimum floor area of 100 square feet. Multiple occupancy rooms should have not less than 80 square feet per bed. If only one delivery room is required, one labor room should be arranged as an emergency delivery room and should have a minimum floor area of 180 square feet.

A toilet and lavatory for each labor room provides privacy for the ambulant patient, and reduces bedpan services; however, patient's use of the toilet should be controlled.

One shower and dressing cubicle is sufficient for the labor room area. If admittance, preparation, and shower facilities are located outside the unit, the labor area shower may be omitted. Each labor room should have a lavatory with gooseneck-type spout and foot- or wrist-operated controls, soap dispenser, and paper towel dispenser for hand-washing by the patient, the nurse, and the physician.

The minimum width for labor room doors is 3 feet-8 inches. However, to provide for the passage of beds or stretchers, 4 feet is recommended. Each labor bed should be furnished with oxygen and vacuum outlets and nurses' calling stations. Controls to provide adjustment of the level of general room lighting and the bed light are required.

**Delivery Room**

In designing and equipping the delivery room, every facility for the welfare and safety of the mother and the newborn child should be incorporated. Basic considerations include the immediate availability of equipment and supplies, built-in protection against anesthetic explosion along with auxiliary electrical systems in case of power failure.

Space allowance for equipment and for the staff to circulate freely is a primary factor in determining the size of a delivery room.

The position of the anesthesiologist in the delivery room is determined by the arrangement of the backup table in the delivery room. This table is located in the cleanest area of the delivery room, away from all traffic and opposite the entrance to the sterilizer and scrub areas. The feet of the patient are usually located nearest the backup table with the obstetrician at that end and the anesthesiologist at the opposite end. Since most anesthesiologists are right-handed, their equipment is located on the right, and it is desirable to place the door so that the anesthesiologist's equipment can be located where it need not be moved when the patient is brought in.

The view box should be located behind the anesthesiologist so that the circulating nurse may insert or remove films and the obstetrician may observe it without turning.

Cesarean sections are performed within the suite in separate C-Section Rooms. These rooms are treated as OR rooms, and require the same level of air-exchange, medical gasses, and finish requirements. Minimum size for these rooms is 400 square feet.

A minimum ceiling height of 9 feet is required for an obstetrical light. Additional height is advantageous and may be required for some types of lighting fixtures.

Oxygen and vacuum wall outlets should be installed near the bassinet location for use in resuscitation. Built-in cabinets in the delivery room should be kept to a minimum and used for storage of such supplies as sutures and special instruments.

The minimum width for the delivery room door is 3 feet-8 inches; however, 4 feet is recommended since patients will often be moved to the delivery room on a labor bed.

An emergency call system must have stations in each delivery room with a dome light and indicator in the corridor over each delivery room door and in locker rooms, lounge, nurses' station, and other such areas. A nurses' intercom system must be provided between these same areas.

### Recovery Room

The recovery period, after delivery, is critical and may last from one to three hours. During this period the mother requires close observation and special care by the labor/delivery nursing staff. Some hospitals insist on continuous bedside attendance during this time. Various locations may be used for patients during the recovery period: a delivery room, a labor room, a bed in the maternity nursing unit, or a recovery room used exclusively for this purpose.

The recovery room has generally been accepted as a necessary facility in the delivery suite and should be considered for any hospital requiring three or more labor beds. A recovery room provides a location for recovering patients, frees the delivery or labor room for cleanup prior to occupancy by another patient, concentrates patients in similar condition, and facilitates the special nursing care required.

In designing the recovery room, provision should be made for easy movement of stretchers or beds. If a number of patients will be cared for, a separate entrance and an exit may be advisable. Space should be provided for a nurse's desk, an instrument cart or table, a clean supply cart, a soiled linen hamper, and a waste receptacle. The nurse's desk should be large enough for a telephone, charts, a nurses' calling station, and forms and writing material. Cubicle curtains at each stretcher location should allow clearance for attending the patient from either side. Oxygen and suction outlets and a nurses' calling station should be installed at each stretcher position. Glass view panels between the room and the corridor facilitate observation. A handwashing sink is also required.

### LDRs (Labor, Delivery, and Recovery Rooms)

Some hospitals provide LDR rooms; a single bed room for both labor, delivery, and recovery functions (Fig 2). Each of these rooms is sized larger than a typical single bed room to allow for the additional equipment and bassinet area. Each room has a toilet/shower room. After birth and recovery, the patient is transferred to the Post-Partum Nursing Unit.

Another variation of this is the LDRP room (Labor, Delivery, Recovery, and Post-Partum Room. Essentially the same room as described above, the patient remains in the same room for the entire birthing and recovery process until she leaves the hospital. This is usually considered a premium service provided by the hospital, and can cost the patient additional money, since it may not be covered by the patient's health insurance.

### Nurses' Station

The nurses' station is the administrative and control center of the labor/delivery unit. Its size, complexity, and location will be determined by the extent of responsibilities charged to the obstetrical supervisor as well as by the size and staffing of the suite.

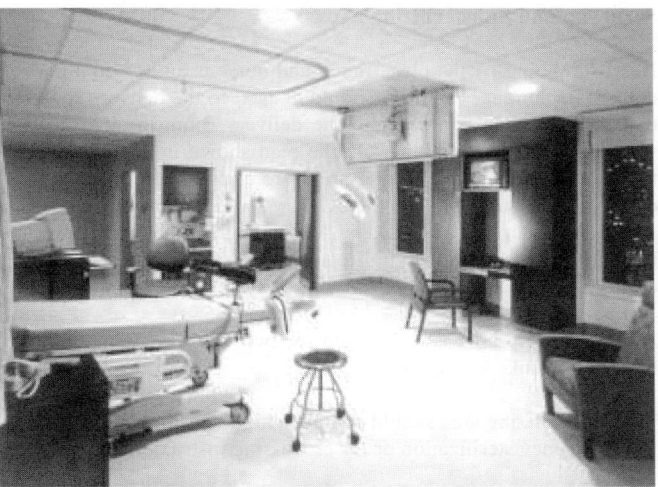

**Fig. 2. Labor delivery recovery room (Taylor Clark Architects; photo: Walter Dufresne)**

If patients are admitted directly to the labor/delivery unit, the nurses' station may be responsible for admitting procedures. Inventory and requisitioning of supplies may be handled at the nurses' station, although central service would assume this responsibility under a complement system.

If office records are extensive, file storage may be necessary. In large units, an office for the obstetrical supervisor may be required. A bulletin board should be provided for work schedules and hospital bulletins. A desk-height counter for the master station of the nurses' calling system, medical records, and a telephone may be adequate if the daily workload is small.

### Doctors' Lockers and Lounge

This area should contain a locker room, a toilet and shower room, a lounge, and sleeping accommodations. If the staff is not large enough to warrant separate facilities, a toilet-shower room and combined locker-lounge-sleeping room may serve staff needs.

In hospitals with only one delivery room, a minimum of 6 lockers is recommended; in those with more than one delivery room, a minimum of 5 lockers per delivery room is recommended. The minimum size recommended for a locker is 12 by 18 by 60 inches. Space should be provided in the locker room for a cart for clean scrub suits and a hamper for soiled linen.

The lounge should accommodate a couch, chairs, bookcase, and a television set. A recessed film illuminator should also be provided. If dictation booths are not provided, a suitable desk and chair for this purpose should be included in the lounge.

Sleeping accommodations for the attending staff should be provided. For flexibility of use by either male or female doctors, it is preferable to provide single occupancy rooms for this purpose. In addition to the bed, furnishings should include chair and night table. If only a combined locker-lounge-sleeping room is required, the couch should open to make a bed.

## Scrub-up and Substerilizing Areas

Hand scrubbing by the obstetrician and nurse is an essential part of delivery technique. Facilities should be next to the delivery room so that the physician can see into the delivery room through a glass view-panel while scrubbing. On the plan shown in this publication the scrub-up and substerilizing areas are combined in one room. A door between this room and the delivery room is recommended. The area used for scrubbing should be deep enough so that persons scrubbing will not interfere with traffic and so that splashed water will not constitute a hazard.

If one scrub-up area is to be used for two delivery rooms, at least three scrub sinks should be provided.

The substerilizing area should contain a high-speed washer-sterilizer for emergency sterilization or for processing instruments.

## Supply and Equipment Storage

*Supplies*

The main factor in determining the space allocation for supply storage in the labor-delivery unit is the method and frequency of issuing supplies from central supply areas. Supplies include all items processed by the laundry and central sterile supply and those issued from central service. Excluded are pharmacy, anesthetic, or equipment items. All supplies should be kept in hospital central service and issued to the labor-delivery unit only after the required processing.

A more recent storage method uses the same carts on which supplies are delivered from storage of clean and sterile items. Supplies used only in the delivery room are packed on one cart and those for other use on other carts. Clean supply carts may also be assigned to doctors' and nurses' locker rooms for scrub clothes and towels. This method requires a clean supply room near the delivery rooms for carts containing clean or sterile items.

*Equipment Storage*

Equipment that is infrequently used, such as delivery table parts and duplicate equipment not in use, should be stored in an equipment storage room in the unit. This room should have shelves for small items and floor space for larger equipment.

## Medications

A medication preparation room or unit should be located near labor and delivery rooms for storage and preparation of drugs, including narcotics.

Medication preparation requires uninterrupted concentration by the nurse, and an enclosure or room with glass viewing panels is suggested for this function. A work counter with storage for syringes and accessories and a sink with gooseneck-type spout and foot or wrist controls for hand-washing are recommended. If stepped shelves, sized for the smaller medicine bottles, are provided, the nurse can read labels quickly and arrange medicines in the order desired. A wall cabinet is suggested for bottles of solutions, and an eye-level, locked cabinet is required. Since some medicines must be maintained below room temperature, a refrigerator is also required.

## Anesthesia Facilities

The head anesthesiologist should be consulted early in the planning stage to determine design requirements for anesthesia facilities including what gases are to be utilized; the number, size, and location of gas cylinders to be stored; and space required for cleaning and checking the anesthesia equipment. Piping oxygen and vacuum to delivery rooms and other areas of the hospital is standard practice. In some hospitals, nitrous oxide is piped to the delivery room.

A room should be provided in the unit for storing gas cylinders. Flammable gases should be stored separately from oxygen and nitrous oxide, which may be stored in any location since there are no hazards involved. Small cylinders sized to fit the anesthesia apparatus may be stored in racks. Cans of volatile liquids may be stored on shelves in the same storage area. Shelves should be provided for equipment such as pressure gauges. Large cylinders should be stored upright in racks. Space for a gas cylinder truck or carrier may be necessary. The primary purpose of storage for these gases and volatile liquids within the unit is to assure availability over weekends and at night when main hospital supply rooms may be closed. Storage space for a 48-hour supply of gas is considered maximum, and additional storage space on the unit is not desirable.

## Instrument Processing

The processing of instruments includes washing, preferably in a washer-sterilizer or by hand, disassembling where necessary, arranging for future use, and sterilizing.

One of several methods may be followed for instrument processing:

1. Soiled instruments are washed in the washer-sterilizer and sent to central sterile supply for processing. The plan shown is based on this assumption.
2. Soiled instruments are sent directly to central supply for processing. The washer-sterilizer is required for emergency sterilization.
3. Processing may take place in the unit under the direction of the obstetrical supervisor. In this case a workroom is required.

## Soiled Holding Room

All cleanup techniques including housekeeping are originated in this area, and soiled materials are placed here for disposal or return to central sterile supply for processing. This room will require a sink with drainboards for gross cleaning, a flushing rim sink for disposal of liquid wastes, a cart for storage of cleaning materials, carts and hampers to receive soiled articles, and a waste receptacle. Germicidal solutions and utensils used in cleaning should be stored here. If placentas are saved, a domestic-type deep freeze will be required.

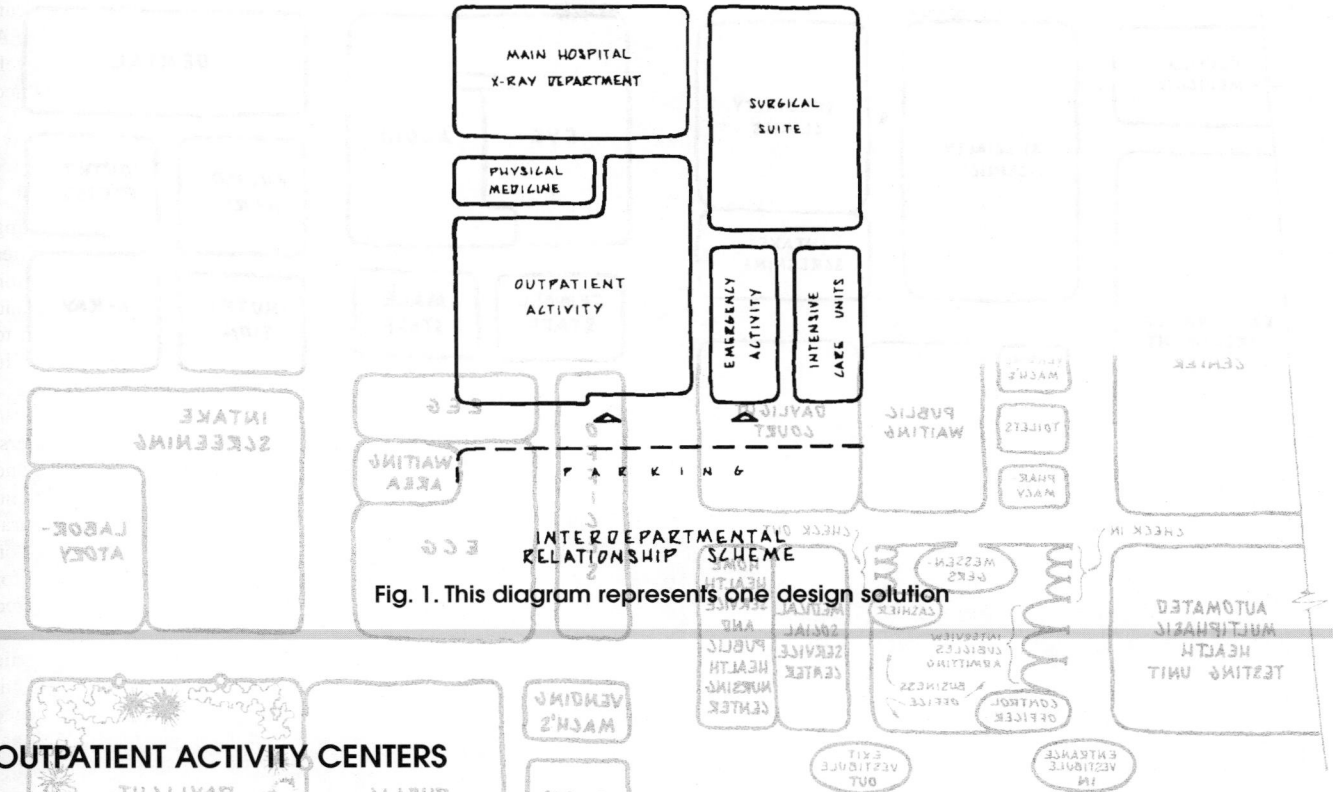

**Fig. 1. This diagram represents one design solution**

# OUTPATIENT ACTIVITY CENTERS

Because physical medicine in the Outpatient Activity is used by both inpatients and outpatients, it is situated for the convenience and accessibility of both types of patients. Patients arriving at the Emergency Activity are evaluated (triage), and appropriate disposition is made of each case. The surgical suite is located close to the Emergency Activity to ensure the most rapid conveyance of a patient in a life-threatening situation. Cardiac arrest patients will receive immediate treatment by the code blue alert team within the Emergency Activity. After the crisis, the patient will be transferred to an adjoining intensive coronary care unit.

Since patients entering the Emergency Activity are frequently assigned elsewhere, close working relationships should exist with other areas of the hospital such as the surgical suite, intensive care units, and the main x-ray department.

Some additional working relationships between the Outpatient Activity and other hospital services are indicated in Fig. 1. Since these do not require immediate adjacency, they assume less importance on the relative scale of values established by either the overall planners or the designer.

### Intradepartmental Relationships

Although the program of functions may delineate certain specific constraints and preferences as to disposition of the elements of an Outpatient Activity, the final outcome often is a compromise that represents the best acceptable solution to all parties concerned (see Figs. 2 and 3).

In one example, elements of the Outpatient Activity are arranged along the main circulation route. Since considerable traffic is expected, this corridor is 10 feet wide and forms the spine of the scheme. Branch corridors, each 8 feet wide, which separate other elements from each other, originate from the spine and provide access for people and goods to respective elements.

Since new patients do not know locations of the various clinics, some method must be devised to assist them. The architect can help by incorporating into the physical design a simple, easily understood system of signs. They might be either wall-mounted or incorporated into the floor surface, adding what can be an exciting physical design element to relieve the monotony of a long hospital corridor.

Becoming oriented within a modern hospital can be difficult even for a well person and especially confusing to a patient who is debilitated. Ability to control the internal environment has resulted in many windowless spaces in a hospital which are interconnected by a maze of corridors, especially in the diagnostic and treatment areas. To help resolve the orientation problem, specialty clinics (except pediatric) are grouped in one area. The pediatric clinic is in close proximity to the entrance to reduce travel distance for the mother carrying an infant.

The control and administration or business office should be the primary contact between the patient and the institution. This is the point of origin of the service where disposition is made as to what is appropriate for the patient.

*References: Guidelines to Functional Programming, Equipping, and Designing Hospital Outpatient & Emergency Activities*, DHEW Publication No. (HRA) 77-4002, US Department of Health and Human Services, Washington D.C.

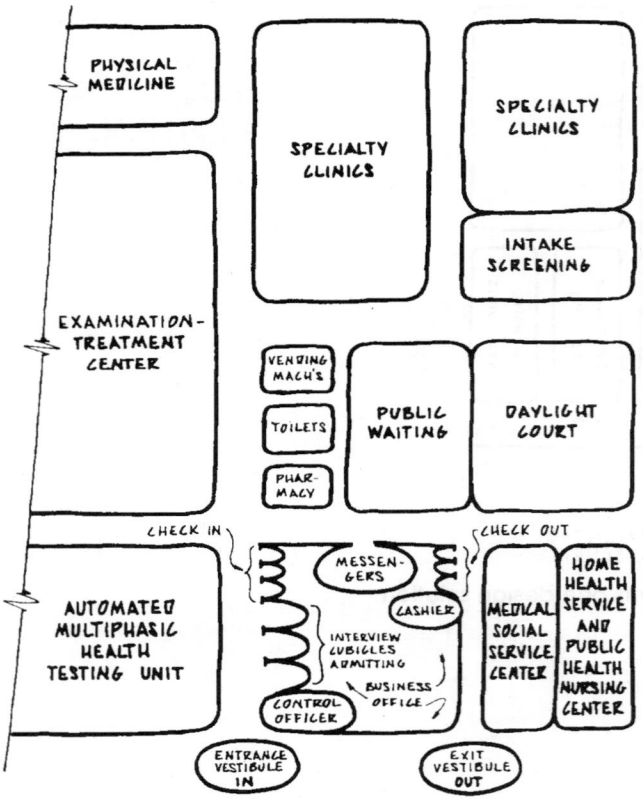

Fig. 2. Intradepartmental relationship scheme

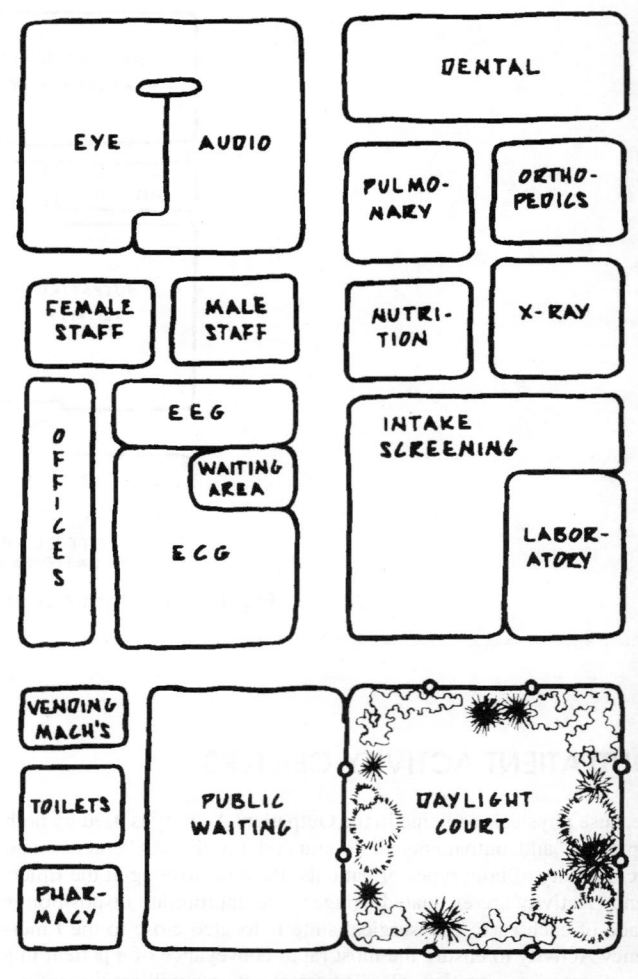

Fig. 3. Relationships of specialty clinics scheme

The two categories of outpatients are:

1. New patients for whom admission records and other documentation must be prepared;
2. Repeat patients whose documentation is on file.

**Administration**

All patients enter the facility through a vestibule which provides protection from inclement weather. They are greeted by a control officer in the business office who has an overview of all incoming people and orients patients to processing (see Fig. 12).

*Admitting*

On the first visit, the patient is directed to one of the admitting interview cubicles which form an integral part of the business office. On completion of the admitting procedure, a clerk summons a messenger whose station, which should be large enough to store wheelchairs, is adjacent and connected to the business office. He escorts the patient directly to the intake screening center or, if it is fully occupied, to the public waiting area.

The repeat patient who has an appointment to a specific clinic stops at the check-in station where she receives instruction. She may go directly to the clinic or wait in the public waiting space until notified by the control officer. (The business office is responsible for checking patients in and out and for collecting fees, if applicable.)

Despite rigorous efforts and best intentions in establishing schedules and appointments, delays due to unforeseen circumstances will occur. Hence, patients and family members must be afforded an appropriate waiting place also needed by patients awaiting prescriptions issued from the pharmacy dispensary. This suggests that the dispensary be directly accessible from the public waiting area and that visual signals be installed near the issue windows indicating when the prescription is ready.

All patients, upon completing their visit, report to the check-out station where they are issued instructions for a repeat visit, if necessary. The architectural design accommodates these requirements.

*Medical Record Unit*

The medical record room is strategically placed near the business office and adjacent to the examination-treatment center for easy access. It may be served by a pneumatic tube station and messenger service.

*Medical Social Service Center*

An important outpatient service is health education and follow-up care that may extend into the patient's home. The center provides a base of operations for medical social service for evaluation and future follow-up, if indicated. The follow-up extends patient care into home and community.

A large multipurpose room is provided for large-group health education. Conveniently placed near the entrance, it can be used when the rest of the Outpatient Activity is closed.

*Home Health and Public Health Nursing Center*

Adjacent and interconnected to medical social service is the home health and public health nursing center. Both have reception and patient subwaiting areas.

**Specialty Clinics**

Adjacent to both the Administration and the Examination and Treatment Center are the clinics designed and equipped for special procedures (see Figs. 2 and 3; see also Fig. 11).

All new patients pass through the intake screening center where medical evaluation and disposition are made regarding subsequent medical treatment. Medical history and documentation are initiated and routine laboratory testing performed. Therefore, provision must be made for separate specimen collection spaces for men and women, a routine testing laboratory, and a submitting area with a registered nurse in attendance. Appropriate spaces and fixtures are provided for disabled persons.

The laboratory and x-ray unit will serve the Outpatient and Emergency Activities. The laboratory, with pass-through windows for specimens, may use pneumatic tubes for forwarding specimens to the main hospital's laboratory. An x-ray unit for diagnostic purposes should be large enough to accommodate stretcher patients.

Patients requiring extensive diagnostic tests can be referred to the main hospital's radiology department and pathological and pulmonary function laboratories. While the EEG and ECG clinics are located within the Outpatient Activity, they serve the entire hospital.

**Examination-Treatment Center**

A large portion of outpatient workload will be handled in the examination-treatment center rather than in the specialty clinics. Hence, a waiting room with public conveniences is provided. The layout of the center, Fig. 4, was called for by the program of functions which designates three work components herein called clusters. Each cluster consisting of ten examination-treatment rooms surrounds its own central utility work space designated as a personnel corridor (see Fig. 5). Other configurations may be equally appropriate (see Figs. 7 and 8).

In the first phase, 30 examination-treatment rooms are provided. Future expansion to add 30 rooms must, of necessity, be linear along the utility work space. This corridor must be limited in length to approximately 100 feet because experience shows greater distance to be undesirable. All the examination-treatment rooms are accessible from a system of patients' corridors stemming from the waiting room. In addition, personnel corridors are accessible from the outside corridor.

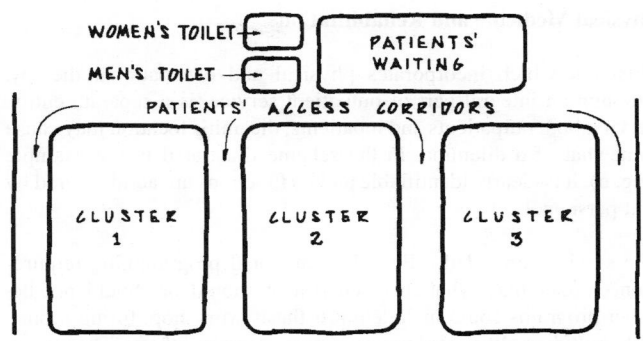

**Fig. 4. Examination-Treatment Center relationship scheme**

With the exception of general and special surgery, proctology, and urology, all examination rooms are similar in size and design.

No special provision is made for patient disrobing since either a ceiling track curtain or a folding screen may be used. It is assumed that the physician examines one patient while another undresses in an adjacent examination room. In most cases, allocation of two or more examination rooms per physician allows economic use of her time.

The following scheme will apply throughout:

- Each examination room will have not less than 80 net square feet of usable floor area. Rooms also used for treatment shall not have less than 120 net square feet of usable floor space.
- Examination or treatment tables are to be accessible on three sides allowing for working space of not less than 30 in clear on each side. Hand-washing facilities for attending staff must be provided.
- The clinics of the center are grouped by similarities of medical specialties. All are identically equipped except those listed below which have individual needs:

  General and special surgery
  Proctology
  Urology
  Diabetic
  Metabolic
  Neurology
  Allergy-Dermatology
  Cardiovascular

See also Fig. 9 for specific equipment recommendations.

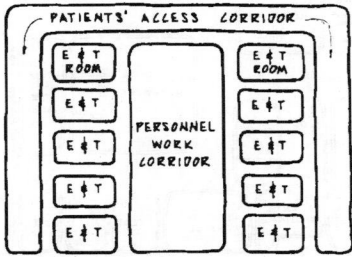

**Fig. 5. Examination-Treatment Center individual cluster scheme**

## Physical Medicine and Rehabilitation

This unit which incorporates physical and occupational therapy, although an integral part of outpatient service, is a separate entity. Serving both outpatients and inpatients, the unit's location may cause somewhat of a dilemma. In the scheme illustrated in the example (Fig. 6), it is clearly identifiable and its functions are administered by unit personnel.

The services provided reflect the functional programming requirements rather than what this department should or should not be. Other programs could include a prosthesis workshop, fitting rooms, and multidiscipline conference rooms, among others. That every individual situation or program requires an individual planning solution to meet specific local needs cannot be overemphasized.

Although an element of outpatient service, Physical Medicine and Rehabilitation (PM&R) also serves the inpatient hospital population. Accessibility from outside as well as from inside the hospital without impeding outpatient services requires the designer's special consideration.

PM&R consists of two principal elements: physical therapy and occupational therapy. While these activities are subject to interpretation, the elements and equipment provided are expected to constitute a comprehensive approach to the normally recognized concept of an Occupational Therapy Department. The two departments are adjacent but separate with their own staffs; administration and control may be shared. Figure 6 illustrates the relationships between individual spaces within the departments and reasons for them as understood by an architect.

PM&R is under the physiatrist-director whose office is accessible from the outside corridor, the secretary's office, and from within the department, thus facilitating overall supervisory duties.

Special attention is given to the fact that many patients are physically incapacitated and use prosthetic appliances or wheelchairs. Some inpatients may be brought in on stretchers. Therefore, corridors are a minimum of 6 feet wide. Wheelchair patients are provided special plumbing fixtures, drinking fountains, and large cubicles for dressing and undressing.

Corridor wall handrails are controversial. Those against maintain that patients should learn to be independent and not have handrails. Those for believe that the weak, uncertain patient needs assistance which he can ignore later. Because patients in PM&R should be under continuous supervision or attended by staff, the decision must be made by the institution. To be a useful aid for disabled persons, the handrail must be designed to meet the users' anthropometric requirements. It must be substantial, offset from the wall, and well secured to prevent anchorage failure and possible injury.

Opinions differ regarding provision of a tank in hydrotherapy for total immersion of the patient's body. Some authorities recommend elimination of the tank. Others advocate provision of a swimming pool. Obviously, the latter cost implications are so great that the issue can only be resolved by each individual program.

Hydrotherapy produces a large volume of soiled wet linen which is often overlooked or given insufficient recognition. Adequate provision should be made either for collecting, temporarily holding, and transporting this linen to the hospital laundry or for processing in the physical medicine department.

The spaces indicated in Fig. 6 accommodate the equipment recommended (see Fig. 10). The physical therapy entity is based on the racetrack corridor principle, facilitating movement of people and equipment from one part of the facility to another. Wet activities such as hydrotherapy are purposefully placed in an enclosed room. The exercise area is placed apart from other activities to help preserve patients' dignity and alleviate their apprehension and self-consciousness as they try to regain their previous mobility or agility.

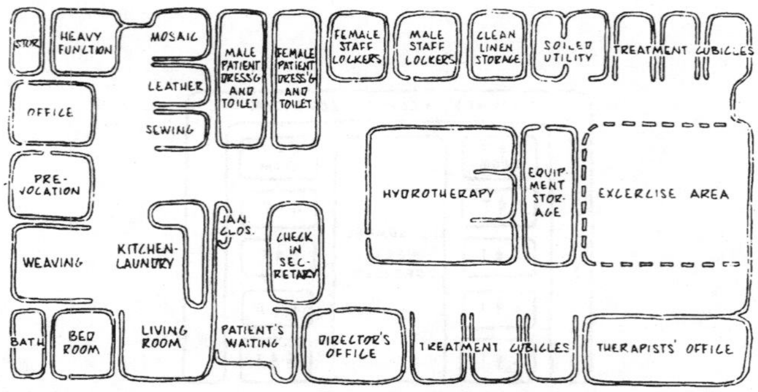

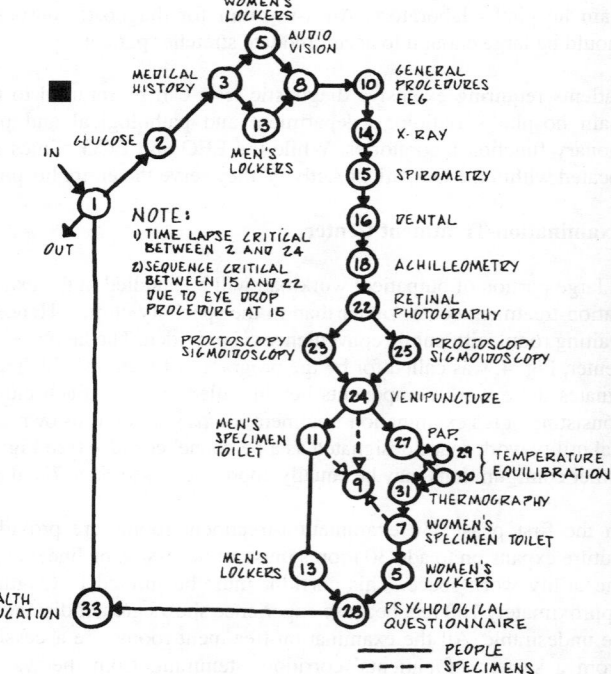

**Fig. 7. Automated multiphasic health-testing sequence**

**Fig. 6. Physical medicine and rehabilitation relationship scheme**

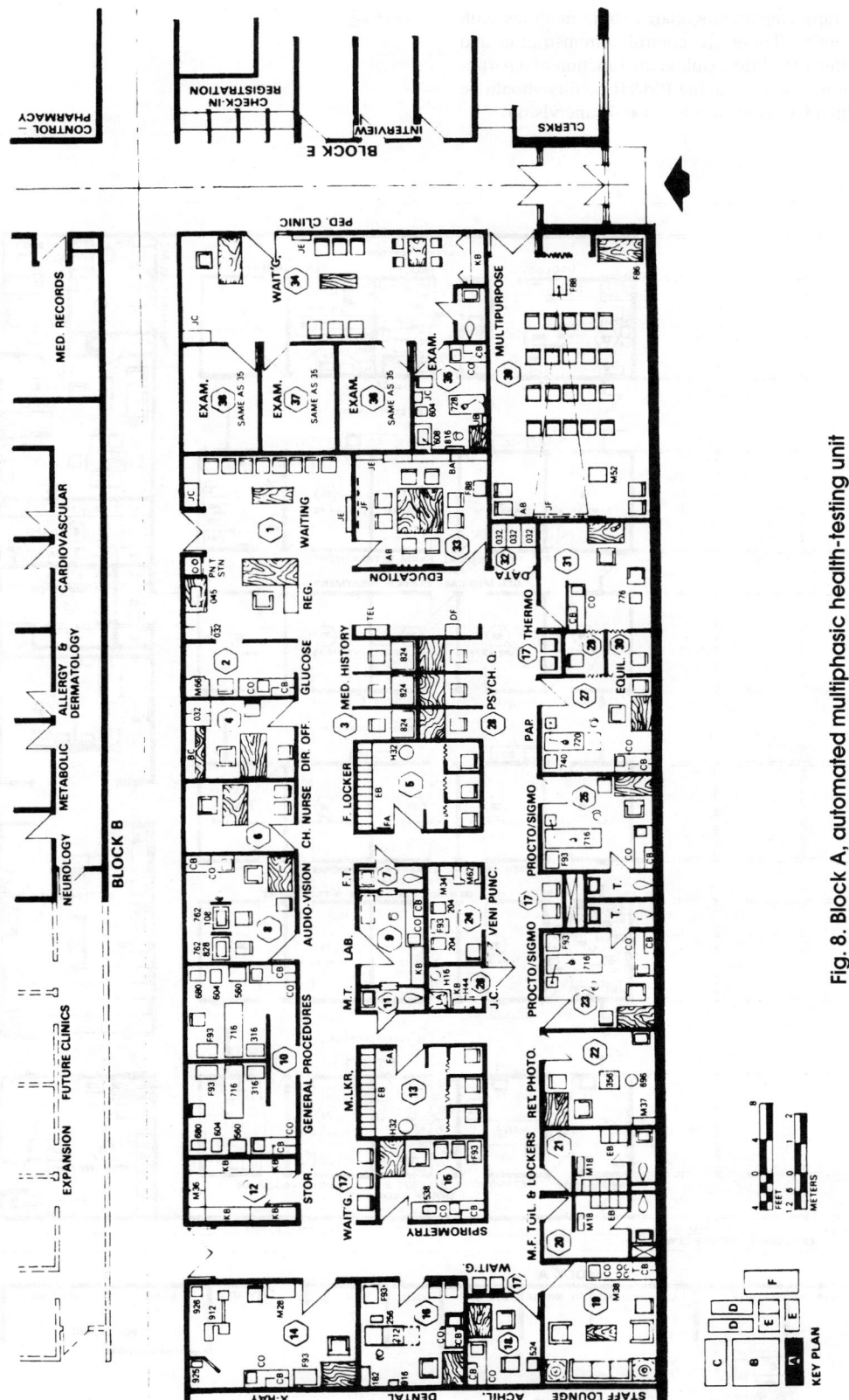

Fig. 8. Block A, automated multiphasic health-testing unit

The Occupational Therapy Department shares some facilities with the physical therapy entity. These are control-administration and patients' dressing and toilet facilities. Unless the function of a particular space dictated that it be enclosed, the PM&R facility should be as open as possible which facilitates needed visual supervision.

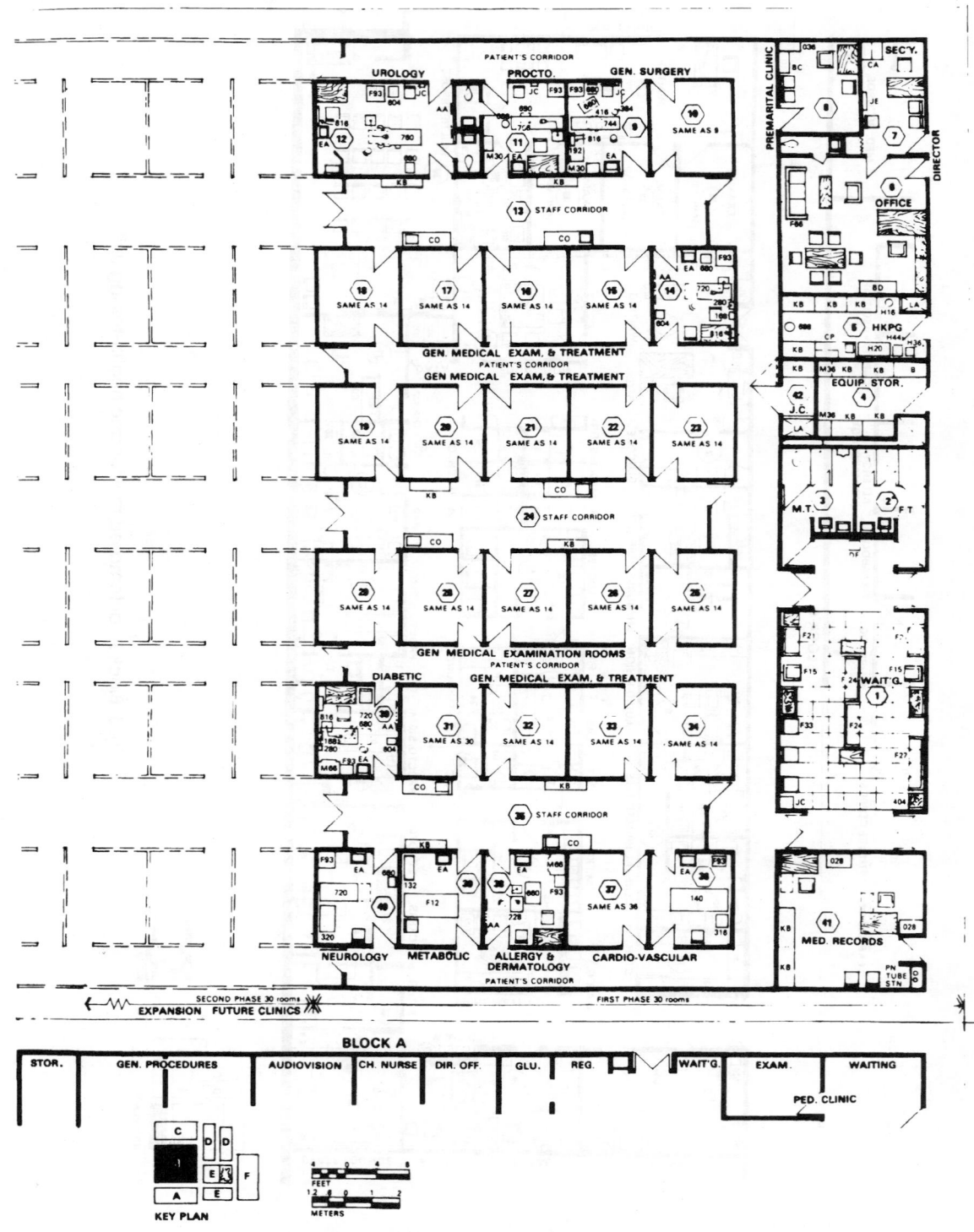

**Fig 9. Block B, Examination-Treatment Center**

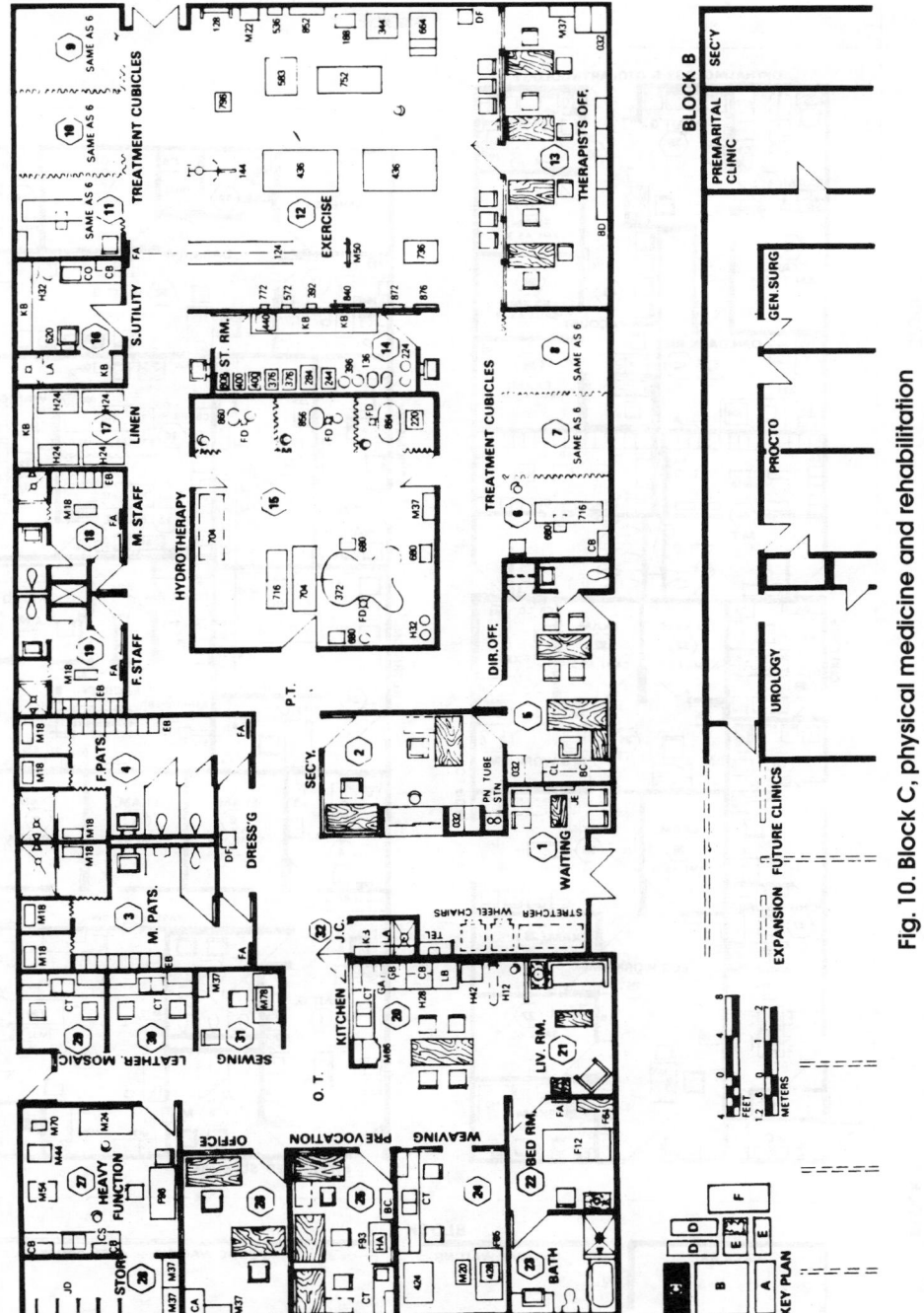

Fig. 10. Block C, physical medicine and rehabilitation

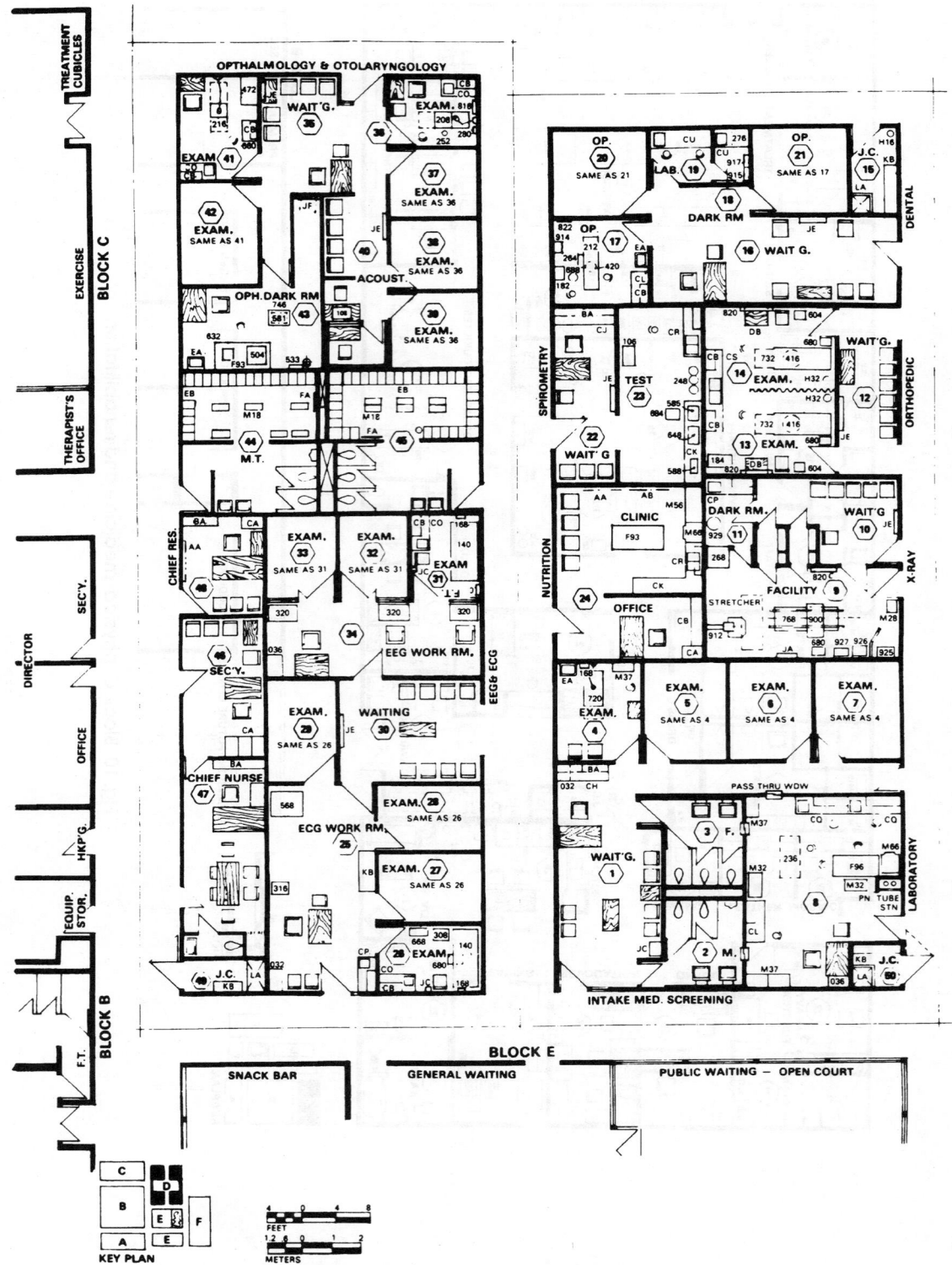

**Fig. 11. Block D, specialty clinics**

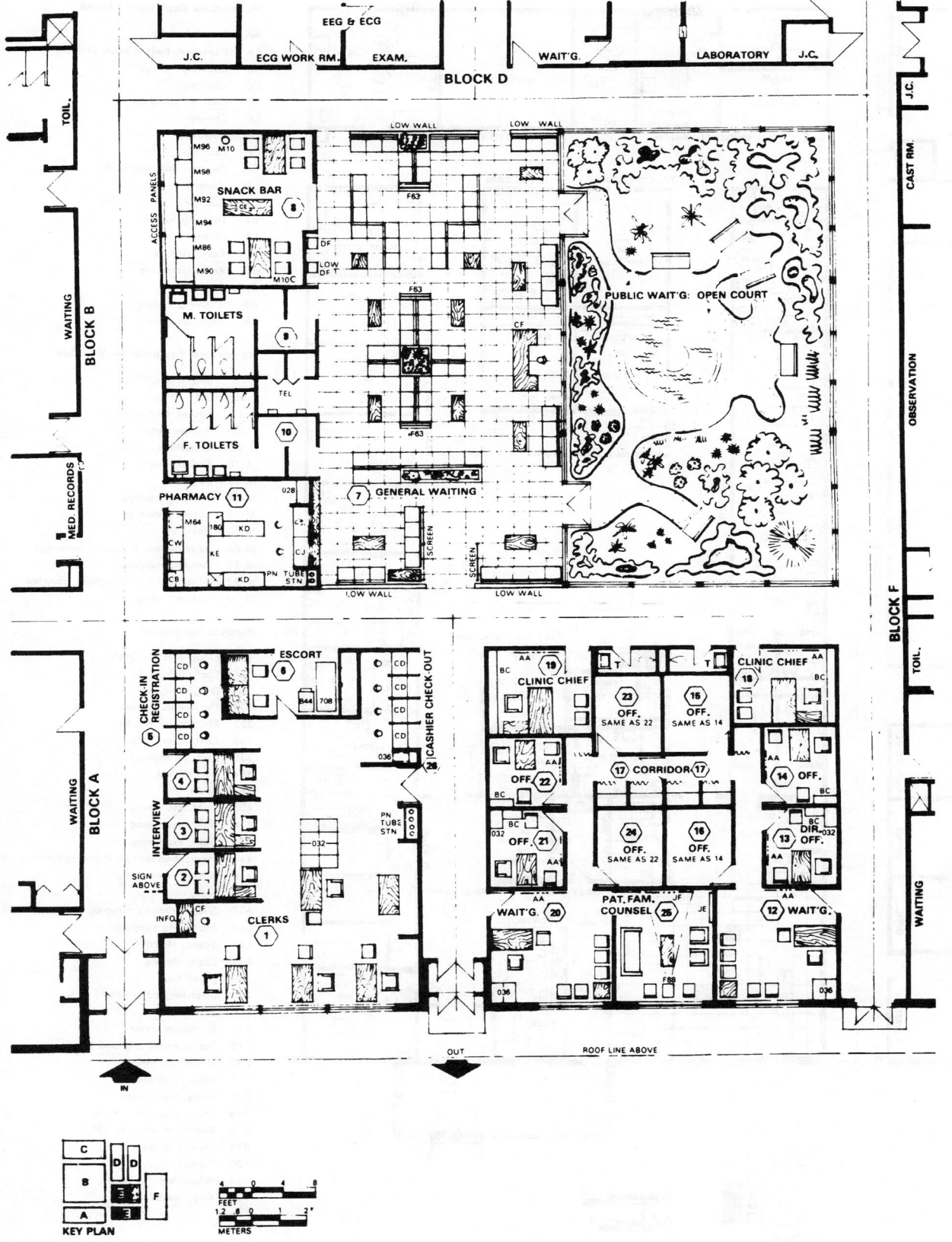

**Fig. 12. Block E, administration**

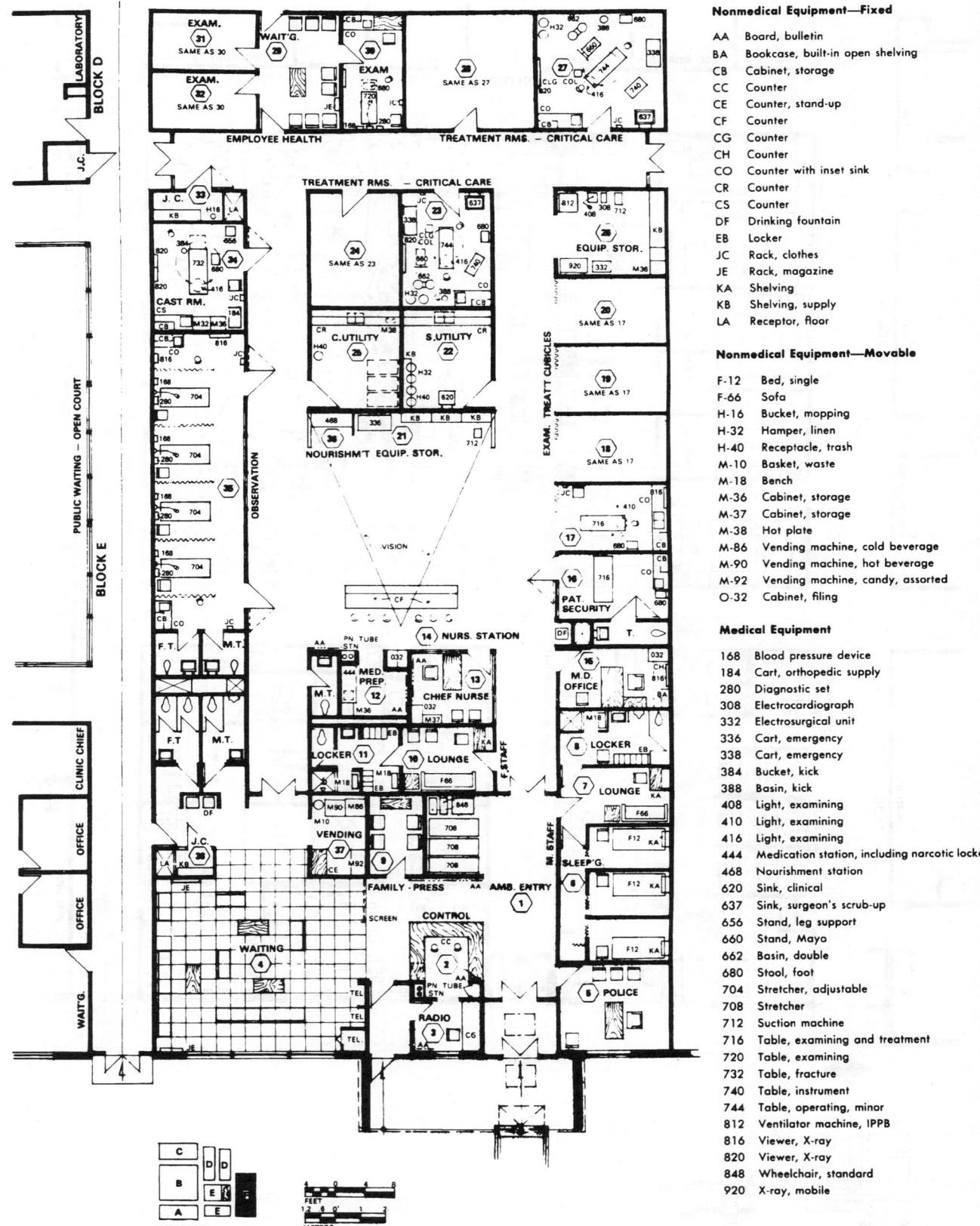

**Nonmedical Equipment—Fixed**

AA   Board, bulletin
BA   Bookcase, built-in open shelving
CB   Cabinet, storage
CC   Counter
CE   Counter, stand-up
CF   Counter
CG   Counter
CH   Counter
CO   Counter with inset sink
CR   Counter
CS   Counter
DF   Drinking fountain
EB   Locker
JC   Rack, clothes
JE   Rack, magazine
KA   Shelving
KB   Shelving, supply
LA   Receptor, floor

**Nonmedical Equipment—Movable**

F-12   Bed, single
F-66   Sofa
H-16   Bucket, mopping
H-32   Hamper, linen
H-40   Receptacle, trash
M-10   Basket, waste
M-18   Bench
M-36   Cabinet, storage
M-37   Cabinet, storage
M-38   Hot plate
M-86   Vending machine, cold beverage
M-90   Vending machine, hot beverage
M-92   Vending machine, candy, assorted
O-32   Cabinet, filing

**Medical Equipment**

168   Blood pressure device
184   Cart, orthopedic supply
280   Diagnostic set
308   Electrocardiograph
332   Electrosurgical unit
336   Cart, emergency
338   Cart, emergency
384   Bucket, kick
388   Basin, kick
408   Light, examining
410   Light, examining
416   Light, examining
444   Medication station, including narcotic locker
468   Nourishment station
620   Sink, clinical
637   Sink, surgeon's scrub-up
656   Stand, leg support
660   Stand, Mayo
662   Basin, double
680   Stool, foot
704   Stretcher, adjustable
708   Stretcher
712   Suction machine
716   Table, examining and treatment
720   Table, examining
732   Table, fracture
740   Table, instrument
744   Table, operating, minor
812   Ventilator machine, IPPB
816   Viewer, X-ray
820   Viewer, X-ray
848   Wheelchair, standard
920   X-ray, mobile

**Fig. 1. Block F, Emergency Activity Center**

# EMERGENCY ACTIVITY CENTERS

## EMERGENCY ACTIVITY

In planning Emergency Activity Centers, particular attention must be paid to movements of people (patients and staff) and material (equipment and supplies). The first priority, of course, must be the movement of those patients who require immediate or urgent medical attention and the responding members of the medical staff. The time factor in terms of minutes can make the difference between life and death. All necessary equipment and lifesaving apparatus must be located in designated spaces so as not to impede the movement of staff, yet be readily accessible when needed.

According to the pro forma example (Fig. 1), the Emergency Activity is intended to be a casualty center offering services 24 hours per day. Medical, surgical, and nursing services as well as first aid are provided. A main premise is that dignity of patients and their families will be respected and protected at all times. Supportive services such as laboratory, diagnostic radiology, electrocardiographic and pulmonary function facilities should be located as close to the unit as possible.

The Emergency Activity Center should be located at a street level to ensure easy access for patients arriving by ambulance or auto. A separate entry for walk-in patients is required. These entrances, which are separate from the Outpatient Activity Center, must be easily identifiable, protected from inclement weather, and accessible to disabled patients. The emergency facility also must be easily accessible from the hospital to patients and to the house staff performing their routine duties or being summoned for consultation or emergency action.

## Intradepartmental Relationships

Good planning practice requires that the Emergency Activity Center be easily accessible to the hospital's surgical suite, coronary intensive care unit, and the primary radiological facilities (see Fig. 1).

The relationships within any Emergency Activity Center may be arranged according to individual preference and needs. The following should be considered for any complete emergency activity:

## Public Sector Areas

- Entrance for patients arriving by ambulance, other modes of transportation, or conveyances
- Entrance for walk-in patients
- Control station
- Public waiting space with appropriate public amenities

## Treatment Facilities

- Patients' observation room
- Treatment cubicles
- Examination rooms
- Trauma rooms (if required)
- Critical care rooms

An Emergency Activity Center may also include a patient's security room and areas providing supportive services and staff accommodations.

Fig. 2 is a graphic interpretation showing space relationships. As stated earlier, the first priority is the movement of patients requiring immediate medical attention. The patient brought by ambulance is conveyed on the ambulance stretcher directly to either a treatment cubicle or to a critical care room. An alcove holds stretchers and wheelchairs for patients arriving by vehicles. If the situation requires use of an operating room, the patient is admitted administratively to the Emergency Activity Center and conveyed through the door by the critical care room to the surgical suite. If a Trauma Room is provided, then immediate extensive attention is provided for.

### Public Sector Area

The admitting procedure is accomplished at the control center either by a family member or another individual accompanying the patient. The walk-in patient enters through the vestibule to the control center

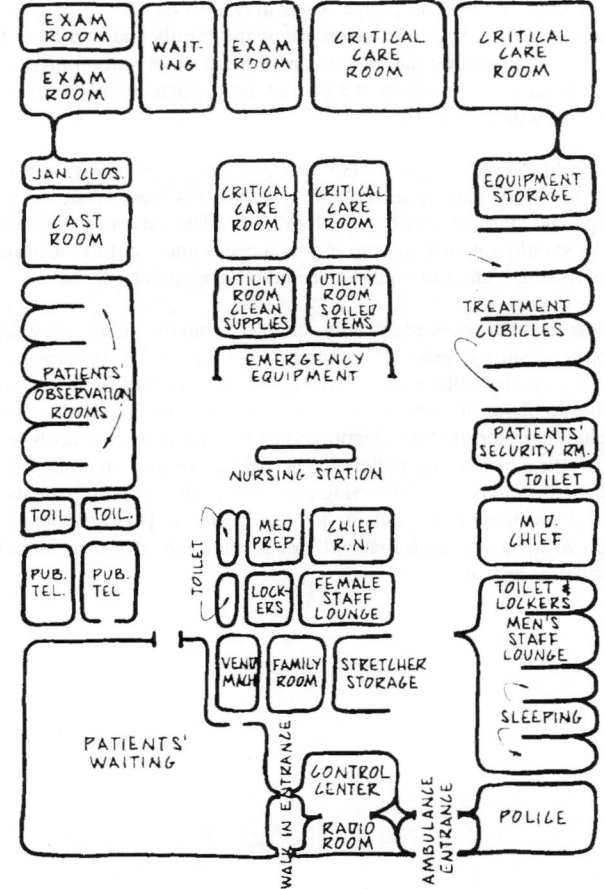

**Fig. 2. Emergency Activity Center intradepartmental relationship scheme**

References: Guidelines to Functional Programming, Equipping, and Designing Hospital Outpatient & Emergency Activities, DHEW Publication No. (HRA) 77-4002, U.S. Department of Health and Human Services, Washington, D.C.

and registers for admission at the center. Afterwards they may be asked to wait until called in public waiting space with their escort or family member. Admitting personnel exercise their medical judgments in each case as to the degree of medical urgency and, if necessary, request a physician to make a disposition. In some cases, the patient may be referred to the adjacent Outpatient Activity Center.

The control center is placed strategically to provide visual control of all incoming traffic and observation of the public waiting area so personnel may be aware of any medical emergency that may arise there. Near the entrance, the control center has an external window so an approaching ambulance may be observed. Vestibules to eliminate drafts at the entrances provide a certain amount of comfort for control center personnel. The center could be enclosed with a glazed partition but, although transparent, it is perceived by patients as a physical barrier. The counter at the control center also serves as a barrier against cold drafts. It must be emphasized that the response the patient receives at admission leaves lasting impressions. Thus, special attention should be given to provide an atmosphere of professional competency.

The communication room, incorporated with the control center, serves as a communication link with ambulance crews or rescue units in the community. The police room may also be used by reporters and attorneys. Immediate members of the family may retire to the family room pending the outcome of medical intervention involving a life-threatening situation of a patient; here, doctors and clergy may converse with the family.

Waiting in an Emergency Activity Center is a particularly difficult time for every patient since each perceives his medical urgency as unique. A state of anxiety predominates. The environment, obviously, should not only cater to physical needs and comfort but should also instill a feeling of confidence and relieve anxiety or fear.

Toilets for both sexes adequately screened from the public view, telephones ensuring privacy, vending machines with beverages or snacks, comfortable seating arrangements (not benches) all contribute to physical comfort. The general design of the waiting space (including color, texture, decor, acoustical control) all contribute to the welfare of waiting patients. The public waiting area should be screened visually from incoming ambulances discharging patients. A daylight window to the outside is often desirable but care should be taken to avoid location that will focus attention of the patients on ambulance arrivals.

## Treatment Facilities

Patients are treated in spaces surrounding the nursing station, the hub of all activities. This station is backed up by the medical preparation room and the office of the chief nurse who supervises all operations. Therefore, a glazed partition is provided which ensures acoustical privacy and affords visual control.

Staff amenities include toilets, lounge, and locker room for staff. Lounge and sleeping accommodations are provided for full-time physicians and resident medical staff who often work long hours and, although not continuously, are on call. Emergency equipment, to be readily accessible in case of urgent need, is deliberately placed in an alcove in front of the nursing station.

The patient's security room, with an unbreakable view window for observation, is placed close to the nursing station. Curtains may be installed outside the room, if necessary, to eliminate a view from the room itself. The door to the room and to its toilet must open outward to prevent the patient from locking himself in. To prevent self-injury, the room should be devoid of any sharp-edged appurtenances, and the light fixture, preferably tamperproof, should be flush with mounting surface. Surfaces should be smooth without any crevices with coved wall bases to facilitate easy cleaning in case of gross soiling by a disturbed patient. It is important to emphasize that this is not a prison cell. The patient confined in this security room is there for medical treatment although he may be under police control or may be mentally unstable. Physical design that provides a pleasant atmosphere is of paramount significance.

Treatment cubicles have curtains for privacy, if necessary, and are equipped to handle examinations and minor treatments. Minimum clear floor area is 80 square feet each. More severe injuries are treated in Trauma rooms which require a minimum clear floor area of 300 square feet. For a coronary patient, the emergency team may consist of a number of specialists using numerous kinds of portable equipment: therefore, larger space is required to accommodate both. Each trauma room is provided with a scrub sink. Special attention should be given to the scrub sink area because of the hazards of infection and a slippery floor.

The patient's observation room must be in full view of the nursing station. Privacy between patients may be achieved by cubicle curtains. Toilets for both genders are provided. Nurses' work counters are at each end of the room.

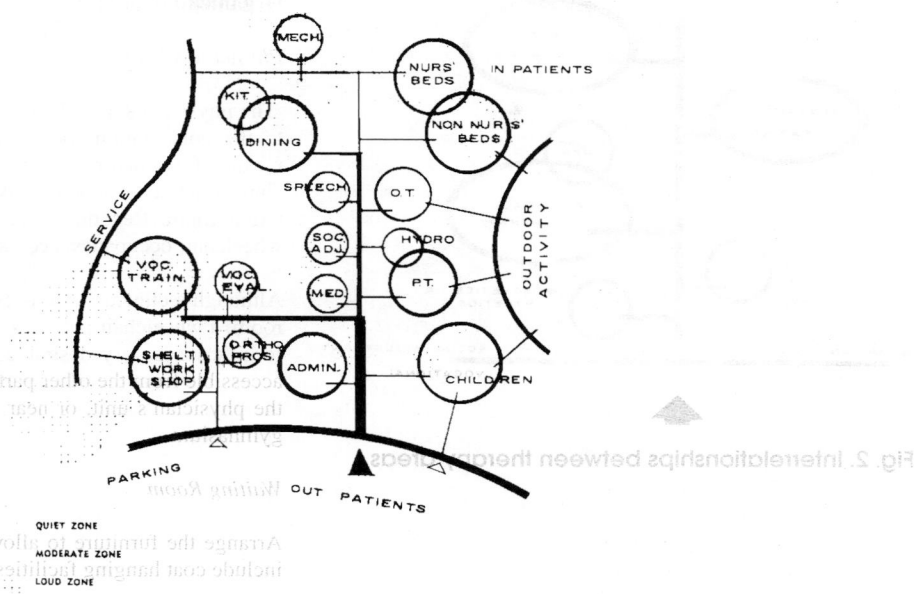

QUIET ZONE
MODERATE ZONE
LOUD ZONE

**Fig. 1. Interrelations of main elements of space of a rehabilitation center. Activities may be grouped according to relative noise levels.**

## REHABILITATION CENTERS

Planning means thinking in terms of spatial and human interrelationships.

The interrelationships between the several areas of activities are varied and complex; add to these the problems of site selection, considerations of finance, and provision for future expansion, and it becomes apparent that sound planning requires rigor and thoroughness (see Fig. 1).

One of the most basic planning principles is organization: the best organization for the purpose intended. When that purpose is rehabilitation, one must take into account the limited mobility and acute sensitivity to physical environment of those for whom the building is intended.

With limited mobility, the wheelchair becomes a basic unit or module of design. The range of the dimensions of a standard wheelchair must be borne in mind. Design is governed not only by these basic dimensions, but also by the dimensions of the paths of action of the chair. Variations in disability permit variable limits of maneuverability, and the relationship of the wheelchair to basic equipment must also be recognized in the development of the planning data. Refer to ADA requirements for minimum wheelchair clearances and approaches.

*Authors:* F. Cuthbert Salmon, AIA, and Christine F. Salmon, AIA
*Reviewer:* James H. Ogden, R.A.

## MEDICAL

The medical area of a rehabilitation center provides the following services: medical evaluation, performed by the physician and her staff; physical therapy, including hydrotherapy; occupational therapy; speech and hearing therapy. It also furnishes the services of a prosthetic and/or orthetic appliance shop. The detailed character of the medical area will vary with the program of the center itself. The emphases in the medical program will be determined by the needs of the patients and by already existent community medical facilities.

The medical area provides the basis for the patients' total program at the center. It must be accessible to all other areas and be well integrated with the administration and admissions services (see Fig. 2).

This section will contain much specialized examination, treatment, and therapy equipment. Some of this will be heavy, requiring a floor designed to accommodate such concentrated loads; the electrical service to these machines is important.

Patients will be wearing lightweight examination or treatment gowns here, and the HVAC system will have to compensate for this. The records for all sections of this area are extensive; therefore, adequate storage for them is mandatory. Conferences with patients and staff

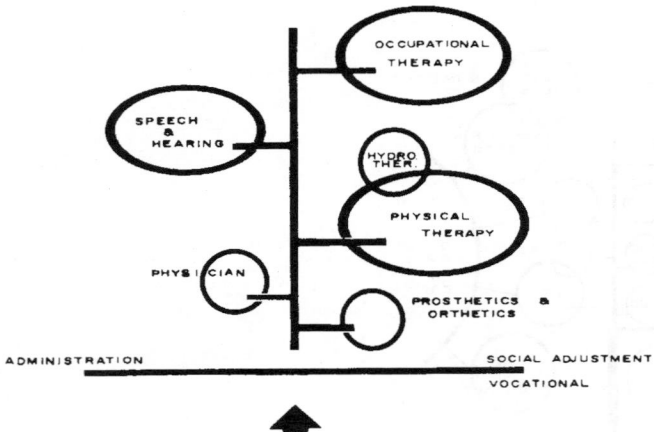

**Fig. 2. Interrelationships between therapy areas**

make further demands on the available space. Many different kinds of activities will be housed here and the space needs to be adjustable accordingly. Accessibility to all other areas is also essential for the medical area of activity.

### Physician

Medical diagnosis is the basis for development of the patient's successful rehabilitation program.

On admission, a medical examination is essential, whether the patient is prescribed a program in one or several of the center's areas of activity: physical medicine, social adjustment, or vocational rehabilitation. A nurse is usually present during the examination.

Complete evaluation of the patient may require the services of consulting medical specialists, staff specialists in the several medical therapies, psychologists, social workers, and vocational counselors. A total integrated program is developed for the patient, with medical considerations as the initial frame of reference.

### Location Within Building

As all patients receive medical evaluation, the physician's unit should be near the center's main entrance. For purposes of admission, and for the keeping of records, location of the unit near the administrative department is desirable.

If an inpatient nursing unit is included, the physician should have, if possible, convenient access to the nursing unit. In smaller centers, the main waiting room for the building may serve as the waiting area for the physician's unit. Place the unit in a quiet zone.

### Staff/Patient Ratios

The physician/patient ratio will depend entirely on the nature of the program. Centers accommodating inpatients will necessarily need a greater amount of physician service per patient than the outpatient type of center. Physician/patient ratios can be established only on an individual basis.

### Organization of Space

*Physician's Unit*

The physician's unit should form a self-contained area, with access to the consultation room and the medical examination room by means of a subcorridor, if possible. To make full use of the physician's time, there should be two examination rooms for each consultation room. Recommended for the area is a toilet designed for wheelchair occupancy, accessible from the examination room.

Although a clinical scale is essential equipment for the examination room, a wheelchair patient's scale constructed from a modified platform scale is very desirable. These scales should be conveniently accessible from the other parts of the building and may be placed in the physician's unit, or near the physical therapy exercise room or gymnasium.

*Waiting Room*

Arrange the furniture to allow space for wheelchair patients. Also, include coat hanging facilities.

*Secretary*

Provide proper work surfaces, computer capabilities, and filing storage, to be determined by program requirements. As certain records must be available to department heads in other areas of the center, placement of such files in the central records room of the administrative area is the usual practice. However, some centers prefer to keep medical records in the physician's unit. A physician's records are traditionally privileged communications, and, if kept in the central records room, should be made available only to the responsible professional personnel.

*Consultation Room*

Include in the furnishings for the physician's office and consultation room an executive desk and chair, bookshelves, and film illuminator. Allow space for two visitors' chairs and a wheelchair. Provide a convenient coat closet (see Fig. 3).

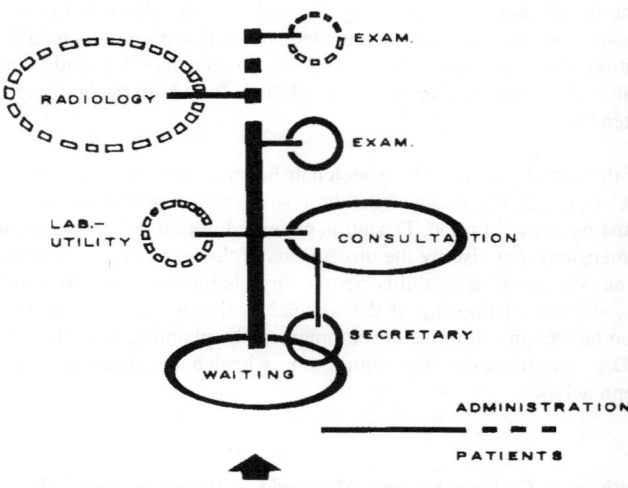

**Fig. 3. Consultation room adjacencies**

### Examination Room

Include in the furnishings for this room an examination table with clearance on all sides, an examination light, a lavatory and mirror, clinical scales, a film illuminator, an instrument and supply closet, a small electric pressure sterilizer (if no lab-utility room is provided), and a chair. Standing bars are optional equipment.

### Lab-Utility Room

If a lab-utility room is needed, it will be equipped with a pressure sterilizer, sink, plaster cart, work counter, and storage cabinets.

### Radiology

Radiology is usually provided for rehabilitation centers by x-ray departments of hospitals, clinics, and other institutions. If radiology is to form a part of the center's services, standard practice in the design and construction of the department should be followed (see Fig. 4).

## PHYSICAL THERAPY

Physical therapy is administered under medical supervision and performed by graduates of a school or course approved by the Council on Medical Education and Hospitals of the American Medical Association.

The objectives of physical therapy are to correct or alleviate bone and joint or neuromuscular disabilities. This entails a concern with all types of physical disabilities, such as neurological diseases, arthritis, amputation, paralysis, spasticity, structural and postural malalignments, crippling accidents, postsurgical conditions, etc. Measures are used to retain or reestablish circulation, muscle tone, coordination, joint motion leading to mobility, ambulation, and activities of daily living.

In carrying out his aim, the therapist will make use of heat, cold, water, light, and electricity as well as the training effects of active, passive, resistive, and reeducation exercises.

There should be two major treatment areas, dry and wet. The dry area includes the exercise room or gym and treatment cubicles; whereas the wet area includes all hydrotherapy treatment, tanks, pools, and related facilities.

Hydrotherapy equipment should be grouped in one area, separate from, but adjacent and accessible to other treatment areas.

Space considerations for a physical therapy department must take into account circulation areas for patients and staff. Situate the equipment for efficient and safe use, and provide storage space for equipment and supplies. Flexibility and expansion of facilities should be considered in basic planning to meet changes in requirements.

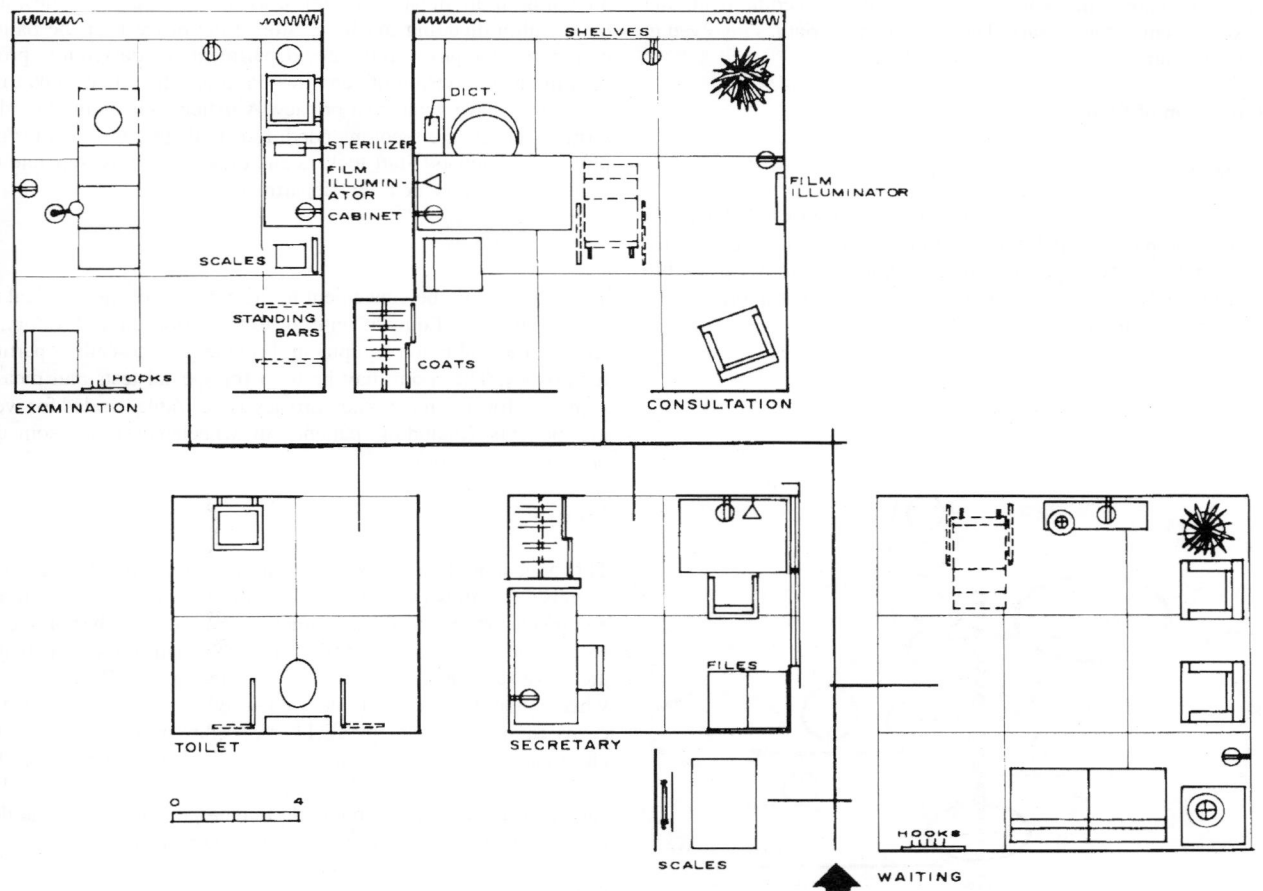

**Fig. 4. Radiology**

It is advisable to consult with the chief physical therapist, the center's director, and the center's physician to determine equipment needs and the program of activity for this department.

**Location Within Building**

The place for physical and occupational therapy, as well as for activities of daily living, should be in close proximity, as many patients will receive treatment and training in all three areas. Arrange the areas so that scheduled patients may proceed directly to physical therapy without interfering with circulation to other departments.

As physical therapy may take advantage of certain outdoor activity, place the exercise room or gym near the outdoors. As physical therapy involves some noisy activity, this area should be removed from quiet zones, such as the place where speech and hearing therapy is administered, or the nursing unit (see Fig. 5).

The area should be convenient to the center's physician and the nursing unit (if provided).

**Staff/Patient Ratios**

One physical therapist can treat an average of 10 to 15 patients per day. Group services may increase this to 20 a day. If the physical therapist is assisted by nonprofessionals and if the work space and scheduling are well planned, a maximum staff/patient ratio may be achieved. Nonprofessional assistants, paid or volunteer, can be trained to prepare patients for treatments, attend to equipment, and transport patients, if necessary. There are many variables involved in staff/patient ratios.

**Organization of Space**

*Treatment Cubicles*

Divide the cubicles with curtain tracks for easy access by wheelchair and stretcher patients and for flexibility in use of space, as for instructional activity or gait training. Curtains should not extend to the ceiling or floor, so that when drawn, they may not interfere with ventilation (see Fig. 6).

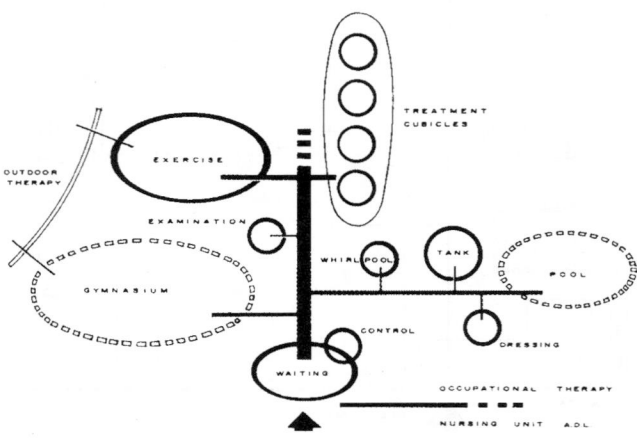

**Fig. 5. Therapy relationships**

Equip cubicles with a treatment table with adequate work space on each side and at the head. Treatment tables with drawers or shelving provide convenient storage space for sheets and other requirements. Provide in the cubicles a place for the patients' outer clothing, such as hooks or lockers. Provide a lavatory convenient for the therapist's use.

Equipment for this department may include infrared and ultraviolet lamps, diathermy, hot pack and electrical stimulation apparatus, ultrasonic equipment, suspension apparatus (Guthrie-Smith), electrical diagnostic apparatus, moist heat equipment, sand bags, powder boards, powder, oil or lotion, alcohol, and linen.

Ceiling lighting should be indirect or semi-direct to avoid glare; in many cases patients will be lying on their backs during treatments. Therapists conducting tests or examinations require shaded or nonglare spotlights.

*Waiting Area*

Provide space for wheelchair and ambulant patients; and if there is a nursing unit, space also for a stretcher. Place the therapist's office near the waiting area for control. From the waiting area, the patient should be able to go to the exercise room, hydrotherapy, or treatment cubicles with a minimum interference of activities.

*Therapist's Office*

There should be staff office space for interviewing patients and attending to administrative duties, as well as space for files, and a desk with a dictating machine. Situate the office near the patients' entrance to the physical therapy department and design it to provide maximum supervision of activities. Partition the office so that interviews may have acoustical privacy. A patient scheduling board and writing surface are recommended. Locate them conveniently for all physical therapists. Staff lockers and dressing rooms (separate from patients) should be near this department.

*Examining Room*

The room should be convenient to the entrance of the physical therapy department. Equip it with an examination table, lavatory, and space for examination equipment. Provide floor-to-ceiling partition for privacy. The room may be used for special tests and measurements, or for treatment when privacy is desirable. Scales for weighing patients (including patients in wheelchairs) are sometimes provided in this room.

*Exercise Area*

This area should be a flexible, clear space for individual and group exercise activities (see Fig. 7). The most frequently used items of equipment are exercise mats, sometimes raised 24 inches off the floor for the convenience of therapists and wheelchair or crutch patients. If area is of sufficient size, mats may remain in place. Provide shoulder wheel, shoulder overhead and wall weights, shoulder ladder, steps, curbs, ramps, stall bars, parallel bars, posture mirror, stationary bicycle, treadmills, counterbalanced and individual weights, sand bags, and paraffin bath. Some of this equipment may be made by a skilled carpenter rather than purchased. Purchased equipment should be accompanied by satisfactory repair and maintenance service.

Certain equipment relationships should be maintained. Place the posture mirror 4 feet from the end of the parallel bars. When mats are

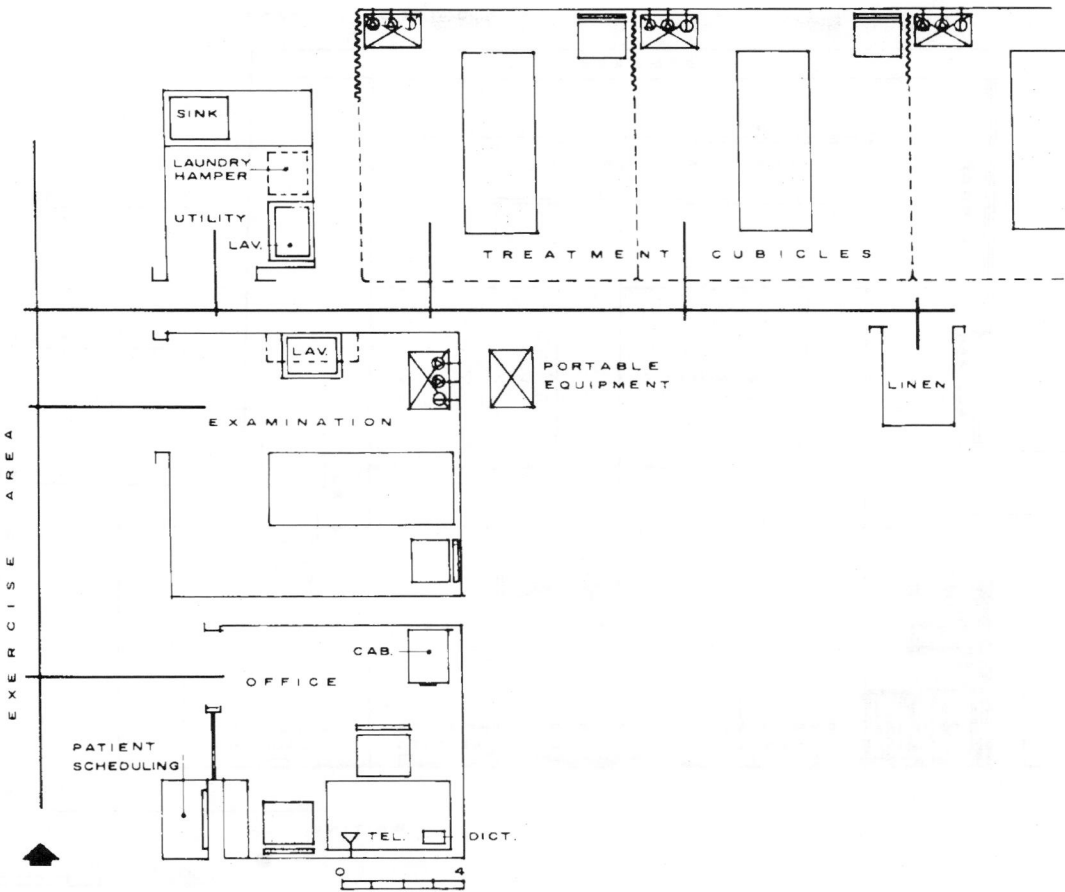

**Fig. 6. Treatment cubicles and examination room**

other movable equipment are removed, there should be sufficient space for gait training, also related to a posture mirror.

The layout shown suggests a minimum exercise area for a physical therapy department with one therapist and an aid. For an expansion of the exercise area see Gymnasium in this section. The exercise area may be divided by open partitions that allow for the attachment of equipment and subdividing of activities, yet which permit circulation of air and easy supervision of the total area. Doors to the exercise area should be wide enough to accommodate not only patients but also equipment. Double doors, each 3 feet wide, are recommended. An observation cubicle with one-way vision glass may sometimes be used to advantage in order that visitors will not interfere with patients' activities.

Reinforce the walls for installation of exercise equipment, such as stall bars. Provide storage for equipment not in use. Toilets should be accessible to the patients and designed for those who are confined to wheelchairs. A wall clock in the room for timing exercises is recommended. Vinyl wall covering to a minimum height of 5 feet will protect walls and ease maintenance.

There should be adequate ventilation. Proper air requirements without drafts in the exercise and treatment cubicles are very important. Windows or room exposure should be designed to provide privacy within the exercise room.

*Gymnasium*

In larger centers or centers with inpatients, a gymnasium is recommended. It serves a variety of uses, such as individual and group exercises, recreational programs, and meetings.

The gymnasium will augment the program of the physical therapy exercise room, permitting the therapist to conduct group wheelchair and mat classes. The room should be furnished with parallel bars, wall bars, stairs, curbs, gradients, wall mirrors, etc., for individual instruction.

The room will also be used for recreational activity such as group volleyball, basketball, moving pictures, and wheelchair square dancing. A minimum clear ceiling height of 14 feet is recommended. If the gymnasium meets standard space requirements, rental of its use to community athletic organizations will be facilitated. Providing a recreational program is particularly important where inpatients are involved.

The gymnasium will also be used by the social group worker in the social adjustment program for some patients. As the gymnasium is a multipurpose room, equipment and furniture within the area should be movable. Provision for its storage is essential.

As a meeting room to be used by selected groups within the community, this facility provides an excellent opportunity to acquaint the

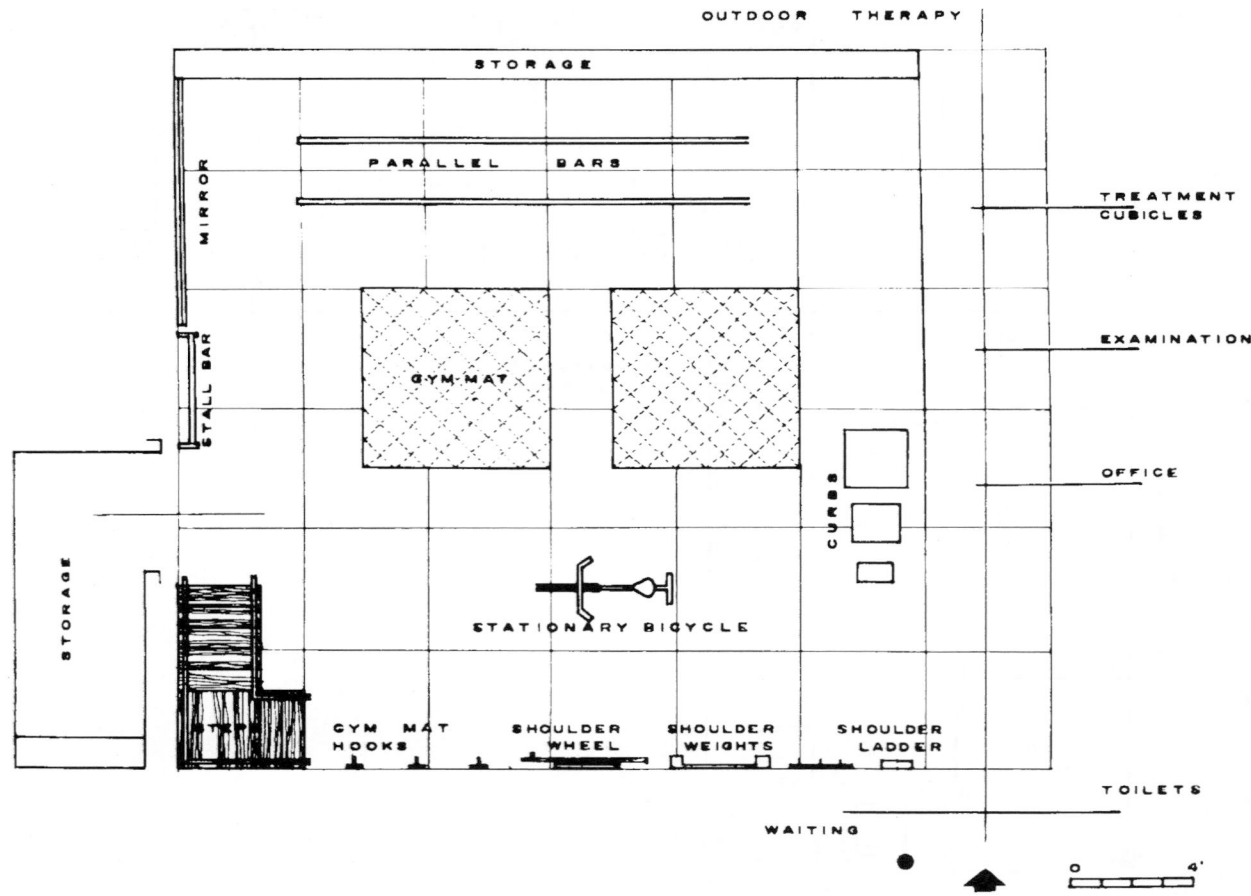

**Fig. 7. Exercise area**

public with the problems of rehabilitation and to arouse interest in the center's program. For this purpose, the gymnasium should be easily accessible to the public.

*Hydrotherapy*

The space for hydrotherapy is frequently the most expensive area of the center; consequently, it should be planned with considerable selectivity. Whirlpool tanks for arm, foot, hip, and leg immersion are considered inadequate by many centers serving multiple disabilities unless augmented with facilities for complete body immersion (see Fig. 8). Almost all exercises and treatments can be conducted with a Hubbard tank and a wading pool and tank. Combinations of Hubbard tanks with wading facilities are available where space is limited.

Therapeutic pools are expensive to construct; consequently, they are usually considered only for larger centers.

All hydrotherapy activities require linen and towel storage. Also provide a wringer and dryer for bathing suits and a storage space for wet and dry bathing suits of both staff and patients. Tank and pool areas require storage space for wheelchairs and stretchers, adequate dressing cubicles, or dressing rooms to permit maximum use of pool, showers, and toilet facilities.

As hydrotherapy is a moderately noisy activity, it should be removed from areas requiring sound control. Floors should be of unglazed ceramic tile with drains for spilled water and tank overflow. As equipment is heavy when filled with water, a structure must be designed for these additional loads. Overhead monorails with lift mechanism are essential for efficient use of Hubbard tanks and waders. Ceilings should be a minimum of 9 feet-6 inches. The location of the monorail with proper relationship to equipment is essential.

All pipes for hydrotherapy should be accessible but concealed. Waste lines should be adequate for rapid changes of water. All hydrotherapy equipment should have thermostatically controlled mixing valves. Adequate pressure and an ample source of 160°F water are essential. Humidity reduction is a major concern in planning the hydrotherapy department. Adequate air conditioning is essential for the comfort of patients and staff.

*Whirlpools*

This includes equipment for the treatment of arms, hips, and legs. Some models are available as movable units, in which case a sink or lavatory is required in the cubicle for drainage of the unit. Provide space for chair, table, and a stool of adjustable height. In small centers where hydrotherapy equipment consists only of whirlpool tanks,

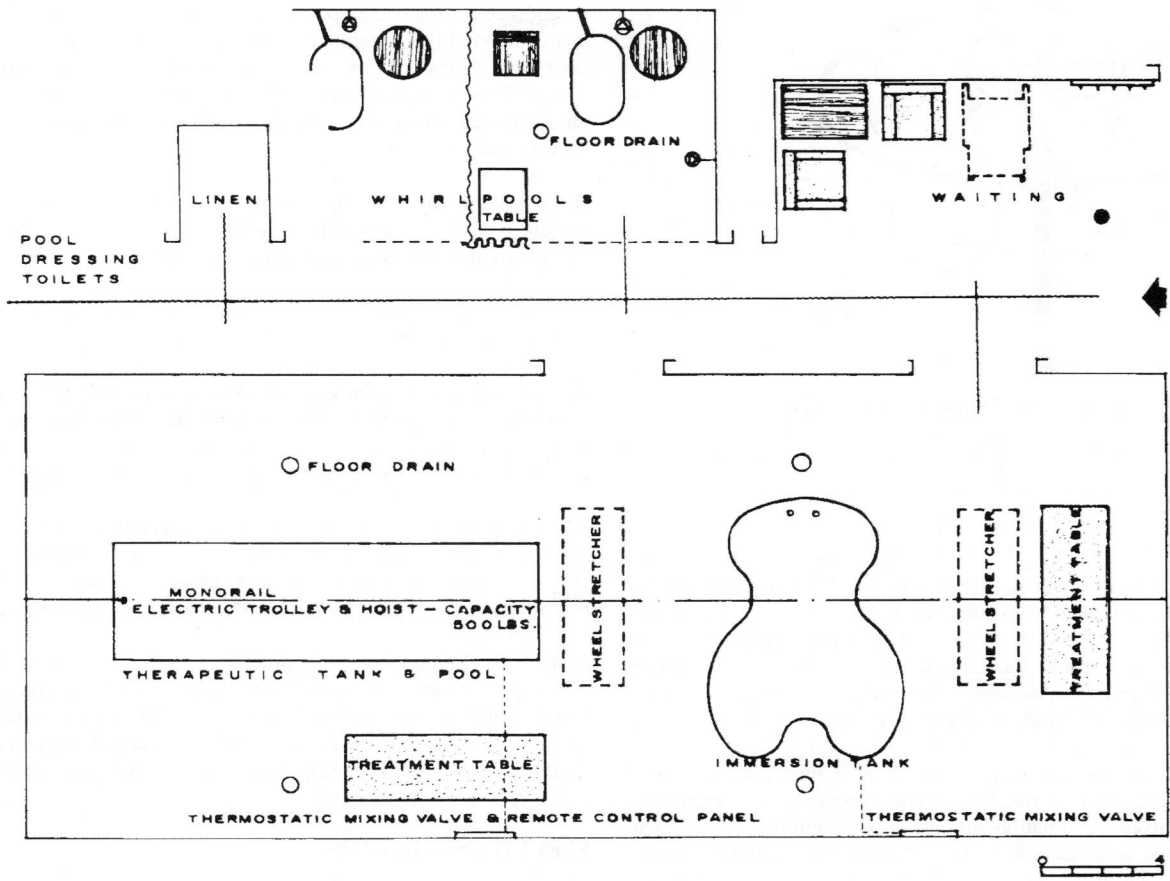

**Fig. 8. Whirlpools and tank room**

place them near treatment cubicles and near the exercise room for easy supervision by the therapist.

*Tank Room*

A treatment table with storage space is an essential requirement. Allow space for wheel stretchers and provide 44-inch-wide doors. (A 56-inch-wide opening is necessary to install combination treatment and wading tank.) Allow space for stretcher and wheelchair storage.

*Showers and Dressing Rooms*

Directly related to the efficient use of a hydrotherapy pool is the provision of adequate dressing room facilities. Dressing facilities do not necessarily have a size relationship to the pool indicated. For example, some programs will require several dressing tables in order to accommodate the patients.

*Hydrotherapy Pool*

Many variations in size are possible. The depth of the pool should be graduated. Variations of depth in 5-inch increments are recommended. For children the shallow end should be 2 feet deep, for adults, 3 feet. The deep end of the pool should be 5 feet.

There should be a continuous gutter around the pool for the use of the patients and for the purpose of attaching plinths. A portion of the

floor surrounding the pool may be depressed to form an observation area for the therapist.

**OCCUPATIONAL THERAPY**

Occupational therapy is administered under medical supervision and performed by graduates of schools of occupational therapy approved by the Council on Medical Education and Hospitals of the American Medical Association.

The objectives of occupational therapists are to assist in the mental and physical restoration of the disabled person, enabling him to adjust to his disability, increase his work capacity, and to want to become a productive member of his community. In addition, the occupational therapist is concerned with the training of patients in the activities of daily living.

To achieve these goals, occupational therapy utilizes, on an individual basis, remedial activities that are found in creative skills and manual arts (see Fig. 9).

**Location Within Building**

Occupational therapy should be adjacent to the physical therapy department, since many patients will use both areas. Locate the area so that scheduled patients may proceed directly to occupational therapy without interfering with the circulation of other departments.

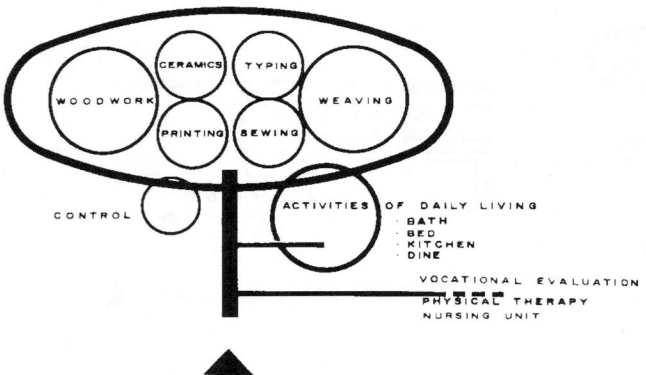

**Fig. 9. Occupational therapy area**

As some phases of occupational therapy involve noisy activity, this area should be removed from quiet zones in the building, or provision should be made for acoustic control. Certain occupational therapy activities, such as those characteristic of daily living, may be conducted out of doors in favorable weather. It is recommended that, if possible, access to an outdoor area be provided.

The area should be accessible to the center's physician, the social adjustment area, and the vocational counseling area. As occupational therapy involves coordination with the nursing unit (for dressing particularly), the occupational therapy department should be conveniently related to it.

**Staff/Patient Ratios**

One occupational therapist can treat 8 to 15 patients per day. The number of patients depends upon types of disabilities and the severity of the cases.

Where highly individual treatments are required, the daily load will decrease. Also, if the therapist is relieved of administrative responsibilities and assisted by nonprofessional persons, the daily load will increase. For orthopedic patients, special equipment must frequently be devised under close supervision of the occupational therapist.

There are many variables applicable to staff/patient ratios.

**Organization of Space**

*Activities of Daily Living*

The activities of daily living (ADL) area, which is used to teach the patient how to live self-sufficiently in his home environment, should be closely related to the main occupational therapy treatment room. The activities which are indicated include most situations found in the home (see Fig. 10). The activity area may be so planned that each activity has a separate unit, or it may be planned to separate quiet from noisy and dusty from clean activity. The unit system facilitates assignment of special instructors to special activities and is also a more orderly arrangement of the space. However, this method increases the number of staff, makes supervision more difficult, and can be considered only in larger departments.

As the occupational therapist works closely with the social adjustment staff and the vocational counselors, the office should be near their areas. Some training, particularly bathroom and bedroom activities, will require cooperation with physical therapists. Consequently, the ADL area should be easily accessible from the physical therapy department.

A gadget board containing numerous items of hardware, light switches, faucets, and other items frequently used should be included. The board should be adjustable in height.

The bathroom should be arranged to accommodate wheelchair patients (see Inpatients).

The kitchen plan may include, in addition to the type illustrated for wheelchair use, standard counter and cabinet arrangements to test the patient's ability to cope with normal situations. Counters of adjustable height may be used to advantage in training patients.

A front loading washer and dryer are desirable for wheelchair patients. Controls at the front of the range are recommended. However, the purpose of this training is to show the patient how he may use, if possible, appliances that are standard in his community.

A standard clothes closet is recommended as a part of the training in dressing. A broom closet, vacuum cleaner, and adjustable ironing board should also be included. Table space should be provided for training in eating and for use as a writing surface. A rug can also be used to test the patient's ability to cope with that type of floor covering.

**SPEECH AND HEARING**

The speech and hearing unit serves those with disabilities of deafness, stuttering, or delayed speech and voice disorders that may result from various basic abnormalities, diseases, or injuries.

A wide variety of programs are possible. Some provide for treatment of postoperative disorders resulting from tonsillectomies and ear operations, cerebral palsy, meningitis, cleft palate, hemiplegia, and vocal cord anomalies.

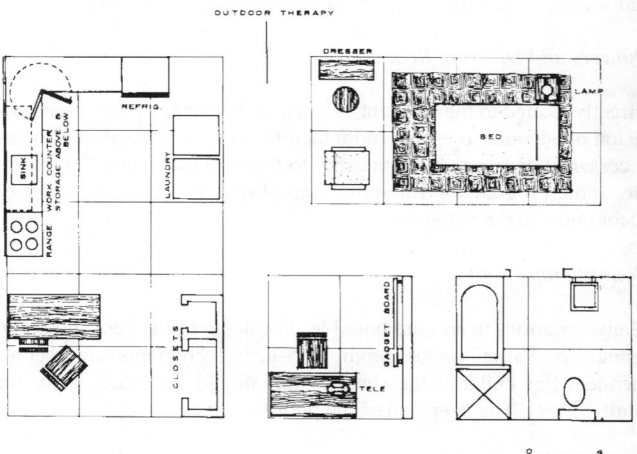

**Fig. 10. Activities of daily living**

Services may range from testing and treating of all conditions to emphasis on disorders associated with certain specific disabilities. The center may include speech therapy only or audiological testing as well. The program may serve adults or children, or both. The center may include a teaching and research program in speech and hearing.

### Staff/Patient Ratios

Although ratios vary widely with different patients, an approximation of staff/patient ratios is as follows:

- For audiometric screening: 1 audiometric technician may screen 1 patient every 5 to 8 minutes.
- For audiometric testing: the audiologist may test 4 to 8 patients per day during the initial screening process. For a complete test for hearing aid evaluation, 3 hours is needed per patient, and the test is usually conducted in 2 visits.
- For individual therapy: 1 therapist for 6 to 10 patients per day (½-hour to 1-hour periods). The audiologist may also act as therapist.
- For group therapy: 5 to 8 persons per therapist; 1 therapist for 24 patients per day.

### Organization of Space

It is recommended that the sound control room, test room, and audiometric testing rooms be located on a subcorridor off the waiting room in order to reduce noise. In a children's program, a play and examination room near the test room is recommended. Patients' toilet facilities and coat racks should be accessible from the waiting room.

*Audiometric Testing*

The audiometric testing room (or, in some cases, booths) is a facility for pure-tone threshold testing and short form hearing screening tests (see Fig. 11).

Space should be provided for the audiologist's desk with an audiometer and one patient's chair or wheel chair. Furniture should be arranged so that the audiologist may face the patient and operate the audiometer. Provide storage and shelving.

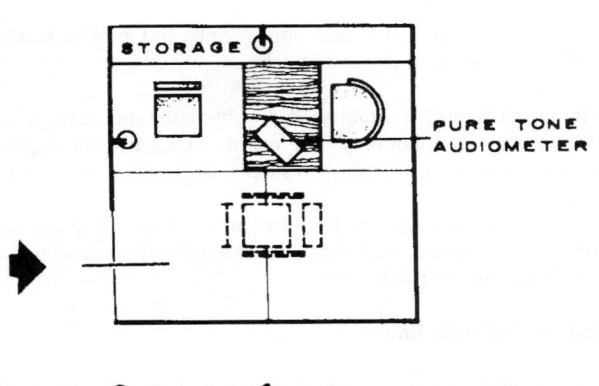

**Fig. 11. Audiometric testing booth**

The room should be treated acoustically for an overall residual noise level of not more than 40 decibels as measured on the "C" scale. This involves the treatment of walls, ceilings, and floors (see Fig. 12).

*Control Room and Test Room*

This facility is essential for an audiology program. It is preferable to place these rooms off the subcorridor or hall, and to control the activity in surrounding rooms in order that extraneous noises be eliminated.

For a children's program it is highly desirable that, outside the test room, a play and examination room be provided to accustom the child to his environment and to make the transition to the test room as easy as possible. This room should be equipped with children's furniture and toys.

Equipment for the control room will include a work surface for the audiometer, earphones and microphone, tape recorder, and tape and record storage, and may include other equipment such as a Bekesy audiometer. If hearing aid evaluation is part of the program, provide storage space for hearing aids either in the test room or the control room.

The control room should be treated acoustically to achieve an overall residual noise level of not more than 40 decibels on the "C" scale. An observation window approximately 18 by 20 inches is required. For adequate control of sound transmission, three pieces of glass of different thicknesses and nonparallel in construction are recommended. One-way vision glass in the control room is optional.

Equipment for the test room includes a speaker, microphone, and headphone. Microphone and headphone jacks should be located near the patient's chair. Additional auxiliary wall- or ceiling-mounted speakers are sometimes provided, particularly for the testing of children. These speakers should be separately switched. All this equipment is wired to the audiometer. Additional spare jacks in both the control and the test room are recommended for other items of equipment. Conduits between the jacks should be installed in a manner that avoids sound transmission.

For complete diagnostic service, a galvanic skin response audiometer may be used in the test room. For diagnostic testing, delayed auditory feedback equipment may be used. For a children's program, children's furniture and toys should be part of the test room.

The test rooms should be acoustically treated to achieve an overall residual noise level of not more than 30 decibels on the "C" scale. This requires carefully supervised construction of a floating room. The subfloor may be depressed to eliminate the high step or ramp at the entrance to the test room. If built on grade, the floating slab for the room may be placed on a sand bed. To achieve this degree of acoustic control, it is essential that the floating room have adequate mass and that all necessary precautions are taken to avoid the conduction of sound.

Proper air circulation should be provided.

### Orthetic and/or Prosthetic Appliance Shop

Orthetic appliances are medically prescribed for the support of weakened parts of the body and to increase or control their function. Prosthetic appliances are medically prescribed artificial substitutes for a

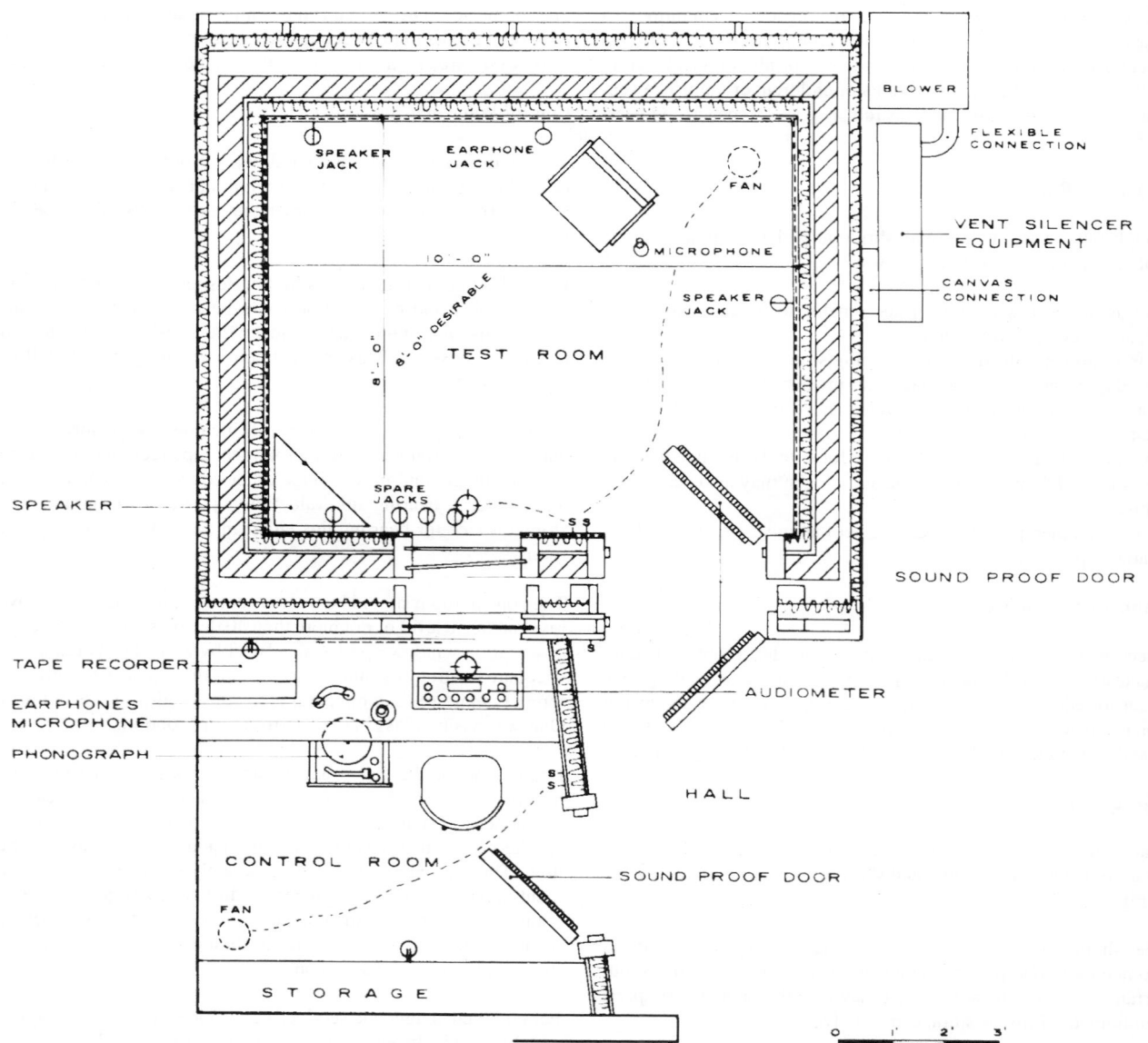

**Fig. 12. Plan of typical audio-testing area**

missing body part. Such devices are constructed by orthetists and prosthetists in cooperation with the physician, the physical therapist, and the occupational therapist (see Fig. 13).

The type of facility for orthetic and prosthetic services will vary widely with rehabilitation centers and is dictated at times by the availability of commercial services. Frequently, arrangements are made for a representative of a commercial firm to visit the center. For this purpose a fitting room is recommended as a minimum facility, although an office or treatment cubicle is sometimes used and minor adjustments and repairs to appliances are made in the occupational therapy department.

However, a small shop (as illustrated) within the center provides close liaison between the patient, the medical team, and the orthetist or prosthetist. In such a shop, small devices such as feeders and page

turners may be fabricated and adjustments and repairs made to wheelchairs, braces, limbs, and crutches.

If a minimum facility is established, consideration should be given to its future expansion, not only in terms of space, but with respect to electrical services, ventilation, gas supply, etc.

The fabrication of major appliances requires much heavy and noisy equipment. Isolation of such a shop is essential to the control of noise and reduction of the fire hazard.

**Location Within Building**

As the orthetic and/or prosthetic appliance shop will serve outpatients requiring minor adjustments or repairs to their devices, the unit should be easily accessible to entrances. The unit should be located

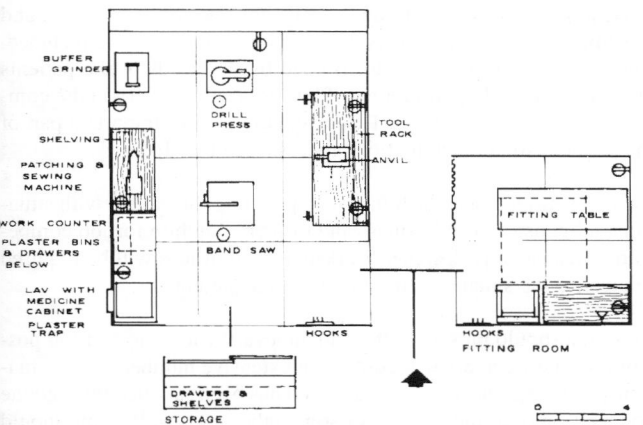

**Fig. 13. Orthetic and/or prosthetic appliance shop (minimum facility)**

n a noisy zone, and, if possible, near the gymnasium, so that the patient may try out his prostheses or braces. The fitting room, however, may be made sufficiently large for this purpose.

## SOCIAL ADJUSTMENT SERVICES

Social adjustment services include psychiatric and social services for the treatment of social and emotional problems.

### Psychiatric Service

Frequently the psychiatrist is employed on a part-time basis and is primarily called upon to provide the following services:

- Psychiatric screening to diagnose emotional problems.
- Staff consultations on how these problems should be managed in relation to the patient's total rehabilitation program.
- In-service staff training for the purpose of developing greater understanding of the psychological factors in disability.

### Psychological services include:

- Psychological evaluation, accomplished by means of various psychological testing procedures and interviews which evaluate the patient's intelligence and personality.
- Interpretation of clinical findings to members of the staff.
- Counseling (therapy) on either an individual or a group basis, usually carried out with the psychiatrist and social service staff.
- In-service training of psychologists and participation in psychological research.

The minimum recommended psychological facilities would include a psychologist's counseling room and test room.

### Social services include the following:

- Social study and evaluation, including the collection of relevant information from the patient, his family, and other agencies, and the appraisal of such information with respect to the patient's rehabilitation potential.
- Social casework, where the social worker (medical social worker or psychiatric social worker) works with the patient to improve attitudes toward self-support and motivation toward treatment and work.

- Social group work, including the correction of abnormal living patterns by using planned group activities, recreational in nature but therapeutic in value. It may include hobby activities, group discussions, and activities of an adult education nature.

### Location Within Building

The services should be administered in a quiet area of the building. As most incoming patients will receive some services in this area, it should be readily accessible from the main entrance of the building. If the program involves large numbers of children, the psychological therapy room for children should be in the children's treatment training unit (see Fig. 14).

### Organization of Space

The flow pattern for patients within this area will vary considerably. A typical pattern for the evaluation of a new patient would have the sequence of receptionist, waiting room, social worker (for case history of patient), medical evaluation (for all incoming patients), psychological testing, and psychiatric screening. The two latter services are not needed by all patients.

Vocational counseling, and appraisal of the patient's employment potential in the vocational evaluation unit may also be included in the initial evaluation. Also for this purpose, audiometric screening and speech evaluation are often helpful.

### Staff/Patient Ratios

As psychiatric screening and psychological therapy will vary widely with individual patients, no approximation of staff/patient ratios is possible.

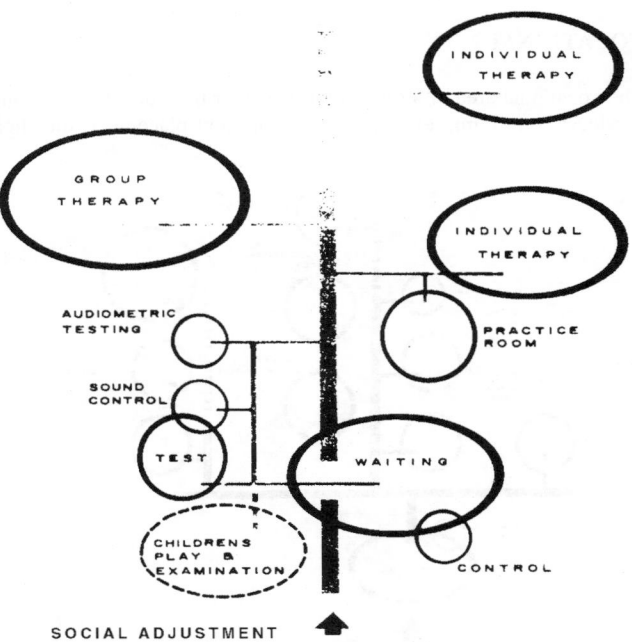

**Fig. 14. Hierarchy of psychology services**

For psychological testing a recommended average is two patients a day per psychologist for brief psychological evaluations. This includes the time required for interpretation and writing reports. Extensive psychological evaluation requires one work day per patient, including time for preparation of the report. Other activities such as training, research, and therapy will detract from these averages. This does not provide for evaluation of vocational skills, aptitudes, and interests, which is a function of vocational services.

For social caseworkers, the number of cases per worker will vary with the number of intake studies and the number receiving continuing service. Where there is a balance between these two types of service, an individual caseworker may handle a caseload of from 25 to 35 patients.

*Waiting Room*

If the program is of sufficient scope, provide a separate waiting area with a receptionist for the psychological-social unit. In smaller centers, this facility may be incorporated in the main waiting room for the center. The receptionist schedules patient interviews with the psychological-social staff.

Access to interview and test rooms by means of a subcorridor will provide privacy and reduce extraneous noise from the rest of the building.

**Psychological Training and Research Programs**

For a training program, provide observation facilities in the children's play therapy and activity group rooms, such as observation cubicles with one-way vision glass or, preferably, television cameras with screens in a central viewing room (see Fig. 15).

Provide a separate office for each psychological trainee.

Research programs are of a wide variety. Some involve much equipment; others, no equipment. Provide a separate area for this facility.

**VOCATIONAL**

The vocational area of a rehabilitation center provides the following services: counseling, evaluation, training, and placement; the shel-

tered workshop (or rehabilitation workshop) is part of this area, and in some cases, certain aspects of special education will be included. The vocational program is determined by the needs of the patients and the needs and opportunities of business and industry in the community served by the center. This program is a most important part of the patient's total rehabilitation process. (See Fig. 16.)

This area has the responsibility of acquainting the patient with situations in industry or in business and of preparing him for job competition. Realistically designed workshops and offices will be required to create a job situation atmosphere for the patient.

This area should present to the patient a very wide range of job possibilities. Few centers will contain an extensive number of job situations; some may have none if this need has been satisfied through the cooperation of a trade school or some other agency. Patients should not be trained for jobs which they cannot obtain later.

Changing types and techniques in industry make it essential that this area have maximum flexibility, especially in heating, ventilating, plumbing, lighting, electrical installation, and equipment placement. The vocational area must offer training in small segments of a job operation and present advanced types of vocational opportunities.

*Vocational counseling* provides an opportunity for the patient to obtain an understanding of his vocational abilities and potential, and to learn the scope of their possible application. The center may choose to work with cooperating counselors already established in the community, if it does not provide this service within the center. Sometimes counselors are loaned to centers by the State Vocational Rehabilitation Agency and conduct their work at the center.

*Vocational evaluation* is the process of collecting and appraising data on the patient's interests, aptitudes, and ability in work situations. This section needs to be quite broad in scope in order to find the vocation best suited and most satisfying to the disabled person. This section of the center's program is frequently referred to as a prevocational unit.

*Vocational training* provides the discipline necessary for the patient to attain his job potential established in vocational evaluation. Voca-

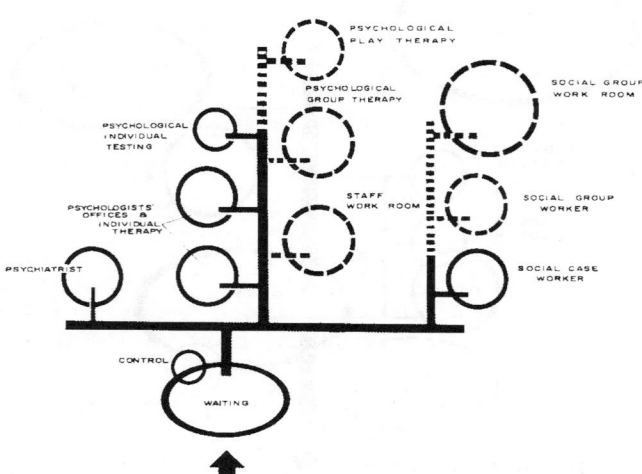

**Fig. 15. Hierarchy of psychological facility**

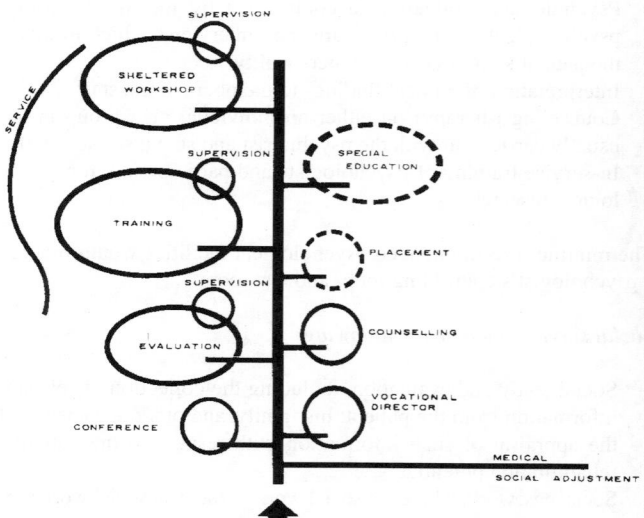

**Fig. 16. Hierarchy of vocational services**

ional training requires carefully supervised instruction in vocations est serving the patient's needs with full regard to employment possibilities.

*Sheltered workshop* provides employment for disabled persons within the center. This is productive work for which wages are paid; he work is usually obtained on a contract or subcontract basis. In this area, further vocational evaluation and training are possible.

*Special Education* will be found in this area when enough patients have difficulties with certain areas of academic or vocational achievement. If children need this service, it may be located in their area. Frequently, this is provided through cooperation with the public schools.

*Placement service* is to be offered when the number of job placements and contacts warrants it; otherwise this service is performed by other agencies. In smaller centers placements may be handled by the vocational counselor. Placement may mean the patient's return to his former job, full employment by selective placement or partial or special employment either at home or in the sheltered workshop.

*Supervisors* will be in charge of the separate units of this area and will be responsible for integrating their unit with the total vocational effort. The *director* will be in charge of the total vocational area and responsible for integrating this area with the rest of the rehabilitation center program.

### Vocational Training

Vocational training is prescribed after evaluation of the patient's abilities, interests, and job training has begun. The vocational training unit provides opportunity for growth in ability and assurance in actual job situations or experiences as close to reality as possible. During this period of training, the patient may continue to receive services from the medical unit, the social adjustment unit, or any other part of the rehabilitation center (see Fig. 17).

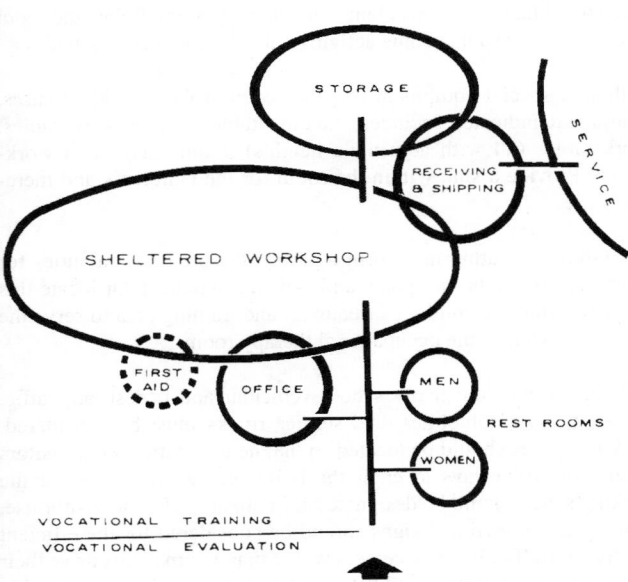

**Fig. 17. Hierarchy of vocational training**

Differences in disabilities and the nature of the community will dictate differences in the kind of training program to be employed. In addition to working with local industry, the local training resources will supplement the center's training programs whenever practicable and suitable. Trade schools may accept only the more capable candidates who do not have emotional or medical problems, and in some cases, they may not be able to give the personal attention needed. The rehabilitation center deals with complex problems and disabilities; therefore, its vocational training unit will need to give greater emphasis to limited training objectives which are often more suitable to the restricted educational and cultural backgrounds of many of its patients.

Training in a range of vocations should be offered to accommodate several levels of abilities, skills, and interests. In addition, the changing personnel needs of industry make a representative range important.

There follows a sampling of some of the vocational training fields that the architect may be called upon to plan for (see Fig. 18):

> Commercial
> Computer repair
> Drafting
> Watch repair
> Shoe repair
> Furniture repair and upholstering
> Machine shop operation
> Video, television, and appliance repair

### Sheltered Workshop

The sheltered workshop provides additional opportunities for further evaluation, training, and eventual employment of the handicapped individual. The sheltered workshop was once thought of as a place for terminal employment of those who could not benefit from further training. Today this concept has changed, and it is established as one of the steps in the rehabilitation process. There will, perhaps, always be some patients who, because of extensive or complicated disabilities, require the environment of the sheltered workshop as the only means of permanent employment.

The sheltered workshop is never an isolated unit in terms of program, but is part of the total vocational area that in turn is an integral part of the center. For selected patients, it is the best means of developing work tolerance, work habits, confidence, and skill. It also provides a means for the development of industrial quantity standards. The added incentive of pay for work done is often the motivation needed to help the disabled person carry through his rehabilitation program. This work is most frequently secured from industry or other sources on a subcontract basis.

This work must be done within the most businesslike atmosphere and framework, yet without undue pressures of time; however, it must meet the standards of quality and guarantee delivery of the required quantities on time schedules. It must provide payment for services rendered and rewards in terms of individual growth and development.

### Location Within Building

The sheltered workshop should be conveniently related to the other areas of vocational services. It may be a detached or semidetached unit with a separate patient entrance, as patients engaged in the shop usually work an eight-hour-day program and no longer require the intensive services of the medical department.

Depending upon its closeness to the medical department of the center, the shop may require a first-aid room. In the larger workshop a full-time nurse may be required.

As work within the shop may be noisy, separation from quiet areas in the center is recommended.

For delivery and shipment of goods, it is essential that the unit be adjacent to a loading area.

**Organization of Space**

This area will closely resemble industrial space and will house industrial operations. The heating, ventilating, and dust collection systems will need to be planned accordingly, with floors designed for adequate loads and an electrical system to meet many different kinds of demands.

The type of work carried out in the shop will be subject to frequent change. Flexibility in organizing the space is, therefore, essential: the area should have a high ceiling and be free of columns. Floors should be designed to take heavy loads of equipment and stacked materials. Much of the work under contract in the shop will be of an assembly line nature. However, the products may merely require work surfaces for their assembly or they may require special equipment (frequently supplied to the center by the contracting firm if it is for a particular job). In laying out equipment in the shop, it is advisable to obtain expert industrial advice in order to assure efficient flow patterns and simplified handling and storage of materials and products.

Some work surfaces should be adjustable in height and all should be designed for the use of wheelchair patients.

Electrical power outlets should be frequently spotted along bench walls and/or the ceiling grid. Floor outlets for power tool use in the central area of the shop are recommended. Wiring should be sized to take a varying power demand. Adequate general illumination should be provided with increased intensity at work stations as dictated by the task. A time clock for the patients' use is sometimes provided in the workshop to encourage punctuality and to determine the patients' production rate.

All necessary safety precautions should be taken to protect the patient from power tool hazards, fire hazards, falls, and other mishaps. A potential hazard exists when there is insufficient space for the storage of materials and products. Ample storage space should be provided for the orderly, safe arrangement of bulky items. A sprinkler system installed in the shop will reduce fire risk.

Storage is a major problem and is related to the volume of items handled. The space for storage will vary from 15 percent to 50 percent of the work area. Receiving, shipping, and handling of bulk items require additional space. This space should be related to a loading dock and truck service area. The service area should be planned so that it does not interfere with other vehicular or pedestrian circulation.

As patients working in the shop will usually work an eight-hour day, facilities for their comfort should not be overlooked. If the center has no dining facilities, a lunchroom convenient to the shop is recommended, as some patients will bring their lunches with them. Provision of a cafeteria is also considered a desirable facility where the number of patients warrants it.

Most states have specific requirements for rest areas for men and women. These requirements should be checked carefully before planning lounges, toilet facilities, and lockers for the patients in the workshop.

A small office for the workshop supervisor should be provided, and so designed that there is maximum supervision of the shop activity from the office. Additional office space will be required for records, cost accounting, and estimating. The size of this area will be determined essentially by the volume of work and number of contracts handled by the workshop.

## PHYSICAL THERAPY CHILDREN'S EXERCISE ROOM

The requirements for this space are similar to those needed in the exercise room for adults, except that the equipment is selected for the child's size and interests (see Fig. 19).

The space indicates a minimum exercise area staffed by one therapist. Treatment cubicle requirements are the same for children as adults; equip them with treatment tables and ceiling-mounted mirrors above. Relate the area to outdoor therapy for outdoor exercises.

Provide a sink for the therapist's and children's use. Toilet facilities for children should be immediately convenient to the exercise room and outdoor therapy.

Special equipment may have to be designed for individual cases. Figure 19 illustrates a movable stall bar and parallel bars adjustable in height and width for children of varying ages.

**Occupational Therapy**

Equipment should be selected for the child's physical and mental age level. The plan indicates an area staffed by one therapist.

Place toilet facilities convenient to the therapy room. Relate the room to the outdoors so that some activities may be conducted outside.

Although special equipment may be required for individual cases, equipment indicated includes standing tables, office work tables, work tables (all with adjustable heights), loom, easel, and workbench. Provide a sink within the room for the children's and therapist's use.

As training in eating may form a part of the program, facilities for snacks; refrigerator, hot plate, and sink are indicated. Or locate this facility within the children's treatment and training area to serve the nursery as well as the occupational therapy room.

Exterior circulation involves both vehicular and pedestrian traffic. Buses, taxis, automobiles, and service trucks must be considered. Parking spaces should be located so that neither patients nor visitors need cross driveways to enter the building. Separate areas of the parking space should be designated for patient, staff, and visitor use. Appropriate directional signs should be considered for the efficient control of traffic. In some centers where many outpatients drive their own cars, a carport designed for wheelchair patients is a considerable convenience (see Fig. 20).

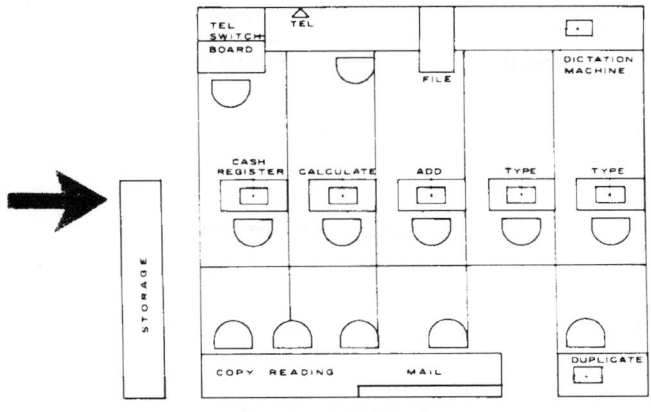

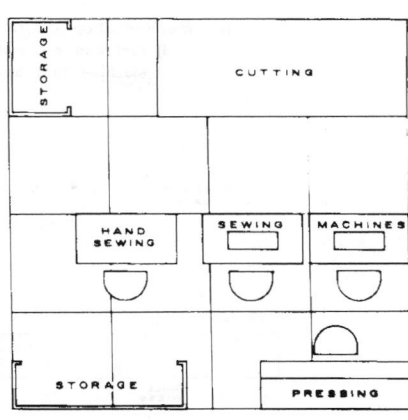

**I. Commercial**

    i) typists;
    ii) secretaries;
    iii) bookkeepers;
    iv) telephone operators;
    v) cashiers;
    vi) business machine operator;
    vii) copy readers;

    viii) bank tellers;
    ix) ticket agents;
    x) receptionists;
    xi) shipping and receiving clerks;
    xii) file clerks;
    xiii) sales clerks.

**II. Skilled and Semiskilled**
  **A. Sewing and Tailoring**

    i) spreaders;
    ii) markers;
    iii) cutter;
    iv) trimmers;
    v) pattern makers;
    vi) pattern graders;

    vii) tailors;
    viii) pressers;
    ix) hand sewers;
    x) sewing machine operators;
    xi) weave-bac specialists;
    xii) chair cover makers.

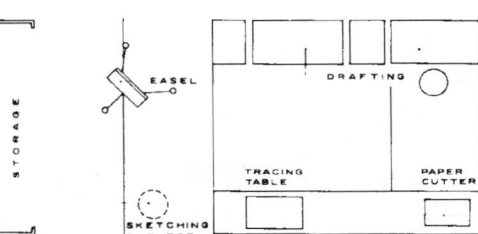

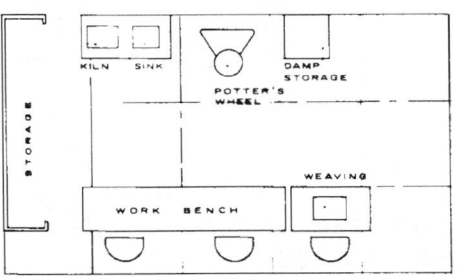

**Skilled and Semiskilled**
  **B. Drafting:**

    i) electrical draftsmen;
    ii) automotive draftsmen;
    iii) architectural draftsmen;
    iv) mechanical draftsmen.

  **C. Commercial Art:**

    i) layout men;
    ii) illustrators;
    iii) letterers;
    iv) window display artists;
    v) show card layout.

**Skilled and Semiskilled**
  **D. Arts and Crafts:**

    i) ceramics;
    ii) leather;
    iii) metal work;

    iv) weaving;
    v) jewelry;
    vi) electroplating.

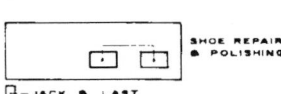

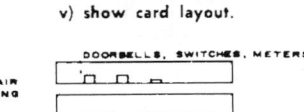

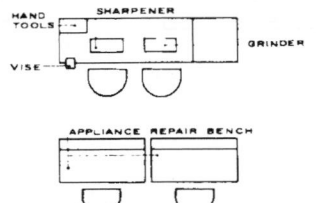

**Skilled and Semiskilled**
  **E. Repairmen:**

    i) business machines;
    ii) watch repairing;
    iii) assemblers;
    iv) tool sharpening;
    v) camera repairing;
    vi) shoe repairing.

  **F. Electric Light, Power, and Electronics:**

    i) meter readers;
    ii) meter men;
    iii) assemblers;
    iv) inspectors and testers;
    v) radio, television, electronic machine repairmen.

**Skilled and Semiskilled**
  **G. Building Trades:**

    i) carpenters;
    ii) painters;
    iii) plumbers;
    iv) masons;
    v) electricians.

  **H. Woodwork Trades:**

    i) patternmakers;
    ii) cabinet makers;
    iii) furniture repairmen.

  **I. Plastics Production:**

    i) bench grinders;
    ii) hand filers;
    iii) drill press operators;
    iv) assemblers.

**Fig. 18. Possible vocational training fields**

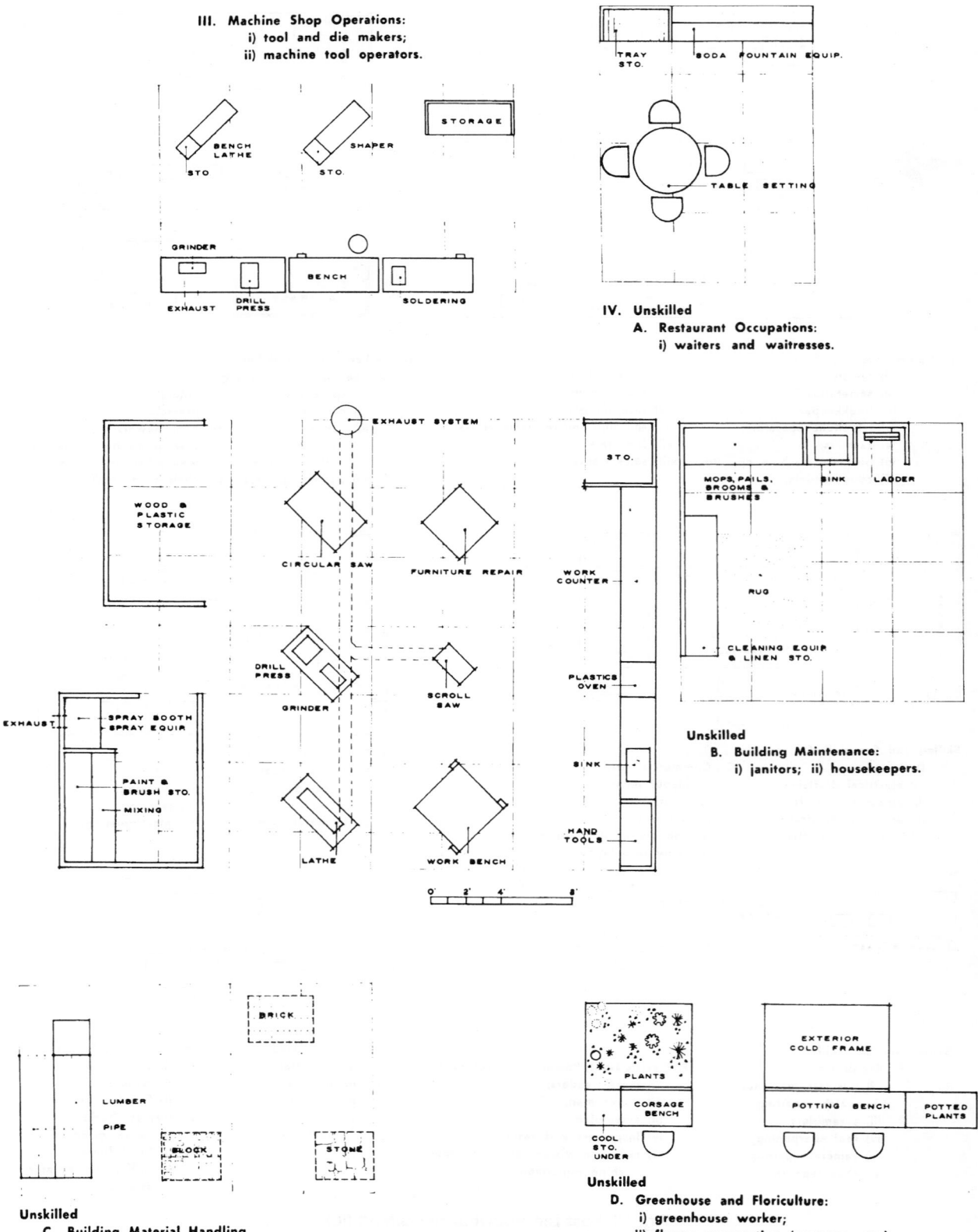

III. Machine Shop Operations:
i) tool and die makers;
ii) machine tool operators.

IV. Unskilled
A. Restaurant Occupations:
i) waiters and waitresses.

Unskilled
B. Building Maintenance:
i) janitors; ii) housekeepers.

Unskilled
C. Building Material Handling

Unskilled
D. Greenhouse and Floriculture:
i) greenhouse worker;
ii) flower preparation (corsages, etc.).

Fig. 18. (cont.)

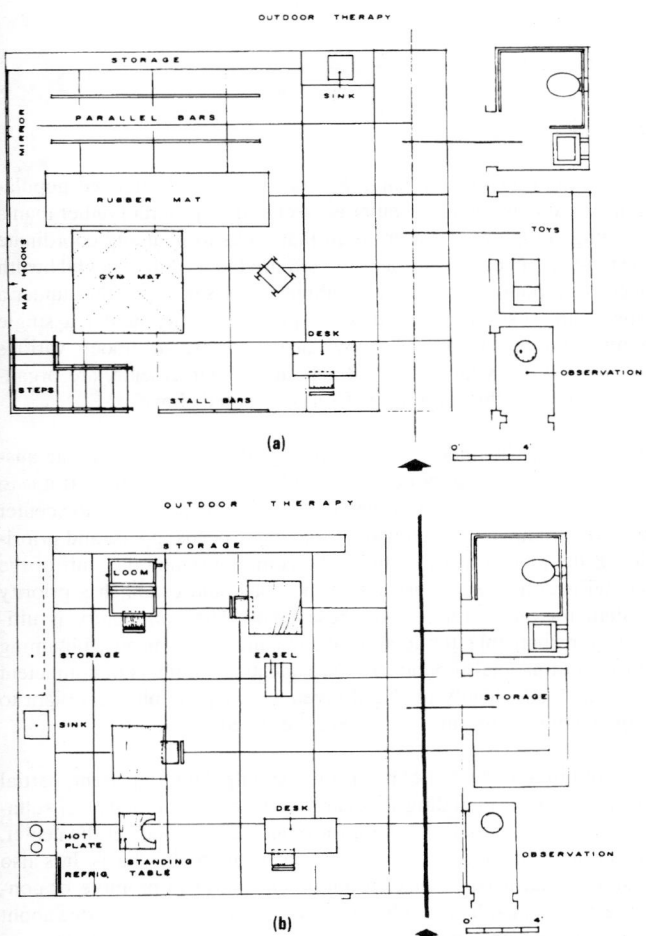

**Fig. 19. (a) Children's physical therapy; (b) Children's occupational therapy**

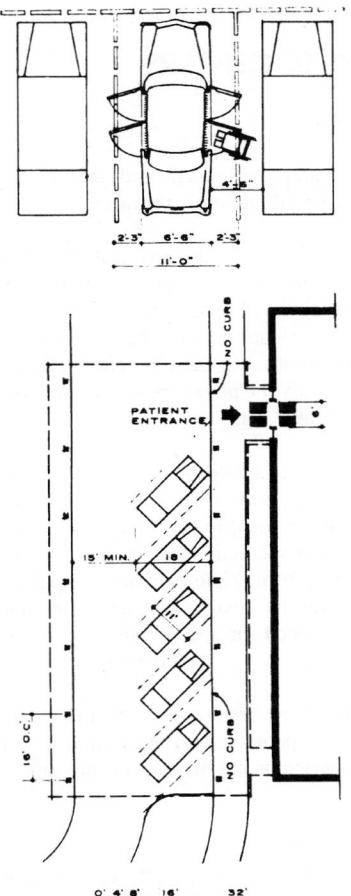

**Fig. 20. Parking space for cars operated by disabled persons**

All centers will require a service area for the delivery of equipment, supplies, and fuel. However, centers with kitchen facilities, vocational training programs, and a sheltered workshop will have a greatly increased service problem; and the service area and its relation to other traffic must be studied accordingly.

Adequate maintenance shop facilities are essential. The shop not only will serve general maintenance purposes, but frequently will be used for the repair, modification, or fabrication of furniture and equipment used in the center.

# MENTAL HEALTH CENTERS

## PHYSICAL PLANT

The physical plant shall provide a safe and sanitary environment with adequate diagnostic and therapeutic resources.

The design and construction of the physical plant should be appropriate to the type of services it houses, to the staffing and organizational pattern of the facility, and to local geography and style. It will, therefore, be unique for each facility, but it must be safe and must make a positive contribution to the efficient attainment of the facility's goals. It must satisfy the physiological as well as the psychological needs of patients and staff.

Sleeping units for patients are designed to promote comfort and dignity and to ensure privacy consistent with the patients' welfare. In the absence of other state or local requirements, there is a minimum of 100 square feet of floor space in single rooms and 80 square feet of floor space per person in multiple patient rooms. It is desirable that multiple patient rooms be designed to accommodate two patients only. There may be a need for appropriate security measures incorporated into the physical design of some units.

There is a minimum of one lavatory and toilet for each room, one tub or shower for each 15 patients, and one drinking fountain on each unit. Appropriate provisions are made to ensure privacy in toilet and bathing areas.

Since psychiatric patients are generally ambulatory and need to associate with other patients and with staff, there is provision for day rooms and recreational areas. At least 50 square feet of floor space per patient is required for dayrooms. There are also usually solaria, a dining room or cafeteria where many patients take their meals, a visitors' room, a gymnasium, an exercise area in the building or perhaps on the grounds, and rooms for special treatment, interviewing of patients, group and individual therapy, etc. Other facilities for patients might include a locker room or individual lockers in the sleeping units, a small laundry room, a snack kitchen on each ward, and a coffee shop, clothing shop, and cosmetic shop for patients as well as employees.

Offices are provided for physicians, psychologists, social workers, nursing administrators, dietitian, and other staff members, and these are conveniently located to encourage effective communication with patients and other staff. Nurses' stations should be centrally located to permit full view of recreation areas and immediate access to patients and to treatment areas. Appropriate conference rooms are also provided, and there are suitable arrangements for clerical staff for each department or unit.

## TYPES OF PSYCHIATRIC FACILITIES

### Community Mental Health Centers

The community mental health center represents the formal reflection of the professional objectives of providing comprehensive services and continuity of care for the prevention, early detection, treatment, and follow-up care of mental disorder within a designated population. The comprehensive center is essentially a program rather than a building complex; it is a program that seeks to plan and coordinate the range of mental health services required to meet the mental health needs of a population. It is a combination of services either under a single administration in a discrete physical entity, under a single administration in multiple physical facilities, or under various administrations which, by contracts and/or agreements, are organized to provide the continuity of services noted above.

A center may be under governmental, philanthropic, or private auspices, or it may be supported by a combination of resources. If it is to be an effective agency, however, the community served by the center should participate in establishing the major needs, goals, and priorities of the mental health center. The community and the staff of the mental health center must define the goals and establish a priority system for the attainment of these goals. The community is ultimately responsible for identifying resources and needs, obtaining sufficient financial support to assure adequate numbers of competent personnel, adequately paid and given an adequate physical plant to implement the programs to achieve the stated goals.

As a minimum, the center must provide outpatient, inpatient, partial hospitalization (including day care) services, community consultation and professional education for other than the staff of the center, and clinical diagnosis and treatment on an emergency basis. It is also desirable that it participate in public education to promote or conserve mental health research to increase the body of knowledge about mental illness and the effectiveness of services utilized; home care and follow-up, nursing home care, vocational rehabilitation, guidance for the families of emotionally disturbed persons, and otherwise contribute to maintaining the optimal functioning of individuals with residual *sequelae* or complications of mental disorders. Services of the center should be easily accessible and widely publicized to the community served.

To provide comprehensive services and continuity of care, the community mental health center should have easy relationships with other agencies, and particularly with the public psychiatric hospital serving the area. Patient care must be coordinated between the center and other agencies, and patients must move from one element of service to another within the center with ease, as treatment needs indicate. For example, in mental health centers that are part of or closely related to general hospitals, the necessary inpatient, dietetic, laboratory, pharmacy, medical, and surgical services might be provided by the general hospital. Arrangements need only be made to ensure availability and ready accessibility for patients in the mental health center.

To be truly comprehensive, the mental health center must be responsible for the adequacy of services provided to persons with special problem mental disorders or to populations facing unusually chronic and severe emotional stress and who are alienated from their community or the broader community's supportive social systems. It may

---

*References: Standards for Psychiatric Facilities* The American Psychiatric Association, Washington, D.C.

not be feasible for the center to provide all of the clinical services necessary in managing the difficult biological and social problems presented by drug dependency, alcoholism, aging, delinquency, mental retardation, or the many other special problems included among the mental disorders or in which mental disorder is suspected of playing a significant part. The center should, however, identify the population at risk for each of the special problems and plan a program to provide preventive, diagnostic, therapeutic, rehabilitative, or supportive services for each of these populations. It should identify the community's most likely agents for early intervention to assist or support individuals in each of these populations or identify agents who are providing therapeutic and rehabilitative care. The program should indicate the ways in which the center would be most useful to these community agents.

The responsibility for the mental health needs of a population implies that the mental health center should help various social systems of the community function in ways that develop and sustain effectiveness of individuals participating in these systems. The center should aid these systems in their support of persons with mental disorder. The implications for prevention, diagnosis, treatment, and rehabilitation are obvious; the recipient of mental health services includes the patient but the services extend to his family and to a variety of social systems. Consultation and education in the community are important functions of any center. In these ways the center responds to the community's need for interlocking, strengthening, and expansion of all its resources that have a bearing on mental health. Community consultation and education offer possibilities for influencing mental health beyond the confines of hospitals and offices and thus contribute to the prevention of mental disorder.

To deliver this broad range of services, a flexible organization with a multidisciplinary staff is required. In addition to the usual professional staff of psychiatrists, psychologists, social workers, nurses, and activity therapists, there may be a variety of nonprofessional personnel, volunteers, and social scientists to add new perspectives to the center. Staff may be organized by services (prevention, diagnosis, intensive treatment, extended treatment, rehabilitation, etc.), by programs for specific population groups (children, adolescents, the aged, substance abuse, mentally retarded, etc.), or by geographic areas of the community served. Regardless of the organization, there must be adequate qualified leadership, administrative and clinical, to assure thoughtful supervision, planning, evaluation, and coordination required to blend the array of available talents and resources into an effective center of services.

Responsibility and commensurate authority should be delegated to ensure optimal utilization of each person's skills, respecting principles of ultimate legal and clinical responsibility. As stated elsewhere by the APA, "The need for cooperatively defining the area of activity and responsibility for professionals who participate in the care of patients requires that physicians or their designees be recognized as having the ultimate responsibility for patient care. They, and they alone, are trained to assume this responsibility. In the public interest, other professionals or nonprofessionals, when contributing to patient care, must recognize and respect this ultimate responsibility."

## Psychiatric Outpatient Clinics

In a psychiatric outpatient clinic, a psychiatrist assumes responsibility for providing diagnostic, consulting, and therapeutic services for outpatients with the help of a professional staff that includes at least the disciplines of psychiatry, psychology, and social work. This staff

nucleus may be supplemented as needed by representatives of related disciplines, such as pediatrics, internal medicine, neurology, mental health nursing, speech therapy, remedial techniques, physical and occupational therapy, and rehabilitation.

Members of the various disciplines not only work on the staff but also function on the team in daily practice, coordinating their skills to meet the needs of patients. The psychiatrist who serves as director sees that this coordination is effective. She assumes responsibility for all clinical functions and is on duty sufficient time, on a regularly scheduled basis, to adequately discharge her responsibility. She assures adequate evaluation of all new patients, supervision of the staff, and sustained direction of the total program of services. The psychiatrist in-charge retains overall authority, but may delegate administrative, as distinct from clinical, responsibility to a nonmedical executive or administrator.

In addition to diagnosing and treating patients, the clinic provides training for professional psychiatric personnel and those of other disciplines as well as education for the public; it participates in various community endeavors related to the mentally ill and carries out research. The methods of implementation and the proportionate emphasis given to the various functions differ according to local circumstances, community needs, and clinic policy.

The clinic may serve patients for whom appropriate psychiatric assistance in a convenient outpatient clinic may prevent more prolonged illness, those recovering from a stage of illness that required hospitalization and who may need further outpatient care as they resume a regular way of life, those who are referred for pre-hospitalization evaluation, and those who can benefit from temporary therapeutic intervention to overcome a life crisis.

Admission policies for outpatient clinics vary. Many clinics have an open door, or walk-in policy, indicating that they accept both self-referrals and referrals from community agents. Others accept only those cases that have been referred by another professional source. Some clinics specialize in the diagnosis and treatment of children, adults, or special populations, such as people with substance abuse problems. Each clinic has a written plan indicating the scope of its admission policy and referral plan, and the plan is well known to all referring sources.

The services of a clinic may be offered on either a full- or part-time basis, according to local circumstances. Whatever its arrangement, the clinic should be accessible to the members of the community it serves.

The clinic's participation in community service plans is an important responsibility. Some individuals may have a problem that can best be removed or alleviated by another agency, and the clinic cooperates with other community resources wherever possible. Some patients need help from several sources, and the professionals involved must clarify the needs and outline areas in which each can be most effective. Working relationships with surrounding inpatient facilities are maintained to achieve easy flow of patients in and out of inpatient services and to avoid administrative delays and failure of communication about patients.

The clinic may be affiliated with a medical school, hospital, welfare or public health department, or other appropriate professional organizations for the exchange of services, scientific advancement, and professional and administrative support. If not, it achieves these aims through the use of qualified consultants or by establishing a professional advisory board of appropriately qualified persons.

The psychiatric outpatient clinic is often asked to furnish an evaluative report regarding a patient. The content of a report is determined by the purposes of the agency for which it is prepared and it is in keeping with ethical practice.

### Psychiatric Services in General Hospitals

All general hospitals should have a well known plan for receiving, management, and disposition of psychiatric patients. If the general hospital has a psychiatric service or department, there must be a qualified psychiatrist in charge, with appropriate allied personnel, particularly nursing personnel who have had training in the management of psychiatric patients.

Every general hospital must think through its responsibilities for the person presenting himself with psychiatric symptoms, in order either to admit the patient or to assist in quickly referring him to the nearest treatment resource capable of providing prompt diagnosis and treatment for the particular case. The feasibility of establishing a psychiatric service in a general hospital as a part of the network of the total community health program will depend upon many factors, including local needs, the availability of other facilities, the availability of staff, and the orientation of the medical professional in the hospital and community.

Whether a separate psychiatric service can or cannot be provided, it is frequently possible to use some general medical, minimal care, or other beds for psychiatric patients and to secure the services of a consultant psychiatrist. All good general hospitals have a plan for handling psychiatric emergencies, such as acute toxic reactions, suicide attempts, and acute behavioral disturbances. Small hospitals may have two or more rooms for such patients, pending their transfer to a hospital where special psychiatric facilities are available. It is advisable that no patient with suicidal tendencies be released without psychiatric consultation.

When the general hospital has a psychiatric service, the service provides for the care and treatment of patients admitted for psychiatric disorders and also for those patients who, in the course of hospitalization for another reason, experience a psychiatric illness. Most patients are admitted voluntarily, although occasionally the hospital seeks legal authority for detaining one who is very disturbed. Any limitations on admissions, such as those imposed by the physical construction of the unit or by the training and experience of its staff, are clearly stated in the plan of the hospital.

Because of the small size of the psychiatric unit in most general hospitals, the unit usually focuses on intensive short-term therapy and diagnostic services. Some general hospitals have, however, found it possible to develop suitable facilities and staffing to admit and treat psychiatric patients who are expected to remain over 30 days. Some hospitals also have provision for partial hospitalization, in addition to round-the-clock services, and for outpatient services to former patients and others who do not need full-time hospitalization.

A capacity of 20 to 26 beds in one nursing unit seems to be most efficient. When a hospital is capable of supporting more than this number of beds, they are usually provided in two or more nursing units. Experience has shown that men and women may be treated in one unit if adequate facilities are available.

Since the psychiatric service operates as an integral part of the hospital, many of its functional services are provided by the hospital administration. These might include most of the general professional services: i.e., medical, surgical, and dental; dietetic, laboratory, x-ray, pharmacy, library, chaplaincy, and medical records; and administrative and maintenance services.

### Private Psychiatric Hospitals

Private psychiatric hospitals are nongovernmental specialty hospitals. Like general hospitals, they may be operated on either a nonprofit or for-profit basis. They have the responsibility of providing treatment programs with definitive goals for the welfare of the patient, with the realization that the period of hospitalization may be only a segment of the total treatment plan.

The medical staff should make use of the opportunity provided by a high ratio of medical staff to patients to regulate the therapeutic program and to observe the processes of illness and the response to therapy. The most advanced approaches to treatment, and individualization of program to meet each patient's needs, should be employed. The hospital should take advantage of around-the-clock observation by many trained observers, and multidisciplinary views in conference, in the evaluation of therapy and the integration of theory and practice. There should be a periodic evaluation of the effectiveness of the hospital therapeutic program. Although the primary function of the hospital is to maintain excellence in psychiatric treatment, the professional and administrative staff should be encouraged to utilize the unique opportunities for education and research.

Most private psychiatric hospitals serve their geographic communities: local, state, and regional, although a number of them, because of their special or unique treatment programs for specific categories of patients, receive referrals from wherever in the world these patients come.

Private psychiatric hospitals, therefore, vary greatly. Each follows the program determined by its medical staff, its approach to treatment and its goals. Each private psychiatric hospital must have established written procedures by which it will either admit a patient or quickly refer her to the nearest, most appropriate, treatment facility. A qualified psychiatrist must be responsible for the treatment of the patient, and there must be other mental health professionals, including nursing personnel with training in psychiatric nursing.

The length of stay in a private psychiatric hospital should be commensurate with the goals of therapy and the patient's illness. In keeping with the concept that early and effective intervention may result in the return of the patient to her community after a very short period of hospitalization, the average length of stay is less than 60 days in three-fourths of the private psychiatric hospitals. To meet the ultimate needs of the patient, many hospitals maintain medium- or long-term intensive treatment programs as well. The primary goal of hospital treatment is not the shortest possible stay but the most effective therapy. Within the limits of therapeutic goals, the hospital should provide the type and amount of treatment that will result in the patient's resumption of healthy functioning.

### Public Psychiatric Hospitals

A public psychiatric hospital is defined as an institution provided by the community whether city, county, state, provincial, or federal government for the diagnosis, treatment, and care of patients with psy hiatric and neurological disorders. Most hospitals in this group are state or provincial hospitals. They provide both short-term and long-term treatment and admit patients both voluntarily and by legal commitment.

While it is recognized that variations in the usual type of state hospital organization are suitable in certain localities, the essential professional, diagnostic, treatment, and administrative and maintenance services described in the preceding section on general standards can be applied to all public hospitals by individual interpretation. Each public hospital has an important function to perform in providing necessary psychiatric services to its community and in promoting psychiatric education and research. Recognizing the advantages of affiliation with medical schools and other medical centers in their areas, many public hospitals have established formal programs of participation in cooperative educational and research efforts.

Whether the total treatment program of the hospital is separated into discrete units depends upon its size, its type of organization, and the medical administrative philosophy. However, patients have individual and differing needs, and the treatment program, however administratively organized, seeks to serve these various needs.

The hospital should be large enough to meet the community's needs for psychiatric services, but not so large as to compromise its ability to meet the needs of each patient for individual treatment. Optimal size might be described as the most efficient and effective balance between the facility's ability to meet the unique needs of the community and its ability to meet the unique needs of each patient. One method that has been devised to achieve this balance is the unit system.

Larger hospitals may operate under this system, with several semiautonomous patient care units making up the complex. The treatment programs are organized into separate units of similar size, staffing, and types of patients. Regardless of how long he stays, each patient is admitted, treated, and discharged within the same unit. His treatment is the responsibility of the same group of staff members from admission to discharge and aftercare. In some instances, the units represent specific geographical areas; this enables the professional staff to work closely and continuously with professional and lay community agencies from that region. Other facilities do not find this geographic admission plan practical and prefer to admit patients to each unit in rotation. Regardless of how admissions are handled, the goal of each unit is appropriate treatment for each patient at the most appropriate site.

The treatment program may include separate units for certain types of patients with special treatment, educational, and rehabilitation needs, such as children, adolescents, substance abuse, and others who require intensive medical treatment in addition to psychiatric care.

Increasingly, public hospitals are following the mental health center concepts of comprehensive service and continuity of care. They are, therefore, developing a range of services, including programs of varying degrees of partial hospitalization, outpatient services, rehabilitation, vocational guidance, and aftercare in addition to the intensive inpatient treatment programs. A proper balance of these other programs allows for the more efficient use of the inpatient services.

The concept of the open door has been applied to the majority of wards in most psychiatric hospitals. The open hospital encourages early treatment by emphasizing the voluntary nature of hospitalization and the expressed confidence of the staff that the patient can accept responsibility for his own management. Freedom of movement enables patients to do many things for themselves that might have to be done by staff members under other conditions, and thus allows more staff time available for the promotion of active treatment. It is necessary for some facilities to maintain a closed unit or units, however, for those patients who may be likely to endanger the safety and welfare of themselves and/or others. Confidence in the facility can best be maintained if appropriate precautions are taken to protect the community from the exceptional patient who has in the past caused it concern.

The hospital encourages and participates in community planning for the development of appropriate alternative resources and facilities to deal with social problems that have in the past often been assigned to the public psychiatric hospital due to the lack of available alternatives. The most appropriate and efficient use of scarce psychiatric resources requires that all possibilities for securing the best treatment and care for each individual patient be explored by the patient's family, the family physician, and community social agencies, and that a broad range of resources be available in the community to meet the multiplicity of needs.

The hospital encourages community provision for diagnostic, treatment, rehabilitation, and educational and preventive mental hygiene services for former patients, and for those for whom hospitalization may be averted, to ensure a comprehensive network of mental health care services. Within this network some services may be provided by the hospital's mental health clinic, which functions on a regular, scheduled basis, either in a fixed location or on a traveling basis. The clinic assists in the rehabilitation of former hospital patients, advises those about to enter the hospital, offers treatment to those who do not need hospitalization, and diagnoses and/or treats children with behavioral or educational problems. The staff of the clinic includes as a minimum a psychiatrist, a social worker, and a psychologist, and, if the hospital has adopted the unit system, the same team follows the patient from preadmission interview to discharge and follow-up care. The services of the clinic also include follow-up counseling, evaluation of adjustment after discharge, and medical supervision of drug dosage.

## SERVICES FOR THE DEVELOPMENTALLY DISABLED

First of all, the care, treatment, education and training of mentally retarded persons in the low borderline and educable range have shifted from residential facilities to day schools. Trained or qualified educators along with other specialists (medicine, audiology, speech, and physical therapy) provide meaningful and adequate services within the public school system or in schools.

Secondly, the care, treatment, and training for more severely disabled children (trainables) are being provided in many communities in a manner similar to that in which these services are rendered for the youngsters who are educable.

As a third observation, there is an observable trend for those persons who suffer from the rather severe to severest degrees of mental disabilities to outnumber either the educable or the trainable in state institutions. Their demand upon the availability of total lifelong care has become a dominant factor.

The complexities of needed services can best be dealt with by projecting various life-span requirements as known to us. However, we shall not attempt to make specific recommendations for those services that are nonmedical in nature.

### Infants and Small Children

Most developmentally disabled children are disabled at birth, although it may not be evident at the time. They require diagnostic, prognostic, and treatment services.

The preschool-age medical clinic may operate as an independent agency, a part of a general hospital, or a part of the state hospital training school system. In any event, utilization of existing services and efforts at integration in regional areas will be made and standards must be established and maintained to meet existing needs.

It is desirable that the director of the clinic be a well-qualified pediatrician. She will have medical consultants on her staff (neurologist, child psychiatrist, ophthalmologist, dentist, nutritionists, public health nurses, and others as needed). Essential are full-time or part-time qualified social workers, clinical or developmental psychologists, audiologists, speech, occupational, and physical therapists and medical secretaries. The number of staff employed must correspond to the needs of the patients referred to the clinic.

The clinic must have adequate space to function. It must have available all diagnostic tools and procedures that are necessary to establish an inclusive and comprehensive diagnosis, such as roentgenology, clinical and anatomic pathology, biochemistry, genetics, and electroencephalography.

All personnel must meet licensing and/or certification requirements of their respective professions. The clinic, if it is eligible, must meet the standards of the Joint Commission on Accreditation of Hospitals.

### Young School-Age Children

Developmentally disabled children, once properly diagnosed, will require a broad range of varying services:

Children who are ambulatory and without significant adjustment problems are, generally, entered into nursery schools with subsequent promotion into subprimary and appropriate grades of the public school system. State licensing procedures establish necessary standards for personnel and facilities.

Children who are not ambulatory or who have major adjustment problems that cannot be dealt with in the public school system or the private home may require in-residence facilities that provide special orthopedic or psychiatric services or services to the blind, deaf, or others. All children in this category will be given the required additional diagnostic, treatment, rehabilitative, and educational services that are needed to assist them to develop their optimal potential. Such programs must be multidisciplinary, under qualified medical direction. Thus, they must meet the requirements of the Joint Commission on Accreditation of Hospitals.

As the process of treatment and rehabilitation progresses, a differentiation of each child's long-range needs will become evident. It may lead to discharge into the community and referral to a child guidance clinic and to the public special school system. It may require prolonged hospitalization because of specific medical requirements. Or, it may result in providing lifelong protective care in an accredited institution for the chronically ill (extended care unit), a licensed nursing home, or a licensed boarding home. In any event, local, state, and/or federal licensing requirements must be met and the facility should be accredited by the Joint Commission on Accreditation of Hospitals if it is eligible.

### Progressing Preadolescents and Adolescents

Most of the developmentally disabled youngsters in the educational and training programs will reach the limit of their academic potential before the age of 16. Therefore, it is necessary that meaningful and adequate prevocational programs be available at the appropriate time. Whether such a program is part of a public school system or an integral part of a private or public residential care facility, it must meet the licensing and certification requirements of the state and/or federal government. Under the current legal definition, a youngster capable of rehabilitation, as interpreted by the Division of Vocational Rehabilitation, qualifies at age 16 to participate in this program.

Adequate day care programs and/or domiciliary facilities must meet the program needs of the clients. Also, they must meet licensing or certification requirements of each licensing body (department of health, department of labor, department of education, the fire marshal, department of insurance, etc.).

### Young Adults and Adults

By the time a developmentally disabled person is 18 years of age, his future role in our society can be assessed fairly accurately, in most instances. The need may range from living more or less independently in the community or in a supervised group living program, to residence in a licensed boarding home, a licensed nursing home, or in an institution for chronically disabled or ill persons. Correspondingly, he may be economically independent, partially self-supporting, or receive public support through Medicare, Medicaid, Social Security, or aid to the permanently and totally disabled.

In any event, adequate legal and social provisions must be made to protect the person against physical, emotional, social, or economic exploitation and abuse. Also, regardless of where the adult lives, he must have adequate access to all community resources that he may need at any given time in his life span. This will require programmed supervisory services that can be included in an adequate protective mechanism (Guardianship Act).

## SPATIAL NEEDS OF PROGRAM ELEMENTS

Design of all spaces should be noninstitutional. The following are suggestions for consideration in all program element needs indicated below:

Openers in space-planning
Live plants
Design for groupings of 4 to 8 persons
Comfortable light level (natural light, desk lamps, etc.)
Freedom for hanging pictures
Warm surface finishes in natural materials
Views outside
Contact with outdoors
Visual access to mainstream of activity.

The following does not assume that all services must be located under one roof (see Location of Services).

## Inpatient Unit

This is a short-term residential facility for living under a supervised therapeutic program, requiring a domestic or college-dormitory rather than a hospital atmosphere. Architectural Section, NIMH, recommends this area be classified residential occupancy (NFPA No. 101) where permitted by local authorities. Each group of 16 to 24 patients requires the spaces discussed below. Design should allow natural groupings of 4 to 8 persons.

### Patient Needs

- Privacy for sleeping, dressing, and bathing
- Provision for personal grooming needs
- As few regulations for use of facility as possible
- Patients should be able to rearrange furniture, hang pictures on wall, etc.
- Patient belongings should not be out of reach; lockable storage space should be provided in each patient's bedroom unless specifically prohibited by program

### Domestic Needs to Be Provided

Laundry and small kitchen for use by each living group (16 to 24 patients).

### Socialization Areas

- Space for small conversational groupings or quiet individual use (2 to 4 persons). Example: small living space in a suite of two or four bedrooms.
- Activity spaces for games, dancing, music, group living (16 to 24 persons). Two living areas are desirable to allow noisy and quiet activities to occur simultaneously. Quiet activity space could also be used for group therapy. Example: a large living room as the focus of living group activities with a smaller, comfortably furnished lounge adjacent.

### Visiting Area

Space should be provided for private visiting with family and friends. Example: an out-of-the-way alcove for 6 persons, located near the entrance to the unit and the nurse's station, allowing visual and conversation level acoustical privacy.

### Recreation

Physical exercise space in the form of an exercise room, gymnasium, or outdoor space (especially in warm climates) should be provided. Example: small exercise room for group setting up exercise program with agreement to use high school gym and playing fields located within easy walking distance.

### Staff Needs

- Lounge area
- Storage for personal property
- Staff toilet
- Area for charting/private discussion with therapists
- Security for drugs
- Multi-use patient interview space, family discussion, etc.
- Minimal barriers to interaction with patients. Example: desks are preferable to glazed nursing stations.

### Housekeeping Needs

Domestic housekeeping
  Linens in patients' bedrooms or locate for central distribution
  Each bedroom unit to have own linen supply
  Bathroom and personal items
Central janitor's closet

### Dietary Services

Snacks, patients' activities in kitchen
Feeding; hospital cafeteria and kitchen service on units; storage for dishes, linens, etc.
Icemakers
Complete domestic kitchen; exhaust system must be adequate

### Intensive Care

- Acoustical privacy
- Social space for contact with staff and freedom to leave confined room
- Close supervision by staff
- Controlled access to toilet, wardrobe, light switches outside patient's room
- Security
- Tamper-proof equipment and fixtures within patient's room and toilet
- Tempered plate glass or removable-type detention screens
- Treatment room; first aid, emergency physical examination items for special programs such as drugs, alcohol, etc.
- Laboratory with storage

*References:* Physical Planning Guidelines for Community Mental Health Centers, Clyde H. Dorsett, AIA, Architectural Consultant, National Institute of Mental Health, Bethesda, Md.

- Direct access from nurses' station and from emergency rooms in general hospitals
- Audio communications between nurses' station and patient's room
- Patient rooms may be used for medical care when needed
- Necessary equipment not removable from the room must be lockable and concealable

We recommend occupancy for this area be institutional.

## Emergencies

Emergencies can occur in any element of service at any time. The most common are walk-in and escorted emergency patients.

- Walk-in: arriving at any element of service for the first time to get help. This person may come in alone or with others. He is ambulant and functioning.
- Escorted emergency: ambulant but not functioning.

### Physical Space for Walk-in

- Inviting entrance
- Must have immediate relationship to outside while patient is in waiting-reception area
- Privacy with receptionist in stating his needs

### Note

All spaces for walk-in interview, initial treatment, and admitting of walk-in emergency patients can be those used by outpatients.

### Escorted Emergency

- Will utilize all staff and space in emergency suite of general hospital.
- Additional spaces may be needed in general hospital emergency.
- Space:
  Interview space that promotes communication between patient and physician.
  Holding space; waiting bed space; for patient to wait while disposition for treatment is considered (i.e., sedated patient).
- Entrance available directly to intensive care area for escorted emergencies.

### Note

Design and location should motivate interaction and communication between all agencies and elements of service utilizing the facility.

## Outpatient Unit

### Admitting Offices

Should be convenient to receptionist.

### Ancillary Services

- Waiting areas
- Secretarial space
- Public and staff toilets, lounge (coffee, sink, refrigerator), and library-workroom

### Waiting Areas

- Limited to 8 to 12 patients
- Distributed throughout office areas
- Receptionist by front door—open, friendly, encourage contact between receptionist and patient

### Children's Treatment

- Adjacent to entrance and child therapist's office
- Provide for observation
- Provide for work sink (as part of messy area), and locked storage
- Provide for separate toilet available to children; separate waiting area, with possibility of observation by parent; outdoor play space; scaled for children; cleanable surfaces

### Office Space

Should motivate communication between patient and therapist, should contain doctor (staff) and at least four or more patients and be flexible in arrangement of furniture.

### Conference Spaces

- Sufficient to accommodate required people
- Suitable for audiovisual presentations, staff meetings, staff work area
- Accessible to main entrance and/or office spaces and rest rooms
- Suitable for group therapy
- Provides storage closet

### Staff Lounge

Adjacent to staff toilets, storage, and small kitchenette (coffeemaker, refrigerator); also adjacent to staff library and workroom.

| Office space | Conference and interview | Meetings (with consultation and educational service) |
|---|---|---|
| Play therapy | Group therapy* | Larger groups |
| Individual | Staff conferences | Community groups |
| Family | Interagency professional groups | General meetings |

*Group therapy rooms to be utilized through total programs

*Meeting Room*

Need for large meeting room depends on availability of space in the community. Such a room needs audiovisual facilities, storage space, and sufficient toilet areas; it should be located between central facilities and community.

## Partial Hospitalization

*Day Care*

This requires a primary social area (living-room-type space)

*Staff Needs*

- Office space for day program director
- Work area for staff
- Medications
- Nurses' lockers and toilet
- (All located in position for information and control for particular hospital program)

*Patient's Needs*

- Storage for wraps and for personal articles
- Telephone, drinking fountain
- Toilets
- Kitchen suitable for social groups and therapy

*Occupational Therapy*

This consists of quiet and noisy activities and depends on the program. The most flexible design requires at least two rooms of classroom size with two kinds of storage for patients' projects and materials, and for equipment. The office for the program director is mostly program space for patient occupational therapy activities with the occupational therapist as part of the therapy team. It may be without staff offices and consist of large rooms divided by movable storage cabinets.

*Social Recreational Therapy*

- Large social space
- Outdoor terrace for gardening, outdoor games, and an inactive outdoor area for quiet
- TV and music
- Quiet indoor space
- Movies/video/computer
- Kitchen
- Library (quiet)
- Quiet social area
- Not minimal but desirable are a swimming pool with its own dressing rooms and toilets; and table games.

Structured recreational therapy programs require a small gym, for 8 to 12 patients at one time, with its own showers, dressing rooms, and lockers. One should inventory the community facilities that can be used: YMCA, schools, shopping centers, public parks, public pools, and other mental health related programs in the community. An active outdoor area must be available with a playing field, large space for active games, etc.

The R.T. office can be same as for O.T. weekend and night-evening program can be held within the same space as the inpatient program.

## Children's Day Care

General needs include a staff office, a central reception room-gathering place, and classrooms. The program could utilize the adult gym. Toilets and a small snack kitchen should be available. (They could be used for other parts of the center's program.)

Classrooms need an area for messy (wet area) work (sink, etc.), an outdoor area, a teacher's work area with a desk (no desk in classroom), and also, for problem kids, quiet study; this class is separated from main classroom area by a curtain. Children's outdoor play space must be separated from adult outdoor areas.

*Administration*

- Reception-waiting area
- Director's office-meeting room nearby
- Offices for program directors
- Volunteers and part-time office and lounge with lockers and toilets
- Conference room
- Library-workroom-staff lounge
- Business-secretarial pool
- Central records for all service elements

*Consultation and Education*

Meeting rooms and office spaces are located adjacent to or within central office groupings. Center can multiuse spaces for other elements of program for this purpose. (Basis of operations for C&S is out in the community and will use facility only to conduct business and for meetings.)

## CIRCULATION

### Use for Socialization

Circulation space can be used for more than transportation from one area to another. Informal contacts, pausing along the way to look at views, and stopping for a cup of coffee are activities that also encourage social contact.

*Entry/Waiting Area*

Entrance through the front door to all program elements located in the facility should be possible. Arriving persons should be greeted by a staff person. Example: volunteer behind a desk located in sight of front door. Waiting areas should be small groups in sight of receptionist. Waiting area allows view of mainstream of activity, but is located in well-defined area out of main traffic pattern.

Drinking fountain, toilets, and pay telephone are adjacent to entry-waiting area.

*Contact with Staff*

Staff persons (volunteers, secretaries) should be located to be visible to persons moving in circulation pattern of building. Example: secretary for outpatient offices located in alcove with chairs for waiting adjacent to circulation space.

Provide informal social areas as part of circulation space leading to meeting rooms, partial hospitalization, etc. places where numbers of people congregate, and also at nodes in circulation system-places where people are likely to pause. Example: gathering space with area for coats, bathrooms outside community meeting room.

Waiting for outpatient appointments should be adjacent to outpatient staff offices. Director of Center should be located adjacent to other staff offices to encourage interstaff contact.

*Orientation*

- Use views of outdoors and natural light; clear inside/outside circulation.
- Clear relation of program spaces to front door.
- Provide privacy or separation by single turn in corridor or by screens; minimum of closed doors.
- Staff person to greet arrival to program area secretary for outpatient area, nurse or volunteer located by entrance to inpatient unit, etc.
- Use staff and design of circulation space rather than barriers (locked doors) for control.

*Time of Use*

- Locate community meeting areas near front door for night-time use; lock off rest of facility.
- Partial hospitalization/inpatient section could have its own entrance for day/night use.

*Variety*

Circulation spaces should contrast light, dark, outside, inside, narrow, wide, free, controlled, stimulating (warm colors), subdued (cool colors) to provide cues to kind of activities associated with nearby program spaces and to maintain orientation. Example: corridor to outside day program area widens to allow informal socialization and use of lockers located against one wall and is lit by skylight.

*Zoning*

Program elements should be related to:

- Public accessibility
- Acoustical separation
- Heavy circulation/noisy activities
- Quiet/private activities
- Scheduled use/nonscheduled use
- Frequency of use
- Day/night use
- Unique or common use
- Sole staff use
- Sole patient use
- Joint use by staff and patients
- Relation to other program spaces
- Relation to front door
- Need for outdoor space and natural light
- Need for privacy/controlled access

*Note*

The prevalent dichotomy between circulation/service spaces and program spaces should be minimized where possible.

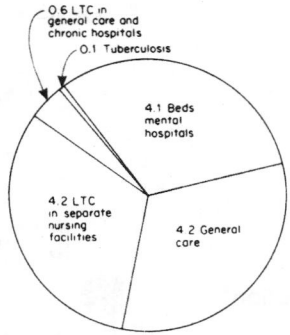

0.6 LTC in
general care and
chronic hospitals
0.1 Tuberculosis

4.1 Beds
mental
hospitals

4.2 LTC
in separate
nursing
facilities

4.2 General
care

**Fig. 1. Ratio of beds to population served**

# LONG-TERM CARE FACILITIES

## INTRODUCTION

Health planning for long-term care facilities (hereafter referred to as LTC) should emphasize the concept of providing a spectrum of care which serves the health needs of the entire community. This spectrum includes general medical and surgical facilities, mental, rehabilitation hospitals, and LTCs that provide care beyond acute, short-term medical and nursing care and may be in either chronic hospitals or nursing homes.

While the functions of a chronic hospital are relatively clear, what is understood by a nursing home can be somewhat ambiguous. For our purposes, an LTC may be defined as a facility which is operated either independently or in connection with a hospital and provides nursing care and medical services under the general direction of persons licensed to practice medicine or surgery. Furthermore, unlike the chronic hospital, the LTC generally does not have resident physicians and limits its medical services to minor treatment, diagnostic x-ray, and minor laboratory analysis. Although good medical practice should be available wherever and whenever a patient needs it, the fact is that major medical and surgical treatments are almost always performed in other facilities.

Eight categories of LTC facilities are readily identifiable: general hospitals with long-term care beds; voluntary chronic hospitals; local government chronic hospitals; public home facilities; convalescent homes; voluntary nursing homes; proprietary nursing homes; and homes for the aged. Other nomenclature for the categories listed above are extended care facilities, intermediate care facilities, shelter homes for the aged, geriatric homes for the aged, long-term care facilities, homes for adults, foster homes, boarding homes, etc.

Each type has its own criteria for admission based for the most part on the type of care required; but reimbursement, whether through private payment, private medical insurance, Medicare or Medicaid, etc., may as well be a determining factor in patient placement. Whatever problems are involved, the fact is that patients often require a wide range of services beyond initial acute medical care, and these services may cross several institutional lines, from intensive nursing and rehabilitative care through lesser degrees of nursing care to perhaps simply convalescent attention.

## SOCIAL PLANNING CRITERIA

The basic criterion used in determining the needs for all health care facilities is the ratio of beds to the population served. A characteristic distribution of these beds is shown in Fig. 1. Their age characteristics are indicated in Fig. 2.

According to Dr. Michael Miller,* studies of this aging population in terms of their characteristics from a medical viewpoint indicate that terminal cancer is seen in only 3 to 5 percent of the patient population. Varying degrees of organic brain syndrome, as manifested by memory, intellectual, and judgmental deficits associated with confusion and disorientation, with or without locomotion disability, constitute at least 70 to 75 percent of the patient population. Studies indicate that 20 to 30 percent of a nursing home population may be expected to have experienced a significant psychiatric decompensation in the pre-aged period. Of the whole, 40 to 50 percent will demonstrate significant cardio-renal-vascular disease in varying degrees of decompensation. Arthropathies are virtually a universal occurrence, although only 20 to 30 percent may require specific management techniques. Fifteen to 20 percent of the patient population will present significant visual deficits, and there will be approximately the same number with auditory deficits. Other organ system involvement in the same patient is the rule rather than exception, such as gastrointestinal, pulmonary, neurological, and metabolic disorders. Multiorgan pathology in the chronically aged is a distinguishing characteristic of disability in contrast to other age groups.

*"Synthesis of a Therapeutic Community for the Aged III," published in *Geriatrics* vol. 21. pp. 151-163.

*Author:* William Breger, AIA
*Reviewer:* James H. Ogden, R.A.
*References:* Hospital statistics from Health and Hospital Statistics Planning Council of Southern New York, and Long-Term Care, (LTC) Projection. Illustrations from Michael B. Miller and William N. Breger, "How to Plan for Extended Care Service," *Modern Hospital.*

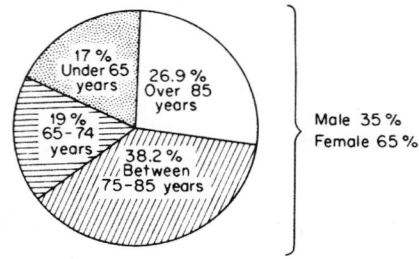

**Fig. 2. Age characteristics of patient population***

One can conclude as well both from the demographic changes in a society that is proportionately growing elderly and the societal changes of placing the elderly members of society in medically oriented facilities that the LTC facility would have a greater percentage of beds allotted to it proportionately in the future and that this area of health concern would experience real as well as proportional growth.

Another aspect of social planning is the translation of social data into the architectural program. We have found that the ideal method of determining the physical facilities of the building is in terms of the proposed patient population rated by their capacities to perform activities, including daily living, both in terms of their physical capabilities and their behavioral capacities. Tables 1 to 4 describe the clinical nature of the patient population under study and give some index of the percentage of patient population in each group. At the conclusion, we will indicate the physical configuration of the nursing units that each group generates.

**Group I: Physically Disabled (15 to 25 percent)***

Patients having significant physical disabilities but with emotional and intellectual intactness and the ability to socialize in an open, unsupervised environment (see Fig. 3).

**Group II: Mentally and Physically Disabled (25 to 30 percent)**

Patients with severe physical disabilities with superimposed substantial handicaps of organic brain disease, thus requiring total nursing care for physical disabilities and major supervision for social activities (see Fig. 4).

**Group III: Custodial (15 to 25 percent)**

Patients presenting moderate or no physical disabilities with either no or minimal emotional or social disabilities, thus able to function in an uncontrolled social milieu. However, they function best in a professionally supervised environment (see Fig. 5).

**Group IV: Mentally Disabled (30 to 50 percent)**

Patients having minimal to mild physical disabilities with major emotional and social disabilities, who therefore require minimal nursing care on a purely physical level but because of the advanced degree of organic brain disease (dementia) these patients are essentially totally and permanently disabled (see Fig. 6).

*Based on 1,050 patient survey by W. Breger at Columbia School of Public Health and Hospital Administration.

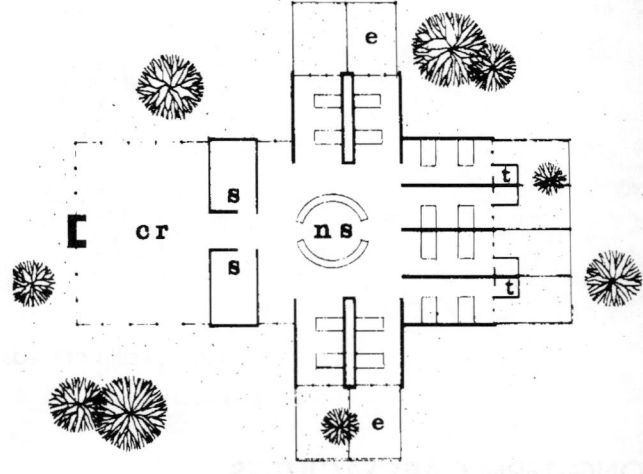

**Fig. 3. Group I: physically disabled.** Symbols represent the following facilities: CR: community room NS: nursing station T: toilet S: services (i.e., utility rooms, treatment, bathing, pantry, nonpatient storage) P: pantry E: outdoor environment

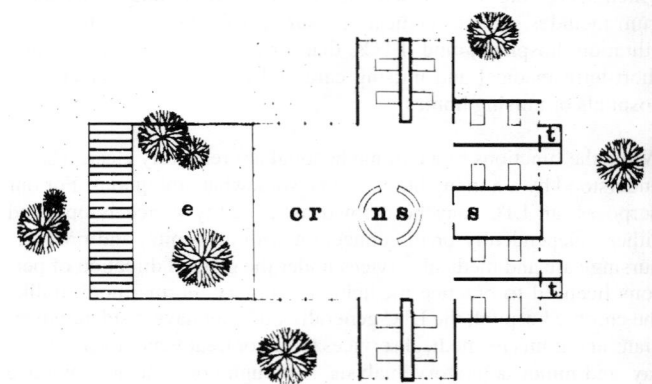

**Fig. 4. Group II: mentally and physically disabled.** Symbols represent the following facilities: CR: community room NS: nursing station T: toilet S: services (i.e., utility rooms, treatment, bathing, pantry, nonpatient storage) P: pantry E: outdoor environment

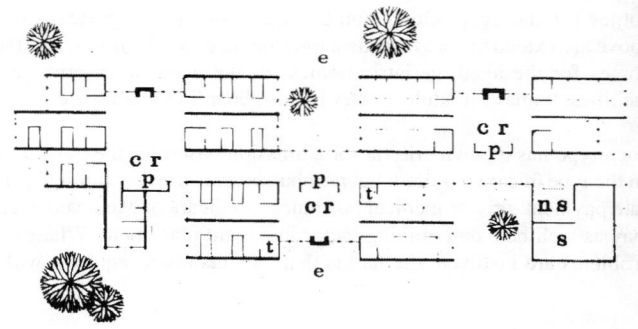

**Fig. 5. Group III: custodial.** Symbols represent the following facilities: CR: community room NS: nursing station T: toilet S: services (i.e., utility rooms, treatment, bathing, pantry, non-patient storage) P: pantry E: outdoor environment

**Table 1**  Group I facilities*

| Area | Design requirements |
|---|---|
| Community room | Unsupervised |
| Physical therapy | Combined with community living |
| Exterior environment | Unsupervised |
| Bedrooms | Sufficient area for wheelchairs, walkers, crutches; half of rooms with bedside flush toilets |
| Toilets | 20–22 inches from floor |
| Bathing | Near nurses' station, must be supervised |
| Utility room | Near nurses' station |
| Pantry | Supervised, near nurses' station |
| Storage area, personal | Limited vertical storage; increase in horizontal storage |
| Nonpersonal storage | Limited vertical storage, increase in horizontal storage |
| Treatment room | Near nurses' station |
| Family counseling | Near nurses' station |
| Nurses' station | Located for convenience of nurses |

*Group I patients suffer severe physical handicaps but are emotionally and physically intact.

**Table 2**  Group II facilities*

| Area | Design requirements |
|---|---|
| Community room | Supervised |
| Physical therapy | Combined with community living |
| Exterior environment | Supervised |
| Bedrooms | Sufficient area for wheelchairs, walkers, crutches; half of rooms with bedside flush toilets |
| Toilets | 20–22 inches from floor |
| Bathing | Near nurses' station, must be supervised |
| Utility room | Near nurses' station |
| Pantry | Supervised, near nurses' station |
| Storage area, personal | Limited vertical storage; increase in horizontal storage |
| Nonpersonal storage | Limited vertical storage, increase in horizontal storage |
| Treatment room | Near nurses' station |
| Family counseling | Near nurses' station |
| Nurses' station | Located for convenience of nurses |

*Group II patients suffer severe and behavioral disability. Therefore they require total nursing care as well as major supervision of social activities.

**Table 3**  Group III facilities*

| Area | Design requirements |
|---|---|
| Community room | Unsupervised |
| Physical therapy | Not indicated |
| Exterior environment | Unsupervised |
| Bedrooms | Conventional |
| Toilets | Conventional |
| Bathing | May be located conveniently; nonsupervision possible |
| Utility room | Not indicated |
| Pantry | Unsupervised, near community room |
| Storage area, personal | Increase in vertical storage; conventional horizontal storage space |
| Nonpersonal storage | Increase in vertical storage, conventional horizontal storage space |
| Treatment room | Not indicated |
| Family counseling | Near nurses' station |
| Nurses' station | Located for convenience of nurses |

*Group III patients require little supervision because they present no, or very moderate, physical and emotional and social disability.

**Table 4**  Group IV facilities*

| Area | Design requirements |
|---|---|
| Community room | Supervised |
| Physical therapy | Not indicated |
| Exterior environment | Supervised |
| Bedrooms | Conventional |
| Toilets | Conventional |
| Bathing | Supervised, but located conveniently for patient |
| Utility room | Not indicated |
| Pantry | Supervised, near nurses' station |
| Storage area, personal | Increase in vertical storage; increase in horizontal storage |
| Nonpersonal storage | Increase in vertical storage, increase in horizontal storage |
| Treatment room | Not indicated |
| Family counseling | Near nurses' station |
| Nurses' station | Located to permit control of patient areas |

*On the purely physical level, patients in Group IV need little nursing care but require maximum supervision because of emotional disability.

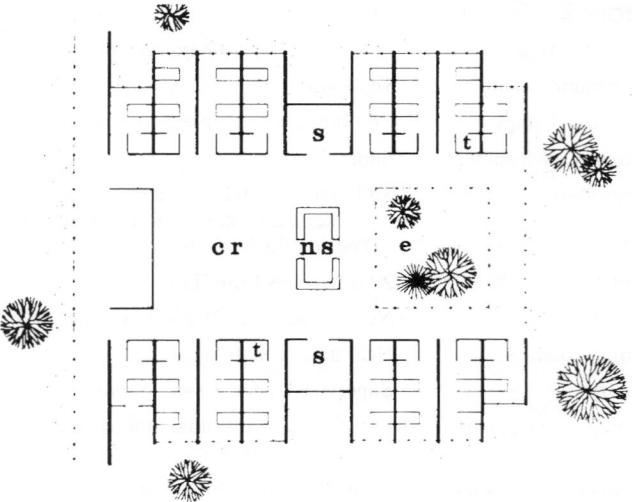

**Fig. 6. Group IV: mentally disabled. Symbols represent the following facilities: CR: community room NS: nursing station T: toilet S: services (i.e., utility rooms, treatment, bathing, pantry, nonpatient storage) P: pantry E: outdoor environment**

## DESIGN CRITERIA

The design problems unique in this facility mainly involve the nursing units and supportive facilities that are required in terms of the projected patient population. The problems inherent in dietary, mechanical maintenance, and general and building storage facilities are fairly uniform regardless of the type of projected patient population and have a basic similarity to medical facilities of the same size, such as general hospitals. It should be noted that supply storage facilities, linens, equipment, etc., would depend to some extent on the projected patient population.

Because, generally speaking, LTC facility administrators cannot determine patient population beforehand or they choose because of administrative and economic patterns to have a wide mix of patients, the common interpretation of the structure is to have the nursing and activity functions not flexible. This type of building is in a great degree determined by the relevant codes and the most economical means of construction. Another factor that should be explored is that operational care could be improved even in the uniform nursing unit if the design were determined to a greater extent by an awareness of the proposed patient population.

In most instances the program delineates the size of the LTC facilities. It is determined by such factors as available money for construction; the need within a community as determined by demographic factors or methods of health care, code requirements, site limitations; and, finally, the kind of operation as foreseen by the administrator or nursing home operator. The nursing unit is a prime factor in operational cost, and thus the size of the facility is usually a multiple of the number of nursing units. Because of the cost of operation of feeding, therapy, and administration, the larger the facility, usually the more economically efficient it will be, although too large a unit might not allow for adequate patient service functions. Once the number of beds has been determined, the areas of the building can be calculated, bearing in mind such factors as the care given, the stipulation of single-bedded or multi-bedded rooms, and the commu-

nity facilities provided. Again, in the typical facility at present, community functions are nonexistent or minimal and the number of single- and multi-bedded rooms is determined by code or FHA regulations.

Although, as previously noted, it is desirable that the inter- and intra-configuration be determined by the medical and social patterns of patient care, there are common facilities that are required for operation by codes and public agencies. Thus, in an overall sense, the design of all independent long-term care buildings will contain the following component parts:

1. Administrative facilities
2. Staff facilities
3. Public facilities
4. Medical, treatment, and morgue facilities
5. Dietary service
6. Storage areas
7. Work area and maintenance areas
8. Mechanical facilities such as boiler, air conditioner, pump
9. Patient, staff and visitor circulation patterns
10. Nursing units including ancillary facilities; i.e., nurses' station, nursing unit dayroom
11. Supportive and rehabilitative facilities for patients, such as recreation, dining, therapy areas

The component parts listed above, except for items 10 and 11, the nursing unit and supportive facilities, are similar to those of general hospitals, and thus criteria developed for general medical facilities, as indicated in the section on Hospitals, may be applied to the LTC facilities. Some indication of the ways in which the areas of the LTC differ from those of the general hospital are listed below.

### Administrative Facilities

LTC facilities sometimes provide fewer medical, surgical, and laboratory services; administrative problems are reduced by the lower turnover of patients (less record keeping and billing); and, usually, there are fewer visitors per patient per day, although there may be more family counseling. However, with the administrative and bookkeeping problems involved in government aid programs and other funding, there has been a remarkable increase in the required area for administrative purposes in recent years, and it is expected that this trend will continue. Generally speaking, there are the following areas: a business office; a lobby and information center; an administrator's office; an admitting and medical records area; an administrative staff toilet room, supervising nurses' areas; social service office; and staff conference room.

### Staff Facilities

As stated above, the reduced medical services provided, as well as the usual absence of staff physicians, results in a concomitant reduction of staff in an LTC facility as compared with a general hospital. Often the staffing is determined by patient population and is indicated in administrative codes.*

---

*Another way of interpreting staff requirements is by using the New York State Code which requires of staffing time one hour of nursing care for ambulatory patients, two hours of nursing care for the semiambulatory, and four hours per day for the bedridden or wheelchair-confined patient.

The facilities needed are locker rooms, toilet and shower facilities, and dining room. There is some question as to the location of these facilities; whether they should be grouped in a separate area or distributed on each nursing floor with a smaller central grouping. There should be a central lounge, and it should be accessible to the employees' dining room.

## Public Facilities

The type and size of the public facilities depend to some extent on the type of sponsorship of the LTC facility; but one factor is constant: the number of visitors in the LTC facility is much smaller per patient than in an acute general hospital. This is often reflected in parking criteria and internal visiting areas. Architectural features that are desirable are a visitors' lavatory on each nursing floor and, when the building is large enough, a small lobby with perhaps a snack and gift shop. When an LTC facility is community sponsored, a variety of public functions may be provided for it, but these would be similar to what is provided in a community supported general hospital.

## Medical, Treatment, and Morgue Facilities

As mentioned, both legislative requirements and medical practice require that major treatment of the acutely ill patient in the LTC be available within general medical and surgical hospitals. This gives the community an economical use of both staffing and facilities. Sometimes chronic hospitals in nonurban areas provide as part of their facilities intensive medical and surgical units; but with the notion of regional health care, this is not considered by most health planning agencies to be desirable today. The facilities in the LTC which are provided, where the law permits, are a diagnostic x-ray unit, a laboratory for hematology, biochemistry, etc., and, usually as part of the nursing unit, treatment rooms. It is desirable that spaces for dentistry, podiatry, and, on occasion, optometry, be provided if the patient population can support them. However, all these operations can usually be carried out in comparatively small areas.

The requirements for a morgue facility have varied with different localities and different regulations. It is ultimately a problem of operation whether they should be provided or not, but if required because of geographic or administrative reasons, the morgue is at best a small area used for storage of bodies for a few hours or a day or two at most. The autopsy procedure is a hospital function.

## Dietary Facilities

In the LTC as in the general hospital, the dietary requirements and the space and equipment required to support them are extensive and the basis for involved research and analysis.

Feeding is required for nourishment and as a patient activity, and, quite understandably, the social functions of dining are important therapeutically. Feeding is accomplished in five different methods in medical facilities: (1) Intravenous infusions, naso-gastric tube feeding, gastrostomy feeding; (2) with trays in bed; (3) at tables in patient rooms; (4) with trays in a controlled recreation room on the patient floor; and (5) family style in a controlled dayroom, in the nursing unit, or on a separate floor. It is understandable that methods 4 and 5 will be favored and used more frequently in the LTC. Here the social dynamics of group situations can be developed, and it is also a more efficient way of providing patient dining. Many have held that feeding intravenously or with trays in bed are undesirable in terms of an LTC facility, but they are occasionally used, depending on patient conditions. Feeding at tables in patient rooms is used more often because it is possible to control behavioral problems in this dining context. The size of the facility, however, is smaller, as the number of employees is much lower than in a general hospital.

## Storage Facilities

In the recent past considerable thought has been given to ways of resolving the storage problems of LTC facilities. Storage areas are about 5 square feet per patient for personal storage and 5 square feet for general hospital supplies and goods. The latter is less than what is allotted in a general hospital, because, as previously mentioned, the type of care required in a nursing home does not demand as many linens, pharmaceuticals, and supplies. However, the elements of hospital storage should be provided, and the importance of ensuring the flexibility of the compartments for this cannot be overemphasized.

## Work Area and Maintenance Areas

In general these are quite similar to those of the community hospitals, except that there is a minimum of medical equipment to maintain and that, although the number of patients may be similar to the general hospital, the total amount of equipment in the LTC requiring maintenance or repair is considerably less.

## Structural and Mechanical Factors

LTC facilities are usually designed to meet the structural and mechanical standards of the general hospital. As in most other medical facilities, problems, particularly of fire safety, have required fireproof buildings, with sprinkler protection, smoke detectors, zoned floor areas, and rigid standards of fire resistance in terms of flooring, surfaces, and materials used. It is, of course, a fact that fire safety in a building housing many patients with behavioral problems (often involving carelessness and disorientation) is one of the major, if not the major factor in construction. While this appears evident, there are also other aspects of mechanical equipment criteria that are somewhat different than those for the short-term general hospital:

### Lighting

The level of illumination required for the LTC, bearing in mind the elderly patient population and their reduced sensory awareness and perception, is somewhat higher than that required in the patient areas of the general hospital. Furthermore, the problems of safety require that all electric lamps and fixtures be firmly connected to a surface to avoid tipping.

### Heating and Cooling

Code-compliant HVAC systems are to be provided to allow for proper heating, cooling, and ventilation.

## Circulation Patterns

The movement of people, goods, and equipment in the LTC is for the most part similar in nature, if not in intensity, to that in general hospitals. The one special problem is the need of adequate control for the circulation of the behaviorally difficult patient, for often the need to control the movement of this type of patient comes into conflict with the need to provide free movement in terms of fire department regulations. The use of mechanical devices such as buzzers attached to fire doors, the shortening of corridors, the visual control of elevator doors, and controlled exits from the building are some of the factors that can help control the traffic problems involved with this patient population.

**Nursing Units and Supportive Facilities**

An almost seminal practice in the design of LTC facilities is the placement of patients in autonomous nursing units, as it is believed that the control and management of patients can best be achieved in this manner. This nursing unit can be defined as a self-contained grouping of rooms, supportive facilities with unified control, all on one level. A basic decision is the size of the nursing unit, and while ideally the size of the unit will have a direct relationship to the degree and type of patient care provided in the unit, nursing home codes and governmental regulations generally set the number of patients cared for in a nursing unit between 30 and 60. In principle, the range could be even greater, as the spectrum of patients in LTC facilities is so varied. As Table 3 shows, patients in Group III (custodial patients) could be in units of up to 100 beds, while patients in Group II (mentally and physically disabled patients) might be in units of 20 beds.

Concomitant with the decision as to the number of beds per nursing unit is the determination of the number of beds per room. Here the guidelines are medical operational criteria, hospital and administrative codes, and financial mechanisms. But also a very important consideration is the aesthetic and social values that the patient may have, and, even more important, those of the people placing him in the home.

The two-bedded room with adjoining or private bath should be the basic room pattern regardless of nursing unit size or type of care required, and that there should be a certain number of single rooms as well within the unit for medical and behavioral problems.

Codes require at least one single room per patient unit as an isolation suite with its own toilet, but often the requirements are that single rooms be available for 10 to 33 percent of the patients. However, the problem of the single or the multi-bedded room, as well as the other functions of the nursing unit, should (once the minimum code requirements are resolved) be determined by the criterion of what patient population would be served in the program given to the architect, and, as pointed out above, the criteria can range from minimum requirements to aesthetic and social values.

Supporting the idea of the autonomy of the nursing unit are the types of ancillary facilities that are part of it. The functions that must be provided are the control of the unit from the nurses' station, the preparation of medicines, the cleaning and providing of the entire range of supplies necessary for the patients, the supplying of supplementary food, and whatever bathing, recreation, dining, and training facilities are required. The question of whether patient treatment (e.g., surgical dressings, etc.) should be done in the room or in a separate treatment room depends on the choices that the nurses make. All of these functions are usually translated into representative areas as determined by the relevant codes. Listed in Tables 1 through 4 is an analysis of the types of areas, the required equipment, the minimum size, the function, and the relationships that seem to be generic in terms of regulations. The fact, of course, is that, depending on the projected patient population, the types and sizes of these facilities would vary. Thus, in Group III, medical preparation and treatment might be eliminated and the pantry might be made much larger than for other patient populations. However, most codes do allow, if not flexibility in the type of function required, a fairly wide range in terms of the size required.

The essential thrust in the design of the LTC is ultimately in the configuration of the nursing unit, and, as mentioned, the genesis of the choices available for this is in the operational program initially presented to the architect, or, even more salutary, when developed with the architect. In the overwhelming percentage of buildings most of the plans are made for a variable patient population, ideally with a central nursing station adjacent to ancillary nursing functions that the nurse directly uses, with visual control of the patient corridors, recreation area, and means of entrance and egress. The size of the units, both for economy of structure and operation, is as large as the relevant code would allow. On a theoretical basis, Figs. 3 to 6 illustrate the correlation of possible unit configurations based on the patient population. While these designs would obviously be modified by code, medical practice, economy, and a difficult problem of determining the projected patient population, we believe they are valuable as abstractions indicating the correlation of care and planning.

**Rehabilitative Facilities**

Rehabilitation and physical medicine is the primary medical discipline involved in LTC facilities. Present thinking is that, in terms of the aged patient population, rehabilitation should properly be both a physical and behavioral therapeutic process. For the most part, this therapy is not centered on making the patient operational in society but rather on providing adjustments for the patients to live with their disabilities. Just as difficult an aspect of this adjustment as the physically based problems are those problems generated by behavioral disabilities. While, broadly speaking, spaces for therapy have meant facilities for physiotherapy, hydrotherapy, and heat therapy, the fact is that facilities for social therapy or facilities for developing social groupings should be part of the overall planning.

The areas for physically based rehabilitation are required by code, but the type of medical care given in these spaces is usually determined by the medical staff and administration. Often, physiotherapy, both in exercise and manipulation, has been considered sufficient for the patient population, and the location of this space has been both in separate rooms and as part of the dayroom, as this would induce a greater incentive for the individual patient to perform in terms of a peer group. Whether this area is separate or part of other areas, the fact remains that the use of such apparatus as parallel bars, exercise wheels, etc., under proper supervision, is a vital part of the patients' care. The need for hydro and heat therapies in the LTC facility has often been questioned. Ultimately, the decision to use these latter therapies is either an administrative or governing regulation.

Recreational spaces are needed for the behaviorally based therapies or what is sometimes called occupational therapy, which can be considered both physical and behavioral therapy. Whereas a central area is desired, often the actual therapy takes place within the nursing unit dayroom.

Often considered the best behaviorally based therapy is participation in a social community, whereby, as it has been demonstrated, many of the anxieties and much of the loneliness that is a concomitant of the aging process can be reduced. These group situations may take the forms of religious services, lectures, group games, group teas; even a bar has been used. However, the most important aspect that generates one of the most difficult planning decisions is the development of a community within the LTC, whereby patients will be providing support for others. In terms of architectural configurations, spaces for this activity have been arranged so that sleeping rooms open directly onto living rooms, or they have been provided by eliminating halls and having spaces open into large community areas. It is through the exploration of this problem that architectural planning may be considered an aid of therapy as well. Again, the only rule we can recommend would be to arrive at this through the analysis of the particular patient population of the proposed facility. Listed in Table 5, in terms of the usual codes and regulations, are the typical patient activity areas, their size, the equipment they usually contain, and their relationships.

## CONCLUSION

The preceding is only the rough planning data of the design of LTC facilities. Microscopic analyses based on the kind of hardware patients with reduced manipulative ability can use, the types of furniture (such as seating that would allow easy access without strain, beds that would be sufficiently protective, and tables that would be sufficiently sturdy), the kind of plumbing fixtures that the elderly patient needs, and the kinds of interior surfaces are part of the literature of professional magazines and should be examined in detail. The essential basis, though, for understanding these aspects of the LTC is the understanding of the patient.

Nor is it our intention to discuss the major problem of aesthetic values in terms of this patient population. The range of what aesthetic an LTC facility should generate, whether the criterion should be what society wants, what the employees want, what the children of the patient want, or what the patients want is a question that individual decisions must resolve, and these can, it is hoped, be based on some empirical data. It is believed as well that the LTC program should generate a building that emphasizes the quality of space required for a longer patient stay and that this quality should be different from that of the community hospital in both plan and form, visually and functionally. Finally, we should arrive at an architectural expression for this space that would be a rejection of institutional forms, such as long hallways, sterile color schemes, mechanistic furniture, purely utilitarian finishes, and an acceptance of the fact that sunlight, casualness, and comfort not only are desirable patterns but also are part of the therapy and well-being of the LTC patient.

The task of resolving this fundamental social problem of providing support for the ill aged is a social action that we have just begun to explore and to which architects can make a most meaningful contribution.

## 5 Typical regulatory requirements for LTC facilities

| | | Nursing Unit | | |
|---|---|---|---|---|
| nd size of room | Activity | Equipment and sizes | Relationship | Comments |
| (125 sq ft) edded (100 sq ft ed), cubicle ins required | Depends on patient population<br><br>Will serve for both sleeping and general activity, and may also include dining, recreation and therapy | Beds (usually gatch type) with side rails, 36 by 86 in.; overbed tables (usually not required); side cabinet, 18 by 20 in.; chairs, straight back and arms (at least one chair per bed)<br><br>Storage Space:<br>Vertical storage—robes, outdoor clothing in closets or wardrobes, 1 ft 8 in. wide by 1 ft 10 in. deep, should contain shoe rack and shelf<br><br>Horizontal storage—cabinets or built-in drawers, 1 ft 6 in. deep<br><br>(Note: Ideally, vertical storage areas should be increased for ambulatory patients and horizontal storage increased for nonambulatory patients.)<br><br>Optional Equipment:<br>Small table, ideally round with a heavy pedestal base; platform rocking chairs, where patient conditions permit; lavatory; cabinet for storing patient toiletries<br><br>(Note: Where private toilet is used, lavatory may be placed in toilet.) | Not more than 120 ft from nurses' station | See plans; desirable distribution should be based on administrative practices |
| (3 by 6 ft) and lavatory y 8 ft and/or 5 ft) | | Required:<br>Grab bars, toiletry cabinet and/or space for toiletries, mirror<br>(Note: Lavatory should be accessible to wheelchair patients.)<br><br>Optional:<br>Divert-a-valve, bedpan washer | | |
| s' station imum 6 lin ft of nter with access e on both sides | Control of nursing unit charting communications, storage of supplies and nurses' personal effects | Patient charts (9 by 12 in.—May be movable or set into the desk), chart rack for 40 charts (4 ft wide by 16 in. deep), writing desk, legal files, cabinet storage area, outlets for nurses' call system, telephones | | |

**Table 5** Typical regulatory requirements for LTC facilities (cont.)

*Nursing Unit (cont.)*

| Type and size of room | Activity | Equipment and sizes | Relationship | Comments |
|---|---|---|---|---|
| Nurses' toilet room (5 ft by 4 ft 6 in.) | | Toilet, lavatory, toiletry cabinet, mirror | Convenient to nurses' station | Although not desirable used as visitors' toilet |
| Clean workroom (minimum 8 by 6 ft) | Storage and assembly of clean supplies such as instruments, etc. | 12-ft-minimum work counter with back splash instrument sterilizer, 2 sinks, drawer and cabinet storage | No more than 120 ft from patients' rooms | |
| Medicine room 1 ft 6 in. by 5 ft cabinet (mediprep unit) | Storage and preparation of medicine | Sink, refrigerator, locked storage (Note: Facilities for preparation of medication can be in mediprep unit.) | Adjacent to nurses' station | May be a designated a within clean workroon self-contained cabinet provided |
| Soiled workroom (minimum 8 by 6 ft) | Cleaning of supplies and equipment | Clinical sink-bedpan flusher, work counter, waste and soiled linen receptacles | No more than 120 ft from patients' rooms | |
| Enclosed storage space (4 by 4 ft) | Clean linen storage | | | May be a designated a within the clean workr |
| Nourishment station 5 lin ft of counter and work space in front | Supplemental food for patients during nondining hours | Storage area, stove, sink, refrigerator  Optional: Icemaker, coffeemaker | | May serve more than nursing unit |
| Equipment storage room (4 by 6 ft) | Storage of intravenous stands, air mattresses, walkers, similar bulky equipment | | | |
| Patient baths (showers not less than 4 sq ft) | | One shower stall or bathtub for each 15 beds, not individually served, grab bars at bathing fixtures, recessed soapdishes | | At least one bathtub in nursing unit |
| Stretcher and wheelchair parking area (8 by 5 ft) | | Open space | Easily accessible from hall, near exit and entrance of nursing unit | |
| Janitor's closet | Storage and cleaning of house equipment | Housekeeping supplies and equipment, floor receptor or service sink | | Larger cleaning area d with garbage and liner in vertical-type buildir |

*Nursing Unit and Patient Activity Areas*

| Type and size of room | Activity | Equipment and sizes | Relationship | Comments |
|---|---|---|---|---|
| Dayroom total area for patient activities, 30 sq ft per patient Minimum size, 300 sq ft | Controlled and multigroup activities, religious services, lectures, group games, group teas, dining (most frequently this is combined with the dayroom, but it can be separate). Recreational therapy often combined with this area | Upholstered sofas and armchairs, preferably with straight backs and designed for ability of patients to sit and get up; straight chairs similar to those in patient rooms; rocking chairs similar to those in patient rooms; tables with firm supports and round or rounded edges, accessible to and of a height for wheelchair patients (preferably with pedestal supports and round tops); television sets on low tables or ceiling-mounted lectern | Required floor day room ideally to be controlled by nurses' station; different medical programs generate different relationships | Generally nursing unit room is 15 sq ft per pa common day and dinin is 15 sq ft per patient |
| Physiotherapy minimum 300 sq ft, (approximately 3 sq ft per patient) | | | Central to LTC circulation from nursing units | |
| a. Exercise space | Exercising, treatment and training in ambulation, stair-climbing, and activities of daily living | Parallel bars, exercise wheel, ambulation track shoulder ladder, convertible exercise steps | | Structural reinforceme necessary for ceiling m ambulation track and v mounted exercise whe |
| b. Examination and massage space | Manipulations and massaging | Treatment tables with pads (3 by 6 ft) | | |
| Hydro and heat therapy area may be combined with physiotherapy Size included in area above | Use of water movement and heat as massage | Mobile stands, hydrocollater (2 by 3 ft high) infrared lamp, whirlpools (partial- and full-immersion tanks), paraffin bath, patient lift, ultrasonic generator, microwave diathermy unit | | Not usually required b |
| Occupational or recreational therapy | Social and physical support in terms of creative actions | Hand looms, potter's wheel, painting equipment, easels, leatherworking tools, woodworking tools, sewing machines | | Size of room varies de on where activity is do Often area is used prin as a storage facility an fixed equipment (i.e., I etc.) |

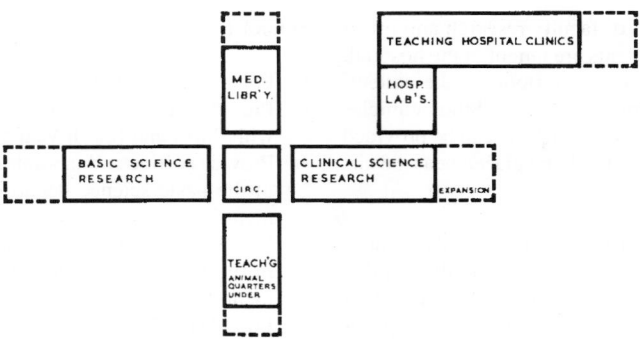

**Fig. 1. Functional relationship of medical school elements**

# MEDICAL SCHOOLS

## SITE AND PLANNING CONSIDERATIONS

The modern medical center is so large and so complex that it should be located on the edge of the university campus rather than within it. This location will emphasize the fact that the medical center is a satellite in the university orbit, but has a degree of autonomy. It is important that students and staff in the medical center have easy access to the main university campus, and that the medical center be accessible to all areas of the university.

The site should be large enough to accommodate growth of the school programs and concurrent parking for at least 20 years. Buildings should be placed on the site so that additions can be made as programs develop and as enrollment increases.

The service functions of the medical school involve patient care in hospitals and outpatient clinics. Growth of research and service responsibilities frequently leads to the development of specialized hospitals, such as children's, veterans', psychiatric, chronic disease, rehabilitation, or others. The site should permit location of these facilities in relation to the major teaching hospital so that staff and students can be within a five- to ten-minute walk. The teaching hospital and clinical science facilities should be placed on the site so that the educational functions relate to and connect with the basic science facilities. Outdoor facilities for rehabilitation of patients related to the clinic and recreation facilities for students related to housing should, be provided. The extent of these facilities varies widely among schools. Adequate space for housing should be provided nearby. Apartment-type housing with play areas for children, within five minutes' walking distance of the hospital, is preferable.

Adequate parking facilities should be provided for students, staff, patients, and public convenient to each element of the medical center including housing. This may take the form of divided shopping-center-type parking, preferably with trees, various types of paved surface parking, or multilevel parking garages.

If possible, the site should be sloping so that more than one level of entrance to the buildings can be obtained and horizontal movement of supplies can take place at one level without conflicting with horizontal movement of people at another level.

### Functional Relationships

Of prime importance in planning medical schools is the relationship of its three major components: the basic science facilities, the clinical science facilities, and the teaching hospital. For the most efficient movement of students, faculty, patients, and supplies, the three should be interconnected, but for maximum flexibility in expansion each should be an independent element. Figure 1 illustrates this relationship.

The basic science and the clinical teaching and research facilities, in turn, should be attached to the hospital to permit easy access to patient units and other hospital facilities. The diagram also shows the possibility of expansion inherent in this relationship.

In the basic science facilities, the departments can be stacked above each other with teaching laboratories, faculty, research and office space, and lecture rooms for each department located on the same floor. The cadaver preparation and storage department is usually located on a floor accessible to grade for convenience in handling cadavers. Central animal quarters serve teaching and research areas for both basic science and clinical departments. A location with direct connection to the circulation center and at grade level for access to a delivery entrance for animals is important.

Other common-use areas should be located where they are accessible to both the basic science and clinical departments. Thus, a basement location for such facilities as the radioisotope laboratory and technical shops is acceptable. Administrative facilities, school post office, dining facilities, student lounge, and media/bookstore should be accessible from a circulation center and are generally placed on the first floor. Study cubicles for basic science students should be convenient to both the medical library and teaching laboratories. The medical illustration area should be located for north light if possible.

Locating the clinical science facilities in connection with the circulation center provides access to the common-use facilities mentioned above. These clinical science facilities, similar to those provided in

*References: Medical School Facilities Public Health Service,* US. Department of Health and Human Services, Washington, D.C.

the basic science departments, consist of faculty research and office space, since third- and fourth-year students are taught in the hospital. Individual departments should be on the same floors as the patient-care units which they serve in the adjoining hospital. Study cubicles for third- and fourth-year students and house officers can be provided in the teaching hospital. Lecture rooms should be placed near the circulation center for greater flexibility of use.

The arrangements and relationships of the elements of the departments in both the basic and clinical sciences are generally similar. Facilities for an individual department should be on the same floor insofar as possible. Teaching laboratories and their auxiliary spaces in basic science departments should be separate from but near faculty offices and research laboratories.

Elements such as floor animal rooms and cold rooms, which are found in each department, should be stacked for economy. These facilities, together with lecture rooms, should be sized initially and located to take care of later expansion.

Toilet facilities should be designed to accommodate expansion. If located on a circulation center they will be accessible to adjacent departments. Separate elevators for passengers and supplies are recommended.

### Program Assumptions

Because of the variations among present schools and programs, it is apparent that space requirements for a new school cannot be stated dogmatically. There is great need, however, for some benchmark for planning a new school.

In this section, it is assumed that the basic science facilities, clinical science facilities, and teaching hospital are contiguous.

The space considerations and requirements presented in this section are for two hypothetical schools including basic science facilities, clinical science facilities, and a teaching hospital. The first is School A, with an entering class of 64 students and a hospital of 500 beds; the second is School B, with an entering class of 96 students and a hospital of 700 beds.

### School A

- Four-year university-based school.
- Provides space to house an entering class of 64 medical students, with a planned expansion to an entering class of 96 students. Enrollment in third- and fourth-year classes will be 60, with future expansion to 90.
- Provides office and laboratory space for a full-time faculty of 35 in the basic science departments and 60 in the clinical departments.
- Provides space for 40 graduate students and postdoctoral fellows in the basic science departments and 30 in the clinical departments.
- Provides either conventional or multidiscipline teaching laboratories for the basic sciences.
- Has its own library, with ultimate capacity of 100,000 volumes.
- Has its own teaching hospital of 500 beds.
- Has its own technical and maintenance shops, but heat is supplied from a central source.
- Does not provide space for teaching students in other health professions such as dentistry or nursing.

### School B

- Four-year university-based school.
- Provides space to house an entering class of 96 medical students with third- and fourth-year enrollment of 90 per class.
- Provides office and laboratory space for a full-time faculty of 50 in the basic science departments and 85 in the clinical departments.
- Provides space for 55 graduate students and postdoctoral fellows in the basic science departments and 40 in the clinical departments.
- Provides either conventional or multidiscipline teaching laboratories for the basic sciences.
- Has its own library with ultimate capacity of 100,000 volumes.
- Has its own teaching hospital of 700 beds.
- Has its own technical and maintenance shops, but heat is supplied from a central source.
- Does not provide space for teaching students in other health professions such as dentistry or nursing.

## GENERAL ADMINISTRATION AND SUPPORTING FACILITIES

### General Administration

The dean of the medical school is responsible for the formulation and execution of policies of the teaching programs and for the general administration of the basic sciences, the clinical sciences, and the teaching hospital. Because of the magnitude and complexities of these programs, the dean will require assistance from competent persons in these fields.

### Medical School Library

The medical school library includes the offices, work areas, stacks, carrels, vaults, reading rooms, alcoves, conference rooms, audiovisual rooms, and other related spaces required by the maintenance and service responsibilities connected with the care and use of recorded medical information. In programming and designing the medical school library, consideration should be given to the probable impact of future regional branches.

The medical school library should be located so that its resources are quickly available to students, research workers, faculty members, hospital staff, and practicing physicians. Unless there are large medical research collections nearby, the library should be equipped to accommodate 100,000 volumes and 1,600 scientific periodicals.

Table 1 gives the net area for a medical school library of 100,000 volumes and 1,600 periodicals. Since medical library collections tend to increase rapidly, the library should be planned for future expansion.

In designing the library, maximum flexibility should be a prime consideration with necessary divisions in the form of partitions which can be moved.

Shelving, whether in stacks or in reading areas, should be standard library equipment, with standard interchangeable parts. Standard sections, usually 3 feet long, should be used throughout, with only such exceptions as floor layout may demand. Those for medical books have a shelf depth of 10 inches. One 3-foot-long single-faced section will accommodate approximately 100 volumes.

Service aisles between stacks should not be less than 3 feet wide. Main aisles should be at least 3 feet-6 inches wide. If bookstacks are on more than one level, or are not on the level where books are received, vertical transportation must be provided.

Students and faculty members should have free access to stack areas, which should be provided with carrels for work and study. These are usually alcoves, preferably adjacent to windows, each equipped with a desk, reading light, and chair. They should be provided at the rate of one for each ten students. However, fewer may be required if individual study cubicles for students are provided elsewhere.

Other rooms often associated with the stack area are a microfilm storage and viewing room and a room for the storage of motion-picture films and slides. A relatively soundproof room for photocopy equipment is necessary. An area for general reading and open-shelf reference work may be supplemented by a number of smaller reading areas, rooms, or alcoves. The main reading area should be near the main catalog and circulation desk. If individual student study cubicles are not provided in the school, student reading areas in the library should accommodate from 25 to 50 percent of the total enrollment of the medical school and students from other programs who require access to the collection. Students seated at tables require a minimum of 25 square feet of space each. Additional seating allowance should be made for faculty and research staff and other users.

A separate alcove with shelves, or a section of shelving in the main reading area, should be provided for unbound journals. If sloping display shelves are used for current issues of journals, open shelving underneath for housing unbound earlier issues are more convenient than closed compartments.

A room may be provided for the use of those on call. Small study rooms for group conferences of four to six persons each should also be included. An area should be provided in the lobby or near the reference desk containing nontechnical books for browsing. A video/audio room to accommodate 16 students and an instructor, may be required depending on the program. Both rooms should be soundproofed and designed so as not to distract readers in other areas. A microfilm reading room is necessary. A medical history room may be required and may be a combined medical history and rare medical book room, in which case protected windows, doors with locks, a fireproof vault, and special air conditioning will be required. Well-lighted exhibit cases should be provided adjacent to the entrance to the library and its main lanes of traffic. Public toilets, rest rooms, coat rooms, and janitor services should be convenient to the reading areas.

The book charging desk, located near the entrance, should control the exits from reading areas, workrooms, and stacks to minimize book loss. The card catalog should be close to the main entrance and near the circulation desk and the acquisition and cataloging rooms. In the staff workroom a sink should be provided. Provisions should be made so that noise generated by activities at these areas does not distract readers.

One workroom subdivided into alcoves by double-faced bookshelves may be provided, instead of separate workrooms, for acquisition and cataloging. These rooms should be near the public catalog and should have direct access to the stacks; 100 square feet should be allowed for each staff member.

The reception-secretary's office should be adjacent to the head librarian's office. A departmental conference room may be required. The

**Table 1**  Net area (in square feet) of facilities required for a medical school library of 100,000 volumes and 1,600 periodicals

| Type of facility | Schools A and B (entering classes of 64 and 96 students) |
|---|---|
| | *Square feet* |
| Total net area | 29,560 |
| Public services: | |
| Total | 24,950 |
| Vestibule | 100 |
| Reception area and display | 400 |
| Charging and reserve areas | 450 |
| Card catalog area | 150 |
| Information and reference areas | 400 |
| Browsing collection | 150 |
| Main reading area | 6,070 |
| Microreading area | 200 |
| Paging-reading area | 400 |
| Periodicals area including indexes | 1,200 |
| Seminar-study areas | 1,350 |
| Historical collection room | 630 |
| Sound demonstration room | 450 |
| Slides and movie room | 450 |
| Bookstack areas | 10,000 |
| Unenclosed carrels | 1,200 |
| Closed carrels | 200 |
| Audiovisual storage | 400 |
| Microfilm storage | 200 |
| Food vending machine area | 300 |
| Public toilets | 250 |
| Work area: | |
| Total | 4,610 |
| Receiving and mailing room | 500 |
| Acquisitions department | 600 |
| Cataloging department | 520 |
| Preparation room | 150 |
| Photoduplication | 800 |
| Binding and mending | 240 |
| Serials work area | 200 |
| Chief librarian's office | 200 |
| Reception-secretary's office | 200 |
| Assistant librarian's offices | 120 |
| Historical librarian's office | 120 |
| Office storage | 80 |
| Staff room | 400 |
| Staff toilets and lockers | 240 |
| Housekeeping | 240 |

head librarian's office should be accessible both to the staff work-rooms and library clientele.

The receiving room is best located on the ground floor with access to an unloading platform. A work table, shelving, and shipping equipment should be provided. Lift service, preferably an elevator which will hold loaded book carts, between the receiving room and the acquisitions department should be provided where these areas are on different floors. Vending machines for food and drink should be located outside the library proper and be provided with space for tables.

## Animal Quarters

The need for controlled care of animals to meet teaching and research requirements is reflected in the provision of a central animal service in an increasing number of medical schools.

The location of animal quarters on the ground floor, where direct-connected outdoor animal runs and truck unloading facilities can be provided with complete separation from any other function, has many advantages. A separate entrance to serve the animal quarters is essential. Provision should be made for expansion in the initial planning.

However, a vivarium in an adjacent wing with its own vertical transportation for animals, animal supplies, and personnel may serve the needs of research better than an animal facility at grade level. The floors of the vivarium should communicate with those of the adjoining structure so that animal rooms are horizontally contiguous to the research and teaching laboratories using them and so that animals can be transferred to the laboratories without traversing corridors of other areas. If a vivarium is provided, animal-holding rooms are not usually required within research areas.

Animal quarters are composed of a number of different kinds of areas. Each has its own requirements in terms of space and location. In animal areas, provision must be made for the reception, quarantine, and isolation of incoming animals near the animal entrance; for housing different species; for exercising animals; and for specific research projects. Isolation rooms for infected animals, each with a vestibule containing facilities for gowning and scrubbing, are required.

Animal rooms should be isolated from each other with no connecting openings and arranged to separate clean and contaminated functions. A service corridor may be provided in addition to the main access corridor to allow the removal of soiled bedding and other material at the rear of a range of cages rather than through the main corridor.

## Departmental Offices

Each basic science and clinical science department faculty member requires office space for his departmental activities and laboratories or research. The head of each department requires an office with a desk, reference table, and space for a conference of several persons located near his research laboratory and adjacent to a secretary's office (see Fig. 2).

The conference room, which will be used for meetings of groups of students, should accommodate about 20 persons. Shelving for departmental books and periodicals and storage space for slide projectors, models, and other visual-aid equipment, chalk boards, and

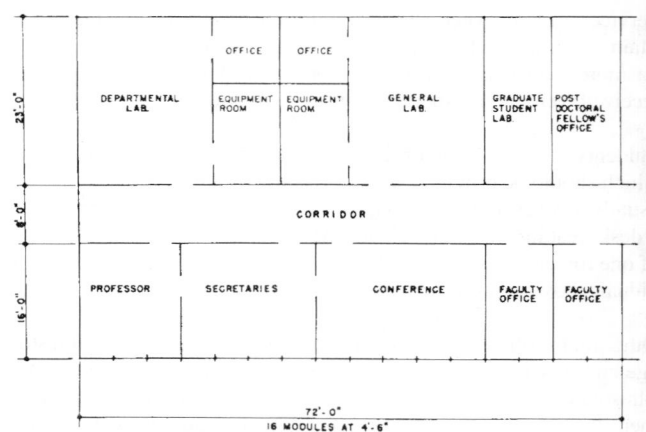

**Fig. 2. Diagram of departmental office and research area**

rollup projection screens should be provided. In the clinical departments, x-ray view boxes are required.

The secretary's office may handle the secretarial work for the entire department and should be sized for the ultimate expansion of the department.

For space estimating, a unit of 16 modules may be used as the primary unit for each department. The balance of the staff can be housed in additional eight-module units each accommodating five or six people and providing laboratory, office space, and supporting facilities. An additional two-module space is required for each additional faculty member.

## Research Facilities

Research laboratories should be provided for faculty members, post-doctoral fellows, and graduate students in each department.

The use of modules in planning laboratory facilities permits flexibility in utilization of space where changes in space requirements are common. Utilities and duct connections should be so provided that when space is changed utilities are available without undue pipe runs or perforations of walls or ceilings.

The equipment of research laboratories will vary with the kind of activity performed in them. It should be possible to rearrange work counters, microscope benches, and sinks, and to vary the size of the room as required without undue labor, inconvenience, or expense. This is most easily accomplished if all utilities and ducts are properly sized and located so as to make them available to all parts of the laboratory wing. This includes space not designed originally for laboratory use.

Some possible arrangements of research laboratories are shown on Fig. 3. The fume hood is shown on the corridor wall for convenient relation to the duct space.

Counter heights will vary—31 inches for sit-down work and 37 inches for stand-up work are most commonly used. The choice of a peninsula or island counter in larger laboratories may vary with the research project. Island counters can be used on all sides but are more expensive to install and alter; peninsula counters are more flexible with respect to air, vacuum, water, gas, drainage, and electrical services required.

An additional two-module space adjacent to the large laboratory can be divided to provide an office for an instructor and a special instrument or storage room. A two-module space may be used for four study cubicles for postdoctoral fellows.

Cold rooms are required in the laboratory wing of each department. They are refrigerated rooms for several workers who do procedures at low temperatures. A counter with sink, undercounter cabinets, and shelving are usual equipment. Electrical, air, and vacuum connections are required. All safety features such as safety door latches and warning lights should be installed.

The term animal-holding room is used to designate areas within a basic science or clinical department where small animals are held for a short time. These holding rooms, located close to an elevator which also serves the central animal quarters, eliminate the hauling of animal cages through public corridors. The animals are assigned to a staff member conducting studies requiring close, periodic observation or experimentation over a short time for a limited number of animals. These rooms may also be available to medical students performing animal experiments. Space is required for racks of cages, often placed back to back in the center of the room, with a single line of racks placed against the walls.

Animal operating and recovery rooms should be located in central animal quarters. Where vivaria are provided on each floor adjacent to departments, they should substitute for animal-holding rooms.

If properly located and provided with the necessary utilities, storage rooms can be used for expanded research activities. Those shown on the accompanying space diagrams are located and sized to allow for expansion. A four-module central equipment room should be provided in each department.

### Auditorium and Lecture Rooms

The auditorium and lecture rooms are important teaching facilities for all the medical school departments and the teaching hospital. They should be located for convenient use by faculty and students from the clinical departments, the teaching hospital, the basic science facilities, and by outside groups.

#### Auditorium

The hospital auditorium is necessary to any medical education program. It is used for demonstrating patients to students and should be attached to the teaching hospital so as to provide maximum convenience and the least movement of patients. Ramps should be provided for bringing in wheelchair and stretcher patients.

The minimum seating capacity required for teaching in a university hospital auditorium is equal to the total number of students in the third- and fourth-year classes plus 50 percent additional seats.

A second auditorium or additional lecture rooms may be required since prolonged use of the lecture facilities may conflict with regular undergraduate teaching schedules.

For auditoriums, most authorities prefer fixed seats with drop-leaf tablet arms, arranged in theater fashion with a sloping floor. The auditorium should have a low stage to facilitate the demonstration of patients and should be equipped for the installation of closed-circuit television. Projection facilities for sound films and slides, lighting controls, chalkboards, public-address systems, and closed-circuit television for doctors' paging should be provided.

#### Lecture Rooms

A significant portion of the instruction in a medical school involves the use of lecture rooms.

A minimum of three lecture rooms should be provided in the *basic science facilities* as follows: two sloping or stepped-floor lecture rooms of 120 to 150 seats each for use primarily in basic science courses, and one sloping or stepped-floor lecture room of 80 seats for graduate-student instruction, continuation education, and other programs. Table 13 gives the area for lecture rooms for a hypothetical basic science facility.

Two 150-seat lecture rooms of sloping or step-floor type should be provided as part of the clinical department facilities and the teaching hospital.

Lecture rooms included in the tables are sized to accommodate a class of 96 students, with 25 percent additional seats. Although a class size of less than 96 students may be contemplated in the initial planning of a new medical school, it will be advantageous to construct lecture rooms on the basis of the maximum class size.

The main entrances to lecture rooms should be located at the rear, although corridor access to the demonstration areas of lecture rooms is essential for bringing in tables and other large equipment. A minimum distance of 10 to 12 feet should be provided between the first row of seats and the back wall of the demonstration space.

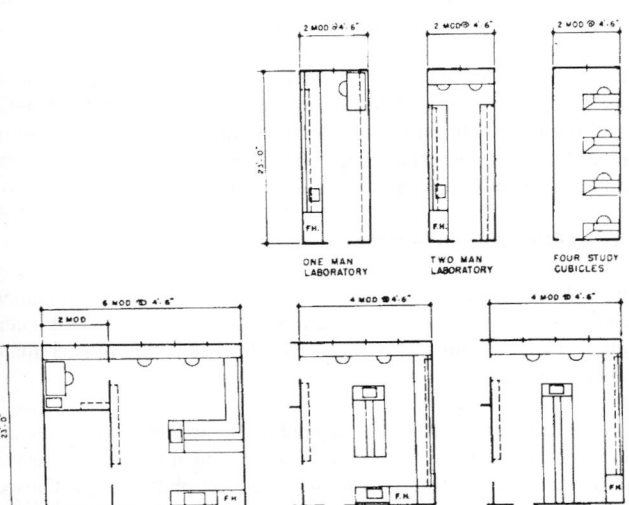

**Fig. 3. Layouts for research laboratories**

Fixed seats with drop-leaf tablet arms are generally preferred for lecture rooms. Such seats are usually 26 inches in width and require a minimum back-to-back spacing of 36 inches. For a rough estimate of lecture-room seating-area size, including aisles and crossovers, 10 square feet per person may be used.

Demonstration areas in all lecture rooms should be equipped with markerboard, x-ray film illuminators, and roll-up projection screens. A lavatory may be necessary for the demonstration areas. A projection area with platform, projector table, and convenient electrical outlets should be provided in each lecture room. Sound amplification equipment with conduits for loudspeakers for sound movies should be installed. Projectors are noisy and some sound-absorbent baffling may be required if a separate booth is not provided.

Auxiliary spaces that may be required for the use of the lecture rooms, such as storage rooms for visual aids and portable equipment, coat-rooms, toilet rooms, and telephone booths, will be determined by the individual school. Public toilets should be convenient to lecture rooms.

### Study Cubicles

Consideration should be given to the use of study cubicles within the basic science and clinical departments for postdoctoral fellows, and in the teaching hospital for the house staff.

Cubicles for medical students in the first two years should be located in the basic science area. For third- and fourth-year students, cubicles should be in the teaching hospital. Table 13 gives the net area for cubicles for hypothetical schools.

Each cubicle contains a desk with drawers on one side; a cabinet above the desk for books with a built-in fluorescent study light underneath; and a locker which, in addition to hanging clothes, may be used for microscope storage. A duplex outlet is necessary to attach the microscope. The locker not only provides privacy by forming a barrier, but also eliminates the necessity for separate locker rooms.

An allowance of 50 square feet per cubicle is adequate. This includes desk, locker, chair space, and adjacent aisle. If aisles are double loaded (cubicles on either side), privacy for the student may be obtained by staggering the cubicles so that desks are not directly opposite each other.

It is desirable to have a lounge area nearby where discussions among small groups can be held without disturbing students in the study cubicle. Marker boards and tack boards should be provided in this area and vending machines should be available.

If the study cubicle-clothes locker combination is not used, separate student locker rooms for male and female students should be provided. To conserve students' time and to ease elevator traffic, locker rooms should be located close to the line of travel to teaching areas. The proximity of the hospital should determine the necessity for separate locker rooms for third- and fourth-year students.

A toilet room should be connected to each locker room or study cubicle area and showers should be provided in the basic science area. If study cubicles with lockers are installed, a dressing room is required adjacent to toilet and shower room in the basic science facilities. A rest room for women should be included.

## Student Activity Facilities

### Lounge

Space may be provided for such activities as ping-pong, billiards, computer use, and game playing (Table 2). A recessed or screened area with vending machines is desirable. A kitchenette for preparing coffee and snacks is provided in some schools. Shelving for books and current magazines, and a storage closet adequate for card tables and other equipment should be provided. Public and house telephones should be available.

### Activities Office

A student activities office near the student lounge may serve as headquarters for such activities as student organizations, honor medical societies, student publications, and student council, and may be the center of inquiry regarding athletic, recreational, and social events. There should be space for computers, file cabinets, and shelving. If the activities office is to serve as an information center, a service counter and bulletin board would be desirable. If the office is to be used for student publications, space for duplicating machines will be required.

### Laundry Collection

The medical student often wears more than one coat per day in the basic science courses. To maintain a supply of clean linen, a laundry collection station convenient to the student lounge or locker room should be provided with a pickup and delivery counter.

### Bookstore

The bookstore, although primarily for students, should be available to all persons using the building. Its location on a main floor of the medical school is preferable.

### Health Office

A student health office will serve the entire four-year student body, half of which will be studying in the basic science areas, the other half in the hospital. Locating the health office adjacent to medical school administrative offices may be desirable if they are near the hospital. Otherwise, a hospital location is suggested.

The health office should have a waiting area, an office area, and an examining room and should provide space for a medical cabinet, a small domestic refrigerator for storing pharmaceuticals, an examining table, a portable examining light, weighing scales, storage cabinet for incidentals, a clothes rack, and a lavatory.

## Medical Illustration Service

The demand in medical schools for visual material to implement teaching, research, and patient-care programs is so great that a centralized medical illustration service for the production of such material is required.

Space required (Table 3) will depend on the extent of activities and number of personnel. The activities of a medical illustration service are divided into graphic arts, plastic arts, and photography. Closed-circuit television as a teaching aid is usually a separate service but may be a part of the medical illustration service. The medical illus-

## Table 2  Net area for student activities

| Type of facility | School A (entering class of 64 students) | School B (entering class of 96 students) |
|---|---|---|
| | Square feet | |
| Total | 1,850 | 2,400 |
| Lounge and toilets | 1,000 | 1,200 |
| Student activities office | 200 | 200 |
| Laundry collection | 200 | 400 |
| Bookstore | 450 | 600 |
| Health office and examination area* | | |

*May be in hospital or part of general university health service.

tration service usually is responsible for maintaining the slides, CDs, DVDs, and videos used throughout the school and facilities for repair and storage of such equipment should be provided.

The emergence of the Internet is providing opportunities for widespread sharing of information wordwide. Computer areas are necessary to provide student access to this service.

## BASIC SCIENCE FACILITIES

Ideally, basic science, clinical science, and teaching hospital facilities are contiguous because of the close interrelationship of their functions in the teaching of clinical medicine. Table 4 gives areas for service facilities.

## Conventional and Multidiscipline Laboratories

Basic science departments have certain common elements, the most outstanding of which are the teaching laboratories. Two types of laboratories are in use in medical schools today: conventional laboratories, where each department has its own laboratories or shares laboratories with another department requiring similar facilities and students move from one laboratory to another; and multidiscipline laboratories where students are assigned work spaces and all disciplines except gross anatomy are taught in this laboratory.

With the exception of gross anatomy, the basic sciences may be taught in either conventional or multidiscipline laboratories.

*Conventional Laboratories*

If conventional laboratories are used, the following considerations must be taken into account:

- Laboratories are usually sized to accommodate an entire entering class. They are sometimes arranged for division, by means of folding partitions, into groups usually of 16 students (Figs. 4 and 5). One laboratory is usually assigned to each of the disciplines in the basic sciences, although in some instances several departments for example, physiology and pharmacology, and pathology and microbiology may use the same laboratory.
- Laboratories are generally referred to as sit-down or stand-up laboratories. Sit-down laboratories are provided for microbiology, microanatomy and neuroanatomy, and pathology. In physiology, pharmacology, and biochemistry, most of the work is done standing up. In sit-down laboratories, however, some stand-up work is done, and it is customary to provide stand-up counters for special instruments and reagents which may be shared by groups of students.

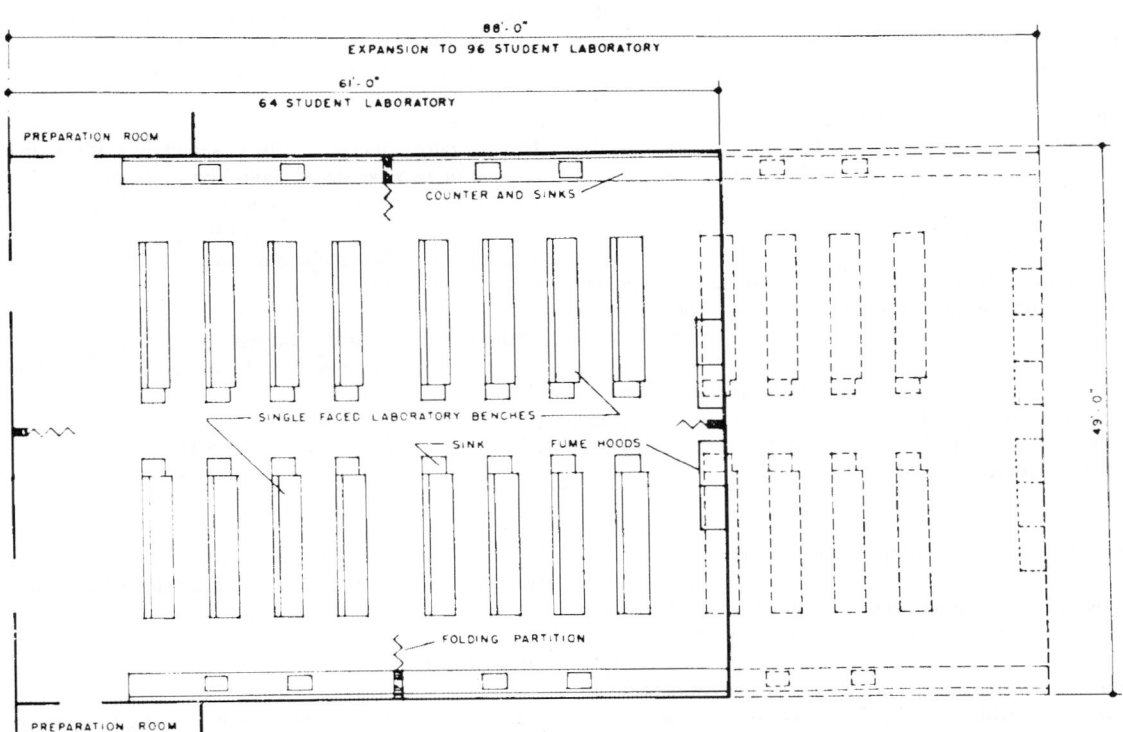

**Fig. 4. Layout for a conventional teaching laboratory with single-faced benches**

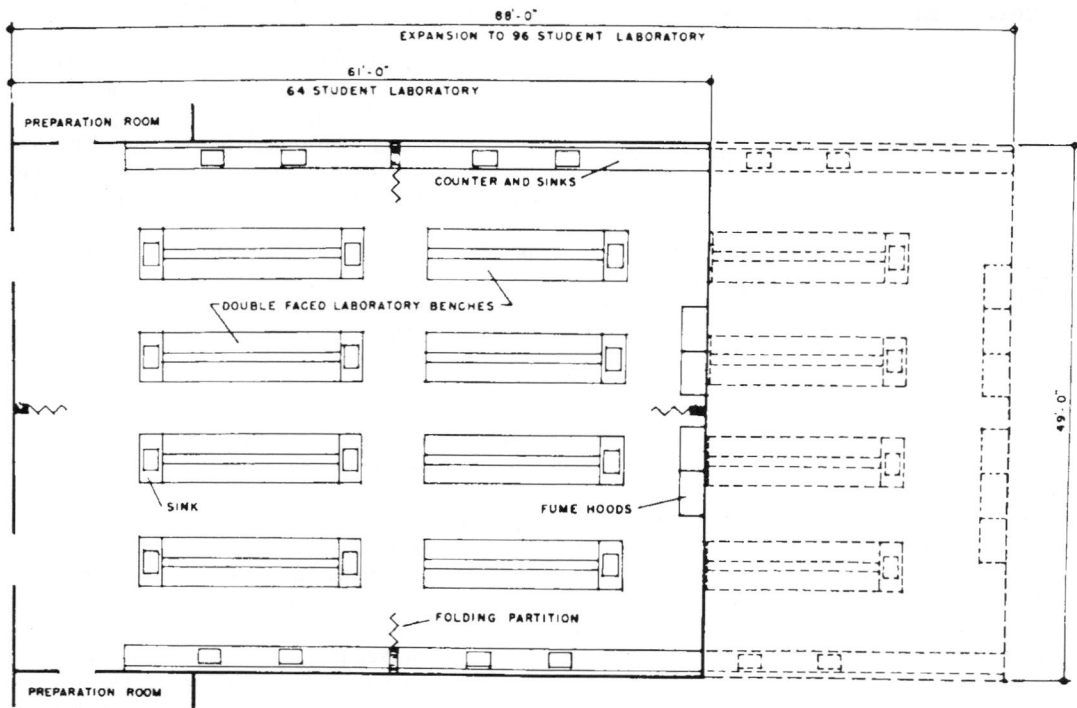

**Fig. 5. Layout for a conventional teaching laboratory with double-faced benches**

- Auxiliary rooms are required. These include preparation and issuing rooms, glassware processing rooms, storage rooms, and media-preparation rooms. Some schools place large and noisy pieces of equipment shared by groups of students in a separate instrument room.
- Graduate students usually use the same laboratories as medical students for classroom laboratory work. If separate facilities are provided, they are located close to the auxiliary rooms. The design is similar but size will vary with the teaching program.

*Multidiscipline Laboratories*

The multidiscipline laboratory is sized to take the number of students assigned to one teacher, usually 16 students, although some schools assign 24.

Except for dissection, the student will do all his laboratory work in this room; therefore, both sit-down counters, 31 inches high, and standup counters, 37 inches high, are required. In addition, movable tables 37 inches high are required for animal work for physiology (Figs. 6 and 7).

Table 5 gives the area for multidiscipline laboratories.

Each student is assigned a space containing about 4 feet of stand-up counter and the same length of sit-down counter opposite.

Utilities, storage, sinks, and general design and finishes of both stand-up and sit-down space will be similar to that for conventional laboratories. Marker boards should be visible from each student space. Bulletin boards should be located near the entrance.

An equipment room is provided adjacent to or between each pair of multidiscipline laboratories in some designs. Equipped with a fume hood, counter space with utilities, and cabinet space, it houses equipment required for the work in adjoining laboratories. Equipment such as centrifuge, freezers, and refrigerators are available to more than one laboratory.

The laboratory manager's office, secretary's office, and office space for one or two assistants should be provided. In addition, a ready storage room, a student issuing and supply room, a chemical storage room, cold room, and glass-washing room are required. If media preparation or slide preparation are to be done here, space for these should be provided.

Additional unassigned conference rooms sized to accommodate 20 persons may be provided in the basic science facilities for use by unscheduled groups.

## BASIC SCIENCE DEPARTMENTS

### Anatomy

Figure 8 shows a space diagram for a minimum department of anatomy. Table 6 provides a list of net areas for an anatomy department.

*Dissecting Room*

The teaching area for gross anatomy is usually one large room with stand-up height dissecting tables to accommodate all the students in the course. Convenience for faculty and students and proximity of

## Table 3  Net area for medical illustration

| Type of facility | School A (entering class of 64 students) | School B (entering class of 96 students) |
|---|---|---|
| | Square feet | |
| Total net area | 2,020 | 3,170 |
| Administration: | | |
| Total | 370 | 370 |
| Chief's office | 140 | 140 |
| Secretary and files | 140 | 140 |
| Equipment and supply room | 90 | 90 |
| Medical illustration: Artists' work area | 600 | 950 |
| Photography: | | |
| Total | 1,050 | 1,050 |
| Photo studio and dressing | 420 | 420 |
| Photomicrography room | 90 | 90 |
| Light lock | 50 | 50 |
| Darkrooms | (2) 140 | (2) 140 |
| Loading room | 30 | 30 |
| Mixing room | 60 | 60 |
| Laboratory | 190 | 190 |
| Finishing room | 70 | 70 |
| Audiovisual: TV studio (including control area) | | 800 |

## Table 4  Net area for service facilities

| Type of facility | School A (entering class of 64 students) | School B (entering class of 96 students) |
|---|---|---|
| | Square feet | |
| Total net area | 13,700 | 16,050 |
| Total | 6,000 | 8,350 |
| Telephone equipment room | 800 | 1,100 |
| Post office | 550 | 1,000 |
| Personnel and purchasing[1] | 400 | 400 |
| Employees' lockers and toilet facilities | 2,000 | 3,000 |
| Maintenance shops | 900 | 1,100 |
| Plant engineer | 150 | 150 |
| Housekeeping | 600 | 600 |
| Duplicating | 200 | 400 |
| Snark bar | 400 | 600 |
| Central storage[2] | | |
| Total | 7,700 | 7,700 |
| Basic science departments: | 1,000 | 1,000 |
| Anatomy | 1,000 | 1,000 |
| Biochemistry | 500 | 500 |
| Physiology | 500 | 500 |
| Microbiology | 500 | 500 |
| Pathology | 1,500 | 1,500 |
| Pharmacology | 500 | 500 |
| Clinical departments: | | |
| Medicine | 500 | 500 |
| Surgery | 500 | 500 |
| Pediatrics | 500 | 500 |
| Obstetrics-gynecology | 500 | 500 |
| Psychiatry | 300 | 300 |
| Radiology | 600 | 600 |
| Preventive medicine | 300 | 300 |

[1]2 offices and secretaries

[2]Central storage spaces for each department are listed on the department tables. However, areas for this storage are grouped here.

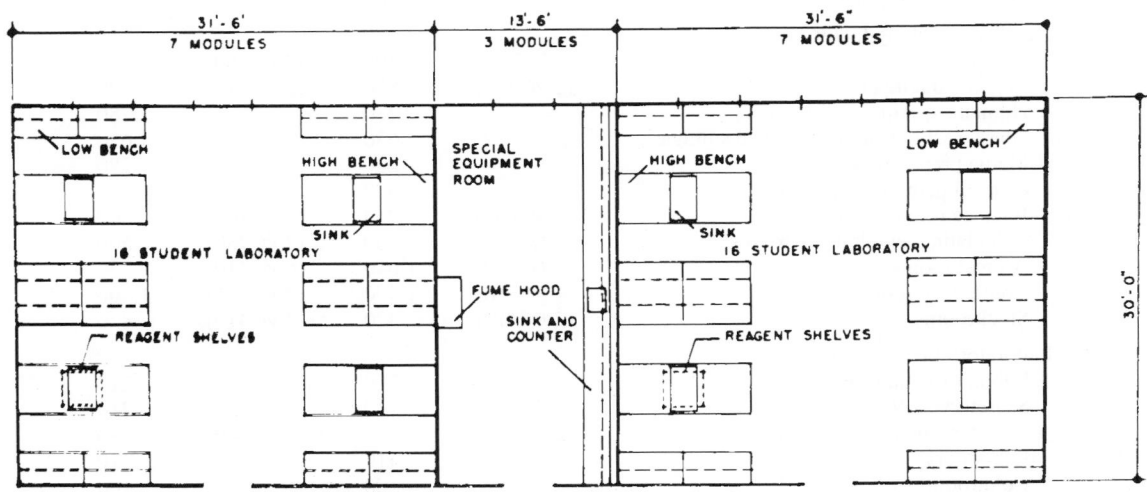

**Fig. 6. Layout for multidiscipline laboratories**

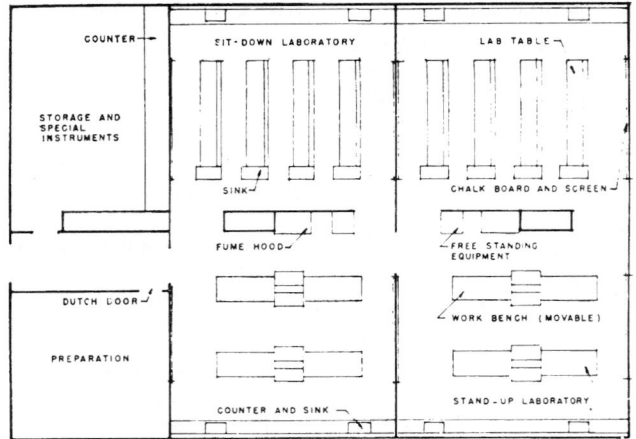

**Fig. 7. Floor plan for multidiscipline laboratories**

**Table 5**   Net area for hypothetical multidiscipline laboratories

| Type of facility | School A (entering class of 64 students) | | School B (entering class of 96 students) | |
|---|---|---|---|---|
| | *Square feet* | | | |
| Total | | 22,500 | | 29,960 |
| Gross dissecting rooms (4 students/table): | | | | |
|   Medical students | | 2,560 | | 3,840 |
|   Graduate students | | 720 | | 720 |
|   Utility room | | 160 | | 160 |
|   Storage room | | 250 | | 250 |
|   Neuroanatomy | | 280 | | 280 |
| Multidiscipline laboratories: | | | | |
|   1st year medical students | (4 @ 940) | 3,760 | (6 @ 940) | 5,640 |
|   "Interlab" equipment rooms | (2 @ 400) | 800 | (3 @ 400) | 1,200 |
|   2d year medical students | (4 @ 940) | 3,760 | (6 @ 940) | 5,640 |
|   "Interlab" equipment rooms | (2 @ 400) | 800 | (3 @ 400) | 1,200 |
| Ancillary teaching facilities: | | | | |
|   Cold rooms | 2 @ 200) | 400 | (2 @ 200) | 400 |
|   Regulated temperature rooms | (2 @ 410) | 820 | (2 @ 410) | 820 |
|   Human experiments laboratory | | 780 | | 780 |
|   Glass washing, sterilizing, and storage | | 630 | | 630 |
|   Media preparation room | | 280 | | 280 |
|   Clinical pathology tissue room | | 570 | | 570 |
|   Balance rooms | (2 @ 100) | 200 | (3 @ 100) | 300 |
|   Calculating and drafting rooms | (2 @ 280) | 560 | (2 @ 280) | 560 |
|   Animal rooms | (4 @ 410) | 1,640 | (6 @ 410) | 2,460 |
|   Conference rooms | (4 @ 350) | 1,400 | (4 @ 350) | 1,400 |
|   Stockrooms | (2 @ 410) | 820 | (2 @ 410) | 820 |
| Laboratory management: | | | | |
|   Laboratory manager's office | | 210 | | 210 |
|   Secretary's office | | 210 | | 210 |
|   Assistant managers' offices | (2 @ 140) | 280 | (2 @ 140) | 280 |
|   Laboratory | | 410 | | 410 |
|   Cold room | | 100 | | 100 |
|   Animal room | | 100 | | 100 |

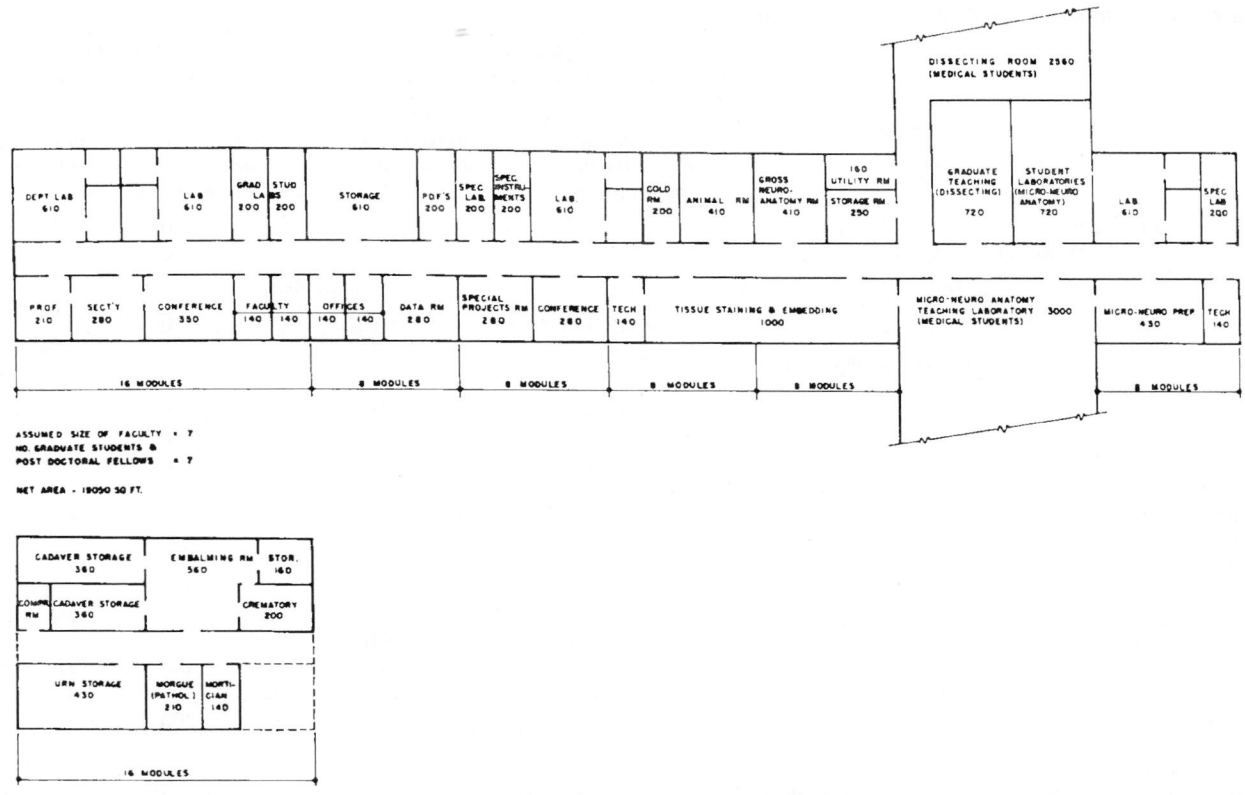

**Fig. 8. Diagram for a department of anatomy**

elevator service to be used for transporting cadavers are important considerations in the location. Provisions should be made to prevent viewing of dissection procedures by unauthorized persons. One dissecting table for each four students is usually required.

Tables should be arranged to allow ample work space on all sides. Additional space to accommodate one or two portable tables for use in demonstrations or by special students may be required. If dissecting tables are movable, a folding partition may be installed to provide a screen behind which the tables may be stacked during off-semesters, freeing the room for other uses.

Hand-washing facilities for students should be provided in the dissecting room. Surgical scrub-up sinks, three for each 16 students, with wrist- or foot-action valves or industrial-type fixtures are recommended. Counter units should have reagent ledges, knee spaces, and under-counter drawers and cabinets for storage of student's dissecting equipment and demonstration microscopes. Electrical service outlets for microscope illuminators should be provided. Counter tops should have resilient surfaces.

Wall-mounted x-ray illuminators, one for each 16 students, a bank of four to eight, should be located for easy viewing by a group. Markerboards located for easy viewing by each 16-student group should also be provided.

Storage for fixed specimens and models used in demonstrations and for x-ray film should be provided. Cabinets in a connecting area, such as a utility room, may suffice.

The utility room, which may serve as a cleaner's work room, should have a flushing-rim service sink accessible to the dissecting area. The sink should have flush valve and wrist-operated valves.

*Graduate-Student Dissecting Room*

It should be adjacent to auxiliary rooms of the medical students' dissecting room. Fixed equipment and mechanical facilities should be similar to those furnished the medical student.

*Microneuroanatomy Teaching Laboratory*

A conventional student teaching laboratory for microanatomy and neuroanatomy instruction usually requires a demonstration area with a table, marker board, projection screen, and sit-down laboratory benches to accommodate all the students of either course. Benches should seat four students on the same side to face in the same direction for an unobstructed view of the demonstration area.

Each bench position should have knee space, drawers, and a cabinet for storing slides and microscope case. Water, air, gas, electrical outlets, and vacuum should be provided at each position. Liquid waste receptors in bench tops may be either lead cup sinks or continuous drain troughs with stone end sinks. Bench top material should be resilient and alcohol- and stain-resistant.

In addition to sit-down benches, some standup bench space should be provided for each 16 students. Bulletin boards and tack boards should be provided.

**Table 6**  Net area for department of anatomy

| Type of facility | | School A (entering class of 64 students) | | | School B (entering class of 96 students) | |
| --- | --- | --- | --- | --- | --- | --- |
| | | With conventional departmental laboratories | With multidiscipline laboratories | | With conventional departmental laboratories | With multidiscipline laboratories |
| Assumed size of faculty | | 7 | 7 | | 10 | 10 |
| Number of graduate students and postdoctoral fellows | | 7 | 7 | | 10 | 10 |
| | | | Square feet | | | |
| Total net area | | 19,330 | (¹) | | 22,950 | (¹) |
| Faculty offices, research laboratories, and related facilities: | | | | | | |
| Total | | 11,640 | 11,510 | | 12,660 | 12,530 |
| Professor's office | | 210 | 210 | | 210 | 210 |
| Secretary's office | | 280 | 280 | | 280 | 280 |
| Conference room | | 350 | 350 | | 350 | 350 |
| Faculty offices | (4) | 560 | (4) 560 | (4) | 560 | (4) 560 |
| Postdoctoral fellows' office | | 200 | 200 | | 200 | 200 |
| Data room | | 280 | 280 | | 280 | 280 |
| Special-projects room | | 280 | 280 | | 280 | 280 |
| Research laboratories: | | | | | | |
| Departmental | | 610 | 610 | | 610 | 610 |
| General | (3) | 1,830 | (3) 1,830 | (4) | 2,440 | (4) 2,440 |
| Graduate students | (2) | 400 | (2) 400 | (3) | 600 | (3) 600 |
| Special | (2) | 400 | (2) 400 | (1) | 200 | (1) 200 |
| Electron microscopy rooms | | 610 | 610 | | 610 | 610 |
| Storage room | | 280 | 280 | | 280 | 280 |
| Tissuestaining and embedding and technician's office | | 1,140 | 1,140 | | 1,140 | 1,140 |
| Microneuro preparation and technician's office | | 570 | 570 | | 570 | 570 |
| Special instrument storage | | 200 | 200 | | 200 | 200 |
| Coldroom | | 200 | 200 | | 200 | 200 |
| Animal room | (1) | 410 | (1) 410 | (2) | 820 | (2) 820 |
| Gross neuroanatomy and neurological storage room | | 410 | 280 | | 410 | 280 |
| Cadaver storage rooms (60 bodies) and compressor room | (2) | 720 | (2) 720 | (2) | 720 | (20) 720 |
| Embalming room | | 560 | 560 | | 560 | 560 |
| Embalming room storage | | 160 | 160 | | 160 | 160 |
| Crematory | | 200 | 200 | | 200 | 200 |
| Morgue (pathology) | | 210 | 210 | | 210 | 210 |
| Mortician's office | | 140 | 140 | | 140 | 140 |
| Urn storage room | | 430 | 430 | | 430 | 430 |
| Departmental central storage² | | | | | | |
| Conventional teaching: | | | | | | |
| Total | | 7,690 | (¹) | | 10,290 | (¹) |
| Gross dissecting rooms (4 students/table): | | | | | | |
| Undergraduate students | | 2,560 | | | 3,840 | |
| Graduate students | | 720 | | | 720 | |
| Utility room | | 160 | | | 160 | |
| Storage room | | 250 | | | 250 | |
| Microneuroanatomy teaching laboratories: | | | | | | |
| Undergraduate students | | 3,000 | | | 4,320 | |
| Graduate students | | 720 | | | 720 | |
| Conference room | | 280 | | | 280 | |

¹For total net area for multidiscipline laboratories, see Table 5.

²For central storage areas, see Table 13.

*Graduate-Student Teaching Laboratory*

It should be adjacent to auxiliary rooms of the medical students' Microneuroanatomy teaching laboratory. Fixed equipment and mechanical facilities should be similar to those furnished the medical student.

*Gross Neuroanatomy Room*

This room is a supplementary teaching area. Usually the area serves also as a departmental storage center for specimens, in which case adjustable shelving for supporting a number of jars of formalin is required.

The demonstration table, located at the center of the room to accommodate four students on each side, is usually provided with a stainless-steel top with raised edge and an integral sink at one end. Lighting should be designed for close observation at tabletop level. Hand-washing facilities, an x-ray film illuminator, and a chalkboard should be provided. Storage for formalin should be considered.

*Tissue Staining and Embedding*

This unit may be subdivided into a head technician's office, an embedding area, a sectioning and tissue-staining area, and a slide storage-and-issue area with access to the teaching laboratory, preferably by way of a dutch door for issuing slides and materials.

In the embedding room small tissue specimens are prepared, processed through a number of solutions by hand or in an automatic tissue-processing machine, then embedded in small cubes of paraffin or celloidin. Preparing the specimens requires the use of a refrigerator for gross tissue storage and a sit-down counter with sink.

For processing specimens and mixing solutions, a stand-up counter with sink, undercounter cabinets for equipment, and wall cabinets for chemicals and reagents are usually sufficient. For embedding procedures, an island bench of stand-up height with paraffin oven at or near one end should be provided.

Cabinets with drawers for paraffin molds and mounting blocks and for filing embedments in frequent use should be provided. A storage room for embedments and for fixed gross tissue specimens not frequently used should be provided in the general storage area of the building. Glazed partitions may be installed to separate sectioning and mounting activities from the staining procedures.

Sectioning and mounting activities require sit-down counters with knee space and drawers for storing slides and equipment. Counters for tissue staining and stain mixing should be of sit-down height. Each work position should have a sink, knee space, cabinets for equipment, and chemical storage. For attaching cover glasses and labels, a sit-down counter with knee space and drawers is satisfactory. Hand-washing facilities should be provided. Counter-top surfaces should be resilient and stain and alcohol resistant.

The slide storage-and-issue area requires standard microscope slide file cabinets, and cabinets for storage of boxed sets of slides.

*Microneuro Preparation*

To prepare microscope slides used in the neuroanatomy course, a microneuro preparation unit is required similar in design and equip-

ment to the tissue staining and embedding unit for microanatomy. The head technician's office should have access to the unit and to the corridor.

*Electron Microscopy*

In the preparation room, stand-up and sit-down counters and a fume hood are required. Air, gas, vacuum, and electrical outlets should be available. A refrigerator is necessary for chemical storage. The electron microscope should be located away from electric motors, elevators, fans, and other equipment that may generate vibration and stray magnetic fields. The room should be shielded to minimize dust, and the room should be windowless (Table 7).

*Cadaver Preparation and Storage*

The unit should be so located and designed that no unauthorized persons may enter. Its location relative to the dissecting and autopsy rooms should not require transportation through any public areas. It should be located at grade with a receiving entrance accessible to a low loading platform. Where design permits, the platform may also serve the animal-receiving entrance.

The mortician's work area or embalming room should permit working on all sides of the embalming table and handling by stretcher cart, portable lift, or other means. An embalming table with built-in sink at one end is generally preferred. A combination instrument and scrub sink with knee- or foot-operated valve, service sink, and a floor drain should be provided. Floor and wall materials should be washable.

A connected storage room for supplies and equipment is necessary. Shower and dressing facilities for use of the mortician should be provided. A mortician's office should be adjacent to the area.

*Cadaver Storage*

This should be adjacent to the embalming room. There are several methods of storing cadavers, some more demanding of space than others. An efficient method is storage on individual tray shelves on both sides of a service aisle. Thirty-five tray positions are usually adequate for a school with a 64-student entering class; provision should be made in the original planning for approximately 60 tray positions to accommodate enrollment increases up to 96 students.

A crematory, if provided, should be located in the cadaver preparation and storage unit.

**Table 7**  Net area for electron microscope suite

| Type of supporting area | | School A (entering class of 64 students), square feet |
|---|---|---|
| Total | | 610 |
| Electron microscope rooms | (2) | 230 |
| Darkroom | | 70 |
| Preparation area | | 280 |
| Entry | | 30 |

The department will require storage space for tissue embedments and gross organs. The same type storage as that described for pathology should be provided.

## Biochemistry

Figure 9 shows a space diagram for a minimum department of biochemistry. Table 8 gives the area for the department for the 64- and 96-student class hypothetical schools.

The conventional teaching laboratory is similar to those of other basic sciences. Island-type laboratory benches approximately 16 feet long will accommodate 8 students, 4 on either side. The bench should have a stone sink at one or preferably both ends and a continuous drain trough or cup sinks (1 for each 2 students), a continuous reagent shelf, and individual service outlets for each student. Services required are gas, air, vacuum, cold water, and electricity. Bench tops should be stone or acid-resistant composition surfaces.

A large marker board, smaller marker boards for each of the 16 students, a retractable projection screen, and a bulletin board should be provided. An instructor's table of desk height with knee space, cabinets, cup sink, electrical outlets, cold water, and gas should be provided for demonstration to the class.

The teaching laboratory should be adjacent to auxiliary rooms of the medical student teaching laboratory. Fixed equipment and mechanical facilities should be similar to those furnished the medical student.

### Preparation Room

A preparation room adjacent to the teaching laboratory is used for mixing reagents and for storing chemicals and glassware. It may be divided by partitions into alcoves for separating issue, storage, and preparation. These alcoves should have laboratory benches, sinks, and cabinets for use as a research area. The storage of glassware, chemicals, and other stocked items requires adjustable shelving. The issuing area requires cabinets with small drawers and an issue window or door opening into the teaching laboratory.

### Glassware Washing and Storage

Commercial glass washing and drying machines are often employed. In addition, a large sink with drainboards is required, with space for glassware carts, a worktable for glassware sorting, and shelves for storage.

## Physiology

Figure 10 shows a space diagram for a minimum department of physiology. Table 9 gives the net area for a physiology department.

### Teaching Laboratory

A conventional teaching laboratory may be used by more than one department. The laboratory described here is a conventional laboratory designed for specific use by the department of physiology. With only minimal additional equipment this laboratory is suitable for pharmacology teaching.

Many animals are used in physiology teaching and stand-up tables 37 inches high with casters to accommodate four students, two on each side, are suggested. A shelf under the top should be provided as storage space for animal boards. A service island may be provided with gas, electrical, air, and vacuum outlets. Distilled water should be piped into one place in each laboratory or preparation area and carboys should be used at work stations. A floor drain should be installed between each pair of service islands.

A 4-foot fume hood should suffice for 8 students. Space for incubators should be considered unless they can be placed on counters.

Marker boards, a bulletin board, and a retractable projection screen should be furnished similar in size and number to those in other teaching laboratories. Space for an instructor's table at the front of the laboratory is required.

### Graduate Student Teaching Laboratory

This should be located adjacent to auxiliary rooms of the teaching laboratory. Fixed equipment and mechanical facilities should be similar to those furnished the medical student.

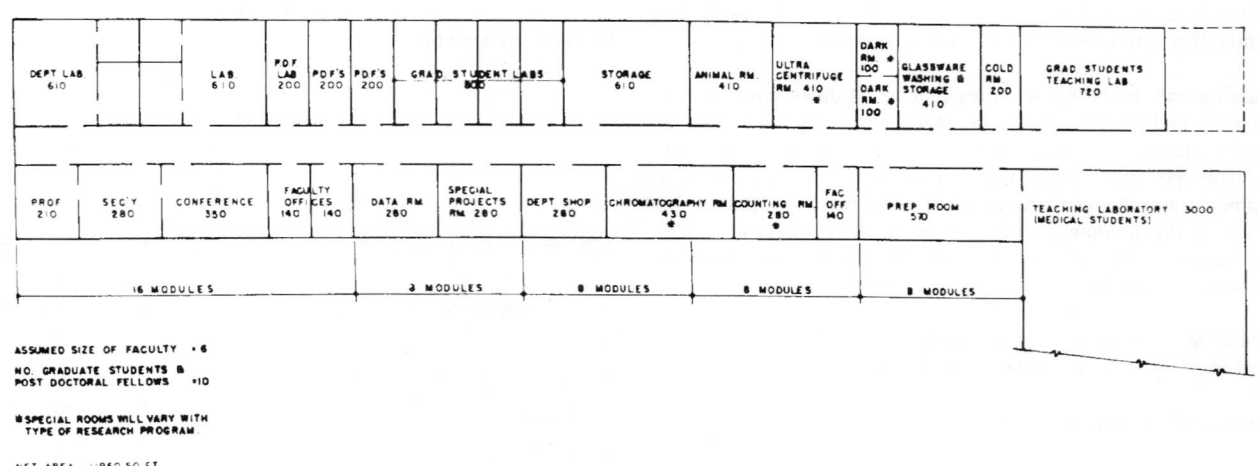

**Fig. 9. Diagram for a department of biochemistry**

**Table 8**   Net area for a department of biochemistry

*Teaching laboratory*

| Type of facility | | School A (entering class of 64 students) | | School B (entering class of 96 students) | |
| --- | --- | --- | --- | --- | --- |
| | | *With conventional departmental laboratories* | *With multidiscipline laboratories* | *With conventional departmental laboratories* | *With multidiscipline laboratories* |
| Assumed size of faculty | | 6 | 6 | 9 | 9 |
| Number of graduate students and postdoctoral fellows | | 10 | 10 | 14 | 14 |
| | | *Square feet* | | | |
| Total net area | | 12,240 | (1) | 14,980 | (1) |
| Faculty offices, research laboratories, and related facilities: | | | | | |
| Total | | 8,670 | 8,670 | 10,090 | 10,090 |
| Professor's office | | 210 | 210 | 210 | 210 |
| Secretary's office | | 280 | 280 | 280 | 280 |
| Conference room | | 350 | 350 | 350 | 350 |
| Faculty offices | (3) | 420 | (3) 420 | (3) 420 | (3) 420 |
| Postdoctoral fellows' offices | (2) | 400 | (2) 400 | (2) 400 | (2) 400 |
| Data room | | 280 | 280 | 280 | 280 |
| Special-projects room | | 280 | 280 | 280 | 280 |
| Research laboratories: | | | | | |
| Departmental | | 610 | 610 | 610 | 610 |
| General | | 610 | 610 | (3) 1,830 | (3) 1,830 |
| Postdoctoral fellows | | 200 | 200 | 200 | 200 |
| Graduate students | (4) | 800 | (4) 800 | (5) 1,000 | (5) 1,000 |
| Storage room (future laboratory) | | 610 | 610 | 610 | 610 |
| Storage room | | 280 | 280 | 280 | 280 |
| Glassware washing and storage | | 410 | 410 | 410 | 410 |
| Cold room | | 200 | 200 | 200 | 200 |
| Special-equipment room[2] | | 430 | 430 | 430 | 430 |
| Centrifuge room[2] | | 410 | 410 | 410 | 410 |
| Darkrooms[2] | (2) | 200 | (2) 200 | (2) 200 | (2) 200 |
| Counting room[2] | | 280 | 280 | 280 | 280 |
| Departmental shop | | 280 | 280 | 280 | 280 |
| Animal room | | 410 | 410 | 410 | 410 |
| Graduate students' teaching laboratory | | 720 | 720 | 720 | 720 |
| Departmental storage[3] | | | | | |
| Conventional teaching: | | | | | |
| Total | | 3,570 | (1) | 4,890 | (1) |
| Teaching laboratory | | 3,000 | | 4,320 | |
| Preparation room | | 570 | | 570 | |

[1]For total net area for multidiscipline laboratories, see Table 5.

[2]Special rooms will vary with type of research.

[3]For central storage areas, see Table 13.

*Student Research Laboratory*

Furniture and mechanical facilities may be similar to those of a typical research laboratory.

*Equipment Storage*

An equipment storage area, adjacent to the teaching laboratory, is needed, as is desk space for a stock clerk and technician. A 31-inch-high counter with gas, air, vacuum, and electrical outlets and cabinets should be installed for testing and preparing equipment. An issue window or door opening into the teaching laboratory is desirable.

Space for assembly of equipment to be issued and for glassblowing and soldering should be provided.

*Shielded Room*

If required by the program, a shielded room distant from obvious electrostatic interference must be provided.

*Audio Room*

If an audio room is provided, it should consist of a test room and a control room with a triple-glazed clear-glass observation window between and with acoustical treatment, including reduction of floor vibration.

The test room should have a microphone and a speaker cabinet. The control room should have a sit-down counter with cabinets located on the observation window side.

*Physio-optics Room*

If the student curriculum includes exercises in physio-optics, a special room will be needed with 20-feet separation between the subject and the vision chart. A sink for hand washing and a sit-down counter for recording are necessary.

*Treadmill and Gas Analysis*

A room close to the laboratory is preferable. The room should also contain a cot and table for recording.

*Supply Room*

This room should be near the teaching laboratory. Shelving and racks for volatile solvent storage should be within a fire-resistive closet off the mixing and issue areas. Counter tops, 37 inches high, with gas, air, vacuum, and electrical outlets, cabinets with varying sized drawers, and a sink are required for mixing solutions and preparations for student use. Glassware washing and storage require a large sink, drainboard, provision for distilled water, and base cabinets for glassware. An issue window is suggested. Space should be allocated for solution carts and assembly of materials to be issued. A head technician's office may be required depending on the quantity of material handled.

*Department Shop*

A minimum machine shop should contain a drill press, a metal lathe, a milling machine, and wood and metal bandsaws. A workbench, stock racks, and tool bin are required.

In the electronics area, a sit-down work counter with electrical outlets of appropriate voltages, drawers, and locked storage cabinets for electronic equipment and space to bring in floor-mounted equipment for testing will be required. Noise and vibration associated with technical shops should be considered in their relation to other areas.

*Constant Temperature Rooms*

Constant temperature rooms should have access to the corridor and to a work area. Doors from the corridor should accommodate beds or animal racks. Floor and wall surfaces should be similar to those suggested for animal quarters.

The work area associated with these rooms should have 31-inch-high work counters, a sink, and gas, air, vacuum, and electrical outlets.

## Microbiology

Figure 11 shows a space diagram for a minimum department of microbiology. The net area for a microbiology department is given in Table 10.

*Teaching Laboratory*

The conventional teaching laboratory is usually designed to accommodate the second-year class. Satisfactory results can be obtained with the use of an island-type laboratory bench to position four students all on the same side facing demonstrations.

Laboratory benches may be 31 inches high for sit-down work with microscopes. Each student should have knee space, drawers for supplies, and a cabinet for microscope storage. Bench service outlets should be water, gas, air, vacuum, and electrical for each position. A cup sink at each position, or continuous drain trough, and a shelf for storing bottles above are required. Bench tops should be resilient and strainproof.

In addition to island benches, it is desirable to have counters 37 inches high, with reagent shelves equipped with gas, air, vacuum, electrical outlets, and sinks with wrist-action valves for hand washing.

A marker board, a bulletin board, a retractable projection screen, and space for the instructor's desk at the front of the laboratory are required. Space in the teaching laboratory may be required for incubators and refrigerators. One domestic refrigerator per 16 students and one stationary incubator per 8 students should be provided. A stationary centrifuge, one per 16 students, may be provided depending on the curriculum.

Facilities should be available to maintain and observe such small animals as rabbits, guinea pigs, and mice close to the teaching laboratories.

*Graduate Student Teaching Laboratory*

It should be adjacent to auxiliary rooms of the teaching laboratory. Fixed equipment and mechanical facilities should be similar to those furnished the medical student.

*Research Laboratories*

The microbiology research laboratories will, in many instances, be similar in equipment and design to laboratories in other basic sciences. However, laboratories used for bacteriological and virus research have additional requirements. Glassware of an unusually large size is often used. One sink in each laboratory should be sized to wash this glassware.

Separate animal rooms are provided in the microbiology department to prevent cross-contamination. If highly contagious material is to be handled, a vestibule may be needed at the entrance to microbiology animal rooms to permit the attendant to change clothes and shoes to reduce infection and cross-contamination.

*Electron Microscopy*

Facilities for this purpose would be similar to those described for the department of anatomy.

*Media Preparation*

Media preparation areas should be adjacent to teaching areas and designed to eliminate through traffic to prevent drafts and the introduction of contaminating organisms. A media kitchen requires a range, or portable hot plates on a counter 37 inches high, for cooking the material. Counter-top sinks and cabinets with drawers ranging in width from 6 inches to 2 feet-6 inches and wall cabinets with shelves for storage are desirable. Counters should have air, gas, vacuum, and electrical outlets. Distilled water should be piped to one location over a sink and distributed in carboys.

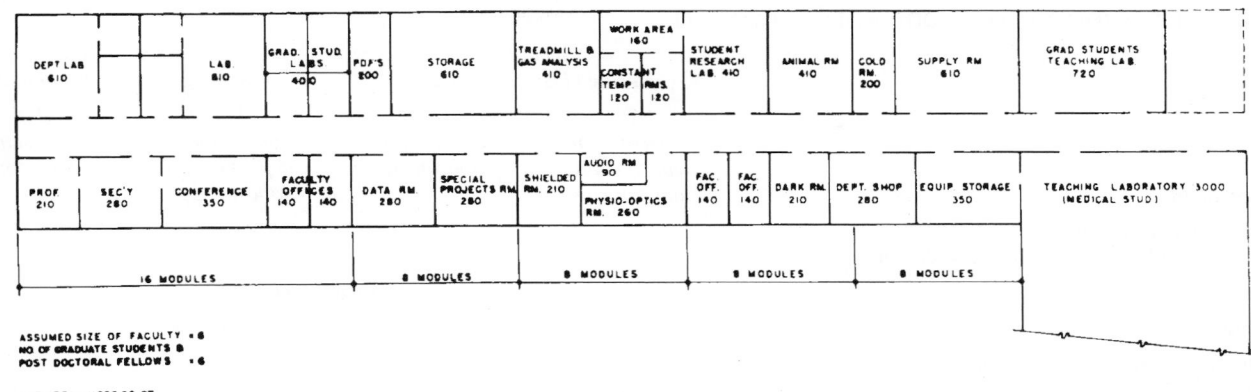

**Fig. 10. Diagram for a department of physiology**

After the unsterile liquid culture media has been prepared in bulk quantities, it is dispensed into test tubes or plates. This requires counter space similar to the media kitchen, including wall and base cabinets and service outlets.

An autoclave is required for sterilizing prepared culture media after it is poured into previously sterilized petri dishes. A flushing-rim sink near the autoclave is desirable for disposal of spoiled media.

The issue room will contain glassware and equipment storage, shelving and cabinets for glassware and equipment, and an issue window opening into the laboratory.

*Glassware Washing and Storage*

If this is to be done as a central unit for the department, it should be divided into sterilizing, sterile storage, glassware washing, and clean glass storage.

An autoclave to sterilize glassware prior to washing, a sink and drainboard area, and space for chemical jars and for soaking extra dirty glassware are required. Commercial glass washers and dryers may be employed and space for these should be provided beside the sink. Space should be available at sink and washer area for glassware and petri dish carts and cart storage.

Storage areas should be furnished with adjustable shelving, as some glassware may be exceptionally long or high. An issue window or door from sterile storage to corridor should be provided.

*Chemical Storage*

Bulk storage of chemicals should be provided for in basement areas.

**Pathology**

Figure 12 shows a space diagram for a minimum department of pathology. Table 11 gives the net area for a pathology department.

*Teaching Laboratory*

A conventional teaching laboratory similar to that described for micro- and neuroanatomy is usually adequate for teaching the second-year pathology course.

*Graduate Student Teaching Laboratories*

These should be adjacent to auxiliary rooms of the medical students' pathology teaching laboratory.

*Tissue Staining and Embedding Technician's Office*

A unit similar in design and equipment to the tissue staining and embedding unit described for microanatomy should be provided.

*Clinical Pathology Preparation Unit*

This unit usually has a head technician's office and a preparation room with direct access to the teaching laboratory, preferably by a dutch door. For preparing some types of specimens as well as stains and reagents for direct issue, a stand-up counter 37 inches high is desirable. For other types of specimens, particularly those such as blood and bone marrow, a sit-down counter 31 inches high is more convenient. Both counters should have reagent shelves, countertop sinks, air, gas, vacuum, and electrical service outlets, knee spaces, cabinets for storing equipment and chemicals and reagents. Work surfaces should be alcohol- and stain-resistant and resilient to minimize glass breakage. A refrigerator for storage of clinical material and a lavatory with wrist-action valves for handwashing are necessary. Space for parking a specimen cart should be provided.

*Autopsy Room*

This should be located convenient both to the teaching hospital and to the pathology department and arranged so as to prevent unnecessary contact of unauthorized persons with autopsy procedures. If the basic science building is separated from the teaching hospital, autopsy facilities should be located in the hospital to avoid transporting bodies from one building to another.

Each autopsy room should be equipped with a scrub-up sink with knee- or foot-action valve; a sink with drainboards, cold-water manifold, and gas and electrical service outlets; an adjacent work counter with drawers and cabinets for storage of supplies; a flushing-rim clinical sink; wall cabinets with adjustable shelves and glazed doors for storing instruments; a wall-mounted four-bank x-ray film illuminator; and a marker board. An instrument sterilizer and a storage cabinet for fixed specimens should also be pro-

**Table 9** Net area for a department of physiology

| Type of facility | School A (entering class of 64 students) | | | | School B (entering class of 96 students) | | | |
|---|---|---|---|---|---|---|---|---|
| | With conventional departmental laboratories | | With multidiscipline laboratories | | With conventional departmental laboratories | | With multidiscipline laboratories | |
| Assumed size of faculty | | 6 | | 6 | | 8 | | 8 |
| Number of graduate students and postdoctoral fellows | | 6 | | 6 | | 8 | | 8 |
| | | | | *Square feet* | | | | |
| Total net area | | 12,230 | | (1) | | 14,160 | | (1) |
| Faculty offices, research laboratories, and related facilities: | | | | | | | | |
| Total | | 6,940 | | 6,940 | | 7,550 | | 7,550 |
| Professor's office | | 210 | | 210 | | 210 | | 210 |
| Secretary's office | | 280 | | 280 | | 280 | | 280 |
| Conference room | | 350 | | 350 | | 350 | | 350 |
| Faculty offices | (4) | 560 | (4) | 560 | (4) | 560 | (4) | 560 |
| Postdoctoral fellows' office | | 200 | | 200 | | 200 | | 200 |
| Data room | | 280 | | 280 | | 280 | | 280 |
| Special-projects room | | 280 | | 280 | | 280 | | 280 |
| Research laboratories: | | | | | | | | |
| Departmental | | 610 | | 610 | | 610 | | 610 |
| General | | 610 | | 610 | (2) | 1,220 | (2) | 1,220 |
| Graduate students | (2) | 400 | (2) | 400 | (2) | 400 | (2) | 400 |
| Storage room (future laboratory) | | 610 | | 610 | | 610 | | 610 |
| Storage room | | 280 | | 280 | | 280 | | 280 |
| Constant-temperature rooms | (2) | 240 | (2) | 240 | (2) | 240 | (2) | 240 |
| Shielded room | | 210 | | 210 | | 210 | | 210 |
| Dark room | | 210 | | 210 | | 210 | | 210 |
| Departmental shop | | 280 | | 280 | | 280 | | 280 |
| Animal room | | 410 | | 410 | | 410 | | 410 |
| Cold room | | 200 | | 200 | | 200 | | 200 |
| Graduate students' teaching laboratory | | 720 | | 720 | | 720 | | 720 |
| Departmental central storage[2] | | | | | | | | |
| Conventional teaching: | | | | | | | | |
| Total | | 5,290 | | (1) | | 6,610 | | (1) |
| Teaching laboratory | | 3,000 | | | | 4,320 | | |
| Equipment storage room | | 350 | | | | 350 | | |
| Supply room | | 610 | | | | 610 | | |
| Student research laboratory and work area | | 570 | | | | 570 | | |
| Audio room | | 90 | | | | 90 | | |
| Physio-optics room | | 260 | | | | 260 | | |
| Treadmill and gas analysis room | | 410 | | | | 410 | | |

[1]For total net area for multidiscipline laboratories see Table 5.

[2]For central storage area, see Table 13.

vided if they are not available in an adjoining utility or clean-up room.

Water and AC electrical service outlets with waterproof caps are required. A table with downdraft top for removal of contamination and odors directly at their source, with an integral sink at one end of the top, and service outlets, is generally preferred. Access for video/audio recording of observations is required. The same mount may provide for TV to remote monitors.

Space to accommodate a portable observation stand opposite the table for convenient viewing of autopsy procedures by students and house staff should be provided.

Floor and walls should be of water-resistant material, and a floor drain should be installed.

*Autopsy and X-ray Room*

A mobile x-ray machine should be provided. X-ray protection should be in accordance with the recommendations of the applicable handbooks of the National Institute for Standards and Technology.

*Utility and Clean-up Room*

This room should be located between two autopsy rooms with direct access to each and to the corridor. Equipment for this area includes a

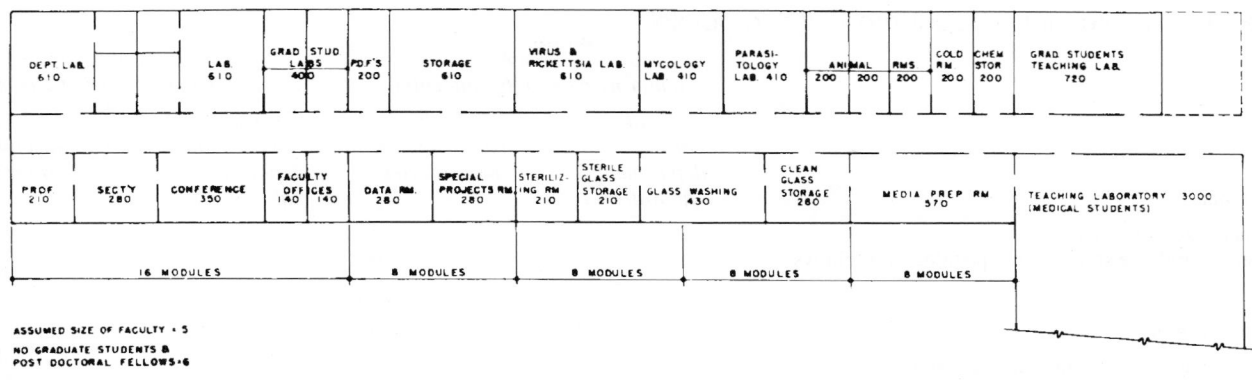

**Fig. 11. Diagram for a department of microbiology**

sink with drainboard; a flushing-rim service sink; provisions for storage of glass jars, formalin, and alcohol; wall cabinets for fixed specimen storage; and an instrument washer—sterilizer unless provided in each autopsy room.

*Photo Room*

The photo room should adjoin the autopsy room.

Fixed equipment in a photo room usually includes a stand-up counter with sink and electrical outlets, a cabinet for instruments and supplies, and shelves for photographic accessories.

For photographing gross specimens, a 3-foot-square light box is used. Electric outlets for table and floodlamps should be 30 amperes.

*Darkroom*

Wet and dry areas of the darkroom should be separated. A refrigerator for storing color film should be provided, and water supply at all processing sinks is required.

Bench tops should be chemically inert, watertight, and wear resistant. Floor surfaces should be waterproof, resistant to chemicals, resilient for foot comfort, and not slippery when wet.

*Cold Room*

A cold room separate from the research cold room but adjacent to the autopsy areas for holding tissue and organs for later study is required. A deep-freeze unit and adjustable metal shelving may be provided for preservation of fresh gross material for class use. Stand-up counters with sinks and air, vacuum, and electrical service outlets are required. Floor surface should be smooth, waterproof, and wear resistant.

A separate room for storing gross pathological specimens should be provided.

*Gross Pathology Conference Rooms*

A stand-up table with sink at one end and downdraft top similar to that described for the gross neuroanatomy room is appropriate. Other equipment includes adjustable shelving, x-ray film illuminators, bul-

letin board, and scrub sink with knee or foot controls. Where possible, this area should have direct access to the cold room.

*Dictating Room*

This is a small room equipped with desk and equipment for writing or dictating autopsy records.

*Record Storage*

Open-faced shelving with shelf dividers designed for vertical stacking of the records with a reference table and chairs should be provided. A storage room for records of less frequent reference should be provided in basement storage.

The pathology department requires areas for storage of embedments, fixed tissue, gross organs, microscope slides, and protocol records not in frequent use. Tissue in solution is kept in glass jars, paraffin sealed, and stored on wood shelving designed for jar height.

Microscope slides are usually contained in metal slide files, and this area should be separated from areas where formalin vapors are present. Protocol records are often bound and placed on shelving or in legal-size file cabinets.

**Pharmacology**

Figure 13 shows a space diagram for a minimum department of pharmacology. Net area for a pharmacology department is given in Table 12.

*Teaching Laboratory*

The conventional pharmacology teaching laboratory may be similar to the physiology teaching laboratory.

*Graduate Student Teaching Laboratory*

This should be adjacent to auxiliary rooms of the medical student teaching laboratory. Fixed equipment and mechanical facilities should be similar to those furnished the medical student.

**Table 10**   Net area for a department of microbiology

| Type of facility | | School A (entering class of 64 students) | | School B (entering class of 96 students) | |
| --- | --- | --- | --- | --- | --- |
| | | With conventional departmental laboratories | With multidiscipline laboratories | With conventional departmental laboratories | With multidiscipline laboratories |
| Assumed size of faculty | | 5 | 5 | 7 | 7 |
| Number of graduate students and postdoctoral fellows | | 6 | 6 | 8 | 8 |
| | | Square feet | | | |
| Total net area | | 12,240 | (¹) | 14,170 | (¹) |
| Faculty offices, research laboratories, and associated facilities: | | | | | |
| Total | | 9,240 | 8,970 | 9,850 | 9,580 |
| Professor's office | | 210 | 210 | 210 | 210 |
| Secretary's office | | 280 | 280 | 280 | 280 |
| Conference room | | 350 | 350 | 350 | 350 |
| Faculty offices | (2) | 280 | (2) 280 | (2) 280 | (2) 280 |
| Postdoctoral fellows' office | | 200 | 200 | 200 | 200 |
| Data room | | 280 | 280 | 280 | 280 |
| Special-projects room | | 280 | 280 | 280 | 280 |
| Research laboratories: | | | | | |
| Departmental | | 610 | 610 | 610 | 610 |
| General | | 610 | 610 | (2) 1,220 | (2) 1,220 |
| Graduate students | (2) | 400 | (2) 400 | (2) 400 | (2) 400 |
| Storage room (fugure laboratory) | | 610 | 610 | 610 | 610 |
| Storage room | | 280 | 280 | 280 | 280 |
| Media preparation room | | 570 | 430 | 570 | 430 |
| Sterilizing room | | 210 | 210 | 210 | 210 |
| Sterile glass storage | | 210 | 210 | 210 | 210 |
| Glass washing | | 430 | 430 | 430 | 430 |
| Clean glass storage | | 280 | 210 | 280 | 210 |
| Chemical storage | | 200 | 140 | 200 | 140 |
| Virus and rickettsia laboratory | | 610 | 610 | 610 | 610 |
| Mycology laboratory | | 410 | 410 | 410 | 410 |
| Parasitology laboratory | | 410 | 410 | 410 | 410 |
| Animal rooms | (3) | 600 | (3) 600 | (3) 600 | (3) 600 |
| Cold room | | 200 | 200 | 200 | 200 |
| Graduate students' teaching laboratory | | 720 | 720 | 720 | 720 |
| Departmental central storage² | | | | | |
| Conventional teaching: | | | | | |
| Total | | 3,000 | (¹) | 4,320 | (¹) |
| Teaching laboratory | | 3,000 | | 4,320 | |

¹For total net area for multidiscipline laboratories see Table 5.

²For central storage areas, see Table 13.

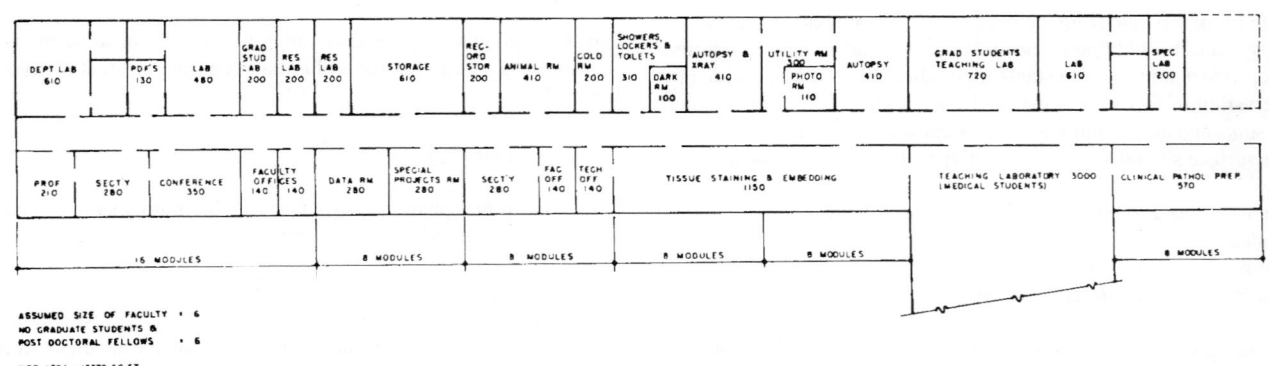

**Fig. 12. Diagram for a department of pathology**

## Table 11  Net area for a department of pathology

| Type of facility | | School A (entering class of 64 students) | | | School B (entering class of 96 students) | | |
| --- | --- | --- | --- | --- | --- | --- | --- |
| | | With conventional departmental laboratories | With multidiscipline laboratories | | With conventional departmental laboratories | | With multidiscipline laboratories |
| Assumed size of faculty[1] | | 6 | 6 | | 9 | | 9 |
| Number of graduate students, postdoctoral fellows and residents | | 6 | 6 | | 8 | | 8 |
| | | | *Square feet* | | | | |
| Total net area | | 14,100 | (²) | | 17,390 | | (²) |
| Faculty offices, research laboratories, and associated facilities: | | | | | | | |
| Total | | 11,100 | 11,100 | | 13,070 | | 13,070 |
| Professor's office | | 210 | 210 | | 210 | | 210 |
| Secretary's offices | (2) | 560 | (2) 560 | (2) | 560 | (2) | 560 |
| Conference room | | 350 | 350 | | 350 | | 350 |
| Faculty offices | (3) | 420 | (3) 420 | (3) | 420 | (3) | 420 |
| Postdoctoral fellows' office | | 130 | 130 | | 200 | | 200 |
| Data room | | 280 | 280 | | 280 | | 280 |
| Special-projects room | | 280 | 280 | | 280 | | 280 |
| Research laboratories: | | | | | | | |
| Departmental | | 610 | 610 | | 610 | | 160 |
| General | (2) | 1,099 | (2) 1,090 | (3) | 1,830 | (3) | 1,830 |
| Graduate students | | 200 | 200 | | 200 | | 200 |
| Special | | 200 | 200 | | 200 | | 200 |
| Residents' laboratories | (2) | 400 | (2) 400 | (3) | 530 | (3) | 530 |
| Electron microscope | | 610 | 610 | | 610 | | 610 |
| Storage room | | 280 | 280 | | 280 | | 280 |
| Tissue staining and embedding and technician's office | | 1,290 | 1,290 | | 1,290 | | 1,290 |
| Clinical pathology preparation | | 570 | 570 | | 570 | | 570 |
| Record storage | | 200 | 200 | | 410 | | 410 |
| Autopsy rooms | | 410 | 410 | (2) | 820 | (2) | 820 |
| Darkroom | | 100 | 100 | | 100 | | 100 |
| Utility room | | 300 | 300 | | 300 | | 300 |
| Photo room | | 110 | 110 | | 110 | | 110 |
| Autopsy and x-ray | | 410 | 410 | | 410 | | 410 |
| Gross pathology conference room | | 310 | 310 | | 310 | | 310 |
| Dictation room | | 140 | 140 | | 140 | | 140 |
| Showers, lockers and toilets | | 310 | 310 | | 310 | | 310 |
| Morgue (see department of anatomy) | | | | | | | |
| Animal rooms | | 410 | 410 | (2) | 820 | (2) | 820 |
| Cold rooms | | 200 | 200 | | 200 | | 200 |
| Graduate students' teaching laboratory | | 720 | 720 | | 720 | | 720 |
| Departmental central storage[3] | | | | | | | |
| Conventional teaching: | | | | | | | |
| Total | | 3,000 | (²) | | 4,320 | | (²) |
| Teaching laboratory | | 3,000 | | | 4,320 | | |

[1] For teaching responsibility only.

[2] For total net area for multidiscipline laboratories see Table 5.

[3] For central storage areas, see Table 13.

Note: These areas do not provide for the permanent professional or resident staffs performing services for clinical pathology in the teaching hospital.

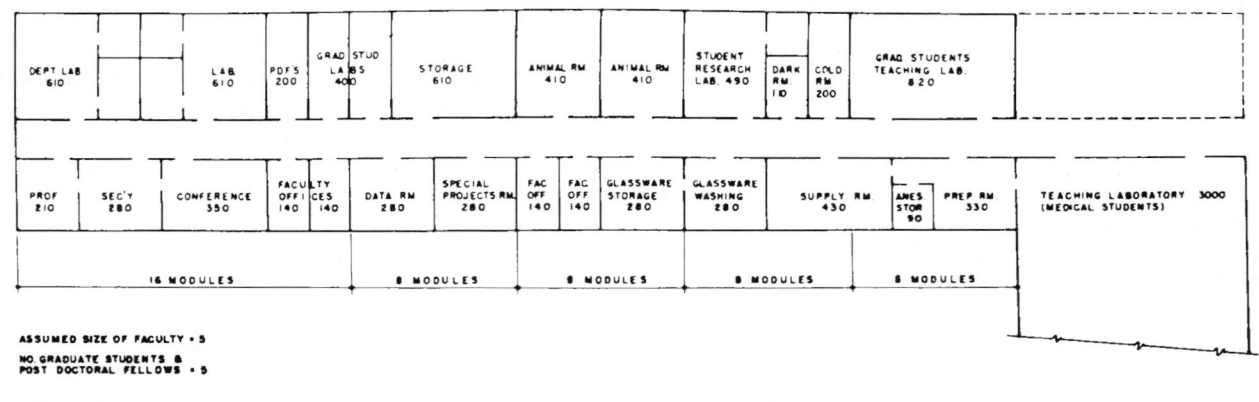

ASSUMED SIZE OF FACULTY = 5

NO. GRADUATE STUDENTS. &
POST DOCTORAL FELLOWS = 5

NET AREA = 11240 SQ FT.

**Fig. 13. Diagram for a department of pharmacology**

**Table 12**  Net area for a department of pharmacology

| | | School A (entering class of 64 students) | | School B (entering class of 96 students) | |
| --- | --- | --- | --- | --- | --- |
| Type of facility | | With conventional departmental laboratories | With multidiscipline laboratories | With conventional departmental laboratories | With multidiscipline laboratories |
| Assumed size of faculty | | 5 | 5 | 7 | 7 |
| Number of graduate students and postdoctoral fellows | | 5 | 5 | 7 | 7 |
| | | | Square feet | | |
| Total net area | | 11,520 | (¹) | 13,450 | (¹) |
| Faculty offices, research laboratories, and associated facilities: | | | | | |
|   Total | | 7,700 | 7,700 | 8,310 | 8,310 |
|   Professor's office | | 210 | 210 | 210 | 210 |
|   Secretary's office | | 280 | 280 | 280 | 280 |
|   Conference room | | 350 | 350 | 350 | 350 |
|   Faculty offices | (4) | 560 | (4) 560 | (4) 560 | (4) 560 |
|   Postdoctoral fellows' office | | 200 | 200 | 200 | 200 |
|   Data room | | 280 | 280 | 280 | 280 |
|   Special-projects room | | 280 | 280 | 280 | 280 |
|   Research laboratories: | | | | | |
|     Departmental | | 610 | 610 | 610 | 610 |
|     General | | 610 | 610 | (2) 1,220 | (2) 1,220 |
|     Graduate students | (2) | 400 | (2) 400 | (2) 400 | (2) 400 |
|   Storage room (future laboratory) | | 610 | 610 | 610 | 610 |
|   Storage room | | 280 | 280 | 280 | 280 |
|   Supply room | | 430 | 430 | 430 | 430 |
|   Glassware washing and storage | | 560 | 560 | 560 | 560 |
|   Anesthesia storage | | 90 | 90 | 90 | 90 |
|   Darkroom | | 110 | 110 | 110 | 110 |
|   Animal rooms | (2) | 820 | (2) 820 | (2) 820 | (2) 820 |
|   Cold room | | 200 | 200 | 200 | 200 |
|   Graduate students' teaching laboratory | | 820 | 820 | 820 | 820 |
|   Departmental central storage² | | | | | |
| Conventional teaching: | | | | | |
|   Total | | 3,820 | (¹) | 5,140 | (¹) |
|   Teaching laboratory | | 3,000 | | 4,320 | |
|   Preparation room | | 330 | 330 | | |
|   Students' research laboratory | | 490 | | 490 | |

¹For total net area for multidiscipline laboratories, see Table 5.

²For central storage areas, see Table 13.

*Student Research Laboratory*

A student research laboratory, if provided, should contain facilities similar to those in typical pharmacology research laboratories. Where possible, it should be located within the teaching area but adjacent to research areas.

*Glassware Washing and Storage*

Glassware washing and storage facilities similar to those indicated for the biochemistry department are adequate in the pharmacology department; they should be located near the teaching laboratory.

*Preparation Room*

This should be adjacent to the pharmacology teaching laboratory.

*Anesthesia Storage*

An anesthesia storage room should be provided with cylinder storage racks to lock cylinders in an upright position and shelving for pressure gauges and other anesthetic equipment. Space at ground level should be provided for bulk storage of cylinders.

*Supply Room*

A supply room in pharmacology may be divided into two areas: one for instruments and general supplies and the other for chemicals used in research.

Some instruments require floor space while others should be placed on shelving. A desk-high counter with drawers and file cabinet is needed. Since some instruments may be used here, electrical outlets should be provided.

If narcotics are to be stored, a built-in safe should be provided.

Space must be provided for the care of animals used in experimental work in pharmacology.

A summary of space estimates for all basic science facilities is given in Table 13.

**Clinical Science Facilities**

The departments generally include internal medicine, surgery, pediatrics, obstetrics and gynecology, psychiatry, preventive medicine, and radiology. Pathology, although usually considered a basic science department, nevertheless has many of the characteristics of a clinical department and, therefore, functionally and structurally, usually bridges both.

Space diagrams for the departments of medicine, surgery, pediatrics, obstetrics-gynecology, psychiatry, and preventive medicine are shown in Figs. 14 through 19 for a hypothetical school with an entering class of 64 students (60 in the third and fourth year). Table 14 gives a summary of space estimates for all clinical science departments.

For convenience of operation, clinical department facilities should be located between, and connecting with, the basic science building and the teaching hospital. This allows for joint use of teaching, research,

and supporting facilities provided in the basic science building and makes it convenient for the medical staff to take care of their hospital responsibilities. Departments should be located on the same floor or floors as the patient-care units they serve.

Research facilities in the form of laboratories should be provided for each department member.

Teaching activities of all departments will be carried out, for the most part, in common lecture rooms, on the units of the hospital, and in the outpatient department.

**Medicine**

The department of medicine consists of physicians specializing in internal medicine and includes the subspecialties of allergy, cardiology, dermatology, gastroenterology, hematology, infectious diseases and immunology, metabolism, neurology, and pulmonary diseases. The members of the department will have responsibility for the care of hospitalized patients, for ambulatory patients in the medical clinics of the outpatient department, and for medical consultations on patients under the care of other clinical services. They will have major teaching duties for second-, third-, and fourth-year medical students, interns, residents, and clinical fellows.

**Surgery**

The department of surgery consists of physicians specializing in general surgery or in one of the surgical specialties, which include anesthesiology, ophthalmology, otolaryngology, orthopedics, neurosurgery, plastic surgery, thoracic surgery, and urology. The members of this department will have responsibility for the care of patients who are hospitalized on the surgical service; who visit the surgical clinics of the outpatient department; and who require surgical consultation while on some other service. Often the emergency service of a hospital is under the direction of the department of surgery, as may be the professional aspects of disaster planning. The department of surgery will have teaching responsibilities for second-, third-, and fourth year medical students, interns, residents, and surgical fellows. Each full-time member of the department may be expected to engage in research.

**Pediatrics**

The department of pediatrics consists of physicians specializing in the developmental aspects of physiological processes and expressions of disease. They are as concerned about the long-term health effects of early disease and with their prevention as with the immediate care of infants and children. In most university hospitals, the age range extends to the 14th or 16th year. Pediatrics is a nonsurgical specialty. Consequently, surgery on patients in the pediatrics age is generally handled by the department of surgery. As in internal medicine, a number of subspecialties generally based on organ systems such as cardiology, neurology, and endocrinology are usually represented in the department of pediatrics.

The general requirements for departmental offices, teaching spaces, and laboratories are the same in pediatrics as in other clinical departments. Teaching is generally concentrated within one or both of the last two clinical years. In addition, there are teaching responsibilities for interns, residents, and postdoctoral fellows in pediatric training.

**Table 13** Summary of space estimates for basic science facilities for hypothetical 4-year medical schools with entering classes of 64 and 96 students[1]

| Type of facility | School A (entering class of 64 students) | | School B (entering class of 96 students) | |
| --- | --- | --- | --- | --- |
| | With conventional departmental laboratories | With multidiscipline laboratories | With conventional departmental laboratories | With multidiscipline laboratories |
| | Square feet | | | |
| Total gross square feet[2] (rounded) | 152,000 | 135,000 | 183,000 | 158,000 |
| Total net square feet (rounded) | 99,000 | 88,000 | 119,000 | 103,000 |
| Department facilities | | | | |
| Anatomy | 19,330 | 11,510 | 22,950 | 12,530 |
| Biochemistry | 12,240 | 8,670 | 14,980 | 10,090 |
| Physiology | 12,230 | 6,940 | 14,160 | 7,550 |
| Microbiology | 12,240 | 8,970 | 14,170 | 9,580 |
| Pathology[3] | 14,100 | 11,100 | 17,390 | 13,070 |
| Pharmacology | 11,520 | 7,700 | 13,450 | 8,310 |
| Multidiscipline laboratories and adjunctive areas | | 22,500 | | 29,960 |
| Lecture rooms | 3,780 | 3,780 | 3,780 | 3,780 |
| Unassigned conference rooms | (2 @ 350) 700 | | (3 @ 350) 1,050 | |
| Study cubicles[4] | 6,110 | ([5]) | 9,400 | ([5]) |
| Technical shops | 1,500 | 1,500 | 2,000 | 2,000 |
| Departmental central storage | 4,500 | 4,500 | 4,500 | 4,500 |
| Toilets | 1,200 | 1,200 | 1,200 | 1,200 |

[1]This table does not include the supporting facilities which are a necessary part of both the basic science and clinical science facilities.

[2]To compute gross area, it is estimated that 65 percent of the total gross area is available as usable space, and the remaining 35 percent will provide space for exterior walls, partitions, corridors, stairs, elevators, and duct ways and chases for mechanical and electrical requirements.

[3]Space for service functions in the teaching hospital is not included.

[4]Study cubicles for 3d- and 4th-year students and for house officers in teaching hospital.

[5]Optional.

## Obstetrics and Gynecology

Obstetrics concerns itself with the processes of conception, gestation, and delivery in women, whereas gynecology deals with the specific diseases of the female reproductive tract.

Requirements of the department of obstetrics and gynecology for administrative office, teaching and research space are not essentially different from those of any other clinical department. Usually this department confines its teaching activities to students in one or both of the third and fourth years. Teaching activities may expand to include such courses as reproductive biology. In addition, there are

teaching responsibilities for residents and fellows. Interns are generally not assigned to this service except as part of a rotating program. Student groups may be smaller than in some services and, therefore, teaching space should be sized accordingly.

## Psychiatry

The department of psychiatry consists of specialists concerned with the functions and disfunctions of the mind and emotions.

Offices for members of the department of psychiatry may be used for somewhat different purposes than staff offices of other clinical depart-

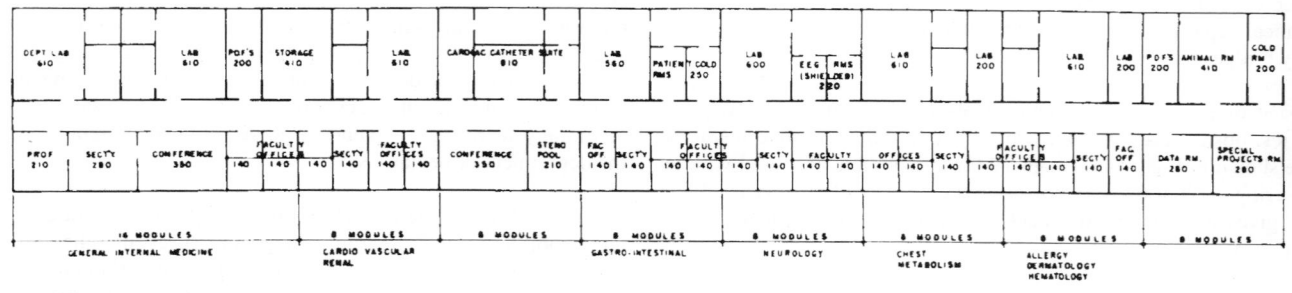

Fig. 14. Diagram for a department of medicine

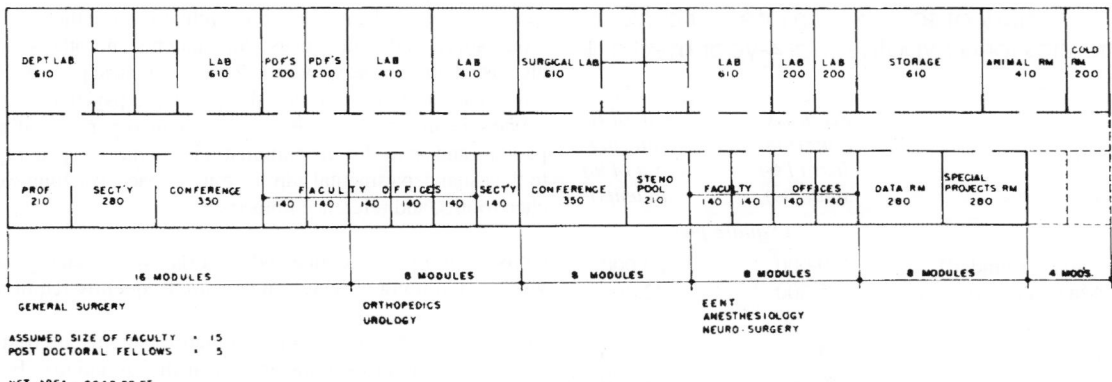

Fig. 15. Diagram for a department of surgery

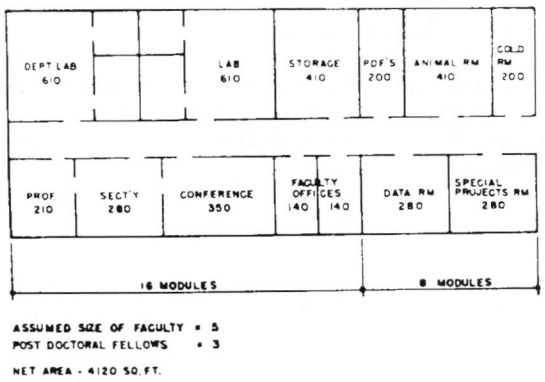

Fig. 16. Diagram for a department of pediatrics

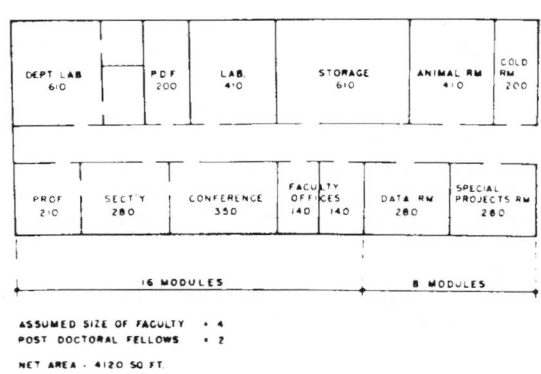

Fig. 18. Diagram for a department of preventive medicine

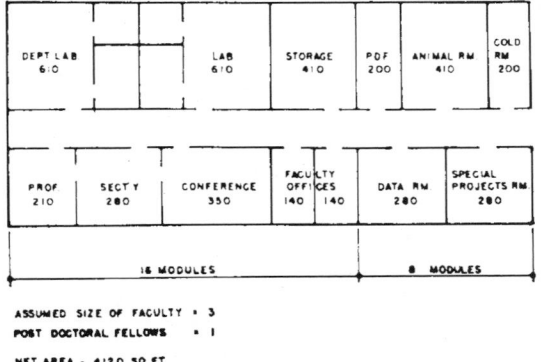

Fig. 17. Diagram for a department of obstetrics-gynecology

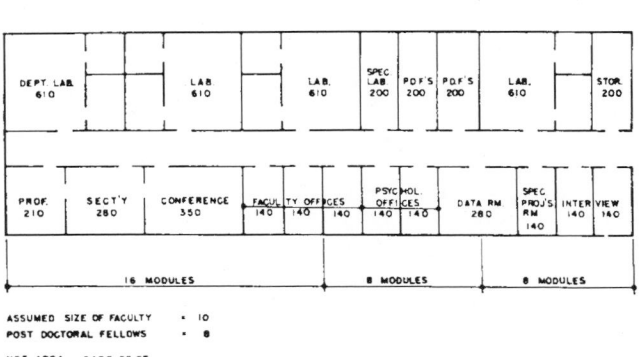

Fig. 19. Diagram for a department of psychiatry

**Table 14** Summary of space estimates for clinical science facilities for a hypothetical 4-year medical school[1]

| Type of facility | School A (entering class of 64 students) | School B (entering class of 96 students) |
|---|---|---|
| | Square feet | |
| Total gross area[2] (rounded) | 69,000 | 80,000 |
| Total net area (rounded) | 45,000 | 52,000 |
| Departmental facilities: | | |
| Medicine | 13,440 | 15,490 |
| Surgery | 8,840 | 11,120 |
| Pediatrics | 4,260 | 5,010 |
| Obstetrics and gynecology | 4,390 | 4,390 |
| Psychiatry | 5,480 | 6,660 |
| Preventive medicine | 4,260 | 4,870 |
| Auditorium[3] | | |
| Lecture rooms[3] | | |
| Central storage | 3,200 | 3,200 |
| Toilet rooms | 1,200 | 1,200 |
| Radiology[3] | | |
| Anesthesiology[3] | | |
| Pathology[4] | | |

[1]This table does not include the supporting facilities which are a necessary part of both the basic science and clinical science facilities.

[2]To compute the gross area, it is estimated that 65 percent of the total gross area is available as usable space, while the remaining 35 percent will provide space for exterior walls, partitions, corridors, stairs, elevators, and duct ways and chases for mechanical and electrical requirements.

[3]In the teaching hospital.

[4]Preclinical pathology is taught in the basic science facilities. Space for clinical pathology may be provided in the teaching hospital.

ments, For example, not only do psychiatrists use their offices for desk work, study, and conferences with students and others, but they may also use them as interview rooms for psychiatric patients. Clearly, this will have an effect upon the design of the psychiatric departmental office suite in that it may be necessary to incorporate waiting rooms for patients and space for the administrative control of patients in addition to the usual departmental administrative space, teaching space, conference rooms, and reference libraries.

Consultation rooms connected by a one-way viewing screen or TV with an adjoining observation area are frequently required.

In general, studies involving psychiatric patients are best carried out in research facilities associated with the psychiatric bed area, and laboratory studies not involving patients are best carried out in departmental research laboratories.

**Preventive Medicine**

In general, the discipline of preventive medicine comprises physicians who are concerned with the natural history of disease and the factors in the environment which have an effect upon morbidity and mortality. They are interested in reducing the incidence of avoidable disease and premature death through control of those factors which may contribute to disability and incapacity.

There is usually a close relationship between the staffs of pediatrics, medicine, obstetrics gynecology, psychiatry, and preventive medicine, and this should be borne in mind in the location and assignment of office space.

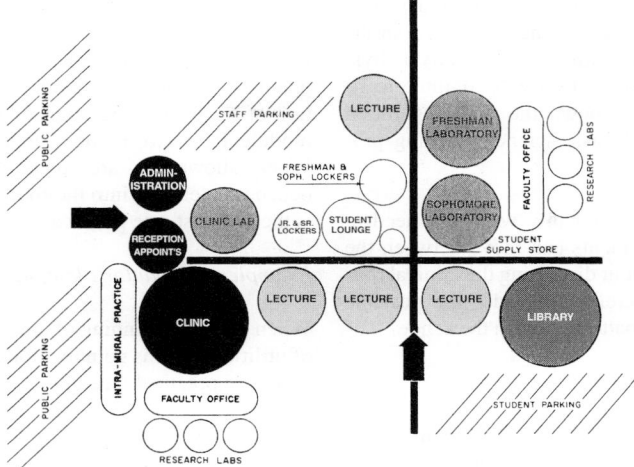

**Fig. 1. Space relationships: preclinical and clinical dental science areas**

# DENTAL SCHOOLS

## SELECTING THE SITE

### Preferred Locations

Dental educators generally prefer certain locations for a dental school. The obvious choice, a university campus, has impressive advantages. It offers students and faculty a richer cultural life and often a more pleasant environment. Adequate housing and student facilities may be more readily available than in other locations. If the university also has a medical school on campus, students and faculty can enjoy a close association with other health professions.

Location in a health center is also advantageous, since it offers access to a complex of health facilities and provides day-to-day opportunity for close cooperation between the health professions. A metropolitan location generally assures the school an ample supply of patients for teaching clinics.

### About the Site

*Topography and Dimensions*

High ground with natural drainage is desirable, but the elevation should not be so high that approach on foot is difficult. A patient entrance at ground level and a service drive to the basement area should be feasible. A gently sloping lot has advantages, since it offers entrances on two levels; traffic in and out of the building is automatically divided between them, and the movement of people and supplies can more easily be diverted over separate routes within the building. The site selected should be of sufficient site to permit later expansion.

*Utilities*

Sewerage, water, electricity, telephone, and gas must be available on the site or be extendible to it at reasonable cost. Utilities must also have adequate capacity.

*Transportation and Parking*

Convenient public transportation is a necessity. Runs should be frequent, with adequate peak-hour service. Good public transportation materially reduces the parking problem. It also makes it easier for the school to secure and retain service and clerical employees. Even with good public transportation, first-class roads should connect the school directly with local traffic arteries.

The site should permit adequate parking areas for students, faculty, and patients. Generally, one parking place for each full-time faculty member and one for every two part-time members is advisable. A site in a suburban area should also allow two parking places per entering class student (ECS) for students, if possible, and another two places per ECS for clinic patients.

## SPACE RELATIONSHIPS

### The Effect of Traffic Patterns

The arrangement of the many elements of a school is determined largely by the movement of students, faculty, patients, and materials.

*Clinics*

The most common and effective way of reducing traffic within the school is by physical separation of the clinical facilities from the

*References:* Public Health Service, U.S. Department of Health and Human Services.

remainder of the school. Staffed by a separate faculty and visited daily by large numbers of patients whose presence elsewhere in the school could be disruptive, the clinical facilities are logically a physical entity. For this reason, physical separation will continue to be advisable even though efforts to break down the rigid separation which exists between the clinical and basic science teaching programs are successful.

However, if they are successful, there probably will be a need to locate certain clinical areas so that students can move between the clinics and the basic science areas without disturbing the clinical routine. Planning committees should therefore consider the possible implications of this change for traffic patterns within the school.

*Basic Science and Preclinical Laboratories*

The activities of freshmen and sophomores are largely confined to these areas; by locating them in reasonable proximity, with other facilities used by these students nearby, traffic within the school could be materially reduced. However, since laboratory sessions are normally scheduled for a full half day, with students shifting between laboratories only once a day, locating these areas on separate floors or in separate wings may well resolve a particular school's problems of space arrangement.

**A Design Which Controls Traffic Flow**

Figure 1 is a space diagram showing the relationships between and within the clinical and preclinical dental science areas of a school which will locate its basic science facilities in another wing or on another floor.

All student facilities are located close to their major areas of activity. Note the proximity of student lounges and locker rooms to the teaching facilities used by the students. Freshmen and sophomore locker rooms are adjacent to the preclinical laboratories, while locker rooms for junior and seniors are close to the clinic. Locker rooms for both groups adjoin the student lounge and bookstore and are located near the student entrance. Lecture rooms, used by both preclinical and clinical students, are readily accessible from all student areas.

The need for a location as free of vibration as possible makes the basement the preferred site for the electron microscope suite, for example, though this location is seldom convenient for users of the laboratory. Facilities which will be used after normal school hours—auditorium, libraries, and study areas—provide another example. Ideally, they should be located so that they can be left open after the remainder of the school is locked.

**THE PHYSICAL PLANT: DESIGN AND STRUCTURE**

**Modular Planning for Flexibility and Efficient Use of Space**

Modular planning is particularly adaptable to the design of schools, hospitals, and other buildings in which repetitive elements lend themselves to the systematic and uniform spacing of certain structural features. The module should be a multiple of the basic 4-inch module recommended by the American Standards Association Project A62.

Many building components are prefabricated on this basis, and the floor plans in this section are based on modular design, using a module of 4 feet-8 inches.

*In Laboratory and Office Planning*

In the dental school, modular design is particularly applicable to the planning of research laboratories and offices. Figure 2 shows a section of a typical basic science laboratory based on the 4 feet-8 inch module. It is a two-module laboratory, approximately 9 feet in width. When allowances are made for the equipment and laboratory benches extending into the room from the wall, the two-module unit is the smallest size practical but yet adequate for its function.

*Examples of Modular Planning*

When modular planning of areas is combined with modular planning of utilities, various combinations of offices, laboratories, and storage space are practical (see Fig. 3).

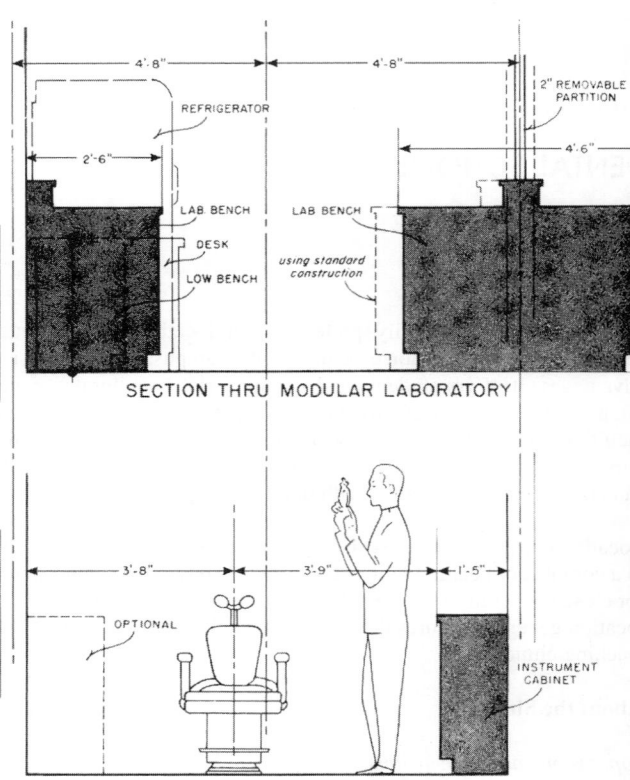

SECTION THRU MODULAR LABORATORY

SECTION THRU OPERATORY

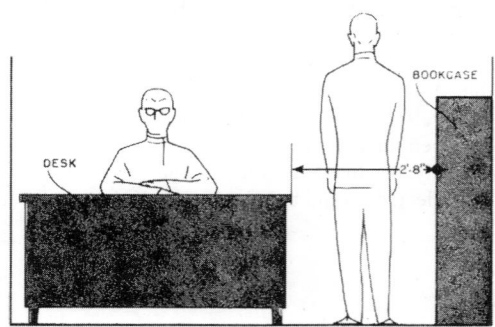

SECTION THRU OFFICE UNIT

**Fig. 2. Building module**

Figure 3b is a sectional drawing of a research floor of a school. Figure 3c is a partial plan of the corridor wall. Columns are located at every fifth module. Vertical utility shafts, which supply the laboratories with water, drainage, gas, and other utilities, are located at every fourth module.

Figure 3a shows the arrangements of laboratories, office, and equipment storage areas possible with this design. For example, if a series of laboratories of four-module width is desired, either index A or B can be followed. Index A has the laboratory bench at the side walls, while index B shows a center island or peninsula type of laboratory. If an office and equipment room is desired with each laboratory, these can be substituted for alternate laboratories.

Indexes C and D illustrate smaller laboratories suitable for one or two researchers. Index C is a series of laboratories only, and index D is a combination of two-module laboratories, offices, and equipment storage rooms. One or more four-module laboratories can easily be provided in combination with two-module laboratories.

*Advantages and Limitations*

Modular design can be applied to structures in which utilities are located at or in the exterior walls. It can also be used, and with perhaps greater flexibility, in research laboratories in which a central utility core is utilized (Fig. 4).

Modular design provides a basis for determining the width of laboratories and offices. In estimating depth, at least 24 or 25 feet should be allowed. In Fig. 18 the bay depth is 28 feet—the equivalent of six modules; a sufficient allowance when utility shafts are located along the corridor wall.

Caution should be used in following modular planning for other elements of the dental school. Where location of columns is important, strict adherence to the selected planning module may result in obstacles in aisles and other areas. This is a particular problem in the clinics, where chair layout may be adversely affected by a lack of coordination with the structural and mechanical features of the building. In the clinic area, modular design is of lesser importance in those plans in which operatories, laboratories, offices, and other small rooms are not located along the exterior walls.

## BASIC SCIENCE LABORATORY FACILITIES IN GENERAL

Few decisions made in the initial stages of programming will have a greater influence on the space and structural requirements of the dental school than those reached in defining the school's teaching and research objectives in the basic sciences.

### Departmental Facilities

The head of every department needs a private office with space enough to accommodate small staff or student conferences. An adjoining office should be provided for the department secretary. A conference room and a seminar room accommodating a 16-student group should also be provided. In addition to chalkboards and book-

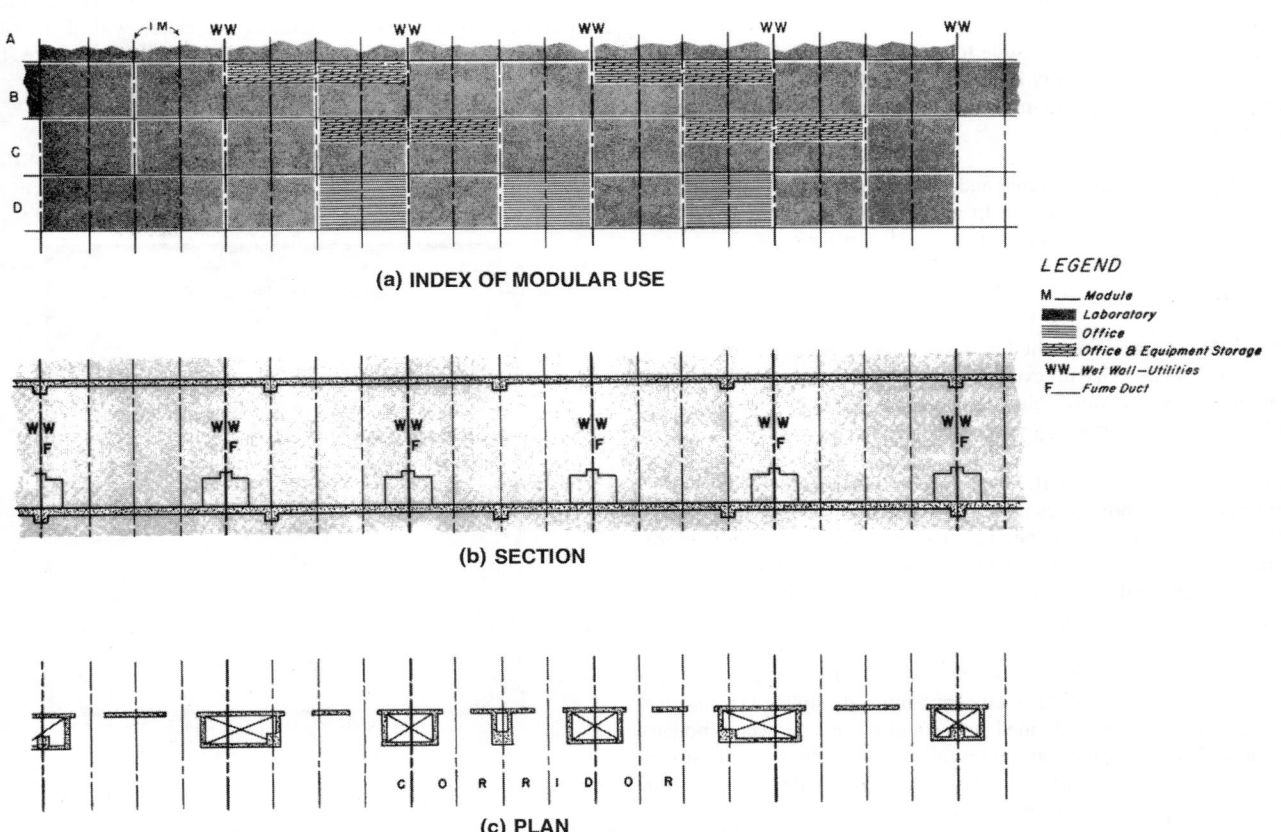

**(a) INDEX OF MODULAR USE**

*LEGEND*

M ____ Module
▨▨▨ Laboratory
▥▥▥ Office
▤▤▤ Office & Equipment Storage
WW__Wet Wall—Utilities
F ____ Fume Duct

**(b) SECTION**

**(c) PLAN**

**Fig. 3. Modular planning of areas**

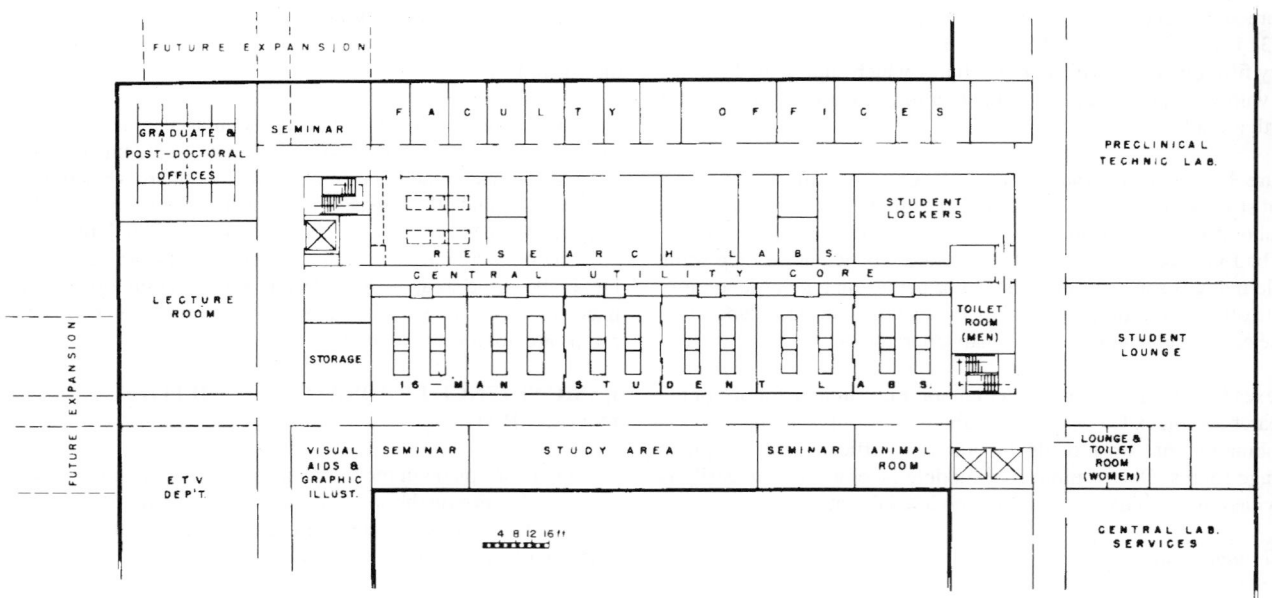

**Fig. 4. Plan for a basic science area utilizing a central utility core**

shelves, each room should be equipped with or adaptable to the use of slide and film projectors and ETV. Both can be used for staff or student conferences, or for formal but unscheduled classes or seminars. A data processing room for use both by faculty and graduate students is also an advantage.

A storage room easily accessible to staff offices and research facilities is a major convenience. Properly planned, it can always be converted into office space—a much-needed insurance against eventual overcrowding.

Every full-time faculty member and graduate student will need office and research laboratory space. In addition, an unassigned research laboratory should be considered for each department.

**Laboratories**

The traditional arrangement for basic science teaching provides a laboratory of class size for every department. This calls for a separate laboratory for anatomy, biochemistry, physiology, microbiology, pathology, and pharmacology.

Considerably less space will be needed for undergraduate teaching if multidiscipline laboratories are used, and dental schools have generally found that more than one discipline can easily be scheduled for a single laboratory. Schools which use integrated systems of instruction or which need to assure a marked degree of flexibility will necessarily plan multidiscipline laboratories.

If they are equipped with movable partitions and four- or eight-person position benches, both departmental and multi-discipline laboratories of class size are easily divided into smaller units to accommodate research projects or small-group teaching. Many educators, however, look with increasing favor on the laboratory designed specifically for the smaller number of students. Figure 5 is a floor plan showing how items of equipment are placed. Sophomore laboratories have no anatomy table but are otherwise similar.

Unit laboratories accommodating a larger number of students and designed for teaching only the basic science disciplines are more widely favored. Figure 6 is a floor plan of a 16-student laboratory in which physiology, biochemistry, and pharmacology are taught. More detailed information on the arrangement and equipment of teaching laboratories, and the special facilities associated with them will be found in a following section. Suggested space allowances are shown in Table 1.

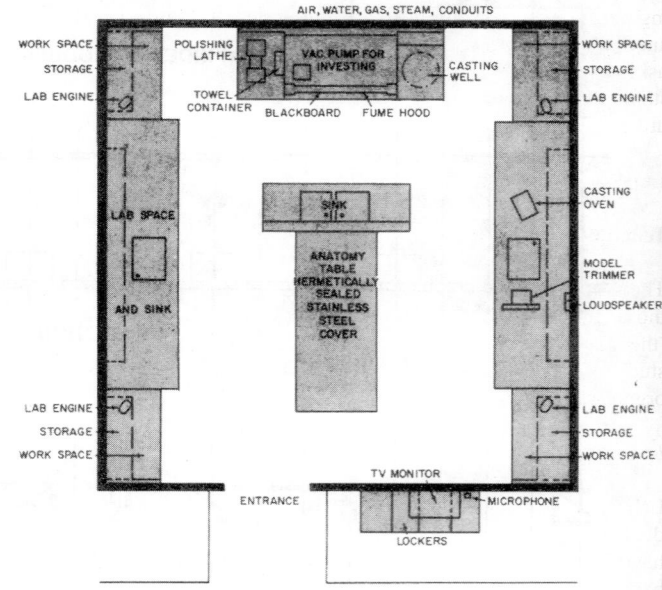

**Fig. 5. Layout and equipment of unit laboratory for both basic and preclinical sciences**

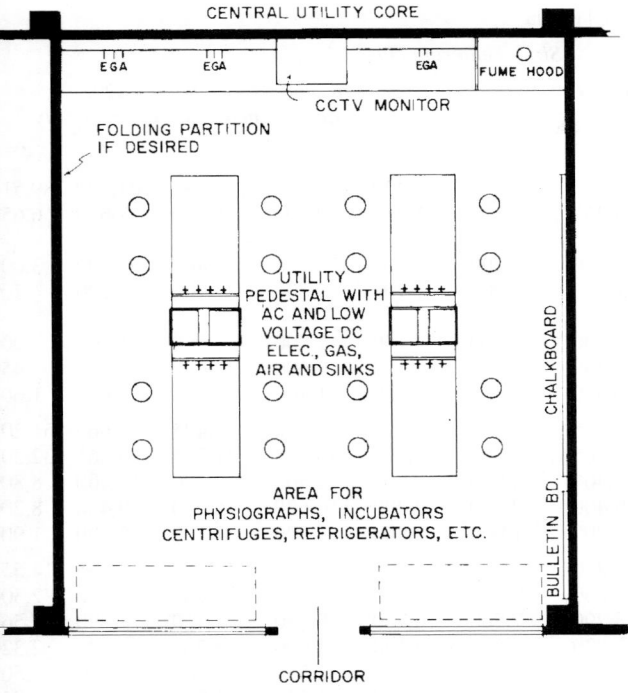

**Fig. 6. Sixteen-student teaching laboratory**

## BASIC SCIENCE LABORATORY FACILITIES

Three teaching laboratories—two multidiscipline and one single discipline—are described in this section. Together, the three can accommodate all of the basic laboratory sciences taught in a dental school.

Each of the multidiscipline laboratories described may be laid out as a series of self-contained units accommodating small groups of students, or retained as a class-size laboratory and equipped with folding partitions to permit division of the room into smaller units. The ancillary and special facilities required by the different disciplines using these laboratories are generally described, and they are substantially the same whether small-group or class-size laboratories are utilized.

## LOW-BENCH DISCIPLINES

### Teaching Laboratory

The disciplines which share the low-bench teaching laboratory are those employing microscopy as their principal technique—histology (the microscopic study of normal tissue), pathology (the microscopic study of diseased tissue), and microbiology (the study of microorganisms).

*Laboratory Benches and Arrangement*

Laboratory benches are usually 30 to 32 inches high to permit students to sit comfortably for long sessions at the microscope. Stools have back rests and adjustable seats. Either single or double-width benches may be used. However, because all students sit along one side of single-width benches, these can be more easily arranged to permit all students to face the demonstration area. A four-position

bench is particularly desirable in the class-size laboratory, since it permits the division of the class into groups of 16 or less without splitting the group at any bench. If double benches are used, the eight-position bench is preferred.

Clearances of 3 feet between single-width benches and 4 feet-6 inches between double-width benches are required. Side aisles, center aisle, and main cross aisle should be 6 feet wide.

*Work Station at the Bench*

Each position at the bench should be at least 42 inches wide to allow both adequate knee space and room for a base cabinet containing drawers for storing slides and supplies and a cupboard for storing a microscope. Water, gas, and electricity should be available at each position. The need for an air outlet is limited, and a vacuum is seldom used. A lead cup sink at each position (or a bench-long drain trough with a sink at one end) is necessary.

*Bench Tops*

Bench-top surfacing should be resilient, to minimize slide breakage, as well as stain and alcohol resistant. Bench tops should be as free of joints as possible.

*Stand-up Work Areas*

Wall counters (37 inches high) are located along the sides of the laboratory area. These provide bench space of stand up height, where students may set up portable equipment, conduct experiments with animals, or take part in other assigned projects. Counter-top hand washing sinks with knee- or foot-operated valves should be installed and supplied with hot and cold running water. Gas, air, and electricity outlets will also be needed. One set of outlets for every four work stations at the counter is adequate.

*Demonstration*

The demonstration area should have a table, retractable projection screen, and a chalkboard at least 4 feet high and as long as the supporting wall permits. Additional small marker boards—3 by 4 feet—should be available throughout the laboratory. At least one for every 16 students should be provided, and all marker boards should have adequate illumination. A bulletin board is also advisable. Because small-group laboratories easily accommodate demonstrations, no separate areas are needed for this purpose in schools employing the unit arrangement. Each of the small-group laboratories will require its own projection screens, marker boards, and a bulletin board.

*Stationary Equipment*

One noncorrosive fume hood should be provided for every 16 students. Stationary centrifuges in the same ratio are desirable for microbiology. Space will be needed for incubators—one for every 8 students—and for refrigerators—one for every 16 students.

*Ancillary Facilities*

Each discipline sharing the low-bench teaching laboratory must have certain ancillary facilities available.

Space for the preparation of microscope slides is necessary for any laboratory in which histology and pathology are taught. Preferably,

**Table 1**   Summary space allocations—10 hypothetical schools

| | Size of entering class | | | | | | | | | |
| | In schools with facilities for all basic sciences | | | | | In schools with facilities for clinically oriented basic sciences only | | | | |
| Type of area | 112 | 96 | 80 | 64 | 48 | 112 | 97 | 80 | 64 | 48 |
|---|---|---|---|---|---|---|---|---|---|---|
| Net square feet—all areas | 215,545 | 185,875 | 165,205 | 141,135 | 122,175 | 156,220 | 134,400 | 120,230 | 104,700 | 89,51( |
| Basic science facilities | 60,600 | 53,750 | 47,200 | 39,250 | 25,500 | 11,250 | 9,900 | 8,750 | 7,650 | 6,65( |
| Teaching laboratory and ancillary facilities | 22,600 | 19,950 | 17,300 | 14,550 | 12,200 | 5,900 | 5,100 | 4,400 | 3,700 | 3,00( |
| Special laboratory facilities | 1,900 | 1,900 | 1,900 | 1,900 | 1,900 | 700 | 700 | 700 | 700 | 70( |
| Faculty offices and research laboratories | 17,100 | 14,400 | 12,300 | 9,000 | 8,100 | 2,100 | 1,800 | 1,500 | 1,200 | 90( |
| Graduate study and research areas | 6,100 | 5,400 | 4,600 | 3,400 | 2,800 | 750 | 600 | 450 | 450 | 45( |
| Other departmental facilities | 12,900 | 12,300 | 11,100 | 10,500 | 10,500 | 1,800 | 1,700 | 1,700 | 1,600 | 1,60( |
| Clinical (and preclinical) facilities | 88,375 | 73,585 | 67,425 | 59,665 | 51,205 | 88,375 | 73,585 | 67,425 | 59,665 | 51,20: |
| Operatories and ancillary facilities | 53,475 | 44,385 | 40,325 | 36,865 | 32,305 | 53,475 | 44,385 | 41,325 | 36,865 | 32,30! |
| Laboratories and ancillary facilities | 18,800 | 16,400 | 14,000 | 11,400 | 8,800 | 18,800 | 16,400 | 14,000 | 11,400 | 8,80( |
| Faculty offices and research areas | 13,200 | 10,600 | 10,600 | 9,400 | 8,200 | 13,200 | 10,600 | 10,000 | 9,400 | 8,20( |
| Graduate study and research areas | 2,900 | 2,200 | 2,100 | 2,000 | 1,900 | 2,900 | 2,200 | 2,100 | 2,000 | 1,90( |
| Common facilities | 31,570 | 28,440 | 23,780 | 19,820 | 16,670 | 24,395 | 22,615 | 19,455 | 16,985 | 14,55: |
| Lecture rooms | 7,100 | 6,200 | 4,900 | 4,000 | 3,100 | 5,300 | 4,600 | 3,700 | 3,000 | 2,30( |
| Library | 10,780 | 9,950 | 9,120 | 8,290 | 7,560 | 10,780 | 9,950 | 9,120 | 8,290 | 7,56( |
| ETV and visual aids | 4,790 | 4,590 | 3,660 | 2,830 | 2,510 | 4,190 | 4,090 | 3,260 | 2,520 | 2,32( |
| ETV | 2,650 | 2,550 | 2,200 | 1,650 | 1,500 | 2,550 | 2,550 | 2,200 | 1,650 | 1,50( |
| Visual aids | 2,140 | 2,040 | q,460 | 1,180 | 1,010 | 1,640 | 1,540 | 1,060 | 870 | 82( |
| Special supporting facilities for laboratories and clinics | 8,900 | 7,700 | 6,100 | 4,700 | 3,500 | 4,125 | 3,975 | 3,375 | 3,175 | 2,37: |
| Animal quarters | 6,900 | 5,700 | 4,700 | 3,500 | 2,500 | 2,525 | 2,375 | 2,275 | 2,175 | 1,57: |
| Technical shops | 2,000 | 2,000 | 1,400 | 1,200 | 1,000 | 1,600 | 1,600 | 1,100 | 1,000 | 80( |
| General supporting facilities | 35,000 | 20,900 | 26,800 | 22,300 | 18,800 | 32,200 | 28,300 | 24,600 | 20,400 | 17,10( |
| Administration | 5,700 | 5,300 | 4,900 | 4,300 | 3,800 | 5,500 | 5,100 | 4,700 | 4,100 | 3,60( |
| Special facilities for students and faculty | 13,600 | 12,100 | 10,300 | 8,700 | 7,300 | 12,000 | 10,700 | 9,100 | 7,700 | 6,50( |
| General maintenance and building services | 15,700 | 13,500 | 11,600 | 9,300 | 7,700 | 14,700 | 12,500 | 10,800 | 8,600 | 7,00( |

this area consists of two interconnecting rooms. In one, the embedding room, tissue is processed and embedded in paraffin. This room should have two counters, 31 inches in height, one to be used as a workbench for preparing and processing specimens and the other for mixing solutions. Placing a plain worktable at one end of the paraffin oven provides an efficient arrangement for the embedding procedures. For easy access from either side, the worktable should be located near the center of the room. Wall cabinets for storing solutions and other supplies should be provided.

The second room is used for sectioning, staining, and storing the completed slides. Counters 31 inches high and 2 feet wide should be provided in this room. Each work station at the counter should have knee space of sufficient width and a base unit with drawers for storing blank slides. All of the countertops in these slide preparation rooms should be resilient and stain-resistant.

For microbiology, a media preparation room should be provided adjacent to the teaching laboratory. Usually the work of a trained technician, media preparation requires space for several items of equipment, including a range or hot plates for cooking the material, an autoclave for sterilizing test tubes and media, a refrigerator for storage of culture media, and often an incubator for testing the steril ity of media prior to use. This area should be dust free. Wall counter: 37 inches high, equipped with base cabinets and air, gas, distille( water and electrical outlets, are needed both in the kitchen area an( in the area where media are transferred to test tubes. In the latte burette stands are normally placed on the counter top.

A fairly large area for glassware washing and sterilization shoul( adjoin the teaching laboratory. Commercial glass-washing and dry ing machines, an autoclave, and often a hot air sterilizer must be accommodated, as well as sink and drainboards, space for storing the carts which carry glassware and Petri dishes to and from the area, an( a worktable for glassware storage.

Storage rooms for chemicals, glassware, equipment, and other mate rials are necessary. Among the items of portable equipment whicl may be used and will require space for storage are water baths, incu bators, and spectrophotometers.

An animal holding room where small animals may be held for obser vation or experimentation completes the list of the larger ancillar areas required in conjunction with this laboratory.

### Special Facilities

Additional facilities which are of special value for research and teaching in the low-bench disciplines include a cold room and electron microscope setup.

The cold room is essentially a refrigerator room. It contains counter space and sink for work that must be done at low temperatures. Safety door latches and warning lights are mandatory features.

An electron microscope unit requires at least three rooms: one to house the microscope itself, another for slide preparation, and a darkroom for developing, enlarging, and printing electron micrographs.

## HIGH-BENCH DISCIPLINES

### Teaching Laboratory

The disciplines which share the high-bench teaching laboratory are those for which laboratory work requires that the student stand and move about to perform experiments. These include physiology (the study of the process of living organisms), pharmacology (the science of drugs), and biochemistry (the study of the chemical compounds and processes occurring in organisms).

### Laboratory Benches and Arrangement

Laboratory benches are usually 37 inches high. Stools of adjustable height are provided. Except for their height, benches may be similar in design and arrangement to those in the low-bench laboratory. The four-position bench has particular merit because much of the work, especially in physiology, consists of special projects undertaken by a team of four students.

### Work Station at the Bench

The student's work station is also similar to that in the low bench lab. Each station should have a base cabinet with both drawer and cupboard space. Adequate knee room should be provided, even though students stand a good share of the time.

Hot, cold, and distilled water should be available at each bench position. Gas and electricity are also required. In addition, low-voltage direct current and control circuits should be available from a central panel.

### Bench Tops

Bench tops should be of stone or of acid-resistant composition stone because of the reagents used in biochemistry.

### Sit-down Work Area

Low counters, with resilient counter tops, and under-counter cabinets are placed along one or more of the laboratory walls. Gas, hot and cold water, air, and electric outlets will be needed, and countertop sinks should be equipped with knee- or foot-operated valves for hand-washing. Stools with adjustable seats should be provided.

### Demonstration Area

The demonstration space and equipment are like that of the low-bench lab. In addition, physiology teaching makes extensive use of electric polygraphs and the Van Slyke machines, often to the extent of one to each four students. If the unit laboratory is used, no demonstration area is necessary since each unit can easily accommodate demonstrations.

### Stationary Equipment

For every 16 students one fume hood should be provided. Because flammable and explosive chemicals are used, the hoods should be installed a safe distance from fire exits. Burette stands, approximately 5 feet in length, are used by both biochemistry and pharmacology students. One to every 16 students is an accepted ratio.

### Movable Equipment

A great variety of movable equipment may be used. A few movable tables of stand-up height may be required for some of the experiments in pharmacology and physiology involving animals. Table tops are of laminated wood with a stain resistant finish, and a shelf is provided for storing animal boards. In addition, a deep-freeze unit, centrifuges, refrigerators, incubators, and much of the electronic apparatus used in physiology are part of the movable equipment used in the laboratory for which space is required. First aid kits and blankets are necessary, although these generally occupy no floor space but are mounted on the wall.

### Ancillary Facilities

Both biochemistry and pharmacology require a preparation room adjacent to the teaching laboratory for mixing reagents and storing chemicals and glassware. Storage and washing facilities are included in this room. Wall counters similar to those in the teaching laboratory and wall cabinets permit this room to be used as a research area during off periods.

Each discipline requires storage and supply areas, some of them special in nature. Special provisions must be made, for example, for storing anesthetics. Although only a limited supply of cylinders holding oxygen or anesthetics should be kept here (additional storage should be allotted at ground level), the storage area should be located along an exterior wall, with floor and ceiling louvers installed to provide gravity ventilation. The room should be locked. For chemical storage areas, fire hazards must be minimized. Narcotics require locked storage. Generally, rooms used to store instruments and equipment should be amply supplied with electrical outlets so that equipment can be used without being removed from the room.

Animal rooms and cold rooms are among the other facilities used regularly in conjunction with the teaching program of the high-bench laboratory.

### Special Facilities

Many of the special facilities used for research and teaching in the high-bench disciplines require unusual construction or safety features.

The *chromatography* room is a biochemistry research laboratory where various processes are employed to separate organic substances. In laboratories where paper or column chromatography is performed, fume hoods capable of exhausting toxic or inflammable vapors are required, and the laboratory must be maintained under negative air pressure to prevent the spread of vapors. Where gas chromatography is used, it must also be possible to seal off the laboratory in the event of fire. Some instruments used in this laboratory depend upon radioactivity as an ionization source; if these are installed, safeguards must be provided, even though the radioactivity level is low.

In the *ultracentrifuge* room, another small laboratory often used in biochemistry research, the selection of equipment will largely determine the requirements. Depending upon its anticipated use, the ultracentrifuge may be either electrically powered or air driven. At least part of the housing for this equipment is of heavy armor plate. Additional cooling may be needed in the room to offset heat produced by operation of the equipment.

*Constant-temperature* rooms, or controlled temperature rooms, as they are sometimes called, are used to house small animals under constant temperature and humidity conditions. The work area in this room usually consists of 31-inch-high counters, with a sink and outlet for gas, air, and electricity. Space may be needed for counter-top food storage. At least one floor drain will be required so that the room may be completely washed down.

## Anatomy

### Dissection Room

Dissection tables are the basic laboratory equipment. They are approximately 24 by 78 inches. Aisles at the table sides should be 5 feet wide and those at the ends 3 feet-6 inches.

Dissection rooms are, as a rule, planned to accommodate full classes. Though class size largely determines room size, space should be allowed to accommodate a few additional tables for use by graduate students and for demonstrations (see Fig. 7).

Good table lighting is essential. Often, adjustable lighting fixtures are attached to both sides of each table. If tables are on casters cleaning of the room will be considerably easier.

The dissection room should be equipped with an adequate number of hand basins.

Round, industrial sinks are a good choice, since they accommodate more students simultaneously than those of standard design. One sink for every four tables is an accepted ratio.

The dissection room should include counter units with drawers and cupboards for storing students' instruments. Storage space should also be provided for such supplies as wood blocks, mallets, arm rests, and embalming fluids.

Because of the odor of the preserving fluids, air conditioning with a 100 percent air exhaust should be provided in the dissection room.

As the anatomy dissection room is frequently washed down, durable, waterproof flooring is required. Providing storage space for the dissection tables will make it possible to use the dissection room for other purposes.

### Ancillary Facilities

Several additional rooms either near or adjacent to the dissection room are required. Storage space for cadavers must be provided and bone storage space will also be needed. If neuroanatomy is taught in the dissection room, storage for gross specimens must be available, too.

Generally, schools will need sufficient storage capacity for 1.5 cadavers for every four ECS. If the school policy is to hold cadavers for one year prior to use, storage requirements will double. Cadavers are commonly stored in large walk-in refrigerators. Because the method of preservation and storage affects ancillary space requirements, the system to be used should be determined early in the programming stage, and specifics should be worked out with the aid of qualified consultants.

A room equipped for embalming is often provided, though dental schools with access to medical school facilities will probably need only a minimum of space for this purpose. As for final disposal, cadavers are usually cremated. The dental school can either provide its own crematory for this purpose, share facilities with a medical school, or arrange periodic transfer of cadavers to public facilities for cremation.

Because it should never be necessary to move cadavers through public areas, facilities for cadaver storage and embalming should be as near as possible to the dissection room, and all three should be located at ground level. Wherever practical, loading platforms should open directly into the cadaver storage area to facilitate delivery and removal.

## PRECLINICAL FACILITIES

### The Preclinical Laboratory

The preclinical laboratory is designed to accommodate the entire class of freshman or sophomore students in a single session (see Fig. 8).

Though it is not often so-called, the preclinical laboratory is actually a multidiscipline laboratory, for all the preclinical dental science courses are taught here: the instructors of the several subjects take over the laboratory in turn while the students remain in their assigned places.

### Seating

In the arrangement most common to preclinical laboratories, students sit on each side of a bench, their backs to those of students at the next row of benches. The aisles separating the rows are at least 4 feet-6 inches wide, so that the instructor may move easily between the benches as he inspects the students' work.

In some of the newer laboratories, benches are arranged so that all students face in one direction—usually toward the instructor's podium. The aisles between benches—a 3-foot-minimum is satisfactory—are not as wide as those required for back-to-back seating. On the other hand, back-to-back seating is economical. It conserves floor space and reduces the cost of bench work and utilities.

In either of the two seating plans, high or low benches can be used, but the low bench—32 inches in height—will perhaps be the more satisfactory. With low benches, a standard adjustable typing chair on casters can be used and is less costly than the laboratory stool. All benches should be equipped with gas, air, and duplex electrical receptacles. Each student station at the bench should be at least 3 feet wide, and 3 feet-6 inches is actually more satisfactory. If the latter figure is used, an over-all allowance of 38 square feet per student position will provide adequately for the teaching facilities.

Every preclinical technic laboratory should provide the instructor with a table or desk, equipped with gas, air, and electricity for demon-

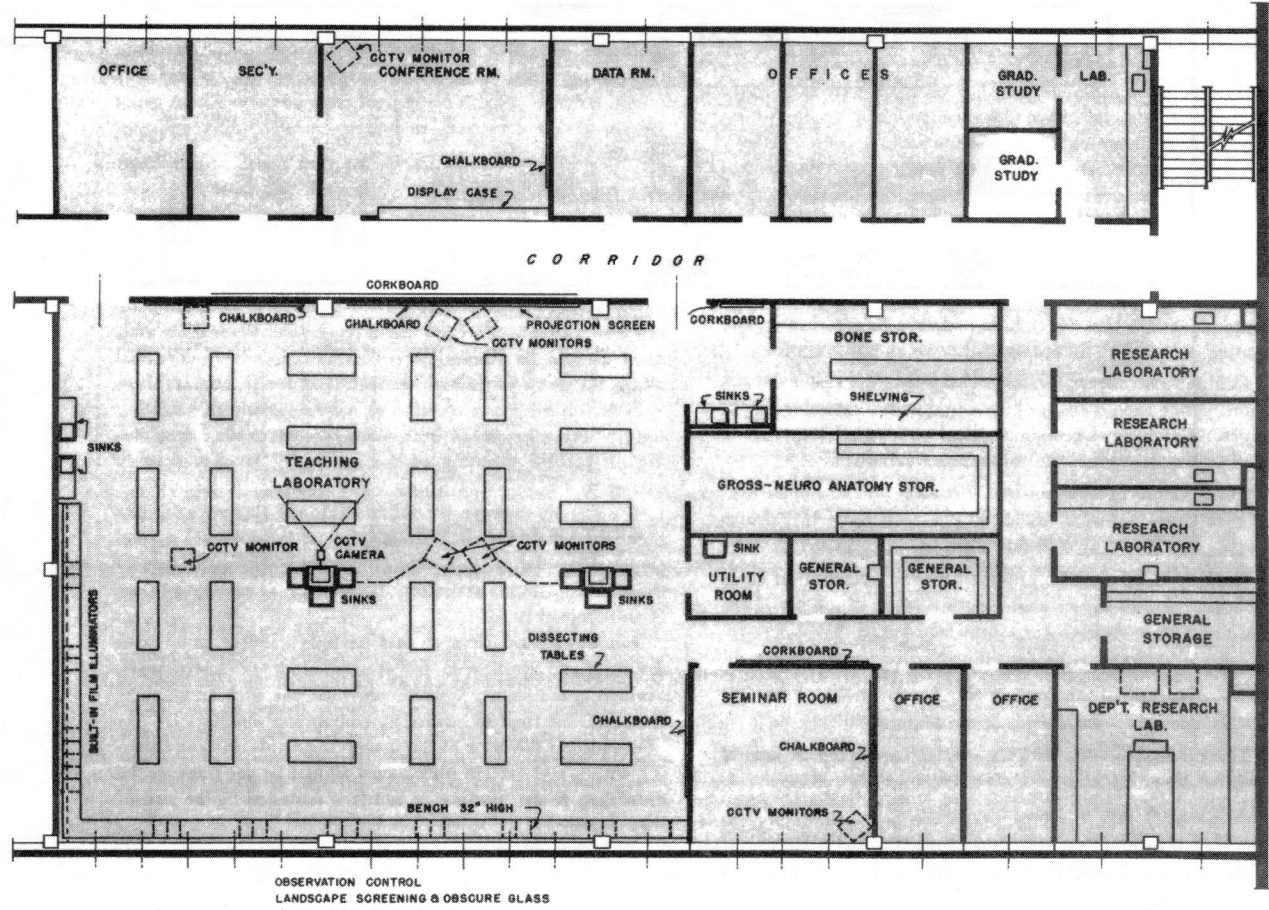

**Fig. 7. Layout of anatomy laboratory of class size**

stration purposes. In large classes which require more than one instructor, each should be allotted desk space.

*Ancillary Facilities*

To reduce the tracking of plaster from the laboratory into the public corridors, the processing room, which is used for pouring wax forms, molds, impressions, and flasks for denture processing, can be located adjacent to the preclinical technic laboratory. Also nearby should be a small storeroom.

*ETV in the Preclinical Laboratory*

Figure 8 shows a preclinical dental technic laboratory of 96 student positions together with an adjoining processing room. Demonstrations within the laboratory are given with closed-circuit television. There are 16 students per monitor. The monitors are also coupled to the television studio of the school.

This layout is also adaptable to the monitoring of students' work by closed-circuit television. In such a system, the picture is relayed to the console at the demonstration position.

While the principal medium of demonstration is ETV, facilities for chalk talks and for projection of motion pictures or slides are provided. Display cases, some of which permit viewing from both sides,

should be provided for models and examples of student work. The laboratory shown has the equipment used in common by students, such as lathes, model trimmers, sinks, ovens and casting machines, located at the perimeter walls.

## THE CLINICS: FUNCTION AND OPERATION

In the clinics, dental students gain experience in the correction and control of dental diseases and disorders. Here, too, the community finds an additional source of dental services, some of which are frequently unobtainable outside the dental school.

*Patient Movement in the Clinics*

Figure 9 illustrates patient movement through the clinics. The new patient first reports to the information desk located in the lobby or main waiting room of the clinic area. He then proceeds to the registration desk, where a case record is opened for him. At the appointment desk, his next stop, he is scheduled for an oral examination.

The patient then undergoes, either on the initial visit or a subsequent one, a screening examination. This procedure enables the school to select patients with varied dental problems.

Following the screening examination, the patient goes to the radiology clinic for full-mouth roentgenograms and then to the diagnostic

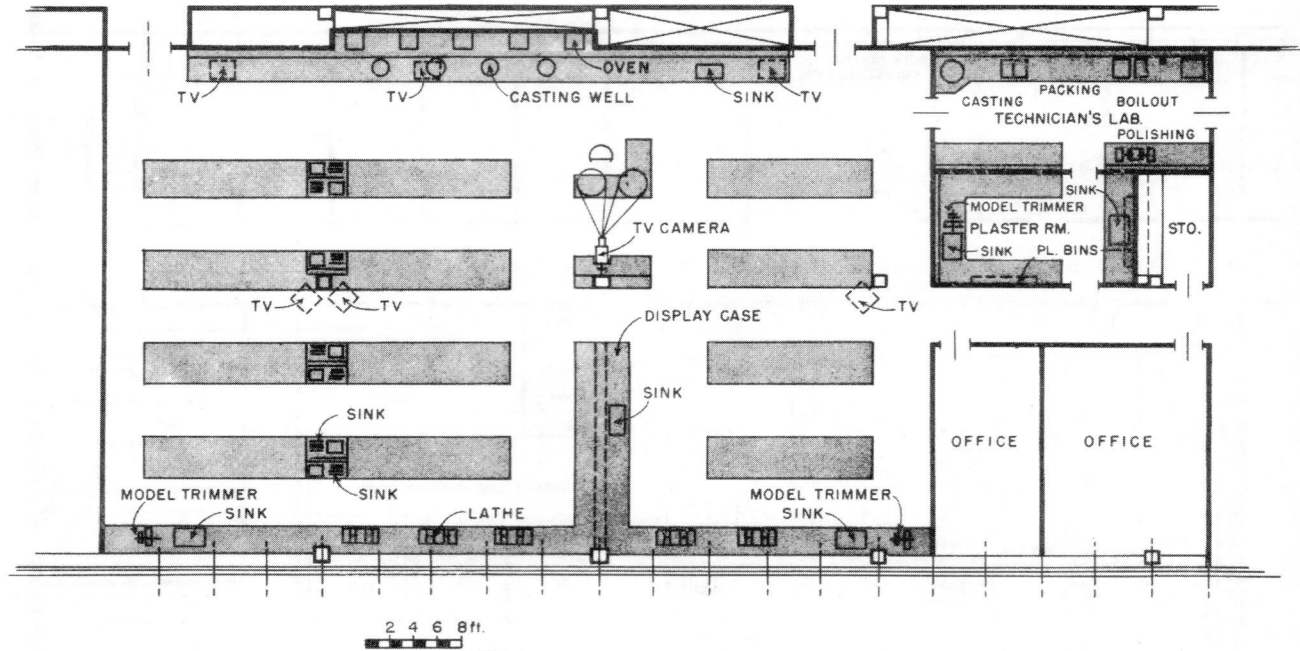

**Fig. 8. Preclinical laboratory of 96 student positions utilizing closed-circuit television for demonstrations**

clinic for a thorough oral examination, performed by a dental student working under the direction of an instructor. When the examination is completed, the patient returns to the appointment desk where he is referred for subsequent visits either to the general dental clinic or to one of the special clinics. On later visits, the patient reports directly to the waiting room of the clinic where he will receive treatment.

*Reception and Screening Area*

The reception area in the main waiting room is the control center of the clinics, coordinating the flow of patients and records to clinics in the treatment area. In addition, the work of the appointment desk is closely coordinated with that of the clinic business off ice.

Frequently the information, registration, and appointment desks are combined, but they may be separate in large schools, or information and registration may be handled at one desk while appointments are

made at a second. Similarly, one or more of these desks may be located either in the main waiting room or in adjacent rooms.

The reception area will require a records office. The convenience with which records can be dispatched to the clinics is an important consideration in the location of the area. However, storage space for inactive records need not be provided here, as these are frequently microfilmed or moved after two years to storage rooms in other areas of the school.

For the screening of new patients, an examination room separate from the diagnostic clinic is desirable. This room should be equipped with dental chairs. Dental units are not necessary unless the room will also be used for emergency treatment.

Emergency treatment rooms function as a part of the reception and screening area. Either a series of single-chair rooms or a large room with two or three dental chairs is practical. Although emergency treatment rooms are sometimes included in each of the clinics in the treatment area, the provision of central facilities is more likely to assure that the rooms are not preempted for some other purpose.

## EXAMINATION, DIAGNOSIS, AND TREATMENT

### Planning Area

It is in the diagnostic and radiology clinics that the incoming patient's need for dental care is determined and a plan of treatment formulated.

### The Diagnostic Clinic

Essential facilities in the diagnostic clinic include operatories or examination rooms, a clinical diagnostic laboratory, and a treatment planning and consultation room. Faculty offices and faculty research areas should be provided nearby.

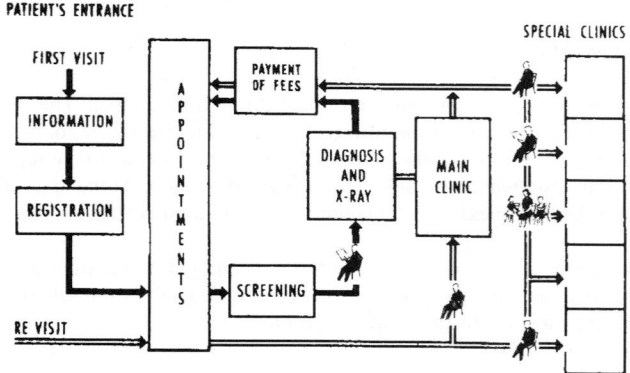

**Fig. 9. Dental clinic flow diagram**

Although multiple-chair rooms are sometimes used for examinations, a series of single-chair rooms assures privacy for the recording of patients' case histories. Each position should be equipped with an x-ray viewer. Estimating that 16 patients can be accommodated daily in each chair, an 8-chair facility could handle over 120 patients each day. In addition to dental chairs, the examination rooms should be furnished with desks for the convenience of those students who are recording case histories.

The clinical diagnostic laboratory is used for hematological and other diagnostic procedures. It is equipped with laboratory benches similar to those used for the low-bench basic science disciplines, but since students are assigned here in blocs, eight positions are usually sufficient. Air, gas, and electricity should be available at each position, and both hot and cold water are desirable. A hand washing sink should also be provided. One stand-up laboratory bench should be located at the outer wall. Because patients seen in this laboratory are referred directly from the diagnostic clinic, no waiting room is needed.

The treatment planning and consultation room, where students and instructors meet to discuss cases, should be equipped with a marker board, demonstration table, projection screen, and x-ray viewer, in addition to a dental chair and unit. The room can also be used for small-group demonstrations.

**Radiology Clinic**

Because roentgenograms are made for every incoming patient, the radiology clinic is included in the examination and diagnostic area. However, the radiology clinic also serves all the other clinics,

and patients undergoing treatment are directed here for additional roentgenograms.

*Shielding Against Radiation*

Rooms containing x-ray machines must be shielded through the use of lead-lined walls and partitions or appropriate building materials of an adequate thickness. In addition, controls for x-ray machines should be located behind shielded partitions.

In general, shielding should be sufficient to limit the exposure of personnel to a minimum amount of radiation, certainly no more than 0.1 roentgen per week. In rooms equipped with 90 kvp x-ray machines, for example, the walls should be shielded with 1.2-mm sheet lead (3 pounds per square foot) to a height of 7 feet. Stone concrete at least 3 inches thick should be used for ceiling and floor.

*Layout of the Clinic*

Figure 10 shows the components and equipment of the radiology clinic. This plan includes eight rooms where the roentgenograms utilized in routine oral examinations are taken, and one extraoral radiology room.

In the radiology rooms, the machine is located behind the dental chair and up to 20 degrees to either side, the recommended position. Observation of the patient is made through a lead glass viewing window which has a speaking slot. Each of the rooms is equipped with a small chalkboard, illuminator, lavatory, and shelf. Room A, slightly larger than the others, has a 4-foot-wide opening to facilitate handling of wheelchair and stretcher patients. The extraoral radiology

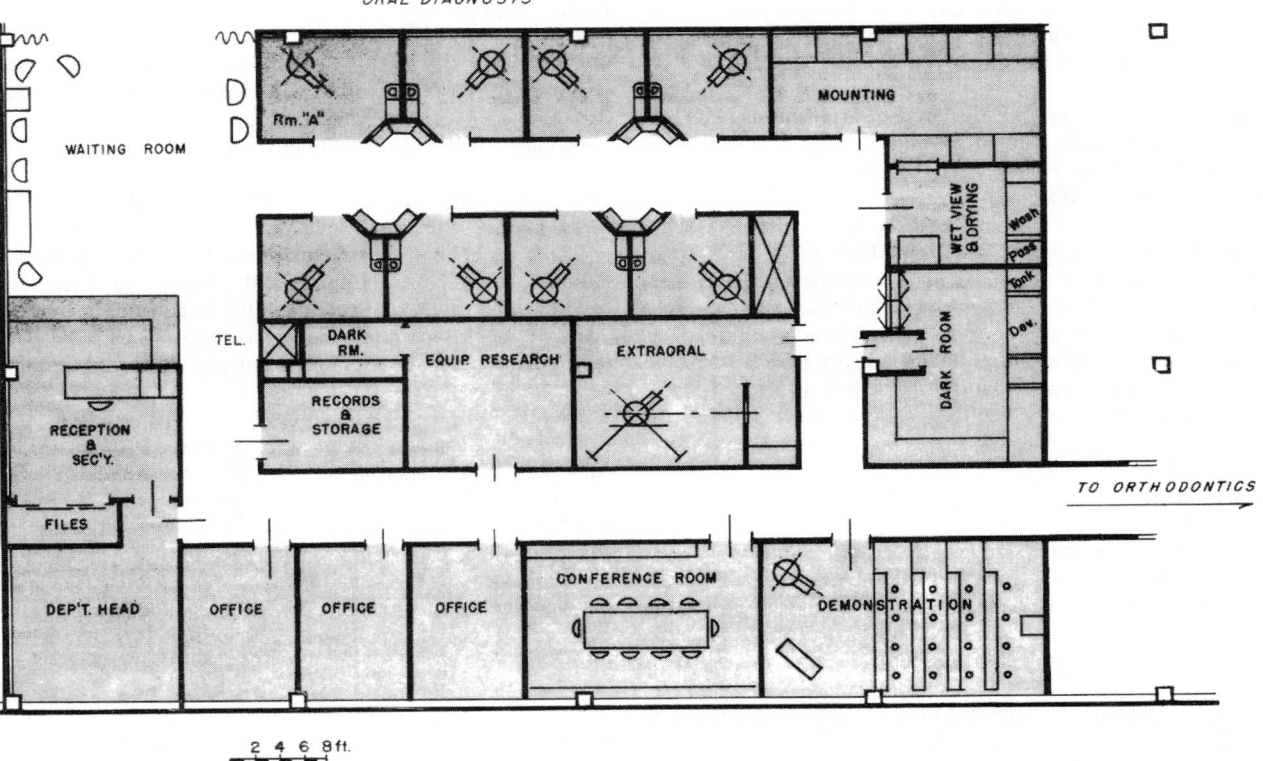

**Fig. 10. Radiology clinic**

room is of slightly greater depth than the intraoral, because a long-focus film distance is required for the facial-profile roentgenogram.

Each of these rooms is lead-shielded, and the x-ray machine controls are located behind lead-protected partitions.

*Film Processing*

A suite of rooms for film processing includes a darkroom, oversized to permit group instruction, a wet viewing and drying room, and a mounting room. A framed opening in the wall between the drying and mounting rooms is used for passage of film. The mounting room accommodates eight students. Each student position has a 14-inch by 17-inch view box built into the surface of the bench.

*Ancillary Facilities*

The special demonstration room, which accommodates 16 students, has provisions for movie and slide projection and closed-circuit television monitors. An exodontist's chair, a mobile x-ray unit, and a mobile lead screen are available for demonstrations. If ETV is used extensively for demonstrations, this room could be converted to a film library.

The departmental research area includes a small darkroom. A conference room, suitable for seminars and equipped with marker board, projection equipment, and an illuminated viewer, and a group of faculty offices complete the radiology clinic.

## TREATMENT AREA

### General Clinic

Because the general clinic is typically the largest and busiest of all the clinics, the main waiting room and control desks and many of the other elements already described are considered a part of it.

Treatment components include operatories, treatment planning and consultation rooms, supply and dispensing services, and sterilization and sterile supply facilities. Study and laboratory areas for the use of graduate students should adjoin.

The operatories, or work stations, into which all the clinics are divided, consist of dental chairs and units, instrument cabinets, sterilization units, and other necessary equipment. Each station should be large enough to accommodate the patient, the student who is treating him, the supervising instructor, and frequently a dental assistant. Several fully partitioned work stations should be provided to accommodate patients whose emotional reaction to dental care makes privacy mandatory.

### Special Clinics

The special clinics—periodontic-endodontic, orthodontic, and others— are differentiated primarily by the type of treatment rendered. One, however, is distinguished by the type of patient treated—the chronically ill, the mentally disturbed, and others who are unable to receive treatment under regular clinical conditions.

The same departmental facilities and most of the treatment facilities required in the general clinic are needed for each of the special clinics. Every special clinic should have at least one fully partitioned work station. Generally, each will have a small waiting room with

control desks separate from the main waiting room. However, related specialties such as pedodontics and orthodontics often share a waiting room.

*Specific Requirements*

Except for some variations in the design of the instrument cabinet, the basic equipment of the special clinics is the same as that of the general clinic. Most of the special clinics are equipped with standard dental chairs and units. The pedodontic clinic, however, requires a smaller chair and the oral surgery clinic special chairs or operating tables. And a few of the special clinics require additional components and highly specialized equipment. Clinics where general anesthetics are administered must have recovery rooms and toilets. A ceramics laboratory is sometimes maintained in the crown and bridge clinic.

The orthodontic clinic requires a number of special facilities. Among these are a measure room, a record room, a tracing room with a light table for routine tracing, and an office for technical personnel. This clinic usually contains two or more rooms with specialized equipment. At least one dental chair which can be used when general anesthetics are administered is required.

Frequently facilities for periodontic and endodontic treatment and for oral medicines are combined in one clinic. If x-ray machines are provided, the clinic must be shielded in the same manner as the radiology clinic or a lead-lined partition provided around the x-ray machines.

## Oral Surgery Clinic: A Special Case

Perhaps the greatest variation in the components and equipment is found in the oral surgery clinic.

Figure 11 illustrates an oral surgery department planned to accommodate blocs of eight students. Eight of its nine operatories are equipped for surgery requiring local anesthetics. Six of these, grouped in threes, are semienclosed. Folding partitions make full enclosure possible.

Of the three remaining operatories, the largest is equipped with an x-ray machine. Centrally located to the other operatories, this room is lead-lined. The demonstration operatory is equipped for cases requiring general anesthesia as well as local. So is the adjacent operatory (upper right). In addition, the demonstration operatory is designed for closed-circuit television. A glass-enclosed gallery can be used for observation of treatment procedures, or as a control booth for television.

Both of the operatories equipped for general anesthesia are located adjacent to their supporting facilities. A scrub-up area is provided at the entrances. Nearby is the recovery area containing bunks and toilet facilities. A glass partitioned nurses station permits observation of patients. Also conveniently located are the sterilizing and sterile supply rooms, which serve only this clinic. Of the two rooms provided for storage of medication, one is used for narcotics and other medicines which must be kept locked.

*Ancillary Facilities*

Student facilities include a locker room with toilet, located near the secondary exit from the main operational area. The combination graduate student study area and laboratory accommodates four students. It

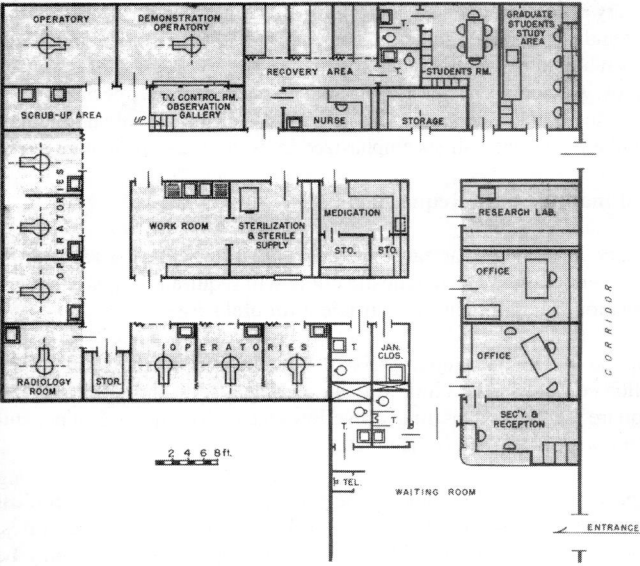

**Fig. 11. Oral surgery department**

contains desks, lockers, and a laboratory bench with a sink and electrical outlets. Locating the two administrative offices at the entrance to the clinic permits greater control and accessibility. A departmental research laboratory is provided, as in other clinical departments.

A patient waiting room seating 16 people would be adequate in a clinic of this type. Toilet rooms should be provided nearby. Although patients would normally enter and leave the clinic through the main waiting room, a secondary exit is provided for those requiring assistance after surgery.

*Central Supply and Dispensing Services*

Although each clinic in the treatment area will have its own small supply facilities, centralized service is necessary for the receiving and distribution of bulk supplies. Locating the central service near the clinics will permit greater efficiency. In a multistory building, stacking the smaller units on different floors will simplify the placement of service elevators and dumbwaiters.

*Clinical Laboratories*

Most schools today believe the provision of two large general laboratories of full-class size—one for the juniors, one for the seniors—to be the most effective. Small separate laboratories in each of the special clinics are also a possibility. Schools should make every effort to see to it that each junior and senior student is provided with assigned, individually locked cupboards and supply drawers.

If the full-class laboratory for each of the upper classes can be provided, the design and layout will be approximately the same as that of the freshman-sophomore preclinical laboratories. Though no special demonstration position need be set aside, facilities for ETV should be included.

The processing laboratory, which contains special equipment such as heavy duty ovens, boil out tanks, and packing and curing units, must be large enough to accommodate not only students but the dental laboratory technicians employed by the school.

## CLINICS: SPACE ALLOCATIONS AND RELATIONSHIP

Dental educators today favor the adoption of the cubicle clinic. The privacy of the cubicle, a factor appreciated by patients as well as students, and the overall atmosphere of the cubicle clinic engender self-confidence and efficiency on the part of the student (see Figs. 12 and 13).

### Planning the Cubicle Clinic

*Influence of Dental Assistants*

Cubicles accommodating the student-assistant team must be narrower and deeper than those in which a student works alone. The size (7 feet-6 inches by 7 feet-6 inches) and the arrangement of the cubicle in Fig. 15a, with the instrument panel at the right of the operator, is satisfactory for the dental student working alone.

The cubicles in Figs. 15b and c are planned for utilization of assistants. The cubicle in Fig. 15b, which is 6 feet-9 inches by 9 feet-2 inches, is slightly narrower and deeper than the one in Fig. 15a. The added depth of the cubicle in Fig. 15b permits the location of the instrument cabinet and sink at the rear of the cubicle, convenient to the operator and the assistant. Figure 15c is another variation, adaptable to the 4-feet-8-inch planning module.

A cubicle clinic designed for utilization of auxiliary personnel is illustrated by Fig. 14. The location of the main and secondary aisles permits the instructor to move from one work station to another without retracing his steps.

### Cubicle Dimensions

Cubicles in existing dental schools range in size from 6 feet-4 inches by 7 feet to 7 feet-8 inches by 9 feet-6 inches. Where dental assistants will be used, a cubicle of 6 feet-9 inches by 9 feet-6 inches is desirable. For students working alone, a cubicle of 7 feet 6 inches by 7 feet-6 inches is adequate.

Cubicles may be either partially or fully enclosed. A partition height of approximately 5 feet is recommended for most cubicles. This provides privacy, yet allows for supervision and gives an impression of

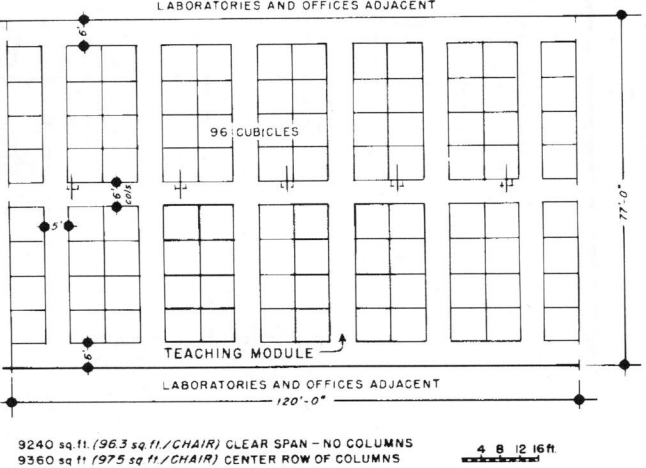

**Fig. 12. Cubicle clinic**

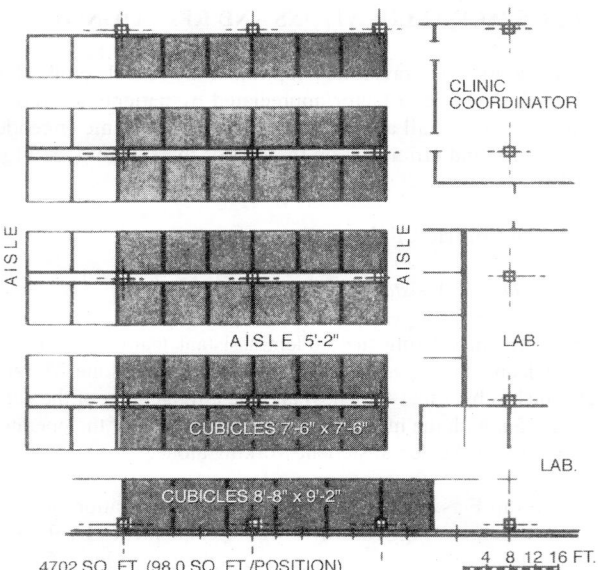

**Fig. 13. Variation of cubicle clinic**

spaciousness. A 4-foot partition topped by a 1-foot-high glazed panel may be used. Allowing an open space between partition and floor facilitates cleaning. However, one or two fully enclosed cubicles are desirable in every clinic.

### Determining the Number of Clinic Positions

For the clinics as a whole, at least two operating positions should be provided for every entering class student—one in the general clinic and one in the group of special clinics.

Every school should also plan additional clinic positions for its graduate and postgraduate students. The equivalent of one student module is desirable in the general clinic for even a modest program of advanced study. Additional positions will also be needed in the special clinics, with the number dependent upon the goals of the school and the particular dental specialities emphasized in its graduate curriculum.

### Estimating Space Requirements

Space allowances for each operating position will also vary in the different clinics. The diagnostic clinic will require 85 square feet per position, an allotment also sufficient for oral surgery.

In the radiology clinic, 115 square feet per position should be allowed, and in the clinic for the chronically ill and disabled, 125 square feet. For other clinics, an allowance of 100 square feet per student position should be adequate.

Space allowance for some of the supporting facilities of the clinical departments will be fairly standard. For demonstration operatories, for example, a uniform allowance of 200 square feet each may be used.

## INSTRUCTION ROOMS, STUDY AREAS, AND LIBRARY FACILITIES

### Seminars

The seminar is a room especially planned to accommodate small-group instruction for 16 students or less, usually at an advanced level of training.

In most schools, one or more seminar rooms will be needed for the use of each basic science department—at least one for instruction and perhaps one for departmental conferences.

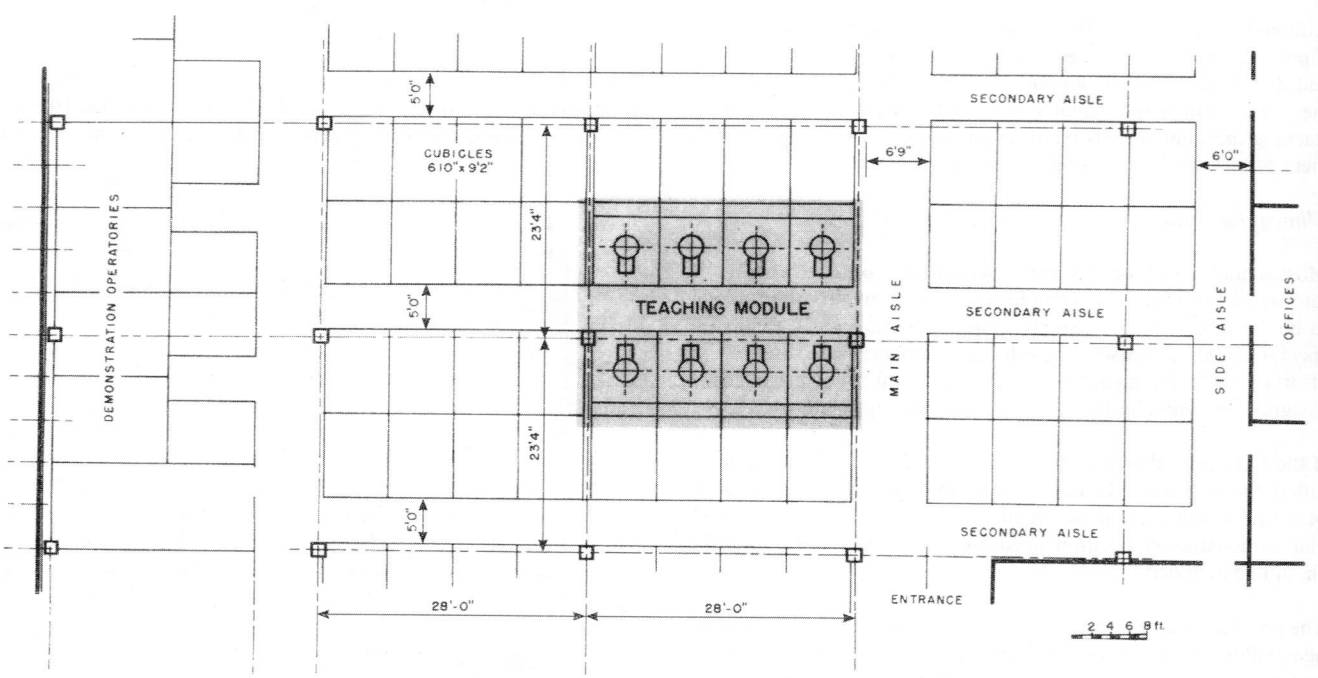

**Fig. 14. Cubicle clinic for utilizing dental auxiliary personnel**

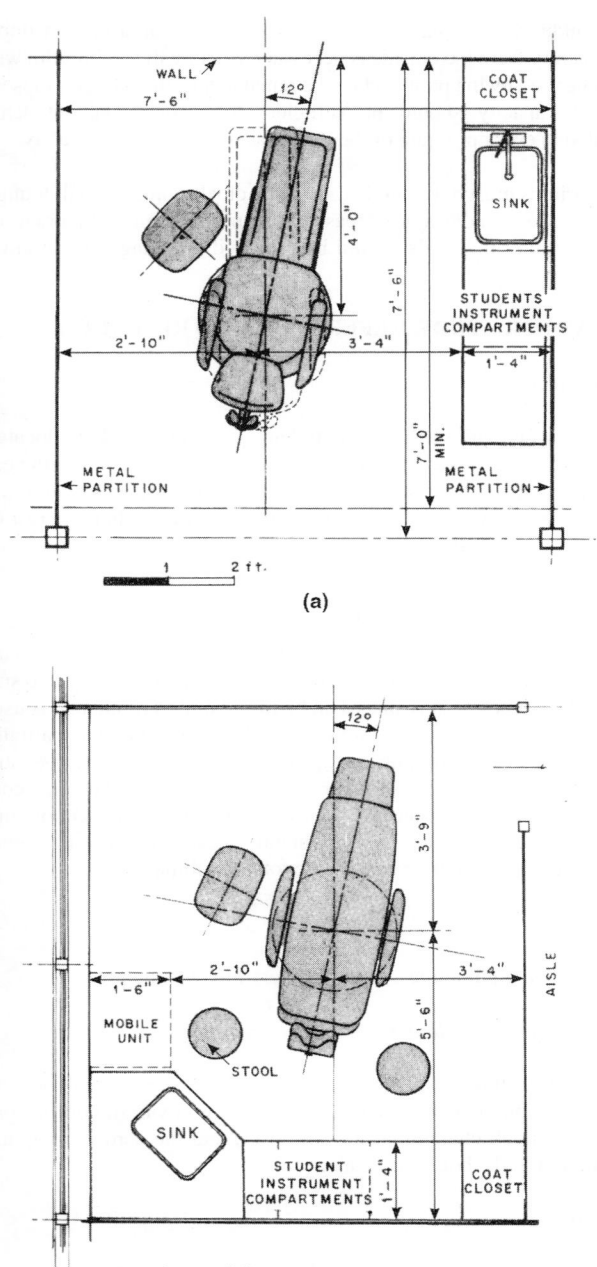

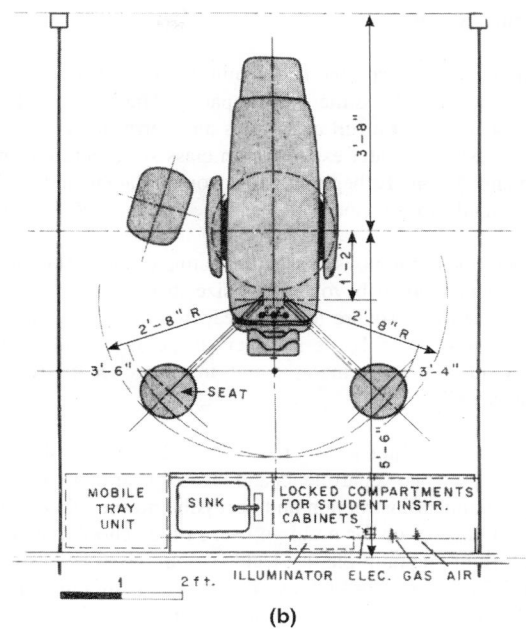

**Fig. 15.** (*a*) Cubicle for student working alone; (*b*) Cubicle for student and assistant; (*c*) Variation for student assistant team

In the clinical facilities of most schools, each of the special clinics will need one seminar room for treatment planning and consultation, and the general clinic will need more than one. In programming, a reasonable standard for the general clinic would allow four rooms for a class size of 96, increasing or decreasing the number by one for each 16-student module added or subtracted.

Allow a minimum of 300 square feet for each seminar room, with increments of 75 square feet for every four students beyond the 16 accommodated in the standard room.

Seating arrangements in seminar rooms are a matter of choice. Usually the instructor and his students sit around a central table, but some seminar rooms are furnished with standard tablet-arm chairs. Unitized folding tables and folding chairs permit maximum flexibility in seating arrangements, however, and their use is increasing, especially in the seminar room used for showing slides, 16 mm films, and other visual aids. If it is so used, a small adjoining room for storage of visual aid materials is also helpful. A seminar, like any other instruction room, should be equipped with a chalkboard.

## Lecture Rooms

Although they accommodate a minimum of 50 people, all lecture rooms need not have the same capacity. The smallest should, however, seat at least a full class, plus an overrun of 20 percent. If the school expects a later expansion in class size, lecture rooms should be planned from the beginning to accommodate it, and the 20 percent overrun allowance should also be based on the larger figure.

A good rule of thumb is to provide seating capacity for one additional 16-student module beyond class size in schools with 96 ECS. An allowance of 12 square feet per seat (roughly 200 square feet for a student module of 16) is sufficient to permit an adequate aisle on either side of the seating area and, in a large lecture room, a center aisle as well.

A minimum of three lecture rooms should be provided, one for use of the basic science departments and located near them, one for clinical and preclinical instruction and accessible to the clinics, and one for special courses or for multiple use. In the school that will have no auditorium, the multiple-use lecture room might be designed to provide 2.5 positions per ECS. All lecture rooms should be located so as to minimize noise and traffic congestion in the corridors.

### Layout

It may be difficult to decide whether the lecture room should be long and relatively narrow, like the usual hall, or wider and shallower, like an amphitheater. Because of its wide viewing angle, the amphitheater is not particularly suitable for the showing of slides and films. On the other hand, instructors favoring the chalk talk technique often dislike a long room. Television monitors can be used in either type.

Every lecture room should be equipped with a large marker board; a minimum of 12 linear feet is recommended. If, because of the size of the room, a raised platform is provided, it should be long enough to extend 2 feet beyond each end of the chalkboard. Projection screens which can be automatically lowered and raised may also be a part of the permanent equipment.

The floors of lecture rooms should be sloped or terraced slightly to provide a good view of the marker boards and projection screen.

Some larger lecture rooms are split level or have a balcony. Whenever possible, students should enter from the rear.

### Furnishings

Fixed or movable tablet-arm chairs, or auditorium seats equipped with tablet arms, are commonly found in lecture rooms. If the latter are used, the aisle seat at the left of each row can be fitted with an outside tablet arm for the use of left-handed students. Writing counters with individual seats are also frequently used.

### Auditoriums

For schools that have ready access to them, auditoriums sometimes serve as lecture or examination rooms. As a rule, however, programming committees will find it difficult to justify a large auditorium solely for the use of a dental school, since it is generally more economical to rent a hall for occasions such as graduations which require large seating capacity.

If an auditorium is planned, it should be located on a ground floor. Direct entry from the outside is necessary, because the auditorium will often be used by the public when the remainder of the school is closed. Seating capacity should be sufficient to accommodate students enrolled in every program of the school as well as the total faculty.

Auditoriums must have public toilets and cloakrooms; a small lounge off the foyer is advisable. Areas for the preparation and storage of demonstration materials should be provided backstage, as should a toilet room.

## AREAS FOR STUDY, REFERENCE, AND RESEARCH

### Study Areas

Places for first and second year students should probably be located near the basic science laboratories, and those for third and fourth year students near the clinics. If possible, they should be so situated that students will have access to them at all times, even when the rest of the school is closed.

### Space

About 19 square feet per ECS should be allowed in planning standard study places for a school providing one study place for every two students. This type of study place can be in a common room and is usually unassigned. However, some schools may prefer the partially partitioned cubicle. Requiring approximately 48 square feet per student position, the cubicles are furnished with a desk and chair, a coat locker, and storage space for books, microscopes, and school supplies. Because a cubicle is permanently assigned to each student, space requirements are based on the total enrollment.

### Library Facilities

The following guidelines, though general, may be helpful.

### Reading and Study Rooms

The main reading room should accommodate from 25 to 50 percent of the total number of students. Reading room exits should be controlled by book charge-out or loan desks, and the card catalog and circulation desk should be nearby.

### Carrels

Unenclosed desk areas of about 12 square feet are useful for individual study and should be available in the ratio of one for every 10 students. Small study rooms reserved for graduate and postdoctoral students are also an advantage. Either they should be soundproofed or located far enough away from the main reading room to permit students to use computers without disturbing others.

### Microfilm

Auxiliary facilities such as a microfilm reading room, a sound tape room, and a rare book room are also desirable.

### Stacks

Stacks should be arranged to facilitate both storage and use of books. The stacks should be located as close to reading rooms as possible, preferably at or below the level of the main reading room.

Stack area varies in proportion to volumes. Generous allowances should always be made for future expansion. Stack sections are usually 3 feet in length and 7 feet-6 inches in height, with a shelf depth of at least 10 inches. One single-faced section 3 feet long will accommodate approximately 100 volumes. Service aisles between stacks should be at least 3 feet wide, and the main aisles at least 3 feet-8 inches wide. A microfilm room for processing and storage may be associated with the stack area.

*Other Facilities*

Acquisition and catalog rooms should be near the public card catalog and have direct access to the stacks.

Offices should be provided for the head librarian and an assistant, with the head librarian's office accessible both to staff rooms and to readers. Storage space for office supplies should be available.

A library stocked with 25,000 volumes and amply supplied with space for reading rooms and auxiliary facilities would require approximately 10,000 square feet for a school with 96 ECS.

## EDUCATIONAL TELEVISION AND OTHER VISUAL AIDS

The location of the ETV department should be carefully chosen to hold distribution distances to a minimum. A top floor or penthouse would be a logical location. Preferably, the visual aids department should be nearby. The studio should not be less than 1,300 square feet, completely visible from the control room. The ceiling height of the studio (13 to 14 feet) is another factor that must be considered in planning. One area of the studio should contain a dental operatory setup, with chair, unit, and instrument cabinet. A movable (on casters) laboratory demonstration bench will be required for demonstrations of experiments in the basic sciences. The televising of anatomical dissection will require a large overhead mirror. A smaller bench for dental technic demonstration, chalkboards, flip stand, and tack boards are additional requirements. Ample maneuvering area for the television cameras and operators must also be provided. Figure 16 shows an ETV department of approximately 2,500 square feet.

The control room should be elevated and built as close to the ceiling as possible for maximum visibility. Entry into the control room should be possible without going through the studio.

Provision should be made for a film chain installation requiring a room approximately 12 by 15 feet. Kinescope recorders and videotape recorders should be planned for in areas adjoining the control room.

The amount of prop storage space required will vary with the emphasis placed on television and on the availability of other storage areas.

The director and assistant director will require office areas.

**Visual Aids Department**

The increasing use of ETV has not eliminated the need for a complete visual aids department, but has increased it. Figure 16 shows a visual aids department. In larger schools, 18 to 20 square feet per ECS would provide centralized visual aids facilities for both the basic sciences and the dental science divisions.

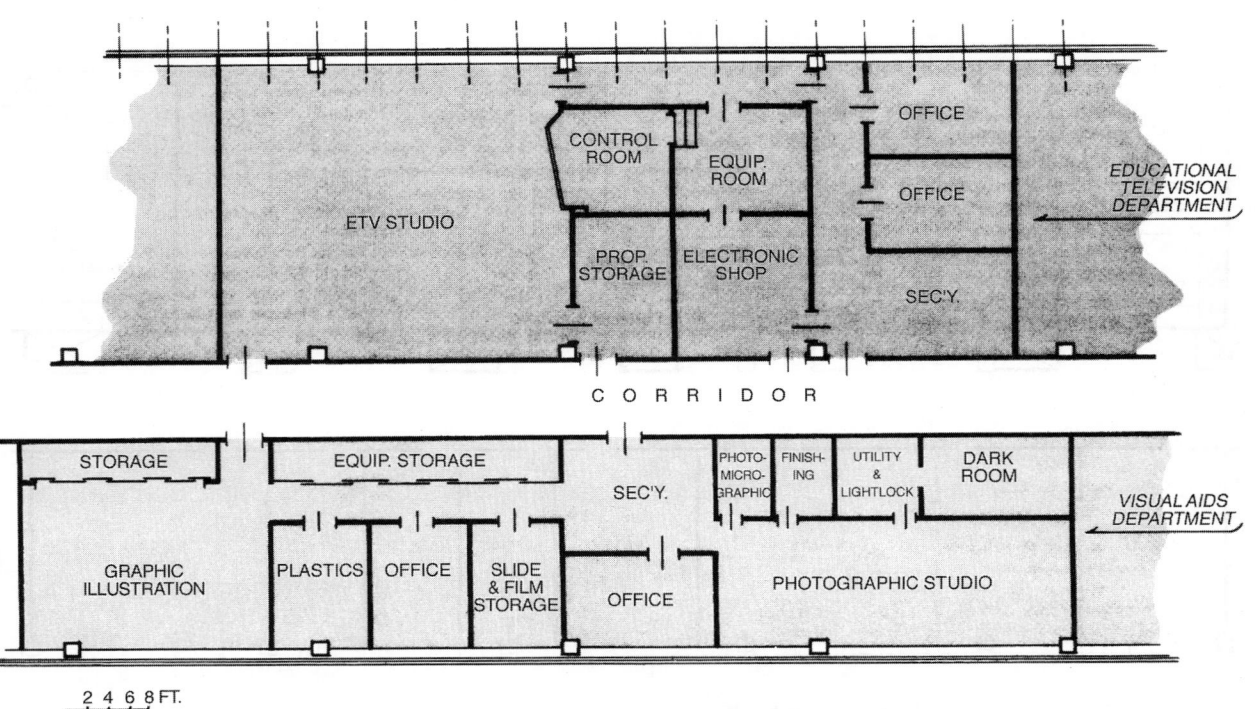

**Fig. 16. ETV and visual aids departments**

*Graphic Arts*

Drafting tables, plan file cabinets, and a sink or lavatory should be provided. Another room is needed for production of the three-dimensional models. A workbench with sink and utilities is required.

*Photography*

The room provided for the photographic section should be large enough to permit the photographing of patients, photomicrography, copying, videotaping, and print and slide finishing. It might also include equipment for preparing and projecting printed pages and similar opaque materials. The studio should be not less than 12 feet wide and approximately 35 feet long for making videos and for their projection.

*Distribution and Storage of Visual Aids*

Administrative offices are required for the maintenance of files and cataloging of material, control of distribution and the requisitioning of visual aids materials, and adequate space should be provided for storage of slides and videos and for the storage, maintenance, and operation of all projectors.

## FACULTY FACILITIES

### Office Facilities

A uniform allowance of 200 square feet for each full time faculty member will provide enough space to assure an individual office for each teacher with the rank of instructor or above as well as sufficient additional space for department heads and others with administrative responsibility.

### Research Facilities

Space requirements for faculty research are particularly difficult to anticipate. An allowance of 100 square feet for each full-time faculty member represents the equivalent of one small laboratory for each two teachers.

### Function and Location

Faculty facilities are usually included in the area of major dental school activities, a location with obvious functional advantages (Fig. 17). If they are housed separately from undergraduate areas, however, future expansion of offices and research space is simplified. Also, if faculty facilities are grouped together in a separate area and their assignments controlled by the office of the dean, rather than by the department, the problem of transferring assigned facilities from one activity or faculty to another will be simplified. The relative merit of separate or departmentally integrated facilities should be carefully weighed before final decisions on exact locations are made.

## GRADUATE AND POSTGRADUATE FACILITIES

In the basic science departments, an allowance of 150 square feet per student will permit a two-module office and a four-module laboratory for each four graduate students. In the clinical departments, an allowance of 100 square feet per student will permit one small combination study and research area for each four students. Additional operatories will also be needed.

Graduate programs should also be adequately provided with study cubicles and reserved library study rooms for the specific use of their students.

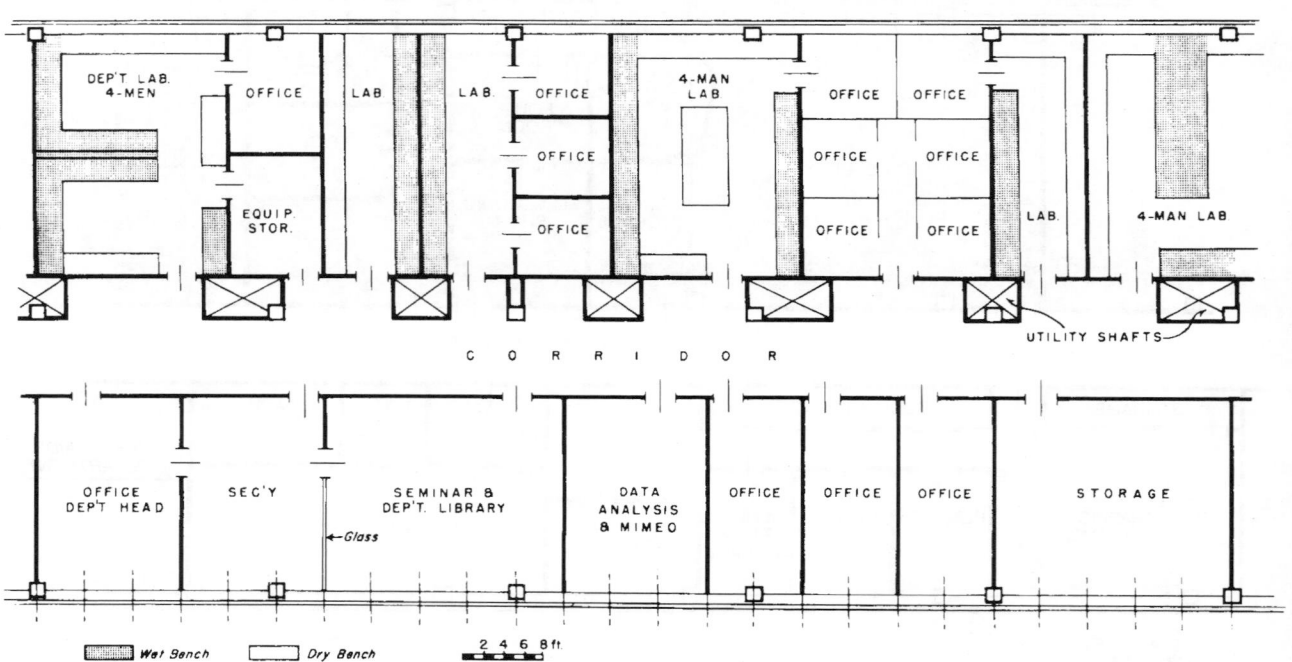

**Fig. 17. Departmental office and research area**

## Auxiliary Personnel

### Training Facilities for Dental Hygienists

Dental hygiene students may share classroom space, facilities of the x-ray department, and the library, for example, with dental students. If ample laboratory space is available in the dental school, this, too, may be shared, although a separate laboratory for hygiene students facilitates class scheduling for courses like dental anatomy and prophylaxis technics, which have heavy clock-hour laboratory requirements. The laboratory should be equipped with low benches having electricity, gas, and air outlets. Sufficient laboratory positions to accommodate an entire class are needed. A space allotment of 600 square feet per 16-student module should be adequate.

The clinic space for the dental hygiene program may be either in a section of the main clinic or in a separate clinic.

If any increase in enrollments is planned for a later date, enough space should be allocated originally and utilities installed to provide for the added students, even though all space is not immediately equipped.

Hygienists will require lounge, locker, and toilet facilities. In some schools, they will share these facilities with other students.

The careful location of a hygiene clinic is one way of providing flexibility in school planning. If, at some later date, it should become necessary to expand the school's clinical facilities, the dental hygiene clinic can be relocated and its former facilities incorporated into other clinics.

## ADMINISTRATIVE FACILITIES

One of the focal points of dental school activity is the administrative area. Though it should be readily accessible to visitors, it need not be in a predominant location. In some schools, it is located on an upper floor, convenient to an elevator or stairway.

In general most dental schools will to some extent undertake duties which fall into three broad categories—academic policy, student affairs, and business and personnel management.

### Academic Offices

In planning the office of the dean, space must be allotted for the dean's private study and for her secretary—with due regard paid to the need for bookshelves, filing space, and office supply storage. A conference room may also be necessary. In addition, offices will be required for an assistant or associate dean and his secretary. Whether or not the dean's offices should be grouped so that the secretarial staff may share a large single office is a decision for the individual school. In programming, approximately 1,500 square feet should be adequate for these rooms. In larger schools, an office for another assistant dean may be needed.

Where the programs warrant it, graduate and postgraduate divisions will have their own officers and offices, and extensive research activity will require a research coordinator, who will also need an office. Schools training dental hygienists or dental assistants will need office accommodations for the director of these programs. Some schools also include an office for part-time faculty members in the administrative area. In programming, allow 200 square feet for each office and 300 square feet for each conference room required in connection with these programs.

## Student Affairs

Schools which do not depend upon the university for such services will require a registrar's office to process applications for admission, to supervise registrations, and to maintain student records.

Many schools also offer active programs of student assistance, including counseling and advisory services, and office space is required for the professional personnel who conduct them. In some schools, offices are provided for the chaplains appointed to serve their students. All schools will probably need space to house expanding scholarship and loan activities, and, in some, additional space will be needed to handle student housing services. In small schools or in schools with very limited responsibilities for directing student affairs, these activities will probably be combined with those of a business or personnel office.

### Business and Personnel Management

Some schools have little more than a cashier's office and a minimum of clerical help. Others maintain a complex accounting and fiscal operation, headed by the office of the bursar.

A public relations department, personnel offices, and staff work areas may also be needed in larger institutions. Adequate space for stock rooms and administrative records is always essential. The advisability of employing an administrative director of clinics should be considered, and some schools today strengthen this service by adding a social worker.

In some activities—printing and publications is one—the type of equipment largely determines space needs.

Mail rooms which consistently handle bulk mailing require a special space allotment.

The actual allocation of space for the various business functions and for the administration of student affairs will vary widely. For the average school, however, total space needs for these two groups of functions will probably be adequately met by an allowance of 25 square feet per ECS.

## STUDENT FACILITIES

### Bookstores

For most schools, an allowance of from 8 to 10 square feet per ECS—with a minimum of 500 square feet—is a good preliminary estimate of bookstore space. This will provide room enough both for open displays and for some storage. If possible, the store should be located near the student lounge or the cafeteria.

### Student Lounges

The student lounge is important—perhaps indispensable—to a dental school, and the availability of similar facilities elsewhere on the campus does not, in this case, reduce the need for a lounge in the dental school itself. The lounge is the students' social center.

Although the number of women enrolled in undergraduate dental schools is small, schools should provide separate lounges for their convenience. In some schools, women dental students will be able to share the lounges provided for student dental hygienists and dental assistants.

In programming, the committee should estimate lounge space at 23 square feet per ECS for a class size of 96. For classes of different sizes, 200 square feet should be added or subtracted for each group of 16 students. These amounts permit simultaneous occupancy by approximately 25 percent of the total enrollment.

**Locker Rooms**

Adjoining the lounge areas should be adequate toilet facilities and—if feasible—the student locker rooms. Locker rooms should at least be convenient to the part of the school where the student spends most of his academic day—near the basic science and preclinical technic laboratories for freshmen and sophomores, near the clinics and associated clinical laboratories for juniors and seniors.

The locker room area required for male students can be estimated at 1,800 square feet for an entering class of 48 (or three 16-student modules); this amount should be increased by 500 square feet for each additional group of 16 students.

As to the lockers themselves, the types chosen should depend on the use to which they are put. If dental students are expected to keep their instrument cases in clothing lockers, the size of the case should be established and a prototype made so that the suitability of the lockers can be tested before they are purchased. The lockers chosen should also be large enough to accommodate other dental equipment.

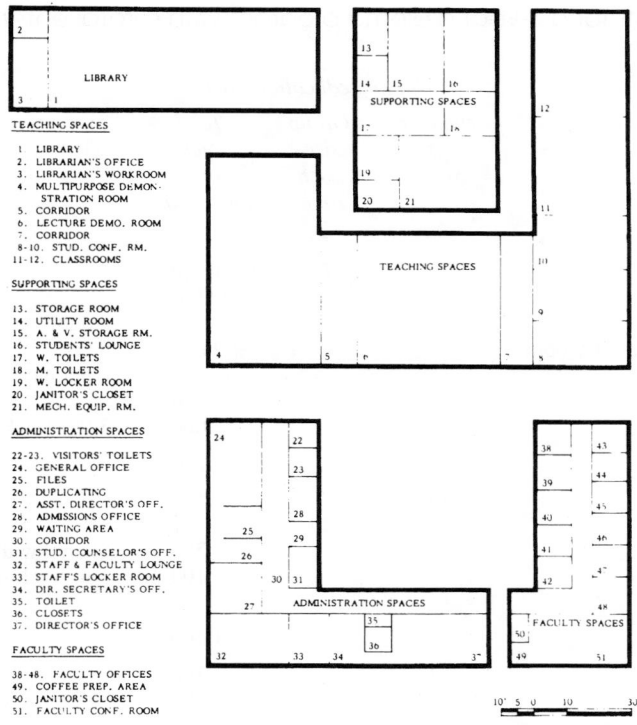

**TEACHING SPACES**

1. LIBRARY
2. LIBRARIAN'S OFFICE
3. LIBRARIAN'S WORKROOM
4. MULTIPURPOSE DEMON-
   STRATION ROOM
5. CORRIDOR
6. LECTURE DEMO. ROOM
7. CORRIDOR
8-10. STUD. CONF. RM.
11-12. CLASSROOMS

**SUPPORTING SPACES**

13. STORAGE ROOM
14. UTILITY ROOM
15. A. & V. STORAGE RM.
16. STUDENTS' LOUNGE
17. W. TOILETS
18. M. TOILETS
19. W. LOCKER ROOM
20. JANITOR'S CLOSET
21. MECH. EQUIP. RM.

**ADMINISTRATION SPACES**

22-23. VISITORS' TOILETS
24. GENERAL OFFICE
25. FILES
26. DUPLICATING
27. ASST. DIRECTOR'S OFF.
28. ADMISSIONS OFFICE
29. WAITING AREA
30. CORRIDOR
31. STUD. COUNSELOR'S OFF.
32. STAFF & FACULTY LOUNGE
33. STAFF'S LOCKER ROOM
34. DIR. SECRETARY'S OFF.
35. TOILET
36. CLOSETS
37. DIRECTOR'S OFFICE

**FACULTY SPACES**

38-48. FACULTY OFFICES
49. COFFEE PREP. AREA
50. JANITOR'S CLOSET
51. FACULTY CONF. ROOM

**Fig. 1. Space relationships in the diploma program**

# NURSING SCHOOLS

## INTRODUCTION

This section deals with design for the following nursing programs, respectively: the diploma, associate degree, baccalaureate and graduate degrees, and practical nursing. In each section, a description is presented of special aspects of each program. A hypothetical school has been described and space requirements determined. No attempt was made to compare the space requirements of one program with another, since each has its special needs, precluding a common basis for comparative purposes. For example, each program differs in purpose, curriculum, and graduation requirements.

The second half of this chapter sets forth planning considerations which will affect the architectural design of a facility. No attempt is made to outline finished plans since this should be the decision of the individual school, after a careful evaluation of various alternatives. Moreover, before the architect begins to develop his plans, the school must first establish its educational program.

## DIPLOMA NURSING PROGRAM

The diploma nursing program is conducted by a single-purpose school and may be either hospital-sponsored or independently incorporated. This program serves the interests and needs of qualified high school graduates who want (1) an education centered in a

hospital, and (2) an early and continuing opportunity to be with patients and with personnel who provide health services (see Fig. 1 and Table 1).

### Program Characteristics

Diploma programs emphasize the basic scientific principles of nursing care and of recognizing indications of diseases, disabilities, and patient needs. The curriculum is planned to equip graduates with the skills necessary to organize and implement a nursing plan that will meet the immediate needs of one or more patients, to be responsible for the direction of other members of the nursing team, and, to the degree possible, to promote the restoration of the patient's health.

Some graduates of diploma programs may wish to fulfill requirements for a baccalaureate degree in nursing. Admission is granted in accordance with the admission policies of the particular college or university they wish to attend.

## ASSOCIATE DEGREE NURSING PROGRAM

The associate degree nursing program is generally established as a division or department of a community junior college, although some are in four-year colleges or universities. This program is designed to fulfill the educational needs of qualified high school graduates who want (1) to prepare to practice nursing as registered nurses, and (2) to study in a college where they may share responsibilities and privi-

*Nursing Education Facilities,* Public Health Service, Department of Health and Human Services, Washington, D.C.

**Table 1**   Space requirements for a 3-year diploma program with a total entering class of 64 and a total enrollment of 148

| Spaces | Number of rooms | Group size, each room | Total net area (sq. ft.) | Remarks |
|---|---|---|---|---|
| Teaching | — | — | 9,330 | |
| Lecture-demonstration room | 1 | 75 | 1,940 | |
| Classrooms | 2 | 28 | 1,370 | |
| Conference rooms | 3 | 16 | 900 | Additional required in hospital |
| Multipurpose room with storage and utility room | 1 | | 2,000 | 8 beds |
| Science laboratories | | | | Optional |
| Storage—teaching aids | 1 | | 120 | |
| Library | 1 | | 3,000 | 3,000 books; 1,000 bound periodical volumes |
| Faculty | | | 2,277 | |
| Offices | 15 | 1 | 1,500 | |
| Conference room | 1 | 20 | 377 | |
| Lounge | 1 | | 300 | Shared with administrative staff |
| Washrooms, toilets | 1 | | 100 | 1 watercloset and 2 lavatories |
| Lockers | | | | |
| Administration | | | 1,660 | |
| Lobby—reception area | 1 | | 100 | |
| General office | 1 | 5 | 400 | |
| Secretary-receptionist | | | | |
| Clerk-typists | | | | |
| Storage area | 1 | | 120 | |
| Duplicating area | 1 | | 100 | |
| Director's office | 1 | | 340 | With coat closet and toilet |
| Director's secretary office | 1 | 1 | 100 | |
| Assistant director's office | 1 | 1 | 120 | |
| Registrar's office and admissions office | 1 | | 140 | Combined function |
| Student's health service | | | | Shared with hospital employees' health service |
| Staff lounge | | | | Shared with faculty |
| Visitors' toilets | | | | |
| Men | 1 | | 40 | 1 watercloset, 1 lavatory |
| Women | 1 | | 40 | 1 watercloset, 1 lavatory |
| Supporting | | | 1,580 | |
| Students' toilets | | | | |
| Men | 1 | | 120 | 1 watercloset, 1 lavatory, including 10 full-size lockers |
| Women | 1 | | 280 | 7 waterclosets, 7 lavatories |
| Students' lounge | 1 | | 300 | |
| Lockers | | | 240 | 30 full-size lockers |
| Janitor's closets | 1 | | 40 | Or as required |
| Coat alcoves | 1 | | 40 | As required |
| Vending machines | | | | As required |
| Telephone booths | | | | As required |
| Drinking fountains | | | | Minimum of 4—recessed or as required |
| General storage | 1 | | 600 | |
| | | | 14,847 | Net area |
| | | | 9,898 | For walls, partitions, corridors, stairs, and mechanical space |
| | | | 24,745 | Total gross area |
| | | | 167.2 | Area per enrolled student |

**Table 1** Space requirements for a 3-year diploma program with a total entering class of 64 and a total enrollment of 148 (cont.)

| Spaces | Number of rooms | Group size, each room | Total net area (sq. ft.) | Remarks |
|---|---|---|---|---|
| If the sciences are taught in the home school, add the following: | | | | |
| Teaching | | | 4,368 | |
| Classrooms | 1 | 38 | 648 | |
| Science laboratories | 2 | | 3,600 | |
| Storage and preparation room | 1 | | 120 | |
| Faculty | | | 500 | |
| Offices | 5 | 1 | 500 | |
| | | | 19,215 | Total net area |
| | | | 12,810 | For walls, partitions, corridors, stairs, and mechanical space |
| | | | 32,025 | Total gross area |
| | | | 216.4 | Area per enrolled student |
| Assembly room | 1 | 200 | 3,000 | Flat floor |
| | | | 22,215 | Total net area |
| | | | 14,810 | For walls, partitions, corridors, stairs, and mechanical space |
| | | | 37,025 | Total gross area |
| | | | 250.2 | Area per enrolled student |

eges as well as intellectual and social experiences with students in other educational programs (see Fig. 2 and Table 2).

## Program Characteristics

The following characteristics identify associate degree nursing programs:

- The college controls, finances, and administers the program.
- The program conforms with the overall standards and policies of the college and operates within the framework of its organization, administration, interdisciplinary curriculum committees, and the student personnel program.
- The policies and procedures promulgated for faculty in other college departments also apply to the nursing faculty.
- Members of the nursing faculty plan, organize, implement, and teach the nursing courses. They select, guide, and evaluate all learning experiences including those in the patient care areas.
- The college, by means of written agreements with hospitals and other agencies in the community, provides clinical facilities essential to nursing education.
- Students meet the requirements of the college and its nursing department for admission, continuation of study, and graduation.
- The nursing program is organized within the framework of the community junior college curriculum pattern leading to an associate degree.

Graduates of the associate degree nursing program are prepared to give patient-centered nursing care in beginning general-duty nurse positions. They are prepared to draw upon a background from the physical, biological, and social sciences in administering nursing care to patients. They relate well with people and are self-directive in learning from experience as practicing nurses. They are prepared to cooperate and share responsibility for the patients' welfare with other general-duty nurses, head nurses, supervisors, attending physicians, and others. As all other beginning practitioners, these graduates need to be oriented to new work situations and given time and opportunity to become increasingly effective in the practice of nursing.

The program is complete for its purpose. Some graduates from associate degree programs may later wish to fulfill requirements for a baccalaureate degree in nursing.

## BACCALAUREATE AND GRADUATE NURSING PROGRAMS

### Program Characteristics

*Undergraduate Programs*

A nursing program leading to a baccalaureate degree is conducted by an educational unit in nursing (department, division, school, or college) that is an integral part of a college or university and is organized and controlled in the same way as other units in the institution (see Table 3).

The baccalaureate degree program is designed to serve the needs and purposes of persons who want (1) to learn and practice the humanistic and scientific bases for care of patients, (2) to prepare for nursing at the baccalaureate level, (3) to share with students preparing for other occupations all the general advantages of a college or university preparation, and (4) to acquire a baccalaureate education as a prerequisite for graduate study to prepare to practice in such specialties as teaching, administration, or research.

Graduates of baccalaureate programs are prepared for nursing positions in community health services and may advance without further formal education to positions, such as head nurse and team leader, which require administrative skills. Graduates also have a foundation for continuing personal and professional development and for graduate study in nursing.

Some graduates of associate degree and diploma programs in nursing may wish to fulfill requirements for a baccalaureate degree in nursing. Admission requirements vary with different colleges and universities.

*Graduate Programs*

A graduate nursing program is organized similar to other graduate programs within the university. With only few exceptions, these are offered in conjunction with a baccalaureate nursing program (see Table 4).

The graduate program is designed to prepare nurses for leadership positions in teaching and administration in all types of educational programs. Such a program also provides an opportunity to study for supervisory and administrative positions in nursing service. Consultants, clinical specialists, and research workers also require graduate study (see Fig. 3).

## PRACTICAL NURSING PROGRAMS

Seventy-five percent of the state-approved nursing programs leading to a practical nurse certificate are controlled by educational institutions or agencies. The majority are under state and local boards of education. The remainder are mostly under the control of hospitals, with the exception of about six which are under other community agencies (see Tables 5 and 6 and Figs. 4 and 5).

### Program Characteristics

The practical nursing program which leads to a certificate or diploma is usually one year in length, self-contained, complete, and satisfactory for its own purpose, providing preparation exclusively for practical nursing. (California and Texas call these program "Vocational Nurse Programs" and license the graduates as Licensed Vocational Nurses.) This program's objective is to prepare a needed worker in nursing service who will share in giving direct care to patients. Graduates of practical nursing programs perform two major functions:

1. Under the direction of a registered nurse or physician, they administer nursing care in situations relatively free of scientific complexity.
2. In a close working relationship, they assist registered nurses in providing nursing care in more complex situations.

### ARCHITECTURAL CONSIDERATIONS

The physical essentials of the various spaces required for any type of program of nursing education are briefly described in this section. All the spaces noted, however, are not necessarily required for all programs. Moreover, many of the spaces may be used in conjunction with other departments of a community college, a university, or institution to which the nursing education program is related. Where possible, variations are noted.

The diagrams of teaching spaces are only suggestive of one method of arranging these spaces. The final scheme used by a nursing education program will depend on its particular needs expressed in the written program. The degree to which the architect can effectively design a facility depends largely on how thoroughly the functional program of the proposed facility was prepared.

Although each nursing education facility will find it necessary to determine its own space requirements in light of its own needs, the spaces required by most schools might be grouped under seven categories. These categories include teaching spaces, research facilities, faculty offices, administrative unit, students' facilities, supporting areas, and continuing education.

## TEACHING SPACES

### Lecture-Demonstration Rooms

The lecture-demonstration room (Fig. 6) is used for the purpose implied in its name. Factors to be considered in determining physical dimensions are requirements for the following: (1) teaching station, (2) demonstration area, (3) seating area, (4) projection space or room, and (5) storage closets. A brief description of each follows:

*Teaching Station*

The teaching station should be equipped with marker boards, tack boards, projection screens, and map rails above to support diagrams and charts.

*Demonstration Area*

The demonstration area in front of the teaching station should be large enough to permit the use of equipment such as an adult-size bed or movable sectional counter units which have locking wheels. These units, which have storage space underneath, provide greater flexibility than fixed counters, since they can be assembled into any arrangement or length and can be stored elsewhere when not in use.

A lavatory will be needed in the lecture/demonstration area for use whenever a patient care demonstration is presented. The doors into this room should be a minimum of 3 feet-8 inches wide to provide an adequate passageway for a bed and other equipment used during a demonstration.

*Seating Area*

Since good visibility of the instruction and demonstration area should be assured from all seats, a stepped floor should be considered. Steps should be so designed that each sight line misses the row ahead by 4 inches. Fixed seats equipped with hinged or removable tablet supports for writing are recommended. Ten percent of the seats should be for left-handed students.

*Projection Room*

A projection room separated from the classroom is desirable because it eliminates such disturbing factors as noise and light. However, certain disadvantages of a separate projection room such as the need for an operator and for communication facilities between the operator and the instructor should be considered.

In lieu of a projection room, a console for projection equipment is a good compromise. This console will contain all lighting and projection controls and will have locked storage space for equipment when not in use.

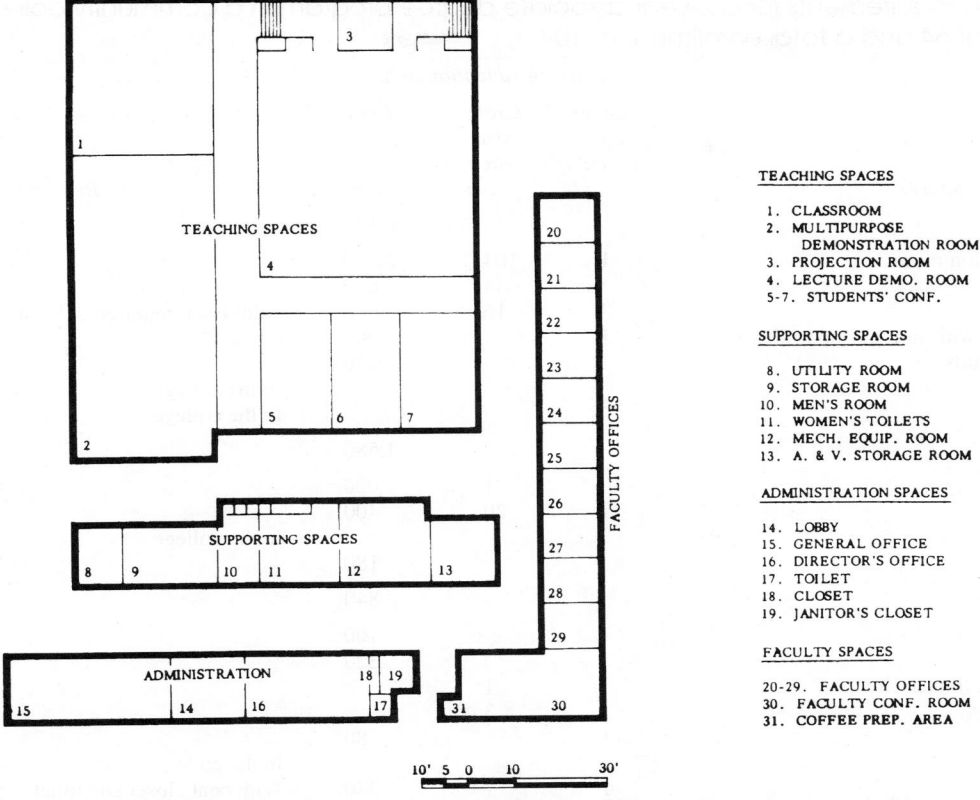

TEACHING SPACES

1. CLASSROOM
2. MULTIPURPOSE
   DEMONSTRATION ROOM
3. PROJECTION ROOM
4. LECTURE DEMO. ROOM
5-7. STUDENTS' CONF.

SUPPORTING SPACES

8. UTILITY ROOM
9. STORAGE ROOM
10. MEN'S ROOM
11. WOMEN'S TOILETS
12. MECH. EQUIP. ROOM
13. A. & V. STORAGE ROOM

ADMINISTRATION SPACES

14. LOBBY
15. GENERAL OFFICE
16. DIRECTOR'S OFFICE
17. TOILET
18. CLOSET
19. JANITOR'S CLOSET

FACULTY SPACES

20-29. FACULTY OFFICES
30. FACULTY CONF. ROOM
31. COFFEE PREP. AREA

**Fig. 2. Space relationships in an associate degree nursing program**

If such a room is provided, it may also be used for editing and storing material to be projected. Provision, therefore, should be made for counters with storage space underneath. One of the counters should have a sink. Open shelves or wall cabinets with glazed doors may be provided above the counters.

The projection wall should have two small windows so that two projectors can show two images on the screens simultaneously. The width of the screen should be approximately equal to one-sixth of the distance to the last row of seats. Projection screens can be the roll-up type, either manually or mechanically operated, or the fixed type. Mechanical operation, although noisy, prevents accidental damage to the screen.

*Storage Closets*

Storage closets with standard-height doors may be provided. Among other things, skeletons and full-scale models of the human body may be stored here if there is no centralized storage.

**Classrooms**

The classroom (see Fig. 7) should provide an optimum setting for communication between the instructor and the students.

The room's shape and size should permit easy visibility of written material on the chalkboard as well as the projected image on the screen. The need to maintain as close a verbal distance as possible between students and the instructor should also be considered.

Acoustical treatment to support verbal communication and sound insulation to prevent the penetration of outside noises must be considered in selecting structural and finish materials.

In addition to the floor area required for seating, space should be allocated for teaching and demonstration and for mounting a projector.

If central storage of such teaching aids as skeletons and full-scale models of the human body is not provided, storage closets will be required in classrooms.

A lavatory should be provided in the room near the teaching station so that it will be easily accessible for use whenever patient care is being demonstrated.

The classroom door should be a minimum of 3 feet 8 in. wide to permit easy transportation of an adult-size bed which may be required for demonstration.

Equipment which will be needed for classrooms includes chalkboards, tack boards, and projection screens. X-ray film illuminators, either portable or wall mounted, may also be used.

**Multipurpose Room**

The multipurpose room (see Fig. 8) may be used for student practice of patient care as well as for classroom functions. Thus, the room should accommodate:

**Table 2**  Space requirements for a 2-year associate degree program in a community college with an entering class of 64 and a total enrollment of 104

| Spaces | Number of rooms | Group size, each room | Total net area (sq. ft.) | Remarks |
|---|---|---|---|---|
| Teaching | | | 6,120 | |
| Lecture-demonstration room | 1 | 104 | 2,300 | |
| Classrooms | 1 | 44 | 800 | |
| Conference rooms | 3 | 16 | 900 | Additional required in hospital |
| Multipurpose room with storage and utility rooms | 1 | | 2,000 | 8 beds |
| Storage—teaching aids | 1 | | 120 | |
| Science laboratories | | | | In the college |
| Library | | | | In the college |
| Faculty | | | 1,580 | |
| Offices | 10 | 1 | 1,000 | |
| Conference room | 1 | 20 | 400 | |
| Lounge | | | | In the college |
| Washroom and toilets | | | 180 | |
| Administration | | | 840 | |
| Lobby-reception | 1 | | 100 | |
| General office | 1 | | 320 | |
| Secretary-receptionist | | 1 | | |
| Clerk-typists | | 3 | | |
| Storage area | 1 | | 80 | |
| Duplicating area | | | | In the college |
| Director's office | 1 | 1 | 340 | With coat closet and toilet |
| Registrar's office | | | | In the college |
| Admissions office | | | | In the college |
| Student counselor's office | | | | In the college |
| Students' health service | | | | In the college |
| Staff lounge—washroom and toilet | | | | In the college |
| Visitors' toilets | | | | |
| Men | | | | In the college |
| Women | | | | In the college |
| Supporting | | | 1,300 | |
| Students' toilets | | | 420 | |
| Men's toilet | | | | 1 watercloset, 1 lavatory, 1 urinal |
| Women's toilets | | | | 5 waterclosets, 5 lavatories |
| Students' lounge | | | | Located in college |
| Lockers | | | 240 | 104 full-size lockers (Additional may be needed in the hospital.) |
| Janitors' closets | 1 | | 40 | Or as required |
| Coat alcoves | | | | As required |
| Vending machines | | | | As required |
| Telephone booths | | | | As required |
| Drinking fountains | | | | Minimum of 3—recessed or as required |
| General storage | 1 | | 600 | |
| | | | 9,840 | Net area |
| | | | 6,560 | For walls, partitions, corridors, stairs, and mechanical space |
| | | | 16,400 | Total gross area |
| | | | 157.7 | Area per enrolled student |

- Adult-size beds which may be separated by curtains suspended from ceiling curtain tracks.
- A medicine preparation area including movable sectional counter units and fixed counters located at the wall, with sink and storage cabinets underneath and wall cabinets with glazed doors above.
- A hand washing demonstration unit and a minimum of three lavatory basins, with foot, wrist, or knee control.
- Dressing cubicles. One method for providing privacy is through the use of curtains suspended from ceiling curtain tracks.
- Storage closets for small equipment, linen, charts, and diagrams. These closets should have a full-size door and should be large enough to store skeletons and full-size models of the human body, if necessary.
- Marker boards, tack boards, projection screens.
- Seating around tables for seminar-type lectures for 16 students.
- Space for projector mounting.

*X-ray Film Illuminators*

These may be used in all teaching areas. They can be either wall mounted or portable. If portable, storage space should be allocated for them when not in use.

*Utility Room*

The utility room can either be a part of the multipurpose demonstration room or may be separated by a solid partition.

Although each facility must determine its own specific equipment needs, the following built-in features are recommended:

- A counter with sink and storage underneath with wall cabinets above.
- Roughed-in plumbing to accommodate future fixtures.

**Students' Conference Rooms (Teaching)**

Student conference rooms will be required in all programs (see Fig. 7). The number of such rooms will depend on the anticipated enrollment. Major planning considerations include:

- Seating arrangement at tables for group discussions or lectures.
- Placement of marker boards and tackboards.
- Adequate sound isolation from one room space to another.

**Science Laboratories**

Students enrolled in associate and baccalaureate degree programs in nursing attend science courses with other undergraduates. The trend in diploma programs is to purchase instruction in the sciences from a local junior college, a college, or a university. To avoid the unnecessary duplication of expensive facilities, diploma programs should plan science laboratories only if such facilities are not available from other institutions (see Fig. 9).

**Library**

Library facilities are required in all nursing education programs. Wherever feasible, a library may be shared with other types of programs; however, the diploma school will usually have its own library. An example of library facilities for a diploma program is shown in Fig. 10.

The information presented is considered minimum for the needs of a nursing education facility whether it is part of a larger library or an independent library. In any event, future expansion should be a major planning consideration.

Principal elements to be considered in designing a library include (1) the library room; (2) the librarian's office; (3) the librarian's workroom; and (4) the storage area for audiovisual equipment and models.

*Reference and Study Area*

Study space should accommodate a minimum of one-third of the total student body. Reference tables may be provided for one-half of these students and carrels for the other half. Teaching machines may be used in carrels.

The reference and study area should occupy 55 to 60 percent of the total floor space of the library room.

*Service Area*

Card catalog and circulation activities should be located near the library entrance and reading area.

*Storage Area*

All nursing programs should have an adequate amount of space for stacks to accommodate necessary titles and bound volumes of periodicals. Appropriate filing arrangements should be provided for reports, pamphlets, bulletins, microfilms, and programmed material for teaching machines. For the diploma program, stacks should be provided for a minimum of 3,000 titles and 1,000 bound periodical volumes.

*Librarian's Office*

The librarian's office should be separated from the library room by a glazed wall partition or a view window to enable the librarian to oversee activity in the library. The office should be sufficiently large to accommodate several people for an informal conference and should be equipped with necessary furniture including bookshelves, desk, and computer stand.

*Librarian's Workroom*

The workroom should be adjacent to the library room and to the librarian's office. Direct access should be provided into the corridor to permit easy deliveries by either a 3-feet 8-inch clear opening or double doors. The room should include:

- Counter worktop with sink and storage cabinets underneath; part of the counter should have knee space underneath.
- Storage shelves or wall cabinets above.
- Adequate number of electrical outlets.
- Space allocation for desk, worktables, movable book carts.

*Reference Reading Room*

Nursing education programs which use adjacent library facilities may need only a small reference-reading room in the nursing education facility. Standard references and professional periodicals should be kept in this room, where study space should also be provided.

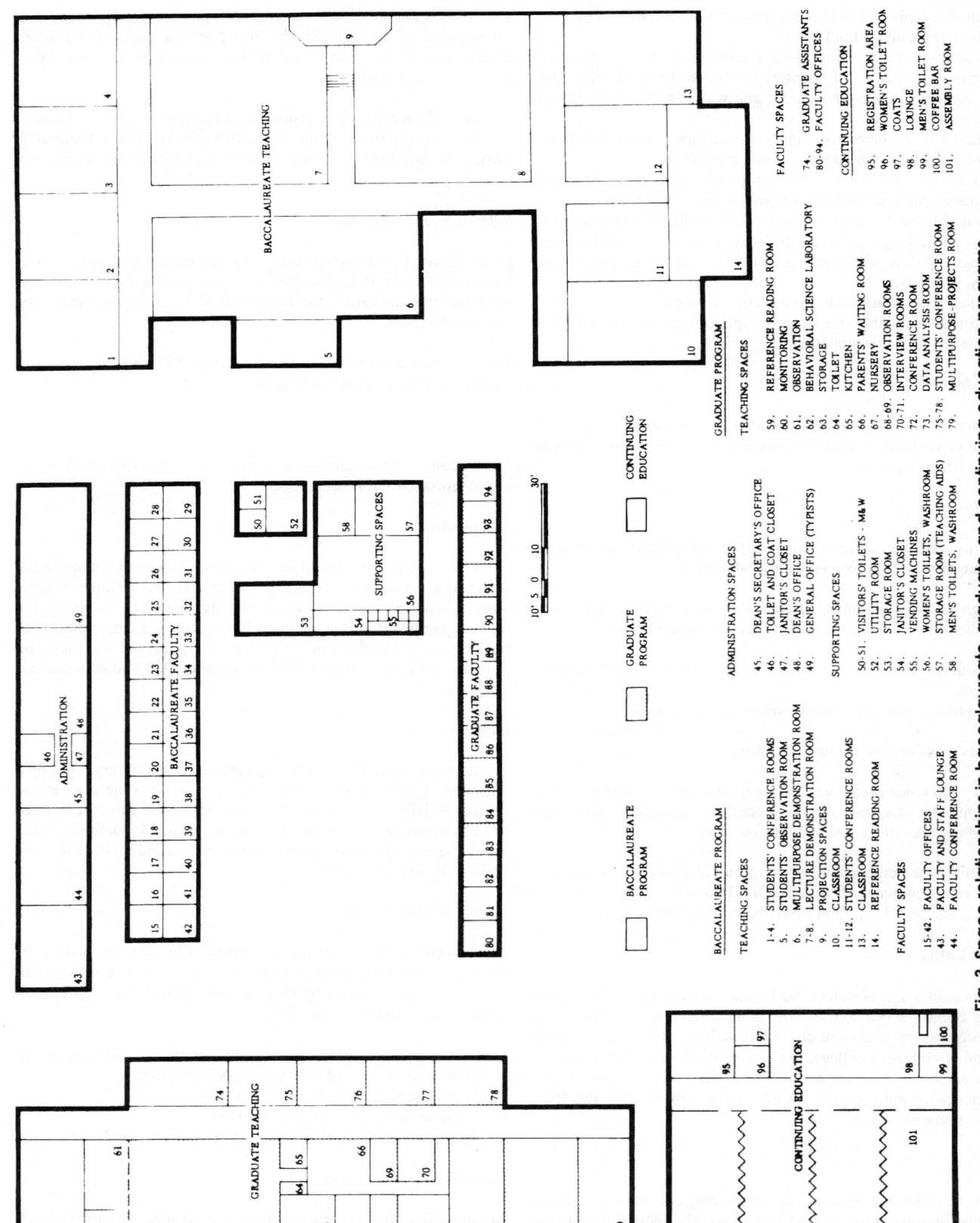

**BACCALAUREATE TEACHING**

**GRADUATE TEACHING**

**ADMINISTRATION**

**BACCALAUREATE FACULTY**

**SUPPORTING SPACES**

**GRADUATE FACULTY**

**CONTINUING EDUCATION**

□ BACCALAUREATE PROGRAM

□ GRADUATE PROGRAM

□ CONTINUING EDUCATION

10' 5 0 10     30'

**BACCALAUREATE PROGRAM**

TEACHING SPACES
1-4.  STUDENTS' CONFERENCE ROOMS
5.  STUDENTS' OBSERVATION ROOM
6.  MULTIPURPOSE DEMONSTRATION ROOM
7-8.  LECTURE DEMONSTRATION ROOM
9.  PROJECTION SPACES
10.  CLASSROOM
11-12.  STUDENTS' CONFERENCE ROOMS
13.  CLASSROOM
14.  REFERENCE READING ROOM

FACULTY SPACES
15-42.  FACULTY OFFICES
43.  FACULTY AND STAFF LOUNGE
44.  FACULTY CONFERENCE ROOM

ADMINISTRATION SPACES
45.  DEAN'S SECRETARY'S OFFICE
46.  TOILET AND COAT CLOSET
47.  JANITOR'S CLOSET
48.  DEAN'S OFFICE
49.  GENERAL OFFICE (TYPISTS)

SUPPORTING SPACES
50-51.  VISITORS' TOILETS - M & W
52.  UTILITY ROOM
53.  STORAGE ROOM
54.  JANITOR'S CLOSET
55.  VENDING MACHINES
56.  WOMEN'S TOILETS, WASHROOM
57.  STORAGE ROOM (TEACHING AIDS)
58.  MEN'S TOILETS, WASHROOM

**GRADUATE PROGRAM**

TEACHING SPACES
59.  REFERENCE READING ROOM
60.  MONITORING
61.  OBSERVATION
62.  BEHAVIORAL SCIENCE LABORATORY
63.  STORAGE
64.  TOILET
65.  KITCHEN
66.  PARENTS' WAITING ROOM
67.  NURSERY
68-69.  OBSERVATION ROOMS
70-71.  INTERVIEW ROOMS
72.  CONFERENCE ROOM
73.  DATA ANALYSIS ROOM
75-78.  STUDENTS' CONFERENCE ROOM
79.  MULTIPURPOSE-PROJECTS ROOM

FACULTY SPACES
74.  GRADUATE ASSISTANT'S
80-94.  FACULTY OFFICES

CONTINUING EDUCATION
95.  REGISTRATION AREA
96.  WOMEN'S TOILET ROOM
97.  COATS
98.  LOUNGE
99.  MEN'S TOILET ROOM
100.  COFFEE BAR
101.  ASSEMBLY ROOM

**Fig. 3. Space relationships in baccalaureate, graduate, and continuing education programs**

**Table 3** Space requirements for a 4-year basic baccalaureate nursing program with an entering class of 96 and a total enrollment of 240

| Spaces | Number of rooms | Group size, each room | Total net area (sq. ft.) | Remarks |
|---|---|---|---|---|
| Teaching | | | 14,064 | |
| Lecture-demonstration rooms | 2 | 120 | 4,608 | |
| Classrooms | 2 | 60 | 2,200 | |
| Conference rooms | 6 | 25 | 3,696 | Additional required in the hospital |
| Multipurpose room with storage, utility, and observation rooms | 1 | | 3,000 | 8 beds |
| Science laboratories | | | | In the college |
| Storage-teaching aids | 1 | | 160 | |
| Reference reading room | 1 | 16 | 400 | |
| Library | | | | In the college |
| Faculty | | | 3,980 | |
| Offices | 27 | 1 | 2,700 | |
| Research space added | | | | Depending on the program |
| Graduate assistants' office | 1 | 4 | 240 | |
| Conference room | 1 | 40 | 720 | |
| Lounge | 1 | | 320 | Shared with administrative staff—with 5 lockers |
| Administration | | | 1,500 | |
| Lobby-reception | 1 | | 100 | |
| General office | 1 | 9 | 720 | |
|    Secretary-receptionist | | | | |
|    Clerk-typists | | | | |
| Storage areas | 1 | | 80 | |
| Duplicating area | 1 | | 80 | |
| Dean's office | 1 | | 340 | With coat closet and toilet |
| Dean's secretary's office | 1 | 1 | 100 | |
| Registrar's office | | | | In the college |
| Admissions office | | | | In the college |
| Student counselor's office | | | | In the college |
| Students' health center | | | | In the college |
| Visitors' toilets | | | | |
|    Men | | | 40 | 1 watercloset, 1 lavatory |
|    Women | | | 40 | 1 watercloset, 1 lavatory |
| Supporting | | | 1,940 | |
| Students' toilets | | | 660 | 1 lavatory |
|    Men | | | | 1 watercloset; 1 urinal |
|    Women | 2 | | | 13 waterclosets; 13 lavatories |
| Students' lounge | | | | In the college |
|    Lockers | | | 600 | 250 full-size lockers or as required |
| Janitors' closets | 2 | | 80 | As required |
| Coat alcoves | | | | As required |
| Vending machines | | | | As required |
| Telephone booths | | | | As required |
| Drinking fountains | | | | Minimum of 7—recessed or as required |
| General storage | 1 | | 600 | |
| Continuing education | | | 2,560 | |
| Assembly room | 1 | 100 | 1,600 | Folding partitions to divide the room into 4 spaces (optional) |
| Conference room | | | | Optional |
| Lounge and reception area | | | 700 | |

**Table 3** Space requirements for a 4-year basic baccalaureate nursing program with an entering class of 96 and a total enrollment of 240 (cont.)

| Spaces | Number of rooms | Group size, each room | Total net area (sq. ft.) | Remarks |
|---|---|---|---|---|
| Toilets | | | | |
| Men | 1 | | 130 | |
| Women | 1 | | 130 | 1 watercloset; 2 lavatories |
| Drinking fountains | | | | |
| | | | 24,044 | Total net area |
| | | | 16,029 | For walls, partitions, corridors, stairs, and mechanical space |
| | | | 40,073 | Total gross area |
| | | | 166.97 | Area per enrolled student, approximately 167 sq. ft. |

Equipment such as shelves, storage cabinets, reference tables, and seats around tables for 16 people should be provided.

*Storage Area*

Some nursing education programs may wish to centralize all teaching aids under the librarian's supervision. Such a center is sometimes referred to as the Instructional Materials Center (IMC). If provisions for storing skeletons and full-scale models of the human body are not made elsewhere (i.e., lecture-demonstration room, classrooms, or multipurpose demonstration room), a central storage facility should be provided. This room should be placed close to the library and should be equipped with sturdy open shelving to hold heavy equipment. In planning the space to be provided for storing charts and diagrams, consideration should be given the need for easy identification and accessibility.

Full-scale skeletons and models of the human body, preferably mounted on a small cart for easy transportation, should be stored in full-size closets. Small models of parts of the human body may be stored in wall cabinets with glazed doors for easy identification. It may be preferable to store certain audiovisual items within the room in which they are used. In addition, a general storage area or room is required, and provision for storing teaching machines should be made.

A building with more than one story will need at least one service elevator for transporting heavy equipment.

**RESEARCH FACILITIES**

Research facilities will be required only by the baccalaureate and graduate nursing education programs. Typical laboratory arrangements are shown in Fig. 11.

In some instances, nursing education programs will need to develop research facilities either for graduate students or faculty members. The amount of laboratory space required depends upon the type of research program offered. Therefore, before architectural plans are developed, the needs should be carefully evaluated and defined by the faculty members and others who will use the laboratory facilities.

The building program for research facilities will vary among schools since it must be based on each school's individual requirements. Research facilities may include:

- Biological science laboratories
- Behavioral science laboratories
- The data analysis room including offices and conference room
- Multipurpose project room(s)

Biological science laboratories will need the following spaces:

- Separate offices for each researcher
- Storage or supply preparation room to serve several laboratories, for equipment, glassware, and supplies
- Deluge shower and eye bath for emergencies

Design factors to be considered for these laboratories are:

- Counters of different heights with knee space underneath and reagent shelf. These may be located along the walls or, if the space permits, an island-type counter similar to others should be provided.
- Chemical-resistant sinks with hot and cold water.
- Gas, air, and electrical outlets.
- Fume hoods with adequate exhaust system and sprinkler heads.
- A refrigerator or freezer may be needed for these laboratories.

It is assumed that the animals needed for research will be supplied from a central location, since it would not be economically feasible to construct special animal housing facilities within the nursing education unit.

**Behavioral Science Laboratory**

The primary requirement in the behavioral science laboratory is that the human subject be observed unobtrusively by the students (see Fig. 12). Thus, the following design factors should be considered:

1. The laboratory should be large enough to accommodate a bed and various patient care activities. Space is also needed for research personnel and equipment.

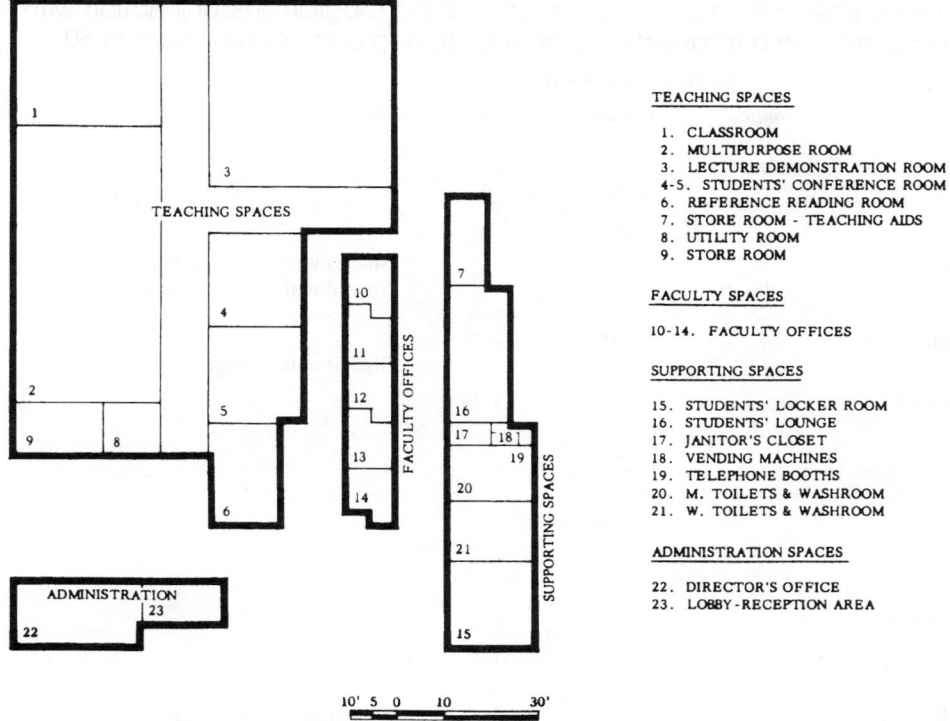

TEACHING SPACES

1. CLASSROOM
2. MULTIPURPOSE ROOM
3. LECTURE DEMONSTRATION ROOM
4-5. STUDENTS' CONFERENCE ROOM
6. REFERENCE READING ROOM
7. STORE ROOM - TEACHING AIDS
8. UTILITY ROOM
9. STORE ROOM

FACULTY SPACES

10-14. FACULTY OFFICES

SUPPORTING SPACES

15. STUDENTS' LOCKER ROOM
16. STUDENTS' LOUNGE
17. JANITOR'S CLOSET
18. VENDING MACHINES
19. TELEPHONE BOOTHS
20. M. TOILETS & WASHROOM
21. W. TOILETS & WASHROOM

ADMINISTRATION SPACES

22. DIRECTOR'S OFFICE
23. LOBBY - RECEPTION AREA

**Fig. 4. Space relationships of a practical nursing program in a vocational school**

2. An adjacent observation room with a one-way viewing glass partition will provide an overall view of the laboratory. The one-way viewing glass partition should be double glazed with sealed airspace between the glass to ensure sound isolation between the two rooms. The viewing screen should be unobtrusive floor-to-ceiling panels rather than a view window which in itself may suggest its purpose. Not all panels need be two-way glass—only those necessary for viewing.

3. The observation room should accommodate 16 students. A stepped seating platform, either permanent or temporary, might be considered to assure all the participants a good overall view of activities within the laboratory. Since the subject should not be disturbed while being observed, observation rooms should be carpeted and should have sound-absorbing materials on walls and ceilings.

4. Provision should be made for communication facilities between the two rooms as well as for concealed recording and audio and physiological factor monitoring equipment.

5. Both the behavioral science laboratory room and the observation room should be equipped with a dimmer switch to control the illumination level. Temperature and humidity controls are also important.

6. Facilities which should be directly accessible from the behavioral science laboratory include:

• Toilet room with lavatory for hand-washing.
• Kitchenette or alcove with kitchen accommodations.
• Storage room for storing equipment such as children's toys.

In conjunction with behavioral science laboratories, the following should be considered:

1. Waiting room or area, suitably furnished for adults or adults with children.
2. Play nursery for children with provision to oversee the activities from the waiting room. Special attention should be paid to acoustical treatment of this room and its decor.
3. Interviewing rooms, with adjacent observation room, separated by one-way glass viewing partition. (Items 2-5 cited above also apply here.)

**Faculty Offices**

Faculty offices may be grouped together to form the faculty offices suite. In programs having a small faculty, administrative, and business offices may be grouped together with faculty offices forming a unit that is separate in character from the teaching spaces (see Fig. 7). In addition to offices for each faculty member, one or more offices might be provided for guest lecturers or visiting faculty.

The faculty offices suite should include:

• Individual offices for each faculty member. Each office should have ample space for furniture, bookcases or shelves, and files.
• Conference room or rooms. The size of the conference room depends on the number of people to be accommodated. Chalkboards and tack boards are necessary in these rooms.

**Table 4**  Space requirements for a 2-year graduate nursing program in conjunction with a basic baccalaureate program with a total entering class of 30 and a total enrollment of 60

| Spaces | Nursing education area | | | Remarks |
| | Number of rooms | Group size, each room | Total net area (sq. ft.) | |
| --- | --- | --- | --- | --- |
| Teaching | | 1,280 | | |
| Lecture-demonstration room | | 80 | | Shared with undergraduate program |
| Classrooms | 40 | | | Shared with undergraduate program |
| Seminar rooms | 4 | 12 | 880 | |
| Reference-reading room | 1 | 16 | 400 | |
| Library | | | | Shared with college |
| Research laboratories | | 7,735 | | |
| Behavioral science | | | | |
| Waiting area | | | | |
| Nursery | | | | |
| Observation rooms | | | | |
| Interview rooms | | | | |
| Conference room | | | | |
| Data analysis room | | | | |
| Multipurpose projects room | | | | |
| Faculty | | 2,726 | | |
| Offices | 15 | 1 | 1,500 | |
| Research space added | | | | Depending on program |
| Graduate assistants' office | 1 | 8 | 576 | |
| Secretaries' office | 1 | 5 | 400 | |
| Toilets | | | | |
| Men | 1 | | 100 | 1 water closet, 1 urinal, 1 lavatory |
| Women | 1 | | 150 | 3 waterclosets, 3 lavatories |
| Supporting | | | | Shared with undergraduate program |
| | | 11,741 | | Total net area |
| | | 7,827 | | For walls, partitions, corridors, stairs, and mechanical space |
| | | 19,568 | | Total gross area |
| | | 326.1 | | Area per enrolled student |

- Faculty lounge. An alcove or small room off the lounge may be provided to accommodate a kitchenette unit and a counter with sink and storage cabinets underneath.
- Toilet facilities including a washroom and locker room or lockers, located in proximity to the lounge or adjoining it. An alcove off the washroom or small room accommodating a sofa, cot, or other suitable furniture might be considered.
- Graduate assistants' office. This room should be furnished with desks for use of teaching assistants or graduate assistants.

In addition to the teaching machines located elsewhere in the school for students' use, some teaching machines may be needed in the faculty office suite for use by members of the faculty who may be engaged in developing programmed materials.

*Data Analysis Room*

The data analysis room will require space for calculating machines, tables, and office-type furniture. Area allocation should be made for storing data. Other requirements include individual offices and a conference room that can be used by research personnel.

*Offices and Ancillary Supporting Areas*

Requirements for office space and for supporting areas and services will vary from school to school. Each program, therefore, should determine its particular needs. Some of the spaces to be considered include:

1. A lobby and reception area with an information desk as a point of control. The information desk or counter may be incorporated in the general office. In small schools the lobby or reception area may also be the secretary's office and the secretary may also be the receptionist. Toilet facilities for visitors should be conveniently located.
2. General office including space for secretarial staff. The amount of space needed will be based on the ratio of secretaries to faculty members established by the school's policy.

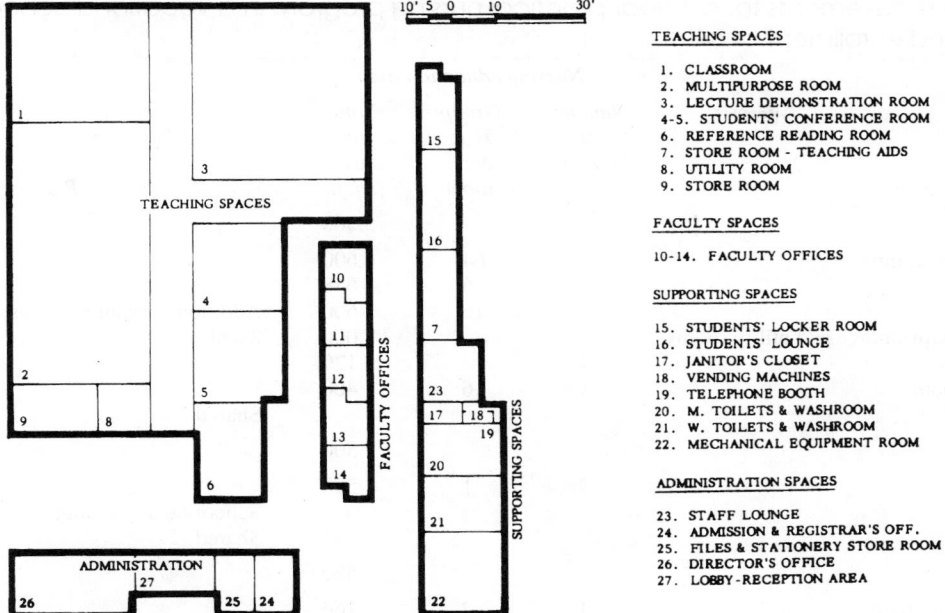

TEACHING SPACES

1. CLASSROOM
2. MULTIPURPOSE ROOM
3. LECTURE DEMONSTRATION ROOM
4-5. STUDENTS' CONFERENCE ROOM
6. REFERENCE READING ROOM
7. STORE ROOM - TEACHING AIDS
8. UTILITY ROOM
9. STORE ROOM

FACULTY SPACES

10-14. FACULTY OFFICES

SUPPORTING SPACES

15. STUDENTS' LOCKER ROOM
16. STUDENTS' LOUNGE
17. JANITOR'S CLOSET
18. VENDING MACHINES
19. TELEPHONE BOOTH
20. M. TOILETS & WASHROOM
21. W. TOILETS & WASHROOM
22. MECHANICAL EQUIPMENT ROOM

ADMINISTRATION SPACES

23. STAFF LOUNGE
24. ADMISSION & REGISTRAR'S OFF.
25. FILES & STATIONERY STORE ROOM
26. DIRECTOR'S OFFICE
27. LOBBY-RECEPTION AREA

**Fig. 5. Space relationships of a practical nursing program in a hospital**

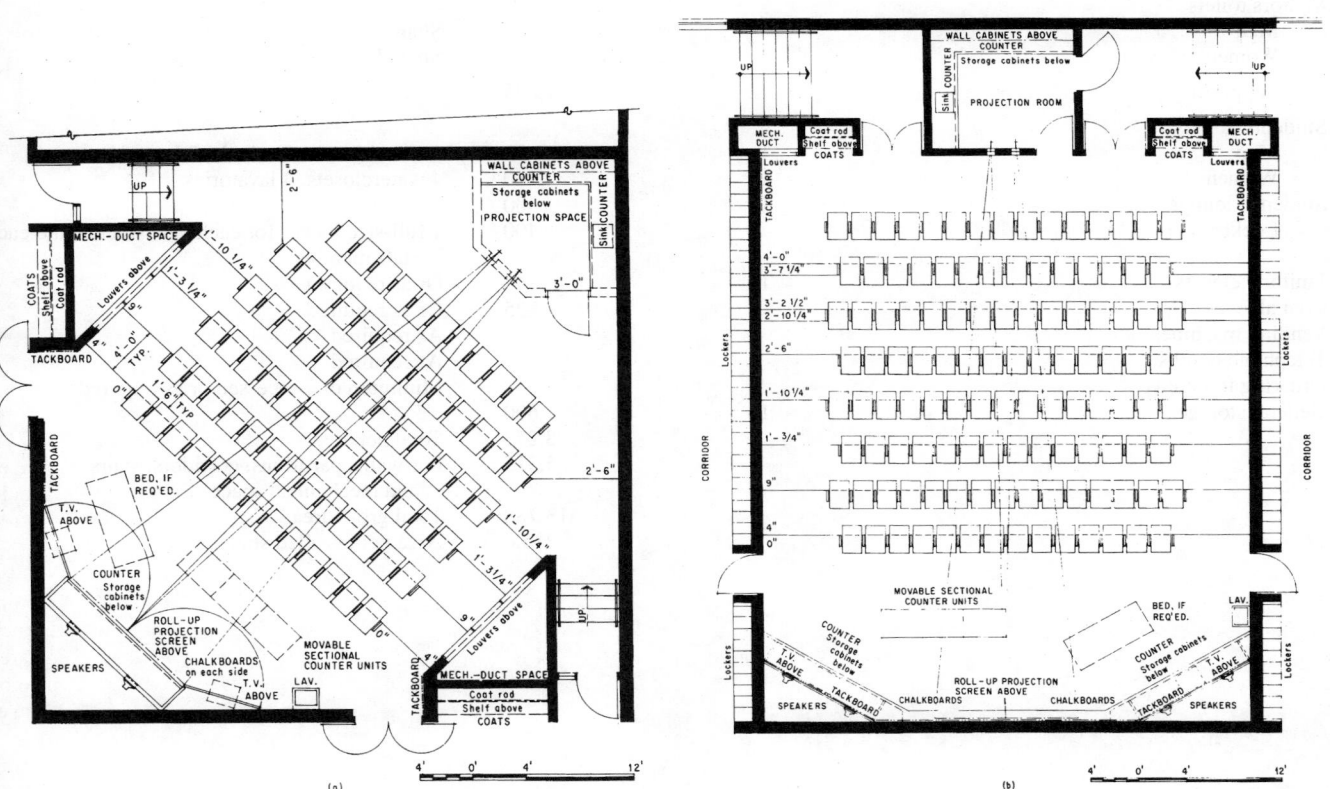

**Fig. 6. Lecture-demonstration rooms**

**Table 5**  Space requirements for a 1-year practical nursing program in a vocational school with an entering class and enrollment of 64

| | Nursing education area | | | |
|---|---|---|---|---|
| Spaces | Number of rooms | Group size, each room | Total net area (sq. ft.) | Remarks |
| Teaching | | | 5,368 | |
| Lecture-demonstration room | 1 | 64 | 1,600 | |
| Classrooms | 1 | 36 | 648 | |
| Conference rooms | 2 | 16 | 600 | Additional required in hospital |
| Multipurpose room with storage and utility rooms | 1 | | 2,000 | 8 beds |
| Storage-teaching aids | 1 | | 120 | |
| Reference-reading room | 1 | 16 | 400 | |
| Library | | | | Shared |
| Faculty | | | 500 | |
| Offices | 5 | 1 | 500 | |
| Lounge | | | | School faculty lounge |
| Toilets and lockers | | | | Shared |
| Administration | | | 580 | |
| Reception and general office | 1 | 2 | 160 | |
| Storage area | 1 | | 80 | |
| Duplicating area | | | | Shared |
| Director's office | 1 | 1 | 340 | With coat closet and toilet |
| Registrar's office | | | | Shared |
| Admissions office | | | | Shared |
| Student counselor's office | | | | Shared |
| Students' health service | | | | Shared |
| Staff lounge | | | | Shared |
| Washroom, toilets, and lockers | | | | Shared |
| Visitors toilets | | | | |
| Men | | | | Shared |
| Women | | | | Shared |
| Supporting | | | 1,825 | |
| Students' toilets | | | | |
| Men | 1 | | 180 | 2 waterclosets, 2 urinals, 2 lavatories |
| Women | 1 | | 180 | 4 waterclosets, 4 lavatories |
| Students' lounge | 1 | | 400 | |
| Lockers | | | 400 | 1 full-size locker for each new student and each staff member |
| Janitors' closets | 1 | | 40 | Or as required |
| Coat alcoves | | | 25 | Or as required |
| Vending machines | | | | As required |
| Telephone booths | | | | As required |
| Drinking fountains | | | | Minimum of 2 recessed or as required |
| General storage | 1 | | 600 | |
| | | | 8,273 | Total net area |
| | | | 5,515 | For walls, partitions, corridors, stairs, and mechanical space |
| | | | 13,788 | Total gross area |
| | | | 215.4 | Area per enrolled student |

**Table 6** Space requirements for a 1-year practical nursing program in a hospital with an entering class and total enrollment of 64

| Spaces | Nursing education area | | | Remarks |
| --- | --- | --- | --- | --- |
| | Number of rooms | Group size, each room | Total net area (sq. ft.) | |
| Teaching | | | 5,368 | |
| Lecture-demonstration room | 1 | 64 | 1,600 | |
| Classrooms | 1 | 36 | 648 | |
| Conference rooms | 2 | 16 | 600 | |
| Multipurpose room with storage and utility rooms | 1 | | 2,000 | 8 beds |
| Storage-teaching aids | 1 | | 120 | |
| Reference-reading room | 1 | 16 | 400 | |
| Library | | | | Shared with a hospital |
| Faculty | | | 500 | |
| Offices | | | 500 | |
| Administration | | | 780 | |
| Lobby-reception area | 1 | 2 | 160 | |
| Storage area | 1 | | 80 | |
| Duplicating area | | | | Shared with hospital |
| Director's office | 1 | 1 | 340 | With coat closet and toilet |
| Staff lounge and washroom | 1 | | 200 | |
| Toilets and lockers | | | | |
| Supporting | | | 1,265 | |
| Students' toilets | | | | |
| Men | 1 | | 180 | 2 waterclosets, 2 urinals, 2 lavatories |
| Women | 1 | | 180 | 4 waterclosets, 4 lavatories |
| Students' lounge | 1 | | 140 | |
| Lockers | | | 100 | |
| Janitor's closets | 1 | | 40 | Or as required |
| Coat alcoves | | | 25 | Or as required |
| Vending machines | | | | As required |
| Telephone booths | | | | As required |
| Drinking fountains | | | | Minimum of 2 recessed or as required |
| General storage | 1 | | 600 | |
| | | | 7,913 | Total net area |
| | | | 5,275 | For walls, corridors, partitions, stairs, and mechanical space |
| | | | 13,188 | Total gross area |
| | | | 206.06 | Area per enrolled student |

3. Space for filing cabinets for the students' active records. This may be either a part of the general office or a small room directly accessible from the general office. A storage area should be provided for inactive files. Programs organized under hospital control must provide space for permanent storage of student and school records.

4. Space for duplicating equipment including a counter with sink and storage cabinets underneath. This space may be either an alcove in the general office or a small room directly accessible from the general office.

5. Storage room for stationery directly accessible from the general office.

6. Small room for receiving, dispatching, and distributing mail and packages. This room also may serve as a message center for faculty members.

7. An intercommunication control system (switchboard) within the general office. Intercommunication between the rooms within the facility for nursing education is highly desirable. Outside calls should be handled by one person who would transfer them to the party concerned or, when necessary, take messages.

8. Wall space should be allocated for official bulletin boards either in the lobby waiting area or outside the general office.

9. Storage room for miscellaneous office equipment or furniture.

10. An office for the dean or director. The office should be large enough to accommodate several people for small conferences. A private toilet room with handwashing facilities and a coat closet adjacent to this office is highly desirable. (See Fig. 7.)

11. An office for a secretary adjoining or accessible to the office of the dean or director.

12. Office or offices for assistants or associates of the dean or director. These offices should either be adjacent or in proximity to the office of the dean or director.

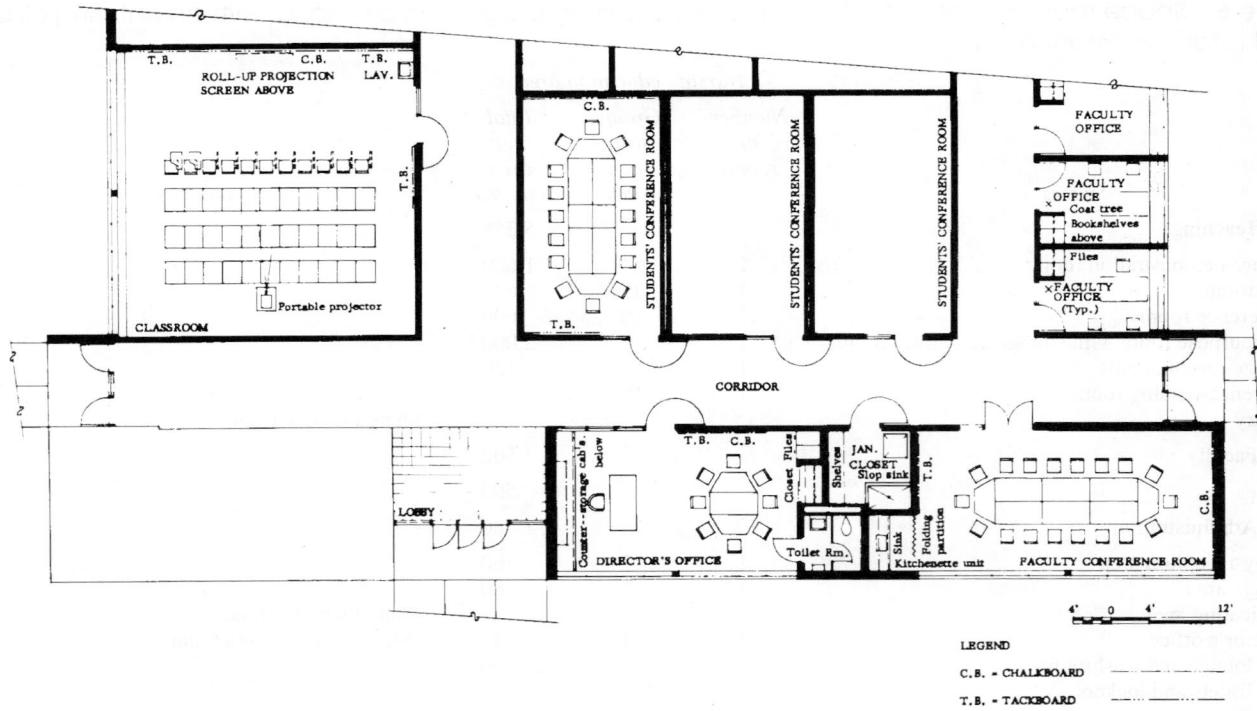

**Fig. 7. Student-faculty areas**

13. Office for registrar with ample space for filing cabinets.
14. Office for admissions officer with ample space for filing cabinets.
15. Students' health service and observation area.
16. Office for students' counselor, incorporating waiting area.
17. Office for graduate assistants and fellows, each of whom should have a desk.
18. Janitors' closets and storage space of housekeeping supplies.

### Students' Facilities

Provision of student facilities should be governed by such factors as enrollment and the school's physical setting. Whether the facility is a self-contained unit or is a part of a larger education complex is an important consideration. The needs should be evaluated and established individually for each program.

Spaces for the following should be considered:

- Toilet room and washroom for women students with adjoining room or alcove to accommodate a sofa or cot.
- Toilet room and washroom for male students.
- Locker rooms or lockers in corridors.
- A student lounge may be found desirable, particularly if no other lounges in the facility are available to nursing students. A lounge may be provided in the students' residence, which may be physically connected with the nursing education facility. In some facilities, students' lounge or lounges are provided, either in the student union building or elsewhere on the college or university campus.

### Supporting Areas

Listed below are planning considerations for supporting areas:

- The provision of coat alcoves in corridors may be desirable.
- The need for general storage rooms should be determined by each program.
- Housekeeping and maintenance rooms, including janitors' closets and storage areas for housekeeping supplies and equipment will be needed.
- Space should be allocated for vending machines either in alcoves of corridor or centralized in one room assigned for this purpose.
- An adequate number of public pay telephone booths should be located in strategic locations in alcoves off corridors so that traffic will not be obstructed.
- An adequate number of drinking fountains or water coolers should be placed in alcoves off corridors or recessed in the wall so that traffic flow will not be obstructed.

### Continuing Education

Continuing education is usually a part of the overall school facility. However, for the purposes of nursing education, it would have the following elements:

- Assembly room to seat a large group
- Conference rooms
- Lounge room and space for coffee service

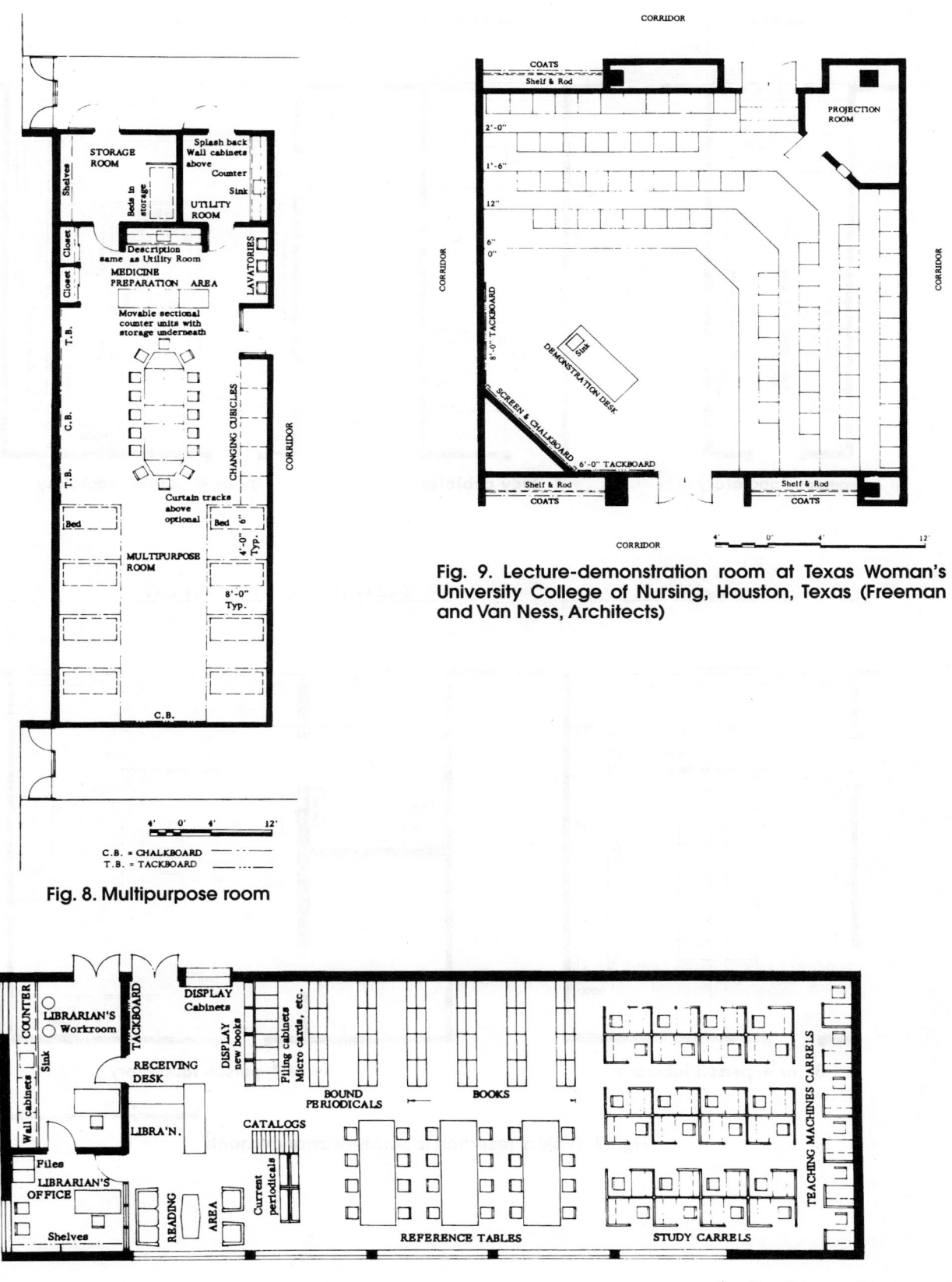

Fig. 8. Multipurpose room

C.B. = CHALKBOARD
T.B. = TACKBOARD

**Fig. 9.** Lecture-demonstration room at Texas Woman's University College of Nursing, Houston, Texas (Freeman and Van Ness, Architects)

Fig. 10. Library facilities for a diploma nursing program

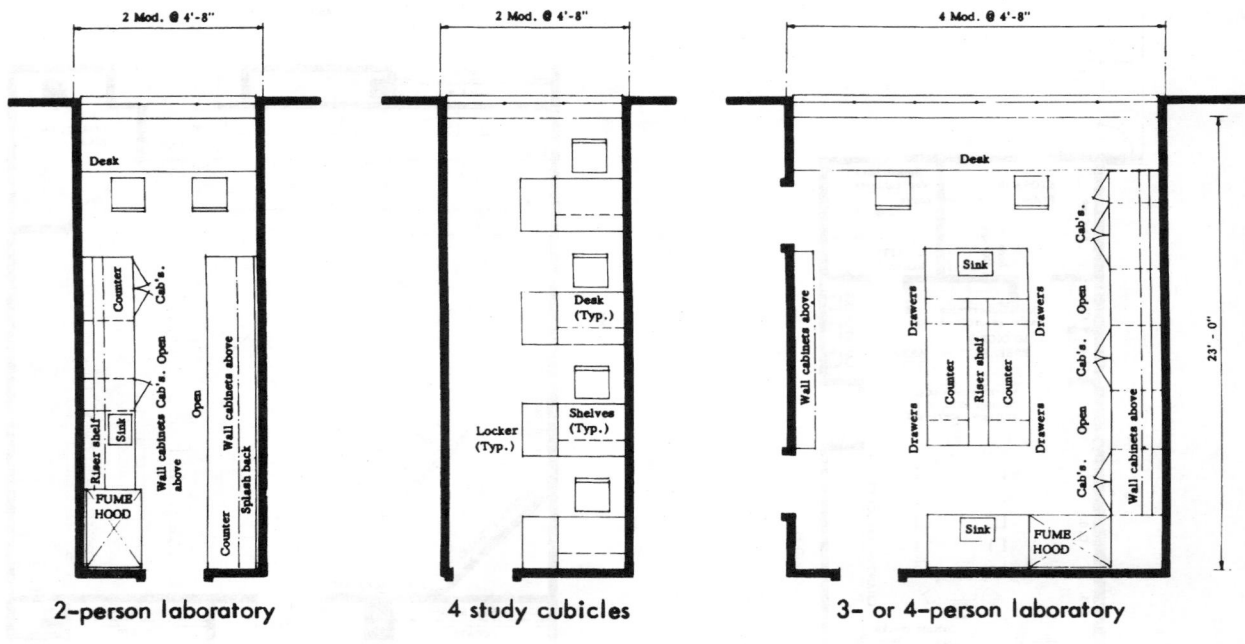

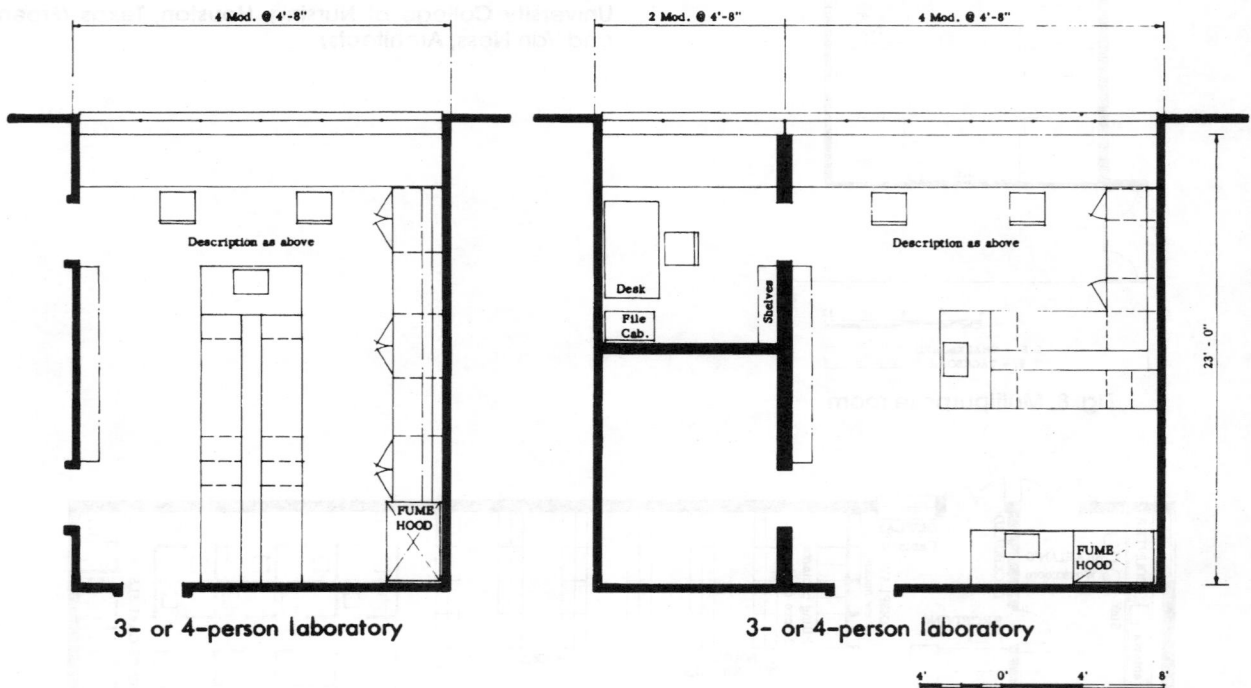

Fig. 11. Typical research laboratory arrangements

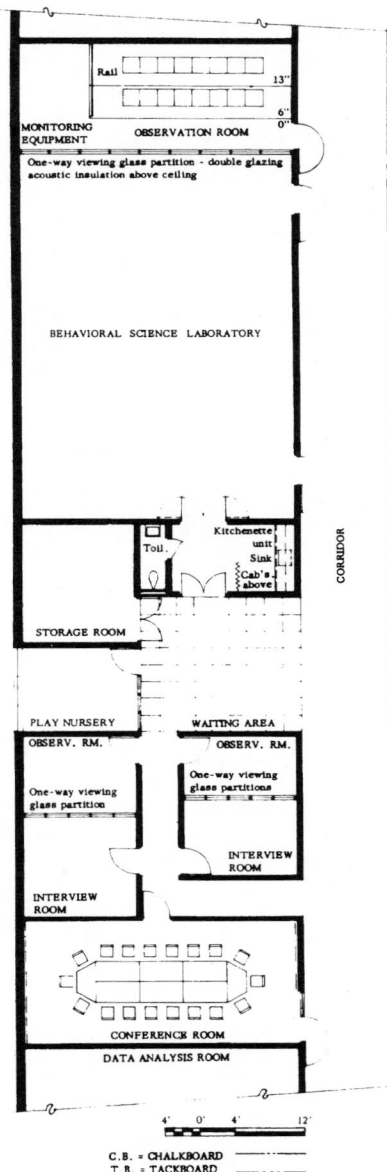

C.B. = CHALKBOARD
T.B. = TACKBOARD

**Fig. 12. Behavioral science laboratory for a nursing graduate program**

- Reception and registration area
- Men's and women's toilets
- If warranted, offices for the continuing education director and staff

*Assembly Room*

The number of people to be accommodated in the assembly room will depend upon the individual facility. In general, provision should be made for 100 or more persons, seated along rows of tables or groups of sectional tables. A movable platform to elevate the speaker should be considered.

If found desirable, this room may be subdivided into from two to four conference spaces by means of folding partitions which should preferably stack up in a wall alcove designed for this purpose. They should be selected for maximum sound-retardant properties to limit the passage of sound from one space to the other. Sound reduction of at least 25 to 30 decibels is considered minimum. These conference spaces should have marker boards and tack boards.

*Conference Rooms*

In some institutions it may be desirable not to subdivide the assembly room, in which case four or five small conference-type rooms should be provided, each to accommodate from 20 to 25 persons. These rooms should have separate entrances, should be equipped with marker boards and tack boards, and should be arranged with seats around tables for face-to-face conferences.

*Reception and Registration Area*

Definite allocation for the reception and registration area should be made. Coat room or alcove for depositing the outer garments should be incorporated.

*Lounge Room*

A lounge room should be provided large enough to accommodate the anticipated number of participants in the Continuing Education Program. An alcove accommodating a kitchenette unit, counter for coffee service, and vending machines may be considered desirable.

An adequate number of toilets should be convenient to this area.

# 6
## Cultural and Entertainment

Pennsylvania State University, Palmer Museum of Art (Arbonies King Vlock Architects with Charles W. Moore; photo: Timothy Hursley, courtesy of architect)

# MUSEUMS

## INTRODUCTION

These guidelines are written for museums of medium size or larger. However, they are also applicable to smaller museums. Smaller institutions tend to have smaller facilities, staffs, and exhibition programs. They do perform the same functions and have the same organizational needs, but are scaled differently.

Museums continue to evolve and change. New technologies, emerging art forms and collections, and diverse audiences have given rise to new museums and exhibition environments. The functional and operational requirements that are unique to this building type are the focus of this section.

Traditionally, the primary mission of a museum is to safeguard its collection. Two of the most important functional requirements are physical security and maintaining constant temperature and relative humidity to unusually high standards.

## MUSEUM GOVERNANCE

The governing structure of museums has a significant affect on their operations and values. Here again there is tremendous variation. Some museums are independent institutions, generally non-profit corporations. These will tend to have their own boards of trustees. Others are a branch of government such as a state history museum. Some museums are related to an institution such as a university museum or gallery.

## MUSEUM MISSION STATEMENT

Museums usually have clear statements of their reason for being. The traditional statement includes the mission "to preserve, protect, and exhibit." However, there are significant variations between institutions beyond this. Some are "collecting" institutions, some have a static collection, others do not collect as a core activity.

Some museums have a strong emphasis on education, with art schools or classrooms being an integral part of the facility. Others emphasize community services and include accessory uses for social and community functions and special events.

Here is an actual mission statement: "The mission of the Austin Museum of Art is to educate, entertain, inspire, and challenge our audience about visual art and its creative, intellectual, and culturally diverse aspects. In an atmosphere of inclusion, excellence, and collaboration, the Museum enhances the quality of life, cross-cultural understanding, and visual literacy of the broad public we serve."

## STRATEGIC PLAN

As a method of moving forward from a mission statement, museums develop strategic plans. The strategic plan is the first step towards defining the programs and activities necessary to achieve the museum's stated purpose. It describes audiences, accessory services, special community requirements, staffing, facilities, and financial resources.

*Authors:* Glenn Arbonies, AIA and Sandra Vlock, AIA, Arbonies King Vlock Architects

### Integration with the Community

Contrary to the idea of museum as an elitist institution, most contemporary museums aspire to become an integral part of their community. This message should be clear and visible—from the initial encounter with the building all the way to the exhibition.

Architecturally, the museum may aspire to integrate itself into its surrounding urban fabric and respond to the community's circulation pattern, or it may stand in stark contrast to its context.

The museum is often seen as an important civic building and cultural landmark. However, the visitor's experience of the building should also be welcoming and comfortable. Familiar forms can be used to give a comfortable, human dimension to the building and streetscape. Free forms can be used to command attention, such as Frank Gehry's design for the Guggenheim in Bilbao, Spain. The choreography of arrival, the relationship of building form and massing, materials and details, and landscaping all contribute to its civic presence and human scale.

Some museums use entertainment to further change the public perception of the museum and to extend visitation. Although entertainment can be a welcome alternative to exhibitions, most museums are concerned that this should not be the dominant image nor diminish the primacy and dignity of the collections.

Museums have a unique role in our society. The architectural design for a museum is often expressive of its role in our culture. It can reflect the museum's mission. As a result, museums tend to be "design statements."

### ARCHITECTURAL PROGRAM

Typically the architectural program develops a net floor area in square feet (nsf). However, this needs to be converted to gross square feet (gsf) to understand the project size and construction cost. A conversion factor in the range of 1.60 to 1.80 is common for new construction. For renovations or additions this factor will not apply.

The actual floor area will vary depending on the efficiency of the architectural design (Fig. 1). The major variable will be circulation space, for both public and collections handling.

The architectural program should include the following:

- Space allocation
- Relationships of rooms/functions
- Organizational diagrams
- Museum's design aspirations
- Construction cost estimate

### Site

Museum sites vary from downtown urban locations to suburban and rural. Some museums are located on campuses, whether higher education or a cultural center complex serving a city or region. The qual-

1. Freight Elevator
2. Collections Handling
3. Platform Lift
4. Loading Dock
5. Gallery
6. Passenger Elevator
7. Security Desk
8. Entrance Lobby
9. Coatroom
10. Kitchen/Food Service
11. Lounge
12. Orientation
13. Library
14. Main Entrance
15. Parking Lot Entrance
16. School Bus Drop-Off Entrance

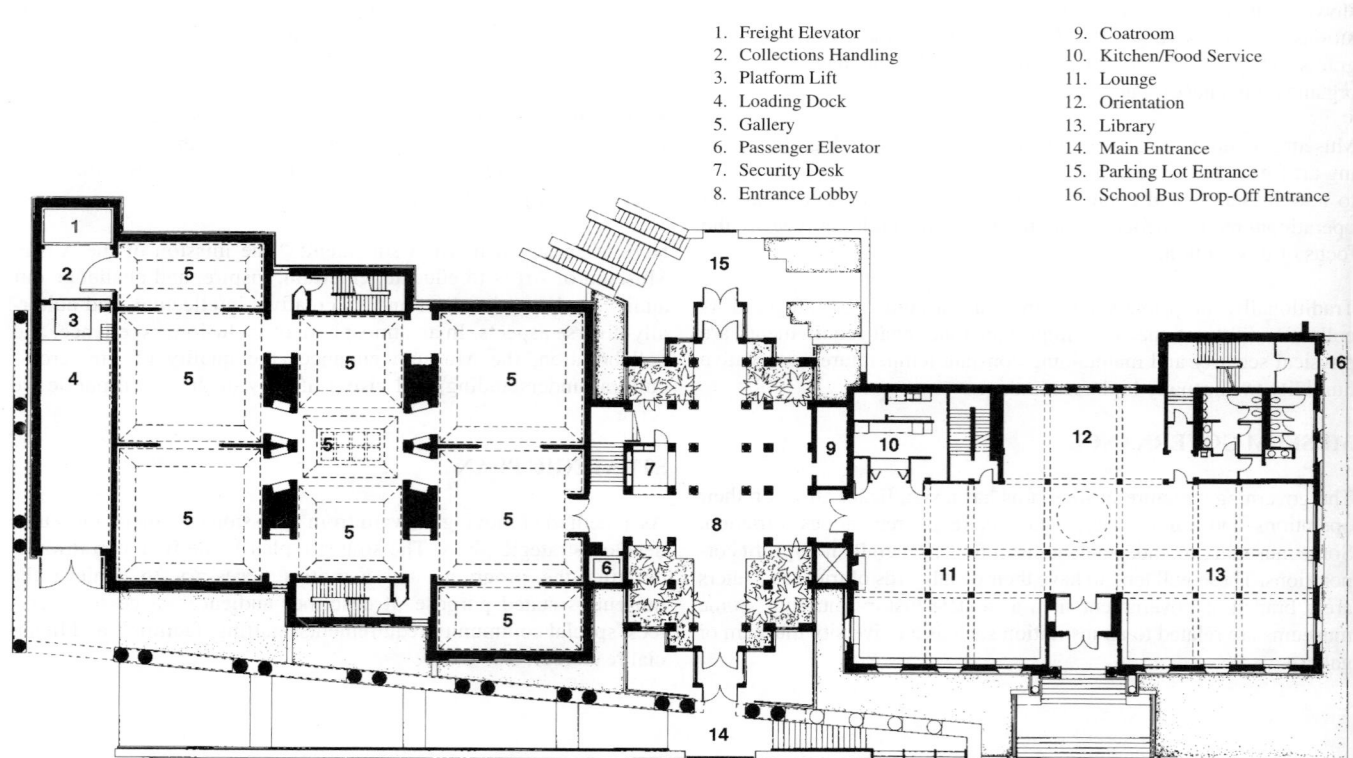

**Fig 1. Plan, Cedar Rapids Museum of Art (Glenn Arbonies, AIA, at Centerbrook Architects with Charles W. Moore)**

ties of the site will have a significant effect on the museum's design and eventual success.

Designs that make the main entrance highly visible, welcoming, and convenient to the public are best (Fig. 2).

Most museums must provide visitor and staff parking, on-site or at a nearby off-site location.

The site should be large enough to allow the museum floors to be of an effective operational size. Other desired site development should be possible, such as outdoor courtyard space for sculpture and events. Ideally the site (and design) is large enough to allow horizontal expansion.

There can be a variety of uses and activities planned for areas outside the building, particularly social gatherings, special events celebrations, and possibly performances and temporary exhibit installations. The location and proximity of service, vehicular circulation, and mechanical elements such as loading dock driveways, receiving for food service, dumpsters, and cooling towers must be carefully planned to be visually and acoustically separate from these public-use outdoor spaces.

The design of the outdoor space may provide a visual focal point or organizing element to the spaces within the Museum. As such, it should provide a visual and functional complement to similar spaces inside, including public circulation, the lobby, food service, retail, and in some cases, the exhibition spaces (Fig. 3).

For rooftop terraces or ground-level courtyards, appropriate paving, landscaping, lighting for evening use, sun and wind protection, power and water, exiting, and floor loading capacities should be anticipated. Proximity to public circulation, rest rooms, catering, and other support facilities as well as public access must be controllable.

The site plan should also recognize adjacent development, whether existing, pending, or likely.

**Fig. 2. Cedar Rapids Museum of Art (Glenn Arbonies, AIA, at Centerbrook Architects with Charles W. Moore; photo: Peter Mauss/ESTO courtesy of Arbonies King Vlock Architects)**

**Fig. 3. Cedar Rapids Museum of Art (Glenn Arbonies, AIA, at Centerbrook Architects with Charles W. Moore; photo: Peter Mauss/ESTO courtesy of Arbonies King Vlock Architects)**

**Spatial Organization**

Museums operate best with a simple and clear floor plan. The primary organizational diagram (Fig. 4) should be based on five basic zones, according to public exposure and the presence of collections.

1. Public/no collections
2. Public/collections
3. Non Public/no collections
4. Non Public/collections
5. Collections storage

Museums have very specific operational needs in each of these zones. Two of the most important operational needs are security for the collections and the HVAC system maintaining nearly constant temperature and relative humidity in all collections-containing spaces year-round, 24 hours per day. Meeting both will require the architectural design to be "zoned" in a manner that facilitates the operation of both security and HVAC systems.

The choreography of arrival, welcome, and circulation inside the museum will be central to the ceremony and drama of the museum visit. Circulation inside the museum will choreograph the entire visitor experience. This experience should be welcoming and coherent. Public circulation—pedestrian and vehicular, exterior and interior—should be logical and clear (Fig. 5).

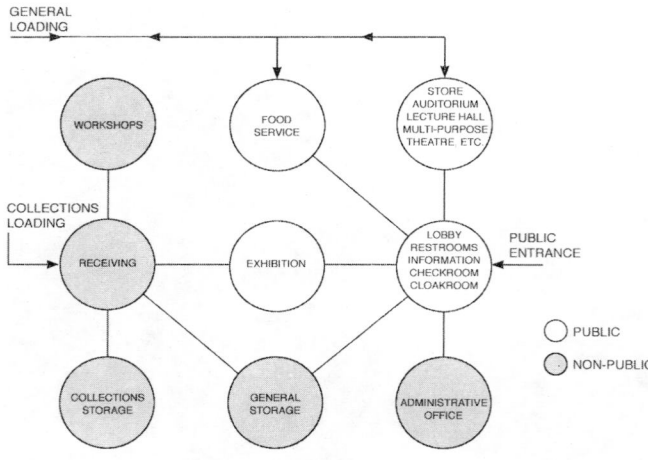

ORGANIZATIONAL DIAGRAM

**Fig. 4. Organizational diagram**

The entrance and lobby will be the public's introduction and welcome to the museum experience. Some museums will charge admission, necessitating an admissions sales point at the entrance or lobby. Some areas may be in a "free zone."

By way of illustrating which zones certain functions would ideally be located in:

| Public Areas | Non-Public Areas |
|---|---|
| **Non-Collection** | **Collections—Related** |
| Checkroom | Workshop |
| Theater | Crating/Uncrating |
| Food Services | Freight Elevator |
| Information Desk | Collections Loading Dock |
| Main Public Toilets | Receiving |
| Museum Lobby | **Non-Collections-Related** |
| Retail (Museum Store) | Catering Kitchen |
| **Collection Spaces** | Electrical Room |
| Classrooms | Food Service/Kitchen |
| Exhibition Galleries | General Storage |
| Orientation | Mechanical Room |
| | Museum Store Office |
| | Offices |
| | Conference Rooms |
| | Security Office |
| | **Super-Secure Spaces** |
| | Collections Storage |
| | Computer Network Room |
| | Security Equipment Room |

**Flexibility**

Museums need flexibility to evolve and respond to constituencies as well as to new technologies, exhibition ideas, and information. Accordingly, the design should provide spaces and relationships that are no more specific than necessary.

The organization of spaces and the resulting circulation pattern should anticipate potential changes in use. Designing for flexibility in the exhibition spaces is discussed elsewhere.

## ACCESSORY FUNCTIONS

Accessory uses may increase the value of the museum to its visitors. Examples of these include auditorium, performance space, film theater, outdoor amphitheater, pond/fountain, coffee bar, café, cafeteria, restaurant, bar, members' lounge, roof terrace, etc.

Many museums prefer to include such spaces as a theater or auditorium if budget allows. This is used in conjunction with the exhibition program. These spaces may also serve as an important revenue-producing space, rented by other groups. This rental use would affect entrance and access.

Museum stores are capable of bringing in significant revenue. Location, scale, visibility, and proximity to the lobby and other public, high-use areas is critical to its success. A retail operation may be important to the museum visit and a special retail destination for the community.

The museum may intend to provide on-site food service. This is desirable because it tends to extend the length of visitor's stays. The range of options and style—sit down, cafeteria, self-service, fast food, etc. will affect design. The museum may also provide catering facilities to support its rental and revenue-producing objectives.

The museum lobby often serves as an event space where important civic, institutional, and private gatherings and celebrations can be held. The architectural design should allow for this space to be easily transformed to accommodate various functions.

## MUSEUM ENTRANCE

Museum visitors most often arrive as individuals and small groups, or as large groups such as a bus of school children or tourists. The intended sequence of entrance, welcome, and orientation are different for these two situations and must be coordinated with the external location of visitor and bus drop-off areas.

A single entrance and exit for all visitors is ideal (Fig. 6). This will allow the museum to provide security efficiently. The clarity of this entrance is of the utmost concern. The entrance should face the direction of approach. If visitors will arrive by multiple modes of transportation, the design should reconcile these to a single entrance.

A separate museum staff entrance may be used and is often located near the collections loading dock, if possible. This entrance should also be used for mail, courier, office supply, and similar deliveries.

A museum's store and food service operations should be served via a separate loading dock, which is effectively another entry that must be secure.

Other special use rooms or accessory spaces (such as an auditorium or theater used for non-museum functions at times) should be accessible when the museum is closed.

All entrances should have vestibules that are deep enough so that the exterior door will close before the next (interior) door is encountered. This is to minimize dust and particulate air pollution (as well as outdoor temperature/humidity infiltration) from affecting the interior.

The design must provide a facility that is inclusive of all peoples. This specifically means that all visitors, regardless of disability or culture, will be provided access to the same experience. All areas, features,

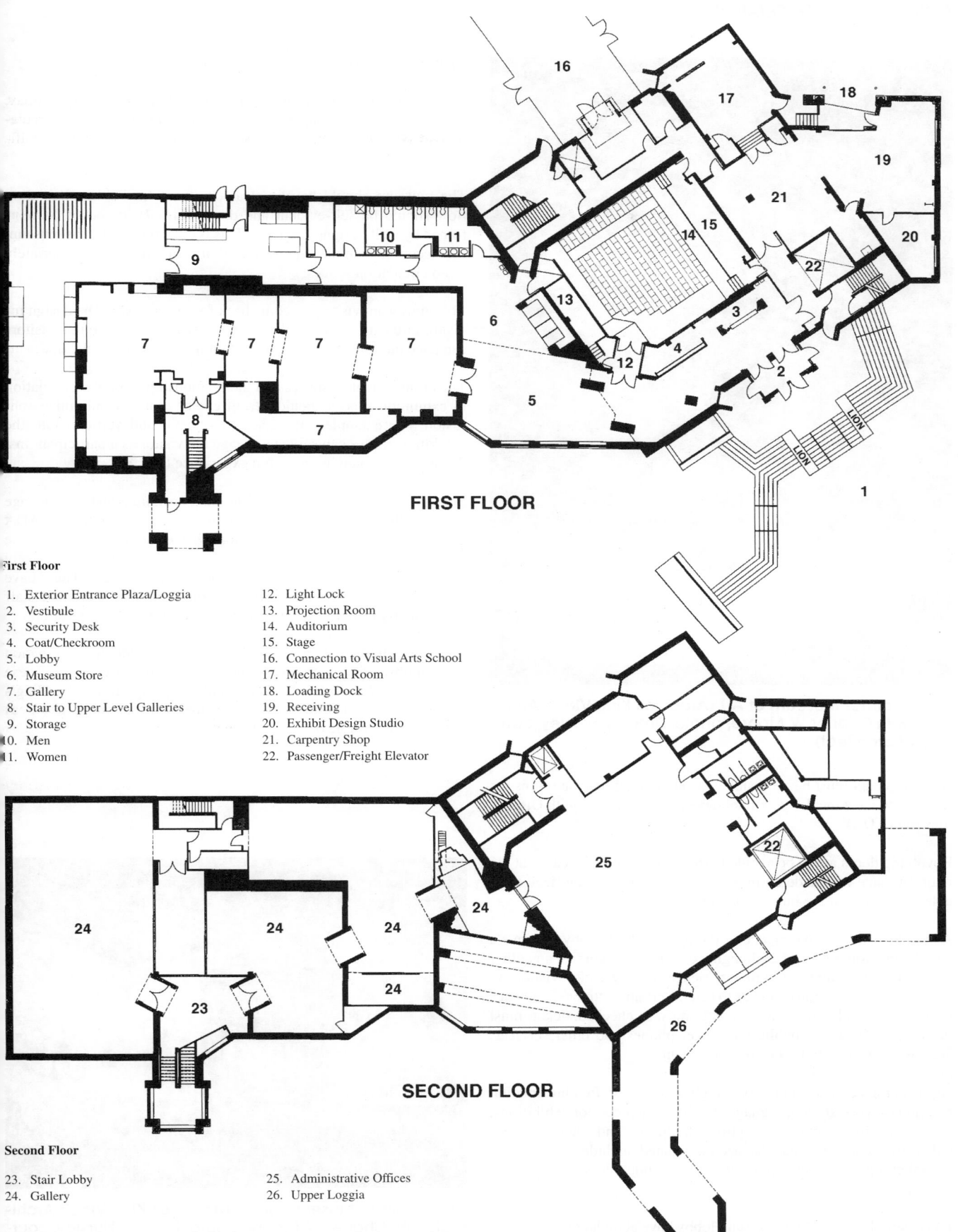

**FIRST FLOOR**

**First Floor**

1. Exterior Entrance Plaza/Loggia
2. Vestibule
3. Security Desk
4. Coat/Checkroom
5. Lobby
6. Museum Store
7. Gallery
8. Stair to Upper Level Galleries
9. Storage
10. Men
11. Women

12. Light Lock
13. Projection Room
14. Auditorium
15. Stage
16. Connection to Visual Arts School
17. Mechanical Room
18. Loading Dock
19. Receiving
20. Exhibit Design Studio
21. Carpentry Shop
22. Passenger/Freight Elevator

**SECOND FLOOR**

**Second Floor**

23. Stair Lobby
24. Gallery

25. Administrative Offices
26. Upper Loggia

**Fig. 5. Plans, Palmer Museum of Art (Arbonies King Vlock Architects with Charles W. Moore)**

**Fig. 6. Palmer Museum of Art (Arbonies King Vlock Architects with Charles W. Moore; photo: Timothy Hursley, courtesy of architect)**

and equipment must be accessible. As public facilities, museums are required to meet the design guidelines of the Americans with Disabilities Act (ADA).

Revolving doors are to be avoided. The number of door leaves at the main entrance will be determined by code (doors must be sized to be able to exit half of the building occupant load).

As the first interior experience of the museum, the lobby presents a significant moment and a challenging one. It may be unlike any other place, unique to this museum experience. It may entice visitors to discover all that the museum has to offer. Certain "entrance" logistics must also be dealt with: coats and bags must be checked, tickets must be bought. Access to public toilets, telephones and other services, and visitor information must be convenient.

At the entrance, there should be a highly visible, staffed information position or work-station. Signage should be included for exhibitions, events, openings, lectures, receptions, weddings, and other activities. Other functions that may be accommodated include: checkroom, school groups, membership service, main public toilets, first aid, and security desk.

It is desirable that the entrance and lobby have abundant natural light and windows. The lobby should be inviting, day or night.

## Visitor Circulation

The number of people to be accommodated in a year, a typical day, and on peak days during a month is significant to designing circulation spaces. Of that figure, school children may represent a significant portion of the museum's audience.

The museum should have a clear organization. Public circulation flow should be self-evident and direct (Fig. 7). It should be reinforced by well designed signage. This is essential so that the museum can accommodate the expected level of visitation with appropriately sized circulation spaces.

Museums want visitors to come back for repeat visits. The design for visitor circulation should allow flexibility and choice so that visitors can pace themselves, seek out the familiar, and explore the new.

The arrangement of spaces and the relationship of public circulation to exhibition spaces should permit choice, but also minimize confusion. For example, view axes (horizontal and vertical) into the exhibition spaces can serve to engage the visitor as a participant in a dynamic and changing museum experience (Fig. 8).

Signage is an important aspect of museum operations and use. Signage must function for both disabled and non-disabled visitors, per ADA requirements. This applies to exterior signage and interior signage.

Information and/or security desks should be well placed. These have a role in guiding visitors through the museum, and also make staff conveniently available to respond to any visitor need or question.

The spaces immediately within the entrance include the information desk, lobby, orientation areas, and major public circulation. These spaces should facilitate visitors' understanding of the building's major elements and how to easily seek them out. All public-use areas should be accessible or visible from the lobby.

**Fig. 7. Palmer Museum of Art (Arbonies King Vlock Architects with Charles W. Moore; photo: Timothy Hursley, courtesy of architect)**

Vistas indicate circulation through galleries and exhibitions, suggest options, and create anticipation of what comes next. Vistas through public circulation spaces are also desirable. Public lobbies, stairs, and other circulation spaces are usually more architecturally expressive than exhibition spaces.

Ideally, all exhibition spaces will be located together, or as nearly together as is practical. This will facilitate maintaining security and environmental conditions. There may be exceptions to this if the design is multi-story or an exhibition space occupies a very special role in the museum and is to be located in a particular location. It is desirable that visitor circulation patterns to and through exhibition spaces be clear and direct. If there are major groups of exhibition spaces or focal points, these can be treated as "anchors" to draw visitors past other exhibition spaces located in between. Vistas may be developed by aligning openings between galleries. Flexibility in changing exhibits should be provided.

Exhibition needs vary substantially by the type of museum. For instance, an art museum is very concerned with display surfaces on walls, while a natural history museum may have casework that completely covers walls.

Exhibition spaces within a museum can have distinct architectural typologies. Light quality, room proportion, finishes, and materials can be tailored for each to suit the nature and scale of works being presented (Fig. 10). With variation, several different types of exhibition can be well shown at any given time. Also, some exhibition spaces will change more frequently and completely than others. The key to managing an active exhibition program is an architecture that facilitates change and promotes installation efficiency.

Defining the exhibition environment for the contemporary artist will challenge the architect to set new standards for the audience experience. Designing for contemporary art involves new ways of seeing and interacting with the art. Exhibition spaces must be flexible to accommodate tremendous variation in size, scale, weight, and technology.

Some museums may require exhibition spaces that are specifically scaled to the collection. For some, this means "room-like" spaces; for others it means grand halls. Permanent collection galleries are typically a series or suite of contiguous exhibition spaces that open into one another.

Fig. 8. Cedar Rapids Museum of Art (Glenn Arbonies, AIA, at Centerbrook Architects with Charles W. Moore; photo: Peter Mauss/ESTO courtesy of Arbonies King Vlock Architects)

**Restrooms**

Public restrooms should be accessed from the lobby. These may also need to serve other facilities, including accessory uses such as auditorium, theater, retail, and the food service operations. For convenience, other restroom facilities may be located on upper floors, but piping for these can be a water-damage risk to collections on exhibit or in storage.

**Exhibition Spaces**

The design of the exhibition spaces should reinforce and promote the audience's engagement with the collection (Fig. 9). Some museums will want vistas and visual connections between areas (vertical and horizontal) to create excitement and anticipation for the visitor.

Visitor choice is essential to attract different audiences. The physical arrangement and relationship of exhibition spaces needs to offer visitors options. The layout of exhibition spaces and the main circulation to these should be flexible and provide opportunities for the visitor to select multiple routes tailored to the duration and intensity of his or her visit. By being so configured, the exhibition experience becomes an active dimension of the whole museum experience, encouraging repeat visits.

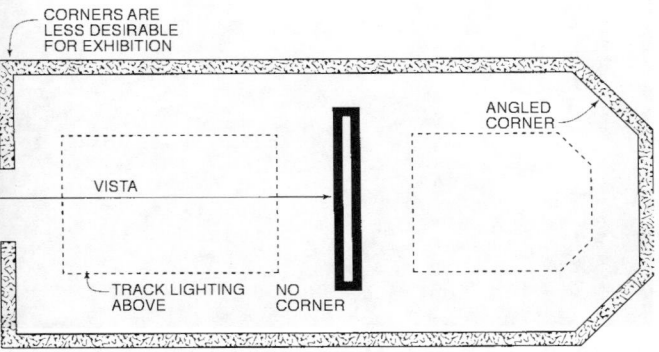

CORNERS ARE LESS DESIRABLE FOR EXHIBITION

ANGLED CORNER

VISTA

TRACK LIGHTING ABOVE

NO CORNER

EXHIBITION CONSIDERATIONS

Fig. 9. Exhibition space features

Fig. 10. Palmer Museum of Art (Arbonies King Vlock Architects with Charles W. Moore; photo: Timothy Hursley, courtesy of architect)

Spaces designed for traveling or temporary exhibitions, organized by the museum to keep interest levels high should be large flexible spaces capable of handling varied layouts and highly diverse exhibit forms. There may be service areas for acoustic-guide rental and book or exhibition-related sales.

Convenient storage for movable seating should be considered in the design to accommodate educational programs in exhibition spaces.

Some museums may feature site-specific installations and special projects devoted to exhibitions by emerging artists not yet ready for full-scale museum showings, but whose work represents new, exciting ideas in the visual arts. High ceilings would be flexible to accommodate cutting-edge art formats and be designed for technologies currently available and some not yet known.

A "hands-on" exhibition space is usually administered by the education department and used for exhibitions geared toward young people and related to those exhibitions on view in other areas. The creative process as well as work may be exhibited.

Some museums should not have any natural light in exhibition areas. Most will accept low levels of natural light if it is filtered to remove harmful wavelengths. If natural light is desired, it must be controlled depending on the contents of the exhibition. Skylights or clerestories are typically preferred over windows (as windows take up much needed wall display surface area).

In some museums, the display surfaces are a part of the architectural design. In others, the entire exhibition space is finished by the museum, often using an exhibit design consultant and exhibit construction firm to out-source the actual fabrication. Natural history museums tend to have installations that do not change often, as compared with an art museum that may change a gallery several times a year.

Gallery and exhibition spaces should be visually pure environments, without visual clutter (thermostats, temperature/humidity recorders, fire extinguishers, access panels, signage, etc.). The display surface material should not be identifiable (by pattern or texture). This surface may be easily paintable to allow the museum to control its color to suit each exhibition. A minimum display wall height of 12 feet is required for most new art museum galleries; however, those dedicated to contemporary art should have considerably higher ceilings, 20 feet is a reasonably flexible height (Figs. 11, 12).

Exhibition finishes should vary to reflect the nature of the art being displayed, while maintaining some cohesion in design. Unifying themes or elements are desirable. Spaces for one type of collection may have uniform finishes and treatments.

Some museums will build temporary walls to implement an exhibition design (Fig. 13). While the architect's design may not include these, it should reflect the most likely or common locations for these as advised by the museum.

For flexibility, museums may prefer rectangular room shapes.

A minimum width for subdividing by temporary walls is about 40 to 50 feet. Dimensions less than this should not be considered subdividable. Care should be taken to ensure that there is space in the gallery width for viewing on opposite sides, with circulation in the middle.

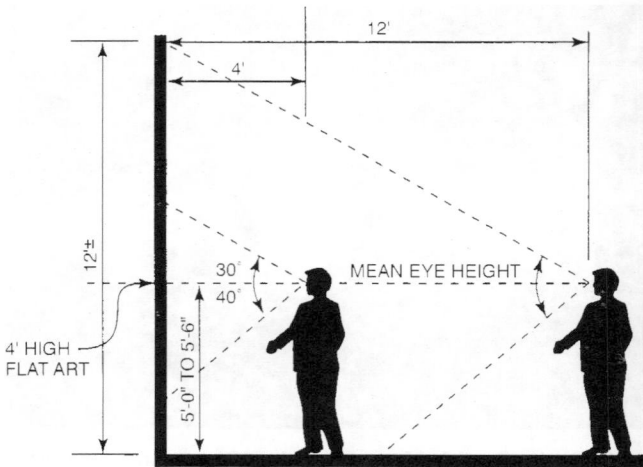

**Fig. 11. Viewing distances**

**Fig. 12. Cedar Rapids Museum of Art (Glenn Arbonies, AIA, at Centerbrook Architects with Charles W. Moore; photo: courtesy of Arbonies King Vlock Architects)**

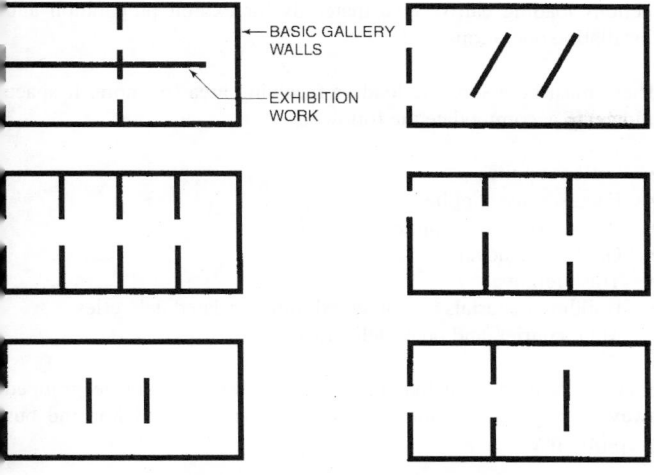

BASIC GALLERY WALLS

EXHIBITION WORK

**Fig. 13. Exhibition space configurations**

The museum may want visitors to experience its collections throughout the museum, not only in dedicated exhibition spaces. There can be exhibition in the lobby. In addition, site-specific works (sculpture or other 3-D pieces) of durable materials could be semi-permanently or permanently displayed. Administrative areas, the boardroom, and main public circulation areas may also contain material from the permanent collection, but not the most valuable works. Ceiling design should not limit exhibition flexibility.

Two exits are required from nearly all exhibition spaces. This is an important consideration in the design of galleries and establishment of circulation patterns.

## EXHIBITION POLICY

Exhibition policy will vary greatly according to the type of museum and its operating budget. Art museums tend to change at least a portion of the exhibition on a regular basis. These tend to be moving an object into positions — a painting or sculpture against a wall. There is also a tradition of change. Some may have a gallery or wing that is devoted to several changes per year, using both its collections and borrowed works. Some may have a gallery devoted to new artists or site-specific installations. This could change five to ten times per year depending on the museum's role in the community. For other types of museums there is less need to change. Natural history museums tend to invest heavily in elaborate permanent display cases.

Another type, such as a presidential history museum, has a relatively defined and fixed story to tell.

### Collections

Collections is a generic term used to designate the valuable artifacts that are stored, preserved or exhibited. A museum's own collection is referred to as its "permanent collection." It may also borrow artifacts or artwork from other museums, galleries, and collectors. These may be exhibited independent of the permanent collection or in combination with it (Fig. 14).

Collections spaces are critical to a museum's mission. They must be designed for moving large objects safely, and have clear circulation

paths. Windows are not desirable. There is typically substantial movement of materials into and out of the museum. Collections movement must be kept entirely separate from other types. Collections loading operations must be separated from other loading or delivery areas by the greatest distance possible.

The collections handling department is responsible for the care and safe handling, shipping/receiving, and storage of all collections and exhibition materials, whether on loan or in the permanent collection. Collections handling and collections storage functions are closely related.

For moving collections and exhibition materials, doorways and openings should have a minimum of clearance established by the museum; typically this is 12 feet high by 8 feet wide. This is a critical requirement. These routes should be carefully planned within the museum to extend from the loading dock to exhibition spaces, including all collections handling areas and collections storage areas. This clear-opening requirement applies to doors, hallway piping and ductwork, wall and overhead devices, freight elevators, and archway-type openings.

For security and environmental reasons, it is very desirable to have an enclosed loading dock for one tractor-trailer truck to park off-street. This dock is not to be used for any purpose other than collections receiving except receipt of large construction materials that will be used for exhibition construction, and collections storage furniture and equipment. This area is to be environmentally conditioned. Exhaust fumes should be vented outside. Truck cabs should not be parked in the building.

The museum floor elevation should minimize the need to use a platform lift. The tongue of any such lift should be long enough to lap over the truck (or trailer) bed, with the truck hard against the dock bumpers. This will affect the museum floor elevation design relative to the street elevations.

Collections will be unpacked or packed in crating/uncrating space. A registrar's remote workstation should be located here. Packing materials and unpacking tools should be close at hand for efficiency. The minimum size for this room is equal to a single truckload of crates, with sufficient space to move around. Collection items will be fully removed from crates and packing materials at this location and inspected. The design and operation of this area must insure that no pests (animal or insects) will enter and cause damage to collections. If there is a pest risk, the object should be sent to an isolation area for an extended period. If it is to proceed to a gallery space for exhibition (and the space is ready), the object can go there directly. If not, it should go to a holding room. On-site pedestal and crate storage is desirable. However, the museum may rent space to store these off-site.

There is often a dedicated freight elevator used only to move collections and exhibit construction materials through the building. Size is critical. It may need to accommodate a large collection object carried by a fork-lift.

### Collections Storage

The function of this department is to preserve in good condition the collections material (objects), especially the permanent collection in long-term storage. This function should be managed by the registrar, with designated staff support.

**Fig. 14. Cedar Rapids Museum of Art (Glenn Arbonies, AIA, at Centerbrook Architects with Charles W. Moore; photo: Peter Mauss/ESTO courtesy of Arbonies King Vlock Architects)**

This area should be located in the core of the building, ideally with no exposure to an outside wall or roof. Stored works are to be inspected on a regular basis.

The types of storage needed will vary depending on the collections and the exhibition program. The specific storage devices depend on the items to be stored. High density systems can be used, but must be vibration-free. There is an unfortunate tendency to undersize these rooms to reduce initial costs.

This area needs to have generously sized hallways to move collections safely. Oversize doors are necessary. An opening 8 feet wide by 12 feet high is a typical minimum (for use and flexibility). Plumbing is not to be located in these spaces.

Fire protection is to be provided. Collections storage areas should have dry-pipe systems that set off a system alarm (audible and electronic) if any loss of pressure is detected. This area will also have the highest level of security in the museum.

This area should have the greatest control and most stable environment. To minimize light damage to collections, lighting should be automatically turned off if the space is not in use. Maximum general lighting levels of objects should be limited to 5 to 7 footcandles (sufficient to move objects around safely and to identify specific pieces). Task lighting should be provided at worktables.

In collections storage, walls should not be easily removable due to security concerns. Utility services should avoid these rooms. Collections storage is likely to be expanded. Metal shelving and cabinets should be used. Painting storage racks are operable systems. Textiles, costumes, and other fabric objects need custom storage to suit each type. Open floor area is used for large sculptures and similar objects. Finishes must be sealed at all joints to be completely airtight, vapor tight, and secure. Finishes should be non-dusting.

## Loading

There is substantial movement of materials into and out of most museums. Collections loading operations must be separated from other loading or delivery areas by the greatest distance possible. Collections loading can receive materials for exhibit preparation and installation operations.

There must be a separate loading/receiving area (or more, if space allows) to accommodate the following:

- Office supplies
- Food service supplies
- Retail stock and supplies
- Garbage removal
- Trash removal
- Building materials and other exhibition-related deliveries
- Mail, courier, and other deliveries

Service, delivery, and loading dock driveways should be grouped away from public entrance(s), outdoor space, and visitor and bus drop-off zones.

### Conservation

Some museums will have "conservation departments," possibly including staffs that are specialists in restoring and re-conditioning collection materials. This would be a very secured area, with laboratory-like work areas and ventilation.

### Education

Some museums provide broad-based educational programs. These may include docent tours of exhibitions (Fig. 15), class-visit programs for schools' special programs (for adults and young people), and creative opportunities for people of all ages. This department may serve a crucial function in providing innovative programming that reflects the museum's mission in reaching out to the community, and can generate a significant portion of a museum's audience.

There are several different types of spaces that are typically included for this department, such as classrooms, docents/volunteers rooms, orientation, special galleries, offices, storage, and hallway circulation.

Classrooms are often intended to accommodate many activities including object-making and demonstrations. The orientation area is a significant space within museums. For student groups especially, this environment will set the tone for the museum experience. The orientation area will be the place where appropriate museum behavior (do's and don'ts) are explained. It is often acoustically separate from the lobby and other public areas of the museum. Docents/volunteers rooms are frequently used as informal gathering places, with some work stations available.

Consideration is sometimes given to a separate entrance for education functions – to keep noisy school children from disrupting other's experiences, in the lobby especially.

### Environmental Systems

Any museum's role is to preserve and protect its collections. An essential requirement for preservation and conservation is the maintenance of an unusually stable interior environment, including maintaining an extremely constant temperature and relative humidity (RH), year-round, day and night. Accordingly, the design of the HVAC system is critical to the museum's ability to operate effectively.

**Fig. 15. Cedar Rapids Museum of Art (Centerbrook Architects; photo: courtesy of Arbonies King Vlock Architects)**

Areas in which collections are to be handled, stored, and exhibited are environmentally critical and the HVAC system(s) is required to maintain the atmosphere in these spaces and other spaces opening directly into them in a state of constant temperature and relative humidity.

Other factors will be important in maintaining a constant environment in these critical spaces. These include, as a minimum, the architectural design, the location of spaces relative to the exterior, continuous vapor barriers, pressurization of critical areas, and filtering and treating all airflows.

The design must comply with applicable building codes, including energy usage and conservation requirements, and with current ASHRAE standards as applicable.

Buffer systems may be designed for "occupied" and "unoccupied" modes. This would allow the systems to condition to the lower portion of the range in the "unoccupied" mode to save energy. For non-collection spaces (also called "non-critical" spaces, such as offices, the museum store, café, and film theater), the HVAC design should comply with building codes, their energy usage guidelines, and

ASHRAE for air changes. Non-critical systems should provide basic humidification and well-filtered air.

**Temperature Standards**

Some museums may allow a slow transition for temperature and relative humidity setpoints. Museum collections are generally more tolerant of temperature variations than of RH variation. However, RH is extremely temperature sensitive and therefore temperature must be held more constant than RH—so that the RH can be controlled within a narrow (2 percent) range from the design setpoint. It is clear from the literature that lower temperatures are better for collections conservation. Although people may be most comfortable in the range of 72 to 76°F, 68 to 70°F is the range generally recommended for exhibition spaces used by the public. A setpoint in the range of 60 to 68°F is recommended for collections storage.

**Relative Humidity Standards**

Generally, the museum profession recommends constant, year-round RH levels of 50%. Constant RH is required because the materials of which collections are made typically are very sensitive to slight changes in RH. In unfavorable conditions, those works made of different materials will expand (each material moving at a different rate), rub, abrade, acidify, etc., thereby causing deterioration.

This 50 percent RH ±2 percent (year-around, 24 hours per day) is an extremely high standard that both the architect and engineer must acknowledge in the design. Architecturally, to have any possibility of meeting this performance level, the design must use other spaces (likely the main public circulation and lobby spaces) as a buffer between collections–containing spaces and the exterior. For the engineering design to work, it will need to treat a single air volume with minimum leakage. This point is stressed for the architect's benefit as it must inform the architectural design. The requirements for HVAC system(s) serving critical spaces in museums are not standard building practice—they are exceptional.

There may be exceptions to maintaining this 50 percent RH level.

In fact, each object in the collection and loaned to the museum may have its own specific needs.

In locations where a museum can be exposed to cold weather and has a high interior relative humidity, significant condensation can occur. A "dew point" calculation should be done to ensure that the dew point is reached outside of a continuous vapor barrier. Vapor leaks (into cold roof and wall spaces) are very problematic. Thermal bridges are also to be avoided. Also see "Exterior Envelope."

**HVAC System Layout**

The space and economical location requirements for the HVAC system(s) should be considered early in the design process. The location of air-handling units will have a major impact on design. Main distribution piping should be run in or above non-critical spaces. Consideration should be given to the possibility of future building expansion and equipment additions. Such flexibility is highly recommended.

Dust is present both inside and outside the building. Outside dust entry should be minimized. Particles in combination with interior humid air can become acidic and cause corrosion and deterioration. Interior dust must be kept from spreading. Dust-producing activities must be segregated from the HVAC systems serving collections spaces.

There are gaseous pollutants in outdoor air. These cannot be allowed to affect the collection and exhibitions. Pollutant molecules may directly attack the collection, or may combine with the water in the humidified environment to form acid.

The location of the intake air supply louver(s) is significant. It must be away from the loading docks, dumpsters, street traffic, restaurant exhaust, building exhaust fan outlets, equipment and chemical exhausts, and building plumbing vents.

The critical HVAC system(s), including humidity control, must have emergency electric power for operation in the event of power loss. The design should also provide for component failure within the system with alarms in the event of any failure.

Consideration should be given to designing components and control systems (such as boiler, chiller, converters, circulation pumps, air compressor) to have built-in redundancy, to the extent this is practically and economically achievable.

### HVAC Criteria for Collections-Containing Spaces

Conceptually, there are four layers to the architectural and HVAC design, all of which require partitions and doors to divide the interior space:

- Zone #A: The core area is the most effectively controlled and includes collections storage.
- Zone #B: The exhibition area (Fig. 16) in which the HVAC requirements are extremely stringent, so much so that exposure to the exterior or any space that directly or indirectly connects to the exterior will cause the conditioning requirements to not be met. This zone includes exhibition and other spaces in which collections are handled, moved, and temporarily stored.
- Zone #C: The buffer layer, in which doors open directly into collections-containing areas or indirectly to the exterior. In this layer, doors and partitions will need to create spaces that are possible to condition to a higher level than spaces with direct exterior exposure.
- Zone #D: The outer layer, in which doors open directly to the exterior. This includes the vestibule, and may include the lobby and main public circulation, food service, retail store, loading docks, and staff entrance, depending on the design.

### Preservation

Preservation is central to a museum's mission statement. The primary requirements are for security to prevent theft and abuse and that the HVAC system maintain a museum-quality environment.

Materials should not off-gas harmful chemicals (such as formaldehyde). Interior materials should not be susceptible to micro-organism, insect, or rodent infestation. Walls in receiving and handling areas should extend to and seal at structure to contain potential infestations. Floors must have nonskid qualities.

Spaces above ceilings and below the superstructure must not be used to run liquid-containing piping of any type above collection-containing spaces.

Interior doors and partitions should be located to create zones for the HVAC system and security system to operate as programmed.

Interior walls may also need to have vapor barriers to separate any non-humidified zones or lower-humidity-level zones from higher ones.

**Fig. 16. Palmer Museum of Art (Arbonies King Vlock Architects wtih Charles W. Moore; photo: courtesy of architect)**

## STRUCTURE

For flexibility in use, museums are typically designed with more than the minimum floor loading capacity. Museum programs seem to vary between 125 pounds per square foot for all spaces and 200 pounds per square foot for exhibition areas. These are well above the code minimums to provide flexibility.

Individual objects in the collection storage and exhibition areas may be extremely heavy. High-density storage is sometimes used. Heavy art objects and exhibition installation materials are moved using equipment that may, in the case of forklifts, weigh far more than the object (8,000 to 10,000 pounds is possible).

Some of the collections may be wall-supported, some may be floor-supported, and others may be suspended from ceilings or other overhead structure. For flexibility, the structural design should accommodate all of these exhibition conditions and storage situations.

The museum should advise as to where the heaviest installations are anticipated.

### Exterior Envelope

Materials for the exterior should be selected for durability and appearance (Fig. 17). Exterior walls and roofs must meet code standards for energy conservation.

Wall and roof construction should avoid thermal bridges. A continuous vapor barrier is required at exterior walls, roofs, and lowest floor. Any discontinuity may result in substantial condensation and water damage.

Windows and skylights should have filtering to eliminate all ultraviolet and infrared light wavelengths. There must also be blocking layers or mechanisms to allow the museum to prevent natural light from entering any space. Operable windows should not be used. Areas without collections may have abundant natural light.

### Artificial and Natural Lighting

For flexibility in use, museums are typically designed with more than the minimum lighting capacity, especially in exhibition spaces.

Lighting needs and systems will vary by the function of the space and type of display (Fig. 18). For example, a natural history museum may only need minimal general distribution where the exhibit cases provide display lighting. At the exterior, lighting and exterior space lighting can be used to dramatize and make visible the museum offering.

Deterioration caused by light is cumulative and irreversible. Making a collection look inviting while following conservation standards is difficult and requires compromise. Energy from light accelerates other kinds of deterioration. It can raise the surface temperature of the object and thereby create a micro-climate of varying relative humidity and chemical reactivity. The museum must be able to control light levels and the length of exposure in the gallery (or other critical space) as well as on each artwork. Lighting can cause fading, darkening, and accelerated aging of collections.

Visible light is a combination of red, orange, yellow, green, blue, and violet. Its wavelength is 400–700 nanometers (nm). The ultraviolet range is 300–400 nm. Light in the blue range and ultraviolet end of the spectrum has more energy and can be more damaging to objects.

**Fig. 17. Cedar Rapids Museum of Art (Glenn Arbonies, AIA, at Centerbrook Architects with Charles W. Moore; photo: courtesy of Arbonies King Vlock Architects)**

**Fig. 18. Palmer Museum of Art (Arbonies King Vlock Architects with Charles W. Moore; photo: Timothy Hursley, courtesy of architect)**

Since neither ultraviolet (UV) nor infrared (IR) light affects viewing, these should be eliminated entirely from exhibition and collection storage and handling areas. The two major sources of UV light are sunlight and fluorescent light.

In most museums, all lighting fixtures in exhibition areas (Fig. 19) and other collection areas should be UV shielded to less than 75 microwatts per lumen and enclosed to avoid damage to objects in the event of lamp breakage.

In general, conform to the illuminance values given in the Illuminating Engineers Society of North America (IESNA), *Lighting Handbook for General Use.* However, in collection areas, light levels are most significant on the surfaces of the collections material itself. On the surfaces of the most sensitive works, including things with paper (such as prints and photographs), the lighting level should not exceed 5 footcandles (fc).

Exhibition lighting needs will vary by exhibit, type and size of works, and layout of each exhibition (Table 1). The goal may be to

**Table 1** Required lighting levels

| Space | Exhibition materials | Light level (fc) |
|---|---|---|
| Exhibition (very sensitive) | works on paper, prints, textiles, dyed leather | 5–10 |
| Exhibition (sensitive) | oil and tempera paintings, wood | 15–20 |
| Exhibition (less sensitive) | glass, stone, ceramics, metals | 30–50 |
| Collections Storage | | 5 |
| Collections Handling | | 20–50 |

light individual objects, not whole rooms. The location of the lighting devices relative to the exhibition material is critical, requiring multiple track locations as well as various types of fixtures, lamping, filters, doors, and grilles.

Exhibition spaces usually have a flexible grid of high-quality track lighting. The final layout should consider temporary wall locations. The track layout should accommodate the following for both permanent and temporary wall locations:

- The angle measured from a point at the wall and 5 feet-4 inches above the floor (which is an average eye-level for adults) should be between 45 and 75 degrees (up) from horizontal to the lamp position in the light fixture (Fig. 20).
- For permanent walls, the ideal angle is usually 65 to 70 degrees.
- The more sensitive the collection material, the less lighting is to be provided.

Natural light can be used to great affect to dramatize and enliven the design of any building (Fig. 21). Some architects use natural light as a form giver to the building design.

**Fig. 19. Cedar Rapids Museum of Art (Glenn Arbonies, AIA, at Centerbrook Architects with Charles W. Moore; photo: Peter Mauss/ESTO courtesy of Arbonies King Vlock Architects)**

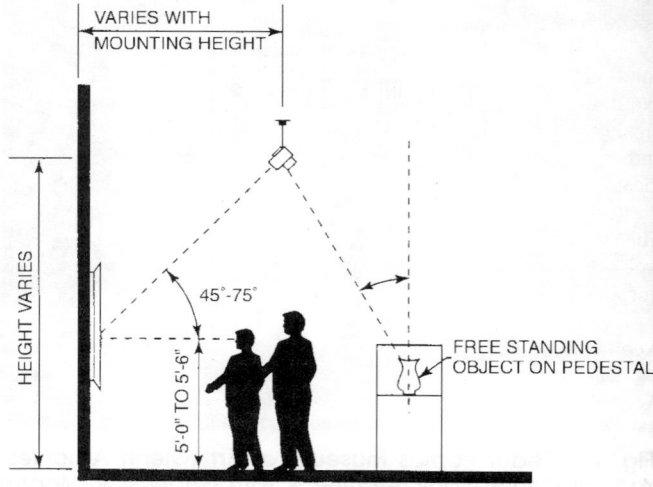

**Fig. 20. Techniques for artificial lighting**

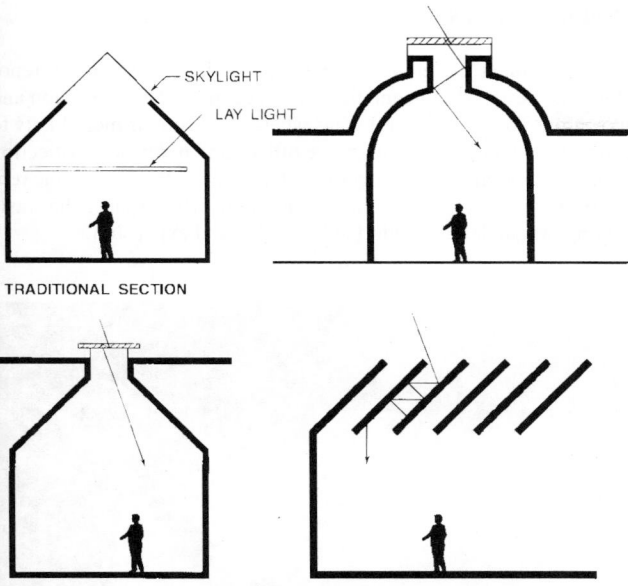

SECTIONS ILLUSTRATING APPROACHES FOR INTRODUCING NATURAL LIGHT INTO EXHIBITION SPACES

**Fig. 21. Techniques for natural lighting**

Designers of museums should understand and accept that most museum professionals value the presentation and preservation of their collections over the architectural benefit of abundant natural light in collections areas. Too much light and particularly certain wavelengths do cause real damage to irreplaceable collections.

## COMMUNICATIONS SYSTEMS

Communication systems that may be incorporated include the following:

Security system
Building management system
Information technology (voice and data)
Audio-visual systems

Technology must be readily available for flexibility in operations as well as for exhibition programming. Technology should be readily available in public-use spaces, including the lobby and main circulation areas, auditorium/theater, conference rooms, and some exterior spaces (e.g., courtyard, rooftop terrace, entrance court, and kiosks). This affects administrative operations, member services, and art-related information seeking by the public at designated locations.

This system may extend to and incorporate the museum's Internet web-site and other operations, such as e-mail, personal communications, security measures, and messaging systems.

### Acoustics

Acoustic needs vary substantially in museums. Acoustics in all spaces must be comfortable for individuals and groups. It is important for docents leading tours to be heard by their group without disturbing other visitors. Some rooms and functions such as conference rooms, orientation, auditorium (or theater) must be designed by a specialist.

Other spaces such as major circulation areas and exhibition spaces may need acoustical treatment to prevent their being so acoustically "live" that the museum experience is inhibited.

### Security

The museum operation must be made entirely secure, not just by an active system of guards and electronics, but also by appropriate layout and design. All aspects of the museum must be designed to maintain security of the collection. The collections must be protected from harm, theft, and abuse. This applies to the visiting public, staff handling, and staff theft.

There should be a single public entrance and typically a separate staff entrance (though this depends on the size of the museum). The priority is collections security, which is different from standard building security.

Five security zones should be contemplated:

| Zone #1: Highest Security | Collections Storage |
| Zone #2: High Security | No public access with collections |
| Zone #3: High Security | Public access with collections |
| Zone #4: Secure | No public access, no collections |
| Zone #5: Secure | Public access, no collections |

The architectural design must provide an organization that segregates these zones for security and efficient operation. Various aspects of the building design and construction are also involved in satisfying security needs. These include HVAC design, doors and hardware, wall construction, and roof and skylight construction.

### Fire Protection

The preservation and stewardship of museum collections require a state-of-the-art fire detection and suppression system that utilizes early-warning detection devices for maximum protection. Such protection and preservation is critical to the museum's mission.

This system must be integrated with the security system to report alarms as well as conditions that could lead to alarms in time for corrective action by trained staff. The most effective protection is an automatic fire protection (sprinkler) system throughout. However, many museum professional are resistant to using such a system, fearing the water-damage caused by actuation, leaks, and false alarms.

### Plumbing

The plumbing system, including the architectural location of toilet rooms, must avoid damage to collections caused by leaks and condensation.

All plumbing systems should be routed to rise and drain through and above service corridors or non-collection areas only. No plumbing piping and storm and roof drainage should be routed through or above any collection-containing or exhibit areas. There should be no plumbing or drainage piping in any collections storage areas.

### Technology

Technology is likely to have a dramatic impact on museums in the next decade. Flexibility to incorporate new technologies is an essential design consideration. Depending on the museum, exhibition and other spaces must be outfitted to accommodate innovative signage, information, visitor interaction, "distance" visits, and exhibitions. Technological systems may be expressed or concealed.

Technology is a very exciting component of exhibit design. It has become an integral aspect of the visual arts and of cutting-edge art forms. It is becoming more accepted in providing exhibition background information to museum visitors as they enjoy the exhibition.

**MUSEUM EXPANSION**

Eventually, most museums will be expanded or substantially renovated. The design should anticipate and accommodate expansion and renovation. There are several areas where expansion is more likely to occur. These include administrative offices and permanent collection storage. Although some changes may be incremental, such as the renovation of classroom or storage space into office space, the basic building organization should facilitate physical expansion.

Fig. 22. Palmer Museum of Art (Arbonies King Vlock Architects with Charles W. Moore; photo: Timothy Hursley, courtesy of architect)

**Chicago Public Library, Mabel Manning Branch (Ross Barney + Jankowski Architects)**

# LIBRARIES

## DIAGRAMS OF ESSENTIAL LIBRARY ELEMENTS

Three diagrams have been prepared as an aid to visualizing the functional relationships of the principal areas in typical small libraries. These diagrams are for libraries for towns of 5,000, 10,000, and 25,000 persons, respectively.

They are meant to clarify relationships and circulation patterns. They definitely are *not* building plans, nor do they constitute the only possible relationships between the program elements. It is intended that they assist in understanding the interrelationships between the major program elements.

They are intended to suggest a starting point for the planning of the library and represent *minimum standards*. They are derived from "Interim Standards for Small Public Libraries: Guidelines Toward Achieving the Goals of Public Library Service." ALA-Public Library Association, Chicago (see Table 2).

## LIBRARY FOR A TOWN OF 5,000 POPULATION

The basic principles when planning for the library (Fig. 1) are:

1. Location to insure maximum accessibility for the community.
2. Clarity of design concept (collections, seating for readers, and staff space require adjacencies to each other that are clear to the user).
3. Ease of supervision by library staff.
4. Provision for future expansion (addition of compact shelving within existing footprint and/or building expansion).

The basic statistics of the library are (in net square feet)

| | |
|---|---|
| Book collection | 15,000 volumes |
| Space for book collection | 1,000 square feet |
| Space for readers | 700 square feet |
| Staff work space | 500 square feet |
| Estimated additional space for toilets, utilities, circulation, and miscellaneous | 800 square feet |
| Total estimated net floor space | 3,000 square feet |

These are approximates only and will, of course, vary with each community.

Staff: One and one-half persons, including a professional librarian and a part-time assistant.

## LIBRARY FOR A TOWN OF 10,000 POPULATION

This library (Fig. 2) in many respects is an expanded version of the first one. The basic principles and relationships are the same. The staff and space requirements are approximately twice those of the first.

The larger size permits the development of special areas that add to the usefulness of the library and enable it to provide better services. Some of these may be: a special area in the children's section for story-telling and related activities, expanded reference, and separate periodical areas. A small meeting room may be a useful addition to the program.

---

*Reviewer:* Perry Dean Rogers & Partners
*Reference:* A. Anthony Tappé ALA., *Guide to Planning a Library Building,* Huggens and Tappé Inc., Boston.

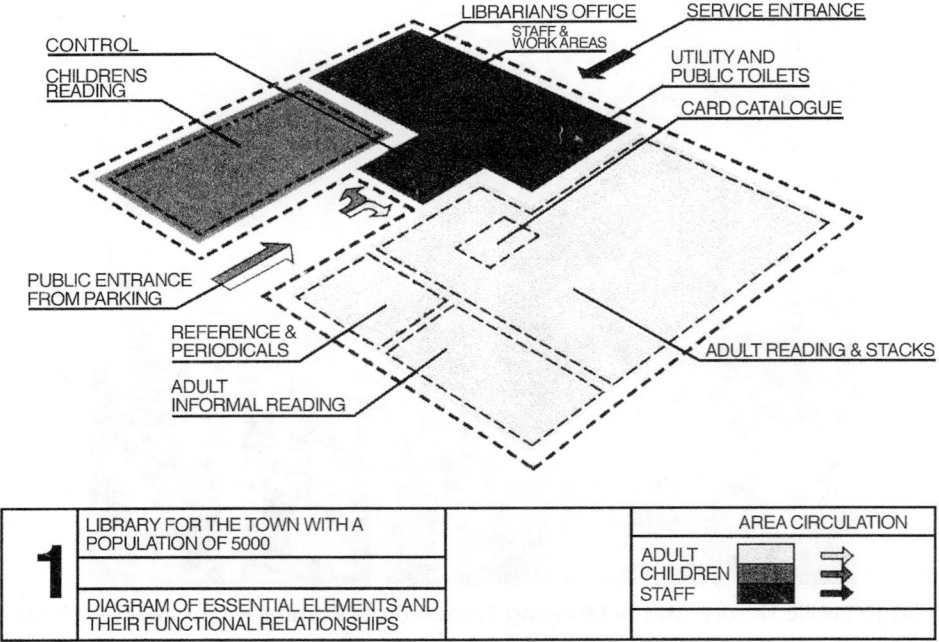

| **1** | LIBRARY FOR THE TOWN WITH A POPULATION OF 5000 | | AREA CIRCULATION |
|---|---|---|---|
| | DIAGRAM OF ESSENTIAL ELEMENTS AND THEIR FUNCTIONAL RELATIONSHIPS | | ADULT CHILDREN STAFF |

**Fig. 1. Library for town with population of 5,000**

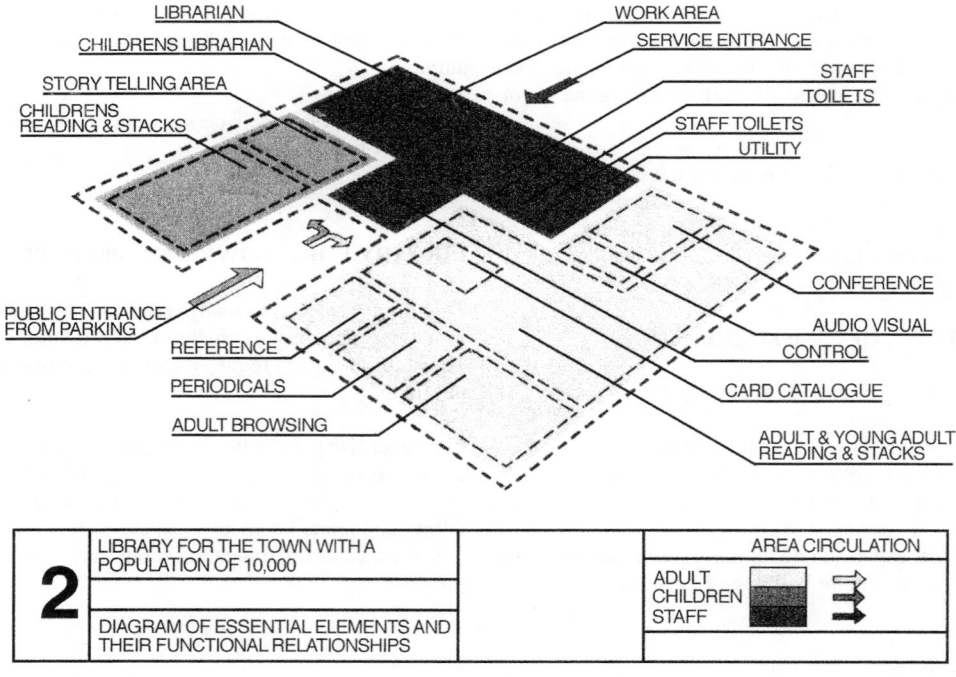

| **2** | LIBRARY FOR THE TOWN WITH A POPULATION OF 10,000 | | AREA CIRCULATION |
|---|---|---|---|
| | DIAGRAM OF ESSENTIAL ELEMENTS AND THEIR FUNCTIONAL RELATIONSHIPS | | ADULT CHILDREN STAFF |

**Fig. 2. Library for population of 10,000**

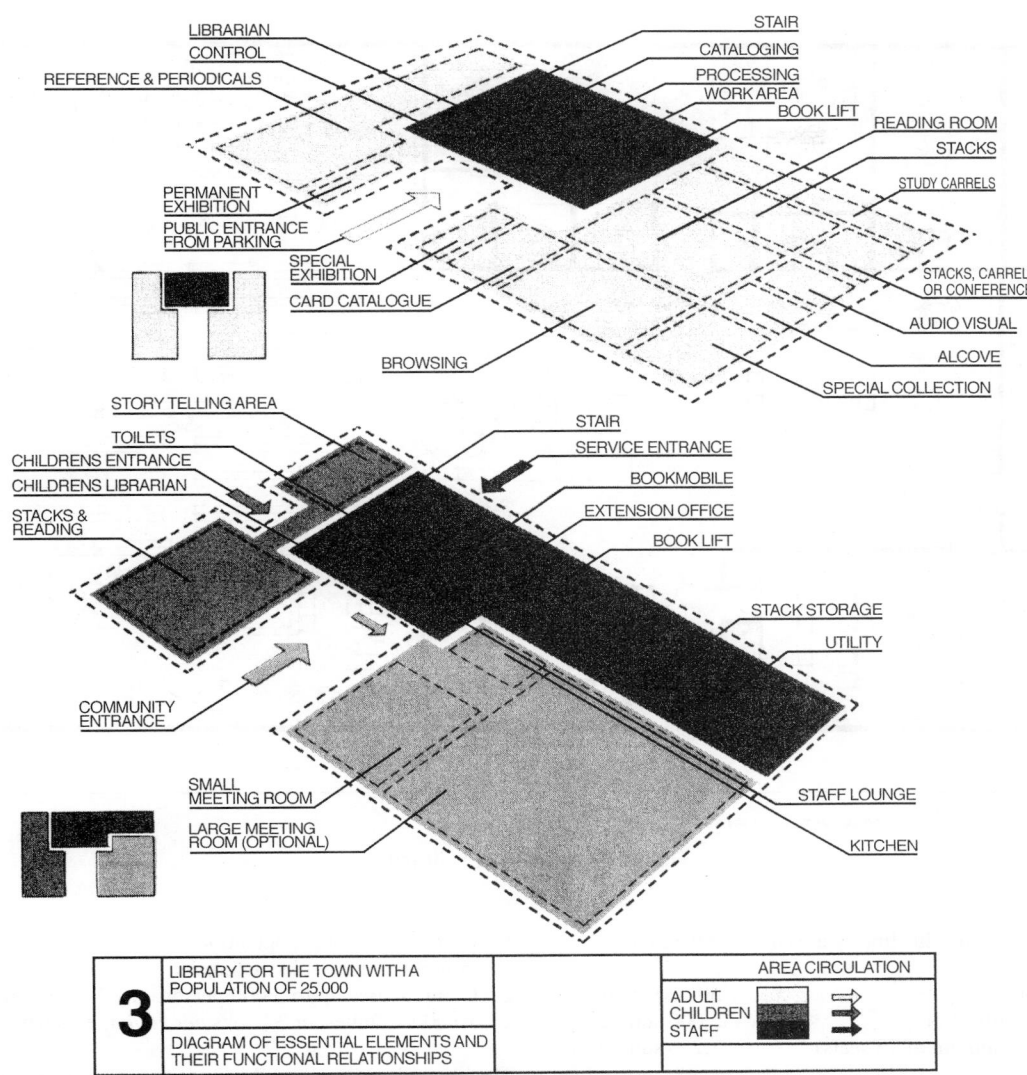

Fig. 3. Library for population of 25,000

The basic requirements for this library are (in net square feet)

| | |
|---|---|
| Book collection | 20,000 volumes |
| Space for the book collection | 2,000 square feet |
| Space for readers (40 seats min.) | 1,600 square feet |
| Staff work space | 1,000 square feet |
| Estimated additional space for utilities, circulation, and miscellaneous | 2,800 square feet |
| Total estimated net floor space | 7,400 square feet |

Staff: Three persons: a professional librarian, an assistant, and part-time clerical staff help equivalent to one full-time person.

## LIBRARY FOR A TOWN OF 25,000 POPULATION

This library (Fig. 3) in function is more complex than the previous libraries. To the three basic functional areas of the library, which are expanded and elaborated on, there usually is added a fourth, a community function, often in the form of a meeting room or small auditorium. There may also be (Fig. 4):

- Special exhibition space
- Special exhibition rooms
- Study area with carrels near the book stacks
- Small meeting rooms
- Audiovisual rooms or booths

The circulation pattern is more complex. A separate entrance for children is highly desirable. Access to the community facility by the public after normal library hours is required. A library of this size may be a two-level structure. On the diagram (Fig. 3) we have indicated these circulation requirements. Note the separate staff and public circulation between levels.

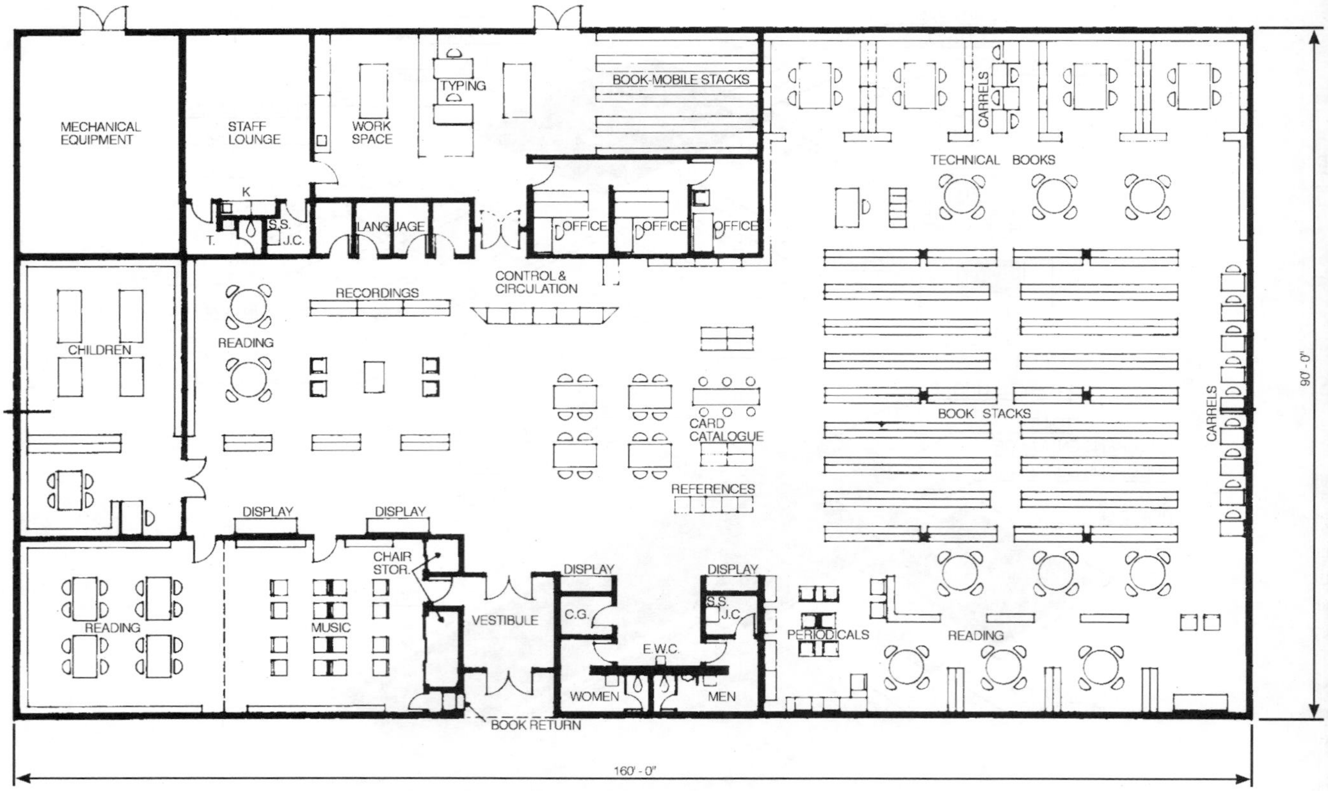

AREA SHOWN: 14,364 SQ. FT.

**Fig. 4. Floor plan of a library**

The basic requirements for this library are (in net square feet)

| | |
|---|---|
| Book collection | 50,000 volumes |
| Space for book collection | 5,000 square feet |
| Reader space (minimum of 75 seats) | 2,250 square feet |
| Staff work space | 1,500 square feet |
| Estimated additional space required for special uses, utilities, and miscellaneous | 6,250 square feet |
| Total estimated floor space | 15,000 square feet |

Staff: Ten, broken down to include two professional librarians, four assistants, and four other persons for clerical staff.

### BRANCH LIBRARIES

A branch library can play an important role as a cultural center. In addition to providing books, it can provide record and tape, video, compact disc, and DVD lending, music listening facilities, visual-aid facilities, and lecture series as well as act as a general information center. With such an expanded role, the library or cultural center will be an important element in the neighborhood. Figs. 5 and 6 are possible floor plans.

Regardless of the size of the community, the library should provide access to enough books to cover the interests of the whole population.

*References: Manual of Housing/Planning and Design Criteria,* De Chiara and Koppelman, Prentice-Hall, Inc., Englewood Cliffs, NJ.

1. Libraries serving populations from 5,000 to 50,000 require a minimum of 2 books *per capita*.
2. Communities up to 5,000 persons need access to a minimum of 10,000 volumes, or 3 books *per capita*, whichever is greater.

The library building should provide space for the full range of library services. All libraries should have designated areas for children, young adult, and adult materials.

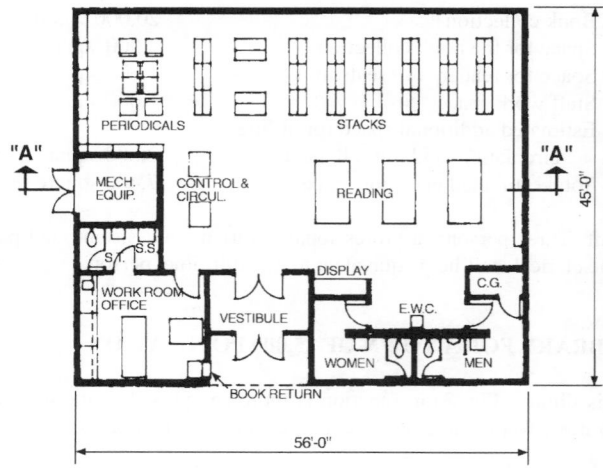

**Fig. 5. Branch library floor plan**

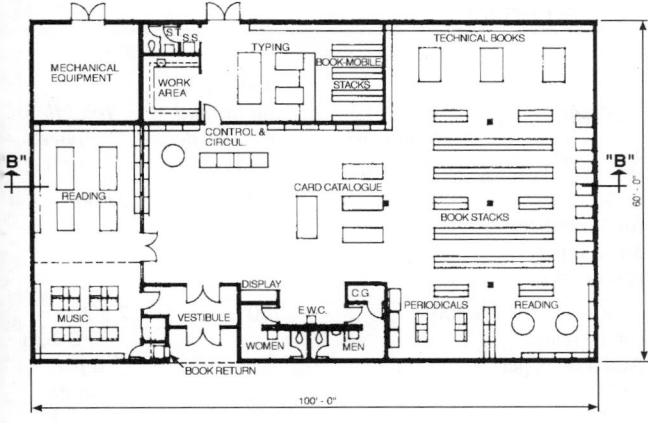

**Fig. 6. Branch library floor plan**

Multipurpose rooms should be provided for meeting, viewing, and listening by cultural, educational, and civic groups unless such facilities are readily available elsewhere in the community. They should be located for easy supervision so that they may be used for quiet reading and study when not needed by groups.

No single type of building is satisfactory for all public libraries. Each building is likely to be different, and its differences should be directly related to its service program.

The library building should be located in or near the community shopping center and at street level if possible. Adequate parking should be available nearby.

## SPACE REQUIREMENTS

The program statement, which includes objectives, activities, and requirements, will spell out total needs in terms of square feet of floor space. Generally speaking, the total need may be divided into five categories: space for (1) books, (2) readers, (3) staff, (4) group meetings, and (5) mechanical operations and all other (stairways, elevators, toilets, etc.). Actual space allocations will tend to vary in accordance with the library service program in relationship to community needs. Table 1 provides general guidelines for programming the total build-

ing, and Table 2 provides guidelines for interior space in relation to population and size of the book collection.

### Space for Books

To a large extent the amount of book shelving required will depend on the size of the library service area and whether the library is a member of a library system. Most library planners, when estimating the size of the book collection, apply a standard which ranges from three books per capita (smallest communities) to one and one-half books per capita (largest cities). In any event enough book shelving should be provided to plan for 20 years' anticipated growth.

The program statement should also include a detailed analysis of the amount of shelving needed. It should be presented in terms of category, location, and linear feet. Categories found in nearly all public libraries include space for computer terminals, adult fiction and nonfiction; children's books; books for young adults; reference books; bound, unbound, and microfilmed newspapers, bound, unbound, and microfilmed periodicals; local history books; less used books for the bookstacks; special subject collections, and space for interlibrary loan (usually with the circulation desk). Allowances should be made also for non-book materials (i.e., LPs, CDs, DVDs, and videos) which are often accommodated on library shelving.

Despite the fact that there is considerable variation in the size of books, there are several reliable formulas which may be used to estimate the amount of space required for books (Figs. 7 to 9). Book stacks are typically 3 feet wide, 12 inches deep, and 6 or 7 shelves high. A 6-shelf stack yields 126 volumes per single faced section, and 147 volumes for the 7-shelf stack. In children's areas, shelving could be 3 or 4 shelves high. ADA requires that aisles be 36 inches clear. Ideally, aisle space in children's areas would be wider than 36 inches. It is important to note that these formulas are given for full capacity. Under normal conditions, one-third of each shelf should be left for future expansion.

### Space for Readers

Reader seating requirements should be determined for at least 20 years ahead. Two principal sources of information which library building planners will find equally useful for this purpose are first, a careful analysis of purely local needs, and second, existing, time proven formulas applied as a basic guide.

**Table 1**  Experience formulas for library size

| Population size | Book stock– volumes per capita | No. of seats per 1,000 population | Circulation– volumes per capita | Total sq ft per capita | Desirable, first floor, sq ft per capita |
|---|---|---|---|---|---|
| Under 10,000 | 3½–5 | 10 | 10 | 0.7–0.8 | 0.5–0.7 |
| 10,000–35,000 | 2¾–3 | 5 | 9.5 | 0.6–0.65 | 0.4–0.45 |
| 35,000–100,000 | 2½–2¾ | 3 | 9 | 0.5–0.6 | 0.25–0.3 |
| 100,000–200,000 | 1¾–2 | 2 | 8 | 0.4–0.5 | 0.15–0.2 |
| 200,000–500,000 | 1¼–1½ | 1¼ | 7 | 0.35–0.4 | 0.1–0.125 |
| 500,000 and up | 1–1¼ | 1 | 6.5 | 0.3 | 0.06–0.08 |

Source: Joseph L. Wheeler and Herbert Goldhor, Practical Administration of Public Libraries (New York: Harper and Row) p. 554.

*References:* Local Public Library Administration, International City Managers Association, Chicago, Ill. With illustrations from Harold L. Roth, Ed., *Planning Library Buildings for Service,* American Library Association, Chicago.

**Table 2**  Guidelines for Determining Minimum Space Requirements

| Population served | Shelving Space | | | Reader space, sq ft | Staff work space, sq ft | Estimated additional space needed, sq ft** | Total floor space sq ft |
|---|---|---|---|---|---|---|---|
| | Size of book collection, volumes | Linear feet of shelving† | Amount of floor space, sq ft | | | | |
| Under 2,499 | 10,000 | 1,300 | 1,000 | Min. 400 for 13 seats at 30 sq ft per reader space | 300 | 300 | 2,000 |
| 2,500–4,999 | 10,000 plus 3 per capita for pop. over 3,500 | 1,300 Add 1 ft of shelving for every 8 vols. over 15,000 | 1,000 Add 1 sq ft for every 10 vols. over 15,000 | Min. 500 for 16 seats. Add 5 seats per 1,000 over 3,500 pop. served, at 30 sq ft per reader space | 300 | 700 | 2,500 or 0.7 sq ft per capita, which-ever is greater |
| 5,000–9,999 | 15,000 plus 2 per capita for pop. over 5,000 | 1,875 Add 1 ft of shelving for every 8 vols. over 15,000 | 1,500 Add 1 sq ft for every 10 vols. over 15,000 | Min. 700 for 23 seats. Add 4 seats per 1,000 over 5,000 pop. served, at 30 sq ft per reader space | 500 Add 150 sq ft for each full-time staff member over 7 | 1,000 | 3,500, or 0.7 sq ft per capita, which-ever is greater |
| 10,000–24,999 | 20,000 plus 2 per capita for pop. over 10,000 | 2,500 Add 1 ft of shelving for every 8 vols. over 20,000 | 2,000 Add 1 sq ft for every 10 vols. over 20,000 | Min. 1,200 for 40 seats. Add 4 seats per 1,000 over 10,000 pop. served, at 30 sq ft per reader space | 1,000 Add 150 sq ft for each full-time staff member over 7 | 1,800 | 7,000 or 0.7 sq ft per capita, which-ever is greater |
| 25,000–49,999 | 50,000 plus 2 per capita for pop. over 25000 | 6,300 Add 1 ft of of shelving for every 8 vols. over 50,000 | 5,000 Add 1 sq ft for every 10 vols. over 50,000 | Min. 2,500 for 75 seats. Add 3 seats per 1,000 over 25,000 pop. served, at 30 sq ft per reader space | 1,500 Add 150 sq ft for each full-time staff member over 13 | 5,250 | 15,000 or 0.6 sq ft per capita, which-ever is greater |

Source: American Library Association, Subcommittee on Standards for Small Libraries, Public Library Association, Interim Standards for Small Public Libraries: Guidelines Toward Achieving the Goals of Public Library Service (Chicago: The Association), p. 15. This brief 16-page report is based on standards set forth in ALA's Public Library Service; A Guide to Evaluation with Minimum Standards. It is intended to provide interim standards for libraries serving populations less than 50,000 until these libraries can meet the standards of ALA's Public Library Service.

*Libraries in systems need only to provide shelving for basic collection plus number of books on loan from resource center at any one time.

†A standard library shelf equals 3 lin ft.

**Space for circulation desk, heating and cooling equipment, multipurpose room, stairways, supplies, toilets, etc., as required by community needs and the program of library services.

The most important factor in determining reader space needs is of course the reading potential of the people who will use the library. A conveniently located, attractive library will stimulate dramatically increased library use (Figs. 10 to 11). Serious errors can result when estimates are based on use of the old, existing library.

As noted earlier an additional problem that must be carefully evaluated is providing an adequate number of seats for use by readers during peak periods. This problem has been intensified in recent years due to the increase in school attendance and the newer methods of instruction which involve extensive use of reference and supplementary materials by students of all ages. Since these periods of peak use occur irregularly, it is not economical to provide reading rooms which will be large enough to accommodate abnormally large crowds. Therefore, some libraries have attempted to solve this problem by locating multipurpose rooms adjacent to

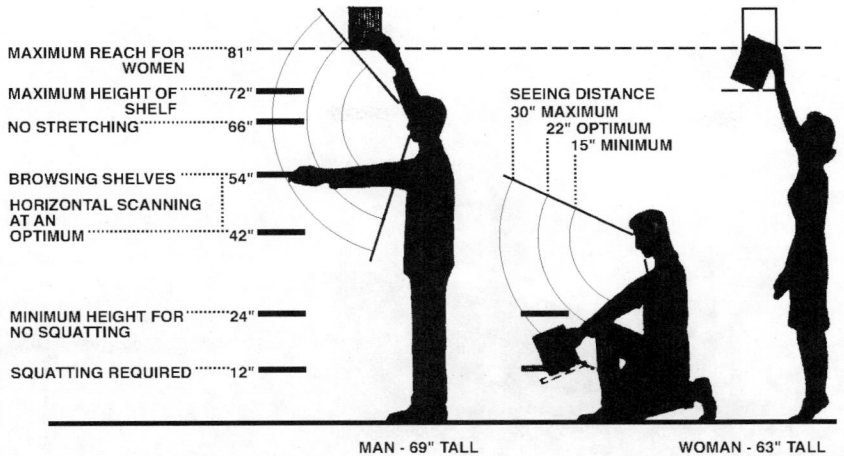

MAXIMUM REACH FOR WOMEN ⋯⋯ 81"
MAXIMUM HEIGHT OF SHELF ⋯⋯ 72"
NO STRETCHING ⋯⋯ 66"
BROWSING SHELVES ⋯⋯ 54"
HORIZONTAL SCANNING AT AN OPTIMUM ⋯⋯ 42"
MINIMUM HEIGHT FOR NO SQUATTING ⋯⋯ 24"
SQUATTING REQUIRED ⋯⋯ 12"

SEEING DISTANCE
30" MAXIMUM
22" OPTIMUM
15" MINIMUM

MAN - 69" TALL          WOMAN - 63" TALL

**Fig. 7. Optimum shelving conditions for adults**

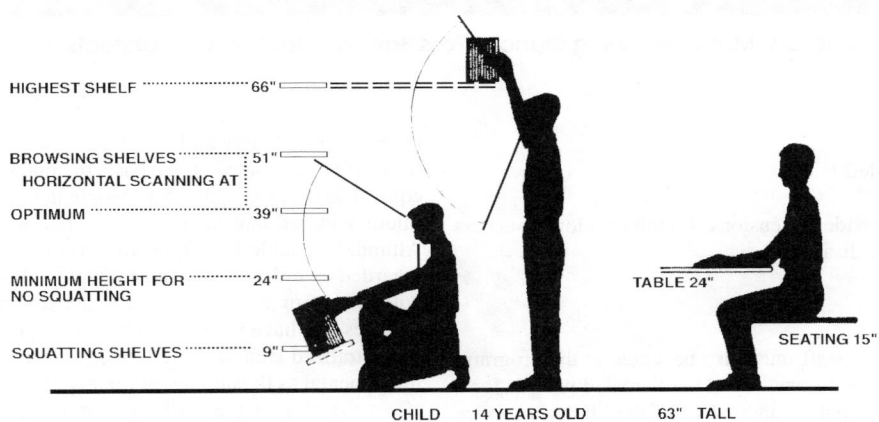

HIGHEST SHELF ⋯⋯ 66"
BROWSING SHELVES ⋯⋯ 51"
HORIZONTAL SCANNING AT OPTIMUM ⋯⋯ 39"
MINIMUM HEIGHT FOR NO SQUATTING ⋯⋯ 24"
SQUATTING SHELVES ⋯⋯ 9"

TABLE 24"
SEATING 15"

CHILD    14 YEARS OLD    63"  TALL

**Fig. 8. Optimum shelving conditions for teenagers**

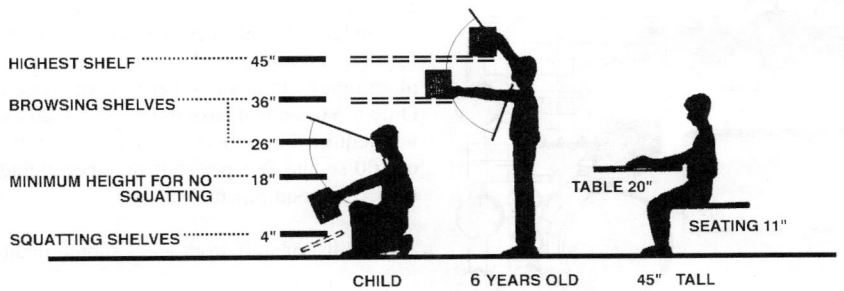

HIGHEST SHELF ⋯⋯ 45"
BROWSING SHELVES ⋯⋯ 36"
⋯⋯ 26"
MINIMUM HEIGHT FOR NO SQUATTING ⋯⋯ 18"
SQUATTING SHELVES ⋯⋯ 4"

TABLE 20"
SEATING 11"

CHILD    6 YEARS OLD    45"  TALL

**Fig. 9. Optimum shelving conditions for children**

adult reference and study areas. Arrangements of this type have proved to be most effective in smaller libraries and in branch library buildings.

The following formulas, developed by Joseph L. Wheeler, are based on building analyses made over a period of more than 30 years. If the estimated future population is less than 10,000, allow 10 seats per thousand; if more than 10,000 but less than 35,000, allow 5 seats per thousand; between 35,000 and 100,000, 3 seats per thousand; between 100,000 and 200,000, 2 seats per thousand; between 200,000 and 500,000, allow 1 1/4 seats per thousand; and 500,000 and up, 1 seat per thousand.

As an established rule of thumb, minimum allowances are made of 35 square feet per adult reader and 20 square feet per child. These allocations for reader seating are in terms of net space for readers, chairs, tables, aisles, and service desk. Seating requirements should be listed according to the several areas of the building. In addition, the program statement should estimate the proportion of table seating to informal seating (see Figs. 13 to 15).

Fig. 10. Chicago Public Library, Mabel Manning Branch (Ross Barney + Jankowski Architects; Steve Hall, Hedrich Blessing Photo)

**Accessible to the Disabled**

Figures 16 through 18 provide dimensions and information for access to library facilities for the disabled.

**Space for Staff**

Space requirements for the staff must also be stated in the program. These estimates will be conditioned by (1) anticipated growth for a 20-year period and (2) the nature and extent of the library's service program. The American Library Association recommends that space for staff be calculated on the basis of "one staff member (full-time or equivalent) . . . for each 2,500 people in the service area." It is a minimum standard that includes pages but not maintenance personnel. Although suitable for application to most situations, it must not be regarded as inflexible. As an example, a library that is not affiliated with a system will probably require a somewhat larger staff than libraries that have joined together in cooperative arrangements, such as centralized technical processing centers. Moreover, something as fundamental as the number of hours per week the library is open will affect the size of the staff and, consequently, space requirements. There are striking differences in staff requirements between libraries open 20, 38, or 72 hours per week.

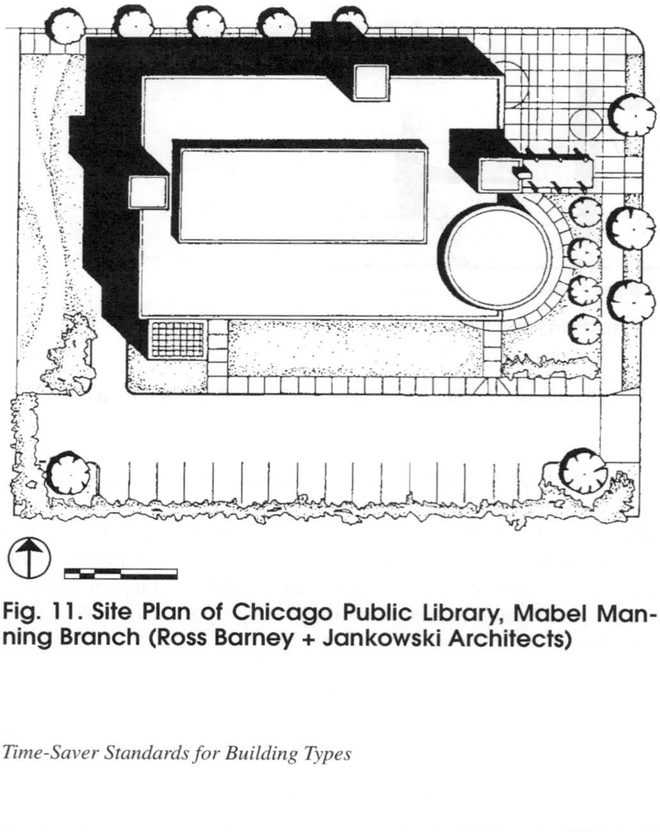

Staff space requirements should be calculated on the basis of 100 square feet per staff member. It is important that this standard be met for there is ample evidence that space for staff has been outgrown more rapidly than any other type of space in most library buildings. Only too often is it easy to forget that an expanding service program will require the support of an enlarged staff. The unit of measurement of 100 square feet per staff member includes space for desk, chair, books, and equipment.

A checklist of staff work areas should include:

- administrative offices
- work rooms
- staff lunch and lounge rooms

Administrative offices should include a combination librarian's office-trustee room; spaces for the assistant librarian and a secretary-receptionist; business office; and other related offices. Work room areas should be provided for receiving technical processing; reference, circulation, extension, and other departments; subject specialists; supply storage; and trash/recycling space. Comfort facilities for the staff should include cooking and lunchroom areas as well as appropriate locker, lounge, and toilet facilities for both men and women. Comfortable working conditions contribute to

Fig. 11. Site Plan of Chicago Public Library, Mabel Manning Branch (Ross Barney + Jankowski Architects)

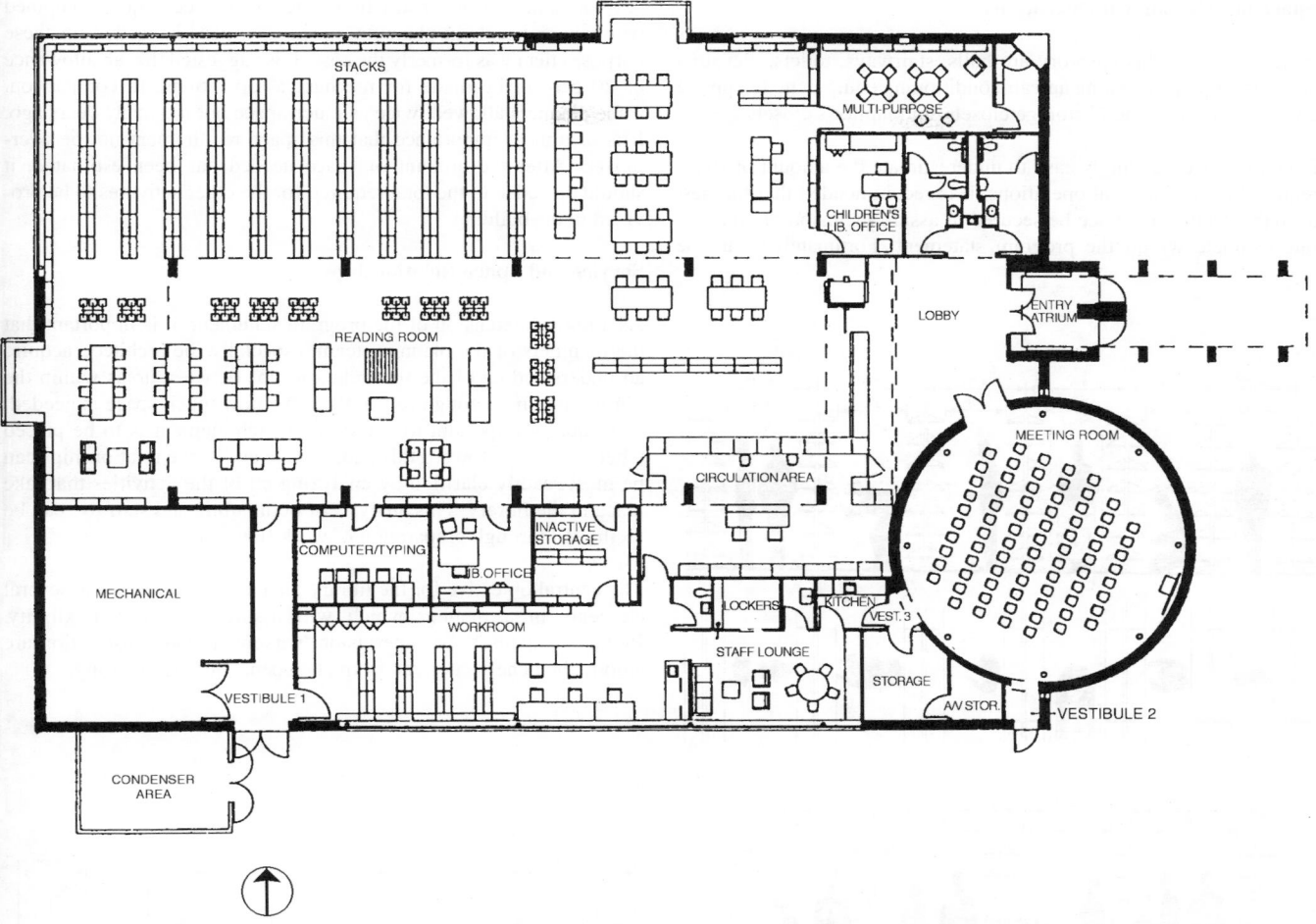

**Fig. 12. Floor Plan of Chicago Public Library, Mabel Manning Branch (Ross Barney + Jankowski Architects)**

effective personnel administration as well as to efficient library service.

## Meeting Rooms

With the exception of the very smallest libraries, most public libraries should provide some group meeting space; at least one multipurpose meeting room. At the other extreme, a small auditorium and a series of conference rooms may be required. The services proposed by the library together with community needs for facilities of this type will be the final determinants.

Multipurpose rooms meet two general classes of need. First, they can be utilized for children's story hours, discussion groups, staff meetings, and other library-sponsored activities. Second, various community, educational, cultural, and local government groups will make frequent and varied use of a multipurpose room. To be of maximum value, however, the room should be arranged for easy and effective use of audiovisual equipment. In addition, there should be adjacent closet space for storage of blackboards, flip charts, white boards, folding tables, chairs, and related equipment.

Many libraries provide a small kitchen in an area adjoining group meeting rooms. Serious consideration should be given to including this facility since there are many occasions when it is highly appropriate to serve simple refreshments. A kitchen featuring a compact combination stove-sink-refrigerator unit will not cause administrative or maintenance problems provided regulations governing its use are stated clearly. Separate provisions should be made for staff kitchen and lounge facilities.

Small auditoriums may feature sloping floors along with elaborate lighting, stage, and projection equipment, or they may be austere with major emphasis placed on flexibility. It is recommended that no auditorium ever be included in a library building program statement without first consulting community leaders. Such facilities are expensive to maintain and, as a result, can place an invisible but dangerous strain on the library's budget unless fully justified. Whenever group meeting spaces are provided, it is important that they be located where there can be access for community use without opening the rest of the building. It is customary to allow from 7 to 10 square feet per seat for meeting room and auditorium seating.

### Space for Mechanical Operations

Included within this category are halls, stairways, toilets, elevators and lifts, air ducts, heating and air conditioning equipment, telephone and data closets, general storage closets, and janitor's closets.

Because it is exceedingly easy to underestimate the amount of space required for mechanical operations, it is recommended that the best available technical advice be secured to assure inclusion of an accurate estimate within the program statement. Fortunately, with the development of new construction materials and techniques combined with new concepts in planning, much less space is needed for these purposes than was formerly the case. It is suggested that an allowance of 20 percent be made for mechanical operations. In comparison, some planners allowed twice as much space not too many years ago. It is of utmost importance that this space requirement not be overlooked. After the amount of space needed has been estimated, it should be added to the total required for the other activities to be provided in the building.

### Service and Space Relationships

As a logical extension of the program statement, it is important that the members of the planning team, especially the architect, acquire an understanding of the interrelationships between areas within the library. It is not enough to simply know how much space is needed; it is equally important to determine which element is to be placed where and why. Toward this end, service and space relationships can be most readily clarified by analyzing all of the activities that take place in the library. This analysis of both public and staff use can be facilitated through preparation of work flow studies.

The central objective for the library planner is to arrange the several elements in a manner which will assure maximum flexibility. Reduced expenses for supervision, personnel, and construction are among the benefits derived from an "open," flexible building.

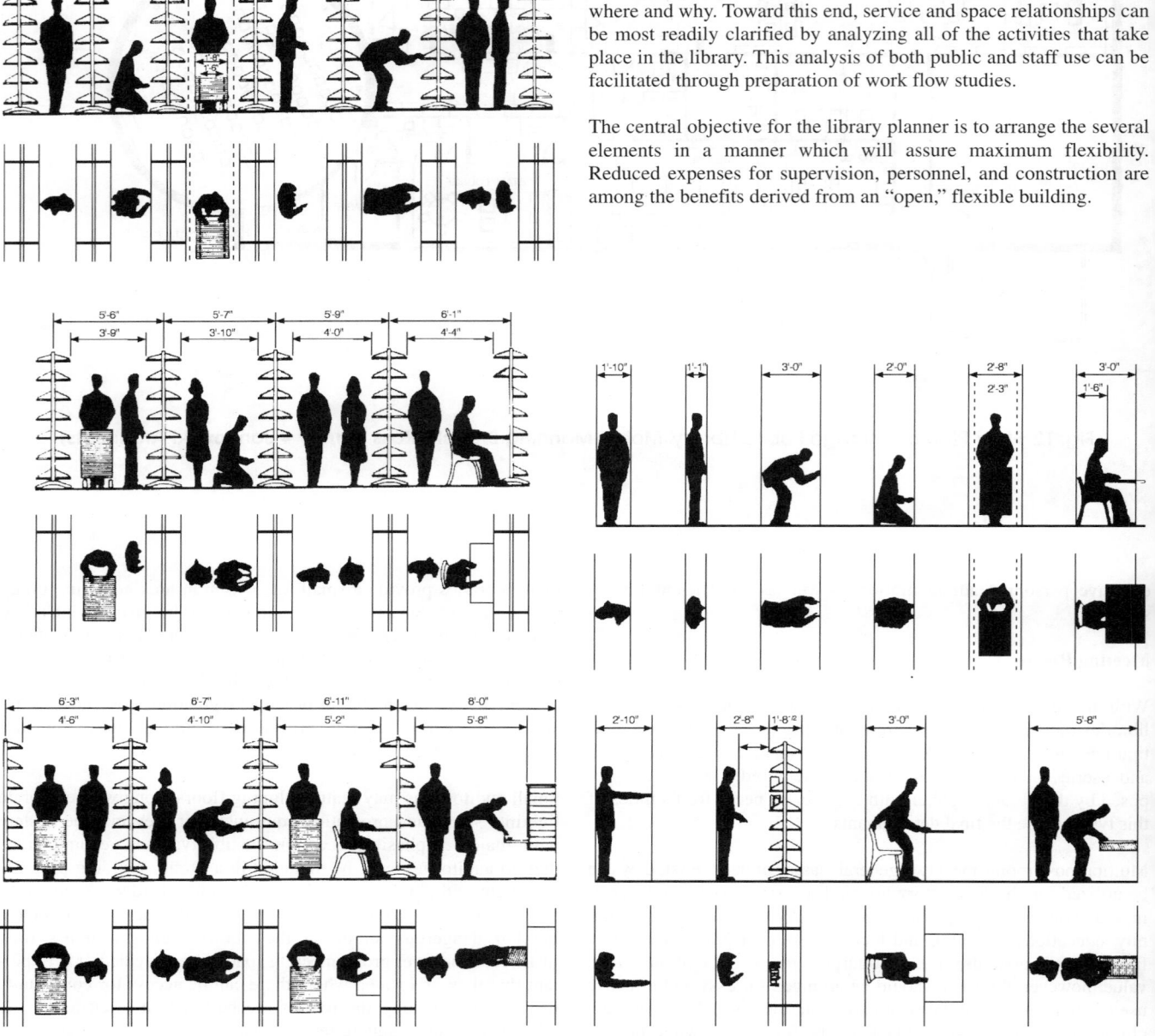

**Fig. 13. Minimum clearances for various body positions in library stack areas**

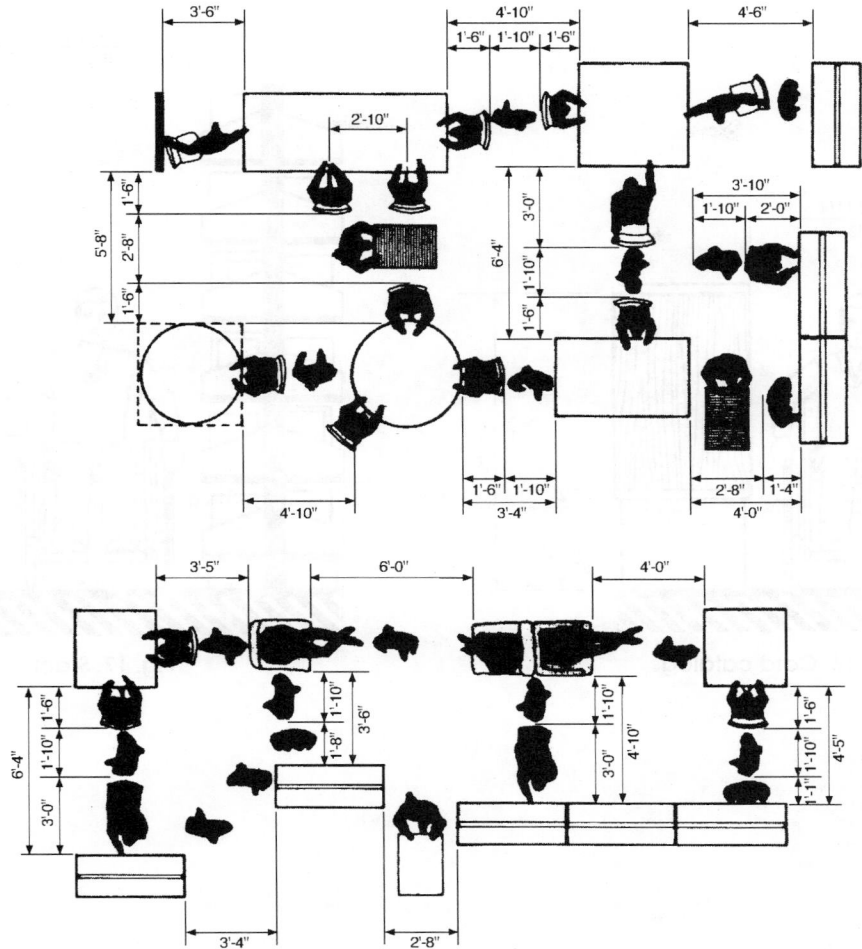

Fig. 14. Minimum clearances for various body positions in library stack areas

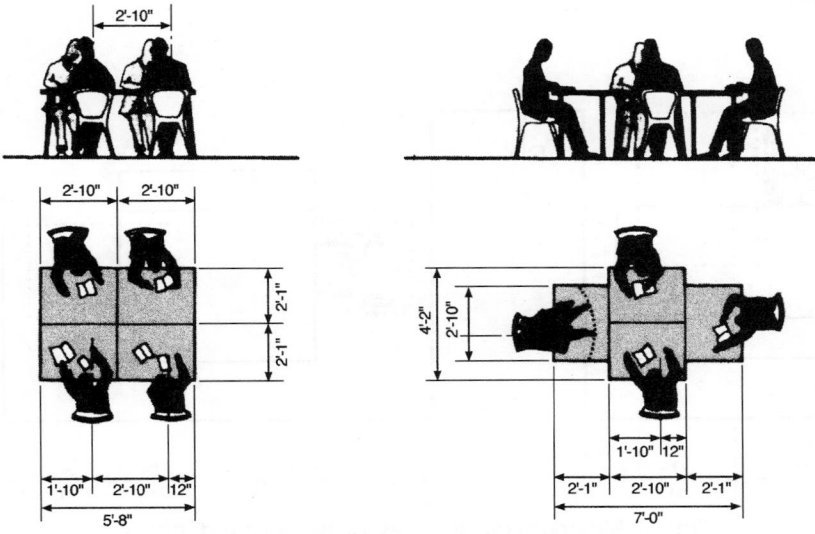

Fig. 15. Table space requirements for readers

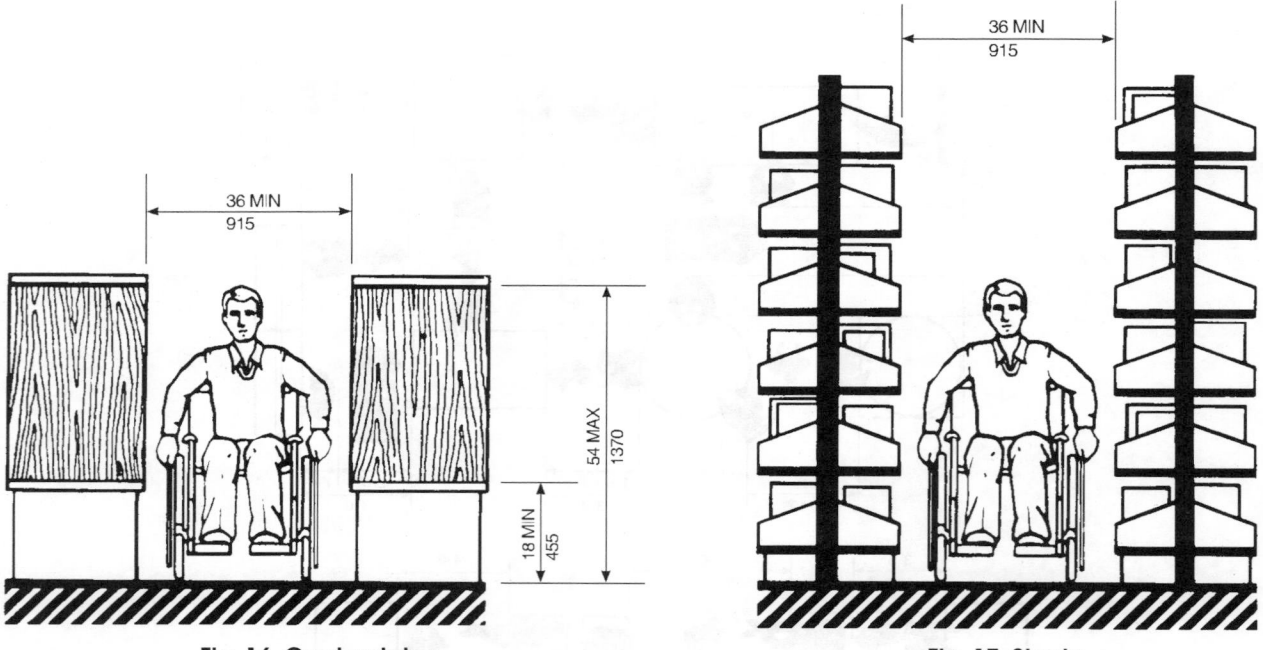

Fig. 16. Card catalog

Fig. 17. Stacks

ACCESSIBLE PATH OF TRAVEL

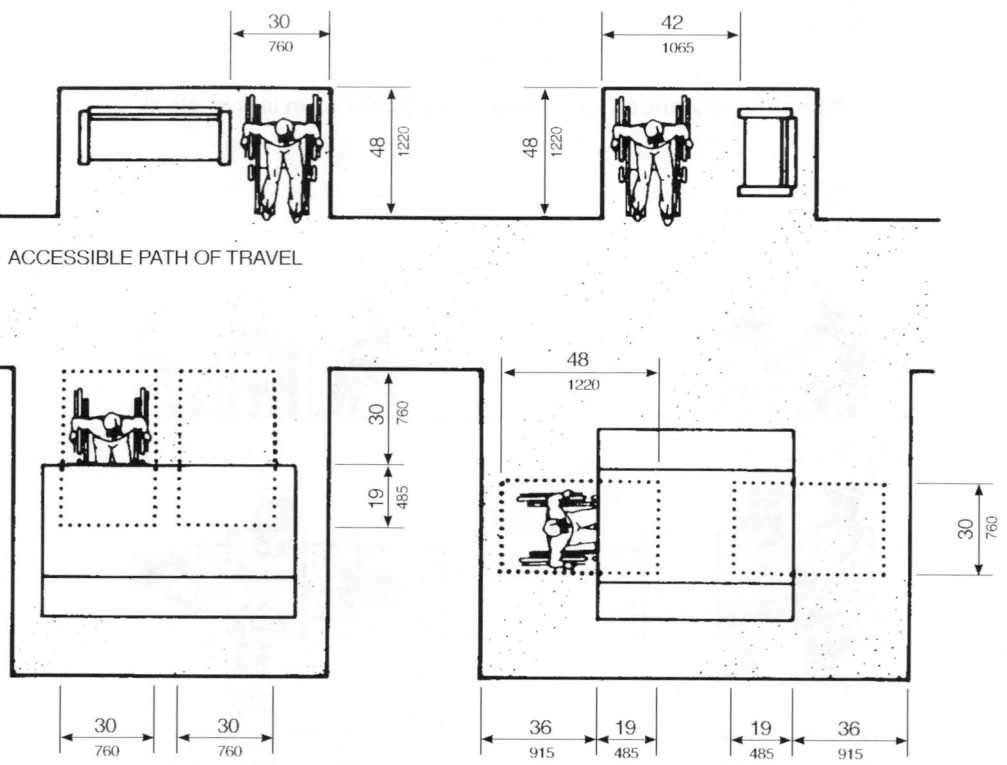

Fig. 18. Minimum clearances for seating and tables

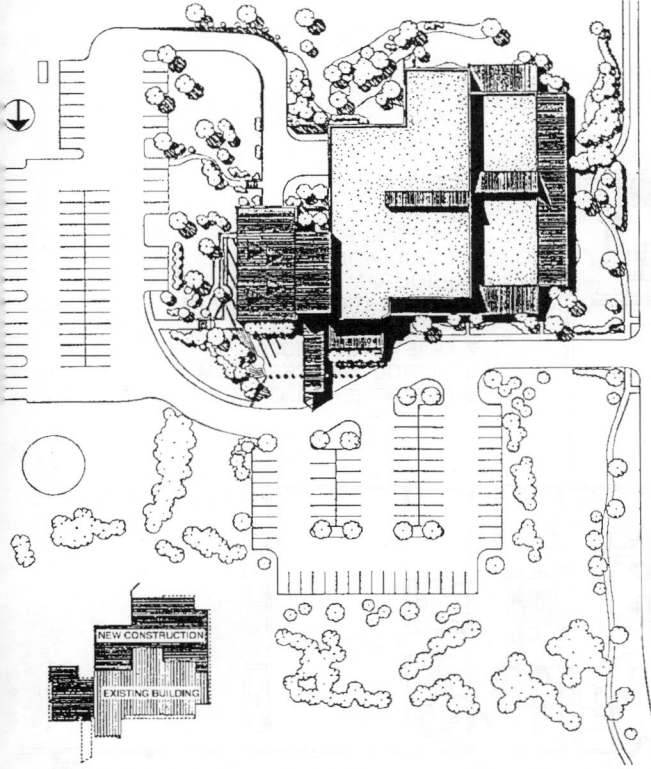

**Fig. 19. Site Plan, Barrington Area Library (Ross Barney + Jankowski Architects)**

More specifically, flexibility implies successful, long-time use of the building. The same area may be used for one or more purposes at different times. The amount of space allocated for a certain use may be shrunk or expanded without structural changes. Furniture and equipment are not fixed and may be relocated.

Ideally, all public services should be located on the main floor of a library in the interests of user convenience, economy, and simplification of operation. Where this is impossible, as in the case of libraries in large cities, every effort should be made to visualize the vertical movement of persons and materials. Under any circumstances, a careful study of the flow of traffic and material is basic to the development of successful service and space relationships. Members of the planning team will find it useful to visualize the traffic flow of library users according to age and purpose of their visit to the library from the point of entrance into the building to the time of departure. Another test that will help to clarify space relationships is to trace a book from the placement of its order to the time it is placed on the public shelves and the notation is entered into the catalog.

In addition to locating a maximum number of public services on the main floor, the following points should be kept in mind:

- Except for large libraries, there should not be more than one circulation desk. It should be near the main entrance where there will be direct visual control of the movement of both children and adults.

- There should be a single public entrance within short distance of the circulation desk. Auditoriums and meeting rooms need not be directly accessible from the main entrance.
- Public toilets, telephone, lockers, and display cases should be located where they can be supervised by circulation desk personnel.
- Every public service area should be supported by book storage, office, and work areas. Reading rooms should be grouped so that they may be served by common book storage, office, and work area.
- Load-bearing walls should be kept to a minimum and maximum use of shelving and furniture made to separate different service areas.

Other factors, such as exterior light and noise, also may influence the location of various areas within the building.

Finally, it may be said that the success or failure of a building is measured by the degree to which planners succeed in applying the foregoing principles of desirable interrelationships. Whether it is a simple village library or a complex large-city library, every effort should be made to facilitate supervisory control, flexibility, and convenience of readers. Careful attention to supervisory control together with a flexible layout of public services will pay off in savings in staff time and ability to handle peak loads with a minimum staff. By the same token, failure to achieve effective service and space relationships can be a financial burden for many years and the source of continuing inconvenience for countless readers.

## LIBRARY LOCATION

### Central Location

A library is a service organization intended to serve people. Therefore, it should be centrally located where it will be accessible to the largest number of potential readers and information seekers.

This principle is neither new nor revolutionary. It has been advocated by a vast majority of experienced public library administrators for well over a half century. The concept of a centrally located library is just as valid now as it was a century ago.

A central location is usually associated with a heavy concentration of retail stores, office buildings, banks, public transportation points, and parking facilities. "This means that it [the public library] should be near the center of general community activity, i.e., the shopping and business district. Just as convenience store operators study the flow of pedestrian traffic before locating one of their units, so should library planners consider carefully the best location to reach the public. A building located just around the corner from the most advantageous spot can lose a great deal of its potential patronage."

The importance of a central location is reaffirmed in this statement: "A prominent, easily accessible location is required to attract a large number of persons." Therefore the library should be placed where people naturally converge—in the heart of the shopping and business district, rather than in a remote location such as a park, civic center, or quiet side street. The American Library Association's standards for public library service also emphasize the need of "maximum accessibility."

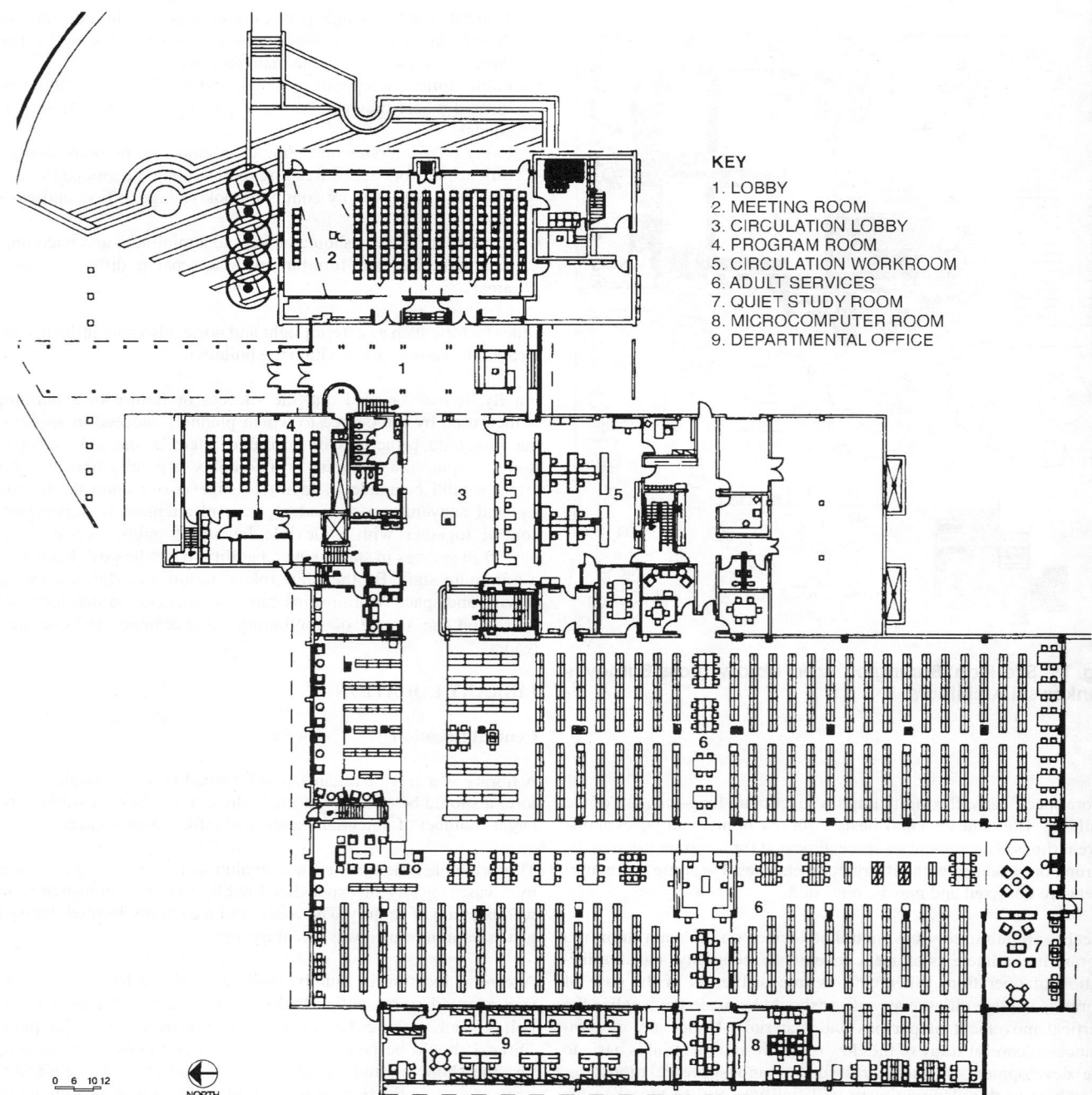

KEY

1. LOBBY
2. MEETING ROOM
3. CIRCULATION LOBBY
4. PROGRAM ROOM
5. CIRCULATION WORKROOM
6. ADULT SERVICES
7. QUIET STUDY ROOM
8. MICROCOMPUTER ROOM
9. DEPARTMENTAL OFFICE

**Fig. 20. First Floor Plan, Barrington Area Library (Ross Barney + Jankowski Architects)**

Unquestionably, a location which affords maximum accessibility to the greatest number of people is fundamental to the success of every new public library, be it the central library or a branch. It is equally true that a site which is located in the heart of a shopping and business district will usually cost far more than a site which is located in a remote or secondary area. Once confronted with the reality of the high cost usually associated with the acquisition of a prime location, there is a tendency toward "instant" compromise. Fortunately, ever increasing numbers of municipal officials, architects, and citizens recognize that the public library cannot fulfill its functions in a second-rate location and that operating costs are proportionately higher for an off-center library than for one which is

**Fig. 21. Barrington Area Library (Ross Barney + Jankowski Architects)**

centrally located. Maximum use is synonymous with lower service unit costs, and strategically located sites are synonymous with maximum use.

In addition to central location, several other important criteria should be considered in library site selection:

- The site should be prominent. A corner site at a busy intersection where the library can easily be seen is preferred. Maximum use should be made of display windows and views of the interior.
- The site should permit street level entrance. The public entrance must be accessible to the disabled. Although a site that slopes to the rear has certain advantages, a level site should be acquired if possible.
- The site should be large enough for expansion (Fig. 19), accessibility for service vehicles and bookmobiles, and a modest amount of landscaping.
- The site should permit orientation of the front of the building to the north in order to minimize glare from the sun. When this is not possible, orientation to the east is the second choice. However, an otherwise excellent, centrally located site should not be eliminated for lack of appropriate orientation. HVAC control devices and artificial light can be used effectively to minimize sun exposure problems.
- Ideally, a site should have uniform foundation conditions, either rock or soil. Test borings should be made, preferably before a site is purchased.

Certain other conditions should be met if the community is to be adequately served. First, the library should be located reasonably near adequate automobile parking. Second, parking provisions should be made for bookmobiles, other official library vehicles, and library staff members. Third, automobile access to drive-in service windows should be provided where this feature has been incorporated into the library building design.

Although emphasis has been placed on acquiring a site which would be large enough to permit easy horizontal expansion, it is important to note that under certain conditions purchase of a strategically located smaller site can be justified provided there is enough space to locate primary adult public service areas at street level. Both Norfolk and Dallas acted accordingly when they acquired their choice downtown sites. In both instances, multistory buildings were erected with provision made for vertical expansion.

**Where Not to Locate a Library**

Despite the overwhelming evidence that can be offered in support of central locations for central libraries and branches in cities both large and small, library planners continue to encounter seemingly plausible arguments from those who believe that libraries should be located in civic or cultural centers, parks, or on sites where avoidance of noise or provision for parking is the major consideration. Usually these misconceptions are held by those who are not qualified to choose a library site. They do not understand the significance of the library in the daily life of its constituents. Quite to the contrary, they associate the library with a setting of monumental buildings, large landscaped grounds, and quiet, aloof surroundings. Libraries are not mausoleums, they are dynamic educational centers whose services and resources must be easily accessible to the greatest number of potential readers.

Specifically, then, remote locations should be avoided. By definition, "remote" means (either literally or psychologically) to be situated at a distance, out of the way, secluded, separate, not primary. Hence the aloof and inaccessible civic and cultural center fits this definition because it is separated from the daily life of the community and is used principally for attendance at special events. How much more satisfactory it is to be where there are bright lights at night rather than in a civic center where governmental offices close at 5 P.M. and there is little activity at night or on weekends.

By the same token, it is almost always a serious mistake to place a library in the geographic or population center of a community. Except in those rare instances where there is coincidence between trade center and geographic or population center, such centers are remote and unrelated to the everyday activities within the life of the community.

Another argument that may be encountered is that the library should be located away from noise. Again, if this point is heeded, it will mean placing the building in a remote location. Fortunately, today's acoustical materials, air conditioning, and lighting methods have completely invalidated this argument.

The argument encountered most often, however, is the one that the library should be placed where there is ample parking space for the library's public. Again, the implication is clear, for if the library is to assume full responsibility for providing enough parking, it will be necessary to locate the building in a secondary location where land is cheap.

Although there are some individuals for whom parking is the main consideration in using the library, numerous surveys have reaffirmed the point of view that a downtown, pedestrian-oriented location in the thick of things is the most important consideration affecting use of the public library.

As another comparison, a well-stocked bookmobile will lend many more books at a busy suburban shopping center than will secluded nearby community libraries that offer the very same books plus parking, peacefulness, and higher service unit costs.

**KEY**
1. GRAPHICS
2. TECHNICAL SERVICES
3. CONFERENCE ROOM
4. ADMINISTRATION
5. STAFF LOUNGE
6. PRESCHOOL
7. DEPARTMENTAL OFFICES
8. JUNIOR HIGH
9. STORYTIME ROOM

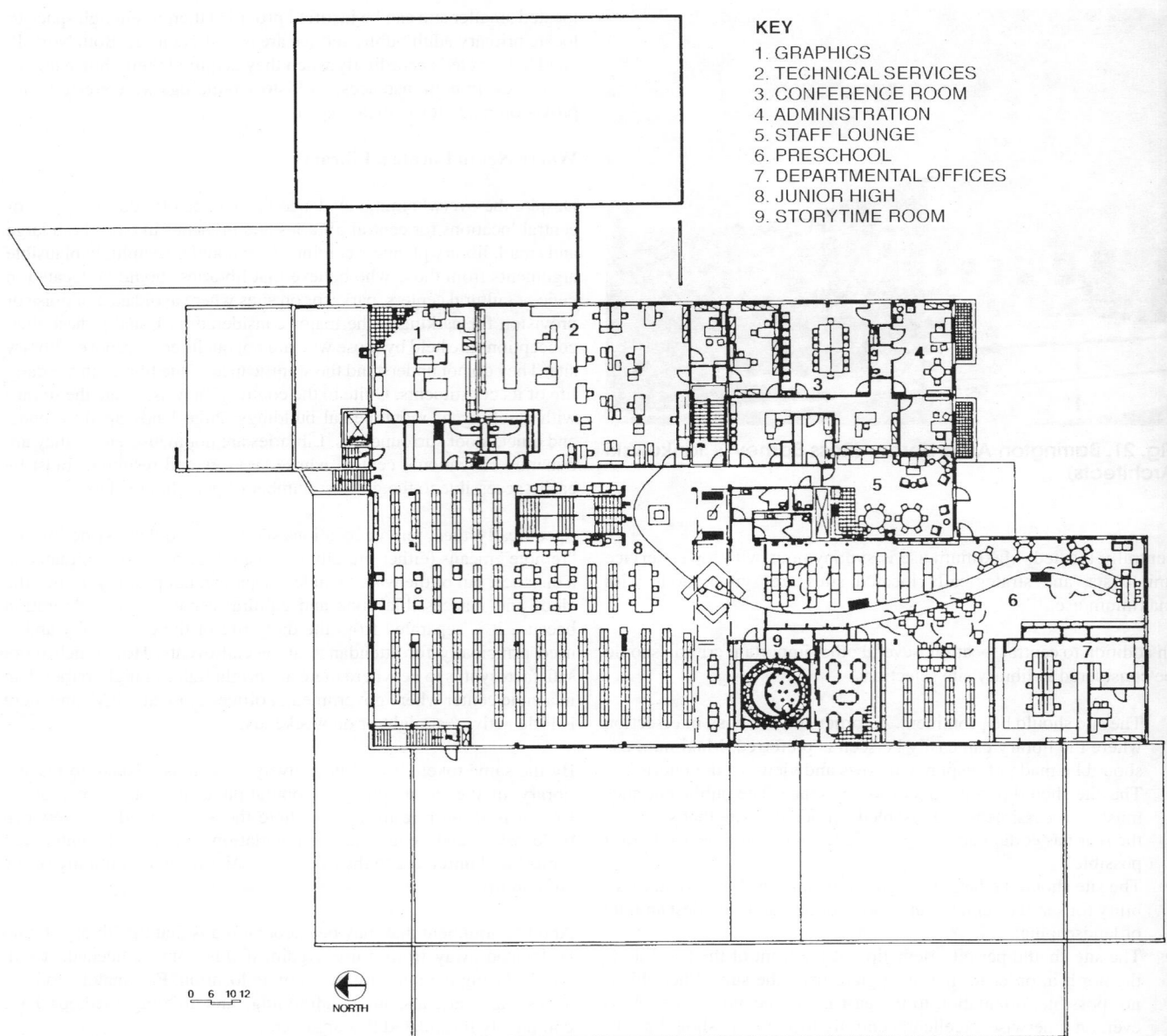

0  6  10 12

NORTH

**Fig. 22. Second Floor Plan, Barrington Area Library (Ross Barney + Jankowski Architects)**

The parking problem cannot be overlooked. On the other hand, it is a community-wide problem that must be solved by the community rather than by the library alone. In fact, choked highways and over-taxed parking facilities are matters of increasing concern to all governments. Perhaps expansion and renovation of mass transit systems will help to alleviate parking problems throughout the nation. In the meantime, many libraries have attempted to ease the parking problem through provision of curbside book return boxes. (Even in small communities, these have become safety hazards.) Drive-in return and "will call" windows similar to those used by banks are other options.

**Branch Buildings**

Branch libraries usually are established as a result of population growth and community expansion (Figs. 20 to 22). Generally, it is their purpose to provide books and services which will meet the everyday reading needs of children and adult general readers who live within the local neighborhood. The person who requires more advanced information and special materials will use the collection at the headquarters library. On-line Internet services have made vast amounts of information available to the smallest branch library.

**Fig. 23. Maywood Public Library (Ross Barney + Jankowski Architects; Steve Hall, Hedrich Blessing Photo)**

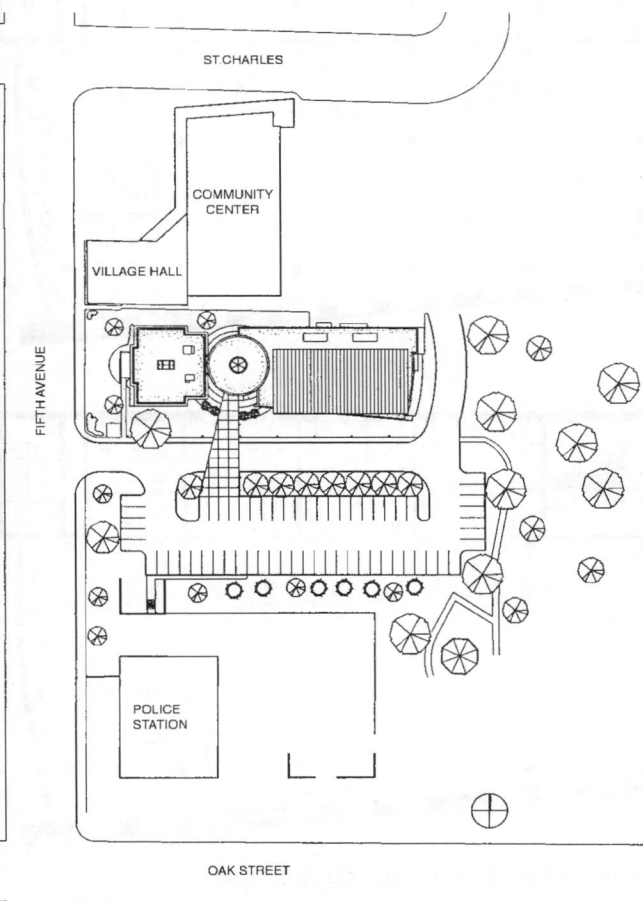

**Fig. 24. Site Plan, Maywood Public Library (Ross Barney + Jankowski Architects)**

Although there is a definite trend toward the establishment of larger and fewer branch libraries, there are hundreds of branch libraries which vary widely in both size and responsibility. They range from the small sub-branch, open for a few hours each week, to large regional centers which provide a full range of library services (Figs. 23 to 26).

Branch libraries may be found in busy urban shopping centers and quiet rural communities. Many are housed in their own buildings while others occupy rented quarters. In smaller communities, branch libraries sometimes share space in public buildings planned for joint municipal use.

Whether small or large, rural or urban, owned or rented, branch library buildings should be planned with great care. The object of this planning is a building strategically located for the area which it is to serve. It should be attractive, functional, flexible, and economical to operate. Toward this end, it is essential that a written program statement be prepared for the guidance of the architect. This statement should include objectives, services and their interrelationships, physical requirements, electronic data needs, and operational procedures. Physical requirements specify the spaces which will be needed for books (Figs. 27 and Tables 3 and 4), readers, staff, meeting and community service rooms, and other auxiliary spaces.

Of equal or even greater importance is the need for adhering to accepted location and site selection standards. The most functional attractive building can never realize its full potential unless it is located where it will be easily accessible to the largest number of people. The following criteria are suggested as a basis for evaluating sites for a new branch building:

- A branch library usually should serve a minimum of 25,000 to 30,000 people within a 1- to 1 1/2-mi. radius of the branch, subject to topographic conditions.

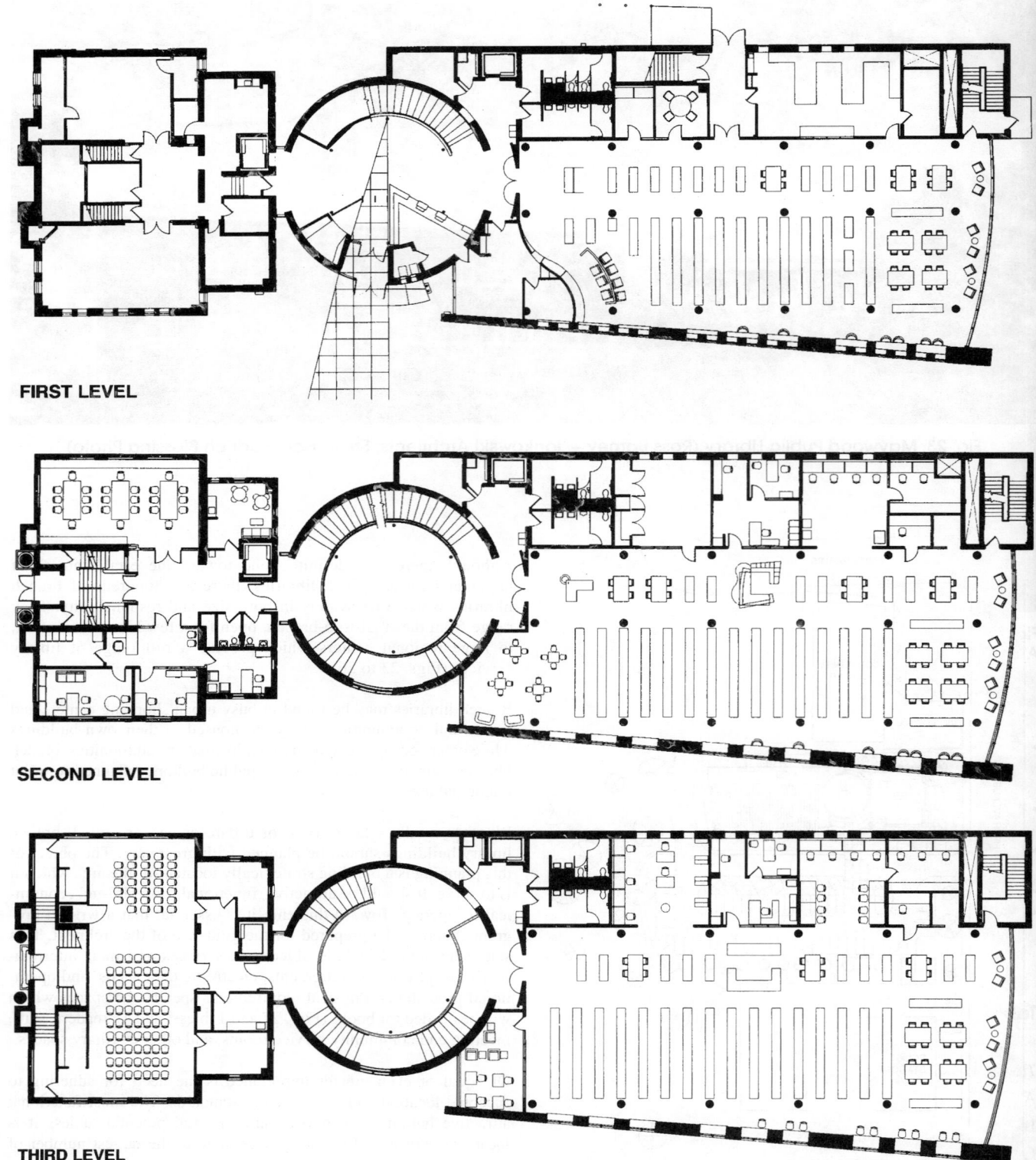

**FIRST LEVEL**

**SECOND LEVEL**

**THIRD LEVEL**

Fig. 25. Floor Plans, Maywood Public Library (Ross Barney + Jankowski Architects)

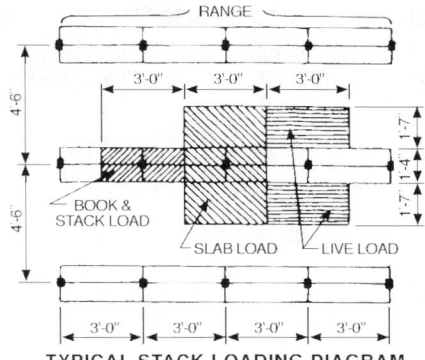

Fig. 27. Typical stack loading diagram

Fig. 26. Maywood Public Library (Ross Barney + Jankowski Architects; Steve Hall, Hedrich Blessing Photo)

Other factors to be considered by the planning team are parking space for bicycles and space for delivery trucks. In certain communities where bicycles are used heavily, it will be necessary to make appropriate provisions. Where the terrain is rugged, the use of bicycles may be limited. Planners must also make allowances for library system delivery and repair vehicles. The latter may be van types, full-size trucks, or both.

In addition to a highly accessible location, a branch library building should use the same basic design principles found in a headquarters or central library building.

- A branch library should be at street level entrance.
- The library's design and construction must comply with ADA.
- When space permits, it should be a one-floor plan with all public service at ground level.
- It should have a minimum number of fixed partitions.
- A branch library should be planned to permit easy expansion.
- It should have enough windows on its street frontage so that the books and people within can serve as a living advertisement and constant invitation to use the library.
- Collections, seating for readers, and staff space require adjacencies to each other that are clear to the user.
- It should not have more than one single control desk, thereby reducing operating costs.
- It should be air conditioned and adequately illuminated.
- It should have one multipurpose meeting room available for both library and community purposes if such use is anticipated.

- A branch library should be located within reasonable proximity of a residential area so that a sizable number of children and adults will be within walking distance.
- A branch library should be near an important street or highway intersection, especially wherever public transportation is available.
- A branch library should be either within or on the fringe of a major neighborhood or regional shopping center.
- A branch library should be located where it can be clearly seen.
- A branch library should provide parking space if general parking facilities are not available.

**Table 3** Stack loads: General variation of stack loads for from 1 to 12 tiers

| Tiers | 1 | 2 | 3 | 4 | 5 | 6 | 7 | 8 | 9 | 10 | 11 | 12 |
|---|---|---|---|---|---|---|---|---|---|---|---|---|
| | | | | | *8-in. shelving* | | | | | | | |
| A | 495 | 2,320 | 4,120 | 5,890 | 7,630 | 9,340 | 11,029 | 12,670 | 14,290 | 15,880 | 17,440 | 18,970 |
| B | 990 | 3,000 | 4,990 | 6,960 | 8,910 | 10,840 | 12,750 | 14,840 | 16,510 | 18,360 | 20,190 | 22,000 |
| C | 495 | 1,500 | 2,600 | 3,590 | 4,570 | 5,540 | 6,500 | 7,450 | 8,390 | 9,320 | 10,240 | 11,150 |
| | | | | | *10-in. shelving* | | | | | | | |
| A | 620 | 2,570 | 4,490 | 6,380 | 8,240 | 10,070 | 11,870 | 13,640 | 15,380 | 17,090 | 18,770 | 20,420 |
| B | 1,240 | 4,000 | 6,240 | 8,460 | 10,660 | 12,849 | 15,000 | 17,140 | 19,260 | 21,360 | 23,440 | 25,500 |
| C | 620 | 1,750 | 2,870 | 3,980 | 5,080 | 6,170 | 7,250 | 8,320 | 9,480 | 10,530 | 11,570 | 12,600 |

Including stocks, books, live load, and 3½-in. concrete deck floor. (A = typical aisle and support; B = typical intermediate support; C = typical wall end support.)

**Table 4**    Shelving data for special collections*

| Type of book | Vols. per foot of shelf | Vols. per foot of single-faced range | Vols. per shelf | Maximum vols. per single-faced section | Shelf depth, in. | Shelves per section |
|---|---|---|---|---|---|---|
| Circulating (non-fiction) | 8 | 56 | 24 | 168 | 8 | 7 |
| Fiction | 8 | 56 | 24 | 168 | 8 | 7 |
| Economics | 8 | 56 | 24 | 168 | 8 | 7 |
| General literature | 7 | 49 | 21 | 147 | 8 | 7 |
| Reference | 7 | 49 | 21 | 147 | 8 & 10 | 6–7 |
| History | 7 | 49 | 21 | 147 | 8 | 7 |
| Technical and scientific | 6 | 42 | 18 | 126 | 10 & 12 | 7 |
| Medical | 5 | 35 | 15 | 105 | 8 & 10 | 6–7 |
| Law | 4 | 28 | 12 | 84 | 8 | 7 |
| Public documents | 5 | 35 | 15 | 105 | 8 | 7 |
| Bound periodicals | 5 | 35 | 15 | 105 | 10 & 12 | 5–7 |
| U.S. patent specifications | 2 | 14 | 6 | 42 | 8 | 7 |
| Art | 7 | 42 | 21 | 126 | 10 & 12 | 5–6 |
| Braille | 4 | 24 | 12 | 72 | 15 | 5–6 |

*To be consistent with cubook method, figures shown should be reduced by 10 percent to avoid overcrowding shelves.

Branch library buildings, as well as central libraries, should be located in the heart of retail shopping districts in order to serve the greatest numbers at the lowest cost, for the more who are served the less each service performed will cost. In other words, there are certain fixed operating costs which pertain wherever the library may be located. With the maximum exposure gained from a good location, unit costs are reduced accordingly.

It can be safely assumed that the most successful branch library will be the one that is based on a carefully stated written program and is located in the thick of things. It is of great importance that the accepted principles of planning and site selection not be overlooked merely because a "small branch" is being planned. To bypass any of these steps in planning is to invite mistakes which might prove to be costly. This holds true for new branches, rented storerooms, leased branch buildings built according to library specifications, and branch facilities incorporated into other public service buildings.

**Bookmobiles**

Because of obvious space restrictions, a bookmobile is a book distribution service which cannot serve as a substitute for a branch library, since there are neither reference nor study facilities. Known to many as "one-room libraries on wheels," bookmobiles have become a widely and enthusiastically accepted form of library service.

Although they principally serve sparsely populated fringe and pocket areas where a full-scale library cannot be justified, they can also serve densely populated areas until branch libraries can be planned, financed, and built. As a natural by-product and added benefit deriving from their mobility, bookmobiles pretest the validity of potential branch library locations.

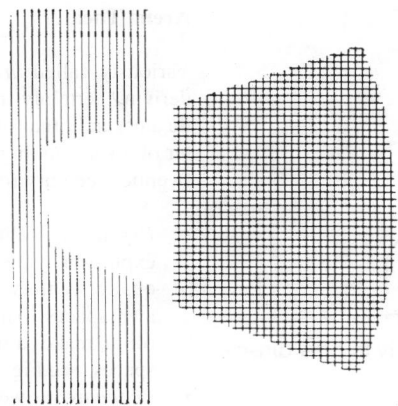

Fig. 1. The proscenium shape

# PERFORMING ARTS SPACES

## INTRODUCTION

As with any building, the design of all performing arts spaces is driven by the program of activities that are housed within. Because of this specialized function, an architect who has been commissioned to design a performing arts building is well advised to engage the services of specialty consultants, particularly in the areas of theater planning, theatrical equipment, acoustics, sound systems, and code analysis.

Performing arts spaces fall broadly into two categories. The first includes spaces that are intended primarily to house one type of performance activity, such as the following:

- Drama theaters
- Opera houses
- Concert halls
- Ballet and other dance theaters
- Film theaters
- Musical theaters

The second category of spaces includes those designed to accommodate two or more such activities within a single space. Such spaces are typically referred to as *multipurpose* or *multiple-use* performing arts theaters. These can take many forms, from 2,500-seat performing arts centers in major urban centers to small-scale community theaters seating a few hundred persons.

## ISSUE OF FORM

One of the first issues a designer confronts in approaching the design of any performing arts space is the issue of form—that is, the relationship between the audience members in their seats and the performers on stage. Issues of form are influenced by a number of forces, including the type of performance, seating capacity, and historical precedents. It is therefore helpful for the designer to have a basic understanding of the different forms of relationship between audience and performer.

The 20th century brought an entirely new attitude toward shaping our theaters. Whereas in the past, a consistent, developing production technique gave rise to a single, if gradually developing theater shape for each period, during the 20th century several theater shapes were discovered or rediscovered and came into common use. Due partly, no doubt, to 19th-century historicism and scholarship, a revival of earlier stage forms sprang up to accompany the mainstream tradition of the proscenium stage. There began to be a multiple choice of theater shapes for plays in the twentieth century—a situation that was unknown in previous times. This movement clearly underscored the tremendous activity in theater arts—the thinking and lack of it—being done by all people involved.

### Proscenium Theaters

From the turn of the 20th century to the present day, the proscenium theater—a direct descendent of the horseshoe opera house that originated in the Renaissance—has continued as the most generally accepted and widely built theater shape in this country. By definition, a proscenium theater is a shape in which the audience faces the performing area on one side only and sees the performing area through an architectural opening that often has an elaborated architectural frame—although that is not an essential element. The performing area is not always limited by that opening; it can project out a nominal distance into the auditorium in the form of what is called a *forestage* or *apron*. The proscenium form can sometimes fail to produce an intimate theater space, since the audience and the actors are each in separate, although connected, interior rooms (see Fig. 1).

This has been the conventional arrangement of 20th-century theater in the U.S. It has the following attributes:

- It establishes a limited range of orientation between performers and audience. Because the audience is disposed largely in one direction from the stage, the performers can relate their actions to the whole audience simultaneously (see Fig. 2).
- It creates a limited, unified, fixed frame for the pictorial composition of the performance. Scenery often approaches the quality of fine art in the refinement of its design elements.

*Reviewers*: Paul Scarbrough and Robert Campbell

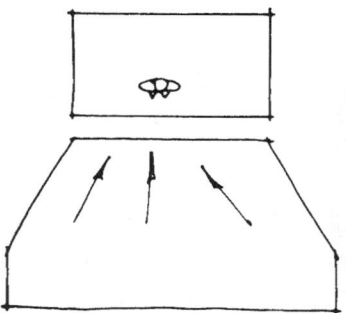

**Fig. 2. Proscenium shape—audience largely in one direction from stage**

- It permits the director and designer to relate performers to scenery, secure in the knowledge that the whole audience will perceive the relationships in substantially the same way.

Theatrical production refuses to be contained within a strictly limited space behind a rectangular opening. The existing proscenium form (Fig. 3) has been called the *picture-frame stage* and the *peep-show stage,* and even during its introduction and rise to prevalence there were objections to its restrictive character. The theory of theater admits, and numerous modern plays contain, instances where the contact between performance and audience must be more intimate than the formal frame permits. The history of theater shows 24 centuries in which the picture frame was either nonexistent or modified by the use of acting areas in front of it, against the last century-and-a-half during which the proscenium developed in prominence. Modern theatrical practice contains frequent instances of the performance's attempting to come through the frame, into, about, and around the audience.

**Fig. 3. The theater in the Whitaker Center for Arts and Sciences in Harrisburg, Pennsylvania, typifies the proscenium form of drama theater (Architect: Hardy Holzman Pfeiffer Associates; photo courtesy of the architect)**

## Arena Theaters

Variously called *arena, theater-in-the-round,* or *circle theater* and deriving certainly from the circus and ancient amphitheater (double theater) and ritual sites, the arrangement of the acting area in the center of a surrounding ring of audience has gained in popularity in the twentieth century for a number of reasons:

- *Expediency:* The soaring cost of building formal theaters and an explosion in the number of theater companies that occurred in the quarter century after 1950 created a demand for many new theater spaces. The arena arrangement, achievable in any large room, makes a rudimentary theater possible in a variety of found spaces (see Fig. 4).
- *Economy.* As well as seating maximum audience in the minimum enclosure, this arrangement seats the largest audience within the shortest distance from the acting area. It is therefore attractive to the performer and also to the spectator who attaches value to proximity to the stage (see Figs. 5 and 6). Economy is also achieved by the effective limitation of scenery—there can be no scenery or properties that the audience cannot see over, under, or through. This restricts scenic elements to paint or other coverings on the stage floor, very low platforms, devices suspended above the acting area, outline representations of such objects as must be set on the stage for use by the actors (doors, windows, and similar architectural details), and low pieces of furniture.

*Disadvantages:* Because the audience is seated all around the acting area, it is unavoidable that viewpoints will be maximally different, and it becomes impossible for director and actors to compose the performance so as to produce a uniform effect. Furthermore, because the conditions of one actor blocking audience vision of another actor are also maximized, it is necessary to prevent this by increasing the pitch of the seating area.

As early as 1914, a group at Teachers College in New York used the simplest bleachers and seats on four sides of a medium-sized room to create an arena stage. An ancient theater shape, the arena stage was used in the great coliseums and arenas of Greece and Rome—but never specifically for drama. This new usage marked the revival of an ancient form but adapted its use and scale to serve contemporary ideas about dramatic performance.

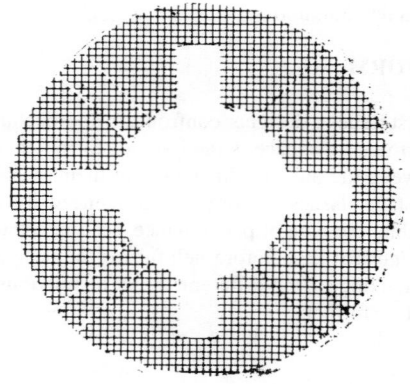

**Fig. 4. Arena shape**

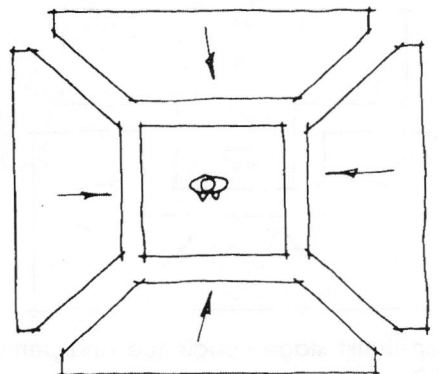

**Fig. 5. Arena shape—audience surrounds stage**

### The Thrust or Open Stage

The period following World War I was exciting in both Europe and America. Inspired by a fresh approach to writing and the new European expressionistic stage designers and producers—Adolphe Appia in Switzerland, Max Reinhardt and Leopold Jessner in Germany—America's best young playwrights, Eugene O'Neill, Elmer Rice, and John Howard Lawson, helped launch and stimulate a new attitude toward stagecraft in the United States.

Expressionistic scene development in Germany and Russia was also reflected in America. Lee Simonson, Norman Bel Geddes, and Robert Edmond Jones produced designs of dramatic imagination for scenery and stage. However, since they were not in the mainstream of commercial thinking, few of these new stages were actually built.

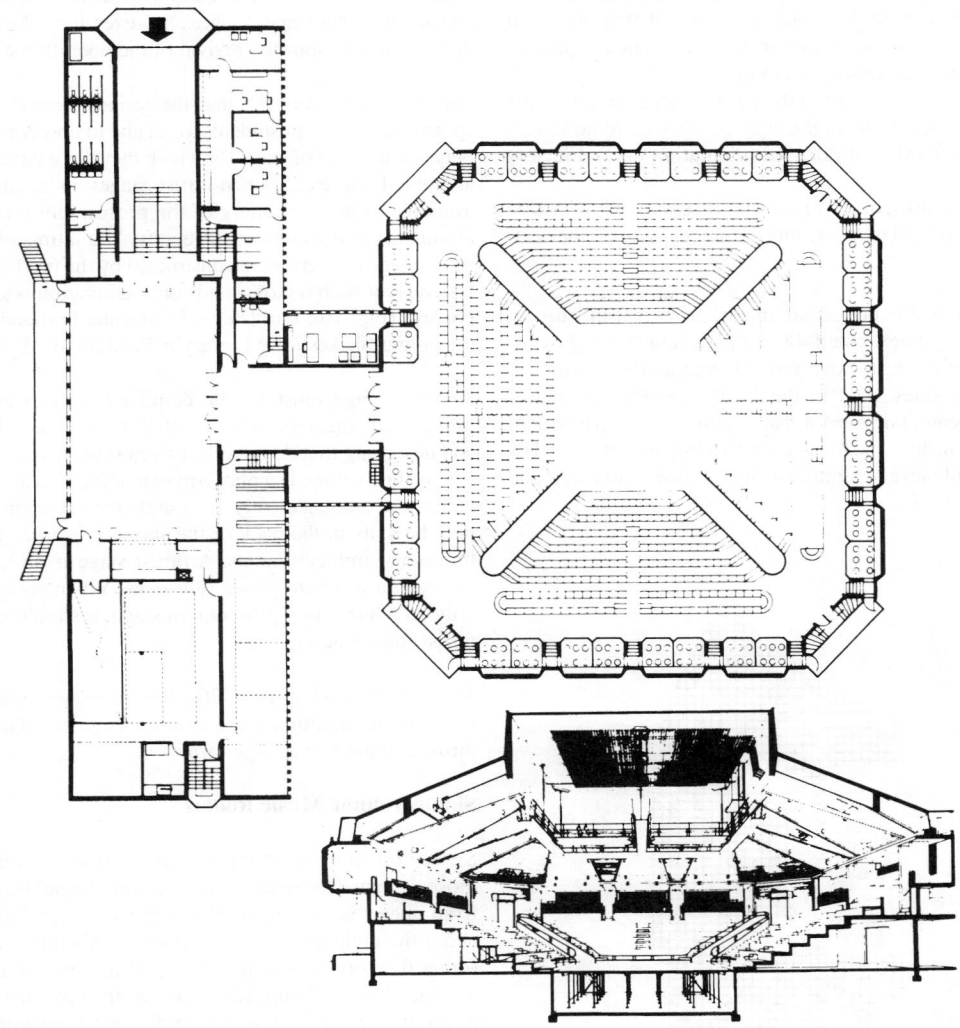

**Fig. 6. Arena stage, Washington, D.C. (Architects: Harry Weese & Associates; consultants: Bolt, Beranek & Newman). The Fichandler Theater (capacity 752) is an octagonal-shaped theater-in-the-round with a rectangular performing area. One of the four tiers of seats is removable to permit a three-quarter arena form. The stage floor is trapped to provide additional staging flexibility and to provide an orchestra pit when the three-quarter arrangement is used for musicals. The height of the catwalk–lighting grid from the stage floor is also adjustable. The building was designed for a resident professional repertory company.**

In the United States, Broadway was not the only vital place for theater; community and college playhouses sprang up all over the country. But the problems associated with producing scenery in conventional proscenium theaters (in terms of cost and time) led directors to bypass traditional approaches to stagecraft and to investigate other techniques.

Early in the 20th century, the ancient open-thrust stage, which had been used before the development of the proscenium theater, was revived by several directors and producers. High costs of proscenium productions, which required elaborate and sometimes complicated scenery as well as high operating costs, led to this revival. Coupled with this was a desire to bring greater intimacy to the theater again (see Fig. 7).

Essentially an old arrangement descended from Greek, Roman, Renaissance, and Elizabethan theaters, the open-thrust shape has been readopted for several reasons:

- It places the performers in the same space envelope as the audience. This is said to produce a unity of experience between performers and audience, though the authors believe that the essential dichotomy of function between performers and audience persists regardless of spatial relationship (see Fig. 8).
- It places more spectators closer to the performance than does the proscenium arrangement and in this way contributes to good seeing, but it places a burden of diffused orientation upon directors and performers.
- It contains inherent difficulties in the entrance and exit of actors which are usually solved by providing entrances beneath the seating area.

The open-thrust stage had experienced an earlier revival in Europe. Davioud and Bourdais' unexecuted 1875 opera house design proposed a stage of extreme thrust, extending 50 feet into the auditorium with seating on three sides. And in the 1920s, the Parisian actor-director Jacques Copeau conceived a truly open theater chamber of intimate proportions in his Theatre Vieux Colombier (Fig. 9). His open stage had multiple levels, a number of entrances and exits, and

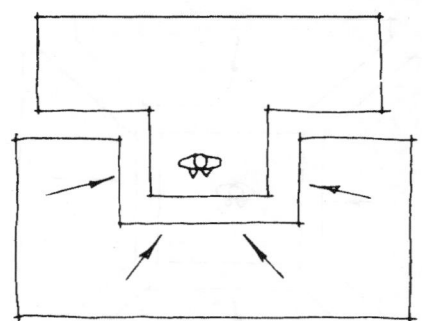

**Fig. 8. Open-thrust stage—audience and performers in same space**

a flexible architectural set, which was permanent and therefore cost-cutting. Neither of these European theater designs directly influenced American stage designs, however, until the educational theater did so much to spur the revival of the open-thrust stage.

American educators felt that the proper method of teaching Shakespeare was to permit students to act and to observe performances of his plays on the type of stage for which they were written. Educators often attempted makeshift open-thrust stages in whatever theaters were available to them. Scenery of the proscenium tradition was virtually eliminated in open-thrust stagecraft. And ultimately permanent open-thrust stage theaters were constructed by the producers of Shakespeare festivals for such regional and community groups as those at Stratford, Ontario (Fig. 10); San Diego, California; Portland, Oregon; and later the Folger Shakespeare Library in Washington, D.C.

A thrust stage must not be confused with extended forestages in proscenium theaters, which utilize techniques of acting, direction, and designing that do not differ from standard proscenium stagecraft. A true thrust stage is a platform extending into an open auditorium in which the audience truly surrounds the stage on three sides. There may be exits in the back of the stage, as well as under the audience through vomitory tunnels. A thrust stage is an area deep and wide enough on which to play a full scene. When an apron or forestage is only an adjunct to a proscenium stage, it should not be considered a thrust stage (see Fig. 11).

Thus, by the end of the 1920s, theater professionals had a choice of not only the traditional proscenium stage but also the revived open-thrust and the arena stage forms.

**Single-Volume Music Rooms**

Spaces for music performance evolved along a different path from those designed for drama. The concept of a public concert (as distinct from opera) is actually a relatively recent development, dating from about the eighteenth century. Prior to this time, most serious music (other than opera) was primarily the preserve of the court (nobility) and the church. Composers were retained by the court or by bishops to produce works of music for a variety of occasions. In court situations, most concerts of such music were for the private pleasure of the monarch and his or her retinue. Works for the church had a more specific purpose, that is, to support the liturgical life of the community. In this sense, the music produced under the aegis of the church can be thought of as being for the public in a way that music for the court only rarely was.

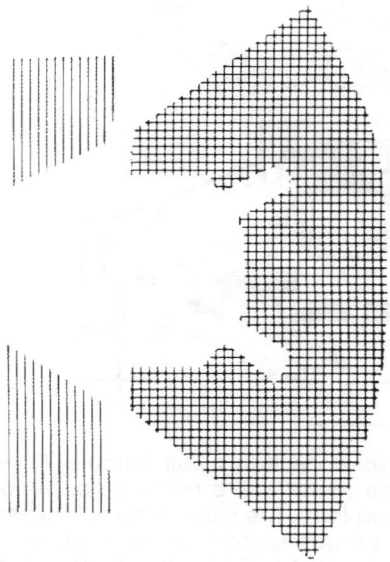

**Fig. 7. Open-thrust shape**

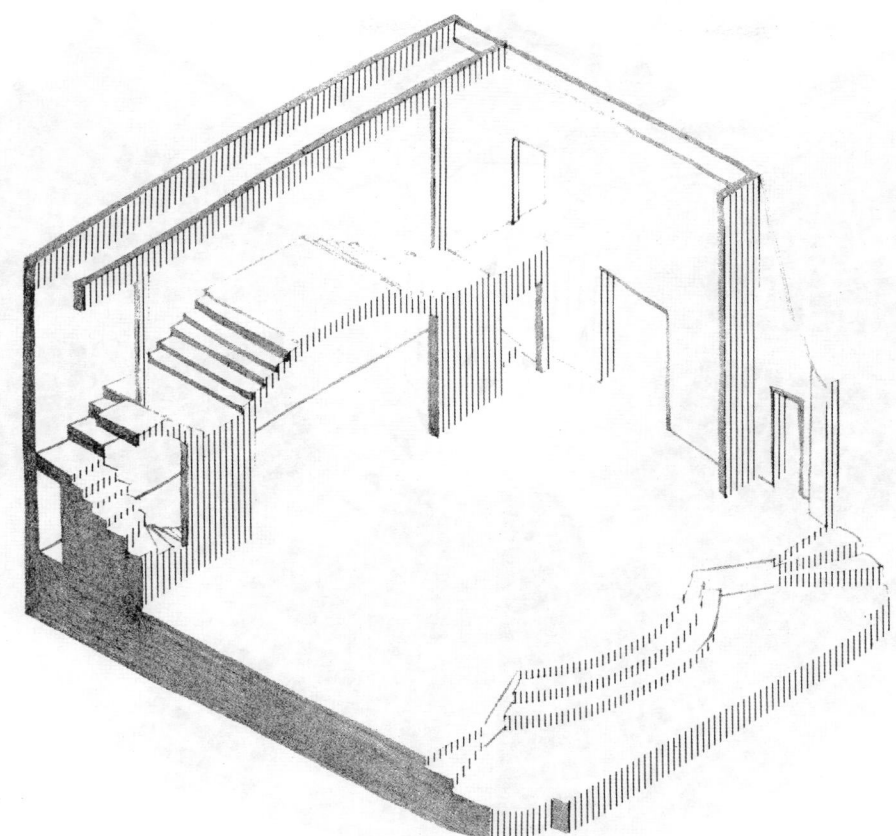

**Fig. 9. The open stage of Jacques Copeau's Vieux Colombier, Paris, had multiple levels and a flexible but permanent architectural set**

In time, composers and musicians began to seek other outlets for their talents. Court composers sought wider audiences for their works and church composers sought to write music not directly dependent on religious themes. These influences gave rise to public performances first in taverns and other public spaces. Eventually the demand for such performances led to the creation of spaces specifically for music events.

Unlike drama and opera, both of which had evolved complex staging techniques that required extensive stage machinery, concerts could be simple affairs. There was no need to provide separate volumes for audience and performer. A concert requires only a platform for the performers and a simple seating area for the audience. This resulted in the creation of single-volume music rooms, spaces where the audience and performer share the same volume, spaces that today we refer to as *concert* or *recital halls* (see Fig. 12).

The earliest of these halls were small, typically seating no more than a few hundred people (at a time when new opera houses such as La Scala in Milan were built with seating capacities well above 2,000). In the nineteenth century, as the popularity of public concerts grew, these smaller halls were replaced by much larger spaces. By the last quarter of the century, concert halls attained the scale and form that we associate with modern concert halls. Buildings like the Grosser Musikvereinssaal in Vienna, McDermott Concert Hall in Dallas (Fig. 13), and Symphony Hall in Boston typify this form.

## RELATIONSHIPS BETWEEN FORM AND PERFORMANCE TYPE

Many performance types are presented in theaters that have evolved with one or more of the specific forms just discussed. Table 1 illustrates the forms commonly associated with specific performance types.

### Evolution of Multipurpose Performing Arts Spaces

The multipurpose auditorium (Fig. 14) is an approach to theaters, born of twentieth century cultural and economic influences. It is an attempt to satisfy the client who wants an auditorium that can adapt to serve a diverse range of the performing arts. Not only do performing groups want a theater to house plays, but they also hope to use their new auditoriums for opera and musical productions, concerts, and recitals. Since each of these performance types is best experienced in a particular acoustical environment, multipurpose rooms require acoustical characteristics that can be adjusted to suit each performance activity. Over the years various approaches to this adjustability have been developed with varying degrees of success. These approaches include everything from varying the cubic volume of the auditorium and sophisticated orchestra shells to moving acoustical banners and subtle electronic acoustical enhancement systems.

Colleges and universities have led the race in building such facilities. High schools have built structures that attempt to accommodate the

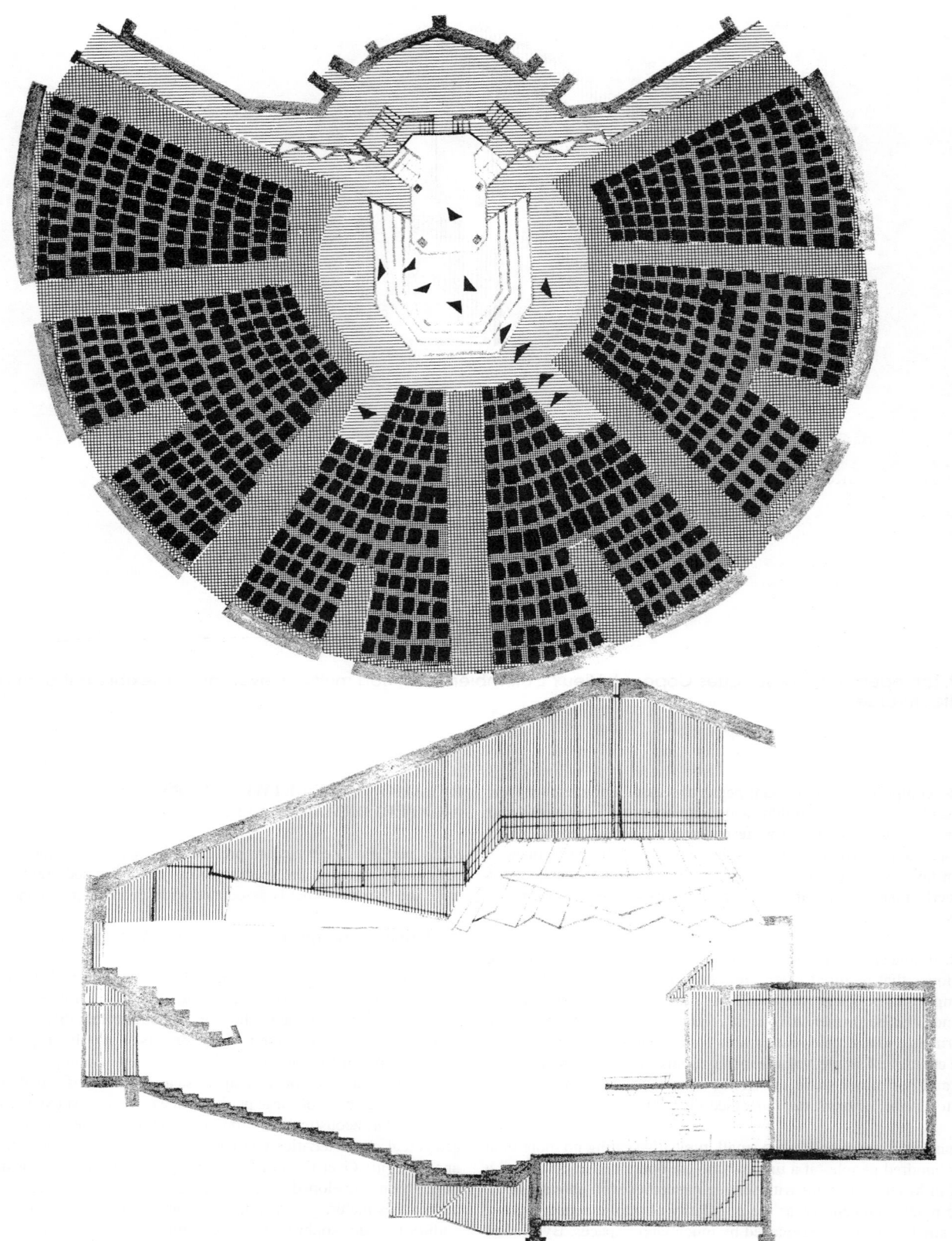

**Fig. 10.** The Stratford, Ontario, Shakespeare Festival Theatre has been an influential interpretation of the open-thrust stage. It combines an Elizabethan stage with a Greco-Roman audience seating plan.

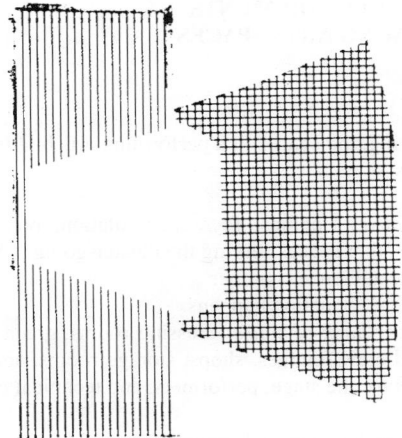

**Fig. 11. Apron shape**

basketball court as well as the performance of Ibsen and the choral society recital. Combinations such as the gymnatorium and the cafetorium have been tried as a means of saving space and construction funds. Such schemes appealed equally to builders, architects, engineers, and clients. The multipurpose theater thus spread to fantastic degrees. It became a byword of confusion in the 1960s. Not only the idea, but the definition of the words *multiuse* or *multipurpose* became confused, even by theater experts.

It is understandable that civic leaders, members of boards of trustees, and college regents cried out for a single design to meet the needs of all performing arts. Even in affluent times, it is not easy for a small city, large university, or regional theater group to raise enough money to build more than one good theater. And there will inevitably be an avid army of architects, engineers, and acoustical specialists willing to take on that challenging desire of clients to accommodate all the performing arts in a single auditorium. Even when the architects or consultants are people of integrity and theater experience, they may find difficulty in persuading building committees that however well an auditorium may suit the combined needs of the choral society and the music school opera, it cannot possibly be used for intimate drama as well.

This is when the dangerous plea is made to bring in the engineering magic that we see in so many regional and college theaters today, and in such community auditoriums as the Jesse Jones Hall in Houston.

During the 1960s, engineering firms devised astounding mechanized systems that changed the very shape of an auditorium, pitching the

**Fig. 13. McDermott Concert Hall in the Morton H. Meyerson Symphony Center in Dallas, Texas, is a modern example of the shoe-box-shaped concert hall form that evolved in the latter half of the 19th century (Architect: I. M. Pei & Partners; photo: David Greenberg)**

floor, tipping the ceiling and cutting off the balconies, pivoting the walls, and rolling banks of seating across the floor and stage. In too many cases, these mechanical tails wagged the theatrical dogs (see Figs. 15, 16, and 17).

Not all engineering developments were futile, however. Certainly in terms of stagecraft, electronic controls for rigging and lighting systems, which were often developed for such auditoriums, have been astonishing in their programs of complicated presentational prob-

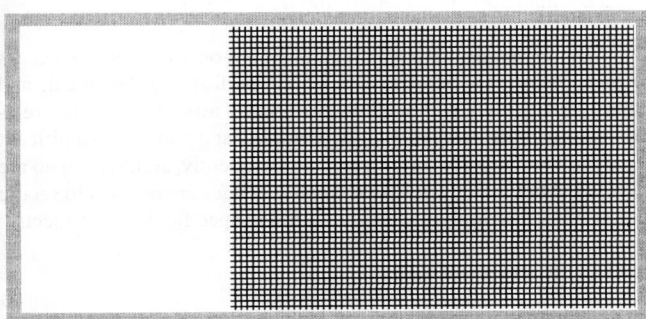

**Fig. 12. Music room**

**Table 1** Form and Performance Type

| Performance type | Common forms |
|---|---|
| Drama | Proscenium, arena, thrust stage |
| Opera | Proscenium |
| Music (concerts) | Single-volume music room (traditional), arena (20-century innovation) |
| Ballet and other dance | Proscenium |
| Musical theater | Proscenium |
| Film | Own archetype |

**Fig. 14. The Nancy Lee and Perry R. Bass Performance Hall in Fort Worth, Texas, is an example of a successful multi-purpose performing arts hall. This view shows the hall in orchestra performance configuration for concerts of the Fort Worth Symphony or the Van Cliburn International Piano Competition. (Design architect: David M. Schwarz Architectural Services; photo: Len Allington, courtesy of Jaffe Holden Acoustics)**

lems, but these are mechanical contributions to the backstage area and are not to be confused with the mechanical manipulation of the architectural front-of-the-house arrangements.

It is certainly human on the part of an owner or manager to feel that a single auditorium with adjustable elements serves in place of what might otherwise be a complex of two or three separate theaters. But every medium in the dramatic and musical arts cries for a specific scale for the performing area and the audience. With the spoken word in drama, the sense of intimacy is essential both visually and aurally. Add music and singing from a musical comedy, and the scale of the auditorium can increase appreciably.

An auditorium that is good for the actor's voice is generally not suitable for the singing voice and for musical instruments. The reverse is equally true. On an everyday level, we know that when we want to say something intimate to a friend, we do not shout it across a courtyard. We approach closely, eye-to-eye, and speak quietly in close contact, as in intimate drama. If we want to sing an aria to that same friend, we would back away or choose a room of sufficient size. The same principle holds in choosing a theater shape.

Specifically, the distance between the last viewer and the performer can increase because when acting is augmented by broader techniques, the audience can be much farther away from the performer and still enjoy an acceptable contact. From operetta to grand opera, an even greater change in scale is acceptable. In fact, the patron who enjoys second-row-center seats at a drama would find grand opera completely unacceptable at this close range. To many followers of opera, of course, the aural appreciation is almost complete without the visual.

The scale that has been referred to is not only the distance between the audience and the forestage but also the width of the playing stage or proscenium opening. As an example, a good width for a legitimate play is not much more than 35 feet; whereas opera stages may open to as much as 60 feet in width.

## TECHNICAL REQUIREMENTS IN PERFORMING ARTS SPACES

### Introduction

Broadly speaking, the spaces in a performing arts buildings fall into four categories:

- *Front-of-house:* Lobbies, foyers, circulation, box office, rest rooms and other spaces serving the theater-going public
- *House:* The audience chamber
- *Stage:* Where the action happens
- *Backstage or back-of-house:* dressing rooms, green rooms, performer and crew lounges, shops, storage rooms, and other support spaces for the stage, performers, and technical crew

The quantity, size, location, and features associated with spaces in each of these categories will vary depending on the unique requirements of the companies, ensembles, producers, or presenters that use a particular performance room. These requirements are most directly influenced by the types of performances and seating capacity (Figs. 18 and 19).

### Americans with Disabilities Act

Before considering the technical requirements of different types of performance spaces, it is important to appreciate the importance of barrier-free design in contemporary facilities. Theater planning changed significantly with the introduction of new requirements for disabled persons in the early 1990s. The Americans with Disabilities Act (ADA) created a new standard of accommodation for persons with mobility and other impairments. The ADA is intended to enable persons with disabilities to have access equal to that afforded other persons at a wide variety of events and in most public facilities and transportation systems. For performing arts centers, two fundamental principles tend to shape the guidelines and interpretations in the ADA Accessibility Guidelines published by the U.S. Architectural and Transportation Barriers Compliance Board and enforced by the U.S. Department of Justice. These principles are as follows:

- *Choice:* Persons with disabilities must be given a range of choices of seating locations and ticket prices similar to those of other patrons, and their ability to actually see the event must be equivalent.
- *Integration:* Persons with disabilities must be accommodated in ways that integrate them with other patrons and do not create isolated or segregated "disabled areas" that are different in appearance and location from other seating. Patrons with and without disabilities should be able to attend events in mixed couples or groups without being separated or distanced by the seating accommodation provided for them (see Fig. 20).

The ADA Accessibility Guidelines affect not only the public's access to these buildings, but also that of the performing, technical, and administrative staff who work in performing arts centers. Interpretation of the guidelines tends to be complex and can have significant legal ramifications for an architect. Consequently, architects who are charged with the design of performance venues are advised to secure expert advice in applying the guidelines to specific design projects.

### Cost Estimates and Design

Unlike typical commercial and institutional buildings, performing arts facilities tend to have rather high net-to-gross multipliers. Heavy

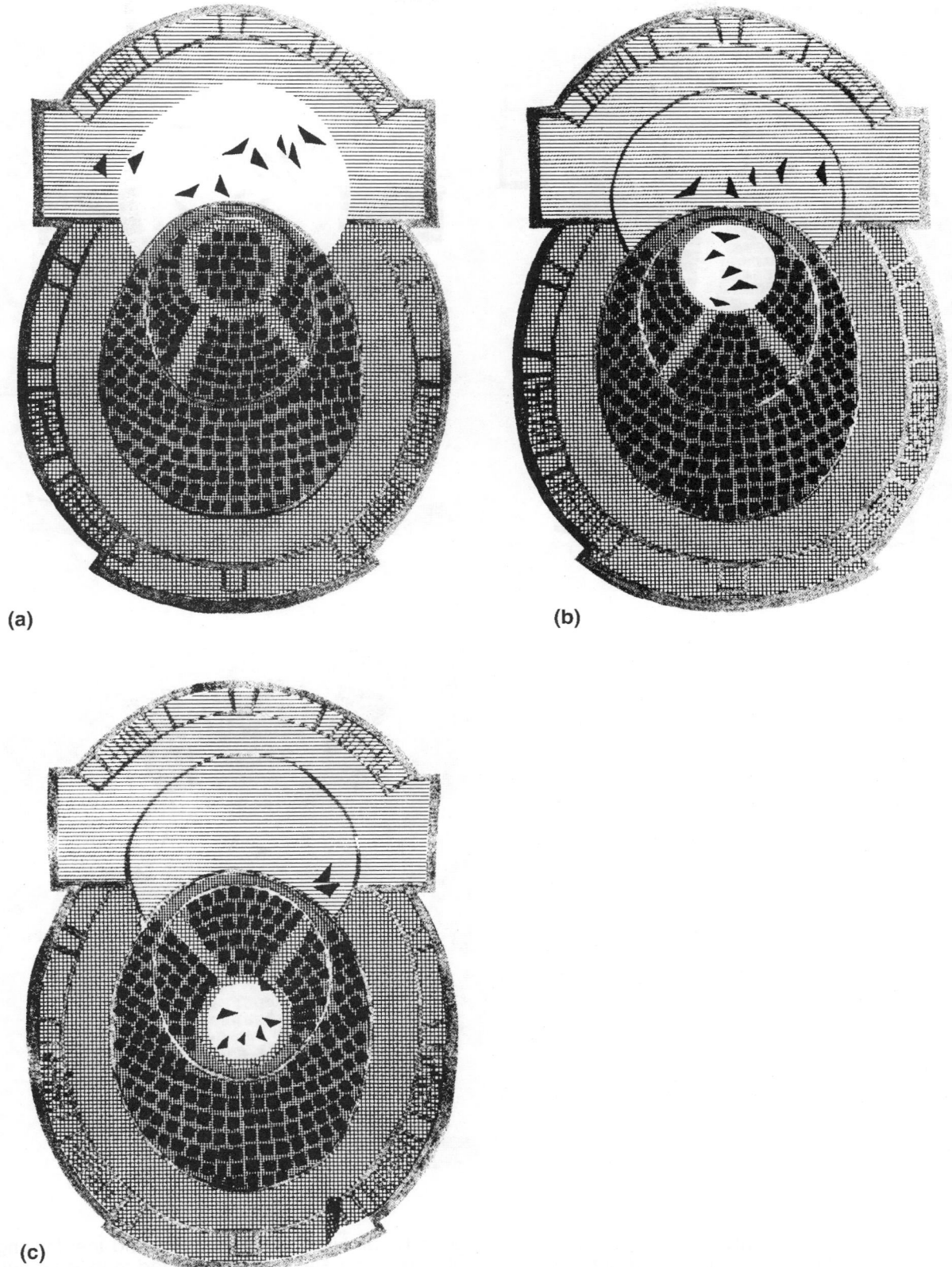

**(a)**

**(b)**

**(c)**

Fig. 15. The total theater scheme, designed by Walter Gropius in 1929, is a chimera holding forth the elusive promise of a multiform stage. It could be changed from (*a*) the proscenium shape to (*b*) the open-thrust shape and (*c*) the arena shape.

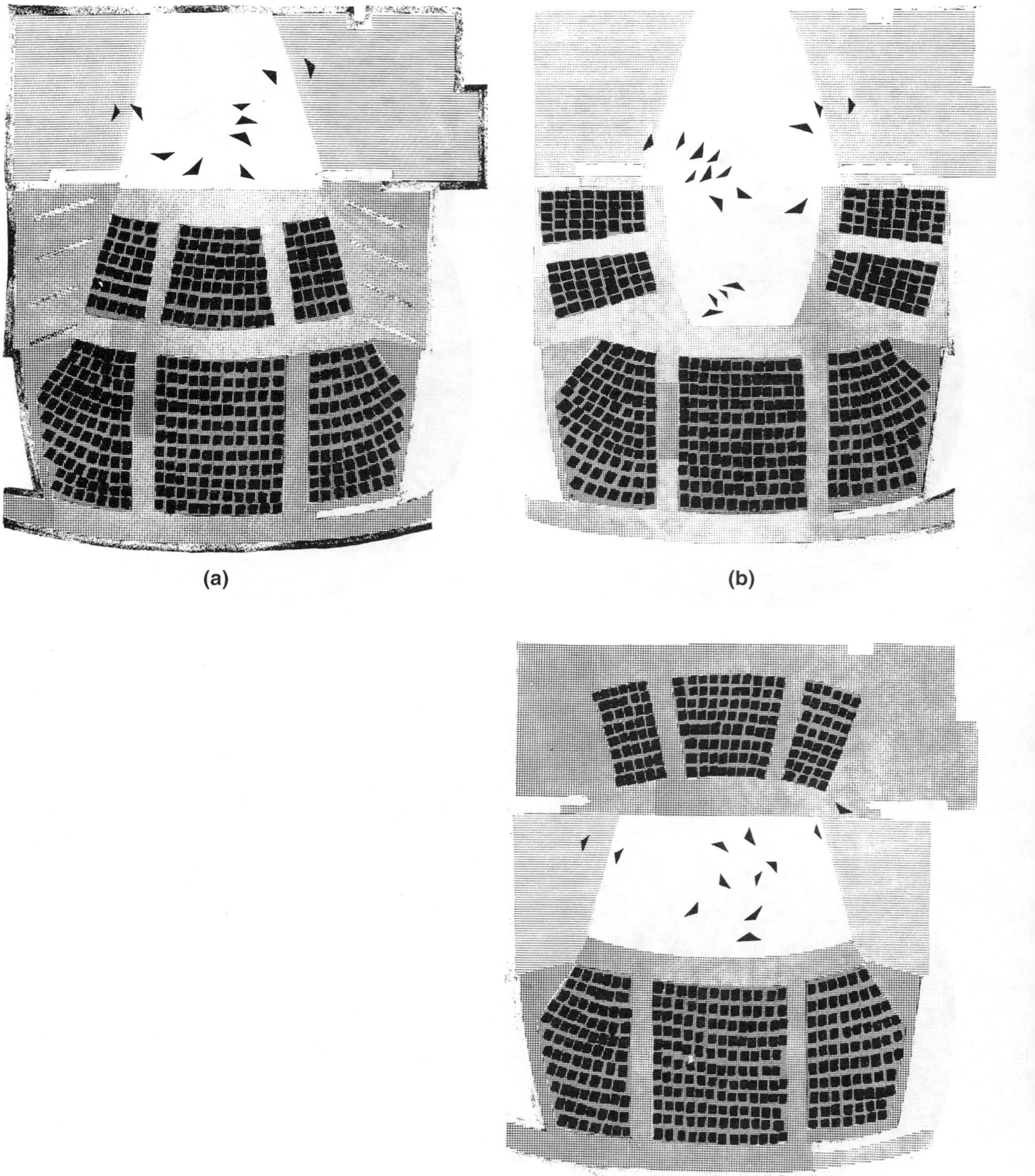

(a)

(b)

(c)

Fig. 16. The Loeb Drama Center at Harvard University, designed by architect Hugh Stubbins and theater engineer George Izenour in 1960, is a small-scale realization of the multiform stage. Electrically operated mobile seating units and stage sections can be rearranged to create (*a*) a basic proscenium shape, (*b*) a basic open-thrust shape, and (*c*) a modified arena or center stage shape.

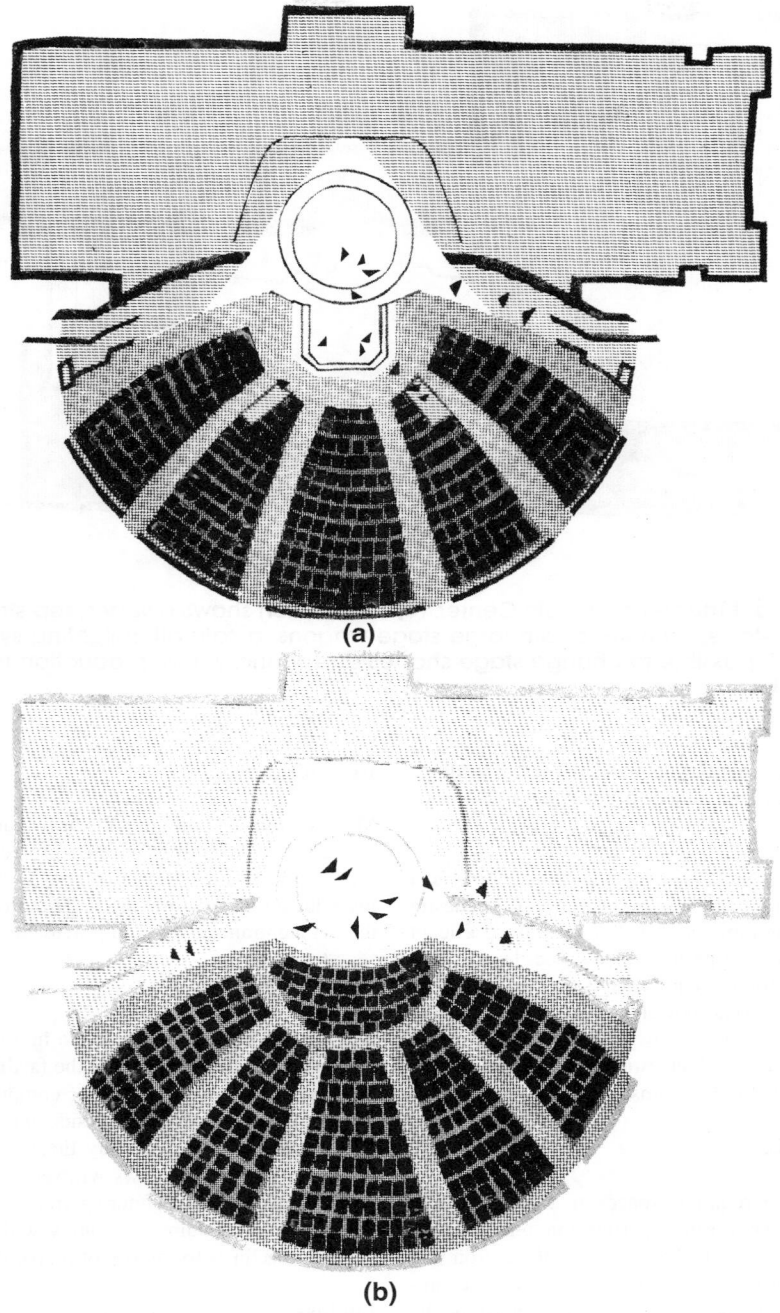

(a)

(b)

Fig. 17. The Beaumont Theater at Lincoln Center, designed by Eero Saarinen and Jo Mielziner in 1960, can change its shape from (a) an open-thrust stage to (b) a proscenium stage with a modified apron

and thick sound-isolating wall constructions, oversized ducts, and substantial circulation space add substantially to the gross floor area in performing arts centers. It is common for the net-to-gross multiplier for such facilities to be in the range of 1.5 to 1.7. Since cost estimates during early planning efforts are sometimes calculated on the basis of gross floor area, it is essential that appropriate grossing factors are applied to the net usable area that results from a typical facility program. Building programs must identify specific net areas for lobbies, major vertical circulation (public stairs), and rest rooms. Do

not rely on the grossing factor to provide adequate allowances for such facilities.

Another factor to consider in budget estimates is the large amount of multiheight space in performing arts facilities. A stage house in a multipurpose performance hall may represent only 6,600 square feet in plan, but that stage house will typically rise to a height of 100 feet or more. This concern also applies to the house and frequently applies to the public lobbies in a performance venue.

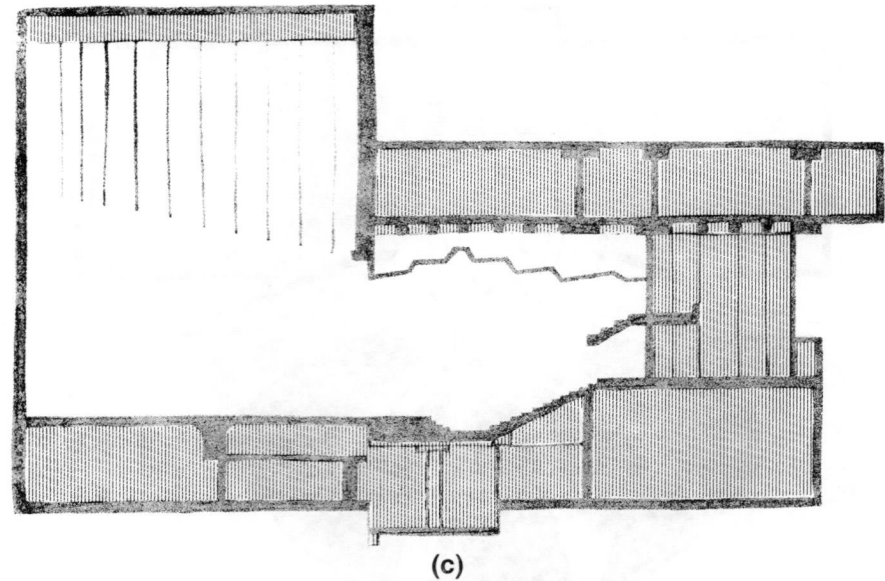

**(c)**

**Fig. 17. (cont.) The Beaumont Theater at Lincoln Center.** (*c*) The section shows a very deep stage planned for a repertory schedule. The deep stage, combined with large stage wagons, a saturation lighting system, and the multiform stage mechanism make it possible to change stage shapes and scenery from production to production in a matter of hours with minimum labor

Because such spaces are an essential feature of these buildings budget estimates that are developed on a cost-per-square-foot basis can be misleading.

Finally, there is the issue of specialized acoustical and theatrical equipment. Theatrical lighting systems, sound systems, orchestra shells, and other specialized equipment will represent a significant percentage of the total budget for a performance space. In addition, these systems will impose additional requirements on the building in terms of storage space and electrical power or heat loads. Separate budget allowances should be reserved for such equipment and appropriate provisions included in the budget estimates for a building's electrical, mechanical, and structural systems.

### FRONT-OF-HOUSE SPACES

Front-of-house spaces are the required spaces that serve theater patrons prior to the performance, during intermission, and after the performance. These spaces typically include all areas the patron will encounter from the parking lot to the interior of the audience chamber. Much care should be given to these spaces, as they determine the initial impression of the patron's theatrical experience. Careful consideration must be made of how the patron gets into the building to the box office, and eventually to the seat.

### Parking

Parking must be ample for all patrons with vehicles. The determination of the size of the lot(s) will depend on the location of the venue, the demographics of the patrons, the number of venues (if more than one), and the number of seats in each theater. Local laws and current ADA guidelines must be followed to determine the number of handicap spaces and their locations. Consideration should be given to the number of performers and staff that will need parking near the facility.

### Drop-off

Many patrons arriving in taxis or by car will want easy access to the facility via a covered or weather-protected car drop-off. During daytime hours this area may also serve as drop-off for school buses serving educational performances. The drop-off should lead directly to the main entrance foyer and provide direct vehicle access to parking

### Box Office

The box office will be one of the first spaces the patron approaches Depending on the operation of the facility, the box office may require multiple windows and areas for computer workstations. Some windows may be located on the outside of the building or just immediately inside where patrons can buy tickets without having to access the building. Multiple windows will serve patrons buying tickets for the evening's performance, future performances and "will call" pickup for prepaid tickets. Future technology will see the need to locate ticket vending machines for pickup of prepaid tickets.

### Lobbies

Lobbies and foyers mediate between the outdoors and the performance space itself and so serve an important role in preparing the patron for the performance experience. Successful lobby spaces invite people to socialize and create a sense of arrival and anticipation. Generously proportioned spaces, ceremonial staircases, and careful architectural detailing are examples of elements that can be combined to create the appropriate atmosphere.

The lobbies of the facility must be sized to allow comfortable circulation and milling space for all patrons. Lobbies will have a number of patron amenities immediately accessible. Rest rooms, donor's lounges, public phones, drinking fountains, concessions, and merchandising should be provided and located within easy access.

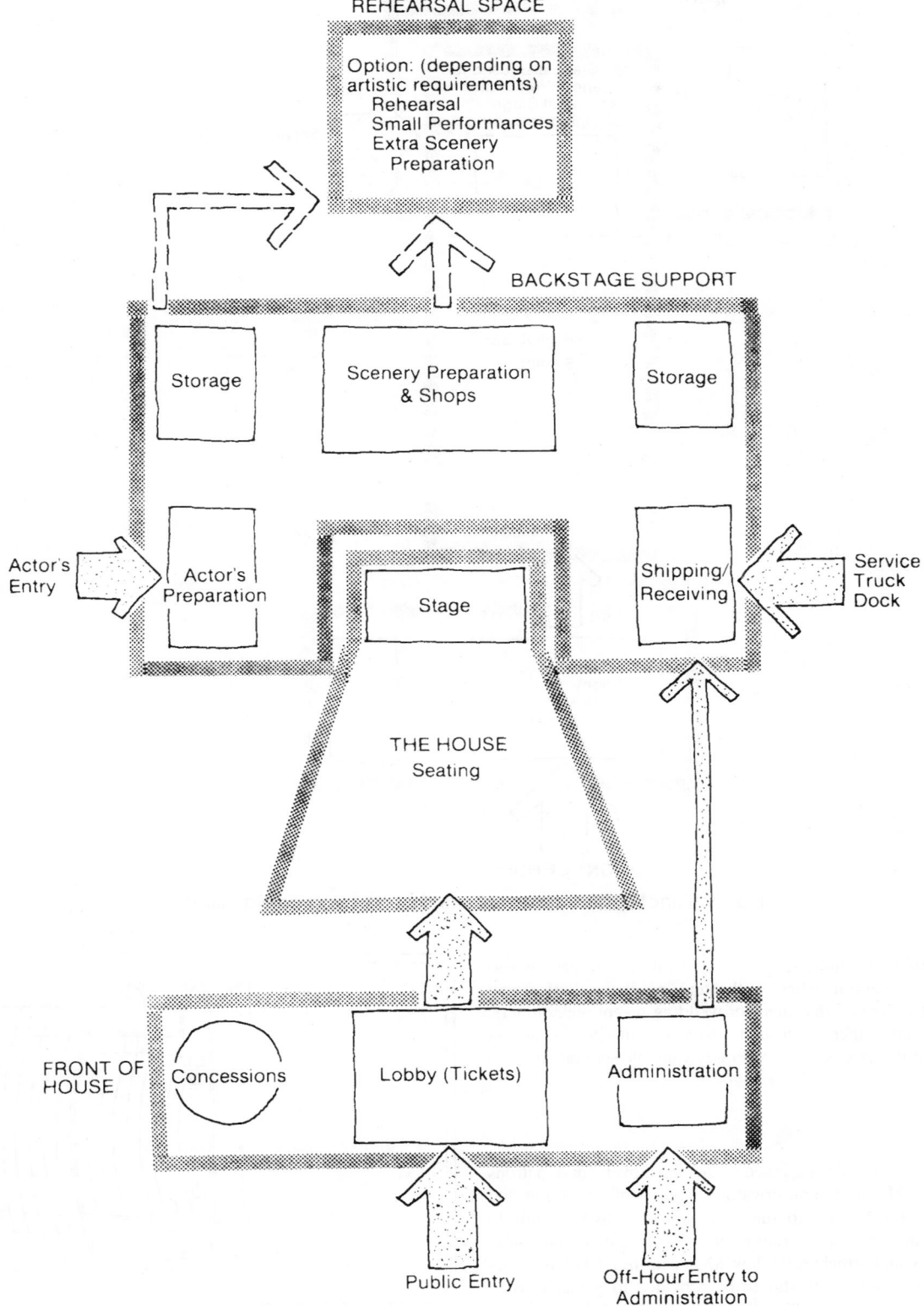

**Fig. 18. Functional diagram of large performing arts facilities**

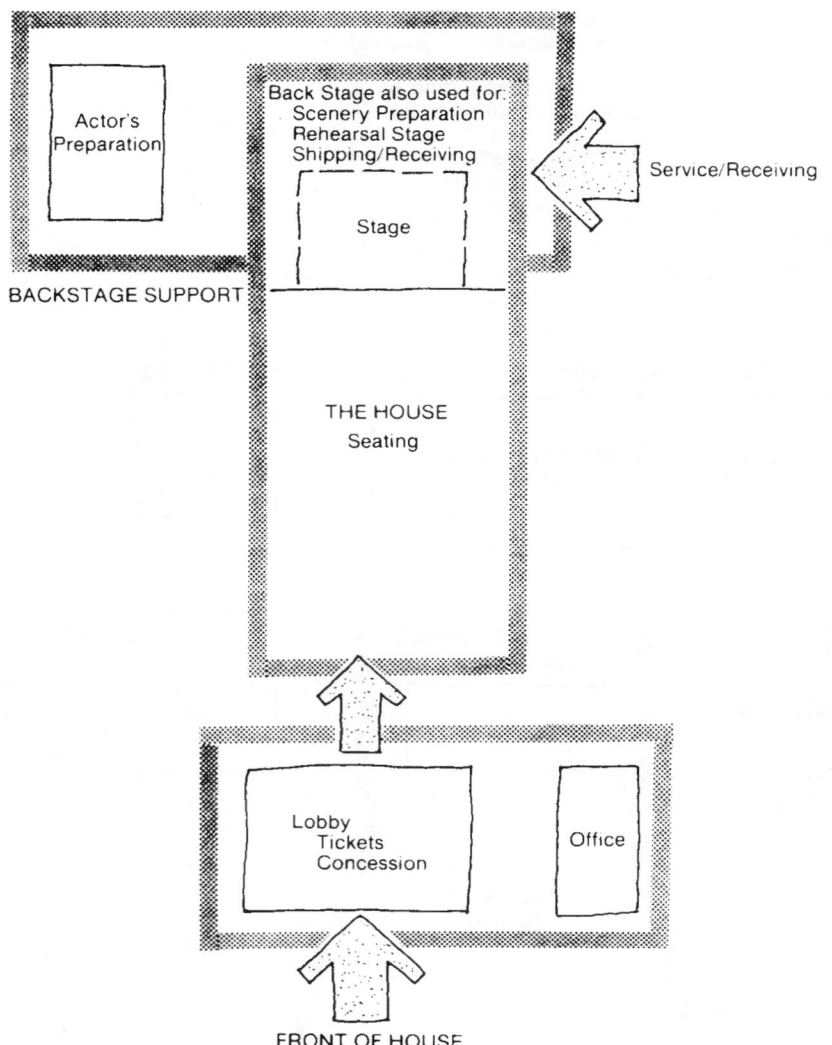

**Fig. 19. Functional diagram of small performing arts facilities**

Since lobbies are large public spaces (Fig. 21), they also serve as significant revenue generators when the theater is not in use. Performing arts center lobbies are often rented for wedding receptions, dinners, formal dances, and other social and business gatherings. Catering kitchens or warming ovens offer extremely valuable support for such functions.

**Circulation**

Public traffic flow should be designed so that the movement of patrons throughout the lobby is straightforward. Locations of rest rooms and concessions should be easy to find. Layouts have to be carefully devised so that queuing for rest rooms, elevators, and house entrances do not interfere with normal traffic flow. Most patrons tend to use stairs whenever possible. Elevators should be provided to get patrons to upper levels and persons with disabilities to all levels. Whenever possible sound and light locks should be designed into the entry of the auditorium. These areas are small vestibules with two sets of doors. When patrons enter the hall they can open the first set of doors and allow them to close before opening the second set. This prevents undesirable light and sound from entering the hall during a performance.

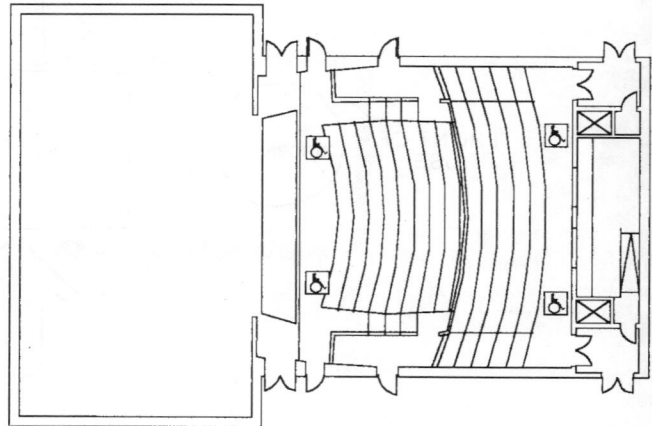

**Fig. 20. Floor plan of a typical orchestra level in a theater showing wheelchair seating positions that are well distributed, offering persons with mobility impairments both choice and integration with their fellow audience members (courtesy of Fisher Dachs Associates)**

**Fig. 21. The generous lobbies for Morton H. Meyerson Symphony Center in Dallas, Texas, offer patrons a high level of comfort and amenity (Architect: I. M. Pei & Partners; photo: David Greenberg)**

### Concessions and Merchandising

Concessions and merchandising are essential to the contemporary performing company as they offer opportunities to earn income over and above ticket revenue through food, beverage, and other sales. The quality and type of concessions depend on the venue, the performance, and the demographics of the audience. They can range from cans of soda and candy bars to champagne and caviar. Typically one large concession area can serve the theater. If there are multiple levels, portable bars can be practically located.

### Area Requirements for Lobby, Circulation, and Concession Spaces

Design practice with respect to the area devoted to these front-of-house functions has varied substantially over the years. In recent decades, there has been a move toward increased patron amenities in the front-of-house with consequent increases in the area allocated to such functions.

While there are no hard-and-fast rules concerning the area for front-of-house functions, one can derive a helpful gauge from an area-per-patron comparison in different types of spaces. Table 2 illustrates how much space is devoted to lobby and circulation for a selected range of facility types.

### Rest Rooms

Rest rooms are another key front-of-house facility. Building codes generally specify minimum fixture counts for public assembly spaces. Oftentimes the code minimum fixture counts do not account for the unique rest room loading that occurs in performance buildings, resulting in fixture counts that are woefully short of what is needed. An inadequate number of fixtures leads to long lines at intermission (particularly at women's rest rooms) which in turn negatively affects the patron experience and reduces opportunities for earned income through concession and merchandising sales.

Contemporary theater design practice calls for a minimum of 1 fixture for every 25 patrons. These should be allocated 65 pecent to women and the remainder to men. Rest rooms should be distributed in proportion to the seats at each level of the house and must provide accessible fixtures in compliance with applicable codes or regulations. Patrons should not have to travel more than one level up or down to get to a rest room.

### HOUSE

The performance experience is fundamentally about the relationship between the performers and the audience. The audience wants to hear and see the show without distraction and in comfort and safety, but its ultimate objective in attending the show is to receive the utmost sensory stimulation toward the maximum emotional and intellectual experience.

The design of the house therefore is driven by a number of considerations, including the performance type or types, the seating capacity, visual criteria, acoustical criteria, and architectural goals.

#### Principles That Influence House Design

A large number of factors influence the design of the house. These include the following:

- Seat count
- Plan arrangement

### Table 2 Lobby and circulation space

| Facility or facility type | Area (per patron), sq ft |
|---|---|
| Broadway theaters* (New York City) | 4–5 |
| New performing arts buildings, minimal | 12–16 |
| New performing arts buildings, standard | 18–22† |

*This refers specifically to the theaters that were built for legitimate theater in New York City from about 1900 to 1930. The handful of theaters built on Broadway after World War II generally devote larger areas to front-of-house functions than their cousins from the first third of the 20th century.

†While this is the typical range, it is in no way representative of the extreme. Morton Meyerson Symphony Center in Dallas, for example, features over 30 square feet per patron.

- Vertical arrangement
- Scale
- Alternate theater forms
- Acoustics
- Americans with Disabilities Act

**Seat Count**

The number and arrangement of seats define the net floor area of the house (an aspect of size). At the earliest stages of a project, the area for seating may be expressed in terms of square feet per seat. This criterion includes an allowance for circulation aisles inside the house and may vary from 6 to 10 square feet per seat. This variation is caused less by differing seat dimensions than by the efficiency of the seating layout and aisles. Generally, a figure of 8 to 9 square feet is good for first estimates, although a higher number is usually needed for spaces with smaller seating capacities. If seating is moveable, additional allowance must be made for imprecision and maneuvering clearances (13 to 15 square feet is commonly used).

As the seat count of a space rises, it becomes difficult and eventually impossible to keep the average patron within a reasonable viewing distance to the performer on a single level. The obvious way to resolve this is to introduce an additional seating level or levels. The use of balconies to vertically distribute seating and preserve a more intimate audience experience of the performance introduces both challenges and opportunities to theater planning.

- Distributing the audience vertically brings a larger percentage of the audience closer to the stage since balconies can overhang the orchestra level seating and one another.
- The distance that a balcony overhangs the seating below must be carefully studied. When a balcony overhang is excessively deep, patrons sitting underneath can have the impression that they are sitting in an area that is visually or acoustically separate from the rest of the house. This is highly undesirable and should be avoided. Generally, the rearmost row under the balcony should at least be able to see the top of the proscenium. In spaces where music is a key program element, acoustics may require extremely shallow overhang distances.
- Houses with more than one level allow upper levels to be closed or darkened, reducing the negative impression created by large areas of empty seats. This can effectively focus the attention of the audience and performer on a smaller (i.e., the occupied) part of the house.
- Front-of-house design becomes more complex as it now must accommodate vertical circulation involving stairs, elevators, and upper-level lobbies and amenities.

**Plan Arrangement**

Vision and acoustic criteria define the horizontal proportions (plan shape) of the room with reference to the stage configuration and proscenium width (Fig. 22). Sight lines need to balance the desire to keep as many patrons as possible close to the centerline of the room with the goal of minimizing the average viewing distance to the stage. The objective logically should be to maximize the number of seats in the center front region.

*Distances*

Performer expressions are difficult to see beyond 40 feet, gestures past 65 feet, and only large body movements can be seen between 65

**Fig. 22. Although designed to house a variety of performing arts events, Bass Performance Hall is derived from the classical horseshoe-shaped European opera houses of the 18th and 19th centuries. The multiple tiers and side box galleries create an intensely intimate space for both audience and performer. (Architect: David M. Schwarz; photo: Len Allington, courtesy of Jaffe Holden Acoustics)**

and 110 feet. Locate drama audiences within 65 feet, if possible. Viewing at an oblique angle foreshortens the image and may require neck craning. The normal cone of optimum vision covers 30 degrees vertically and 40 degrees horizontally. Front corner seats are generally least desirable, as the viewing angle from this location provides an oblique view in which portions of the acting area may be obscured. For that matter, any front row seat requires a lot of head movement to take in the entire acting area. A 45-degree pivot is considered the maximum tolerable (see Fig. 23).

If the foregoing limitations are applied in the horizontal plane for any given proscenium opening, they will limit an area of maximum value as seating space which is approximately elliptical. It is interesting to note that this shape for an auditorium plan was pioneered by the late architect Joseph Urban, who had little of the present data to work with and may safely be assumed to have chosen the shape largely on esthetic grounds. A fan shape provides additional seating space at

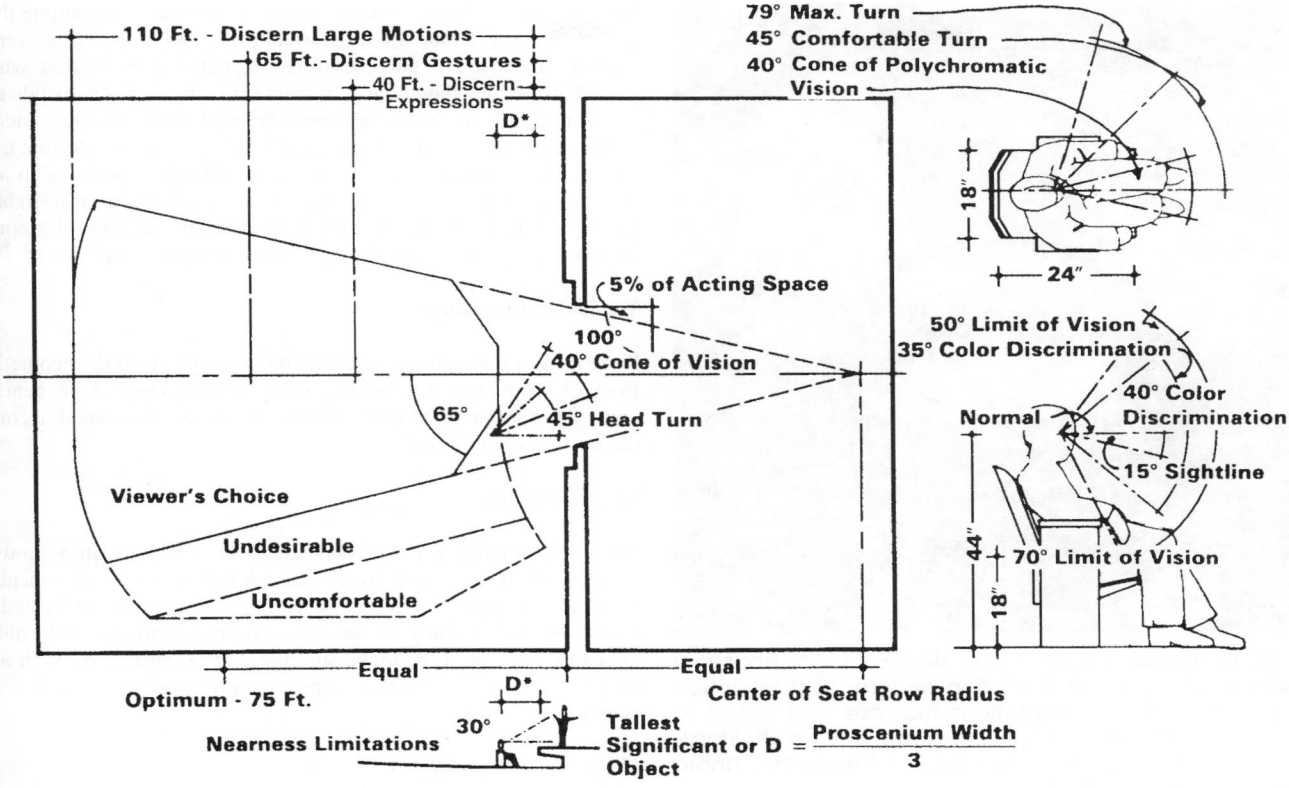

Fig. 23. Critical dimensions for plan arrangements in a theater

minimum sacrifice of sight lines, but the seats in the extreme rear corners are undesirable.

In theatrical entertainment, which has as its chief visual component human actors (live shows), the degree to which these performers must be seen to satisfy the audience and put the show across varies.

1. Details of facial expression and small gestures are important in legitimate drama, vaudeville and burlesque, intimate revue, and cabaret.
2. Broad gestures by single individuals are important in grand opera presentation, musical comedy, and dance.
3. Gestures by individuals are unimportant and movement of individuals from place to place is the smallest significant movement in pageant.

It follows then that theaters planned for the types of entertainment listed under 1 must be limited in depth of auditorium so that visibility from the remotest seat still allows the occupant to perceive facial expressions.

Theaters planned for the types listed under 2 may have greater distance from the stage to the remotest seat, but this distance is set at a maximum beyond which the individual actor is diminished to insignificance.

For spectators in the last rows at Radio City Music Hall in New York (Fig. 24), looking through a distance ranging from 160 to over 200 feet, an individual performer, even with the dramatic enhancement of a follow spot, is a very insignificant figure indeed.

*House Width*

Sight lines from the side seats limit the practical distance between the side walls. Width of the house therefore is related to the proscenium width. The width of the proscenium opening is a function of the kind of production contemplated for the theater. The dimensions given in Table 3 are derived from the requirements of the types of production noted when the performances are staged so as to assure maximum effectiveness.

*Row Curvature*

Occupants of all seats are visually related to the performance when the seats are oriented toward the stage. This necessitates curving the rows of seats. The center of curvature is located on the centerline of the auditorium approximately the depth of the house behind the proscenium. Budgetary limitations may dictate that seats be in straight rows to simplify construction; these rows can at least be related to the center of attention on stage by being placed on chords of the optimum row curvature (see Fig. 25).

*Stagger*

To provide best visibility from any seat, no patron should sit exactly in front of any other patron unless more than one row distant. This requirement makes it necessary to stagger seats. Staggering is accomplished by the nonuniform placement of seats of varying widths in succeeding rows. Unless the walls of the theater are parallel, it is extremely unlikely that more than a very few rows can be made up of seats of uniform width. The lack of uniformity thereby introduced

**Fig. 24.** Radio City Music Hall in New York City houses a variety of entertainment, motion picture, and television broadcast events, presentations that are well suited to the scale of this magnificent art-deco palace (Restoration architect: Hardy Holzman Pfeiffer Associates; photo courtesy of the architect)

provides the means by which staggering can be accomplished. Seats are made with uniform standards and interchangeable backs and seats so that a wide variation of seat width is possible; a variation from seat to seat of an inch or two, cumulative enough to accomplish satisfactory stagger and make rows even, is not noticed by the patron.

Various seating companies have their own schemes and formulas for seat stagger, some of them patented. The client may ask a seating company for a seating plan and should examine it critically for (1) insufficient stagger in occasional areas of the house and (2) the introduction of seats narrower than the acceptable minimum.

*Aisles*

Aisles are of questionable desirability except in the largest houses. They must, however, be employed in many localities because of building codes which make no provision for continuous-row or so-called continental seating in which all rows are widely spaced and serve as

**Table 3** Proscenium widths for kinds of theatrical productions, in feet

| | Minimum | Usual | Reasonable maximum |
|---|---|---|---|
| Drama | 26 | 30 to 35 | 40 |
| Vaudeville, revue | 30 | 35 | 45 |
| Musical comedy, operetta | 30 | 40 | 50 |
| Presentation, opera | 40 | 50 to 55 | 65 |

transverse aisles. Many a bad sight line has resulted from putting the maximum legal number of seats, usually 14, into each row in every section. Obviously, for purposes of seeing, radial aisles are best, with curved aisles only slightly less efficient (Fig. 26). Aisles perpendicular to the curtain line often have the accidental result of making side-section seats undesirable because people using the aisles interrupt the view toward the stage. The box office would like a theater with all seats in the center section. A center aisle wastes the most desirable seating area in the theater and inevitably causes the objectionable condition of seats near the aisle being directly in front of each other.

**Vertical Arrangement**

If the floor is flat, patrons have a hard time seeing over the people in front of them. For this reason, most theater floors slope gently upward toward the back of the house. Floors may be ramped (a continuous slope) or stepped.

*Elevation of Stage*

The stage should always be below eye level of patrons sitting in the first row. Ideal height is between 2 feet-6 inches and 3 feet-6 inches from the floor at the first row of seats. The viewing angle of the audience varies with art form. In dance, for example, patrons must be able to see the dancers' feet. Make sure the stage floor is level with all support spaces backstage to expedite movement of scenery and equipment (see Fig. 27).

*House Floor Slope (Rake)*

Sight-line criteria in the vertical dimension help define floor slope. Flat-floor rooms are limited in capacity by the problem of seeing past a few rows of people. A straight-rake (ramped) floor improves conditions for a short distance only. With each successive row, the steepness of slope must increase in order to accomplish the same geometric sight-line clearance from row to row—optimum 5 or 6 inches every two rows if seats are staggered. The relative stage level is a factor here—a lower stage favors a steeper floor (see Fig. 28).

Since concern for comfort and safety limits the maximum ramp slope and discourages single risers in aisles, a limit is implied for the number of rows before a cross aisle or other device breaks the pattern. Where steps are necessary, they should be between 4.5 and 8 inches high and clearly marked or illuminated. General design practice suggests that slopes less than 1:10 are judged to be comfortable, while a slope of 1:8 is the practical upper limit for nonstepped aisles. Steeper rises must be stepped. Step height and slopes must be reviewed in the context of applicable codes, which vary from locale to locale.

*Relationship Between Seat Stagger and Slope*

The positioning of seats in the rows depends on the degree of the rake. One-row vision, in which seats in each row line up directly with those in front, requires a very steep rake to allow for proper viewing angles. Two-row vision involves staggered seating and permits an unobstructed view between the two seats in front of the patron. Because this arrangement does not involve a steep rake, it is highly recommended (see Fig. 29).

*Relationship Between Row Curvature and Slope*

The planning of the floor slope is not completed when pitch of orchestra and balcony has been laid out on the centerline. It depends

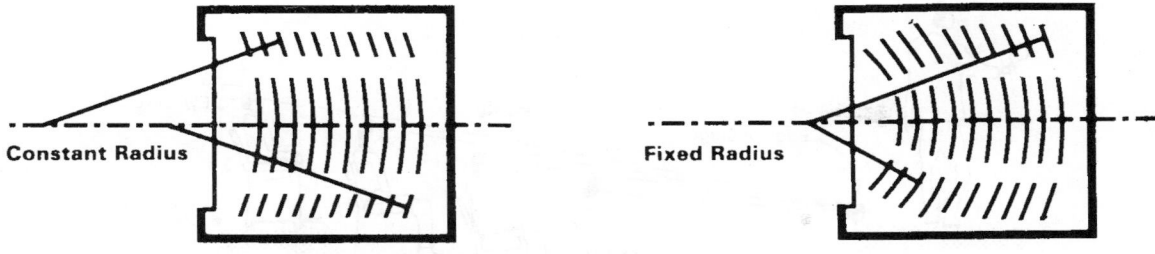

**Fig. 25. Different approaches to row curvature**

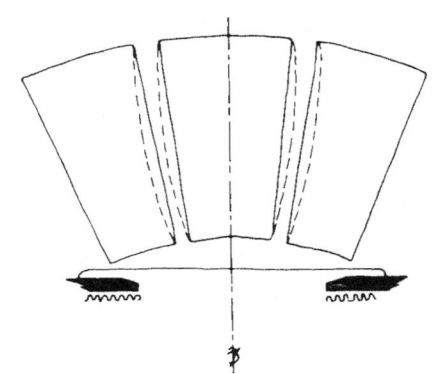

**Fig. 26. Straight radial aisles are better than aisles which curve or bend**

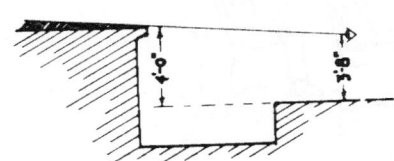

**Fig. 27. Zone of invisibility—causes: stage too high, front seats too low**

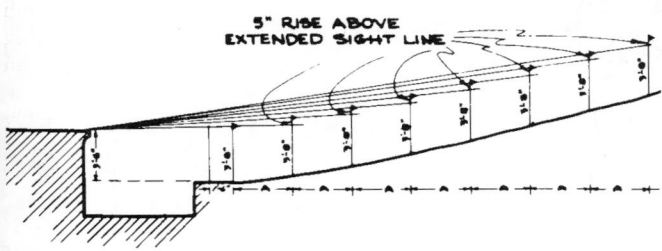

**Fig. 28. Developed floor slope for unobstructed vision**

also on the curve of the rows of seats. The whole row must be at the same elevation if the seats are to be level. The floor therefore is not a sloped plane, but a dished surface in which horizontal contours follow the seat row curve. The floor section at the centerline, rotated horizontally about the center of curvature of the rows of seats, will determine the orchestra floor shape. The balcony is planned the same way save that the floor is terraced to take the seats (see Fig. 30).

*Section*

The vertical angle of 30 degrees at the spectator's position establishes the distance from the closest seat to the screen or to the highest significant object on the stage. The lowest seat in the orchestra (typically the first row) must be located where the patron can just see the stage floor (or the bottom of a movie screen). The highest seat in the balcony must be on a line which is not more than 30 degrees to the horizontal from the stage floor at the curtain line. The standing patron at the back of the orchestra level should be able to see the top of a screen or as high as any significant portion of a stage setting. Each spectator must see the whole stage or screen over the heads of those in front. Within these limits the floor slope of orchestra and balcony can be laid out: the first step in determining auditorium section (see Fig. 31).

Several methods have been offered heretofore for developing the floor slope. Doubtless others will be offered in the future. The authors present the following method as one which ensures unobstructed vision from all seats. It may be noted that this system produces a floor slope considerably steeper than that in many existing theaters. It also produces better seeing conditions.

To determine floor slope, establish eye position of spectator in first row on centerline by approximately a 30-degree vertical angle above. For live performances, the stage floor will be approximately 2 inches below this level. The height of stage floor above the first row typically ranges from 30 to 42 inches. For theaters designed solely for motion pictures, the bottom of the screen is critical (see Fig. 32).

The eye point of the first row is established at 3 feet-8 inches above the floor level. In new construction it is necessary to consider that the first few rows may have to be wheelchair accessible, thereby requiring the first few rows to be flat. The following procedure can be executed after the second or third row of seats.

- *Step 1:* Draw a sight line from the downstage edge of the stage to the eye point for the second or third row. Step off horizontal seat spacing (back to back), and draw vertical lines at the points thus established for subsequent seating rows (typically 34 to 38 inches).

**One-Row Vision**

Rake of floor is steep enough for row A to see over heads of row B

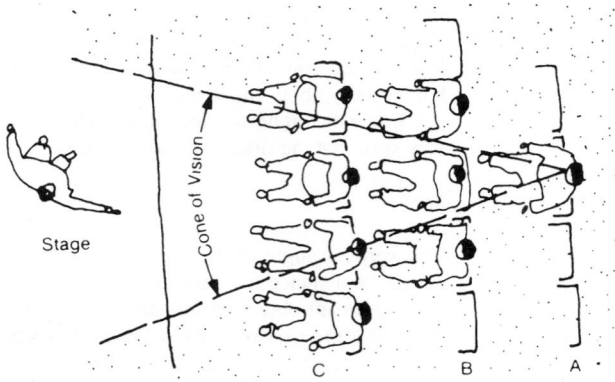

**Plan of One-Row Vision**

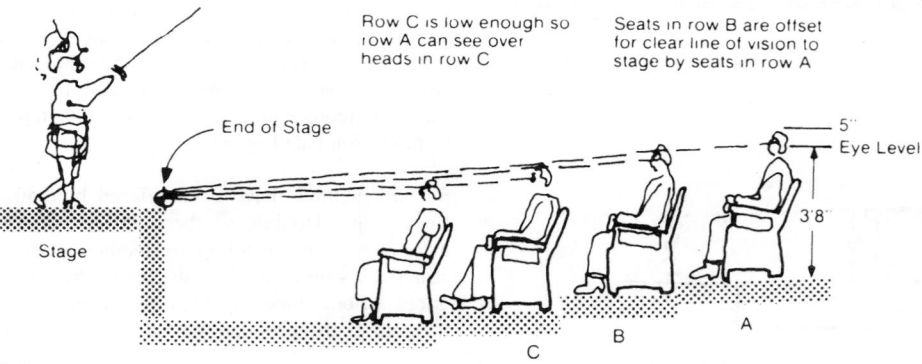

Row C is low enough so row A can see over heads in row C

Seats in row B are offset for clear line of vision to stage by seats in row A

**Two-Row Vision**

Requires the Lowest Angle Rake

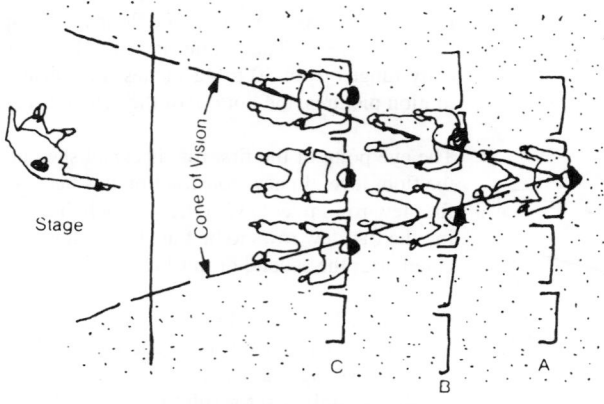

**Fig. 29. Comparison of one-row and two-row vision**

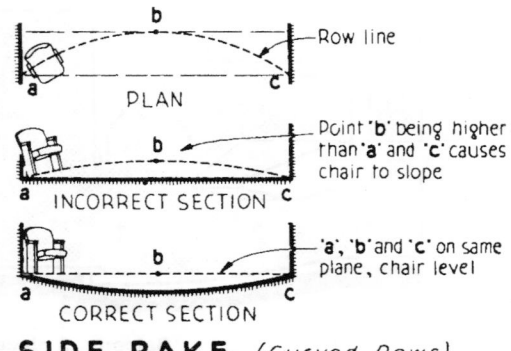

**SIDE RAKE** *(Curved Rows)*

**Fig. 30. Illustration of slab dish caused by row curvature**

- *Step 2:* Establish a point 5 inches above the intersection of the sight line and the eye point and extend to the next vertical line.
- *Step 3:* The intersection of these lines is the eye point for the next seat row and the floor level at this row is 3 feet-8 inches below the eye point.
- Repeat steps 1, 2, and 3 to the last seating row and draw in the floor slope.

Where the number of rows exceeds more than 10, the slope of the orchestra floor could become excessive. A simple compromise to reduce the slope is to horizontally stagger the seats. In this way a viewer would never sit directly behind the head of a person in the row in front. To complete the procedure, establish the vertical line spacing for every other row.

Per most building codes, where the slope exceeds 1:8, steps are required and steps can be no less than 4 inches. A cross aisle that divides the orchestra into front and back sections necessitates raising the elevation of the first row of seats behind it to make up for horizontal depth of the aisle.

Raising the stage will make it possible to reduce the floor slope but at the penalty of producing upward sight lines in the first two or three rows, which are uncomfortable and unnatural for viewing stage setting and action. If the stage floor is above the elevation of the first-row eye position, the upstage floor can be out of sight by perhaps as much as 6 inches. The compromised view from the first row is gen-

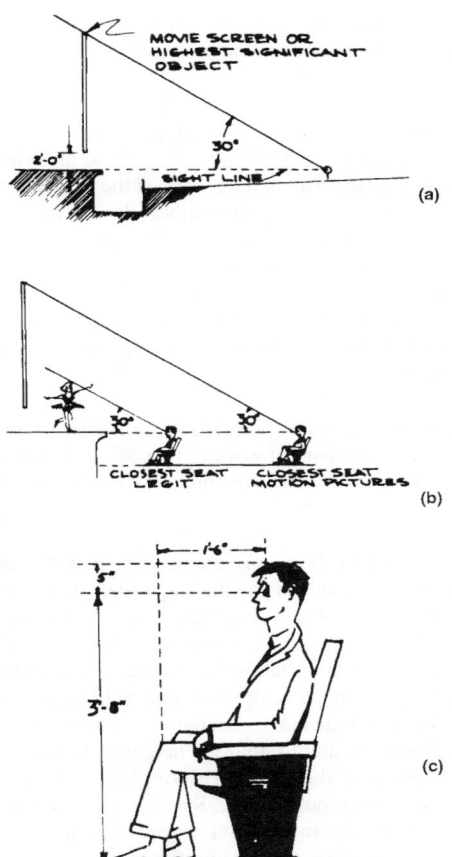

**Fig. 32. (*a*) Maximum tolerable upward sight-line angle for top of the stage picture or motion picture screen; (*b*) maximum angle determines location of closest seats; (*c*) basic dimensions for plotting floor slope**

erally preferable to having an excessive floor slope, especially if more than one balcony is used.

The standing spectator's eye level behind the rear row of seats is assumed to be 5 feet-6 inches above the floor level of the last row. The sight line from this position to the top of the screen or highest probable curtain trim establishes the minimum height for ceiling under balcony (see Fig. 33). Where acoustics are a concern, the height of the balcony may be determined by the number of rows under the balcony and the required opening.

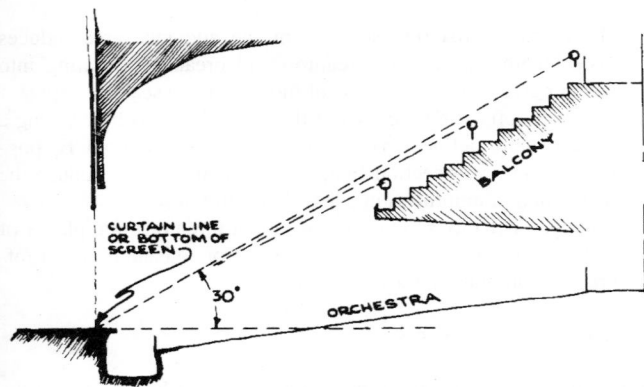

**Fig. 31. Maximum tolerable downward sight-line angle from balcony**

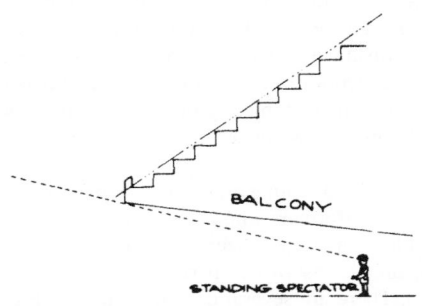

**Fig. 33. The sight line of the standing patron limits the balcony overhang**

When planning for movies only, the lower sight line from the first row will come to the bottom of the projected picture, approximately 24 inches above the stage floor.

The balcony slope can be determined by a similar procedure. It should be noted that most building codes, while allowing for variances in slopes and step riser heights, restrict the amount of variation. The focal point onstage is the point farthest downstage at which visibility is critical (i.e., dancers' toes), or in the case of movies, the bottom of the screen. The maximum forward point of the balcony is then determined when the location of the spectator's eye position has been moved forward to a point at which the floor and supporting structure would intersect the upper sight line of the spectator standing at the rear of the orchestra.

To maintain constant pitch in the balcony, sight lines should be determined for the last row using the above procedure. If vision from the rear row in the balcony is adequate, the rest of the balcony will be satisfactory.

In theaters designed to show only movies, the first row need not be located so that the patron can see the stage floor. It is satisfactory if the patron sees without obstruction the bottom of the screen, which is seldom placed less than 2 feet above the stage floor. Raising the screen makes it possible to flatten the contour of the orchestra floor. The reversed floor slope developed by Ben Schlanger makes use of this relationship to get the maximum number of seats into the zone of least visual distortion, and to hold the height of movie theaters to a minimum. A result of the reversed floor slope is placing balcony seats in the zone of optimum seeing. Special consideration should be given that a reverse slope in the first few rows does not prevent access to that location by patrons with disabilities.

### Scale

Larger-scale spaces generate other design challenges, particularly how to give an intimate sense of scale to a sea of people. It makes the performance seem more remote, the individual less important, and the experience less intense.

A large area of seating without aisles can heighten this impression, although such arrangements can be more efficient at large capacities because cross aisles are not needed. Aisles do help define smaller units of seating, which may make the room seem smaller.

As distances increase, the effects of floor slope are amplified. Differences in the elevation of the various entries to the house can make the planning of adjacent lobby and circulation spaces particularly challenging. Further, as aisle length increases with conventional seating, good design practice and building codes generally require that cross aisles be added to the seating plan to ensure reasonable travel distance to exits. A cross aisle is a means of collecting the audience from more than one aisle, and it is consequently quite wide. Cross aisles typically occupy the space normally allocated to two or more rows of seats.

Large undifferentiated seating areas can also have a negative psychological effect on performers when the house is less than full. A small audience in a large house can seem even smaller if the apparent size of the seating area is vast by comparison to the number of seats actually occupied. There are several design strategies (Fig. 34) that can be employed to counter the impact of large seating capacities and thereby promote greater intimacy for performer and audience:

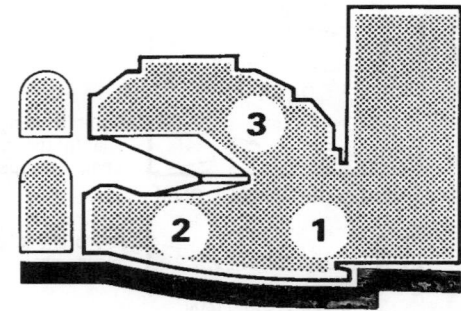

**Balcony: 3 places**

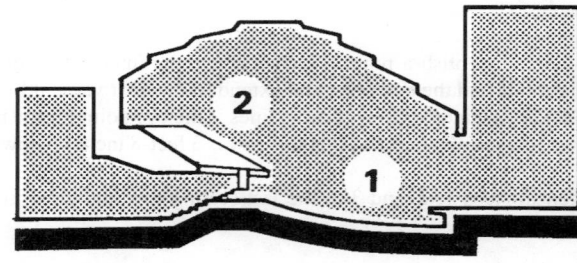

**Ledge: 2 places**

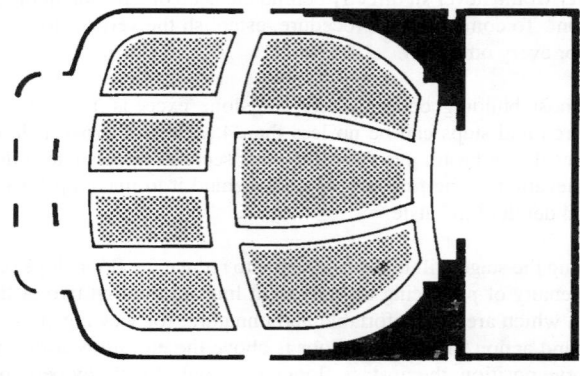

**Berry Patch**

**Fig. 34. Larger house subdivisions**

- Horizontally offsetting sections of the audience area reduces aisle lengths (a desirable feature) and breaks the seating into smaller areas creating a sense of more intimate scale.
- Vertically offsetting sections of the audience areas by creating a parterre helps define two distinct places within the room. By populating the lower section first, a house manager can reduce the perception of emptiness in a less-than-full house.
- Finally, a balcony solution brings about three or more places of different flavor. Each place provides a strong visual frame of reference more intimate than the whole.

### Alternate Theater Forms

In the thrust or open-stage form, sight lines must be directed to the edge of the acting area, requiring steeper balconies. The balcony of a theater that is convertible from proscenium to open-stage form must ollow the requirements for thrust configuration. Any theater in which performance extends beyond the proscenium onto either forestage, open stage, or extended stage requires very careful planning to provide good seeing from all balcony seats to all parts of the acting area.

Few, if any, arena-form theaters have balconies, since the in-the-round seating of the arena form seems best suited to a single level. In addition, acoustical constraints related to the power and the directional nature of the human voice place a practical limit on the size of such spaces. Such constraints tend to keep seating capacities small enough to preclude a need for a balcony. Moreover, to satisfy the requirements of good seeing in arena forms, it is necessary to elevate successive rows of seats more than in proscenium form to minimize the problem of actors covering other actors from some points in the room (see Fig. 35).

If seat rows are successively and sufficiently elevated, the audience may see over the heads of near actors to the heads, and partially the bodies, of actors farther away.

## Acoustics

Acoustical design plays an important role in developing many features in a performance facility. Acoustics impact everything from the size and shape of the house, the location of mechanical rooms, and the selection of sound equipment to the density of materials enclosing the performance hall, the sizes of ducts, and the requirements for floors and windows. Acoustical issues can be broken down into several subdisciplines:

*Room acoustics:* This aspect of acoustics deals with how the interior of the house and stage are designed to promote the proper acoustical environment for the performances planned in the theater. Where a theater must accommodate more than one type of performance, adjustable acoustic features need to be incorporated into the room acoustic design for a building.

*Sound and vibration isolation:* A quiet environment is essential to our enjoyment of most performances. This area of acoustics determines how a building should be built to ensure that noise sources both within the building and in the external environment do not intrude on the house or stage.

*Mechanical services noise and vibration control:* Contemporary buildings feature extensive mechanical plants to maintain comfort and distribute power and water. Such systems must be carefully designed to ensure that they do not introduce noise into the performance space.

*Electroacoustics:* Many types of contemporary music and Broadway-style musical theater require sound amplification as an essential part of the art form. These systems must be carefully designed to provide excellent intelligibility for speech and definition for music. A successful design combines the proper equipment with a sensitive understanding of the acoustical environment.

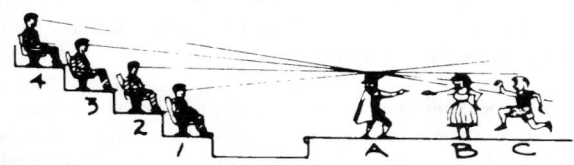

**Fig. 35. The sight-line problem inherent in the arena form: A hides B and C from first two rows**

The following sections offer conceptual approaches that might be helpful during early programming or predesign efforts. Ideally, an experienced acoustical consultant should be engaged to assist the client and architect in the development of the program, initial building concepts, and budgets. This can help ensure that the initial design assumptions are in line with a building's intended uses.

### Room Acoustics

The program of performances in a theater will establish a design direction for room acoustics in any space. It is essential to realize that each performance type is best experienced in a particular acoustical environment. Each of these different acoustical environments imposes a different set of constraints on issues such as the cubic volume contained within the theater, width of the house, depth of balcony overhangs, and materials of construction. Table 4 illustrates how acoustical requirements vary for different types of performances.

Spaces that are used for more than one type of performance require an acoustical environment that can be varied to serve each performance appropriately. While there are a number of approaches to providing this kind of adjustable acoustical control in multiple-use performance halls, the various approaches reflect one of two basic strategies:

- The base acoustics are designed to meet the needs of orchestral and choral performances. Physically adjustable acoustic devices (Fig. 36) are employed to reduce the acoustical "liveness" for opera, ballet, and amplified performances.
- The base acoustics are designed to meet the needs of amplified music and speech. An electronically adjustable acoustic system is used to increase the acoustical "liveness" for opera, ballet, orchestral, and choral performances.

Of the two strategies, the former is far more common than the latter. The latter approach is still greeted with some skepticism by classically trained musicians despite the fact that electronic acoustical enhancement technology has made tremendous advances in recent years.

Humidity should be carefully controlled in performance spaces. From an acoustic standpoint, the relative humidity in spaces for music should be 40 percent. This includes the stage, house, dressing spaces, and instrument storage room. Low humidity makes air more absorptive of high-frequency sound, which should be avoided. Low humidity also creates an uncomfortable environment for singers and actors. The control systems for the mechanical systems should be able to maintain relative humidity within a narrow band (±5 percent). Wide swings in humidity must be avoided as many instruments are wood and therefore sensitive to moisture changes.

### Sound and Vibration Isolation

The need to exclude unwanted sound from the interior of a performance space means that such buildings are more substantially constructed than other common building types. The degree of sound isolation needed in a specific building will vary depending on the nature of the performance type (spaces for orchestral and choral music demand greater quiet than those designed exclusively for amplified music), the amount of noise in the zone around the building (noisy urban settings create more demanding isolation requirements than pastoral rural settings), and site constraints (tight sites may require that noise producing equipment rooms be closer to sensitive spaces than in more generous sites).

**Table 4**  Acoustical requirements for different performance types

| Performance type | Acoustical environment | Architectural impact |
| --- | --- | --- |
| Symphonic and choral music | Very live and resonant with good definition, brilliance, and warmth | House encloses a very large cubic volume of some 350–450 cubic feet per audience seat (even higher for halls seating less than 1,000 persons); hall width is narrow (preferably 80–90 feet or less). Materials of construction are heavy, dense and acoustically reflective. |
| Opera and ballet | Moderately live with some resonance, good definition, brilliance, and warmth | House encloses about 20 to 40 percent less cubic volume than spaces for symphonic music. Materials still tend toward those that are heavy, dense, and acoustically reflective. |
| Drama | Dry and articulate to foster good speech intelligibility | House encloses the smallest cubic volume consistent with seating requirements and architectural aesthetics. Construction may include a mixture of acoustically reflective and acoustically absorptive materials. |
| Amplified music and speech | Very dry to foster good intelligibility and definition | House encloses the smallest cubic volume consistent with seating requirements, architectural aesthetics, or other uses. Construction will include a high percentage of acoustically absorptive materials. |

In developing proper isolation details, one must consider that sound may be either airborne or structure-borne. Vibration is primarily a structure-borne problem. Airborne sound is defeated through the use of massive walls and ceilings and special sound-isolation doors. Structure-borne sound and vibration is defeated primarily through the use of massive, rigid structures, as well as separated and/or isolated structural systems. When separate structural systems are required, the two or more parts of a building may literally employ structural frames that are independent of one another from foundation level through to the roof. The separated structural systems abut at an acoustic-isolation joint, where special construction details are needed to prevent vibration from being transmitted across the gap between the adjacent structures.

Concert halls for orchestral and choral music in large urban centers have the most stringent isolation requirements. Isolation of such buildings will typically require massive multiple-wythe masonry walls, double-slab roofs, acoustic-isolation joints, and other special constructions to buffer the interior of the concert space from exterior noise. If light-rail, subsurface transit, or heavy-rail lines pass in close proximity to the site, it is not uncommon for the structural systems of such buildings to be fully isolated at their foundations to ensure that vibration from these sources does not enter the structure and produce audible noise inside the concert venue. Even in spaces with less stringent requirements, an architect should expect to use heavy masonry constructions around the performance spaces (house, stage, and other critical spaces).

Sound and vibration isolation are two related concerns. In a building with diverse uses or multiple performance spaces, one must consider isolation in two contexts. The first context is the isolation of the theaters from noise and vibration sources which are external to the building. The second is the isolation of the theaters from each other and from other activities in the building.

*Mechanical Services Noise and Vibration Control*

The mechanical, electrical, and plumbing systems that serve contemporary buildings are major sources of noise and vibration. Their design must be carefully considered so as not to introduce unwanted noise and vibration into the performance space. Again, the nature of the performances presented in a theater will determine how stringent the equipment isolation must be.

Generally speaking, it is advisable that mechanical, electrical, and plumbing equipment be remote from critical listening spaces (house and stage). Heavy equipment, such as chillers and boilers, should be located in a central mechanical room remote from the theater component. The best location for mechanical rooms is generally at grade

**Fig. 36. This photograph illustrates the setting of the orchestra shell ceiling at the Bass Performance Hall in Fort Worth, Texas. The shell ceiling is shown as it folds out from the wall. At the end of this process, the ceiling will segment the stagehouse into two parts: an upper volume where the sound absorptive scenery is stored and a lower empty volume that creates a resonant chamber for the orchestra to perform within. A series of moving wall towers are positioned around the orchestra to create an attractive architectural setting for the performance. (Photo: Glen Ellman, courtesy of Jaffe Holden Acoustics)**

a a portion of the building that is structurally separate from the por-
on of the building containing the theater itself.

: is important to minimize the amount of vibration transmitted to the
tructure by mechanical equipment. Equipment, ductwork, and
ipework will generally need to be designed with appropriate vibration
solation in mind. Such isolation may include inertia bases, isolation
nounts and hangers, floating floors, and other isolation devices. In the
nost sensitive buildings, structural breaks (acoustic-isolation joints)
nay also be needed between the mechanical rooms and the theater.

o minimize the amount of noise transmitted into critical spaces by
ne mechanical and other systems, following are some helpful guide-
nes for programming or conceptual design work:

Employ ducts with large cross-sectional area and sound-absorptive
lining.
Use the lowest possible air velocities consistent with air-change
requirements. The following velocity guidelines are useful for initial planning (these are maximum velocities, expressed in feet per
minute):

| | |
|---|---|
| Trunk ducts | 1,000 |
| Branch ducts | 700 |
| Terminal ducts | 400 |
| Slot speed at terminal | 300 |

Locate mechanical rooms remote from the theaters. Long duct
runs are the easiest and cheapest means of attenuating noise from
HVAC systems.
Avoid locating rest rooms or other major plumbed facilities adjacent to the walls of the house or stage.
Do not route conduit, pipes, or ducts in or through a noise-sensitive
space unless they actually serve or supply the sensitive space.
Transformers can be particularly problematic. Place large transformers (i.e., those which step down utility power to typical
building voltages) in vaults that are outside the building. Internal
transformers should be carefully located to ensure that audible
hum does not intrude on the performance space. Transformers
must not be located in or adjacent to the house or stage.
Seal around conduits, pipes, and ducts where they penetrate into
sensitive areas to preserve the isolation characteristics of these
assemblies.

*Electroacoustics*

Sound reinforcement and reproduction systems have become ex-
remely sophisticated in recent years. Specialist designers should be
employed to ensure that the designs for a particular theater meet the
needs of the performers and are integrated with the room acoustic
design of the space.

The electroacoustic systems have a variety of infrastructure requirements. In the house, a control room is typically required. This space
s best located at the rear of the orchestra level as close to the center-
ine as possible. The control room must be elevated above the last
ow of seats in the orchestra level to ensure that the operator has an
unobstructed view of the stage. An operable (sliding) acoustical win-
low isolates the interior of house from conversations in the control
room but can be opened if the operator wants to hear what is happen-
ng in the house. This space should be separate from control spaces
provided for theatrical lighting or stage management purposes.

Sound engineers generally prefer to mix the sound for a show from a
position in the house itself. An area of removable seats is usually pro-

vided for this purpose. This feature is generally called an *in-house
mix position*. Power and audio wiring are routed to an electrical box
at the in-house mix position so that sound equipment can be set at
this location with minimal effort. Since the operator and the equipment will typically be taller than the surrounding seats, the location
and design of this area needs to be carefully considered to eliminate
sight-line problems for audience members behind. In some instances,
it makes sense to depress the area of the in-house mix location. In
others, the position can be located just below a vertical break
(parterre) in the orchestra seating. Generally speaking, mix engineers
prefer to be out from under any balcony overhang and as close to the
center of the room as possible. Sometimes an auxiliary in-house mix
position is provided at the very rear of the orchestra level (in front of
the control room) because some presenters do not like to lose seats in
the center of the orchestra floor for this function.

In addition, the electroacoustic systems generally need an equipment
rack room and audio equipment storage room. The former is generally positioned close to the stage on an upper level. The latter is generally backstage, ideally at stage level, and close to other crew and
equipment storage spaces.

Control and equipment rack rooms must be air-conditioned to
remove the heat of people and equipment. The heat loads produced in
these areas need to be considered by the mechanical engineers in the
overall assessment of building loads.

A stable electrical supply is essential to dependable and reliable
operation of the electroacoustic systems in theaters. Audio equipment is sensitive to line surges and drop-outs, as well as interference from radio-wave sources [radio-frequency interference (RFI)]
and electromotive sources [electromagnetic interference (EMI)].
To minimize potential operational difficulties and to protect the
client's investment in expensive audio equipment, an isolated electrical supply for the audio systems is essential. In addition to the
electrical systems, the sensitive low-voltage cabling network for
the audio systems must be designed to minimize potential problems
from RFI and EMI sources.

## STAGE

The stage is easily defined: it is that part of the theater where the performance takes place. Its size, shape, arrangement, and equipment
must therefore logically develop from the nature of the performance.
Requirements for the stage depend on the performances planned for
the building and the resulting operational, visual, and acoustical criteria associated with each performance type.

Virtually any stage consists of two parts: the *performing area* and the
*working areas*. The former is that part of the stage which is typically
visible to the audience and where the performer presents his or her
activity so as to be seen and heard by the audience. The latter are
those spaces that are adjacent to the performing area and which provide space for the performer to get onto the stage and operating and
storage space for scenic elements, theatrical lighting, and all of the
other support equipment or features that support the performer.

Broadly speaking, stages fall into two types: proscenium stages and
open stages. *Proscenium stages* refer to those where the performing
area is predominantly in a space which is separate from the house, a
space typically referred to as the *stagehouse. Open stages* refer to
those where the performing area largely or wholly shares the same
space as the audience.

### Stage Space

For all production types, the visual components divide into two categories: *performers* and *scenic elements*. These indicate the functional divisions of the stage:

- Space in which the performers work, which, though actually three-dimensional, is usually referred to as the *performing area.*
- Space wherein the scenic elements are arranged, which will be called hereafter the *scenery space.* Scenic elements also need room to be operated and stored, creating a third functional division of the stage: *working and storage space.*

There is a functional relationship between performing area, scenery space, and working and storage space. The size, shape, and arrangement of the performing area must be determined before the other spaces can be logically developed (see Figs. 37 and 38).

### Orchestra Pit

Performance venues that present opera, musical theater, or dance need an adequate orchestra pit. While not technically part of the stage, it has an important relationship to the proscenium arch and backstage support functions and so its design must be considered in relation to the stage. The size of the pit is driven by the number of musicians required for the productions anticipated in a space. Grand opera from the late 19th century is frequently scored for an orchestra of 100 or more musicians. Musical theater (such as the typical Broadway-style musical comedy) rarely requires more than 26 to 30 players. Pit orchestras for dance ensembles can fall anywhere between these two extremes. The area for an orchestra pit will typically fall between 18 and 20 square feet per musician tending toward the higher figure for pits with smaller capacities and the lower number for pits with large capacities.

Pit size will also be influenced to a lesser degree by the scale of the venue. The stage with a 45-foot proscenium would probably have an orchestra pit of sufficient size to seat 60 to 75 players. Likewise, a stage with a 60-foot proscenium would have a pit large enough to accommodate a 100-piece orchestra.

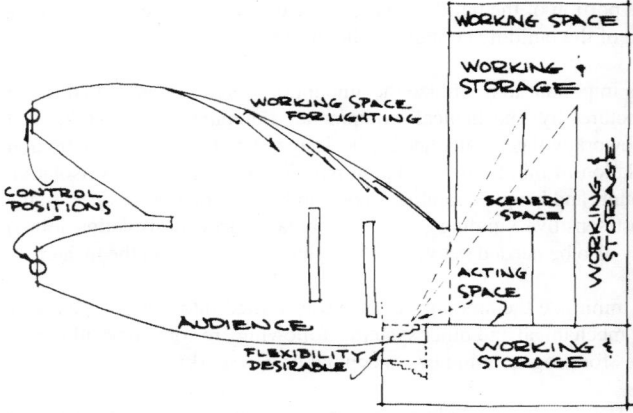

**Fig. 38. Position of stage spaces**

One perennial argument is the degree to which the area of an orchestra pit extends under the lip of the stage. Unfortunately, there is little consensus of opinion among opera and ballet conductors on this matter. Most acousticians believe that if a pit is to be used for opera, at least a portion of its area should extend under the stage lip. The space under the lip is typically intended to seat the high-energy brass and percussion sections so that their sound has less chance of overpowering the singers on stage. How much of the pit should extend under the stage is a matter of some debate. Some allow as little as 8 feet of depth. Others permit as much as 30 percent of the entire floor area. The authors suggest that the larger the pit, the more of its area may be under the lip. In no event should more than 30 percent of the area or 12 feet of pit depth extend under the stage lip, however.

Conductors and artistic directors in dance ensembles typically prefer the orchestra pit to be totally open (none of its area falls under the stage lip). This is to allow the maximum amount of sound from the orchestra to fill the house and increase its potential for dynamic impact.

The pit should be deep enough so that the orchestra is completely out of sight of the audience. The director's podium should be high enough for him to be able to see the stage floor all the way to the upstage wall of the stage yet remain in full view of the orchestra (see Fig. 39).

A movable pit floor, usually known as a *pit lift,* is a highly desirable feature. The pit lift should be able to travel from the lowest pit level to the stage level and have multiple stops at pit level, orchestra floor level, and stage level. Large pits may be equipped with two or in some cases three lifts. This allows the pit to be set in a variety of size and step configurations. Multiple-lift configurations can also create a flexible pit that extends partially under the stage for opera but is totally open for dance. Such solutions, while technically practical, are extremely expensive.

In many contemporary multiuse theaters, the pit lifts also communicate with seat wagon storage areas. When a production does not require a pit, the pit lift is lowered to the wagon storage level, and the wagons are moved onto the lift and raised back up to orchestra floor level to provide additional audience seating. The pit lift will act as a good sound reflector when not being used as an orchestra pit. For such uses, the pit will probably be located slightly below the stage level.

The railing around the entire orchestra pit must be high enough to hide the orchestra yet low enough not to interfere with the sight lines

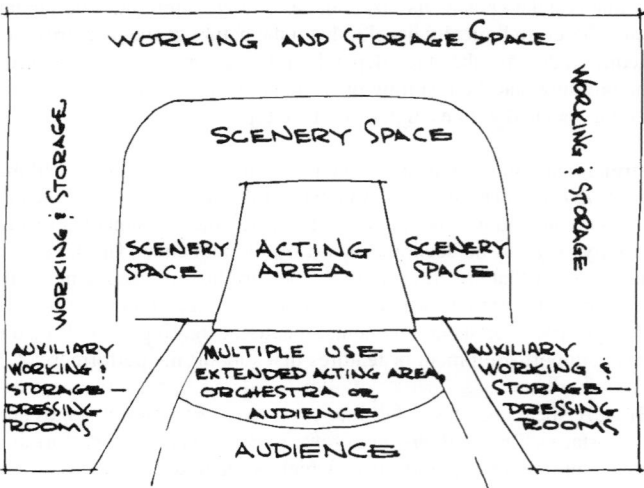

**Fig. 37. Position of stage areas relative to each other. This diagram must not be interpreted in terms of size or shape.**

**Fig. 39.** Section through a typical orchestra pit. The conductor must be able to see every member of the orchestra and all of the performers on stage without interfering with audience sight-lines. When the pit extends under the stage, no more than 30 percent of its total area should be under the overhang. The thickness of the stage lip must be minimized to avoid exaggerating the depth of the pit.

of the audience. The head and the shoulders of the director may be visible over this orchestra pit railing. The railing is typically a pipe frame with a mixture of visually solid, sound-transparent material and sound-diffusing elements. The sound-diffusing elements help reflect some sound back to the pit orchestra so the musicians can hear one another more clearly. The diffusing panels also reflect sound up to the singers or dancers on stage so that they can hear the orchestra. The sound-transparent materials allow some of the orchestra's energy to pass through into the house (see Fig. 40).

**Fig. 40.** Close-up view of the new orchestra pit at the Wang Center for the Performing Arts in Boston (Photo: Roger Farrington)

**Basic Stage Mechanics and Support Spaces**

To gain an understanding of technical and spatial requirements for different types of stages, it is helpful to have a basic grounding in stage terminology as well as the function of the equipment or features to which such terms refer.

**proscenium or proscenium arch**   The opening in the wall between the stagehouse and the audience chamber. The architectural and structural frame of the proscenium is typically set by the event that requires the widest or tallest opening. Productions that do not require the maximum architectural opening will reduce the size of the opening through the use of masking. Masking can be either hard (wood panels or the like) or soft (velour drapes or panels, for example).

**stage directions**   All stage directions are given from the performer's perspective (with an assumption that the performer is facing the audience). *Stage right* is to the performer's right and *stage left* to the left. *Downstage* is moving toward the proscenium opening, i.e., toward the audience. *Upstage* is moving away from the audience.

**side stage**   The area to the left and right of the performing area. This area is used variously to store scenery and as a holding area for performers before they enter or after they leave the performing area.

**rear stage**   An area upstage of the performing area, usually intended for scenery storage. Most commonly found in large opera houses.

**fly loft or fly tower**   The volume above the proscenium opening where scenery is stored when not in use.

**grid**   A steel framework over the stage used to support theatrical rigging. The grid typically covers the entire footprint of the stage and provides a walking surface as well as a sturdy frame to support theatrical rigging elements.

**theatrical rigging**   The means by which scenery can be raised out of view of the audience for storage purposes or lowered to the stage for use. Rigging can be of the following types:

- *Counterweight rigging* typically consists of pipes or battens to which scenery can be attached so that it can be lowered (flown in) or raised (flown out). A series of cables attach the battens to an arbor on which steel plates (counterweights) can be loaded to balance the load of the scenic elements attached to the batten. Battens typically run left and right across the stage. Each batten, its associated lines, and arbor are called a *line set*. The typical stagehouse will have many line sets to offer flexibility in placing a particular scenic element on stage. Counterweight rigging is operated manually and is the most common form of rigging in North American theaters (see Fig. 41).
- *Spot* or *point rigging* is used to support single point loads such as a chandelier or other scenic element that does not require a full-length batten.
- *Winch rigging* is an electromechanical variation on counterweight rigging. Winch rigging may consist of either battens or spot lines, but in both cases the lifting is accomplished by means of an electrically operated winch as opposed to a manually operated counterweight line set. Winch rigging is more common in Europe than North America.

**rigging wall**   In a stage with counterweight rigging, the arbors and their guides will all be mounted on one wall (at either stage left or stage right). It is important to establish the location of the rigging wall early in the planning process since it is not desirable to interrupt any portion of the rigging wall with doors, duct openings, or other penetrations.

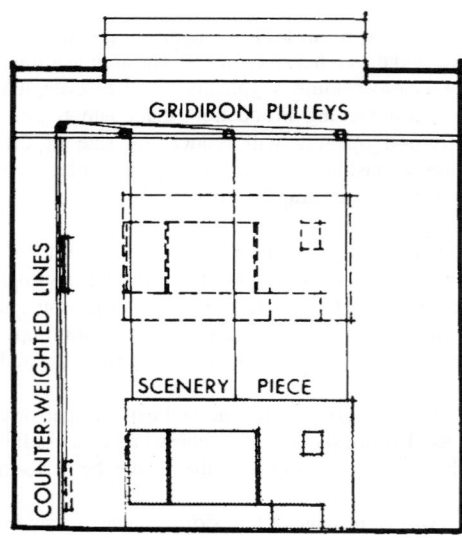

**Rigging Diagram**

**Fig. 41. A simplified diagram of counterweight rigging**

**counterweight pit**   A pit along the rigging wall down into which counterweights can descend to extend the travel distance of the battens in a counterweight rigging system.

**loading gallery**   An elevated platform adjacent to the rigging wall which gives access to the arbors so that the counterweights can be loaded and unloaded as scenery is added to or removed from a batten.

**locking rail**   The position from which counterweight rigging is operated. After a line set is moved, it is locked to prevent further movement, hence the name. The locking rail can be either at stage level or on a running gallery elevated above stage level.

**trap room**   A room located under the stage. The stage floor over the trap room is structured so that openings can easily be cut into the floor to accommodate dramatic effects involving performers or scenery appearing from beneath the stage or disappearing into it.

**house curtain**   The decorative curtain that closes the proscenium off from the audience prior to a performance, during intermissions, or at the end of a performance.

**fire curtain**   fireproof barrier that closes off the proscenium to protect the audience from a fire on stage.

**deluge system**   A variation on the fire curtain, a system that releases a curtain of water at the proscenium to contain a fire on stage.

**blacks** or **velours**   A set of black velour drapes that are used to provide basic dressing for a stage.

**theatrical lighting**   The system of lighting used to highlight all or portions of the performing area. The light sources are typically referred to as *instruments*. Lighting instruments come in a variety of types and sizes, each suited to a particular function or location.

**lighting positions**   Theatrical lighting designers will employ a variety of locations from both onstage positions and house positions to achieve desired lighting effects. Stage positions will generally be supported via the rigging system. House positions will generally be provided in a number of locations including one or more front-lighting positions in the ceiling (or on catwalks suspended under the ceiling), on the faces of balconies (balcony rail), and on the side walls near the proscenium (sometimes referred to as *box boom* positions).

**lighting control room**   A lighting control room is typically required. This space is best located at the rear of the orchestra level as close to the centerline as possible. The control room must be elevated above the last row of seats in the orchestra level to ensure that the operator has an unobstructed view of the stage. This space should be separate from but adjacent to the sound control room or stage manager booth.

**dimmer room**   The dimmers for the theatrical lighting systems are typically housed in a central location near to the stage (but not necessarily at stage level). This space will have a large AC power load and a significant heat load that will have to be exhausted by the mechanical systems. Most dimmer racks feature cooling fans which can be noisy, so this space should be appropriately isolated from the house and stage.

## Stage Dimensions

Stage dimensions and volumetric relationships of the house and stage are inter-related. The specific physical characteristics of the stage depend on its intended use. Several performance types are examined to demonstrate how each influences stage characteristics.

### General Considerations

Variations among stage forms have two levels of impact on room design: *vision parameters* (location of audience) and *hearing parameters* (location of boundary surfaces).

#### Vision Parameters

These are related to the dimensions of the performing area:

- Width, depth, and shape of acting area
- Height of the proscenium (if any)
- Elevation and/or rake of the stage
- Location of the acting area relative to the proscenium

#### Hearing Parameters

These are related to the boundaries of the stage enclosure:

- Size and shape of the enclosing shell (if any)
- Nature of coupled volumes (if any)
- Absorptive properties of the enclosure
- Location of sound source relative to the enclosure

The corresponding functional elements depend on the use for which the stage is designed. A few categorical terms will be of help in comparative treatments of stage types. The stage floor may be stepped or sloped (*raked*) although this is rarely done as a permanent feature, but rather as a production-specific scenic element.

Orchestral and choral music (and small recitals) require a sound-reflecting enclosure within the stagehouse, often called an *orchestra* or *concert shell*. The enclosure includes walls and a ceiling. If the ceiling extends into the house, this element is called a *forestage canopy*. If the shell is designed such that a portion of the remaining stagehouse volume communicates with the interior of the shell and the house, the stagehouse is said to be *acoustically coupled*.

For drama, musical theater, dance, and opera, scene space surrounds the performing area, which is in turn surrounded by working space within the stagehouse—around, above, or below. Both proscenium and open stages can have scene and working space. On a proscenium stage, all of the working areas (i.e., the performing area behind the proscenium, the fly space, and the trap room) must be separated from the house by a suitable fire enclosure. The orchestra pit is on the audience side of this separation.

### Functional Requirements

The following are desirable stage characteristics for various performance types. Discussion here stresses key functions and design rationale.

#### Legitimate Drama

The medium includes speech, action, and scenic context. The human figure is extremely important; scenic illusion refers to this for dimensional scale. Dominant movement across the acting area, entering left and right, makes other entries special events. Drama usually works through sustained continuity over a series of unfolding, developing events and situations; the ability to control changes in context, pace, center of attention and atmospheric tone is essential (see Fig. 42).

*Performance space:* Acting area is approximately 35 feet wide by 20 feet deep (40 by 25 feet usual maximum). This defines the downstage zone of most action; however, the full stage depth is utilized. It has a level floor that can be built upon. Traps are recommended in key performing areas.

*Enclosure:* A stagehouse is recommended, with a proscenium portal 35 feet wide x 26 feet (can be larger). Stagehouse configuration is related to scene-handling methods; fly loft is strongly recommended.

*Scene and working space:* Wraparound scene space is required for flats, drops, and wagons. Allow ample horizontal working space for the largest set piece plus actors' passage, waiting areas, technicians' workspace, counterweights and pinrail, curtain space, and switchgear. Use inside clearances and keep the plan shape compact and rectangular. Overhead working space must accept the longest flown piece plus borders plus gridiron and line space plus person-high passage above grid. Understage working space should be at least 8 feet clear height.

#### Dance

The medium consists of action with music and some scenic context. Large movements of dancers in two directions (to-fro, side-side). Dancers' entry from scene space on all sides is important. Scenery is often minimal, but stage lighting is generally extensive. Although recorded music can be used, a dance facility should provide for a live orchestra. A dance concert usually consists of a series of separate pieces or events with rest periods between during which the stage is reset and the audience must be otherwise occupied. The technical qualities that help sustain continuity during performance should be versatile and sophisticated, especially lighting controls. Also, the music must be heard on stage distinctly (see Fig. 43).

*Performance space:* Acting area is typically 50 feet wide by 40 feet deep, although a 40-foot width will accommodate modern dance and small troupes. A resilient dance floor is essential. Such a floor is typically comprised of criss-crossed sleepers with neoprene pads under the sleeper, a plywood subfloor, and hardwood finish floor. Often, a removable vinyl mat called a *marley floor* is put down on the stage floor and any seams are taped.

While each company stages dance in accordance with its own artistic vision, most companies consider a performing area 45 feet wide by 40 feet deep the minimum necessary. Many prefer a wider space.

A dance stage must be wider than the actual performance space. A proper stage includes a minimum of 10 to 15 feet of wing space on each side. These are transition zones between the performing area and offstage. Performers preparing for an entrance need wing space in which to warm up, to catch their breath, or to concentrate on a difficult passage. An entrance or exit can be ruined if the dancer is bumped by another performer or a stagehand as he or she prepares to move on or off stage. At one New York theater, where wing space is almost nil, dancers are said to lean mattresses against the walls, and to station themselves in the wings to catch colleagues making fast

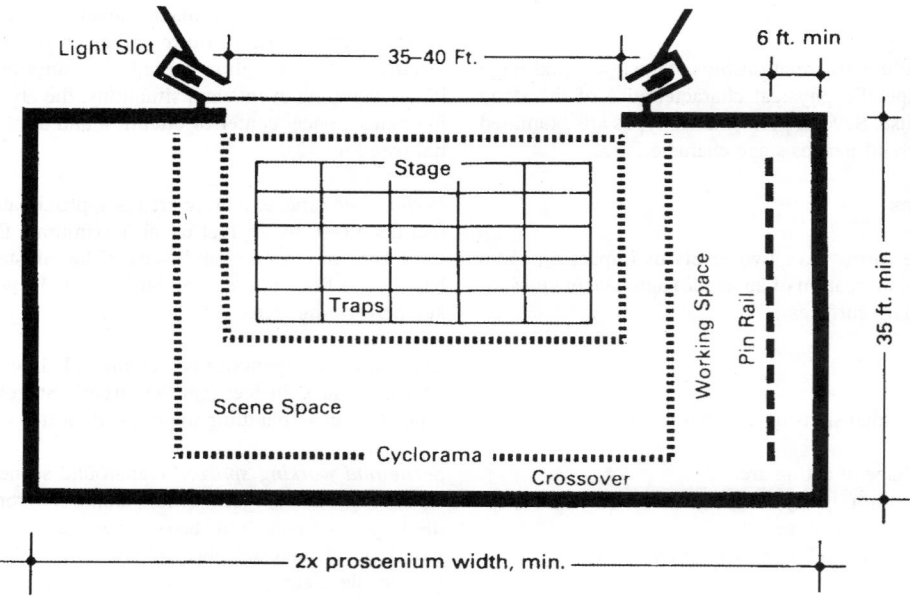

**Fig. 42. Typical drama stage**

exits. Dance is demanding, but leaping offstage into a mattress seems one demand too many.

The wing space is occupied by more than dancers entering and exiting. Lighting equipment mounted on vertical steel booms (known as *torms, trees,* or *ladders*) is positioned in the wings for sidelighting effects. Dancers expect to cope with booms; but ample wing space can minimize potential conflicts between performers and equipment.

*Enclosure:* A high proscenium is needed in large rooms to provide a clear view of the dancers' space (Fig. 44). Intimate rooms may have

no proscenium at all. Stagehouse requirements relate to scenery components.

*Scene and working space:* Scene space at each side is usually devoted to entry legs and tabs for the depth of the stage. A cyclorama or backdrop is frequently used. Unimpeded crossover passage is very important, preferably wide enough for costumed dancers to pass each other without disturbing drapery and the like. Wing space must accommodate assembled dancers. An orchestra pit is generally essential. Its size is dictated by the dance ensemble's requirements.

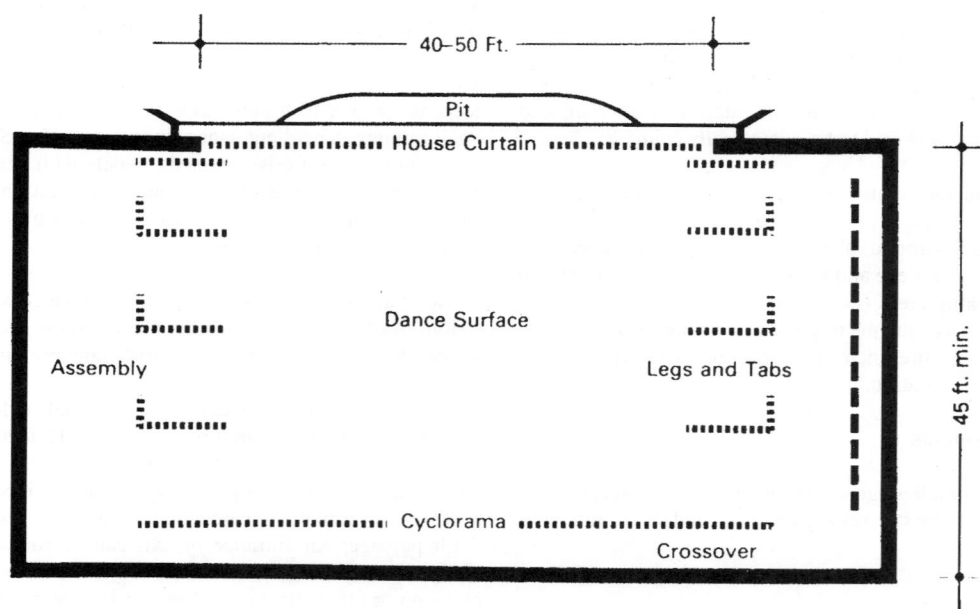

**Fig. 43. Typical dance stage**

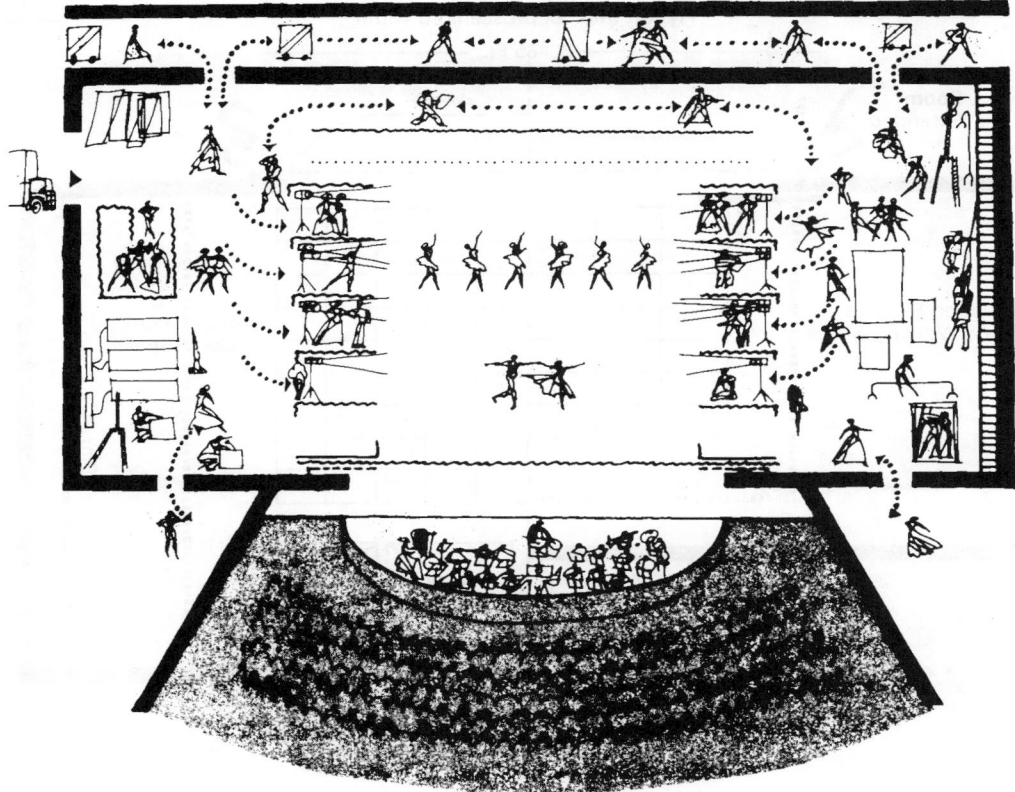

**Fig. 44. Proscenium stage in full operation for dance**

*Music-Drama*

Speech, music, action, and scenic components are all incorporated in this form of presentation, sometimes called *light opera* or *musical comedy*. It is similar to straight drama in its storyline continuity, which demands directorial skill in successfully alternating speech, song and dance, and also relies heavily on stagecraft and technical support. The musical component is a key feature of transitions, requiring expert control. A relatively large cast and crew are typical, with up to 50 people on stage at once and quantities of scenery to manage. Coordinating all this activity is a major problem requiring, besides extensive preparations, an excellent communications system during performance (see Fig. 45).

*Performance space:* Although principal attention is generally focused downstage, background chorus activity and the ability to have cross talk at the same time makes a wide, deep acting area desirable, maximum 60 feet by 50 feet deep. For most productions, this will be masked down. The floor should be danceable, although it needn't be very sophisticated in construction; the ability to build on and anchor to it is as important. Traps are sometimes desirable.

*Enclosure:* A 30- to 35-foot-high proscenium arch is recommended, along with fly loft stagehouse. Stagehouse proportions recognize that wing space is as important as loft space.

*Scene and working space:* Wraparound scene space must accept a large variety of rather elaborate scenery. The dimension of this zone must allow for structural support of stand-up sets with recesses and

overhangs, often in combination with flown portions. Wagon sets are very useful as well, but require substantial working space in addition to that for cast assembly, other properties and technicians. Symmetrical working space is advised, to simplify maneuvering during scene changes. Since live music is essential, provide an orchestra pit for 15 to 30 musicians.

*Opera*

Opera consists of song, music, action, and spectacle. The storyline is often well known and sometimes is less important than the calibre of musical execution. Traditionally lavish costumes and settings are involved, along with a large cast of singers and musicians supporting lead soloists. Grand opera involves a great deal of background movement, multiple entry points, stagecraft, special effects, and scene changes.

*Performance space:* Generally comparable to that for music drama although it can be larger, it is typically 60 feet x 50 feet deep. Traps, multilevel constructions, stage elevators, and lifts are used extensively. Dramatic part-singing demands a great deal of movement on stage, reassembling of voices, and accommodation of a large chorus. Since it is difficult to sing while moving, the cast moves to new relationships with the soloists.

*Enclosure:* The opera proscenium is typically 50 to 60 feet wide and 35 to 50 feet high. This promotes acoustic coupling of the deep stage to the house and recognizes the probable height of a multitiered audience requiring good sight lines. The enormity of stage and stage-

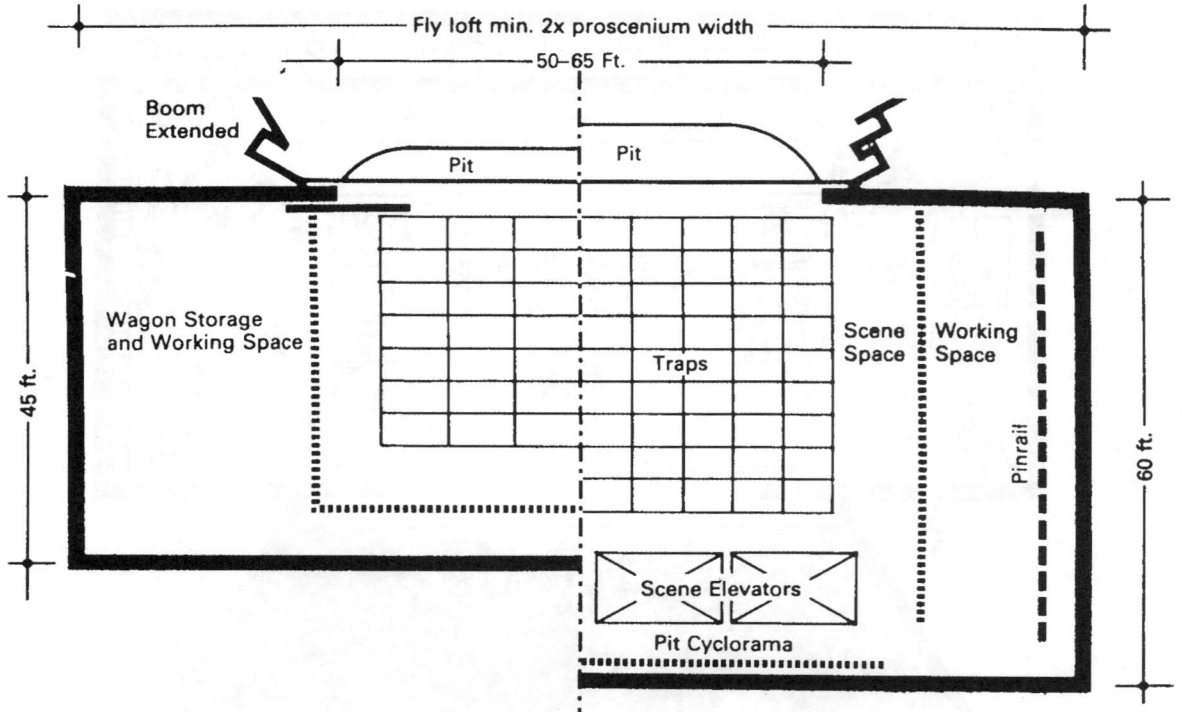

**Fig. 45. Typical stage for opera or music-drama**

house places premium value on trained, powerful voices and dramatic presence.

*Scene and working space:* Opera stages are often the most technically sophisticated, the scenery vast and expensive because of its importance to performance. A person on an empty opera stage is dwarfed. He must move from prop to carefully selected prop, in order to maintain continuity of scale. Grand opera requires substantial scene space and offstage working space on all sides. A large, fully equipped fly loft, or a combination with scene elevators from below the stage, is also needed. The fly loft must furnish generous flexible lighting points behind the proscenium and above the stage, often including sidelighting towers in the wings.

Grand opera requires an especially large pit (upwards of 100 musicians or more, depending on work and the company's resources) and careful acoustic design. This design often reflects the nature of opera music; the pit should be designed so as not to overpower vocal intelligibility.

*Orchestral and Choral Music*

The stage in dedicated music spaces (i.e., concert halls) will tend to be a fixed arrangement, whereas the stage of a multiuse hall will need to be adapted to the needs of such music through the use of an orchestra shell. As a first step, it is important to identify the kind and size of orchestral and choral ensembles that will use a particular stage. While the basic accommodations are designed around its most likely users, it is important to provide tolerances for variations. Music concerts consist of a series of uninterrupted performance periods of varying length. In the intervals between works, instrumental forces may be changed or reorganized while the audience refreshes itself. The sometimes subtle alterations must be carefully prearranged in a rehearsal situation as similar to concert conditions as possible.

*Performance space:* Orchestra arrangements are best when they are as compact as practicable. Tight arrangements allow the musicians to hear and see one another better. Stage area averages 20 to 24 square feet per instrumental musician plus an additional 3 to 4 square feet per chorister. Stage or proscenium widths range from 56 to 70 feet.

- Ensemble or band: 30 to 50 musicians, 800 to 1,200 square feet
- Medium orchestra: 50 to 80 musicians, 1,200 to 1,900 square feet
- Medium orchestra and chorus: 50 to 100 voices, 1,400 to 2,300 square feet
- Symphony: 90 to 105 musicians and large chorus of 200 voices, 2,600 to 3,300 square feet

A flat floor with portable riser platforms is common in multiuse stages, while a dedicated concert hall stage may be fitted with permanent or semipermanent risers. In dedicated concert halls, the chorus is often accommodated in a band of seats above and to the rear of the orchestra. These seats can be sold as audience seating for programs without a chorus.

Sometimes, especially in multiuse houses, variations in the required floor area are accommodated (i.e., for large orchestra and chorus) by raising the pit lift to stage level and allowing the orchestra to move downstage onto the extended stage. Moving the orchestra forward alters the relationship to the orchestra shell, and appropriate provisions for this must be included in the acoustical design of the shell, the forestage canopy, and the side walls of the house adjacent to the proscenium. To accommodate smaller ensembles, the orchestra shell should employ a modular layout that allows the enclosure size to be scaled down as required for chamber orchestras or even solo recitals.

*Enclosure:* The enclosure around a music ensemble will typically comprise a mixture of sound-reflective, sound-diffusing, and occaionally sound-absorbing materials. The shape of the enclosure must be carefully designed to blend and balance the different sections of an ensemble. The enclosure will primarily project the sound of the ensemble out to the audience; however, it must also be able to direct a portion of the sound energy back to the musicians to enable them hear themselves and one another.

*Scene and working space:* Stagehouse functions, if any, are minimal for music; most support activity takes place backstage or from control areas in the house. However, space adjoining the performance area should be allotted for performers' assembly and temporary instrument standby (pianos and extra chairs and stands). There may also be separate rooms for broadcasting, recording equipment, and lighting equipment.

### Functional Relationship of Stage to Room

It is difficult for a single stage form to satisfy all of the functional requirements for every performance type. But a given stage form can often accommodate more than one performance type.

While single-purpose rooms (Fig. 46) are typically best suited to their uses, the likelihood is that some degree of multiuse will exist (Fig. 47).

Performance types can be grouped according to similarity of stage requirements as a first step, but it is important to bear in mind that both stage and house are interdependent parts of the total room. Any alteration of selection criteria for one has impact on the other particularly with regard to vision and hearing parameters. The audience arrangement in the house is based on the task of seeing and hearing action on the stage, and this changes with the stage form and type of perform-

ance. The enclosure construction for both house and stage is typically governed by acoustical criteria and obviously the enclosure must vary to suit different types of performances with varying acoustical criteria.

### BACKSTAGE

Backstage support spaces comprise the wide variety of dressing rooms, work rooms, and storage spaces needed to support what happens on stage.

### Dressing Rooms

Requirements for individual dressing rooms vary, depending on the nature of performances housed in a theater. Dressing rooms can be of different types; star dressing rooms are generally reserved for principal performers and accommodate one person. Some of these will be large enough to accommodate a piano in addition to lounge, shower, and lavatory spaces. General-purpose dressing rooms will come in various sizes and generally accommodate 2, 4, or 8 people. Chorus dressing rooms may accommodate larger numbers. Separate chorus rooms are often provided for men and women. Orchestra changing rooms can accommodate quite large numbers (50 or more) and again are provided for men and women.

### Green Rooms

Green rooms are of two types. In the drama world, the green room generally refers to an informal space which is used by the cast and crew for lounging. In the orchestral world, the green room is a formal space that is used by the artist to greet the public after a performance. Multiuse performing arts centers may need both types of green rooms.

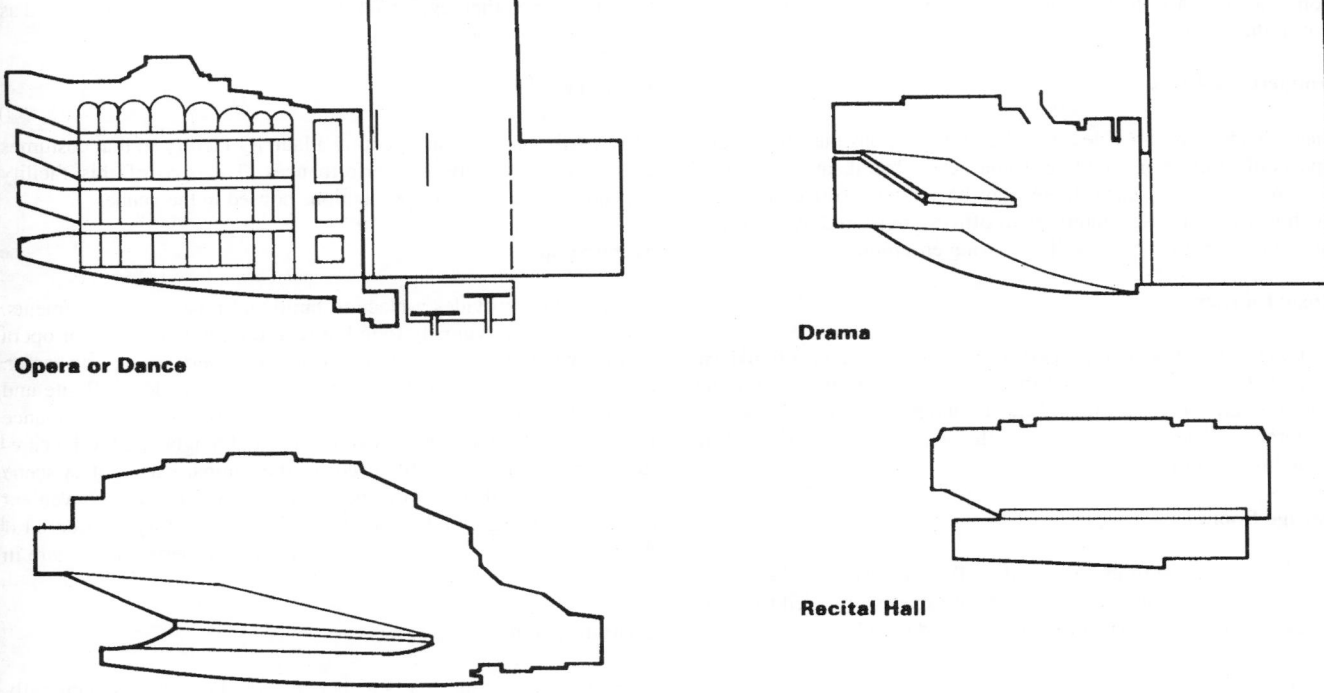

**Opera or Dance**

**Drama**

**Orchestral**

**Recital Hall**

**Fig. 46. Four kinds of single-purpose rooms**

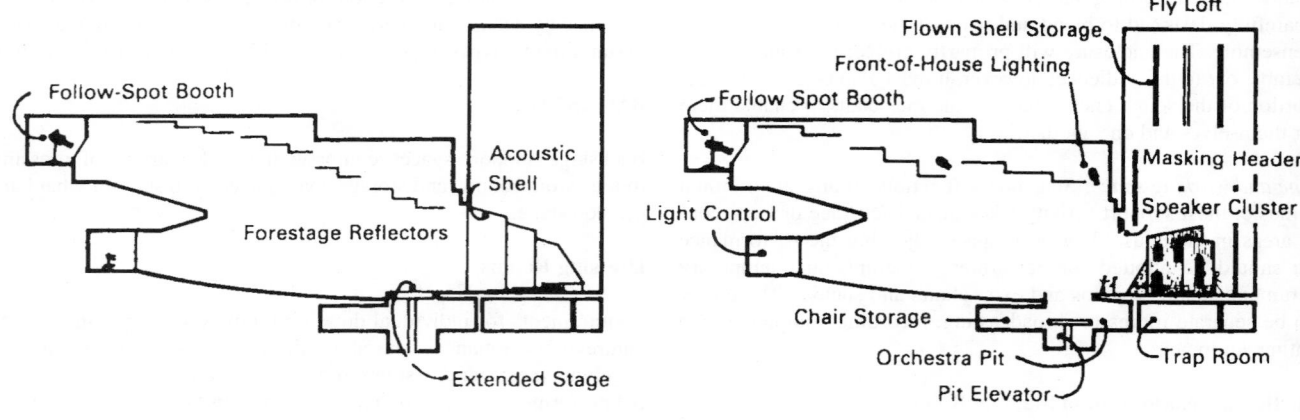

**Fig. 47. Multiuse room**

**Stage Door**

This is the control point for access to backstage areas and the stage from outside the building. Performers and crew enter the building through this space. Security is usually provided at this point to keep unauthorized persons from entering nonpublic backstage areas.

**Crew Rooms**

Depending on how a facility is used and the size of the crew, such spaces may include locker rooms, showers, lounge, and office.

**Rest Rooms**

In addition to the facilities provided in crew areas or in dressing rooms, there is a need for general-purpose restrooms at stage level near to the stage.

**Production Offices**

These spaces are provided for the staff responsible for specific aspects of production (lighting, sound, etc.). If a theater has one or more resident companies, there may be multiple offices for these functions. In multiuse centers, such offices are shared by the different resident companies as well as touring ensembles.

**Music Library**

If an orchestra is resident in a performing arts center, it is often desirable for the orchestra's music library to be located in the building. This facilitates access during rehearsals and performance. The size of the library will depend on the size of the orchestra's collection and its music library staff.

**Storage Rooms**

A variety of storage rooms are needed. Typically these will be segregated according to function, with separate spaces provided for lighting, audio, rigging, musical instruments, and the like.

**Work Rooms**

A small number of work rooms are needed for minor repairs and maintenance to the equipment in a venue. As with storage spaces, these will be segregated according to function, such as lighting and audio.

**Loading or Scene Dock**

Loading access is a critical concern in practically any performance venue. The size and location of the dock (number of truck bays, storage space, communication to the stage and other backstage areas) will be driven by the use program of the building and site constraints.

**Freight Elevator**

Since it is only rarely possible for all of the backstage support spaces to be at stage level, a freight elevator is generally required to move equipment, instruments, costumes, and other gear between loading-dock level and other levels backstage. The elevator should be sized as generously as resources allow.

**Laundry**

Most performance venues require a laundry facility so that costumes can be cleaned between performances. The size of this facility depends on the nature of productions housed in the venue.

**Scene Shop**

A scene shop provides a place to build and repair scenic elements. Scene shops are typically found in repertory drama theater or opera houses but are not usually found in multiuse performing arts center. At multiuse centers, most scenery construction is done off-site and the finished material transferred to the facility for the performance run. If a scene shop is provided, its size and height need to be carefully considered to meet the needs of the company using it. A scene shop should be adjacent to scene-storage rooms and have convenient access to the stage. Sound isolation must be carefully considered if the scene shop is to be used while rehearsals or performances are in progress.

**Costume Shop**

Like the scene shop, this is a specialty facility which is generally provided only in a building occupied for large periods by a single resident company. Costume-storage space should adjoin the costume shop.

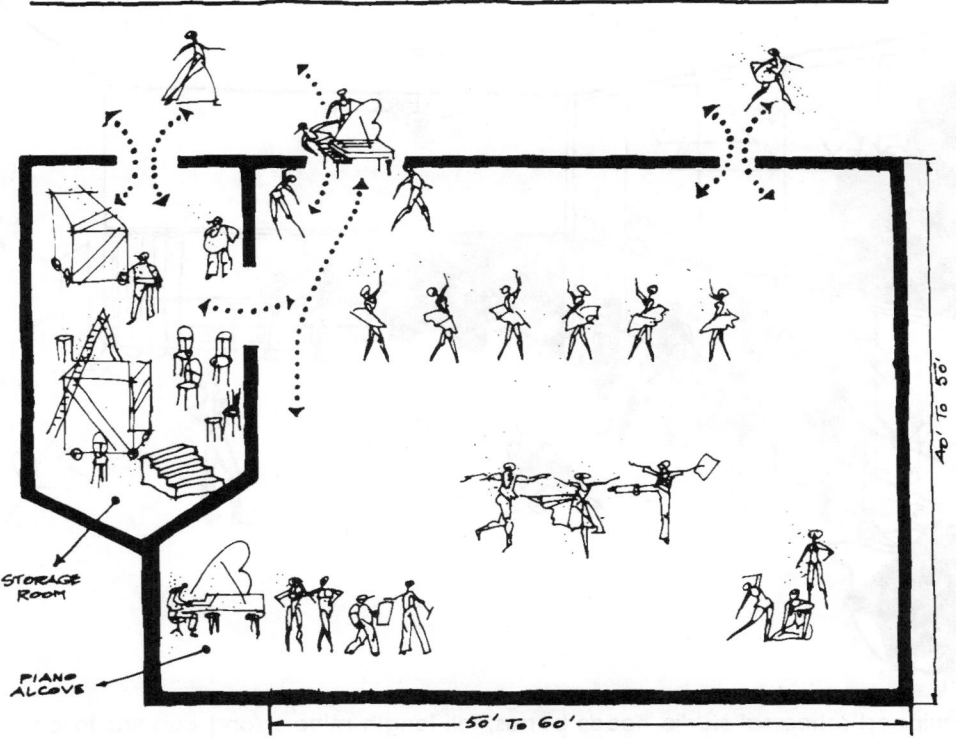

STORAGE
ROOM

PIANO
ALCOVE

50' TO 60'

40' TO 50'

**Fig. 48.** The rehearsal studio must be larger than the performing area on stage in order to allow space for entrances and exits, for dancers waiting their turn to rehearse, for rehearsal instruments or sound equipment, and for the choreographer and rehearsal director to have an adequate view of the work in progress

## Rehearsal Rooms

The number of rehearsal rooms (Figs. 48 to 50) is determined entirely by how much use is made of the building and how often the stage is available for rehearsal. Rehearsal rooms should be in the same proportion and somewhat larger than the performing area of the stage; acoustically, they should reproduce stage conditions as closely as possible. The public lounge, adjacent to the auditorium lobby, may also serve for rehearsals. The height of a rehearsal room is determined by its use. Rooms intended for orchestral rehearsal need a large amount of cubic volume. Such rooms should be planned to have 30 to 40 feet of height.

## COMMUNITY THEATERS

The community theater usually contains 500 to 1,000 seats and serves amateurs, semiprofessionals, and visiting professional groups. Most of the scenery and costumes are designed and made at the theater; therefore, such theaters require scene and costume shops. Because of its varied use, and the rather indeterminate responsibility of its management, its planning should be as simple and as foolproof as possible.

## MUSIC FACILITIES*

### Room and Area Requirements

Music facilities can be divided into two general classifications depending on their function: those used for *instructional activities* and those serving in an *auxiliary capacity,* such as storage areas,

workrooms, and offices. A typical large music facility for an institution of higher education will require a wide variety of rooms and work areas. The needs of elementary and secondary schools will probably be somewhat less but will incorporate many of these functional areas (see Fig. 51).

- Instructional areas
    Rehearsal halls
    Practice rooms
    Class piano rooms
    Regular classrooms
    Listening facilities
    Studios and recital halls
    Combinations

- Auxiliary areas
    Storage areas
    Music library
    Workrooms
    Broadcast control booth
    Additional facilities

### Instructional Areas

*Rehearsal Halls—Instrumental Rooms*

An instrumental rehearsal room obviously should be large enough to accommodate the largest band, orchestra, or combined group expected

---

*Reference: Music Buildings, Rooms and Equipment,* Music Educators National Conference, 1902 Association Drive, Reston, Va.

**Fig. 49. A well-equipped rehearsal studio needs barres, full-length mirrors (and curtains to cover them), a piano alcove, windows for fresh air and natural light, and ceiling fans for circulation**

to use the facility. The needs may vary from one institution to another, but 80 to 120 pupils may be taken as the normal range. In some areas which emphasize large bands it is not unusual, however, to find groups containing up to 180 pupils. The use of the school for community music activities should also be considered. Combined school and community groups may make it desirable to construct somewhat larger rehearsal facilities and provide additional storage space.

*Room size:* In estimating the approximate number of square feet of floor space that should be provided for instrumental groups, one should allow a live area of 20 to 24 square feet per student (i.e., 1,600 to 1,920 square feet of floor space for an 80-piece band or a 60-piece orchestra) plus a band of space 5 feet wide around the perimeter of this live area. This will provide the necessary space for aisles, music stands, and other equipment. No musician should sit against a wall. This is especially true of the basses and percussion instruments, which are frequently placed on the highest riser in the back of the ensemble. Area calculations should also include provisions for the types of wall shaping that are typically needed to provide acoustical diffusion in rehearsal halls.

*Room height:* The height of an instrumental rehearsal hall depends on the number of students involved, the floor area of the room, and the type of ensemble. One of the common faults of music facilities is the lack of sufficient ceiling height. Ceiling height must be planned for acoustic purposes even if a split-level effect is created on the floor above the music suite. Not all such rooms will be designed with a ceiling that is parallel to the floor, so that an average ceiling height figure may be more meaningful than a simple number. This average will be in the neighborhood of 25 to 40 feet. Anything less than a 20-foot ceiling in an instrumental rehearsal room should be questioned. Large ensembles, such as full symphony orchestras and large brass bands, benefit from additional cubic volume and hence should be designed to be as tall as possible. Rehearsal rooms without adequate cubic volume can be dangerous for students and instructors since exposure to high sound-pressure levels in such spaces can exceed recommended doses, leading to hearing damage.

**Fig. 50. Typical dimensions for rehearsal studio barres, mirrors, and draperies**

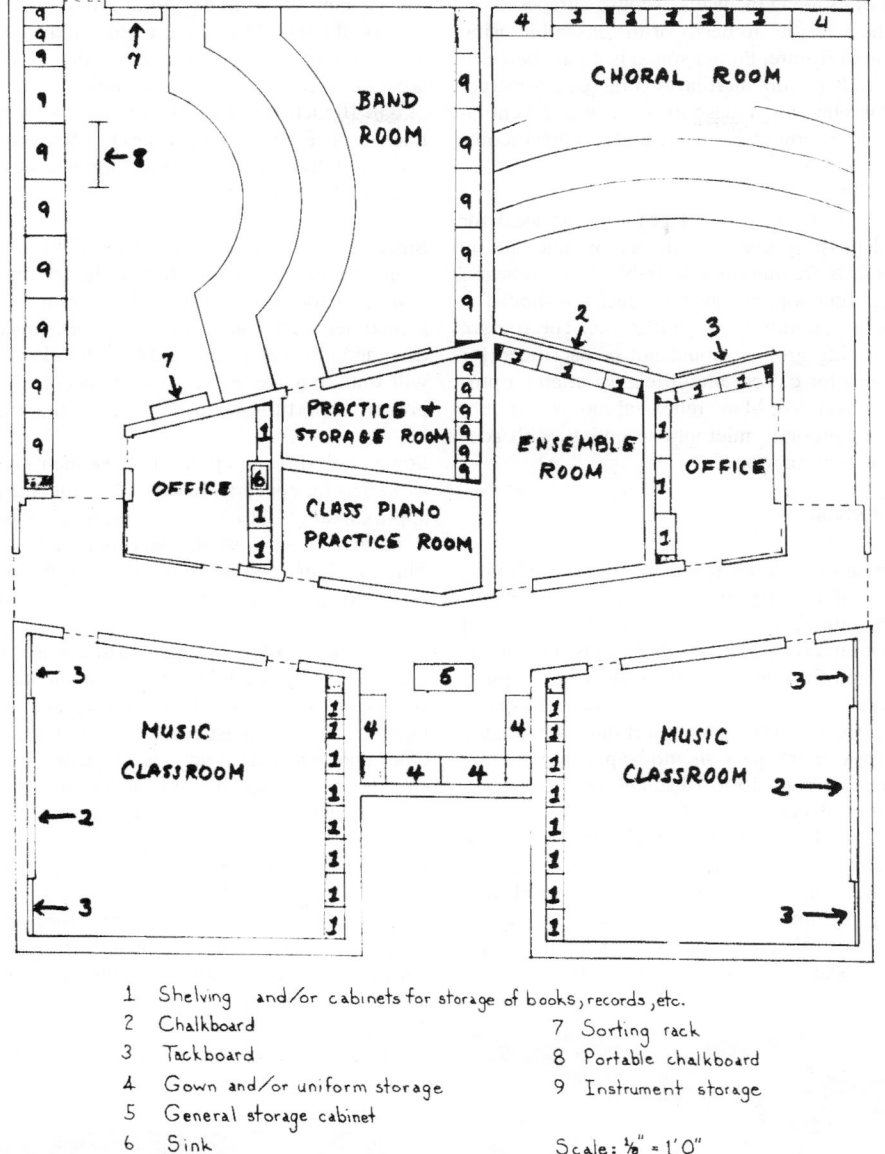

1 Shelving and/or cabinets for storage of books, records, etc.
2 Chalkboard
3 Tackboard            7 Sorting rack
4 Gown and/or uniform storage      8 Portable chalkboard
5 General storage cabinet         9 Instrument storage
6 Sink

Scale: ⅛" = 1'0"

**Fig. 51. Governor Thomas Johnson High School, Frederick, Maryland (Henry Powell Hopkins and Associates, architects)**

*Risers:* Differences of opinion will be found concerning the desirability of providing risers in instrumental rooms. Musicians sitting in the back of the room and the far sides may have some difficulty in seeing the conductor unless they are elevated somewhat. No decided preference for flat floors or for risers has been demonstrated. Architects are currently designing music rooms of both types according to the preference of those planning the facilities. With the use of risers, additional room height will be needed. Some groups feel that semipermanent or portable risers solve the problem and provide room flexibility. The provision of sets of risers—one to be kept in the auditorium and another for the rehearsal hall—avoids some of the logistical problems, but many directors who have risers in the rehearsal room find the flat floor of the stage satisfactory.

If risers are used, a width of 48 to 60 inches for most terraces will prove adequate. A 48- to 60-inch step will be wide enough for a single row of instrumentalists. The top riser should be wider (up to 120 inches) since the back of the room ordinarily accommodates the larger percussion and bass instruments. Ordinarily, an elevation of 6 to 8 inches is adequate (sight line is a good indication of ear line). A white strip of paint or a rubberized nonskid tread on the edge of all risers provides an element of safety. The number of terraces will range from one to five, depending on the size of the room and the needs of the organizations using the rehearsal facilities.

*Other considerations:* Acoustical issues influence the shaping of walls and ceilings as well as the selection of finish materials. Most rehearsal halls feature a mixture of sound-reflective and sound-absorptive materials. The mix of shaping and different materials helps to soften the power of large ensembles and distribute sound energy evenly around the room. Adjustable acoustics are usually provided with a simple system of heavy velour drapes, which can be moved from pockets to various points along the walls. Acoustic drapes allow the instructor to adjust the acoustics to needs of the ensemble using the room and are an essential feature. Proper sound isolation between rehearsal rooms will generally require multilayer composite construction assemblies using a combination of masonry and drywall. Ventilation systems will require close scrutiny to ensure that rehearsal rooms are free from noise.

Instrumental rehearsal rooms (Fig. 52) will probably be used for instrumental classes and possibly even for theory or other music classes. Mounted chalkboards are therefore desirable. Since rehearsing is the room's principal function, however, no decision should be made that will detract from its ability to fulfill that role. The straight chairs required for performing groups should not be sacrificed for tablet armchairs. Provisions for closed-circuit television and a projection screen should be considered. Many rehearsal rooms currently being planned and built incorporate microphone outlets with adequate wiring leading to the control room.

*Rehearsal Halls—Choral Rooms*

The specialized requirements of choral rehearsal rooms are somewhat different from those of facilities used exclusively for instrumental groups. Space requirements are simplified since it is not necessary to provide floor area for music stands and instruments. If the vocal groups are to stand for rehearsals, 6 square feet per pupil will suffice. The use of fixed chairs on risers will require more space; at least 10 square feet is necessary for each pupil if the risers are the minimum width of 30 inches. Extra space should be planned if wider (36- or 40-inch) risers are preferred, 15 to 18 square feet per person being not unusual. Choral room ceilings need not be as high as those in instrumental rehearsal halls, but should be in the region of 16 to 24 feet, depending on the size of the choral groups using the space. Large, well-trained choruses can produce sound-pressure levels that approach those of large of instrumental ensembles. For this reason, it is important to incorporate sufficient cubic volume in the choral rehearsal rooms to accommodate the acoustic power of the group.

*Risers:* Few if any large choral groups rehearse or perform without the use of risers. They are used to avoid having the tone of singers in the back rows obstructed by the bodies of the singers in front. They are also essential for easy observation of the conductor. An elevation of 6 to 10 inches and a width of 30 to 40 inches are adequate for permanent or semipermanent choral risers where seating for the chorus is desired. In rooms where the chorus stands for rehearsal, risers can be 24 inches wide.

Since the choral room is most likely to be used as a general classroom in nonchoral hours, folding tablet armchairs will be useful for both classroom and rehearsal functions. Fixed theater chairs are sometimes employed in choral rooms, especially when the room is designed to serve as a recital hall. In all probability choral directors will want to make recommendations concerning the chairs to ensure proper support for the lower backs of the singers.

Some choir directors prefer to have their groups stand for rehearsals as well as for concerts. In such cases the risers should have a width of approximately 16 to 24 inches and a height of 8 or 10 inches per step. A permanent or portable stage is an advantage for a choral room. Three or four steps from the floor of the room to the stage can be designed to serve as permanent standing risers.

*Other considerations:* As in instrumental rooms, choral rehearsal rooms (Fig. 53) need the same close attention to acoustics, including consideration of wall shaping, finish materials, sound isolation, ventilation noise, and adjustable acoustics. The use of the choral room for other than rehearsal functions suggests the advisability of providing chalkboards, a projection screen, and closed-circuit television. Microphone outlets for recording and broadcasting should be considered.

*Rehearsal Halls—Combined Vocal-Instrumental*

Acoustically, one room cannot serve for both vocal and instrumental rehearsals with completely satisfactory results. Some communities, however, find it economically unfeasible to provide space for both instrumental and vocal groups while employing only one teacher. It is therefore expedient to consider space for combined vocal-instrumental situations. Provisions for changing the reverberation characteristics of such a room with drapes or other materials are a possibility.

Fig. 52. An instrumental rehearsal room at the new school of music at the University of Georgia in Athens. The lower grid ceiling provides diffusion close to the performers, while openings in the grid (black squares) acoustically couple a large volume above the grid. Other acoustical features include a drapery system along the walls which allows the instructor to adjust the acoustics. (Architect: Thompson Ventulett Stainbach & Associates; photo courtesy of the architect)

Fig. 53. A choral rehearsal room at the new school of music at the University of Georgia. It has features quite similar to those for the previously illustrated instrumental rehearsal room. (Architect: Thompson Ventulett Stainbach & Associates; photo courtesy of the architect)

In many one-teacher situations, one room is the nucleus of all music activities. In the smallest of music departments, a single all-purpose room can be planned in terms of space to accommodate the vocal and instrumental group rehearsals, small ensembles and individual rehearsals, library, instrument and equipment storage, instrument repair facilities, office, and teaching studio, as well as various other music classes insofar as the scheduled school day permits. Although space can be provided for this multipurpose situation, few of these activities can be adequately housed in one room without creating undesirable acoustical conditions for the other activities.

Space and accommodations in such a combination room will have to be figured on the basis of the guidelines for instrumental rehearsal halls. The room might be thought of as the future instrumental room, when funds to create a separate vocal rehearsal room become available.

*Practice Rooms*

Practice rooms are a facility peculiar to the teaching of music, with some special problems not encountered by administrators or architects in planning other elements of the school. Among the factors which must be considered are acoustics, size, ventilation, amount of use, and supervision. The acoustical issues are particularly important and include consideration of interior finish materials, construction assemblies for sound isolation, ventilation system noise, and acoustical doors and windows.

*Number:* The number of practice rooms needed by a music department should be related to the number of musicians involved and the administrative policies concerned with their use. Some authorities recommend that students practice as much as possible in school, so that assistance and supervision are possible. Many feel that it is particularly important that practice room facilities be available for those students who play the larger instruments because of the difficulty in carrying the instruments home. These practice rooms should be convenient to the large rehearsal room, so that the moving of heavy, large instruments is minimized. In determining the number of practice rooms needed by a collegiate school or department of music, a calculation similar to that shown in Table 5 might be used.

*Size:* Practice rooms vary in size according to their various functions. Individual practice rooms are quite satisfactory in the 55 to 65-square-foot range. This provides sufficient space for an upright piano, a chair, and a music stand, but little more. Public schools, once planned with several rooms of this size in the music suite, are now being built with slightly larger rooms for ensemble practice, reflecting the increased emphasis on small groups, both vocal and instrumental (Fig. 54). Colleges that plan large blocks of small practice

**Fig. 54. In addition to small practice rooms for one or two people, some schools require special practice facilities for particular instrument groups. Shown here is the percussion practice room at the School of Music at the University of Georgia. (Architect: Thompson Ventulett Stainbach & Associates, photo courtesy of the architect)**

rooms will also want to provide a number of larger rooms for ensemble practice, or to accommodate two grand pianos or organs.

*Other considerations:* Practice rooms are often arranged in blocks. While natural light is certainly desirable, windows can create sound-isolation problems, particularly if they are operable. Ventilation sys-

**Table 5** Estimating the number of required practice rooms

| | | | |
|---|---|---|---|
| 50 music majors | x | 16 hr per week = | 800 hr per week |
| 40 on secondary instruments | x | 6 hr per week = | 240 hr per week |
| 80 theory students | x | 2 hr per week = | 160 hr per week |
| 150 elementary education students | x | 2 hr per week = | 300 hr per week |
| | | | 1,500 hr per week |

$$\frac{\text{Practice hours per week}}{\text{Hours available for use per week}} = \frac{1,500}{60} = 25 \text{ practice rooms needed}$$

tems need to be carefully designed to be sufficiently quiet and so that sound is not transmitted from room to room via the ducts. Dedicated return-air systems are needed since the acoustic doors used in practice rooms preclude the use of undercut doors for return-air purposes. The construction employed between practice rooms will generally be composite multilayer assemblies to ensure adequate sound isolation. Vertical isolation (floor to floor) must be considered in additional to horizontal isolation (room to room).

Prefabricated practice rooms are available. These have the advantage of being preengineered from an acoustics standpoint and hence come with certain guarantees regarding acoustical performance. Another advantage of prefabricated rooms is the availability of electronic acoustic enhancement as an optional feature. This enhancement allows the musician to rehearse in an acoustical environment which is akin to the larger spaces where performances occur (i.e., a recital or concert hall). This gives the musician valuable experience rehearsing in a performance acoustic that would not otherwise generally be available. The economics of the local building market will determine whether prefabricated rooms or scratch-built rooms are more cost effective for a particular building.

Nonparallel walls have been widely used to avoid unpleasant acoustical anomalies in small practice rooms. Double-paned windows in the doors, or opening on the rehearsal hall or teacher's office in schools, permit supervision without interruption. Electronic monitoring devices are sometimes incorporated.

### Class Piano Rooms

Many conservatories and school systems provide class instruction in piano as well as in the band and orchestra instruments. Some have constructed specially designed rooms for this type of instruction. These rooms should be as near as possible to the other music rooms in order to realize complete utilization in a coordinated music program. There should be acoustical treatment of the walls and ceilings, and insulation against sound transmission to and from other classrooms as prescribed by the acoustical consultant. The front wall should be equipped with blackboards (plain and with music staves), bulletin board space, music cabinet, and electrical outlets. Space should be provided for television, CD players, and recording facilities.

### Regular Classrooms

Regular academic classrooms are used by many schools for classes in music history, appreciation, theory, composition, arranging, and other music education classes. Though the acoustical treatment may not need to be as extensive or expensive as in some other parts of the music suite, if the learning to take place in the room is to involve listening to music, more than ordinary care must be taken to block out extraneous sounds. A classroom that will be used primarily for general music classes needs ample storage space for books, records, rhythm instruments, autoharps, piano keyboards, pictures, and similar equipment. Provide accommodations for a ceiling-mounted projection screen.

In some situations it may be possible to provide a projection room adjoining the classroom, or even between two classrooms, so that the projector can be prepared without losing class time. If a classroom is to be used primarily for theory classes, it will be desirable to have staff lines painted on the chalkboard. Conversely, if music literature

classes are to be the principal occupants, painted staff lines are less desirable. If a college classroom is to be used largely for music education classes, it will need adequate locked shelf space or will need to be planned adjacent to a storage room (with shelves) for the large amount of material used in such classes. In a campus school situation, classrooms may need to be provided with rows of coat hooks and shelf space.

### Listening Facilities

Several types of listening facilities are in common use in collegiate music schools today, and each presents specific planning problems. As independent study becomes more common in secondary schools, some similar facilities will become desirable in the music department or in the school library. The principal systems include the following:

1. A number of soundproofed listening rooms or cubicles are each provided with playback equipment. The student receives recordings from a central location (often the departmental office) and listens when convenient.
2. A bank of playback devices is placed in a central control room. Worktables in an adjoining room are supplied with a number of receiving channels and sets of headphones. The student requests a particular recording, which is played by the monitor in charge of the control room, and the student listens through headphones.

The planning of a listening facility is dictated first of all by the kind of equipment the department uses, or the kind to which it wishes to change. The number of listening rooms or cubicles, the size of the control room and the number of channels available, and the number of places at the worktables can be calculated by a method similar to that employed in the case of practice rooms. The design of the system, if method 2 is used, must of course precede the planning of the area. Other than providing for adequate space and convenient location in relationship to other music areas, no general observations will be needed in this section.

In many cases certain classrooms will be set aside as theory laboratories. It may be desirable to provide cubicles in which students may work with individual tape recorders, CD players, or similar equipment. Certain storage and control requirements must also be planned in such situations.

### Studios and Recital Halls

Traditionally, much of the teaching of music has been done on a one-to-one basis. Though this country has accomplished much through group instruction, it is still true that advanced instruction is almost always given to a single student. In colleges and conservatories this is carried on in studios which also serve as the faculty members' offices. It is desirable also for schools to provide an office for each full-time music instructor. Most frequently it is located adjacent to the teacher's rehearsal hall and is provided with windows that enable the instructor to keep an eye on ensemble rehearsals being conducted by students in the hall or in practice rooms.

In a college it is not difficult to determine the proper number of office-studios, since the figure corresponds directly with the number of applied music teachers. More difficult is the matter of assuring the responsible authorities that space devoted to the studios will be fully used. College instructors teaching applied music are likely to have teaching schedules of 18 to 24 hours per week, and they will wish to do their own practicing and professional work in their studios. Occupancy of somewhere between 30 and 40 hours per week may thus be expected. Administrators may expect a 50- to 60-hour-per-week occupancy as they do in the case of classrooms and practice rooms. They may need help to see that music teachers cannot work effectively if they have to share a studio.

As in virtually all music school spaces, faculty studios need close attention to acoustics, including finish materials, sound isolation, and ventilation noise.

*Size:* Music teachers' offices need to be larger than a small practice room since they will, in all probability, have their desk and files here. There should be enough additional space for group lessons if they have the need. Music files, instrument storage, and work areas frequented by students should not be in the office-studio.

College studios will vary in size with the instructor's specialty. Studios for the senior piano staff will ideally be large enough to accommodate two grand pianos and the usual office furniture of desk, file cabinets, and bookshelves. Studios for instructors of voice and other instruments, traditionally requiring only one piano, can be a bit smaller if acoustic conditions are otherwise met. Nonparallel walls are recommended, but the studios should not be designed in such a way that piano placement and disposition of furniture are made difficult.

The size of the individual studios may also be determined by faculty members' other duties. As academic advisers, they may need additional space for file cabinets; if they use the room for seminars, they may require space for a table and chairs. In virtually all cases a small mounted chalkboard in each studio will be a valuable asset.

### Combinations

Many schools are adopting the administrative policy of establishing fine arts departments and housing art, drama, and music in units separate from the classroom area. Buildings of this nature usually consist of a music complex, a drama complex, and a visual arts complex. Dance may sometimes be included (see Fig. 55).

The music complex has been described earlier. The drama complex consists of a small theater with a capacity of 300 to 500, workroom, dressing areas, one or more classrooms, storage rooms, radio and television control and listening areas, costume storage and work areas, and library.

## Auxiliary Areas

### Storage Areas

Adequate storage areas, planned with traffic patterns in mind, are important to the proper functioning of a music facility. Storage, with proper heat and humidity control, is necessary for musical instruments; robes and uniforms; music, records, tapes, and CDs; and various types of equipment. With careful planning, the storage areas can be conveniently placed and at the same time serve as a buffer between two sound-producing areas, such as the instrumental and choral rehearsal halls (see Fig. 56).

*Instrument storage:* Instrument-storage facilities should be located so as to minimize the moving of instruments. Sufficient free floor space should be provided to permit smooth flow of traffic. Storage cabinets located within the rehearsal areas are inaccessible during rehearsal periods and frequently cause congestion during period changes.

*Uniform and robe storage:* Storage facilities should be planned for the school-owned band and orchestra uniforms, choir robes, or vestments. This closet space should be cedar lined. A well-constructed, close-fitting door will help protect against moths and dust. The closet space should be high enough so that the uniforms and robes will not touch the floor when hanging on the racks. Some provision should be made to space the uniforms and robes at equal intervals and to facilitate identification. A separate (pigeonhole) compartment for the caps, belts, and other miscellaneous equipment should also be provided.

### Music Library

Music libraries will range from a single set of filing cabinets in the music room to the school of music library complete with stacks, reading rooms, charging desk, listening facilities, and work areas. In most colleges there will also be smaller libraries (band, orchestra, choral) which are more like the school situations described here.

### Workrooms

*Instrument repair:* Some sort of facility should be provided for emergency instrument repairs. A special room is recommended, although many schools will use a section of the music library room or director's office for this purpose. Larger school systems will employ specially trained technicians to take care of all instrument and equipment repairs. The minimum provision should be a workbench, stool, and a supply of tools for repairs. Cabinet space with small drawers should be provided to hold pads, pad cement, springs, cork, and other miscellaneous equipment. If a great deal of repair work is done in the school, the workbench should have a gas connection, electrical outlets, wood and steel vises, and other specialized equipment. Running water and a large sink for cleaning brass instruments should be included.

*Copy center:* School music departments will have the facilities of the general office at their disposal in most cases and may not need copy equipment in the music suite itself. Most collegiate departments or schools of music and some school departments housed separately in a campus-type school will find a copy center invaluable. There are many times when the music department needs items copied—rehearsal schedules, instrumental parts of a student composition, football show routines, trip itineraries, vocalizes for the choir, songs in the public domain—that equipment should be readily available. The room should include enough counter space for several machines, space for collating, and a sink.

*Offices:* A music program that functions smoothly should provide a well-located director's office. The size of the office and the types of equipment included in it will depend on the size and organization of the school. The room need not be especially large unless it is also to serve as a studio in which small-group instruction may be carried on. It should, however, be able to accommodate a desk, two or three chairs, filing cabinets for correspondence, cabinets for miscellaneous storage, and any special equipment such as electronic tuners, piano, CD player, radio, and tape recorder.

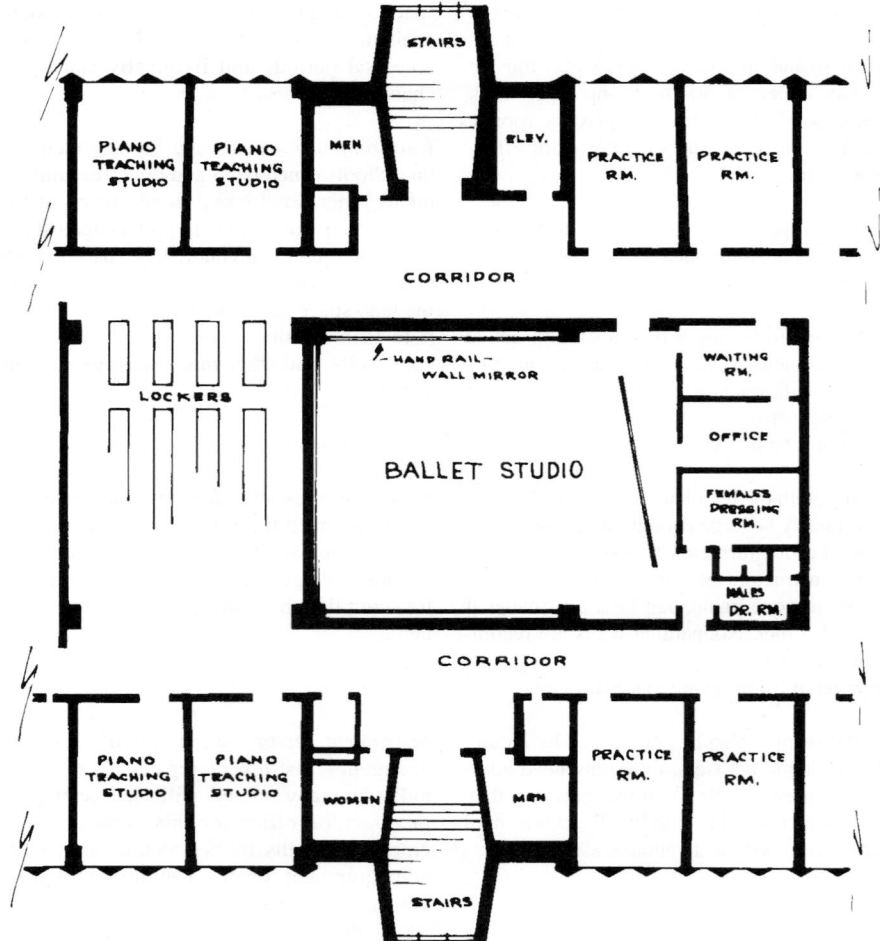

**Fig. 55. Provisions for instruction in dance may be included in some buildings (College Conservatory of Music, University of Cincinnati; architect: Edward J. Schulte and Associates)**

Music teachers who teach in several locations in a school (e.g., harmony in a classroom, choir in the recital hall, general music in a specially equipped center) need an office to organize the many materials and instruments and pieces of equipment with which they work. Offices are also essential for the department head or the director of performing groups because of the frequent contact they have with members of the community.

*Broadcast Control Booth*

The recent improvements in recording equipment and television education have resulted in many schools being constructed with facilities to make possible the use of these new techniques. Educational programs of all types are made available to the school and community; therefore, school space should be allowed for both receiving and broadcasting of music. The control booth should be well insulated for sound and should have slanted double-glass windows for viewing the performing groups. Such a control booth is sometimes located adjacent to the stage of the auditorium or recital hall and sometimes between the rehearsal halls.

*Additional Facilities*

*Washroom and toilet facilities:* Because the music suite is frequently used at night when the remainder of the building is locked, washroom, toilet facilities, and custodial work areas must be provided within the music unit. In many instances they may be necessary for the changing of uniforms and must be convenient to the rest of the department. These facilities require about 15 percent of the total floor space if adequate room is to be provided. If recitals to which the public is invited are given within the music unit, additional rest room space may be needed.

*Lounge:* Collegiate music departments may need to consider the desirability of a lounge in which students can relax. If other study areas on the campus are some distance from the music facilities, one portion of the lounge might provide desk or table space. An area might also be provided for vending machines.

*Elevator:* Because of the heavy instruments and equipment that it is frequently necessary to move in a music department, an elevator is a

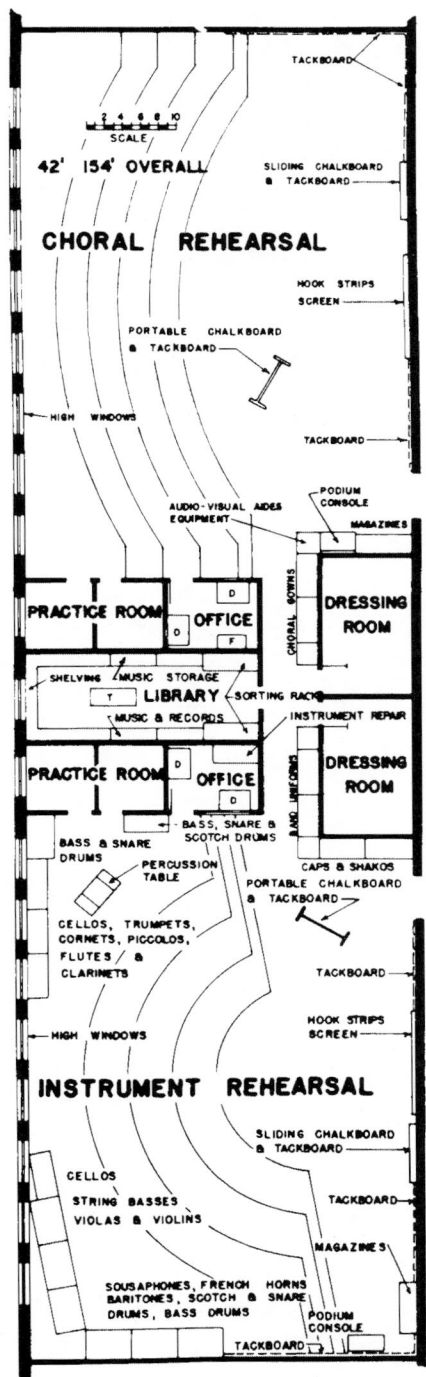

**Fig. 56. Plan for a two-teacher music department**

most desirable feature in a building of two or more floors. Also recommended is a loading dock adjacent to the parking area.

## Performance Spaces in Music Education Facilities

From a technical point of view, the performance spaces in a music education center differ little from those built for professional or commercial purposes. The major differences in education centers relate to the mix of performances and the seating capacities.

Seating capacities in education performance centers tend to be much more modest than those in professional facilities. While a concert hall serving a major metropolitan orchestra will typically seat 2,000 to 3,000 people, most university concert halls seat 600 to 1,500 people. The acoustic, theater planning, and equipment issues remain much the same as in professional performance venues. It is common, however, for university administrators to reduce the area devoted to public lobby areas and some backstage support functions in the interest of focusing scarce resources on the interior of the performance space and other teaching facilities.

Educational institutions sometimes require two or more performance venues to satisfy the full range of their program. It is quite common for a school to build a 300- to 600-seat recital hall for solo recitals and chamber music concerts along with an 800- to 1,500-seat concert hall for large ensemble performances (Fig. 57). Although schools generally build single-volume concert and recital halls, schools with a focus on opera may build a proscenium theater with multiuse features to serve both its opera program and instrumental ensembles.

It has become common for local universities or secondary schools to work jointly with a local municipality to create a performance center that serves both the school's teaching mission and the community's need for performance space. These "town-gown" projects have the advantage of being able to tap multiple funding sources to complete projects that the university or municipality might not be able to accomplish alone.

Because a school's mission and pedagogy influence its need for performance space and a town-gown element adds additional requirements, the programming effort for such facilities is critically important. The mixing of requirements from disparate users introduces considerable complexity into the planning process for such buildings. It is particularly important for issues such as priority of use, ownership, and management to be investigated and resolved during the programming phase so that the architectural designs are more likely to respond to the various ways that the building will ultimately be used.

**Fig. 57. The concert hall in the School of Music at the University of Georgia, Athens. While seating only slightly more than 1,100 people, the stage of this space can accommodate a full symphony orchestra and chorus. (Architect: Thompson Ventulett Stainbach & Associates; photo courtesy of the architect)**

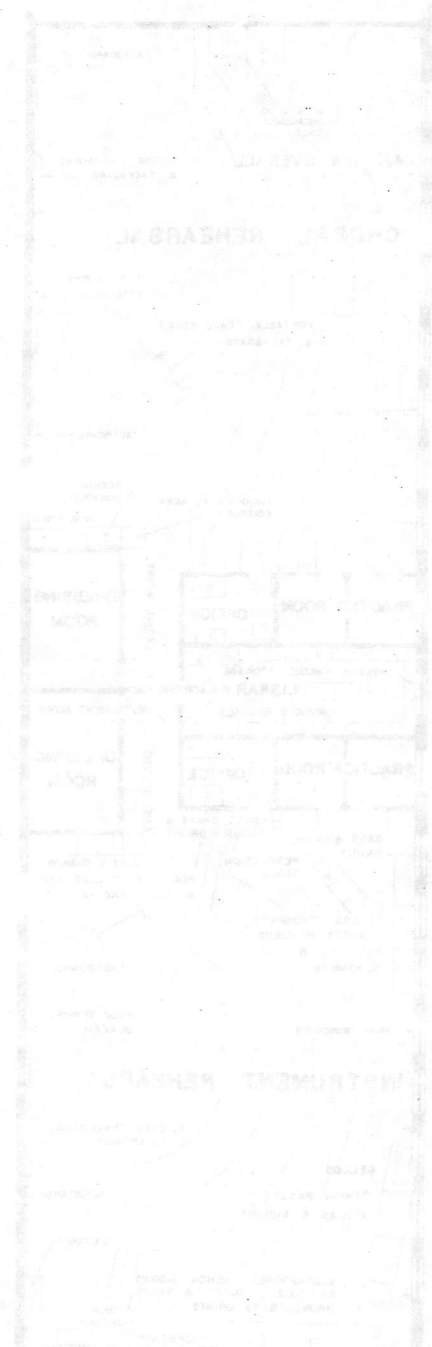

# 7

# Governmental and Public

**Fig. 1. Fire station, Essex, Connecticut (Photo: Ken Sasso)**

# MUNICIPAL BUILDINGS

## CITY AND TOWN HALLS

Steps to be taken in planning and constructing a city hall are:

1. determining need
2. determining space requirements
3. selecting an architect
4. acquiring a site
5. approving layout, design, and architectural features, and
6. developing a financial plan.

These steps are not a one-two-three process; frequently they must be done simultaneously. It is important to have an idea of what is wanted before selecting an architect, but the architect can be helpful in delineating the program. It is important to remember that the city hall should last 60 years or more. The following "dos and don'ts" provide a guide to officials engaged in planning a new city hall.

*Do:*

- Locate the city hall where it will be most convenient and, if possible, where land values are reasonable.
- Be clear on departments to be housed, the number of employees, types of furnishings and equipment, and special requirements such as vault and storage space.
- Provide ample off-street parking space for both employees and the public.
- Put most or all city department headquarters in the city hall.
- Provide for structural expansion and flexibility in office layout.
- Plan the city hall from the inside out with emphasis on work flow, convenience to the public, and convenience for employees.

- Provide for the comfort and efficiency of employees with controlled ventilation and adequate lighting.
- Provide for employee lounges and rest rooms.
- Use materials, construction, and furnishings which make the city hall easy to maintain.
- Provide open, unobstructed counters for transactions with the public.

*Don't:*

- Don't locate in an area of declining property values except when part of a program.
- Don't try to remodel an old post office, school building, convention hall, or other building designed for some other special use.
- Don't forget that the city hall is an office building, not a monument or an ornament.
- Don't underestimate space needs.
- Don't tie up valuable space with indoor pistol ranges, drive-through garages, private exits, wide corridors, and other gadgets.
- Don't cut up the city hall into cubbyholes for minor officials.
- Don't build the city hall over two stories in height if at all possible.
- Don't let the public come in contact with police or criminal activities.
- Don't provide in the main lobby any facilities that encourage loitering.

### Determining Need

The need for a new city hall may seem obvious to those who spend their working hours at the city hall. Ceilings are high; heating costs are twice what they should be; space originally meant for storage has been converted to offices; electrical wiring violates code provisions; and the present facility is just old. All of this—and more besides—

*Reviewer:* Schoenhardt Architects, Inc.
*Credits: Planning the New City Hall,* Report #212 Management Information Service, International City Managers' Association, Washington, D.C.

may be true, but what is not known is how extensive the need is. This must be determined by careful study. In determining the need for a city hall alternate courses of action should be studied.

Determining the extent of need involves two areas: (1) condition of building, and (2) space needs.

The condition of the building is the easiest to evaluate. Things to be considered are type of construction, structural condition, electrical wiring, heating and ventilating, and facilities such as rest rooms. Nothing may be seriously wrong and a new facility still needed, but it is important to know these points. Careful and professional review may bring factors to light heretofore not considered.

At an early stage it is important to have some idea of space needs. This can be determined in general terms by having each department submit their space needs for review and study. If departments are already crowded, additional space needed now is not hard to estimate. The real problem in determining space needs is what will be needed in the future. The building may be adequate now, but how will it be in 5, 10, 20 years? Few cities decide to build a new city hall and do so almost immediately. Experience seems to indicate that a new city hall is the outgrowth of a number of years of careful planning and, once built, lasts a long time.

In estimating future needs not only must traditional services such as police and building inspection be considered but also what future services the city may be required to provide. One of the "dos" is to provide for structural expansion. However, provision for such expansion must be in reason, and should be based on projections of future needs. Knowledge of the community and its people is essential to space planning. City officials should know the population projections for the next 20 or 25 years, the economic level of the community, and present and probable social and economic characteristics.

## SELECTING THE LOCATION OF THE CITY HALL

### Civic Centers

In selecting the location for a city hall, the first consideration is whether it should be placed on a site by itself or whether it should be combined with a group of related buildings in a civic center. The civic center has had great appeal to the city planner because it offers certain advantages and at the same time provides for latitude in design. The buildings that are included in civic centers range from a grouping of strictly administrative offices and service buildings to a complex of office buildings, auditoriums, libraries, and so on.

The great advantage of a civic center is that the grouping of public buildings may prove to be convenient to the public in transacting business that requires visits to more than one public agency. It also may result in one or more governmental units being able to use the facilities of the other. Finally, it is often convenient to have certain facilities grouped together in order to expedite interagency and governmental relations.

Obviously if a city hall is to be part of a civic center, it must be planned in relation to the other facilities. For instance, one city hall is part of a civic center consisting of a health building, communications building, police garage, county office building, sheriff's department and jail, criminal-legal building, and a juvenile center. Some of the facilities, such as the administrative offices in the health building, did not have to be repeated in the city hall.

Site selection for a civic center must consider the factors listed below for locating a city hall. In addition, several other points are important. The site for a civic center must permit flexibility in building arrangement. Since more land is necessary, street patterns may have to be altered, and additional land will be needed for parking. Once the site has been selected, means must be found to preserve it for gradual development of all the units. Also, the site must be located so as not to interfere with the normal development of the business district.

On the surface the civic center idea has great appeal, but there are those who feel that center concept has limitations.

Government buildings—the city hall, fire station (Fig. 1), and police stations—which were long the nucleus of most civic centers, tend themselves to be dispersed today. The reason is obvious. Fire and police buildings, for example, are best located at a central point in the street network, and with the building of expressways, this point rarely intersects with the best location for the mayor's office or the council chamber. Service agencies (such as the water and park departments) increasingly favor headquarters locations adjacent to their operating facilities.

### City-County Building

The county-seat city should investigate the possibility of constructing one building to serve the needs of both the city and the county.

The city-county building has two major advantages. First, local governmental facilities are together, which is frequently a convenience to the public and to city and county agencies that have contact with each other. The second advantage is cost savings. Depending on conditions, a joint building can be constructed for less money than two separate facilities when all costs are considered: land, engineering and architectural fees, financing charges, and so on. Joint occupancy can result in operating savings.

The majority of cities that occupy office space with the county feel that the arrangement is very satisfactory. The most often stated disadvantage is lack of room for expansion. A joint city-county building must be carefully planned so that both governmental units have area to expand in. A city and a county have different as well as similar needs. When the differences are too great, a city-county building can cause problems. The other drawback is that expenses and responsibilities for operating the building are not always distributed equitably. It is thus extremely important that an agreement for building operation and maintenance be worked out in advance of construction.

### Location

The selection of a site (Fig. 2) for a city hall will be influenced by a number of circumstances. Some of these conditions are limiting in nature, such as the availability of land. There are, however, certain guiding principles that should be considered. Some applicable principles for a city hall location are as follows:

1. "Government must serve and be accessible to the people . . ." Efficiency of service is related to how convenient governmental facilities are for the majority of those citizens using the facility.
2. "Since public services must serve every citizen as well as, and as conveniently as possible, those activities must be located near the center of transportation and the center of business activity." In a large city public transportation comes to a head in the central business district. Major arterial streets are planned to bring peo-

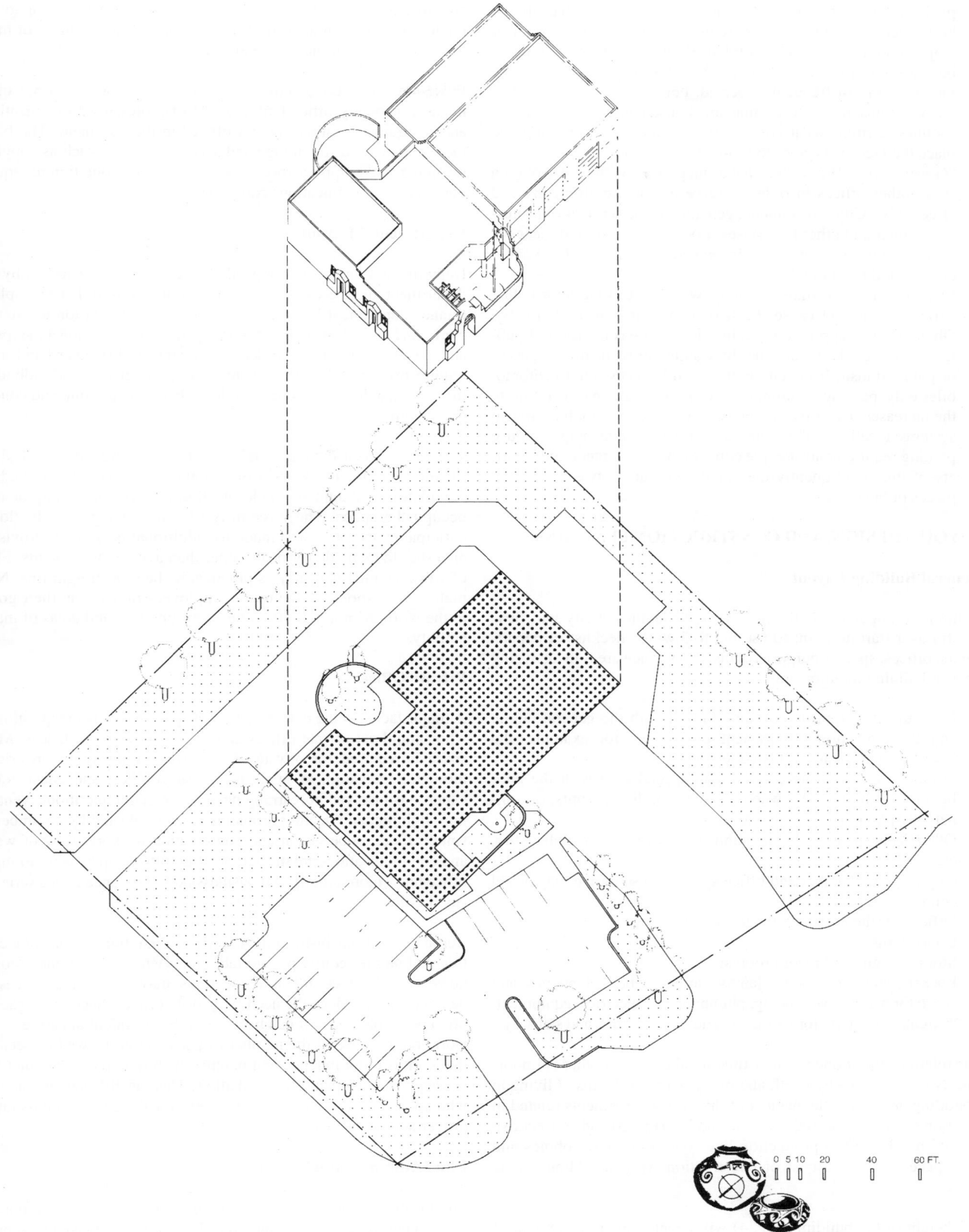

0  5 10    20        40        60 FT.

**Fig. 2. Site plan, Village Hall, Los Ranchos de Albuquerque, New Mexico (Westwork Architects)**

ple in and out of the city center. In most cases the city hall should be located near public transportation, if any, and certainly near major arterial streets. The city hall should be near the center of business activity because this is where the principal users of the facility are most frequently located. For example, attorneys frequently must use records that are housed in city hall. A city should determine what groups most often come to city hall and place the facility as close to those groups as possible.

3. "Government offices must have integration with, not isolation from, other offices in order to serve the public efficiently and effectively." City government agencies use the services of professional men and other businesses. Locating the city hall near the center of business activity helps expedite the work of the agencies located in city hall.

4. "Maximum use of transit systems will result in the least public parking areas and cause the least congestion on city streets." Obviously this applies only to the city having some form of public transit. People travel either by walking or by using cars, taxis, or public transit. If the city hall is readily accessible to automobiles only, parking requirements would increase in direct ratio to the increased use of the car. For the city that does not have transit systems, location in the center area of the city may help to reduce parking requirements. People come to the city center to do a variety of things; frequently they park and walk between different places of business.

## LAYOUT, DESIGN, AND CONSTRUCTION FEATURES

### General Building Layout

Building arrangement is the next step in planning a city hall. It is helpful as a starting point to use the following checklist of departments, offices, special-purpose rooms, and service areas in analyzing interior building requirements:

1. Departments requiring constant contact with the general public and the collection or payment of money—for example, the finance department and tax collector;
2. Departments requiring contact with special classes of the public—for example, city-owned utilities, building permits, personnel, city planning, and city clerk;
3. Other departments including public works, recreation, police, fire, etc.;
4. City council chamber and office space for use by the mayor and council members;
5. Offices for the chief administrator;
6. Courtrooms;
7. Storage vaults and record rooms;
8. Locker rooms, rest rooms, janitor closets, public telephones, and space for heating, ventilating, plumbing, and electrical equipment;
9. "Circulating areas" for lobbies, corridors, elevators, and stairways.

The relationship of one room or functional area to another is important. No room exists by itself, and many of the problems of living in a building arise from the neglect of this fact. Departments related in function should be located near one another (Fig. 3) and consecutive operations planned in production-line style. Excessive lobbies and hall space add to the cost of construction without adding usable space.

The height of the building (Fig. 4) will depend upon the amount of ground available and the amount of office space needed. Land generally is cheaper than additional height. Taller buildings are more diffi-

cult to maintain and require more planning of the interior to get related functions on adjacent floors. Also, any city building of more than two floors will need an elevator.

Provision for a full basement housing general offices is not often made in new city office buildings. Most professional organizations advise against locating general offices in the basement. The basement can be used for storage and service activities such as copying, receiving and shipping rooms, heating and air conditioning equipment, and communications equipment.

### Departmental Layout

Departmental layout will depend on the activities carried on by the department and the tools or special equipment used. For example, a finance department layout may require an open area for accounting clerks and collectors with one or two private offices, a machine room, and a vault. The public works department, on the other hand, may require private offices for the director, the engineer, and individual inspectors, a drafting room, a vault, a plan or map room, and conference rooms.

The first step in departmental layout is to survey the work done by the department. Work flow should be especially studied. A complete list should be made of all employees and equipment to occupy the space. The possibility of future expansion should be anticipated and provision made for additional personnel. Provision also should be made for peak rather than average work loads. Flow of work should, as nearly as practicable, be in a straight line. Normally, work should come to the employees rather than their going to the work. Minor activities can be grouped around areas of major activity.

### Private Offices

A major factor in the determination of space needs is the question of who should get private offices and under what circumstances. More space is required for private offices; space utilization is restricted through segregation of areas for private offices; and considerable expense is involved in rearranging and re-erecting partitions. Ventilation, lighting, and heating problems are complicated by a number of small offices; supervision and coordination of work, flow of work, and communications are made more difficult. An open, well-arranged office has a more orderly and businesslike appearance than a series of small offices.

Certain conditions justify private offices. First, transactions of a confidential nature require private facilities. General conference rooms, however, where confidential meetings may be held as occasion demands, may reduce the need for private offices. Second, privacy is often desirable not so much because of the confidential nature of the work, but because of the number of persons interviewed or because the work is of an independent nature which requires more quiet and privacy than the open office will allow. There is little agreement as to who should have private offices except for the chief administrative officer and department heads.

### Chief Administrator's Office

The location of the chief administrator's office (Fig. 5) is important to good public relations. It should be located so as to give the impression of being easily reached and open to any caller, but it should not be too prominent. The second floor ordinarily is a good location

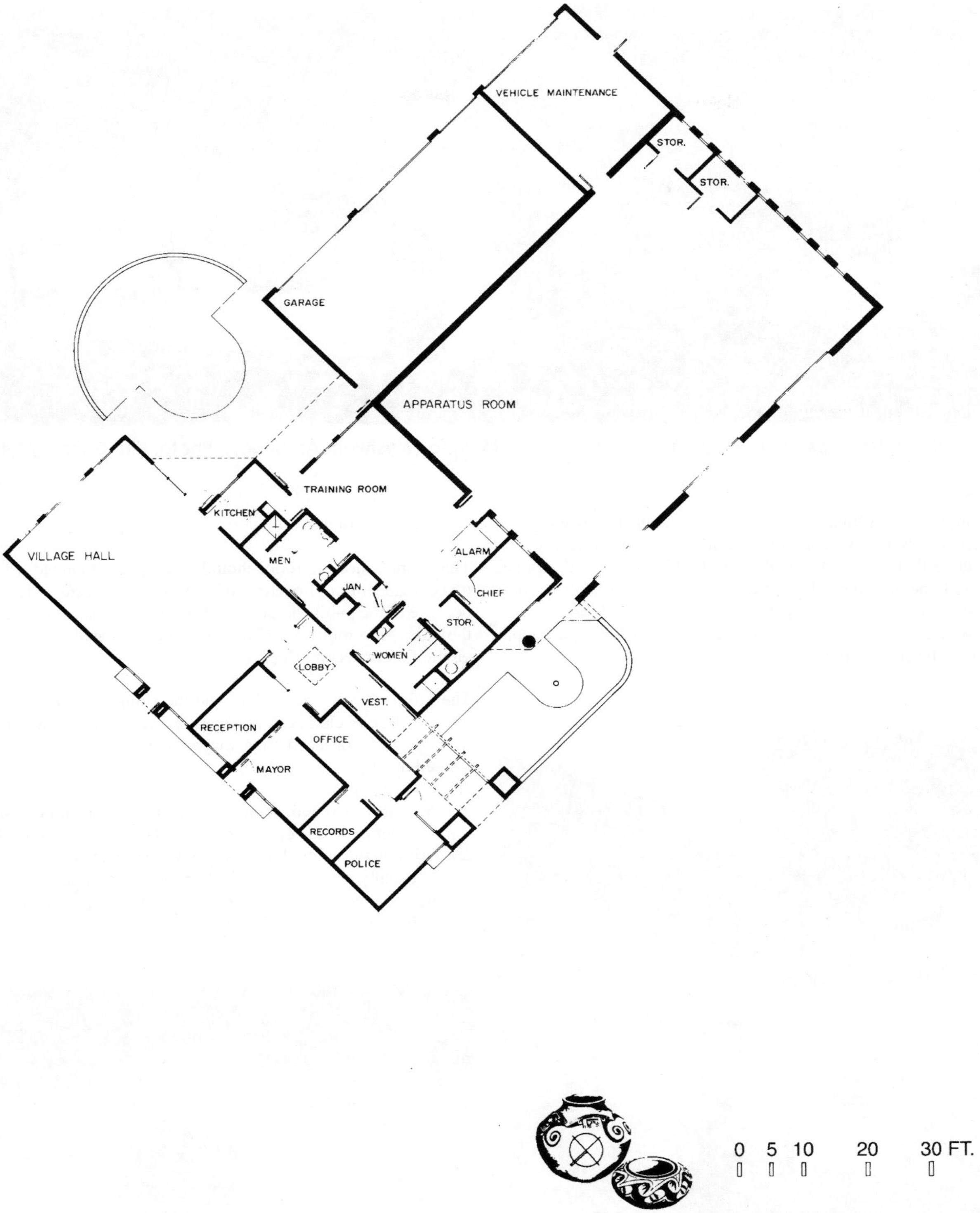

VEHICLE MAINTENANCE

STOR.

STOR.

GARAGE

APPARATUS ROOM

TRAINING ROOM

KITCHEN

VILLAGE HALL

MEN

ALARM

JAN.

CHIEF

STOR.

WOMEN

LOBBY

VEST.

RECEPTION

OFFICE

MAYOR

RECORDS

POLICE

0  5  10     20     30 FT.

**Fig. 3. Plan, Village Hall, Los Ranchos de Albuquerque, New Mexico (Westwork Architects)**

since some effort must be expended to visit it, and the casual or merely curious individual is less likely to intrude.

A first-floor location, however, can be just as good if callers are properly screened by a secretary or receptionist. It has the additional advan-

tage of being close to the offices most frequented by the public (Fig. 6). Of interest to council-manager cities is the fact that the mayor has an office in the majority of cases located very close to the city manager's office. See the second-floor plan of the Alhambra, California, city hall (Fig. 7) for a typical executive layout.

Fig. 4. Village Hall, Los Ranchos de Albuquerque, New Mexico (Westwork Architects; Photo: Kirk Gittings/Syntax)

The administrator's office should be large enough for meetings of department heads unless a conference room adjoins his office. A conference table that will accommodate up to 12 people is desirable. Space should be provided adjacent to the administrator's office for a support staff of two or three, depending upon the size of the city. The support staff office would also serve as a reception room for people who call on the administrator.

**Council Chamber**

The council meeting room should be carefully planned if full use is to be made of it. Location of the council chamber is important because of the public nature of the business transacted there. Most of the cities with multistoried buildings have located the council room on the first or second floor.

The offices located near or around the council chamber are usually those of the city clerk, city attorney, and city manager. Small meeting rooms and an office for the mayor and council members may be located nearby.

In most cities surveyed, council members sit at separate desks or at a semicircular table, the open end of which faces the citizens. In only a few cities do the council members have their backs to the public. The mayor usually sits in the center flanked by the manager, clerk, and attorney. The council table often is put on a dais 18 inches or 2 feet above the main floor (see Fig. 8).

Fig. 5. Village Hall, Los Ranchos de Albuquerque, New Mexico (Westwork Architects; Photo: Kirk Gittings/Syntax)

Fig. 6. Village Hall, Los Ranchos de Albuquerque, New Mexico (Westwork Architects; Photo: Kirk Gittings/Syntax)

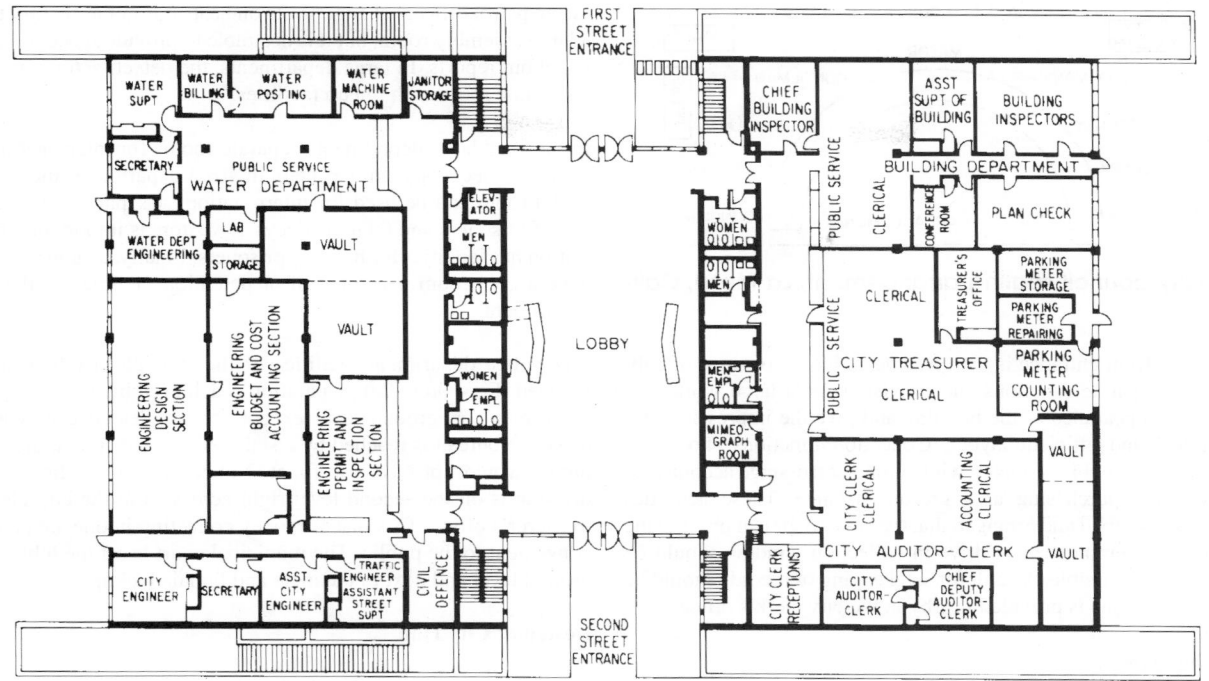

FIRST FLOOR PLAN

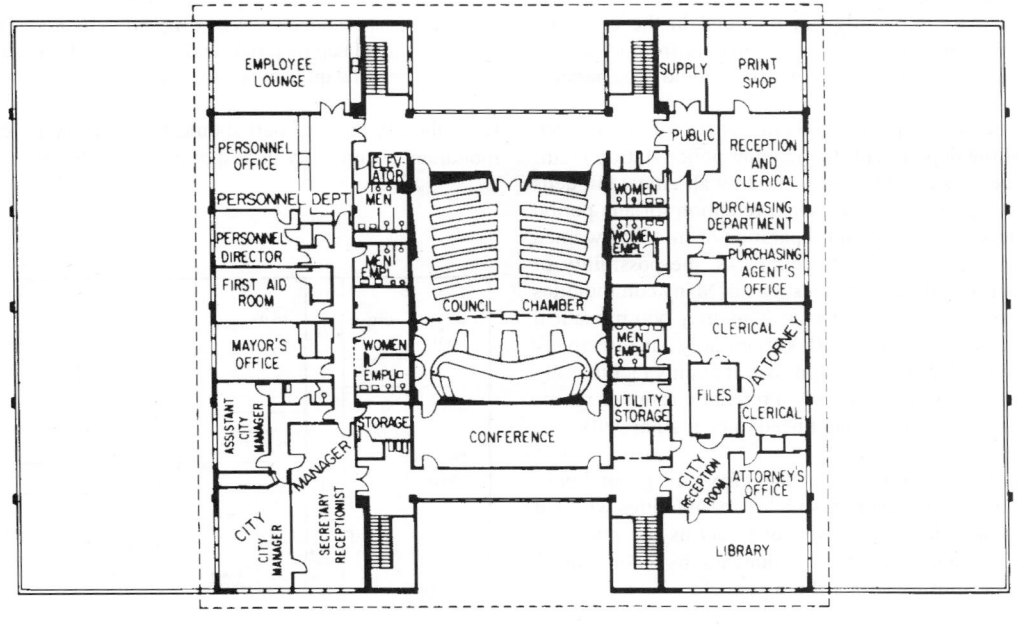

SECOND FLOOR PLAN

**Fig. 7. Alhambra, California, City Hall**

It is well to plan the council chamber so that it also can be used for other purposes. In many cities it is used as a general courtroom for public hearings held by city agencies, as a meeting room for the city planning or zoning commission, for general conferences, and as a public meeting room.

**Finance Activities**

The collection activities of the finance department have more contact with the public than any other municipal activity with the possible exception of the police and building departments. A prominent loca-

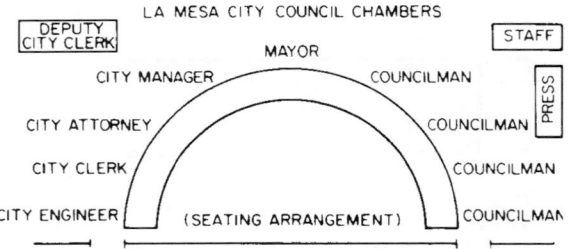

**Fig. 8. City council seating arrangement, La Mesa, California**

tion near the front entrance is therefore desirable. Avoidance of cubbyholes for separate functions and provision for a large work area enhance the appearance of the building and give the impression of a well-planned and efficient layout. Collection functions should be located near the public counter with billing, assessing, accounting, budgeting, and purchasing at a greater distance. These activities should be so grouped and arranged that the supervisor can observe the work of all his employees. A drive-in collection window should be provided where possible. A vault for safekeeping of records should be provided unless one is provided nearby in the city clerk's office.

**Police Department**

The police department is singled out for discussion because of the special facilities it needs other than regular office space. As noted, the police department is frequently not included in the city hall. When it is, however, it should be basically separate from other city hall activities, and public and criminal activities should be separated.

The extent of facilities will depend largely on the size of the community and the size of the department. In planning police station facilities, several basic needs should be considered by all cities. Jail cells should be away from public areas. Prisoner retention for any period requires toilets, kitchen facilities, and separation of men and women prisoners. Because of the expense of cellblocks, the possibility of using county jail facilities should be investigated. Many communities contract with the county for prisoner care. This may be impractical for very large cities, but cities up to 100,000 certainly can effectively use this method of reducing police station cost. If county facilities are used, it is then necessary only to provide a retention room or rooms with toilet facilities. Such rooms do not need to be regular cells.

The communications center should be isolated from the general public and other work areas. However, in smaller communities where it is necessary for communications personnel to act as receptionists, this is not possible. In such a case the communications section might be located in a glass enclosure with a sliding panel.

Fingerprinting, photographic, identification, and booking areas should be located together, although not necessarily in the same room. Where possible, a separate prisoner entrance leading directly into the area for booking should be provided. The essential element is to provide a continuous process of booking, fingerprinting, photographing, and identifying of prisoners in the same area of the building. Where possible, it is desirable to have the area near the jail or retention area.

Provide plenty of space for storage. Firearms and other equipment should be stored in locked cabinets. Room for confiscated, lost, and abandoned articles is necessary.

When patrol officers change shifts on beats it is not necessary to have a large assembly room, but it is desirable to provide space for officers to fill out reports. In large departments, the detective force will need a separate room with lineup facilities.

In the very large departments separate rooms for interrogating prisoners are necessary. In the medium-sized department, the detective squad room can be used for interrogation. A separate room for the use of prisoners and their attorneys or visitors is important when the station has facilities for housing prisoners. Finally, a large city should have a courtroom near the jail or detention facilities of the police department.

The police department facilities of the Raleigh city hall are well planned (Figs. 9a to 9c). Separation is achieved by having the police department on ground level except for the detective bureau. The detective bureau is reached by a stairwell located so that the general public would not have use for it. Notice that the traffic violations division is on the second level right across from the city clerk and treasurer's office. This places money collecting in one area and very convenient to the public. The municipal court is off the lobby on the ground level and next to the male and female lockups.

**Design of City Hall**

The city hall is essentially an office building, not a monument or an ornament. The building should be designed so as to be economical in construction and maintenance. *True long-range economy is achieved by a judicious balance between original cost and maintenance cost.* A building with cheap materials and equipment for the sake of initial low cost may become quite expensive in maintenance and replacement.

Even though the city hall should be basically functional and not a monument, originality in design is not precluded.

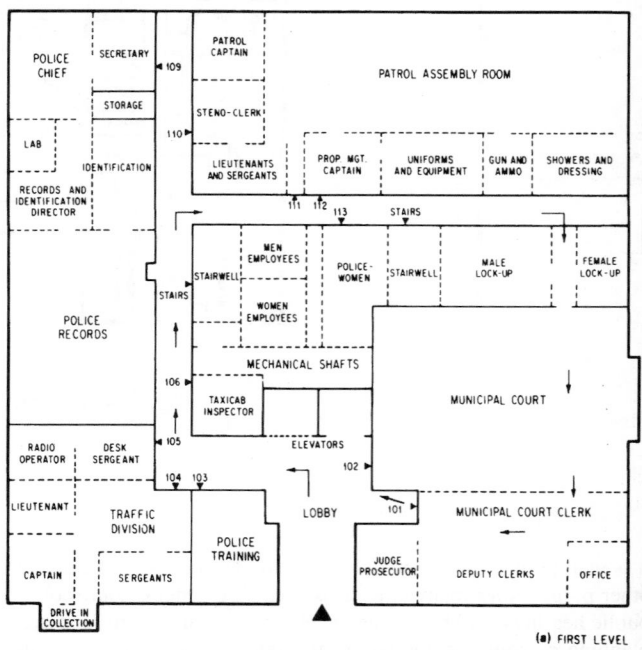

**Fig. 9. Raleigh, North Carolina, City Hall**

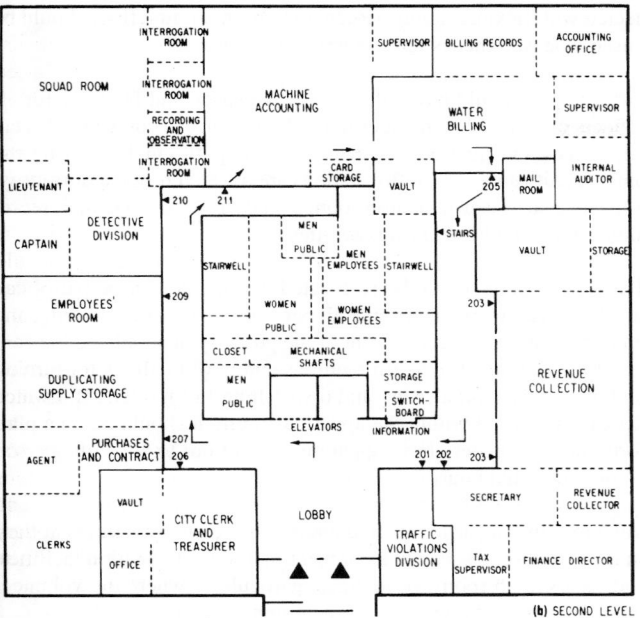

**(b)** SECOND LEVEL

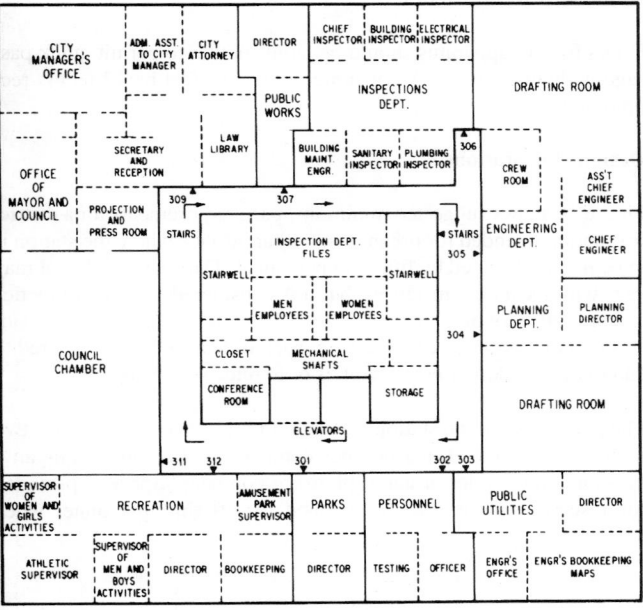

**(c)** THIRD LEVEL

**Fig. 9. (cont.) Raleigh, North Carolina, City Hall**

## FIRE STATIONS

### Fire Department Stations and Buildings

Fire department buildings include administrative offices; "stations," "houses," or "halls" housing the apparatus and equipment; fire alarm

*Authors:* George H. Tryon and Gordon P. McKinnon
*Reviewer:* Schoenhardt Architects, Inc.
*Credits: Fire Protection Handbook,* National Fire Protection Association-International, Boston, Massachusetts.

and communications centers; fire training facilities; and maintenance and supply facilities, including shops and storerooms. In some relatively small fire departments, all or several of these functions, insofar as provided, may be housed in one facility.

### Administrative Offices

The administrative offices may be housed in a municipal office building or city hall, or at a headquarters or central fire station. Headquarters may include offices and facilities for the chief of department, the fire prevention division, the planning and research staff, the budget or fiscal bureau, the personnel department, the fire investigation bureau, and the medical officer. The exact facilities needed will vary with the organization of the individual department. It is desirable to arrange the headquarters offices so that the general public will not have to pass through the apparatus room or fire fighters' quarters to reach the offices.

### Fire Stations

There are two types of fire houses: one is operated by a paid fire department, the other by volunteers. Equipment for both is essentially the same. Differences occur in facilities provided for personnel.

Practice is to group companies and apparatus needed to protect a given neighborhood in order to provide better teamwork and administrative control. Most fire stations house at least one pumper company, with its assigned first line and reserve apparatus, and other companies, including aerial ladder, aerial platform, squad, rescue, salvage, and various auxiliary types of apparatus. Ample space is needed for reserve apparatus, both to provide a replacement when needed and as equipment for use by off-duty personnel recalled in an emergency.

Far too many fire stations have outgrown their usefulness because inadequate consideration was given to the future needs of the district. The cost of providing adequate apparatus storage space is relatively modest when compared with the total cost of a fire station facility. A desirable policy is to provide an apparatus room large enough to house at least six major fire department vehicles. Even where it is intended initially to house a single first line piece of apparatus, a prudent minimum would be a two-track station capable of housing two first line and two reserve or special-duty pieces. Space should also be provided for additional men, who will be needed when further apparatus is obtained.

Elements of firehouse design are shown in Fig. 10. All facilities indicated are desirable but not mandatory. In paid departments, one company generally consists of 14 people; in a volunteer department, quarters are provided for paid drivers only.

#### Apparatus Rooms

It is preferable that the apparatus floor be unobstructed by columns. Future use of the space should not be circumscribed by having major rooms protrude into the apparatus storage area. For multi-track stations, a minimum width of 20 feet per track is recommended. This should be increased to at least 24 feet for a single-track station. A suggested desirable unobstructed depth is 80 feet, with ceiling height of 14 feet (minimum).

Ample space is needed to permit work around the apparatus, changing of hose, putting on fire clothing when responding, and to permit

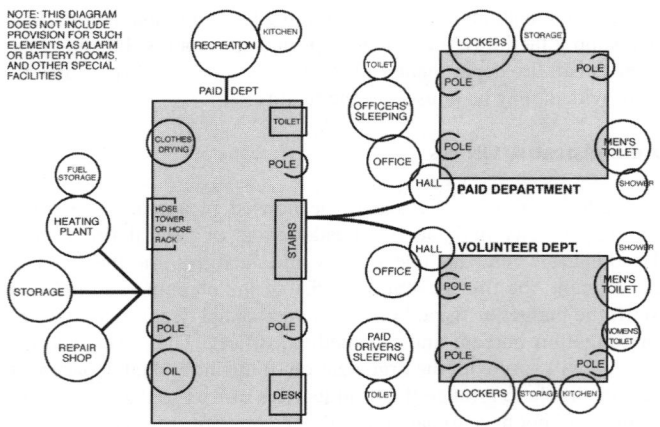

**Fig. 10. Elements of a firehouse**

free movement of personnel when answering alarms. Space is needed along walls for clothing racks, slop sinks, battery chargers, water tank fill connections, etc. Space should be provided for hose storage racks without obstructing access to apparatus. Table 1 gives sizes of apparatus.

Floor should be of concrete, designed to carry a load of 125 pounds per square feet.

Wall surfaces should be of an easily cleaned material, and floor should have sufficient drains to permit flushing with hose. Hot and cold water connections are needed at center of side walls.

If apparatus room is to be used for repairs, provide a repair pit. Also, carbon monoxide gases have to be exhausted to outside, usually by means of under-floor piping to which motor exhaust may be con-

nected with flexible tubing. (Recreation room on first floor should be raised at least 6 inches for protection against gas.)

Fire stations should have adequate office space and facilities for all officers on duty. This includes not only the various company officers but offices and quarters for district and deputy chiefs. Among the other facilities needed in fire stations are a watch room, a dormitory, a locker and washroom, storerooms, study rooms, a kitchen, recreation room, and hose drying facilities.

The watch room should be so located that the person on patrol can see the apparatus floor, observe all persons entering the building, and preferably see the street in front of the property. It should be the center of the station's fire alarm facilities and have facilities for turning on house lights and alerting and dispatching fire fighters. If a watch desk is to be used within the apparatus room, it should be on a platform raised 6 inches above apparatus room floor to allow the person on duty to remain during cleaning.

Volunteer fire departments frequently require other facilities at their stations including social halls or meeting rooms, recreation facilities, and ladies' club rooms or lounges, particularly where the volunteer fire company's quarters serve as a community center.

**Apparatus Room Doors**

Doors for fire apparatus should be large enough to permit quick passage without accident. An opening at least 12 feet by 12 feet is recommended.

**Designs for Stations**

Figure 11 shows suggested minimum space requirements for a district fire station intended for urban or suburban service where the station is to be mainly manned by full-paid personnel. The shape of the lot may vary with local circumstances, but it is considered very poor practice to start with a lot of inadequate size. A larger lot tends to have considerably more reuse or resale value at such time as it may be desired to add to the fire department facilities or to relocate the station.

The plan for an urban station shown in Fig. 11 provides space for two pumper companies (or a pumper company and a squad company) plus an aerial ladder or aerial platform company. Space is provided for reserve apparatus to be manned by off-shift personnel when

## Table 1 Fire apparatus sizes

| | |
|---|---|
| Village-size pumping enigne, 500 g.p.m. | |
| Length Overall | 24′–0″ |
| Width Overall | 7′–6″ |
| Height Overall | 6′–5″ |
| | |
| Triple combination pumping engine, 750 g.p.m. (most used) | |
| Length Overall | 28′–0″ |
| Width Overall | 8′–0″ |
| Height Overall | 6′–11″ |
| | |
| Hook-and-ladder truck (removed hand-raised ladders) | |
| Length Overall | 41′–3″ |
| Width Overall | 8′–0″ |
| Height Overall | 7′–3″ |
| | |
| Hook-and-ladder aerial truck (4-wheel type) | |
| Length Overall | 58′–9″ |
| Width Overall | 8′–0″ |
| Height Overall | 8′–7″ |
| | |
| Hook-and-ladder aerial truck (tractor-drawn type, 6-wheel) | |
| Length Overall | 63′–60″ |
| Width Overall | 8′–0″ |
| Height Overall | 8′–7″ |
| Clearance Required | 12′–0″ |

Note: Turning radius varies from 26 to 48 feet according to type and make. "Cab-over-engine" type of apparatus is slightly shorter overall.

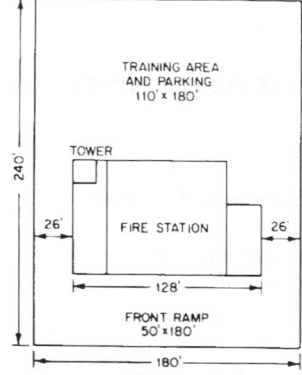

**Fig. 11. Plot plan for a typical district fire station for urban and suburban services. Minimum recommended plot size is 43,200 square feet.**

eeded. If desired, two-piece engine or truck companies can be oper-
ted out of such a station. Separate quarters with a garage are pro-
ided for the district fire chief so that he or she can come and go
without opening up or lighting the main station and so that major
apparatus can be taken out without moving the chief's car.

Unless required by the terrain or grade, a basement is not recommended under the main apparatus room as this tends to add materially to the cost. However, where the terrain makes a basement
necessary, the main apparatus room may be reduced in size and a
garage for reserve apparatus provided on the lower level. A basement
may be desirable under the living quarters to provide room for heating equipment, storage, and other facilities.

The apparatus area should be of modern garage-type construction. It is
good practice to provide automatic sprinklers for a fire department station. This has training value as well as providing fire protection for a
type of garage occupancy which has a rather poor fire record. The heat
for the garage area (where required) may be controlled by a separate
thermostat from the company quarters. Where a hose drying tower is
provided (see NFPA No. 198) it may also be equipped as a drill tower.

For a rural fire station manned chiefly by call or volunteer firefight-
rs (Fig. 12), space should be provided initially for not less than four
pieces of major apparatus including a pumper, water tanker, booster
squad or forest fire truck, and a reserve pumper or second tanker.
Often a rescue truck or ambulance also must be housed. Far too many
rural fire departments have quickly outgrown their stations and have
been forced to leave part of their apparatus outside or in a private
garage where it is not readily available for use or under close fire
department supervision.

Adequate meeting room space is needed, with proper exit facilities.
The station should be located on a plot large enough to permit doubling the apparatus room when the department grows and to provide
future office space and quarters for paid apparatus drivers who may
be subsequently employed.

It is bad practice to crowd three pieces of apparatus abreast in space
designed for two trucks; this slows response and makes it difficult to
properly service apparatus.

In Figs. 13 and 14 apparatus doors are shown at the front and rear of
the stations. These are desirable so that the apparatus in the second
line can leave the building in event of mechanical failure of a first-
line piece. In some cases, where the lot has a long road frontage, it
may be desirable to provide more apparatus doors facing the road and
to reduce the depth of the building to about 50 feet (Figs. 15 to 17).
However, care should be taken to allow ample depth for major apparatus which may be purchased, such as large "nurse tankers" or apparatus with long ladders or an aerial platform. Normally, fire stations
are expected to give 50 to 60 years of service, and what starts as a
purely rural district fire station often has major properties to protect
as business and industry move into the area. This may require facilities to house additional major apparatus and manpower.

**Parking Facilities**

Parking areas for firefighters' cars should not be overlooked. The station should have a parking area large enough to provide off-street parking for each firefighter on duty or scheduled to respond to fires. Where
call or volunteer firefighters are to respond to the station, ample parking space should be provided adjacent to the front of the station. With
paid departments, parking should be at the sides or rear. Additional
yard space should be provided for company drill work. Figures 11 and
12 show plot plans for urban and rural stations respectively.

The apron or ramp in front of the station should be large enough to
permit washing of apparatus and safe entry of vehicles into traffic.

**Fire Alarm and Communications Buildings**

The communications building or fire alarm office should be of fire-
resistive construction and isolated from all hazards that might interfere with the prompt transmission of alarms. Where the fire alarm
office is part of a fire station or administration building, it should be
isolated from the rest of the structure and protected against all hazards both internal and external. Ample emergency power should be
provided so that the station and communications equipment can continue to operate should outside power fail.

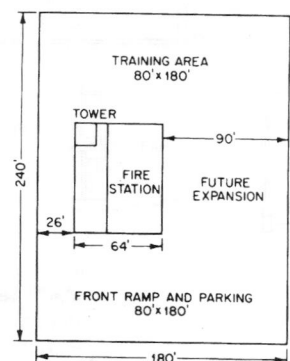

**Fig. 12. Plot plan for a typical rural fire station. Minimum recommended plot size is 43,200 square feet**

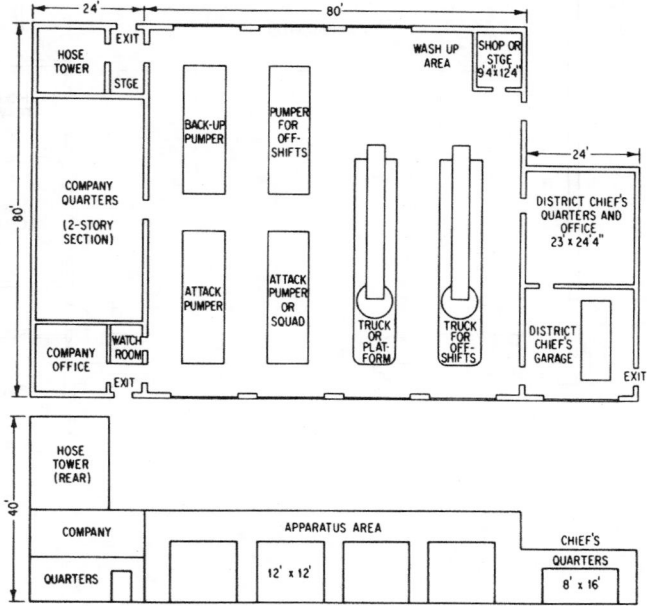

**Fig. 13. Elevation and plan view of a typical urban fire station**

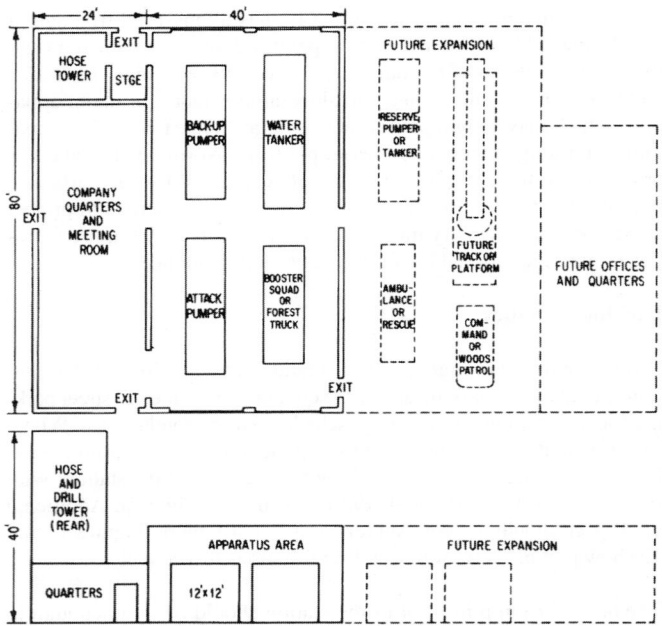

**Fig. 14. Elevation and plan view of a typical rural fire station**

The communications office includes the operating room where all alarms are received and transmitted to the department. It also should have the communications room for the department, the radio control console, fire alarm circuit panels, and test equipment. Frequently, a central console is provided containing all communications controls and information needed by the dispatchers. There should be an office for the fire alarm superintendent, drafting room for plans, battery room, storerooms for fire alarm supplies, garage for fire alarm vehicles, and facilities for fire alarm personnel.

### Fire Training Facilities

Facilities needed for the fire department training program include study rooms and library facilities in each fire station. A fire training center should include adequate classrooms and training aids. The better training centers have an apparatus room where major apparatus can be brought indoors for instruction purposes, and the operation of various items of fire protection equipment (hydrants, fire alarm, and automatic sprinklers) can be demonstrated. Other desirable features include an auditorium where various fire protection conferences and training meetings can be held, facilities for preparation and reproduction of training manuals and bulletins, and a fire protection library.

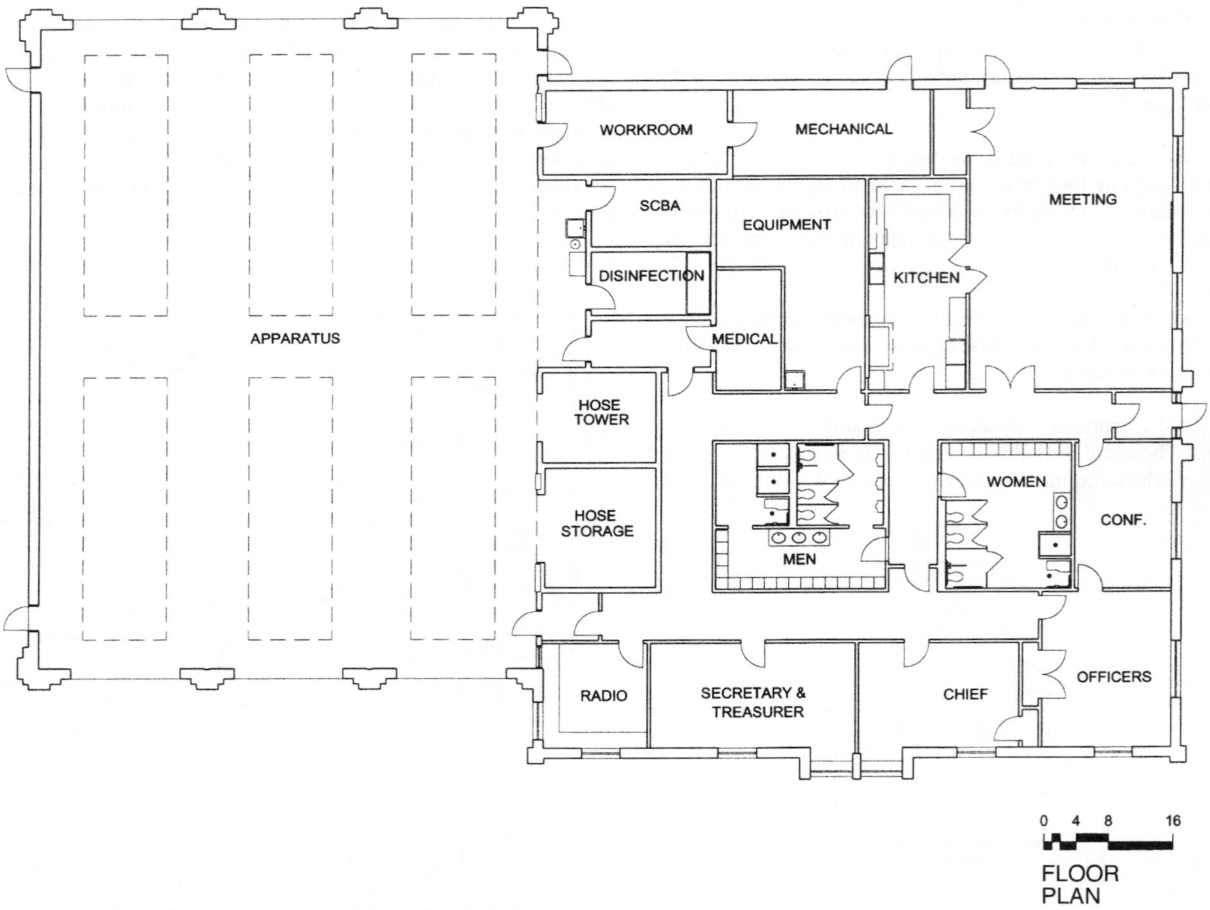

**Fig. 15. Plan of 12,108-square-foot Essex, Connecticut, fire station designed for a volunteer department, including a multipurpose room to be used for training, meeting, and as a community emergency shelter (Schoenhardt Architects, Inc.**

**Fig. 16. Front elevation, Essex, Connecticut, fire station (Schoenhardt Architects, Inc.)**

Outdoor training facilities should include large grounds with various structures for demonstrations and practice fires, a drill tower for hose and ladder evolutions, tanks for practice on flammable liquids fires, electrical and gas utility installations for fire training purposes, hydrants and pumper suction facilities, and other equipment duplicating situations that may be encountered at fires. When an individual fire department is too small to provide all the necessary training facilities, the practice is to supplement the local training program by use of regional or state fire schools which do provide more adequate facilities and curricula.

**Maintenance Facilities and Shops**

Facilities for maintenance and repair work on fire apparatus should be provided. A repair shop includes an area where major apparatus, including ladder trucks, can be serviced and repaired.

**Fig. 17. Essex, Connecticut, fire station (Schoenhardt Architects, Inc.)**

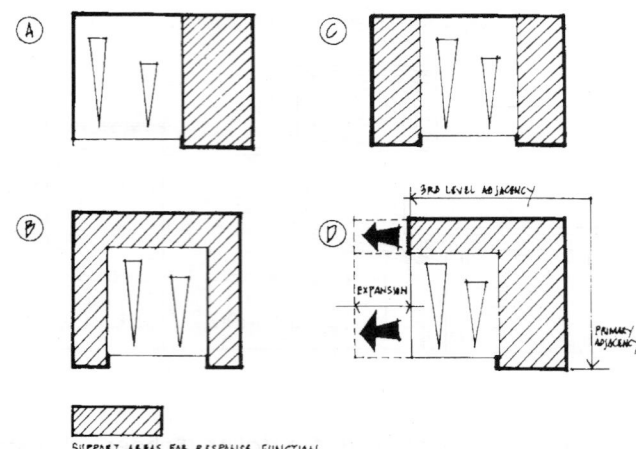

**Fig. 1. Floor plans show the various planning concepts of a fire station and the various adjacencies in the individual floor plans, as they relate to fire fighting response action and turnout time**

# FIRE STATIONS

### FIREHOUSE PLANNING

Firehouse planning and design has become increasingly sophisticated and complex. Years of study and experience have made it apparent that by planning a firehouse properly, a safer and quicker turnout can be made. This is accomplished primarily by arranging traffic flow patterns within the firehouse to be as direct as possible. The integration of the "primary adjacency" concept for planning the firehouse will deduct considerably from the turnout time by "grouping" the firefighting personnel in the "highest activity" areas of the firehouse. Turnout time along with dispatching time and travel time are three of the key elements in the successful containment of fire which is one of the primary goals of a firefighting unit.

The improvements in firehouse planning have created a total upgrading of human comforts with great emphasis on physical fitness. These include well-planned kitchens, air conditioning, better lighting, well-planned toilet-shower facilities and dormitory spaces, acoustical improvements, safety features in building planning and the integration of a small gymnasium-like area, for physical fitness purposes in firefighting needs, into the firehouse plan.

### Concept Planning for the Firehouse and Plan Types

Turnout time is the key element in firehouse planning. When planning the firehouse the most important feature is to group various functional spaces in a primary adjacency pattern so that movements to exit from the firehouse are minimized. Dispatching, travel, and turnout time are the key elements in the successful containment of the fire.

The one-story firehouse has a series of plan types which can be categorized in the following manner (see Fig. 1):

### One-Way Straddle of the Apparatus Area

All of the support functions for this plan type (Fig. 1a) are located to the left or right of the apparatus area. This plan type is the least desirable in that the plan has the longest travel distances to reach the apparatus area and therefore adds to the turnout time of the fire company. This plan type by its nature creates a circulation pattern which can be eliminated in other plan types. Other plan types have supporting areas responding directly onto the apparatus area.

### Two-Way, U Wraparound of Apparatus Area

This plan type (Fig. 1b) is the most desirable for purposes of minimizing the turnout time in firehouse planning. Using the same gross area for the standard two-company unit, it places all areas at the shortest possible distance from the responding apparatus. Another key element in this type of planning concept is that it separates the noisy areas of the firehouse from the quiet areas by the natural separation of the apparatus area.

### Two-Way Straddle of the Apparatus Area

This plan type (Fig. 1c) is the second most desirable for purposes of minimizing the turnout time in firehouse planning. The plan clearly separates the noisy areas of the firehouse from the quiet areas and may create circulation patterns in the support areas by not taking advantage of the back of the firehouse for support area use. This plan type is the same for the two-story firehouse with the quiet volume stacked over the apparatus area (see Figs. 2 and 3).

### L-Wraparound of the Apparatus Area

This plan type (Fig. 1d) is unique in that the location of the L-arrangement allows for the natural progression in locating the primary

*Author:* Emmanuel Mesagna AIA NCARB, Registered Architect Principal, Fire Service Buildings Design Consultant, Syosset, New York and formerly Chief Architect, Fire Department of the City of New York.
*Reviewer:* Schoenhardt Architects, Inc.

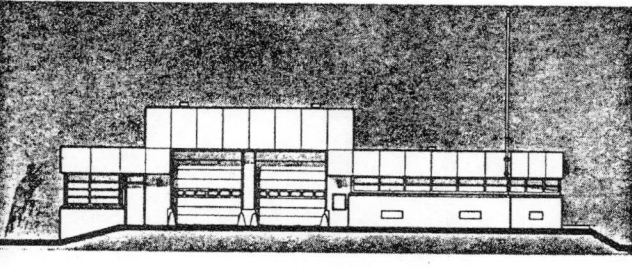

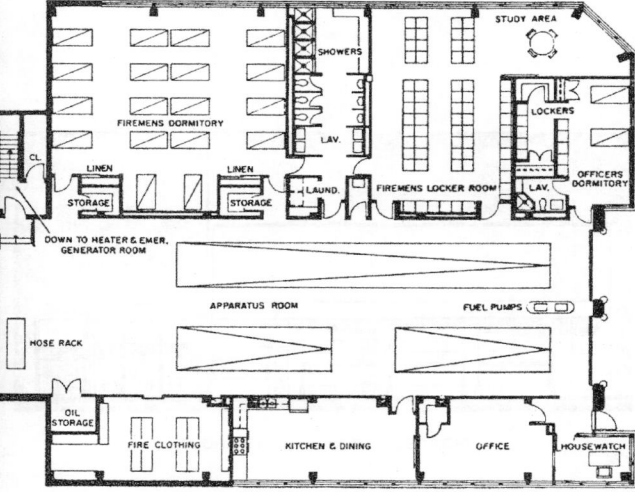

**ig. 2. Typical plan and elevation of a one-story firehouse.**
**ront elevation and floor plan of one-story firehouse, which**
**eatures "active" and "quiet" sections divided by the**
**apparatus floor, a good example of the two-way straddle**
**of the apparatus area**

djacency areas through the third-level adjacency areas as the L wraps round the apparatus area from the leg of the L to the toe. The key urnout spaces are placed in normal sequence by virtue of its form. One of the advantages of this plan type is the flexibility for expansion ilong the apparatus area and the toe of the L. This plan type is the hird most desirable with the advantage of potential for expansion.

## Adjacency Relationships for Space Planning of a Firehouse

The key concept in planning a firehouse for the shortest turnout time possible is the development of an adjacency planning concept. The main purpose of this concept is an in-depth study of spaces in a firehouse which require an "adjacency rating" for purposes of functional planning of the firehouse to verify where the greatest amounts of activity occur. These "activity locations" will then be joined in such a manner that a minimum amount of grouping time is required for the firefighting personnel to respond to the fire. This grouping time is extremely valuable to the response action. At this time the company officers develop a response strategy for the shortest route to the fire ocation and the problems of the fire condition.

### Primary Adjacency

Spaces in this category must be directly connected in a physical manner to each other or directly to the apparatus area which is the key urnout location in the response action.

### Secondary Adjacency

Spaces in this category must be placed at a midway location in the firehouse plan because of the dependency of function during day-to-day operations that are not of primary importance.

### Third-Level Adjacency

Spaces in this category are the least used in a firehouse and have no direct day-to-day operational relationship to the primary and secondary adjacency spaces.

### Primary Adjacency Spaces

Dispatcher-housewatch area, lobby area
Administrative-company offices
Kitchen/recreation area/gym area/training area
Lounge area
Classroom facility with accommodations for television, video-
tape teaching
Basic toilet area (close to high-use areas)
Dormitory areas
Turnout gear storage (can be third-level adjacency according to
response action strategy)

### Secondary Adjacency Spaces

General shop, storage, repair area
Cleanup areas
Hose storage/drying area

### Third-Level Adjacency Spaces

Apparatus parts storage
Boiler plant, utilities, and emergency generator area
Locker room area
Miscellaneous storage areas
Major toilet-shower area, clothes washing and drying area
Administrative area—not related to the response action
Conference/public areas
Any other function not directly related to the response action

*Note:* Adjacency levels must be ascertained through in-depth interviews with fire department administrators and may change accordingly.

### Space-Planning Analysis

Prior to site selection it is essential that an architect/space-planning analyst be retained for purposes of ascertaining the gross area requirements for the firehouse. A space-planning analyst's main responsibility is to arrive at the most efficient total gross space required for the building. High building costs have necessitated the use of a space-planning analyst to obtain the least gross area for the building function with maximum efficiency.

The space-planning analyst will make in-depth studies of equipment, personnel, utility needs, and circulation and arrive at the optimum gross area requirements for the building. Prior to planning a firehouse, it is essential that all equipment and personnel needs are clearly delineated in numbers and size so that proper circulation allowances can be made for the proper functioning of the firehouse; these in turn will give the gross area requirements. As part of the study by the space-planning analyst many options will be offered

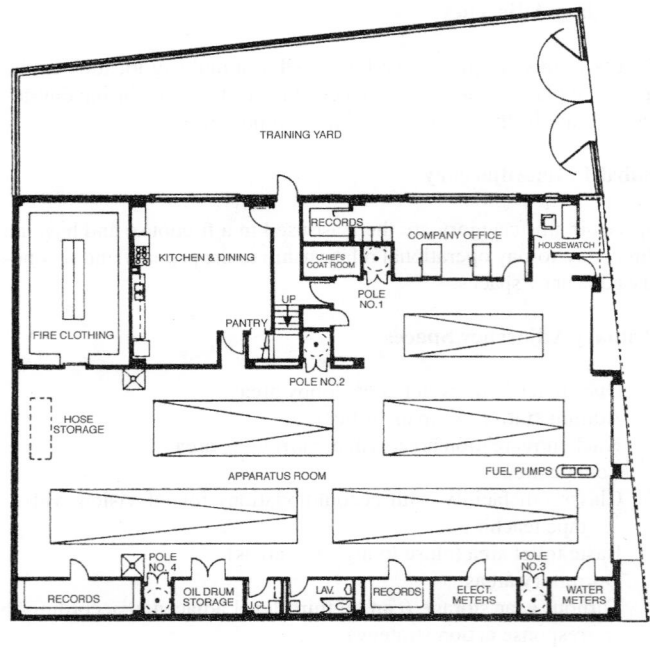

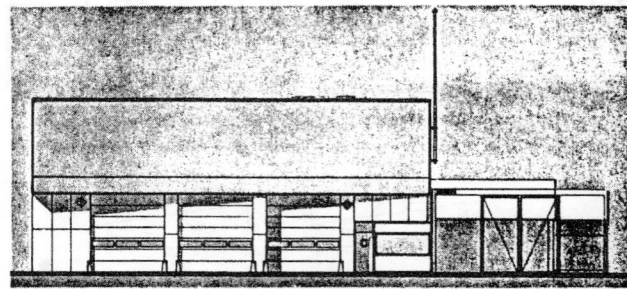

FRONT ELEVATION OF THE FIREHOUSE

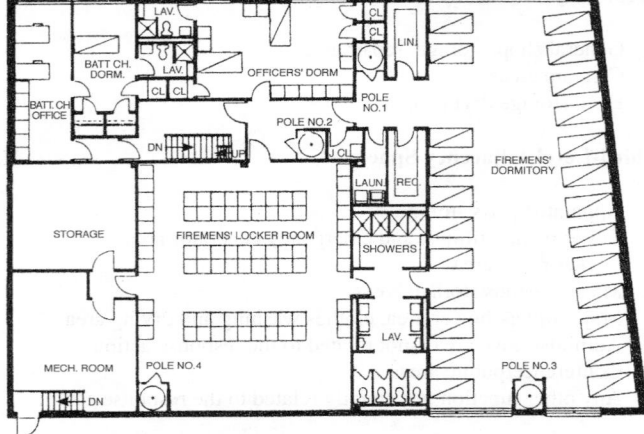

SECOND-STORY PLAN OF THE TWO-STORY FIREHOUSE

**Fig. 3. Typical plans and elevation of a two-story firehouse, a good example of a two-way straddle of the apparatus area with the "quiet" section stacked over the apparatus area**

which will examine the level of maximizing or minimizing the space needs and the ultimate advantage and disadvantage of each as they relate to the function of the building.

**Building and Site Relationship**

Three of the major considerations related to the building and site relationship are the building setback, training area requirements, and the on-site parking requirement for firefighting personnel. The minimum setback is 30 feet and should ideally be standard at 65 feet to accommodate the largest piece of apparatus in the fire service. This will give optimum visibility for apparatus exiting from the firehouse (Fig. 4). The apron area shall have the smallest possible slope to drain water and may include a hot-water underground piping system or electrical cable de-icing system to clear the apron for response purposes. All building sites require an open area to one side of the

firehouse for purposes of training with the largest piece of apparatus available to the firefighting unit. A parking area to accommodate all personnel on duty at any one time is absolutely necessary, plus a minimum of 50 percent more as extra space for administrative personnel. Beyond this point the parking requirement is a subjective judgment which may include parking spaces for public and social functions. The parking area is to be located adjacent to the dispatcher-housewatch area with visual control of the activity in the parking area.

The main arterial street shall be wide enough to accommodate the apparatus with the largest turning radius. It is also essential that traffic controls be installed on extreme ends of the front property line to stop traffic during a response action.

As a secondary consideration, any responding of apparatus directly into the low sun orientations shall be eliminated to do away with the

Fig. 4. Fire station, Essex, Connecticut (Schoenhardt Architects, Inc.)

vision problem of the quick transition from basic darkness to brightness and the ensuing accident potential by orienting the building properly.

Wherever possible additional land should be allocated to the site footage for purposes of integrating the drive-through apparatus area arrangement in the floor plan. This method of returning from the response action creates less disruption in the street and potential for accident during the backing up of apparatus.

## VARIOUS SPACE COMPONENTS IN FIREHOUSE PLANNING

### Dispatcher-Housewatch Area

This key communications area is being formed as an independent operating space, completely sound-controlled for optimum hearing ability. It must be completely air conditioned and have maximum visual control of the quarters and street conditions. Glass areas in the front of the housewatch are arranged in such a manner, that 180 degrees of visibility in front of the firehouse is possible. The alarm lights button at the fire communications console is not limited to activating the alarm lights as in the post. The alarm button also activates the apparatus fume-exhaust system and a series of floodlights mounted on the front face of the building. These lights illuminate the apron area and street for a safer response. An adjustable timer turns off the floodlights and the fume-exhaust system after the overhead doors have been electrically secured shut. They can be activated manually through an override switch by the housewatchman in other than response situations.

### Control Functions of the Dispatcher-Housewatch Area

This key communication area is also the center of all electronic switching devices which control the security and functioning of the firehouse and include:

Gasoline and diesel pump operation

Manual operation of floodlights mounted on the front of the building

Security lights surrounding the problem areas of the building

Manual control of fume-exhaust system

Alarm lights for various parts of the building during response action

Daily-use light control

Control of overhead doors with up and stop buttons only for safety purposes; down button located at overhead door location only

A complete intercom system for immediate verbal communication to all areas of the firehouse plan

### Management Adjacency

The planned adjacency of the housewatch and the company offices affords excellent audible communication between the dispatcher-housewatch area and the company offices—the management arm of the firehouse. Both areas also face the apparatus storage area and have glass walls, allowing for visual control of the apparatus floor. This adjacency of space is ideal for all aspects of communication and decision making during initial turnout action.

### Apparatus Storage Area

This is the heart of every firehouse; its location, shape, flexibility, size, layout, and column-free approach will provide for easy, quick access from all areas in the four major concepts in planning a firehouse. These factors will provide the firefighting units with a good functional design for response purposes. The integration of the large areas such as the apparatus area and hose storage area into one large, open apparatus area and the elimination of the turnout gear storage from the apparatus area have allowed for "clear space" mobility. The single open space now offers greater flexibility in the apparatus storage area and may also function as an area for training and for storage of spare or down apparatus.

Apparatus storage areas must be equipped with fume-exhaust systems. The fume-exhaust system is activated from the alarm lights button located on the fire communications console unit. The fume-exhaust system shall have the capability of exhausting contaminated air at a rate between 12 to 15 air changes per hour or an average air change of the complete volume of the space every 4 to 5 minutes. It has been ascertained of OSHA and NIOSH that diesel fumes are carcinogenic and must be removed or diluted and the interior air diluted to 50 PPM or lower carbon monoxide, with total particulate and poly aromatic hydrocarbons level kept below 1 PPM. There is monitoring equipment available to insure that the apparatus bays comply with these levels.

A timer will automatically shut the system down after a set time lapse. Provisions have been made for the manual control of the fume-exhaust system when companies are not in a response action. A study of fume-exhaust pipe locations on the apparatus has allowed the placement of intake grilles at optimum locations for greatest intake pull. The goal is for the maximum elimination of fume-exhaust gases on the apparatus floor. Upon the return of the apparatus to quarters, a manual switch operation can be utilized and the fumes can be exhausted as long as required for the comfort of the personnel.

It is recommended that all apparatus areas utilize single apparatus doors approximately 12 feet wide by 12 feet high. Wide, single-opening apparatus doors are not recommended because of the possibility of having the door frozen closed due to a breakdown in the mechanized door operation. This situation will put the responding apparatus out of service and increase the response time of first-due apparatus. A pair of doors is more functional in that a breakdown in one door will allow the responding apparatus to maneuver through the other door. This will eliminate the turnout problem in case of an emergency breakdown of one of the mechanized overhead doors. It is essential to include a totalizer on all apparatus doors so that tension springs may be replaced on a preventive maintenance schedule based on predictive breakdown of the equipment. This standardization of door-opening size will simplify the storage of spare parts for repair purposes. All door operators, springs, track, turning shafts, and other accessory equipment of a single size will simplify the storage of parts while minimizing the inventory burden. It is recommended that all overhead doors be opened with electrical operators for purposes of decreasing the turnout time. Electrical operators shall have the capability of manual operation in case of breakdown of the motorized equipment. It is essential that the overhead-door-operating equipment be put on the emergency generator in case of electrical failure in the community.

Generally throughout the fire service, the hose tower is being eliminated as a functional need in the operation of a firehouse. With the use of sophisticated hose drying equipment and the use of polyester hose which does not require drying, the hose tower is being phased out in both new and existing firehouses.

### Turnout Gear Storage

A well-planned firehouse shall have facilities for storing helmets, coats, and boots with accommodation for washing and drying out, as well as a floor drain system. The turnout gear storage area shall be secured with a pull-down see-through mesh gate arrangement and locking device to secure the area while the company is out of quar-

ters. Included as part of the equipment for this area shall be an electric heater for drying and an exhaust fan to clear out the humidity in the area. The wall and ceiling finishes in this area are critical for maintenance and shall include maintenance-free finishes such as permanently glazed surfaces.

### Slide Pole and Enclosures

There is a movement in the fire service to generally eliminate the slide pole as a means of circulation from the second floor of a firehouse. Serious injuries have occurred in the use of slide poles. Their use is generally discouraged in favor of a stairway or the trend toward the one-story firehouse, wherever the land value permits, in all areas of the country. In some areas of the country, particularly in the urban areas, the air rights over firehouses have been sold to developers to offset the high land cost.

### Classroom—TV Amphitheater for Training Purposes

Training programs in the firehouse through the medium of closed-circuit television and videotape are more and more common. For this purpose space is required in order to create a positive environment for learning. The space will require complete acoustical treatment, theater-type viewing chairs, a sloped floor arrangement for viewing purposes, and a desk top writing surface. In terms of adjacency level, this space is classified as a primary adjacency and shall have direct access to the firefighting apparatus area.

### Kitchen—Dining Room—Recreation Area

The kitchen-dining room area is completely planned for reduction of maintenance and efficiency of operation. Each component shall be planned for the level of commercial use completely in stainless steel. Included also are a large refrigerator and a six-burner range (commercial type) with a grill unit and oven. This is a heavy-duty commercial range with a proven successful performance. Included is a stainless steel range hood with removable and washable stainless steel filters. The ceilings are of washable acoustical file and the floor and wall are finished in a ceramic or quarry tile, which has eliminated maintenance except for simple cleaning.

### Dormitory—Locker Room

New planning concepts have the dormitory and locker-room spaces straddling the toilet-shower and clothes-washing core areas. This provides sound isolation between the noisy locker room and quiet dormitory area. In cases where the dormitory area faces onto a traffic street it is best not to provide any windows on the dormitory walls facing the street. This type of planning will give maximum sound isolation and privacy for this quiet area of the firehouse.

### Chief's Quarters

A refinement of the planning of the chief's quarters has produced a unique privacy aspect and efficiency of response. The chief's car and turnout gear storage closet are located at the base of the egress stair or circulation corridor of the apparatus floor level, with the chief's office and dormitory having direct access to the response vehicle. In the typical two-story firehouse illustrated (Fig. 3), the chief's quarters are located at the head of the stairs at the second floor, and the chief goes directly into a suite of rooms from the egress stair. This eliminates many unnecessary steps by giving the responding chief direct access to the response vehicle. This will eliminate circulation

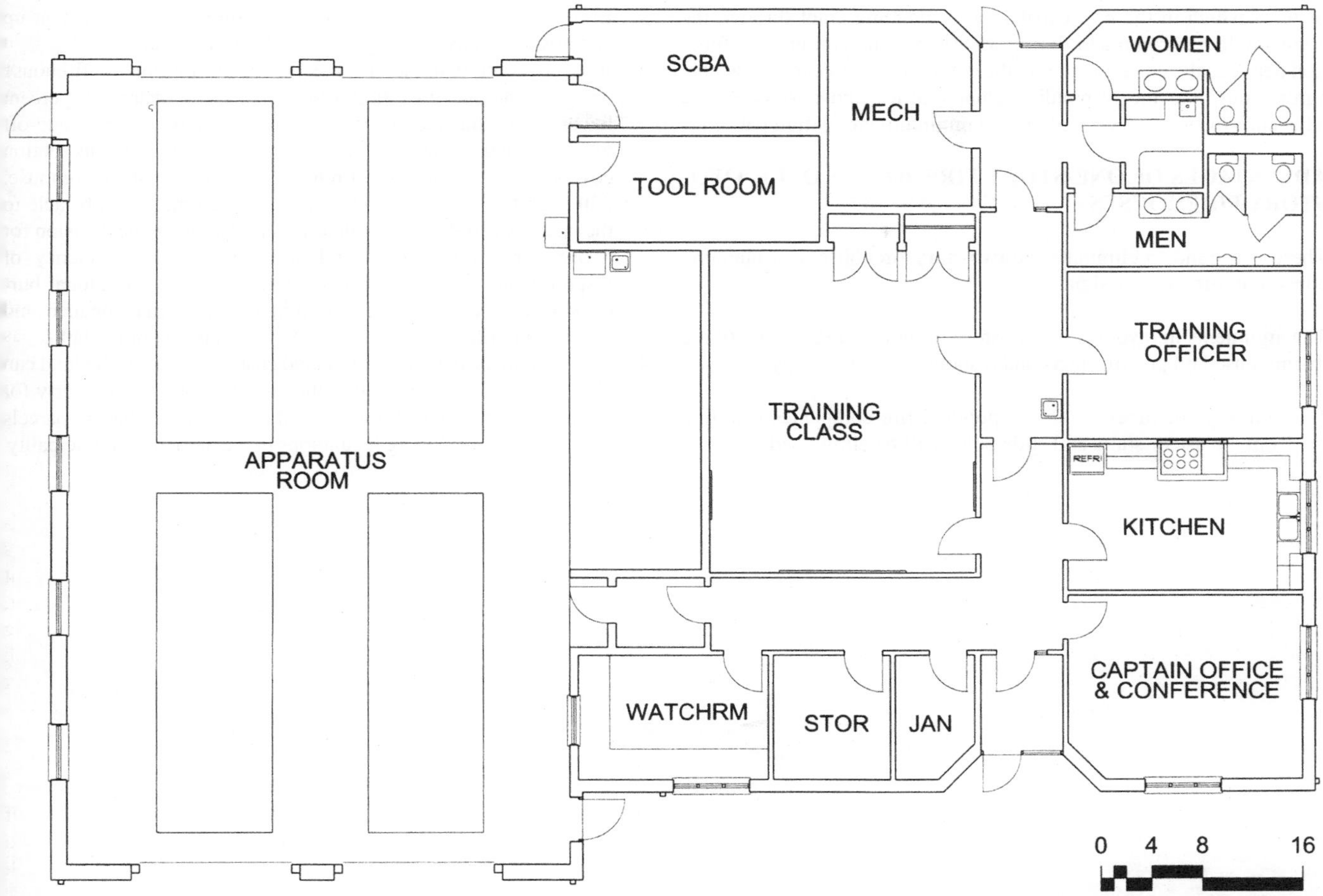

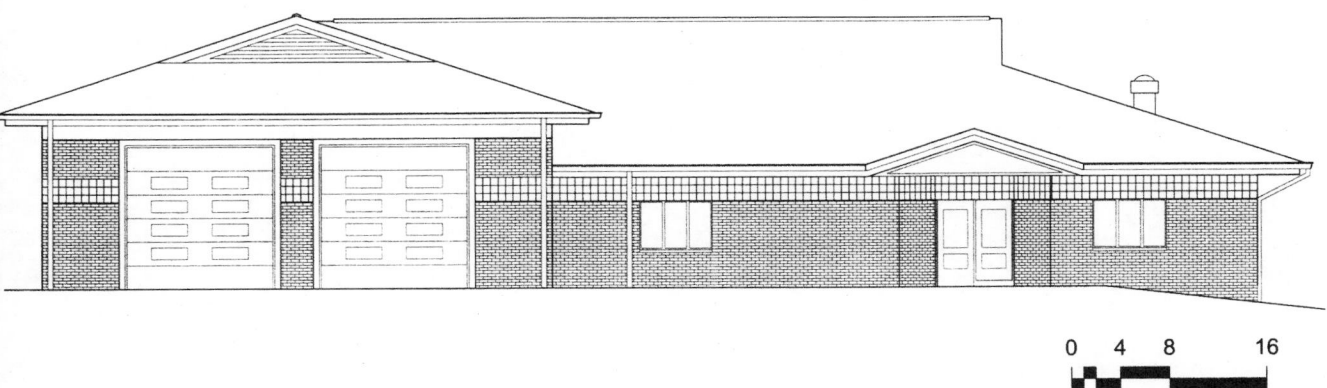

**Fig. 5.** Plan of two-bay 6,530-square-foot fire station, Weatogue, Connecticut, including training support facilities for Simsbury town-wide fire department (Schoenhardt Architects, Inc.)

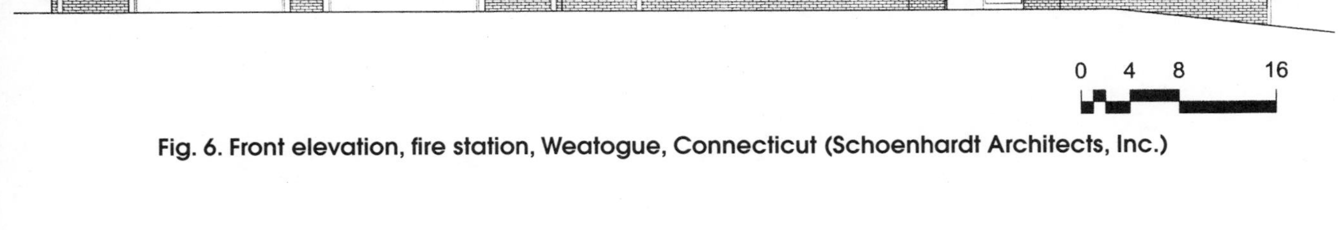

**Fig. 6.** Front elevation, fire station, Weatogue, Connecticut (Schoenhardt Architects, Inc.)

patterns which in the past carried the responding chief through the company locker room and dormitory. There is a continuity of function between the chief's car area, the chief's turnout gear storage, the egress stair, and the responding chief's office and dormitory; the adjacency of these spaces indicates a minimum circulation pattern.

## ADVANTAGES OF ONE-STORY FIREHOUSES OVER TWO-STORY FIREHOUSES

There is a trend to eliminate the two-story firehouse as a planning concept in firehouse design.

The arguments in favor of the one-story firehouse (Figs. 5 and 6) are mainly based on positive facts and response action strategy:

1. Injuries to members of the responding fire companies resulting from the use of stairs and slide poles will be eliminated.

2. Elimination of the physical exertion required in the constant up and down activity of a high activity firefighting unit.

3. It is apparent that the most economical solution to firehouse design is the one-story firehouse. It is approximately 10 percent lower in cost than the two-story firehouse and becomes a trade-off when evaluating low land cost and the difference in construction cost between the one-story firehouse and the two-story firehouse. Although the one-time land costs have been made an obstacle to the one-story firehouse, the determining factors in the decision for a one-story or two-story firehouse shall be the efficiency of response and the reduction of maintenance and operational burdens which are life/cycle determinants. This maintenance and operation burden will far exceed the original cost of the land.

4. As a secondary option for high land cost, the value of the land can always be recouped by selling the air rights over the property for future development or for additional floor area to adjacent parcels as allowed by the zoning regulations in the particular municipality.

**Fig. 1. Police Services Building, Branford, Connecticut**

# POLICE STATIONS

## PLANNING CONTEXT

Perhaps no item of police equipment or property has the potential for providing or denying optimal utilization of command and supportive services personnel in any greater degree than the police headquarters building itself (Fig. 1). In the early 1900s the automobile reduced the need for large numbers of officers to provide on-street police service or for emergency standby purposes, but no such dramatic invention has reduced the non-line personnel requirements of a police agency. Indeed, the complexities of staff and auxiliary services and the utilization of sophisticated automated data processing equipment and systems, the growth of planning and research activities, the increase in training requirements—all emphasize the need for sound planning of police facilities if both space and personnel are to be used effectively and economically.

When an old building is recognized as inadequate several alternative responses to the problem may be identified:

* Doing nothing about the building or its floor plan and employing additional personnel in numbers sufficient to overcome the operational handicaps of the existing facility;
* Reducing service to the public and to the line or field elements of the department whenever the physical and functional relationships of people and their work are such that they require more time and/or personnel than is presently available;
* Researching the departmental and public needs and redesigning and modifying those portions of the structure which present operational or administrative problems; or
* Designing and constructing a new facility.

Whenever a new building or a major restructuring of an old one is under consideration, the key decision to be made does not concern building design at all; it is analysis and appraisal of departmental programs and organization. All too often a building is designed to fit an antiquated, unrealistic agency structure. Thus a review of department organization should be made, accompanied by necessary changes, before a new building design or modification of an old one is attempted.

In some situations, the handicap of a poorly arranged building may be overcome by minimal reconstruction or relocation of offices and work areas, though this approach may not always be used to great advantage in cases where unusual problems exist. It is generally unwise, however, to attempt to redesign the police station in an existing structure. Experience has shown that such moves may eventually cost more than new construction, and the results are seldom satisfactory. The most economical approach, if viewed from a 20- to 40-year vantage point, probably will be in the design and construction of a new facility. This is true because the expenses of reconstruction are essentially a one-time cost, but the personnel costs of employees whose work performance is limited or wasted through poor building design continue year after year. Moreover, delaying new buildings when the need is apparent can be costly because of rising construction costs.

If only one unnecessary 24-hour per day position is saved or eliminated by such a move, the annual salary savings amounts to approximately five times the cost of one person's salary and fringe benefits. Unnecessary recurring personnel expenditures are a major consideration in building design. The luxury of poor working quarters is beyond the reach of most police departments in the United States. Given an already undermanned field force, the additional cost burden for personal services occasioned by poor building design is a major consideration. Fortunately, there is a developing awareness of the impact of poor design on police efficiency and costs for personal services.

## DESIGN OF A POLICE STATION

In designing modifications of an existing structure, or when a new police facility is designed, many factors should be considered. These involve functional relationships, economy of space, public convenience, security, etc.

### Functional Relationships

Offices and work areas of elements performing essentially the same tasks should be grouped so as to achieve maximum use of physical facilities, thereby avoiding duplication of equipment or furnishings. For example, the work of records and communication units are so interrelated and mutually supportive that space arrangements should

*Reviewer:* Schoenhardt Architects, Inc.
*Credits: Municipal Police Administration*, International City Management Association, Washington, D.C.

assure direct access from one to the other. Further, temporary reassignments of personnel could easily be made between the integrated elements as work loads vary between the two. Administrative line officers should be grouped closely. Booking, identification, and detention operations must be so related that time and travel distance are shortened to conserve personnel resources and to avoid security problems.

**Public Considerations**

Public access (Fig. 2) should not conflict with prisoner passageways or areas; this will avoid exposure of prisoners to the public and will eliminate the possibility of harm to either. The public, of course, must be restricted in its movement within designated areas of the building. Avoidance of prisoners' public contact eliminates the possibility of embarrassment, particularly to women and children, and criticism of the agency and its procedures. Also eliminated is the possibility of passing weapons to prisoners and escape efforts.

Public counters or business windows should be within reasonable distance of the building entrance to avoid public confusion and to limit the public's need to move about the police buildings. The public information and complaint desk should be adjacent to the communications or dispatch area. This is particularly important in the smaller departments. Equally important is provision of a single complaint counter or center; this avoids duplication of services or permits better administrative control and convenience. Public telephones for the use of attorneys, bonds persons, visitors, and the public should be located away from the main counter to avoid confusion and disruption of ongoing police services.

**General Design Considerations**

Building design should make possible the use of only one floor, or a section of one floor, during those hours when the administrative offices

**Fig. 2. Entrance, Police Services Building, Branford, Connecticut**

are closed. This concept has full applicability to both small and large agencies. Such design tends to keep operating costs low and improve general security. Whenever possible, walls for offices, rooms, and assembly areas should be of modular construction which permits expansion and flexibility of operation. Metal and glass partitions, and even file cabinet dividers should be used for functional allocation of space whenever privacy is not a major consideration; open space should predominate. Lighting, decor, and acoustical treatment should be planned carefully to increase comfort and efficiency of personnel.

Adequate parking facilities should be provided, including space for vehicles belonging to all agencies using the building, on-duty personnel, and clients and visitors, plus reasonable space for emergency needs. A distinction should be made between official and public needs. Location of parking space should provide for close access to the building by kinds of use.

**Communications, Records, and Evidence**

The communications operation, including computers, radio consoles, monitoring units, alarm systems, and telephones, should be housed in an air-conditioned, acoustically treated room. The room should be designed to assure privacy and security; only police personnel on duty in communications and records and certain other authorized personnel should have access to it. In addition, the communications center should be on a raised, paneled floor to allow for adequate conduits and wiring and to provide flexibility when rearrangement is necessary.

Design of the records facility should provide for utilization of under-the-counter files in appropriate locations. In addition, vertical shelf files should be used whenever practicable to reduce storage space; closed shelf files provide all the features of standard file cabinets but require less room. As suggested earlier, file cabinets of five or more drawers can be used effectively as space dividers which provide for a measure of privacy. Acoustical treatment, false floors, and air conditioning are essential in the design of space for electronic data processing equipment.

Provision for the safekeeping of evidence and recovered property should be made within the services offices and should be separate from those facilities used for prisoners' property.

**Detention and Related Facilities**

All prisoner facilities should be located near the services element to enable personnel to perform booking and turnkey duties whenever possible, thus minimizing the need for jail-keeping staff. Provisions should be established whereby prisoners may be held in separate security areas prior to being booked. This will prevent prisoners not yet booked from disposing of possible evidence in their possession or from passing dangerous weapons through cells to prisoners already in custody.

The outside entrance to the jail and detention facilities should open to a drive-in garage. Police vehicles should be able to drive into the interior of the police building, with the outer garage door opened and closed remotely from within the area, and still remain outside the main detention and booking area. A second door which separates the unloading area from passage to the jail, also electrically controlled from within, should be provided. Means of providing security for the transportation of prisoners or material witnesses to court from the detention areas should be planned carefully, and conflicts with routes of nonpolice traffic within the building avoided.

visitors' and attorneys' rooms must maintain all but audible and visual separation between prisoner and visitor.

A separate, secure storage area for prisoners' personal property should be provided within the booking area, preferably under a counter. It should contain enough cubicles to allow each to be numbered to correspond to the cells and bunks within each cell. For example, the first compartment logically would be 1-A, meaning Cell Number 1, Bunk A. It would contain property only if a prisoner were occupying that cell and bunk. This procedure would permit booking or detention personnel to immediately return property to a prisoner as he is released, avoiding unfortunate loss or destruction of property which has been mislaid or forgotten at the time of his release.

Closed-circuit television may be installed at various vantage points within the security areas for protection of police and detention personnel and for observation of prisoners, if direct observation of prisoners cannot be accomplished because of jail location or design without additional station personnel. A special cordless or cell phone should be provided for prisoner use and located in a secure and private area within the detention facility. A gun reception and storage area should also be provided near the jail entrance where police officers may turn in their weapons to the officer in charge before entering the detention areas.

## Provisions for Multiple Use

Often classrooms, assembly, and other rooms may be designed to form a complex of interrelated multipurpose areas, giving sufficient flexibility to allow use for roll call, training classes, police community relations meetings, public hearings, scout troop meetings, and other purposes. A little foresight in the design of this section of the building can save a considerable amount of wasted space that is used only sporadically. Coupled with careful planning of class or meeting schedules, the same space can often be used for almost the entire day.

## Service Facilities

It is important to the progressive police administrator that staffing requirements of the department's administrative and service elements be kept at the lowest level, consistent with continued high-quality service to other elements within the department and to the public. This is possible only when the design and physical layout of the police facility are responsive to this need.

Important in the design of any building is the location of the records and identification files and the communications center. These are intimately related in function and purpose. If possible, the communications center and the records office should be located back-to-back, with facilities provided to allow for the direct exchange of information during those hours when clerks are on duty in the records office. In those departments where records clerks normally are not on duty around the clock, direct access to current records must be provided for the communications personnel; otherwise the lack of immediate availability of previously gathered information will handicap field forces.

The property room should also be located in or near the records center and close to the public information counter or desk. The communications center should be a room of sufficient size to provide an adequate number of dispatchers' positions, status boards, a supervisor's monitoring and backup position (perhaps only a desk initially, later to be replaced by a complete radio console), and communica-

tions equipment. The records staff should be trained so that its personnel can provide additional personnel in the communications center during periods of maximum dispatching need. Unless appropriate physical facilities are provided to allow mutual assistance, additional personnel must be assigned to the communications section to allow it to handle overloads as well.

Provisions for rest rooms, filing cabinets, and space for additional personnel during peak work periods should be provided near the communications center. It is axiomatic that the greater the distance to these areas, the greater the cost to the department.

### Administrative and Investigative Offices

The location of offices for the chief of police, division command offices, and the working offices and areas for criminal investigators, vice officers, youth officers, and administrative and staff support personnel, while not perhaps as critical as that of the records and communications center, has far-reaching operational and public relations implications.

Depending upon the size of the department, the chief of police and top-level command officers should have some freedom of movement and privacy. Some chiefs find it nearly impossible to function effectively while in their offices because of constant interruption by visitors who should normally be assisted by desk officers or other personnel. Frequently a visitor will demand to see the chief, rather than the proper officer or employee, simply because of inadequate provision for privacy. Too few persons see this as a design or office layout problem, insisting that "with proper control the interruptions will be kept at a minimum." The chief of a small or medium-sized department will soon find that a view into his or her office, with no one else in the room, indicates to many citizens that he or she should be available to talk to anyone. Therefore, certain offices should not be located immediately adjacent to the main public entrance unless some screening or physical separation is provided which allows privacy and freedom of movement to and from the offices.

For the same reasons, offices of the youth unit, the vice unit, and the intelligence unit should be located away from the normal public traffic flow areas. However, they should be relatively close to the police officers' entrance to the records area. Often the desired degree of isolation can be provided by rear entrances or alternate routes of exit. Informants, victims of potentially embarrassing crimes, parents of youths apprehended for offenses, and cooperating officers from other agencies generally do not wish to expose themselves to persons in the building for fear of recognition, injury, or other reasons. The feeling that the department is concerned with their privacy or their personal safety frequently assists investigators in persuading citizens to cooperate in investigations in which they would normally maintain silence. Further, the damage caused by the unexpected exposure of a witness, informant, criminal partner, or an otherwise unknown officer to a suspect who happened to be in the station for some other reason is often irreparable.

The layout of investigators' work areas should be kept simple and free of the honeycomb or cubbyhole design found in many stations. Private offices should be provided only for the commander of the unit in small and medium-sized departments and only for the top-level subordinate commanders in the larger agencies. Investigators should have individual lockers for clothing and equipment required for normal work, with nominal filing cabinet space for paperwork associated with current cases.

Good investigators can seldom justify a private desk and file cabinets, for most of their work will be in the field, in the preparation of reports, and in attendance at court, inquests, and hearings. Many agencies utilize a series of tables or desks for the investigators' use while reading records, taking notes, or dictating reports, thus minimizing the need for furniture and space. In such situations, a number of semiprivate interview areas are sometimes provided for questioning witnesses, informants, and other persons. However, responsibility for providing interview facilities for prisoners remains with the auxiliary services element so that prisoners need not be removed from within the security area. The same precautions apply for line-up or show-up rooms, and they should not be placed in the investigative office areas.

The offices of division commanders need not be removed from the general area of their subordinates' work areas, but patrol and traffic personnel assembly and roll-call rooms may be multipurpose facilities some distance from the division offices. Whenever possible, the highest ranking commanders' offices should be close to the chief's office and the conference room.

Other administrative offices such as those used by training personnel, planning, and internal affairs personnel also should be located in the same area so that the command staff will be close to these support units. These working areas also should be predominantly open space with a minimum of private offices or rooms. Modular wall dividers and desk or filing cabinet separators are sufficient to divide space among several major elements performing similar or related work.

**Vehicle Storage**

One major consideration involves the location, design, and use of the police garage. Generally speaking, no attempt should be made to combine the auto maintenance or storage garage with a prisoner unloading area except in smaller departments. The garage and prisoner entrance may use the some door, but there should be a secure "tunnel" or section set aside which would allow the vehicle carrying prisoners to be completely isolated inside the security area after the door is closed. Sufficient space must be allowed so that several prisoners may be taken from the prisoner van without endangering the officers involved. Preferably, this area should not be visible from within the remainder of the garage.

Vehicle storage facilities located inside the garage should provide enough space to house most vehicles not in use, especially in areas where the weather is severe. The garage entrance should not open directly onto a public street or a heavily used alley unless sufficient space is provided so that police vehicles need not be backed out into oncoming traffic. If also used for maintenance and repair of departmental vehicles, the garage should be provided with additional space for a small office, parts and storage, and the actual repair and maintenance area. If possible, the garage should not occupy prime first-floor space, especially in larger communities where the police building is situated in the congested downtown area.

**Firearms Facilities**

A final matter of building design involves the departments' firearms program. A department often will need an indoor as well as an outdoor target range, but careful planning minimizes the space required. If properly designed and constructed, the range may sometimes be combined with other training facilities, especially in smaller agencies where the shooting program does not require full-time use of the area.

## POLICE STATIONS

Police stations represent one of the necessary governmental functions requiring careful planning. One of the most serious administrative problems confronting most police forces is lack of adequate or proper space and facilities for a police headquarters and jail.

There are two main objectives to be considered in the construction of the police department building: first, the handling and processing of the prisoners; second, the service to the public. The arrangement should be such that prisoners may be handled within the police department itself, without allowing those prisoners to be in contact with the public generally.

## PLANS DEVELOPED FOR THIS SECTION

The plans shown (Figs. 4 to 6) represent the results of the field survey and study by the police chiefs' advisory committee and subcommittees. Particular attention was given to room sizes and the arrangement in the plan of these various spaces in relation to one another, so as to ensure safe flow of traffic within the building by the public and security control of the prisoners by the police force without unnecessary duplication of staff.

The ideas reflected are based on past experiences with similar police stations now in use, and the explanation which follows each plan directs attention to some of the important elements suggested for inclusion in new structures.

## SITE REQUIREMENTS

### General

Police stations should be planned as if they are to be in a separate location from other structures. If analysis of site locations for a police station permits other structures housing other city functions (such as city hall or fire station) to be erected on the same site without interfering with the proper discharge of functions, then one central site can be chosen.

The jail section of a building should be above the ground and set back far enough from the property line to prevent contact between prisoners and persons outside of the building. Jail quarters should be accessible to a loading space at, or within, the building for the transportation of prisoners. It should be located where the vehicular traffic is not too heavy.

Off-street parking (Fig. 3), space for expansion, light and air on all sides, and separate entrances must be provided whenever possible.

### Small Cities and Towns

It has been found in small, compactly built cities and towns that one location will serve all city departments under one roof. When the city or town area extends only a few blocks in any direction, access to arterial streets is readily possible. Such a central site, however, should be so laid out that it gives an opportunity for the public to

*Author:* Joshua H. Vogel, AIA
*Reviewer:* Schoenhardt Architects, Inc.
*Credits: Police Stations, Planning and Specifications*, Bureau of Governmental Research and Services, University of Washington, Seattle, Washington.

**Fig. 3. Off-street parking, Police Services Building, Branford, Connecticut**

enter the administration rooms from one street, the fire department from another side street, and the police department from a third side or from the rear.

In all these cases, the location in relationship to the various land uses, the street pattern, and size of the site itself makes it possible that this central site can have all the governmental units in one location and still meet all the site requirements of the individual functions separately.

## GENERAL DESIGN INFORMATION

### Horizontal Plan

A building with the least number of floors is more economical to supervise because less personnel is required to supervise it. While a building of several floors may cost less in construction and be a saving in site costs, the extra outlay for administrative personnel, year after year, will never cease; in time it may be far greater than the additional cost of the desirable horizontal plan.

### Construction Building Code

The building should be fire resistant, properly lighted, heated, and ventilated. The plans should be arranged to prevent smoke and hot gases, from cooking or heating units, from passing through the building at any time.

Fire safety devices such as standpipes, fire hose, extinguishers, and alarms should be amply provided.

If the building is of two stories or more, two or more enclosed stairways should be provided according to building regulations for fire hazards.

### Facilities

Windows adjacent to jail quarters should have steel bars or steel detention sash with screening devices and be inaccessible to prison-

ers. All parts of detention quarters should be separated from exterior walls by a mesh partition, parallel to outside walls and 3 feet inside them, to prevent passing of contraband, exhibitionism, and to give passage for supervising personnel.

A safe storage place should be provided for cash and valuable articles.

Firearms, weapons, and medicines should be stored in strong, securely locked cabinets inaccessible to prisoners; they should be kept in locations removed from jail quarters and corridors.

All fire hazards should be guarded against. Avoid exposed electrical installations, wood partitions, straw ticks, paper, rags, and other combustible materials. Fire hose in locked cabinets should be easily accessible for inspection, for jail personnel to have for drilling, and for use in event of fire or emergency.

Telephone and radio service should include equipment for fire calls and auxiliary fire alarm as well as provision for right-of-way calls, conference calls, watch calls from stations of duty, and supervisory calls.

The location of a detective division will depend upon the workload involved and the number of detectives employed. There should be a main detective office large enough to permit all detectives to get together for briefing and instructions. In addition, there should be small rooms located adjacent to the main detective office, which can be used for interrogation purposes. These need not be elaborate and require only a desk and two or three chairs.

In case a show-up room is desired, it should be located in such a manner as to permit the shuttling back and forth of prisoners from the confinement quarters to the show-up room without coming into contact with the public.

A visiting room should be provided so as to promote informal interviews under adequate supervision. This visitors' room can serve for visitors for the prisoners or as a conference room between an attorney and a prisoner. It should be so located that the prisoners' entrance is on the jail side and the visitors' and attorneys' entrance is from the public side. A separation between prisoners and visitors inside the room should be provided by at least a fine meshed double screening or heavy plate glass windows. Another type of separation is the use of a table at least 3 feet wide with a partition extending to the floor and the partition above the table running to the ceiling so that it is impossible to pass even the smallest item of contraband.

A separate interview room should be provided for the use of attorneys, probation officers, and social welfare workers. This same room, if properly located, can also serve as an examination room for the medical officer. For medical facilities, a locked steel cabinet for the medical equipment can be placed on the wall in one of the examination rooms.

When the jail averages more than 15 prisoners a day, a properly equipped kitchen has been found advisable. There should be a refrigerator room and locked storage closet. The kitchen should be equipped with a stove for top and oven cooking. If it is a two-story building, one kitchen only on the first floor is recommended and dumbwaiters may be used, with a pantry on the second floor. In cases where the food is brought from the outside and not cooked on the premises, the kitchen or pantry should at least have modern sterilizing dishwashing equipment.

A laundry should be included in the jail, with modern-type equipment and a sterilizer for clothing and bedding.

A janitor's stop sink should be placed in an open space large enough so that mops and cleaning gear can be hung on racks exposed to sun and air. This janitor's room should be well ventilated and inaccessible to prisoners.

Male and female prisoners must be kept separate. Other segregations are necessary, such as separations of juveniles, sentenced from unsentenced prisoners, those with crime records and disciplinary cases separated from more serious perpetrators. Prisoners with medical problems must be isolated. Plans should provide close and readily maintained supervision of the jail sections housing intoxicated prisoners or the mentally disturbed.

Cells should be arranged so that maximum security is provided for prisoners serving time, and these cells must be separated from those housing material witnesses. The maximum number of individual cells makes possible segregation of prisoners. Individual cells are advised for small jails where accommodations are limited. Cells for women prisoners, where women prisoners are rarely housed, can be used for juveniles. One cell should be capable of heavy padding for violent prisoners and should be unfurnished.

Cells should be equipped with toilet, washbowl, a locker or cabinet (preferably an under-bed type), a table, and a chair or stool. The cell beds should be metal, equipped with a clean mattress, clean sheets, mattress cover, blankets, pillow, and pillowcase. The bed should have a rigid bedspring frame bracketed to the wall. The washbowl and toilet should be prison type.

Dormitories should have at least 75 square feet of floor space per prisoner, have 10-foot ceiling height, and there should be at least one toilet and one washbowl for each eight inmates or fraction thereof.

Tanks can be equipped with a fastened bench and open toilet and urinal for prisoners. Tanks should be limited to accommodate not more than 15 prisoners each.

All the various portions of the building should contain floor drains to make it possible to flush out the floors to avoid odors.

It is desirable, where possible, that the prisoners' living quarters be accessible to the entrance of natural light, and the walls should be painted in light colors. Where light is dependent upon electrical fixtures, the fixtures should be the built-in, tamperproof type with tempered plate glass front for protection of the lamp.

Adequate water and sewage systems should be provided. Provision for prisoners to obtain drinking water should be provided by the installation of recessed sanitary drinking fountains installed throughout the jail. Bathing facilities (showers) should be available for daily use. In the larger police stations, some tub baths for women are recommended. Thermostatically controlled, concealed mixing valves should be provided for all showers and hot water supply to lavatories. For flushing devices, the control should be vandalproof, pushbutton-operated, and flushing type valve adjustable for flushing time. Toilets and urinals should have a similar type of pushbutton valve. Lavatories should be equipped with self-closing, pushbutton-operated valves and integral supply spout and nozzle and an integral slow-draining strainer. Hand-operated valves, which are easily damaged, should not be used. Waste and vent stacks, as well as supply and exhaust ducts, must be property constructed so that the prisoners cannot use them for communication. Plumbing fixtures should be wall-mounted in the tanks and individual cells. For padded cells, a flushing-rim floor drain is the only toilet fixture which can be used, and its flushing valve should be located in the pipe space to be operated only by supervisory personnel outside the cell. Showers shall have vandalproof head with concealed pushbutton-operated flushing-type valve with adjustable flushing time, and, as mentioned above, all hot water should be thermostatically controlled to prevent scalding.

A receiving garage should be built immediately adjacent to the building or made a part of it, so that cars can drive in off the street or alley directly into the garage. This garage should not be used for parking purposes but merely for the discharge of prisoners when they are brought to the police station. The jail elevator should be in such a position as to be easily available directly from this garage.

## POLICE STATIONS FOR CITIES OF 3,500 AND 7,000 POPULATION

### General Needs

Although a city with 3,500 or 7,000 population requires less jail space, nevertheless, space for traffic reports and courtroom is needed, and it is most important to have a one-story plan well arranged, as personnel is very limited.

The same requirements for circulation, isolation, and public and private entrances, as described for the larger cities, are equally important.

The prisoner booking room, jail, and general office should be arranged so that one officer can book and supervise prisoners, handle communications, and serve the public without leaving the main office. The entrance to the jail and routing of prisoner traffic must be separate from the public area traffic. There should be an enclosed, escape-proof hallway or area for conducting prisoners from the jail to the courtroom.

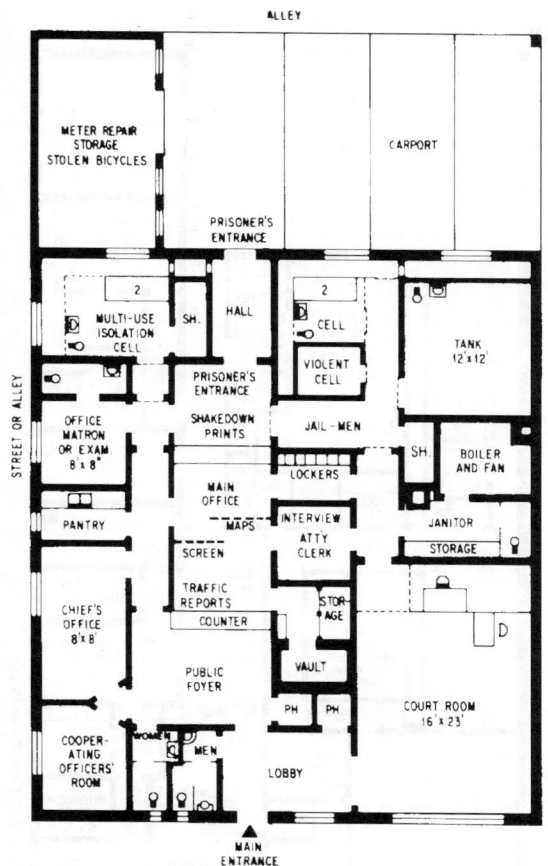

**ig. 4. Plan of police station for city of 3,500 population. One story, lot 48 by 74 feet, building 2,784 square feet.**

**Police Station for City of 3,500 Population**

The floor plan for 3,500 or less population on a small lot on a corner street has all the needed central control but has few offices and a small jail (see Fig. 4).

The courtroom is located so as to be accessible to men prisoners, while women prisoners can be brought through the office to court. As the courtroom is sometimes used for special meetings, it is planned to have a separate entrance lobby so the public need not pass through the police station foyer and disturb the office at night.

Men's cells, one padded cell, one two-bed cell, and a large tank are provided. The tank can serve as a dayroom in this plan. Beds could be placed in the tank.

A multi-use isolation cell with two beds can be for isolation, for two inmates, for juveniles, or, in rare cases, it can be used as a women's cell, in which latter case a matron must be called in and the examination room is for her use. The multipurpose cell could be arranged for two two-beds so that altogether six inmates could be accommodated. If beds are placed in the tank, up to ten inmates could be housed.

The pantry is for service and dishwashing in case meals are so arranged. It can be used as a small laboratory if not used as a pantry.

If the particular city has a greater maximum number of prisoners, it should be noted that the men's jail could be expanded into the carport space by placing the carport space farther back on the lot and building more cells on the cell side of the corridor. A dayroom in back of the tank side of the corridor could be provided.

**Summary of Requirements**

*Population:* Less than 3,500. See Fig. 4 for plan.

*Number of Persons in Police Department:* 4 Officers

*Parking:* Space for police officials' cars and public's vehicles, 4 (minimum)

**Estimate of Space and Facilities Requirements for:**

I. *General Police Administration Operations*
A. Executive's Requirements (Room or space sizes in feet)
  1. Chief's office: 8 by 14
  2. Private entrance
  3. Conference room: combined with courtroom
  4. Cooperating officer's room: 8 by 10
B. Records and Clerical
  1. Central records maintenance: combined with main office, traffic records, and personnel records.
  2. Map space: in main office
C. Communications
  1. Telephone and radio: in main office
D. Training
  1. Classroom: combined with court room
  2. Library: combined with chief's office
  3. Supplies storage: combined with main office
E. Identification
  1. Prints: combined with shakedown room
II. *Prisoners and Jail Facilities*
A. Receiving, Processing, and Confinement
  1. Drive-in garage: 12 by 25
  2. Booking, searching room: 10 by 10
  3. Medical examination room: 8 by 8
  4. Isolation cell: one, 7 by 8
  5. Violent cell: one, 7 by 7
  6. Tank: 12 by 12
  7. Dayroom: combined with tank
  8. Toilet: in cells
  9. Shower: 3 by 7
  10. Attorneys' interview room: 9 by 9
  11. Storage: Combined with janitor's room
  12. Storage prisoners' property: vault 4 by 6
  13. Prisoners' waiting space to courtroom: 4 by 8
  14. Pantry: 6 by 8
B. Separate Rooms, Facilities for Women Prisoners
  1. One multi-use isolation cell: 12 by 12
  2. Shower, toilet: 3 by 8
  3. Matron's room, combined with examination room: 8 by 8
  4. Matron's toilet: 3 by 8
C. Separate Rooms for Juvenile Prisoners
  1. Use multi-use isolation cell
III. *Receiving and Assisting Public*
  1. Separate entrance foyer: 10 by 14
  2. Public toilets: mens and womens, each 5 by 10
  3. Public telephone: in foyer
  4. Complaint counter: combined with main office, traffic violations and reporting accidents

IV. *Police Personnel Requirements*
    1. Locker rooms: 6 by 8
    2. Toilet: combined with janitor's room
V. *Police Property Requirements:*
    1. Storage of recovered stolen bicycles: combined with meter repair, 12 by 24
    2. Storage of recovered stolen property
    3. Storage of police department supplies: 8 by 8, near vault
VI. *Police Building Maintenance Requirements*
    1. Janitor's room: 6 by 10
    2. Boiler and fans: 10 by 10
    3. Heating, ventilating: combined with boiler room
    4. Repairs: combined with meter repair room
VII. *Courts*
    1. Police courtroom: 16 by 23
    2. Clerk's office: combined with attorney's room, 9 by 9
    3. Attorney's room: combined with interview room
VII. *Public Safety Education*
    1. Safety: combined with main office

### Police Station—City of 7,000 Population

The plan shown in Fig. 5 for 7,000 population is for a narrow site on a street corner.

Offices for officers and the central record office and courtroom are provided. A 4-foot wall space is needed for the intercommunication system in the office. The attorney-clerk's room must serve also as visitors' room in conjunction with prisoners' waiting hall back of the courtroom. The matron's office must serve for visitors' room for women; and the attorney-clerk's office, in conjunction with the corridor for men prisoners, must serve for visitors' room for men.

The women's cell for four inmates and adjacent cell for two inmates could be used for juvenile or isolation cells.

The kitchenette is a pantry for serving food brought in from outside and placed in trays, and for dishwashing.

For men there are two isolation cells, one padded cell, and four four-bed cells, thus housing 18 inmates besides those in the tank. Dayroom for the privileged is provided.

### Summary of Requirements

*Population:* Less than 7,000. See Fig. 5 for plan.

*Number of Persons in Police Department:* 8 to 10 Officers

*Parking:* Off-street parking area for police vehicles adjacent to the police building; 2 cars. Area required for parking cars of persons who visit police headquarters; 2 cars. Total, 4 cars (minimum).

*Location of Police Headquarters Facilities:* In the business district or manufacturing district. The building should be by itself if possible—if not, with the city hall. If it is combined, the lights, heating, and ventilation for the police department are to be operated separately. The police station should have separate entrances, one for the public and one for prisoners.

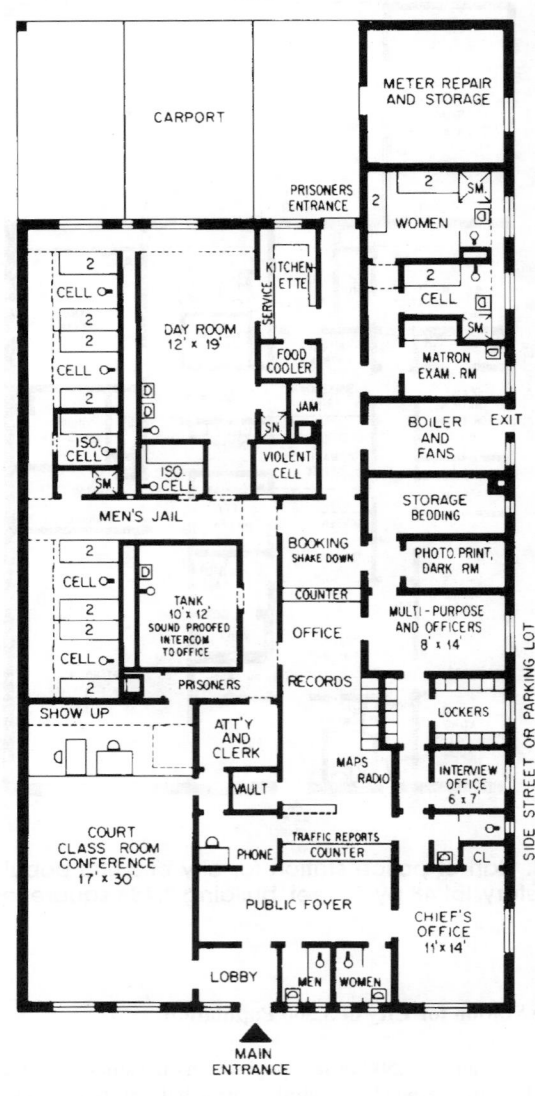

**Fig. 5. Plan of police station for city of 7,000 population. One story, lot 50 by 100 feet; building 4,300 square feet.**

### Estimate of Space and Facilities Requirements for:

I. *General Police Administrative Operations*
A. Executive's Requirements (Room or space sizes in feet)
    1. Chief's office: 11 by 14
    2. Private entrance: Yes
    3. Conference Room and classroom: combined with courtroom
    4. Chief's office toilet: 3 by 8
    5. Chief's office clothes closet: 2 by 4
B. Records and Clerical
    1. Central records maintenance: combined with main office traffic records, and personnel records

2. Map space in main office
3. Copy machine in main office
. Communications
  1. Telephone and radio in main office
  2. Public telephone in foyer
. Training
  1. Classroom: combined with courtroom
  2. Library: in chief's office
  3. Firearms range: at shared facility
  4. Supplies storage: combined with main office
. Identification
  1. Photographing and fingerprinting room
  2. Darkroom: 6 by 10
  3. Lineup or show-up: combined with courtroom
. *Prisoners and Jail Facilities*
.. Receiving, Processing and Confinement
  1. Drive-in garage: 12 by 24
  2. Booking and searching room: 10 by 10
  3. Medical examination room: combined with booking room
  4. Isolation cells: two, 7 by 8 each
  5. Violent cells: one, 7 by 7
  6. Group cells: Four, four bunks each
  7. Tank: 10 by 12
  8. Dayroom: 12 by 19
  9. Toilet and shower room: one in dayroom
  10. Attorneys' interrogation room: 8 by 8
  11. Prisoners' visiting: space in corner courtroom
  12. Matron's room: 7 by 10
  13. Storage, bedding: 7 by 14
  14. Storage, prisoners' property: vault, 5 by 5
  15. Enclosed vestibule to prisoners' waiting space: 3 by 12
  16. Prisoners' waiting space adjacent to courtroom: 3 by 10
  17. Kitchenette-pantry: 7 by 12
  18. Food storage: 4 by 7
. Separate Rooms for Women Prisoners
  1. One group cell: 12 by 12, four bunks
  2. One isolation call: 8 by 10
  3. Shower, toilet
  4. Matron's room: combined with examination room, 7 by 10
III. *Receiving and Assisting the Public*
  1. Separate entrance foyer: 8 by 15
  2. Public toilets—mens and womens: 6 by 6, each
  3. Public telephone: in anteroom
  4. Complaint counter: combined with traffic violations' bureau and traffic accident reporting counter
V. *Police Personnel Requirements*
  1. Locker rooms: 8 by 10
  2. Coffee bar: combined with kitchenette
. *Police Property Requirements*
  1. Storage of recovered stolen bicycles: 14 by 14
  2. Storage of recovered stolen property
VI. *Police Building Maintenance Requirements*
  1. Janitor's room: 4 by 7
  2. Boiler and fans: 8 by 14
  3. Heating and ventilating system
  4. Electrical controls
  5. Water controls
VII. *Courts*
  1. Police courtroom: 17 by 30
  2. Court clerk's office and city attorney's office: 8 by 8
VIII. *Public Safety Education*
  1. Safety education office: combined with main office

## POLICE STATION FOR CITY OF 15,000 POPULATION

The plan illustrates how arrangements provide for central control with public and private entrances and separated, isolated quarters for juveniles, men, and women without any necessity for different classes of prisoners to cross each others' quarters or intermingle.

For 15,000 population or less, a plan of a one-story building is shown in Fig. 6.

All the necessary offices for administrative functions are provided. Offices for chief and assistant officers are accessible to the jail or to the public. The public, however, is separated from prisoner areas. The main office oversees the whole first floor with a minimum of personnel on duty at any one time.

The courtroom has the public entrance at one end, and at the other end the prisoners' waiting room adjoins. In this case the prisoners' waiting room is also arranged to be used in conjunction with the visitors' room.

The booking room is central to the men's jail and the juveniles' or women's quarters. The interrogation room can also be used as a matron's office as needed.

There are cells for four juveniles. For the women's jail, there is a cell for four inmates and a small tank, which can also serve as an isolation cell.

For the men's jail there is one eight-bed group cell which can be used for trusties, two isolation cells, one padded cell, and one sixteen-bed and one eight-bed group cell with dayrooms. A maximum number of 34 men can be housed, besides those in the tank.

It should be noted that if the men's jail is on the second floor, the jail quarters are not over the juveniles' or women's jail quarters. Intercommunication thus is impossible and there are no special construction problems. The second floor, however, requires one more officer on duty than would be required in the case of the one-story plan.

The enclosed passage and/or stairs to the courtroom for men prisoners is provided for whether a one-story or a two-story plan is adopted.

### Summary of Requirements

*Population:* Less than 15,000. See Fig. 6 for plans.

*Parking:* Off-street parking area for police vehicles adjacent to the police building: 6 cars. Area required for parking cars of persons who visit police headquarters; 3 to 6 cars. Total, 9 to 12 cars (minimum).

### Estimate of Space and Facilities Requirements for:

I. *General Police Administration Operations*
A. Executive's Requirements (Room or space sizes in feet)
  1. Chief's office: 12 by 12 to 12 by 15
  2. Private entrance: 3 by 6
  3. Conference room: 10 by 10
  4. Chief's office toilet: 6 by 8
  5. Chief's office clothes closet: 2 by 4
  6. Assistant chief's office: 9 by 10
  7. Chief's secretary's office: combined with main record room, 10 by 17
  8. Other: waiting room or public lobby: 15 by 20

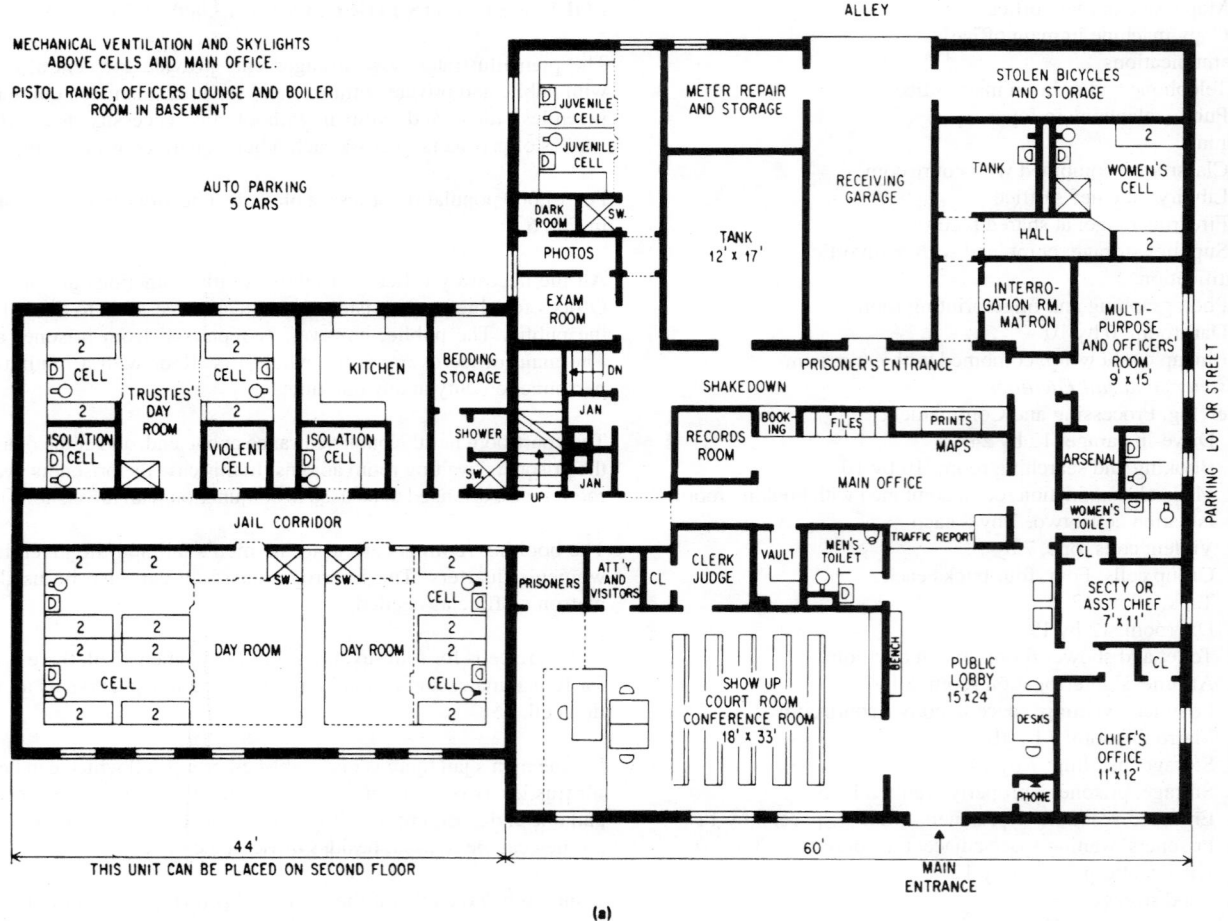

MECHANICAL VENTILATION AND SKYLIGHTS
ABOVE CELLS AND MAIN OFFICE.

PISTOL RANGE, OFFICERS LOUNGE AND BOILER
ROOM IN BASEMENT

AUTO PARKING
5 CARS

**Fig. 6. Plan of police station for city of 15,000 population. Building 6,000 square feet. (*a*) First floor plan**

B.  Records and Clerical
1. Central records maintenance: in main office, 12 by 18
2. Map room and library (accidents and crime data): combined with officers' briefing room, 9 by 15
3. Old records storage: 4 by 6
4. Men staff toilets and lockers: 8 by 10
5. Women staff toilets and lockers: 8 by 10
6. Motor repair room: 10 by 12
C. Communications: combined with general office
D. Training
1. Classroom: combined with courtroom, 17 by 24
2. Library: optional, 10 by 12
3. Firearms range: 15 by 70
4. Supplies storage: 6 by 6
E. Identification
1. Photographing and fingerprinting rooms: combined with record room, 9 by 12
2. Photographic dark room: 6 by 8
3. Identification records: combined with main office
4. Storage: 6 by 6 or combined with hall lockers
5. Lineup or show-up: combined with courtroom
F. Office for Use of Other Enforcement Agencies' Representatives (Military Police, Federal Agents, Parole Officers): 10 by 10, optional

II.  *Prisoners and Jail Facilities*
A. Receiving, Processing, and Confinement
1. Drive-in, escape-proof garage: 15 by 25
2. Booking and searching rooms: 10 by 12
3. Physician's office and medical examination and treatment rooms: combined with interrogation room
4. Isolation cells: two, 7 by 8 each
5. Violent cells: one, 6 by 7
6. Group cells: two, 8 by 13
7. Cellblock: one 10 by 24; one 15 by 24
8. Tank: 12 by 17
9. Dayroom: two, 9 by 20 and 12 by 20
10. Toilet in cells and shower room: two, 4 by 6
11. Attorneys' interrogation room: 9 by 10
12. Prisoners' visiting room: 8 by 8
13. Delousing room: 6 by 6
14. Laundry: 8 by 8
15. Storage, cleaning utensils: 9 by 13, combined with storage
16. Storage, bedding: 6 by 8
17. Storage, prisoners' property: 4 by 6, or lockers
18. Prisoners' waiting room adjacent to courtroom: 7 by 8
19. Kitchen: 8 by 10
20. Refrigerator: 4 by 6, optional
21. Food storage: 4 by 6

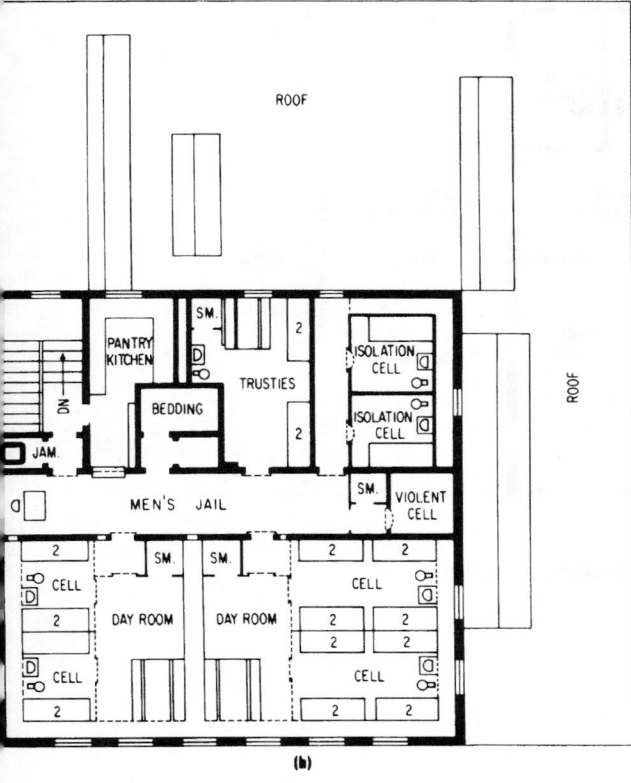

**g. 6. (cont.) Plan of police station for city of 15,000 opulation. Building 6,000 square feet. (b) Second floor lan**

. Separate Rooms for Women Prisoners
   1. One isolation cell: 8 by 12
   2. One violent cell: 7 by 7, optional
   3. One tank: 9 by 10
   4. One shower in tank, one in cell, toilet in each cell
   5. Matron's room: 10 by 14, plus 4 by 6 toilet optional
. Separate Rooms for Juvenile Offenders
   1. Two cells: 7 by 8
   2. One shower, one toilet in cell
II. *Receiving and Assisting Public*
   1. Separate entrance
   2. Public waiting room: 10 by 14 to 15 by 24
   3. Public toilets: men's and women's, 8 by 8 each
   4. Public telephone: one pay phone, 3 by 3
   5. Information center: desk sergeant
   6. Complaint counter: combined with general office, 12 by 18
   7. Traffic violations bureau: combined with complaint counter
   8. Traffic accident reporting counter: one 3 by 5 desk
V. *Police Personnel Requirements*
   1. Male employees' lounge: 10 by 12, optional in basement
   2. Locker rooms: 9 by 12
   3. Shower and toilet rooms: two toilets, one shower combined with lounge
   4. Gymnasium: 27 by 23, in basement
   5. Lunchroom and coffee bar: 9 by 10, in squad room in basement

V. *Police Property Requirements*
   1. Storage of uniforms: lockers in basement
   2. Storage of guns and ammunition: 5 by 6
   3. Storage of police vehicles: two cars, 20 by 24
   4. Storage of recovered stolen bicycles: 10 by 12
   5. Storage of recovered stolen property: combined with storage
   6. Storage of police department supplies: two cupboards in officers' room
VI. *Police Building Maintenance Requirements*
   1. Janitor's room and lockers: closets on each floor
   2. Boiler and fuel: 14 by 16
   3. Heating and ventilating system
   4. Electrical controls: emergency electric generator unit for radio and lights
   5. Repair and construction: 12 by 15
VII. *Courts*
   1. Police courtroom: 18 by 33, combined with courtroom
   2. Judge's chambers: 9 by 9
   3. Court clerk's office: combined with item 2
VIII. *Police Divisional Operations*
A. Detective Division
   1. Office of officer-in-charge: 8 by 10, combined with interrogation or assistant chief
   2. Interrogation rooms: 8 by 8, combined with examining room
B. Women's Bureau
   Office of officer-in-charge: 9 by 15, combined with interrogation room
C. Juvenile Division
   Office of officer-in-charge: 8 by 10, combined with interrogation room
D. Public Safety Education
   Bicycle licensing room: 8 by 10

## DESCRIPTION OF PLAN FOR A SMALL TOWN HALL WITH POLICE STATION

### Site Location

The site location can be any place centrally located in town. Distances across a small town are too short to present special problems. Usually the fire department is a rural fire district with the fire station located on separate property, although it could be on the same lot. In some cases the library can be planned on the same site if the entrance is on the opposite side from the prisoners' entrance.

### Plans

A plan of a small town hall is shown in Fig. 7.

### Spaces

1. For a small town in a rural fire district, with few utilities to operate, a combined city hall and police station is desirable, as the council room can serve as a courtroom, and only one heating unit is needed.
2. To provide for best use of personnel, since the clerk-treasurer may serve only part time, the marshal's office is located to oversee the town hall's public lobby as well as the prisoners' entrance and jail. The requirement of reporting traffic accidents warrants the office being kept open daily.

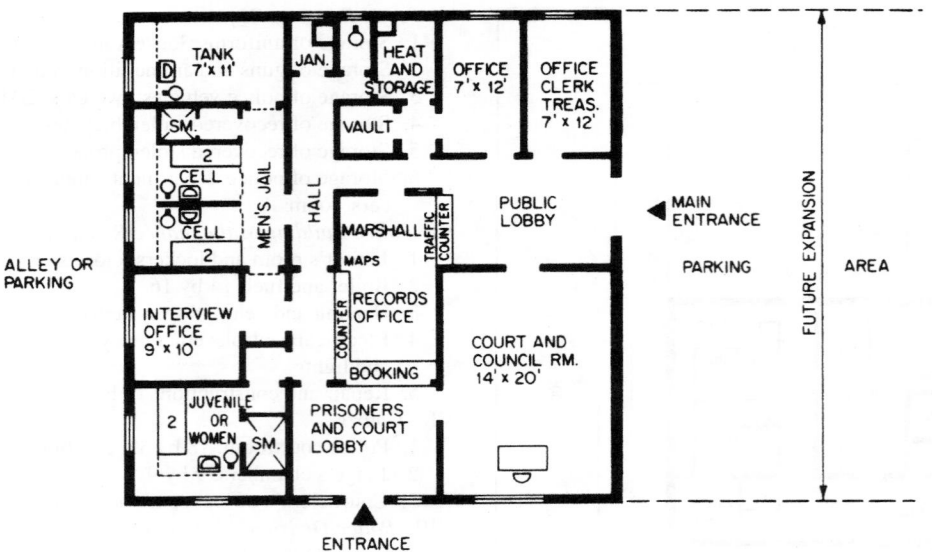

**Fig. 7. Small town hall with police station**

3. This small plan has an office for the mayor or conference room, one clerk-treasurer office, a vault used by the marshal and city clerk, and a court-council room. The records room and the marshal's office are in one unit.

4. One two-bed isolated cell can serve for juvenile or women prisoners, or as an isolation cell. Seldom is it needed for all such uses at the same time.

5. The men's jail includes the tank and two two-bed cells. Altogether 6 inmates, besides those in the tank, can be housed. Toilets and heating plant are included.

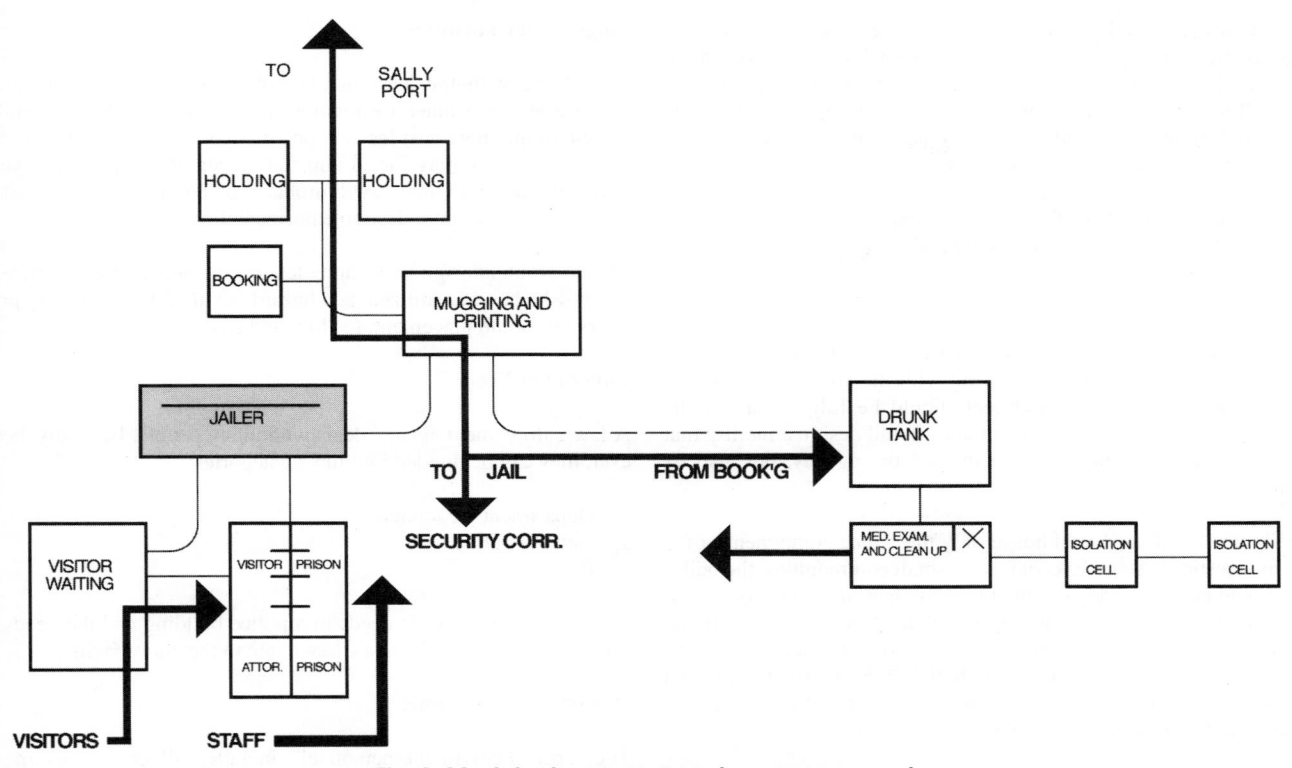

**Fig. 1. Model prisoner-processing arrangement**

# POLICE FACILITIES

## SITE SELECTION

### Accessibility

From a total program standpoint, several possible sites should be inspected for a proposed police facility. Several factors should be taken into consideration when selecting the site including location, available land area, configuration, and relationship of the site to major arteries and main highways that extend throughout the area. Additionally, the relationship of the proposed building to existing governmental structures should be considered, with particular emphasis placed on the relative proximity to the existing courts, jails, and prisons.

Primary consideration should be given to the selection of a site that will provide maximum accessibility to the community being served. The facility should be as close to the centers of business, industries, schools, welfare agencies, and the courts as circumstances permit and in an area which can be served by public transportation. Not only will this facilitate the use of such resources, but problems in staffing are simplified when there are not tiring and complicated daily trips to and from the facility. For prisoners who are selected to participate in programs of work release, study release, clinical services, or other community activities, transportation problems can contribute heavily to the success of such programs.

The facility should be easily accessible to the public and not hidden on a side street or on a site with very limited street frontages. The building should be related to one or two of the main streets connecting both north and south and east and west portions of the city. The building should not face an extremely busy highway or through-city thoroughfare, which might make access into the traffic lanes difficult.

The site should be accessible to two streets, rather than one. Several entrances and exits should be provided for police vehicles to ensure immediate access and egress to and from the site in the event one of the entrances might be temporarily blocked.

Residents can best be served by the central location of all criminal justice components and activities in a centralized design concept.

### Parking

The site should be adequate, not only for the building itself, but to accommodate a police motor-court activity, staff parking area, and public off-street parking requirements. The parking space allocated for employee vehicles and for police vehicles is important when making shift changes and removing prisoners to and from jail. In the case of a combined police/jail facility, a private jail booking entrance (sallyport) and prisoner processing area, easily accessible to automobiles, should be included in the plans.

*Credits: Police Facility Design,* Bureau of Operations and Research, International Association of Chiefs of Police, Gaithersburg, Maryland.

In some instances, a basement-level parking garage for police vehicles may be desirable. A ramp leading from the basement level would provide adequate street access. Placing the garage and official parking facilities in the basement will reduce noise levels at shift change times and during the conduct of daily activities, thereby avoiding inconvenience to adjacent land owners.

The parking lot or roof of the structure should also be considered as a possible site for a helicopter landing pad.

## FACILITY

A police building should be regarded as a viable and flexible structure. It should be capable of growing with the community and the department it serves. The architect should be fully aware of the growth potential of the department and should design a facility that will meet not only the present needs of the agency, but also its future needs.

Ideally, the building should house only the police component of the criminal justice system. Except in very small communities, the building should be exclusively oriented to the police function. Consideration should be given to separating the police from the incarceration function and the associated stringent design features necessary when the jail is made a part of the police building. Similarly, the judicial functions would best serve the needs of the people if they were not located in the same building as the police.

### Exterior Design

To the public, the police building should represent a friendly, businesslike, professional building complex. Security provisions must, of course, be incorporated into the design; however, it is possible to artfully disguise them so that the fortress image is not the predominant feature of the structure.

The police facility should be constructed of noncombustible materials. The design of the building, including the exterior surfaces, landscaping, and other elements, should be planned to reduce the number of areas where explosives may be hidden. Reinforced masonry on the exterior walls and either concrete or a lightweight concrete layer on the roof, will improve the building's resistance to civil or natural disasters. Many refinements to increase building safety and security can be provided at little additional cost. All or most of the glass areas, both interior and exterior, should be of bullet-resistant material. An interior garden court could be one of the methods used to create a quiet, beautiful, and serene atmosphere that could psychologically benefit the entire staff and eliminate the feeling of being enclosed in a windowless fortress.

The so-called "windowless" building may contain considerable glass, but the glass is positioned in such a manner that none of the interior activities can be viewed from the exterior areas. Psychologically, glass used in this manner can completely eliminate the feeling by the staff that they are working in a windowless facility.

The police building should be designed to provide services to the public as well as to fulfill the everyday working needs of the police. The structure should be readily accessible with ample public and private parking space. Properly designed landscaping, flagpoles, and identifying illuminated signs can and should be attractive and functional components of the building.

### Single-Story Facilities

A building with the least number of floors is more economical because less personnel are required to supervise it. While a multi-story building may cost less in construction and be a saving in land costs, the extra outlay for administrative personnel, year after year, will never cease. In time, it will probably be far greater than the additional cost of the more desirable horizontal plan.

The horizontal design philosophy lessens the need for stairs and elevators which, when utilized, add hazard potential when moving prisoners, for bomb placement, for fire, and so on.

### Functional Needs

A law enforcement agency deals with many people. Basically, however, they can be divided into three categories:

1. Department personnel
2. General public
3. Prisoners

Each group has specific needs in a police building and the needs of each should be considered as they relate to the entire facility.

### Department Personnel

The term "department personnel" includes all employees of an agency: executives, managers, supervisors, officers (both uniformed and plainclothed), clerical, and special employees.

Uniformed personnel who constitute the bulk of employees usually report to a central location which should include lockers, showers, and physical exercise area. A briefing room with the capacity to accommodate approximately two-thirds of the patrol force should be located near the locker rooms. A separate entrance into the building should be provided for use by police employees only. Unnecessary mingling of police officers, the public, and prisoners should be avoided in the police facility.

### General Public

The majority of persons visiting the police headquarters will have business only at the central information center. Therefore, the public information lobby should be a part of the information center operation and should be easily accessible from the main entrance. Employees in the information center can then handle inquiries and refer callers to the proper official or office. As a general rule, the building should be planned and equipped to avoid confusing the public. Offices should be plainly designated by functional titles on the doors. A conveniently placed building directory in the lobby is also an important feature that should not be overlooked.

### Prisoners

When the jail facility is located within the police building and/or when prisoner booking is done at police headquarters, special design features must be incorporated to accommodate this function. Prisoners should enter the building through a separate secure entrance. A sallyport with automatic doors and drive-in provision should be part of the security entrance. A model prisoner-processing arrangement is shown in Fig. 1.

The reader should refer to Fig. 2 to better understand the relationship of the three separate entrances, public parking, employee parking, and police vehicle parking. Note in Fig. 2 the security feature of the gate separating the police vehicles from public access. Whenever the police facility is located in a residential area, high shrubbery and, more preferably, a masonry wall surrounding the police parking area should protect the adjacent residents from the glare of vehicle lights at night.

### Interior Design Features

One of the basic requirements of a functional floor plan in a modern police facility is the control of internal circulation. Efficiency and safety dictate that the public enter the building through a single entrance into a controlled lobby. The public should not penetrate beyond the lobby and should be allowed further access only after the need has been demonstrated. Fig. 2 shows the functional relationships of the three entrances.

### Space Allocation

The functional policy facility should be as flexible as possible for efficiency and economy. A flexible building is one in which the interior space is adaptable to a broad variety of occupancies and the exterior walls are expandable to meet future growth needs.

In some cases, interior flexibility may be attained by the installation of movable partitions that can provide necessary privacy and also may be shifted to meet future functional space needs. Partitions approximately 6 feet in height afford sufficient privacy without affecting light or air conditioning. Private offices and small rooms should be kept to a minimum.

Private offices make supervision more difficult; occupants are tempted to turn their attention to outside matters and to engage in activity not strictly police-related. The potential for this situation is lessened when the partitions forming the offices are glass and, in some instances, the partitions may be less than ceiling height.

Glass partitions facilitate supervision and tend to assist in maintaining a businesslike appearance on the part of personnel by providing an unobstructed view for supervisors. Each area that must be kept secure, such as places where prisoners are confined or moved, the

communications center, and areas for property and evidence storage, require special design features. Permanent partitions should be used in these areas and wherever the need is justified.

The building should contain large open floor areas in which a broad variety of furniture and equipment may be arranged. These areas may be subdivided with a minimum of structural or mechanical operation and expense through the use of standardized, movable, and interchangeable nonstructural elements.

Space can also be separated effectively by counters. The counters can also serve as receptacles for file cabinets.

### ADMINISTRATIVE AREA

One portion of the police facility should be reserved exclusively for the administrative command staff. This staff includes the chief of police, planning and inspectional services commanders, and the commanders of the primary organizational entities with department-wide jurisdiction, such as the uniformed division, criminal investigation division, administrative services division, and technical services division.

#### Chief of Police

Immediate public access to the chief of police is not always necessary or desirable. Many citizens with minor problems, who at first demand to see the chief, can have their problems adequately resolved by talking to subordinate personnel. Constant interruptions of this sort would distract the chief from his or her primary obligations to the department. The chief's office (Fig. 3) is best located away from the mainstream of public and staff, preferably near the rear of a one-story building or on the second floor of a two-story building. It is customary and worthwhile for the chief to have a private entrance, private toilet facility, closet, and a conference room immediately adjacent to the office. The normal space allowance for the chief's private office should be approximately 300 square feet. The separate conference room (Fig. 4) should be large enough to seat all officers above the rank of lieutenant, i.e., the executive staff. Access to the conference room should be from both the chief's office and from a common hallway for staff use.

The chief should be provided with a private secretary and, in larger agencies, an administrative officer. These two staff assistants should, of course, be provided sufficient office space immediately adjacent to the chief's offices.

#### Executive Command Staff

The chief's executive staff should occupy offices which surround his own. Each staff office should be approximately 200 square feet in size. These staff offices could conceivably share secretarial services, e.g., one secretary for every two staff commanders.

### CENTRAL RECORDS AREA

The public entrance into a police facility should be primarily through a single main entranceway into a common lobby. This single public entrance should be controlled and supervised from the central records center.

This central records center should be placed in full view of the main facility entrance. The location should be such that records personnel

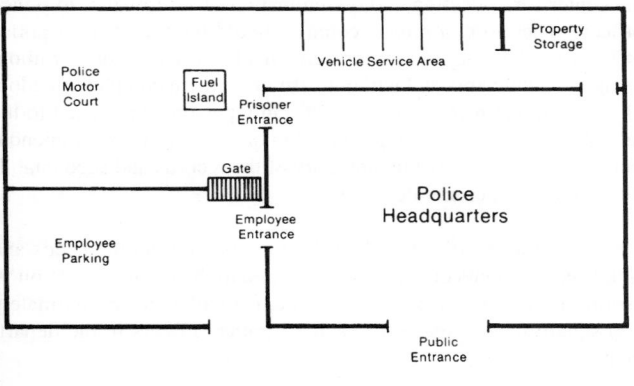

**Fig. 2. Exterior design relationship**

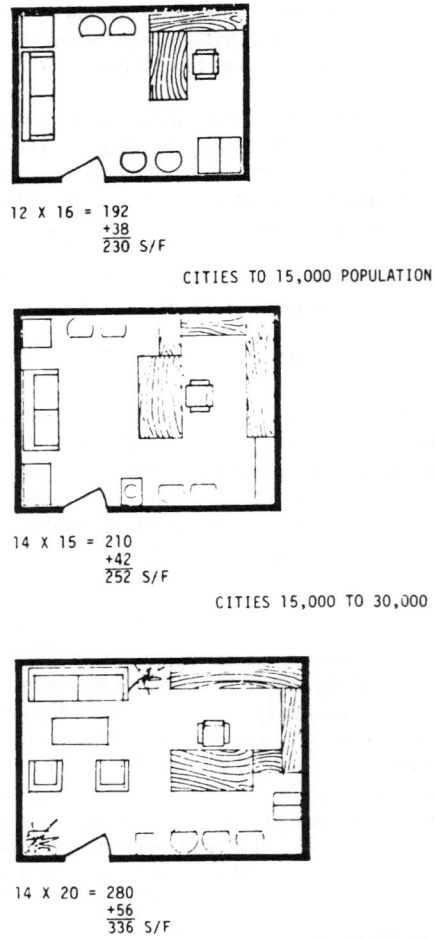

12 X 16 = 192
+38
230 S/F

CITIES TO 15,000 POPULATION

14 X 15 = 210
+42
252 S/F

CITIES 15,000 TO 30,000

14 X 20 = 280
+56
336 S/F

CITIES 30,000 TO 75,000

**Fig. 3. Office for police chief**

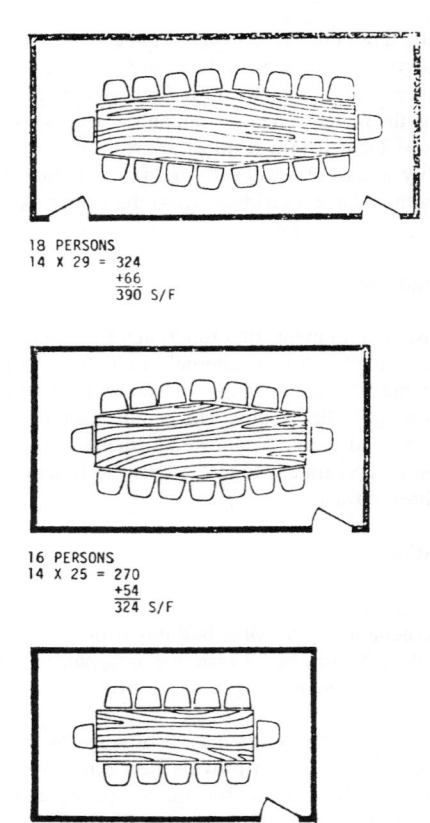

18 PERSONS
14 X 29 = 324
+66
390 S/F

16 PERSONS
14 X 25 = 270
+54
324 S/F

12 PERSONS
12 X 21 = 252
+50
302 S/F

**Fig. 4. Conference rooms**

can individually screen all those entering the building. Provision should be made in the lobby area for public seating, public telephones, showcases for display of exhibits, and public restrooms. The public restrooms should be constructed of materials that would limit damage to the building in the event of a concealed, incendiary explosion.

The records area should be separated by glass from the public areas and staff access counter to ensure complete security of the entire records area.

The majority of persons visiting the police station will have business at the records center (Fig. 5). Therefore, a public counter should be part of the records center. The employees in the records center can then handle inquiries or refer callers to the proper official or office. As a general rule, the building should be planned to reduce the necessity of having the public wander about the building seeking assistance. Public circulation within the building should be controlled and limited by separating the public lobby area from other corridors and doors that should be controlled electrically.

The interior of a police facility should be decorated in a professional manner. Bright, warm, but soft colors combined with careful use of complementary accents should greet the public. Rotary records systems should enhance the appearance of the records center as well as provide for a functional records storage and retrieval operation.

The records room, in addition to serving the public, should also be the center for collection and dissemination of information to police officers. Therefore, a private counter should be provided for police officers so that they may more effectively utilize records without using the public area and without permitting them complete freedom of access to the records room itself. Only personnel assigned to the records function should be permitted in the room. This recommendation is made to preserve the integrity of the records and accountability for their proper maintenance.

The size of a records area should, of course, reflect the needs and space requirements of personnel assigned to the records function. A useful guide, when in doubt as to size, is to allocate approximately 100 square feet of space for each 15 police officers in the department.

Because of the heavy floor weight that will be required in the records area of the building as a result of files and other equipment, structural design requires that the floor be reinforced.

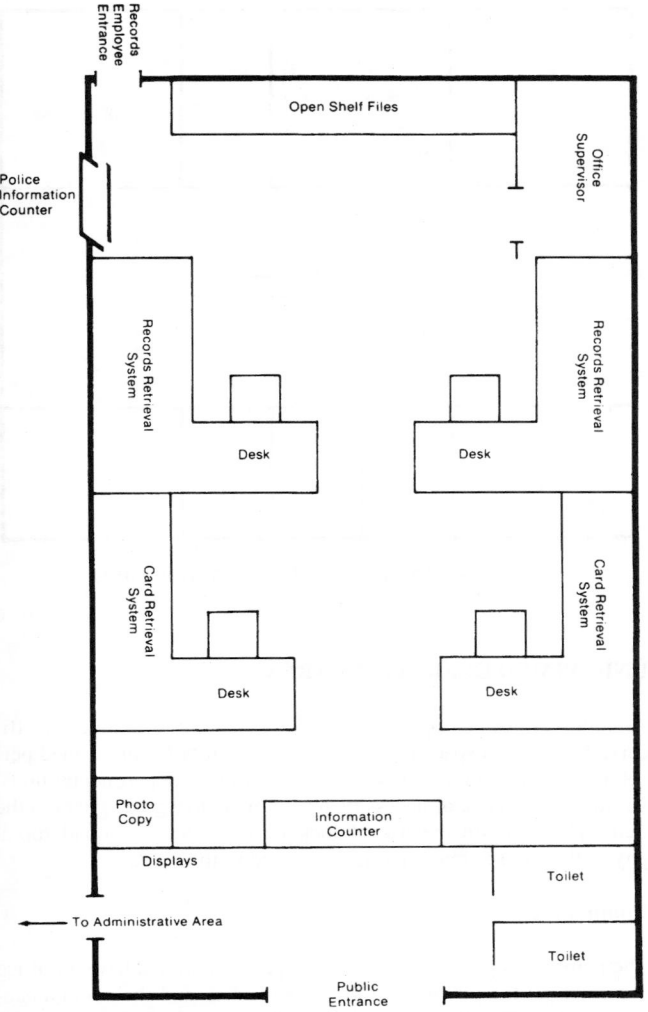

**Fig. 5. Model functional space design, police records center**

## COMMUNICATIONS

### Dispatching Facilities

The police communications command center (Fig. 6) and its related equipment should be isolated from public contact in one of the more secure areas of the building. Other electrical and mechanical systems should also be protected to reduce the possibility of sabotage or vandalism.

Most police practitioners would agree that locating the dispatching and records units in close proximity offers advantages of expediting the flow of information and makes more efficient use of personnel. This philosophy is most practical in small agencies where a minimum number of persons on a late tour of duty could conceivably handle both communications and records responsibilities. When this arrangement is necessitated by department size, we recommend that the entire records and communications area be bullet-resistant.

In addition to radio, the dispatch console should contain all electronic systems such as television surveillance of the jail and outside

of the building, smoke and fire detection and warning devices, detention area audio surveillance, remote control for doors, and vehicle status boards, recorders, intercom, and TV monitors.

Status boards are devices used to indicate the availability of field units. Such a device is justified as a dispatching aid in the smaller as well as the larger departments. Switch control pilot lights may be used, with indicators at each dispatching position, on a large map visible to all positions. The switches must be wired so that actuation in any position causes the same indication at all other positions. Placing of pilot lights on a large map showing beat boundaries is particularly valuable to dispatchers responsible for deployment of large numbers of field units. Each unit's status cannot be accurately recalled from memory, nor can time usually be taken to query a number of units to determine which is the closest to the assignment at hand.

### Complaint Operator/Dispatcher

Two types of complaint/dispatch operations are generally acceptable, depending upon the size of a particular agency. In the smaller departments, a single person usually can handle both the complaint-reception function as well as the dispatch operation. Whereas, in the larger agencies, complaint processing may require extensive specialization, perhaps with operators subdivided for geographical areas of responsibility. An alternate approach to the latter is to combine the complaint operator's and dispatcher's duties in one position and add personnel as message volume demands. Difficulties arise in this method, however, when the message volume would justify either a separate complaint operator and a dispatcher or two combined operators/dispatchers (or any multiple thereof). The architect and the agency consultant will have to make the decision as to individual agency needs regarding communications according to the volume of complaint traffic, prior to the design of the command center.

### Command Center Supervision

The function of supervising a police communications center should not pose any unusual problems arising out of the nature of the task. The sensitive nature of the process demands at least constant availability of supervision. In larger installations, provision should be made for the supervisor to monitor both landline and radio communications as they are carried on; performance of complaint operators and dispatchers may thus be evaluated to determine training needs and to correct improper procedures. A monitoring position is also useful for instruction of newly assigned personnel, and for intercepting and/or assisting in high priority calls.

### Environmental Considerations

The communications command center should be made adequate in terms of sound conditioning, lighting, air conditioning, room configuration ability to expand facilities, and total security from potential sabotage. This area should be a complete self-contained unit with toilet, lunch room, locker space, and supervisor's area.

### Emergency Power Supplies

Radio and landline communications are vulnerable to several influencing factors, the most important of which is electrical power. In the event of failure of normal power sources, the communications center should have some method of obtaining standby electrical service to the base station to insure its continued operations; therefore, the base station should be equipped with an emergency power source. This equipment should be capable of supporting not only all communications equipment, but also lighting requirements for the command center and primary operational portions of the building.

Figure 6 is intended to provide the reader with a visual display of a conceptual design model for a communications command center where telephone reception and dispatching are performed by the same person.

## CRIMINAL INVESTIGATION AREA

Several design features should be considered when allocating floor space for criminal investigators (Fig. 7). Investigators make extensive and constant use of records; therefore, it is practical to place investigators as near as possible to the records center. A great number of people coming to the police facility do so in order to confer with investigators; public access is an important feature that must be considered when physically locating detectives.

The area allocated to detectives should provide for individual work space and a degree of privacy for each officer. Collectively, however, detectives should be in constant contact with one another. Therefore, a single spacious room is recommended to house all detectives. The room could then be divided into individual office areas by movable partitions.

Interrogation rooms (Fig. 8) are another important feature that should be located near the detectives.

Again, in the same general vicinity, the architect should provide for office space for both the unit commander and supervisors.

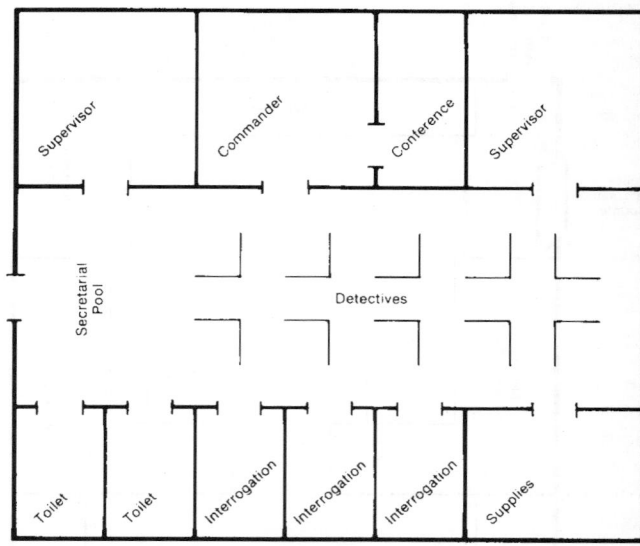

**Fig. 7. Model criminal investigation area**

## UNIFORMED OPERATIONS AREA

Although uniformed operations requires the largest number of officers, the physical space needs in a police facility for uniformed personnel are substantially less than those of other departmental units. Uniformed officers, of necessity, must remain to a great extent in the field. They require the use of locker rooms, toilets, squad room, physical exercise area, briefing room, and writing area.

### Commander/Supervisor

The patrol commander and/or shift supervisor should have an office accessible to the public, uniformed personnel, and the communications center. The close proximity to the communications center is important so that the commander can assist dispatchers, or take over the operation when necessary, under emergency conditions.

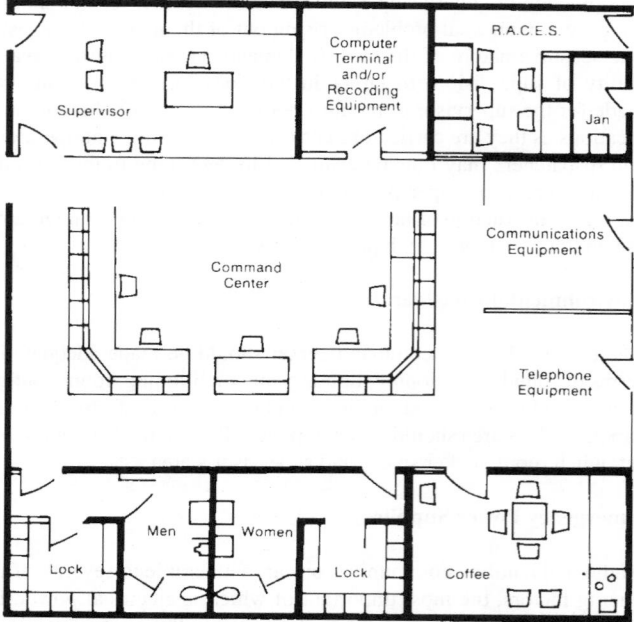

**Fig. 6. Model communications command center**

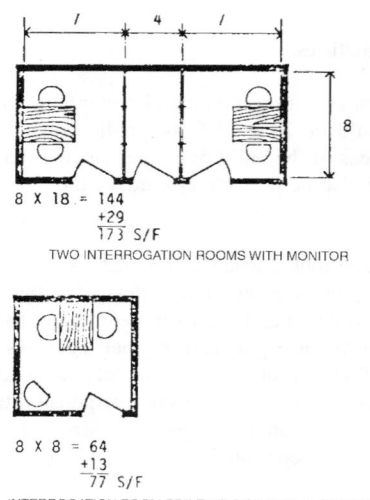

8 X 18 = 144
+29
173 S/F
TWO INTERROGATION ROOMS WITH MONITOR

8 X 8 = 64
+13
77 S/F
INTERROGATION ROOM FOR TWO OR THREE PERSONS

**Fig. 8. Interrogation rooms**

## Special Operations

Office space should also be provided for traffic and tactical supervisors. These offices should be of sufficient size to accommodate crime and traffic accident location maps, charts, and other crime, accident, and special event analysis materials.

## Roll-Call Room

Uniformed personnel, who constitute the bulk of employees, will report for roll call (briefing) prior to going on their assignments. Special features of a roll-call room should be planned by the architect. It is wise policy to have this room as private as possible. The public, upon seeing numerous members about an office (especially uniformed members), inevitably concludes that they are nonproductive. Roll call, with its attendant inspection, training, reading of orders, and special instructions, should be conducted in a place out of public view. It is equally important to provide space, which cannot be seen by the public, where officers may prepare reports that are not completed in the field because of time or importance.

## Special Features

It is wise to plan for a recreation area and lunch area with commissary provisions. The recreation area should be large enough to accommodate a universal gym and other physical exercise equipment that would encourage officers to maintain excellent physical condition, as well as provide space for defensive tactics and other training.

Squad or roll-call rooms should be designed so that desired privacy can be maintained during roll call and training sessions. Lockers should not be placed in these rooms thereby making it necessary for officers to change clothes or use lockers while the roll call for the next shift is in session. The squad room should not serve as a traffic path to other portions of the building.

Movable seating should be provided where roll-call and training is conducted. The room should be acoustically treated and equipped with wall-mounted bulletin boards, chalk boards, individual mail slots for distribution of printed material, and wall-mounted clothes and hat racks. An ideal work flow pattern would show the locker room adjacent to the roll-call room.

## Locker Facilities

An individual clothes locker should be provided for each uniformed officer in the department. The locker facility should be coupled with shower room accommodations.

## Training

Where possible, a training room should be separate from the roll-call room. This would allow uninterrupted training sessions. In the event that space is at a premium, the roll-call room could be designed as a multipurpose room large enough to conduct training sessions.

## Library

A police library is a reflection of the philosophy of a police administrator and his agency to achieve the best possible law enforcement through constant staff study and improvement.

A library should be provided with a sufficient number of bookshelves and seating capacity to accommodate approximately 5 percent of the work force. Tables in the library should be at least 5 to 6 feet from each other if the chairs are to be placed back to back. Between the tables and the walls, there should be an aisle approximately 5 feet wide. The length of the shelving should not be more than 3 feet per section.

## PROPERTY ROOMS

### Department Property

Department-owned property such as report forms, stationery, blank books, pencils, and other office equipment should be stored in a single room. Likewise, the department armament and munitions should be stored in a dustproof, moistureproof, secure room. It is recognized that armament must be immediately available to operational personnel; however, the supervisor in charge of property management must have the armament under his or her immediate control and provide for routine inspections and inventory of such equipment. Both of these factors must be considered when planning for the location of the armory.

### Evidence Room

An evidence storage room should be included in any planning for a police facility. The room should be secured against unauthorized intrusion and should allow for four different types of storage modes:

1. Open bins
2. File cabinets
3. Safe
4. Refrigerator

Open bins should constitute the majority of the room area. The bins should be approximately 3 feet wide and should be designed to allow for expansion upward. The balance of the evidence room can best be utilized by installing standard, letter-sized file cabinets. Small items that are more subject to loss are better stored in cabinets.

A good-sized safe should constitute the third storage mode for inclusion in an evidence room. This receptacle should be used to safeguard monies, jewelry, and other such valuables.

A refrigerator should be used to store narcotics, blood samples, and other perishables.

Since the evidence room would not normally be open 24 hours a day, it is necessary to establish temporary holding lockers into which evidence can be placed until it can be secured by the department evidence custodian. These lockers should be either self-locking or equipped with open padlocks. Officers coming into possession of evidence should properly mark it and deposit it in a locker. The door can then be snapped shut or padlocked. It should thereafter be opened only by the duly designated evidence custodian.

All evidence should be kept in the evidence storage room when not otherwise being examined or presented at trial.

### Laboratory Facilities

The location of the laboratory in a police building is relatively unimportant, and some advantages are gained in having it in a remote area.

Space requirements and utility connections are the principal considerations; space needs are strongly influenced by the size of the laboratory staff and the equipment used. A police laboratory should be designed to meet future requirements.

Every agency should have at least a rudimentary laboratory. Depending upon the department's expertise and size, a laboratory could range in size from a single photography darkroom to a complex facility with separate rooms to accommodate a darkroom; copy and other photographic work; chemical examinations; other laboratory instruments; evidence storage; a repository of standards for comparison; a director's office; a reception room; and a polygraph room.

Needless to say, those agencies that are physically located near a county, regional, state, or federal laboratory facility would require less laboratory space.

**Firearms Range**

An indoor firearms range should be considered as a very necessary component of every police facility. Such a range would most likely be situated in the basement or, in the case of only one floor, adjacent to the main facility. A minimum area for a range should be approximately 100 feet in length with a minimum of 4 feet in width for each shooting position desired.

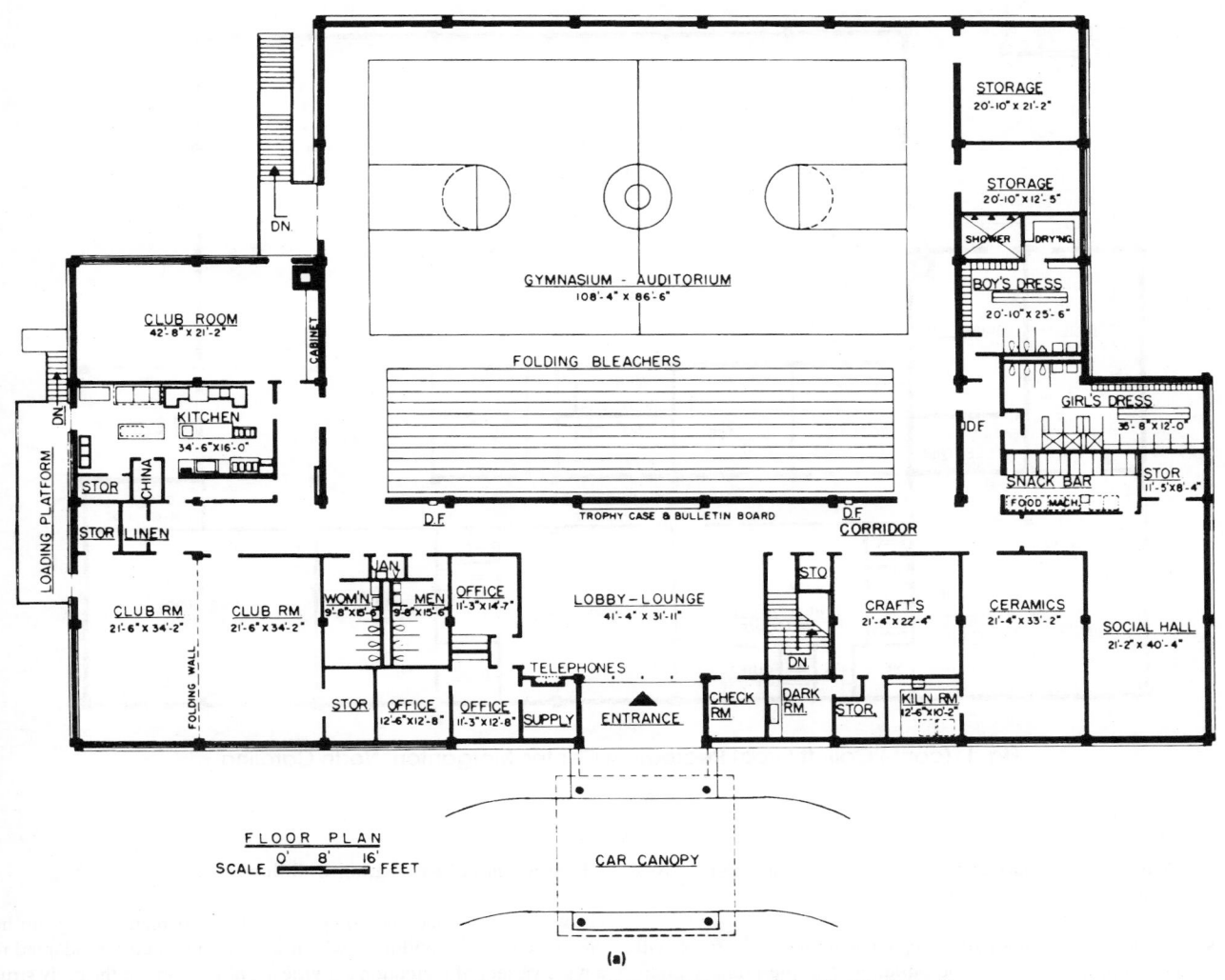

**Fig. 1. Collett Street Recreation Center, Morganton, North Carolina**

# RECREATION CENTERS

Recreation buildings should be functionally designed to make possible a varied program of activities. These buildings should be designed and dedicated to meet the needs of all people in their respective neighborhoods and communities.

Recreation buildings should provide a safe, healthful, and attractive atmosphere in which every person in the community or neighborhood has the opportunity to enjoy his leisure by participation in activities of a social, creative, cultural, or physical nature.

Almost without exception, recreation areas require some type of structure which will fulfill program needs and yet blend aesthetically into their surroundings. In terms of function, building types may range from the simple picnic shelter to the complex community recreation building with its variety of special service facilities.

In many neighborhoods and communities, school facilities are adequately equipped to provide recreation programs for youth, but other existing age groups are not always served. In such instances, the community must depend upon public recreation facilities which are planned and operated independently to accommodate a recreation program for the total community. Since the school is an integral part of the community, it should have a part in the planning of public recreation facilities. Conversely, when school buildings are being designed, cooperative planning with community recreation authorities is essential in order to assure that the new structures will include facilities needed for joint school and community use.

## PLANNING OBJECTIVES

The planning and design of a recreation building demand a precise and logical approach. Since a recreation building reflects the unique needs of a neighborhood or community, the specific plans and design

*Credits: Planning Areas and Facilities for Health, Physical Education, and Recreation,* rev., The Athletic Institute, Merchandise Mart, Chicago, Illinois, American Association for Health, Physical Education, and Recreation, Washington, D.C.

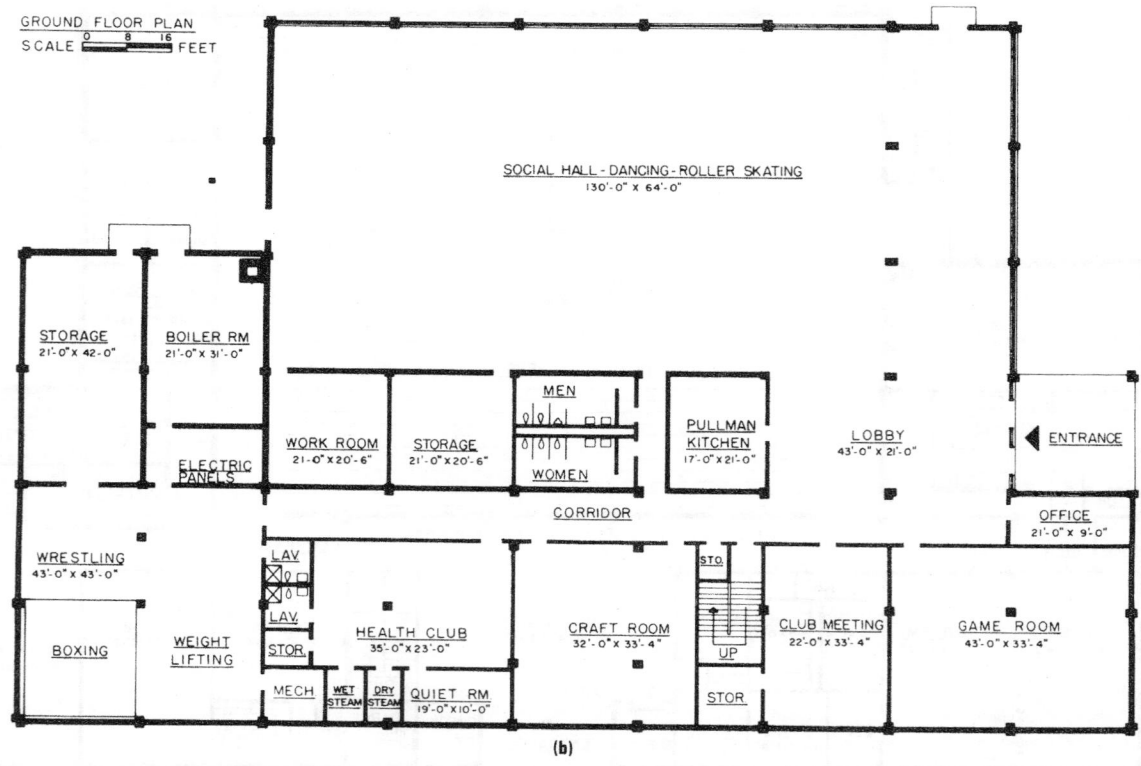

**Fig. 1. (cont.) Collett Street Recreation Center, Morganton, North Carolina**

will vary, but the preliminary considerations and planning objectives will be the same.

The successful incorporation of accepted planning objectives will ensure maximum utilization of the building. The preliminary plans and the continuous reevaluation of the functional design of the building prior to its construction should be considered in terms of the following questions:

- Has the most effective use of the entire area been determined, and does it utilize all of the natural resources?
- Does the preliminary plan include all of the essential areas and facilities necessary to fulfill the program objectives?
- Does the design provide for flexibility in use and for future expansion?
- Does the floor plan permit convenient access to, and facilitate circulation within, the building?
- Does the floor plan provide for ease in supervision and administration of the building?
- Have individual rooms been located and designed so as to encourage multiple use within safety limits?
- Has the building been designed so as to ensure opportunity for its use by all members of the community, including the aging and disabled?
- Does the design encompass accepted aesthetic qualities that relate harmoniously with the surroundings?
- Is the building designed and constructed so as to ensure joint use with other public or private agencies?
- Is the building so designed that it will permit economy in construction and maintenance?

## Classification of Recreation Buildings

Growth in the scope and complexity of the recreation program has created a need for buildings which will provide facilities adapted for a wide variety of recreation activities. Unlike many of the early structures, present-day buildings provide for adaptability and multiple use. This change from the simple to the complex has stimulated the development of a variety of recreation buildings. These are classified by function and then categorized by size.

The standards used for determining the size requirements of recreation buildings are usually based upon a square-footage-to-population ratio. This may be determined by allowing 1 to 2 square feet per person to be served. For example, if the building is to serve 8,000 persons, it should be approximately 12,000 square feet in size. This footage ratio may vary where cities build one center to accommodate the entire population.

## Type I Recreation Buildings

The plan in Fig. 1 illustrates a Type I recreation building. This type of building is usually constructed in larger subdivisions or suburban areas of a metropolitan center. However, many smaller cities (30,000 or less) have constructed such facilities to serve the total community.

This type of building encloses 20,000 square feet or more and usually includes the following facilities:

Multipurpose
Game room

Gymnasium
Shower and locker rooms
Office (administration) rooms
Office (staff)
Club rooms
Rest rooms
Arts and crafts room
Kitchen
Lounge and lobby
Large storage areas

## Type II Recreation Buildings

The Type II recreation building is illustrated in Fig. 2. This is the most common type and can be used in any city or community. It is believed by many recreation experts that the most efficiently operated building is the one designed to accommodate a neighborhood or area of approximately 8,000 people.

This building encloses 10,000 to 20,000 square feet and includes basically the same facilities as the Type I structure. Room sizes may vary and emphasis may be placed on those facilities that will best serve the program objectives.

## Type III Recreation Buildings

These buildings are used in many communities to satisfy the needs of less populated areas and usually include most of the following facilities (Fig. 3):

Social hall or gymnasium
Shower-dressing room
Club room
Lobby-lounge
Office
Rest rooms
Kitchenette
Adequate storage areas

**Social Hall-Gymnasium**

In order to obtain maximum benefit from the social hall-gymnasium, this facility is ordinarily used for a variety of social activities, such as dancing, banquets, and roller skating, in addition to basketball and other forms of athletics.

The size of a community recreation building's social hall-gymnasium should be at least 90 by 100 feet, with a minimum height of 22 feet. This will permit a basketball court of 50 by 84 feet.

These dimensions will permit seven tiers of telescopic bleachers on one side of the social hall-gymnasium, seating approximately 325 spectators.

Provision should be made for a mechanical ventilating system (forced air). The wainscoting should provide clear, unobstructed wall space from the floor to a height of 12 feet. If the room contains windows, they should be placed above the wainscoting on the sides and should be provided with protective guards. There should be no windows at either end of the social hall-gymnasium.

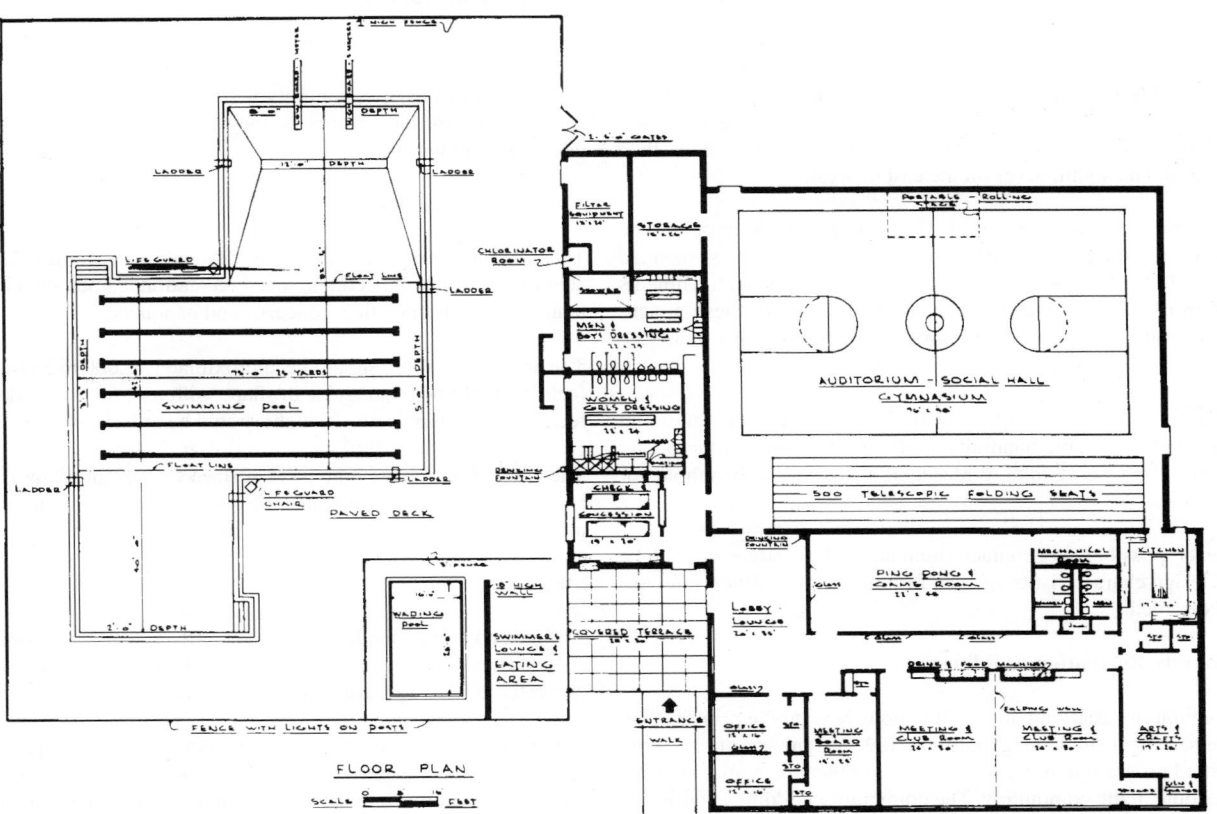

**Fig. 2. Thomaston-Upson County Recreation Center, Thomaston, Georgia**

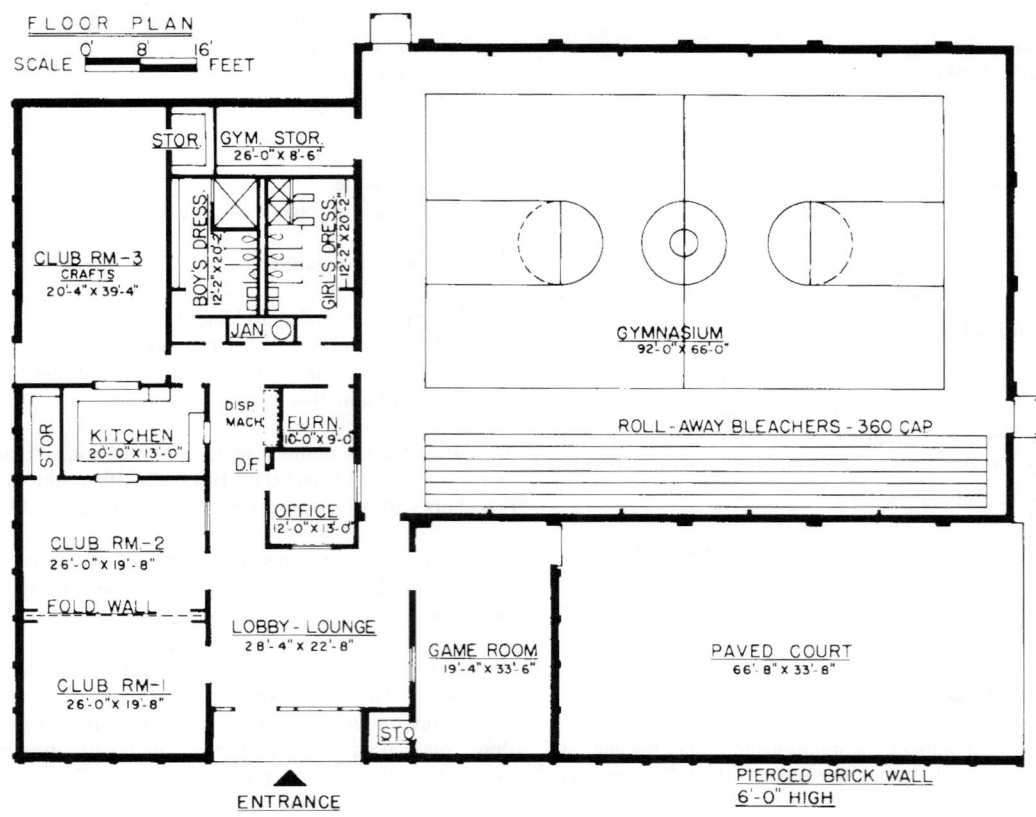

**Fig. 3. Glenwood Community Center, Greensboro, North Carolina**

It is preferable to have no windows in a social hall-gymnasium as they have little functional value. If it is necessary to use windows, they should be placed on the north side, or if used on two sides, then on the north and south, never on the east or west.

Maple flooring is commonly used. The cork spring clip or other type expansion joint should be installed on all four sides. If suspended apparatus is used in the social hall-gymnasium and wall attachments for control ropes and chains are affixed to the wall, these attachments should be at least 7 feet above the floor level and should be recessed.

This room should be equipped with stainless steel or aluminum portable and removable handrails attached to all wall surfaces, and also along the face of folding bleachers to provide a handhold for roller skaters.

Whenever possible, noncontact (nonmarring) furniture should be used. Design characteristics of such furniture also facilitate safer use by the disabled.

**Community Recreation Buildings**

A community recreation building functions beyond the primary purpose of serving a single neighborhood. It is designed to offer a more diversified program in order to meet the complete recreational needs of all people in the community. The community building is normally larger than a neighborhood building and is usually located in a major recreation area such as a community park or playing field.

As stated previously, community recreation buildings vary in function and design, but, generally, they contain most of the facilities described on the following pages.

**Multipurpose Room**

The multipurpose room should be designed to accommodate such activities as general meetings, social recreation, games, dancing, dramatics, orchestra practice, concerts, and banquets.

The area of this room should be approximately 2,000 to 3,000 square feet. It should be rectangular in shape with a minimum width of 40 feet. The minimum ceiling height should be at least 16 feet.

The floor should have a nonskid surface to prevent many common accidents. The floor should also be level in order to permit multiple use for meetings, dancing, dramatic presentations, etc.

**Stage**

A stage and related facilities are frequently included in a community center. They may be built in conjunction with the multipurpose room or, preferably, as a separate unit.

The stage proper should be about 20 feet in depth, and the proscenium opening should be at least two-thirds the width of the room. It is desirable that the approach to the stage from the floor of the main room be by inclined ramp with a nonskid surface to accommodate the physically disabled and aging and to facilitate the movement of equipment.

consideration might be given to the construction of an outdoor
[st]age contiguous to the multipurpose room. Some buildings have
[be]en successfully constructed with a revolving stage for outdoor
[an]d indoor programs. Portable or recessed stages might also be
[co]nsidered.

## [D]ressing-Locker Room

[A] room for the purpose of changing clothes is necessary and should
[b]e in close proximity to the social hall-gymnasium. There are
[t]wo accepted plans for checking personal apparel: (1) the use of
[lo]cker rooms with metal lockers; and (2) the use of dressing rooms
[w]ith a checkroom for checking clothing in wire baskets or nylon
[b]ags.

[If] the lockers are to be used in connection with outdoor sports, they
[sh]ould be located so the players will have access to them without
[go]ing through the entire building. The suggested requirements for
[th]e locker room in a community recreation building are as follows for
[m]en and boys, 200 lockers; for women and girls, 150 lockers. The
[pl]acement of lockers should take into account the space requirements
[o]f the disabled.

[T]he floor of the locker room should pitch to a central drain or drains
[to] facilitate cleaning and washing. The junction of the wall and floor
[sh]ould be coved. In the women's locker room, dressing booths
[sh]ould be supplied in the ratio of 10 percent of the total number of
[lo]ckers. Hair dryers and nonbreakable liquid-soap dispensers are also
[re]commended.

[T]he use of galvanized-wire baskets or nylon or plastic bags is another
[o]ption. This system will accommodate the same number of users in
[a]bout one-quarter of the space required for metal lockers. However,
[th]ere is no saving of space required for dressing.

[If] there is a possibility of a swimming pool being constructed on this
[s]ite at some future time, dressing rooms should be located and
[ar]ranged so as to serve both the gymnasium and the pool.

## [S]hower Rooms

[T]he size of shower rooms is dependent upon the extent of the facili-
[ti]es and the number of persons to be served at one time. Adequate
[v]entilation should be a primary consideration.

[F]or mens facilities, it is suggested that approximately 12 shower
[h]eads be provided, spaced a minimum of 4 feet apart and 6 feet above
[th]e floor level. For women and girls, it is recommended that a mini-
[m]um of 6 group shower heads and 3 individual shower-and-dressing
[b]ooths be provided. Shower heads should be 4½ feet above the floor
[le]vel. Nonbreakable liquid-soap dispensers are recommended, and
[h]air dryers are suggested for the ladies' locker room.

[T]o accommodate the disabled, two folding "L" seats should be placed
[i]n opposite corners of each group shower to facilitate both right-hand
[an]d left-hand approaches.

[I]n the construction of the shower-room floor, drainage gutters 4
[i]nches deep and 8 to 10 inches wide placed around the perimeter of
[th]e shower room will provide a sanitary means of drainage. The cen-
[tr]al portion of the shower floor, raised above the depressed area,
[sh]ould drain toward the shower drains. A carborundum-impregnated
[ce]ramic tile, or its equal, will provide a nonslip surface.

The temperature of water feeding into the shower heads should be
120°F, controlled by means of a mixing chamber rather than by individual control. Vandalproof shower heads should be used.

## Club Rooms

Experience indicates the desirability of providing a minimum of 500
square feet of floor space per club room. For community recreation
buildings, at least three to five club rooms should be provided for
multiple use. At least one large club room should be located adjoining the kitchen.

When windows in club rooms and lounges are placed high in a wall,
they are not broken as often as low windows and they also provide
more space for furniture, bulletin boards, pegboards, chalkboards,
and exhibits. Since broken window glass is a major problem, a nonbreakable type of windowpane is preferable.

A chair rail or wainscoting to prevent the marring of walls should be
installed to a height of 3 feet above the floor. Whenever possible,
noncontact (nonmarring) furniture should be used.

## Arts and Crafts Room

A separate arts and crafts room is desirable. However, if this is not
possible, then at least one club room should be equipped for crafts,
with provision for gas, compressed air, and a sink with hot and cold
water. The sink should have a clay trap.

Ample storage cabinets, closets, or lockers should be included for the
safe storage of craft materials, unfinished projects, and exhibit materials. If a kiln is used, it should be placed in an adjoining room for
reasons of safety and should be equipped with a heavy-duty 220-volt
electrical outlet. Bulletin boards and exhibit cases may be used to
display completed projects.

## Lounge and Lobby

The lobby of the community recreation building is the space just
inside the entrance. The lounge should open off the lobby, and, if
possible, should be close to the central office and to the multipurpose
room and/or social hall-gymnasium. The lounge and lobby are often
combined into one room. When they are combined, it is suggested
that the size of the lobby-lounge be about 600 to 800 square feet.

This facility should be attractively lighted and should contain a wall-
mounted, recessed drinking fountain and a lighted trophy case and bulletin board. Appropriate space should be allowed for public telephones.
Provision should also be made for aquariums and for growing plants
and flowers. Adequate space, preferably recessed, and electrical and
water connections for automatic vending machines should be included.

The office, club rooms, game room, and rest rooms are usually adjacent to the lobby-lounge.

## Game Room

The game room, approximately 30 by 64 feet in size, is designed for
a variety of games, including billiards and table tennis. In planning
this room, sufficient storage space should be provided for various
items of game equipment and supplies to be used. This room should
be in close proximity to office supervision. It should also be acoustically treated, due to the noise factor.

The choice of floor material should be carefully considered because of the heavy traffic usually prevalent in this room. Windows should be placed high in the walls to reduce glass breakage. A chair rail or wainscoting to prevent the marring of walls should be installed to a height of 3 feet above the floor. Whenever possible, noncontact (non-marring) furniture should be used.

## Photography Room

A special room can be provided and equipped as a darkroom. Ventilation should be provided through the use of lightproof ventilators. Hot and cold running water, special light plugs—both wall and base—and photographic sinks for developing and washing prints should also be provided. A mixer is desirable to accurately control the water temperature. A filter should also be provided if the water quality is not good. Doors should be lightproof.

## Director's Office

An office of approximately 120 square feet in size is suggested, with sufficient window space to provide maximum supervision of the lobby, lounge, club rooms, and social hall-gymnasium. At least three walls should have windows. If there is a window connected to the social hall-gymnasium, a nonbreakable-type glass is preferable.

It is often recommended that there be an adjoining shower-dressing unit with a floor surface area of not less than 100 square feet. This unit should contain a shower, toilet and lavatory, clothes closet, and first-aid supply cabinet.

Opening off the director's office should be a storage closet with a burglarproof door for storing valuable supplies and equipment, such as the motion-picture projector and public address system.

## Rest Rooms

Rest room facilities should be designed to serve both indoor and outdoor areas. Provision should be made for direct access from the exterior of the building at a point adjacent to such activity areas.

Rest rooms should include multipurpose units, combining automatic towel and soap dispensers, mirror and shelf, and a combination paper-towel dispenser and waste receptacle. These units should be recessed in the wall. Mirrors should have metal frames and be recessed into the wall so they cannot be torn off. The preferred soap dispenser is built into the lavatory since this type is less subject to vandalism than the wall-installed type.

Dressing-room benches should be of a permanent type and should be securely anchored to the floor so they cannot be turned over, stacked against the wall, broken, or removed from the building. Toilet fixtures should be hung from the wall for ease in cleaning. In rest rooms where several fixtures are used, one fixture of proper height for young children and the disabled should be included. Lavatories should be of enamel-coated iron or other unbreakable material rather than vitreous china.

A flush-valve water closet with the valve 24 inches above the top of the fixture—or 3 feet above the floor—is preferred over a tank-type toilet fixture. Automatic valves for water taps in showers and lavatories are recommended to reduce water loss caused by taps being left open. Hose bibbs should be installed in each rest room and/or shower room, at a proper height so buckets can be placed under them.

Toilet facilities should be designed in accordance with the Americans with Disabilities Act Accessibility Guidelines.

## Kitchen

The Pullman or kitchenette-type kitchen is usually desirable for most community and neighborhood recreation buildings. If large dinners or banquets are to be served, provision should be made for a full-size modern kitchen that conforms to local health regulations and has a free floor space at least 54 inches wide.

The kitchen should be located near the club rooms and the social hall-gymnasium. This will make the kitchen available to small gatherings in the club rooms and to large banquet gatherings in the social hall-gymnasium. The kitchen is often placed between two club rooms and made available to both rooms by the use of aluminum roll-up doors.

Adequate storage space, cabinet space, and electrical outlets for such appliances as the refrigerator, the range, the dishwasher, and can openers should be provided. Exhaust fans should also be installed.

## Storage Areas

One of the most common errors found in many recreation buildings is the lack of sufficient storage space for equipment, maintenance, and custodial purposes.

## Equipment Storage

Provision should be made for storing apparatus and equipment. There should be an opening 6 feet wide with louvered flush doors between the social hall-gymnasium and the storage room. This will permit passage of the most bulky equipment. There should be no raised threshold.

The minimum size of the storage room should be approximately 250 square feet. Provision should be made for storage of inflated balls, bats, softballs, and other supplies, either in separate cabinets or a special closet. Appropriate bins, shelves, and racks are suggested. In addition, a recessed alcove for the storage of a piano is desirable.

## Maintenance Storage Room

The maintenance storage room varies in size, depending upon the adjacent outdoor space and the size of the building. The room is ordinarily located on the ground level, adjacent to the outdoor areas. An outside entrance should be provided by means of a burglar-proof door sufficiently large to permit the passage of motorized and other maintenance equipment.

This facility is used as a headquarters for all outdoor maintenance. It may have to house rakes, shovels, hose, marking equipment and supplies, hand tools, power tools, and other equipment. A repair shop and its facilities are usually incorporated in this area. The room should have sufficient base and wall outlets to serve both the workbench and power-equipment needs.

Recessed wall shelving and cabinet storage should be provided for tools, supplies, and equipment. This space should also contain hot

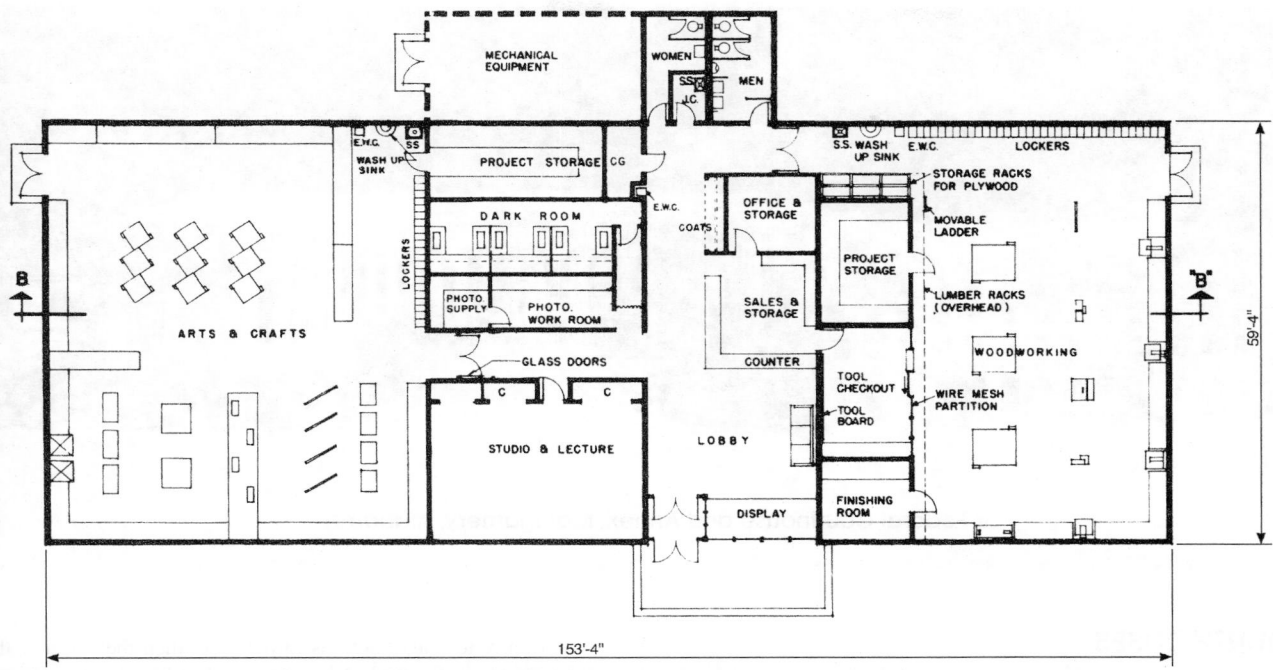

**Fig. 4. Recreation center. U.S. Naval Facilities Engineering Command, Department of the Navy, Washington D.C.**

nd cold water, a slop sink, a lavatory, a water closet, and a clothes loset. The floor should be concrete and should be pitched to a cen- ral drain. The junction of the floor and wall should be coved.

**Custodial Storage Rooms**

A supply closet equipped with a slop sink and space for mops, pails, rooms, and cleaning supplies should be centrally located on each loor level.

**Neighborhood Recreation Buildings**

The neighborhood recreation building (Fig. 4) will include many of the features of the community recreation building, as previously described. The neighborhood building, however, is usually intended to serve a smaller number of people. The size of the facility will ordinarily fall into the Type III (under 10,000 square feet) or Type II (10,000 to 20,000 square feet) classification. In all cases, the building should be so designed that rooms can be easily added.

**Federal Courthouse and Annex, Montgomery, Alabama**

# COURTHOUSES

There are two judicial systems throughout the United States. One system consists of state and local courts established under the authority of the state governments. These local courts may also include county, city, and municipal courts, depending on the jurisdictions and state guidelines. The other system is the federal court system.

State courts have general, unlimited authority over nearly every type of case, and are the courts with which the public has most interactions. Both civil and criminal cases are handled at this court level. However, they are subject to the particular limitations of their state laws and constitutions, and those of the U.S. Constitution.

In particular cases where the U.S. Constitution gives them authority, the federal courts have power to decide over those cases. In addition, the federal court may decide cases which might be between states or which question the jurisdiction or impartiality of a state court.

## GENERAL TRIAL COURT

### Trial Operations

Jury trials, whether civil or criminal, involve five general operations: opening preliminaries (including impaneling of the jury), opening statements, presentation of evidence by each side, closing statements, and deliberation and decision.

1. The opening preliminaries start with the bailiff's announcement that the court is in session and the naming of the presiding judge, who enters and calls the first case. The attorneys first have the opportunity to make motions in the case, then they signify that they are ready for trial. After the jury has been impaneled and sworn, an attorney may ask that all witnesses other than the parties be excluded from the courtroom. If the judge so rules, the witnesses are informed where they should wait. The court may recess a number of times, and it may adjourn to reconvene the following day or at some later time.

2. The prosecutor or the attorney for the plaintiff generally presents the first opening statement, followed by the defendant's opening statement. Each attorney tries to present the strong points of their case in their statement, defining the issues and describing the evidence they intend to present in support of their contentions. Motions may be made during or at the end of the opening statements.

3. The attorneys for each side then present their evidence. The prosecution in a criminal case, or the plaintiff in a civil action, goes first. Evidence consists of all exhibits and testimony by witnesses, including parties. Absent a priori stipulation on its admissibility, the opposing attorney may challenge the admissibility of any exhibit. The jury may be dismissed while the attorneys present their arguments to the judge on the matter, or the arguments may occur at the judge's bench or outside the courtroom. Each exhibit received in evidence is given an identifying number by the reporter or clerk. When the attorneys request the isolation of witnesses, private and secure waiting facilities outside the courtroom are necessary. After each witness is called and sworn by the clerk, the attorney who called the witness proceeds with direct examination. The opposing attorney then cross-examines the witness and the first attorney may then examine on redirect.

4. Attorneys make a closing statement to present the merits of their case forcefully and persuasively. Although practices vary, the

*Author:* Luis F. Pitarque, RA, NCARB

*References:* (Fig. 1.) *The American Courthouse: Planning and Design for the Judicial Process,* The American Bar Association and The American Institute of Architects Joint Committee on the Design of Courtrooms and Court Facilities, The Institute of Continuing Legal Education Ann Arbor, Michigan.

*Photo:* Model of the Federal Courthouse & Annex, Montgomery, AL. Barganier Davis Sims Architects, General Services Administration.

judge usually has had an earlier conference with the attorneys about the length of these statements and the content of instructions to be given to the jury. Generally, each attorney prepares the instructions that they wish the judge to give to the jury. The judge may use any of these or, in most jurisdictions, may frame their own instructions. Opposing counsel may object to specific instructions given by the judge. A growing number of states are adopting pattern jury instructions, which are standardized expositions of points of law to be used in every case where they are applicable. Such instructions should reduce the number of inconsistent and conflicting decisions in the trial courts of the state and eventually reduce the number of appeals.

Jury deliberation and decision continues until agreement is reached or the jury informs the bailiff that it cannot agree upon a verdict. Deliberations can continue for days, and unless facilities are planned so that the trial courtroom can be utilized for other proceedings during this period, the space is not being used efficiently. After the jury returns a verdict, the losing attorney may ask that the jury be polled; the judge then asks jurors if the verdict properly states their decision. Judgment may be entered on the verdict forthwith, or judgment may be reserved until the judge has ruled on post-trial motions filed by counsel.

These operations illustrate the need for separate circulation systems, one for general use by the public and one for restricted use by court support staff and the judiciary (Fig. 1). In addition, a secure circulation system would be provided for use by prisoners and law enforcement officers.

## Space Requirements

Table 1 shows the areas for movement and furniture (including working and seating surfaces) which each person in the courtroom requires. The nonencroachment distance of 5-6 feet for the judge insures a degree of privacy commensurate with their role. A nonencroachment distance surrounding jurors and witnesses helps prevent violation of the jurors' impartial role by attorneys and lessens the impact of attempts to intimidate witnesses.

Numerous cases involve several parties and more than one attorney for each side. Space should be provided for four attorneys and four parties, an area of 192-240 square feet. In addition, a space of 112-140 square feet must be provided for 12 jurors and two alternates.

Thirty jurors are usually called for examination (voir dire); if 30 spectators are assumed, the total public and observation seating area required would be 180-240 square feet, with perhaps an additional 50-75 square feet for the media. A total space of 534-695 square feet is required to accommodate all active (304-380 square feet) and passive (230-315 square feet) participants. This does not include general circulation space.

## Communication and Spatial Patterns

The four types of communications in every courtroom are visible, audio, movement of people, and document transfer. By studying the frequency and importance of communications, a communication pattern is developed for each person in relation to every other person in the courtroom. The communication pattern is then utilized to show how each person should be spatially related to every other person. The patterns for the four types of communications, together with the unit space requirements, provide the analytical basis for a courtroom plan.

*A Total Communication System*

By combining the separate analyses of visual and audio communications, movement of people and document transfer, a total pattern of communications is achieved (Fig. 2). The attorneys and judge are the main nodes of communication, followed in importance by the witness and the jury.

Figure 3 is the final composite spatial disposition diagram resulting from a superimposition of separate diagrams. This diagram reveals that if the visual requirements of the active participants are met, most of the other requirements are fulfilled. The bailiff can move unobtrusively to judge, witness, and jury; easily supervise and escort witnesses and jurors; and keep the public and press under constant surveillance.

The witness is located within the private conversation zone of the judge. To keep the witness out of this zone and still meet the visual requirements, the space around which the active participants are grouped must be expanded. Failing this, the judge's bench should be designed so that the end farthest from the witness box can be used for private talks (or "sidebar") between judge and counsel with the reporter present.

Only visual and audio requirements need be considered in the location of the public and media. No satisfactory visual location of the observation area permits it to fall wholly within the desirable audio zone.

*Observation Space Problems*

The space allocated to public and media in Fig. 3 may not be sufficient for cases that attract a large attendance. However, the ability to satisfy visual and audio requirements decreases as the observation space expands beyond its optimum position. With an extension sideways, the public and media move behind the primary participants and are less able to see faces clearly. If the public and media space is extended around the rear of the attorneys' and parties' stations, the public and press would see the attorney only from behind when they address the court. Such extension would also conflict with any expansion of the area for attorneys and parties in cases involving several of each. Where there is a problem and those areas cannot be extended or expanded, it may be necessary to move the case to a larger courtroom.

Providing a large public observation space in every courtroom to accommodate an occasional well-publicized case is unrealistic and expensive. Most courtrooms require only sufficient space to accommodate relatives and friends of the defendant or people directly related to the case.

In jurisdictions where the impaneling of jurors, including the voir dire questioning, is performed in the courtroom, there should be adequate space for the seating of prospective jurors. The observation area is the natural place for this purpose. If 30 persons are required from which to impanel a jury, the observation area should provide seating for this number plus some observers, perhaps a total of 40. If the jurors are impaneled outside the courtroom, 20 seats would be quite adequate for observers.

In each jurisdiction, average and maximum public attendance for each type of case should be recorded and analyzed to assist in the formulation of space requirements for future facilities. Occasional cases for which a large public attendance is anticipated can be assigned to

**COURT AS A WHOLE**

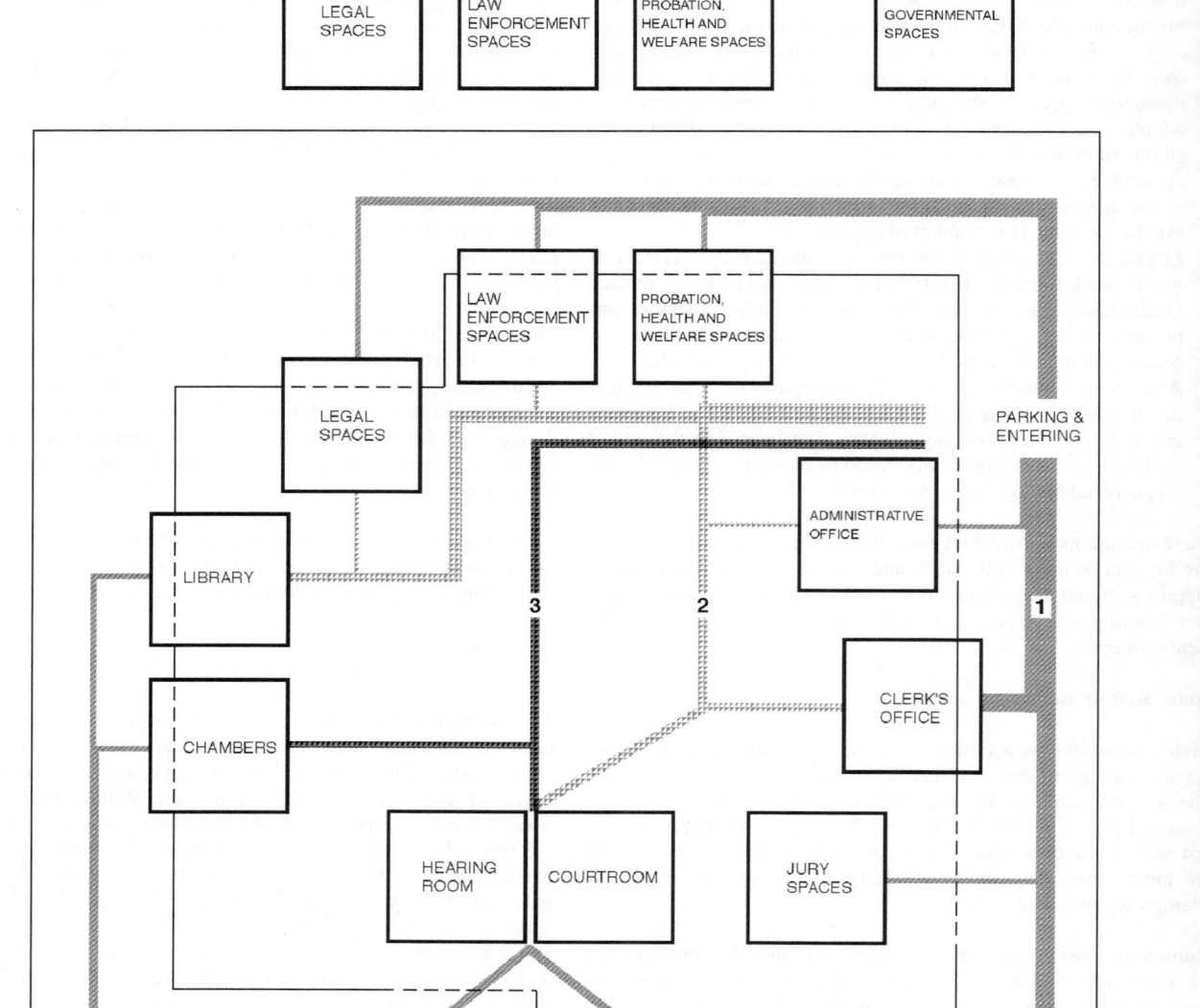

**Fig. 1. Movement and access to internal spaces in the general trial court**

## Table 1 Unit space requirements of the courtroom

| PARTICIPANTS | FURNITURE AREA PER PERSON, SQ. FT. | MOVEMENT AREA PER PERSON, SQ. FT. | TOTAL AREA PER PERSON, SQ. FT. |
|---|---|---|---|
| JUDGE | 20-25* | 25-30 | 45-55 |
| CLERK | 15-18 | 15-17 | 30-35 |
| REPORTER | 8-9 | 3-6 | 11-15 |
| BAILIFF | 8-9 | 3-6 | 11-15 |
| ATTORNEY | 15-18† | 17-22 | 32-40 |
| PARTY | 11-13 | 5-7 | 16-20 |
| WITNESS | 7-9* | 8-11 | 15-20 |
| JUROR | 4-5* | 4-5 | 8-10 |
| PRESS | 6-7 | 4-8 | 10-15 |
| PUBLIC | 3-4 | 3-4 | 6-8 |

\* ADD A NONENCROACHMENT DISTANCE OF 5-6 FT.
† ADD 4-5 SQ. FT. FOR A MOVABLE PODIUM.

courtrooms equipped with larger public observation spaces. One judge writes: "With respect to courtrooms for jury trials, I believe they must be basically of one size. The need for larger space for the public during an important trial would have its drawbacks. Basically, we are interested in the litigants, their witnesses and relatives and friends—not to provide an amphitheater for those interested in watching a particular procedure."

A recent survey indicates that most news reporters want a court location where they can clearly see and hear the primary participants; leave the courtroom with minimum disturbance; have adequate writing surfaces, have an unobstructed frontal view of all participants and a clear close-up view of all exhibits; and be close enough to the witness to hear every word. With the increased use of new technology such as assisted listening systems and electronic evidence display systems, several of the issues addressed above may be mitigated.

Because they fear it would set a precedent for excluding the media from the courtroom, most news reporters see little merit in seating the press in another room behind a one-way window with a view of the proceedings. However, there is some interest in an enclosed press area behind a one-way window that would permit the use of phones and possibly courtroom photography. A one-way window would give news reporters maximum freedom to converse and move about and enable them to have instant communication with their offices in order to meet deadlines. Some news reporters, on the other hand, think that a courtroom should be designed primarily for the trial proceedings and that no special provisions should be made for the press.

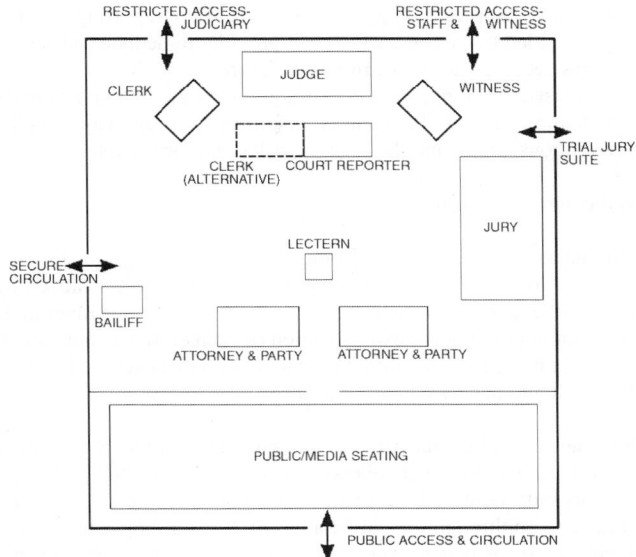

**Fig. 3. Spatial disposition for jury trials, based on a total communication system**

In most general trial courtrooms today, the space ratio between the action area and the public observation space is approximately two to one, with the latter being a physical part of the court room. The public is usually placed behind the attorneys and parties as a visually integrated part of the courtroom.

If the observation space were separated from the courtroom by a glass wall and a sound system were installed, there would still be a possibility of visual distraction from the audience. This would not be the case, however, if one-way glass were used as the separating wall. Depending on the number of people to be accommodated, the observation area could be placed in two or more locations. Whatever its size and location, this area requires different spatial and other environmental considerations than does the courtroom action area.

Closed-circuit television (CCTV) is being accepted more and more in a public trial, which affects the spatial relationship between the public observation space and the courtroom. The public observation space would no longer have to adjoin the courtroom, which could lead to several drastic design and planning changes:

- There would be a significant reduction in the size of the courtroom. Few jury courtrooms would need to exceed 1,500 square feet, and the area of nonjury courtrooms could be considerably smaller.
- In a multilevel courthouse, more courtrooms could be grouped together on each floor. Public traffic could be more readily separated from the traffic of courtroom participants; thus, more courtrooms on each floor would not necessarily mean greater traffic congestion.
- Public observation spaces could be centralized on the lower floors of a multilevel building, concentrating the public traffic to avoid overload of the vertical transportation system and minimizing unnecessary movement throughout the building.
- Public access TV could provide the ability for the public to view court proceedings through local cable TV channels, or through major media channels in a case attracting national attention.

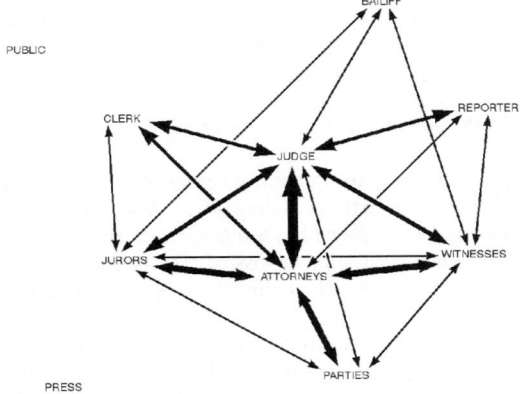

**Fig. 2. A total communication system for jury trials**

- Court reporter technology allows for real-time reporting or computer-aided transcripts, which can provide immediate transcripts of proceedings at remote monitors/locations.
- Increased use of remote video arraignments and first appearances will allow several of the courts' functions to occur away from the courthouse, reducing the security risk of the prisoners.

**Courtroom Accessibility**

Participants entering the courtroom should be able to get to their respective locations as directly as possible, a goal best achieved by placing access points close to their locations (Fig. 3). The diagram is not meant to pinpoint the exact location of each entrance, but simply to indicate its general position; nor is it implied that each type of participant should have a separate entrance.

Movement of participants from spaces outside the courtroom to their points of access should also be as direct as possible. The judge and the court staff, coming from their chambers and staff offices, should not have to go through the public areas of the courthouse to get into the courtroom. This is not merely a matter of convenience. Personal contact between jurors and the public should be avoided under all circumstances to minimize the risk of mistrial. Separate public, private, and security zones must be established in the courthouse, with similar zones of access to the courtroom.

An alternate plan may be possible that allows the judge, court staff, and jurors coming directly from their outside private zone and going directly to their stations within the courtroom. However, this takes away from the flexibility of use for that particular courtroom by tying it in to the respective judge's chambers. The public and the media should be able to enter their observation area directly from the public zone. Attorneys, parties, and witnesses should be able to enter their waiting areas from the public zone and from there go directly to their stations in the courtroom. Prisoners should come directly through a separate security zone to a detention space near the bailiff's station.

All these plans indicate the need for three separate and distinct circulation systems within the courthouse: public circulation for use by the general public, including attorneys, parties, witnesses, and the media; restricted or private circulation to be used by the judge, court staff, jurors, and attorneys/parties/witnesses on a controlled basis; and secure circulation to be used by prisoners and bailiffs/detention officers.

## NONJURY TRIALS, HEARINGS AND ANCILLARY FUNCTIONS

The current trend in the court system is toward achievement of a speedier and more effective administration of justice. In the nonjury trial, participants are few and the operations are simple; in formal and informal hearings, the participants are even fewer and the operations simpler. Thus, the physical requirements of these proceedings are modified accordingly from those of the jury trial.

Courtrooms equipped for full jury trials can, of course, be used for nonjury trials and hearings. A flexible arrangement of furniture, with a movable spectator rail and front rows of seating which can double as attorneys' tables, is desirable.

Certain cases are being heard in mediation and arbitration hearings, where a neutral third-party attempts to resolve a dispute through meetings with the disputing parties. The purpose is to facilitate communication in seeking resolution, and as an alternative to trial in a wide variety of cases. Many jurisdictions are putting an emphasis on this type of hearing, which may be required as the first step in some cases, and may alternately be identified as the alternate dispute resolution program. However, the mediator is not generally authorized to impose a settlement or issue a decision.

**Objectives**

*Nonjury Trials*

In comparison with jury trials, nonjury trials reduce the emotional and monetary costs; they also require less time for disposition. The nonjury trial encourages a substantial reduction in the real or apparent hostility of attorneys and allows the judge to dispose of many more disputes. The time for impaneling a jury is eliminated, and opening and closing statements can be much briefer since the judge is presumed to be an expert. Arguments can be heard immediately because repeated recesses for discussion out of hearing of the jury are not required. There is no need for the preparation of instructions to the jury, and the time for jury deliberation and decision is eliminated.

The needs of news reporters and the general public are essentially the same as in jury trials. However, there is generally much less public interest in nonjury trials; the physical facilities for news reporters and public observers can be reduced without impairing any privileges.

*Hearings*

Whether a hearing is formal or informal, its primary characteristic is variety. There is a broad spectrum of legal proceedings ranging from adoption to bankruptcy to arraignment to general motion practice. There is an equivalent range in the extent to which hearings can dispose of cases. A hearing may result in final disposition, temporary resolution, resolution of one part of a larger proceeding or a temporary postponement. The degree to which a hearing is an adversary proceeding can also range widely within the same type of hearing, whether formal or informal. The same is true of the number and types of persons involved, as well as the degree of simplicity or complexity of their activities. Despite this, courtrooms should be designed primarily for the trial proceedings and no special provisions should be made for the press.

Formal hearings require flexibility seasoned with appropriate solemnity and restraint. Flexibility is needed because of the variety of matters which may come before the presiding officers, who may or may not be judges. Appropriate solemnity and restraint are needed because of the hostility which may be present.

Informal hearings require flexibility seasoned with kindly or businesslike responses from the presiding officer. The hearing should aim at maximum interchange within a quasiprivate environment. Informality can be achieved without loss of dignity and with minimum restraint on all participants, including the presiding officers. Flexibility is required because of the great variety of legal proceedings heard informally. When personal problems are involved, an atmosphere of calm and friendly concern is needed. For fiscal matters like bankruptcy or small claims, an atmosphere of efficiency and businesslike involvement is desirable.

## Operations

### Nonjury Trials

The general operations of the nonjury trial include the opening preliminaries, opening statements, presentation of evidence, closing statements, and deliberation and decision by the judge.

With the elimination of a jury, activities are simplified. Opening preliminaries involve only convening of the court and determining that all parties or their representatives are ready for trial. Opening and closing statements tend to be briefer. Presentation of evidence may evoke objections, but these can be argued and ruled upon immediately by the judge. Closing statements are usually confined to questions of law raised by the case. The judge either gives a decision immediately or takes the case under advisement. In the latter instance, the judge often asks for briefs from each side. After the decision, post-trial motions are filed and later considered by the judge, and a judgment, final unless appealed, is given.

### Hearings

Certain hearings are almost indistinguishable from trials without a jury and, further, the dividing line between formal and informal hearings is as nebulous as the line of demarcation between informal hearings and conferences.

Hearings, both formal and informal, may be related to a trial or may be used as a substitute for a trial to dispose of cases in certain specialized legal proceedings involving, for example, minors, incompetents, injunctions or probate matters.

Most hearings related to trials involve motions, which are typically requests that the court decide a single issue such as jurisdiction or a change of venue, discovery requests, a motion for a new trial or postponement of sentencing. Motions can be made verbally at the hearing or presented in writing, and arguments can be verbal or in the form of briefs. Decisions can be expressed as an opinion or a verbal assent or dissent.

The operations in the formal hearing include the opening preliminaries; presentation and argument, in which the presiding officer may play an active role; and decision by the presiding officer. They are not too different from nonjury trials—somewhat less elaborate but still retaining the formal qualities of a trial. The presiding officer may be a judge or a court officer such as a referee in bankruptcy cases. Typically, a clerk and a court reporter make an official transcript of the proceeding.

Opening preliminaries include convening the hearing and determining that all necessary parties or their representatives are ready to proceed. Depending on the type of hearing, the presiding officer may actively participate in examination of a party or witness or may sit as a disinterested overseer of the proceeding. In the latter instance, the hearing operates in much the same fashion as a nonjury trial. Decision by the presiding officer may be made immediately, or they may take the matter under advisement and hand down a decision at a later date.

Informal hearings are similar, but less stylized and often private. Attorneys are frequently not present and usually a small number of persons attend. Very often court reporters are not necessary and in some instances the presiding officer does not use a clerk or bailiff. Official orders are either prepared and signed during the hearing by the presiding officer or prepared, signed, and transmitted at a later date.

Exploration of the problem and its possible solutions may involve ordered presentations by the parties or their attorneys, or it may only be a conversation between the presiding officer and someone who has a problem. The problem can be extremely complicated, or it may only require a necessary signing of a document. Usually, the decision of the presiding officer is made immediately.

### Requirements of Nonjury Trials and Formal Hearings

Each nonjury trial and formal hearing exhibits different characteristics, but even in the largest metropolitan areas it is impractical to design a formal hearing room to serve each type of case. Instead, it is more practical to have one room which can be adapted to fewer participants and differing degrees of formality. Furniture should be movable and adjustable in height, so that its arrangement can conform to the degree of formality. Adjustable partitions and ceilings allow for change in the size and character of the room as needed. The bench or seating area for the presiding officer and support staff should still retain and enforce the authority and respect due a representative of the court.

Except for the elimination of jury activities and the space required for the jury box, the activity, space, and communication (visual, audio, movement, and document transfer) relationships in nonjury trials and formal hearings are the same as in jury trials. There is only a slight variation in the degree of importance of the bailiff.

### Composite Spatial Disposition

As might be expected, the composite spatial disposition for communications (Fig. 4) is much the same as that for the jury trial (Fig. 3). The absence of a jury enables the participants to be closer to each other, and the attorneys and parties can be moved toward the judge. The diameter of the trial area is also reduced by approximately 5 feet.

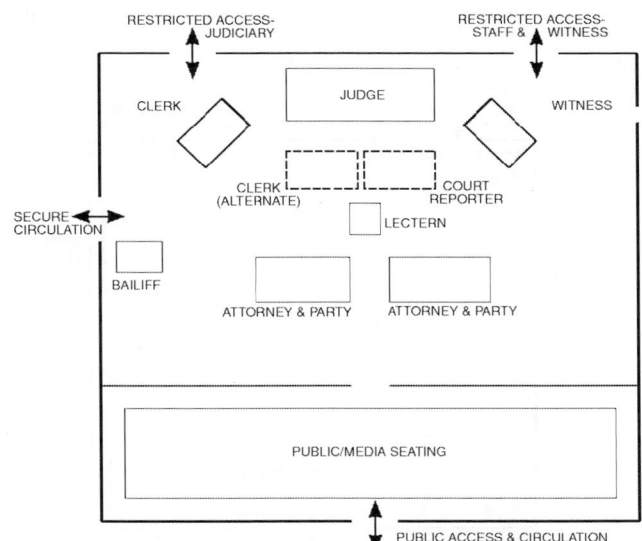

**Fig. 4. Spatial disposition based on a total communication system (nonjury trials, formal hearings)**

## Optimum Access to the Nonjury Trial Courtroom

The use of movable furniture in the trial area in front or below the judge's bench will allow rearrangements to conform to proceedings of differing complexity and formality. With fewer participants, the distance between them can be reduced or they can be brought into a less formal relation to each other.

Figure 5 shows the location of television cameras related to a videotape system. The camera behind the clerk is capable of panning 180 degrees while the second camera is fixed on the judge and the witnesses. The only variation from the jury trial is that the exhibits display board is now within the range of the first camera. In a jury trial courtroom, only the fixed camera would be used, to provide protection to the jurors selected to hear the evidence in that case.

## Requirements of Informal Hearings

Compared with trials and formal hearings, everything is simplified and condensed in the informal hearing. Frequently, the only participants are the judge or hearing officer, the clerk, and the party or parties, although attorneys or other representatives of the parties, a court reporter, and witnesses also attend at times. Even if open to the public and press, the degree of public interest is so low that observers can readily be accommodated with a few extra chairs.

The communication patterns among participants in such hearings are similar to those in trials, but simplified by the absence of the bailiff, jury, public, press, and others.

The smaller number of people and the informality require a more intimate arrangement of participants. A spatial disposition for visual communication based on the maximum visual angle of 150 degrees reduces the distance between the judge and the attorneys to less than 15 feet and between the court reporter and the farthest party to less than 25 feet.

Movement during informal hearings is minimal, although sometimes the judge and the attorneys may discuss matters privately at the bench outside the hearing range of the parties and witnesses, with the reporter also moving to the bench. Occasionally attorneys and their respective clients may have private conferences. For the most part, however, all remain seated throughout the proceedings (Fig. 4).

To emphasize their role, the judges bench should be raised, but not so high as to prevent informality in the proceeding. Since all participants remain seated when speaking, it is generally sufficient for the judge to be one step above the eye level of the other participants. The nonencroachment distance between attorneys and the judge and between the witness and attorney during examination should be maintained at a minimum of 5 to 6 feet.

Ideally, there should be three separate points of access into the informal hearing room, as shown in Fig. 4. The judge and the court staff, including the clerk and the court reporter, should have separate private entrances into the room. The attorneys and the parties can enter either from their waiting spaces or from the public waiting space. Witnesses involved in informal hearings do not normally require isolation, so seating space could be provided for them within the room.

## Ancillary Functions

Several ancillary functions primarily identified with trials and hearings may also have some relation to other court functions. Conferences between attorneys and parties call for conference rooms. Attorneys should be able to relax and work in the privacy of an attorneys' lounge, while the public and news media should have separate facilities. When witnesses are isolated, they are the responsibility of the bailiff and must remain in witness isolation spaces until called to testify. Temporary detention of the accused or defendant in detention facilities is the responsibility of the law enforcement officers, but the security and safety of jurors during jury deliberation and sequestering are the responsibility of the bailiff.

Analysis of movement among these activities shows their relative importance to be in the following descending order: trial and hearing, waiting, working and relaxing, public waiting, conference, news reporting, jury deliberation, detention, witness isolation, and jury sequestering.

Figure 6 shows the interspatial movement pattern for ancillary functions. Witness isolation and jury deliberation and sequestering spaces should be located in close proximity to the witness stand and to the jury box, respectively. The other ancillary activities are related to each other and should be grouped together near the courtroom. The attorneys' lounge should preferably have a separate access into the courtroom and be readily accessible to the detention space. In addition, the detention space should be close to the defendant's station in the courtroom, with direct access. Media facilities should be located near the courtroom and reasonably near the conference and waiting spaces. The public waiting space should provide access to the conference and waiting spaces, media facilities and the attorneys' lounge, as well as to the public observation space in the courtroom. If audiovisual devices are used, however, the public observation space does not have to be located in the courtroom. Table 2 shows unit space requirements for each ancillary activity both on a per person basis and as modules for minimum requirements.

## THE DISTRICT COURT

Court spaces most frequently required in federal buildings are for the United States District Court which holds sessions in the principal cities of its judicial district and generally has its headquarters in the largest or most centrally located city in the district.

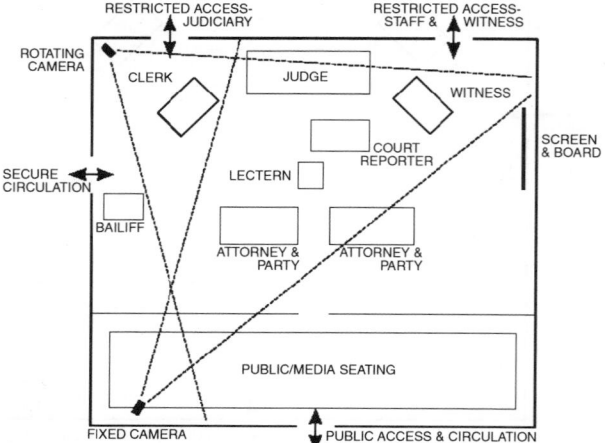

**Fig. 5. Location of visual equipment and display board (nonjury trials, formal hearings)**

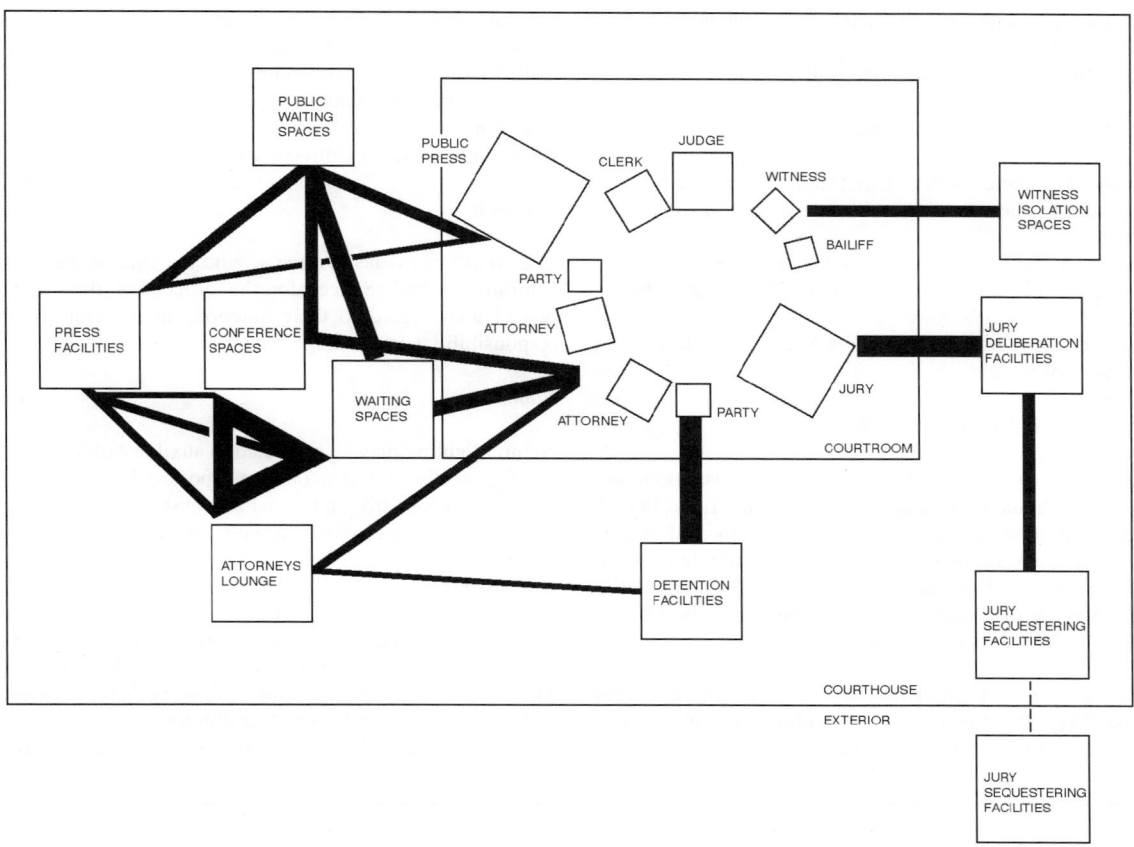

**Fig. 6. Interspatial movement pattern for ancillary functions**

## Part 1. Description

*Jurisdiction*

The U.S. District Court is the federal court of original jurisdiction where cases are given their initial trial. Each state comprises at least one judicial district and, depending upon the volume of business and its geographical distribution, a state may be divided into two or more judicial districts.

*Spaces Required*

With a few exceptions, a U.S. District Court sits at more than one place within each judicial district. The following spaces are always required:

> Courtroom
> Judge's chambers suite
> Trial jury suite
> Attorney conference/witness rooms
> Grand jury suite

In some instances, a court library, jury assembly room, and media/press room will also be required.

*Court Officers Requiring Spaces*

At each place of holding court, space will be required for the following officers:

> United States District Judge (one or more, depending upon the volume of business within the district)
> Clerk of the Court
> United States Attorney's Office
> United States Marshals Service

**Table 2** Unit space requirements of ancillary functions

| SPACE | AREA PER PERSON, SQ. FT. | AREA OF COMBINED SPACES, SQ. FT. |
|---|---|---|
| **CONFERENCE SPACE** | 20-27 | 80-108 (4 PERSONS) |
| **WAITING SPACE** | 13-20 | 260-400 (20 PERSONS) |
| **WITNESS ISOLATION** | 44-63 | |
| **ATTORNEY'S LOUNGE** | | |
|    LOUNGE SPACE | 13-20 | 130-200 (10 PERSONS) |
|    WORK SPACE | 44-63 | |
| **PRESS ROOM** | | |
|    INTERVIEW SPACE | 20-25 | 200-250 (10 PERSONS) |
|    OFFICES | 69-75 | |

U.S. Probation Office/Pretrial Services office (one or more)
Court Reporter (one or more)
Alternative Dispute Resolution (ADR) suite

*Additional Offices at Major Installations*

Wherever a major installation of the District Court is required, facilities will be needed in it for the following additional officers, if specified:

Visiting (non-resident) District Judges' Chambers Suites
District Court Magistrate Judges' Chambers Suites, and Clerk of the Court support functions
Bankruptcy Court – Judges' Chambers Suites and Clerk of the Court (one or more)

*Space Arrangements in District Court Suite*

Certain parts of the court must be closely connected. Courtrooms and their related rooms should ordinarily be above the first floor. In multistory buildings, all of the court activities should be located on consecutive floors. It is not desirable to place agencies unrelated to the court on the same floor with it. The need for simple, direct circulation for the public and for the court officers will influence the location and arrangement of the units of the court.

Three separate and distinct circulation systems are required within the courthouse (Fig. 7): public circulation/waiting and support areas for use by the general public, including attorneys, parties, witnesses,

and the media; restricted or private circulation to be used by the judge, court staff, jurors, and attorneys/parties/witnesses on a controlled basis; and secure holding and circulation to be used by prisoners and bailiffs/detention officers.

**Part 2. The District Courtroom**

*Location*

The court's activities revolve around the courtroom, so it should be centrally located. Spaces for the officers of the court should be placed with regard to their functions in the courtroom and their responsibilities to the judge.

*Illumination*

Natural lighting may be restricted to auxiliary offices, the courtroom itself generally having no outside exposure. If natural lighting is provided in the courtroom, provisions must be made for lighting controls for evidence display and presentations.

*Dimensions*

The minimum size of a District courtroom is 40 feet in width by 60 feet in length, for an approximate area of 2,400 net square feet (NSF). The ceiling height of a courtroom should be proportionate to its size and to the requirements of proper illumination, ventilation or air conditioning, and acoustics. A minimum ceiling height for the courtroom

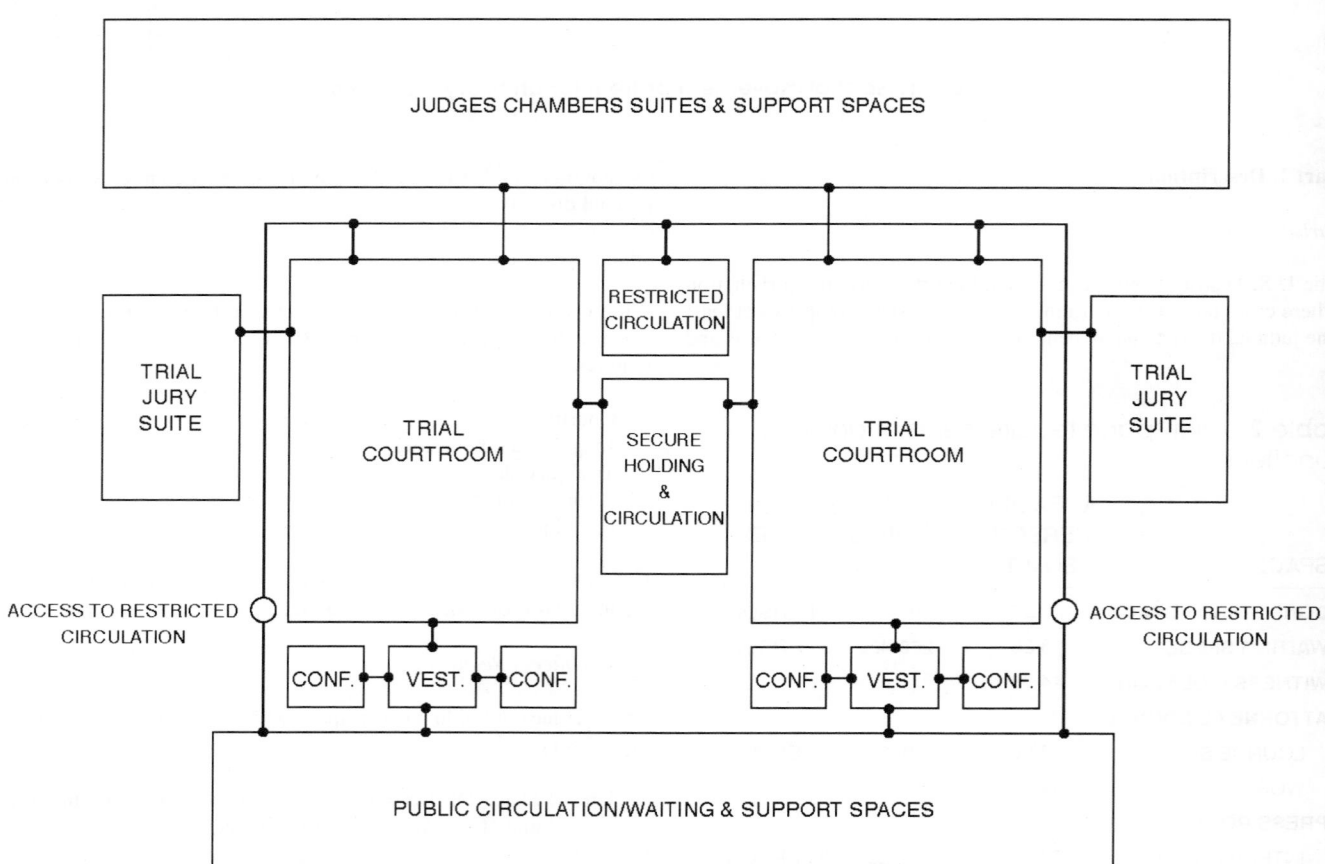

**Fig. 7. Circulation systems within the courthouse**

16 feet, but the areas over the spectator seating and room perimeter may be lower. In a large installation with many courtrooms, most of them should be of minimum size. One or more courtrooms with additional space for the audience may be necessary to accommodate trials that attract the public and are attended by many representatives of the press. The Special Proceedings Courtroom should be of an approximate area of 3,000 net square feet and a ceiling height of 18 feet, to accommodate multi-defendant trials, increased jury box capacity, and additional spectator seating.

The judge's bench and support functions are generally the focal point of the courtroom, but the witness box and jury box are elements necessary for the administration of justice. The layout, location, and arrangement of courtroom built-in furniture will be finalized by the court officers of the respective jurisdiction, and several options (See Figs. 8 through 10) have been developed for use.

Figure 8 illustrates a courtroom with a centrally-located Judges Bench and an adjacent witness box. The jury box is adjacent to the witness box, and the jurors and witness are in the same line of sight to the judge. Figure 9 illustrates a courtroom with a corner judge's bench. The witness box is centrally-located, and the jury box is adjacent to but more distant from the witness box. Fig. 10 illustrates a courtroom with a centrally-located judge's bench, and the witness box and jury box are located at opposing sides of the courtroom.

## Courtroom Entrances

### Public Entrance

This is located at the end of the courtroom opposite the judge's bench and fitted with double doors swinging out into a courtroom vestibule/soundlock, and then to the courtroom lobby and public circulation corridor. Attorney conference/witness rooms may be accommodated either off the courtroom vestibule/soundlock or off the public circulation corridor (Fig. 7).

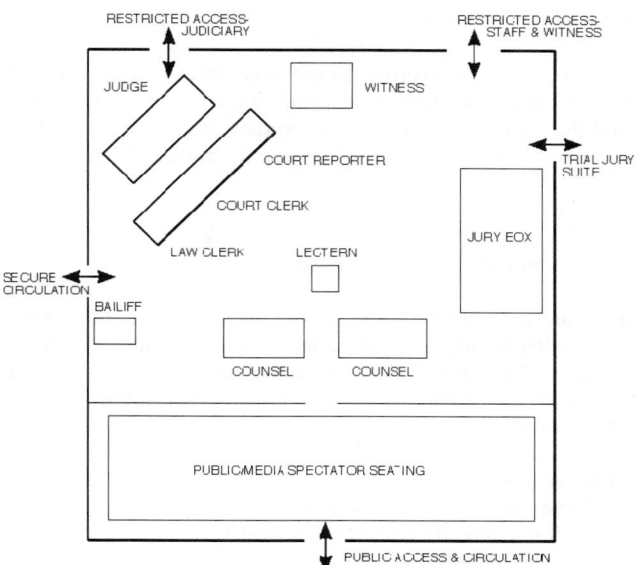

**Fig. 9. Courtroom with corner judge's bench and central witness box**

### Jury Entrance

This entrance should permit the jury to pass directly from the courtroom to the jury rooms, preferably without crossing the courtroom or passing through any public corridor or space, and through restricted circulation (Fig. 7).

### Prisoner Entrance

Provide an entrance for secure access of prisoners, through which they may be taken to the detention holding cells and secure circulation (Fig. 7).

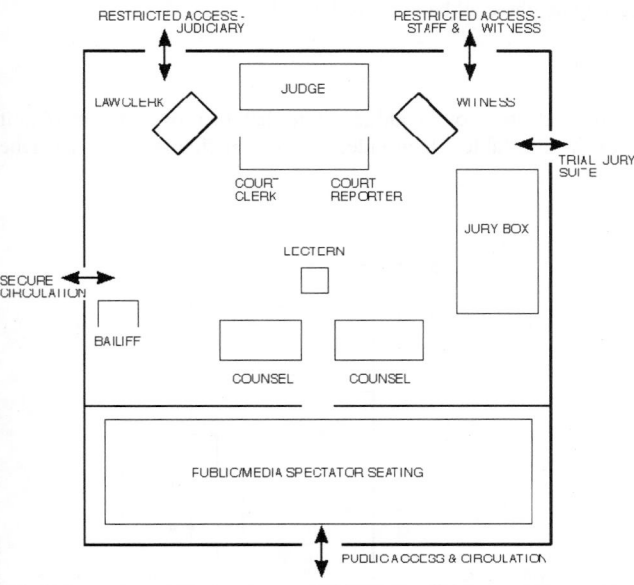

**Fig. 8. Courtroom with central judge's bench and adjacent witness box**

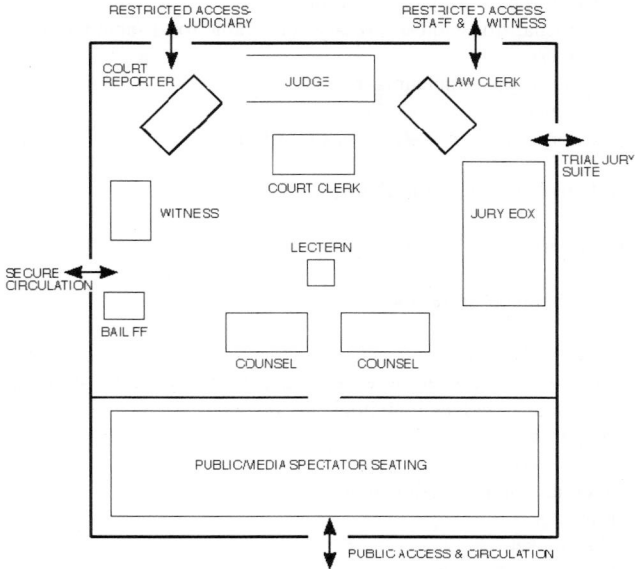

**Fig. 10. Courtroom with central judge's bench and opposing witness box**

*Staff/Witness/Judiciary Entrances*

These entrances should permit the staff and witnesses to pass directly to the courtroom from the restricted circulation corridors, and similarly permit the judiciary to pass directly to the courtroom from judges' chambers suites through restricted circulation corridors (Fig. 7).

## Furniture

*Built-in Furniture*

Courtroom areas used by the public must be accessible, which includes witness box, jury box, lectern, counsel seating, and spectator seating. The judge's bench and support areas must be adaptable for accessibility or made accessible initially. The following items must be provided:

> 1 Judge's bench
> 1 Witness box
> 1 Clerk of court and court reporter bench
> 1 Law clerk bench
> 1 Jury box
> 12 benches for spectator seating, with gate and railings

*Fixed Chairs*

The jury type courtroom must accommodate the following fixed chairs:

> 18 Armchairs for jurors, rotary – fixed, with 1 removable for disabled access

*Movable Furniture*

Limited to the following:

> 1 Judge's chair (3 may be provided at special proceedings courtroom)
> 1 Clerk of court armchair—rotary
> 1 Court reporter armchair—rotary
> 1 Armchair for witness—rotary, removable for disabled access
> 1 Lectern
> 10 Attorneys' armchairs—rotary
> 10 Armchairs for general use
> 2 Attorneys' tables—42 inches by 84 inches

## Part 3. Judge's Chambers Suite

*Components*

Judge's chambers suites include the following rooms:

> Judge's chambers
> Judge's conference/reference/library (with 18 units of 3-feet-wide, 7-shelves-high bookcases)
> Judge's toilet
> Judge's coat closet
> Secretary and reception area
> Law clerks' offices
> Coat closet
> Mail/fax/copy room
> Service unit (w/sink and base/wall cabinets)
> Supply/storage room
> Files storage

Courtroom deputy clerk may be included within the suite.
If there are five or more active judges in the district, the chief judge may have a third law clerk or a second secretary.

*Location*

The judge's suite must be located with access through a restricted circulation corridor to the courtroom. A corner office for the judge is generally preferred, with appropriate sound isolation to get maximum freedom from street noises. Locate the judge's chambers to provide access to the bench through a private vestibule to restricted circulation so that the judge will not have to go through any public space. The judge's office private vestibule will also permit the judge to enter or leave without passing through any other office or area of the chambers suite (Fig. 11).

*Entrances*

The entrances required for circulation within the judge's chambers are shown on Fig. 11. Where several courtrooms are grouped on a floor, judges will pass to the courtrooms through a common private, restricted circulation corridor. In multistory buildings, it is desirable to have the judges' suites as adjacent as possible to the courtrooms so that the judges do not have to go through public spaces or use public elevators when going to or from court. Controlled public entrance must be provided for access to the secretary/reception area and chambers suite. An alternative arrangement locates chambers suites in a group or "collegial" layout in an area or floor separate from the courtrooms, accessible by secure restricted elevators and corridors.

## Judge's Chambers

*Area and Furniture*

As informal meetings hearings are often held in the judge's office, the minimum area shall be 500 net square feet.

*Height*

Ceiling height shall be not less than 9 feet.

*Shelving*

Usable wall space of the judge's suite shall be provided with 18 units of flush, adjustable 3-feet-wide, 7-shelves-high bookcases, 10 inches

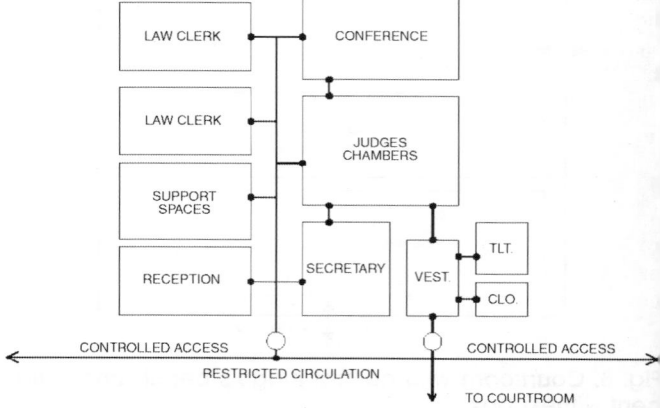

**Fig. 11. Judge's chambers suite**

eep and extending from the floor to the top of the doors. The walls bove shall be furred out to the face of the shelves.

*rivate Toilet*

 is desirable to locate the judge's toilet room so that the entrance is ot directly from their chambers. The toilet shall be equipped with a oiseless type water closet, a lavatory, a medicine cabinet with mir- or, paper holder, towel dispenser/disposal, soap dispenser, and base abinet with drawers. The fixtures shall not be mounted on the court- oom wall (refer to Fig. 11).

*oat Closet*

 is desirable to locate the judge's coat closet off a passage or estibule outside their office, adjacent to the toilet room and accessi- le off the restricted circulation corridor. The closet shall be not less an 5 feet wide and 2 feet deep; it shall be equipped with 1-foot-6- ches-deep shelves and a coat rod.

**ecretary and Reception Room**

*ocation*

he secretary and reception area may be located between the judge's hambers office and the law clerks' offices (refer to Fig. 11). The first oint of entrance to the suite by the public is through the reception rea, which may be occupied by a court bailiff.

*rea and Furniture*

he room shall have a minimum area of 220 net square feet and the ecretary's space shall be accessible to coat closet, mail/fax/copy oom, service unit (w/sink and base/wall cabinets), supply/storage oom, and files storage areas.

*ntrances*

ig. 11 shows the preferred arrangement of entrances between the ooms. It is not desirable to put closets, copy areas, or toilets between ne secretary's space and the judge's chambers.

**aw Clerks' Offices**

he law clerks' offices usually should adjoin the secretary's area so nat the secretary can receive the clerks' visitors as well as those for ne judge. Usable wall space shall be provided with five units of lush, adjustable 3-feet-wide, 7-shelves high bookcases, 10 inches eep and extending from the floor to the top of the doors. The offices hall have a minimum area of 150 net square feet.

**udge's Conference/Reference/Library**

Jsable wall space shall be provided with 18 units of flush, adjustable -feet-wide, 7-shelves high bookcases, 10 inches deep and extending rom the floor to the top of the doors. The library shall have a mini- num area of 400 net square feet, and is best located adjoining the udge's chambers and internal circulation corridor.

**upport Spaces**

oat closet should be located immediately accessible to reception rea, for staff and visitor use. Mail/fax/copy room and service unit (w/sink and base/wall cabinets) may be co-located, and supply/stor- age room and files storage areas should be centrally located in the chambers suite.

**Part 4. Trial Jury Suite**

*Description*

The trial jury usually consists of 12 jurors, but there may be up to six alternates. It is assumed that in actual practice the number of jurors and alternates in the jury box during a trial will not exceed 14. At the end of the trial, the alternates, if any, withdraw, and the jury retires to the jury deliberation room to consider its verdict. The jury later returns to the courtroom to report to the court the jury's verdict or disagreement. The jury panel from which the jury is selected consists of persons chosen by the clerk of the court according to law. The names of those constituting the panel from which the jury is selected have been drawn from the jury pool and summoned by the court to report as jurors. If the court has a Jury Assembly Room, the prospec- tive jurors assemble there and do not go into the courtroom until a case is called for a trial in which a jury is required. Prospective jurors are selected, staged in the jury assembly room, and then proceed to the courtroom. The jurors who are finally accepted for the trial of the case remain in the courtroom and sit in the jury box, and those who are not accepted withdraw and return to the jury assembly room.

*Location of Jury Rooms*

Locate jury rooms so that jurors may go to them from the courtroom without going through a public corridor or going across the court- room. It is desirable to have jury rooms on the same floor as the courtroom, adjacent to the courtroom as indicated on Fig. 7, for the security, convenience, and ease of access of jurors. Frequently two jury rooms are required where there is but one courtroom in the building. When there are two or more courtrooms, one jury room is usually provided for each courtroom.

*Area and Furniture*

Jury rooms shall have a minimum area of 350 net square feet and must be proportioned to accommodate a table, 120 by 48 inches, and 18 armchairs.

*Coat Closet and Toilet Rooms*

Each jury room must have a coat/storage closet, a service unit with sink and wall/base cabinets, and 2 separate handicap accessible toilet rooms for men and women.

*Entrances*

Jury rooms shall be accessed off a soundlock entry, under the control of a bailiff, and adjacent to the restricted circulation corridor.

*Signaling Equipment*

Each jury room shall have equipment installed to operate a flashing signal or other communications system to the bailiff, the judge's sec- retary area, and the courtroom.

*Panic Exits*

If entrance to a jury room is directly from a common lobby, such a jury room or common lobby must have a second exit door of panic type, equipped with suitable panic hardware, local alarm signal, and explanatory sign on the jury side of the door.

*Soundproofing*

The walls of the jury room must be soundproofed, as the jurors' discussions would otherwise be audible in adjoining rooms. The jury room should have an acoustic ceiling.

*Auxiliary Occupancy*

When court is not in session, the jury room often serves as a waiting room, a conference room, or for additional jurors hearing another case for another courtroom.

**Part 5. Attorney Conference/Witness Rooms**

*Locations*

These rooms are for the use of attorneys for client meetings or for witnesses waiting to testify before the court and should be located as near the courtroom as possible, preferably off the courtroom soundlock/vestibule. A deputy marshal or bailiff calls the witnesses into the courtroom. Refer to Fig. 7.

*Area*

The room shall have a minimum area of 150 net square feet, and there shall be two provided per courtroom.

**Part 6. Jury Assembly**

*Description/Location*

The size of the juror orientation area shall be determined by allowing 10 net square feet per occupant. There shall be separate toilet rooms for men and women, all accessible, and vending/service unit areas for juror use only. Provide an entrance with controlled access from the public circulation corridors, preferably on the ground or main public access floor. The jury assembly area will have reception/check-in areas and equipment/supply/file support areas, as well as lounge or "quiet" area for juror work.

*Furniture*

The number of selected jurors will determine the number of varied style chairs, tables, magazine racks, etc., to be installed in this jury assembly orientation assembly and lounge areas.

**Part 7. Grand Jury Suite**

*Description, Location, and Components*

The grand jury is impaneled by the court and consists of not less than 16 nor more than 23 jurors. The grand jury hears evidence presented to it and conducts investigations to determine if charges or violation of federal criminal statutes shall be prosecuted. It is presided over by a foreperson, named by the court, and usually the cases considered by it are presented by the United States Attorney's Office. Outsiders must not be able to overhear or observe grand jury proceedings. The plan of the grand jury suite shown in Fig. 12 indicates the relationship of the rooms and the entrances required. The grand jury suite includes the following rooms:

Grand jury hearing room
Witness rooms
Bailiff's vestibule, security area, and secure sallyport
Toilets for men and women
Service unit
Coat closet/video storage

*Grand Jury Hearing Room*

The grand jurors' chairs are in either three or four rows, depending upon the width of the room. This room shall have a minimum area of 600 net square feet to accommodate:

23 jurors' armchairs—rotary, 1 removable for handicap access
1 U.S. Attorney/court reporter bench
1 Witness/foreperson/secretary bench

*Witness Rooms*

These rooms are for the use of witnesses until called by the bailiff to testify in the grand jury hearing room and should have limited, controlled access to the secure circulation system. The two witness rooms shall have minimum areas of 120 net square feet and 200 net square feet.

*Bailiff's Security/Vestibule*

This area shall have a work area of 50 net square feet to accommodate a desk and one armchair, and an entry vestibule area of 50 net square feet, to be located adjacent to the entry off the restricted corridor.

*Support Spaces*

Figure 12 shows a desirable combination of coat closet, a service unit with sink and wall/base cabinets, and separate toilet rooms for men and women, all of which must be accessible.

**Part 8. United States Attorney's Office**

*Duties and Location*

The United States Attorney's Office represents the government in all cases, both civil and criminal, to which the government is a party or in which it has an interest. Since much of the time of the United States Attorney and the Assistant United States Attorney is spent in

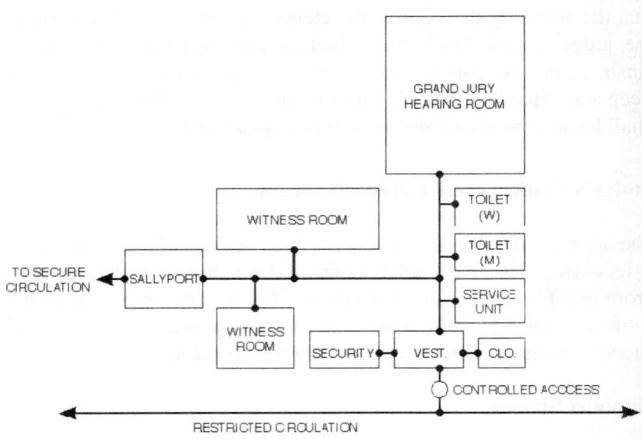

**Fig. 12. Grand jury suite**

e courtroom, their offices should be located convenient to it, but not
cessarily on the same floor.

*mponents*

e United States Attorney's Office has a headquarters at some des-
nated city in the judicial district, not necessarily the same city
here the judge's headquarters are located. Their suite in a court
ilding varies in size in accordance with the amount of work they
ust handle. A typical suite will include the following:

United States Attorney's office (with coat closet/toilet)
Reception room
Witness/interview room
Secretary's office
Chief Assistant United States Attorney's office
Assistant United States Attorneys' office
Visiting attorneys' room
Conference room
Library
Trial preparation room
Administrative assistant's office (with vault)
Secretary workstations
Mail/copy/supply work room and break room with service unit
Clerks and files room
Secure storage room

*nited States Attorney's Office*

e office of the United States Attorney shall have a minimum area
300 net square feet, and be provided with a private toilet room and
at closet.

*ception Room*

large installations a public reception room, readily accessible to vis-
rs, shall be provided. It shall adjoin the secretary's office and should
located between the office of the United States Attorney and that of
e administrative assistant. The minimum area of the reception room
all be 300 net square feet. It shall be planned to seat visitors and to
rmit control of intercommunicating doors by the receptionist. This
ea is generally of ballistic-resistant construction and has glazing
th speakerholes and document pass-throughs at the counters. The
tness/interview room should be located off this reception.

*tness/Interview Room*

is room should be located immediately adjacent to the reception
om, with controlled visitor access from one side and secure staff
cess from the other side. Witnesses may be held here prior to a court-
om or grand jury appearance, or may be used for interviewing.

*cretary's Office*

e secretary's office is adjacent to the office of the United States
torney and in close proximity to the reception room, centrally
cated to the support staff and spaces.

*hief Assistant United States Attorney's Office*

e office of the Chief Assistant United States Attorney shall have a
inimum area of 250 net square feet and should be located adjoining
e office of the United States Attorney.

*Assistant United States Attorney's Offices*

Offices of the Assistant United States Attorney should be adjacent
and convenient to the Chief Assistant United States Attorney. Each
office shall have a minimum area of 180 net square feet.

*Visiting Attorney's Offices*

Offices of the visiting United States Attorneys should be adjacent and
convenient to the Chief Assistant United States Attorney. Each office
shall have a minimum area of 180 net square feet.

*Conference Room*

The conference room shall have a minimum area of 250 net square
feet. A large installation may require several conference rooms,
located for the convenient use of the attorneys. This room should be
sound isolated.

*Library*

The library is used by all of the attorneys in the suite and therefore
should open off an internal circulation corridor.

*Trial Preparation Room*

This space shall be sound isolated for use in trial preparation, and
shall be provided with sufficient shelf and layout/worksurface areas
for this function.

*Administrative Assistant's Office*

The office of the administrative assistant should be located adjoining
the reception room on the side opposite the United States Attorney's
Office and shall have a minimum area of 230 net square feet. A vault
for use by the administrative assistant, opening into their office, shall
have a minimum size of 6 feet by 9 feet.

*Secretary Workstations*

Provide administrative secretary open office workstations between
the offices of Assistant United States Attorneys, allowing a minimum
area of 80 net square feet per area. Generally there will be a ratio of
one secretary for two attorneys.

*Mail/Copy/Supply Work Room*

A general work room centrally located and convenient to staff shall
have a minimum area of 120 net square feet. It may be necessary to
combine areas for mail, copy, and supply within this room. Co-locate
with break room and service unit.

*Break Room/Service Unit*

A break room with service unit, with sink and base/wall cabinets, centrally located and convenient to staff shall have a minimum area of 120
net square feet. Co-locate with mail/copy/supply work room.

*Clerks and Files Room*

The room for the clerks and files shall adjoin and connect with the administrative assistant's office.

*Secure Storage Room*

A storage room for secure evidence, records, and files, convenient to the administrative assistant's office shall have a minimum area of 80 net square feet.

*Smaller Installations*

United States Attorney's Office suites differ in size and requirements in accordance with the work in the district. They may be as small as three rooms in cities where court is held for a very short period or where no Assistant United States Attorney is regularly stationed. Where no United States Attorney is regularly stationed at a place of holding court, those offices will not have a private toilet or coat closet and the rooms may be used for conference or committee rooms when court is not in session. Room sizes will average about 200 net square feet each and furniture will correspond with that of similar rooms in a major installation.

## Part 9. United States Marshal's Suite

*Duties*

The United States Marshal is charged with the custody of prisoners and their production in court, the maintenance of order in the courtroom, the service of processes, the appearance of witnesses, the collection and disbursement of certain monies and fees, the custody of certain property in the possession of the court, and other special duties assigned by the court.

*Location*

The United States Marshal's Suite should be so located with relation to the courtroom that prisoners can pass directly to it from the detention holding cells without exposure to public contact or view. If the suite is located one floor above or below the courtroom, a private elevator and stair which offers no opportunity for escape must be provided for prisoners. In multistory buildings with courtrooms on different floors, a private elevator to transport prisoners from a lower floor or basement sallyport entrance to the Marshal's detention holding cells and to and from the courtrooms is required. On large installations, detention holding cells may be put in the basement, in addition to the detention holding cells provided on the courtroom floors.

*Components*

The United States Marshal has a headquarters at some designated city in the judicial district, not necessarily the same city where the judge's headquarters are located. The Marshal's suite varies in size according to the amount of work in the district. A typical suite for large installations includes:

Marshal's office (w/coat closet/toilet)
Chief Deputy Marshal's office
General office
Vault
Deputy Marshal's office/squad room
Processing area

Interviewing room
Vehicle sallyport
Fitness room/lockers/showers for staff
Central detention holding cells for men and for women
Courtroom holding cells
Command and control center
Evidence storage room (may be in basement)

*Marshal's Office*

This office shall have a minimum area of 450 net square feet. Provide an adjacent private toilet of not less than 50 net square feet.

*Chief Deputy Marshal's Office*

This office shall have a minimum area of 325 net square feet, and be located adjacent to the Marshal's Office.

*General Office*

Provide a general office with a minimum area of 500 net square feet adjacent to the public reception area, for support staff and functions. This counter area is of ballistic-resistant construction and has glazing with speakerholes and document pass-throughs at the counters. Witness/interview room should be located off this reception, as well as non-contact attorney/prisoner conference rooms.

*Vault*

Provide a vault opening into the general office, with a minimum area of 100 net square feet and accommodating a money safe. Locate the vault so that the interior is not visible from the public space.

*Deputy Marshal's Office/Squad Room*

Adjacent to general office area, provide an open office area/squad room with a minimum area of 100 net square feet for each Deputy Marshal workstation. One workstation is required for each Deputy.

*Processing Area*

Provide fingerprinting, photographic, and processing equipment in room of a minimum of 120 net square feet, adjoining and connecting with the Deputy Marshal's office. Provide adjacent areas for shower, prisoner intake, and staging.

*Interviewing Room*

Provide non-contact interviewing room with a minimum area of 7 net square feet, located so that prisoners can be brought from the detention cells as directly as possible, for staff and attorney use.

*Vehicle Sallyport*

The vehicle sallyport is the first point of entry into the prisoner secure circulation system, when transport vehicles arrive at the courthouse. It is for the exclusive use of the Marshal's Service and must accommodate a variety of vehicle sizes and types.

*Fitness Room/Lockers/Showers for Staff*

In support of the Marshal's Service fitness program initiative an exercise training room should be provided, with separate, adja

nt lockers and shower areas for male and female staff. It should
e accessible off the restricted circulation system, and may be
ed by other court personnel if authorized by the Marshal's Ser-
ce.

### entral Detention Cells for Men and for Women

#### ells for Men

rovide a minimum of three detention cells with sallyport/sound-
ck/passage. The cells shall be not less than 12 feet wide and be
rge enough to accommodate the maximum number of prisoners
tained at one time. The size of a two-person cell shall be a mini-
um of 120 net square feet, and a multi-person cell shall be a mini-
um of 200 net square feet. Provide detention-resistant lighting,
umbing, furniture, and door hardware in all cells, and construction
all be of glazed CMU walls, acoustical security ceilings, and epoxy
olymer integral floors and base.

#### ells for Women

milar to detention cells for men, and must be located separate.

#### ourtroom Holding Cells

rovide two courtroom holding cells per courtroom, or three court-
om holding cells per each two courtrooms, with sallyport/sound-
ck/passage and access to the secure circulation system. They
ould be located toward the back of the courtroom adjacent to the
isoners' entrance.

#### ommand and Control Center

his is the central monitoring station for the courthouse, both for
aces within and for the building perimeter. All surveillance cam-
as and duress alarms are monitored at this location, and is generally
cated adjacent to the central holding and sallyport areas.

#### vidence Storage

t times Deputy Marshals have custody of bulky evidence, requiring
large storage area. A storage room (preferably in the basement) of
0 net square feet minimum should be provided.

#### naller Installation

his suite will require fewer and perhaps smaller rooms than the
eadquarters suite in the same district, but the arrangement and rela-
onship of its rooms will be similar to that of the corresponding
oms in a major installation.

### art 10. Clerk of the District Court

#### uties

he Clerk of the Court is the administrative officer of the court.
he Clerk receives cases for filing in the court, maintains the
cords of its proceedings and actions, organizes its calendar,
ceives and disburses its money, and gives information to attor-
eys and interested parties regarding the disposition of cases as
corded in this office.

#### Location

It is desirable to locate the Clerk of the Court near the courtroom and
convenient to the judiciary. In multiple courts, the Clerk of the Court
should be easily accessible to the public.

#### Components

The offices of the Clerk of the Court vary in size and number in
accordance with the volume of business. The rooms include:

Clerk's office (with toilet)
Chief Deputy Clerk's office
General office, with public access counter and files
Examination room
Supply room
Work room
Vault
Exhibit room
File rooms as required

#### Clerk's Office

This shall have a minimum area of 300 net square feet and be connected with a private toilet with a minimum area of 50 net square feet.

#### Deputy Clerk's Office

This shall have a minimum area of 250 net square feet and be located
between the clerk's office and the general office.

#### General Office with Public Access Counter and Files

The size of the general open-office area ordinarily will be determined by the number of desks, tables, and file cases used. But if it
requires so many cases for active files that they would cause the general office to be disproportionately large, additional file rooms
should be provided. Preferably they should be connected to the general office: but if located on adjacent floors, provide direct stairways
and dumbwaiters. The public space is separated from the rest of the
general office by a counter with one or more gates. The public space
shall have a minimum width of 8 feet. In a very large general office,
the counter will be U-shaped or L-shaped to accommodate the
required length. Provide a minimum of one cashier's grille with
returns on the counter. If required, high-density shelving units can
be done to accommodate the active records storage, with careful
consideration being made for the structural floor loading requirements of this equipment.

#### Examination Room

This room is provided for attorneys and others who are permitted to
inspect the records. It shall have a minimum area of 150 net square
feet and be connected to the public entry counter and general open-
office area for visual control.

#### Supply Room

This area should be close to the general office and have a minimum
area of 100 net square feet.

*Work Room*

This area should be near the supply room. A general work room centrally located and convenient to staff shall have a minimum area of 300 net square feet. It may be necessary to combine areas for mail, copy, and storage within this room. Co-locate with break room and service unit, with sink and base/wall cabinets.

*Vault*

The vault, which holds a money safe, shall open into the general office and be planned to prevent public view of the interior. It shall have a minimum area of 80 net square feet, lined with steel shelving in sections 3 feet long and 12 inches wide.

*Exhibit Room*

This room shall have a minimum area of 250 net square feet. Entrance shall be from a corridor through double doors. Exhibit and display equipment for courtroom use is usually stored in this room.

**Part 11. Magistrate Judge**

*Duties*

The Magistrate Judge exercises certain judicial functions and before whom persons are arraigned immediately after arrest. They hold preliminary hearings of prisoners to determine whether they shall be held for the grand jury, discharged, or released on bail. They issue warrants and writs, set bail, and sometimes handle juvenile cases.

*Location and Components*

The location of the Magistrate Judge within the building, and the relationship of their courtroom, chambers suites, and clerk of court areas, is determined by the same conditions that govern in the case of the District Court (Figs. 7 and 11).

**Part 12. Probation Office and Pretrial Services Office**

*Duties*

The Probation Office supervises probationers referred to them by the court. For a stated period the probationer is required to report to the officer at specified intervals. To aid the judge in determining a sentence, the probation officer, when requested by the judge, makes presentence investigations of persons convicted of violations of the law and makes recommendations for consideration by judicial officers. The Pretrial Services Office conducts background investigations on all defendants charged with Federal criminal offenses, and provides judicial officers with reports and recommendations for bail and release conditions. The pretrial services officer also supervises released defendants, performs pretrial diversion investigations, and supervises diversion program enrollees. These two different components should be kept separate but may share drug test/lab space.

*Location and Components*

The suites should be located where they are accessible to the public by elevator or stairs, and preferably near the Marshal's Service office, but not necessarily on the courtroom floor. The number of rooms in a suite varies with the amount of work handled by the officer. A suite may consist of the following:

Office for the probation officer or pretrial services officer
Offices for one or more assistant officers
General office, with public space
File room
Urinalysis room/lab

*Probation Officer and Pretrial Services Officer*

These offices shall have a minimum area of 300 net square feet, with private toilet of a minimum area of 50 net square feet. In an office staffed by two or more officers, the area for the chief may be increased. The office should connect to the general office. In the case of a one-person office, it is desirable but not mandatory for the officer to be able to pass directly from his office to the public corridor. Where there are two or more assistant officers, it is mandatory that each officer be able to pass directly from his or her office to the public corridor.

*Offices for Assistant Probation Officer and Assistant Pretrial Services Officer*

Each of these shall have a minimum area of 150 net square feet.

*General Office with Public Space*

This general public access space shall have a minimum area of 275 net square feet when there are no assistant officers and 350 net square feet when there are one or more assistant officers.

*File Room*

This area will be required only when there are two or more assistant probation or pretrial services officers. It shall have a minimum area of 14 net square feet of file space for each assistant.

*Urinalysis Room/Lab*

Both Probation and Pretrial Services perform urinalysis drug testing as part of their supervision activities. Provide a room for equipment and storage, with sink and base/wall cabinets.

**Part 13. Miscellaneous Assignments**

*Chambers Suites for Visiting Judges*

When these are required, the types of spaces shall be generally similar to those provided for the resident judge, but totaling 900 net square feet, subdivided at the discretion of the judge.

**Court Reporter**

*Duties and Location*

The court reporter makes the official verbatim record of the court proceedings and furnishes transcripts when required. Their office may be located anywhere in the building.

*Components and Furniture*

The court reporter's office will include a general office, with file space, having a minimum area of 200 net square feet if the building has one courtroom. For each additional courtroom, add 50 net square feet to the general office.

## Court Library

### General

When there are two or more courtrooms, a general law library may be required, convenient to the judges' chambers.

### Arrangement

Reading tables should be located in front of windows. When window spacing will permit, put tables in small alcoves formed by bookstacks as separating partitions. Provide a main aisle at least 4 feet in width extending the full length of the room and separating the reading section from the general stack section.

### Areas and Furniture

The size of the library will accommodate readers to be seated.

### Bookstacks

Legal volumes average 2 to 2½ inches thick, 6 to 10 inches wide, and 8 to 11 inches high. Thus a typical range or stack section 3 feet long and 7 feet high with 7 adjustable shelves 12 inches on-center will store about 98 legal volumes. Stack sections are made up of single-faced wall sections and double-faced freestanding sections, which must be arranged in rows with the range aisles at least 3 feet wide, and accessible from the main aisle.

### Reading Tables

Each of these seats four people.

### Media/Press Room

The location may be at any place in the building. Telephone booths with coin telephones and media data hookup connections will be installed. This room for news reporters may be required in buildings with two or more courtrooms. The minimum area of the room shall be 200 net square feet.

### Alternative Dispute Resolution (ADR) Suite

The location may be at any place in the building. Certain cases are being heard in mediation and arbitration hearings, where a neutral third-party attempts to resolve a dispute through meetings with the disputing parties. Provide a series of conferencing rooms varying in size from 120 to 180 net square feet, with support staff and work areas.

## BANKRUPTCY COURT

### Duties

The Bankruptcy Judge conducts hearings, holds conferences, makes findings, and disposes of bankruptcy cases.

### Location and Components

The location of the Bankruptcy Judge within the building, and the relationship of their courtroom, chambers suites, and clerk of court areas, is determined by the same conditions that govern in the case of the District Court (Figs. 7 and 11).

## CIRCUIT COURT OF APPEALS

### Description

#### Jurisdiction

The Circuit Court of Appeals and the Court of Appeals for the District of Columbia are the intermediate federal appellate courts, each having the power to review the decisions of the district courts within its judicial circuit and the orders and decisions of certain federal boards, commissions, and other regulatory agencies. There are eleven judicial circuits, each composed of several states. The District of Columbia is a separate jurisdiction. There may be several places of holding court within each judicial circuit, but each circuit court of appeals has a headquarters court within its circuit.

#### Location

The location of the Circuit Court within the building, and the relationship of its areas, is determined by the same conditions that govern in the case of the District Court.

### Courtroom

#### Dimensions

The minimum size of a Court of Appeals Panel courtroom is 40 feet in width by 60 feet in length, for an approximate area of 2,400 net square feet (see Fig. 13). A minimum ceiling height for the courtroom is 16 feet, but the areas over the spectator seating and room perimeter may be lower. The judges' bench shall accommodate 3

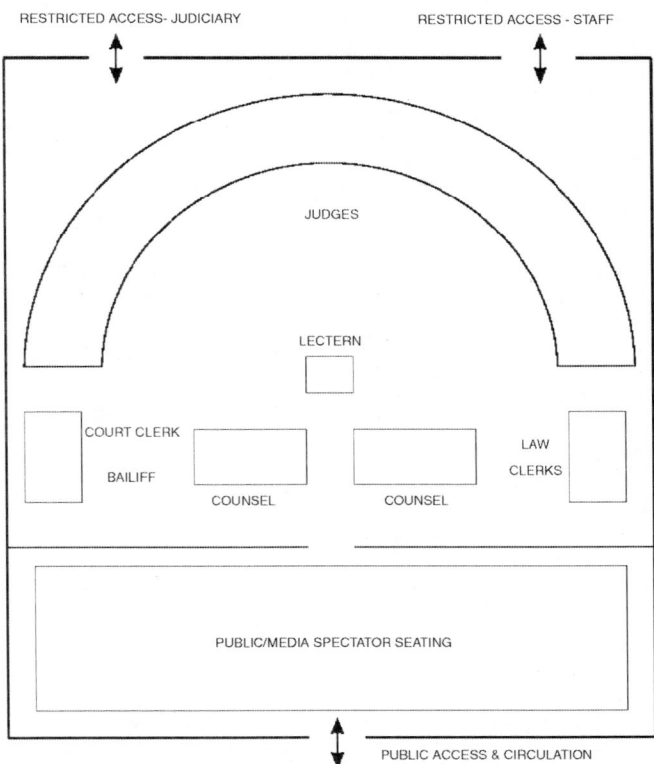

**Fig. 13. Courtroom for Circuit Court of Appeals**

judges. In a large installation with many courtrooms, most of them should be of minimum size. The Court of Appeals en banc courtroom should be of an approximate area of 3,000 net square feet and a ceiling height of 18 feet, to accommodate an expanded judges' bench for 11 judges and additional spectator seating.

*Entrances*

The public entrance, the judges' entrance, and corridor entrances are indicated on Fig. 13.

*Built-in Furniture*

It shall include:

> Combination judge's bench, deputy clerk/bailiff bench, and law clerk bench
> 16 benches for spectator seating, with gates and railings.

## Judge's Suite

*Location*

There will be three or more judge's chambers suites for the Circuit Court of Appeals. Each judge's suite shall be similar in size, arrangement, and equipment to the District Court judge's chambers suite, except that additional areas are provided for larger chambers, a larger reference/conference/library, a study, a second secretary, and a third law clerk. The judges' suites need not adjoin the courtroom, but shall be adjacent to it and preferably on the same floor.

*Judges' Conference Room and Toilet*

This room shall have a minimum area of 400 net square feet, should be provided with a connection to the judges' robing room and toilet, and must accommodate 1 table 120 inches by 48 inches and 10 armchairs.

*Judges' Robing Room and Toilet*

Provide a robing room with a minimum floor area of 200 net square feet so located that judges may enter the courtroom without passing through any circulation corridor. Provide a robe closet for each judge, and a connection to the judges' conference room.

## OTHER SPECIALIZED COURTS

There are several specialized courts that have exclusive jurisdiction over certain kinds and types of cases that a court may hear. In addition to those courts previously identified and described, the following are other courts must commonly encountered by the public:

> Supreme Court
> Court of Appeals for the Federal Circuit
> Court of Federal Claims
> Court of International Trade
> Court of Appeals for the Armed Forces
> Court of Military Appeals
> Court of Veterans Appeals
> Tax Court
> District Court Territorial Courts

# CORRECTIONAL FACILITIES

## INTRODUCTION

Prisons, jails, and detention facilities need to address society's many social, economic, and political factors. Many correctional facilities built well before the 1990s were not designed to meet the soaring prison populations, building codes, correctional standards, programmatic changes, or increasingly diverse needs of the 21st century. Correctional agencies must compete for funding with other pressing demands on public resources. With the passage of state and federal laws mandating longer sentences for a wider variety of crimes, prisons will continue to house greater numbers of inmates for longer terms, resulting in an older and sicker inmate population.

National attention to crime and the criminal justice system has focused on enhanced security in all public buildings. Justice facility architects must be familiar with design, technology, construction methods and materials, project delivery systems, legislative and legal trends to remain aware of what new facilities will require and what clients will expect to see in their buildings.

Between 1980 and 2000, over 1,000 new correctional facilities were built in the United States. The crime rate dropped dramatically in many American cities during the 1990s, but the prison population steadily increased, at a rate of between 50,000 to 100,000 people annually. From 1970 to 1999, the number of people incarcerated in the United States quadrupled to 1.8 million, including about 120,000 in the Federal Bureau of Prisons, 1.1 million in state facilities and 600,000 in municipal jails.

Large state and federal prisons (Figs. 1 to 6) reflect many of the same problems found within urban communities: gang violence, health care issues (AIDS, HIV, tuberculosis, hepatitis), substance abuse, and mental illness, especially with the closure of public psychiatric hospitals. Society's attitudes towards crime and punishment play a role in the growth and development of the correctional facilities, including the sentencing and incarceration of violent offenders who have committed heinous crimes.

## CORRECTIONAL FACILITIES

Correctional facilities refer to jails, prisons, and secure detention facilities. City or county jails hold those awaiting trial or serving sentences of a year or less, and unlike prisons, offer few programs. Prisons incarcerate those convicted of federal or state crimes for a year or longer, provide a variety of staffed rehabilitative programs, treatment and activities, and as a result, have high staffing and operational costs.

*Author:* Barbara A. Nadel, FAIA

Fig. 1. The 1,000-bed Fort Devens Federal Medical Center is located on a closed Army base. The program includes 13: medical beds in a renovated hospital, a new 150-bed psychiatric hospital, low security housing and common facili ties for maintenance, laundry, chapel, and recreation, all within the secure perimeter fence. Administrative function: are located outside the fence for public access and security; visiting is below grade. (Federal Medical Center, For Devens, Massachusetts, The Stubbins Associates, Architects; Barbara Nadel Architect, Correctional Medical Architect

## Jails

Holding cells are secure facilities for temporary detention of those held for investigation or preliminary hearings following arrest. These facilities are usually operated by the local police department. Detention generally does not exceed 48 hours; those held longer are often transferred to a city or county jail. Through computerized data bases, interagency networks and DNA testing, municipal law enforcement agencies can often determine if detained individuals are wanted for crimes in other jurisdictions.

Jail represents an offender's first contact with the criminal justice system. Typically, jails do not provide rehabilitation programs because of the relatively short stays of most detainees. Some city jails with sizable inmate populations offer educational or vocational classes, high school degree programs and public health education classes on preventing the spread of communicable diseases.

Jails are usually located in urban centers due to the need to be close to the courts. Highly visible downtown locations for justice facilities provide architects with urban design opportunities not available when designing large prisons on remote rural sites. As prominent examples of civic architecture, these buildings can revitalize a community by providing increased pedestrian traffic, outdoor public spaces, plazas and parks.

## Multifunctional Municipal Facilities

Many localities provide several municipal programs and services under one roof. Multifunctional facilities can incorporate law enforcement and jail facilities adjacent to or near courthouses. As

downtown real estate becomes costly and scarce in many cities, mul tifunctional facilities save time and resources on site selection, con struction costs, inmate transportation and security for police, judges lawyers and detainees.

Fig. 2. This 824-bed direct supervision county jail has separate zones for minimum, medium and maximum security housing. Individual cells of 16 by 16 feet or 16 by 20 feet are grouped around a day room. An 11- story tower includes intake, detention and substance abuse treatment and protective custody. (Suffolk County House of Correction, Boston Massachusetts, The Stubbins Associates, Architect)

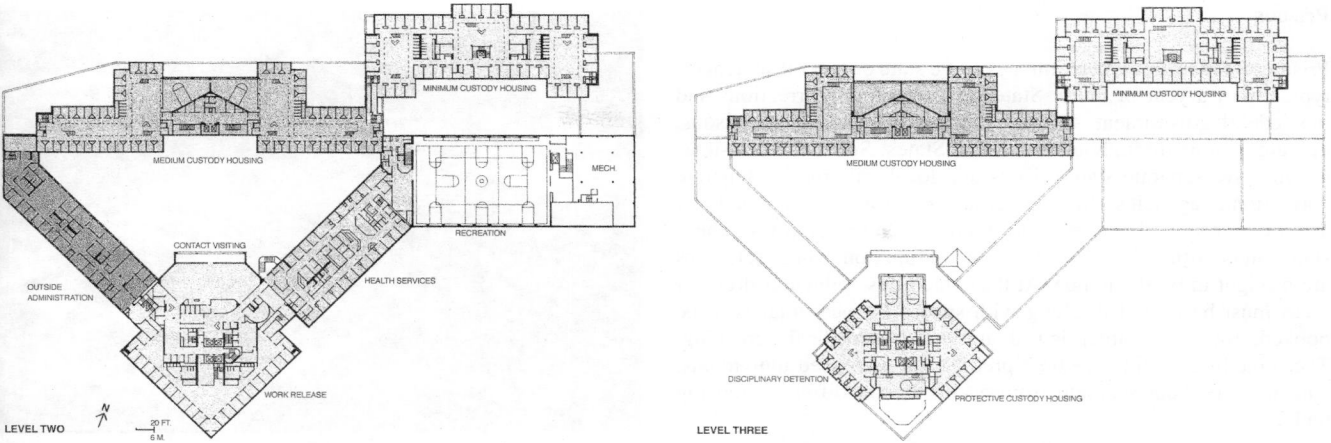

**Fig. 3. Floor plans, levels two and three with housing, administration, health and recreation units (Suffolk County House of Correction, Boston Massachusetts, The Stubbins Associates, Architect)**

Rapid and secure inmate transportation between jails and the courts is required for inmates to stand before a judge. Through on-site video capabilities in jails, video arraignment has reduced the need for inmate transportation outside the correctional facility to local courts. Judges and lawyers can come to the jails, or through video teleconferencing, conduct hearings broadcast between the courts and the jails, simplifying the process, and reducing security risks and operational costs of legal proceedings. Many jails have created an on-site courtroom for this purpose, equipped with the necessary technology capabilities.

As jail populations rise, designers must consider the need for different housing and room types, to reflect and accommodate many different types of inmates in male and female populations. These spaces include single bed and double bed cells, double bunked housing, isolation cells for those with contagious diseases, suicide prevention rooms, handicapped cells, and dormitories. A mix of housing units

(Figs. 7 and 8) for special populations, juveniles and older adolescents, medical and mental health, segregation units for violent offenders, gang members and others who must be separated from the general population, is desirable for flexibility in managing fluctuating inmate populations.

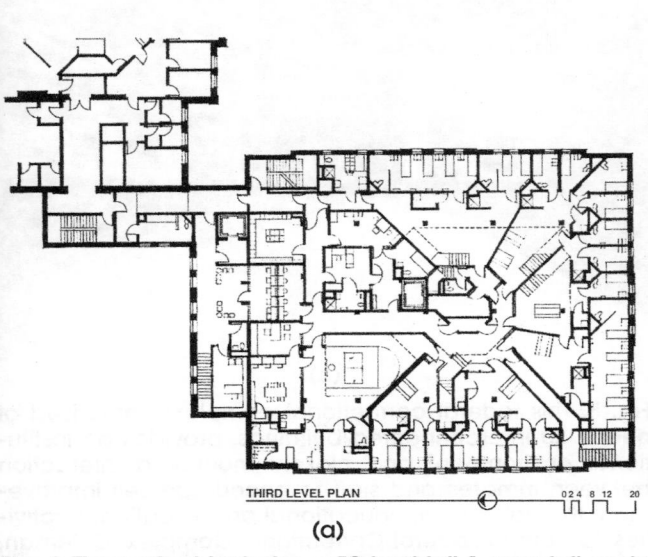

(a)  (b)

**Fig. 4. The project includes a 50-bed jail 1-year jail and County Sheriff's Department and City Police Department Law Enforcement facility (City of New Ulm/Brown County Joint Law Enforcement Center, New Ulm, Minnesota; Klein McCarthy & Co., Architects); (a) plan of third floor; (b) view of main entrance**

## Prisons

Prisons are facilities where inmates serve state or federal sentences, typically of a year or more. State departments of corrections and the federal government, through the Federal Bureau of Prisons, operate prisons throughout the United States. Some smaller states do not have separate state prisons and local jails run by separate correctional agencies. In such cases, the state-run correctional agency manages all correctional facilities and operations. These state-run facilities also serve the local jail function, where detainees are brought in by the police. At these facilities, vehicular drop off areas must be provided, along with spaces for new intakes to be booked, processed, interviewed and receive medical screening. These facilities will house both pretrial and sentenced individuals, who must be kept separate from each other in different housing units.

Some states have created central reception centers as the main entry point to the correctional system, where all inmates are sent after sentencing as they begin their prison term. Upon entering the correctional system, inmates are given security classifications, based on case histories, medical exams and screening for AIDS, HIV, tuberculosis and other communicable diseases. After orientation, inmates are then assigned to another correctional facility, based on security levels, to begin their sentences. Inmates with proven records of good behavior may be assigned to the "cadre" of those who stay at the reception center and perform necessary routine maintenance and operational tasks.

Prisons operate a variety of work details, daily programs, activities and therapeutic services to occupy an inmate's entire day. Common programs include individual and group therapy, substance abuse treatment, counseling, high school equivalency programs, vocational training, facility maintenance, laundry, food service and other chores to keep the facility operating.

Because of large acreage, space requirements, and site development criteria, most state and federal prisons are located on large tracts of publicly owned land, far from downtown areas. Prisons also require good transportation access from highways and major roads for staff, visitors and delivery of goods and services. These institutions are self sufficient communities of administrative and security personnel, responsible for medical, educational, recreational, religious, food and maintenance services.

## Supermax Facilities

Since the 1990s, the trend has been towards building harsher, more secure adult and juvenile facilities, with more bars and less glazing. Many state correctional agencies have one or two supermax facilities for the worst behaving, most violent inmates, those who have committed heinous crimes, or those who are a security risk within the general population.

Supermax prisons enable corrections officials to manage a difficult population in one location. Private cells have their own showers, closed circuit television for education and religious programs, to minimize inmate movement out of the cell and unnecessary security risks. Inmates are allowed an hour of daily outdoor recreation and limited indoor recreation. Some cells feature small individual outdoor areas with controlled doors to prohibit inmate contact with others. These facilities do not have dayrooms and spaces for group activities.

(a)

(b)

(c)

**Fig. 5.** This federal correctional complex, comprised of nearly 30 interconnected buildings, provides an institutional environment and closely monitored interaction between inmates and staff to encourage self-improvement through social, educational and vocational activities (Coleman Federal Correctional Complex, Coleman, Florida; Spillis Candela & Partners, Architects); (*a*) site view entire campus; (*b*) bird's eye perspective of housing complex; (*c*) building detail

## SPECIAL NEEDS

The demand for medical, psychiatric, geriatric, women's, juvenile and sex offender facilities has increased dramatically and is expected to grow. Designing for maximum flexibility is the best way to achieve a balance between changing inmate needs and new or renovated facilities. Users should participate in the planning and design process through a team approach, ensuring that both special needs and security mandates are met. Involving more individuals with diverse perspectives, including architects, administrators, security staff and health care and mental health providers in planning teams results in a more comprehensive, user-responsive project. Key issues concerning special needs design include the following:

### Health Care

With longer sentences and more people in prison, the inmate population will continue to get older, sicker and more expensive to care for. Providing adequate care and code compliant medical facilities for a growing inmate population will remain a challenge for corrections agencies.

At older facilities with double or triple the number of beds from the original design, prison medical facilities and other infrastructure building systems were not designed for large populations, resulting in operational problems. Old infirmaries and outpatient clinics were not designed to meet high patient volumes, modern health care codes and standards, or to deal with contagious diseases requiring negative pressure isolation rooms and other health care facilities.

The need for mental health and mental retardation units, counseling areas, staff offices, and suicide prevention rooms in housing units will also continue to rise. Inmates with substance abuse problems often require staff-intensive treatment programs.

### Juvenile Facilities

As more juveniles commit violent crimes, states and localities must contend with treating juveniles as adults before the law, during sen-

**Fig. 6. View of circulation spine between medical buildings (Federal Medical Center, Fort Devens, Massachusetts, The Stubbins Associates, Architects; Barbara Nadel Architect, Correctional Medical Architect)**

(a)

(b)

**Fig. 7 (a) Exterior view (Scioto Village School for Girls, URS Architects Engineers & Planners); (b) dayroom**

tencing and incarceration. More secure juvenile facilities are needed for violent offenders, instead of sending juveniles to an adult prison. Juvenile facilities must provide education, recreation, and intensive counseling programs within a secure perimeter. These components are often located in separate parts of a campus to replicate a young person's daily life on the outside, of going to school, outdoor recreation and other activities.

Juvenile facilities are often designed with smaller housing units to reflect a normalized, residential setting. For many young people, this intervention is a last chance at rehabilitation before becoming enmeshed in the criminal justice system as a repeat offender and eventually, as an adult inmate. Juvenile detention centers may often be located amid residential communities and thus the building design can be more residential and smaller in scale than for larger institutions.

## Women's Facilities

Between 1970 and 1999, the number of women in American prisons grew twelve-fold, to about 80,000. Most women inmates have children, some are pregnant on entering prison and require prenatal care and training. Many women inmates are violent, with substance abuse and health problems. As more women inmates are sentenced to prison, more maximum security beds will be needed as well.

Women have a number of different needs than men in prison, and the planning and design of women's correctional facilities should reflect these differences (Figs. 7 and 8). Simply converting a design of a men's prison for women is not cost effective or appropriate. Wardens and administrators involved in operating women's facilities should be involved in the planning process early on to determine how these needs will be addressed at each facility. Women need more space than men for storage, education, religion, visiting, personal hygiene, laundry, counseling and health care. They respect their environments more than men, and are less prone to destroy and vandalize their spaces.

## Geriatric Populations

Longer, mandatory sentences and life without parole creates larger aging prison populations. Some facilities maintain handicapped accessible housing units for older inmates, located convenient to medical units. Geriatric inmates have a greater need for more medical services than younger inmates, and age faster when in prison. Inmates are often considered 10 to 15 years older than their chronological age because many did not lead healthy lifestyles before they arrived in prison. Some facilities have hospice programs, to allow aging and terminally ill inmates to die with dignity, removed from the general population. Hospice programs may operate in designated housing units or at the infirmary.

## Sex Offender Facilities

Many states have developed detailed policies, programs and facilities for treating sex offenders. These individuals may have served and completed their prison sentences. In the late 1990s, the Supreme Court ruled sex offenders who have completed their prison sentences may be held involuntarily under civil commitment because they are not fit to be released into society. State laws vary as to whether these individuals are held under the supervision of a corrections department or a mental health agency. Some sex offenders can never be cured and are incarcerated for life, adding to the pool of geriatric inmates. These individuals are generally not considered violent offenders. Design, materials and construction methods to house them need not be as harsh and expensive as those for maximum security prisons.

Types and sizes of housing units for these inmates can range from 24 beds per campus to 200-bed facilities. When minimum security in living areas is appropriate, residential construction materials may be used. Counseling offices, group therapy spaces and program areas are vital to the treatment program.

## Community Correctional Centers

Community correctional centers serve as a transition point for inmates just prior to the end of their sentences. The programs may be operated by public agencies or non-profit organizations working closely with corrections departments. This type of facility is ideally located within the community and serves pretrial and sentenced offenders, those on probation, parole, post-prison supervision, work release, or diverted by the courts to programs instead of serving prison time. They typically provide offenders with job training, education, counseling, substance abuse programs and daily living skills. By using treatment and support programs, community corrections helps preserve public safety while helping offenders make the transition to useful citizenship.

## THE PLANNING PROCESS

Planning for correctional facilities involves many individuals at government agencies, local community leaders and design and construction professionals. The architect's role during the preliminary stage is usually as a consultant to the agency or design/build team planning and building the new facility.

The planning team must determine the purpose of the facility, the size and scope of the project, and the overall goals of the owner. Correctional departments generally are able to project their prison populations over a given planning horizon, based on law enforcement information, sentencing criteria, legislative trends, and demographic projections.

### Needs Assessment

Inmate population projections consist of estimates of the numbers and kinds of people coming into the correctional system. Information is generally classified by age, gender, offense, previous history of incarceration, substance abuse, medical and mental health history. Most correctional departments track these statistics, along with many different types of data, to aid in long range planning and budgeting for facilities, staffing and operations. Local, state and federal laws, such as "Three Strikes and You're Out," and Truth In Sentencing provisions, calling for long sentences after a third offense, and requiring inmates to serve fixed terms of their sentences respectively, are examples of legislative impact on prison populations. With longer sentences, inmates will remain behind bars for longer periods of time, causing new demands for more prison beds, as well as a host of other prison-based and contracted services.

The following is a partial list of typical planning criteria:

1. Number and dates of arrests by major categories:

   a. Felonies. Breakdown by crimes against property, against persons, against public order; drug sale and use, gender.

   b. Misdemeanors. Same breakdown as for felonies. Alcohol and drug related arrests, minor traffic arrests.

2. Number and dates of judicial actions:

   a. Adjudication actions. Number dismissed, transfers to other jurisdictions, pleas as charged, pleas to reduce charges, to trial, convictions.

   b. Sentencing actions. Number of: fines, restitution orders and suspended sentences; jail sentences; probations granted; prison and reformatory sentences; commitments to community correctional centers.

3. Number and movements of sentenced offenders by:

   time served in jail before discharge; time served in state institutions before parole or discharge; time served on probation before discharge; time served on parole before discharge.

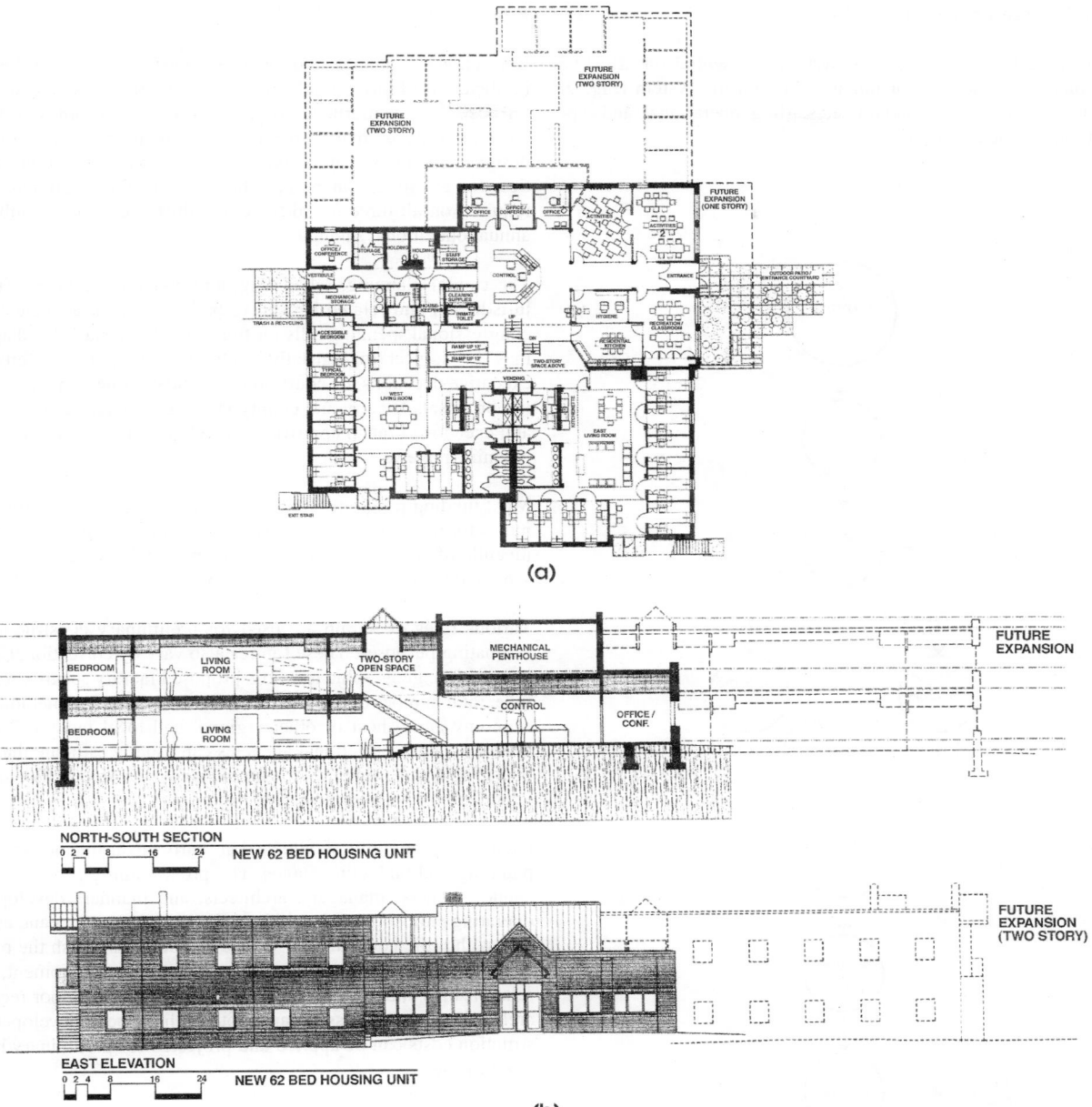

**(a)**

**(b)**

Fig. 8. The Minnesota Correctional Facility at Shakopee is an innovative women's prison designed to create and foster rehabilitative opportunities for women. The campus is located in the heart of a quiet residential community without a perimeter security fence, a unique feature rarely found among correctional facilities in the United States. The design for small group living units includes public and private zones. The goal is to respect women's need for privacy and enhance inmate management.

This 62-bed housing unit configuration includes four units of 8 bedrooms clustered around separate living room, kitchenette, laundry, private showers and toilet room. Activity rooms and a residential kitchen include capacity for future expansion to an additional 62 beds. (MCF Shakopee Housing Unit and Support Facilities Expansion, Shakopee, Minnesota; Klein McCarthy & Co., Architects; Barbara Nadel Architect, Special Needs Programming and Design Consultant); (a) floor plan; (b) section and elevation

### Analysis of Existing Systems

Understanding the criminal justice system is essential for effective facility planning. The flow of inmates through the system (Fig. 9) and the role of each agency and related staffing, operational, and capital costs should be evaluated.

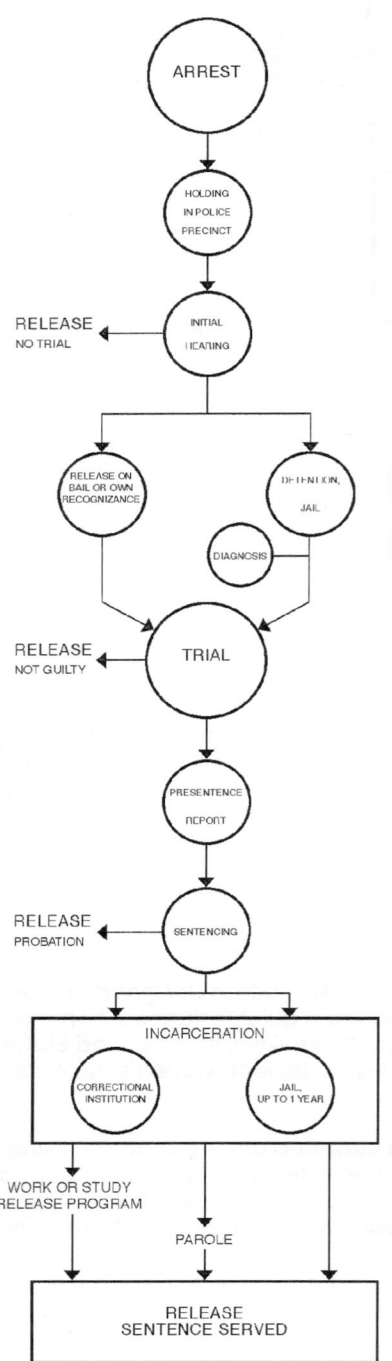

**Fig. 9. Typical offender flow through the criminal justice system**

### Program Planning and Funding

Correctional agencies and planners must evaluate the long-term implications of any capital construction program and annual operating costs. When amortized over 20 to 50 years, one-time construction costs are only a small percentage of annual operating costs. Well designed facilities, with good sight lines and observation capabilities, for example, can reduce the number of correctional officers required on all three round-the-clock shifts, resulting in substantial annual operational savings.

The capital planning, scheduling, and budgeting process varies by jurisdiction and related legislative bodies. Federal agencies rely on congressional spending bills for funds, while state and local agencies may be subject to legislative authorization, public referendums, executive decisions, or court orders mandating new facilities. Funding proposals for city and county jails are also subject to legislative and executive branch approvals, as well as community and land-use planning reviews.

Most funding programs combine several sources, with intricate formulas for matching funds and subsidies for certain programs, such as juvenile offenders, nonviolent offenders, implementation of truth in sentencing laws and drug treatment programs.

Various rules of thumb are used for preliminary construction cost estimating purposes. These figures also vary by correctional agency, jurisdiction, geographic location, proposed facility security level and type, total number of beds, construction materials and methods, local economy and a host of other regional and local factors. Based on available data, correctional agencies can usually estimate the annual operating cost per inmate, construction cost per square foot and construction cost per bed for new facilities.

Facility programming should be done early on during the preliminary planning and budgeting stages. The programming process involves agency owners, managers, architects, and planners developing an operating philosophy that will be reflected in the spaces and adjacencies within the new building. Space programs establish the required number of rooms, spaces, departments, functions, equipment, spatial relationships and site issues, such as parking and outdoor recreation areas. When total gross square footages have been developed, construction costs can be applied and projected for preliminary budgeting purposes.

### Planning for the Future

Comprehensive criminal justice planning integrates data analysis, review of existing facilities, development of options and recommendations for future needs, services and facilities. Long-range system-wide master planning provides a framework for implementing these goals and strategies with phased schedules for capital budget appropriations and construction. As new population and demographic needs emerge, facilities and correctional programs must be ready to adapt to unforeseen situations.

Designing for flexibility and expansion capability is a good way to optimize capital planning budgets, especially for one time appropriation of large expenditures. Many new correctional facilities are designed for double bunking capability in the future to accommodate population spikes. The total maximum number of beds must be factored in throughout the planning process, along with additional staffing needs, building engineering systems and other support services.

## Site Selection

Many factors are considered during the correctional facility site selection process. Available acreage and good road access are primary criteria. Federal, state and municipal jurisdictions have different goals and priorities when locating new facilities. Criteria may include the need to create new jobs in economically depressed areas, proximity to inmate families, seeking jurisdictions and local public officials who truly want the facility in their district, clustering several facilities in one area for convenient sharing of services and minimizing transportation costs.

While correctional facilities once were strictly "Not In My Back-yard" building types, many communities compete for new federal and state prisons in their jurisdictions for the steady stream of new government jobs and the spinoff economic benefits that accrue to localities. These may include increased tax revenues, need for new construction and related jobs for housing, schools, community services, infrastructure, and new jobs for local businesses to support the influx of inmates, staff, families and visitors to the area.

When seeking a site for a new prison, state and federal agencies develop a list of site selection criteria that is applied against potential sites under consideration. Typical factors include:

- sufficient available acreage for building footprint, roads and parking
- proximity and access to major highways
- local public and private support for the project
- favorable subsoil conditions, water supply, and availability of all major utilities
- overall site development costs
- economic climate of the area, available labor pool
- sufficient land and economic climate to develop a new community infrastructure (schools, housing, commercial ) for the prison and its employees within a geographical region.

If there is a strong interest in locating a new facility in a specific area, public officials and private sector community groups may decide to collaborate and work out site acquisition and other mutually beneficial financial and legal arrangements to help the project move forward on a timely basis.

With the construction of so many new prisons since 1990, and the economic benefits that have gone to adjacent communities, the federal government and most state correctional agencies have often been able to build prisons in communities who want them, rather than in areas that don't want them.

## DESIGN

Correctional facility design is an important tool for correctional agencies and managers to maintain a safe and secure facility for inmates and staff. Each design decision made during preliminary planning and design phases can result in operational, staffing and maintenance cost savings over the course of the building life cycle.

### Historical Background

The development of corrections theory in the United States dates from the early 19th century, when punishment and restraint were major components of the criminal justice system. Gradually, criminologists advocated the need to rehabilitate prisoners, but efforts often called for encouraging offenders to contemplate their sins in solitude and silence, as if doing penance. Early penitentiary designs reflected this operational philosophy.

By 1870, some concerned corrections professionals understood that methods used to rehabilitate offenders were not working. They drew up a Declaration of Principles, adopted at the first meeting of the American Correctional Association in Cincinnati. It included the following objectives:

- Reformation, not vindictive suffering, should be the purpose of correctional treatment.
- The prisoner should understand that his destiny was in his own hands.
- Prison discipline should gain the will of the prisoner and conserve self-respect.
- The goals of the prison should be to make industrious free men rather than orderly and obedient prisoners.
- Prisons should be small, and separate; institutions should be constructed for different types of offenders.
- Establishment of a system to collect consistent prison statistics.
- Society at large should understand its responsibility for crime conditions.

One hundred years later, in 1970, the American Correctional Association met in Cincinnati and reconfirmed these recommendations.

As prison conditions improved and reformed during the 1900s, the corrections profession evolved, with an emphasis on vocational training, education, and individual rehabilitation. Group therapy and counseling, the therapeutic community approach, and community-based treatment are widely accepted correctional programs. During the 1990s, public opinion about violent crime and punishment influenced subsequent legislation on prison policies, sentencing and operations. For example, some agencies eliminated weights as a recreational activity and inmate access to taxpayer funded college programs behind bars.

## SECURITY CLASSIFICATION

### Minimum Security

Minimum security housing (Fig. 10) consists of open dormitories. Inmates housed in dormitories are often classified as nonviolent offenders and do not need to be segregated from the general population. This housing type is often cheaper to build, but can pose problems in managing large populations in a single open space. As many as 50 inmates may be housed in one dormitory. Double bunked beds may be used to house more people in a single space. Gang toilets (several stalls rather than individual rooms) and showers are commonly used.

Dormitories are generally not used for housing women and girls, because of the greater privacy needs accorded women in prison.

Minimum security housing and open dormitories are often used for housing juvenile offenders and inmates nearing release. Other minimum security facility examples include open camps, work camps or farms adjacent to higher security prisons, or separate independent camps for reforestation, land reclamation and farming.

### Medium Security

Medium security institutions typically contain a secure perimeter and control system allowing a greater degree of free movement within the

**(a)**

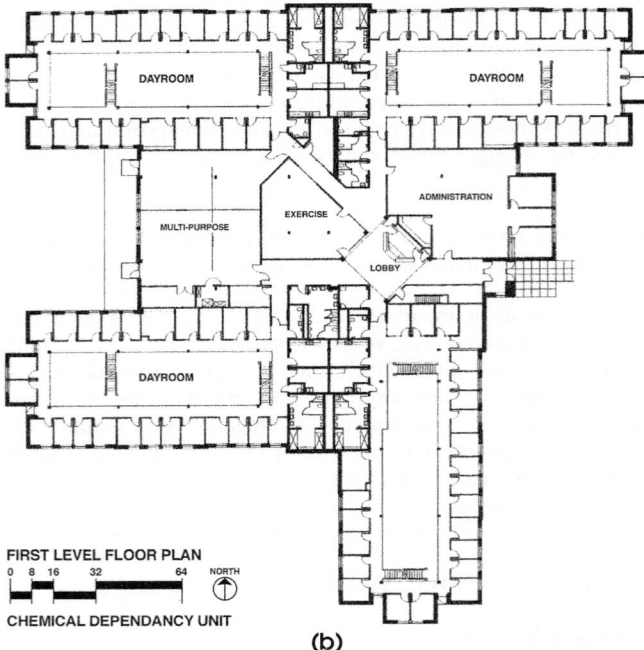

**FIRST LEVEL FLOOR PLAN**

CHEMICAL DEPENDANCY UNIT

**(b)**

**Fig. 10. This 232-bed minimum security building on a correctional facility campus provides inmates with up to 24 months of chemical dependency and sex offender therapy before release to the community. (Minnesota Correctional Facility at Lino Lakes, Chemical Dependency Unit, Lino Lakes, Minnesota; Klein McCarthy & Co., Architects); (a) view of dayroom; (b) floor plan**

facility than at maximum security facilities. Other perimeter surveillance techniques include guard houses, regular vehicular patrols around the facility, and electronic detection systems and security cameras tied to a central monitoring system in the control room. Perimeter control can be extended to include the exterior skins of housing units. Electronic security devices, closed circuit video surveillance and motion detectors, are among the many available options for secure perimeter systems.

Inmate housing in a medium security facility (Figs. 11 and 12) consists of individual cells, rooms, or dormitories, or a combination of each. Some correctional agencies designate a medium security facility or housing unit for older inmates less prone to violence, those nearing the

end of their sentence or other demographic grouping. A variety of housing and rooms types allows flexibility for inmate management.

**Maximum Security**

Maximum security facilities provide the highest level of custody and supervision and consist only of cells. Violent offenders and other inmates who must be separated from the general population are assigned to maximum security housing, if only for their own protection from other inmates.

Maximum security prisons are surrounded by a perimeter wall or fence. Access into and within the prison is closely monitored. While the combination of security systems at each prison may vary, perimeter control is often achieved by strategically located guard towers, closed circuit television cameras, vehicular patrols in constant contact with the control center, motion detectors and other electronic devices.

Housing units are single cells (with one or two beds), and in newer facilities, are often designed for double bunking capability to accommodate more beds without building a new facility. These cells are "wet cells," with a combination stainless steel water closet and lavatory located in the room. "Dry cells" do not have plumbing in the room, and gang toilets and showers are provided. Wet cells are more expensive to build, while housing units with dry cells require greater inmate movement and supervision.

**PHYSICAL IMAGE**

A building's physical appearance communicates its identity and goals to users and the community. Historically, correctional facilities were represented by a monolithic, fortress-like and forbidding appearance, regardless of where the building was sited and its surrounding environment.

As more municipal jails, juvenile facilities, detention centers, and community based programs are located within residential neighborhoods, downtown districts and commercial areas, justice facilities become an important example of civic architecture, representing the American justice system to the local community and public at large. Effective justice facility site planning and building design can respect the character of neighborhoods and reflect local design influences such as scale, colors, materials and landscaping (Fig. 13).

To enhance relations with neighbors, some city and county justice facilities have incorporated a public meeting space into the building for use by local community groups. This meeting space is ideally located near the main public lobby of the building, so that visitors do not have to pass through the interior security checkpoint to enter the secure perimeter. Public toilets, seating and a public telephone should be provided in the lobby.

**Building Massing**

During preliminary programming and planning phases, the project team investigates site subsurface conditions, site selection criteria, housing unit configurations and the proposed facility footprint. These findings, as well as social, economic and demographic factors, drive design and construction decisions.

Urban sites often require vertical stacking of functions, due to limited land availability. High rise design solutions should maintain eff

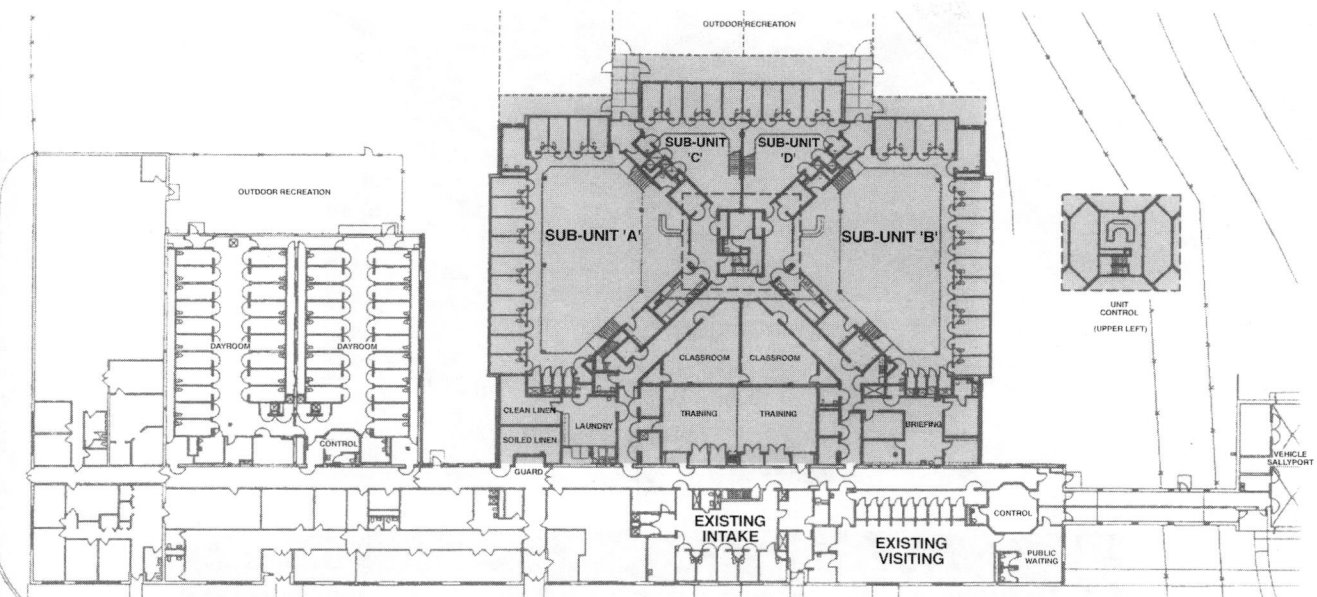

g. 11. floor plan. This 80-cell (160 bed) unit functions as a 'jail within a prison' and houses disruptive inmates within a edium security population, whose actions do not meet criteria for a classification change. The unit contains double unked cells in a two-tier podular plan, directly supervised dayrooms and program spaces. (Minnesota Correctional cility at Lino Lakes, Administrative Segregation Unit, Lino Lakes, Minnesota; Klein McCarthy & Co., Architects)

ent vertical transportation systems for inmates, services and staff. otential design issues to address include avoid placing inmate occu- ed spaces facing the street, clear vehicular circulation to and from e facility, and the creation of outdoor recreation areas. Construction asing and scheduling in busy urban areas can also pose logistical oblems.

here large tracts of land are available (Fig. 14), horizontal arrange- ent of functions allows a more flexible design and construction proach as well as planning for expansion. A building configuration ith connecting corridors works well for high-custody facilities here maximum control of inmate movement is required. Separate

buildings on the site allow greater freedom of movement between units within the secure perimeter.

**Growth and Flexibility**

Correctional facilities must be designed to anticipate increased prison populations and the need to house more beds. Correctional buildings are planned for 20 to 50 year life cycles. Routine mainte- nance for major building systems does not always occur at every facility, due to lack of funds, staff or both. When designing and spec- ifying materials, technology and equipment, architects should con- sider that minimal maintenance, staff and resources will be available at most correctional facilities. Building materials and systems should be durable and built to last over the long term without sophisticated upkeep requirements.

Planning for growth can include the following considerations:

- Site planning: size, location and capacity of parking lots, utility locations, leaving open space available for new buildings, out- door recreation fields and yards.
- Buildings: determine locations and sizes of future additions, housing units; capability of adding additional floors on multi- story buildings; planning cells to be sized and outfitted for dou- ble bunking to double the population, plan for additional support spaces such as dining areas, recreation, program space, medical units, visiting areas and classrooms.
- Building engineering services: Capacity of central building sys- tems and plants to serve new buildings. Design and capacity of existing and new mechanical and electrical systems should be considered if a building addition or replacement facility is planned.
- Housing units can be designated for growth of special popula- tions, such as mental health, mental retardation, geriatrics or the

g. 12. Typical cell block (St. Croix County Government enter, Hudson, Wisconsin; Ayres Associates, Architects)

(a)

(b)

**Fig. 13.** The 114,500-square-foot 124-bed juvenile detention center evokes the silhouette, scale and materials of the neighborhood's residential brownstones and commercial buildings. The facility resembles a community center, has a meeting room for public use, and fits in with the urban fabric. (Crossroads Juvenile Detention Center, Brooklyn, New York; Kaplan McLaughlin Diaz, Architects); (*a*) Courtyard; (*b*) main entrance

(a)

(b)

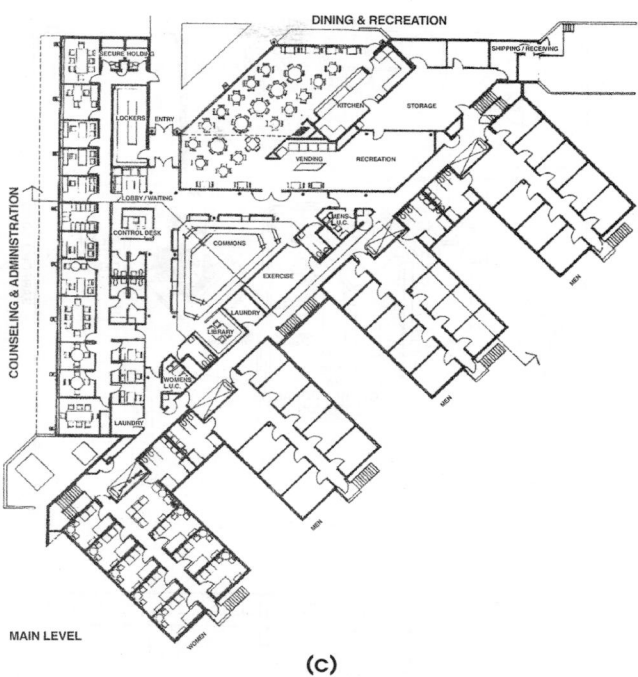

MAIN LEVEL

(c)

g. 14. The building utilizes orientation, shading and earth erming to reduce heat gain and loss. It is designed for xpansion with several additional housing clusters. (Hennepin County Work/Study Release Residence, Plymouth, Iinnesota; Klein McCarthy & Co., Architects); (a) exterior iew; (b) dining hall; (c) plan

handicapped. Housing units with a mix of single and double cells permit administrators to manage populations more effectively and separate inmates as needed. For short-stay co-ed facilities, housing units should be designed to accommodate male or females.

esigning for flexibility should be balanced against the project idget, the appropriate security level required, life cycle costs as ell as the need for increased staffing and operational costs over the ng term. Other considerations include:

- Location of building circulation elements, such as stairs, elevators and visitor, inmate and service entrances.
- Location of fixed service elements (loading docks, storage rooms) and site utilities.
- Structural modules, spans, and column locations.
- Design of mechanical, electrical, plumbing, and lighting systems.
- Design and layout of interior partitions, finishes, and furnishings.
- Economy, performance, maintenance needs, life cycle and sustainability of building systems.
- Housing types: single-bed or double bunk cells; wet (plumbing fixtures in cells) vs. dry cells (no plumbing in cells); cells vs. dormitories.
- Construction materials and methods, such as steel or concrete prefabricated units vs. traditional on-site construction methods.

**Circulation and Security**

Inmate movement within a correctional facility is an important design consideration. Correctional administrators must decide if they want to move inmates to services or move services to where inmates are located. The approach to this issue determines which services and programs will be located in or near housing units and which will be centrally located in other parts of the facility. Greater inmate movement presents more potential problems and security risks, and calls for additional correctional officers, escorts and surveillance within a facility. However, some services, such as sick call, may be best delivered at housing units, while other services, such as dentist visits and work assignments, may require inmate movement to a central location (Fig. 15).

Circulation between housing units, dining halls, work assignments, education, recreation, medical unit, canteen, administration building, and other areas within the facility should provide clear unobstructed sight lines and full observation in corridors and hallways by correctional officers. Blind corners and alcoves where inmates can hide from sight are to be avoided.

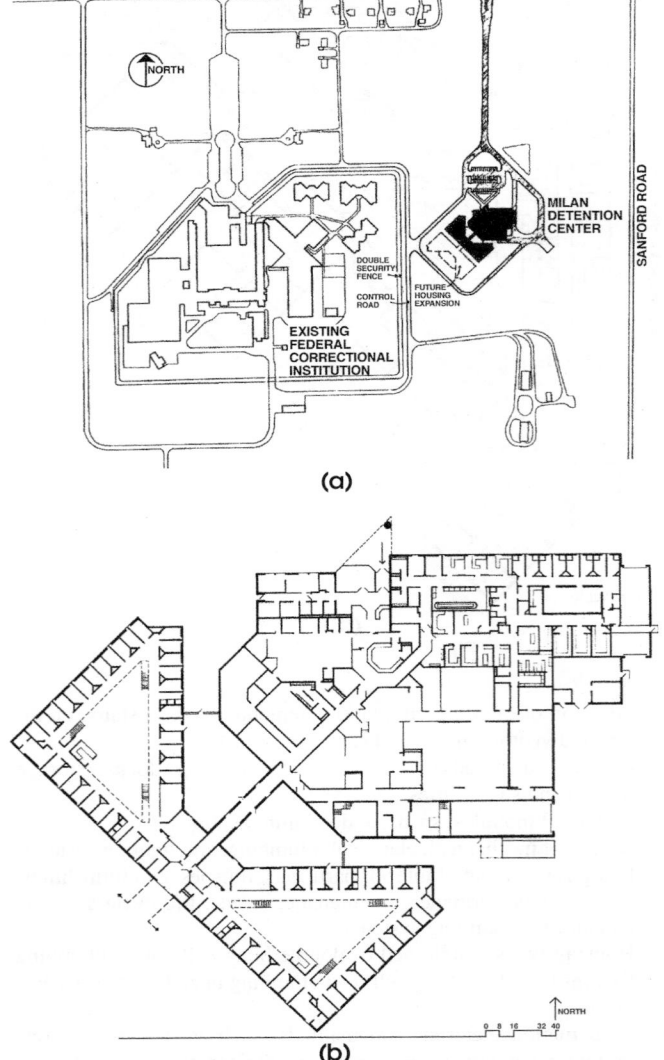

**(a)**

**(b)**

**Fig. 15.** This detention unit house detainees awaiting trial or in transit under the custody of the U.S. Marshals Service. The facility is physically separate from the main institution but shares central functions. The building includes 138 cells with planned expansion to total 268 cells. Peak capacities may require double bunking for a total population of 400-450 inmates. (Detention Unit Addition to the Federal Correctional Institution, Milan, Michigan; Klein McCarthy & Co., Architects); (a) site plan; (b) floor plan

Materials management, or the movement of supplies and materials into and within the facility is also an essential part of good circulation planning. This includes the flow of delivery trucks into the facility, unloading, bulk storage and break out of boxes and goods, delivery to units or departments, and available central and decentralized storage areas throughout the facility.

Comprehensive security is achieved through good planning and design, appropriate use of technology and the facility's staffing and operational plan. Programs and services operating around the clock, 24 hours a day, 7 days a week, require constant security and supervi-

sion, such as housing units, control center, and the main entrance However, some areas, such as the dining hall, may operate from 12 to 16 hours a day, others operate 8 hours a day, 5 days a week, while other activities occur during evening hours. By planning the location and access to these spaces, areas used during certain hours may be grouped together and closed off entirely when not in operation reducing potential security risks.

## CORRECTIONAL FACILITY PROGRAM ELEMENTS

When prison and jail populations increase rapidly, facilities become crowded and may exceed available bed space. The demand for more beds can place corrections departments under tremendous pressure to build and occupy new prisons quickly and within budgets. Fast track project delivery methods, such as design/build, or installation of steel or concrete prefabricated units, are examples of approaches that can expedite project completion and result in occupancy sooner than using traditional bid/build and on-site construction methods.

### Inmate Housing

Inmate housing design and configuration is an important design deci sion. Typically, the architectural planning and design team, working with the client agency and the corrections department, if they are no one and the same, reach consensus on overall project goals and develop the space and functional program. The correctional agency determines the security level, number of beds, correctional officer staffing levels, programs and services required in a new facility Within this framework, the project team determines the housing type design, configuration and construction method that best meets the project goals, budget and schedule.

Some corrections agencies prefer certain configurations based on experience and have developed prototype designs which they repli cate at various facilities and modify only as needs arise. Correctional managers and designers embarking on a project for the first time will benefit from traveling and visiting other facilities to gather new idea about design and operations and see for themselves how building design elements, materials, systems and equipment hold up over time.

A mix of single bed rooms or cells and two bed rooms or cells in each housing unit allows officers the flexibility to segregate inmates from the general population. Housing types are generally classified as fol lows:

- Maximum security housing, or "close security," is exclusively single cells or double bunked cells.
- Medium security housing includes cells, semiprivate rooms, dor mitories and/or a combination of housing types.
- Minimum security and work camp housing is typically open dor mitories, multi-bed rooms.

Inmate housing areas must provide safety for inmates and staff Widely recognized standards are found in the "Standards for Adul Correctional Institutions, 3rd Edition" published by the American Correctional Association (January 1990). The American Correctional Association maintains operational and facility standards for those institutions seeking accreditation status. Accreditation verifies to the public and the courts overseeing correctional facilities that facilitie meet minimum standards. The following are considered guidelines only. Designers should verify all applicable codes and requirement with appropriate governing agencies.

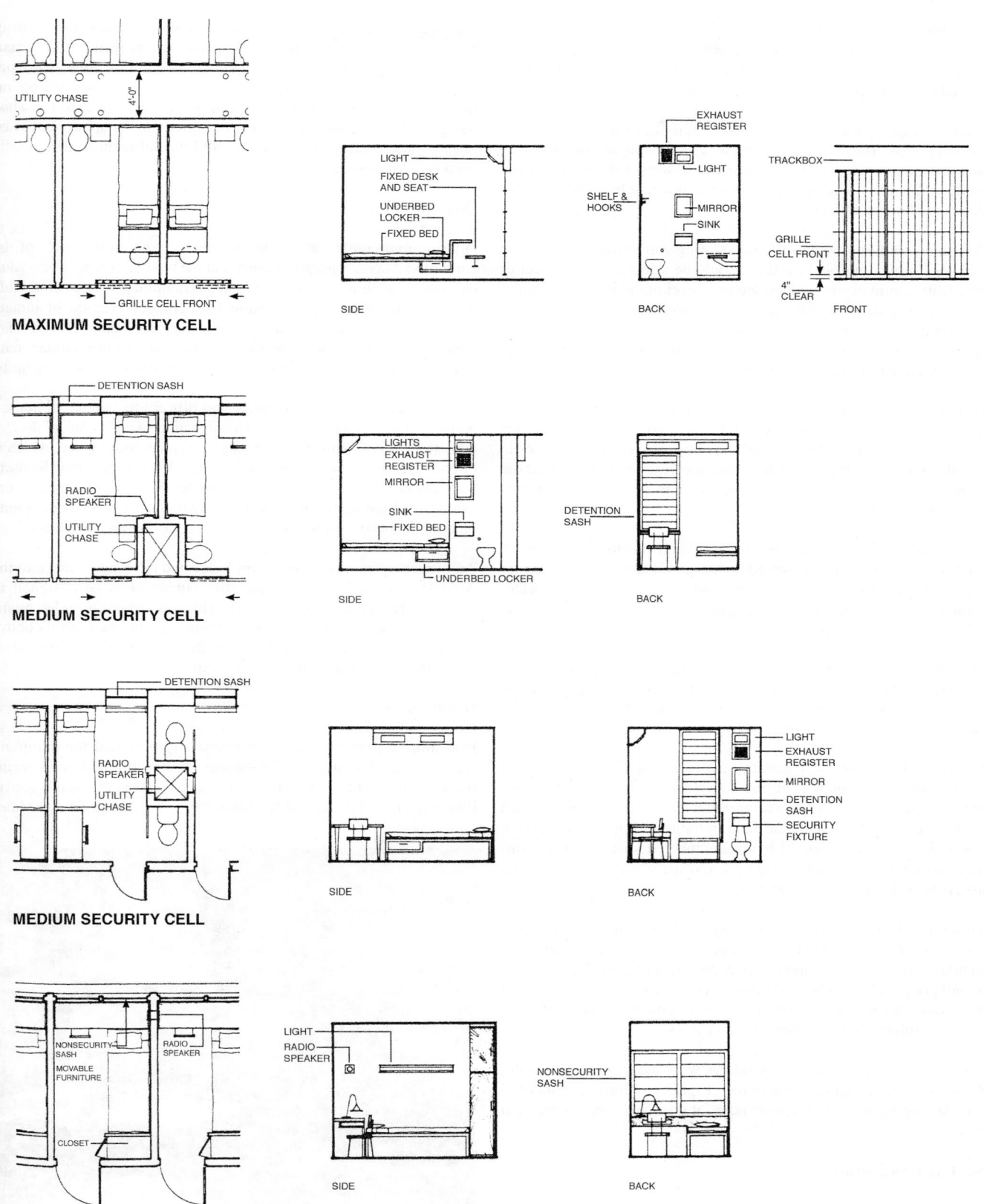

**MAXIMUM SECURITY CELL**

UTILITY CHASE

4'-0"

GRILLE CELL FRONT

SIDE

LIGHT
FIXED DESK AND SEAT
UNDERBED LOCKER
FIXED BED

BACK

EXHAUST REGISTER
LIGHT
SHELF & HOOKS
MIRROR
SINK

FRONT

TRACKBOX
GRILLE CELL FRONT
4" CLEAR

**MEDIUM SECURITY CELL**

DETENTION SASH
RADIO SPEAKER
UTILITY CHASE

SIDE

LIGHTS
EXHAUST REGISTER
MIRROR
SINK
FIXED BED
UNDERBED LOCKER

BACK

DETENTION SASH

**MEDIUM SECURITY CELL**

DETENTION SASH
RADIO SPEAKER
UTILITY CHASE

SIDE

BACK

LIGHT
EXHAUST REGISTER
MIRROR
DETENTION SASH
SECURITY FIXTURE

**INMATE ROOM**

NONSECURITY SASH
RADIO SPEAKER
MOVABLE FURNITURE
CLOSET

SIDE

LIGHT
RADIO SPEAKER

BACK

NONSECURITY SASH

**Fig. 16. Plans and elevations of various living spaces. Layouts and materials should reflect a concern for security, durability, and low maintenance.**

Cells housing inmates for over 10 hours per day should be a minimum of 80 square feet. Cells typically include a bed, toilet and lavatory, desk or writing surface, locker for clothes and personal storage and other fixed equipment for each occupant.

Dayrooms are spaces for varied inmate activities located in or near sleeping areas. They should be designed for a minimum of 35 square feet per inmate (exclusive of lavatories, showers and toilets) for the total number of inmates using the space at once, or be sized at a minimum of 100 square feet.

Dayrooms should provide sufficient seating and writing surfaces for inmates. Furnishings and finishes should be selected with respect to durability, maintenance and the security level of the inmates. Typical dayroom activities include television viewing, reading, recreation, conversation, games, eating and work. Fixed tables and chairs are appropriate for higher security settings, while movable furnishings are preferable in lower security settings.

Inmates must have access to toilet and hand-washing facilities at all times. Generally, toilets are provided at a minimum ratio of one for every 12 inmates in male facilities and one for every eight inmates in female facilities. Urinals may be substituted for up to one half of the male toilet facilities. Housing units with three or more inmates should have a minimum of two toilets.

Designers may consider the use of "dry" cells (without plumbing), provided a toilet room of grouped or "gang" toilets and lavatories are provided. Hand-washing sinks with hot and cold running water should also be located in housing units, cells, sleeping areas, at the minimum of one sink per 12 inmates.

Showers should be provided with temperature controlled hot and cold water, at a minimum ratio of one shower for every eight inmates. Temperature controls should range from 100 to 120°F Fahrenheit, to ensure safety and encourage good hygiene.

Segregation housing units contain cells or rooms similar to those in the general population but confine inmates to their cells for extended periods. These units may require greater security features and staffing levels. All cells should be a minimum of 80 square feet, of which 35 square feet should be unencumbered space, with a minimum dimension of 7 feet. Unencumbered space is available area not occupied by furniture or fixtures.

Correctional facilities must be able to provide housing, programs and activities for handicapped inmates. Local, state and federal codes and standards apply. Some standards may require a minimum percentage of cells in a facility to be handicap accessible. This can be achieved by locating accessible cells on ground level, and ensuring wheelchair access to toilets, sinks, showers or tub rooms.

Rooms and cells should have windows with access to natural light, with a minimum area of 3 square feet. Lighting in inmate rooms and cells should be at least 20 foot-candles at desk level and in personal grooming areas.

## Staffing Considerations

The number of correctional officers per inmate, or the staffing ratio, is another important operational factor influencing the planning and configuration of housing units. Correctional agencies determine the ratios of officers to inmates, or number of officers assigned to each housing unit, as a means of developing housing unit and security plans, and controlling staffing and operational budgets. Each corrections officer post represents an operational cost of three shifts per day, along with salaries and benefits. On an annual basis, the operational cost of a single officer post can be a significant expense. Thus design of housing units, and other occupied inmate areas, should be planned to enhance surveillance, visibility, and security without the need for excessive officer staffing.

## Configuration

Housing unit configurations are generally based on the goals of the correctional agency administrators and the type of inmate supervision envisioned within the housing units. Traditional single or double loaded corridors reflect the indirect supervision method of inmate management. Inmates remain in cells and are supervised from a remote control room or officer post. Officers have limited contact with inmates. Cameras and foot patrols are used to supervise housing units.

Direct supervision allows inmates and officers to mingle within the housing unit with direct contact. Housing units are a "podular" design consisting of cells surrounding a large, open dayroom space, which is often in a triangular configuration. A single level of cells may be used but more commonly, cells on the ground level are stacked with a mezzanine level above, reached by stairs. Swinging or sliding doors may be used in housing pods, with electronic controls and key access.

An officer's post or desk is centrally located near the entrance to the pod. An enclosed control room, or "bubble" can be designed to supervise two or more pods at once. This room contains video monitors, alarms and communication systems tied into the central control room of the facility. An officer's toilet should also be provided, accessible from within the control room.

## Dormitories

Dormitories (Figs. 17 to 19) are generally provided for minimum security facilities, and may be used in some medium security facilities as well. As many as 50 inmates may be housed in a single space. Planning should include observation capability and good sight lines

Fig. 17. Medium security dormitory (Dunn County Judicial Center, Menomonie, Wisconsin; Ayres Associates, Architects)

**Fig 18. Typical cell (St. Croix County Government Center, Hudson, Wisconsin; Ayres Associates, Architects)**

from all vantage points. Each inmate is usually assigned a locker or storage space for personal belongings. Adjacent toilets and showers are also required.

Sleeping area partitions may be used if more than four people are in a single area. Partition height should allow officers to observe inmates, and the open ends of cubicles can be oriented towards a circulation corridor. Dayroom areas and program spaces should also be provided for dormitories, with appropriate types and numbers of furnishings.

### Housing Support Functions

Housing units require the following spaces: sleeping rooms or areas, toilets, lavatories, showers, and a janitor's closet with a slop sink.

Clean and soiled linen rooms for storage and collection should be provided, either within the housing unit, or at a central location.

**Fig. 19. Trusty dormitory (Florence County Detention Center, Effingham, South Carolina; Freeman White, Inc., Architects)**

Some facilities provide a commercial grade washer and dryer within each housing unit so that inmates are responsible for their laundry. Other facilities maintain a central inmate-operated laundry facility and collect linens and clothing on a scheduled basis. Similarly, inmate clothing (winter coats, etc.) may be stored within the housing unit or at a central inmate clothing storage room.

### Administration

Correctional agencies establish their own system-wide chain of command, as well as the operational organization within each correctional facility. Understanding the agency's internal organizational structure and policies is important when planning administrative areas within a correctional facility.

Administrative functions can be grouped to include those functions and spaces to be located outside the secure perimeter and those within the secure perimeter. Typically, functions located outside the secure perimeter are those which need to be accessible to the public and require ease of entry and exit from the institution. They may include the offices of the facility director or warden, business manager, certain deputy wardens whose duties relate to the public; administrative, clerical, and secretarial support staff; public meeting and conference spaces; staff lounge with a kitchenette and lockers and visiting areas.

During programming and planning, designers and administrators should consider if program offices should be centralized in one administrative area or decentralized, near the inmate programs and services they relate to. Security, scheduling, travel distances, space needs and important adjacencies should be considered.

Large prisons may have several deputy wardens responsible for different functions, such as security, administration, facilities operations, and inmate programs.

### INMATE PROGRAMS

Programs include rehabilitative activities and treatment to influence change in attitudes and behavior. Correctional facility programs include mental health services, education, vocational training and work release.

### Mental Health Services

Mental health services are provided by psychiatrists, clinical psychologists, psychiatric nurses, social workers, occupational therapists, and other specially trained professionals. These professionals offer diagnoses and treatment to inmates needing mental health therapy.

Mental health providers need offices or work spaces with phones, secure file storage and access to clerical support functions, including a copier and fax machine. A conference room is recommended for staff meetings. A single meeting room can double for group therapy space as well.

Inmate treatment is provided through individual or group therapy sessions. Personal inmate interviews may be conducted in staff offices, or in a designated unassigned interview room, with sound privacy. Group therapy spaces should also be provided. Some rooms may be designed with one-way glass to permit observation from an adjacent office or staff area. Optimum size for a counseling group ranges from 8 to 15 people. A multi-use space within the housing unit for group therapy activities is desirable. Small residential groupings provide an effective setting for treatment and fostering relationships between staff and inmates.

Some administrators prefer mental health areas and services be provided within or near housing units, convenient to inmates, thus requiring mental health staff to travel and deliver services to units. Another approach calls for centrally located mental health services serving the whole facility, requiring inmate movement to mental health offices. These decisions depend on security levels, available space, staffing concerns and operational procedures within each facility.

### Education

Education in prison enhances an inmate's opportunity to succeed upon release. Many inmates cannot read and lack a high school degree. In most correctional facilities, inmates have access to a variety of educational services and programs. During orientation, inmates are often given a test to determine adult basic education levels. These results are used to place inmates in the appropriate educational programming.

Adult education is offered to those who need to develop basic skills in reading, writing and math. General Educational Development (GED) instruction and testing, which prepares inmates for the high school equivalency certificate, is offered at many facilities.

Classroom design in prisons is similar to other applicable local and state educational design standards. Classrooms may be used for high school equivalency classes, computer instruction, facility orientation meetings, information, public health instruction and vocational training.

The educational unit (Fig. 20) should be located on a major circulation corridor for inmate accessibility. To accommodate outside instructors who visit the prison to teach day and evening classes, classrooms should be conveniently located within the facility secure perimeter without the need for circulation through high security areas.

A library should be located adjacent to classroom areas. Offices for the educational director and staff, locked storage areas and inmate and staff toilets should also be provided within the educational component of the facility.

### Vocational Training

Vocational training programs include activities and skills that provide job training for inmates upon release. When planning vocational training areas, maximum flexibility of interior spaces is important so that a variety of programs may be housed within the space. Due to the long lead times between initial planning and building occupancy, correctional agencies may not be able to finalize the programs that will be offered until building completion. Outside contractors may also arrange to provide training and bring in special equipment for a fixed period of time. A large, open, flexible space with electrical outlets, plumbing and good lighting levels will allow for a range of activities.

Typical spaces may include carpentry shops, maintenance areas, classrooms, offices, toilets, and a janitor's closet (Fig. 21). Vocational instruction and programs may be coordinated with a local technical college. The programs offered may include electronics, desktop publishing, horticulture and construction technology. Creative arts programs in painting and drawing may also be available. Interactive

television connections between the facility and a local community college can provide expanded vocational training and educational programming.

### Industry

Some state correctional agencies maintain a prison industries division where inmates manufacture and sell their products to local and state governments and the public. However, each jurisdiction has its own policy regarding the extent and market for such programs and services.

Industry programs within facilities are designed to provide inmates with opportunities to learn job skills, develop good work habits, and gain work experience that is relevant to the job market. Industry programs vary widely and include data entry, assembly, textiles, market research, telemarketing, scanning, technical services, word processing, computer aided drafting; and soap, clothing and furniture manufacturing. Large, flexible spaces with building utilities, a service entrance and loading area are most adaptable for any type of program that may be implemented.

### Work Release

A state corrections department work release program allows offenders who meet certain criteria the opportunity to serve the last two to eight months of their incarceration in a community facility. A work release coordinator assists inmates in the areas of eligibility, guidance and work release preparation. Most work release participants are placed in correctional "halfway houses" in their communities. Mixing work release inmates with other prison inmates is generally discouraged, because they may be coerced to smuggle contraband inside the prison.

Since the occupants of the work-release units are free to work in the community, the costly and elaborate security elements found in correctional facilities are unnecessary. The housing type resembles a college dormitory with multi-bed rooms and public spaces. Central offices and support services are generally provided near the ground floor entrance, where inmates are often required to sign in. Typical spaces include offices, sleeping rooms, recreation space, dayrooms, kitchen, dining room, laundry, and storage.

Site selection for work release facilities should consider proximity to public transportation, parking and community acceptance of this building type in a neighborhood.

## INMATE SERVICES

### Library

The library is an information center for the facility. Ideally, the library is located convenient to housing units and the educational component. Depending on available resources, staffing and policy, the library may operate during day and evening hours, another factor in location and adjacencies.

In small facilities, such as a small county jail or prison camp, a small reference collection may be supplemented by a book exchange program from a general library. Support facilities can include a librarian's office, workroom, and magazine storage room. Many facilities have programs for transporting books on carts to the segregated maximum security units and infirmary areas to serve inmates who cannot travel to the library.

(a)

(b)

(c)

**Fig. 20.** Classroom for programs and services providing short term inmate management and long term rehabilitative efforts. The 45,000 sq ft building includes space for education and vocational training, chemical dependency counseling, chapel services, recreation, medical care, and industry production. (Hennepin County/Adult Correctional Facility Programs and Services Facility, Plymouth, Minnesota; Klein McCarthy & Co., Architects); (*a*) classroom; (*b*) gym; (*c*) elevation

### Commissary

The commissary (Fig. 22) is where inmates purchase personal items, such as cigarettes, combs, candy, juice, and miscellaneous items. A commissary operation may be centralized, so that inmates come in shifts to make their purchases, or it may be mobile, with a cart moving to and from the housing units. As a variation of the centralized commissary operation, inmates fill out request slips in their housing area, the slips are taken to the central commissary, where orders are placed in containers and marked for the inmates. The containers are then distributed in the housing units.

A central commissary needs sufficient space and display counters for inmates to see the items available. If ice cream or cold drinks are sold, refrigerated storage units are required. Space should be provided for bulk storage, and bookkeeping functions.

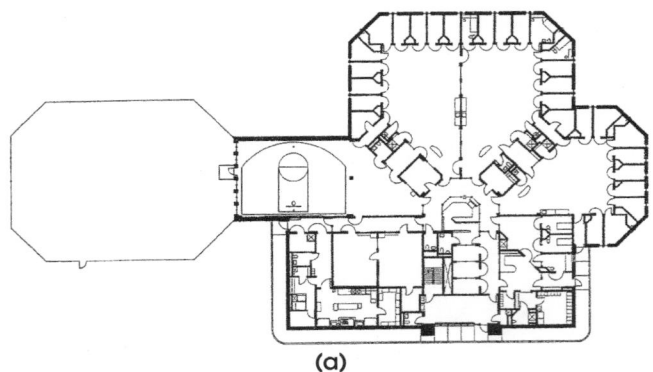

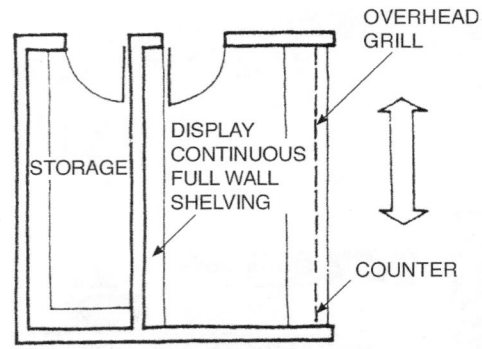

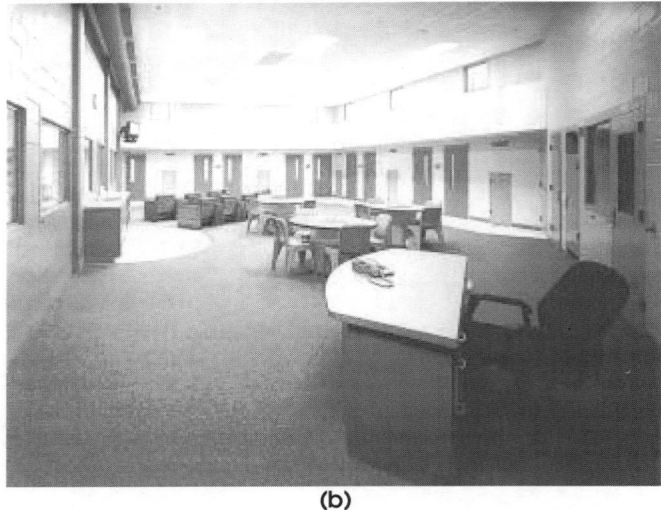

(b)

Fig. 21. This one-story 30-bed juvenile detention facility has three 9-bed direct supervision living units, each with a dayroom, showers, counseling room, janitor's closet and storage space. A 3-bed observation unit is constructed for a higher security level and abuse resistance. Central facilities include an intake processing area, contact visiting, medical exam room, multipurpose exercise room, kitchen and laundry. All areas are organized around a central control station. (Minnesota Correctional Facility - Red Wing Secure De-tention Cottage, Red Wing, Minnesota; Klein McCarthy & Co., Architects); (a) floor plan; (b) dayroom

Fig. 22. A commissary component with adjacent storage room for stock, corridor located for easy access (Guidelines for the Planning and Design of Regional and Community Correctional Centers for Adults, University of Illinois)

**Barber and Beauty Shop**

Barber facilities are located in a convenient location to all housing units. Between one to three chairs may be appropriate, depending on facility population and staffing. In women's facilities, the beauty shop is a popular place and getting an appointment can be difficult. For some women's facilities, locating a beauty shop within or near a housing unit may be considered an amenity available to those on good behavior or in an "honor unit." Special sinks for hairwashing should be provided, along with counterspace, storage and security grade mirrors.

**RECEPTION AND INTAKE**

The reception/intake unit is the point of entry for all new prisoners. The reception process includes booking, strip search, new clothing

issue, classification interview, medical examination, fingerprinting, photographing, and housing assignment (Fig. 23).

Holding areas with benches and toilet facilities should be provided for incoming inmates to wait until the staff is ready to interview them (Fig. 24). Adjacent showers and drying areas should be provided. Rooms are needed for strip searches by one or more officers.

Depending on the average number of new intakes arriving at one time, one or more medical exam rooms and private interview spaces with adjacent offices should be included, where intakes give a health care provider their medical history. The National Commission on Correctional Health Care, an accrediting body for prison health facilities who wish to apply for accreditation, requires new intakes to receive a medical screening within two hours of booking.

The reception process is sequential. Prisoners entering the process should not mix with those who have been screened and are awaiting housing assignments. Many institutions assign new inmates to special reception housing units, where they undergo orientation and classification.

FROM ARRANGEMENT

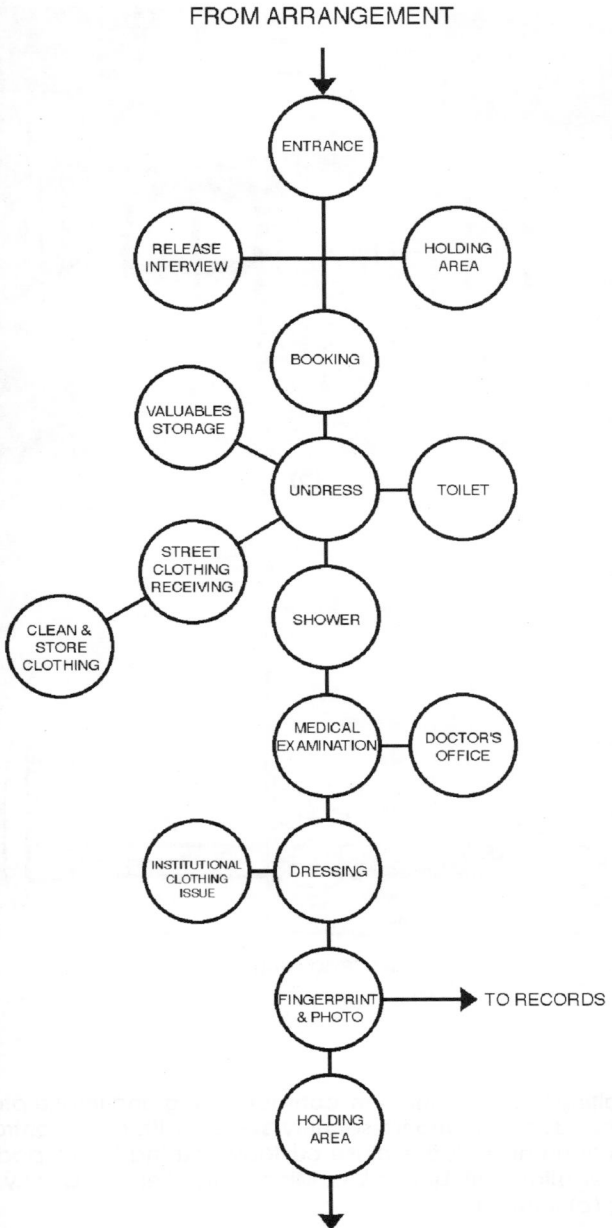

TO DETENTION HOUSING

**Fig. 23. A diagram showing inmate flow through the reception component of a detention facility**

## MEDICAL SERVICES

Correctional facilities have a public responsibility for protecting the health of inmates and staff and preventing the spread of disease among the inmate population and the families of staff members. Correctional health facilities include outpatient and inpatient, or infirmary, services. An officer's post should be provided in the medical unit waiting area, outpatient clinic and infirmary (Figs. 25 to 27).

Outpatient clinics provide daily sick call for inmates who wish to see a doctor or medical provider. A waiting area should be provided with

benches, a toilet and water fountain near the pharmacy for those taking pills and medication. Outpatient spaces generally include exam and treatment rooms, an emergency room, clinical laboratory, x-ray room, pharmacy, offices, medical records room, separate staff and inmate toilets, a janitor's closet, storage, support areas, and conference room.

The emergency room should be readily accessible to a vehicular entrance and ambulance access. All doors and corridors leading to the outdoor vehicular entrance should be wheelchair accessible and wide enough to accommodate a stretcher for emergencies. Medical units are best located on ground level, without stairs at the entry.

At women's correctional facilities, at least one examination room should be designated for ob/gyn exams, with appropriate exam tables and equipment. Some women's facilities may choose to provide prenatal care, and a nursery for newborns up to six months to a year old.

Dentistry is a part of outpatient medical services. The inmate waiting area may be shared by those waiting to see the dentist. The most efficient dental suite includes one space containing between one and three dental operatories, or chairs. Counters, sinks, and storage are required in the room. The dentist and a lab technician need office space, lab work area, and room for dental equipment storage. Daylight in the operatory should be provided where possible.

The infirmary is for inmates requiring overnight medical attention or who have a contagious disease. The total number of beds varies at each facility and depend on the size and nature of the prison population. A mix of single and double bed rooms allows flexibility in treatment. One bed isolation rooms with separate anterooms are required for those inmates with a contagious diseases, such as tuberculosis. Special negative pressure air flow ventilation to the outdoors is required for these rooms so that germs are not recirculated in the facility.

Visibility from the nurse's station to the patient rooms is essential for observation. Design standards for community health facilities are advisable.

Suicide prevention rooms, or psychiatric isolation rooms, are also necessary for those inmates who require mental health attention, but are not medically ill. These rooms may be located in the infirmary for flexibility of use, within the housing units, or in specially designated mental health units. They should be outfitted with tamperproof hardware and finishes to prevent inmates from harming themselves.

## FOOD SERVICE

Like hospitals, hotels and universities, correctional facilities provide three meals a day for hundreds or thousands of people. Food service and dining facilities pose specific challenges due to security concerns. Most food service tasks are performed by inmates. Cooking and food preparation can also be part of a vocational culinary training program.

Food preparation occurs in a central kitchen. Related adjacent spaces include a loading dock, bulk storage, cooking and dishwashing areas, trash collection and disposal. Storage should be provided for dry goods, paper storage, refrigeration, and dairy products. Offices should be provided for the food service director and other staff to meet with outside vendors and plan menus. When food service is also a work program, nearby inmate lockers and toilets should also be

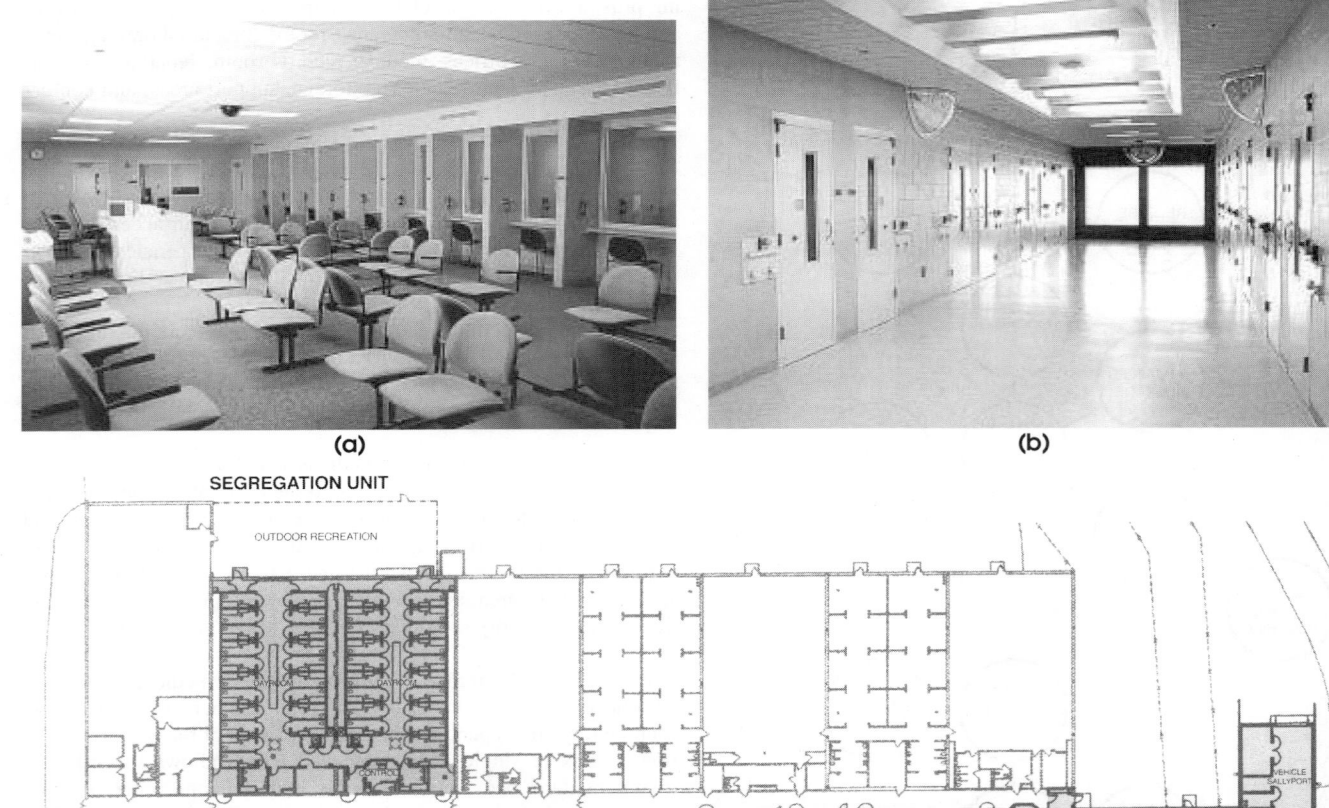

Fig 24. Intake and visiting contains an entry sallyport, visitor waiting, contact and non-contact visiting and intake processing/secure holding area. The central control room commands an electronic security system with door control communications and video surveillance. The 42-bed Segregation Unit includes close custody housing in two pods (Minnesota Correctional Facility at Lino Lakes Reception/Segregation Unit, Lino Lakes, Minnesota; Klein McCarthy & Co., Architects); (a) waiting area; (b) corridor in housing area; (c) floor plan

provided for changing. An adjacent multipurpose space can serve as a conference room, classroom or informal dining area.

Some agencies run prison farms that grow vegetables and raise farm animals. Others may utilize a cook/chill system, where food is prepared off-site and trucked into nearby satellite kitchen facilities for reheating at each institution.

At larger prisons facilities, separate food service areas may be provided for several housing units to minimize inmate movement between buildings. At smaller scale facilities, including women's, mental health and juvenile facilities, cooking and dining within the housing units may be a positive, therapeutic activity to teach inmates daily living and group interaction skills.

Meal service operations can occur in several ways. Typical meal delivery systems include:

- Central dining room adjacent to kitchen
- Local dining rooms in housing units
- Delivery of meals to cells
- A combination of the above

**Central Dining**

Central dining adjacent to the kitchen facilitates delivery of prepared food and return of soiled dishes to the dishwashing area, located in the kitchen. Dining may occur in a single room (Fig. 28) or in subdivided spaces to reduce a large number of inmates congregating in a single space. Dining may occur in shifts or on a continuous basis where inmates leave after they have finished their meals and other inmates take their seats. The facility sound system should be extended into the dining area for broadcasting announcements and music. Acoustics are another consideration for large dining spaces with hard finishes on floors, walls and ceilings.

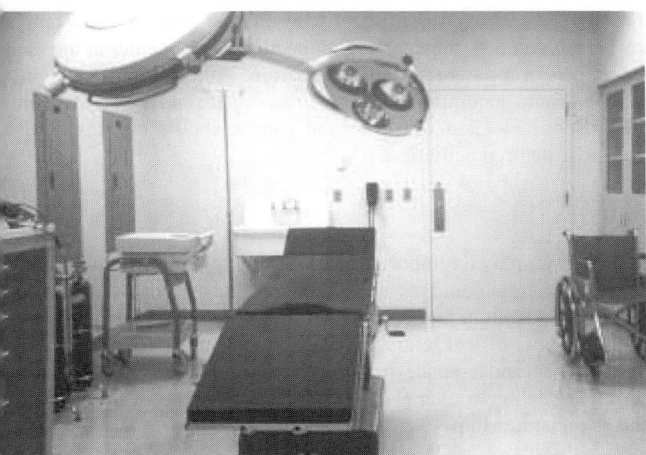

Fig. 25. Treatment room

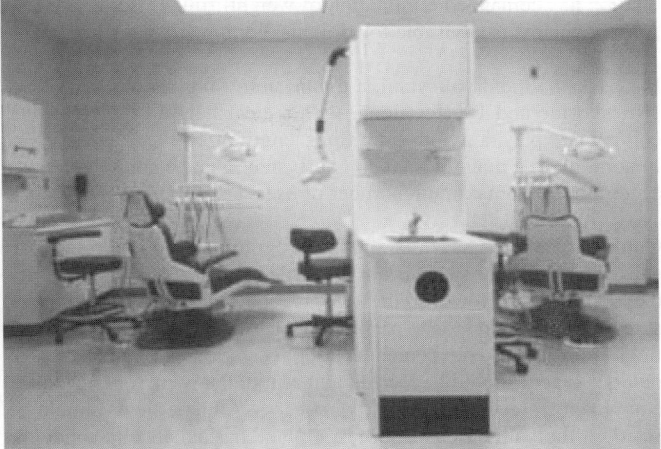

Fig. 27. Dental operatory

**Decentralized Dining in Housing Units**

Dining in housing units eliminates the potential security issues related to large numbers of inmates moving to a single space and congregating together. When designed as a multipurpose space, the dining room area can also be used for other program activities. Prepared food is delivered from the central kitchen by heated food carts, which may be unloaded in the dining area. Unless disposable plates are used, dirty dishes are returned to a central dishwashing facility in the kitchen, where they are cleaned in accordance with health code standards.

**Delivery of Meals to Cells**

Inmates in segregation units or maximum security cells who may not leave their cells will have food trays delivered to them through slots in the cell doors. These trays are delivered and picked up on carts going to the unit from the central kitchen area.

**Staff Dining**

Separate staff dining areas should be provided. In smaller units, or juvenile facilities for example, which seek to promote interaction between inmates and staff, staff may choose to dine with inmates for at least one meal a day.

**RECREATION**

Recreation is an important part of correctional activities and rehabilitative programs. Engaging in sports directs inmate energy from other potentially destructive behavior. A recreation program should include a variety of competitive sports and activities. Indoor facilities are also essential for a full year-round recreation program.

A gymnasium can be multifunctional, for sports, movies and auditorium functions. Basketball is a popular sport. The gym floor should be available for basketball, volleyball, and other floor games. Public

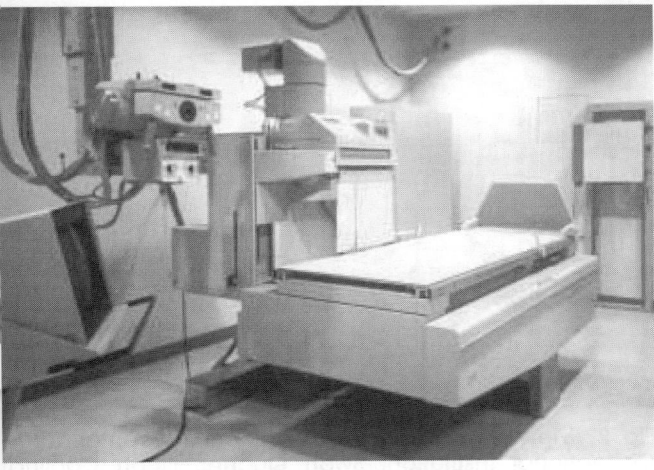

Fig. 26. Radiology room

Fig. 28. Dining room (Coleman Federal Correctional Complex, Coleman, Florida; Spillis Candela & Partners, Architects)

opinion has demanded elimination of weightlifting in some prisons. A separate area is advisable for weights, boxing and wrestling.

For basketball and volleyball, a gymnasium floor should be at least 60 feet wide and 100 feet long, with a clear height of 20 feet. For competitive play, a gymnasium floor length of 100 feet is desirable. In addition to a main basketball court, side practice courts may also accommodate a maximum number of users at a time.

Outdoor recreation space is another program component. On urban sites where outdoor space is not available, enclosed rooftop activities may be feasible. However, these areas require secure fencing enclosures at the sides and top to prevent escapes. Where possible, yard and field areas should supplement indoor recreation programs. Ideally, outdoor spaces should be located adjacent to the gym, for convenient equipment storage and locker room access. Athletic fields should be sized for football, baseball, soccer, softball, basketball, and handball.

## VISITING

Inmate visiting occurs on a scheduled basis. Visits strengthen family ties and inmate morale. Designated visiting areas are located near the public entrance to limit visitor circulation within secure areas. All visits are carefully supervised to ensure contraband is not exchanged between visitors and inmates. Visitors are required to leave packages and purses outside the visiting room. Lockers with keys are often provided in the main lobby for this purpose. The lobby should include public toilets.

Visiting areas are designated as either contact, or non-contact. Contact visits allow inmates and visitors to be in a large room together under officer supervision, while non-contact visits occur in cubicles, with inmates and visitors on opposite sides of a wall. Inmates most often receive visits from family members and attorneys.

For contact visiting, a large room with tables, chairs and a children's play area should be sized for several clusters of two to three people to converse quietly. An officer's post should be strategically located within the space, on a raised platform, to ensure total observation capability. The visiting room should be rectangular or square in shape, without blind spots, alcoves, freestanding columns or any obstructions that will hinder observation by officers. An enclosed outdoor area adjacent to the visiting room may be provided, along with picnic tables and seating areas.

The visiting area is usually accessed by a public corridor from the lobby for visitors and an inmate corridor leading to and from the housing units. Inmates receiving contact visits are often strip searched before and after visiting, and may be required to change clothing to ensure they do not have any contraband. Small cubicles should be provided on the inmate side of the visiting areas for this purpose, along with an inmate toilet and officer area. The circulation flow should be sequential, so inmates do not backtrack after they have been searched prior to visiting, or can avoid a search after visiting.

Non-contact visits occur with the inmate and visitor on separate sides of a physical barrier to prevent passage of contraband, with telephones or speakholes to allow communication. Violent offenders may be limited to non-contact visits for security reasons.

At women's facilities, providing new skills and opportunities for increased interaction with inmates' children can ease reentry into the family upon release. Children of women residing in a parenting unit may be allowed overnight visits with their mother in small bungalows, residential settings, or an independent living center at the facility, as part of a parenting/family program. Pullout trundle beds in a sleeping room accommodate the woman inmate and the child. A children's room, stocked with toys and games, should be provided for play or structured activities.

## RELIGION

Religion can play an important part of an inmate's time in prison. A religion program could include weekly or daily services, counseling religious education, and contact with inmates' families and visitors. Clergy require offices, either separate or a shared space, for administrative work and a space for private counseling sessions. In older facilities, elaborate chapels may be used for large meeting spaces and as an auditorium.

Due to space constraints, chapels are often used by different faiths on a scheduled basis. When planning large new facilities, public agencies prefer to avoid planning traditional chapels or labeling spaces with religious designations. Instead, a multipurpose space can be used for religious services or other group activity. Locked storage closets can hold religious items.

## SECURITY

Security standards at every correctional facility are maintained to ensure the safety of the community, staff and inmates. Outside doors, cell doors, and other access areas are monitored electronically from a central control room (Fig. 29), which is occupied 24 hours a day, 7 days a week by one or more officers.

Security planning begins during the initial design stages. Every design decision—from site planning, perimeter fencing, landscaping, room locations, materials, construction methods, to engineering and building systems—will impact security. Facility operations, staffing patterns, maintenance and use of technology are other important administrative decisions that should be coordinated with the overall security goals, mission and design goals.

**Fig. 29. View of dormitory from open control center (Hyde Correctional Institution, Swan Quarter, North Caolina; FreemanWhite, Inc., Architects)**

g. 30. Direct supervision housing unit (Florence County etention Center, Effingham, South Carolina, Freeman-White, Inc., Architects)

echnological developments have had a tremendous impact on erimeter, building, and interior security in correctional facilities. utdoors, perimeter fencing is often supplemented with infrared evices and motion detectors.

he central control room is the nerve center of the facility. It is deally located near the main public entrance, adjacent to the lobby, r just within the secure perimeter, if there is a separate reception esk to greet visitors (Fig. 30). The central control room is generally quipped with an electronic security system integrating door control, ideo surveillance, security communications and life safety systems. hese systems often require raised floors, climate control, tinted lass, task lighting, vision panels, several phone lines, computer anks, and security features around the room itself. A staff toilet hould be provided adjacent to the control room.

Until the 1990s, prison security often relied on intercoms and paging ystems. As new electronic systems came on the market, security lanning changed dramatically to reflect the age of technology. High ech items include microprocessor-run systems allowing officers to iew any cell, automatically open only that cell door (and not an ntire cell block of doors) and adjust the temperature.

he long rows of cells in older facilities have been replaced with omputerized podular designs, with an average of 24 cells. Advanced ecurity systems are operated by electrical/mechanical control pan-ls, about 4 feet wide by 2.5 feet high. A control room staffed by a ew officers can monitor five pods. The panels control all systems vithin those cells, a stark change from older panels capable of con-rolling only one function and requiring a 30-square-foot room.

Standard prison security elements include closed-circuit television monitoring, access control, paging, visiting and staff room inter-oms, video conferencing, perimeter sensing, man-down systems, listance learning, and even telemedicine.

Graphic panel technology, or touch-screens, are a popular innova-tion. With touch-screens, an inmate call is automatically illuminated on the officer's screen, showing where the call is originating from. The officer touches the light to activate an intercom or video camera where the inmate is located.

Man-down systems are found in an average of one in 12 new facili-ties. The system includes a device carried on a correctional officer and sounds an alarm when the officer falls. Some devices are voice activated, others work with a pull cord.

**Electronic Education and Management Systems**

Electronic systems can provide distance learning through media edu-cation programs for inmates and staff. Most of the systems use disc, tape or satellite media for delivery. Security management is another benefit of increased technology, especially with larger inmate popula-tions. The systems and goals may vary, but the overall goal is to record activity. Typically, each inmate is assigned a number to enter into a keypad or a card to swipe, which monitors the number of times each inmate receives clothing, for example. It can count how often an inmate's door opens and where he goes. The management system thus creates an electronic record of each individual. These systems create an automated record to assist staff with data reporting and documentation, and may also be used to monitor hours and facility access for staff.

**Vehicular Access**

Vehicles entering a correctional facility with a secure perimeter fence must pass through a vehicular sallyport. A sallyport is an entrance vestibule with doors or gates at each end. Only one door or gate should be open at any one time. Large vehicular sallyports are elec-tronically operated from guard posts, a nearby guard tower, or the central control room. All vehicles entering the facility are searched by officers. Sufficient parking space should be provided for queuing at large facilities.

Parking areas should be provided for staff and visitors. Access should be provided for service vehicles making deliveries and pickups of bulk items, such as food and laundry. Facilities may have buses to transport inmates to court appearances, other correctional facilities, or on medical trips to local hospitals. Parking and drop off areas sized to accommodate these vehicles should be provided within the secure perimeter.

**SUMMARY**

Correctional facility design is a form of civic architecture that repre-sents an important part the American justice system plays in urban neighborhoods, suburban towns and rural communities. The varied and complex issues present great challenges for architects and design-ers, from site selection, campus planning, and building massing to interior space planning. Correctional facility design is an opportunity to exercise social responsibility, and create humane, functional, cost efficient facilities that can be built, operated and maintained for years to come.

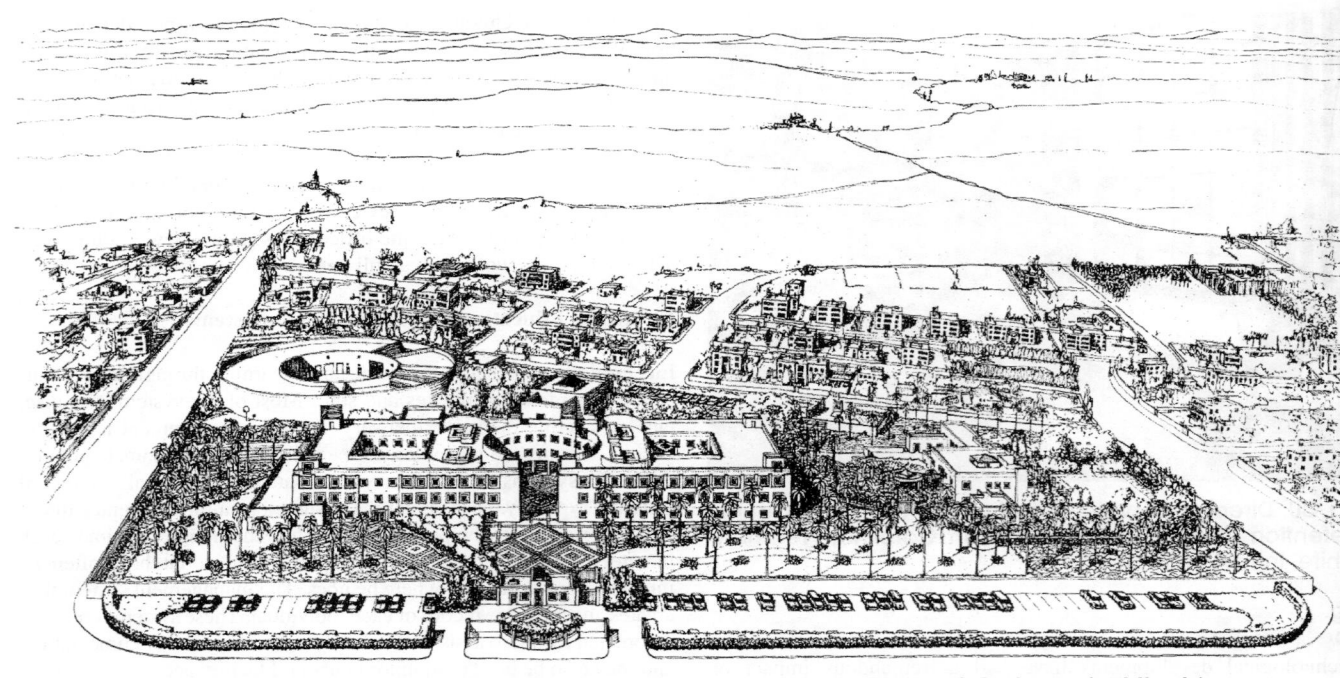

Fig. 1. Perspective, U.S. Embassy, Amman, Jordan (Perry Dean Rogers & Partners, Architects)

# U.S. EMBASSIES/CHANCERIES

### DESIGN CONSIDERATIONS FOR EMBASSY OFFICE BUILDINGS

#### Building Character

Buildings should be representative of their function as a U.S. Diplomatic Mission facility. Embassy office buildings and representational residences should present an unpretentious architectural form representative of the United States and expressing such qualities as dignity, strength, and good will.

#### Host Country Compatibility

Buildings should demonstrate respect for the architectural customs, traditions, and environment of the host country, or the region thereof.

#### Design

Building structure should demonstrate an appropriate building-to-land form relationship (Figs. 1 and 2) and should minimize the effect of construction on the site and surrounding areas. Consideration shall be given to the potential of natural forces and weather conditions within the area (i.e., earthquakes, floods, tornadoes, hurricanes, and temperature extremes). Each design shall embody the principles of

functional simplicity and spatial flexibility. The concept of whole building performance shall be incorporated into the design so that a balance between functional, security, safety, environmental, energy and operational factors is achieved. Sensitivity to the economic cost of a building's initial construction and life-cycle operations shall reflect a commitment to providing high standards for comfort, productivity, and quality of life for its occupants.

#### Culturally Sensitive Design

The quality of significance in a host country's history, architecture, archaeology, and culture is present in its districts, sites, and buildings. These possess the integrity of location, design, setting, materials, and association. Whenever possible the project's site landscaping, the building's architectural character (Fig 3), and the construction materials (Fig. 4) should reflect the cultural heritage of the locality or region. The design of spaces and features shall reflect cultural sensitivity (Figs. 5 and 6) but not be in conflict with the building design policies.

### EMBASSY ORGANIZATION AND FUNCTIONS

#### Embassy

Under the strict definition, an Embassy is people, the Ambassador and his or her staff representing the United States to another country.

*Author:* Foreign Buildings Office, U.S. Department of State

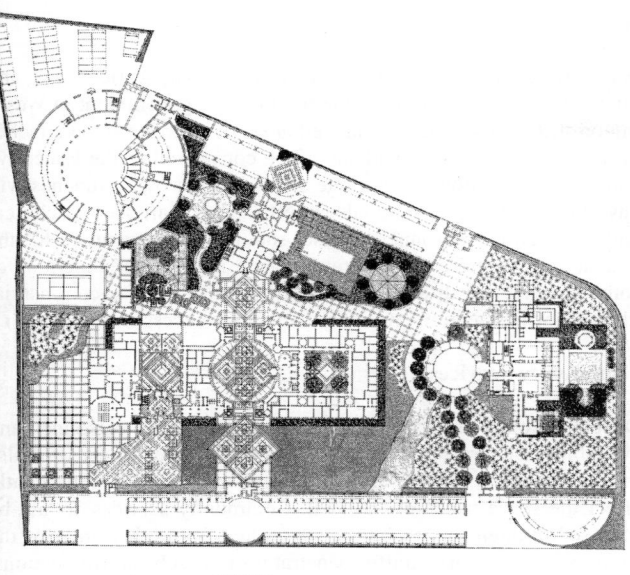

SITE PLAN

g. 2. Plan, U.S. Embassy, Amman, Jordan (Perry Dean ɔgers & Partners, Architects)

Fig. 4. U.S. Embassy, Amman, Jordan (Perry Dean Rogers & Partners, Architects; photo: Richard Mandelkorn, courtesy of architect)

The Chancery is the Embassy office building in which offices of the Ambassador and substantive sections are located along with some or all of the other sections.

In some countries, there are two or more Ambassadors: one for the Embassy, and others heading special missions—permanent or of limited duration—such as those for international organizations (such as the United Nations) or for special negotiations.

**Consulates and Consulate-Generals**

In many countries, the Embassy also has "branch offices" in cities other than the capital. These are called Consulates or Consulates-General. The difference between these is primarily a matter of size, the latter being larger.

ig. 3. U.S. Embassy, Amman, Jordan (Perry Dean Rogers & ʾartners, Architects; photo: Richard Mandelkorn, courʾesy of architect)

Fig. 5. U.S. Embassy, Amman, Jordan (Perry Dean Rogers & Partners, Architects; photo: Richard Mandelkorn, courtesy of architect)

### Embassy sections

Typically, an Embassy consists of the following major sections:

- Executive
- Political
- Economic
- Consular
- Public Diplomacy
- Administrative
- Communications

Other agencies and services which may be in the Embassy include:

- United States Agency for International Development (USAID)
- Military Assistance Advisory Group (MAAG) or Office of Military Cooperation (OMC)
- Federal Bureau of Investigation (FBI)
- Drug Enforcement Agency (DEA)
- Internal Revenue Service (IRS)
- Immigration and Naturalization Service (INS)
- U.S. Trade Center/Export Development Office (USTC/EDO)

It is possible that any U.S. agency or department could have an overseas office.

**Fig. 6. U.S. Embassy, Amman, Jordan (Perry Dean Rogers & Partners, Architects; photo: Richard Mandelkorn, courtesy of architect)**

### Attachés

Attachés, such as Defense, Labor, Commercial, Agricultural, and others, report to the Ambassador and the U.S. government in Washington, D.C. on various specialized areas of interest. Some attachés have sensitive functions and should be convenient to the Executive and Political Sections, in discrete suites of their own. Attachés will have Foreign Service Nationals (FSN) support staff such as clerical and translation personnel. These should be convenient to the attachés, but outside the discrete attaché area. Other functions of some attaches are directed toward the public, such as commercial libraries, which require proximity to a public access control (PAC).

### Community Services

Depending on the size of the mission, the number of personnel, and availability of services in the host country, a wide variety of diplomatic community services may be offered and this will significantly affect the space needs of the Post. Community services should be accessed through a PAC, but be segregated from other areas of the Embassy to minimize traffic penetration into substantive sections. Some examples are:

- Health Unit: This unit provides health care counseling, management, and treatment for Embassy personnel and their dependents. Facilities and services provided are determined based on factors that include the location, nature, and size of the community served and the availability of host country medical services.
- Community Liaison Office (CLO): This office offers assistance and counseling to FSOs (Foreign Service Officers) and their dependents on the local conditions and adaptation thereto.
- Food Service: This can range from simple short-order to full meal facilities, augmented in some cases by cocktail lounges and private VIP dining rooms. While ostensibly for Embassy personnel and dependents, these facilities sometimes become meeting places for a larger community of diplomats, media personnel, host country, and temporary official business travelers.
- Commissary: This is a facility for retail, tax-exempt sales of merchandise to Embassy personnel and dependents. The commissary can range in size from a small alcohol/tobacco sales room to a supermarket.
- Recreation Association: This is an Embassy staff-supported organization sponsoring many functions such as recreational activities. At some posts, it provides contract services to the Embassy for a variety of services such as residential guard services, supplemental vehicles, and TDY quarters. It can be a modest or, at times, extensive unofficial operation that can have substantial effect on space requirements.
- Foreign Service Institute (FSI): This is a facility for language training of Embassy employees and their dependents.
- Personal Services: Examples include barber shop, beauty shop, repair shops, and the like.

### Factors Influencing the Size of a U.S. Foreign Mission

The U.S. presence in a host country ranges from about a dozen Americans and local employees to more than a thousand. There is seldom a direct relationship, however, between the area or population of the host country and the number of persons staffing official U.S. interests. Factors that tend to influence the number of persons at a post include:

- Issues requiring negotiation or administration: These would include treaties or other bilateral and multilateral agreements;

Financial or military assistance or cooperation

Number of U.S. citizens: This would also include relatives of citizens in the host country;

Demand for visas: This often results from economic or social conditions in the host country;

Amount of economic, commercial, social, cultural, military, and political intercourse: This takes place between the United States and host country.

## Locations of Embassy Functions

The Embassy Office Building is organized into four areas of access control: Public Access Area (Fig. 6), General Work Area, Restricted Area, and Core Area. The Restricted Area and Core Area taken together make up the Controlled Access Area (CAA). Planning of these areas is geared to security, functional, and organizational requirements and they are areas of a Foreign Service Post which are separate and distinct from all other elements of the Post in terms of space planning and access controls. The areas of access restriction are listed below with the Embassy offices that are normally located within each area:

Public Access Area: An area designated for protection solely by perimeter security measures. This area is provided for the screening of visitors and employees before admittance into areas behind the Embassy Office Building's public access controls (PAC).

General Work Area: Work spaces occupied by U.S. citizen and Foreign Service National (FSN) personnel in which Sensitive But Unclassified (SBU) information may be handled, stored, discussed, or processed. This area will be located behind the PAC.

Examples of such areas may include: Consular Section, Foreign Commercial Service (FCS), Foreign Agricultural Service (FAS), Administrative Section functions, USAID, and tenant agency offices such as Customs, INS, etc.

- Controlled Access Area (CAA): This is the only area(s) within the building where classified information or materials may be handled, stored, discussed or processed. The CAA is occupied by American staff only.

- Restricted Area: Those areas of the building in which classified information may be handled and stored. Classified discussions and processing are permitted but may be limited to designated areas, depending on the technical security threat. Typically, the Executive Section, Regional Security Office, Political Section, Economic Section, and other similar sections would be included in the restricted area. Routine access to restricted areas is limited to U.S. citizens possessing at least a Secret clearance. Uncleared persons are to be under the continuous escort or surveillance of an appropriately-cleared U.S. citizen employee.

- Core Area: Those areas within the CAA requiring the highest levels of protection where intelligence, cryptographic, security, and other particularly sensitive or compartmentalized information may be handled, stored, discussed, or processed. Unescorted access is limited to authorized U.S. citizen personnel holding a Top Secret clearance. Authorized U.S. citizens with a Secret clearance may have access to core areas, but must be under constant escort and observation.

## Space Allocation

The following page presents space allocations within a typical U.S. Embassy/Chancery.

# Programming/Planning Module Matrix

## Principles

- The space requirements program needs to identify all primary and support type spaces.
- The program size is an area range and is not a literal translation into a building.
- The built office layout will vary from planning size.
- The space requirements program needs to identify all primary and support type spaces.

| Programming Size (SM) | 54.8 | 44.9 | 37.4 | 32.8 | 28.1 | 22.5 | 16.4 | 14.0 | 14.0 | 12.1 | 6.0 |
|---|---|---|---|---|---|---|---|---|---|---|---|
| Internal Circulation (IC) | Internal Circulation (IC) 30% | | | | | | | | Internal Circulation 40% | | |

| SPACE FUNCTION | 54.8 | 44.9 | 37.4 | 32.8 | 28.1 | 22.5 | 16.4 | 14.0 | 14.0 | 12.1 | 6.0 |
|---|---|---|---|---|---|---|---|---|---|---|---|
| Ambassador Office | closed | closed • | closed | closed | closed | closed | closed | closed | open | open | open |
| DCM - CG Office | | | • | | | | | | | | |
| Chief of Section / Agency Head Office | | | | | • | | | | | | |
| Branch Chief Office | | | | | | • | | | | | |
| Standard Closed Office | | | | | | | | closed • | | | |
| Standard Workspace | closed | closed | closed | closed | closed | closed | closed | closed | open • | open | open |
| Standard Workspace II/TDY | | | | | | | | | | • | |
| Consular Workspace | | | | | | | | | | | • |
| Planning Module Size (SM) | 42.12 | 34.56 | 28.80 | 25.20 | 21.60 | 17.28 | 12.60 | 10.80 | 10.80 | 8.64 | 4.32 |

NOTES:

The FBO planning/programming modules are utilized as a guide for programming purposes only. The module utilization shall not be used as an entitlement.

1. The • designates the **typical** Programming/Planning module for US Embassies. The shaded area represents the module options for each function

2. The minimum size for closed offices and workstations is the PM10.8 planning size module.

3. The Planning Modules: For the PM10.8 are either a closed office or open workstation modules. The office functional

   3-a: For the PM10.8 are either a closed office or open workstation modules. The office functional requirement will determine space type utilized, either open or closed workspace.

   3-b: For the PM8.64 or the PM4.32 planning modules utilization is for staff that have a duplicate or multiple work areas, such as functions in the consular sections, or regional operation, and communication centers

**Sample Program**

The following section is a sample program for a U.S. Embassy/Chancery. All areas are given in square meters.

## Program

| Space Description | Net area | | | Comments |
|---|---|---|---|---|
| | Work Area NSM | Internal Circ Percent | Recom'd Unit NSM | |
| **EXECUTIVE SECTION** | | | | |
| **Restricted Access Area:** | | | | |
| Ambassador - Chief of Mission | 34.6 | 30% | 45.0 | |
| Deputy Chief of Mission | 28.8 | 30% | 37.4 | |
| COM Secretary | 10.8 | 30% | 14.0 | |
| DCM Secretary | 10.8 | 30% | 14.0 | |
| Waiting | 13.0 | 30% | 16.9 | Include coat closet. |
| Visitor's Coat Closet | 2.2 | 0% | 2.2 | |
| EXEC Toilet/Lavatory | 4.4 | 0% | 4.4 | |
| Work Room/Files/Supplies | 13.0 | 30% | 16.9 | |
| Kitchenette | 9.0 | 0% | 9.0 | |
| Conference Room | 17.3 | 0% | 17.3 | |
| **Unrestricted Access Area:** | | | | |
| Protocol Asst | 10.8 | 30% | 14.0 | |
| Waiting | 4.4 | 30% | 5.7 | Shared w/other FSNs from CAA sections. |
| Files | 9.0 | 30% | 11.7 | Shared w/other FSNs from CAA sections. |
| Work Room | 10.8 | 30% | 14.0 | Shared w/other FSNs from CAA sections. |
| Chauffeur | 0.0 | 0% | 0.0 | See Drivers' Lounge |

**ADDITIONAL COMMENTS:**
Adjacent to Political and Economic Sections

**CO-LOCATION OF EXECUTIVE/ECONOMIC/POLITICAL/SECURITY:**
The non-CAA staff of all CAA sections (executive, political, economic, defense attache and security) should be co-located and shall share work room, file area, and waiting area.

**POLITICAL SECTION**

| Space Description | Work Area NSM | Internal Circ Percent | Recom'd Unit NSM | Comments |
|---|---|---|---|---|
| **Restricted Access Area:** | | | | |
| Political Counselor | 17.3 | 30% | 22.5 | Need a 2-Drawer Safe |
| Political Officer | 10.8 | 30% | 14.0 | Need a 2-Drawer Safe |
| Secretary | 9.0 | 30% | 11.7 | |
| TDY Space/Ref Area/Meeting Area | 15.1 | 30% | 19.6 | Include an Internet Terminal, small table and 6 bookcases. |
| Work Room | 10.8 | 30% | 14.0 | Include unclass fax, scanner, copier, and printer. |
| Files | 10.8 | 30% | 14.0 | 4 5-Drawer Safes. 1 Supply Cabinet, 1 Storage Cabinet, 4 Bookcases |
| Waiting Area | 4.4 | 30% | 5.7 | |
| **Unrestricted Access Area:** | | | | |
| Translator/Political Assistant | 9.0 | 30% | 11.7 | |

**ADDITIONAL COMMENTS:**

**CO-LOCATION OF EXECUTIVE/ECONOMIC/POLITICAL/SECURITY:**
The non-CAA staff of all CAA sections (executive, political, economic, defense attache and security) should be co-located and shall share work rooms, file area, and waiting area.

## Program (cont.)

| Space Description | Net area | | | Comments |
|---|---|---|---|---|
| | Work Area NSM | Internal Circ Percent | Recom'd Unit NSM | |

**ECONOMIC SECTION**

| | Work Area NSM | Internal Circ Percent | Recom'd Unit NSM | Comments |
|---|---|---|---|---|
| **Restricted Access Area:** | | | | |
| Econ Counselor | 17.3 | 30% | 22.5 | Need a 2-Drawer Safe |
| Econ Officer | 10.8 | 30% | 14.0 | Need a 2-Drawer Safe |
| Secretary | 9.0 | 30% | 11.7 | |
| TDY Space/Ref Area/Meeting Area | 15.1 | 30% | 19.6 | Include an Internet Terminal, small table and 6 bookcases. |
| Work Room | 10.8 | 30% | 14.0 | Include unclass fax, scanner,copier, and printer. |
| Files | 10.8 | 30% | 14.0 | 4 5-Drawer Safes. 1 Supply Cabinet, 1 Storage Cabinet, 4 Bookcases |
| Waiting Area | 4.4 | 30% | 5.7 | |
| **Unrestricted Access Area:** | | | | |
| Economic Specialist | 10.8 | 30% | 14.0 | |

> *ADDITIONAL COMMENTS:*
>
> *CO-LOCATION OF EXECUTIVE/ECONOMIC/POLITICAL/SECURITY:*
> The non-CAA staff of all CAA sections (executive, political, economic, defense attache and security) should be co-located and shall share work rooms, file area, and waiting area.

**DIPLOMATIC SECURITY**

| | Work Area NSM | Internal Circ Percent | Recom'd Unit NSM | Comments |
|---|---|---|---|---|
| **Restricted Access Area:** | | | | |
| Regional Security Officer | 17.3 | 30% | 22.5 | Need a 2-Drawer Safe |
| Asst Security Officer | 10.8 | 30% | 14.0 | Need a 2-Drawer Safe |
| RSO X-Ray Equipment Room | 0.0 | 30% | 0.0 | This area should be located near loading dock. |
| Work Room | 10.8 | 30% | 14.0 | Include unclass fax, scanner, copier, and printer. |
| Files/Supplies | 10.8 | 30% | 14.0 | Includes 6 Moslers, 2 5-drawer cabinets, 1 supply cabinet |
| Waiting Area | 4.4 | 30% | 5.7 | |
| **Unrestricted Access Area:** | | | | |
| Security Investigator | 10.8 | 30% | 14.0 | |
| Local Guards Supervisor | 9.0 | 30% | 11.7 | |
| Local Guards | 0.0 | 0% | 0.0 | No desks assigned, roving assignments |

> *ADDITIONAL COMMENTS :*
>
> *CO-LOCATION OF EXECUTIVE/ECONOMIC/POLITICAL/GLOBAL/SECURITY:*
> The non-CAA staff of all CAA sections (executive, political, economic, and security, not including guards) should be co-located and shall share file area, work rooms, and waiting area.

**DEFENSE ATTACHE OFFICE**

| | Work Area NSM | Internal Circ Percent | Recom'd Unit NSM | |
|---|---|---|---|---|
| **Restricted Access Area:** | | | | |
| Defense & Air Attache | 17.3 | 30% | 22.5 | |
| Army Attache | 13.0 | 30% | 16.9 | |
| Navy Attache | 13.0 | 30% | 16.9 | |

# Program (cont.)

| Space Description | Net area | | | Comments |
|---|---|---|---|---|
| | Work Area NSM | Internal Circ Percent | Recom'd Unit NSM | |
| Secretary | 9.0 | 30% | 11.7 | |
| TDY Space/Meeting Area | 15.1 | 30% | 19.6 | |
| Waiting Area | 4.4 | 0% | 4.4 | |
| Work Room | 10.8 | 30% | 14.0 | Include unclass fax, scanner, copier, and printer. |
| Files | 9.0 | 30% | 11.7 | 6 Moslers, Refrig, and 2 Shelving Units |
| | | | | |
| **Unrestricted Access Area:** | | | | |
| Translator/Protocol | 9.0 | 30% | 11.7 | |
| Partnership for Peace Coord | 9.0 | 30% | 11.7 | |
| Chauffeurs | 0.0 | 30% | 0.0 | See Driver's Lounge |

---

**ADDITIONAL :**

-CO-LOCATION OF EXECUTIVE/ECONOMIC/POLITICAL/SECURITY:
The non-CAA staff of all CAA sections (executive, political, economic, and security, not including guards) should be co-located and shall share file area, work rooms, and waiting area.

---

## CONSULAR SECTION

| Space Description | Work Area NSM | Internal Circ Percent | Recom'd Unit NSM | Comments |
|---|---|---|---|---|
| **Executive Office** | | | | |
| Consular Officer | 17.3 | 30% | 22.5 | |
| Receptionists | 9.0 | 30% | 11.7 | |
| Reception/Waiting | 9.0 | 30% | 11.7 | |
| | | | | |
| **Staff Offices** | | | | |
| Consular Officer | 13.0 | 30% | 16.9 | |
| Consular Officer | 13.0 | 30% | 16.9 | |
| Consular Associate | 9.0 | 30% | 11.7 | |
| Visa Clerk | 9.0 | 30% | 11.7 | |
| Consular Assistant | 9.0 | 30% | 11.7 | |
| Cashier | 9.0 | 30% | 11.7 | |
| | | | | |
| **Common Area:** | | | | |
| Employee Toilets | 6.0 | 0% | 6.0 | Male/Female |
| Consular Affairs Kitchenette | 10.8 | 0% | 10.8 | Adjacent to Meeting Room |
| CA Meeting Room | 15.1 | 30% | 19.6 | |
| Workroom | 13.1 | 30% | 17.0 | Includes 2 copiers, shredder, fax, scanner. |
| | | | | |
| **Consular Public Areas:** | | | | |
| CA applicant toilets | 10.8 | 0% | 10.8 | Male/Female |
| Waiting Area | 83.0 | 0% | 83.0 | Seating for 80. |
| Exterior NIV Waiting | 0.0 | 30% | 0.0 | Factor in exterior area of space program |
| | | | | |
| **Amer. Citizen Services** | | | | |
| Workroom - assembly | 9.0 | 30% | 11.7 | |
| MRP Station | 4.4 | 30% | 5.7 | |
| Teller Service Windows | 6.0 | 0% | 6.0 | |
| | | | | |
| Queue area | 6.0 | 0% | 6.0 | |
| Writing area | 2.2 | 0% | 2.2 | |
| Files | 4.4 | 30% | 5.7 | |
| ACS/Estate Storage | 9.0 | 30% | 11.7 | |

## Program (cont.)

| Space Description | Net area | | | Comments |
|---|---|---|---|---|
| | Work Area NSM | Internal Circ Percent | Recom'd Unit NSM | |
| **NIV Section** | | | | |
| Controlled Storage | 9.0 | 30% | 11.7 | |
| CA Cashier, et al | 16.5 | 0% | 16.5 | |
| Teller Service Windows | 6.0 | 0% | 6.0 | |
| Queue area | 15.1 | 0% | 15.1 | |
| Writing area | 2.2 | 0% | 2.2 | |
| Prescreening windows | 6.0 | 0% | 6.0 | |
| Workroom - assembly | 9.0 | 30% | 11.7 | |
| Files, working | 4.4 | 30% | 5.7 | |
| Files, archive, locked | 9.0 | 30% | 11.7 | |
| MRV Station | 2.2 | 0% | 2.2 | |
| | | | | |
| **IV Section/Diversity Visas** | | | | |
| Teller Service Windows | 6.0 | 0% | 6.0 | |
| Interview Booth | 10.8 | 0% | 10.8 | |
| Queue area | 15.1 | 0% | 15.1 | |
| Writing area | 2.2 | 0% | 2.2 | |
| Files | 9.0 | 30% | 11.7 | |
| Workroom-assembly | 13.0 | 30% | 16.9 | |

**ADDITIONAL COMMENTS:**

*COMMON AREAS:*
- kitchenettes and employee toilets should be accessible to ALL consular section employees; During design, effort should be made to consolidate equpment areas and central space saver filing systems to conserve footprint area

*EXTERIOR CONSULAR WAITING:*
- Requirements for exterior consular applicant waiting. The waiting area should be shielded from the elements and have seating and writing counter areas.

### ADMINISTRATIVE OFFICE

| Unrestricted Access Area: | | | | |
|---|---|---|---|---|
| Administrative Officer | 17.3 | 30% | 22.5 | |
| Administrative Assistant | 9.0 | 30% | 11.7 | |
| Reception/Waiting | 4.4 | 30% | 5.7 | |
| Files | 4.4 | 30% | 5.7 | 12 files |
| Waiting Area | 4.4 | 30% | 5.7 | |
| Work Room | 9.0 | 30% | 11.7 | |

**ADDITIONAL COMMENTS:**
- This section should be located adjacent to the GSO section/Personnel/FMO. The admin work room shall serve as GSO's secondary work room.

- Most visitors are internal. Several outside visitors are accommodated per week. They would be escorted to the area and would likely be by appointment.

## Program (cont.)

| Space Description | Net area | | | Comments |
|---|---|---|---|---|
| | Work Area NSM | Internal Circ Percent | Recom'd Unit NSM | |

**FINANCIAL MANAGEMENT OFFICE**

| Space Description | Work Area NSM | Internal Circ Percent | Recom'd Unit NSM | Comments |
|---|---|---|---|---|
| Financial Management Officer | 15.1 | 30% | 19.6 | |
| Budget Analyst | 9.0 | 30% | 11.7 | |
| Financial Assistant | 9.0 | 30% | 11.7 | |
| Pay Liaison Clerk/Cashier | 9.0 | 30% | 11.7 | |
| Voucher Examiner | 9.0 | 30% | 11.7 | |
| Cashier/Cage | 16.5 | 0% | 16.5 | |
| Budget Files - Archives & Current | 10.8 | 30% | 14.0 | Hanging File System for 400 linear feet of storage. |
| Waiting Area | 4.4 | 30% | 5.7 | |
| Cashier Client Que Area | 4.4 | 0% | 4.4 | |
| Cashier Window | 6.0 | 0% | 6.0 | |

**PERSONNEL OFFICE**

| Space Description | Work Area NSM | Internal Circ Percent | Recom'd Unit NSM | Comments |
|---|---|---|---|---|
| Personnel Assistant | 15.1 | 30% | 19.6 | Include Personnel Files (2 5-drawer file cabinets.) |
| Personnel Specialist | 9.0 | 30% | 11.7 | |
| Personnel Assistant | 9.0 | 30% | 11.7 | |
| Pay Liaison Clerk | 9.0 | 30% | 11.7 | |
| Files/Ref Material | 9.0 | 30% | 11.7 | Include 5 5-drawer cabinets and 2 bookcases. |
| Waiting Area | 4.4 | 30% | 5.7 | |
| Client Interview and Testing Area | 0.0 | 0% | 0.0 | |

**INFORMATION MANAGEMENT**

| Space Description | Work Area NSM | Internal Circ Percent | Recom'd Unit NSM | Comments |
|---|---|---|---|---|
| **Unrestricted Access Area:** | | | | |
| Information Management Officer | 15.1 | 30% | 19.6 | |
| Operator Switchboard | 15.1 | 30% | 19.6 | |
| Receptionist | 0.0 | 30% | 0.0 | Sits in Switchboard room. |
| Telephone/Radio Technician | 0.0 | 30% | 0.0 | Include desk space in workroom. |
| Telephone/Radio Workroom | 15.0 | 30% | 19.5 | Include workbench, shelves, and desk space. |
| Waiting Area | 4.4 | 30% | 5.7 | |
| Files | 4.4 | 30% | 5.7 | |
| **Restricted Access Area:** | | | | |
| PBX Frame Room | 0.0 | 0% | 0.0 | Varies per Building |

- Receptionist is stationed at the lobby next to Post #1 and offers translation assistance to the marines as well as acts as an information booth.

**COMPUTER SERVICES CENTER**

| Space Description | Work Area NSM | Internal Circ Percent | Recom'd Unit NSM | Comments |
|---|---|---|---|---|
| **Unrestricted Access Area:** | | | | |
| Information Systems Manager | 9.0 | 30% | 11.7 | Offices should be adjacent to computer center |
| Assistant Systems Manager | 9.0 | 30% | 11.7 | Sits in Computer Center |
| Waiting Area | 4.4 | 30% | 5.7 | |
| Files | 4.4 | 30% | 5.7 | |

## Program (cont.)

| Space Description | Net area | | | Comments |
|---|---|---|---|---|
| | Work Area NSM | Internal Circ Percent | Recom'd Unit NSM | |
| Computer Center | 18.0 | 0% | 18.0 | |
| Computer Training Room | 25.0 | 0% | 25.0 | |
| PC Testing/Upgrades/Scanning | 13.0 | 30% | 16.9 | |
| Storage Room | 15.1 | 30% | 19.6 | |

- Computer Services Center to be in environmentally controlled with locked entry.

### MAIL ROOM

| Unrestricted Access Area: | | | | |
|---|---|---|---|---|
| Mail Clerks | 6.0 | 30% | 7.8 | Include as desk space in the mailroom. |
| Mail Room | 32.0 | 0% | 32.0 | Include double doors. |
| Window Service | 4.4 | 0% | 4.4 | |
| Package Wrap Area | 4.4 | 0% | 4.4 | |
| Customer queue | 4.4 | 0% | 4.4 | |
| Storage | 10.8 | 0% | 10.8 | |
| Office Distribution Boxes | 9.0 | 0% | 9.0 | Official Mail distrib boxes |

**_ADDITIONAL COMMENTS:_**
- This area is a good basement location candidate. It should be close to the loading dock and/or freight elevator, have a wide and clear path through which to move mail pouches. Entrance to mail room should include double doors.

### GENERAL SERVICES OFFICE

| Unrestricted Access Area: | | | | |
|---|---|---|---|---|
| General Service Officer, Supv | 15.1 | 30% | 19.6 | Locate close to Admin officer |
| General Service Officer | 10.8 | 30% | 14.0 | |
| Translator/Protocol/Receptionist | 9.0 | 30% | 11.7 | |
| Waiting | 9.0 | 0% | 9.0 | During design, may want to combine with Admin waiting area. |
| Files | 9.0 | 30% | 11.7 | |
| Work Room | 9.0 | 30% | 11.7 | Shared w/procurement/customs |
| Visitors Coat Closet | 2.2 | 0% | 2.2 | Shared w/procurement/customs |
| Reference Area/Meeting Area | 17.3 | 30% | 22.5 | Bookcases along perimeter for procurement regulations and vendor catalogues. |
| **Procurement Unit** | | | | |
| Procurement Supervisor | 9.0 | 30% | 11.7 | |
| Procurement/GS Assistant | 9.0 | 30% | 11.7 | |
| Purchasing Agent | 9.0 | 30% | 11.7 | |
| Files | 9.0 | 30% | 11.7 | |
| Waiting | 4.4 | 30% | 5.7 | |
| **Customs & Shipping Unit** | | | | |
| Shipping Assistant | 9.0 | 30% | 11.7 | |
| Shipping Clerk | 9.0 | 30% | 11.7 | |

## Program (cont.)

| Space Description | Net area | | | Comments |
|---|---|---|---|---|
| | Work Area NSM | Internal Circ Percent | Recom'd Unit NSM | |
| Travel Assistant | 9.0 | 30% | 11.7 | |
| Customs Expeditor | 9.0 | 30% | 11.7 | |
| Waiting | 4.4 | 30% | 5.7 | |
| Files | 9.0 | 30% | 11.7 | |

- Reference area will be used to meet with clients and vendors; Large number of catalogues which need to be close to offices and meeting area. Internet stations are used frequently to research procurement issues.

- Customs & Shipping. Need to verify if there is a NEPA clerk w/ NEPA PC. Internet stations are used frequently to research customs & shipping issues. Internet stations are used frequently to research customs and shipping issues.

- Visitors: This section has frequest visitors both internal and external.

### OFFICE OF PUBLIC DIPLOMACY

| Unrestricted Access Area: | | | | |
|---|---|---|---|---|
| **Executive Office** | | | | |
| Public Affairs Officer | 17.3 | 30% | 22.5 | |
| Asst Public Affairs Officer | 13.0 | 30% | 16.9 | |
| Secretary | 9.0 | 30% | 11.7 | |
| Administrative Assistant | 9.0 | 30% | 11.7 | |
| Files | 4.4 | 30% | 5.7 | |
| Waiting | 4.4 | 30% | 5.7 | Shared w/ cultural affairs, information office and management information systems. |
| Work Room | 10.8 | 30% | 14.0 | Shared w/ cultural affairs, information office and management information systems. |
| | | | | |
| **Cultural Affairs Office** | | | | |
| Cultural Affairs Asst | 9.0 | 30% | 11.7 | |
| Cultural Affairs Asst | 9.0 | 30% | 11.7 | |
| Secretary/Receptionist | 9.0 | 30% | 11.7 | Locate adjacent to Public Affairs Officer secretary. |
| Files | 4.4 | 0% | 4.4 | |
| | | | | |
| **Information Office** | | | | |
| Press Assistant | 9.0 | 30% | 11.7 | |
| Press Assistant | 9.0 | 30% | 11.7 | |
| Worldnet Assistant | 9.0 | 30% | 11.7 | |
| AV Equiment Storage | 13.0 | 0% | 13.0 | |
| AV Control | 15.1 | 0% | 15.1 | Newspaper/mags/files |
| Media Storage | 4.4 | 0% | 4.4 | |
| Worldnet TV/Press Room | 13.0 | 0% | 13.0 | |
| AV library(archive) | 4.4 | 30% | 5.7 | |
| Files | 4.4 | 30% | 5.7 | |
| | | | | |
| **Information Resource Center** | | | | |
| IRC Asst | 9.0 | 30% | 11.7 | |
| Book Specialist | 9.0 | 30% | 11.7 | |
| Distribution Clerk/Chauffeur | 0.0 | 0% | 0.0 | Share an office adjacent to distribution center. |
| Reproduction/Desktop Publ Station | 32.0 | 0% | 32.0 | |
| Work Room | 9.0 | 30% | 11.7 | |
| Archives/File | 10.8 | 30% | 14.0 | |
| Storage | 13.0 | 0% | 13.0 | |
| Resource Center (Library) | 120.0 | 0% | 120.0 | |
| | | | | |
| **Management Information Systems** | | | | |
| Computer Systems Manager | 9.0 | 30% | 11.7 | Adjacent but separate from computer room. |
| Computer Room | 0.0 | 30% | 0.0 | Computer system should be incorporated into Computer Center, Section K. |

## Program (cont.)

| | Net area | | | | |
|---|---|---|---|---|---|
| Space Description | Work Area NSM | Internal Circ Percent | Recom'd Unit NSM | Comments | |

| | | | | |
|---|---|---|---|---|
| **ADDITIONAL COMMENTS:** | | | | |
| - This section should be positioned for maximum public accessibility | | | | |
| - Should consider a single file room for executive, cultural affairs, and information offices. | | | | |
| - Resource Center is currently set-up for hard copies of literature.   In the future, many items will be available over the internet; therefore,  provide 6  internet workstations.   The internet stations will also serve chancery personnel. | | | | |

### FOREIGN AGRICULTURAL SERVICE

| Space Description | Work Area NSM | Internal Circ Percent | Recom'd Unit NSM | Comments |
|---|---|---|---|---|
| **Unrestricted Access Area:** | | | | |
| Agricultural Attache | 17.3 | 30% | 22.5 | |
| Agricultural Marketing/Admin Asst | 9.0 | 30% | 11.7 | |
| Files | 4.4 | 30% | 5.7 | |
| Work Room | 9.0 | 30% | 11.7 | |
| Supplies/Equipment Area | 13.0 | 0% | 13.0 | |
| | | | | |
| **Shared (FCS & FAS) Usage Area:** | | | | |
| Reference Area | 0.0 | 0% | 0.0 | See below. |
| Visitors Coat Closet | 0.0 | 0% | 0.0 | See below. |
| Waiting | 0.0 | 0% | 0.0 | See below. |

| |
|---|
| - Locate adjacent to Foreign Commercial Service as they will share some areas.   A common waiting area has been programmed for these 2 sections. |

### FOREIGN COMMERCIAL SERVICE

| Space Description | Work Area NSM | Internal Circ Percent | Recom'd Unit NSM | Comments |
|---|---|---|---|---|
| **Unrestricted Access Area:** | | | | |
| **Office of Commercial Counselor** | | | | |
| Commercial Attache | 17.3 | 30% | 22.5 | |
| Commercial Trade Specialist | 9.0 | 30% | 11.7 | |
| Commercial Assistant | 9.0 | 30% | 11.7 | |
| Supplies/Trade events storage | 13.0 | 0% | 13.0 | Trade event storage |
| Files | 9.0 | 30% | 11.7 | |
| Work Room | 9.0 | 30% | 11.7 | |
| | | | | |
| **Shared (FCS & FAS) Usage Area:** | | | | Shared w/ Foreign Agriculture Service |
| Reference Area | 21.6 | 30% | 28.1 | Include Internet Station, small table, and 8 bookcases. |
| Visitor's Coat Closet | 2.2 | 0% | 2.2 | For visitors - modular in design. |
| Waiting | 9.0 | 30% | 11.7 | |

| |
|---|
| - Locate adjacent to Foreign Agricultural Service as they will share some areas.   A common waiting area has been programmed for these 2 sections. |
| - Large number of visitors.  Needs to be as close to the first floor as they can due to access control;  should be close to the multipurpose room for trade events (+40 people) |

## Program (cont.)

| Space Description | Net area | | | Comments |
|---|---|---|---|---|
| | Work Area NSM | Internal Circ Percent | Recom'd Unit NSM | |
| **USAID** | | | | |
| Executive Office | | | | |
| | | | | |
| USAID Representative | 17.3 | 30% | 22.5 | |
| Secretary | 9.0 | 30% | 11.7 | |
| Waiting Area | 10.8 | 30% | 14.0 | |
| File/Supply Room | 15.1 | 30% | 19.6 | |
| Work Room | 9.0 | 30% | 11.7 | |
| Mail Workstation | 4.4 | 30% | 5.7 | |
| Shipping Area | 13.0 | 30% | 16.9 | |
| Kitchenette | 4.4 | 30% | 5.7 | |
| Storage Room | 13.0 | 30% | 16.8 | Include Shelving along perimeter walls. |
| | | | | |
| **Program Office** | | | | |
| Program Officer | 13.0 | 30% | 16.9 | |
| Development Program Asst | 10.8 | 30% | 14.0 | |
| | | | | |
| **Democracy Office** | | | | |
| Democracy Officer | 13.0 | 30% | 16.9 | |
| Local Government Officer | 10.8 | 30% | 14.0 | |
| | | | | |
| **Economic Growth Office** | | | | |
| Economic Growth Officer | 13.0 | 30% | 16.9 | |
| Office Asst | 9.0 | 30% | 11.7 | |

## Program (cont.)

| Space Description | Net area | | | Comments |
|---|---|---|---|---|
| | Work Area NSM | Internal Circ Percent | Recom'd Unit NSM | |
| | | | | |
| **Administrative/Support Office** | | | | |
| Executive Officer | 13.0 | 30% | 16.9 | |
| Personnel/Admin Asst | 9.0 | 30% | 11.7 | |
| Budget Analyst | 9.0 | 30% | 11.7 | |
| Communications & Records | 9.0 | 30% | 11.7 | |

> *ADDITIONAL COMMENTS:*
> - *Shipping Area:*  Table for collating/wrapping; work station w/ PC; storage for foam peanuts; book trolleys, book storage receiving and distribution.   Access door should be double to allow for large packages to enter and depart the area.
>
> -

### LEGATTE (FBI)

| Space Description | Work Area NSM | Internal Circ Percent | Recom'd Unit NSM | Comments |
|---|---|---|---|---|
| **Restricted Access Area:** | | | | |
| Legal Attache | 23.0 | 30% | 29.9 | |
| Agent | 10.8 | 30% | 14.0 | |
| Office Assistant | 9.0 | 30% | 11.7 | |
| Work Room | 9.0 | 30% | 11.7 | |
| TDY Office | 9.0 | 30% | 11.7 | |
| Waiting | 4.4 | 30% | 5.7 | |

### MARINE SECURITY GUARDS

| Space Description | Work Area NSM | Internal Circ Percent | Recom'd Unit NSM | Comments |
|---|---|---|---|---|
| **Unrestricted Access Area:** | | | | |
| MSG Office | 15.1 | 30% | 19.6 | 1 5-drawer Mosler |
| Marine Guards | 0.0 | 30% | 0.0 | |
| Shared workstations/Internet/Co-lateral duties | 23.0 | 30% | 29.9 | |
| Work Room | 9.0 | 30% | 11.7 | |
| Files | 4.4 | 30% | 5.7 | |
| MSG Change Room - Male | 21.6 | 0% | 21.6 | |
| MSG Change Room - Female | 10.8 | 0% | 10.8 | |
| MSG Toilet/Shower | 6.0 | 0% | 6.0 | unisex |
| Kitchenette | 4.4 | 0% | 4.4 | |

### MAIN ENTRANCE/LOBBY

| Space Description | Work Area NSM | Internal Circ Percent | Recom'd Unit NSM | Comments |
|---|---|---|---|---|
| Local Guard Desk | 4.4 | 0% | 4.4 | |
| Admitting/WTMD | 34.6 | 0% | 34.6 | |
| Reception Booth | 9.0 | 0% | 9.0 | |
| Lobby | 28.8 | 0% | 28.8 | |
| Guard Post #1 (MSG) | 15.1 | 30% | 19.6 | |
| Toilets  (Main entrance) | 4.4 | 0% | 4.4 | Male/Female |
| Electrical Room | 9.0 | 30% | 11.7 | |

# rogram (cont.)

| Space Description | Net area | | | Comments |
|---|---|---|---|---|
| | Work Area NSM | Internal Circ Percent | Recom'd Unit NSM | |

## CONFERENCE CENTER

| Unrestricted Access Area: | | | | |
|---|---|---|---|---|

| Conference Center : | | | | |
|---|---|---|---|---|
| Conference room/Multi-Purpose Room | 120.0 | 0% | 120.0 | |
| Ante Room | 17.3 | 0% | 17.3 | Could be combined w/lobby area in main entrance |
| Coat Room | 13.0 | 0% | 13.0 | Should be off the ante room. |
| Toilets | 15.1 | 0% | 15.1 | Male/Female |
| Kitchen Area | 10.8 | 0% | 10.8 | Full service |
| Tables/Chairs Storage | 10.8 | 0% | 10.8 | |
| A/V Storage | 13.0 | 0% | 13.0 | |
| Conference (World Net) Control Room | 13.0 | 0% | 13.0 | Video/sound equip |

**ADDITIONAL COMMENTS:**
- *The Conference center conference room (WorldNet)* should be fitted with folding partitions which will divide the area into equi-sized rooms when required. The area will require storage for tables and chairs, video equipment, and have a control room attached. The control room will be fitted out with specialized projection,audio,video equipment and have an area capable of supporting two simultaneous translators. The design phase should investigate the possibility of

## SECONDARY (CONSULAR) ENTRANCE

| Local Guard Desk | 4.4 | 0% | 4.4 | |
|---|---|---|---|---|
| Admitting/WTMD #2 | 25.0 | 0% | 25.0 | |
| Waiting | 20.0 | 0% | 20.0 | |
| Guard Post #2 (MSG) | 10.8 | 30% | 14.0 | |
| Pre-Screening Teller Windows | 6.0 | 0% | 6.0 | |
| Passback Teller Windows at CAC | 0.0 | 0% | 0.0 | See CAC. |
| Toilets  (Secondary Entrance) | 4.4 | 0% | 4.4 | Male/Female |
| Interview Room | 10.8 | 20% | 13.0 | |

**ADDITIONAL COMMENTS:**
- *Areas marked #2* are to be located for the Consular applicants. This entrance is optional and dependent upon the design of the building.

## COMMON USE

| Meeting Rooms Shared | 15.1 | 30% | 19.6 | |
|---|---|---|---|---|
| Meeting Room Shared | 21.6 | 30% | 28.1 | |
| Kitchennettes | 4.4 | 0% | 4.4 | |
| TDY Stations | 9.0 | 30% | 11.7 | |

## OTHER SPECIAL REQUIREMENTS

| PBX Room | 15.1 | 0% | 15.1 | |
|---|---|---|---|---|
| Electrical Switchgear Room | 15.1 | 0% | 15.1 | |
| Centralized UPS | 60.0 | 0% | 60.0 | |
| Loading Dock | 40.0 | 0% | 40.0 | Counted at 50%.  Include an overhung roof. |
| Receiving Area | 34.6 | 0% | 34.6 | |
| Temporary Storage | 15.1 | 30% | 19.6 | Double doors. |
| Pouch Vault | 15.1 | 30% | 19.6 | Double doors. |
| RSO Secure Storage | 23.0 | 30% | 29.9 | Include 4 shelving units.  Locate adjacent to x-ray room. |
| RSO X-Ray Equipment Room | 15.1 | 30% | 19.6 | Locate near loading dock. Include double doors. |

**ADDITIONAL COMMENTS:**
- *Loading dock:*  Include overhead door.

## Program (cont.)

| | Net area | | | |
|---|---|---|---|---|
| Space Description | Work Area NSM | Internal Circ Percent | Recom'd Unit NSM | Comments |

**SERVICES/SUPPORT**

| | | | | |
|---|---|---|---|---|
| Custodial Supplies and Equipment | 9.0 | 30% | 11.7 | |
| Janitorial Closet | 2.2 | 30% | 2.9 | |
| Expendable Storage | 17.3 | 30% | 22.5 | |
| Non-expendable Storage | 17.3 | 30% | 22.5 | |
| Maintenance Immediate supplies/tools | 15.1 | 30% | 19.6 | |
| Trash & Sort Area - recycling materials - Temporary | 15.1 | 30% | 19.6 | |

- Trash Sorting and Temporary Holding Area: This is a small, environmentally controlled area. The major trash is programmed to be stored at the perimeter in a trash holding structure. The room should be properly ventilated .

The following sections should be grouped together to form a community area,  The community areas could be located in the main building with a separate entrance or in an annex.

| **COMMUNITY LIAISON** | | | | |
|---|---|---|---|---|
| CLO | 10.8 | 30% | 14.0 | |
| Administrative Assistant | 9.0 | 30% | 11.7 | |
| Waiting Area | 9.0 | 30% | 11.7 | |
| Visitor's Coat Closet | 2.2 | 30% | 2.9 | |
| CLO Reference Materials and Internet Stations | 15.1 | 30% | 19.6 | |
| Work Room | 9.0 | 30% | 11.7 | |
| Storage/Equipment | 13.0 | 30% | 16.9 | |

- Offices for CLO and Housing Unit can be colocated.  CLO offices should be separated from the waiting area, reference area and work room.

| **Housing Unit** | | | | |
|---|---|---|---|---|
| **Housing Unit** | | | | |
| Housing/Procurement Assistant | 9.0 | 30% | 11.7 | |
| Waiting Area | 0.0 | 30% | 0.0 | |
| Visitor's Coat Closet | 0.0 | 30% | 0.0 | |
| Work Room | 0.0 | 30% | 0.0 | |

## Program (cont.)

| Space Description | Net area | | | Comments |
|---|---|---|---|---|
| | Work Area NSM | Internal Circ Percent | Recom'd Unit NSM | |

### HEALTH UNIT

| | | | | |
|---|---|---|---|---|
| **Unrestricted Access Area:** | | | | |
| Nurse Practicioner | 23.0 | 30% | 29.9 | |
| Local Physician - Part Time | 23.0 | 30% | 29.9 | |
| Assistant | 9.0 | 30% | 11.7 | |
| Medical Records | 4.4 | 30% | 5.7 | |
| Waiting Room | 10.8 | 30% | 14.0 | |
| Patient Toilet | 4.4 | 30% | 5.7 | |
| Small Lab | 10.8 | 30% | 14.0 | |
| Pre-screen /Exam Room | 10.8 | 30% | 14.0 | |
| Pharmacy/Medical Supplies | 13.0 | 30% | 16.9 | |
| Observation Room/Equipment | 10.8 | 30% | 14.0 | |
| Work Room | 9.0 | 30% | 11.7 | |
| Storage | 17.3 | 30% | 22.5 | |

**ADDITIONAL COMMENTS:**
- A separate entrance is prefered.   This section should be on ground-level.

### COMMERCIAL TRAVEL OFFICE

| | | | | |
|---|---|---|---|---|
| **Unrestricted Access Area** | | | | |
| Commercial Travel Office | 10.8 | 30% | 14.0 | |

**ADDITIONAL COMMENTS**
- The function of this office is to coordinate, confirm, and makes reservations both for official and personal travel.  Minimal facilities are necessary.

### COMMERCIAL BANK

| | | | | |
|---|---|---|---|---|
| **Unrestricted Access Area** | | | | |
| Bank Facility et al | 10.8 | 30% | 14.0 | |

**ADDITIONAL COMMENTS:**
- Commercial banking facilities are limited.   Therefore, need to verify if they need this space.

    This should contain the following features:
- one service windows for transactions
- no  vault is required  - need to verify
- area for customers to wait, fill out forms and queue

### EXERCISE ROOM

| | | | | |
|---|---|---|---|---|
| **Unrestricted Access Area** | | | | |
| Exercise Room | 65.0 | 30% | 84.5 | |
| Recreational Equipment/Storage Room | 10.9 | 30% | 14.2 | |

## Program (cont.)

| | Net area | | | | |
|---|---|---|---|---|---|
| Space Description | Work Area NSM | Internal Circ Percent | Recom'd Unit NSM | Comments | |

**ADDITIONAL COMMENTS:**

*Exercise Room:* This room is a candidate for the basement. However, due to the fact that families may be using the facility heavily, keeping it out of the main building or in the community area is probably more prudent due to access.

This area should contain the following
- one male / one female shower units/toilet facilities and sink/change area w/lockers and bench
- one exercise floor of approximately 40 SM

### CAFETERIA

| Unrestricted Access Area | | | | |
|---|---|---|---|---|
| Dining, Informal seating | 60.0 | 30% | 78.0 | |
| Cashier | 6.0 | 30% | 7.8 | |
| Serving/Food Prep/Equip Area | 60.0 | 30% | 78.0 | |
| Storage/Receiving | 13.0 | 30% | 16.9 | |
| Refrigerated Storage | 13.0 | 30% | 16.9 | |
| Employee Locker Room | 9.0 | 30% | 11.7 | |
| Employee Toilet Facilities | 4.4 | 30% | 5.7 | |
| Chef/Manager Office | 9.0 | 30% | 11.7 | |

*ADDITIONAL COMMENTS*
- Dining room capacity is 42
- The kitchen should be close to the loading dock.
- All areas of the cafeteria should be properly ventilated.

### COMMISSARY

| Unrestricted Access Area | | | | |
|---|---|---|---|---|
| Sales Room | 60.0 | | | |
| Stock Room | 15.0 | | | |
| Freezer Room | 15.0 | | | |
| Receiving Area | 10.8 | | | |
| Office Area | 10.8 | | | |
| Cashier Area | 6.0 | | | |

## ANNEX BUILDING : Warehouse/Shop

| Warehouse | | | | |
|---|---|---|---|---|
| Loading Dock | 15.1 | | | |
| Receiving/Shipping Area | 50.0 | | | |
| Warehouse Storage | 550.0 | | | |
| Work Room | 9.0 | | | |
| Files | 9.0 | | | |
| Welcome Kits | 21.6 | | | |
| Toilet | 4.4 | | | |

## rogram (cont.)

| Space Description | Net area | | | |
|---|---|---|---|---|
| | Work Area NSM | Internal Circ Percent | Recom'd Unit NSM | Comments |

**Maintenance Shops**

| | | | | |
|---|---|---|---|---|
| Gardener and equipment storage area | 30.0 | | | |
| Appliance Repair | 20.0 | | | |
| HVAC Shop | 34.0 | | | |
| Electricians' Shop and Supplies | 34.0 | | | |
| Carpenters' Shop and Supplies | 60.0 | | | |
| Painters Shop/ Paint Storage and Supplies | 20.0 | | | |
| Plumbers' /Masons' Shop and Supplies | 34.0 | | | |
| Materials Storage | 34.0 | | | |

**MOTOR POOL MAINTENANCE**

| | | | | |
|---|---|---|---|---|
| Mechanic's Maintenance Bay | 13.0 | | | |
| Mechanic's Storage including Tires | 17.3 | | | |
| Mechanic's Car Wash Area | 0.0 | | | |

## ANNEX BUILDING : Offices for Motor Pool

**MOTOR POOL OFFICES**

| | | | | |
|---|---|---|---|---|
| Dispatcher | 9.0 | | | |
| Mechanic | 0.0 | | | |
| Marine Driver's | 0.0 | | | |
| Chauffeurs  Lounge and Lockers | 23.0 | | | |
| Kitchennette | 6.0 | | | |
| Toilets | 4.4 | | | |

**Facility and Maintenance Offices**

| | | | | |
|---|---|---|---|---|
| Facility Maintenance Specialist | 10.8 | | | |
| GSO Maintenance Assistance | 9.0 | | | |
| Maintenance Supervisor | 10.8 | | | |
| Maintenance Inspector | 9.0 | | | |
| Work Control Clerk | 9.0 | | | |
| FF&E Repair Clerk | 9.0 | | | |
| Maintenance Assistant | 9.0 | | | |
| Preventative Maintenance Mechanic | 9.0 | | | |
| Plumbers | 0.0 | | | |
| Maintenance Foreman - Electrical | 9.0 | | | |
| Electricians | 0.0 | | | |
| Maintenance Foreman - Carpenter | 9.0 | | | |
| Carpenters | 0.0 | | | |
| CharForce | 0.0 | | | |
| Custodian | 0.0 | | | |
| Meeting Room | 13.0 | | | |
| Waiting Area - FMS | 9.0 | | | |
| Workroom - FMS | 13.0 | | | |
| File room - FMS | 13.0 | | | |

Offices for Foreman would be used to distribute work to the various tradesmen.   The foreman offices could possible be arranged in the  "bull-pen" type arrangement.

## Program (cont.)

| Space Description | Net area | | | Comments |
|---|---|---|---|---|
| | Work Area NSM | Internal Circ Percent | Recom'd Unit NSM | |

**Supply & Warehouse Offices**

| | | | | |
|---|---|---|---|---|
| General Services Property Management | 10.8 | | | |
| Supply Supervisor | 9.0 | | | |
| Supply Clerk(exp/non-expen) | 9.0 | | | |
| Storekeeper | 9.0 | | | |
| Warehousemen | 0.0 | | | |
| Driver/Laborer | 0.0 | | | |
| Driver/Laborer | 0.0 | | | |

**Shared Areas**

| | | | | |
|---|---|---|---|---|
| Showers and Lockers - Male | 28.8 | | | |
| Showers and Lockers - Female | 17.3 | | | |
| Breakroom/Kitchennette | 34.6 | | | |

**Fig. 1. St. Thomas More Catholic Church (Williamson Pounders Architects; Photo: Jeffery Jacobs)**

# CHURCHES, GENERAL

Church design, which for many years followed long-established rules governing the organization of the space, has been affected by the liturgical renewal all denominations have undergone in recent years. In fact, each particular building committee is confronted by some quite disturbing questions and doubts. There are those who ask "Why build?" as well as being concerned with "fixing the form of worship," so that future change is, at best, difficult.

Assuming that these questions are satisfactorily resolved, the building committee and architect can commence developing a program. The church is essentially a gathering place for worship and other congregational activities (Figs. 1 and 2). There is a functional need not only to provide a comfortable environment but also a special quality that makes worship possible as well as meaningful. It is precisely this search for quality which makes church design so challenging to most architects.

## THE SITE

The "house of worship" is by its very nature an important public building. It speaks to the entire community about the beliefs and aspirations of the congregation. While some congregations worship in churches considerably more "triumphant" than their creed, it is advisable to strive for simplicity and subtlety.

The church's position on the site will be somewhat determined by this "public image," but some functional considerations also exist. On a limited urban site the church may occupy so much of the land that only building entry and egress are possible. However, if there is room on the site for parking spaces, these will be useful even if the majority of the worshipers walk. The possibility of pulling wedding and funeral cars out of the stream of street traffic as well as dropping off worshipers during inclement weather is worth investigation. The suburban or country church site is usually larger (Figs. 3 and 4) and, with a dispersed congregation, the car parking capability is no longer optional, it is indeed essential. Ample parking areas reached by convenient driveways are functional necessities. There is a stronger entrance relationship to the parking areas and driveways than there may be to the street. Many otherwise successfully designed churches are flawed by the fact that most of the congregation is always coming in the back door. The more generous site permits the consideration of outdoor worship as well as other outdoor activities. The building program must consider these possibilities very thoroughly.

## THE PLAN

The basic determinant of the plan is the programmed relationship between the congregation and the area designated as the center for worship action. The emphasis of many faiths is on the involvement of the congregation in the action of the worship service (Fig. 5). Plans

*Authors:* Maria A. Bentel, AIA, and Frederick R. Bentel, AIA
Reviewer: Douglas R. Hoffman, AIA

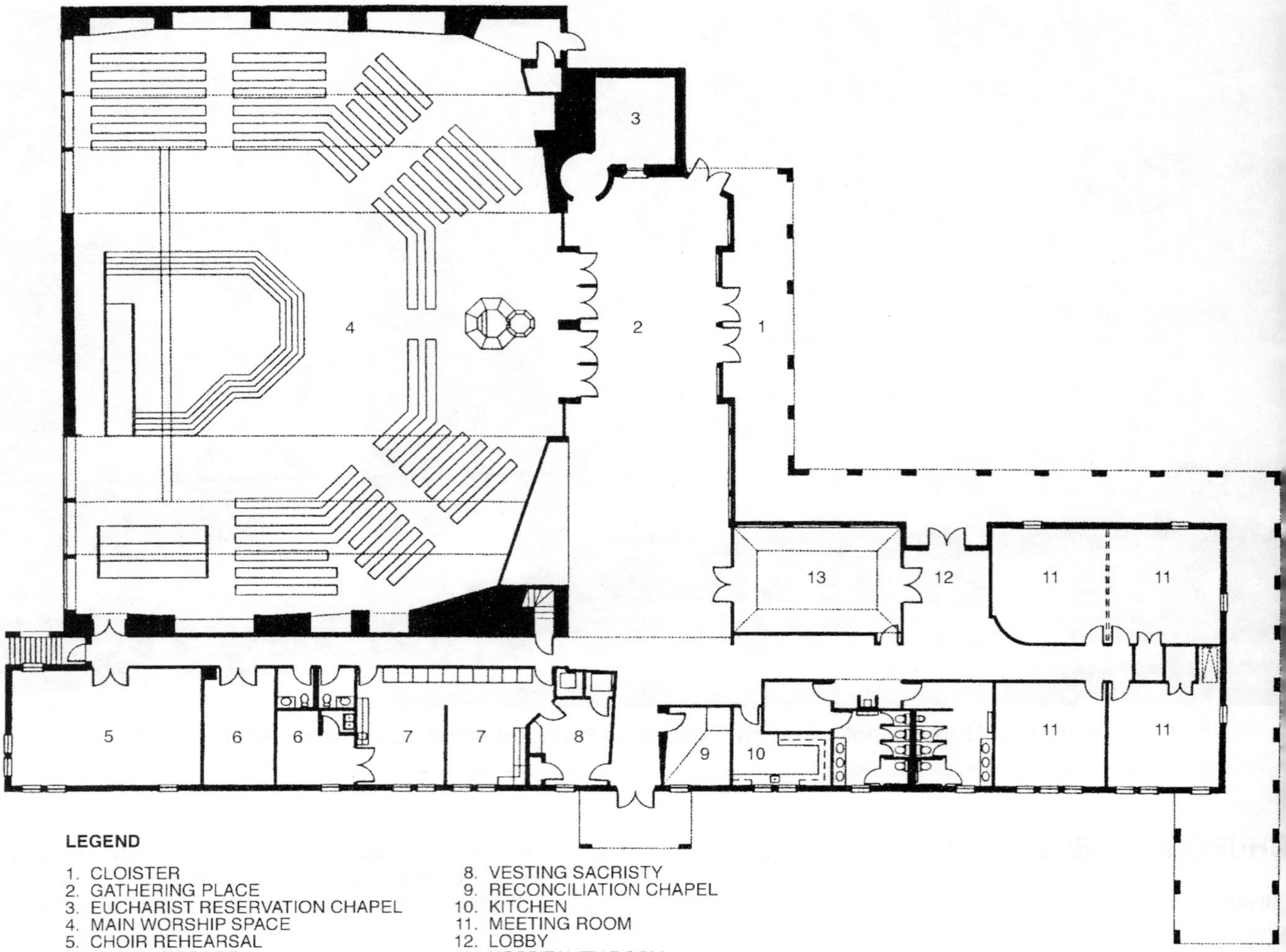

**Fig. 2. Floor Plan, St. Thomas More Catholic Church (Williamson Pounders Architects; Photo: Jeffery Jacobs)**

LEGEND

1. CLOISTER
2. GATHERING PLACE
3. EUCHARIST RESERVATION CHAPEL
4. MAIN WORSHIP SPACE
5. CHOIR REHEARSAL
6. CHAIR STORAGE
7. STORAGE
8. VESTING SACRISTY
9. RECONCILIATION CHAPEL
10. KITCHEN
11. MEETING ROOM
12. LOBBY
13. HOSPITALITY ROOM

**Fig 3. Cloister at St. Thomas More Catholic Church (Williamson Pounders Architects; Photo: Jeffery Jacobs)**

which suggest an auditorium, with the altar platform viewed through a proscenium arch, may be very limiting to this participation, reduce sight lines, and impair acoustics. Likewise, plan forms which destroy the oneness of the congregation are less favored.

Since most faiths place emphasis on the spoken word, it is important to consider the ability of the speaker to maintain eye contact with the congregation. Theater-in-the-round is not a recommended approach for this reason. Great care must be exercised if the structure requires columns or piers within the worship space for obvious reasons having to do with the sight lines. Although there is no liturgical requirement for seating, the length of most services require the utilization of a seating device. It is in this particular aspect that the concept of flexible use collides with reality. The church pew has in its favor its relatively modest cost and its orderly appearance. The much more flexible individual chair generally requires more

Fig. 4. St. Thomas More Catholic Church (Williamson Pounders Architects; Photo: Jeffery Jacobs)

pace per person and, even when ganged, requires straightening by custodial help. The desire of the congregation for non-worship uses f the church will determine the type of seating. It is worth noting nat some church plans, with the assistance of movable altar platorms and chairs, permit more than one arrangement of the congre-

Fig. 5. Worship space of St. Thomas More Catholic Church Williamson Pounders Architects; Photo: Jeffery Jacobs)

gation. This is an attractive possibility for faith groups interested in innovation.

Plan types are discussed below. All other elements of the church building are related to the worship area. Listed below are the required supporting facilities.

### Entry/Gathering Area

The minimum function of the entry area is as a vestibule from the out-of-doors. However, this space must be sized in relation to the number of occupants, as it will oftentimes act as a lobby and gathering area for the congregation before and after worship services. A rule of thumb would be to provide standing space for the average attendance at worship, or about 2.5 square feet per person. Coat storage may be located here, as well as any required toilet facilities or usher's room and janitor's closet. Pamphlet racks, bulletin boards, and memorial plaques or books are wisely located here rather than in the worship room.

### Vesting Room or Sacristy

Although each denomination favors a particular nomenclature, the function remains the same. The celebrant requires a room for robing and the storage of vestments and the ceremonial utensils. It is prudent to consider a toilet connected to this room. Often this room will accommodate a guest speaker or another clergyperson. Vestments should be stored flat or hung no tighter than three per foot.

It is important that this room be located thoughtfully in relation to both the entry and the worship space. While it is convenient to consider a position close to the altar platform, it will work at a disadvantage if the worship ceremony involves procession through the congregation, or if the minister is to greet or bid farewell to the congregation at the entry. Acolytes or altar attendants also require a vesting space, which should be near the vesting room for supervision.

### Work Sacristy

This room may also have many different names, but its function is to provide space for flower arranging, the storage of altar cloths (sometimes also their washing and pressing), ceremonial utensil storage and cleaning, and candle and candlestick storage. A sink is required, as well as storage cupboards or closets. This room is best located near the altar platform if at all possible.

### Choir Robing Room

Depending on the size of the choir, this room may have to be very spacious. Closet space for robes is essential, and it will serve the coats of the choir also. Choir robes should not be stored more densely than four per foot of hanging. Provide a lockable closet for women's handbags.

The choir room can also serve as a rehearsal room if acoustic isolation from the balance of the building is provided. A piano or small electric organ may be necessary.

### Church Meeting Room

Depending on the congregation, the requirements for a meeting or conference room will vary. A small kitchenette is also desirable.

### Expansion Space

The sometimes great fluctuations of attendance at worship can be overcome by programming for expansion space. The relationship to the worship area should be planned to ensure good sight lines when in use. If the two spaces are utilized for separate functions at the same time, an acoustic separation is essential.

## PLAN TYPES

### Rectangular

The most commonly utilized plan form is the rectangular, with the altar platform (or bema) at one end and the seating oriented in rows looking toward the single focal point. A central aisle is usual. This plan is simple, and as long as the altar platform is within the congregational volume, there is no excessive "performance" quality. The primary difficulty arises when the seating capacity exceeds 500, because the viewing distance becomes overly long and worshipers in the rear seats experience a diminished sense of participation. The length of the room in a rectangular plan should not exceed twice the width of the room, to maintain good sight lines and acoustics.

The illustrated plan (Fig. 6a) shows an entry stair within the seating from an on-grade vestibule. The rear pews are on elevated steps for good sight lines. The choir in this case is part of the altar area. The

vesting room is on the vestibule floor level adjacent to the main doors. While the plan is very simple, the movement is almost into the middle of the worship space. This arrangement has some aesthetic impact as well as counteracting the tendency for worshipers to concentrate at the usually more convenient rear seats.

### Cruciform

Plan forms which have symbolic significance are not unusual. The altar area is often in the head of the cross or at the crossing (see Fig. 6b). Depending on the seating arrangement within the arms of the cruciform plan, there may be a loss of a sense of congregational unity.

The church shown in Fig. 6b is constructed with glass walls looking into walled gardens. The altar platform is at the transept. Note that there are numerous entrances, which are related to parking areas.

A fairly large congregation (600) is accommodated without a "gymnasium" effect or very large structural spans. Many times the cruciform plan is chosen less for the inherent symbolism than for the smaller scale imparted to the building exterior.

### Central

Plans based on the concept of an encircling congregation are to be found in quite ancient churches. Liturgical reevaluation has generated renewed interest in this concept. In addition to the previously discussed problem concerning lack of eye contact with the minister, certain nonreligious activities taking place in the church may also suffer. Not all the seats will have good viewing angles for motion pictures or slides. Likewise, a lecturer may also find an audience distributed for a span of 270 feet around the lectern an unusual condition.

Nevertheless, the sense of intimacy and oneness is very great and may overcome all objections. While the accompanying example (Fig. 6c) is hexagonal, many geometric forms are possible. The portion of the space not utilized for seating in this example is used for support facilities. There is the immediate problem that the external form is not internally complete, and this can be a grave fault. The architect should be equally concerned about the deleterious effect of a clearly expressed worship space form when a multitude of small support facility spaces are "tacked on."

### "L" or "T" Expandable

As stated previously, the varying requirements for worship space seating have caused a variety of plans that are expandable to be developed. The most compelling argument for this type of plan is that the space can be tailored to the number of participants. Unfortunately, this argument has resulted in the building of many churches that are flexible, but in which those who worship in the overflow area feel like outsiders. The ceiling height, floor and wall finish, and lighting of the expansion space should be in harmony with those of the smaller worship area to which it is joined. Worshipers in the expansion space should not get the feeling that they are looking through a doorway. Undoubtedly the best approach is to design the total worship area and then to introduce dividing partitions.

Figure 6d illustrates a church for over 600, of which only 120 are accommodated in the permanent chapel. The expansion space is sized for basketball, with a small stage platform at one end. The ori

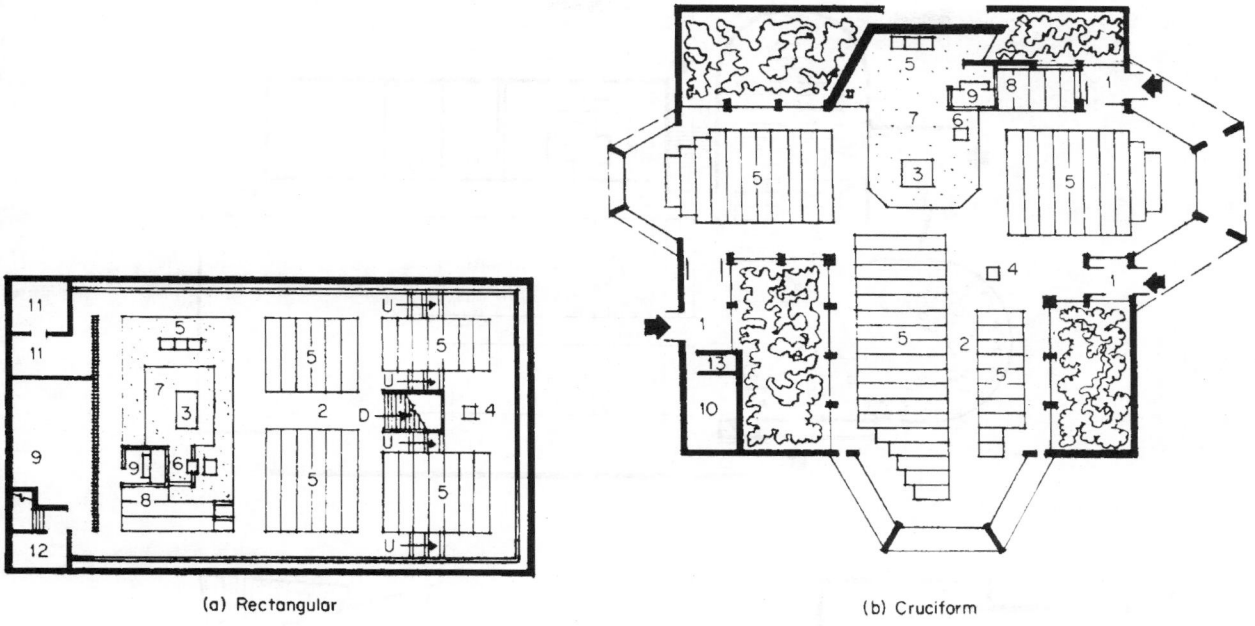

(a) Rectangular

(b) Cruciform

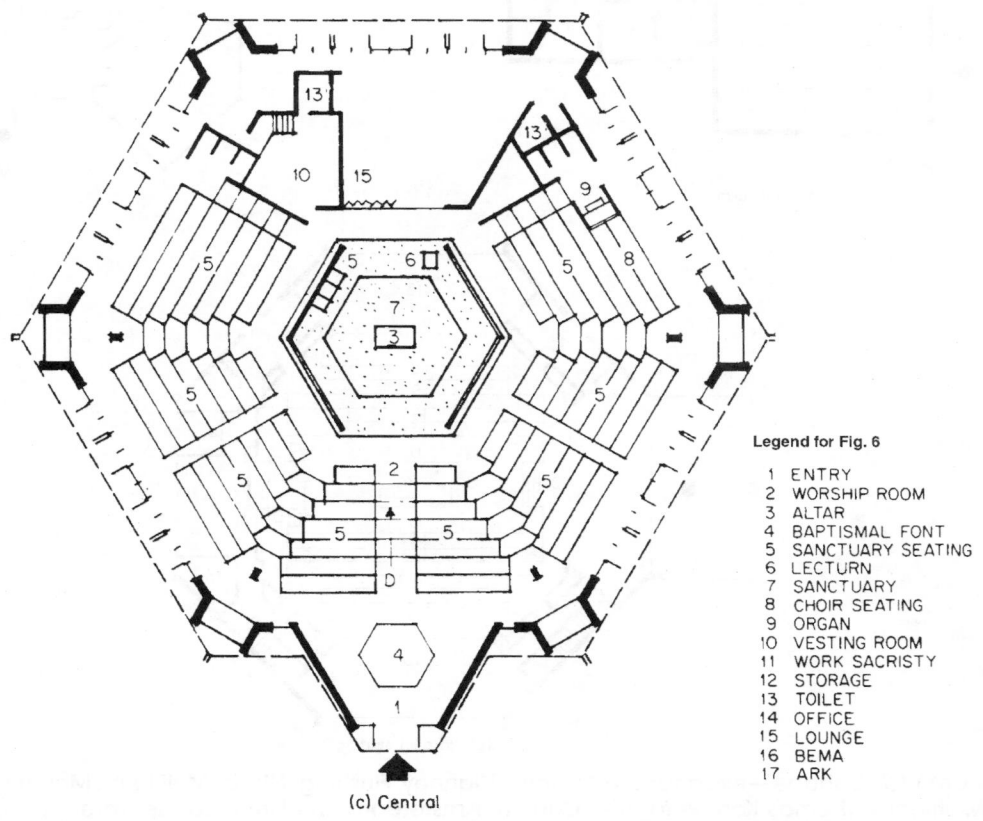

(c) Central

**Legend for Fig. 6**

1 ENTRY
2 WORSHIP ROOM
3 ALTAR
4 BAPTISMAL FONT
5 SANCTUARY SEATING
6 LECTURN
7 SANCTUARY
8 CHOIR SEATING
9 ORGAN
10 VESTING ROOM
11 WORK SACRISTY
12 STORAGE
13 TOILET
14 OFFICE
15 LOUNGE
16 BEMA
17 ARK

**Fig. 6.** (*a*) Rectangular. Church of the Redeemer, Merrick, NY (*b*) Cruciform. St. Anthony, Nanuet, NY (*c*) Central. St. Jude's Church, Napanoch, NY

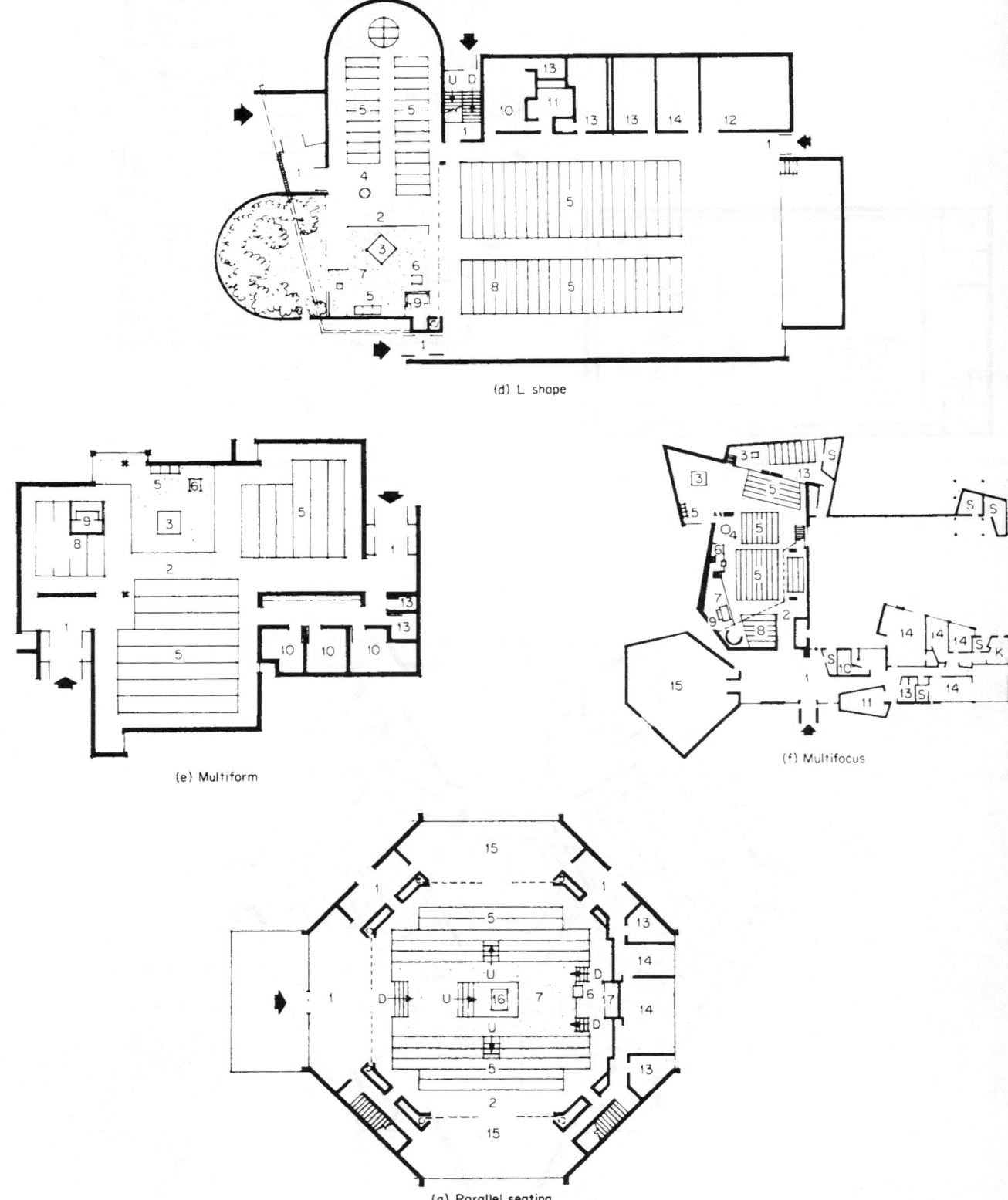

(d) L shape

(e) Multiform

(f) Multifocus

(g) Parallel seating

**Fig. 6. (cont.)** (*d*) L-shape—expandable. St. John-Vianney, Flushing, NY (*e*) Multiform. Mount Snow Chapel, Wilmington, Vt. (*f*) Multifocus. Thomas Kerk Reformed Church. Amsterdam, The Netherlands. Karel Sijmons, Architect. (*g*) Parallel seating. Orthodox Synagogue, Lakewood, NJ. Davis, Brody, & Wisniewski, Architects

tation of the seats is deliberately reversed from performance to worship. The enclosed garden visible from the chapel is related more the expansion space than to the chapel. The altar is rotated depending on the size of the congregation.

**ultiform**

urrent interest is focused on a rather random deployment of the ongregation around the altar platform. The plan then reflects this rangement by articulating each group of pews. This nonrigid plan informal and invites innovation if a movable altar platform and ating are used.

g. 6e is the plan of a small interfaith chapel with parking on two des and vesting space for the three chaplains. Fairly conventional ood framing is supported on columns so located as to avoid interrence with viewing angles.

**ultifocus**

relatively new liturgical innovation has been included in the illusations since it may develop into a significant plan form. Here the ought is to move the focus of interest with the liturgical actions ound the space. Fixed seating is not compatible with this approach, or is it likely to be used for large congregations because of the possbility of confusion.

he Dutch church plan (Fig. 6f) shows the seating used for preaching d singing, with a large standing space about the communion table or that part of the service.

**arallel Seating**

arallel seating is a less common arrangement in churches, but a trational form in orthodox synagogues. As illustrated in the synaogue plan shown (Fig. 6g), this approach is worthy of thoughtful amination. The problem of expansion is also neatly solved by simy adding parallel rows.

## ORGAN AND CHOIR LOCATION

For many years, the choir has been located in the church either in monastic fashion before the altar or in the "voice of angels" position in the choir loft. Due in no small part to the relocation of the altar so that the celebrant can face the congregation, the choir location must be rethought.

Possibly just as the worship service is losing its performance quality, so too the choir is being asked to lead the congregation's singing rather than to perform before it. Hence new locations of the choir within the congregation are being considered.

Illustrated are five alternatives:

1. Behind altar (Fig. 7a), the choir is less visible but still easily heard. Unfortunately the members of the choir are not part of the congregation and have poor opportunity to worship properly or to feel that the spoken word is also directed to them.
2. Before the altar (Fig. 7b). Here, the choir is segregated but part of the congregation.
3. Rear of the church (Fig. 7c). The choir is part of the congregation, but this situation is not much different from that in the choir loft.
4. Choir alcove (Fig. 7d). This arrangement has many variants, and it can be very effective.
5. Within the pews (Fig. 7e). A simpler version of the "before the altar" arrangement. The significance of the choir is very much reduced.

It should be emphasized that in all cases the organ will be best located where the organist can see the action at the altar as well as cue the singers by virtue of being seen when giving signals. The organist is a potential distraction to the rest of the congregation, and it is therefore prudent to construct low walls about the instrument.

Pipe organs should not be treated as an afterthought. A church which expects to install a pipe organ must plan for that instrument, since introducing an instrument later without proper provisions is almost

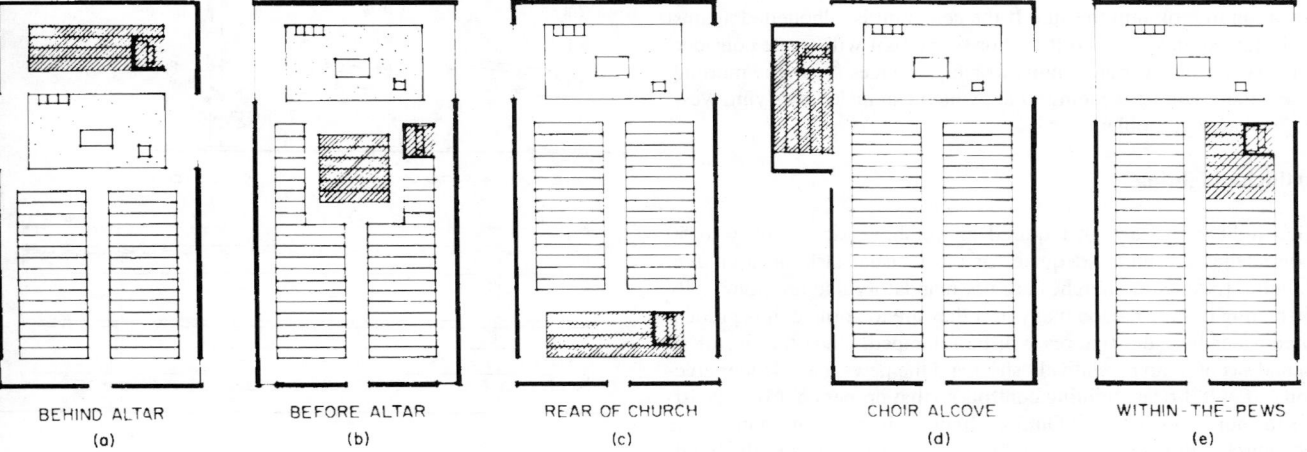

BEHIND ALTAR (a)  BEFORE ALTAR (b)  REAR OF CHURCH (c)  CHOIR ALCOVE (d)  WITHIN-THE-PEWS (e)

**Fig. 7. Possible locations for the choir**

always unsuccessful. While other musical instruments have been successfully used in churches, sophisticated electronic organs permit even very small congregations to consider their use without sacrificing quality.

## OTHER PLANNING CONSIDERATIONS

### Acoustics

Small churches seldom have acoustic problems if the space is "live" (i.e., somewhat reverberant). More errors are committed by excessive use of sound absorbing materials than by restraint in their use.

Echoes and "dead spots" will have to be anticipated in churches sized for more than 600, but even then reasonable precautions will suffice.

Public address systems are recommended for all but the smallest churches. A trained speaker can usually be very well heard, but amplification is a help to the many untrained and unaccustomed speakers using the lectern.

If an ambitious music program (chamber groups or recitals) is programmed, then a competent acoustical consultant is recommended.

### Air Conditioning

In an age when every public space is usually air-conditioned, it is imprudent to overlook this aspect of providing a comfortable environment for worship. The use of the church during the summer months, the hour and length of the worship service, and the anticipated size of the congregation will determine the best type of system. However, it is imperative that the architect and engineering consultants give due consideration to equipment and air noise. A church with a high background noise generated by poor equipment and register selection has failed to provide a proper environment for worship.

### Natural Lighting

The introduction of natural light into a worship area can animate the space and create that sense of the unique which should be part of the architect's goal. The programmatic and liturgical emphasis will dictate how natural light will be admitted and what it is to do.

One word of caution: avoid the common pitfall of forcing the congregation to look into the sun. If the celebrant is silhouetted against back-lighted glass (even diffused or stained), it will create considerable discomfort. Although most worship services are in the morning hours, there will be weddings, etc., which can make low-lying westerly sun a great problem.

### Artificial Lighting

High light levels are not required in worship spaces. Thirty to 50 foot-candles are quite adequate for most visual tasks in a church. Hanging fixtures in churches are not mandatory and are potentially distracting if there are too many or if they are too ornate. It is prudent to consider how the fixtures will be relamped, since the life of an incandescent lamp is relatively short and the pews make ladder erection difficult. Locate lighting controls so that proper control is possible for non-worship uses. Outdoor lighting is also important, since the church will be utilized at night and the access paths to the building must be defined.

Churches have been the targets for some of the increasing vandalism all buildings have experienced. Therefore outdoor security lighting, controlled by a timer, is recommended.

## SIZES

### Gross Area

For purposes of establishing preliminary space requirements, allow 12+ square feet per seat. This would include moderate space for altar, platform, work sacristy, vesting room, and vestibule. If only the seating area is considered (including aisles), allow 8 square feet per person.

### Seating

If pews are utilized, some building codes will gauge capacity on the basis of 18 inches of pew length per person. Actually, this density will only rarely be achieved, and the usual space per person will be 22 to 24 inches. Back-to-back dimension will average 36 inches with a minimum of 33 inches (especially if a kneeler is contemplated) and a maximum of 42 inches. The widest spacing will actually be uncomfortable for kneeler use. It is wise to provide storage space for prayer books or hymnals on a shelf below the seat ahead or mounted on the seat back. The foregoing dimensions will hold true for folding or stacking chairs. Allow space in the aisle for funeral catafalques and candles (see Fig. 8).

### Altar

Size varies from 48 to 96 inches long by 28 to 48 inches wide by 4 inches high. The altar need not be rectangular, but in any event its historical beginning was as a table and it is reasonable to retain some of that image (see Figs. 9 and 10).

### Altar Platform

Four to 6 inches in height is generally sufficient. It is imperative to plan the platform for the furniture and the movements of all those on it. The chancel platform may be raised one 6-inch step for every four

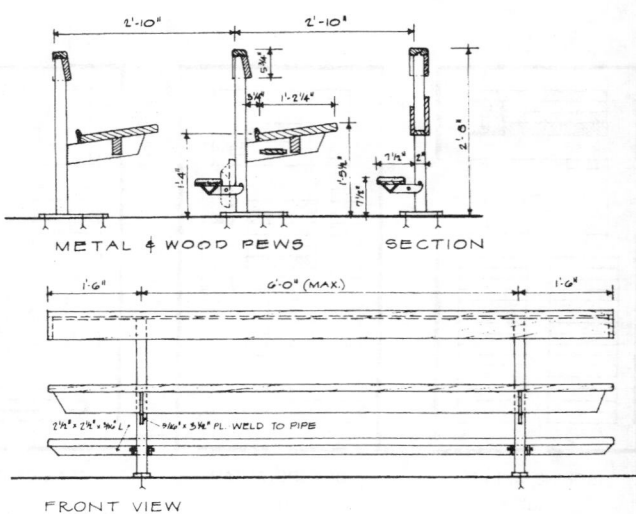

**Fig. 8. Metal and wood pews, section**

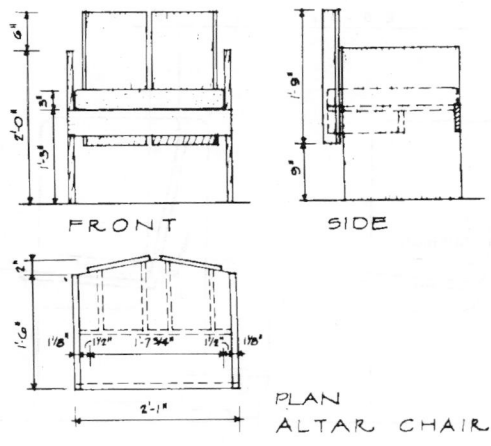

**Fig. 9. Altar chair**

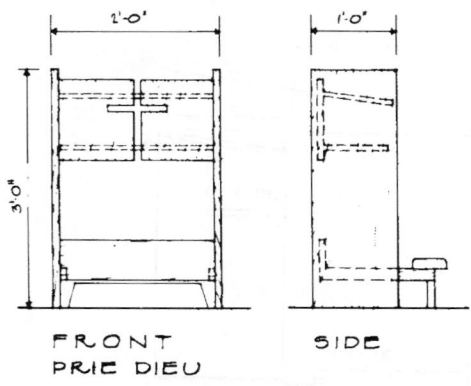

**Fig. 11. Prie-dieu**

rows of seating, but avoid platforms more than 30 inches above the main seating floor height. Worship spaces with less than ten rows of seating may not need to elevate the chancel platform.

Weddings are often performed on the platform and space between the altar and the platform edge will have to accommodate the clergy person and the nuptial couple (sometimes kneeling at a prie dieu or kneeling device; (see Fig. 11).

### Confessional

With the advent of Vatican II, the traditional confessional booth has been in large part replaced by the reconciliation room. In the past the custom was to provide a space for the seated priest with the penitent kneeling within a small cubicle and speaking through a heavily veiled opening at the priest's ear. It is now possible to use a more natural conference room setting, but the arrangement should be such that the penitent may have the option of speaking to the confessor (priest) through a screen, in order to preserve anonymity.

### Candlesticks

Candles vary in size from 1 to 2½ inches in width and in length from 9½ to 33½ inches. The holder can be on the altar or on the floor beside the altar. Overly tall candlestick and holder combinations may obstruct the view of the clergyperson. It should be mentioned that an air stream directed toward the altar will cause annoying flickering of the candle flame and uneven wax burning.

### Lectern or Pulpit

Provide a sloped (adjustable height) surface with lip to retain a book placed on the surface. The pulpit width varies from 24 to 36 inches. Depth measured horizontally is a minimum of 16 inches (see Fig. 12).

### Communion Rail

If a rail is required, the height should not exceed 36 inches. The communion rail is considered to be a symbolic extension of the altar table, and as such it is desirable that it have a broad top (6 to 8 inches).

### Church Pews

See Fig. 13 for illustration.

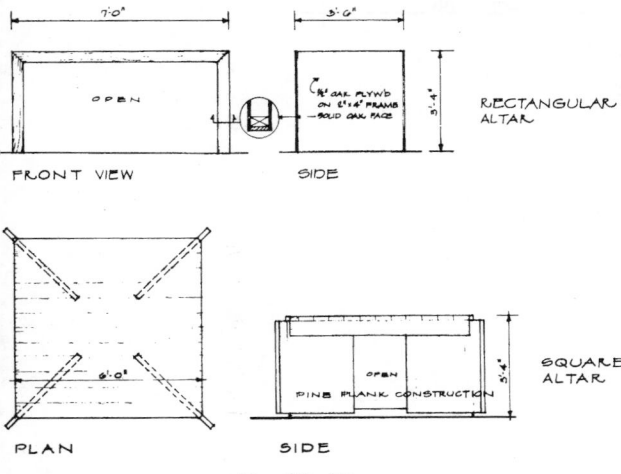

**Fig. 10. Altar**

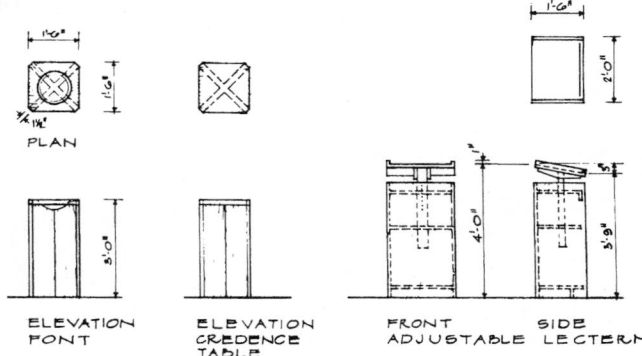

**Fig. 12. Lectern**

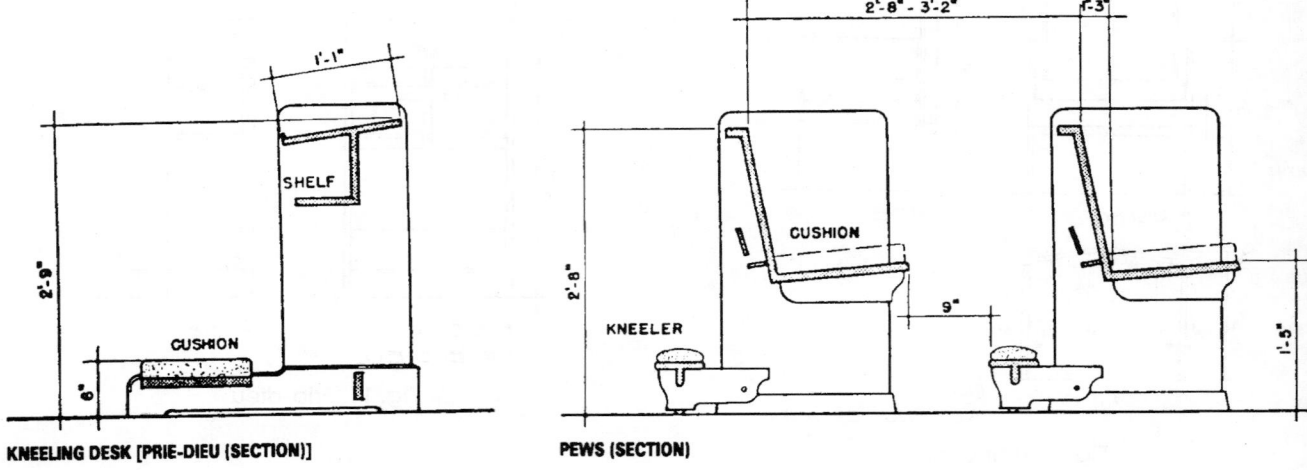

**KNEELING DESK [PRIE-DIEU (SECTION)]**

**PEWS (SECTION)**

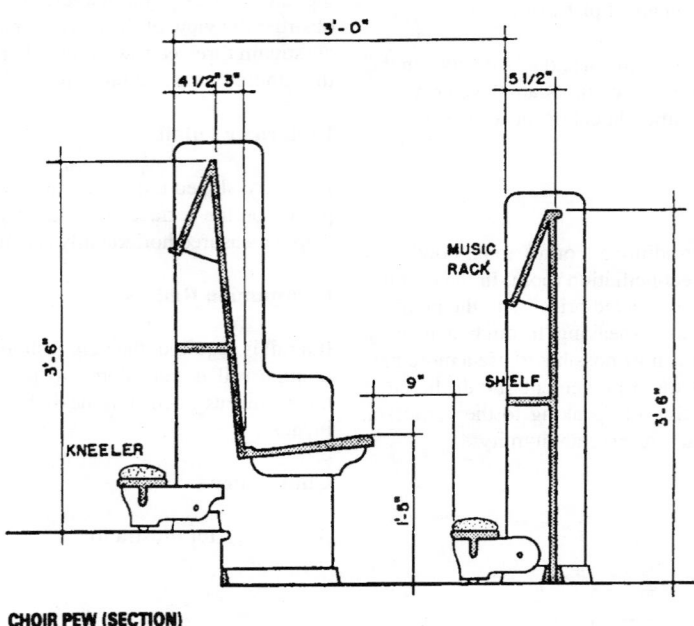

**CHOIR PEW (SECTION)**

Fig. 13.

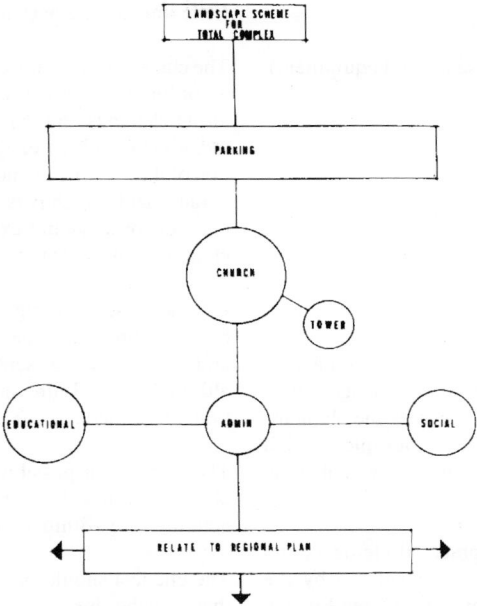

**Fig. 1. Diagrammatic relation of elements of the Lutheran church**

# CHURCHES, LUTHERAN

## SELECTION OF THE SITE

The selection of the site is the most important decision to be made by the building committee, since it sets limitations for the potential area and volume of the proposed church structure and profoundly shapes its character and determines its future growth, development, and importance to the community and parish. The following factors are major considerations:

1. The character and stability of the environs of the site
2. Accessibility to the site for the membership
   a. relationship to highways and secondary roads
   b. coordination into the regional plan and traffic pattern of area affected
   c. provision of ample parking area
   d. general contours of the property
   e. soil characteristics
   f. presence of rock and ledge outcroppings
   g. presence of water problems
   h. availability of utilities

The practical elements and component spaces required by the church are as follows:

1. The church room (liturgical center) areas for intimately related activities
   a. narthex (entrance vestibule)
   b. nave (congregational seating area)
   c. chancel (including altar, pulpit, and lectern)
   d. choir and organ facilities
   e. baptismal font and facilities
   f. sacristy
   g. minister's study
   h. church tower

2. Administration
   a. secretary's office
   b. general office
   c. mailing, printing, and reproduction rooms
   d. minister's office
   e. assistant minister's office

3. Church school
   a. kindergarten
   b. intermediate classes
   c. junior classes
   d. senior classes
   e. college group facilities
   f. adult facilities
   g. family counseling facilities
   h. visual education facilities
   i. Boy Scout rooms
   j. Brownie rooms
   k. library facilities/ media center

4. Social hall
   a. auditorium with portable stage or dais
   b. kitchen facilities

*Author:* Maurice R. Salo, AIA, Consulting Architect to the Lutheran Church in America
*Reviewer:* Douglas R. Hoffman, AIA

c. coat rooms

d. toilet facilities

e. storage rooms (generous for materials, seats, and equipment)

f. lobby or foyer

5. Church parlor with fireplace

6. Kitchenette

7. Parking

8. Landscape—gardens and similar features

Note: The above facilities are desirable for complete church activities. However, each parish has its own special requirements, which are specified in the building committee's brief. There some elements can be omitted and some areas may be assigned to multiple use. All these elements are critical in determining the design and establishing the cost of the building program.

After the selection of the site, the following practical elements and spaces required for a church structure must be considered by the committee and incorporated into their program or brief (see Fig. 1). Administration is centrally located for control. Other elements are related but adapted to dictates of site, to the architect's interpretation of the problem, and to suggestions of building committee.

**Narthex/Gathering Area**

The narthex is the vestibule or entry into the church room, but also serves as a gathering area for the congregation before and after services. Its shape is, of course, suggested by the basic plan of the church complex. It is recommended that it be at least 10 feet wide to permit facile movement of the congregation and the usual personal greetings to the parishioners by the minister. It is well to locate toilet facilities, coat rooms, and similar conveniences discreetly off the narthex or in other accessible areas, since there is no rigid rule except convenience to determine their disposition.

**Church Room**

The church room on the main body of the church today may assume many forms due to the demands of site and the architect's interpretation of the building committee's stated program needs.

Essentially the space must have dignity and strength to carry out the spirit of worship and logically contain the 12 elements outlined subsequently in this article.

A center or direct aisle from the seating area is essential to permit weddings and similar activities to function properly. The center aisle should not be less than 5 feet wide. Side aisles should not be less than 3 feet wide.

Sculpture, painting, and stained glass may be used, but with good taste and properly placed to enhance the room and to express its special character. Art has always been a basic vehicle of man to express the beauty and logic of the universe and for a moment's escape from the sometime prosaic reality, and therefore, it is a fitting agent to bring about the awareness of divine truth.

The church room (liturgical center) and appurtenant areas for intimately related activities are as follows.

**Unicameral Space (Chancel)**

The chancel is the climactic point of the church room and the main center of liturgical activities. Therefore special attention should be given to all its elements and appointments. The chancel or unicameral area in today's church is an integral part of the church room. A distinct separation of these elements should be avoided and any clear separation of celebrants and worshipers should also be avoided. It follows that the chancel space should extend as far as practical limits permit into the church room, so that all can equally participate in corporate worship.

It is the present feeling that all liturgical centers are equally holy. The historic liturgical center with its concentration of worship at the altar and reredos as an essential element in the church room is changing although some Lutherans still preserve an attachment to this traditional treatment.

There are great possibilities in the placement of the chancel and its elements. It may be located centrally or asymmetrically as long as its activities are within a comfortable vision range.

The chancel should be raised three steps, each of which is not more than 6 inches high, with treads a minimum of 16 inches wide. A clear aisle with a minimum width of 5 feet should be provided for convenient circulation around the perimeter of the chancel. We are not illustrating characteristic arrangements since the range of possibilities is too great. However, in the discussion of the choir arrangements some suggestions will be made.

**Altar**

The altar is the most sacred element in the chancel. It usually reflects the concept of the Last Supper and should bear the character of a table. Its design treatment should reflect dignity and should have meticulously thought out details. The special treatment of this element must be the responsibility of the design team. They must properly relate its material and character to the total church room design. Figure 2 is a sketch of an altar, with dimensions to be used solely as a guide.

**Pulpit**

The pulpit is the most actively used element in the chancel. It is dynamic, as opposed to the more static holy appointments. It is a setting from which the preacher brings the Gospel and the word of God to the worshipers. It should be prominently placed in the chancel without obscuring the view of the altar and other elements of the chancel. The centrally placed pulpit in a circular room, in the author's opinion, is not sound, since it does not permit the preacher to be seen by all. It should be comfortably located, seen by all, so that the preacher's visage, movement, and use of hands can be viewed enabling preachers to deliver their messages forcefully and to have complete communication with every worshiper. We suggest that the pulpit be raised two or three steps to raise the preacher's stature to give them greater dignity—for at these moments they are more apostles of God than ordinary humans.

The pulpit must be provided with the following elements:

- Bible rest
- shelf under Bible rest for notes and papers
- a light over the Bible rest for reading purposes
- microphone—with all its conduits and devices shrouded in the construction of the pulpit

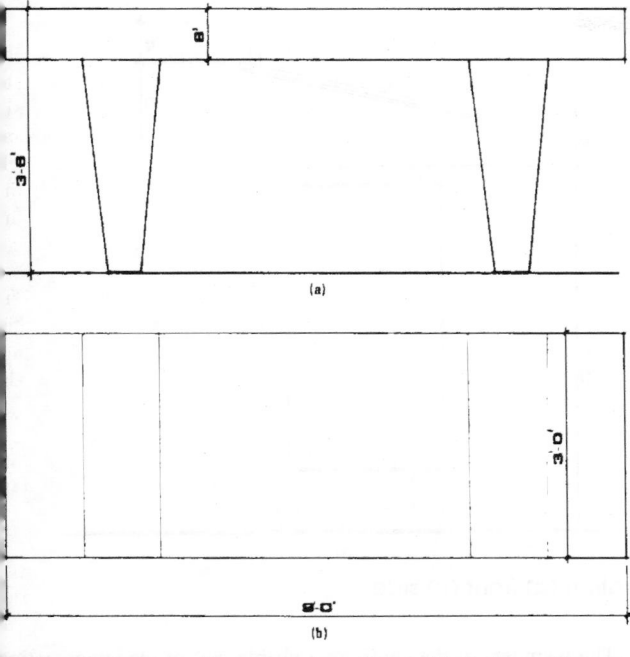

Fig. 2. (a) Schematic altar elevation; (b) Schematic altar plan

The design character should be left to the architect, as a standard form is not possible due to the variability of the church room design. Materials are optional, but they are related to the church design and should have inherent dignity and strength. Figure 3 is a sketch of a pulpit with critical dimensions to be used solely as a guide.

## Lectern

The lectern is a smaller reading desk and is an element in liturgical activities. It is used in conjunction with the pulpit during services.

It may be omitted at the discretion of the building committee. This is particularly true in the design for smaller churches. The following elements are essential to the lectern:

- Bible rest
- reading light over the Bible rest
- microphone (electrical elements to be concealed)

Figure 4 shows the lectern's critical dimensions, but this sketch is not to be taken as a criterion for its design.

### Communion Rail

In many Lutheran churches the communion rail is omitted and the communion elements are served directly from the altar table while the communicants are standing.

In such instances where a communion rail is desired, it should not be more than 2½ feet high and located around the elements of the chancel to permit maximum participation at one time with easy movement flow to the rail and to the pews. The step before the rail should not be less than 2 feet wide. As in the case of the other elements of the chancel, the design should reflect and be in character with the design idiom of the church room. Figure 5 shows critical dimensions, which may be used as a guide.

### Choir and Organ Facilities

The particular location of a choir is usually determined by the minister, choirmaster, and organist for its suitability to the required serv-

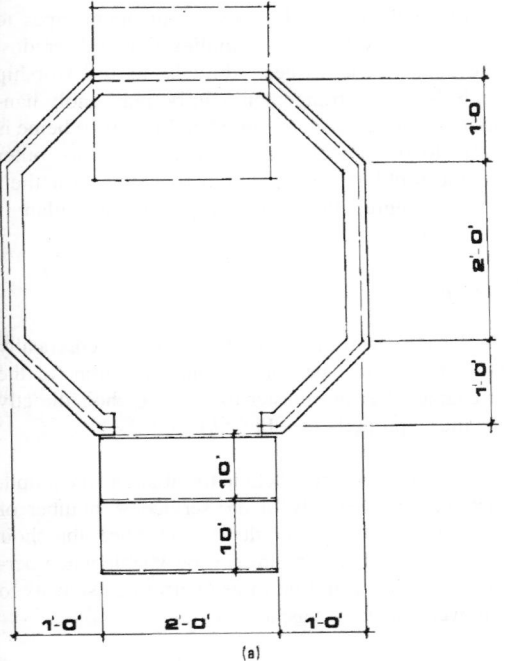

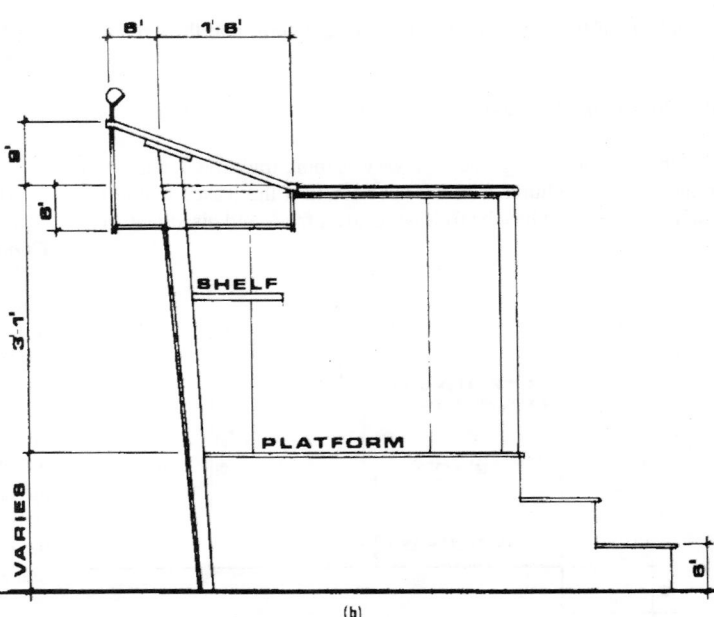

Fig. 3. (a) Schematic plan of pulpit, minimum dimensions; (b) Schematic section of pulpit

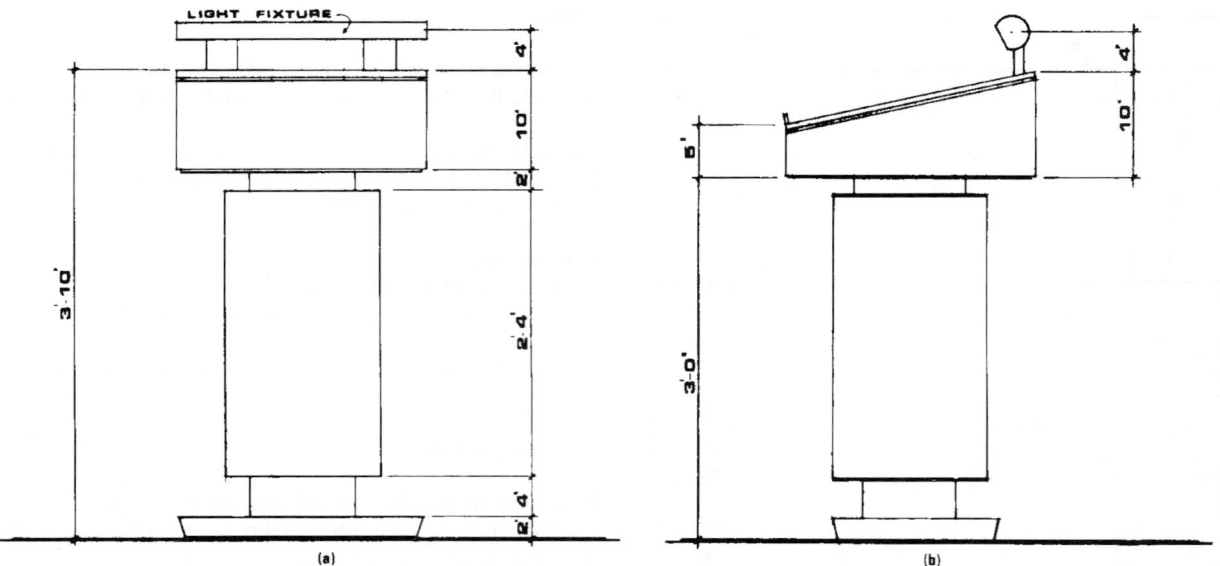

**Fig. 4. Schematic lectern elevation (a) front (b) side**

ices. The decision on its placement must be made by the committee early in its deliberations and the architect must be advised as soon as possible, since the choir is a major element affecting the shape of the church room.

There are five possible arrangements for the choir and many interpretations for each type. These five basic choir locations are as follows:

- split choir in the chancel
- choir centrally located behind the altar
- asymmetrically located choir placed on one or the other side of the chancel
- choir placed in the seating area of the church room
- choir in the rear balcony

An analysis of the five basic locations of the choir and their relative merits follows.

*Split Choir in the Chancel*

This type of choir setting (see Fig. 6a) was more traditional in the past century, but most churches today have found it the least suitable for present-day needs. It has the following advantages and disadvantages:

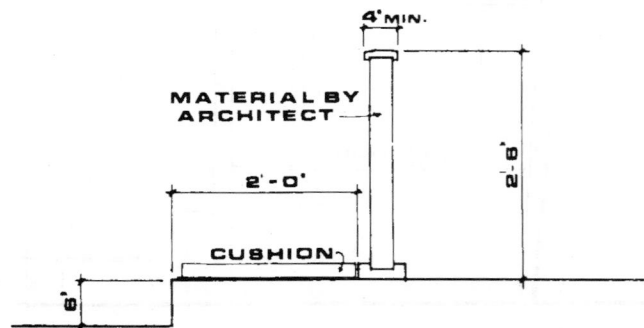

**Fig. 5. Schematic section through communion rail**

- The members of the choir are a visible part of the congregation and participate in the total worship.
- The altar, placed between the ranks of the choir pews, has a dominant focal position.
- The service is enriched by the color of the choristers' vestments, by their trained behavior, and by their organized singing.
- Musically, this arrangement creates some problems, since the singers cannot be centrally directed. The organist needs the aid of mirror devices to see the singers perform in unison.
- It creates further a sense of separation between the singers, the professional clerical celebrants, and the lay worshippers, reflecting the complete separation of these functions which was characteristic of the medieval church.
- This scheme frequently forces the location of organ pipes to be opposed on the side wall, since it implies a central reredos. Musically, the organ should speak directly to the worship room. Although this side arrangement can be reasonably handled, it would be a compromise. As stated earlier, this scheme is not sympathetic to today's church concept. There are other approaches to the problem which should be studied for their suitability to the congregation before type of choir plan is decided upon.

*Choir Centrally Located*

The choir may be located centrally, behind the altar. Theoretically this is sound. This arrangement permits a central position for the organ console. It enables the choirmaster to face the choir directly and to conduct the music properly (see Fig. 6b).

However, it places the choir personnel behind the altar and the pulpit, which can distract from the serenity of the service. A number of devices can be used to offset this difficulty. For instance, the choir stalls may be lowered, so that singers are not too visible when performing. Another possibility would be to use perforated screens to make the choir's movements less conspicuous.

The organ screen, of course, is best located behind the singers, so that it voices directly to the church room. This arrangement has many

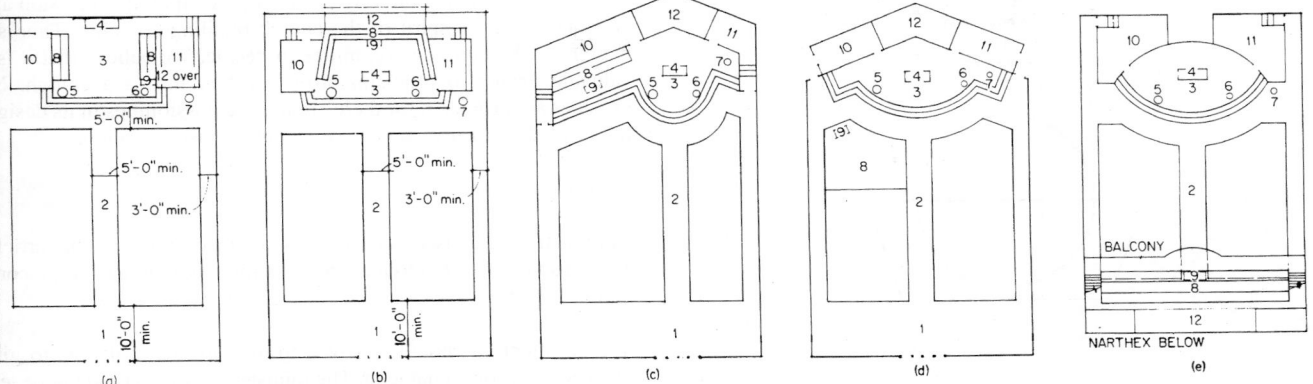

Fig. 6. (a) Split choir in chancel; (b) Choir centrally located; (c) Choir located asymmetrically; (d) Choir located in seating area; (e) Choir located in balcony. (1) Narthex, (2) church room, (3) chancel or unicameral space, (4) altar, (5) pulpit, (6) lectern, (7) baptistry, (8) choir space, (9) organ console, (10) ministers' room, (11) sacristy, (12) organ loft.

advantages, but it makes the organ conflict and compete with the altar and pulpit. With a disciplined choir, however, this plan has interesting possibilities.

### Choir Located Asymmetrically

This arrangement (see Fig 6c) places the choir facilities at the front of the church next to the chancel area. It causes the design of the church itself to be asymmetrical in plan and volume, and it poses a difficult problem for the architect who seeks to develop a design of proper repose with ecclesiastical dignity. This plan has the advantage of avoiding direct competition between the choir and the chancel, and placing all liturgical activities within comfortable vision range of the congregation. It permits good musical direction and provides a control position for the console and organist.

### Choir Placed in the Seating Area of the Church Room

This (see Fig. 6d) is a novel departure from tradition. It has the advantage that the choir and parishioners worship in concert. Perhaps it also de-emphasizes the choir and its colorful role in the worship ritual. The decision for this arrangement must be based on the minister's attitude toward the service and on the feelings of the building committee. The console of the organ can be fitted into the pens of the choir area and arranged so that the organist faces the choir and has complete control of the singing. The organ space and its elements must be closely related to the choir's location.

### Choir in the Rear Balcony

This (see Fig. 6e) arrangement is ideal from the musician's point of view since the direction of the music is good and the organist can be so placed as to be in perfect control of the singing. The organ can be effectively located behind the choir. From the point of view of the worship, the choir is remote from the main church room and not visible.

This arrangement will provide an effective musical background for church services, and many successful examples of this scheme exist. It does, however, conflict with the current understanding of corporate worship and the full and active participation of all the members in the action of worship. The committee must decide to

what extent its ideas on worship conflict with this musically preferable arrangement.

### Organ

The organ is a major element in the design of a church space, and adequate volume for its housing, air supply, and electrical elements must be provided.

Often today, pipes are exposed in the interior walls of the church room and become an interesting part of the church decor. We noted earlier that an organ builder must be consulted in the earliest stage of church planning as the organ cannot be installed as an afterthought. The form of the church must be designed to ensure maximum purity of tone and to provide the proper acoustics. The excessive use of sound-absorbing acoustical material will strip the overtones of the various pipes, particularly double reed sounds, basses, and tones in the treble clef.

### Baptismal Font

This unit is an important part of liturgical activities and must be placed in a prominent area of the church room—that is, in the chancel or in a space conveniently close to it. It must be in the visual range of the congregation so that all can participate in the baptismal rites.

The baptismal font may be a fixed element or it can be a movable unit which can be placed conveniently when required. If it is a fixed unit, a proper setting must be provided.

Figure 7 gives some basic dimensions to be used as a guide for its design. The concept can be simple or elaborate, but it must be related in character to the overall design of the church room.

### Sacristy

The sacristy is a room located adjacent to the chancel. It is a practical space for flow arrangement, for the preparation of communion elements, and for the storage of items required for the activities in the chancel. It generally contains a double sink with hot and cold water, a refrigerator, and base and wall-hung cabinets. Its design may be simple and materials may be chosen as economically as desired as long as they are in good taste.

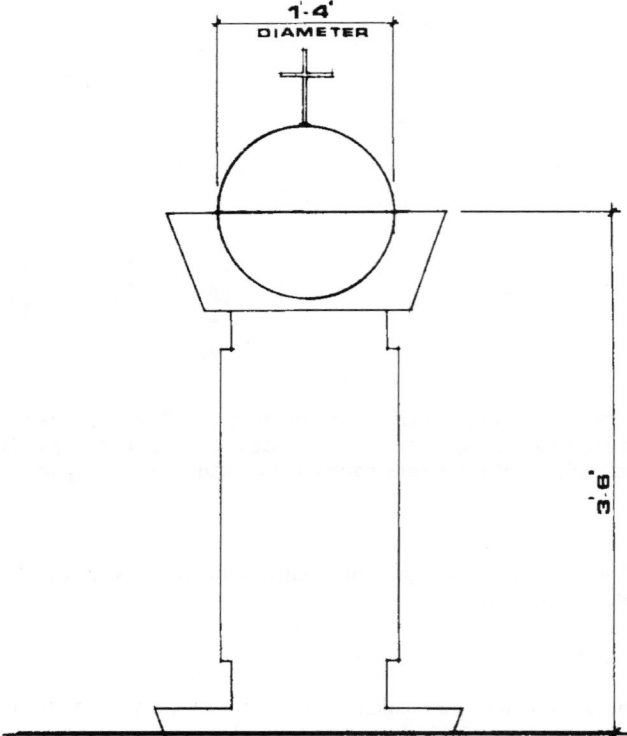

**Fig. 7. Schematic section through baptismal font**

No illustrative drawing is required for this space since it varies in so many instances, but it must function smoothly. At least two people must be able to work here at the same time. It must have direct access to the chancel and a secondary exit to a hall or corridor outside the church area.

### Minister's Study

A minister's study or room is adjacent to the chancel, with direct access to the chancel and egress to a hall or corridor. This room should provide space for a desk and a number of chairs, files, coat closet, toilet, and a shower bath. It is convenient for last-minute reviews of the sermon, guest speakers, conferences, and similar purposes.

This room should be well appointed and have comfortable seating for informal counseling. Since this area varies a great deal in form, no sketches will be provided.

### Church Tower

The church tower, though not an integral part of the church room itself, will be discussed herein since it is a symbol of the church and expresses the religious character of the total church complex.

Today it is often felt that the church tower involves an unnecessary expense and that a properly designed church is sufficient to express the spirit of Christian worship. However, a church tower or campanile has long been associated with ecclesiastical structures and to many it has a symbolic value beyond cost or logic. Perhaps it does conflict with the criteria of present-day attitudes. But it is an understandable symbol of worship and an abstract witness to the Christian spirit; therefore it may justifiably be used.

It does provide an opportunity for abstract sculptural expression an keynotes the total spirit of the church building complex. This is matter for the building committee to decide. We believe that it is valuable device to proclaim positively that this is a church. N sketches are provided, for there are infinite possibilities in its desig It has another positive value in that it can house a carillon.

### Administration

Administration consists of elements outlined earlier in this articl These rooms are sized to meet the specific requirements of the con mittee's brief.

Special attention should be given to the minister's offices, to gi them ecclesiastical character. The minister's office should not be le than 12 by 20 feet clear and should contain closets, bookshelves, ar toilet facilities.

### Church School

Classrooms should not be less than 24 by 32 feet. Small rooms a too restrictive and are not adaptable to program changes. It is be that adequate natural light be provided, and light areas should not I sacrificed for design effects.

The kindergarten should provide at least 30 square feet per pup because of the nature of kindergarten activities.

The architectural treatment should reflect the rhythm and characte of the church building.

### Social Hall

This should provide seating equal to that of the nave. Dining capac ity should be determined by programmatic needs, but should n exceed average attendance at the larger communal dining function since this can be expensive space to build. It should be a pleasant are and well correlated to the exterior landscape features if possible. Th ceiling should not be less than 14 feet clear if possible.

### Church Parlor

This is a very desirable space and serves many functions. It shoul not be less than 24 by 14 feet in plan dimensions and should have ceiling at least 12 feet high. The room should have a formal livin room character with suggestions of its basic religious relationship. should be comfortable and pleasantly furnished and decorated.

### Parking

Required parking will generally be a function of local zoning regula tions, but should provide a minimum of one parking space for ever four persons in the church room seating. Its arrangement should be product of a well coordinated total landscape and site design.

### Landscaping

The landscape is an integral part of the total architectural concept an should properly relate to building plans and mass. It is recommende that a professional landscape architect be retained to achieve the be results.

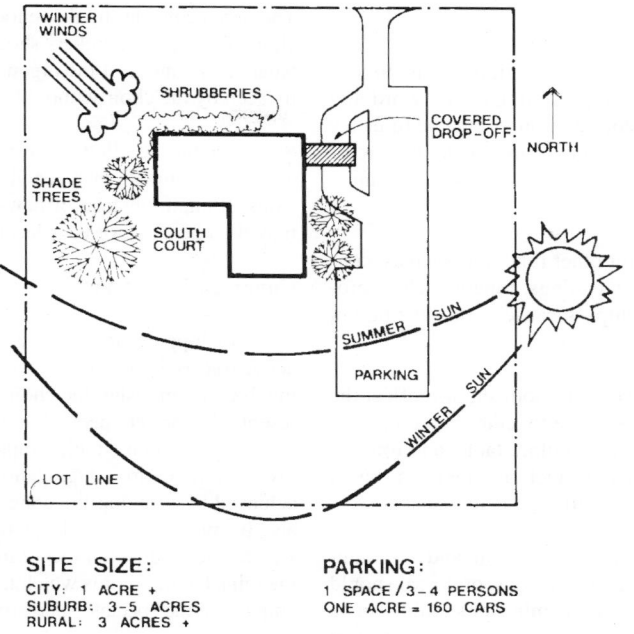

**SITE SIZE:**
CITY: 1 ACRE +
SUBURB: 3-5 ACRES
RURAL: 3 ACRES +

**PARKING:**
1 SPACE / 3-4 PERSONS
ONE ACRE = 160 CARS

**Fig. 1. Site location**

# CHURCHES, UNITED METHODIST

## ORGANIZATION

The main entrance to the building should be easily accessible from the parking area, and should be designed with a drive up and canopy entrance. This permits covered access to the building during inclement weather (Fig. 1).

The building should be organized so that people can easily orient themselves once inside the front doors. A key feature in this kind of arrangement is a large, centrally located gathering area that serves as the circulation hub of the building. A person should be able to proceed directly from the gathering area to the sanctuary, fellowship hall, or classrooms. For convenience, the church offices and restrooms could also be located off this area. Not only does this make them more accessible, but it also enables the church secretary to monitor the main entrance from the church office. Figure 2 illustrates this kind of arrangement.

## SANCTUARY

Basic premises on which the recommendations are based:

The purpose of erecting a building is to provide a place where people may assemble for worship, fellowship, and education and prepare for service.

- People and what they do are the major concern of the church. The building forms a background for the action and is secondary to the gathered congregation and the liturgy.
- The essential elements for worship consist of a place for the preaching of the word and the right enactment of the sacraments.
- The aim of worship is "to focus attention and to suggest and direct appropriate human responses to the divine-human encounter."
- Theology does not directly influence architecture. Theology (or beliefs) does influence liturgy (what we do). Architecture is a result of efforts to provide a setting for the liturgy.
- Methodist church buildings should celebrate the conviction that God is present in our lives in this age.

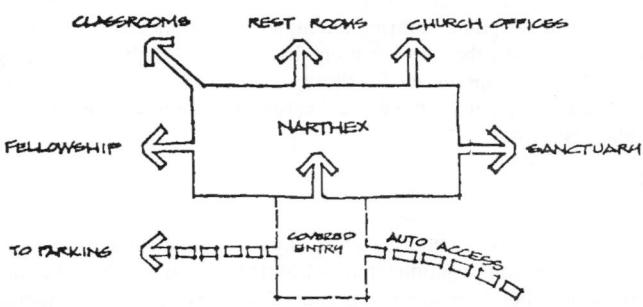

**Fig. 2. Arrangement with centrally located narthex**

*Reference:* Materials taken in part from publications of the General Board of Global Ministries, the United Methodist Church.

## WORSHIP ROOM

The worship room is to be designed to assist the liturgy. The liturgy consists basically of provisions for the preaching of the word and the sacraments of baptism and holy communion. Since the ministry of the word and the sacraments are of equal importance, the architectural plan should give emphasis and stress to the pulpit, table, and font.

The worship room may also be used for other functions such as: confirmation and reception of members, weddings, funerals, choir programs, drama, education, and fellowship. Because of this, the pulpit, table, and font should be portable.

The design and arrangement of the worship room should reflect the fact that the minister and congregation come together in a corporate act of worship. The platform on which the pulpit, table, and font are located is a distinct area because of the functions involved, but it should not be separated from the congregational seating space.

Since the major emphasis is upon preaching, baptism, and communion, architectural features such as windows, reredos, or dossal should not distract from the liturgy. The seats for the minister should also be located so that they do not compete visually with the more liturgical centers unless used as such.

### Sermon

The pulpit is a place designed specifically for the preaching and reading of the word of God. This does not exclude the possibility that in some instances this function may take place elsewhere in the room.

The location of the pulpit affects the relationship between the sermon and the congregation. The minister must be able to see the congregation, and the congregation must be able to hear and see the minister.

Listening to a sermon is a corporate activity. The minister must be aware of the response of the congregation to the sermon even though the response is unspoken. Conversely, the congregation needs to see the minister. They need to see the minister's facial expressions and gestures. This can be achieved by elevating the pulpit, so that even those seated in back of the room can see the minister.

The rapport between the minister and congregation can be destroyed, however, if the pulpit is raised too high or if it is located at too great a distance from the congregation. If raised too high, the viewing angle becomes oppressive for those seated nearby. If placed too far from the congregation, the contact between the minister and the people is lessened.

### Choir

The function of the choir is to lead congregational singing (hymns), to sing to the congregation (anthem), and to sing on behalf of the congregation (choral responses). In addition, many choirs offer sacred concerts on special occasions. The choir should be located so as to best fulfill these functions.

The choir should *not* be placed behind the pulpit or table facing the congregation or in divided choir stalls in a deep chancel where they may be a visual distraction during the service. Their task is to lead worship, not to be performers of musical acts.

The organ console should be located so that the organist can direct the choir. The organ chambers should be located so that the organist may balance the music of the organ and choir. The director should be easily seen by the choir without being conspicuous to the congregation.

Space should be allowed in the design of the worship room for the use of instruments or unusually large choir groups on special occasions. If chairs instead of pews are used in the choir loft, this space may then be used for the placement of musical instruments.

### Congregational Space

The worshipping assembly should be situated so as to suggest their active role as participants in worship. Worship is a corporate activity. It involves the minister, the choir, and the congregation. It does not represent a performer-spectator relationship. The size, shape, and arrangement of the room should emphasize the understanding that worship involves the entire congregation in the service (Fig. 3). This can be achieved by bringing the congregation closer to the liturgical center and by planning for a level floor. Conversely, long, narrow rooms which place a large number of the congregation at a great distance from the minister and rooms which have sloping floors and balconies which emphasize the spectator-performer relationship should be avoided.

In order to provide as much flexibility as possible in adjusting the seating for different occasions, services, numbers of worshipers, and future trends, chairs are recommended instead of pews. The chairs should be comfortable, attractive, durable, and reasonable in cost. They should be firmly linked together when in use and designed to be stacked when not in use.

Chairs are recommended for the following reasons:

- For some services, such as those which emphasize preaching, there may be advantages in eliminating the center aisle so that the congregation sits together as one group, further emphasizing the corporate aspects of worship.
- For those occasions when the attendance is lower, the number of seats may be reduced, the aisles may be made wider, and the spacing of the seats and rows increased.
- For some communion services the church may desire to place the communion table in the congregational seating space with the people grouped around the table.
- The church may desire to use the sanctuary for youth or adult church school classes. Chairs would allow several groups to meet and arrange their seats in a circle or small group.

Different functions require aisles of varying widths. For a choir or offertory processional, a 5-foot aisle is usually sufficient. A wedding processional could use a 6-foot aisle, and a funeral processional needs a 7-foot aisle (see Fig. 4).

### Order of Worship

The normal service for most churches places emphasis on the spoken word: invocation, prayers, reading of the scriptures, responsive reading, affirmations, sermon, and benediction. The worship room should be designed to provide the best possible acoustical environment for these functions. It is imperative that the minister be able to communicate directly with the congregation without having to resort to artificial aids such as a public address system. The size and shape of the room and the materials employed should contribute to the effectiveness of the spoken word.

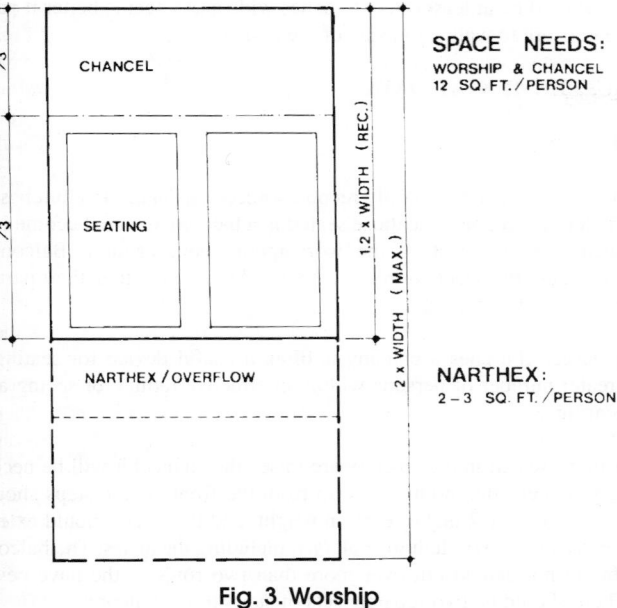

SPACE NEEDS:
WORSHIP & CHANCEL
12 SQ. FT./PERSON

NARTHEX:
2–3 SQ. FT./PERSON

**Fig. 3. Worship**

### Order for the Administration of the Sacrament of Baptism

The baptismal font should be located so that it is convenient for all to see. The ceremony should be visible to the entire congregation. The candidates should be able to approach the font if baptism by pouring is desired, and there should be sufficient space for the minister, parents, and sponsors. The basin should be sufficiently large to make pouring possible (no less than 15 inches in diameter), and the use of water should be visible and audible. The font should be of sufficient size and prominence to remind people of their baptism and to suggest the importance of this sacrament.

### Order for Confirmation and Reception into the Church

The service should take place in view of the entire congregation. It might be helpful if the candidates step up into the raised chancel area so that they may be easily seen when they stand or kneel. There should be sufficient space for a considerable number of candidates to kneel, only one row deep, and space for the minister to conveniently lay his hands upon their heads while they kneel.

### Order for the Administration of the Sacrament of the Lord's Supper or Holy Communion

Traditionally, United Methodists have served the elements to those who kneel at the communion rail. Because of the time this method may consume if individual table dismissals are considered necessary, many large churches serve the elements to those seated in the nave.

Both methods will probably be continued, and in addition it may also be possible to consider serving communion to those who stand around the table. Apparently this was one of the methods used by the early church.

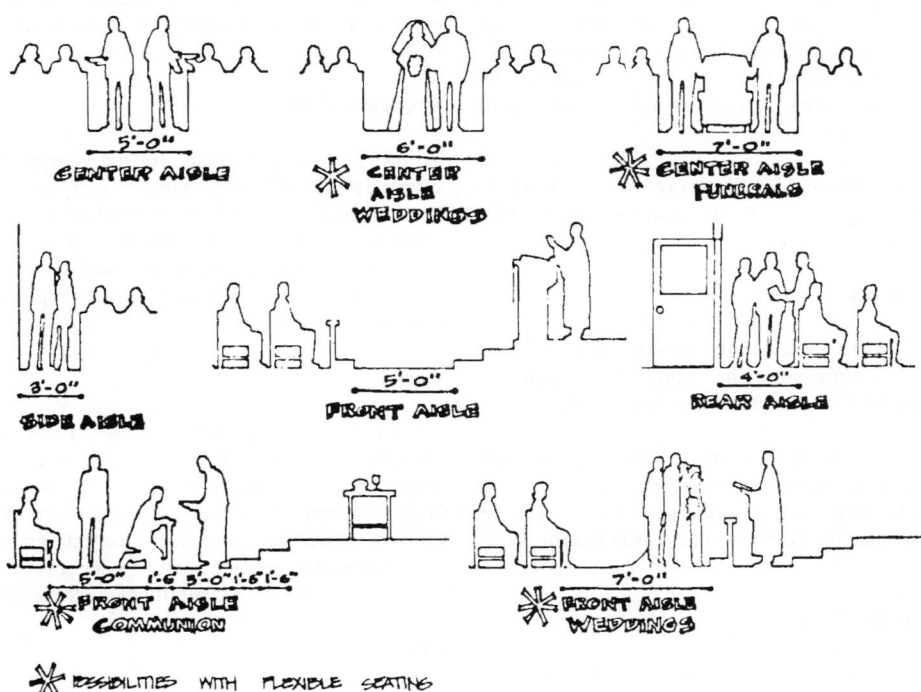

**ig. 4. Aisle widths in the sanctuary: the minimum recommended sanctuary aisle widths needed for the various liturgies**

If communion is to be served to those who stand around the table, a rail is no longer needed. In this case the table should be easily accessible to the congregation, and there must be sufficient space around the table for the minister and assistants as well as a large number of communicants. The entire congregation should be accommodated in at least 10 tables and 5 would be a better goal, either standing or at a rail.

The communion rail was originally designed to protect the table from profane and irreverent treatment. It now serves as a rail for support while people are kneeling and to hold the empty cups. It should no longer be designed as a barrier to prevent one from entering a "holy of holies."

The architectural solution should not determine whether the elements will be offered in the chancel or in the nave seats. The church should decide how the service is to be conducted. The architectural plan should be a result of efforts to provide a meaningful setting for the liturgy.

Ideally, the room should be designed to accommodate both methods of serving communion. This will allow communion to be served in the pews now, if this be the wish of the church, and yet it will permit others to conduct the service in the chancel if this be their desire.

The Commission on Worship of the United Methodist Church does not recommend self-service communion. With this method, the elements are placed at the rail before the start of the service and each person serves himself.

The communion table provides a surface for the placement of the communion elements. It is essentially a table. The size of the table should be scaled to the person or persons involved and the liturgical action about it.

The table should be free-standing so that the minister may stand behind the table and face the congregation for parts of the service. The table may also be used to receive the offering and provide a place for a small, portable book rest. If the table is movable, it can be relocated when not in use for a communion service, or to facilitate another form of worship service.

It is often desirable to provide a small table or credence shelf to hold flowers, empty offering plates, the communion cloth, lids, or other items while not being used.

### Order for the Service of Marriage

The aisle leading to the chancel should be of ample width (6 to 7 feet) for the procession of the wedding party. There should be a way to signal the organist when the bride is ready to make her entrance.

There should be sufficient space at the front cross aisle for the wedding party. If the ceremony takes place on the raised chancel area, the wedding party will not block the congregation's view of the couple. There should be provision for the couple to kneel after the ring ceremony.

### Order for the Burial of the Dead

There should be sufficient space for carrying the casket from the front door of the church with a minimum number of stairs and slopes. The doors should be sufficiently wide. The aisle leading to the chan-

cel should be at least 6 feet 6 inches wide and 7 feet is better if pall bearers are to walk alongside of the casket.

## SUPPLEMENTAL DATA

### Balcony

Balconies are not generally recommended, especially in churches of moderate size, because those seated in a balcony tend to become isolated from the rest of the worshipping congregation. Balconies emphasize the spectator role of the worshiper rather than their participation in the service.

In larger churches a balcony is often a useful device for seating greater number of persons within an effective radius for seeing and hearing.

If those seated in the balcony are to see the chancel it will be necessary to step succeeding rows up from the front. These steps should not exceed 6 1/2 inches each in height, and the risers should extend across the full width of the balcony, including the aisles. The balcony should not extend out over more than two rows of the nave pews. There should be two separate sets of stairs to the balcony.

### Candles

If the communion table is to be free-standing, the candles could be placed on a credence shelf on the rear wall of the chancel, behind the table; but large candles standing free on the floor might be more in scale with the chancel. Candle splicers or joiners may be used, so that only the top part of the candle is burned and replaced when necessary.

### Chancel Rail

There is a trend today to modify or eliminate the chancel rail in order to reduce or eliminate the effect of separation between nave and chancel. Its height is usually the same as the choir screen, approximately 36 inches.

### Credence Shelf

To provide a definite place for the candles, flowers, and/or empty offering plates, etc., we suggest an adaptation of the ancient credence shelf in the chancel. This shelf could be placed on the wall behind the communion table, and it should be large enough to accommodate the above pieces and high enough so that they can be seen by the congregation. The credence shelf does not replace the communion table, but is an addition to it.

### Cross

As late as 1920 the cross was unheard of in nearly all Protestant churches in America, but in a generation it came back into almost general use. The problem today is not *whether* there should be a cross, but rather how many and what size. No church should have more than two crosses—one on the exterior and one in the chancel. The tendency to treat the cross as a decorative symbol to be used with abandon throughout the building is regrettable.

### Flags

It is not recommended to place flags in the chancel for the following reasons:

Flags in the chancel create separate and static centers of interest in competition with the action of the liturgy and such essential physical centers as the cross, table, and pulpit.

Aesthetically, the colors of the flag often clash with the liturgical colors of the paraments and the chancel itself.

## Hymn Boards

Hymn boards have been used to indicate to the congregation the numbers of hymns to be sung and the responsive reading for the day. Since nearly all churches now use a printed bulletin to give this information, hymn boards may no longer necessary. They cost money, and like the flags, create unnecessary centers of interest.

## Lectern

The pulpit, table, and font are all that is needed for worship in most of our churches. There are times, however, when it may be advantageous to have a small portable lectern. Some ministers prefer to reserve the pulpit for preaching only, and use the lectern for the reading of the Scriptures, etc. This leaves the pulpit bookstand free of a large pulpit Bible, more easily usable for sermon notes or manuscript. Announcements and addresses or talks other than sermons are delivered from the lectern. Also if more than one minister is involved in the service, an additional place from which to speak or conduct the service may be helpful.

## Offering Plates

Apparently there are two basic ways of receiving the offering. In most cases the offering plates are in the chancel and the minister hands them to the ushers who come forward to receive them. In other churches the empty offering plates are kept at the rear of the room and are brought forward by the ushers, only after the offering is taken. In any case, empty offering plates should never be placed on the table. After the offering has been received, the minister or ushers places the plates upon the table. If the empty plates are kept in the chancel we suggest that they be placed on the credence shelf, or on a small table provided for that purpose.

## Organ Grille

If the organ pipes are located prominently on the chancel wall (so that they would become the visual center of interest if left exposed), we recommend that the pipes be screened from view by an organ grille. The screening material should be acoustically transparent. If an electronic organ is used, the grille will conceal the speakers and other electronic equipment. Exposed pipes are acceptable on side walls or at the rear.

## Pews

If pews are used, provide for a center aisle and two sections of pews. Local building codes may specify the width of aisles and the seating space per person. We recommend side aisles in all but the smallest churches so as to provide direct access to both ends of the pews. On special occasions when additional seating space is needed, a row of chairs can be placed in the side or cross aisles, providing the local fire regulations are not violated.

Unless local ordinances require otherwise, allow a maximum of 14 persons per pew when both ends open out onto an aisle, and a maximum of 7 persons per pew when there is access to only one aisle. For pews to seat up to 8 persons, the minimum pew spacing is 32 inches back-of-pew to back-of-pew. For pews to seat 9, 10, or 11 persons, allow 33 inches and for 12, 13, or 14 persons per pew, allow a minimum spacing of 34 inches.

| | |
|---|---|
| Width of seat per person: | 18 inches minimum |
| | 20 inches good |
| | 22 inches excellent |
| Spacing of rows of pews: | 32 inches minimum |
| | 34 inches good |
| | 36 inches excellent |
| Spacing of screen in front of first pew: | 36 inches minimum |
| | 38 inches good |
| | 40 inches excellent |
| Height of seat above floor: | 17 inches |

## Aisles

| | |
|---|---|
| Center aisle minimum requirements: | 4 feet small church |
| | 5 feet medium church |
| | 6 feet large church |
| Side aisle minimum requirements: | 2 feet-6 inches small church |
| | 3 feet-6 inches medium church |
| | 4 feet-6 inches large church |
| Front cross aisle minimum requirements: | 5 feet small church |
| | 6 feet medium church |
| | 7 feet large church |
| Rear cross aisle minimum requirements: | 4 feet small church |
| | 5 feet medium church |
| | 6 feet large church |

## Prayer Desk

A prayer desk (prie-dieu) provides a place for the minister to kneel. Since it is portable, it may be placed in front of the clergy seat or out in the chancel in front of the table. Here it is sometimes used for the wedding service. It should not compete with the more important liturgical centers.

## Predella

The predella is a raised floor area or platform beneath the communion table. It is usually 6 inches or so higher than the rest of the chancel floor. Its function is to elevate the table so that it can be seen by the entire worshiping congregation. Many planners forget that virtually everything below head height (approximately 48 inches) will be masked from view by the heads and shoulders of people seated in the first few pews in the nave.

There should be a minimum of 36 inches and preferably 42 inches between the edge of the table and the edge of the predella. In larger churches 48 inches is desirable. This allows ample space for the officiating minister to present the offering or administer holy communion.

The steps leading up to the predella and/or chancel should be broad, 14 to 18 inches in width, with 6-inch risers.

### Reredos and Dossal

The reredos is a vertical screen of wood or carved stone in back of the altar, usually ornate in design and intended to enhance the appearance and focal importance of the altar. The reredos developed in the Middle Ages as a successor to the ciborium when the altar was moved to the rear wall of the chancel.

Since we recommend a free-standing communion table, not an altar, the reredos becomes a distraction and an unnecessary item of expense.

The dossal is a fabric hanging on the wall in back of the altar or table. Like the reredos, its purpose is to give visual prominence to the worship center and its appointments. In fact, it is in fabric what the reredos is in carving.

The main disadvantage of a dossal (beside the danger of drawing attention to itself) is that it creates a large sound-absorbing surface in an area where you would normally want a hard surface to reflect sound out into the nave. We do not recommend its use.

## FELLOWSHIP HALL

The fellowship hall needs to be sized to accommodate the average attendance for social functions and not oversized based on unrealistic expectations for growth. The space needed for dining should be calculated at 12 square feet per person for rectangular tables, with family-style meals. For table service–style meals using round tables, more area is needed per person. Use 12 to 15 square feet per person.

The kitchen size is a function of the fellowship hall and the quantity and style of cooking. Smaller churches without daytime feeding programs may be well served with a residential style kitchen sized at about 20 percent of the floor area of the fellowship hall. Larger churches, or churches with feeding programs, will probably require commercially equipped kitchens, with all the attendant fire-safety precautions. Kitchen floor area will be at least 25 percent of the fellowship hall and could grow to as much as 50 percent, depending on the amount of meals served. If the congregation normally does not prepare meals at the church, then the kitchen design should place emphasis on warming food with ovens and microwaves. If meals are normally prepared at the church, then there is a need for more cooking surfaces, refrigeration, and preparation areas. Both styles require ample storage for dry foods, plates, flatware, cooking utensils, pots, pans, etc.

A well designed fellowship hall can be subdividable and used for education, small group meetings, or other activities. Figure 5 illustrates this point. When using folding walls or movable panel partitions to subdivide a fellowship hall, evaluate acoustical separation in relationship to cost. Panel wall systems provide far better acoustical isolation than accordion partitions. In either event, plan pockets to receive the folded panels to avoid their intrusion on the space when opened for large assembly purposes.

## UTILITY, SIMPLICITY, FLEXIBILITY, AND INTIMACY

*Reference:* Professor James F. White in paper prepared for the Commission on Worship, Dallas, Texas.
*Reviewer:* Douglas R. Hoffman, AIA

In planning buildings designed to meet the needs of present and future generations, it is questionable whether we should continue to treat worship as something apart from the rest of life requiring a special place for this sole purpose. This approach presumes that all other activities are secular in nature and must take place elsewhere. In practice this has led to the building of one room for worship and other rooms for education, fellowship, or community services.

The early Christian church apparently made no such distinction. Homes were used for formal rites as well as a full range of domestic activities. A church building is essentially a house to permit the Lord's people to gather for worship and witness. The building itself is neither sacred nor holy. It is only the relationship between people that can be considered in these terms.

In addition to the more important question of what activities may take place within the church, the demand for adequate facilities for both new and old congregations in the inner city as well as in suburban and rural areas places a heavy burden on funds available for building. In many instances it would be better to invest financial resources in program and additional trained personnel rather than continue to build single purpose structures.

The Commission on Worship suggested that churches be planned around the following axioms:

*Utility:* A church should be designed for the several types of worship which will be used.

*Simplicity:* Concentrate on the essentials and eliminate the superfluous.

*Flexibility:* A church should be adaptable for many different services and occasions.

*Intimacy:* Our buildings should foster a sense of oneness in the doing of our work.

The sketches in Fig. 6 illustrate ways of accomplishing these goals. Apparently maximum use can be made of a rectangular room with level floor. Not shown in the sketches are such facilities as narthex, gathering area, sacristy, organ space, choir room, kitchen, or storage areas which would normally be needed. The size and location of these spaces would vary with each architectural solution. To change the character or atmosphere of the room, movable wall panels, light cloth hangings, or other devices might be used. The following abbreviations are used:

T = Communion table
P = Pulpit
L = Lectern
F = Baptismal font

A. Formal Worship
All furnishings are portable with the possible exception of the organ console. The emphasis is upon the pulpit, table, and font. The nave seats 240 and the choir from 21 to 24.

B. Baptism
The pastor and the one being baptized would stand on the level of the chancel platform so the ceremony could be seen by the congregation. The parents and sponsors would stand before the font on the nave floor.

C. Communion
Communion is served by the pastor to the congregation as they stand around the table. The center aisle has been eliminated and the rows of chairs placed 42 inches apart allowing 20 inches per person.

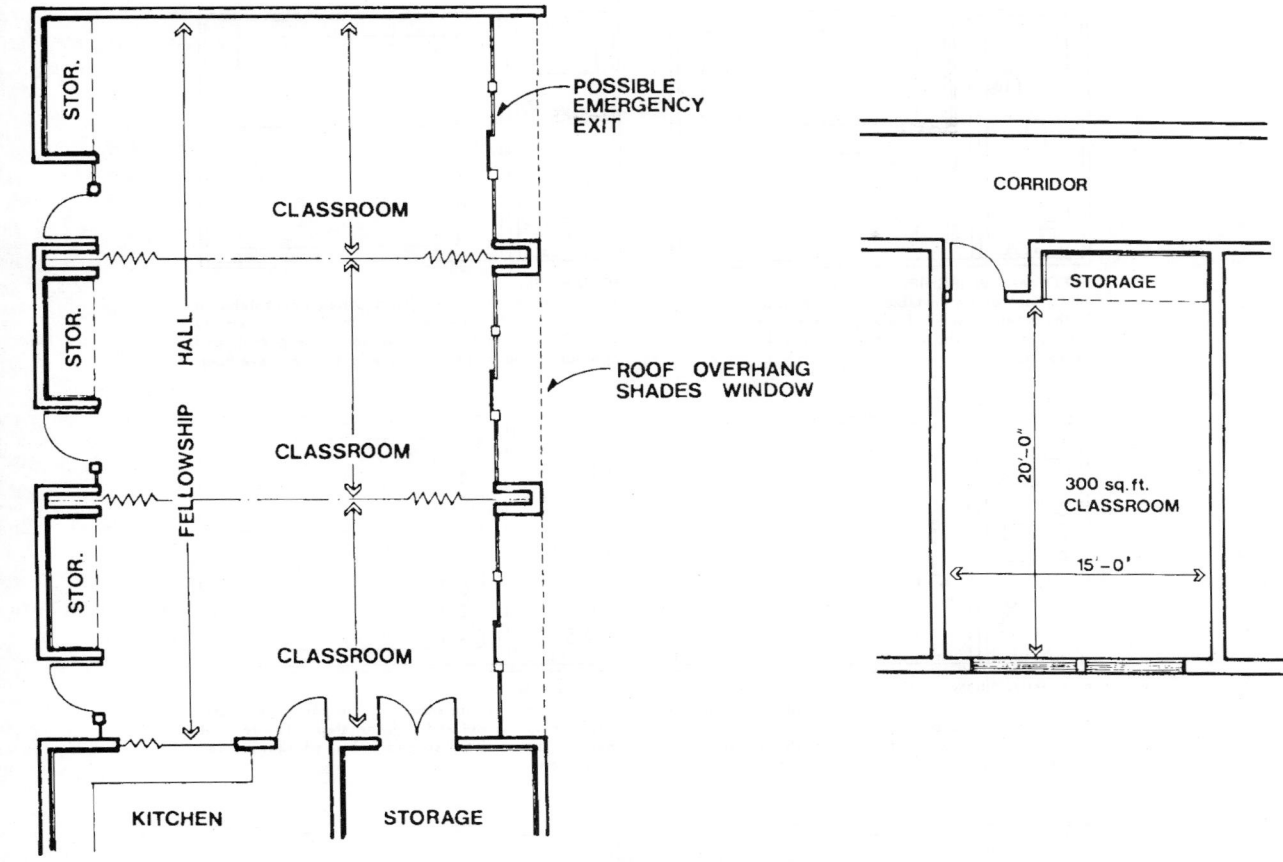

**Fig. 5. Fellowship/classrooms**

D. Communion

The communicants are served by the pastor at a portable communion rail and kneeling step. The rows of chairs in the nave are spaced 32 inches apart, allowing 18 inches per person.

E. Communion

The communion table has been moved down into the nave with the congregation grouped around it. The pulpit has been moved to the center of the chancel platform. Communion could be served standing or the portable rail and kneeling step could be used for kneeling.

F. Wedding

The width of the center aisle has been increased from 5 feet to 7 feet and the width of the front cross aisle increased to allow adequate space for the bridal party and pastor. A prayer desk or prie dieu is used for kneeling. This plan seats 98 although the capacity could be increased.

G. Funeral

The width of the center aisle has been increased to 7 feet to allow the pallbearers to bring in the casket. The actual seating capacity would depend upon the need. The normal practice is to place the casket as indicated, perpendicular to the table.

H. Reception of Members

Those being received in membership are shown at the communion rail. The same arrangement would serve a confirmation service where kneeling is required.

I. Evangelistic Meeting

The congregation has been grouped together in front of the pulpit, which has been placed in the center of the chancel. The choir is grouped in back of the pulpit. The communion table and rail are forward of the pulpit.

J. Choir Program

The choir is grouped together on the platform facing the choir leader and congregation. Special choir programs (cantatas, oratorios, etc.) are popular in many parts of the country. There is considerable freedom in these plans in providing space for instrumentalists near the choir.

K. Concert

Ample space is available in this arrangement for large musical instruments and a piano on the platform.

L. Drama

The chancel platform serves as a stage for drama, interpretative dancing, church school pageants, etc. In this illustration, the organ console is screened from view.

M. Drama

The acting area is in the center of the nave and the chancel is used for seating. This is similar to theater-in-the-round productions.

N. Group Singing

For community or group singing the congregation is grouped around the piano and a song leader.

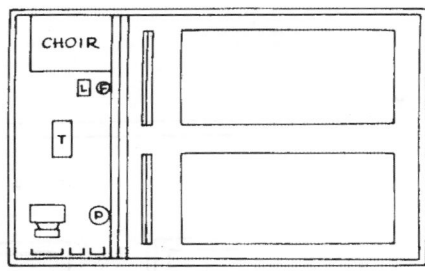

**A. FORMAL WORSHIP**
All furnishings are portable with the possible exception of the organ console. The emphasis is upon the pulpit, table and font. The nave seats 240 and the choir from **21 to 24.**

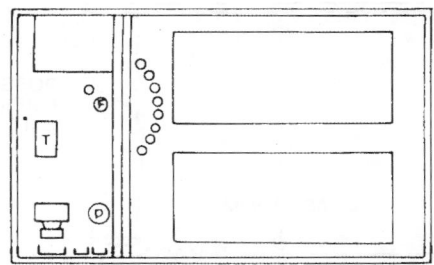

**B. BAPTISM**
The pastor and the one being baptized would stand on the level of the chancel platform so the ceremony could be seen by the congregation. The parents and **sponsors would stand before the font on the nave floor.**

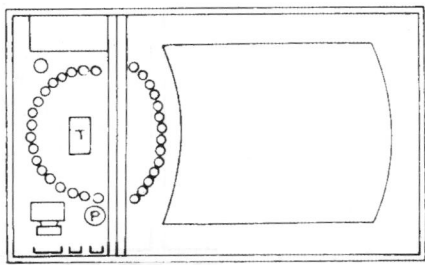

**C. COMMUNION**
Communion is served by the pastor to the congregation as they stand around the table. The center aisle has been eliminated and the rows of chairs placed 42" **apart allowing 20" per person.**

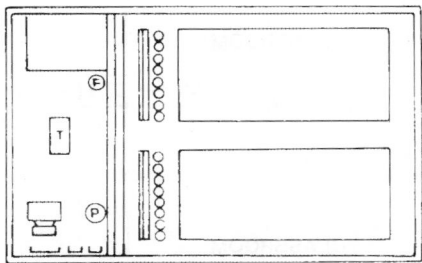

**D. COMMUNION**
The communicants are served by the pastor at a portable communion rail and kneeling step. The rows of chairs in the nave are spaced 32" apart allowing 18" **per person.**

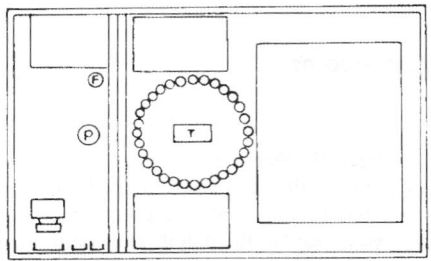

**E. COMMUNION**
The communion table has been moved down into the nave with the congregation grouped around it. The pulpit has been moved to the center of the chancel platform. Communion could be served standing or the portable rail and kneeling step could be used for **kneeling.**

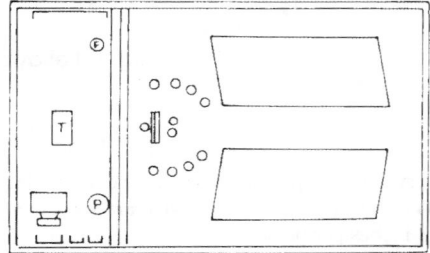

**F. WEDDING**
The width of the center aisle has been increased from 5' to 7' and the width of the front cross aisle increased to allow adequate space for the bridal party and pastor. A prayer desk or prie-dieu is used for kneeling. This plan seats 98 although the capacity could be in-**creased.**

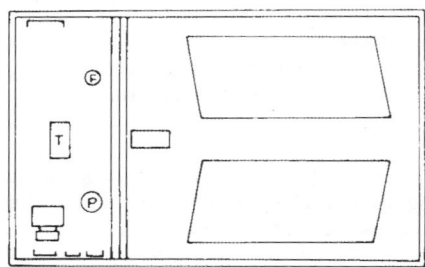

**G. FUNERAL**
The width of the center aisle has been increased to 7' to allow the pallbearers to bring in the casket. The actual seating capacity would depend upon the need. The normal practice is to place the casket as indicated, **perpendicular to the table.**

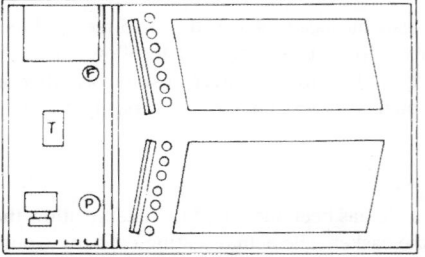

**H. RECEPTION OF MEMBERS**
Those being received in membership are shown at the communion rail. The same arrangement would serve a confirmation service where kneeling is required.

**Fig. 6.**

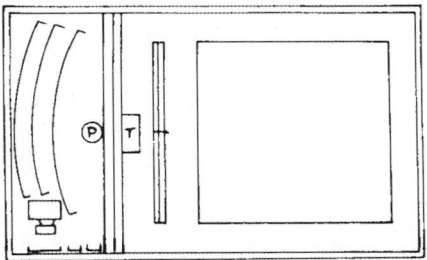

**I. EVANGELISTIC MEETING**
The congregation has been grouped together in front of the pulpit, which has been placed in the center of the chancel. The choir is grouped in back of the pulpit. The communion table and rail are forward of the pulpit.

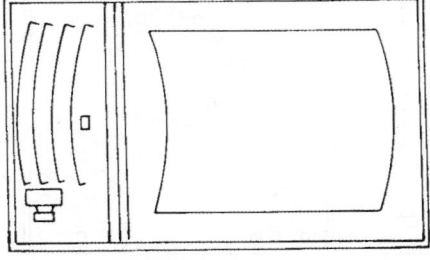

**J. CHOIR PROGRAM**
The choir is grouped together on the platform facing the choir leader and congregation. Special choir programs (cantatas, oratorios, etc.) are popular in many parts of the country. There is considerable freedom in these plans in providing space for instrumentalists near the choir.

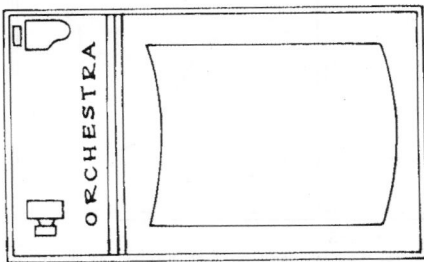

**K. CONCERT**
Ample space is available in this arrangement for large musical instruments and a piano on the platform.

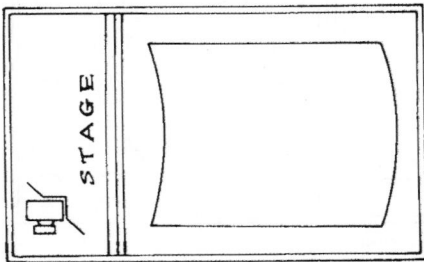

**L. DRAMA**
The chancel platform serves as a stage for drama, interpretative dancing, church school pageants, etc. In this illustration, the organ console is screened from view.

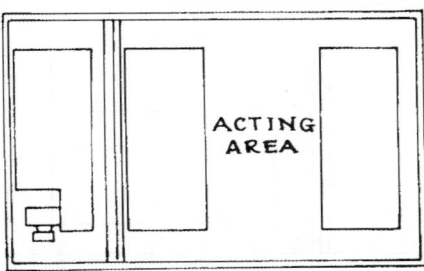

**M. DRAMA**
The acting area is in the center of the nave and the chancel is used for seating. This is similar to theatre-in-the-round productions.

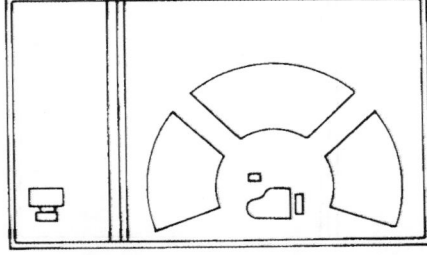

**N. GROUP SINGING**
For community or groups singing the congregation is grouped around the piano and the song leader.

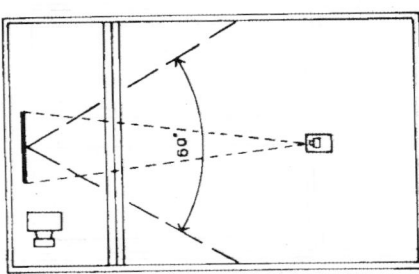

**O. AUDIO-VISUAL**
The screen is located on the platform so that the majority of the audience would be within the recommended 60° viewing angle. Beyond this angle the picture becomes distorted.

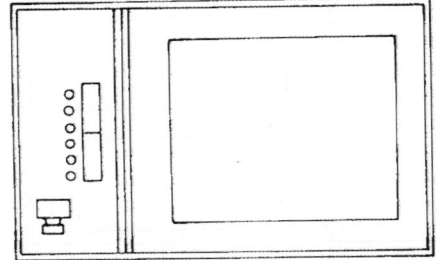

**P. MEETINGS**
In this illustration two tables have been placed in the center of the platform with the leaders seated behind the tables. This could be used for debates, lectures or church or community meetings.

**Fig. 6. (cont.)**

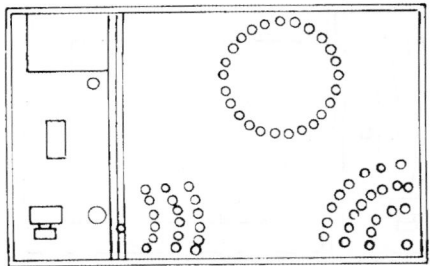

**Q CHURCH SCHOOL**
Three classes for youth or adults are shown in different parts of the room. We are assuming that separate classes would be provided for children.

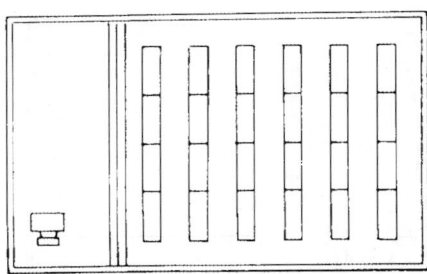

**R. DINING**
Using standard size tables (30" x 96") the room would accommodate 192 persons allowing 8 persons per table. The 15' x 40' platform could serve for the speaker's table, additional tables or for a program.

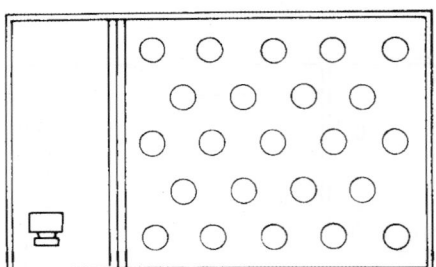

**S. DINING**
Round tables encourage a greater sense of fellowship since all persons are within conversation range of each other. This arrangement around 48" diameter tables seats 138 at 6 persons per table, or 184 at 8 persons per table.

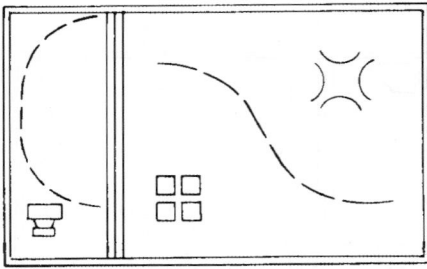

**T. DISPLAYS**
The room is arranged for such displays as paintings, sculpture, book exhibits, schools of mission displays, church school exhibits or any other type of exhibition which requires space for large numbers of people and ample viewing areas. The arrangement is planned to encourage the flow of traffic through the exhibitions.

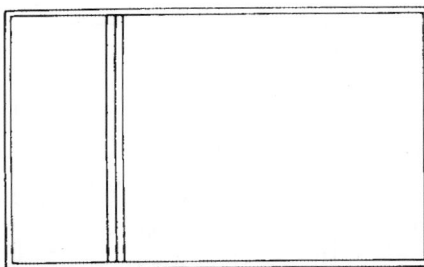

**U. GROUP ACTIVITIES**
If all the furniture in the rooms were movable, the entire area could be cleared for group activities. This would require ample nearby storage space for all furniture.

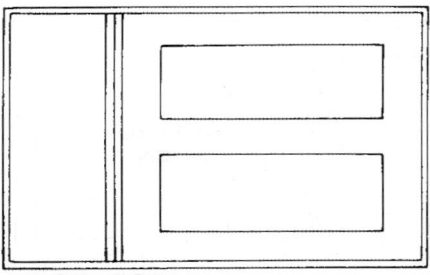

**V. MINIMUM SEATING**
The use of chairs allows the church to set up seats for the anticipated attendance. For each of these arrangements the room would appear to be full. (12 rows of chairs, 24" per person, 36" per row, seats 144).

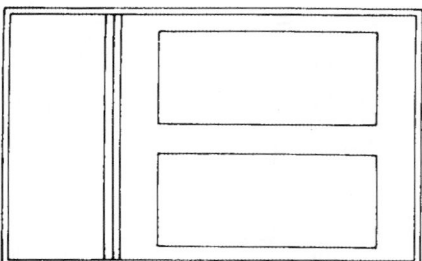

**Y. AVERAGE SEATING**
By reducing the spacing between chairs and between rows and by reducing the width of aisles, the room would seat 234 persons. (13 rows of chairs, 20" per person, 33" per row, seats 234).

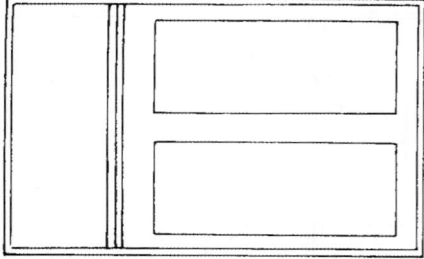

**Z. MAXIMUM SEATING**
For those occasions requiring maximum seating the chairs are placed closer together. This will still allow ample seating space for most individuals. (15 rows of chairs, 18" per person, 32" per row, seats 300).

**Fig. 6. (cont.)**

Audio-Visual

e screen is located on the platform so that the majority of the audi-
e would be within the recommended 60-degree viewing angle.
yond this angle the picture becomes distorted.

Meetings

this illustration two tables have been placed in the center of the
tform with the leaders seated behind the tables. This could be used
debates, lectures, or church or community meetings.

Church School

ree classes for youth or adults are shown in different parts of the
m. We are assuming that separate classes would be provided for
dren.

Dining

ing standard size tables (30 inches by 96 inches), the room would
ommodate 192 persons allowing 8 persons per table. The 15- by
foot platform could serve for the speaker's table, additional
les, or for a program.

Dining

und tables encourage a greater sense of fellowship since all per-
s are within conversation range of each other. This arrangement
und 48-inch-diameter tables seats 138 at 6 persons per table, or
4 at 8 persons per table.

Displays

e room is arranged for such displays as paintings, sculpture, book
ibits, schools of mission displays, church school exhibits, or any
er type of exhibition which requires space for large numbers of
ople and ample viewing areas. The arrangement is planned to
ourage the flow of traffic through the exhibitions.

## U. Group Activities

If all the furniture in the rooms were movable, the entire area could
be cleared for group activities. This would require ample nearby
storage space for all furniture.

## V. Minimum Seating

The use of chairs allows the church to set up seats for the anticipated
attendance. For each of these arrangements the room would appear to
be full (12 rows of chairs, 24 inches per person, 36 inches per row,
seats 144).

## W. Average Seating

By reducing the spacing between chairs and between rows and by
reducing the width of aisles, the room would seat 234 persons (13
rows of chairs, 20 inches per person, 33 inches per row, seats 234).

## X. Maximum Seating

For those occasions requiring maximum seating the chairs are placed
closer together. This will still allow ample seating space for most
individuals (15 rows of chairs, 18 inches per person, 32 inches per
row, seats 300).

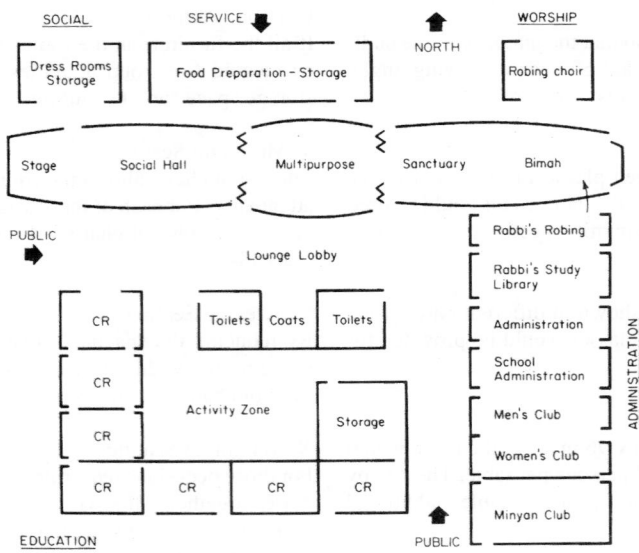

**Fig. 1. Flow diagram**

# TEMPLES AND SYNAGOGUES

### GENERAL

Organized Judaism and the synagogue are found in nearly all of the civilized areas of the world except eastern Asia. Jewish culture, through the ages, has not developed an indigenous architectural style or expression primarily because Jews have been frequently denied social, economic, and educational opportunities, i.e., the owning of property and the establishing of permanent roots. Temple and synagogue designers have, for the most part, emulated regional architecture. Current congregations tend to welcome the best in contemporary architectural design and art work. The architect undertaking a temple or synagogue commission should become familiar with Jewish customs, traditions, art forms, and the magnificent literary expression of the religion.

Religious Judaism in the U.S. today consists of the Orthodox, Conservative, and Reform movements. Each group has readily distinguished ceremonial practices and a divergent approach to programming. Furthermore, within each of the three main divisions there exist considerable variations of viewpoints and practices. Hence, the architect will find it mandatory to collaborate closely with the individual synagogue building, religion, and education committees.

In the U.S., the terms *temple* and *synagogue* are used interchangeably. This text will use the generic terminology *synagogue*.

### Site

If possible, the architect should advise on the selection of a site. Most community zoning and building jurisdictions will permit religious structures within any of their zoned areas. A site location on a secondary street at the approximate center of the congregation neigh-

borhood is desirable. An optimum off-street parking ratio of one c per congregation family is desirable but seldom achieved. It shou be noted that Orthodox congregations prohibit the use of autos public transportation on the Sabbath and hence must be placed close proximity to membership.

### Materials

Since funds are usually limited, the majority of synagogues a designed for conservative initial cost. Construction materials a mechanical equipment should be specified for considerations of pe manence, durability, and low cost of maintenance. The selection better materials and equipment may increase initial cost but c result in considerable long-term maintenance economies.

### Master Plan

Both budget limitations and anticipated congregation growth n mally require a staged program and multiple use of facilities. "ultimate growth" master plan should be designed so that the init and later stages of construction can be readily expanded and int grated into the master plan (final) concept.

### SPACE CRITERIA

Elements shown in Figs. 1 to 3 are those most commonly pr grammed in temple and synagogue buildings.

### WORSHIP AREAS

#### Sanctuary

The sanctuary (Fig. 7) will traditionally, if site use permits, orie with the bema platform to the east. The bema platform height w

*Author:* Keith I. Hibner, AIA
*Reviewer:* Douglas R. Hoffman, AIA

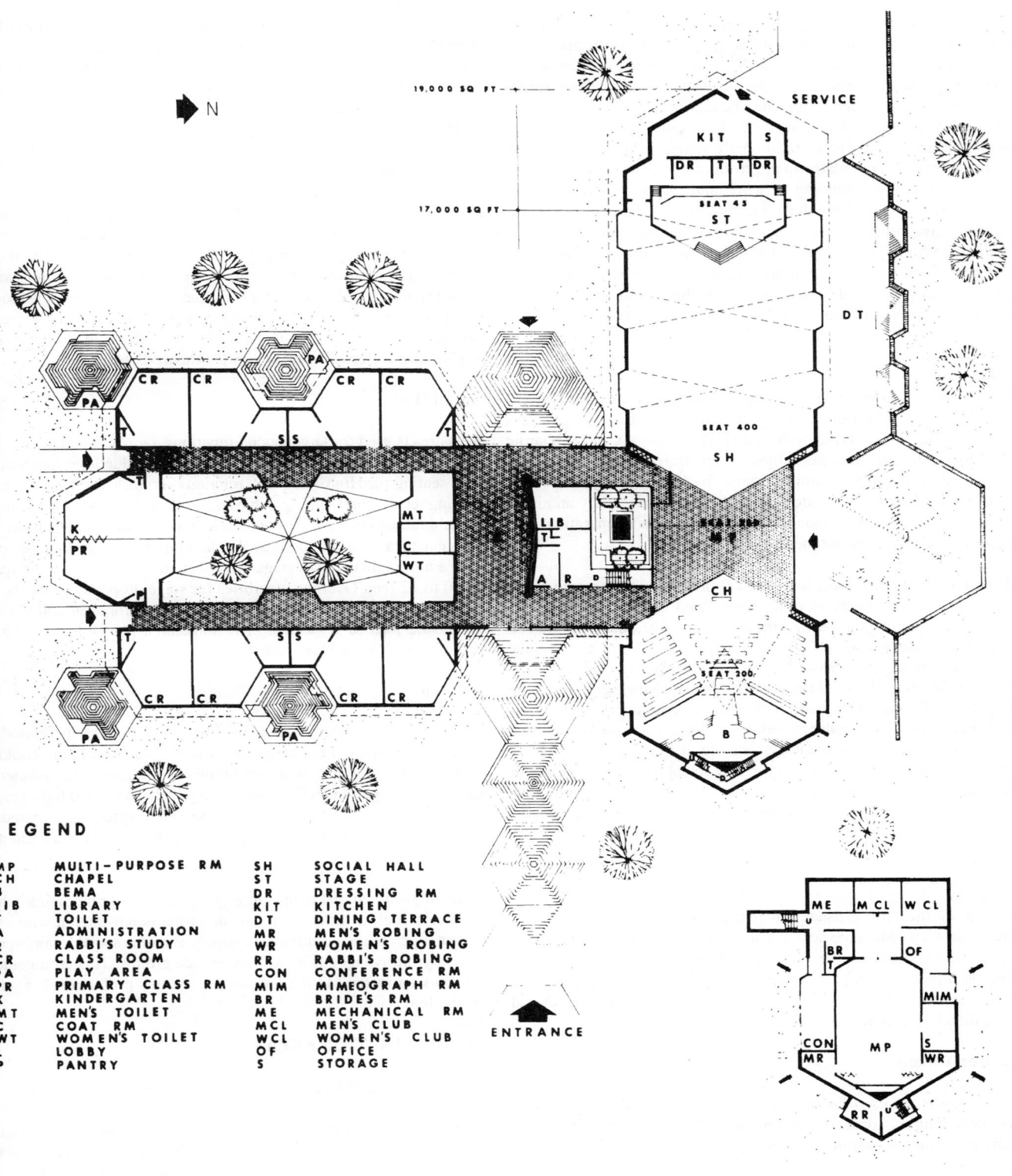

N

SERVICE

19,000 SQ FT

17,000 SQ FT

KIT    S
DR   T   T   DR
SEAT 45
ST

DT

SEAT 400
SH

CR   CR         CR   CR
PA
T                 T
SS

LIB
T
A   R   D

CH

MT
C
WT

SEAT 200
B

K
PR
P

T                 T
SS

CR   CR         CR   CR
PA

## LEGEND

| | | | | |
|---|---|---|---|---|
| MP | MULTI-PURPOSE RM | SH | SOCIAL HALL |
| CH | CHAPEL | ST | STAGE |
| B | BEMA | DR | DRESSING RM |
| LIB | LIBRARY | KIT | KITCHEN |
| T | TOILET | DT | DINING TERRACE |
| A | ADMINISTRATION | MR | MEN'S ROBING |
| ARC | RABBI'S STUDY | WR | WOMEN'S ROBING |
| CR | CLASS ROOM | RR | RABBI'S ROBING |
| PA | PLAY AREA | CON | CONFERENCE RM |
| PR | PRIMARY CLASS RM | MIM | MIMEOGRAPH RM |
| K | KINDERGARTEN | BR | BRIDE'S RM |
| MT | MEN'S TOILET | ME | MECHANICAL RM |
| C | COAT RM | MCL | MEN'S CLUB |
| WT | WOMEN'S TOILET | WCL | WOMEN'S CLUB |
| L | LOBBY | OF | OFFICE |
| P | PANTRY | S | STORAGE |

ENTRANCE

ME   MCL   WCL
BR       OF
MIM
CON
MR      MP      S
RR      WR

LOWER LEVEL

**Fig. 2. Plan for a reform temple (Keith I. Hibner, Architect)**

vary from 24 to 36 inches. Center steps (6-inch rise, 12-inch tread) are normally used. The focal point of the sanctuary is the ark, which is located on the rear wall area of the bema. The ark cabinet houses the congregation's Torah or Scrolls, the written doctrine of the divine rule for Jewish religious life. The ark platform is one or two steps above the bema floor level. Suspended in front of and above the ark is the eternal light, which traditionally remains constantly lighted. Located on the bema platform are reading lecterns for the rabbi and cantor, occasionally standing art work, and chairs for the synagogue officers and trustees. Note that all Orthodox congregations and some Conservative congregations separate the bema area and the cantor's station from the pulpit area and ark. The specific requirements and physical facilities of the religious areas must be thoroughly programmed in the early design stage. The architect should seek advice from the rabbi and the congregation's religious committee.

### Seating Data

Reform and Conservative synagogues commonly use the conventional fan or auditorium seating pattern with the bema platform placed at the front end (preferably east). The Orthodox and Sephardic synagogues traditionally place the bema platform in the center of the U-shaped rectangular seating pattern in the sanctuary. Men and women are seated in separate sections (usually divided by an aisle), and a more Orthodox group will require visual separation also between the men's and women's sections.

The number of permanent seats (pews) provided in the sanctuary is commonly 40 to 50 percent of the anticipated ultimate adult congregation size. A synagogue with 400 to 500 members will provide 200 to 225 permanent seats (10 square feet per person) for the average attendance at weekly services. However, the yearly observance of High Holy Days (Rosh Hashanah, the Jewish New Year; and Yom Kippur, the Day of Atonement) will require maximum seating (of several times more than regular attendance) with direct view to the bema. Hence it is practically mandatory planning that the sanctuary seating area expand into multipurpose areas and social hall areas. Sliding or folding soundproof doors are commonly placed between the religious and social areas. Folding or stacking chairs (6 to 7 square feet per person) are used for the temporary seating requirements.

### Choir

Seating for the choir is usually in an area concealed from direct congregation view. Movable screen partitions are utilized occasionally, so that the choir is visible for various functions such as weddings. The choir members and the organist must have a direct and easy view of the cantor and rabbi. Men's and women's robing rooms should have direct hidden access to the choir seating area or loft.

### Minyan Chapel

Such chapels are used for small groups (10 to 25 male congregants) for daily religious observance. Frequently a multipurpose area will suffice for minyan services where budget does not permit separate facilities.

### EDUCATION

The Hebrew school normally functions in the late afternoon, after the public school sessions. Classes are limited ideally to a maximum of 20 students. Normal public school desk and seating data apply to classroom size. Ample storage and display areas are required. Class-

rooms can also double as meeting rooms for adult game/craft club and education in the evenings. A teenage or secondary social area desirable and should include a small kitchenette facility. Outdoo supervised seminar and play areas are desirable.

### SOCIAL AREAS

### Multipurpose Area

Such a room is desirable when budget and space permit. The area located between the sanctuary and a social hall and will open b means of movable doors to one or both adjoining rooms. The mult purpose room serves for overflow sanctuary seating or for large social functions. Also, the area is frequently used as a smaller soci meeting room (Fig. 6). The multipurpose area acts as an effectiv sound barrier between the chapel and social hall. A small kitchen un for serving coffee and snacks is often incorporated.

### Social Hall

This area is used for larger social functions, i.e., dining, dancing, Ba Mitzvahs and wedding parties, little theater productions, and temp rary seating for High Holy Day religious services. Storage space fc folding chairs and dining tables is a necessity. A permanent c portable stage platform should have a minimum area and facilities fc amateur theatrical productions. If planning a permanent stage, prc vide a minimum depth of stage of 18 feet and a minimum wing spac of 10 to 12 feet. Overhead facilities for stage drop and lights shou be provided. Small dressing rooms and toilets for men and wome should be located backstage. The stage area platform can also b used for High Holy Day seating.

### Kitchen

Requirements for the kitchen facilities vary greatly in individu synagogues. Smaller congregations will program minimum cookin serving areas for use with off-premises catering establishment Larger congregations will require a large self-contained food prepa ration center. The Orthodox and Conservative synagogues manda kosher kitchen facilities with absolute separation between meat an dairy food functions.

It should be noted that many large synagogues will rent their kitche and social hall facilities to an outside professional caterer, who wi in turn, operate the premises and supply food for social affairs spor sored by the synagogue as well as outside groups. This arrangeme provides an income to the temple and assures professional, readil available service.

### ADMINISTRATION AREAS

### Administration Office

An administration office (150 to 170 square feet) should have visu control over the main public entry. Desk and file space is required fc one or two secretaries. The rabbi's study is normally contiguous.

### General Office

A further general office (175 to 200 square feet) is desirable. includes the school administrative area, desks and counter for mai ing and general filing, and storage facilities. A separate but adjacer room is desirable for photocopying, mailing, etc. The school admir

rative portion of this general office should be so located as to have
sual control of the classroom facilities area.

### abbi's Study

room should be provided (175 to 200 square feet) for the rabbi's
sk or work table, plus lounge and seating space for small informal
eetings, and adequate shelf and storage facilities. The rabbi's study
ould have nonpublic access to a robing room and private toilet. It is
ost desirable that the rabbi be able to robe and enter directly to the
ar or side of the bema platform in the sanctuary without walking
rough the sanctuary's public seating aisles.

### brary

room (220 to 250 square feet ) for the housing of religious books is
quired in many programs. The library is frequently used for syna-
gue executive board meetings. Furnishings normally include a table
ating 12 to 16 and informal lounge facilities. The library should
ve access from the rabbi's study and the public lobby.

### Men's Club and Women's (Sisterhood) Club Offices

When required, provide a 120- to 150-square-foot room with desk
and file space and seating for club officer meetings.

## MISCELLANEOUS AREAS

### Bride's Room

This area (120 to 150 square feet) is used for seclusion and final
dressing of a bride prior to a wedding. A private toilet should be provided. It is desirable to locate the bride's room adjacent to a multipurpose room where the bride may receive well-wishers.

### Public Toilets

In a modest budget program, one set of toilet facilities can reasonably
service the school as well as the sanctuary and social areas and hence
should be easily accessible to both. This is possible because educational, religious, and social functions do not normally occur simulta-

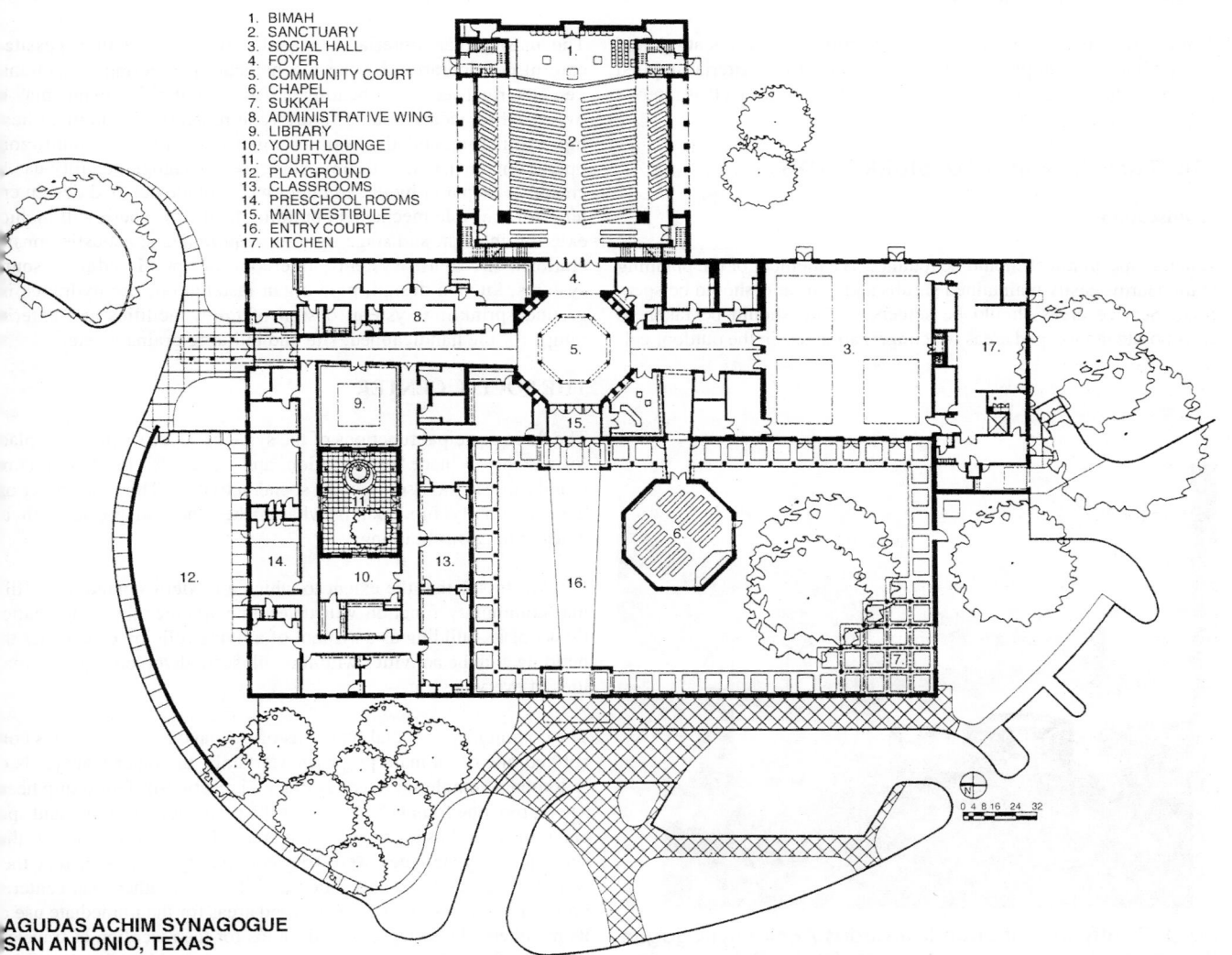

1. BIMAH
2. SANCTUARY
3. SOCIAL HALL
4. FOYER
5. COMMUNITY COURT
6. CHAPEL
7. SUKKAH
8. ADMINISTRATIVE WING
9. LIBRARY
10. YOUTH LOUNGE
11. COURTYARD
12. PLAYGROUND
13. CLASSROOMS
14. PRESCHOOL ROOMS
15. MAIN VESTIBULE
16. ENTRY COURT
17. KITCHEN

AGUDAS ACHIM SYNAGOGUE
SAN ANTONIO, TEXAS

**Fig. 3. Floor Plan, Agudas Achim Synagogue (Finegold Alexander + Associates)**

neously. If budget permits, two separate toilet facilities should be programmed.

### Coat Room

Spaces for coat hanging and shelving should be provided (100 to 150 square feet of floor area is adequate).

### Public Spaces

Lobbies, corridors, and circulation should be designed for direct, easy movement. Large lounge and congregating areas are required for social functions as well as religious recesses (Figs. 4 to 6). Where possible, outdoor courtyards, terraces, and atriums are most desirable.

### Storage Areas

Ample storage space should be provided within the area of the separate synagogue functions (education, social, religious, kitchen, etc.) Provide storage area for the outdoor functions (deck chairs, lawnmowers, landscaping tools, etc.).

### Mechanical Equipment Areas

The location and size of rooms having utility services, heating, and air-conditioning equipment will be determined from criteria supplied by the mechanical engineering consultant. Exterior as well as interior access to these areas is desirable.

## ADDITIONAL DESIGN CONSIDERATIONS

### Landscaping

A landscape architect should be retained as a member of the planning team. Hardy, easily maintained shrubs and plantings should be specified. Service areas should be screened. Care should be taken to incorporate landscaped areas for congregation use in the outdoor cel-

**Fig. 4. Courtyard entrance to Agudas Achim Synagogue (Finegold Alexander + Associates; Photo: Peter Vanderwarker)**

ebration of the festival holidays, i.e., feasts of Shabuoth and Sukkot (Fig. 5).

### Aesthetics—Art Work

Nineteenth-century American synagogues were predominantly routine copies of churches. The six-pointed star (Mogen David) was the distinctive (typical) form of art decoration. Today, however, architects and artists are making significant contributions to Jewish culture by incorporating Jewish religious symbolism in structure and ornament. Ideally, the religious artist will work under the direction of, and collaborate closely with, the architect. The artist should be retained in the preliminary planning stages. The art program will include such items as decorative ark doors, the design of the eternal light, stained glass windows, exterior and interior lettering and sculpture, woodcarvings, weavings, lecterns, choir screens, paintings, mosaics, etc. While Jewish tradition still leans strongly to the omission of the human face or form in the sanctuary and strictly prohibits the depiction of the Deity in any form whatsoever, there has been a decided return to the human and animal form in art work in contemporary buildings.

### Mechanical Design

The master plan criteria of staged construction will necessitate careful consideration by the mechanical engineering consultant, i.e., electrical service or heating and air-conditioning plants may be oversized to accommodate future requirements. Economical heating, ventilating, and air-conditioning design will utilize multi-zone operation consistent with time-staggered synagogue facility use. A checklist prepared by the architect will include detailed design criteria for multiple mechanical building facilities. These will include exterior, interior, and stage lighting requirements; acoustic considerations; fire alarm systems; intercom and public address sound systems; kitchen design; pipe organ installation; fire hydrants; inground sprinkling system; design of toilet facilities and exterior ramps for the handicapped; site and building drainage, etc.

## THE SOCIAL CENTER

The three principal functions of the synagogue are to provide a place for worship, a place for education, and a place for the Jewish community to carry on some of its social activities. The latter function, the community function, is what makes the synagogue such an unusual religious building.

It is fair to say that the extent to which a modern synagogue fulfills that community function will determine whether the congregation thinks of its building as a symbol of a living religion or whether the building and the activities within it will seem divorced from the realities of everyday life.

The community or social functions of a synagogue have always constituted one of its main purposes. Certainly, the outer courtyards of Solomon's Temple served a visiting and meeting-in-fellowship need. There, too, one found chambers for the preparation of food, and special rooms for those with special interests. History also shows us that subsequent synagogues were true community centers in that they were built around a congregation and its needs rather than centered upon a royal priesthood. Even beyond areas for the immediate use of its members, the synagogue had rooms for the reception of travelers who paid for such hospitality many times over with their tales of foreign places and news of the outer world.

**Fig. 5: Sukkah at Agudas Achim Synagogue (Finegold Alexander + Associates; Photo: Peter Vanderwarker)**

So the importance of the synagogue as a community center is not a recent development; only its ways of serving the community are modified; the purposes remain unchanged. The basic need is for a place for friendly, social intercourse; a place to discuss common day-to-day problems in the outer world; a place for healthy common activities, for the young folks to meet and to prepare to assume their places in the community; a place to enjoy the company of those with the same interests; and, finally, a place in which, from time to time, one might be stimulated by considerations beyond the immediate horizon.

Today, these fundamental needs are reflected in the increasing complexity of synagogue plans. Spacious corridors, foyers, and lobbies (Fig. 8) have taken the place of the ancient open courtyards. There are club rooms for men, women, and children. There are kitchens for the preparation of food and large spaces for dinners and suppers. There are areas for dances, plays, lectures, concerts, and exhibitions. There are classrooms for adult education as well as craft and hobby

rooms. And there are offices where the organization and direction of these activities can be guided and publicized to ensure their success.

Naturally, there is a tremendous range in the size and extent of the facilities provided depending upon the size and means of each congregation. Few synagogues have a separate space for every function, and the multi-use of space is the rule rather than the exception.

**Corridors and Vestibules**

The most elementary social function is the meeting, greeting, and visiting with follow congregants before and after religious services (Figs. 6 and 8). This requires generously sized corridors, aisles, lobbies, foyer, and vestibules. If these elements are generous in size, they permit friends to pause and talk without obstructing the flow of traffic. For the same reason there should be wide walks outside the building, and a large paved area or courtyard that invites "stopping to

**Fig. 6: Community Court at Agudas Achim Synagogue (Finegold Alexander + Associates; Photo: Peter Vanderwarker)**

chat" without blocking sidewalks. A few feet added to a corridor makes it useful also as an exhibition space and does much to enhance the dignity and serenity of a structure.

**Social Hall**

The social hall is probably the most important community facility. With a kitchen it becomes a banquet hall; adding a stage makes it a theater or lecture hall; removing chairs and tables makes it a dance hall or game room; by means of folding doors it can become overflow space to be merged with an adjoining sanctuary for High Holy Day services.

In determining its size one can estimate its capacity by allowing about 7 square feet per person for seating on folding chairs in rows and about 12 square feet per person for seating people at long tables. Main aisles from the kitchen to dining tables should be at least 5 feet wide and other spaces between tables can be 3 feet wide. Such approximate standards are useful only for preliminary planning, since each room becomes an individual problem that must take into account the position of entrance doors, the kitchen access, stage platform, exits, and so on. Careful attention to seating arrangements is most important in achieving quick, smooth, and efficient service of meals.

The height of the social hall is an architectural consideration. If the room is to be used for games, such as basketball, that may determine its height; if it is to open into the main sanctuary through folding doors, the merger of these two spaces may be a deciding factor.

Sometimes there will be a projection room for movies; but the wide availability of VHS, DVD, and computer-operated video projection makes such an elaborate installation less necessary. If, however, a projection booth is desired, it should be large enough to make possible the use of color and spot lighting of the stage. Phone, intercom and/or buzzer connection to the stage manager is then essential. Even if it is planned for simple A/V projection, a signal system and conduit connections for sound should be provided.

Plays and movies make light control of windows a serious problem. Windows might be eliminated entirely to escape this problem, but a frequent objection to that is that the same space is used for many different purposes and should therefore be capable of reflecting a number of different moods. The answer is that this can be accomplished effectively by several artificial lighting schemes. For example, one could have a down-light only from the ceiling for dances and lectures; light "washed" by wall brackets over ceiling and walls (and no other lights) for dining; and all the light fixtures turned on for games. Many congregations do not allow their social hall to be used for games that are liable to give the room too much wear and tear. If the room is used for games at all, any windows will have to be specially guarded against breakage; and if large windows are used, care must be taken to have them screened on the outside by planting (or have them look out on an enclosed area) to ensure privacy from anyone passing by. So that, by and large, a good case can be made for a windowless social hall. Alternatively, manually or electrically operated black-out shades could be mounted over windows, especially clerestory windows that provide an indirect natural lighting source.

Specific details that must be considered in planning the social hall:

- As in all public buildings, durability is a prime consideration in the choice of building materials. By using natural materials on which any scratches will uncover the same color (and more or less the same texture) as the original surface, one can make sure that a room will last longer and look better for a longer period of time than if one had used synthetic surface materials and unprotected plaster and paint.
- In a room that is to serve so many functions a rather neutral color scheme will make decoration for specific occasions a good deal easier and more effective than a strong initial decorating scheme.
- There should most certainly be some acoustic treatment to quiet the room, and the designer should investigate the acoustic properties of the room for its use as an auditorium.
- If the room has a large seating capacity, artificial ventilation is needed during some of the events that may take place in it.
- Generally speaking, a hardwood floor is recommended for a social hall.
- Among the drawbacks of multipurpose rooms, which must have level floors, are less comfortable sight lines for stage, lecture, and movie purposes.

**Stage**

The stage itself can vary in elaborateness from a temporary platform at one end of a room to a complete professional setup. But in all stage designs there are certain basic principles that must be followed: The first is to augment the playing area (the part visible from the audience) with space at both sides for the exits and entrances of the players, for temporary placing of props and of scenery necessary for other acts, as well as for positions for stage crew and actors awaiting their parts. Experience suggests that the horizontal handling of scenery is preferred for amateur theatricals. "Flying," the hoisting of backdrops and

**Fig. 7: Sanctuary of Agudas Achim Synagogue (Finegold Alexander + Associates; Photo: Peter Vanderwarker)**

unused scenery, is expensive and relatively dangerous to untrained people. The stage floor should be of soft wood to allow for stage screws to brace the scenery.

A most vital element of the stage design is good, flexible lighting. Folding footlights, border lights above, and a method of lighting the entire proscenium from the front, coupled with heavy-duty outlets for spot and floodlights backstage, should all be included.

Dressing rooms are necessary; but sometimes Sabbath school rooms must double for that purpose. Most needed is storage space. Old scenery, props, makeup material, stage braces, and extra lights should all have a space where they can be kept safely. It must be remembered that several different groups will probably make use of the stage—groups of different ages and degrees of responsibility. In such cases some groups should have space to keep their own accessories under lock and key.

No matter how elementary the stage setup, there will, of necessity, be some making of scenery with its attendant painting and mess. In other words, the stage should not be a "finished" space, but a workshop within which one can simulate a variety of environments.

If the auditorium is to be used for many different purposes, chair storage may be found under the stage. Most often the chairs are stacked on carts which can be pushed into position under the stage. This method requires the stage to be about 3½ feet above the floor. Occasionally, one

or two sections of the stage floor can be made removable, but such a provision is not mandatory. Access from outside to the stage area must be considered in relation to the size of the scenery and props that will be used. This access should be convenient to a service drive.

### Kitchen

The layout should not be that of a commercial kitchen. A greater number of people will have to be accommodated; its use will be rather sporadic; and the kitchen help will not be so well trained to work together—which means that they will need more space than would be provided in a commercial kitchen.

The basic scheme for kitchens usually develops from the route waitresses follow in returning from the dining room. The planning sequence is for them immediately to pass a soiled dish station, behind which is the dishwashing equipment, and (if space permits) the dish storage. Next, the waitresses pass the cook's table which is backed up by ranges, ovens, space for meat and vegetable preparation, and storage, including refrigerators. They then pass a cold table where salads are prepared. At this station, ice cream is picked up—if that is the dessert. Next comes the pastry table where milk as a beverage is usually found as well. Finally the waitress passes by the coffee station.

The synagogue kitchen differs here from the usual commercial kitchen: first, all plates are served with the same menu; second, returned plates all come at the same time, but they do not need immediate washing for immediate reuse. This means there may have to be greater stacking area, but the dishwashing equipment may not have to be so elaborate or work so fast. Finally, attention to special requests is at a minimum, and each waitress need merely pick up plates and portions already prepared and waiting. Checking stations and cashiering can be dispensed with under this arrangement.

If at all possible, kitchens should be planned so that the entering traffic moves from the right to the left. The kitchen should be entered and left through vestibules which deaden the noise so that after-dinner activities in the social hall are not disturbed by the sounds of finishing up in the kitchen. Attention must also be paid to ventilating the kitchen, both to prevent odors from permeating the rest of the building and to ensure comfort for the volunteer workers. In smaller kitchen installations, pass-through openings may be used as pickup stations for the waitresses rather than having them file through the kitchen. A similar slot can be located for the return of used dishes.

Here are some additional points to consider in kitchen planning:

- For congregations adhering to the dietary laws, separate dish storage is demanded, as well as separate sinks for washing the double set of plates.
- Since the kitchen will be used by different groups, glass cupboard doors are often specified so that those unfamiliar with the kitchen can more readily find stored articles.
- Cupboards should be planned for utensils, silver, paper cups and napkins, and linen storage.
- Storage space should also be provided for canned goods, soft drinks and other supplies for special events, as well as lockers or clothes closets and toilet facilities for kitchen help.
- Stainless steel equipment, quarry tile or grease-proof mastic floors, tile walls, and acoustic ceilings are recommended.
- The kitchen should be close to a service entrance, which should give access to a screened, walled-in service court large enough to take care of the necessary refuse.

- A telephone in the kitchen is a necessary convenience and should connect with the administration office.
- In addition to the main kitchen, it is not uncommon to find kitchenettes for use at small teas and for the staff to use for their lunches. If a separate kitchenette is not used, a smaller stove for small occasions should augment the main range.

### Parlors and Lounges

A parlor or lounge can serve many purposes. Teas, coffee and cake refreshments, and visiting after evening affairs, club and committee meetings, as well as weddings and receptions need that kind of space. The relation of such a room to the rest of the temple is important.

Open and flexible planning does not conceive of a synagogue plan as a series of cells strung along corridors but as a series of large spaces that flow into each other. They can still be closed off one from the other whenever a desire for privacy or use by smaller groups makes this necessary.

The parlor or lounge should be near the main kitchen or near a kitchenette.

Changeable lighting effects for different purposes make the room more useful; furniture that can be shifted without too much difficulty is similarly desirable. If this room can be designed to open onto a patio, court, or garden, its charm and usefulness will be tremendously enhanced.

### Club Rooms

Economy usually suggests that the same club room should be shared by a number of organizations. If that is so, individual closets, or even storage rooms, which can be locked up to enable each organization to store its own possessions, will give each the sense that its needs were considered in planning the building.

### Craft Rooms

Art studios, photographic dark rooms, woodworking and sewing rooms, and the like are often used by both adults and children, day and night. This raises several problems: there must be storage space for materials and for projects under way; the rooms must be located in such a way that they can be used independently of the rest of the building; furniture suitable for both children and adults must be provided; there should be plenty of steady, clear light; they should have durable wall and floor finishes; they should be sound-conditioned to keep their noise a way from other rooms; and, in some instances, they should have special safety devices to prevent the use of dangerous equipment without adequate supervision.

### Games and Sports

In the small synagogue, the social hall may, on occasion, be used as a game room. As noted above, such necessarily rough usage demands materials and details which are often not desirable when the room is used for more formal occasions. Ping-Pong and less strenuous (and destructive) games are then indicated.

In some cases basement space can be created quite economically and playrooms can then be located at half grade or below.

If a gymnasium is to be included it should be big enough to house a regulation-size basketball court. In addition to the playing floor,

there must be a locker space, shower and drying rooms for both boys and girls, and storage space for equipment. While it is possible to build one gym for boys and another for girls (or to build one large gym that can be divided into two), a single gym used alternately seems more reasonable.

### Publicity Office

The office space of the synagogue must include space for those who organize, schedule, and publicize the community activities. Desk and work-table space, filing space, space for duplicating devices and for envelope stuffing and kindred tasks must all be provided. Often publicity is taken for granted in a small congregation, since it is informally accomplished by word of mouth. With expansion, this situation often changes and organized publicity is needed to get full advantage of the opportunities offered by a new building. In addition to this office space, bulletin boards in key spots, with adequate space for posters and notices and good illumination, are important. Display space for objects created in art, sewing, and craft classes also provide a stimulus for those taking part in such programs as well as encouragement for others to enroll.

### Storage Facilities

Large closets in each room are often of greater value than large storage rooms somewhere else. Desk drawers, table pedestals, chests and cabinets often turn out to be more flexible and cheaper than built-in equipment.

One of the vexing problems created by large community facilities is the disposition of hats and coats. Lockers that can line the corridors

**Fig. 8. Agudas Achim Synagogue (Finegold Alexander + Associates; Photo: Peter Vanderwarker)**

e probably best, though they are expensive. In more modest plans, ook strips and a shelf have proved to be perfectly satisfactory. A checkroom (supplemented by the use of classrooms for peak loads) offers another sensible solution. In classrooms, wardrobes whose oors open in unison have turned out to be usable. Sometimes the oors can have blackboards on their outer faces.

## ommunity Affairs

he section of the synagogue devoted to community affairs should be ocated and its various entrances should be arranged, so that it can be sed independently of the rest of the building when necessary. This eans, incidentally, that the heating and ventilating system can be one-controlled to reduce operating cost. Any intelligent plan will roup together areas of similar use.

as a principle this is obvious. But in practice there are a number of actors that must be remembered. Though the building may be divisole into zones according to function, each zone must have access to oilets. The office area probably should function in relation to each one; and certain classrooms must be considered both as part of the eligious school and as part of the community center. This is especially true of classrooms that may double as dressing rooms for the tage; of the arts and crafts rooms and the camera studio; and of lassrooms that may on occasion double as coat rooms.

There is a natural temptation for a congregation to try to arrive at a ixed plan. Only rarely will we accept the fact that future generaions may discover new needs—and may wish to abandon some activities. The wisest planning will allow for additions and make uture changes easy. This is accomplished best by the elimination of interior bearing walls, by extending corridors to the full length of any wings, and above all, by starting with a site that will allow for healthy growth. For the community functions of the synagogue have grown and changed radically over the past centuries, and there s no reason to believe that this growth and change will not conlinue.

## THE JEWISH EDUCATIONAL CENTER

In planning the educational facilities of a synagogue, several general considerations must be kept in mind from the very start.

Future expansion is one. This can be accomplished in several ways. One is by horizontal extension, i.e., either by increasing the size of the wing of the building or by constructing an additional wing. In this connection it is important to secure sufficient land at the outset so that there will be adequate space for the extension; or else, there should be an agreement whereby adjoining land may be secured when required. Future expansion may also be provided by vertical extension in the form of adding one or more stories.

While horizontal extension is usually more desirable than the vertical (since it reduces walking up and down stairs), it is frequently impossible to acquire the necessary land. In that case future stories can be planned by slight increase in the foundations and other supporting members. The additional cost is negligible compared to the resulting benefits.

The one-story educational unit is undoubtedly the best arrangement. It permits direct access to the exterior for outdoor play, with quick and easy dismissal in case of an emergency. If conditions require more than one story, then stairways must be introduced and there should be a sufficient number of stairs to permit quick exit. Usually, local building codes are very specific about the number and width of stairs required as well as their location, construction, and arrangement.

Children should not be required to walk more than two flights of stairs; therefore, the school should be limited to a three-story building. Only in extreme cases (where horizontal planning is impossible because of high land cost or for other reasons) is it reasonable to build more than three stories—and that only if an elevator is provided. Although elevators can be expensive to install and costly to operate and maintain, their use in religious buildings has dramatically increased since the passage of the Americans with Disabilities Act (ADA) legislation.

Great care should be given to the exposure of the classrooms. For the academic classroom an east or west orientation is desirable. Special rooms like nature study and science should face south. The ideal exposures for the kindergarten or nursery are south and east.

Here are several specific issues that arise in the design of a synagogue school wing:

### Classrooms

The size of the school, and therefore the number of classrooms, depends on the number of pupils expected to attend and also on the type of school. Classrooms for an all-day school will vary slightly in requirements from those for a part-time school. Since finances are of utmost concern to most institutions, the classrooms are frequently planned to accommodate a large number of pupils in order to reduce the number of teachers. But conditions vary from year to year, so that a large room may be wasted if only a small number of pupils will use it. Good education practice, on the other hand, dictates smaller classes for greater efficiency; between these two extremes a happy medium must be selected. A class of 25 students has proved satisfactory in most instances. Since most schools have shown considerable variation in the size of classes for different grades, it is often possible to construct classrooms of varying sizes to accommodate from 20 to 35 students.

The number of children to be provided for will depend largely on the community. A careful survey must be made to determine how many pupils may be expected to attend the school. From that figure the number of classrooms can be arrived at, using the average-size class as a basis. For an all-day school, provision must be made for at least one classroom for each grade in order to permit a full school curriculum.

The actual size of the classroom is based on a minimum of 15 square feet for each child. This figure provides only for the area devoted to seats and aisles; if the educational program calls for activity space, then the room must be based on a larger amount of between 20 and 25 square feet per child.

The advantages of the larger room can readily be understood. With it an air of informality and spaciousness can easily be achieved. From nearly every point of view it permits greater flexibility in use. It pro-

*Authors:* Max B. Schreiber and T. P. Deis
*Reviewer:* Douglas R. Hoffman, AIA
*Reference:* Peter Blake (ed.), *An American Synagogue for Today and Tomorrow*, The Union of American Hebrew Congregations, New York

vides increased flexibility in the arrangement of furniture and class groups; in the accommodation of changing class sizes; in the education program which can be carried out in the classroom; and in the accommodation of adult activities.

On the other hand, the special suitability of the smaller room for the work of small groups and committees should not be overlooked.

**Movable Partitions**

Various types of movable partitions may be used to separate one room or area from another. One type becoming increasingly popular is the wall panel system of separate acoustically treated panels operated manually on an overhead fixed track. A second type is the flexible accordion partitions, which are hinged so that they may be extended to form a wall or folded back out of the way. A third type is a curtain of cloth, reed, or bamboo, operating in or on a fixed track. A fourth type is the movable area separator, which is really a portable screen generally extending to a height of 6 or 7 feet.

**Multiple Use**

Most of the factors mentioned in the two preceding sections, such as the size and flexibility of classrooms, have a direct bearing on the extent to which classrooms can be used for multiple purposes. If there is no large assembly hall or auditorium available, a row of classrooms separated by folding or accordion type doors can quickly and easily be converted into a large assembly, meeting, or banquet hall. A smaller classroom, however, accommodates the smaller group or committee admirably. In this way, both large and small classrooms can serve subsidiary uses such as for meeting, working, and social gathering places.

In the dual use of a room, the selection of the type of furniture is of utmost importance. If a classroom is also to be used as a meeting room for adults, the fixed type of children's desks and seats will be impractical for the adults. It will be necessary to select the upper grade classroom to be used for adult meetings since there the furniture will be of a larger size and more suitable.

For the afternoon type school, a large space must be set aside for the pupils to gather in inclement weather before time for classes; this is required since the classrooms may be occupied by a previous session and the pupils will not be able to go directly to their classes until the previous period is ended. In the all day schools the problem does not generally exist, since the pupils can go directly to their classrooms.

**Kindergarten/Nursery**

A kindergarten and nursery can be a powerful force in attracting younger families to the synagogue who otherwise would be unwilling to leave their small children at home or who could not all attend at the same time. The kindergarten and nursery may well be combined; in fact, there is a worthwhile advantage in this. In the case of families with two or three children in the nursery and kindergarten age group, keeping them all together helps them adjust much more quickly to the new surroundings, cuts down the fears and insecurities which children naturally feel under the circumstances, and makes the work of the adult attendant much easier.

This kindergarten area should be well soundproofed. Consequently, a movable partition separating this room from another might be inadvisable.

The room should have adequate tackboard area for mounting large colorful posters and displays. For the smallest children, and for those who become sleepy, the necessary number of cots should be provided.

It is important that the kindergarten and nursery be large and roomy. Children of the age to be accommodated here often play on the floor and delight in active games. These demand generous space. Adequate room is needed for the storage of toys, materials, and other play equipment. From a health point of view, congestion in this space particularly ought to be avoided because it encourages the spread of disease. In general, it can be said that an air of attractiveness and commodiousness in the nursery and kindergarten area will return worthwhile dividends in increased family attendance and participation in all the activities of the synagogue.

In order to provide as much sunlight as possible, the kindergarten room should face south and east. The ideal location is on the first floor to avoid steps and also to provide easy access to an outdoor playground, which is of utmost importance to this kind of a class. The area of this room should be based on 30 square feet per child and the class should be limited to a maximum of 20 children.

Window areas should be generous—the more light the better. If the window sills are more than a few feet above the exterior ground, some type of window guard must be provided to protect the youngsters from falling out. Window shades are necessary, since the kindergarten pupils frequently rest during the day and require a darkened room. Also the heat of the sun and strong glare can be minimized by lowering the shades.

Since the kindergarten pupils must be kept under constant observation, it is mandatory to provide the toilet room directly off the main playroom. In this way the teacher can control the children and help those who require assistance without leaving the room itself. At least two water closets and two washbasins should be provided in each kindergarten toilet room, and these fixtures should be of the small low type to suit the age of the children. Soap dispensers and paper towels are provided for purposes of cleanliness and to teach the children good health practices. A wash sink in the playroom itself is standard equipment, since children love to play with water. Drinking facilities must be provided either in the form of a drinking fountain or by means of paper cups adjacent to the sink.

Clothing facilities should be located in the playroom itself or as close to it as possible. The cubicles containing five or six spaces have proved quite satisfactory since they are easy to move from place to place. The top portion of each section is devoted to a blanket or hat, the center portion is for the coat, and the lower part for rubbers or boots.

There should be a sufficient number of movable toy storage cabinets. These cabinets are used not only for the storage of toys and equipment but also to form alcoves of varying sizes and shapes to section off various play activities. Since the children play on the floor a good part of the time, a sanitary material must be provided which is easy to clean, warm to the touch, and colorful.

While many of the rooms in the education center may be used for other purposes, the kindergarten should never be used for any other purpose. Frequently, the children work on a project of building which may take several days or a week, and this must not be disturbed.

Fig. 9. Library of Agudas Achim Synagogue (Finegold Alexander and Associates; Photo: Peter Vanderwarker)

In connection with the kindergarten room, an outdoor playground is necessary since the children spend considerable time outdoors in good weather. Sand pit, swings, slides, and seesaws are the commonly used items of equipment. The playground should be so arranged that the sun will strike it and not be cut off by adjoining buildings.

## Classroom Elements

Research has established that the planning of physical environmental factors of the classroom—such as seating, lighting, decoration, temperature, and sound—contributes greatly to the learning progress and well-being of the children. Coordinating the environment in this way is particularly important where the children spend several hours in sustained visual activity.

The proportions of an academic classroom should be such that the width is about three-fourths of the length. The long, narrow room provides better control for the teacher than a classroom which is wide

and shallow. In the latter room the light from the windows will not penetrate to the far side and thus the last rows of seats will be poorly lighted. The windows should be arranged on the long side so that when the pupils face the front of the room the natural light will come from the left side.

Windows may be as large as possible, starting at approximately 3 feet above the floor and rising to the ceiling or as high as structural members permit; the higher the heads of the windows the farther the light will penetrate toward the opposite side of the room. The areas of the windows should never be less than 10 percent of the floor area of the room. Shades or other sun-control devices should be provided to cut the glare and strong sun and for use if motion pictures are shown.

The following description of a typical classroom should not be taken as a rigid formula, for many variations in design are possible. This is merely one good way of designing such a room: the front of the classroom should be provided with a chalkboard across the entire wall, with a cork tack board above. On the corridor wall toward the front of the room is the door. This door should swing into the room if the local law permits, in order to keep the corridor clear. If the law requires that the door swing outward towards the corridor, then it should be set back into the room in the form of a recess. The door itself should be provided with a glass vision panel, and a glass transom should be provided over the door to admit light into the corridor. On the room side of the corridor wall, beginning at the entrance door, there should be a series of cabinets in this order: teachers' locker, storage cabinet, pupils' wardrobe, material cabinet, exhibit cabinet with a cupboard under, magazine rack. The wardrobe is composed of a series of doors which contain tack board or chalkboard sections. The Austral type wardrobe doors are the most acceptable since they pivot out of the line of travel; they are, however, the most expensive, and if finances are limited, then the sliding or hinged type of wardrobe doors may be used. Within the wardrobe are hooks and a shelf for hats. The wardrobe compartment must be ventilated, either by mechanical means if the building is equipped with an air-conditioning or ventilating system or by means of a grille in several of the doors.

Classroom furniture of the best design and quality is available at moderate cost. Since the equipment will be moved frequently, it is important that it possess the needed strength and durability. The soundest equipment for individual student use is a desk with swivel seat and a top adjustable to 20-foot slope. Depending on the extent to which the room is to be used for different purposes, individual tables with sloped tops and separate chairs provide greater flexibility. These individual tables can easily be grouped to form larger working surfaces. Probably the greatest all-round flexibility can be achieved by the use of larger multi-place tables with adjustable-height steel standards and folding chairs. For kindergarten and primary grades, however, folding chairs are not satisfactory.

Painting the classroom does more than any other single item to make the room attractive and cheerful. The painting scheme should produce high reflectivity without glare and yet maintain the practical quality of easy maintenance.

## Library

Depending again upon the scope of the services the synagogue means to offer, it can provide files of periodicals, newspapers, videos, and recorded music, which might not otherwise be conveniently available to members.

The library (Fig. 9) might also be made available for small meetings, teas, and receptions.

Beauty and attractiveness are just as important as health and usefulness in planning the library. Informality without loss of discipline can be obtained by the proper selection of furniture, equipment, and decoration. The shelves must be suited to the age groups for which they are intended. Best possible natural daylight should be obtained and bilateral fenestration is desirable. Artificial illumination must be carefully worked out. If the library is to be used by outsiders after school hours, then the room should be located in such a position that it is easily accessible from the exterior; yet it should be removed from the noisy side of the building.

Contemporary education is making more extensive use of visual aids in an unending variety of videos, CDs, slides, maps, charts, photographs, and other non-book aids. These items are usually controlled by the school library and are made available for use in such a manner as has been traditionally employed for books. Special provision must be made for storing and handling the items mentioned and cabinets and shelving or special racks are required.

# CHAPELS

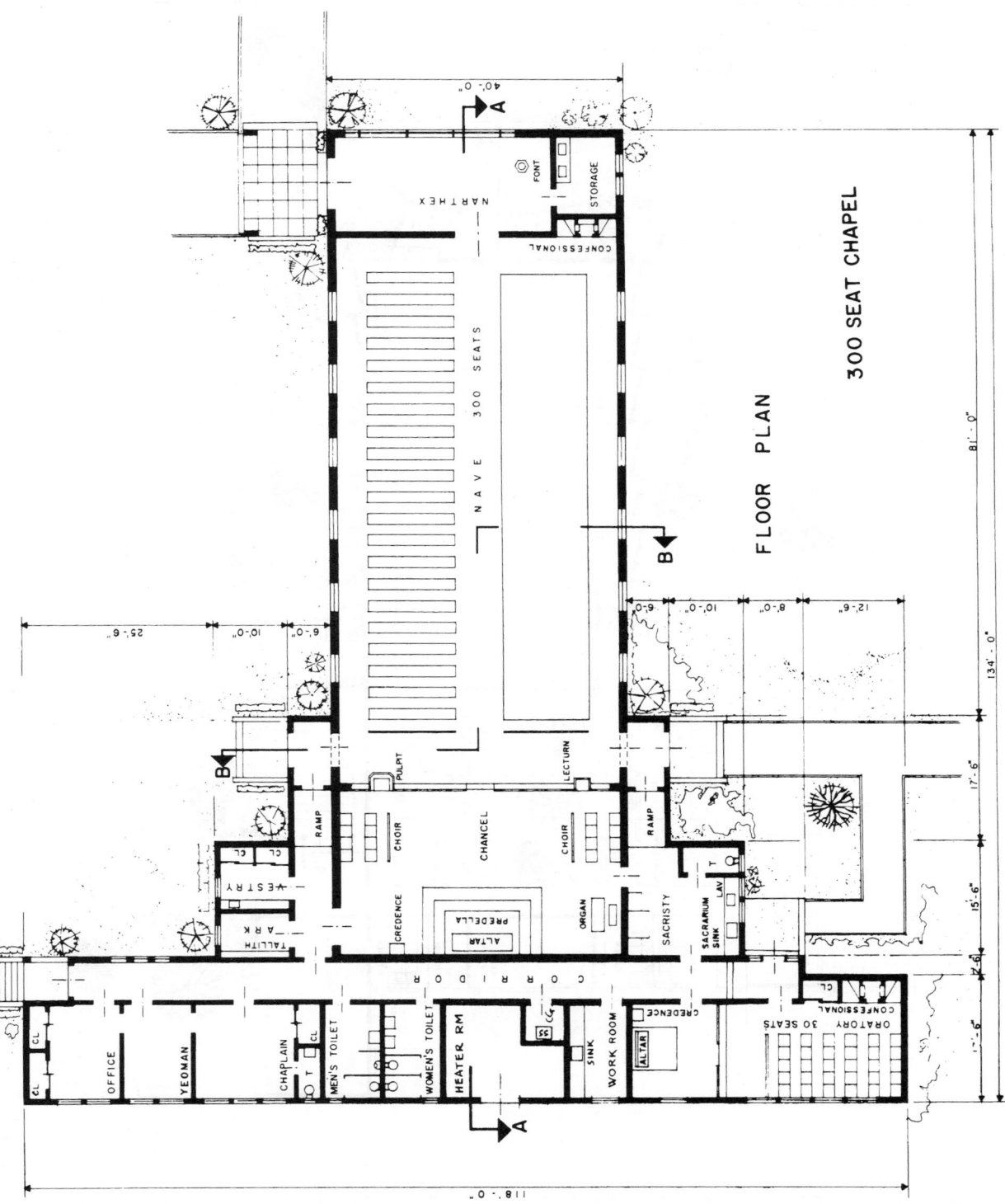

Fig. 1. 300-seat chapel (Department of the Navy, Bureau of Yards & Docks, Washington, D.C., Williams, Coile & Blanchard and Associates Architects, Engineers, Washington, D.C.

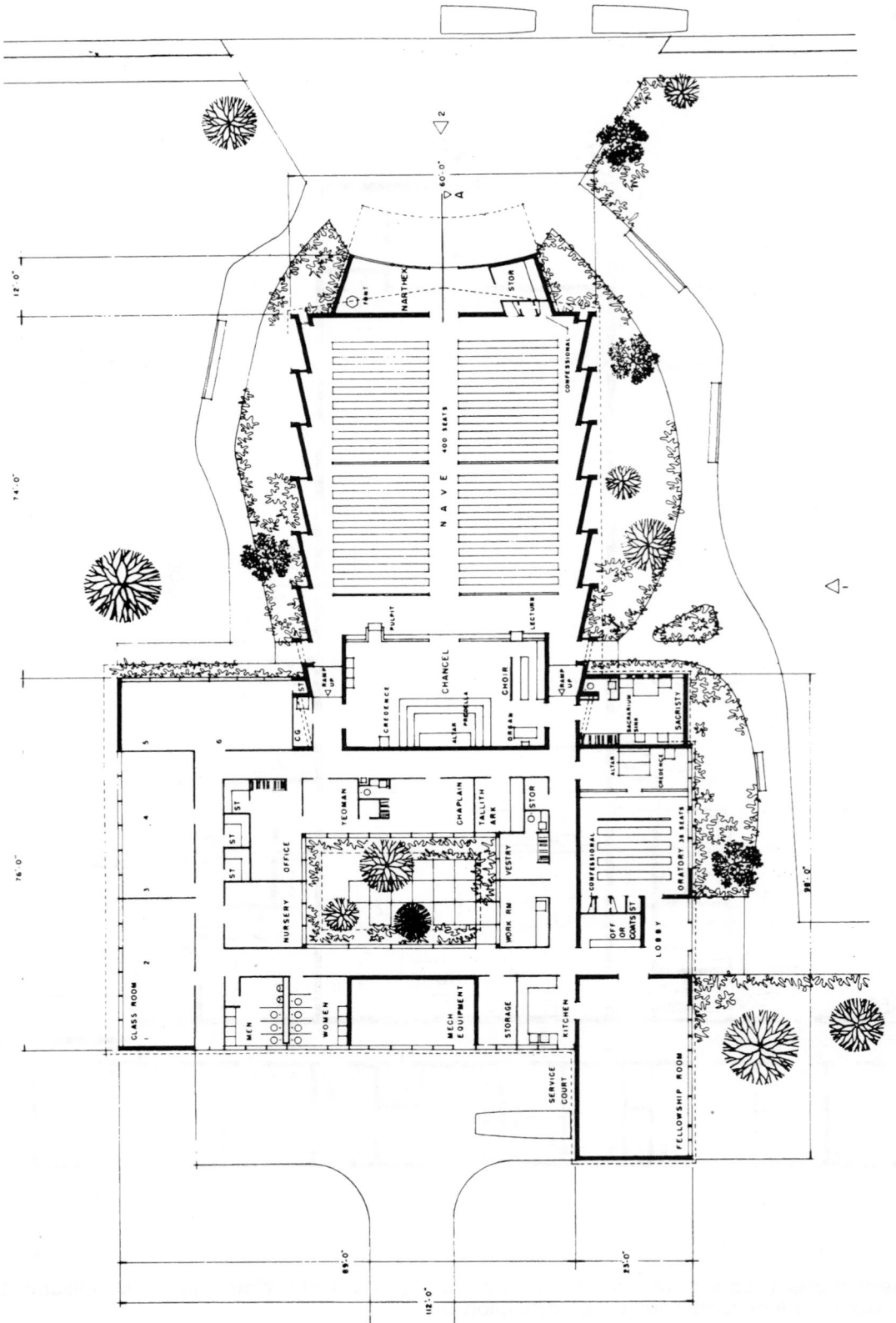

**Fig. 2. Chapel and education center (Department of the Navy, Bureau of Yards & Docks, Washington, D.C., William Coile & Blanchard and Associates Architects, Engineers, Washington, D.C.)**

# CHURCH SCHOOLS

**Table 1** Rooms needed in relation to program and size of church school

| | Very small church school, 1–99 pupils | | Small church school, 100–199 pupils | |
|---|---|---|---|---|
| | Enrollment | Housing facilities | Enrollment | Housing facilities |
| Nursery, infants and toddlers under 18 months | | None unless separate space is available. | | None unless separate space is available. |
| Toddlers, ages 1½ and 2 . . . . | | Same as above. | | Same as above. |
| Nursery class, age 3 . . . . . . | 12 | May be necessary to house several 3-year-olds in same room as kindergarten. Try to keep in a separate area of the room with one helper. | 18 | One room that may be kept just for the 3-year-old group. If church sponsors weekday nursery school, this room and kindergarten room may be used. Rooms should be near each other. |
| Kindergarten, ages 4 and 5 | 12 | Separate room. Do not encourage attendance of 3-year-olds at expense of 4- and 5-year olds. | 20 | One room that may be used both during church school hour and church hour. Limit use by others. |
| Primary, grades 1 and 2 . . . . . | 12 | One room where age group can meet, but if necessary, along with the entire church school session. May meet separately in a large, divided space. | 16–20 | Separate room for each 16–20 pupils. Beyond those numbers, two sessions or additional space needed. Grades one and two may meet together or separately. |
| Grades 3 and 4 . . . . . . . | 10 | Same as for primary. | 16–25 | Separate room, 16–25 in group. Beyond 25, additional space or two sessions needed. |
| Grades 5 and 6 . . . . . . . | 8 | One room or part of room in which juniors may be alone for at least 45 minutes a Sunday.<br>Note: In all cases boys and girls should be grouped together. | 16–25 | Same as above for lower juniors. |
| | | | | Seventh grade |
| Grades 7 and 8 . . . . . . . . . | 6 | If necessary, church school class may meet in church pew or in nearby home. For other types of activity, see below. | 10–20 | One room. (See notes below.) |
| Grades 9 and 10 . . . . . . . . | 6 | Same as for grades 7 and 8. | 8–15 | One room. |
| Grades 11 and 12 . . . . . . . | 10 | Meet in church pews for church school classes.<br>Junior highs and seniors may meet together for activities other than study and discussion. Ordinarily the church sanctuary, a home nearby, or the fellowship room is available for such use. | 8–15 | Same as above<br>Program activities room may be coordinated for use by all junior and senior high groups. (See notes below.) |
| Older youth . . . . . . . . . . | | If older youth are working, they may wish to form a group of their own or they may join with college students. If they are attending college away from home, let the college pastor know. If they are attending college at home, provide for a college-age fellowship. Facilities needed are both those listed in this section and those on chart for adults. In all cases boys and girls should be grouped together. | | |

*Author:* Mildred C. Widber and Scott Turner Ritenour
*Focus: Building for Christian Education,* United Church Press, Philadelphia.

**Table 1** Rooms needed in relation to program and size of church school (cont.)

| Medium church school, 200-299 pupils | | Large church school, 300-599 pupils | | Very large church school 600 or more pupils |
|---|---|---|---|---|
| Enrollment | Housing facilities | Enrollment | Housing facilities | |
| 6-10 | Provide separate room with cribs and play-pens for those under 18 months. | 10 | Separate crib and playpen room. | Similar to large church school, but these usually operate in two or three sessions and so have more adequate space for each age group. |
| 6-10 | Separate room needed for toddlers — or one room for above, with separate spaces for infants and toddlers. | 12 | Separate room for toddlers. | |
| 30-36 | Two rooms or two sessions. No more than 18 children in any one nursery class group. 15 a better figure. | 30-36 | Two rooms to be used by 3-year-olds only, or one room used for two or three sessions. No more than 15-18 in any one group. | |
| 40 | Two rooms, one for 4-year-olds, one for 5-year-olds. 20 limit in any one group. Or, two 4-5-year-old groups, 20 in each. | 50-80 | Four rooms — two for 4-year-olds and two for 5-year-olds or two rooms (one for each age) if there are two or three sessions. 20 limit. | |
| 32-60 | Two or three rooms, one for each 16-20 pupils. Grades may meet together or separately. May come together occasionally for common interests. These rooms may be used during the week by parents or other groups. Should be multipurpose. | 64-80 | Four rooms — or two if there is a second session. 16-20 pupils in one group. Grades 1 and 2 may meet together or separately. | |
| 16-75 | Same as for primary. May have up to 25 in one group. | 64-100 | Same as for primary. May have up to 25 in one group. | |
| 16-25 | Grades 5 and 6 may meet together or separately, boys and girls together. 16-25 the limit for each group. | 32-75 | Two or three rooms depending upon enrollment. See medium church school for further details. | |

through youth

| | | | | |
|---|---|---|---|---|
| 20-30 | One room large enough for entire group. Smaller spaces for conversation and discussion. Class groups, 8-10. Flexible arrangement possible. | 30-60 | Flexible arrangement. One room needed where entire group may gather for sings, recreation, dramatics. Small rooms for conversation and discussion groups of 8-10 each. | Enrollment, 60 — similar to large school. Multiple sessions provide more adequate space for each group. |
| 15-25 | Same as above for middle high, and senior high. | 25-50 | Same as above for middle high and senior high. | |

The important arrangements for all three youth groups are:

1. A large space for the entire group for varied activities, such as recreation, sings, dramatics.

2. Small, intimate class groupings of 8-10 members each, in which there may be vigorous discussion, research, and study. This means use of the large space for two or three such groups (possibly), with use of other smaller rooms when enrollment necessitates. It is better not to have many small groups meeting in a single space. Intimacy and privacy of class groupings are essential at this age.

3. Formal worship provided by attendance at regular church service.

For any church to consider:

When possible, the room used in the church school should be used for the Sunday evening or through-the-week program. Therefore, it should be suited to a variety of activities and provided with ample storage space for supplies and equipment.

Classrooms should be attractive, efficiently designed, and large enough for ample movement.

Recreation, crafts, hobbies, art activities, and drama are part of the ongoing program, and facilities should be provided for them. A kitchenette is desirable.

For a weekday schedule of activities, rooms should be near a building entrance for easy access.

**ble 2**  Summary—school equipment

| Age group | Maximum children per room* | Floor space per child | Toilets, sinks, drinking fountains | Coats | Cabinets |
|---|---|---|---|---|---|
| sery I, babies d toddlers rth to age 2 | 8-10 (Cribs at 3 ft intervals) | 35 sq ft — good; 30 sq ft — fair; under 25 sq ft — poor. Separate room for babies and toddlers. | Toilets and wash basins within pre-school room area preferred. Otherwise, observe strictest sanitation facilities for storing and warming food. | Rod hangers in the room (preferably in storage cabinet with shelf above and below), 30 in. above floor. Full length for teachers. Hooks are hazardous. Not recommended. | Movable, ample for supplies. |
| rsery II, ge 2 | 8 — good 10 — fair 12 — poor | 35 sq ft — good; 30 sq ft — fair; under 25 sq ft — poor. (Warm clean floors for children to sit on. All preschoolers.) | Adjoining room with junior fixtures or wooden step if adult fixtures used. Toilets 10 in., basins 24 in. above floor. | Rod hangers in the room (preferably in storage cabinet with shelf above and below), 30 in. above floor. Full length for teachers. Hooks are hazardous. Not recommended. | Movable, ample for supplies needed. Low open shelves for toys. |
| rsery III, ge 3 | Up to 15 — good; 15-18 — fair Over 18 — poor | 35 sq ft — good; 30 sq ft — fair; under 25 sq ft — poor. | Adjoining room with junior fixtures or wooden step if adult fixtures used. Toilets 10 in., basins 24 in. above floor. | Rod hangers in the room (preferably in storage cabinet with shelf above and below), 36 in. above floor. Full length for teachers. Hooks are hazardous. Not recommended. | Movable, ample for supplies needed. Low open shelves for toys. Space for filing pictures and materials used in room. Open shelves for toys. |
| ndergarten I, II, ages 4 and 5 | Up to 20 — good 20-25 — fair Over 25 — poor | 35 sq ft — good; 30 sq ft — fair; under 25 sq ft poor. | | Rod hangers in the room (preferably in storage cabinet with shelf above and below), 42 in. above floor. Full length for teachers. Hooks are hazardous. Not recommended. | Movable, ample for supplies needed. Low open shelves for toys. Space for filing pictures and for materials used in room. Open shelves for toys. |

Rooms on first floor and above grade level.

**able 3**  Rooms needed in relation to program and to size of church school—preschool children

| Age group | Church school, 1-99 pupils | Church school, 100-299 pupils | Church school, 300-499 pupils | Church school, 500-899 pupils | Church school, 900 or more pupils |
|---|---|---|---|---|---|
| Nursery I, infants and toddlers, under 18 months Nursery II, ages 1½ and 2 | Omit — unless suitable separate space is available. | Omit — unless suitable separate space is available. | Possible here to provide one room for toddlers. If there is a need, consider separate room with cribs and playpens, etc., for those under 18 months. | Separate crib and playpen room. Separate room for toddlers. | Similar to larger church schools. |
| Nursery III, age 3 | May be necessary to house several 3-year-olds in same room as kindergarten. Try to separate parts of the room, using one helper. | Enrollment 8-18. One room that may be kept for just the 3-year-old group. If the church sponsors a weekday nursery school, this room and kindergarten room may be used. Have rooms near each other. | Enrollment 20-30. Two rooms. These may be used during the week by parent groups, etc., particularly if a folding partition separates them. | Enrollment 32-54. Three rooms to be used by 3-year-olds only, or one room used for each of two or three sessions. | These usually operate in two sessions. |
| Kindergarten I, II, ages 4 and 5 | Enrollment up to 12. Separate room. Do not encourage attendance of 3-year-olds at expense of the 4- and 5-year-olds. | Enrollment 16-25. One room to be used both during the church school hour and church hour; limited use by others. | Enrollment 40-50. Two rooms, one for 4-year-olds and one for 5-year-olds. It is helpful to have rooms adjoining for possible use by adults. | Enrollment 64-100. Four rooms, two for 4-year-olds and two for 5-year-olds; or two rooms (one for each age) used for two or three sessions. | Three sessions would provide more adequate space for each age group. |

**Table 3**  Rooms needed in relation to program and to size of church school—preschool children (cont.)

| Age group | Display space | Furniture | Other materials |
|---|---|---|---|
| Nursery I | Grooved picture rail 14 in. above floor. Tack board extending from 14 to 38 in. above the floor. | Cribs — preferably bassinets on metal frames with rubber tires. Playpens, bed linen, plastic mats for playpens. | |
| Nursery II | Grooved picture rail 17 in. above the floor. Tack board extending 17 to 43 in. above the floor. | Chairs 6 in. from floor. Not needed for every child. Tables — height 16 in. — small. Tops 18 by 24 in. A book table — not essential if space limited. | Large blocks (2 x 4 x 8 in. and 2 x 4 x 12 in.); floor toys (peg wagon, wooden, train, cars); books, pictures; a Bible; cuddly toys (stuffed animals, rag dolls); housekeeping toys (doll, doll bed, tea table and dishes); ball; picture rail; offering container; wastebasket; growing plants or other nature materials; a songbook, or collection of songs, recommended in the literature for use by the leaders. Add later (where space permits) walking board; more housekeeping equipment (pans, telephone, small rocking chair); push and pull toys; small wagon, resting mats; washable rug or rugs for floor. |
| Nursery III | Grooved picture rail 20 in. above the floor. Tack board extending from 20 to 48 in. above floor. | Chairs 8 in. from floor. A few 6 in. Tables, height, 18 in. Tops, 24 by 36 in. or 28 by 42 in. Teacher's table, 18 by 24 in. Piano — not essential but desirable. | Large blocks (2 x 4 x 8 in. and 2 x 4 x 12 in.); floor toys (cars, trucks, train, boat); ball, books; a Bible; pictures; housekeeping toys; a songbook, or collection of songs, recommended in the literature for use by the leaders; offering container; wastebasket; growing plants or other nature materials. Add later (where space permits) easels for painting; paint; set of steps; large hollow blocks; more housekeeping toys (broom, ironing board, iron, clothesline, doll carriage — large enough to come to waist of child); large puzzles, sets of wooden animals and people for block play; low bench or stools near place for wraps. |
| Kindergarten I, II | Grooved picture rail 24 in. above floor. Tack board extending from 24 to 54 in. above floor. | Chairs 10 in. from floor. Tables, height 20 in. Tops 24 by 42 in. or 28 by 48 in. Piano desirable. | Large blocks (2 x 4 x 8 in. and 2 x 4 x 12 in.); floor toys for dramatic play; books; a Bible; pictures; housekeeping toys; paper scissors; large crayons; a songbook or collection of songs, recommended in the literature for use by the teachers; offering container; wastebasket; growing plants or other nature materials; display or tack strip space. Add later (where space permits) easels for painting; paint; large hollow blocks; large puzzles; sets of wooden animals and people for block play; small aprons, nurses' caps, pocketbooks, ties, for dramatic play in housekeeping center. |

**Table 4**  Rooms need by elementary children as related to school size

| Age group | Church school, 1–99 pupils | Church school, 100–299 pupils | Church school, 300–499 pupils | Church school, 500–899 pupils | Church school, 900 or more pupils |
|---|---|---|---|---|---|
| Primary, grades 1, 2, and 3 | Enrollment up to 18. One room where age group can meet, but if necessary along with the entire church school session. May be part of large space divided. | Enrollment 24–54. One room; or one large room and one medium size room for approximately 25. Two grades can use large room for all purposes. One grade can use smaller room for all purposes or unite with the other two grades. | Enrollment 60–90. Three rooms — one for each school grade to be treated as separate groups; or may come together occasionally for worship or other purposes. | Enrollment 96–162. Six rooms — or three if there is a second session. Handle as separate groups. | Have more adequate space for each age group. |
| Junior, grades 4, 5, and 6 | Enrollment up to 15. One room or part of room in which juniors may be alone for at least 45 minutes a Sunday. May have to worship some of the time with older groups in the church school. | Enrollment 20–45. Same as requirements for primary children. | Enrollment 50–75. Three rooms, one for each grade; or one large room and one medium size for approximately 30. | Enrollment 80–135. Same as for primary. | |

**Table 5**  Summary of space and equipment for elementary school children

| Age group | Maximum children per room* | Floor space per child | Toilets, basins, drinking facilities | Wraps |
|---|---|---|---|---|
| Primary, grades 1, 2, and 3; ages 6, 7, and 8 | Up to 25 — good 25–30 — fair 30–35 — poor (See comment below for assembly) | 30 sq ft — good 25 sq ft — fair 20 sq ft — poor | Separate toilets for boys, girls. Readily accessible on same floor. Washbasins 28 in. from floor. Toilets 14 in. from floor. Sink with running water and double drain board in room preferred. | Some prefer in room. Use rod hangers 42 to 48 in. above floor, shelf above. |
| Juniors, grades 4, 5, and 6; ages 9, 10 and 11 | Up to 25 — good 25–30 — fair 30–35 — poor Up to 45 pupils, 3 rooms; 1 larger for assembly at times. | 20–30 sq ft — good 25 sq ft — fair 20 sq ft — poor | As above except basins 30 in; toilets 16 in. from floor. | Some prefer in room, otherwise in recessed corridor storage space. Use rod hangers 48–54 in. above floor, shelf above. |

* Preferably on first floor, above grade level.

**Table 6**  Rooms needed in relation to program and to size of church school—youth division

| | Church school, 1–99 pupils | Church school, 100–299 pupils | Church school, 300–499 pupils | Church school, 500–899 pupils | Church school, 900 or more pupils |
|---|---|---|---|---|---|
| Junior high | Enrollment up to 12. Church school class may meet in church pew or in nearby home. For other types of activity, see below. | Enrollment 12–35. Church school classes may be held in sanctuary if necessary but a meeting space is needed for other program activities. | Enrollment 35–60. Department Assembly Room, plus two classrooms large enough for classes of 15–20. Assembly room may be used for through-the-week activities. | Enrollment 60–100. Department Assembly Room with classrooms for groups of 15–20. Assembly room should be available for activities of junior highs throughout the week. | Enrollment 100 or more. Three departments should be provided, one for each grade. Provide each section with an Assembly Room and classrooms. |
| Senior high | Enrollment up to 10. Meet in church pews for church school classes. Junior highs and seniors may meet together for activities other than study and discussion. Ordinarily the church sanctuary, a home nearby, or the fellowship room is available for such use. | Enrollment 10–30. Same as above. Separate room should be available for program activities. | Enrollment 24–40. Assembly Room with two classrooms. A third class may meet in the assembly room itself. Such a room also becomes a headquarters for the Youth Fellowship. | Enrollment 50–90. Department Assembly Room with classrooms for groups of about 20. | Enrollment 90. Department Assembly and Room with classrooms over for groups of not more than 25. |
| Older youth | If older youth are working, they may wish to have a group of their own, or they may join with college students. If they are attending college away from home, let the college pastor know. If they are attending college at home, provide for a college-age fellowship. Facilities needed are both those listed in this section and those under "Adult." | For any church to consider: Where possible the same room should be used for assembly and worship in the church school and also for Sunday evening or through-the-week program. Therefore, it should be suited to a variety of activities and provided with ample storage space for supplies and equipment. Classrooms should be attractive, efficiently designed, and large enough to allow for ample movement. Recreation, crafts, hobbies, and drama are part of the ongoing program and facilities should be provided for them. A kitchenette is desirable. For a weekday schedule of activities, room should be easy of access, near building entrance. | | | |

**Table 6**  Rooms needed in relation to program and to size of church school—youth division (cont.)

| Cabinets | Display space | Furniture | Other materials |
|---|---|---|---|
| Ample space carefully planned for pupils' and teachers' supplies, handiwork, picture storage. Open shelves for books. | Grooved picture rail 30 in. above the floor. Tack board 30 to 62 in. above the floor. Portable blackboards or turnover charts made for handling and tack boards on one or two sides of room. | Chairs 14 in. from floor, some 12 in. Table tops 30 by 48 or 54 in., 24 in. high. Small tables for beauty or worship centers. Piano. CD player. | Recommended literature, one or more Bibles, paper, pencils, crayons, paste, scissors. Songbook for pianist and teacher's use (one recommended in the literature). Pictures, books chosen according to unit being studied; simple reference books. Song charts. Growing plants or other nature materials, wastebasket, picture rail, movable blackboard or large sheets of newsprint on an easel may be desired. |
| Same as above but provide storage for maps, large objects. | Grooved picture rail 36 in. above the floor. Tack board 36 to 72 in. above floor. | Chairs 16 in. from floor. Table tops 30 by 48 or 54 in., 26 in. high. Piano. Small tables for beauty and worship center. CD player. | Recommended literature, a Bible for the department, a Bible for each child. Songbooks for children's use (one recommended in the literature), pictures. Books chosen according to unit being studied, paper, pencils, crayons, paste, scissors; offering container. Wastebasket, growing plants or other nature materials, picture rail, movable blackboard or large sheets of newsprint on an easel may be useful. Add later Bible dictionary; Bible atlas, maps, a globe, reference books, copies of different translations of the Bible, a dictionary. |

**Table 7**  Summary of space and equipment for youth*

| Age group | Maximum pupils per room | Floor space per pupil | Furniture and equipment |
|---|---|---|---|
| Junior high I, II, III, and grades 7, 8, and 9; ages 12, 13, and 14 | 20 pupils — good 10-15 pupils — preferred | 15-18 sq ft — good 12-15 sq ft — fair 10-12 sq ft — poor | Lightweight tables without drawers. Space to store extra tables and chairs. Comfortable, sturdy chairs, blackboard or turn-over chart frames with large sheets of paper. Display board, wall maps, youth library, pianos, record player and record storage, recreational equipment and place to store it. Bibles, textbooks, etc. |
| Senior high and older youth; grades 10, 11, and 12; ages 15, 16, and 17 | 25 pupils maximum | Same as above | Equipped for audiovisuals. Nearby accessible cloak storage space, toilet facilities. Storage cabinets for pictures, hymnals, materials and supplies. Colorful, attractive furnishings in keeping with decor of building. |
| Older youth, 18-23 years | | | |

* Provision should be made for recreation, worship, handicraft and hobbies, dramatics, youth choirs, and refreshments.

**Table 8**  Rooms needed in relation to program and to size of church school—adult division*

| | Church school, 1-99 pupils | Church school, 100-299 pupils | Church school, 300-499 pupils | Church school, 500-899 pupils | Church school, 900 or more pupils |
|---|---|---|---|---|---|
| Young adult | Enrollment up to 10. Church school class may meet in sanctuary or in nearby home. Social, recreation, and service activities of class, and of young adult fellowship, may use church dining room or homes of members. | Enrollment up to 30. One classroom advisable especially for parents' class, or a mixed group. Class may use sanctuary. For other class and young adult fellowship activities use may be made of church fellowship hall, or similar room and homes of members. | Enrollment up to 50. Two classrooms advisable; one for parents' group, one for a mixed group. Sanctuary pews may be used. Young adult fellowship Sunday night and week night activities in fellowship hall or other rooms, or in homes. Provision needed for dramatics, recreation, and audiovisuals. | Enrollment up to 50. Same needs in general as medium church school, except provision for more class groupings according to interest needs. A church hobby room would enlist many young adults. Provision needed also for dramatics, recreation, and audiovisuals. | Enrollment 100 or more. Same needs in general as large church school. More activities on Sunday night and week nights will need church space because homes cannot usually accommodate larger attendance. |
| Middle adult | Enrollment up to 10. Church school class may meet in sanctuary or nearby home. | Enrollment up to 30. One or two class meeting places in sanctuary or available rooms in other parts of the church. | Enrollment up to 50. Same general space and equipment needs as medium church school, with allowance for larger attendance and provision for informal interest groups. | Enrollment up to 90. Same general space and equipment needs as medium church school, with allowance for more classes, especially short-term interest groups. | Enrollment 100 or more. Smaller classes of 20 to 30 preferable to one or two large classes. |
| | Middle adults will also be active in men's fellowships, women's associations, and other organized groups and will need space and equipment for such activities. However, these meeting places will probably be used by other age groups at other times, thus making it unnecessary to build and equip these rooms for adults only. Storage space must thus be provided for equipment that will serve the different age groups. | | | | |
| Older adult | Enrollment up to 7. No special facilities needed. Older adults will probably participate in middle adult study and activities. | Enrollment up to 21. May participate with middle adults. If separate class is needed, a section of the pews in the sanctuary will probably be available | Enrollment up to 35 | Enrollment 65 or more | Enrollment up to 65 |

* The enrollment figures used in this chart are based on a sampling of a variety of church schools. It was found that there were approximately 27 adults to every 100 pupils enrolled in the church school. The figure 27 was broken down into 10 young adults, 10 middle adults, and 7 older adults. However, church school situations are so varied in proportionate age groupings that many exceptions must be made.
   Space should also be considered for meeting of entire adult department of the church school. An office for administration of the adult department, and for records, is desirable. A fellowship hall with stage, kitchenette, provision for audiovisuals, hobbies, recreation, and service activities will provide for a multiplicity of uses for almost every kind of adult need.

**Table 9**  Summary of space equipment for adults*

| Age group | Maximum persons per room | Floor space per person | Furniture and equipment |
|---|---|---|---|
| Young adults, ages 24-35 | 20-25 preferred 50 persons maximum | Lecture type, 8-10 sq ft per person | Facilities for study groups and discussions, tables for discussion groups and study, comfortable chairs, blackboards or turnover charts, lecterns, pictures, Bibles, books, pianos, cabinets for supplies, provision for dramatics and audiovisuals. |
| Adults, ages 36-64 | | 10-12 sq ft for activity-type teaching | Facilities for teas, light refreshments, suppers, hobby and recreation, and informal fellowship weekday clubs, recreation, etc. |
| Older adults, age 65 up | | | Small meditation room apart from the nave or chapel. |

* For adults and older adults, rooms should be on first floor, if possible.

**Table 10**  Rooms needed in relation to program and to size of church school administrative functions

| Persons and functions | Church school, 1-99 pupils | Church school, 100-299 pupils | Church school, 300-499 pupils | Church school, 500-899 pupils | Church school 900 or more pupils |
|---|---|---|---|---|---|
| Pastor . . . . . . . . | Study and work room. Built-in table and shelves with curtain or doors to conceal mimeograph equipment when not in use. | Study and separate work room. Closet for supplies. | Study and office for secretary with equipment for records. Work room with cabinets for supplies. | Study with office for secretary. Office for church secretary. Offices for other staff members and their secretaries. Work room and supply closets. | Same as for 500-899 church school with addition of conference or board room adequate for largest group, should have table, exhibit space, blackboard, A-V equipment. |
| Director of Christian Education | None. | None. | Office large enough for desk, table, bookcases, and chairs. Space for counseling and small committee work. | Office large enough for desk, table, bookcases, chairs, with space for counseling and committee work. A separate office for secretary. | Same as for 500-899 church school plus offices for age group assistants and their secretaries. |
| Church School Supt., Secretary, and Treasurer | Desk space with shelves or chest of drawers for literature, supplies, and records. | Room with desks and cabinets for records, literature and supplies. | Room with desks, cabinets for records, literature, and supplies. | Room with desks, work table, filing cabinet for records. Storeroom for literature and supplies. | Same as for 500-899 church school but with increased space. |
| Choir Director . . . . | Desk or table space. Cabinet for filing church music. Closet or cabinet for choir robes. | Room with desk or table. Cabinets for music and choir robes. Shelves for hymnals used by choir. | Office with desk, cabinet, and piano. Room with table, and cabinets for music, choir robes, hymnals. | Office and studio with piano. Room for robing of choir with cabinets for music, robes, and hymns. | Same as for 500-899 church school but with more ample robe closets and robing space. |
| Library . . . . . . . | Built-in bookcases with locks, or space for movable units. Filing cabinets for records. | Room with bookcases (built-in or movable), table, chairs, filing cabinet for records. Cabinet for picture files. | Room with bookcases, table, chairs, cabinets for records, filing pictures and maps. Exhibit cabinets. | Large room with tables, chairs, with space for reading and study. Picture and files. Cabinet for records. World friendship museum. | Same as for 500-899 church school but with increased space and equipment. |

**Fig. 1. American Airlines Consolidated Terminal, John F. Kennedy International Airport (TAMS Consultants, Inc.)**

# AIRPORTS AND TERMINALS

## INTRODUCTION

The airport plays a vital role in social and economic life and in the quality of human experience. The airport is the point of access, interaction, and interrelationship between the local, regional and global community. The airport is the point of interface and transition between the various modes of surface and air transportation and is of critical importance to the total transportation network.

The planning and design of the airport is a study in the complex, multi-dimensional spatial and temporal movement and flow of aircraft, surface vehicles, travelers and their baggage, service and operational personnel, and cargo. However, the airport is also a study in the aesthetics and symbolism of urban and architectural form (Fig. 1). The airport is an expression of the nature and character of the people and community it serves and the greater environmental context of which it is an integral part.

An airport is like a total city devoted to dynamic movement. It comprises many varied structures that facilitate passenger and cargo movement, maintenance, and aircraft control, and other structures that provide for auxiliary support functions. The very nature of an airport's complexity makes it necessary to isolate its segments for design purposes. It is therefore the intent of this article to isolate primarily the passenger functions and to discuss how they tend to operate at an airport and what their general relationships to a community are.

### Functional Design of the Airport Passenger Terminal

The passenger terminal is one of the most important elements of the airport due to its essential role in providing services to air travelers. The passenger terminal must be designed to perform a number of basic functions:

1. Facilitate the transition of passengers between surface and air modes of transportation.
2. Provide a controlled and orderly environment for the processing and flow of passengers.
3. Create a secure and comfortable environment for passengers to gather and to wait, if necessary, prior to boarding the aircraft.
4. Accommodate and facilitate all of the necessary and often complex work processes associated with the operation and maintenance of the terminal facility.

On the landside, the passenger terminal must be designed to interface with the various modes of transportation providing access to the airport. Personal and commercial vehicle traffic must be analyzed and the access roadways and terminal curbfront must be designed to accommodate the volume of average peak hour vehicle traffic. If train service is provided to the airport, the train stations and passenger platforms must be carefully integrated with the design of the terminal complex to provide smooth and efficient passenger flow to and from the terminal building. The terminal building must be designed to accommodate the projected average peak hour departing and arriving passenger volume. (Average peak hour passenger traffic is defined by the Federal Aviation Administration as the volume of passengers projected for the peak hour of the average day of the peak month.) On the airside, the terminal must be designed to accommodate the airline flight schedules. The terminal apron and airside interface must be designed to accommodate the anticipated number and type of average peak hour aircraft and all necessary ground service vehicles and equipment.

### Users of the Airport Terminal

The airport terminal must be planned and designed to meet the needs of the users of the terminal facility. The primary user groups include the passengers, airlines, airport operator, and concessionaires. The principal purpose of the passenger terminal is to provide transportation services to air travelers. Therefore, it is of the greatest importance to accommodate passenger needs.

*Author:* Richard M. Adler, AIA, President, Brodsky, Hopf & Adler, Architects & Engineers, PC
*Reviewer:* David Karlquist, TAMS Consultants, Inc.

The airlines are the primary providers of services to passengers and are one of the most important operators of the passenger terminal. Therefore, it is especially important that the passenger terminal be designed in accordance with the requirements of the airlines and to facilitate the process of providing passenger services.

The airport operator performs many functions that are essential to the operation and maintenance of the airport terminal. Therefore, it is imperative that the airport terminal must be designed for efficient and economical operations and maintenance. The passenger terminal must accommodate the airport operator's requirements for administrative and support space and must provide an efficient, safe, and healthy work environment for the airport operations and maintenance personnel.

## Airport Operations

First, all movements and functions of the passengers, cargo, and the airline employees to and from an airport are regulated by a printed schedule. That is, the action that each discipline will follow is begun on the basis of this schedule, and the passenger's actions are based on the printed timetable of the airline chosen for flight.

The passenger time actions are accelerated because of the wide use of electronics, computers, and telephones. Passengers can arrive with information to "go directly to your gate, no ticket is required."

The cargo movements to or from the community are based upon the normal working hours of the community. This working schedule is generally in conflict with the flying schedule of the airline. Therefore it requires special correlation by the airline.

Considerable storage or holding area is required to offset the window of shipment.

The employees' working hours are predicated upon the functions of each discipline as it relates to the schedule. Therefore, all major elements of movement to and from the airport tend to take place upon a preestablished, programmed basis. However, the technology of the aviation industry changes so rapidly that a secondary but most important consideration arises. The technology can, overnight, change the preestablished schedules, thereby changing all relationships and movement to and from the airport. This occurs in three ways:

1. The aircraft manufacturer has demonstrated its ability to produce new aircraft with greater speeds, capable of carrying a gross load comparable to that of existing aircraft. Therefore, with the faster aircraft, time zones that had one relationship now have another. This then affects the predetermined schedule and all related disciplines.
2. The ability to change and increase the payload of the aircraft for both passengers and cargo creates a new condition. This requires a revision of function and all disciplines in order to accept greater numbers of passengers and increased cargo movement within a short period of time. It also creates voids during other periods of the day.
3. This condition results from both increased payload and increased speed. This will totally change the predetermined schedule.

Therefore, the constant factor in the development and design program is the on-time record of aircraft as related to the printed schedule. The actual arrival and departure times are subject to weather conditions, mechanical difficulties, and other special considerations that will arise from time to time.

The extent of on-time arrival and departure by aircraft and the extent of deviation from the schedule must be carefully evaluated. The airlines themselves afford the best source of information related to this problem. Although the scheduling and on-time record is good, a 10 or 15 percent deviation can raise havoc at an airport; therefore consideration must be directed toward the capability of handling the peak condition plus an overload factor for deviation from the schedule. No two airports function in the same manner. The overload factor must be evaluated separately. However, the designer must use caution and be aware of the fact that peak capacity may be reached only at two or maybe four hours a day, depending upon the airport and for the remainder of a 24-hour day, selected elements of the airport operate at very low efficiency. Restraint must be exercised to carefully control the amount of structure that is designed so as to provide an economically correct solution.

An airport functions as a transfer point between air vehicles and ground vehicles. There are numerous types of air vehicles designed for various functions.

The ground vehicles at an airport can take many forms. They are motor vehicles utilized as passenger cars, trucks, etc.; rapid transit systems of many descriptions; and special loading vehicles which can be utilized for supplementary transfer with the airport proper. The transfer point (passenger terminal) is generally a building structure or structures, and it is to its activities that we will primarily address ourselves. However, the understanding of the operation of this type building would be incomplete without knowledge of a series of systems that must be correlated to its activity.

The activity is divided into public and nonpublic functions as an operating reality. The public function for both arrival and departure of passengers is described in Figs. 2 to 4. The nonpublic function is described in Figs. 5 to 7.

## Relationship to Community

The operation of the airport is influenced by the fact that, for the traveling passenger, air transportation makes the period of inconvenience considerably shorter than it would be with other conventional systems. An airport has a great impact on a community. The very size of the airport affects the surrounding community. The careful planning of buildings and site location afford the potential for improving the environment and economics of a community.

There are many problems of noise, air pollution, and ecological balance that can be minimized or eliminated by proper site planning and building design. The community is affected by the working population of the airport, by the introduction of the new industry, and by the economic impact of same.

The economic health of the airport and the architect's attempt to stay within bounds cannot be overemphasized. The successful operation of the airport will demand total cooperation with the surrounding community. It thereby follows that every effort to establish proper working relationships among the many varied systems within the airport will be predicated upon a successful relationship with the surrounding community.

## Glossary

*Amenities:* That part of a terminal building housing convenience, service, and diversion facilities for the passengers, tenants, and public.

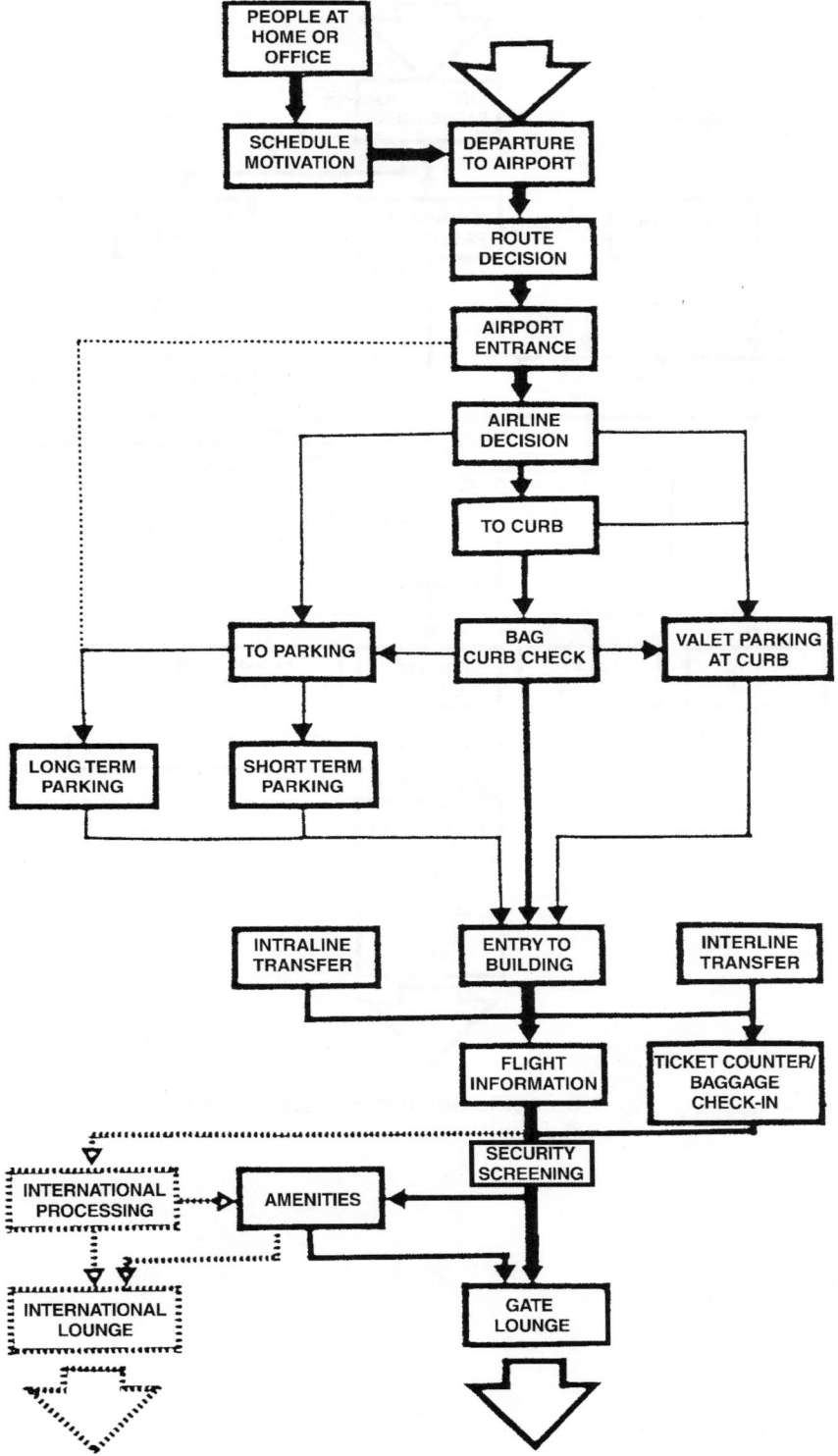

**Fig. 2. Domestic enplaning passenger flow**

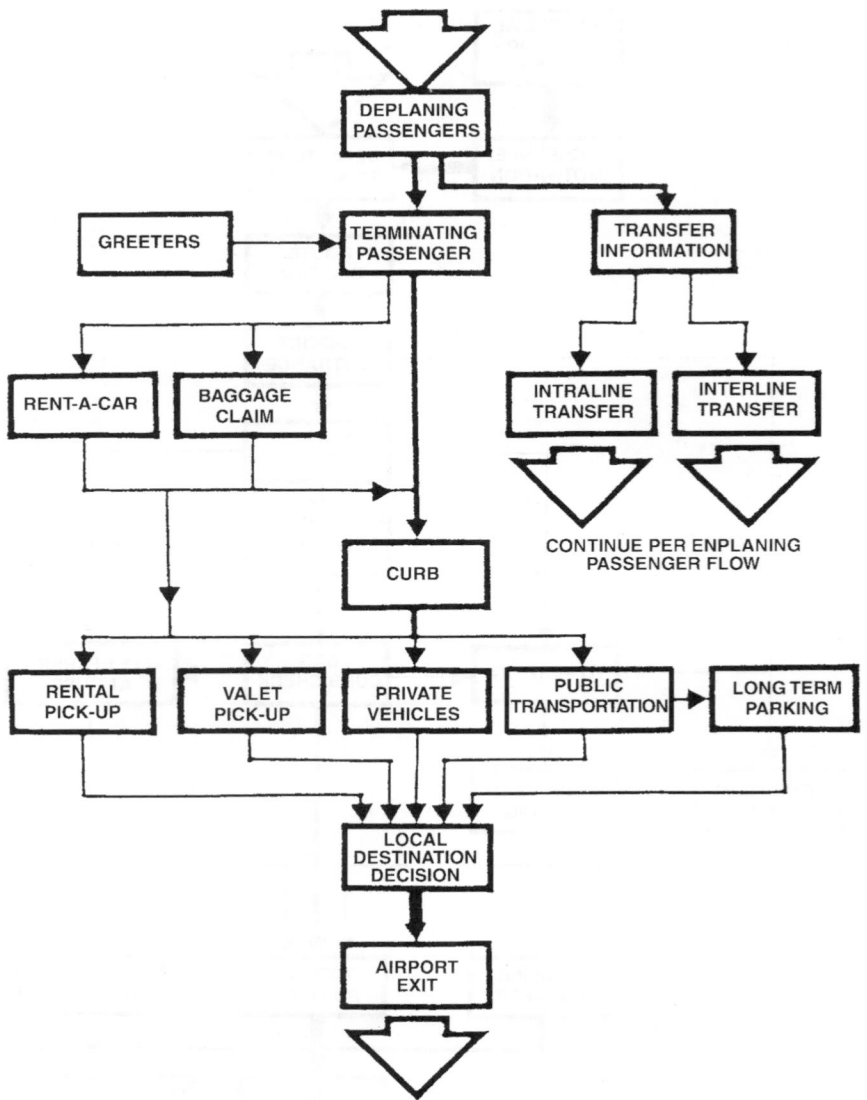

Fig. 3. Domestic deplaning passenger flow

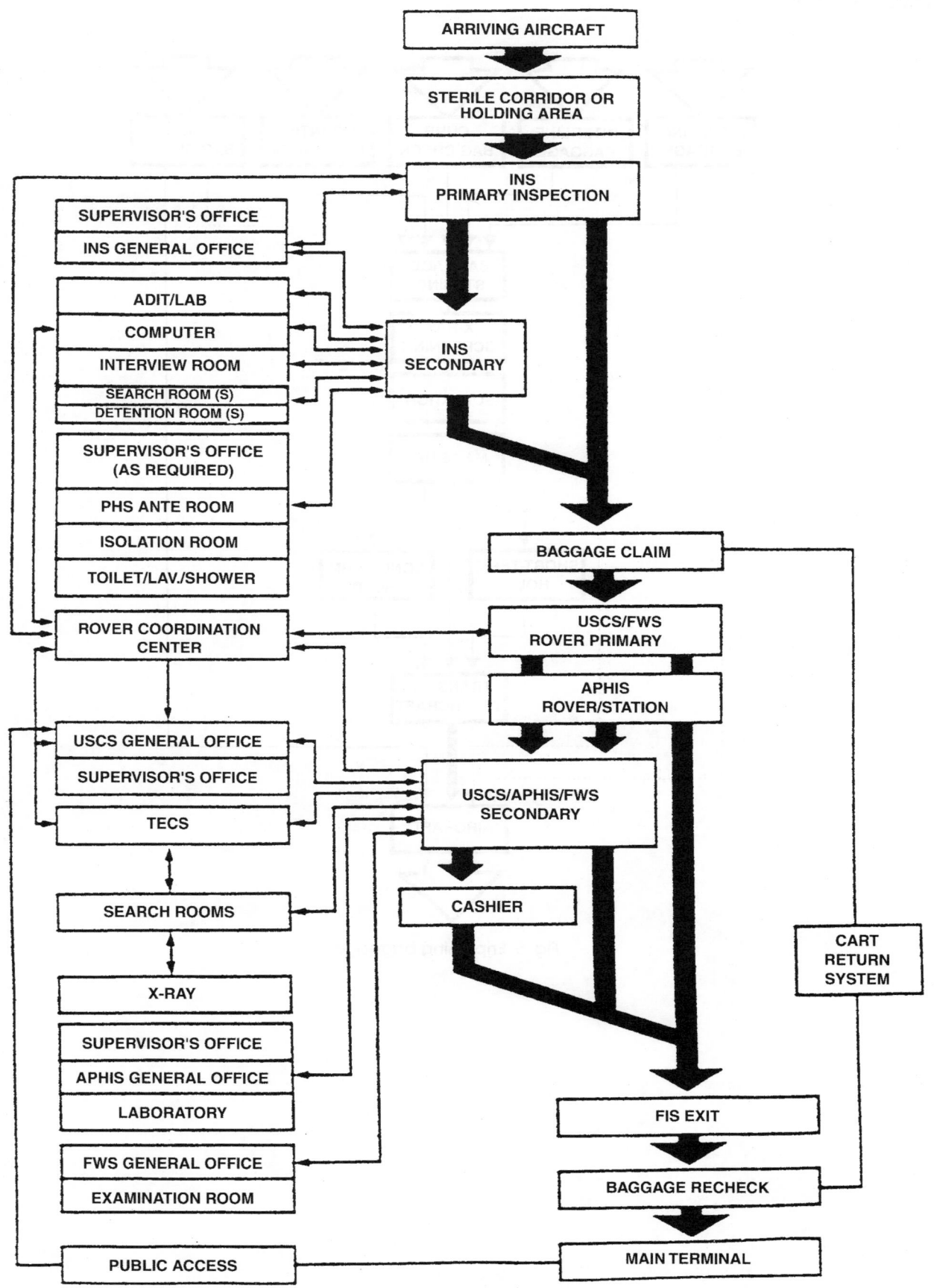

**Fig. 4. International arrival passenger flow**

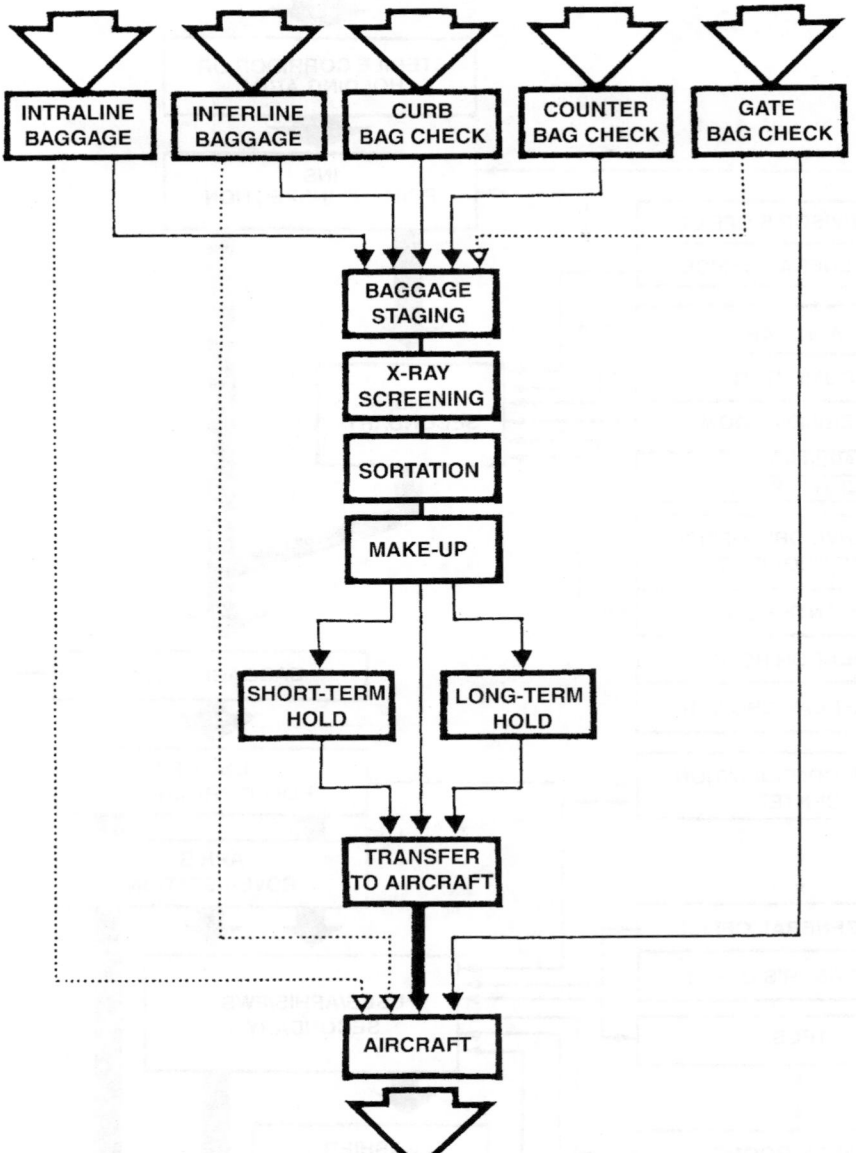

Fig. 5. Enplaning baggage

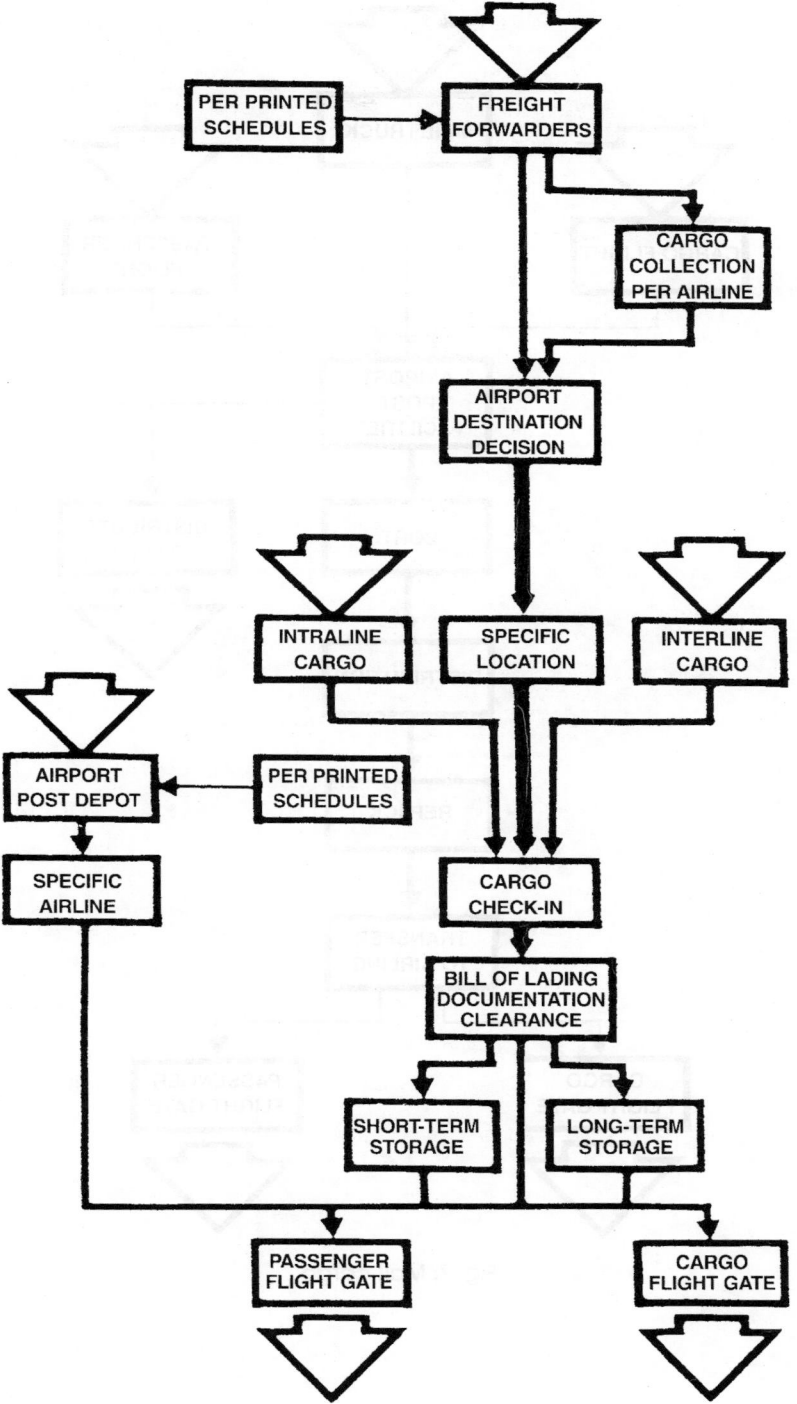

Fig. 6. Enplaning cargo

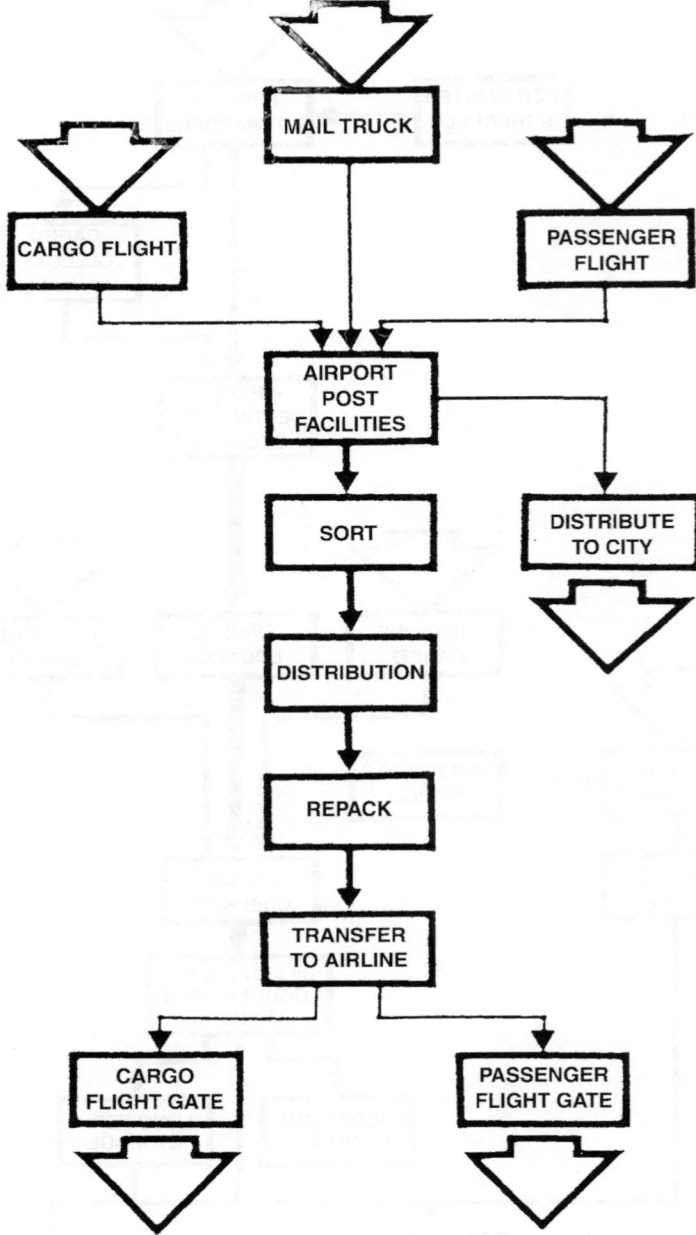

Fig. 7. Mail cargo

*Apron:* The apron comprises the area and facilities used for aircraft gate parking and aircraft support and servicing operations. It includes the following subcomponents:

*Aircraft Gate Parking Positions:* Used for parking aircraft to enplane and deplane passengers. The passenger boarding device is part of the gate position.

*Aircraft Service Areas:* On or adjacent to an aircraft parking position. They are used by airline personnel/equipment for servicing aircraft and the staging of baggage, freight, and mail for loading and unloading of aircraft.

*Taxi Lanes:* Reserved to provide taxiing aircraft with access to and from parking positions.

*Service/ Fire Lanes:* Identified rights-of-way on the apron designated for aircraft ground service vehicles and fire equipment.

*Average Peak Hour:* The peak hour of the average peak day. The peak hour is the one hour period of any peak day during which the highest percentage of the day's traffic is experienced. The average peak day is the average of the top 37 days (10 percent) of a year in terms of traffic volume.

*Baggage Diverter:* A mechanical device for transferring baggage from a moving conveyor belt to a baggage claim counter in such manner that the baggage is evenly distributed along the baggage counter.

*Boarding Control Point:* The point at which a passenger's credentials are inspected to assure that she is authorized to board a particular flight. Normally, this point is located in the vicinity of the gate from which the flight will depart.

*Boarding Passenger:* Any originating or connecting passenger authorized to board a flight.

*Connecting Passenger:* A passenger who arrives on one flight only for the purpose of transferring to another flight to reach her destination. These passengers are broken down into two categories: intraline and interline passengers.

*Connector:* The connector consists of the structure(s) and/or facilities normally located between the aircraft gate position and the main terminal building. At low activity airports, i.e., less than approximately 200,000 annual enplaned passengers, this component is often combined with the terminal building component. It normally contains the following elements:

- *Concourse:* A passageway for circulation between aircraft gate parking positions and the main terminal building.
- *Departing Lounge:* An area for assembling and holding passengers prior to a flight departure. In some instances, it may be a mobile lounge also used to transport passengers to a parked aircraft.
- *Security Inspection Station:* A control point for passenger and baggage inspection and controlling public access to parked aircraft.
- *Airline Operational Areas:* Areas set aside for airline personnel, equipment, and servicing activities related to aircraft arrivals and departures.
- *Passenger Amenities:* Areas normally provided in both the connector as well as the terminal components, particularly at the busier airports with relatively long connectors. These amenities include rest rooms, snack bars, beverage lounges, and other concessions and passenger services.
- *Building Maintenance and Utilities:* Areas often included in the connector component to provide terminal building maintenance and utilities.

*Customs:* This is an area under federal jurisdiction through which passengers arriving from foreign countries are required by law to pass, in order to make a declaration related to baggage which is accompanying them upon entry to the United States. This area is used for receipt of a declaration and/or examination of baggage. If duty is required, the customs agent will receive same in the customs area. Special attention must be paid to the design of this area because of changing techniques of operation.

*Departure Room:* An assembly area, including the boarding control point, located at a gate position(s) for passengers pending availability of aircraft for boarding.

*Deplaning:* Any passenger, cargo, baggage, visitor, etc., which is related to the unloading from an arriving flight.

*Domestic Passengers:* All passengers traveling in the territorial limits of a country or its territories are considered as domestic. Foreign nationals within the confines and territory require no special checking and operate as domestics.

*Enplaning:* Any passenger, cargo, baggage, visitor, etc., which is related to the boarding of a departing flight.

*FIS:* Abbreviation for Federal Inspection Services. It is utilized as an all-inclusive term for the U.S. Public Health, Immigration, and Naturalization Service, the Department of Agriculture, and U.S. Customs.

*Gate:* A location to which aircraft are brought for the purpose of discharging and loading passengers and their baggage.

*Gate Concourse:* An extension from the main terminal building primarily intended to provide protected access for passengers and the gates. In addition to the passenger between the main terminal building corridor, the concourse may include airline functional areas and minimum consumer services.

*Ground Transportation:* The independently operated transportation vehicles scheduled for passenger's use between airports and the areas served thereby is called ground transportation.

*Immigration:* This area is devoted to the examination of passports of U.S. nationals and aliens seeking to enter the U.S. Consideration for design and function of this area must be correlated with federal authorities.

*Interline Connecting(ion):* A term used to describe passengers and baggage which arrive on the flight of one airline and depart on the flight of another.

*Intown Terminal:* A facility located apart from the airport, usually in the downtown area of the city, at which passengers may be processed, baggage checked to passengers' destinations, and from which ground transportation is provided.

*Intraline Connecting(ion):* A term used to describe passengers and baggage which arrive on one flight and depart on another flight of the same airline.

*In-Transit Passenger:* If an internationally bound aircraft stops at an airport for refueling or discharge of passengers and a remaining number of passengers are to be detained in the aircraft for another destination, the convenience of providing a totally segregated lounge facility may be warranted for the continuing passengers. This facility is referred to as an in-transit area. No FIS inspection is required, but security of the area is important.

*Long-Haul:*   A term used to define flights or traffic which travel over a relatively long distance as opposed to those which travel over a shorter distance. Normally, long-haul passengers arrive at the originating airport earlier than short-haul passengers, carry more baggage than short-haul passengers, and are accompanied to or are met at the airport by more persons than short-haul passengers.

*Originating Passenger:*   A passenger who is starting a trip.

*Outbound Baggage Room:*   The area to which checked baggage of originating passengers is delivered for sorting by flights prior to its being dispatched to the aircraft for loading.

*Public Health Service:*   The function of the Public Health Service is to determine whether an arriving passenger will present a health hazard to the general population. Design requires correlation with federal authorities. This may require inoculation, special examination, and possibly quarantine.

*Ready Room:*   An area adjacent to the normal work areas in which personnel whose duties are performed out-of-doors may assemble, be protected, and from which they may receive their work assignments. These rooms should be concealed from public view.

*Self-Claim Baggage:*   A method under which passengers have direct access to terminating baggage in a controlled area. As passengers leave the area, an attendant retrieves baggage claim checks and matches them to strap checks to assure that passengers have selected only baggage to which they are entitled.

*Short-Haul:*   A term used to define flights or traffic which travel over a relatively short distance as opposed to those which travel over a long distance. Normally, passengers arrive at the airport of origin later, carry less baggage than long-haul passengers, and are accompanied to or met at the airport by fewer persons.

*Standby Passenger:*   A passenger not holding confirmed space but who is on hand at departure time for space that might become available.

*Terminating Passenger:*   A passenger who has arrived at her destination.

*Through Passenger:*   A passenger who arrives and departs on the same flight.

*Transfer Baggage Room:*   The area to which checked baggage of connecting passengers is delivered for sorting by flights prior to its being dispatched to the aircraft for loading. This may be combined with outbound baggage room at some locations.

*Unit Terminal:*   One of several functionally complete terminal areas (which may be in the same or several buildings) each of which houses the activities of one or more airlines.

## PRELIMINARY DESIGN PROGRAM AND DEVELOPMENT CONSIDERATIONS

Before planning in any form can proceed, the architect must establish a data bank and an ability to retrieve pieces of information in the most rapid manner. This includes all information from participating airlines and all programs on studies that may have been completed by the airport authority. General economic considerations must be examined and the geographical site location evaluated. The acquisition of data, its analysis, and the request for supplementary information must be made at this time.

The architect must also make inquiries to the governing agency as to the requirements of the Federal Aviation Administration and all other government agencies. The architect must further recognize the assistance, advice, and guidance by organizations such as Air Transport Association, Airline Pilots Association, and the International Air Transport Association.

The most important single element that the architect must provide for in her design is *flexibility*, so that all elements of the system may grow as required. In design and planning, the following must have *growth capability* on an individual basis without jeopardizing the total relationship of the master plan. Parking lots must be capable of growth within any specific area as demands require, and public transportation systems must be capable of individual growth. Curb frontage must grow on an independent basis. Baggage claim areas, check-in areas, gate lounge areas, aircraft positions, the number of aircraft positions—any or all of these elements and the airline operational areas must offer the capability of independent growth to meet the changing demands of the future.

The prime reason for this independence and flexibility relates to the problem of aircraft technology and the fact that the preestablished schedules may change and, as a result, congestion may become a problem at almost any point in the terminal system. These two factors make it mandatory that each element have a built-in potential for expansion.

Security at airport terminals creates constraint on access, and the back-up that results causes the displeasure of passengers. This can be most difficult if an amenities area is located outside of a secured passenger area and a delayed flight is then announced for departure.

Flexibility must be inherent in each of the elements, yet both good design and economy must be maintained. When all program information has been collected and expansion flexibility has been planned for, the architect must establish a first-stage program based upon the scheduled opening date for the airport. She must then relate this program to an ultimate date of operation. The best method for this is through the use of a computer model simulation.

The computer simulation can be established by examining the maximum number of aircraft movements that air saturation will allow and correlating this with the maximum ground area that may be available for the airport under consideration. This data can now be related back to the terminal building area for all functional disciplines that pertain. The summation of maximums and minimums will now serve as a guide for the master plan of the terminal building area. Since this analysis is extremely complex, the architect should retain specialists in this area of endeavor.

Using the computer simulation as a working tool, the architect can establish a preliminary design concept or concepts and, in addition, preliminary expansion stages for planning can be established. The architect should not take this preliminary work back to the computer at this time. Instead, he must now test and evaluate critical conditions that can occur due to changing technology, passenger growth, and expansion, and the computer will allow him to check each discipline all functional aspects of the terminal area. This would include all functions with the terminal building, curb-side accessibility, parking requirements (both public and employees), road access and capabilities, public transportation, etc. Either computer simulation or analytical methods will establish time periods of congestion traditionally referred to as Average Peak Hours. The architect will carefully examine the average peak hour so as to ascertain simple, direct, and logical routes for all passengers, including their baggage and their vehicular transportation. She should then take these movements to the computer for analysis.

For example, assume that in the design of the terminal, average peak-hour traffic problems relate to a time span of 11 A.M. and 2 P.M. for arriving passenger flights. What will happen if, operating on the present city relationships, new aircraft traveling at considerably greater speeds become operational at this airport? It is very possible that the computer simulation will show there is no effect, or quite the contrary, it may show that the average peaking conditions may double up.

Taking into account the time frame, the architect will be further required to work with each of the airlines to ascertain their method of operation. How do they handle passengers, baggage, cargo, amenities, food service, ramp operations, maintenance, and their own personnel? He will then attempt to provide space utilization compatible with the different users. He will also establish those space needs required by the FAA, the airport administration, etc.

Another essential requirement related to the terminal building is that of providing parking space for automobiles. The architect must acquire from the operator of the parking area a system of tariffs, including those that will be applied to short-term, long term, and valet parking. Without the tariff indication, it is impossible to determine the accrual rate of vehicular parking. The accrual rate is the factor that determines the number of parking spaces that will be required. Any change in the tariff or relationships of tariffs will change the accrual rate and therefore will change the parking space requirements.

As an additional factor, the architect must consider employee parking and the congestion that occurs during the shift changes. It therefore becomes necessary for the architect to ascertain the general character of employment practices by the airlines involved as it relates to the schedule of time. Care must be exercised in developing access for employees to the terminal building.

In developing the passenger terminal the architect is advised to relate only to "Terminal." The expression of passenger is inaccurate as the terminal serves to enplane and deplane cargo, mail, and people.

In the best interests of the operation of airline, airport and amenity operators, adequate space relationships must be provided for storage, waiting room and access paths which will satisfy average peak hour needs.

Terminals, small or large, will need the same elements. Since the passenger terminal is the transfer point between land and air, consideration must be given to the geometries of the aircraft apron. It should afford a great degree of flexibility to include larger aircraft, aircraft mix (different types of aircraft), space required for ground equipment, the storage of cargo, and the techniques for loading people from the building to aircraft.

Any passenger terminal system will rely heavily upon the ability of the public to secure information. It is, therefore, incumbent upon the architect to give consideration as early as possible to the nature and types of information systems that will be made available to the general public, so as to guide them to their desired locations.

Early planning must take into account fire safety and access to the structure as well as the probabilities of insurance premiums. The fire hazards relating to the terminal structure can be most readily identified as aircraft, fueling operations on the aircraft apron, public area hazards, baggage room areas, and cargo storage areas.

It is not unusual, in the smaller terminals, for secondary functions of the airline to be incorporated into the terminal building. These may fall into categories such as in-flight feeding, line maintenance, and general office use.

The designer of the terminal building must at an early date include significant analyses of engineering considerations, as this will involve boiler plants, air conditioning, electrical distribution, communications systems, waste removal, and maintenance areas. Any mechanical system that is utilized must of necessity have an alternate or redundant system so that reliability of operation is guaranteed at the airport.

## Airport Passenger Terminal Design Concepts

The design of the airport passenger terminal is dependent upon many interrelated factors that must be carefully considered in developing the passenger terminal design concept. These factors include the volume and nature of passenger demand, passenger characteristics, the number and type of airlines providing service, the type and quality of service to be provided, whether passenger travel is international, domestic or a combination of both, and whether service is scheduled or chartered. The types of surface transportation providing access to the airport, the physical conditions and constraints of the site and the nature and quality of the environmental context must also be carefully considered in the development of the passenger terminal design concept.

Passenger processing is one of the most basic and important considerations in the development of the passenger terminal concept. Basic passenger processing includes ticketing, passenger and baggage check-in, security screening, immigration, customs, and baggage claim. A principal objective in the design of the airport terminal is for passenger processing to be as simple, efficient, and pleasant as possible while, at the same time, accomplishing all of the necessary formalities and observing the governmental regulations associated with air travel.

One of the principal considerations in the design of the airport passenger terminal is the sequence and distribution of passenger processing throughout the terminal. The degree of centralization versus decentralization of passenger processing must be taken into consideration. As passenger volumes have grown, there have been many design and technological innovations in passenger processing such as electronic ticketing, curbside check-in, gate check-in, automated check-in, and immigration and customs pre-clearance. These innovations have help to streamline passenger processing and have helped to minimize crowding, congestion and waiting time in passenger processing areas.

An appropriate design philosophy and concept must be developed for each passenger terminal taking into consideration its unique requirements and potentials. The following discussion illustrates a range of concepts that have been developed for the design of the airport passenger terminal.

## Linear Terminal

The linear terminal is one of the most basic passenger terminal concepts. The linear terminal may be a single level or multi-level building. The linear plan may accommodate a single airline or may be a consolidated terminal for multiple airlines. In the linear terminal concept, passenger processing is primarily centralized.

For single level terminals, the aircraft are parked adjacent to the terminal building with access from the terminal to the aircraft at apron level. The single level, linear terminal concept (Figs. 8a, 9, and 10) is normally used for airport terminals with lower passenger volumes. The single level apron loading concept provides a fairly minimal level of passenger service and providing adequate services for passengers in need of assistance to board and deboard the aircraft is of concern with this concept. In the two-level terminal, access may be provided to the aircraft via passenger boarding bridges from an upper level. The two-level linear terminal provides more convenient access to the aircraft (Figs. 8b, 11).

The linear terminal concept has also been utilized for large, high volume passenger terminals. The larger terminals are complex, multi-level facilities. The airside of the terminal may be designed with aircraft gates and passenger boarding lounges. The terminal building may also be extended along the airside to increase the number of aircraft gates and passenger waiting areas. Essentially, an attached linear concourse is created along the airside of the terminal building (Figs. 8c, 8d, 12, 13).

## Central Terminal with Finger Piers

The number of gates and capacity of the linear terminal may be increased through the use of finger piers (Figs. 14a, b, c). The finger piers increase the airside perimeter providing additional aircraft gates and passenger boarding lounges. The gates may be assigned to an airline on a permanent basis to simplify ramp operations. In this concept, as the piers become extended to provide additional gates, walking distances are increased which may become especially problematic for connecting passengers.

As a variant of this concept, nodes or satellites may be created at the ends of the finger piers, which provide the capability of providing additional aircraft gates and passenger boarding lounges, as well as decentralized passenger services such as passenger check-in and concessions (Fig. 14d). The new central terminal at Lester B. Pearson International Airport in Toronto, Ontario, Canada is an excellent example of this terminal concept.

## Central Terminal with Remote Satellites

The central terminal with remote satellites was developed, in part, to overcome the problem of walking distances and inefficiencies in the movement of aircraft and ground service vehicles associated with finger pier terminals. In larger terminals with greater distances to the satellites, automated transportation systems provide passenger access from the central terminal to the remote satellites. Initially, the terminals utilizing this concept, such as Tampa and Orlando, Florida International Airport (Fig. 15), were highly centralized with most passenger processing occurring in the central terminal building. As these terminals have been further developed there has been a somewhat greater degree of decentralized passenger processing.

## Central Terminal with Remote Piers

In this concept, the terminal complex includes a central terminal building with access provided to remote piers via a corridor beneath

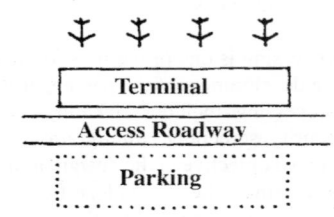

**(a) Single level terminal–
open apron**

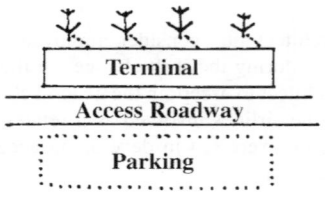

**(b) Two level terminal–
passenger boarding bridges**

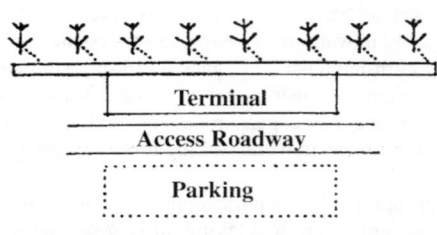

**(c) Two level terminal–
linear airside concourse**

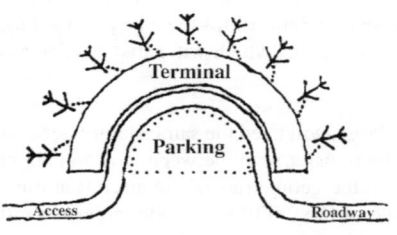

**(d) Curvilinear two-level terminal**

**Fig. 8. Linear terminal concepts**

Fig. 9. Martha's Vineyard Airport, passenger terminal (TAMS Consultants, Inc.)

Fig. 10. Martha's Vineyard Airport, passenger terminal, airside (TAMS Consultants, Inc.)

Fig. 11. Mid America Airport and Passenger Terminal (TAMS Consultants, Inc.)

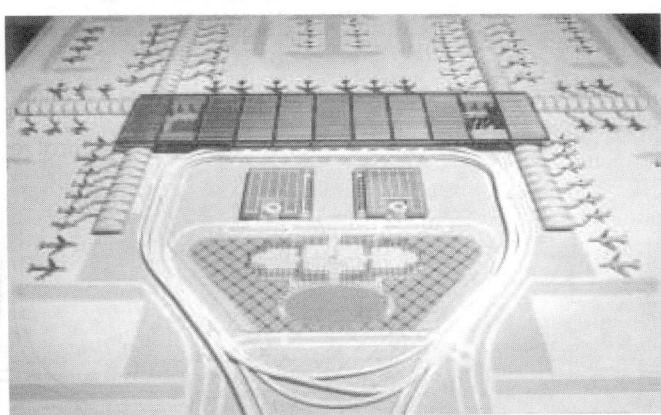

Fig. 12. Second Bangkok International Airport passenger terminal complex (MJTA Joint Venture: Murphy/Jahn Architects; TAMS Consultants, Inc.; ACT Consultants)

Fig. 13. Second Bangkok International Airport passenger terminal complex (MJTA Joint Venture: Murphy/Jahn Architects; TAMS Consultants, Inc.; ACT Consultants)

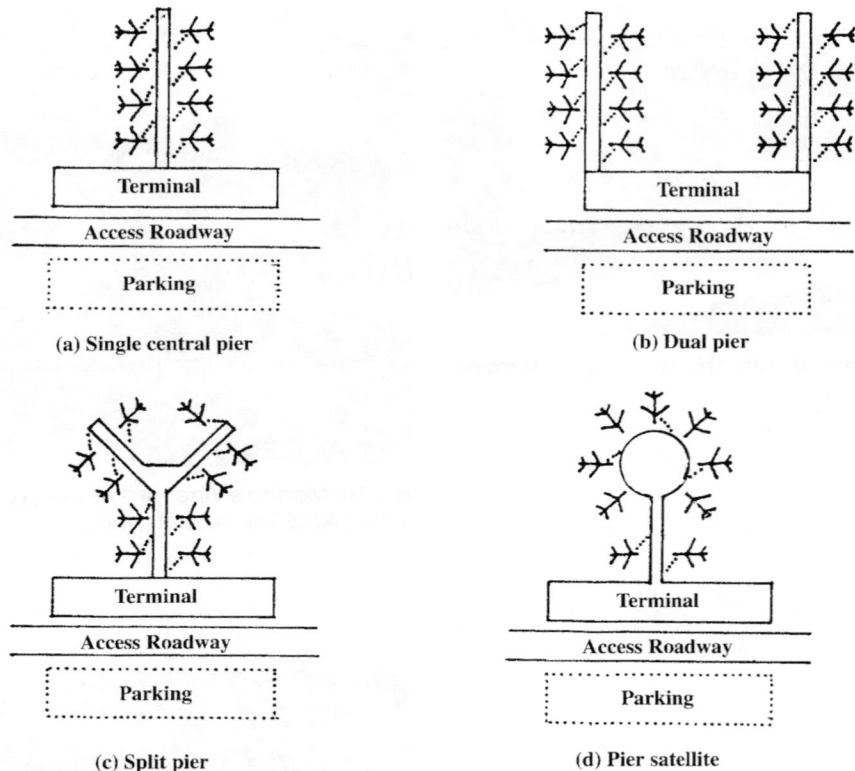

(a) Single central pier

(b) Dual pier

(c) Split pier

(d) Pier satellite

**Fig. 14. Central terminal pier concepts**

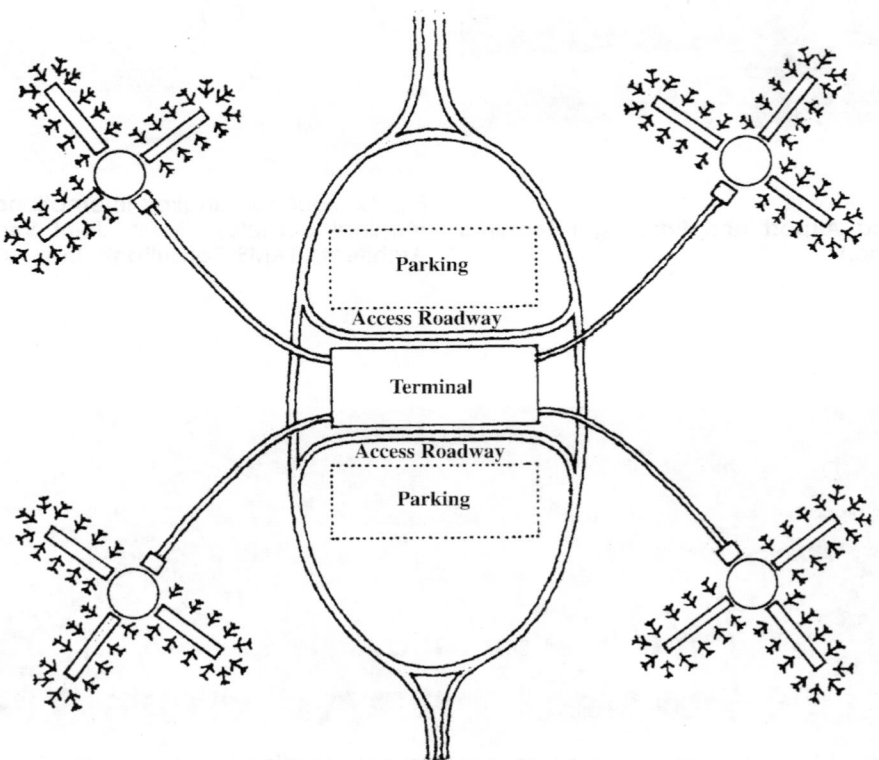

**Fig. 15. Central terminal with remote satellites**

aircraft apron (Fig. 16). The terminal complex may include one or more remote piers. Multiple piers are normally designed parallel to each other to simplify airside geometry and operations. This concept has been utilized primarily at airports with high passenger volumes. The remote piers have a very high capacity providing a large number of aircraft gates with very efficient airside operations. Due to the considerable distance to the remote piers, the access corridor is usually designed with moving walkways or an automated people mover system. Passenger processing and services may be provided both in the central terminal building and in the remote piers. This concept may be especially appropriate at airports with aircraft hub operations having a significant number of transfer passengers. The Atlanta Hartsfield, Denver Jeppeson, and proposed Chicago Third Airport (Fig. ) are examples of this design concept.

### Central Terminal with Airside Transporters

The concept of using airside transporters to provide passenger access to remote aircraft stands has been widely used in the U.S. and Europe. The airside transporters may be specially designed apron buses or mobile lounges (Figs. 18a, b). The mobile lounges are equipped with hydraulic lifts to accomplish the vertical transition at the terminal and concourse. The primary advantage to this concept is the flexibility of airside operations. Ground traffic on the airside is increased which may cause ground traffic flow problems on the aircraft apron. The maneuvering and docking of the mobile lounges may be problematic. Passenger boarding and deboarding of the buses complicates the airside transition for many passengers. Some passengers will require special assistance boarding and leaving the apron buses. Also, there is the potential for considerable delays due to the operation of the transporters.

### Unit Terminal

In the unit terminal concept, a single airline or a number of airlines are accommodated in individual, stand alone terminal buildings (Fig. 19). The individual terminal buildings are linked together by a terminal area access roadway. The unit terminal concept provides a high degree of individual identity and operational autonomy to the airlines. Transferring between airlines and between unit terminal buildings may be very difficult for passengers at unit terminal airports. London Heathrow, John F. Kennedy Airport in New York (Fig. 20), and the Chicago O'Hare International Airports are examples of the unit terminal concept implemented on a large scale. The Dallas Fort Worth International airport is a famous example of the unit terminal concept in which the designers tried to provide for more efficient interline transfers.

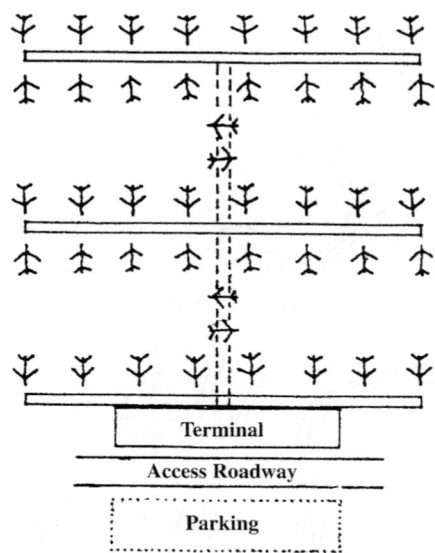

Fig. 16. Central terminal with remote piers

Fig. 17. Proposed Chicago Third Airport (TAMS Consultants, Inc.)

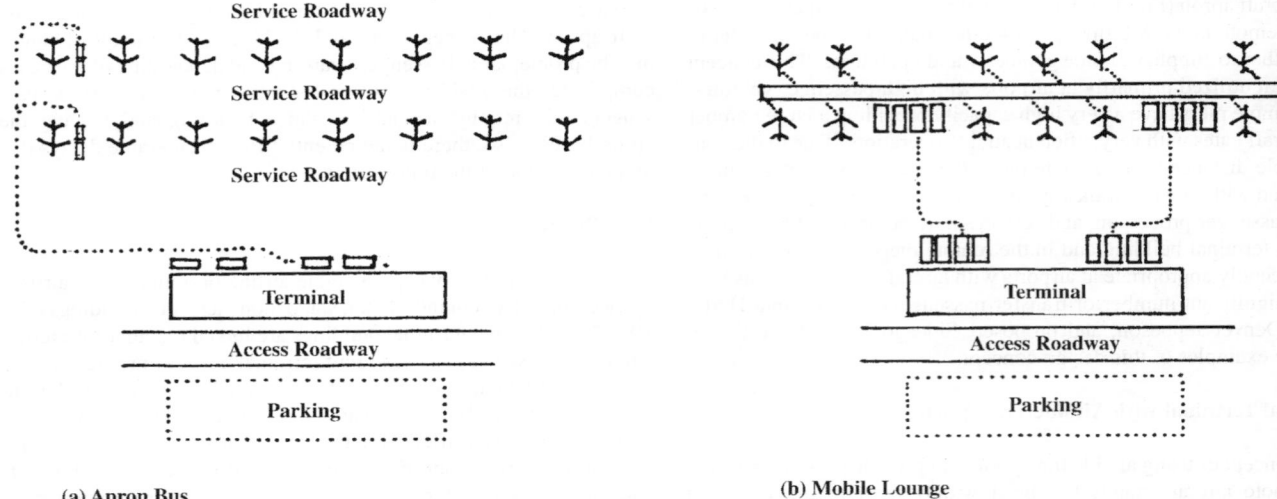

(a) Apron Bus          (b) Mobile Lounge

**Fig. 18. Central terminal with airside transporters**

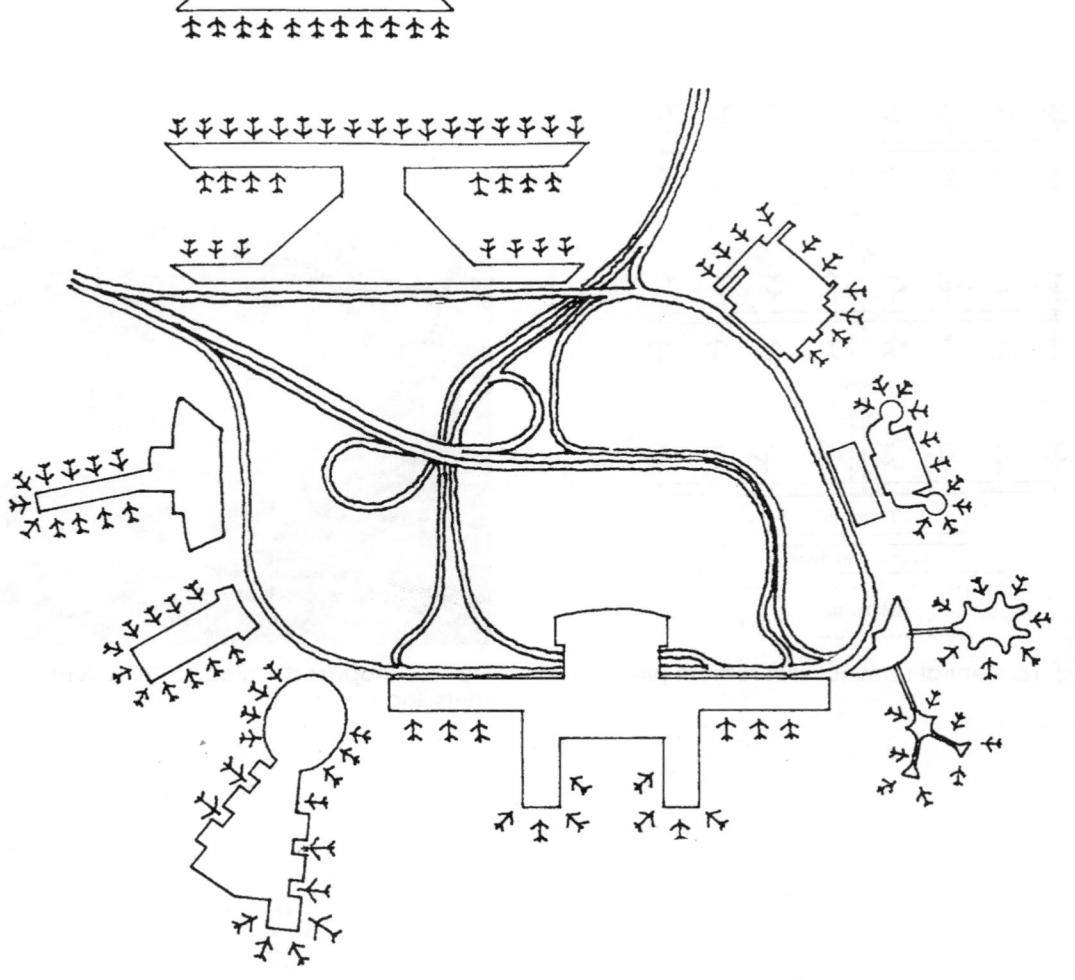

**Fig. 19. Unit terminal concept, John F. Kennedy International Airport**

g. 20. Pan American Airlines World Port (foreground), ohn F. Kennedy International Airport (TAMS Consultants, c.)

## IRLINE REQUIREMENTS

he architect will carefully ascertain from the individual carriers eir specific needs. This information should be correlated to the year f operations, the anticipated level of passenger and cargo, opera- onal growth, the potential of changing route structures, and an ini- al and future projected flight schedule. Table 1 lists the basic data formation that is required from the airlines. There are many addi- onal technical information items which are not listed here, but the esigner will determine these by inference.

ach airline demands a distinctive visual character that will make it eadily identifiable to the public. All too frequently the architect ends to dismiss this requirement. The careful integration of individ- al airline identification in a total building design will assist the pas- enger. An airline will retain many professional consultants in ttempting to carry a corporate image system wide, and it will spend onsiderable sums of money in order to achieve this.

Undoubtedly, not all corporate identity systems are in good taste. Iowever, one should not dismiss the very special effort to achieve a imple visual image that the airlines attempt to achieve. Design judg- nent at this point is of paramount importance.

## AIRCRAFT PARKING SYSTEMS

The placement of aircraft on the aircraft apron may be divided into wo categories: push-out operations and power-out operations. The rchitect should determine the general technique that the airlines will utilize. The system they select will have a great effect on the aircraft apron area as well as the passenger loading system that can be uti- ized.

Power-out operations will involve special design considerations with regard to the wall surfaces of terminal buildings and they will require greater apron area. They will also call for blast protection in the oper- ational areas of the terminal. This method of operation will generally mean that fewer ground personnel and less equipment are required.

## Table 1 Airline statistical data requirements

1. Estimated enplaning and deplaning traffic:
   Figures on enplaning and deplaning passengers should be given separately.

   a. Passengers—total number per year
   Passengers—average day, peak month
   Passengers—peak hour and time
   Passenger characteristic (business, vacation, student)

   b. Interline passengers

   c. Intraline passengers

   d. Originating passengers

   e. Air freight cargo—total tons

   f. Mail—total tons

   g. Baggage—total number per year
   Baggage—average day, peak month

2. Projected flight schedule:

   a. City pairs

   b. Originating and terminating

   c. Time frame

   d. Aircraft type

3. Aircraft:

   a. Number of gate positions

   b. Number and type of aircraft for gate size design

   c. Aircraft parking attitude

4. Terminal building spaces:

   a. Gate lounge—number and sizes

   b. Baggage claim type and size

   c. Amenities area

   d. Operational facilities—type and sizes

   e. Central ticketing facilities

5. Automobile parking requirements (airline experience):

   a. Public

   b. Valet

   c. Taxis

   d. Limousines

   e. Car rental

   f. Employees

The push-out operation requires the use of tractors and personnel to move the aircraft out of its gate position before it powers away from the terminal area. The push-out operation does offer the advantage of requiring less apron area. It also requires less square footage at the terminal building because of a reduced linear length.

Included in the data sheets is general information related to the major types of aircraft (Figs. 21 to 24).

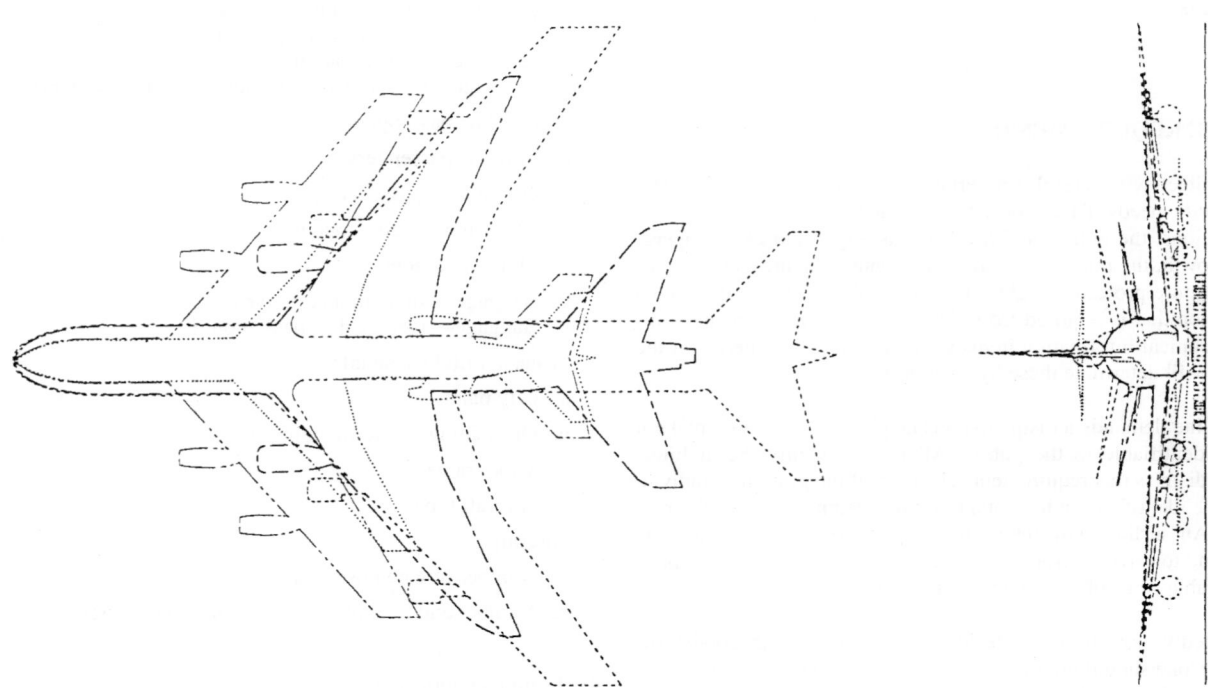

**Fig. 21. Aircraft composite**

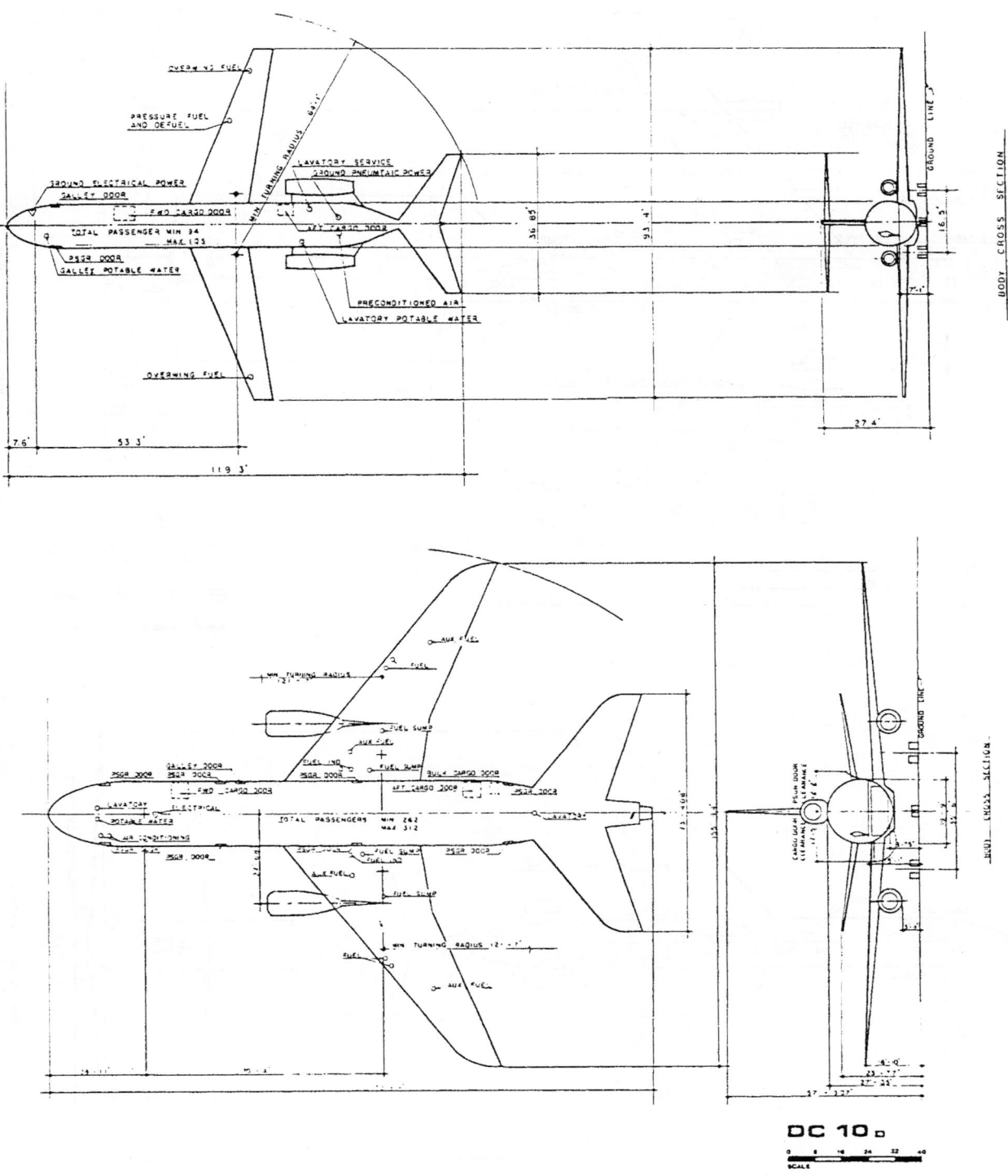

**Fig. 22**

DC 10 D

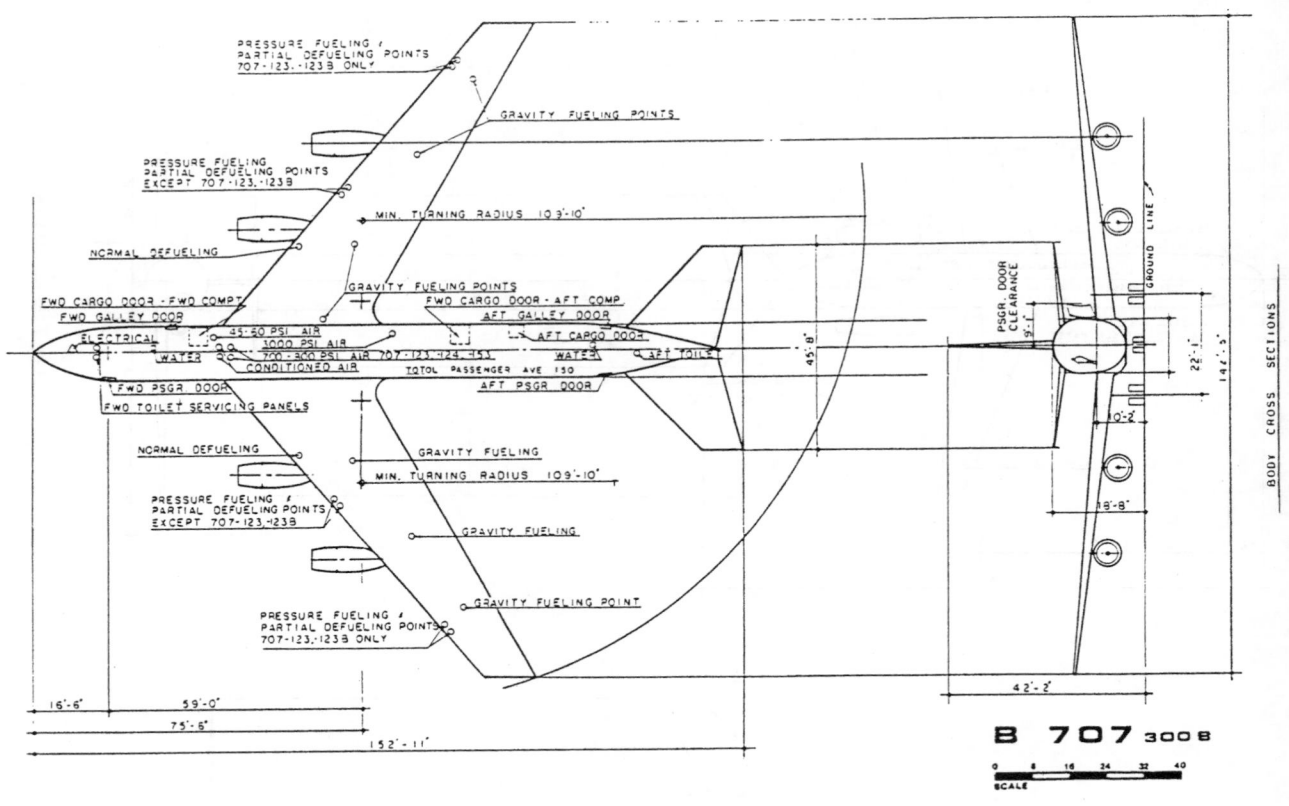

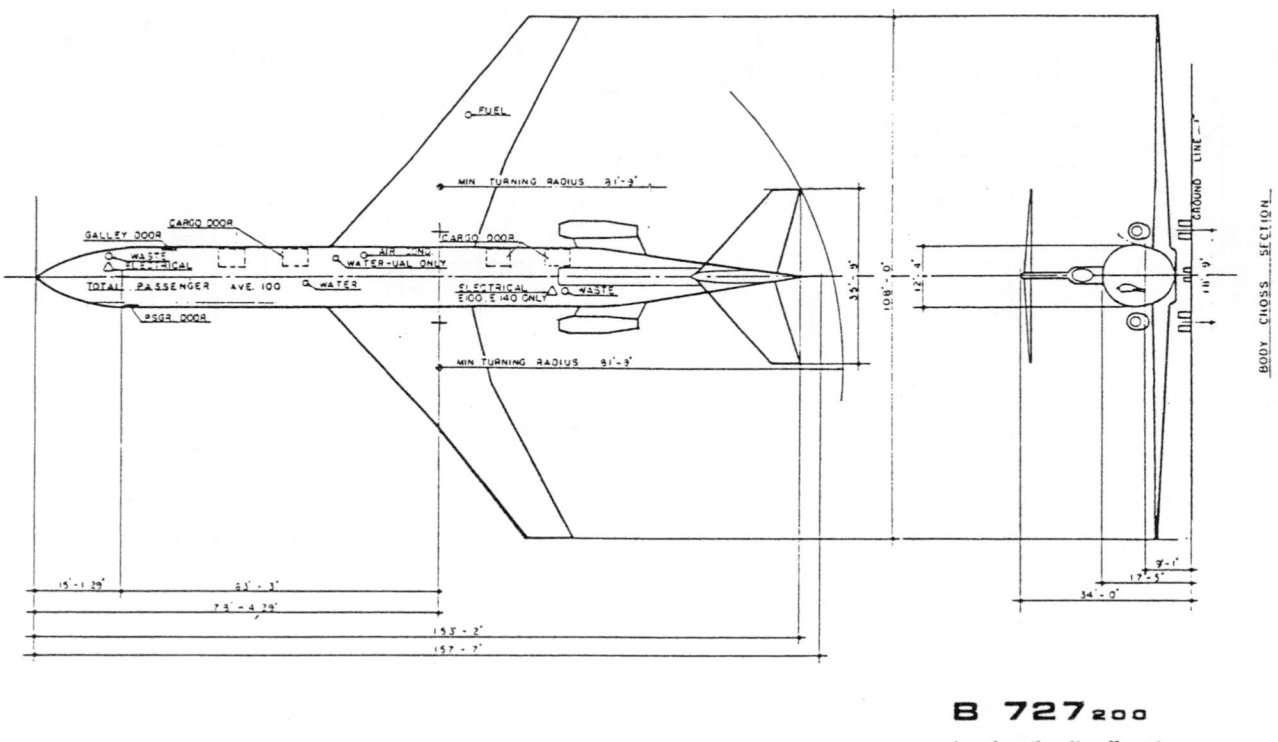

**Fig. 23**

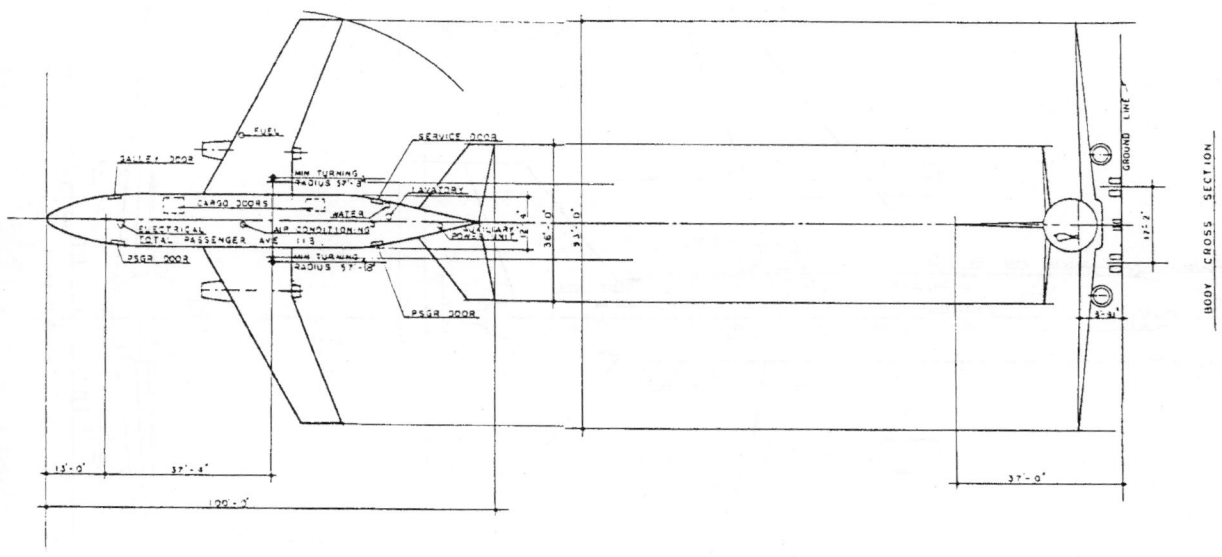

B 737 200

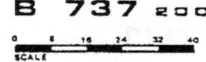

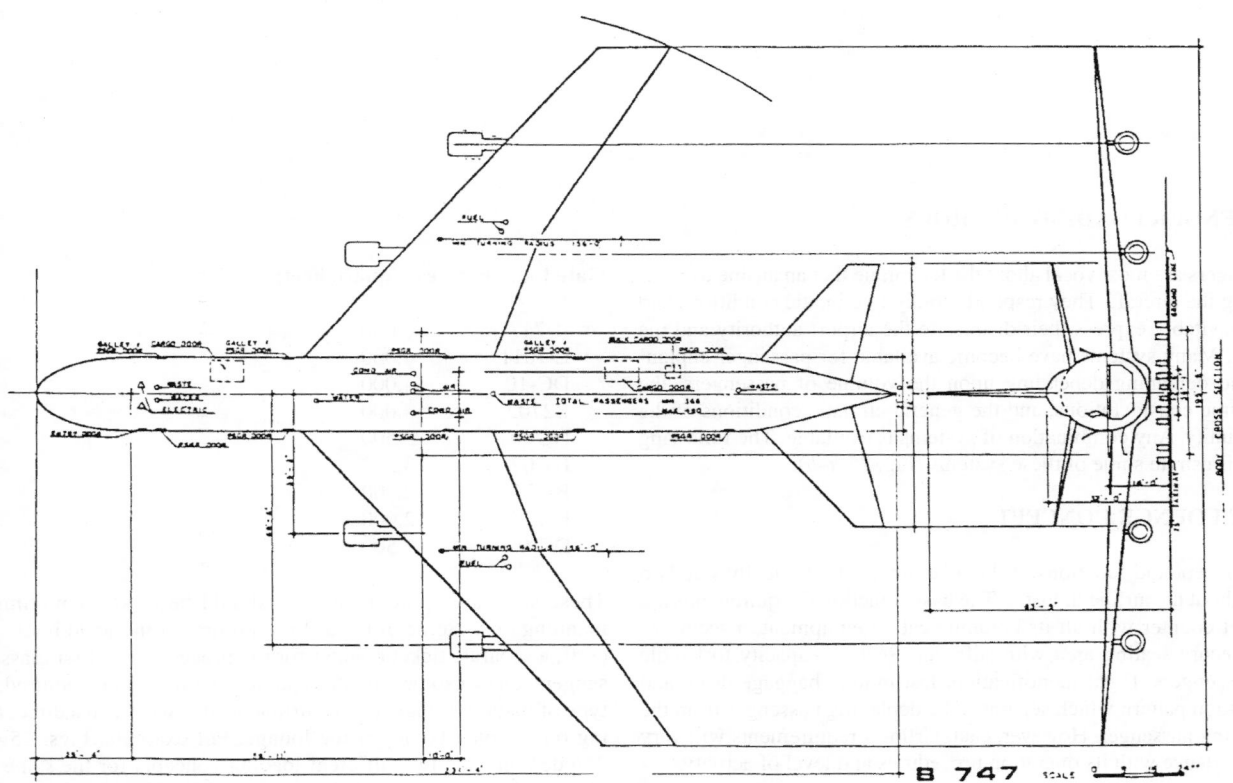

B 747

**Fig. 23 (cont.)**

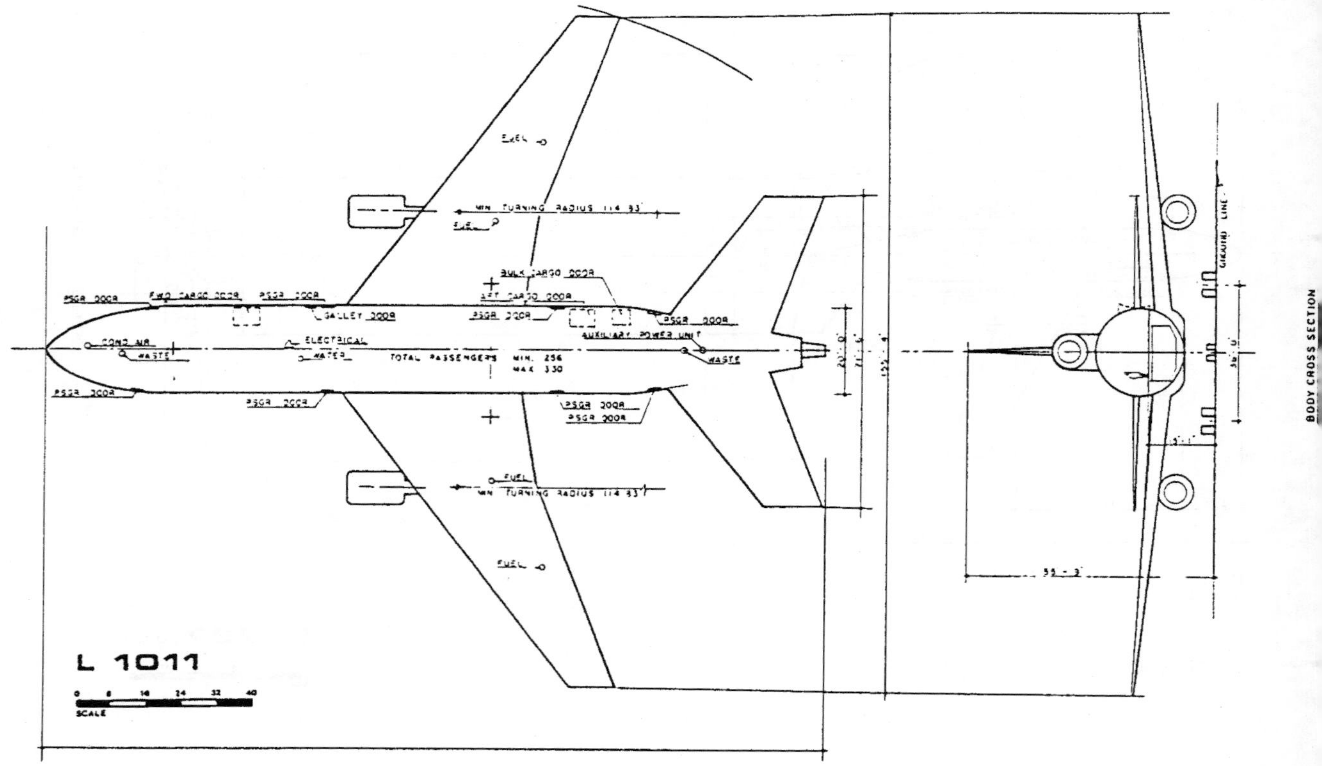

L 1011

**Fig. 24**

## PASSENGER LOADING METHODS

Passengers are most vocal about the technique that an airline uses for loading the aircraft. They respond rapidly to climatic conditions and will inevitably express their distress to the airport authority and the airline. Many systems have become available for passenger enplaning and deplaning depending upon the volume of passengers, the economic considerations, and the general climatic conditions of the community. Any combination of systems is available. The following pages illustrate some of these systems (Fig. 25 a–h).

## GATE LOUNGE CONCEPT

The concept and functions of the gate lounge are basically standard throughout the airline industry. The basic functional requirements are a ticket counter with all its communication equipment, a secure or semi-secure seating area with sufficient seating capacity to handle the passengers, flight identification, last-minute baggage drop, and circulation pattern which separates the deplaning passenger from the enplaning passenger. However, each airline's requirements will vary in accordance with its operation procedures and level of activity.

Following are average sizes for gate lounges as required by each type of aircraft.

**Gate Lounge Sizes, Square Feet:**

| | |
|---|---|
| B-747 | 6,000 |
| L-1011 | 4,000 |
| DC-10 | 4,000 |
| B2702 | 4,000 |
| DC-8 | 3,500 |
| B-707 | 3,500 |
| B-737 | 2,000 |
| B-727 | 2,000 |
| DC-9 | 1,500 |

These sizes are approximate and should be used for preliminary planning only. Some of the airlines prefer, for the wide-bodied aircraft, a separate ticket counter for the processing of first-class passengers, and in some cases a separate seating area is required. The type of loading bridge that an airline desires will have a direct bearing on the plan layout of the lounge. For example, Figs. 25g and 25h demonstrate two different loading concepts for the same type of aircraft. It is obvious that the circulation pattern within the gate lounge for these two types of loading bridges will be completely different.

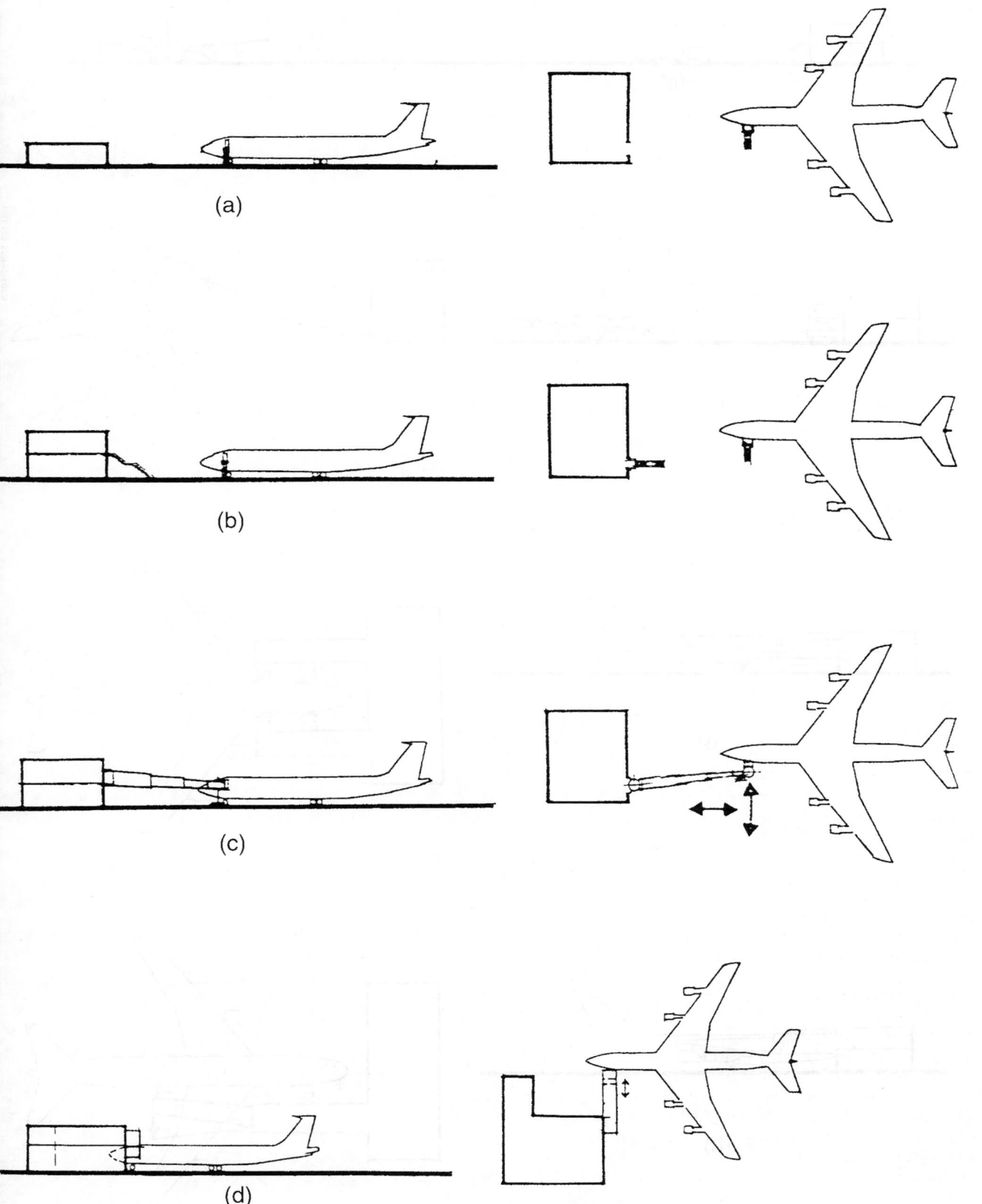

**Fig. 25. Typical loading methods**

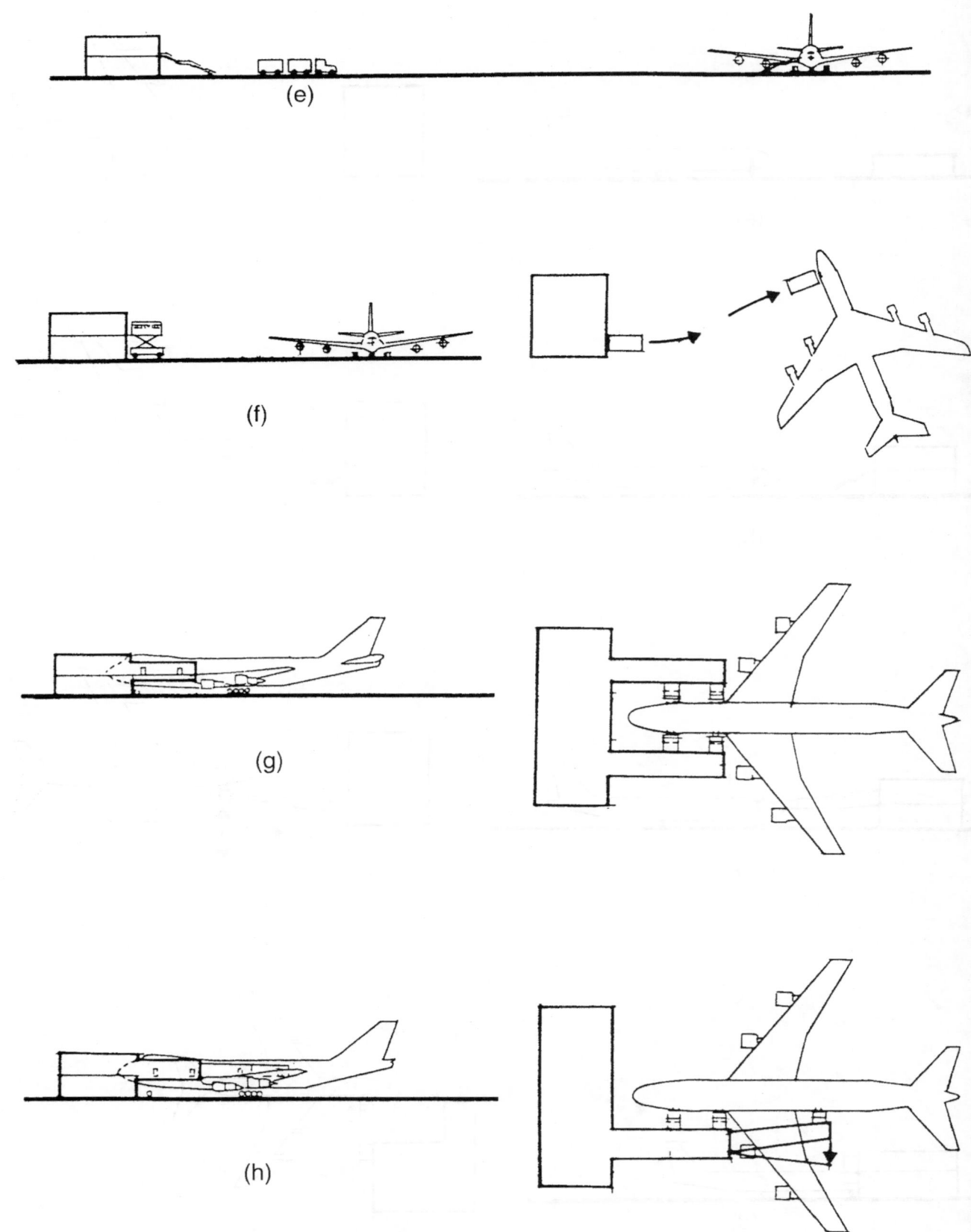

**Fig. 25. (cont.) Typical loading methods**

## BAGGAGE HANDLING SYSTEMS

Baggage handling is of critical importance to the operation of an airport terminal.

Typically business travelers will carry on one suitcase which will fit below an airline seat and a garment bag of reasonable dimension that can be hung in a wardrobe on the aircraft. The use of such carry-ons allows business and other travelers to bypass the baggage system. Transfer baggage also bypasses the check-in and claim part of the system.

Is not unusual for the volume of business travelers at a given airport to reach 30 percent, and it can be anticipated that at least 80 percent of these business travelers will not require any baggage check-in system. Nor is it unusual for the volume of transfer passengers to vary from 10 to 45 percent of the total passenger load. Therefore, the selection of the desired system will require a complete understanding of what percentage of the passengers utilize the terminal facilities for the particular airport.

The average number of baggage pieces handled by the airlines ranges from 1.6 to 1.9 bags per passenger. This will vary depending upon the airport and the airline for the type of route structure that exists. For example, the longer the flight the greater the probability that passengers will take several pieces of luggage—although very long international stage lengths show a reduction. Therefore, an airline that has a route structure built basically of long flight lengths will handle a much greater number of bags than an airline with a route structure based upon short stage lengths.

In providing space for baggage handling system, the architect must have a complete understanding of each airline operation and the relationship of all the airlines combined. This understanding should encompass the percentage of baggage per passenger for originating, terminating, and transfer (both interline and intraline). It also should be related to the time schedule and the peak conditions.

A baggage check-in system can incorporate check-in points at a central ticketing counter, at the gate lounge, at the curbside, and in a parking lot. The parking lot or curbside check-in provides the greatest amount of convenience for the passenger and allows for quick acceptance of the baggage. This means that the rest of the public space in the terminal area will not be congested by baggage, taking floor space while waiting to be checked in. The curbside check-in isolates the major portion of the baggage handling with sky cap personnel and not with airline agents.

A check-in system can be serviced by a simple conveyor or a gravity chute. For large terminal facilities where there can be many check-in points and more than one baggage makeup space, a system can comprise fully automated cars or pallets that move bags to many destinations. This type of sophisticated system is costly and, in order to justify its use, it should be considered as a total system of all baggage movement, from aircraft to passenger and from passenger to aircraft.

The acceptance of baggage from the originating passenger at the terminal is complicated by the acceptance of interline and intraline baggage for the transferring of passengers. A large number of employees, for the amount of baggage handled, are utilized in interline transfers. Their route of travel by vehicle is frequently time-consuming. The transferred baggage is processed in the same backup area as the originating and terminating baggage, therefore space must

be allowed in order to accomplish this handling. The volume of bags that is to be transferred and processed must be determined in cooperation with the airline user. The precise system used and its building space must have the capability of expansion from the initial operational level.

The selection of the correct baggage system must also be correlated to the reverse flow of baggage from aircraft to baggage claim. The baggage claim system, by its very nature, produces an acute problem of baggage handling. Terminating passengers from an arriving flight expect to claim their baggage within a short period of time. A peaking condition occurs when a combination of flights arrives within the same time frame. In contrast, the originating passengers will generally arrive at the airport over an extended period of time, therefore dispersing the handling of baggage over the same time period.

As larger aircraft, such as the 747, have been utilized in greater numbers, the peaking conditions increase and decentralization of the baggage claim system becomes more desirable for the sake of passenger convenience and the elimination of congestion.

Baggage claim devices can involve many different shapes, forms, and methods of mechanical or manual handling of baggage. Figure 26 demonstrates the basic concepts that are available. The designer can see from these illustrations that the basic general technique is to produce a great display of linear feet of frontage so that passengers can readily identify their bags and claim same.

The interface between the aircraft and the claim area is still generally accomplished by towing the baggage to the terminal building, where a manual operation accomplishes the placement of baggage on the claiming device (Fig. 27).

The ability to retrieve bags from the aircraft and transfer them to the terminal baggage handling system is a key element in rapid and efficient baggage dispersal.

The design of an automated system to transfer the baggage modules to the building system is technically feasible. This would eliminate the towing operation and provide a faster method of producing the baggage at the claim area. It would also mean that the baggage could be claimed in many different locations. However, this will depend upon the airline's required time frame, passenger convenience, and financial capabilities.

Baggage rooms must be handled with special caution to make sure that sufficient quantities of fresh air are provided if diesel-power tractors are used. Sprinkler protection must be provided and careful fire cutoff must be made between the terminal proper and baggage areas. Doors leading from the baggage room to the outside should be automated and must use rapid-acting equipment. However, it is important to provide, on all doors, safety edges that will prevent closure should an obstacle be in the way. The design concept must incorporate the capability of future expansion, and preferably this should be accomplished without disturbing the existing claiming facilities.

### Area Considerations for Baggage Systems

In the consideration of a baggage system the designer must insist on redundancy in the event of power failure or basic mechanical failure. This aspect of another method for baggage movement cannot be over emphasized.

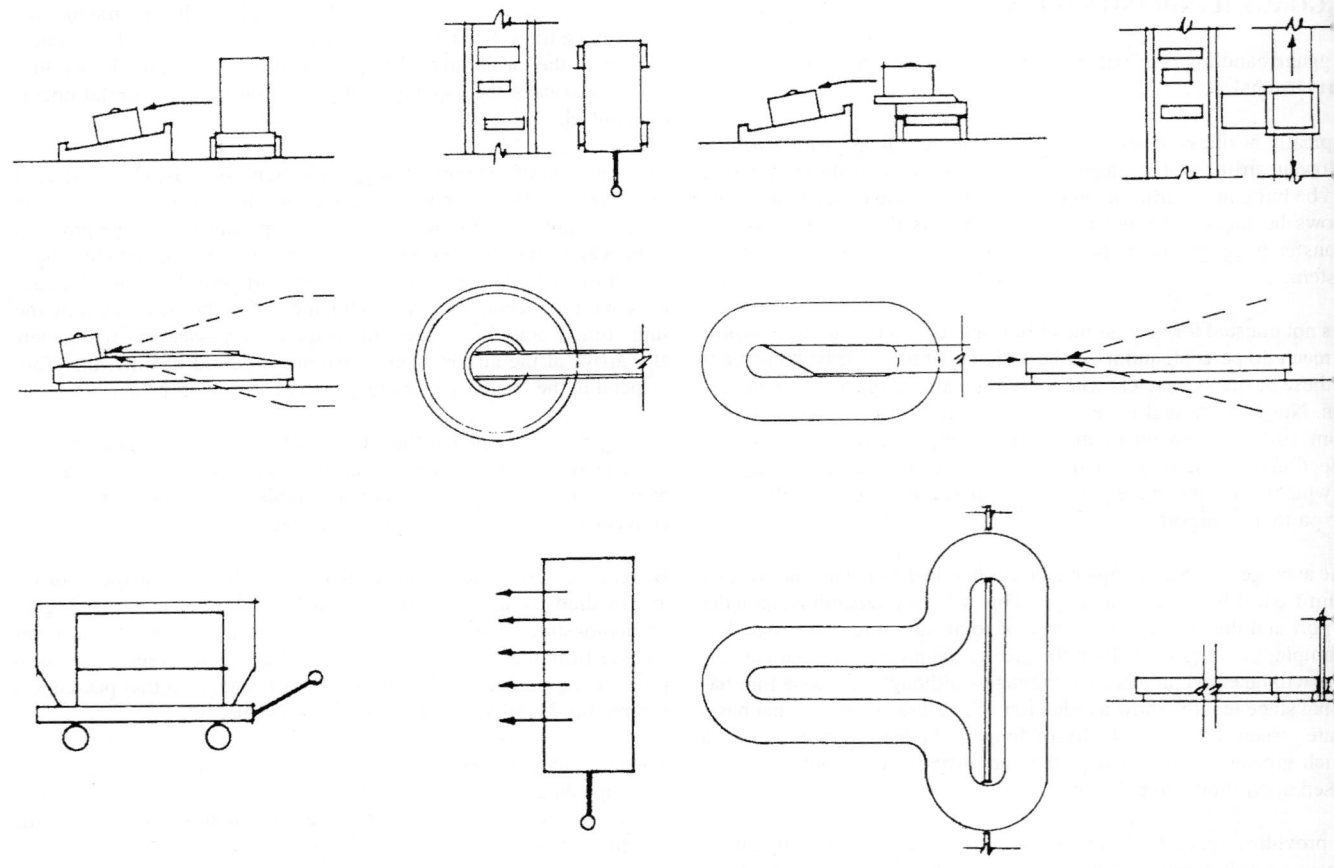

**Fig. 26. Baggage claim systems**

Even as alternate means of power, i.e., automatic-switch gear for basic service, or mechanical failure can occur; the designer must always provide other access or retrieval methods.

Aircraft and air traffic move at a rapid pace and a baggage system failure will cause chaos with scheduled air traffic.

**Enplaning Baggage**

As indicated in the flow diagram (Fig. 5), baggage may be received from four possible sources:

1. *Curbside Check-in.* This area must provide convenience of tagging and usually some mechanical conveyance back to a central bag room.

2. *Counter Check-in.* This will coincide with the usual tick counter in the main terminal area. It is customary to provi mechanization from an area directly in the back of the tick counter to the central baggage room.

3. *Gate Check-in.* In small quantities, bags are received at the gat Bags must be checked in at this point because many passenge mistakenly believe that their suitcases will be accepted for sto age in the passenger portion of the plane. A significant number airline passengers frequently use carry-on suitcases, but unle such luggage can be stored below the seat and out of aisle spac it must be carried in the baggage compartment.

4. *Transfer Baggage.* Additional bags will be received at a conve ient location adjacent to the baggage room for transfer from oth airlines or the same carrier. All baggage rooms which utili mechanized equipment must be provided with sufficient room f

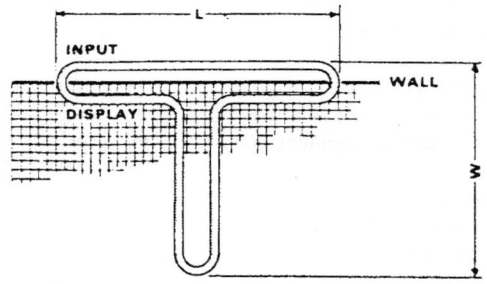

**FLATBED — DIRECT FEED**

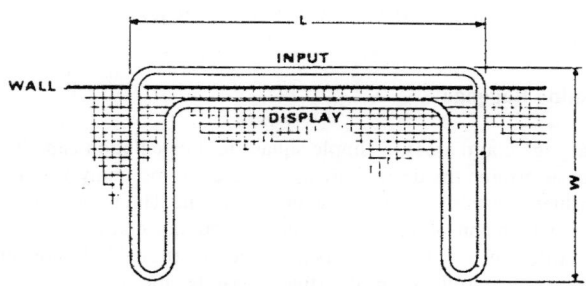

**FLATBED — DIRECT FEED**

| SHAPE | L FT (M) | W FT (M) | CLAIM FRONTAGE FT (M) | BAG STORAGE ① |
|-------|----------|----------|------------------------|----------------|
| ⊂⊃ | 65 (20) | 5 (1.5) | 65 (20) | 78 |
| ⊥ | 85 (26) | 45 (13.7) | 180 (55) | 216 |
| ⊥ | 85 (26) | 65 (20) | 220 (67) | 264 |
| ⊔ | 50 (15) | 45 (13.7) | 190 (58) | 228 |

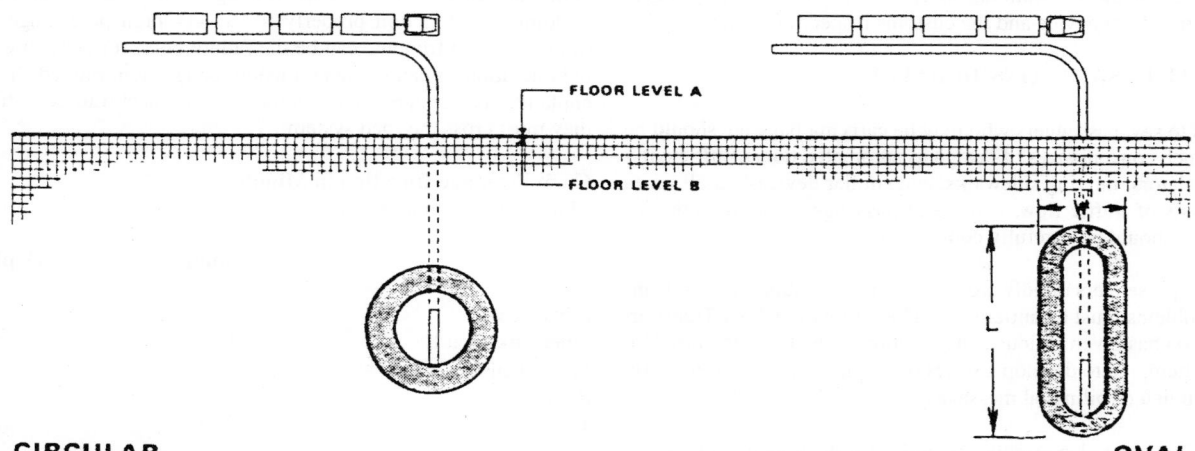

**CIRCULAR**
**REMOTE FEED SLOPING BED**

**OVAL**
**REMOTE FEED SLOPING BED**

| DIAMETER FT (M) | CLAIM FRONTAGE FT (M) | BAG STORAGE ① |
|------------------|------------------------|----------------|
| 20 (6) | 63 (19) | 94 |
| 25 (7.5) | 78 (24) | 132 |
| 30 (9) | 94 (29) | 169 |

| L FT (M) | W FT (M) | CLAIM FRONTAGE FT (M) | BAG STORAGE ① |
|----------|----------|------------------------|----------------|
| 36 (11) | 20 (6) | 95 (29) | 170 |
| 52 (16) | 20 (6) | 128 (39) | 247 |
| 68 (21) | 18 (5.5) | 156 (48) | 318 |

① THEORETICAL BAG STORAGE — PRACTICAL BAG STORAGE CAPABILITY IS 1/3 LESS

Fig. 27. Mechanical claim devices (Source: *Planning and Design Considerations for Airport Terminal Building Development*, Advisory Circular AC 150/5360-7, DOT, FAA)

manual handling in the event that service requirements cause a shutdown.

### Deplaning Baggage

For baggage claim areas, a simple square foot calculation cannot be used to determine the desired area, for there are too many variables that influence establishment of the proper layout. The basic terminal building which consolidates all the airlines into one claim area establishes a different set of parameters than does a terminal building concept where decentralization of airlines separates the baggage claims for each airline. In some decentralized concepts, airlines are now developing more than one claim area for each traffic level. A terminal building which processes international arrivals requires another set of parameters for the establishment of the claim area.

In order to size a baggage claim area, the architect must have the following information: the number of passengers and the amount of baggage that will be claimed with the peak condition, the type of claiming device and its physical size, its capacity, and its linear feet of frontage. Care should be taken to determine the actual working capacity of the claiming device and not the theoretical capacity as advertised by manufacturers. The architect should also determine the desired type of operation and degree of security required by either the airline or the authority. With the correlation of this material, the architect should allow additional space for the queuing of passengers between the claim device and the customs inspection system.

### GENERAL DESIGN CONSIDERATIONS

Needless to say, passengers who may be carrying baggage should be offered such conveniences of design as automated doors, sufficiently wide escalators, moving sidewalks, and similar devices. At all times the analysis of traffic flow, volume of passengers, and direction of movement should be carefully considered.

Air traffic passengers rapidly cross international boundaries, and language problems must be anticipated. The International Air Transport Association has given serious consideration to the language problem and has attempted to develop a series of glyphs which can frequently be used in lieu of bilingual messages.

The terminal must also provide amenities for the traveling public. In fact, current trends are to make shopping part of the travel experience, and some terminals have become akin to mini shopping malls. Amenities may include any of the following list and such other items as may be determined by a particular locale:

Airline priority travel lounge
Bank
Barber shop
Camera shop
Candy store
Car rental agencies
Chapel
Clothing store
Drug store
Duty-free shop
Employee snack bar and cafeteria
Flowershop
Gift shop
Haberdashery
Hotel

Insurance vending
Money exchange
Newsstand
Observation deck
Parcel lockers
Restaurant, bar, and supplementary eating facilities
Shoe shine
Showers/dressing rooms
Telecommunication center
Television lounge
Valet

In addition to the amenities, consideration should be given to traveler's aid in large installations and nursery facilities adjacent to the rest rooms in the main portion of the facility. Medical and first-aid facilities should be included in the passenger terminal if they are not provided elsewhere in the airport.

Communications systems will be required between the airlines, the operating authority, and/or police authorities. The size of the terminal building and the complex needs of each user should receive consideration when planning the communications system.

### CURB FRONTAGE UTILIZATION

When designed correctly, curb frontage at the face of the terminal building will function properly for a very high percentage of the time. The curb frontage can be the failure point for the entire terminal operation. It can cause confusion, congestion, missed flights by enplaning passengers, and become a safety hazard to pedestrians as they must cross the road system.

**Curb Frontage Duration in Minutes**
(if no survey data is available)

|  | Enplaning | Deplaning |
|---|---|---|
| Private cars | 2 | 3 |
| Valet cars at curb | 3 | 3 |
| Valet queuing | 5 | |
| Rental cars | 3 | 3 |
| Taxis | 5 | 5 |

The architect should devote considerable time and effort to designing the curbside frontage and the road system to it. Present design trends and concepts have separated the enplaning and deplaning road systems but very few have eliminated pedestrian traffic across these roads.

In the design of the curb frontage, the architect must consider all the forms of vehicular movement, such as private passenger vehicles, chauffeur-driven cars, rental cars, taxis, and public transportation (especially buses).

To determine the quantity of curb frontage, the following factors and assumptions must be considered:

1. All vehicles will require approximately 35 linear feet at the curb. This is a realistic interpretation of the indiscriminate manner in which vehicles tend to be parked.
2. The average time required at the curb for passenger vehicles should be surveyed for passengers by type of vehicle.
3. Duration time for valet parking will exceed the standard for passenger cars in order to provide time for an attendant to queue the

vehicle prior to its being parked and so as not to impose a penalty on the need for curb frontage. The total of parking queuing time is estimated at five minutes.

In order to compensate for heavy congestion periods resulting from holidays, delays, etc., it is recommended that the working frontage be increased by 30 percent beyond normal calculations. The system of curb frontage must be allowed for in the total master plan and thereby its expansion from the initial operation.

Under no circumstances should the prime arterial circulation road be tied to curb frontage. Rather, a spur from the main road network should be extended to the curb frontage.

The curb frontage should be divided into private and commercial curb. The passive curb is utilized for valet queuing or other long-term uses such as bus connections.

It is necessary to determine the average peak vehicular traffic for both enplaning and deplaning passengers. A graph or summation sheet should be prepared. It is helpful if this is done by 20-minute increments, and the cumulative total peaking can be determined if there is no separation of enplaning and deplaning traffic. In the event that the enplaning and deplaning functions are totally separated, the summation peak will result in isolating the time frame for the maximum parking demand as well as vehicle peak of appropriate road.

## TERMINAL BUILDING SPACE AND FACILITY GUIDELINES

### Gross Terminal Area per Gate

The relationship between annual enplaned passengers and gross terminal area per gate for a 10-year and 20-year forecast can be approximated. The profile of the curves is based on predicted growth in seats per aircraft for each forecast period: specifically, the growth in predicted aircraft mix during the peak hour of the average day of the peak month of the design year.

### Rule-of-Thumb

A rule-of-thumb of about 150 square feet of gross terminal building area per design peak-hour passenger is sometimes used for rough estimating purposes. Another rule using 0.08 to 0.12 square feet per annual enplanement at airports with less than 250,000 annual enplanements can similarly be applied. At small airports with less than 250,000 enplanements, estimates should be based on peak hour considerations and simple sketches.

### Space Allocations

The terminal building area is comprised of both usable and unusable space. Unusable space involves those areas required for building columns and exterior and interior walls, about 5 percent of the total gross area. The usable space can be classified into the two broad categories of rentable and nonrentable space. Usually, 50 to 55 percent is allocated to rentable space and 45 to 50 percent to nonrentable space. Figure 28 presents a further breakdown of these basic categories.

### Public Lobby Areas

Lobbies provide public circulation and access for carrying out the following functions: passenger ticketing; passenger and visitor waiting; housing concession areas and other passenger services; and baggage claim.

### Ticketing Lobby

As the initial objective of most passengers, the ticketing lobby should be arranged so that the enplaning passenger has immediate access and clear visibility to the individual airline ticket counters upon entering the building. Circulation patterns should allow the option of bypassing counters with minimum interference. Provisions for seating should be minimal to avoid congestion and encourage passengers to proceed to the gate area.

Ticket lobby sizing is a function of total length of airline counter frontage; queuing space in front of counters; and, additional space for lateral circulation to facilitate passenger movements. Queuing space requires a minimum of 12 to 15 feet. Lobby depths in front of the ticket counter range from 20 to 30 feet for a ticket area serving 50 gates or more.

### Waiting Lobby

Apart from providing for passenger and visitor circulation, a centralized waiting area usually provides public seating and access to passenger amenities, including rest rooms, retail shops, food service, etc. The sizing of a central waiting lobby is influenced by the number, seating capacity, and location of individual gate waiting areas. If all gate areas have seating, the central waiting lobby may be sized to seat 15 to 25 percent of the design peak hour enplaning passengers plus visitors. However, if no gate seating areas are provided or planned, seating for 60 to 70 percent of design peak hour enplanements plus visitors should be provided.

Visitor-passenger ratios are best determined by means of local surveys. In the absence of such data, an assumption of one visitor per peak hour originating passenger is reasonable for planning purposes.

### Baggage Claim Lobby

This lobby provides public circulation space for access to baggage claim facilities and for egress from the claim area to the deplaning curb and ground transportation. It also furnishes space for such passenger amenities and services as car rental counters, telephones, rest rooms, limousine service, etc.

Allowance for public circulation and passenger amenities outside the claim area ranges from 15 to 20 feet in depth at small hub airports, 20 to

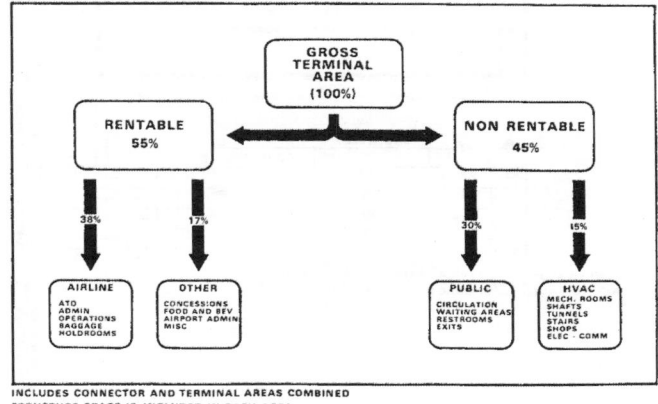

Fig. 28. Gross terminal area space distribution

30 feet at medium hubs, and 30 to 35 feet at those airports serving large hubs. Lobby lengths range from 50 to 75 feet for each baggage claim device. For approximating lobby length and area, one claim device per 100 to 125 feet of baggage claim frontage should be assumed.

### Airline Ticket Counter/ Offices

The airline ticket counter (ATO) area is the primary location for passengers to complete ticket transactions and check-in baggage. It includes the airline counters, space and/or conveyors for handling outbound baggage, counter agent service areas, and related administrative/support offices. In almost all cases, ticket counter areas are leased by an airline for its exclusive use. Therefore, the planning, design, and sizing of these areas should be closely coordinated with individual airlines.

### Ticket Counter Configurations

Three ticket counter configurations are in general use. They include:

*Linear:* Linear configuration is the most frequently used one (see Fig. 29). Multipurpose positions indicated are those in which the agent performs several functions such as ticketing, baggage check-in, and the other services an airline may consider appropriate. During peak periods, multipurpose positions may be utilized for a single function to expedite passenger processing for those requiring only one type of service. At high-volume airports, permanent special-purpose positions may be justified.

*Flow-Through Counters:* Flow-through counters, as depicted in Fig. 30, are used by some airlines, particularly at high-volume locations with a relatively high percentage of "baggage only" transactions. This configuration permits the passenger to check-in baggage before completing ticketing transaction and increases outbound baggage handling capability by providing additional belt conveyors. This type of counter requires more floor space, an additional 50 to 70 square feet than the linear type and involves increased investment and maintenance costs. Future application will probably be limited to relatively few airports.

*Island Counter:* The island counter shown in Fig. 31 combines som features of the flow-through and linear arrangements. The agent pos tions form a "U" around a single baggage conveyor belt (or pair belts) permitting interchangeability between multipurpose or sp cialized positions. As with flow-through counters, this configuratic has relatively limited application.

### Office Support

The airline ticket counter/office provides space for a number of ai line support activities. These activities include: accounting and saf keeping of receipts; agent supervision; communications; informatic display equipment; and personnel areas for rest, personal groomin, and training. At low activity locations, the ticket counter area m provide space for all company administrative and operational fun tions, including outbound baggage. Figure 32 depicts two typic layouts for low-activity airports with single-level terminals. At hig activity locations, there is more likelihood that additional space f airline support activities will be remotely located from the tick counters.

### Outbound Baggage Facilities

The outbound baggage facility is that area where baggage is receive by mechanical conveyor from the ticket counters, online and offli connecting flights, and curb-side check-in. It is sorted and loade into containers or carts for subsequent delivery to aircraft. At lo volume airports, bags may be manually moved through a wall ope ing.

At most airports, outbound baggage areas are located in buildir spaces leased by the tenant airlines for exclusive use. Each airlir provides its own baggage processing equipment and conveyors. Tł outbound baggage area should be located in reasonably close prox imity to the ticket counters to facilitate the movement of baggag between these locations. The area should also have convenient acce to the aircraft parking apron by means of carts or other mobile mechanical conveyors.

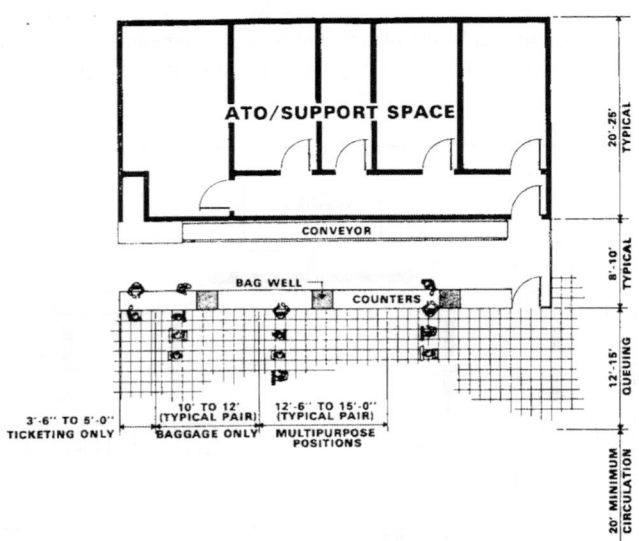

**Fig. 29. Linear counter**

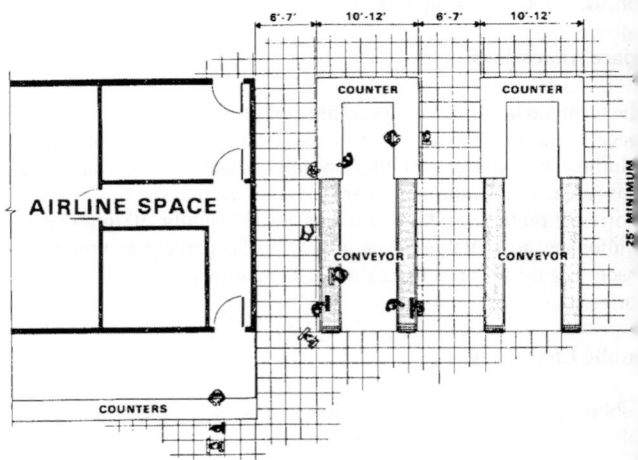

**Fig. 30. Flow-through counter**

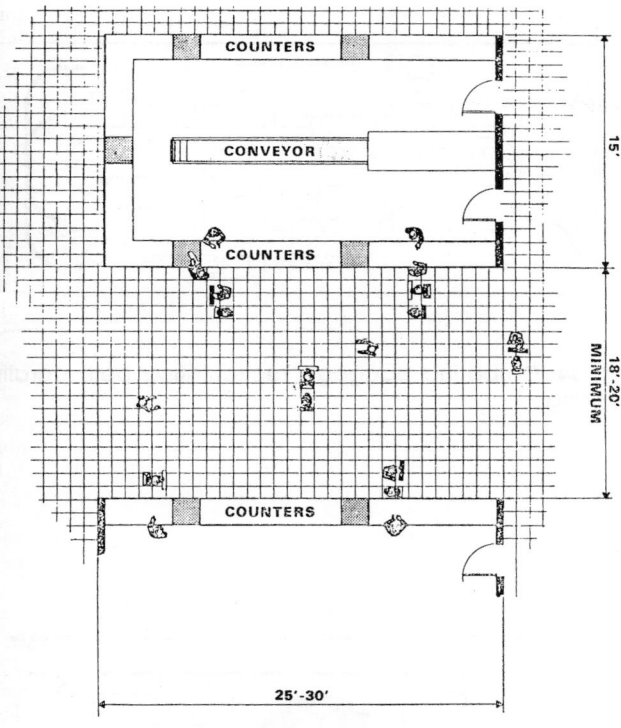

**Fig. 31. Island counter**

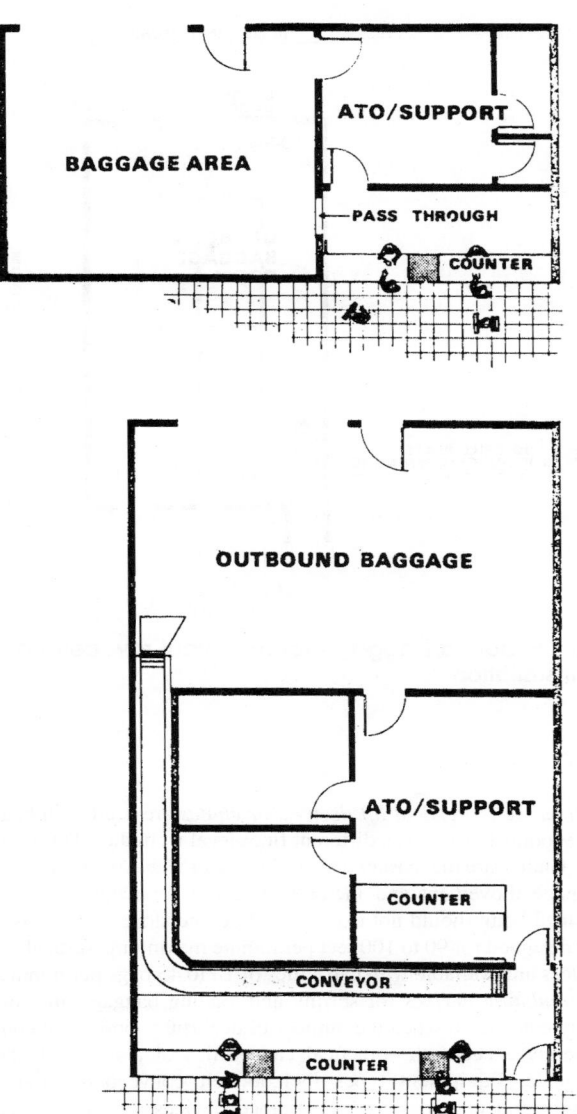

**Fig. 32. Typical ATO layouts—single-level terminals**

On-line and interline transfer baggage is best handled in the same area with other outbound baggage for optimal use of personnel, space, and equipment. An area or conveyor for receiving transfer baggage from other airlines should be considered. Often, this area is adjacent to a primary traffic aisle. Security for delivered baggage makes a conveyor or pass-through into the outbound baggage area advisable. At stations where the airlines contract with a third party for all interline deliveries, a pickup area for baggage to be delivered to other carriers should be provided with similar provisions for baggage security and control.

Since outbound baggage area requirements are determined by individual airline policy, early input from the airlines is essential. The minimum size for an outbound baggage room is approximately 400 to 450 square feet per airline.

At locations where an airline proposes using some type of automated sorting, additional area will be necessary. The required area should be increased by at least 150 to 200 percent for tilt tray sorting systems and 100 percent for destination-coded vehicle systems.

Following are some common types of outbound baggage equipment:

*Belt conveyors* represent the most commonly used mechanized component for baggage systems, operating at speeds of 80 to 150 feet per minute over short distances, and providing transport capacities of 26 to 50 bags per minute. Raw belt conveyors with spill plates (Fig. 33) tend to become less efficient as the length of unloading section is increased to process simultaneous departures. In such cases, bags not removed by the baggage handler at his normal working position must be retrieved later from the end

of the spill plate. That end becomes progressively more distant as the number of flights and size of aircraft increase. This condition may be alleviated somewhat by using belt conveyors with indexing features activated by photoelectric switches. Belt conveyor capacities can be increased by adding conveyors between counter inputs and outbound baggage rooms or, marginally, by merging multiple input conveyors into a higher-speed mainline conveyor. Long segments may operate at speeds up to 30 feet per minute with acceleration and deceleration belts at each end. This represents a practical maximum for current technology and maintenance. Accordingly, high-speed belts are primarily used to reduce transport times for long conveyor runs and seldom, if ever, increase system capacity.

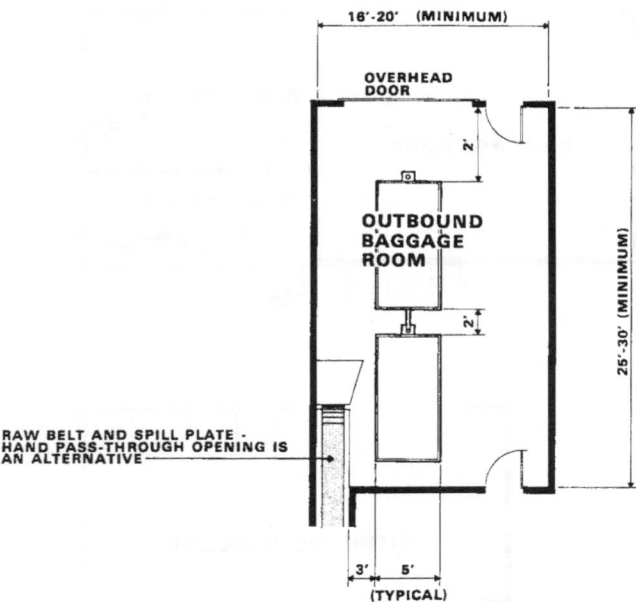

**Fig. 33. Outbound baggage room typical raw belt conveyor installation**

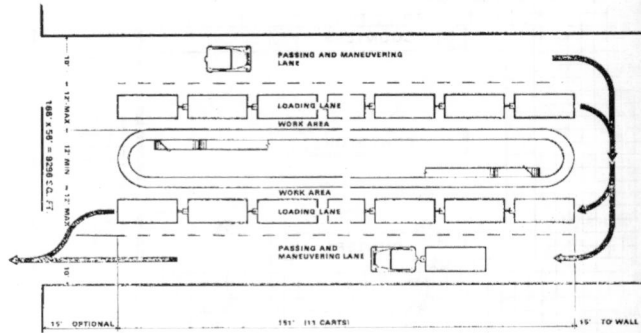

**Fig. 34. Outbound baggage recirculating belt: parallel parking**

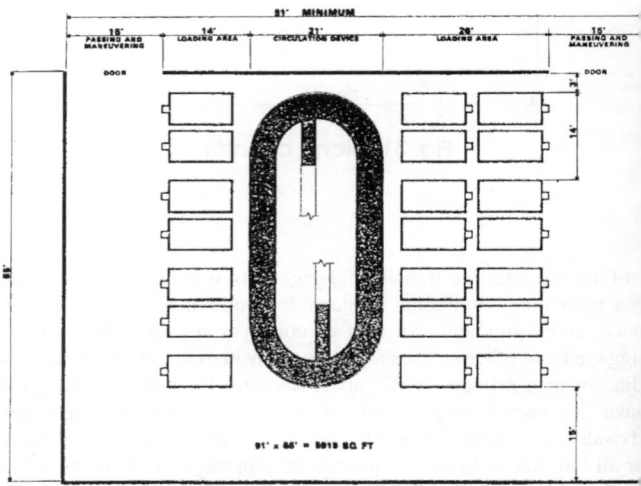

**Fig. 35. Outbound baggage recirculating sloping bed perpendicular parking**

- *Inclined belts, vertical lift devices, or chutes* are used with baggage rooms located on a different floor level from the ATO counters. Chutes are the least expensive but lack means for controlling baggage movement and increase potential for damaged bags. Inclined belts should not exceed a 22-degree slope and are usually designed for 90 to 100 feet per minute maximum. Vertical lift devices are available with capacities of 18 to 45 bags per minute.

- *Recirculating devices* for sorting and loading baggage are normally considered when the number of departures processed concurrently exceeds the practical capabilities of a raw belt and spillplate. Equipment types include belt conveyors utilizing straight and curved segments, flatbed devices, or sloping-bed plates devices. Each of these may be fed by more than one input conveyor and may require indexing belts and accumulators to control input flow. The recirculating feature facilitates sorting bags into carts for more flights and larger aircraft by fixing relatively stationary work positions for baggage handlers with "dynamic storage" of bags until they can be sorted into carts or containers.

- *Elongated oval configurations* tend to be used in lieu of circular devices as the number of carts increases. Figure 34 shows carts and container dollies parked parallel to a belt loop or flatbed sorting device. Figure 35 shows the same carts parked at right angles to a sloping-bed device. The sloping bed may accommodate two rows of bags to increase overall storage capacity. This can offset the reduction in perimeter frontage from that afforded with parallel parking. Although right-angle parking can reduce floor space by 30 to 50 percent, some carriers prefer this to minimize time and manpower for maneuvering and positioning of carts. In either case, the input conveyors need to be elevated to permit passage of carts and containers within the space.

- *Semi-automated sorting* utilizes mechanical equipment to move bags onto a lateral slide or conveyor designated for concurrently processing separate departures. Figure 36 shows a linear belt

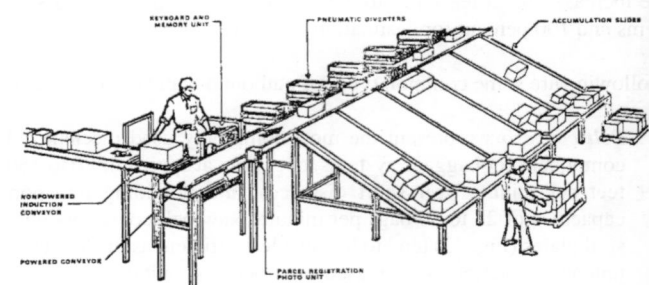

**Fig. 36. Semiautomated linear belt sorter**

sorter capable of handling about 30 bags per minute, where the maximum number of concurrent departures processed does not exceed 12 to 15. The operator designates the appropriate lateral slide after reading the tag on each passing bag. A separate sorter is needed for each input conveyor line from the ATO.

*Tilt-tray sorters* are considered appropriate for very high-volume stations requiring multiple inputs and greater capacities than possible with preceding types. These systems are custom designed with relatively sophisticated coding and sorting features as well as lateral conveyors accumulating baggage for each departing flight. Terminal designs should allow the flexibility for future installation of such systems.

*Destination-coded vehicle systems* can handle the higher volumes, longer distances, interline transfers, and elevation changes encountered in terminals serving large hubs. Although the vehicles and propulsion methods vary, all have similar design criteria. These are: speeds up to 880 feet per minute; elevation change capability (up to 33 degrees); fixed rights-of-way; programmable control systems and vehicle encoding; and interface with load/unload stations.

### Security Inspection Stations

Air carriers using over 60 passenger seat aircraft in scheduled or public charter operations are required by Federal Aviation Regulations (FAR) 121.538 to screen all passengers prior to boarding in accordance with the provisions of FAR Part 108. This activity is normally handled inside the terminal building at a security screening station.

There are three types of passenger inspection stations, depending on the location of the station in relation to the aircraft boarding area. These include:

. Boarding Gate Station;
. Holding Area Station; and
. Sterile Concourse Station.

A Sterile Concourse Station, from both the standpoint of passenger security facilitation and economics, is the most desirable type of screening station. It is generally located in a concourse or corridor leading to one or several pier finger(s) or satellite terminal(s) and permits the screening and control of all passengers and visitors passing beyond the screening location. It thus can control a considerable number of aircraft gates with a minimum amount of inspection equipment and personnel. Pier and satellite terminal concepts are well suited for application of the Sterile Concourse Station since the single-point entrance connector element facilitates isolation of boarding areas.

Because of building geometry, especially that associated with linear and transporter terminal concepts, the Sterile Concourse Station is not always feasible. Under these circumstances, several inspection stations may be required to control a number of holding areas or departure lounges. In the worst situation, a screening station may be required at each boarding gate.

Except at low-activity airports, where manual search procedures may be employed, a security inspection station will generally include a minimum of one walk-through weapons detector and one x-ray device. Such a station has a capacity of 500 to 600 persons per hour and requires an area ranging from 100 to 150 square feet. Examples of security inspection station layouts are illustrated in Fig. 37.

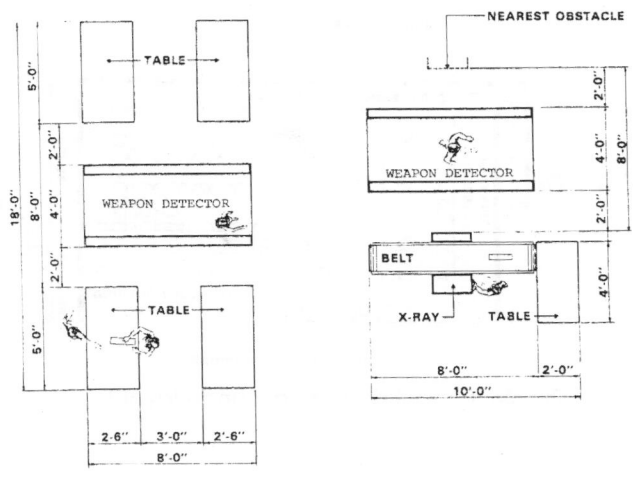

MANUAL SEARCH (144 SQ FT)    X-RAY SEARCH (120 SQ FT)

**Fig. 37. Security inspection station layouts**

Space leading to the security inspection station should allow room for queuing as the flow of passengers through security is often interrupted when a passenger requires a rescreening or physical search. Queuing space should not extend into or block other circulation elements.

The boarding area beyond a security screening checkpoint, whether a holding area concourse or departure lounge, requires a design which will enable security to be maintained. In this respect, the design and location of entrances, exits, fire doors, concessions, etc., require special consideration.

### Departure Lounges

The departure lounge is the waiting or holding area for passengers immediately prior to boarding an aircraft. At most airports (excepting some low-activity airports), departure lounges are normally included in the space leased and controlled by individual airlines.

The departure lounge normally includes: space for one or more airline agent positions for ticket collections, aircraft seat assignment, and baggage check-in; a seating and waiting area; a queuing area for aircraft boarding; and an aisle or separate corridor for aircraft deplaning. Figures 38 and 39 illustrate typical departure lounge layouts.

The number of agent positions/desks is determined by the user airlines on the basis of individual airline standards for passenger waiting, processing, and boarding procedures. A queue length of at least 10 feet in front of agent positions should be provided in departure lounges at larger airports.

The departure lounge area is a function of the number of passengers anticipated to be in the lounge 15 minutes prior to aircraft boarding. Table 2 presents information for estimating departure lounge areas on the basis of aircraft seating capacity and load factors. The average depth of lounge area generally considered to be reasonable is 25 to 30 feet.

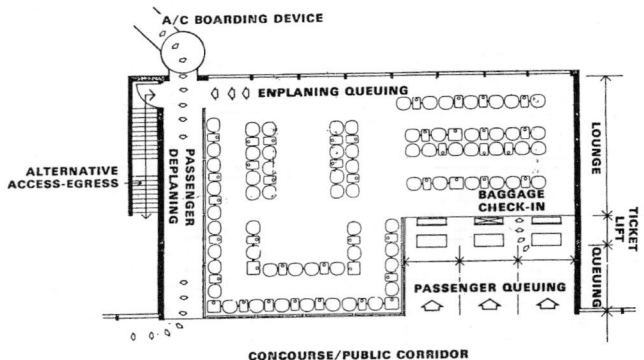

**Fig. 38. Typical departure lounge layout**

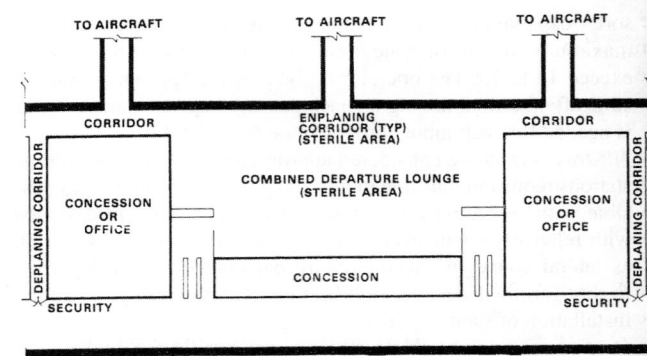

**Fig. 39. Typical combined security/departure lounge layout**

When a lounge area serves more than one aircraft gate position, the estimated total lounge area shown in Table 2 may be reduced 5 percent for each aircraft gate position, up to a maximum of six gates.

Departure lounge seats are not generally provided to accommodate all passengers boarding an aircraft. A number of passengers will elect to remain standing in the waiting area while others will only arrive shortly before or during the boarding process. Between 15 and 20 square feet, including aisle space, is required per seat.

The deplaning area is generally a roped aisle or separate corridor directly leading deplaning passengers from the loading bridge or apron gate to a public corridor. Separation from the rest of the departure lounge is provided to avoid interference and congestion between deplaning passengers and those waiting to board the aircraft. Six feet is an acceptable width for this area.

**Baggage Claim Facilities**

Inbound baggage handling requires both public and nonpublic building areas. The public space (claiming area) is that in which passengers and visitors have access to checked baggage displayed for identification and claiming. Nonpublic space is used to off-load bags from carts and containers onto claim devices or conveyor systems for moving into the public area.

The claiming area should be located adjacent to a deplaning curb and have convenient access to ground transportation service and auto parking facilities. Passenger access from arriving flights should be direct and avoid conflicting with enplaning passengers. The claim area should also be readily accessible from the aircraft apron by means of carts, tractors or mechanical conveyors for quick and direct baggage delivery.

At low-activity airports, a simple claim shelf is the most common baggage claim scheme. As passenger activity increases, several types of mechanical claim devices, as illustrated in Fig. 27, may be utilized to help reduce the overall required claim area length. A discussion of the more common claim schemes follows.

The simple shelf or counter is merely a shelf or counter provided in a public area on which baggage from an arriving aircraft is placed for passenger identification and retrieval. Width of the shelf is generally 30 to 36 inches. Passengers merely move laterally along the shelf until their baggage is located and claimed.

Flat-bed plate devices are particularly applicable when direct feed loading areas are immediately adjacent and parallel to the claiming area and on the same floor level.

Sloping-bed devices are somewhat more adaptable for remote feed situations where the loading area cannot be immediately adjacent to

**Table 2**   Departure lounge area space requirements

| | Departure lounge area, square feet (square meters) | | |
| | Boarding load factors | | |
| Aircraft seating capacity | 35–45 percent | 55–65 percent | 75–85 percent |
|---|---|---|---|
| Up to 80 | 350 (33) | 515 (48) | 675 (63) |
| 81 to 110 | 600 (56) | 850 (79) | 1,110 (102) |
| 111 to 160 | 850 (79) | 1,175 (109) | 1,500 (139) |
| 161 to 220 | 1,200 (111) | 1,600 (149) | 2,000 (186) |
| 221 to 280 | 1,500 (139) | 2,000 (186) | 2,500 (232) |
| 281 to 420 | 2,200 (204) | 3,000 (279) | 3,800 (353) |

claiming area or must be located on a different floor level. In some cases, the width of the sloping bed is sufficient to provide storage of two rows of bags.

low-volume airports, exclusive-use facilities are not usually economically justified and claim facilities are shared or assigned preferentially to several airlines. The use of a Design Day Activity Analysis recommended to size baggage claim facilities. In this analysis, passenger arrivals in periods of peak 20 minutes are used as the basis for sizing. However, when exclusive facilities are planned, each airline determines its baggage claim frontage and space requirements according to its own criteria for sizing space, systems, and staffing.

public claiming area may require railings or similar separation from other public space and controlled egress to enable inspection of removed baggage for assurance of "positive claim." At some terminals, additional space may be needed adjacent to the claiming area for storage and security of unclaimed baggage and for airline baggage service facilities (Lost and Found).

### Food and Beverage Services

These services include snack bars, coffee shops, restaurants, and bar lounges. The basic service offered at small airports is the coffee shop, although separate restaurants at some smaller city airports can be successful, depending on the community and restaurant management. Large airports usually can justify several locations for snack bars, coffee shops, bar lounges, and restaurants. Requirements for more than one of each type are highly influenced by the airport size and terminal concept involved. Unit terminals, for instance, may require coffee shops and/or snack bars at each separate terminal.

Generally speaking, a coffee shop seating less than 80 is considered an uneconomical operation at airports enplaning over one million passengers annually. At smaller airports, the seating capacity minimum may be somewhat lower, depending on such factors as local labor costs and concessionaire lease arrangements.

The following ranges appear representative for food and beverage services:

Turnover rates: 10 to 19 average daily per seat. Some operators appear satisfied averaging 10 to 14 daily.
Space per seat: 35 to 40 square feet per coffee shop/restaurant seat, including support space.
Snack bars: 15 to 25 percent of coffee shop/restaurant overall space requirements.
Bar lounges: 25 to 35 percent of coffee shop/restaurant overall space requirements.

The sizing of food and beverage services involves applying "use factors." Use factors are determined by dividing the average daily transactions by average daily enplanements.

For estimating and for initial planning purposes, the following average daily use factors are suggested:

40 to 60 percent at terminal airports with a high percentage of long-haul flights;
20 to 40 percent at transfer airports and through airports; and
15 to 25 percent at terminal airports with a low percentage of long-haul flights.

### Concessionaire and Building Services

The following building and concessionaire services are provided at airport terminals as appropriate for the size and activity of the airport. General area ranges for many of these services are presented for planning purposes. Larger areas may be required.

- Newsstands are physically separate at most airports where annual enplanements exceed 200,000 per year, and may be combined with other services at airports with lesser traffic. Space allowance: 150 square feet minimum, and averaging 600 to 700 square feet per million annual enplanements.
- Gift and apparel shops operations are combined with a newsstand at smaller airports. Separate facilities normally become feasible when annual enplanements exceed one million. Space allowance: 600 to 700 square feet per million annual enplanements.
- Drug store, including sale of books, cards, and liquor, may be feasible as separate operation when annual enplanements exceed 1.5 million. Space allowance: 700 square feet minimum and averaging 600 to 700 square feet per million enplanements.
- Barber and shoe-shine operations at some large airports allow one chair per million annual enplanements. The most successful operations range from three to seven chairs. Space allowance: 110 to 120 square feet per chair with 150 square feet for a minimum facility.
- Auto rental counters vary according to the number of companies. Space allowance: 350 to 400 square feet per million annual enplanements.
- Florist shop operation as a separate function may become feasible when annual enplanements exceed 2 million. The usual space allowed is 350 to 400 square feet per terminal.
- Displays (including courtesy phones for hotels). Space allowance: 90 to 100 square feet per million annual enplanements.
- Insurance (including counters and machines). Space allowance: 150 to 175 square feet per million annual enplanements.
- Public lockers require in the range of 70 to 80 square feet per million annual enplanements.
- Public telephones space requirement is 100 to 110 square feet per million annual enplanements.
- Automated post offices may be found desirable to the extent of providing one station, 125 square feet for each terminal serving at least 2.75 million annual enplanements.
- Vending machine items supplement staffed facilities, especially when extended hours of operation are not justified by low volumes or multiplicity of locations. When vending machines are provided, they should be grouped and/or recessed to avoid encroaching upon circulation space for primary traffic flows. Space allowance: 50 square feet minimum or 150 square feet per million annual enplanements.
- Public toilets are sized for building occupancy in accordance with local codes. Space allowances applied at airports vary greatly. They range from 1,500 to 1,800 square feet per 500 peak-hour passengers (in and out) down to 1,333 square feet per million annual enplanements at large hub airports.
- Airport management offices' space requirements vary greatly according to the size of staff and the extent to which airport authority headquarters are located in the terminal.
- Airport Police/Security Office space needs vary according to based staff and nature of arrangements with local community law enforcement agencies.
- Medical aid facilities' space requirements range from that needed for first-aid service provided by airport police to that for branch operations at off-airport clinics.

- USO/Travelers Aid facilities vary considerably. Space requirements are relatively minor, 80 to 100 square feet, except at airports with annual enplanements of over one million.

- Nursery facilities for travelers with small infants have been provided at airports with annual enplanements of over 1 million. The most practical solutions include a private toilet room of 50 to 60 square feet with facilities for changing and feeding. The number of such facilities may range from two up, depending upon terminal size and configuration.

- Building maintenance and storage varies, depending upon the types of maintenance (contracted versus authority operated) and storage facilities available in other authority-owned buildings.

- Building mechanical systems (HVAC) space ranges from 12 to 15 percent of the gross total space approximated for all other terminal functions. A value of 10 to 12 percent is used in relation to the connector element space. This allowance does not cover separate facilities for primary source heating and refrigeration (H&R plants).

- Building structure space allowance for columns and walls is 5 percent of the total gross area approximated for all other functions.

- Other space, as determined on a case-by-case basis, may be required at some airports for information services, government offices, contract service facilities and the like.

## AIRPORT ACCESS SYSTEMS

### Airport Roads

The five types of airport roads are primary airport access roads, terminal area access roads, terminal frontage roads, recirculation roads and service roads. Fig. 40 shows the location of these road types with different terminal site configurations.

*Primary airport access roads:* These provide access to the airport from the neighboring community road system. A capacity per lane of 700 to 800 vehicles per hour should be provided for at-grade interrupted flow conditions. This value approximates the flow relationship for urban arterial highways with signalized intersections, average speed range of 20 to 25 miles per hour; and a demand volume to capacity ratio of approximately 0.80. For limited access highways with grade separations under uninterrupted flow conditions, the recommended design is one lane for each 1,200 to 1,600 vehicles per hour. This value approximates the flow relationship for urban freeways; average speeds from 40 to 50 miles per hour; and a demand volume to capacity ratio approximating 0.60. A lane width of 12 feet, with a minimum of two lanes in each direction, is recommended.

*Terminal area access roads:* These roads service airport passengers, visitors, and employees and connect primary airport access roads with terminal buildings and parking facilities. Terminal area access roads should be sufficiently long to permit smooth channeling of traffic into appropriate lanes for safe access to terminal curb, parking lots, and other public facilities. To avoid driver confusion, ample separation should be provided at locations where drivers must make directional choices. Not more than two choices should be required of a driver at any location. Traffic circulation in front of the terminal should, normally, be one-way and counter-clockwise for convenience of right-side loading and unloading of vehicles. Recirculation of vehicles to the passenger terminal should be permitted by providing road sections to link the ingress and egress lanes of the access road. When several buildings exist, it may be advisable to provide more than one terminal road.

Traffic streams should be separated at an early stage with appropriate signing to avoid congestion and assure lower traffic volumes on each of the terminal frontage roads. Terminal area access roads should be planned to accommodate 900 to 1,000 vehicles per lane per hour. A minimum of two 12-foot lanes should be provided. For recirculation roads, each lane should serve 600 vehicles per hour. If only one recirculation lane is provided, its width should be 20 feet to accommodate stalled vehicles. For multiple recirculation lanes, the standard lane width is 12 feet.

*Terminal frontage roads:* These distribute vehicles directly to terminal buildings. Since considerable merging from through lanes to and from the curb front occurs on these roadways, at least two lanes should be provided adjacent to the curb. The inside lane, sized at 12 feet, provides terminal curb frontage and the 12-foot outside lane serves through traffic and maneuvering to the terminal curb frontage. While planned capacity for the outside lane should be 300 vehicles per hour, the inside lane is considered to have no throughput capacity. Additional 12-foot through lanes should be provided at a rate of 600 vehicles per lane per hour. The terminal frontage is a critical element in the performance of the airport ground access system. Accordingly, to avoid the congestion caused by the inevitable double parking, a minimum of four lanes adjacent to the terminal curb is recommended. Four lanes are also recommended when terminal arrivals and departures are on the same level (see Figs. 41 and 42).

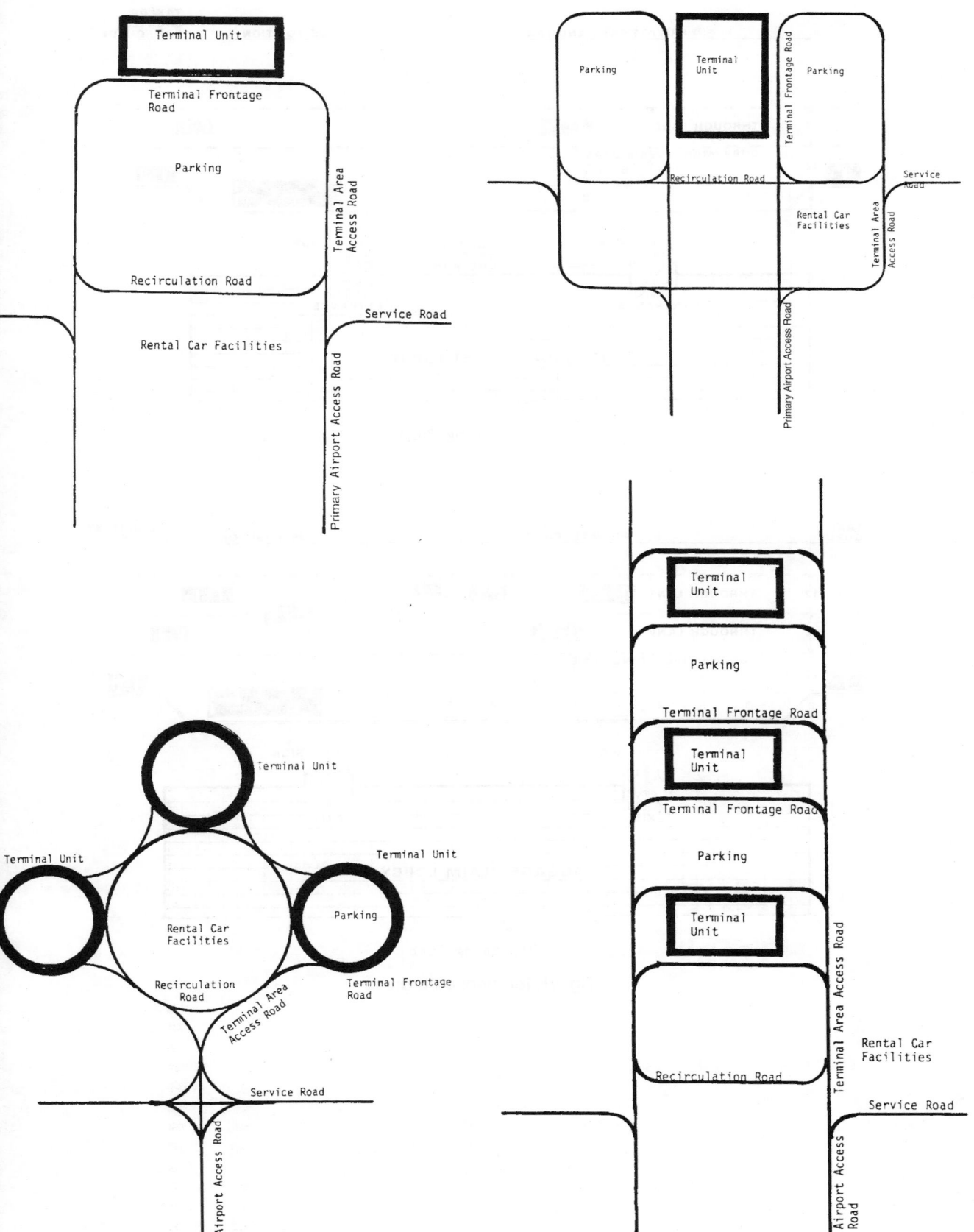

**Fig. 40. Airport road types**

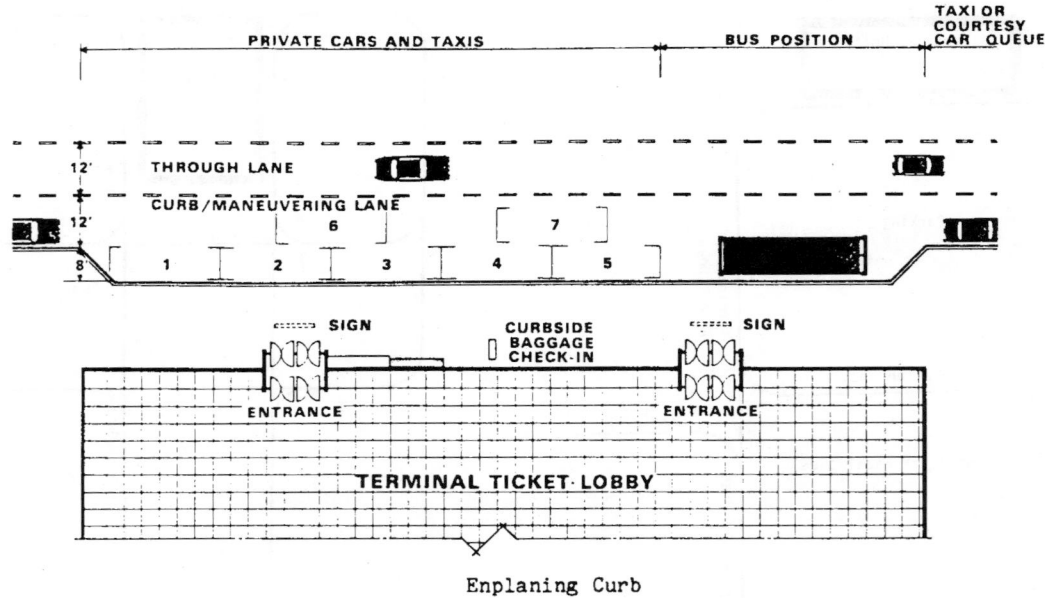

Enplaning Curb

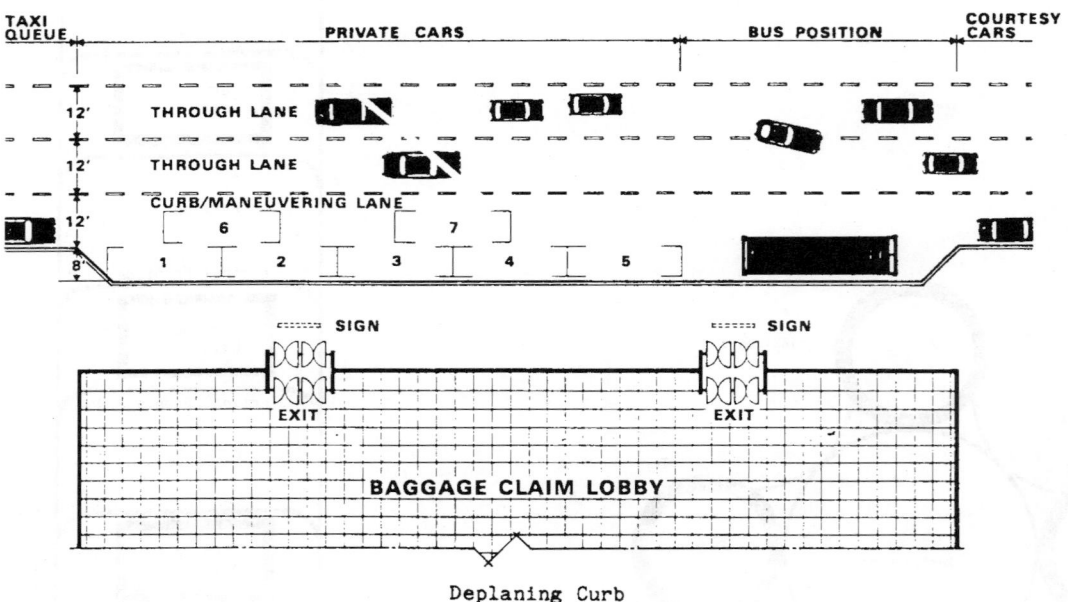

Deplaning Curb

**Fig. 41. Terminal curb areas**

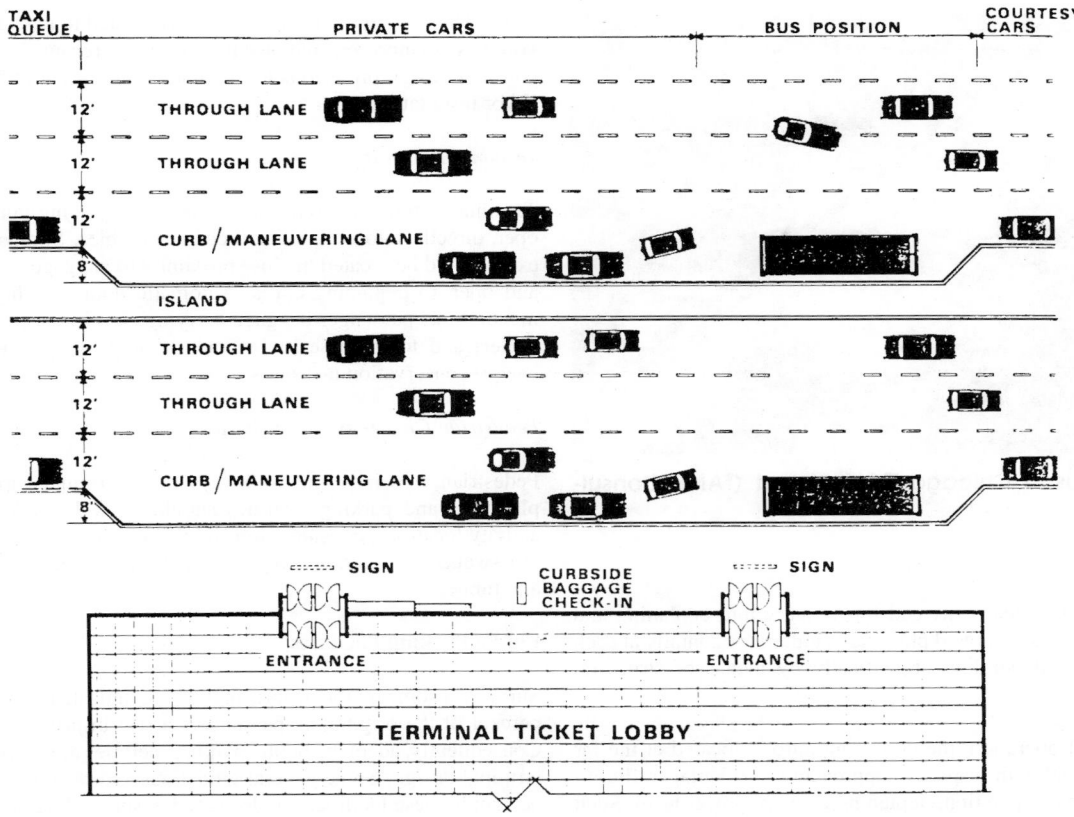

**Fig. 42. Vehicular island curb**

*circulation roads:* These allow all traffic, both private and commercial, to recirculate through the terminal frontage road in front of the terminal. Recirculation roads are usually single level, but may be served by double-level terminal frontage roads.

*service roads:* These roads are divided into two user categories—general and restricted. General-use service roads are used for the delivery of goods, services, air cargo, flight kitchen supplies, and the like. At very large airports, to relieve congestion on airport terminal access roads, it is desirable to provide service road entrances and interchanges either before or shortly after entering the airport site. At low activity airports, the service and primary airport access roads may be coincidental.

Restricted-use service roads and traffic lanes are limited to such traffic as maintenance, fire and rescue, fuel, baggage, freight, and aircraft service vehicles. Those roads or sections of roads providing access to aircraft operating and parking areas require control points for adequate area security.

The recommended hourly lane capacity is 600 to 1,200 vehicles. Since a major portion of the road traffic is from trucks, the lower value should be used in preliminary design. The typical vehicle speed is 15 to 20 miles per hour and frequent curb cuts are required for access to airport service facilities. Usually, these roads are two-way in nature with 12-foot lane widths.

**Terminal Curb Areas**

Curb areas are required at terminals for loading and unloading of passengers and their baggage (Fig. 43).

*Curb Frontage*

The length of curb to be provided is related to the mix of vehicle types and expected curb dwell time. Table 3 shows typical curb dwell times and required vehicle slot lengths for different types of vehicles. It should be noted that, in the case of deplaning passengers, larger volumes of passengers, baggage, and ground transportation requirements peak over shorter periods of time. Strict policing is highly effective in optimizing the vehicle curb slot occupancy rate.

*Sidewalk Platforms*

Sidewalk platforms are located immediately adjacent to curb/maneuvering lanes and terminal building entrances and exits to provide passenger walkways and safety areas for loading and unloading of vehicles.

At high activity airports, traffic curb islands are often provided to increase the curb area and, in some cases, to segregate different types of ground transportation vehicles. Airports with relatively low passenger levels may be able to accommodate both enplaning and deplaning passengers from one curb face.

**Fig. 43. Proposed Chicago Third Airport (TAMS Consultants, Inc.)**

Generally, the curb area is divided functionally into enplaning and deplaning curbs. It is separated physically, either horizontally at each end of the terminal building or vertically by means of structural vehicular ramps.

With a one-level operation, the deplaning curb is located at the far end of the terminal with respect to approaching vehicular traffic. In the case of vertical separation, deplaning is on the lower level. Such separation minimizes the congestion which will result if opposing flows and volumes of persons, baggage, and ground vehicles are concentrated in the same curb area.

At most terminals, specific curb areas are designated for buses, limousines, courtesy cars, and taxi queues. These designated areas should be located at reasonable distances from terminal exits to reduce congestion. Overhead coverings are desirable to protect disembarking passengers from inclement weather.

*Curbside Baggage Check-in*

Curbside baggage check-in permits baggage to be checked directly to the appropriate airline flight. The area which accommodates this service normally requires space for a baggage check-in desk (usually portable), baggage handtrucks, and a baggage conveyor or belt. Baggage may be either taken by handtruck to the ticket counter or transported directly by an adjacent conveyor belt to the outbound baggage

room. The system used is economically related to passenger activi volumes, manpower, and installation cost. Terminal plans shou consider design provisions to facilitate both present and future co veyor installations.

*Terminal Entryways*

Terminal entrances should be located at enplaning curb areas ar open directly into airline ticket counter lobbies. Similarly, termin exits should be located in close proximity to baggage claim faciliti and open to deplaning curbs. Automatic doors are highly recon mended for: passenger baggage carrying convenience; as a weath buffer; and to increase the efficiency of passenger movement energy conservation measures.

*Pedestrian Crossings and Walkways*

Pedestrian crossings and walkways from terminal curbs to islar platforms and parking facilities should be well marked. At higl activity locations, consideration should be given to traffic-controlle crosswalks or, preferably, to grade separation by means of overpass and tunnels.

**Public Parking Facilities**

Surveys at some major airports in the U.S. indicate that from 40 to 8 percent of the originating passengers arrive in private automobile Consequently, adequate public parking facilities are essential to goc terminal design. Some general guidelines and recommendations fe designing these facilities are discussed in succeeding paragraphs.

*Location*

Public parking lots should be located to provide walking distance from parked automobiles to terminals to no more than 1,000 feet. larger airports, large volume parking needs may require provision remote parking facilities served by shuttle bus or people mover sy tems.

*Size*

The number of public parking spaces available per million originatir passengers varies between airports, particularly at airports with ov 1.5 million originations. While the range at existing airports may va from under 1,000 to as high as 3,300 parking spaces per million ori inations, the suggested range is from 1,000 to 1,400. Another metho ology provides parking spaces for 1.5 times the number of peak hou passengers. A better way for estimating parking needs is through

**Table 3** Typical curbfrontage dwell times and vehicle slot lengths

| Vehicle | Curb dwell time (minutes) | | Vehicle slot length (feet/meters) |
|---|---|---|---|
| | Enplane | Deplane | |
| Private auto | 1.0 to 3.0 | 2.0 to 4.0 | 25.0/7.5 |
| Rental car | 1.0 to 3.0 | 2.0 to 4.0 | 25.0/7.5 |
| Taxi | 1.0 to 2.0 | 1.0 to 3.0 | 20.0/6.0 |
| Limousine | 2.0 to 4.0 | 2.0 to 5.0 | 35.0/10.5 |
| Bus | 2.0 to 5.0 | 5.0 to 10.0 | 50.0/15.0 |

ulation based on existing parking characteristics and forecasted
ure needs. Simulation is expensive and time consuming, but can be
tified where expansion space is severely limited or the cost of addi-
nal spaces is very high. A rule-of-thumb suggests an increase of 15
rcent in the number of estimated parking spaces to minimize the
ount of time required to find a parking space. In developing a park-
g lot plan, approximately 350 to 400 square feet, including lanes,
ould be allowed for each parked automobile. This is the equivalent
109 to 124 parked cars per acre for on-grade parking.

*ort-term Versus Long-term Parking*

le generally accepted definition for short-term parking is anything
ss than three hours. Approximately 70 to 85 percent of all airport
rking lot users are short-term parkers, mainly drop-off or pick-up.
owever, this amounts to full-time use of only 20 to 30 percent of the
tal parking requirements. Long-term parkers, the remaining 15 to
) percent of parking lot users, are almost all travelers and occupy 70
80 percent of the available parking spaces. Through actual surveys
d analysis of parking stubs conducted over several consecutive
ys, utilization charts can be developed showing vehicle volumes
d length of stay. Short-term parking is usually provided nearest the
rminal, since its turnover rate is often at least three times as much
for long-term lots. Short-term rates are high to discourage long-
rm parkers from clogging close-in lots. A rule-of-thumb suggests
at separate parking should be provided when the total annual pas-
nger volume exceeds 150,000 to 200,000.

*rking Lot Entrances and Exits*

arking lot entrances and exits can easily become points of conges-
on. This congestion can be minimized by providing appropriate
cket dispensing and fee collection facilities and queuing lanes to
duce vehicle interference with access roads and parking lot circula-
on. Entrance and exit points should be clearly identified and suffi-
ently separated to avoid confusion. The total in and out airport
arking lot flow can approach 25 percent of capacity in peak periods.
Vhile automatic ticket dispensers can process up to 400 vehicles per
our, a design capacity of 240 is recommended. At least two ticket-
ispensing machines per entrance should be provided to permit
quipment maintenance without severely restricting parking opera-
ons. Attendant parking fee collection booths can process 120 to 150
ehicles hourly with variable fee parking and about 250 vehicles per
our with a flat fee. One collection position should be provided per
05 vehicles hourly in manual mode and one position per 185 vehi-
les per hour in a computerized operation.

*Circulation*

Counter-clockwise circulation within the parking lot is usually
referable and one-way traffic control is recommended to minimize

congestion and hazards. Aisle widths should be generous and parking
stalls clearly marked. The layout should be designed to minimize the
number of turns and both vehicular and pedestrian travel distances.
Parking lot aisles should be laid out in the direction of pedestrian-
parker destination. Perpendicular parking is frequently used, since it
permits parking from each side of the aisle and maximizes the number of stalls in a given area. However, parking stall layout mainly
depends on the area's shape and, to a lesser extent, on local parking
habits.

*Parking Structures*

Multilevel parking structures are used at high activity airports, albeit
with higher construction costs, to increase the number of parking
slots in a given area and to reduce walking distances. This parking
arrangement also furnishes users with protection from inclement
weather.

**Employee and Tenant Parking**

Surveys show that approximately 90 percent of airport employees
travel to work in private automobiles. Due to the variation among airports for aircraft maintenance, air cargo, and other servicing activities, a consistent relationship between numbers of employees and
passengers has not been established. The number of employee/tenant
parking spaces should be obtained by surveying airport management
and terminal tenants. Employee and tenant parking should be provided near working areas which are not in or near terminal buildings.
Otherwise, remote parking with a shuttle service to work areas is
required.

**Public Transportation and Rental Car Areas**

Parking facilities are also required for taxis, vans, limousines, buses,
and for rental car ready and storage lots. Discussions should be held
with the various service operators to establish parking requirements.
Approximately 750 originating passengers are accommodated per
rental car ready stall. The space required for taxi parking and rental
car storage facilities is less than for public parking or rental car
ready lots, since these vehicles are driven by professional drivers.
Space for 160 vehicles per acre is recommended. Land in the immediate terminal area is at a premium. Accordingly, a trend is that on-
airport rental car agencies are basing vehicles at remote locations
and using vans to shuttle customers to and from these areas. Usually,
short-term parking areas for buses, taxis, vans, and limousines are
located away from the terminal curbfront to increase curbside operational efficiency. These vehicles can be called to the curb in a
demand responsive mode and curbfront dwell time considerably
reduced. Similarly, provisions can be made for exclusive lanes or
dedicated auxiliary curbs for high occupancy vehicles such as vans,
limousines, and buses.

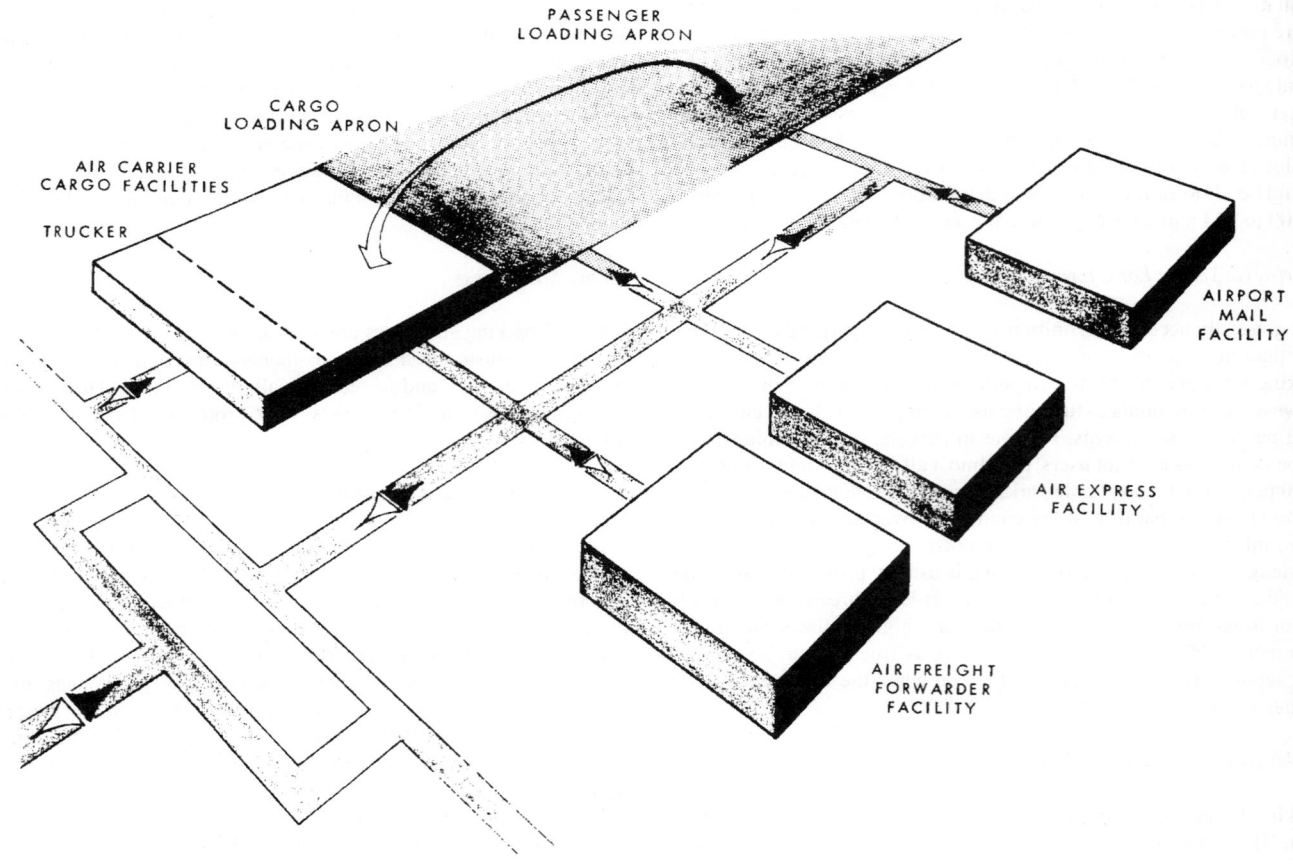

**Fig. 1. Relationships of cargo facilities**

# AIRPORT CARGO FACILITIES

### INTERRELATIONSHIPS OF FACILITIES

As the air cargo industry grows, the complex on the airport designed to handle air cargo becomes a significant element in airport planning and design. These facilities must provide for the efficient transfer of air cargo between surface transportation and aircraft. For larger airports, the complex may include a number of air carrier cargo facilities or multiple-occupancy buildings.

**Design Considerations**

The elements that compose the airport cargo center facilities and establish their character, size, and configuration will depend on the level of activity of the air cargo industry in the community served. The architect-engineer should work closely with the air carriers, air freight forwarders, truckers, and airport management to determine what is needed, including any special requirements peculiar to these facilities. The resulting design must satisfy present requirements and provide the flexibility necessary for future expansion. Buildings should be oriented, and land should be available, to enable a logical expansion plan.

The air carrier cargo facility is the core of the cargo center, and the emphasis in this article is on that facility. It may be treated as a single building or combination of elements under one roof sufficiently integrated to permit operation as a single entity.

The design program, in the architect's vocabulary, denotes the building user's space requirements. It is one of the basic essentials for successful solution to the design of any building. Fundamental considerations in developing a program are the elements of the building, the amount of space needed by each element, and the relationships between the spaces.

### AIRPORT CARGO CENTER LOCATION

**Importance of Site Planning**

The complex on the airport specifically designed for the handling of air cargo is one of the major elements on the airport. The airport cargo center must be sited in a location that will contribute to the eff

*Airport Cargo Facilities*, Federal Aviation Agency, Washington, D.C.

ent transfer of cargo between surface and air transport. The selection of an appropriate site is the decision which determines to a large extent the effectiveness of the air cargo operation. The location of the elements of the complex in proper relationship to each other is of equal importance.

## Location at the Airport

Four primary considerations dictate the selection of the site at an airport for the cargo complex.

Taxi distance from the most used runways should be as short as possible, and yet there should not be interference with passenger operations.

The site should be readily accessible by surface vehicles from the passenger aircraft loading positions for efficient servicing of aircraft carrying both passengers and cargo.

The complex should be readily reached from all access roads to the airport to assure noninterference of vehicular traffic with aircraft movement areas.

Adequate space should be allowed for expansion of air cargo operations without encroaching on other airport functions, particularly without interfering with the expansion of the passenger terminal.

These four primary considerations indicate the general relationships with other functions and activities. They require extensive study to determine the degree to which they can be met on any individual airport. This study can best be made through the medium of an airport layout plan in which the advantages of possible locations and their effect on other airport facilities and operational activities can be objectively weighed.

## Planning Considerations

The general location of the cargo complex having been established, a number of other factors should also be studied prior to adoption of a siting plan.

The arrangement of buildings and associated support facilities is important to satisfactory and efficient use, and it also affects future expansion of individual buildings. Important in this regard is consideration of spacing of buildings for access, vehicular circulation, and fire and safety clearances. Vehicular access, roadways, and parking areas are discussed in detail in the paragraphs that follow. Proper orientation of buildings, with respect to these factors and the prevailing winds, is essential to the functional operation of the buildings. Economical design dictates the need for balance of requirements for paved areas with other considerations discussed heretofore. Good drainage, consistent with driveway, parking, and pedestrian access requirements, is a necessary design consideration.

Noise is a consideration which must not be overlooked. Acoustical control can be achieved through proper landscape planting for sound absorption.

## Cargo Center Site Plan

To illustrate the application of functional relationships discussed in this article, a diagrammatic site plan has been developed. Figure 1 indicates the relationships of facilities for a number of air carrier cargo operators, truckers, air freight forwarders, air express (REA), and airport mail facility (AMF).

The site plan orientation on the airport establishes optimum relationships of aircraft parking apron, and access and service roads discussed in the following paragraphs.

### Aircraft Parking Aprons

Paved apron requirements for aircraft parking and loading positions adjoining air carrier cargo facilities are dependent upon the type and size of aircraft used, airline schedules, and the type of materials handling system used. The need for direct access from certain facilities to the passenger loading apron, for access to both combination and all-cargo aircraft aprons for others, and for completely integrated building-apron relationships for certain materials handling systems are all important. Information on space requirements for aircraft apron parking positions can be found in the article dealing with airport design.

### Access, Circulation, and Parking

Discussion of ground vehicle movement considerations is presented in general terms.

#### Roads

Access to and egress from the airport cargo complex and circulatory roads within it should be direct and unimpeded. There should be as little interference as possible with airport passenger vehicular traffic. In those cases where the number and types of trucks using the access roads will cause frequent passenger traffic congestion, separate roads should be designed specifically for truck traffic leading directly to the cargo center. Visitors, passengers, and customers should be provided convenient access from the passenger terminal area.

#### Truck Parking

Parking areas required include those designed to serve the trucker, the customer and visitor, and the employee. Planning of truck parking spaces and maneuvering areas will probably present a difficult problem because of the many variables. Maximum truck sizes vary from state to state. Trucks bringing freight to the cargo center will be of many types and sizes. Parking areas and truck-dock facilities with adequate maneuvering space must be provided for movement of vehicles without creating bottlenecks during peak loading and unloading hours.

Generally, the recommended distance for maneuvering from the loading platform to the nearest obstruction is twice the length of the largest road vehicle expected to use the facility. The Air Transport Association suggests a minimum overall depth of 100 feet for the terminal-truck apron which will allow 75 feet for maneuvering of trucks plus a 25-foot-wide access roadway. Minimum interference distances may in effect be less when tractors with smaller turning radii are used, when the spacing between trailers is increased, or when a loading platform design is used.

#### Customer and Visitor Parking

Those seeking service should have the most direct access possible to the reception areas of individual air carriers, freight forwarders, and other service facilities. These parking spaces may be adjacent to the building in conjunction with the truck parking area. Permanent parking areas should not be located where expansion of buildings is being contemplated.

*Employee Parking*

Sufficient parking should be provided for employees' cars which are generally parked for a period equal to the length of the working day. Since the employee does not usually require ready access to his car during this period, it is not necessary to locate the employee parking area directly adjacent to the freight handling facilities. Where the airport is relatively small, an employee parking area common to all operational functions on the airport may be adequate for parking needs. For the larger airport, strategically located parking spaces which may be used by all employees of the airport cargo complex should be considered. There may be just one of these areas planned near the center of activity, or there may be several dependent upon the size and spread of the airport cargo complex. Administrative personnel usually require parking spaces adjacent to the office area because they may have to use their cars frequently during the working day.

## AIR CARRIER CARGO BUILDINGS

### Elements of the Building

An air carrier cargo building may be planned for single or multiple occupancy. The type of occupancy normally will depend on the potential for air cargo industry growth in the community being served and the volume of business generated by each of the airlines. At airports where there are a number of carriers, each generating only nominal amounts of freight daily, a multiple-occupancy building can provide adequate space to satisfy the needs of all. Single- or double-occupancy buildings with adequate aircraft apron space should be considered for those air carriers that operate all-cargo schedules and handle larger amounts of air freight.

There are four major functional elements to consider in the design of the air carrier cargo building:

1. Freight-handling areas
2. Administration areas
3. Personnel and customer accommodations
4. Service facilities

Figure 2 indicates diagrammatically the space relationships for functions within the air carrier cargo facilities. Airport cargo buildings should be designed for planned expansion in both length and depth, where economically feasible, and fixed support facilities so located to avoid interference with such expansion.

### Truck Dock Facilities

There must be a sufficient number of truck stations to serve truckers, air freight forwarders, and others for both incoming and outgoing shipments. In addition to truck dock positions, consideration should be given to providing facilities for the airport-to-airport customers who use other than trucks to deliver or pick up small shipments.

The number of truck dock spaces will vary with the airline operation and the community. To determine the optimum number requires detailed analysis of truck arrival in a peak hour, the service time at the dock, and the acceptable waiting time for those experiencing delays.

The minimum number of dock spaces required for incoming trucks can readily be determined. Assume for example a normal "stripping"

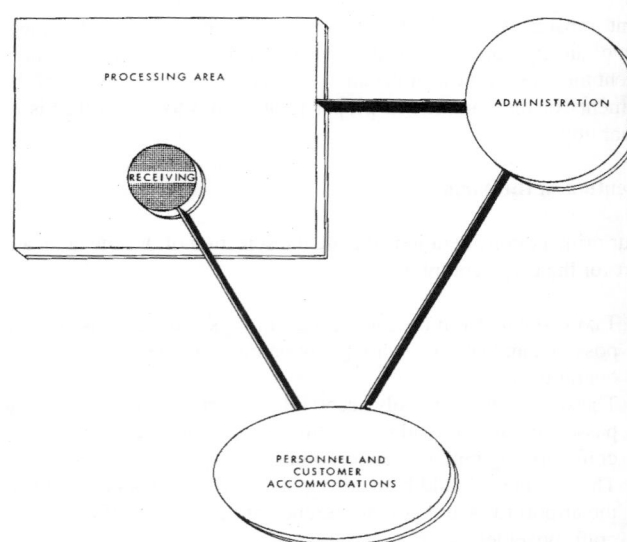

**Fig. 2. Space relationships within buildings**

or unloading rate at each dock space of approximately 5,000 pe hour. This rate includes time allowed for delays and spotting of veh cles. For an inbound volume from trucks of 90,000 of freight and time allowed for "stripping" vehicles of three hours, the unloadin would have to be accomplished at the rate of 30,000 per hour. Thu there would be a requirement for six truck spaces at the dock for th operation.

The width of each truck station should be a minimum of 12 feet t allow for parking of large vehicles. Building door openings at eac station should be a minimum of 10 feet wide by 10 feet high. Exten sive open platforms are not recommended because freight left in th open is subject to pilferage and damage from inclement weather. Pro tection from the weather for freight and personnel during stripping loading operations should be provided by an overhang canopy of least 5 feet. Clearance above the top of the parked freight van shoul be approximately 18 inches.

Building floor heights may vary from 44 to 47 inches above grade There are a number of leveling devices for accommodating truck be heights ranging from 30 inches for a pickup truck to 50 inches for large tractor-trailer.

### Processing Area

Receiving, sorting, weighing, labeling, and building up of loads fc shipment are the major activities in the processing of freight from th truck to the aircraft. There are a number of factors which have a pro found effect on total space requirements.

1. Cargo turnover is affected by such variables as types of aircraf frequency of service, time of day of arrivals and departure inbound, outbound, and directional preponderance of cargo.
2. Density of cargo accounts for considerable dimensional dispar ity. A ton of cut flowers occupies many times more space than ton of machine parts.
3. Character of cargo creates a need for specific space allocatior Refrigerated storage is required for perishable cargo, and othe

temperature controlled areas are needed for live cargo. Bonded storage is needed for customs, import/export control, as well as security accommodations for valuable cargo.

Methods of handling and storing cause variations in space requirements. Operations utilizing forklifts and pallets require more square footage for circulation and maneuvering.

he arrangement of space in the load buildup areas is also influenced / aircraft loading characteristics. Space should be planned for quence loading to provide for distribution of weight in the aircraft d for easy removal of loads at destinations. Freight to be loaded on ombination aircraft should be kept separate from freight to be aded on all-cargo aircraft. Loads to be unitized on pallets, loads to e unitized in containers, and those to be loaded on aircraft manually iould be controlled by providing separate but adequate space for ich. The types of aircraft and the numbers of each type being served / the facility should be given careful study.

onsultation with the users as to the type of materials handling sys-ms to be employed is essential and will be most helpful in this area : design. As materials handling systems for the air cargo industry e developed and improved, space requirements for the load build-o area and other operations may be reduced substantially. Figure 3 idicates diagrammatically suggested space requirements for receiv-ıg and processing areas.

### dministrative Area, and Customer and Personnel ccommodations

dequate administrative space is necessary for efficient management f cargo operations. A thorough analysis of the duties and responsi-lities of the administrative personnel should be made prior to

preparing the design program of the building. The number of employees that may ultimately be employed in the management of operations should be studied.

Reception areas should be provided to handle customers. In addition to serving as a receiving point for visitors, small packages may be claimed or bills may be paid here. There should be sufficient space for a counter, accommodations for customers, and cases for display of brochures and other sales material.

Sales offices may be required by some airlines. Space in the sales office should provide for desks, files, and facilities for telecommuni-cations. Files should be readily accessible to all the salespeople. The sales office may serve also as a customer service center or clearing-house for telephone inquiries. Close communication must be main-tained between this office, receiving, aircraft space control, and accounting.

Management and general office space requirements are dependent upon variables such as the type of operation, the amount and type of freight processed, and the community being served. Accounting and records offices may be necessary facilities for operations of any siz-able magnitude. The space required varies with the type of record keeping and accounting equipment that may be used such as auto-matic filing systems and data processing equipment.

Communications centers assist management in the efficient move-ment of freight. Each facility component must be kept informed of changes in schedule, cargo space available, and of special shipments requiring unusual attention. The communications center can serve as the central nerve system. It can provide the link between administra-tion and operations. Space may be required for teletype machines and closed-circuit television facilities in addition to sufficient desk space for communications personnel.

Aircraft space control office requirements are dependent upon the amount of freight handling activity. This office may be placed in the receiving area or in the administration offices. Space must be pro-vided for computing and communications equipment and for aircraft charts indicating cargo space available on the aircraft. These func-tions are closely related to those of receiving and processing and to those of the communications center. Provisions should be made to facilitate close liaison with these interrelated functions.

The number of personnel employed in cargo operations will vary not only with the type and volume of freight handled but also with the materials handling system used and the scheduling of aircraft loading operations. A careful study should be made of all factors including local codes and state labor laws to assure adequate provision for employee needs. Figure 3 indicates suggested space requirements. This overall area may be allocated to administration, customer accommodations, and personnel accommodations such as rest rooms, locker rooms, and lunchrooms. A first-aid room, pilot-ready room, or other specialized area may be included dependent on cir-cumstances peculiar to proposed facilities.

### Maintenance, Services, and Storage

In order to provide for an efficient operation, equipment must be kept in good working order at all times. Maintenance and storage of mate-rials handling equipment, such as containers, should not be over-looked. The functions of maintenance and storage may be joined, or they may be completely separated. The manner in which these func-

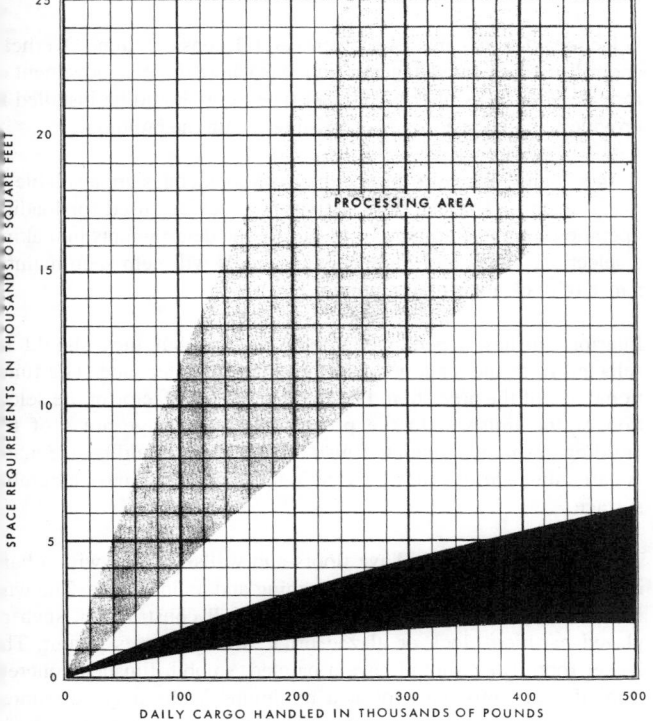

**Fig. 3. Building area space requirements**

tions are handled depends largely on the type and amount of equipment used.

For large operations, maintenance and servicing shops may be necessary to provide repairs for such items as pallets and containers, forklift trucks, conveyors, and other materials handling equipment. Webbing used to secure freight against dislodgment in aircraft requires periodic repair. The maintenance and the servicing shops may be centrally located in the cargo complex, or they may be constructed as a part of the air carrier's individual freight handling facilities.

Garage or hangar space may be required for larger pieces of equipment, such as scissors lifts, mobile freight loaders, or other vehicles used in the freight loading operations. (In some cases, it may be economically more practical for the air carriers if this space and this type of equipment are furnished by the airport management on a rental basis.)

Space required for building utilities, such as plumbing, heating, ventilating, air conditioning, electricity, and gas depends primarily on the geographical location of the airport. Other factors, such as requirements of servicing equipment, type of fuel available in the area, and accessibility of public utilities to the airport cargo center, also must be considered. All utilities may be centrally located on the airport and furnished to users by airport management. Each building may house its own space for the provision of these utilities.

### Special Handling

Some types of freight require special handling, that is, facilities and techniques not ordinarily used for normal items. Requirements depend on the policy of the air carrier in accepting shipments that require special techniques. Basically, three types of shipments which fall into the special handling category are live animals, perishables (pharmaceuticals, meats produce, and flowers), and bonded and valuable shipments.

If the volume of live animal shipments is expected to be large, special provisions for them should be given consideration. Heating, ventilation, cleaning facilities, fresh water supply, cages and stables, and storage facilities for handling, cleaning, and feeding equipment will require study. Consultation with the local chapter of the Society for Prevention of Cruelty to Animals (SPCA) is suggested.

Perishables are being shipped in increasing quantities. Bonded and other valuable freight processed varies not only with the economic character of the community but also with the seasons.

### Facilities at International Airports

Air carriers providing service for overseas shipments at international airports will require space for inspection of deplaned freight. Consultation with Bureau of Customs, Agricultural Research Service, and Public Health Service officials in addition to the airlines is essential in developing a proper design program for this area.

### Building Construction

Building design consistent with functional requirements and the need for economical construction and maintenance cannot be overemphasized. Airport buildings are often constructed in areas beyond the jurisdiction of a city building code. Materials and methods of construction and design of an airport cargo building may or may not be governed by a building code of the local community or regulations established in state labor laws. When local codes are applicable, particularly in small communities, the standards designated in such codes are sometimes below those acceptable as good architectural or engineering practice for buildings on airports.

Selection of the structural system to be used for the building should be based on careful consideration of the insurance rates for various classes of building construction and occupancy. The initial cost of fire-resistant construction may be higher than other types of construction, but a lower insurance rate will often offset this higher initial cost. Fire is not the only hazard about which the designer must be concerned. Protection against pilferage, vandalism, or possible sabotage in time of emergency should be considered in choosing materials of construction. The location of the building and the types of commodities moved through the facility will also influence the type of construction.

Structural systems having the capability of economically spanning as much as 100 feet provide greater flexibility in building design and space arrangement. Clear-span structures (Fig. 4) are desirable because they allow for greater maneuverability of forklift trucks and other freight handling equipment. Large-space areas, free of columns and bearing walls, can be divided and adapted to satisfy the changing demands of functional operations. Roof construction and roof design loads vary with the area of the country.

Floor construction, according to the NBFU recommended National Building Code, should be designed and constructed for the greatest loads that are anticipated by the user. Provision should be made for such items as floor scales, pit elevators, and tracks for conveyor systems (Fig. 5). Floors in the office areas, where extensive filing systems are maintained, should be designed to carry a minimum uniformly distributed load of 125 pounds per square foot.

Selection of doors must be given careful consideration. Overhead and roll-up doors are suggested in areas where there is movement of freight. The tracks of the overhead-type door should be installed to provide as much headroom as possible within the building.

Bumpers and guards for protecting truckdock edges are available in many designs. The nature of activity, the devices used for loading operations, and the amount of traffic are the determinants in making a selection. The use of bumpers and guards will help keep maintenance of dock areas to a minimum.

Interior finishes depend upon local factors, but they should be selected from the standpoint of minimum maintenance. The functional use of the area should be the determining factor in the selection of the finishes. In the processing and storage areas of the building, a smooth concrete finish for the floor should be adequate. A hardening additive may be used in the concrete to make a durable surface.

The toilet rooms should have floors and walls finished with a hard impervious material for ease of cleaning and maintenance. The wall finishes may be an integral part of the wall construction, such as glazed partition block or glazed brick where budgets permit. The locker room floor should have a painted, smooth finished concrete floor if costs must be kept at a minimum. Walls may be painted masonry units or plaster. Since locker rooms are generally noisy places, an acoustic ceiling should be considered for this area.

**tilities**

eating and ventilating requirements vary with the climate and the
quirements of the user. It may be possible to integrate systems with
e humidity and temperature control required for handling special
mmodities. A system which will provide proper year-round condi-
oning of air particularly in administrative areas is important.

lectrical and lighting systems should be adequate for the designed
nctions. The requirements of the electrical service vary with the
ze and character of the facility. Much will depend upon the nature
f the materials handling system used. Minimum required lighting
vels may be governed by local codes or state labor laws; however,
ese may sometimes be below those acceptable as good architec-
ral or engineering practice for buildings on airports. It is recom-
ended that airport owners voluntarily adopt the standards from one
f several recognized sources.

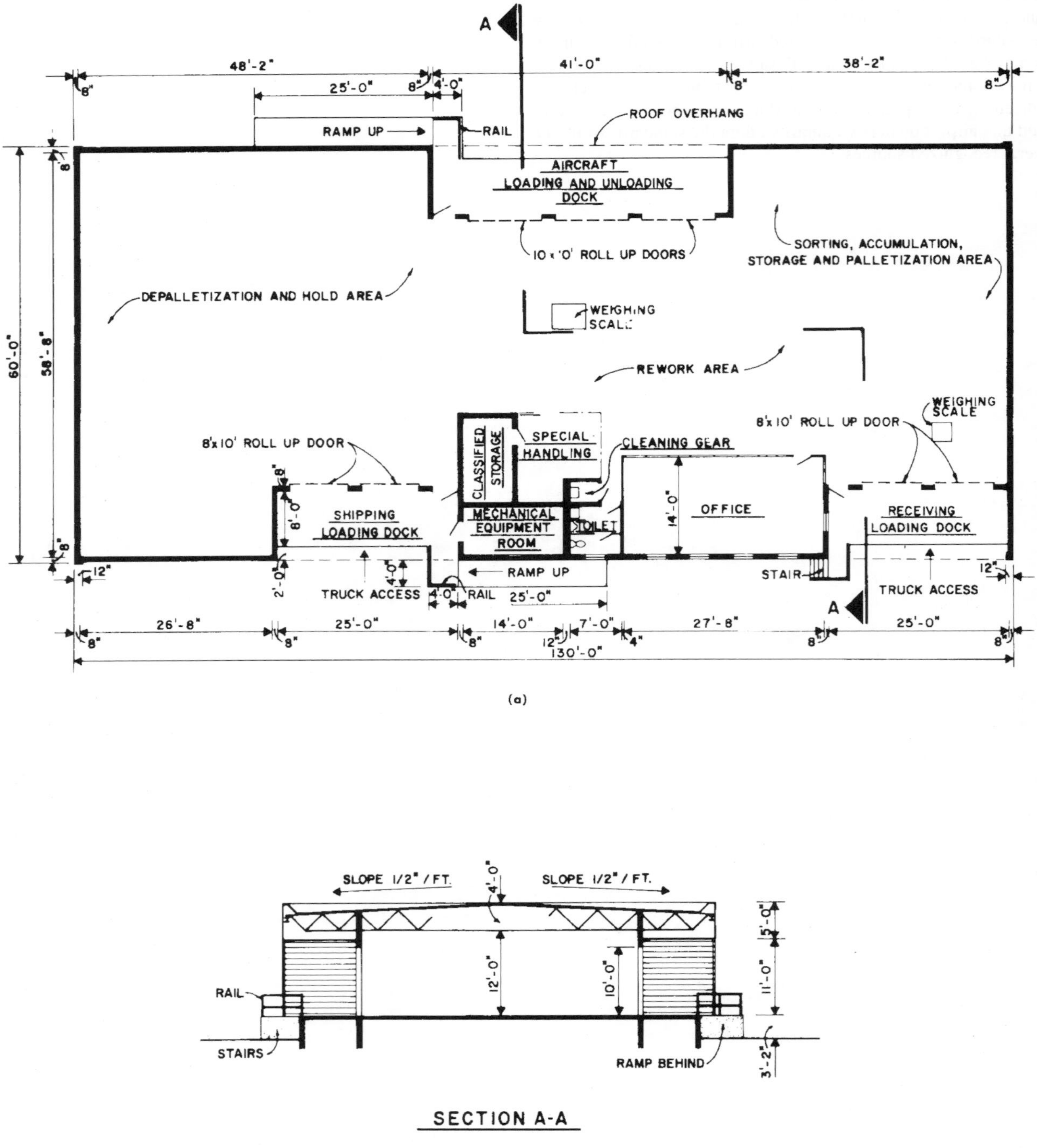

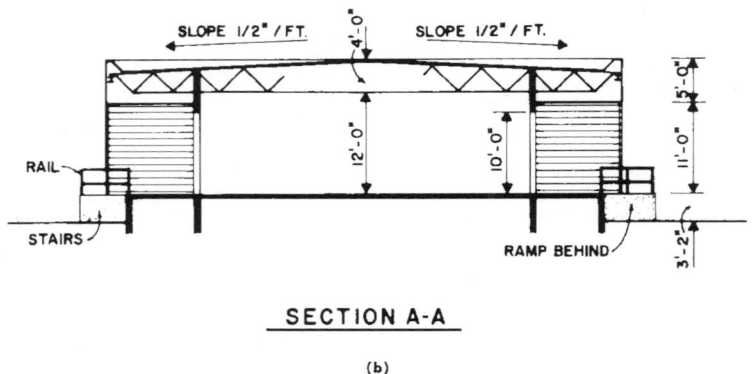

(a)

SECTION A-A

(b)

**Fig. 4. Typical air cargo terminal (Naval Facilities Engineering Command, Department of the Navy, Washington, D.C.**

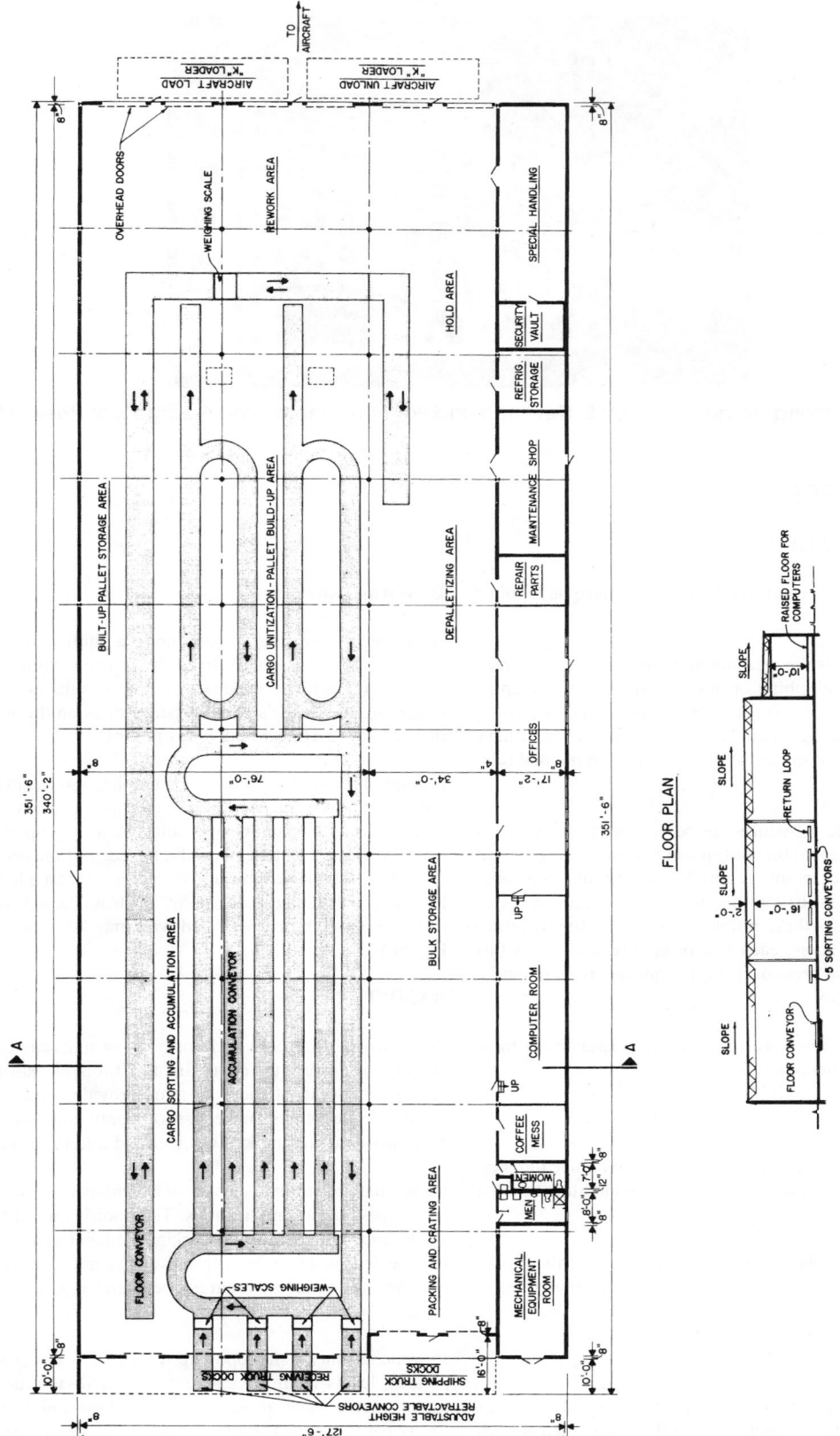

FLOOR PLAN

SECTION A-A

Fig. 5. Typical air cargo terminal with conveyors (Naval Facilities Engineering Command, Department of the Navy, Washington, D.C.)

**Fig. 1. Union Station parking garage (Herbert S. Newman and Partners; photo: Fred George, courtesy of the architect**

# PARKING GARAGES

### RAMP BREAKOVER ANGLE

Parking garages large (Fig. 1) and small must all be designed around their ramp systems.

The ramp breakover angle is the measure of ability of the car to break over a steep ramp, either climbing or descending, without scraping (see Fig. 2). The Society of Automotive Engineers calls for a minimum of 10 degrees as a design standard. A number of models have not met this standard. The average for all groups has remained relatively constant.

The ramp breakover angle influence can be altered through use of design techniques. Transitional blends top and bottom of ramps composed of two or more break points can multiply the ramp steepness, with workable break angles, beyond the normal capacities of car or driver. In existing structures these problems are overcome by building a pad of asphalt or concrete each side of the break point. In this manner cars having a low breakover angle can negotiate potential critical points without scraping.

Long wheelbase cars combined with low center clearance are most susceptible to inadequate breakover angles.

### Angle of Departure

A reasonable minimum value (Fig. 3) is necessary to reduce the incidence of tailpipe and rear bumper dragging. The standard calls for a minimum of 10 degrees.

Most cars are substantially above 10 degrees. The most critical condition is at driveways where the apron is steep, or a combination of excessive crown to gutter and apron slope.

### Ramp Slopes

The maximum ramp slope should be 15 percent. For slopes over 10 percent, a transition at least 8 feet long should be provided at each end of the ramp at one half the slope of the ramp itself (see Fig. 4).

### Driveway Exits

A ramped driveway exit rising up to a public sidewalk must have a transition section that is almost level (maximum slope: 5 percent before intersecting the sidewalk to prevent the hood of the car from obscuring the driver's view of pedestrians on the walk. This transition should be 16 feet long (see Fig. 5a).

Property line walls should also be regulated so as not to interfere with the driver's view of pedestrians on a public sidewalk. Wherever an exit driveway is parallel and adjacent to a property line wall that extends all the way to a sidewalk, the edge of the driveway should be physically established, by curb or railing, at least 6 feet from that wall. For each foot that the wall is held back from the sidewalk, the required distance between driveway and wall may be reduced by 1 foot (see Fig. 5b).

### RAMP TYPES

A number of different interfloor ramp systems can be used to enable vehicles to traverse the approximate 10-foot elevation between parking levels. Some of these systems provide separate and exclusive ramps, while others make use of continuous sloping floors that accommodate both parked vehicles and interfloor travel.

Ramps may be straight, curved, or a combination. No single ramp system is best for all applications. The choice should be based on site shape and dimensions and parking demand characteristics. Ramps may be designed for one-way or two-way traffic movement. However, one-lane-wide ramps should not be operated on a reversible two-way basis.

In some instances, site topography will allow direct access to several parking levels from the street system. This is a desirable arrangement, since it leaves more space for parking and provides more flexibility for traffic distribution between the street system and parking facility.

*Reference: Parking Garage Planning and Operation, Eno Foundation for Transportation, Inc., Westport, Connecticut.*

Fig. 2. Ramp breakover angle

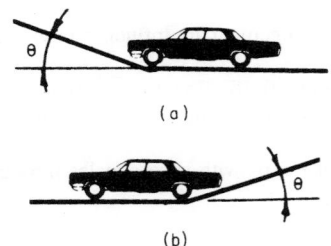

Fig. 3. (*a*) Angle of approach (*b*) Angle of departure

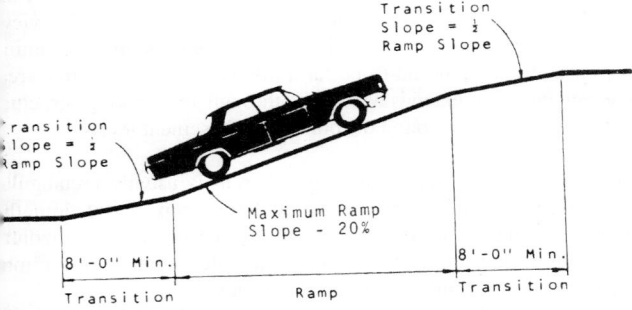

Fig. 4. Ramp slopes (transitions are required only if ramp slope exceeds 10 percent)

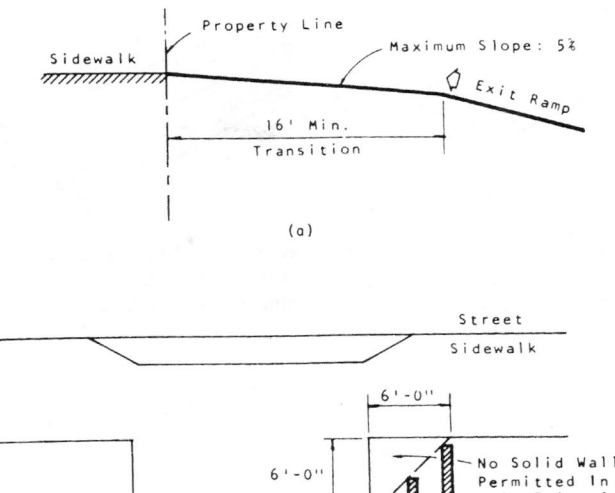

Fig. 5. Driveway exits

Time and convenience are important to ramp travel and should be considered in any comparison of ramp types. Actual travel time on ramps varies little among different ramp system types; however, some ramp systems have more potential for delay caused by conflicting traffic movements that limit ramp capacity. Other factors influencing ramp design include accident hazards, construction cost, and ability to accommodate vehicles and drivers conveniently.

**Analysis of Ramp Movements**

A ramp system includes any portion of storage floors used by vehicles moving between levels. Nearly every successful ramp system requires vehicles to follow an approximately circular path when traveling between parking levels. The number of 360-degree rotations required to circulate through the garage and parking structure height are major concerns.

It is generally desirable to limit the maximum number of complete rotations to five or six. Depending on ramp system type, this will control the maximum desirable number of parking levels and limit the number of parking spaces a driver must pass during garage travel.

Drivers are sometimes distracted or disturbed by the awareness of height when traveling on upper parking levels, a condition that can be accentuated if parking levels extend higher than adjacent buildings. To reduce driver distraction, parapet walls (Fig. 6) along driving ramps should be designed to limit the driver's view of surroundings outside the parking structure.

**Clearway and Adjacent Ramp Types**

Ramp systems may be divided into two types, based on the amount of interference between ramp traffic and parking-unparking operations. Ramp systems designed on the "clearway" principle provide interfloor travel paths completely separated from potentially conflicting parking-unparking movements. Ramp systems in which part or all of the ramp travel is performed on access aisles may be called the "adjacent parking" type. The number of parking stalls adjacent to the ramp may vary from a small number to the total capacity of the facility (see Fig. 7).

Fig. 6. Ninth Square District parking garage (Herbert S. Newman and Partners; photo: Norman McGrath, courtesy of the architect)

**Fig. 7. Parking garage examples that incorporate adjacent-parking ramp systems for traffic entering and clearway ramp systems for traffic exiting the facilities**

Clearway ramp systems provide the safest movement with least delay and, except for sloping floor designs, are preferred for self-park designs. However, the clearway ramp system is seldom feasible for small garage sites.

An adjacent-parking layout requires less area per parking stall because of the twofold use of travel paths, and consequently can be used to advantage on smaller land parcels. However, adjacent-parking ramp designs are more susceptible to traffic movement delays and potential accident-causing situations.

The actual travel speeds for free-moving vehicles on the two types of ramps do not vary greatly. Delays on the adjacent-parking type ramp system caused by parking-unparking maneuvers are difficult to measure but must be recognized as a sizable quantity. Delays will be greater on parking levels nearest the street level, since these levels always have larger numbers of vehicles in the circulation system.

**Concentric Versus Tandem Ramp Design**

Ramp systems also can be classified as concentric or tandem, depending on whether the travel paths of vehicles moving up and down between parking levels revolve about the same or separate centers. Helically-curved (spiral) ramps are usually built concentrically to save space and to provide flatter grades. Straight ramp systems are designed in either concentric or tandem configurations.

Vehicles traveling on a ramp system may move either clockwise or counterclockwise. Counterclockwise rotation is generally preferred in the United States and other countries where drivers customarily sit on the left side in vehicles since it places drivers on the inside of turns, enabling better vehicle handling.

**Parallel Versus Opposed Ramp Design**

For vehicles to rotate in the same direction on a ramp system, up and down ramps must slope in opposite directions, requiring ramp surfaces to be opposed. If up and down ramps slope in the same direction, ramp surfaces are parallel and vehicles must rotate in opposite directions.

While no significant difference has been observed in operational ease, it is obvious that opposed ramp types are safer, since all vehicles must travel in the same direction. Parallel ramp systems are considerably cheaper to construct, however.

**Geometric Ramp Types**

For safety, convenience, and traffic operating efficiency, the path followed by the ramp through traffic on any floor of a parking garage should be short, with minimum turns and traffic crossings. Ramp arrangements within a garage should be consistent, in order to be as simple and comprehensible as possible.

Ramp design and arrangement are influenced by:

- orientation of ramp traffic flow to main floor street entrance and exit points and to other ramp systems that might exist in large garages
- conformance of ramps with access aisles throughout each floor area
- site dimensions

**Straight-Ramp Systems**

Ramps within a straight-ramp system usually should be "stacked" one over another for construction economy and traffic circulation uniformity. The stacking of ramps creates a "ramp-well." From a plan view the sum of the system's ramp-well areas and the floor area containing aisles used by ramp portal-to-portal traffic is the ramp system's area or envelope. This extends vertically through the parking structure (with the possible exception of roof and/ or basement levels).

For straight-ramp garages, the ramp system is usually rectangular shaped (ignoring curved ramp ends), with the ramp well(s) along the structure's longer-side dimension. This is because more horizontal distance is required to satisfy ramp grade criteria than to accommodate vehicular movement between ramp ends.

Figure 8 illustrates a basic straight-ramp system having a ramp-well on one side only. In this system, vehicles follow an elliptical path most of which is on flat surfaces. Figure 9 is a parallel straight-ramp system, with ramp-wells on two sides of the structure. Turning movements for the up and down ramps are performed in different areas while the floor travel is performed in a two-way movement along the same aisle. Depending on structure width, the floor travel could be directionally separated. The systems represented in Figs. 8 and 9 are both very adaptable to entrance and exit points on the same street.

Figure 10 is an adjacent-parking type opposed straight-ramp system. Travel paths for through up and down movements fall in the same aisle, eliminating traffic crossing points. Figure 11 illustrates a clearway type opposed straight-ramp system. Ends of opposed ramps on the main floor are pointed in opposite directions, making this type suited to structures with entrance and exit points on separate streets. This design can be adapted to entrance and exit points on the same street, but requires a 180-degree turn on the main floor necessitating additional space.

Straight-ramp systems are advantageous in relatively narrow buildings. They require less floor area than helically-curved ramps and are simple to construct, particularly in existing structures being converted to parking garages. However, sharp turns, necessary to get on and off straight ramps, are disadvantages.

**Split-Level or Staggered-Floor Systems**

The staggered-floor parking garage, invented by Fernand E. d'Humy, is generally referred to as a split-level garage. It is constructed in two

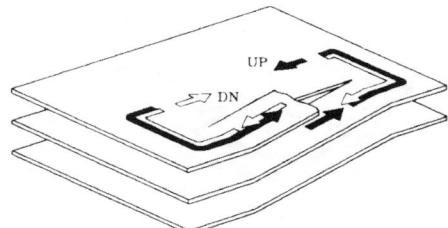

**Fig. 8. Straight-ramp system with one ramp-well**

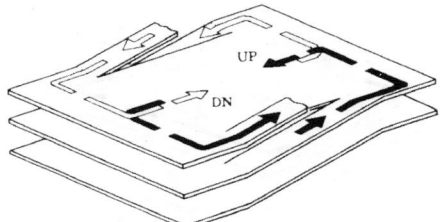

**Fig. 9. Parallel straight-ramp system with ramp-wells on two structure sides**

...tions, with floor levels in one section staggered vertically by one-...lf story from those in adjacent sections. Short straight ramps, ...ped in alternate directions and separated by the distance required ...easily make a 180-degree turn between ramps, connect the half-...ories.

...ny combination of straight ramps can be applied to the split-level ...or systems. Traffic rotation direction may be the same, in which ...se the aisles are one-way, thereby reducing conflicts. Turning ...ths may overlap, requiring less space for the ramp system. Rota-...n can be provided also in opposite directions, which simplifies ...mp construction by having up and down ramps on the same ...ane.

...e division between split-level structure halves may be perpendicu-... to the street or parallel. In the latter case, either the front or back ...lf may be elevated. Split-level floors can overlap as much as 5 to 6 ...et to increase space efficiency and make narrow sites workable.

...gures 12 through 15 illustrate various types of split-level configu-...tions. Figure 14 is the most common type.

...lit-level designs are particularly applicable to small, high-cost ...es where maximum use of space must be achieved. Construction is ...latively simple, and the design fits well on rectangular sites. This ...stem is efficient in terms of floor space per vehicle parking stall ...t, like all ramp systems employing adjacent parking, frequent con-...cts may arise between circulating traffic and parking-unparking ...hicles.

...ne variation in the split-level system uses three separate sections, ...ith the two end sections at equal elevations and staggered one-half ...ory with respect to the center section (see Fig. 15). Fifty percent ...wer turns are required, thereby reducing travel time. However, ...hicles parked on the end sections must be driven an extra half-floor

when entering or leaving. "Wrong way" ramp travel is also a greater possibility with this type of design.

**Sloping-Floor Systems**

The sloping-floor parking garage, in its simplest form, contains two adjacent parking modules tilted in opposite directions, with cross-aisles at each end so that vehicles traveling the length of both aisles make a 360-degree turn to move up or down one complete parking level (Fig. 16). Thus, there is no area set aside for ramps in the ordinary sense. The cross-aisles may be sloped or level.

Parking industry experience indicates that the sloping-floor design is well-suited to self-park operations. The relatively flat floor slope (customarily ranging between 3 and 5 percent) permits comfortable parking and pedestrian walking. Because parking is adjacent to the interfloor circulation system, each entering customer has an opportunity to park in the first available space. However, the operational problems in adjacent parking can cause congestion during peak outbound movements if clearway-type express ramps are not used.

Floor-to-floor travel distance is greater in sloping-floor garages than in other types of ramp garages. However, this is offset somewhat by the opportunity for greater travel speeds due to flat slopes and longer tangents.

For large structures it is desirable to have only part of the floor area sloped, with level floor sections at ends to form cross-aisles. Ramp connections at midpoints of opposite sloping floors permit one-way traffic circulation (Fig. 17). It is possible to achieve one-way traffic circulation in sloping-floor layouts, with parking along aisles on every level, by using two sloping-floor garage units placed end-to-end. In the level center section where the two units meet, traffic flow can change from up to down and vice versa. This permits flexibility for angled parking, limited only by available site width (Fig. 18).

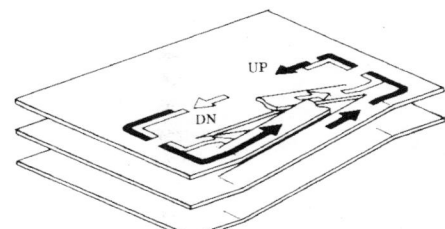

**ig. 10. Adjacent-parking type opposed straight-ramp ystem**

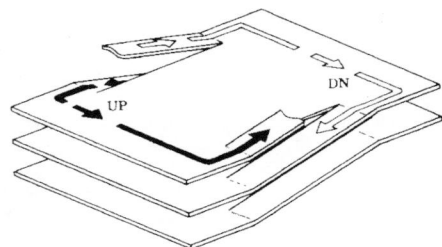

**Fig. 11. Clearway-type opposed straight-ramp system**

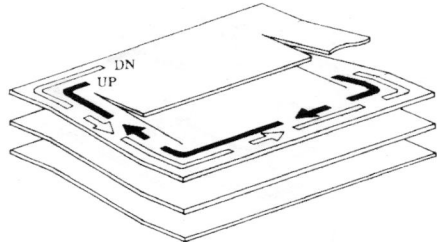

Fig. 12. Two-way staggered-floor ramp system

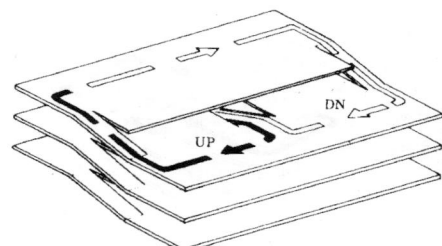

Fig. 13. Tandem staggered-floor ramp system

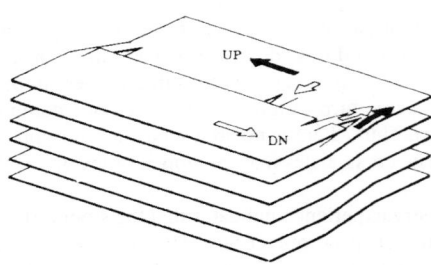

**Fig. 14. This staggered-floor system provides parking on level floors and desirable one-way traffic flow**

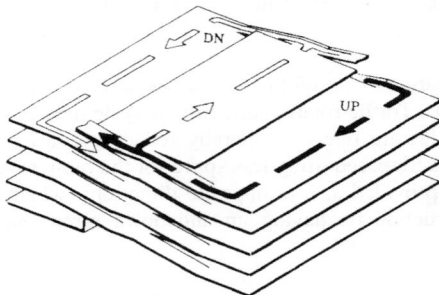

Fig. 15. Three-level staggered-floor ramp system

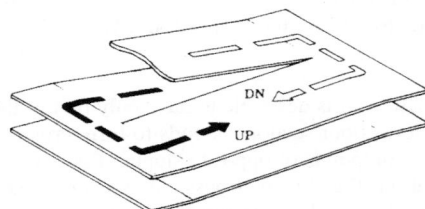

Fig. 16. Basic sloping-floor concept

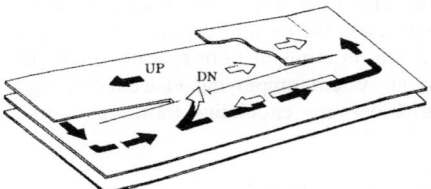

Fig. 17. Sloping-floor system with crossover ramp of mid point

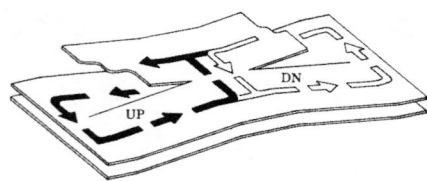

**Fig. 18. Double sloping-floor system with midpoint crossover**

### ·lically Curved Ramp Systems

·e helix (spiral) ramp can be a single surface that permits vehicles ·travel on a continuous helical path between parking levels. When ·o-way traffic is handled on a single helix, the outer lane is used for · movements, since it has a larger radius of curvature and lower ·de. Up movements are usually counterclockwise and down move-·nts clockwise.

·lical-ramp entrance and exit points can be located on the same ·le or opposite sides of the ramp coil. In either case, ramp access ·nts are located directly above each other on each succeeding floor. ·lically curved ramps should be of the clearway type. Examples are ·istrated in Figs. 19 and 20.

·e double helix system (Fig. 20) uses two helical-path surfaces that ·e sloped in opposite directions. One surface can be used for up ·vements, the other for down movements. The two sloping helical ·rfaces may be separated or they may be interwoven. Vehicle move-·nts for both up and down travel directions are made in the same ·rection of rotation. In the U.S. and other countries using left-side ·ive vehicles, counterclockwise rotation is preferred.

·terwoven double helix systems are popular in tall structures (10 to · parking levels) because the number of 360-degree turns can be ·duced by using two separated helical surfaces to serve alternate ·rking levels.

·aditionally, curving ramps are said to be continuous where they ·ovide 360 degrees of rotation between two parking levels. The non-·ntinuous helically curved ramps that provide rotation through 180 ·grees are commonly referred to as semicircular although this defi-·tion is not quite correct, since the curved section is helical in shape.

·lically curved ramps are most often located in corners of rect-·gular structures to minimize floor-space loss, or they are located ·itside the structure when additional site area is available. Helically ·irved ramps require more space than straight ramps, but they can ·fer better traffic operation by providing gradual turning as com-·ired to sharp turning movements usually required at ends of straight ·mps. In addition, superelevation at ends of straight ramps may ·quire undesirable warping of floor areas.

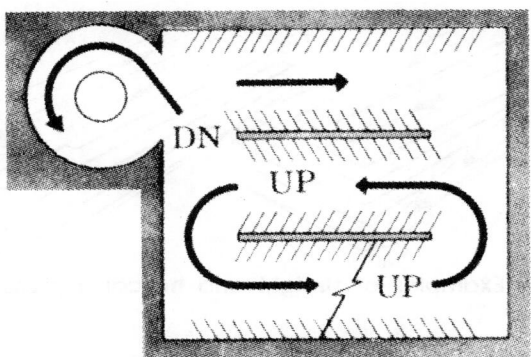

**Fig. 19. Helical ramps such as this one can be used effec-tively for express exiting**

### Express Exit Ramps

Large parking structures with frequent high-turnover conditions may be served best with an express ramp for one direction of travel usu-ally for exiting traffic. Express exits can be curved or straight, and are designed always on the clearway principle, providing one-way traffic movement (Fig. 21). They are generally desirable to serve high-turnover transient patronage. They improve operating efficiency by reducing travel time and conflicts but may add significantly to struc-ture costs, since they increase the area prorated to each parking space in determinations of space-use efficiency.

### RAMP STANDARDS

Ramp design parameters governing the acceptability of such ramp features as maximum gradient and minimum radius of curvature have evolved from garage operating experience. The following dis-cussion presents standards generally used by the parking industry.

### Ramp Grades

Ramp grade (slope) is computed by multiplying floor-to-floor height by 100 and dividing by the ramp length. The difference between ramp length measured along the slope or horizontally is negligible.

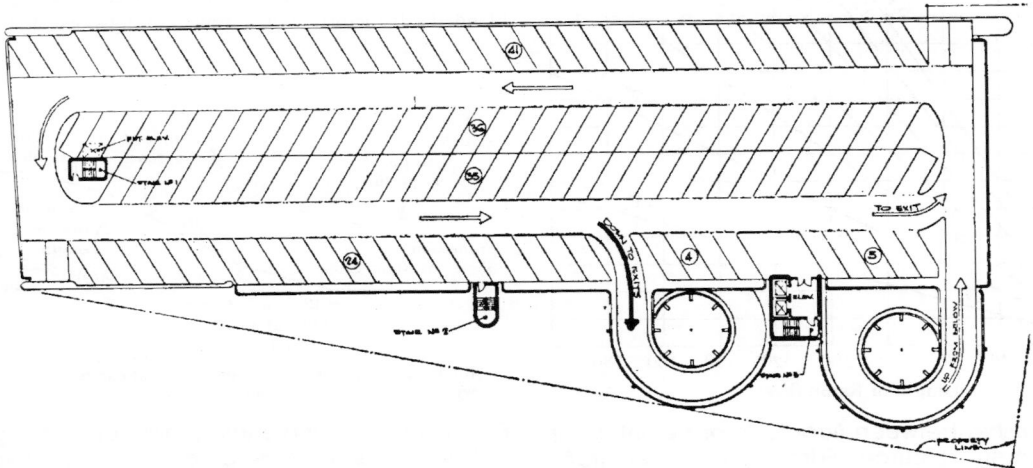

**Fig. 20. Helical ramp systems can often be advantageous for structures situated on odd-shaped sites**

**Fig. 21. Examples of straight and helical express exit ramps**

Grades on curving ramps are measured along the outer ramp pavement edge.

Maximum practical ramp grades are principally limited by safety considerations and the psychological effect on drivers, with hill-climbing and braking abilities of automobiles being a secondary factor. Steep ramps slow traffic movement and can be particularly hazardous when wet, requiring drivers to be excessively cautious.

For self-park designs, maximum ramp grades should not exceed 15 percent; however, 20 percent maximum ramp grades for attendant-parking garages are acceptable. In parking structures where pedestrians are expected to walk on vehicle ramps, grades preferably should be no more than 10 percent.

Figure 22 graphically relates ramp grade and length with floor-to-floor heights. For instance, this graph shows that for a slope of 13 percent and a rise of 9 feet (floor-to-floor height), a ramp length of 70 feet long is required. Similarly, a floor-to-floor height of 11 and a ramp length of 90 feet results in a slope (ramp grade) of 12 percent.

The maximum preferable grade for sloping floor self-park garages is 4 percent, and in attendant-park garages, 10 percent. Angle parking in sloping-floor garages should be 60 degrees or greater, to minimize gravity roll-back of vehicles.

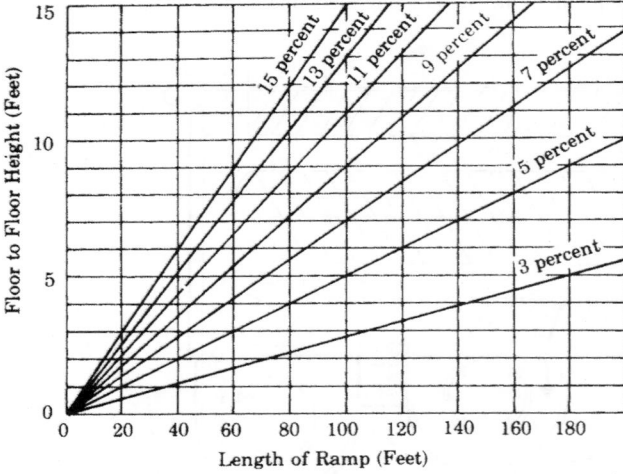

**Fig. 22. Relationship between floor-to-floor height, ramp grade, and length** (Source: Edmund R. Ricker, *Traffic Design of Parking Garages,* The Eno Foundation for Highway Traffic Control)

### Ramp Grade Transition Design

Critical vehicle clearances, driver comfort, and safety consideration influence the design of ramp ends where they meet flatter floor surfaces. Ramp breakover angle, and the angles of approach (affecting front overhang of vehicles) and departure (affecting rear overhang) are critical vehicle clearance points. These angles are established for stationary vehicles with normal equipment and load, including passengers and fuel.

The ramp breakover angle is limited by wheelbase and vehicle ground clearance, and is a measure of an automobile's ability to be driven over the crest formed by two converging surfaces without scraping its underside. Ramp breakover angle varies inversely with wheelbase.

Angles of approach and departure are limited by vehicle front and rear overhang and ground clearance. These vehicle clearance angles determine an automobile's ability to roll over the sag point (lower end of ramp) formed by different grades without scraping or touching the pavement surface. The angle of departure is more critical because the rear overhang of vehicles is generally longer than the front overhang.

Standards established by the Society of Automotive Engineers limit the ramp breakover angle to no less than 10 degrees; angle of departure, no less than 10 degrees; and angle of approach, no less than 10 degrees. Vehicles designed to these minimum standards theoretically are able to traverse sag and crest sections at the bottom and top of 17.6 percent ramp grade, and to move to flat floor grades without need for a grade transitioning (blending) area.

However, centrifugal force, causing vehicle suspension to compress when crossing a sag point, even at low speed, can result in vehicle scraping pavement surfaces. Without grade transitioning at the ramp crest, driver sight-distance can be limited momentarily, and crossing abrupt grade changes can be uncomfortable for drivers and passengers. Therefore, ramp grades should be blended gradually or transitioned to flatter floor surfaces.

A practical method of blending ramp grades to relatively flat floor levels involves using a minimum 12-foot-long transition slope equal to one-half of the ramp grade. Figure 23 illustrates this ramp grade transitioning method. Ramp grades of less than 10 percent can be blended satisfactorily with a transitioning slope shorter than 12 feet.

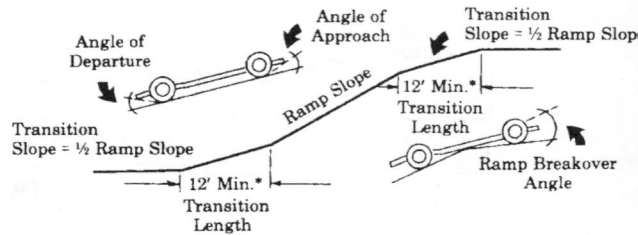

*Ramp slopes (grades) less than 10 percent can be blended satisfactorily with an 8-foot transition length.

**Fig. 23. Method of blending ramp and floor grades. Vertical scale is exaggerated to show detail. (Source: Adapted from Edmund R. Ricker, *Traffic Design of Parking Garages,* The Eno Foundation for Highway Traffic Control)**

## Ramp Width and Radii

For one-way straight ramps, minimum acceptable width is 12 feet; and for two-way straight ramps, where opposing traffic flows are not separated, 22 feet is the recommended minimum width. Where a barrier is used between lanes to separate traffic flows, each lane should be at least 12 feet wide for tangent lengths. Circular ramp lanes generally should be 14 to 18 feet wide.

The repeated turning movements of vehicles traveling between parking levels is a primary design consideration. The spiraling path radius must be kept minimal to conserve space and reduce travel distance. However, very sharp and unrelieved turning will produce a dizzying effect on drivers. To minimize this effect, ramp systems can be laid out with sharp curves separated by short tangents or less sharply curved sections (Fig. 24).

Lateral clearance for a vehicle traveling a curved path is determined by a vehicle's outermost corner point radius (usually the front bumper) when it is turning on a minimum radius. The inside edge of travel lane radius must be less than the minimum inside rear-wheel radius but not much smaller, or drivers will attempt to enter the ramp at too sharp an angle. The relationship between these radii depends on relative vehicle position, which is determined by maximum steering angle and driver steering input, extreme corner dimensions, and speed. Clearance is usually provided for the vehicle with the largest outermost corner point radius.

Minimum outside radius for a single-lane helical ramp is 32 feet; however, an outer radius of 35 to 37 feet is desirable. With helically curved two-lane ramp surfaces, the outer lane need not be as wide as the lane used on the inside path. The outer lane radius is less restrictive, allowing drivers to turn at a flatter angle that requires less effective width for a travel path (Fig. 25).

## Ramp Turn Superelevation

Vehicles traveling on curved paths are acted upon by centrifugal force proportional to the square of the velocity and inversely proportional to the radius of curvature. This centrifugal force must be balanced by other forces that are developed by side-friction of the tires on pavement, and superelevation (banking) of the ramp surface. Although speeds in parking garages are low, turning radii are much smaller than those required for street or highways, thus resulting in rather large centrifugal forces. Ramp curves should not be superelevated too steeply, because very slow drivers may have difficulty in keeping away from the inside edge of the ramp pavement and fast drivers may be encouraged to drive at speeds greater than conditions of grade and sight-distance safely permit.

Garage ramp superelevation should be approximately 1/2-inch/foot of ramp width at the point of sharpest turning, with lesser amounts adjacent to straight sections or storage floors.

## Ramp Appearance

Some motorists are reluctant to use ramp garages because travel paths in parking garages may combine narrow lanes, steep grades, and sharp turns. Even drivers accustomed to garage parking depend on appearance and "feel" in maneuvering their vehicles.

Consequently it is desirable to use architectural and optical effects that will give drivers confidence and reduce possible adverse psychological effects of driving in restricted spaces. An obvious means is to make sight distances as great as possible and to provide abundant illumination.

The optical trick of obscuring horizontal and vertical lines of reference may be used to reduce the apparent steepness of ramp grades. Ramp walls can be painted with stripes contrasting to wall color, parallel to ramp surface or at steeper angles. The normal angles between vertical columns and the travel way can be obscured by paint markings, or adjacent structural features may be built with architectural lines parallel or perpendicular to ramp surfaces.

Ramp structures should be as open as practicable to provide sight distances and to reduce closed-in impressions. In locations where icing conditions are common, ramp systems should be placed in building interiors or otherwise protected from weather.

Ramp illumination should be given special attention. Wall openings should not be allowed where outside light sources could blind drivers. Artificial lighting should take the form of diffused illumination, and reflectors should be pointed away from the direction of travel.

## TYPICAL DESIGNS

In the following pages the functional plans and design features of five self-parking facilities are presented.

In Fig. 26, the plan for a twin-spiral garage is shown. The ramps, situated in opposite corners, are angled to facilitate the movement from the floors to the ramps. Entrances and exits have been provided on two streets on separate levels to take advantage of the different elevations.

**Fig. 24. Curved ramp system with tangent sections**

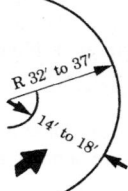

Minimum radius is 32 feet to outer pavement edge for helical ramp or other turning path. A 35- to 37-foot radius is most desirable.

R 32' to 37'

14' to 18'

**Fig. 25. Helical ramp dimension standards (Source: *Parking Principles*, Special Report 125 Highway Research Board)**

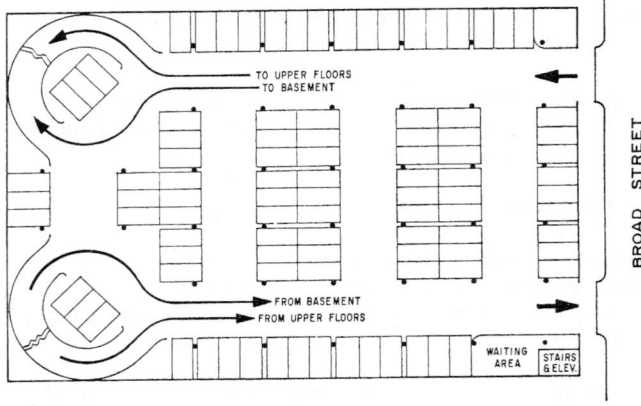

MAIN FLOOR

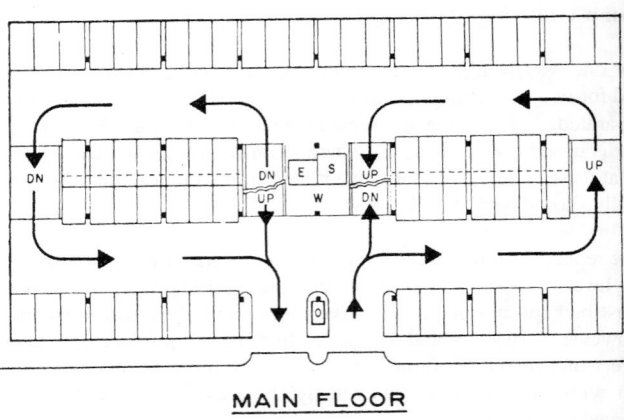

MAIN FLOOR

TYPICAL FLOOR

**Fig. 26. Functional plan for twin-spiral garage**

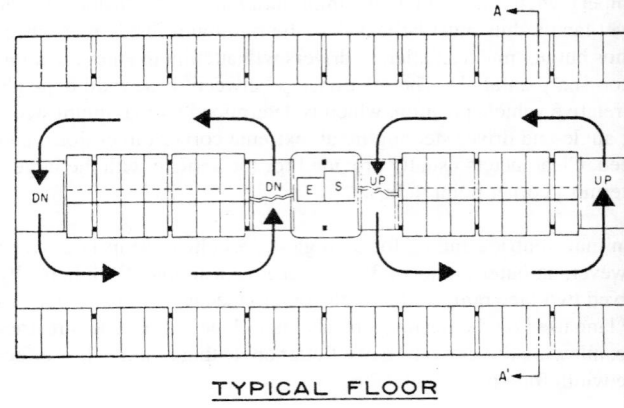

TYPICAL FLOOR

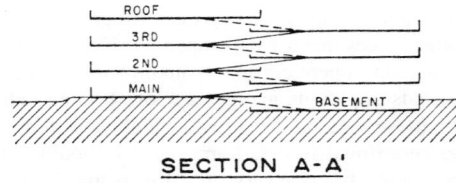

SECTION A-A'

**Fig. 27. Functional plan for staggered-floor garage**

The waiting area—two elevators, rest rooms, cashier's booths, and vending machines—is in the center of the garage. A retail area extends along the entire frontage of one of the streets and has a depth of about 85 feet. The fourth level of the garage, or roof deck, extends over the retail area. Ninety-degree parking is employed throughout the facility.

A staggered-floor or split-level garage is shown in Fig. 27. The ramp systems feature separated one-way operation, and access is on only one street. The overall dimensions of the 352-space facility are 120 by 240 feet. Ninety-degree parking is utilized throughout the four floors. The cashier's booth is at the entrance, and the stairs and elevators are strategically located in the center of the facility to take advantage of the split-level and to afford minimum walking distances.

In Fig. 28 a functional plan is presented for a facility with straig ramps. The garage has one-way aisles and angle parking. Actually, portion of the aisles is used in the floor-to-floor circulation. There ar three pedestrian elevators and four stairways to serve the eight floor Though the entrance and exit were on the same street, they are wide separated to reduce conflicts. The overall dimensions of the facili are 183 by 165 feet.

In a sloping-floor or continuous-ramp garage, the aisles serve tw purposes: access to the parking stalls, and floor-to-floor circulatio In Fig. 29, a typical garage is shown which provides 90-degree park ing. One pedestrian elevator and three stairways have been provide for the five-level facility. The entrance and exit are on one street. Th

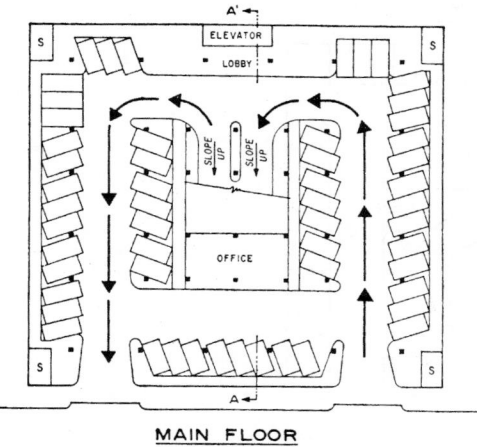

MAIN FLOOR

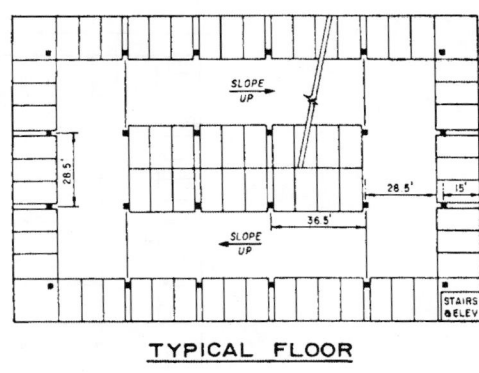

TYPICAL FLOOR

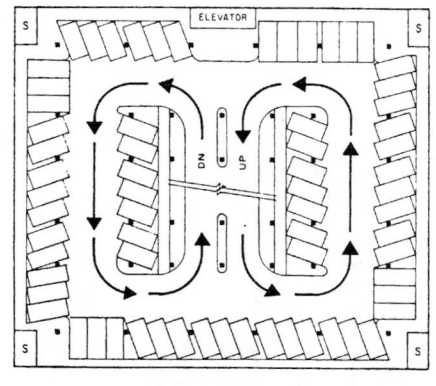

TYPICAL FLOOR

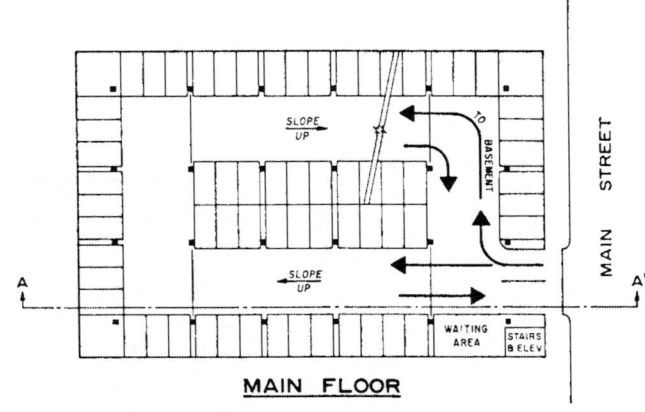

MAIN FLOOR

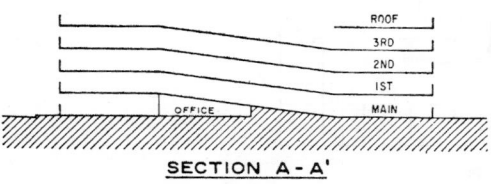

SECTION A - A'

**Fig. 28. Functional plan for straight-ramp garage**

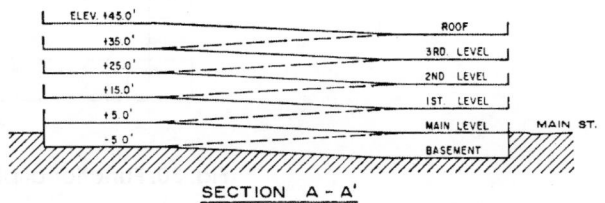

SECTION A - A'

**Fig. 29. Functional plan for sloping-floor garage**

irection of travel on the ramps has been reversed to reduce the con-
lict at the contact with the one-way street. Overall dimensions are
22 by 157 feet.

he preparation of a design for an irregular-shape site presents many
roblems, especially when self-parking is to be provided. An exam-
le of a good design is presented in Fig. 30 where a spiral ramp is in
he center of the garage. The aisles are one-way and two-way, and 90-
egree parking is used throughout the facility.

For the three-floor garage, there is one pedestrian elevator available
at present. Plans and areas are provided for an additional elevator
when warranted. There are four stairways. In the operation of the
facility, an entrance has been provided on one street and two streets
are used for exiting.

Many variations may be used in garage design. The previous examples are typical designs. Design criteria and standards were assembled in a study.[1] The designs must be tailored to the available land.

[1]Ricker, *Traffic Design of Parking Garages*, Eno Foundation.

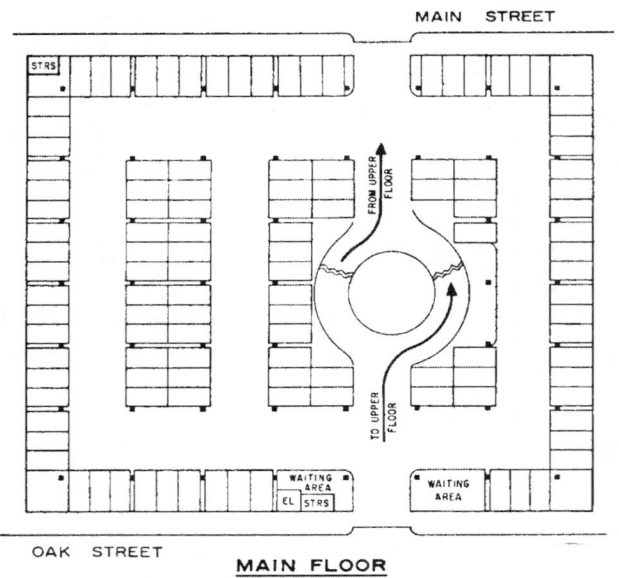

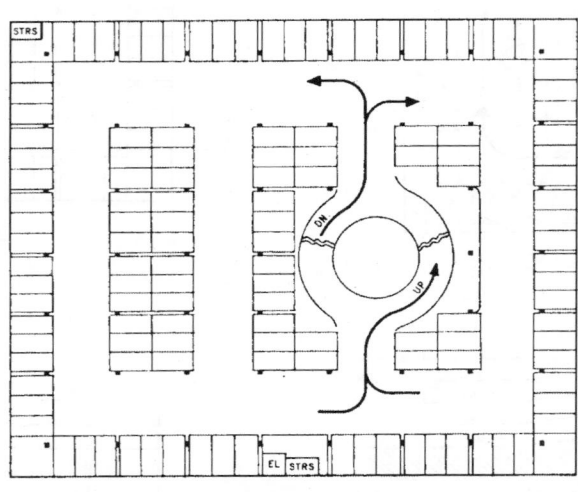

**Fig. 30. Functional plan for concentric-spiral garage**

## RAMP GARAGES

Ramp garages do not simply multiply the parking capacity of a lot by the number of parking levels added. Considerable space on each level will be occupied by ramps and circulation ways which must be kept free of parked cars. Only on the uppermost level (or the lowermost in the case of an underground garage) can cars be temporarily stored in the aisles as they normally are in an attendant-operated parking lot.

On a sloping lot, developed with only two or three parking levels, space normally required for ramps may be reduced. By connecting adjacent streets to the different parking levels, the street system is, i effect, incorporated into the garage ramp system.

As most garages henceforth will be designed, we believe, for cus tomer self-parking, we have taken 12 percent (i.e., a rise of 12 feet i every 100, or a 7-degree angle of slope) as the maximum convenier ramp grade.

Public use and acceptance of a ramp slope depends less upon th mechanical power and body dimensions of the car than upon th apparent hazards to the timid driver of steep narrow slopes and shar

*Authors:* Geoffrey Baker and Bruno Funaro
*Reference: Parking*, Reinhold Pubishing Corp., New York, Van Nostrand Reinhold Company.

ind turns. For some also the terror of coming down a ramp is likely be greater than that of going up.

o make a ramp seem less confined and hazardous, it should be one-ay, well-lighted but without distracting glare, and separated from pposing traffic with a wide divider strip. Camouflage painting evices may be used to make the slope appear less steep. Horizontal nes of reference can be obscured with wall stripes parallel to, or at steeper angle than, the roadway. A long sight line, particularly at e upper end of a ramp, will guard against drivers hesitating. This in irn will increase speeds (without decreasing safety), and so increase e ramp's traffic capacity.

he shallower and longer the ramp, the more space it requires on ach parking level. The only exception to this is where the whole arage becomes in effect a shallow-angled ramp, a wide roadway ith a line of 90-degree parking on each side. This spirals up and round in a continuous line of warped rectangles fitted into the rect-ngular shell of the building.

he second factor governing ramp length is floor-to-floor height. The maller this dimension, the shorter can be the ramps. However, the oor-to-ceiling clear height should not be less than 7 feet-6 inches, nd even this will require many car antennas (especially on sport-tility vehicles) to be retracted or tied down at the garage entrance. hin-floor structural slabs are particularly worthwhile in garage con-truction.

ach end of the ramp, where it joins the parking level, must be lended into the floor grade over a minimum distance of 12 feet. The ections of a modern car most likely to scrape ground at top or bot-om of a slope are the long overhangs in front and rear beyond the vheelbase.

he area required for a ramp system will be most important in deter-nining whether a given piece of land can be profitably developed vith a multistory garage structure. A floor-to-floor height of 8 feet-6 nches requires a 12-percent ramp 71 feet long (see Table 1). Another 5 feet beyond this will be needed for a reasonably convenient turn-ng radius in circulation lanes on each parking floor. So the minimum ength needed for the simplest form of parking deck, with a straight

ramp and on more than two levels, is 90 feet in addition to the ramp length, which will vary according to steepness.

Minimum economical width totals 108 feet. Still, even with these minimum dimensions, there is a quite uneconomical ratio of circula-tion space to storage space on each parking floor. Only by enlarging the floor areas, which usually means enlarging the available lot size, can more storage space be served by the same amount of circulation space.

Ramp length, of course, can only be reduced by steepening the ramp angle or reducing the floor-to-floor height between parking floors. The shape of a ramp can be changed and condensed by coiling it into a helix.

Location and shape of the ramp system is particularly important on the entrance floor of attendant-operated garages. The further away the ramp from the street entrances, the larger the reservoir space, and the better the cushion against delay and congestion at periods of peak arrival.

In general, as we have seen above, the larger each parking floor, the more advantageous the ratio between storage space and circulation ways. The upper limit on floor area in attendant-operated garages will be set by the time required to walk between the farthest parked car and the central interfloor lift that connects with the entrance check-in point where cars are collected and delivered.

This interfloor communication point should be as near as possible to the centroid of the parking floor. For attendants' average walking speed is found to be 5 feet per second; their driving speed averages 13 feet per second.

The layout of parking stalls should be designed to minimize travel time. One-hundred feet of extra travel distance to and from a parking stall will add 7 1/2 seconds to driving time and 20 seconds to walk-ing time, thus reducing each attendant's parking rate by one car per hour. In a large operation with high turnover, this will be revealed by either an increase of labor costs, or by long delays in the delivery of cars to outgoing customers, or by need for a larger reservoir to pre-vent delay in reception of incoming cars.

**Table 1**  Ramp length for straight ramps (to the nearest foot)

| Angle, degrees | Ramp grade, percent | Floor-to-floor height | | | | | Split-level floors | |
|---|---|---|---|---|---|---|---|---|
| | | 8 ft | 9 ft | 10 ft | 11 ft | 12 ft | 4 ft | 5 ft |
| 3 | 5 | 160 | 180 | 200 | 220 | 240 | 80 | 100 |
| 3½ | 6 | 133 | 150 | 167 | 183 | 200 | 67 | 88 |
| 4 | 7 | 114 | 128 | 143 | 157 | 172 | 57 | 77 |
| 4½ | 8 | 100 | 112 | 125 | 138 | 150 | 50 | 63 |
| 5 | 9 | 89 | 100 | 111 | 122 | 134 | 45 | 55 |
| 6 | 10 | 80 | 90 | 100 | 110 | 120 | 40 | 50 |
| 6½ | 11 | 73 | 82 | 91 | 100 | 109 | 37 | 46 |
| 7 | 12 | 67 | 75 | 83 | 92 | 100 | 34 | 42 |
| 7½ | 13 | 61 | 69 | 77 | 85 | 92 | 31 | 39 |
| 8 | 14 | 57 | 64 | 72 | 79 | 86 | 29 | 36 |
| 8½ | 15 | 53 | 60 | 66 | 73 | 80 | 27 | 33 |

For customer-parking garages (Fig. 31), the same standards of walking distance should apply as in parking lots: a maximum walk of 300 feet from parked car to garage entrance. Most important here is allowance for peak periods of interfloor travel by customers entering or leaving.

In a large garage, customer-operated elevators may be insufficient for these peak periods. Escalators will give much better service under these conditions; but they will probably be justified only in a very large garage.

In a parking garage of three floors or less, stairs are still accepted by the public. It will, however, generally be wiser to fill the top floor with long-term parkers, who (perhaps tempted by lower monthly rates) will be more willing to make the climb.

**Types of Ramp Garages**

Types of ramp garages vary widely. No one plan is best for all sites or all types of garage. The shape of the lot, anticipated parking demand, whether the garage is to be designed for parking by customers or by attendants, limitations of cost and of structure (particularly if the garage is part of another building such as an office block or an auditorium)—all are important factors when deciding what is the most efficient type of ramp design for the job.

To improve the ratio between ramp area and parking area, the ramp can be steepened, a one-way ramp can be used for two-way traffic, the ramp can be designed to double as a parking aisle with stalls on each side, cars may be parked in the aisles, and more rows may be double-parked. Every one of these will lower operating efficiency. None of them (except possibly the ramp which doubles as a parking aisle) are even to be considered in a customer-parking garage.

All ramp systems except the helical need circulation lanes kept clear on each parking floor for a continuous path upward and downward through the building.

All ramp systems must circle in order to gain sufficient length within the building to go upward at a reasonable slope. In helical ramps this circling is confined to the ramp. In all other types the turning move-

ment (through 360 or 180, according to ramp type and floor layout is made not on the ramp but on the parking floors. This turning move ment can be made more easily on a banked helical ramp than on th flat parking floors.

Minimum site width required for a ramp garage is 100 to 110 feet, a shown below; even then, there is a quite uneconomical ratio betwee parking area and ramp space. A helical ramp would fit a narrower sit but waste even more space. For a narrow site, particularly a corne lot, the elevator garage may be most economical. Minimum width c the structure alone may be as little as 60 feet. But there must b access on both sides of this, for entrance and exit. There should als be off-street reservoir space. So minimum site width, with a street o the front and one side, is 80 feet (see Fig. 32). If there is no sid street, another 20 feet must be added to the frontage for exit lanes.

Of helical ramp types the least costly to construct is usually tha shown in Fig. 33. One-way up and down lanes are on a single-banke surface. The outer lane is used for up traffic, usually counterclock wise, so that cars keep to the right in normal fashion.

The diameter of the ramp is controlled by the required turning radiu a minimum of 45 feet to the face of the outside curb of the outer lan (see Table 2). There is crossing of traffic at each parking floor con nection, but drivers have a clear view each way.

In the circular ramp shown in Fig. 33 there is no crossing of up an down traffic, even at the parking floor connections. Each traffi stream is confined to its own ramp all the way from top to bottom c the building.

As entrance and exit points are at opposite sides of the ramp cylinde the best position for this type of ramp will be near the center of th parking floor.

The surface of these ramps can be fully banked between floors, but the must be flattened at the point of connection with each parking floor, s that cars can turn off and on without too sharp a break in grade.

To avoid scraping the floor with front or rear overhangs or some pa of the underbody of the car, change of grade between floor and ram must not be too sudden. The blending distance must be at least a long as most wheelbase lengths—about 10 feet. As precise construc tion in concrete is not to be expected, it is wiser to set 12 feet as mir imum. A simple rule of thumb is to make this transition grade half th ramp grade (see Fig. 34).

Halfway between the circular and the straight ramp is what may b called the rectangular circle. This is so large and so shallow that normally fills the whole building, and so wide that there is a line c right-angle parking along each side. The floors of the garage becom tilted planes. A basic disadvantage of this plan is that a two-way ci culation road must also serve as a parking aisle—and a very long or too. The inevitable result is congestion and delay, particularly at th lower levels during outgoing rush hours.

Probably the simplest types of ramp in structure, planning, and ope ation are the two-way divided ramps set one above the other at or edge or in the center of the parking floor (see Fig. 35).

This is quite economical of space, particularly on a lot that is rathe long and narrow. Two-way circulation lanes on the parking floor ma be hazardous.

**Fig. 31. Ninth Square District parking garage (Herbert S. Newman and Partners; photo: Norman McGrath, courtesy of the architect)**

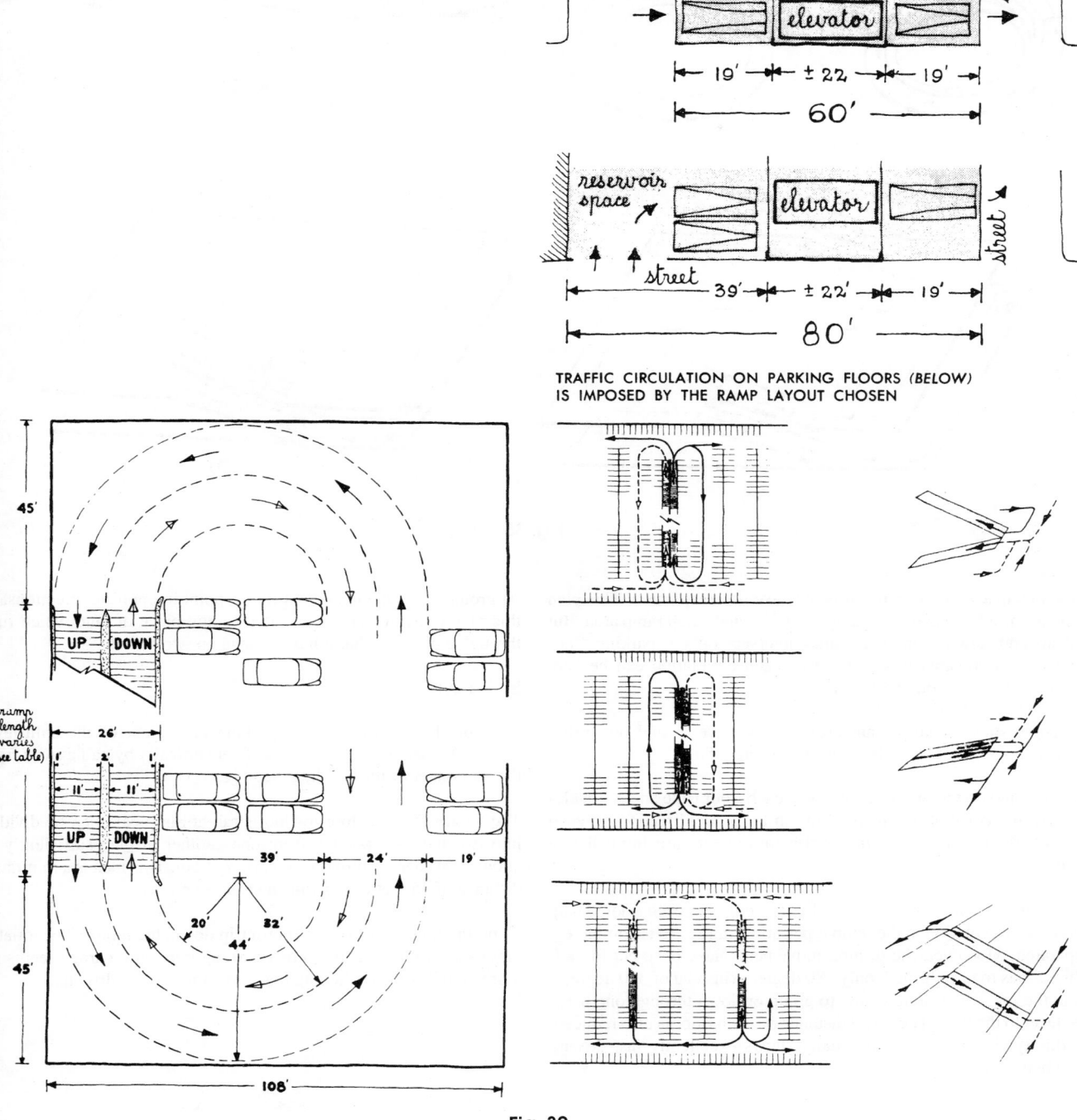

TRAFFIC CIRCULATION ON PARKING FLOORS (BELOW)
IS IMPOSED BY THE RAMP LAYOUT CHOSEN

Fig. 32

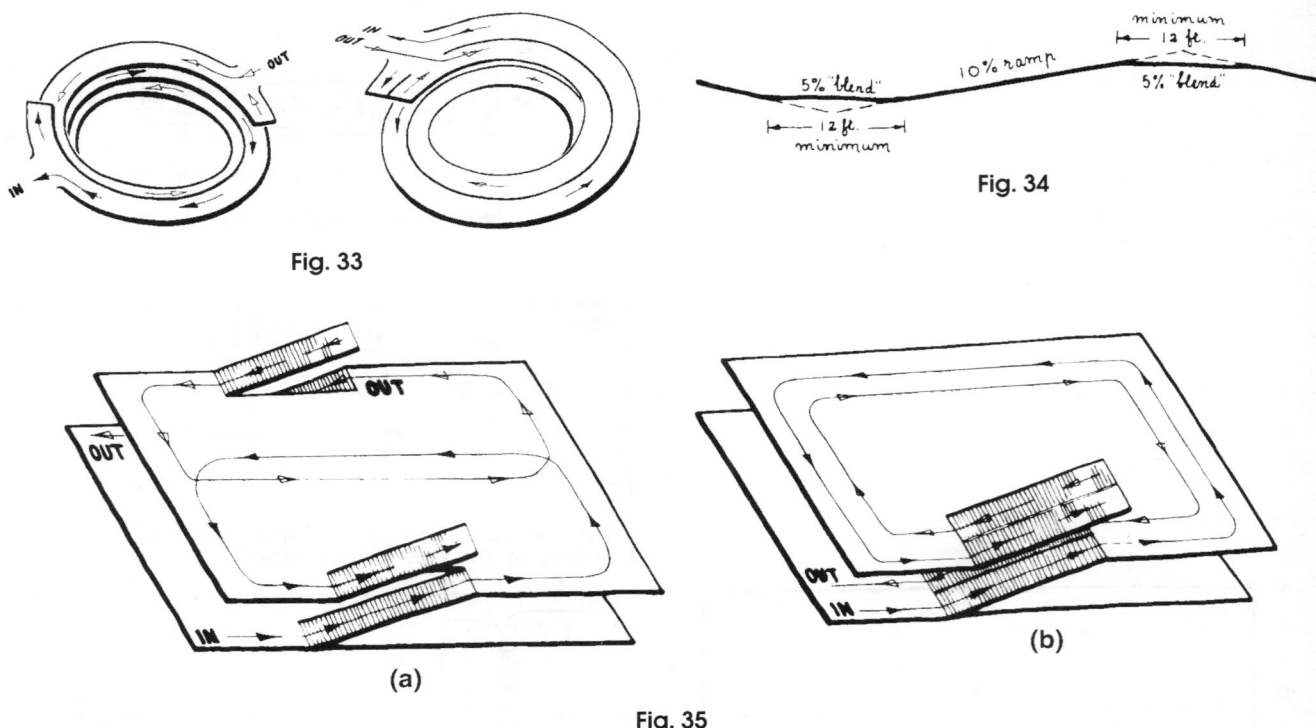

**Fig. 33**

**Fig. 34**

**(a)**

**(b)**

**Fig. 35**

Here the up and down traffic streams have been separated. This plan still has the advantages of rectangular shape and small ramp area. But the up and down circulation lanes intersect on the parking floor unless the floor area is so large that each circulation can be kept within its own half on one-way lanes.

On some sites it may be an advantage to have in and out traffic widely separated at street level, as it is in Fig. 35a.

If the up and down ramps crisscross at each floor (like an "X" in elevation), the two traffic streams flow in the same direction on each parking floor, and conflicting traffic movements are immediately reduced.

By placing up and down ramps at alternate edges of each floor, the up and down circulation in the ramp type shown in Fig. 36 is completely separated. Moreover, the turning movements have been cut in half. The car has to turn through only 180 degrees (instead of 360 degrees, as in the preceding ramp plans) to go up or down through one parking level to the next. The travel distance on each floor is also reduced, so this type of ramp layout usually shows excellently fast driving time between floors.

At ground level the in and out ramps point in opposite directions, s this plan is particularly well fitted to any piece of land which run through a block so that it has frontage on two streets.

**Split-Level Garage**

The split-level garage is the parking equivalent of the split-leve house. One section of a garage is offset vertically by half a story from the remainder of the building (see Fig. 37).

The length of each floor-to-floor straight ramp can then be divide into two halves separated from one another in plan sufficiently t allow a 180-degree turn on the parking floor. This means a minimum distance of 45 feet center-to-center of the ramps.

Climbing upward, or on the return trip down, the motorist negotiate these short ramps easily, so that parking in a ramp garage seems n more complex or frightening than any other sort of driving.

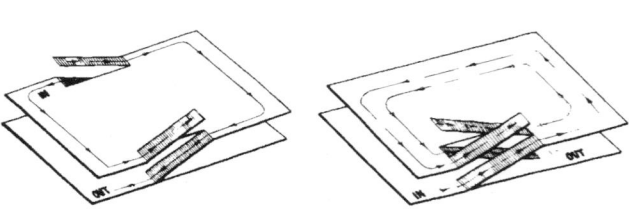

**Fig. 36**

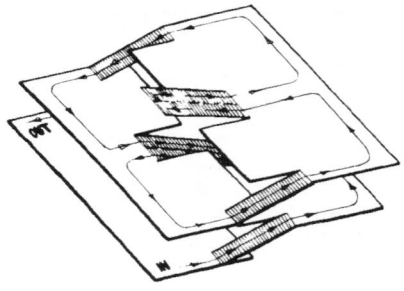

**Fig. 37**

**Table 2**  Helical ramps—minimum dimensions for two lanes side by side, feet

| | |
|---|---|
| Radius to inside face of outer curb of outer lane | 45 |
| Radius to inside lane to inside face of outer curb | 32 |
| Width of inside lane between curbs | 12 |
| Width of outside lane between curbs | 11 |
| Width of border curbs (curb height: 6 in.) | 1 |
| Width of median curb (curb height: 6 in.) | 2 |
| Maximum super-elevation on ramp turns | 0.1 ft per ft of width |

at the junction point between the two sections of the building, where the floors are offset vertically, they also overlap horizontally. In these few feet along the edge of each floor there is only half the normal floor-to-ceiling height found in the rest of the building; but this is sufficient height for the end few feet of a car, front or rear. Here the parked cars actually overlap one above the other, to give a saving of perhaps 4 to 5 feet in the overall width of the structure. On a narrow lot these may be the few extra feet necessary to accommodate minimum parking lot dimensions to the dimension of the lot.

Any of the ramp and circulation systems discussed earlier can be applied to the split-level garage structure.

**Mechanical Elevator Garages**

Mechanical elevator garages are most suitable on expensive sites which are too small for economical development with a ramp garage. They are the only practical means of developing garage space on deep lots with narrow frontage.

Mechanical elevator garages can be structurally very light and open if local building codes allow.

The two principal makes—Bowser and Pigeon Hole—both impose similar circulation patterns. Cars enter the central elevator hoistway

on one side and exit on the other. This type of garage is particularly well suited to corner sites, or any interior lot where the long side abuts on an alley which can be used for exit. In such cases the main street frontage required will be only 80 feet.

If entrance and exit must be on the same frontage, the minimum width required will be approximately 100 feet. On a structure above 10 stories in height, however, if sufficient reservoir space is provided at ground level to cushion peak arrival periods (without cars having to line up on the street outside), the lot size may have to be greater than this minimum.

Up to a point this will depend also upon the number of elevators used (the more elevators, the higher the speed of storage and delivery), which in turn will affect the capital cost of such a garage structure.

In mechanical elevator garages a minimum of one quarter of each parking level area is occupied by circulation. When there is no double-row parking (which may entail moving front-row cars to reach those in the back), circulation space, i.e. the elevator hoistway, occupies one third of the area on each parking level. On the other hand, on a site 100 by 100 feet a circular ramp (the most condensed type) would occupy almost two-thirds of the area on each level.

The Pigeon Hole hydraulic elevator equipment moves on rails set on the ground; the Bowser electric elevators are hung from an overhead crane track. In both systems the elevator car moves simultaneously in a horizontal and a vertical direction.

Pigeon Hole uses a dolly, controlled by the elevator operator, for moving the car in and out of the elevator. Bowser elevator operators drive the car on and off. The elevator control panel is within easy reach of the operator as he sits in the car. An intercom and signal light system connects the elevators with the cashier's control booth.

The Bowser elevators are counterweighted so that, if the electric power fails, the garage can still be unloaded. These elevators will rise without power when empty. Loaded with a car, they descend at a controlled rate.

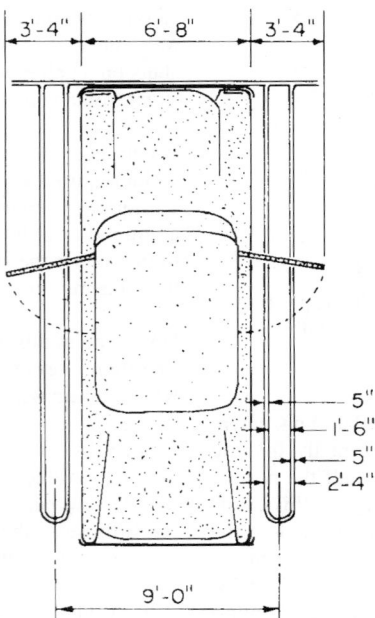

**Fig. 1. Single parking stall**

## PARKING LOTS

Parking stalls should be built to accommodate the larger cars frequently used, although not necessarily the very largest. Planning in hopes of just medium and compact cars invites difficulties. The larger cars (such as sport utility vehicles) have an over-all length of 19 feet, over-all width 6 feet-8 inches, with a wide open door projecting 3 feet-4 inches beyond the over-all width. The ramp angle must not exceed 7 degrees. The limit of the front approach angle is 14 degrees, while the corresponding angle at the rear is limited to 9 degrees. When parked at right angles to a curb or buffer, the front overhang generally does not exceed 2 feet-10 inches, and the rear overhang seldom exceeds 4 feet-6 inches. These dimensions need consideration when planning widths of sidewalks affected by the overhang. A 5-foot sidewalk would have its usable width reduced almost to zero by the rear overhang. The front overhang may be taken at 1 foot-6 inches when figuring closely the minimum feasible spacing between buffers for a minimum width parking lot. When a central driveway is used with 90-degree parking on both sides, the space required is 62 feet wide, but the space between buffers need only be 59 feet because of the overhang.

A single stripe, 4 to 6 inches wide, may be used to mark the parking stalls. Better results in centering the car are obtained by using two 5-inch stripes, separated by 1 foot-6 inches, to mark the stalls. The stripes, about 18 feet long, are joined by a semicircular arc at the incoming end to form an elongated U (Fig. 1). Experience has shown this method to be very satisfactory and fully worth the extra painting.

Parking stalls should be at least 9 feet wide; 10 feet wide if space is not too restricted. Parking stalls 8 feet-6 inches wide are unsatisfac-

tory because with the car 6 feet-8 inches wide, there is only 1 foot-10 inches between cars. If an adjacent car is only 6 inches off center and the car door is 4 inches thick, only 1 foot remains through which to squeeze, if possible.

Motel parking lots planned for maximum guest convenience mark of parking stalls 11 feet wide and 23 feet long, allowing 4 feet behind the 19-foot car for unloading space, which is advisably clear of the driveway.

Parking lots, exclusive of drives for entering them, require 350 square feet per car as a very rough, preliminary figure. The width of the available space and the desired angle of parking are determining factors in economy. The area per car varies from 279 to 585 square feet under conditions covered in the tabulation of parking lot dimensions (Table 1). A central driveway with two rows of cars and 90 degree parking gives the best economy. Diagonal parking is easier for the driver, reduces the necessary driveway width, but requires more total space (Fig. 2).

In designing parking spaces, end stalls should be about 1 foot wider than usual, especially if bounded by a building or other obstruction or a driveway. Parking spaces under buildings should be 11 feet wide, watching out for columns, and should have 7 feet height in the clear.

The parking pattern that will be most satisfactory fully warrants careful thought. It depends upon many factors including the possible locations of access drives. These should be 20 feet wide for two-way traffic or 12 feet wide for one-way traffic (Fig. 3 ). If a restricted site

*Author:* Frank Harrison Randolph, P.E

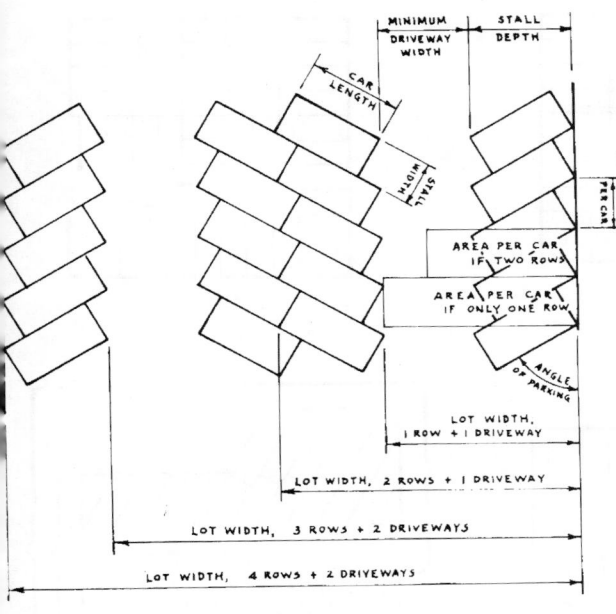

**Fig. 2. Diagonal parking**

frontage requires a right-angle turnoff, the driveway should be 25 feet wide and the curb should have a 30-foot radius. A curb radius of less than 18 feet is inadvisable.

A slope of 6 percent is the usual maximum for state highways. A slope of 12 percent is customary for ramps, but may be as much as 15 percent. The parking lot should be nearly level. The central driveway may be crowned, with a 1 percent slope draining to the edges so that persons on foot will find the driveway relatively free from water after rain or from ice in cold weather.

The following drawings provide guidance on terms used in parking lot design (Fig. 4), as well as dimensions for rows of stalls (Fig. 5), and dimensions for 90-, 45-, and 60-degree parking (Figs. 6 to 8).

**Table 1**  Parking lot dimensions

| Angle of parking | Stall width | Curb length per car | Stall depth | Minimum driveway width | Lot width 1 row + 1 driveway | Sq ft per car | Lot width 2 rows + 1 driveway | Sq ft per car | Lot width 3 rows + 2 driveways | sq ft per car | Lot width 4 rows + 2 driveways | Sq ft per car |
|---|---|---|---|---|---|---|---|---|---|---|---|---|
| Along curb = 0° | 9′ | 23′ | 9′ | 12′ | 21′ | 483 | 30′ | 345 | 51′ | 391 | 60′ | 345 |
| | 10′ | 23′ | 10′ | 12′ | 22′ | 506 | 32′ | 368 | 54′ | 414 | 64′ | 368 |
| 30° | 9′ | 18′ | 17′4″ | 11′ | 28′4″ | 510 | 45′8″ | 411 | 66′2″ | 397 | 83′6″ | 376 |
| | 10′ | 20′ | 18′3″ | 11′ | 29′3″ | 585 | 47′6″ | 475 | 68′0″ | 453 | 86′2″ | 431 |
| 45° | 9′ | 12′9″ | 19′10″ | 13′ | 32′10″ | 420 | 52′8″ | 336 | 79′0″ | 376 | 98′10″ | 315 |
| | 10′ | 14′2″ | 20′6″ | 13′ | 33′6″ | 490 | 54′0″ | 383 | 80′4″ | 379 | 100′10″ | 358 |
| 60° | 9′ | 10′5″ | 21′0″ | 18′ | 39′0″ | 407 | 60′ | 313 | 95′0″ | 330 | 116′0″ | 305 |
| | 10′ | 11′6″ | 21′6″ | 18′ | 39′6″ | 455 | 61′ | 351 | 95′6″ | 366 | 116′6″ | 335 |
| 90° | 9′ | 9′ | 19′ | 24′ | 43′ | 387 | 62′ | 279 | 105′ | 315 | 124′ | 279 |
| | 10′ | 10′ | 19′ | 24′ | 43′ | 430 | 62′ | 310 | 105′ | 350 | 124′ | 310 |

Refer to Fig. 2

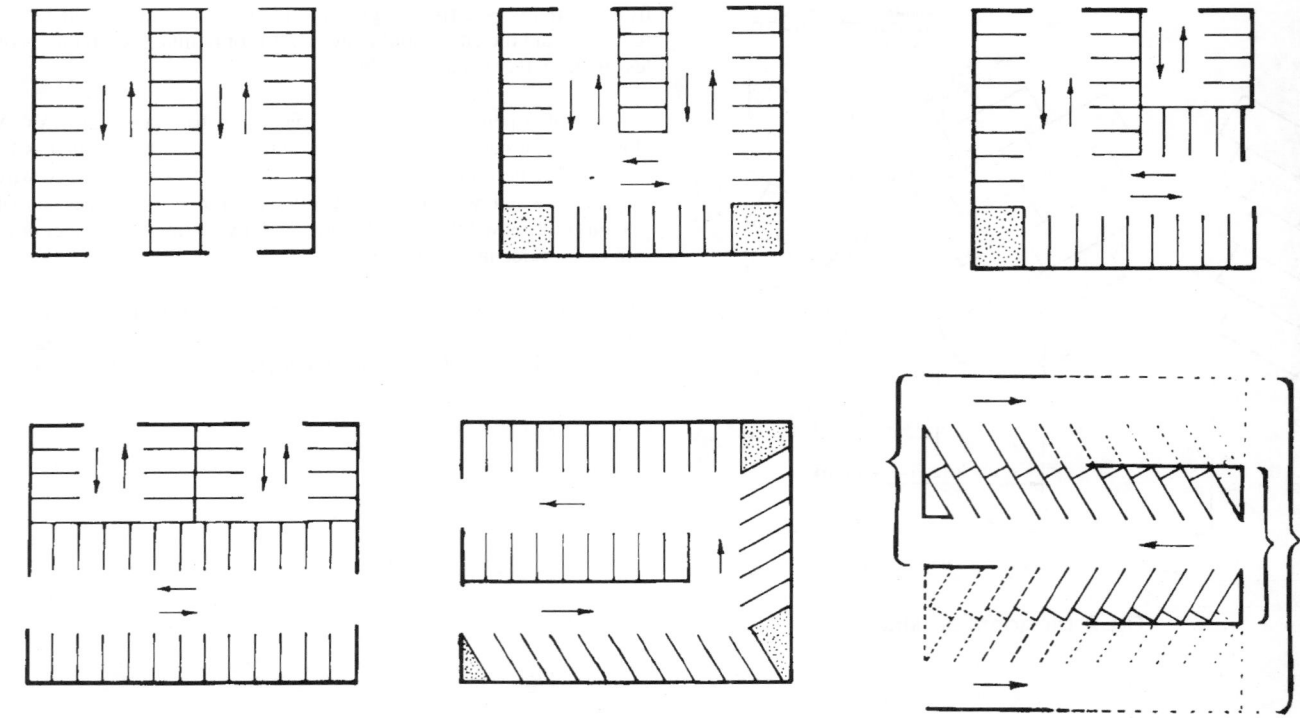

**Fig. 3. Lot access**

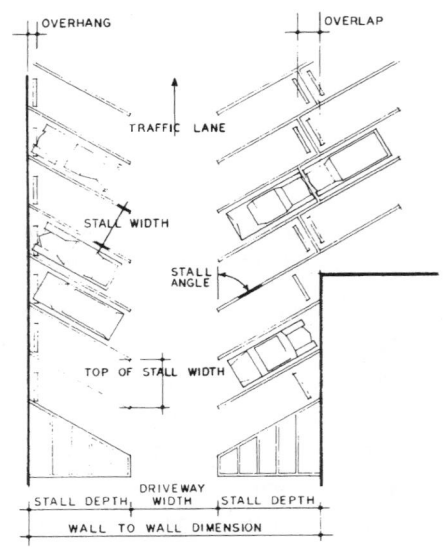

**Fig. 4. Definitions**

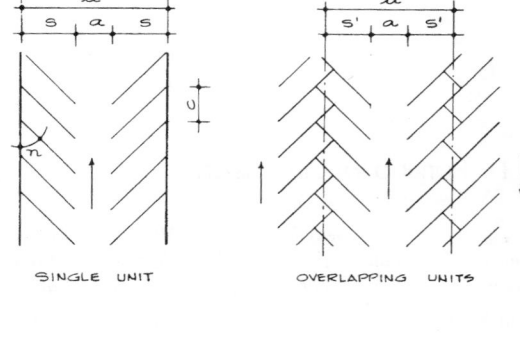

SINGLE UNIT          OVERLAPPING UNITS

| $n$ | $s$ | $a$ | $c$ | $u$ | $s'$ | $u'$ |
|------|--------|--------|--------|--------|--------|--------|
| 90° | 19' 0" | 24' 0" | 9' 0" | 62' 0" | 19' 0" | 62' 0" |
| 60° | 21' 0" | 18' 0" | 10' 5" | 60' 0" | 18' 9" | 55' 6" |
| 45° | 19' 10" | 13' 0" | 12' 9" | 52' 8" | 16' 7" | 46' 2" |

**Fig. 5. Parking layout dimensions**

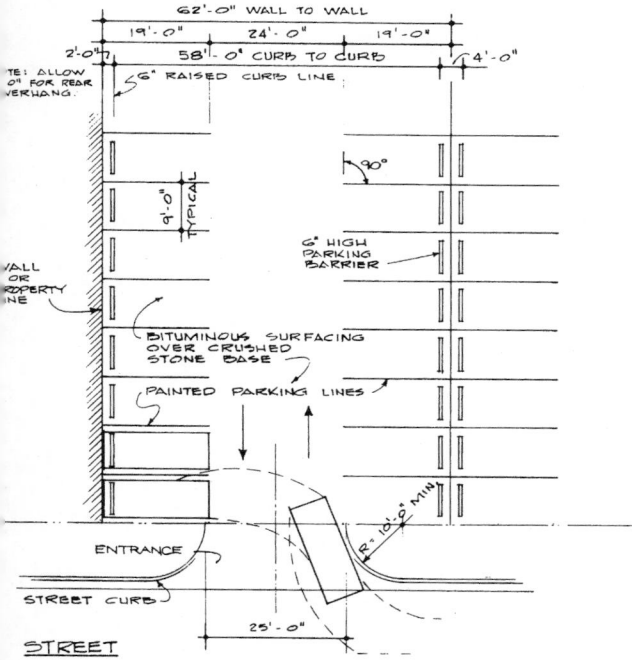

Fig. 6. Parking plan—90-degree parking (*Design Guide for Permanent Parking Areas,* National Crushed Stone Association, Washington, D.C.)

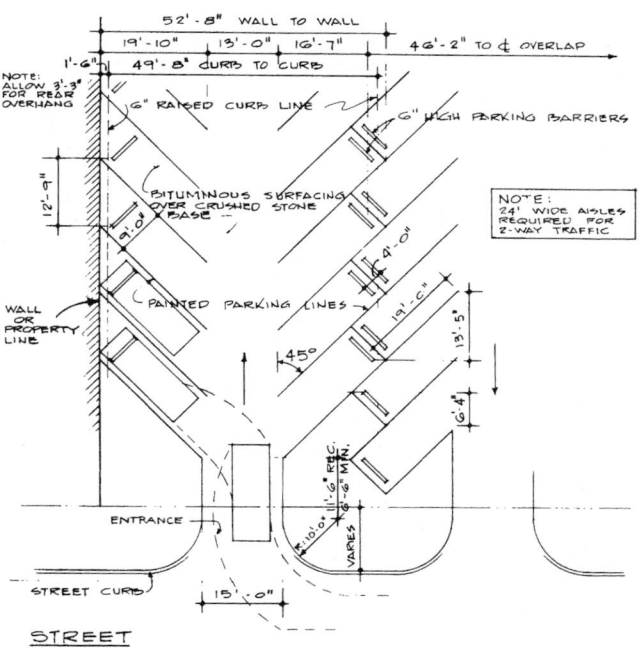

Fig. 7. Parking plan—45-degree parking

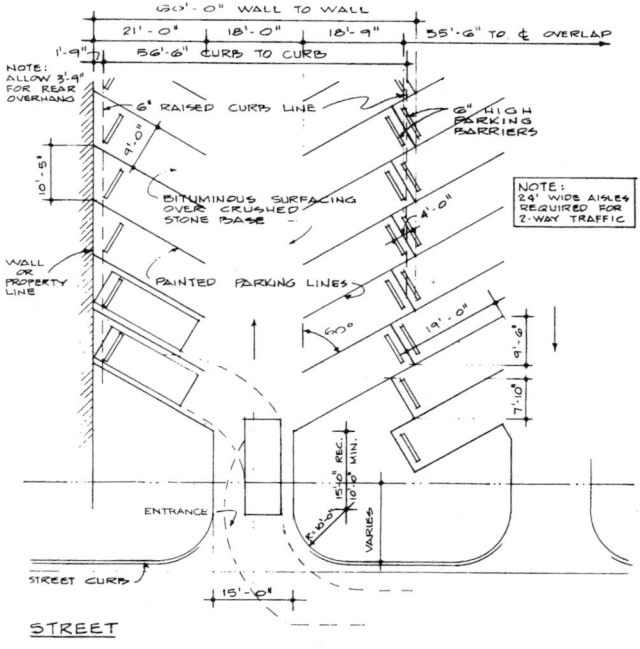

Fig. 8. Parking plan—60-degree parking

Academic libraries. *See* Colleges and universities, libraries

ADA. *See* Americans with Disabilities Act (ADA) Accessibility Guidelines

Adults (human figures, dimensions of), 3–4

Aged, housing for. *See* Senior housing

Airport cargo facilities:
buildings, 968–971
general considerations, 966
interrelationship of facilities, 966
parking
aircraft, 967
vehicles, 967–968
site selection and location, 966–968
terminals, 972–973

Airport passenger terminals:
access systems, 960–965
airline requirements, 941
baggage handling systems, 949–952
curb frontage utilization, 952–953, 963–964
design and development programs, 934–940
flow diagrams, 927–932
food service facilities, 959–960
gate lounge concepts, 946–948
general considerations, 925–926, 952
glossary, 926, 933–934
parking
aircraft, 941–945
vehicles, 964–965
passenger loading methods, 946–948
terminal space guidelines and plans, 953–960

Americans with Disabilities Act (ADA) Accessibility Guidelines:
dimensions, human figures and wheelchairs, 3–5, 81–82, 84–86
disabled persons, housing for, 78–87
educational buildings, 367–368
hospitals, 520
libraries, 700, 704

Americans with Disabilities Act (ADA) Accessibility Guidelines (*Cont.*):
museums, 680, 682
performing arts spaces, 720, 726

Apartment buildings:
commercial space, 61
configuration, 55–56
design process models, 51
floor plans and layouts, 58–62
general considerations, 51
group homes (*see* Group homes)
laundry areas, 61–62
plans and layouts, 58–62
program elements, 51–52
seniors housing (*see* Seniors housing)
site selection and location, 54–55
structural systems, 56–58
types, 55, 60
zoning and building codes, 52–54

Apartments:
balconies, 46
bathrooms, 47
bedrooms, 47
closets, 47
combined areas
efficiency apartments, 48–50
living-dining, 44–46
dining areas, 44–46
efficiency, 48–50
entry halls, 48–49
exposure types, 44
general considerations, 43–44
kitchens, 46–47
living areas, 44–46
seniors, 50 (*see also* Seniors housing)
standards, minimum
dimensions, 50
room sizes, 45

Auditoriums. *See* Performing arts spaces

Automobile dealer and service centers:
 body shops, 169–171
 dealerships, 145–156
 service stations, 163–168

Balconies:
 apartments, 46
 senior housing, 73
Ballet theaters. *See* Performing arts spaces
Bathrooms, residential buildings:
 apartments, 47
 group homes, 89
 seniors housing, 71–72, 75–77
 single-family homes, 33–38
Bedrooms, residential buildings:
 apartments, 47
 disabled person, housing for, 85
 group homes, 89
 seniors housing, 69–71
 single-family homes, 15–18
Body shops. *See* Vehicle dealer and service centers

Cargo (air) facilities. *See* Airport cargo facilities
Chanceries. *See* Embassies and chanceries
Chapels:
 educational centers with, 914
 300-seat, 913
Child care facilities. *See* Early childhood education
 facilities
Children (human figures, dimensions of), 5
Churches:
 chapels
  educational centers with, 914
  300-seat, 913
 general
  general considerations, 873, 880
  organ and choir location, 879–880
  plans, 873–876, 879–882
  plan types, 876–879
  site selection, 873
  sizes, 880–882
 Lutheran
  elements of, 883
  parking, 888
  plans, 884–888
  site selection, 883–884
 schools
  equipment, requirements, 917, 919–921
  rooms, requirements, 915–922
  space, requirements, 919–921
 United Methodist
  fellowship halls and classrooms, 894–895
  organization, 889
  plans, 889–894
  site selection, 889

Churches (*Cont.*):
 utility, simplicity, flexibility, and intimacy,
  incorporation of, 894–899
City and town halls:
 fire departments within, 767–771 (*see also* Fire
  services buildings)
 general considerations, 759
 layout, design, and construction features,
  762–766
 needs assessments, 759–760
 plans, 761, 763, 765–766
 police departments within, 766, 789–790 (*see also*
  Police services buildings)
 site plans, 761
 site selection and location, 760–762
Closets, residential buildings:
 apartments, 47
 disabled persons, housing for, 81–85
 seniors housing, 63, 69–70, 75
 single-family homes, 39–42
College and university buildings:
 classrooms
  front platforms, 463
  general considerations, 462
  large group facilities, 468–478
  projection facilities, 468–478
  projection systems, 463
  seating, 462–464, 478
  theater arts laboratory teaching stations, 465–468
 gymnasiums and recreational centers
  auxiliary facilities, 501–504
  field houses, 504–505
  general considerations, 497–498
  site selection and location, 497–498
  space requirements, 498–501
  student recreational centers, 505
 laboratories
  equivalent linear footage (ELF) factors, 515
  requirements, 506, 509–514
  total area calculations, 507–508
  types, 508–514
 libraries
  book storage and stack capacity, 479–480, 493–496
  ceiling heights and floor areas, 483
  column spacing, 479–482
  general considerations, 479 (*see also* Libraries)
  plans and layouts, 485–489, 492, 495
  seating capacity and accommodations, 482,
   484–493
 residence halls
  facilities, 452–453
  general considerations, 446
  interior environments, 450–452
  planning types, 453–454
  plans and layouts, 447–450, 454

college and university buildings (*Cont.*):
    space allocation and requirements, 450–451
    student rooms, 446–450, 454
  student centers
    functions, 455–456
    general considerations, 455–456
    integration of areas, 460–461
    organization, 455
    space requirements, 456–460
combined areas, residential buildings:
  apartments
    efficiency, 48–50
    living-dining, 44–46
  single-family homes
    dining-kitchen, 13–14
    living-dining, 12–13
    living-sleeping, 18–19
commercial buildings:
  airport facilities, 925–973 (*see also* Airport facilities)
  apartment buildings, space within, 61
  funeral homes, 265–269
  hospitality buildings, 273–356 (*see also* Hospitality buildings)
  media facilities
    radio stations, 255–264
    television stations, 248–254
  offices
    general, 172–199
    law, 225–231
    medical, 200–212
  parking facilities, 974–993 (*see also* Parking facilities)
  research laboratories, 232–247
  retail shops, 105–116
  shopping centers, 119–144
  supermarkets, 117–118
  vehicle dealer and service centers
    body shops, 169–171
    dealerships, 145–157
    service stations, 163–168
    truck dealer and service facilities, 157–162
Concert halls. *See* Performing arts spaces
Conference centers:
  characteristics, 299
  plans and layouts, 298–299
  programs, establishing, 300–301
  types of centers, 298–299
  types of rooms, 301–304
Correctional facilities:
  classifications, security
    maximum, 833–834
    medium, 833–834
    minimum, 833
    supermax, 828
  design considerations, 833

Correctional facilities (*Cont.*):
  educational and vocational training, 842
  food service, 845–847
  general considerations, 825, 849
  health care services, 844, 847
  inmate programs and services, 841–844
  libraries, 842–843
  parking, 849
  physical image, 834–838
  planning process, 830–833
  plans and layouts, 831, 834–839
  program elements, 838–841
  reception and intake, 844–846
  recreation, 847–848
  religious facilities, 848
  security standards, 848–849
  site selection and location, 833
  special needs
    community correctional facilities, 830
    general considerations, 829
    geriatric populations, 830
    health care, 829
    juvenile facilities, 829, 844
    sex offender facilities, 830
    women's facilities, 830–831
  types
    definitions, 825–826
    jails, 826
    military, 826
    multifunctional municipal facilities, 826–827
    prisons, 827
    supermax facilities, 828
  visitation facilities, 846, 848
Courthouses:
  bankruptcy courts, 823
  district courts
    clerk of the court areas, 821–822
    courtrooms, 814–815
    general considerations, 813–814
    jury suites and assembly areas, 817–820
    probation and pretrial services areas, 822–823
    United States Marshal suite, 820–821
  general considerations, 806
  libraries, law, 823
  movement and access diagram, 808
  plans and layouts, 808–809, 811–816, 818, 823
  police services. *See* Police services buildings
  space requirements, 807–809, 813
  specialized courts, 824
  trial court functions, 806–812
Cultural and entertainment facilities:
  libraries, 693–712
  museums, 677–692
  performing arts spaces, 713–755
  recreational centers, municipal, 799–805

Dance theaters. *See* Performing arts spaces
Day care centers. *See* Early childhood education
    facilities
Dealerships, automobile and truck. *See* vehicle dealer and
    service centers
Dental schools:
    administrative areas, 653–654
    faculty areas, 652
    general considerations, 635–636
    graduate and postgraduate facilities, 652–653
    high-bench disciplines, 641–642
    laboratories, 637–641, 643
    libraries, 648–652
    plans and layouts, 636–654
    practice offices, 213–220
    preclinical and clinical facilities, 642–648
    site selection and location, 635
    space allocation and relationships, 635–636, 640
    teaching areas, 648–652
Detention centers. *See* Correctional facilities
Developments, manufactured homes. *See* Manufactured
    home developments
Dining areas, residential buildings:
    apartments, 44–46
    group homes, 88–89
    seniors housing, 65–67
    single-family homes, 9–11
Disabled persons, housing for:
    bedrooms, 85
    closets and storage areas, 81–85
    community spaces, 86–87
    dwelling structures, 79–86
    general considerations, 78
    health clinic areas, 87
    kitchens, 82–85, 87
    laundry areas, 80–81
    libraries, 87
    lighting, 79
    living areas, 81–82
    outdoor areas, 79
    parking, 79
    plantings, 79
    ramps and walkways, 78–79
    recreation areas, 87
    seniors housing (*see* Seniors housing)
    site selection and location, 78
    (*See also* Americans with Disabilities Act (ADA)
        Accessibility Guidelines)

Early childhood education facilities:
    ancillary classroom areas, 373–375
    common areas, 375–377
    educational areas, 370–376
    general considerations, 369–370
    plans and layouts, 375–379

Early childhood education facilities (*Cont.*):
    site selection and location, 377
    staff-child ratios, 370
Eateries. *See* Restaurants and eateries
Educational buildings:
    colleges and universities
        classrooms, 462–478
        gymnasiums and recreation centers, 497–505
        laboratories, 506–515
        libraries, 479–496
        residence halls, 446–454
        student centers, 455–462
    conference centers, 298–304
    early childhood facilities, 369–379
    elementary and secondary schools, 380–386
    health care schools
        dental, 635–654
        medical, 609–635
        nursing, 655–673
    libraries, 693–712, 910–911
    museums, 677–692
    organization and design of schools
        administrative suites, 404–407
        art facilities, 413–415
        auditoriums, 431–434
        buses, 402–403
        capacities, classrooms and pupil, 388–389
        classrooms, 412
        elementary schools, 389–390, 395–400, 403–404,
            409, 411, 413, 415, 434, 440
        food service facilities, 441–445
        general considerations, 387
        glossary, 387–388
        gymnasiums, 434–440
        international schools, 395–399, 423
        K–12 campuses, 397–403
        laboratories, general science and biology, 418–422
        language facilities, 423
        libraries and resource centers, 423–425
        life skills facilities, 427–429
        multipurpose rooms, 430–431
        music facilities, 415–418
        organizational types, 387
        parking, 402–403
        plans and layouts, 390–402, 404–407, 410–420,
            423–443, 445
        recreational facilities, 403–404
        secondary schools, 387, 391–400, 403, 411–414, 527
        site selection and location, 401–403
        space allocation and requirements, 389, 401
        student services offices, 404–407
        vocational and technology facilities, 426–427
    performing arts spaces. *See* Performing arts spaces
    religious buildings with educational facilities
        chapels, 914

Educational buildings (*Cont.*):
   churches with classrooms, 894–895
   church schools, 915–922
   temples and synagogues, 909–912
  research laboratories, 232–247
  safety and security issues
   accessibility provisions, 367–368
   active concepts, 365–366
   general considerations, 364
   life safety considerations, 357
   passive concepts, 364–365
  technology, planning for
   general considerations, 359–360
   learning environments, typical, 360–363
   media centers and libraries, 361
Elderly, housing for. *See* Seniors housing
Elementary and secondary school buildings:
  early childhood education facilities, 369–379
  economics and financing, 381–382, 384–386
  general considerations, 380–381
  organization and design of schools, 387–445
  planning for, 380–386
  safety and security
   accessibility issues, 367–368
   active concepts, 365–366
   general considerations, 364, 366
   life-safety considerations, 367
   passive concepts, 364–365
  space allocation and requirements, 382–384
  strategic planning, 381
  technology, educational and administrative,
   359–363
Embassies and chanceries:
  cultural sensitivity, 850
  general considerations, 850
  organization and functions, 850–853
  space allocation
   general considerations, 853
   programming and planning modules matrix, 854
   sample program, 855–870

Film theaters. *See* Performing arts spaces
Firehouses. *See* Fire services buildings
Fire services buildings:
  city and town halls, within, 767–771 (*see also* City and
    town halls)
  fire apparatus sizes, 768
  general considerations, 767, 772
  parking, 769
  planning
   elements and components, 767–771, 775–778
   general considerations, 772
  plans and layouts, 767–774, 777
  site selection and location, 774–775
  types, 772–773, 778

Food service facilities, restaurants, eateries, and kitchens:
  commercial kitchens
   cafes, 296
   general considerations, 292
   hotels and motels, 292–294
   personnel and functions, 292
   restaurants, 292–297
   self-service facilities, 294–295
   snack bars, 294
   student dining halls and cafeterias, 297
   tea room, 296
  correctional facilities, 845–847
  elementary and secondary schools, 441–445
  food service facilities
   bar sizes, 284–285, 290
   dining areas, 282–284
   general considerations, 279, 281, 291
   lunch counters, 289–290
   other areas, 285, 291
   receiving areas, 281
   serving areas, 282
   space estimates, 279–281
   storage areas, 281–282
   table and chairs sizes, shapes, and arrangements,
    283–291
  hotels and motels
   banquet facilities, 323–324
   food and beverage services, 309–312
   restaurants, 314–315
  passenger airports and terminals, 959–960
  restaurants and eateries
   dining areas, 273–275
   general considerations, 273
   meal production areas, 275–277
   receiving and storage areas, 277–278
   sanitation areas, 278
   serving areas, 277
Funeral homes:
  elements, 266–269
  flow diagrams, 268
  general considerations, 265
  parking, 265, 269
  site selection and location, 265–266

Garages, parking. *See* Parking facilities, garages
Governmental and public buildings:
  city and town halls, 759–766
  correctional facilities, 825–849
  courthouses, 806–824
  embassies and chanceries, 850–870
  fire services buildings, 767–778
  police services buildings
   police facilities, 791–798
   police stations, 779–790
  recreation centers, 799–805

Group homes:
  plans and layouts, 89–91
  space requirements
    bathrooms, 89
    bedrooms, 89
    buildings, 88
    dining areas, 88–89
    entries and exits, 88
    kitchens, 88–89
    living areas, 88
    recreation areas, 88

Halls, residential buildings, 48–49
Handicapped persons, housing for. *See* Disabled
      persons, housing for
  (*See also* Americans with Disabilities Act (ADA)
      Accessibility Guidelines)
Health care buildings:
  clinics
    in correctional facilities, 844, 847
    in housing for disabled persons, 87
  educational facilities
    dental schools, 635–655
    medical schools, 609–634
    nursing, 655–673
  hospitals
    diagnostic x-ray suites, 536–544
    emergency activity centers, 572–574
    general, 519–527
    laboratories, 555–558
    labor-delivery suites, 559–563
    long-term care facilities, 601–608
    nurseries and pediatric facilities, 531–535
    occupational therapy departments,
      549–552
    outpatient activity centers, 563–571
    pharmacies, 543–544
    physical therapy departments, 545–548
    rehabilitation centers, 575–591
    surgical suites, 528–531
  mental health centers
    community, 553–554
    general, 592–600
  practice offices
    dental, 213–220
    medical, 200–212
    ophthalmological, 221–224
Home offices:
  group homes, 89
  single-family homes, 19
Homes, single-family. *See* Single-family homes
Hospitality facilities:
  commercial kitchens, 292–297
  conference centers, 298–304
  food service facilities, 279–291

Hospitality facilities (*Cont.*):
  hotels, 305–336
  motels, 337–356
  restaurants and eateries, 273–279
Hospitals:
  diagnostic x-ray suites, 536–542
  emergency activities, 572–574
  general
    admitting departments, 524–526
    flow charts, 519
    general considerations, 519–520
    nursing units, 526–527
    patient rooms, 521–524
  laboratories, 555–558
  labor-delivery suites, 559–562
  long-term care facilities, 601–608
  mental health facilities, 553–554, 592–600
  nurseries and pediatric units, 531–535
  occupational therapy departments, 549–552
  outpatient activities, 559–571
  pharmacies, 543–544
  physical therapy departments, 545–548
  rehabilitation centers, 575–591
  surgical suites, 528–531
  (*See also* Americans with Disabilities Act (ADA)
      Accessibility Guidelines)
Hotels and motels:
  conference centers
    characteristics, 299
    plans and layouts, 298–299
    programs, establishing, 300–301
    types of centers, 298–299
    types of rooms, 301–304
  hotels
    food service facilities
      banquet facilities, 323–324
      food and beverage services, 309–312
      restaurants, 314–315
    general considerations, 305–306
    guest characteristics, 332
    house, the
      back of, 306–312
      front of, 312–324
    plan and layout, theories, 305–306
    plans and layouts, theories, 305–306
    space allotments
      floor analysis, 329
      guest room designs, 331–333
      guest room dimensions, 333–336
      guest room floors, 326–331
      100-room facilities, typical, 327–328
      schedule, 325–326
      slab configurations, 325
      suites, 334–336
      tower plans, 331

otels and motels (*Cont.*):
  motels
    general considerations, 337–338, 353
    parking, 346–349, 351, 355–356
    planning considerations, 340–341
    prototypes, 337–339
    room groups, 346–349
    site plans, 343–349, 353–356
    site selection and location, 341–349, 353–356
    space allotments, 349–352
    types, 342
ousing. *See* Residential buildings
uman figures, dimensions of, 3–5

ils. *See* Correctional facilities
uvenile detention centers. *See* Correctional facilities

itchens:
  apartments, 46–47
  disabled persons, housing for, 82–85, 87
  group homes, 88–89
  seniors housing, 63–65, 73–76
  single-family homes, 19–30

aboratories:
  colleges and universities, 506–515
  dental schools, 637–641, 643
  hospitals, 555–558
  medical schools, 616–632
  nursing schools, 664–665, 672–673
  research, 232–247. *See also* Research laboratories
aundry areas:
  apartment buildings, 61–62
  disabled persons, housing for, 80–81
  single-family homes, 30–32
aw offices. *See* Offices, law
ibraries:
  Americans with Disabilities Act (ADA) Accessibility
      Guidelines, 700, 704
  bookmobiles, 712
  branches, 696–697, 708–709, 711–712
  correctional facilities, 842–843
  disabled persons, housing for, 87
  elementary and secondary schools
    general considerations, 693
    population sizes, 693–696
  floor plans, 696–697, 701, 706, 708, 710
  law
    courthouses, 823
    police services buildings, 797
  medical
    dental schools, 648–652
    medical schools, 610–612
    nursing schools, 656–657, 660–664, 668–669, 671
  meeting areas, 701

Libraries (*Cont.*):
  music facilities, 753
  sites
    plans, 700, 705, 709
    selection and location, 705–709, 711–712
  space requirements
    books, 697
    general considerations, 697
    guidelines, 698
    handicapped access, 700, 704
    mechanical operations, 702
    readers, 697–700
    service and space relationships, 702, 705
    shelving conditions, optimum, 699
    size, experience formulas, 697
    stack areas and stack loads, 702, 704, 711–712
    staff, 700–701
    tables, 703–704
  temples and synagogues, 903, 910–911
Living areas:
  apartments, 44–46
  disabled persons, housing for, 81–82
  group homes, 88
  seniors housing, 67–69
  single-family homes, 6–8
Lots, parking. *See* Parking facilities, lots
Lutheran churches. *See* Churches, Lutheran

Manufactured home developments:
  circulation and streets, 94–96
  cluster plans, 99–101
  community facilities, 96–99
  individual lots, 93–96
  plans and layouts, 92–101
  site selection and location, 92
Media facilities:
  radio stations
    facilities, 256–259
    general considerations, 255–256
    plans and layouts, 259–262
    site selection and location, 263–264
    transmitters, 262–263
    utilities and services, 262
  television stations
    broadcasting facilities, 248–252
    planning considerations, 252–254
    site selection and location, 249
    transmitters, 254
Media resource centers. *See* Libraries
Medical care buildings. *See* Health-care buildings
Medical schools:
  administration and supporting facilities, 610–616
  basic science departments, 616–632
  clinical science facilities, 631–634
  elements, functional relationships, 609

Medical schools (*Cont.*):
  general considerations, 609–610
  health care buildings. *See* Health-care buildings
  libraries, 610–612
  parking, 609
  practice offices
    dental, 213–220
    medical, 200–212
    ophthalmological, 221–224
  site selection and location, 609–610
Mortuaries. *See* Funeral homes
Motels. *See* Hotels and motels
Municipal buildings. *See* Governmental and public
    buildings
Museums:
  accessory functions, 680
  Americans with Disabilities Act (ADA), Accessibility
    Guidelines, 680, 682
  architectural programs, 678–680
  collections environmental considerations, 685–688
  communication systems, 691–692
  entrances, 680–682
  exhibition policies and considerations, 683–688
  expansion considerations, 692
  general considerations, 677
  governance and mission statements, 677
  organizational diagrams, 680–682
  parking, 679
  plans and layouts, 681–685
  public versus nonpublic areas, 680
  site selection and location, 678–679
  strategic plans, 677–678
  structures, 689–691
Musical theaters. *See* Performing arts spaces

Nursing schools:
  faculty spaces, 665–670
  general considerations, 655, 658
  libraries, 656–657, 660–664, 668–669, 671
  programs
    associate degree, 655–657, 659–660, 666
    baccalaureate and graduate degree, 657–658,
      662–664, 666
    diploma, 655
    practical and vocational, 658, 665, 667–669
  research facilities, 664–665, 672–673
  student spaces, 670–673
  teaching spaces, 658–664, 667, 671–673

Offices:
  general
    conference and training centers, 197–199
    core locations, 172–173
    design principles and elements, 173–177
    functions, 187–189

Offices (*Cont.*):
  plans and layouts
    conference rooms, 184, 197–199
    open plans, 197–199, 178
    private offices, 182–183
    shared offices with multiple workstations,
      185–186
    space allowances, 189–197
    workstations, 177, 179–181, 185–186
  home. *See* Home offices
  law
    elements, 228–231
    general considerations, 225
    large offices, 228
    medium-size offices, 228
    plans and layouts, 225–231
    small offices, 227
  medical practice offices
    general
      general considerations, 200
      pediatric offices, 210
      practice areas, 209
      radiology areas, 205–208
      reception and business office areas, 200
      treatment and consultation rooms,
        202–206
      waiting rooms, 200–202
    plans and layouts, 205–224
    specialties
      dental, 212–220
      internal medicine, 210
      ophthalmological, 221–224
      pediatrics, 210
      radiology, 205–208
      surgery, general, 212
      surgery, orthopedic, 212
      surgery, plastic, 211
Opera houses. *See* Performing arts spaces
Ophthalmological practice offices, 221–224

Parking facilities:
  airport facilities
    aircraft, 941–945, 967–968
    vehicles, 964–965, 967–968
  correctional facilities, 849
  educational buildings
    medical schools, 609
  elementary and secondary schools, 402–403
  fire services buildings, 769
  funeral homes, 265, 269
  garages
    designs and plans, 975–989
    ramps
      breakover angles, 974–975
      helical, 989

Parking facilities (*Cont.*):
    ramp garages, 984–989
    standards, 979–981
    straight, lengths of, 985
    systems, 974–979
    types, 986–989
  hotels and motels, 346–349, 351, 355–356
  lots
    diagonal, 991–993
    dimensions, 991
    general considerations, 990–991
    plans, 990–993
  museums, 679
  performing arts spaces, 725
  police services buildings, 782, 791–792
  shopping centers, 124, 128–129, 134–139
  vehicle dealer and service centers
    body shops, 169–171
    dealerships, 145–156
    service stations, 163–168
    truck dealer and service facilities, 157–162
Passenger airports and terminals. *See* Airport, passenger
    terminals
Performing arts spaces:
  backstage areas, 745–747
  community theaters, 747
  dimensions, critical, 729
  forms
    apron shapes, 719
    arena theaters, 714–715, 722
    general considerations, 713
    open-thrust theaters, 715–719, 721–723
    performance types, relationships with, 717,
      719–720
    proscenium theaters, 713–714, 721–723, 730
    single-volume music rooms, 716–717, 719
    total theater schemes, 721
  functional diagrams, 725–726
  general considerations, 713
  house, the
    design influences, 727–737
    front, 724–727
    general considerations, 727
  music facilities
    area requirements, 747–755
    libraries, 753
    music education facilities, 755
  parking, 724
  performance types, 717, 719–720
  plans and layouts, 713–726, 729, 731–735, 738–740,
    742–751, 754–755
  requirements, technical
    acoustical, 735–737
    Americans with Disabilities Act (ADA) Accessibility
      Guidelines, 720

Performing arts spaces (*Cont.*):
    cost estimates and design, 721, 723–724
    general considerations, 720
  stages and orchestra pits, 737–745
Police services buildings:
  police facilities
    administrative areas, 793–794
    central records areas, 793–794
    communications, 795–796
    criminal investigation areas, 796–797
    facility elements, 792–793
    firearms ranges, 798
    laboratory areas, 798
    libraries, 797
    parking, 791–792
    plans and layouts, 791, 793–796
    prisoner processing and detention areas, 791–793
      (*see also* Correctional facilities)
    property rooms, 797–798
    site selection and location, 791–792
    space allocation, 793
  police stations
    courtrooms, 785–788 (*see also* Courthouses)
    general considerations, 779–784
    detention facilities, 780–781. *See also* Correctional
      facilities
    general considerations, 779, 782
    plans and layouts, 782, 785–786, 788–790
    site selection and location, 782–783
    small town halls with police stations, 789–790 (*see
      also* City and town halls)
    town populations of 3,500–7,000, 784–787
    town populations of 15,000, 787–789
    vehicle storage and garages, 782
Preschools. *See* Early childhood education facilities
Prisons. *See* Correctional facilities
Private outdoor areas, seniors housing, 72–73
Public buildings:
  municipal and government buildings (*see* Governmental
    and public buildings)
  schools (*see* Elementary and secondary school buildings)

Radio stations. *See* Media facilities, radio stations
Recreational centers:
  classifications
    community centers, 802–805
    general considerations, 800
    social halls and gymnasiums, 801–802
    type I, 800–801
    type II, 801
    type III, 801
  elements, 802–805
  general considerations, 799
  planning objectives, 799–800
  plans and layouts, 799–802, 805

Religious buildings:
  chapels, 913–914
  churches
    general, 873–882
    Lutheran, 883–888
    United Methodist, 889–899
  church schools, 915–922
  correctional facilities, 848
  temples and synagogues, 900–912
Research laboratories:
  finishes and materials, 241–244
  general considerations, 232–233
  programs and functions, 233–239
  space allocation, 234–238
  structural considerations, 246–247
  support areas, 239–241
  systems, 244–246
  types, 239
  utilities, 244
Residential buildings:
  apartment buildings, 51–62
  apartments, 43–50
  disabled persons, housing for, 78–87
  group homes, 88–91
  human figures, dimensions of, 3–5
  manufactured home developments, 92–101
  seniors housing, 63–77
  single-family homes, 6–42
Resource centers. *See* Libraries
Retail shops:
  design principles, 105–106
  general considerations, 105
  interiors, 107–110
  layouts and dimensions, 110–116

Schools. *See* Educational buildings
Secondary schools. *See* Elementary and secondary school
    buildings
Secure detention facilities. *See* Correctional facilities
Seniors housing:
  balconies, 73
  bathrooms
    personal hygiene equipment, 75–77
    plans and layouts, 71–72
  bedrooms, 69–71
  closets, 63, 69–70, 75
  dining areas, 65–67
  entries and exits, 63–64
  general considerations, 50, 63
  kitchens and food preparation areas
    food preparation equipment, 73–76
    plans and layouts, 63–65
  living areas, 67–69
  private outdoor areas, 72–73
  (*see also* Americans with Disabilities Act (ADA)
    Accessibility Guidelines)

Service stations. *See* vehicle dealer and service centers
Shopping centers:
  design and planning criteria, 123–124
  development and financing, 120–121
  general considerations, 119
  leasing arrangements, 124–125
  malls, 125–131
  parking, 124, 128–129, 134–139
  patterns, 142–144
  planning teams, 133–134
  regional shopping centers, 131–133
  schematic planning, 122–123
  site selection and location, 121
  space allotments, 134–142
  types, 119–120, 140–142
Single-family homes:
  Americans with Disabilities Act (ADA) Accessibility
    Guidelines, 19, 26–30, 33–38 (*see also*
    Americans with Disabilities Act (ADA)
    Accessibility Guidelines)
  bathrooms, 33–38
  bedrooms, 15–18
  closets, 39–42
  combined areas
    dining-kitchen, 13–14
    living-dining, 12–13
    living-sleeping, 18–19
  dining areas, 9–11
  home offices, 19
  kitchens, 19–30
  laundry areas, 30–32
  living areas, 6–8
Stations:
  fire (*see* Fire services buildings)
  police (*see* Police services buildings)
  radio (*see* Media facilities, radio stations)
  television (*see* Media facilities, television stations)
Supermarkets:
  displays, 118
  general considerations, 117
  plans and layouts, 117–118
  refrigeration equipment, 118
  store sizes, 117
Synagogues. *See* Temples and synagogues

Television stations. *See* Media facilities, television
    stations
Temples and synagogues:
  educational centers, 909–912
  general considerations, 900
  libraries, 903, 910–911
  plans, 900–912
  site selection, 900
  space criteria, 900
Terminals, airport. *See* Airport cargo facilities, Airport
    passenger terminals

heaters. *See* Performing arts spaces

own halls. *See* City and town halls

ransmitters, media facilities:
  radio stations, 262–263
  television stations, 254

ransportation buildings:
  airport facilities
    cargo facilities, 966–973
    passenger airports and terminals, 925–965
  parking facilities
    garages, 974–989
    lots, 990–993

ruck dealer and service facilities, 157–162

United Methodist churches. *See* Churches, United
  Methodist

University buildings. *See* College and university
  buildings

Vehicle dealer and service centers:
  body shops, 169–171
  dealerships, 145–156
  service stations, 163–168
  truck dealer and service facilities,
    157–162

Worship buildings. *See* Religious buildings